CLYMER®

HARLEY-DAVIDSON

FLH/FLT/FXR EVOLUTION • 1984-1998

The world's finest publisher of mechanical how-to manuals

PRIMEDIA
Information Data Products
P.O. Box 12901, Overland Park, Kansas 66282-2901

FIRST EDITION
First Printing August, 1992
Second Printing August, 1993

SECOND EDITION
First Printing June, 1995
Second Printing May, 1997
Third Printing September, 1998
Fourth Printing October, 2000
Fifth Printing January, 2002
Sixth Printing September, 2003

THIRD EDITION
First Printing June, 2005

Printed in U.S.A.

CLYMER and colophon are registered trademarks of PRIMEDIA Business Magazines & Media Inc.

ISBN: 0-89287-916-5

Library of Congress: 2004117389

AUTHOR: Ed Scott.

TECHNICAL PHOTOGRAPHY: Ed Scott with assistance from Jordan Engineering, Oceanside, CA. Motorcycles courtesy of San Diego Harley-Davidson (www.sandiegoharley.com).

TECHNICAL ILLUSTRATIONS: Steve Amos and Errol McCarthy.

WIRING DIAGRAMS: Bob Meyer and Lee Buell.

EDITOR: Lee Buell.

PRODUCTION: Justin Marciniak.

TOOLS AND EQUIPMENT: K&L Supply Co. at www.klsupply.com. Engine and transmission special tools provided by JIMS Tools (www.jimsusa.com).

COVER: Mark Clifford Photography at www.markclifford.com. 1998 FLHRC-I courtesy of Bob Ferra.

PRIMEDIA
Business Magazines & Media
P.O. Box 12901, Overland Park, KS 66282-2901 • 800-262-1954 • 913-967-1719

The following books and guides are published by PRIMEDIA Information Data Products.

More information available at *primediabooks.com*

Contents

CHAPTER FOUR

CHAPTER FIVE

CHAPTER SIX

CHAPTER SEVEN

CHAPTER EIGHT

CHAPTER NINE

CHAPTER TEN

QUICK REFERENCE DATA

MODEL:____________________ YEAR:__________
VIN NUMBER:____________________
ENGINE SERIAL NUMBER:____________________
CARBURETOR SERIAL NUMBER OR IDENTIFICATION MARK:____________________

TIRE INFLATION PRESSURE (FXR, FLH AND FLT [COLD])[1]

Item	psi	kPa
Front (rider only)		
1984-1985		
FXRS (K291T[2])	30	207
FXRT (K291T[2])	30	207
FLT/FLTC	–	–
FLHT/FLHTC (K101A[2])	28	193
1986-1998		
FXR series models	30	207
FLH and FLT series models	36	248
Front (rider with one passenger)		
1984-1985		
FXRS	30	207
FXRT	30	207
FLT/FLTC and FLHT/FLHTC	28	193
FLT with sidecar	28	193
1986-1998		
FXR series models	30	207
FLH and FLT series models	36	248
Rear (rider only)		
1984-1985		
FXRS (K291T[2])	36	248
FXRT (K291T[2])	36	248
FLT/FLTC	–	–
FLHT/FLHTC (K101A[2])	36	248
1986-1998		
FXR series	36	248
FLH and FLT series models	36	248
Rear (rider with one passenger)		
1984-1985		
FXRS	40	275
FXRT	40	275

(continued)

TIRE INFLATION PRESSURE (FXR, FLH AND FLT [COLD])[1] (continued)

Item	psi	kPa
Rear (rider with one passenger) (continued)		
1984-1985		
FLT/FLTC and FLHT/FLHTC	36	248
FLT with sidecar	40	275
1986-1998		
FXR series models	40	275
FLH and FLT series models	40	275

1. Tire inflation pressure is for OEM tires. Aftermarket tires might require different inflation pressure. The use of tires other than those specified by Harley-Davidson can cause instability.
2. Indicates the OEM Dunlop tire designation.

TIRE INFLATION PRESSURE (FXWG, FXSB AND FXEF [COLD])[1]

Item	psi	kPa
Front (rider only)		
FXWG	30	207
FXEF and FXSB		
K181[2]	30	207
K291T[2]	36	248
Front (rider with one passenger)		
FXWG		
F rib	30	207
K101A	–	–
FXEF and FXSB		
K181[2]	30	207
K291T[2]	36	248
Rear (rider only)		
FXWG	32	221
FXEF and FXSB		
K181[2]	32	221
K291T[2]	36	248
Rear (rider with one passenger)		
FXWG		
F rib	32	221
K101A	28	193
FXEF and FXSB		
K181[2]	32	221

1. Tire inflation pressure is for OEM tires. Aftermarket tires might require different inflation pressure. The use of tires other than those specified by Harley-Davidson can cause instability.
2. Indicates the OEM Dunlop tire designation.

RECOMMENDED LUBRICANTS AND FLUIDS

Brake fluid	DOT 5 silicone
Fork oil	HD Type E or an equivalent
Battery	Purified or distilled water
Transmission	HD Transmission Lubricant or an equivalent
Clutch	HD Transmission Lubricant or an equivalent
Drive chain	
Enclosed drive chain	SAE 50 or SAE 60
Open drive chain (without O-rings)	Commercial drive chain lubricant
Open drive chain (with O-rings)	Commercial drive chain lubricant recommended for O-ring chains

ENGINE AND PRIMARY DRIVE/TRANSMISSION OIL CAPACITIES

Engine oil tank	
FXR series models	3.0 qts. (2.8 L)
FLT/FLH series models	4.0 qts. (3.8 L)
FXWG, FXSB and FXEF	4.0 qts. (3.8 L)
Transmission	
1984-1990	16 oz. (473 mL)
1991-1998	20-24 oz. (591-710 mL)
Primary chaincase	
Early 1984	N.A.
Late 1984-1990	1.5 qt. (1.4 L)
1991-1996	38-44 oz. (1.1-1.3 L)
1997-1998	32 oz. (946 mL)
Rear chaincase (1984-1985)	6 oz. (177 mL)

FRONT FORK OIL CAPACITY

Model and year	Oil Change oz.	Oil Change cc	Rebuild oz.	Rebuild cc
FXR				
1984-1987 FXR and FXRS	6.25	184.8	7.0	206.9
1984-1987 FXRD and FXRT	7.0	206.9	7.75	229.2
1987-1994 FXLR	9.2	272	10.2	300.9
1988-1994 FXR and FXRS	9.2	272	10.2	300.9
1988-1994 FXRT and FXRS-SP and FXRS-Con	10.5	310.5	11.5	339.2
1999 FXR2 and FXR3	9.2	272	10.2	300.9
FXWG	10.2	300.9	11.2	330.4
FXSB	7.5	221.8	6.75	199.6
FXEF	5.0	147.8	6.5	192.2
FLT and FLH series models	7.75	229.2	8.5	251.3

TUNE-UP SPECIFICATIONS

Engine compression	90 psi (620 kPa)
Spark plugs	
Type	HD 5R6A
Gap	0.038-0.043 in. (0.97-1.09 mm)
Ignition timing	
Type	Electronic
Timing specifications	
Early 1984	
Range	5-50° BTDC
Start	5° BTDC
Fast idle at 1800-2800 rpm	35° BTDC
Late 1984-1994	
Range	0-35° BTDC
Start	0° BTDC
Fast idle at 1800-2800 rpm	35° BTDC
1995 domestic	
Range	0-35° BTDC
Start	TDC
Fast idle at 1050-1500 rpm	35° BTDC
1995 HDI	
Range	0-42.5° BTDC
Start	TDC
Fast idle at 1050-1500 rpm	20° BTDC

(continued)

TUNE-UP SPECIFICATIONS (continued)

Timing specifications (continued)	
1996-1998	
Range	0-42.5° BTDC
Start	TDC
Fast idle at 1050-1500 rpm	20° BTDC

IDLE SPEED SPECIFICATIONS

Model and year	Speed
FXR, FLH and FLT series	
1984-1987	
Slow idle	900-950 rpm
Fast idle	1500 rpm
1988-1989	
Slow idle	1000 rpm
Fast idle	1500 rpm
1990	1000 rpm
1991-1996	1000-1050 rpm
1997-1998	1050-1500 rpm
FXR2 and FXR3	1000-1050 rpm
FXWG, FXSB and FXEF	
Slow idle	1000-1050 rpm
Fast idle	1500-1550 rpm

CLUTCH ADJUSTMENT

Clutch hand lever free play	
Dry clutch (early 1984)	1/16 in. (1.59 mm)
Wet clutch	
Late 1984-1989	1/8-3/16 in. (3.17-4.76 mm)
1990	1/8-3/16 in. (3.17-4.76 mm)
1991-1999	1/16-1/8 in. (1.59-3.17 mm)

CARBURETOR SPECIFICATIONS

Model and year	Main jet	Pilot jet
FXR series models		
1984-1985	160	50
1986	170	50
1987	165	50
1988-1989		
49-state	165	52
California	140	42
1990-1991		
49-state	185	52
California	165	42
1992-1993		
49-state	165	40
California	160	40
1994		
49-state	165	42
California	165	42
HDI*	165	40

(continued)

CARBURETOR SPECIFICATIONS (continued)

Model and year	Main jet	Pilot jet
FXWG		
1985	165	50
1986	170	50
FXEF and FXSB		
1985	165	50
FLH and FLT series models		
Early 1984	165	50
Late 1984-1986	175	50
1987	170	50
1988-1989		
49-state	165	52
California	140	42
1990-1991		
49-state	185	45
California	165	42
1992-1993		
49-state	175	40
California	160	40
1994		
49-state	175	42
California	165	42
HDI*	175	40
1995		
49-state	175	42
California	175	42
HDI*	180	42
Swiss HDI*	175	40
1996		
49-state	175	42
California	180	42
HDI*	175	42
FLH and FLT series models		
1996 (continued)		
Swiss HDI*	175	40
1997-1998		
49-state	175	42
California	180	42
HDI*	180	42
Swiss HDI*	180	42
1999		
49-state	170	N.A.
California	175	N.A.
Float level (refer to text in Chapter Eight)		

*HDI indicates International models.

REPLACEMENT BULBS (1984-1994 MODELS)

Item	Size-amperage (all 12-volt) × quantity
Headlight	
FXWG, FXSB and FXEF	3.9
FLTC	3.57/2.5 × 2
FLHTC and FLHS	4.28/3.93
Passing lamp	2.34 × 2
Instrument panel/gauges lamps	
FXSB and FXEF	0.27 × 5

(continued)

REPLACEMENT BULBS (1984-1994 MODELS) (continued)

Item	Size-amperage (all 12-volt) × quantity
Instrument panel/gauges lamps (continued)	
FXWG	
High beam	0.04
Oil pressure	0.08
Neutral indicator	0.08
Speedometer	0.27
FLT	0.12 × 9
FXRT	
Fuel gauge	
1984-1990	0.27
1991-1992	0.12
High beam indicator	0.12
Neutral indicator	0.08
Oil pressure gauge	0.08
Speedometer	0.12 × 2
Tachometer	0.12
Turn signal indicator	0.27
FXR, FXLR, FXRS-SP and FXRS-Con	
Fuel gauge	0.12
High beam indicator	0.27
Neutral indicator	0.08
Oil pressure gauge	0.08
Speedometer	0.27
Tachometer	0.27
Turn signal indicator	0.27 × 2
Tail lamp	0.59
Stop lamp	
FXR, FXLR, FSRS-SP and FXRS-Con	2.25
All other models	2.1
Front turn signal/running	
FXWG, FXSB and FXEF	2.1 × 2
All other models	0.59/2.25 × 2
Rear turn signal	
FXR, FXLR, FSRS-SP and FXRS-Con	2.25 × 2
All other models	2.1 × 2
Tour-Pak lamps	0.10 × 4
Fender tip lamp	0.10 × 2

REPLACEMENT BULBS (1995-1998 MODELS)

Item	Size-wattage (all 12-volt) × quantity
Headlight	
FLTC-UI and FLTR	55/60 × 2
All other models	55/60
Passing lamp	
Domestic	30 × 2
HDI*	35 × 2
Position lamp (HDI)*	3.9
Instrument panel/gauges lamps	
1995-1997 FLHR	
Engine check light (EFI)	2.1
Fuel gauge	2.7
High beam indicator	2.1
Neutral indicator	2.1
Oil pressure gauge	2.1

(continued)

REPLACEMENT BULBS (1995-1998 MODELS) (continued)

Item	Size-wattage (all 12-volt) × quantity
Instrument panel/gauges lamps	
1995-1997 FLHR (continued)	
Speedometer	3.7 × 2
Odometer	2.7
Turn signal indicator	2.1 × 2
1995 FLHT, FLHTC, FLHTC-U and 1996 FLTC-UI	
Cruise	2.7
Engine check light (EFI)	3.7
Fuel gauge	2.7
High beam indicator	2.7
Neutral indicator	3.7
Odometer	2.7
Oil pressure gauge	2
Speedometer	3.7 × 2
Tachometer	3.7 × 2
Turn signal indicator	3.7 × 2
Voltmeter	2
1996-1998 FLHT, FLHTC, FLHTC-I, FLHTC-U and FLHTC-UI	
Air temperature gauge (EFI)	3.4
Engine check light (EFI)	2.1
Fuel gauge	3.4
High beam indicator	2.1
Neutral indicator	2.1
Odometer	2.7
Oil pressure gauge	3.4
Speedometer	1.7 × 2
Tachometer	3.4
Turn signal indicator	2.1 × 2
Voltmeter	3.4
1998 FLTR and FLTR-I	
Air temperature gauge (EFI)	3.4
Engine check light (EFI)	2.1
Fuel gauge	3.4
High beam indicator	2.1
Neutral indicator	2.1
Oil pressure gauge	3.4
Speedometer	1.7 × 2
Tachometer	3.4
Turn signal indicator	2.1 × 2
1999 FXR2 and FXR3	
Fuel gauge	2.7
High beam indicator	1.1
Neutral indicator	1.1
Odometer	2.7
Oil pressure gauge	1.1
Speedometer	3.7
Tachometer	4.9
Turn signal indicator	1.1 × 2
Tail lamp	
Domestic	7
HDI*	5
Stop lamp	
Domestic	27
HDI*	21
Front turn signal/running	27/7
Rear turn signal	
Domestic	27
HDI*	21

(continued)

REPLACEMENT BULBS (1995-1998 MODELS) (continued)

Item	Size-wattage (all 12-volt) × quantity
License plate lamp (HDI)*	5.2
Fender tip lamp	3.7 × 2
Tour-Pak	3.7 × 4

*HDI indicates International models.

BLADE TYPE FUSES (1994-1998 FLH AND FLT SERIES)

Circuit	Rating (amps)	Color code
CB power	3	Violet
CB memory	1	Charcoal
Cruise and brake (1997-1998)	15	Blue
Fender tip light		
1994-1998 FLHT and FLHR series models	1	Charcoal
Instruments (1997-1998)	15	Blue
P & A (1997-1998)	10	Red
Pod power	5	Tan
Radio (Ultra models)	10	Red
Radio memory	1	Charcoal
Fuel pump (EFI)	15	Blue
Electronic control module (EFI)	5	Tan

MAINTENANCE AND TUNE UP TORQUE SPECIFICATIONS

Item	ft.-lb.	in.-lb.	N•m
Clutch diaphragm spring bolts			
Late 1984-1989 wet clutch	–	71-97	8-11
Engine front mounting bracket			
Side bolts	33-38	–	45-52
Center bolt	35-45	–	47-61
Front fork air pipe hex bolts (1997-1998 models)	–	97-106	11-12
Primary drive chain shoe nut or bolt	22-29	–	30-39
Rear axle nut			
1984-1988	60-65	–	81-88
1989-1998	60	–	81
Spark plugs	14	–	19
Swing arm anchor bolt (enclosed chain models)	20	–	27
Valve lifter screen plug	–	89-124	10-14

FRONT WHEEL TORQUE SPECIFICATIONS

Item	ft.-lb.	in.-lb.	N•m
Axle nut			
FXR series			
1984-1992	50	–	68
1993-1998	50-55	–	68-75
FXWG, FXSB and FXEF	50-55	–	68-75
FLH and FLT series	50-55	–	68-75

(continued)

FRONT WHEEL TORQUE SPECIFICATIONS (continued)

Item	ft.-lb.	in.-lb.	N•m
Axle slider cap nuts			
FXR series			
FXLR	–	85-110	10-12
All other models	–	110-156	12-18
FXWG, FXSB and FXEF	–	110-156	12-18
FLH and FLT series	–	110-156	12-18
Front brake caliper	25-30	–	34-41
Spoke nipple	–	40-50	4-6

REAR WHEEL TORQUE SPECIFICATIONS

Item	ft.-lb.	in.-lb.	N•m
Axle nut	60-65	–	81-88
Driven sprocket bolts (belt drive)	55-65	–	75-88
Driven sprocket bolts (chain drive)			
FXR, FLH and FLT series			
1984-1991			
Grade No. 5 bolts	45-50	–	61-68
Grade No. 8 bolts	65-70	–	88-95
1992	45-55	–	61-75
1993-1998	55-65	–	75-88
FXWG, FXSB and FXEF			
Laced wheel			
FXWG	40-55	–	54-75
FXSB and FXEF	35	–	47
Alloy wheel			
Grade No. 5 bolts	45-50	–	61-68
Grade No. 8 bolts	65-70	–	88-95
Spoke nipple	–	40-50	4-6

FRONT SUSPENSION TORQUE SPECIFICATIONS

Item	ft.-lb.	in.-lb.	N•m
Fork air control system			
Air tubes banjo bolts			
1984-1994 FXRD, FXRT and FXRS-SP models	25-30	–	34-41
Air accumulator bracket bolts			
1984-1987 FXRD and FXRT models	30-35	–	41-47
Antidive solenoid housing bolts			
1984-1987 FXRD and FXRT models	–	155-190	17-21
Air tubes flange nuts			
1988-1994 FXRT and FXRS-SP	17	–	23
Antidive switch bolts			
1986-1996 FLH and FLT series models	25-30	–	34-41
1986-1996 FLHT series models	25-30	–	34-41
Air tube assembly hex bolts			
1997-1998 FLH and FLT series models	–	97-142	11-16
Antidive solenoid banjo bolts	–	97-124	11-14
Fork tube pinch bolts			
FXR series models			
1984-1987 FXR, FXRS, FXRD and FXRT			
Upper	21-27	–	28-37
Lower	30-35	–	41-47

(continued)

FRONT SUSPENSION TORQUE SPECIFICATIONS (continued)

Item	ft.-lb.	in.-lb.	N•m
Fork tube pinch bolts			
FXR series models (continued)			
1987 FXLR, FXRS and 1988-1992 FXR			
Upper and lower	25-30	–	34-41
1993-1994 FXR, 1999 FXR2 and FXR3			
Upper and lower	30-35	–	41-47
FXWG, FXSB and FXEF	25-30	–	34-41
FLH and FLT series models			
1984-1990	25	–	34
1991-1998	40	–	54
Fork tube plug (FLH and FLT series models)	50-55	–	68-75
Fork stem and bracket			
FXR series models			
Fork stem nut or bolt	Refer to text		
Upper bracket-to-fork stem pinch bolt			
1984-1987 FXR, FXRS, FXRD and FXRT	21-27	–	28-37
1987 FXLR, FXRS and 1988-1992 FXR	25-30	–	34-41
1993-1994 FXR	30-35	–	41-47
FXWG, FXR2 and FXR3			
Fork stem nut	35-40	–	47-54
Brake hose-to-lower steering stem bracket	–	133	15
FXSB and FXEF			
Fork stem nut	Refer to text		
Upper bracket-to-fork stem pinch bolt	20-25	–	27-34
FLH and FLT series models			
Fork stem nut	35-40	–	47-54
Steering stem nut	35-40	–	41-54

REAR SUSPENSION TORQUE SPECIFICATIONS

Item	ft.-lb.	in.-lb.	N•m
Swing arm pivot bolt			
FXR, FLH and FLT series models			
1984-early 1986 pivot shaft nut	45	–	61
Late 1986-1988 (12-point head pivot bolt)	85	–	115
1989-1998 pivot shaft nut	45	–	61
FXWG, FXSB and FXEF	Refer to text		
Rear axle nut	60-65	–	81-88
Rear shock absorber bolts or nuts			
FXR series models			
1984	N.A.		
1985-1998			
Upper and lower	33-35	–	45-47
FXWG, FXSB and FXEF	N.A.		
FLH and FLT series models			
Upper			
1984-early 1988	35-40	–	47-54
Late 1988-1998	33-35	–	45-47
Lower	35-40	–	47-54
Passenger footpeg bolts	20-25	–	27-34

CHAPTER ONE

GENERAL INFORMATION

This detailed and comprehensive manual covers the Harley-Davidson FLH, FLT and FXR series models from 1984-1998, the FXSB and FXEF models from 1985 and FXWG models from 1985-1986.

The text provides complete information on maintenance, tune-up, repair and overhaul. Hundreds of photographs and illustrations created during the complete disassembly of the motorcycle guide the reader through every job. All procedures are in step-by-step format and designed for the reader who may be working on the motorcycle for the first time.

MANUAL ORGANIZATION

A shop manual is a tool and, as in all Clymer manuals, the chapters are thumb tabbed for easy reference. Main headings are listed in the table of contents and the index. Frequently used specifications and capacities from the tables at the end of each individual chapter are listed in the Quick Reference Data section at the front of the manual. Specifications and capacities are provided in U.S. standard and metric units of measure.

During some of the procedures, there will be references to headings in other chapters or sections of the manual. When a specific heading is called out in a step it will be *italicized* as it appears in the manual. If a subheading is indicated as being "in this section" it is located within the same main heading. For example, the subheading *Handling Gasoline Safely* is located within the main heading *Safety.*

This chapter provides general information on shop safety, tools and tool usage, service fundamentals and shop supplies. **Tables 1-12**, at the end of the chapter, list the following:

Table 1 lists model identification.

Table 2 lists general specifications (FLH, FLT and FXR series models).

Table 3 lists general specifications (FXSB, FXEF and FXWG).

Table 4 lists motorcycle weight (dry).

Table 5 lists motorcycle weight ratings.

Table 6 lists fuel tank capacity.

Table 7 lists decimal and metric equivalents.

Table 8 lists general torque specifications.

Table 9 lists conversion tables.

Table 10 lists technical abbreviations.

Table 11 lists American tap and drill sizes.

Table 12 lists special tools.

Chapter Two provides methods for quick and accurate diagnosis of problems. Troubleshooting procedures present typical symptoms and logical methods to pinpoint and repair the problem.

Chapter Three explains all routine maintenance necessary to keep the motorcycle running well. Chapter Three also includes recommended tune-up procedures, eliminating the need to constantly consult the chapters on the various assemblies.

Subsequent chapters describe specific systems such as engine, transmission, clutch, drive system, fuel system, suspension, brakes, cruise control, fairing and exhaust system. Each disassembly, repair and assembly procedure is discussed in step-by-step form.

WARNINGS, CAUTIONS AND NOTES

The terms WARNING, CAUTION and NOTE have specific meanings in this manual.

A WARNING emphasizes areas where injury or even death could result from negligence. Mechanical damage may also occur. WARNINGS are to be taken seriously.

A CAUTION emphasizes areas where equipment damage could result. Disregarding a CAUTION could cause permanent mechanical damage, though injury is unlikely.

A NOTE provides additional information to make a step or procedure easier or clearer. Disregarding a NOTE could cause inconvenience but would not cause equipment damage or injury.

SAFETY

Professional mechanics can work for years and never sustain a serious injury or mishap. Follow these guidelines and practice common sense to safely service the motorcycle.

1. Do not operate the motorcycle in an enclosed area. The exhaust gasses contain carbon monoxide, an odorless, colorless and tasteless poisonous gas. Carbon monoxide levels build quickly in small enclosed areas and can cause unconsciousness and death in a short time. Make sure to properly ventilate the work area or operate the motorcycle outside.
2. Never use gasoline or any extremely flammable liquid to clean parts. Refer to *Cleaning Parts* and *Handling Gasoline Safely* in this section.
3. Never smoke or use a torch in the vicinity of flammable liquids such as gasoline or cleaning solvent.

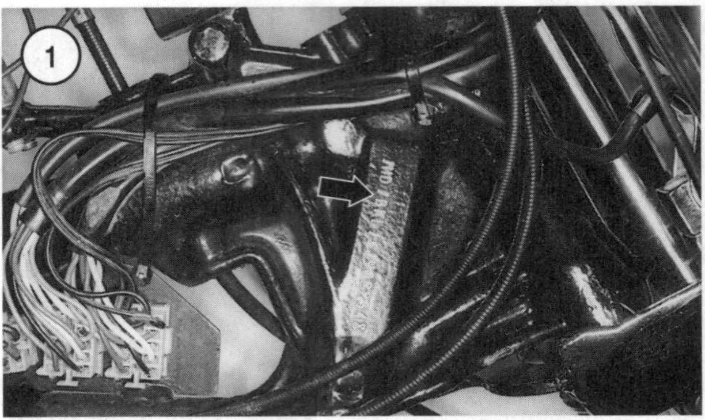

4. If welding or brazing on the motorcycle, move the fuel tank to a safe distance at least 50 ft. (15 m) away.
5. Use the correct type and size of tools to avoid damaging fasteners.
6. Keep tools clean and in good condition. Replace or repair worn or damaged equipment.
7. When loosening a tight fastener, be guided by what would happen if the tool slips.
8. When replacing fasteners, make sure the new fasteners are the same size and strength as the original ones.
9. Keep the work area clean and organized.
10. Wear eye protection anytime the safety of the eyes is in question. This includes procedures that involve drilling, grinding, hammering, compressed air and chemicals.
11. Wear the correct clothing for the job. Tie up or cover long hair so it does not get caught in moving equipment.
12. Do not carry sharp tools in clothing pockets.
13. Always have an approved fire extinguisher available. Make sure it is rated for gasoline (Class B) and electrical (Class C) fires.
14. Do not use compressed air to clean clothes, the motorcycle or the work area. Debris may be blown into the eyes or skin. Never direct compressed air at anyone. Do not allow children to use or play with any compressed air equipment.
15. When using compressed air to dry rotating parts, hold the part so it does not rotate. Do not allow the force of the air to spin the part. The air jet is capable of rotating parts at extreme speed. The part may disintegrate or become damaged and cause serious injury.
16. Do not inhale the dust created by brake pad and clutch wear. These particles may contain asbestos. In addition, some types of insulating materials and gaskets may contain asbestos. Inhaling asbestos particles is hazardous to health.
17. Never work on the motorcycle while someone is working under it.

18. When placing the motorcycle on a stand, make sure it is secure before walking away.

Handling Gasoline Safely

Gasoline is a volatile flammable liquid and is one of the most dangerous items in the shop. Because gasoline is used so often, many people forget it is hazardous. Only use gasoline as fuel for gasoline internal combustion engines. When working on the machine, keep in mind gasoline is always present in the fuel tank, fuel line and throttle body. To avoid a disastrous accident when working around the fuel system, carefully observe the following precautions:

1. Never use gasoline to clean parts. Refer to *Cleaning Parts* in this section.
2. When working on the fuel system, work outside or in a well-ventilated area.
3. Do not add fuel to the fuel tank or service the fuel system while the motorcycle is near open flames, sparks or where someone is smoking. Gasoline vapor is heavier than air; it collects in low areas and is more easily ignited than liquid gasoline.
4. Allow the engine to cool completely before working on any fuel system component.
5. Do not store gasoline in glass containers. If the glass breaks, a serious explosion or fire may occur.
6. Immediately wipe up spilled gasoline with rags. Store the rags in a metal container with a lid until they can be properly disposed of, or place them outside in a safe place for the fuel to evaporate.
7. Do not pour water onto a gasoline fire. Water spreads the fire and makes it more difficult to put out. Use a class B, BC or ABC fire extinguisher to extinguish the fire.
8. Always turn off the engine before refueling. Do not spill fuel onto the engine or exhaust system. Do not overfill the fuel tank. Leave an air space at the top of the tank to allow room for the fuel to expand due to temperature fluctuations.

Cleaning Parts

Cleaning parts is one of the more tedious and difficult service jobs performed in the home garage. Many types of chemical cleaners and solvents are available for shop use. Most are poisonous and extremely flammable. To prevent chemical exposure, vapor buildup, fire and serious injury, read each product warning label and note the following:

1. Read and observe the entire product label before using any chemical. Always know what type of chemical is being used and whether it is poisonous and/or flammable.
2. Do not use more than one type of cleaning solvent at a time. If mixing chemicals is required, measure the proper amounts according to the manufacturer.
3. Work in a well-ventilated area.
4. Wear chemical-resistant gloves.
5. Wear safety glasses.
6. Wear a vapor respirator if the instructions call for it.
7. Wash hands and arms thoroughly after cleaning parts.
8. Keep chemical products away from children and pets.
9. Thoroughly clean all oil, grease and cleaner residue from any part that must be heated.
10. Use a nylon brush when cleaning parts. Metal brushes can cause a spark.
11. When using a parts washer, only use the solvent recommended by the manufacturer. Make sure the parts washer is equipped with a metal lid that will lower in case of fire.

Warning Labels

Most manufacturers attach information and warning labels to the motorcycle. These labels contain instructions that are important to personal safety when operating, servicing, transporting and storing the motorcycle. Refer to the owner's manual for the description and location of labels. Order replacement labels from the manufacturer if they are missing or damaged.

SERIAL NUMBERS

Serial numbers are stamped on various locations on the frame, engine, transmission and carburetor. Record these numbers in the *Quick Reference Data* section in the front of the manual. Have these numbers available when ordering parts.

The frame serial number (**Figure 1**) is stamped on the right side of the frame down tube.

The VIN number label is located just below the frame number on the right side frame down tube.

The engine serial number is stamped on a pad on the left side of the crankcase (**Figure 2**) at the base of the rear cylinder block.

Table 1 lists model identification.

NOTE
Harley-Davidson makes running changes during a production year. Depending on when this change was made, the models are then identified, as an example, as either an Early 1985 or Late 1985 model. All of these models are so identified in this manual. The 17-digit VIN number will also give the correct identity to these models.

FASTENERS

Proper fastener selection and installation is important to make sure the motorcycle operates as designed and can be serviced efficiently. The choice of original equipment fasteners is not arrived at by chance. Make sure replacement fasteners meet all the same requirements as the originals.

Threaded Fasteners

Threaded fasteners secure most of the components on the motorcycle. Most are tightened by turning them clockwise (right-hand threads). If the normal rotation of the component being tightened would loosen the fastener, it might have left-hand threads. If a left-hand threaded fastener is used, it is noted in the text.

Two dimensions are required to match the thread size of the fastener: the number of threads in a given distance and the outside diameter of the threads.

The two systems currently used to specify threaded fastener dimensions are the U.S. standard system and the metric system (**Figure 3**). Pay particular attention when working with unidentified fasteners; mismatching thread types can damage threads.

NOTE
To make sure that the fastener threads are not mismatched or cross-threaded, start all fasteners by hand. If a fastener is hard to start or turn, determine the cause before tightening with a wrench.

The length (L, **Figure 4**), diameter (D) and distance between thread crests (pitch) (T) classify metric screws and bolts. A typical bolt may be identified by the numbers, 8—1.25 × 130. This indicates the bolt has a diameter of 8 mm, the distance between thread crests is 1.25 mm, and the length is 130 mm. Always measure bolt length as shown in L, **Figure 4** to avoid purchasing replacements of the wrong length.

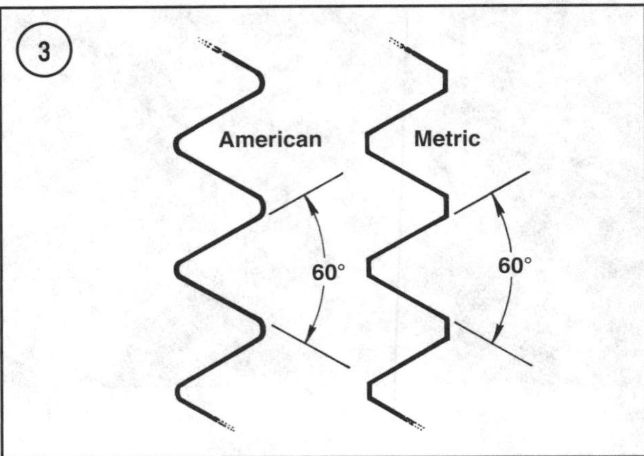

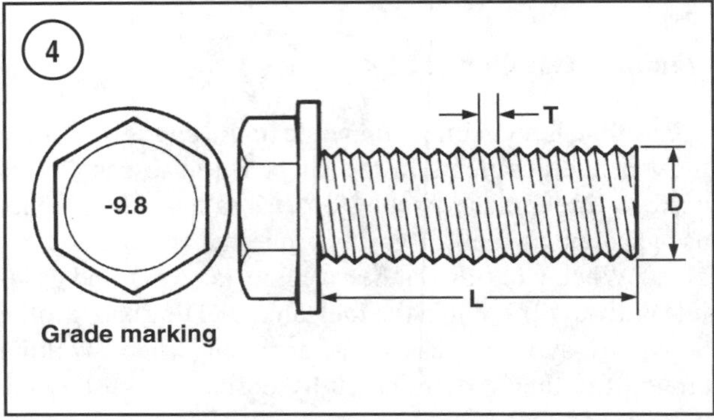

The numbers on the top of the fastener (**Figure 4**) indicate the strength of screws and bolts. The higher the number, the stronger the fastener is. Typically, unnumbered fasteners are the weakest.

Many screws, bolts and studs are combined with nuts to secure particular components. To indicate the size of a nut, manufacturers specify the internal diameter and the thread pitch.

The measurement across two flats on a nut or bolt indicates the wrench size.

WARNING
Do not install fasteners with a strength classification lower than what was originally installed by the manufacturer. Doing so may cause equipment failure and/or damage.

Torque Specifications

The materials used in the manufacturing of the motorcycle may be subjected to uneven stresses if the fasteners of the various subassemblies are not installed and tightened correctly. Fasteners that are improperly installed or

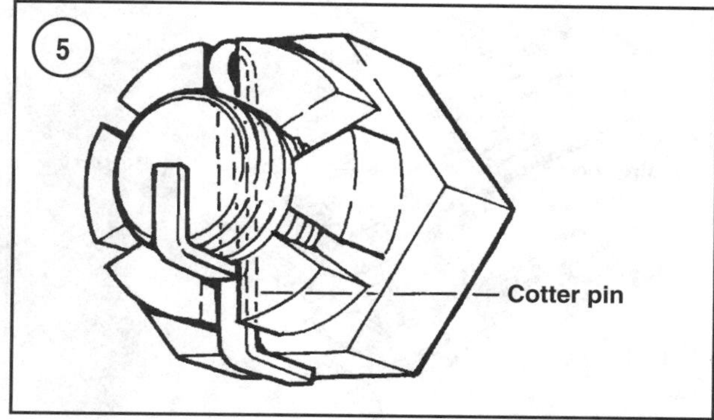

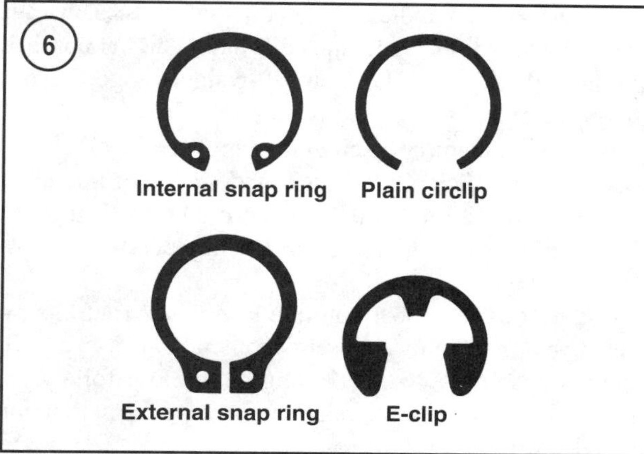

work loose can cause extensive damage. It is essential to use an accurate torque wrench as described in this chapter.

Specifications for torque are provided in Newton-meters (N•m), foot-pounds (ft.-lb.) and inch-pounds (in.-lb.). Refer to **Table 8** for general torque specifications. To determine the torque requirement, first determine the size of the fastener as described in *Threaded Fasteners* in this section. Torque specifications for specific components are at the end of the appropriate chapters. Torque wrenches are covered in *Basic Tools* in this chapter.

Self-Locking Fasteners

Several types of bolts, screws and nuts incorporate a system that creates interference between the two fasteners. Interference is achieved in various ways. The most common types are the nylon insert nut and a dry adhesive coating on the threads of a bolt.

Self-locking fasteners offer greater holding strength than standard fasteners and improve their resistance to vibration. All self-locking fasteners cannot be reused. The materials used to form the lock become distorted after the initial installation and removal. Discard and replace self-locking fasteners after removing them. Do not replace self-locking fasteners with standard fasteners.

Washers

The two basic types of washers are flat washers and lockwashers. Flat washers are simple discs with a hole to fit a screw or bolt. Lockwashers are used to prevent a fastener from working loose. Washers can be used as spacers and seals, or can help distribute fastener load and prevent the fastener from damaging the component.

As with fasteners, when replacing washers make sure the replacement washers are of the same design and quality.

Cotter Pins

A cotter pin is a split metal pin inserted into a hole or slot to prevent a fastener from loosening. In certain applications, such as the rear axle on an ATV or motorcycle, the fastener must be secured in this way. For these applications, a cotter pin and castellated (slotted) nut is used.

To use a cotter pin, first make sure the diameter is correct for the hole in the fastener. After correctly tightening the fastener and aligning the holes, insert the cotter pin through the hole and bend the ends over the fastener (**Figure 5**). Unless instructed to do so, never loosen a tightened fastener to align the holes. If the holes do not align, tighten the fastener enough to achieve alignment.

Cotter pins are available in various diameters and lengths. Measure the length from the bottom of the head to the tip of the shortest pin.

Snap Rings and E-clips

Snap rings (**Figure 6**) are circular-shaped metal retaining clips. They are required to secure parts and gears in place on parts such as shafts, pins or rods. External snap rings are used to retain items on shafts. Internal snap rings secure parts within housing bores. In some applications, in addition to securing the component(s), snap rings of varying thicknesses also determine endplay. These are usually called selective snap rings.

The two basic types of snap rings are machined and stamped snap rings. Machined snap rings (**Figure 7**) can be installed in either direction, because both faces have sharp edges. Stamped snap rings (**Figure 8**) are manufactured with a sharp and a round edge. When installing a stamped snap ring in a thrust application, install the sharp edge facing away from the part producing the thrust.

E-clips are used when it is not practical to use a snap ring. Remove E-clips with a flat blade screwdriver by prying between the shaft and E-clip. To install an E-clip, center it over the shaft groove and push or tap it into place.

Observe the following when installing snap rings:

1. Remove and install snap rings with snap ring pliers. Refer to *Basic Tools* in this chapter.
2. In some applications, it may be necessary to replace snap rings after removing them.
3. Compress or expand snap rings only enough to install them. If overly expanded, they lose retaining ability.
4. After installing a snap ring, make sure it seats completely.
5. Wear eye protection when removing and installing snap rings.

SHOP SUPPLIES

Lubricants and Fluids

Periodic lubrication helps ensure a long service life for any type of equipment. Using the correct type of lubricant is as important as performing the lubrication service, though in an emergency, the wrong type is better than not using one. The following section describes the types of lubricants most often required. Make sure to follow the manufacturer's recommendations for lubricant types.

Engine oils

Engine oil for four-stroke motorcycle engine use is classified by three standards: the American Petroleum Institute (API) service classification, the Society of Automotive Engineers (SAE) viscosity rating and the Japanese Automobile Standards Organization (JASO) T 903 Standard rating.

The API and SAE information is on all oil container labels. The JASO information is found on oil containers sold by the oil manufacturer specifically for motorcycle use. Two letters indicate the API service classification. The number or sequence of numbers and letter (10W-40, for example) is the oil viscosity rating. The API service classification and the SAE viscosity index are not indications of oil quality.

The API service classification indicates that the oil meets specific lubrication standards. The first letter in the classification, *S*, indicates that the oil is for gasoline engines. The second letter indicates the standard the oil satisfies.

Always use an oil with a classification recommended by the manufacturer. Using an oil with a different classification can cause engine damage.

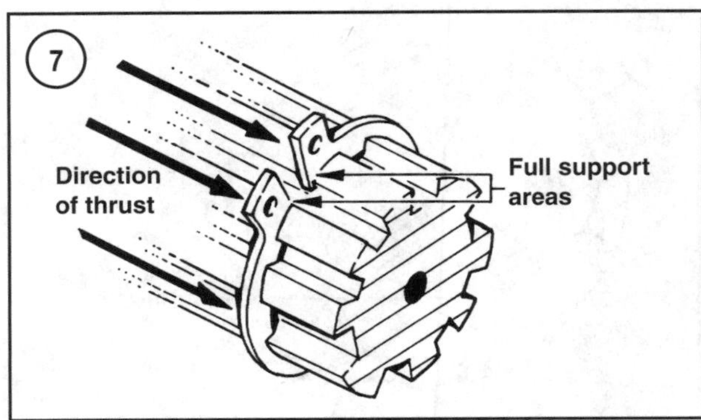

Viscosity is an indication of oil thickness. Thin oils have a lower number, and thick oils have a higher number. Engine oils fall into the 5- to 50-weight range for single-grade oils.

Most manufacturers recommend multigrade oil. These oils perform efficiently across a wide range of operating conditions. Multigrade oils are identified by a *W* after the first number, which indicates the low-temperature viscosity.

Engine oils are most commonly mineral (petroleum) based, but synthetic and semisynthetic types are used more frequently. When selecting engine oil, follow the manufacturer's recommendation for type, classification and viscosity.

Greases

Grease is lubricating oil with thickening agents added to it. The National Lubricating Grease Institute (NLGI) grades grease. Grades range from No. 000 to No. 6 with No. 6 being the thickest. Typical multipurpose grease is NLGI No. 2. For specific applications, manufacturers may recommend water-resistant grease or one with an additive such as molybdenum disulfide (MoS_2).

Brake fluid

Brake fluid is the hydraulic fluid used to transmit hydraulic pressure (force) to the wheel brakes. Brake fluid is classified by the Department of Transportation (DOT). Current designations for brake fluid are DOT 3, DOT 4 and DOT 5. This classification appears on the fluid container.

Each type of brake fluid has its own definite characteristics. The Harley-Davidson models use the silicone-based DOT 5 brake fluid. Do not mix DOT 3 or DOT 4 with DOT 5 brake fluid. Mixing may cause brake system failure because the DOT 5 brake fluid is not com-

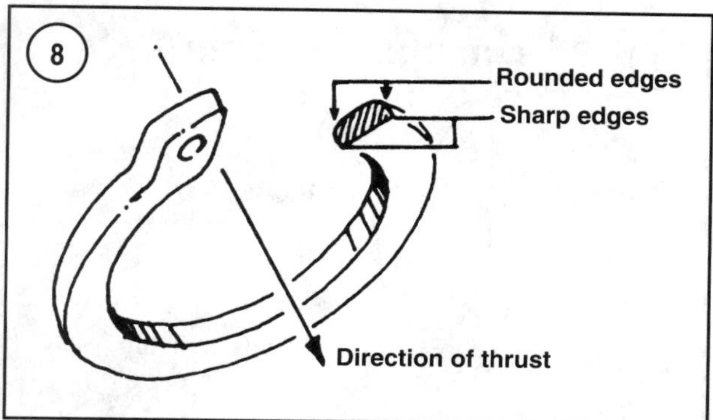

patible with other brake fluids. When adding brake fluid, *only* use the fluid recommended by the manufacturer.

Brake fluid will damage any plastic, painted or plated surface it contacts. Use extreme care when working with brake fluid and remove any spills immediately with soap and water.

Hydraulic brake systems require clean and moisture-free brake fluid. Never reuse brake fluid. Keep containers and reservoirs properly sealed.

WARNING
Never put a mineral-based (petroleum) oil into the brake system. Mineral oil causes rubber parts in the system to swell and break apart, which causes complete brake failure.

Cleaners, Degreasers and Solvents

Many chemicals are available to remove oil, grease and other residue from the motorcycle. Before using cleaning solvents, consider how they will be used and disposed of, particularly if they are not water-soluble. Local ordinances might require special procedures for the disposal of many types of cleaning chemicals. Refer to *Safety* in this chapter.

Use brake parts cleaner to clean brake system components. Brake parts cleaner leaves no residue. Use electrical contact cleaner to clean electrical connections and components without leaving any residue. Carburetor cleaner is a powerful solvent used to remove fuel deposits and varnish from fuel system components. Use this cleaner carefully. It can damage finishes.

Generally, degreasers are strong cleaners used to remove heavy accumulations of grease from engine and frame components.

Most solvents are designed to be used with a parts washing cabinet for individual component cleaning. For safety, use only nonflammable or high flash point solvents.

Gasket Sealant

Sealant is used in combination with a gasket or seal. In other applications, such as between crankcase halves, only a sealant is used. Follow the manufacturer's recommendation when using a sealant. Use extreme care when choosing a sealant different from the type originally recommended. Choose sealant based on its resistance to heat, various fluids and its sealing capabilities.

A common sealant is room temperature vulcanization sealant, or RTV. This sealant cures at room temperature over a specific time period. This allows the repositioning of components without damaging gaskets.

Moisture in the air causes the RTV sealant to cure. Always install the tube cap as soon as possible after applying RTV sealant. RTV sealant has a limited shelf life and will not cure properly if the shelf life has expired. Keep partial tubes sealed and discard them if they have surpassed the expiration date.

Applying RTV sealant

Clean all old gasket residue from the mating surfaces. Remove all gasket material from blind threaded holes to avoid inaccurate bolt torque. Spray the mating surfaces with aerosol parts cleaner. Then wipe with a lint-free cloth. The area must be clean for the sealant to adhere.

Apply RTV sealant in a continuous bead 0.08-0.12 in. (2-3 mm) thick. Circle all the fastener holes unless otherwise specified. Do not allow any sealant to enter these holes. Assemble and tighten the fasteners to the specified torque within the time frame recommended by the sealant manufacturer.

Gasket Remover

Aerosol gasket remover can help remove stubborn gaskets. This product can speed up the removal process and prevent damage to the mating surface that may be caused by using a scraping tool. Most of these types of products are very caustic. Follow the gasket remover manufacturer's instructions for use.

Threadlocking Compound

A threadlocking compound is a fluid applied to the threads of fasteners. After tightening the fastener, the fluid dries and becomes a solid filler between the threads.

This makes it difficult for the fastener to work loose from vibration or heat expansion and contraction. Some threadlocking compounds also provide a seal against fluid leaks.

Before applying a threadlocking compound, remove any old compound from both thread areas and clean them with aerosol parts cleaner. Use the compound sparingly. Excess fluid can run into adjoining parts.

CAUTION

Threadlocking compounds are anaerobic and will stress, crack and attack most plastics. Use caution when using these products in areas where there are plastic components.

Threadlocking compounds are available in a wide range of compounds for various strength, temperature and repair applications. Follow the manufacturer's recommendations regarding compound selection.

BASIC TOOLS

Most of the procedures in this manual can be carried out with simple hand tools and test equipment familiar to the home mechanic. Always use the correct tools for the job at hand. Keep tools organized and clean. Store them in a tool chest with related tools organized together.

Quality tools are essential. The best are constructed of high-strength alloy steel. These tools are light, easy to use and resistant to wear. The working surfaces are devoid of sharp edges and carefully polished. They have an easy-to-clean finish and are comfortable to use. Quality tools are a good investment.

Some of the procedures in this manual specify special tools. In many cases, the tool is illustrated in use. Those with a large tool kit may be able to use a suitable substitute or fabricate a suitable replacement. However, in some cases, the specialized equipment or expertise may make it impractical for the home mechanic to attempt the procedure. When necessary, such operations come with the recommendation to have a dealership or specialist perform the task. It may be less expensive to have a professional perform these jobs, especially when considering the cost of equipment.

When purchasing tools to perform the procedures covered in this manual, consider the potential frequency of use. If a tool kit is just now being started, consider purchasing a basic tool set from a quality tool supplier. These sets are available in many tool combinations and offer substantial savings when compared to individually purchased tools. As work experience grows and tasks become more complicated, specialized tools can be added.

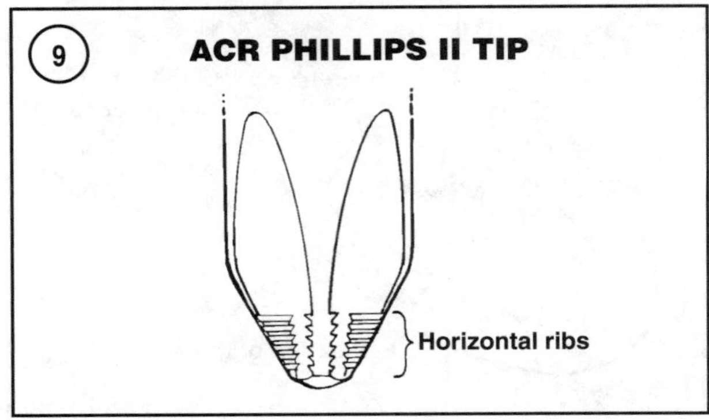

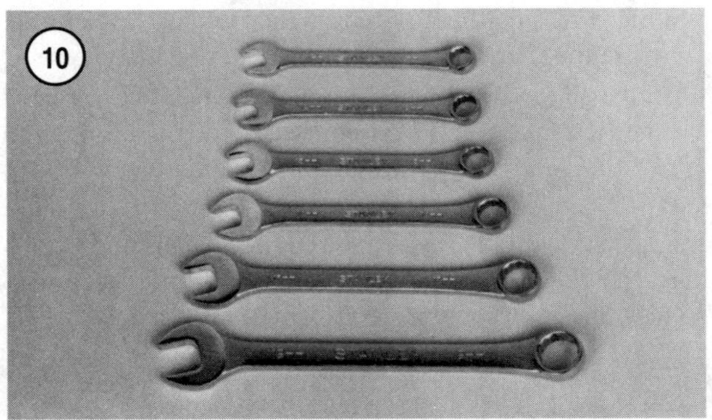

Screwdrivers

Screwdrivers of various lengths and types are mandatory for the simplest tool kit. The two basic types are the slotted tip (flat blade) and the Phillips tip. These are available in sets that often include an assortment of tip sizes and shaft lengths.

As with all tools, use a screwdriver designed for the job. Make sure the size of the tip conforms to the size and shape of the fastener. Use them only for driving screws. Never use a screwdriver for prying or chiseling metal. Repair or replace worn or damaged screwdrivers. A worn tip may damage the fastener and make it difficult to remove.

Phillips-head screws are often damaged by incorrectly fitting screwdrivers. Quality Phillips screwdrivers are manufactured with their crosshead tip machined to Phillips Screw Company specifications. Poor quality or damaged Phillips screwdrivers can back out (camout) and round over the screw head. In addition, weak or soft screw materials can make removal difficult.

The best type of screwdriver to use on Phillips screws is the ACR Phillips II screwdriver, patented by the Phillips Screw Company. ACR stands for the horizontal anti-camout ribs found on the driving faces or flutes of the screwdriver tip (**Figure 9**). ACR Phillips II screwdrivers

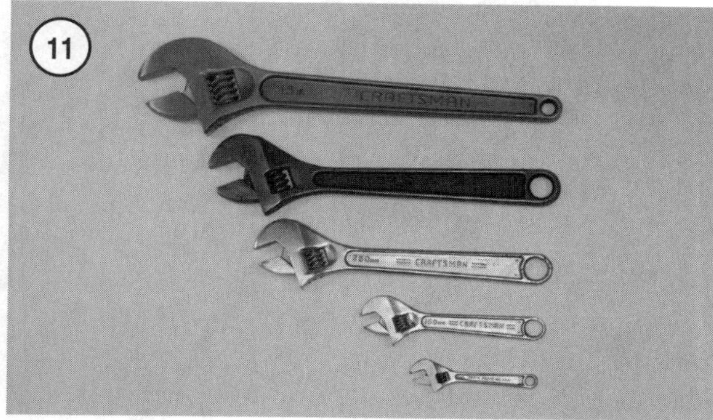
11

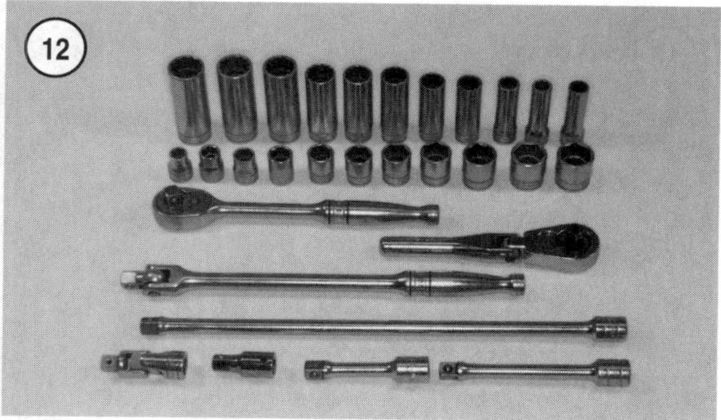
12

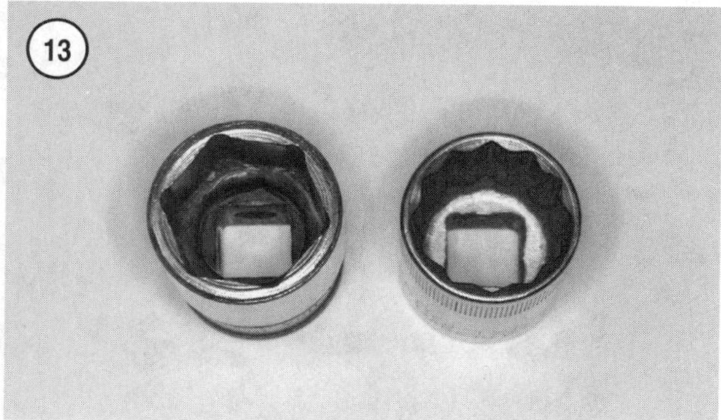
13

were designed as part of a manufacturing drive system to be used with ACR Phillips II screws, but they work well on all common Phillips screws. A number of tool companies offer ACR Phillips II screwdrivers in different tip sizes and interchangeable bits to fit screwdriver bit holders.

NOTE

Another way to prevent camout and to increase the grip of a Phillips screwdriver is to apply valve-grinding compound or Permatex Screw & Socket Gripper to the screwdriver tip. After loosening/tightening the screw, clean the screw recess to prevent engine oil contamination.

Wrenches

Open-end, box-end and combination wrenches (**Figure 10**) are available in a variety of types and sizes.

The number stamped on the wrench refers to the distance between the work areas. This size must match the size of the fastener head.

The box-end wrench is an excellent tool because it grips the fastener on all sides. This reduces the chance of the tool slipping. The box-end wrench is designed with either a 6- or 12-point opening. For stubborn or damaged fasteners, the 6-point provides superior holding because it contacts the fastener across a wider area at all six edges. For general use, the 12-point works well. It allows the wrench to be removed and reinstalled without moving the handle over such a wide arc.

An open-end wrench is fast and works best in areas with limited overhead access. It contacts the fastener at only two points and is subject to slipping if under heavy force, or if the tool or fastener is worn. A box-end wrench is preferred in most instances, especially when breaking loose and applying the final tightness to a fastener.

The combination wrench has a box-end on one end and an open-end on the other. This combination makes it a convenient tool.

Adjustable Wrenches

An adjustable wrench or Crescent wrench (**Figure 11**) can fit nearly any nut or bolt head that has clear access around its entire perimeter. An adjustable wrench is best used as a backup wrench to keep a large nut or bolt from turning while the other end is being loosened or tightened with a box-end or socket wrench.

Adjustable wrenches contact the fastener at only two points, which makes them more subject to slipping off the fastener. Because one jaw is adjustable and may become loose, this shortcoming is aggravated. Make certain the solid jaw is the one transmitting the force.

Socket Wrenches, Ratchets and Handles

Sockets that attach to a ratchet handle (**Figure 12**) are available with 6-point or 12-point openings (**Figure 13**) and different drive sizes. The drive size indicates the size of the square hole that accepts the ratchet handle. The

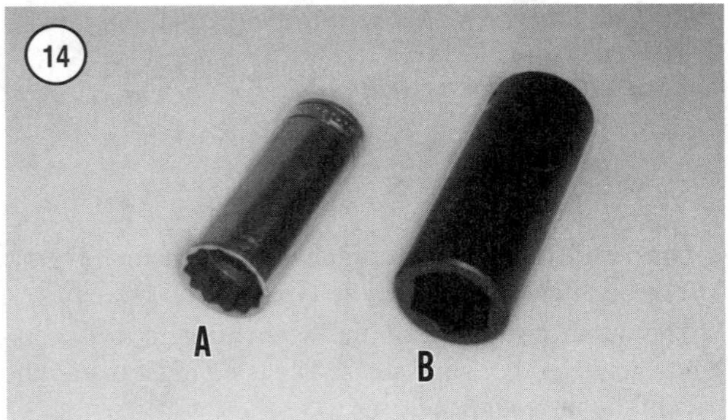

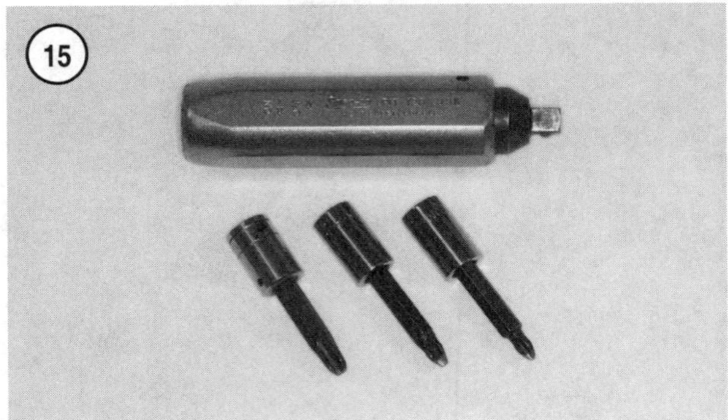

number stamped on the socket is the size of the work area and must match the fastener head.

As with wrenches, a 6-point socket provides superior holding ability, but a 12-point socket needs to be moved only half as far to reposition it on the fastener.

Sockets are designated for either hand or impact use. Impact sockets are made of thicker material for more durability. Compare the size and wall thickness of a 19-mm hand socket (A, **Figure 14**) and the 19-mm impact socket (B). Use impact sockets when using an impact driver or air tools. Use hand sockets with hand-driven attachments.

WARNING
Do not use hand sockets with air or impact tools because they can shatter and cause injury. Always wear eye protection when using impact or air tools.

Various handles are available for sockets. Use the speed handle for fast operation. Flexible ratchet heads in varying lengths allow the socket to be turned with varying force and at odd angles. Extension bars allow the socket setup to reach difficult areas. The ratchet is the most versatile. It allows the user to install or remove the nut without removing the socket.

Sockets combined with any number of drivers make them undoubtedly the fastest, safest and most convenient tool for fastener removal and installation.

Impact Drivers

An impact driver provides extra force for removing fasteners by converting the impact of a hammer into a turning motion. This makes it possible to remove stubborn fasteners without damaging them. Impact drivers and interchangeable bits (**Figure 15**) are available from most tool suppliers. When using a socket with an impact driver, make sure the socket is designed for impact use. Refer to *Socket Wrenches, Ratchets and Handles* in this section.

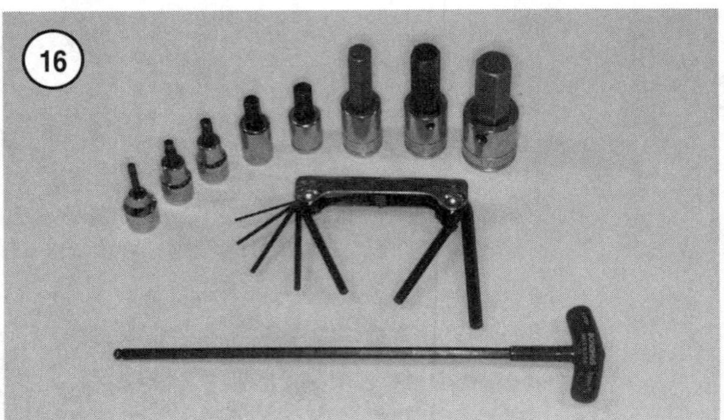

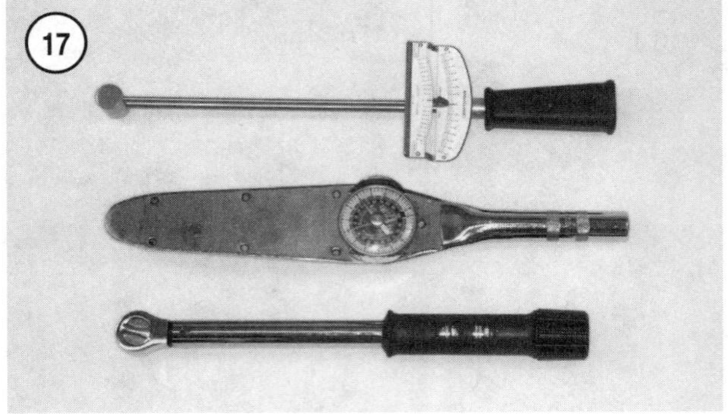

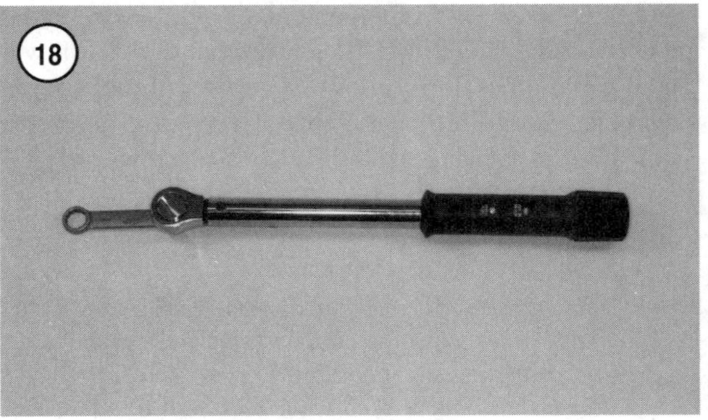

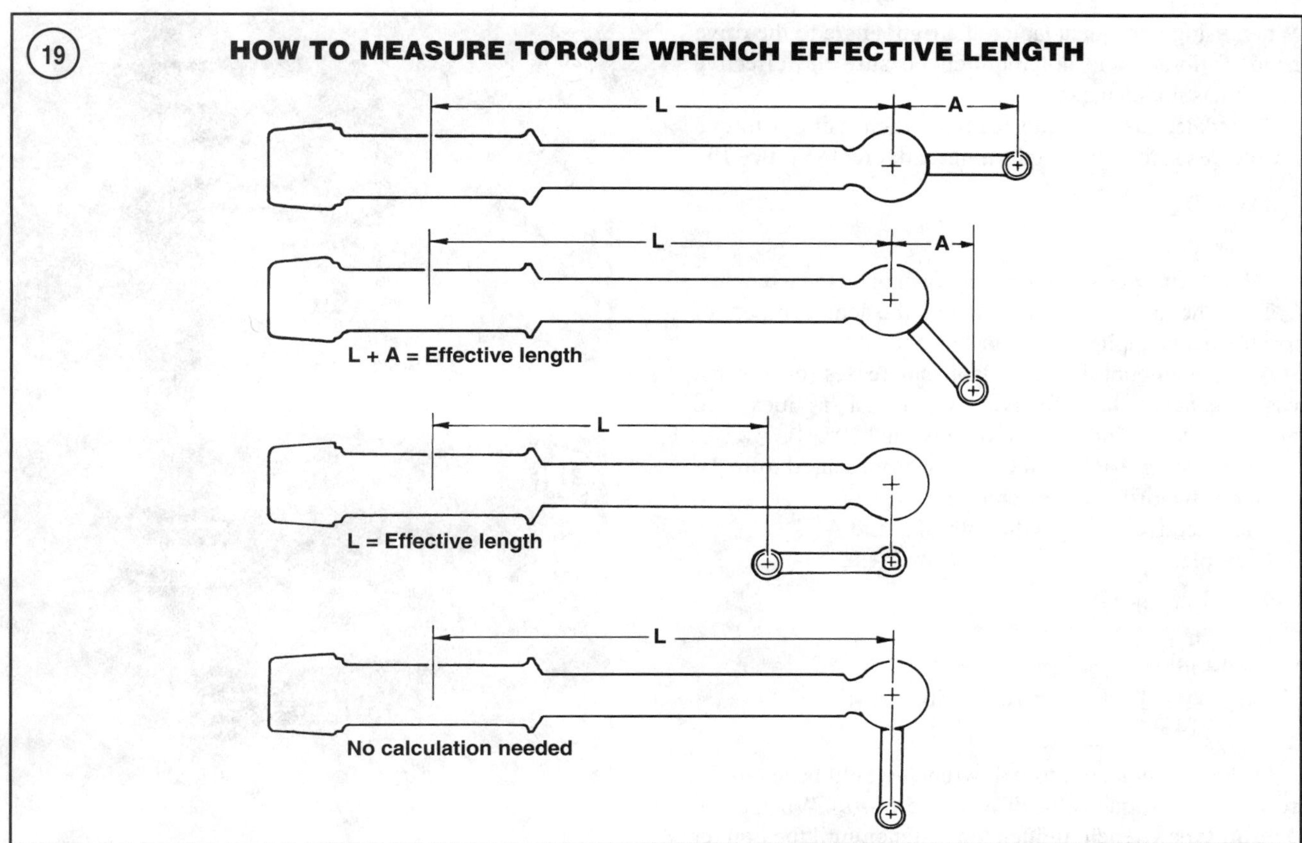

WARNING
Do not use hand sockets with air or impact tools because they can shatter and cause injury. Always wear eye protection when using impact or air tools.

Allen Wrenches

Use Allen or setscrew wrenches (**Figure 16**) on fasteners with hexagonal recesses in the fastener head. These wrenches are available in L-shaped bar, socket and T-handle types. An inch and metric set is required when working on Harley-Davidson motorcycles. Allen bolts are sometimes called socket bolts.

Torque Wrenches

Use a torque wrench with a socket, torque adapter or similar extension to tighten a fastener to a measured torque. Torque wrenches come in several drive sizes (1/4, 3/8, 1/2 and 3/4) and have various methods of reading the torque value. The drive size indicates the size of the square drive that accepts the socket, adapter or extension. Common methods of reading the torque value are the deflecting beam, the dial indicator and the audible click (**Figure 17**).

When choosing a torque wrench, consider the torque range, drive size and accuracy. The torque specifications in this manual provide an indication of the range required.

A torque wrench is a precision tool that must be properly cared for to remain accurate. Store torque wrenches in cases or separate padded drawers within a toolbox. Follow the manufacturer's instructions for care and calibration.

Torque Adapters

Torque adapters or extensions extend or reduce the reach of a torque wrench. The torque adapter shown in **Figure 18** is used to tighten a fastener that cannot be reached because of the size of the torque wrench head, drive and socket. If a torque adapter changes the effective lever length (**Figure 19**), the torque reading on the wrench will not equal the actual torque applied to the fastener. It is necessary to recalibrate the torque setting on the wrench to compensate for the change of lever length.

When using a torque adapter at a right angle to the drive head, calibration is not required because the effective length has not changed.

To recalculate a torque reading when using a torque adapter, use the following formula and refer to **Figure 19**:

$$TW = \frac{TA \times L}{L + A}$$

TW is the torque setting or dial reading on the wrench.

TA is the torque specification and the actual amount of torque that is applied to the fastener.

A is the amount that the adapter increases (or in some cases reduces) the effective lever length as measured along the centerline of the torque wrench.

L is the lever length of the wrench as measured from the center of the drive to the center of the grip.

The effective length is the sum of L and A.

Example:

TA = 20 ft.-lb.
A = 3 in.
L = 14 in.

$$TW = \frac{20 \times 14}{14 + 3} = \frac{280}{17} = 16.5 \text{ ft. lb.}$$

In this example, the torque wrench would be set to the recalculated torque value (TW = 16.5 ft.-lb.). When using a beam-type wrench, tighten the fastener until the pointer aligns with 16.5 ft.-lb. In this example, although the torque wrench is preset to 16.5 ft.-lb., the actual torque is 20 ft.-lb.

Pliers

Pliers come in a wide range of types and sizes. Pliers are useful for holding, cutting, bending and crimping. Do not use them to turn fasteners. **Figure 20** and **Figure 21** show several types of useful pliers. Each design has a specialized function. Slip-joint pliers are general-purpose pliers used for gripping and bending. Diagonal cutting pliers are needed to cut wire and can be used to remove cotter pins. Use needlenose pliers to hold or bend small objects. Locking pliers (**Figure 21**), sometimes called Vise-Grips, are used to hold objects very tightly. They have many uses ranging from holding two parts together to gripping the end of a broken stud. Use caution when using locking pliers. The sharp jaws will damage the objects they hold.

Snap Ring Pliers

Snap ring pliers are specialized pliers with tips that fit into the ends of snap rings to remove and install them.

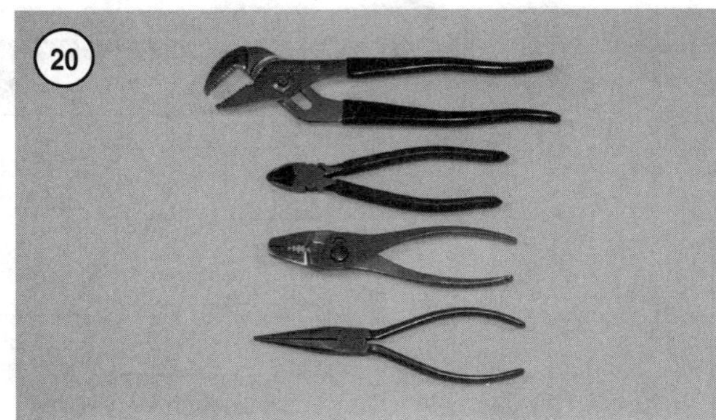

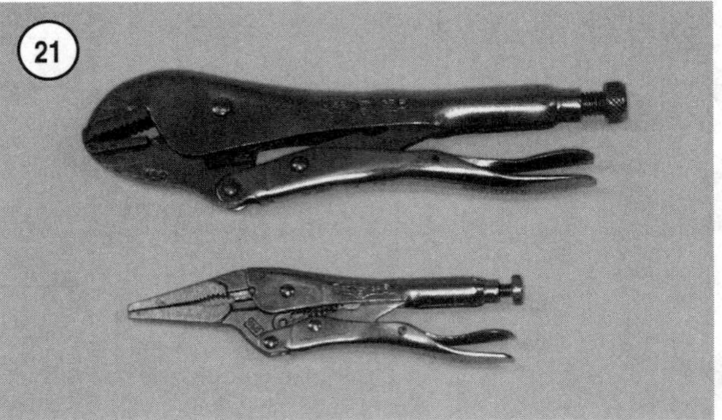

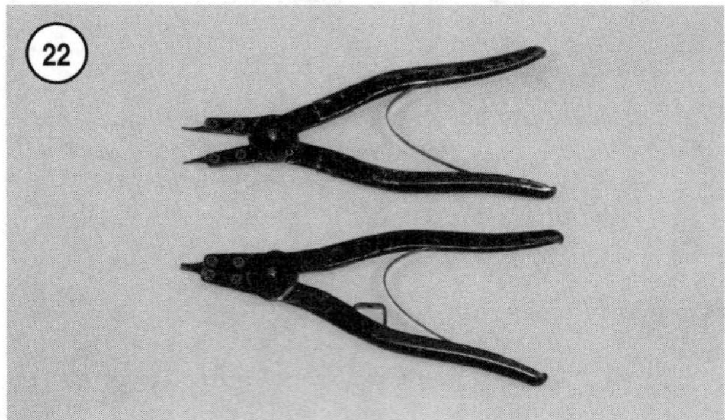

Snap ring pliers (**Figure 22**) are available with a fixed action (either internal or external) or are convertible (one tool works on both internal and external snap rings). They may have fixed tips or interchangeable ones of various sizes and angles. For general use, select convertible pliers with interchangeable tips (**Figure 22**).

WARNING
Snap rings can slip and fly off when removing and installing them. Also, snap ring pliers tips can break. Always wear eye protection when using snap ring pliers.

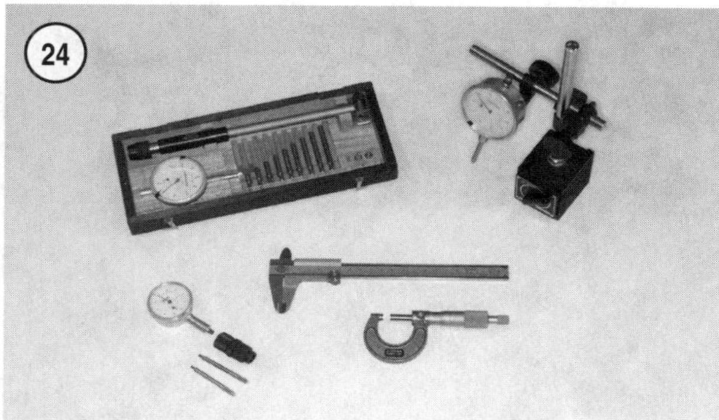

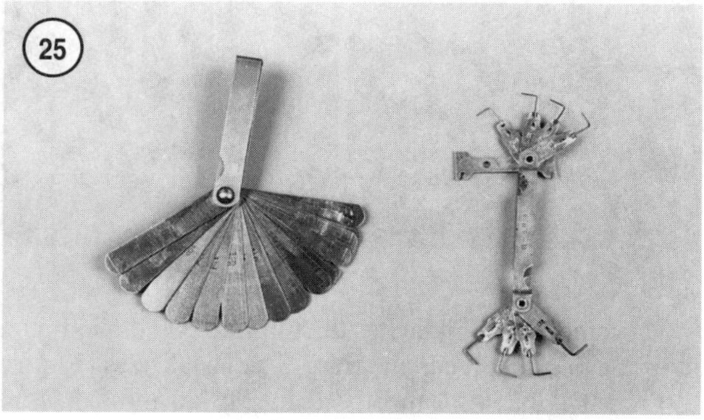

Hammers

Various types of hammers are available to fit a number of applications. Use a ball-peen hammer to strike another tool, such as a punch or chisel. Use soft-faced hammers when a metal object must be struck without damaging it. Never use a metal-faced hammer on engine and suspension components because damage occurs in most cases.

Always wear eye protection when using hammers. Make sure the hammer face is in good condition and the handle is not cracked. Select the correct hammer for the job and make sure to strike the object squarely. Do not use the handle or the side of the hammer to strike an object.

SPECIAL TOOLS

Many of the procedures in this manual require special tools. These are described in the appropriate chapter and are available from either the manufacturer or a tool supplier. Always follow the manufacturer's instructions when using the special tools (**Figure 23**). See **Table 12**.

In many cases, an acceptable substitute may be found in an existing tool kit. Another alternative is to make the tool. Many schools with a machine shop curriculum welcome outside work that can be used as practical shop applications for students.

PRECISION MEASURING TOOLS

The ability to accurately measure components is essential to perform many of the procedures described in this manual. Equipment is manufactured to close tolerances, and obtaining consistently accurate measurements is essential to determine which components require replacement or further service.

Each type of measuring instrument (**Figure 24**) is designed to measure a dimension with a certain degree of accuracy and within a certain range. When selecting the measuring tool, make sure it is applicable to the task.

As with all tools, measuring tools provide the best results if cared for properly. Improper use can damage the tool and cause inaccurate results. If any measurement is questionable, verify the measurement using another tool. A standard gauge is usually provided with micrometers to check accuracy and calibrate the tool if necessary.

Precision measurements can vary according to the experience of the person performing the procedure. Accurate results are only possible if the mechanic possesses a feel for using the tool. Heavy-handed use of measuring tools produces less accurate results. Hold the tool gently by the fingertips to easily feel the point at which the tool contacts the object. This feel for the equipment produces more accurate measurements and reduces the risk of damaging the tool or component. Refer to the following sections for specific measuring tools.

Feeler Gauge

Use feeler or thickness gauges (**Figure 25**) for measuring the distance between two surfaces.

A feeler gauge set consists of an assortment of steel strips of graduated thickness. Each blade is marked with its thickness. Blades can be of various lengths and angles for different procedures.

A common use for a feeler gauge is to measure valve clearance. Use wire (round) gauges to measure spark plug gaps.

Calipers

Calipers (**Figure 26**) are excellent tools for obtaining inside, outside and depth measurements. Although not as precise as a micrometer, they allow reasonable precision, typically to within 0.001 in. (0.05 mm). Most calipers have a range up to 6 in. (150 mm).

Calipers are available in dial, vernier or digital versions. Dial calipers have a dial readout that provides convenient reading. Vernier calipers have marked scales that must be compared to determine the measurement. The digital caliper uses a liquid-crystal display (LCD) to show the measurement.

Properly maintain the measuring surfaces of the caliper. There must not be any dirt or burrs between the tool and the object being measured. Never force the caliper to close around an object. Close the caliper around the highest point so it can be removed with a slight drag. Some calipers require calibration. Always refer to the manufacturer's instructions when using a new or unfamiliar caliper.

To read a vernier caliper refer to **Figure 27**. The fixed scale is marked in 1-mm increments. Ten individual lines on the fixed scale equal 1 cm. The movable scale is marked in 0.05 mm (five-hundredth) increments. To obtain a reading, establish the first number by the location of the 0 line on the movable scale in relation to the first line to the left on the fixed scale. In this example, the number is 10 mm. To determine the next number, note which of the lines on the movable scale align with a mark on the fixed scale. A number of lines will seem close, but only one will align exactly. In this case, 0.50 mm is the reading to add to the first number. Adding 10 mm and 0.50 mm equals a measurement of 10.50 mm.

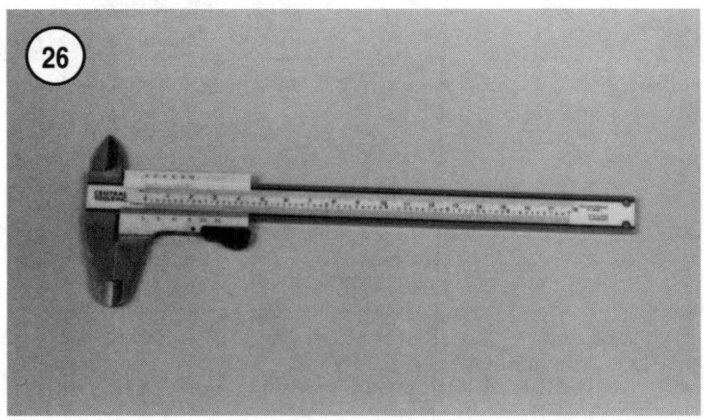

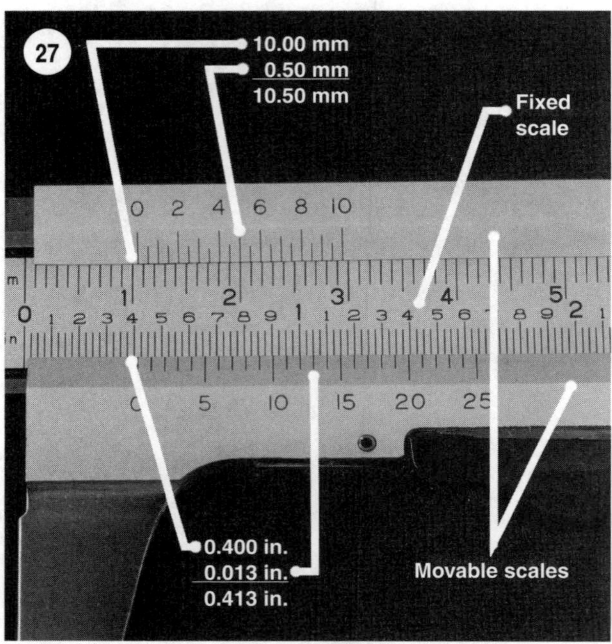

Micrometers

A micrometer is an instrument designed for linear measurement using the decimal divisions of the inch or meter (**Figure 28**). While there are many types and styles of micrometers, most of the procedures in this manual call for an outside micrometer. Use the outside micrometer to measure the outside diameter of cylindrical forms and the thickness of materials.

Micrometer size indicates the minimum and maximum size of a part that it can measure. The usual sizes (**Figure 29**) are 0-1 in. (0-25 mm), 1-2 in. (25-50 mm), 2-3 in. (50-75 mm) and 3-4 in. (75-100 mm).

Micrometers that cover a wider range of measurements are available. These use a large frame with interchangeable anvils of various lengths. This type of micrometer offers a cost savings, but its overall size may make it less convenient.

Adjustment

Before using a micrometer, check its adjustment as follows:

1. Clean the anvil and spindle faces.
2A. To check a 0-1 in. or 0-25 mm micrometer:

28

DECIMAL PLACE VALUES*

0.1	Indicates 1/10 (one tenth of an inch or millimeter)
0.010	Indicates 1/100 (one one-hundreth of an inch or millimeter)
0.001	Indicates 1/1,000 (one one-thousandth of an inch or millimeter)

*This chart represents the values of figures placed to the right of the decimal point. Use it when reading decimals from one-tenth to one one-thousandth of an inch or millimeter. It is not a conversion chart (for example: 0.001 in. is not equal to 0.001 mm).

a. Turn the thimble until the spindle contacts the anvil. If the micrometer has a ratchet stop, use it to make sure that the proper amount of pressure is applied.

b. If the adjustment is correct, the 0 mark on the thimble will align exactly with the 0 mark on the sleeve line. If the marks do not align, the micrometer is out of adjustment.

c. Follow the manufacturer's instructions to adjust the micrometer.

2B. To check a micrometer larger than 1 in. or 25 mm use the standard gauge supplied by the manufacturer. A standard gauge is a steel block, disc or rod that is machined to an exact size.

a. Place the standard gauge between the spindle and anvil, and measure its outside diameter or length. If the micrometer has a ratchet stop, use it to make sure that the proper amount of pressure is applied.

b. If the adjustment is correct, the 0 mark on the thimble will align exactly with the 0 mark on the sleeve line. If the marks do not align, the micrometer is out of adjustment.

c. Follow the manufacturer's instructions to adjust the micrometer.

Care

Micrometers are precision instruments. They must be used and maintained with great care. Note the following:

1. Store micrometers in protective cases or separate padded drawers in a toolbox.
2. When in storage, make sure the spindle and anvil faces do not contact each other or an other object. If they do, temperature changes and corrosion may damage the contact faces.
3. Do not clean a micrometer with compressed air. Dirt forced into the tool will cause wear.
4. Lubricate micrometers with WD-40 to prevent corrosion.

Reading

When reading a micrometer, numbers are taken from different scales and added together. The following sections describe how to read the measurements of various types of outside micrometers.

For accurate results, properly maintain the measuring surfaces of the micrometer. There cannot be any dirt or burrs between the tool and the measured object. Never force the micrometer to close around an object. Close the micrometer around the highest point so it can be removed with a slight drag.

Metric micrometer

The standard metric micrometer (**Figure 30**) is accurate to one hundredth of a millimeter (0.01 mm). The sleeve line is graduated in millimeter and half-millimeter increments. The marks on the upper half of the sleeve line equal 1.00 mm. Each fifth mark above the sleeve line is identified with a number. The number sequence depends on the size of the micrometer. A 0-25 mm micrometer, for example, will have sleeve marks numbered 0 through 25 in 5 mm increments. This numbering sequence continues with larger micrometers. On all metric micrometers, each mark on the lower half of the sleeve equals 0.50 mm.

The tapered end of the thimble has 50 lines marked around it. Each mark equals 0.01 mm. One complete turn of the thimble aligns its 0 mark with the first line on the lower half of the sleeve line or 0.50 mm.

When reading a metric micrometer, add the number of millimeters and half millimeters on the sleeve line to the number of hundredths of millimeters on the thimble. Perform the following steps while referring to **Figure 30**.

1. Read the upper half of the sleeve line and count the number of lines visible. Each upper line equals 1 mm.
2. See if the half-millimeter line is visible on the lower sleeve line. If so, add 0.50 mm to the reading in Step 1.
3. Read the thimble mark that aligns with the sleeve line. Each thimble mark equals 0.01 mm.

NOTE

If a thimble mark does not align exactly with the sleeve line, estimate the amount between the lines. For accurate readings in two-thousandths of a millimeter (0.002 mm), use a metric vernier micrometer.

4. Add the readings from Steps 1-3.

Standard inch micrometer

The standard inch micrometer (**Figure 31**) is accurate to one thousandth of an inch or 0.001 in. The sleeve is marked in 0.025 in. increments. Every fourth sleeve mark is numbered 1, 2, 3, 4, 5, 6, 7, 8, 9. These numbers indicate 0.100 in., 0.200 in., 0.300 in. and so on.

The tapered end of the thimble has 25 lines marked around it. Each mark equals 0.001 in. One complete turn of the thimble will align its zero mark with the first mark on the sleeve or 0.025 in.

To read a standard inch micrometer, perform the following steps and refer to **Figure 31**.

1. Read the sleeve and find the largest number visible. Each sleeve number equals 0.100 in.
2. Count the number of lines between the numbered sleeve mark and the edge of the thimble. Each sleeve mark equals 0.025 in.
3. Read the thimble mark that aligns with the sleeve line. Each thimble mark equals 0.001 in.

NOTE

If a thimble mark does not align exactly with the sleeve line, estimate the amount between the lines. For accurate readings in ten-thousandths of an inch (0.0001 in.), use a vernier inch micrometer.

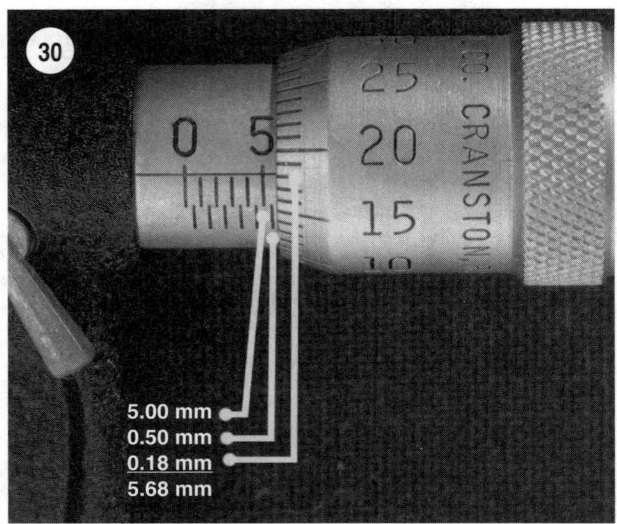

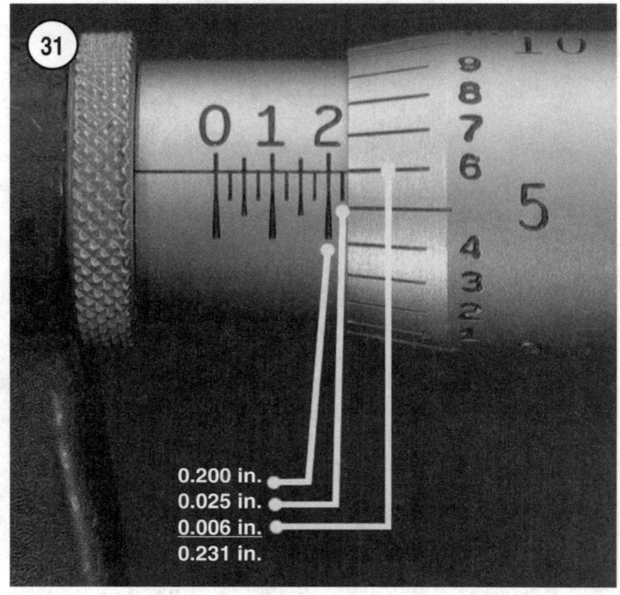

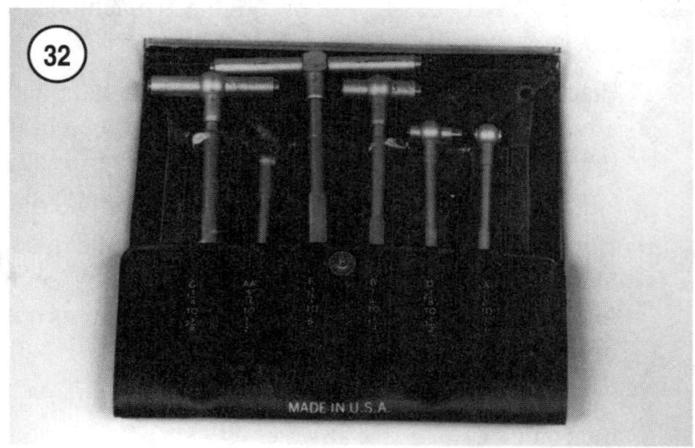

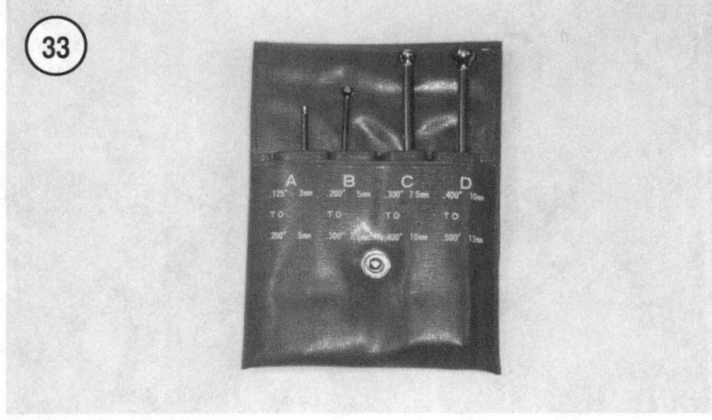
33

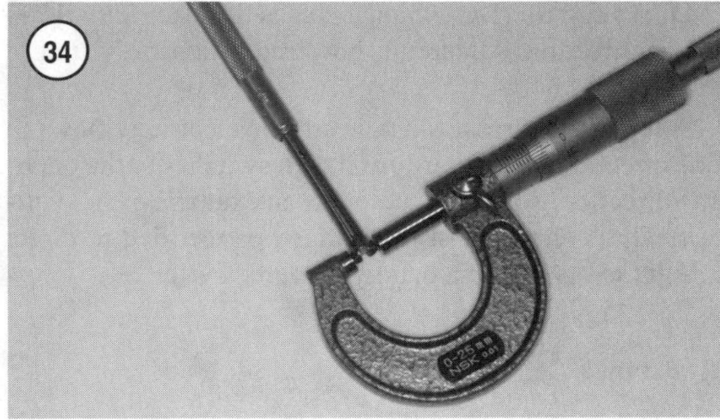
34

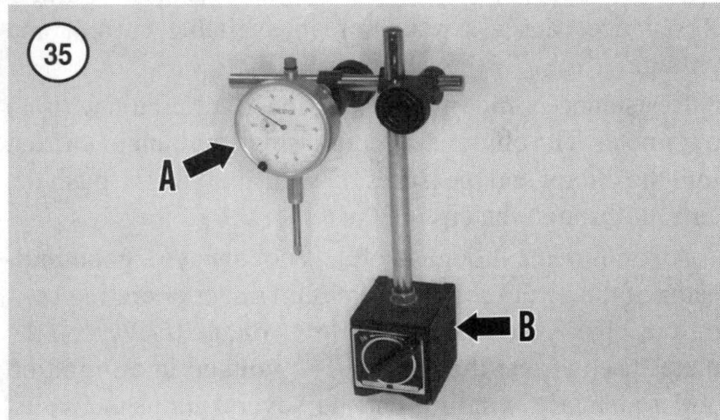

35

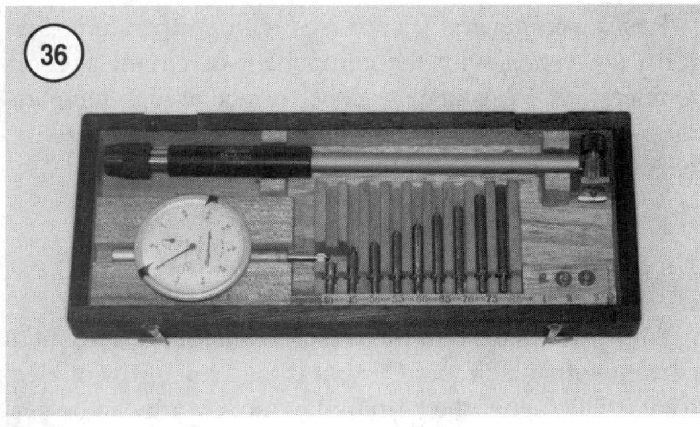
36

4. Add the readings from Steps 1-3.

Telescoping and Small-Bore Gauges

Use telescoping gauges (**Figure 32**) and small-bore gauges (**Figure 33**) to measure bores. Neither gauge has a scale for direct readings. Use an outside micrometer to determine the reading.

To use a telescoping gauge, select the correct size gauge for the bore. Compress the movable post and carefully insert the gauge into the bore. Carefully move the gauge in the bore to make sure it is centered. Tighten the knurled end of the gauge to hold the movable post in position. Remove the gauge and measure the length of the posts. Telescoping gauges are typically used to measure cylinder bores.

To use a small-bore gauge, select the correctly sized gauge for the bore. Carefully insert the gauge into the bore. Tighten the knurled end of the gauge to carefully expand the gauge fingers to the limit within the bore. Do not overtighten the gauge because there is no built-in release. Excessive tightening can damage the bore surface and damage the tool. Remove the gauge and measure the outside dimension (**Figure 34**). Small bore gauges are typically used to measure valve guides.

Dial Indicator

A dial indicator (A, **Figure 35**) is a gauge with a dial face and needle used to measure variations in dimensions and movements. Measuring brake rotor runout is a typical use for a dial indicator.

Dial indicators are available in various ranges and graduations and with three basic types of mounting bases: magnetic (B, **Figure 35**), clamp or screw-in stud. When purchasing a dial indicator, select one with a continuous dial (A, **Figure 35**).

Cylinder-Bore Gauge

A cylinder-bore gauge is similar to a dial indicator. The gauge set shown in **Figure 36** consists of a dial indicator, handle, and different length adapters (anvils) to fit the gauge to various bore sizes. The bore gauge is used to measure bore size, taper and out-of-round. When using a bore gauge, follow the manufacturer's instructions.

Compression Gauge

A compression gauge (**Figure 37**) measures combustion chamber (cylinder) pressure, usually in psi or kg/cm^2.

The gauge adapter is either inserted or screwed into the spark plug hole to obtain the reading. Disable the engine so it will not start, and hold the throttle in the wide-open position when performing a compression test. An engine that does not have adequate compression cannot be properly tuned. See Chapter Three.

Multimeter

A multimeter (**Figure 38**) is an essential tool for electrical system diagnosis. The voltage function indicates the voltage applied or available to various electrical components. The ohmmeter function tests circuits for continuity or lack of continuity and measures the resistance of a circuit.

Some manufacturers' specifications for electrical components are based on results using a specific test meter. Results may vary if using a meter not recommended by the manufacturer. Such requirements are noted when applicable.

Ohmmeter (Analog) Calibration

Each time an analog ohmmeter is used, or if the scale is changed, the ohmmeter must be calibrated.

Digital ohmmeters do not require calibration.

1. Make sure the meter battery is in good condition.
2. Make sure the meter probes are in good condition.
3. Touch the two probes together and observe the needle location on the ohms scale. The needle must align with the 0 mark to obtain accurate measurements.
4. If necessary, rotate the meter ohms adjust knob until the needle and 0 mark align.

ELECTRICAL SYSTEM FUNDAMENTALS

A thorough study of the many types of electrical systems used in today's motorcycles is beyond the scope of this manual. However, an understanding of electrical basics is necessary to perform simple diagnostic tests.

Refer to *Electrical Testing* in Chapter Two for typical test procedures and equipment. Refer to Chapter Nine for specific system test procedures.

Voltage

Voltage is the electrical potential or pressure in an electrical circuit and is expressed in volts. The more pressure (voltage) in a circuit, the more work can be performed.

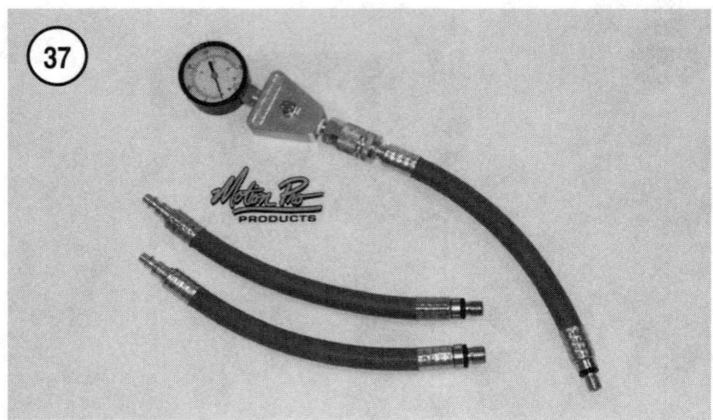

Direct current (DC) voltage means the electricity flows in one direction. All circuits powered by a battery are DC circuits.

Alternating current (AC) means the electricity flows in one direction momentarily and then switches to the opposite direction. Alternator output is an example of AC voltage. This voltage must be changed or rectified to direct current to operate in a battery powered system.

Resistance

Resistance is the opposition to the flow of electricity within a circuit or component and is measured in ohms. Resistance causes a reduction in available current and voltage.

Resistance is measured in an inactive circuit with an ohmmeter. The ohmmeter sends a small amount of current into the circuit and measures how difficult it is to push the current through the circuit.

An ohmmeter, though useful, is not always a good indicator of the actual ability of a circuit under operating conditions. This is because of the low voltage (6-9 volts) the meter uses to test the circuit. The voltage in an ignition coil secondary winding can be several thousand volts. Such high voltage can cause the coil to malfunction, even though it tests acceptable during a resistance test.

Resistance generally increases with temperature. Perform all testing with the component or circuit at room temperature. Resistance tests performed at high temperatures can indicate high resistance readings and cause unnecessary replacement of a component.

Amperage

Amperage is the unit of measurement for the amount of current within a circuit. Current is the actual flow of electricity. The higher the current, the more work can be per-

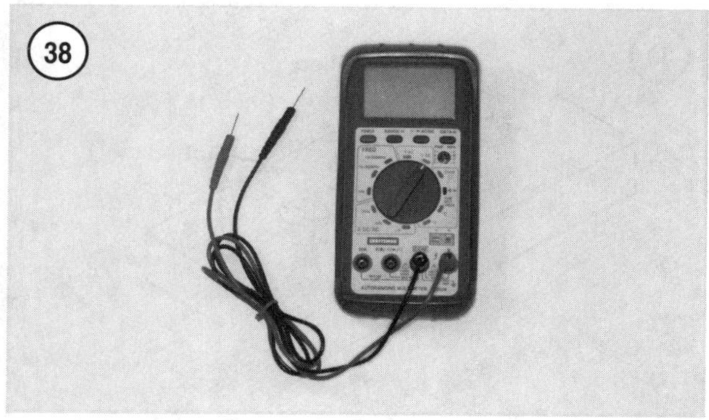

38

formed up to a given point. If the current flow exceeds the circuit or component capacity, it will damage the system.

BASIC SERVICE METHODS

Most of the procedures in this manual are straightforward and can be performed by anyone reasonably competent with tools. However, consider personal capabilities carefully before attempting any operation involving major disassembly.

1. In this manual, *front* refers to the front of the motorcycle. The front of any component is the end closest to the front of the motorcycle. The left and right sides refer to the position of the parts as viewed by the rider sitting on the seat facing forward.

2. Whenever servicing an engine or suspension component, secure the motorcycle in a safe manner.

3. Tag all similar parts for location and mark all mating parts for position. Record the number and thickness of any shims when removing them. Identify parts by placing them in sealed and labeled plastic sandwich bags.

4. Tag disconnected wires and connectors with masking tape and a marking pen. Do not rely on memory alone.

5. Protect finished surfaces from physical damage or corrosion. Keep gasoline and other chemicals off painted surfaces.

6. Use penetrating oil on frozen or tight bolts. Avoid using heat where possible. Heat can warp, melt or affect the temper of parts. Heat also damages the finish of paint and plastics.

7. When a part is a press fit or requires a special tool for removal, the information or type of tool is identified in the text. Otherwise, if a part is difficult to remove or install, determine the cause before proceeding.

8. To prevent objects or debris from falling into the engine, cover all openings.

9. Read each procedure thoroughly and compare the illustrations to the actual components before starting the procedure. Perform the procedure in sequence.

10. Recommendations are occasionally made to refer service to a dealership or specialist. In these cases, the work can be performed more economically by the specialist than by the home mechanic.

11. The term *replace* means to discard a defective part and replace it with a new part. *Overhaul* means to remove, disassemble, inspect, measure, repair and/or replace parts as required to recondition an assembly.

12. Some operations require using a hydraulic press. If a press is not available, have these operations performed by a shop equipped with the necessary equipment. Do not use makeshift equipment that can damage the motorcycle.

13. Repairs are much faster and easier if the motorcycle is clean before starting work. Degrease the motorcycle with a commercial degreaser; follow the directions on the container for the best results. Clean all parts with cleaning solvent when removing them.

CAUTION

Do not direct high-pressure water at steering bearings, fuel hoses, wheel bearings, suspension and electrical components. Water can force grease out of the bearings and possibly damage the seals.

14. If special tools are required, have them available before starting the procedure. When special tools are required, they are described at the beginning of the procedure.

15. Make diagrams of similar-appearing parts. For instance, crankcase bolts are often not the same lengths. Do not rely on memory alone. Carefully laid out parts can become disturbed and make it difficult to reassemble the components correctly.

16. Make sure all shims and washers are reinstalled in the same locations and positions.

17. Whenever rotating parts contact a stationary part, look for a shim or washer.

18. Use new gaskets if there is any doubt about the condition of old ones.

19. If using self-locking fasteners, replace them with new ones. Do not install standard fasteners in place of self-locking ones.

20. Use grease to hold small parts in place if they tend to fall out during assembly. Do not apply grease to electrical or brake components.

Removing Frozen Fasteners

If a fastener cannot be removed, several methods may be used to loosen it. First, apply penetrating oil such as Liquid Wrench or WD-40. Apply it liberally and let it penetrate for 10-15 minutes. Rap the fastener several times with a small hammer. Do not hit it hard enough to cause damage. Reapply the penetrating oil if necessary.

For frozen screws, apply penetrating oil as described. Then insert a screwdriver in the slot and rap the top of the screwdriver with a hammer. This loosens the rust so the screw can be removed in the normal way. If the screw head is too damaged to use this method, grip the head with locking pliers and twist the screw out.

Avoid applying heat unless specifically instructed. Heat can melt, warp or remove the temper from parts.

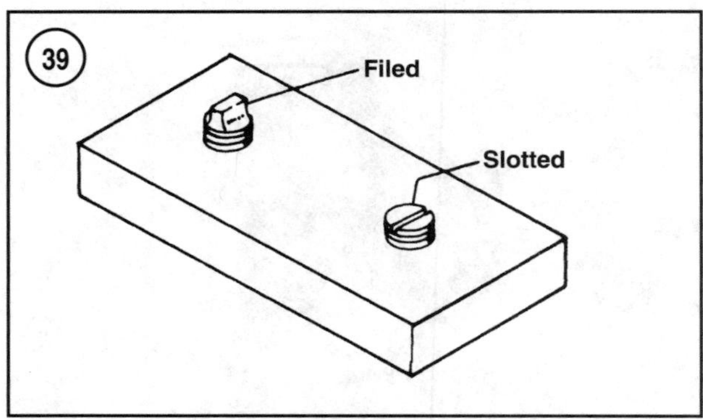

Removing Broken Fasteners

If the head breaks off a screw or bolt, several methods are available for removing the remaining portion. If a large portion of the remainder projects out, try gripping it with locking pliers. If the projecting portion is too small, file it to fit a wrench, or cut a slot in it to fit a screwdriver (**Figure 39**).

If the head breaks off flush, use a screw extractor. To do this, center punch the exact center of the remaining portion of the screw or bolt. Drill a small hole in the screw and tap the extractor into the hole. Back the screw out with a wrench on the extractor (**Figure 40**).

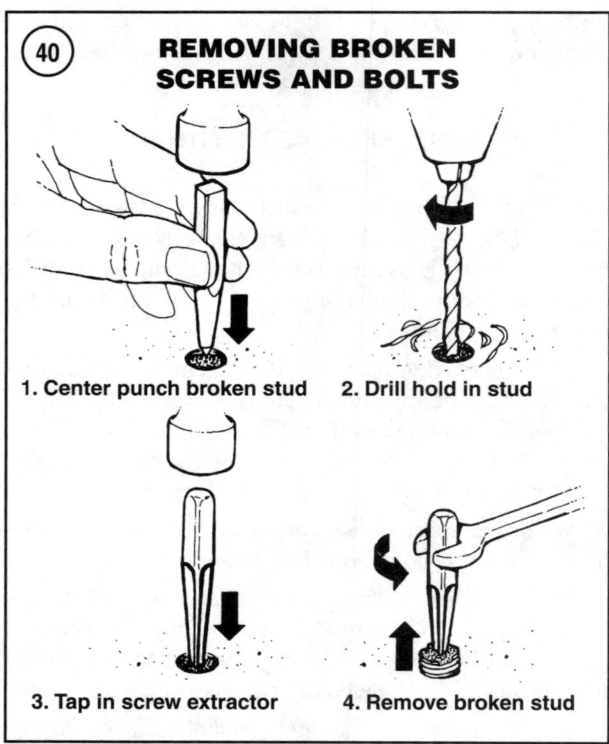

Repairing Damaged Threads

Occasionally, threads are stripped through carelessness or impact damage. Often the threads can be repaired by running a tap (for internal threads on nuts) or die (for external threads on bolts) through the threads (**Figure 41**). To clean or repair spark plug threads, use a spark plug tap.

If an internal thread is damaged, it may be necessary to install a Helicoil or some other thread insert. Follow the manufacturer's instructions when installing the insert.

If it is necessary to drill and tap a hole, refer to **Table 11** for American tap and drill sizes.

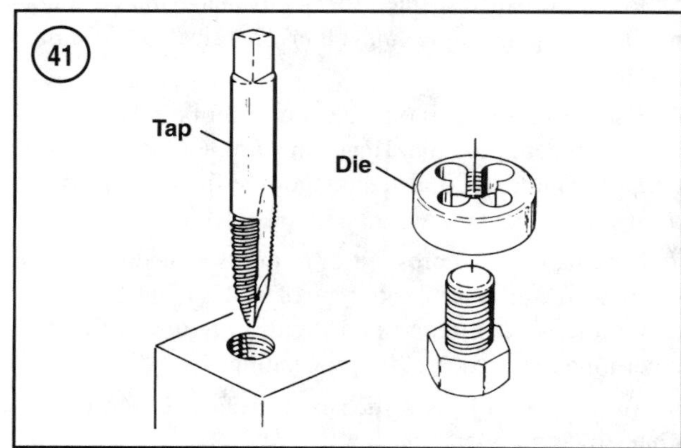

Stud Removal/Installation

A stud removal tool is available from most tool suppliers. This tool makes the removal and installation of studs easier. If one is not available, thread two nuts onto the stud and tighten them against each other. Remove the stud by turning the lower nut (**Figure 42**).

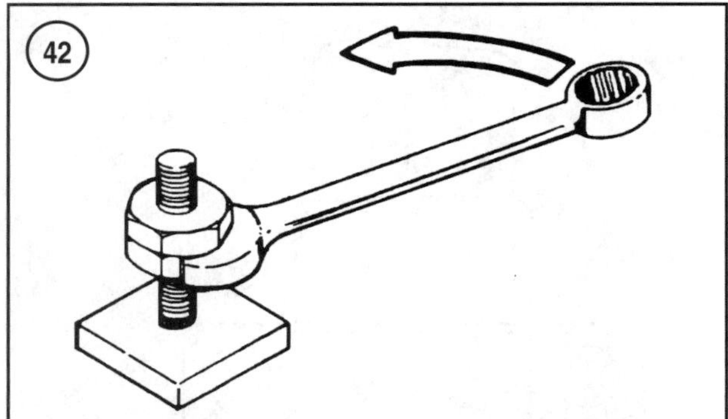

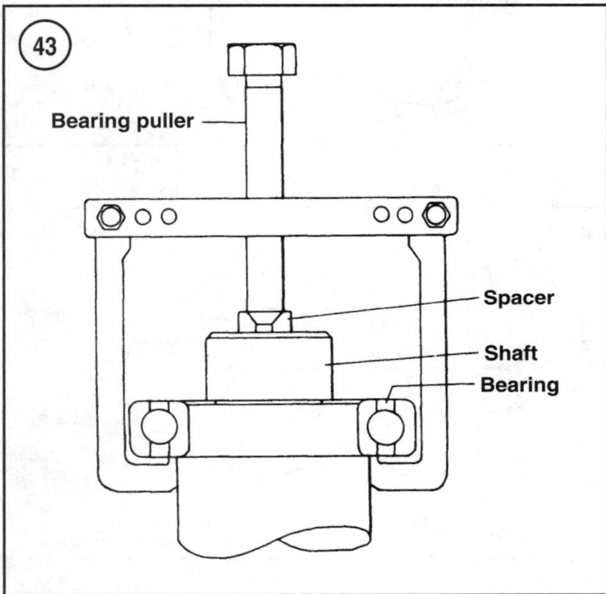

1. Measure the height of the stud above the surface.
2. Thread the stud removal tool onto the stud and tighten it, or thread two nuts onto the stud.
3. Remove the stud by turning the stud remover or the lower nut.
4. Remove any threadlocking compound from the threaded hole. Clean the threads with an aerosol parts cleaner.
5. Install the stud removal tool onto the new stud or thread two nuts onto the stud.
6. Apply threadlocking compound to the threads of the stud.
7. Install the stud and tighten with the stud removal tool or the top nut.
8. Install the stud to the height noted in Step 1 or its torque specification.
9. Remove the stud removal tool or the two nuts.

Removing Hoses

When removing a stubborn hose, do not exert excessive force on the hose or fitting. Remove the hose clamp and carefully insert a small screwdriver or pick tool between the fitting and hose. Apply a spray lubricant under the hose and carefully twist the hose off the fitting. Clean the fitting of any corrosion or rubber hose material with a wire brush. Clean the inside of the hose thoroughly. Do not use any lubricant when installing the hose (new or old). The lubricant may allow the hose to come off the fitting, even with the clamp secure.

Bearings

Bearings are used in the engine and transmission assembly to reduce power loss, heat and noise resulting from friction. Because bearings are precision parts, they must be maintained with proper lubrication and maintenance. If a bearing is damaged, replace it immediately. When installing a new bearing, take care to prevent damaging it. Bearing replacement procedures are included in the individual chapters where applicable; however, use the following sections as a guideline.

NOTE
Unless otherwise specified, install bearings with the manufacturer's mark or number facing outward.

Removal

While bearings are normally removed only when damaged, there may be times when it is necessary to remove a bearing that is in good condition. However, improper bearing removal will damage the bearing and possibly the shaft or case. Note the following when removing bearings:

1. When using a puller to remove a bearing from a shaft, take care that the shaft is not damaged. Always place a piece of metal between the end of the shaft and the puller screw. In addition, place the puller arms next to the inner bearing race. See **Figure 43**.
2. When using a hammer to remove a bearing from a shaft, do not strike the hammer directly against the shaft. Instead, use a brass or aluminum rod between the hammer and shaft (**Figure 44**) and make sure to support both bearing races with wooden blocks as shown.
3. The ideal method of bearing removal is with a hydraulic press. Note the following when using a press:
   a. Always support the inner and outer bearing races with a suitably sized wooden or aluminum spacer

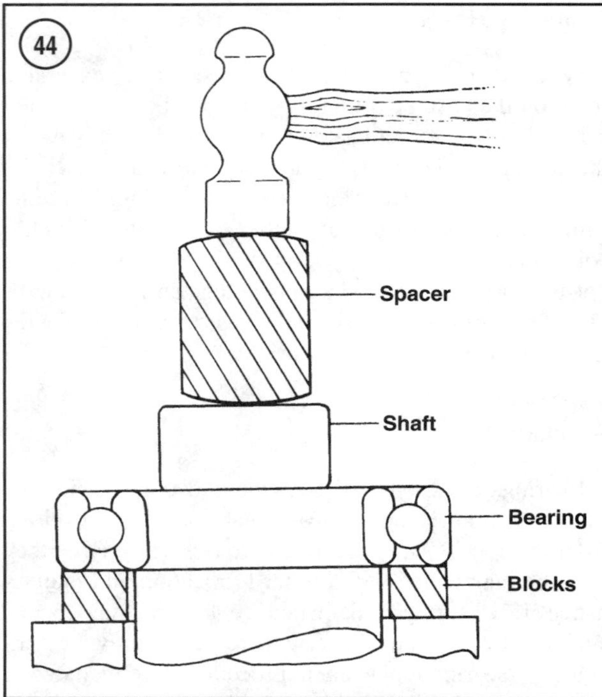

(**Figure 45**). If only the outer race is supported, pressure applied against the balls and/or the inner race will damage them.

b. Always make sure the press arm (**Figure 45**) aligns with the center of the shaft. If the arm is not centered, it can damage the bearing and/or shaft.
c. The moment the shaft is free of the bearing, it drops to the floor. Secure or hold the shaft to prevent it from falling.

Installation

1. When installing a bearing in a housing, apply pressure to the outer bearing race (**Figure 46**). When installing a bearing on a shaft, apply pressure to the inner bearing race (**Figure 47**).
2. When installing a bearing as described in Step 1, some type of driver is required. Never strike the bearing directly with a hammer, or it will damage the bearing. When installing a bearing, use a piece of pipe or a driver with a diameter that matches the bearing inner race. **Figure 48** shows the correct way to use a driver and hammer to install a bearing.
3. Step 1 describes how to install a bearing in a case half or over a shaft. However, when installing a bearing over a shaft and into the housing at the same time, a tight fit is required for both outer and inner bearing races. In this situation, install a spacer underneath the driver tool so that pressure is applied evenly across both races. See **Figure 49**. If the outer race is not supported as shown, the balls will push against the outer bearing race and damage it.

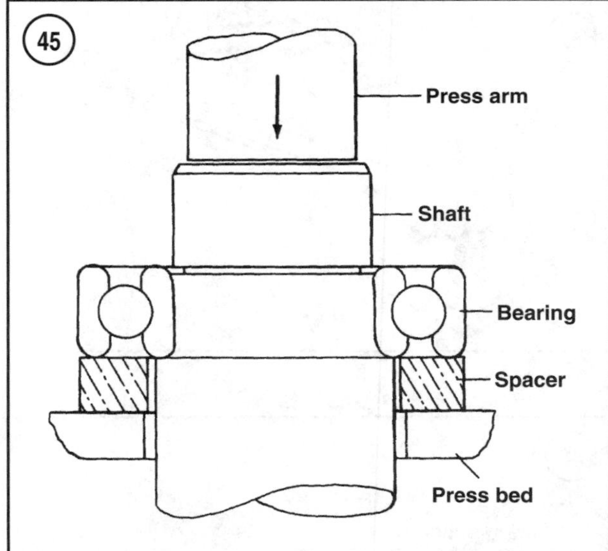

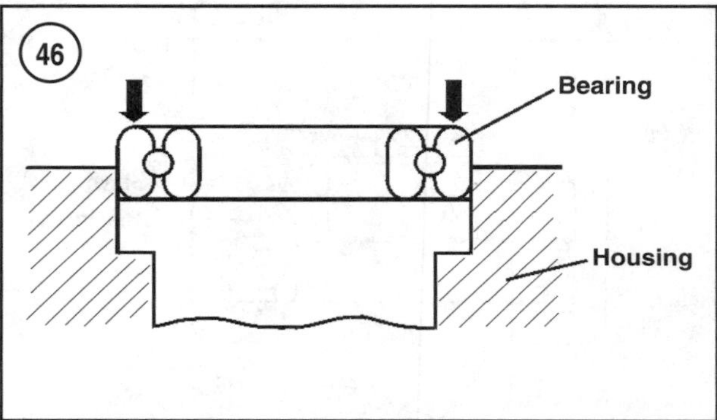

Interference fit

1. Follow this procedure when installing a bearing over a shaft. When a tight fit is required, the bearing inside diameter is smaller than the shaft. In this case, driving the bearing on the shaft using normal methods may cause bearing damage. Instead, heat the bearing before installation. Note the following:
   a. Secure the shaft so it is ready for bearing installation.
   b. Clean all residues from the bearing surface of the shaft. Remove burrs with a file or sandpaper.

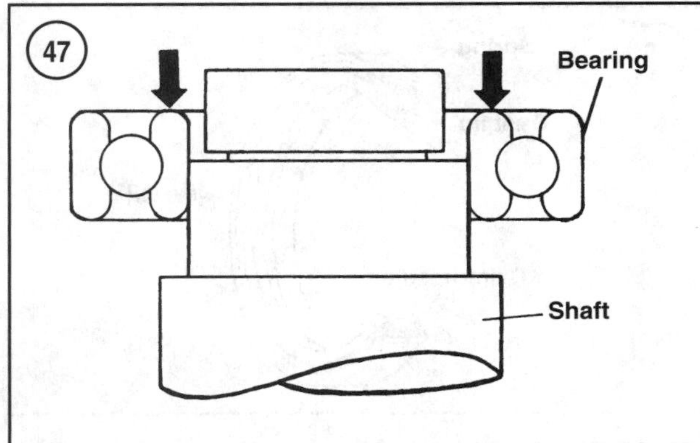

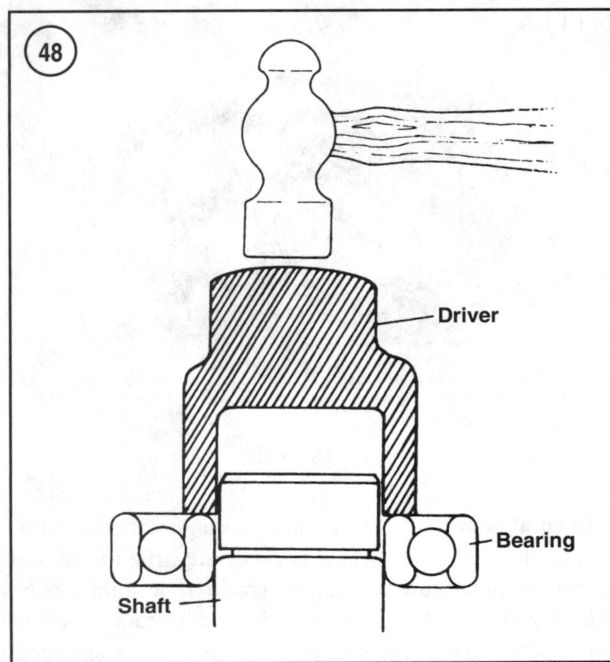

c. Fill a suitable pot or beaker with clean mineral oil. Place a thermometer rated above 248° F (120° C) in the oil. Support the thermometer so it does not rest on the bottom or side of the pot.

d. Remove the bearing from its wrapper and secure it with a piece of heavy wire bent to hold it in the pot. Hang the bearing in the pot so it does not touch the bottom or sides of the pot.

e. Turn on the heat and monitor the thermometer. When the oil temperature rises to approximately 248° F (120° C), remove the bearing from the pot and quickly install it. If necessary, place a socket on the inner bearing race and tap the bearing into place. As the bearing chills, it will tighten on the shaft, so

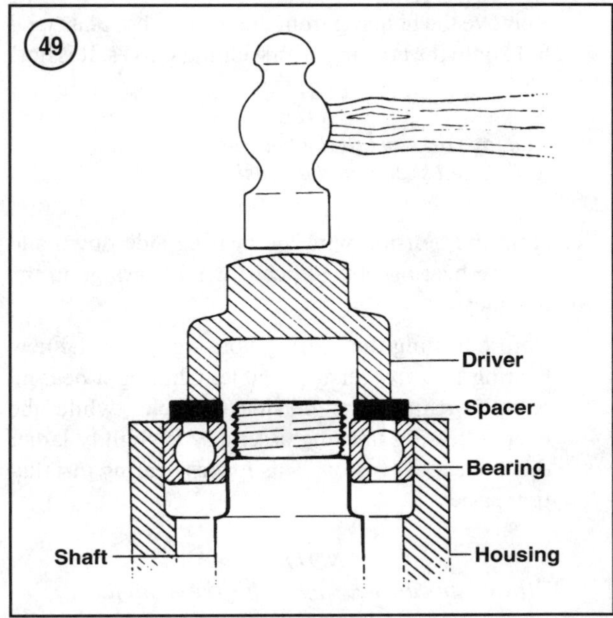

installation must be done quickly. Make sure the bearing is installed completely.

2. Follow this step when installing a bearing in a housing. Bearings are generally installed in a housing with a slight interference fit. Driving the bearing into the housing using normal methods can damage the housing or cause bearing damage. Instead, heat the housing before the bearing is installed. Note the following:

CAUTION
Before heating the housing in this procedure, wash the housing thoroughly with detergent and water. Rinse and rewash the cases as required to remove all traces of oil and other chemical deposits.

a. Heat the housing to approximately 212° F (100° C) in an oven or on a hot plate. An easy way to check that it is the proper temperature is to place tiny drops of water on the housing; if they sizzle and evaporate immediately, the temperature is correct. Heat only one housing at a time.

CAUTION
Do not heat the housing with a propane or acetylene torch. Never bring a flame into contact with the bearing or housing. The direct heat will destroy the case hardening of the bearing and will likely warp the housing.

b. Remove the housing from the oven or hot plate, and hold onto the housing with welding gloves. It is hot!

NOTE
Remove and install the bearings with a suitably sized socket and extension.

c. Hold the housing with the bearing side down and tap the bearing out. Repeat for all bearings in the housing.

d. Before heating the bearing housing, place the new bearing in a freezer if possible. Chilling a bearing slightly reduces its outside diameter while the heated bearing housing assembly is slightly larger due to heat expansion. This makes bearing installation easier.

NOTE
Always install bearings with the manufacturer's mark or number facing outward.

e. While the housing is still hot, install the new bearing(s) into the housing. Install the bearings by hand, if possible. If necessary, lightly tap the bearing(s) into the housing with a driver placed on the outer bearing race (**Figure 46**). Do not install new bearings by driving on the inner-bearing race. Install the bearing(s) until it seats completely.

Seal Replacement

Seals (**Figure 50**) contain oil, water, grease or combustion gasses in a housing or shaft. Improperly removing a seal can damage the housing or shaft. Improperly installing the seal can damage the seal. Note the following:

1. Prying is generally the easiest and most effective method of removing a seal from the housing. However, always place a rag underneath the pry tool (**Figure 51**) to prevent damage to the housing. Note the installed depth of the seal or whether it is installed flush.

2. Pack waterproof grease in the seal lips before the seal is installed.

3. In most cases, install seals with the manufacturer's numbers or marks facing out.

4. Install seals with a socket or driver placed on the outside of the seal as shown in **Figure 52**. Drive the seal squarely into the housing until it is to the correct depth or flush as noted during removal. Never install a seal by hitting the top of it with a hammer.

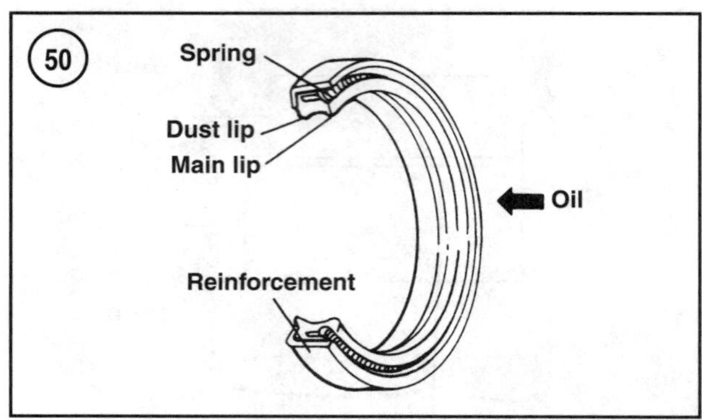

STORAGE

Several months of disuse can cause a general deterioration of the motorcycle. This is especially true in areas of extreme temperature variations. This deterioration can be minimized with careful preparation for storage. A properly stored motorcycle is much easier to return to service.

Storage Area Selection

When selecting a storage area, consider the following:

1. The storage area must be dry. A heated area is best but not necessary. It should be insulated to minimize extreme temperature variations.

2. If the building has large window areas, mask them to keep sunlight off the motorcycle.

3. Avoid buildings in industrial areas where corrosive emissions may be present. Avoid areas close to saltwater.

4. Consider the risk of fire, theft or vandalism in the area. Check with an insurer regarding motorcycle coverage while in storage.

Preparing the Motorcycle for Storage

The amount of preparation a motorcycle should undergo before storage depends on the expected length of disuse, storage area conditions and personal preference. Consider the following list of minimum requirements:

1. Wash the motorcycle thoroughly. Make sure all dirt, mud and road debris are removed.
2. Start the engine and allow it to reach operating temperature. Drain the engine oil regardless of the riding time since the last service. Fill the engine with the recommended type of oil.
3. Fill the fuel tank completely. There is no need to try to empty the fuel delivery or return lines since they are not vented to the atmosphere.
4. Remove the spark plugs and pour a teaspoon (15-20 ml) of engine oil into the cylinders. Place a rag over the openings and slowly turn the engine over to distribute the oil. Reinstall the spark plugs.
5. Remove the battery. Store the battery in a cool and dry location. Charge the battery once a month.
6. Cover the exhaust and intake openings.
7. Apply a protective substance to the plastic and rubber components. Make sure to follow the manufacturer's instructions for each product being used.
8. Place the motorcycle on a stand or wooden blocks so the wheels are off the ground. If this is not possible, place a piece of plywood between the tires and the ground. Inflate the tires to the recommended pressure if the motorcycle cannot be elevated.
9. Cover the motorcycle with old bed sheets or something similar. Do not cover it with any plastic material that will trap moisture.

Returning the Motorcycle to Service

The amount of service required when returning a motorcycle to service after storage depends on the length of disuse and storage conditions. In addition to performing the reverse of the above procedure, make sure the brakes, clutch, throttle and engine stop switch work properly before operating the motorcycle. Refer to Chapter Three and evaluate the service intervals to determine which areas require service.

Table 1 MODEL IDENTIFICATION

Model Description	Years Produced
FXR Super Glide	1986-1994
FXRS Low Rider and Convertible	1984-1992
FXRS-SP Low Rider Sports Edition	1988-1993
FXLR Low Rider Custom and Anniversary Edition	1987-1994
FXRD Super Glide Grand Touring	1986
FXRT Sports Glide	1984-1992
FXRS-Con Low Rider-Convertible	1991-1993
FXWG Wide Glide	1985-1986
FXSB Low Rider	1985
FXEF Fat Bob	1985
FXR2 and FXR3 Super Glide	1999
FLHT Electra Glide	1995-1998
FLHTC Electra Glide Classic and Anniversary Edition	1984-1998
FLHTC-I* Electra Glide Classic	1996-1998
FLHTC-U Electra Glide Classic-Ultra and Anniversary Edition	1989-1997
FLHTC-UI* Electra Glide Classic-Ultra and Anniversary Edition	1996-1998
FLHS Electra Glide-Sport	1988-1993
FLHR Road King	1995-1998
FLHR-I* Road King	1996-1997

(continued)

Table 1 MODEL IDENTIFICATION (continued)

Model Description	Years Produced
FLHRC-I* Road King	1998
FLTC Tour Glide	1984-1991
FLTC-U Tour Glide Classic-Ultra	1989-1995
FLTC-UI* Tour Glide	1996
FLTR Road Glide	1998
FLTR-I* Road Glide	1998
*Indicates models equipped with electronic fuel injection.	

Table 2 GENERAL SPECIFICATIONS (FXR, FLH AND FLT)*

Item and model	in.	mm
Wheel base		
1984-1985		
FXRT	64.7	1643.4
FXRS	63.13	1603.5
FLHTC	62.9	1597.6
FLTC	62.9	1597.6
1986-1990		
FXR and FXRS	63.13	1603.5
FLHTC and FLHS	62.94	1598.7
FLTC	62.94	1598.7
1991-1994		
FXR, FXRS and FXLR	63.13	1603.5
FXRT, FXRS-SP and FXRS-Con	64.7	1643.4
FLH and FLT series models	62.94	1598.7
1995-1996		
FLH and FLT series models	62.94	1598.7
1997-1998		
FLH and FLT series models	62.94	1598.7
1999 FXR2 and FXR3	63.13	1603.5
Length		
1984-1985		
FXRS	91.65	2327.9
All models except FXRS	94.2	2392.7
1986-1990		
FXR and FXRS	91.65	2327.9
FXLR	91.6	2326.6
FXRD	98.0	2489.2
FXRT	94.2	2392.7
FXRS and FXRS-SP	93.2	2367.3
FLHTC	94.25	2393.9
FLTC	94.25	2393.9
1991-1992		
FXR and FXRS	91.65	2327.9
FXRT	94.2	2392.7
FXLR	91.6	2326.6
FXRS-SP and FXRS-Con	93.2	2367.3
FLT	94.25	2393.9
1993		
FXLR	91.63	2327.8
FXRS-SP and FXRS-Con	93.2	2367.3
FLHS	94.25	2394.0
1993-1996		
FXR	91.6	2326.6
FLH and FLT series models	94.25	2393.9

(continued)

Table 2 GENERAL SPECIFICATIONS (FXR, FLH AND FLT)* (continued)

Item and model	in.	mm
Length (continued)		
1997-1998		
FLHTC	97.5	2476.5
FLHTU	98.3	2496.8
FLHT, FLHRC and FLTR	93.7	2380.0
1999		
FXR2	92.75	2355.9
FXR3	92.34	2345.4
Width		
1984-1985		
FXRT	34.5	876.3
FXRS	31.0	787.4
FLHT and FLHTC	37.0	939.8
FLT	37.0	939.8
1986-1992		
FXR and FXRS	31.0	787.4
FXRT and FXRD	34.5	876.3
FXLR, FXRS, FXRS-SP and FXRS-Con	31.0	787.4
FLHTC and FLHS	39.0	990.6
FLTC	37.0	939.9
1993		
FXRS-SP and FXRS-Con	31.0	787.4
FLHS	39.0	990.6
1993-1994		
FXR	31.0	787.4
FXLR	31.0	787.4
FLHTC and FLHTC-U	39.0	990.6
FLTC-U	37.0	939.9
1995-1996		
FLTC-U and FLTC-UI	37.0	939.9
FLHTC, FLHTC-U, FLHTC-UI and FLHTC-I	39.0	990.6
FLHR	34.45	875.0
1997-1998		
FLHR, FLHR-I and FLHRC-I	34.45	875.0
FLHTC, FLHTC-U, FLHTC-UI and FLHTC-I	39.0	990.6
1999 FXR2 and FXR3	33.50	850.9
Overall height		
1984-1985		
FLHTC	60.5	1536.7
FLTC	59.0	1498.6
FXRT	59.5	1511.3
FXRS	48.0	1219.2
1986-1992		
FLHTC and FLHS	61.0	1549.4
FLTC	58.75	1492.3
FXR, FXRS and FXLR	48.0	1219.2
FXRT and FXRD	59.5	1511.3
FXRS, FXRS-SP and FXRS-Con	50.0	1270.0
1993		
FXRS-SP and FXRS-Con	50.0	1270.0
FLHS	61.0	1549.4
1993-1994		
FXR	48.0	1219.2
FXLR	48.0	1219.0
FLTC-U	58.75	1492.3
FLHTC and FLHTC-U	61.0	1549.4
1995-1998		
FLTC-U	58.75	1492.3

(continued)

Table 2 GENERAL SPECIFICATIONS (FXR, FLH AND FLT)* (continued)

Item and model	in.	mm
Overall height		
1995-1998 (continued)		
FLHT, FLHTC, FLHTC-U, FLHTC-UI and FLHTC-I	61.0	1549.4
FLHR, FLHR-I and FLHRC-I	55.06	1398.5
1999 FXR2 and FXR3	49.63	1260.6
Seat height		
1984-1985		
FXRS	28.1	713.7
All models except FXRS	28.0	711.2
1986-1992		
FLHTC and FLHS	28.0	711.2
FLTC	29.6	751.8
FXR, FXRS and FXLR	26.5	673.1
FXRT	27.75	704.8
FXRD	28.25	717.6
FXRS, FXRS-SP and FXRS-Con	27.5	698.5
1993	27.0	685.8
FXRS-SP and FXRS-Con	27.5	698.5
FLHS	27.0	685.8
1993-1994		
FXR	26.0	660.4
FXLR	26.5	673.1
FLHTC and FLHTC-U	28.0	711.2
FLTC-U	29.62	752.3
1995-1996		
FLTC-U	28.5	723.9
FLHT, FLHTC, FLHTC-U, FLHTC-UI and FLHTC-I	28.0	711.2
FLHR	28.20	716.3
1997-1998		
FLHT, FLHTC, FLHTC-U, FLHTC-UI, FLHTC-I and FLHR	27.25	692.2
1999		
FXR2	25.50	647.7
FXR3	25.80	655.3
Ground clearance		
1984-1985		
FXRT	6.0	152.4
FXRS	5.25	133.4
FLHTC and FLTC	5.1	129.5
1986-1994		
FXR, FXRS and FXLR	5.25	133.4
FXRT, FXRD, FXRS, FXRS-SP and FXRS-Con	6.0	152.4
1995-1998		
FLH and FLT series models	5.12	130.0
1999		
FXR2	4.56	115.8
FXR3	4.48	113.8

*Dimensions are identical for both fuel-injected and carbureted models.

Table 3 GENERAL SPECIFICATIONS (FXWG, FXSB AND FXEF)

Item and model	in.	mm
Wheel base		
FXEF	63.0	1600.0
FXSB	63.50	1612.9

(continued)

Table 3 GENERAL SPECIFICATIONS (FXWG, FXSB AND FXEF) (continued)

Item and model	in.	mm
Wheel base (continued)		
FXWG	65.0	1651.0
Length		
FXEF	91.50	2324.1
FXSB	92.0	2336.8
FXWG	93.0	2362.2
Width		
FXEF	33.75	857.25
FXSB	29.0	736.6
FXWG	27.50	698.5
Overall height		
FXEF	47.75	1212.85
FXSB	41.75	1060.45
FXWG	47.0	1193.8

Table 4 MOTORCYCLE WEIGHT (DRY)*

Model	lb.	kg
1994-1995		
FXRT	640	290.3
FXRS	575	260.8
FLHTC	712	322.9
FLTC	741	336.1
1986-1992		
FXR, FXRS and FXLR	575	260.8
FXRT	640	290.4
FXRD	672	304.8
FLHTC and FLHS	722	327.5
FLTC	741	336.1
1993-1994		
FXR and FXLR	575	260.8
FLHTC-U and FLTC-U	765	347.0
FLHTC	741	336.1
FLHS	692	313.9
1995-1996		
FLHTC-U and FLTC-U	765	347.0
FLHTC	741	336.1
FLHT	711	322.5
1997-1998		
FLHT	742	336.6
FLHTC	760	344.7
FLHT-U	772	350.2
FLHR	707	320.7
FLHRC	694	314.8
FLTR	715	324.3
1999		
FXR2	560	254.0
FXR3	605	274.4

*Dimensions are identical for both fuel-injected and carbureted models.

Table 5 MOTORCYCLE WEIGHT RATINGS[1]

Model and year	lb.	kg
Gross motorcycle weight rating (GVWR)[2]		
1984-1985		
FXR series models	1085	492.1
FLH and FLT series models	1180	535.2
FXEF, FXSB and FXWG	1085	492.1
1986-1992		
FXR series models	1085	492.1
FLH and FLT series models	1180	535.2
FXWG	1085	492.1
1993-1994		
FXR and FXLR	1085	492.6
FLH series models	1197	542.9
1995-1996 FLH and FLT series models	1260	571.5
1997-1998 FLH and FLT series models	1179	534.8
1999 FXR2 and FXR3	1085	492.6
Gross axle weight rating (GAWR)		
Front axle		
1986-1992		
FXR	390	176.9
FXEF, FXSB and FXWG	390	176.9
FLT and FLH series models	410	186.0
1993-1994		
FXR	390	176.9
FLH and FLT series models	427	193.7
1995-1998 FLH and FLT series models	410	186.0
1999 FXR2 and FXR3	390	176.9
Rear axle		
1984-1994		
FXR series models	695	315.2
FXEF, FXSB and FXWG	695	315.2
FLH and FLT series models	770	349.3
1995-1998 FLH and FLT series models	769	348.8
1999 FXR2 and FXR3	695	315.2

1. Dimensions are identical for both fuel-injected and carbureted models.
2. GVWR is the maximum allowable vehicle weight. This includes combined vehicle weight, rider(s) and accessory weight.

Table 6 FUEL TANK CAPACITY

Model and year	U.S. gal.	Liters
Total		
FXR series models	4.2	15.9
FXEF and FXSB	4.2	15.9
FXWG	5.2	19.7
FXR2 and FXR3	4.2	15.9
FLH and FLT series models		
1984-1990	5.0	18.9
1991-1998	5.0	18.9
Reserve		
FXR series models	0.4	1.5
FXEF and FXSB	1.0	3.8
FXWG	1.2	4.5
FXR2 and FXR3	0.4	1.5
FLH and FLT series models		
1984-1988	0.7	2.6
1989-1999	0.9	3.4

Table 7 DECIMAL AND METRIC EQUIVALENTS

Fractions	Decimal in.	Metric mm	Fractions	Decimal in.	Metric mm
1/64	0.015625	0.39688	33/64	0.515625	13.09687
1/32	0.03125	0.79375	17/32	0.53125	13.49375
3/64	0.046875	1.19062	35/64	0.546875	13.89062
1/16	0.0625	1.58750	9/16	0.5625	14.28750
5/64	0.078125	1.98437	37/64	0.578125	14.68437
3/32	0.09375	2.38125	19/32	0.59375	15.08125
7/64	0.109375	2.77812	39/64	0.609375	15.47812
1/8	0.125	3.1750	5/8	0.625	15.87500
9/64	0.140625	3.57187	41/64	0.640625	16.27187
5/32	0.15625	3.96875	21/32	0.65625	16.66875
11/64	0.171875	4.36562	43/64	0.671875	17.06562
3/16	0.1875	4.76250	11/16	0.6875	17.46250
13/64	0.203125	5.15937	45/64	0.703125	17.85937
7/32	0.21875	5.55625	23/32	0.71875	18.25625
15/64	0.234375	5.95312	47/64	0.734375	18.65312
1/4	0.250	6.35000	3/4	0.750	19.05000
17/64	0.265625	6.74687	49/64	0.765625	19.44687
9/32	0.28125	7.14375	25/32	0.78125	19.84375
19/64	0.296875	7.54062	51/64	0.796875	20.24062
5/16	0.3125	7.93750	13/16	0.8125	20.63750
21/64	0.328125	8.33437	53/64	0.828125	21.03437
11/32	0.34375	8.73125	27/32	0.84375	21.43125
23/64	0.359375	9.12812	55/64	0.859375	22.82812
3/8	0.375	9.52500	7/8	0.875	22.22500
25/64	0.390625	9.92187	57/64	0.890625	22.62187
13/32	0.40625	10.31875	29/32	0.90625	23.01875
27/64	0.421875	10.71562	59/64	0.921875	23.41562
7/16	0.4375	11.11250	15/16	0.9375	23.81250
29/64	0.453125	11.50937	61/64	0.953125	24.20937
15/32	0.46875	11.90625	31/32	0.96875	24.60625
31/64	0.484375	12.30312	63/64	0.984375	25.00312
1/2	0.500	12.70000	1	1.00	25.40000

Table 8 GENERAL TORQUE SPECIFICATIONS (FT.-LB.)[1]

	Body Size or Outside Diameter									
Type[2]	1/4	5/16	3/8	7/16	1/2	9/16	5/8	3/4	7/8	1
SAE 2	6	12	20	32	47	69	96	155	206	310
SAE 5	10	19	33	54	78	114	154	257	382	587
SAE 7	13	25	44	71	110	154	215	360	570	840
SAE 8	14	29	47	78	119	169	230	380	600	700

1. Convert ft.-lb. specification to N•m by multiplying by 1.3558.
2. Fastener strength to SAE bolts can be determined by the bolt head grade markings. Unmarked bolt heads and cap screws are usually mild steel. More grade markings indicate higher fastener quality.

Table 9 CONVERSION TABLES

Multiply:	By:	To get the equivalent of:
Length		
Inches	25.4	Millimeter
Inches	2.54	Centimeter
Miles	1.609	Kilometer

(continued)

Table 9 CONVERSION TABLES (continued)

Multiply:	By:	To get the equivalent of:
Length (continued)		
Feet	0.3048	Meter
Millimeter	0.03937	Inches
Centimeter	0.3937	Inches
Kilometer	0.6214	Mile
Meter	0.0006214	Mile
Fluid volume		
U.S. quarts	0.9463	Liters
U.S. gallons	3.785	Liters
U.S. ounces	29.573529	Milliliters
Imperial gallons	4.54609	Liters
Imperial quarts	1.1365	Liters
Liters	0.2641721	U.S. gallons
Liters	1.0566882	U.S. quarts
Liters	33.814023	U.S. ounces
Liters	0.22	Imperial gallons
Liters	0.8799	Imperial quarts
Milliliters	0.033814	U.S. ounces
Milliliters	1.0	Cubic centimeters
Milliliters	0.001	Liters
Torque		
Foot-pounds	1.3558	Newton-meters
Foot-pounds	0.138255	Meters-kilograms
Inch-pounds	0.11299	Newton-meters
Newton-meters	0.7375622	Foot-pounds
Newton-meters	8.8507	Inch-pounds
Meters-kilograms	7.2330139	Foot-pounds
Volume		
Cubic inches	16.387064	Cubic centimeters
Cubic centimeters	0.0610237	Cubic inches
Temperature		
Fahrenheit	$(F - 32°) \times 0.556$	Centigrade
Centigrade	$(C \times 1.8) + 32°$	Fahrenheit
Weight		
Ounces	28.3495	Grams
Pounds	0.4535924	Kilograms
Grams	0.035274	Ounces
Kilograms	2.2046224	Pounds
Pressure		
Pounds per square inch	0.070307	Kilograms per square centimeter
Kilograms per square centimeter	14.223343	Pounds per square inch
Kilopascals	0.1450	Pounds per square inch
Pounds per square inch	6.895	Kilopascals
Speed		
Miles per hour	1.609344	Kilometers per hour
Kilometers per hour	0.6213712	Miles per hour

Table 10 TECHNICAL ABBREVIATIONS

ABDC	After bottom dead center
ATDC	After top dead center
BBDC	Before bottom dead center
BDC	Bottom dead center
BTDC	Before top dead center

(continued)

Table 10 TECHNICAL ABBREVIATIONS (continued)

C	Celsius (centigrade)
cc	Cubic centimeters
CCA	Cold-cranking amps
CDI	Capacitor discharge ignition
cid	Cubic inch displacement
CKP	Crankshaft position sensor
CMP	Camshaft position sensor
cu. in.	Cubic inches
ECM	Electronic control module
EFI	Electronic fuel injection
ET	Engine temperature sensor
F	Fahrenheit
ft.	Feet
ft.-lb.	Foot-pounds
gal.	Gallons
H/A	High altitude
HDI	Harley-Davidson International
hp	Horsepower
IAC	Idle air control
IAT	Intake air temperature sensor
in.	Inches
in.-lb.	Inch-pounds
I.D.	Inside diameter
kg	Kilograms
kgm	Kilogram meters
km	Kilometer
kPa	Kilopascals
L	Liter
m	Meter
µF	Microfarad
mL	Milliliter
mm	Millimeter
NAL	North American Lighting
N•m	Newton-meters
O.D.	Outside diameter
oz.	Ounces
psi	Pounds per square inch
pt.	Pint
qt.	Quart
rpm	Revolutions per minute
TP	Throttle position sensor
TSM	Turn signal module
VAS	Vehicle attitude sensor
VOES	Vacuum-operated electric switch
VOV	Vacuum-operated valve

Table 11 AMERICAN TAP AND DRILL SIZES

Metric size	Drill equivalent	Decimal fraction	Nearest fraction
3 × 0.50	No. 39	0.0995	3/32
3 × 0.60	3/32	0.0937	3/32
4 × 0.70	No. 30	0.1285	1/8
4 × 0.75	1/8	0.125	1/8
5 × 0.80	No. 19	0.166	11/64
5 × 0.90	No. 20	0.161	5/32
6 × 1.00	No. 9	0.196	13/64

(continued)

Table 11 AMERICAN TAP AND DRILL SIZES (continued)

Metric size	Drill equivalent	Decimal fraction	Nearest fraction
7 × 1.00	16/64	0.234	15/64
8 × 1.00	J	0.277	9/32
8 × 1.25	17/64	0.265	17/64
9 × 1.00	5/16	0.3125	5/16
9 × 1.25	5/16	0.3125	5/16
10 × 1.25	11/32	0.3437	11/32
10 × 1.50	R	0.339	11/32
11 × 1.50	3/8	0.375	3/8
12 × 1.50	13/32	0.406	13/32
12 × 1.75	13/32	0.406	13/32

Table 12 SPECIAL TOOLS

Tool Description	Part No.	Manufacturer
Belt tensioner tool	HD-355381-64	H-D
Camshaft inner bearing installer	1288	JIMS
Camshaft inner bearing remover	95760-TB	JIMS
Clutch hub puller	95960-52C	JIMS
Clutch spring compressor	38515-90	JIMS
Connecting rod bushing hone	HD-422569	H-D
Connecting rod bushing reamer tool	1726-1	JIMS
Connecting rod holding tool	1284	JIMS
Crankcase stud installer	08-0148	Motion Pro
Crankshaft assembly removing tool	1047-TP	JIMS
Crankshaft bearing snap ring remover	1719	JIMS
Crankshaft pinion gear puller	96830-51	JIMS
Crankshaft pinion shaft nut sprocket	94555-55A	JIMS
Crankshaft seal installation tool	39361-69	JIMS
Crankshaft sprocket shaft bearing installation tool	97225-55	JIMS
Cylinder chamfering cone	2078	JIMS
Cylinder head stand	39782	JIMS
Cylinder torque plates	1287	JIMS
Drive sprocket lock	2260	JIMS
Engine stand for Big Twin	1006T	JIMS
Fork seal/cap installer	2046	JIMS
Hose clamp pliers	1171	JIMS
Hydraulic brake bleeder	–	Mityvac
Oil pump seal tool	1053	JIMS
Piston pin keeper tool	34623-83	JIMS
Primary chain case boot remover	HD-97101-81	H-D
Primary drive locking tool	2234	JIMS
Snap ring remover and installer	1710	JIMS
Steering head bearing race installer	1725	JIMS
Swing arm cleveblock bushing		
Assembly tool	HD-96200-80	H-D
Assembly tool	1743	JIMS
Spreading tool	1707	JIMS
Timken bearing race installer	2246	JIMS
Transmission tools (four-speed transmission)		
Countershaft bearing tool	34733-77	JIMS
Mainshaft bearing tool	34902-84	JIMS
Mainshaft gear bushing tool	1005	JIMS
Main drive gear bushing tool	1005	JIMS
Mainshaft gear puller	1700	JIMS

(continued)

Table 12 SPECIAL TOOLS (continued)

Tool Description	Part No.	Manufacturer
Transmission tools (four-speed transmission) (continued)		
Main drive gear seal driver tool	95660-77	JIMS
Main drive gear seal tool	95660-42	JIMS
Shift fork gauge	96385-78A	JIMS
Transmission tools (five-speed transmission)		
Bearing and race installer tool handle	33416-80	JIMS
Door assembly remover	1078	JIMS
Main drive gear bearing tool	37842-91	JIMS
Main drive gear bearing remover set	1720	JIMS
Main drive gear tool set	3516-80	JIMS
Mainshaft sprocket nut wrench	94660-37A	JIMS
Shaft installers	2189	JIMS
Vacuum hose identifier kit	74600	Lisle
Valve cutter set (Neway)	HD-082454	H-D
Valve guide alignment tool	HD-33443	H-D
Valve guide brush	HD-34751	H-D
Valve guide driver	HD-34740	H-D
Valve guide hone	HD-34723	H-D
Valve guide installation sleeve	HD-34731	H-D
Valve guide reamer	HD-39932	H-D
Valve guide reamer T-handle	HD-39847	H-D
Valve guide reamer and honing lube	HD-39064	H-D
Valve guide seal tool	34643-84	JIMS
Wheel bearing race remover/installer	33071-73	JIMS
Wheel rim protectors	HD-01289	H-D

CHAPTER TWO

TROUBLESHOOTING

Diagnosing mechanical problems is relatively simple if an orderly procedure is used. The first step in any troubleshooting procedure is to define the symptoms closely and then localize the problem. Subsequent steps involve testing and analyzing those areas that could cause the symptoms. A haphazard approach may eventually solve the problem, but it can be very costly with wasted time and unnecessary parts replacement.

Proper lubrication, maintenance and periodic tune-ups as described in Chapter Three will reduce the necessity for troubleshooting. Even with the best of care, however, the motorcycle may require troubleshooting.

Never assume anything; do not overlook the obvious. If the engine will not start, the engine stop switch or start button may be shorted out or damaged. When trying to start the engine, it may be flooded.

If the engine suddenly quits, consider the easiest, most accessible system first. If the engine sounded as if it ran out of fuel, make sure there is fuel in the tank and that it is reaching the carburetor. On carbureted models, make sure the fuel shutoff valve is turned on.

If a quick check does not reveal the problem, proceed with one of the troubleshooting procedures described in this chapter. Gather as many symptoms as possible to determine where to start. For example, note whether the engine lost power gradually or all at once, what color came from the exhaust, etc.

After defining the symptoms, follow the procedure that most closely relates to the condition(s). Guessing at the cause of the problem might provide a solution, but it can easily lead to wasted time and unnecessary parts replacement.

Expensive equipment or complicated test gear is not required to determine whether repairs can be attempted at home. A few simple checks could save a large repair bill and lost time while the motorcycle sits in a dealership service department. On the other hand, be realistic and do not attempt repairs beyond personal capabilities. Dealership service departments tend to charge heavily when working on equipment that has been abused. Some will not even take on such a job. Use common sense to avoid getting involved in a procedure that cannot be completed satisfactorily. If referring troubleshooting to a repair facility, describe problems accurately and fully.

Table 1 and **Table 2** list electrical specifications. **Tables 1-4** are located at the end of this chapter.

ENGINE PRINCIPLES

Figure 1 explains the basic four-stroke engine operation. This information is helpful when troubleshooting or repairing the engine.

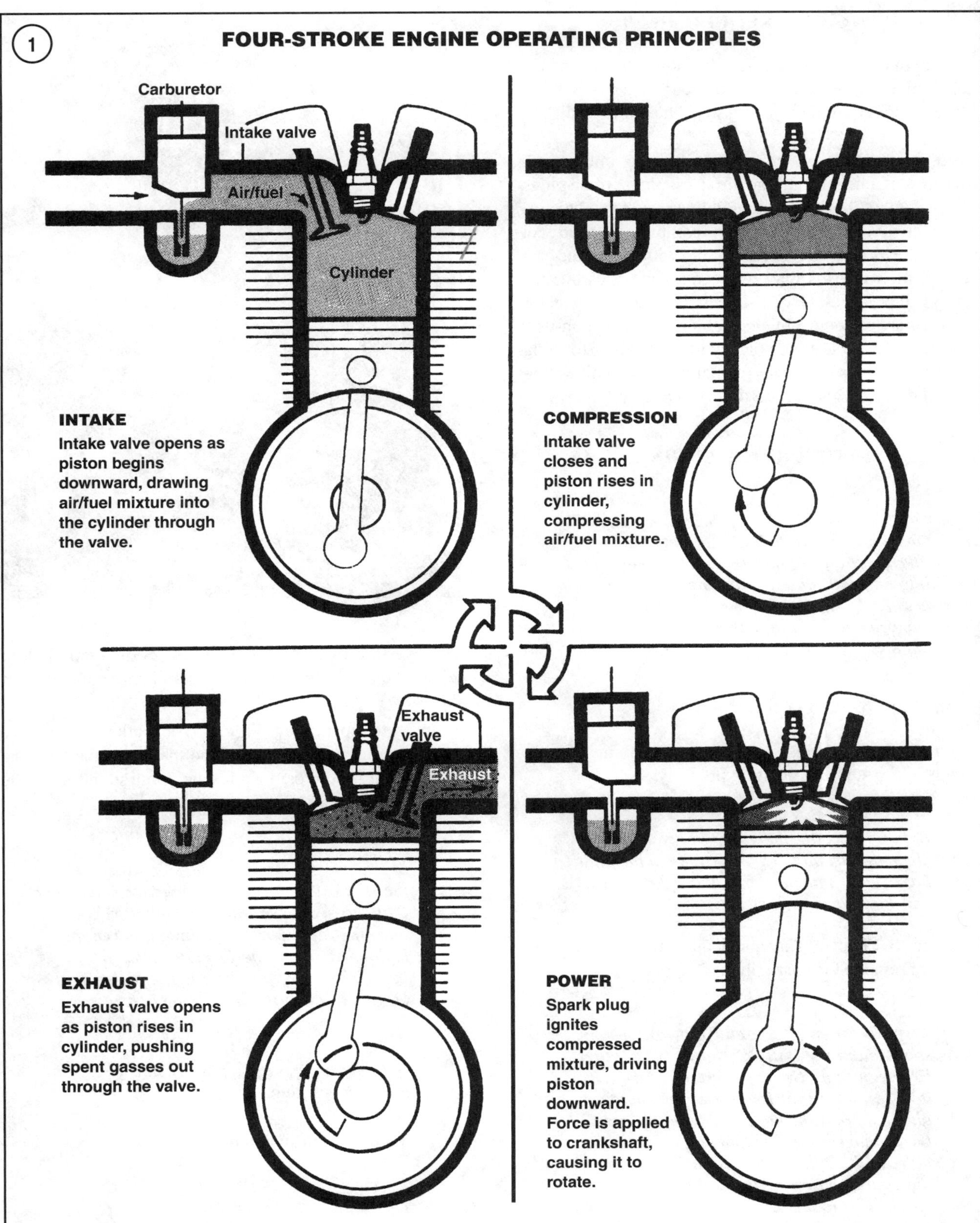
1
FOUR-STROKE ENGINE OPERATING PRINCIPLES
Carburetor
Intake valve
Air/fuel
Cylinder
INTAKE
Intake valve opens as piston begins downward, drawing air/fuel mixture into the cylinder through the valve.
COMPRESSION
Intake valve closes and piston rises in cylinder, compressing air/fuel mixture.
Exhaust valve
Exhaust
EXHAUST
Exhaust valve opens as piston rises in cylinder, pushing spent gasses out through the valve.
POWER
Spark plug ignites compressed mixture, driving piston downward. Force is applied to crankshaft, causing it to rotate.

OPERATING REQUIREMENTS

An engine needs three basics to run properly: correct fuel/air mixture, compression and a spark at the right time. If one basic requirement is missing, the engine will not run.

If the motorcycle has been sitting for any time and refuses to start, check and clean the spark plugs. If the plugs are not fouled, look to the fuel delivery system. This includes the fuel tank, fuel shutoff valve, fuel filter and fuel lines. If the motorcycle sat for a while with fuel in the carburetor, fuel deposits may have gummed up carburetor jets and air passages. On fuel-injected models, the injector nozzles may become plugged after prolonged non-use. Gasoline tends to lose its potency after standing for long periods. Condensation may contaminate it with water. Drain the old gas and try starting with a fresh tank.

STARTING THE ENGINE

NOTE
On fuel-injected models, there is no starter enrichener valve to assist in cold starting. The electronic control module takes that into consideration during the starting procedure. Do not pump or roll the throttle lever prior to starting either a cold or warm engine.

Engine Fails to Start (Spark Test)

Perform the following spark test to determine whether the ignition system is operating properly.

CAUTION
Before removing the spark plugs in Step 1, clean all dirt and debris away from the plug base. Dirt that falls into the cylinder will cause rapid engine wear.

1. Refer to Chapter Three, disconnect the spark plug wire, and remove the spark plug.

NOTE
A spark tester is a useful tool for testing spark output. ***Figure 2*** *shows the Motion Pro Ignition System Tester (part No. 08-122). This tool is inserted in the spark plug cap, and the base is grounded against the cylinder head. The tool air gap is adjustable, and it allows the visual inspection of the spark while testing the intensity of the spark. This tool is available through motorcycle repair shops.*

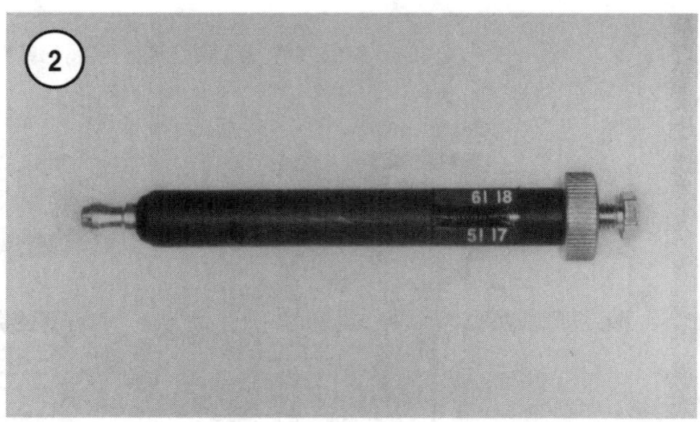

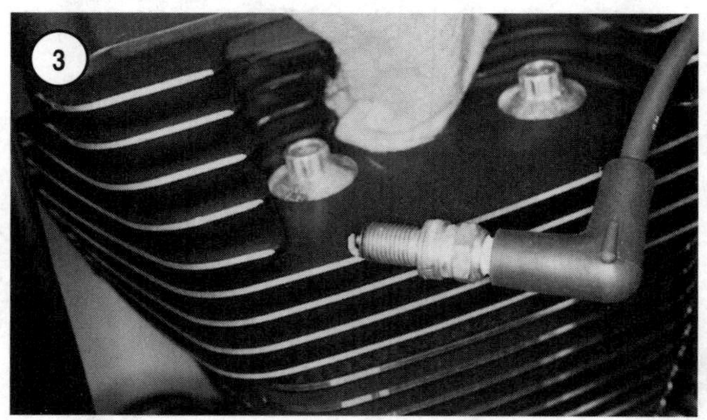

2. Cover the spark plug hole with a clean shop cloth to lessen the chance of gasoline vapors being emitted from the hole.

3. Insert the spark plug (**Figure 3**) or spark tester (**Figure 4**) into its plug cap and ground the spark plug base against the cylinder head. Position the spark plug so the electrode is visible.

WARNING
Mount the spark plug, or tester, away from the spark plug hole in the cylinder head so that the spark or tester cannot ignite the gasoline vapors in the cylinder. If the engine is flooded, do not perform this test. The firing of the spark plug can ignite fuel that is ejected through the spark plug hole.

NOTE
If a spark plug is used, perform this test with a new spark plug.

4. Turn the ignition switch on.

WARNING
Do ***not*** *hold the spark plug, wire or connector, or a serious electrical shock may result.*

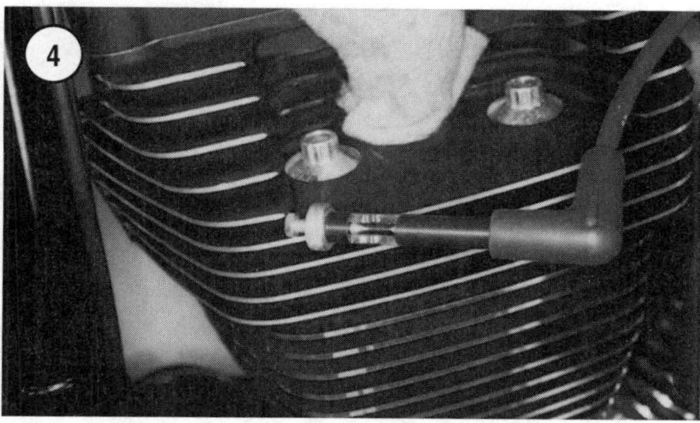

5. Turn the engine over with the electric starter. A crisp blue spark should be evident across the spark plug electrode or spark tester terminals. If there is strong sunlight on the plug, shade the plug by hand to see the spark better.
6. If the spark is good, check for one or more of the following possible malfunctions:
   a. Obstructed fuel line or fuel filter.
   b. Malfunctioning fuel pump or fuel pump circuit (fuel-injected models).
   c. Low compression or engine damage.
   d. Flooded engine.
7. If the spark is weak, or if there is no spark, refer to *Engine Is Difficult to Start* in this section.

NOTE

If the engine backfires during starting, the ignition timing may be incorrect due to a defective ignition component. Refer to ***Ignition Timing*** *in Chapter Three for more information.*

Engine Is Difficult to Start

Check for one or more of the following possible malfunctions:

1. Fouled spark plug(s).
2. Improperly adjusted starting enrichment valve (carbureted models).
3. Intake manifold air leak.
4. Plugged fuel tank filler cap.
5. Clogged fuel line.
6. Contaminated fuel system.
7. An improperly adjusted carburetor (carbureted models).
8. Malfunctioning fuel pump or fuel pump circuit (fuel-injected models).
9. A defective ignition module.
10. A defective ignition coil.
11. Damaged ignition coil primary and secondary wires.
12. Incorrect ignition timing.
13. Low engine compression.
14. Engine oil too heavy (winter temperatures).
15. Discharged battery.
16. Defective kickstarter assembly (four-speed transmission).
17. A defective starter motor (five-speed transmission).
18. Loose or corroded starter and/or battery cables (five-speed transmission).
19. A loose ignition sensor and module electrical connector.
20. Incorrect pushrod length (intake and exhaust valve pushrods interchanged).

Engine Will Not Crank

Check for one or more of the following possible malfunctions:

1. Ignition switch turned off.
2. A faulty ignition switch.
3. Engine run switch off.
4. A defective engine run switch.
5. Loose or corroded starter and battery cables (solenoid chatters). (Five-speed transmission models.)
6. Discharged or defective battery.
7. Defective kickstarter assembly (four-speed transmission).
8. A defective starter (five-speed transmission).
9. A defective starter solenoid (five-speed transmission).
10. A defective starter shaft pinion gear.
11. Slipping overrunning clutch assembly.
12. A seized piston(s).
13. Seized crankshaft bearings.
14. A broken connecting rod(s).

ENGINE PERFORMANCE

In the following checklist, it is assumed that the engine runs but is not operating at peak performance. This will serve as a starting point from which to isolate a performance malfunction.

Fouled Spark Plugs

If the spark plugs continually foul, check for the following:

1. Severely contaminated air filter element.
2. Incorrect spark plug heat range. See Chapter Three.
3. Rich fuel mixture.
4. Worn or damaged piston rings.
5. Worn or damaged valve guide oil seals.
6. Excessive valve stem-to-guide clearance.
7. Incorrect carburetor float level (carbureted models).

Engine Runs but Misfires

1. Fouled or improperly gapped spark plugs.
2. Damaged spark plug cables.
3. Incorrect ignition timing.
4. Defective ignition components.
5. An obstructed fuel line or fuel shutoff valve (carbureted models).
6. Obstructed fuel filter.
7. Clogged carburetor jets (carbureted models).
8. Malfunctioning fuel pump or fuel pump circuit (fuel-injected models).
9. Loose battery connection.
10. Wiring or connector damage.
11. Water or other contaminants in the fuel.
12. Weak or damaged valve springs.
13. Incorrect camshaft/valve timing.
14. A damaged valve(s).
15. Dirty electrical connections.
16. Intake manifold or carburetor air leak (carbureted models).
17. Induction module air leak (fuel-injected models).
18. A plugged carburetor vent hose.
19. Plugged fuel tank vent system.

Engine Overheating

1. Incorrect carburetor adjustment or jet selection.
2. Incorrect ignition timing or defective ignition system components.
3. Improper spark plug heat range.
4. Damaged or blocked cooling fins.
5. Low oil level.
6. Oil not circulating properly.
7. Leaking valves.
8. Heavy engine carbon deposits.

Engine Runs Roughly with Excessive Exhaust Smoke

1. Clogged air filter element.
2. Incorrect rich carburetor adjustment (carbureted models).
3. Choke not operating correctly (carbureted models).
4. Water or other fuel contaminants.
5. Clogged fuel line and/or filter.
6. Spark plugs fouled.
7. A defective ignition coil.
8. A defective ignition module or sensor(s).
9. Loose or defective ignition circuit wire.
10. Short circuits from damaged wire insulation.
11. Loose battery cable connections.
12. Incorrect camshaft/valve timing.

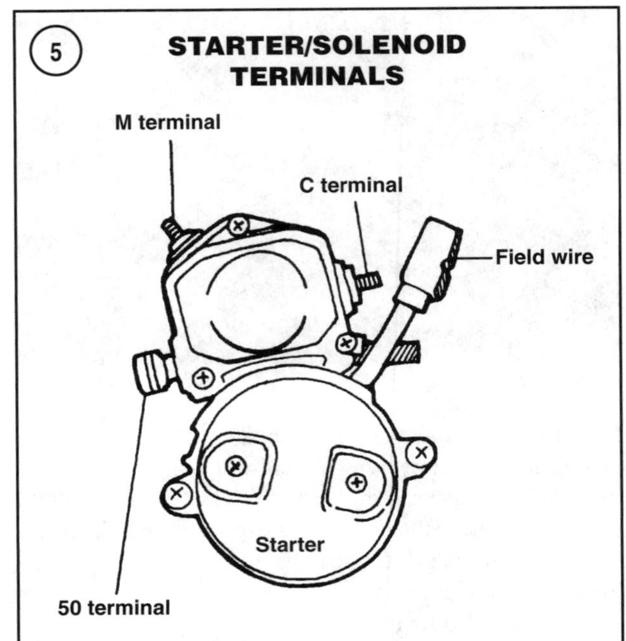

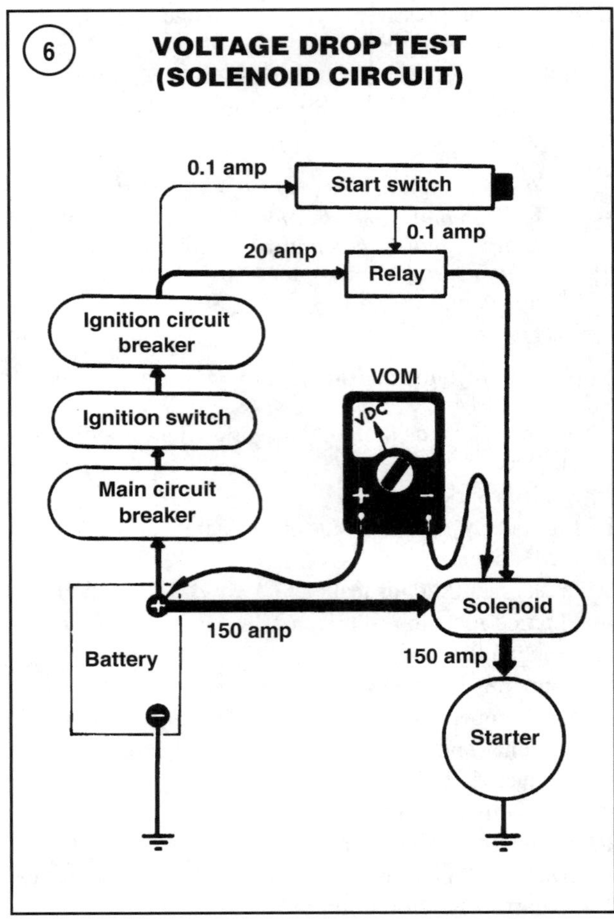

13. Intake manifold or air filter air leaks.

Engine Loses Power

1. Incorrect carburetor adjustment (carbureted models).
2. Engine overheating.
3. Incorrect ignition timing.
4. Incorrectly gapped spark plugs.
5. An obstructed muffler(s).
6. Dragging brake(s).

Engine Lacks Acceleration

1. Incorrect carburetor adjustment (carbureted models).
2. Clogged fuel line.
3. Incorrect ignition timing.
4. Dragging brake(s).

Valve Train Noise

1. A bent pushrod(s).
2. A defective hydraulic lifter(s).
3. A bent valve.
4. Rocker arm seizure or damage (binding on shaft).
5. Worn or damaged camshaft gear bushing(s).
6. Worn or damaged camshaft gear(s).

STARTING SYSTEM (FIVE-SPEED TRANSMISSION MODELS)

The starting system consists of the battery, starter, starter relay, solenoid, start switch, starter mechanism and related wiring.

When the ignition switch is turned on and the start button pushed in, current is transmitted from the battery to the starter relay. When the relay is activated, it in turn activates the starter solenoid that mechanically engages the starter with the engine.

Starting system problems are relatively easy to find. In most cases, the trouble is a loose or corroded electrical connection.

Refer to **Figure 5** for starter and solenoid terminal identification.

Troubleshooting Preparation

Before troubleshooting the starting system, make sure that:

1. The battery is fully charged.
2. Battery cables have proper size and length. Replace cables that are damaged, severely corroded or undersized.
3. All electrical connections are clean and tight.
4. The wiring harness is in good condition with no worn or frayed insulation or loose harness sockets.
5. The fuel tank is filled with an adequate supply of fresh gasoline.
6. The spark plugs are in good condition and properly gapped.
7. The ignition system is working correctly.

Voltage Drop Test

Before performing the steps listed under *Troubleshooting*, perform this voltage drop test. These steps will help find weak or damaged electrical components that may be causing the starting system problem. A multimeter is required to test voltage drop.

1. To check voltage drop in the solenoid circuit, connect the positive multimeter lead to the positive battery terminal; connect the negative multimeter lead to the solenoid (**Figure 6**).

NOTE

The multimeter lead must not touch the starter-to-solenoid terminal. ***Figure 7*** *shows the solenoid terminal with the starter/solenoid removed to better illustrate the step.*

2. Turn the ignition switch on and push the starter button while reading the multimeter scale. Note the following:
   a. The circuit is operating correctly if the multimeter reading is 0.2 volts or less. A multimeter reading of 12 volts indicates an open circuit.
   b. A voltage drop of more than 0.2 volts shows a problem in the solenoid circuit.
   c. If the voltage drop reading is correct, continue with Step 3.

3. To check the starter ground circuit, connect the negative multimeter lead to the negative battery terminal; connect the positive multimeter lead to the starter housing (**Figure 8**).
4. Turn the ignition switch on and push the starter button while reading the multimeter scale. The voltage drop must not exceed 0.2 volts. If it does, check the ground connections between the meter leads.
5. If the problem is not found, refer to *Troubleshooting Basics* in the following section.

NOTE
Steps 3 and 4 check the voltage drop across the starter ground circuit. Repeat this test to check any ground circuit in the starting circuit. To do so, leave the negative multimeter lead connected to the battery and connect the positive multimeter lead to the ground in question.

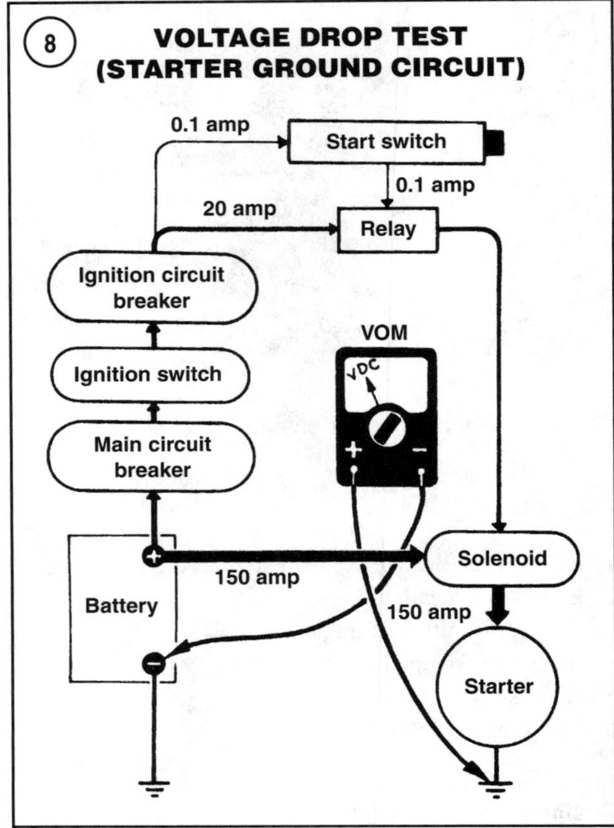

Troubleshooting Basics

The basic starter-related troubles are:
1. Starter does not spin.
2. Starter spins but does not engage.
3. The starter will not disengage after the start button is released.
4. Loud grinding noises when starter turns.
5. Starter stalls or spins too slowly.

Perform the steps listed under *Troubleshooting Preparation*.

CAUTION
Never operate the starter for more than 30 seconds at a time. Allow the starter to cool before reusing it. Failing to allow the starter to cool after continuous starting attempts can damage the starter.

Troubleshooting

Perform the steps listed under *Troubleshooting Preparation*. When making the following voltage checks, test results must be within 1/2 volt of battery voltage.

1984 and late 1985-1988 models

When making the following voltage tests, isolate the individual components to check voltage flow into a component (input side) and voltage through the component (output side).
1. Turn on the ignition switch and depress the start button. If the solenoid and relay do not click, perform Step 2. If only the solenoid clicks, perform Step 3. If only the relay clicks, perform Step 4.
2. If the solenoid and relay did not click when performing Step 1, perform the following checks. When making the following checks, first connect the negative multimeter lead to a good ground. Then connect the positive multimeter lead to the point in the circuit described in each of the following tests. With both multimeter leads connected, turn the ignition switch on; depress the start button and check the multimeter reading. Turn the ignition switch off and check the multimeter reading.

NOTE
*Refer to **Figure 9** for starter relay terminal contact numbers.*

a. Connect the negative multimeter lead across the No. 85 (FX series models) or the No. 86 (FLH and FLT series models) starter relay terminal (ground). Then connect the positive multimeter lead across the No. 86 (FX series models) or the No. 85 (FLH and FLT series models) starter terminal. If the voltage reading is low, check for loose or damaged wiring at the starter relay and start switch. If battery

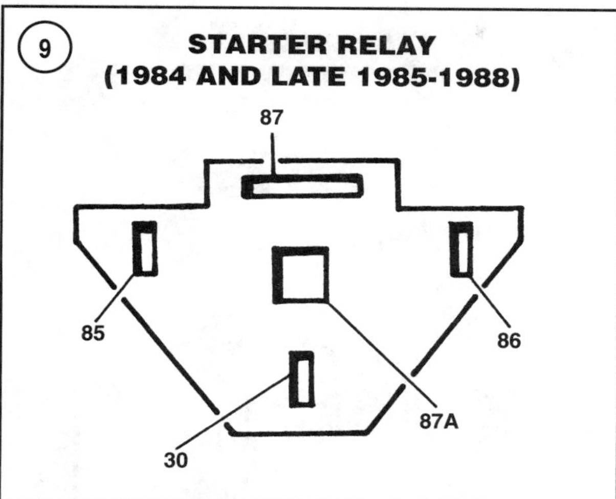

voltage is indicated, the starter relay is defective. Confirm by bench testing the starter relay as described in this chapter.

b. Connect the negative multimeter lead to ground. Then connect the positive multimeter lead separately across the start switch input and output terminals; there should be battery voltage during each test. Low input voltage indicates a damaged stop switch. Low output voltage indicates a damaged start switch.
c. Connect the negative multimeter lead to ground. Then check input and output voltage at the stop switch; there should be battery voltage during each test. Low input voltage indicates damaged or faulty wiring to the ignition switch. Low output voltage indicates a faulty stop switch.
d. Connect the negative multimeter lead to ground and the positive multimeter lead to the ignition circuit breaker input side (copper stud). Repeat to check voltage on circuit breaker output side. There should be battery voltage during each test. Low input voltage indicates a problem in the wiring from the ignition switch and circuit breaker. Low output voltage indicates a damaged ignition circuit breaker.
e. Connect the negative multimeter lead to ground and the positive multimeter lead to the main circuit breaker input side (copper stud). Repeat voltage check on output side. There should be battery voltage during each test. Low input voltage indicates a problem in the wiring from the main circuit breaker to the battery. Low output voltage indicates a damaged main circuit breaker.
f. Connect the negative multimeter lead to ground and the positive lead to the ignition terminal on the ignition switch. A low reading indicates a damaged ignition switch.
g. Connect the negative lead to ground and the positive lead to the battery terminal on the ignition switch. Low voltage indicates a problem in the wiring from the main circuit to the switch.

3. If only the solenoid clicked when performing Step 1, perform the following checks. When making the following tests, first connect the negative multimeter lead to a good ground. Then connect the positive multimeter lead to the point in the circuit described in each of the following tests. When both multimeter leads are connected, turn the ignition switch on; depress the start button and check the multimeter reading. Turn the ignition switch off and disconnect the multimeter.
   a. Connect the negative multimeter lead to ground and the positive lead to the starter wire at the starter; there should be battery voltage. A low reading indicates a problem in the wiring from the solenoid to the starter.
   b. Connect the negative multimeter lead to ground and the positive lead to the long solenoid terminal; battery voltage should be indicated. A low reading indicates a problem in the wiring from the battery to the solenoid.
   c. Connect the negative multimeter lead to ground and the positive lead to the short solenoid terminal; battery voltage should be indicated. A low reading indicates a damaged solenoid or faulty starter drive system.
4. If only the starter relay clicked when performing Step 1, perform the following checks. When making the following tests, first connect the negative multimeter lead to a good ground. Then connect the positive multimeter lead to the point in the circuit described in each of the following tests. When both multimeter leads are connected, turn the ignition switch on; depress the start button and check the multimeter reading. Turn the ignition switch off and disconnect the multimeter.
   a. Connect the negative multimeter lead to ground and the positive lead to the starter relay No. 30 terminal (**Figure 9**); meter should read battery voltage. A low reading indicates a problem in the main circuit breaker wiring.
   b. Connect the negative multimeter lead to ground and the positive lead to the starter relay No. 87 terminal (**Figure 9**); meter should show battery voltage. A low reading indicates a damaged starter relay. Confirm by bench testing the starter relay as described in this chapter.
   c. Connect the negative multimeter to ground and the positive lead to the center solenoid terminal; meter

should show battery voltage. A low reading indicates a problem in the wiring between the solenoid and starter relay.

Early 1985 models

When making the following voltage tests, isolate the individual components to check voltage flow into a component (input side) and voltage through the component (output side).

1. Turn the ignition switch on and depress the start button. If the solenoid and relay do not click, perform Step 2. If only the solenoid clicks, perform Step 3. If only the relay clicks, perform Step 4.

2. If the solenoid and relay did not click when performing Step 1, perform the following checks. When making the following checks, first connect the negative multimeter lead to a good ground. Then connect the positive multimeter lead to the point in the circuit described in each of the following tests. When both multimeter leads are connected, turn the ignition switch on; depress the start button and check the multimeter reading. Turn the ignition switch off and disconnect the multimeter. Refer to **Figure 10** for starter relay test points.

   a. Connect the negative multimeter lead across the starter relay base (ground) and the positive lead across the small starter relay terminal. A low reading indicates a problem in the wiring at the relay base (ground), on the small terminal on the relay or at the start switch. If battery voltage is indicated, the starter relay is defective. Confirm by bench testing the starter relay as described in this chapter.

   b. Connect the negative multimeter lead to ground and the positive multimeter lead separately across the start switch input and output sides; battery voltage should be shown during each test. Low input voltage indicates a damaged stop switch. Low output voltage indicates a damaged start switch.

   c. Connect the negative multimeter lead to ground. Then check input and output voltage at the stop switch; battery voltage should be shown during each test. Low input voltage indicates damaged or faulty wiring to the ignition switch. Low output voltage indicates a faulty stop switch.

   d. Connect the negative multimeter lead to ground and the positive multimeter lead to the ignition circuit breaker input side (copper stud). Repeat to check voltage on circuit breaker output side. Battery voltage should be shown when making each test. Low input voltage indicates a problem in the wiring from the ignition switch and circuit breaker. Low output voltage indicates a damaged ignition circuit breaker.

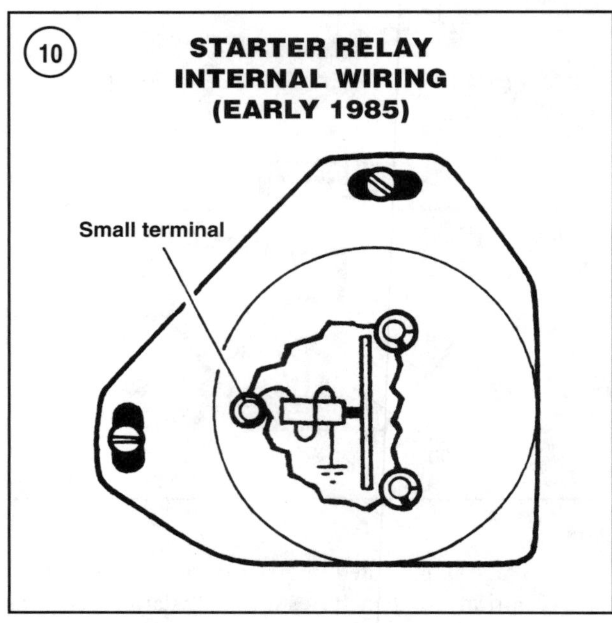

   e. Connect the negative multimeter lead to ground and the positive multimeter lead to the main circuit breaker input side (copper stud). Repeat to check voltage on output side. Battery voltage should be shown when making each test. Low input voltage indicates a problem in the wiring from the main circuit breaker to the battery. Low output voltage indicates a damaged main circuit breaker.

   f. Connect the negative multimeter lead to ground and the positive lead to the ignition terminal on the ignition switch. A low reading indicates a damaged ignition switch.

   g. Connect the negative multimeter lead to the battery terminal on the ignition switch. Low voltage indicates a problem in the wiring from the main circuit to the switch.

3. If only the solenoid clicked when performing Step 1, perform the following checks. When making the following checks, first connect the negative multimeter lead to a good ground. Then connect the positive multimeter lead to the point in the circuit described in each of the following tests. When both multimeter leads are connected, turn the ignition switch on; depress the start button and check the multimeter reading. Turn the ignition switch off and disconnect the multimeter.

   a. Connect the negative multimeter lead to ground and the positive lead to the starter wire at the starter; battery voltage should be indicated. A low reading in-

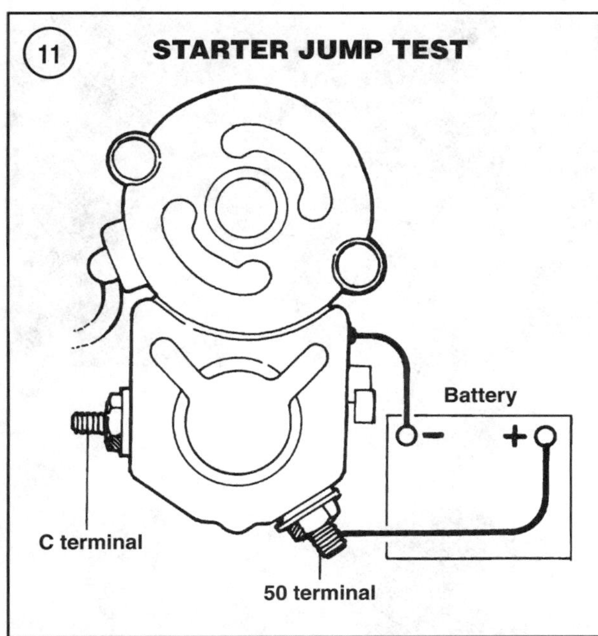

dicates a problem in the wiring from the solenoid to the starter.

b. Connect the negative multimeter lead to ground and the positive lead to the short/large solenoid terminal; battery voltage should be indicated. A low reading indicates solenoid damage. Confirm by bench testing the solenoid as described in this chapter. If the solenoid tests correctly, check the starter drive system for damage.

4. If only the starter relay clicked when performing Step 1, perform the following checks. During testing, first connect the negative multimeter lead to a good ground. Then connect the positive multimeter lead to the point in the circuit described in each of the following tests. When both multimeter leads are connected, turn the ignition switch on; depress the start button and check the multimeter reading. Turn the ignition switch off and disconnect the multimeter.

a. Connect the negative multimeter lead to ground and the positive lead to the starter relay battery terminal; the meter should read battery voltage. A low reading indicates a problem in the wiring between the starter relay and battery.

b. Connect the negative multimeter lead to ground and the positive lead to the starter relay-to-solenoid terminal at the starter relay. No battery voltage indicates a damaged starter relay.

c. Connect the negative multimeter lead to ground and the positive lead to the long/large solenoid terminal. Low battery voltage indicates a problem in the wiring from the solenoid to the starter relay.

d. Connect the negative multimeter lead to ground and the positive lead to the small solenoid terminal. A low voltage reading indicates a problem between the jumper wire at the solenoid.

1989-1998 models

The basic starter-related troubles are:

1. Engine cranks very slowly or not at all.
2. Starter spins but does not crank engine.
3. Starter will not disengage when start button is released.
4. Loud grinding noises when starter runs.

Starter system problems are relatively easy to find. In most cases, the trouble is a loose or dirty electrical connection.

Starter does not spin

1. Turn the ignition switch on and push the starter button while listening for a click at the starter relay in the electrical panel. Turn the ignition switch off and note the following:

a. If the starter relay clicks, test the starter relay as described under *Component Testing* in this section. If the starter relay test readings are correct, continue with Step 2.

b. If the solenoid clicks, go to Step 3.

c. If there is no click, go to Step 6.

2. Check the wiring connectors between the starter relay and solenoid. Note the following:

a. Repair any dirty, loose-fitting or damaged connectors or wiring.

b. If the wiring is good, remove the starter as described in Chapter Nine. Perform the solenoid and starter bench tests described in this section.

3. Perform a voltage drop test between the battery and solenoid terminals as described under *Voltage Drop Tests* in this section. The normal voltage drop is less than 0.2 volts. Note the following:

a. If the voltage drop is less than 0.2 volts, perform Step 4.

b. If the voltage drop is more than 0.2 volts, check the solenoid and battery wires and connections for dirty or loose-fitting terminals; clean and repair as required.

4. Remove the starter as described in Chapter Nine. Momentarily connect a fully charged 12-volt battery to the starter as shown in **Figure 11**. If the starter is operational,

it will turn when connected to the battery. Disconnect the battery and note the following:

a. If the starter turns, perform the solenoid pull-in and hold-in tests as described under *Solenoid Testing (Bench Tests)* in this section.
b. If the starter does not turn, disassemble the starter as described in Chapter Nine, and check it for opens, shorts and grounds.

5. If the problem is not evident after performing Steps 3 and 4, check the starter shaft to see if it is binding at the jackshaft. Check the jackshaft for binding or damage. Refer to *Starter Jackshaft* in Chapter Five.
6. If there is no click when performing Step 1, measure voltage between the starter button and the starter relay. The multimeter must read battery voltage. Note the following:
   a. If battery voltage is noted, continue with Step 7.
   b. If there is no voltage, go to Step 8.
7. Check the starter relay ground at the starter relay. Note the following:
   a. If the starter relay is properly grounded, test the starter relay as described in this section.
   b. If the starter relay is not grounded, check the ground connection. Repair the ground connection. Then retest.
8. Check for voltage at the starter button. Note the following:
   a. If there is voltage at the starter button, test the starter relay as described in this section.
   b. If there is no voltage at the starter button, check continuity across the starter button. If there is voltage leading to the starter button but no voltage leaving the starter button, replace the button switch and retest. If there is no voltage leading to the starter button, check the starter button wiring for dirty or loose-fitting terminals or damaged wiring; clean and/or repair as required.

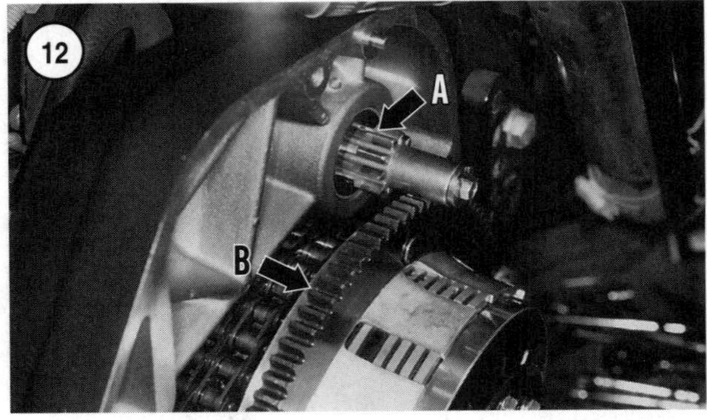

Starter spins but does not engage

If the starter spins, but the pinion gear does not engage the ring gear, perform the following:

1. Remove the outer primary cover as described in Chapter Five.
2. Check the pinion gear (A, **Figure 12**) mounted on the end of the jackshaft. If the teeth are chipped or worn, inspect the clutch ring gear (B, **Figure 12**) for the same problems. Note the following:
   a. If the pinion gear and ring gear are damaged, service these parts as described in Chapter Five.
   b. If the pinion gear and ring gear are not damaged, continue with Step 3.
3. Remove and disassemble the starter as described in Chapter Nine. Then check the overrunning clutch assembly (**Figure 13**) for:
   a. Roller damage (**Figure 14**).
   b. Compression spring damage (A, **Figure 15**).
   c. Excessively worn or damaged pinion teeth.
   d. Pinion not running in overrunning direction.
   e. Damaged clutch shaft splines (B, **Figure 15**).
   f. Damaged overrunning clutch assembly (**Figure 16**).
4. Replace worn or damaged parts as required.

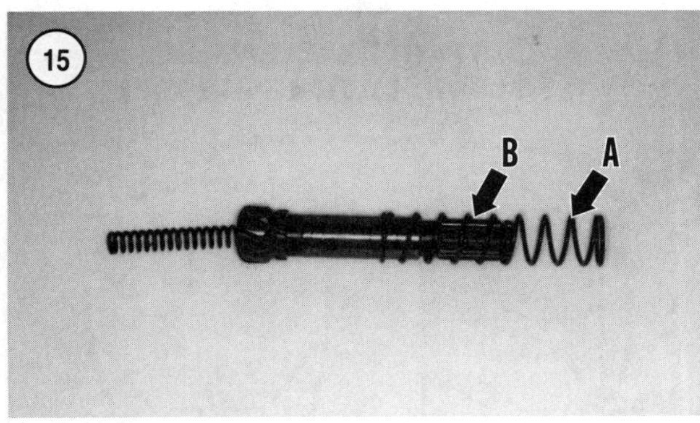

Starter will not disengage after the start button is released

1. A sticking solenoid, caused by a worn solenoid compression spring (A, **Figure 15**), can cause this problem. Replace the solenoid if damaged.

2. On high-mileage machines, the pinion gear (A, **Figure 12**) can jam on a worn clutch ring gear (B). Unable to return, the starter will continue to run. This condition usually requires ring gear replacement.

3. Check the start switch and starter relay for internal damage. Test the start switch as described under *Switches* in Chapter Nine. Test the starter relay as described in this chapter.

Loud grinding noises when the starter turns

Incorrect pinion gear and clutch ring gear engagement (B, **Figure 12**) or a broken overrunning clutch mechanism (**Figure 16**) can cause this problem. Remove and inspect the starter as described in Chapter Nine.

Starter stalls or spins too slowly

1. Perform a voltage drop test between the battery and solenoid terminals as described under *Voltage Drop Tests* in this section. The normal voltage drop is less than 0.2 volts. Note the following:
   a. If the voltage drop is less than 0.2 volts, continue with Step 2.
   b. If the voltage drop exceeds 0.2 volts, check the solenoid and battery wires and connections for dirty or loose-fitting terminals; clean and repair as required.

2. Perform a voltage drop test between the solenoid terminals and the starter motor as described under *Voltage Drop Tests* in this section. The normal voltage drop is less than 0.2 volts. Note the following:
   a. If the voltage drop is less than 0.2 volts, continue with Step 3.
   b. If the voltage drop exceeds 0.2 volts, check the solenoid and starter motor wires and connections for dirty or loose-fitting terminals; clean and repair as required.

3. Perform a voltage drop test between the battery ground wire and the starter motor as described under *Voltage Drop Tests* in this section. The normal voltage drop is less than 0.2 volts. Note the following:
   a. If the voltage drop is less than 0.2 volts, continue with Step 4.
   b. If the voltage drop exceeds 0.2 volts, check the battery ground wire connections for dirty or loose-fitting terminals; clean and repair as required.

4. Perform the *Starter Current Draw Test* in this section. Note the following:
   a. If the current draw is excessive, check for a damaged starter or starter drive assembly. Remove the starter as described in Chapter Nine and perform the *Current draw test (starter removed from the engine)* in this section.
   b. If the current draw reading is correct, continue with Step 5.

5. Remove the outer primary cover as described in Chapter Five. Check the pinion gear (A, **Figure 12**). If the teeth are chipped or worn, inspect the clutch ring gear (B, **Figure 12**) for the same problem.
   a. If the pinion gear and ring gears are damaged, service these parts as described in Chapter Five.
   b. If the pinion gear and ring gears are not damaged, continue with Step 6.

6. Remove and disassemble the starter as described in Chapter Nine. Check the disassembled starter for opens, shorts and grounds.

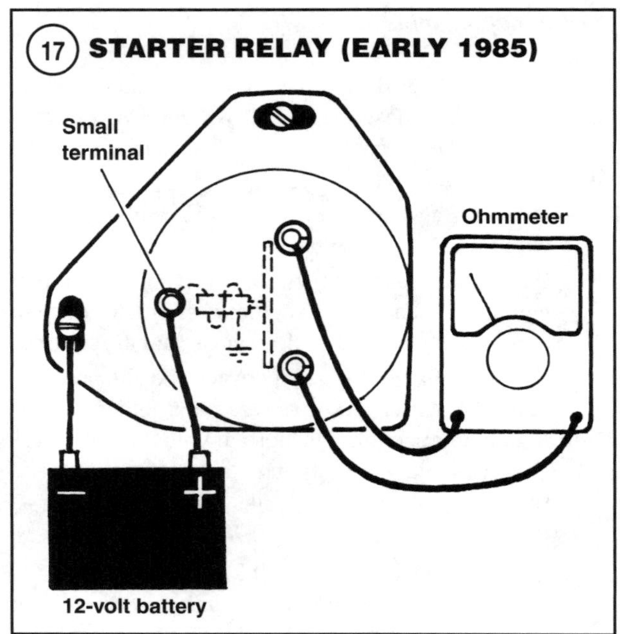

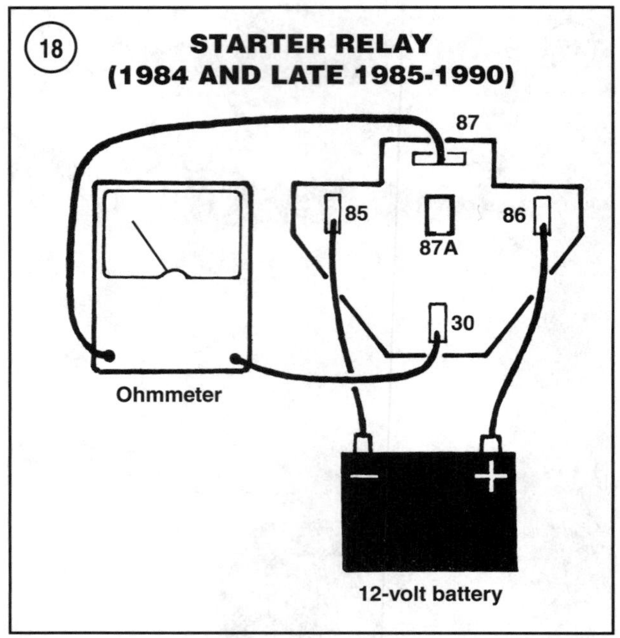

Component Testing

The following sections describe how to test individual starting system components. Refer to Chapter Nine for starter service.

Starter Relay Testing

Check the starter relay operation with a multimeter, jumper wires and a fully charged 12-volt battery.

1. Disconnect and remove the starter relay from the starting circuit on the motorcycle. See Chapter Nine.

2. To energize the relay, refer to **Figures 17-19** and connect a multimeter and 12-volt battery between the relay terminals.

CAUTION
*On 1991-1998 models, the negative battery terminal must be connected to the No. 85 terminal as shown in **Figure 19**. Otherwise, the diode connected across the relay winding will be damaged.*

3. Use the multimeter and check for continuity through the relay contacts (**Figures 17-19**) with the relay coil energized. There should be continuity. Replace the relay if there is no continuity.

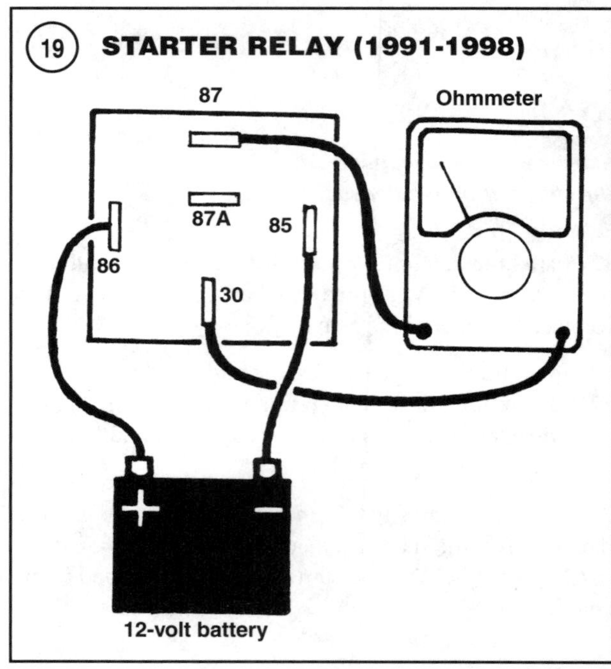

Starter Current Draw Tests

The following current draw test measures current (amperage) that the starter circuit requires to crank the engine. Refer to **Table 1** for current draw specifications.

A short circuit in the starter or a damaged pinion gear assembly can cause excessive current draw. If the current

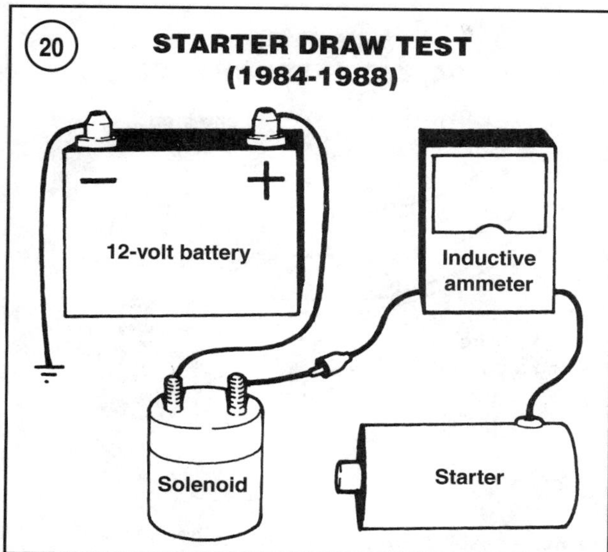

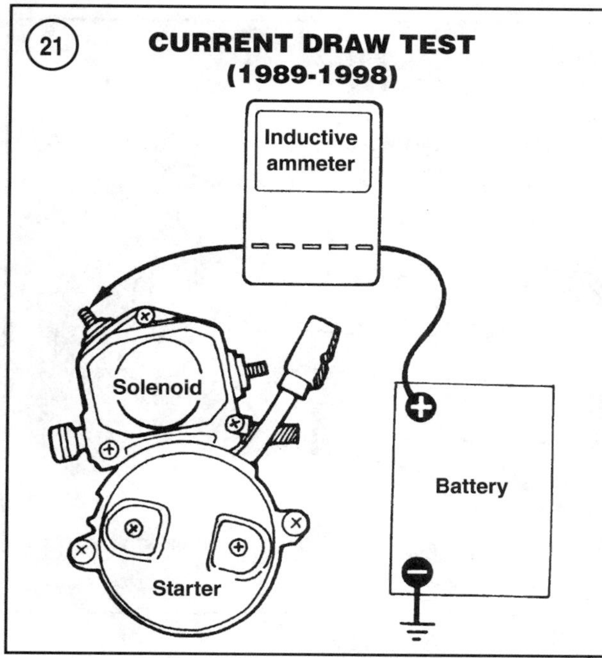

draw is low, suspect an undercharged battery or an open circuit in the starting circuit.

Current draw test (starter mounted on the engine)

NOTE
This test requires a fully charged battery and an inductive ammeter.

1. Shift the transmission into NEUTRAL.
2. Disconnect the two spark plug caps from the spark plugs. Then ground the plug caps with two extra spark plugs. Do *not* remove the spark plugs from the cylinder heads.
3A. On 1984-1988 models, connect an inductive ammeter between the starter terminal and positive battery terminal (**Figure 20**). Connect a jumper cable from the negative battery terminal to ground (**Figure 20**).
3B. On 1989-1998 models, connect an inductive ammeter between the starter terminal and positive battery terminal (**Figure 21**). Connect a jumper cable from the negative battery terminal to ground (**Figure 21**).
4. Turn the ignition switch on and press the start button for approximately 10 seconds. Note the ammeter reading.

NOTE
The current draw is high when the start button is first pressed. Then it will drop and stabilize at a lower reading. Refer to the lower stabilized reading during this test.

5. If the current draw exceeds the current draw specification in **Table 1**, check for a defective starter or starter drive mechanism. Remove and service these components as described in Chapter Eight.
6. Disconnect the ammeter and jumper cables.

Current draw test (starter removed from the engine)

This test requires a fully charged 12-volt battery, an inductive ammeter, a jumper wire (14-gauge minimum) and three jumper cables (6-gauge minimum).
1. Remove the starter as described in Chapter Nine.

NOTE
The solenoid must be installed on the starter motor during the following tests.

2. Mount the starter in a vise with soft jaws.
3. Connect the 14-gauge jumper cable between the positive battery terminal and the solenoid 50 terminal (**Figure 22**).
4. Connect a jumper cable (6-gauge minimum) between the positive battery terminal and the ammeter (**Figure 22**).
5. Connect the second jumper cable between the ammeter and the M terminal on the starter solenoid (**Figure 22**).
6. Connect the third jumper cable between the battery ground terminal and the starter motor mounting flange (**Figure 22**).
7. Read the ammeter. The correct ammeter reading is 90 amps. A damaged pinion gear assembly will cause an ex-

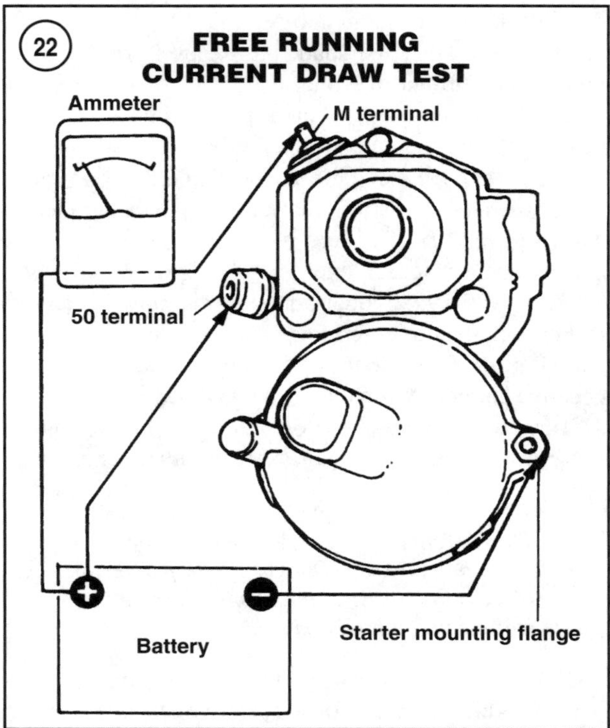

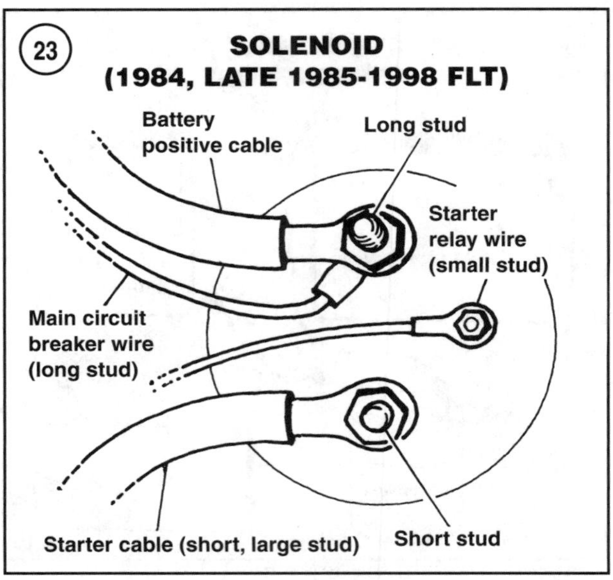

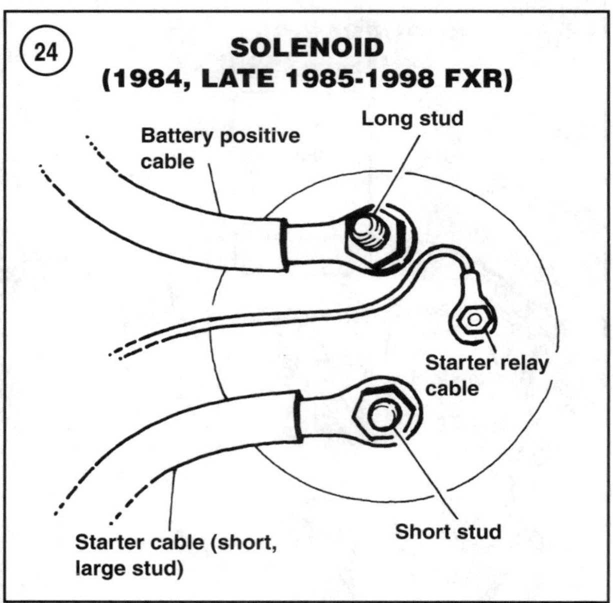

cessively high current draw reading. If the current draw reading is low, check for an undercharged battery or an open field winding or armature in the starter.

Solenoid Test (1984-1988 Models)

The solenoid can be tested while mounted on the motorcycle. Refer to **Figures 23-27** for solenoid wire locations.

1. Disconnect the negative battery cable from the battery.
2. Refer to Chapter Nine and locate the solenoid. Label and disconnect all of the cables at the solenoid.
3. Pull-in coil test: Connect an ohmmeter between the small and the short/large terminal on the solenoid (**Figure 28**). There should be continuity (no measurable resistance).
4. Hold-in coil test: Connect one ohmmeter lead to the small-diameter solenoid terminal and touch the opposite lead to the solenoid body (**Figure 29**). There should be continuity (no measurable resistance).
5. Connect a battery to the solenoid as shown in **Figure 30**. The solenoid should click when both battery cables are connected. With the battery still connected, connect an ohmmeter between the two large coil terminals. There should be continuity (no measurable resistance).
6. Replace the solenoid if it failed any one test in Steps 3-5.
7. Reverse Steps 1 and 2 after testing or replacing the solenoid.

Solenoid Test (1989-1998 Models) (Bench Tests)

This test requires a fully charged 12-volt battery and three jumper wires.

1. Remove the starter (A, **Figure 31**) as described in Chapter Eight.

NOTE

*The solenoid (B, **Figure 31**) must be installed on the starter during the following tests. Do not remove it.*

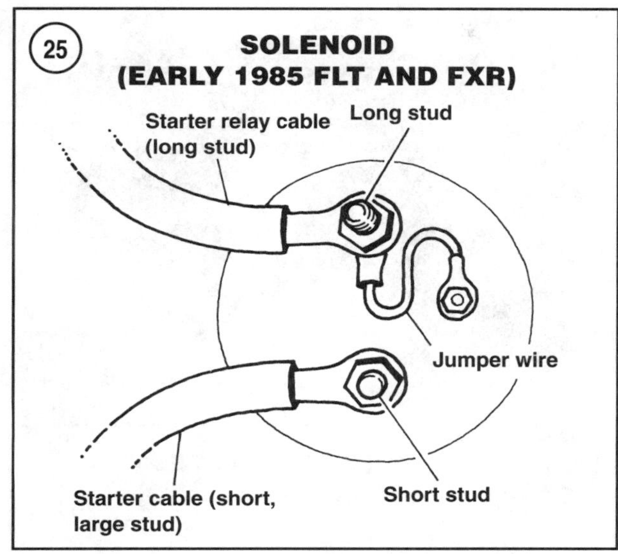
25
SOLENOID
(EARLY 1985 FLT AND FXR)
Starter relay cable
(long stud)
Long stud
Jumper wire
Starter cable (short,
large stud)
Short stud

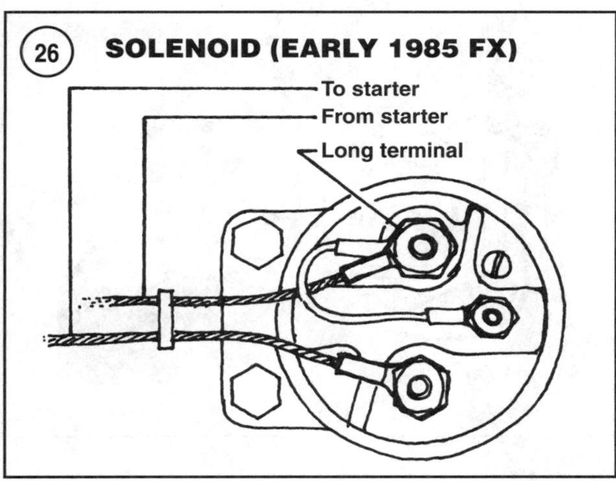
26
SOLENOID (EARLY 1985 FX)
To starter
From starter
Long terminal

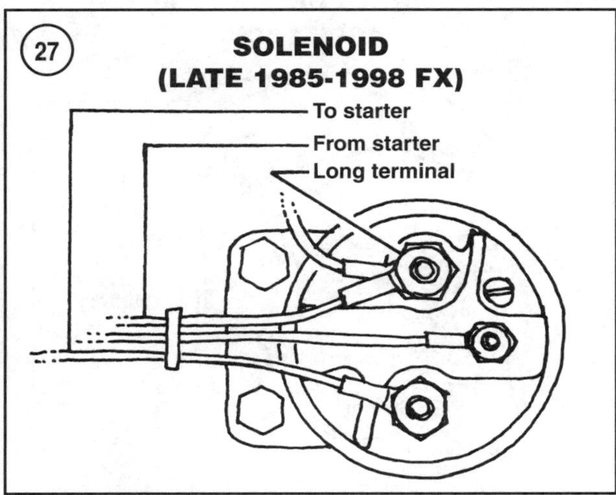
27
SOLENOID
(LATE 1985-1998 FX)
To starter
From starter
Long terminal

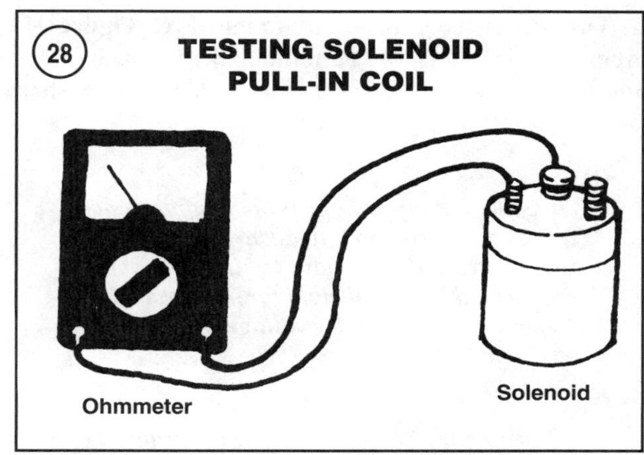
28
TESTING SOLENOID
PULL-IN COIL
Ohmmeter
Solenoid

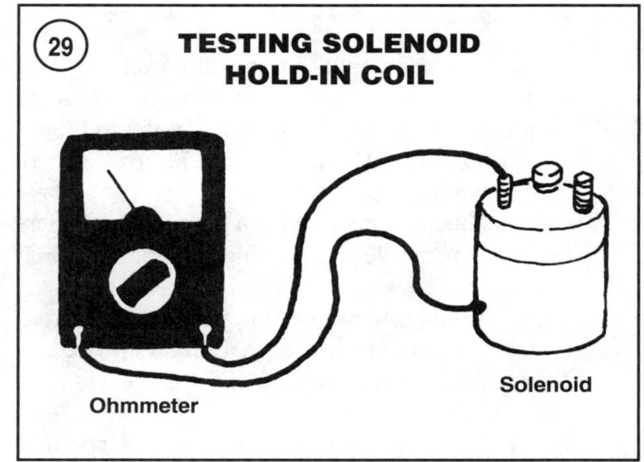
29
TESTING SOLENOID
HOLD-IN COIL
Ohmmeter
Solenoid

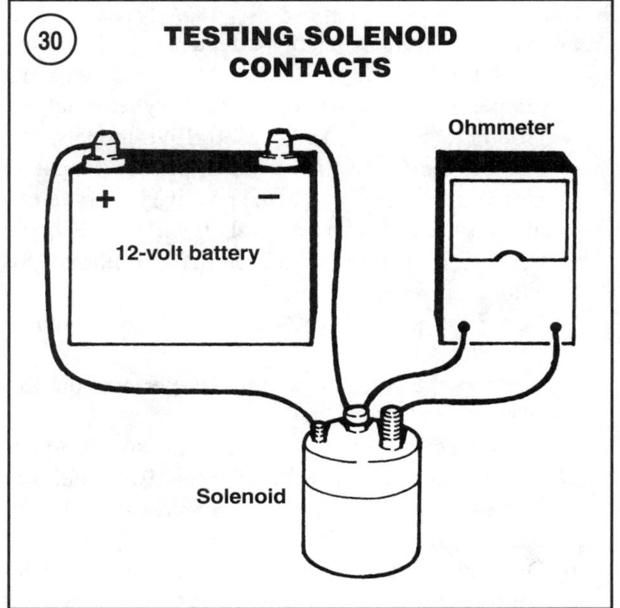
30
TESTING SOLENOID
CONTACTS
Ohmmeter
+
−
12-volt battery
Solenoid

2. Disconnect the C field wire terminal (C, **Figure 31**) from the solenoid before performing the following tests. Insulate the end of the wire terminal so that it cannot short out on any of the test connectors.

CAUTION
Because battery voltage is being applied directly to the solenoid and starter in the following tests, do not leave the jumper cables connected to the solenoid for more than 3-5 seconds; otherwise, the voltage will damage the solenoid.

NOTE
Thoroughly read the following procedure to familiarize and understand the procedures and test connections. Then perform the tests in the order listed and without interruption.

3. Perform the solenoid pull-in test as follows:
   a. Connect one jumper wire from the negative battery terminal to the solenoid C terminal. Refer to **Figure 32** for 1989-1994 models or **Figure 33** for 1995-1998 models.
   b. Connect one jumper wire from the negative battery terminal to the solenoid housing (ground). See **Figure 32** or **Figure 33**.
   c. Touch a jumper wire from the positive battery terminal to the starter 50 terminal. See **Figure 32** or **Figure 33**. The pinion shaft (D, **Figure 31**) must pull into the housing.
   d. Leave the jumper wires connected and continue with Step 4.
4. To perform the solenoid hold-in test, perform the following:
   a. With the pinion shaft extended (Step 3) on 1989-1990 models, disconnect the C terminal jumper wire from the negative battery terminal and ground it (**Figure 34**). On 1991-1998 models, disconnect the C terminal from the battery negative terminal and connect it to the positive battery terminal (**Figure 35**). The pinion shaft will remain in the housing. If the pinion shaft returns to its normal position, replace the solenoid.
   b. Leave the jumper wires connected and continue with Step 5.
5. To perform the solenoid return test, perform the following:
   a. Disconnect the jumper wire from the starter 50 terminal. Refer to **Figure 36** for 1989-1994 models or **Figure 37** for 1995-1998 models; the pinion shaft must return to its original position.
   b. Disconnect all of the jumper wires from the solenoid and battery.

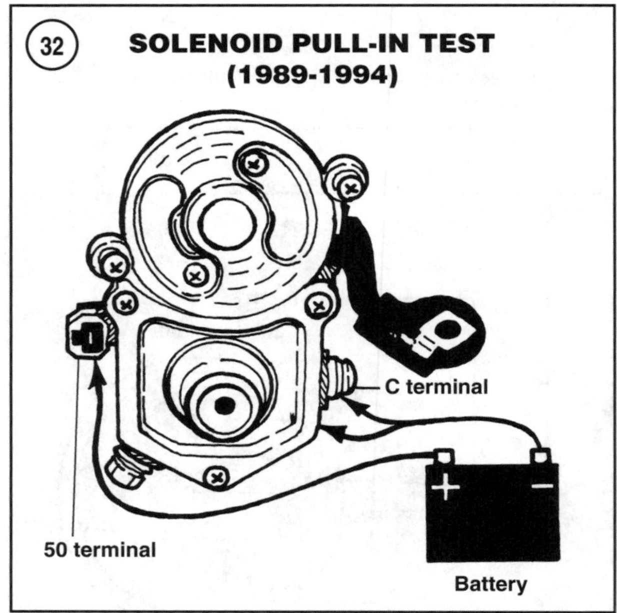

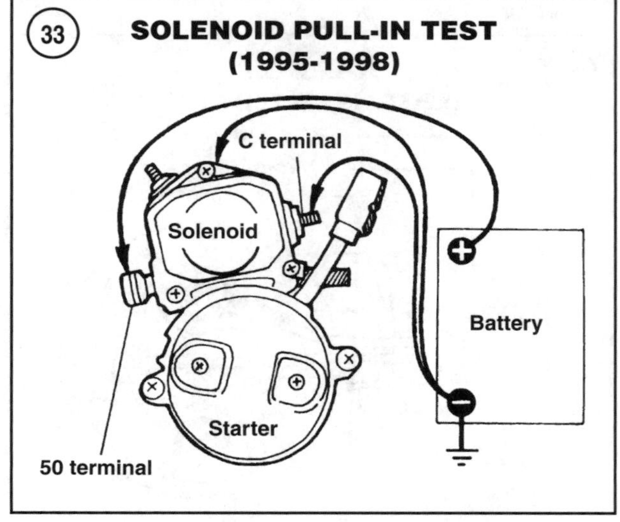

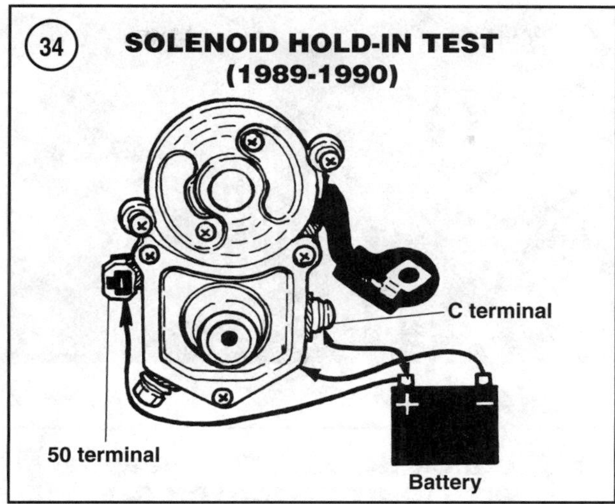

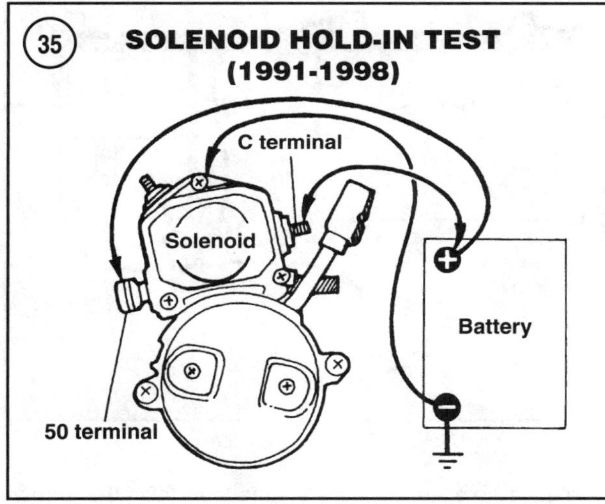

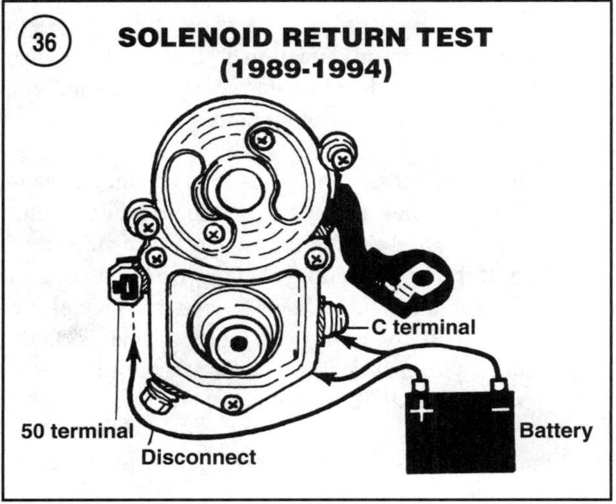

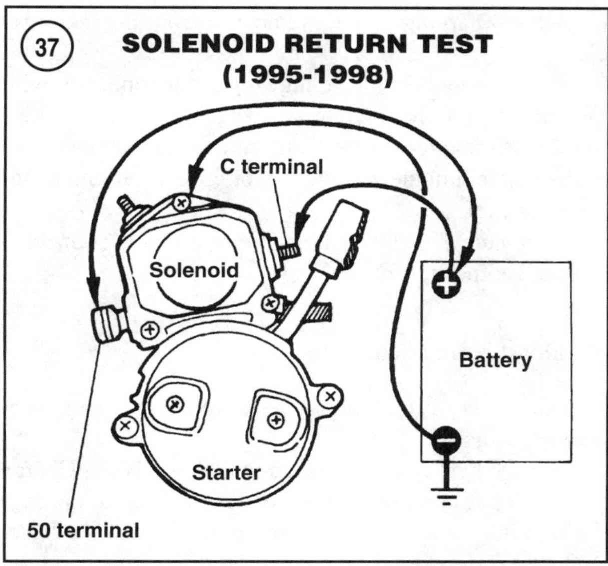

6. Replace the solenoid if the starter shaft failed to operate as described in Steps 3-5. Refer to *Solenoid Replacement* in Chapter Eight.

CHARGING SYSTEM

The charging system consists of the battery, alternator and a solid-state rectifier/voltage regulator.

The alternator generates an alternating current (AC), which the rectifier converts to direct current (DC). The regulator maintains the voltage to the battery and load (lights, ignition and accessories) at a constant voltage regardless of variations in engine speed and load.

A malfunction in the charging system generally causes the battery to remain undercharged.

Service Precautions

Before servicing the charging system, observe the following precautions to prevent damage to any charging system component.

1. Never reverse battery connections.
2. Do not short across any connection.
3. Never start the engine with the alternator disconnected from the voltage regulator/rectifier, unless instructed to do so in testing.
4. Never start or run the engine with the battery disconnected.
5. Never attempt to use a high-output battery charger to assist in engine starting.

6. Before charging battery, remove it from the motorcycle.
7. Never disconnect the voltage regulator connector with the engine running. The voltage regulator/rectifier (**Figure 38**) is mounted on the front frame crossmember.
8. Do not mount the voltage regulator/rectifier unit at another location.
9. Make sure the battery negative terminal is connected to both engine and frame.

Troubleshooting Sequence

If the battery is discharged, perform the following procedures as listed.

1. Test the battery as described in Chapter Nine. Charge the battery if necessary. If the battery will hold a charge while riding, perform the *Charging System Output Test.*
2. If the charging system output is within specification, determine the amount of current demand by the electrical system and all accessories as described under *Electrical System Current Load Test.*
3. If the charging system output exceeds the current demand, and the battery continues not to hold a charge, perform the *Current Draw Test.*
4. If the charging system output is not within specification, test the stator and voltage regulator as described in this section.
5. If the battery will not hold a charge when the motorcycle is not use, perform the *Current Draw Test.*

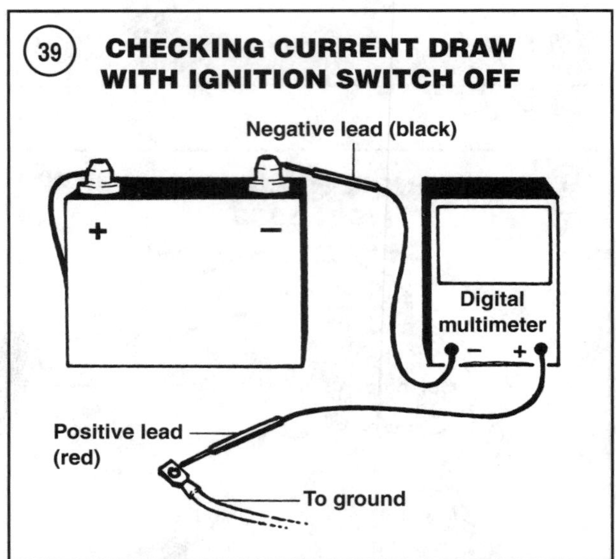

Current Draw Test (Battery Discharges When Motorcycle Not in Use)

NOTE
Because the clock and radio memory (if so equipped) are energized at all times, the battery may run down if the motorcycle is not run during a one- to two-week time period. To prevent battery drain, disconnect the negative battery cable or trickle charge the battery.

1. To perform this test, the battery must be fully charged.
2. Turn the ignition switch off.
3. Disconnect the negative battery cable from the battery.
4. Set the ammeter to the highest setting. Connect the positive ammeter lead to the negative battery terminal and the negative lead to the battery ground cable (**Figure 39**).
5. With the ignition switch and all lights and accessories turned off, read the current draw and compare it to the specification in **Table 2**. A reading exceeding the specification indicates excessive current draw.
6. If excessive current draw is noted, perform the following. If the motorcycle is not equipped with a clock, radio or CB, the regulator is probably faulty.
   a. Refer to the wiring diagram at the end of this manual and check the charging system wires and connectors for shorts or other damage.
   b. Check the radio, clock, CB and voltage regulator wiring. Unplug each of these electrical connectors separately and check for a change in the meter reading. If the meter reading changes when one of these connectors has been disconnected from the electrical system, one of these components is faulty. Check the electrical connections carefully before testing the individual component.
7. After completing the test, disconnect the ammeter and reconnect the negative battery cable.

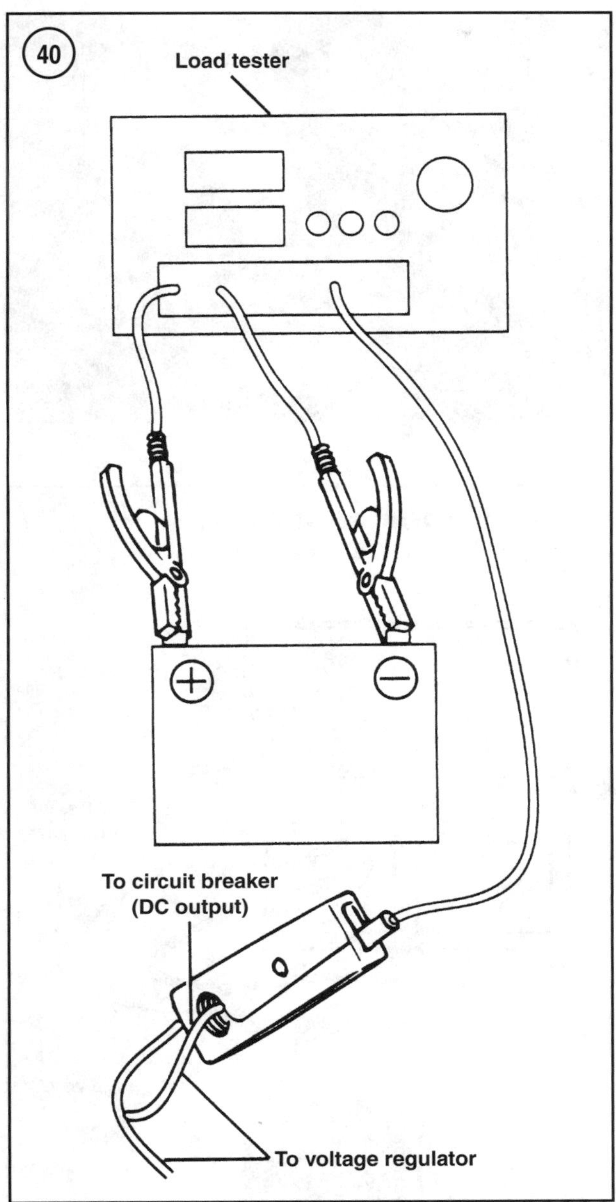

Current Draw Test (Battery Discharges When Motorcycle in Use)

This test measures the current draw or load of the motorcycle electrical system. A load tester is required for this test. Perform this test if the battery keeps discharging, yet the charging system is working correctly.

The charging system is designed to provide current to meet the demands of the original equipment installed on the motorcycle. If aftermarket accessories have been installed, the increased current demand can exceed the charging system capacity and result in a discharged battery.

NOTE
When using a load tester, read and follow the manufacturer's instructions. To prevent tester damage from overheating, do not leave the load switch on for more than 20 seconds at a time.

1. Connect a load tester to the battery as shown in **Figure 40**.
2. Turn the ignition switch on, but do not start the engine. Then turn on *all* electrical accessories and switch the headlight beam to HIGH.
3. Read the ampere reading (current draw) on the load tester and compare it to the alternator output listed in **Table 1**. The ampere reading registering on the load tester should be 3.5 amps less than the alternator output specification in **Table 1**. If the current draw exceeds the charging system output, the battery will continually run down.
4. If aftermarket accessories have been added to the motorcycle, disconnect them and repeat Step 2. If the current draw is now within the specification, the problem is with the additional accessories.
5. If no accessories have been added to the motorcycle, a short circuit may be causing the battery to discharge.

Voltage Regulator Ground Test

The voltage regulator base (**Figure 41**, typical) must be grounded to the frame for proper operation.

1. Connect one ohmmeter lead to a good engine or frame ground and the other ohmmeter lead to the regulator base. Read the scale. The correct reading is 0 ohm. Note the following:
   a. If there is low resistance (0 ohm), the voltage regulator is properly grounded.
   b. If there is high resistance, remove the voltage regulator and clean its frame mounting points.
2. Check the voltage regulator connector plug. Cut the wire clamp, lower the connector, and check that it is clean

and tightly connected. Reposition the connector onto the frame and secure it with a new wire clamp.

Voltage Regulator Bleed Test

This test requires a 12-volt test lamp. This tool relies on the vehicle battery to supply power to the component being tested.

1. Disconnect the voltage regulator connector (**Figure 42**) from the engine crankcase.

NOTE
Do not disconnect the wire from the voltage regulator to the circuit breaker.

2. Connect one test lamp probe to a good frame or engine ground.
3. Connect the other test lamp probe to one of the voltage regulator pins and then to the other pin.
4. If the test lamp lights, replace the voltage regulator.
5. If voltage regulator passes this test, reconnect the voltage regulator connector at the engine crankcase.

Charging System Output Test

This test requires a load tester.

1. To perform this test, the battery must be fully charged.

NOTE
When using a load tester, read and follow the manufacturer's instructions. To prevent tester damage from overheating, do not leave the load switch on for more than 20 seconds at a time.

2. Connect an induction load tester as shown in **Figure 43**.
3. Start the engine and slowly bring its speed up to 2000 rpm while reading the load tester scale. With the engine idling at 2000 rpm, operate the load tester switch until the voltage scale reads 13.0 volts. Then read the current output scale and refer to the specifications listed in **Table 1**.
4. With the engine still running at 2000 rpm, turn the load switch off and read the load tester voltage scale. Battery voltage must not exceed 15 volts. If volt reading exceeds 15 volts, the voltage regulator is damaged.
5. Turn the engine off and then disconnect the load tester from the motorcycle.
6. If output voltage is incorrect, test the stator as described under *Stator Test* in this chapter.

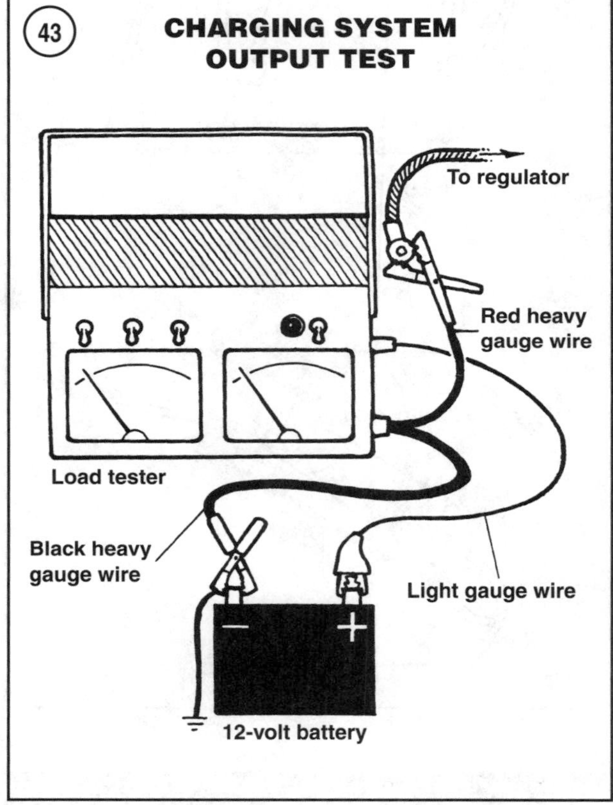

Stator Test

1. With the ignition turned off, disconnect the regulator/rectifier connector (**Figure 42**) from the stator at the crankcase.
2. Connect an ohmmeter between either stator pin and ground (**Figure 44**). The ohmmeter should read infinity (no continuity). If the reading is incorrect, the stator is grounded and must be replaced.

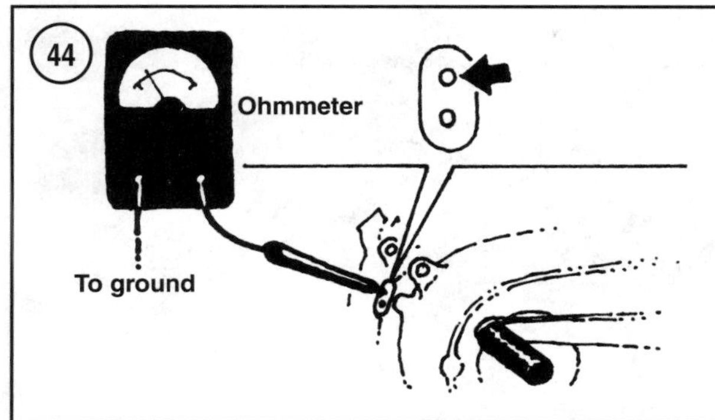

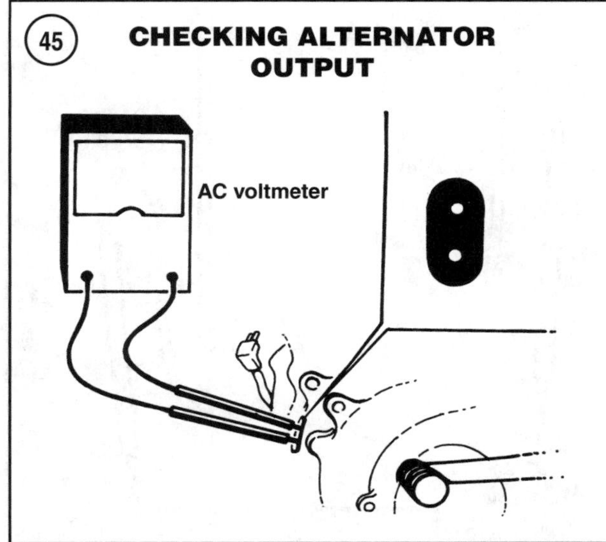

3. Connect the ohmmeter between both stator pins. The correct ohmmeter reading should be 0.2-0.4 ohm (1984-1988 models) or 0.10-0.12 ohm (1989-1998 models). If the resistance is not as specified, replace the stator.
4. Check the stator AC output as follows:
   a. Disconnect the regulator/rectifier connector (**Figure 42**).
   b. Connect an AC voltmeter across the stator pins as shown in **Figure 45**.
   c. Start the engine and slowly increase idle speed. Refer to **Table 1** for specified AC output.
   d. If the AC voltage output reading is below the specified range, the trouble is probably a defective stator (**Figure 42**) or rotor. If these parts are not damaged, perform the *Charging System Output Test* in this section.
5. Reconnect the regulator/rectifier connector.

IGNITION SYSTEM (CARBURETED MODELS)

All models are equipped with a transistorized ignition system. This solid state system uses no contact breaker points or other moving parts. Refer to the wiring diagrams at the end of this manual for the specific model and year.

Because of the solid-state design, problems with the transistorized system are rare. If a problem occurs, it generally causes a weak spark or no spark at all. An ignition system with a weak spark or no spark is relatively easy to troubleshoot. It is difficult, however, to troubleshoot an ignition system that only malfunctions when the engine is hot or under load.

Ignition System Precautions

Certain measures must be taken to protect the ignition system.

1. Never disconnect any of the electrical connectors while the engine is running.
2. Apply dielectric grease to all electrical connectors prior to reconnecting them. This will help seal out moisture.
3. Make sure all electrical connectors are free of corrosion and are completely coupled to each other.
4. The ignition control module must always be mounted securely to the back side of the electrical panel.

Troubleshooting Preparation

1. Refer to the wiring diagrams at the end of this manual for the specific model.
2. Check the wiring harness for visible signs of damage.
3. Make sure all connectors are properly attached to each other and locked in place.
4. Check all electrical components for a good ground to the engine.
5. Check all wiring for short circuits or open circuits.
6. Remove the seat as described in Chapter Fifteen.
7. Check for a damaged ignition circuit breaker.
8. Make sure the fuel tank has an adequate supply of fresh gasoline.
9. Check spark plug cable routing and the connections at the spark plugs. If there is no spark or only a weak one, repeat the test with new spark plugs. If the condition remains the same with new spark plugs, and if all external wiring connections are good, the problem is most likely in the ignition system. If a strong spark is present, the problem is probably not in the ignition system. Check the fuel system.

10. Remove the spark plugs and examine them as described in Chapter Three.

Ignition Test (No Spark at Spark Plug)

1. Check the battery charge as described in Chapter Nine. If good, proceed to Step 2.
2. Check that the ignition module (black) lead is fastened securely. Check also that the battery ground lead is fastened and in good condition.

NOTE
*When performing the following test procedures, it will be necessary to fabricate a test jumper from two lengths of 16-gauge wire, three alligator clips and a 0.33 μF capacitor (**Figure 46**). The test jumper should be long enough to reach from the ignition coil to a good engine ground.*

3. Perform the following:
   a. Connect the multimeter positive lead to the white/black wire (1994-1999 FLH and FLT series models, FXR2 and FXR3 models) or white wire (all other models) and the multimeter negative lead to ground (**Figure 47**).
   b. Turn the ignition switch on. The multimeter should read 11-13 volts. Turn the ignition switch off. Interpret results as follows.
   c. Voltage correct: Proceed to Step 4.
   d. Voltage incorrect: Check the main and ignition circuit breakers. Also check for loose or damaged ignition system wiring.
4. Perform the following:
   a. Disconnect the blue (1984-1990 models) or pink (1991-1998 models) wire from the ignition coil terminal (**Figure 48**).
   b. Turn the ignition switch on.
   c. Connect the multimeter negative lead to ground. Connect the multimeter positive lead alternately to the white/black wire (1994-1998 FLH and FLT series models) or white wire (all other models) and then to the blue or pink ignition coil terminals (**Figure 48**). The voltmeter should read 12 volts at each wire. Turn the ignition switch off. Interpret results as follows.
   d. Voltage correct: Proceed to Step 5.
   e. Voltage incorrect: Check the ignition coil resistance as described in *Ignition Coil Testing* in this section. If the resistance is within specification, proceed to Step 5.
5. Perform the following:

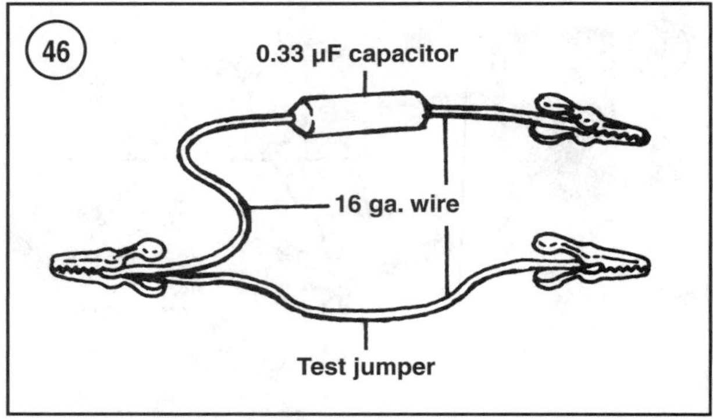

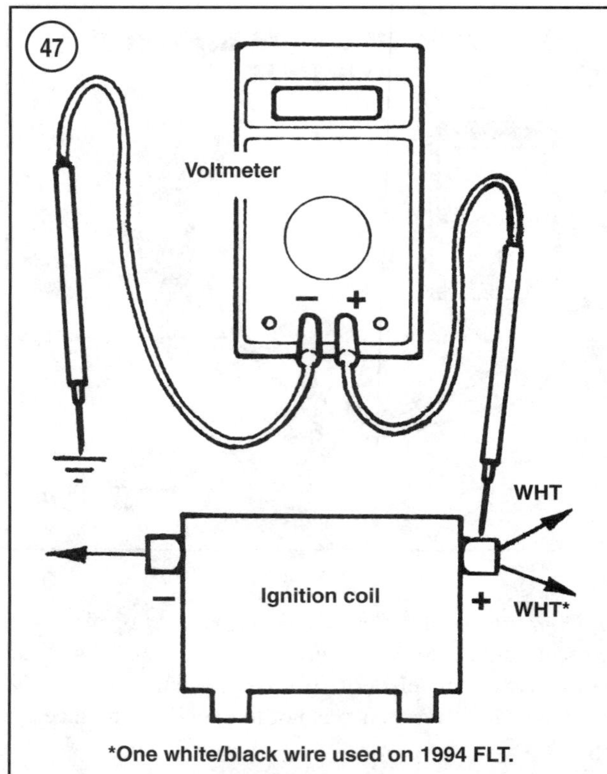

*One white/black wire used on 1994 FLT.

   a. Disconnect the blue (1984-1990 models) or pink (1991-1998 models) wire from the ignition coil terminal (**Figure 49**).
   b. Remove one of the spark plugs. Then connect the spark plug wire and connector to the spark plug and touch the spark plug base to a good ground. Position the spark plug so you can see the electrodes.
   c. Turn the ignition switch on.
   d. Connect the two jumper wires to a good engine ground (**Figure 49**). Then momentarily touch the jumper wire with the capacitor to the ignition coil

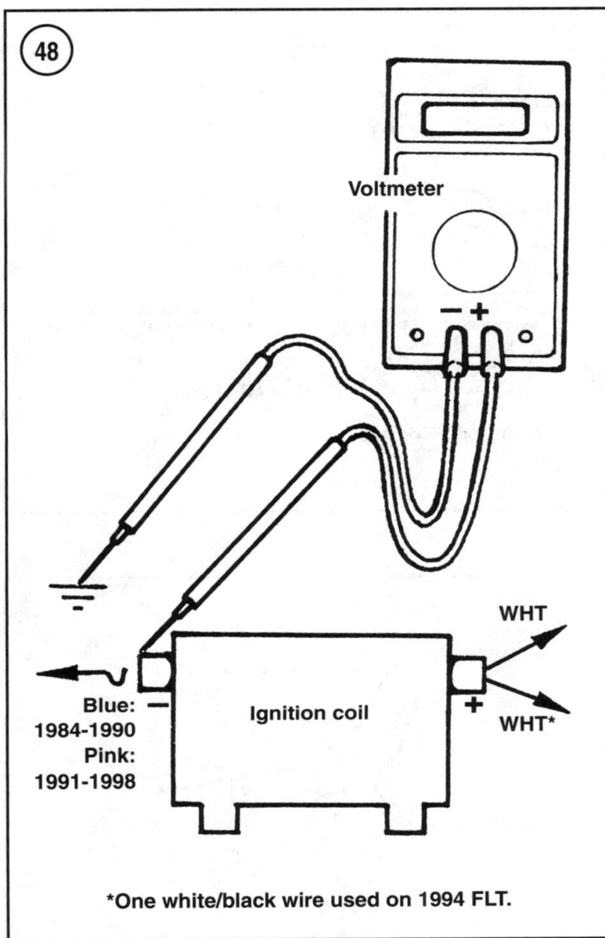

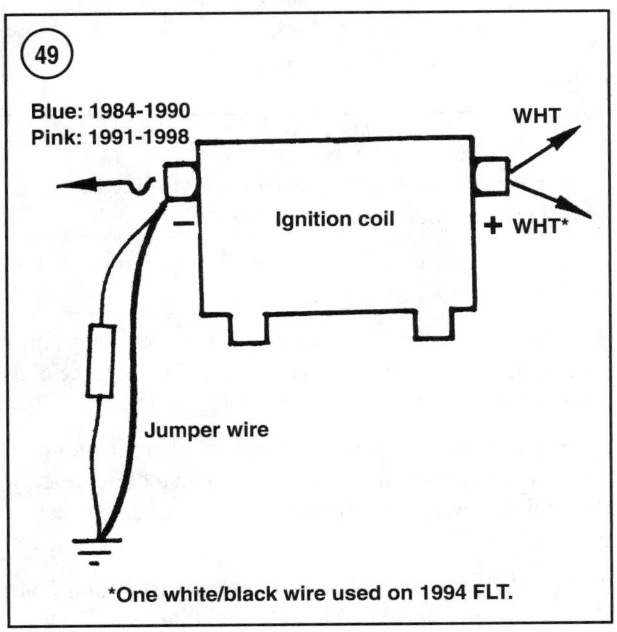

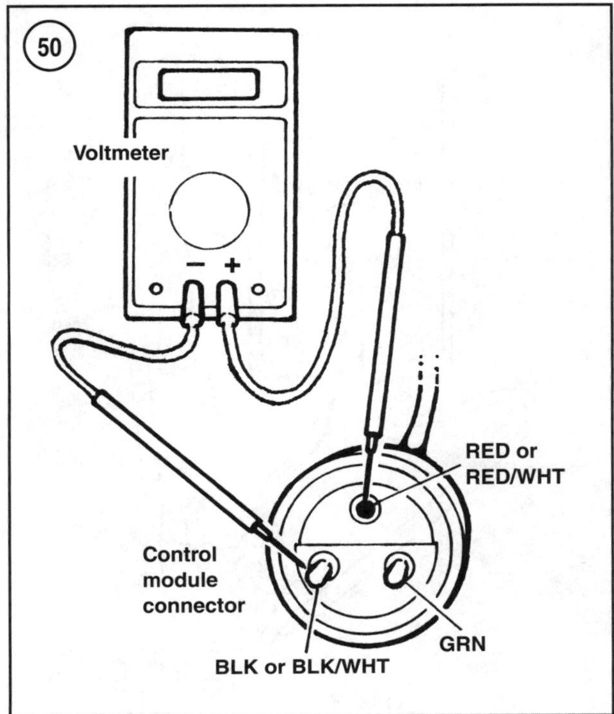

blue or pink terminal while observing the spark plug firing tip. The spark plug should spark. Turn the ignition switch off and remove the jumper wire assembly. Interpret results as follows.

e. Spark: Proceed to Step 6.
f. No spark: Replace the ignition coil.
g. Do not reinstall the spark plug at this time.

6. Perform the following:
   a. Reconnect the ignition coil blue (1984-1990 models) or pink (1991-1998 models) wire to its terminal on the ignition coil.
   b. Turn the ignition switch on.
   c. Disconnect the control module electrical connector.
   d. Connect the multimeter positive lead to the ignition module red/white wire (1994-1998 FLH and FLT series models) or red wire (all other models) and the multimeter negative lead to the ignition module black (1984-1990 models) or black/white (1991-1998 models) pin. Refer to **Figure 50** for 1984-1994 models or **Figure 51** for 1995-1998 models. The multimeter should read 4.5-5.5 volts. Disconnect the multimeter and turn the ignition switch off. Interpret results as follows.
   e. Voltage correct: Proceed to Step 7.
   f. Voltage incorrect: Check the ignition module ground wire and the module for loose connections or damage. If good, proceed to Step 7.

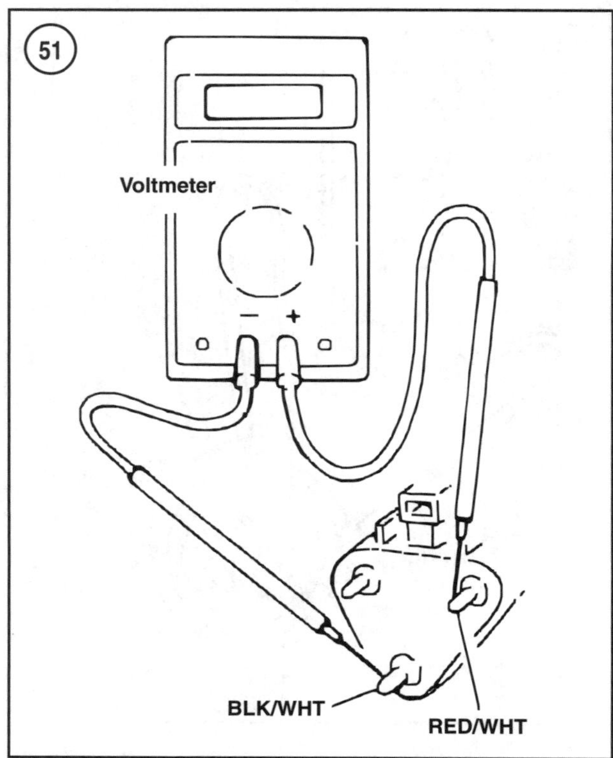

7. Turn the ignition switch on. Then momentarily ground a screwdriver across the ignition module green or green/white and the black or black/white connector pins. Refer to **Figure 52** for 1984-1994 models or **Figure 53** for 1995-1998 models. There should be a strong spark at the spark plug firing tip as the screwdriver is removed from the connector pins. Interpret results as follows:
   a. Spark: Check the sensor resistance as described in this chapter.
   b. No spark: Check the ignition module resistance as described in this chapter.

8. Install and reconnect all parts removed for this procedure. If there is still no spark, either retest or have a Harley-Davidson dealership check the ignition system.

Ignition Test (Intermittent Ignition Problems)

Intermittent problems are usually caused by temperature or vibration.

Temperature test

NOTE
Steps 1-4 must be performed while the engine is cold (95° F [35° C]).

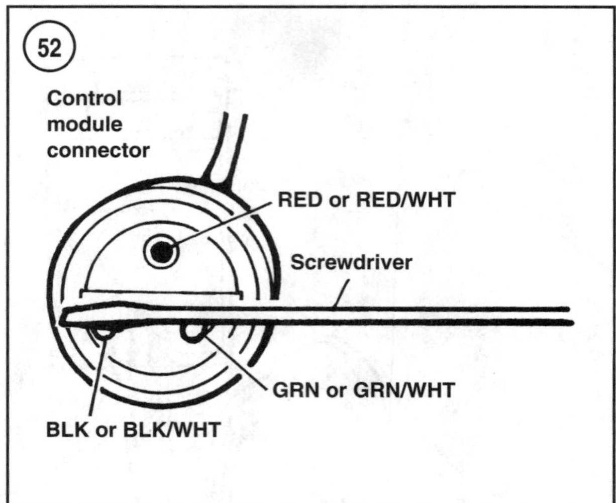

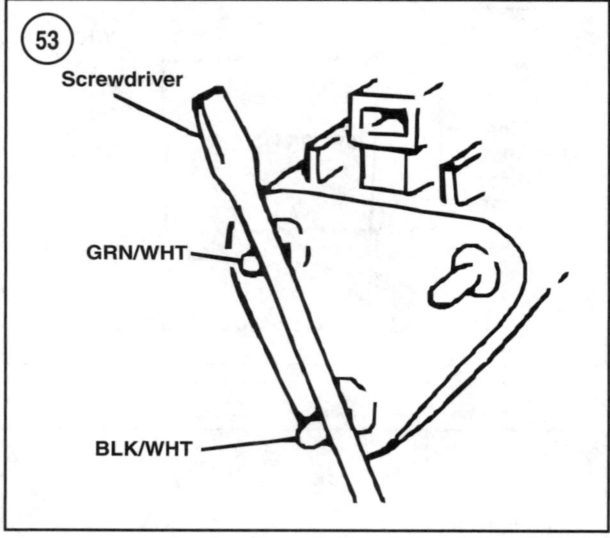

1. Remove the outer timing cover, inner timing cover and gasket as described in Chapter Nine.

2. Start the engine and allow it to idle (do not allow it to reach normal operating temperature).

3. Spray the sensor (**Figure 54**) with a cooling spray (available at electronic supply stores). If the engine dies, replace the sensor as described in Chapter Nine.

4. Allow the engine to warm to normal operating temperature. Then apply heat to the sensor with a blow dryer. If the engine dies, replace the sensor as described in Chapter Nine.

5. Install the inner timing cover, *new* gasket and outer timing cover as described in Chapter Nine.

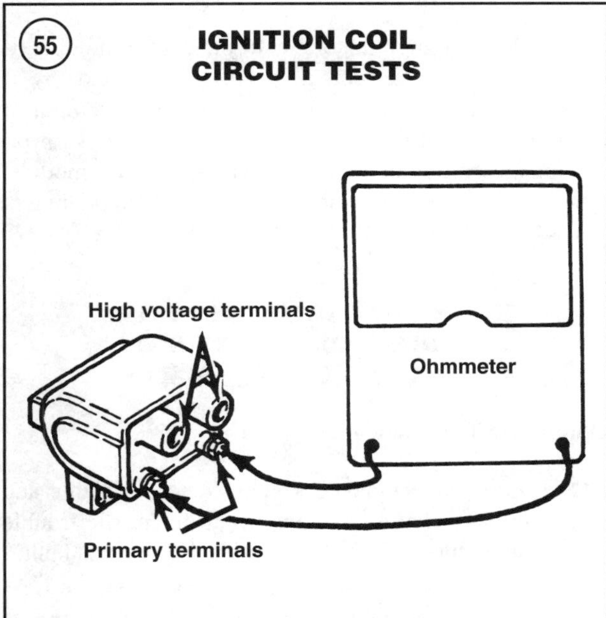

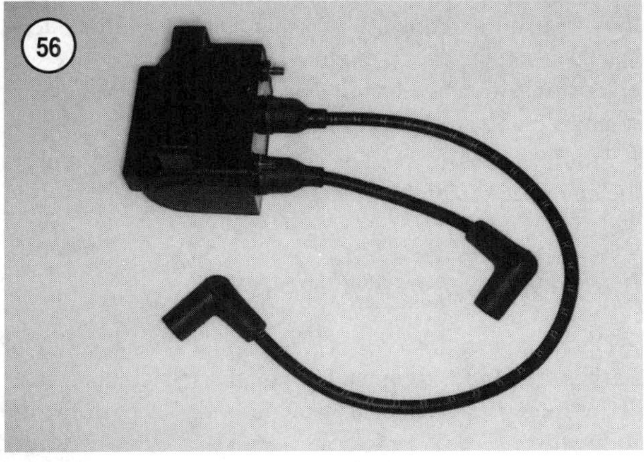

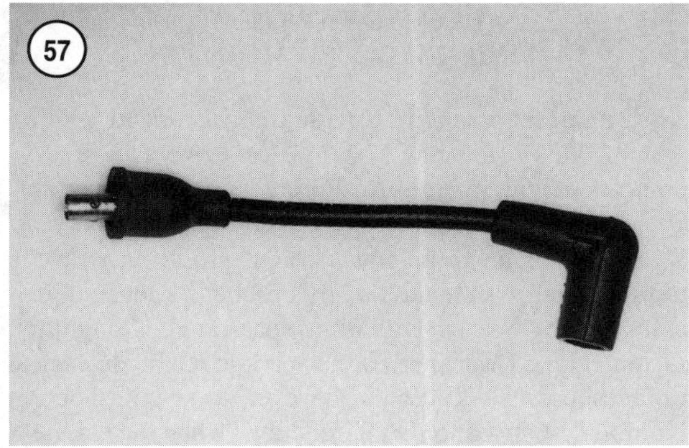

Ignition Coil Testing

Use an ohmmeter to check the ignition coil secondary and primary resistance. Test the coil twice: first when it is cold (room temperature) and then at normal operating temperature. If the engine will not start, heat the coil with a blow dryer, then test it.

1. Disconnect the primary wire connector and the secondary wires from the ignition coil.
2. Measure the ignition coil primary resistance between the coil primary terminals (**Figure 55**). Compare the reading to the specification listed in **Table 1**. Replace the ignition coil if the reading is not within specification.
3. Measure the resistance between the secondary terminals (**Figure 55**). Compare the reading to the specification listed in **Table 1**. Replace the ignition coil if the reading is not within specification. Refer to Chapter Nine.

Ignition Coil Cables and Caps Inspection

All models are equipped with resistor- or suppression-type spark plug cables (**Figure 56**, typical). These cables reduce radio interference. The cable conductor consists of a carbon-impregnated fabric core material instead of solid wire.

If a plug cable becomes damaged, either due to corrosion or conductor breaks, its resistance increases. Excessive cable resistance will cause engine misfire and other ignition or drivability problems.

When troubleshooting the ignition system, inspect the spark plug cables (**Figure 57**, typical) for:

1. Corroded or damaged connector ends.
2. Breaks in the cable insulation that could allow arcing.
3. Split or damaged plug caps that could allow arcing to the cylinder heads.

Replace damaged or questionable spark plug cables.

IGNITION SYSTEM (FUEL-INJECTED MODELS)

All models are equipped with a transistorized ignition system. This solid-state system uses no contact breaker points or other moving parts. Refer to the wiring diagrams at the end of this manual for the specific model and year.

Because of the solid-state design, problems with the transistorized system are rare. If a problem occurs, it generally causes a weak spark or no spark at all. An ignition system with a weak spark or no spark is relatively easy to troubleshoot. It is difficult, however, to troubleshoot an ignition system that only malfunctions when the engine is hot or under load.

All 1995-1998 models are equipped with an on-board diagnostic system. Troubleshooting this system by non-Harley-Davidson personnel is limited to trouble code retrieval and clearing.

Retrieving the trouble code(s) will indicate where a fault(s) has occurred. Further testing requires several special Harley-Davidson tools that are available *only* to Harley-Davidson dealerships.

If a fault has occurred, have the diagnostic procedures performed at a Harley-Davidson dealership.

Ignition System Precautions

Certain measures must be taken to protect the ignition system.

1. Never disconnect any of the electrical connectors while the engine is running.
2. Apply dielectric grease to all electrical connectors prior to reconnecting them. This will help seal out moisture.
3. Make sure all electrical connectors are free of corrosion and are completely coupled to each other.
4. The ignition control module must always be mounted securely to the back side of the electrical panel.

Troubleshooting Preparation

1. Refer to the wiring diagrams at the end of this manual for the specific model.
2. Check the wiring harness for visible signs of damage.
3. Make sure all connectors are properly attached to each other and locked in place.
4. Check all electrical components for a good ground to the engine.
5. Check all wiring for short circuits or open circuits.
6. Remove the seat as described in Chapter Fifteen.
7. Check for a damaged ignition circuit breaker.
8. Make sure the fuel tank has an adequate supply of fresh gasoline.
9. Check spark plug cable routing and the connections at the spark plugs. If there is no spark or only a weak one, repeat the test with new spark plugs. If the condition remains the same with new spark plugs and if all external wiring connections are good, the problem is most likely in the ignition system. If a strong spark is present, the problem is probably not in the ignition system. Check the fuel system.
10. Remove the spark plugs and examine them as described in Chapter Three.

Electronic Control Module Testing and Replacement

If the ignition module, or electronic control module, is suspected of being defective, have it tested by a Harley-Davidson dealership before purchasing a replacement. The cost of the test will not exceed the cost of replacing an ignition module, or electronic control module, that may not repair the problem. Most parts suppliers will not accept returns on electrical components.

ENGINE MANAGEMENT SYSTEM DIAGNOSTIC CODES (FUEL-INJECTED MODELS)

Diagnostic Trouble Codes

The on-board diagnostic system identifies faults and stores this information as a two-digit diagnostic trouble code. If more than one fault is found it also sets that fault.

If a trouble code has been set, the check-engine light will come on. During normal operation, the check-engine light will illuminate for approximately four seconds when the ignition is turned on. The check-engine light then turns off and remains off. If a diagnostic trouble code(s) has been set, the check-engine light turns on for four seconds, turns off, and then turns back on for eight seconds or remains on beyond the eight second period.

Trouble codes are read by counting the number of times the check-engine light flashes.

Retrieving diagnostic trouble codes

Diagnostic trouble codes are displayed as a series of flashes at the check-engine light on the speedometer face. To retrieve the diagnostic trouble code(s), perform the following:

1. Turn the ignition/light key switch to ignition for three seconds.
2. Pause for one second after the fuel pump stops running.
3. Turn the engine stop switch to run.
4. Turn the ignition/light key switch off or to lock for three seconds.
5. Repeat Steps 1-4 one more time.
6. Turn the ignition/light key switch to ignition and wait for approximately eight seconds for the check-engine light to start flashing as follows:
   a. The check-engine light begins with a ready signal, which is a series of six rapid flashes, approximately three per second. The ready signal indicates that the check-engine light is ready to flash a diagnostic trouble code.
   b. This is followed by a two-second pause in which the light is off.
   c. The system then flashes the first digit of the stored diagnostic trouble code. The check-engine light will illuminate for one second and then turn off for one second. Count the number of flashes and record the number. For example, two blinks indicates the first digit is 2.
   d. The system will pause for two seconds and then flash the second digit of the diagnostic trouble code. Count the number of flashes and record this number. For example, five blinks indicates the second digit is 5. This indicates that the first trouble code is 25, which indicates a problem with the rear ignition coil.
   e. If more than one trouble code is present, the system will pause for two seconds and then flash the ready signal, which is a series of six rapid flashes. It is now ready to flash the next trouble code.
   f. The system will pause for two seconds and then flash the first digit of the next diagnostic trouble code followed by the second digit.
7. The check-engine light displays the stored codes sequentially and one at a time until each diagnostic trouble code has been displayed. The system then repeats. The check-engine light will continue to flash out stored codes until the ignition/light key switch moves to the following position:
   a. Turn the ignition/light key switch off or to lock.
   b. Wait for ten seconds for the ECM relay to click. After this time the motorcycle can be started.
8. Refer to **Table 3** for information on diagnostic trouble codes to locate the problem.

Clearing diagnostic trouble codes

The trouble codes may be cleared by disconnecting the battery.

CRUISE CONTROL SYSTEM DIAGNOSTIC CODES

The 1997-1998 models on-board diagnostic system identifies faults within the system and stores this information as a three-digit diagnostic trouble code. If more than one fault is found, it also sets that fault with the maximum of eight trouble codes that can be set.

Trouble codes are retrieved by counting the number of times the cruise control engagement *C* light flashes on the tachometer face.

To retrieve the diagnostic trouble code(s), perform the following:

1. Turn off the engine.
2. On the front fairing cap, turn the Cruise ON/OFF switch to off. The light in the switch is extinguished.
3. On the right handlebar switch, push the Cruise SET/RESUME switch to set and hold it in this position.
4. Turn the ignition key switch to ignition, but do not start the engine.
5. On the right handlebar switch, release the Cruise SET/RESUME switch from the set position while looking at the cruise control engagement *C* light. The light will begin transmitting the cruise dropout codes. Each code consists of three digits.
6. The system will flash the first digit of the stored diagnostic trouble code. The cruise control engagement *C* light will illuminate for about 1/4 of a second and then turn off for about 1/4 of a second. Count the number of flashes and record the number. For example, three blinks indicates the first digit is 3.
7. The system will pause for one second and then flash the second digit of the diagnostic trouble code. Count the number of flashes and record this number. For example, five blinks indicates the second digit is 5.
8. The system will again pause for one second and then flash the third digit of the diagnostic trouble code. Count the number of flashes and record this number. For example, three blinks indicates the third digit is 3. This indicates that the first trouble code is 353, which signals an internal failure.
9. If more than one trouble code is present, the system will pause for two seconds and then flash the ready signal, which is a series of six rapid flashes. It is now ready to flash the next trouble code.
10. Refer to the information in **Table 4** about diagnostic trouble codes to locate the problem.

11. To exit the diagnostic mode, turn the ignition key switch off.

12. The trouble codes can only be cleared by a Harley-Davidson dealership.

FUEL SYSTEM (CARBURETED MODELS)

Begin fuel system troubleshooting with the fuel tank and work through the system, reserving the carburetor as the final point. Most fuel system problems result from an empty fuel tank, a plugged fuel filter or fuel valve, sour fuel, a dirty air filter or clogged carburetor jets. Do not assume the carburetor is the problem. Unnecessary carburetor adjustment can compound the problem.

Identifying Carburetor Conditions

Refer to the following conditions to identify whether the engine is running lean or rich.

Rich

1. Fouled spark plugs.
2. Engine misfires and runs rough under load.
3. Excessive exhaust smoke as the throttle is increased.
4. An extreme rich condition results in a choked or dull sound from the exhaust and an inability to clear the exhaust with the throttle held wide open.

Lean

1. Blistered or very white spark plug electrodes.
2. Engine overheats.
3. Slow acceleration; engine power is reduced.
4. Flat spots on acceleration that are similar in feel to when the engine starts to run out of gas.
5. Engine speed fluctuates at full throttle.

Troubleshooting

Isolate fuel system problems to the fuel tank, fuel shutoff valve and filter, fuel hoses, external fuel filter (if used) or carburetor. The following procedures assume that the ignition system is working properly and is correctly adjusted.

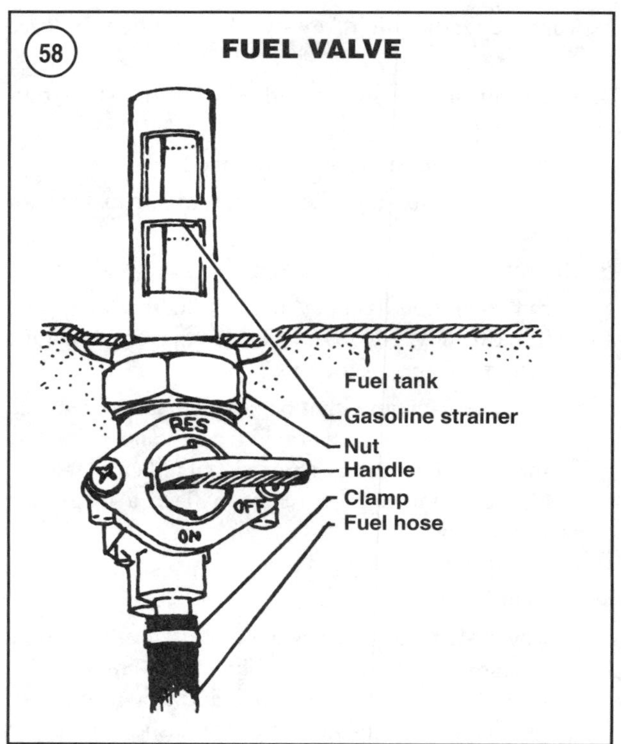

Fuel delivery system

Check fuel flow. Remove the fuel filler cap(s) and look into the tank. If fuel is present, disconnect the battery ground cable as a safety precaution. Then check that the fuel valve is turned off. Disconnect the fuel hose at the carburetor and put the hose into a container to catch any discharged fuel.

WARNING
Make sure there are no open flames in the area when performing the following.

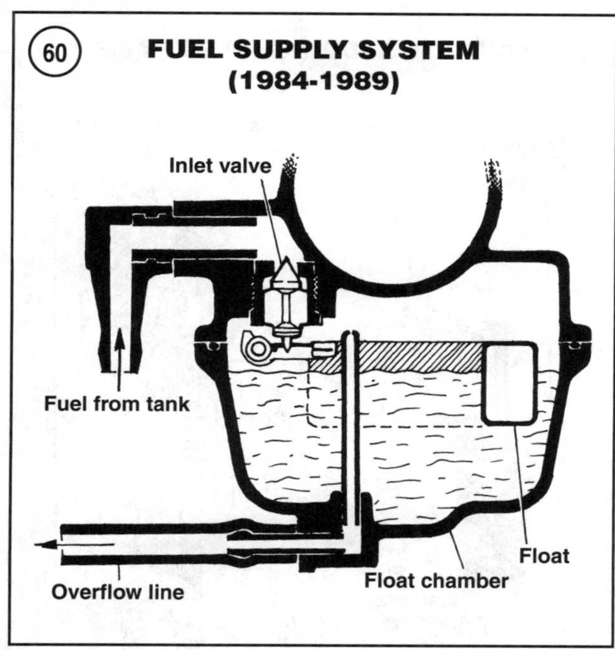

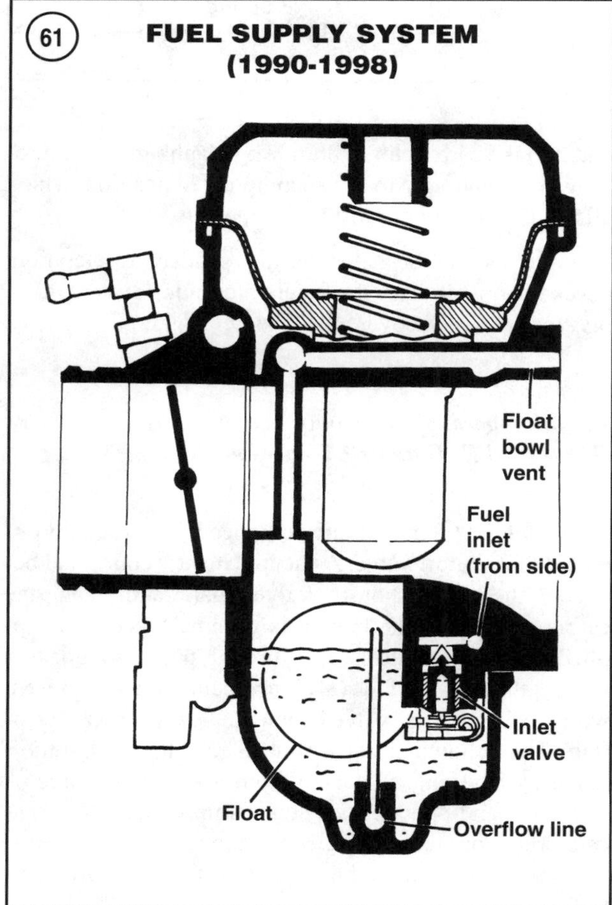

NOTE
Make sure there is a sufficient supply of fuel in each tank to allow the fuel valve to work in its normal operating position.

The fuel valve controls fuel flow from the fuel tank to the carburetor. The fuel valve on all models is a three-position valve (**Figure 58**). Because a gravity-feed fuel delivery system is used, fuel should always be present at the fuel valve. Turn the fuel valve so that the end of the handle faces down (valve in normal operating position). Fuel should flow into the container. Turn the fuel valve so that the end of the handle faces up (valve in reserve). Fuel should flow into the container.

If fuel flow is present, fuel is reaching the carburetor. Examine the fuel in the container for rust or dirt that could clog or restrict the fuel valve filter and the carburetor jets. If there is evidence of contamination, it will be necessary to clean and flush the fuel tanks, fuel valve assembly, hoses and carburetor. Refer to Chapter Nine for fuel system service.

If there is no fuel present at the hose, check the following:

1. The fuel valve may be shut off or blocked by rust or foreign matter. If fuel flows in the reserve but not in the on position, the fuel level in the tank may be too low. If the fuel level is high enough to flow in the on position, the on side of the valve is clogged. This would also hold true if the reserve side failed to work properly.
2. The fuel hose may be plugged or kinked. Remove the fuel hose and then clear the hose by passing a stiff piece of wire or a rod (less than 1/4 in. [6.35 mm] in diameter) through the hose.

WARNING
*When reconnecting the fuel hose, make sure the hose is inserted through the nylon hose insulator (**Figure 59**). Do not operate the engine without the insulator properly installed.*

3. The fuel tank is not properly vented. Check by opening the fuel tank cap. If fuel flows with the cap open, check for a plugged vent.

Fuel level system

The fuel level system is shown in **Figure 60** and **Figure 61**. Proper carburetor operation depends on a constant and correct carburetor fuel level. As fuel is drawn from the float bowl during engine operation, the float level in the bowl drops. As the float drops, the fuel valve moves away from its seat and allows fuel to flow through the seat into the float bowl. Fuel entering the float bowl will cause the float to rise and push against the fuel valve. When the fuel level reaches a predetermined level, the fuel valve is pushed against the seat to prevent the float bowl from overfilling.

If the fuel valve fails to close, the engine will run too rich or flood with fuel. Symptoms of this problem are rough running, excessive black smoke and poor acceleration. This condition will sometimes clear up when the engine is run at wide-open throttle as the fuel is being drawn into the engine before the float bowl can overfill. As the engine speed is reduced, however, the rich running condition returns.

Several things can cause fuel overflow. In most instances, it can be as simple as a small piece of dirt trapped between the fuel valve and seat or an incorrect float level. If fuel is flowing out of the overflow tube connected to the bottom of the float bowl, the fuel valve inside the carburetor is being held open. First check the position of the fuel shutoff valve lever. Turn the fuel shutoff valve lever off. Then lightly tap on the carburetor float bowl and turn the fuel shutoff valve lever on. If the fuel flow stops running out of the overflow tube, whatever was holding the fuel valve off of its seat now has been dislodged. If fuel continues to flow from the overflow tube, remove and service the carburetor. Refer to Chapter Seven.

NOTE

Fuel will not flow from the vacuum-operated fuel shutoff valve until the engine is running.

Starting enrichment (choke) system

A cold engine requires a rich mixture to start and run properly. On all models, a cable-actuated starter enrichment valve is used for cold starting.

If the engine is difficult to start when cold, check the starting enrichment (choke) cable adjustment described in Chapter Three.

Accelerator pump system

During sudden throttle openings the diaphragm accelerator pump system provides additional fuel to the engine. Refer to **Figure 62** and **Figure 63**. Without this system, the carburetor would not be able to provide a sufficient amount of fuel.

The system consists of a spring-loaded neoprene diaphragm that is compressed during sudden acceleration by the pump lever. This movement causes the diaphragm to force fuel from the pump chamber, through a check valve

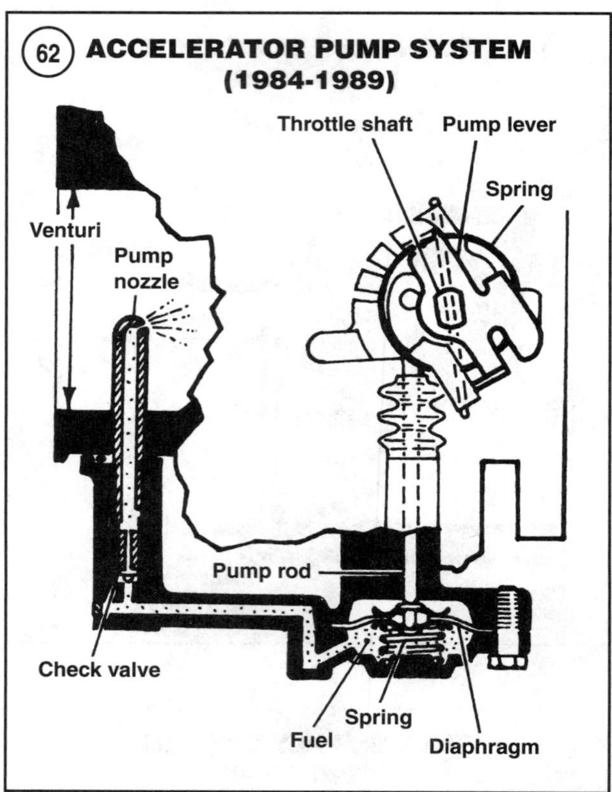

and into the carburetor venturi. The diaphragm spring returns the diaphragm to the uncompressed position, which allows the chamber to refill with fuel.

If the engine hesitates during sudden acceleration, check the operation of the accelerator pump system. *Carburetor Service* is covered in Chapter Eight.

Vacuum-operated fuel shutoff valve testing (1994-1998 FLH and FLT series models)

All 1994-1998 models are equipped with a vacuum-operated fuel shutoff valve. A vacuum hose is connected between the fuel shutoff valve diaphragm and the carburetor. When the engine is running, vacuum is applied to the fuel shutoff valve through this hose. For fuel to flow through the fuel valve, a vacuum must be present with the fuel shutoff valve handle in the ON or RES position. The following steps troubleshoot the fuel shutoff valve by applying a vacuum from a separate source. A Mityvac hand-operated vacuum pump (**Figure 64**), gas can, drain hose that is long enough to reach from the fuel valve to the gas can and hose clamp are required for this test.

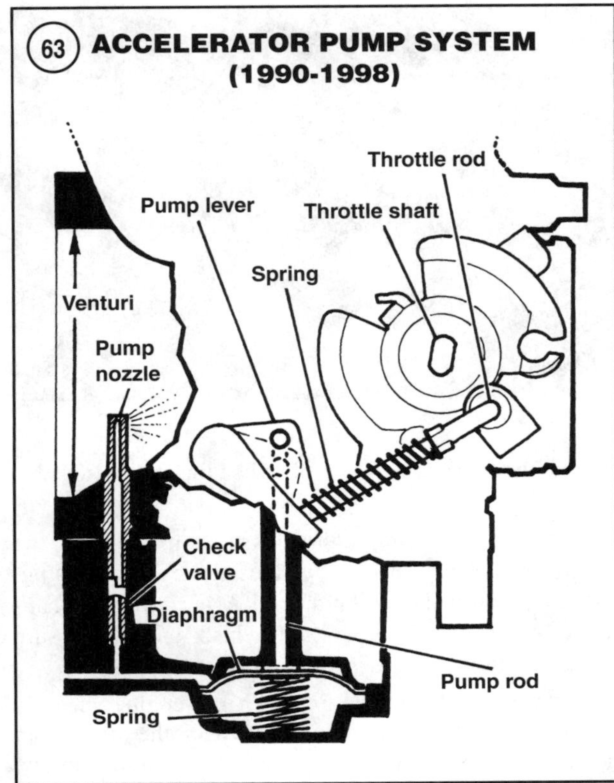

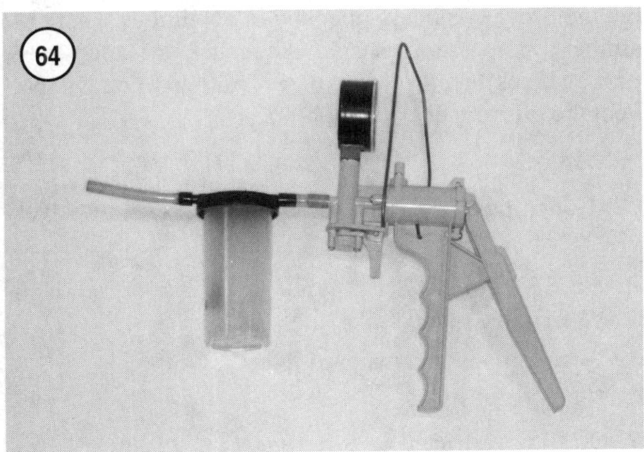

WARNING
Gasoline is highly flammable. When servicing the fuel system in the following sections, work in a well-ventilated area. Do not expose gasoline and gasoline vapors to sparks or other ignition sources.

1. Disconnect the negative battery cable from the battery.
2. Visually check the amount of fuel in the tank. Add fuel if necessary.
3. Turn the fuel shutoff valve off and disconnect the fuel hose from the fuel shutoff valve. Plug the open end of the hose.
4. Connect the drain hose to the fuel shutoff valve and secure it with a hose clamp. Insert the end of the drain hose into a gas can.

WARNING
Do not perform this test if there are open flames or sparks in the area.

5. Disconnect the vacuum hose from the fuel shutoff valve.
6. Connect a hand-operated vacuum pump to the fuel shutoff valve vacuum hose nozzle.
7. Turn the fuel shutoff valve lever on.

CAUTION
In Step 8, do not apply more than 25 in. (635 mm) Hg vacuum or the fuel shutoff valve diaphragm will be damaged.

8. Apply 25 in. Hg of vacuum to the valve. Fuel must flow through the fuel shutoff valve when the vacuum is applied.
9. With the vacuum still applied, turn the fuel shutoff valve lever to reserve. Fuel must continue to flow through the valve.
10. Release the vacuum and check that fuel flow stops.
11. Repeat Steps 8-10 five times and check that fuel flows with vacuum applied and stops flowing when the vacuum is released.
12. Turn the fuel shutoff valve off. Disconnect the vacuum pump and drain hoses.
13. Reconnect the fuel hose to the fuel shutoff valve.
14. If the fuel valve failed this test, replace the fuel shutoff valve as described in Chapter Eight.

FUEL SYSTEM (ELECTRONIC FUEL INJECTION)

Start troubleshooting the fuel system at the fuel tank and work throughout the fuel system reserving the fuel injecting system to the final point. Most fuel system problems result from an empty fuel tank, a plugged filter, fuel pump failure, sour fuel or a clogged air filter element. Refer to the *Starting the Engine* and *Engine Performance* procedures in this chapter.

The fuel injection system is controlled by the engine management system via the ignition control module. Other than the previously mentioned possible problems, troubleshooting must be performed by a Harley-Davidson dealership.

ENGINE NOISES

1. Knocking or pinging during acceleration can be caused by using a lower octane fuel than recommended or a poor grade of fuel. Incorrect carburetor jetting (carbureted models) and an incorrect (hot) spark plug heat range can cause pinging. Refer to *Spark Plug Heat Range* in Chapter Three. Check also for excessive carbon buildup in the combustion chamber or a defective ignition module.
2. Slapping or rattling noises at low speed or during acceleration can be caused by excessive piston-to-cylinder wall clearance. Check also for a bent connecting rod(s) or worn piston pin and/or piston pin hole in the piston(s).
3. Knocking or rapping while decelerating is usually caused by excessive connecting rod bearing clearance.
4. Persistent knocking and vibration or other noises are usually caused by worn main bearings. If the main bearings are in good condition, consider the following:
   a. Loose engine mounts.
   b. Cracked frame.
   c. Leaking cylinder head gasket(s).
   d. Exhaust pipe leakage at cylinder head(s).
   e. Stuck piston ring(s).
   f. Broken piston ring(s).
   g. Partial engine seizure.
   h. Excessive connecting rod bearing clearance.
   i. Excessive connecting rod side clearance.
   j. Excessive crankshaft runout.
5. Rapid on-off squeal indicates a compression leak around the cylinder head gasket or spark plug.
6. If valve train noise is a factor, check for the following:
   a. Bent pushrod(s).
   b. Defective lifter(s).
   c. Valve sticking in guide.
   d. Worn cam gears and/or cam.
   e. Damaged rocker arm or shaft. Rocker arm might be binding on shaft.

ENGINE LUBRICATION

An improperly operating engine lubrication system will quickly lead to serious engine damage. Check the engine oil level weekly as described in Chapter Three. Oil pump service is covered in Chapter Four.

Low Oil Warning Light

The low oil warning light, mounted on the indicator light panel, will come on when the ignition switch is turned on before starting the engine. After the engine is started, the oil light will turn off when the engine speed is above idle.

If the low oil warning light does not come on when the ignition switch is turned on and the engine is not running, check for a burned out oil light bulb as described in Chapter Nine. If the bulb is working, check the oil pressure switch (**Figure 65**) as described in Chapter Nine.

If the oil light remains on when the engine speed is above idle, turn the engine off and check the oil level in the oil tank. If the oil level is satisfactory, oil may not be returning to the oil tank from the return line. Check for a clogged or damaged return line or a damaged oil pump. If the motorcycle is being operated in conditions where the ambient temperature is below freezing, ice and sludge may be blocking the oil feed pipe. This condition will prevent the oil from circulating properly.

Oil Consumption High or Engine Smokes Excessively

1. Worn valve guides.
2. Worn valve guide seals.
3. Worn or damaged piston rings.
4. Oil pan overfilled.
5. Oil filter restricted.
6. Leaking cylinder head surfaces.

Oil Fails to Return to Oil Tank

1. Oil lines or fittings restricted or damaged.
2. Oil pump damaged or operating incorrectly.
3. Oil tank pan empty.
4. Oil filter restricted.
5. Damaged oil feed pump.

Engine Oil Leaks

1. Clogged air filter breather hose.
2. Restricted or damaged oil return line to oil tank.
3. Loose engine parts.
4. Damaged gasket sealing surfaces.
5. Oil pan tank overfilled.
6. Restricted oil filter.
7. Plugged air filter-to-breather system hose.

CLUTCH

All clutch troubles except adjustments require partial clutch disassembly to identify and cure the problem. Refer to Chapter Five for clutch service procedures.

Clutch Chatter or Noise

This problem is usually caused by worn or warped friction and steel plates.

Clutch Slip

1. Incorrect clutch adjustment.
2. Worn friction plates.
3. Weak or damaged diaphragm spring.
4. Damaged pressure plate.

Clutch Drag

1. Incorrect clutch adjustment.
2. Warped clutch plates.
3. Worn or damaged clutch shell or clutch hub.
4. Worn or incorrectly assembled clutch ball and ramp mechanism.
5. Incorrect primary chain alignment.
6. Weak or damaged diaphragm spring.

TRANSMISSION

Transmission symptoms are sometimes hard to distinguish from clutch symptoms. Refer to Chapter Six or Chapter Seven for transmission service procedures.

Jumping Out of Gear

1. Worn or damaged shifter parts.
2. Incorrect shifter rod adjustment.
3. Incorrect shifter drum adjustment.
4. Severely worn or damaged gears and/or shift forks.

Difficult Shifting

1. Worn or damaged shift forks.
2. Worn or damaged shifter clutch dogs.
3. Weak or damaged shifter return spring.
4. Clutch drag.

Excessive Gear Noise

1. Worn or damaged bearings.
2. Worn or damaged gears.
3. Excessive gear backlash.

LIGHTING SYSTEM

If bulbs burn out frequently, check for excessive vibration, loose connections that permit sudden current surges, or the installation of the wrong type of bulb.

Most light and ignition problems are caused by loose or corroded ground connections. Check these prior to replacing a bulb or electrical component.

EXCESSIVE VIBRATION

Excessive vibration is usually caused by loose engine mounting hardware. A bent axle shaft or loose suspension component will cause high-speed vibration problems. Vibration can also be caused by the following conditions:

1. Cracked or broken frame.
2. Severely worn primary chain.
3. Tight primary chain links.
4. Loose, worn or damaged engine stabilizer link.
5. Loose or damaged rubber mounts.
6. Improperly balanced wheel(s).
7. Defective or damaged wheel(s).
8. Defective or damaged tire(s).
9. Internal engine wear or damage.
10. Loose or worn steering head bearings.
11. Loose swing arm pivot shaft nut.

FRONT SUSPENSION AND STEERING

Poor handling may be caused by improper tire inflation pressure, a damaged or bent frame or front steering component, worn wheel bearings or dragging brakes. Possible causes for suspension and steering malfunctions are listed in the following sections.

Irregular or Wobbly Steering

1. Loose wheel axle nut(s).

2. Loose or worn steering head bearings.
3. Excessive wheel bearing play.
4. Damaged alloy wheel.
5. Laced wheel out of alignment.
6. Unbalanced wheel assembly.
7. Incorrect vehicle alignment.
8. Bent or damaged steering stem or frame at steering neck.
9. Tire incorrectly seated on rim.
10. Excessive front end loading from non-standard equipment.

Stiff Steering

1. Low front tire air pressure.
2. Bent or damaged steering stem or frame.
3. Loose or worn steering head bearings.
4. Incorrect steering head adjustment.

Stiff or Heavy Fork Operation

1. Incorrect fork springs.
2. Incorrect fork oil viscosity.
3. Excessive amount of fork oil.
4. Bent fork tubes.
5. Incorrect fork air pressure.

Poor Fork Operation

1. Worn or damaged fork tubes.
2. Fork oil capacity low due to leaking fork seals.
3. Bent or damaged fork tubes.
4. Contaminated fork oil.
5. Incorrect fork springs.
6. Heavy front end loading from nonstandard equipment.
7. Incorrect fork air pressure.

Poor Rear Shock Absorber Operation

1. Weak or worn springs.
2. Damper unit leaking.
3. Shock shaft worn or bent.
4. Incorrect rear shock springs.
5. Rear shocks adjusted incorrectly.
6. Heavy rear-end loading from nonstandard equipment.
7. Incorrect loading.
8. Incorrect rear shock air pressure.

BRAKE PROBLEMS

All models are equipped with front and rear disc brakes. Good brakes are vital to the safe operation of any vehicle. Perform the maintenance specified in Chapter Three to minimize brake system problems. Brake system service is covered in Chapter Twelve. When refilling the front and rear master cylinders, use only DOT 5 silicone-based brake fluid.

Insufficient Braking Power

Worn brake pads or disc, air in the hydraulic system, glazed or contaminated pads, low brake fluid level, or a leaking brake line or hose can cause this problem. Visually check for leaks. Check for worn brake pads. Check also for a leaking or damaged primary cup seal in the master cylinder. Bleed and adjust the brakes. Rebuild a leaking master cylinder or brake caliper. Brake drag will result in excessive heat and brake fade. See *Brake Drag* in this section.

Spongy Brake Feel

This problem is generally caused by air in the hydraulic system. Bleed and adjust the brakes.

Brake Drag

Check the brake adjustment while checking for insufficient brake pedal and/or hand lever free play. Also check for worn, loose or missing parts in the brake calipers. Check the brake disc for excessive runout.

Brakes Squeal or Chatter

Check brake pad thickness and disc condition. Check that the caliper antirattle springs are properly installed and in good condition. Clean off any dirt on the pads. Loose components can also cause this. Check for:
1. Warped brake disc.
2. Loose brake disc.
3. Loose caliper mounting bolts.
4. Loose front axle nut.
5. Worn wheel bearings.
6. Damaged hub.

Table 1 ELECTRICAL SPECIFICATIONS

Item	Specification
Battery capacity	
1984-1990	12 volts, 19 amp hours
1991-1996	
FXR series models	12 volts, 19 amp hours
FLH and FLT series models	12 volts, 20 amp hours
1997-1998	
FLH and FLT series models	12 volts, 30 amp hours
1999	
FXR2 and FXR3 models	12 volts, 19 amp hours
Ignition coil	
Primary resistance	2.5-3.1 ohms
Secondary resistance	
1986-1992	11250-13750 ohms
1993-1998	10000-12500 ohms
Alternator	
Stator coil resistance	
1984-1988	0.2-0.4 ohm
1989-1998	0.1-0.2 ohm
AC output	
FXR, FLH and FLT series models	
1984-1988	19-23 amps at 2000 rpm
1989-1990	29-32 amps at 2000 rpm
1991-1994	26-32 amps at 3000 rpm
1995-1998	
Carbureted models	32-40 amps at 3000 rpm
Fuel-injected models	41-48 amps at 3000 rpm
FXWG, FXSB and FXEF models	19-26 amps at 2000 rpm
Starter draw test	
1984-1988	45 amps maximum at 10.0 volts
1989-1998	90 amps maximum at 11.5 volts
Starter current draw test	
1984-1988	40-50 amps maximum
1989-1992	150 amps maximum
1993-1998	
Range	160-180 amps
Maximum	200 amps

Table 2 CURRENT DRAW (FXR, FLH AND FLT)

Model	Meter reading (milliamperes)
1986-1987	
FLTC and FLHTC	Less than 40
FXR series models	Less than 40
1988-1998	
FLTC and FLHTC[1]	Less than 10
1989-1998	
FLTC Ultra and FLHTC Ultra[2]	Less than 15
1984-1998 (without clock and radio)	Less than 3

1. Radio memory only.
2. Radio and CB memory.

Table 3 ENGINE MANAGEMENT DIAGNOSTIC CODES

Diagnostic code No.	Fault condition
11	Throttle position sensor
12	Barometric pressure sensor
14	Engine temperature sensor
15	Intake air temperature sensor
16	Battery voltage
23	Front cylinder fuel injector
24	Front cylinder ignition coil
25	Rear cylinder ignition coil
32	Rear cylinder fuel injector
33	Fuel pump relay
52	RAM error or failure
54	EE-PROM error or failure
55	Ignition module failure
56	Camshaft position sensor and crankshaft position sensor timing or signal error

Table 4 CRUISE CONTROL DIAGNOSTIC TROUBLE CODES

Diagnostic code No.	Fault condition
111	No code recorded
112	Throttle roll off
113	Cruise control switch turned off
121	Short between wiring harness SET/RESUME
122	Application of front or rear brakes
211	Coast (S/C button engaged) interval longer than six seconds
212	Speed drops below 30 mph (48 km/h) while in coast (S/C button engaged)
213	Speed drops below 26 mph (42 km/h) or exceeds 90 mph (145 km/h)
221	Speed drops 15 mph (24 km/h) below set speed (such as while climbing a steep hill)
222	Speed decreases greater than 20 mph (32 km/h) per second
223	Vehicle speed sensor input
231	Engine speed over 5000 rpm
232	Loss of tachometer signal
242	High rate of change of RPM detected (such as when contacting a slippery surface)
311	Internal failure
312	Internal failure
313	Internal failure
321	Internal failure
323	Internal failure
331	Internal failure
332	Internal failure
333	Internal failure
341	Low voltage
342	Internal failure
343	Internal failure
351	Internal failure
352	Internal failure
353	Internal failure
361	Internal failure
362	Internal failure
363	Internal failure
371	Internal failure
423	Internal failure
432	Internal failure
777	Internal failure

CHAPTER THREE

LUBRICATION, MAINTENANCE AND TUNE-UP

This chapter covers lubrication, maintenance and tune-up procedures. If a procedure requires more than minor disassembly, reference to the appropriate chapter is listed. Maintenance intervals, capacities, recommendations and specification are in **Tables 1-13** at the end of this chapter.

To maximize the service life of the motorcycle and gain maximum safety and performance, it is necessary to perform periodic inspections and maintenance. Minor problems found during routine service can be corrected before they develop into major ones.

Consider the maintenance schedule a guide. Harder than normal use and exposure to mud, water or high humidity indicates the need for more frequent servicing to most maintenance items.

ROUTINE SAFETY CHECKS

Pre-Ride Inspection

1. Check wheel and tire condition. Check tire pressure. Refer to *Tires and Wheels* in this section.
2. Make sure all lights work. Refer to *Lights and Horn* in this section.
3. Check engine, transmission and primary drive chaincase for oil leakage. If necessary, add oil as described in this chapter.
4. Check brake fluid level and condition. If necessary, add fluid as described in this chapter.
5. Check the operation of the front and rear brakes.
6. Check clutch operation. If necessary, adjust the clutch as described in this chapter.
7. Check the throttle operation. The throttle should move smoothly and return quickly when released. If necessary, adjust throttle free play as described in this chapter.
8. Inspect the front and rear suspension. They should have a solid feel with no looseness.
9. Check the exhaust system for leaks or damage.
10. Inspect the fuel system for leaks.
11. Check the fuel level in fuel tank.
12. Check drive belt tension as described in this chapter.

CAUTION
When checking the tightness of the exposed fasteners, do not check the cylinder head

bolts without following the procedure described in Chapter Four.

Lights and Horn

With the ignition on, check the following:

1. Pull the front brake lever and make sure the brake light works.
2. Push the rear brake pedal down and check that the brake light comes on soon after the pedal has been depressed.
3. Make sure the headlight and taillight work.
4. Move the dimmer switch up and down between the high and low positions. Make sure both headlight elements are working.
5. Push the turn signal switch to the left and right positions, and make sure all four turn signal lights are working.
6. Make sure all accessory lights work properly, if so equipped.
7. Check the horn button operation.
8. If the horn or any light fails to work properly, refer to Chapter Nine.

TIRES AND WHEELS

Tire Pressure

Check the tire pressure often to maintain tire profile, traction and handling, and to get the maximum life out of the tire. Carry a tire gauge in the motorcycle tool kit. **Table 2** and **Table 3** lists the cold tire pressures for the original equipment tires.

Tire Inspection

Inspect the tires periodically for excessive wear, deep cuts and embedded objects such as stones or nails. If a nail or other object is found in a tire, mark its location with a light crayon prior to removing it. This will help locate the hole for repair.

Measure the depth (**Figure 1**) with a tread depth gauge or a small ruler. As a guideline, replace tires when the tread depth is 5/16 in. (8.0 mm) or less. Refer to Chapter Ten for tire changing and repair information.

Laced Wheel Spoke Tension

On models with laced wheels, check for loose or damaged spokes. Refer to Chapter Ten for spoke service.

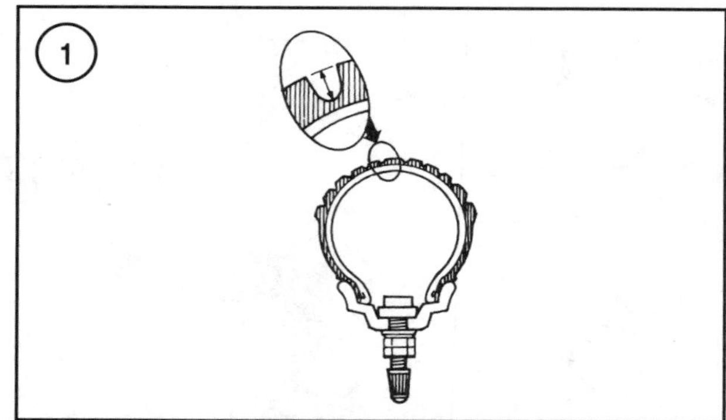

Rim Inspection

Check the wheel rims for cracks and other damage. If they are damaged, a rim can make the motorcycle handle poorly. Refer to Chapter Ten for wheel service.

PERIODIC LUBRICATION

Oil Tank Inspection

Before checking the oil level, inspect the oil tank for cracks or other damage. If oil seepage is noted on or near the tank, find and repair the problem. Check all of the oil tank mounting bolts for loose or missing fasteners; replace or tighten fasteners as required. Check the hose connections on the tank. Each hose should be secured with a hose clamp. Check each hose for swelling, cracks or damage and replace immediately; otherwise, oil leakage may occur and cause engine damage. Refer to **Figures 2-8**.

Oil Tank Level Check (All Models Except 1993-1998 FLH and FLT Series Models)

Check the engine oil level with the dipstick mounted in the tank filler cap.

1. Start and run the engine for approximately ten minutes or until the engine has reached normal operating temperature. Then turn the engine off and allow the oil to settle in the tank.

2A. On FXR models, place the motorcycle on a level surface and park it on the jiffy stand. Do not check the oil level with the motorcycle standing straight up as it will result in an incorrect reading.

2B. On all models except FXR models, have an assistant support the motorcycle standing straight up. Do not check the oil level with the motorcycle on the jiffy stand because it will result in an incorrect reading.

2 **OIL HOSE ROUTING (EARLY 1984 FXR, FLH AND FLT SERIES MODELS)**

Air cleaner (top)
Crankcase vent
Oil tank (right side)
Oil tank return
Main oil feed
To oil filler
Engine (left side)
Oil pump
Front chain oiler return
Front chain oiler

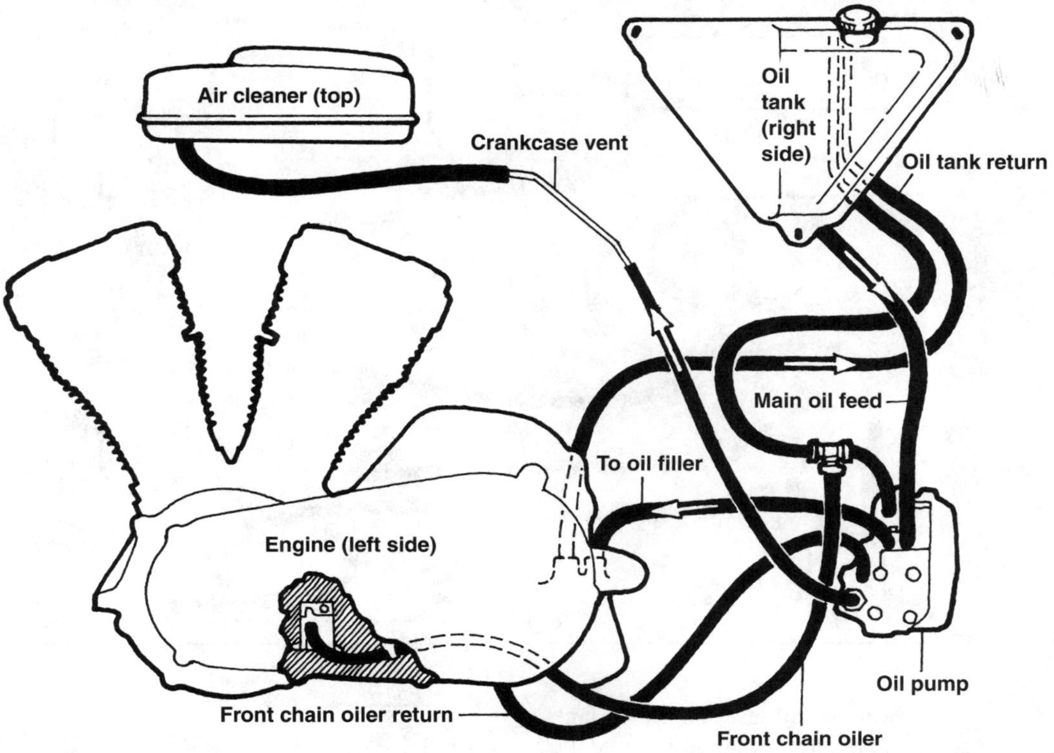

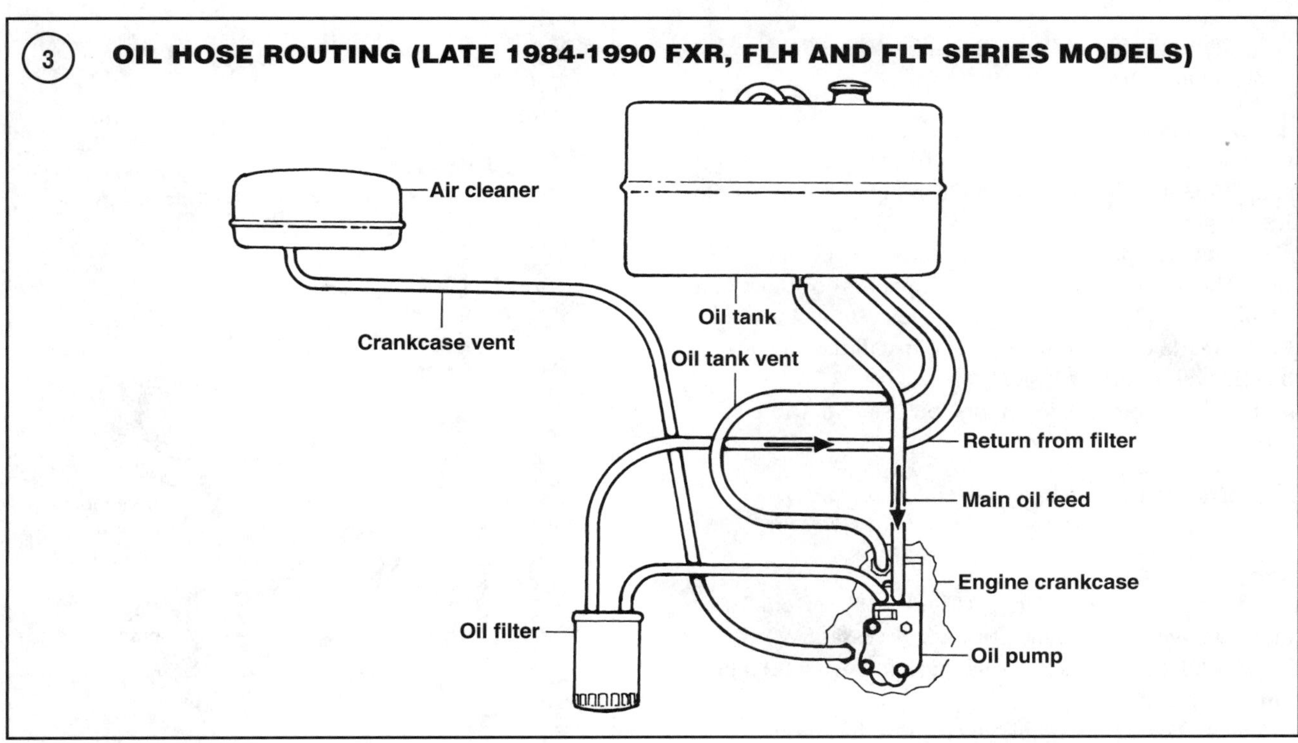

3 **OIL HOSE ROUTING (LATE 1984-1990 FXR, FLH AND FLT SERIES MODELS)**

Air cleaner
Oil tank
Crankcase vent
Oil tank vent
Return from filter
Main oil feed
Engine crankcase
Oil filter
Oil pump

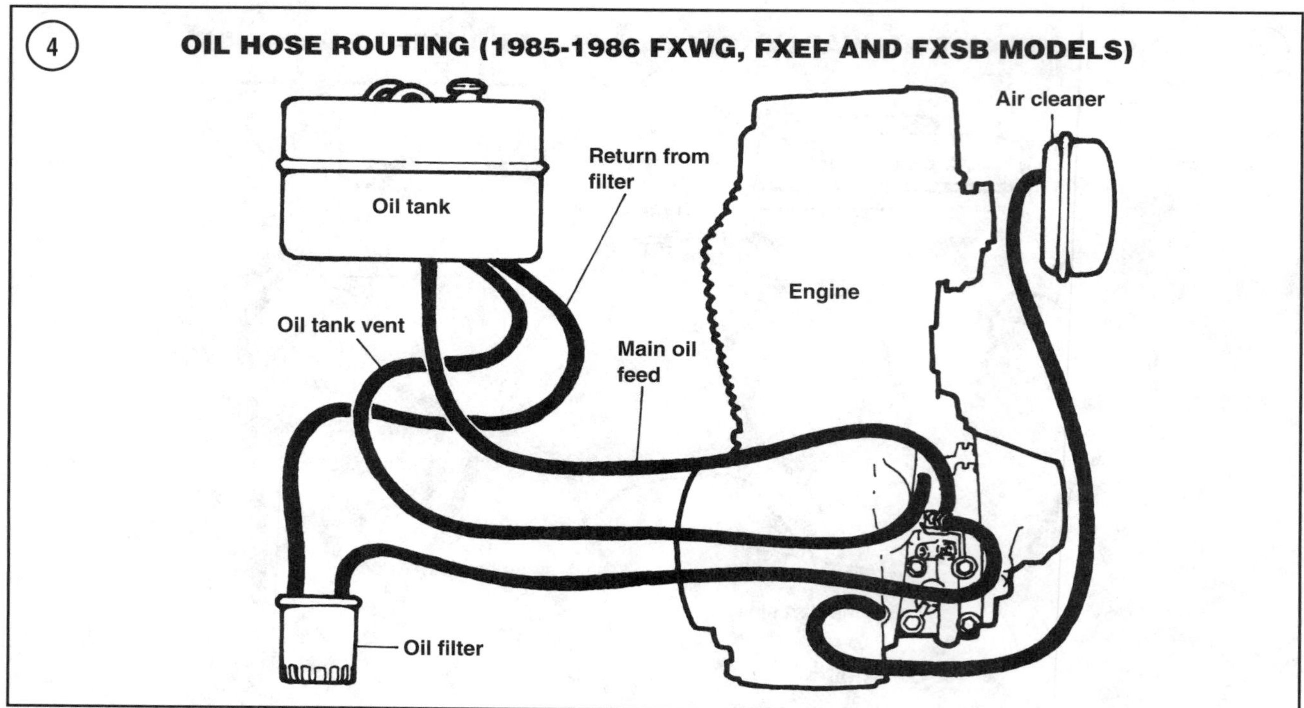

3A. On FXR models, check the oil level on the oil tank sight gauge. The oil level is correct when it is above the top of the sight gauge.

NOTE
On FXR models, raise the seat to check the oil level with the dipstick.

3B. On all models, wipe the area around the oil filler cap with a clean rag. Then pull the oil filler cap out of the oil tank. Wipe the dipstick with a clean rag and reinsert the filler cap all the way into the oil tank until it bottoms. Withdraw the filler cap and check the oil level on the dipstick. The oil level should be at the upper groove mark on the dipstick (**Figure 9**). If the oil level is at the lower groove mark, continue with Step 4. Install the dipstick. If the oil level is correct, go to Step 5.

4. Add the recommended engine oil listed in **Table 4**.

CAUTION
Do not overfill the oil level in the oil tank, or the oil filler cap will be forced out when the oil gets hot.

5. Check the dipstick O-ring (**Figure 10**) for cracks or other damage. Replace the O-ring if necessary.
6. Reinstall the oil filler cap and push it down until it bottoms.
7. Check the oil tank drain plug or hose for tightness.

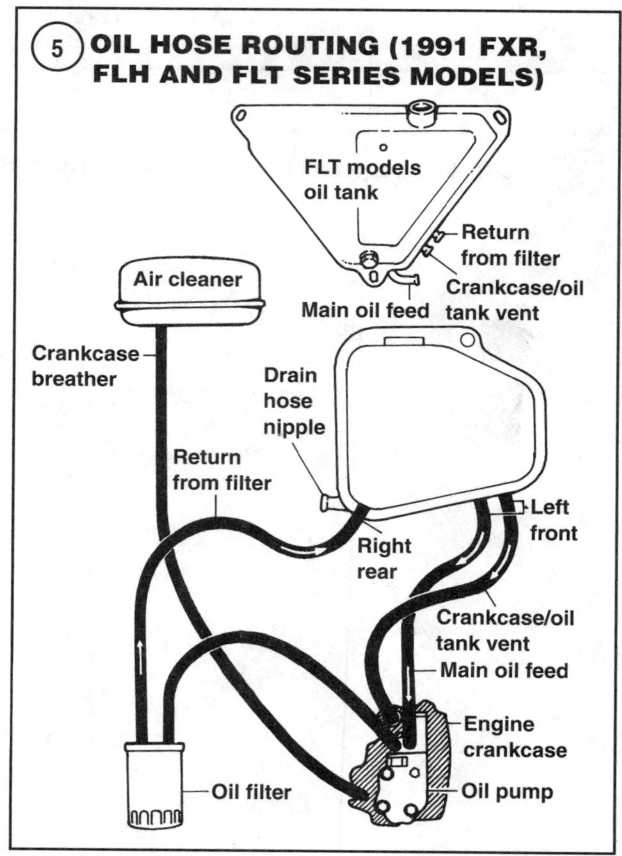

6

OIL HOSE ROUTING (1992-1998 FXR SERIES MODELS)

Crankcase
breather
Oil
tank
vent
Drain hose nipple
Transmission vent hose
Air
cleaner
Oil filter
To oil filter
Main oil
feed hose
Oil return hose
from filter
Clip

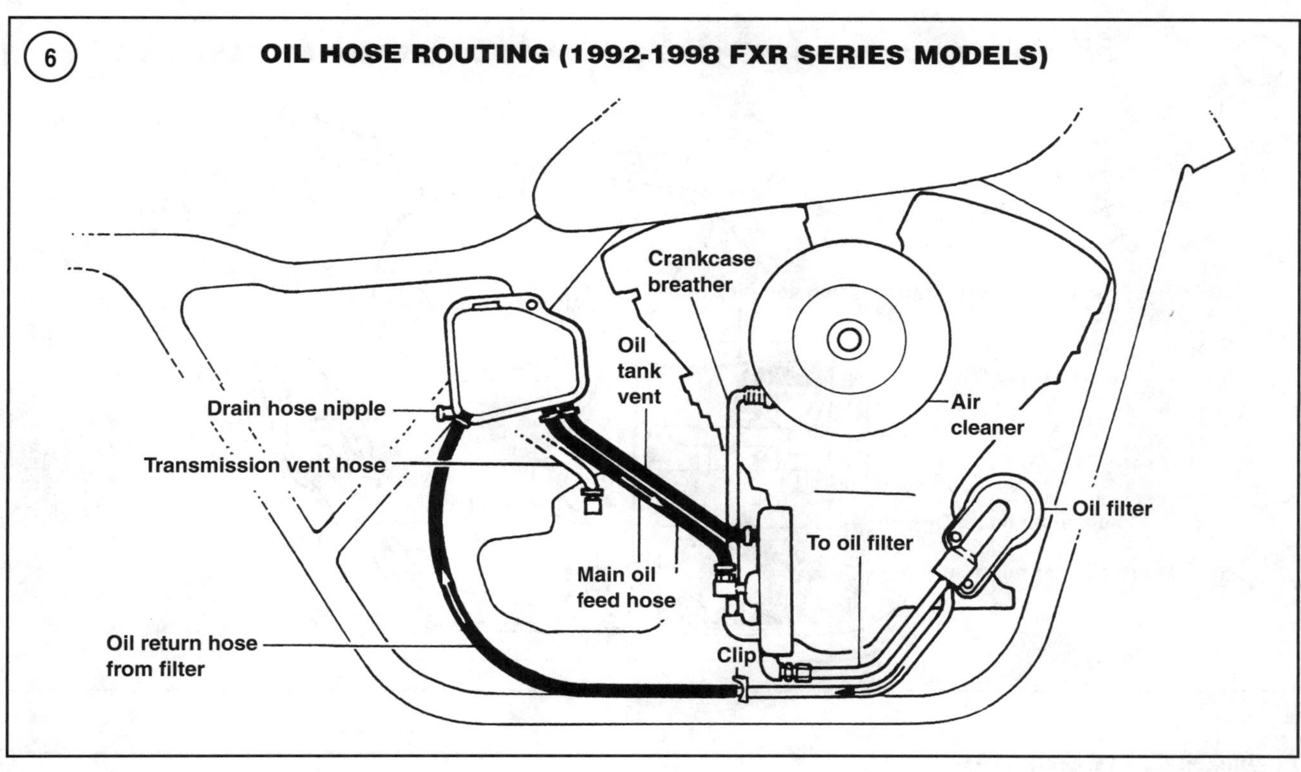

7

OIL HOSE ROUTING (1992 FLH AND FLT SERIES MODELS)

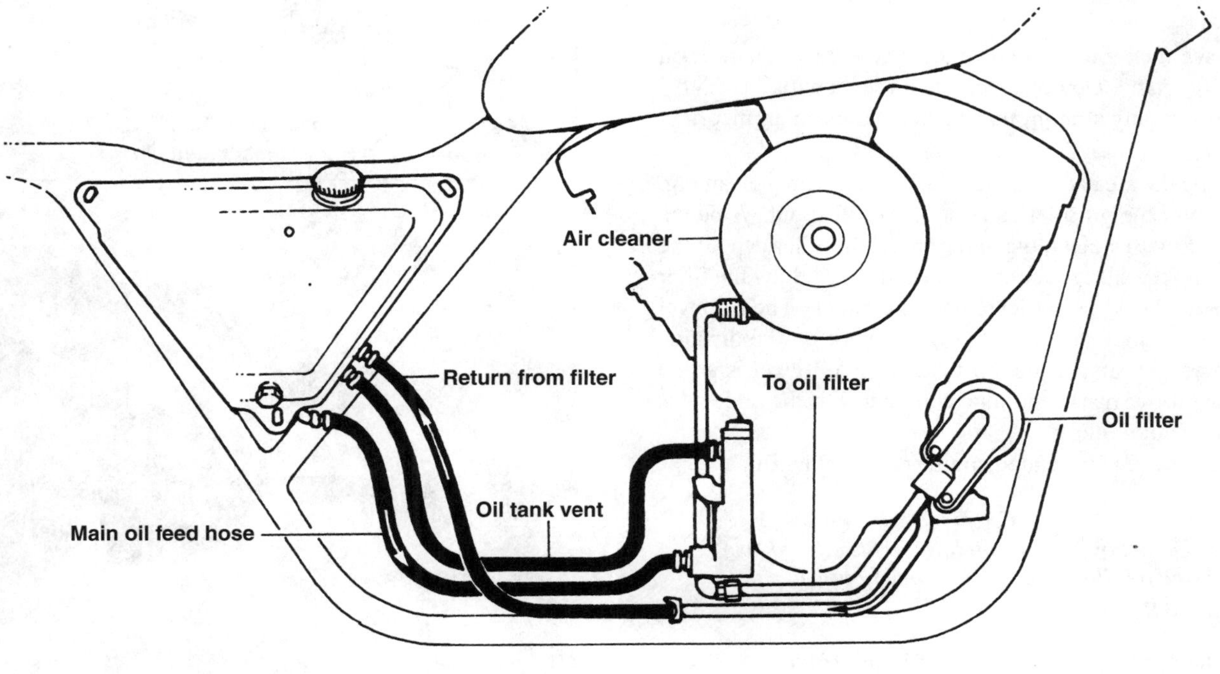

Air cleaner
Return from filter
To oil filter
Oil filter
Oil tank vent
Main oil feed hose

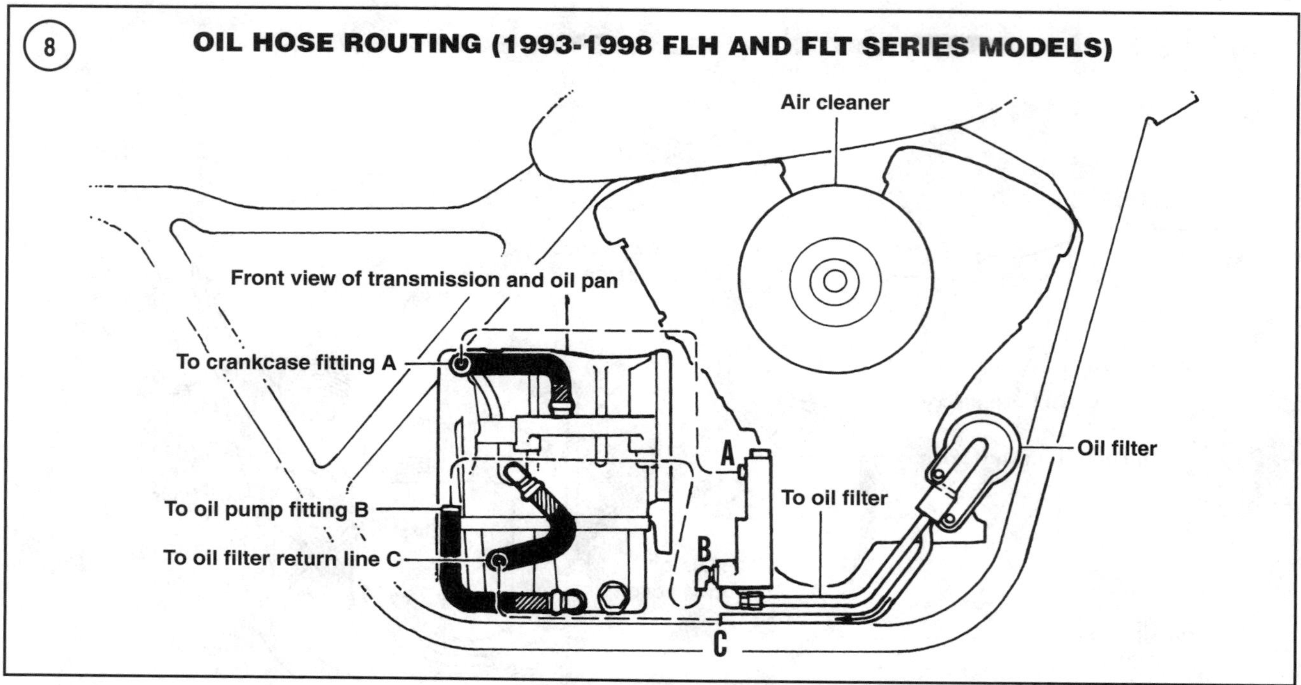

Engine Oil Level Check (1993-1998 FLH and FLT Series Models)

1. Start and run the engine for approximately ten minutes or until the engine has reached normal operating temperature. Then turn the engine off and allow the oil to settle in the tank.
2. Place the motorcycle on a level surface and park it on the jiffy stand. Do not check the oil level with the motorcycle standing straight up as it will result in an incorrect reading.
3. Wipe the area around the oil filler cap with a clean rag. Then pull the oil filler cap out of the fill spout. Wipe the dipstick with a clean rag and reinsert the filler cap all the way into the fill spout until it bottoms. Withdraw the filler cap and check the oil level on the dipstick. The oil level should be above the *ADD QUART* mark on the dipstick (**Figure 11**). Install the dipstick. If the oil level is at the lower groove mark, continue with Step 4. If the oil level is correct, go to Step 5.
4. Add the recommended engine oil listed in **Table 4**.

CAUTION
Do not overfill the oil level in the oil tank, or the oil filler cap will be forced out when the oil gets hot.

5. Check the dipstick O-ring (**Figure 10**) for cracks or other damage. Replace the O-ring if necessary.

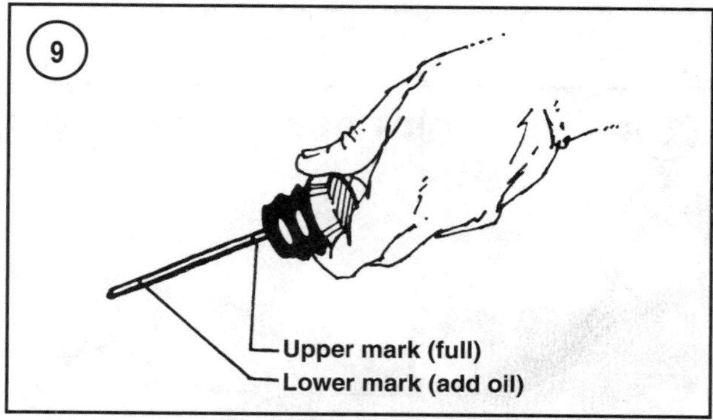

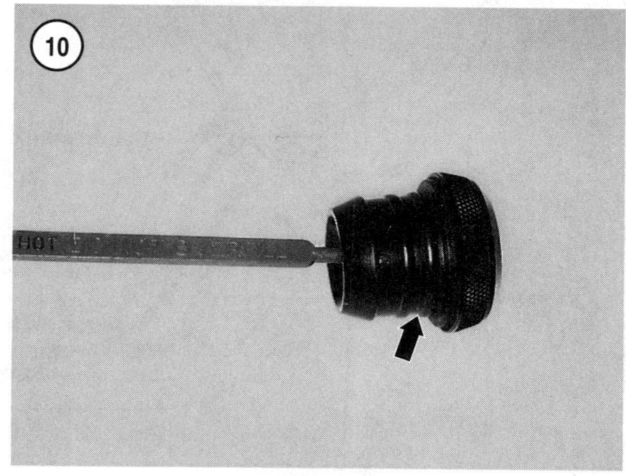

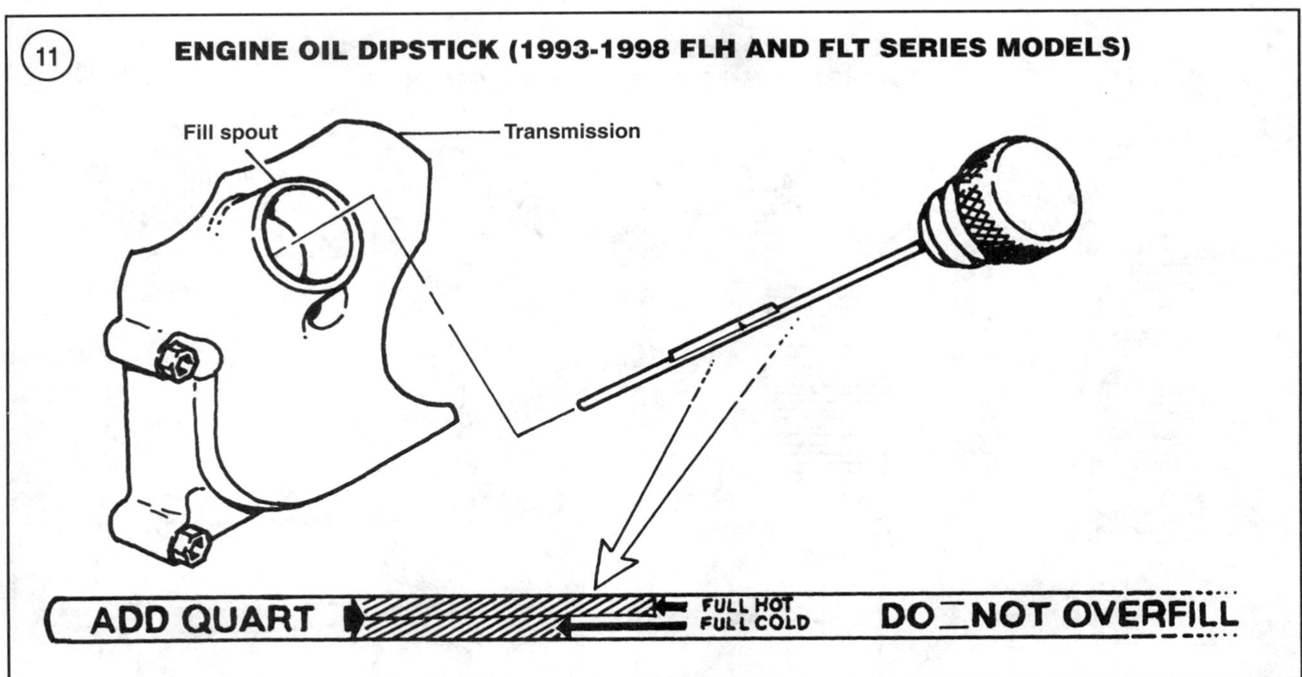

6. Reinstall the oil filler cap and push it down until it bottoms.
7. Check the oil tank drain plug or hose for tightness.

Engine Oil and Filter Change (All Models)

Regular oil and filter changes contribute more to engine longevity than any other maintenance performed. **Table 1** lists the recommended oil and filter change intervals for motorcycles operated in moderate climates. If the motorcycle is operated under dusty conditions, the oil becomes contaminated more quickly and should be changed more frequently than recommended.

Use a motorcycle oil with an API classification of *SF* or *SG*. The classification is printed on the container. Always use the same brand of oil at each change. Refer to **Table 4** for correct oil viscosity to use under anticipated ambient temperatures, not engine oil temperature. Using oil additives is not recommended because they can cause clutch slip.

WARNING

Contact with oil can cause skin cancer. Wash oil from hands with soap and water as soon as possible after handling engine oil.

CAUTION

Do not use the current SH and SJ automotive oils in motorcycle engines. The SH and SJ oils contain friction modifiers that reduce frictional losses on engine components. Specifically designed for automotive engines, these oils can damage motorcycle engines and clutches.

NOTE

Never dispose of motor oil in the trash, on the ground or down a storm drain. Many service stations and oil retailers accept used oil for recycling. Do not combine other fluids with motor oil to be recycled. To locate a recycler, contact the American Petroleum Institute (API) at ***www.recycleoil.org****.*

1. Start and run the engine for approximately 10 minutes or until the engine has reached normal operating temperature. Turn the engine off and allow the oil to settle in the oil tank. Support the motorcycle so that the oil can drain completely.
2. Clean off all dirt and debris around the oil filler cap. Remove the oil filler cap to speed up the flow of oil.

WARNING

The exhaust system is hot and the engine oil will be hot. Work quickly and carefully when removing the oil tank plug to avoid burning your hand and arm.

3A. On 1993-1998 FLH and FLT series models, place a drain pan underneath the oil pan. Remove the engine

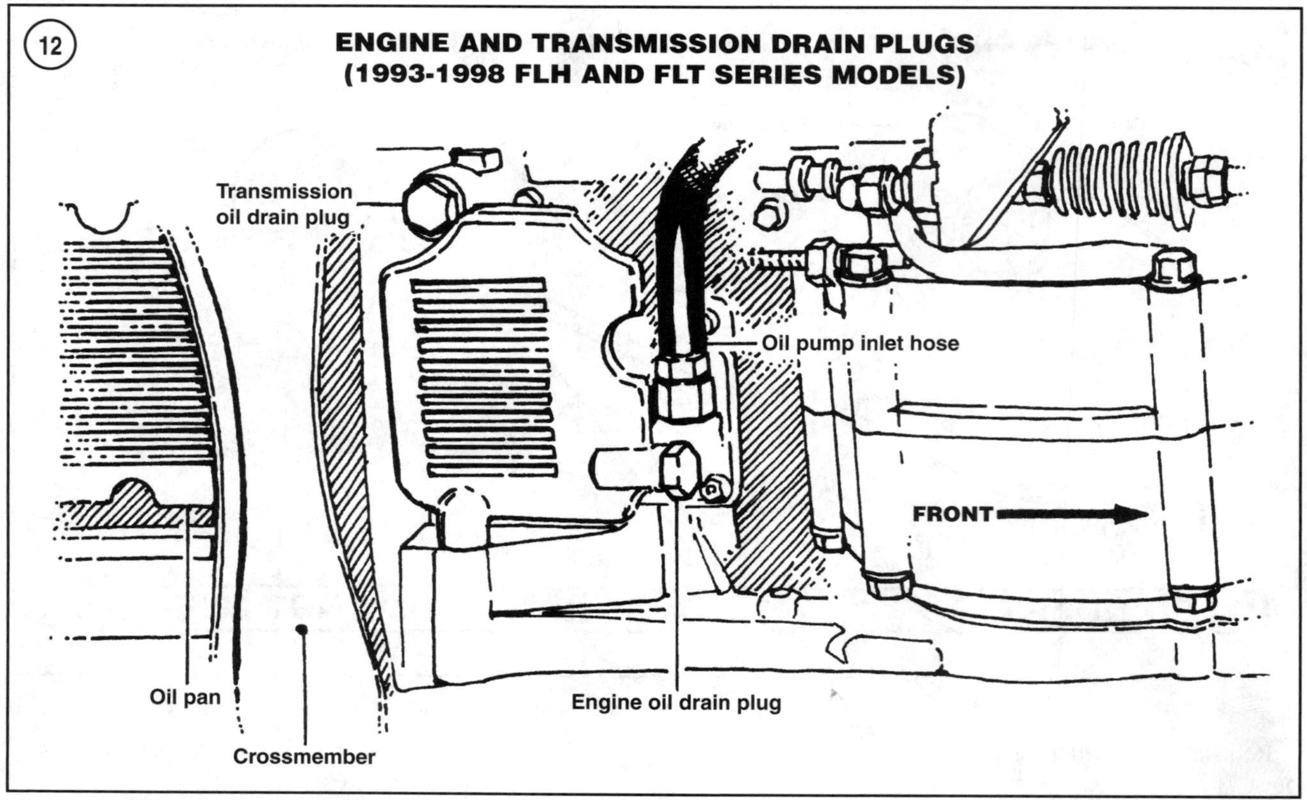

drain plug and gasket at the front of the oil pan (**Figure 12**). Allow the oil to drain completely.

3B. On all other models, place a drain pan beside the motorcycle. Then remove the oil tank drain plug and gasket (**Figure 13**) or remove the drain hose clamp at the drain hose connected to the bottom of the oil tank (**Figure 14**).

4. On models with a dry clutch, remove the primary case drain plug located underneath the clutch cover and drain the primary case. Reinstall the drain plug and washer.

5. Allow the oil to drain completely.

6. To replace the oil filter, perform the following:

   a. Temporarily install the drain plug and gasket, and tighten finger-tight. Then move the drain pan underneath the front portion of the crankcase and the oil filter.

   b. On 1984-1991 models, under the transmission housing, install a socket oil filter wrench squarely over the oil filter and loosen it *counterclockwise.* Quickly remove the oil filter because oil will begin to run out of it.

   c. On 1992-on models, at the front left side of the engine, install a socket oil filter wrench squarely over the oil filter (**Figure 15**) and loosen it *counterclockwise*. Quickly remove the oil filter because oil will begin to run out of it.

   d. Hold the filter over the drain pan and pour out the remaining oil. Place the filter in a plastic bag, seal the bag and dispose of it properly.

   e. Thoroughly wipe off all oil that drained onto the top surface of the left crankcase half. Wipe with a clean, lint-free cloth to eliminate all oil residue from the engine prior to installing the new oil filter.

   f. Coat the gasket on the new filter with clean oil.

CAUTION

Tighten the oil filter by hand. Do not overtighten.

   g. Screw the oil filter onto its mount by hand and tighten it until the filter gasket touches the sealing surface. Then tighten the filter by hand an additional 1/2 to 3/4 turn.

7. On models with an oil tank, after rebuilding the engine and at every second oil change during warm riding weather, flush the oil tank as described in this section. During colder weather, the oil tank should be flushed at each oil change.

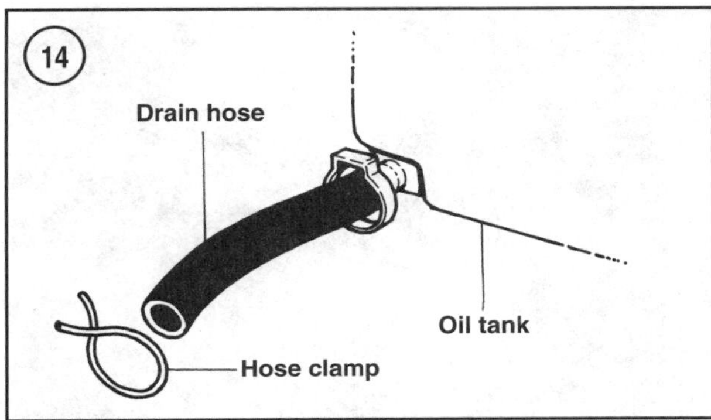

8A. On 1993-1998 FLH and FLT series models, reinstall the oil pan drain plug and gasket. Tighten securely.

8B. On all other models, reinstall the oil tank drain plug and gasket or reinstall the drain hose clamp onto the drain hose.

9. Clean the tappet oil screen as described under *Valve Lifter Oil Screen Cleaning* in this chapter.

10. Fill the oil pan (1993-1998 FLH and FLT series models) or oil tank (all other models) with the correct viscosity (**Table 4**) and quantity (**Table 6**) of oil.

11. Insert the filler cap into the oil tank or oil pan. Push it down until it bottoms.

NOTE
After oil has been added, the oil level will register above the upper groove dipstick mark until the engine runs and the filter fills with oil. To obtain a correct reading after adding oil and installing a new oil filter, follow the procedure in Step 12.

12. After changing the engine oil and filter, check the oil level as follows:
   a. Start and run the engine for 1 minute. Then shut it off.
   b. Check the oil level on the dipstick as described in this section.
   c. If the oil level is correct, it will register in the dipstick safe operating level range. If so, *do not* top off or add oil to bring it to the upper groove level on the dipstick.

13. Check the oil filter and drain plug for leaks.
14. Dispose of the used oil properly.

Oil Tank Flushing (Except 1993-1998 FLH and FLT Series Models)

After rebuilding the engine and at every second oil change during warm riding weather, flush the oil tank before refilling it with new oil. During colder weather, flush the oil tank at each oil change.

1. Drain the oil tank as previously described.
2. Remove the oil tank as described in Chapter Four.

CAUTION
Do not try to totally flush the oil tank while it is mounted in the frame. Any sludge not removed during this procedure will clog oil passages and cause engine seizure.

3. Reinstall the oil tank drain plug (if used) and plug all tank hose openings.
4. Fill the oil tank 3/4 full with kerosene.
5. Secure the dipstick in place and vigorously move the tank side-to-side and top-to-bottom to break loose accumulated sludge and sediment within the tank.
6. Remove the dipstick and drain the tank into a suitable container. Use a small flashlight and check for any large deposits of sludge and sediment that did not drain out. If necessary, *carefully* break any hard deposits loose with a wooden dowel or similar tool inserted into the tank. Remove these deposits.
7. Repeat Steps 4-6 until all deposits are removed and the interior of the oil tank is clean.

8. After the tank is clean, pour a small amount of clean engine oil into the tank and shake the tank to cover the walls with the oil. Drain and discard the oil.

9. Clean the filler cap/dipstick assembly before installing it back into the tank.

10. Remove the plugs from the oil tank hoses and reinstall the oil tank as described in Chapter Four.

11. Dispose of the used kerosene and oil properly.

Transmission Oil Check

Table 1 lists the recommended transmission oil inspection intervals. When checking the transmission oil level, do not allow any dirt or debris to enter the transmission/oil tank case opening.

WARNING
Contact with oil can cause skin cancer. Wash oil from hands with soap and water as soon as possible after handling engine oil.

1. Ride the motorcycle for approximately 10 minutes and shift through all gears until the transmission oil has reached normal operating temperature. Turn the engine off and allow the oil to settle in the tank.

2. Park the motorcycle on a level surface and support it standing straight up.

3. Wipe the area around the transmission filler cap. Refer to **Figures 16-18**.

4A. On four-speed models with an oil level plug, remove the oil level plug from the transmission cover. The oil should be level with the oil level plug opening. If not, perform Step 5. Reinstall the oil level plug.

4B. On four-speed models without an oil level plug, remove the filler cap (**Figure 17**). The oil should be level with the filler cap opening. If not, perform Step 5. Reinstall the plug

4C. On five-speed models, wipe the dipstick off and reinsert it into the transmission housing; do not screw the cap in place. Rest it on the housing and then withdraw it. The oil level should be between the two dipstick marks. See **Figure 19**.

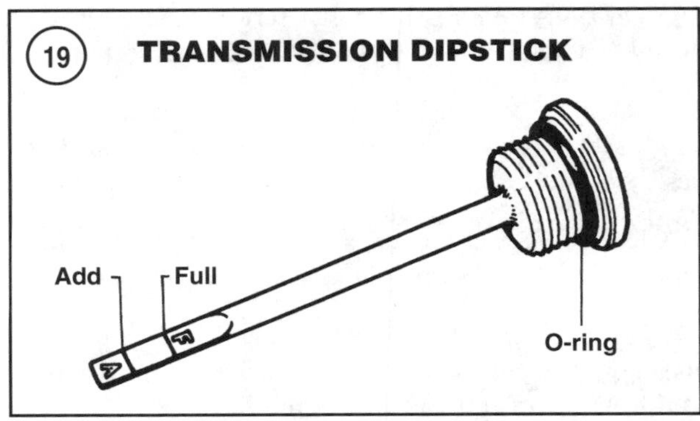

5. If the oil level is low, add the recommended type of oil listed in **Table 5**. Do not overfill.

6. On five-speed models, inspect the filler cap O-ring. Replace if worn or damaged.

7. On five-speed models, install the oil filler cap and screw it into place.

8. Wipe off any spilled oil from the transmission case.

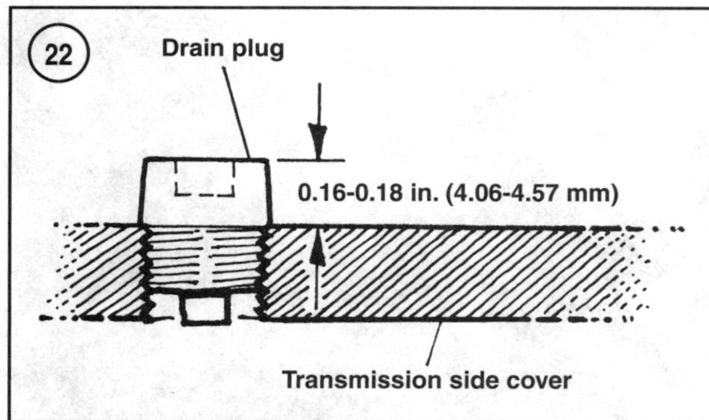

Transmission Oil Change

Table 1 lists the recommended transmission change intervals.

1. Ride the motorcycle for approximately 10 minutes and shift through all four or five gears until the transmission oil has reached normal operating temperature. Turn off the engine and allow the oil to settle in the tank.
2. Park the motorcycle on a level surface and support it standing straight up.
3. Wipe the area around the transmission filler cap. Refer to **Figures 16-18**.

NOTE
*On 1993-1998 FLH and FLT series models, the oil tank pan is equipped with two drain plugs. Make sure to remove the transmission oil drain plug at the rear and not the engine oil drain plug at the front. Refer to **Figure 12**.*

4. Place a drain pan underneath the transmission drain plug.

WARNING
If any oil spills onto the ground, wipe it up immediately before it contacts the rear tire.

5A. On four-speed models, remove the drain plug and gasket from the bottom of the transmission case. Allow the oil to drain for 10 minutes.
5B. On 1993-1998 FLH and FLT series models, remove the rear drain plug and gasket from underneath the transmission housing. Allow the oil to drain for 10 minutes.
5C. On all other five-speed models, remove the drain plug from the transmission side cover (**Figure 20**). Allow the oil to drain for 10 minutes.
6. Check the drain plug gasket for damage and replace if necessary.
7. The drain plug is magnetic. Check the plug (**Figure 21**) for metal debris that may indicate transmission damage. Then thoroughly clean it of all debris. Replace the plug if damaged.
8A. On 1993-1998 FLH and FLT series models, install the drain plug and its gasket into the bottom of the transmission housing and tighten securely.

CAUTION
*On models where the drain plug screws into the side cover (**Figure 20**), the plug has tapered threads. Do not overtighten the plug because it can lock into the cover.*

8B. On all other five-speed transmissions, install and tighten the drain plug until the top of the drain plug is 0.16-0.18 in. (4.06-4.57 mm) above the top surface of the transmission side cover (**Figure 22**).

CAUTION
*Do not add engine oil. Add only the recommended transmission oil in **Table 5**. Make sure to add the oil into the correct oil filler hole.*

9. Refill the transmission through the side cover hole (**Figures 16-18**) with the recommended type (**Table 5**) and quantity (**Table 6**) of transmission oil.
10. Install the filler cap and *new* O-ring. Tighten securely.

11. Remove the oil drain pan from underneath the transmission and dispose of the oil as outlined under *Engine Oil and Filter Change* in this section.
12. Ride the motorcycle until the transmission oil reaches normal operating temperature. Then shut off the engine.
13. Check the transmission oil level as described in this chapter and readjust the level if necessary.
14. Check the transmission drain plug for leaks.
15. Check the transmission oil level as described in this section. Readjust the level if necessary.

Primary Chaincase Lubrication Check (Dry Clutch Models)

The primary chain is lubricated through a metering tube (**Figure 23**) that is connected to an oil line from the oil pump. A fixed (nonadjustable) metering orifice controls the oil flow. Any excess oil that collects in the primary cover is drawn back into the engine through the gearcase breather. Whenever the primary chain is adjusted, check to make sure that oil drops from the metering tube as follows.
1. Remove the clutch inspection cover (**Figure 24**).
2. Start the engine and check that oil comes out of the metering tube (**Figure 23**).
3. Turn off the engine.
4. If oil did not flow out of the metering tube in Step 2, check and clean the metering tube and the oil hose located behind the primary chaincase.

Primary Chaincase Oil Level Check (Wet Clutch Models)

The primary chaincase oil lubricates the clutch, primary chain and sprockets. **Table 1** lists the intervals for checking the chaincase oil level. When checking the primary chaincase oil level, do not allow any dirt or debris to enter the housing.
1. Park the motorcycle on a level surface and support it so that it is standing straight up. Do not support it on the jiffy stand.

CAUTION
Do not check the oil level with the motorcycle supported on its jiffy stand or the reading will be incorrect.

2. Remove the screws securing the clutch inspection cover and O-ring (**Figure 25**). Remove the cover.
3A. On 1984-1997 models, the oil level is correct when it is even with the bottom of the clutch opening or at the bottom of the clutch diaphragm spring (**Figure 26**).

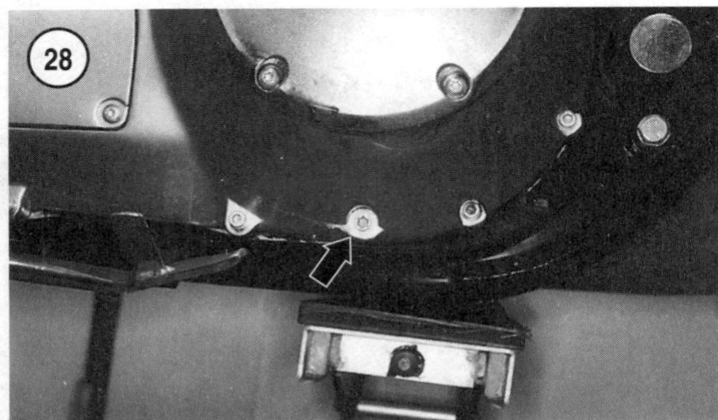

3B. On 1998 models, the oil level is correct when it is even with the bottom of the clutch opening or at the bottom of the clutch diaphragm spring (**Figure 27**).

CAUTION
Do not add engine oil. Add only the recommended primary chaincase lubricant listed in Table 5.

4. If necessary, add Harley-Davidson Primary Chaincase Lubricant or an equivalent through the opening to correct the level.
5. Install the clutch inspection cover O-ring onto the primary chaincase cover.
6. Install the clutch inspection cover and tighten the screws securely.

Primary Chaincase Oil Change (Wet Clutch Models)

Table 1 lists the recommended primary chaincase lubricant replacement intervals.

1. Ride the motorcycle for approximately 10 minutes and shift through all gears until the transmission oil has reached normal operating temperature. Turn off the engine and allow the oil to settle.
2. Park the motorcycle on a level surface and support it standing straight up.
3. Place a drain pan under the chaincase and remove the drain plug (**Figure 28**).
4. Allow the oil to drain for at least 10 minutes.
5. The drain plug is magnetic (models so equipped). Check the plug for metal debris that can indicate drive component or clutch damage. Then wipe off the plug. Replace the plug if damaged.
6. Reinstall the drain plug and tighten securely.
7. Remove the screws securing the clutch inspection cover and O-ring (**Figure 25**). Remove the cover.

CAUTION
*Do not add engine oil. Add only the recommended primary chaincase lubricant listed in **Table** 5.*

8. Refill the primary chaincase through the clutch opening with the recommended type (**Table 5**) and quantity (**Table 6**) of primary chaincase oil. Do not overfill. The oil level must be even with the bottom of the clutch opening or at the bottom of the clutch diaphragm spring.
9. Install the clutch inspection cover O-ring (**Figure 25**) onto the primary chaincase cover.
10. Ride the motorcycle until the primary chaincase oil reaches normal operating temperature. Then shut off the engine.
11. Check the primary chaincase drain plug for leaks.

Drive Chain Lubrication (Enclosed Drive Chain Models)

The drive chain is enclosed in a housing/cover assembly (**Figure 29**). The drive chain is lubricated by the oil held in the housing assembly. Oil capacity used in the rear cover is not specified but is determined by the oil level in the rear cover.

1. Park the motorcycle on level ground in the upright position.
2. To check chain housing oil level, remove the oil level bolt and O-ring from the lower cover (**Figure 30**).
3. The oil level is correct if the oil is level with the bottom of the hole. If the oil level is correct, install the oil level bolt and O-ring and tighten securely. If the oil level is low, proceed to Step 4.
4. Fill the drive chain housing as follows:
   a. Wipe the top cover area around the oil filler cap.
   b. Carefully pry the oil filler plug out with a small screwdriver (**Figure 31**). Do not gouge the upper cover when removing the plug.
   c. Slowly fill the housing with SAE 50 or SAE 60 engine oil until it begins to drain out of the oil level hole. Install the oil level bolt and O-ring and tighten securely.

CAUTION
Do not install transmission oil into the chain housing because it will damage the chain boots and seals.

   d. Wipe off the lower cover with a shop rag after installing the plug.
   e. Install the oil filler plug into the top cover. Make sure the plug completely seats in the cover hole.
5. Check the chain housing for oil leaks.
6. Check the tire for oil that may have contacted it during checking or filling the rear cover. Thoroughly wipe the tire clean prior to riding the motorcycle.

Drive Chain Lubrication (Open Drive Chain Models)

1. Ride the motorcycle a few miles to warm the drive chain. A warm chain increases lubricant penetration.
2. Park the motorcycle on level ground. Support the motorcycle securely on a swing arm stand with the rear wheel off the ground.
3. Shift the transmission to neutral.

CAUTION
If the motorcycle is equipped with an O-ring drive chain, lubricate it with a chain lubricant specified for use on O-ring chains. Using another type of lubricant can cause the O-rings to swell and deteriorate.

NOTE
On an O-ring drive chain, the chain lubricant is used mainly to keep the O-rings pliable and to prevent the side plates and rollers from rusting. The actual chain lubricant is enclosed within the O-rings.

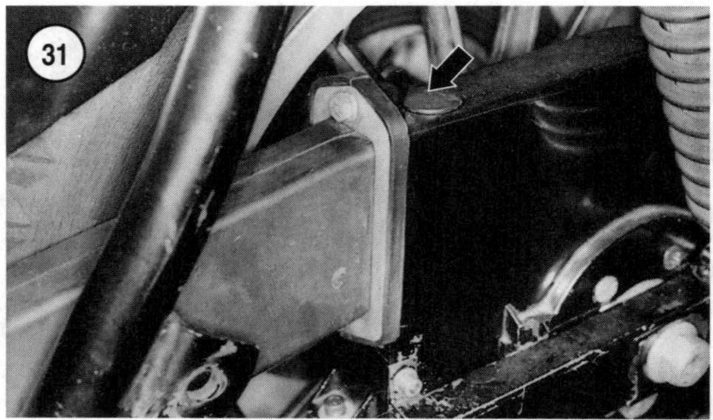

4. Oil the bottom chain run with a commercial chain lubricant. Concentrate on getting the lubricant down between the side plates, pins, bushings and rollers of each chain link.
5. Rotate the chain and continue lubricating until the entire chain has been lubricated.
6. Turn the rear wheel slowly and wipe off excess oil from the chain with a shop cloth. Also wipe off lubricant from the rear hub, wheel and tire.
7. Remove the auxiliary stand.

Front Fork Oil Change (1984-1996 and 1999 Models)

Table 1 lists the recommended front fork oil change intervals.

1. On FLT models, remove the instrument panel and handlebar.
2. On 1986-1997 FLHT models, remove the front fairing as described in Chapter Fifteen.

WARNING
Use caution when releasing the air from the front fork air valve. Moisture and/or fork oil may spurt out when the air pressure is released. Protect eyes accordingly.

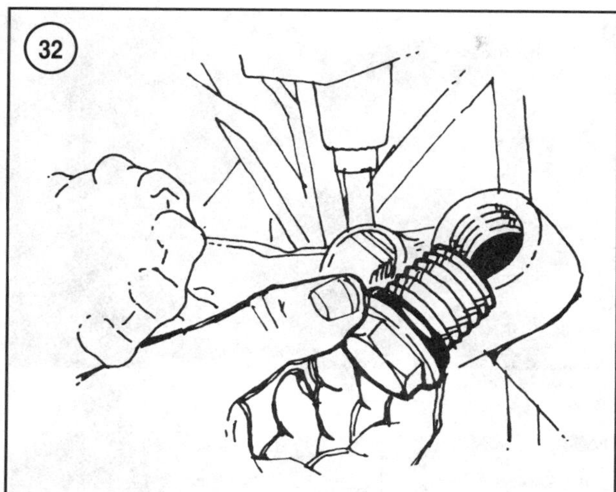

3A. On all FXR and FLT models with air fork, bleed the air from the front fork. Then remove the banjo bolt from the fork tube.

WARNING
The fork caps on non-air forks are under pressure from the fork springs. Remove the caps slowly and carefully in Step 3B.

3B. On all other models, remove the fork cap from one fork tube. See **Figure 32**, typical.

4. Place a drain pan beside one fork tube and remove the drain screw and washer (**Figure 33**, typical).

5. Apply the front brake lever and push down on the fork and release. Repeat this procedure until all of the fork oil is drained.

6. Inspect the sealing washer on the drain screw; replace if necessary.

7. Reinstall the drain screw and washer. Tighten securely.

8. Repeat Steps 4-7 for the opposite fork tube.

CAUTION
Do not allow the fork oil to contact any of the brake components.

9. Support the motorcycle with the front wheel off the ground. Both fork tubes should be fully extended. Refer to *Motorcycle Stands* in Chapter 10.

10. Insert a small clear plastic tube into the opening in the fork cap bolt opening. Attach a funnel to the plastic tube and refill each fork leg with the correct viscosity and quantity of fork oil. Refer to **Table 5** and **Table 7**.

11. Repeat Step 10 for the opposite fork tube.

12. Check the fork cap O-ring (if so equipped) and replace it if necessary.

13. Reinstall the fork cap and O-ring or banjo bolt.

14. Repeat for the opposite fork tube.

15. Pressurize the front fork tubes to the air pressure in **Tables 10-12** (models so equipped).

16. Install all parts previously removed.

17. Road test the motorcycle and check for leaks.

Front Fork Oil Change (1997-1998 Models)

Table 1 lists the recommended fork oil change intervals.

1. Disconnect the negative battery cable from the battery as described Chapter Nine.

2A. On FLHT, FLHTC and FLHTC-UI models, remove the outer fairing and radio. On FLHT models, also remove the glove box as described in Chapter Fifteen.

2B. On FLHR, FLHR-I and FLHRC-I models, remove the headlight nacelle as described in Chapter Fifteen.

2C. On FLTR and FLTR-I models, remove the instrument nacelle as described in Chapter Fifteen.

3. On models so equipped, remove the right side saddlebag as described in Chapter Fifteen.

WARNING
Use caution when releasing the air from the front fork air valve. Moisture and/or fork oil may spurt out when the air pressure is released. Protect eyes accordingly.

4. Cover the rear brake assembly and wheel prior to releasing the compressed air from the front air valve. If necessary, wipe any oil residue that might have been ejected from the air valve.

5. Remove the cap from the front fork air valve (**Figure 34**). Then slowly depress the air valve to evacuate the air from the front fork air pipe system. Unscrew and remove the core from the air valve. Place the air valve core and cap in a reclosable plastic bag to avoid misplacing them.

6. Place a drain pan beside one fork tube. Then remove the drain screw and washer (**Figure 33**, typical) from the slider.
7. Straddle the motorcycle and apply the front brake lever. Push down on the fork and release. Repeat to force as much oil as possible out of the fork tube.

CAUTION
Do not allow the fork oil to contact any of the brake components.

8. Replace the drain screw washer if damaged.
9. Repeat Steps 6-8 for the opposite fork tube.
10. Support the motorcycle on a stand or floor jack. Refer to *Motorcycle Stands* in Chapter Ten.
11. Unscrew and remove the hex bolt (**Figure 35**) securing the banjo fitting to the top of each fork tube.
12. Carefully move the air pipe assembly from the top of the fork tubes.
13. After the fork oil has thoroughly drained, install the drain screw and washer into the fork slider. Tighten the drain screw securely.
14. Insert a clear plastic tube into the fork cap bolt opening (**Figure 36**). Attach a funnel to the plastic tube and refill each fork leg with the correct viscosity and quantity of fork oil. Refer to **Table 5** and **Table 7**. Remove the small funnel and plastic tube.
15. Repeat for the opposite fork tube.
16. Install the valve core and tighten it securely into the front fork air valve (**Figure 34**)
17. Apply clean fork oil to *new* O-rings on the banjo fittings (**Figure 37**). Then install them onto the banjo fitting.
18. Carefully install the air pipe assembly onto the top of the fork tubes.
19. Slowly screw the hex bolt (**Figure 35**) securing the banjo fitting to the top of the fork tube. Hold the air pipe assembly to keep it from turning. Then tighten the hex bolt to 97-106 in.-lbs. (11-12 N•m).
20. Pressurize the front forks to the air pressure in **Table 12**.
21. Install all items removed in Steps 2 and 3.
22. Reconnect the negative battery cable as described in Chapter Eight.
23. Road test the motorcycle and check for leaks.

Control Cable Lubrication (Non-Nylon Lined Cables Only)

Lubricate the *non-nylon lined* control cables at the intervals specified in **Table 1** or when they become stiff or sluggish. At this time, inspect each cable for fraying and cable sheath damage. Cables are relatively inexpensive and should be replaced if faulty. Lubricate the cables with a cable lubricant.

CAUTION
*If the cables have been replaced with nylon-lined cables, do **not** lubricate them as described in this procedure. Oil and most cable lubricants will cause the cable liner to expand, pushing the liner against the cable sheath. Nylon-lined cables are normally used dry. When servicing nylon-lined and*

37

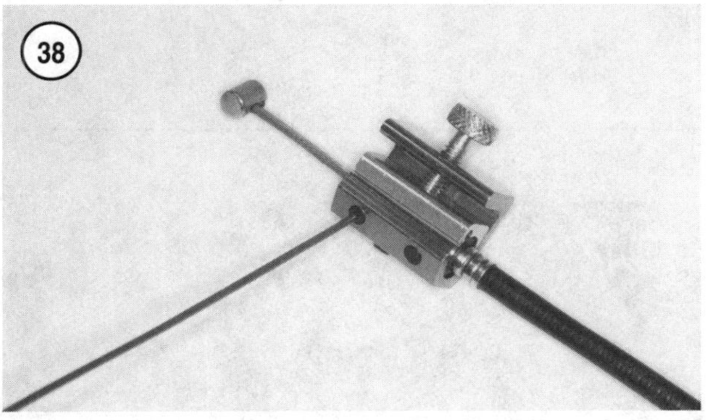

38

other aftermarket cables, follow the manufacturer's instructions.

CAUTION
Do not use chain lubricant to lubricate control cables.

CAUTION
*The starting enrichment valve (choke) cable on 1990-on models is designed to operate with a certain amount of cable resistance. Do **not** lubricate the starting enrichment cable or its conduit.*

NOTE
The major cause of cable breakage or cable stiffness is improper lubrication. Maintaining the cables as described in this section will ensure long service life.

1A. Disconnect the clutch cable ends as described under *Clutch Cable Replacement* in Chapter Five.

1B. Disconnect both throttle cable ends as described under *Throttle and Idle Cables* in Chapter Eight.

2. Attach a lubricator tool to the cable following its manufacturer's instructions (**Figure 38**).

NOTE
Place a shop cloth at the end of the cable to catch all excess lubricant.

3. Insert the lubricant nozzle tube into the lubricator, press the button on the can, and hold it down until the lubricant begins to flow out of the other end of the cable. If the lubricant squirts out from around the lubricator, it is not properly clamped to the cable. Loosen and reposition the cable lubricator.

NOTE
If the lubricant does not flow out of the other end of the cable, check the cable for fraying, bending or other damage. Replace damaged cables.

4. Remove the lubricator tool and wipe off both ends of the cable.

5A. Reconnect the clutch cable ends as described under *Clutch Cable Replacement* in Chapter Five.

5B. Reconnect both the throttle cable ends as described under *Throttle and Idle Cable Replacement* in Chapter Eight.

6. Adjust the cables as described in this chapter.

Throttle Control Grip Lubrication

Table 1 lists the recommended throttle control grip lubrication intervals. To remove and install the throttle grip, refer to *Throttle and Idle Cable Replacement* in Chapter Eight. Lubricate the throttle control grip (where it contacts the handlebar) with graphite.

Speedometer Cable Lubrication

Lubricate the cable every year or whenever needle operation is erratic.

1. Disconnect the speedometer cable from underneath the speedometer.

2. Pull the cable from the sheath.

3. Thoroughly clean off all old grease if it is contaminated.

4. Thoroughly coat the cable with a multipurpose grease and reinstall into the sheath.

5. Make sure the cable is correctly seated into the drive unit. If not, it will be necessary to disconnect the cable at its lower connection and reattach.

Steering Head Lubrication (1991-1998 FLH and FLT and 1992-1998 FXR Series Models)

Table 1 lists the recommended steering head lubrication intervals.

On 1991-1998 FLH and FLT and 1992 FXR series models, a grease fitting (**Figure 39**) is located on the left side of the steering head. All 1993-1998 FXR series models have a grease-fitting hole in the right side of the steering head. The hole is tapped and sealed with a removable plug.

Wipe the grease fitting clean prior to installing the grease gun. Wipe off any excess grease from the fitting.

1. On 1993-1998 FXR models, remove the grease-fitting plug and install a grease fitting.
2. On FLHTC and FLHS models, remove the front fairing as described in Chapter Fifteen.
3. Snap the grease gun nozzle onto the fitting. Slowly pump the gun until grease starts to ooze out between the upper and lower steering head bearings.
4. Remove the grease gun and wipe off all excess grease.
5. On 1993-1998 FXR models, remove the grease fitting and reinstall the plug.
6. On FLHTC and FLHS models, install the headlight assembly as described in Chapter Nine.

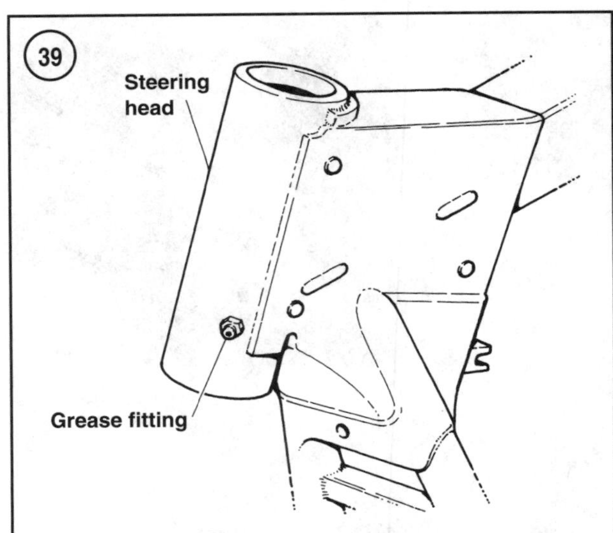

NOTE
If the grease fitting will not take the grease, it may be plugged. Remove the fitting and clean or replace it.

Steering Head Lubrication (All Models Except 1991-1998 FLH and FLT and 1992-1998 FXR Series Models)

Table 1 lists the recommended steering head lubrication intervals.

At the prescribed intervals, the steering bearings must be removed from the steering head, cleaned and lubricated. Complete lubrication will require removal of the steering head assembly as described in Chapter Eleven.

Rear Swing Arm Pivot Shaft Lubrication (FXWG, FXSB and FXEF Models)

Table 1 lists the recommended rear swing arm pivot shaft lubrication intervals.

A grease fitting is located in the middle of the swing arm on the bottom side. Wipe the grease fitting clean prior to installing the grease gun. Wipe off any excess grease from the fitting.

1. Park the motorcycle on a level surface and support it on the jiffy stand.
2. Snap the grease gun nozzle onto the fitting. Slowly pump the gun until grease fills the area between the bearings.
3. Remove the grease gun.

Rear Brake Pedal and Shift Linkage Lubrication

On some models, a grease fitting is installed on the brake pedal and/or shift linkage mounting bracket that allows periodic lubrication of the respective pivot shaft.

Wipe the grease fitting clean prior to installing the grease gun. Wipe off any excess grease from the fitting.

1. Park the motorcycle on a level surface and support it on the jiffy stand.
2. Snap the grease gun nozzle onto the fitting. Slowly pump the gun until grease starts to ooze out of the pivot shaft area.

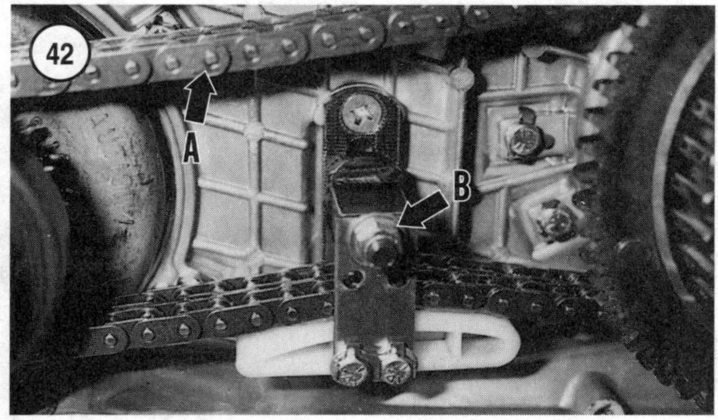

NOTE
If the grease fitting will not take the grease, it is probably plugged. Remove the fitting and clean or replace it.

3. Remove the grease gun.

Miscellaneous Lubrication Points

Lubricate the clutch lever, front brake lever, rear brake lever, jiffy stand pivot and footrest pivot points. Use SAE 10W/30 motor oil.

PERIODIC MAINTENANCE

This section describes the periodic inspection, adjustment and replacement of various operational items. Perform these procedures at the intervals in **Table 1** or earlier, if necessary.

Front Rubber Mount Inspection (FXR, FLH and FLT Series Models)

Check the front rubber engine mount for cracks or damage. Check the area between the large metal washer and the frame for damage. If the rubber mount is damaged, it must be replaced.

After replacing the front rubber mount, adjust the vehicle alignment as described in this chapter.

Engine Stabilizer Links (FXR, FLH and FLT Series Models)

Check the engine stabilizer links (**Figure 40**) for looseness or damage. Check end play by moving the links along the mounting axis. Replace the links if end play is 0.025 in. (0.63 mm) or more as described in Chapter Four.

Primary Chain Adjustment

As the primary chain stretches and wears, free play movement increases. Excessive free play will cause premature chain and sprocket wear and increase chain noise. If the free play is adjusted too tightly, the chain will wear prematurely.

1. Park the motorcycle on level ground. Support the motorcycle securely on a swing arm stand with the rear wheel off the ground.
2. Disconnect the negative battery cable as described in Chapter Nine.

NOTE
Note the locations of the inspection cover screws. On some models, there are two different-length screws, and they must be reinstalled in the correct locations.

3. Remove the primary chain inspection cover and gasket (**Figure 41**).
4. Turn the primary chain to find the tightest point on the chain. Measure chain free play at this point.

NOTE
***Figure 40** is shown with the primary chain cover removed to better illustrate the steps.*

5. Check primary chain free play at the upper chain run midway between the sprockets (A, **Figure 42**). The correct primary chain free play specifications are:
   a. Cold engine: 5/8 to 7/8 in. (15.9-22.3 mm).
   b. Hot engine: 3/8 to 5/8 in. (9.5-15.9 mm).

If the primary chain free play is incorrect, continue with Step 6. If the free play is correct, go to Step 7.

6. To adjust free play, perform the following:
   a. Loosen the primary chain adjuster shoe nut or bolt (B, **Figure 42**).
   b. Move the shoe assembly up or down to correct free play.

c. Tighten the primary chain adjuster shoe nut or bolt to 22-29 ft.-lb. (30-39 N•m). Then recheck free play.

7. Install the primary chain inspection cover (**Figure 41**) and *new* gasket. Tighten the cover screws securely.
8. Lower the motorcycle to the ground.

Enclosed Drive Chain Adjustment

When adjusting the chain, check the free play at several places along its length by rotating the rear wheel. The chain will rarely wear uniformly and as a result will be tighter at some places than others. Make sure the chain free play at the tightest place on the chain is not less than the specification.

1. Remove the bolts holding the upper chain cover (**Figure 43**). Slide the cover forward to expose as much of the upper chain run as possible. Secure the cover with a bungee cord.
2. Park the motorcycle on level ground. Support the motorcycle securely on a swing arm stand with the rear wheel off the ground.
3. Turn the rear wheel and check the chain for its tightest point. Mark this spot and turn the wheel so that the mark is located midway between both sprockets on the upper chain run.
4. Push the chain up midway between the sprockets on the upper chain run and check free play. The correct free play is 1/2 in. (12.7 mm) with an assistant sitting on the seat.
5. If chain adjustment is incorrect, adjust it as follows:
   a. Support the motorcycle securely on a swing arm stand with the rear wheel off the ground.
   b. Loosen the rear axle nut (**Figure 44**).
   c. Loosen the anchor bolt locknut and loosen the anchor bolt (**Figure 44**) if so equipped.
   d. Turn each axle adjuster in or out to achieve the correct chain free play. Turn both axle adjusters in equal amounts to maintain rear wheel alignment.
   e. When the chain free play is correct, check chain alignment with the tool shown in **Figure 45**. Measure from the center of the swing arm pivot shaft to the center of the rear axle. Slide the rubber grommet along the tool until it aligns with the center of the axle. Now check alignment on the opposite side. Compare the rubber grommet position with the center of the axle. The alignment on both sides of the axle must be within 0.32 in. (0.8 mm) of each other. If necessary, adjust the axle with the axle adjusters while maintaining correct chain free play at the same time.
   f. Tighten the axle nut to the specification in **Table 13**. Tighten the chain adjuster locknuts securely.

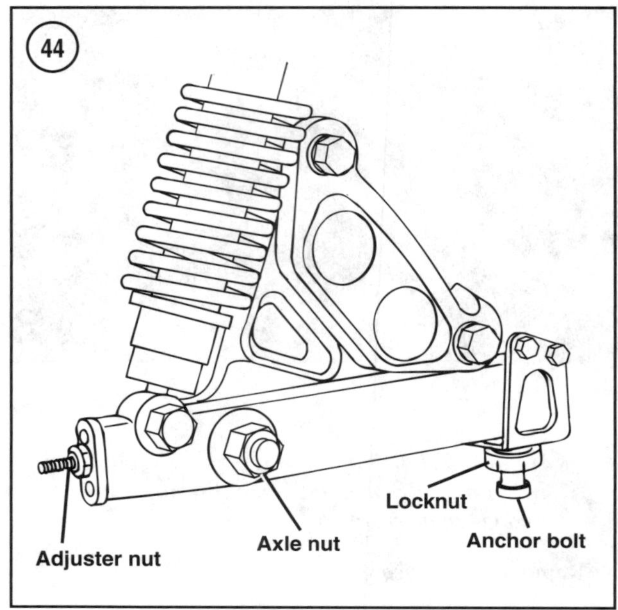

   g. Tighten the anchor bolt (**Figure 44**) until the rubber plug in the center of the bolt just starts to compress, then stop. Secure the bolt with a wrench when tightening the locknut to 20 ft.-lb. (27 N•m).

6. If the drive chain cannot be adjusted within the limits of the chain adjusters, the chain has stretched and must be replaced. Replace the drive chain and both sprockets as a set. If only the drive chain is replaced, the worn sprockets will cause rapid chain wear.

7. Release the chain cover and apply a coating of RTV silicone sealant to the chain cover and to the chain housing mating surface. Secure the cover with its screws and tighten securely.

8. Remove the swing arm stand.

9. After adjusting the drive chain, adjust the rear brake pedal free play as described in this chapter.

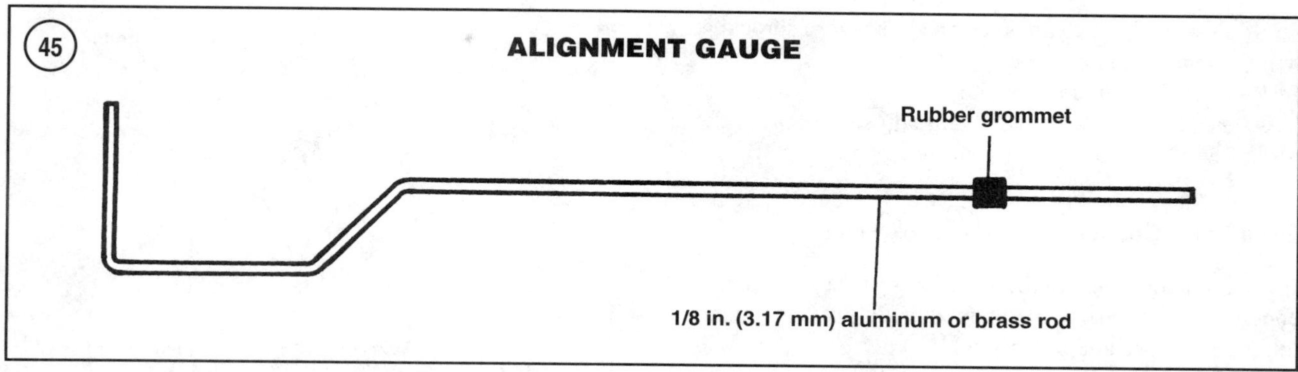

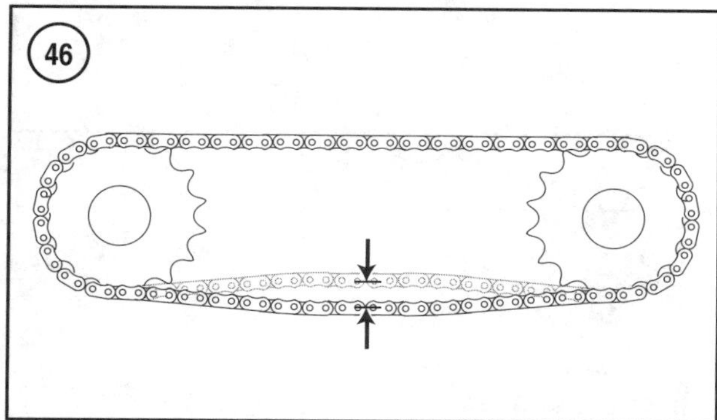

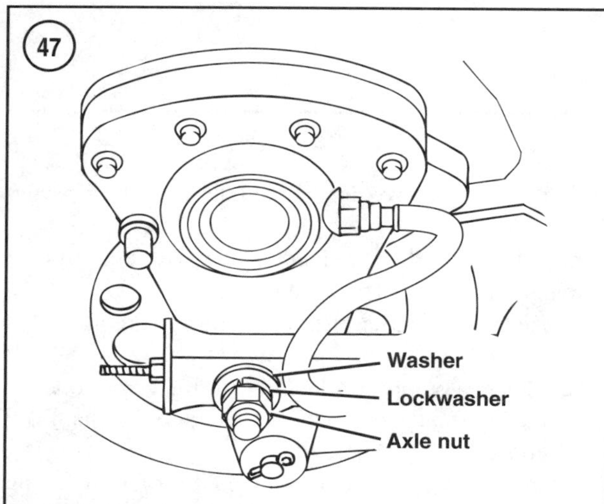

Open Drive Chain Adjustment

Clean the drive chain after riding over dusty or sandy conditions. A properly maintained chain provides maximum service life and reliability.

When adjusting the chain, check the free play at several places along its length by rotating the rear wheel. The chain will rarely wear uniformly and as a result will be tighter at some places than others. Make sure the chain free play at the tightest place on the chain is not less than the specification.

1. Park the motorcycle on level ground. Support the motorcycle securely on a swing arm stand with the rear wheel off the ground.
2. Turn the rear wheel and check the chain for its tightest point. Mark this spot and turn the wheel so that the mark is located midway between both sprockets on the lower chain run.
3. Push the chain up midway between the sprockets on the lower chain run and check free play (**Figure 46**). The correct free play is 1/2-5/8 in. (12.7-15.87 mm) with an assistant sitting on the seat.
4. If chain adjustment is incorrect, adjust it as follows:
   a. Loosen the rear axle nut (**Figure 47**).
   b. Loosen the axle adjuster locknut.
   c. Turn each axle adjuster (**Figure 48**) in or out to adjust chain free play. Turn axle adjusters in equal amounts to maintain rear wheel alignment.
   d. When the chain free play is correct, check chain alignment with the tool shown in **Figure 49**. Measure from the center of the swing arm pivot shaft to the center of the rear axle. Slide the rubber grommet along the tool until it aligns with the center of the axle. Now check alignment on the opposite side. Compare the rubber grommet position with the center of the axle. The alignment on both sides of the axle must be within 0.32 in. (0.8 mm) of each other. If necessary, adjust the axle with the axle adjusters while maintaining correct chain free play at the same time.
   e. Tighten the axle nut to 60-65 ft.-lb. (81-88 N•m). Tighten the chain adjuster locknuts securely.
5. If the drive chain cannot be adjusted within the limits of the chain adjusters, the chain has stretched and must be replaced. Replace the drive chain and both sprockets as a

set. If only the drive chain is replaced, the worn sprockets will cause rapid chain wear.

6. Remove the swing arm stand.
7. After adjusting the drive chain, adjust the rear brake pedal free play as described in this chapter.

Open Drive Chain Cleaning and Inspection

Clean the drive chain after riding over dusty or sandy conditions. A properly maintained chain provides maximum service life and reliability.

CAUTION

Some models are equipped with an O-ring drive chain. Clean the chain with kerosene only. Solvents and gasoline cause the rubber O-rings to swell. The drive chain then becomes so stiff it cannot move or flex. If this happens, the drive chain must be replaced. High-pressure washers and steam cleaning can also damage the O-rings.

1. Ride the motorcycle a few miles to warm the drive chain. A warm chain increases lubricant penetration.
2. Park the motorcycle on level ground. Support the motorcycle securely on a swing arm stand with the rear wheel off the ground.
3. Remove the drive chain as follows:
   a. Loosen the rear axle nut and the chain adjusters and push the rear wheel forward.
   b. Locate the master link. Then remove the outer link clip.
   c. Remove the master link with a chain breaking tool and separate the drive chain.
   d. Using the master link, connect one end of an old chain to the existing chain. Then pull the existing chain out from around the front drive sprocket. Disconnect and remove the existing chain from the old chain. Leave the old chain in place.

NOTE

Wear rubber gloves when cleaning the drive chain in the following steps.

4A. On O-ring chains, perform the following:
   a. Do not soak O-ring chains in any type of solvent.
   b. Soak a thick rag in kerosene. Then wipe it against a short section of the chain run. Repeat until all of the chain is clean. To remove stubborn dirt, scrub the rollers and side plates with a soft brush. Clean one section of the chain at a time.

4B. On chains without O-rings, perform the following:
   a. Soak the chain in a pan of kerosene or solvent for approximately 15-30 minutes. Move it around and flex it to remove dirt trapped between the pins and rollers.
   b. Scrub the rollers and side plates with a stiff brush and rinse away loosened grit.
   c. Rinse it a couple of times to make sure all dirt is washed out.
   d. Place an empty can underneath the chain to catch the kerosene or solvent and hang up the chain and allow it to dry thoroughly.

5. After cleaning the chain, examine it for the following conditions (**Figure 50**). If the chain is damaged or severely worn, replace it.
   a. Excessive wear.
   b. Loose pins.
   c. Damaged rollers.
   d. Damaged plates.
   e. Dry plates.
   f. On O-ring chains, check for worn, damaged or missing O-rings (**Figure 51**).

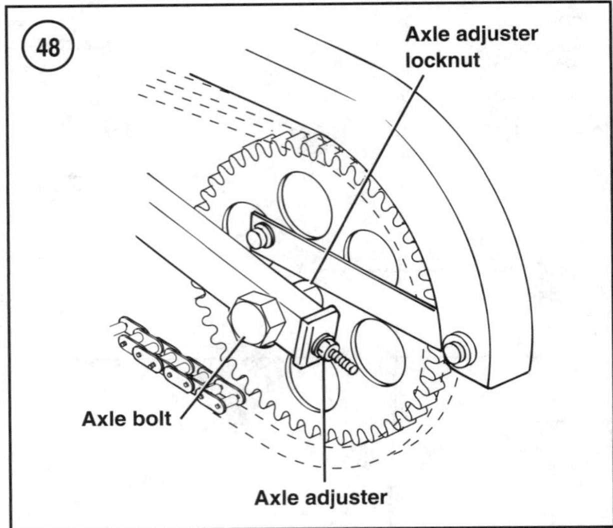

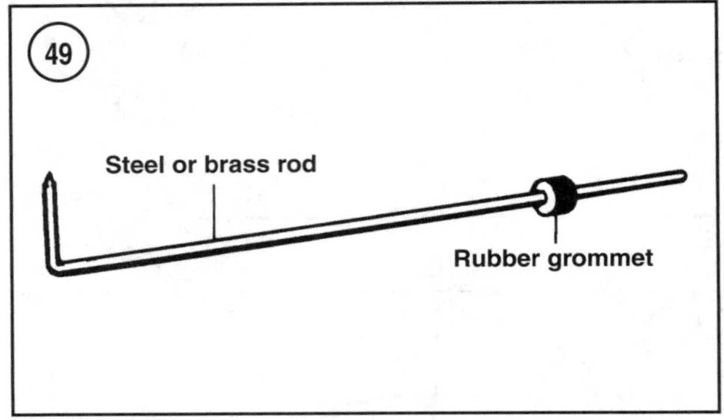

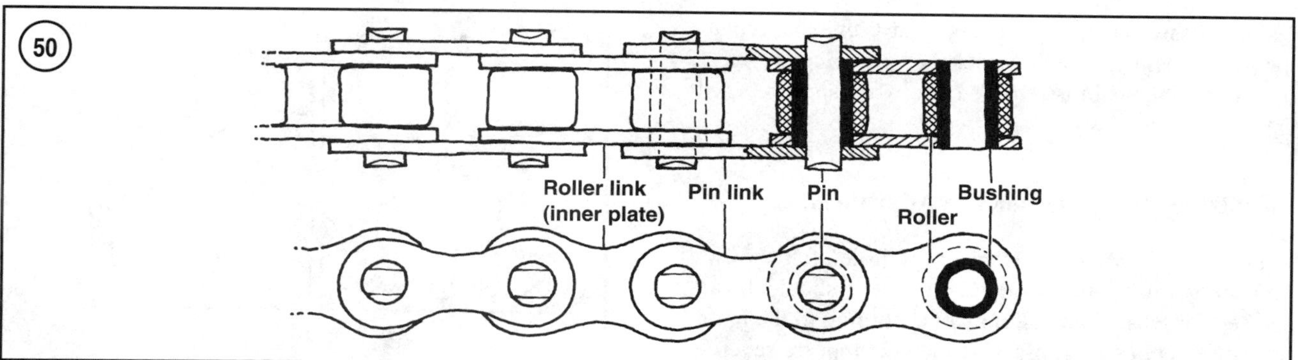

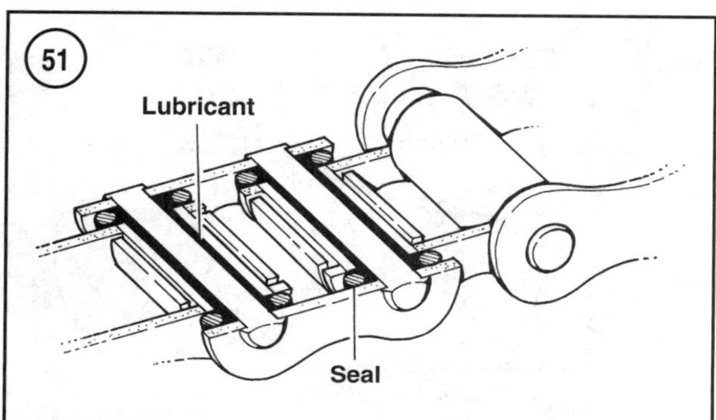

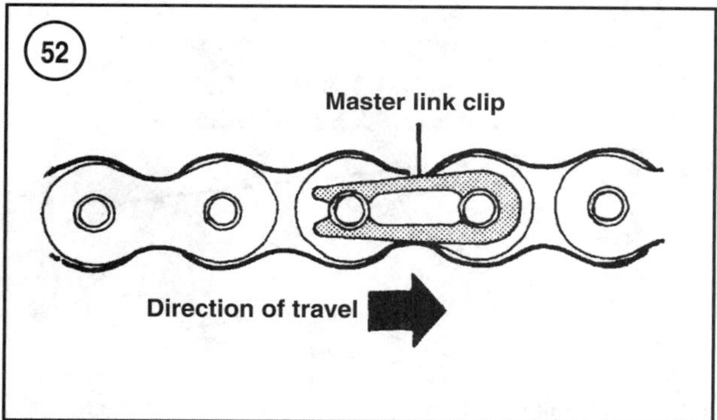

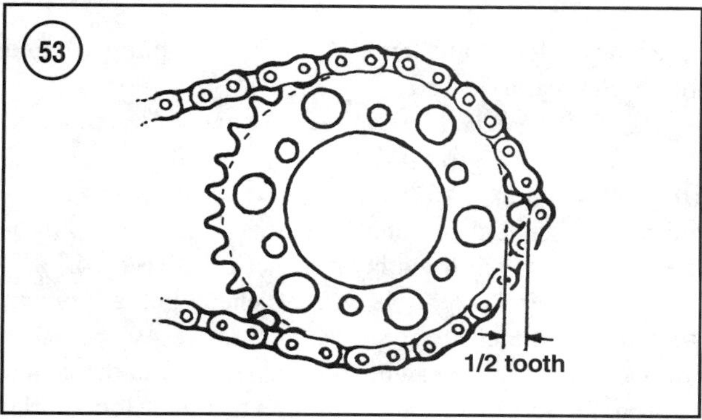

CAUTION

Always check both sprockets when the drive chain is removed. If wear is visible on the teeth, replace the chain and both sprockets as a set. Never install a new chain over worn sprockets or a worn chain over new sprockets.

6. Reverse Step 3 to install the drive chain. Reconnect the drive chain with a new master link and side plate. Then install the master link spring clip with the closed end facing in the direction of chain travel (**Figure 52**). Make sure the clip seats completely in the link grooves.
7. Lubricate the drive chain as previously described in this section.

Drive Chain and Sprocket Inspection

Frequently check the chain and both sprockets for excessive wear and damage.

1. Clean the drive chain as described in this chapter.
2. Park the motorcycle on level ground. Support the motorcycle securely on a swing arm stand with the rear wheel off the ground.
3. Turn the rear wheel and inspect both sides of the chain for missing or damaged O-rings.
4. At the rear sprocket, pull one of the links away from the driven sprocket. If the link pulls away more than 1/2 the height of the sprocket tooth (**Figure 53**), the chain is excessively worn.
5. Inspect the inner plate chain faces. They should be polished on both sides. If they show considerable uneven wear on one side, the sprockets are not aligned properly. Severe wear requires replacement of not only the drive chain but also the drive and driven sprockets.
6. Inspect the drive and driven sprockets for the following defects:
   a. Undercut or sharp teeth (**Figure 54**).
   b. Broken teeth.

7. If excessive chain or sprocket wear is evident, replace the drive chain and both sprockets as a complete set. If only the drive chain is replaced, the worn sprockets will cause rapid chain wear.

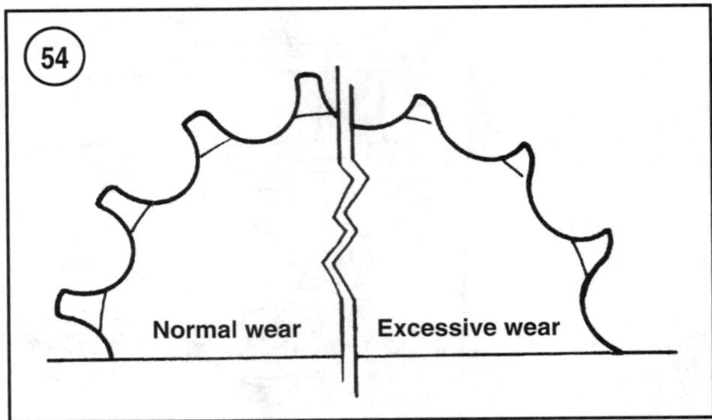

Final Drive Belt Deflection and Adjustment

The final drive belt stretches very little after the first 500 miles (800 km) of operation, but it should be inspected for tension and alignment according to the maintenance intervals in **Table 1**. If the belt appears severely worn or wearing incorrectly, inspect it as described in Chapter Twelve.

NOTE
Check the drive belt defection and alignment when the belt is cold.

1. On models so equipped, remove the left side saddlebag as described in Chapter Fifteen.
2. Remove the drive belt debris cover.
3. Support the motorcycle with the rear wheel off the ground. Then turn the rear wheel and check the drive belt for its tightest point. When this point is located, turn the wheel so that the tight spot is midway between the front and rear sprockets on the lower belt run.
4. Lower the motorcycle to the ground.
5. Position the motorcycle so that both wheels are on the ground. Check and adjust drive belt deflection in the following steps with an assistant sitting on the motorcycle seat facing forward.

NOTE
Use the Harley-Davidson belt tension gauge (part No. HD-35381) or equivalent to apply pressure to the drive belt in Step 6.

6A. On FXWG and FXSB models, perform the following:
   a. Apply a force of 10 lbs. (4.5 kg) to the middle of the lower belt strand while measuring the deflection of the upper belt (**Figure 55**).
   b. The top belt strand should deflect 3/8-1/2 in. (9.5-13 mm).

6B. On all models except FXWG and FXSB models, perform the following:
   a. Apply a force of 10 lbs. (4.5 kg) to the middle of the lower strand while measuring the deflection at the same point (**Figure 56**).
   b. The bottom belt strand should deflect 5/16-3/8 in. (8-9.5 mm).

7. Support the motorcycle with the rear wheel off the ground.

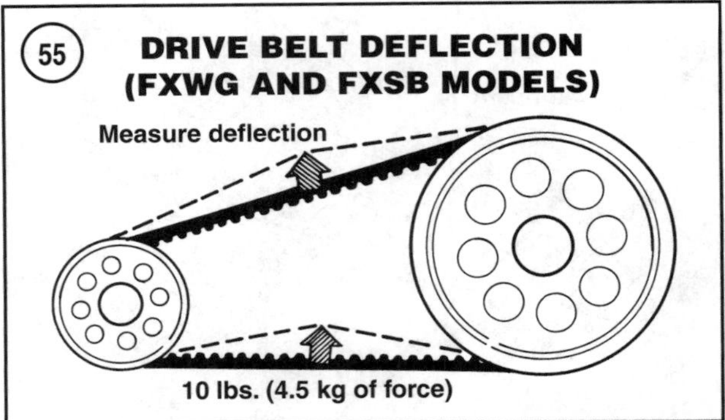

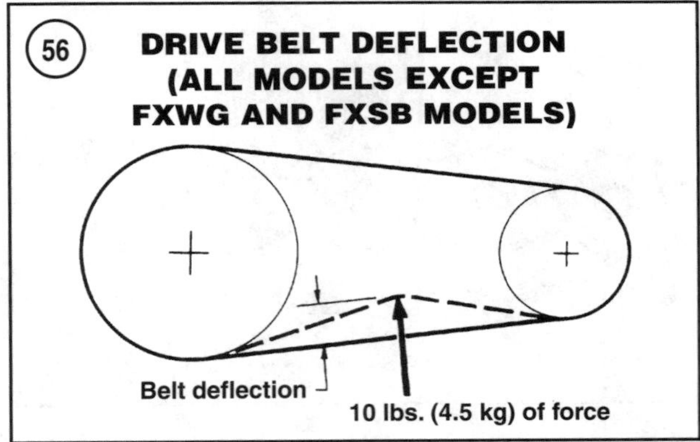

8. Remove the cotter pin (models so equipped) and loosen the rear axle nut.
9. On 1985 models, loosen the brake anchor locknut and the anchor nut (**Figure 44**).
10. Turn each axle adjuster (**Figure 48**) in or out as required and in equal amounts to maintain rear wheel alignment. Recheck belt free play as described in Step 4.
11. When belt free play is correct, check belt alignment with the alignment tool shown in **Figure 49**. Measure from the center of the swing arm pivot shaft to the center of the axle. Slide the rubber grommet along the tool until it

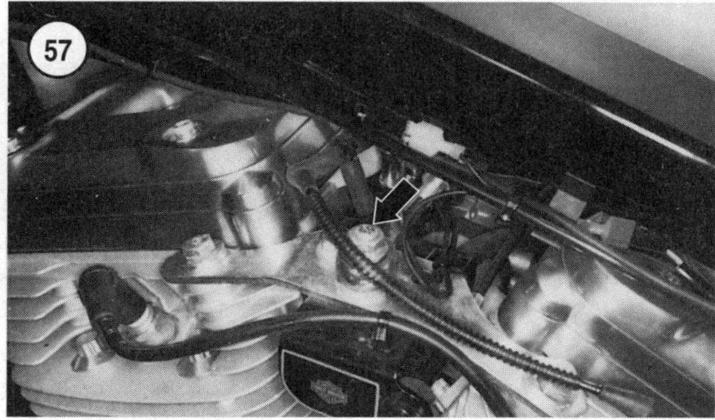

aligns with the center of the axle. Now check alignment on the opposite side. Compare the rubber grommet position with the center of the axle. The alignment on both sides of the axle must within 0.32 in. (0.8 mm) of each other. If necessary, adjust the belt with the adjusters, while at the same time maintaining correct belt free play as described in Step 4.

12A. On 1984-1988 models, tighten the axle nut to 60-65 ft.-lb. (81-88 N•m).

12B. On 1989-1998 models, tighten the axle nut to 60 ft.-lb. (81 N•m). If necessary, tighten the nut to align the hole in the axle with the slot in the nut. Do not exceed 65 ft.-lb. (88 N•m); do not loosen the nut to align the hole and slot. Install a *new* cotter pin and bend the end over completely.

13. On 1985 models, tighten the anchor bolt (**Figure 44**) until the rubber plug in the center of the bolt just starts to compress. Then stop. Secure the bolt with a wrench when tightening the locknut to 20 ft.-lb. (27 N•m).

14. Lower the rear wheel to the ground.

15. Install the drive belt debris cover.

16. On models so equipped, install the left side saddlebag as described in Chapter Fifteen.

Vehicle Alignment

This procedure checks the alignment of the rear axle with the swing arm pivot shaft. It also checks the engine stabilizer adjustment that aligns the engine in the frame. These checks determine the condition and alignment of the components that hold the motorcycle together: steering stem, front axle, engine, swing arm pivot shaft and rear axle. If any of these items are out of alignment, the motorcycle will not handle properly. Bad handling will increase the vibration level while reducing overall performance and drivability.

Preliminary inspection

Before checking vehicle alignment, make the following checks to spot problems caused from normal wear. Adjust, repair or replace any component as required.

1. The engine top stabilizer (**Figure 57**), mounted between the cylinder heads and upper frame tube, aligns the top portion of the engine in the frame.
2. The engine bottom stabilizer (**Figure 58**), connecting the engine front mounting bracket with the frame via the front engine mount, aligns the bottom portion of the engine in the frame.
3. Check both engine stabilizers for loose or damaged parts. To adjust the engine stabilizer, perform the *Alignment* procedure in this section.
4. Check the steering head bearing adjustment as described under *Steering Play Adjustment* in Chapter Eleven.
5. Check the runout of each wheel as described in Chapter Ten.

Alignment

Each alignment step, check and adjustment affects the next one. Work carefully and accurately when performing the following steps.

1. Perform all of the checks listed under *Preliminary Inspection* in this section. When all of the checks are within the specifications, continue with Step 2. If the motorcycle has been involved in a crash, refer frame alignment to a Harley-Davidson dealership or motorcycle frame alignment specialist.
2. Disconnect the negative battery cable from the battery as described in Chapter Nine.
3. On models so equipped, remove both saddlebags as described in Chapter Fifteen.
4. Remove the fuel tank as described in Chapter Eight.
5. Remove the mufflers as described in Chapter Eight.

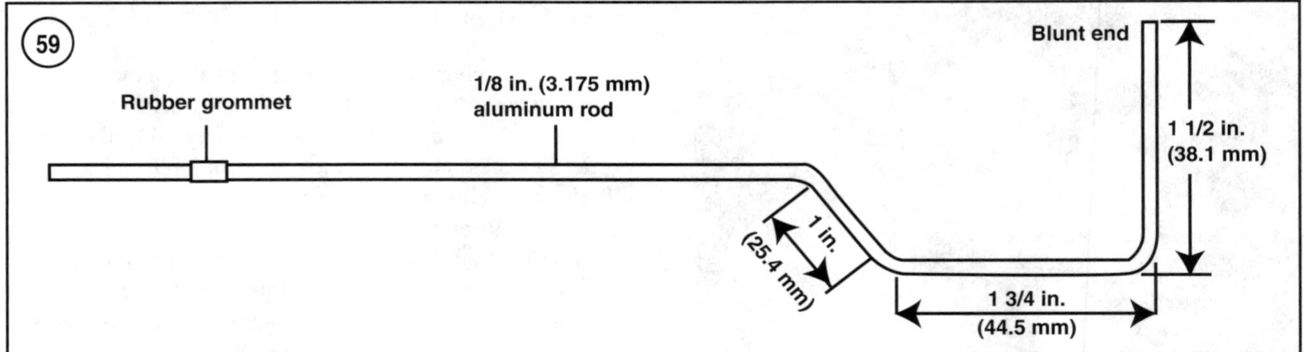

6. On models so equipped, remove both passenger footboards as described in Chapter Fifteen.
7. On models so equipped, remove the chrome trim cap from the swing arm passenger footrest brackets.
8. Insert the blunt end of the alignment tool (**Figure 59**) into the center of the swing arm pivot shaft. Slide the rubber grommet down the length of the tool until it is aligned with the center of the rear axle.
9. Without repositioning the grommet, remove the tool and repeat Step 8 for the opposite swing arm side, comparing this position with the first measurement. The measurement must be equal. If the alignment is incorrect, perform the following. When the drive chain or drive belt adjustment is correct, continue with Step 10:
   a. *Open Drive Chain Adjustment* in this section.
   b. *Enclosed Drive Chain Adjustment* in this section.
   c. *Final Drive Belt Deflection and Adjustment* in this section.

NOTE
The following steps must be performed with the rear wheel off the ground.

10. Park the motorcycle on level ground. Support the motorcycle securely on a swing arm stand with the rear wheel off the ground.
11. At the top stabilizer on the left side of the vehicle, remove the bolt securing the stabilizer link to the top engine mounting bracket (**Figure 57**).
12. On 1995-1998 models, remove the flange locknuts securing the voltage regulator to the frame. Remove the voltage regulator from the mounting studs and move it out of the way. Suspend it with a piece of wire, do not suspend it with the electrical harness.
13. At the bottom stabilizer on the front of the motorcycle, thoroughly loosen the center throughbolt and the two mount-to-frame bolts securing the mount to the frame and engine bracket. Refer to **Figure 60**, typical.

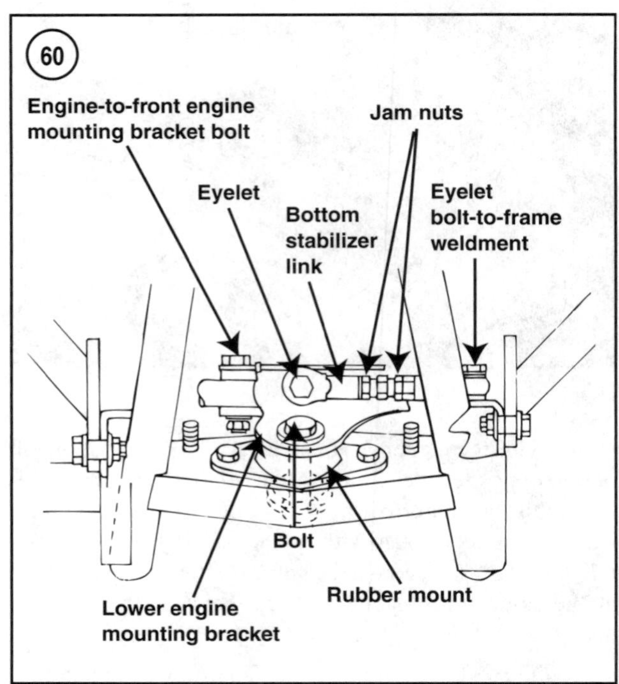

14. Verify that the front and rear wheels are aligned as follows:
    a. Place a straightedge along each side of the rear wheel and check that the front wheel is centered between the two straightedges (**Figure 61**). Dimension A must be equal to Dimension C, and Dimension B must be equal to Dimension D.
    b. If alignment is incorrect, use an open-end crowfoot wrench and loosen the two jam nuts on the bottom stabilizer link (**Figure 60**).
    c. Use an open-end crowfoot wrench and loosen the two jam nuts on the top stabilizer link (**Figure 62**).
    d. Adjust the top stabilizer until the bolt removed in Step 11 can be reinstalled without pushing the en-

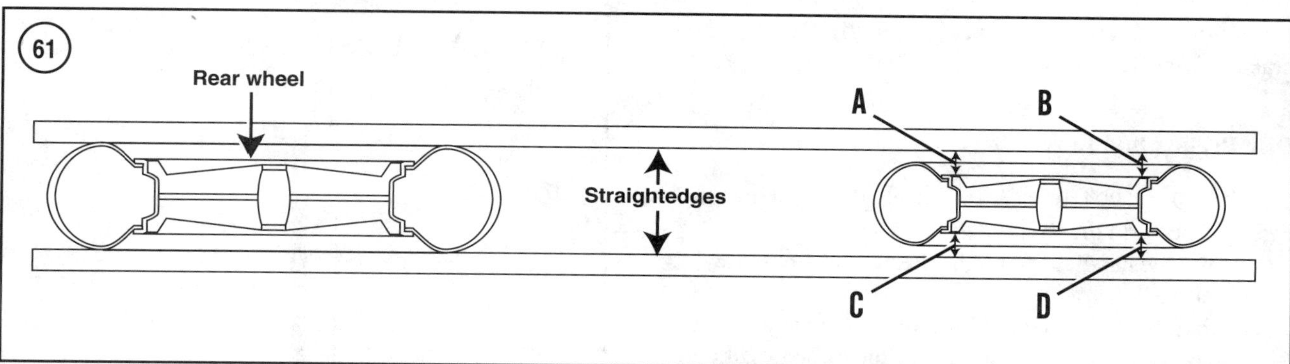

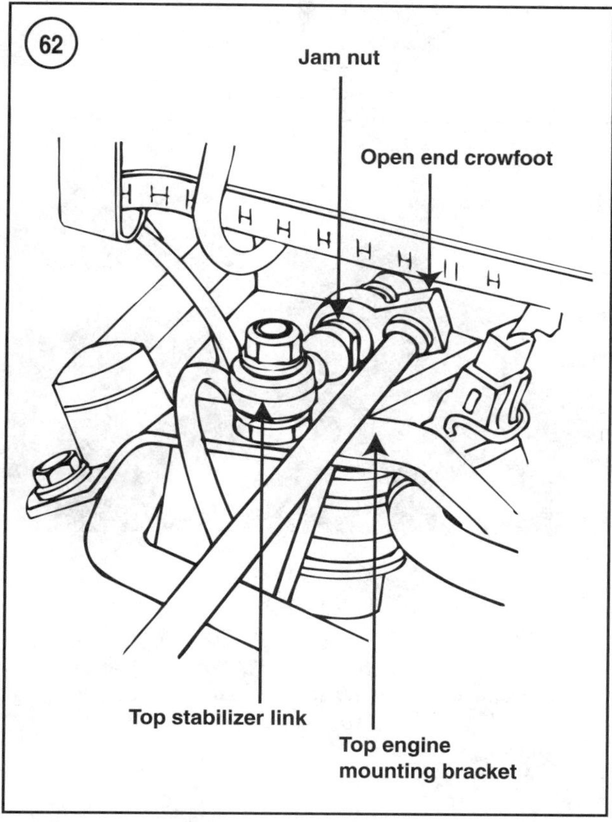

gine either to the left or right. Install the bolt and washer and tighten securely.

15. Tighten the jam nuts on both the top and bottom stabilizer links.

16. With the engine weight on the front rubber mount, verify that the two front rubber mount-to-frame mount bolts are loose.

17. Push the rubber mount plate from side to side until the rubber bulge, below the frame crossmember, is centered with the plate and equally compressed from side to side. Tighten the two front rubber mount-to-frame side mount bolts to 33-38 ft.-lb. (45-52 N•m).

18. Remove the front engine mounting bracket-to-rubber long center mount bolt, washer and nut (**Figure 60**).

19. With the engine weight on the front rubber mount, push the rubber mount plate forward and rearward until the rubber bulge, below the frame crossmember, is centered with the plate and equally compressed forward and rearward.

20. With the rubber mount centered, install the front engine mounting bracket-to-rubber mount bolt, washer and nut. Make sure the bolt does not bind while traveling through the rubber mount and the front engine mount.

21. Tighten the front engine mounting bracket-to-rubber center mount bolt to 35-45 ft.-lb. (47-61 N•m). Check the alignment of the rubber mount after the bolts are tightened in Step 17 and Step 18.

22. On 1995-1998 models, install the voltage regulator onto the mounting studs and tighten the flange locknuts securely.

23. On models so equipped, install the chrome trim cap onto the passenger footrest brackets.

24. On models so equipped, install both passenger footboards as described in Chapter Fifteen.

25. Install the mufflers as described in Chapter Eight.

26. Install the fuel tank as described in Chapter Eight.

27. On models so equipped, install both saddlebags as described in Chapter Fifteen.

28. Connect the negative battery cable as described in Chapter Nine.

Brake Pad Inspection

1. Without removing the front or rear brake calipers, inspect the brake pads for damage.

2. Measure the thickness of each brake pad lining (**Figure 63**) with a ruler. Replace the brake pad if it is worn to the

minimum thickness of 1/16 in. (1.58 mm). Replace the brake pads as described in Chapter Thirteen.

Disc Brake Fluid Level Check

1A. On 1984-1994 models, to check the front master cylinder, perform the following:

a. Turn the handlebar straight ahead so the master cylinder is level.
b. Observe the brake fluid level by looking at the sight glass (**Figure 64**) on the side of the master cylinder reservoir. If the fluid level is correct, the sight glass will appear dark purple. If the level is low, the sight glass will have a lightened, clear appearance.

1B. On 1995-on models, to check the front master cylinder, perform the following:

a. Turn the handlebar straight ahead so the master cylinder is level.
b. Observe the brake fluid level by looking at the sight glass (**Figure 65**) on the master cylinder reservoir top cover. If the fluid level is correct, the sight glass will appear dark purple. If the level is low, the sight glass will have a lightened, clear appearance.

2A. On 1984-1994 models, to check the rear master cylinder, perform the following:

a. Support the motorcycle so that the rear master cylinder is level.
b. Remove the screws securing the top cover and remove the top cover and diaphragm.
c. The brake fluid level should be 1/8 in. (3.17 mm) below the gasket surface.
d. If the fluid level is correct, reinstall the diaphragm and top cover. Tighten the screws securely.

2B. On 1995-on models, to check the rear master cylinder, perform the following:

a. Support the motorcycle so that the rear master cylinder is level.
b. Observe the brake fluid level by looking at the sight glass (**Figure 66**) on the side of the master cylinder reservoir. If the fluid level is correct, the sight glass will appear dark purple. If the level is low, the sight glass will have a lightened, clear appearance.

WARNING
*Do not use brake fluid labeled **DOT 5.1**. This is a glycol-based fluid that is **not compatible** with silicone-based DOT 5. DOT 5 brake fluid is purple while DOT 5.1 is an amber/clear color. Do not mix these two completely different types of brake fluid. Doing so will lead to brake component damage and possible brake failure.*

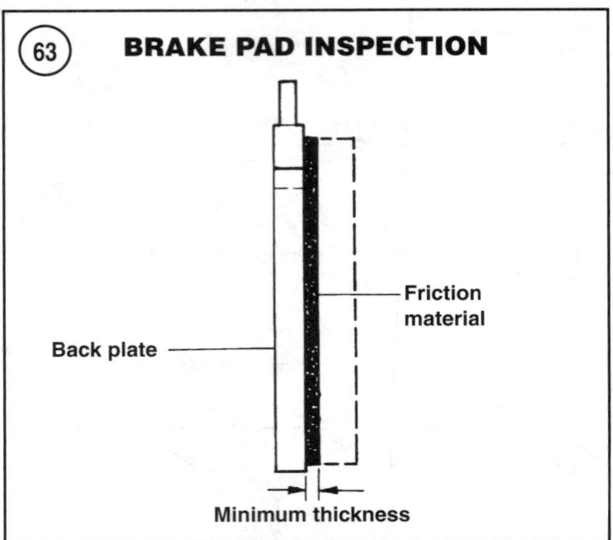

CAUTION
Be careful when handling brake fluid. Do not spill it on painted or plastic surfaces because it damages them. Wash the area immediately with soap and water and thoroughly rinse it.

NOTE
To control the flow of brake fluid, punch a small hole in the seal of a new container of brake fluid next to the edge of the pour spout. This helps eliminate the fluid spillage, especially while adding fluid to the small reservoir.

3. If the brake fluid level is low, perform the following:

a. If necessary, remove the front cylinder muffler as described in Chapter Eight to access the rear master cylinder.
b. Clean any dirt from the master cylinder cover prior to removing it.

65

66

67

c. Remove the top cover and lift the diaphragm out of the reservoir.

d. Add fresh DOT 5 brake fluid to correct the level.

e. Reinstall the diaphragm and top cover. Tighten the screws securely.

WARNING
If the brake fluid level is low enough to allow air in the hydraulic system, bleed the brakes as described in Chapter Thirteen.

Front and Rear Brake Disc Inspection

Visually inspect the front and rear brake discs (**Figure 67**, typical) for scoring, cracks or other damage. Measure the brake disc thickness and, if necessary, service the brake discs as described in Chapter Thirteen.

Disc Brake Lines and Seals

Check brake lines between the master cylinders and the brake calipers. If there is any leakage, tighten the connections and bleed the brakes as described in Chapter Thirteen. If this does not stop the leak or if a line is damaged, cracked or chafed, replace the line and seals and bleed the brake.

Disc Brake Fluid Change

Every time the reservoir cover is removed, a small amount of dirt and moisture enters the brake fluid. The same thing happens if a leak occurs or if any part of the hydraulic system is loosened or disconnected. Dirt can clog the system and cause unnecessary wear. Water in the fluid vaporizes at high temperatures, impairing the hydraulic action and reducing brake performance.

To change brake fluid, follow the brake bleeding procedure in Chapter Thirteen. Continue adding new fluid to the master cylinder until the fluid leaving the caliper is clean and free of contaminants and air bubbles.

WARNING
*Do not use brake fluid labeled **DOT 5.1**. This is a glycol-based fluid that is **not compatible** with silicone-based DOT 5. DOT 5 brake fluid is purple while DOT 5.1 is an amber/clear color. Do not mix these two completely different types of brake fluid. Doing so will lead to brake component damage and possible brake failure.*

Front Disc Brake Adjustment (All Models)

The front disc brake does not require periodic adjustment.

Rear Disc Brake Adjustment (All 1984-1996 and 1999 Models)

NOTE
On 1997-1998 models, the rear disc brake does not require periodic adjustment.

1984-early 1987 FXR series models (except FXRD) and 1999 FXR2 and FXR3

The brake pedal adjustment is a two-part procedure consisting of brake pedal height and pushrod free play.

1. Park the motorcycle on a level surface on the jiffy stand.
2. Place the brake pedal in the at-rest position.
3. Determine brake pedal height as follows:
   a. Place a ruler on the ground next to the brake pedal pivot shaft. Measure the distance from the ground up to the center of the brake pedal pivot shaft; record the measurement.
   b. Measure the distance from the ground up to the top of the brake pedal; record the measurement.
   c. Subtract substep a from substep b. The difference should be 4 1/8-4 3/8 in. (105-111 mm). If the difference is correct, perform Step 7. If the difference is incorrect, perform Step 4.
4. Measure the distance from the center of the footpeg rubber to the brake pedal pivot shaft centerline (**Figure 68**); the correct distance is 7/8-1 3/16 in. (22-30 mm). If necessary, loosen the footpeg mounting bolts and adjust footpeg position to obtain the correct distance measurement. Tighten bolts and recheck. Make sure that the brake pedal arm does not contact the footpeg mounting bracket. Perform Step 5.
5. Measure the distance from the top of the brake pedal to the brake pedal pivot shaft centerline (**Figure 68**); the correct distance is 4 1/8-4 3/8 in. (105-111 mm). If the distance is incorrect, perform the following:
   a. Loosen the rear brake pedal stop bolt locknut and turn the stop bolt in either direction until the correct brake pedal height is achieved.
   b. Hold the stop bolt and tighten the locknut securely.
   c. Recheck the height distance and readjust if necessary.

WARNING
The brake pedal cannot make contact with the exhaust pipe in the normal range of operation. If sufficient clearance is not maintained, complete brake application cannot be achieved.

6. Measure pushrod free play between the brake pedal arm and the brake pedal stop bolt as shown in **Figure 69**. The correct free play is 1/16 in. (1.58 mm). If the free play is incorrect, perform the following.
   a. Loosen the pushrod locknut and turn the pushrod in either direction until the free play is correct.
   b. Hold the pushrod and tighten the locknut securely.
   c. Recheck the free play and readjust if necessary.

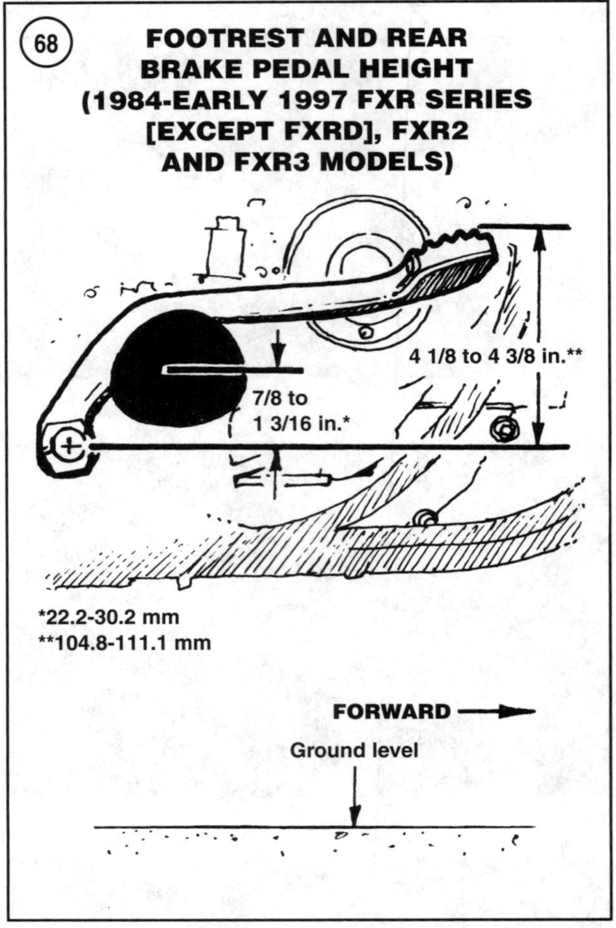

WARNING
Insufficient pushrod free play can cause brake drag and incorrect brake operation.

FXRD models

There is no specified brake pedal height specification. It is strictly rider preference, but sufficient clearance must be maintained.

Brake pedal adjustment is a two-part procedure consisting of the brake pedal height and the pushrod free play.

1. Park the motorcycle on level ground on the jiffy stand.
2. Place the brake pedal in the at-rest position.

WARNING
The brake pedal cannot make contact with the floorboard in the normal range of operation. If sufficient clearance is not maintained, complete brake application cannot be achieved.

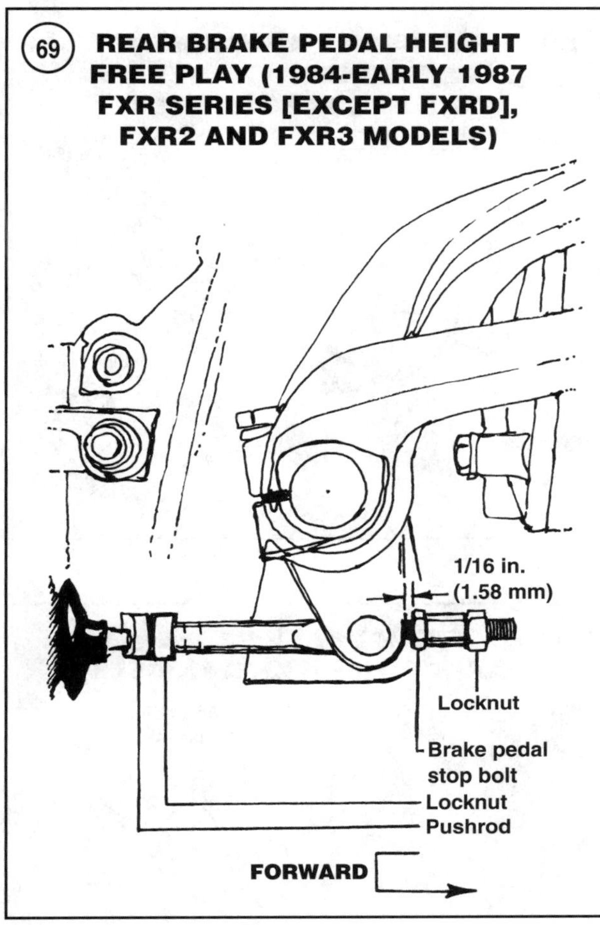

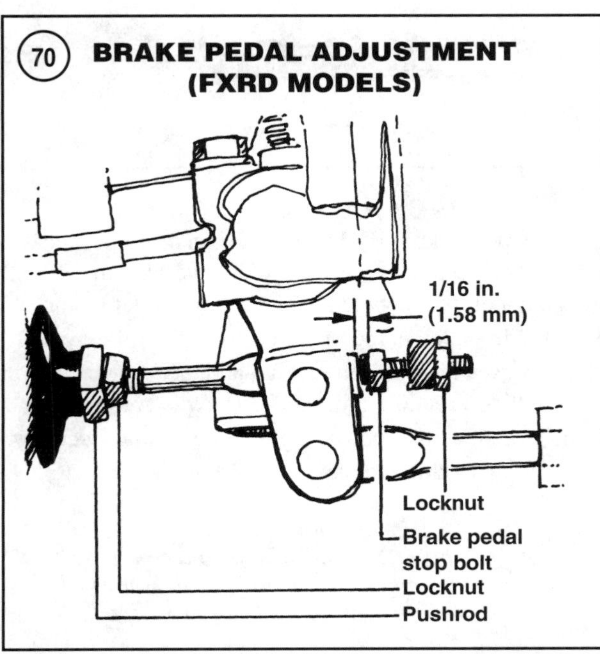

3. To adjust the brake pedal height, perform the following:
   a. Sit on the motorcycle and operate the rear brake pedal. Determine at what position the brake pedal feels the most comfortable.
   b. If adjustment is necessary, loosen the brake pedal stop bolt locknut (**Figure 70**) and turn the stop bolt in either direction until the desired brake pedal height is achieved.
   c. Hold the stop bolt and tighten the locknut securely.
   d. Recheck the height distance and readjust if necessary.

4. Measure free play between the brake pedal arm and the brake pedal stop bolt as shown in **Figure 70**. The correct free play is 1/16 in. (2 mm). If the free play is incorrect, perform the following:
   a. Loosen the pushrod locknut and turn the pushrod in either direction until the free play is correct.
   b. Hold the pushrod and tighten the locknut securely.
   c. Recheck the free play and readjust if necessary.

WARNING

If 1/16 in. (1.58 mm) pushrod free play cannot be achieved, the brake pedal might be positioned incorrectly. Check the brake pedal position and readjust if necessary. Insufficient pushrod free play can cause brake drag.

Late 1987-1998 FXR series, FXR2 and FXR3

Rear brake adjustment on these models consists of setting the brake pedal height in the proper relationship with the footpeg.

1. Park the motorcycle on level ground on the jiffy stand.
2. Place the brake pedal in the at-rest position.
3. Determine brake pedal height as follows:
   a. Place a ruler on the ground next to the brake pedal pivot shaft. Measure the distance from the ground up to the center of the brake pedal pivot shaft; record the measurement.
   b. Measure the distance from the ground up to the top of the brake pedal; record the measurement.
   c. Subtract substep a from substep b. The difference should be 4 1/8-4 3/8 in. (105-111 mm). If the difference is incorrect, perform Step 5. If the difference is correct, perform Step 7.

WARNING

When adjusting the master cylinder pushrod in Step 4, sufficient thread engagement between the brake rod and pushrod must be maintained. Otherwise, these parts could disconnect and cause complete loss of the rear brake.

4. Loosen the pushrod locknut and turn the pushrod (**Figure 71**) in either direction until the brake pedal height is correct. Hold the pushrod and tighten the locknut securely. Recheck the brake pedal height and readjust if necessary.
5. Measure the distance from the center of the footpeg rubber to the brake pedal pivot shaft centerline (**Figure 68**); the correct distance is 7/8-1 3/16 in. (22-30 mm). If necessary, loosen the footpeg mounting bolts and adjust footpeg position to obtain the correct distance measurement. Tighten bolts and recheck. Make sure that the brake pedal arm does not contact the footpeg bracket.
6. There is no rear brake free play adjustment on these models. Free play is built into the master cylinder. To check free play, push the brake pedal down by hand. A small amount of free play should be felt. If there is no free play, check the brake pedal assembly for damage. If the pedal assembly is OK, the rear master cylinder might require service; refer to Chapter Fifteen.

FXWG models

1. Park the motorcycle on level ground on the jiffy stand.
2. Place the brake pedal in the at-rest position.
3. Measure the distance between the brake pedal and the footrest (**Figure 72**). The correct distance is 17/64-1/2 in. (7-13 mm).
4. To adjust, loosen the locknut and turn the stop bolt in either direction until the correct distance is achieved. Tighten the locknut and recheck.
5. Work the brake pedal by hand. When the brake pedal is adjusted correctly, the pushrod will move approximately 1/16 in. (2 mm) before it contacts the master cylinder piston. If necessary, adjust as follows:
   a. Loosen the brake pedal locknut (**Figure 72**).
   b. Loosen the locknut and turn the clevis rod (**Figure 72**) counterclockwise to increase free play or clockwise to decrease it.
   c. Tighten the locknut and recheck the adjustment.

WARNING
Do not test-ride the motorcycle until the rear brake adjustment is correct and the pedal does not interfere with the rear exhaust system or footboard (if so equipped).

FXEF and FXSB models

1. Place the brake pedal in the at-rest position.

71 REAR BRAKE ADJUSTMENT (LATE 1987-1998 FXR SERIES, FXR2 AND FXR3 MODELS)

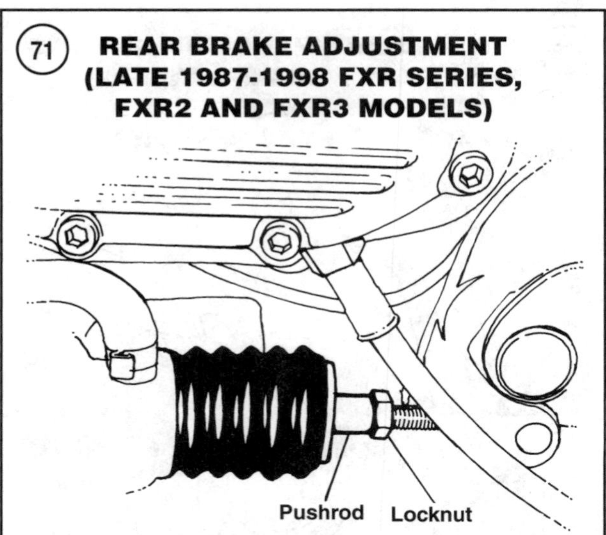

72 REAR BRAKE PEDAL ADJUSTMENT (FXWG MODELS)

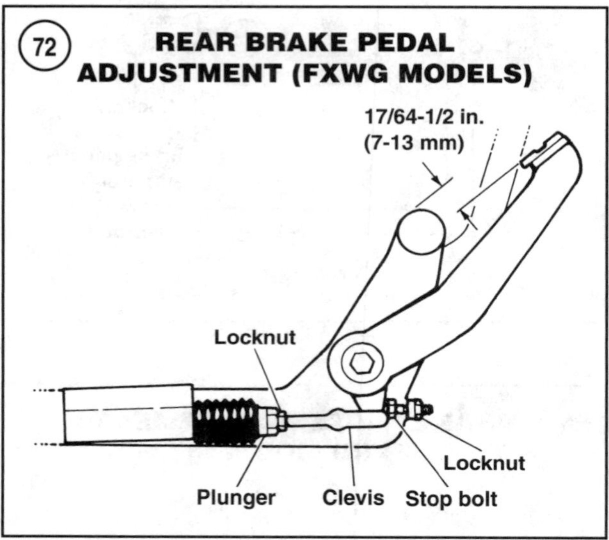

2. Work the brake pedal by hand. When the brake pedal is adjusted correctly, the pushrod will have 1/16 in. (2 mm) free play before it contacts the master cylinder piston.
3. If the free play is incorrect, perform the following:
   a. Loosen the pushrod locknut and turn the pushrod in either direction until the free play is correct.
   b. Hold the pushrod and tighten the locknut securely.
   c. Recheck the free play and readjust if necessary.

WARNING
If 1/16 in. (1.58 mm) of pushrod free play cannot be achieved, the brake pedal may be positioned incorrectly. Check brake pedal position and readjust if necessary. Insuffi-

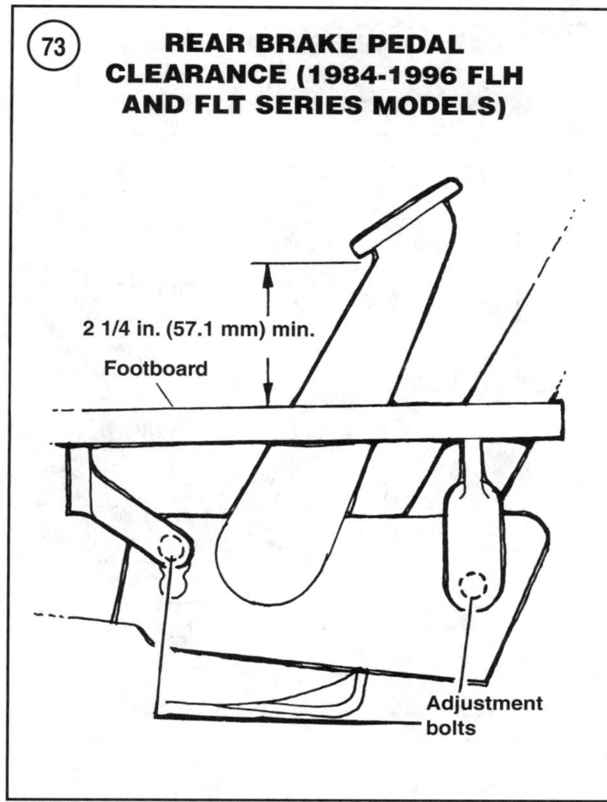

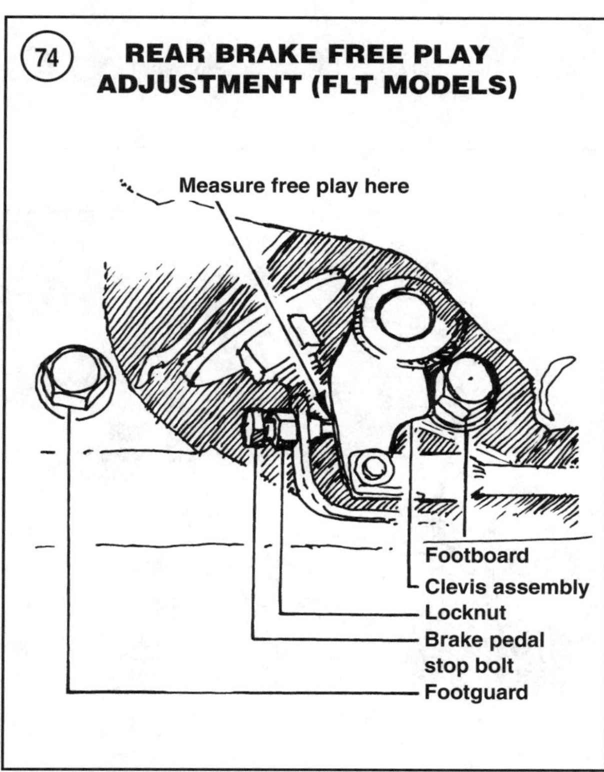

cient pushrod free play can cause brake drag.

FLH and FLT series models

On 1984-1991 models, the brake pedal adjustment is a two-part procedure consisting of brake pedal height and pushrod free play. On 1992-1996 models, the brake pedal adjustment consists of brake pedal height only because the pushrod free play is built into the master cylinder.

Maintain a minimum clearance of 2 1/4 in. (57 mm) between the brake pedal and footboard at all times. Maintain this clearance whenever the brake pedal height, footboard position or master cylinder pushrod free play is changed.

WARNING
The brake pedal cannot make contact with the floorboard in the normal range of operation. If sufficient clearance is not maintained, complete brake application cannot be achieved.

1. Park the motorcycle on level ground.

2A. To adjust footboard position and clearance, loosen the footboard adjustment bolts (**Figure 73**) and reposition the footboard within the guide slots. Tighten the bolts securely and recheck adjustment. Apply the rear brake pedal to ensure correct brake pedal-to-floorboard clearance; readjust if necessary.

2B. To change brake pedal height, remove the clevis screw and pull the clevis off of the brake pedal shaft. Rotate the clevis on the brake rod in either direction to change the brake pedal position on the brake rod. Reinstall the clevis onto the brake pedal shaft and remeasure pedal clearance (Step 2A). If pedal clearance is correct, install clevis screw and tighten securely.

3A. On 1984-1991 models, after the brake pedal clearance is correct, check and adjust pushrod free play as follows:

   a. Place the brake pedal in the at-rest position. Measure the clearance between the end of the stop bolt and the clevis assembly as shown in **Figure 74**. Correct pushrod free play is 3/32-1/8 in. (2.4-3.2 mm).
   b. To adjust free play, loosen the stop bolt locknut and turn the stop bolt in either direction. Tighten locknut and recheck clearance.

WARNING
Insufficient pushrod free play can cause brake drag and incorrect brake operation.

3B. On 1992-1996 models, make brake pedal minor height adjustments as follows:

a. Loosen the pushrod locknut (**Figure 75**).
b. Turn the pushrod in either direction to change pedal height. Tighten the locknut securely.
c. Measure the length of the exposed threads on the brake rod as shown in **Figure 75**. The maximum amount of exposed threads is 1/2 in. (12.7 mm). If necessary, loosen the pushrod locknut and readjust the pushrod until less than 1/2 in. (12.7 mm) of threads are exposed. Tighten the locknut and remeasure.

WARNING

If more than 1/2 in. (12.7 mm) of threads are exposed on the brake rod, there is insufficient thread engagement between the brake rod and pushrod. This can allow the brake rod and pushrod to disengage and cause loss of rear brake action.

4. Recheck the brake pedal height.

Clutch Adjustment (Dry Clutch Models)

Table 1 lists the recommended clutch inspection and adjustment intervals. If the clutch slips when engaged, or if the motorcycle creeps forward when in gear, the clutch release mechanism must be adjusted.

Refer to **Figure 76**.

1. At the clutch release arm end of the clutch cable, perform the following:
   a. Loosen the locknut next to the swivel nut.
   b. Turn the adjust sleeve in either direction to achieve approximately 1/16 in. (1.58 mm) clutch lever free play before the clutch starts to release (**Figure 77**).
   c. Tighten the locknut securely.
   d. If the correct amount of free play cannot be achieved, perform Step 2.
2. Loosen the locknut, next to the swivel nut, and turn the adjust sleeve clockwise to allow slack in the clutch cable. Then disconnect the clutch cable from the release arm.
3. Remove the clutch inspection cover and O-ring (**Figure 78**).
4. Loosen the pushrod locknut (1, **Figure 79**).
5. Turn the clutch adjusting screw (2, **Figure 79**) *clockwise* until all free play is removed from the release arm, then back it out 1/4 turn. Tighten the locknut securely.
6. Install a *new* O-ring and the clutch inspection cover. Tighten the screws securely.
7. Reconnect the clutch cable at the release arm.
8. Perform Step 1 and adjust the clutch cable.

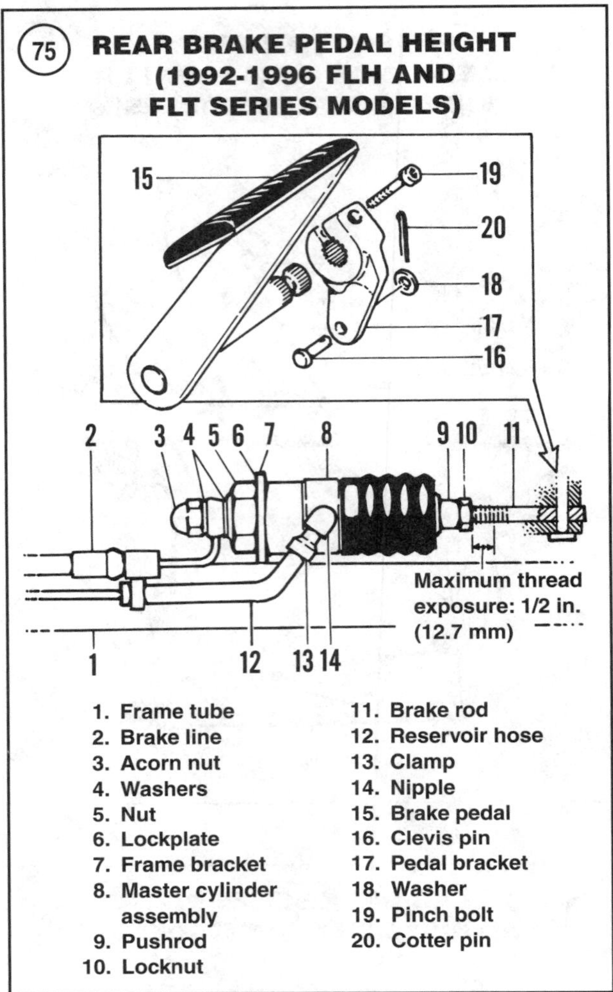

1. Frame tube
2. Brake line
3. Acorn nut
4. Washers
5. Nut
6. Lockplate
7. Frame bracket
8. Master cylinder assembly
9. Pushrod
10. Locknut
11. Brake rod
12. Reservoir hose
13. Clamp
14. Nipple
15. Brake pedal
16. Clevis pin
17. Pedal bracket
18. Washer
19. Pinch bolt
20. Cotter pin

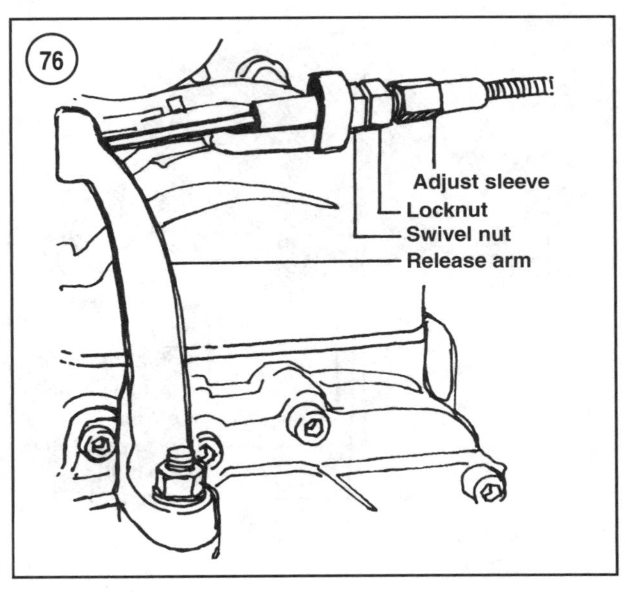

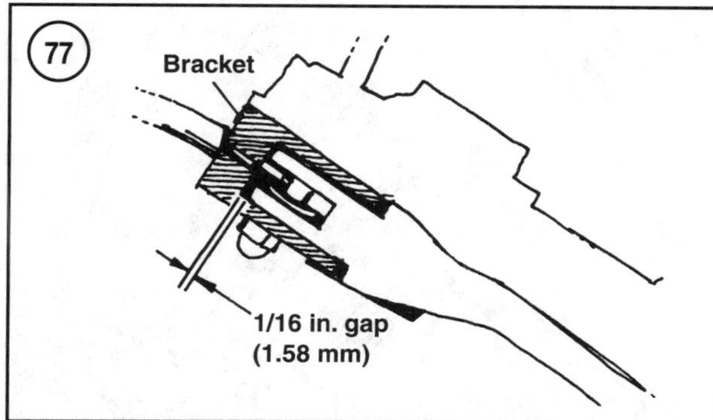

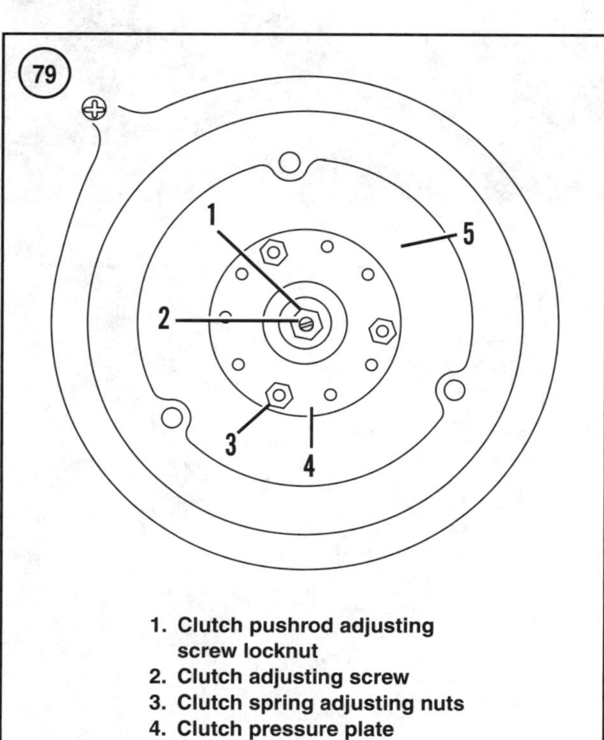

1. Clutch pushrod adjusting screw locknut
2. Clutch adjusting screw
3. Clutch spring adjusting nuts
4. Clutch pressure plate
5. Clutch outer disc

9. If the clutch still slips after making this adjustment, perform the *Clutch Disc Adjustment* in this section.

Clutch Disc Adjustment (Dry Clutch Models)

1. Shift the transmission into neutral.
2. Remove the clutch inspection cover and O-ring (**Figure 78**).
3. Turn the clutch spring adjusting nuts (3, **Figure 79**) *clockwise* 1/2 turn.
4. Temporarily install the clutch inspection cover and O-ring. Tighten the screws.
5. Start the engine and allow it to idle. Then test the clutch by shifting transmission into gear. If clutch slips or drags, repeat Step 3. Turn the engine off.

CAUTION
Do not increase clutch spring tension any more than necessary.

6. Remove the clutch inspection cover and O-ring.
7. Measure the distance between the clutch pressure plate and the outer disc (**Figure 79**) at each of the adjusting nut positions. The distance should be 7/8 in. (22 mm) or more. If the distance is equal to or less than 7/8 in. (22 mm), the clutch might not disengage. Adjust a new clutch to 1 1/32 in. (26 mm).
8. If the clutch disc cannot be adjusted to this specification, refer to Chapter Five and service the clutch and/or clutch cable.
9. Install the clutch inspection cover and *new* O-ring. Tighten the screws securely.

Clutch Adjustment (Wet Clutch with Four-Speed Transmission)

Refer to **Figure 80**.

1. Park the motorcycle on a level surface and support it standing straight up.
2. Disconnect the clutch cable at the release lever at the engine.
3. Remove the clutch inspection cover (**Figure 78**).
4. Loosen the clutch adjuster screw locknut (**Figure 81**).

NOTE
When performing Step 5, lightly push on the release lever to remove any pushrod free play.

5. Turn the adjuster Allen screw (**Figure 80**) and position the release lever 13/16 in. (21 mm) from the transmission cover as shown in **Figure 82**.

6. Secure the adjuster screw with an Allen wrench to keep it from turning. Then tighten the locknut (**Figure 80**) securely.
7. Connect the clutch cable at the release lever.
8. Loosen the clutch cable adjusting screw locknut (**Figure 83**). Turn the adjusting screw in either direction to obtain 1/16 in. (1.58 mm) free play at the clutch hand lever (**Figure 77**). Tighten the locknut securely.
9. Before reinstalling the clutch inspection cover, check the primary chaincase oil level as described in this chapter.
10. Install the clutch inspection cover and *new* O-ring. Tighten the screws securely.

Clutch Adjustment (Late 1984-1989 Wet Clutch with Five-Speed Transmission)

1. Park the motorcycle on a level surface and support it standing straight up.

2A. On late 1984-1986 models, loosen the locknut and turn the adjust sleeve clockwise to loosen the clutch cable (**Figure 76**).

2B. On 1987-1989 models, perform the following:
   a. At the clutch cable in-line adjuster, slide the rubber boot away from the adjuster (**Figure 84**).
   b. Loosen the cable locknut and turn the adjuster to provide as much cable slack as possible.

3. Remove the clutch inspection cover (**Figure 78**).
4. Refer to **Figure 80** and perform the following:
   a. Loosen the clutch pushrod adjusting screw locknut.
   b. Turn the clutch adjusting screw *clockwise* and remove all pushrod free play.
   c. Turn the clutch adjusting screw three-fourths of a turn *counterclockwise.*
   d. Secure the adjuster screw to keep it from turning. Then tighten the locknut securely.
5. Check the primary chaincase oil level as described in this chapter before reinstalling the clutch inspection cover.
6. Reinstall the clutch inspection cover and *new* O-ring. Tighten the screws securely.
7. Pull the handlebar clutch lever three to four times to seat the clutch release mechanism.

NOTE

When turning the clutch cable adjuster in Step 8, pull the clutch cable away from the clutch hand lever bracket.

8. Turn the clutch cable adjuster (**Figure 83** or **Figure 84**) until there is 1/8-3/16 in. (3-5 mm) free play between

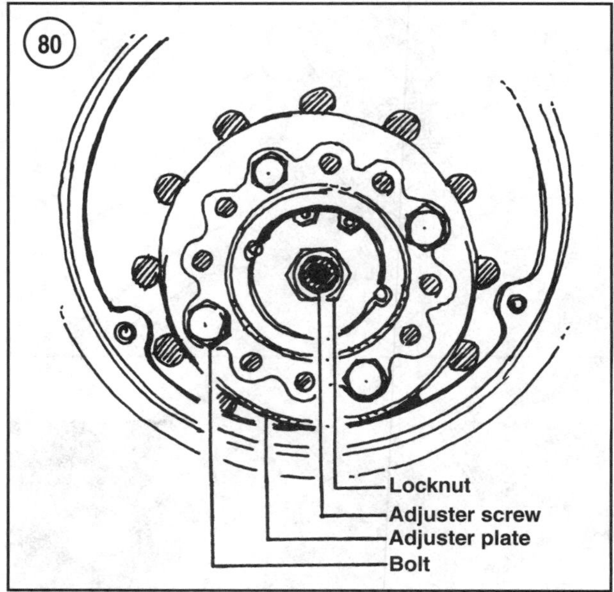

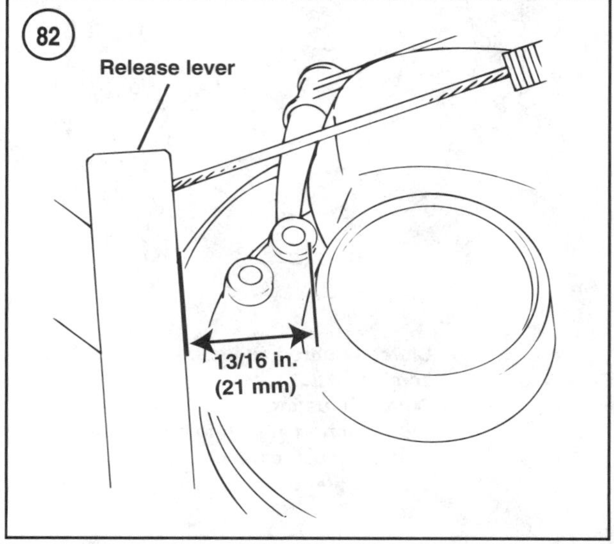

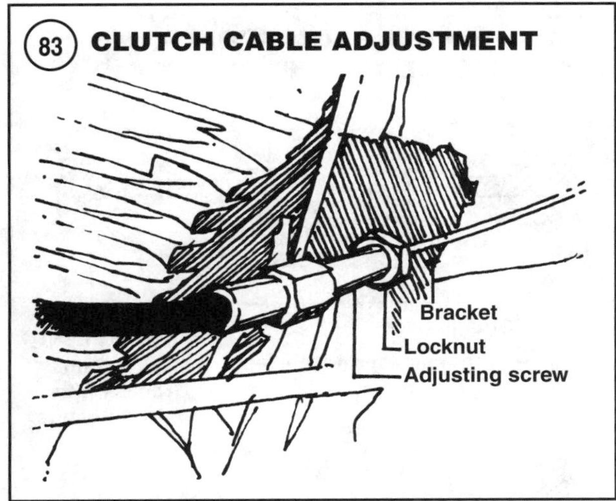

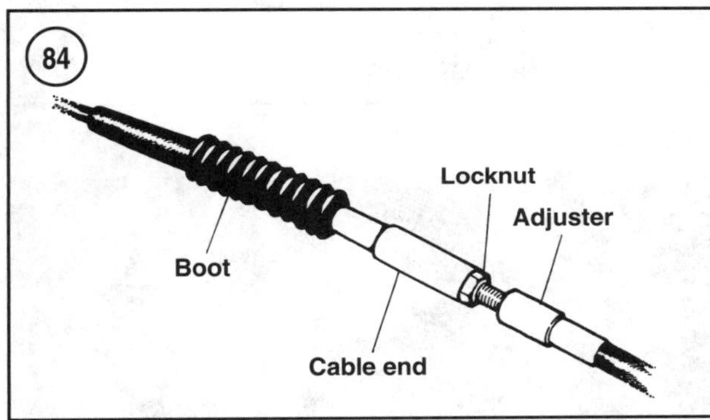

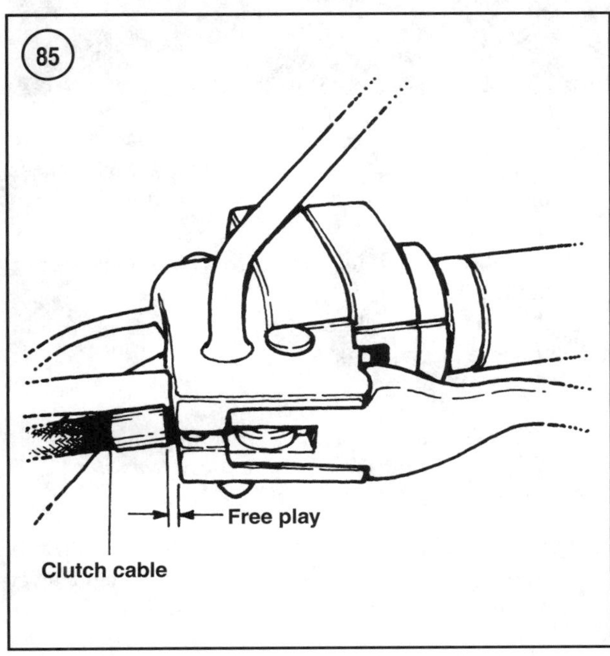

the clutch hand lever bracket and the outer clutch cable end as shown in **Figure 85**.

9. Tighten the clutch cable locknut. On 1987-1989 models, slide the rubber boot over the cable adjuster.

10. If clutch slips or drags, perform *Clutch Diaphragm Spring Adjustment* in this section.

Clutch Diaphragm Spring Adjustment (Late 1984-1989 Wet Clutch with Five-Speed Transmission)

1. Park the motorcycle on a level surface and support it standing straight up.

2A. On late 1984-1986 models, loosen the locknut and turn the adjust sleeve clockwise to loosen the clutch cable (**Figure 76**).

2B. On 1987-1989 models, perform the following:

   a. At the clutch cable in-line adjuster, slide the rubber boot away from the adjuster (**Figure 84**).
   b. Loosen the cable locknut and turn the adjuster to provide as much cable slack as possible.

3. Remove the clutch inspection cover (**Figure 78**).

4. Refer to **Figure 80** and perform the following:

   a. Loosen the clutch pushrod adjusting screw locknut.
   b. Turn the clutch adjusting screw *clockwise* and remove all pushrod free play.

5. Lay a straightedge across the diaphragm spring (**Figure 86**) and perform the following:

   a. Use a flat feeler gauge and measure the distance between the straightedge and spring.
   b. There should be a gap of more than 0.010 in. (0.25 mm) (**Figure 87**).
   c. If the gap is greater than 0.010 in. (0.25 mm), the spring must be adjusted.

NOTE

*To adjust spring compression in the following steps, remove the adjuster plate (**Figure 88**). Then reinstall it using one of the three different hole positions (**Figure 89**).*

6. Loosen the four adjuster plate bolts (**Figure 88**) in a crisscross pattern one-half to one turn at a time. Continue until all spring tension is removed. Then remove the bolts and spring adjuster.

7. Install the spring adjuster plate at the mounting holes that will accomplish the correct clutch adjustment (**Figure 89**). Note the following:

   a. If the spring is bowed outward more than 0.010 in. (0.25 mm), position the adjuster plate at the next hole that offers greater compression.
   b. If the spring is dished inward more than 0.010 in. (0.25 mm), position the adjuster plate at the next hole that offers less compression.
   c. The factory spring position is flat to 0.010 in. (0.25 mm) concave. No adjustment required at this position (**Figure 87**).

8. Install the four adjuster plate bolts. Tighten in a crisscross pattern to 71-97 ft.-lb. (8-11 N•m). Recheck the adjustment as described in Step 5. If adjustment is correct, remove the four adjuster plate bolts and apply a medium strength threadlocking compound to the bolt threads. Reinstall the bolts and tighten to 71-97 ft.-lb. (8-11 N•m).

9. Adjust clutch as previously described in this section.

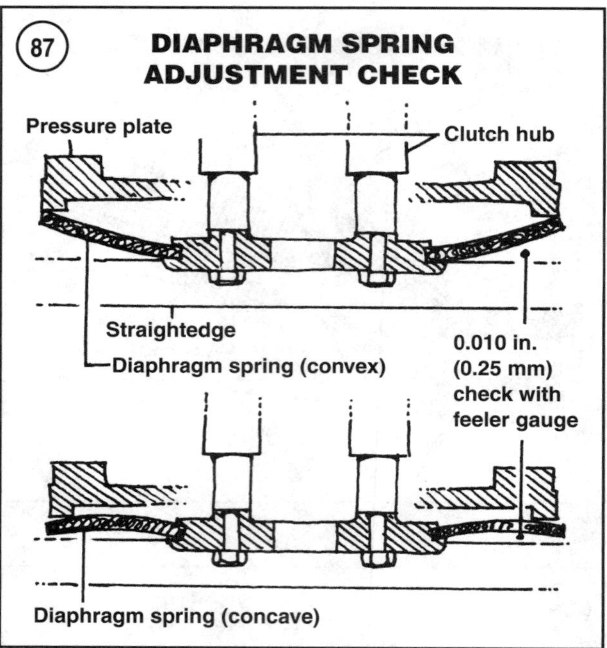

Clutch Adjustment (1990-1994 Models)

CAUTION

Because the clutch adjuster clearance increases with engine temperature, adjust the clutch when the clutch is cold. If the clutch is adjusted when the engine is hot, insufficient pushrod clearance can cause the clutch to slip.

1. Park the motorcycle on a level surface and support it standing straight up.
2. At the clutch cable in-line adjuster, slide the rubber boot away from the adjuster (**Figure 84**).
3. Loosen the cable locknut and turn the adjuster to provide as much cable slack as possible.
4. Remove the clutch inspection cover (**Figure 78**).
5. Adjust the clutch pushrod free play as follows:
   a. Loosen the clutch pushrod adjusting screw locknut (A, **Figure 90**).
   b. Turn the clutch adjuster screw (B, **Figure 90**) *clockwise* to remove all pushrod free play.
   c. Turn the clutch adjuster screw one-half to three-fourths of a turn *counterclockwise*. Then secure the screw from turning and tighten the locknut securely.
6. Before reinstalling the clutch inspection cover, check the primary chaincase oil level as described in this chapter.
7. Reinstall the clutch inspection cover and *new* O-ring. Tighten the screws securely.
8. Pull the handlebar clutch lever three times to seat the clutch release mechanism.

NOTE

When turning the clutch cable adjuster in Step 9, pull the clutch cable away from the clutch hand lever bracket.

9. Turn the clutch cable adjuster (**Figure 84**) until there is the following free play between the clutch hand lever bracket and the outer clutch cable end as shown in **Figure 85**):

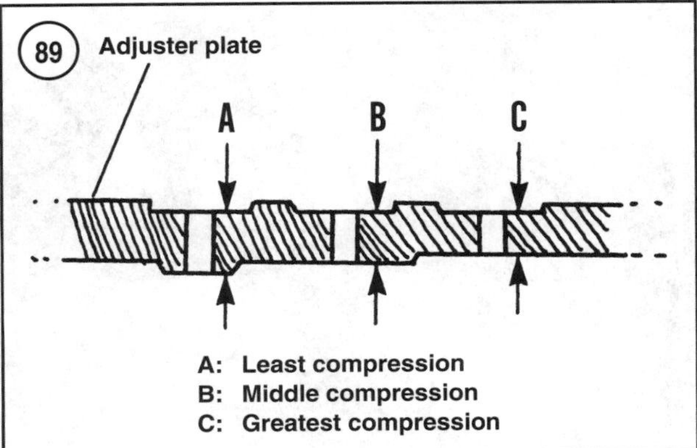

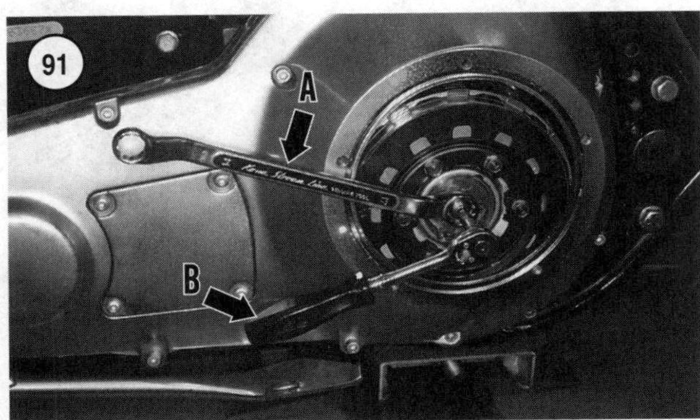

a. 1990 models: 1/8-3/16 in. (3-5 mm).
b. 1991-1994 models: 1/16-1/8 in. (2-3 mm).

10. Tighten the clutch cable locknut (**Figure 84**) and slide the rubber boot over the cable adjuster.

Clutch Adjustment (1995-1998 Models)

CAUTION
Because the clutch cable adjuster clearance increases with engine temperature, adjust the clutch when the engine is cold. If the clutch is adjusted when the engine is hot, insufficient pushrod clearance can cause the clutch to slip.

1. Park the motorcycle on a level surface and support it standing straight up.
2. At the clutch cable in-line adjuster, slide the rubber boot away from the adjuster (**Figure 84**).
3. Loosen the cable locknut and turn the adjuster to provide as much cable slack as possible.
4. Remove the clutch inspection cover (**Figure 78**).
5. Check that the clutch cable seats squarely in its perch at the handlebar.
6. At the clutch mechanism, loosen the clutch adjusting screw locknut (A, **Figure 91**) and turn the adjusting screw (B) *clockwise* until it is lightly seated.
7. Squeeze the clutch lever three times to verify the clutch balls are seated in the ramp release mechanism located behind the transmission side cover.
8. Back out the adjusting screw (B, **Figure 91**) *counterclockwise* one-half to one full turn. Then hold the adjusting screw and tighten the locknut (A, **Figure 91**) securely.
9. Once again, squeeze the clutch lever to its maximum limit three times to set the clutch ball and ramp release mechanism.
10. Check the free play as follows:
   a. At the in-line cable adjuster, turn the adjuster away from the locknut until slack is eliminated at the clutch hand lever.
   b. Pull the clutch cable sheath away from the clutch lever. Then turn the clutch cable adjuster to obtain the clearance gap (**Figure 85**) of 1/16-1/8 in. (2-3 mm).
   c. When the adjustment is correct, tighten the clutch in-line cable locknut and slide the rubber boot over the cable adjuster.
11. Install the clutch inspection cover and *new* O-ring. Tighten the screws securely.

Throttle Cables Inspection

Inspect the throttle cables from grip to carburetor or fuel injector module. Make sure they are not kinked or chafed. Replace them if necessary as described in Chapter Seven.

Make sure that the throttle grip rotates smoothly from fully closed to fully open. Check with the handlebar at center, full left and full right positions.

Throttle Cable Adjustment (Cruise Control Models)

Refer to Chapter Fourteen.

Throttle Cables Adjustment (Carbureted Models)

There are two different throttle cables. At the throttle grip, the front cable is the throttle control cable (A, **Figure 92**) and the rear cable is the idle control cable (B). At the carburetor, the outboard cable is the throttle control cable (A, **Figure 93**), and the inboard cable is the idle control cable (B).

1. Remove the air filter and back plate as described in Chapter Eight.
2. At the handlebar, loosen both control cable adjuster locknuts (C, **Figure 92**). Then turn the cable adjusters (A and B, **Figure 92**) *clockwise* as far as possible to increase cable slack.
3. Turn the handlebars so that the front wheel points straight ahead. Then turn the throttle grip to open the throttle completely and hold it in this position.

NOTE
***Figure 94** is shown with the carburetor body removed to better illustrate the steps.*

4. At the handlebar, turn the throttle control cable adjuster (A, **Figure 92**) *counterclockwise* until the throttle cam (A, **Figure 94**) stop just touches the stop boss (B) on the carburetor body. Then tighten the throttle cable adjuster locknut and release the throttle grip.
5. Turn the front wheel all the way to the full right lock position and hold it there.
6. At the handlebar, turn the idle cable (B, **Figure 92**) adjuster until the lower end of the idle control cable just contacts the spring in the carburetor cable guide (C, **Figure 94**). Tighten the idle cable locknut.
7. Shift the transmission into neutral and start the engine.
8. Increase engine speed several times. Release the throttle and make sure engine speed returns to idle. If engine speed does not return to idle, at the handlebar, loosen the idle control cable adjuster locknut and turn the cable adjuster *clockwise* as required. Tighten the idle control cable adjuster locknut.
9. Allow the engine to idle in neutral. Then turn the handlebar from side to side. Do not operate the throttle. If the engine speed increases when the handlebar assembly is turned, the throttle cables are routed incorrectly or damaged. Turn off the engine. Recheck cable routing and adjustment.
10. Install the air filter and back plate as described in Chapter Eight.

WARNING
Do not ride the motorcycle until the throttle cables are properly adjusted. Likewise, the cables must not catch or pull when the han-

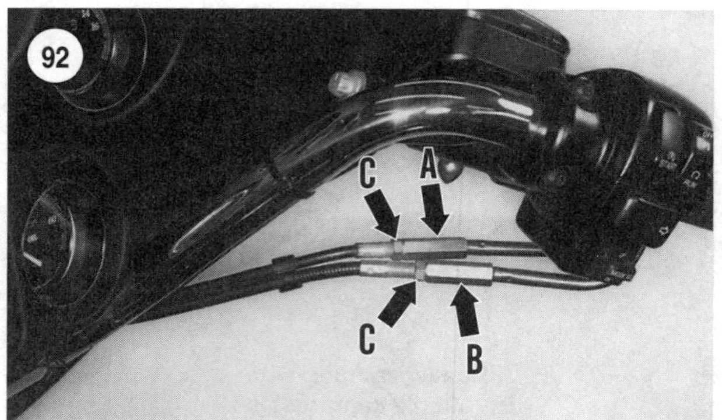

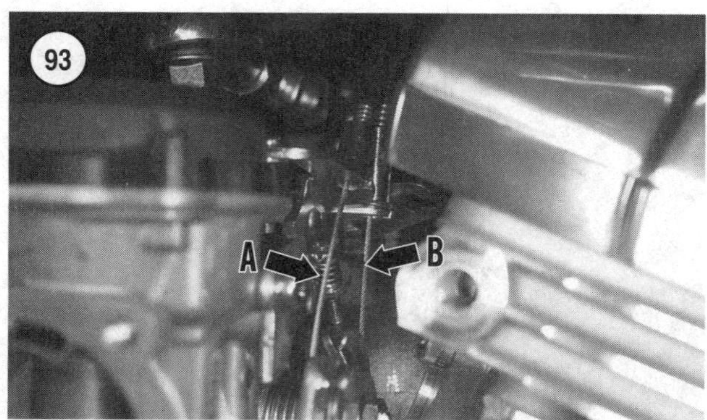

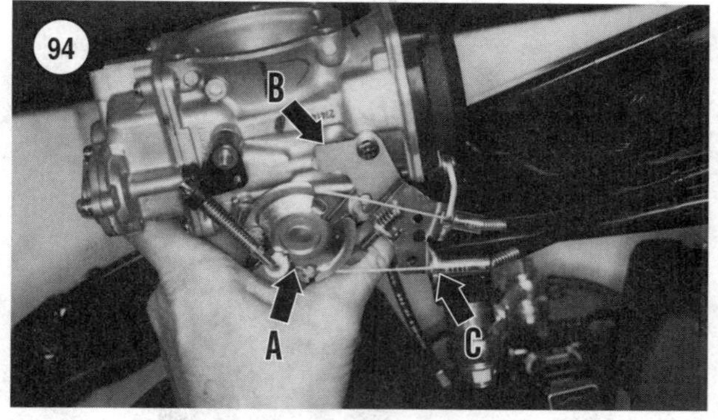

96

97

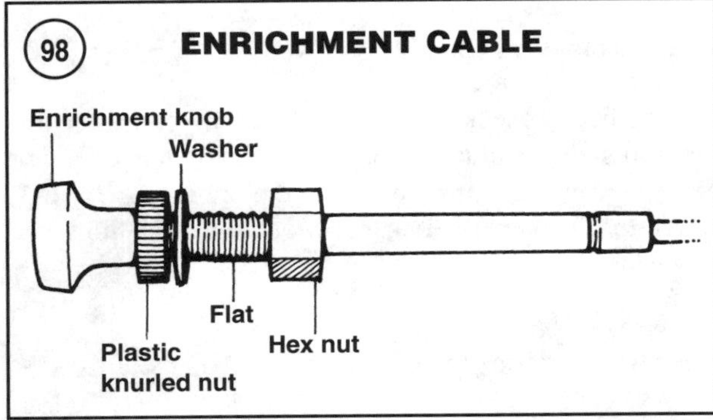

98

dlebar is turned from side to side. Improper cable routing and adjustment can cause the throttle to stick open. This could cause loss of control and a possible crash. Recheck this adjustment before riding the motorcycle.

Throttle Cables Adjustment (Fuel-Injected Models)

The throttle cable adjustment must be performed by a Harley-Davidson dealership using the Scanalyzer tool.

Choke Cable Adjustment (1984-1989 Carbureted Models)

1. Remove the air filter and back plate as described in Chapter Eight.
2. Operate the choke lever (**Figure 95**) and check for smooth operation of the cable and choke mechanism.
3. Move the lever (**Figure 95**) all the way to the closed position. Then pull the choke arm (**Figure 96**) at the carburetor to make sure it is at the end of its travel. If the choke lever can move an additional amount, it must be adjusted as follows.
4. Loosen the choke cable clamping screw (**Figure 96**) and move the cable sheath up until the choke lever is fully closed. Hold the choke lever in this position and tighten the cable clamping screw.
5. Slide the choke lever all the way to the fully open position.
6. If proper adjustment cannot be achieved using this procedure, the choke cable has stretched and must be replaced.
7. Install the air filter and back plate as described in Chapter Eight.

Starting Enrichment Valve (Choke) Cable Adjustment (1990-on Carbureted Models)

The starting enrichment (choke) knob (**Figure 97**) must move from fully open to fully closed without any sign of binding. The knob must also stay in its fully closed or fully open position without creeping. If the knob does not stay in position, adjust tension on the cable by turning the knurled plastic nut behind the knob (**Figure 98**) as follows:

CAUTION

The starting enrichment (choke) cable must have sufficient cable resistance to work properly. Do not lubricate the enricher cable or its conduit.

1. Loosen the hex nut behind the mounting bracket. Then move the cable to free it from its mounting bracket slot.
2. Hold the cable across its flats with a wrench and turn the knurled plastic nut *counterclockwise* to reduce cable resistance. The knob must slide inward freely.
3. Turn the knurled plastic nut (**Figure 98**) *clockwise* to increase cable resistance. Continue adjustment until the knob remains stationary when pulled all the way out. The knob must move without any roughness or binding.
4. Reinstall the cable into the slot in its mounting bracket with the star washer located between the bracket and hex nut. Tighten the hex nut securely.

5. Recheck the knob movement and readjust if necessary.

Fuel Line Inspection

Inspect the fuel lines from the fuel tank to the carburetor or fuel injection module. Replace leaking or damaged fuel lines. Make sure the hose clamps are in place and holding securely. Check the hose fittings for looseness.

WARNING
A damaged or deteriorated fuel line can cause a fire or explosion if fuel spills onto a hot engine or exhaust pipe.

Fuel Shutoff Valve/Filter

Refer to Chapter Eight for complete details on removal, cleaning and installation of the fuel shutoff valve.

Exhaust System

Check all fittings for exhaust leaks. Do not forget the crossover pipe connections. Tighten all bolts and nuts; replace any gaskets as necessary. Removal and installation procedures are described in Chapter Eight.

Valve Lifter Screen Cleaning

Clean the valve lifter oil screen at each oil change. The valve lifter screen (**Figure 99**) is located in the right crankcase above the oil pump.

1. Remove the lifter screen plug and O-ring (**Figure 99**) from the crankcase.
2. Remove the oil screen and spring (**Figure 100**).
3. Clean the screen and spring in solvent and dry with compressed air.
4. Replace the screen if damaged.
5. If removed, install the spring over the oil screen (**Figure 101**).
6. Install the oil screen (**Figure 100**) into the crankcase with the open end facing down.
7. Install the lifter screen plug and O-ring (**Figure 99**) and tighten to 89-124 in.-lb. (10-14 N•m).

Wheel Bearings

Table 1 lists the recommended wheel bearing cleaning and repacking intervals.

Refer to Chapter Ten for complete service procedures.

Steering Play

Table 1 lists the recommended steering head inspection for looseness and adjustment intervals.

Refer to Chapter Eleven for the adjustment procedures.

Front Suspension Check

Periodically check the front fork mounting bolts for tightness. Refer to Chapter Eleven for torque specifications.

Rear Suspension Check

Periodically check the rear shock absorber and rear suspension swing arm pivot shaft bolts for tightness. Lubricate the rear swing arm bearing at the interval in **Table 1**. Refer to Chapter Twelve for torque specifications and procedures.

Rear Shock Absorber Check

Table 1 lists the recommended rear shock absorber inspection intervals.

1. Check the rear shock absorbers for fluid leaks. If a shock is leaking, it must be replaced.
2. Grasp the shock absorber and twist it from side to side while checking for excessive bushing movement. If the bushings are worn, replace the bushings and/or the shock absorber(s).

Air Shock Adjustment

Refer to Chapter Twelve for air shock adjustment procedures.

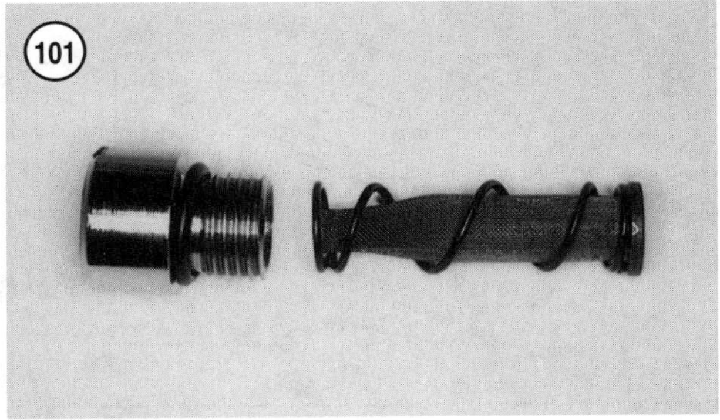

Fasteners

Vibration can loosen many fasteners on a motorcycle. Check the tightness of all fasteners, especially those on:

1. Engine mounting hardware.
2. Engine and primary covers.
3. Handlebar and front fork.
4. Gearshift lever.
5. Sprocket bolts and nuts.
6. Brake pedal and lever.
7. Exhaust system.
8. Lighting equipment.

Electrical Equipment and Switches

Check all of the electrical equipment and switches for proper operation. Refer to Chapter Nine.

Rear Brake Caliper Pins and Boots

Table 1 lists the recommended lubrication intervals for the caliper pins.

Check the brake caliper boots for tearing or other damage. The caliper pins should be removed and lubricated. Refer to Chapter Thirteen for service procedures.

TUNE-UP

Perform the following tune-up procedures at the intervals in **Table 1**. Perform a complete tune-up in the following order:

1. Clean or replace the air filter element.
2. Check engine compression.
3. Check or replace the spark plugs.
4. Check the ignition timing.
5. On carbureted models, adjust idle speed.

Air Filter Element Removal/Installation

Remove and clean the air filter at the interval in **Table 1**. Replace the element at the interval in **Table 1** or whenever it is damaged or starts to deteriorate.

The air filter removes dust and abrasive particles before the air enters the carburetor or fuel injection module and the engine. Without the air filter, very fine particles could enter the engine and cause rapid wear of the piston rings, cylinder bores and bearings. They also might clog small passages in the carburetor. Never run the motorcycle without the element installed.

Refer to **Figures 102-107** (carbureted models) or **Figure 108** (fuel-injected models).

1. Remove the air filter cover screw(s) and washer(s) (A, **Figure 109**, typical) and remove the cover (B).

2A. On 1984-1992 models, remove the air filter element (**Figure 110**, typical).

2B. On 1993-1998 domestic carbureted models, gently pull the air filter element away from the back plate and disconnect the two breather hoses (**Figure 111**) from the breather hollow bolts on the back plate. Remove the air filter element.

2C. On 1993-1998 international carbureted models, remove the four screws and washers securing the air filter element to the back plate. Remove the air filter element.

2D. On 1995-1998 fuel-injected models, remove the screws securing the air filter element to the back plate. Remove the air filter element.

3. Clean the air filter as described in the following procedure. If the element cannot be cleaned satisfactorily, replace it.

4. Inspect the gasket for damage. Replace if necessary.

5. On models so equipped, inspect the breather hoses (**Figure 112**) for tears or deterioration. Replace if necessary.

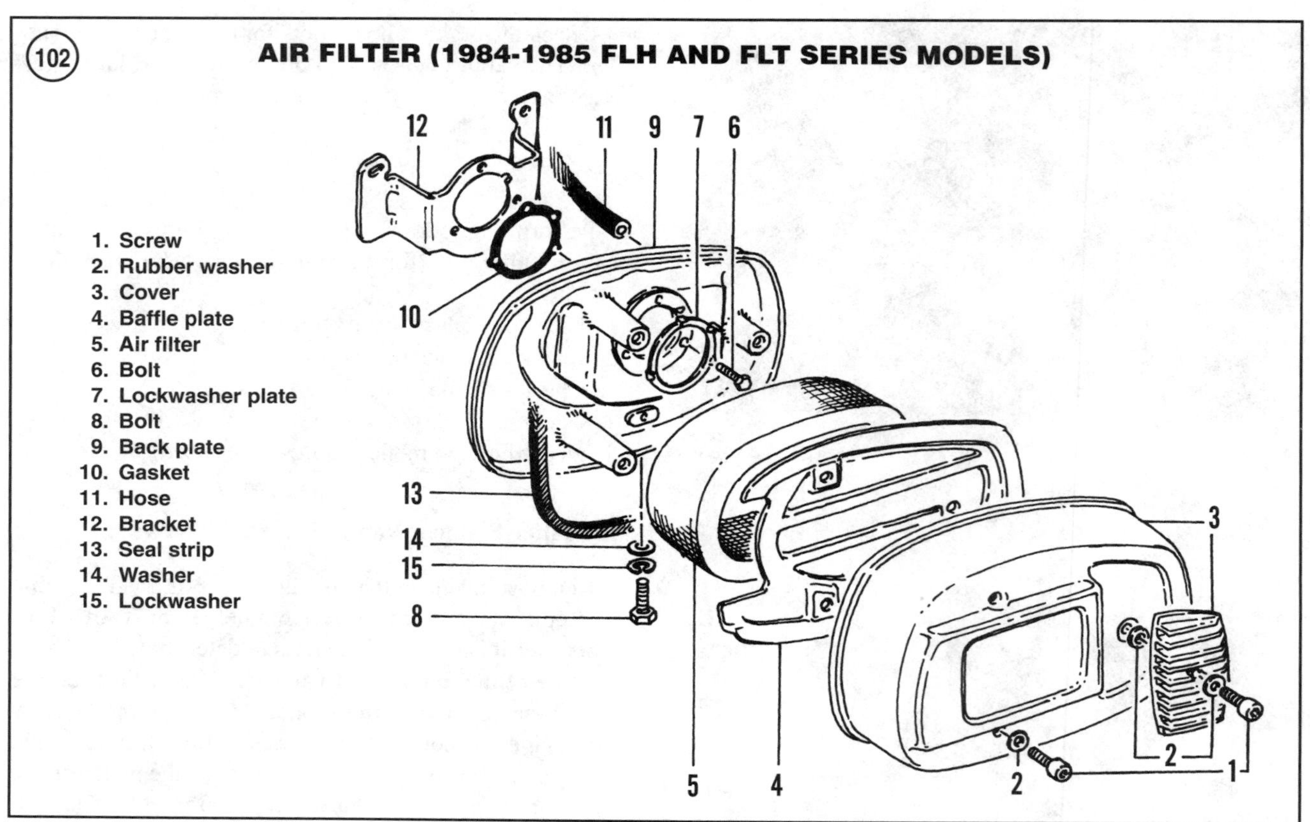
102
AIR FILTER (1984-1985 FLH AND FLT SERIES MODELS)
1. Screw
2. Rubber washer
3. Cover
4. Baffle plate
5. Air filter
6. Bolt
7. Lockwasher plate
8. Bolt
9. Back plate
10. Gasket
11. Hose
12. Bracket
13. Seal strip
14. Washer
15. Lockwasher

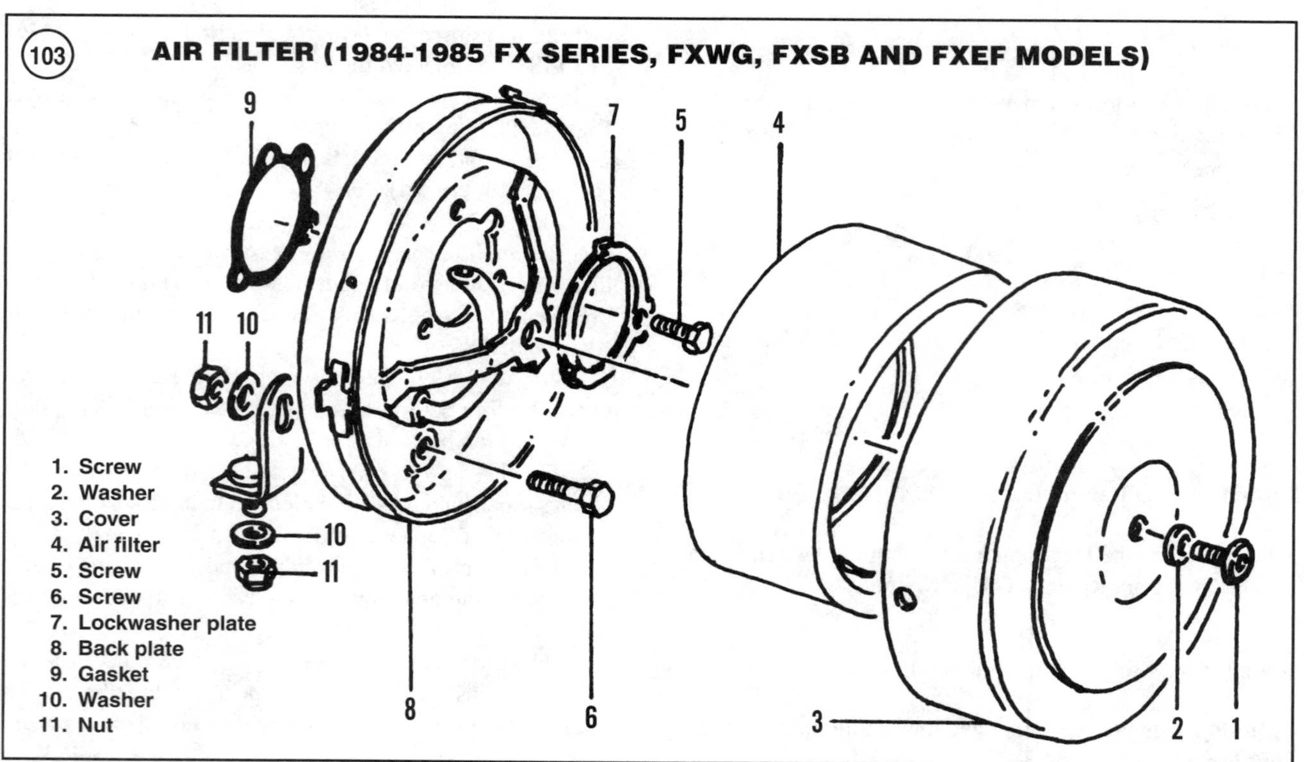
103
AIR FILTER (1984-1985 FX SERIES, FXWG, FXSB AND FXEF MODELS)
1. Screw
2. Washer
3. Cover
4. Air filter
5. Screw
6. Screw
7. Lockwasher plate
8. Back plate
9. Gasket
10. Washer
11. Nut

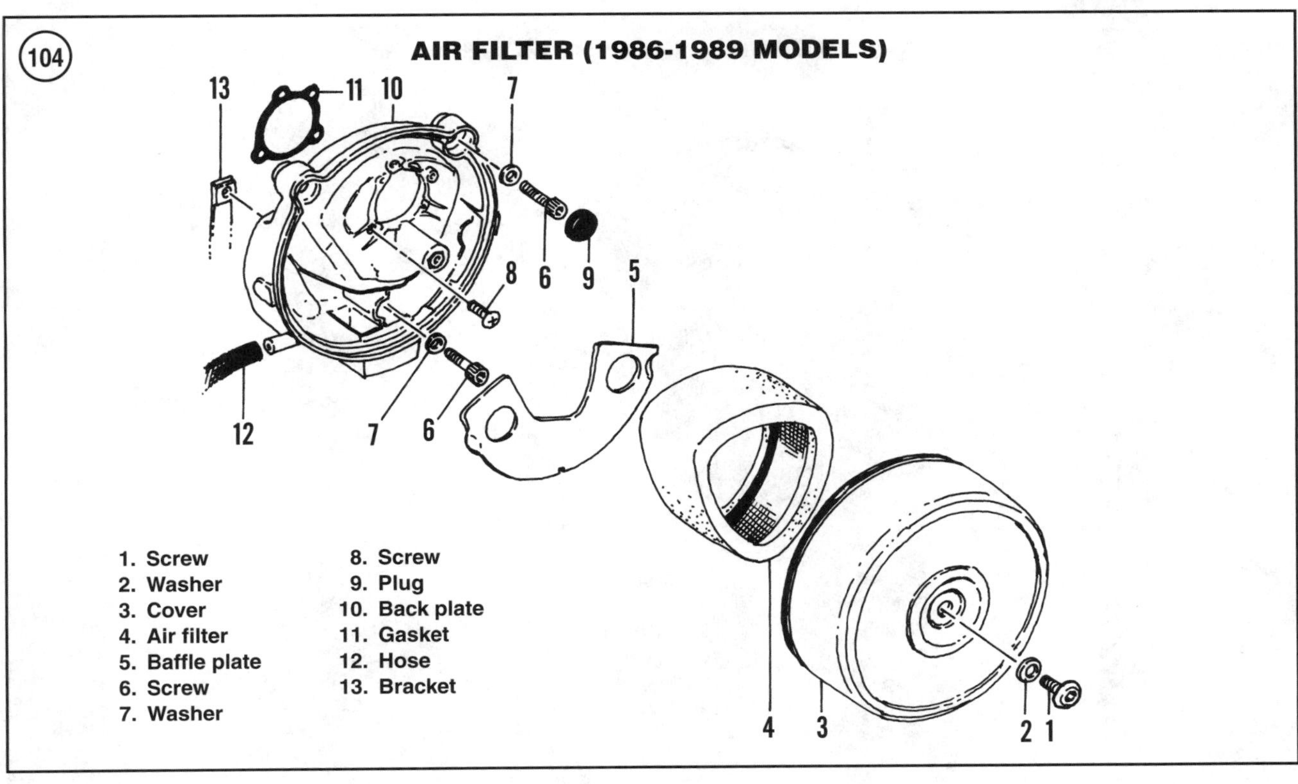
104
AIR FILTER (1986-1989 MODELS)
13
11
10
7
8
6
9
5
12
7
6
4
3
2
1
1. Screw
2. Washer
3. Cover
4. Air filter
5. Baffle plate
6. Screw
7. Washer
8. Screw
9. Plug
10. Back plate
11. Gasket
12. Hose
13. Bracket

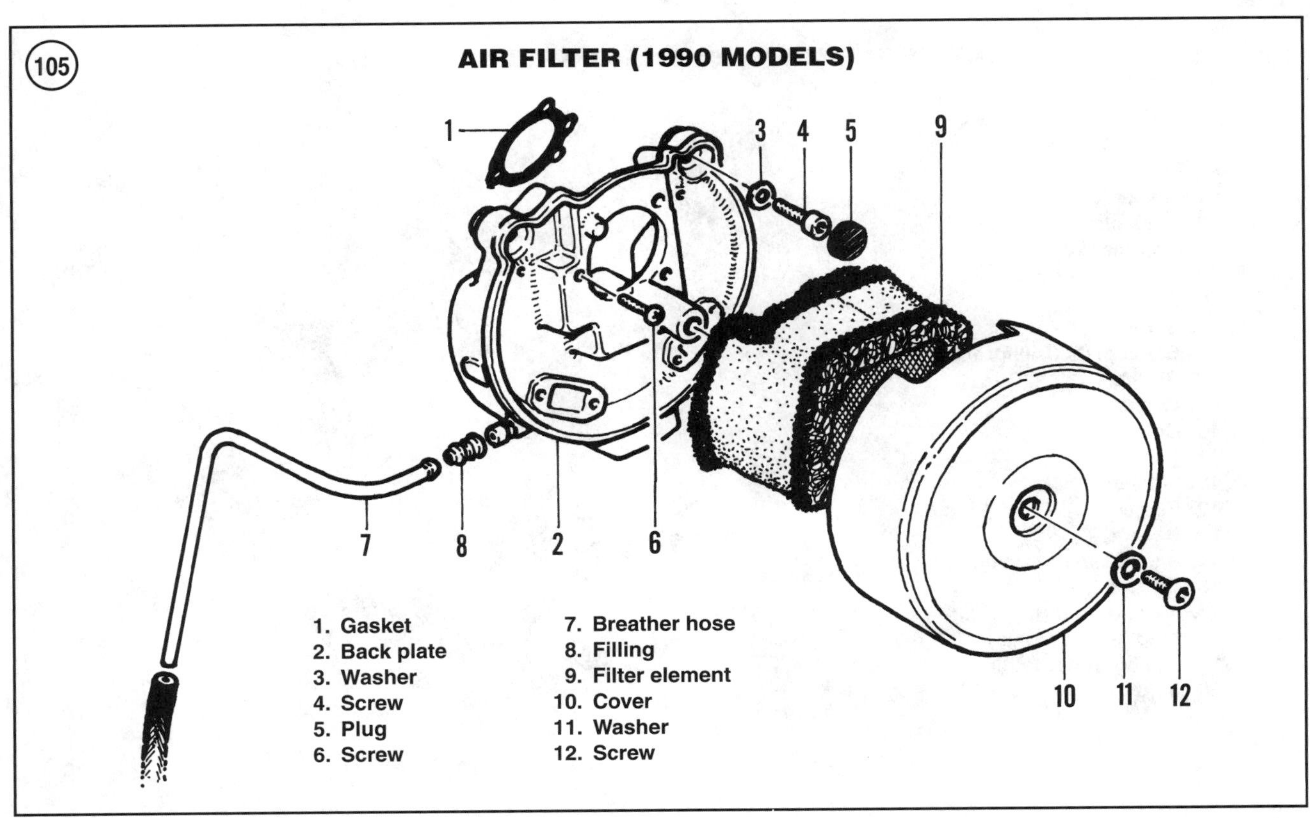
105
AIR FILTER (1990 MODELS)
1
3
4
5
9
7
8
2
6
10
11
12
1. Gasket
2. Back plate
3. Washer
4. Screw
5. Plug
6. Screw
7. Breather hose
8. Filling
9. Filter element
10. Cover
11. Washer
12. Screw

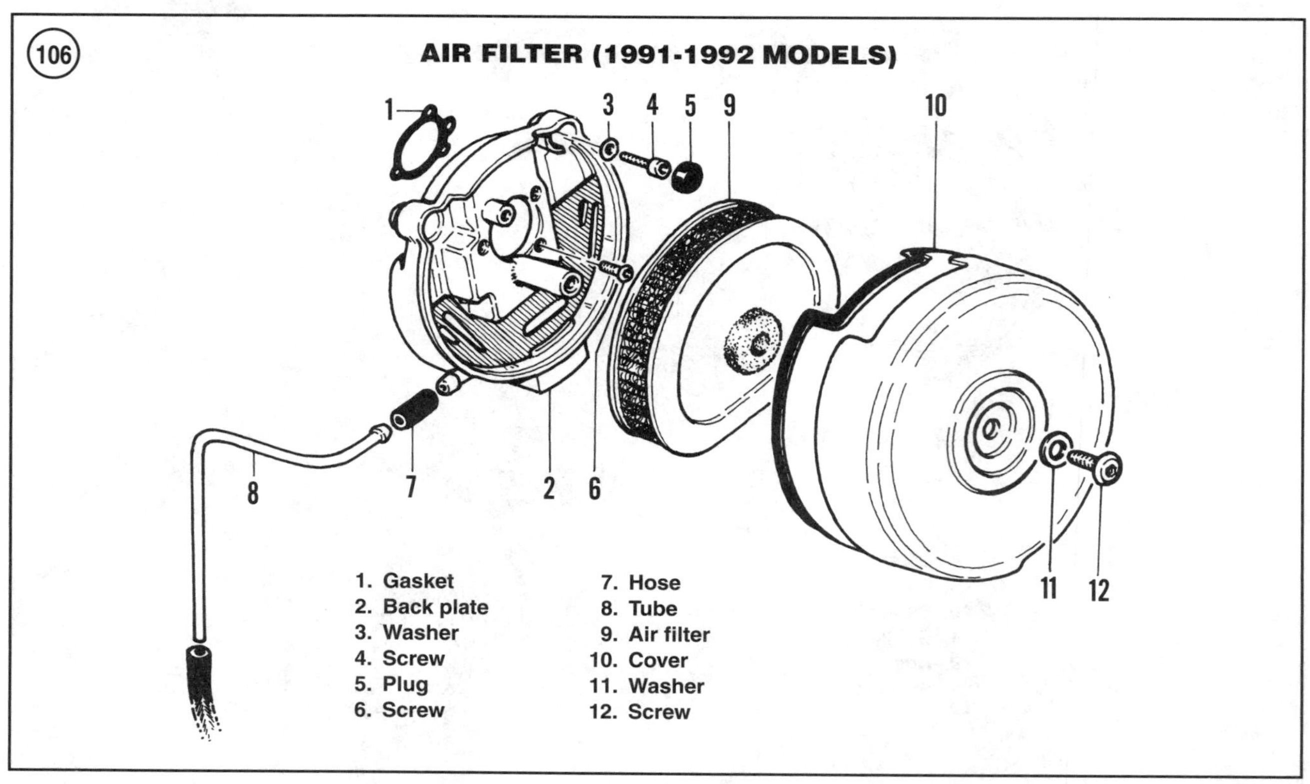
106
AIR FILTER (1991-1992 MODELS)
1
3
4
5
9
10
8
7
2
6
11
12
1. Gasket
2. Back plate
3. Washer
4. Screw
5. Plug
6. Screw
7. Hose
8. Tube
9. Air filter
10. Cover
11. Washer
12. Screw

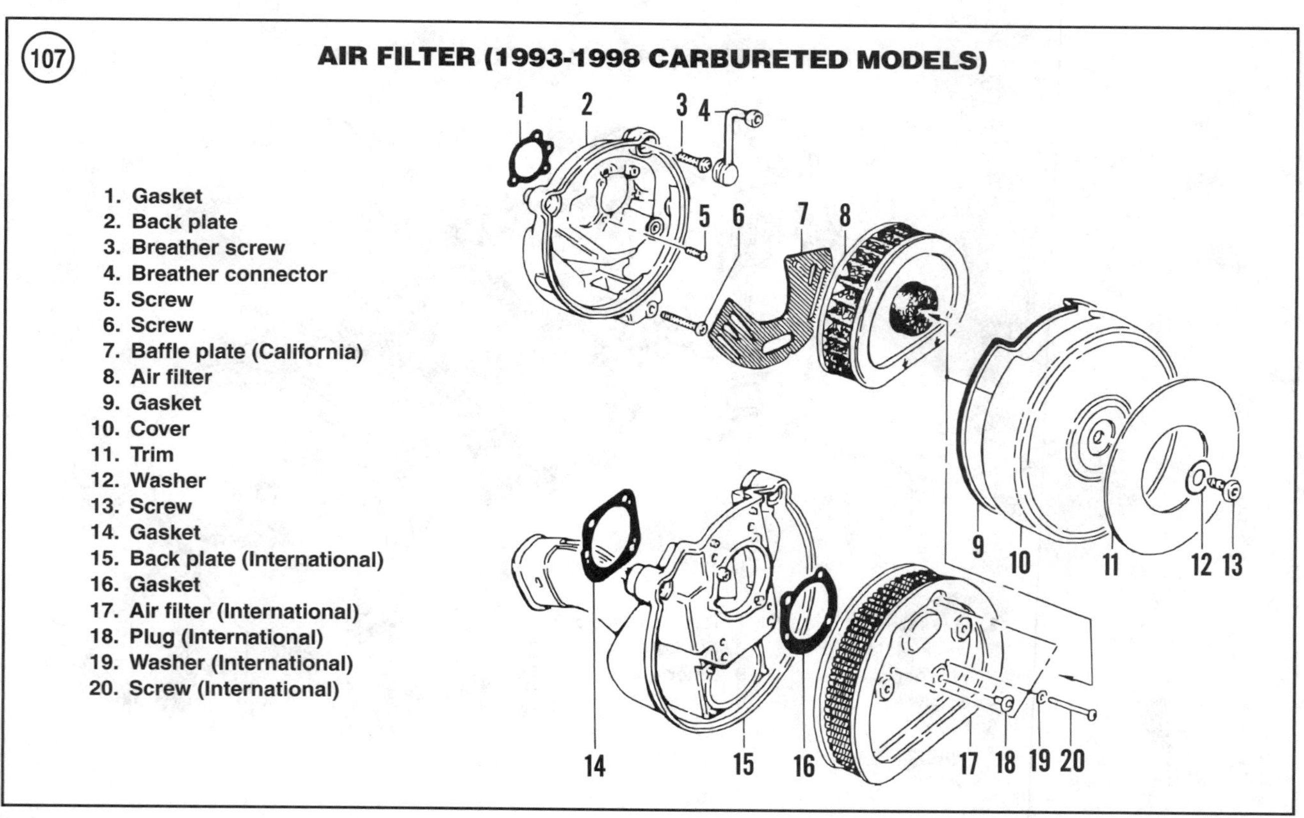
107
AIR FILTER (1993-1998 CARBURETED MODELS)
1. Gasket
2. Back plate
3. Breather screw
4. Breather connector
5. Screw
6. Screw
7. Baffle plate (California)
8. Air filter
9. Gasket
10. Cover
11. Trim
12. Washer
13. Screw
14. Gasket
15. Back plate (International)
16. Gasket
17. Air filter (International)
18. Plug (International)
19. Washer (International)
20. Screw (International)

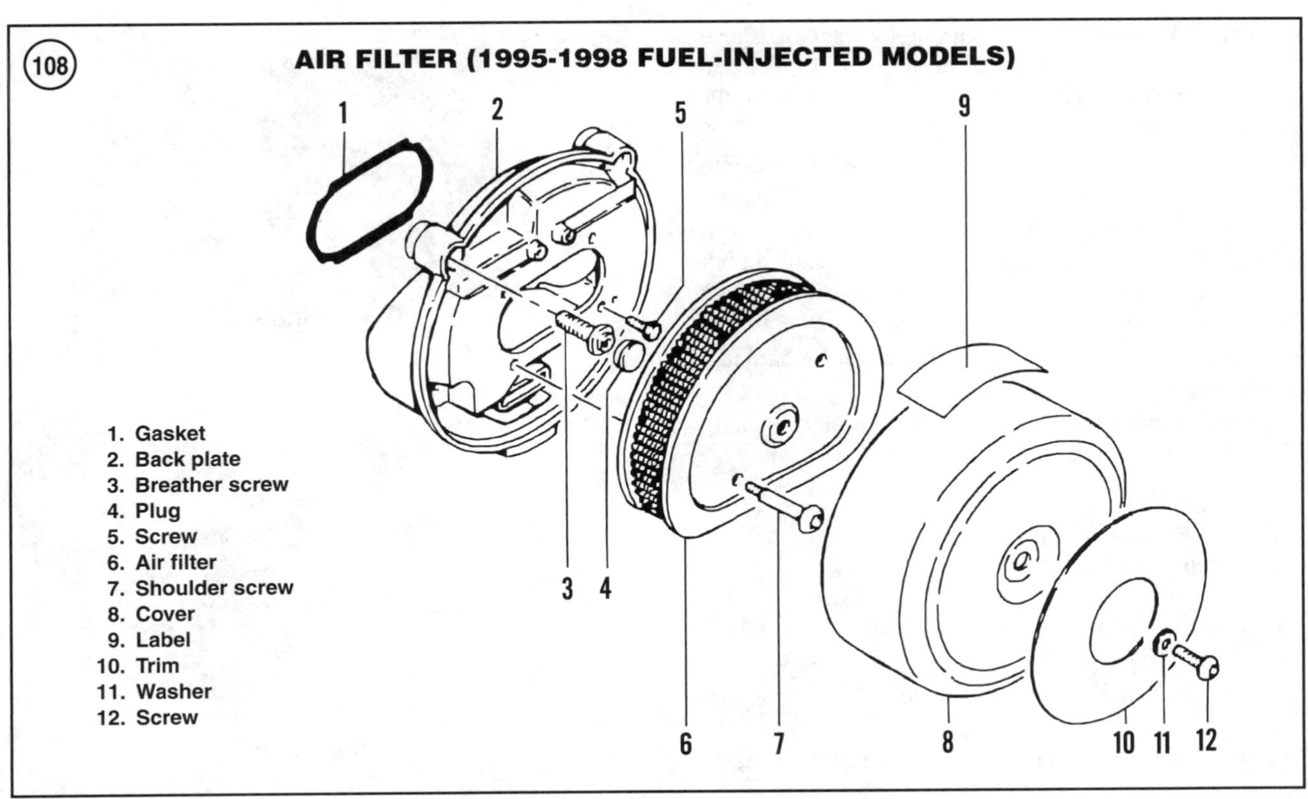

6. If removed, install a new gasket and breather hoses (**Figure 112**) (models so equipped) to backside of the element.

7. Position the element with the flat side and arrows (**Figure 113**) facing down.

NOTE
If an aftermarket air filter element is being installed, position it onto the back plate following the manufacturer's instructions.

8A. On 1984-1992 models, install the air filter element (**Figure 110**, typical).

8B. On 1993-1998 domestic carbureted models, move the air filter element into position on the back plate and connect the two breather hoses (**Figure 111**) to the breather hollow bolts on the back plate.

8C. On 1993-1998 international carbureted models, install the air filter element into position and install the four screws and washers. Tighten the screws securely.

8D. On 1995-1998 fuel-injected models, install the air filter element into position and install the screws. Tighten the screws securely.

9. Inspect the seal ring on the air filter cover for hardness or deterioration. Replace if necessary.

10. Install the air filter cover (B, **Figure 109**, typical), washer(s) and the screw(s). Tighten the screw securely.

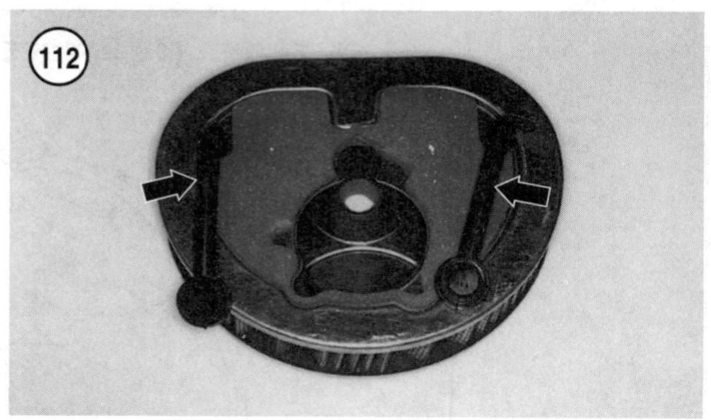
112

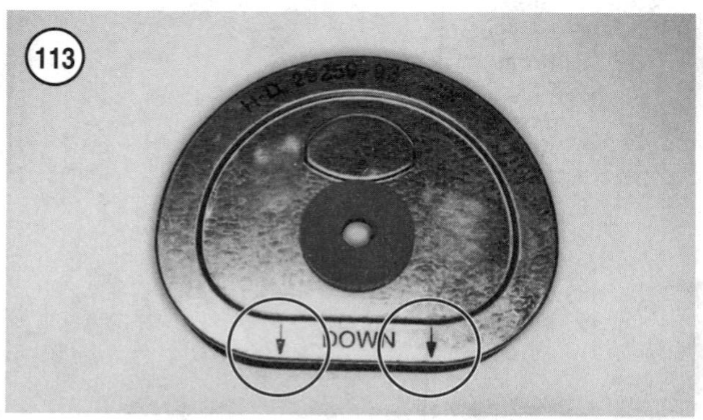

113

Air Filter Element Cleaning and Re-Oiling (1984-1990 Models)

Service the air filter element in a well-ventilated area, away from all sparks and flames

1. Remove the air filter element as described in this section.
2. Remove the wire mesh from inside the filter element.

WARNING
Do not clean the filter element in gasoline.

3. Clean the filter element with a filter solvent to remove oil and dirt.
4. Inspect the filter element. Replace if it is torn or broken in any area.
5. Fill a clean pan with liquid detergent and warm water.
6. Submerge the filter element in the cleaning solution and gently work the solution into the filter pores. Soak and gently squeeze the filter element to clean it.

CAUTION
Do not wring or twist the filter element when cleaning it. This could damage a filter pore or tear the filter loose at a seam. This would allow unfiltered air to enter the engine and cause severe and rapid wear.

7. Rinse the filter element under warm water while soaking and gently squeezing it.
8. Repeat Step 6 and Step 7 two or three times or until there are no signs of dirt being rinsed from the filter.
9. After cleaning the element, inspect it again carefully. If it is torn or broken in any area, replace it. Do not run the engine with a damaged filter element.
10. Set the filter aside and allow it to dry thoroughly.

CAUTION
Make sure the filter element is completely dry before oiling it.

11. Properly oiling the filter element is a messy but important job. Wear a pair of disposable rubber gloves when performing this procedure. Oil the filter as follows:
    a. Purchase a box of gallon size storage bags. The bags can be used when cleaning the filter as well as for storing engine and carburetor parts during disassembly.
    b. Place the filter element into a storage bag.
    c. Pour foam filter oil or clean engine oil onto the filter to soak it.
    d. Gently squeeze and release the filter element to soak oil into the filter pores. Repeat until all of the filter pores are saturated with oil.
    e. Remove the filter element from the bag and check the pores for uneven oiling. Uneven oiling is shown by light or dark areas on the filter element. If necessary, soak the filter element and squeeze it again.
    f. When the filter oiling is even, squeeze the filter element a final time to remove excess oil.
    g. Pour the leftover filter oil from the bag back into the bottle for reuse.

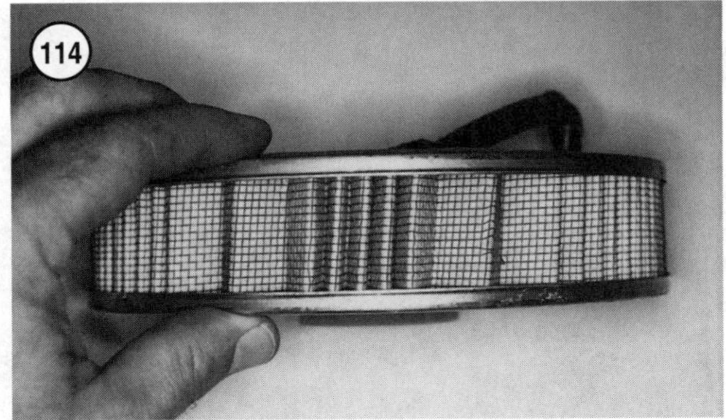

h. Dispose of the plastic storage bag.

12. Install the air filter element as described in this section.

Air Filter Element Cleaning (1991-1998 Models)

1. Remove the air filter element as described in this section.
2. Replace the filter element if damaged.

WARNING
Do not clean the filter element in gasoline.

CAUTION
Do not tap or strike the air filter element on a hard surface to dislodge dirt. Doing so will damage the element.

3. Place the air filter in a pan filled with lukewarm water and mild detergent. Move the filter element back and forth to help dislodge trapped dirt. Thoroughly rinse it in clean water to remove all detergent residue.
4. Hold the air filter up to a strong light. Check the filter pores for dirt and oil. Repeat Step 3 until there is no dirt or oil in the filter pores. If the air filter cannot be cleaned, or if the filter is saturated with oil or other chemicals, replace it.

CAUTION
Do not use high air pressure to dry the filter because this will damage it. Maximum air pressure is 32 psi (221 kPa).

CAUTION
In the next step, do not blow compressed air through the outer surface of the filter element. Doing so can force dirt trapped on the outer filter surface deeper into the filter element and restrict airflow and damage the filter element.

5. Gently apply compressed air through the inside surface of the filter element to remove loosened dirt and dust trapped in the filter.
6. Inspect the air filter element (**Figure 114**). Replace it if it is torn or damaged. Do not ride the motorcycle with a damaged air filter element because it will allow dirt to enter the engine.
7. Clean the breather hoses in the same lukewarm water and mild detergent. Make sure both hoses are clean and clear. Clean them out with a pipe cleaner if necessary.
8. Wipe the inside of the cover and back plate with a clean damp shop rag.

CAUTION
Air will not pass through a wet or damp filter element. Make sure the filter element is dry before installing it.

9. Allow the filter element to dry completely. Then reinstall it as described in this section.

Compression Test

A compression test is one of the most effective ways to check the condition of the engine. If possible, check the compression at each tune-up and record and compare it with the readings at subsequent tune-ups. This will help spot any developing problems.

1. Prior to starting the compression test, check for the following:
   a. The cylinder head bolts are tightened as specified in Chapter Four.
   b. The battery is fully charged to ensure proper engine cranking speed.
2. Warm the engine to normal operating temperature. Shut off the engine.
3. Remove both spark plugs (**Figure 115**) and reinstall them in their caps. Place the spark plugs against the cylinder heads to ground them.
4. Connect the compression tester to one cylinder following the manufacturer's instructions (**Figure 116**).

5. Place the throttle in the wide-open position.
6. On carbureted models, make sure the starting enrichment (choke) knob is off.
7. Crank the engine over until there is no further rise in pressure.
8. Record the reading and remove the tester.
9. Repeat Steps 4-8 for the other cylinder.
10. Reinstall the spark plugs and reconnect their caps.

Results

When interpreting the results, note the difference between the readings and compare the readings to the specification. **Table 8** lists the standard engine compression specification. Pressure must not vary between the cylinders by more than 10 percent. Greater differences indicate worn or broken rings, leaky or sticky valves, a blown head gasket or a combination of all.

If compression readings do not differ between cylinders by more than 10 percent, the rings and valves are in good condition. A low reading (10 percent or more) on one cylinder indicates valve or ring trouble. To decide which, pour about a teaspoon of engine oil into the spark plug hole. Turn the engine over once to distribute the oil. Then take another compression test and record the reading. If the compression increases significantly, the valves are good, but the rings are defective on that cylinder. If compression does not increase, the valves require servicing.

NOTE
An engine cannot be tuned to maximum performance with low compression.

Cylinder Leakdown Test

A cylinder leakdown test can determine engine problems from leaking valves; blown head gaskets; or broken, worn or stuck piston rings. A cylinder leakage test is performed by applying compressed air to the cylinder and then measuring the percent of leakage. A cylinder leakdown tester (**Figure 117**) and an air compressor are required to perform this test.

Follow the manufacturer's directions and the following information when performing a cylinder leakdown test.
1. Start and run the engine until it reaches normal operating temperature.
2. Remove the air filter assembly. Then set the throttle and choke valves in their wide-open position.
3. Remove the ignition timing inspection plug from the crankcase (**Figure 118**).

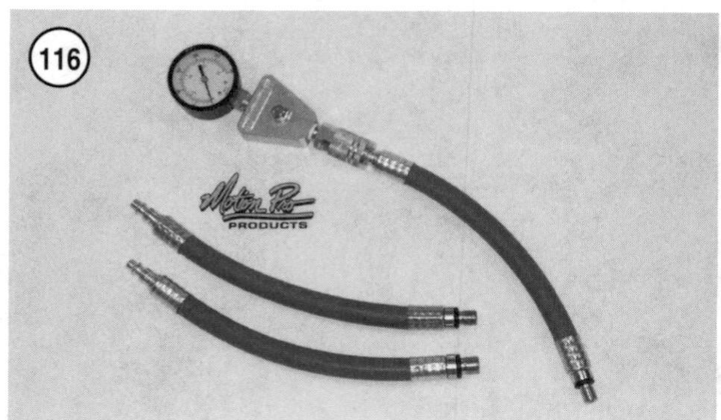

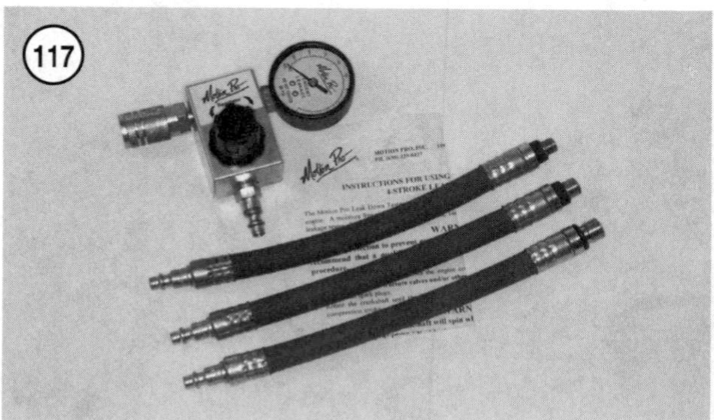

4. Set the piston for the cylinder being tested to TDC on its compression stroke. Reinstall the timing plug.
5. Remove both spark plugs (**Figure 115**).

NOTE
The engine might turn over when air pressure is applied to the cylinder. To prevent this from happening, shift the transmission into fifth gear and lock the rear brake pedal so that the rear brake is applied.

6. Listen for leaking air while noting the following:

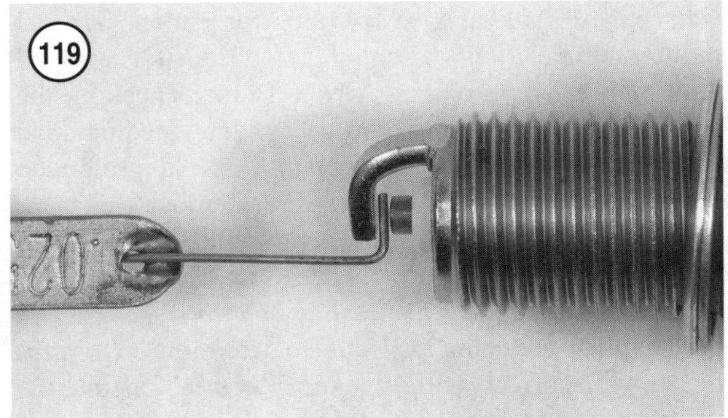

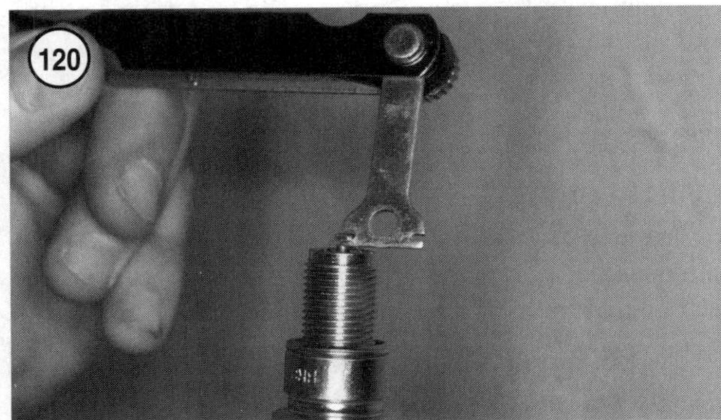

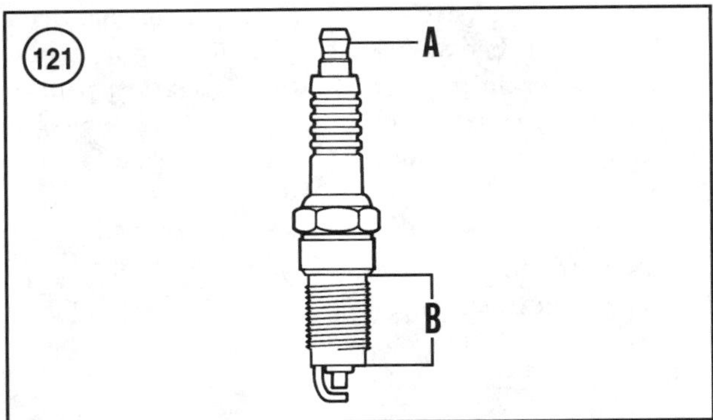

a. Air leaking through the exhaust pipe indicates a leaking exhaust valve.

b. Air leaking through the carburetor or fuel induction module indicates a leaking intake valve.

NOTE
Air leaking through the valves can also be caused by pushrods that are too long.

c. Air leaking through the ignition timing inspection hole indicates worn or broken piston rings, a leaking cylinder head gasket or a worn piston.

7. Repeat for the other cylinder.

Spark Plug Removal

CAUTION
Whenever the spark plug is removed, dirt around it can fall into the plug hole. This can cause serious engine damage.

1. Blow away loose dirt or debris that might have accumulated around the base of the spark plug and could fall into the cylinder head.
2. Grasp the spark plug lead (**Figure 115**) and twist it from side to side to break the seal. Then pull the cap off the spark plug. If the cap is stuck to the plug, twist it slightly to break it loose.

NOTE
Use a special spark plug socket equipped with a rubber insert that holds the spark plug. This type of socket is necessary for both removal and installation because the spark plugs are recessed in the cylinder head.

3. Install the spark plug socket onto the spark plug. Make sure it is correctly seated. Install an open-end wrench or socket handle and remove the spark plug. Mark the spark plug with the cylinder number from which it was removed.
4. Repeat Steps 1-3 for the remaining spark plug.
5. Thoroughly inspect each plug. Look for broken center porcelain, excessively eroded electrodes and excessive carbon or oil fouling.
6. Inspect the spark plug caps and secondary wires for damage or hardness. If any portion is damaged, replace the cap and secondary wire as an assembly. The front and rear cylinder assemblies have different part numbers.

Spark Plug Gapping and Installation

Carefully gap the spark plugs to ensure a reliable, consistent spark. Use a special spark plug gapping tool and a wire feeler gauge.

1. Insert a wire feeler gauge between the center and side electrode of the plug (**Figure 119**). The correct gap is in **Table 8**. If the gap is correct, a slight drag will be felt as the wire gauge is pulled through. If there is no drag, or if the gauge will not pass through, bend the side electrode with a gapping tool (**Figure 120**) to adjust to the proper gap in **Table 8**.
2. Install the terminal nut (A, **Figure 121**).

3. Apply a *light* coat of antiseize lubricant to the threads of the spark plug before installing it. Do *not* use engine oil on the plug threads.

CAUTION
The cylinder head is aluminum, and the spark plug hole is easily damaged if the spark plug is cross-threaded.

4. Slowly screw the spark plug into the cylinder head by hand until it seats. Very little effort is required. If force is necessary, the plug is cross-threaded; unscrew it and try again.

CAUTION
Do not overtighten. This will only distort the gasket and destroy its sealing ability.

5. Hand-tighten the plug until it seats against the cylinder head. Then tighten it to 14 ft.-lb. (19 N•m).
6. Install the spark plug cap and lead to the correct spark plug. Rotate the cap slightly in both directions and make sure it is attached to the spark plug.
7. Repeat for the other spark plug.

Spark Plug Heat Range

Spark plugs are available in various heat ranges that are hotter or colder than the plugs originally installed by the manufacturer.

Select a plug with a heat range designed for the loads and conditions under which the motorcycle will be operated. A plug with an incorrect heat range can foul, overheat and cause piston damage.

In general, use a hot plug for low speeds and low temperatures. Use a cold plug for high speeds, high engine loads and high temperatures. The plug should operate hot enough to burn off unwanted deposits but not so hot that it is damaged or causes preignition. To determine if plug heat range is correct, remove each spark plug and examine the insulator.

Do not change the spark plug heat range to compensate for adverse engine or air/fuel conditions.

When replacing plugs, make sure the reach or thread length (B, **Figure 121**) is correct. A longer than standard plug could interfere with the piston and cause engine damage.

Refer to **Table 8** for recommended spark plugs.

Spark Plug Reading

Reading the spark plugs can provide information regarding engine performance. Reading plugs that have been in use indicates spark plug operation, air/fuel mixture composition and engine conditions (such as oil consumption or piston ring wear). Before checking the spark plugs, operate the motorcycle under a medium load for approximately 6 miles (10 km). Avoid prolonged idling before shutting off the engine. Remove the spark plugs as described in this section. Examine each plug and compare it to those in **Figure 122**. Refer to the following sections to determine the operating conditions.

If the plugs are being inspected to determine if carburetor jetting is correct, start with new plugs and operate the motorcycle at the load that corresponds to the jetting information desired. For example, on carbureted models, if the main jet is in question, operate the motorcycle at full throttle, shut the engine off and coast to a stop.

Normal condition

If the plug has a light tan or gray deposit and no abnormal gap wear or erosion, the engine, air/fuel mixture and ignition conditions are good. The plug in use is of the proper heat range and may be serviced and returned to use.

Carbon-fouled

Soft, dry, sooty deposits covering the entire firing end of the plug are evidence of incomplete combustion. Even though the firing end of the plug is dry, the plug insulation decreases when in this condition. An electrical path is formed that bypasses the electrodes and causes a misfire condition. Carbon fouling can be caused by one or more of the following:
1. Rich fuel mixture.
2. Cold spark plug heat range.
3. Clogged air filter.
4. Improperly operating ignition component.
5. Ignition component failure.
6. Low engine compression.
7. Prolonged idling.

Oil-fouled

The tip of an oil-fouled plug has a black insulator tip, a damp oily film over the firing end and a carbon layer over the entire nose. The electrodes are not worn. Oil-fouled spark plugs may be cleaned in an emergency, but it is better to replace them. Correct the cause of fouling before returning the engine to service. Common causes for this condition are as follows:
1. Incorrect air/fuel mixture.
2. Low idle speed or prolonged idling.

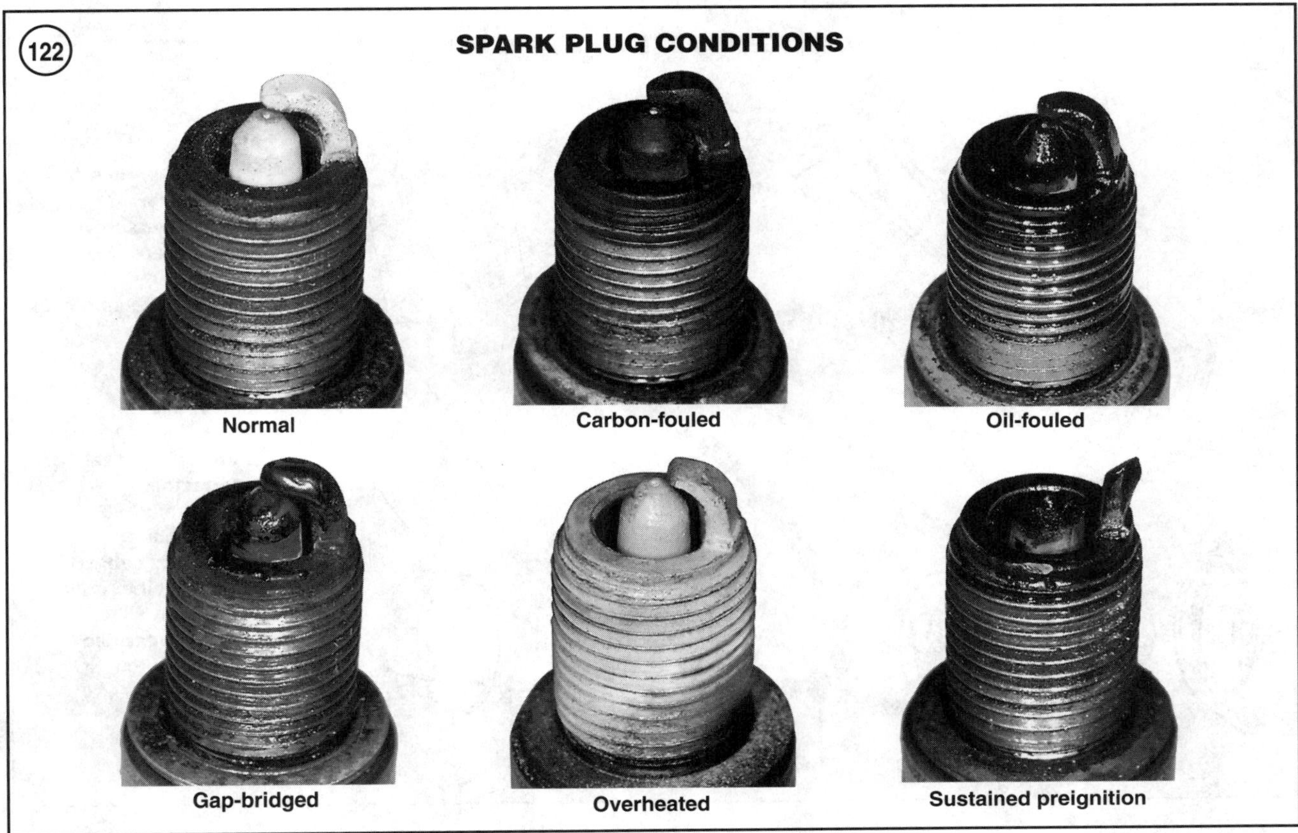

3. Ignition component failure.
4. Cold spark plug heat range.
5. Engine still being broken in.
6. Valve guides worn.
7. Piston rings worn or broken.

Gap bridging

Plugs with gap bridging have gaps shorted out by combustion deposits between the electrodes. If this condition is encountered, check for excessive carbon or oil in the combustion chamber. Be sure to locate and correct the cause of this condition.

Overheating

Badly worn electrodes, premature gap wear and a gray or white blistered porcelain insulator surface are signs of overheating. The most common cause is a spark plug of the wrong heat range (too hot). If the spark plug is the correct heat range and is overheated, consider the following causes:

1. Lean air/fuel mixture.
2. Improperly operating ignition component.
3. Engine lubrication system malfunction.
4. Cooling system malfunction.
5. Engine air leak.
6. Improper spark plug installation (overtightened).
7. No spark plug gasket.

Worn out

Corrosive gases formed by combustion and high-voltage sparks have eroded the electrodes. A spark plug in this condition requires more voltage to fire under hard acceleration. Replace it with a new spark plug.

Preignition

If the electrodes are melted, preignition is almost certainly the cause. Check for intake air leaks at the manifold and carburetor, or throttle body, and advanced ignition timing. It is also possible that the plug is the wrong heat range (too hot). Find the cause of the preignition before returning the engine to service. For additional information on preignition, refer to *Preignition* in Chapter Two.

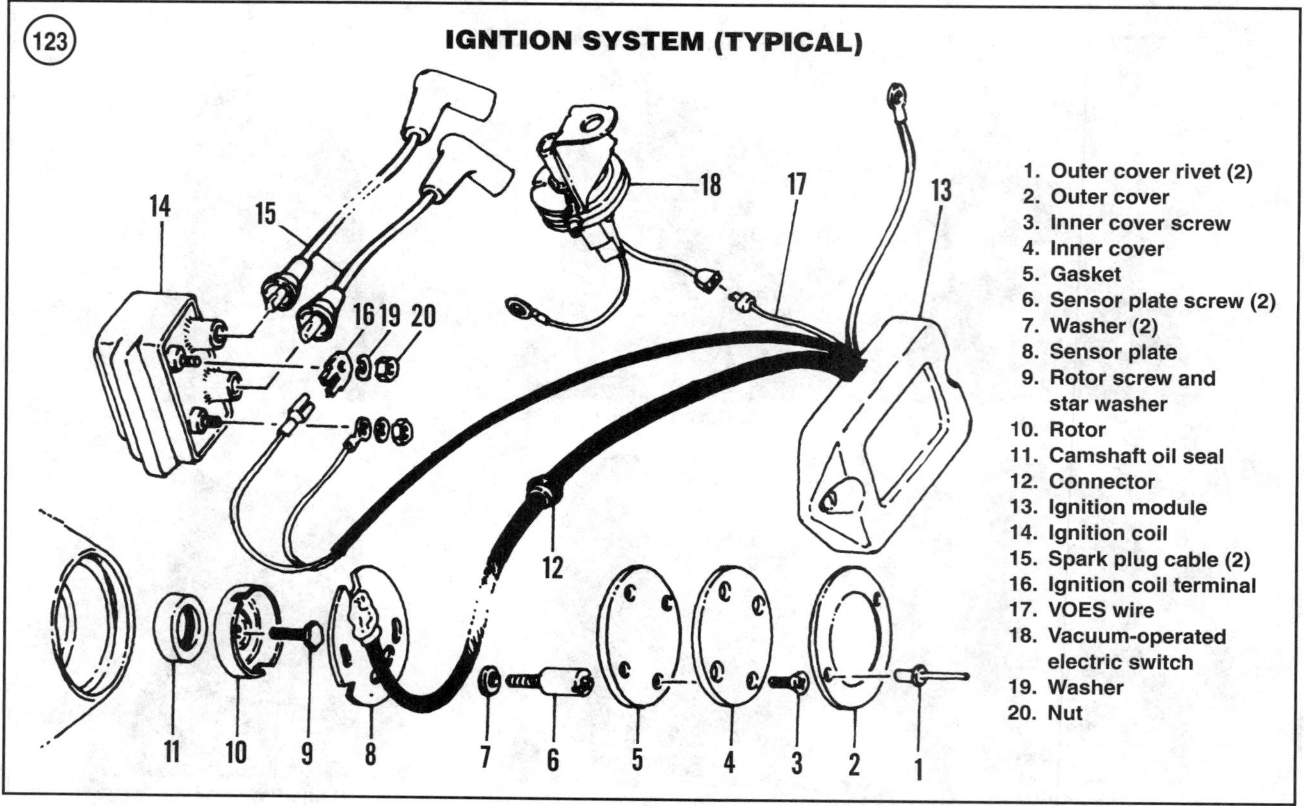

IGNITION SERVICE

Ignition Timing Inspection and Adjustment (Carbureted Models)

Refer to **Figure 123**.

1. Park the motorcycle on a level surface on the jiffy stand.

2. Remove the plug from the timing hole on the left side of the engine (**Figure 118**). A clear plastic viewing plug is available from Harley-Davidson dealers to minimize oil spray. Make sure the plug does not contact the crankshaft flywheel.

3. Connect a portable tachometer following the manufacturer's instructions. The motorcycle tachometer (models so equipped) is not accurate enough in the low rpm range for this adjustment.

4. Connect an inductive clamp-on timing light to the front cylinder spark plug wire following the manufacturer's instructions.

NOTE
Make sure the vacuum hose is connected to the carburetor and the vacuum-operated

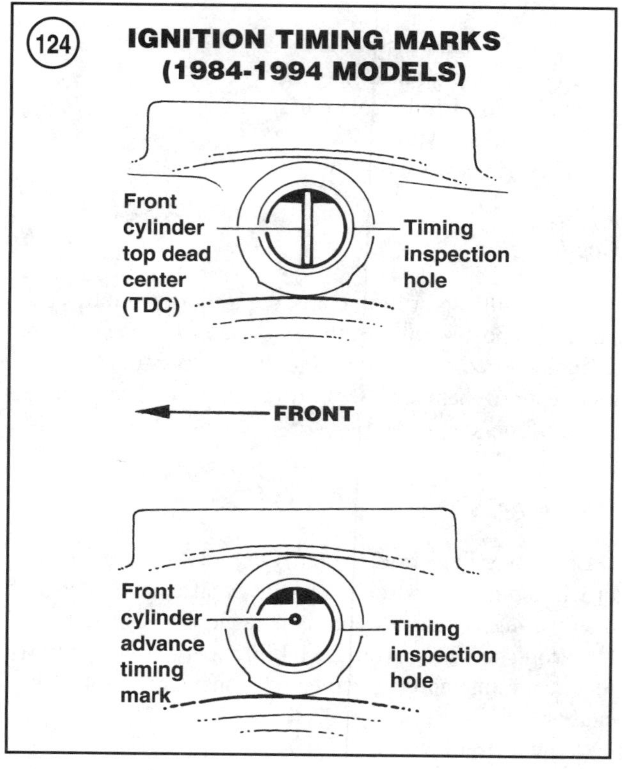

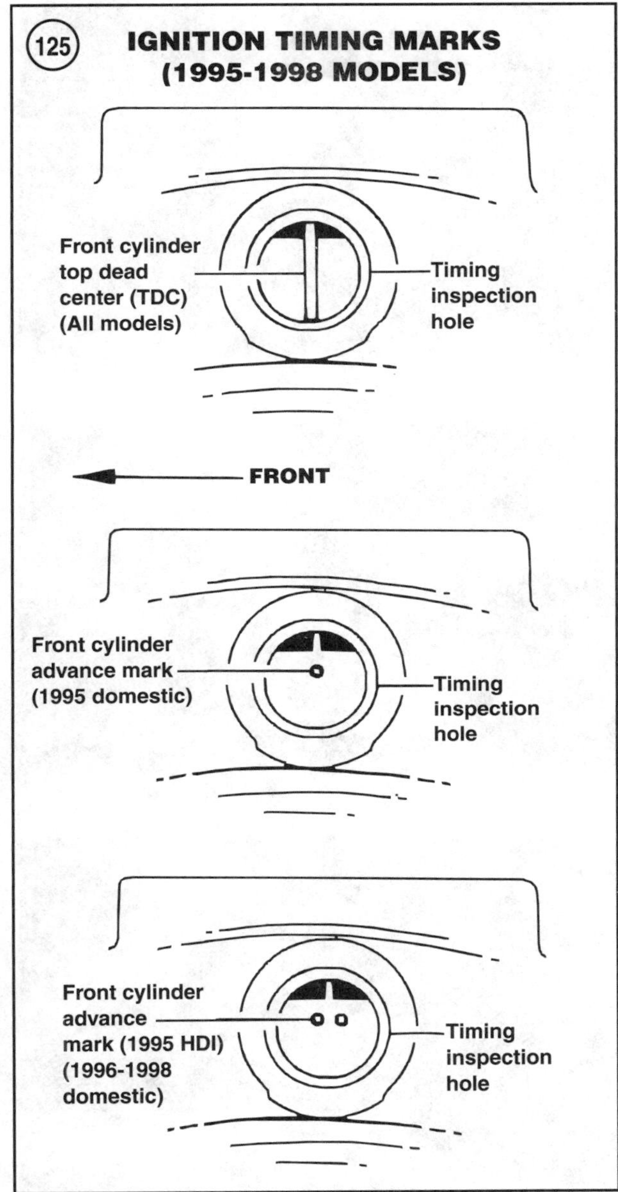

electric switch (VOES) when checking ignition timing.

5. Start the engine and allow to idle at the engine speed listed in **Table 9**. If necessary, adjust idle as described in this chapter.
6. Aim the timing light at the timing inspection hole. At the specified idle rpm, the front cylinder advance mark should appear in the center of the inspection window. Refer to **Figure 124** for 1983-1994 models or **Figure 125** for 1995-1998 models for ignition timing mark(s). If the mark(s) does not align, stop the engine and adjust the ignition timing, starting with Step 8.
7. If the ignition timing is incorrect, reinstall the timing hole plug (**Figure 118**) and proceed to Step 8.
8. Drill out the outer cover pop rivets (**Figure 126**) with a 3/8-in. (9.5 mm) drill bit.
9. Using a punch, lightly tap the rivets out of the outer cover (**Figure 127**).
10. Remove the outer cover (**Figure 128**).
11. If necessary, lightly tap the rivets out of the inner cover (**Figure 129**).
12. Remove the inner cover screws and remove the inner cover (**Figure 130**).
13. Remove the gasket (**Figure 131**).

14. Remove any remaining rivet bits from the ignition housing.
15. Loosen the timing plate sensor plate screws (**Figure 132**) just enough to allow the plate to rotate. Start the engine and turn the plate as required so that the advanced mark is aligned as described in Step 6. Make sure idle speed specified in Step 6 is maintained when checking timing. Tighten the screws and recheck ignition timing.
16. Install the gasket and inner cover.

NOTE
*When installing pop rivets to secure the outer cover, make sure to use the headless type shown in **Figure 133**. The end of a normal pop rivet will break off on installation and damage the timing mechanism.*

17. Install the outer cover and secure with the new rivets (**Figure 134**).
18. As part of the tune-up, check the vacuum-operated electric switch (VOES) as follows:
  a. Start the engine and allow to idle.
  b. Disconnect the vacuum line at the carburetor.

NOTE
*The carburetor VOES port is identified in **Figure 135** (1984-1989 models) and **Figure 136** (1990-on models).*

NOTE
***Figure 135** and **Figure 136** are shown with the carburetor removed to better illustrate the step.*

  c. Plug the carburetor VOES port with a finger. With the port blocked, the engine speed should decrease, and the ignition timing should retard. When the vacuum hose is reconnected to the VOES port, the engine speed should increase and the ignition timing should advance.
  d. If the engine failed to operate as described in substep c, check the VOES wire connection (**Figure 123**) at the ignition module. Also check the VOES ground wire for looseness or damage. If the wire connections are good, have the VOES tested by a Harley-Davidson dealership.

CAUTION
The vacuum-operated electric switch (VOES) must be tested at each tune-up and replaced if malfunctioning. A damaged VOES switch will allow too high a spark advance and will cause severe engine knock and damage.

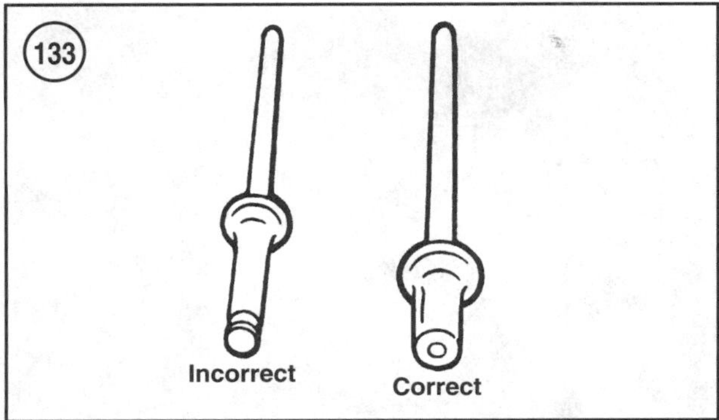

3

Ignition Timing Inspection (Fuel-Injected Models)

The fuel-injected models are equipped with a fully transistorized ignition system and are controlled by the electronic control module. Harley-Davidson does not provide any ignition timing procedures for these models If an ignition related problem is suspected, inspect the ignition components as described in Chapter Nine.

CARBURETOR ADJUSTMENTS

Slow and Fast Idle Adjustment (1984-1989 Models)

1. Park the motorcycle on a level surface and support it standing straight up.
2. Attach a tachometer to the engine following the manufacturer's instructions.
3. Start the engine and warm it to normal operating temperature. When the engine can run without the enrichment (choke) being applied, proceed to Step 3.

NOTE
Figure 137 *is shown with the air filter assembly removed to better illustrate the step.*

4. With the engine at idle speed, compare the engine rpm reading to the idle speed specification listed in **Table 9**. If the slow idle speed is incorrect, turn the throttle stop screw (**Figure 137**) to achieve the correct slow idle speed.
5. The idle mixture is set and sealed and cannot be adjusted.
6. Rev the engine a couple of times and release the throttle. Engine rpm should return to the idle speed set in Step 3. Readjust if necessary.
7. Pull the choke knob (**Figure 138**) out to its first detent and compare the tachometer reading to the fast idle speed specification listed in **Table 9**. If the fast idle speed is incorrect, turn the fast idle screw to achieve the correct fast idle speed.

Then push the choke knob all the way in and check that the idle drops to the slow idle speed (**Table 9**). If the choke does not operate correctly, adjust it as described in this chapter.

8. Disconnect the tachometer.

Idle Speed Adjustment (1990-1998 Models)

1. Park the motorcycle on a level surface and support it standing straight up.
2. Attach a tachometer to the engine following the manufacturer's instructions.
3. Start the engine and warm it to normal operating temperature. When the engine can run without the enrichment (choke) being applied, proceed to Step 3. Make sure the enrichment valve is pushed all the way in to the closed position.

NOTE
Figure 139 *is shown with the carburetor removed to better illustrate the step.*

4. With the engine at idle speed, compare the engine rpm reading to the idle speed specification listed in **Table 9**. If the slow idle speed is incorrect, turn the throttle stop screw (**Figure 139**) to achieve the correct slow idle speed.
5. The idle mixture is set and sealed and cannot be adjusted.
6. Rev the engine a couple of times and release the throttle. Engine rpm should return to the idle speed set in Step 3. Readjust if necessary.
7. Disconnect and remove the tachometer.

Table 1 MAINTENANCE SCHEDULE[1]

Pre-ride check	
	Check tire condition and inflation pressure
	Check wheel rim condition
	Check light and horn operation
	Check engine oil level; add oil if necessary
	Check brake fluid level and condition; add fluid if necessary
	Check the operation of the front and rear brake lever and pedal
	Check throttle operation
	Check enricher (choke) cable operation (carbureted models)
	Check clutch lever operation
	Check drive chain condition (models so equipped)
	Check drive belt condition (models so equipped)
	Check fuel level in fuel tank; top off if necessary
	Check fuel system for leaks
Initial 500 miles (800 km)	
	Change engine oil and filter
	Check tappet oil screen
	Check battery condition; clean cable connections if necessary
	Check brake fluid level and condition; add fluid if necessary
	Check front and rear brake pads and discs for wear

(continued)

Table 1 MAINTENANCE SCHEDULE[1] (continued)

Interval	Service
Initial 500 miles (800 km) (continued)	
	Check tire condition and inflation pressure
	Check primary chain deflection; adjust if necessary
	Change primary chaincase lubricant
	Change transmission lubricant
	Check clutch lever operation; adjust if necessary
	Check drive chain tension; adjust if necessary (models so equipped)
	Check drive belt tension and alignment; adjust if necessary (models so equipped)
	Check drive belt and sprockets condition (models so equipped)
	Inspect spark plugs
	Check vacuum-operated electric switch (VOES)
	Inspect air filter element
	Lubricate front brake and clutch lever pivot pin
	Lubricate brake cable if necessary
	Lubricate clutch cable if necessary
	Check throttle cable operation
	Check enricher (choke) cable operation (carbureted models)
	Check engine idle speed; adjust if necessary
	Check fuel system for leaks
	Check electrical switches and equipment for proper operation
	Check cruise control throttle disengagement switch operation (models so equipped)
	Check oil and brake lines for leakage
	Check engine mounting hardware for tightness
	Check all fasteners for tightness[2]
	Lubricate swing arm pivot shaft and bearings (FX series models)
	Road test the motorcycle
Every 2500 miles (4000 km)	
	Check transmission lubricant level; add lubricant if necessary
	Check drive belt tension and alignment; adjust if necessary
	Inspect air filter element
	Check throttle operation
	Check enricher (choke) cable operation (carbureted models)
	Check fuel system for leaks
	Check oil and brake lines for leakage
	Check electrical switches and equipment for proper operation
	Road test the motorcycle
Every 5000 miles (8000 km)	
	Change engine oil and filter
	Check tappet oil screen
	Change primary chaincase lubricant
	Change transmission lubricant
	Check battery condition; clean cable connections if necessary
	Check brake fluid level and condition; add fluid if necessary
	Check front and rear brake pads and discs for wear
	Check tire condition and inflation pressure
	Check wire wheel spoke nipple tightness; adjust if necessary (models so equipped)
	Check primary chain deflection; adjust if necessary
	Check drive belt tension and alignment; adjust if necessary (models so equipped)
	Check drive chain tension; adjust if necessary (models so equipped)
	Check clutch lever operation; adjust if necessary
	Check drive belt and sprockets condition (models so equipped)
	Check drive and driven sprockets condition (models so equipped)
	Check steering head bearing adjustment; adjust if necessary
	Inspect spark plugs
	Inspect ignition timing
	Check vacuum-operated electric switch (VOES)

(continued)

Table 1 MAINTENANCE SCHEDULE[1] (continued)

Every 5000 miles (8000 km) (continued)	Inspect and oil the air filter element (1984-1991) Inspect air filter element (1992-1998) Lubricate front brake and clutch lever pivot pin Lubricate clutch cable if necessary Lubricate speedometer cable Lubricate fitting on rear brake linkage (models so equipped) Check throttle cable operation Check enricher (choke) cable operation (carbureted models) Check engine idle speed; adjust if necessary Check fuel system for leaks Check electrical switches and equipment for proper operation Check oil and brake lines for leakage Check air suspension components and hoses (models so equipped) Check rubber engine mounts (models so equipped) Check all fasteners for tightness[2] Lubricate swing arm pivot shaft and bearings (FX series models) Lubricate non-nylon lined control cables Perform a tune-up Lubricate throttle grip Check solenoid-operated butterfly valve for proper operation Road test the motorcycle
Every 10,000 miles (16,000 km)	Replace spark plugs Perform a compression test Change front fork oil Lubricate rear swing arm bearings Inspect engine mounts for wear or damage; replace if necessary Check stabilizer links Lubricate brake caliper pins Clean and repack wheel bearings Road test the motorcycle
Every 20,000 miles (32,000 km)	Lubricate steering head bearings Inspect fuel tank filter; replace if necessary Inspect fuel supply valve filter screen

1. Consider this maintenance schedule a guide to general maintenance and lubrication intervals. Harder than normal use and exposure to mud, water, high humidity indicate more frequent servicing to most of the maintenance items.
2. Except cylinder head bolts. Cylinder head bolts must be tightened following the procedure listed in Chapter Four. Improper tightening of the cylinder head bolts can cause cylinder gasket damage and/or cylinder head leakage.

Table 2 TIRE INFLATION PRESSURE (FXR, FLH AND FLT [COLD])[1]

Item	psi	kPa
Front (rider only)		
1984-1985		
FXRS (K291T[2])	30	207
FXRT (K291T[2])	30	207
FLT/FLTC	–	–
FLHT/FLHTC (K101A[2])	28	193
1986-1998		
FXR series models	30	207
FLH and FLT series models	36	248
Front (rider with one passenger)		
1984-1985		
FXRS	30	207
FXRT	30	207
FLT/FLTC and FLHT/FLHTC	28	193

(continued)

Table 2 TIRE INFLATION PRESSURE (FXR, FLH AND FLT [COLD])[1] (continued)

Item	psi	kPa
Front (rider with one passenger)		
1984-1985 (continued)		
FLT with sidecar	28	193
1986-1998		
FXR series models	30	207
FLH and FLT series models	36	248
Rear (rider only)		
1984-1985		
FXRS (K291T[2])	36	248
FXRT (K291T[2])	36	248
FLT/FLTC	–	–
FLHT/FLHTC (K101A[2])	36	248
1986-1998		
FXR series	36	248
FLH and FLT series models	36	248
Rear (rider with one passenger)		
1984-1985		
FXRS	40	275
FXRT	40	275
FLT/FLTC and FLHT/FLHTC	36	248
FLT with sidecar	40	275
1986-1998		
FXR series models	40	275
FLH and FLT series models	40	275

1. Tire inflation pressure is for OE tires. Aftermarket tires might require different inflation pressure. The use of tires other than those specified by Harley-Davidson can cause instability.
2. Indicates the OE Dunlop tire designation.

Table 3 TIRE INFLATION PRESSURE (FXWG, FXSB AND FXEF [COLD])[1]

Item	psi	kPa
Front (rider only)		
FXWG	30	207
FXEF and FXSB		
K181[2]	30	207
K291T[2]	36	248
Front (rider with one passenger)		
FXWG		
F rib	30	207
K101A	–	–
FXEF and FXSB		
K181[2]	30	207
K291T[2]	36	248
Rear (rider only)		
FXWG	32	221
FXEF and FXSB		
K181[2]	32	221
K291T[2]	36	248
Rear (rider with one passenger)		
FXWG		
F rib	32	221
K101A	28	193
FXEF and FXSB		
K181[2]	32	221

1. Tire inflation pressure is for OE tires. Aftermarket tires might require different inflation pressure. The use of tires other than those specified by Harley-Davidson can cause instability.
2. Indicates the OE Dunlop tire designation.

Table 4 ENGINE OIL

Type	HD rating	Viscosity	Ambient operating temperature
HD Multigrade	HD360	SAE 10W/40	Below 40°F (4° C)
HD Multigrade	HD360	SAE 20W/50	Above 40°F (4° C)
HD Regular heavy	HD360	SAE 50	Above 60°F (16° C)
HD Extra heavy	HD360	SAE 60	Above 80°F (27° C)

Table 5 RECOMMENDED LUBRICANTS AND FLUIDS

Brake fluid	DOT 5 silicone
Fork oil	HD Type E or an equivalent
Battery	Purified or distilled water
Transmission	HD Transmission Lubricant or an equivalent
Clutch	HD Transmission Lubricant or an equivalent
Drive chain	
Enclosed drive chain	SAE 50 or SAE 60
Open drive chain (without O-rings)	Commercial drive chain lubricant
Open drive chain (with O-rings)	Commercial drive chain lubricant recommended for O-ring chains

Table 6 ENGINE AND PRIMARY DRIVE/TRANSMISSION OIL CAPACITIES

Engine oil tank	
FXR series models	3.0 qts. (2.8 L)
FLT/FLH series models	4.0 qts. (3.8 L)
FXWG, FXSB and FXEF	4.0 qts. (3.8 L)
Transmission	
1984-1990	16 oz. (473 mL)
1991-1998	20-24 oz. (591-710 mL)
Primary chaincase	
Early 1984	N.A.
Late 1984-1990	1.5 qt. (1.4 L)
1991-1996	38-44 oz. (1.1-1.3 L)
1997-1998	32 oz. (946 mL)
Rear chaincase (1984-1985)	6 oz. (177 mL)

Table 7 FRONT FORK OIL CAPACITY

Model and year	Oil Change oz.	Oil Change cc	Rebuild oz.	Rebuild cc
FXR				
1984-1987 FXR and FXRS	6.25	184.8	7.0	206.9
1984-1987 FXRD and FXRT	7.0	206.9	7.75	229.2
1987-1994 FXLR	9.2	272	10.2	300.9
1988-1994 FXR and FXRS	9.2	272	10.2	300.9
1988-1994 FXRT and FXRS-SP and FXRS-Con	10.5	310.5	11.5	339.2
1999 FXR2 and FXR3	9.2	272	10.2	300.9
FXWG	10.2	300.9	11.2	330.4
FXSB	7.5	221.8	6.75	199.6
FXEF	5.0	147.8	6.5	192.2
FLT and FLH series models	7.75	229.2	8.5	251.3

Table 8 TUNE-UP SPECIFICATIONS

Engine compression	90 psi (620 kPa)
Spark plugs	
Type	HD 5R6A
Gap	0.038-0.043 in. (0.97-1.09 mm)
Ignition timing	
Type	Electronic
Timing specifications	
Early 1984	
Range	5-50° BTDC
Start	5° BTDC
Fast idle at 1800-2800 rpm	35° BTDC
Late 1984-1994	
Range	0-35° BTDC
Start	0° BTDC
Fast idle at 1800-2800 rpm	35° BTDC
1995 domestic	
Range	0-35° BTDC
Start	TDC
Fast idle at 1050-1500 rpm	35° BTDC
1995 HDI	
Range	0-42.5° BTDC
Start	TDC
Fast idle at 1050-1500 rpm	20° BTDC
1996-1998	
Range	0-42.5° BTDC
Start	TDC
Fast idle at 1050-1500 rpm	20° BTDC

Table 9 IDLE SPEED SPECIFICATIONS

Model and year	Speed
FXR, FLH and FLT series models	
1984-1987	
Slow idle	900-950 rpm
Fast idle	1500 rpm
1988-1989	
Slow idle	1000 rpm
Fast idle	1500 rpm
1990	1000 rpm
1991-1996	1000-1050 rpm
1997-1998	1050-1500 rpm
FXR2 and FXR3	1000-1050 rpm
FXWG, FXSB and FXEF	
Slow idle	1000-1050 rpm
Fast idle	1500-1550 rpm

Table 10 FRONT FORK AIR CONTROL (FXR SERIES MODELS 1984-1994)

	Recommended air pressure psi (kPa)	
Vehicle load	Front fork	Accumulator 1984-1987 FXRD and FXRT
Rider weight up to 150 lbs. (68 kg)	4-8 (28-55)	5-30 (34-207)
Each additional 25 lbs. (11 kg), add	2.0 (14)	
Passenger weight: For each 50 lbs. (23 kg), add	1.0 (7)	
Maximum pressure	20 (138)	30 (207)

Table 11 FRONT FORK AIR CONTROL (1984-1994 FLH AND FLT SERIES MODELS)

Ride	Amount of antidive	Recommended pressure psi (kPa)
Firm	Stiff	20 (138)
Normal	Normal	15 (103)
Soft	Soft	10 (69)

Table 12 AIR SUSPENSION ADJUSTMENTS (1995-1998 FLH AND FLT SERIES MODELS)

	Recommended pressure psi (kPa)	
Load	Front fork	Rear shock absorber
Rider weight		
Up to 150 lbs. (68 kg)	–	–
For each additional 25 lbs. (11 kg), add	1.0 (7)	1.0 (7)
Passenger weight: For each additional 50 lbs. (23 kg), add	–	1.5 (10)
Luggage weight: For each additional 10 lbs. (6 kg), add	1.0 (7)	3.0 (21)
Maximum pressure	25 (172)	35 (241)

Table 13 MAINTENANCE AND TUNE-UP TORQUE SPECIFICATIONS

Item	ft.-lb.	in.-lb.	N•m
Clutch diaphragm spring bolts late 1984-1989 wet clutch	–	71-97	8-11
Engine front mounting bracket			
Side bolts	33-38	–	45-52
Center bolt	35-45	–	47-61
Front fork air pipe hex bolts (1997-1998 models)	–	97-106	11-12
Primary drive chain shoe nut or bolt	22-29	–	30-39
Rear axle nut			
1984-1988	60-65	–	81-88
1989-1998	60	–	81
Spark plugs	14	–	19
Swing arm anchor bolt (enclosed chain models)	20	–	27
Valve lifter screen plug	–	89-124	10-14

CHAPTER FOUR

ENGINE

This chapter provides complete service and overhaul procedures, including information for disassembly, removal, inspection, service and engine reassembly.

Refer to **Tables 1-5** at the end of the chapter for specifications.

All models covered in this manual are equipped with the V-2 Evolution, an air-cooled four-stroke overhead-valve V-twin engine. The engine consists of three major assemblies: engine, crankcase and gearcase. Viewed from the right side of the engine, engine rotation is clockwise.

Both cylinders fire once in 720° of crankshaft rotation. The rear cylinder fires 315° after the front cylinder. The front cylinder fires again in another 405°. Note that one cylinder is always on its exhaust stroke when the other fires on its compression stroke.

SERVICE PRECAUTIONS

Before servicing the engine, note the following:

1. Review the information in Chapter One, especially the *Service Methods and Precision Measuring Tools* sections. Accurate measurements are critical to a successful engine rebuild.
2. Throughout the text, there are references to the left and right sides of the engine. These refer to the engine as it is mounted in the frame, not how it may sit on the workbench.
3. Always replace worn or damaged fasteners with those of the same size, type and torque requirements. Make sure to identify each bolt before replacing it. Lubricate bolt threads with engine oil, unless otherwise specified, before tightening. If a specific torque value is not listed in **Table 5**, refer to the general torque specifications in Chapter One.

CAUTION

The engine is assembled with hardened fasteners. Do not install fasteners with a lower strength grade classification.

4. Use special tools where noted.
5. Store parts in boxes, plastic bags and containers (**Figure 1**). Use masking tape and a permanent, waterproof marking pen to label parts.

6. Use a box of assorted size and color vacuum hose identifiers (Lisle part No. 74600) (**Figure 2**) for identifying hoses and fittings during engine removal and disassembly.
7. Use a vise with protective jaws to hold parts.
8. Use a press or special tools when force is required to remove and install parts. Do not try to pry, hammer or otherwise force them on or off.
9. Replace all O-rings and oil seals during reassembly. Apply a small amount of grease to the inner lips of each new seal to prevent damage when the engine is first started.
10. Record the location, position and thickness of all shims as they are removed.

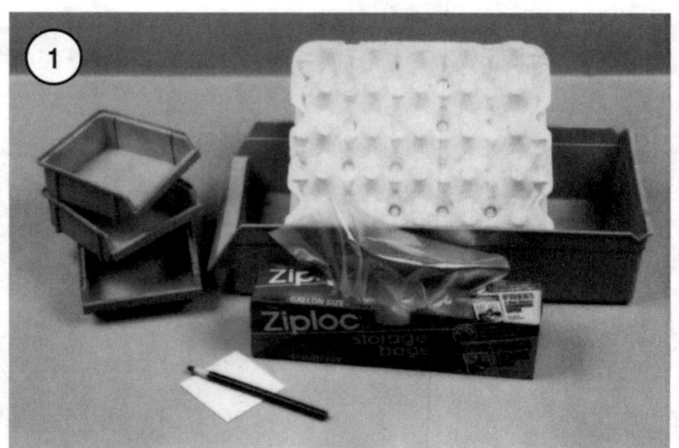

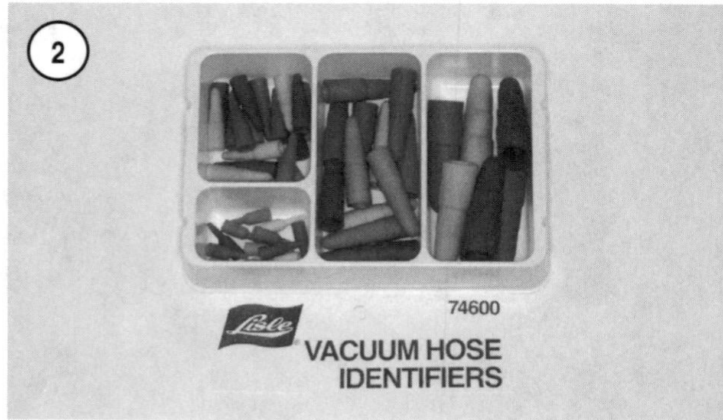

SPECIAL TOOLS

Engine service requires a number of special tools. These tools and their part numbers are listed with the individual procedures. For a complete list of the special tools mentioned in this manual, refer to **Table 12** in Chapter One. The engine tools used in this chapter are either H-D or JIMS special tools. JIMS special tools are available through many aftermarket motorcycle suppliers.

When purchasing special tools, make sure to specify that the tools required are for the specific year and model number motorcycle being worked on. Many of the tools are specific to this engine. Tools for other engine models might be slightly different.

SERVICING ENGINE IN FRAME

Many components can be serviced while the engine is mounted in the frame:

1. Rocker arm cover.
2. Cylinder head.
3. Cylinders and pistons.
4. Camshafts.
5. Gearshift mechanism.
6. Clutch.
7. Transmission.
8. Carburetor or fuel injection induction module.
9. Starter and gears.
10. Alternator and electrical systems.

ENGINE

Removal

1. Thoroughly clean the engine of all dirt and debris.
2. Remove the seat as described in Chapter Fifteen.
3. Disconnect the negative battery cable as described in Chapter Nine.
4. Support the motorcycle on a stand or floor jack. See *Motorcycle Stands* in Chapter Ten.
5. Remove the fuel tank as described in Chapter Nine.
6. On models so equipped, remove both saddlebags as described in Chapter Fifteen.
7. Remove both frame side covers as described in Chapter Fifteen.
8. On models so equipped, remove the inner front fairing as described in Chapter Fifteen.
9. Remove the air filter and backing plate as described in Chapter Eight.

10A. On carbureted models, remove the carburetor as described in Chapter Eight.

10B. On fuel-injected models, remove the fuel injection induction module as described in Chapter Eight.

11. Remove the exhaust system as described in Chapter Eight.
12. Remove the rear brake pedal as described in Chapter Thirteen.
13. Remove all four footboards as described in Chapter Fifteen.

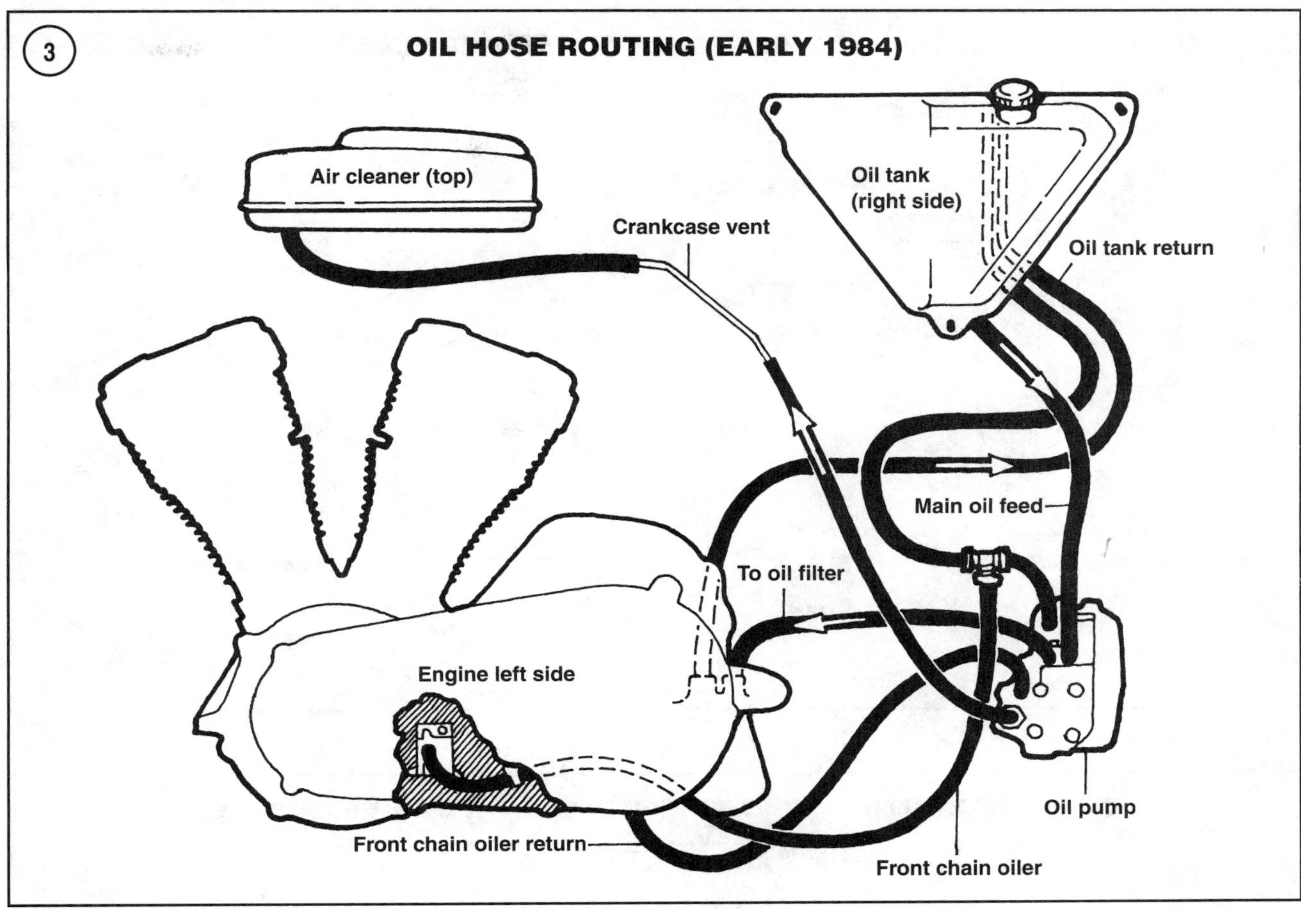

14. Drain the engine oil and oil tank as described in Chapter Three.
15. Label and disconnect the engine-to-oil tank oil lines. Refer to **Figures 3-9**. Plug the ends to prevent the entry of debris.
16. Disconnect the wire from the oil pressure switch (**Figure 10**).
17. Disconnect the alternator connector from the crankcase (**Figure 11**).
18. On FXR series models, perform the following:
   a. Disconnect the choke knob and cable from the upper cylinder stabilizer bar and bracket.
   b. Disconnect spark plug wires and cap assemblies and move them out of the way.
   c. Remove the ignition switch and the ignition coil as described in Chapter Nine.
19. On FLH and FLT series models, remove the ignition coil and spark plug assembly as described in Chapter Nine.
20. On models so equipped, remove the screws securing the crankshaft position sensor (**Figure 12**) and remove it from the crankcase.
21. On models so equipped, disconnect the wires from the engine temperature sensor (**Figure 13**).
22. Remove the primary chaincase assembly, including the inner housing, as described in Chapter Five.
23. Remove the alternator rotor and stator as described in Chapter Nine.
24A. On FXWG, FXSB and FXEF models, remove the upper cylinder head stabilizer bar and bracket assembly (**Figure 14**).
24B. On all other models, remove the upper cylinder head stabilizer bar and bracket assembly (**Figure 15**).
25. On the left side, remove the front stabilizer and outer end bolt.
26. Disconnect the hose from the breather cover and move the hose out of the way.
27. Remove the voltage regulator as described in Chapter Nine.
28. Remove the clutch cable from the lower portion of the crankcase as described under *Clutch Cable Replacement* in Chapter Six.

4 **OIL HOSE ROUTING (LATE 1984-1990 FXR, FLH AND FLT SERIES MODELS)**

Air cleaner
Crankcase vent
Oil tank
Oil vent
Return from filter
Main oil feed
Engine crankcase
Oil filter
Oil pump

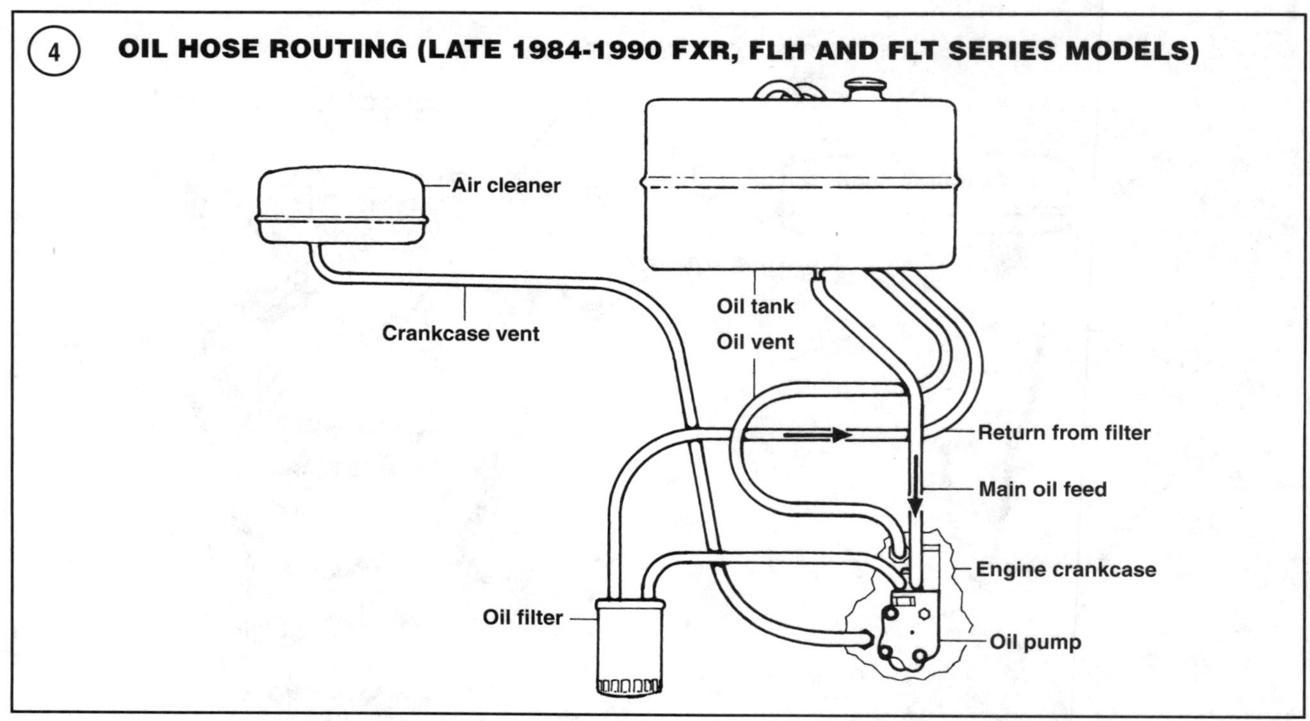

5 **OIL HOSE ROUTING (1991 FXR, FLH AND FLT SERIES MODELS)**

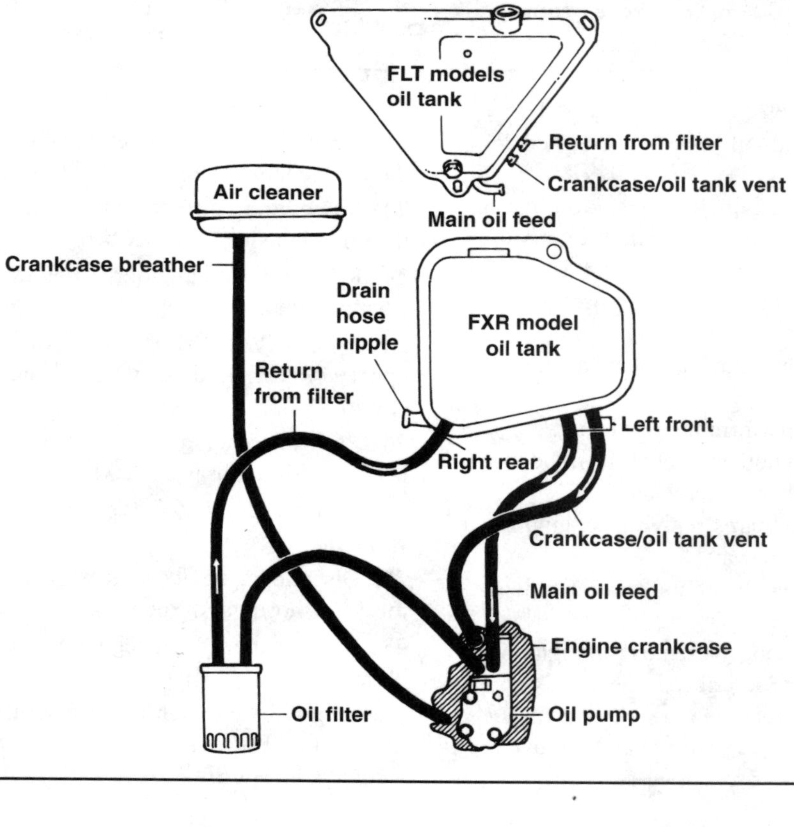

FLT models
oil tank
Return from filter
Crankcase/oil tank vent
Air cleaner
Main oil feed
Crankcase breather
Drain
hose
nipple
FXR model
oil tank
Return
from filter
Left front
Right rear
Crankcase/oil tank vent
Main oil feed
Engine crankcase
Oil filter
Oil pump

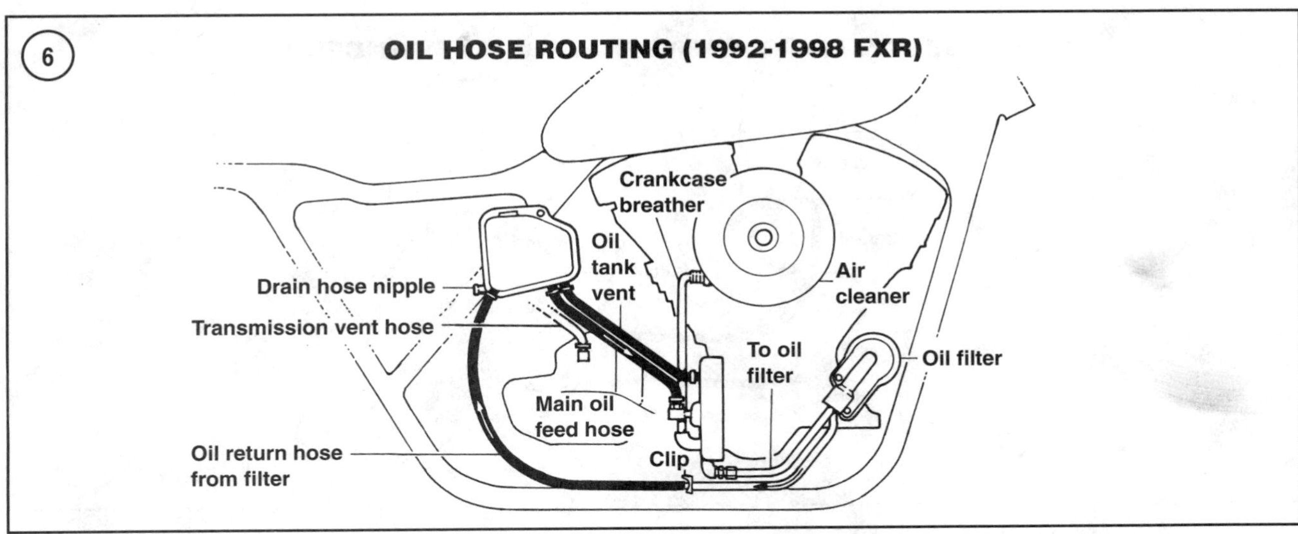
6
OIL HOSE ROUTING (1992-1998 FXR)
Crankcase breather
Oil tank vent
Drain hose nipple
Transmission vent hose
Air cleaner
To oil filter
Oil filter
Main oil feed hose
Oil return hose from filter
Clip

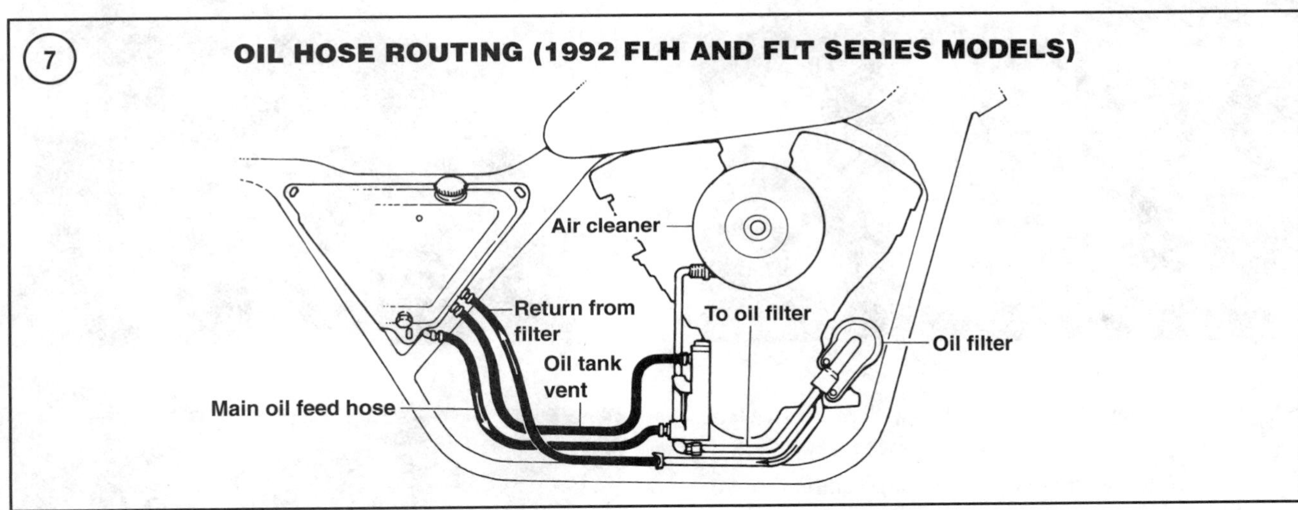
7
OIL HOSE ROUTING (1992 FLH AND FLT SERIES MODELS)
Air cleaner
Return from filter
To oil filter
Oil filter
Oil tank vent
Main oil feed hose

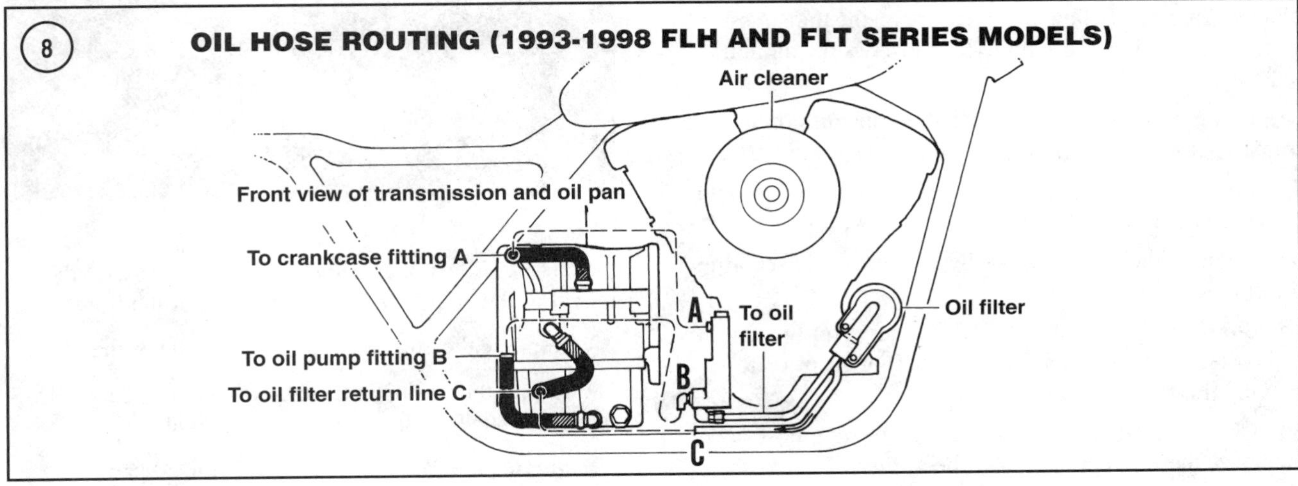
8
OIL HOSE ROUTING (1993-1998 FLH AND FLT SERIES MODELS)
Air cleaner
Front view of transmission and oil pan
To crankcase fitting A
A
To oil filter
Oil filter
To oil pump fitting B
B
To oil filter return line C
C

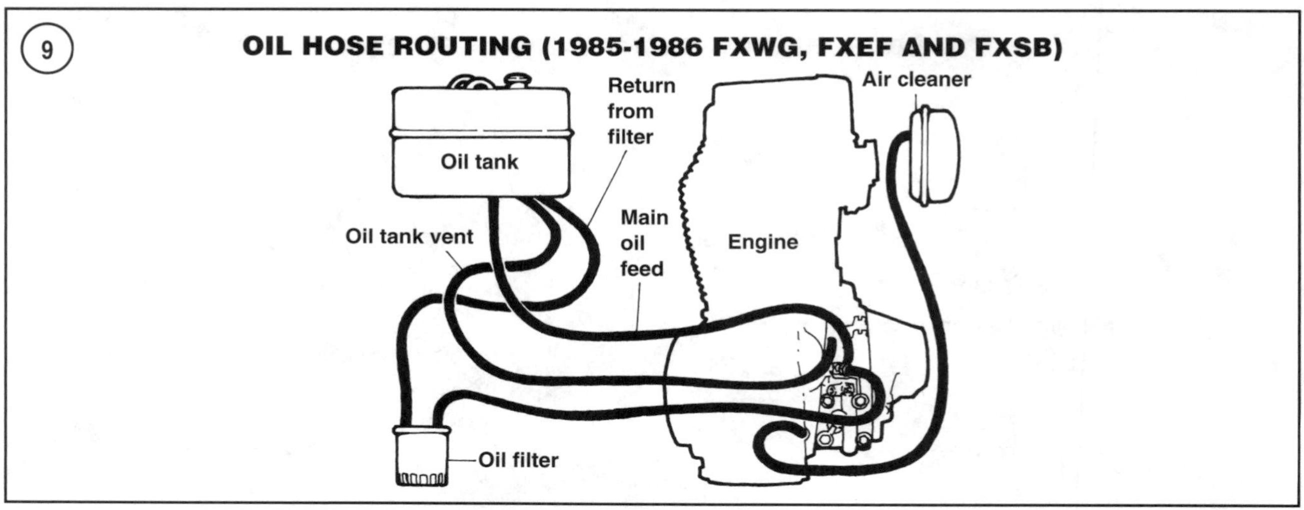

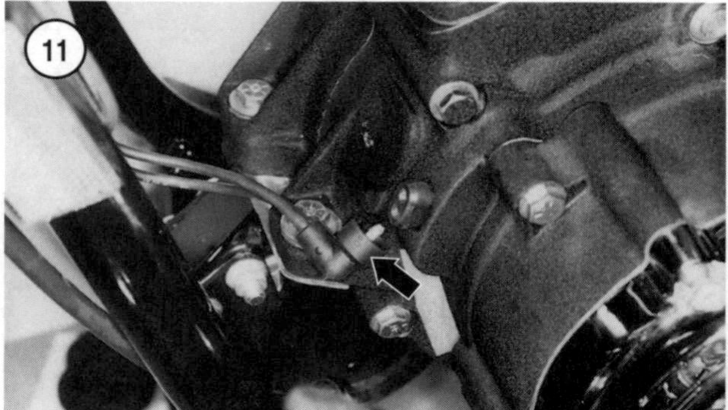

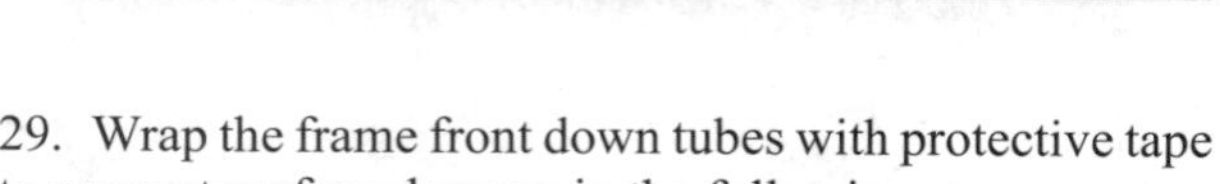

29. Wrap the frame front down tubes with protective tape to prevent surface damage in the following steps.

30. Cover both rocker covers with foam padding to protect the finish.

31. Support the transmission case with a jack or wooden blocks. Apply sufficient jack pressure on the transmission prior to removing the engine-to-transmission mounting bolts.

32. Using a ratchet strap, secure the transmission to the frame so it will not shift after the engine is removed.

33. Remove the front engine mount bolts, washers and nuts (**Figure 16**).

34. Remove the bolts and washers (**Figure 17**) securing the engine to the transmission.

35. Support the engine with a floor jack. Apply enough jack pressure on the crankcase to support it prior to removing the engine mounting bolts.

36. Check the engine to make sure all wiring, hoses and other related components have been disconnected from the engine. Check that nothing will interfere with the removal of the engine from the right side of the frame.

37. Remove the engine from the right side of the frame.

38. Mount the engine in the big twin engine stand (JIMS part No. 1006T) (**Figure 18**) or an equivalent.

39. Service the front engine mount, if necessary.

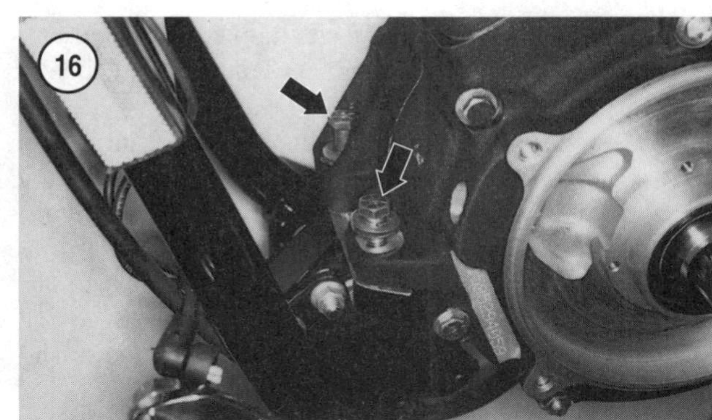

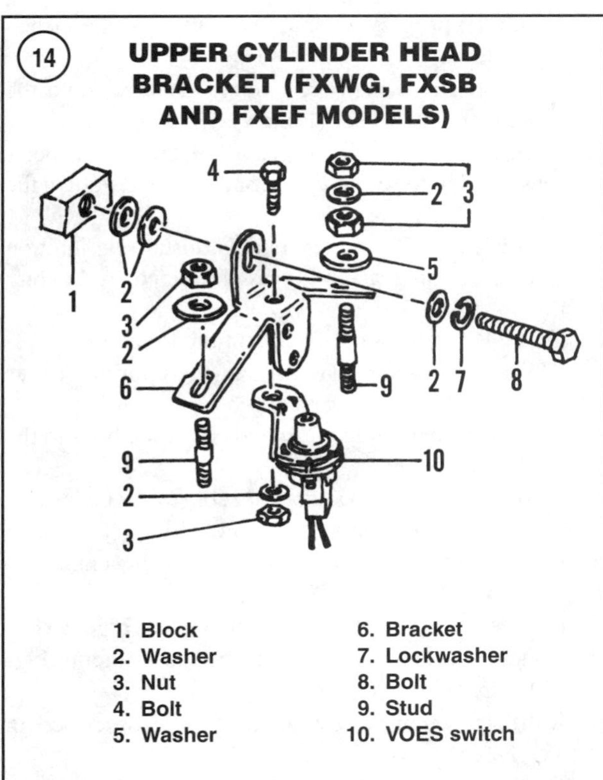

40. Clean the front and rear engine mount bolts and washers in solvent and dry thoroughly.

41. Replace leaking or damaged oil hoses.

Installation

1. Recheck that all wiring, hoses and other related components are out of the way and will not interfere with engine installation.

2. Correctly position a floor jack and piece of wood under the frame to support the engine when it is installed into the frame.
3. Install the engine from the right side of the frame and place it on the floor jack. Apply enough jack pressure on the crankcase to support it prior to installing the engine mounting bolts.
4. Slide the engine assembly toward the rear next to the transmission.
5. Install the rear engine-to-transmission bolts and washers (**Figure 17**) hand-tight at this time.
6. Install the front two bolts, washers and nuts (**Figure 16**) securing the engine to the lower mounting bracket front isolator. Tighten finger-tight at this time.
7. Tighten the engine-to-transmission bolts 33-38 ft.-lb. (45-52 N•m).
8. Tighten the engine front lower mounting bolts and nuts to 33-38 ft.-lb. (45-52 N•m).
9. Remove the ratchet strap from the transmission and frame.
10. Remove the floor jack.
11. Remove the protective tape from the frame front down tubes.
12. Remove the foam padding from the rocker covers.
13. Install the clutch cable onto the lower portion of the crankcase as described under *Clutch Cable Replacement* in Chapter Five.
14. Connect the hose to the breather cover.
15A. On FXWG, FXSB and FXEF models, from the left side of the engine, install the upper cylinder head stabilizer bar and bracket assembly (**Figure 14**). Tighten the bolts and nuts securely.
15B. On all other models, from the left side of the engine stabilizer, perform the following:
   a. Install the stabilizer link and upper mounting bracket assembly onto the frame and engine.
   b. Install the two bolts and washers securing the upper mounting bracket to the cylinder heads. Tighten to 28-35 ft.-lb. (38-47 N•m).
   c. Install the bolt and nut securing the inboard end of the stabilizing link to the frame and tighten securely.
16. Install the voltage regulator as described in Chapter Nine.
17. Install the alternator stator and rotor assembly as described in Chapter Nine.
18. Install a *new* O-ring (**Figure 19**) onto the crankcase shoulder.
19. Install the primary chaincase inner housing and assembly as described in Chapter Five.
20. Adjust the clutch and primary chain as described in Chapter Three.

21. Install the primary chain outer housing as described in Chapter Five.
22. On models so equipped, connect the wires onto the engine temperature sensor (**Figure 13**).
23. On models so equipped, install the crankshaft position sensor (**Figure 12**) onto the crankcase and tighten the screws securely.
24. On FLH and FLT series models, install the ignition coil and spark plug assembly as described in Chapter Nine.
25. On FXR series models, perform the following:
   a. Install the ignition switch and the ignition coil as described in Chapter Nine.
   b. Connect spark plug wires and cap assemblies to the spark plugs.
   c. Connect the choke knob and cable to the upper cylinder stabilizer bar and bracket.
26. Connect the alternator connector to the crankcase (**Figure 11**).
27. Connect the wire to the oil pressure switch (**Figure 10**).
28. Connect the engine-to-oil tank oil lines. Refer to **Figures 3-9**). Install *new* clamps.
29. Refill the engine oil and oil tank as described in Chapter Three.
30. On wet-clutch models, refill the primary chaincase as described in Chapter Three.
31. Install all four footboards as described in Chapter Fifteen.
32. Install the rear brake pedal as described in Chapter Thirteen.
33. Install the exhaust system as described in Chapter Eight.
34A. On carbureted models, install the carburetor as described in Chapter Eight.
34B. On fuel-injected models, install the fuel injection induction module as described in Chapter Eight.
35. Install the air filter and backing plate as described in Chapter Eight.

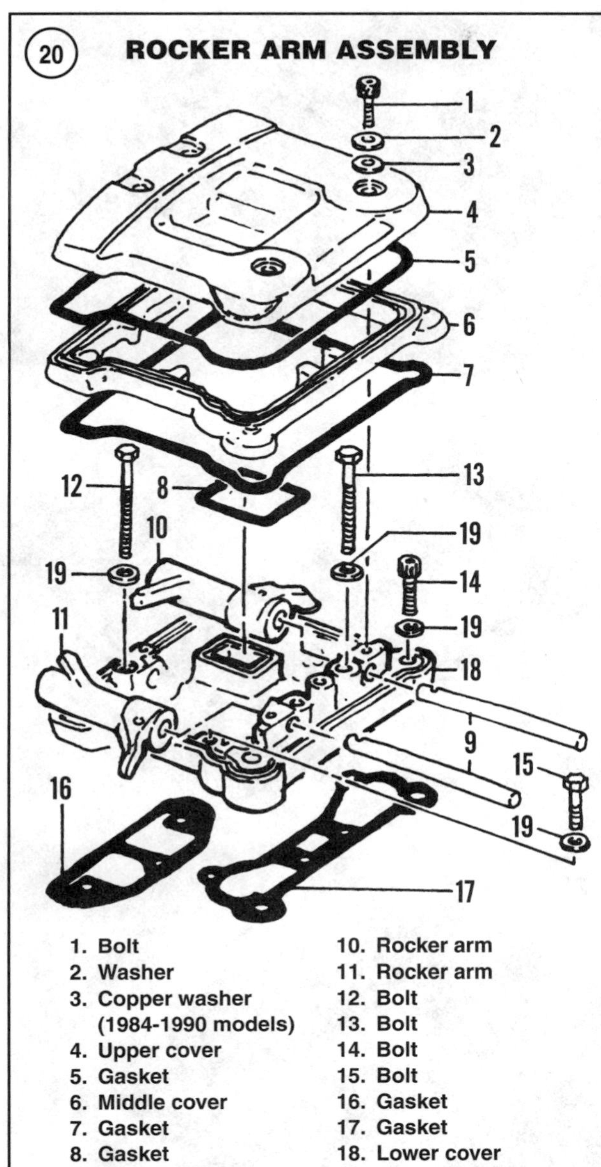

36. On models so equipped, install the inner front fairing as described in Chapter Fifteen.
37. Install both frame side covers as described in Chapter Fifteen.
38. On models so equipped, install both saddlebags as described in Chapter Fifteen.
39. Install the fuel tank as described in Chapter Nine.
40. Remove the motorcycle stand or floor jack.
41. Connect the negative battery cable as described in Chapter Nine.
42. Remove the seat as described in Chapter Fifteen.
43. Check vehicle alignment as described in Chapter Nine.
44. Start the engine and check for leaks.

ROCKER ARMS AND ROCKER ARM COVERS

Refer to **Figure 20**.

Removal

1. If the engine is mounted in the frame, perform the following:
   a. Perform Steps 1-11 under *Engine Removal* in this chapter.
   b. Remove the upper cylinder head mounting bracket (**Figure 15**).
2. On FXR series models, remove the ignition coil bracket assembly (**Figure 21**) and move it out of the way.
3. Remove the bolts and washers securing the upper rocker cover and remove the cover and gasket.
4. Remove the middle rocker cover and gasket.
5. Remove both spark plugs as described in Chapter Three to make it easier to rotate the engine by hand.

CAUTION
The piston must be at top dead center (TDC) to avoid damage to the pushrods and rocker arms in the following steps.

6A. With the primary chain cover in place, position the piston for the cylinder being worked on at top dead center (TDC) on the compression stroke as follows:
   a. Support the motorcycle on a stand with the rear wheel off the ground. Refer to *Motorcycle Stands* in Chapter Ten.
   b. Shift the transmission into fourth or fifth gear.
   c. Rotate the rear wheel in the direction of normal rotation.
   d. Stop rotating the rear wheel when both the intake and exhaust valves are closed.

4

e. Wiggle both rocker arms. There should be free play indicating that both valves are closed. This indicates that the piston is at top dead center (TDC) on the compression stroke and both valves are closed. Also, the pushrods are in the unloaded position.

f. Look into the spark plug hole with a flashlight and verify that the piston is at TDC.

6B. With the primary chain cover removed, position the piston for the cylinder being worked on at top dead center (TDC) on the compression stroke as follows:

a. Shift the transmission into neutral.

b. Install the sprocket shaft nut onto the end of the left side of the crankshaft.

c. Place a socket or wrench on the compensating sprocket shaft nut.

d. Rotate the compensating sprocket shaft *counter-clockwise* until both the intake and exhaust valves are closed.

e. Wiggle both rocker arms. There should be free play indicating that both valves are closed. This indicates that the piston is at top dead center (TDC) on the compression stroke and both valves are closed. Also, the pushrods are in the unloaded position.

f. Look into the spark plug hole with a flashlight and verify that the piston is at TDC.

7. Remove the pushrod covers as follows:

a. Using a screwdriver, pry the spring cap retainer (**Figure 22**) out from between the cylinder head and spring cap. Remove the spring cap retainer.

b. Slide the upper cover down (A, **Figure 23**).

c. Repeat for the opposite pushrod cover.

8. Mark each pushrod as to its top and bottom position and its position in the cylinder head. The pushrods must be installed in their original positions during assembly.

CAUTION

When removing the pushrods in the following steps, do not mix the parts from each set. When reinstalling the original pushrods, install them so that each end faces in its original operating position. The pushrods develop a set wear pattern and installing them upside down may cause rapid wear to the pushrod, lifter and rocker arm.

9. Remove the bolts (A, **Figure 24**) securing the lower rocker cover and rocker arms.

10. Remove the rocker arms and the lower rocker cover (B, **Figure 24**) as an assembly (**Figure 25**).

11. Remove the intake (A, **Figure 26**) and exhaust (B) pushrods up through the cylinder head.

12. Remove the pushrod cover assemblies (B, **Figure 23**).
13. Remove the upper (**Figure 27**) and lower (**Figure 28**) pushrod cover O-ring and washer.
14. Disassemble and inspect the rocker arm/cylinder head assembly as described in this chapter.

Installation

1. Install the valve lifters as described in this chapter if they were removed.
2. If the engine has been rotated since it was originally set on TDC, rotate the engine until both lifters (**Figure 29**) for the cylinder head being worked on seat onto the lowest camshaft position (base circle).
3. Install the pushrod covers (B, **Figure 23**) as follows:
   a. Install a *new* lower O-ring and washer (**Figure 28**) into the lifter block (**Figure 30**).
   b. Install a *new* upper O-ring (**Figure 27**) into the cutout in the bottom of the cylinder head.
   c. If the pushrod covers were disassembled, assemble them as described under *Pushrods and Pushrod Covers* in this chapter.
   d. Refer to the marks made during removal and install the pushrod sets (**Figure 31**) in the correct locations in the crankcase.
   e. Install the pushrod cover into the valve lifter block (**Figure 32**) and O-ring.
4. If installing *new* pushrods, refer to the following identification marks:
   a. Purple: rear exhaust (A, **Figure 33**).
   b. Blue: rear intake (B, **Figure 33**).
   c. Yellow: front intake (C, **Figure 33**).
   d. Green: front exhaust (D, **Figure 33**).
5. Install the pushrods as follows:
   a. Center the pushrod cover in between the cylinder head and valve lifter block.

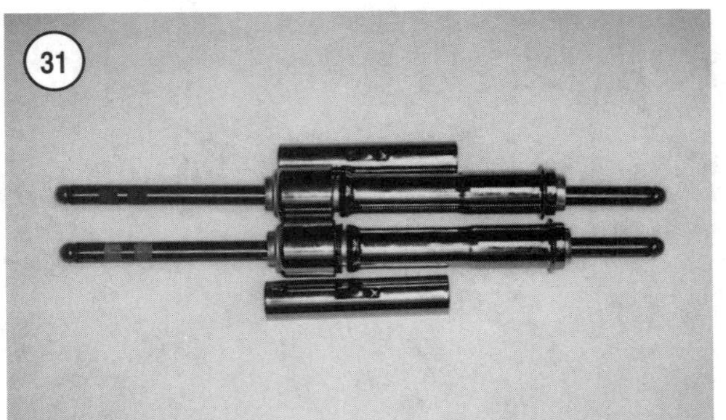

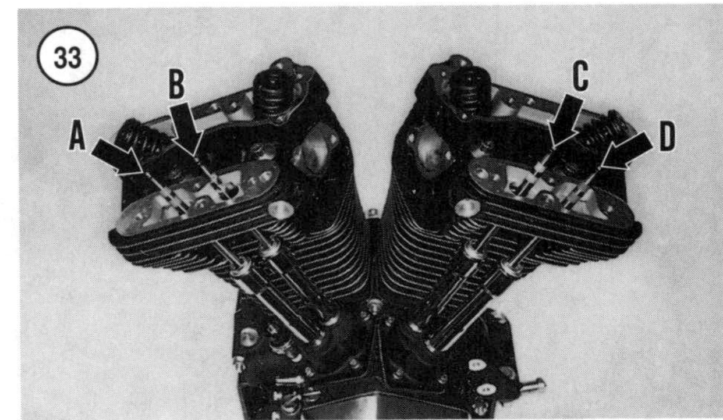

b. If the pushrods were labeled during removal, install each pushrod in the original location in the cylinder head.

c. If the pushrods were not labeled during removal, refer to Step 12 and install each pushrod in the original location in the cylinder head.

6. Install *new* lower rocker cover gaskets (**Figure 34**) onto the cylinder head.

7. Install the lower rocker cover and rocker arm assembly (B, **Figure 24**) onto the cylinder head while guiding the pushrod ends into the rocker arm sockets (A, **Figure 35**).

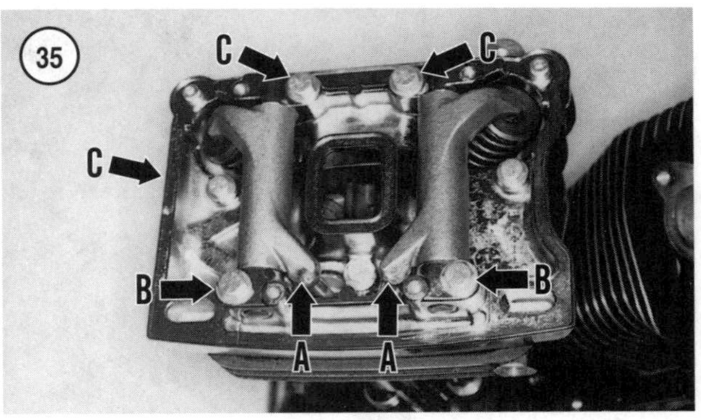

NOTE

*If the right side bolts will not pass through the rocker arm, the notch in the rocker arm shaft is not properly aligned with the mating bolt hole (**Figure 36**). Realign if necessary.*

8. Install the lower rocker arm cover bolts as follows. The longer bolts (B, **Figure 35**) on the right side (pushrod side) and the shorter bolts (C) on the left side of the engine.

CAUTION

To avoid damaging a pushrod, rocker arms or valves, tighten the lower rocker arm cover bolts evenly and in a crisscross pat-

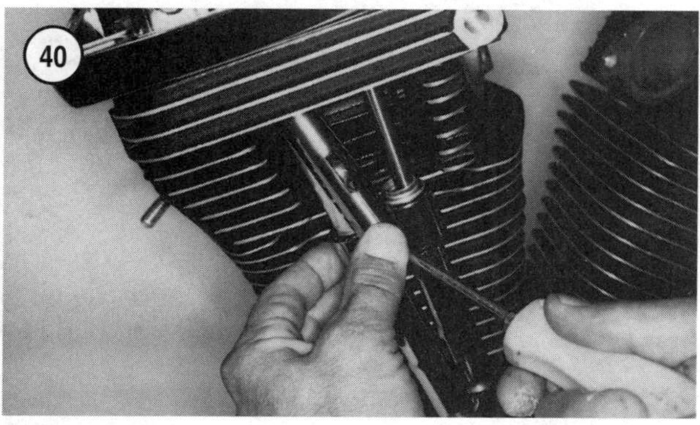

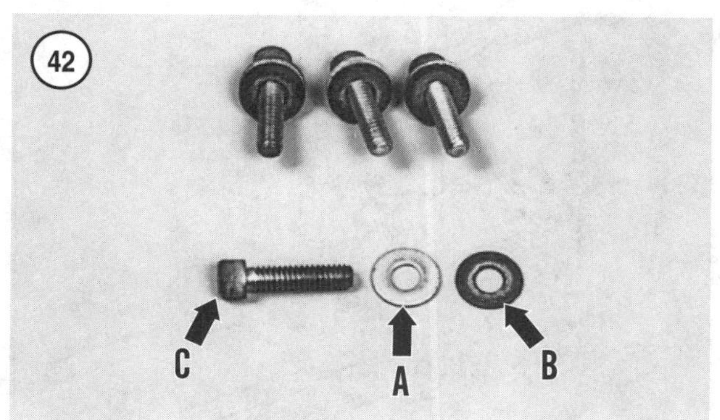

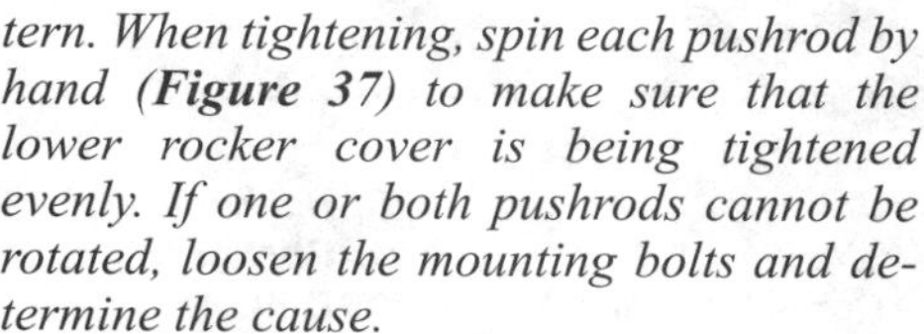

*tern. When tightening, spin each pushrod by hand (**Figure 37**) to make sure that the lower rocker cover is being tightened evenly. If one or both pushrods cannot be rotated, loosen the mounting bolts and determine the cause.*

9. Tighten the lower rocker cover bolts in a crisscross pattern to 15-18 ft.-lb. (20-25 N•m). Tighten the bolts in small increments to help bleed the lifters.

10. Push the upper pushrod cover up (**Figure 38**) and seat it in the cylinder head with a screwdriver (**Figure 39**).

11. Position the spring cap retainer between the cap and the cylinder head and pry it into place with a screwdriver (**Figure 40**).

12. Repeat Step 10 and 11 for the other pushrod cover (**Figure 41**).

13. Install a *new* gasket (C, **Figure 35**) onto the lower pushrod cover and install the middle pushrod cover.

14. Install a *new* gasket onto the middle pushrod cover.

15. Install the upper pushrod cover onto the middle pushrod cover.

16A. On 1984-1990 models, install the steel washer (A, **Figure 42**) followed by the copper washer (B) onto the bolt (C) on the upper pushrod cover.

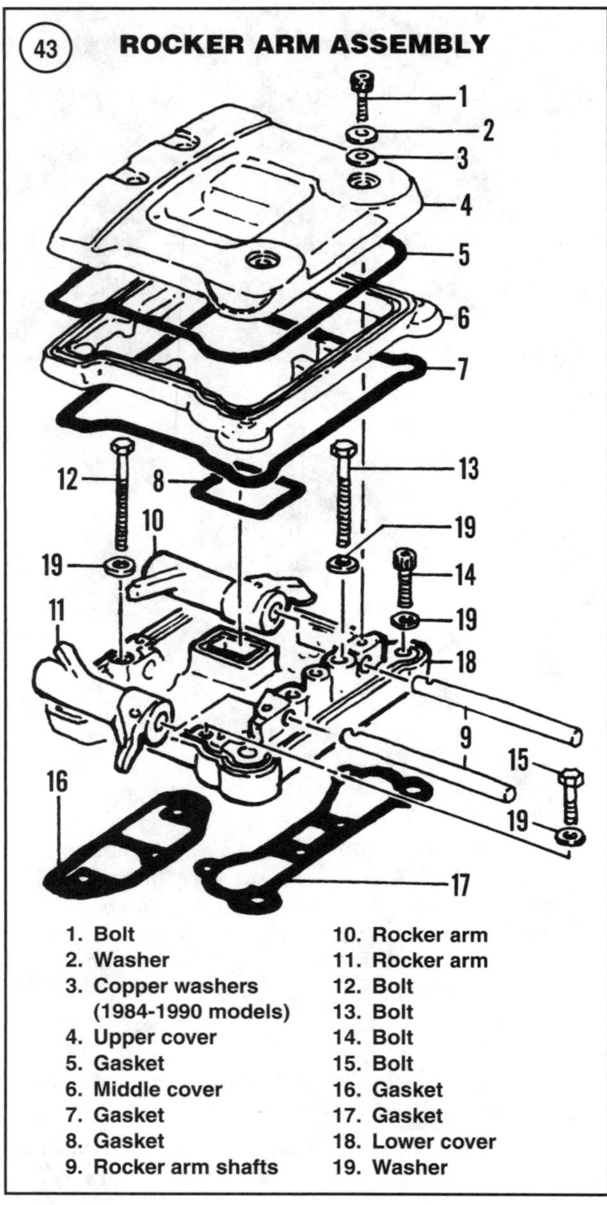

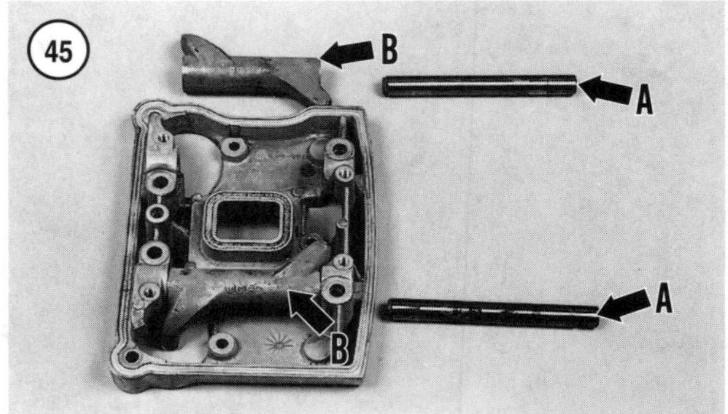

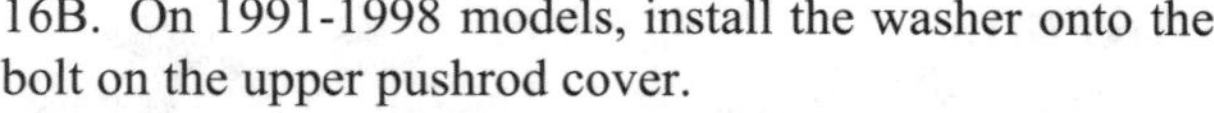

16B. On 1991-1998 models, install the washer onto the bolt on the upper pushrod cover.

17. Check that the middle rocker cover is spaced evenly on all sides. Then tighten the upper cover 1/4-in. bolts to 124-159 in.-lb. (13-18 N•m) in a crisscross pattern.

Rocker Arm Disassembly/Assembly

Refer to **Figure 43**.

1. Remove the lower rocker cover as described in this section.

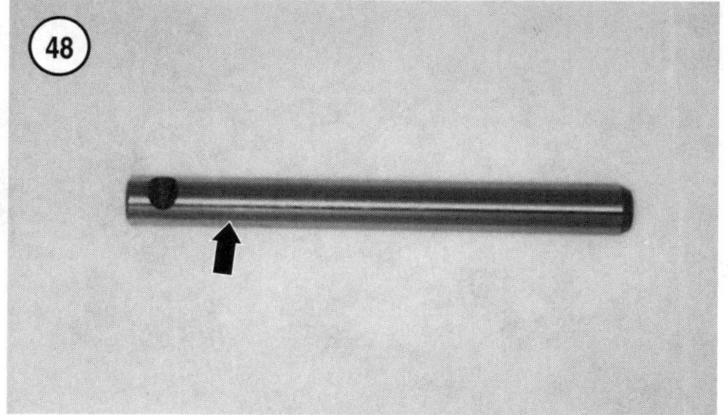

48

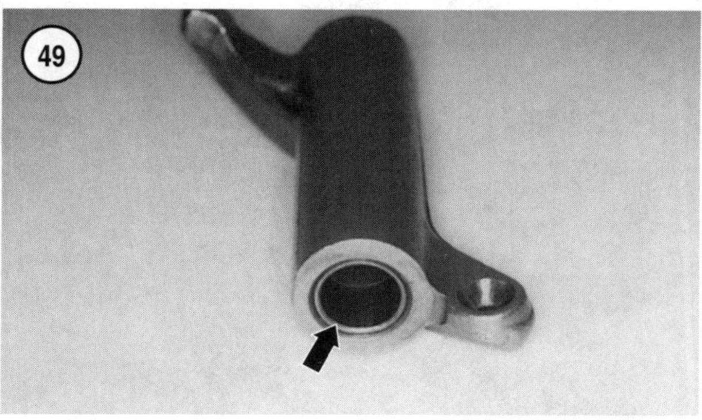

49

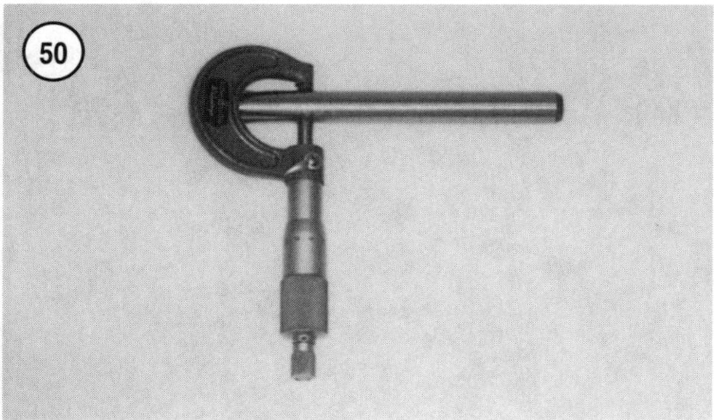

50

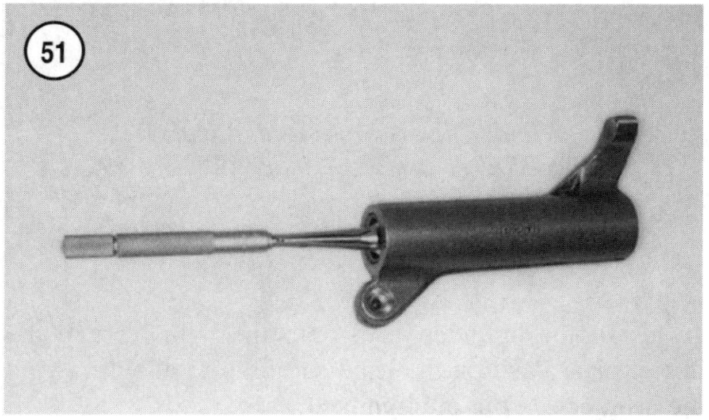

51

2. Before disassembling the rocker arms, measure the rocker arm side clearance as follows:
   a. Insert a flat feeler gauge between the rocker arm end and the side of the lower rocker cover (**Figure 44**).
   b. Record the dimension.
   c. Repeat for each rocker arm.
   d. Replace the rocker arm and/or the lower rocker cover if the end clearance is not within the specification in **Table 2**.

3. Prior to disassembling the rocker arms, mark each one with an IN (intake) or EX (exhaust) to ensure they will be installed in their original positions.
4. Remove the rocker arm shafts (A, **Figure 45**) and remove the rocker arms (B).
5. Thoroughly clean all parts in solvent and dry with compressed air. Blow through all oil passages.
6. Inspect all parts as described in this section.
7. Install the rocker arm in its original position (**Figure 46**).
8. Install the rocker arm shaft partway into the lower rocker cover and rocker arm.
9. Align the notch in the rocker arm shaft (A, **Figure 47**) with the mating bolt hole (B) in the lower rocker cover and install the shaft all the way. Check for correct alignment. Realign if necessary.
10. Repeat Steps 7-9 for the remaining rocker arm and shaft.

4

Rocker Arm Component Inspection

1. Examine the rocker arm pads and ball sockets for pitting and excessive wear; replace the rocker arms if necessary.
2. Examine the rocker arm shaft (**Figure 48**) for scoring, ridge wear or other damage. If these conditions are present, replace the rocker arm shaft. If the shaft does not show any wear or damage, continue with Step 8.
3. Check the rocker arm bushing (**Figure 49**) for wear or scoring.
4. Measure the rocker arm shaft diameter (**Figure 50**) where it contacts the rocker arm bushings and lower rocker cover. Measure both ends of the shaft. Record each measurement.
5. Measure the rocker arm bushing inside diameter (**Figure 51**) and the lower rocker cover bore diameter. Record each measurement.
6. Subtract the measurements taken in Step 4 from those taken in Step 5 to obtain the following rocker arm shaft measurements:
   a. Shaft-to-lower rocker cover.
   b. Shaft-to-rocker arm bushing.

7. Replace the rocker arm, the bushing or the lower rocker cover if the clearance exceeds the specifications in **Table 2**.

8. Inspect the rocker arm shaft contact surfaces (**Figure 52**) on the lower rocker cover for wear or elongation.
9. Inspect the gasket surfaces of the upper rocker cover (A, **Figure 53**) and the middle rocker cover (B) for damage or warp.
10. Inspect the gasket surfaces of the lower rocker cover (**Figure 54**) for damage or warp.

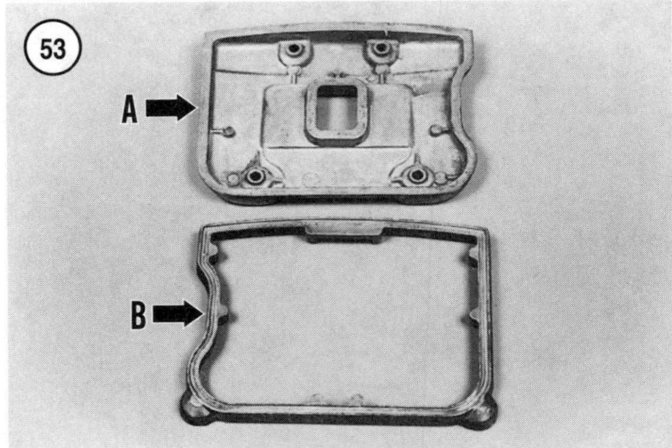

CYLINDER HEAD

Removal

Refer to **Figure 55**.

1. Remove the rocker arm assembly as described in this chapter.
2. Remove the bolts (**Figure 56**) securing the cylinder head one-eighth turn at a time in the pattern shown in **Figure 57**.
3. Tap the cylinder head with a plastic mallet to loosen it. Then lift it off the cylinder.
4. Remove and discard the cylinder head gasket.
5. Remove the O-rings and dowel pins (**Figure 58**) from the cylinder.
6. Repeat these steps for the opposite cylinder head.
7. Repeat Steps 1-6 and remove the opposite cylinder head assembly.
8. Inspect the cylinder head assembly as described in this section.

Installation

1. If removed, install the piston and cylinder as described in this chapter.
2. Assemble and inspect the rocker arm/cylinder head assembly as described in this chapter.
3. Install the two dowel pins (**Figure 58**) into the top of the cylinder.
4. Install a *new* O-ring over each dowel pin. Apply a light coat of clean engine oil to the O-rings.

CAUTION
Because the O-rings center the head gasket on the cylinder, install them before installing the head gasket.

5. Install a *new* cylinder head gasket onto the cylinder.

CAUTION
Do not use sealer on the cylinder head gasket. If using an aftermarket head gasket, follow the manufacturer's instructions for gasket installation.

NOTE
The cylinder heads are ***not identical****. Refer to the FRONT or REAR mark (**Figure 59**) cast into the top surface of the cylinder head.*

6. Install the cylinder head onto the cylinder and the dowel pins. Position the head carefully to avoid moving the head gasket out of alignment.

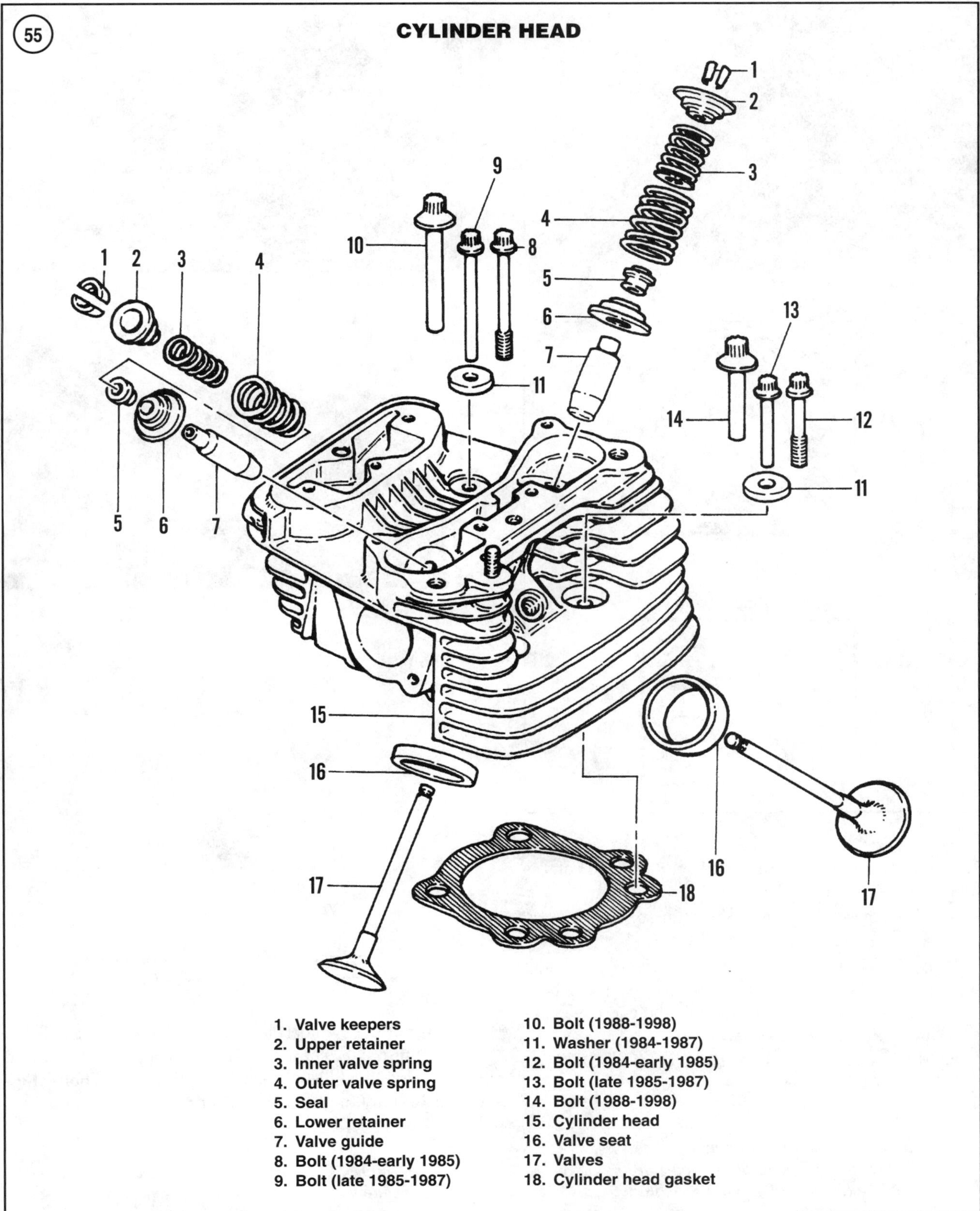

1. Valve keepers
2. Upper retainer
3. Inner valve spring
4. Outer valve spring
5. Seal
6. Lower retainer
7. Valve guide
8. Bolt (1984-early 1985)
9. Bolt (late 1985-1987)
10. Bolt (1988-1998)
11. Washer (1984-1987)
12. Bolt (1984-early 1985)
13. Bolt (late 1985-1987)
14. Bolt (1988-1998)
15. Cylinder head
16. Valve seat
17. Valves
18. Cylinder head gasket

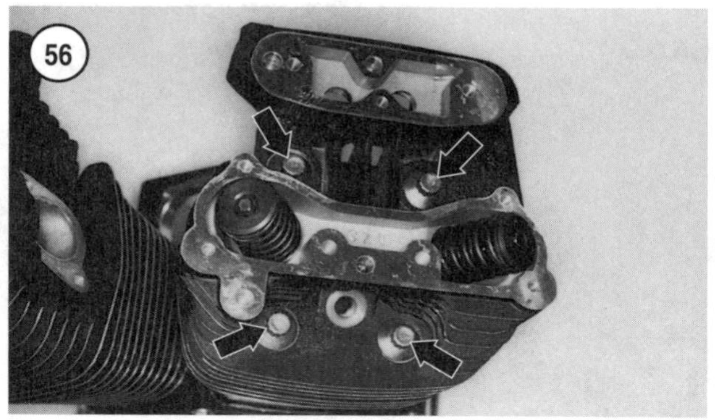
56

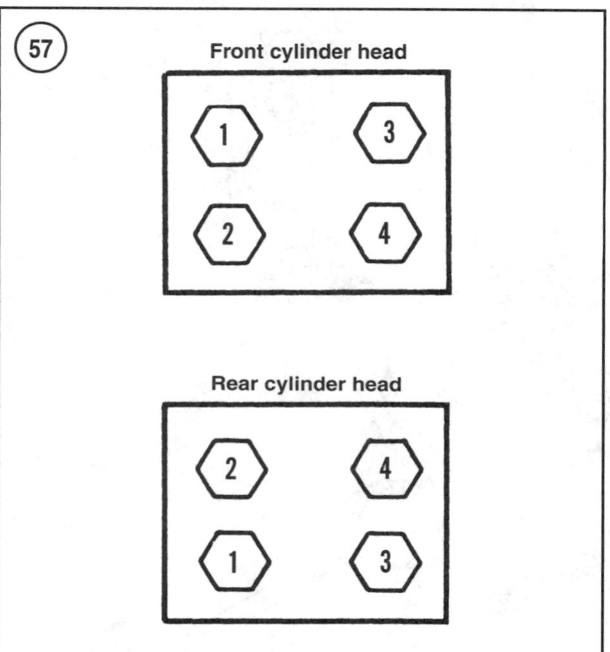

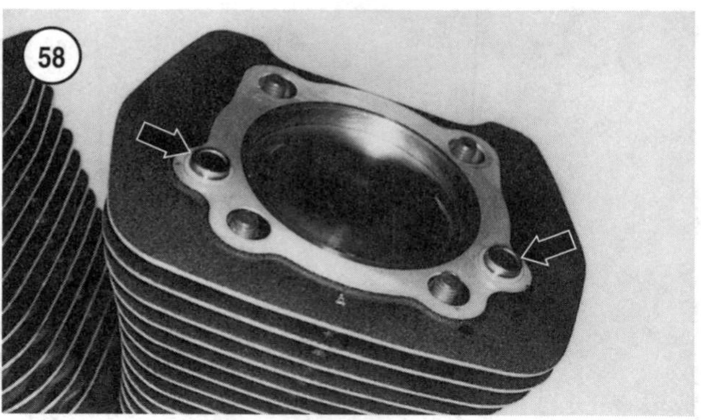
58

59

60

7. Lubricate the cylinder studs and cylinder head bolts as follows:
   a. Clean the cylinder head bolts in solvent and dry with compressed air.
   b. Apply clean engine oil to the cylinder head bolt threads and to the flat shoulder surface on each bolt. Wipe off any excess oil from the bolts. Leave only an oil film on these surfaces.
   c. Make sure to install washers onto the bolts on 1984-1987 models.

NOTE
*The original equipment cylinder head bolts and washers (**Figure 60**, typical) are made of Grade 8 material. Do not substitute these items with a part of lesser strength. Late style cylinder head washers **cannot** be used on early style cylinder head bolts.*

8. Install the cylinder head long bolts in the center bolt holes; install the short bolts in the outer bolt holes next to the spark plug hole. Tighten the cylinder head bolts (**Figure 56**) only finger-tight at this time.

CAUTION
Failure to follow the tightening pattern and sequence in Step 8 may cause cylinder head distortion and gasket leakage.

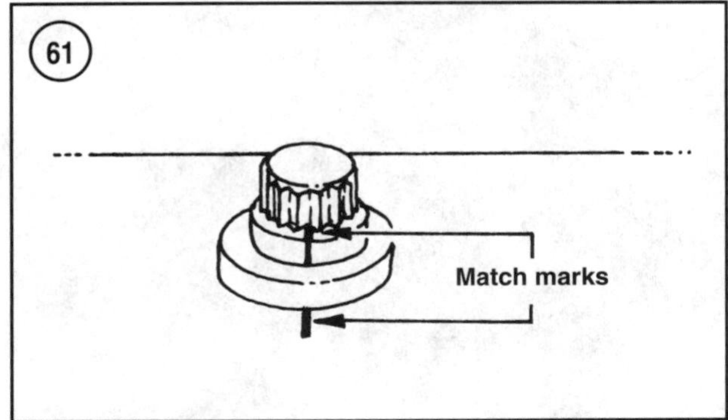

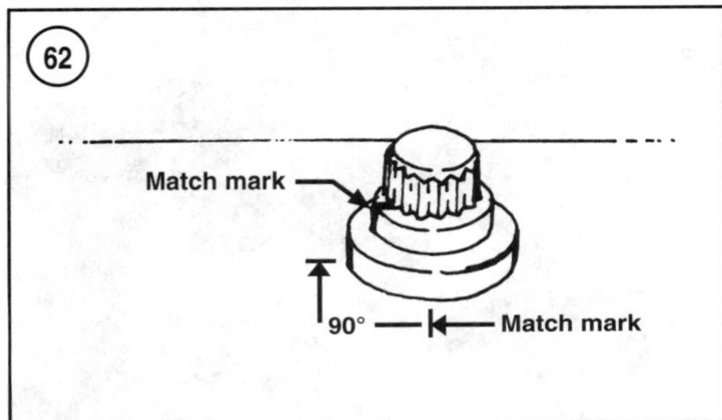

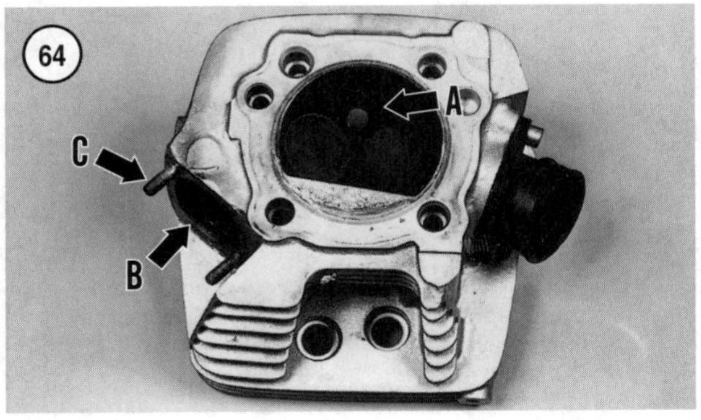

9. Refer to **Figure 57** for the front and rear cylinder head bolt tightening sequence. Tighten the cylinder head bolts as follows:

a. Starting with bolt No. 1, tighten each bolt in order to 80-106 in.-lb. (9-12 N•m).
b. Then once again, starting with bolt No. 1, tighten each bolt in order to 142-168 in.-lb. (16-19 N•m).
c. Make a vertical mark with a permanent marker on each bolt head (**Figure 61**). Make another mark on the cylinder head.
d. Following the tightening sequence in **Figure 57**, turn each bolt head a quarter turn *clockwise* using the match marks as a guide (**Figure 62**).
e. When the marks appear as shown in **Figure 62**, the tightening sequence is complete.
f. Repeat for the opposite cylinder head.

4

Inspection

Refer to **Figure 55**.

1. Thoroughly clean the outside of the cylinder head. Use a stiff brush, soap and water and remove all debris from the cooling fins (A, **Figure 63**). If necessary, use a piece of wood and scrape away any lodged dirt. Clogged cooling fins can cause overheating, leading to possible engine damage.
2. Without removing the valves, use a wire brush to remove all carbon deposits from the combustion chamber (A, **Figure 64**). Use a fine wire brush dipped in solvent or make a scraper from hard wood. Take care not to damage the head, valves or spark plug threads.

CAUTION
Cleaning the combustion chamber with the valves removed can damage the surfaces of the valve seat. A damaged or even slightly scratched valve seat will cause poor valve seating.

3. Examine the spark plug threads (B, **Figure 63**) in the cylinder head for damage. If damage is minor, or if the threads are dirty or clogged with carbon, use a spark plug thread tap (**Figure 65**) to clean the threads following the manufacturer's instructions. If thread damage is severe, restore the threads by installing a steel thread insert. Purchase thread insert kits at automotive supply stores or have them installed by a Harley-Davidson dealership or machine shop.

CAUTION
Aluminum spark plug threads commonly are damaged due to galling, cross-threading and overtightening. To prevent galling, apply an antiseize compound to the plug

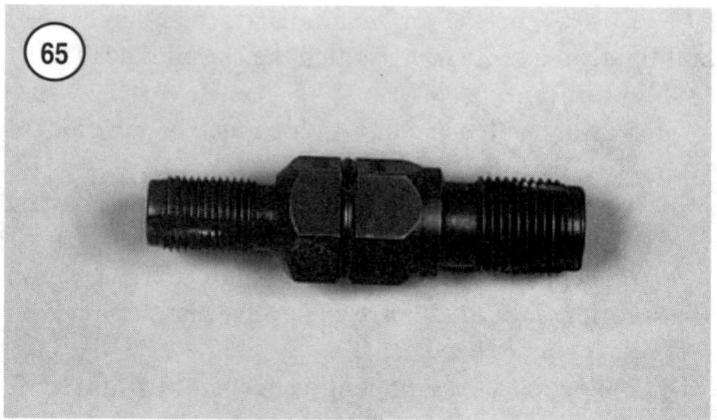

65

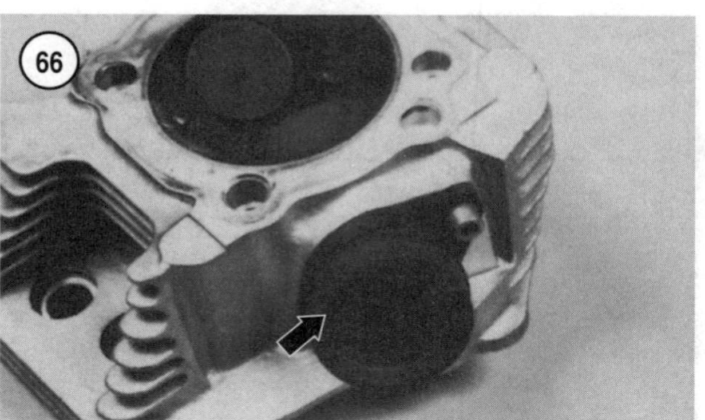

66

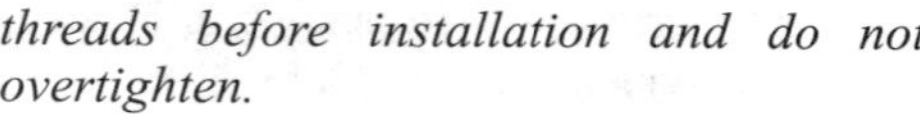

threads before installation and do not overtighten.

NOTE

When using a tap to clean spark plug threads, coat the tap with an aluminum tap-cutting fluid or kerosene.

4. After all carbon is removed from combustion chambers and valve ports and, if necessary, the spark plug thread hole is repaired, clean the entire head in solvent. Blow dry with compressed air.
5. Examine the crown on the piston. The crown should show no signs of wear or damage. If the crown appears pecked or spongy, also check the spark plug, valves and combustion chamber for aluminum deposits. If these deposits are found, the cylinder has overheated. Check for a lean fuel mixture or other conditions that could result in preignition.
6. On 1984-1989 models, check the intake manifolds (**Figure 66**) for cracks or tear damage that could allow unfiltered air to enter the engine. Also check the manifold bolts for tightness. If you removed the manifold, install it with a new gasket.
7. Check for cracks in the combustion chamber, the intake port and the exhaust port (B, **Figure 64**). Replace a cracked head if welding cannot repair it.
8. Inspect the exhaust pipe mounting bolt threads (C, **Figure 64**) for damage. Repair with a thread die if damaged.

CAUTION

If the cylinder head is bead-blasted, clean the head thoroughly with solvent and then with hot soapy water. Residual grit seats in small crevices and other areas and can be hard to remove. Also run a tap through each exposed thread to remove grit from the threads. Residue grit left in the engine will cause premature wear.

67

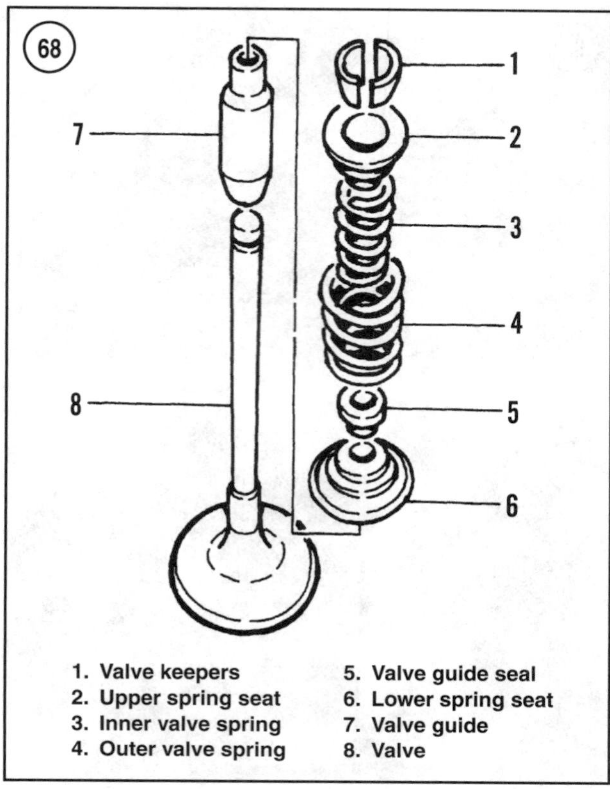

1. Valve keepers
2. Upper spring seat
3. Inner valve spring
4. Outer valve spring
5. Valve guide seal
6. Lower spring seat
7. Valve guide
8. Valve

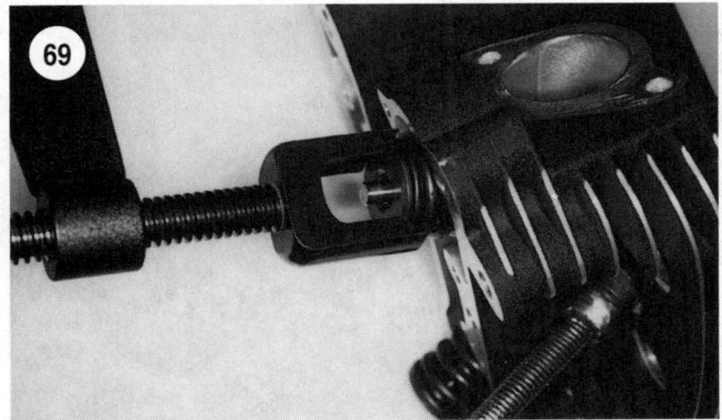

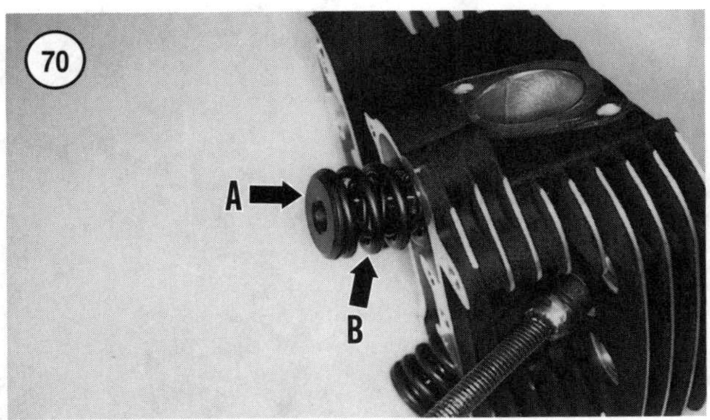

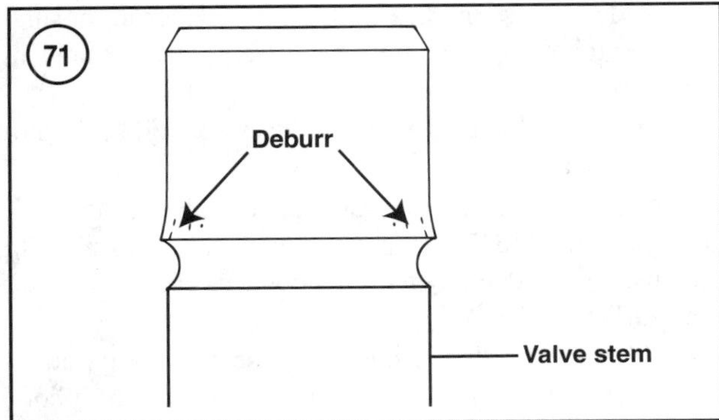

9. Thoroughly clean the cylinder head.

10. Place a straightedge across the gasket surface at several points and measure for warp by attempting to insert a feeler gauge between the straightedge and cylinder head at each location (**Figure 67**). Maximum allowable warp is listed in **Table 2**. Distortion or nicks in the cylinder head surface could cause an air leak and result in overheating. If warp exceeds the limit, the cylinder head must be resurfaced or replaced. Consult with a Harley-Davidson dealership or machine shop experienced in this type of work.

11. Check the lower rocker housing mating surfaces for warp using the procedure in Step 10.

12. Check the valves and valve guides as described under *Valves and Valve Components* in this chapter.

4

VALVES AND VALVE COMPONENTS

Complete valve service requires a number of special tools, including a valve spring compressor to remove and install the valves. The following procedures describe how to check for valve component wear and to determine what type of service is required.

Refer to **Figure 68**.

Valve Removal

1. Remove the cylinder head as described in this chapter.
2. Install the valve spring compressor squarely over the valve spring upper retainer (**Figure 69**) and against the valve head.

CAUTION
To avoid loss of spring tension, compress the spring only enough to remove the valve keepers.

3. Tighten the valve spring compressor until the valve keepers separate from the valve stem. Lift the valve keepers out through the valve spring compressor with a magnet or needlenose pliers.
4. Gradually loosen the valve spring compressor and remove it from the cylinder head.
5. Remove the spring retainer (A, **Figure 70**) and the valve springs (B).

CAUTION
*Remove any burrs from the valve stem groove (**Figure 71**) before removing the valve (**Figure 72**); otherwise, the valve guide will be damaged as the valve stem passes through it.*

6. Remove the valve from the cylinder while rotating it slightly.
7. Remove the valve guide oil seal (**Figure 73**).
8. Remove the valve spring lower retainer (**Figure 74**).

CAUTION
Keep the components of each valve assembly together by placing each set in a divided carton, or into separate small boxes or small reclosable plastic bags. Identify the components as either intake or exhaust. If both cylinders are disassembled, also label the components as front and rear. Do not mix components from the valves, or excessive wear may result.

9. Repeat Steps 3-8 and remove the remaining valve.

Valve Installation

1. Clean the end of the valve guide.
2. Install the spring lower retainer (**Figure 74**). Push it down until it is seated on the cylinder head surface.
3. Coat a valve stem with Torco MPZ, molybdenum disulfide paste or equivalent. Install the valve partway into the guide. Then, slowly turn the valve as it enters the oil seal and continue turning it until the valve is installed all the way.
4. Work the valve back and forth in the valve guide to make sure the lubricant is distributed evenly within the valve guide.
5. Withdraw the valve and apply an additional coat of the lubricant.
6. Reinstall the valve into the valve guide but do not push the valve past the top of the valve guide.
7. Use isopropyl alcohol and thoroughly clean all traces of lubricant from the outer surface of the valve guide.

CAUTION
Do not allow any of the retaining compound to enter the valve guide bore.

8. Apply Loctite Retaining Compound RC 620 or an equivalent to the oil seal seating surface and to the outer surface of the valve guide.
9. Push the valve all the way into the cylinder head until it bottoms.

CAUTION
The oil seal will be torn as it passes the valve stem keeper groove if the plastic capsule is not installed in Step 10. The capsule is included in the top end gasket set.

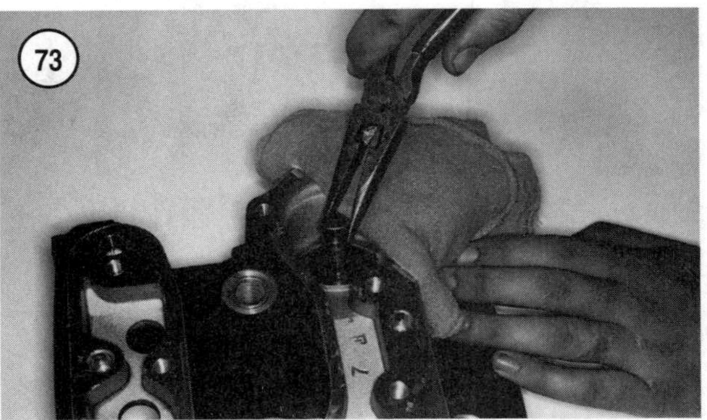
73

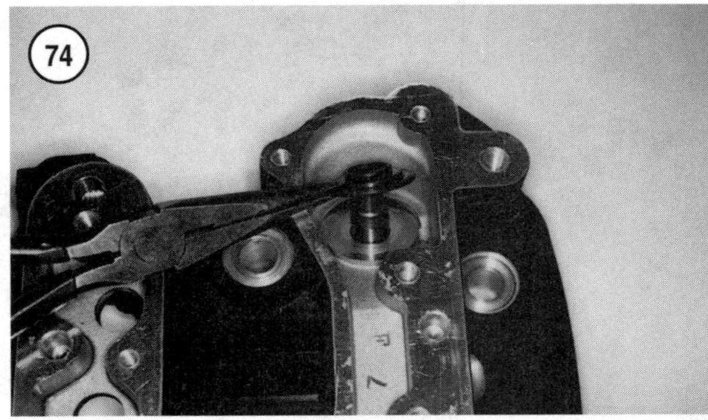
74

10. Hold the valve in place and install the plastic capsule onto the end of the valve stem. Apply a light coat of clean engine oil to the outer surface of the capsule.
11. With the valve held in place, install the oil seal onto the valve stem.

12A. If special tools are used, use JIMS Valve Guide Seal tool (part No. 34643-84) and driver handle (**Figure 75**) and push the oil seal down until it bottoms on the cylinder head surface.

12B. If special tools are not used, use an appropriately sized deep socket and push the oil seal down until it bottoms on the cylinder head surface.

13. Remove the plastic capsule from the valve stem. Keep the capsule as it will be used on the remaining valves.
14. Install the inner valve spring and make sure it is properly seated on the lower spring retainer.
15. Install the outer valve spring and make sure it is properly seated on the lower spring retainer.
16. Install the upper spring retainer on top of the valve springs.

CAUTION
To avoid loss of spring tension, compress the springs only enough to install the valve keepers.

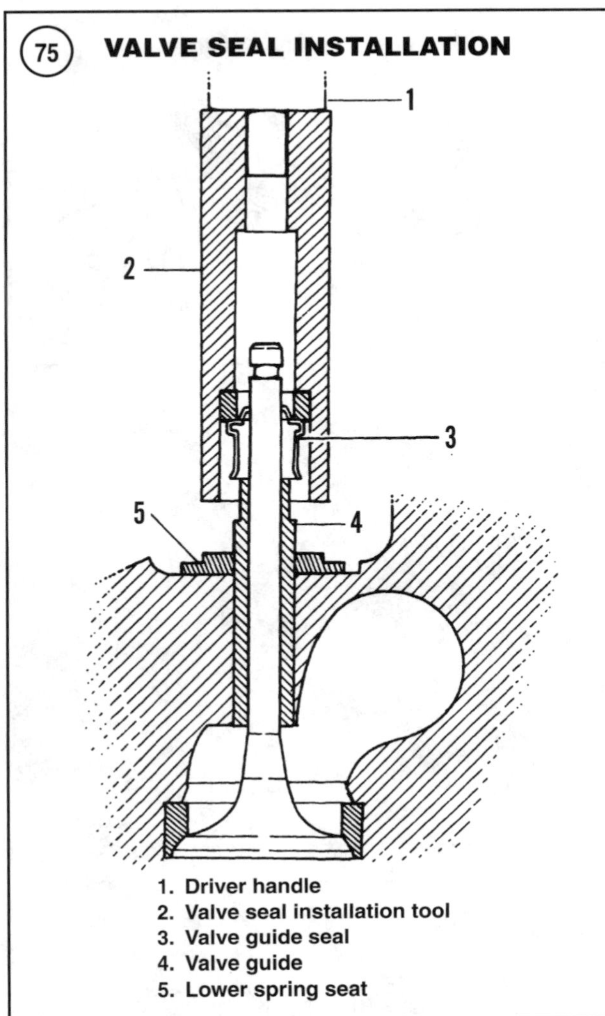

17. Compress the valve springs with a valve spring compressor (**Figure 69**) and install the valve keepers.

18. Make sure both keepers are seated around the valve stem prior to releasing the compressor.

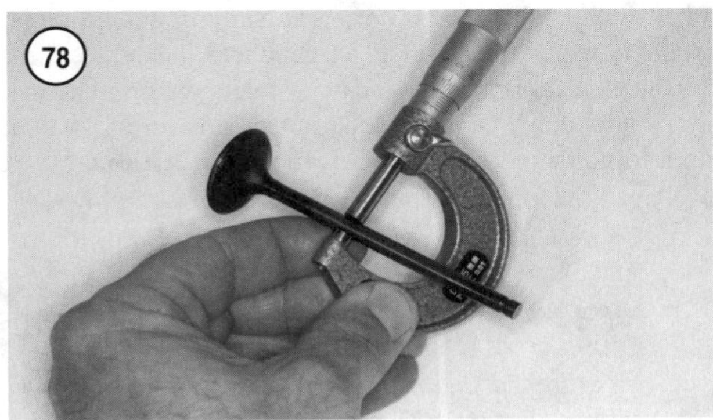

19. Slowly release tension from the compressor and remove it. After removing the compressor, inspect the valve keepers to make sure they are properly seated (**Figure 76**). Tap the end of the valve stem with a *soft-faced* hammer to ensure that the keepers are properly seated.
20. Repeat Steps 1-19 for the remaining valves.
21. Install the cylinder head as described in this chapter.

Valve Inspection

When measuring the valves and valve components in this section, compare the actual measurements to the new and wear limit specifications in **Table 2**. Replace parts that are out of specification or show damage as described in this section.

1. Clean valves in solvent. Do not gouge or damage the valve seating surface.
2. Inspect the valve face. Minor roughness and pitting (**Figure 77**) can be removed by lapping the valve as described in this chapter. Excessive unevenness to the contact surface is an indication that the valve is not serviceable.
3. Inspect the valve stem for wear and roughness. Then measure the valve stem outside diameter with a micrometer (**Figure 78**).

4

4. Remove all carbon and varnish from the valve guides with a stiff spiral wire brush before measuring wear.
5. Measure the valve guide inside diameter with a small hole gauge. Measure at the top, center and bottom positions. Then measure the small hole gauge.
6. Determine the valve stem-to-valve guide clearance by subtracting the valve stem outside diameter from the valve guide inner diameter. Compare this measurement to the specification listed in **Table 2**.
7. If a small hole gauge is not available, insert each valve into its guide. Attach a dial indicator to the valve stem next to the head (**Figure 79**). Hold the valve slightly off its seat and rock it sideways in both directions 90° to each other. If the valve rocks more than slightly, the guide is probably worn. However, as a final check, take the cylinder head to a Harley-Davidson dealership or machine shop and have the valve guides measured. Valve stem-to-guide clearance specifications are in **Table 2**.
8. Check the inner and outer valve springs as follows:
   a. Check each of the valve springs (**Figure 80**) for visual damage.
   b. Use a square and visually check the spring for distortion or tilt (**Figure 81**).
   c. Measure the valve spring free length with a vernier caliper (**Figure 82**) and check against the dimension in **Table 2**.
   d. Repeat for each valve spring.
   e. Replace defective springs as a set (inner and outer).
9. Check the valve spring upper and lower retainers seats for cracks or other damage.
10. Check the fit of the valve keepers on the valve stem end (**Figure 83**). The valve keepers must index tightly into the valve stem groove.
11. Inspect the valve seats (**Figure 84**) in the cylinder head. If worn or burned, they can be reconditioned as described in this chapter. Seats and valves in near-perfect condition can be reconditioned by lapping with fine Carborundum paste. Check as follows:
   a. Clean the valve seat and corresponding valve mating areas with contact cleaner.
   b. Coat the valve seat with layout fluid.
   c. Install the valve into its guide and rotate it against its seat with a valve lapping tool. Refer to *Valve Lapping* in this chapter.
   d. Lift the valve out of the guide and measure the seat width at various points around the seat with a vernier caliper.
   e. Compare the seat width with the specification in **Table 2**. If the seat width is less than specified or uneven, resurface the seats as described in this chapter.

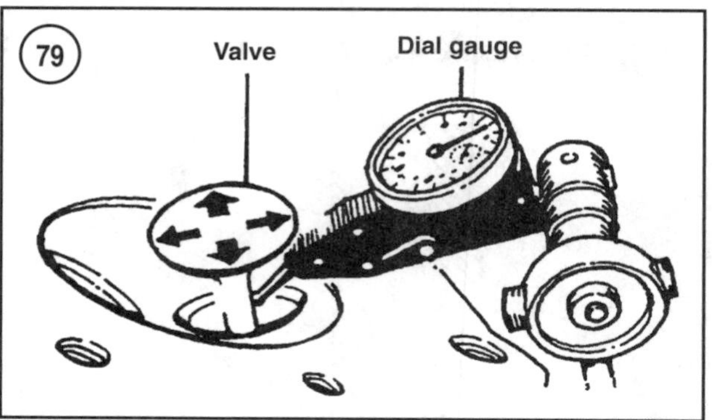

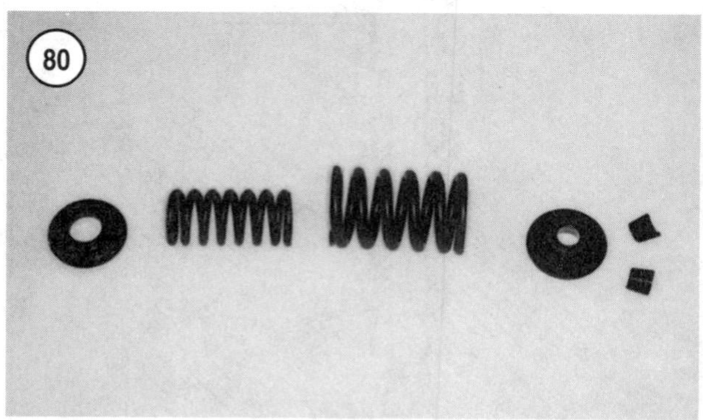

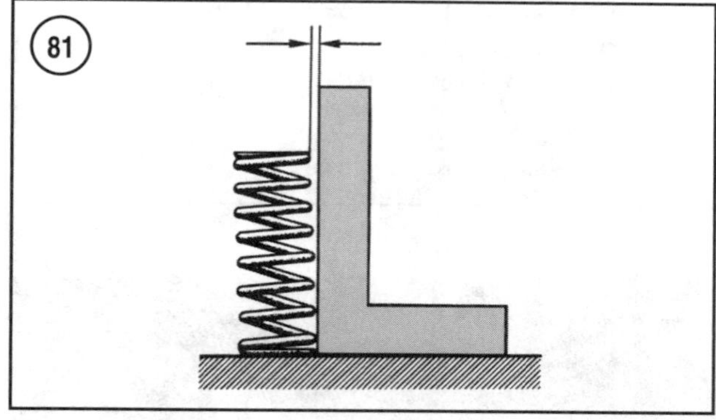

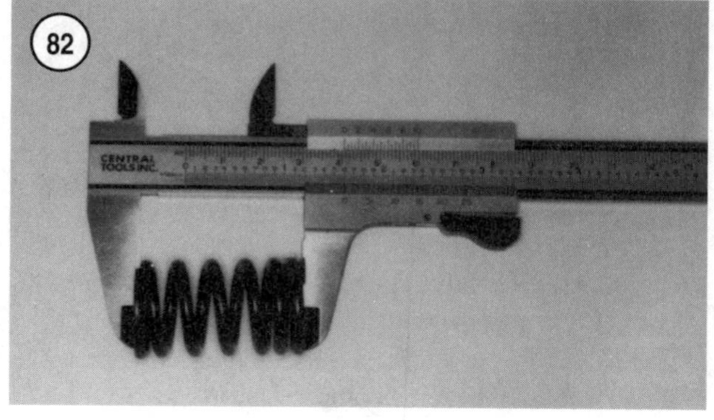

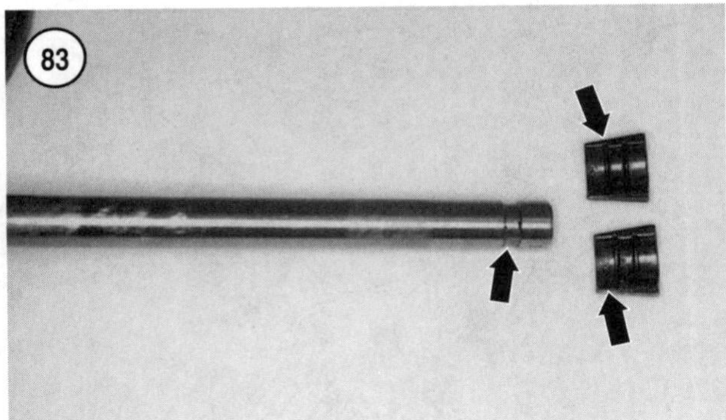

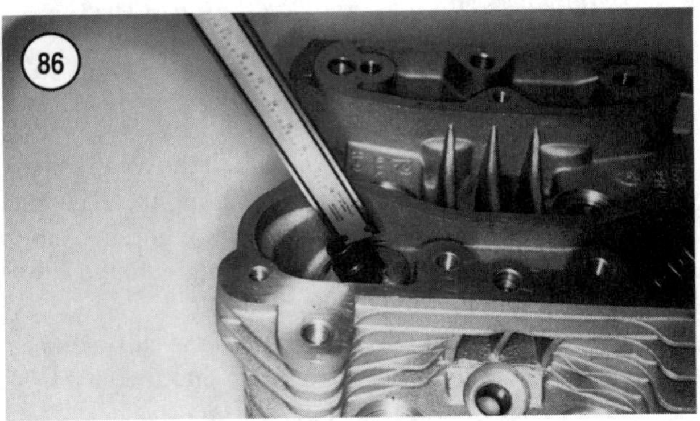

f. Remove all layout fluid residue from the seats and valves.

Valve Guide Replacement

Tools

The following tools or the equivalents are required to replace the valve guides.

1. Driver handle and remover (part No. HD-34740).
2. Valve guide installation sleeve (part No. HD-34741).
3. Valve guide reamer (part No. HD-39932) and T-handle (part No. HD-39847).
4. Valve guide reamer honing lubricant (part No. HD-39964).
5. Valve guide hone (part No. HD-34723).
6. Valve guide brush (part No. HD-34751).

Procedure

1. Place the cylinder head on a wooden surface with the combustion chamber side facing down.
2. Shoulderless valve guides (**Figure 85**) are used. Before the valve guides are removed, note and record the shape of the guide that projects into the combustion chamber. If the valve guide installation tool is *not* going to be used, measure the distance from the face of the guide to the cylinder head surface with a vernier caliper (**Figure 86**). Record the distance for each valve guide. The new valve guides must be installed to this *exact* same height dimension.
3. Remove the valve guides as follows:

CAUTION

Use the valve guide removal tool of the correct size when removing the valve guides; otherwise, the tool might expand the end of the guide. An expanded guide will widen and damage the guide bore in the cylinder head as it passes through it.

NOTE

The valve guides can either be pressed out or driven out. Pressing out is recommended because it lessens the chance of cylinder head damage.

a. Support the cylinder head so that the combustion chamber faces down.
b. If driving the guides out, place the cylinder head on a piece of wood.
c. If pressing the guides out, support the cylinder head in the press so that the valve guide is perpendicular

to the press table with a cylinder head stand (JIMS part No. 39782).

d. Insert the driver handle and remover into the top of the valve guide.

e. Press or drive the valve guide out through the combustion chamber.

f. Repeat substeps a-e for the remaining valve guides.

4. Clean the valve guide bores in the cylinder head.

5. Because the valve guide bores in the cylinder head might have enlarged during removal of the old guides, measure each valve guide bore prior to purchasing the new guides. Then purchase the new valve guides to match its respective bore diameter. Determine the bore diameter as follows:

a. Measure the valve guide bore diameter in the cylinder head with a bore gauge or snap gauge. Record the bore diameter.

b. The new valve guide outside diameter must be 0.0020-0.0033 in. (0.050-0.084 mm) larger than the guide bore in the cylinder head. When purchasing new valve guides, measure the outside of the new guide diameter with a micrometer. If the outside diameter is not within this specification, oversize valve guide(s) must be installed. See a Harley-Davidson dealership for available sizes.

6. Apply a thin coating of molylube or white grease to the entire outer surface of the valve guide before installing it in the cylinder head.

CAUTION

When installing oversize valve guides, make sure to match each guide to its respective bore in the cylinder head.

7. Install the new guide using the driver handle and valve guide installation tools. Press or drive the guide into the cylinder head until the valve guide installation tool bottoms out on the cylinder head surface. When the tool bottoms on the cylinder head surface, the valve guide is installed to the correct height. If the driver handle tool is not used, install the valve guide to the same height recorded prior to removing the valve guide; measure the valve guide installed height using a vernier caliper (**Figure 86**) when installing it.

NOTE

Replacement valve guides are sold with a smaller inside diameter than the valve stem, so the guide must be reamed to fit the valve stem.

8. Ream the new valve guide as follows:

a. Apply a liberal amount of reamer lubricant to the ream bit and to the valve guide bore.

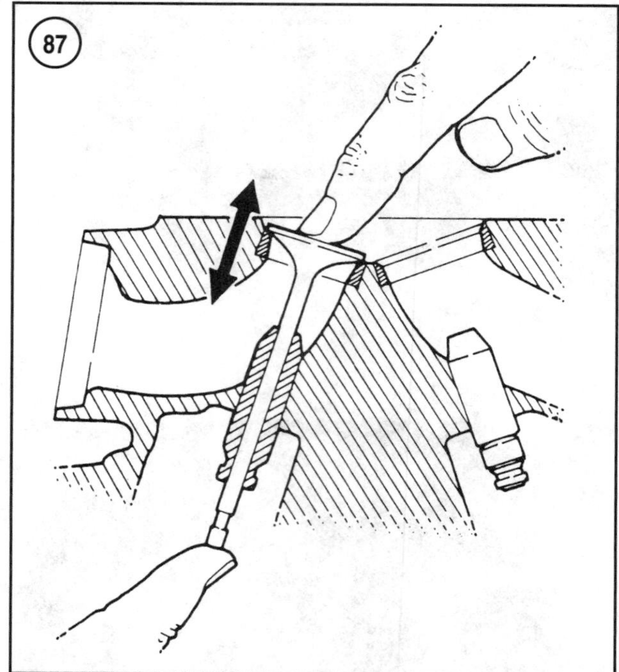

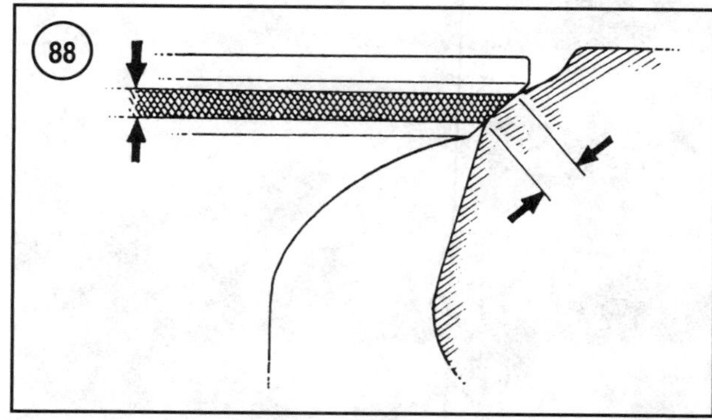

b. Start the reamer straight into the valve guide bore.

CAUTION

Apply pressure only to the end of the drive socket. If pressure is applied to the T-handle, it will result in an uneven, rough cut and a tapered bore.

c. Apply thumb pressure to the end of the drive socket portion of the T-handle while rotating the T-handle *clockwise*. Only *light* pressure is required. Apply additional lubricant to the reamer and into the valve guide while rotating the reamer.

d. Continue to rotate the reamer until the entire bit has traveled through the valve guide and the shank of the reamer rotates freely.

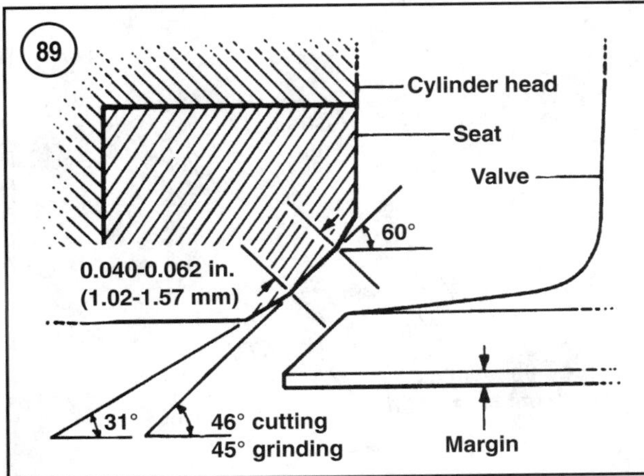

CAUTION
Never back the reamer out through the valve guide because the guide will be damaged.

e. Remove the T-handle from the reamer. Remove the reamer from the combustion side of the cylinder head.
f. Apply low-pressure compressed air and clean the small shavings from the valve guide bore. Then clean the valve guide bore with the small spiral brush.

9. Hone the valve guide as follows:
   a. Install the valve guide hone into a high-speed electric drill.
   b. Lubricate the valve guide bore and hone stones with the reamer lubricant. *Do not* use motor oil.
   c. Carefully insert the hone stones into the valve guide bore.
   d. Start the drill and move the hone back and forth in the valve guide bore for ten to 12 complete strokes. Work for a 60° crosshatch pattern.
10. Repeat Steps 8 and 9 for each valve guide.
11. Soak the cylinder head in a container filled with hot soapy water. Then clean the valve guides with a valve guide brush or an equivalent bristle brush. *Do not* use a steel brush. Do not use cleaning solvent, kerosene or gasoline because these chemicals will not remove all of the abrasive particles produced during the honing operation. Repeat this step until all of the valve guides are thoroughly cleaned. Then rinse the cylinder head and valve guides in clear, cold water and dry with compressed air.
12. After cleaning and drying the valve guides, apply clean engine oil to the guides to prevent rust.
13. Resurface the valve seats as described in *Valve Seat Reconditioning* in this section.

Valve Seat Inspection

1. Remove all carbon residue from each valve seat. Then clean the cylinder head as described under *Valve Inspection* in this section.

NOTE
The most accurate method of checking the valve seat width and position is with machinist's dye.

2. Check the valve seats in their original locations with machinist's dye as follows:
   a. Thoroughly clean the valve face and valve seat with contact cleaner.
   b. Spread a thin layer of Prussian Blue or machinist's dye evenly on the valve face.
   c. Insert the valve into its guide.
   d. Support the valve by hand (**Figure 87**) and tap the valve up and down in the cylinder head. Do not rotate the valve, or a false reading will result.
   e. Remove the valve and examine the impression left by the machinist's dye. The impressions on the valve and the seat must be even around their circumferences, and the width (**Figure 88**) must be within the specifications in **Table 2**. If the width is beyond the specification, or if the impression is uneven, recondition the valve seats.
3. Closely examine the valve seat in the cylinder head (**Figure 84**). It must be smooth and even with a polished seating surface.
4. If the valve seat is in good condition, install the valve as described in this chapter.
5. If the valve seat is not correct, recondition the valve seat as described in this section.

Valve Seat Reconditioning

Valve seat reconditioning requires considerable expertise and special tools. In most cases, it is more economical and practical to have these procedures performed by an experienced machinist.

The following procedure is provided for those equipped to perform the task. A Neway Valve seat cutter set (part No. HD-082454) or equivalent is required. Follow the manufacturer's instructions.

Refer to **Figure 89** for valve seat angles. Although the valve seat angles for both the intake and exhaust valves are the same, different cutter sizes are required. Also note that a 45° seat angle is specified when grinding the seats, but a 46° seat angle is specified when cutting seats.

1. Clean the valve guides as described under *Valve Inspection* in this section.

2. Carefully rotate and insert the solid pilot into the valve guide. Make sure the pilot is correctly seated.

CAUTION
Valve seat accuracy depends on a correctly sized and installed pilot.

3. Using the 45° grinding stone or 46° cutter, descale and clean the valve seat with one or two turns.

CAUTION
*Measure the valve seat contact area in the cylinder head (**Figure 88**) after each cut to make sure its size and area are correct. Overgrinding will sink the valves too far into the cylinder head and require replacement of the valve seat.*

4. If the seat is still pitted or burned, turn the cutter until the surface is clean. Work slowly and carefully to avoid removing too much material from the valve seat.
5. Remove the pilot from the valve guide.
6. Apply a small amount of valve lapping compound to the valve face and install the valve. Using a valve lapping tool, rotate the valve against the valve seat. Remove the valve.
7. Measure the valve seat with a vernier caliper (**Figure 88**). Record the measurement to use as a reference point when performing the following.

CAUTION
The 31° cutter removes material quickly. Work carefully and check the progress often.

8. Reinsert the solid pilot into the valve guide. Be certain the pilot is properly seated. Install the 31° cutter onto the solid pilot and lightly cut the seat to remove one fourth of the existing valve seat.
9. Install the 60° cutter onto the solid pilot and lightly cut the seat to remove the lower fourth of the existing valve seat.
10. Measure the valve seat with a vernier caliper. Then fit the 45° grinding stone or 46° cutter onto the solid pilot and cut the valve seat to the specified seat width in **Table 2**.
11. When the valve seat width is correct, check valve seating as follows.
12. Remove the solid pilot from the cylinder head.
13. Inspect the valve seat-to-valve face impression as follows:
   a. Clean the valve seat with contact cleaner.
   b. Spread a thin layer of Prussian Blue or machinist's dye evenly on the valve face.
   c. Insert the valve into its guide.

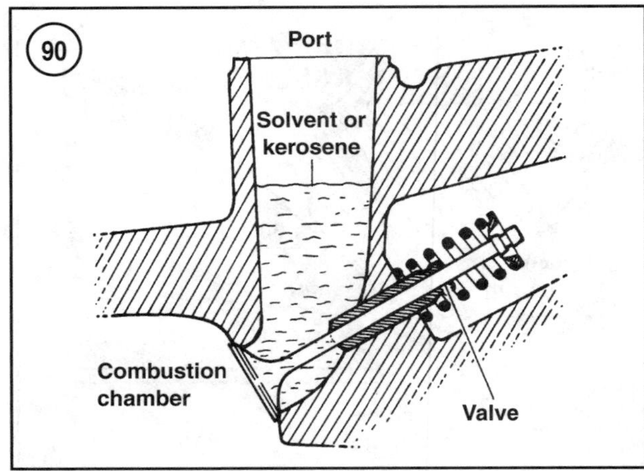

   d. Support the valve with two fingers and turn it with the valve lapping tool.
   e. Remove the valve and examine the impression left by the Prussian Blue or machinist's dye.
   f. Measure the valve seat width (**Figure 88**). Refer to **Table 2** for the correct seat width.
   g. The valve seat contact area must be in the center of the valve face area.
14. If the contact area is too high on the valve, or if it is too wide, cut the seat with the 31° cutter. This will remove part of the top valve seat area to lower or narrow the contact area.
15. If the contact area is too low on the valve, or if it is too wide, use the 60° cutter and remove part of the lower area to raise and widen the contact area.
16. After obtaining the desired valve seat position and angle, use the 45° grinding stone or the 46° cutter and very lightly clean off any burrs caused by the previous cuts.
17. When the contact area is correct, lap the valve as described in this chapter.
18. Repeat Steps 1-17 for the remaining valve seats.
19. Thoroughly clean the cylinder head and all valve components in solvent. Then clean with detergent and hot water and rinse in cold water. Dry with compressed air. Then apply a light coat of engine oil to all nonaluminum metal surfaces to prevent rust formation.

Valve Lapping

If valve wear or distortion is not excessive, attempt to restore the valve seal by lapping the valve to the seat.

After lapping the valves, install the valve assemblies and test each valve seat for a good seal by pouring solvent into the ports (**Figure 90**). If the seal is good, no solvent will leak past the seat surface. If solvent leaks past any

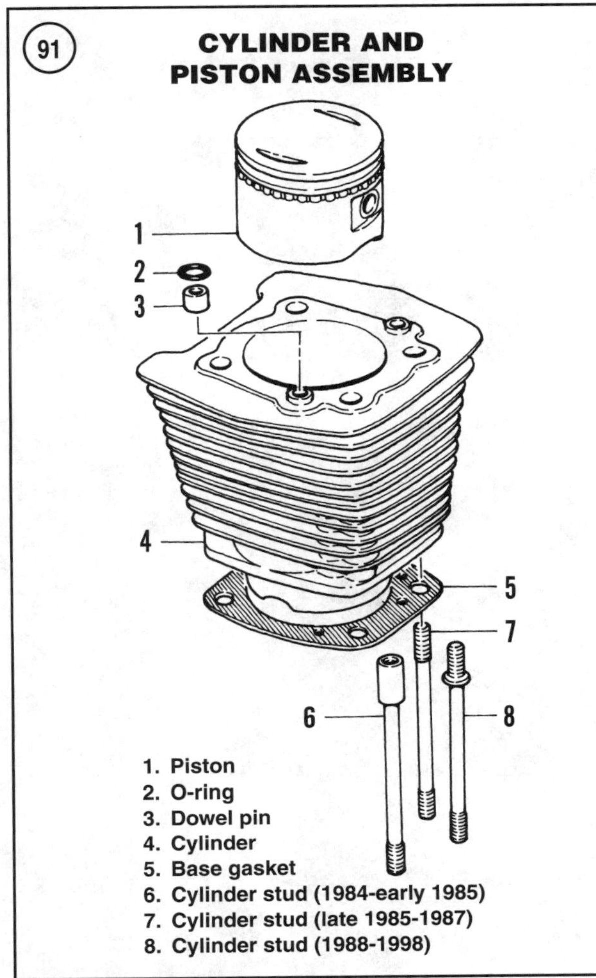

seat, the combustion chamber will appear wet. Disassemble the leaking valve and repeat the lapping procedure or recondition the valve as described in this chapter.

1. Smear a light coating of fine-grade valve lapping compound on the seating surface of the valve.
2. Insert the valve into the head.
3. Wet the suction cup of the lapping tool and stick it to the head of the valve. Lap the valve to the seat by spinning the tool between both hands while lifting and moving the valve around the seat one-fourth turn at a time.
4. Wipe off the valve and seat frequently to check the progress. Lap only enough to achieve a precise seating ring around valve head.
5. Closely examine the valve seat in the cylinder head. The seat must be smooth and even with a polished seating ring.
6. Thoroughly clean the valves and cylinder head in solvent to remove all grinding compound residue. Compound left on the valves or the cylinder head will cause rapid engine wear.
7. After installing the valves into the cylinder head, test each valve for proper seating. Check by pouring solvent into the intake and exhaust ports. Solvent must not leak past the valve seats. If leakage occurs, the combustion chamber will appear wet. If solvent leaks past any of the seats, disassemble that valve assembly and repeat the lapping procedure until there are no leaks.

Valve Seat Replacement

Valve seat replacement requires considerable experience and equipment. Refer this work to a Harley-Davidson dealership or machine shop.

CYLINDER

Removal

Refer to **Figure 91**.

1. Remove the cylinder head as described in this chapter.
2. Remove all dirt and foreign material from the cylinder base.
3. Remove the two dowel pins and O-rings (**Figure 92**) from the top of the cylinder.
4. Turn the engine until the piston is at bottom dead center (BDC).

NOTE

The front and rear cylinders are identical (same part number). Mark each cylinder so they will be installed in their original positions.

5. Loosen the cylinder by tapping around the perimeter with a plastic mallet.
6. Pull the cylinder straight up (**Figure 93**) and off the piston and cylinder studs.

7. Stuff clean shop rags into the crankcase opening to prevent objects from falling into the crankcase.
8. Install a vinyl or rubber hose over the studs (A, **Figure 94**). This will protect both the piston and studs from damage.

CAUTION
After removing the cylinder, be careful when working around the cylinder studs to avoid bending or damaging them. The slightest bend could cause a stud to fail.

9. Repeat Steps 1-8 for the other cylinder.

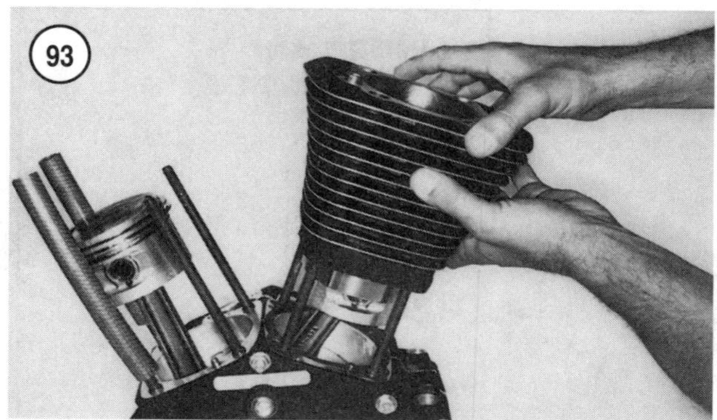
93

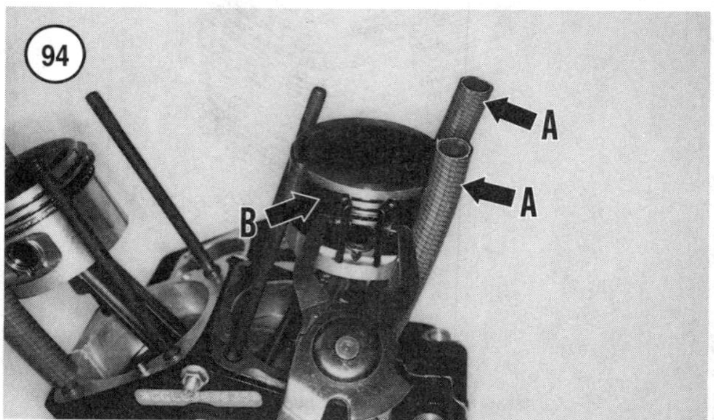

94

Installation

NOTE
*When a cylinder has been bored oversize, the inner lead-in angle at the base of the bore skirt (**Figure 95**) has been eliminated. This lead-in angle is necessary so the piston rings can safely enter the cylinder bore. If necessary, use a chamfering cone (JIMS part No. 2078) or a hand grinder with a fine stone and grind in a new lead-in angle. The finished surface must be smooth so it will not catch and damage the piston rings during installation.*

1. If removed, install the pistons and rings as described in this chapter.
2. Remove all gasket residue and clean the cylinder as described under *Inspection* in this chapter.
3. Remove the vinyl or rubber hose from each stud.
4. If removed, install the locating dowels into the crankcase.
5. Turn the crankshaft until the piston is at top dead center (TDC).
6. Lubricate the cylinder bore, piston and piston rings liberally with clean engine oil.
7. Correctly position the piston ring end gaps as described under *Piston Ring Replacement* in this chapter.
8. Compress the piston rings with a ring compressor (B, **Figure 94**).

NOTE
Install the cylinder in its original position as noted during removal.

9. Carefully align the cylinder (front facing forward) with the cylinder studs and slide it down until it is over the top of the piston. Then continue sliding the cylinder down and past the rings. Remove the ring compressor once the piston rings enter the cylinder bore. Remove the shop rag from the crankcase opening.

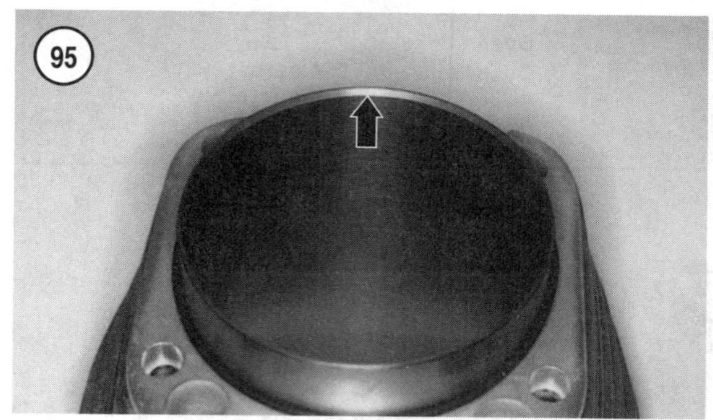
95

96

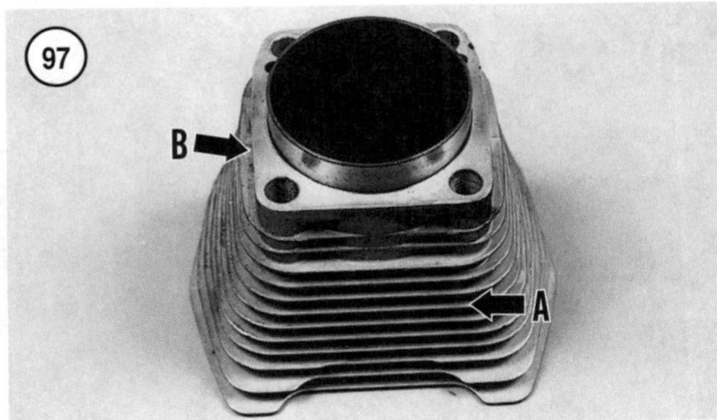

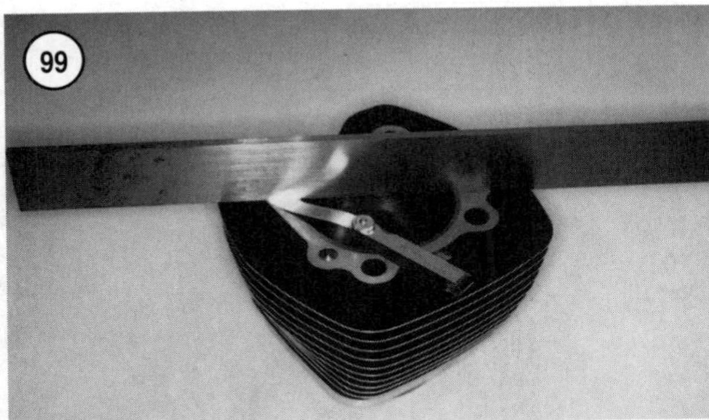

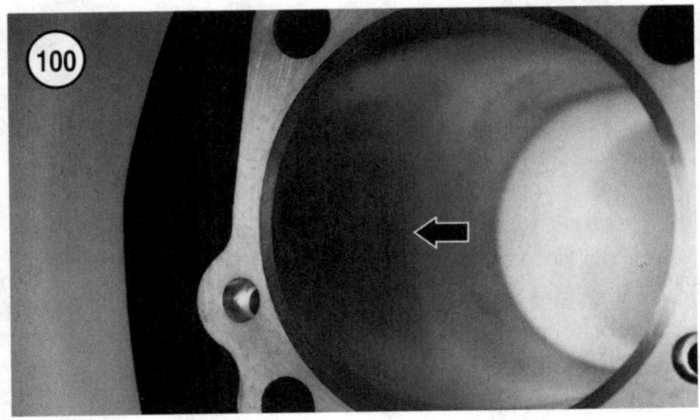

10. Continue to slide the cylinder down (**Figure 93**) until it bottoms out on the crankcase (**Figure 96**).
11. Repeat to install the other cylinder.
12. Install the cylinder heads as described in this chapter.

Inspection

The pistons on all models cannot be accurately measured with standard measuring instruments and techniques. This is because the piston has a complex shape due to its design and manufacturing.

Piston-to-cylinder clearance is checked by measuring the cylinder bore only. If a cylinder is worn, the cylinder must be bored to specific factory specifications and not to match a particular piston size as with conventional methods. Refer piston-to-cylinder matching to a Harley-Davidson dealership.

The following procedure requires the use of highly specialized and expensive measuring instruments. If such instruments are not readily available, have the measurements performed by a Harley-Davidson dealership or qualified machine shop.

To obtain an accurate cylinder bore measurement, the cylinder must be tightened between torque plates (JIMS part No. 1287). Measurements made without the torque plates will be inaccurate and may vary by as much as 0.001 in. (0.025 mm). Refer this procedure to a shop equipped and experienced with this procedure if the tools are not available. The cylinder bore must be thoroughly clean and at room temperature to obtain accurate measurements. Do not measure the cylinder immediately after it has been honed because it will still be warm. Measurements can vary by as much as 0.002 in. (0.051 mm) if the cylinder block is not at room temperature.

1. Thoroughly clean the outside of the cylinder. Use a stiff brush, soap and water and clean all debris from the cooling fins (A, **Figure 97**). If necessary, use a piece of wood and scrape away any lodged dirt. Clogged cooling fins can cause overheating leading to possible engine damage.
2. Carefully remove all gasket residue from the top (**Figure 98**) and bottom (B, **Figure 97**) cylinder block gasket surfaces.
3. Thoroughly clean the cylinder with solvent and dry with compressed air. Lightly oil the cylinder block bore to prevent rust.
4. Check the top and bottom cylinder gasket surfaces with a straightedge and feeler gauge (**Figure 99**). Replace the cylinder if warp exceeds the limit in **Table 2**.
5. Check the cylinder bore (**Figure 100**) for scuff marks, scratches or other damage.

6. Install the torque plate onto the cylinder (**Figure 101**) following the manufacturer's instructions.

7. Measure the cylinder bore with a bore gauge or inside micrometer at the positions indicated in **Figure 102**. Perform the first measurement 0.500 in. (12.7 mm) below the top of the cylinder (**Figure 103**). Do not measure areas where the rings do not travel.

8. Measure in two axes: aligned with the piston pin and at 90° to the pin. If the taper or out-of-round measurements exceed the service limits in **Table 2**, bore both cylinders to the next oversize and install oversize pistons and rings. Confirm the accuracy of all measurements and consult with a parts supplier on the availability of replacement parts before having the cylinder serviced.

9. Remove the torque plates.

10. If the cylinders were serviced, wash each cylinder in hot soapy water to remove the fine gritty material left from the boring or honing process. After washing, run a clean white cloth through the cylinder bore. If the cloth shows traces of grit or oil, the bore is not clean. Repeat until the cloth passes through cleanly. When the bore is clean, dry with compressed air. Then lubricate with clean engine oil to prevent the bore from rusting.

CAUTION
The use of hot soapy water is the only procedure that will completely clean the cylinder bore. Solvent and kerosene cannot wash fine grit out of the cylinder crevices. Abrasive grit left in the cylinder will cause premature engine wear.

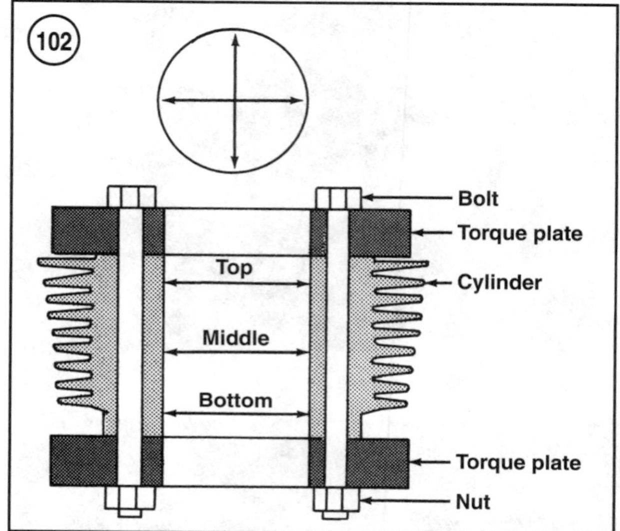

Cylinder Studs and Cylinder Head Bolts Inspection and Cleaning

The cylinder studs and cylinder head bolts must be in good condition and properly cleaned prior to installing the cylinder and cylinder heads. Damaged or dirty studs may cause cylinder head distortion and gasket leakage.

CAUTION
The cylinder studs, cylinder head bolts and washers consist of hardened material. Do not substitute these items with a part made of a lower grade material. If replacement is required, purchase the parts from the manufacturer.

1. Inspect the cylinder head bolts. Replace any that are damaged.

2. Examine the cylinder studs for bending, looseness or damage. Replace studs as described under *Cylinder Stud Replacement* in this chapter. If the studs are in good condition, perform Step 3.

3. Cover both crankcase openings with shop rags to prevent debris from falling into the engine.

4. Remove all carbon residue from the cylinder studs and cylinder head bolts as follows:

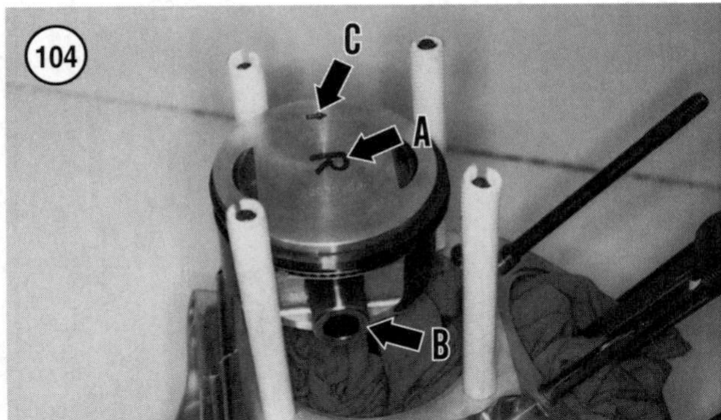

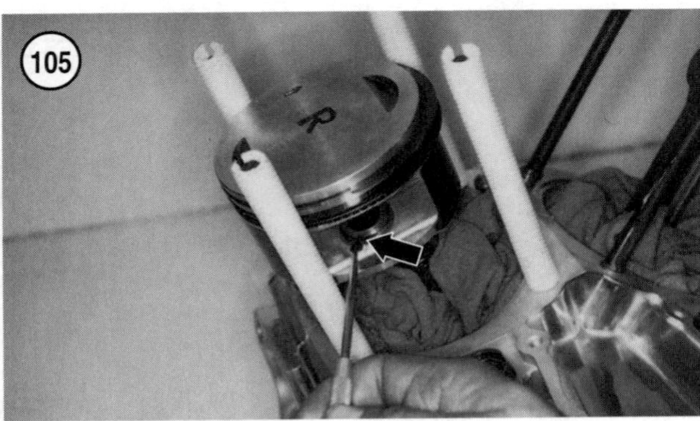

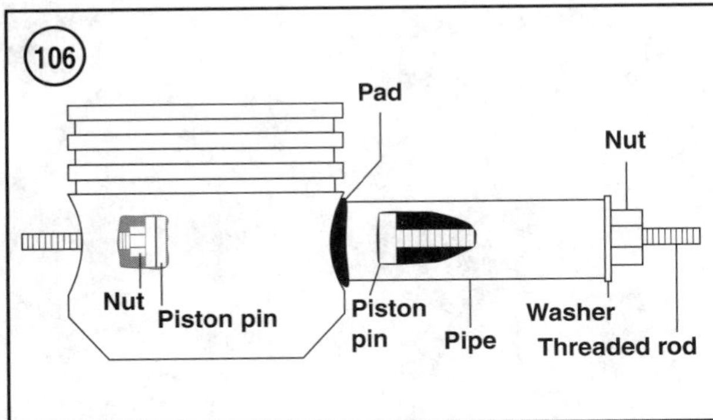

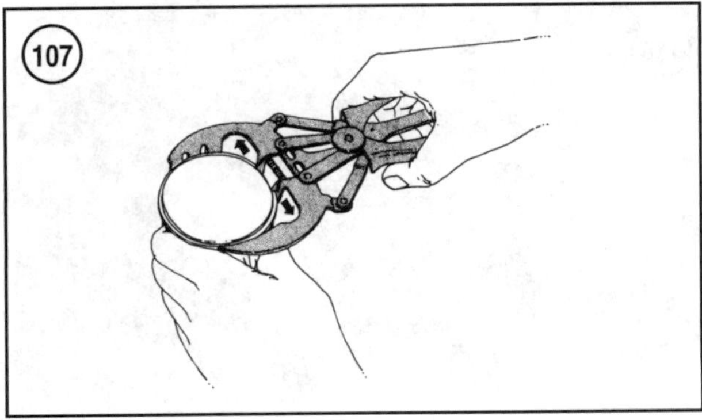

a. Apply solvent to the cylinder stud and mating cylinder head bolt threads and thread the bolt onto the stud.
b. Turn the cylinder head bolt back and forth to loosen and remove the carbon residue from the threads. Remove the bolt from the stud. Wipe off the residue with a shop rag moistened in cleaning solvent.
c. Repeat until both thread sets are free of all carbon residues.
d. Spray the cylinder stud and cylinder head bolt with an aerosol parts cleaner and allow them to dry.
e. Set the cleaned bolt aside and install it on the same stud when installing the cylinder head.

5. Repeat Step 4 for each cylinder stud and cylinder head bolt set.

PISTONS AND PISTON RINGS

Refer to **Figure 91**.

Piston and Piston Rings Removal

1. Remove the cylinder as described in this chapter.
2. Cover the crankcase with clean shop rags.
3. Lightly mark the pistons with an *F* (front) or *R* (rear) (A, **Figure 104**).

WARNING

The piston pin retaining rings may spring out of the piston during removal. Wear safety glasses when removing them in Step 4.

4. Using an awl, pry the piston pin retaining rings (**Figure 105**) out of the piston. Place a thumb over the hole to help prevent the rings from flying out during removal.

NOTE

Mark the piston pins so they can be reinstalled into their original pistons.

5. Support the piston and push out the piston pin (B, **Figure 104**). If the piston is difficult to remove, use a piston pin removal tool (**Figure 106**).
6. Remove the piston from the connecting rod.
7. Remove the piston rings using a ring expander tool (**Figure 107**) or spread them by hand (**Figure 108**) and remove them.
8. Inspect the pistons, piston pins and piston rings as described in this chapter.

Piston Inspection

1. If necessary, remove the piston rings as described in this chapter.

2. Carefully clean the carbon from the piston crown (**Figure 109**) with a soft scraper. Large carbon accumulations reduce piston cooling and result in detonation and piston damage. Re-letter the piston as soon as it is cleaned to keep it properly identified.

CAUTION
Be very careful not to gouge or otherwise damage the piston when removing carbon. Never use a wire brush to clean the piston ring grooves. Do not attempt to remove carbon from the sides of the piston above the top ring or from the cylinder bore near the top. Removal of carbon from these two areas may cause increased oil consumption.

3. After cleaning the piston, examine the crown. The crown should show no signs of wear or damage. If the crown appears pecked or spongy-looking, also check the spark plug, valves and combustion chamber for aluminum deposits. If these deposits are found, the engine is overheating.
4. Examine each ring groove for burrs, dented edges or other damage. Pay particular attention to the top compression ring groove as it usually wears more than the others. The oil rings and grooves generally wear less than compression rings and their grooves. If there is evidence of oil ring groove wear, or if the oil ring assembly is tight and difficult to remove, the piston skirt might have collapsed due to excessive heat and become permanently deformed. Replace the piston.
5. Check the piston skirt for cracks or other damage. If a piston shows signs of partial seizure (bits of aluminum buildup on the piston skirt), the piston should be replaced to reduce the possibility of engine noise and further piston seizure.

NOTE
If the piston skirt is worn or scuffed unevenly from side-to-side, the connecting rod might be bent or twisted.

6. Check the circlip groove (**Figure 110**) on each side for wear, cracks or other damage. If the grooves are questionable, check the circlip fit by installing a new circlip into each groove and then attempt to move the circlip from side to side. If the circlip has any side play, the groove is worn, and the piston must be replaced.
7. Measure piston-to-cylinder clearance as described under *Cylinder Inspection* in this chapter.
8. If damage or wear indicates piston replacement, select a new piston as described under *Piston Clearance* in this chapter. If the piston, rings and cylinder are not damaged and are dimensionally correct, they can be reused.

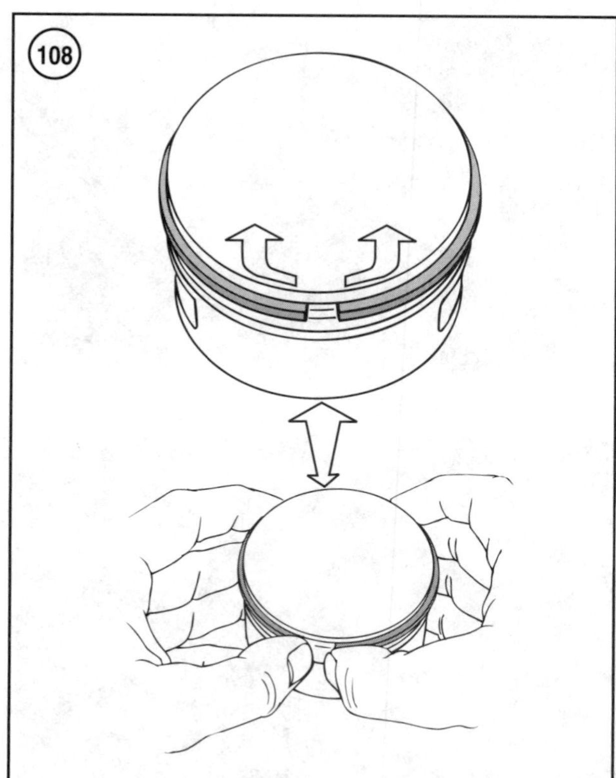

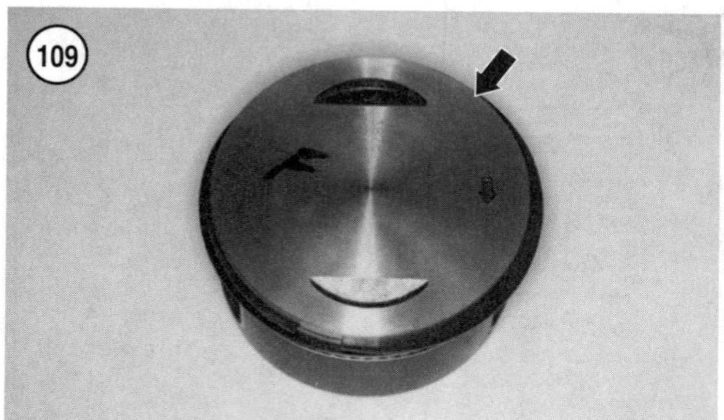

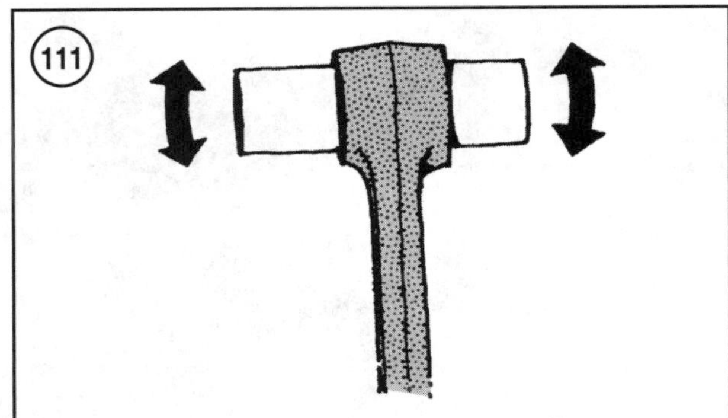

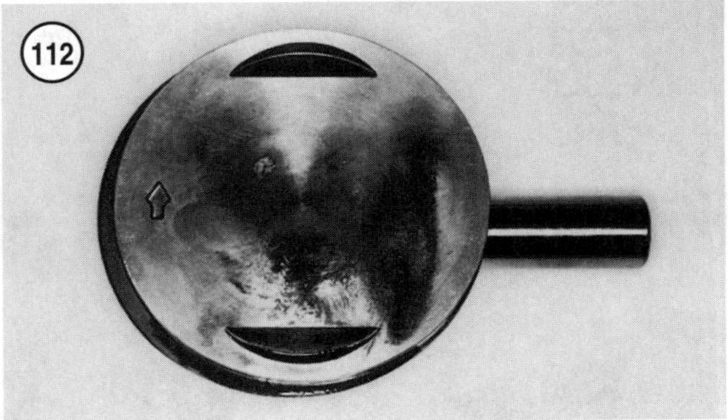

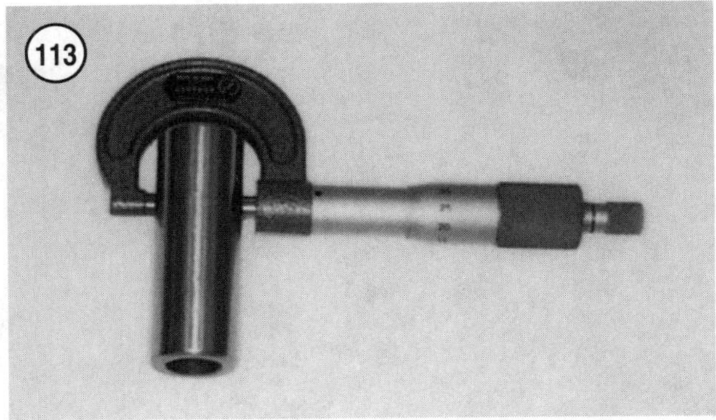

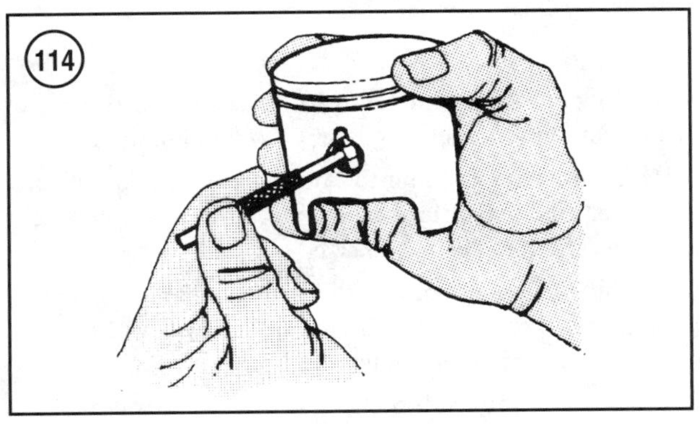

Piston Pin Inspection and Clearance

1. Clean the piston pin in solvent and dry thoroughly.
2. Inspect the piston pin for chrome flaking or cracks. Replace if necessary.
3. Oil the piston pin and install it in the connecting rod (**Figure 111**). Slowly rotate the piston pin and check for radial play.
4. Oil the piston pin and install it in the piston (**Figure 112**). Check the piston pin for excessive play.
5. To measure piston pin-to-piston clearance, perform the following:
   a. Measure the piston pin outer diameter with a micrometer (**Figure 113**).
   b. Measure the inside diameter of the piston pin bore (**Figure 114**) with a snap gauge. Measure the snap gauge with a micrometer.
   c. Subtract the piston pin outer diameter from the piston pin bore to obtain the clearance dimension. Check against the specification in **Table 2**.
   d. If out of specification, replace the piston and/or the piston pin.
6. Replace the piston pin and/or piston or connecting rod if necessary.

Piston Pin Bushing in Connecting Rod Inspection and Replacement

The piston pin bushings are reamed to provide correct piston pin-to-bushing clearance. This clearance is critical in preventing pin knock and top-end damage.

1. Inspect the piston pin bushings (**Figure 115**) for excessive wear or damage (pit marks, scoring or wear grooves). Then check to make sure the bushing is not loose. The bushing must be a tight fit in the connecting rods.
2. Measure the piston pin diameter (**Figure 113**) where it contacts the bushing.

3. Measure the piston pin bushing inside diameter using a snap gauge (**Figure 116**).
4. Subtract the piston pin outer diameter from bushing inner diameter to determine piston pin clearance. Replace the pin and bushing if they are worn to the service limit in **Table 2**.

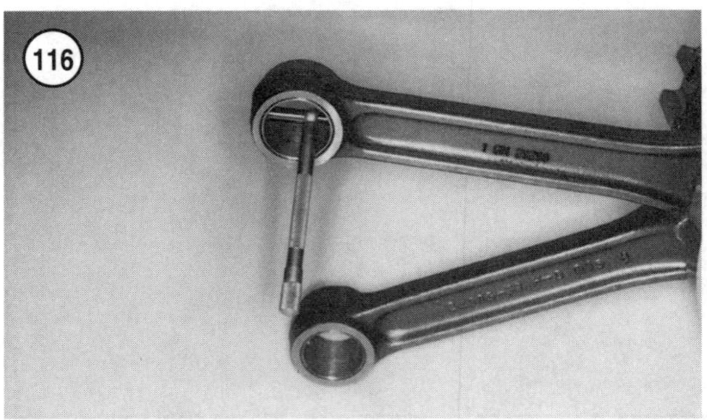

Piston Pin Bushing Replacement

Tools

The following special tools are required to replace and ream the piston pin bushings. The clamp tool is required only if the bushing is being replaced with the crankcase assembled. If these tools are not available, have a shop with the proper equipment perform the procedure.
1. Connecting rod clamp tool (JIMS part No. 1248).
2. Connecting rod bushing tool (JIMS part No. 95970-32C).
3. Connecting rod bushing reamer tool (JIMS part No. 1726-1).
4. Connecting rod bushing hone (HD-422569).

Procedure

1. Remove two of the plastic hoses protecting the cylinder studs.
2. Install the connecting rod clamping tool as follows:
   a. Install the clamp portion of the connecting rod clamping tool over the connecting rod so the slots engage the cylinder head studs. Do not scratch or bend the studs.
   b. Position the threaded cylinders with the knurled end facing up and install the cylinders onto the studs. Tighten securely to hold the clamp in place.
   c. Alternately tighten the thumbscrews onto the side of the connecting rod. Do not turn only one thumbscrew, as this will move the connecting rod off center and when tightening the other thumbscrew will cause the connecting rod to flex or bend.
3. Cover the crankcase opening to keep bushing particles from falling into the engine.

NOTE

When installing the new bushing, align the oil slot in the bushing with the oil hole in the connecting rod.

4. Following the tool manufacturer's instructions, replace the bushing using the connecting rod bushing tool (**Figure 117**). The new bushing must be flush with both sides of the connecting rod.

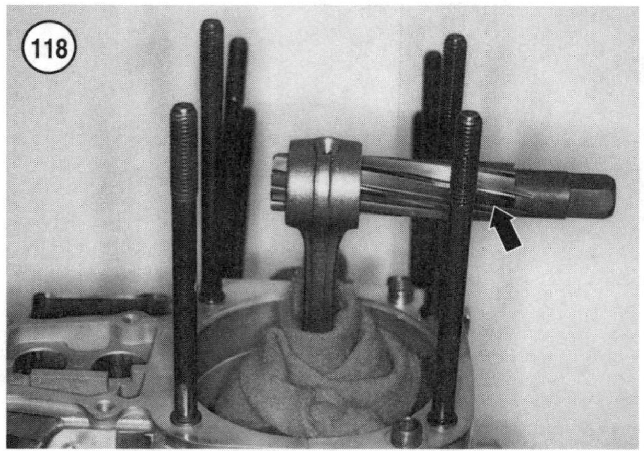

5. Following the manufacturer's instructions, ream the piston pin with the bushing reamer tool (**Figure 118**).
6. Hone the new bushing to obtain the piston pin clearance specified in **Table 2**. Use honing oil, not engine oil, when honing the bushing to size.
7. Install the piston pin through the bushing. The pin must move through the bushing smoothly. Confirm pin clearance using a micrometer and bore gauge.
8. Carefully remove all metal debris from the crankcase.

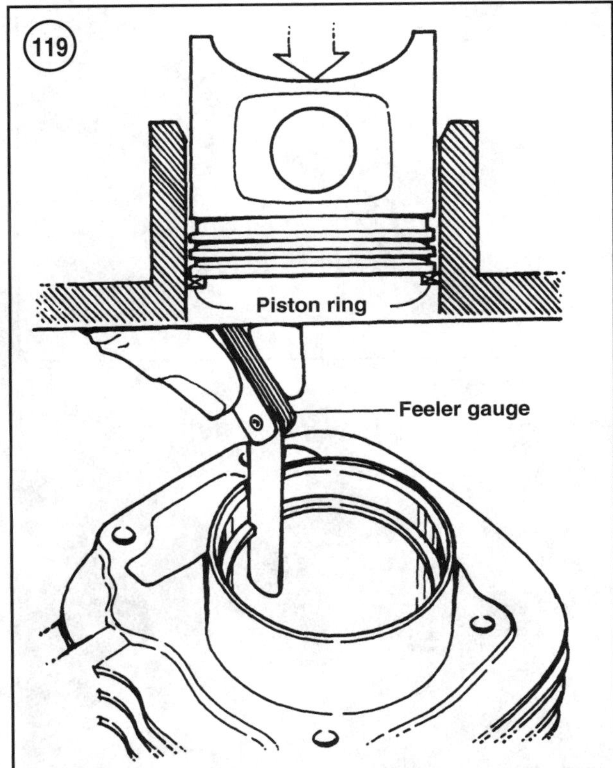

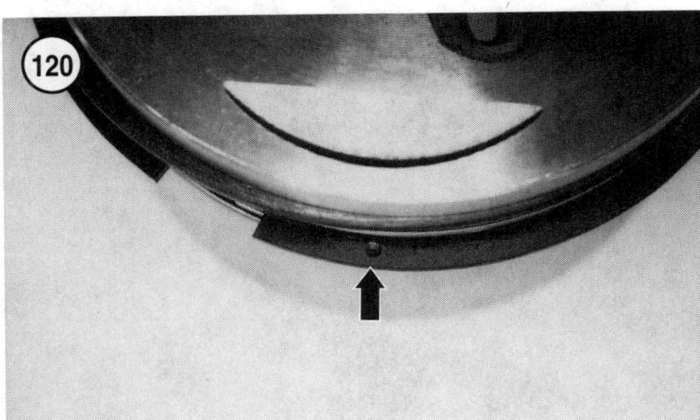

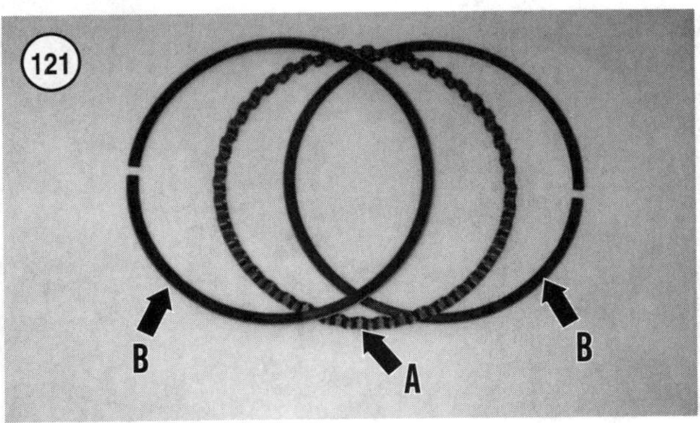

Piston Ring Inspection

1. Clean the piston ring grooves as described under *Piston Inspection*.
2. Inspect the ring grooves for burrs, nicks, or broken or cracked lands. Replace the piston if necessary.
3. Insert one piston ring into the top of its cylinder and tap it down approximately 1/2 in. (12.7 mm) while using the piston to square it in the bore. Measure the ring end gap (**Figure 119**) with a feeler gauge and compare with the specification in **Table 2**. Replace the piston rings as a set if any one ring end gap measurement is excessive. Repeat for each ring.
4. Roll each compression ring around its piston groove. The ring must move smoothly with no binding. If a ring binds in its groove, check the groove for damage. Replace the piston if necessary.

4

Piston Ring Installation

Each piston is equipped with three piston rings: two compression rings and one oil ring assembly. The top compression ring is not marked. The lower compression is marked with a dot (**Figure 120**).

Harley-Davidson recommends that *new* piston rings be installed every time the piston is removed. Always lightly hone the cylinder before installing new piston rings.

1. Wash the piston in hot soapy water. Then rinse with cold water and dry with compressed air. Make sure the oil control holes in the lower ring groove are clear.
2. Install the oil ring assembly as follows:
   a. The oil ring consists of three rings: a ribbed spacer ring (A, **Figure 121**) and two steel rings (B).
   b. Install the spacer ring into the lower ring groove. Butt the spacer ring ends together. Do not overlap the ring ends.
   c. Insert one end of the first steel ring into the lower groove so that it is below the spacer ring. Then spiral the other end over the piston crown and into the lower groove. To protect the ring end from scratching the side of the piston, place a piece of shim stock or a thin flat feeler gauge between the ring and piston.
   d. Repeat substep c to install the other steel ring above the spacer ring.

NOTE

*When installing the compression rings, use a ring expander as shown in **Figure 107**. Do not expand the rings any more than necessary to install them.*

3. Install the lower compression ring as follows:

a. A dot mark is located on one side of the lower compression ring.
b. Install the *new* lower compression ring with the dot mark facing up (**Figure 120**).

4. Install the top compression ring as follows:
a. The top compression ring is not marked.
b. Install the *new* top compression ring with either side facing up.

5. Check the ring side clearance with a feeler gauge as shown in **Figure 122**. Check the side clearance in several spots around the piston. If the clearance is larger than the service limit in **Table 2**, replace the piston.
6. Stagger the ring gaps around the piston.

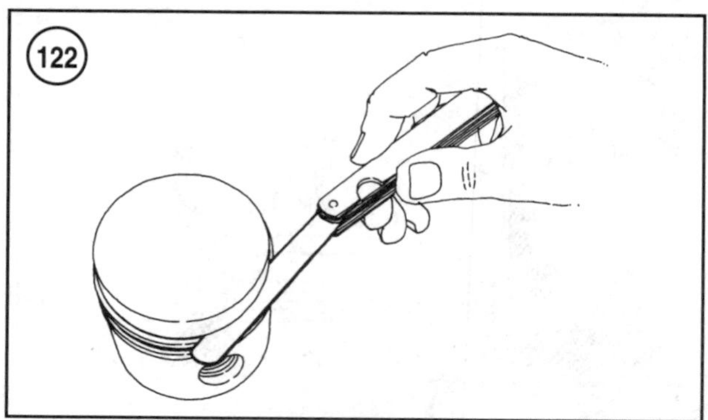

122

Piston Installation

1. Cover the crankcase openings to avoid dropping a retaining ring into the engine.

CAUTION
Use the JIMS Piston Pin Keeper Tool (part No. 34623-83) ***(Figure 123)*** *to avoid distorting the very rigid retaining rings during installation.*

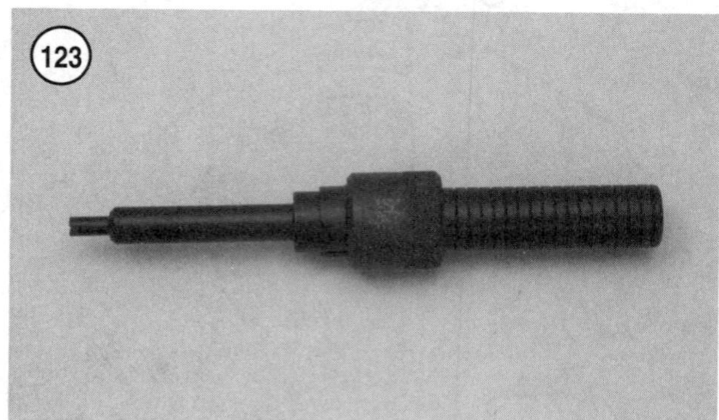

123

2. Install a *new* piston pin retaining ring into one groove in the piston. Make sure the pin seats in the groove completely.
3. Coat the connecting rod bushing and piston pin with assembly oil.
4. Slide the piston pin into the piston until its end is flush with the piston pin boss.

NOTE
The piston markings described in Step 5 are for original equipment pistons. If using aftermarket pistons, follow the manufacturer's directions for piston alignment and installation.

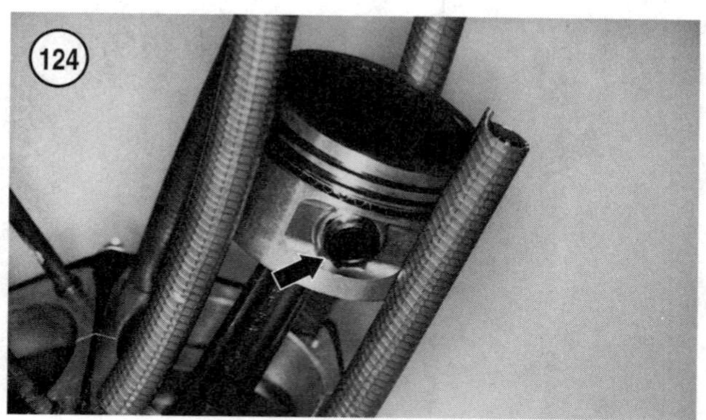

124

5. Place the piston over the connecting rod with its arrow mark (C, **Figure 104**) facing toward the front of the engine. Install used pistons on their original connecting rods; refer to the marks made on the piston during removal.
6. Push the piston pin (**Figure 124**) through the connecting rod bushing and into the other side of the piston. Push the piston pin in until it bottoms on the retaining ring.
7. Install the other *new* piston pin retaining ring into the piston groove using the special tool. Make sure it seats properly in the piston groove (**Figure 125**).
8. Repeat for the other piston.
9. Install the cylinders as described in this chapter.

125

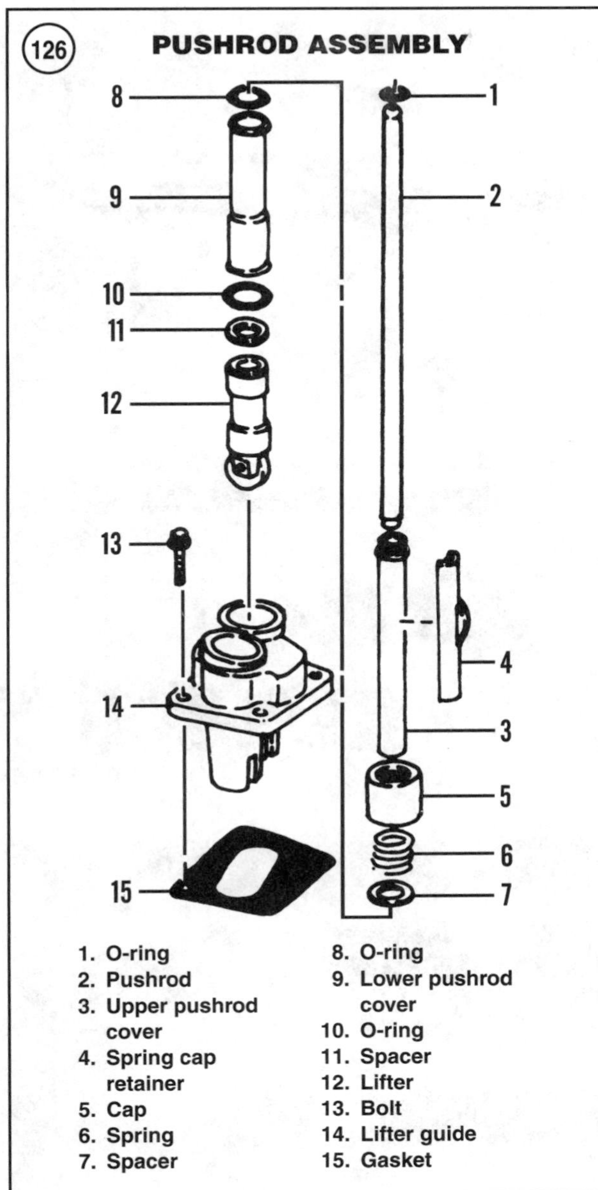

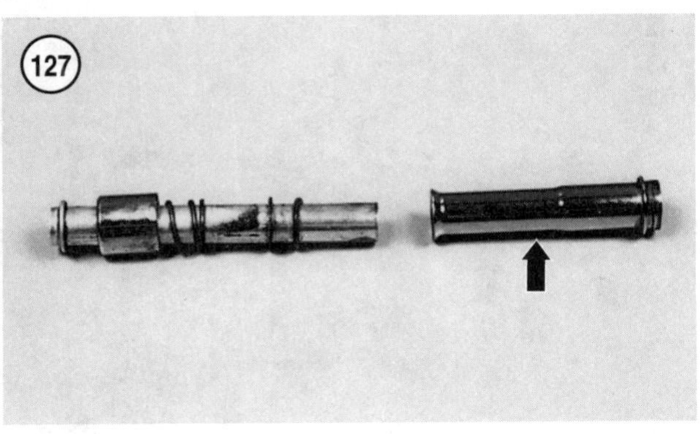

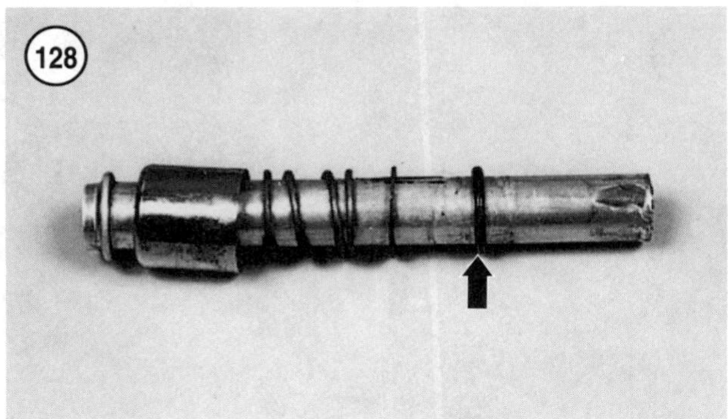

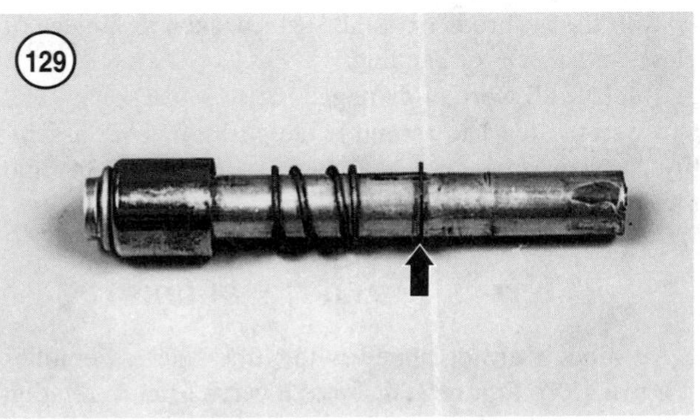

PUSHRODS AND PUSHROD COVERS

Removal/Installation

Remove and install the pushrods as described under *Rocker Arms and Rocker Arm Covers Removal* in this chapter.

Inspection

1. Disassemble the pushrod cover (**Figure 126**) as follows:
   a. Remove the lower pushrod cover (**Figure 127**).
   b. Remove the O-ring (**Figure 128**).
   c. Remove the spacer (**Figure 129**).
   d. Remove the spring (**Figure 130**).
   e. Remove the cap (**Figure 131**).
2. Inspect the pushrod cover assembly (**Figure 132**) as follows:
   a. Check the spring for sagging or cracking.
   b. Check the spacer for deformation or damage.
   c. Check the O-ring for cracking or wear.
   d. Check the pushrod covers for cracking or damage.
3. Check the pushrod ends (**Figure 133**) for wear.

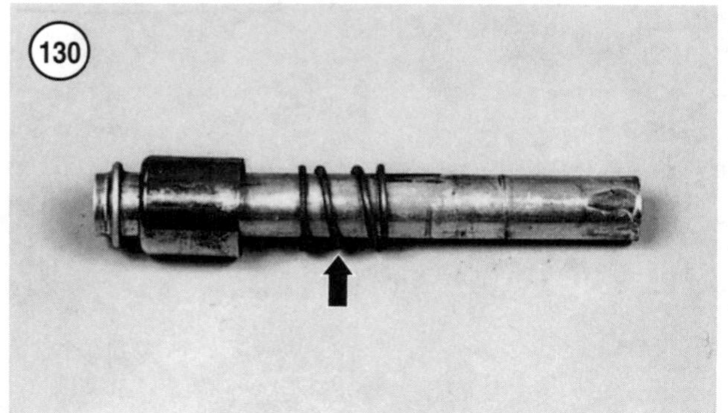

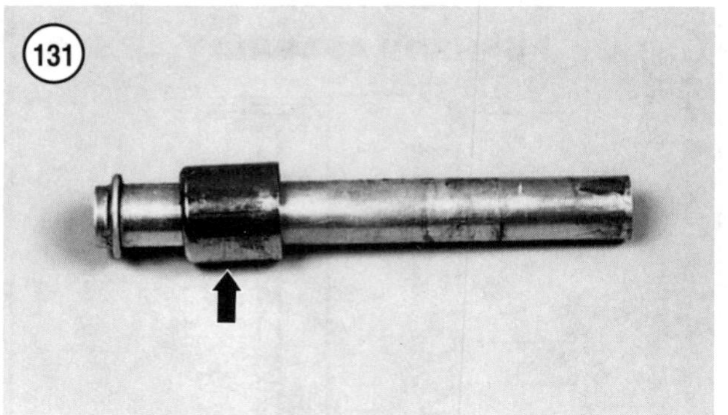

4. Roll the pushrods on a flat surface, such as a piece of glass, and check for bending.
5. Replace all worn or damaged parts as necessary.
6. Reverse Step 1 to assemble the pushrod cover assembly. Push the lower pushrod cover (A, **Figure 134**) into the cap (B) to seat the O-ring (C).

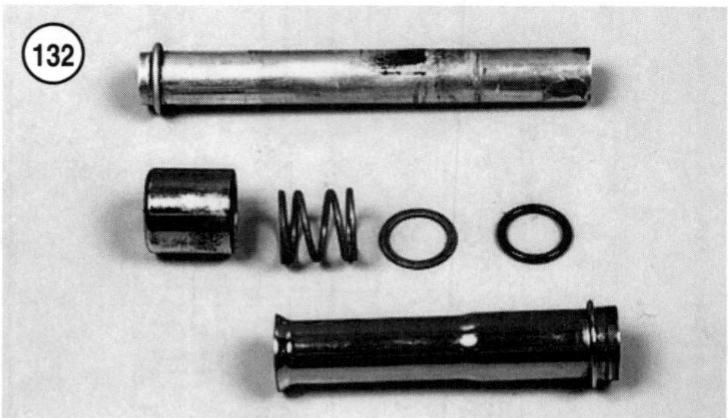

LIFTERS AND LIFTER GUIDES

All models are equipped with lifter/roller assemblies (**Figure 135**). **Figure 126** shows a valve lifter in relation to the pushrod and valve lifter guide. The valve lifters and guides are installed on the right side of the engine crankcase. During engine operation, the lifters are pumped full with engine oil, thus taking up all play in the valve train. When the engine is turned off, the lifters will leak down after a period of time as some of the oil drains out. When the engine is started, the lifters will click until they completely refill with oil. The lifters are working properly when they stop clicking after the engine runs for a few minutes. If the clicking persists it may indicate a problem with the lifter(s).

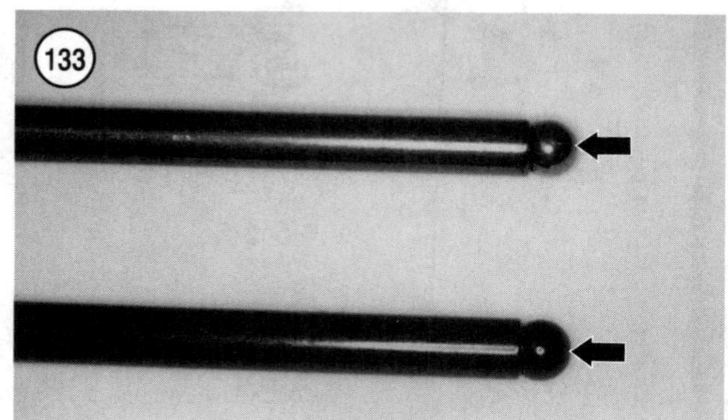

Removal

During removal, store lifters in proper sequence so they will be installed in their original positions in the crankcase.

1. Remove the pushrods as described under *Rocker Arms and Rocker Arm Covers Removal* in this chapter.
2. Remove the bolts securing the lifter guide (**Figure 136**). Loosen the lifter guide by striking it lightly with a plastic-tipped hammer.

3A. To remove the lifter guide with gearcase installed on the crankcase, perform the following:

a. Bend a piece of stiff wire into a U shape. Then insert the ends into the holes in the top of each lifter (**Figure 137**).

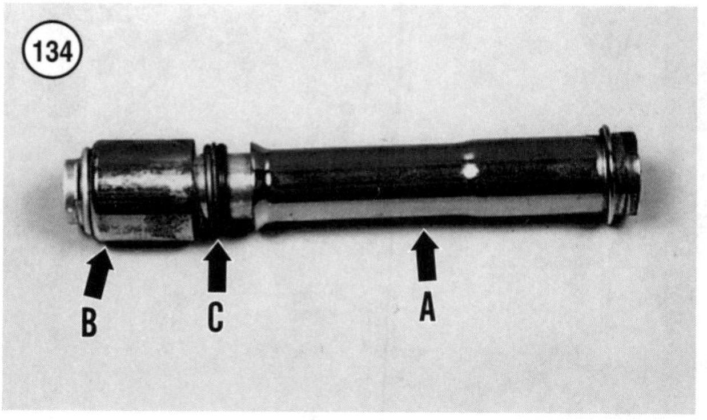

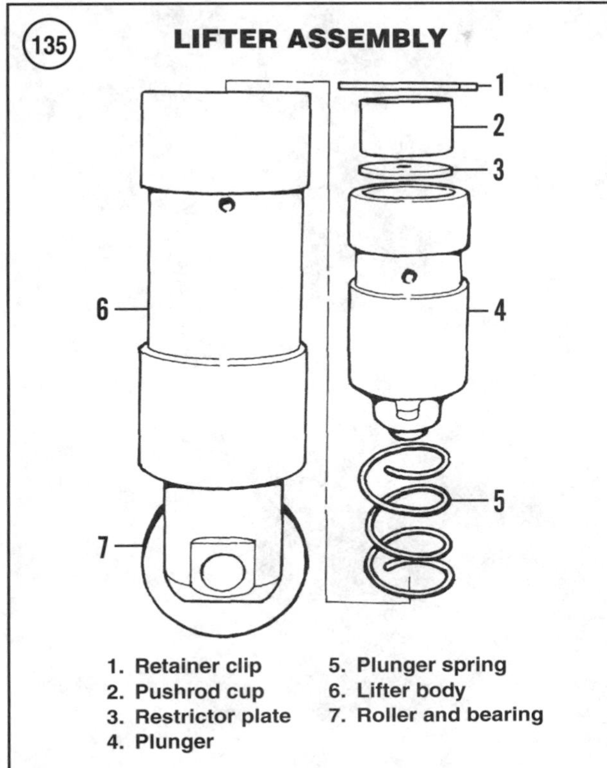

1. Retainer clip
2. Pushrod cup
3. Restrictor plate
4. Plunger
5. Plunger spring
6. Lifter body
7. Roller and bearing

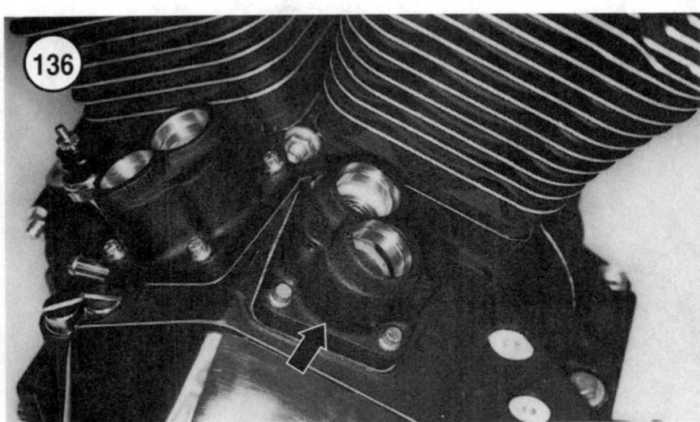

b. Pull the wire back to bind the lifters in the guide and then remove the guide and lifters from the engine as an assembly (**Figure 138**).

3B. If the gearcase is removed from the engine, perform the following:

a. Push the lifters against the side of the guide and hold in this position.

b. Lift the lifter guide away from the crankcase while still holding the lifters in position.

NOTE
Do not mix the lifters when removing them in Step 4. Mark them so they will be installed in their original positions in the crankcase.

4. Remove the lifters through the bottom of the lifter guide (**Figure 139**).

5. If the lifters are not going to be inspected, store them in a container filled with new engine oil until they are installed.

6. Remove the lifter guide gasket from the gearcase or lifter guide.

Disassembly/Inspection

NOTE
Place the lifters on a clean, lint-free cloth during inspection. Place inspected lifters in a container of clean engine oil.

1. Check the pushrod socket (**Figure 140**) in the top of the lifter for wear or damage.
2. Check the lifter roller (**Figure 141**) for pitting, scoring, galling or excessive wear. If the rollers are worn excessively, check the mating cam lobes (**Figure 142**) for the same wear condition.
3. Clean the lifter rollers with contact cleaner. Then measure roller fit and end clearance and compare to the specification in **Table 2**. Replace the lifter assembly if either measurement is worn to the service limit.
4. Determine the lifter-to-guide clearance as follows:
   a. Measure the inside diameter of the lifter bore receptacle (A, **Figure 143**) in the lifter guide and record the measurement.
   b. Measure the lifter outside diameter (**Figure 144**) and record the measurement.
   c. Subtract substep b from substep a to determine the lifter-to-crankcase bore clearance. Then compare the measurement to the service limit in **Table 2**. Replace the lifter or crankcase if the clearance is worn to the service limit.
5. If a lifter does not show visual damage, it may be contaminated with dirt or have internal damage. If so, replace it. The lifters are not serviceable and must be replaced as a unit.
6. After inspecting the lifters, store them in a container filled with clean engine oil until installation.
7. If most of the oil has drained out of the lifter, refill it with a pump-type oil can through the oil hole in the side of the lifter.
8. Clean all old gasket residue from the mating surfaces of the gearcase and the lifter cover.

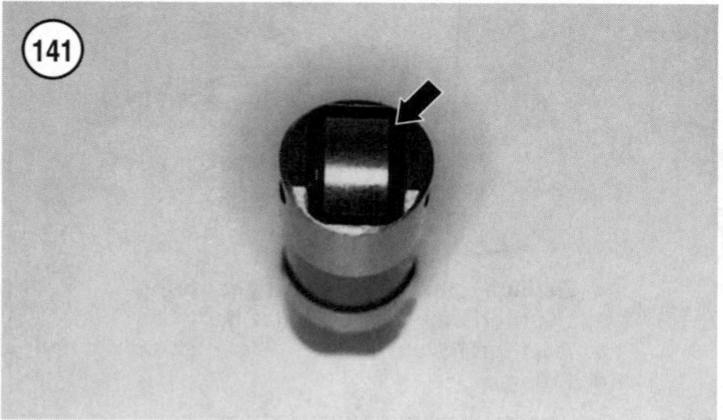

Installation

NOTE
*The oil hole in the lifter (**Figure 145**) does not have to be installed in the lifter guide facing in any specific direction.*

1. Install a *new* lifter guide gasket (A, **Figure 146**). Do not install any type of sealer on the gasket.
2. Remove the lifters from the oil-filled container and slide the lifters through the bottom of the lifter guide (**Figure 147**).

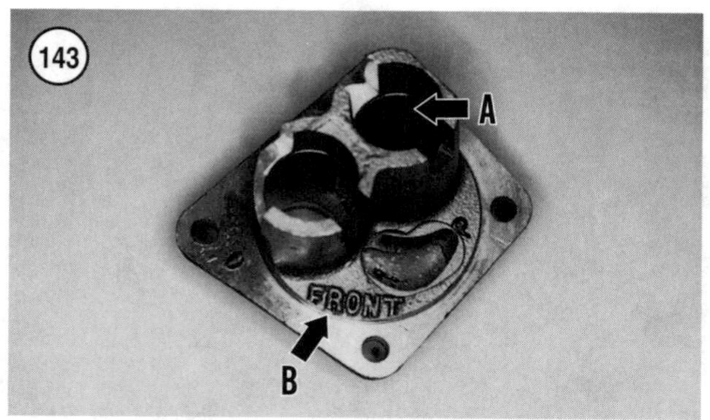

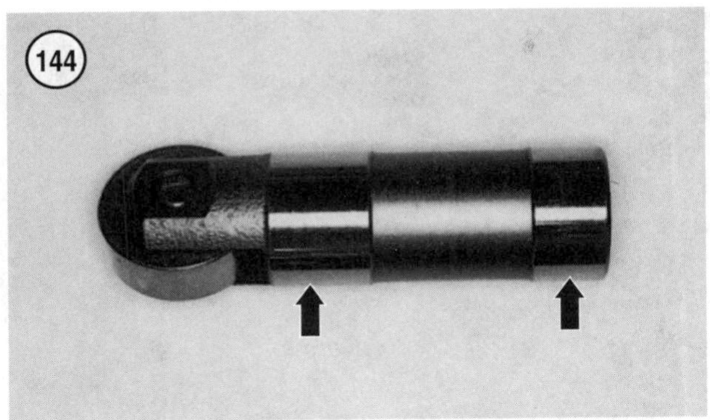
144

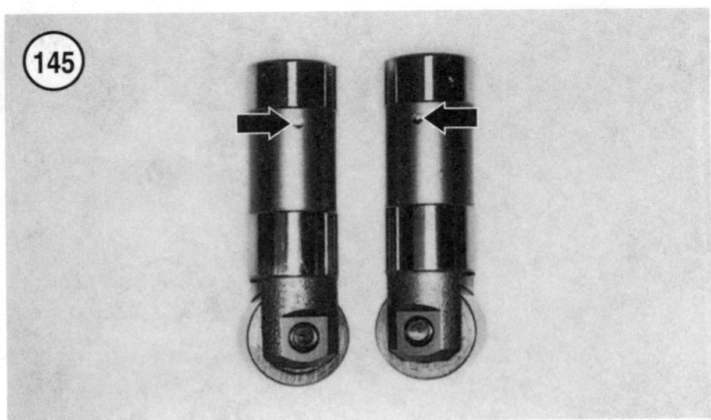
145

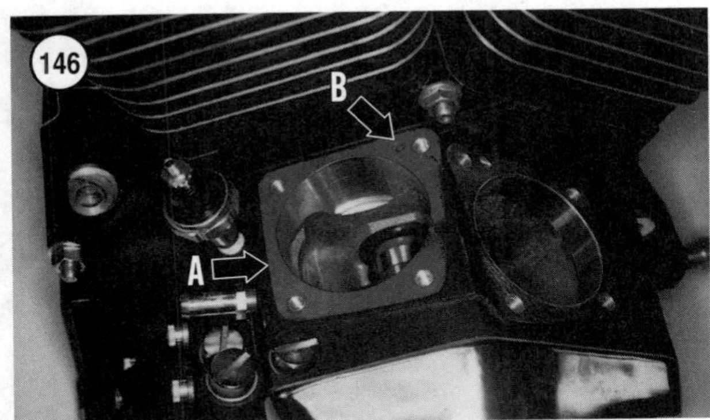

146

147

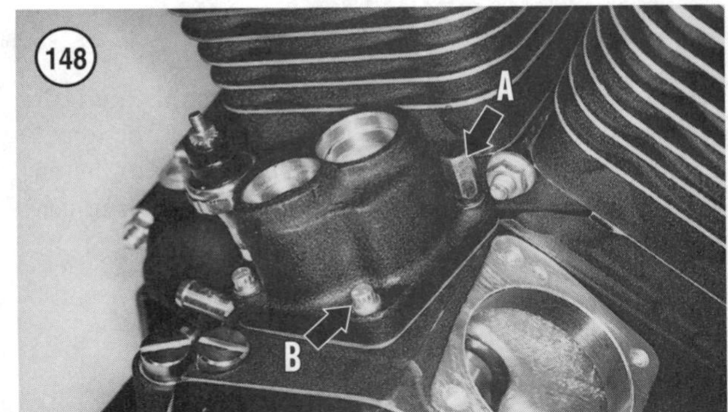

148

NOTE
*The front and rear lifter guides are not symmetrical and are marked with a FRONT (B, **Figure 143**) or REAR on the lower surface of the guide.*

3A. To install the lifter guide and lifters with the gearcase installed on the crankcase, perform the following:

a. Pour clean engine oil onto the camshaft lobes (**Figure 142**).
b. Bend a piece of stiff wire into a U shape. Then insert the ends into the holes in the top of each lifter (**Figure 138**).
c. Pull the wire back to bind the lifters in the guide and then install the guide and lifters into the engine as an assembly (**Figure 137**).

3B. If the gearcase is removed from the crankcase, perform the following:

a. Push the lifters against the side of the guide and hold in this position.
b. Install the lifter guide into the crankcase. Release the lifters and allow them to contact the camshaft lobes.

NOTE
*The oil feed hole location is shown in B, **Figure 146**.*

4. Install the Lifter Guide Alignment Tool (part No. HD-33443) into the lifter screw hole closest to the lifter oil feed hole (A, **Figure 148**). Then install the three lifter block mounting bolts (B, **Figure 148**) and tighten them securely. Remove the alignment tool and then install and tighten the remaining lifter block mounting bolt.
5. Tighten the lifter guide retaining bolts securely.
6. Repeat Steps 1-6 and install the opposite lifter guide and lifters (**Figure 149**).
7. Install the pushrods as described under *Rocker Arms and Rocker Arm Covers Installation* in this chapter.

OIL PUMP

The oil pump (**Figure 150**) is located behind the gearcase cover. The oil pump consists of two sections: a feed pump, which supplies oil under pressure to the engine components, and a scavenger pump, which returns oil to the oil tank from the engine.

Refer to **Figure 151**.

Removal/Disassembly

The oil pump can be disassembled with the gearcase cover installed on the engine and the engine in the frame. This procedure is shown with the engine removed to better illustrate the steps.

NOTE
Label all gears and Woodruff keys during removal to make sure they can be installed in the original positions.

1. Drain the engine oil as described in Chapter Three.

NOTE
When disconnecting the oil hoses in Step 2, make sure to tag each hose and fitting so that the hoses can be returned to the original positions. Refer to ***Figures 152-158****.*

2. If the engine is installed in the frame, perform the following:
   a. Remove the exhaust system as described in Chapter Eight.
   b. Remove the rear brake pedal as described in Chapter Thirteen.
   c. On 1984-1991 models, cut the hose clamp securing the oil hose to the oil pump. Then disconnect the hoses. Plug the hose ends to prevent the entry of debris. Discard the clamps.
   d. On 1992-1998 models, disconnect the oil hoses from the oil pump as described under *Oil Filter Mount* in this chapter. Plug the hose ends to prevent the entry of debris.
3. Remove the relief valve assembly as follows:
   a. Remove the relief valve plug and O-ring (**Figure 159**).
   b. Remove the spring and relief valve (**Figure 160**).
4. Remove the check valve assembly as follows:
   a. Remove the check valve plug and O-ring (**Figure 161**).
   b. Remove the check valve spring (**Figure 162**).
   c. Remove the check valve ball (**Figure 163**).

149

150

5A. On 1984-1991 models, remove the oil pump cover mounting bolts and remove the cover (**Figure 164**) and gasket.

5B. On 1992-on models, remove the oil pump cover mounting bolts and remove the oil pump cover (**Figure 165**) and gasket.

6. Remove the drive (A, **Figure 166**) and idler (B) feed gears as follows:

NOTE
Do not push the drive gear shaft into the gearcase housing when removing the drive gear in the following steps. If pushed on, the inner key will fall inside the gearcase housing. To retrieve and install the key, the gearcase cover must be removed.

   a. Remove the snap ring (**Figure 167**) from the groove in the end of the drive shaft (A, **Figure 166**).
   b. Remove the drive (A, **Figure 166**) and idler (B) feed gears.
   c. Remove the Woodruff key from the drive gear shaft keyway.

7. Remove the bolts (A, **Figure 168**) securing the oil pump housing.

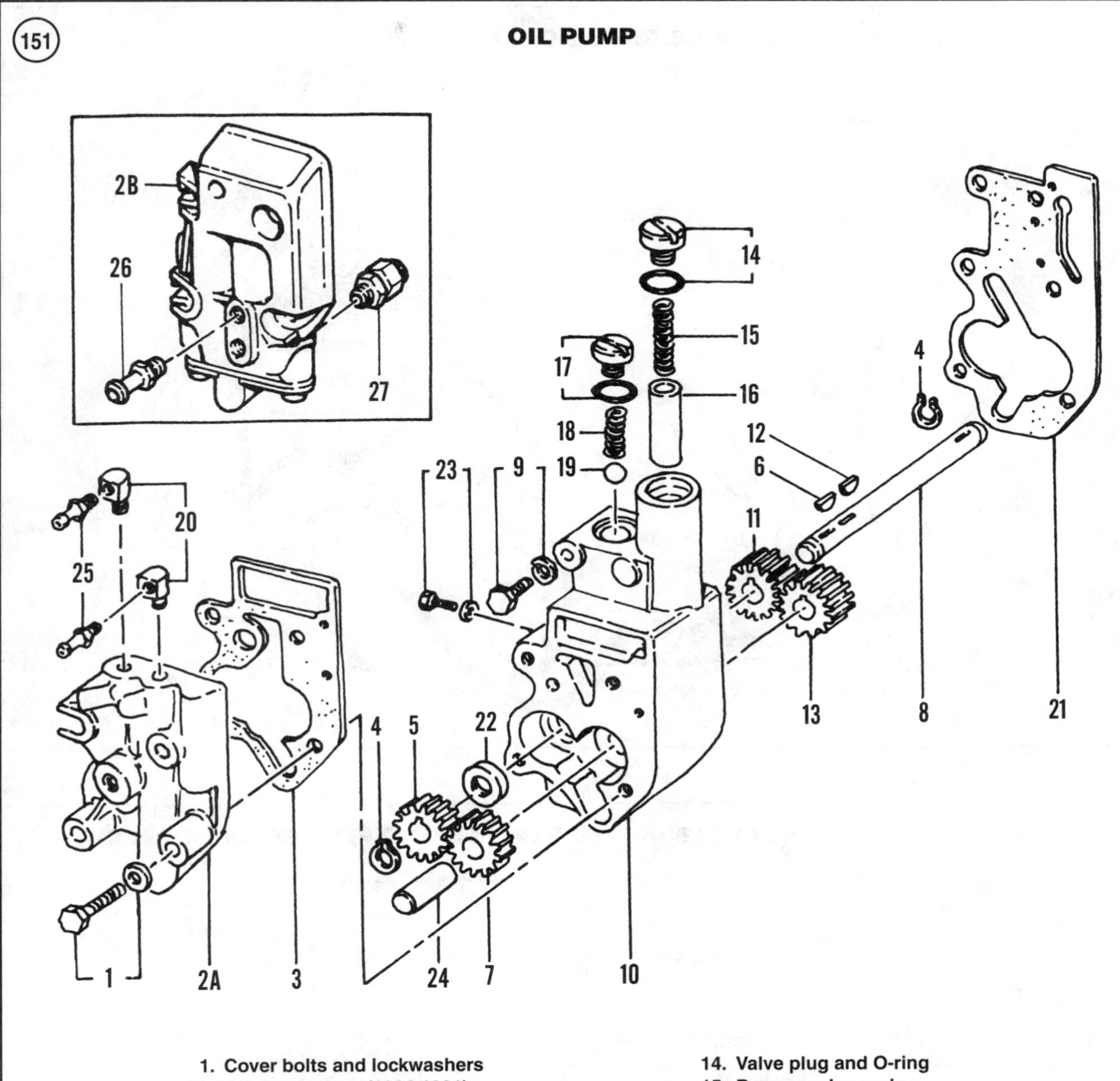

1. Cover bolts and lockwashers
2A. Oil pump cover (1984-1991)
2B. Oil pump cover (1992-1998)
3. Cover gasket
4. Snap ring
5. Drive gear
6. Woodruff key
7. Idler gear
8. Oil pump gear drive shaft
9. Oil pump body mounting bolts/lockwashers
10. Oil pump body
11. Drive gear
12. Gear key
13. Idler gear
14. Valve plug and O-ring
15. Bypass valve spring
16. Bypass valve
17. Check valve spring cover
18. Check valve spring
19. Check valve ball
20. Oil line elbow
21. Gasket
22. Seal
23. Plug and gasket
24. Idler shaft
25. Oil line nipple
26. Hose nipple
27. Compression nut filling

(152) **OIL HOSE ROUTING (EARLY 1984)**

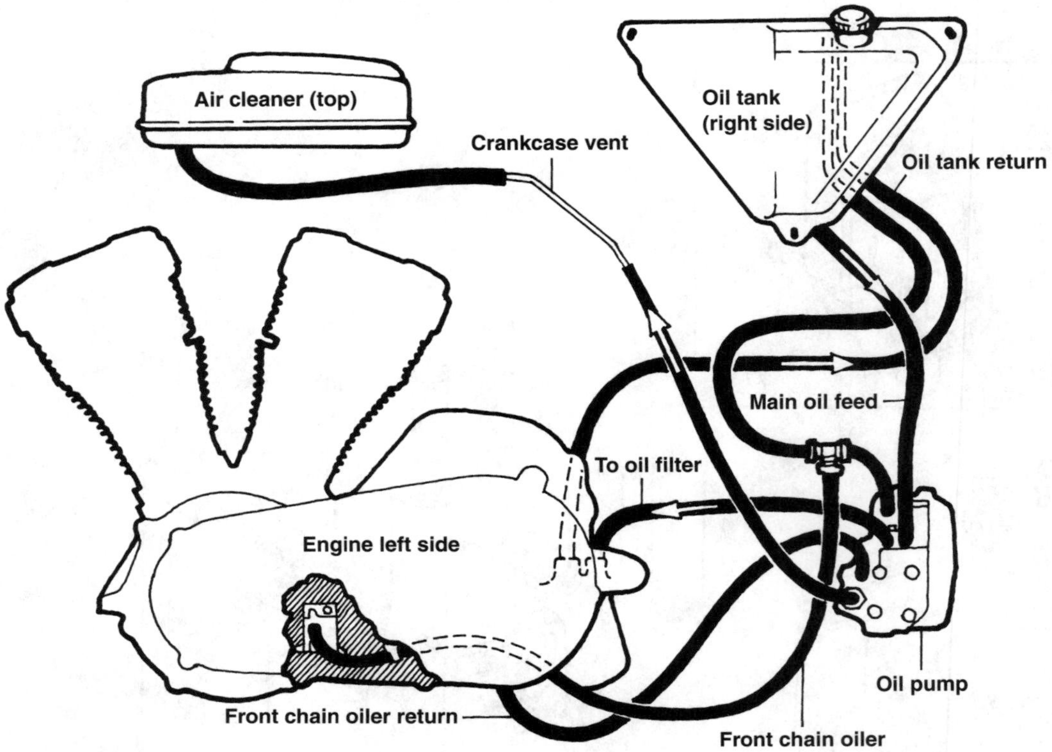

Air cleaner (top)
Crankcase vent
Oil tank
(right side)
Oil tank return
Main oil feed
To oil filter
Engine left side
Oil pump
Front chain oiler return
Front chain oiler

(153) **OIL HOSE ROUTING (LATE 1984-1990 FXR, FLH AND FLT SERIES MODELS)**

Air cleaner
Crankcase vent
Oil tank
Oil vent
Return from filter
Main oil feed
Engine crankcase
Oil filter
Oil pump

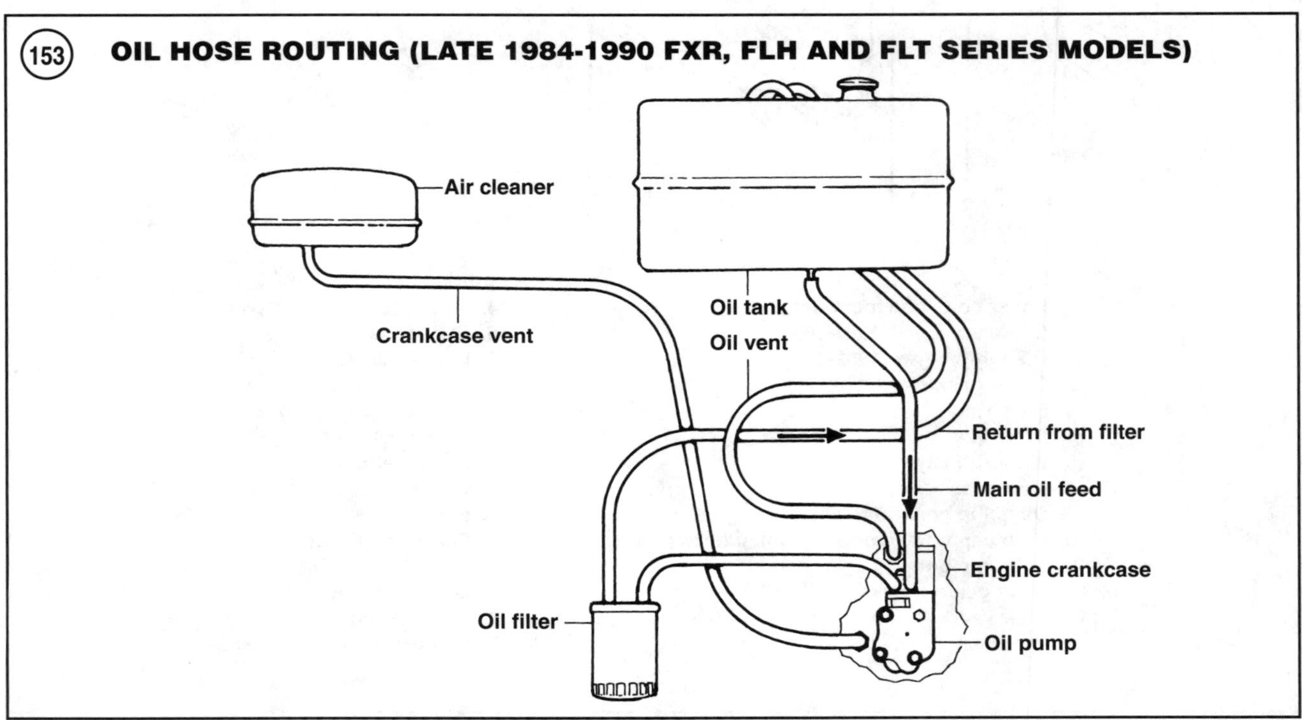

154

OIL HOSE ROUTING (1991 FXR, FLH AND FLT SERIES MODELS)

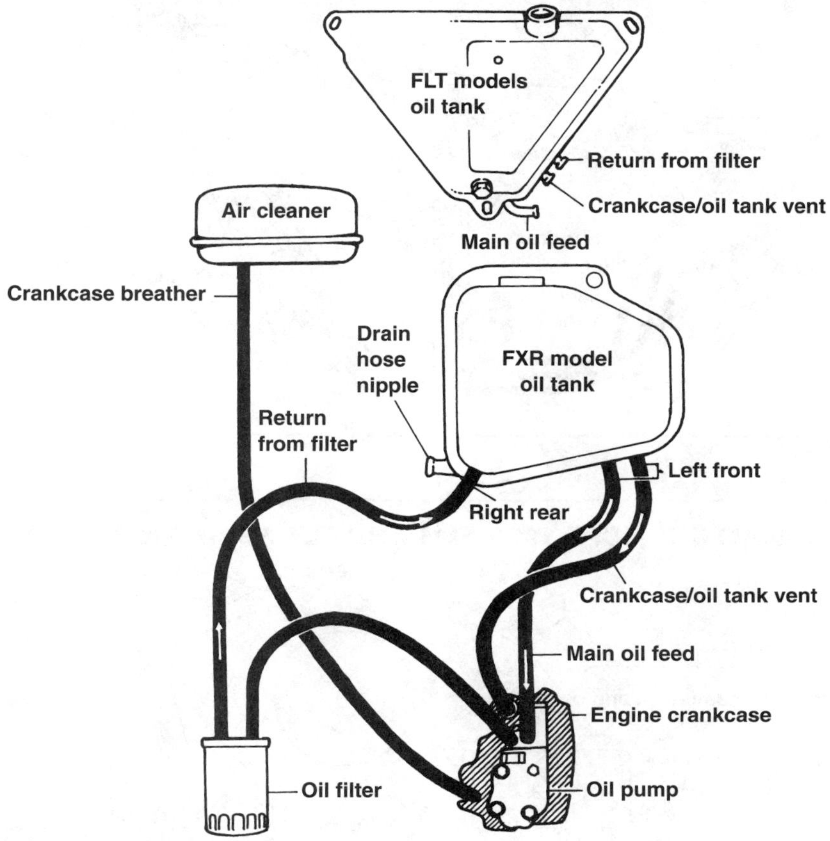

FLT models oil tank
Return from filter
Crankcase/oil tank vent
Main oil feed
Air cleaner
Crankcase breather
Drain hose nipple
FXR model oil tank
Return from filter
Left front
Right rear
Crankcase/oil tank vent
Main oil feed
Engine crankcase
Oil filter
Oil pump

155

OIL HOSE ROUTING (1992-1998 FXR)

Crankcase breather
Oil tank vent
Drain hose nipple
Transmission vent hose
Air cleaner
Oil filter
To oil filter
Main oil feed hose
Oil return hose from filter
Clip

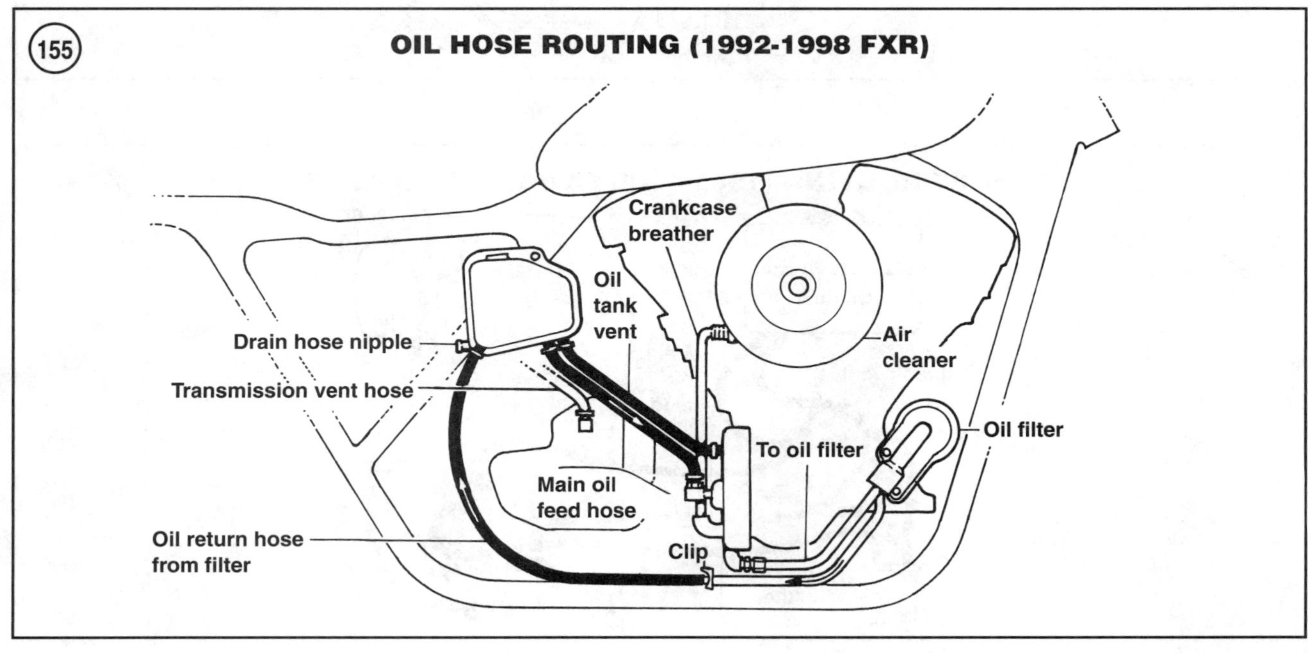

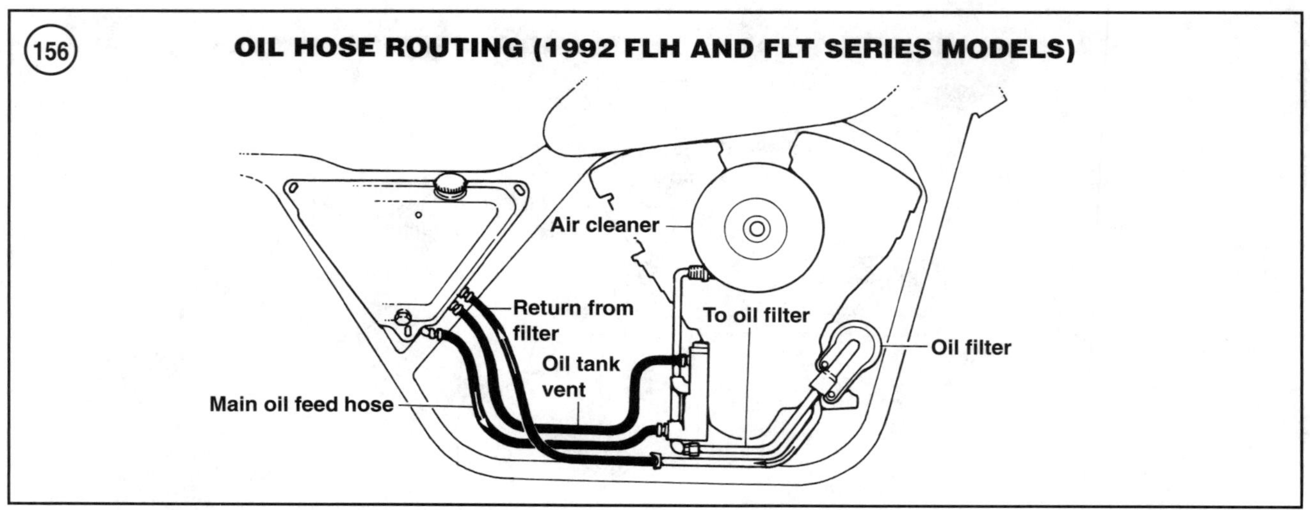
156
OIL HOSE ROUTING (1992 FLH AND FLT SERIES MODELS)
Air cleaner
Return from filter
To oil filter
Oil filter
Oil tank vent
Main oil feed hose

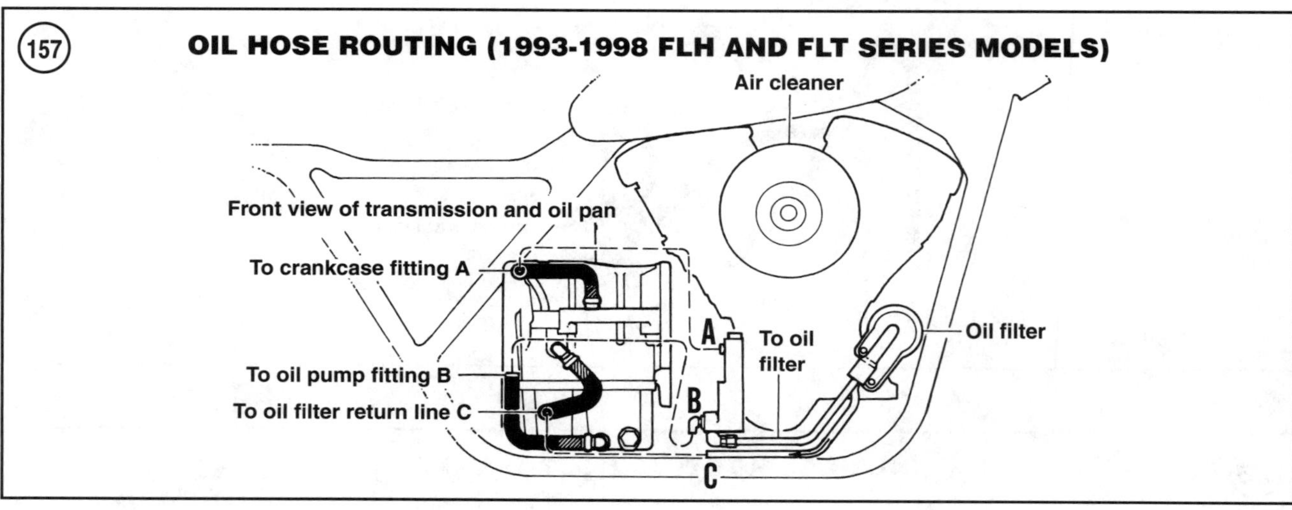
157
OIL HOSE ROUTING (1993-1998 FLH AND FLT SERIES MODELS)
Air cleaner
Front view of transmission and oil pan
To crankcase fitting A
A
To oil filter
Oil filter
To oil pump fitting B
B
To oil filter return line C
C

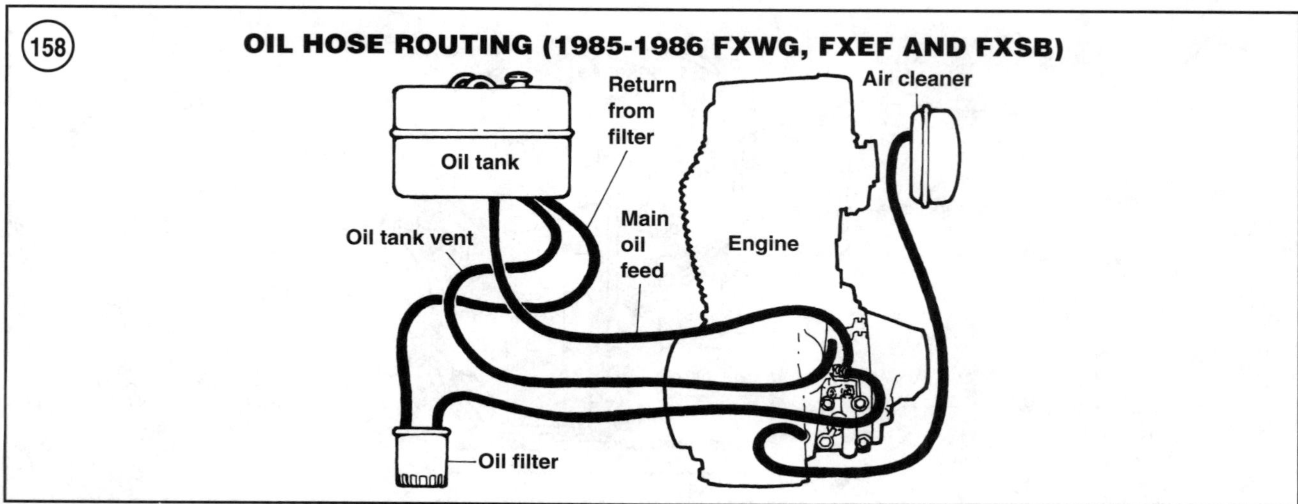
158
OIL HOSE ROUTING (1985-1986 FXWG, FXEF AND FXSB)
Return from filter
Air cleaner
Oil tank
Oil tank vent
Main oil feed
Engine
Oil filter

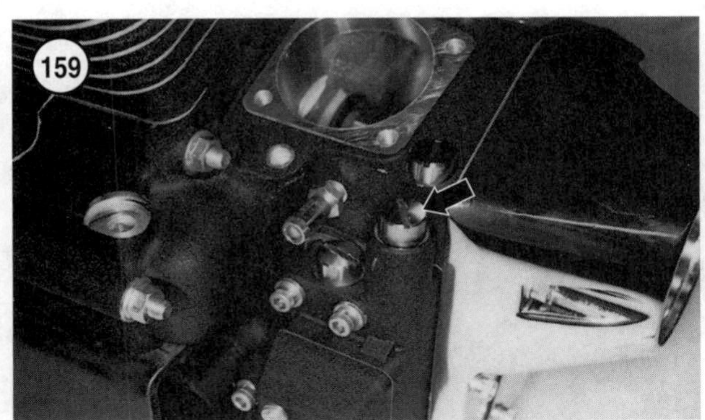
159

163

160

164

161

165

162

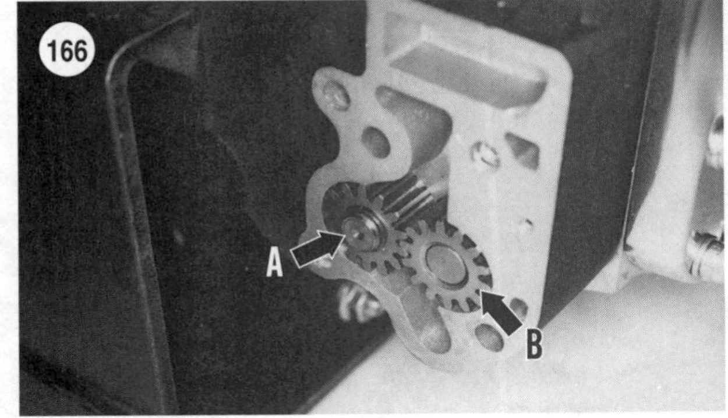
166
A
B

8. Slide the oil pump housing (B, **Figure 168**) off the drive gear shaft and remove the housing.
9. Remove the scavenger pump gears as follows:
   a. Remove the idler gear (**Figure 169**) from the pump housing.
   b. Remove the drive gear (**Figure 170**) and key (**Figure 171**) from the drive gear shaft.
10. Remove the oil pump housing gasket.
11. To remove the oil pump drive gear and drive gear shaft, remove the timing gears as described under *Gearcase Cover and Timing Gears* in this chapter.

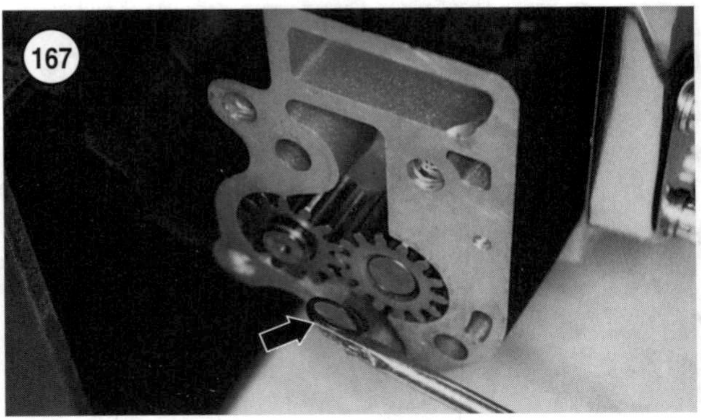
167

Assembly/Installation

NOTE
Install all gears and Woodruff keys in the original positions as noted during removal and disassembly.

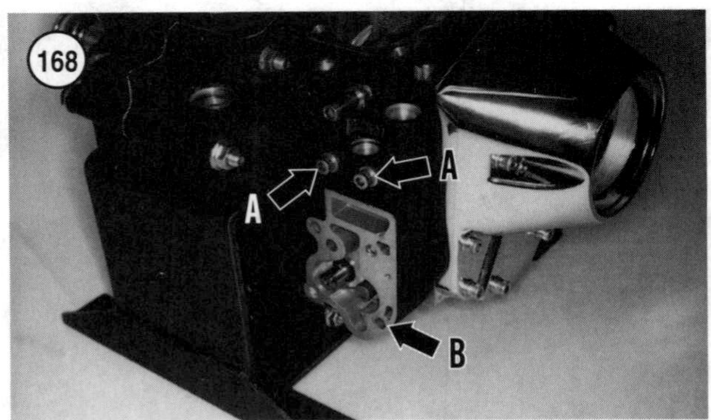

168

CAUTION
Always use original equipment gaskets during oil pump reassembly. OE gaskets are made to a specified thickness with holes placed accurately to pass oil through the oil pump. Gaskets of the incorrect thickness can cause loss of oil pressure and severe engine damage.

1. If removed, install the drive gear shaft, oil pump drive gear and timing gears as described under *Gearcase Cover and Timing Gears* in this chapter.
2. Coat all parts in clean engine oil prior to installation.
3. Install a *new* gasket (**Figure 172**) onto the crankcase.
4. Install the scavenger pump gears as follows:
   a. Install the Woodruff key (**Figure 171**) onto the drive gear shaft.
   b. Install the drive gear (**Figure 170**) and Woodruff key on the drive gear shaft. Seat the gear against the crankcase.
5. Install the idler gear (**Figure 169**) into the pump housing.
6. Install the oil pump housing (B, **Figure 168**) over the drive gear shaft and seat it against the crankcase.
7. Install the oil pump housing bolts (A, **Figure 168**) and tighten to 62-88 in.-lb. (7-10 N•m).

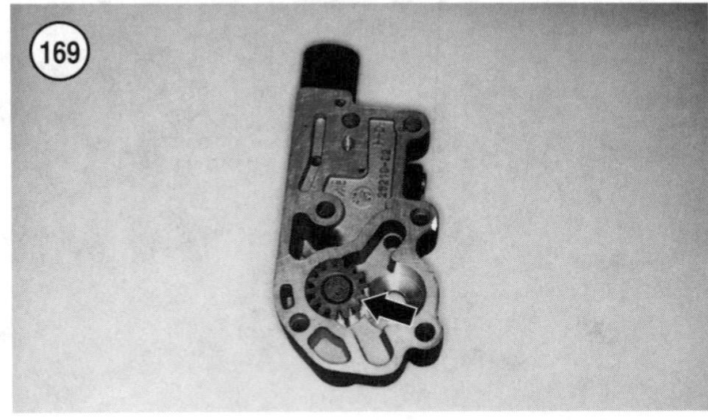
169

NOTE
Do not push the drive gear shaft into the gearcase housing when installing the drive gear and its spiral retaining ring in the following steps. If pushed on, the inner key will fall inside the gearcase housing. To retrieve and install the key, the gearcase cover must be removed.

170

171

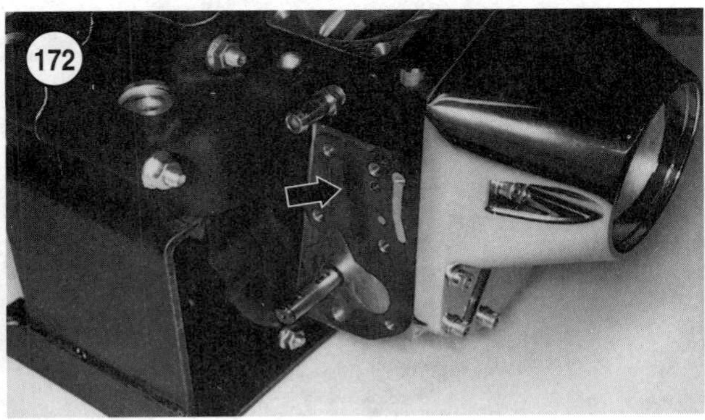
172

173

8. Install the feed gears as follows:
   a. Install the Woodruff key onto the drive gear shaft keyway.
   b. Install the drive gear (A, **Figure 166**) over the keyway and drive gear shaft.
   c. Install the idler gear (B, **Figure 166**) over the idler shaft.
   d. Install a *new* snap ring (**Figure 167**) into the groove in the end of the drive gear shaft. Make sure it is correctly seated in the groove.

9. Install a *new* gasket (**Figure 173**) onto the oil pump cover.

CAUTION
Do not overtighten the oil pump cover mounting bolts. If overtightened, the gear-side clearance will be decreased and cause oil pump seizure.

10A. On 1984-1991 models, install the oil pump cover (**Figure 164**) and the mounting bolts and lockwashers. Tighten the oil pump cover mounting bolts to 62-88 in.-lb. (7-10 N•m).
10B. On 1992-1998 models, install the oil pump cover (**Figure 165**) and mounting bolts. Tighten the oil pump cover mounting bolts to 88-124 in.-lb. (10-14 N•m).

CAUTION
If the pump will not turn after tightening the housing and cover mounting bolts, loosen both sets of bolts and reposition the pump to remove binding. Then tighten the housing and cover bolts to 115-120 in.-lb. (13-13.6 N•m).

11. Install the check valve assembly as follows:
    a. Install the check valve ball (**Figure 163**).
    b. Install the check valve spring (**Figure 162**).
    c. Install the check valve plug and *new* O-ring (**Figure 161**). Tighten the plug securely.
12. Install the relief valve assembly as follows:
    a. Install the spring and relief valve (**Figure 160**).
    b. Install the relief valve plug and O-ring (**Figure 159**).
    c. Tighten the valve plug to 80-106 in.-lb. (9-12 N•m).

NOTE
On 1984-1991 models, replace damaged hose clamps as required and tighten securely. On 1992-1998 models, install new original equipment one-piece band clamps. Tighten the hose clamp with a JIMS pinch hose clamp tool (part No. 1171) or an equivalent.

13A. On 1984-1991 models, connect the hoses to the oil pump. Install *new* hose clamps securing the oil hoses to the oil pump. Refer to **Figures 152-158**.
13B. On 1992-1998 models, connect the oil hoses to the oil pump as described under *Oil Filter Mount* in this chapter.
14. If the engine is installed in the frame, perform the following:
    a. Install the rear brake pedal as described in Chapter Thirteen.

b. Install the exhaust system as described in Chapter Eight.

15. Refill the engine oil as described in Chapter Three.

Inspection

Inspect all parts, and if any part is damaged or out of specification, replace those part(s).

1. Clean all parts thoroughly in solvent and dry with compressed air.
2. Apply low-pressure compressed air through all of the oil pump cover and housing passages (**Figure 174**).
3. Remove the old oil pump housing seal (A, **Figure 175**). Replace the oil seal as described in this section, if necessary.
4. Check the oil pump idler gear shaft (B, **Figure 175**). If it is loose, replace the oil pump body because slippage will allow metal shavings in the oil pump. A new shaft can be pressed in, but in most cases, the shaft is now loose in the shaft bore in the housing.
5. Inspect each gear for chipped or missing teeth or other damage.
6. Inspect the feed gears and drive gear shaft keyways (**Figure 176**) for wear or damage.
7. Inspect the check valve ball and spring (A, **Figure 177**) for wear or damage.
8. Check the bypass valve plunger and spring (B, **Figure 177**) for wear or damage.
9. Assemble the scavenger gears into the oil pump housing (**Figure 178**). Place a straightedge across the gears and measure the end clearance with a flat feeler gauge (**Figure 179**). Refer to **Table 2** for specifications.
10. Repeat Step 9 for the feed gears (**Figure 180**).

Oil Pump Seal Replacement

1. Carefully remove the oil seal (A, **Figure 175**) from the housing.
2. Coat the seal and housing receptacle with clean engine oil.
3. Position the *new* seal with the lips facing toward the feed gears.
4. Install the new seal using a JIMS Oil Seal Installation Tool (part No. 1053) (**Figure 181**) following the manufacturer's instructions.
5. Remove the special tool and check for correct seal installation.

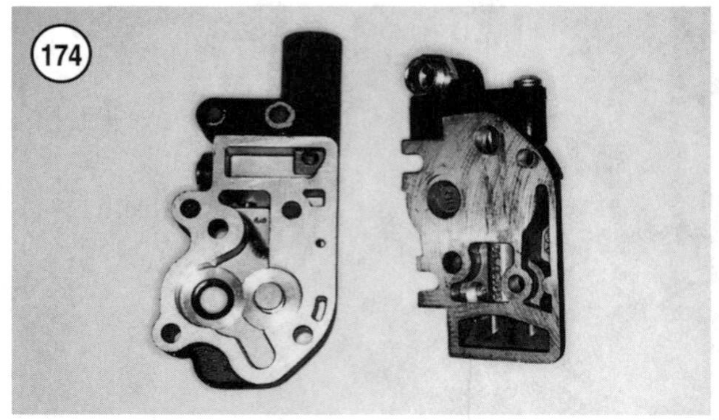

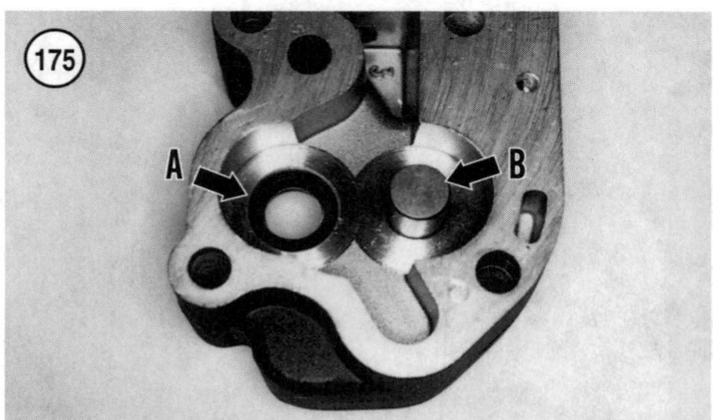

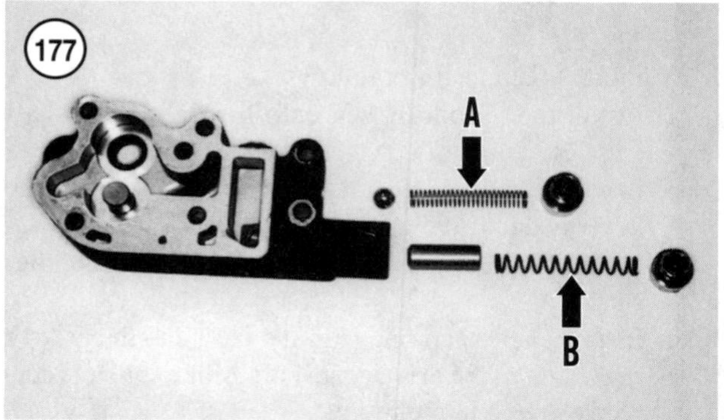

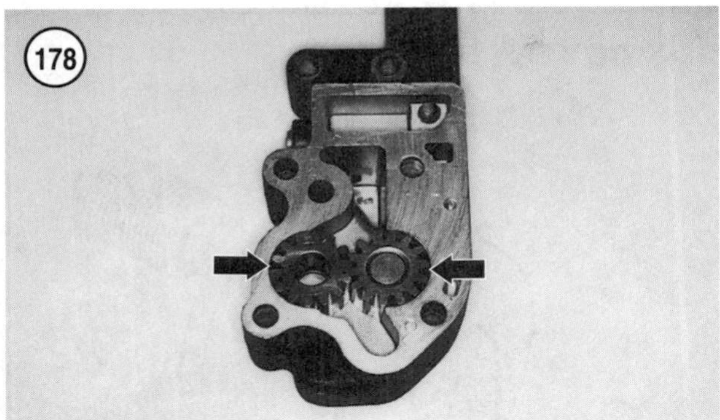

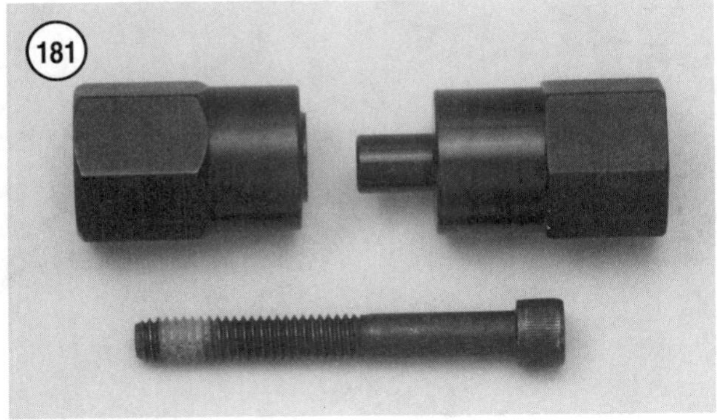

OIL FILTER MOUNT (1992-1998 MODELS)

The oil filter mount is located on the front of the engine on the right side. Refer to **Figure 182**.

Removal

1. Park the motorcycle on a level surface on the jiffy stand.
2. Drain the oil tank or engine oil (oil pan) and remove the oil filter as described in Chapter Three.
3. Loosen the oil filter line compression nut at the oil pump cover manifold until it sets on the oil line.
4. Remove the oil pump cover manifold mounting bolts and washers and remove the manifold and O-rings from the oil pump cover.
5. Remove the oil line clamp nut, washer and spacer.
6. Loosen the oil line compression fittings at the oil filter mount. Then remove the oil lines from the oil filter mount.
7. Remove the oil filter mount screws and washers and remove the oil filter mount.
8. Remove the upper compression nut seals from the oil lines. If necessary, remove the upper compression nuts.
9. Loosen and then remove the compression nut fitting from the oil pump cover manifold.
10. Remove the lower seal and compression nut from the oil line.
11. If necessary, remove the oil filter adapter from the oil filter mount.
12. If necessary, remove the hose nipple from the oil pump cover.

Installation

1. Make sure all parts are clean and dry prior to installing them.
2. If removed, install the hose nipple (2, **Figure 182**) as follows:
   a. On FXR series models, install the hose nipple in the upper pump cover hole (1, **Figure 182**).
   b. On FLH and FLT series models, install the hose nipple in the lower pump cover hole (1, **Figure 182**).
3. If removed, install the compression nut fitting (7, **Figure 182**) as follows:
   a. Apply Loctite 242 (blue) to the compression nut fitting threads prior to installation.
   b. Install the compression nut fitting and tighten to 97-142 in.-lb. (11-16 N•m).
4. If removed, install the oil filter adapter into the oil filter mount.

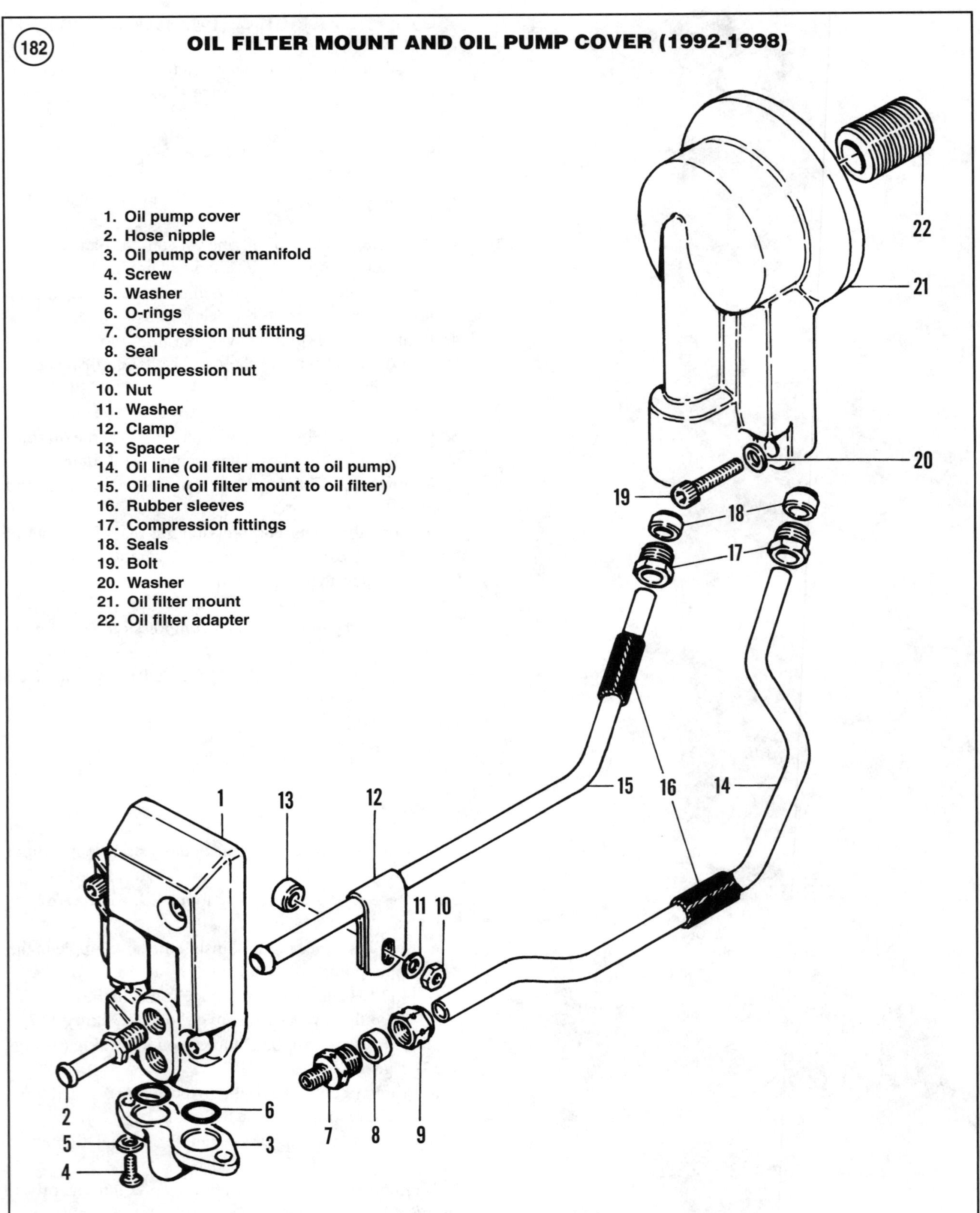
182
OIL FILTER MOUNT AND OIL PUMP COVER (1992-1998)
1. Oil pump cover
2. Hose nipple
3. Oil pump cover manifold
4. Screw
5. Washer
6. O-rings
7. Compression nut fitting
8. Seal
9. Compression nut
10. Nut
11. Washer
12. Clamp
13. Spacer
14. Oil line (oil filter mount to oil pump)
15. Oil line (oil filter mount to oil filter)
16. Rubber sleeves
17. Compression fittings
18. Seals
19. Bolt
20. Washer
21. Oil filter mount
22. Oil filter adapter
22
21
20
19
18
17
15
16
14
1
13
12
11
10
2
6
5
3
4
7
8
9

5. Install the oil filter mount and its mounting screws and washers. Tighten the oil filter mount screws to 13-17 ft.-lb. (18-23 N•m).
6. Slide the oil line compression nut (9, **Figure 182**) and seal (8, **Figure 182**) onto the oil line.
7. Install the two compression fitting oil seals (18, **Figure 182**) into the oil filter mount.
8. Install the upper oil line compression nut fittings (17, **Figure 182**) into the oil filter mount. Tighten the fittings finger-tight only.
9. Insert the oil lines (14 and 15, **Figure 182**) into their respective compression nut fittings until they bottom out.
10. Assemble the oil line clamp, spacer, washer and nut as shown in **Figure 182**; do not tighten the nut at this time.
11. Slide the oil pump manifold compression nut onto the oil line (15, **Figure 182**).
12. Install two *new* O-ring seals onto the oil pump cover manifold and place the manifold onto the bottom of the oil pump cover. Install the manifold screws and washers and tighten to 71-80 in.-lb. (8-9 N•m).
13. Thread the compression nut (9, **Figure 182**) onto the compression nut fitting; tighten the nut until it bottoms out on the fitting.
14. Tighten the upper oil line compression fittings (17, **Figure 182**) until the hex portion on fittings seats against the oil filter mount.
15. Securely tighten the oil line securing nut (10, **Figure 182**).
16. Install the oil filter and fill the oil tank or oil pan as described in Chapter Three.
17. Start the engine and check for leaks.

Inspection

1. Inspect the oil lines for cracks or other damage.
2. If the oil lines were replaced, remove the rubber sleeves from the old oil lines and install them on the new lines in the same position.
3. Clean the compression nuts and compression nut fitting in solvent and dry thoroughly.
4. Replace worn or damaged parts as required.

OIL TANK (1984-1992 MODELS)

Refer to **Figures 183-185**.

Removal/Installation

1. Park the motorcycle on a level surface.
2. Drain the oil tank and engine oil as described in Chapter Three.
3. Remove the seat and right side cover as described in Chapter Fifteen.
4. Remove the exhaust system as described in Chapter Eight.
5. Remove the oil tank dipstick.
6. On models so equipped, disconnect the electrical connector from the oil temperature sender.

NOTE
When disconnecting the oil hoses in Step 7, make sure to tag each hose and fitting so that the hoses can be returned to the original positions.

7. Cut the hose clamp securing the oil hose to the oil tank fittings. Then disconnect the hoses. Plug the hose ends to prevent the entry of debris. Discard the clamps.
8. Remove all mounting hardware securing the oil tank to the frame.
9. Slowly remove the oil tank from the right side of the frame. Make sure no electrical wires are interfering with removal of the oil tank.
10. Install by reversing these removal steps while noting the following:
   a. Tighten all bolts and nuts securely.
   b. Install *new* original equipment one-piece band clamps. Tighten hose clamp with a JIMS pinch hose clamp tool (part No. 1171) or an equivalent.
   c. Refill the engine and oil tank as described in Chapter Three.

GEARCASE COVER AND TIMING GEARS

Refer to **Figure 186** and **Figure 187**.

Removal

1. Remove the pushrods, valve lifters and guides as described in this chapter.
2. Remove the lifter oil screen cap and O-ring (**Figure 188**). Then remove the spring and screen (**Figure 189**).
3. Remove the ignition sensor plate and rotor as described in Chapter Nine.
4. Place an oil drain pan underneath the gearcase cover.

NOTE
The gearcase cover screws are different lengths. Note the lengths and locations during removal to make sure they are installed in the proper positions during installation.

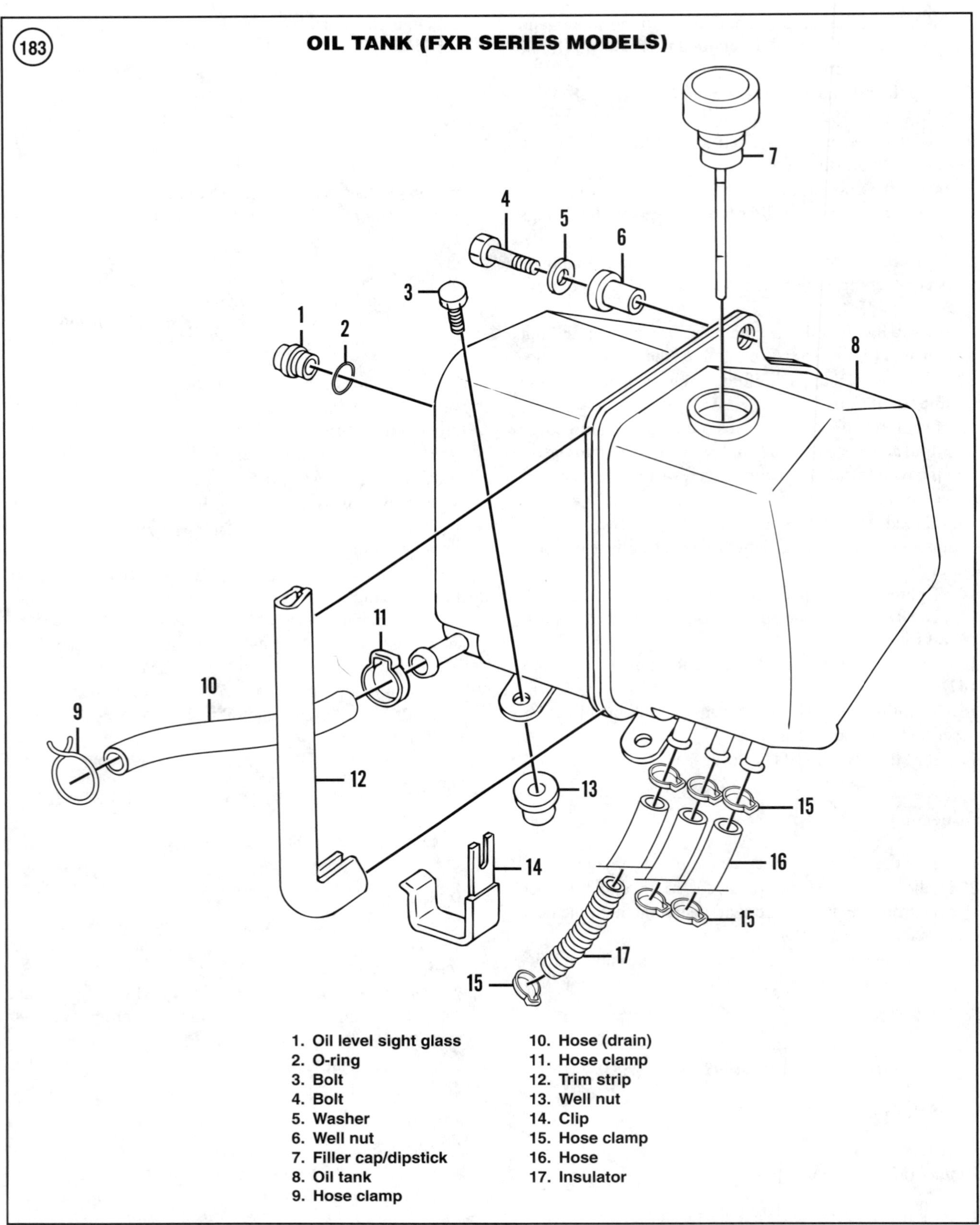
183
OIL TANK (FXR SERIES MODELS)
1
2
3
4
5
6
7
8
9
10
11
12
13
14
15
16
17
1. Oil level sight glass
2. O-ring
3. Bolt
4. Bolt
5. Washer
6. Well nut
7. Filler cap/dipstick
8. Oil tank
9. Hose clamp
10. Hose (drain)
11. Hose clamp
12. Trim strip
13. Well nut
14. Clip
15. Hose clamp
16. Hose
17. Insulator

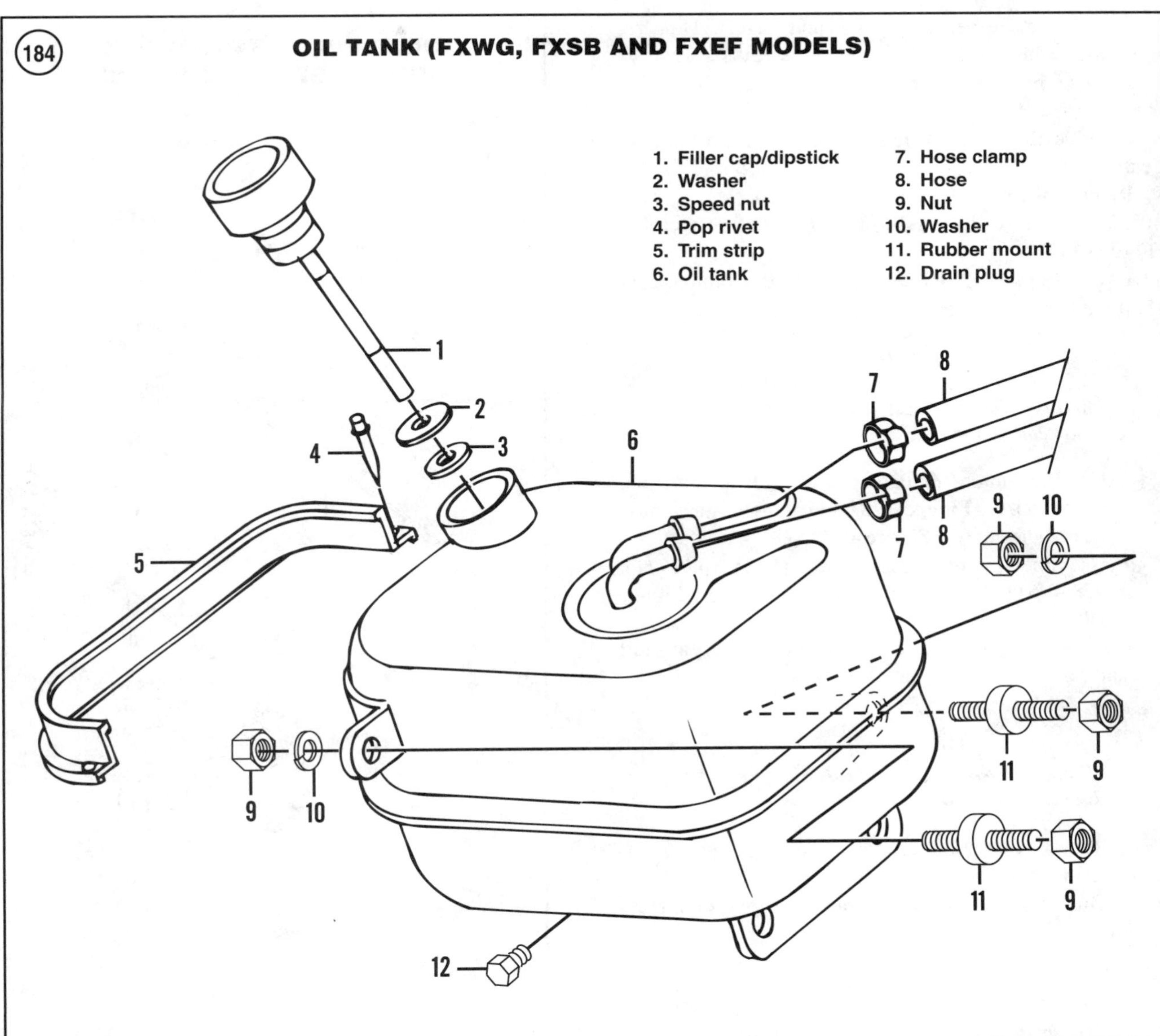

5. Loosen and remove the screws securing the gearcase cover (**Figure 190**).

NOTE
Snug-fitting dowel pins locate the gearcase cover to the crankcase. The cover must be removed carefully. Do not pry the gearcase cover off with any sharp metal tools. Doing so will result in an oil leak. If necessary, tap on the cover with a plastic hammer to break it loose.

6A. At the point where the cover projects beyond the crankcase, tap the gearcase cover lightly with a plastic hammer and remove the cover (**Figure 190**) and gasket. If the cover will not release from the dowel pins, perform Step 6B.

6B. If the gearcase was not removed in Step 6A, perform the following:

a. Fabricate the puller shown in **Figure 191**. The outside diameter of the puller must be the same size as the ignition sensor plate outside diameter.
b. Install the puller onto the gearcase cover and secure it with the two screws (**Figure 192**).
c. Tighten the puller center screw against the crankshaft to force the gearcase cover away from the crankcase.

d. Remove the gearcase cover and gasket. Then remove the puller from the gearcase cover.

7. If loose, remove the two dowel pins from the crankcase (**Figure 193**).

8. Remove the spacer (**Figure 194**) from the breather gear.

9. Remove the breather gear (**Figure 195**).

10. Remove the camshaft (**Figure 196**) and thrust washer (**Figure 197**).

11A. On 1984-1992 models, remove the pinion gear shaft nut and pinion gear shaft as follows:

NOTE

*The pinion gear shaft nut has left-hand threads. Turn the nut **clockwise** to loosen and remove the nut.*

a. Use the Pinion Shaft Nut Socket (JIMS part No. 94555-55A) (**Figure 198**) and remove the pinion gear shaft nut (A, **Figure 199**).

b. Use the pinion gear puller (JIMS part No. 96830-51) and remove the pinion gear (B, **Figure 199**).

11B. On 1993-1998 models, remove the pinion gear shaft nut and pinion shaft gear as follows:

NOTE

*The pinion gear shaft nut has right-hand threads. Turn the nut **counterclockwise** to loosen and remove it.*

a. Remove the pinion gear shaft nut (A, **Figure 199**).

b. Remove the pinion gear (B, **Figure 199**).

12A. On 1984-1992 models, remove the following parts in order:

NOTE

On 1990-1992 models, there is a single Woodruff key for both the pinion and oil pump gears.

a. On 1984-1989 models: Woodruff key.

b. Pinion gear spacer.

c. Oil pump pinion shaft gear.

d. Woodruff key.

12B. On 1993-1998 models, remove the following parts in order:

a. Oil pump drive gear (**Figure 200**).

b. Woodruff key (**Figure 201**).

13. To remove the oil pump drive gear and drive gear shaft, perform the following:

a. Remove the oil pump as described in this chapter.

b. Remove the oil pump drive gear snap ring (A, **Figure 202**).

185 OIL TANK (1984-1992 FLH AND FLT SERIES MODELS)

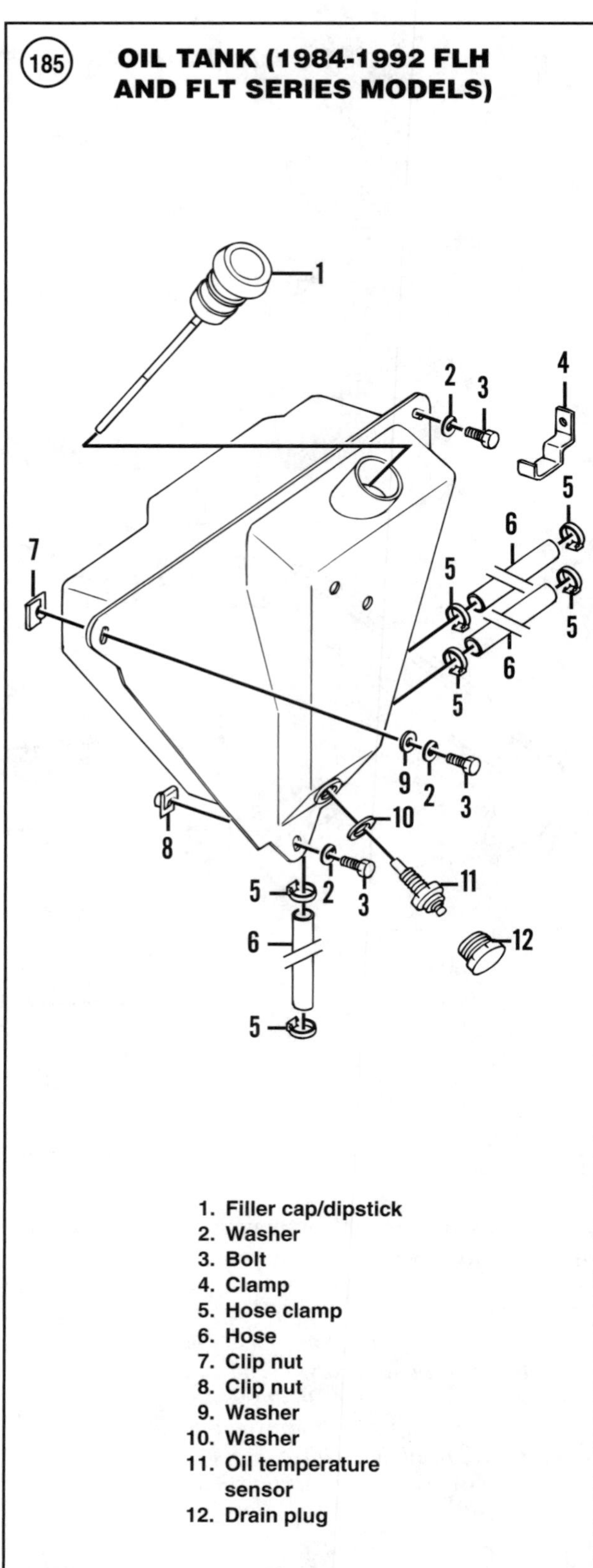

1. Filler cap/dipstick
2. Washer
3. Bolt
4. Clamp
5. Hose clamp
6. Hose
7. Clip nut
8. Clip nut
9. Washer
10. Washer
11. Oil temperature sensor
12. Drain plug

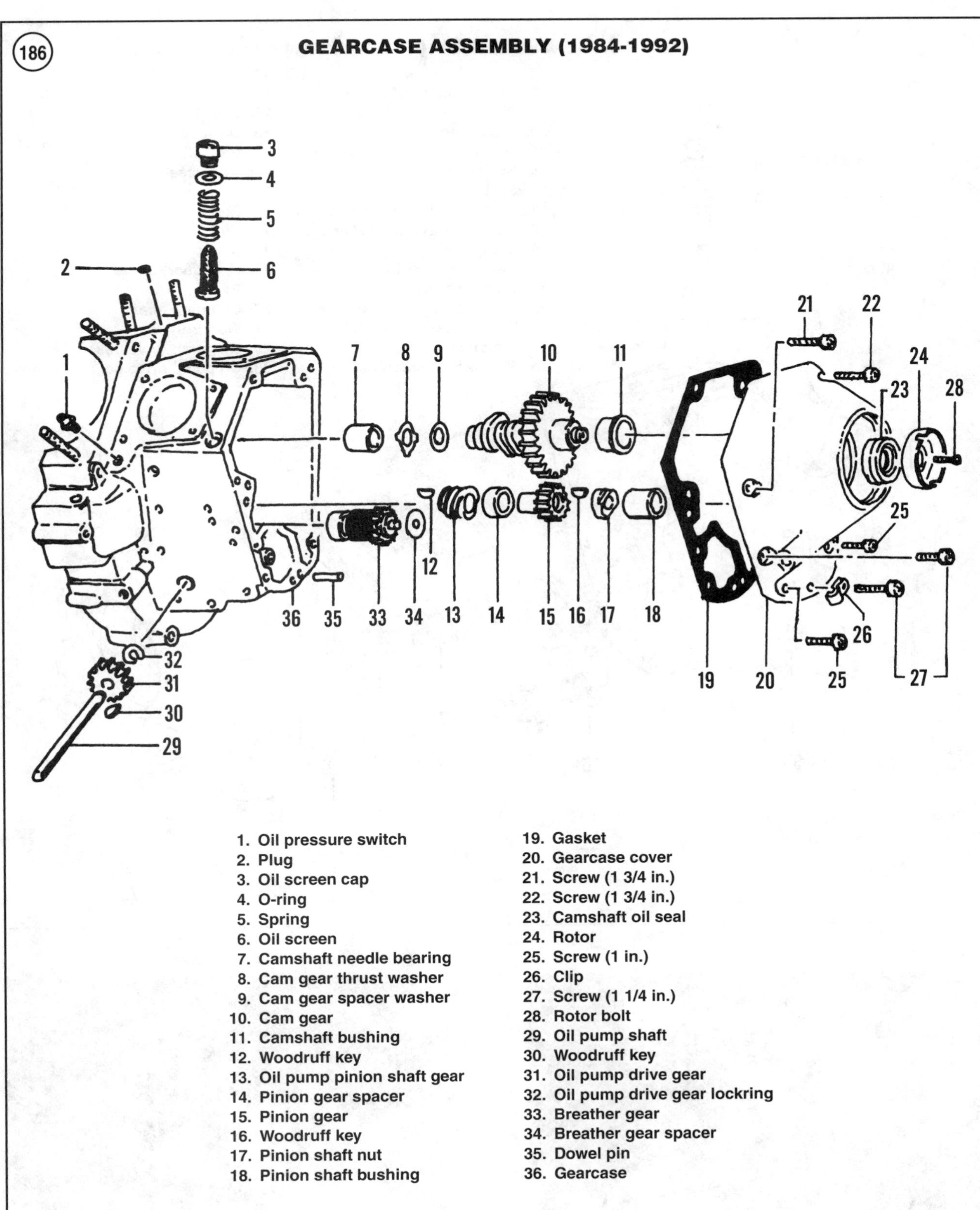

1. Oil pressure switch
2. Plug
3. Oil screen cap
4. O-ring
5. Spring
6. Oil screen
7. Camshaft needle bearing
8. Cam gear thrust washer
9. Cam gear spacer washer
10. Cam gear
11. Camshaft bushing
12. Woodruff key
13. Oil pump pinion shaft gear
14. Pinion gear spacer
15. Pinion gear
16. Woodruff key
17. Pinion shaft nut
18. Pinion shaft bushing
19. Gasket
20. Gearcase cover
21. Screw (1 3/4 in.)
22. Screw (1 3/4 in.)
23. Camshaft oil seal
24. Rotor
25. Screw (1 in.)
26. Clip
27. Screw (1 1/4 in.)
28. Rotor bolt
29. Oil pump shaft
30. Woodruff key
31. Oil pump drive gear
32. Oil pump drive gear lockring
33. Breather gear
34. Breather gear spacer
35. Dowel pin
36. Gearcase

187

GEARCASE ASSEMBLY (1993-1998)

1. Oil pressure switch
2. Plug
3. Oil screen cap
4. O-ring
5. Spring
6. Screen
7. Cam gear needle bearing
8. Cam gear thrust washer
9. Cam gear
10. Cam gear bushing
11. Woodruff key
12. Oil pump pinion shaft gear
13. Pinion gear
14. Pinion shaft nut
15. Pinion shaft bushing
16. Breather gear
17. Breather gear spacer
18. Dowel pin
19. Gasket
20. Gearcase cover
21. Screw
22. Screw
23. Clip
24. Screw
25. Cam gear oil seal
26. Rotor
27. Oil pump shaft
28. Woodruff key
29. Oil pump drive gear
30. Oil pump drive gear lockring

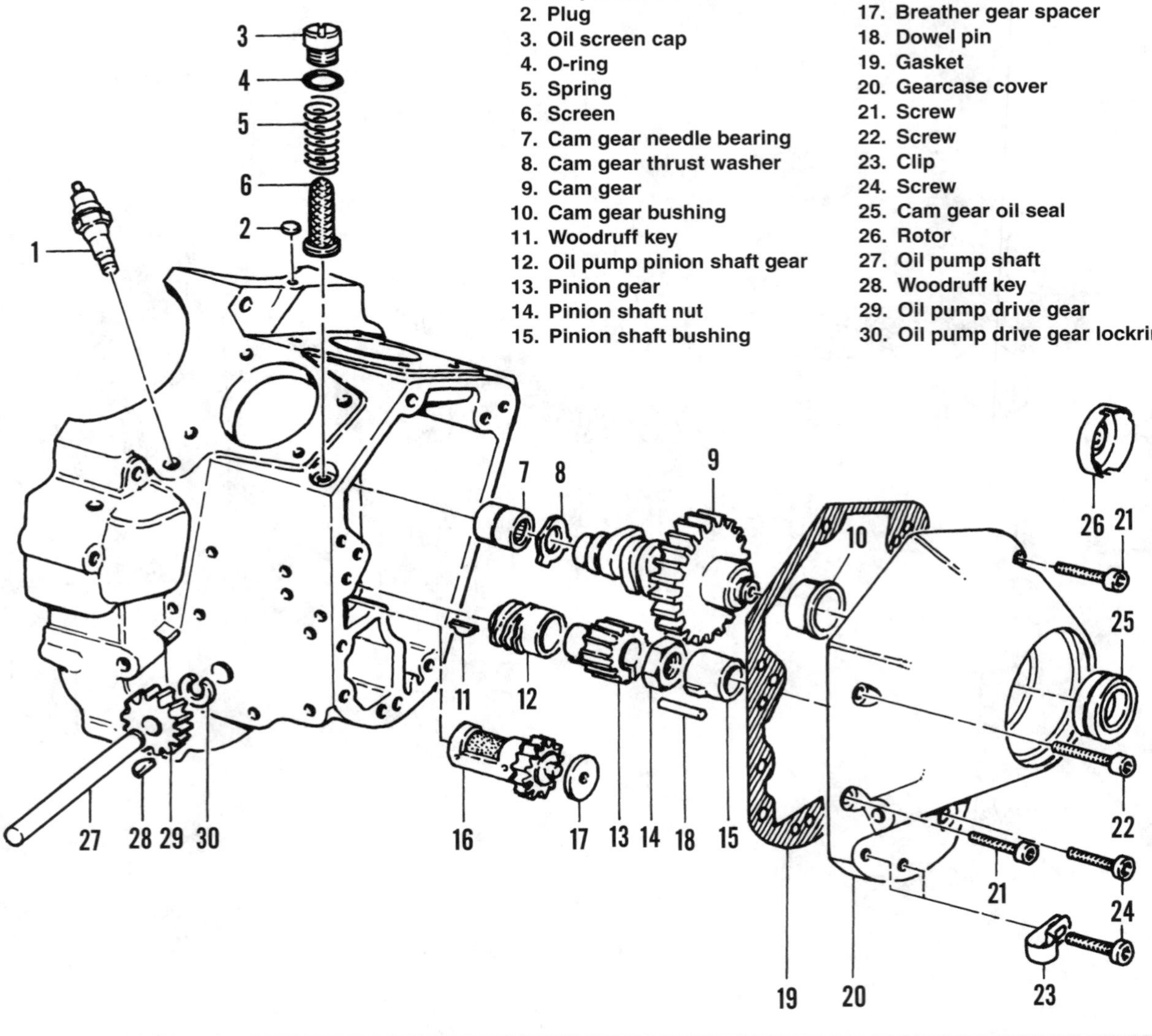

188

189

190

193

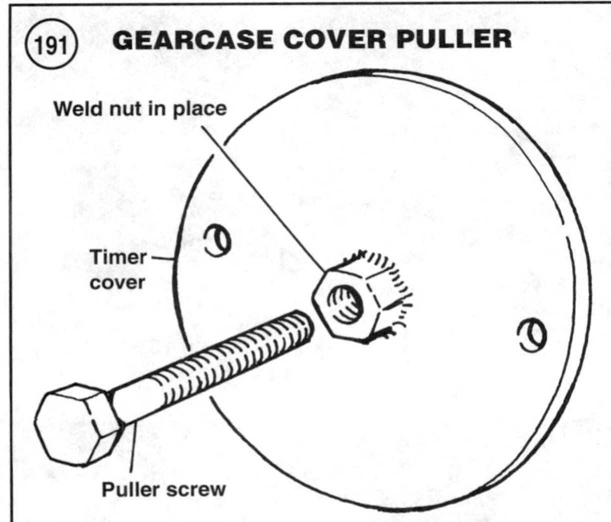
191
GEARCASE COVER PULLER
Weld nut in place
Timer cover
Puller screw

194

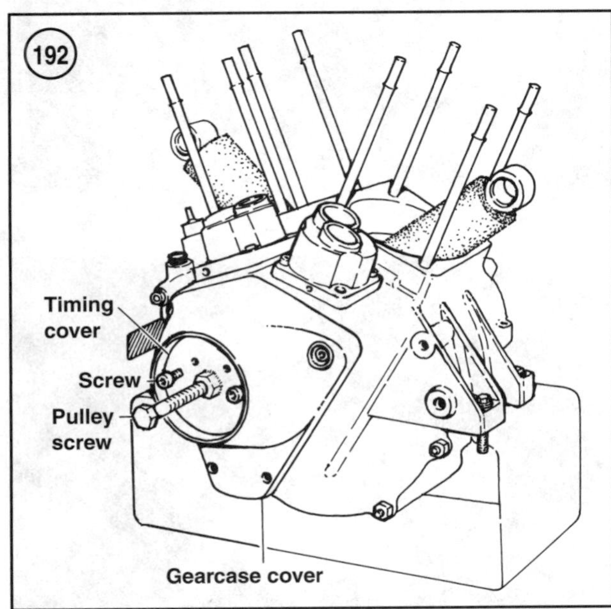
192
Timing cover
Screw
Pulley screw
Gearcase cover

195

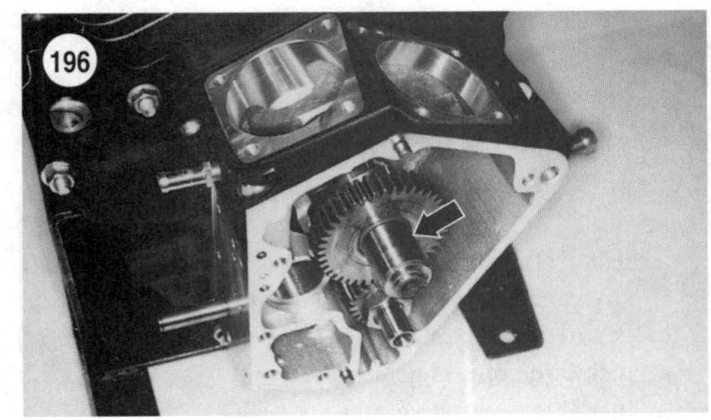
196

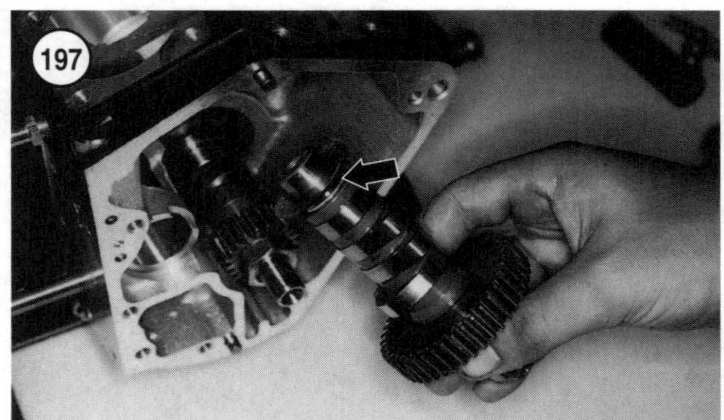

c. Remove the oil pump drive gear (B, **Figure 202**).
d. Remove the Woodruff key (**Figure 203**).
e. Remove the oil pump drive gear shaft (A, **Figure 204**).

Installation

1. Prior to final assembly of the gearcase components, perform the following:
   a. Check the breather gear end play as described in this section.
   b. Check the camshaft gear end play as described in this section.
2. Install the oil pump drive gear shaft and drive gear as follows:
   a. Position the drive gear shaft having the two Woodruff keyways (B, **Figure 204**) going in last and install the drive gear shaft (A) through the crankcase.
   b. Install the Woodruff key onto the shaft (**Figure 203**). Make sure it is centered in the keyway.
   c. Align the keyway of the gear with the Woodruff key on the shaft and install the drive gear (**Figure 201**).
   d. Hold onto the end of the shaft and install a *new* snap ring onto the end of the shaft. Make sure the snap ring is correctly seated in the shaft groove.

NOTE
At this point, the oil pump assembly may be installed. It may also be installed after the completion of this procedure.

3A. On 1984-1992 models, install the following parts in this order:
   a. Install the Woodruff key into the pinion shaft keyway. Make sure it is centered in the keyway.
   b. Install the oil pump pinion shaft gear onto the shaft.
   c. Install the pinion gear spacer.
   d. Install the pinion gear.

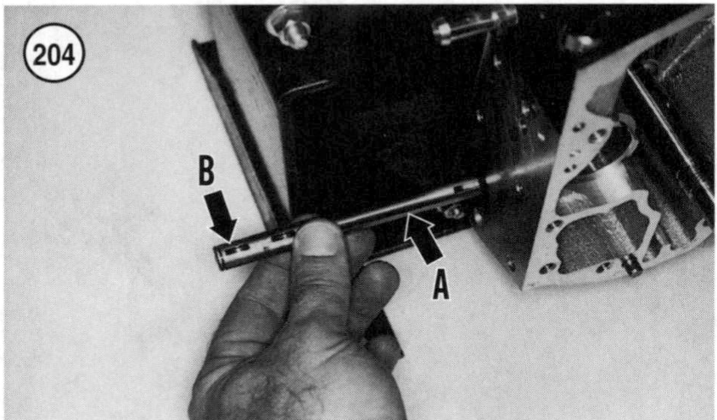

NOTE

*The pinion gear shaft nut has left-hand threads. Turn the nut **counterclockwise** to tighten the nut.*

e. Apply high strength threadlocking compound to the pinion shaft threads and install the pinion gear shaft nut. Tighten the nut to 35-45 ft.-lb. (46-61 N•m).

3B. On 1993-1998 models, install the following parts in order:

a. Install the Woodruff key (**Figure 201**) onto the pinion shaft keyway. Make sure it is centered in the keyway.

b. Position the oil pump drive gear with the shoulder side facing out and install the oil pump drive gear (**Figure 200**).

c. Install the pinion gear (B, **Figure 199**) onto the pinion shaft. Engage the keyway in the gear with the Woodruff key.

NOTE

*The pinion gear shaft nut has right-hand threads. Turn the nut **clockwise** to tighten the nut.*

d. Apply high-strength threadlocking compound to the pinion shaft threads and install the pinion gear shaft nut (A, **Figure 199**). Tighten the nut to 35-45 ft.-lb. (46-61 N•m).

4. Install the thrust washer onto the camshaft gear (**Figure 197**).

5. Align the index timing mark on the camshaft gear with the index mark on the pinion gear (A, **Figure 205**) and install the camshaft gear onto the crankcase (**Figure 196**).

6. Align the index timing mark on the breather gear with the index mark on the camshaft gear (B, **Figure 205**) and install the breather gear (C) into the crankcase receptacle.

CAUTION

At this time, the index timing marks in Step 5 and 6 must be aligned correctly. Otherwise, camshaft timing will be incorrect. Do not proceed if the timing marks are not aligned correctly. Readjust the gear(s) at this time if necessary.

7. Install the breather gear spacer onto the breather gear (**Figure 194**).

8. Rotate the crankcase several complete revolutions to make sure the gears rotate with no binding. Correct any problem at this time if necessary.

9. Install the two dowel pins (**Figure 193**) if removed.

10. Install a *new* gasket onto the crankcase.

4

11. Install the gearcase cover and push it on until it is seated correctly. Do not try to correctly seat the cover with the mounting screws.
12. Install the cover screws and tighten to the following:
   a. 1984-1992 models: 62-88 in.-lb. (7-10 N•m).
   b. 1993-1998 models: 88-124 in.-lb. (10-14 N•m).
13. Pour about 1/4 pint of clean engine oil through the lifter guide hole to provide initial gear train lubrication.
14. Install the electronic sensor plate and rotor as described in Chapter Nine.
15. Install the valve lifters, guides and pushrods as described in this chapter.
16. Install the lifter oil screen (**Figure 189**), cap and O-ring (**Figure 188**). Tighten the cap to 90-120 in.-lb. (10-14 N•m).

Breather Gear End Play Check and Adjustment

Prior to final assembly of the gearcase components, check the breather gear end play as follows:
1. Install the breather gear (**Figure 195**) and the spacer (**Figure 194**).
2. Install a *new* gearcase cover gasket onto the crankcase. Hold it in place with several small dabs of cold grease.
3. Place a straightedge across the gearcase and gasket adjacent to the breather gear spacer. Measure the clearance with a flat feeler gauge (**Figure 206**). Note the dimension.
4. Subtract 0.006 in. (0.15 mm) from the clearance dimension in Step 3. This is the existing end play clearance. **Table 2** lists the specified breather gear clearance.
5. Replace the spacer if necessary. Spacers with several different thicknesses are available from Harley-Davidson dealerships.
6. Remove the gasket and put it aside for installation.

Camshaft Gear End Play Check and Adjustment

Prior to final assembly of the gearcase components, check the camshaft gear end play as follows:
1. Install the camshaft gear thrust washer, cam gear spacer washer (1984-1987 models) and the camshaft gear (**Figure 196**).
2. Install a *new* gasket and the gearcase cover. Install a minimum of four gearcase cover screws and tighten securely.
3. Insert a feeler gauge through the gearcase valve lifter hole (**Figure 207**) and measure the camshaft gear end play between the gear shaft and the thrust washer.
4. **Table 2** lists the specified camshaft gear end play.
5A. On 1984-1987 models, replace the washer if necessary. Washers with several different thicknesses are available from Harley-Davidson dealerships.

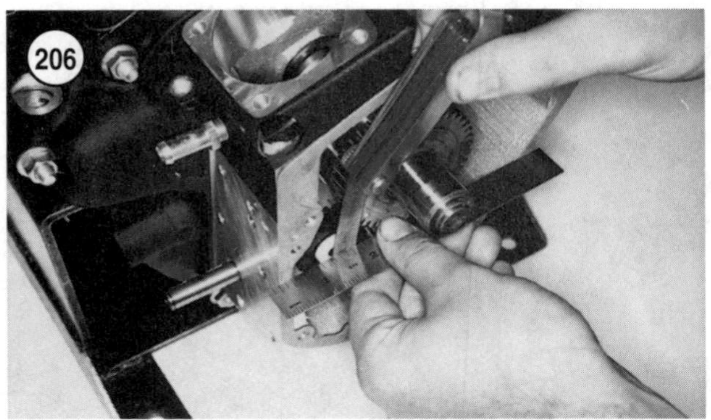
206

207

208

5B. On 1998 models, washers with different thicknesses are not available. If the clearance exceeds the specifications, check for worn or damaged parts and replace as necessary.

Inspection

1. Thoroughly clean gearcase compartment, cover and components with solvent. Blow out all oil passages with low pressure compressed air. Remove all traces of gasket compound from the gasket mating surfaces.

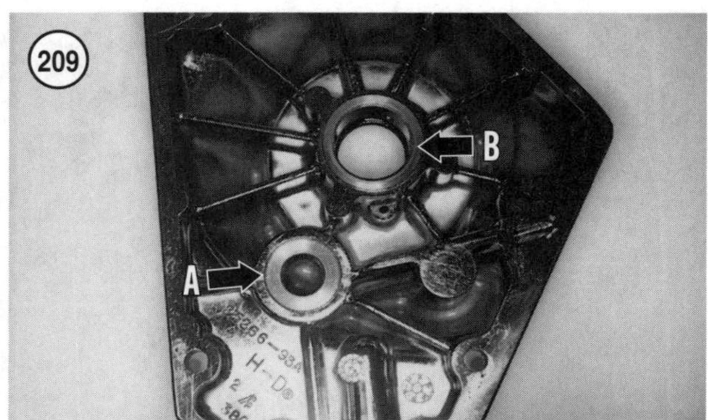

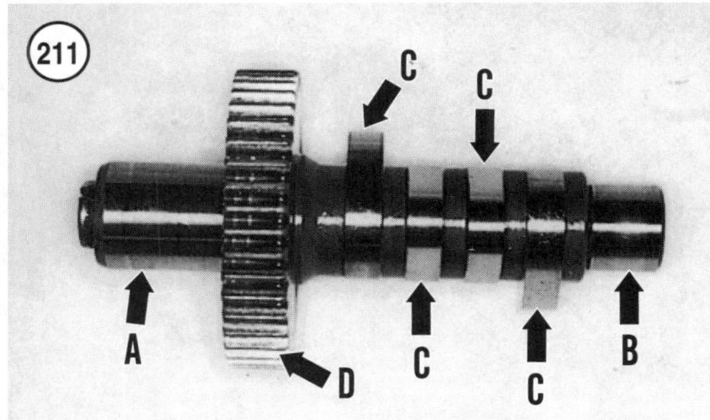

2. Check the oil screen (**Figure 208**) for damage and/or contamination. Hold the screen upside down and fill it with engine oil. Watch the screen to see that the oil flows evenly through the screen. If not, replace the screen.

3. Check the pinion gear shaft and camshaft gear bushings in the gearcase cover for grooving, pitting or other wear. If the bushings appear visibly worn, refer replacement to a Harley-Davidson dealership. If the bushings are good, continue to Step 4.

4. Determine the pinion shaft bushing (A, **Figure 209**) clearance as follows:

   a. Measure the pinion shaft bushing inside diameter. Record the measurement.
   b. Measure the pinion shaft (A, **Figure 210**) outside diameter where it rides in the bushing. Record the measurement.
   c. Subtract substep b from substep a to determine pin shaft bushing clearance. Replace the bushing if worn to the service limit in **Table 2**.

5. Determine camshaft gear bushing (B, **Figure 209**) clearance as follows:

   a. Measure the camshaft gear bushing inside diameter. Record the measurement.
   b. Measure the camshaft gear (A, **Figure 211**) outside diameter where it rides in the bushing. Record the measurement.
   c. Subtract substep b from substep a to determine pin shaft bushing clearance. Replace the bushing if worn to the service limit in **Table 2**. Refer this service to a Harley-Davidson dealership.

6. Inspect the camshaft gear needle bearing (B, **Figure 210**) for wear or damage. If the bearing is good, perform Step 7. If worn or damaged, replace it as described in this chapter.

7. Measure the camshaft gear as follows:

   a. Measure the end (B, **Figure 211**) where it rides in the crankcase needle bearing.
   b. Repeat substep a measuring closer to the camshaft lobe where it does *not* ride in the needle bearing.
   c. If the difference between substep a and b exceeds 0.003 in. (0.08 mm), replace the camshaft gear and the needle bearing.

8. Measure the camshaft lobes (C, **Figure 211**) with a micrometer and compare to the lobes on a *new* Evolution cam. If the camshaft lobes are worn more than 0.006 in. (0.15 mm), replace the camshaft gear.

NOTE

*Camshafts used in pre-1984 V-twin models are **not interchangeable** with 1984-1998 Evolution engines and vice versa. Do not use a non-Evolution camshaft when comparing lobe wear in Step 8.*

9. Inspect the camshaft gear for chipped or missing teeth (D, **Figure 211**).

10. Inspect the pinion gear and the oil pump pinion shaft for wear or damage.

NOTE

Color codes identify the camshaft and pinion gear pitch diameters. The diameters of both replacement gears must be matched, or

4

abnormal gear noise will result. Refer this service to a Harley-Davidson dealership.

11. Mount a dial indicator to the pinion shaft as shown in (**Figure 212**). Slowly rotate the sprocket shaft on the other side and measure the pinion shaft runout. If the runout is worn to the service limit, either the crankshaft must be trued, or the pinion shaft bearing in the crankcase is worn. Refer this procedure to a Harley-Davidson dealership.
12. Check the camshaft gear oil seal (**Figure 213**) in the gearcase cover. If worn, carefully pry it out of the case. Install a new seal. Refer to the typical procedure described in Chapter One.
13. Inspect the breather gear (**Figure 214**) for chipped or missing teeth. Also check the oil screen for debris or damage and clean with solvent if necessary. Replace the breather gear if necessary.

212

213

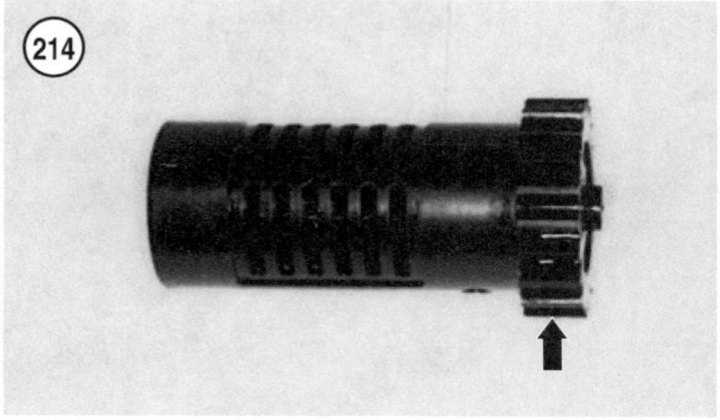
214

CRANKCASE AND CRANKSHAFT

Crankshaft End Play Check

Measure the crankshaft end play prior to disassembling the crankcase. Crankshaft end play is a measure of sprocket shaft bearing wear.

1. Remove the engine from the frame as described in this chapter.
2. Remove the gearcase cover as described in this chapter.
3. Mount the crankcase in an engine stand (JIMS part No. 1006T) (**Figure 215**).
4. Install the bearing installation tool (JIMS part No. 97225-55) onto the sprocket shaft to preload the bearing races (**Figure 216**).
5. Attach a dial indicator so that the probe touches against the end of the crankshaft (**Figure 216**).
6. Turn and pull on the sprocket shaft while noting the end play registering on the dial indicator. If end play exceeds the limit in **Table 2**, the inner bearing spacer (4, **Figure 217**) or (4, **Figure 218**) must be replaced. Adjust end play by installing a different spacer selected from the chart in **Table 5**.

215

Disassembly

Refer to **Figure 217** and **Figure 218**.

1. Remove the engine from the frame as described in this chapter.

CAUTION

After removing the cylinders, slip a 1/2-in. diameter vinyl or rubber hose over each cyl-

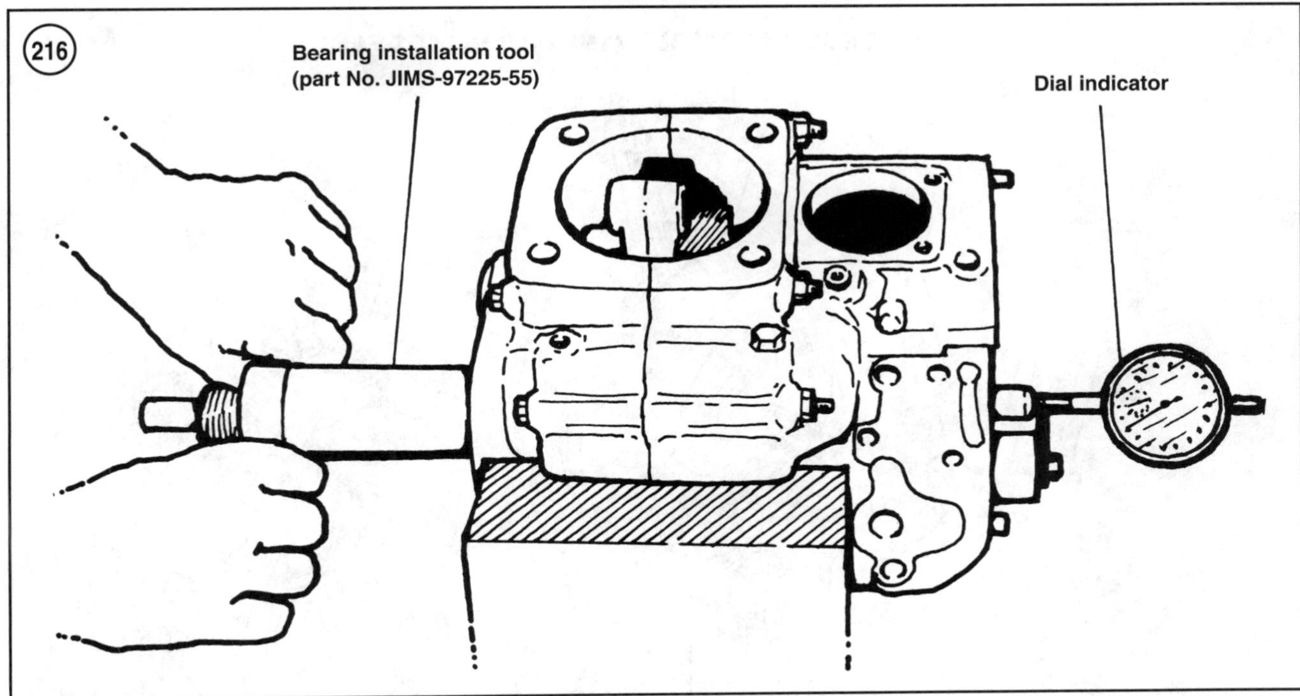

217

CRANKCASE ASSEMBLY (1984-1986 MODELS)

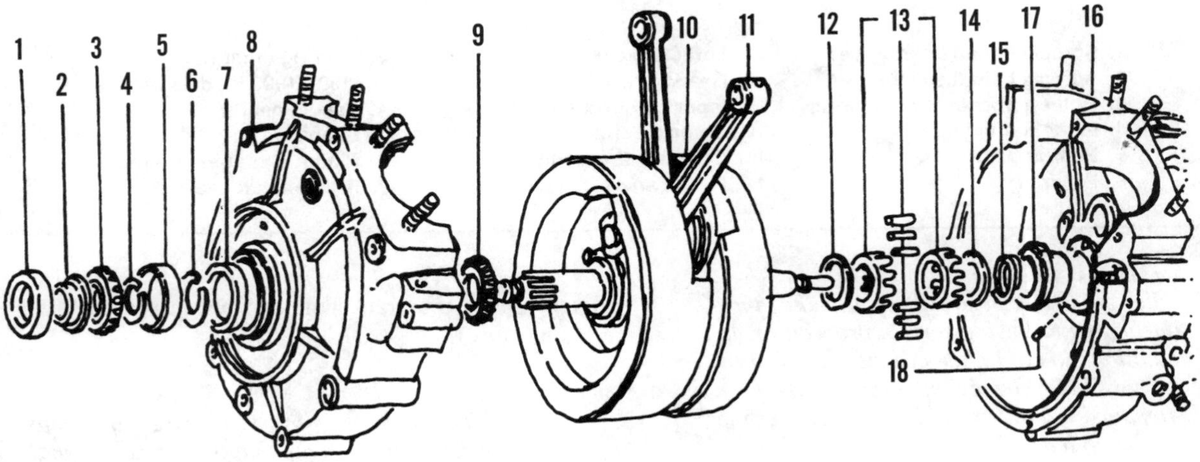

1. Sprocket shaft bearing seal
2. Sprocket shaft spacer
3. Sprocket bearing half
4. Inner bearing spacer
5. Bearing outer race
6. Lockring
7. Bearing outer race
8. Left crankcase half
9. Sprocket bearing half
10. Crankshaft assembly
11. Connecting rod
12. Bearing washer
13. Bearings and retainer
14. Bearing washer
15. Snap ring
16. Right crankcase half
17. Pinion shaft bearing race
18. Lock screw

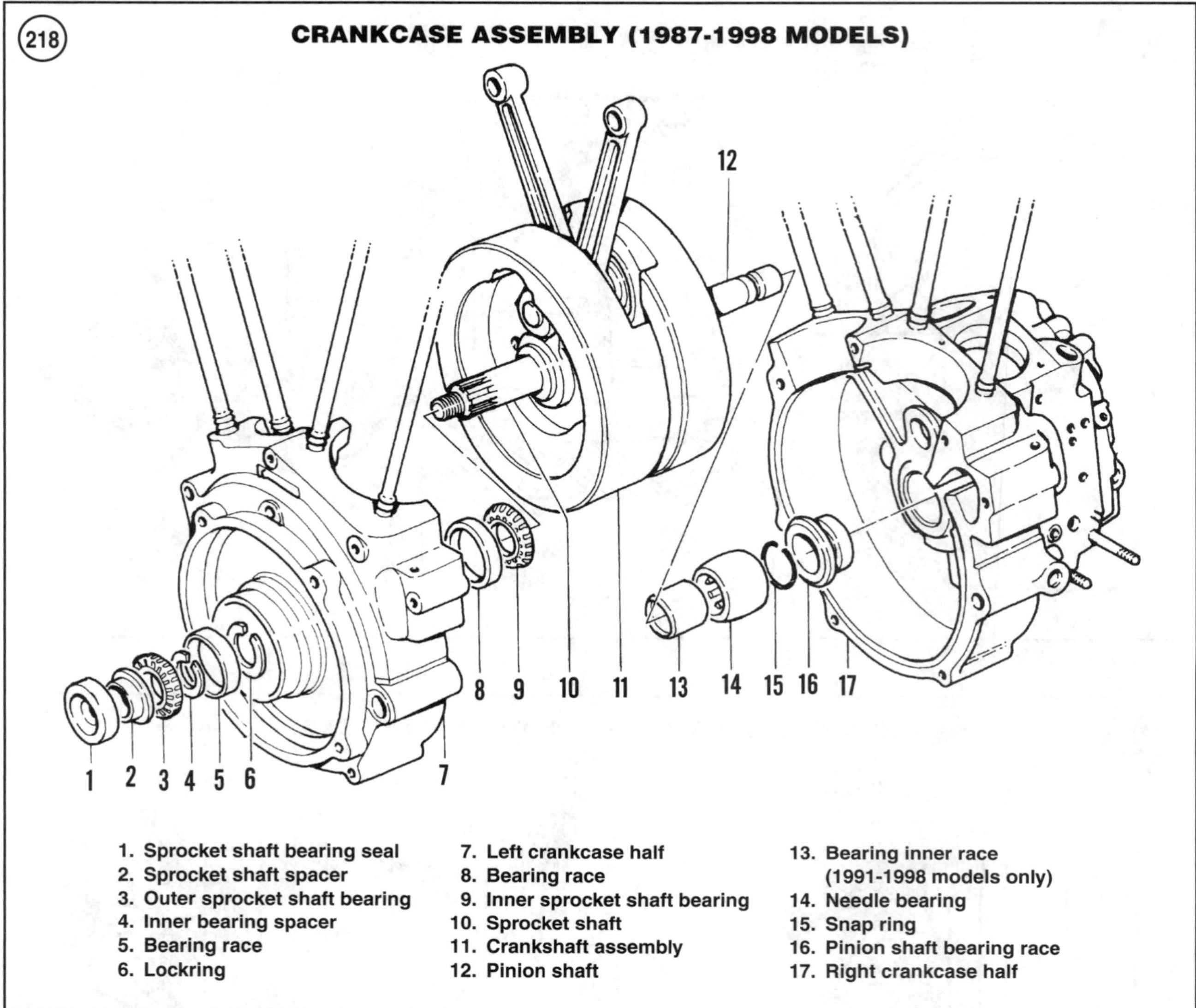

1. Sprocket shaft bearing seal
2. Sprocket shaft spacer
3. Outer sprocket shaft bearing
4. Inner bearing spacer
5. Bearing race
6. Lockring
7. Left crankcase half
8. Bearing race
9. Inner sprocket shaft bearing
10. Sprocket shaft
11. Crankshaft assembly
12. Pinion shaft
13. Bearing inner race (1991-1998 models only)
14. Needle bearing
15. Snap ring
16. Pinion shaft bearing race
17. Right crankcase half

inder stud. The hose will protect the studs during the following service procedures. In addition, do not lift the crankcase assembly by grabbing the cylinder studs. Bent or damaged cylinder studs may cause the engine to leak oil.

2. Remove the following components as described in this chapter:
   a. Cylinder heads and cylinders.
   b. Pistons.
   c. Pushrods, valve lifters and lifter guides.
3. Disassemble and remove the gearcase assembly as described in this chapter.
4. Check the crankshaft end play as described in this chapter.

NOTE
When removing the crankcase bolts and studs in Step 4, note that the top center stud and the right bottom studs are matched and fitted to the crankcase holes for correct crankcase alignment. Mark these bolts so they can be reinstalled in their original positions.

5. Using a crisscross pattern, loosen and remove the crankcase bolts, threaded studs and nuts (**Figure 219**).
6. Lay the crankcase assembly on wooden blocks so the right side faces up.

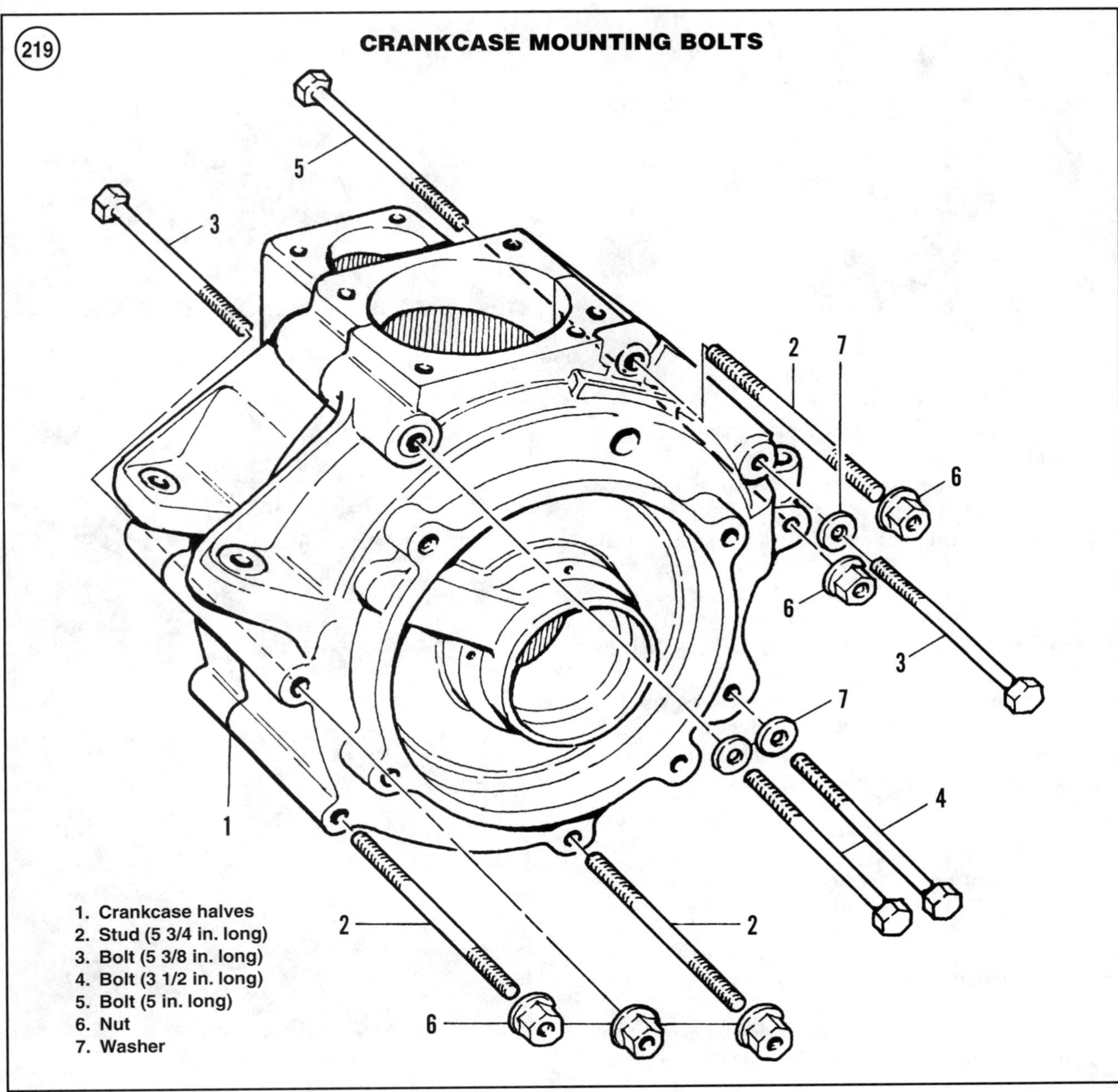

7. Tap the crankcase with a plastic mallet and remove the right crankcase half (**Figure 220**).

8. Remove the pinion shaft snap ring (**Figure 221**).

9A. On 1984-1986 models, grasp the two bearing washers and remove the washers, bearings and retainers as an assembly from the pinion shaft. Store the complete assembly in a plastic bag.

9B. On 1997-1998 models, remove the needle bearing (**Figure 222**) from the pinion shaft.

WARNING
Wear safety glasses to press out the crankshaft in Step 9.

CAUTION
Do not drive the crankshaft out of the crankcase with a hammer.

10A. If a hydraulic press is available, press the crankshaft out of the left crankcase half as follows:

220

221

a. Support the left crankcase half on the press bed on wooden blocks (**Figure 223**).
b. Center the press ram on the sprocket shaft and apply slight pressure.
c. Have an assistant secure the crankshaft as it is being pressed out.
d. Press the crankshaft out of the left crankcase half and place it on workbench for further service.

10B. If a hydraulic press is not available, use the JIMS Crank Disassembly Removing Tool (part No. 1047-TP) and press the crankshaft out of the left crankcase half as follows:

a. Following the manufacturer's instructions, install a flywheel press onto the left side of the crankcase.
b. Apply clean engine oil or press lube to the end of the center screw and install it into the tool.

CAUTION
Do not use a hand impact driver or air impact wrench on the center screw. They will damage the crankcase as well as the tool.

c. Secure the right side of the crankshaft with a wrench to prevent it from rotating in the following step.
d. Slowly turn the center screw with a wrench a half turn at a time. After each turn, tap on the end of the center screw with a brass mallet to relieve the stress on the center screw and the tool.
e. Repeat substep d until the center screw pushes the crankshaft out of the left crankcase half.
f. Remove the special tool from the left crankcase half.

11. To remove the outer sprocket shaft bearing assembly, perform the following:

a. Carefully pry the sprocket shaft spacer (**Figure 224**) out of the oil seal (**Figure 225**).
b. Carefully pry the oil seal (**Figure 226**) out of the left crankcase with a wide blade screwdriver. Place a

222

223

224

rag under the screwdriver to prevent damage to the crankcase (**Figure 227**).

c. Lift out the outer sprocket shaft bearing half (B, **Figure 227**).

Assembly

Refer to **Figure 217** and **Figure 218**.

The JIMS Big Twin Sprocket Shaft Bearing Installation Tool (part No. 97225-55) is required to assemble the crankcase halves.

1. If removed, install the spacer onto the crankshaft next to the inner bearing.
2. Position the crankshaft with the left side facing up.
3. Apply clean engine oil or assembly lube to the inner bearing and to the left-side crankcase inner bearing race.
4. Place the left crankcase half (A, **Figure 228**) over the sprocket shaft (B).
5. Make sure the connecting rods are correctly positioned within the crankcase openings.
6. Make sure the crankcase is located correctly on the crankshaft inner bearing.
7. Install the outer sprocket shaft bearing over the sprocket shaft (**Figure 229**) and push it into the outer bearing race.
8. Install the sprocket shaft bearing installation tool onto the crankshaft following the manufacturer's instructions.
9. Hold onto the handle (A, **Figure 230**) and tighten the large nut with a wrench (B). Tighten the large nut until the outer bearing is seated correctly and makes firm contact with the spacer installed in Step 1.
10. Remove the special tools and make sure the outer bearing is seated correctly (**Figure 231**).
11. Check crankshaft end play as follows:
    a. Securely attach a dial indicator to the left crankcase half.
    b. Position the dial indicator contact pointer on the end of the crankshaft.

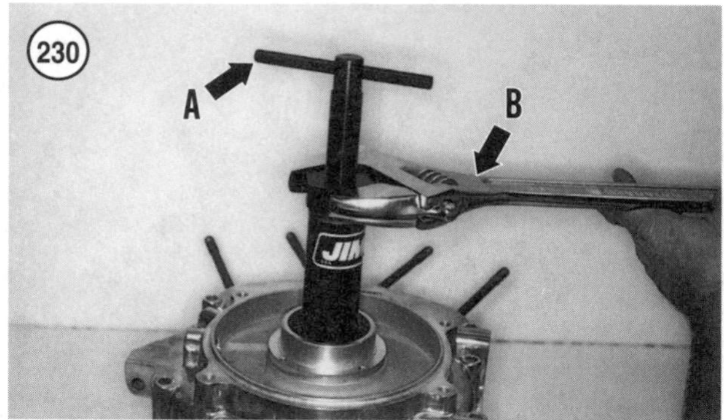

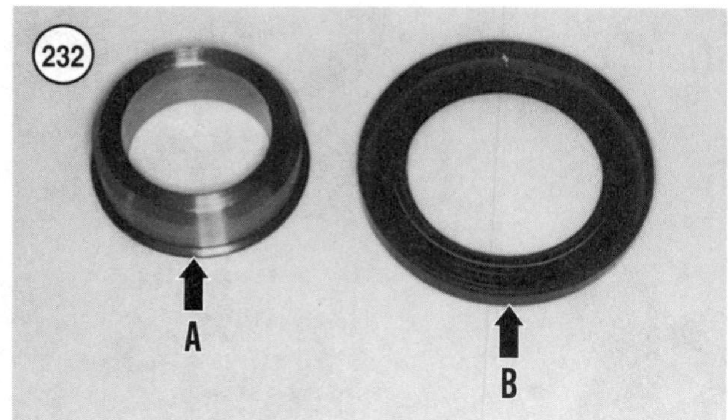

c. Push down hard on the crankcase while turning it back and forth.
d. Hold the crankcase down and zero the dial gauge.
e. Pull up on the crankcase as far as it will go while turning it back and forth. Note the dial indicator reading.
f. Repeat this step several times and note the readings. They should all be the same.
g. The end play must be within 0.001-0.005 in. (0.025-0.127 mm). If the end play is incorrect, the spacer must be replaced using a shim of a different thickness. **Table 4** lists the spacers with various thicknesses and the part numbers.
h. Remove the dial indicator.

12. Turn the crankcase assembly over and place it on wooden blocks thick enough so the left side of the crankshaft clears the workbench surface.
13. Install the sprocket spacer (A, **Figure 232**) onto the *new* oil seal (B) so the spacer shoulder seats against the closed side of the oil seal (**Figure 233**).
14. Install the spacer and oil seal assembly into the crankcase half so the oil seal lip faces out (**Figure 234**).
15. Press the oil seal into the crankcase with the shaft seal install tool (JIMS part No.39361-69) (**Figure 235**) as follows:

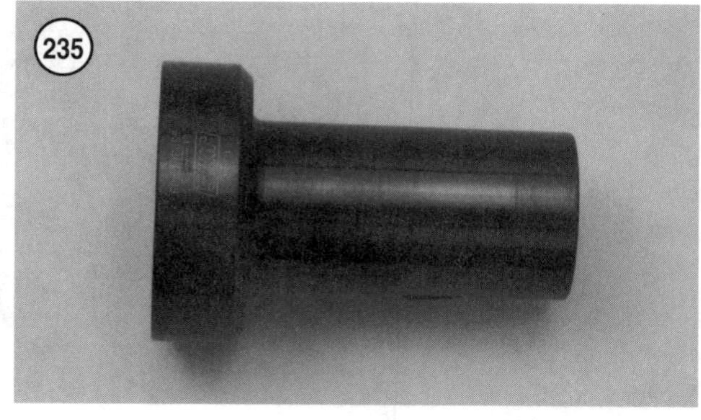

236

240

237

241

238

239

a. Apply clean engine oil or press lube to the special tool threads, both washers and the radial bearing.

b. Install the shaft seal installer tool following the manufacturer's instructions.

c. Install the main body onto the crankshaft and screw it on until it stops (**Figure 236**).

d. Hold onto the handle (A, **Figure 237**) of the main body and tighten the large nut (B) with a wrench. Tighten the large nut slowly and check that the oil seal (**Figure 238**) is entering straight into the bearing bore.

e. Tighten the large nut slowly until the shaft seal installer tool makes contact with the crankcase surface (**Figure 239**).

f. Remove the special tools.

16. Support the left crankcase half assembly on wooden blocks as shown in **Figure 240**.

17. Clean the bearing inner race (**Figure 241**), then apply clean engine oil to it.

18A. On 1984-1986 models, install the retainers, bearings and washers as an assembly onto the pinion shaft.

18B. On 1997-1998 models, apply clean engine oil to the needle bearing. Then slide it over the inner race (**Figure 242**).

19. Install a *new* snap ring (**Figure 243**) and make sure it is seated correctly in the shaft groove.
20. Thoroughly clean and dry both crankcase gasket surfaces before applying gasket sealer in Step 21.
21. Apply a thin coat of a nonhardening gasket sealer to the crankcase mating surfaces. Use one of the following gasket sealers:
   a. Harley-Davidson crankcase sealant (part No. HD-99650-81).
   b. 3M #800 sealant.
   c. ThreeBond Liquid Gasket 1104.
22. Align the crankcase halves and carefully lower the right crankcase half onto the crankshaft and left crankcase half (**Figure 244**). Press it down until it is seated correctly on the locating dowels. If necessary, carefully tap the perimeter of the right crankcase half until it is seated around the entire perimeter.

CAUTION
When properly aligned, the crankcase halves will fit snugly against each other around the entire perimeter. If they do not meet correctly, do not attempt to pull the case halves together with the mounting bolts. Separate the crankcase assembly and investigate the cause of the interference.

23. Carefully tap the three crankcase studs (marked during disassembly) into the crankcase halves (**Figure 245**). Center the studs. Then install the nuts onto each end of the studs and tighten hand-tight.
24. Install the remaining bolts and nuts.
25. Place the crankcase assembly in an engine stand (**Figure 246**). Secure the engine stand to the workbench so it cannot move.
26. Tighten the crankcase fasteners as follows:
   a. Tighten the fasteners to 10 ft.-lb. (14 N•m) in the sequence shown in **Figure 247**.
   b. Install the pistons, cylinders and cylinder heads as described in this chapter.
   c. Tighten the fasteners to 15-17 ft.-lb. (20-23 N•m) in the sequence shown in **Figure 247**.
27. Recheck the flywheel end play as described in this chapter.
28. Install and assemble the gearcase assembly as described in this chapter.
29. Install the following components as described in this chapter:
   a. Alternator rotor and stator assembly (Chapter Nine).
   b. Oil pump.
   c. Camshaft assembly.

242

243

244

30. Install the engine into the frame as described in this chapter.

Crankcase Cleaning and Inspection

1. Clean both case halves in solvent and dry with compressed air.
2. Apply a light coat of oil to the races to prevent rust.
3. Inspect the right (**Figure 248**) and left (A, **Figure 249**) case halves for cracks or other damage.

245

CRANKCASE MOUNTING BOLTS

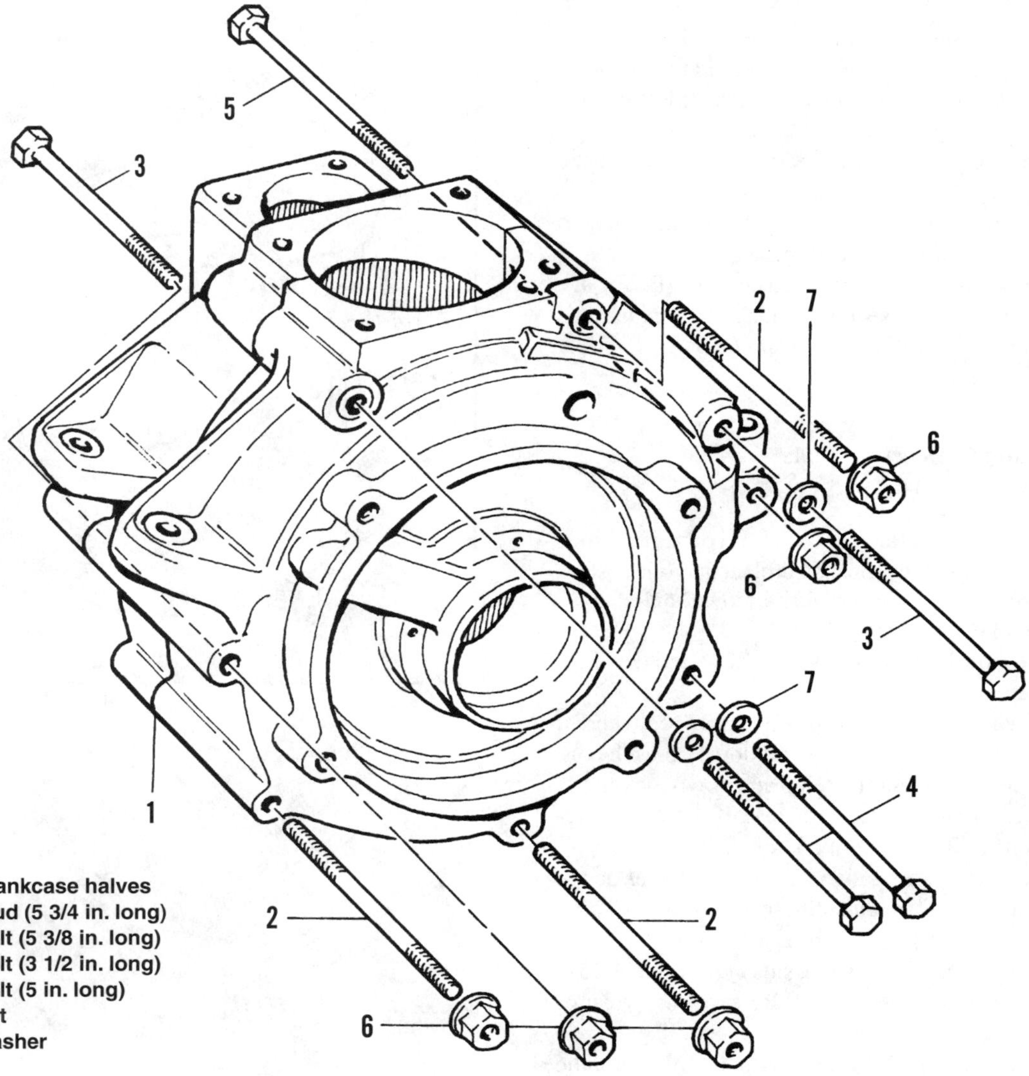

1. Crankcase halves
2. Stud (5 3/4 in. long)
3. Bolt (5 3/8 in. long)
4. Bolt (3 1/2 in. long)
5. Bolt (5 in. long)
6. Nut
7. Washer

246

4. Inspect the case studs for bending, cracks or other damage. If necessary, replace studs as described under *Cylinder Stud Replacement* in this section.

5. Inspect the left main bearing races (B, **Figure 249**) for wear or damage. Replace the bearing assembly as described under *Left Main Bearing Replacement* in this section.

NOTE

Harley-Davidson has determined that there is a possible problem with the inner race and has established a program to replace the inner race on 1993-1998 models. Refer any questions regarding a possible problem to a Harley-Davidson dealership.

6. Inspect the pinion shaft bearing race (A, **Figure 250**) for wear or damage. If damaged, inspect the needle bearing (**Figure 242**) and its inner race (**Figure 251**) for damage. Note the following:
   a. Replace the pinion shaft bearing and races at the same time as a complete set.
   b. Refer pinion shaft inner bearing race replacement to a Harley-Davidson dealership.
7. Inspect the camshaft gear needle bearing (B, **Figure 250**) in the right crankcase for damage. To replace this bearing, refer to *Camshaft Gear Needle Bearing Replacement* in this section.

Crankshaft and Connecting Rods Cleaning and Inspection

If any portion of the crankshaft and/or connecting rods are worn or damaged, they must be replaced as one assembly. If necessary, have the crankshaft overhauled by a Harley-Davidson dealership.

1. Clean the crankshaft assembly in solvent and dry thoroughly with compressed air.
2. Hold the shank portion of each connecting rod where it attaches to the crankshaft. Pull up and down on each connecting rod. Any slight amount of up and down movement indicates excessive lower bearing wear. If there is movement, the crankshaft must be overhauled.
3. Measure connecting rod side play with a feeler gauge (**Figure 252**) and check against the service limit in **Table 2**.
4. Inspect the pinion shaft (right side) (A, **Figure 253**) and the sprocket shaft (left side) (B) for excessive wear or damage.
5. Support the crankshaft on a truing stand or in a lathe and check runout at the flywheel outer rim (C, **Figure 253**) and at the shaft adjacent to the flywheel (D) with a dial indicator. Check against the service limit in **Table 2**.

Camshaft Gear Needle Bearing Replacement

The camshaft needle bearing (B, **Figure 250**) can be removed from the crankcase with the engine mounted in the frame and the camshaft gearcase assembly removed.

Tools

The following tools or the equivalents are required to replace the camshaft gear needle bearing:

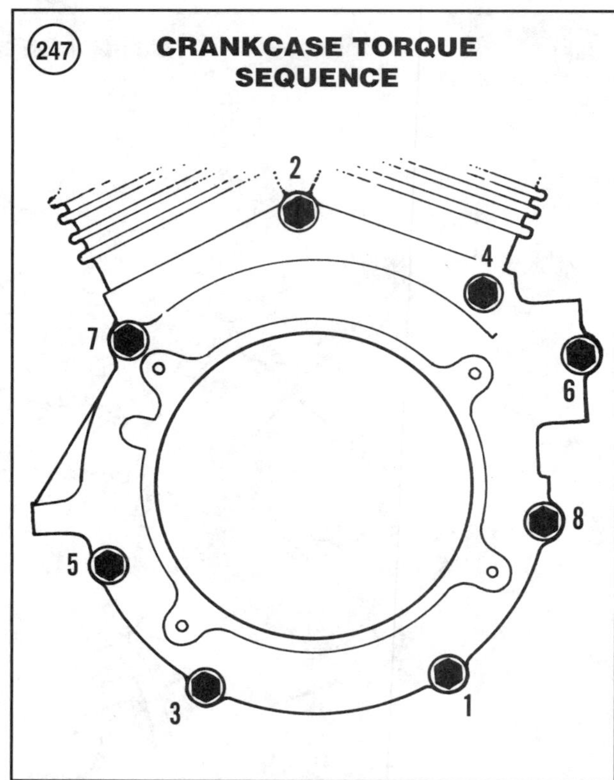

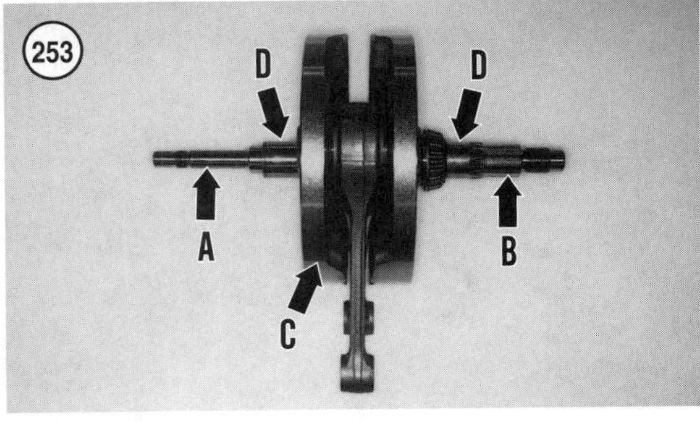

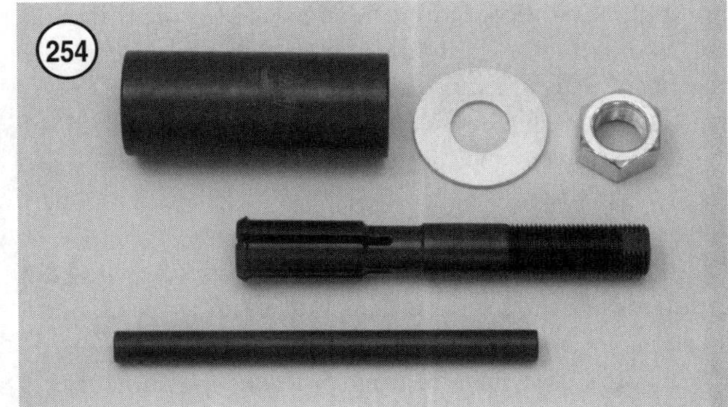

1. Engine stand (JIMS part No. 1006T) (if engine is removed from frame).
2. Needle bearing puller (JIMS part No. 95760-TB) (**Figure 254**).
3. Needle bearing installer (JIMS part No. 2188).

Procedure

1. Remove the camshaft gearcase assembly from the engine as described in this chapter.
2. Rotate the crankshaft and verify that the crankpin is *not* visible through the camshaft needle bearing bore. Rotate the engine if necessary to obtain clearance.
3. Install the puller portion of the tool set partway into the needle bearing. Install a small hose clamp onto the end, closer to the needle bearing, and tighten. This will close the end of the tool so it can pass through the needle bearing. Push the puller all the way through the needle bearing. Then remove the hose clamp to grab the back side of the needle bearing.
4. Following the manufacturer's instructions, assemble the remainder of the tool components onto the puller portion.
5. Place a 5/8-in. wrench on the flats of the puller.
6. Place a 1 1/8-in. wrench or an adjustable wrench on the large nut.

CAUTION
Do not turn the 5/8-in. wrench because this will damage the special tool and the crankcase receptacle.

7. Hold onto the 5/8-in. wrench to keep the puller from rotating. Turn the 1 1/8-in. wrench *clockwise* on the large nut. Tighten the large nut and pull the needle bearing out of the crankcase receptacle.
8. Disassemble the special tool and remove the needle bearing from it.

9. Apply a light coat of clean engine oil or press lube to the outer surface of the ball bearings, the crankcase needle bearing (A, **Figure 255**) and bearing receptacle (B).
10. Apply a light coat of clean engine oil to the threads of the screw portion and to the installer plate.
11. Insert the center screw portion of the special tool part way into the installer plate.
12. Following the manufacturer's instructions, install the installer onto the screw and push it on until it locks into place.
13. Position the new bearing with the manufacturer's marks facing out on the installer.
14. Install the installer plate onto the crankcase and align the tool to the bearing receptacle.
15. Install the thumb screws through the installer plate and onto the crankcase threaded holes. Tighten the screws securely.
16. Slowly tighten the center screw until the bearing starts to enter the crankcase receptacle. Continue to tighten until the installer contacts the crankcase surface. This will correctly locate the needle bearing within the crankcase.
17. Remove the special tools and make sure the needle bearing (**Figure 256**) is seated correctly.

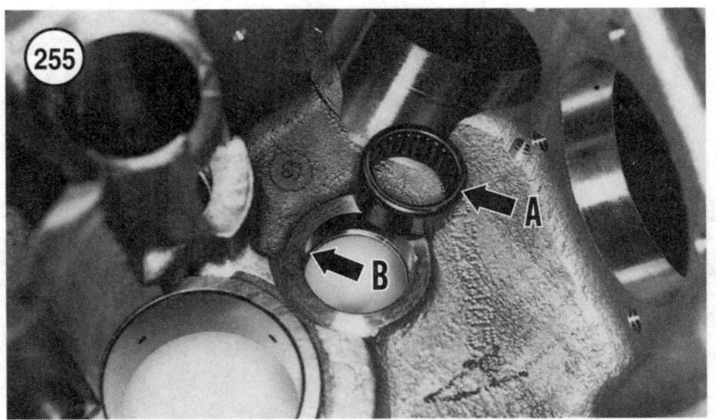

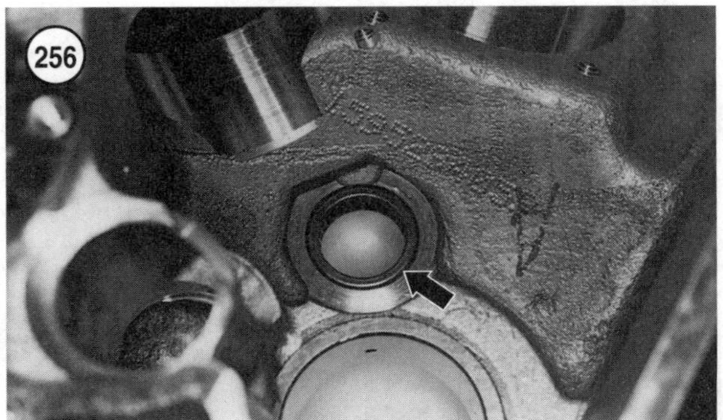

Left Side Main Bearing Assembly Replacement

The left main bearing assembly must be replaced as a complete set even if one bearing or race is damaged.

Tools

The following tools or the equivalents are required to remove and install the left side main bearing:
1. Hydraulic press.
2. Sprocket shaft bearing race tool (JIMS part No. 94547-80A) (A, **Figure 257**).
3. Race and bearing installation tool handle (JIMS part No. 33416-80) (B, **Figure 257**).
4. Snap ring removal and installation tool (JIMS part No. 1710) (**Figure 258**).
5. Sprocket bearing race installation tool (JIMS part No. 2246) (**Figure 259**).

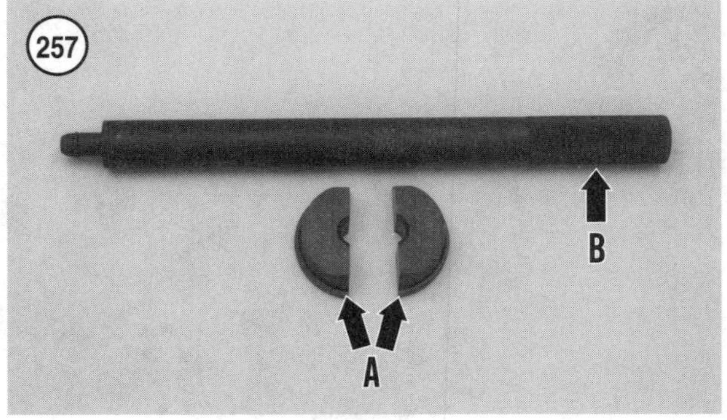

Inner and outer bearing race replacement

CAUTION
When replacing the bearing races in the following steps, do not remove the lockring installed between the inner and outer bearing races unless it is loose or damaged. This

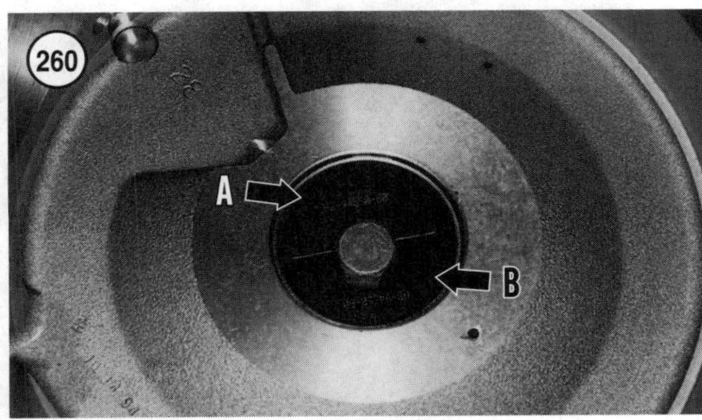

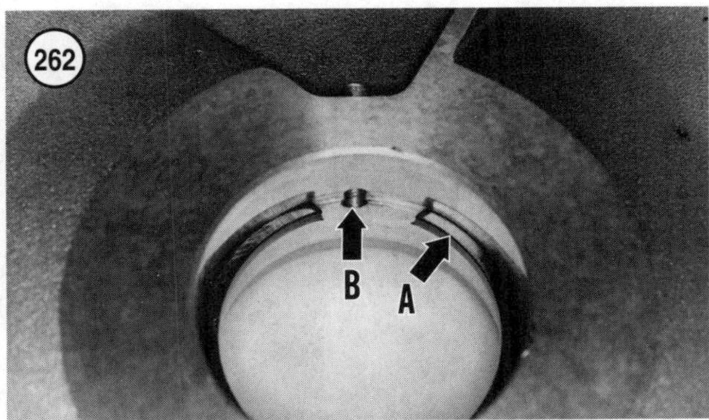

ring is under heavy tension and will damage the bearing bore as it passes through it.

1. Disassemble the crankcase as described in this section.
2. Place the crankcase on the workbench with the inboard surface facing up.
3. Install one half of the bearing race remover tool into the crankcase and push it against the inner bearing race (A, **Figure 260**).
4. Install the other half of the bearing race remover tool into the crankcase and push it against the inner bearing race (B, **Figure 260**).
5. Hold the bearing race remover tools in place and turn the crankcase over.
6. Insert the tool handle into the center (**Figure 261**) of both race remover tools. Press it into place until the ring is locked into both bearing race remover tools.
7. Support the left crankcase half on wooden blocks on the press bed with the tool handle facing up.
8. Center the press ram directly over the tool handle and slowly press the inner bearing race out of the crankcase.
9. Remove the crankcase and special tools from the press bed.
10. Place the crankcase on the workbench with the outboard surface facing up.
11. Repeat Steps 3-9 for the bearing on the other side.
12. Clean the crankcase half in solvent and dry with compressed air.
13. Check the lockring (A, **Figure 262**) for looseness or damage. If the lockring is loose or damaged, perform the following:
    a. Place the crankcase on a workbench with the outboard side facing up.
    b. With the gap of the lockring at the 12 o'clock position, install the special tool clamps onto each side of the lockring at the 10 o'clock and 2 o'clock positions.
    c. Securely tighten the 9/16-in. Allen screws securing the clamps to the lockring.
    d. Use snap ring pliers with straight tips and install them in one of the holes in each clamp.
    e. Squeeze the pliers, compress the lockring and withdraw it from the crankcase groove.
    f. Remove the clamps from the old lockring and install them onto the new lockring.
    g. Squeeze the pliers (**Figure 263**) and insert the lockring into the crankcase groove.
    h. Check that the lockring gap is centered with the crankcase oil hole as shown in B, **Figure 262**. Do not block the oil hole with the ring.

NOTE

Install both races with the larger diameter sides facing out. Install the bearing races

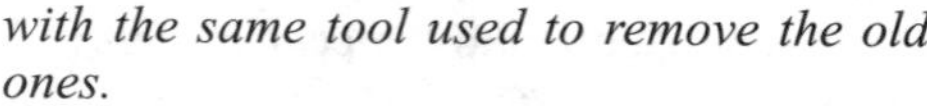

with the same tool used to remove the old ones.

14. Apply clean engine oil or press lube to the bearing receptacles in the crankcase and to the outer surface of the inner bearing races.
15. Position the installer base with the large end facing up and place it on the press bed.
16. Position the crankcase with the outboard surface facing up.
17. Install the crankcase onto the installer base until the crankcase retaining ring rests on top of the installer base.
18. Install the outboard outer race into position on the crankcase receptacle.
19. Apply clean engine oil or press lube to the shaft of the pressing plug and install the pressing plug into the installer base. Push it down onto the bearing outer race.
20. Center the press ram directly over the pressing plug and slowly press the outer bearing race into the outboard surface of the crankcase until it touches the retaining ring.
21. Remove the crankcase and special tools from the press.
22. Turn the crankcase over and repeat Steps 14-21 for the inboard outer bearing race.

Crankshaft inner sprocket shaft bearing replacement

A sprocket shaft bearing cone installer (JIMS part No. 97225-55) is required to install the sprocket shaft bearing.

1. Support the crankshaft with the sprocket shaft bearing side facing up.
2. Remove the bearing spacer (**Figure 264**) from the sprocket shaft.
3. Install the bearing splitter under the bearing and tighten securely.
4. Attach a bearing puller to the splitter (**Figure 265**).
5. Slowly tighten the center screw and withdraw the bearing from the crankshaft shoulder.

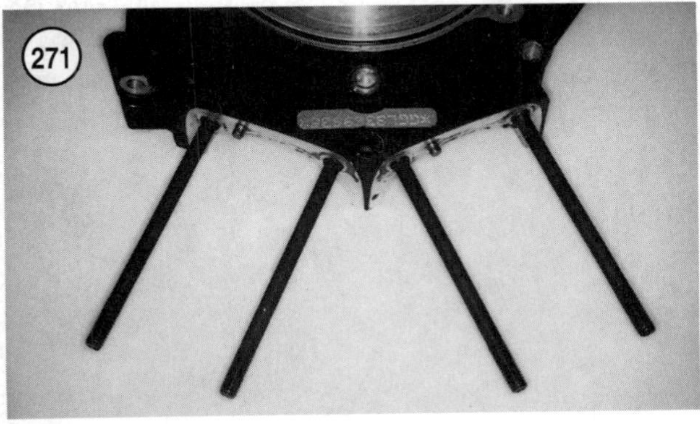

6. Remove the bearing remover, splitter and bearing from the crankshaft.
7. Clean the sprocket shaft with contact cleaner. Check the sprocket shaft (**Figure 266**) for cracks or other damage. If damaged, refer service to a Harley-Davidson dealership.
8. Slide the new bearing (**Figure 267**) over the sprocket shaft.
9. Install the new bearing with the bearing installation tool (**Figure 268**). Remove the special tool.
10. Make sure the bearing is correctly seated (**Figure 269**) against the crankshaft.
11. Install the inner bearing spacer and seat it against the bearing (**Figure 270**).

Cylinder Stud Replacement

Replace bent or otherwise damaged cylinder studs (**Figure 271**) to prevent cylinder block and cylinder head leaks.

1. If the engine lower end is assembled, block off the lower crankcase opening with clean shop cloths.

2A. If the stud has broken off with the top surface of the crankcase, remove it with a stud remover. Refer to Chapter One for typical procedures.

2B. If the stud is still in place, perform the following:
   a. Thread a 3/8 in.–16 nut onto the top of the stud.
   b. Thread an additional screw onto the stud and tighten it against the first nut so that they are locked.
   c. Turn the bottom nut counterclockwise and unscrew the stud.

3. Clean the stud threads in the crankcase with a spiral brush. Then clean with an aerosol parts cleaner. If necessary, clean the threads with an appropriately sized tap.

NOTE

*On late 1987-1998 models, the cylinder studs have a shoulder on the upper end (**Figure 272**).*

4. On 1984-early 1987 models, measuring from the top of the stud and paint a mark that is 5.75 in. (146.05 mm) down from the top of the stud (**Figure 273**).

NOTE

New studs may have a threadlocking compound patch already applied to the lower stud threads. If so, do not apply any additional locking compound to these studs.

5. If the new stud does not have the threadlocking compound patch, apply ThreeBond TB1360 or an equivalent to the lower stud threads.

NOTE
The cylinder studs have a shoulder on one end, and this end must be installed next to the crankcase surface.

6. Place a 0.313 in. diameter steel ball (H-D part No. 8860) into a cylinder head bolt. Then thread the bolt onto the end of the new stud without the collar.
7. Position the stud with the shoulder end going in first and hand-thread the new stud into the crankcase.

CAUTION
Do not use a breaker bar, ratchet or similar tool to install the studs. These tools can bend the stud and cause the engine to leak oil.

8A. On 1984-early 1987 models, perform the following:

a. Hold the air impact wrench directly in line with the stud. *Slowly* tighten the new stud with an air impact wrench until the paint mark on the stud aligns with the gasket surface of the crankcase.
b. Measure the installed height of the stud with a vernier caliper. The installed height must be 5.670-5.770 in. (144.02-146.56 mm).

8B. On late 1987-1998 models, hold the air impact wrench directly in line with the stud. *Slowly* tighten the new stud with an air impact wrench until the stud shoulder contacts the top surface of the crankcase.
9. Use a torque wrench and hand-tighten the stud to 120 in.-lb. (14 N•m).
10. Remove the cylinder head bolt and steel ball from the cylinder stud.
11. Repeat for any additional studs.

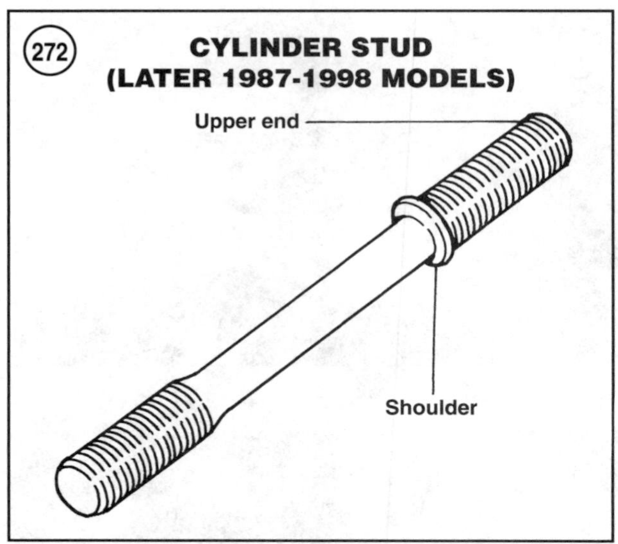

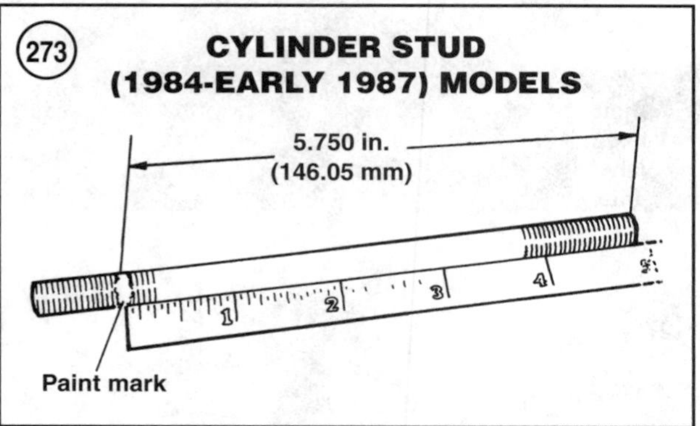

ENGINE BREAK-IN

Following cylinder service (boring, honing, new rings) and major lower end work, the engine must be broken in just as though it were new. The service and performance life of the engine depends on a careful and sensible break-in.

1. For the first 50 mi. (80 km), maintain engine speed below 2500 rpm in any gear. However, do not lug the engine. Do not exceed 50 mph during this period.
2. From 50-500 mi. (80-804 km), vary the engine speed. Avoid prolonged steady running at one engine speed. During this period, increase engine speed to 3000 rpm. Do not exceed 55 mph during this period.
3. After the first 500 mi. (804 km), the engine break-in is complete.

Table 1 ENGINE GENERAL SPECIFICATIONS

Item	Specification
Engine type	Four-stroke, 45° OHV V twin
Bore × stroke	3.498 × 4.250 in. (88.85 × 107.95 mm)
Displacement	81.6 cubic inch (1340 cc)
Compression ratio	8.5 to 1
Cooling system	Air-cooled

Table 2 ENGINE SERVICE SPECIFICATIONS

Item	New in. (mm)	Service limit in. (mm)
Cylinder head		
Warp	–	0.006 (0.15)
Valve seat fit in head	0.0020-0.0045 (0.051-0.1143)	0.0020 (0.051)
Valve guide fit in head	0.0020-0.0033 (0.051-0.084)	0.0020 (0.051)
Rocker arm		
Bushing fit in rocker arm	0.002-0.004 (0.05-0.102)	0.0035 (0.089)
Shaft-to-rocker arm bushing clearance	0.0005-0.002 (0.013-0.050)	0.0035 (0.089)
End clearance	0.003-0.013 (0.08-0.33)	0.025 (0.63)
Rocker arm shaft		
Shaft-to-rocker arm cover	0.0007-0.0022 (0.018-0.056)	0.0035 (0.089)
Valves		
Valve stem-to-guide clearance		
Intake	0.0008-0.0026 (0.020-0.066)	0.0035 (0.89)
Exhaust	0.0015-0.0033 (0.038-0.084)	0.0040 (0.102)
Seat width		
1984	0.040-0.062 (0.102-0.157)	0.062 (0.157)
1985-1998	0.040-0.062 (0.102-0.157)	0.090 (2.29)
Valve stem protrusion	1.990-2.024 (50.55-51.41)	2.034 (51.66)
Valve springs free length		
Outer spring	2.105-2.177 (53.47-55.3)	–
Inner spring	1.926-1.996 (48.92-50.70)	–
Piston-to-cylinder clearance		
1984, early 1995	0.0008-0.0023 (0.020-0.058)	0.0053 (0.135)
Late 1995-1998*	0.00075-0.00175 (0.019-0.044)	0.0053 (0.135)
Piston pin-to-piston clearance	0.0002-0.0006 (0.005-0.015)	0.001 (0.02)
Piston rings		
Compression ring end gap	0.007-0.020 (0.18-0.51)	0.030 (0.76)
Oil control ring end gap	0.009-0.052 (0.23-1.32)	0.065 (1.65)
Compression ring side clearance		
Top ring	0.002-0.0045 (0.05-0.11)	0.006 (0.15)
Second ring	0.0016-0.0041 (0.041-0.104)	0.006 (0.15)
Oil control ring side clearance	0.0016-0.0076 (0.041-0.193)	0.008 (0.20)
Cylinder		
Taper	–	0.002 (0.05)
Out-of-round	–	0.002 (0.05)
Warp		
At top (cylinder head)	–	0.006 (0.15)
At base (crankcase)	–	0.008 (0.20)
Cylinder bore		
Standard	–	3.501 (88.925)
Oversize 0.005 in. (0.13 mm)	–	3.506 (89.052)
Oversize 0.010 in. (0.25 mm)	–	3.511 (89.179)
Oversize 0.020 in. (0.51 mm)	–	3.521 (89.433)
Oversize 0.030 in. (0.76 mm)	–	3.531 (89.687)

(continued)

Table 2 ENGINE SERVICE SPECIFICATIONS (continued)

Item	New in. (mm)	Service limit in. (mm)
Connecting rods		
Connecting rod-to-crankpin clearance	0.0004-0.0017 (0.010-0.043)	0.002 (0.05)
Piston pin clearance in connecting rod	0.0003-0.0007 (0.008-0.018)	0.001 (0.03)
Side play at crankshaft	0.005-0.025 (0.13-0.63)	0.030 (0.76)
Valve lifters		
Lifter-to-guide clearance	0.0008-0.002 (0.020-0.051)	0.003 (0.08)
Roller end clearance	–	0.015 (0.38)
Guide-to-crankcase fit	0.000-0.004 (0.00-0.10)	–
Gearcase		
Breather gear end play	0.001-0.011 (0.025-0.28)	0.016 (0.41)
Cam gear shaft-to-bushing clearance	0.00075-0.00175 (0.0190-0.0444)	0.003 (0.08)
Cam gear shaft-to-bearing clearance	0.0005-0.0025 (0.013-0.063)	0.005 (0.13)
Cam gear end play	0.001-0.050 (0.025-1.27)	0.050 (1.27)
Oil pump drive shaft-to-crankcase bushing	0.0004-0.0025 (0.010-0.063)	0.0035 (0.089)
Crankshaft		
Runout at rim	0.000-0.010 (0.00-0.25)	0.015 (0.38)
Runout at pivot shaft end	0.000-0.002 (0.00-0.05)	0.003 (0.08)
End play	0.001-0.005 (0.02-0.13)	0.006 (0.15)
Sprocket shaft bearing		
Cup fit in crankcase	0.0032-0.0012 (0.081-0.030)	–
Cone fit on crankshaft	0.0005-0.0015 (0.013-0.038)	–
Pinion shaft bearing and bushing		
Roller bearing fit	0.0002-0.0009 (0.005-0.023)	–
Cover bushing fit	0.001-0.0025 (0.025-0.063)	0.0035 (0.089)
Oil pump gears end clearance	–	0.003-0.004 (0.08-0.10)

*Specifies clearance for KSG pistons.

Table 3 PUSHROD AND LIFTER LOCATION

Cylinder	Lifter bore	Cylinder head/ rocker housing bore
Front		
Intake (yellow)	Inside	Rear
Exhaust (green)	Outside	Front
Rear		
Intake (blue)	Inside	Front
Exhaust (purple)	Outside	Rear

Table 4 CRANKSHAFT INNER BEARING SPACER SHIM SIZE

Shim part number	in.	mm
9120	0.0915-0.0925	2.324-2.350
9121	0.0935-0.0945	2.375-2.400
9122	0.0955-0.0965	2.426-2.451
9123	0.0975-0.0985	2.476-2.502
9124	0.0995-0.1005	2.527-2.553
9125	0.1015-0.1025	2.578-2.602
9126	0.1035-0.1045	2.629-2.654
9127	0.1055-0.1065	2.680-2.705
9128	0.1075-0.1085	2.731-2.756
9129	0.1095-0.1101	2.781-2.800

(continued)

Table 4 CRANKSHAFT INNER BEARING SPACER SHIM SIZE (continued)

Shim part number	in.	mm
9130	0.1115-0.1125	2.832-2.858
9131	0.1135-0.1145	2.883-2.908
9132	0.1155-0.1165	2.934-2.959
9133	0.1175-0.1185	2.985-3.010
9134	0.1195-0.1205	3.035-3.061

Table 5 ENGINE TORQUE SPECIFICATIONS

Item	ft.-lb.	in.-lb.	N•m
Crankcase fasteners			
Initial	–	124	14
Final	15-17	–	20-23
Crankcase studs	–	124	14
Cylinder head bolts	See text		
Cylinder studs	–	124	14
Engine mounting bolts			
Front lower	33-38	–	45-52
Rear at transmission	33-38	–	45-52
Upper mount bracket bolts	28-35	–	38-47
Gearcase cover screw			
1984-1992	–	60-65	6.8-7.3
1993-1998	–	88-124	10-14
Lifter oil screen cap	–	88-124	10-14
Oil filter mount screws			
1992-1998	13-17	–	18-23
Oil pump			
Housing bolts	–	62-88	7-10
Compression nut fitting			
1992-1998	–	97-142	11-16
Cover bolts (1984-1991)	–	62-88	7-10
Cover (1992-1998)			
Bolts	–	88-124	10-14
Manifold screw	–	71-80	8-9
Relief valve plug	–	80-106	9-12
Pinion gear shaft nut	35-45	–	47-61
Rocker cover bolts			
Upper and lower cover 1/4 in. bolts	–	124-159	14-18
Lower cover 5/16 in. bolts	15-18	–	20-25
Spark plug	18-22	–	25-30
Timing screws	–	15-30	1.7-3.4
Valve lifter oil screen plug	–	88-124	10-14

CHAPTER FIVE

CLUTCH AND PRIMARY DRIVE

This chapter describes service procedures for the clutch and primary drive assembly.

Specifications are in **Tables 1-6** at the end of this chapter.

PRIMARY CHAINCASE OUTER COVER

Removal

Refer to **Figure 1**.

1. Disconnect the negative battery cable from the battery.

WARNING
Disconnect the negative battery cable before working on the clutch or any primary drive component to avoid accidentally activating the starter.

2. Thoroughly clean the primary chaincase cover of all dirt, oil and road debris before removing it.
3. On early models, remove the gearshift pedal (A, **Figure 2**).
4. On models so equipped, remove the left footboard (B, **Figure 2**) as described in Chapter Fifteen.
5. Drain the primary chain oil as described in Chapter Three.

NOTE
Note the location of the outer cover screws. There are two screws with different lengths, and they must be reinstalled in the correct locations.

6. Remove the bolts and captive washers securing the chaincase outer cover (**Figure 3**) and remove the chaincase outer cover.
7. Remove the chaincase outer cover gasket.
8. Remove the dowel pins, if necessary.

Installation

1. If removed, install the dowel pins (**Figure 4** and **Figure 5**) onto the chaincase inner housing.

CAUTION
*Harley-Davidson specifies that a **new** Print-O-Seal gasket must be installed every time the chaincase outer cover is removed.*

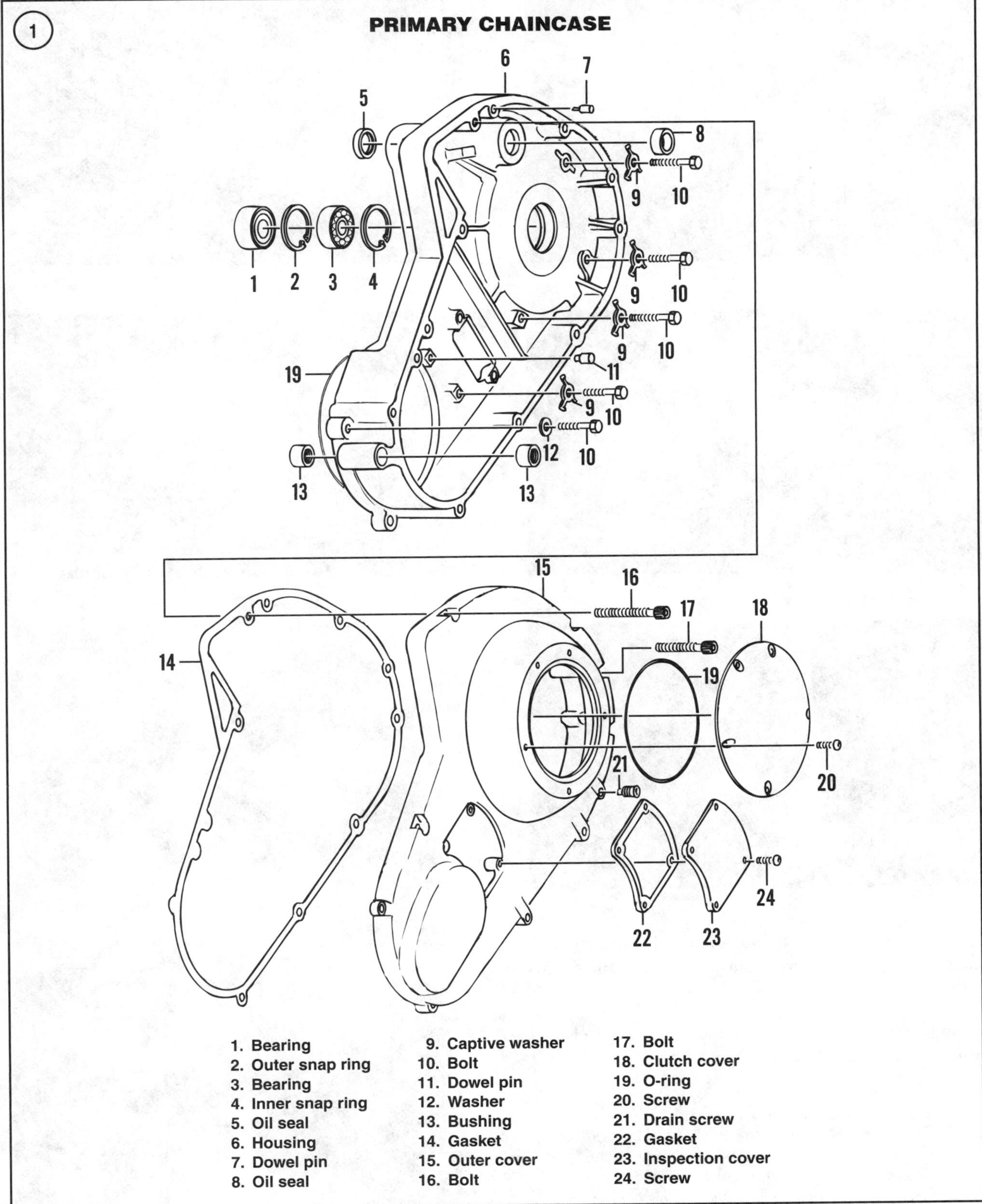
1
PRIMARY CHAINCASE
1
2
3
4
5
6
7
8
9
10
11
12
13
14
15
16
17
18
19
20
21
22
23
24
1. Bearing
2. Outer snap ring
3. Bearing
4. Inner snap ring
5. Oil seal
6. Housing
7. Dowel pin
8. Oil seal
9. Captive washer
10. Bolt
11. Dowel pin
12. Washer
13. Bushing
14. Gasket
15. Outer cover
16. Bolt
17. Bolt
18. Clutch cover
19. O-ring
20. Screw
21. Drain screw
22. Gasket
23. Inspection cover
24. Screw

2. Install a *new* gasket (**Figure 6**) over the locating pins and seat it against the gasket surface of the chaincase inner housing.

3. Slide the primary cover over the locating dowels and seat it flush against the gasket.

NOTE
The gasket sealing surface is very thin, and the overall size of the gasket is very large. The gasket might shift prior to installing the cover bolts, so make sure the gasket is posi-

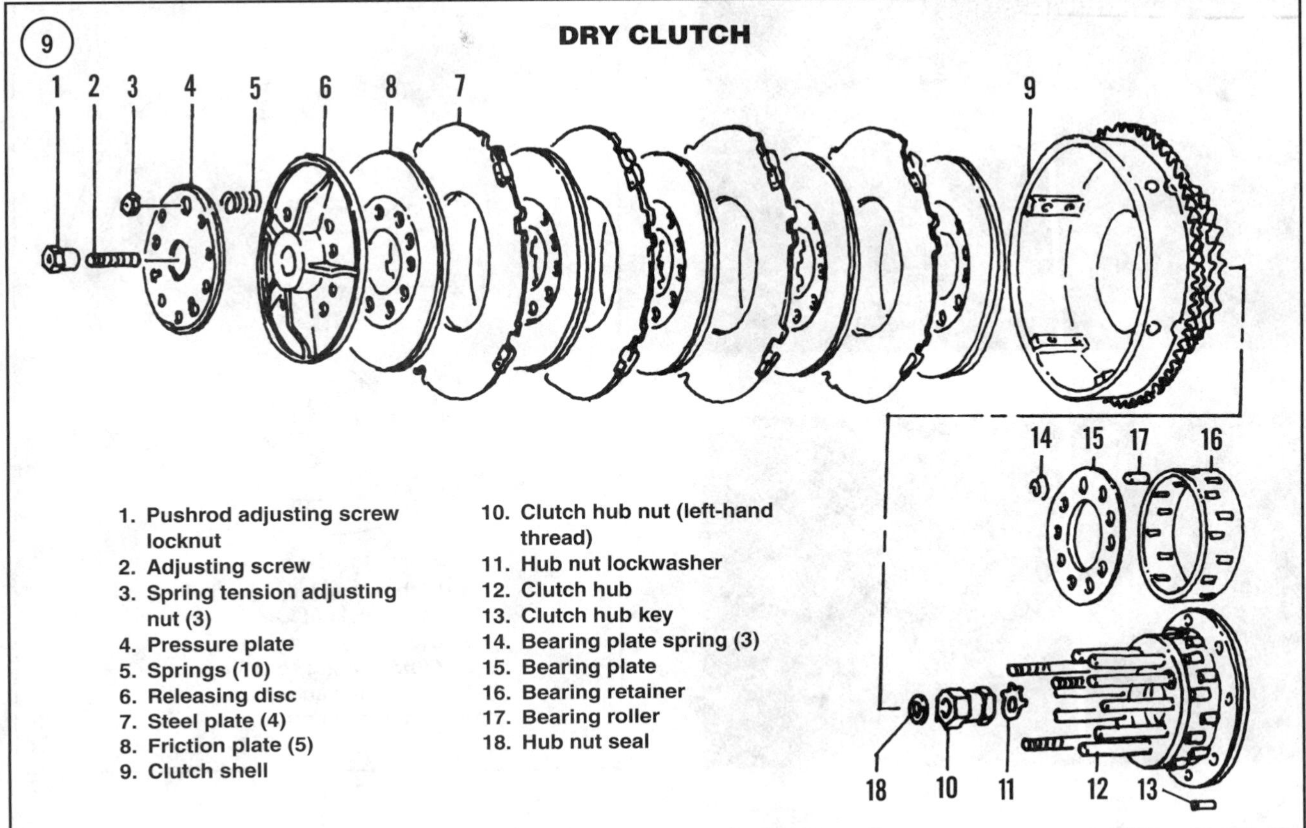

1. Pushrod adjusting screw locknut
2. Adjusting screw
3. Spring tension adjusting nut (3)
4. Pressure plate
5. Springs (10)
6. Releasing disc
7. Steel plate (4)
8. Friction plate (5)
9. Clutch shell
10. Clutch hub nut (left-hand thread)
11. Hub nut lockwasher
12. Clutch hub
13. Clutch hub key
14. Bearing plate spring (3)
15. Bearing plate
16. Bearing retainer
17. Bearing roller
18. Hub nut seal

tioned correctly while installing the cover bolts in Step 4.

4. Install the primary chaincase outer cover bolts and captive washers into the correct locations noted during removal. Tighten the cover bolts to the torque in **Table 5** and **Table 6**. Check that the gasket seats flush around the cover.
5. On early models, install the gearshift pedal (A, **Figure 2**).
6. On models so equipped, install the left footboard (B, **Figure 2**) as described in Chapter Fifteen.
7. Refill the primary chaincase with the type and quantity of oil specified under *Primary Chain Lubrication* in Chapter Three.
8. Connect the negative battery cable.

Inspection

1. Remove all gasket residue from the chaincase outer cover (**Figure 7**) and chaincase inner housing gasket surfaces.
2. Clean the primary cover in solvent and dry with compressed air.
3. Inspect the primary chaincase outer cover for cracks or damage.
4. Inspect the starter jackshaft bushing (**Figure 8**) for excessive wear or damage. To replace the bushing, perform the following:
   a. Remove the bushing with a blind bearing removal tool.
   b. Clean the bushing bore in the housing.
   c. Press in the new bushing until its outer surface is flush with the edge of the bushing bore.

DRY CLUTCH

Refer to **Figure 9**.

Removal

1. Disconnect the negative battery cable from the battery.
2. Remove the primary chaincase outer cover as described in this chapter.

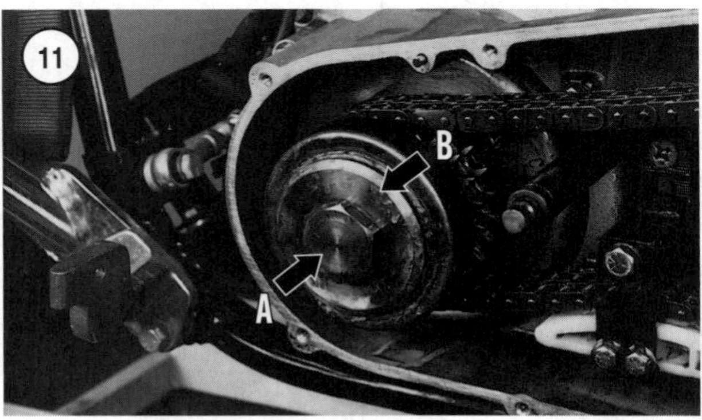

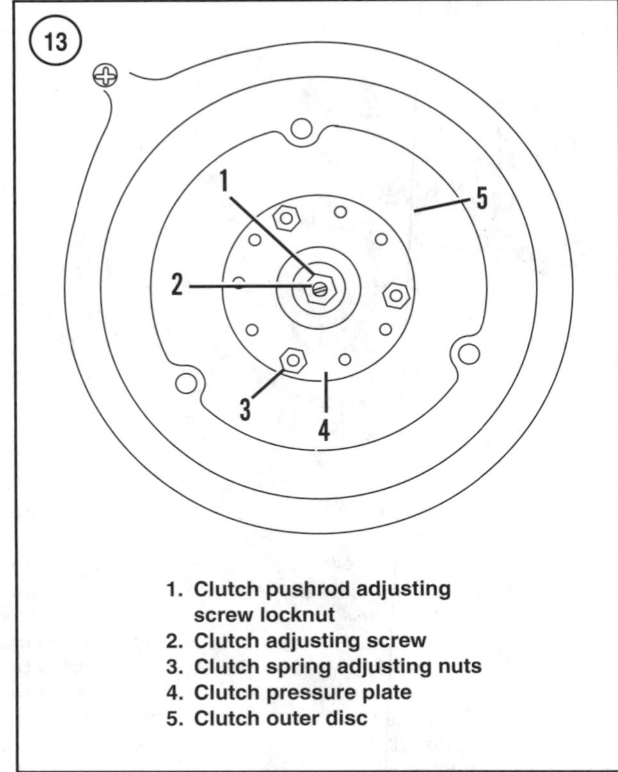

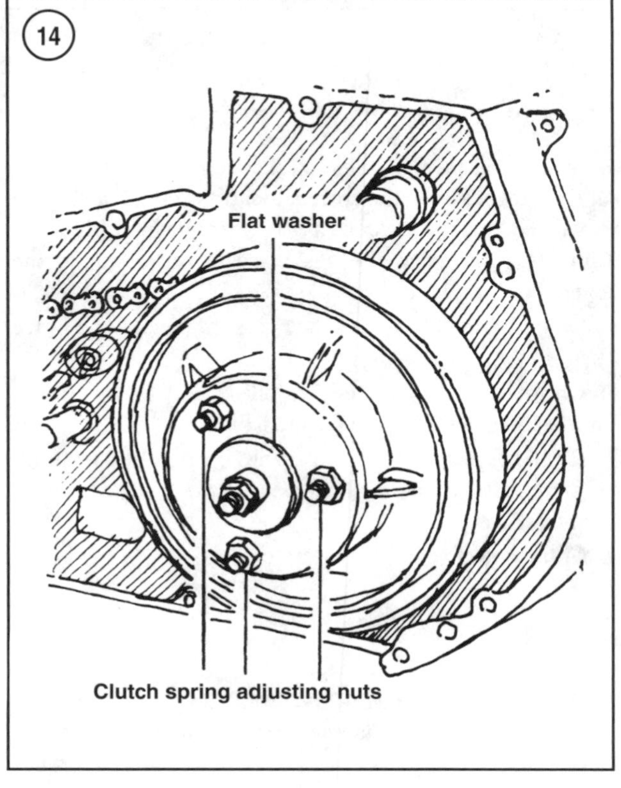

3A. If a special tool is available, place the primary drive locking tool (JIMS part No. 2234) onto the primary chain next to the clutch housing (**Figure 10**).

3B. If the special tool is not available, shift the transmission into fifth gear. Have an assistant apply the rear brake.

4. Loosen the compensating sprocket nut (A, **Figure 11**) with an impact wrench. Then remove the nut.

5. Remove the cover (B, **Figure 11**) and the sliding cam (**Figure 12**).

6. Remove the pushrod adjuster screw locknut (**Figure 13**).

7. Place a flat washer (1/8 in. thick, 1 3/4-in. outer diameter and 3/8-in. inner diameter) over the pushrod adjusting screw (**Figure 14**). Reinstall the adjuster screw locknut removed in Step 6.

8. Tighten the pushrod adjusting screw locknut until the clutch spring adjusting nuts are loose.

9. Remove the clutch spring adjusting nuts (**Figure 14**).

NOTE
Do not disassemble the parts in Step 10 unless replacement is required. Disassembly is described under ***Clutch, Inspection*** *in this chapter.*

10. Remove the pressure plate, clutch springs and the releasing disc as an assembly.

11. Remove the friction (**Figure 15**) and steel (**Figure 16**) clutch plates in order.

12. Remove the primary chain adjuster bolt (A, **Figure 17**) and remove the chain adjuster assembly (B).

13. Remove the oil hose from the primary chain adjuster fitting.

14. Remove the clutch shell, compensating sprocket and primary chain as an assembly (**Figure 18**).

NOTE
The clutch nut has ***left-hand threads****. Turn the clutch nut* ***clockwise*** *to loosen it.*

15. Pry back the clutch hub lockwasher tab. Then loosen the clutch nut (A, **Figure 19**) by turning it clockwise. Remove the nut and the lockwasher.

16. Attach the clutch hub puller (JIMS part No. 95960-52C) to the clutch hub (**Figure 20**). Turn the center bolt on the puller *clockwise* and remove the clutch hub (B, **Figure 19**).

17. Remove the clutch hub Woodruff key (**Figure 21**) from the groove in the transmission mainshaft.

Installation

1. If the pressure plate unit was disassembled, assemble as follows:
   a. Place the clutch hub on the workbench with the bolts face up.
   b. Install the retaining disc on the hub.
   c. Install the clutch springs on the hub pins and studs.
   d. Place the pressure plate over the clutch springs. Because of stud hole arrangement, the plate collar in the pressure plate will fit only one way.
   e. Screw the pushrod adjuster locknut onto the adjuster screw until the screw is flush with the top of the nut. Install a 1 3/4-in. washer under the nut and thread the adjust screw into the releasing disc.
   f. Tighten the nut to compress the clutch springs.
   g. Install the three clutch spring adjusting nuts.
   h. Remove the adjust screw locknut and remove the 1 3/4-in. washer. Then reinstall the locknut.
   i. Tighten the three adjusting nuts in a crisscross pattern until the distance from the releasing disc to the pressure plate is exactly 1 1/32 in. (26.19 mm). Tighten the adjust locknut to maintain this distance.
2. If removed, install the Woodruff key (**Figure 21**) into the mainshaft keyway.
3. If removed, install the pushrod.
4. Install the clutch hub assembly (B, **Figure 19**) onto the mainshaft.

NOTE
*The clutch nut has **left-hand threads**. Turn the clutch nut **counterclockwise** to tighten it.*

5. Install a *new* lockwasher and then the clutch nut onto the mainshaft.
6. Use the same tool setup to prevent the mainshaft from turning as used during disassembly.
7. Turn the nut *counterclockwise* and tighten to 50-60 ft.-lb. (67-81 N•m). Bend the lockwasher tab against the nut to lock it.

NOTE
Grease the clutch shell bearing prior to installing the clutch shell in Step 7.

8. Assemble the clutch shell, primary chain and the compensating sprocket as an assembly on the workbench.
9. Install the clutch shell, primary chain and the compensating sprocket as an assembly onto the crankshaft and transmission shaft as shown in **Figure 18**.
10. Install the washer (if removed), shaft extension (if removed), sliding cam (**Figure 12**) and cover.

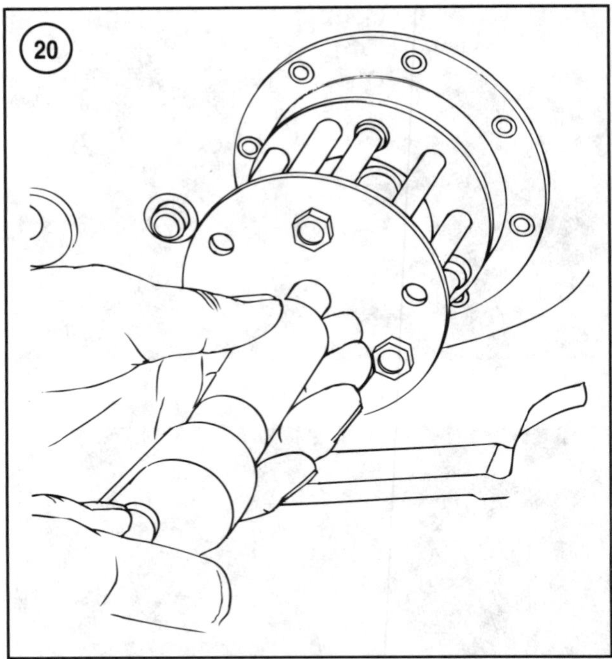

CAUTION
The compensating sprocket nut is tightened to a high torque specification. Make sure to hold the sprocket securely when tightening the nut in Step 10.

11. Apply a few drops of medium-strength threadlocking compound on the sprocket nut threads prior to installation.
12. Install the compensating sprocket nut (**Figure 11**) and tighten it to 90-100 ft.-lb. (122-136 N•m). Use the same tools and procedures to prevent the crankshaft from turning as used during disassembly. Remove the special tool at this time.
13. Position the steel clutch plates with the side stamped OUT facing outward.

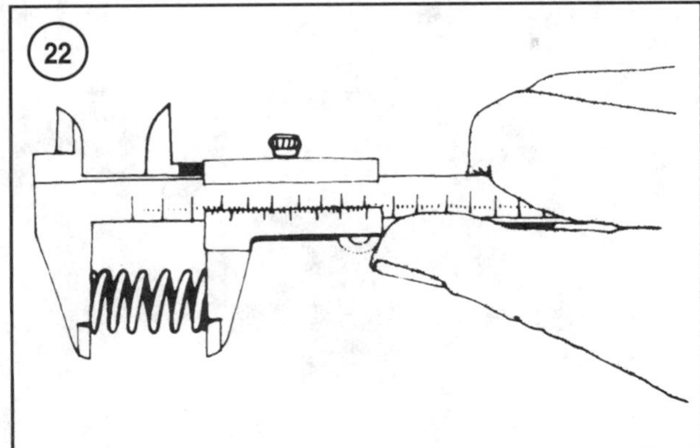
22

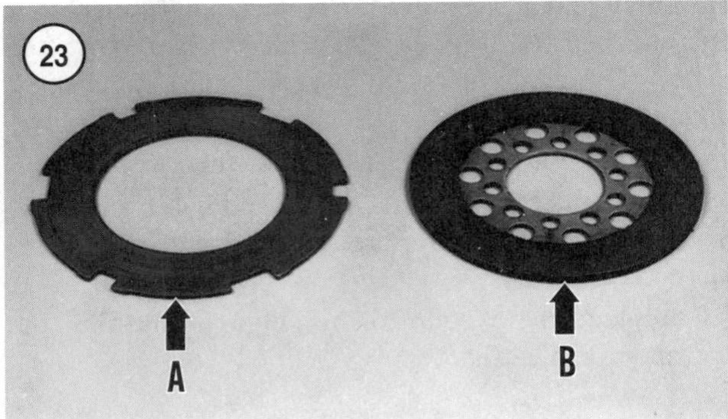

23

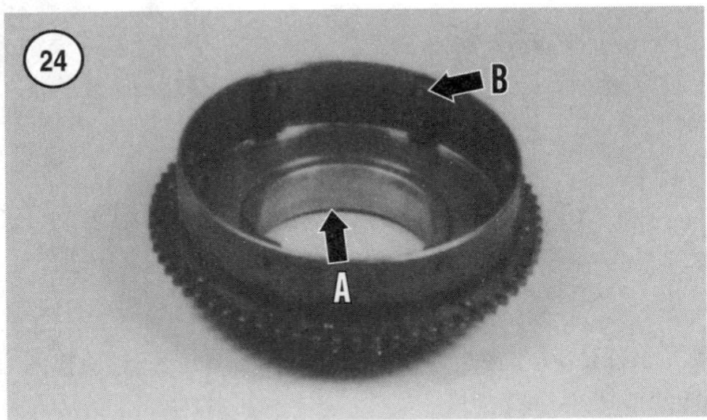

24

14. Install a friction plate (**Figure 15**) and then a steel plate (**Figure 16**). Continue to alternately install the friction plates and steel plates. The last part installed is a friction plate.

15. Install the primary chain adjuster assembly (B, **Figure 17**) and the adjuster bolt (A).

16. Adjust the primary drive chain as described in Chapter Three.

17. Check primary chain alignment as described in this chapter.

18. Install the primary chaincase outer cover as described in this section.
19. Connect the negative battery cable to the battery.
20. Perform the *Primary Housing Vacuum Check (Early 1984 Models With Dry Clutch)* as described in this chapter.
21. Ride the motorcycle a short distance and check the cover for oil leaks.

Inspection

When measuring the clutch components, compare the actual measurement to the specifications in **Table 1**. Replace parts that are out of specification or show damage as described in this section.

1. Clean all clutch parts in non-oil-based solvent and thoroughly dry with compressed air.
2. To disassemble the pressure plate assembly:
   a. Install three bolts through the original pressure plate-to-clutch hub bolt holes. The bolts must be long enough to allow removal of the parts while under compression.
   b. Secure each nut with a flat washer and nut. Tighten all nuts in a crisscross pattern until the clutch springs compress slightly.
   c. Remove the adjuster locknut and remove the adjuster screw.
   d. Loosen the nuts one-half to one turn at a time in a crisscross pattern and release the spring tension evenly.
   e. After loosening the nuts, remove the washers and three bolts.
   f. Separate the pressure plate and remove the clutch springs.
3. Measure the free length of each clutch spring (**Figure 22**).
4. Inspect steel clutch plates (A, **Figure 23**) for warping or wear grooves.
5. Inspect friction plates (B, **Figure 23**) for a shiny appearance or signs of oil soaking. Also check the plates for worn or grooved lining surfaces. Measure each plate.
6. Check for loose clutch plate rivets; replace if necessary.
7. Check the clutch shell inner bearing race (A, **Figure 24**) for grooves, wear or damage. Also check the clutch shell plate tabs (B, **Figure 24**) for looseness or damage. If found, replace the clutch shell.
8. Check both sets of gear teeth on the clutch shell (**Figure 25**). If the teeth are visibly worn or undercut, replace the clutch shell.
9. Spin the clutch hub roller bearing assembly by hand. If bearing assembly appears rough, remove the three bear-

ing plate springs. Then slide the bearing plate off the hub pins and remove the bearing retainer. Check all parts for wear or damage; replace parts as required.

10. Pry the pushrod seal out of the hub nut. Carefully tap a *new* seal into place.

WET CLUTCH (LATE 1984-1989)

Refer to **Figure 26**.

Removal

1. Disconnect the negative battery cable from the battery.
2. Remove the primary chaincase cover as described in this chapter.

3A. If a special tool is available, such as the primary drive locking tool (JIMS part No. 2234), place it onto the primary chain next to the clutch housing (**Figure 10**).

3B. If the special tool is not available, shift the transmission into fifth gear. Have an assistant apply the rear brake.

4. Loosen and remove the adjuster plate bolts (A, **Figure 27**) in a crisscross pattern.
5. Remove the adjuster plate (B, **Figure 27**) and the diaphragm spring (C).
6. Remove the snap ring and the release plate (A, **Figure 28**) from the pressure plate.
7. Remove the pressure plate (B, **Figure 28**).
8. Remove the steel clutch plate (**Figure 29**) and friction clutch plate (A, **Figure 30**) plates.
9. Remove the pushrod (B, **Figure 30**).

10A. If a special tool is available, place the primary drive locking tool (JIMS part No. 2234) onto the primary chain next to the clutch housing (**Figure 10**).

10B. If the special tool is not available, shift the transmission into fifth gear. Have an assistant apply the rear brake.

NOTE
The clutch nut has left-hand threads. Turn the nut ***clockwise*** *to loosen it.*

11. Turn the clutch nut (**Figure 31**) clockwise and remove it. Do not remove the special tool at this time.
12. Remove the primary chain adjuster bolt (A, **Figure 32**) and remove the chain adjuster assembly (B).
13. The engine is still locked from Step 10.
14. Loosen the compensating sprocket nut (A, **Figure 33**) with an impact wrench. Then remove the nut.
15. Remove the cover (B, **Figure 33**) and the sliding cam (**Figure 34**).
16. Following the manufacturer's instructions, attach the puller (JIMS part No. 95960-52C) to the clutch hub (**Figure 35**).

17. Turn the clutch hub puller pressure screw to pull the clutch hub and remove the clutch shell (with clutch hub attached) (C, **Figure 32**), primary chain (with adjuster) (D) and compensating sprocket (E) at the same time.
18. Remove the shaft extension and washer, if necessary.
19. Disassembly of the clutch shell and hub assembly is not required unless parts are damaged and require replacement.
20. Remove the Woodruff key (**Figure 36**) from the transmission mainshaft.

Installation

Refer to **Figure 26**.

1. If removed, install the Woodruff key (**Figure 36**) into the transmission mainshaft.

NOTE
Make sure that the Woodruff key is parallel with the mainshaft taper and is completely seated.

2. Refer to **Figure 37** and install the washer and shaft extension (if removed).
3. Install the clutch shell, hub (C, **Figure 32**), primary chain (D), compensating sprocket and cam (E) as an assembly. Make sure the Woodruff key was not knocked out of alignment during installation.

CAUTION
Do not overtighten the clutch nut because overtightening can damage the clutch hub and pilot bearing.

NOTE
The clutch nut has left-hand threads. Turn the nut ***counterclockwise*** *to tighten.*

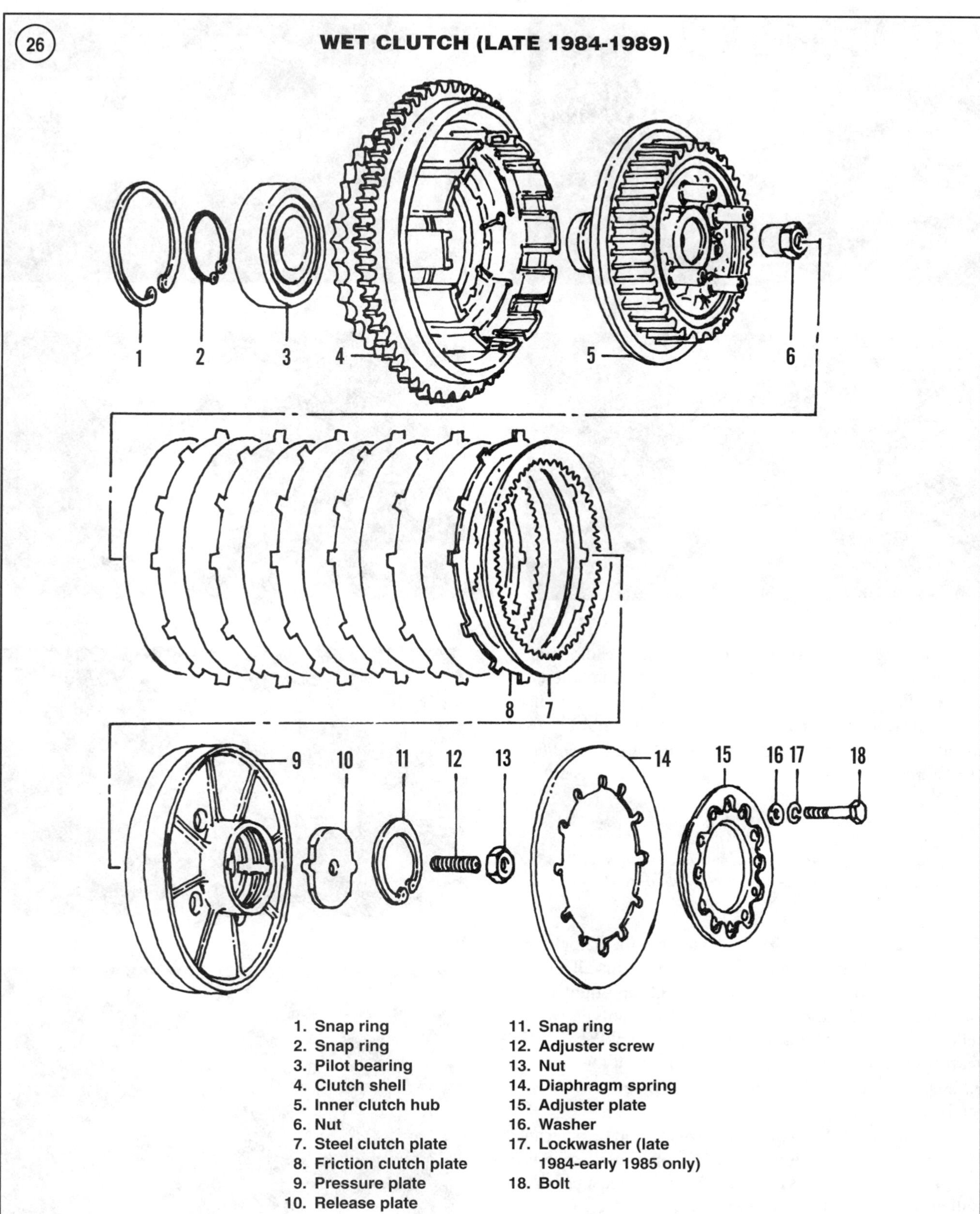
26
WET CLUTCH (LATE 1984-1989)
1
2
3
4
5
6
8
7
9
10
11
12
13
14
15
16
17
18
1. Snap ring
2. Snap ring
3. Pilot bearing
4. Clutch shell
5. Inner clutch hub
6. Nut
7. Steel clutch plate
8. Friction clutch plate
9. Pressure plate
10. Release plate
11. Snap ring
12. Adjuster screw
13. Nut
14. Diaphragm spring
15. Adjuster plate
16. Washer
17. Lockwasher (late 1984-early 1985 only)
18. Bolt

4. Apply a few drops of medium-strength threadlocking compound to the clutch nut threads prior to installation.
5. Use the same tools and procedures to prevent the mainshaft from turning as used during disassembly.
6. Install the nut onto the mainshaft and turn it *counterclockwise*. Tighten the nut to 50-60 ft.-lb. (67-81 N•m).

CAUTION
The compensating sprocket nut is tightened to a high torque specification. Make sure you hold the sprocket securely when tightening the nut in Step 5.

7. Apply a few drops of medium-strength threadlocking compound to the sprocket nut threads prior to installation.
8. Install the sprocket nut (A, **Figure 33**) and tighten to 90-100 ft.-lb. (122-136 N•m). Use the same tools and procedures as used during disassembly to prevent the crankshaft from turning. Remove the special tool at this time.
9. Soak all friction plates in clean engine oil before assembly.
10. Install a steel clutch plate (**Figure 29**) and then a friction clutch plate (A, **Figure 30**). Continue to alternately install the friction plates and steel plates. The last part installed is a steel clutch plate (**Figure 29**).
11. If removed, install the pushrod into the release plate.

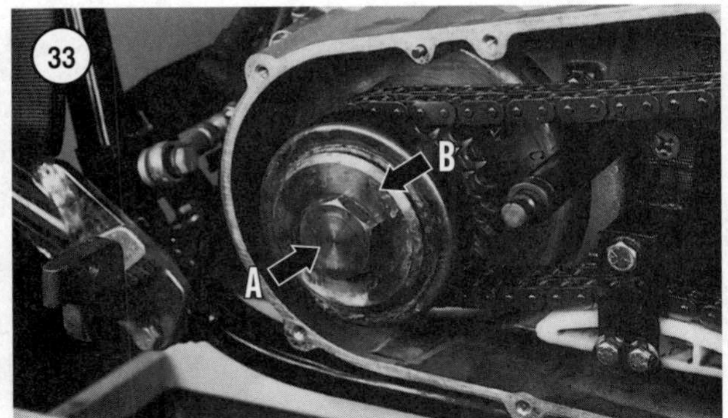

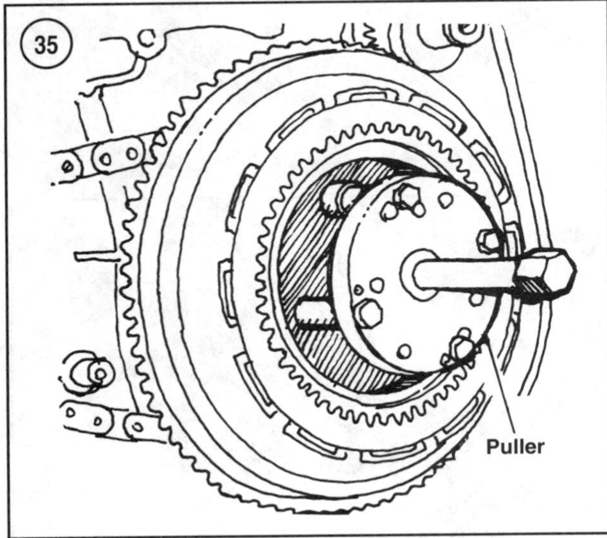

12. If the release plate was removed from the pressure plate, perform the following:
   a. Install the release plate (A, **Figure 38**) into the pressure plate (B).
   b. Position the snap ring with the beveled edge faces inward.

   c. Install the beveled snap ring and make sure it seats correctly in the pressure plate groove.

13. Install the pressure plate (B, **Figure 28**).
14. Position the diaphragm spring (C, **Figure 27**) with its convex side facing outward and install it onto the pressure plate.
15. Install the adjuster plate (B, **Figure 27**).

NOTE
Late 1984-early 1985 models use a flat washer and a lockwasher on each of the clutch hub bolts. Late 1985 and later models use only the washer, not the lockwasher.

16. Install the washer(s) onto each of the clutch hub bolts.

NOTE
Use only Loctite 222 (purple) threadlocking compound in Step 17.

17. Thoroughly clean the bolt threads with Loctite primer. Apply a few drops of Loctite 222 (purple) to threads on each of the clutch hub bolts.
18. Install the bolts (A, **Figure 27**) through the adjuster plate (B) and pressure plate. Then screw the bolts into the clutch hub. Tighten the bolts in a crisscross pattern to 80-97 in.-lb. (9-11 N•m).
19. Adjust the clutch as described in Chapter Three.

NOTE
If new clutch components were installed, readjust the clutch at the first 500-mile (800 km) interval.

20. Assemble and secure the primary chain adjust shoe assembly as described in this chapter.
21. Adjust the primary chain as described in Chapter Three.
22. Check primary chain alignment as described in this chapter.

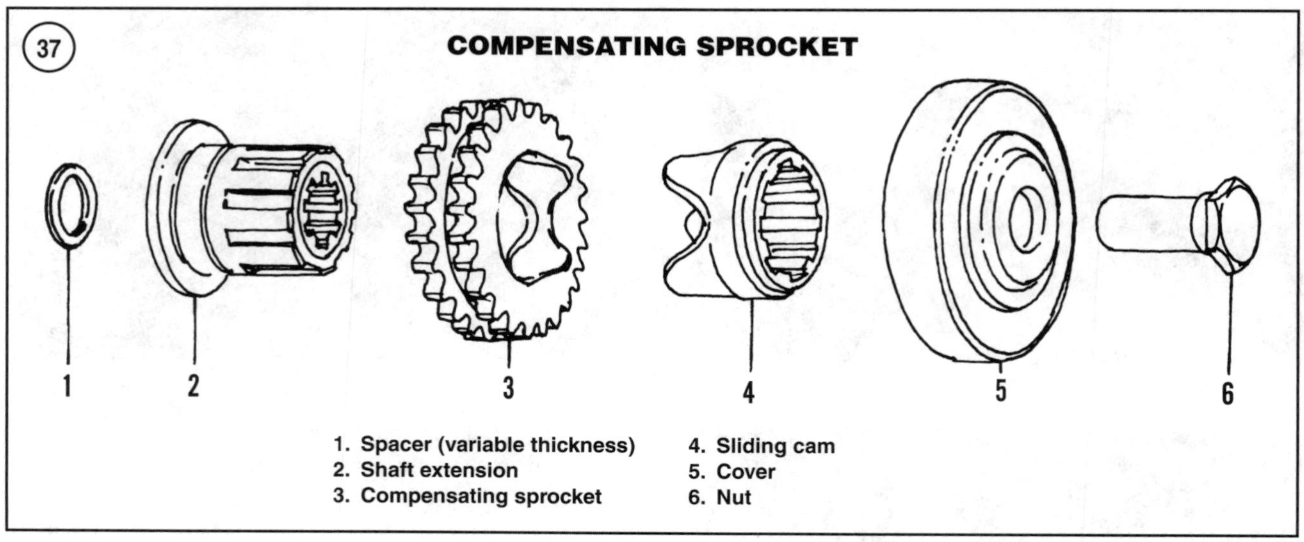

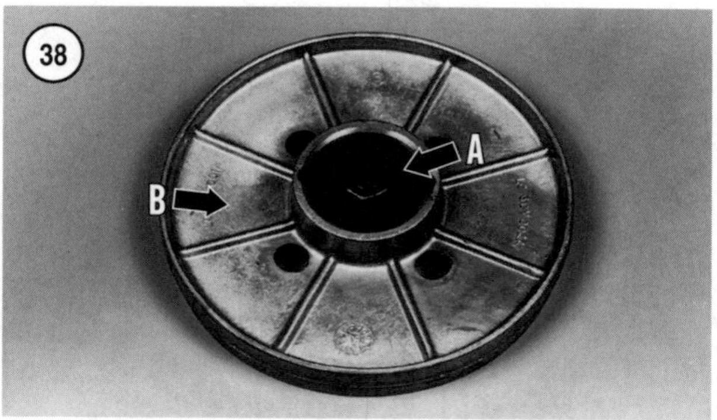

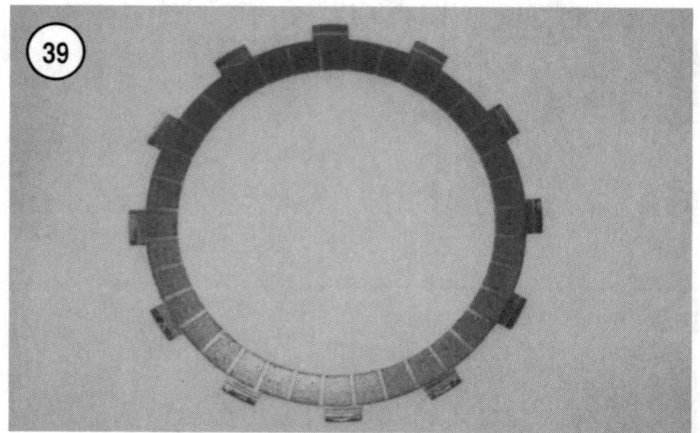

23. Install the primary chaincase outer cover as described in this chapter.

24. Refill the primary chain housing with the correct type and quantity of oil as described in Chapter Three.

25. Connect the negative battery cable to the battery.

26. Ride the motorcycle a short distance and check the cover for oil leaks.

Inspection

When measuring the clutch components, compare the actual measurement to the specifications in **Table 2**. Replace parts that are out of specification or show damage as described in this section.

1. Clean all clutch parts in a non-oil-based solvent and thoroughly dry with compressed air.

2. Inspect the friction plates (**Figure 39**) for worn or grooved lining surfaces. Measure each plate (**Figure 40**).

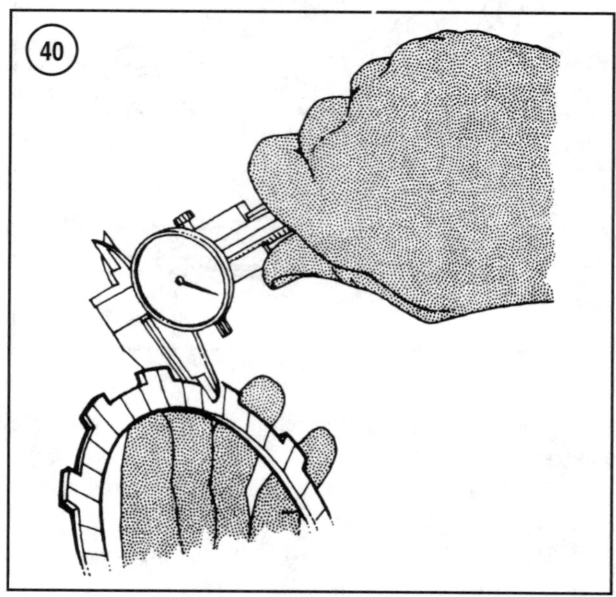

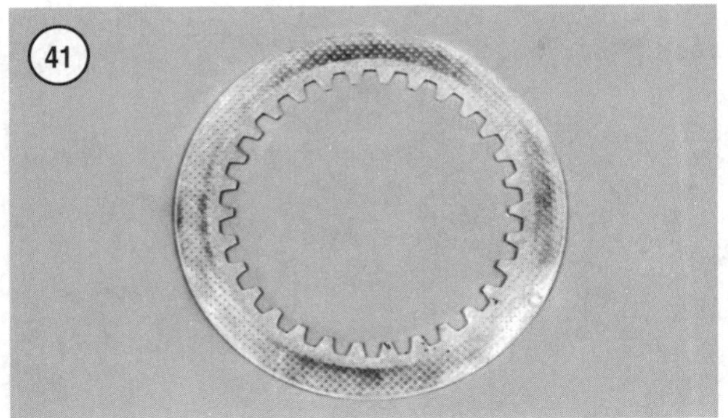

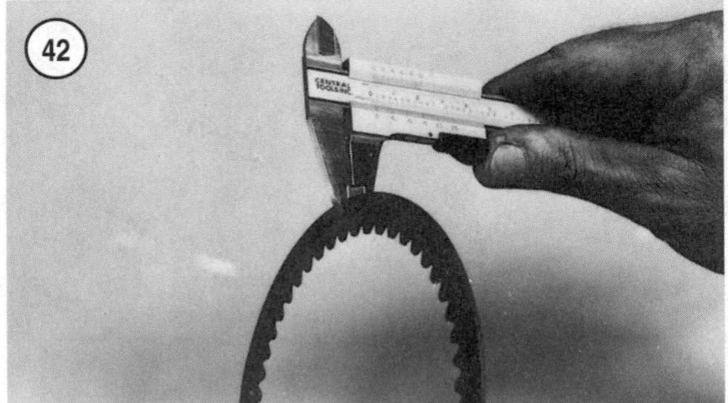

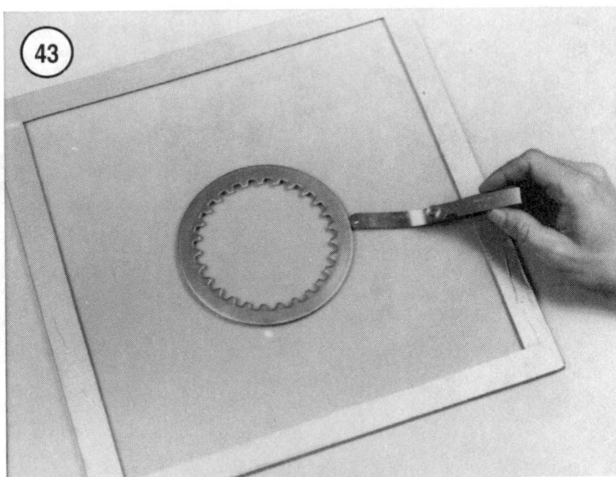

Replace the friction plates as a set if one plate is found too thin.

3. Check each steel plate (**Figure 41**) for thickness with a vernier caliper (**Figure 42**). Also check each steel plate for flatness with a feeler gauge and straightedge in several places (**Figure 43**).

4. Check the diaphragm spring (**Figure 44**) for wear or damage. Replace if necessary.

5. Check the pressure plate surfaces (B, **Figure 38** and **Figure 45**) for wear or cracking. Replace if necessary.

CAUTION

The clutch shell assembly consists of the inner clutch hub, clutch shell and pilot bearing. Because of the possibility of damaging the pilot bearing when removing it, do not disassemble these parts unless it is necessary to replace worn or damaged parts or to access the parts for closer inspection. A press is required for disassembly and assembly.

6. Check the pilot bearing (A, **Figure 46**) for wear by holding the clutch hub and turning the clutch shell by hand. If the bearing appears worn, replace it as described in this section.

7. Check both sets of gear teeth on the clutch shell (B, **Figure 46**). If the teeth are visibly worn or undercut (**Figure 47**), replace the clutch shell.

8. Check the inner clutch hub splines (**Figure 48**) for wear or damage. If worn or damaged parts are detected, disassemble the clutch shell assembly as described under *Clutch Shell, Clutch Hub and Sprocket (All Wet Clutch Models)* in this chapter.

WET CLUTCH ASSEMBLY (1990-1997 MODELS)

This section describes removal, inspection and installation of the clutch plates. If the clutch requires additional service, refer to the clutch shell procedures in this chapter.

In order to remove the clutch plates from the clutch hub, a special tool is necessary to safely compress the diaphragm spring and remove the snap ring. Use the clutch spring compressor (JIMS part No. 38515-90) (**Figure 49**) or an equivalent tool.

If the correct tool is not available, remove the clutch unit intact from the motorcycle and take it to a Harley-Davidson dealership or independent repair shop for disassembly, service and assembly. Do not attempt to disassemble the clutch without the correct tool.

Removal

Refer to **Figure 50**.

1. Disconnect the negative battery cable from the battery.
2. Remove the primary chaincase cover as described in this chapter.
3. Loosen the clutch adjust screw locknut with a socket (**Figure 51**). Then remove the adjusting screw and locknut.

WARNING
The previously described tool ***must be used*** *in the following step. The clutch diaphragm spring is under considerable pressure and, when released, will come off rapidly and possibly cause injury.*

4. Install the spring compressor tool as follows:
   a. Align the tool with the clutch assembly and thread the forcing screw on the tool into the release plate until the hex head on the forcing screw bottoms out against the release plate (**Figure 52**).
   b. Turn the tool handle clockwise to compress the diaphragm tool while at the same time moving the clutch spring seat inward and away from the large snap ring.
   c. When the clutch spring seat has been moved away from the snap ring, remove the snap ring with snap ring pliers or carefully pry it out with a small screwdriver (**Figure 53**).
5. After removing the snap ring in Step 4, remove the tool from the clutch with the diaphragm spring and pressure plate still attached (**Figure 54**).

46

47

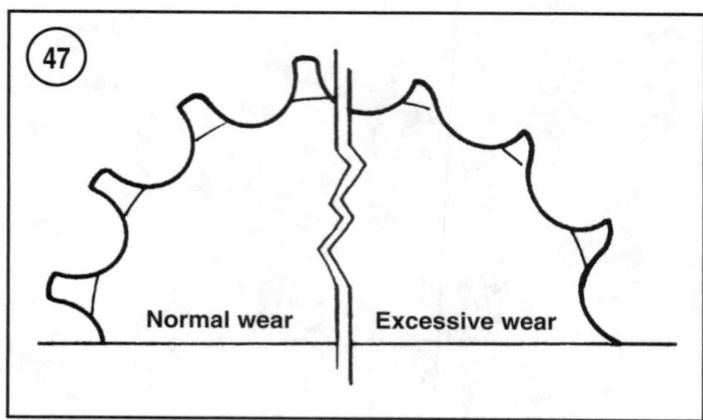

48

49

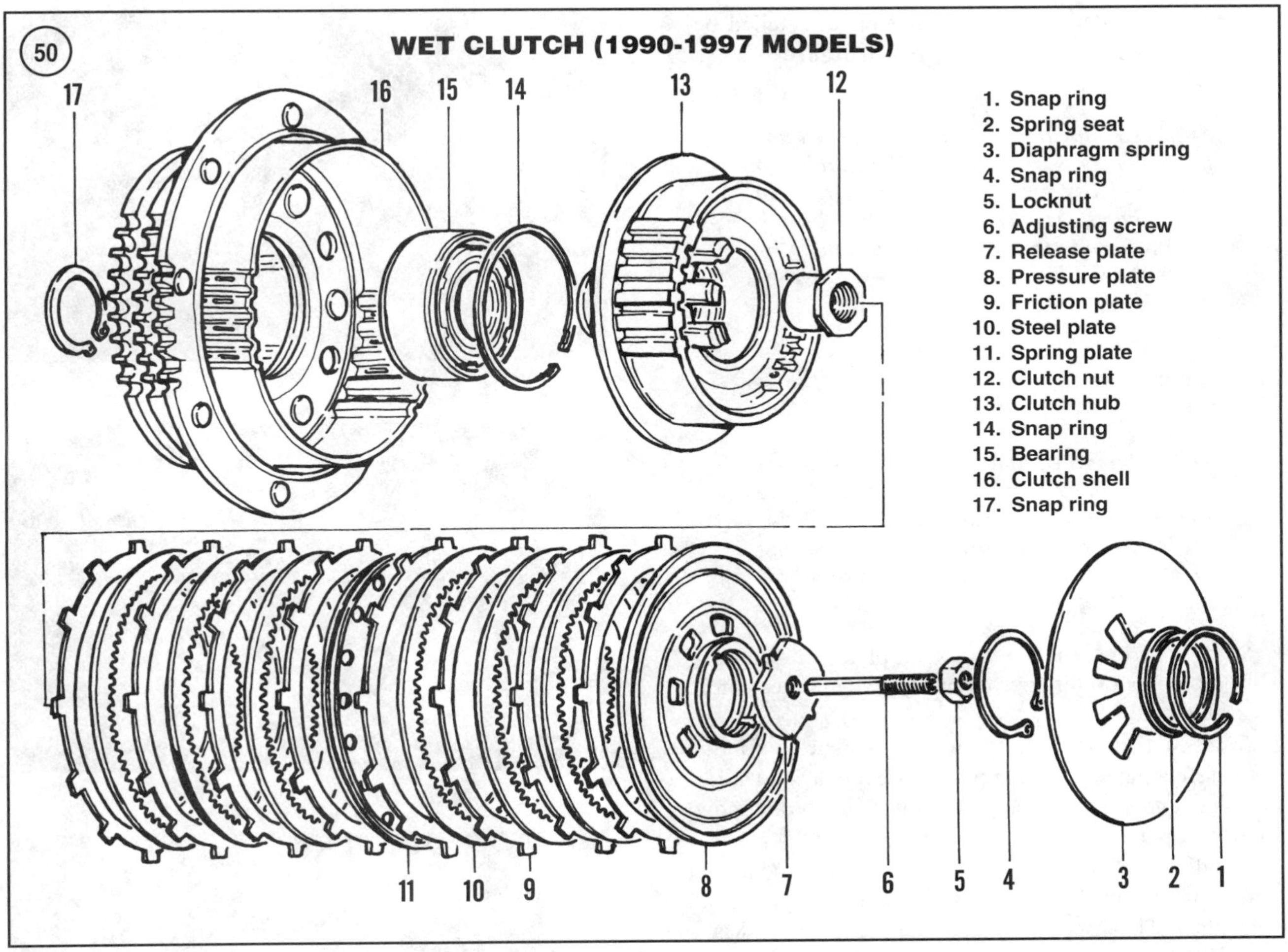

50

WET CLUTCH (1990-1997 MODELS)

1. Snap ring
2. Spring seat
3. Diaphragm spring
4. Snap ring
5. Locknut
6. Adjusting screw
7. Release plate
8. Pressure plate
9. Friction plate
10. Steel plate
11. Spring plate
12. Clutch nut
13. Clutch hub
14. Snap ring
15. Bearing
16. Clutch shell
17. Snap ring

NOTE

Do not loosen the spring compressor tool to remove the diaphragm spring or pressure plate unless these parts require inspection or replacement. Loosening and removing the tool will require repositioning of the diaphragm spring during assembly. This step will not be required as long as the tool is not removed from these parts.

6. Remove the friction and steel clutch plates (and the spring plate) from the clutch assembly (**Figure 55**) and

keep them in order. Note the spring plate installed between the fourth and fifth friction plate (**Figure 56**).

NOTE

*Further removal steps are not required unless it is necessary to remove the clutch hub and shell assembly. If necessary, remove these parts as described under **Clutch Shell, Compensating Sprocket and Primary Drive Chain** in this chapter. See **Figure 57**.*

Installation

NOTE

The original equipment clutch has eight friction plates, six steel plates and one spring plate. Make sure each part is installed in the correct order. When installing an aftermarket clutch plate assembly, follow the manufacturer's instructions.

1. Soak the friction plates and steel plates in clean primary chaincase oil for approximately five minutes before installing them.
2. Install a friction plate, then a steel plate, a friction plate, a steel plate, a friction plate, a steel plate and a friction plate and stop. At this point, four friction plates and three steel plates have been installed.
3. Install the spring plate, then a friction plate and a steel plate. Continue to alternately install the friction plates and steel plates. The last part installed is a friction plate. Make sure it is locked into place in the clutch shell.

NOTE

If the diaphragm spring and pressure plate were removed from the compression tool, proceed to Step 4. If they were not removed from the tool, proceed to Step 5.

4. Assemble the pressure plate and diaphragm spring as follows:
   a. Align the release plate tabs with the slots in the pressure plate and install it into the pressure plate.
   b. Install the snap ring and secure the release plate in the pressure plate. Make sure the snap ring seats in the groove completely. Do not thread the adjusting screw and locknut into the release plate at this time.
   c. Align the teeth on the pressure plate with the clutch hub. Then insert the pressure plate into the clutch hub.
   d. Position the diaphragm spring with the convex side facing out from the pressure plate and install it onto the pressure plate. The diaphragm spring has room to move around within the pressure plate. This is normal. Center the diaphragm spring by hand and hold it in position.
   e. Position the clutch spring seat with the lip side facing out and install it onto the diaphragm spring.

WARNING

*The previously described tool **must be used** in the following step. The clutch diaphragm spring is under considerable pressure and must be held in place during snap ring in-*

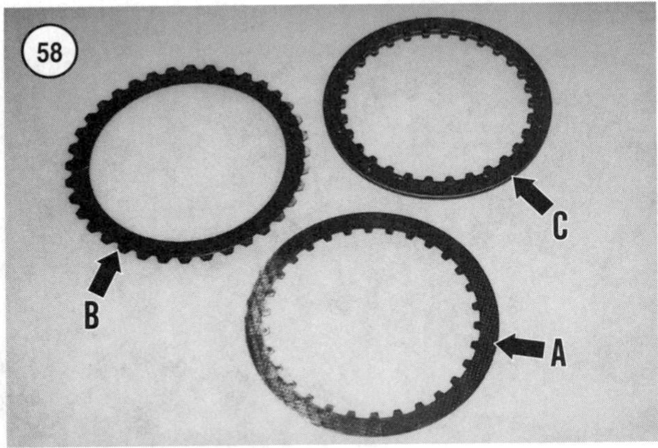

stallation. Personal injury could occur if the correct tool is not used.

f. Align the spring compressor tool with the clutch hub and thread the center screw on the tool into the release plate until the hex head on the forcing screw bottoms out against the release plate (**Figure 52**). Then check that the diaphragm spring is still centered within the clutch hub spring pocket as described in substep d. If necessary, reposition the diaphragm spring.

g. Turn the tool handle *clockwise*. Compress the diaphragm spring moving the clutch spring seat inward to access the clutch hub snap ring groove.

h. Install the diaphragm spring snap ring into the clutch hub groove. Make sure the ends of the snap ring do not hang over the bosses or posts on the end of the clutch hub.

i. After making sure the snap ring is seated completely in the clutch hub groove and that it is positioned as described in substep h, *slowly* turn the tool handle *counterclockwise* while making sure that the clutch spring seat lip seats inside the snap ring. After all tension has been removed from the tool, remove it from the release plate.

j. Install the adjust screw and locknut into the release plate (**Figure 51**).

5. If the tool was not removed from the diaphragm spring, install the diaphragm spring as follows:

a. Align the teeth on the pressure plate (**Figure 52**) with the clutch hub. Then insert the pressure plate into the clutch hub.

b. Thread the forcing screw on the tool into the release plate until the hex head on the forcing screw bottoms out against the release plate.

c. Turn the tool handle *clockwise* to compress the diaphragm spring and move the clutch spring seat inward to access the clutch hub snap ring groove.

d. Install the diaphragm spring snap ring into the clutch hub groove while making sure the ends of the snap ring do not overhang the bosses or posts on the end of the clutch hub.

e. After making sure the snap ring is seated completely in the clutch hub groove and positioned as described in substep d, slowly turn the tool handle *counterclockwise* while checking that the clutch spring seat lip seats inside the snap ring. After all tension has been removed from the tool, remove it from the release plate.

Inspection

When measuring the clutch components, compare the actual measurement to the specifications in **Table 3**. Replace parts that are out of specification or show damage as described in this section.

1. Clean all clutch parts in a non-oil-based solvent and thoroughly dry with compressed air.
2. Check each steel plate (A, **Figure 58**) for visual damage such as cracks or wear grooves.

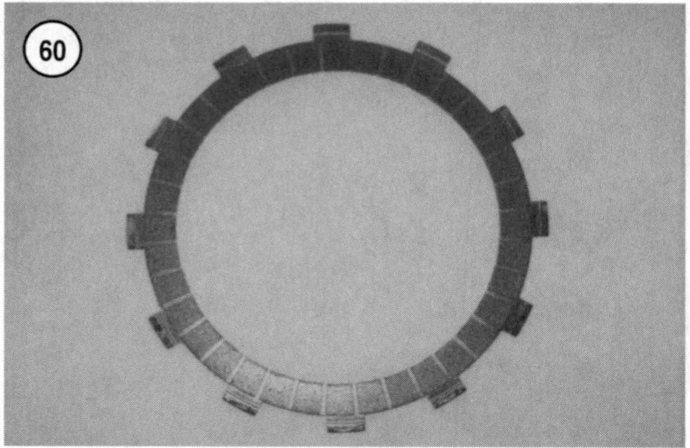

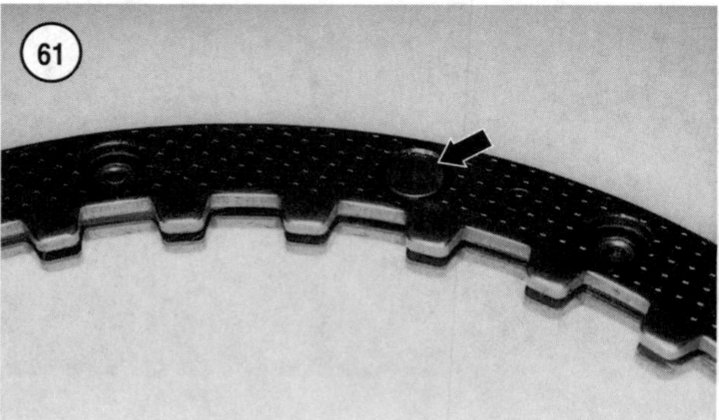

3. Also check each steel plate for flatness with a feeler gauge and straightedge in several places (**Figure 59**).
4. Inspect the friction plates (**Figure 60**) for worn or grooved lining surfaces. Replace the friction plates as a set if any one plate is damaged.
5. Clean each friction plate thoroughly with a lint-free cloth to remove as much oil from the plates as possible. Then stack each of the eight friction plates on top of each other and measure the thickness of the plate assembly with a vernier caliper or micrometer. Replace the friction plates as an assembly if the combined minimum thickness of the eight plates is less than the specification in **Table 3**.
6. Inspect the friction plates (B, **Figure 58**) for worn or grooved lining surfaces.
7. Check the spring plate (C, **Figure 58**) for cracks or damage. Check each of the rivets (**Figure 61**) for looseness or damage. Replace the spring plate if necessary.
8. Check the diaphragm spring for cracks or damage. Check also for bent or damaged tabs. Replace the diaphragm spring if necessary.

CLUTCH SHELL, COMPENSATING SPROCKET AND PRIMARY DRIVE CHAIN (WET CLUTCH ASSEMBLY [1990-1997 MODELS])

Removal

This procedure describes clutch shell, primary chain and compensating sprocket removal. These components must be removed from the engine and transmission as an assembly.

1. Disconnect the negative battery cable from the battery.
2. Remove the primary chaincase cover as described in this chapter.
3. Remove the clutch components from the clutch shell and hub as previously described.

4A. If a special tool is available, such as the primary drive locking tool (JIMS part No. 2234), place it onto the primary chain next to the clutch housing (**Figure 62**).

4B. If the special tool is not available, shift the transmission into fifth gear. Have an assistant apply the rear brake.

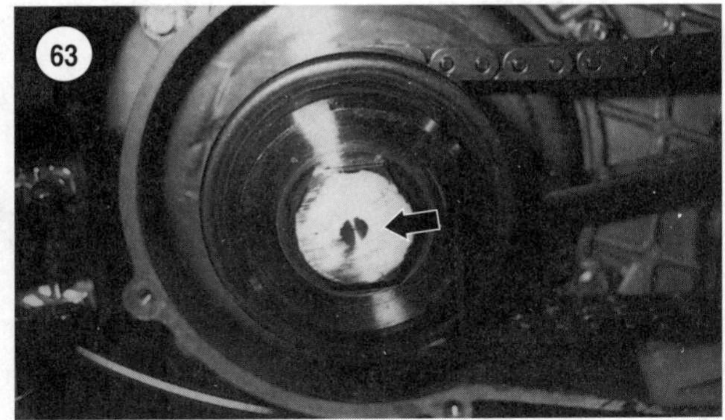
63

64

65

66

5. Loosen the compensating sprocket nut (**Figure 63**) with an impact wrench. Then remove the nut.

CAUTION
*The clutch hub nut has **left-hand threads**. Turn the clutch nut **clockwise** to loosen it.*

6. Loosen the clutch nut with an impact wrench. Remove the clutch nut.
7. Remove the nut and washer from the center bolt on the primary chain adjusting shoe assembly (**Figure 64**).
8. Remove the special tool installed in Step 4A.
9. Remove the clutch assembly, compensating sprocket, primary chain and chain adjuster bracket as an assembly (**Figure 57**).
10. Inspect the clutch shell as described in this chapter.

5

Installation

1. Remove all threadlocking compound residue from the crankshaft and mainshaft threads, compensating sprocket nut and clutch nut.
2. Remove all gasket residue from the inner primary housing gasket surface.
3. If removed, install the sprocket shaft spacer (**Figure 65**) and the compensating sprocket shaft extension (**Figure 66**).
4. Assemble the clutch, compensating sprocket, primary chain and chain adjuster bracket.
5. Install the clutch assembly, compensating sprocket, primary chain and chain adjuster bracket as an assembly (**Figure 57**). Make sure the chain tension assembly is still attached to the chain.
6A. Use the same tool setup used during removal to prevent the compensating sprocket and clutch shell from rotating during the following steps.
6B. If the special tool is not available, shift the transmission into fifth gear. Have an assistant apply the rear brake.

CAUTION
*The clutch hub nut has **left-hand threads**. Turn the clutch nut **counterclockwise** to tighten it.*

7. Apply two drops of medium-strength threadlocking compound to the clutch hub nut threads. Install the nut and tighten it to 70-80 ft.-lb. (95-108 N•m).
8. Apply two drops of medium-strength threadlocking compound to the compensating sprocket nut threads and thread the nut onto the crankshaft.
9. Use the same tools and procedures to prevent the compensating sprocket from turning. Tighten the nut to 150-165 ft.-lb. (203-224 N•m).

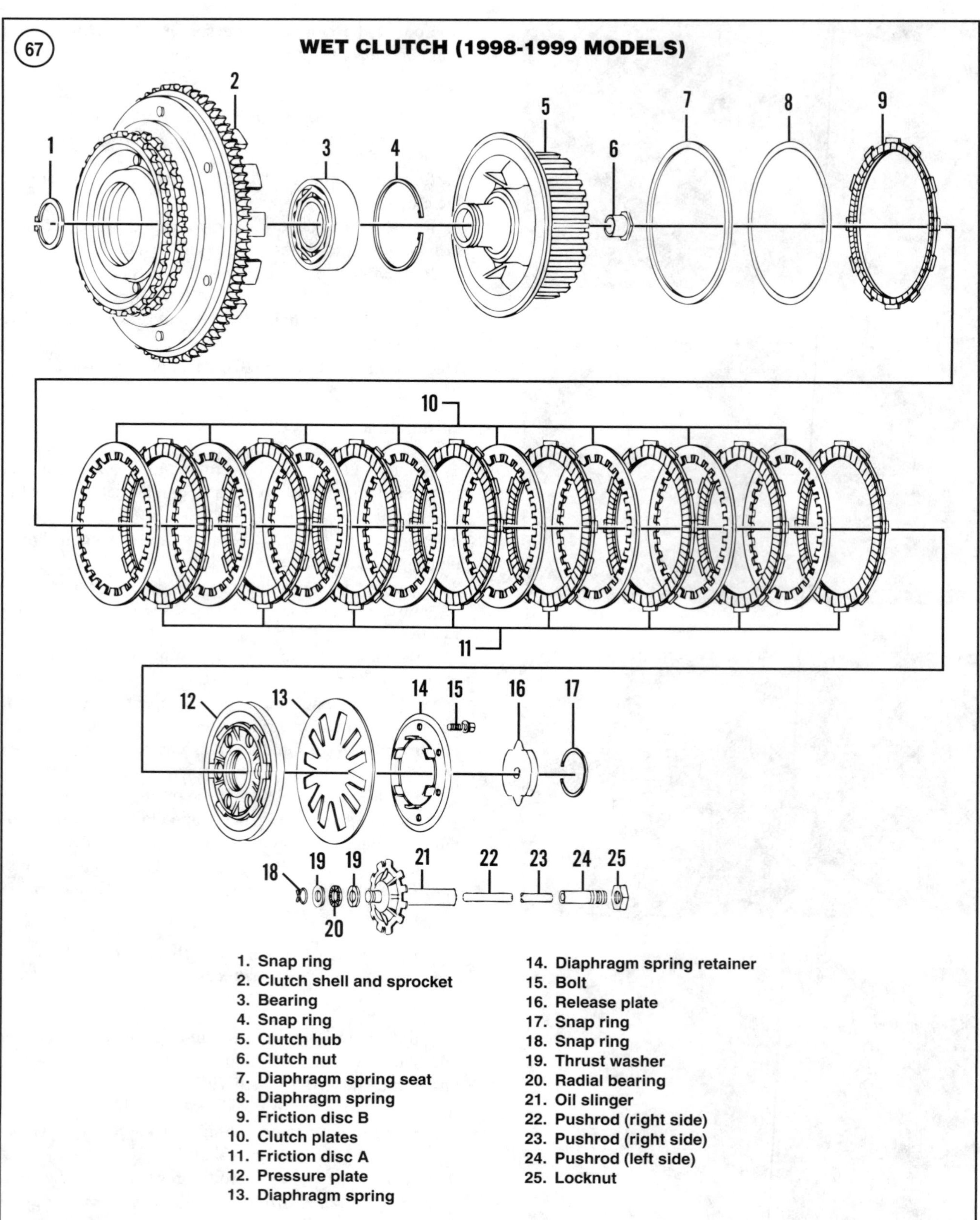
67
WET CLUTCH (1998-1999 MODELS)
1
2
3
4
5
6
7
8
9
10
11
12
13
14
15
16
17
18
19
19
20
21
22
23
24
25
1. Snap ring
2. Clutch shell and sprocket
3. Bearing
4. Snap ring
5. Clutch hub
6. Clutch nut
7. Diaphragm spring seat
8. Diaphragm spring
9. Friction disc B
10. Clutch plates
11. Friction disc A
12. Pressure plate
13. Diaphragm spring
14. Diaphragm spring retainer
15. Bolt
16. Release plate
17. Snap ring
18. Snap ring
19. Thrust washer
20. Radial bearing
21. Oil slinger
22. Pushrod (right side)
23. Pushrod (right side)
24. Pushrod (left side)
25. Locknut

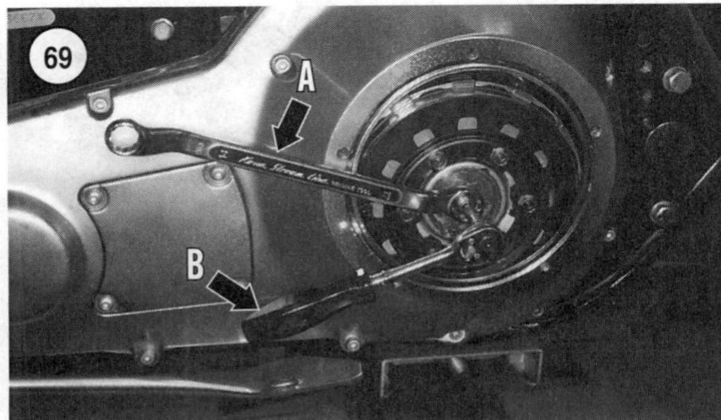

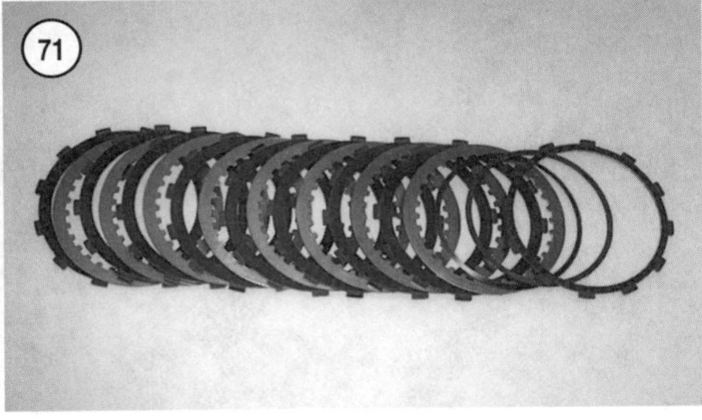

10. Adjust the clutch as described in Chapter Three.

NOTE
If new clutch components were installed, re-adjust the clutch at the first 500-mile (800 km) interval.

11. Assemble and secure the primary chain adjust shoe assembly as described in this chapter.

12. Adjust the primary chain as described in Chapter Three.

13. Check the primary chain alignment as described under *Primary Chain and Guide Alignment* in this chapter.

14. Install the primary chaincase cover as described in this chapter.

15. Ride the motorcycle a short distance and check the cover for oil leaks.

5

WET CLUTCH (1998-1999 MODELS)

This section describes removal, inspection and installation of the clutch plates. If the clutch requires additional service, refer to *Clutch Shell, Clutch Hub and Sprocket* in this chapter.

Refer to **Figure 67**.

Removal

1. Disconnect the negative battery cable from the battery.

2. Remove the clutch mechanism inspection cover and O-ring (**Figure 68**).

3. At the clutch mechanism, loosen the clutch adjusting screw locknut (A, **Figure 69**) and turn the adjusting screw (B) *counterclockwise* to allow slack against the diaphragm spring.

4. Remove the primary chaincase outer cover as described in this chapter.

5. Loosen the bolts securing the diaphragm spring retainer (A, **Figure 70**) in a crisscross pattern. Remove the bolts and the retainer and diaphragm spring (B, **Figure 70**).

6. Remove the pressure plate.

7. Remove the clutch plates and friction discs from the clutch shell.

8. Remove the damper spring and damper spring seat from the clutch shell. Keep all parts in order as shown in **Figure 71**.

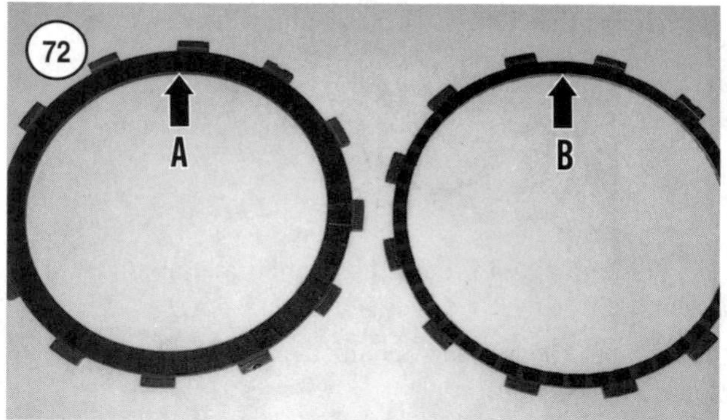

Installation

NOTE
*The original equipment clutch (**Figure 71**) has nine friction plates, eight steel plates, one damper spring and one damper spring seat. Make sure each part is installed. If installing an aftermarket clutch plate assembly, follow the manufacturer's instructions for plate quantity, alignment and installation sequence.*

1. Soak the clutch friction disc and clutch plates in new primary drive oil for approximately five minutes before installing them.

NOTE
*There are two different types of clutch friction discs (**Figure 72**). The wider friction disc A is the normal width disc. The narrow width disc B is installed first because it works in conjunction with the damper spring and damper spring seat.*

2. Install the clutch friction disc B (**Figure 73**) onto the clutch shell and clutch hub. Push it on all the way until it bottoms within the clutch hub.

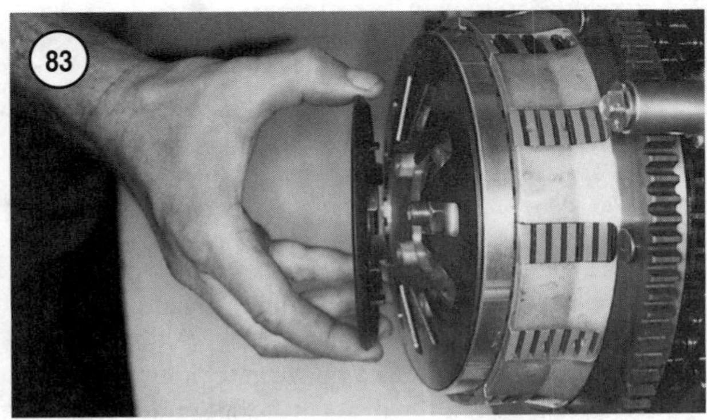

3. Install the damper spring seat (**Figure 74**) onto the clutch hub and push it in until it seats within the clutch friction disc B.

4. Position the damper spring with the concave side facing out (**Figure 75**) and install it onto the clutch hub against the damper spring seat (**Figure 76**).

5. Install a clutch plate (**Figure 77**) and then friction disc A (**Figure 78**). Continue to alternately install the clutch plates and friction discs. The last part installed is friction disc A (**Figure 79**).

6. Make sure the left pushrod assembly (**Figure 80**) is in place in the pressure plate. Install the pressure plate onto the clutch hub.

7. Position the diaphragm spring with the convex side facing out (**Figure 81**) and install it onto the pressure plate (**Figure 82**). Hold the pressure plate in place.

8. Position the diaphragm spring retainer with the finger side (**Figure 83**) facing in toward the diaphragm spring (B, **Figure 70**). Install the diaphragm spring retainer (A) and bolts.

9. Tighten the bolts in a crisscross pattern to 90-110 in.-lb. (10-12 N•m).

10. Install the primary chaincase outer cover as described in this chapter.

11. Install the clutch mechanism inspection cover and O-ring.
12. Connect the negative battery cable.

Inspection

When measuring the clutch components, compare the actual measurements to the specifications in **Table 4**. Replace parts that are out of specification or show damage as described in this section.

1. Clean all parts in solvent and thoroughly dry with compressed air.
2. Inspect the friction discs as follows:

NOTE
*If any friction disc is damaged or out of specification as described in the following steps, replace **all** of the friction discs as a set. Never replace only one or two discs.*

a. The friction material used on the friction discs (**Figure 84**) is bonded to an aluminum plate for warp resistance and durability. Inspect the friction material for excessive or uneven wear, cracks and other damage. Check the disc tangs for surface damage. The sides of the disc tangs must be smooth where they contact the clutch shell finger; otherwise, the discs cannot engage and disengage correctly.

NOTE
If the disc tangs are damaged, carefully inspect the clutch shell fingers as described later in this section.

b. Measure the thickness of each friction disc with a vernier caliper (**Figure 85**). Measure at several places around the disc.

3. Inspect the clutch plates (**Figure 86**) as follows:
   a. Inspect the clutch plates for cracks, damage or color change. Overheated clutch plates will have a blue discoloration.
   b. Check the clutch plates for oil glaze buildup. Remove by lightly sanding both sides of each plate with 400-grit sandpaper placed on a surface plate or piece of glass.
   c. Place each clutch plate on a flat surface and check for warp with a feeler gauge (**Figure 87**).
   d. The clutch plate inner teeth mesh with the clutch hub splines. Check the clutch plate teeth for any roughness or damage. The teeth contact surfaces must be smooth; otherwise, the plates cannot engage and disengage correctly.

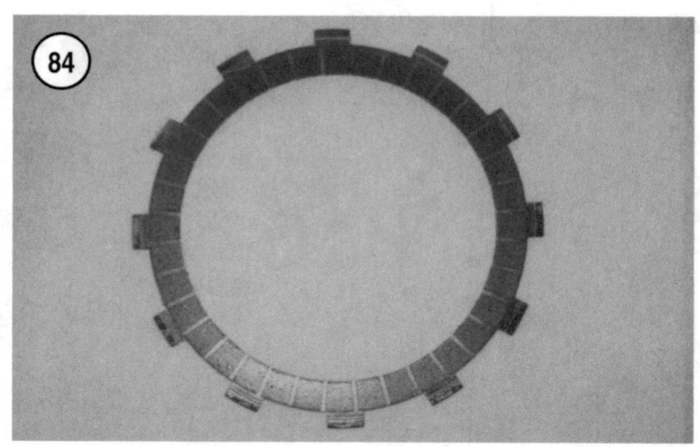
84

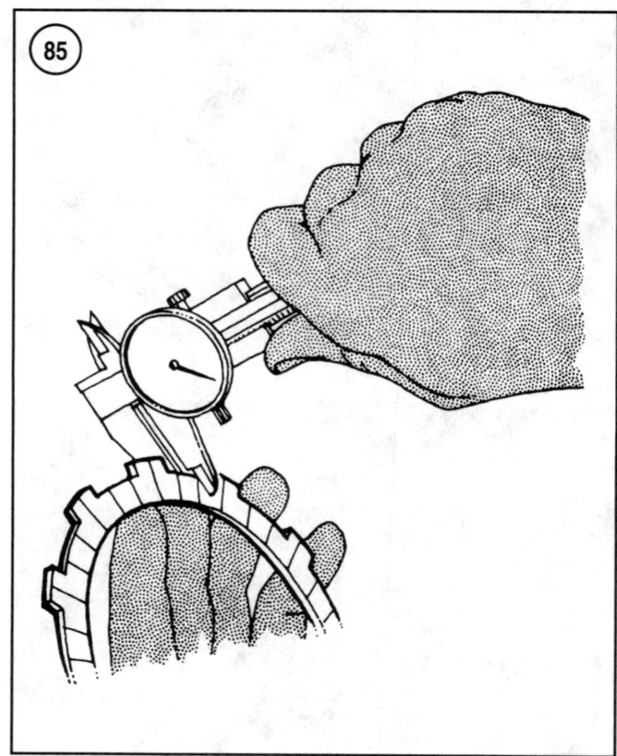
85

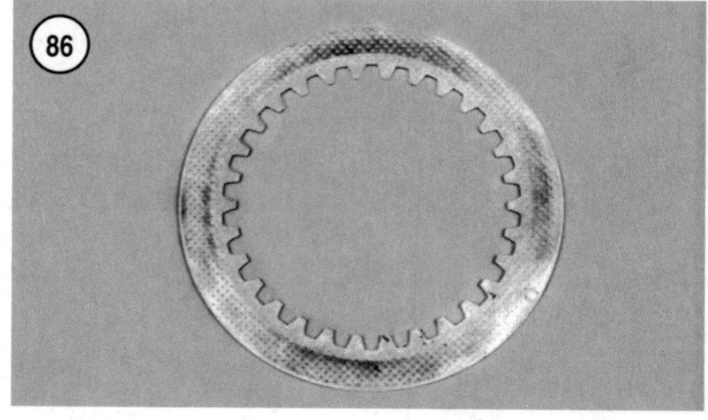
86

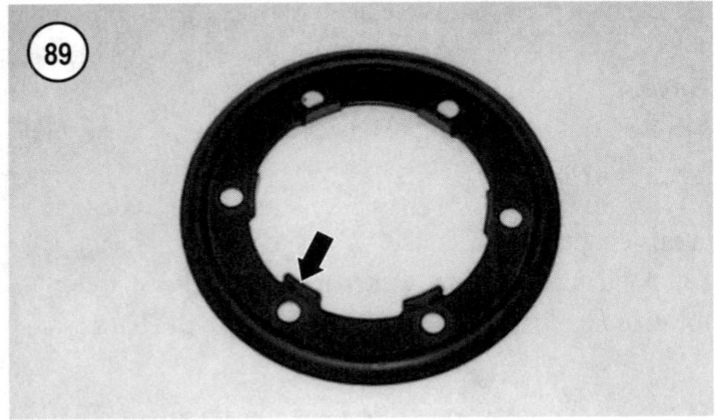

NOTE
If the clutch plate teeth are damaged, carefully inspect the clutch hub splines as described later in this section.

4. Inspect the diaphragm spring (**Figure 88**) for cracks or damage.
5. Inspect the diaphragm spring retainer for cracks or damage. Check also for bent or damaged tabs (**Figure 89**).

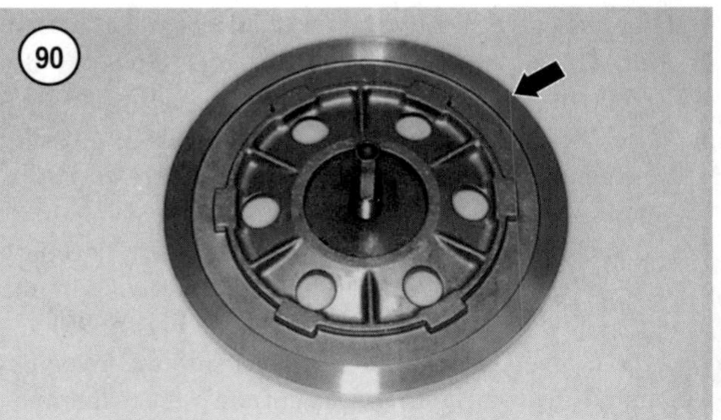

6. Inspect the pressure plate contact surface (**Figure 90**) for cracks or other damage.
7. If necessary, disassemble the pressure plate as follows:
   a. Remove the snap ring and remove the release plate, left pushrod and locknut (**Figure 91**) from the pressure plate.
   b. Inspect the release plate, left pushrod and locknut for wear or damage.
   c. Inspect the snap ring groove for damage.
   d. Position the release plate with the OUT mark facing out (**Figure 92**) and install the assembly into the pressure plate.
   e. Install the snap ring and make sure it is correctly seated in the pressure plate groove.

CLUTCH SHELL, COMPENSATING SPROCKET AND PRIMARY DRIVE CHAIN (WET CLUTCH ASSEMBLY [1998-1999 MODELS])

Removal

This procedure describes clutch shell **Figure 93**, primary chain and compensating sprocket removal (**Figure 94**). These components must be removed as an assembly.

5

1. Disconnect the negative battery cable from the battery.
2. Remove the primary chaincase outer cover as described in this chapter.
3. If necessary, remove the diaphragm spring, pressure plate, clutch plates and friction discs as described in this chapter.
4A. If the special tool is available, such as the primary drive locking tool (JIMS part No. 2234), place it onto the primary chain next to the clutch housing (**Figure 95**).
4B. If the special tool is not available, shift the transmission into fifth gear. Have an assistant apply the rear brake.

CAUTION
*The clutch nut has **left-hand threads**. Turn the clutch nut **clockwise** to loosen it.*

5. Loosen the clutch nut with an impact wrench. Remove the clutch nut (**Figure 96**).
6. Loosen the compensating sprocket nut (**Figure 97**) with an impact wrench.
7. Remove the compensating sprocket nut (**Figure 97**), washer, cover (**Figure 98**) and sliding cam (**Figure 99**).
8. Remove the primary chain shoe adjuster locknut (**Figure 100**).
9. Remove the compensating sprocket, primary chain, chain adjuster and clutch assembly at the same time (**Figure 101**).
10. Remove the shaft extension (**Figure 102**) and the spacer.
11. Inspect the various components as described in this chapter.

Installation

1. Remove all residue from the crankshaft and mainshaft threads and from the compensating sprocket nut and the clutch nut.
2. Remove all gasket residue from the inner primary housing gasket surfaces.
3. Install the spacer and the shaft extension (**Figure 102**) onto the crankshaft.
4. Assemble the compensating sprocket, primary chain, chain adjuster and clutch as shown in **Figure 101**.
5. Install the compensating sprocket, primary chain, chain adjuster and clutch. Insert the chain adjuster bolt through the chain adjuster hole as shown in **Figure 103**.
6. Install the primary chain shoe adjuster locknut (**Figure 100**) and tighten finger-tight at this time.
7. Install the compensating sprocket (**Figure 99**) and the cover (**Figure 98**).
8. Install the washer.

9. Install the same tool setup (**Figure 95**) used during removal or shift the transmission into fifth gear to prevent the compensating sprocket and clutch shell from rotating during the following steps.
10. Apply two drops of medium-strength threadlocking compound to the compensating sprocket nut threads. Install the nut (**Figure 97**) and tighten to 150-165 ft.-lb. (203-224 N•m).

NOTE
*The clutch nut has **left-hand threads**. Turn the nut **counterclockwise** to tighten it.*

11. Apply two drops of medium-strength threadlocking compound to the clutch nut threads. Install the nut (**Figure 96**) and tighten (**Figure 104**) to 70-80 ft.-lb. (95-108 N•m).
12. If used, remove the special tool from the clutch shell.
13. Adjust the primary chain as described in Chapter Three.
14. Install the clutch plates, friction discs, pressure plate and diaphragm spring as described in this chapter.
15. Install the primary chaincase outer cover as described in this chapter.
16. Adjust the clutch as described in Chapter Three.
17. Connect the negative battery cable to the battery.

CLUTCH SHELL, CLUTCH HUB AND SPROCKET (ALL WET CLUTCH MODELS)

Disassembly/Assembly

Do not separate the clutch hub and shell unless the bearing or either part is going to be replaced. If the two parts are separated, the bearing will be damaged. Removal and installation of the bearing requires the use of a hydraulic press.

Refer to **Figure 93**.

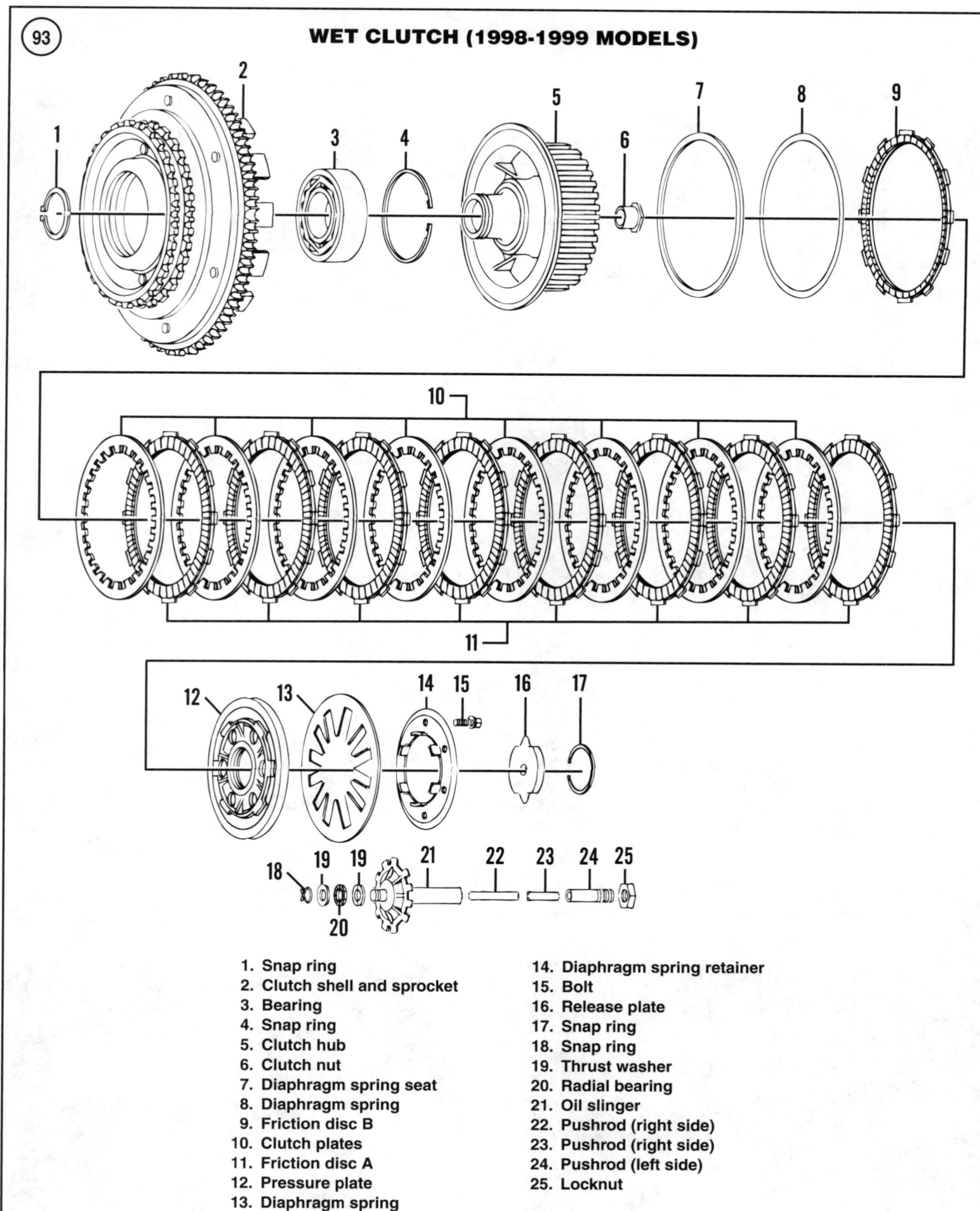
93
WET CLUTCH (1998-1999 MODELS)
1
2
3
4
5
6
7
8
9
10
11
12
13
14
15
16
17
18
19
19
20
21
22
23
24
25
1. Snap ring
2. Clutch shell and sprocket
3. Bearing
4. Snap ring
5. Clutch hub
6. Clutch nut
7. Diaphragm spring seat
8. Diaphragm spring
9. Friction disc B
10. Clutch plates
11. Friction disc A
12. Pressure plate
13. Diaphragm spring
14. Diaphragm spring retainer
15. Bolt
16. Release plate
17. Snap ring
18. Snap ring
19. Thrust washer
20. Radial bearing
21. Oil slinger
22. Pushrod (right side)
23. Pushrod (right side)
24. Pushrod (left side)
25. Locknut

94

COMPENSATING SPROCKET

1 2 3 4 5 6 7

8 9 10 11

12

13 14 15 16 17 18

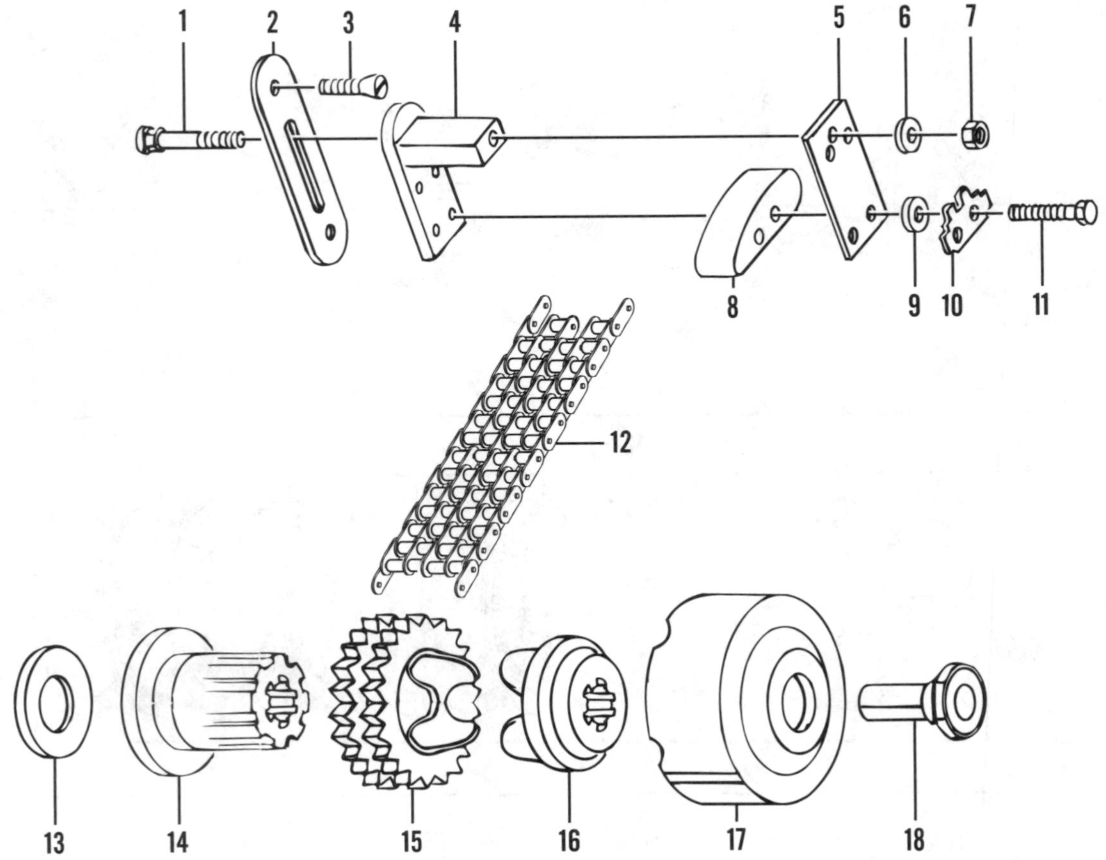

1. Bolt
2. Anchor plate
3. Screw
4. Chain tensioner
5. Plate
6. Washer
7. Nut
8. Tensioner pad
9. Washer
10. Lockwasher
11. Bolt
12. Primary drive chain
13. Spacer
14. Shaft extension
15. Compensating sprocket
16. Sliding cam
17. Cover assembly with springs*
18. Nut*

*Spacer between No. 17 and No. 18 for 1999 models not shown.

95

96

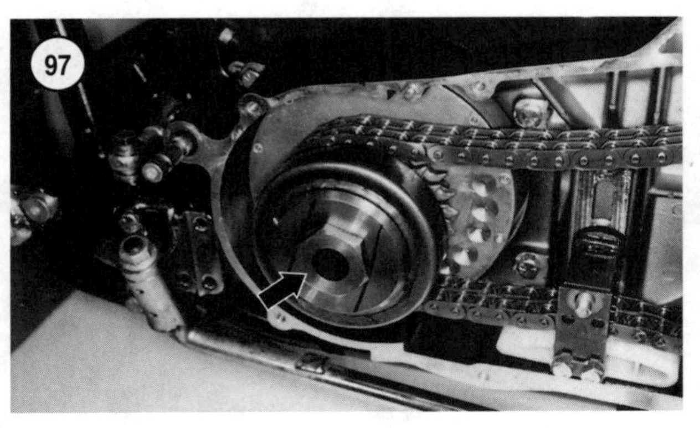
97

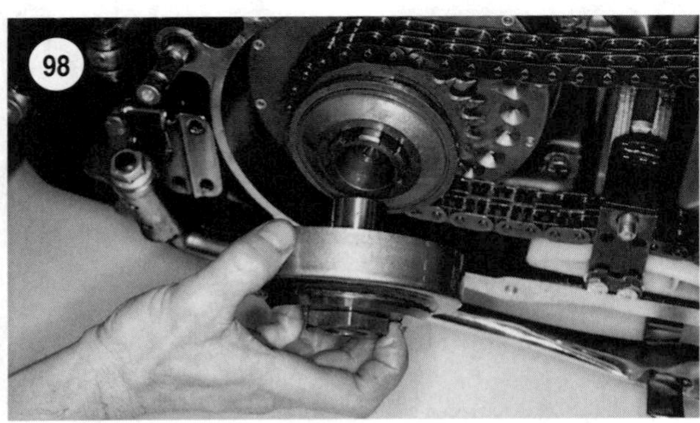
98

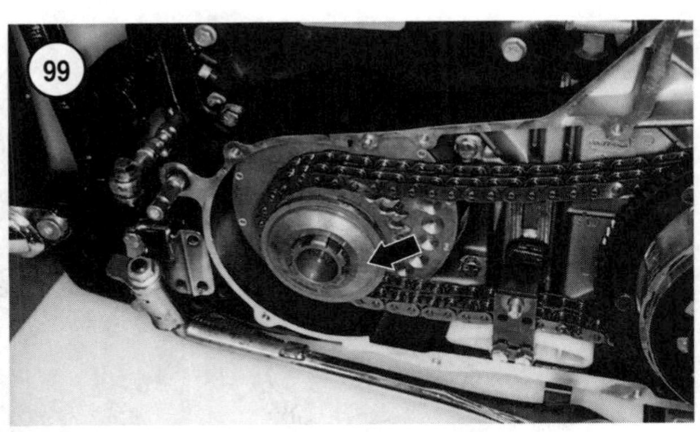
99

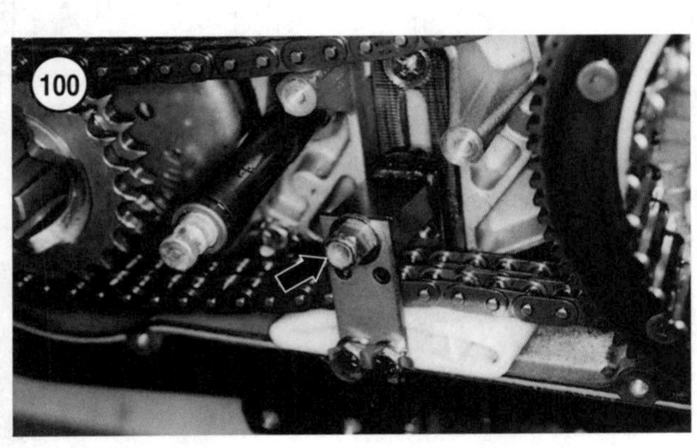
100

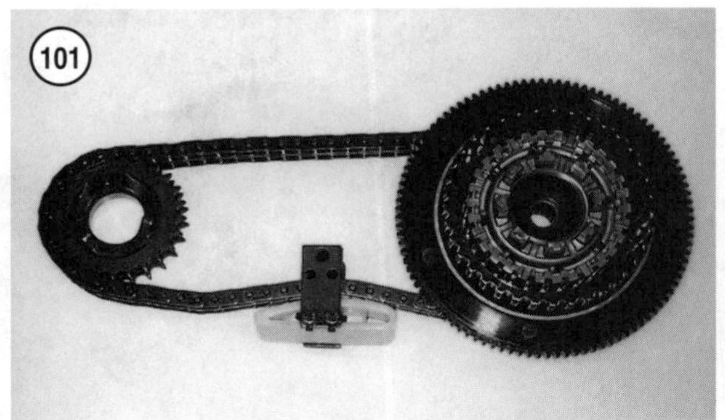
101

102

103

104

1. Remove the clutch as described in this chapter. Remove the clutch shell assembly from the primary drive chain.
2. Remove the snap ring (**Figure 105**) from the clutch hub groove.
3. Position the clutch hub and shell with the primary chain sprocket side *facing up*.
4. Support the clutch hub and clutch shell in a press (**Figure 106**).
5. Place a suitable size arbor in the clutch hub surface and press the clutch hub (A, **Figure 107**) out of the bearing.
6. Remove the clutch shell from the press (B, **Figure 107**).
7. On the inner surface of the clutch shell, remove the bearing retaining snap ring (**Figure 108**) from the groove in the middle of the clutch shell.

CAUTION

Press the bearing out from the primary chain sprocket side of the clutch shell. The bearing bore has a shoulder on the primary chain side.

8. Support the clutch shell in the press with the primary chain sprocket side *facing up*.
9. Place a suitable size arbor on the bearing inner race and press the bearing out of the clutch shell (**Figure 109**).
10. Thoroughly clean the clutch hub and shell in solvent and dry with compressed air.
11. Inspect the bearing bore in the clutch shell for damage or burrs. Clean off any burrs that would interfere with new bearing installation.
12. Support the clutch shell in the press with the primary chain sprocket side *facing down*.
13. Apply chaincase lubricant to the clutch shell bearing receptacle and to the outer surface of the bearing.
14. Align the bearing with the clutch shell receptacle.
15. Place a suitable size arbor on the bearing outer race and slowly press the bearing into the clutch shell until it

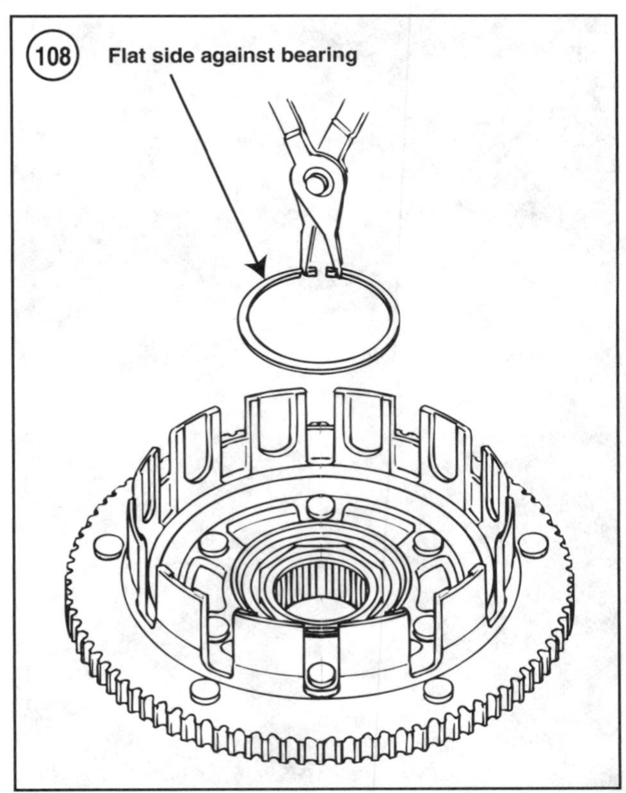

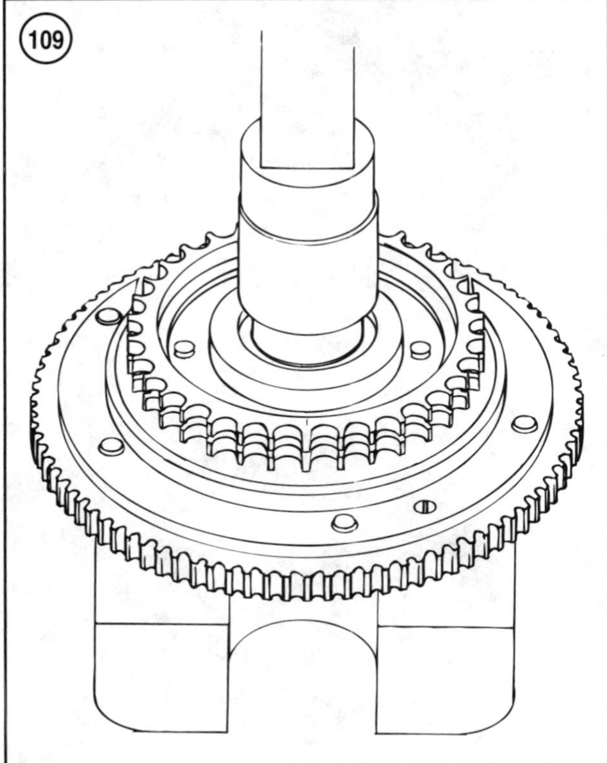

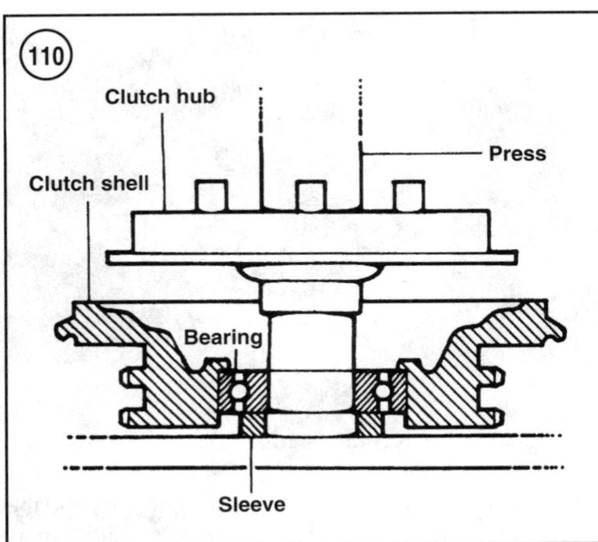

bottoms on the lower shoulder. Press only on the outer bearing race. Applying force to the bearing inner race will damage the bearing. Refer to *Bearing Replacement* in Chapter One for additional information.

16. Position the new snap ring with the flat side against the bearing and install the snap ring into the clutch shell

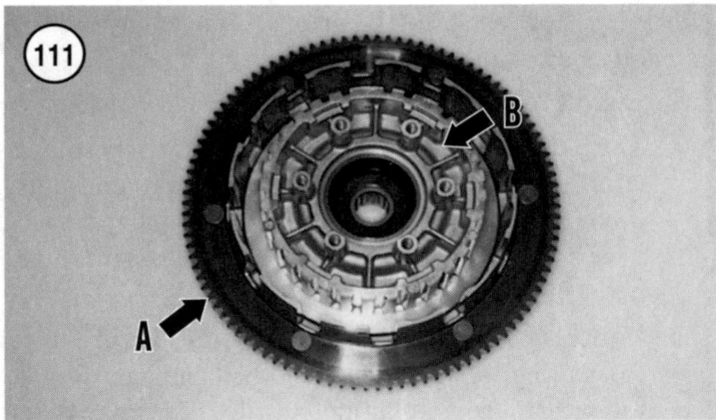

groove (**Figure 108**). Make sure the snap ring is seated correctly in the clutch shell groove.

17. Press the clutch hub into the clutch shell as follows:

CAUTION
Failure to support the inner bearing race properly will cause bearing and clutch shell damage.

a. Place the clutch shell in a press. Support the inner bearing race with a sleeve as shown in **Figure 110**.
b. Align the clutch hub with the bearing and slowly press the clutch hub into the bearing until the clutch hub shoulder seats against the bearing inner race.
c. Install a *new* snap ring (**Figure 105**) into the clutch hub. Make sure the snap ring is seated correctly in the clutch hub groove.

18. After completing assembly, hold the clutch shell (A, **Figure 111**) and rotate the clutch hub (B) by hand. The shell must turn smoothly with no roughness or binding. If the clutch shell binds or turns roughly, the bearing was installed incorrectly. Repeat this procedure until this problem is corrected.

Inspection

The clutch shell is a subassembly consisting of the clutch shell, the clutch hub, the bearing and two snap rings.

1. Remove the clutch shell as described in this chapter.
2. Hold the clutch shell and rotate the clutch hub by hand. The bearing is damaged if the clutch hub binds or turns roughly.
3. Check the sprocket (A, **Figure 112**) and the starter ring gear (B) on the clutch shell for cracks, deep scoring, excessive wear or heat discoloration.
4. If the sprocket or the ring gear are worn or damaged, replace the clutch shell. If the primary chain sprocket is

worn, also check the primary chain and the compensating sprocket as described in this chapter.

5. Inspect the clutch hub for the following conditions:
   a. The clutch plate teeth slide in the clutch hub splines (A, **Figure 113**). Inspect the splines for rough spots, grooves or other damage. Repair minor damage with a file or oil stone. If the damage is severe, replace the clutch hub.
   b. Inspect the clutch hub inner splines (**Figure 114**) for galling, severe wear or other damage. Repair minor damage with a fine-cut file. If damage is severe, replace the clutch hub.
   c. Inspect the bolt towers and threads (B, **Figure 113**) for thread damage or cracks at the base of the tower. Repair thread damage with the correctly sized metric tap. If the tower(s) is cracked or damaged, replace the clutch hub.
6. Check the clutch shell. The friction disc tangs slide in the clutch housing grooves (C, **Figure 113**). Inspect the grooves for cracks or galling. Repair minor damage with a file. If the damage is severe, replace the clutch housing.
7. If the clutch hub, the clutch shell or the bearing is damaged, replace it as described in the following procedure.

PRIMARY CHAIN AND GUIDE

Removal/Inspection/Installation

1. Remove the primary chain as described under the *Clutch, Compensating Sprocket and Primary Drive Chain Removal and Installation* procedure in this chapter.
2. Clean the primary chain in solvent and dry thoroughly.
3. Inspect the primary chain (A, **Figure 115**) for excessive wear, cracks or other damage. If the chain is worn or damaged, check both the compensating sprocket (B, **Figure 115**) and the clutch shell-driven sprocket (C) for wear or damage. Replace parts as necessary.

NOTE
If the primary chain is near the end of its adjustment level, or if no more adjustment is available, and the adjusting guide is not worn or damaged, the primary chain is excessively worn. Service specifications for chain wear are not available.

4. Inspect the adjusting guide for cracks, severe wear or other damage. Replace the adjusting shoe if necessary.

Adjustment Shoe Replacement

If the primary chain cannot be adjusted properly and the adjustment shoe (**Figure 116**) appears worn, replace it as follows.

1. Remove the primary chaincase outer cover as described under clutch removal in this chapter.
2. Remove the top shoe bracket bolt and remove the bracket.
3. Pry back the locking tabs and remove the adjusting shoe mounting bolts. Remove the old adjusting shoe and

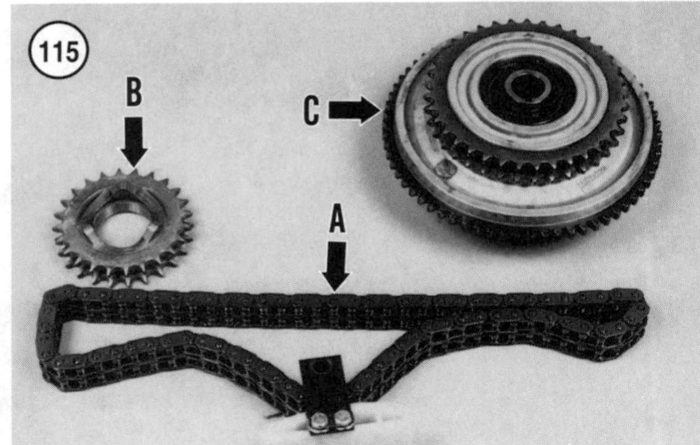

install a new one. Lock the new adjusting shoe in place by bending the lockwasher tabs over the mounting bolts.

4. Adjust the primary chain as described in Chapter Three.

5. Install the primary chaincase outer cover as described under the *Clutch Inspection* in this chapter.

Alignment

The compensating sprocket is aligned with the clutch sprocket by a spacer placed between the alternator rotor and the shaft extension (**Figure 94**). The same spacer should be reinstalled any time the compensating sprocket is removed. However, if the primary chain is wearing on one side, or if new clutch components were installed that could affect alignment, perform the following.

Dry clutch models

1. Remove the primary chaincase outer cover as described under *Clutch Removal* in this chapter.

2. Check and adjust the primary chain tension as described in Chapter Three.

3. Push the primary chain toward the engine as far as it will go at the sprockets as shown in **Figure 117**. This pushes the chain clearance to the inside of the sprockets.

4. Place a straightedge across the primary cover gasket surface near the engine compensating sprocket and measure the distance from the chain-link side plates to the straightedge. Record this measurement.

5. Repeat Step 4 by measuring the distance at the clutch sprocket.

6. The difference between Step 4 and Step 5 should be within 0.030 in. (0.76 mm). If the clearance exceeds 0.030 in. (0.76 mm), replace the spacer (13, **Figure 94**) with a suitably sized spacer.

Wet clutch models

1. Remove the primary chaincase outer cover as described in this chapter.

2. Adjust the primary chain tension so the chain is snug against both the compensating sprocket and clutch shell sprocket.

3. Push the primary chain toward the engine and transmission (at both sprockets) as far as it will go.

4. Place a straightedge across the primary chain side plates as close to the compensating sprocket as possible.

5. Close to the compensating sprocket, measure the distance from the chain-link side plates to the primary chaincase housing gasket surface (**Figure 118**). Record the measurement.

6. Repeat Steps 4 and 5 with the end of the straightedge as close to the clutch sprocket as possible (**Figure 119**). Record the measurement.

7. The difference between the two measurements must be within 0.030 in. (0.76 mm) of each other. If the difference exceeds this amount, replace the spacer (**Figure 120**) with a suitably sized spacer. Refer to **Table 3** and **Table 4** for spacer thickness.

8. To replace the spacer, perform the *Clutch, Compensating Sprocket and Primary Drive Chain Removal and Installation* procedure in this chapter.
9. Install the primary chaincase outer cover as described in this chapter.
10. Check and adjust the primary chain tension as described in Chapter Three.

COMPENSATING SPROCKET INSPECTION

Refer to **Figure 121**.
1. Remove the compensating sprocket assembly as described in this chapter.
2. Clean all parts in solvent and dry with compressed air.
3. Check the cam surfaces (**Figure 122**) for cracks, deep scoring or wear.
4. Check the compensating sprocket gear teeth (**Figure 123**) for cracks or wear.

NOTE
If the compensating sprocket teeth are worn, also check the primary chain and the clutch shell gear teeth for wear.

5. Check the compensating sprocket inner bushing (**Figure 124**) for wear.
6. Check the sliding cam inner splines (**Figure 125**) for wear.
7. Check the shaft extension splines for wear or galling.
8. Check the cover (**Figure 126**) for damage.
9. Inspect the inner threads (**Figure 127**) of the nut for damage.
10. If any of these components were replaced, check the primary chain alignment as described in this chapter.

PRIMARY CHAINCASE (1984-1988 MODELS)

The primary chaincase houses the compensating sprocket assembly, primary chain, chain adjuster and clutch.

Removal (FXWG, FXSB and FXEF Models)

1. Remove the clutch, primary chain and compensating sprocket as described in this chapter.
2. Remove the solenoid and plunger as described in Chapter Nine.

3. Remove the electric starter drive housing as described in this chapter.
4. Loosen the lower engine-to-frame mounting bolts and nuts.
5. Loosen the transmission-to-frame mounting bolts and nuts.
6. Remove the primary chaincase-to-transmission bolts.
7. On models so equipped, remove the two upper bolts (A, **Figure 128**) at the rear of the housing. Then remove the two lower bolts (B, **Figure 128**) from behind the case (not shown).

(121)

COMPENSATING SPROCKET

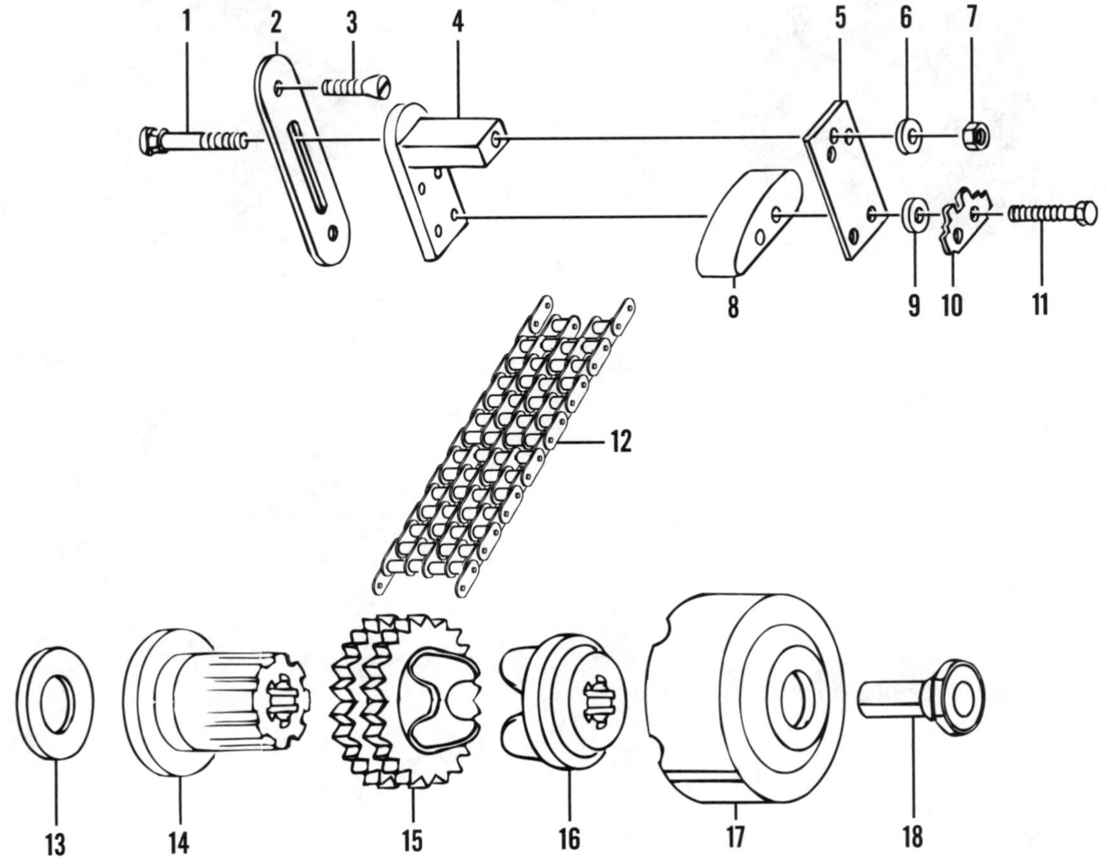

1. Bolt
2. Anchor plate
3. Screw
4. Chain tensioner
5. Plate
6. Washer
7. Nut
8. Tensioner pad
9. Washer
10. Lockwasher
11. Bolt
12. Primary drive chain
13. Spacer
14. Shaft extension
15. Compensating sprocket
16. Sliding cam
17. Cover assembly with springs*
18. Nut*

*Spacer between No. 17 and No. 18 for 1999 models not shown.

8. Remove the primary housing-to-engine case bolts. See **Figure 129** or **Figure 130**.

9. Pull the primary chaincase (**Figure 131**) away from the engine and remove it.

10. Inspect the primary chaincase assembly as described in this chapter.

Installation (FXWG, FXSB and FXEF Models)

1. Replace the alternator O-ring (**Figure 132**) if worn or damaged.

NOTE
Wipe the inner chaincase oil seal lip with chaincase oil before installing the chaincase in Step 2. When installing the chaincase, work the oil seal carefully along the mainshaft to prevent damage.

2. Carefully align the chaincase with the mainshaft and slide the chaincase onto the mainshaft.

CAUTION
The following procedures should be followed to make sure that the transmission is properly aligned with the engine. Improper alignment could cause chain and transmission failure.

3. Loosen the engine and transmission frame mounting fasteners if they were not loosened during removal.

4. Install the primary chaincase-to-transmission mounting bolts finger-tight.

NOTE
*Install into the rear engine mounting holes the two primary chaincase-to-engine mounting bolts (**Figure 133**) with the drilled heads.*

129

133

130

134

131

132

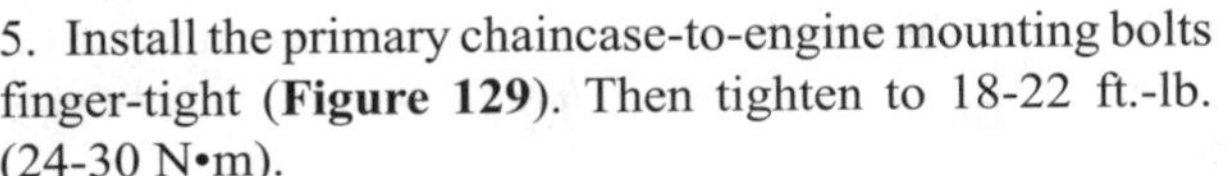

5. Install the primary chaincase-to-engine mounting bolts finger-tight (**Figure 129**). Then tighten to 18-22 ft.-lb. (24-30 N•m).

6. Align the primary case with the transmission housing.

NOTE

*Before tightening the primary chaincase-to-transmission bolts, check the bolts for binding by screwing them in and out by hand. Likewise, check the mainshaft (**Figure 134**) for binding by turning it by hand. If the bolts or mainshaft show any sign of binding, the primary chaincase must be repositioned where it mounts on the transmission. If necessary, loosen the primary case-to-engine mounting bolts and start over. When there is no apparent binding when the engine mounting bolts are tight, proceed to Step 8.*

7. Tighten the primary chaincase-to-transmission mounting bolts to 18-22 ft.-lb. (24-30 N•m). Bend the lockwasher tab over the bolt head to lock it.

8. Tighten the lower engine-to-frame mounting bolts and nuts to 35-38 ft.-lb. (47-52 N•m).

9. Tighten the transmission-to-frame mounting bolts to 35-38 ft.-lb. (47-52 N•m).

NOTE
*Recheck that the mainshaft (**Figure 134**) turns freely with no sign of binding.*

10. Safety wire the rear primary chaincase-to-engine bolts as shown in **Figure 135** and **Figure 136**.

CAUTION
*Always install safety wire so that it tightens the bolt. **Figure 137** shows the correct way to safety-wire two bolts by the double-twist method. Always use stainless steel wire approved for safety wiring.*

11. Install the starter and starter drive housing as described in this chapter.
12. Install the solenoid and plunger as described in Chapter Nine.
13. Install the clutch, engine compensating sprocket, chain adjuster, primary chain and primary chaincase cover as described in this chapter.

135

136

Removal (1984-1988 FXR, FLH and FLT Series Models)

1. Remove the clutch, primary chain and compensating sprocket as described under *Clutch Removal* in this chapter.
2. Remove the solenoid and plunger as described in Chapter Nine.
3. Remove the starter and starter drive housing as described in this chapter.
4. On 1984 models, use the Rear Chain Boot Remover tool (Harley-Davidson part No. HD-97101-81). Remove the screws securing the chain boot to the primary chaincase.
5. On early 1984 models, perform the following:
   a. Label the vent hoses before disconnecting them in the following steps.
   b. Disconnect the chain oil hose at the oil pump.
   c. Locate the T-fitting next to the oil pump with two vent hoses. Disconnect the crankcase and oil pump vent hoses from the T-fitting.
6. Cut any safety wire from the two engine case bolts. Refer to **Figure 135** and **Figure 136**.
7. Remove the primary chaincase-to-transmission bolts.
8. On models so equipped, remove the two bolts (A, **Figure 128**) at the rear of the housing. Then remove the two lower bolts (B, **Figure 128**) from behind the case (not shown).
9. Remove the primary housing-to-engine case bolts. See **Figure 129** or **Figure 130**.
10. On early 1984 models, pull the primary chaincase out slightly and disconnect the remaining vent hose from the rear of the primary case.
11. On all models, rotate the primary chaincase clockwise on the mainshaft and remove it.
12. On 1985-1988 models, pull the primary chaincase away from the engine and remove it (**Figure 131**).
13. Inspect the primary chaincase assembly as described in this chapter.

Installation (1984-1988 FXR, FLH and FLT Series Models)

1. Replace the alternator O-ring (**Figure 132**) if worn or damaged.
2. On models where the mainshaft bearing is not held in place with snap rings, wipe the outer bearing surface with Loctite Retaining Compound No. 601 and install the bearing into the primary chaincase. On later models, install the bearing and secure it with the two snap rings.
3. On early models, install a *new* inner chaincase gasket.
4. Carefully align the chaincase with the mainshaft and slide the chaincase partially onto the mainshaft.

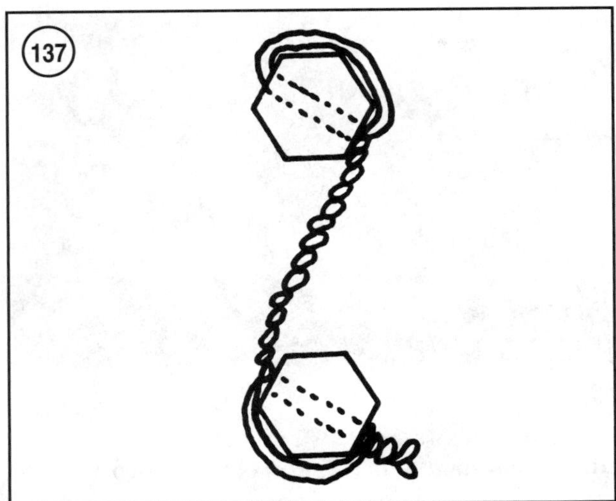

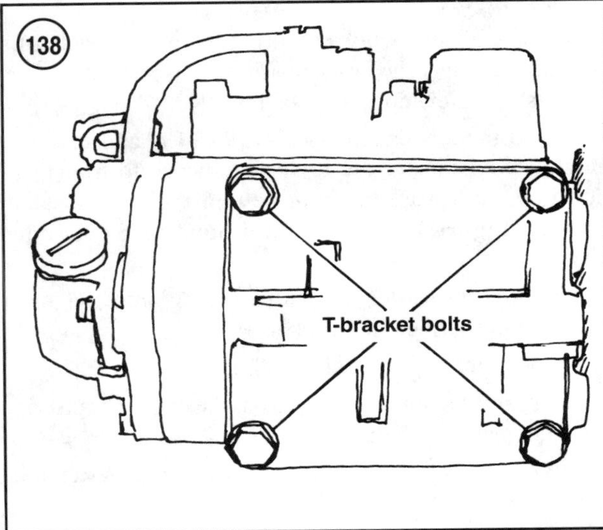

NOTE
Refer to the marks made on the vent hoses prior to disassembly in Step 5 of ***Removal****.*

5. On early 1984 models, perform the following:
   a. Connect the vent hose removed in Step 10 to the rear of the primary chaincase.
   b. Connect the oil return hose to the fitting on the bottom/rear of the primary housing. Then route the chain oiler and vent hoses between the engine and transmission housings.
   c. Connect the chain oil hose to the fitting on the oil pump.
   d. Connect the vent hoses from the oil tank and oil pump to the fitting on the primary vent hose.

CAUTION
The following procedures should be followed to make sure that the transmission is properly aligned with the engine. Improper alignment could cause chain and transmission failure.

6. Install the inner primary chaincase to transmission bolts and lock tabs and tighten to the following:
   a. Tighten the 3/8-in. bolts to 21-27 ft.-lb. (29-37 N•m).
   b. Tighten the 5/16-in. bolts to 13-16 ft.-lb. (18-22 N•m).
7. After tightening bolts, check that the mainshaft (**Figure 134**) turns freely. When mainshaft is turning properly, bend the lock tabs over the bolt heads to lock the bolts.
8. Install the chaincase to engine mounting bolts finger-tight.

9A. On 1984-1986 models, loosen the four engine T-bracket-to-transmission bolts (**Figure 138**).

9B. On 1987-1988 models, loosen the two engine-to-transmission 3/8-in. bolts.

10. Tighten the chaincase-to-engine bolts to 16-18 ft.-lb. (22-24 N•m).
11. On 1984 models, safety wire the two inner bolts. See **Figure 135** and **Figure 136**.

NOTE
Always install safety wire so that it tightens the bolt. ***Figure 137*** *shows how to safety-wire two bolts by the double-twist method. Always use stainless steel wire approved for safety wiring.*

12A. On 1984-1986 models, tighten the four engine T-bracket-to-transmission bolts to 13-16 ft.-lb. (18-22 N•m).

12B. On 1987-1988 models, tighten the two engine-to-transmission 3/8-in. bolts to 35-38 ft.-lb. (47-52 N•m).

13. Install the starter and starter drive housing as described in this chapter.
14. Install the solenoid as described in this chapter.
15. Coat the rear chain boots and the chaincase and transmission case mating surfaces with 3M 750 Silicone Sealant. Install the housing bolts and tighten securely in a crisscross pattern.
16. Install the clutch, primary chain and compensating sprocket as described in this chapter.
17. On dry clutch models, perform the *Primary Housing Vacuum Check (Early 1984 Models with Dry Clutch)* in this section.

Primary Housing Vacuum Check (Early 1984 Models with Dry Clutch)

The primary housing must be checked for air tightness after assembly.

1. Remove one of the clutch inspection cover screws (**Figure 139**) and thread the vacuum gauge (part No. HD 96950-68) or an equivalent into the screw hole.
2. Start the engine and allow it to idle. The vacuum gauge should read 9 in. of water vacuum (minimum).
3. Locate the 3/8-in. (9.5 mm) vent hose connected between the chaincase and the T connector. Pinch this hose closed and increase engine idle speed to 1500 rpm. The vacuum gauge should now read 25 in. of water vacuum.
4. If the vacuum gauge shows a lower reading, there is an air leak into the primary housing.
5. Pinch all of the oil lines running to the primary housing. Pinch the hoses as close to the housing as possible.

CAUTION
Do not apply more than 10 psi (0.7 kg/cm^2) of compressed air into the primary housing.

6. Pressurize the housing with 10 psi (0.7 kg/cm^2) of compressed air. Now listen for air leaks at the following locations:
   a. All O-ring and gasket surfaces.
   b. All hose and oil seal fittings.
   c. Starter drive and solenoid mounting areas.
   d. Timing inspection hole.
   e. Transmission filler hole.
   f. Along the primary chaincase housing and cover (possible cracks or casting defects).
7. Leaking areas must be repaired before putting the motorcycle back into service.
8. Install the clutch inspection cover screw and tighten securely.

PRIMARY CHAINCASE (1989-1998 MODELS)

Removal (1989-1998 FXR, FLH and FLT Series Models)

Refer to **Figure 140**.

1. Disconnect the negative battery cable from the battery.
2. Remove the shift lever assembly as described under *Shifter Assembly* in Chapter Six.
3. Remove the primary chaincase outer cover as described in this chapter.
4. Remove the compensating sprocket, primary chain and clutch assembly as described in this chapter.
5. Remove the starter as described in Chapter Nine.

6. Pry the lockwasher tabs away from the five inner primary housing bolts (**Figure 141**). Loosen the five bolts.
7. Loosen the front two inner housing bolts with flat washers (**Figure 142**).
8. Remove all seven bolts securing the inner housing to the engine and the transmission. Discard the five lockwashers. New ones must be installed.
9. On all models except 1993-1998 FLH and FLT series models, remove the lower chaincase-to-transmission bolts and washers from behind the transmission housing (**Figure 143**). Move the ground strap out of the way.
10. Remove the starter jackshaft assembly from the inner housing as described in this chapter.
11. Tap the inner primary housing loose.
12. Remove the inner housing from the engine, transmission and gearshift shaft.
13. Remove the O-ring (**Figure 144**) from the engine crankcase shoulder.
14. Inspect the inner housing as described in this chapter.

Installation (1989-1992 FXR, FLH and FLT Series Models)

1. Replace the alternator O-ring (**Figure 144**) if worn or damaged.

CAUTION
Wipe the inner chaincase oil seal lip with chaincase oil before installing the chaincase in Step 2. When installing the chaincase, work the oil seal carefully along the mainshaft so that it will not be damaged. Wrap the mainshaft splines with tape to protect the inner chaincase oil seal when installing it over the mainshaft.

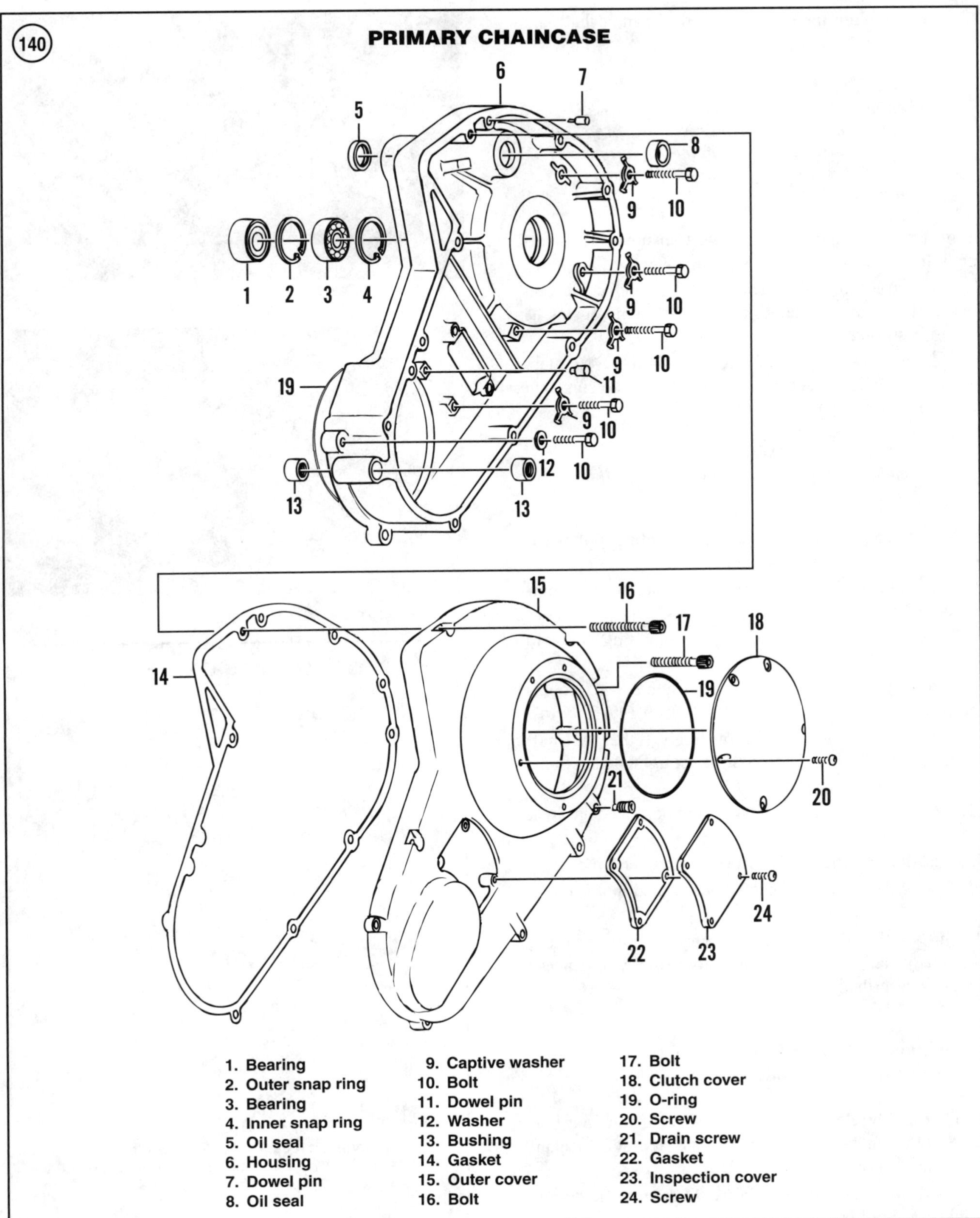

1. Bearing
2. Outer snap ring
3. Bearing
4. Inner snap ring
5. Oil seal
6. Housing
7. Dowel pin
8. Oil seal
9. Captive washer
10. Bolt
11. Dowel pin
12. Washer
13. Bushing
14. Gasket
15. Outer cover
16. Bolt
17. Bolt
18. Clutch cover
19. O-ring
20. Screw
21. Drain screw
22. Gasket
23. Inspection cover
24. Screw

2. Carefully align the chaincase with the mainshaft and slide the chaincase onto the mainshaft.

CAUTION
The following procedures must be followed to make sure that the transmission is properly aligned with the engine. Improper alignment could cause chain and transmission failure.

3. Install the primary chaincase-to-transmission mounting bolts finger-tight.
4. Install the bolt, *new* lockwasher, ground cable and lockwasher onto the back of the transmission housing as shown in **Figure 143**. Tighten finger-tight.
5. Tighten bolts installed in Steps 3 and 4 to 13-16 ft.-lb. (18-22 N•m). After tightening the bolts, make sure that the mainshaft turns freely.

NOTE
Recheck that the alternator O-ring is still in position.

6. Install the chaincase-to-engine mounting bolts and lockwashers. Tighten bolts finger-tight.
7. Loosen the two engine-to-transmission 3/8-in. mounting bolts (**Figure 143**).
8. Tighten the chaincase-to-engine mounting bolts to 16-18 ft.-lb. (22-24 N•m).
9. Tighten the two engine-to-transmission 3/8-in. mounting bolts (loosened in Step 7) to 35-38 ft.-lb. (47-52 N•m).
10. Check that the mainshaft turns freely. If the mainshaft binds or turns roughly, loosen the bolts tightened in Steps 8 and 9 and retighten them.
11. Bend the lockwasher tab over the bolt heads to lock them in place.
12. Install the starter as described in Chapter Nine.
13. Install the starter jackshaft as described in this chapter.
14. Install the clutch, engine compensating sprocket, chain adjuster, primary chain and primary chaincase cover as described in this chapter.

Installation (1993-1998 FXR, FLH and FLT Series Models)

1. Thoroughly clean the *outer surface* of the five bolt holes of the inner cover. Apply a light coat of RTV sealant to the inner surfaces.
2. Install the *new* O-ring (**Figure 144**) onto the engine crankcase shoulder.

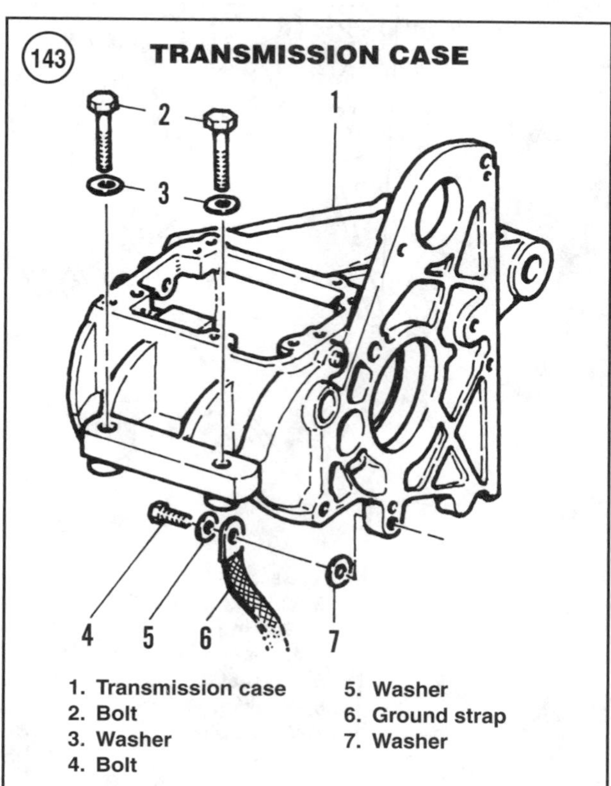

1. Transmission case
2. Bolt
3. Washer
4. Bolt
5. Washer
6. Ground strap
7. Washer

144

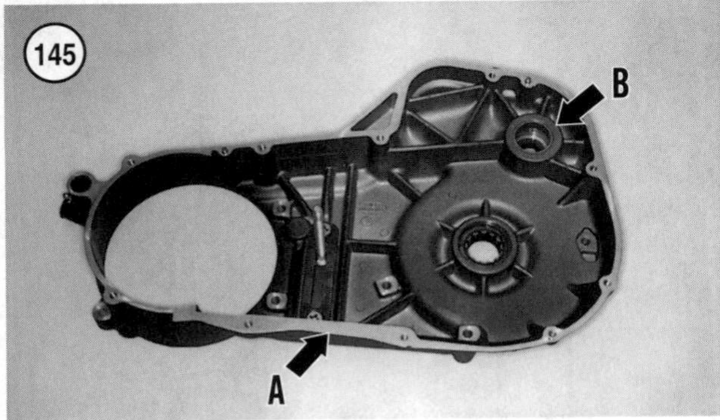

145

3. To prevent the transmission mainshaft splines from damaging the inner cover oil seal, wrap the mainshaft splines with tape.
4. If removed, install the drive belt prior to installing the inner housing.
5. Align the inner housing with the engine and transmission and install it over the gearshift lever shaft. Push the inner housing on until it stops.
6. Apply a bead of RTV sealant to the threads of the five mounting bolts that are used with the lockwashers.
7. Install the five inner housing bolts (**Figure 141**) and *new* lockwashers.
8. Install the front two inner housing bolts with flat washers (**Figure 142**).
9. Tighten the inner housing bolts in the following order:
   a. Tighten the four inner housing-to-engine mounting bolts to 18-21 ft.-lb. (24-28 N•m).
   b. Bend the lockwasher tabs against the two rear bolt heads.
10. Tighten the three inner housing-to-transmission mounting bolts to 18-21 ft.-lb. (24-28 N•m). Bend the lockwasher tabs against the three bolt heads.
11. Install the starter jackshaft as described in this chapter.
12. Install the starter as described in Chapter Nine.
13. Install the compensating sprocket, primary chain and clutch assembly as described in this chapter.
14. Install the primary chaincase outer cover as described in this chapter.
15. Connect the negative battery cable.

CHAINCASE INSPECTION (ALL MODELS)

5

Early Models with Dry Clutch

1. Clean the primary chaincase in solvent and dry thoroughly with compressed air.
2. Check the gasket surface on both sides of the housing for cracks or other damage.
3. Check the primary chaincase bearing. Turn the bearing inner race by hand. The bearing should turn smoothly with no roughness. To replace the bearing perform the following:

NOTE
The bearing is held in position with a chemical locking compound.

   a. Remove the bearing. Refer to Chapter One.
   b. Thoroughly clean the bearing mounting area in the case to remove all chemical residue.
   c. Apply Loctite Retaining Compound No. 601 to the bearing outer surface and press the bearing into the housing. Refer to Chapter One.

NOTE
Follow the manufacturer's cure time before reassembling the primary housing.

Late Models with Wet Clutch

1. Remove all gasket residue from the inner housing gasket surfaces (A, **Figure 145**).
2. Clean the inner housing in solvent and dry thoroughly.
3. Check the inner housing (A, **Figure 146**) for cracks or other damage.
4. Check the starter jackshaft oil seal for excessive wear or damage. To replace the oil seal, perform the following:
   a. Note the direction the oil seal lip faces in the housing.
   b. Pry the oil seal out of the inner primary housing.
   c. Pack the new oil seal lips with grease.
   d. Carefully drive the *new* oil seal into the housing until it seats against the housing shoulder.

5A. On 1989 models, inspect the starter jackshaft bushing (B, **Figure 145**) for wear, cracks or other damage. To replace the bushing, perform the following:

a. Remove the bushing with a suitable driver or press. Then press the new bushing into the housing so that it is flush or within 0.010 in. (0.25 mm) below its mounting boss.

b. To replace the oil seal, first drive the oil seal and scraper out of the housing and discard both parts. Install a *new* seal to the dimensions shown in **Figure 147**.The oil scraper is no longer used.

5B. On 1990-1998 models, check the starter jackshaft bushing and oil seal for damage. If worn or damaged, remove the oil seal and bushing and discard them both. Install *new* parts to the dimensions shown in **Figure 147**.

6. Inspect the shift lever bushings (**Figure 148**) for wear, cracks or other damage. To replace the bushing, perform the following:

a. Remove the bushing with a blind bearing removal tool. Refer to Chapter One.

b. Clean the bushing bore in the housing.

c. Press in the *new* bushing until its outer surface is flush or within 0.030 in. (0.76 mm) below the edge of the bushing bore.

d. Repeat for the other bushing.

7. Turn the bearing inner race (**Figure 149**) by hand. The bearing should turn smoothly with no roughness. Replace the bearing as follows:

a. Remove the oil seal (**Figure 150**) as described in Step 7.

b. Remove the inner and outer bearing snap rings.

c. Support the inner primary housing and press the bearing out.

d. Install the outer snap ring (clutch side). Make sure the snap ring is correctly seated in the groove.

CAUTION

When pressing the bearing into the housing, support the outer snap ring. The force required to press the bearing into the inner primary housing can force the snap ring out of its groove and damage the housing.

e. Support the inner housing and outer snap ring.

f. Press the bearing into the inner housing until it seats against the snap ring.

g. Install the inner snap ring. Make sure the snap ring is seated correctly in the groove.

h. Install a *new* oil seal as described in Step 8.

8. Inspect the inner primary cover oil seal (**Figure 150**) for excessive wear, tearing or other damage. To replace the oil seal, perform the following:

a. Remove the oil seal with a wide-blade screwdriver.

b. Clean the oil seal bore.

c. Pack the oil seal lip with a waterproof bearing grease.

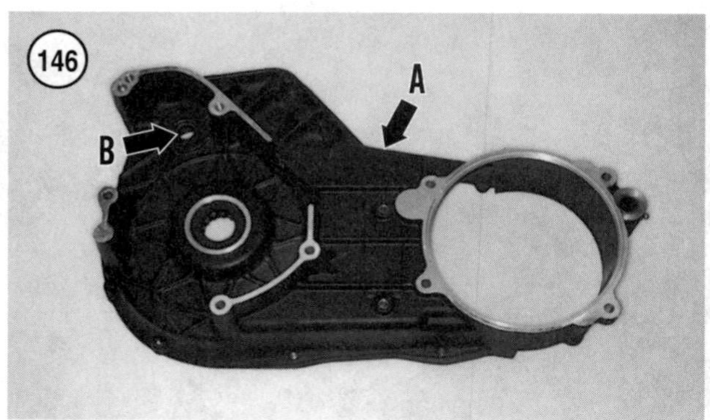

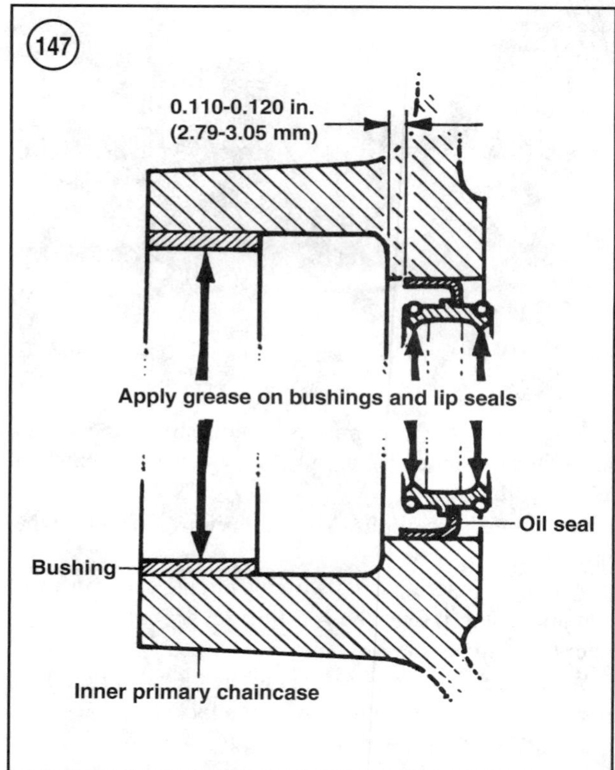

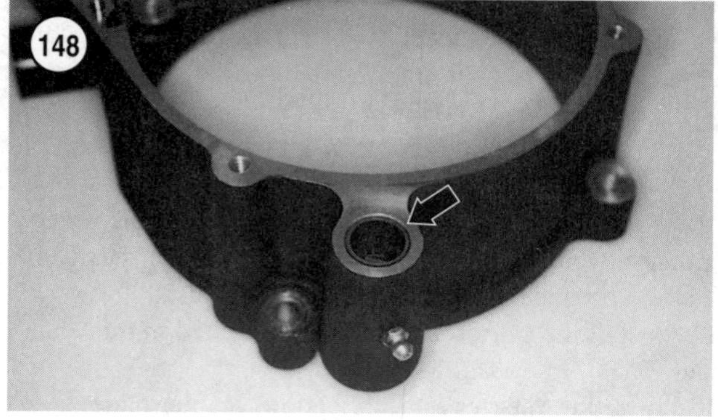

149

150

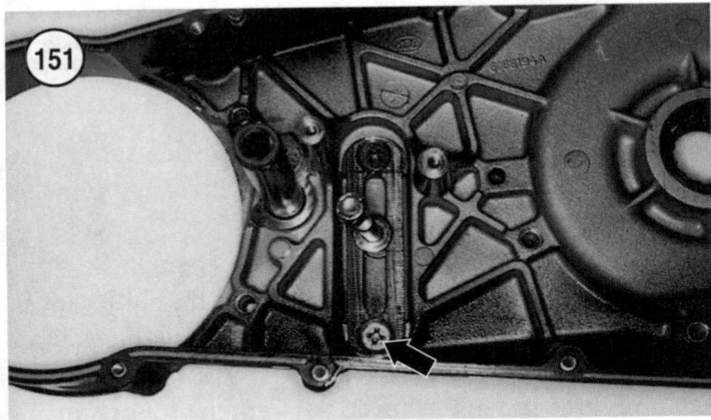
151

d. Position the oil seal with its closed side facing out. Press in the *new* oil seal until its outer surface is flush with the edge of the bearing bore.

9. Check the primary chain adjuster rack screws (**Figure 151**) for looseness. Tighten the screws, if necessary.

ELECTRIC STARTER DRIVE (1984-1988 FLT, FLH AND FXR MODELS)

Refer to **Figure 152**.

Removal

1. Disconnect the negative battery cable from the battery.
2. Remove the primary chaincase cover as described in this chapter.
3. Remove the starter solenoid as described in Chapter Nine.
4. Remove the thrust washer and remove the starter shaft.
5. Remove the hex plug, shaft and shifter arm.

Installation

1. Assemble the pinion gear and shaft assembly as described under *Inspection*.
2. Install the starter shaft assembly and the thrust washer.
3. If the shifter arm was removed, lightly grease the pivot shaft with high-temperature grease.
4. Install the shifter arm pivot shaft and hex plug.
5. Install the starter solenoid as described in Chapter Nine.
6. Install the starter and starter shaft housing as described in Chapter Nine.
7. Install the primary chaincase cover as described in this chapter.

Inspection

1. Check the pinion gear for worn, chipped or broken teeth. Replace the gear if necessary.
2. Check pinion gear operation by attempting to turn the gear in both directions. It should only rotate in one direction.
3. Check the needle bearings in the cover and starter housing for wear or damage. Rotate the bearings by hand. The bearing should turn smoothly with no roughness. To replace the bearings, refer to Chapter One.
4. Lubricate the needle bearings with high-temperature grease.
5. To disassemble the pinion gear shaft assembly, perform the following:
   a. Secure the pinion shaft in a vise with soft jaws.

   NOTE
   The pinion shaft nut has left-hand threads. Turn the nut ***clockwise*** *to loosen it.*

   b. Turn the pinion shaft nut *clockwise* and remove it.
   c. Remove the bearing race.
   d. Remove the pinion gear and collar as one assembly. If necessary, remove the snap ring and separate them.
   e. On chain drive models, remove the spacer.

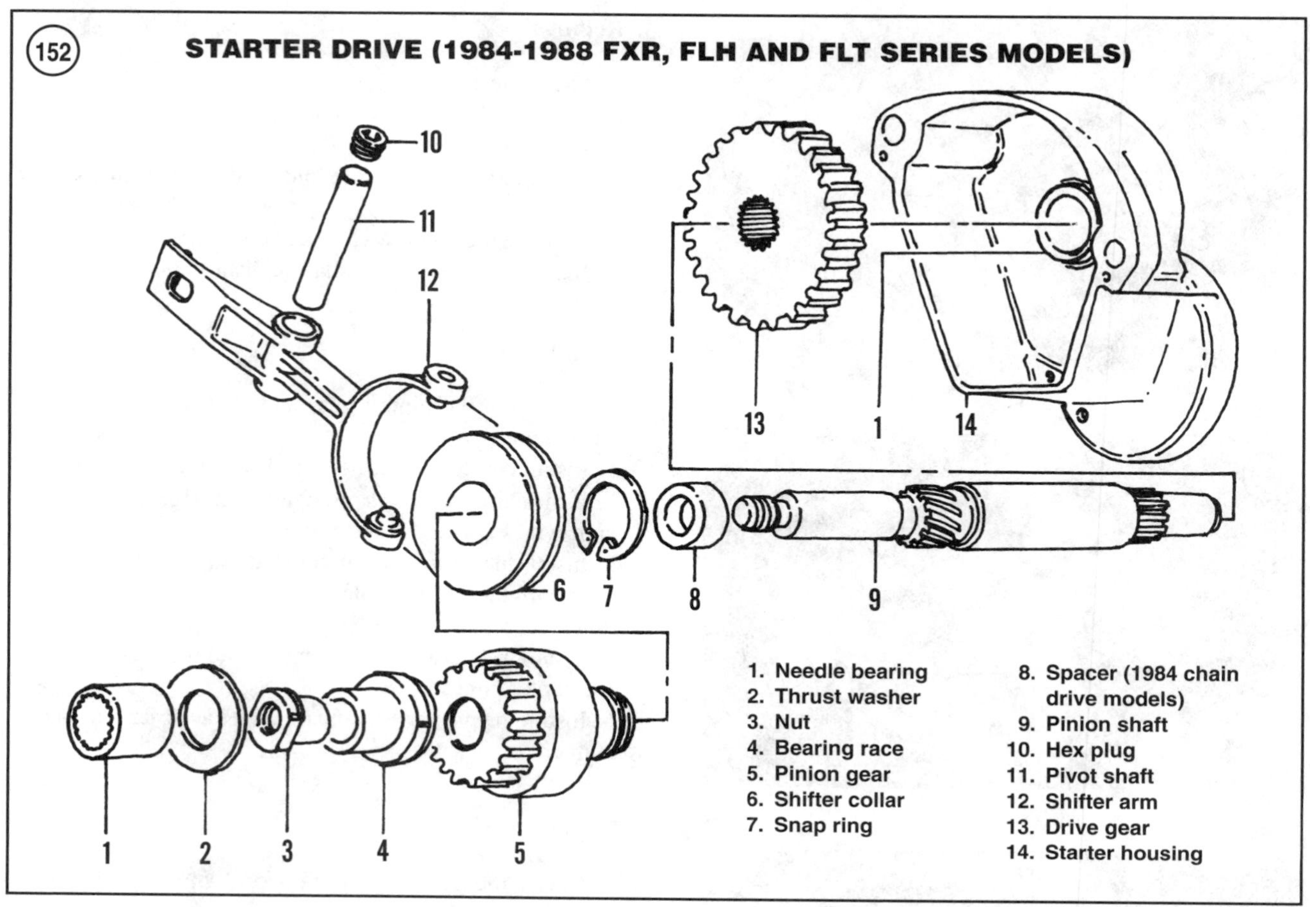

f. Inspect the components as described in this section.

6. Reverse Step 5 and assemble the pinion gear and shaft assembly, while noting the following:
   a. Lubricate all parts with high-temperature grease.
   b. Install the bearing race so that its lip faces against the pinion gear.
   c. Tighten the pinion shaft nut securely.

ELECTRIC STARTER DRIVE (1985 CHAIN DRIVE FXWG, FXSB AND FXEF MODELS)

Refer to **Figure 153**.

Removal

1. Disconnect the negative battery cable from the battery.
2. Remove the starter as described in Chapter Nine.
3. Remove the primary chaincase cover as described in this chapter.
4. Remove the mounting bolts, or threaded studs, nuts and lockwashers securing the drive gear housing. Remove the drive gear housing.
5. Remove the oil deflector, gasket and O-ring.
6. Working from the left side, disengage the shifter lever fingers from the shifter collar. Then remove the pinion gear and shaft assembly.
7. To remove the shifter lever, perform the following:
   a. Remove the battery and battery carrier.
   b. Remove the oil tank mounting brackets.
   c. Remove the starter solenoid as described in Chapter Nine.
   d. Remove the shifter lever screw and remove the shifter lever.

Installation

1. If disassembled, assemble the pinion gear and shaft assembly as described under *Inspection* in this section.
2. Install the pinion shaft assembly. Engage the shifter lever fingers with the shifter collar drum.

(153) **STARTER DRIVE (1985 CHAIN DRIVE FXWG, FXSB AND FXEF MODELS)**

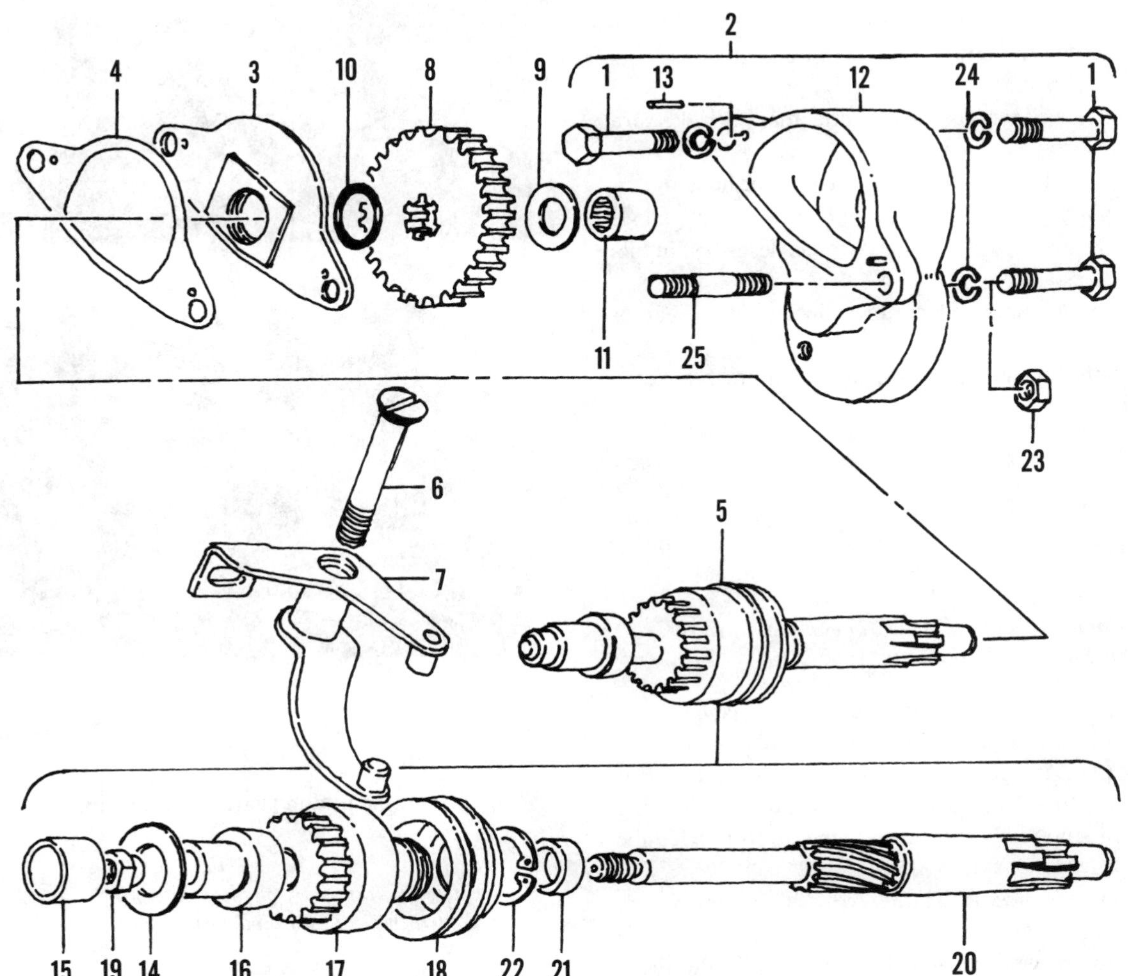

1. Bolt
2. Drive gear housing assembly
3. Oil deflector
4. Gasket
5. Pinion gear and shaft assembly
6. Shifter lever screw
7. Shifter lever
8. Drive gear
9. Thrust washer
10. O-ring
11. Bearing (in drive gear housing)
12. Drive gear housing
13. Locating pin
14. Thrust washer
15. Bearing (in primary cover)
16. Pinion shaft collar
17. Pinion gear
18. Shifter collar
19. Pinion shaft nut (left-hand thread)
20. Pinion shaft
21. Spacer
22. Snap ring
23. Nut
24. Lockwasher
25. Stud

3. Install the shifter lever assembly into the inner primary chaincase. Lubricate the shifter lever screw with high-temperature grease and install it through the shifter lever. Tighten the screw securely.
4. Install the drive gear housing and drive gear (**Figure 154**). Install the mounting bolts, or threaded studs, nuts and lockwashers and tighten securely.
5. Install a *new* O-ring in the oil deflector and make sure it is seated correctly.
6. Install the oil deflector into the drive gear housing.
7. Install a *new* gasket on the oil deflector.
8. Install the primary chaincase cover as described in this chapter.
9. Install the solenoid and starter as described in Chapter Nine.
10. Install the battery and the oil tank mounting brackets.

Inspection

1. Check the drive gear for worn, chipped or broken teeth. Replace the gear if necessary.

NOTE
If the drive gear is worn, check the starter gear for wear or damage.

2. Check the drive gear thrust washer for damage or cupping. Replace the washer if necessary.
3. Check the drive gear housing needle bearing for wear or damage. Rotate the bearings by hand. The bearing should turn smoothly with no roughness. To replace the bearings, refer to Chapter One.
4. Lubricate the needle bearing with high-temperature grease.
5. Install the drive gear and thrust washer in the drive housing.
6. Inspect the pinion gear needle bearing (**Figure 155**) in the primary cover. Rotate the bearings by hand. The bearing should turn smoothly with no roughness. To replace the bearings, refer to Chapter One.
7. Inspect the bearing surface of the pinion shaft collar. If the bearing or collar is worn, replace it as described in Chapter One.
8. Check the pinion gear for worn, chipped or broken teeth. Replace the gear if necessary.

NOTE
If the pinion gear is worn, check the clutch ring gear as described in this chapter.

9. Check the shifter collar groove and the shifter lever fingers for wear. Replace both parts if either is worn.

10. To disassemble the pinion gear shaft assembly, perform the following:
    a. Secure the pinion shaft in a vise with soft jaws.

    NOTE
    *The pinion shaft nut has left-hand threads. Turn the nut **clockwise** to loosen it.*

    b. Loosen and remove the pinion shaft nut.
    c. Remove the washer and pinion shaft collar from the pinion shaft.
    d. Remove the slide pinion gear and shifter collar as one unit from the pinion shaft.
    e. Remove the spacer from the pinion shaft.
    f. If necessary, remove the snap ring and separate the pinion gear and shifter collar.
    g. Inspect components as described in this section.
11. Reverse Step 10, and assemble the pinion gear and shaft assembly.
12. Inspect all parts for wear and damage as described in this procedure. Replace parts as necessary.
13. Lubricate all parts with high-temperature grease.

(156) STARTER DRIVE (1985-1986 BELT DRIVE FXWG, FXSB AND FXEF MODELS)

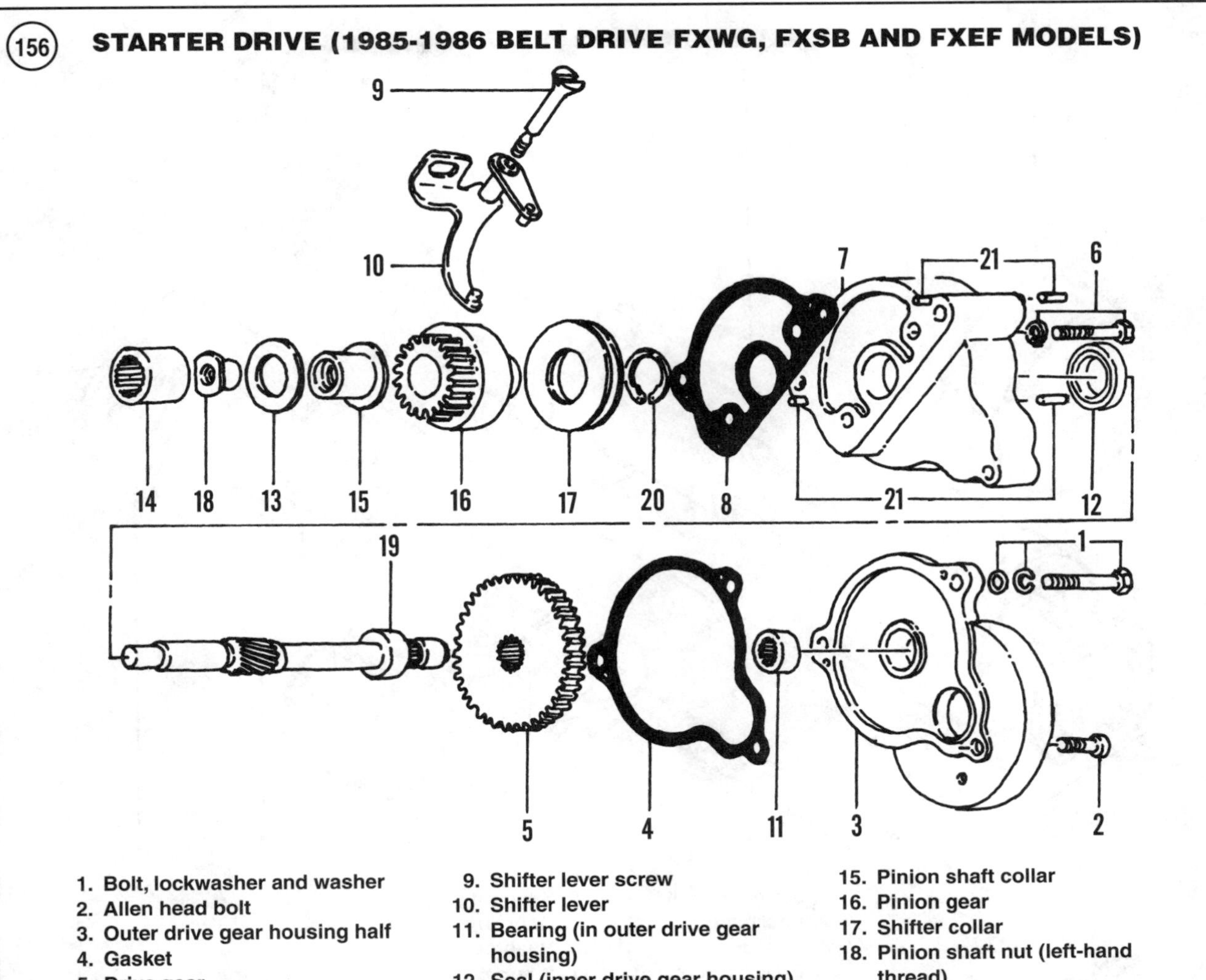

1. Bolt, lockwasher and washer
2. Allen head bolt
3. Outer drive gear housing half
4. Gasket
5. Drive gear
6. Bolt and lockwasher
7. Inner drive gear housing half
8. Gasket
9. Shifter lever screw
10. Shifter lever
11. Bearing (in outer drive gear housing)
12. Seal (inner drive gear housing)
13. Thrust washer
14. Bearing (in outer primary cover)
15. Pinion shaft collar
16. Pinion gear
17. Shifter collar
18. Pinion shaft nut (left-hand thread)
19. Pinion shaft (1985)
20. Snap ring
21. Locating pins

ELECTRIC STARTER DRIVE (1985-1986 BELT DRIVE FXWG, FXSB AND FXEF MODELS)

Refer to **Figure 156**.

Removal

1. Disconnect the negative battery cable from the battery.
2. Remove the starter as described in Chapter Nine.
3. Remove the primary chaincase cover as described in this chapter.
4. Remove the outer drive gear housing bolts and the Allen screw.
5. Remove the outer drive housing, gasket and drive gear.
6. Remove the inner drive housing bolts and remove the housing, and gasket.
7. Working from the left side, disengage the shifter lever fingers from the shifter collar. Then remove the pinion gear and shaft assembly.
8. Remove the solenoid as described in Chapter Nine and the shifter lever screw to remove the shifter lever.

Installation

1. Assemble the pinion gear and shaft assembly as described under *Inspection*.

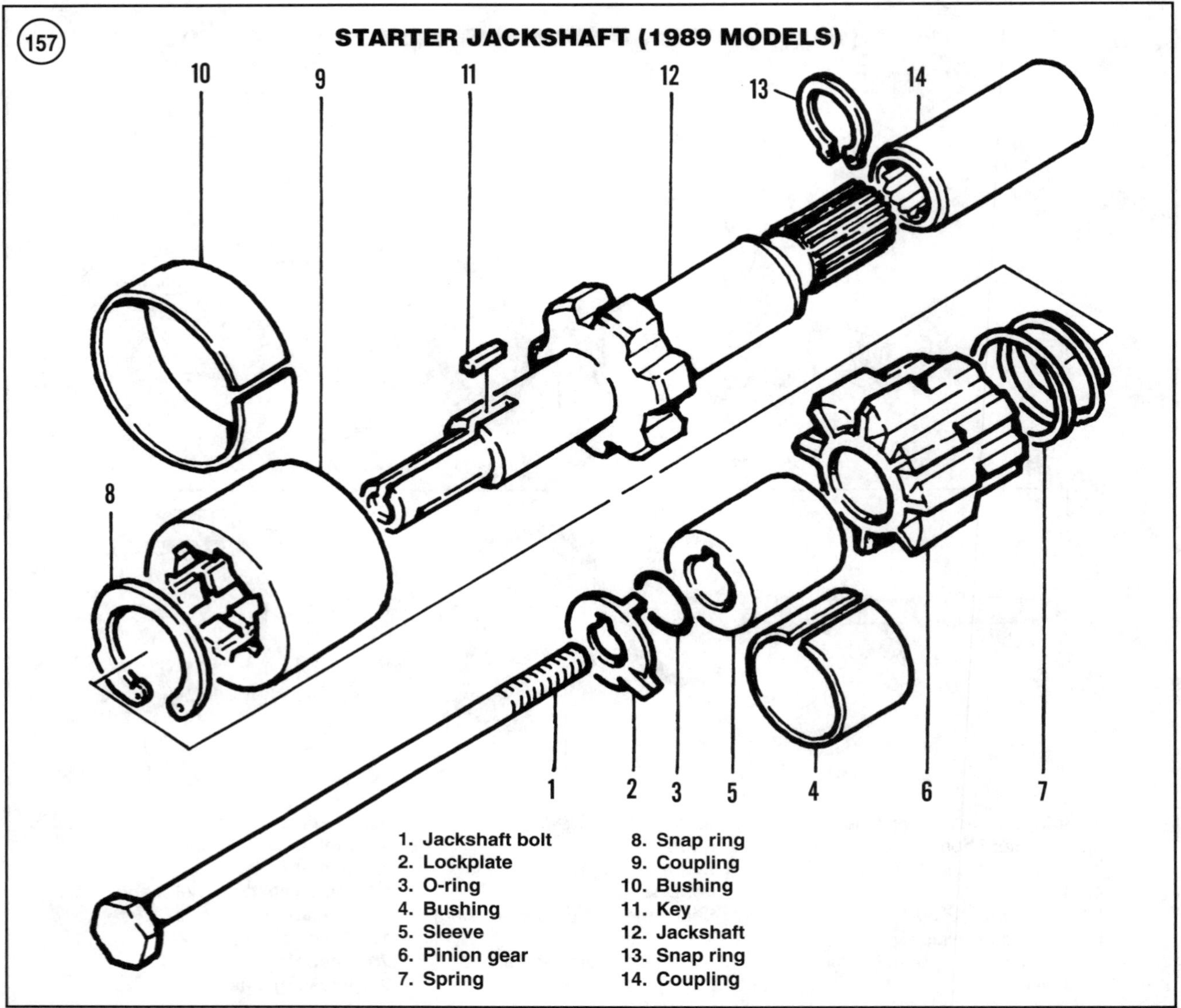

2. Install the shifter lever assembly into the inner primary case. Lubricate the shifter lever screw with high-temperature grease and install it through the shifter lever. Securely tighten the screw.

3. Install the pinion shaft assembly. Engage the shifter lever fingers with the shifter collar.

4. Use ThreeBond 1104 to hold a new gasket onto the inner drive gear housing.

5. Install the inner drive gear housing over the pinion shaft assembly and install onto the primary case. Install the mounting bolts and tighten securely.

6. Lubricate the drive gear with high-temperature grease and slide it onto the pinion shaft.

7. Use ThreeBond 1104 to hold a new gasket onto the outer drive gear housing. Then install the housing and securely tighten the mounting bolts and the Allen screw.

8. Install the starter as described in Chapter Nine.

9. Wipe the thrust washer with grease and slide it onto the pinion shaft collar.

10. Install the primary cover as described in this chapter.

11. Install the solenoid as described in Chapter Nine.

Inspection

1. Check the drive gear for worn, chipped or broken teeth. Replace the gear if necessary.

NOTE
If the drive gear is worn, check the starter gear.

2. Inspect the inner drive gear housing seal for wear or damage. If necessary, remove the seal by prying it out of the housing with a screwdriver. Install the new seal with a large socket placed on the outside seal surface. Install the seal with the lip side facing toward the drive gear.
3. Grasp the locating pins on both sides of the inner drive gear housing. The pins should be tight. If not, check the pin locations to make sure the housing is not cracked.
4. Check the inner drive gear housing needle bearing for wear or damage. Rotate the bearing by hand and check for noise, roughness or looseness. If the bearing condition is doubtful, replace it. Replace the bearing with a press.
5. Lubricate the needle bearings with high-temperature grease.
6. Inspect the pinion gear needle bearing installed in the outer drive gear housing as described in Step 4. Also check the pinion shaft collar bearing surface. If the bearing or collar is worn, replace them both. Replace the bearing as described in Step 4.
7. Check the pinion gear for worn, chipped or broken teeth. Replace the gear if necessary.

NOTE
If the pinion gear is worn, check the clutch ring gear as described in this chapter.

8. Check the shifter collar groove and the shifter lever fingers for wear. Replace both parts if any one part is worn.
9. To disassemble the pinion gear shaft assembly, perform the following:
   a. Secure the pinion shaft in a vise with soft jaws.

NOTE
*The pinion shaft nut has left-hand threads. Turn the nut **clockwise** to loosen it.*

   b. Loosen and remove the pinion shaft nut.
   c. Remove the washer and pinion shaft collar.
   d. Remove the slide pinion gear and shifter collar as one unit.
   e. If necessary, remove the snap ring and separate the pinion gear and shifter collar.
   f. Inspect components as described in this section.
10. Assemble the pinion gear and shaft assembly by reversing Step 9. Note the following:
   a. Inspect all parts for wear and damage as described in this procedure. Replace parts as necessary.
   b. Install a *new* snap ring.
   c. Lubricate all parts with high-temperature grease.

STARTER JACKSHAFT (1989-1998 MODELS)

NOTE
The 1989 starter jackshaft assembly is not interchangeable with 1990-1998 models.

Removal/Disassembly (1989 Models)

Refer to **Figure 157**.

1. Disconnect the negative battery cable from the battery.
2. Remove the primary chaincase cover as described in this chapter.
3. Remove the clutch as described in this chapter.
4. Remove the starter-to-jackshaft coupling if it did not come off with the starter.
5. Pry the lockplate tab away from the jackshaft bolt. Then hold the pinion gear and loosen the jackshaft bolt. Withdraw the jackshaft bolt, lockplate and O-ring from the jackshaft.
6. Slide the jackshaft assembly out of the primary housing.
7. Disassemble the jackshaft as follows:
   a. Slide the sleeve off of the jackshaft and remove the key from the jackshaft if it did not come off with the sleeve.
   b. Remove the pinion gear.
   c. Slide the coupling off the jackshaft. Then remove the spring from inside the coupling. If necessary, remove the snap ring from inside the coupling.
   d. If necessary, remove the snap ring from the jackshaft.
8. Clean and inspect the starter jackshaft assembly as described in this chapter.

Assembly/Installation (1989 Models)

NOTE
Before installing the coupling in Step 4, note the snap ring installed inside the coupling. The coupling side with the snap ring closest to the end slides over the jackshaft.

1. Install the *new* snap ring onto the jackshaft, if previously removed.
2. Install the *new* snap ring into the coupling.
3. Place the spring inside the coupling and slide the coupling onto the jackshaft.

NOTE
Make sure that the side of the coupling with the snap ring faces toward the starter after installing it. If the coupling is reversed, the

5

pinion gear cannot engage the clutch ring gear.

4. Position the pinion gear with the small outer diameter end going on first and slide the pinion gear onto the jackshaft.
5. Install the key in the jackshaft keyway. Make sure it is correctly seated in the groove.
6. Align the keyway in the sleeve with the key and slide the sleeve onto the jackshaft.
7. Slide the lockplate and O-ring onto the jackshaft bolt. Then insert the jackshaft bolt into the jackshaft.

CAUTION
*The inner lockplate tab must be installed in the jackshaft keyway. The lockplate serves two purposes; it prevents the key from sliding out of the sleeve and locks the jackshaft bolt to prevent it from backing out of the jackshaft. Always install a **new** lockplate.*

8. Align the inner tab on the lockplate with the keyway in the sleeve. Then tighten the bolt finger-tight.
9. Slide the jackshaft-to-starter coupling onto the other end of the jackshaft.
10. Slide the jackshaft into the primary chaincase with the pinion gear facing outward. Make sure the coupling engages the starter motor shaft as the jackshaft assembly is installed.
11. Hold the pinion gear and tighten the jackshaft bolt to 80-106 in.-lb. (9-12 N•m). Bend the lockplate tab against the jackshaft bolt head to lock it. If the lockplate tab does not align with one of the bolt head flats, tighten the bolt until the two parts align with each other; do not loosen the bolt to align the tab.
12. Install the clutch as described in this chapter.
13. Install the primary chaincase cover as described in this chapter.
14. Connect the negative battery cable.

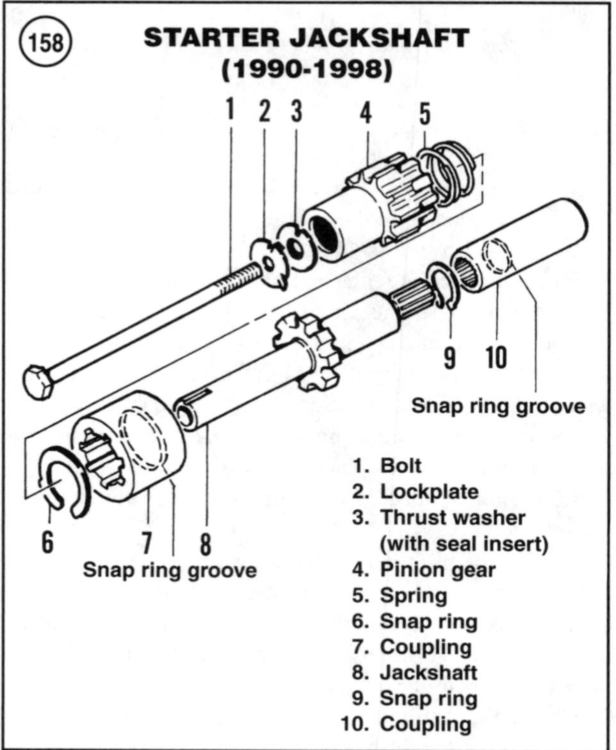

Removal (1990-1998 Models)

Refer to **Figure 158**.

1. Disconnect the negative battery cable from the battery.
2. Remove the primary chaincase outer cover as described in this chapter.

NOTE
*If only removing parts 1-5 listed in **Figure 158**, do not perform Step 3.*

3. Remove the clutch assembly as described in this chapter.
4. Straighten the tab on the lockplate (**Figure 159**).
5. Wrap the pinion gear with a cloth to protect the finish. Then secure it with pliers (A, **Figure 160**).
6. Loosen and remove the bolt (B, **Figure 160**), lockplate, thrust washer and O-ring (1990-1992 models) from the starter jackshaft assembly and the end of the starter motor.
7. Remove the pinion gear (**Figure 161**) and spring from the jackshaft.
8. Remove the outer coupling from the chaincase inner housing.

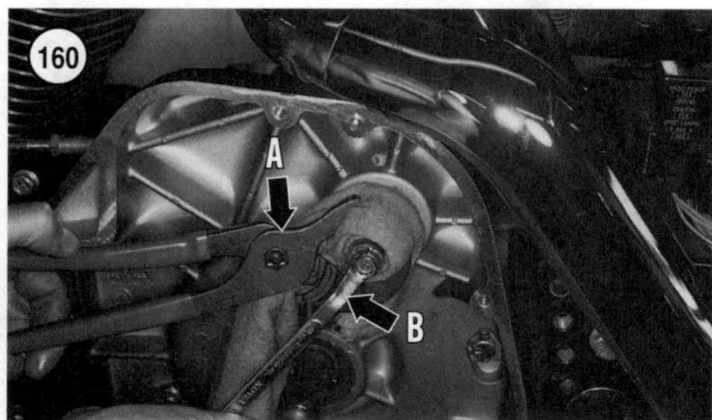

CAUTION

On 1994-1998 models, if the starter is not removed prior to removing the output shaft coupling and snap ring, the primary chaincase oil seal will be damaged when the jackshaft is withdrawn.

9A. On 1990-1993 models, remove the jackshaft assembly and the inner coupling from the chaincase inner housing.

9B. On 1994-1998 models, perform the following:

a. Remove the starter as described in Chapter Nine.
b. Remove the output shaft coupling and snap ring from the starter motor output shaft.
c. Withdraw the jackshaft from the chaincase inner housing.

10. Clean and inspect the starter jackshaft assembly as described in this chapter.

5

Installation (1990-1998 Models)

1A. On 1990-1993 models, install the jackshaft and the inner output shaft coupling into the chaincase inner housing. Push it in until it stops.

CAUTION

*On 1994-1998 models, the inner coupling must **not** be installed on the jackshaft before installing the jackshaft into the chaincase inner housing. If installed, it will damage the inner housing oil seal.*

1B. On 1994-1998 models, perform the following:

a. Install the output shaft coupling and snap ring onto the starter output shaft.
b. Install the starter as described in Chapter Nine.
c. Install the jackshaft into the chaincase inner housing (**Figure 162**) *without* the output shaft coupling in place. Push it in until it stops.

NOTE

*Before installing the outer coupling in Step 2, note the location of the snap ring (**Figure 163**) within the outer coupling. The outer coupling side with the snap ring closest to its end slides over the jackshaft.*

2. Position the outer coupling with the snap ring closest to its end slides going in first. Install the outer coupling over the jackshaft and into the housing bushing (**Figure 164**). Push it in until it bottoms.
3. Install the spring (**Figure 165**) onto the jackshaft.
4. Install the pinion gear (**Figure 166**) onto the jackshaft. Push it in until it bottoms.

5. Push in on the pinion gear (A, **Figure 167**) and install the bolt, lockplate and thrust washer (B) onto the jackshaft.

6. Push the assembly on until it bottoms.

7. Align the lockplate tab with the thrust washer. Then insert the tab into the notch in the end of the jackshaft.

8. Screw the bolt into the starter output shaft by hand.

9. Wrap the pinion gear with a cloth to protect the finish. Then secure it with pliers (A, **Figure 160**).

10. Tighten the bolt (B, **Figure 160**) onto the starter motor to 80-106 in.-lb. (9-12 N•m). Bend the outer lockplate tab against the bolt head (**Figure 159**).

11. To make sure that are components have been installed correctly, perform the following:

   a. Install the clutch shell onto the transmission mainshaft.
   b. With the starter not engaged, the pinion gear (A, **Figure 168**) must not engage the clutch shell gear (B).
   c. To check for proper engagement, pull out on the pinion gear and engage it with the clutch shell gear. Then rotate the clutch shell in either direction and make sure the pinion gear rotated with it.
   d. If engagement is incorrect, remove the clutch shell and correct the problem.
   e. Remove the clutch shell.

12. Install the clutch assembly as described in this chapter.

13. Install the primary chaincase outer cover as described in this chapter.

14. Connect the negative battery cable.

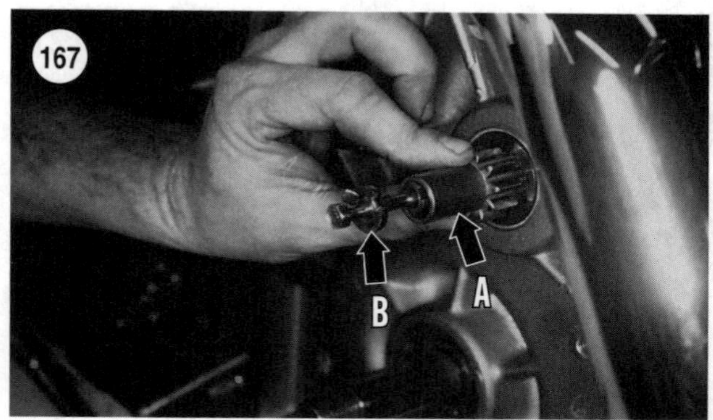

Inspection (All Models)

1. Clean all jackshaft components thoroughly in solvent. Dry with compressed air.

2. Check the snap ring in each coupling (**Figure 163** and **Figure 169**). Replace any loose or damaged snap rings.

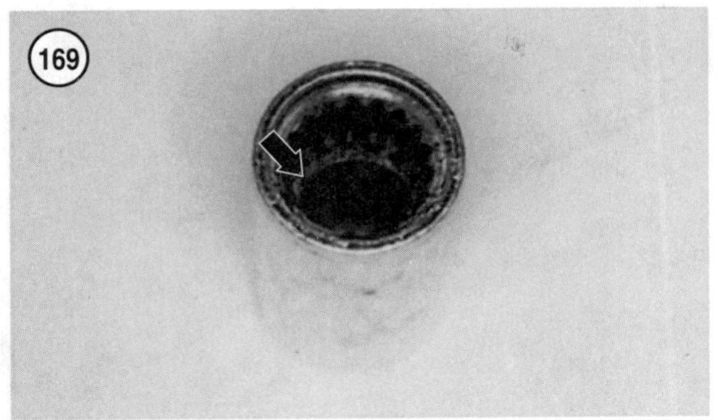

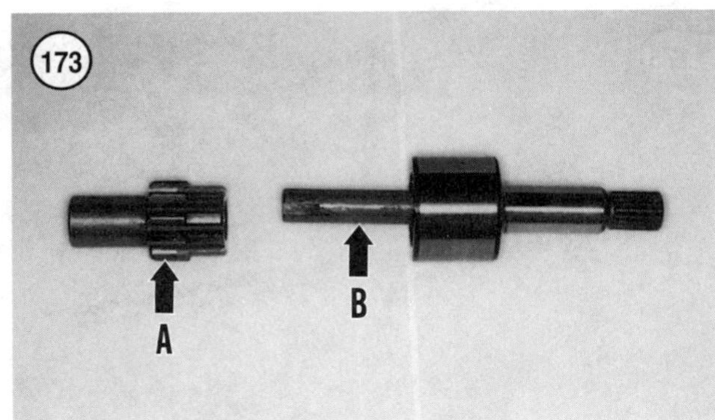

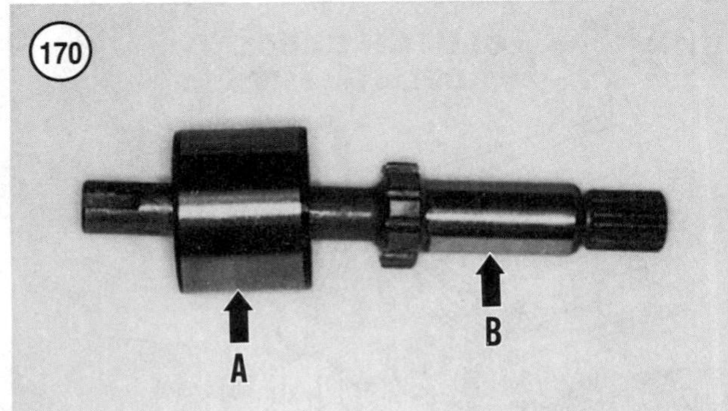

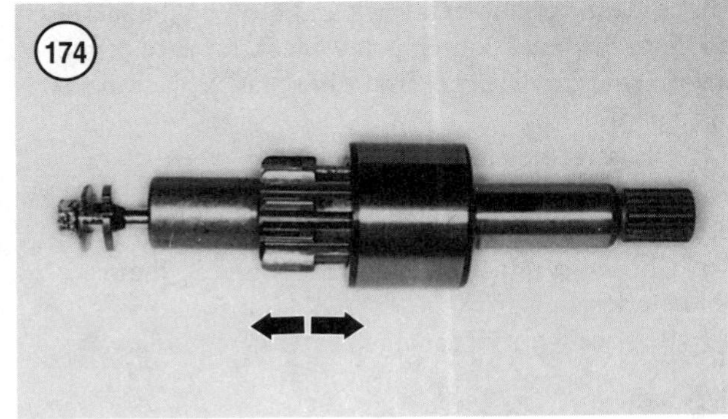

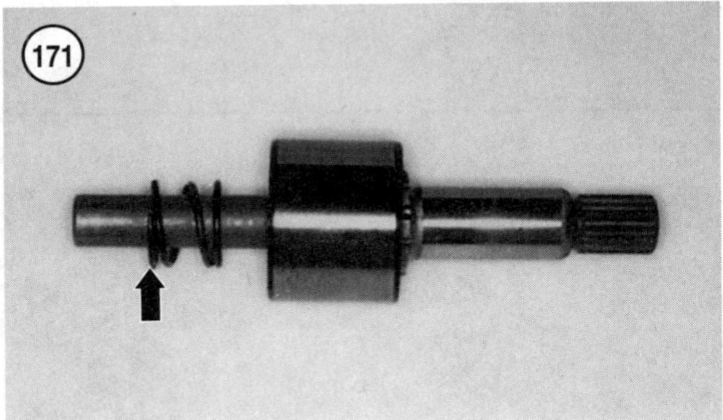

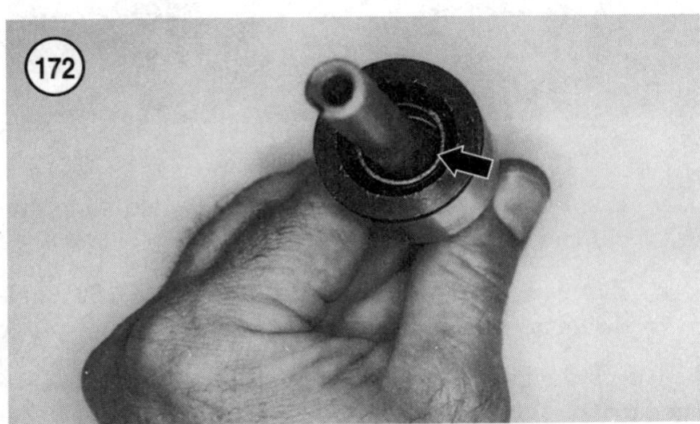

3. Visually check the jackshaft surfaces for cracks, deep scoring, excessive wear or discoloration. Check the keyway slot and snap ring grooves for damage.

4. Check the jackshaft and pinion gear teeth for cracks, severe wear or damage.

5. Check the spring for stretching or damage.

6. Check the jackshaft bolt and jackshaft threads for stripping, cross-threading or deposit buildup. If necessary, use a tap to true up jackshaft threads and remove any deposits. Replace the jackshaft bolt if threads or the bolt head is damaged.

7. Check the large coupling for surface damage. Check the spline and the snap ring groove inside the coupling for damage.

8. On 1989 models, inspect the small sleeve for surface damage. Check the keyway inside the sleeve for damage. Check the key for damage.

9. Install the outer coupling (A, **Figure 170**) onto the jackshaft (B) with the snap ring side going on first.

10. Install the spring (**Figure 171**) onto the jackshaft and inside the outer coupling (**Figure 172**).

11. Slide the pinion gear (A, **Figure 173**) onto the jackshaft (B).

12. Temporarily install the bolt, lockplate and thrust washer into the jackshaft (**Figure 174**).

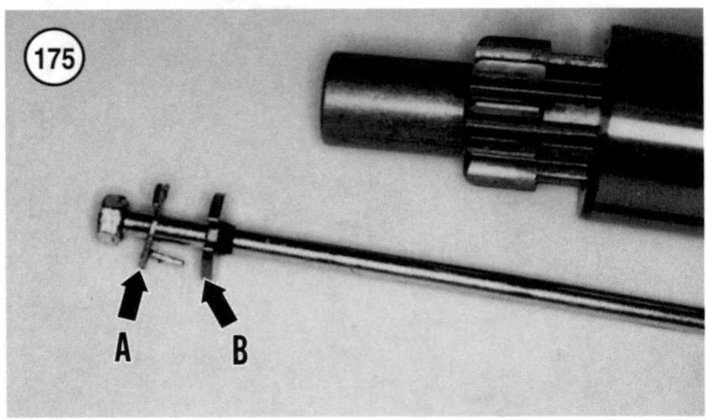

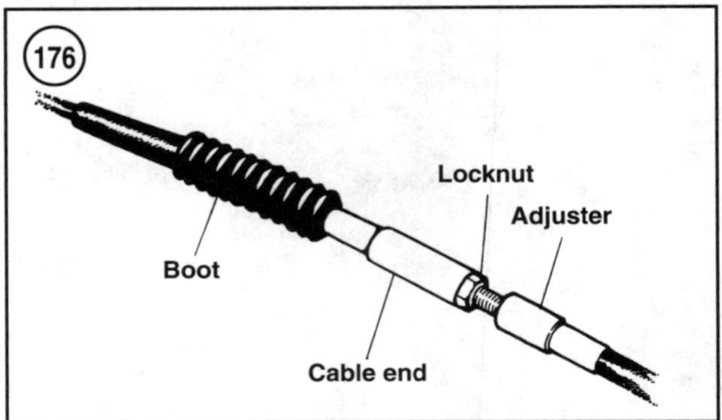

13. Slide the pinion gear back and forth on the jackshaft and into the outer coupling and check for ease of movement. If the movement is erratic or binds, replace the damaged part(s).
14. Disassemble all parts assembled in Steps 10-13.
15. Inspect the lockplate (A, **Figure 175**) for cracked, broken or weak alignment and locktabs.
16. Check the thrust washer and O-ring (B, **Figure 175**) for deterioration.
17. Replace worn or damaged parts as required.

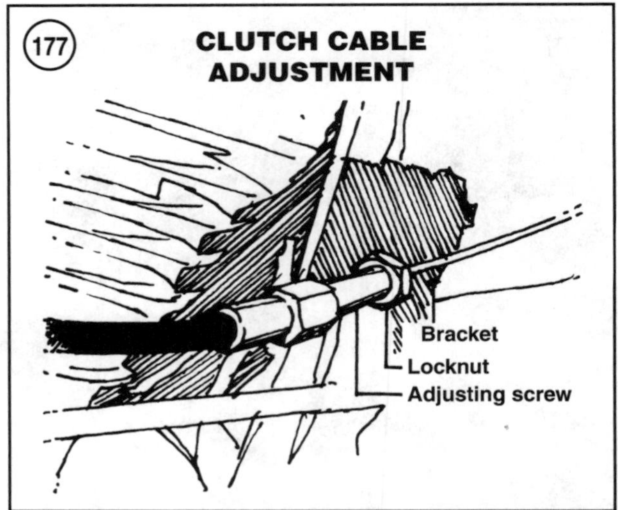

CLUTCH CABLE REPLACEMENT

1. Disconnect the negative battery cable from the battery.
2. Remove the seat as described in Chapter Fifteen.
3. Before removing the clutch cable, make a drawing of its routing path from the handlebar to the transmission side door.
4. At the clutch cable in-line adjuster, slide the rubber boot off the adjuster (**Figure 176**). Loosen the locknut and turn the adjuster to provide as much cable slack as possible.

5A. On FXWG, FXSB and FXEF models, perform the following:
   a. Disconnect the clutch cable from the release lever bracket (**Figure 177**).
   b. Remove the E-clip from the clutch lever pivot pin and withdraw the pivot pin.
   c. Release the cable from the clutch lever mounting bracket. Then disconnect the cable from the anchor pin in the lever.
   d. Remove the clutch cable from the frame.

5B. On all other models, perform the following:
   a. Disconnect the clutch cable from the clutch release mechanism (**Figure 178**) as described under *Transmission Side Cover* in Chapter Seven.
   b. Remove the snap ring from the base of the clutch lever pivot pin.

   c. Remove the pivot pin (**Figure 179**) and slide the clutch lever out of its perch.
   d. Remove the plastic anchor pin (**Figure 180**) and disconnect the clutch cable from the lever.

6. Check the clutch lever components for worn or damaged parts.

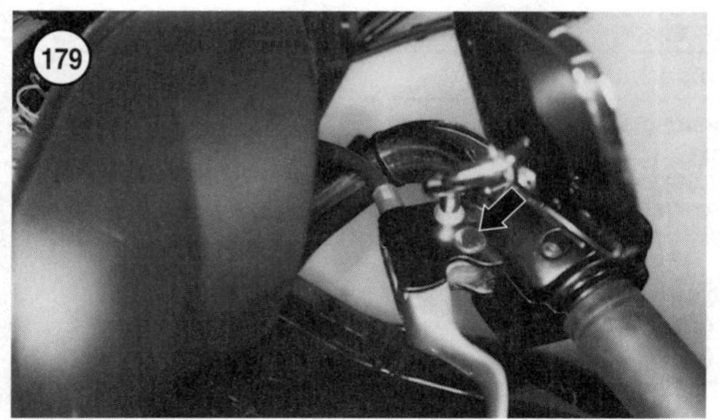
179

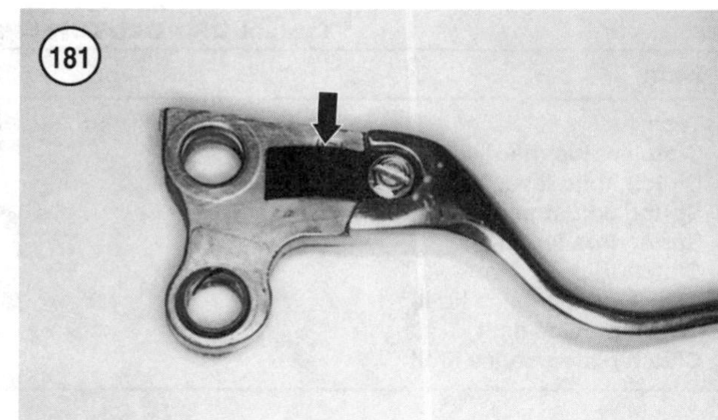
181

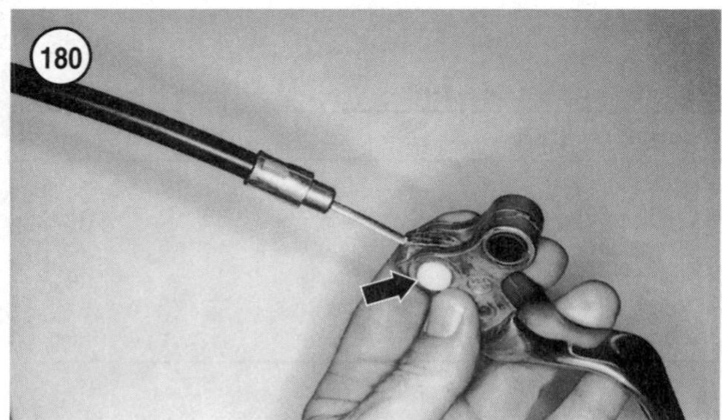
180

182

7. Check that the antislack spring screw (**Figure 181**) on the bottom of the clutch lever is tight.
8. On models so equipped, withdraw the clutch cable from the inner fairing rubber grommet (**Figure 182**). Move the clutch cable forward and out of the fairing.
9. Route the new clutch cable from the handlebar to the transmission side cover. Following the drawing made in Step 3.
10. Fit the clutch cable into its lever and secure with the plastic anchor pin (**Figure 180**).
11. Slide the clutch lever into the perch and install the pivot pin (**Figure 179**).
12. Secure the pivot pin with the snap ring.
13A. On FXWG, FXSB and FXEF models, perform the following:

a. Connect the clutch cable to the anchor pin and insert the pin in the clutch lever.
b. Hook the clutch cable into the clutch lever mounting bracket.
c. Install the clutch lever into the mounting bracket and install the pivot pin.
d. Install the E-clip onto the pivot pin and make sure it is seated correctly in the pivot pin groove.
e. Connect the clutch cable onto the release lever bracket (**Figure 177**).

13B. On all other models, connect the clutch cable to the clutch release mechanism as described under *Transmission Side Cover* in Chapter Seven.
14. Adjust the clutch as described in Chapter Three.

Tables 1 through 6 are on the following pages.

5

Table 1 DRY CLUTCH SPECIFICATIONS (EARLY 1984)

Item	Specification in. (mm)
Type	Dry multiplate disc
Clutch adjustment screw	See text
Clutch hand lever free play	1/16 (1.59)
Spring adjustment	1 1/32-1 7/8 (26.2-47.6) from spring collar edge
Spring free length	1 45/64-1 47/64 (43.26-44.04)
Clutch friction disc	
Thickness service limit	1/32 (0.8)
Warp service limit	0.010 (0.25)
Clutch plate service limit	0.010 (0.25)

Table 2 WET CLUTCH SPECIFICATIONS (LATE 1984-1989)

Item	Specification in. (mm)
Type	Wet multiplate disc
Clutch hand lever free play	1/8-3/16 (3.17-4.76)
Clutch friction discs	
Thickness service limit	0.044 (1.12)
Warp service limit	0.011 (0.28)
Clutch plate service limit	0.078 (1.98)

Table 3 WET CLUTCH SPECIFICATIONS (1990-1997)

Item	Specification in. (mm)
Type	Wet multiplate disc
Clutch hand lever free play	
1990	1/8-3/16 (3.17-4.76)
1991-1997	1/16-1/8 (1.6-3.2)
Clutch friction disc assembly	
Lining thickness service limit (assembly)	0.661 (16.8)*
Clutch plate warp service limit	0.006 (0.15)
Compensating sprocket shim thickness	0.010 (0.25), 0.020 (0.51), 0.030 (0.76), 0.060 (1.52)

*See text for measuring procedure.

Table 4 WET CLUTCH SPECIFICATIONS (1998-1999)

Item	Specification in. (mm)
Type	Wet multiplate disc
Clutch hand lever free play	1/16-1/8 (1.6-3.2)
Clutch friction disc	
Thickness service limit	0.143 (3.62)
Clutch plate thickness service limit	0.006 (0.15)
Compensating sprocket shim thickness	0.010 (0.25), 0.020 (0.51), 0.030 (0.76), 0.060 (1.52)

Table 5 CLUTCH TORQUE SPECIFICATIONS (1984-1997)

Item	ft.-lb.	in.-lb.	N•m
All 1/4-in. fasteners	–	80-106	9-12
Clutch hub nut			
Dry clutch	50-60	–	67-81
Wet clutch			
1984-1989	50-60	–	67-81
1990-1997	70-80	–	95-108
Clutch pressure plate-to-clutch hub bolts			
1984-1989	–	80-97	9-11
Compensating sprocket nut			
1984-1989	90-100	–	122-136
1990-1999	150-165	–	203-224
Jackshaft bolt (1989-1997)	–	88-106	10-12
Primary chaincase cover bolts	–	80-106	9-12
Primary chaincase to engine and transmission			
1984-1992 FXR, FLH and FLT series models			
Chaincase-to-transmission bolts			
3/8-in. bolts	21-27	–	29-37
5/16-in. bolts	13-16	–	18-22
Chaincase-to-engine bolts	16-18	–	22-24
1984-1986 T-bracket-to-transmission bolts	13-16	–	18-22
1987-1992 engine-to-transmission bolts	35-38	–	47-52
FXWG, FXSB and FXEF			
Chaincase-to-transmission bolts	18-22	–	24-30
Lower engine-to-frame bolts	35-38	–	47-52
Transmission-to-frame bolts	35-38	–	47-52
1993-1998 all models	18-21	–	24-28

Table 6 CLUTCH TORQUE SPECIFICATIONS (1998-1999)

Item	ft.-lb.	in.-lb.	N•m
All 1/4-in. fasteners	–	80-106	9-12
Clutch hub nut	70-80	–	95-108
Compensating sprocket nut	150-165	–	203-224
Diaphragm spring bolts	–	90-110	10-12
Jackshaft bolt	–	80-106	9-12
Primary cover screws	–	80-106	9-12
Primary chaincase to engine and transmission	18-21	–	24-28

CHAPTER SIX

FOUR-SPEED TRANSMISSION

This chapter covers procedures for the four-speed transmission, shift linkage and kickstarter installed on the FXWG, FXSB and FXEF models. Special tool requirements are described in the procedures.

All models are equipped with a four-speed transmission that is a separate unit attached to the rear of the engine. The transmission shaft and shifter assemblies can be serviced with the transmission case mounted in the frame.

A ratchet-type kickstarter assembly is mounted in the side cover. The kickstarter mechanism can be removed with the transmission mounted on the motorcycle.

Table 1 and **Table 2** are at the end of the chapter.

SPECIAL TOOLS

The four-speed transmission requires a number of special tools. These tools and the part numbers are listed with the individual procedures. For a complete list of the special tools mentioned in this manual, refer to **Table 12** in Chapter One. The transmission tools used in this chapter are either Harley-Davidson or JIMS special tools. JIMS special tools are available through many aftermarket motorcycle suppliers.

When purchasing special tools, make sure to specify that the tools required are for the 1985-1986 FXWG, FXSB and FXEF models. Many of the tools are specific to this transmission. Tools for other transmissions and years may be slightly different.

SHIFTER ASSEMBLY

The shifter assembly consists of the external shift linkage and internal shift cam and shift arm components. The internal components can be serviced with the transmission case installed in the frame by removing the top cover.

If a shift problem is encountered, refer to the troubleshooting procedures in Chapter Two and eliminate all clutch and shifter mechanism possibilities *before* considering transmission repairs. Improper clutch adjustment is often a cause of poor shifting. Refer to Chapter Three for adjustment procedures.

The external shift linkage assembly (**Figure 1**) connects the foot-operated shift rod and levers. The shift linkage does not require adjustment unless it is replaced, or the transmission gears do not engage properly.

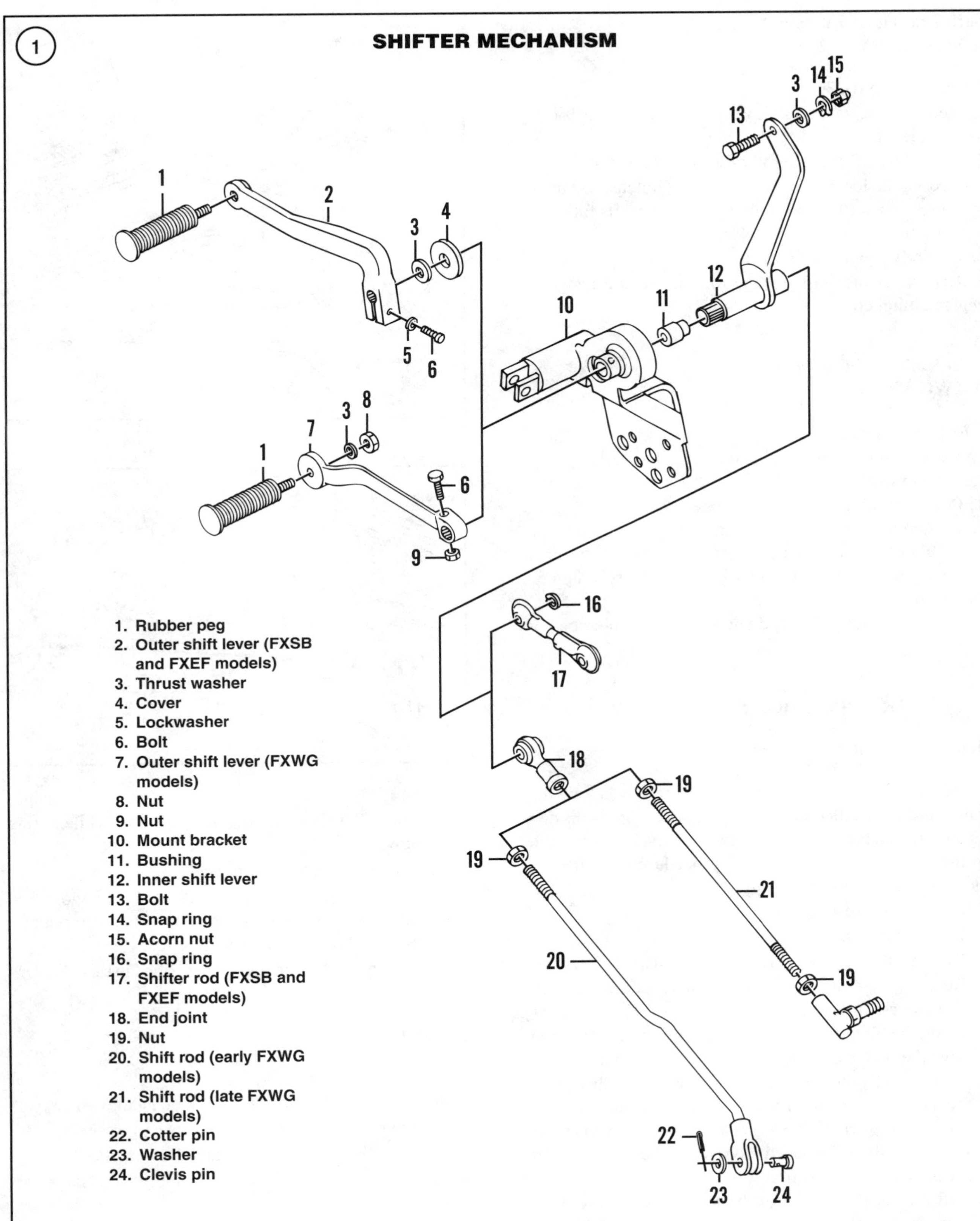
1
SHIFTER MECHANISM
1
2
3
4
5
6
7
8
9
10
11
12
13
14
15
16
17
18
19
20
21
22
23
24
1. Rubber peg
2. Outer shift lever (FXSB and FXEF models)
3. Thrust washer
4. Cover
5. Lockwasher
6. Bolt
7. Outer shift lever (FXWG models)
8. Nut
9. Nut
10. Mount bracket
11. Bushing
12. Inner shift lever
13. Bolt
14. Snap ring
15. Acorn nut
16. Snap ring
17. Shifter rod (FXSB and FXEF models)
18. End joint
19. Nut
20. Shift rod (early FXWG models)
21. Shift rod (late FXWG models)
22. Cotter pin
23. Washer
24. Clevis pin

6

Shift Linkage Adjustment (FXSB and FXEF Models)

Refer to **Figure 2**.

1. Remove the retaining clip securing the shifter rod to the shift lever.
2. Slide the shift linkage rod off of the clevis pin.
3. Loosen the locknut and turn the shift linkage rod in either direction until the shift linkage can travel its full limit without interference.
4. Securely tighten the locknut.
5. Reconnect the shift linkage rod and secure it with a *new* retaining clip.

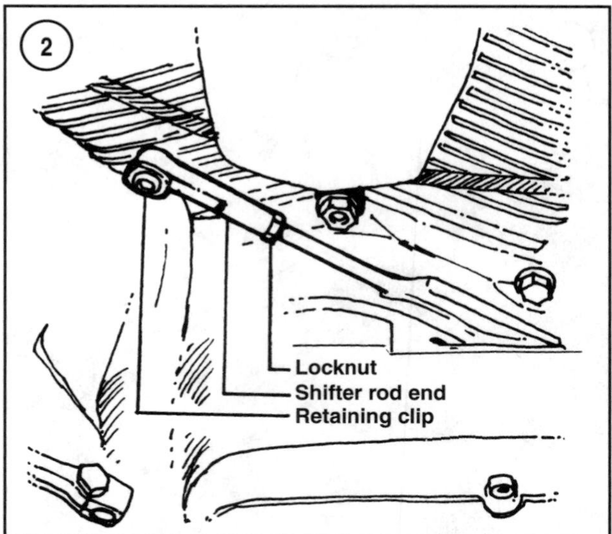

Shift Linkage Adjustment (FXWG Models)

Refer to **Figure 3**.

1. Remove the retaining clip securing the shifter rod to the clevis pin.
2. Pull the shifter rod off of the clevis pin.
3. Loosen the shifter rod locknut and turn the shifter rod end in either direction until the shift pedal travels through all gear positions without interference. Securely tighten the locknut.
4. Reconnect the shifter rod and secure it with a *new* retaining clip.

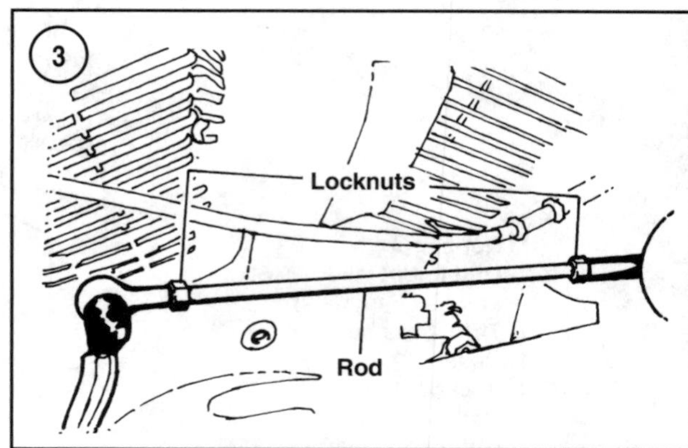

TRANSMISSION SHIFT COVER

Removal/Installation

The shift cam cover assembly can be removed with the transmission installed on the motorcycle. If transmission repairs are also required, remove the transmission and shift cam cover as one unit. This procedure describes removal of the shifter cover only.

Refer to **Figure 4**.

1. Shift the transmission into neutral.
2. Remove the battery as described in Chapter Three.
3. Remove the bolts, washers and nuts securing the battery carrier and remove the carrier.
4. Drain the oil tank as described in Chapter Three. Then remove the oil tank as described in Chapter Four.
5. Remove the bolts and washers attaching the shift cover to the transmission. Refer to the arrow directed to the circled bolt in **Figure 4**. This bolt cannot be removed at this time; it can only be loosened. To remove the bolt, the shift cover must be removed first.
6. Lift the shift cover off of the transmission case. Discard the shifter cover gasket.
7. Install by reversing these removal steps, while noting the following:
   a. Install a *new* shift cover gasket.
   b. Apply a light coat of threadlocking compound to the cover mounting bolts. Tighten the mounting bolts to 13-16 ft.-lb. (18-22 N•m).
   c. Adjust the shift linkage as described in this chapter.

Disassembly

Refer to **Figure 4**.

1. Remove the neutral indicator switch and washer.
2. Remove the shift shaft cover bolts and washers.
3. Remove the shift lever bolt and washer.
4. Remove the shifter linkage assembly from the transmission cover.
5. Remove the remaining shifter cover bolt.

(4) **SHIFTCAM ASSEMBLY**

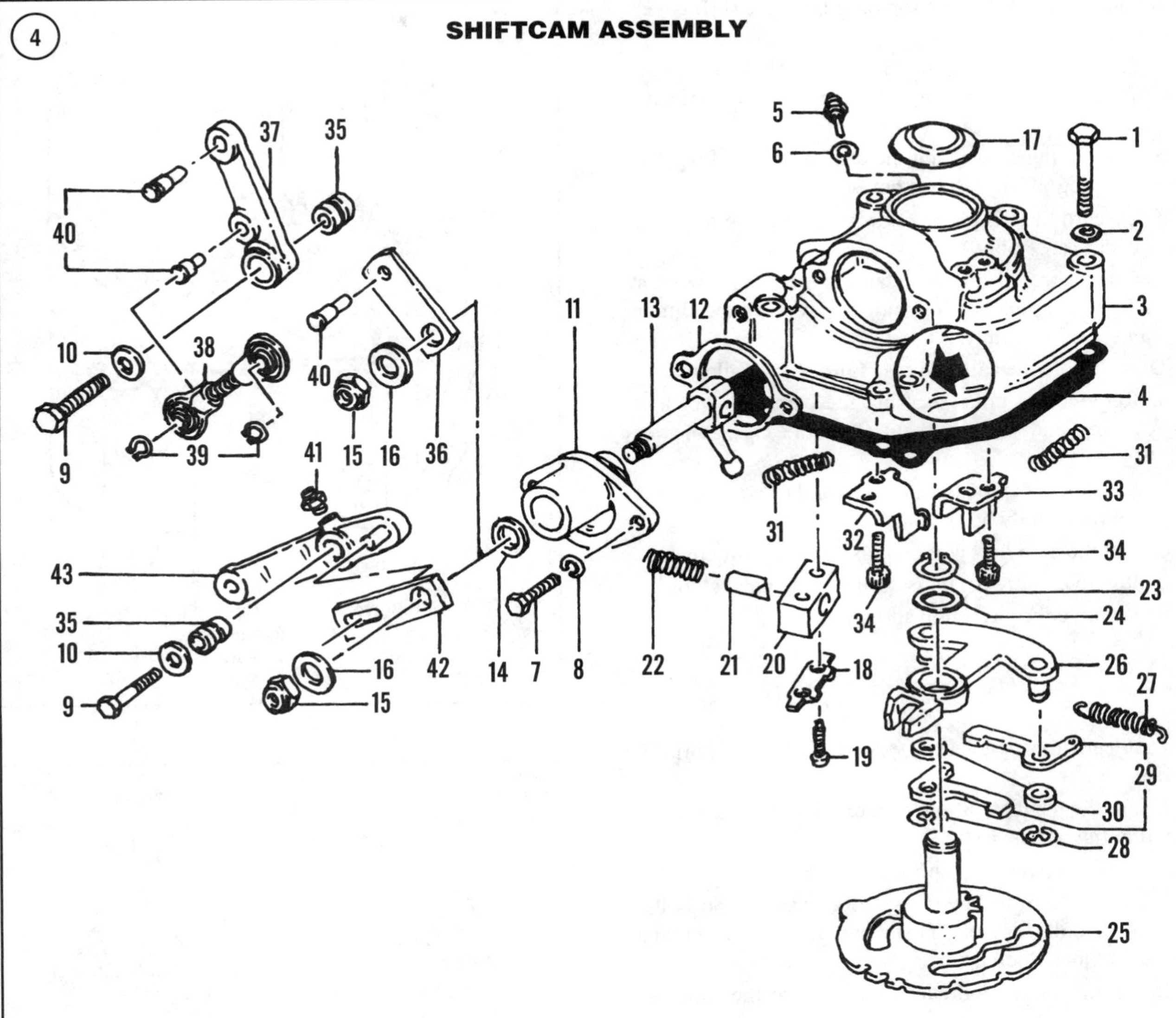

1. Bolt
2. Washer
3. Shift cover
4. Gasket
5. Neutral indicator switch
6. Washer
7. Bolt
8. Lockwasher
9. Bolt
10. Washer
11. Shifter shaft cover
12. Gasket
13. Shifter shaft
14. Oil seal
15. Nut
16. Washer
17. Plug
18. Lockplate
19. Bolt
20. Plunger body
21. Plunger
22. Spring
23. Retaining ring
24. Thrust washer
25. Shifter cam
26. Pawl carrier
27. Shifter pawl spring
28. Retaining rings
29. Pawls
30. Spacers
31. Pawl carrier spring
32. Shift pawl stop, rear
33. Shift pawl stop, front
34. Socket head screw
35. Bushing
36. Shift lever arm (FXEF and FXSB)
37. Shift lever (FXEF and FXSB)
38. Shift linkage arm (FXEF and FXSB)
39. Retaining ring (2) (FXEF and FXSB)
40. Pivot pin (3) (FXEF and FXSB)
41. Grease fitting
42. Shift lever arm (FXWG)
43. Shift lever (1985 FXWG)

6. If necessary, remove the top plug from the shift cover as follows:
   a. Drill a 1/4-in. (6.35 mm) hole through the top plug. Drill only far enough to penetrate completely through the top plug material.
   b. Insert a punch through the drilled hole and pry the top plug off of the shift cover.
   c. Discard the top plug; a new plug must be installed during assembly.
7. Remove the shift cam retaining ring and washer through the top plug hole opening and remove the shifter cam and pawl assembly.
8. Disassemble the shift cover (**Figure 5**) as follows:
   a. Remove the bolts securing the cam follower and spring and remove them from the cam follower body.
   b. Straighten the lockwasher tabs and remove the cam follower body bolts.
   c. Lift the cam follower body out of the shift cover.
   d. Remove the Allen bolts securing the pawl stops.
   e. Remove the pawl stop springs.

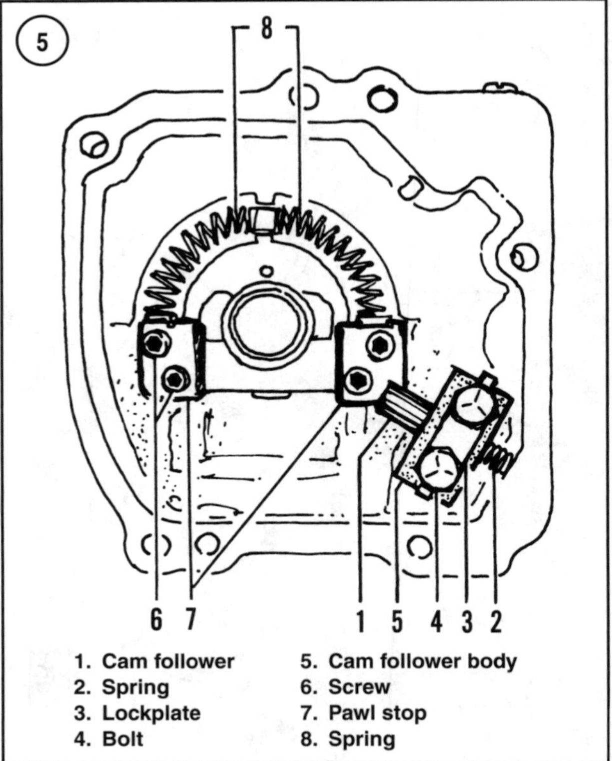

1. Cam follower
2. Spring
3. Lockplate
4. Bolt
5. Cam follower body
6. Screw
7. Pawl stop
8. Spring

Assembly

1. Lubricate the pawl stop springs with multipurpose grease.
2. Install the pawl stops and secure with the Allen bolts. Securely tighten the bolts.
3. Install both pawl stop springs.
4. Install the cam follower body, lockwasher and bolts. Tighten the bolts securely. Then bend the lockwasher tabs over the bolts to lock them.
5. Install the spring and cam follower into the cam follower body.
6. Coat the neutral switch threads with Loctite Pipe Sealant with Teflon. Install the neutral switch and washer and tighten to 62-124 in.-lb. (7-14 N•m).
7. Slide the pawl carrier assembly on the shift cam (**Figure 6**). Engage the pawls with the shift cam gear teeth and make sure they are correctly engaged.
8. Install the shift cam and pawl carrier assembly into the shift cover. Position the tab on the pawl carrier assembly between the pawl stop springs.
9. Install the shift cam washer and a *new* snap ring.
10. Coat a new top plug with Seal-All sealant or an equivalent. Then place the top plug in the cover and tap it into place with a hammer.
11. Assemble the shift linkage using a *new* snap ring. Tighten all linkage bolts securely.

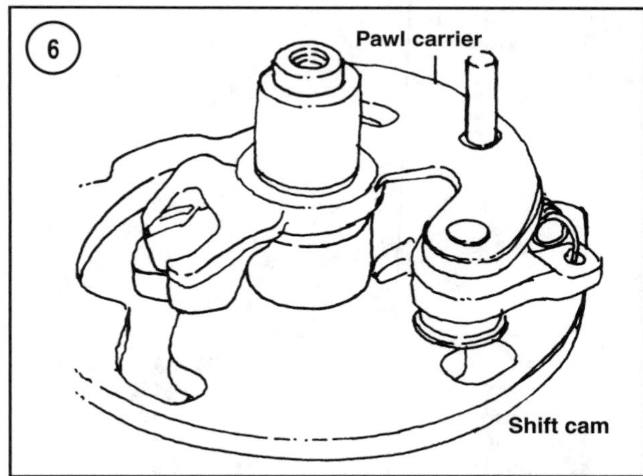

Inspection

1. Thoroughly clean all parts (except neutral switch) in solvent. Then blow dry.
2. Inspect them for any signs of wear, cracks, breakage or other damage. Replace as necessary.
3. Check the shift cam slots for worn or grooved cam slots. Excessive wear will result in difficult shifting.
4. Check pawl stops for breakage or surface cracks.

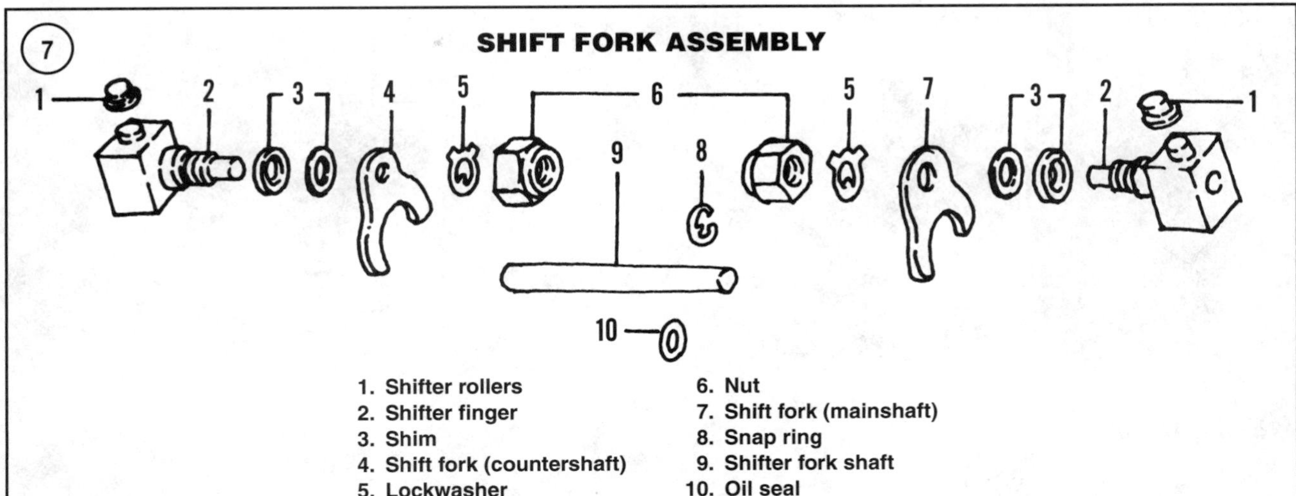

SHIFT FORKS

Removal/Disassembly

Refer to **Figure 7**.

1. Remove the shift cover as described in this section.
2. Remove the rollers (**Figure 8**) from each shift finger.

3. Remove the snap ring (**Figure 9**) from the end of the shift fork shaft.
4. Tap on the end of the shift fork shaft with a drift and remove the shaft from the case (**Figure 10**).
5. Mark the shift forks with an *L* (left side or driven-sprocket side) and *R* (right side). Remove both shift forks (**Figure 11**).

NOTE
Do not disassemble the forks unless a portion requires replacement.

6. Disassemble one shift fork (**Figure 12**) at a time and keep them separate. Do not interchange any of the parts.
7. Straighten the lockwasher tabs (A, **Figure 13**). Loosen and remove the nut (B) and lockwasher securing the shift fork to the shift finger.
8. Remove the shift fork and shims from the shift finger and keep them in order shown in **Figure 7**.
9. Repeat for the other shift fork assembly.

6

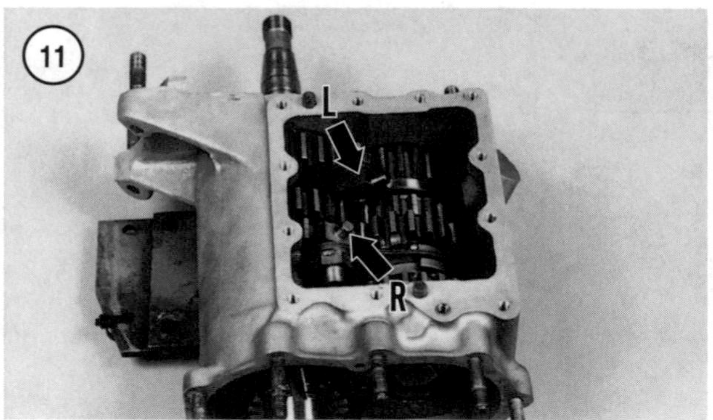

Assembly/Installation

NOTE
If any part was replaced, the shift fork clearance must be checked and adjusted.

1. Coat all bearing and sliding surfaces with assembly oil.

CAUTION
Do not exceed the torque specifications in Step 2 because this could cause the shift finger to bind on the shift shaft.

2. Install the spacer(s), shift fork, *new* lockwasher and then nut on the shift finger. Tighten the nut to 124-150 in.-lb. (14-17 N•m). Bend the lockwasher tab against the nut to lock it.
3. Refer to the marks made in Step 5 of *Removal/Disassembly* and install the shift fork assemblies into the transmission case. Refer to **Figure 14** and **Figure 15**. Engage the shift forks with the respective gears. (**Figure 11**).
4. Insert the shift shaft through the transmission case (**Figure 16**) and through both shift fork assemblies. Push the shaft in until it bottoms in the transmission case.
5. Install a *new* snap ring (**Figure 17**) into the shaft groove and make sure it properly seats (**Figure 9**).
6. Install the shift rollers (**Figure 8**) onto the shift fingers. Press them down until they bottom.
7. If any part was replaced, adjust the shift forks as described in this section.

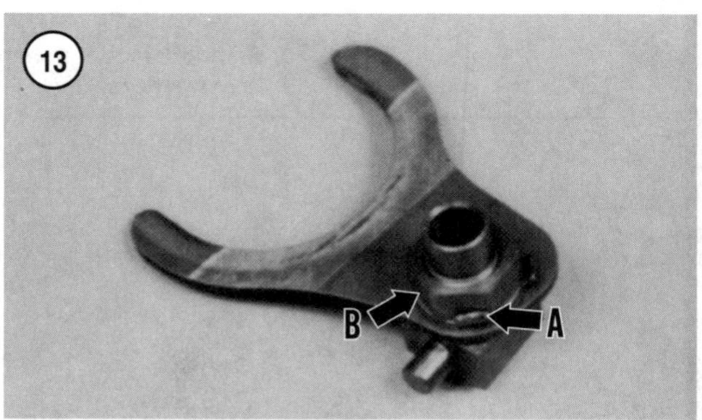

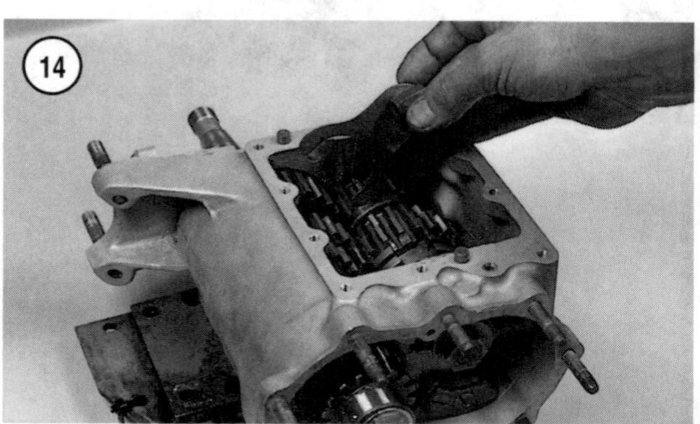

Inspection

1. Clean all parts in solvent and dry.
2. Inspect each shift fork (**Figure 13**) for signs of wear or damage.
3. Make sure the forks slide smoothly on the shifter fork shaft.
4. Check for any arc-shaped wear or burn marks on the shift forks (**Figure 18**). If this is apparent, the shift fork

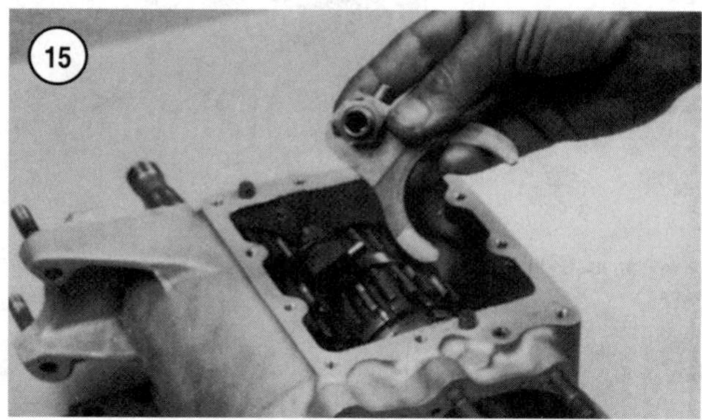

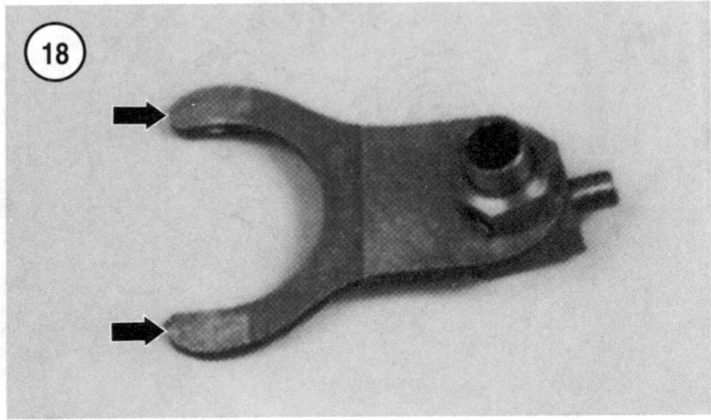

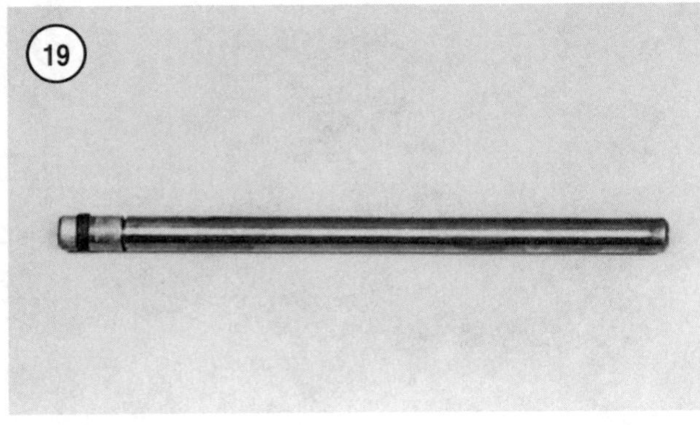

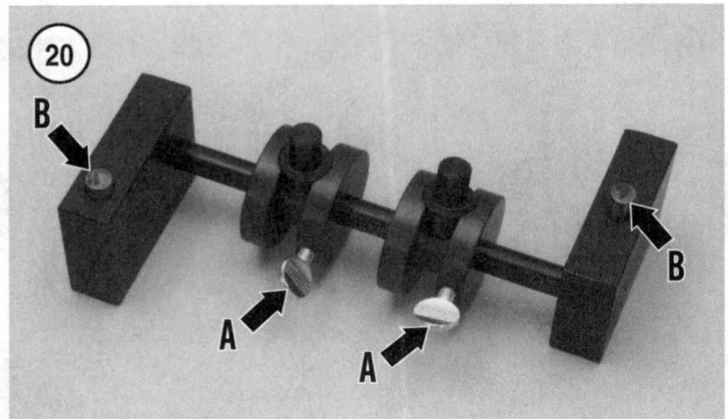

6

has come in contact with the gear, which indicates that the fingers are worn and must be replaced.

5. Roll the shift fork shaft (**Figure 19**) on a flat surface and check for bending. If the shaft is bent, it must be replaced.

6. Install each shift fork on the shift shaft. The shift fork should slide smoothly without any sign of binding.

Shift Fork Adjustment

This procedure requires the Shift Fork Gauge (JIMS part No. 96385-78A) to correctly adjust the shift forks clearance.

1. Turn the shift cover assembly upside down on the workbench.
2. Move the shift cam to the neutral position.
3. Loosen the two thumb screws (A, **Figure 20**) on the sliding blocks on the tool. Move the sliding blocks back and forth to make sure they move freely.
4. Install the tool onto the cover and align the two dowel pins (B, **Figure 20**) into the pin holes in the cover. At the same time, align the sliding blocks into the shift plate located in the neutral position. Tighten the two thumb screws locking both sliding blocks in this position.
5. Pull the tool straight up off the cover and turn it over (dowel pins facing up).
6. Install the tool onto the transmission case. Index the case dowel pins into the tool pin receptacles while aligning the shift fork fingers with the sliding block grooves.
7. Check the clearance between the shift fingers and both sides of the shifter clutches with a flat feeler gauge. The specified clearance is as follows:
   a. Countershaft first and second gears: 0.080-0.090 in. (2.03-2.28 mm).
   b. Mainshaft third and forth gears: 0.100-0.110 in. (2.54-2.79 mm).
8. Remove the special tool from the transmission case.

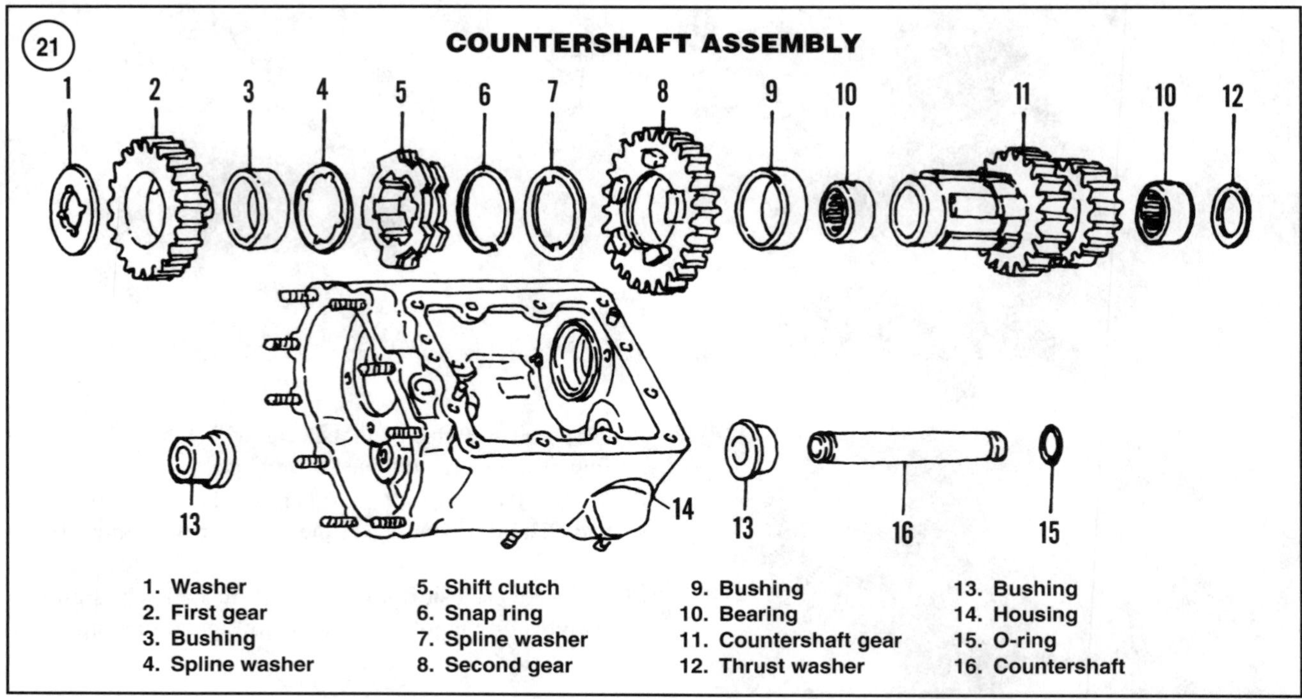

9. If the clearance is not as specified, remove the shift fork assemblies and change the shim(s) with one of a different thickness. The shims are available in sizes from 0.007-0.014 in. (0.178-0.355 mm) from a Harley-Davidson dealership.

TRANSMISSION SHAFTS

Countershaft Removal/Installation

Refer to **Figure 21**.

1. Remove the transmission case as described in this chapter.
2. If the countershaft drive sprocket was not removed during transmission case removal, remove it as follows:
   a. Hold the sprocket with a universal holding tool.
   b. Remove the sprocket nut setscrew.

NOTE
*The sprocket nut has left-hand threads. Turn the wrench **counterclockwise** to loosen and remove it.*

   c. Loosen and remove the sprocket nut.
   d. Remove the lockwasher (models so equipped).
   e. Remove the drive sprocket.
3. Remove the following assemblies from the transmission as described in this chapter:

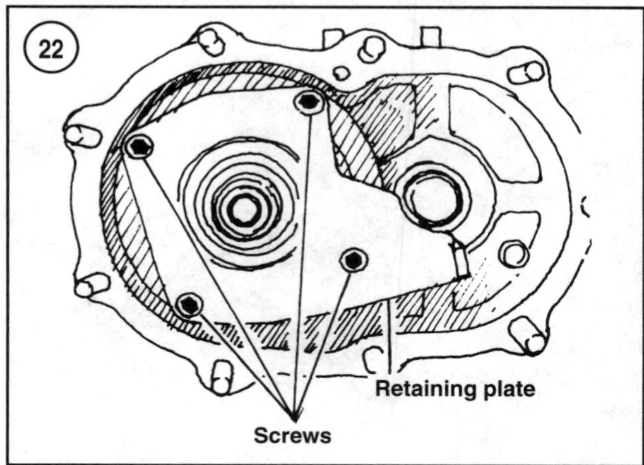

a. Shift cover.
b. Side cover.
c. Shift forks.

4. Remove the retaining plate screws and remove the retaining plate (**Figure 22**).
5. Hold onto the gear cluster (**Figure 23**) with one hand. Then withdraw the countershaft (**Figure 24**) through the side of the case.
6. Lift the gear cluster out of the case (**Figure 25**).

NOTE
In Step 7, the washer and thrust washer may come out with the gear cluster or stick to the side of the transmission case.

7. Remove the washer (A, **Figure 26**) and thrust washer (B) from the transmission case.
8. Coat the countershaft thrust washer (B, **Figure 26**) with grease and install it into the correct location in the transmission case.
9. Install a *new* O-ring on the sprocket end of the countershaft. Apply clean engine oil to the O-ring.
10. Position the gear cluster with the countershaft gear end going in first and install the gear cluster into the transmission case (**Figure 25**). Hold the gear cluster in position with one hand.

11. Position the countershaft with the sprocket side (O-ring) end going in last and insert the countershaft through the gear cluster from the sprocket side of the transmission case.
12. Push the countershaft in until it bottoms and make sure the O-ring is still in place.
13. Measure the countershaft gear end play as follows:
  a. Insert a flat feeler gauge between the washer (1, **Figure 21**) and the countershaft (11, **Figure 21**). Correct end play is listed in **Table 1**.
  b. If the end play is incorrect, replace the washer with a washer of a different thickness. The washers are available in sizes from 0.074-0.100 in. (1.88-2.54 mm) from a Harley-Davidson dealership.
14. Install the retaining plate (**Figure 22**). Tighten the screws to 94-108 in.-lb. (9.5-12.2 N•m).
15. Install the countershaft drive sprocket as follows:
  a. Install the drive sprocket onto the countershaft. Push it on until it bottoms.
  b. On models so equipped, install a *new* lockwasher.
  c. Install the sprocket nut and tighten securely.
  d. Hold the sprocket with a universal holding tool.

NOTE
The sprocket nut has left-hand threads, turn the wrench ***clockwise*** *to tighten it.*

  e. Tighten the sprocket nut to 80-90 ft.-lb. (108-122 N•m).
  f. Tighten the sprocket nut setscrew to 50-60 in.-lb. (6-7 N•m).

Countershaft Disassembly

1. Remove the first gear (**Figure 27**) and slide off the first gear bushing.
2. Remove the spline washer (**Figure 28**).
3. Slide off the shift clutch (**Figure 29**).
4. Remove the snap ring (**Figure 30**) from the gear cluster.

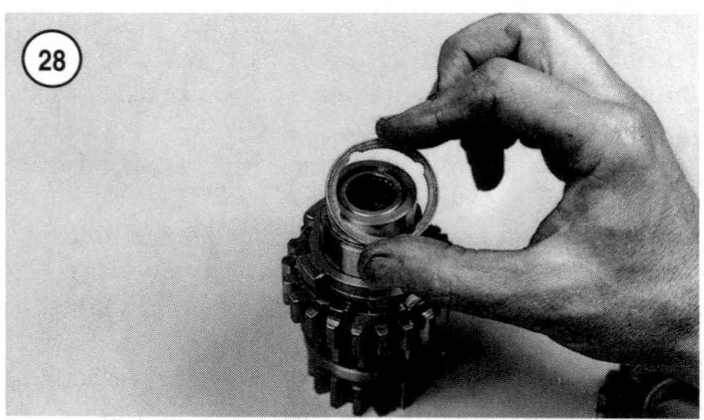

5. Slide off the spline washer (**Figure 31**).
6. Slide off the second gear (**Figure 32**) and slide off the second gear bushing (**Figure 33**).
7. Remove the thrust washer from the other end of the countershaft.

Countershaft Assembly

1. Coat all parts with engine oil prior to assembly.
2. Slide on the second gear bushing (**Figure 33**).

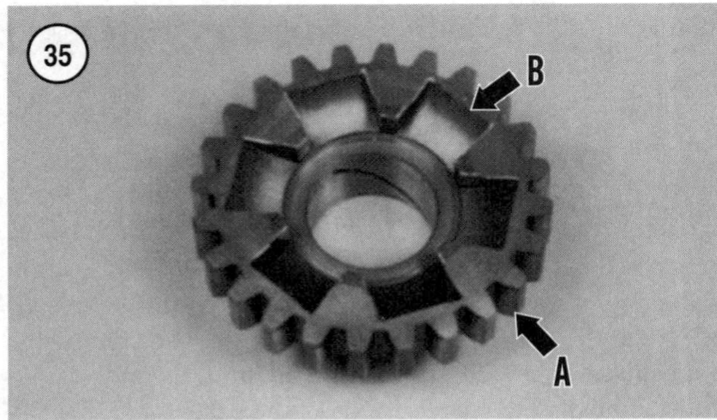

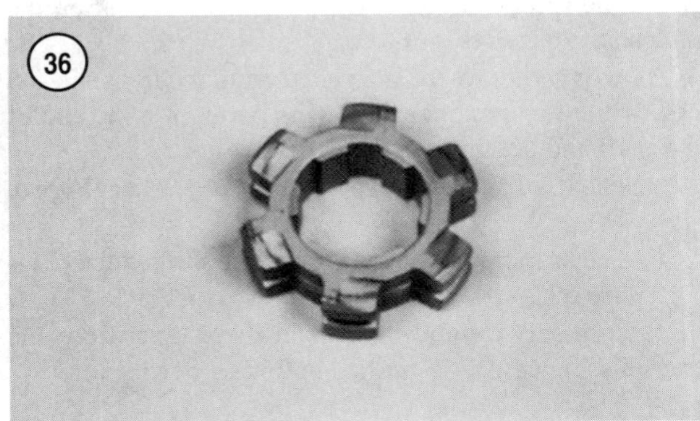

3. Position the second gear with the shift dog side going on last and install the second gear (**Figure 32**).
4. Install the spline washer (**Figure 31**).
5. Install a *new* snap ring (**Figure 30**). Make sure the snap ring seats correctly in the countershaft groove.
6. Install the shift clutch (**Figure 29**) and spline washer (**Figure 28**).
7. Slide on the first gear bushing and the first gear (**Figure 27**).

Inspection

1. Inspect each gear for excessive wear, burrs, pitting or chipped or missing teeth. Refer to **Figure 34** and A, **Figure 35**.
2. Inspect the shift clutch (**Figure 36**) for rounded edges or severe wear. Also check the inner splines for excessive wear or damage.
3. Check dogs on the gears (**Figure 37**) and receptacles (B, **Figure 35**) for excessive wear or rounded edges.
4. Examine gear and shaft splines for wear or rounded edges.
5. Slide the gears onto the shaft in the original positions. The gear should slide back and forth without any binding or excessive play.
6. Check the countershaft gear needle bearing (**Figure 38**) at each end for wear or roughness. If worn or damaged, they must be replaced in the following procedure.
7. Inspect the transmission case bushings and oil seals as described in this section.

Countershaft Gear Needle Bearing Replacement

A hydraulic press and Countershaft Bearing Tool (JIMS part No. 34733-77) (**Figure 39**) are required for this procedure.

1. Support the countershaft gear in a vise with soft jaws.

2A. Remove the old bearings with a blind bearing remover (**Figure 40**).
2B. Remove the old bearings with long drift and hammer.
3. Clean out the countershaft gear bore with solvent and dry with compressed air.
4. Check the bearing bore in the countershaft gear for burrs and remove if necessary.
5. Apply clean engine oil to the bearing bore and to the exterior of the bearings.
6. Place the countershaft gear on the press bed.
7. Position the needle bearing onto the countershaft gear with the manufacturer's mark facing out.
8. Install the bearing installer tool (**Figure 39**) onto the bearing and countershaft gear as shown in **Figure 41**. The tool is double-ended and must be positioned as shown to install the bearing to the correct depth within the countershaft gear.
9. Slowly press the bearing into the countershaft gear. When the tool bottoms on the gear surface, the bearing is installed at the correct depth.
10. Remove the special tool and the countershaft from the press bed.
11. Repeat Steps 5-9 for the remaining bearing.

Mainshaft Removal/Disassembly

Refer to **Figure 42**.

The mainshaft is partially disassembled during the removal procedure.

1. Remove the transmission case as described in this chapter.
2. On late 1984-on models, remove the bearing race from the end of the mainshaft with the Mainshaft Bearing Race Tool (JIMS part No. 34902-84) (**Figure 43**) as follows:
   a. Thread the center screw into the puller bar. Thread the hardened tip onto the end of the center screw and tighten securely.
   b. Place a washer onto the two bolts. Position the bolts onto the puller bar with the washers resting on the puller bar.
   c. Thread the two bolts onto the bearing plate until they are flush with the back side of the bearing plate.
   d. Position the bearing plate behind the bearing and tighten the center screw onto the end of the transmission shaft. Center the hardened tip onto the end of the transmission shaft.

NOTE
If the bearing will not dislodge from the shaft, slowly heat (not to exceed 200° F [93° C]) the bearing until it is free to move on the shaft.

   e. Slowly tighten the center screw and withdraw the bearing from the shaft.
   f. Remove the special tools.
3. Remove countershaft from the transmission case as described in this chapter.
4. Using a plastic mallet, carefully drive the mainshaft (**Figure 44**) part way out through the cover side of the transmission case. Slowly drive it out until second gear almost contacts the inner surface of the case.
5. Release the snap ring (**Figure 45**) from its groove between the spline washer and shift clutch. Slide it on the mainshaft splines (**Figure 46**).
6. Slowly withdraw the mainshaft from the transmission case while removing the following parts from the end of the shaft and out through the case opening:
   a. The third gear (**Figure 47**) and the washer (**Figure 48**).
   b. The snap ring (**Figure 49**) and the shift clutch (**Figure 50**).
7. If necessary, remove the main drive gear from the transmission case as described in this section.

NOTE
Step 8 requires the use of a hydraulic press.

8. If necessary, remove the bearing (A, **Figure 51**) and the first/second combination gear (B) from the mainshaft. Perform the following:
   a. Clamp the mainshaft in a vise with soft jaws.
   b. Straighten the lockwasher tab away from the mainshaft nut. Then remove the nut and the lockwasher.
   c. Place the mainshaft assembly in the hydraulic press.
   d. Position the press plates under the larger gear.
   e. Place a suitably sized driver, or round stock, on the end of the mainshaft. The driver must be small

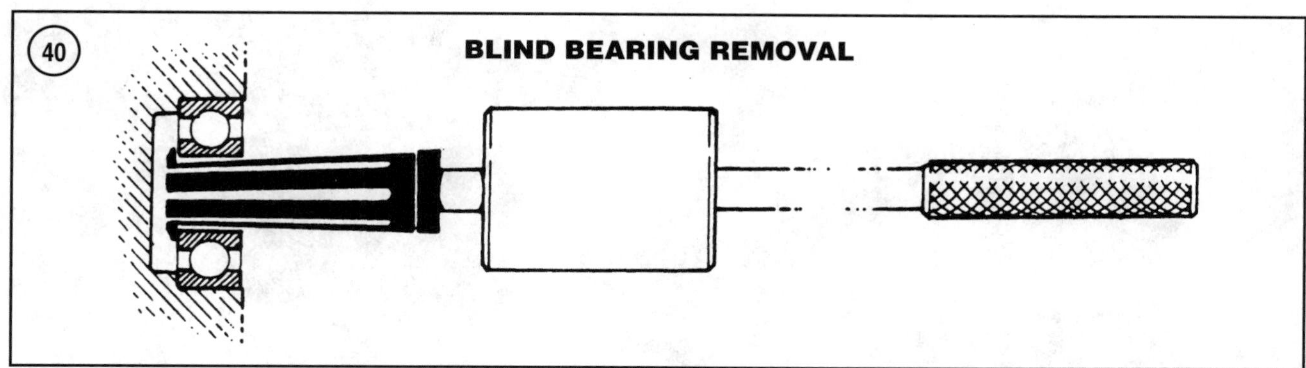
40
BLIND BEARING REMOVAL

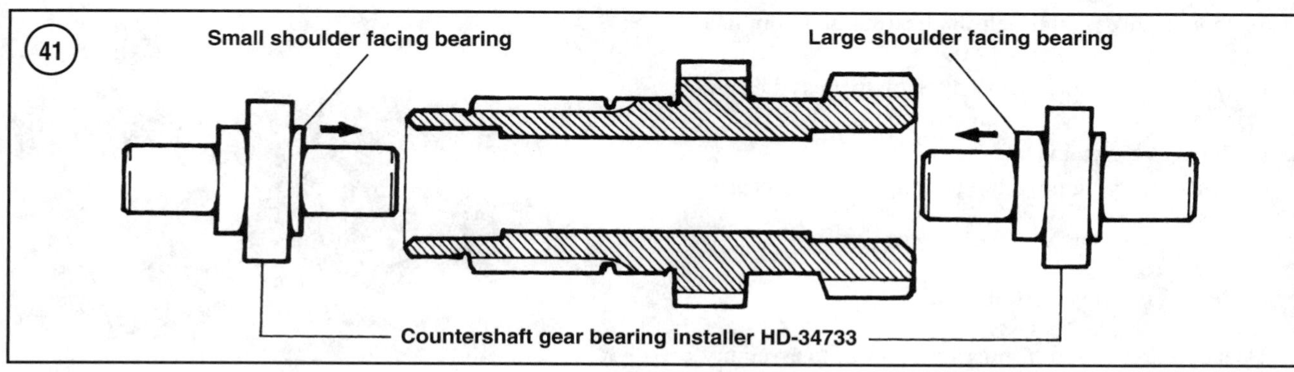
41
Small shoulder facing bearing
Large shoulder facing bearing
Countershaft gear bearing installer HD-34733

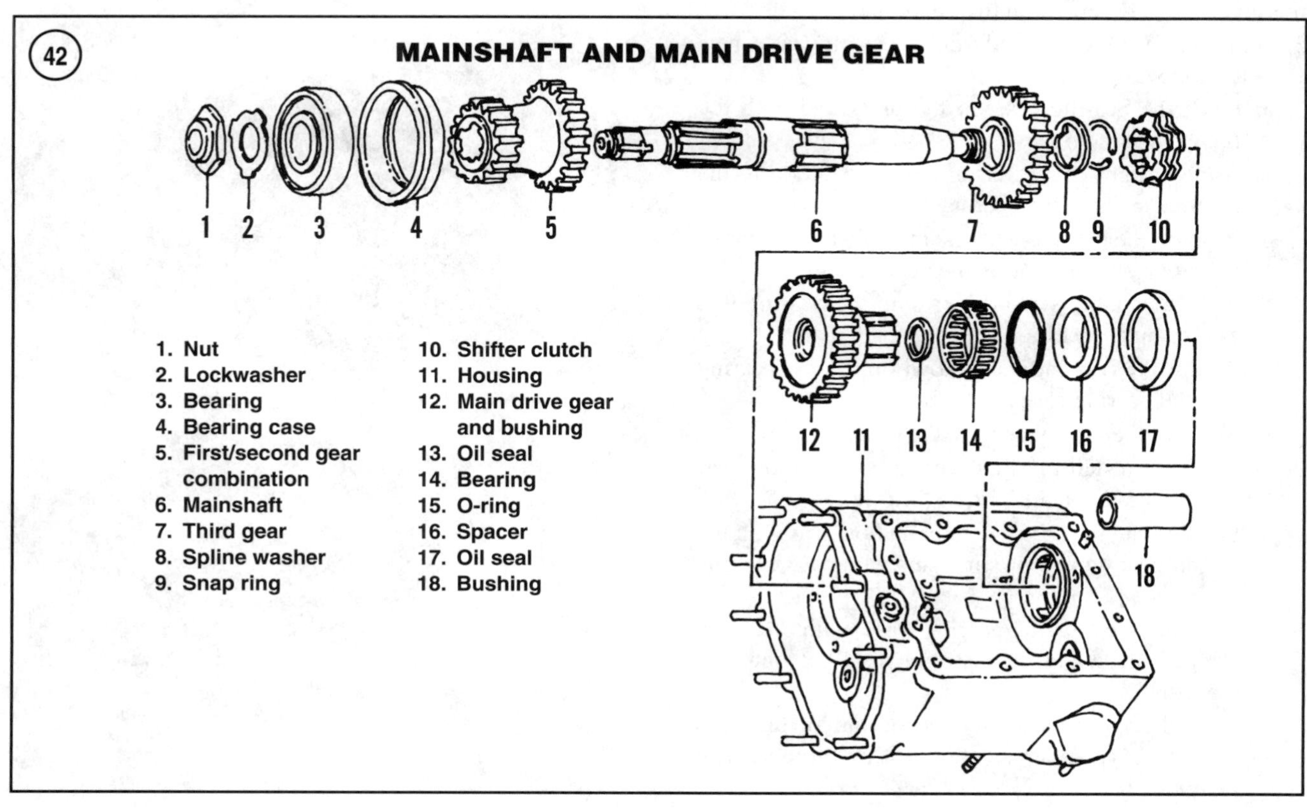
42
MAINSHAFT AND MAIN DRIVE GEAR
1 2 3 4 5 6 7 8 9 10
12 11 13 14 15 16 17
18
1. Nut
2. Lockwasher
3. Bearing
4. Bearing case
5. First/second gear combination
6. Mainshaft
7. Third gear
8. Spline washer
9. Snap ring
10. Shifter clutch
11. Housing
12. Main drive gear and bushing
13. Oil seal
14. Bearing
15. O-ring
16. Spacer
17. Oil seal
18. Bushing

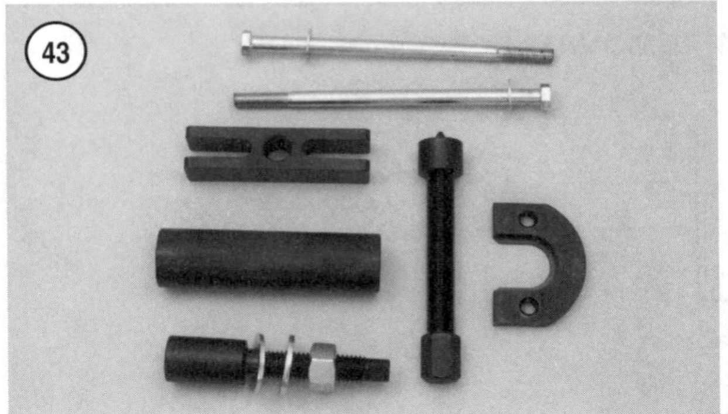

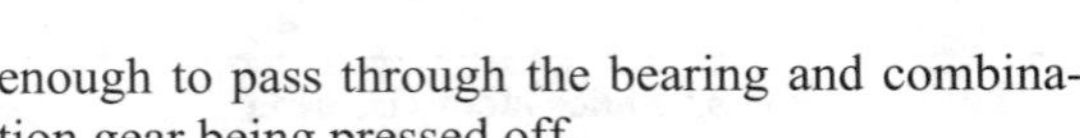

enough to pass through the bearing and combination gear being pressed off.

f. While holding the mainshaft, slowly press the combination gear and bearing off the mainshaft.

g. Remove the mainshaft.

h. If necessary, remove the bearing from the bearing case.

Mainshaft Assembly/Installation

1. Coat all parts with transmission oil prior to assembly.

2. If removed, install the main drive gear into the transmission case as described in this section.

3. If the bearing was removed from the bearing case, perform the following:

   a. Place the bearing case on the press bed with the flange side facing up.

   b. Apply a light coat of clean transmission oil to the external sides of the bearing.

   c. Position the bearing with the manufacturer's marks facing up and place it on the bearing case.

   d. Place a suitably sized driver onto the bearing that fits the outer bearing race.

   e. Secure the two parts and slowly press the bearing into the bearing case until it bottoms.

   f. Remove the assembly from the press bed.

3. If removed, install the first/second combination gear and bearing onto the mainshaft, as follows:

   a. Position the first/second combination gear with the larger gear going on first and slide it onto the mainshaft.

   b. Position the bearing/bearing case with the case flange side going on last and install it onto the mainshaft.

   c. Place the opposite end of the mainshaft on the press bed and have an assistant hold it in a true vertical position.

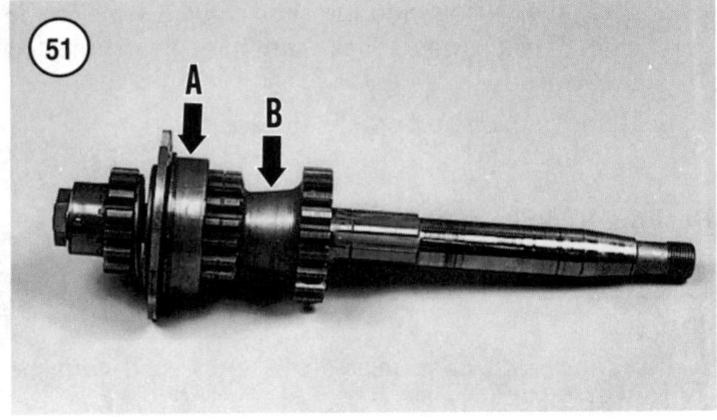

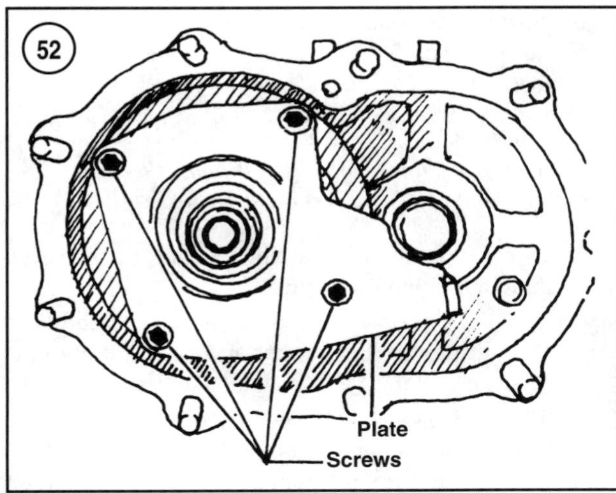

d. Place a suitably sized driver onto the bearing that fits the inner bearing race. The driver must fit the inner race and must also be large enough on the inside to clear the splines on the mainshaft. If the inner surface of the driver touches the shaft, splines will be damaged.

e. Hold onto the mainshaft and slowly press the bearing onto the shaft. Press the bearing on until it stops.

f. Remove the shaft and driver from the hydraulic press.

4. Support the mainshaft in a vise with soft jaws. Install the lockwasher and nut onto the end of the mainshaft. Tighten the nut to 50-60 ft.-lb. (67-81 N•m). Then bend the lockwasher tab against the nut.

5. Install the mainshaft into the transmission case and slide it so that the second gear barely contacts the case.

6. Slide the third gear (**Figure 47**) and then the spline washer (**Figure 48**) onto the mainshaft.

7. Install a *new* snap ring (**Figure 49**) and make sure it seats correctly in the mainshaft groove.

8. Position the shift clutch so that the side with the word HIGH faces toward the main drive gear. Install the shift clutch (**Figure 50**).

9. Move the mainshaft into the other side of the transmission case and lightly tap into place until the bearing case flange seats against the transmission case.

10. Install the countershaft as described in this section.

11. Install the retaining plate (**Figure 52**). Tighten the screws to 84-108 in.-lb. (9.5-12.2 N•m).

12. On late 1984-on models, install the bearing race onto the end of the mainshaft with the Mainshaft Bearing Race Tool (JIMS part No. 34902-84) (**Figure 43**) as follows:

a. Apply transmission oil to the transmission shaft and to the inner surface of the bearing race.

b. Position the bearing race with the chamfered edge side going on first and slide it onto the transmission shaft.

NOTE
*The extension shaft has left-hand threads. Turn the shaft **counterclockwise** to install it.*

c. Thread the extension shaft onto the transmission shaft and tighten securely.
d. Install the pusher tube over the extension shaft. Then install the flat washer and large nut onto the extension shaft. Slowly tighten the nut until the washer is against the pusher tube.
e. Place a wrench on the end of the flat portion of the extension to keep it from turning.
f. Tighten the large nut and press the bearing race onto the mainshaft. Install the bearing race until the inside edge is 0.200 in. (5.08 mm) from the main drive gear. Before measuring the bearing race-to-main drive gear clearance, pull the main drive gear toward the end of the mainshaft.
g. Remove the installation tool.

Mainshaft Inspection

1. Inspect each gear for excessive wear, burrs, pitting or chipped or missing teeth (**Figure 53**).
2. Inspect the shift clutch (**Figure 54**) for rounded edges or severe wear. Also check the inner splines for excessive wear or damage.
3. Slide the gears onto the shaft in the original positions. The gears should slide back and forth without any binding or excessive play.
4. Replace the worn or damaged spline washer.

53

54

MAIN DRIVE GEAR

Removal/Inspection/Installation

Refer to **Figure 42**.
1. Remove the countershaft and mainshaft as described in this chapter.
2. Push the main drive gear (**Figure 55**) into the transmission case. Then remove it through the shift cover opening.
3. Examine the main drive gear for worn or chipped teeth, pitting, scoring or other damage. Replace if necessary. If the gear is damaged, also check the mating gear on the countershaft for wear or damage.
4. Examine gear splines for wear or rounded edges.
5. Examine the needle bearing within the transmission case for wear or damage. Replace if necessary as described in this section.
6. Install the main drive gear onto the end of the countershaft and check for excessive gear bushing-to-shaft clearance. Refer to **Table 1**. If the clearance is excessive, replace the bushing as described in this section.
7. Install by reversing these removal steps while noting the following:
   a. Wrap the main drive gear threads with clear tape to protect the O-ring during installation.
   b. Apply clean transmission oil to the O-ring. Then slide the O-ring over the main drive gear.
   c. Slide the O-ring onto the shaft until it seats in the shaft O-ring groove. Make sure it is correctly seated in the groove.
   d. Remove the tape from the threads.

Bushing Replacement

1. Remove the oil seal from the small end of the main drive gear.
2. Place the main drive gear on the press bed with the gear side facing down.

55

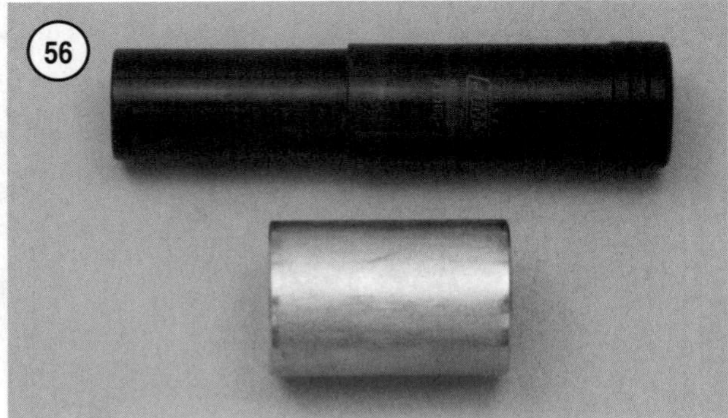
56

3. Install the Main Gear Bushing Tool (JIMS part No. 1005) (**Figure 56**) as follows:
   a. Insert the sleeve into the main drive gear.
   b. Insert the driver into the sleeve and rest it on the bushing.
   c. Carefully press the bushing out of the drive gear.
   d. Remove the special tools.
4. Clean out the bushing bore with solvent and dry with compressed air.
5. Check the bushing bore for burrs and remove if necessary.
6. Apply clean transmission oil to the bushing bore and to the exterior of the bushing.
7. Position the bushing with the tightly spaced grooved end going in last.
8. Position the bushing squarely over the drive gear and position the installer tool onto the bushing.
9. Slowly press the bushing squarely into drive gear until the tool bottoms on the drive gear. The bushing is now installed at the correct depth.
10. Remove tool and the drive gear from the press bed.

CAUTION
Improper bushing-to-shaft clearance can cause bushing and mainshaft failure from improper lubrication.

11. Install the main drive gear onto the end of the countershaft and check for the new gear bushing-to-shaft clearance. Refer to Table 1. If the clearance is excessive, hone the bushing to achieve the correct clearance.
12. Install a *new* seal into the small end of the main drive gear.

TRANSMISSION CASE

Removal/Installation

1. Drain the transmission oil as described in Chapter Three.
2. Remove the battery as described in Chapter Three.
3. Remove the bolts, washers and nuts securing the battery carrier and remove the carrier.
4. Remove the oil tank as described in Chapter Four.
5. Remove the passenger grab strap and the seat.
6. Remove the master cylinder reservoir mount bracket at the transmission end cover.
7. Remove the starter as described in Chapter Nine.
8. Remove the primary case as described in Chapter Five.
9. Disconnect the shift rod end from the shift lever (FXEF and FXSB models) or from the shift linkage (FXWG models).
10. Disconnect the clutch cable from the release lever.
11. Disconnect the wiring at the solenoid.
12. Disconnect the speedometer drive cable and case at the transmission (if so equipped).
13. Disconnect the neutral indicator switch wire at the transmission.
14A. On chain-driven models, disconnect the drive chain master link and remove the drive chain from the drive sprocket.
14B. On belt-driven models, loosen the rear axle and the belt adjusters and remove the drive belt from the drive sprocket.

NOTE
The transmission can be removed with its mounting plate attached.

15. Remove the transmission mounting plate-to-frame bolts.
16. Remove the starter relay and wiring.
17. Remove the rear brake line bracket.
18. Remove the transmission-to-frame mounting bolt from underneath the right side.
19. On FXEF and FXSB models, remove the master cylinder alignment plate, if necessary.
20. On FXWG models, remove the rear brake line clip from the transmission end cover.

21. Remove the transmission and mounting plate from the left side of the frame.
22. Installation is the reverse of these steps while noting the following:
   a. Install the transmission assembly in the frame and install the mounting hardware. Tighten the mounting plate bolt to 30-33 ft.-lb. (41-45 N•m).
   b. Tighten the transmission-to-mounting plate bolts to 21-27 ft.-lb. (28-37 N•m).
   c. Tighten the right transmission-to-frame mounting bolt to 21-27 ft.-lb. (28-37 N•m).
   d. Refill the transmission with the correct type and quantity of oil as described in Chapter Three.
   e. Adjust the primary chain as described in Chapter Three.
   f. Check primary chain alignment as described in Chapter Five.
   g. When reconnecting the drive chain with its master link, make sure the closed end of the master link clip faces toward normal chain travel.
   h. Adjust the rear drive chain or drive belt as described in Chapter Three.
   i. Adjust the clutch as described in Chapter Three.

Transmission Case Needle Bearing and Oil Seal Replacement

1. Check the needle bearing in the transmission case for wear or roughness. If worn or damaged, replace it as follows.
2. Use a flat-tip screwdriver and carefully pry the main drive gear oil seal (**Figure 57**) out of the transmission case. Place a rag underneath the pry tool to prevent damage to the case.
3. Push the spacer in toward the transmission case and out of the needle bearing. Remove the spacer.
4. Carefully press the needle bearing out of the transmission case.
5. Clean out the needle bearing bore with solvent and dry with compressed air.
6. Check the bearing bore in the transmission case for burrs and remove if necessary.
7. Apply clean transmission oil to the bearing bore and to the exterior of the bearing.
8. Place the transmission case on the press bed. Protect the threaded studs on the opposite side of the case. Do not apply any pressure to the studs in the following steps.
9. Position the needle bearing squarely over the transmission case bearing bore with the manufacturer's mark facing out.
10. Install the bearing installer tool (JIMS part No. 33428-78) (**Figure 58**) onto the bearing.

11. Slowly press the bearing squarely into the transmission case until the installer tool bottoms on the transmission case surface. The bearing is now installed at the correct depth.
12. Remove the tool and the transmission case from the press bed.
13. Rotate the bearing to make sure it is installed correctly. It must rotate smoothly with no binding.
14. Position the spacer with the flange side going in last and install the spacer into the inner surface of the transmission case. Push it in until it bottoms.

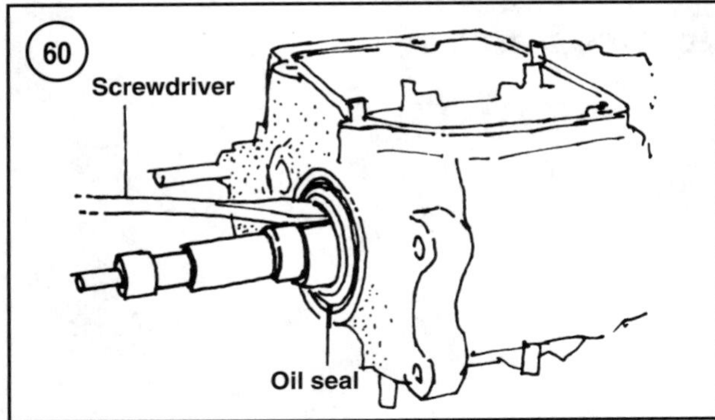

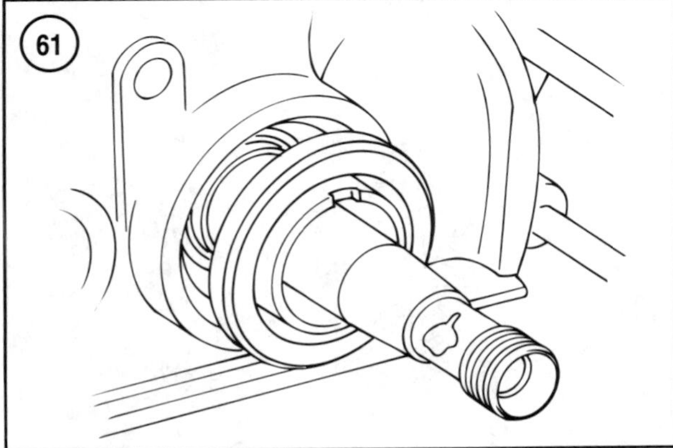

15. Install the main drive gear *new* oil seal (**Figure 57**) squarely into the transmission case. Push it in until it bottoms.

Transmission Case Oil Seal Replacement (with Transmission Installed)

The main drive gear oil seal (**Figure 59**) can be replaced with the transmission installed in the frame.

1. Remove the countershaft sprocket as follows:
   a. Hold the sprocket with a universal holding tool.
   b. Remove the sprocket nut setscrew.

NOTE
The sprocket nut has left-hand threads. Turn the wrench ***clockwise*** *to loosen and remove it.*

   c. Loosen and remove the sprocket nut.
   d. Remove the lockwasher (models so equipped).
   e. Remove the drive sprocket.
2. Remove the primary chaincase as described in Chapter Five.
3. Use a flat-tip screwdriver and carefully pry the main drive gear oil seal (**Figure 60**) out of the transmission case. Place a rag underneath the pry tool to prevent damage to the case.
4. Carefully install the new oil seal over the shaft (**Figure 61**) and align it with the seal bore in the transmission case.
5. Following the manufacturer's instructions, install the Seal Driver Tool (JIMS part No. 95660-77) and Main Seal Tool (JIMS part No. 95660-42) onto the oil seal.
6. Slowly press the oil seal squarely into the transmission case until the tool bottoms on the transmission case surface. The oil seal is now installed at the correct depth.
7. Remove the tool and the transmission case from the press bed.
8. Install the primary chaincase as described in Chapter Five.
9. Install the countershaft drive sprocket as follows:
   a. Install the drive sprocket onto the countershaft. Push it on until it bottoms.
   b. On models so equipped, install a *new* lockwasher.
   c. Install the sprocket nut and tighten securely.
   d. Hold the sprocket with a universal holding tool.

KICKSTARTER, STARTER CLUTCH AND SIDE COVER (FXWG AND FXSB MODELS)

Removal

Refer to **Figure 62**.

1. Disconnect the negative battery cable from the battery.
2. Remove the exhaust pipes as described in Chapter Eight.

3A. On FXWG models, perform the following:
   a. Remove the rear brake line support clip.
   b. Remove the starter motor bracket.
   c. Remove the master cylinder reservoir as described in Chapter Thirteen.

3B. FXSB models, perform the following:
   a. Remove the rear brake pedal assembly as described in Chapter Thirteen.
   b. Remove the master cylinder and reservoir as described in Chapter Thirteen.

4. Drain the transmission oil as described in Chapter Three.
5. Remove the clamp bolt and lockwasher securing the kickstarter pedal. Remove the pedal and install the bolt and lockwasher onto the pedal.
6. Remove the Acorn nuts, or hex nuts, and washers securing the side cover. Remove the side cover and gasket.
7. If necessary, disassemble the side cover as described in this chapter.

Installation

1. Install a *new* side cover gasket.

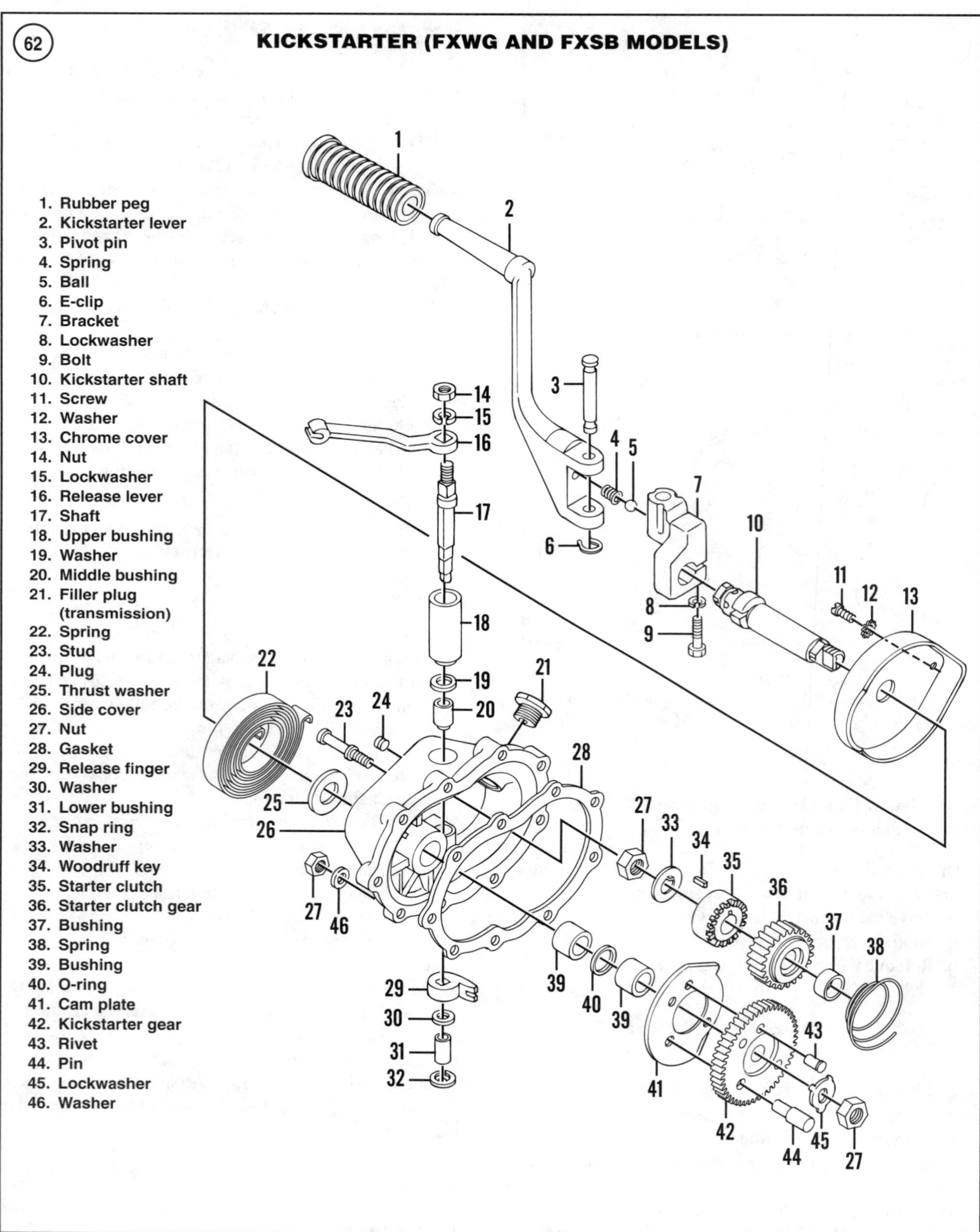
62
KICKSTARTER (FXWG AND FXSB MODELS)
1. Rubber peg
2. Kickstarter lever
3. Pivot pin
4. Spring
5. Ball
6. E-clip
7. Bracket
8. Lockwasher
9. Bolt
10. Kickstarter shaft
11. Screw
12. Washer
13. Chrome cover
14. Nut
15. Lockwasher
16. Release lever
17. Shaft
18. Upper bushing
19. Washer
20. Middle bushing
21. Filler plug (transmission)
22. Spring
23. Stud
24. Plug
25. Thrust washer
26. Side cover
27. Nut
28. Gasket
29. Release finger
30. Washer
31. Lower bushing
32. Snap ring
33. Washer
34. Woodruff key
35. Starter clutch
36. Starter clutch gear
37. Bushing
38. Spring
39. Bushing
40. O-ring
41. Cam plate
42. Kickstarter gear
43. Rivet
44. Pin
45. Lockwasher
46. Washer

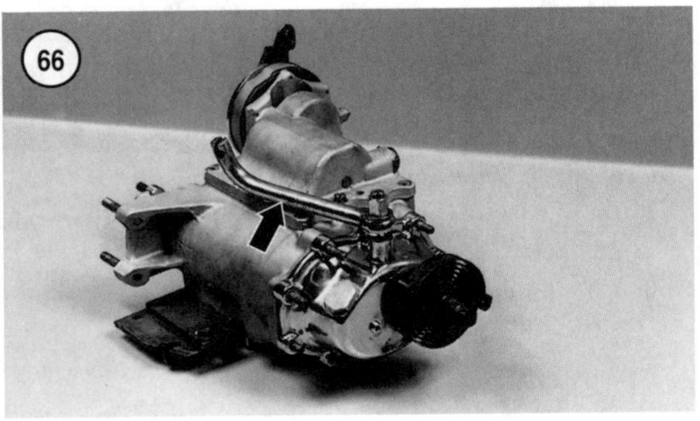

2. Pull the pushrod assembly partway out as shown in **Figure 63**.
3. Position the release lever to the left of the cover as shown in A, **Figure 64**.
4. Align the pushrod oil slinger (**Figure 65**) with the release lever mechanism (B, **Figure 64**) and install the side cover. After installing the side cover, the lever must face in the direction as shown in **Figure 66**.
5. Install the side cover-mounting Acorn nuts, or hex nuts, and washers. Then tighten to 13-16 ft.-lb. (18-22 N•m).
6. Install the kickstarter pedal and secure it with the bolt and lockwasher. Tighten the bolt securely.
7. Refill the transmission with the correct type and quantity of oil as described in Chapter Three.
8A. On FXWG models, perform the following:
   a. Install the master cylinder reservoir as described in Chapter Thirteen.
   b. Install the starter motor bracket.
   c. Install the rear brake line support clip.
8B. On FXSB models, perform the following:
   a. Remove the master cylinder and reservoir as described in Chapter Thirteen.
   b. Remove the rear brake pedal assembly as described in Chapter Thirteen.
9. Bleed the rear brake as described in Chapter Thirteen.
10. Install the exhaust pipes as described in Chapter Eight.
11. Connect the negative battery cable to the battery.

Disassembly

Refer to **Figure 62**.
1. Clamp the end of the kickstarter shaft in a vise with soft jaws.
2. Remove the screw and lockwasher securing the chrome cover. Remove the cover from the side cover.
3. Straighten the lockwasher and remove the kickstarter shaft nut (A, **Figure 67**).

4. Use a two-jaw claw puller (**Figure 68**) and remove the kickstarter gear assembly (B, **Figure 67**).
5. Support the side cover in a vise or on wooden blocks. Do not block the kickstarter shaft or spring. Use a plastic mallet and drive the kickstarter shaft and spring out of the side cover. Remove the thrust washer from the end of the shaft.
6. Remove the release lever as follows:
   a. Remove the nut and washer securing the release lever.
   b. Use a small two-jaw claw puller and remove the release lever.
   c. Remove the E-clip from the lower end of the shaft.
   d. Withdraw the shaft from the side cover.
   e. Remove the release finger and washer from the side cover.
7. Inspect all parts as described in this section.

Assembly

Refer to **Figure 62**.

1. Install the release lever as follows:
   a. Install the washer and release finger into the side cover.
   b. Insert the release lever shaft into the side cover and through the release finger and washer. Secure the shaft with a *new* E-clip.
   c. Install the release lever onto the shaft. Install the lockwasher and nut and tighten the nut until the release lever bottoms on the shaft.
2. Install a *new* O-ring to the kickstarter shaft.
3. Apply clean transmission oil to the kickstarter shaft and the O-ring.
4. Position the washer with the chamfered side facing the spring. Then install the washer onto the kickstarter shaft.
5. Install the kickstarter shaft and spring into the side cover.
6. Refer to **Figure 69** and install the kickstarter gear as follows:
   a. Turn the outer end of the kickstarter shaft so that the flat side is straight up (12 o'clock).
   b. Slide the kickstarter gear onto the shaft. When installed correctly, the kickstarter gear dowel pin is in the 7 o'clock position.
7. Hold the kickstarter shaft in a vise with soft jaws as during disassembly.
8. Engage the end of the kickstarter spring with the stud on the side cover.
9. Press the kickstarter gear onto the kickstarter shaft.
10. Install the kickstarter gear lockwasher and nut. Tighten the nut to 30-41 ft.-lb. (41-55 N•m). Bend the lockwasher tab against the side of the nut.

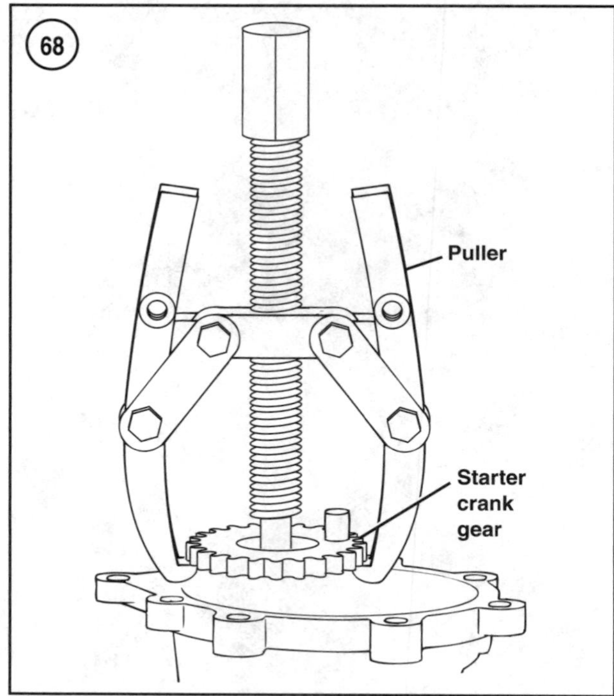

11. Install the chrome cover onto the side cover. Secure it with the screw and lockwasher and tighten the screw securely.

Inspection

1. Clean all components with solvent.
2. Remove any gasket residue from the side cover mating surface.
3. Check the threads in the transmission case for damage. Clean up with a tap or replace as necessary.
4. Check the kickstarter shaft surfaces for cracks, deep scoring, excessive wear or heat discoloration.
5. Check the kickstarter gear for worn, damaged or missing teeth.
6. If oil leaks out of the side cover along the kickstarter shaft, the oil seal requires replacement as described in this section.
7. Check the kickstarter spring. If it is damaged or broken, replace it by performing the following:
   a. Remove the kickstarter shaft as described in this chapter.
   b. Lift the outer spring hook off of the shaft spring stop.
   c. Tap the spring off the kickstarter shaft with a punch and hammer.

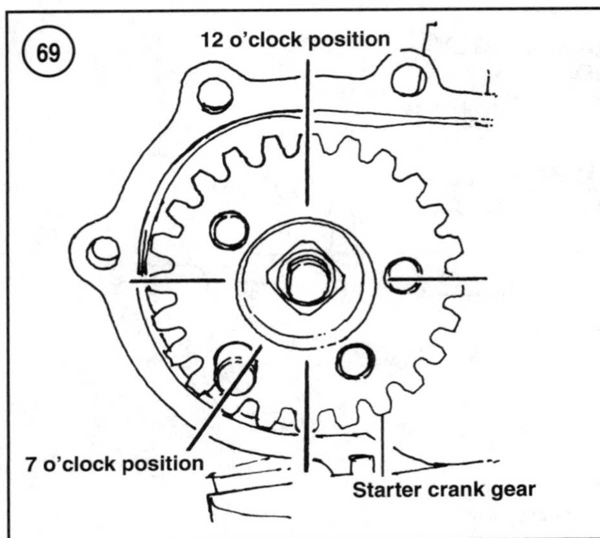

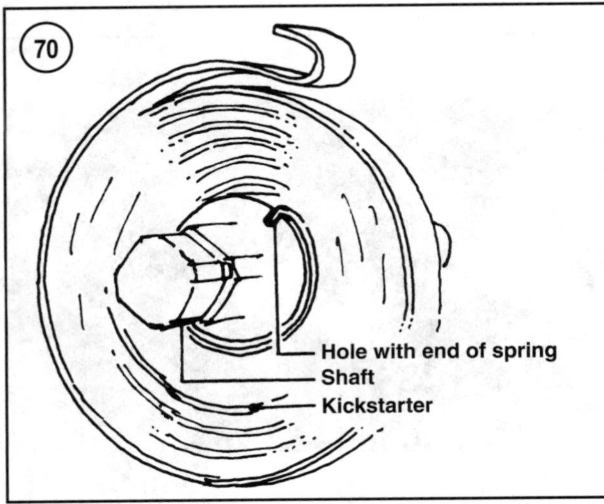

d. Install the new spring, so that the outer spring hook faces the left side when looking at the kickstarter shaft end (**Figure 70**).

Side Cover Bushing Replacement

1. Remove the front bushing with a blind bearing remover and slide hammer.
2. Clean out the bushing bore with solvent and dry with compressed air.
3. Check the bushing bore in the cover for burrs and remove if necessary.
4. Apply clean transmission oil to the bushing bore and to the exterior of the bushing.
5. Place the side cover on the press bed.
6. Position the bushing squarely over the side cover.
7. Press the bushing into the side cover until it is flush with the outer surface of the side cover.

STARTER CLUTCH

Removal/Installation

Refer to **Figure 71**.

1. Remove the kickstarter side cover as described in this chapter.
2. Remove the pushrod (**Figure 63**).
3. Shift the transmission into fourth gear to prevent the mainshaft from rotating.
4. Straighten the lockwasher tab and loosen the starter clutch nut (**Figure 72**). Remove the nut and lockwasher.
5. Install the Mainshaft Clutch Gear Puller (JIMS part No. 1700) (**Figure 73** and **Figure 74**) onto the starter clutch (**Figure 75**) and remove the starter clutch as follows:
   a. Position the gear puller halves with the ridge side going on first and place them onto the back side of the starter clutch. Slide the ring over both puller halves to hold them in place.
   b. Thread the center screw into the puller bar. Thread the hardened tip onto the end of the center screw and tighten securely.
   c. Place a washer onto the two bolts and position the bolts on the puller bar with the washers resting on the puller bar.
   d. Thread the two bolts onto the gear puller halves as far as they will go.
   e. Tighten the center screw onto the end of the transmission shaft. Center the hardened tip onto the end of the transmission shaft.
   f. Secure the puller bar, tighten the center screw, and withdraw the starter clutch from the shaft. If necessary, tap on the end of the center screw with a plastic hammer.
   g. Remove the special tools.
6. Remove the Woodruff key, the starter clutch gear and the spring.
7. Inspect the parts as described in this section.
8. Apply transmission oil to the mainshaft and to the inner surfaces of the starter clutch gear and starter clutch.
9. Install the spring.
10. Position the starter clutch gear with the ratchet side going on last and install the starter clutch gear onto the mainshaft.
11. Install the Woodruff key into the mainshaft slot.
12. Position the starter clutch with the ratchet side going on first and install the starter clutch onto the mainshaft and the Woodruff key.

6

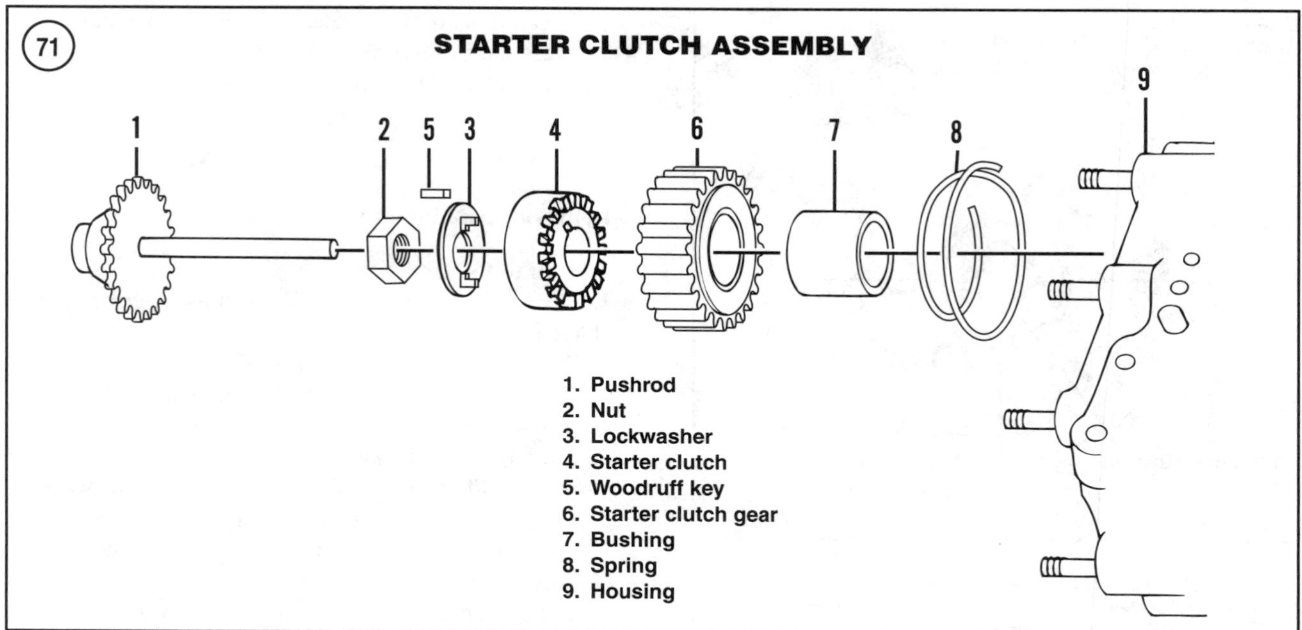

13. Check that the transmission is still in fourth gear to prevent the mainshaft from rotating.

14. Slowly tighten the nut and drive the starter clutch gear onto the mainshaft.

15. Install a *new* lockwasher and the nut (**Figure 72**) onto the mainshaft.

16. Tighten the starter clutch nut to 34-42 ft.-lb. (46-57 N•m). Bend the lockwasher tab up against the flat on the nut.

Inspection

1. Clean all parts in solvent and dry.

2. Inspect the starter clutch gear and starter clutch teeth. The teeth must be sharp and show no signs of cracking, scoring or excessive wear. Replace the starter clutch and starter gear as a set if the teeth are rounded or if the kickstarter has been slipping.

3. Check the starter clutch for cracks, deep scoring and excessive wear.

4. Reinstall the spring and starter gear onto the mainshaft.

5. Slide the gear on the mainshaft and check axial play. The gear should just be loose enough to slide under spring pressure. If the gear is loose, replace the bushing.

SIDE COVER (FXEF ELECTRIC START MODELS)

Removal

Refer to **Figure 76**.

1. Disconnect the negative battery cable from the battery.

2. Drain the transmission oil as described in Chapter Three.

3. Remove the exhaust system as described in Chapter Eight.

4. Remove the rear master cylinder reservoir as described in Chapter Thirteen.

5. Remove the starter bracket.

6. Remove the nuts and washers securing the side cover and remove the side cover and gasket.

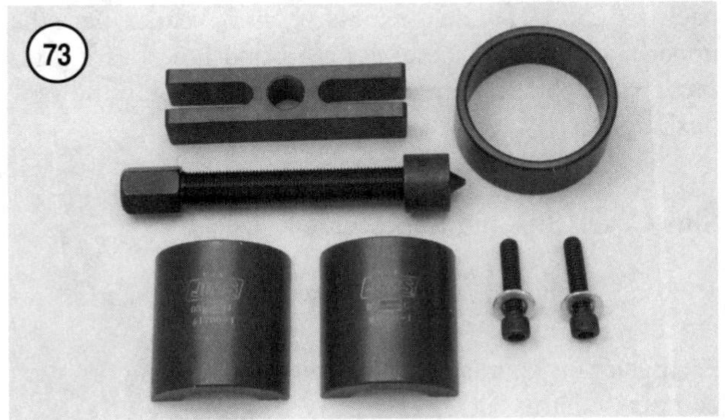

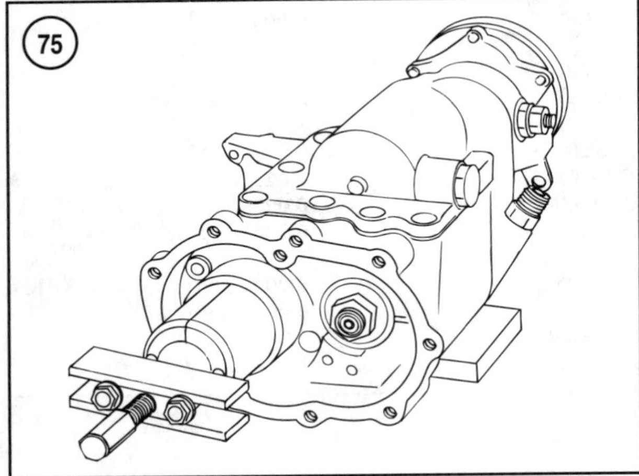

7. If necessary, disassemble the side cover as described in this section.

Installation

1. Install a *new* side cover gasket.
2. Pull the pushrod assembly partway out as shown in **Figure 63**.

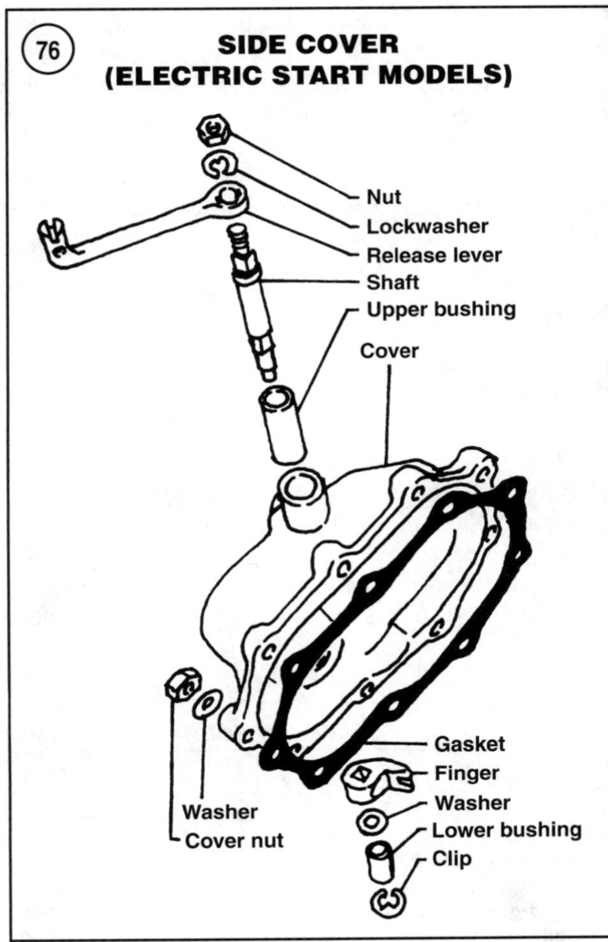

3. Position the release lever to the left of the cover as shown in A, **Figure 64**.
4. Align the pushrod oil slinger (**Figure 65**) with the release lever mechanism (B, **Figure 64**) and install the side cover. After installing the side cover, the lever must face in the direction shown in **Figure 66**.
5. Install the side cover mounting hex nuts and washers. Then tighten to 13-16 ft.-lb. (18-22 N•m).
6. Refill the transmission with the correct type and quantity of oil as described in Chapter Three.

Disassembly/Assembly

1. Remove the release lever nut and washer.
2. Pull the release lever off of the shaft with a universal claw puller.
3. Remove the E-clip. Then remove the shaft from the cover.
4. Remove the release finger and washer.

5. Install the washer and release finger into the side cover.
6. Insert the release lever shaft into the side cover and through the release finger and washer. Secure the shaft with a new snap ring.
7. Install the release lever. Then install the lockwasher and the nut. Tighten the nut until the release lever bottoms on the shaft.

Inspection

1. Clean all components thoroughly with solvent.
2. Remove any gasket residue from the side cover mating surface.
3. Check the threads in the transmission case for damage. Clean up with a tap or replace as necessary.
4. Visually check the shaft surfaces for cracks, deep scoring, excessive wear or heat discoloration.
5. Slide the shaft release lever shaft into the side cover. Check the shaft-to-bushing wear by moving the shaft back and forth. If there is excessive shaft wear, replace the upper and lower bushings with a blind hole bearing remover and slide hammer. Use a press to install the new bushing.

Side Cover Bushing Replacement

1. Remove the upper bushing with a blind bearing remover and slide hammer.
2. Clean out the bushing bore with solvent and dry with compressed air.
3. Check the bushing bore in the cover for burrs and remove if necessary.
4. Apply clean transmission oil to the bushing bore and to the exterior of the bushing.
5. Place the side cover on the press bed.
6. Position the bushing squarely over the side cover.
7. Press the bushing into the side cover until it is flush with the outer surface of the side cover.

Table 1 FOUR-SPEED TRANSMISSION SERVICE SPECIFICATIONS

Item	New in. (mm)	Service limit in. (mm)
Mainshaft main drive gear		
Bushing-to-shaft clearance	0.0018-0.0032 (0.046-081)	0.004 (0.10)
Mainshaft		
Third gear end play	0.005-0.021 (0.13-0.53)	0.021 (0.53)
Shift fork clutch gear spacing	0.100-0.110 (2.54-2.79)	0.110 (2.79)
Countershaft		
Gear end play	0.004-0.012 (0.10-0.30)	0.015 (0.38)
Second gear end play	0.003-0.017 (0.076-0.43)	0.020 (0.51)
Bushing-to-shaft (loose)	0.000-0.0015 (0.00-0.038)	0.002 (0.051)
Bushing in gear (loose)	0.0005-0.0025 (0.013-0.063)	0.002 (0.051)
First gear		
Bushing-to-shaft (loose)	0.000-0.0015 (0.00-0.038)	0.002 (0.051)
Bushing in gear (loose)	0.0005-0.0025 (0.013-0.063)	0.002 (0.051)
Shifter fork clutch gear spacing	0.080-0.090 (2.03-2.286)	0.090 (2.286)
Gear backlash	0.003-0.006 (0.076-0.152)	0.010 (0.254)

Table 2 FOUR-SPEED TRANSMISSION TORQUE SPECIFICATIONS

Item	ft.-lb.	in.-lb.	N•m
Clutch nut	34-42	–	46-57
Drain screw	12-15	–	16-20
Drive sprocket			
Nut	80-90	–	108-122
Nut setscrew	–	50-60	5.6-6.7
Kickstarter			
Gear nut	30-41	–	41-55

(continued)

Table 2 FOUR-SPEED TRANSMISSION TORQUE SPECIFICATIONS (continued)

Item	ft.-lb.	in.-lb.	N•m
Kickstarter (continued)			
Side cover nuts	13-16	–	18-22
Mainshaft ball bearing nut	50-60	–	67-81
Neutral switch	–	62-124	7-14
Retaining plate screws	–	84-108	9.5-12.2
Shifter cover bolts	13-16	–	18-22
Shift clutch nut*	34-42	–	46-57
Shift fork nut	–	124-150	14-17
Side cover (FXEF electric start)	13-16	–	18-22
Sprocket nut	80-90	–	108-122
Sprocket nut setscrew	–	50-60	5.6-6.8
Starter clutch nut	34-42	–	46-57
Starter crankcase nut	18-22	–	24-30
Transmission end cover stud nut	13-16	–	18-22
Transmission mounting plate bolt	30-33	–	41-45
Transmission-to-frame bolts	21-27	–	28-37
Transmission-to-mounting plate	21-27	–	28-37
Transmission top cover bolts	13-16	–	18-22

*Kickstarter-equipped models only.

CHAPTER SEVEN

FIVE-SPEED TRANSMISSION

The five-speed transmission and shifter assembly is mounted in a separate housing and can be completely disassembled and serviced without having to disassemble the engine or remove the transmission housing.

Tables 1-4 are at the end of the chapter.

SPECIAL TOOLS

The five-speed transmission requires a number of special tools. These tools and the part numbers are listed with the individual procedures. For a complete list of the special tools mentioned in this manual, refer to **Table 12** in Chapter One. The tools used in this chapter are either Harley-Davidson or JIMS special tools. JIMS special tools are available through many aftermarket motorcycle suppliers.

When purchasing special tools, make sure to specify that the tools required are for the FXR, FLH and FLT series models from 1984-1999. Many of the tools are specific to this transmission. Tools for other transmissions and years might be slightly different.

PRODUCTION GEARS (1994-1998 FLH AND FLT MODELS)

From 1994-1998, there are two different five-speed transmission assemblies with different gear configurations depending on in which country the motorcycle is sold.

The majority of the motorcycles are equipped with the standard High Contact Ratio (HCR) transmission. The gears do not have a radius groove.

The other transmission has unique gears with a 0.03 in. (0.76 mm) radius groove machined in the center of each gear tooth on the second through fifth gears on both main and countershafts.

The two different transmissions are identified by the model year serial number located on the right side of the transmission case behind the shifter or top cover. The first prefix 9 digit indicates the transmission type. The HRC transmission is identified with a double 99 in the serial number, similar to No. 995172001, and the other transmission is identified with a single 9, similar to No. 95172001.

CAUTION
Do not mix HCR gears with the gears from the other transmission. Meshing both types of gears will cause transmission damage.

NOTE
*On 1994 models, the standard transmission is identified as the Harley-Davidson International (HDI) and is equipped on models sold in the United States, Canada and Japan. On these models, the first and third gear ratios are unique as listed in **Table 1**.*

SHIFTER ASSEMBLY

The shifter assembly (**Figure 1**) consists of the external shift linkage and internal shift cam and shift arm components. The internal components can be serviced with the transmission case installed in the frame by removing the top cover.

If a shift problem is encountered, refer to the troubleshooting procedures in Chapter Two and eliminate all clutch and shifter mechanism possibilities *before* considering transmission repairs. Improper clutch adjustment (Chapter Three) is often a cause of poor shifting.

The shift linkage assembly connects the transmission shift rod lever to the foot-operated shift levers. The shift linkage does not require adjustment unless it is replaced or the transmission gears do not engage properly.

Shift Linkage Adjustment (FXR Series Models)

NOTE
*The ball joint rod at one end (**Figure 2**) has left-hand threads. When the ball joint rod is turned, it will either shorten or lengthen the shifter pedal position.*

1. Hold the ball joint flat with a wrench and loosen the locknuts (**Figure 2**).
2. Turn the ball joint until the gears engage properly.
3. Tighten both locknuts to 20-24 ft.-lb. (28-33 N•m).

Shift Linkage Adjustment (FLH and FLT Series Models)

1. Disconnect one end of the shifter rod (**Figure 3**).
2. Loosen the locknuts on the end of the shifter rod disconnected in Step 1. Then turn the shifter rod until the gears engage properly.
3. Reconnect the shifter rod and tighten the locknuts to 20-24 ft.-lb. (28-33 N•m).

CAUTION
The foot shifter pedal must not contact the footboard when shifting the transmission. Contact would cause incomplete gear engagement or transmission damage. Maintain a minimum clearance of 3/8 in. (9.5 mm) between the shifter pedal and the floorboard.

Gear Engagement Check and Adjustment

When the transmission gears do not engage properly, check and adjust gear engagement as follows:

1. Make sure the clutch is operating properly. Refer to *Clutch Adjustment* in Chapter Three. If the clutch is operating correctly, continue to Step 2.
2. Disconnect the negative battery cable from the battery.
3. Shift the transmission into third gear. Make sure third gear is fully engaged.
4. Remove the transmission top cover as described in this section.
5. Move the shifter lever (**Figure 4**) to check for free play and spring pressure in both directions.
6. The gear engagement is correct if the spring pressure is the same in both directions and there is approximately 0.010 in. (0.25 mm) clearance between the shifter pawl arms and the shift cam pins as shown in **Figure 5**. If necessary, adjust the gear engagement as described in Step 7.
7. To adjust the gear engagement, perform the following:
   a. Loosen the adjusting screw locknut (**Figure 6**) and turn the screw in quarter-turn increments or less (clockwise or counterclockwise) until the shifter lever travel spring pressure is equal on both sides and the 0.010 in. (0.25 mm) clearance is maintained.
   b. Secure the adjusting screw to prevent it from turning and securely tighten the locknut.
   c. Check the engagement and adjustment if necessary.
8. Connect the negative battery cable.

TRANSMISSION SHIFT COVER

Removal/Installation

1. Remove the battery as described in Chapter Nine.
2. Remove the exhaust system as described in Chapter Eight.
3. Drain the engine oil as described in Chapter Three.
4. Remove the engine oil tank as described in Chapter Four.
5. Disconnect the vent hose from the fitting on the top cover.
6. On 1984-1986 models, perform the following:

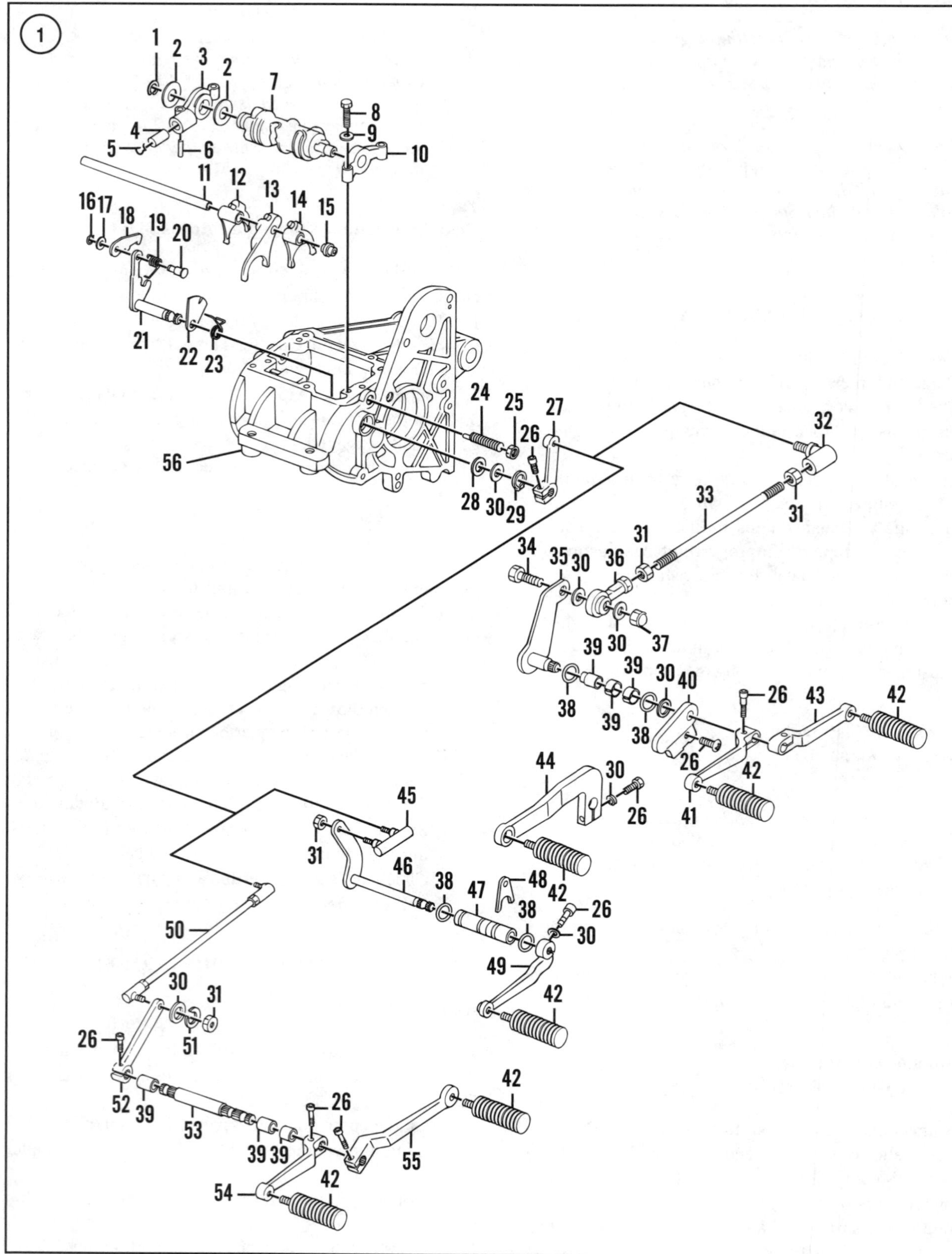
1
1
2
3
2
7
8
9
10
4
5
6
11
12
13
14
15
16
17
18
19
20
21
22
23
24
25
27
26
56
28
30
29
32
33
31
31
34
35
30
36
37
30
39
39
30
40
38
39
38
26
43
42
26
42
41
44
30
26
45
31
46
38
47
48
42
38
26
30
49
42
50
30
31
26
51
52
39
53
39
39
26
42
55
54
42

SHIFT MECHANISM

1. Snap ring
2. Thrust washer
3. Support (right)
4. Cam follower
5. Spring
6. Roll pin
7. Shift cam
8. Bolt
9. Washer
10. Support (left)
11. Shift fork shaft
12. Shift fork No. 3
13. Shift fork No. 2
14. Shift fork No. 1
15. Setscrew
16. Snap ring
17. Seal
18. Shifter cam pawl
19. Spring
20. Pivot pin
21. Shift shaft lever
22. Centering plate
23. Spring
24. Adjusting screw
25. Locknut
26. Screw
27. Shift rod lever
28. Oil seal
29. Snap ring
30. Washer
31. Nut
32. Ball joint
33. Shift rod
34. Bolt
35. Shift lever
36. End piece
37. Acorn nut
38. O-ring
39. Bushing
40. Cover
41. Shift lever
42. Rubber peg
43. Shift lever
44. Shift lever
45. Ball joint
46. Shift lever
47. Sleeve
48. Keeper
49. Shift lever
50. Shift rod
51. Lockwasher
52. Lever
53. Shaft
54. Shift lever
55. Shift lever
56. Transmission housing

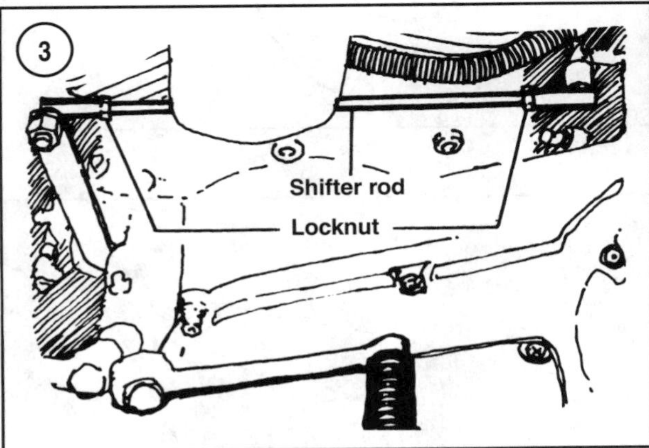

7

a. Disconnect the clutch cable from the release lever (A, **Figure 7**).

b. Remove the bolts and remove the cable mounting bracket (B, **Figure 7**) from the top cover. Move the cable and bracket out of the way.

7. Disconnect the electrical wire from the neutral switch (**Figure 8**).

8. Remove the bolts securing the transmission top cover (**Figure 9**). Remove the cover and gasket.

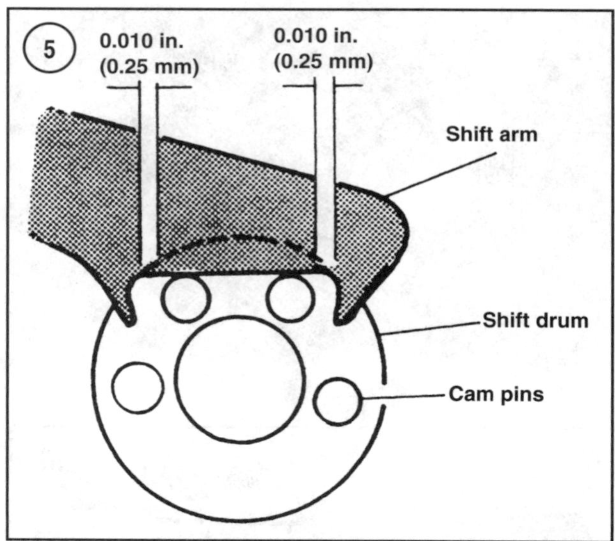

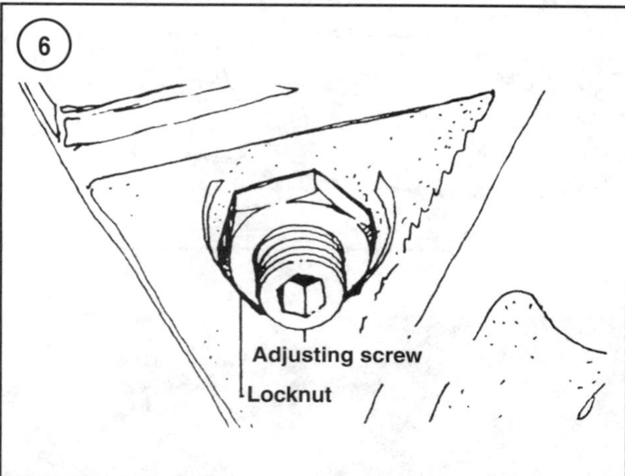

9. Remove the gasket residue from the transmission cover and transmission case gasket surfaces.

10. Install a *new* gasket onto the transmission case.

11. Install the transmission top cover, bolts and washers. Tighten the bolts in a crisscross pattern to 80-106 in.-lb. (9-12 N•m).

12. Reconnect the vent hose to the fitting and install a *new* hose clamp.

13. Connect the wire to the neutral indicator switch.

14. Install the oil tank as described in Chapter Four.

15. Install the exhaust system as described in Chapter Eight.

16. Install the battery as described in Chapter Nine.

17. Refill the engine oil as described in Chapter Three.

SHIFT CAM

The shift cam assembly (**Figure 10**) can be serviced with the transmission case installed in the frame by removing the battery, oil tank and transmission top cover.

Shift Cam Design Change

On 1984-early 1991 models, a variable thickness thrust washer sets the shifter cam position in the transmission in the case. Late 1991 and later models do not use this

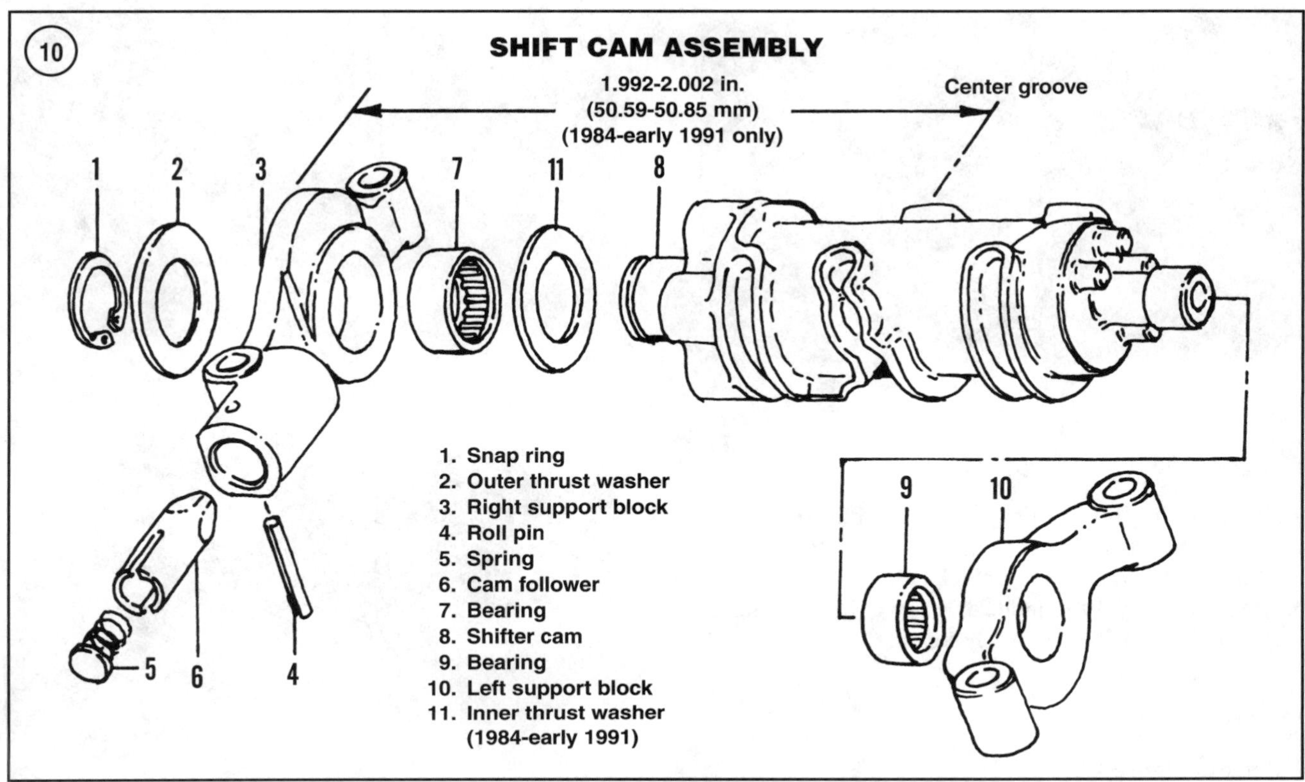

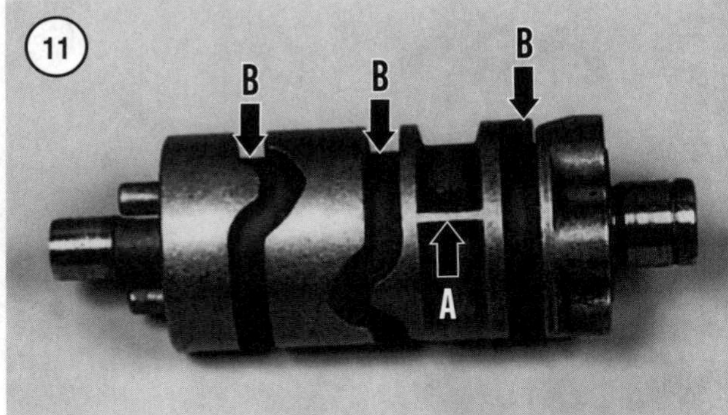

washer. Instead, the cam is machined so that the shift cam position is set when it is installed in the transmission case. Early- and late-style shifter cams are identified by the neutral indicator actuator (A, **Figure 11**) mounted on the shifter cam. A cast neutral indicator actuator is used on early-style shifter cams. Late-style shifter cams use a pressed-in pin. In addition, on models with the late-style shifter cam, two locating dowel pins are used to locate the left support block (10, **Figure 10**) to the transmission case.

Removal

1. Remove the transmission top cover as described in this section.
2. Remove the bolts securing the shift cam (**Figure 12**) and lift the shift cam assembly (**Figure 13**) out of the transmission.
3. Slide the left support block (**Figure 14**) off the shift cam. On late 1991-1998 models, remove the two dowel pins.

NOTE
On 1984-1991 models, label all of the thrust washers removed in the following steps.

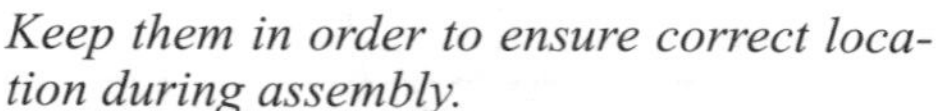

Keep them in order to ensure correct location during assembly.

4. Remove the shift cam snap ring (A, **Figure 15**) and outer thrust washer (B).
5. Remove the right support block (**Figure 16**).
6. On 1984-early 1991 models, remove the inner thrust washer (**Figure 17**) from the shift cam.

Installation

Refer to **Figure 10**.

1. Coat all bearing and sliding surfaces with assembly oil.
2. On 1984-early 1991 models, install the inner thrust washer (**Figure 17**). On all models, install the right support block (**Figure 16**) on the shifter cam.
3. On 1984-early 1991 models, check the shift drum position as follows:
   a. Install the shifter drum/right support block onto the transmission case. Engage the right support block with its dowel pins.
   b. Turn the shifter drum to its neutral position. Use the neutral indicator ramp mounted on the shift drum as a reference point (A, **Figure 11**).
   c. Push the shifter drum so that it fits snugly against the right support block thrust washer.
   d. Measure from the outer bearing support machined surface to the nearest edge of the center shifter cam groove as shown in **Figure 18**. The correct distance is 1.992-2.002 in. (50.59-50.85 mm).
   e. If the distance is incorrect, replace the inner thrust washer (11, **Figure 10**) with a thrust washer of a different thickness. Thrust washers are available from a Harley-Davidson dealership.
   f. Remove the shifter drum/right support block from the transmission case.
4. Install the outer thrust washer (B, **Figure 15**) and *new* snap ring (A). Make sure the snap ring is correctly seated in the groove.

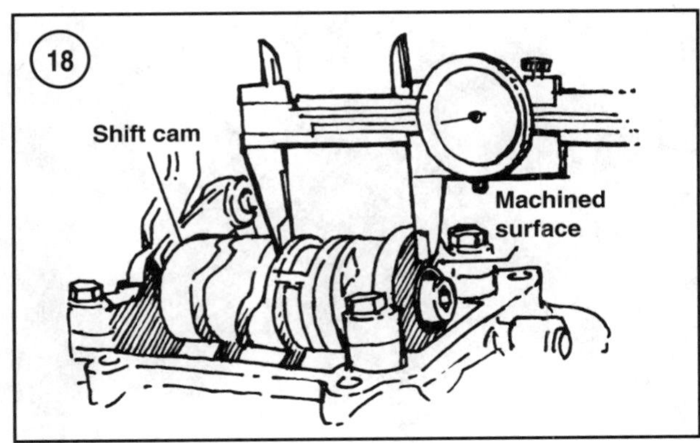

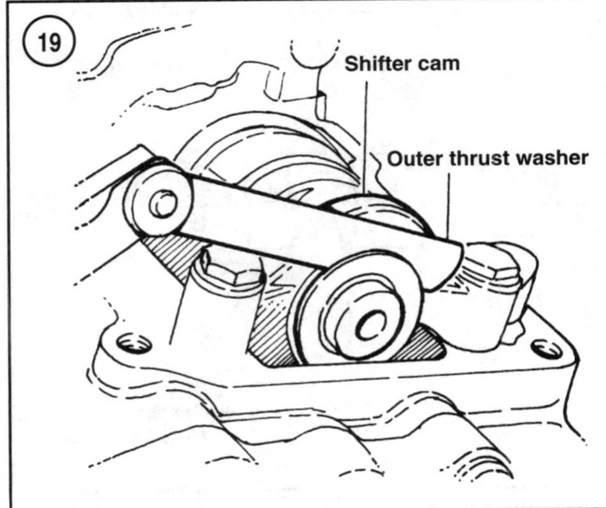

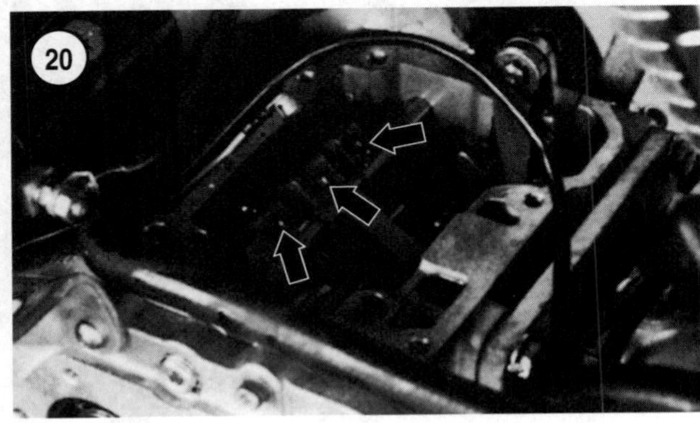

NOTE
*After installing the snap ring, make sure the outer thrust washer (2, **Figure 10**) can be rotated by hand.*

5. Measure shifter cam end play as follows:

a. Install the shifter drum/right support block onto the transmission case. Engage the right support block with its dowel pins.
b. Measure end play between the outer thrust washer and shifter cam (**Figure 19**). Correct end play measurement is 0.001-0.004 in. (0.025-0.010 mm).
c. If the distance is incorrect, replace the outer thrust washer (2, **Figure 10**) with a thrust washer with a different thickness. Thrust washers are available from a Harley-Davidson dealership.

CAUTION
*On 1984-early 1991 models, do not correct shifter cam end play by changing the inner thrust washer (11, **Figure 10**) clearance. This washer is used to set shift cam position only. Late 1991-1998 models do not use the inner thrust washer.*

NOTE
Inner and outer thrust washers are available from a Harley-Davidson dealership in the following thicknesses: 0.017 in. (0.43 mm), 0.020 in. (0.51 mm), 0.022 in. (0.56 mm), 0.025 in. (0.63 mm), 0.028 in. (0.71 mm), 0.031 in. (0.79 mm), 0.035 in. (0.89 mm) and 0.039 in. (0.99 mm).

d. Remove the shifter drum/right support block from the transmission case.

6. Position the left support block (**Figure 14**) onto the shifter cam with the numbers facing down toward the transmission.
7. Align the shift fork pins (**Figure 20**) with the shifter cam slots. Then install the shifter cam into position (**Figure 13**). On 1984-early 1991 models, engage the transmission case dowel pins with the right support block mounting holes. On late 1991-1998 models, engage the left and right support block mounting holes with the transmission case dowel pins.
8. Engage the shift lever with the shifter cam (**Figure 21**).
9. Install the shifter cam mounting bolts (**Figure 12**). Tighten bolts in a crisscross pattern to 84-108 in.-lb. (9-12 N•m).

CAUTION
On all models, overtightening the shifter cam mounting bolts can distort the cam follower and cause shifting problems.

NOTE
On 1984-early 1991 models, check that the left support block is not cocked or binding on its bearing.

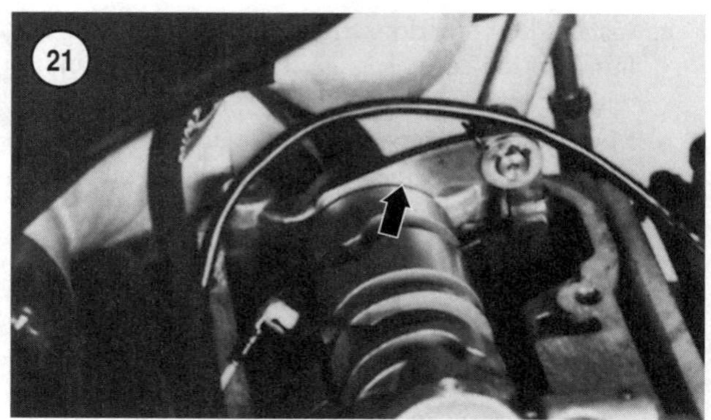

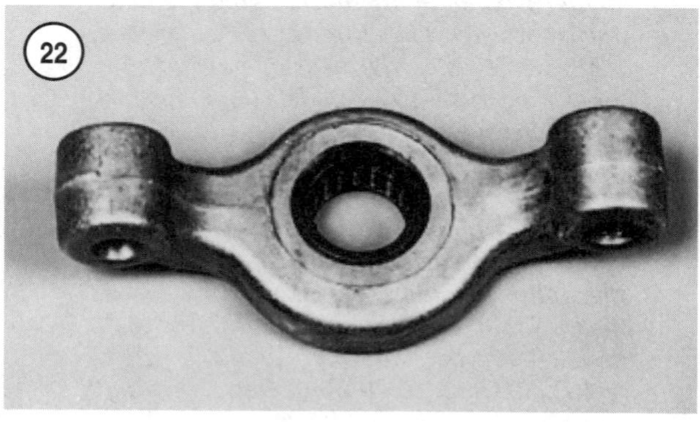

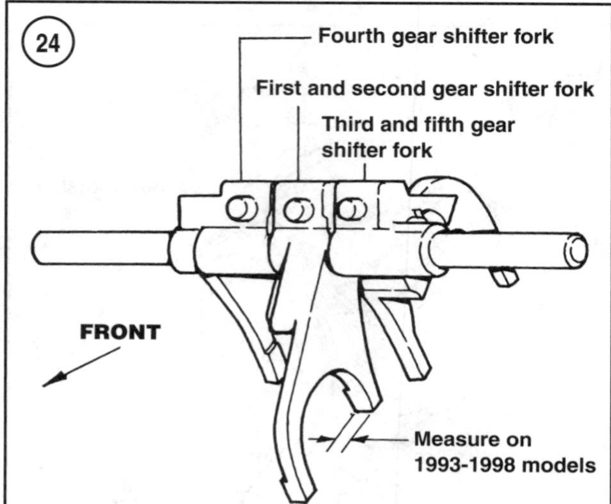

10. Perform the *Gear Engagement Check/Adjustment* procedure in this section.
11. Install the top cover as described in this section.

Inspection

1. Clean all parts, except the support block bearings, in solvent and dry.
2. Check the grooves in the shift cam (B, **Figure 11**) for wear or roughness. If any of the groove profiles have excessive wear or damage, replace the shift cam.
3. Check the support block bearings for excessive wear, cracks or damage . See **Figure 22** and **Figure 23**. If necessary, refer to *Basic Service Methods* in Chapter One to replace the bearings.
4. Check the support blocks for wear, cracks or other damage. Replace the support blocks if necessary.

SHIFT FORKS

The shift forks can be serviced with the transmission case installed in the frame by removing the battery, oil tank and transmission top cover.

Removal

Refer to **Figure 24**.

1. Remove the transmission top cover as described in this section.
2. Remove the shift cam as described in this chapter.

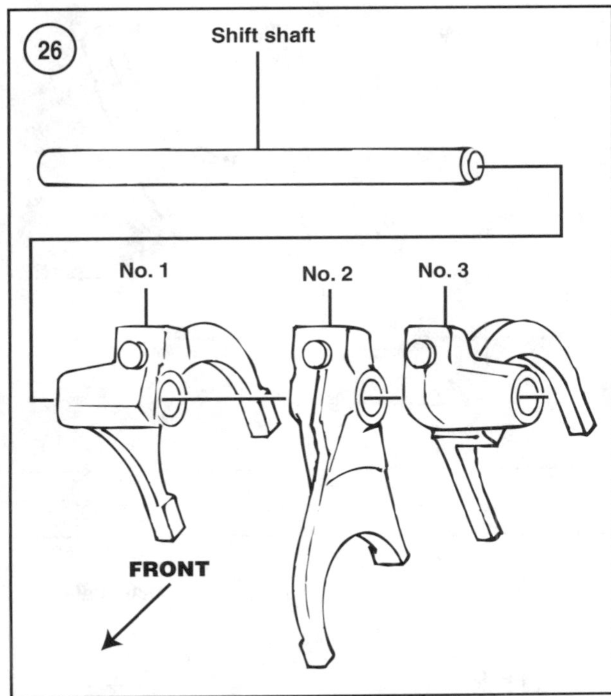

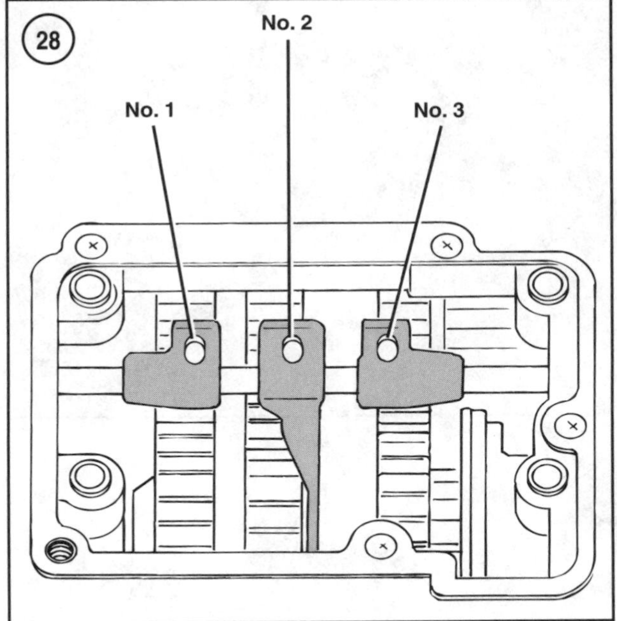

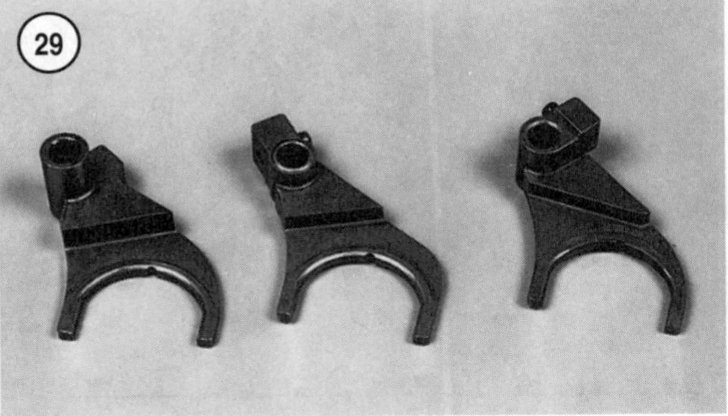

3. Remove the plug (**Figure 25**) from the transmission side door.

NOTE
*Use a waterproof felt-tip pen or scribe to mark the installed position of each shift fork in the transmission (**Figure 26**). All three shift forks are unique and must be reinstalled in the correct positions. The No. 1 shift fork is on the right side, No. 2 is in the middle, and No. 3 is on the left side.*

4. Slide the shift shaft (**Figure 27**) out of the transmission case and remove the shift forks (**Figure 28**) from the transmission.

Inspection

1. Inspect each shift fork (**Figure 29**) for excessive wear or damage. Replace worn or damaged shift forks as required.
2. On 1993-1998 models, measure the thickness of each shift fork finger (A, **Figure 30**) where it contacts the sliding gear groove (**Figure 31**). Replace any shift fork with a finger thickness worn to the specification in **Table 2**.
3. Check the shift forks for arc-shaped wear or burn marks (B, **Figure 30**). Replace damaged shift forks.
4. Roll the shift fork shaft on a flat surface and check for bends. Replace the shaft if it is bent.
5. Install each shift fork on the shift shaft. The shift forks must slide smoothly with no binding or roughness (**Figure 32**).

7

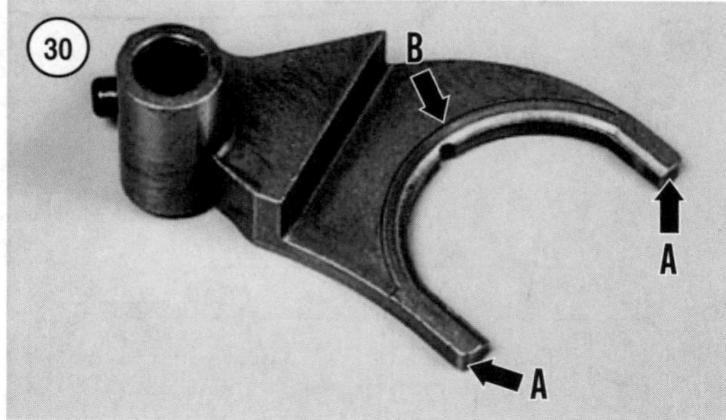

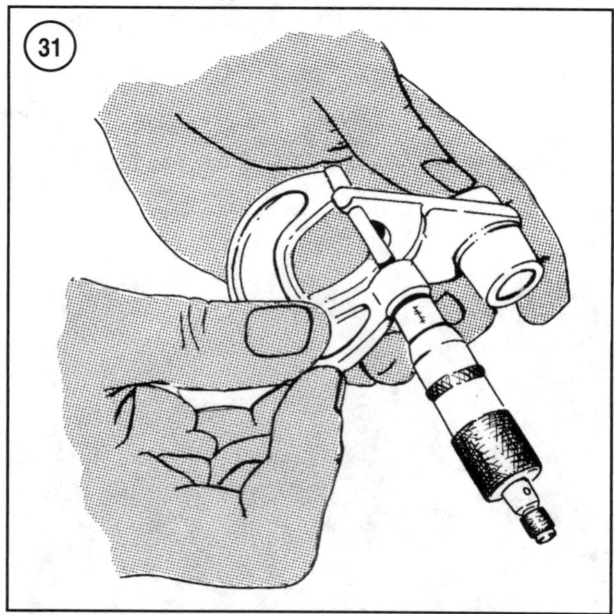

Assembly

Refer to **Figure 33** to identify the transmission gears.

1. Coat all bearing and sliding surfaces with assembly oil.
2. To install the shift forks and shaft (**Figure 20**), perform the following:
   a. Insert the No. 1 shift fork into the mainshaft first gear groove.
   b. Install the No. 2 shift fork into the countershaft third gear groove.
   c. Install the No. 3 shift fork into the mainshaft second gear groove.
3. Insert the shift shaft through the transmission side door (**Figure 27**), through all three shift forks and into the transmission case on the other side. Push the shift shaft in until it bottoms.

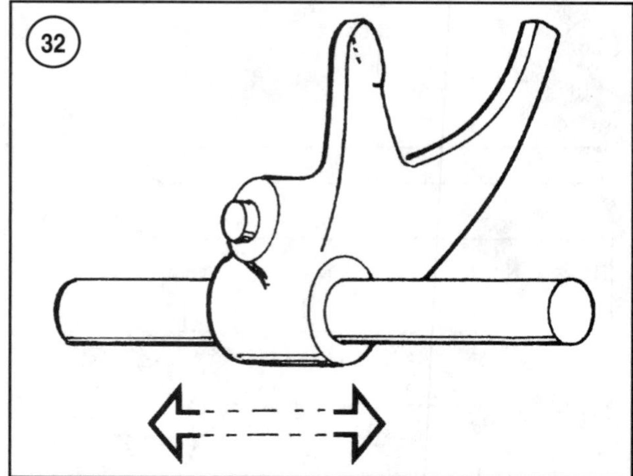

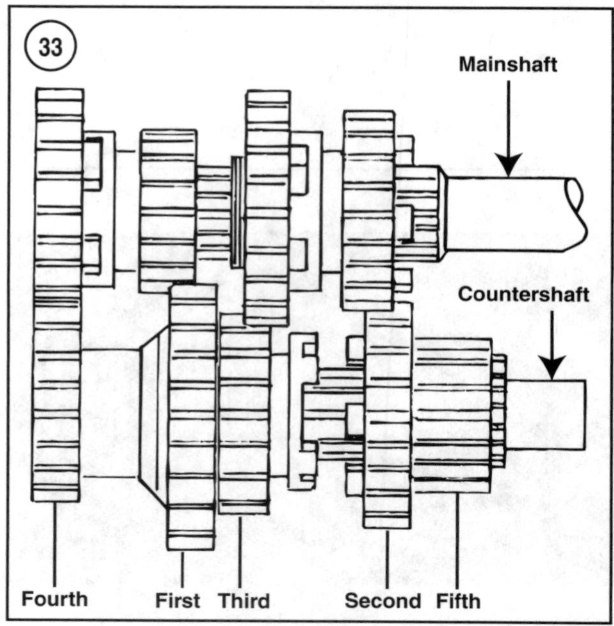

4. Apply a light coat of Loctite Pipe Sealant with Teflon to the shift shaft plug threads. Install the plug (**Figure 25**) into the side door and tighten securely.
5. Check that forks move smoothly when the gear position is changed by hand.
6. Install the shift cam as described in this chapter.

TRANSMISSION SIDE DOOR AND TRANSMISSION SHAFT ASSEMBLIES

The transmission side door and transmission shaft assemblies can be serviced with the transmission case installed in the frame.

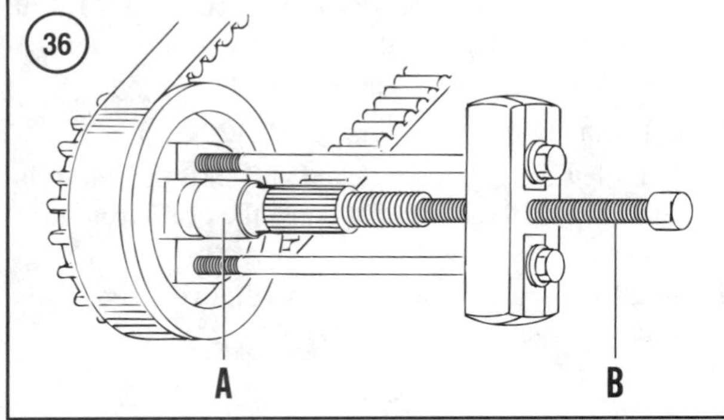

Removal

1. Remove the exhaust system as described in Chapter Eight.
2. Drain the transmission oil as described in Chapter Three.
3. Remove the primary chaincase cover as described in Chapter Five.
4. Remove the clutch release arm (**Figure 34**).
5A. On 1984-1986 models, remove the transmission clutch release cover (**Figure 35**).
5B. On 1987-1998 models, remove the transmission clutch release cover as described in this chapter.
6. Remove the clutch assembly as described in Chapter Five.
7. Remove the primary chaincase housing as described in Chapter Five
8. Remove the shift forks as described in this chapter.
9. Remove the bearing inner race from the mainshaft as follows:
   a. Attach the mainshaft bearing race puller and installation tool (JIMS part No. 34902-84) to the inner bearing race following the manufacturer's instructions.
   b. Tighten the puller bolt and withdraw the inner race from the mainshaft (**Figure 36**).

10A. On 1986-early 1991 models, remove the roller (**Figure 37**) and clutch pushrod (**Figure 38**).
10B. On late 1991-1998 models, remove the oil slinger and clutch pushrod.
11. Turn the transmission by hand and shift the transmission into gear to keep the gears from rotating.

NOTE
*The mainshaft and countershaft nuts have left-hand threads. Turn the nuts **clockwise** to loosen them.*

12. Loosen the countershaft and mainshaft locknuts and spacers (**Figure 39**). Do not remove at this time.

7

13. Remove the drive sprocket as described under *Transmission Drive Sprocket* in this chapter.
14. Remove the bolts securing the transmission side door (**Figure 40**) to the transmission case.

CAUTION
When removing the transmission side door in Step 14, do not tap the transmission shaft from the opposite side. This will damage the side door bearings.

15. Tap the transmission side door to loosen its seal with the transmission case.

NOTE
If the transmission side door will not remove easily from the transmission case, perform Step 16B.

16A. Slowly withdraw the transmission side door and the transmission gear assemblies from the transmission case (**Figure 41**).
16B. To assist in removing the transmission door and the gear assemblies, perform the following:
  a. Following the manufacturer's instructions, install the special five-speed door puller tool (JIMS part No. 2283) onto the door.
  b. Alternating from side to side, tighten the outside screws one-half turn at a time until the door releases from the transmission case. Remove the special tool.
  c. Slowly withdraw the transmission side door and the transmission gear assemblies from the transmission case (**Figure 41**).
17. Remove the transmission side door gasket. Do not lose the locating pins.
18. If necessary, service the side door and transmission assembly as described in this chapter.
19. If necessary, remove the main drive gear as described in this chapter.

Installation

1. If the main drive gear was removed, install it as described in this chapter.
2. Remove all gasket residue from the side door and transmission case mating surfaces.
3. Install a *new* gasket onto the transmission case. If the locating pins were removed, install them.
4. Install the side door and transmission assembly into the transmission case. Make sure the side door fits flush against the transmission case.

5. Install the transmission side door 5/16-in. and 1/4-in. bolts finger-tight. Tighten the bolts to the following:
  a. 5/16-in. bolts: 13-16 ft.-lb. (18-22 N•m).
  b. 1/4-in. bolts: 80-106 in.-lb. (10-12 N•m).
6. Turn the transmission by hand and shift the transmission into two different gears to keep the gears from turning.
7. Install the spacers and locknuts (**Figure 39**) onto the transmission shafts.

NOTE
*The mainshaft and countershaft nut have left-hand threads. Turn the nuts **counterclockwise** to tighten them.*

8. Tighten the countershaft and mainshaft locknuts to the following:
  a. 1984-1995 models: 27-33 ft.-lb. (37-45 N•m).
  b. 1996-1998 models: 45-55 ft.-lb. (61-75 N•m).

CAUTION
Wrap the mainshaft clutch hub splines on 1990 and later models with tape to prevent the splines from damaging the inner primary housing oil seal.

9. Install the bearing inner race onto the mainshaft as follows:
   a. Measure the length of the bearing inner race. On early 1985 models, the race is 0.8125-0.8975 in. (20.637-22.796 mm) long. On late 1985 and later models, the race is 0.9950-1.000 in. (25.273-25.4 mm) long. Length of race will determine its final installation position.
   b. Apply clean oil to the transmission shaft bearing surface, shaft threads and inner surface of the inner race.
   c. Position the bearing with the chamfered edge going on first, toward the transmission case, and slide the bearing inner race on the mainshaft.
   d. Use the same special tool setup used for bearing inner race removal.
   e. Install the extension shaft onto the mainshaft.
   f. Place the pusher tube, two flat washers and nut over the extension shaft.
   g. Place a wrench on the end of the sleeve pilot screw flats.

CAUTION
Install the inner bearing race to the dimension in substeps h and i. This dimension aligns the race with the bearing outer race installed in the primary chaincase. Installing the wrong race or installing it incorrectly will damage the bearing and race assembly.

NOTE
The mainshaft has left-hand threads. Tighten the large nut ***counterclockwise*** *to tighten it in substeps h and i.*

   h. On early 1985 models (with the 0.8125-0.8975 in. [20.637-22.796 mm] long race), tighten the large nut until the inside edge of the bearing inner race is spaced away from the main drive gear by 0.200 in. (5.08 mm).
   i. On late 1985 and later models (with the 0.9950-1.000 in. [25.273-25.4 mm] long race), tighten the large nut until the inside edge of the bearing inner race is spaced away from the main drive gear by 0.100 in. (2.54 mm).
   j. Remove the special tools.

10A. On 1986-early 1991 models, install the clutch pushrod (**Figure 38**) and roller (**Figure 37**).

10B. On late 1991-1998 models, install the oil slinger and clutch pushrod.

11. Install the shift forks as described in this chapter.

12. Install the primary chaincase housing as described in Chapter Five.

13A. On 1986 models, install the transmission clutch release cover (**Figure 35**).

13B. On 1987-1998 models, install the transmission clutch release cover as described in this chapter.

14. Install the primary chaincase cover as described in Chapter Five.

15. Install the drain plug and refill the transmission oil as described in Chapter Three.

16. Install the exhaust system as described in Chapter Eight.

17. Test-ride the motorcycle slowly and check for proper transmission operation.

7

TRANSMISSION SHAFTS

This section describes service to the side door and both transmission shaft assemblies.

Refer to **Figure 42** and **Figure 43**.

Shaft Disassembly

The transmission shaft assemblies must be partially disassembled prior to removing both shafts from the side door. Do not try to remove the shafts with all of the gears in place.

The snap rings are difficult to loosen and remove even with high-quality snap ring pliers. Heavy-duty retaining ring pliers (JIMS part No. 1133) or an equivalent are recommended for this procedure.

Store all of the transmission gears, snap rings, washers and split bearings in the order of removal.

1. Remove the transmission side door and transmission shaft assemblies as described in this chapter.
2. Protect the splines and threads on the mainshaft with tape or a plastic sleeve (**Figure 44**).
3. Remove the mainshaft second gear (**Figure 45**).

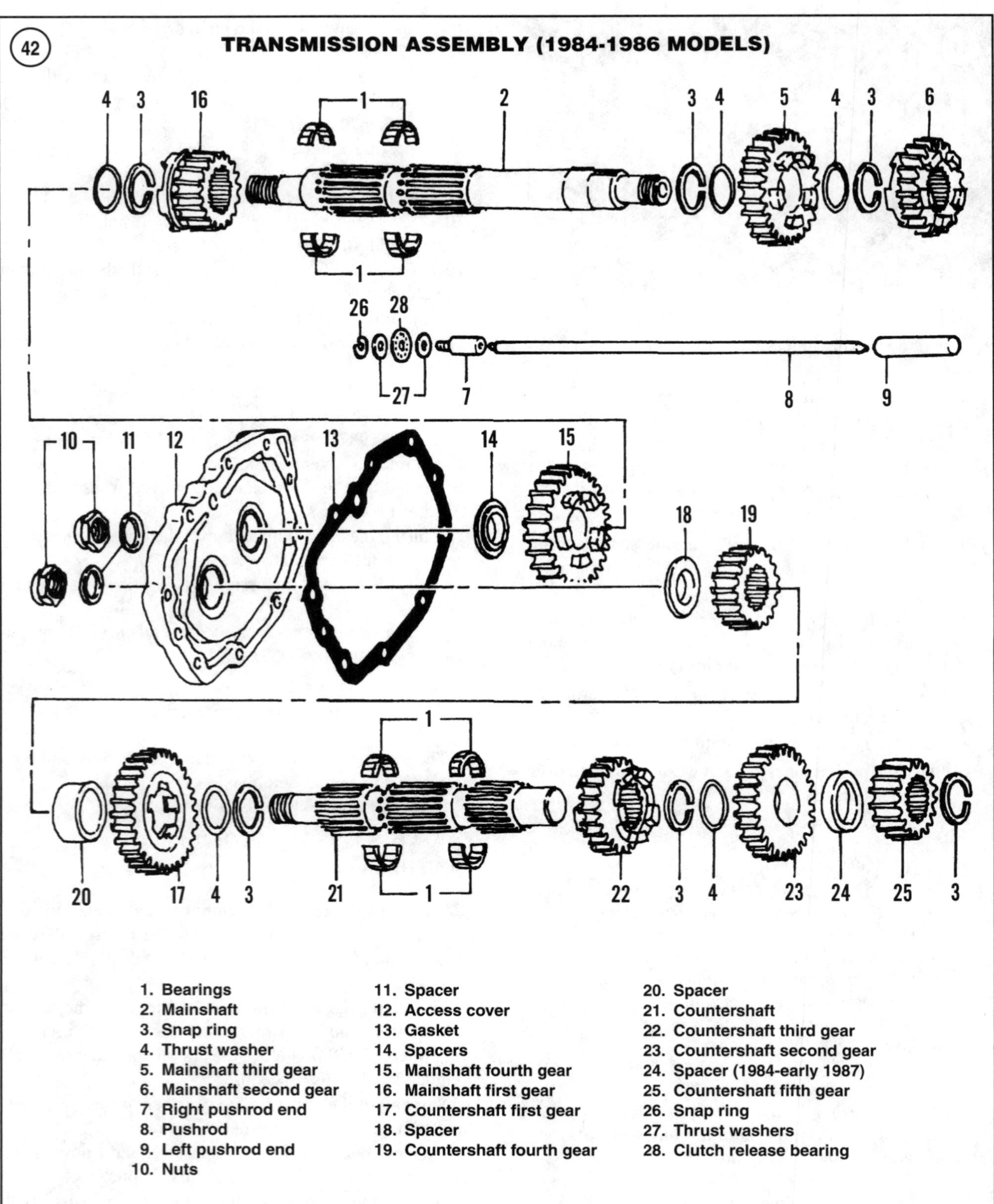

TRANSMISSION ASSEMBLY (1984-1986 MODELS)

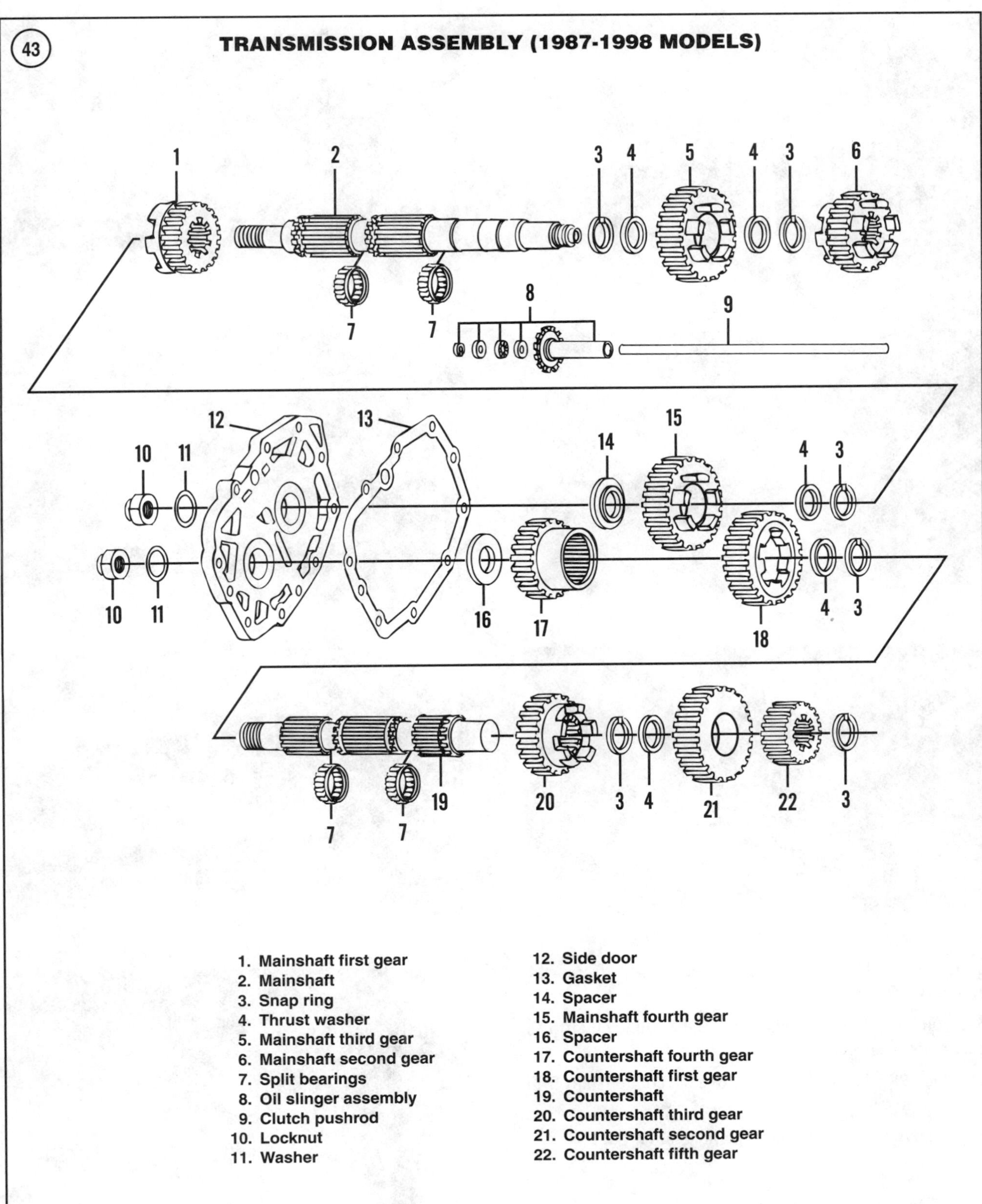

TRANSMISSION ASSEMBLY (1987-1998 MODELS)

1. Mainshaft first gear
2. Mainshaft
3. Snap ring
4. Thrust washer
5. Mainshaft third gear
6. Mainshaft second gear
7. Split bearings
8. Oil slinger assembly
9. Clutch pushrod
10. Locknut
11. Washer
12. Side door
13. Gasket
14. Spacer
15. Mainshaft fourth gear
16. Spacer
17. Countershaft fourth gear
18. Countershaft first gear
19. Countershaft
20. Countershaft third gear
21. Countershaft second gear
22. Countershaft fifth gear

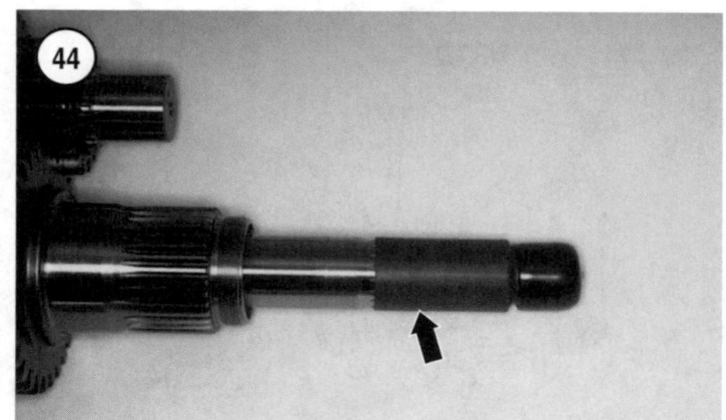

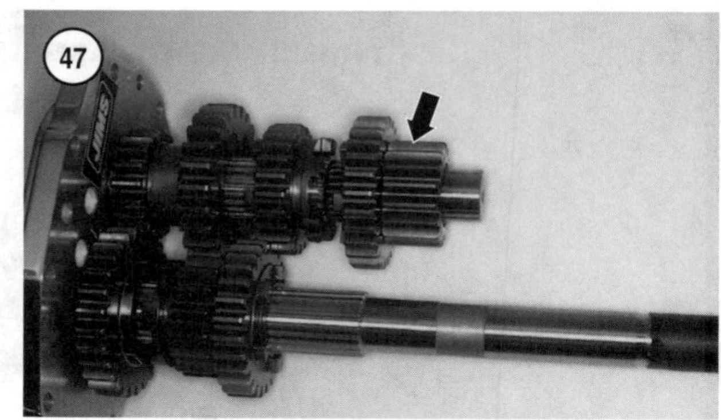

4. Remove the snap ring (**Figure 46**) from the countershaft.

5A. On 1984-1986 models, remove the countershaft fifth gear and the spacer.

5B. On 1987-1998 models, remove the countershaft fifth gear (**Figure 47**).

6. Remove the countershaft second gear (**Figure 48**).

CAUTION
Do not expand the split bearings any more than necessary to slide them off the shaft.

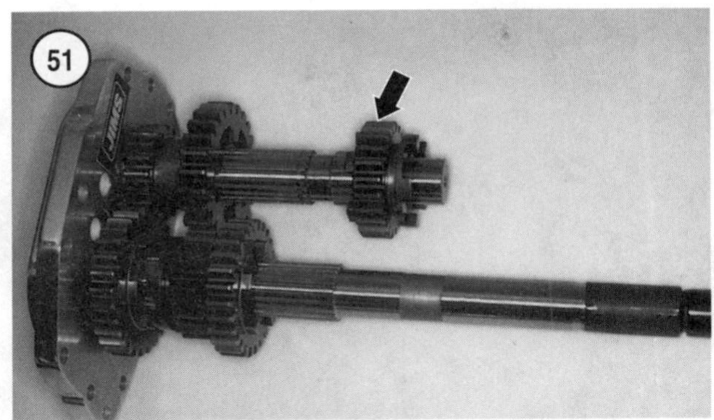
51

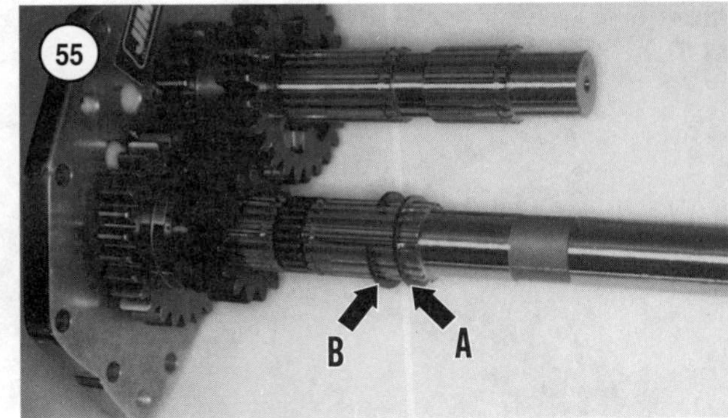

55

52

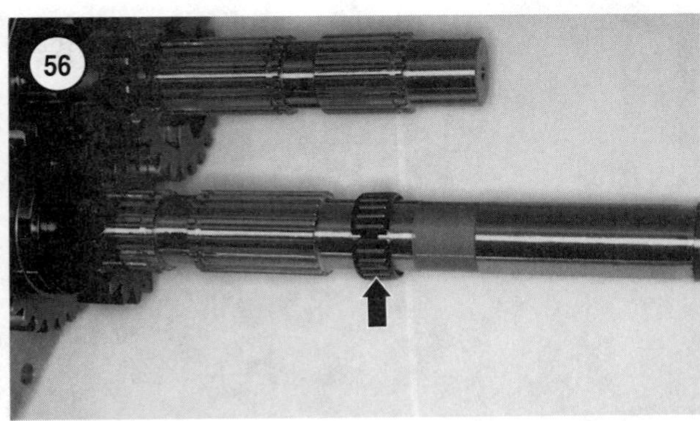
56

53

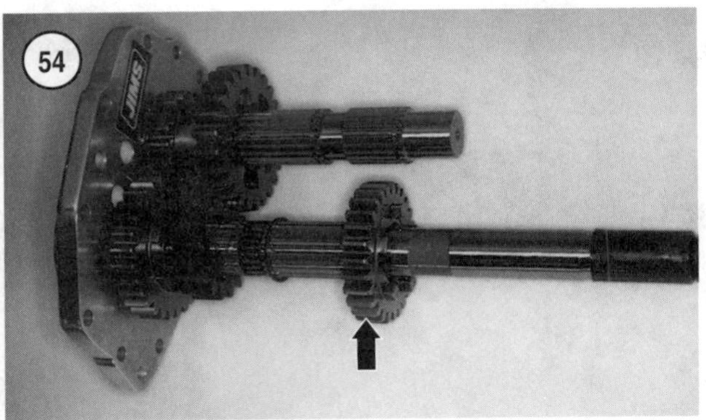
54

The bearing carriers are plastic and will fracture if expanded too far.

7. Remove the split bearing (**Figure 49**) from the countershaft.
8. Slide off the washer and remove the snap ring (**Figure 50**) from the countershaft.
9. Remove the countershaft third gear (**Figure 51**).

NOTE
The snap ring in Step 10 must be released and moved to gain access to the snap ring on the other side of the third gear.

10. Using snap ring pliers, release the snap ring (**Figure 52**) behind the mainshaft third gear. Slide the snap ring away from the third gear.
11. Slide the third gear toward the side door and remove the snap ring (**Figure 53**) and washer.
12. Remove the mainshaft third gear (**Figure 54**).
13. Remove the washer and snap ring (**Figure 55**).
14. Remove the split bearing (**Figure 56**) from the countershaft.
15. Place a brass or aluminum washer (**Figure 57**) between the countershaft fourth gear and the mainshaft

57

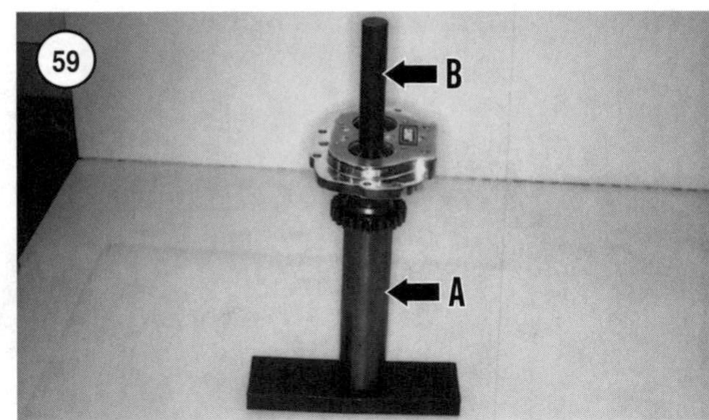

59

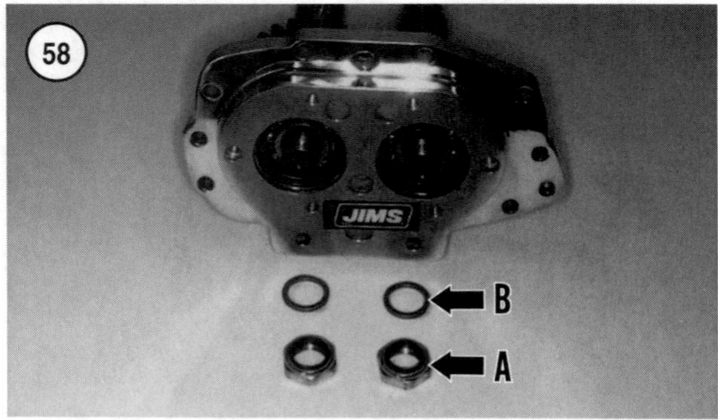

58

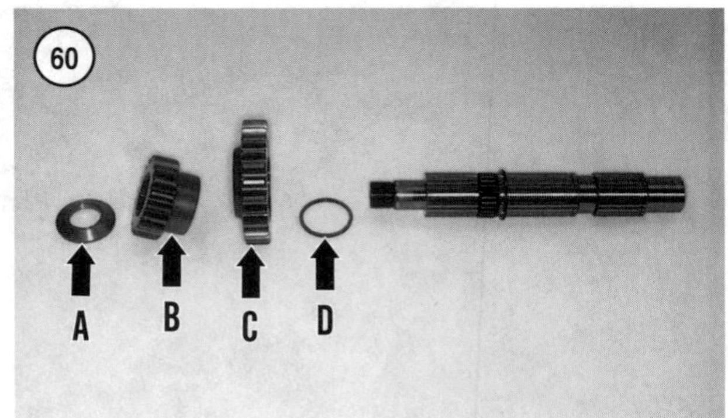

60

fourth gear. This locks both transmission shafts from rotation.

16. If not loosened during removal, loosen and remove the locknuts and washers (**Figure 58**) securing the shaft assemblies to the side door. Remove the brass or aluminum washer from between the shafts. New locknuts must be installed during assembly.

17. Press the countershaft out of its side door bearing as follows:

   a. Support the countershaft first gear in a press with a tube (A, **Figure 59**) so the countershaft can be pressed out without interference. Center the countershaft under the press ram.
   b. Place a mandrel (B, **Figure 59**) on top of the countershaft and press the countershaft out of the side door.

18A. On 1984-1986 models, remove the spacer, fourth gear, spacer, first gear and washer from the countershaft.

18B. On 1987-1998 models, remove the spacer (A, **Figure 60**), fourth gear (B), first gear (C) and washer (D) from the countershaft.

19. Remove the split bearing (A, **Figure 61**) from the countershaft.

20. If necessary, remove the snap ring (B, **Figure 61**) from the countershaft.

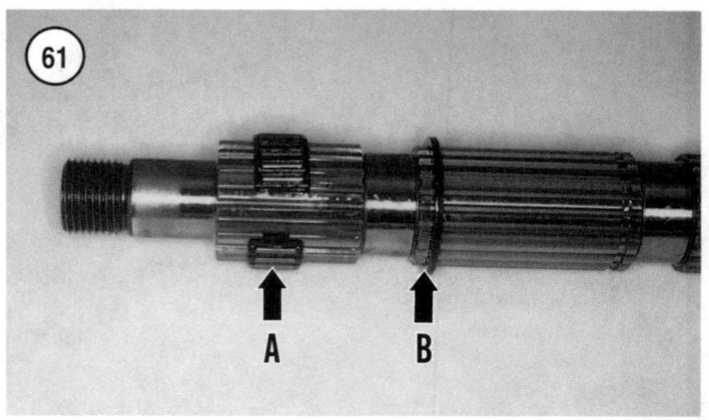

61

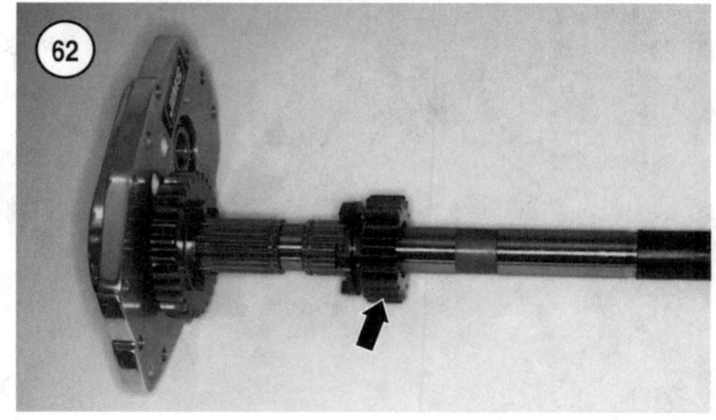
62

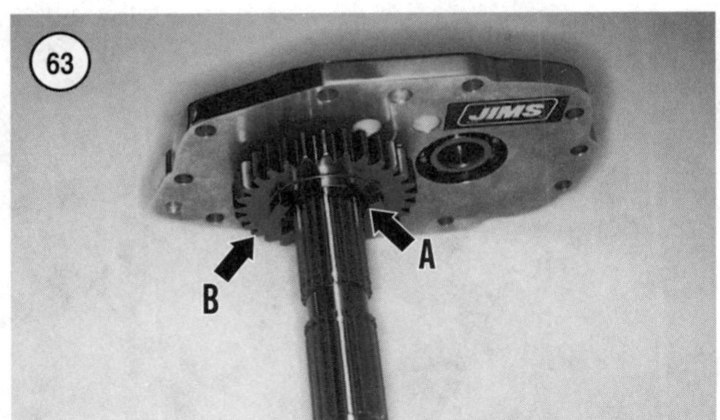

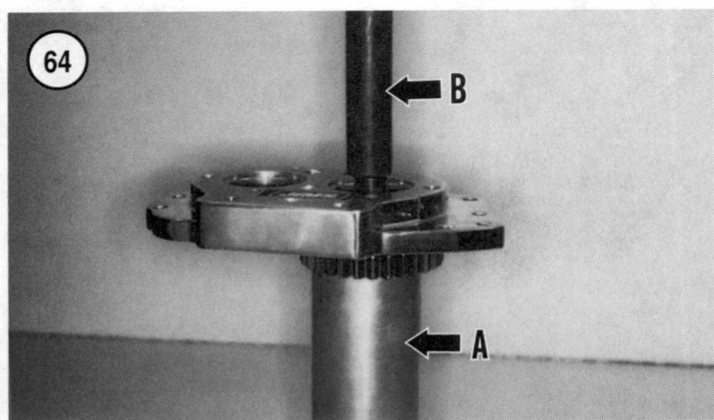

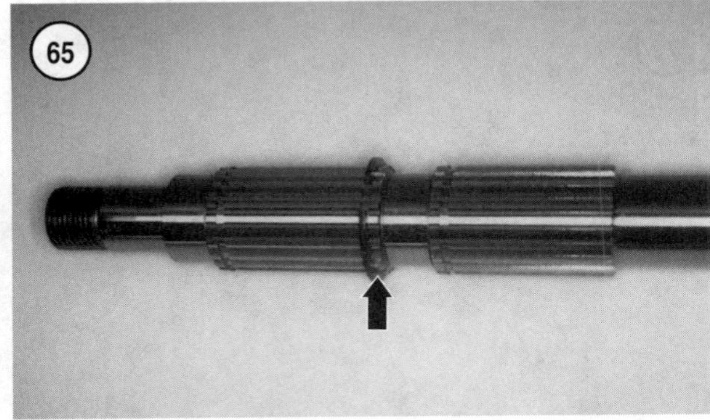

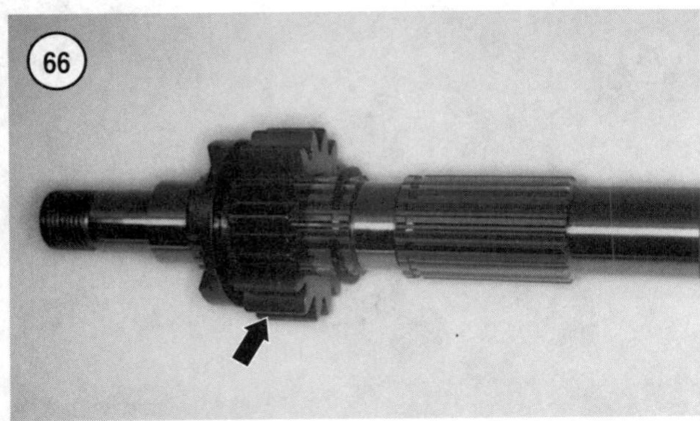

21. Remove the first gear (**Figure 62**) from the mainshaft.
22. Remove the snap ring and washer (A, **Figure 63**) from the mainshaft.
23. Press the mainshaft out of its side door bearing as follows:
    a. Support the mainshaft fourth gear on a tube (A, **Figure 64**) in a press so the mainshaft can be pressed out without interference. Center the mainshaft under the press ram.
    b. Place a mandrel (B, **Figure 64**) on top of the mainshaft and press the mainshaft out of the side door.
24. Remove the fourth gear and spacer (B, **Figure 63**) from the mainshaft.
25. Inspect all parts as described in this section.

7

Shaft Assembly

CAUTION

*Install **new** snap rings at every location to ensure proper gear alignment and engagement. Never reinstall a snap ring that has been removed because it is distorted and weakened, and it may fail. Make sure each **new** snap ring is correctly seated in its respective shaft groove.*

1. Apply a light coat of clean transmission oil to all mating gear surfaces and to all split bearing halves before assembly.
2. If removed, install the side door bearings as described in this chapter.
3. Install the following onto the mainshaft:
    a. If the snap ring was removed, install a *new* snap ring (**Figure 65**).
    b. Position the first gear with the shift dog side going on last and install the first gear (**Figure 66**).
    c. Install the snap ring (A, **Figure 67**) and washer (B).

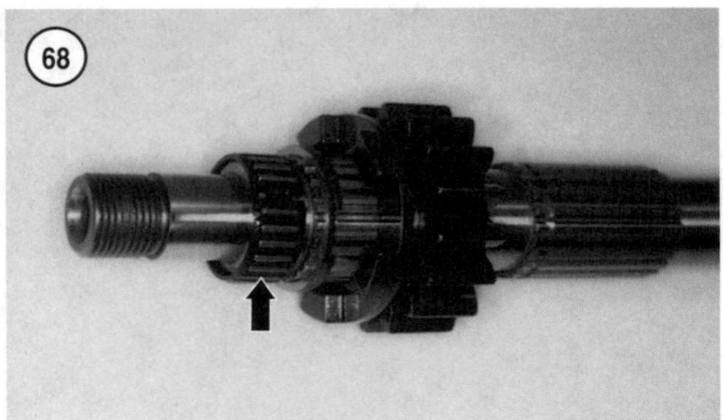

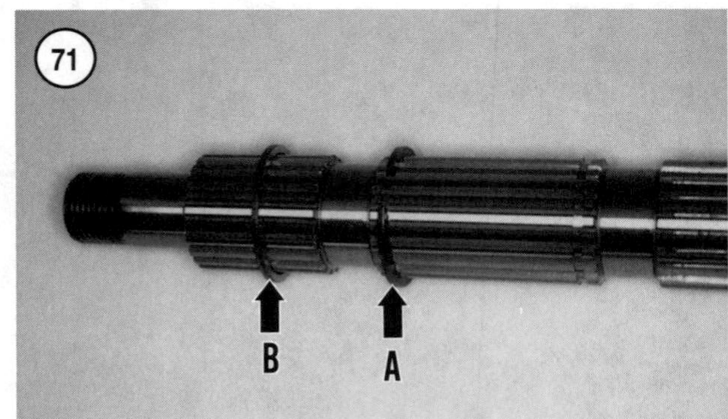

d. Install the split bearing (**Figure 68**).
e. Position the fourth gear with the shift dog side going on first and install the fourth gear (**Figure 69**).
f. Position the spacer with the beveled side facing out (**Figure 70**) and install the spacer.

4A. On 1984-1986 models, install the spacer, fourth gear, spacer, first gear and washer onto the countershaft.

a. If the snap ring was removed, install a *new* snap ring.
b. Install the washer and push it against the snap ring.
c. Install the split bearing.
d. Position the first gear with the shoulder side going on last and install the first gear onto the split bearing.
e. Install the spacer and then the fourth gear and the spacer.

4B. On 1987-1998 models, install the following onto the countershaft:

a. If the snap ring was removed, install a *new* snap ring (A, **Figure 71**).
b. Install the washer (B, **Figure 71**) and push it against the snap ring.
c. Install the split bearing (**Figure 72**).
d. Position the first gear with the shoulder side (**Figure 73**) going on last and install the first gear onto the split bearing (**Figure 74**).

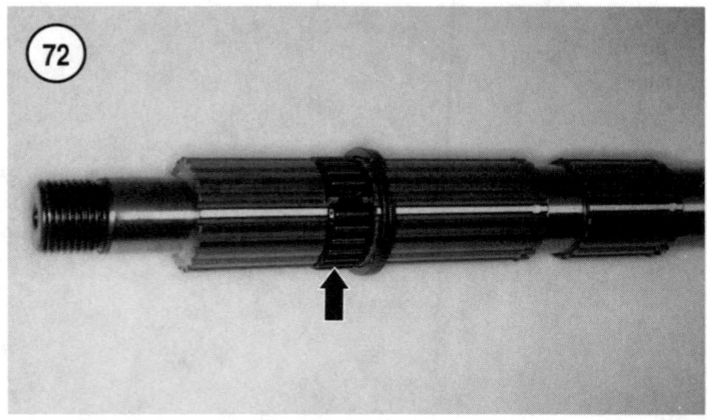

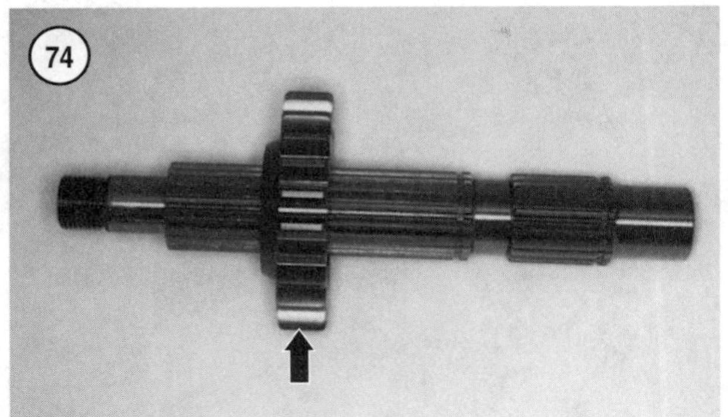

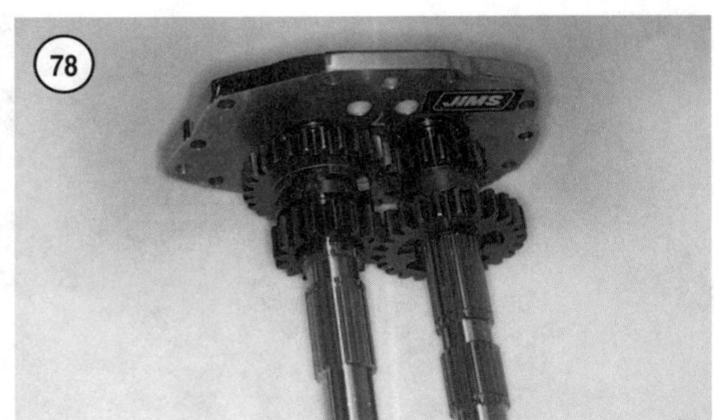

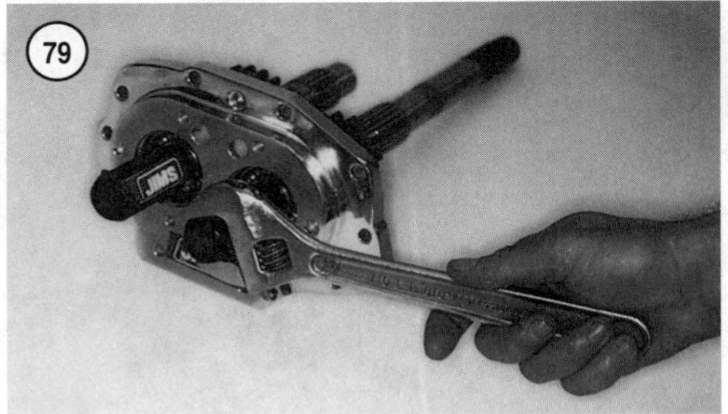

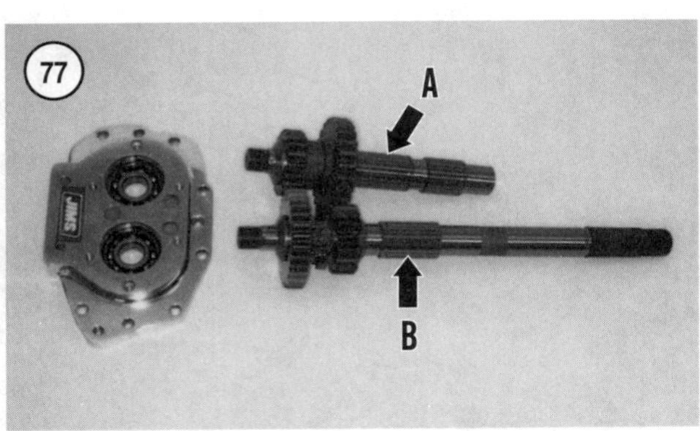

e. Position the fourth gear with the wide shoulder (**Figure 75**) going on first and install the fourth gear.

f. Position the spacer with the beveled side facing out (**Figure 76**) and install the spacer.

5. Apply transmission oil to the inner race of both bearings and to the shoulder of both shaft assemblies. Also apply transmission oil to the inner threads and ends of the special tools used in Step 8.

6. Position the countershaft (A, **Figure 77**) on the left side of the side door. Position the mainshaft (B, **Figure 77**) on the right side of the side door.

7. Mesh the two shaft assemblies together and start them into the side door bearings (**Figure 78**).

8. Attach the shaft installers (JIMS part No. 2189) onto the ends of both shafts.

9. Alternating between both shafts, tighten the shaft installers (**Figure 79**) until both shaft shoulders bottom on the inner race of the side door bearings (**Figure 80**).

10. Unscrew and remove the special tools.

CAUTION

*Always install **new** locknuts. If an old locknut is reinstalled, it may work loose and cause costly transmission damage.*

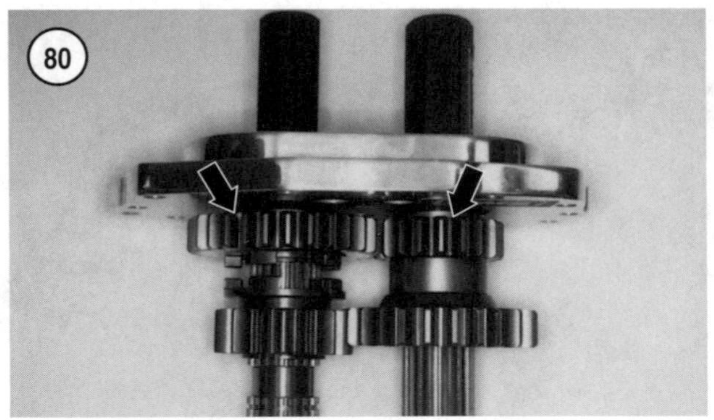

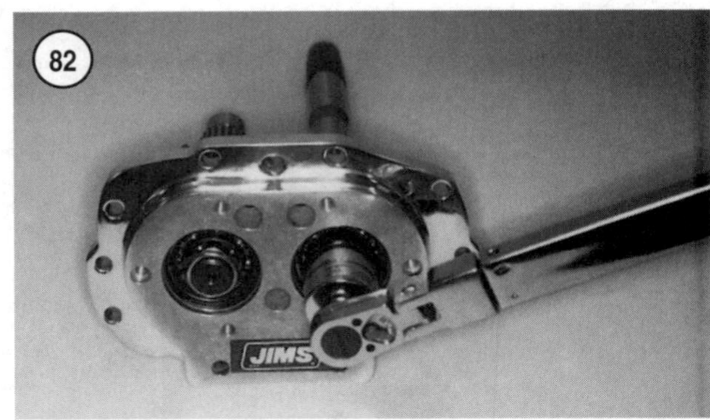

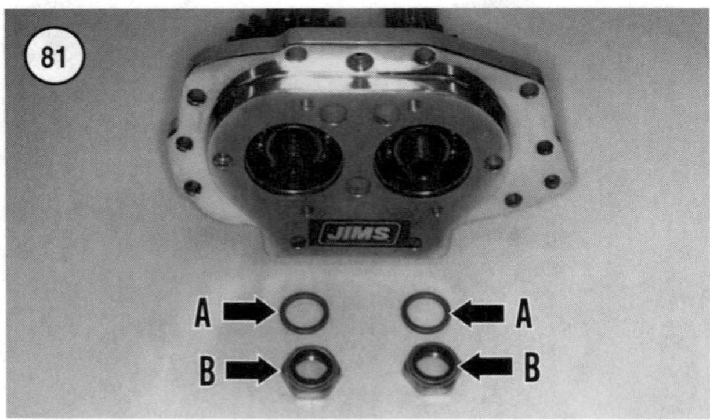

11. Install the spacers (A, **Figure 81**) and *new* locknuts (B).

12. Start the *new* locknuts by hand until the locking portion of the nut touches the end of the transmission shaft.

13. Place a brass or aluminum washer between the countershaft fourth gear and the mainshaft fourth gear. This will lock both transmission shafts.

14. Tighten the countershaft and mainshaft locknuts (**Figure 82**) to the following:

   a. 1984-1994 models: 27-33 ft.-lb. (37-45 N•m).
   b. 1995-1998 models: 45-55 ft.-lb. (61-75 N•m).

15. Install the following onto the mainshaft:

   a. Install the split bearing (**Figure 83**).
   b. Move the snap ring (A, **Figure 84**) installed in Step 3 out of the groove and toward the first gear.
   c. Install the washer (B, **Figure 84**) and slide it against the snap ring (A, **Figure 85**).
   d. Position the third gear with the shift dogs side (B, **Figure 85**) going on last. Install the third gear onto the split bearing (**Figure 86**).
   e. Install the washer (A, **Figure 87**) and snap ring (B). Make sure the snap ring is correctly seated in the mainshaft groove.

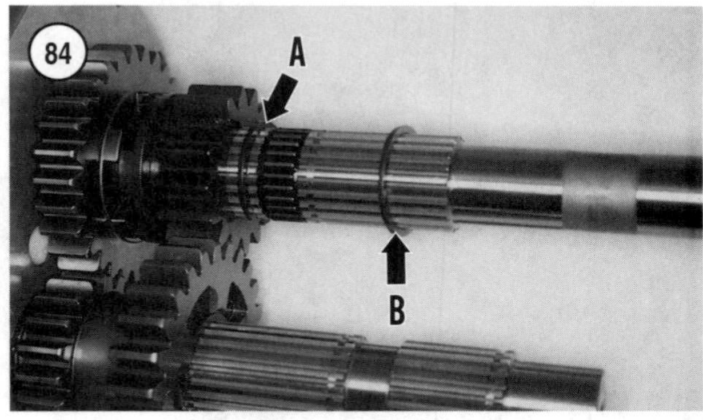

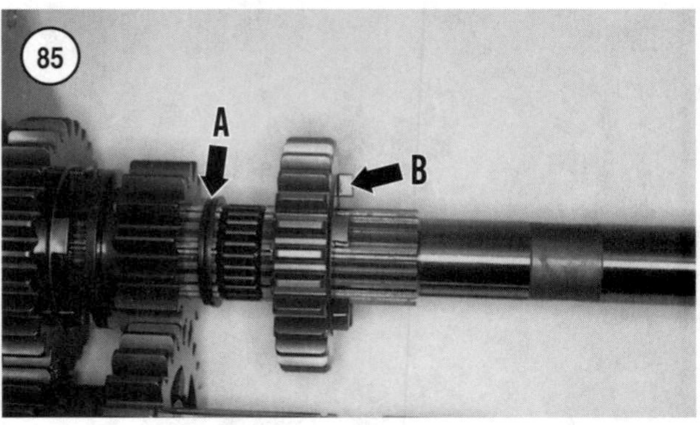

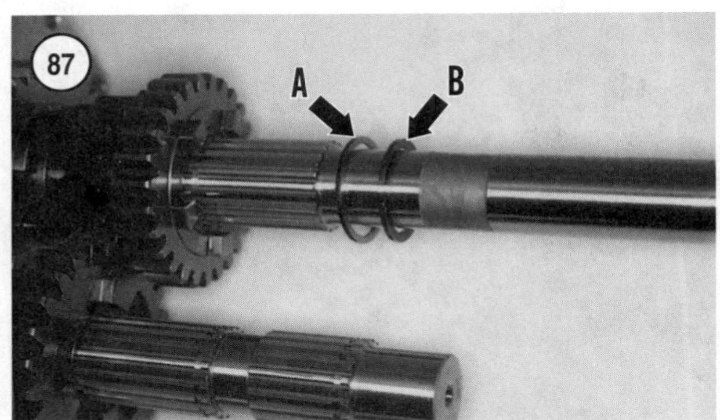

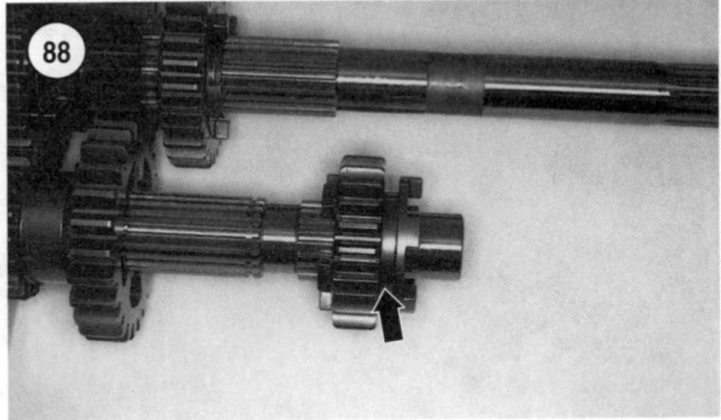

   f. Move third gear away from the first gear and up against the washer and snap ring installed in substep e.
   g. Reposition the washer and snap ring (A, **Figure 84**) behind third gear. Make sure the snap ring is correctly seated in the mainshaft groove.

16. Install the following onto the countershaft:
   a. Position the third gear with the shift fork groove (**Figure 88**) side going on last and install the third gear.
   b. Install the snap ring (A, **Figure 89**) and washer (B).
   c. Install the split bearing (**Figure 90**).
   d. Position the second gear with the shift dog side (**Figure 91**) going on first. Install the second gear onto the split bearing (**Figure 92**).

17. On the mainshaft, position the second gear with the shift fork groove (**Figure 93**) side going on first and install the second gear (**Figure 94**).

18A. On 1984-1986 models, on the countershaft, install the spacer and fifth gear. Install the snap ring. Make sure the snap ring is correctly seated in the countershaft groove.

18B. On 1987-1998 models, on the countershaft, install the fifth gear (**Figure 95**). Then install the snap ring (**Figure 96**). Make sure the snap ring is correctly seated in the countershaft groove.

92

94

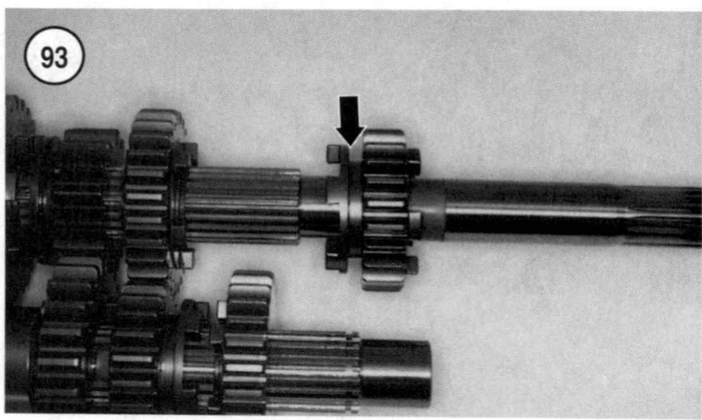

93

95

19. Refer to **Figure 97** for correct placement of all gears. Also make sure the gears mesh properly to the adjoining gears where applicable. Make sure the gears are correctly assembled before installing the shaft assemblies into the transmission case.

96

Shaft Inspection

Maintain the alignment of the transmission components when cleaning and inspecting the individual parts in the following section. To prevent mixing parts, work on only one shaft at a time.

Refer to **Table 2** and inspect the service clearance and end play of the indicated gears and shafts. Replace parts that are excessively worn or damaged as described in this section.

CAUTION
Do not clean the split bearings in solvent. Removing all traces of solvent from the bearing plastic retainers is difficult. Flush the bearings clean with new transmission oil.

1. Clean and dry the shaft assembly.
2. Inspect the mainshaft and countershaft for:

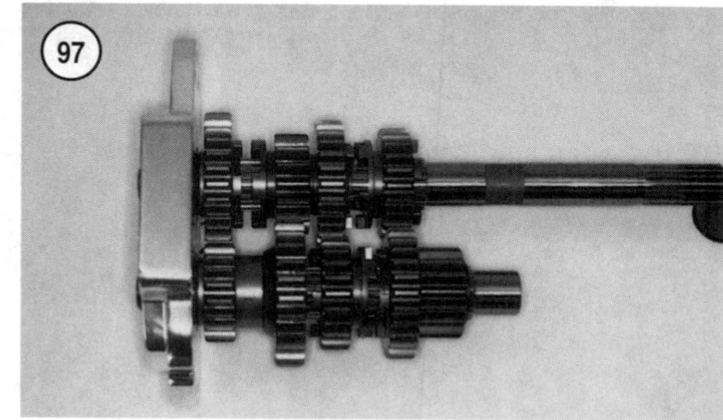

97

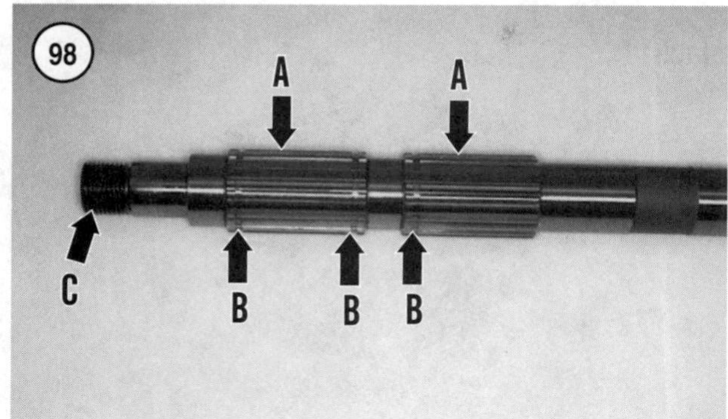

a. Worn or damages splines (A, **Figure 98**).
b. Excessively worn or damaged bearing surfaces.
c. Cracked or rounded-off snap ring grooves (B, **Figure 98**).
d. Worn or damaged threads (C, **Figure 98**).

3. Check each gear for excessive wear, burrs, pitting, or chipped or missing teeth. Check the inner splines (**Figure 99**) on sliding gears and the bore on stationary gears for excessive wear or damage.
4. Check the gear bushings (**Figure 100**) for wear, cracks or other damage.
5. To check stationary gears for wear, install them in their original operating positions. If necessary, use the old snap rings to secure them in place. Then spin the gear by hand. The gear should turn smoothly. A roughly turning gear indicates heat damage. Check for a dark blue color or galling on the operating surfaces. Rocking indicates excessive wear to the gear and/or shaft.
6. To check the sliding gears, install them in the original operating positions. The gear should slide back and forth without any binding or excessive play.
7. Check the shift fork slot (**Figure 101**) for wear or damage.
8. Check the dogs on the gears for excessive wear, rounding, cracks or other damage. Refer to **Figure 102**. When wear is noticeable, make sure it is consistent on each gear dog. If one dog is worn more than the others, the others will be overstressed during operation and will eventually crack and fail. Check engaging gears as described in Step 10.
9. Check each gear dog slot for cracks, rounding and other damage. Check engaging gears as described in Step 10.
10. Check engaging gears by installing the two gears on the respective shafts and in the original operating positions. Mesh the gears together. Twist one gear against the other and check the dog engagement. Then reverse the thrust load to check the other operating position. Make sure the engagement in both directions is positive and

there is no slippage. Make sure there is equal engagement across all of the engagement dogs.

NOTE

*If there is excessive or uneven wear to the gear engagement dogs, check the shift forks carefully for bends and other damage. Refer to **Shifter Assembly** in this chapter.*

NOTE

Replace defective gears and the mating gears, though the mating gears might not show as much wear or damage.

11. Check the spacers (**Figure 103**) for wear or damage.
12. Check the split bearings (**Figure 104**) for excessive wear or damage.
13. Replace all of the snap rings during assembly. Check the washers for burn marks, scoring or cracks. Replace as necessary.

Side Door Bearings Inspection and Replacement

The side door bearings are pressed into place and secured with a snap ring. They can be removed and installed with a transmission door bearing remover and installer (JIMS part No. 1078) (**Figure 105**). If this special tool set is not available, a press is required.

1. Clean the side door and bearings in solvent and dry them with compressed air.
2. Turn each bearing inner race (**Figure 106**) by hand. The bearings must turn smoothly. If they need to be replaced, continue to Step 3.
3. Remove both snap rings (**Figure 107**) from the outer surface of the side door.

4A. To remove the bearings with the special tool set, follow the manufacturer's instructions.

4B. Remove the bearings with a press as follows:
   a. Support the side door on the press bed with the outer surface facing up.
   b. Use a driver or socket to press the bearing out of the back side of the side door.
   c. Repeat substep b for the opposite bearing.

5. Clean the side door in solvent and dry it thoroughly.
6. Inspect the bearing bores in the side cover for cracks or other damage. Replace the side door if it is damaged.

NOTE

Both side door bearings have the same part number.

7A. To install the bearing with the special tool set, follow the manufacturer's instructions.

103

104

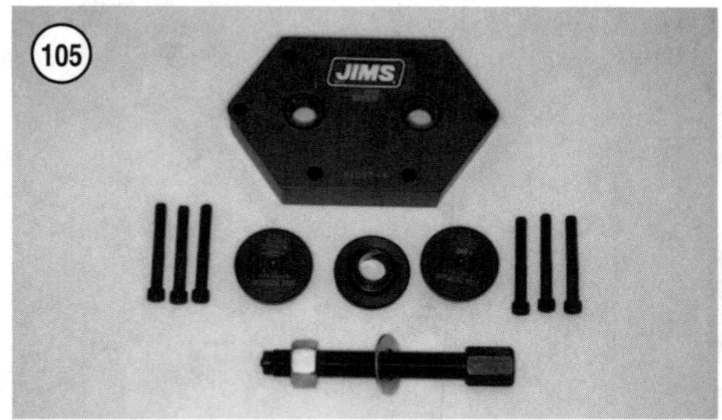

105

7B. Install the bearing with a press as follows:
   a. Support the side door in a press with the back side facing up.
   b. Install bearings with the manufacturer's marks facing out.
   c. Use a driver that matches the bearing outer race. Press the bearing into the side door until it bottoms.
   d. Repeat substeps b and c for the opposite bearing.

8. Position the beveled snap ring with the sharp side (**Figure 108**) facing away from the bearing outer race and in-

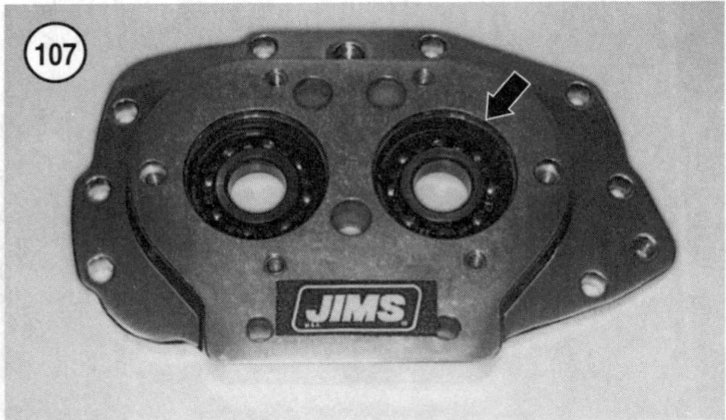

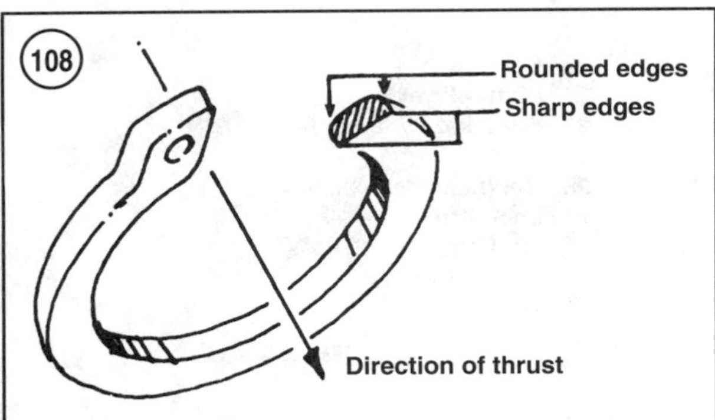

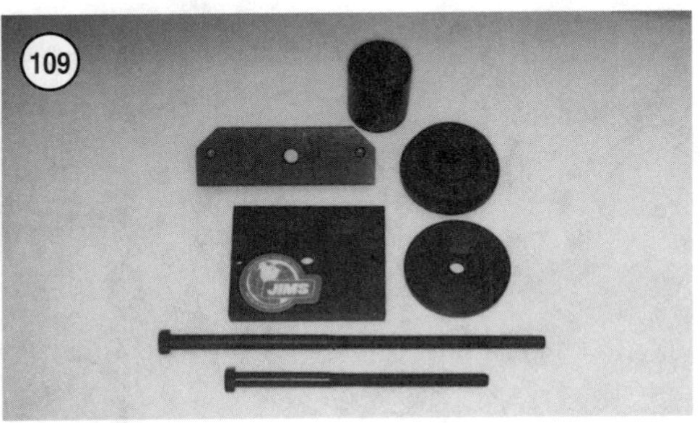

stall the snap ring. Make sure both snap rings are correctly seated in the side door grooves (**Figure 107**).

MAIN DRIVE GEAR

The main drive gear and bearing assembly are pressed into the transmission case. If the transmission case is installed in the frame, a special transmission main drive gear tool set (JIMS part No. 35316-80) (**Figure 109**) is required to remove the main drive gear. If the transmission has been removed, use a press to remove and install the main drive gear.

Whenever the main drive gear is removed, the main drive gear bearing must be replaced at the same time.

Refer to **Figure 110**.

7

Removal

1. Remove the transmission shaft assemblies from the transmission case as described in this chapter.
2. Remove the spacer from the main drive gear oil seal.
3. Remove the circlip behind the bearing.

NOTE

If the main drive gear will not loosen from the bearing in Step 4 due to corrosion, remove the special tools and heat the bearing with a heat gun.

4. Following the manufacturer's instructions, assemble the special tool set onto the main drive gear. Then tighten the puller nut slowly to pull the main drive gear (**Figure 111**) from the bearing in the transmission case (**Figure 112**).
5. Remove the main drive gear bearing from the transmission case as described in this section.

Inspection

1. Clean the main drive gear in solvent and dry it with compressed air, if available.
2. Check each gear tooth (A, **Figure 113**) for excessive wear, burrs, galling and pitting. Check for missing teeth.
3. Check the gear splines (B, **Figure 113**) for excessive wear, galling or other damage.
4. Inspect the two main drive gear needle bearings for excessive wear or damage. Refer to **Figure 114** and **Figure 115**. Insert the mainshaft into the main drive gear to check bearing wear. If necessary, replace the bearings as described in this section.

(110)

MAIN DRIVE GEAR ASSEMBLY

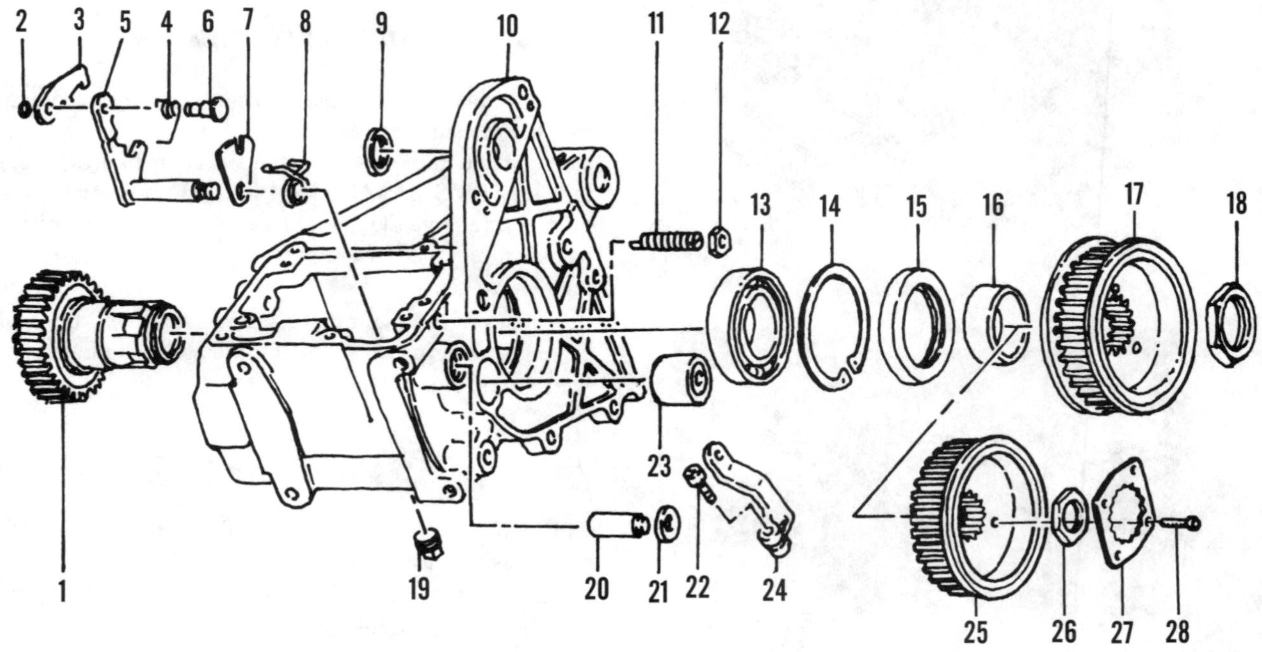

1. Main drive gear
2. Snap ring
3. Pawl
4. Spring
5. Shift arm
6. Pin
7. Centering plate
8. Spring
9. Oil seal
10. Transmission case
11. Spring
12. Nut
13. Bearing
14. Snap ring
15. Oil seal
16. Spacer
17. Sprocket (1984-early 1991)
18. Nut
19. Drain plug
20. Spacer
21. Oil seal
22. Screw
23. Bearing
24. Shifter lever
25. Sprocket (Late 1991-1998)
26. Nut (Late 1991-1998)
27. Lockplate (Late 1991-1998)
28. Screw (Late 1991-1998)

(111)

(112)

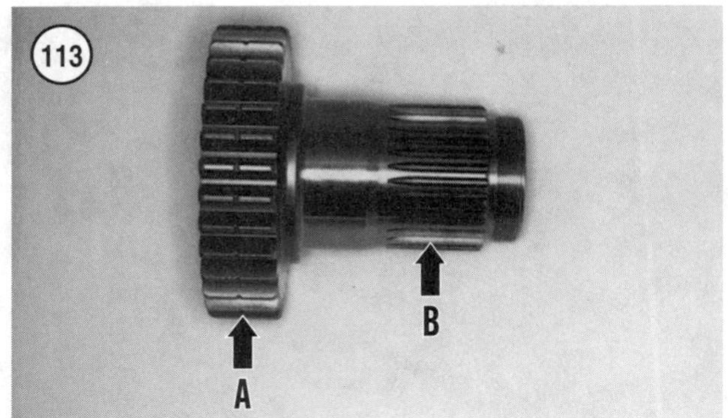

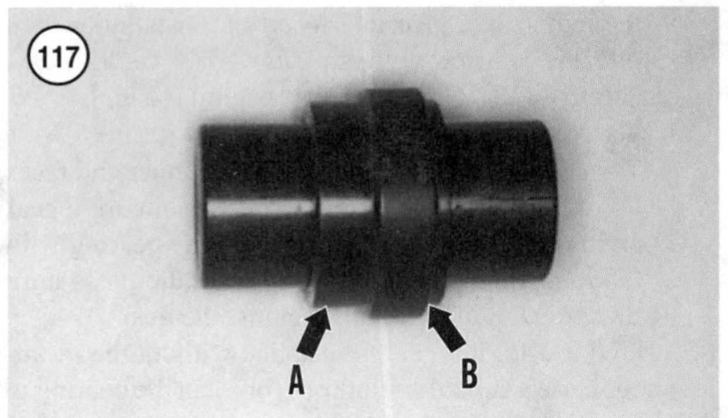

Needle Bearing Replacement

Both main drive gear needle bearings must be installed to a correct depth within the main drive gear. The correct depth is obtained with a main drive gear bearing tool (JIMS part No. 37842-91). This tool also installs the oil seal. If this tool is not available, a press is required.

If the special tool is not available, measure the depth of both bearings before removing them.

Replace both main drive gear needle bearings as a set.

CAUTION
Never reinstall a main drive gear needle bearing because it is distorted during removal.

1. Remove the oil seal (**Figure 116**) from the clutch side of the main drive gear.
2. If the special tool is not used, measure and record the depth of both bearings.
3. Support the main drive gear in a press and press out one needle bearing. Then turn the gear over and press out the opposite bearing.
4. Clean the gear and its bearing bore in solvent and dry them thoroughly.
5. Apply transmission oil to the bearing bore in the main drive gear and to the outer surface of both bearings.

NOTE
Install both needle bearings with the manufacturer's name and size code facing out.

6A. Install the bearings with the special tool as follows:

a. The special tool has two ends with different lengths. The long side (A, **Figure 117**) is for the clutch side of the main drive gear (**Figure 115**). The short side (B, **Figure 117**) is for the transmission side of the main drive gear (**Figure 114**).
b. Install the main drive gear in a press with the transmission end facing up. Align the new bearing with

the main drive gear and insert the installation tool into the bearing with the *short side facing down* (**Figure 118**). Operate the press until the tool shoulder bottoms against the gear.

c. Turn the main drive gear over so the inner end faces up. Align the *new* bearing with the main drive gear and insert the installation tool into the bearing with the *long side facing down*. Operate the press until the tool shoulder bottoms against the gear.

6B. If the bearings are being installed without the installation tool, use a suitable mandrel to press in the bearing to the depth recorded in Step 2.

7. Install a *new* oil seal (**Figure 116**) into the clutch side of the main drive gear.

Main Drive Gear Bearing Replacement

The main drive gear bearing is pressed into the transmission case. If the transmission case is installed in the frame, a transmission main bearing remover set (JIMS part No. 1720) (**Figure 119**), or an equivalent, is required to remove the main drive gear bearing. If the transmission has been removed, use a press to remove the main drive gear bearing.

Whenever the main drive gear is removed, the main drive gear bearing is damaged and must be replaced at the same time.

CAUTION
Failure to use the correct tools to install the bearing will cause premature failure of the bearing and related parts.

1. Remove the main drive gear from the transmission case as described in this chapter.
2. Following the manufacturer's instructions, assemble the special tool set onto the main drive gear bearing. Then tighten the bolt and nut slowly to pull the main drive gear bearing from the transmission case.
3. Clean the bearing bore and dry it with compressed air. Check the bore for nicks or burrs. Check the snap ring groove for damage.

NOTE
Install the bearing into the transmission case with the bearing manufacturer's name and size code facing out.

4. Apply transmission oil to the bearing bore in the transmission case and to the outer surface of the bearing. Also apply oil to the nut and threaded shaft of the installer tool.
5. Following the manufacturer's instructions, install the bearing onto the installation tool and assemble the installation tool.

118

119

6. Slowly tighten the puller nut to pull the bearing into the transmission case. Continue until the bearing bottoms in the case.
7. Disassemble and remove the installation tool.

Installation

1. Replace the main drive gear bearing and oil seal as described in the previous section.
2. Install a *new* snap ring with the flat side facing the bearing.
3. Position the snap ring with the open end facing the rear of the transmission and within a 45° angle to horizontal (**Figure 120**). Make sure it is fully seated in the snap ring groove.
4. Install the *new* oil seal into the case so the closed side faces out.
5. Apply transmission oil to the bearing bore and to the outer surface of the main drive gear. Also apply oil to the nut and threaded shaft of the installer tool.
6. Insert the main drive gear into the main drive gear bearing as far as it will go. Hold it in place and assemble the special tool onto the main drive gear and transmission case by following the manufacturer's instructions.

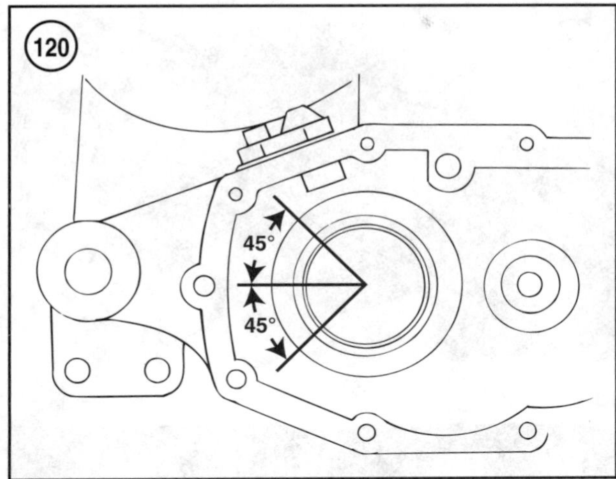

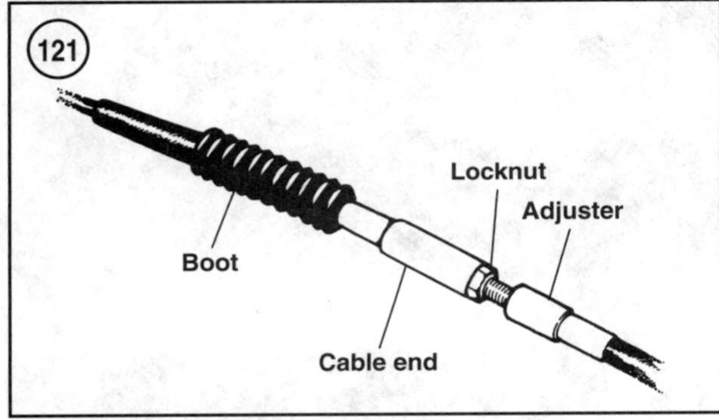

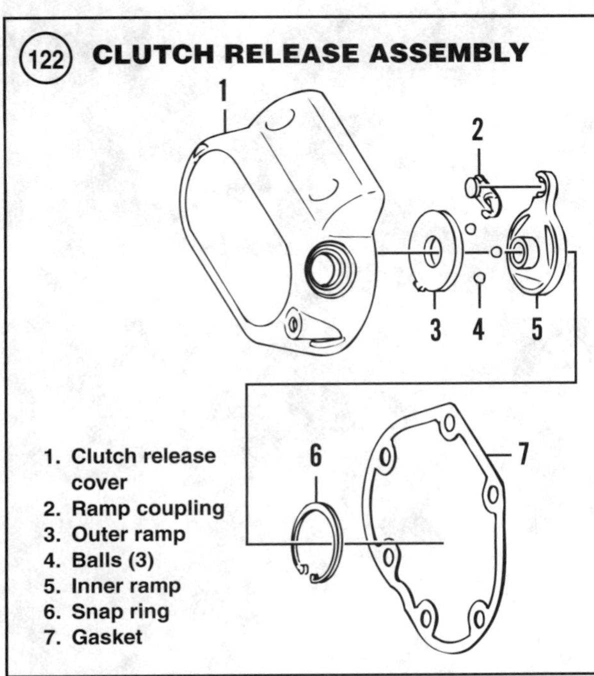

7. Slowly tighten the puller nut to pull the main drive gear into the bearing in the transmission case. Continue until the gear bottoms in the bearings inner race.

8. Disassemble and remove the installation tool.

9. Install the spacer into the main drive gear oil seal.

10. Install the transmission shaft assemblies from the transmission case as described in this chapter.

TRANSMISSION SIDE COVER

Removal

1. Remove the exhaust system as described in Chapter Eight.

2. Drain the transmission oil as described in Chapter Three.

NOTE
If the cover is difficult to remove, apply the clutch lever after the mounting bolts have been removed. This will usually break the cover loose.

3. Remove the side cover mounting bolts and remove the side cover. Remove the gasket. Do not lose the locating dowels.

4. At the clutch cable in-line adjuster, slide the rubber boot away from the adjuster (**Figure 121**). Loosen the cable locknut and turn the adjuster to provide as much cable slack as possible.

Disassembly

Refer to **Figure 122**.

NOTE
Before removing the snap ring in Step 1, note the position of the snap ring opening. The snap ring must be reinstalled with the opening in the same position.

1. Remove the snap ring (A, **Figure 123**) from the groove in the side cover.

2. Lift the inner ramp (A, **Figure 124**) out of the cover and disconnect it from the clutch cable coupling (B).

3. Remove the clutch cable coupling (A, **Figure 125**).

4. Remove the inner ramp and balls (B, **Figure 125**).

5. If necessary, remove the clutch cable (B, **Figure 123**) from the side cover.

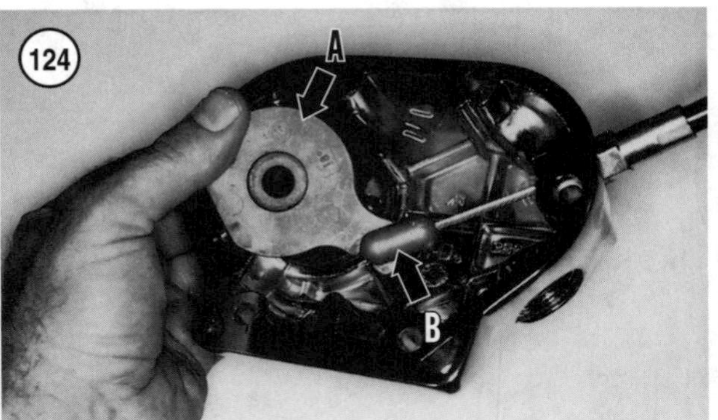

Assembly

1. If removed, screw the clutch cable into the side cover. Do not tighten the cable fitting at this time.
2. Install the inner ramp and balls (B, **Figure 125**). Center a ball in each socket.
3. Install the clutch cable coupling onto the clutch cable as shown in A, **Figure 125**.
4. Connect the inner ramp to the clutch cable coupling (B, **Figure 124**).
5. Align the inner ramp socket with the balls and install the inner ramp as shown in **Figure 126**.
6. Install the snap ring into the side cover groove. Position the snap ring so its opening faces to the right of the outer ramp tang slot as shown in A, **Figure 123**. Make sure the snap ring is seated correctly in the groove.

Installation

1. If removed, install the locating dowels.
2. Install a *new* gasket.
3. Install the side cover and bolts. Tighten the bolts in a crisscross pattern to 80-106 in.-lb. (9-12 N•m).
4. Refill the transmission with oil as described in Chapter Three.
5. Install the exhaust system as described in Chapter Eight.
6. Adjust the clutch as described in Chapter Three.

Inspection

1. Clean the side cover and all components thoroughly in solvent and dry them with compressed air.
2. Check the release mechanism balls and ramp ball sockets for cracks, deep scoring or excessive wear (**Figure 127**).
3. Check the side cover (**Figure 128**) for cracks or damage. Check the clutch cable threads and the coupling snap

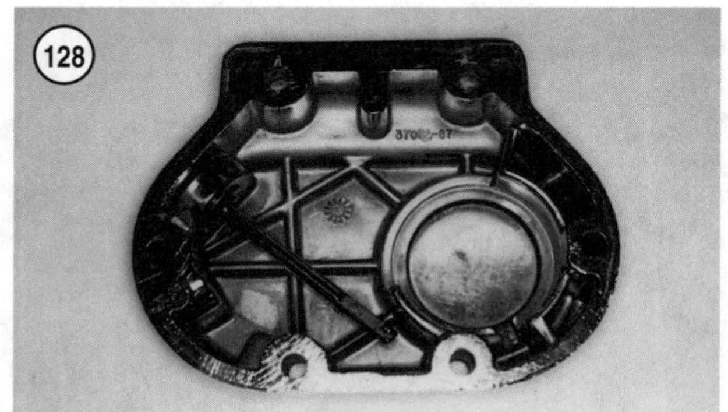

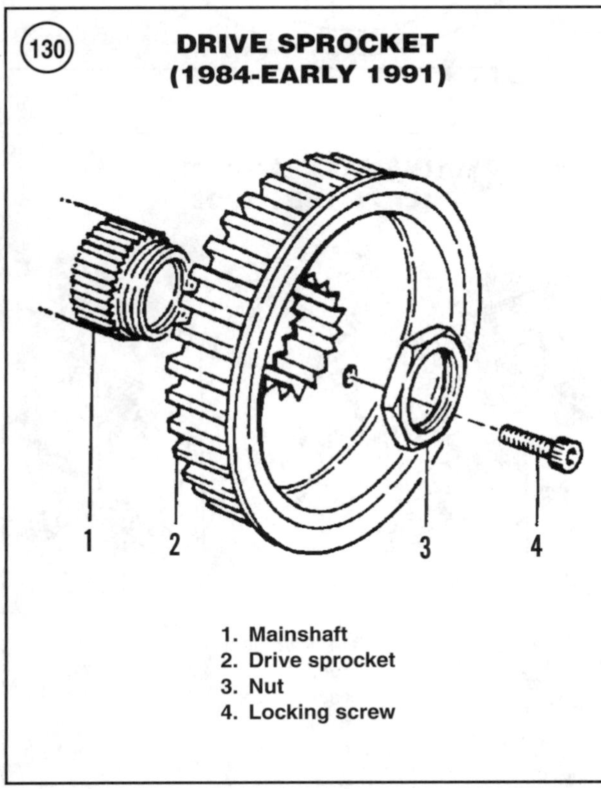

ring groove for damage. Check the ramp bore in the side cover for excessive wear, or lips or grooves that could catch the ramps and bind them sideways, causing improper clutch adjustment.

4. Replace the clutch cable O-ring if it is damaged.
5. Replace all worn or damaged parts.

7

TRANSMISSION DRIVE SPROCKET

Removal

NOTE
The mainshaft bearing race does not need to be removed for the transmission drive sprocket to be removed.

1. Remove the primary chaincase assembly as described in Chapter Five.
2. If necessary, install a Sprocket Locker Tool (JIMS part No. 2260) (**Figure 129**) onto the transmission drive sprocket by following the manufacturer's instructions.

3A. On 1984-early 1991 models, remove the sprocket nut locking screw (**Figure 130**).

3B. On late 1991-1998 models, remove the two Allen bolts and the lockplate (**Figure 131**).

4A. Shift the transmission into gear.

4B. If the drive belt is still in place, have an assistant apply the rear brake.

CAUTION
*The sprocket nut has left-hand threads. Turn the tool **clockwise** to loosen it in Step 5.*

5. Use the Mainshaft Sprocket Nut Wrench (JIMS part No. 94660-37A) as follows:
   a. Install the inner collar (**Figure 132**) onto the end of the mainshaft.
   b. Install the wrench onto the sprocket nut (**Figure 133**), turn it *clockwise* with a 1/2-in. drive, and loosen the nut.

6. Remove the special tools and the nut from the mainshaft.
7. Carefully remove the transmission drive sprocket from the mainshaft. Do not damage the bearing race.

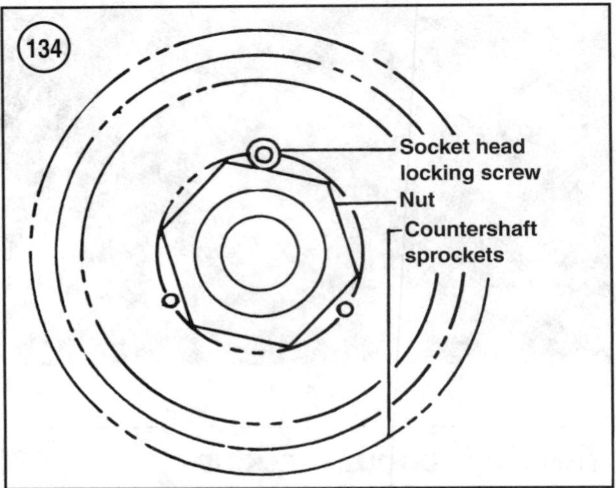

Installation

1. Use the same tool setup used during removal.
2. Carefully install the transmission drive sprocket onto the mainshaft. Do not damage the bearing race.

CAUTION
The sprocket nut has left-hand threads. Turn the tool ***counterclockwise*** *to tighten it in Step 5.*

3. Apply high-strength threadlocking compound to the sprocket nut prior to installation.
4. Position the sprocket nut with the flanged side facing the drive sprocket and install the sprocket nut.

5A. On 1984-early 1991 models, perform the following:
   a. Have an assistant apply the rear brake.
   b. Tighten the sprocket nut to 110-120 ft.-lb. (149-163 N•m).
   c. Locate a lock screw hole in the sprocket that most closely matches that alignment in **Figure 134**. If none of the tapped holes align, turn the sprocket *counterclockwise* to obtain correct alignment. Do not loosen the nut to align the holes. Apply low-strength threadlocking compound to the locking screw threads and install the screw into the sprocket.
   d. Tighten the lock screw to 50-60 in.-lb. (6-7 N•m).

CAUTION
Do not exceed 150 ft.-lb. (203 N•m) when tightening the sprocket nut.

5B. On late 1991-1994 models, perform the following:
   a. Have an assistant apply the rear brake.

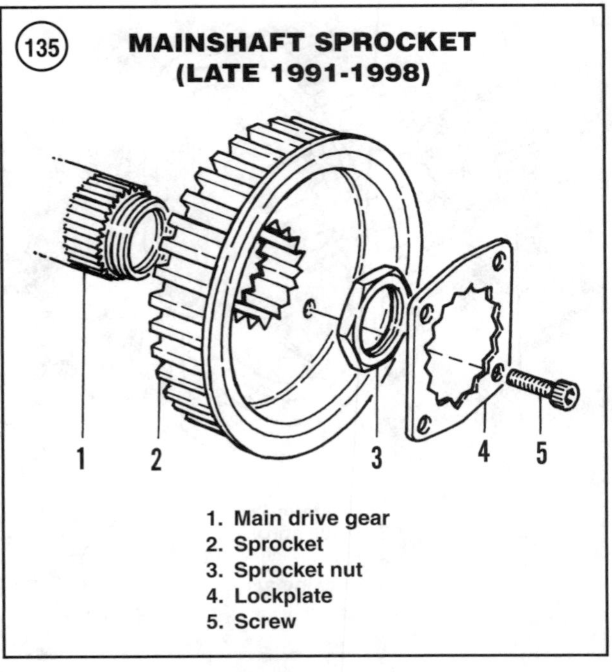

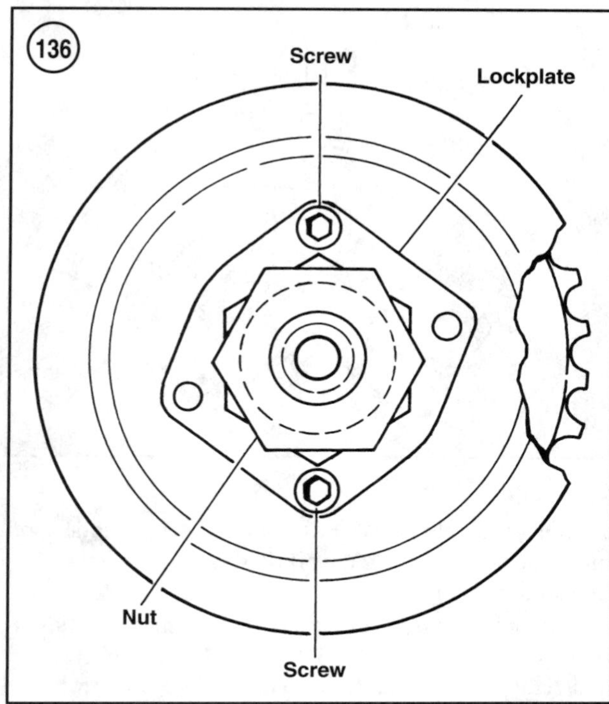

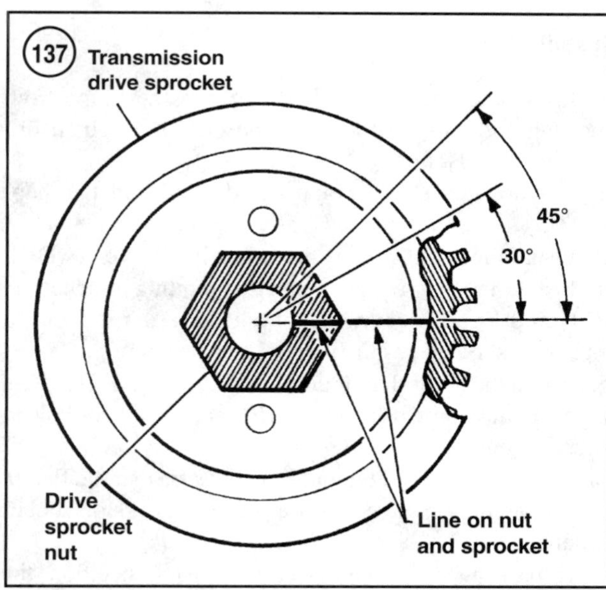

b. Tighten the sprocket nut to 110-120 ft.-lb. (149-163 N•m).

NOTE
Threadlocking compound patches are applied to the locking screw threads. These screws can be reused up to three times. Then either replace the screws, or apply a low-strength threadlocking compound to the threads.

c. Install the lockplate (**Figure 135**) and align two of the lockplate holes with the two tapped holes in the sprocket (**Figure 136**). If the holes do not align, turn the sprocket *counterclockwise* to obtain correct alignment. Do not loosen the nut to align the holes. Apply low-strength threadlocking compound to the locking screw threads and install the screw into the sprocket.

d. Tighten the locking screws to 84-108 in.-lb. (9-12 N•m).

5C. On 1995-1998 models, perform the following:

a. Have an assistant apply the rear brake.

b. Tighten the sprocket nut to 50 ft.-lb. (68 N•m).

c. Scribe a line across the sprocket nut and the sprocket as shown in **Figure 137**. Then tighten the sprocket nut an additional 30-40° (**Figure 137**).

NOTE
Always use two locking screws to secure the lockplate.

d. Install the lockplate (**Figure 135**) and align two of the lockplate holes with the two tapped holes in the sprocket (**Figure 136**). If the holes do not align, turn the sprocket *counterclockwise* to obtain correct alignment. Do not exceed 45°. Do not loosen the nut to align the holes. Apply low-strength threadlocking compound to two locking screw threads and install the screws into the sprocket.

NOTE
Threadlocking compound patches are applied to the locking screw threads. These screws can be reused up to three times. Then either replace the screws, or apply a low-strength threadlocking compound to the threads.

e. Tighten the locking screws to 90-110 in.-lb. (10-12 N•m).

6. Install the primary chaincase assembly as described in Chapter Five.

TRANSMISSION CASE

Only remove the transmission case if it requires replacement or to perform extensive frame repair or replace the frame. All internal transmission components can be removed with the case in the frame.

Removal

1A. On 1993-1998 FLH and FLT series models, drain the engine and transmission oil as described in Chapter Three.

1B. On all other models, drain transmission oil as described in Chapter Three.

2. Remove the primary chaincase assembly as described in Chapter Five.

3. If the transmission is going to be serviced, remove the transmission mainshaft and countershaft assemblies as described in this chapter.

4. If necessary, remove the main drive gear as described in this chapter.

5. Remove the starter as described in Chapter Nine.

6. Disconnect the foot shifter rod from the shifter arm.

7. Remove the shifter lever from the shifter arm.

8. Remove the clamp bolt (A, **Figure 138**) and remove the shift rod lever (B).

9. Loosen the locknut (C, **Figure 138**) and turn the adjuster screw (D) out until it clears the centering plate slot of the shifter pawl assembly within the transmission case.

10. Remove the retaining ring and flat washer from the splined end of the shifter shaft. Push on the end of the shift lever to free the shifter pawl assembly from the transmission case.

11. Label and then disconnect the oil hoses at the transmission case and oil filter mount (on early models).

12A. On 1993-1998 FLH and FLT series models, refer to **Figure 139** and disconnect the following hoses:

   a. Transmission housing-to-crankcase hose.
   b. Oil pan-to-oil pump hose.
   c. Transmission housing-to-oil filter hose.

12B. On all other models, disconnect the transmission vent hose.

13A. On 1984 models, unscrew and remove the oil filter at the bottom of the transmission case.

13B. On 1985-1998 models except the 1993-1998 FLH and FLT series models, label the engine oil hoses at the oil filter mount. Then remove the oil filter mount.

14. Support the engine with wooden blocks and a suitable jack.

CAUTION
On 1993-1998 FLH and FLT series models, do not damage the oil pan when positioning the jack.

15. Remove the swing arm as described in Chapter Twelve.

16. Remove the bolts and washers securing the engine to the transmission.

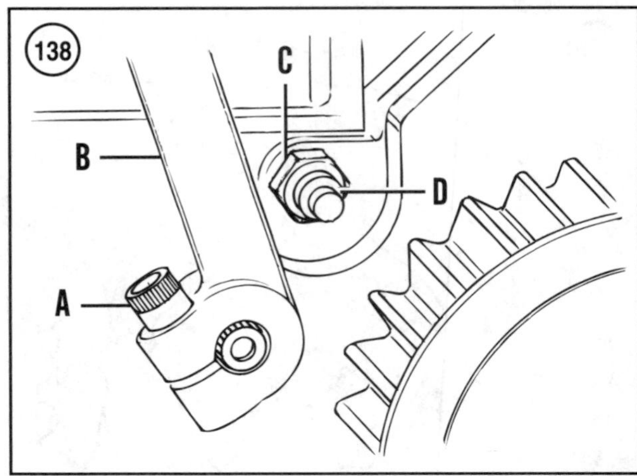

17. On some 1993-1998 FLH and FLT series models, remove the bolts securing the oil fill spout, if necessary. Remove the spout and gasket.

18. Remove the transmission case from the right side. If removal is difficult, use a 3/16-in. ball hex socket driver and remove the Allen bolts securing the oil pan to the transmission case as described in this chapter.

Installation

1. Install the transmission housing into the frame from the right side. Install the bolts and nuts and tighten finger-tight at this time.

2. If removed, install the oil pan as described in this chapter.

3. Install the swing arm as described in Chapter Twelve.

4. Install the passenger footpeg mounting bracket on FLH and FLT series models. Make sure the roll pin in each bracket engages the hole in rubber mount.

5. Install the pivot shaft mounting brackets on FXR series models. Make sure roll pin in each bracket engages hole in rubber mount.

6. On 1984-early 1986 models, make sure that the flat on the pivot shaft engages the flat on the right-side rubber mount.

7. If passenger footpegs were removed, position the footpegs so that they fold at a 45° angle. Then tighten the mounting nuts to 20-25 ft.-lb. (27-35 N•m).

8. If removed, install the shift arm assembly into the transmission housing as described in this chapter.

9. On FLH and FLT series models, install the oil fill spout, if removed, as follows:

   a. Remove gasket residue from mating surfaces.
   b. Install a *new* oil spout gasket and position the cutout side at the bottom.

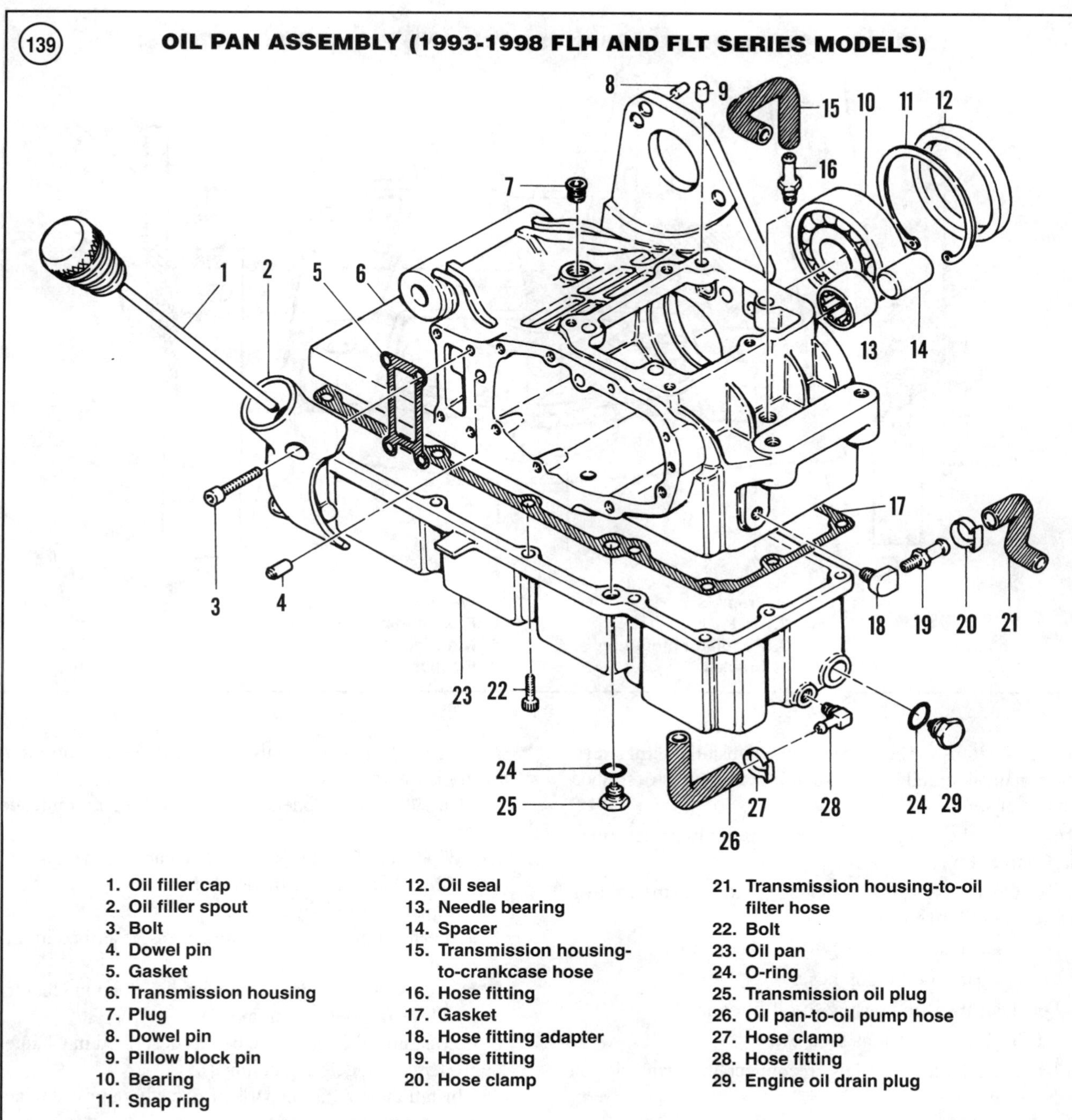

c. Install the oil spout and the bolts and tighten securely.

CAUTION

The oil spout gasket must be installed correctly. Otherwise, there will be an oil spout leak.

10. Install the shift lever rod (B, **Figure 138**) and clamp bolt (A). Securely tighten the bolt.
11. Install the shifter lever onto the shifter arm.
12. Connect the foot shifter rod to the shifter arm.
13. Install the starter as described in Chapter Nine.
14. If removed, install the main drive gear as described in this chapter.

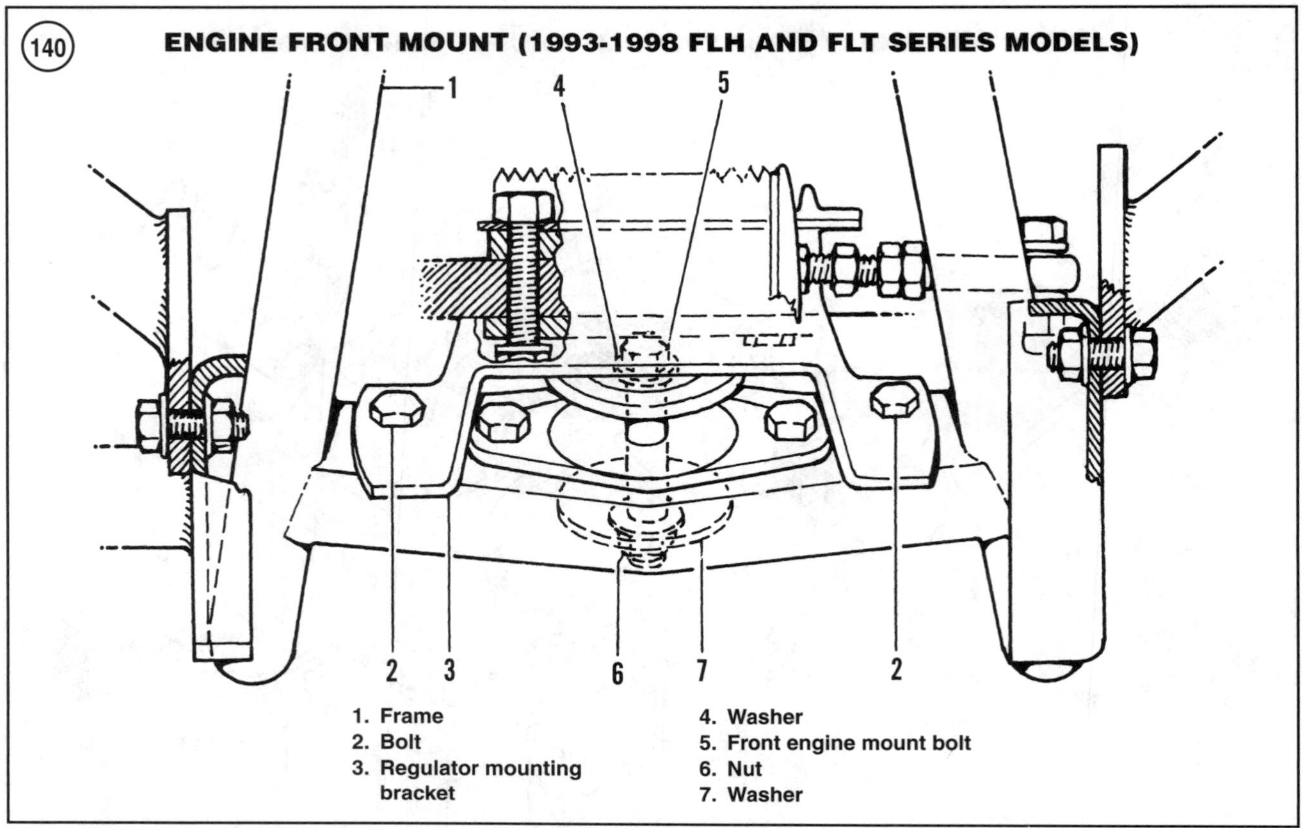

1. Frame
2. Bolt
3. Regulator mounting bracket
4. Washer
5. Front engine mount bolt
6. Nut
7. Washer

15. If the transmission was serviced, install the transmission mainshaft and countershaft assemblies as described in this chapter.

16. Install the primary chaincase assembly as described in Chapter Five.

17A. On 1993-1998 FLT models, reconnect the following hoses (**Figure 139**):

   a. Transmission housing-to-crankcase hose.
   b. Oil pan-to-oil pump hose.
   c. Transmission housing-to-oil filter hose.
   d. Tighten the clamps securely.

17B. On all other models, reconnect the transmission vent hose.

18A. On chain-drive models, coat the rear chain boots (if used) and the mating surfaces on the primary housing and transmission with RTV silicone sealant. Secure the boots to the housing and tighten screws in a crisscross pattern.

18B. On belt-drive models, adjust the drive belt as described in Chapter Three.

19. Tighten the transmission-to-engine mounting bolts to 33-38 ft.-lb. (45-52 N•m).

20. Connect the foot shifter rod to the shifter arm.

21. On 1984 models, install the oil filter to the bottom of the transmission case.

22. On 1985-1998 models, install the oil filter mount and the mounting bolt.

23. Wipe the oil filter seal with clean engine oil and screw the filter onto the filter mount.

24. Adjust the following:

   a. Perform the shifter adjustments as described in this chapter.
   b. Adjust the rear drive chain as described in Chapter Three (models so equipped).
   c. Readjust the rear drive belt as described in Chapter Three (models so equipped).

25. Install the remaining parts previously removed to access the transmission housing.

26. Refill the transmission and primary housings with the correct type and quantity of oil as described in Chapter Three.

27. On 1993-1998 FLH and FLT series models, refill the engine oil as described in Chapter Three.

NOTE
Recheck the pivot shaft nut torque every 5000 miles (8000 km).

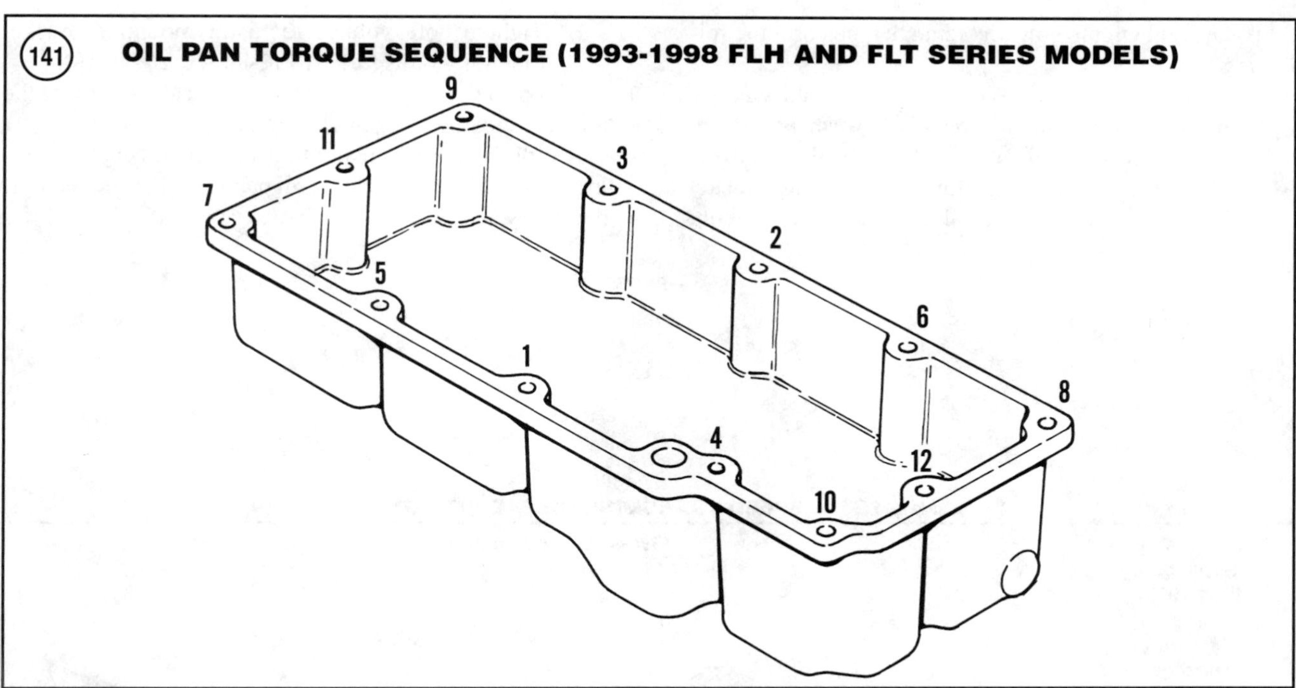

7

TRANSMISSION OIL PAN (1993-1998 FLH AND FLT SERIES MODELS)

Refer to **Figure 139**.

Removal

1. Park the motorcycle on a level surface and support it securely.
2. Drain the engine and transmission oil as described in Chapter Three.
3. Disconnect the oil pan-to-oil pump hose at the front of the oil pan.
4. Use a 3/16-in. ball hex socket driver and remove the Allen bolts securing the oil pan to the transmission case.
5. Remove the engine oil dipstick.

CAUTION
The engine oil dipstick must be removed prior to removing the oil pan. Otherwise, the dipstick will contact the oil pan and be damaged during removal of the pan.

6. Remove the oil pan from the transmission case.

NOTE
If the oil pan contacts the frame crossmember and cannot be removed, the front engine mount must be disconnected as described in Step 7.

7. Disconnect the front engine mount (**Figure 140**) and remove the oil pan as described in the following:
   a. Remove the left voltage regulator bracket bolt.
   b. Loosen the right voltage regulator bracket bolt.
   c. Pivot the left end of the regulator bracket forward.
   d. Remove the front engine nut, bolt and washers.
   e. Carefully raise the front of the engine and support it.
   f. Slide the oil pan forward and remove it.
8. Remove all gasket residue from the oil pan and transmission case gasket surfaces.
9. Clean the oil pan in solvent and dry thoroughly with compressed air.

Installation

1. Apply a thin coat of Hylomar gasket sealer or an equivalent to the oil pan gasket surface.
2. Place a *new* gasket onto the oil pan. Allow the sealer to dry to a slightly tacky feel before installing the oil pan.
3. Install the oil pan and gasket. Install the oil pan mounting bolts; tighten bolts two turns after making initial thread engagement. Check that the gasket is centered correctly on the oil pan.
4. Tighten all oil pan bolts finger-tight. Then tighten bolts in the order shown in **Figure 141** to 80-106 in.-lb. (9-12 N•m).

5. If the front engine bolt was removed, perform the following:
   a. Remove the wooden blocks supporting the engine.
   b. Install the front engine mount bolt, washers and nut. Tighten the bolt and nut to 35-45 ft.-lb. (47-61 N•m).
   c. Move the voltage regulator and mounting bracket back until the bolt holes align. Install the left bolt. Tighten both voltage regulator mounting bracket mounting bolts to 15-19 ft.-lb. (20-26 N•m).

6. Connect the oil pan-to-oil pump hose at the front of the oil pan. Securely tighten the clamp.
7. Refill the engine oil and transmission oil as described in Chapter Three. Check the oil pan for leaks and repair if necessary.

Table 1 FIVE-SPEED TRANSMISSION SPECIFICATIONS

Transmission type	Five-speed, constant mesh
Internal gear ratios	
1984-1993	
First gear	3.24
Second gear	2.21
Third gear	1.60
Fourth gear	1.23
Fifth gear	1.00
1994	
First gear	
Domestic	3.24
HDI	3.21
Second gear	2.21
Third gear	
Domestic	1.60
HDI	1.57
Fourth gear	1.23
Fifth gear	1.00
1995-1999	
First gear	3.21
Second gear	2.21
Third gear	1.57
Fourth gear	1.23
Fifth gear	1.00
Overall gear ratios*	
1991-1992	
First gear	10.93
Second gear	7.46
Third gear	5.40
Fourth gear	4.15
Fifth gear	3.37
1995-1997	
First gear	10.11
Second gear	6.96
Third gear	4.95
Fourth gear	3.86
Fifth gear	3.15
Transmission fluid capacity	
1984-1990	16 oz. (473 mL)
1991-1998	20-24 oz. (591-710 mL)

*Overall gear ratios indicate the number of engine revolutions required to drive the rear wheel one revolution. Not available for all model years.

Table 2 FIVE-SPEED TRANSMISSION SERVICE SPECIFICATIONS

Item	in.	mm
Mainshaft		
Runout	0.000-0.003	0.00-0.08
End play	None	
First gear clearance	0.0000-0.0080	0.000-0.203
Second gear clearance	0.0000-0.0080	0.000-0.203
Third gear		
Clearance	0.0003-0.0019	0.008-0.048
End play	0.0050-0.0420	0.127-1.067
Fourth gear		
Clearance	0.0003-0.0019	0.008-0.048
End play	0.0050-0.0310	0.127-0.787
Mainshaft drive gear (fifth gear)		
End play	None	
Fit on mainshaft	0.0001-0.0009	0.0025-0.023
Fit on bearing		
Loose	0.00010	0.0023
Tight	0.0009	0.023
Bearing fit in transmission case		
1984-1992		
Loose	0.00010	0.0023
Tight	0.0004	0.010
1993-1998		
Loose	0.0003	0.008
Tight	0.0017	0.043
Countershaft		
Runout	0.000-0.003	0.00-0.08
End play	None	
First gear		
Clearance	0.0003-0.0019	0.008-0.048
End play	0.0039-0.0050	0.099-0.127
Second gear		
Clearance	0.0003-0.0019	0.008-0.048
End play	0.0050-0.440	0.127-1.118
Third gear		
Clearance	0.0000-0.0080	0.000-0.203
Fourth gear		
Clearance	0.0000-0.0080	0.000-0.203
End play	0.0050-0.0391	0.127-0.993
Fifth gear		
Clearance	0.0000-0.0080	0.000-0.203
End play	0.0050-0.0040	0.127-0.102
Shifter cam assembly		
Shifter cam end play	0.0001-0.004	0.002-0.102
Right edge of middle fork groove to the right support block	See text	
Shift forks		
Shift fork finger minimum thickness	0.165	4.19
Shift fork-to-cam groove end play	0.0017-0.0019	0.043-0.048
Shift fork-to-gear groove end play	0.0010-0.0110	0.025-0.279
Side door bearing		
Fit on mainshaft		
Loose	0.0001	0.0023
Tight	0.0007	0.018
Fit on countershaft		
Loose	0.00001	0.0002
Tight	0.0008	0.0203
Fit on side door (tight)	0.0001-0.0014	0.002-0.035

7

Table 3 SHIFT DOG CLEARANCE SPECIFICATIONS

Gears	Minimum in. (mm)	Maximum in. (mm)
Second-fifth gear	0.035 (0.89)	0.139 (3.53)
Second-third gear	0.035 (0.89)	0.164 (4.16)
First-fourth gear	0.035 (0.89)	0.152 (3.86)
First-third gear	0.035 (0.89)	0.157 (3.99)

Table 4 FIVE-SPEED TRANSMISSION TORQUE SPECIFICATIONS

Item	ft.-lb.	in.-lb.	N•m
Clutch release arm cover bolts	–	80-106	9-12
Countershaft sprocket nut	110-120	–	149-163
Mainshaft and countershaft			
Oil pan bolts	–	80-106	9-12
Passenger footpeg mount bolts	20-25	–	27-35
Shifter arm adjusting locknut	20-24	–	27-33
Shifter cam mount bolts	–	84-108	9-12
Socket head screws (sprocket lockplate)	–	80-106	9-12
Top cover bolts	–	80-106	9-12
Shift linkage locknuts	20-24	–	27-33
Transmission side door mounting screws			
1/4 in.	–	80-106	9-12
5/16 in.	13-16	–	18-22
Transmission-to-engine mounting bolts	33-38	–	45-52
Transmission side door locknuts			
1984-1995	27-33	–	37-45
1996-1998	45-55	–	61-75
Transmission sprocket nut			
1984-1994	110-120	–	149-163
1995-1998	50 then additional 30-40°		
Transmission sprocket lock screw			
1984-early 1991	–	50-60	6-7
Late 1991-1994	–	84-108	9-12
1995-1998	–	90-110	10-12
Voltage regulator bracket bolts	15-19	–	20-26

CHAPTER EIGHT

FUEL, EXHAUST AND EMISSION CONTROL SYSTEMS

This chapter includes procedures for all carburetors and fuel, exhaust and emission control systems (California models). Electronic fuel injection (EFI) models are also covered. Specifications and carburetor jet sizes are in **Tables 1-3** at the end of the chapter.

WARNING
Gasoline is carcinogenic and extremely flammable and must be handled carefully. Wear latex gloves to avoid skin contact. If gasoline does contact skin, immediately and thoroughly wash the area with soap and warm water.

AIR FILTER BACK PLATE

Removal

1. Remove the air filter cover screw(s) and washer(s) (A, **Figure 1**) and remove the cover (B).

2A. On 1984-1992 models, remove the air filter element (**Figure 2**, typical).

2B. On 1993-1998 domestic carbureted models, gently pull the air filter element away from the back plate and disconnect the two breather hoses (**Figure 3**) from the

breather hollow bolts on the back plate. Remove the air filter element.

2C. On 1993-1998 international carbureted models, remove the four screws and washers securing the air filter element to the back plate. Remove the air filter element.

2D. On 1995-1998 fuel-injected models, remove the screws securing the air filter element to the back plate. Remove the air filter element from the back plate.

3A. On 1984-1986 FXR series, FXWG, FXEF and FXSB models, refer to **Figure 4** and perform the following:

a. Straighten the tabs on the lockwasher plate.
b. Remove the screws securing the washer plate and back plate to the carburetor.
c. Remove the bolt, lockwasher and washer at the base of the back plate.
d. Remove the back plate from the carburetor.
e. Carefully remove the gasket from the carburetor.
f. Carefully remove the gasket from the carburetor flange.

3B. On 1984-1985 FLH and FLT series models, refer to **Figure 5** and perform the following:

a. Straighten the tabs on the lockwasher plate.
b. Remove the screws securing the washer plate and back plate to the mounting bracket.
c. Remove the bolt, lockwasher and washer at the base of the back plate.
d. Partially remove the back plate away from the carburetor. Disconnect the crankcase breather hose from the back plate.
e. Remove the back plate.
f. Carefully remove the gasket from the carburetor flange.

3C. On 1986-1992 all series models, refer to **Figures 6-8** and perform the following:

a. Remove the plugs from the upper two bolts.
b. Remove the two upper bolts and washers securing the back plate to the cylinder heads.

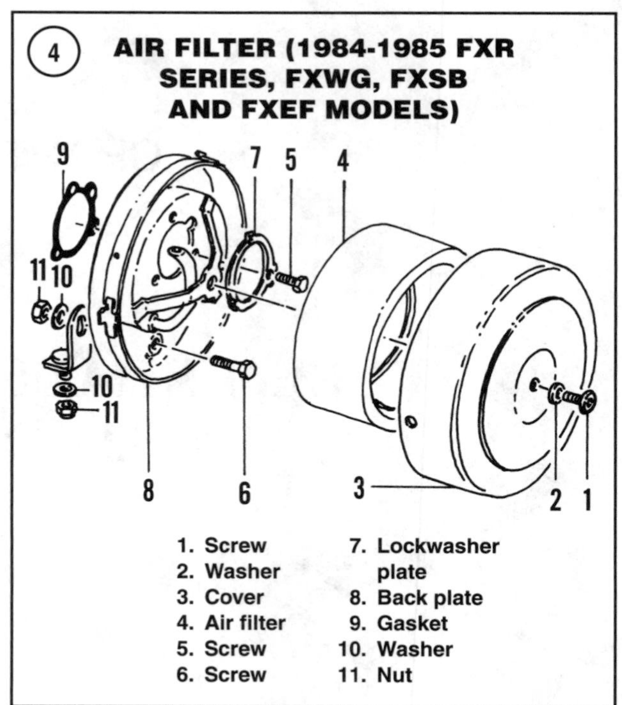

4 **AIR FILTER (1984-1985 FXR SERIES, FXWG, FXSB AND FXEF MODELS)**

1. Screw
2. Washer
3. Cover
4. Air filter
5. Screw
6. Screw
7. Lockwasher plate
8. Back plate
9. Gasket
10. Washer
11. Nut

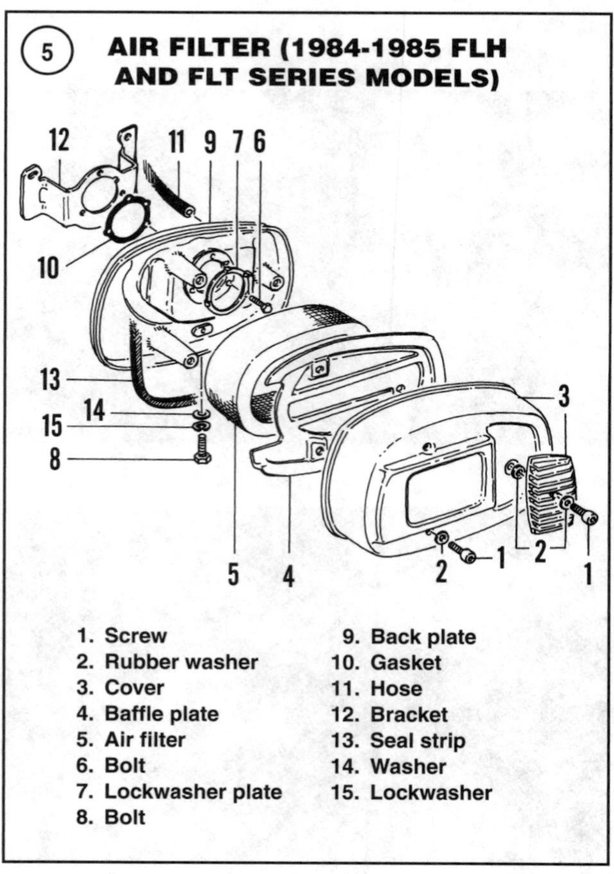

5 **AIR FILTER (1984-1985 FLH AND FLT SERIES MODELS)**

1. Screw
2. Rubber washer
3. Cover
4. Baffle plate
5. Air filter
6. Bolt
7. Lockwasher plate
8. Bolt
9. Back plate
10. Gasket
11. Hose
12. Bracket
13. Seal strip
14. Washer
15. Lockwasher

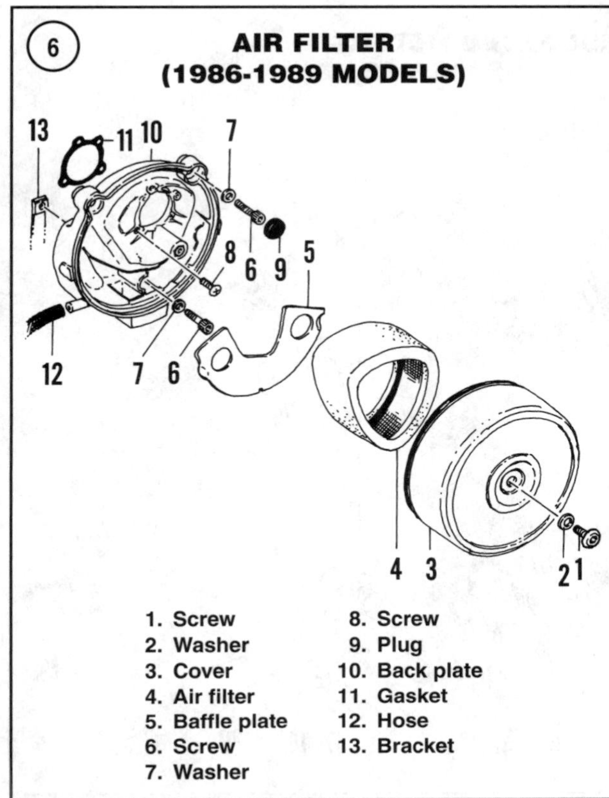

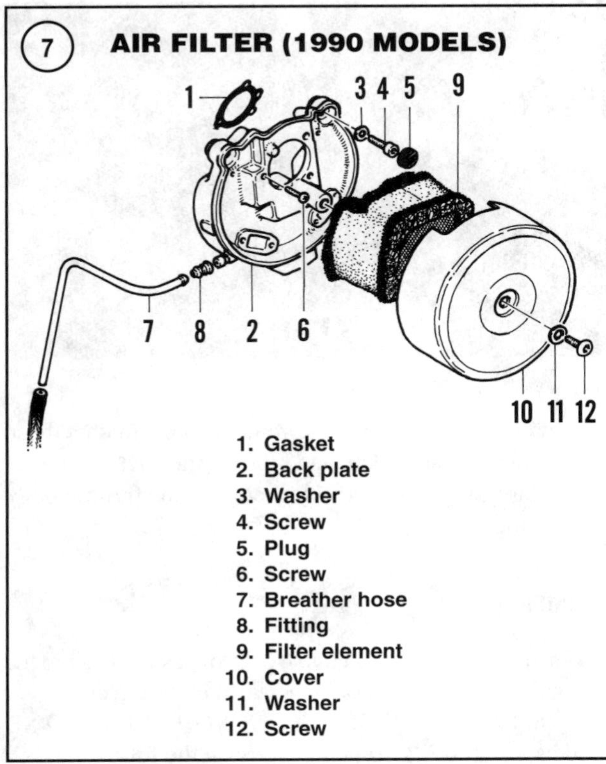

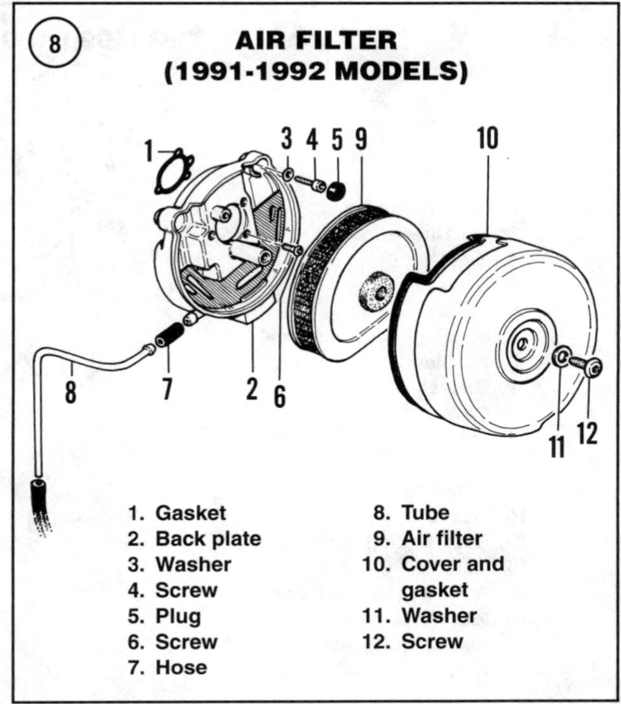

CAUTION
To prevent damage to the back plate, do not allow the captive screw threads to engage the threads of the back plate inserts. The screws remain with the back plate.

c. Loosen the four captive screws in two to three steps in a crisscross pattern while carefully pulling the back plate away from the carburetor.

d. Disconnect the hose from the back plate.

e. On 1992 California models, disconnect the solenoid harness electrical connector.

f. Remove the back plate with the captive screws intact. Do not remove the captive screws unless the back plate is to be replaced.

g. Carefully remove the gasket from the carburetor flange.

3D. On 1993-1998 all series carbureted models, refer to **Figure 9** and perform the following:

a. Remove the breather connectors from the upper two bolts.

b. Remove the upper bolts and washers (A, **Figure 10**) securing the back plate to the cylinder heads.

CAUTION
To prevent damage to the back plate, do not allow the captive screw threads to engage

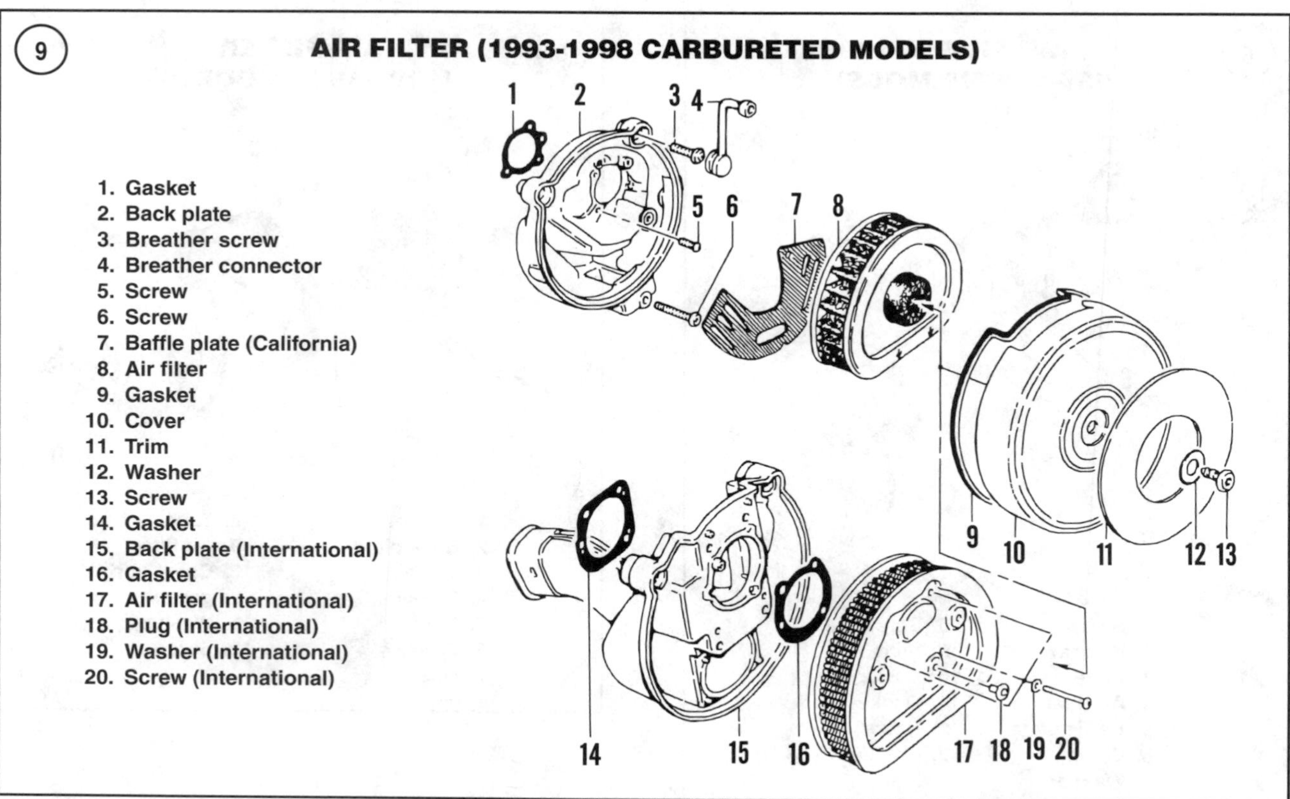

the threads of the back plate inserts. The screws remain with the back plate.

NOTE
The baffle is riveted to the back plate and is not removable.

c. Loosen the captive screws (B, **Figure 10**) in two to three steps in a crisscross pattern while carefully pulling the back plate away from the carburetor.
d. Remove the back plate with the captive screws intact. Do not remove the captive screws unless the back plate is to be replaced.
e. Carefully remove the gasket from the carburetor flange.

3E. On 1995-1998 all series fuel-injected models, refer to **Figure 11** and perform the following:

a. On California models, remove the breather connectors from the upper two bolts.
b. On 49-state models, remove the plugs from the upper two bolts.
c. Remove the two upper bolts securing the back plate to the cylinder heads.
d. Remove the four bolts securing the back plate to the throttle body.

e. On California models, remove the breather hose from the back plate and remove the back plate.
f. Carefully remove the gasket from the throttle body flange.

Installation

1. On all models, apply a couple dabs of gasket sealer to the *new* gasket and install it onto the air filter back plate.

2A. On 1984-1986 FXR series, FXWG, FXEF and FXSB models, refer to **Figure 4** and perform the following:

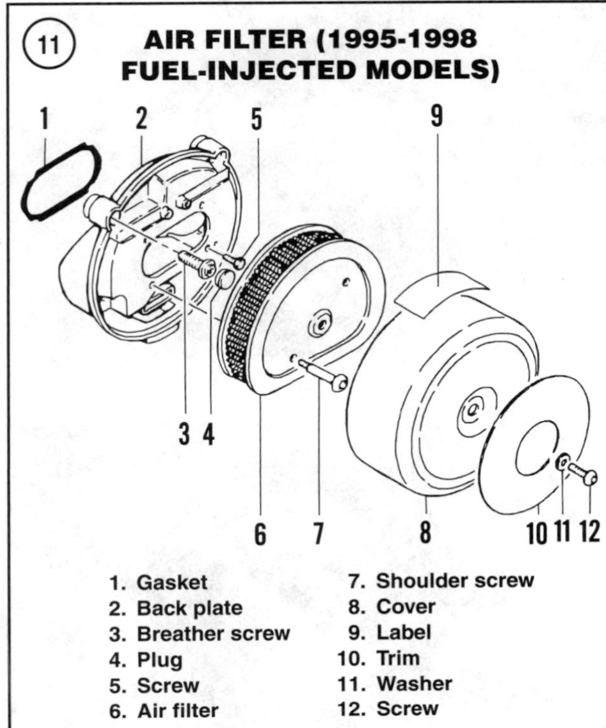

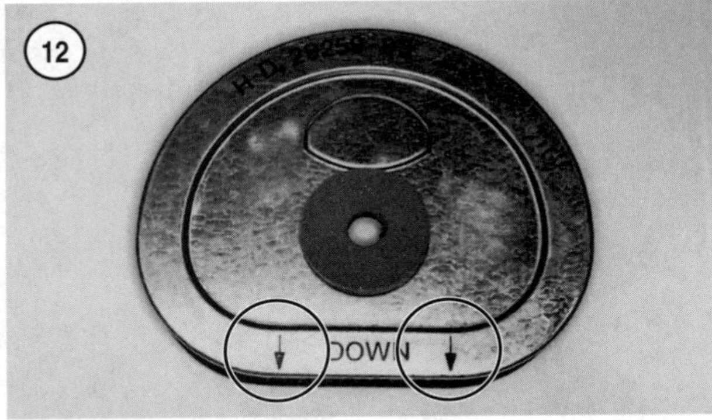

a. Install a *new* gasket onto the carburetor flange.
b. Install the back plate onto the carburetor and install the lockwasher plate and screws.
c. Tighten the screws securely and bend the lockwasher plate tabs against the screws.
d. Install the bolt, lockwasher and washer onto the small bracket and tighten securely.

2B. On 1984 FLH and FLT series models, refer to **Figure 5** and perform the following:

a. Partially install the back plate. Then connect the crankcase breather hose to the back plate.
b. Move the back plate into position and install the lockwasher plate and screws.
c. Install the bolt, lockwasher and washer at the base of the back plate and tighten securely.

2C. On 1986-1992 all series models, refer to **Figures 6-9** and perform the following:

a. Install a *new* gasket onto the carburetor flange.
b. Install the back plate onto the carburetor and tighten the four captive screws in two to three steps in a crisscross pattern. Tighten the screws securely.
c. Connect the hose to the back plate.
d. On 1992-1998 California models, connect the solenoid harness electrical connector.
e. Install the two upper bolts and washers securing the back plate to the cylinder heads. Tighten the bolts securely. Then install the plugs onto the bolts.

2D. On 1993-1998 all series carbureted models, refer to **Figure 9** and perform the following:

a. Install a *new* gasket onto the carburetor flange.
b. Install the back plate and tighten the four captive screws securely in two to three steps in a crisscross pattern.
c. Install the two upper bolts and washers and tighten securely.
d. Install the breather connectors onto the upper two bolts.

2E. On 1995-1998 all series fuel-injected models, refer to **Figure 11** and perform the following:

a. Install a *new* gasket onto the carburetor flange.
b. On California models, attach the breather hose to the back plate and install the back plate.
c. Install the four bolts securing the back plate to the throttle body and tighten securely.
d. Install the two upper bolts and tighten securely.
e. On 49-state models, install the plugs into the upper two bolts.
f. On California models, install the breather connectors into the upper two bolts.

3. Position the element with the flat side and arrows (**Figure 12**) facing down.

NOTE

If an aftermarket air filter element is being installed, follow the manufacturer's instructions to position it onto the back plate.

4A. On 1984-1992 models, install the air filter element (**Figure 2**).

4B. On 1993-1998 domestic carbureted models, move the air filter element into position on the back plate and connect the two breather hoses (**Figure 3**) to the breather hollow bolts on the back plate.

4C. On 1993-1998 international carbureted models, install the air filter element into position and install the four screws and washers. Tighten the screws securely.

8

4D. On 1995-1998 fuel-injected models, install the air filter element into position and install the screws. Tighten the screws securely.
5. Inspect the seal ring on the air filter cover for hardness or deterioration. Replace if necessary.
6. Install the air filter cover (B, **Figure 1**), washer(s) and the screw(s). Tighten the screw securely.

Inspection

1. Inspect the back plate assembly (**Figure 13**, typical) for warp and damage.
2. Always replace the back plate-to-carburetor (throttle body) gasket (**Figure 14**, typical).
3. On models so equipped, inspect the breather hoses (**Figure 15**) for tears or deterioration. Replace if necessary.

CARBURETOR OPERATION

An understanding of the function of each of the carburetor components and the relation to one another is a valuable aid for pinpointing the source of carburetor trouble.

The purpose of the carburetor is to supply and atomize fuel and mix it in correct proportions with the air drawn in through the air intake. At the primary throttle opening (idle), a small amount of fuel is siphoned through the pilot jet by the incoming air. As the throttle is opened farther, the air stream begins to siphon fuel through the main jet and needle jet. The tapered needle increases the effective flow capacity of the needle jet as it is lifted and occupies progressively less of the area of the jet. At full throttle, the carburetor venturi is fully open, and the needle is lifted far enough to permit the main jet to flow at full capacity.

The choke circuit is a starting enrichment valve system. The choke knob under the fuel tank on the left side of the engine opens an enrichment valve rather than closing a butterfly in the venturi area as on some carburetors. In the open position, the slow jet discharges a stream of fuel into the carburetor venturi to enrich the mixture when the engine is cold.

The accelerator pump circuit reduces engine hesitation by injecting a fine spray of fuel into the carburetor intake passage during sudden acceleration.

CARBURETOR (1984-1989 MODELS)

Removal/Installation

1. Remove the air filter assembly as described in this chapter.
2. Turn off the fuel shutoff valve.

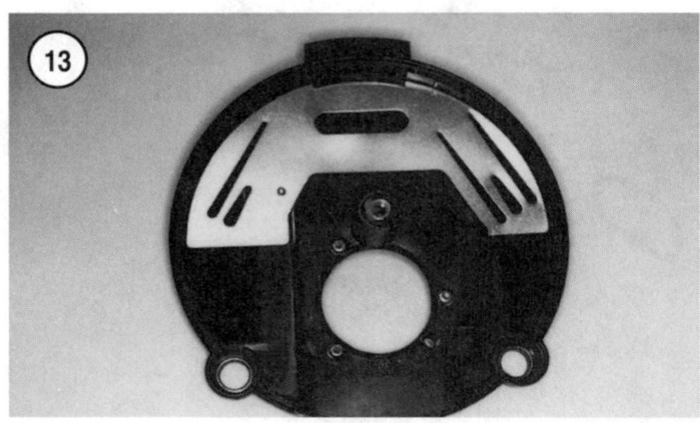

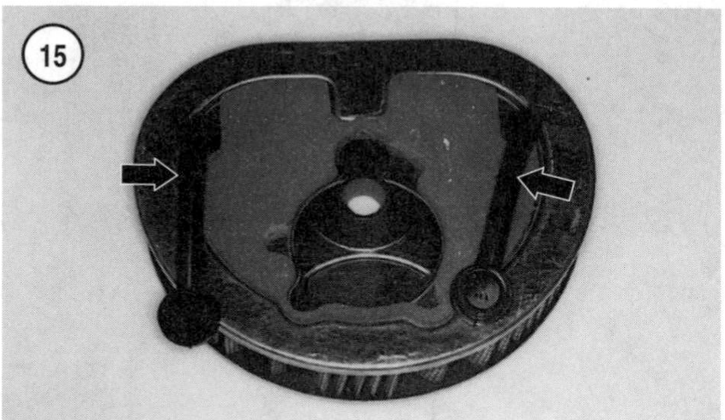

3. Disconnect the throttle (A, **Figure 16**) and choke (**Figure 17**) cables at the carburetor.
4. Disconnect the fuel hose at the fuel shutoff valve (**Figure 18**).
5. Label and disconnect all hoses from the carburetor.
6. Remove the carburetor mounting screws, carburetor (B, **Figure 16**) and insulator block.
7. Examine the intake manifolds on the cylinder head for cracks or damage that would allow unfiltered air to enter the engine. Replace damaged parts.

8. Install by reversing these removal steps while noting the following:
   a. Tighten the carburetor mounting screws securely.

CAUTION
Make sure all carburetor mounting points are well-secured and airtight to avoid engine damage.

   b. Connect the fuel line and turn on the fuel shutoff valve. Check for fuel leaks and correct before starting the engine.
   c. Adjust the throttle and choke cables as described in Chapter Three.

Disassembly

Refer to **Figure 19**.

CAUTION
Residual fuel will remain in the float bowl. Work over a pan on the workbench.

1. Remove the accelerating pump housing at the bottom of the float bowl (**Figure 20**). Then remove the spring (**Figure 21**) and diaphragm (A, **Figure 22**) from the accelerating pump housing.
2. Remove the O-ring from the accelerating pump housing.
3. Remove the screws securing the float bowl (B, **Figure 22**) and remove the float bowl.
4. Remove the overflow hose (**Figure 23**) from the base of the float bowl.
5. Turn the float bowl over and remove the rubber boot (A, **Figure 24**) and O-ring rubber gasket (B).
6. Remove the float pin screw (**Figure 25**) and withdraw the float pin and float (**Figure 26**).
7. Detach the fuel inlet valve (**Figure 27**) from the float and remove the clip (**Figure 28**).
8. Remove the accelerator pump rod from the float bowl.
9. Unscrew and remove the main jet (**Figure 29**).
10. Remove the pilot jet plug (**Figure 30**). Then unscrew and remove the pilot jet (**Figure 31**).
11. If necessary, remove the cable bracket (A, **Figure 32**) at the top of the carburetor housing.
12. The throttle (B, **Figure 32**) and choke (**Figure 33**) valve assemblies are matched to the individual carburetor during manufacturing. Do not remove them from the carburetor. If these parts are damaged, the carburetor must be replaced.

Assembly

1. Install the pilot jet (**Figure 31**) into the passage and tighten securely.
2. Install the pilot jet plug (**Figure 30**). Push it in until it bottoms.
3. Install the main jet (**Figure 29**) and tighten securely.
4. Install the clip (**Figure 28**) and attach the fuel valve (**Figure 27**) onto the float arm.
5. Install the float and fuel valve. Position the float onto the carburetor so that the fuel valve drops into its seat.

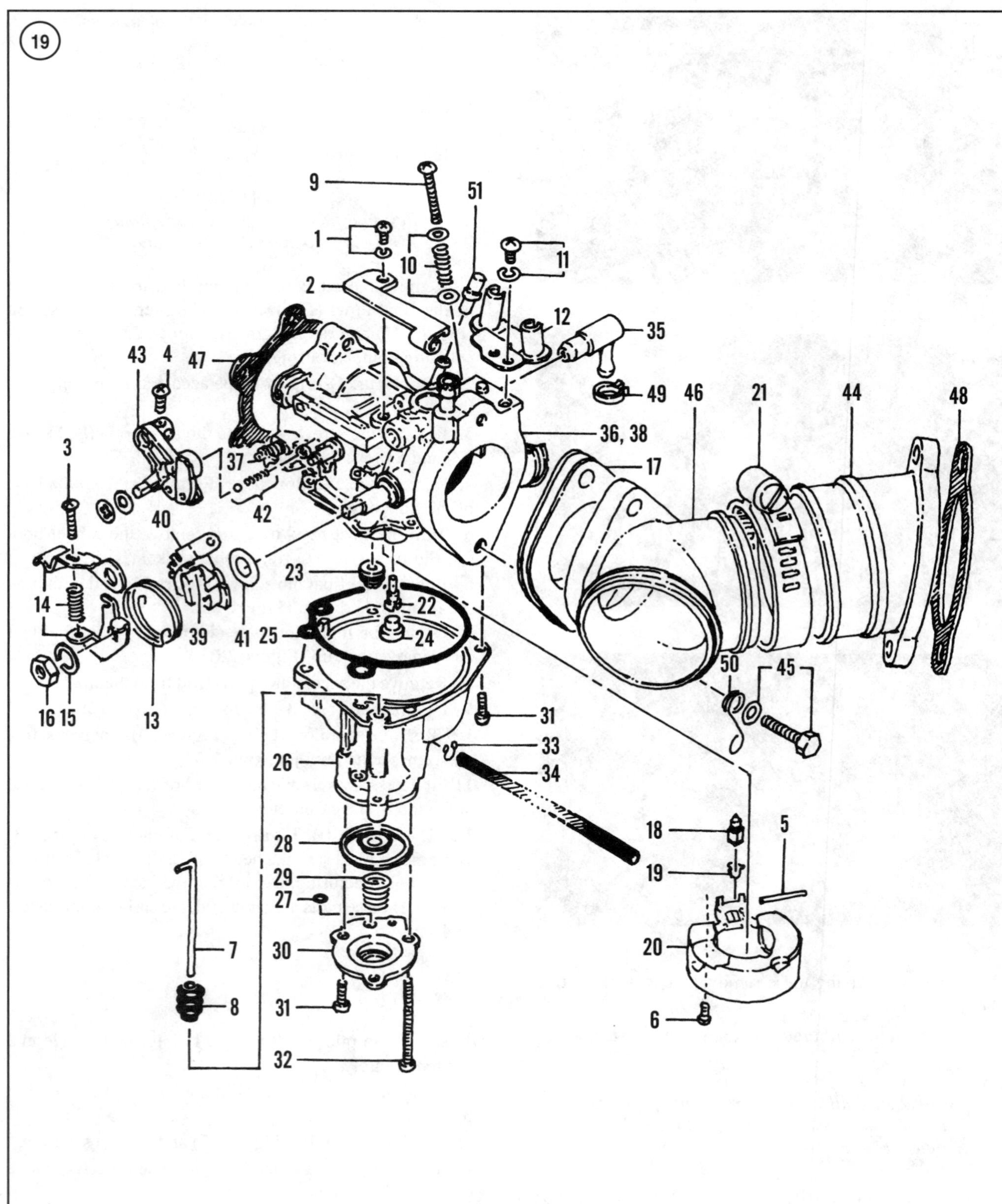
19
9
51
1
10
11
2
12
35
43
4
47
49
46
21
44
48
36, 38
3
37
17
42
40
23
22
14
39
41
25
24
50
45
16
15
13
31
33
26
34
18
5
28
29
19
27
7
30
20
8
31
6
32

CARBURETOR AND INTAKE MANIFOLD (1984-1989 MODELS)

1. Screw and washer
2. Choke cable bracket
3. Fast idle adjusting screw
4. Choke cable screw
5. Float pin
6. Float retaining screw
7. Accelerating pump rod
8. Rubber boot
9. Throttle stop screw
10. Spring and washers
11. Screw and washer
12. Throttle cable bracket
13. Spring
14. Fast idle cam assembly
15. Lockwasher
16. Nut
17. Insulator block
18. Inlet valve
19. Clip
20. Float assembly
21. Clamp
22. Pilot jet
23. Main jet
24. Plug
25. Rubber gasket
26. Float bowl
27. O-ring (accelerating pump)
28. Accelerating pump diaphragm
29. Accelerating pump spring
30. Accelerating pump housing
31. Screw
32. Screw
33. Overflow line clip
34. Overflow line
35. Fuel inlet fitting
36. Choke plate (not shown)
37. Choke lever shaft
38. Housing
39. Accelerating pump rod hole
40. Rocker arm
41. Washer
42. Choke detent ball and spring
43. Fast idle cam
44. Compliance fitting
45. Mounting bolt and lockwasher
46. Intake manifold
47. Gasket
48. Gasket
49. Clamp
50. Cable guide
51. Cap (evap. purge port)

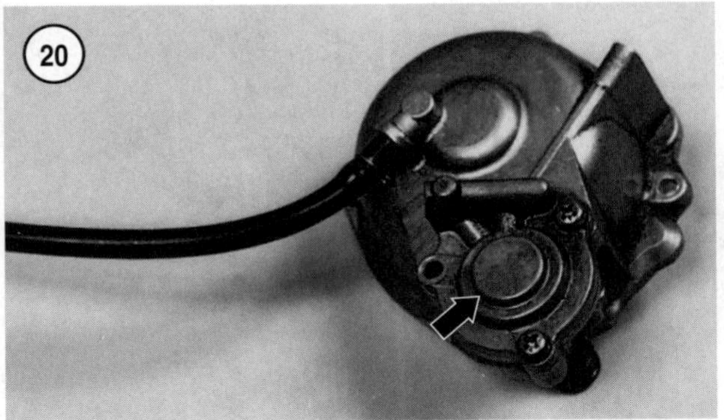

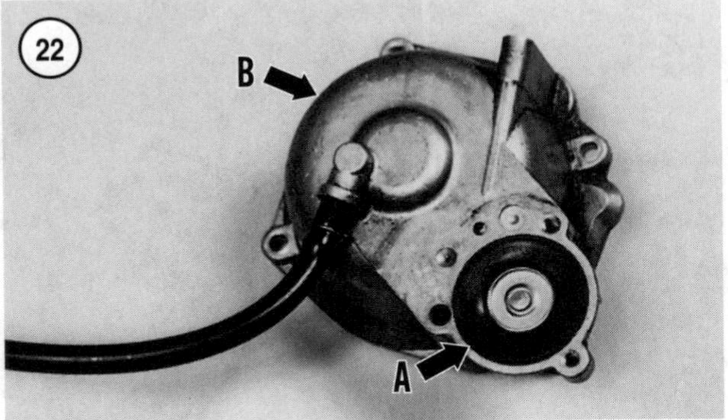

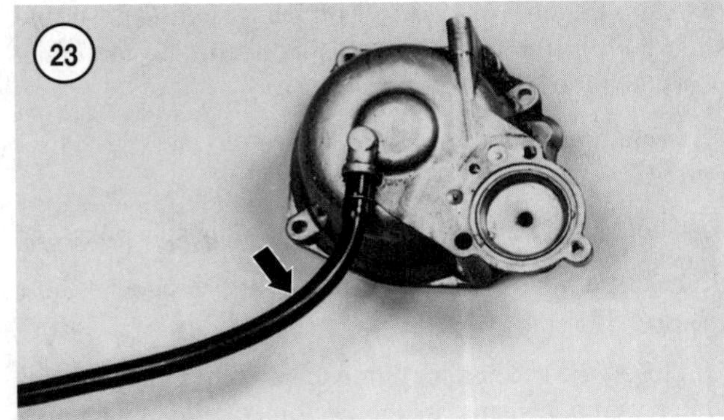

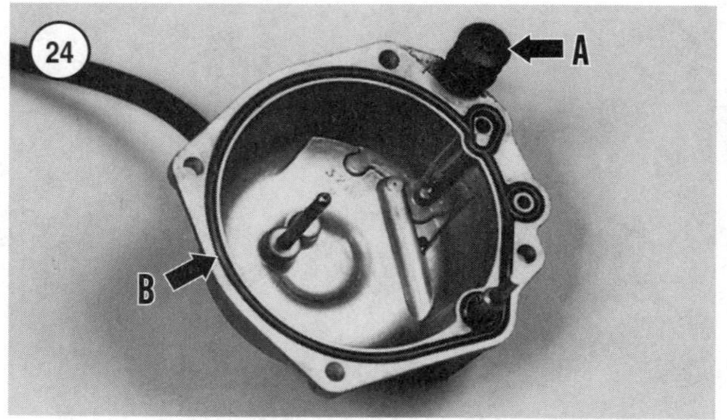

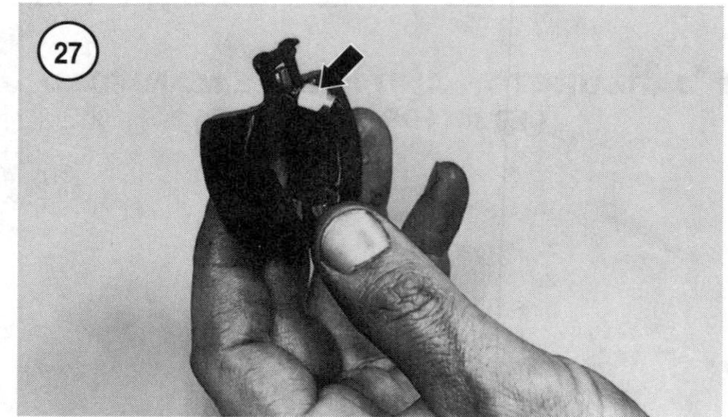

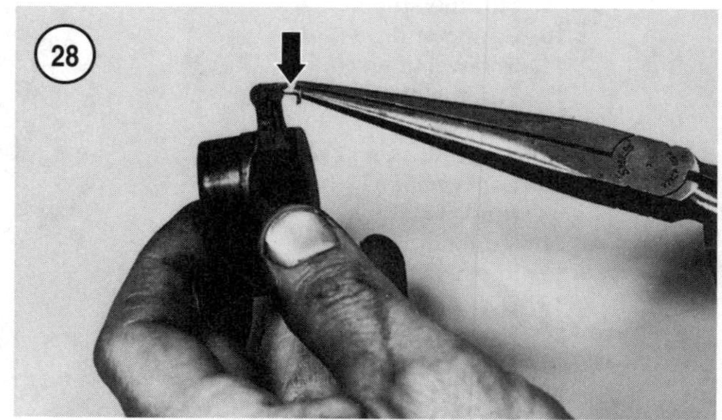

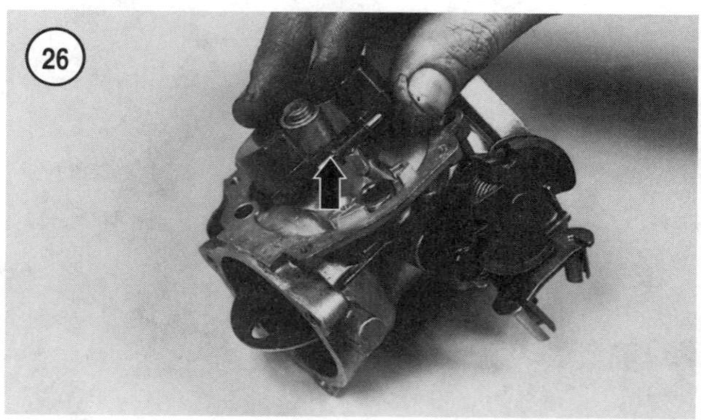

6. Align the float pivot arm with the mounting posts and slide the pin through the float pivot arm and mounting posts (**Figure 26**).

7. Install the float pin screw (**Figure 25**) and tighten securely.

8. Check the float level as described in this chapter.

9. Install a *new* O-ring into the cover passageway hole (**Figure 34**).

10. Insert the accelerator pump diaphragm into the accelerator pump housing in the bottom of the float bowl.

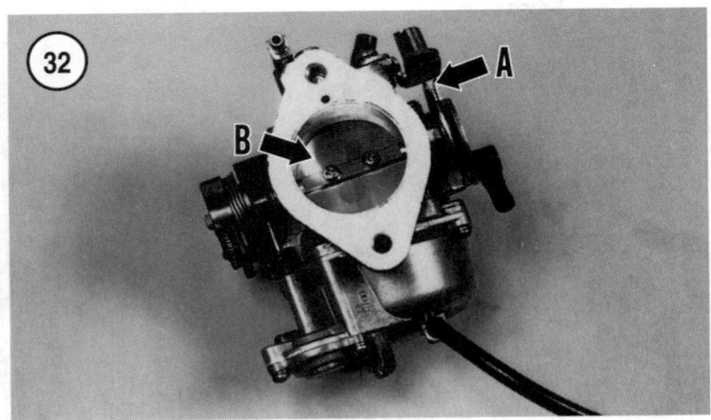

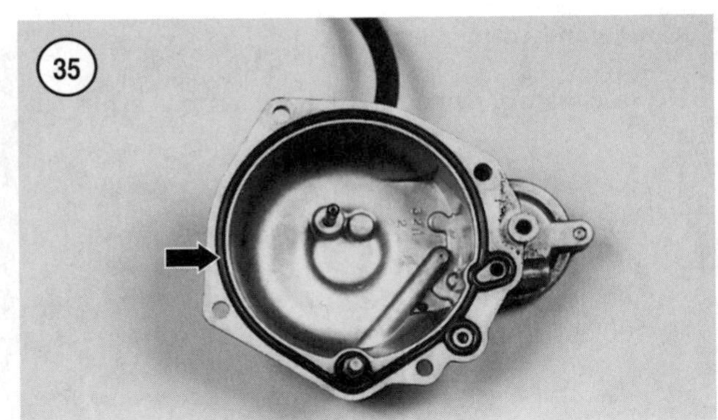

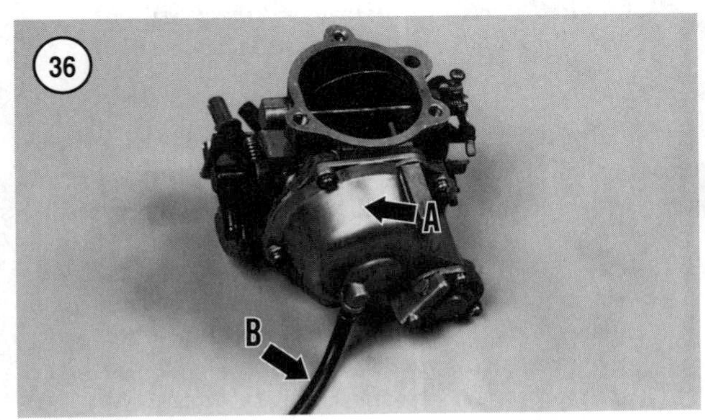

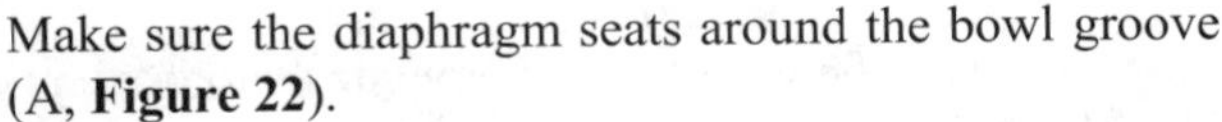

Make sure the diaphragm seats around the bowl groove (A, **Figure 22**).

11. Install the spring (**Figure 21**) onto the accelerator pump diaphragm.

12. Align the cover assembly with the diaphragm and bowl and install the cover assembly (**Figure 20**). Install the screws and lockwashers and tighten securely.

13. If removed, insert the accelerator pump nozzle into the float bowl.

14. Install the rubber boot (A, **Figure 24**) onto the float bowl.

15. Install a *new* rubber O-ring seal (**Figure 35**) onto the float bowl and make sure it is seated correctly.

16. Align the float bowl with the carburetor and install the float bowl (A, **Figure 36**). Install the float bowl screws and lockwasher and tighten them in a crisscross pattern to prevent warp.

17. Insert the pump rod through the boot on the float bowl and engage the rod with the diaphragm. Then connect the pump rod with the lever assembly.

18. Install the drain hose (B, **Figure 36**) onto the float bowl.

Cleaning and Inspection

Replace worn or damaged parts as described in this section.

CAUTION
The carburetor body is equipped with plastic parts that cannot be removed. Do not dip the carburetor body, O-rings, float assembly or float fuel valve in a carburetor cleaner or another harsh solution that can damage these parts. The use of a caustic carburetor cleaning solvent is not recommended. Instead, clean the carburetor and related parts in a petroleum-based solvent or Simple Green. Then rinse them in clean water.

1. Initially, clean all parts in a mild petroleum-based cleaning solution. Then clean them in hot soapy water and rinse with cold water. Blow them dry with compressed air.

CAUTION
*If compressed air is not available, allow the parts to air-dry or use a clean lint-free cloth. Do **not** use a paper towel to dry carburetor parts because small paper particles can plug openings in the carburetor housing or jets.*

2. Allow the carburetors to dry thoroughly before assembly. Blow out the jets with compressed air.

CAUTION
*Do **not** use wire or drill bits to clean jets because minor gouges in the jet can alter the air/fuel mixture.*

3. Inspect the accelerator pump boot (A, **Figure 24**) for hardness or deterioration.
4. Inspect the float bowl O-ring rubber gasket (B, **Figure 24**) for hardness or deterioration.
5. Inspect the float for deterioration or damage. If the float is suspected of leakage, place it in a container of water and push it down. If the float sinks or if bubbles appear, there is a leak, and the float must be replaced.
6. A damaged accelerator pump diaphragm will cause poor acceleration. Hold the diaphragm up to a strong light and check the diaphragm for pin holes, cracks or other damage. Replace if necessary.
7. Make sure the throttle plate (B, **Figure 32**) screws are tight. Tighten them if necessary.
8. Move the throttle wheel back and forth from stop to stop and check for free movement. The throttle lever should move smoothly and return under spring tension.

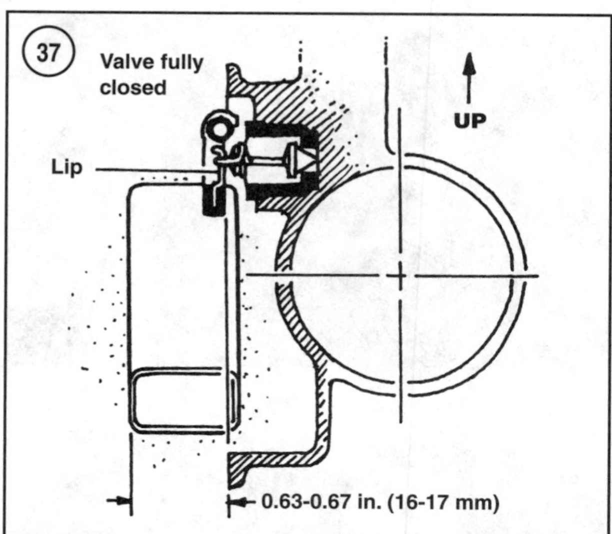

9. Check the throttle wheel return spring for free movement. Make sure it rotates the throttle wheel back to the stop position with no hesitation.
10. Make sure all openings in the carburetor housing are clear. Clean them out if they are plugged. Then apply compressed air to all openings.
11. Inspect the carburetor body for internal or external damage. If there is damage, replace the carburetor assembly because the body cannot be replaced separately.

Float Adjustment

1. Remove the carburetor as described in this section.
2. Remove the float bowl as described in this section.
3. Turn the carburetor to position the float bowl as shown in **Figure 37**. Measure the float height from the face of the bowl mounting flange surface to the bottom float surface (**Figure 38**). Float specified height is 0.63-0.67 in. (16-17 mm).

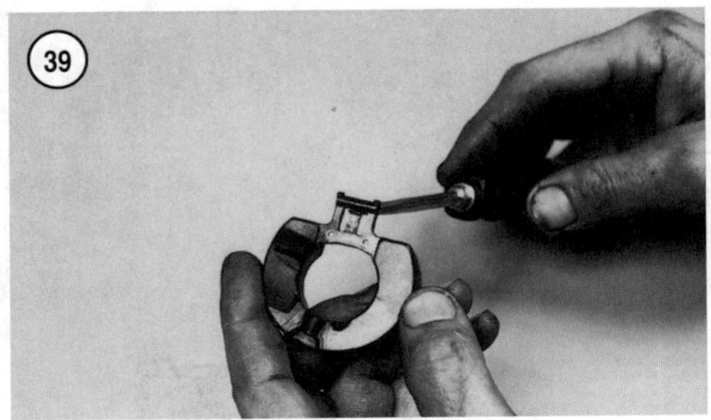

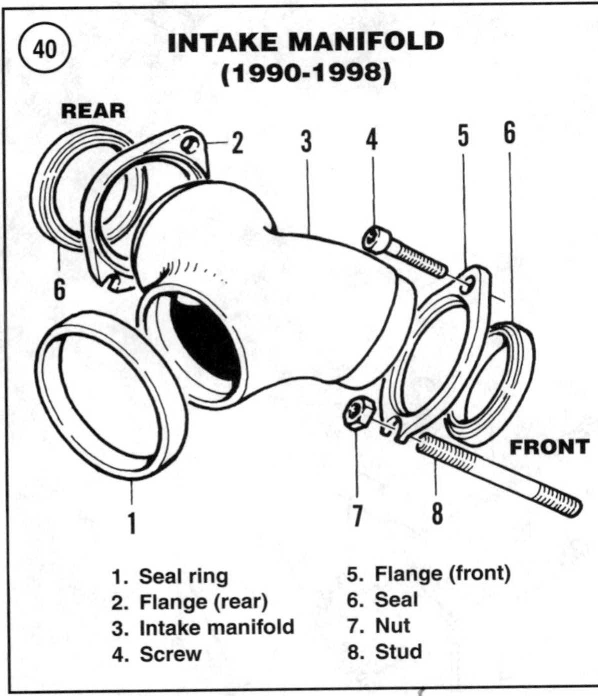

4. If the float level is incorrect, remove the float as described in this section.
5. Slowly bend the float tang with a screwdriver (**Figure 39**) and adjust it to the correct position.
6. Reinstall the float bowl and install the carburetor as described in this section.

CARBURETOR (1990-1998 MODELS)

Removal/Installation

1. Remove the air filter assembly as described in this chapter.
2. Turn off the fuel shutoff valve (**Figure 18**).
3. Label and disconnect the throttle and choke cables at the carburetor.

NOTE
On models so equipped, disconnect the cruise control servo cable at the carburetor.

4. Disconnect the fuel hose at the fuel shutoff valve.
5. Label and disconnect all hoses at the carburetor.
6. Pull the carburetor off of its seal ring and manifold.
7. Inspect the carburetor seal ring (**Figure 40**) and replace it if it is worn or damaged.
8. Install by reversing these removal steps while noting the following:
   a. Route the float bowl overflow hose between the rear cylinder pushrods and then down between the engine oil pump cover and crankcase.

CAUTION
Make sure all carburetor mounting points are well-secured and airtight. Any leaks around the engine manifold or air filter housing can easily cause serious engine damage.

   b. Adjust the throttle and choke cables as described in Chapter Three.

8

Disassembly

Refer to **Figure 41**.

NOTE
*The throttle cable bracket shown in 46, **Figure 41**, is for models without cruise control. Cruise control models have an additional tab that is used to mount the cruise control servo cable.*

1. Disconnect the overflow hose from the float bowl (**Figure 42**).
2. Unscrew and remove the starting enrichment (choke) cable (**Figure 43**).
3. Remove the screws and washers securing the throttle cable bracket to the carburetor. Remove the bracket (**Figure 44**).
4. Remove the remaining cover screws and washers and remove the cover (**Figure 45**) and spring (**Figure 46**).
5. Remove the vacuum piston (**Figure 47**) from the carburetor housing. Do not damage the jet needle sticking out of the bottom of the vacuum piston.

NOTE
Because the accelerator pump is synchronized with the throttle plate, note the posi-

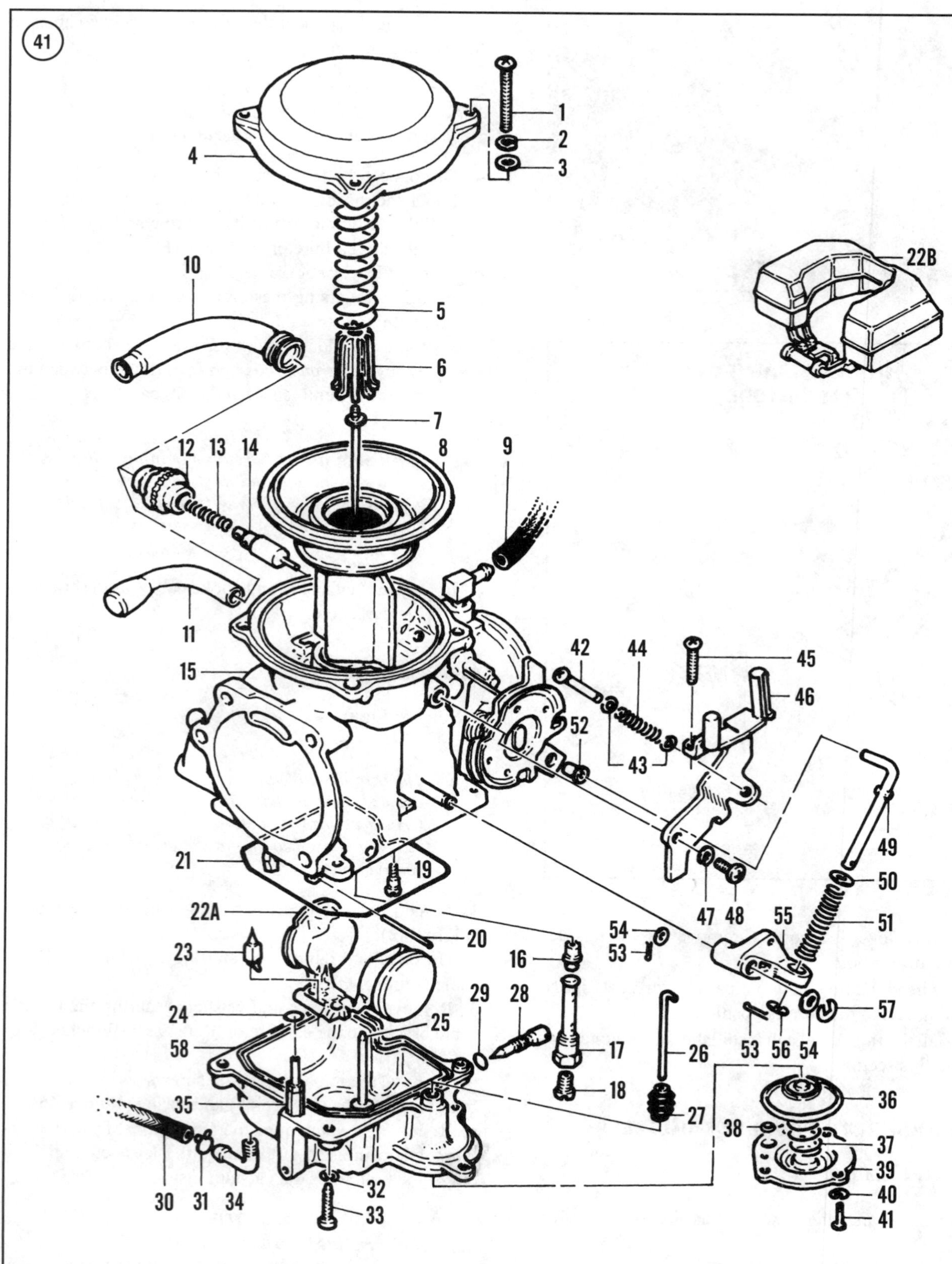
41
1
2
3
4
5
6
7
8
9
10
11
12
13
14
15
16
17
18
19
20
21
22A
22B
23
24
25
26
27
28
29
30
31
32
33
34
35
36
37
38
39
40
41
42
43
44
45
46
47
48
49
50
51
52
53
54
55
56
57
58

CARBURETOR (1990-1998)

1. Screw
2. Lockwasher
3. Flat washer
4. Cover
5. Spring
6. Spring seat
7. Jet needle
8. Vacuum piston
9. Vacuum hose
10. Cable guide
11. Starter cap
12. Cable sealing cap
13. Spring
14. Enricher valve
15. Body
16. Needle jet
17. Needle jet holder
18. Main jet
19. Pilot jet
20. Float pin
21. O-ring

22A. Float (1990-1991)

22B. Float (1992-1998)

23. Fuel valve and clip
24. O-ring
25. Overflow pipe
26. Rod
27. Boot
28. Drain screw
29. O-ring
30. Hose
31. Clamp
32. Washer
33. Screw
34. Fitting
35. Accelerator pump nozzle
36. Diaphragm
37. Spring
38. O-ring
39. Cover
40. Lockwasher
41. Screw
42. Idle adjust screw
43. Washers
44. Spring
45. Screw
46. Throttle cable bracket
47. Washer
48. Screw
49. Rod
50. Washer
51. Spring
52. Collar
53. Collar pin
54. Washer
55. Lever
56. Washer
57. E-clip
58. Float bowl

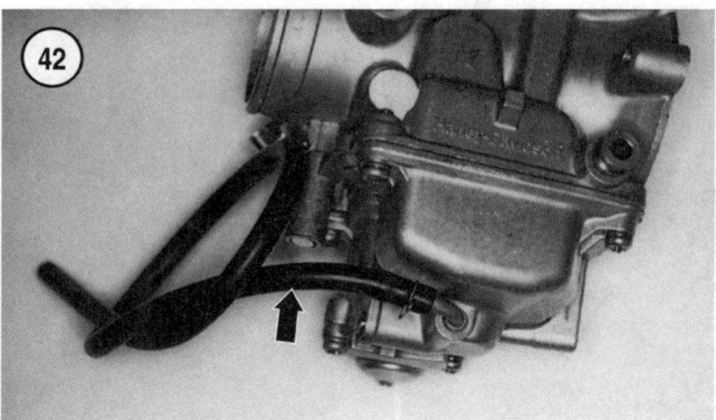

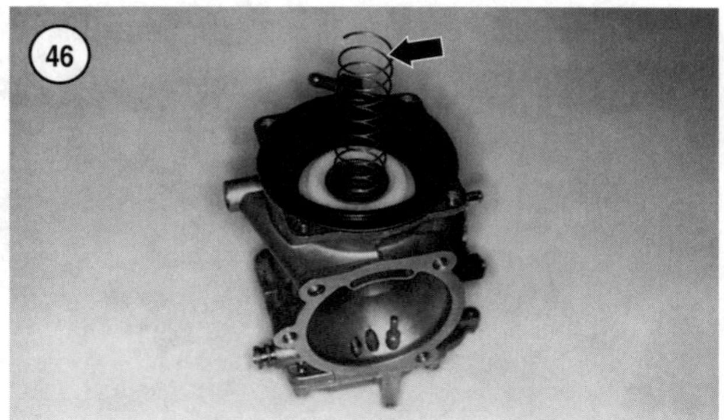

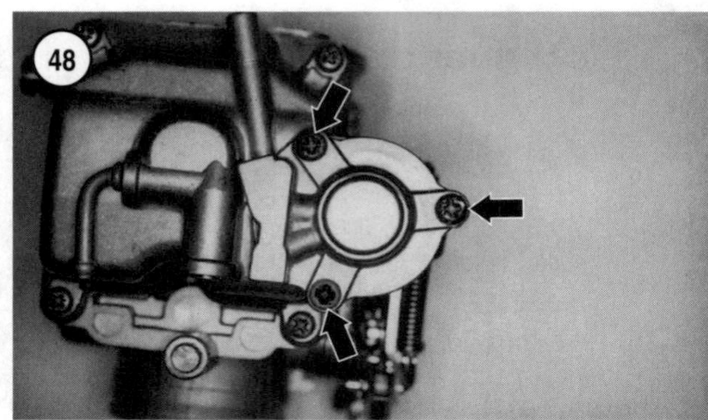

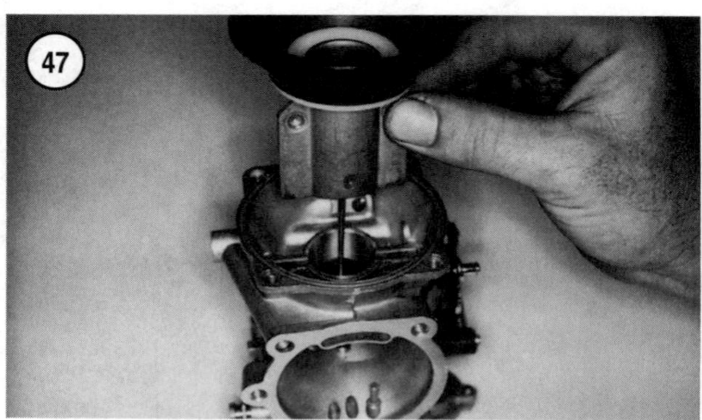

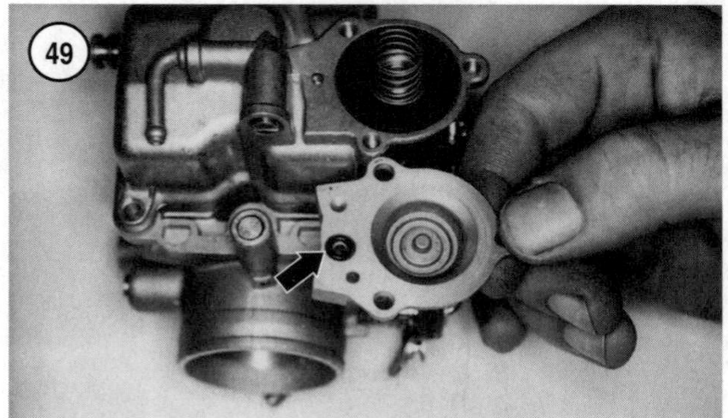

tion of the throttle and pump rods when removing the float bowl in the following steps.

6. Remove the accelerator pump diaphragm as follows:
   a. Remove the screws and lockwashers holding the pump cover (**Figure 48**) to the float bowl and remove the cover.
   b. Remove the small pump cover O-ring (**Figure 49**).
   c. Remove the spring (A, **Figure 50**) and diaphragm (B).
7. Remove the float bowl as follows:
   a. Remove the screws and washers securing the float bowl (C, **Figure 50**).
   b. Pull straight up and remove the float bowl from the carburetor. Guide the pump rod (A, **Figure 51**) up and out of the boot (B) on the bowl.
   c. Disconnect the pump rod (A, **Figure 52**) from the lever assembly (B) on the carburetor.
   d. Carefully pull the boot (**Figure 53**) off of the float bowl.

8A. On 1990-1991 models, remove the float pin (**Figure 54**) and lift off the float and needle valve assembly (**Figure 55**).

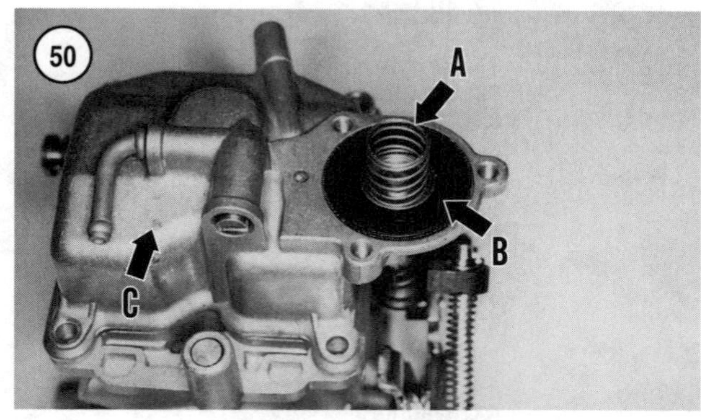

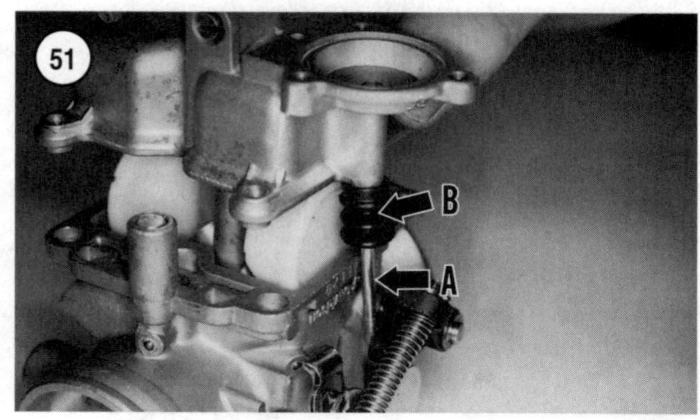

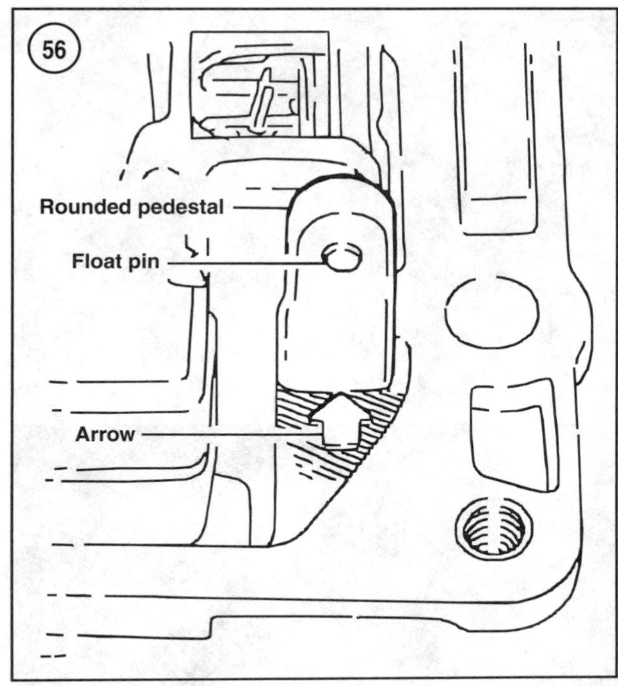

CAUTION

*On 1995-1998 models, one of the float bowl pedestals has an interference fit that holds the float pin in place. The arrow, cast into the carburetor body, points to this pedestal. Tap the float pin out and remove it from this pedestal in the direction of the arrow (**Figure 56**).*

8B. On 1992-1998 models, remove the float pin (**Figure 57**) and lift off the float and needle valve assembly (**Figure 58**).

9. Unscrew and remove the main jet (**Figure 59**) from the top of the needle jet holder.

10. Unscrew and remove the needle jet holder (**Figure 60**).

8

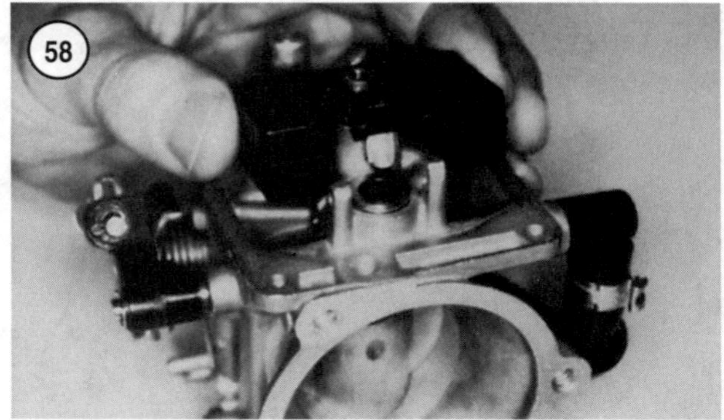

58

60

59

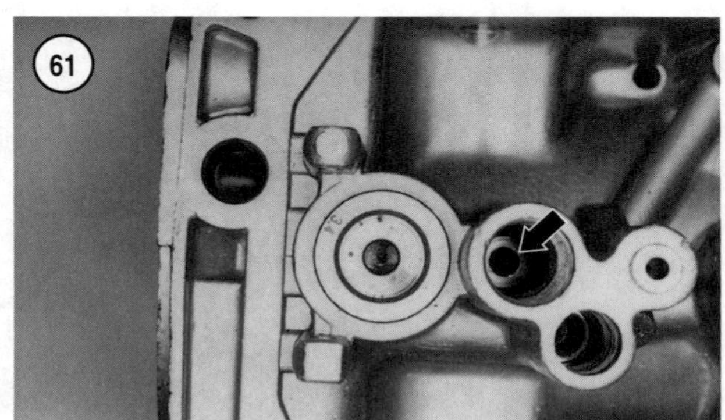

61

11. Remove the needle jet from the needle jet bore in the carburetor (**Figure 61**).
12. Use a narrow flat-tipped screwdriver that fits the pilot jet slot. Loosen, unscrew and remove the pilot jet (**Figure 62**).
13. The throttle plate (**Figure 63**) is matched to the individual carburetor during manufacturing. Do not remove it from the carburetor. If this part is damaged, the carburetor must be replaced.

Assembly

1. Prior to assembly, make sure all worn or damaged parts have been repaired or replaced as described under *Inspection*. Thoroughly clean all parts before assembly.
2. Insert the pilot jet (**Figure 62**) into the passage and tighten with the same screwdriver used during removal.
3. The needle jet is not symmetrical and must be installed correctly. Position the needle jet with the larger opening faces toward the top of the carburetor and install it into its receptacle (**Figure 61**).
4. Install the needle jet holder (**Figure 60**) into the main jet passage and tighten securely.
5. Install the main jet (**Figure 59**) onto the end of the needle jet holder and tighten securely.

62

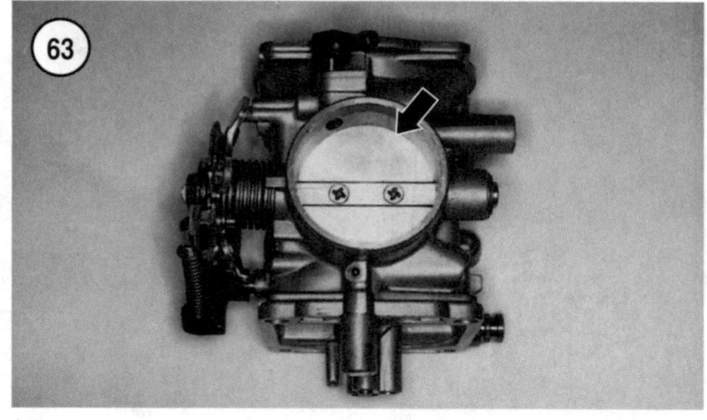

63

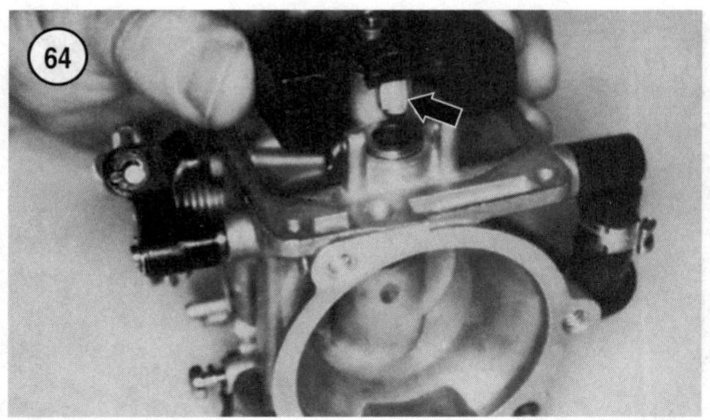
64

65

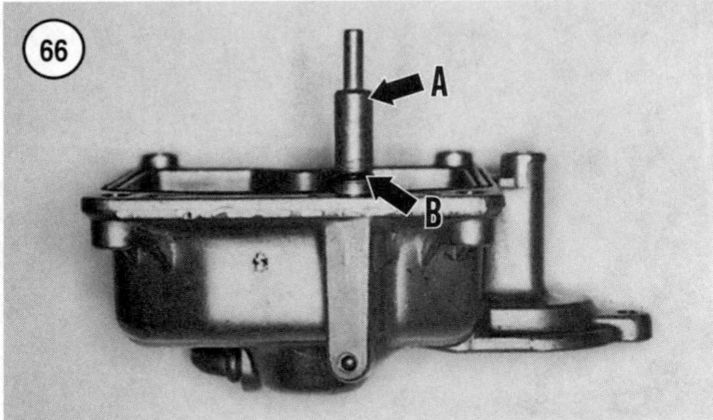

66

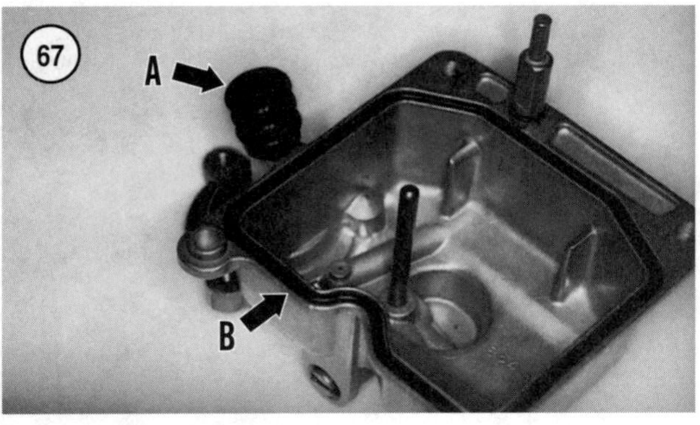

67

68

6A. On 1990-1991 models, install the float as follows:

a. Install the fuel valve onto the float (**Figure 55**) and install the float onto the carburetor. Make sure the fuel valve is seated correctly in its receptacle.
b. Align the float pivot arm with the two carburetor mounting posts and slip the pin through the float pivot arm and mounting posts (**Figure 54**).

NOTE

*On 1995-1998 models, one of the float bowl pedestals has an interference fit that holds the float pin in place. Tap the float pin in from the loose side opposite the arrow (**Figure 56**).*

6B. On 1992-1998 models, install the float as follows:

a. Install the fuel valve onto the float (**Figure 64**) and position the float onto the carburetor so that the valve drops into its seat.
b. Align the float pivot arm with the two carburetor mounting posts and slip the pin through the float pivot arm and mounting posts (**Figure 65**).

7. Check float level as described in this section.
8. Assemble and install the float bowl as follows:

a. Insert the accelerator pump nozzle (A, **Figure 66**) into the float bowl. Install the *new* O-ring (B, **Figure 66**) onto the nozzle.
b. Install the rubber boot (A, **Figure 67**) and *new* O-ring (B) onto the float bowl.
c. Connect the pump rod to the lever assembly on the carburetor (**Figure 68**).
d. Insert the pump rod through the boot (**Figure 69**) on the float bowl and engage the rod with the diaphragm while installing the float bowl. Then check that the pump rod is still attached to the lever assembly as shown in **Figure 70**. Check also to see if the pump rod is visible through the hole in the pump chamber in the float bowl (**Figure 71**). If not, remove and reinstall the float bowl and pump rod.

8

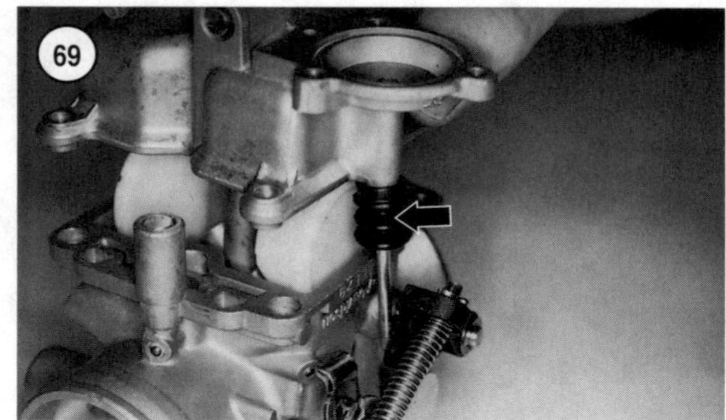

e. Install the float bowl screws and washers and tighten securely in a crisscross pattern.

9. Install the accelerator pump diaphragm assembly as follows:

a. Insert the accelerator pump diaphragm into the bottom of the float bowl. Make sure the diaphragm seats around the bowl groove (**Figure 72**).

b. Install the spring into the center of the accelerator pump diaphragm (**Figure 73**).

c. Install the O-ring into the cover passageway hole (**Figure 74**).

d. Align the cover assembly with the diaphragm and bowl and install the cover assembly. Install the screws (**Figure 75**) and lockwashers and tighten securely.

10. Drop the jet needle through the center hole in the vacuum piston. Install the spring seat over the top of the needle to secure it.

11. Align the slides on the vacuum piston with the grooves in the carburetor bore and install the vacuum piston (**Figure 76**). The slides on the piston are offset, so the piston can only be installed one way. When installing the vacuum piston, make sure the jet needle drops through the needle jet.

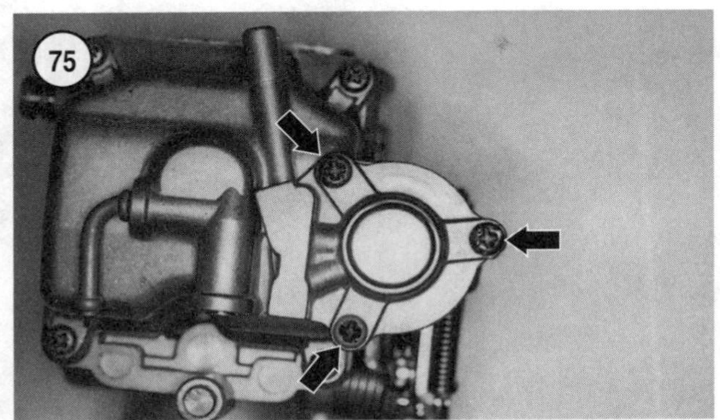

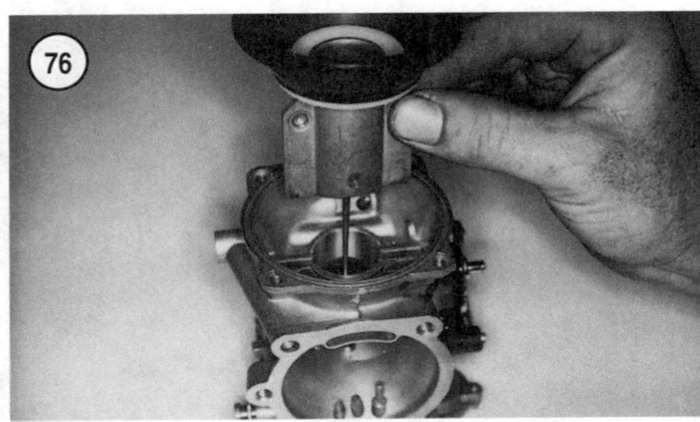

12. Seat the outer edge of the vacuum piston into the groove at the top of the carburetor piston chamber.

13. Insert the spring (**Figure 77**) into the vacuum piston so that the end of the spring fits over the spring seat.

14. Align the free end of the spring with the carburetor top and install the top onto the carburetor, which compresses the spring.

15. Hold the carburetor top in place and lift the vacuum piston (**Figure 78**) by hand. The piston should move smoothly. If the piston movement is rough or sluggish, the spring might be improperly installed. Remove the top and reinstall the spring. Then repeat this step.

16. Install the carburetor top (**Figure 79**) screws, lockwashers and flat washers finger-tight.

17. Install the throttle cable bracket (A, **Figure 80**) onto the carburetor so that the end of the idle speed screw engages the top of the throttle cam stop (B). Hold the bracket in place and install the bracket side mounting screw and washer; securely tighten the screw. Then install the upper bracket mounting screw (**Figure 81**), lockwasher and flat washer finger-tight.

18. Tighten the carburetor cap screws securely in a crisscross pattern.

19. Align the enricher valve needle with the needle passage in the carburetor (**Figure 82**) and install the enricher valve. Tighten the valve nut securely.
20. Install the float bowl overflow hose and secure it with its clamp.

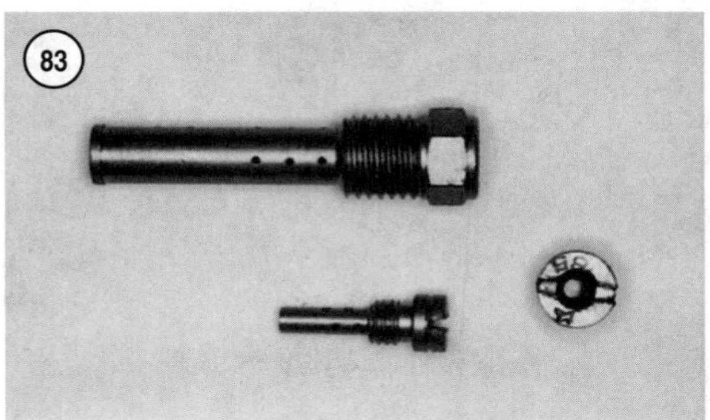

Inspection

Replace worn or damaged parts as described in this section.

CAUTION
The carburetor body is equipped with plastic parts that cannot be removed. Do not dip the carburetor body, O-rings, float assembly or float fuel valve in a carburetor cleaner or another harsh solution that can damage these parts. The use of a caustic carburetor cleaning solvent is not recommended. Instead, clean the carburetor and related parts in a petroleum-based solvent or Simple Green. Then rinse them in clean water.

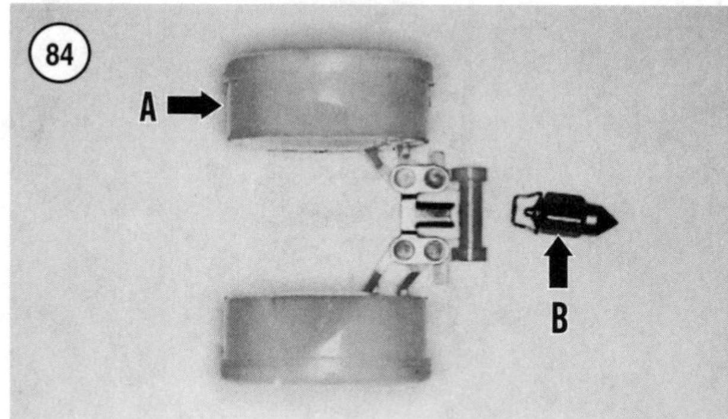

1. Initially, clean all parts in a mild petroleum-based cleaning solution. Then clean them in hot soapy water and rinse with cold water. Blow them dry with compressed air.

CAUTION
*If compressed air is not available, allow the parts to air-dry or use a clean lint-free cloth. Do **not** use a paper towel to dry carburetor parts because small paper particles can plug openings in the carburetor housing or jets.*

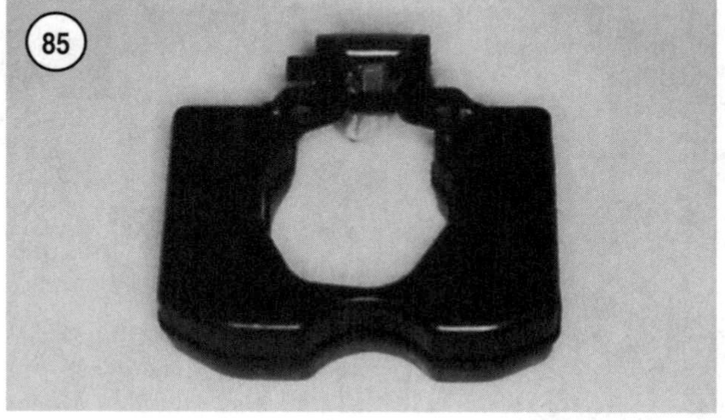

2. Allow the carburetor to dry thoroughly before assembly. Blow out the jets (**Figure 83**) with compressed air. Do not use a piece of wire to clean them because minor gouges in a jet can alter the flow rate and upset the air/fuel mixture.

86

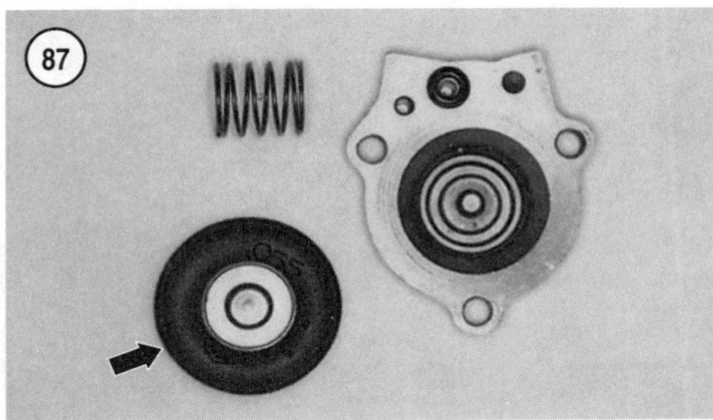

87

88

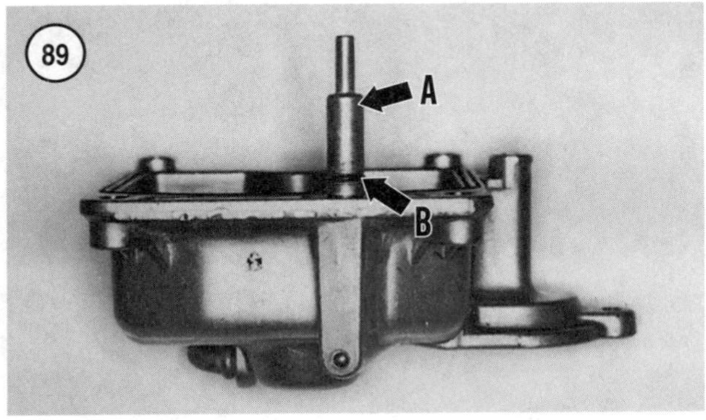

89

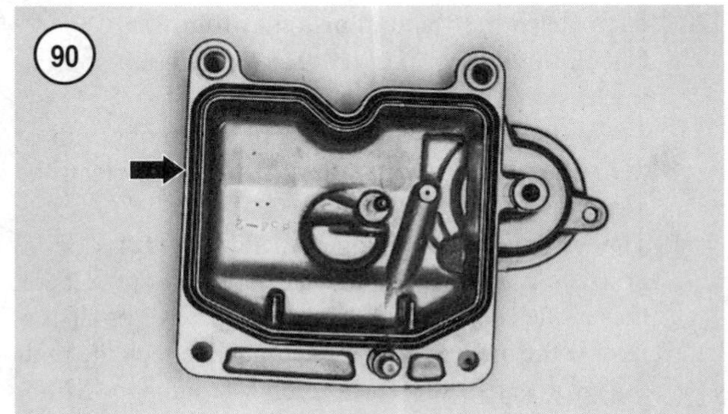

90

3. Make sure the needle jet holder bleed tube orifices are clear.

4. Make sure all fuel and air openings are clear. Blow out with compressed air if necessary.

5. Inspect the float for deterioration or damage. Refer to A, **Figure 84** (1984-1991 models) or **Figure 85** (1992-1998 models). If the float is suspected of leakage, place it in a container of water and push it down. If the float sinks, or if bubbles appear, there is a leak, and the float must be replaced.

6. Check the float needle (B, **Figure 84**) and seat (**Figure 86**) contact areas. Both contact surfaces should appear smooth without any gouging or other apparent damage. Replace the needle if damaged. The seat is a permanent part of the carburetor housing; if damaged, the housing must be replaced.

7. A damaged accelerating pump diaphragm (**Figure 87**) will cause poor acceleration. Hold the diaphragm up to a strong light and check the diaphragm for pinholes, cracks or other damage (**Figure 88**). Replace if necessary.

8. Remove the accelerator pump nozzle (A, **Figure 89**) and its O-ring (B) from the float bowl. Clean the nozzle with compressed air.

9. Replace the pump rod if bent or worn.

10. Inspect the float bowl O-ring (**Figure 90**) for hardness and replace as necessary. Make sure the *new* O-ring fits in its groove properly.

11. Inspect the pilot jet (**Figure 83**) for wear or damage that might have occurred during removal. Check the slot in the top of the jet for cracks or breakage. Do not install a damaged pilot jet.

NOTE

Step 12 describes bench checks that should be performed on the vacuum piston. Operational checks with the vacuum installed in the carburetor and with the engine running are described in this chapter.

8

12. Bench check the vacuum piston as follows:
   a. Check the spring (**Figure 91**) for fatigue, stretching, distortion or other damage.
   b. Check the vacuum passage through the bottom of the piston for contamination. If blocked, clean the passage.
   c. The sides of the piston (A, **Figure 92**) ride in grooves machined in the carburetor bore. Check these sides for roughness, nicks, cracks or distortion. If the piston sides are damaged, check the mating grooves in the carburetor for damage. Minor roughness can be removed with emery cloth or by buffing. If the sides are severely damaged, replace the vacuum piston.
   d. Hold the vacuum piston up to a light and check the diaphragm (B, **Figure 92**) for pinholes, tearing, cracks, age deterioration or other damage. Check the diaphragm where it is mounted against the piston. If the diaphragm is damaged, replace the vacuum piston.
   e. Check jet needle for bending or damage.

13. A plugged, improperly seating or contaminated enricher system will cause hard starting as well as poor low- and high-speed performance. Check the following:
   a. Check for a rough or damaged enricher valve. Check the needle (**Figure 93**) on the end of the enricher valve for bending or contamination.
   b. Check the enricher valve spring for fatigue, stretching or distortion.
   c. The enricher valve chamber (A, **Figure 94**) in the carburetor must be clean. Clean the chamber carefully. Make sure the enricher valve air inlet and the air/fuel passages are clear.
   d. Check the enricher valve cable (**Figure 95**) for kinks or other damage.

14. Check the throttle rod (**Figure 96**) and all external carburetor components for missing or damaged parts.

15. Check that the throttle valve shaft E-clip (B, **Figure 94**) is properly secured in the groove on the end of the shaft.

Float Adjustment (1990-Early 1991 Models)

NOTE
1990-early 1991 model carburetors are equipped with a three-sided fuel valve. Starting with late 1991 models (production date of June 1991), the carburetor is equipped with a four-sided fuel valve.

1. Remove the carburetor as described in this section.
2. Remove the float bowl as described in this section.

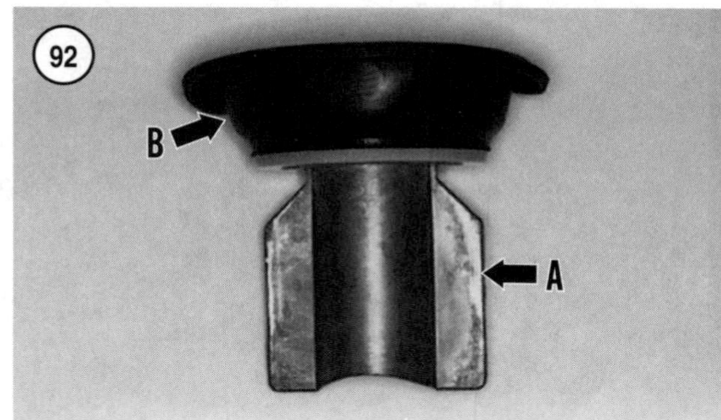

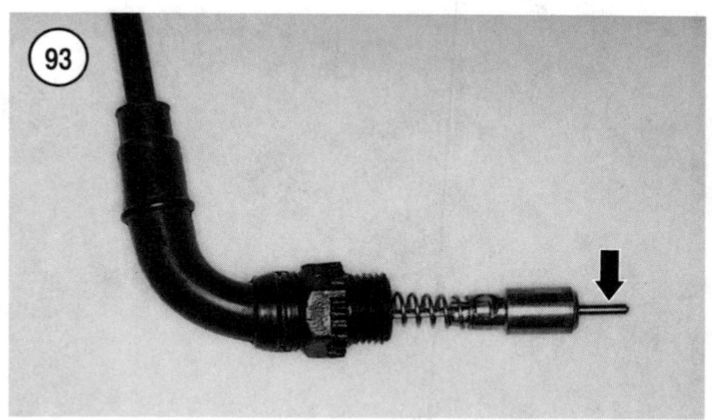

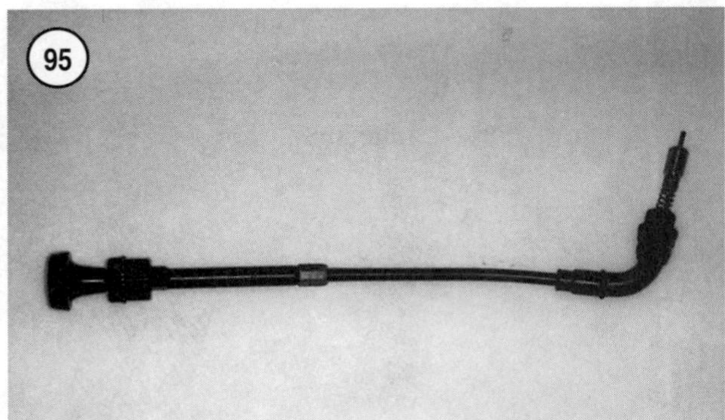

95

96

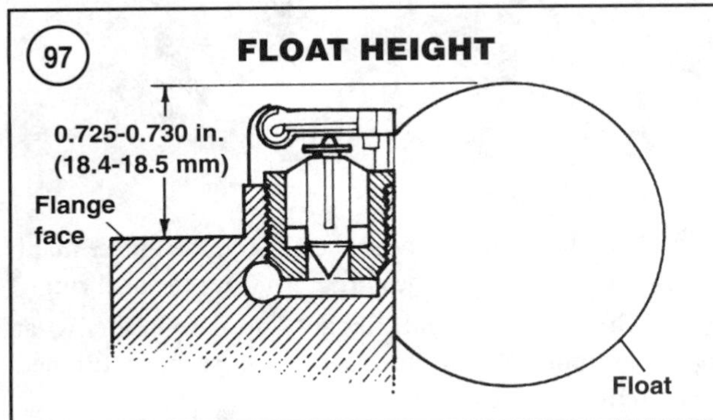

97 FLOAT HEIGHT

98

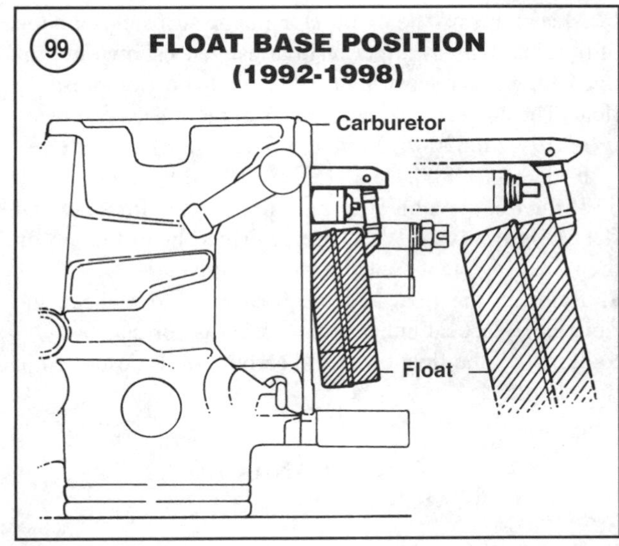

99 FLOAT BASE POSITION (1992-1998)

3. Turn the carburetor to position the float bowl as shown in **Figure 97**. Measure the float height from the face of the bowl mounting flange surface to the bottom float surface (**Figure 97**). Do not apply pressure to the float when measuring. The correct float height is 0.725-0.730 in. (18.4-18.5 mm).
4. If the float height is incorrect, remove the float pin and float (**Figure 98**).
5. Bend the float tang with a screwdriver to adjust.
6. Reinstall the float and the float pin and recheck the float level. Repeat until the float level is correct.
7. Reinstall the float bowl and carburetor as described in this chapter.

Float Adjustment (Late 1991-1998 Models)

An incorrect float level can cause flooding as well as poor fuel economy and acceleration.

The carburetor must be removed and partially disassembled for this adjustment.

1. Remove the carburetor as described in this chapter.
2. Remove the float bowl as described in this chapter.
3. Place the engine manifold side of the carburetor on a flat surface as shown in **Figure 99**. This is the base position.
4. Tilt the carburetor counterclockwise 15-20° as shown in **Figure 100**. At this position, the float will come to rest as the float pin compresses without compressing the pin return spring.

NOTE
If the carburetor is tilted fewer than 15° or more than 20°, the following carburetor measurements will be incorrect.

8

5. Measure from the carburetor flange surface to the top of the float with a caliper or float gauge as shown in **Figure 100**. When measuring float level, do not compress the float. The correct float level measurement is as follows:
   a. 1991: 0.690-0.730 in. (17.5-18.5 mm).
   b. 1992-1998: 0.413-0.453 in. (10.5-11.5 mm).
6. If the float level is incorrect, remove the float pin and float (**Figure 101**). With a screwdriver, bend the tab on the float hinge that contacts the fuel valve.
7. Reinstall the float and the float pin and recheck the float level. Repeat until the float level is correct.
8. Reinstall the float bowl and carburetor as described in this chapter.

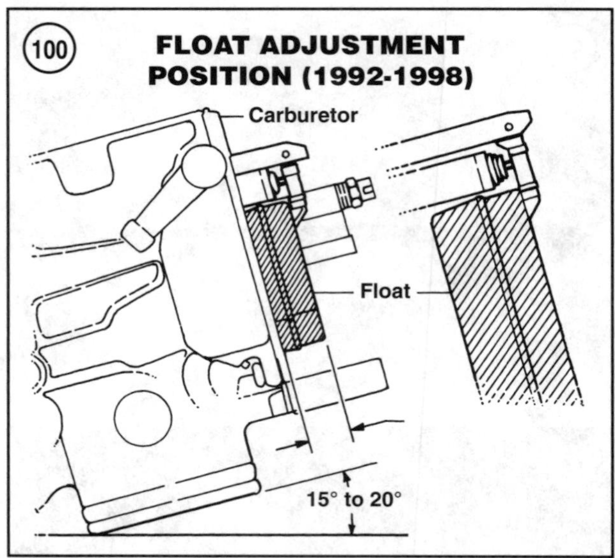

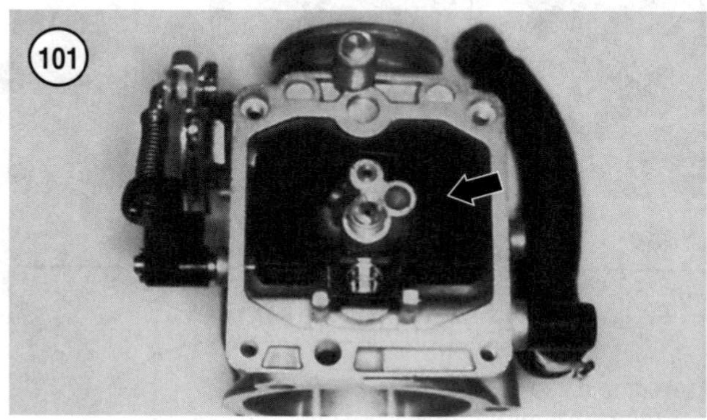

INTAKE MANIFOLD (CARBURETED MODELS)

Removal/Installation

NOTE
*The front and rear intake manifold flanges (**Figure 102**) are different. If the flanges are not marked, label them with an F and R so they will be reinstalled in the correct locations.*

1. Remove the carburetor as described in this chapter.
2. Remove the manifold Allen bolts and nut. Remove the manifold, the two flanges and the two intake manifold seals.
3. Inspect the intake manifold seals (**Figure 103**) for wear, deterioration or other damage. Replace the seals if necessary.
4. Inspect the carburetor seal ring (**Figure 104**) and replace it if it is worn or damaged.
5. Install the intake manifold as follows:
   a. Install the front and rear flanges onto the intake manifold so that the slot in each flange will align with the cylinder head stud.

CAUTION
Do not tighten the manifold nuts and bolts until the manifold, flanges and carburetor are aligned with each other. Attempting to align the assembly after tightening the bolts will damage the manifold seals.

   b. Install an intake manifold seal into the front and rear manifold-to-cylinder head openings.
   c. Install the intake manifold onto the cylinder heads. Then install the washer and nut on each stud. Tighten finger-tight.
   d. Install the intake manifold Allen bolts and washers (if used). Tighten finger-tight.
   e. Install the carburetor seal ring onto the intake manifold. Then insert the carburetor into the seal ring.
   f. Align the manifold, flanges and carburetors as an assembly. When the assembly is properly aligned, remove the carburetor.
   g. Tighten the mounting screws and nuts securely.
6. Install the carburetor as described in this chapter.

ELECTRONIC FUEL INJECTION (EFI)

This section describes the components and operation of the sequential port electronic fuel injection (EFI) system. A map-controlled fuel and ignition system allows the elimination of an inefficient cold-start enrichment device and accurate control of the idle speed. Without a carburetor, there is no periodic adjustment required, and altitude compensation is automatic. Improved torque characteristics are achieved as well as greater fuel economy and low

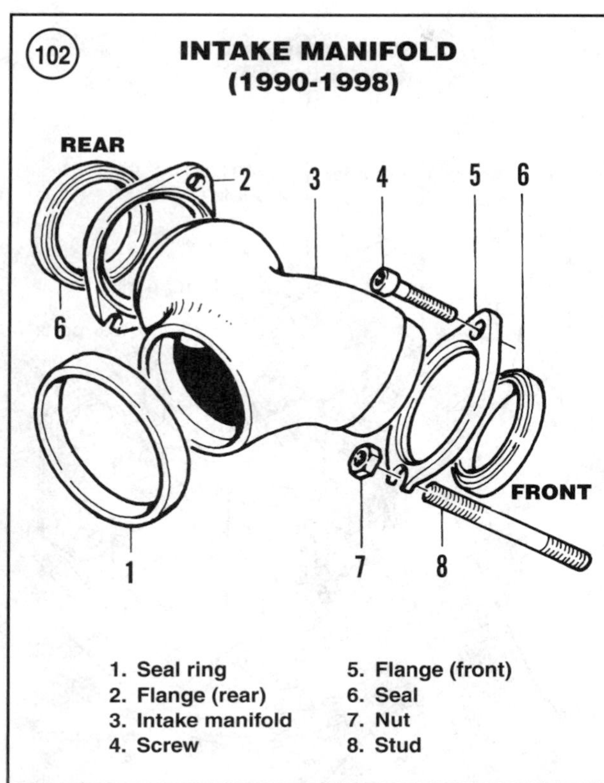

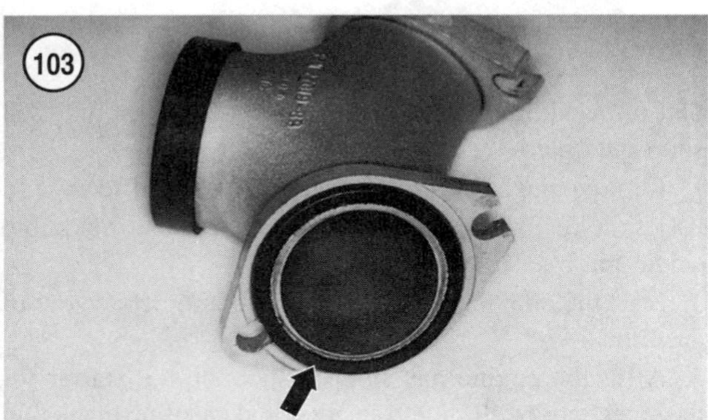

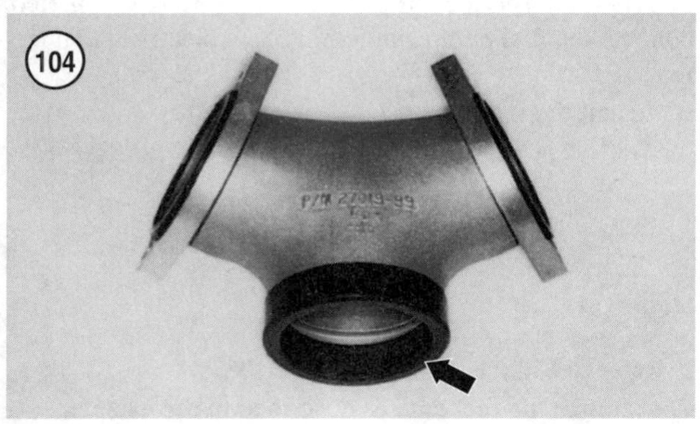

exhaust emissions due to the matching of the air/fuel ratio and ignition point, dependent upon load conditions. Engine performance modification is possible by installing an electronic control module (ECM) with different map characteristics.

Complete service of the system requires a Harley-Davidson Scanalyzer and a number of other specialty tools. However, basic troubleshooting diagnosis is no different on a fuel-injected machine than on a carbureted one. If the check-engine light comes on, or there is a drivability problem, make sure all electrical connections are clean and secure. A high or erratic idle speed can indicate a vacuum leak. Make sure there is an adequate supply of fresh gasoline. If basic tests fail to reveal the cause of a problem, refer service to a Harley-Davidson dealership. Incorrectly performed diagnostic procedures can result in damage to the fuel injection system.

8

Electronic Control Module and Sensors

The electronic control module (ECM), mounted under the right side cover, determines the optimum fuel injection and ignition timing based on input from six or seven sensors. Make sure the ECM is securely mounted on the rubber isolators to prevent damage from vibration. Do not tamper with the ECM; it is sealed to prevent moisture contamination. Refer to **Figure 105** for 1995-1996 models or **Figure 106** for 1997-1998 models. The sensor functions are as follows:

1. The throttle position sensor (TP), located on the front of the induction module and attached directly to the throttle shaft, indicates throttle angle. The ECM indicates the air volume entering the engine based on the throttle angle.
2. The crankshaft position sensor (CKP), located on the forward position of the left crankcase, is an inductive sensor. The ECM determines the engine speed by how fast the machined teeth on the flywheel pass by the sensor.
3. The camshaft position (CMP), located in the chaincase cover on the right side, is also an inductive sensor. The ECM determines the camshaft position when the semicircular ridge on the rear cylinder primary camshaft chain sprocket passes the sensor.
4. The engine temperature sensor (ET) is located on the front cylinder head. The ECM adjusts the injector opening time based on input from this sensor.
5. The intake air temperature sensor (IAT) is located inside the induction module (rear cylinder intake runner). The ECM determines the air density and adjusts the injector opening time based on input from this sensor.
6. Idle air control actuator (IAC) is located on top of the induction module. The ECM controls the engine speed by

moving the IAC to open or close the passage around the throttle plate.

7. The vehicle attitude sensor (VAS), located within the camshaft position sensor assembly, interrupts the ignition and shuts off the engine if the lean angle of the motorcycle is greater than 80° from vertical for more than one second.

Fuel Supply System

Fuel pump and filters

The fuel pump and filter assembly is located inside the fuel tank. This assembly is part of the removable canopy attached to the top of the fuel tank. The canopy provides removal and installation of the attached components without having to work within the fuel tank cavity. An inlet screen on the fuel pump and the secondary fuel filter canister are located downstream from the fuel pump to provide maximum filtration before the fuel reaches the fuel injectors.

Fuel lines

The fuel line is attached to the base of the fuel tank with a quick-disconnect fitting.

The fuel supply line pressure is 58 psi (400 kPa). A check valve is located on the fuel line where it attaches to the fuel tank.

Fuel injectors

The solenoid-actuated constant-stroke pintle-type fuel injectors consist of a solenoid plunger, needle valve and housing. The fuel injector opening is fixed, and fuel pressure is constant.

The ECM controls the time the injectors open and close.

Induction module

The induction module consists of the two fuel injectors, fuel pressure regulator, throttle position sensor, intake air temperature sensor, idle speed lever, fuel supply line fitting and the idle speed control actuator. Refer to **Figure 107** and **Figure 108**.

DEPRESSURIZING THE FUEL SYSTEM (FUEL-INJECTED MODELS)

The fuel system is under pressure at all times, even when the engine is not operating. The system must be depressurized prior to loosening fittings or disconnecting

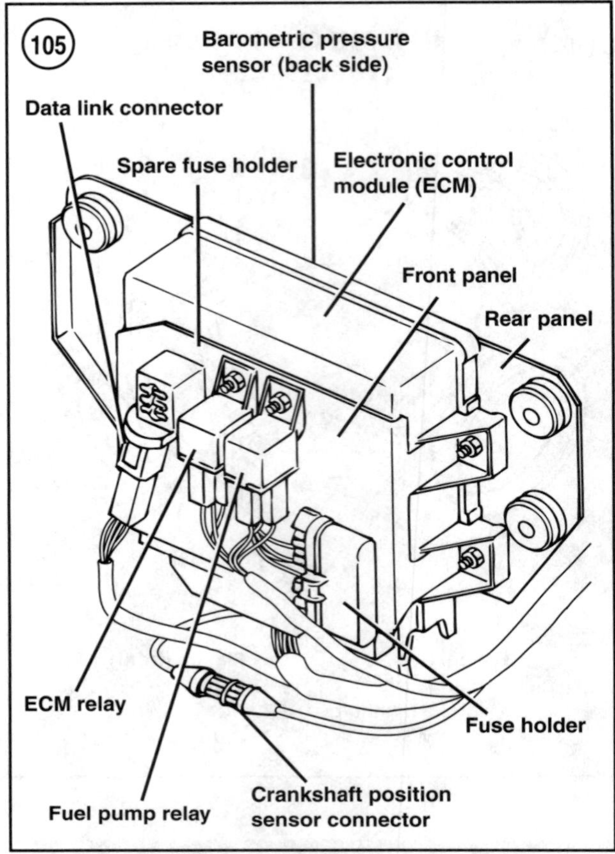

fuel lines within the fuel injection system. Gasoline will spurt out unless the system is depressurized.

1. Remove the seat as described in Chapter Fifteen.
2. At the rear of the fuel tank, disconnect the fuel pump single-pin black electrical connector.
3. Start the engine and allow it to idle until it runs out of gasoline.
4. After the engine has stopped, operate the starter for three seconds to eliminate any residual gasoline in the fuel lines.
5. After all service procedures have been completed, connect the fuel pump single-pin black electrical connector.
6. Install the seat.

INDUCTION MODULE (FUEL-INJECTED MODELS)

Removal

Refer to **Figure 107** and **Figure 108**.

1. Remove the fuel tank as described in this chapter.

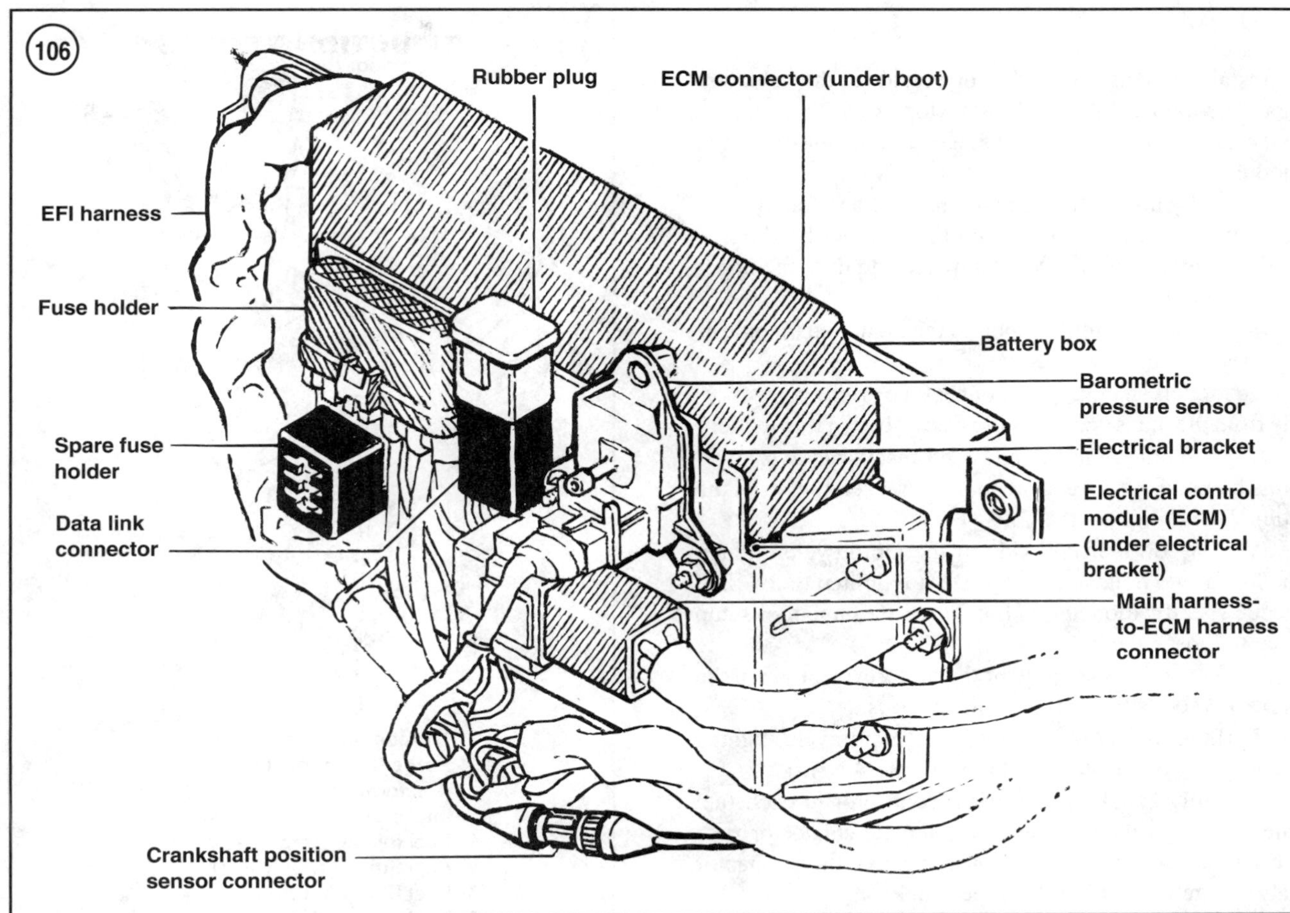

2. Remove the air filter assembly as described in this chapter.

3. Disconnect the throttle cables from the induction module as described in this section.

4. On models so equipped, disconnect the cruise control cable from the induction module as described in this section.

5. On California models, disconnect the EVAP hose from the port on the induction module. Plug the end of the hose to keep out debris.

6. Depress the wire bail and *carefully* disconnect the electrical connector from each fuel injector by rocking the connector back and forth.

7. Disconnect the following electrical connectors from the induction module:

a. Intake air temperature sensor (IAT).

b. Idle air control actuator (IAC).

c. Throttle position sensor (TP).

d. Fuel injectors.

NOTE

The front and rear intake manifold flanges are different. If the flanges are not marked, label them with an F and R so they will be reinstalled in the correct locations.

8. Working on the right side of the motorcycle, loosen and remove the lower two Allen bolts securing the cylinder head mounting flanges to the cylinder heads. Use a 1/4-in. ball Allen bit with a 4-in. extension.

9. Working on the left side of the motorcycle, loosen and remove the lower two 1/2-in. hex bolts securing the cylinder head mounting flanges to the cylinder heads.

10. Slide the induction module partway out of the cylinder head ports past the two 1/2-in. hex bolts.

11. Remove the induction module and fuel line assembly. Be careful not to damage the fuel lines as they pass the horn bracket.

12. Remove the mounting flanges and discard the seals.

13. Inspect the induction module and fuel hoses as described in this section.

8

Installation

1. Install the flanges onto the correct side of the induction module with the slotted hole at the top. Refer to the marks made during *Removal*. Install *new* seals onto the induction module.
2. Carefully install the induction module and fuel line assembly past the horn bracket on the cylinder head ports. Slide the induction module into place and onto the upper two 1/2-in. hex bolts.
3. Connect both throttle cables to the induction module as described in this chapter.
4. On models so equipped, connect the cruise control cable from the induction module as described in this section.
5. Align the mounting flanges and install the two lower bolts by hand. Use the same tool setup used to loosen the bolts. Do not tighten the bolts at this time.
6. Working on the right side of the motorcycle, tighten the lower two bolts until snug. Do not tighten to the final torque specification at this time. Use the same tool setup used to loosen the bolts.
7. Working on the left side of the motorcycle, tighten the upper two bolts to 71-124 in.-lb. (8-14 N•m).
8. Working on the right side of the motorcycle, tighten the lower two bolts to 71-124 in.-lb. (8-14 N•m).
9. Carefully attach the electrical connector to each fuel injector. Align the grooves in the female connector with the tabs in the male space housing. Push the connector halves together until both latches click.

NOTE

In Step 10, push the electrical connector halves together until the female slot connector is fully engaged with the tabs on the male space housing.

10. Connect the following electrical connectors onto the induction module:
    a. Fuel injectors.
    b. Throttle position sensor (TP).
    c. Idle air control actuator (IAC).
    d. Intake air temperature sensor (IAT).
11. On California models, connect the EVAP hose to the port on top of the induction module.
12. Install the air filter assembly as described in this chapter.
13. Install the fuel tank as described in this chapter.

Inspection

Check the induction module assembly for wear, deterioration or other damage. Replace the seals as a set if necessary. The throttle housing is not serviceable and must be replace if damaged.

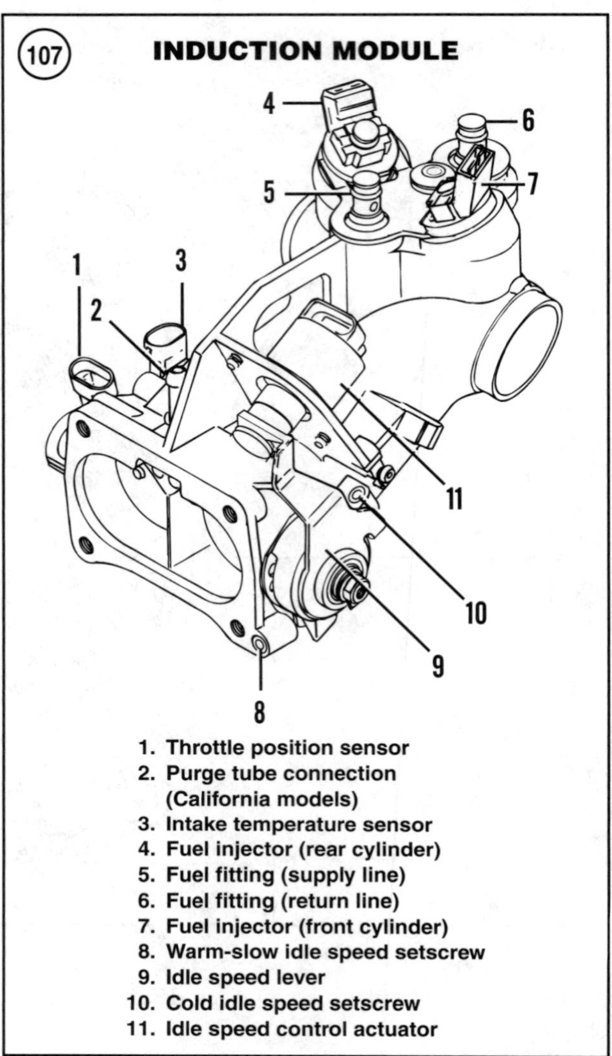

1. Throttle position sensor
2. Purge tube connection (California models)
3. Intake temperature sensor
4. Fuel injector (rear cylinder)
5. Fuel fitting (supply line)
6. Fuel fitting (return line)
7. Fuel injector (front cylinder)
8. Warm-slow idle speed setscrew
9. Idle speed lever
10. Cold idle speed setscrew
11. Idle speed control actuator

THROTTLE AND IDLE CABLE REPLACEMENT (CRUISE CONTROL MODELS)

Refer to Chapter Fourteen.

THROTTLE AND IDLE CABLE REPLACEMENT (CARBURETED MODELS)

There are two different throttle cables. At the throttle grip, the front cable is the throttle control cable (A, **Figure 109**), and the rear cable is the idle control cable (B). At the

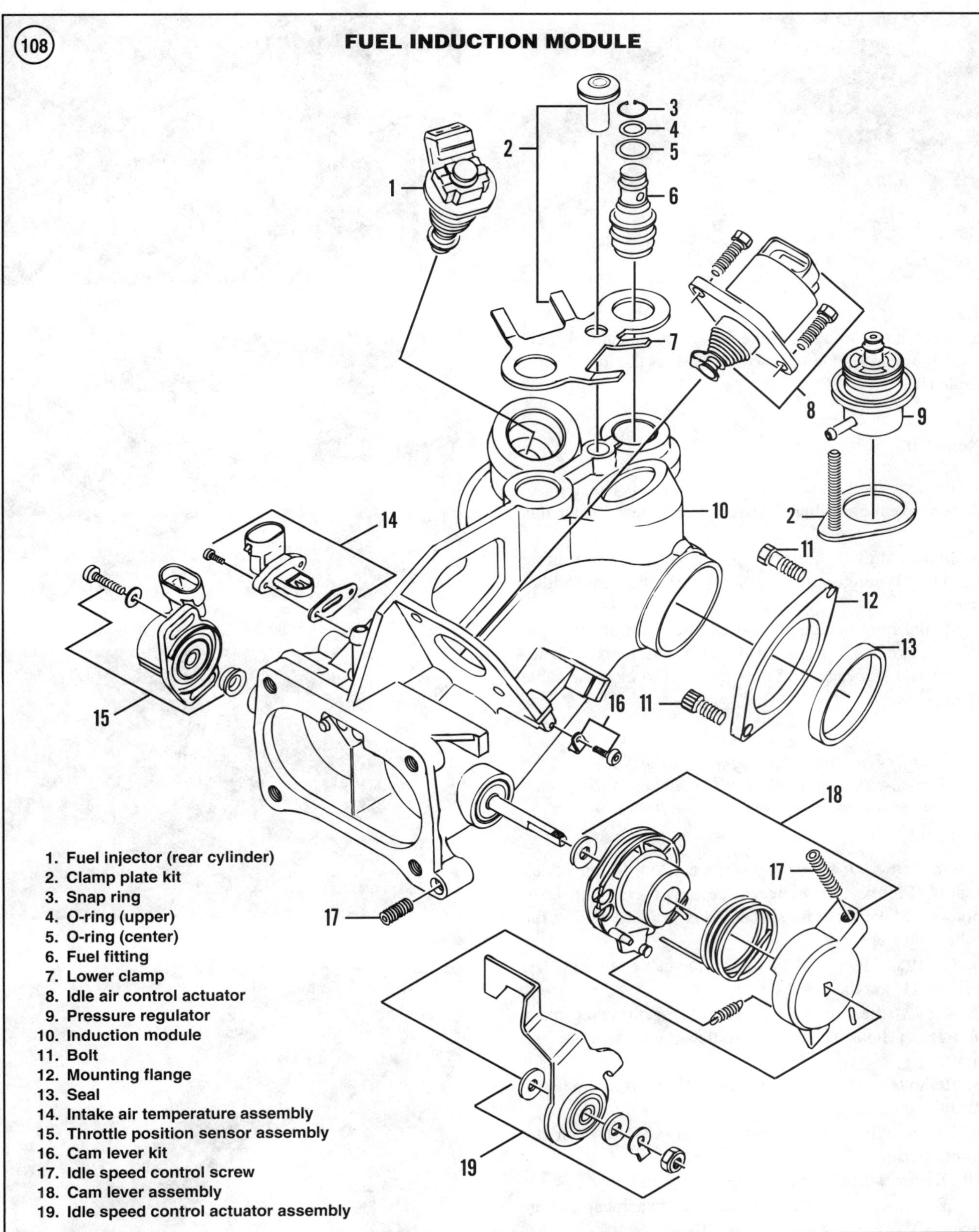
108
FUEL INDUCTION MODULE
1
2
3
4
5
6
7
8
9
10
2
11
12
13
14
15
16
11
17
18
17
19
1. Fuel injector (rear cylinder)
2. Clamp plate kit
3. Snap ring
4. O-ring (upper)
5. O-ring (center)
6. Fuel fitting
7. Lower clamp
8. Idle air control actuator
9. Pressure regulator
10. Induction module
11. Bolt
12. Mounting flange
13. Seal
14. Intake air temperature assembly
15. Throttle position sensor assembly
16. Cam lever kit
17. Idle speed control screw
18. Cam lever assembly
19. Idle speed control actuator assembly

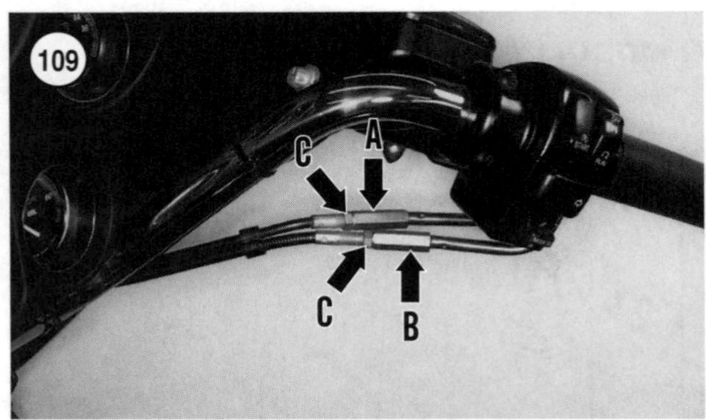

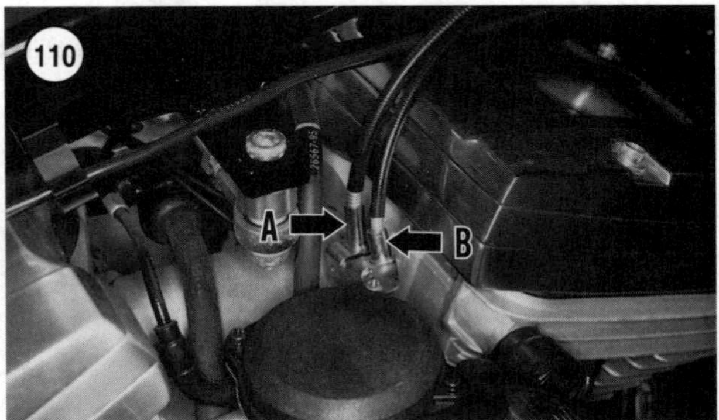

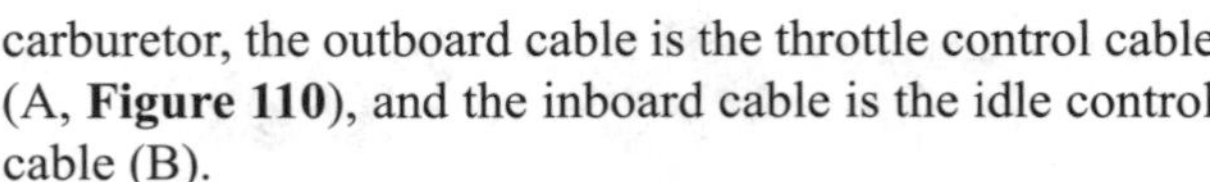

carburetor, the outboard cable is the throttle control cable (A, **Figure 110**), and the inboard cable is the idle control cable (B).

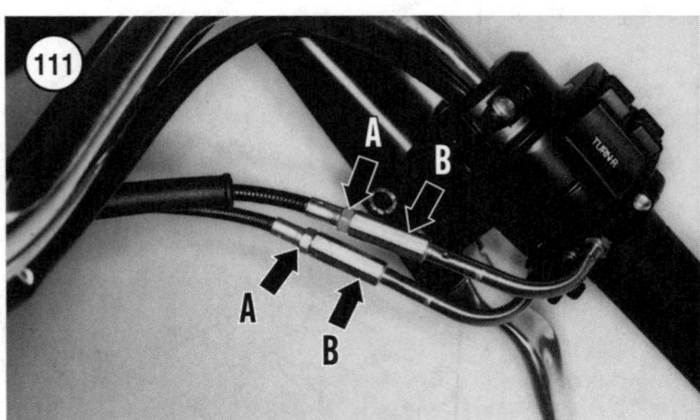

Removal

1. Remove the fuel tank as described in this chapter.
2. Remove the air filter and back plate as described in this chapter.
3. Make a drawing or take a picture of the cable routing from the carburetor through the frame to the right handlebar.
4. At the right handlebar, loosen both control cable adjuster locknuts (A, **Figure 111**). Then turn both cable adjusters (B) *clockwise* as far as possible to increase cable slack.

CAUTION
On 1996-1998 models, failure to install the spacer in Step 5 will result in damage to the rubber boot and plunger on the front brake switch.

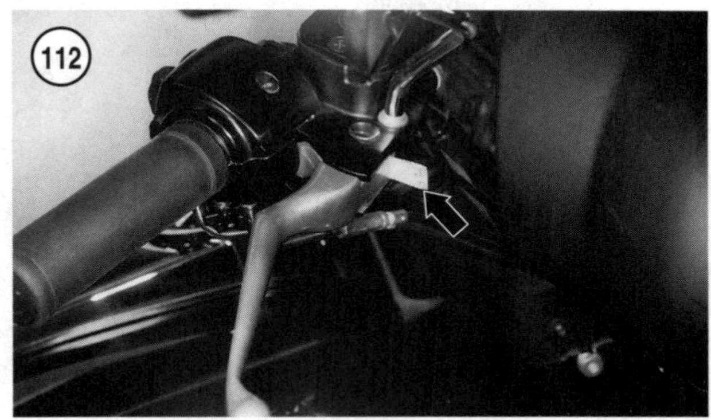

5. On 1996-1998 models, insert a 5/32 in. (4 mm) thick spacer (**Figure 112**) between the brake lever and lever bracket. Make sure the spacer stays in place during the following steps.
6. On 1984-1995 models, loosen the cable jam nuts (A, **Figure 113**) at the throttle housing.
7. Remove the screws (B, **Figure 113**) securing the upper and lower housing to the handlebar and separate the housing.
8. Remove the friction pad (**Figure 114**) from the lower throttle housing.
9. Unhook the throttle cables (**Figure 115**) from the throttle grip.
10. Remove the throttle grip from the handlebar.
11. Remove the ferrule from the end of each cable (**Figure 116**).

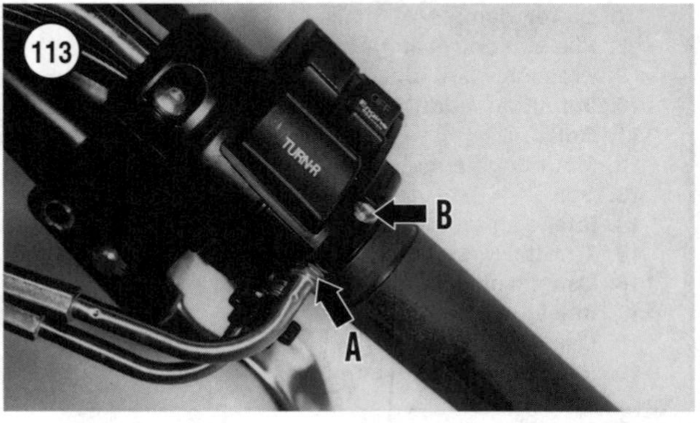

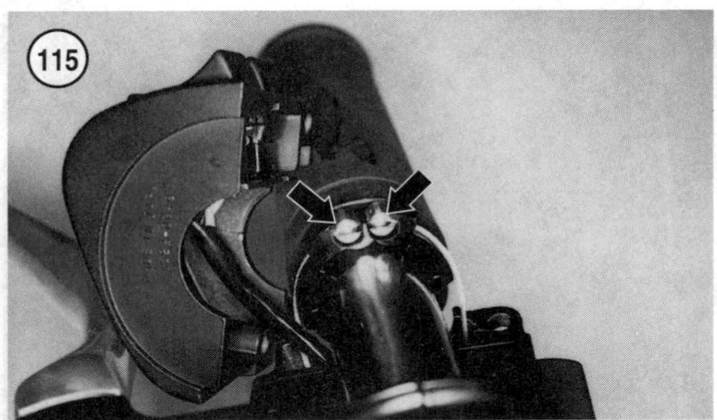

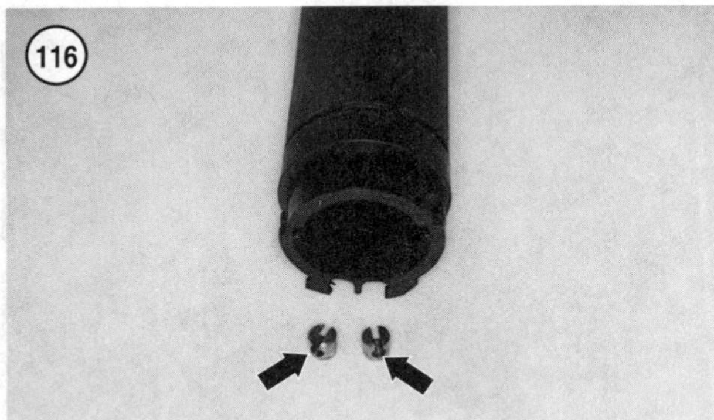

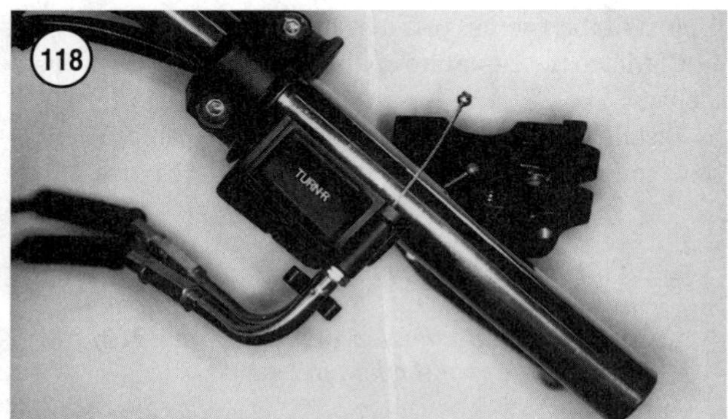

12. Remove each cable from the lower housing assembly.

13. On models so equipped, withdraw the throttle and idle cables from the inner fairing rubber grommet. Move the idle and throttle cables forward and out of the way.

14. Remove all clips and tie-wraps securing the throttle and idle control cables from the frame backbone and ignition coil bracket.

8

NOTE
***Figure 117** is shown with the carburetor partially removed to illustrate the step better.*

15. Disconnect the idle cable (A, **Figure 117**) and throttle cable (B) from the carburetor.

16. Remove the cables from the frame.

17. Clean the throttle grip assembly and dry thoroughly. Check the throttle slots for cracks or other damage. Replace the throttle if necessary.

18. The friction adjust screw is secured to the lower switch housing with a snap ring. If necessary, remove the friction spring, snap ring, spring and friction adjust screw. Check these parts for wear or damage. Replace damaged parts and reverse to install. Make sure the snap ring completely seats in the friction screw groove.

19. Clean the throttle area on the handlebar with solvent.

Installation

1. On models so equipped, insert the throttle and idle cables trough the inner fairing rubber grommet.

2. Apply a light coat of graphite to the housing inside surfaces and to the handlebar.

3. Reconnect the idle and throttle cables to the switch lower housing (**Figure 118**). Do not tighten the jam nuts at this time.

4. Install the friction pad into the lower housing (**Figure 114**). Match the curvature on the friction pad with the handlebar.
5. Install a ferrule (**Figure 116**) onto each cable. Then insert the ferrules into the throttle grip slots (**Figure 115**).

NOTE
*If the master cylinder is not mounted on the handlebar, make sure to fit the throttle housing wiring into the depression (**Figure 119**) in the bottom of the handlebar.*

6. Assemble the upper and lower switch housings and the throttle grip. Rotate the throttle grip until the ferrule notches are at the top. Install the lower screws (B, **Figure 113**) and tighten finger-tight. Operate the throttle and make sure both cables move in and out properly. On 1984-1995 models, tighten the nuts.
7. If not in place, insert the 5/32 in. (4 mm) thick spacer (**Figure 112**) between the brake lever and lever bracket. Make sure the spacer stays in place during the following steps.
8. Securely tighten the switch housing screws.
9. Correctly route the cables from the handlebar to the carburetor. Secure the cables with the clamps and tie-wraps as noted during removal.
10. Connect the idle cable (A, **Figure 117**) to the carburetor as follows:
   a. The idle cable has the small spring (**Figure 120**) on the end of the cable.
   b. Insert the idle cable sheath into the rear cable bracket guide on the carburetor (**Figure 121**).
   c. Attach the end of the idle cable into the throttle wheel (A, **Figure 117**).
11. Connect the throttle cable to the carburetor as follows:
   a. Insert the throttle cable (B, **Figure 117**) sheath into the front cable bracket guide on the carburetor.
   b. Attach the end of the throttle cable to the throttle wheel.
12. At the throttle grip, tighten the cables to keep the cable ends from being disconnected from the throttle wheel.
13. Operate the hand throttle a few times to make sure the idle cable (A, **Figure 122**) and the throttle cable (B) seat squarely in the cable bracket guides.
14. Operate the throttle grip and make sure the throttle linkage operates smoothly with no binding. Also check that both cable ends are seated squarely in the cable bracket guides and in the throttle barrel.
15. Adjust the throttle and idle cables as described in Chapter Three.
16. If partially removed, install the carburetor as described in this chapter.

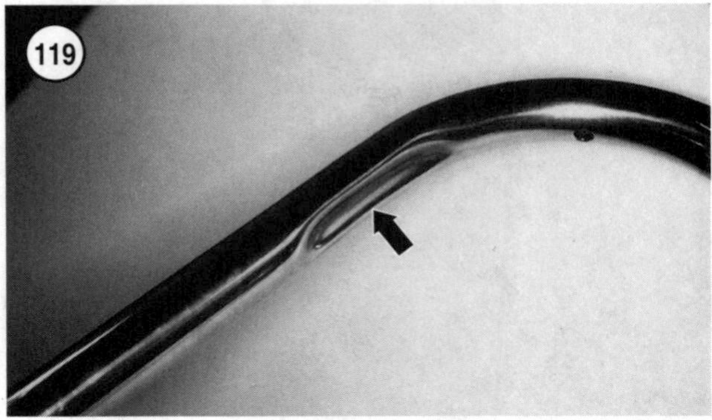
119

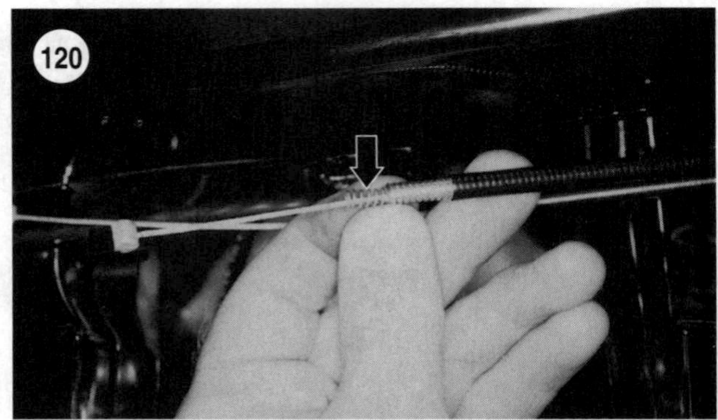
120

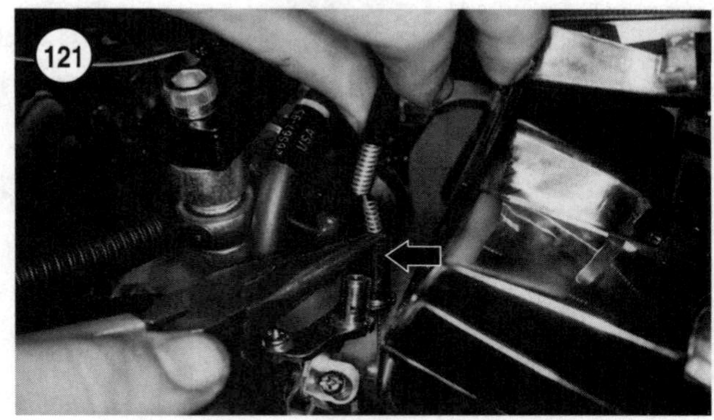
121

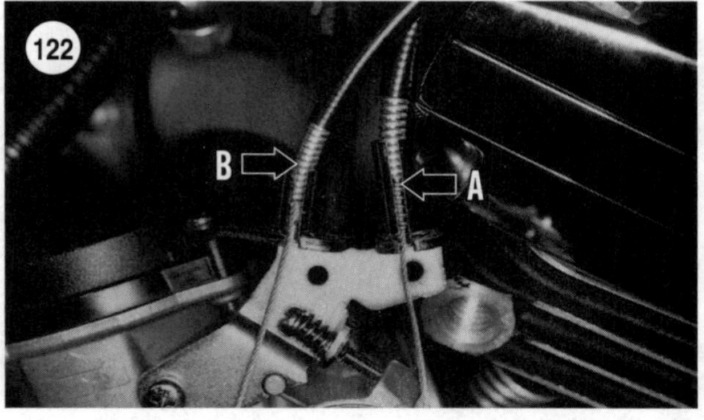

122

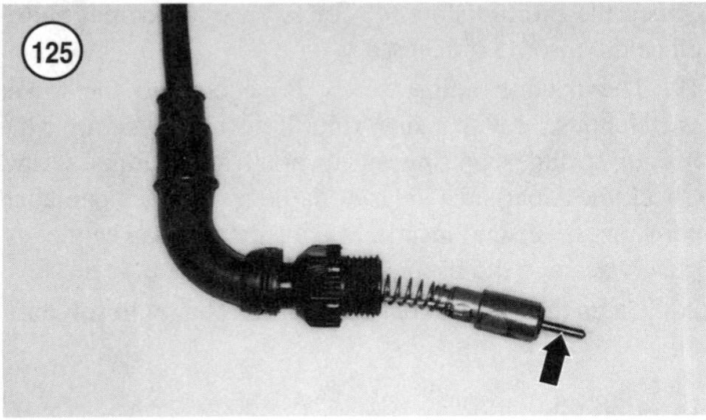

17. Install the air filter back plate and air filter as described in this chapter.

18. Install the fuel tank as described in this chapter.

19. Turn the ignition switch to the on position, operate the brake lever, and make sure the brake light comes on. If not, correct the problem at this time.

20. Shift the transmission into neutral.

21. Start the engine and allow it to idle. Then turn the handlebar from side to side. Do not operate the throttle. If the engine speed increases when turning the handlebar assembly, the throttle cables are routed incorrectly or damaged. Recheck cable routing and adjustment.

WARNING

Do not ride the motorcycle until the throttle cables are properly adjusted. Improper cable routing and adjustment can cause the throttle to stick open. This could cause loss of control. Recheck the work before riding the bike.

CHOKE/ENRICHER CABLE REPLACEMENT (CARBURETED MODELS)

A choke cable is used on 1984-1989 models. An enricher cable is used on 1990-1998 models.

1. Remove the air filter and back plate assembly as described in this chapter.
2. Note the routing of the cable from its mounting bracket to the carburetor.
3. Disconnect the enricher cable (**Figure 123**) nut from the mounting bracket. Move the cable out of the mounting bracket.
4. Partially remove the carburetor as described in this chapter to gain access to the enricher cable at the carburetor.

NOTE

***Figure 124** is shown with the carburetor completely removed to illustrate the step better.*

5. Unscrew the enricher nut (**Figure 124**) from the carburetor.
6. Remove the enricher cable from the motorcycle.
7. Installation is the reverse of these steps while noting the following:
   a. On 1990-1998 models, align the enricher valve needle (**Figure 125**) with the needle passage in the carburetor and install the enricher valve. Securely tighten the valve nut.
   b. Adjust the choke or enricher cable as described in Chapter Three.

THROTTLE AND IDLE CABLES (EFI MODELS)

There are two different throttle cables. At the throttle grip, the front cable is the throttle control cable (A, **Figure 109**) and the rear cable is the idle control cable (B). At the carburetor, the outboard cable is the throttle control cable

8

(A, **Figure 110**) and the inboard cable is the idle control cable (B).

Removal

1. Remove the fuel tank as described in this chapter.
2. Remove the air filter and back plate as described in this chapter.
3. Make a drawing or take a picture of the cable routing from the carburetor through the frame to the right handlebar.
4. At the right handlebar, loosen both control cable adjuster locknuts (A, **Figure 111**). Then turn both cable adjusters (B) *clockwise* as far as possible to increase cable slack.

CAUTION
On 1996-1998 models, failure to install the spacer in Step 5 will result in damage to the rubber boot and plunger on the front brake switch.

5. On 1996-1998 models, insert a 5/32 in. (4 mm) thick spacer (**Figure 112**) between the brake lever and lever bracket. Make sure the spacer stays in place during the following steps.
6. On 1984-1995 models, loosen the cable jam nuts (A, **Figure 113**) at the throttle housing.
7. Remove the screws (B, **Figure 113**) securing the upper and lower housing to the handlebar and separate the housing.
8. Remove the friction pad (**Figure 114**) from the lower throttle housing.
9. Unhook the throttle cables (**Figure 115**) from the throttle grip.
10. Remove the throttle grip from the handlebar.
11. Remove the ferrule from the end of each cable (**Figure 116**).
12. Unscrew and remove each cable from the lower switch housing assembly.
13. On models so equipped, withdraw the throttle and idle cables from the inner fairing rubber grommet. Move the idle and throttle cables forward and out of the way.
14. Remove all clips and tie-wraps securing the throttle and idle control cables from the frame backbone and ignition coil bracket.

NOTE
***Figure 126** is shown with the induction module removed to illustrate the step better.*

15. Disconnect the idle cable (A, **Figure 126**) and throttle cable (B) from the throttle barrel (C).

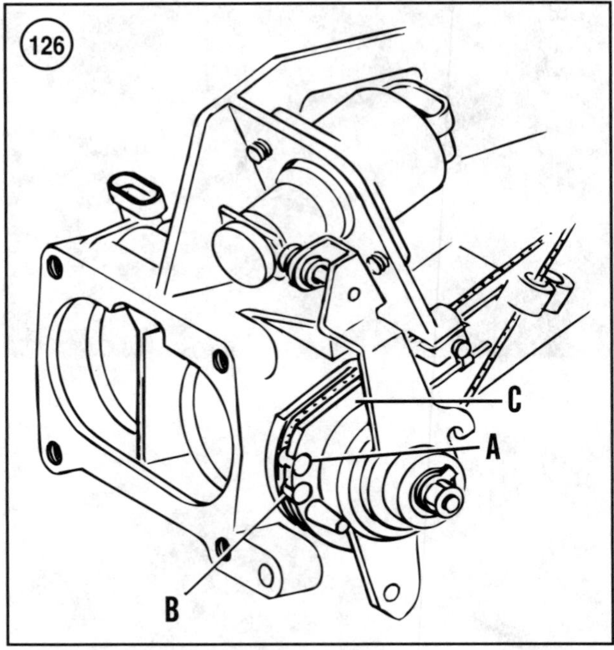

16. Release the cables from the integral cable guides in the induction module.
17. Remove the cables from the frame.
18. Clean the throttle grip assembly and dry thoroughly. Check the throttle slots for cracks or other damage. Replace the throttle if necessary.
19. The friction adjust screw is secured to the lower switch housing with a snap ring. If necessary, remove the friction spring, snap ring, spring and friction adjust screw. Check these parts for wear or damage. Replace damaged parts and reverse to install. Make sure the snap ring completely seats in the friction screw groove.
20. Clean the throttle area on the handlebar with solvent.

Installation

1. On models so equipped, insert the throttle and idle cables trough the inner fairing rubber grommet.
2. Apply a light coat of graphite to the housing inside surfaces and to the handlebar.
3. Reconnect the idle and throttle cables to the switch lower housing (**Figure 118**). Do not tighten the jam nuts at this time.
4. Install the friction pad into the lower housing (**Figure 114**). Match the curvature on the friction pad with the handlebar.
5. Install a ferrule (**Figure 116**) onto each cable. Then insert the ferrules into the throttle grip slots (**Figure 115**).

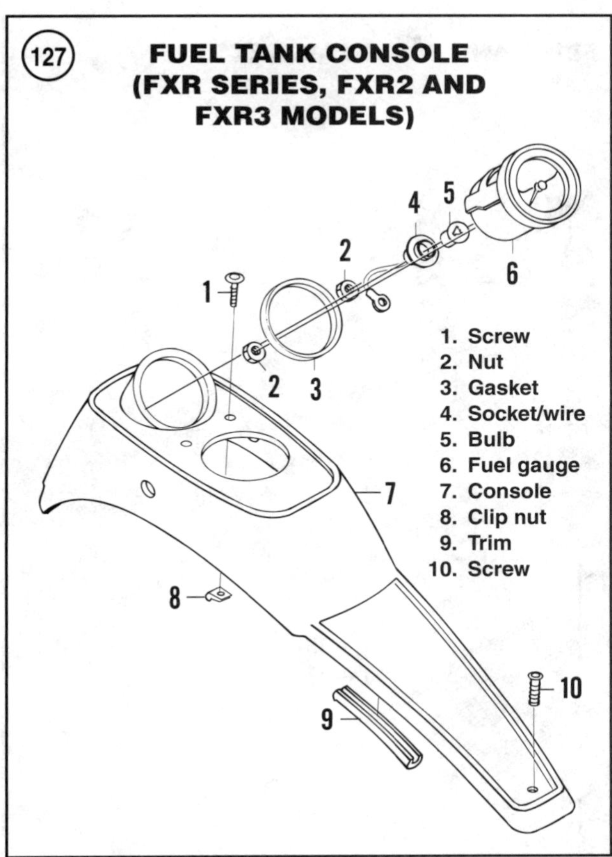

NOTE
*If the master cylinder is not mounted on the handlebar, make sure to fit the throttle housing wiring into the depression (**Figure 119**) in the bottom of the handlebar.*

6. Assemble the upper and lower switch housings and the throttle grip. Rotate the throttle grip until the ferrule notches are at the top. Install the lower screws (B, **Figure 113**) and tighten finger-tight. Operate the throttle and make sure both cables move in and out properly. On 1984-1995 models, tighten the nuts.
7. If not in place, insert the 5/32 in. (4 mm) thick spacer (**Figure 112**) between the brake lever and lever bracket. Make sure the spacer stays in place during the following steps.
8. Securely tighten the switch housing screws.
9. Correctly route the cables from the handlebar to the induction module. Secure the cables with the clamps and tie-wraps as noted during removal.

NOTE
***Figure 126** is shown with the induction module removed to illustrate the step better.*

10. At the induction module, perform the following:
    a. Install the idle cable (A, **Figure 126**) ball end over the top of the throttle barrel (C) and install the cable ball end into the upper hole in the throttle barrel. Make sure it is properly seated.
    b. Install the throttle cable (B, **Figure 126**) ball end over the bottom of the throttle barrel (C) and install the cable ball end into the lower hole in the throttle barrel. Make sure it is properly seated.
    c. Install the cables into the integral cable guides in the induction module.
11. At the throttle grip, tighten the cables to keep the cable ends from being disconnected from the throttle wheel at the induction module.
12. Operate the hand throttle a few times and make sure the idle cable and the throttle cable seat squarely in the cable bracket guides.
13. Operate the throttle grip and make sure the throttle linkage operates smoothly with no binding. Also check that both cable ends are seated squarely in the cable bracket guides and in the throttle barrel.
14. Adjust the throttle and idle cables as described in Chapter Three.
15. If partially removed, install the induction module as described in this chapter.
16. Install the air filter back plate and air filter as described in this chapter.
17. Install the fuel tank as described in this chapter.
18. Turn the ignition switch to the on position, operate the brake lever, and make sure the brake light comes on. If not, correct the problem at this time.
19. Shift the transmission into neutral.
20. Start the engine and allow it to idle. Then turn the handlebar from side to side. Do not operate the throttle. If the engine speed increases when turning the handlebar assembly, the throttle cables are routed incorrectly or damaged. Recheck cable routing and adjustment.

WARNING
Do not ride the motorcycle until the throttle cables are properly adjusted. Improper cable routing and adjustment can cause the throttle to stick open. This could cause loss of control. Recheck the work before riding the bike.

FUEL TANK CONSOLE (FXR SERIES, FXR2 AND FXR3 MODELS)

Refer to **Figure 127**.

1. Disconnect the negative battery cable from the battery.
2. Remove the seat as described in Chapter Fifteen.

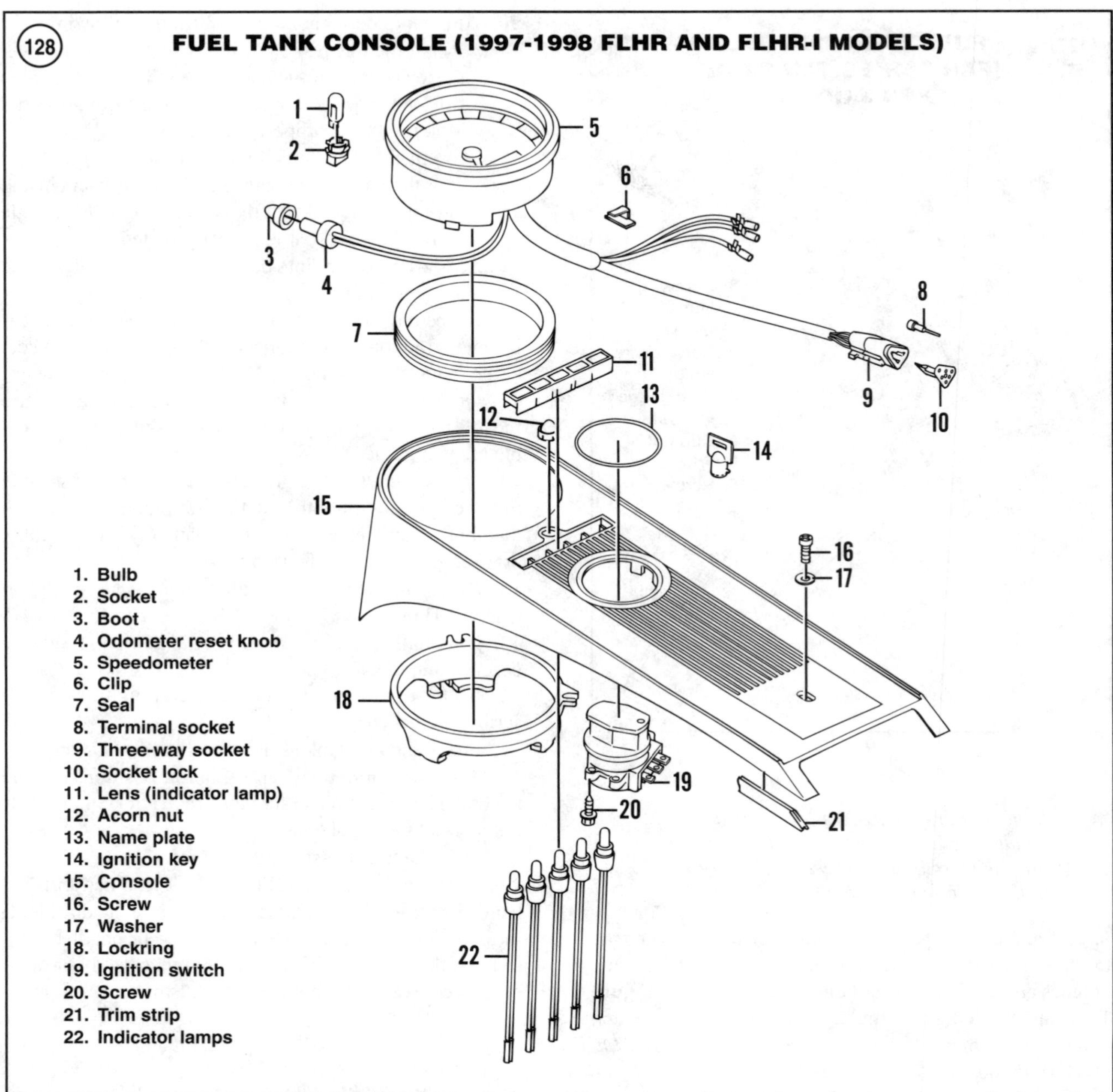

3. Remove the screws securing the console to the fuel tank.

4. Partially lift the console away from the fuel tank and disconnect the electrical connector from the fuel gauge.

5. Remove the fuel console from the fuel tank.

6. Install by reversing these removal steps. Carefully route the electrical cable between the console and fuel tank so it will not get pinched.

FUEL TANK CONSOLE (1997-1998 FLHR, FLHR-I, FLHT, FLHTC, FLHTC-U AND FLHTC-UI MODELS)

Removal/Installation

Refer to **Figure 128** and **Figure 129**.

1. Disconnect the negative battery cable from the battery.
2. Remove the seat as described in Chapter Fifteen.

129

FUEL TANK CONSOLE (FLHT, FLHTC, FLHTC-I, FLHTC-U AND FLHTC-UI MODELS)

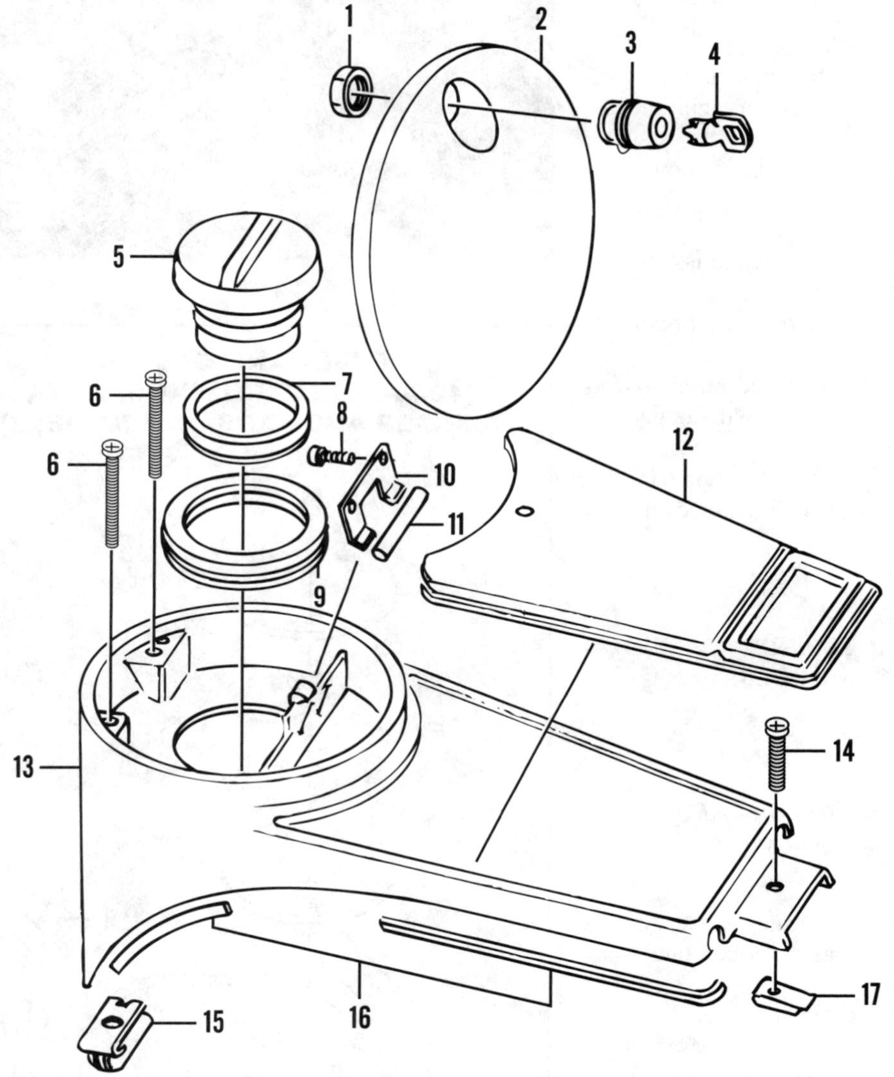

1. Nut
2. Console door
3. Lock
4. Key
5. Fuel filler cap
6. Screw
7. Gasket
8. Screw
9. Rubber boot
10. Clip
11. Hinge pin
12. Trim insert
13. Console
14. Screw
15. Clip nut
16. Trim
17. Staked nut

130

3. On FLHR-I models, perform the following:
   a. Cut the cable strap securing the fuel level sender wires to the main harness on the left frame rail.
   b. At the rear of the fuel tank, disconnect the fuel level sensor two-pin electrical connector from the main harness.

4A. On FLHT series models, perform the following:
   a. Remove the screw (**Figure 130**) securing the console to the fuel tank.
   b. Open the console door.
   c. Remove the two front Allen bolts (A, **Figure 131**) securing the console to the fuel tank mounting brackets.

d. Unscrew the fuel filler cap (B, **Figure 131**).

4B. On FLHR and FLHR-I models, perform the following:

a. Remove the front acorn nut and rear screw and washer securing the console to the fuel tank.

b. Lift the console partially off the fuel tank and disconnect the electrical connector from the ignition switch and the indicator lamp housing.

5. Carefully remove the console and lay it upside down on the shop cloths or towels.

6. Reinstall the fuel filler cap.

7. Install by reversing these removal steps while noting the following:

a. On FLHT series models, make sure the rubber boot is in place prior to installation.

b. Carefully route the electrical cables and hose between the console and fuel tank so they will not get pinched.

c. Reposition fuel-level sender wires to the main harness on the left frame rail and install a *new* cable strap.

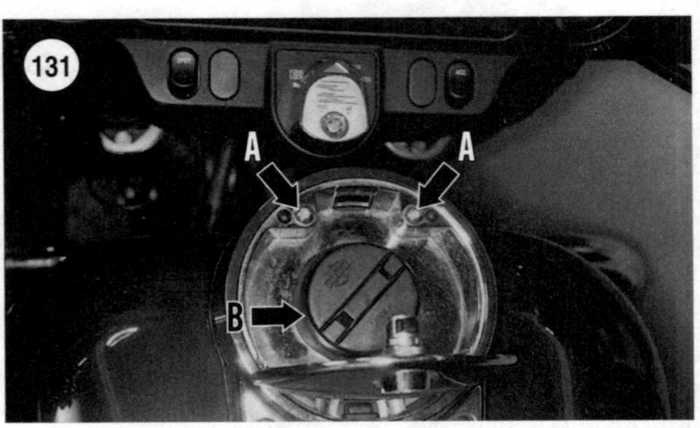

FUEL TANK GAUGE (1984-1999 FXR SERIES AND 1997-1998 FLH SERIES MODELS)

Refer to **Figure 132** and **Figure 133**.

NOTE

Additional fuel tank gauges are covered along with fuel tank removal/installation in this section.

1. Disconnect the negative battery cable from the battery.

2. Drain the fuel from the fuel tank as described under *Fuel Tank Draining* in this section.

3. Remove the seat as described in Chapter Fifteen.

4. Working under the left side of the fuel tank, release the fuel gauge indicator electrical wires from the clamp on the base of the fuel tank. Feed the wires into the fuel tank so there is enough slack to raise the fuel gauge indicator.

WARNING

Do not twist the fuel gauge indicator during removal in the following step.

5. On models so equipped, securely hold onto the fuel gauge indicator and pull straight up until it just clears the fitting on top of the fuel tank. Remove the fuel gauge indicator and gasket.

NOTE

If only the illumination bulb is being replaced, do so at this time because no further

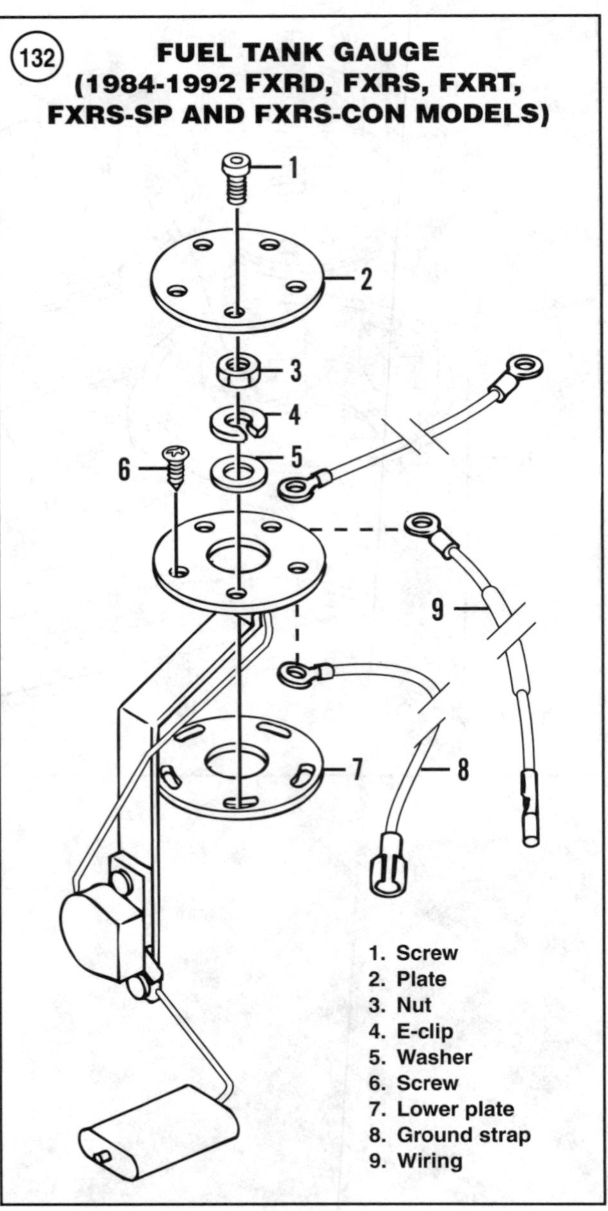

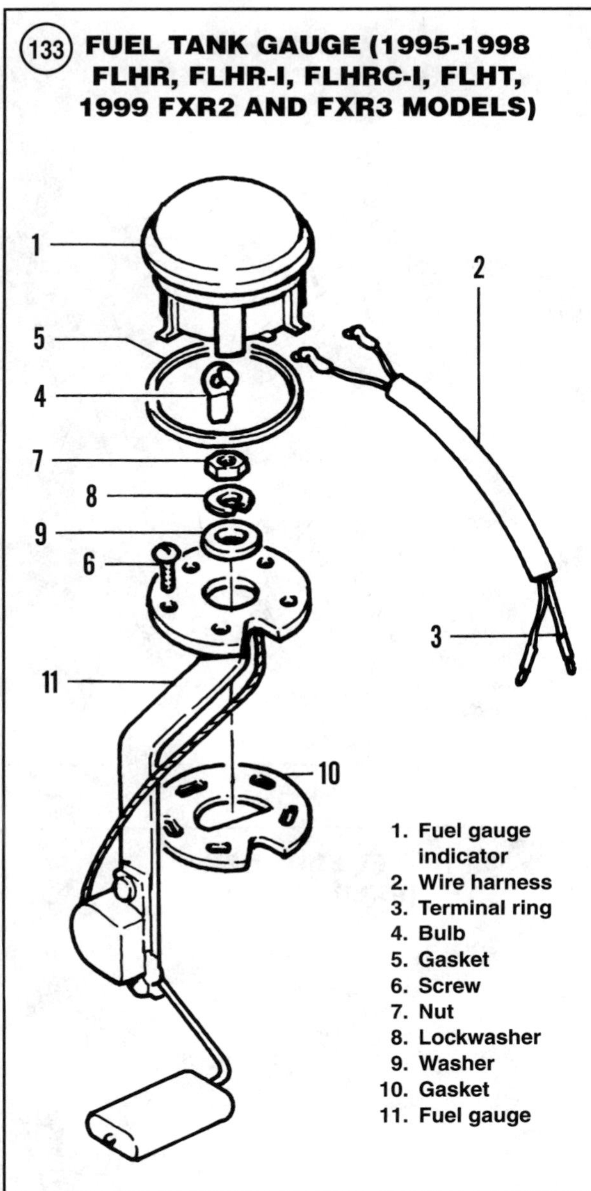

disassembly is required (models so equipped).

6. Mark the location of the electrical wires. Then disconnect the electrical connectors from the fuel gauge indicator.

CAUTION

Do not remove the center nut securing the electrical wire terminal to the top plate of the fuel gauge sending unit. If the nut is removed, the sensor float device will drop into the fuel tank.

7. Remove the screws securing the outer edge of the plate to the fuel tank.

8. Secure the center nut with pliers, carefully raise the unit slightly, and rotate it *counterclockwise* until the cut on the outer edge is facing the left side of the fuel tank.

9. Carefully lift the sending unit out of the fuel tank. If necessary, use a slight rocking motion to ease removal.

10. Remove the gasket from the fuel tank receptacle.

11. Install by reversing these removal steps while noting the following:

   a. Install a *new* gasket and mounting screws.

   b. Tighten the *new* screws securely.

FUEL TANK (CARBURETED MODELS)

8

WARNING

Some fuel might spill from the fuel tank hose(s) during these procedures. Because gasoline is extremely flammable and explosive, perform this procedure away from all open flames (including appliance pilot lights) and sparks. Do not smoke or allow anyone to smoke in the work area because an explosion and fire can occur. Always work in a well-ventilated area. Wipe up any spills immediately.

WARNING

Make sure to route the fuel tank vapor hoses so that they cannot contact any hot engine or exhaust component. These hoses contain flammable vapors. If a hose melts from contacting a hot part, leaking vapors can ignite and cause a fire.

WARNING

Gasoline is a known carcinogen, as well as an extremely flammable liquid, and must be handled carefully. Wear latex gloves to avoid contact. If gasoline does contact skin, immediately and thoroughly wash the area with soap and warm water.

The fuel hoses are secured to the fuel tank with a nonreusable clamp. If the same type of clamp is going to be reinstalled, purchase *new* ones before servicing the fuel tank.

When removing the fuel tank in the following procedures, keep track of all fasteners and rubber bushings to avoid losing them or mixing them up during installation.

Fuel Tank Draining

Prior to removing the fuel tank from the frame, drain the fuel from the tank. If the fuel is drained into a clean container, it may be returned to the fuel tank.

1. Disconnect the negative battery cable from the battery.
2. Turn the fuel shutoff valve to the OFF position (**Figure 134**).
3. Disconnect the carburetor fuel inlet hose from the fuel shutoff valve fitting.
4. Connect a longer drain hose to the shutoff valve fitting and place the open end of the hose in a safety-approved fuel storage tank.

5A. On vacuum-operated fuel shutoff valves, perform the following:

   a. Disconnect the vacuum hose from the fitting on the back side of the shutoff valve.
   b. Turn the shutoff valve to reserve.
   c. Connect a hand-operated vacuum pump to the vacuum hose fitting and apply vacuum to the shutoff valve.
   d. Drain the fuel into the storage tank.
   e. Disconnect the vacuum pump from the shutoff valve.

5B. On all other models, turn the shutoff valve to reserve and drain the fuel into the storage tank. Do not lose the fuel hose insulator.

6. Disconnect the drain hose from the shutoff valve and turn the valve to the OFF position.

Removal/Installation (FXRS, FXLR, FXR2 and FXR3 Models)

Refer to **Figures 135-137**.

1. Disconnect the negative battery cable from the battery.
2. Drain the fuel from the fuel tank as described under *Fuel Tank Draining* in this section.
3. Disconnect the hoses from the fuel tank.

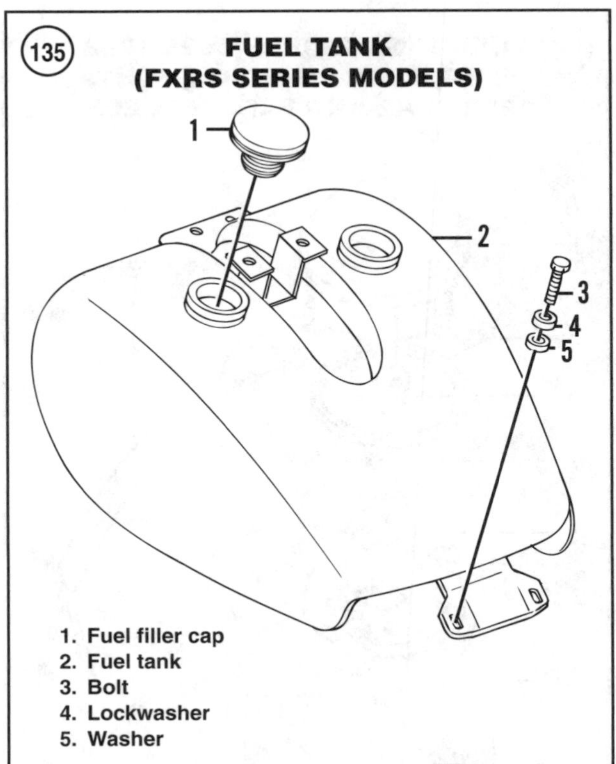

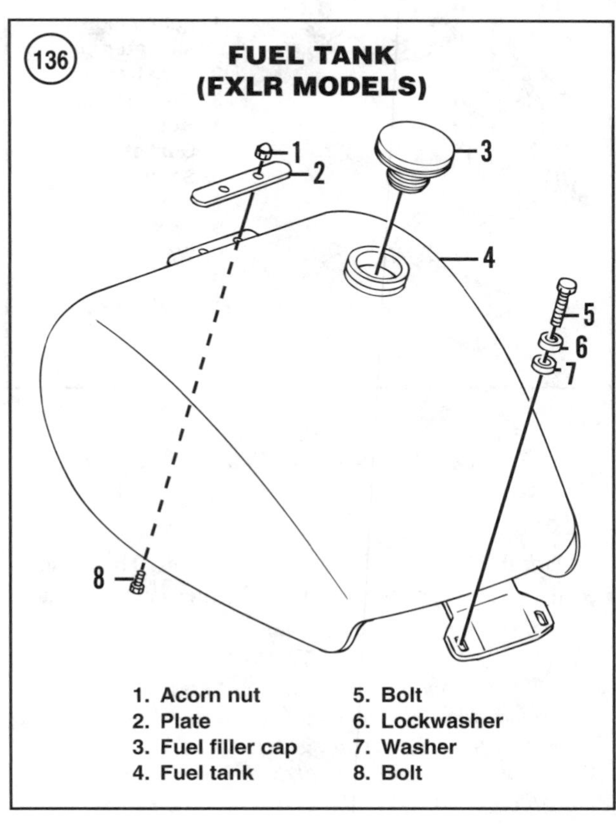

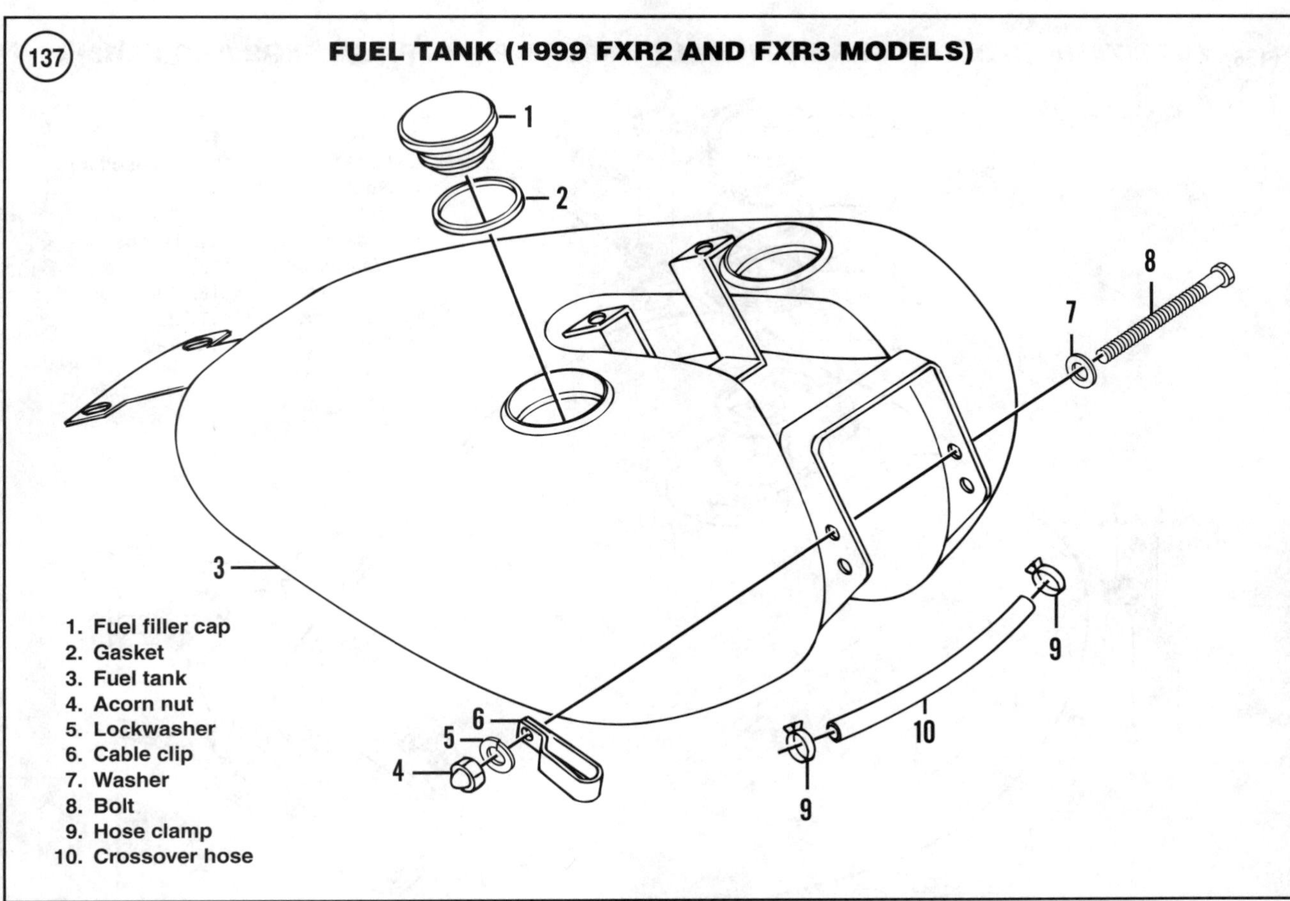

4. Remove the seat as described in Chapter Fifteen.

5. On FXRS models, remove the instrument cluster as described in Chapter Nine.

6A. On FXRS and FXLR models, remove the bolts and nuts.

6B. On FXR2 and FXR3 models, remove the bolt, washer, lockwasher and cable clip securing the front of the fuel tank.

NOTE
Residual fuel will drain from both sides of the fuel tank when the crossover fuel hose is disconnected. Have several golf tees or bolts ready to plug the hose end and fuel tank fitting.

7. Disconnect the crossover hose from the fuel tank. Plug the hose and tank openings.

8. Remove the bolts, lockwashers and washers securing the rear of the fuel tank.

CAUTION
When removing the fuel tank in Step 9, do not pull on or damage the main wiring harness.

9. Carefully remove the fuel tank from the frame.

10. Drain any remaining fuel in the tank into the fuel storage tank.

11. Install by reversing these removal steps while noting the following:

   a. Position the fuel tank on the frame tube and install the washers, bolts and nuts in their original mounting positions.
   b. Secure the fuel line with a *new* hose clamp. Make sure the insulator is placed over the fuel line before reconnecting it.
   c. Refill the tank and check for leaks.

Removal/Installation (FXR Models except FXRS, FXLR, FXR2 and FXR3 Models)

Refer to **Figure 138**.

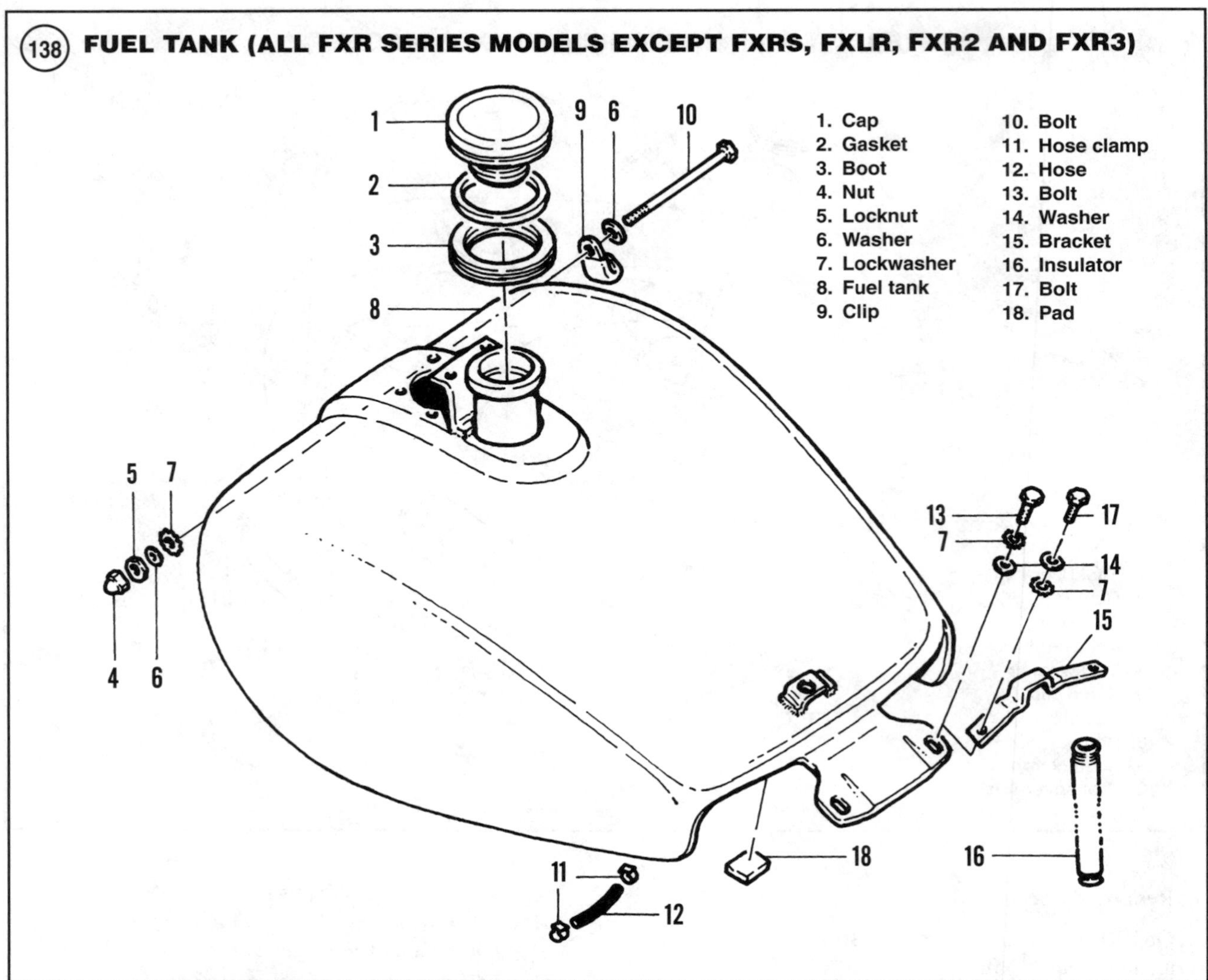

1. Disconnect the negative battery cable from the battery.
2. Drain the fuel from the fuel tank as described under *Fuel Tank Draining* in this section.
3. Disconnect the hoses from the fuel tank.
4. Remove the seat as described in Chapter Fifteen.
5. Disconnect the fuel gauge sending unit wire connector from the main wire harness.
6. On models so equipped, remove the instrument cluster as described in Chapter Nine.

NOTE
Residual fuel will drain from both sides of the fuel tank when the crossover fuel hose is disconnected. Have several golf tees or bolts ready to plug the hose end and fuel tank fitting.

7. Disconnect the crossover hose from the fuel tank. Plug the hose and tank openings.
8. Remove the bolt, lockwashers, washers, locknut and acorn nut securing the front of the fuel tank.
9. Remove the bolts, lockwashers and washers securing the rear of the fuel tank.

CAUTION
When removing the fuel tank in Step 10, do not pull on or damage the main wiring harness.

10. Carefully remove the fuel tank from the frame.
11. Drain any remaining fuel in the tank into the fuel storage tank.
12. Install by reversing these removal steps while noting the following:

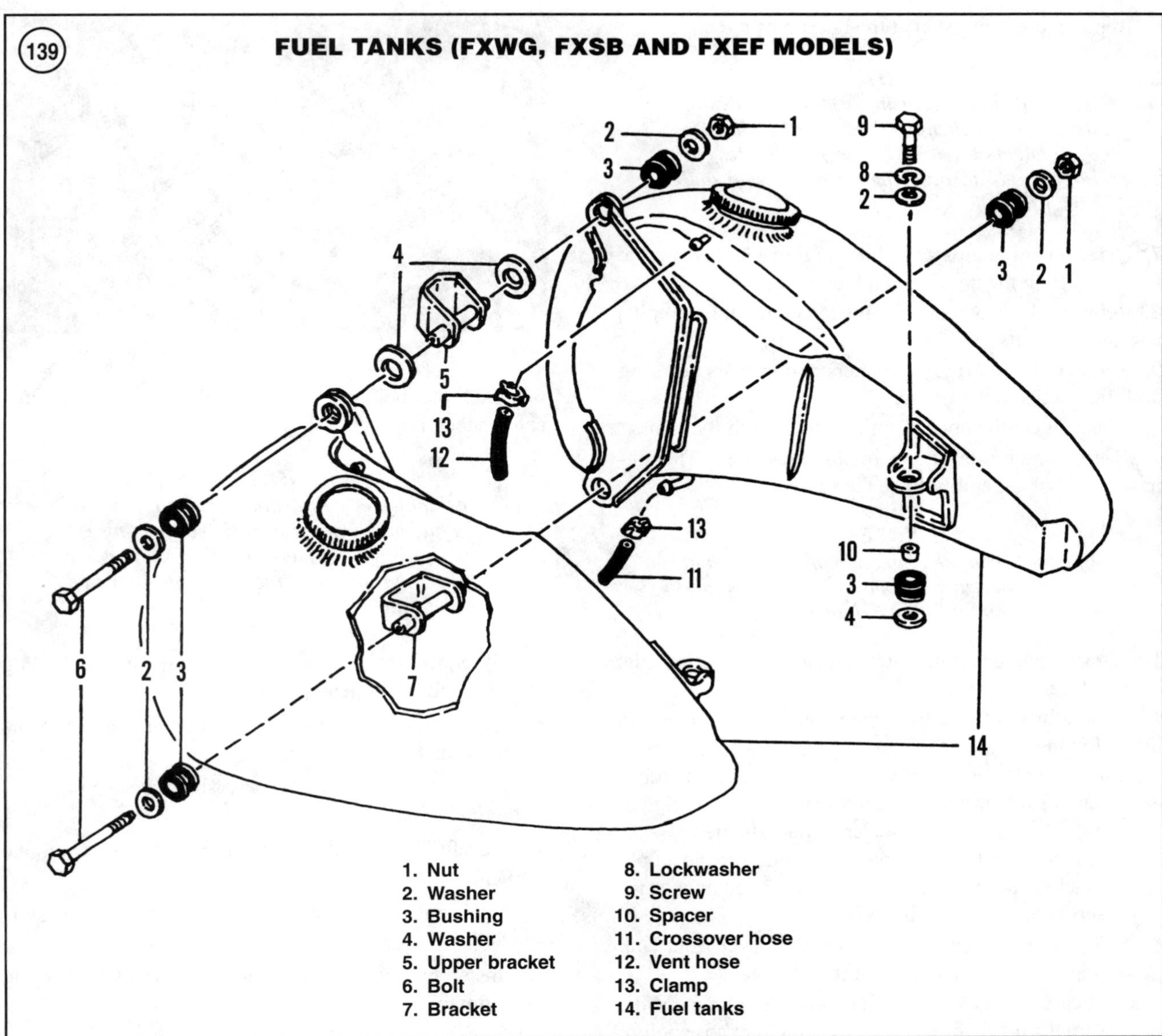

FUEL TANKS (FXWG, FXSB AND FXEF MODELS)

1. Nut
2. Washer
3. Bushing
4. Washer
5. Upper bracket
6. Bolt
7. Bracket
8. Lockwasher
9. Screw
10. Spacer
11. Crossover hose
12. Vent hose
13. Clamp
14. Fuel tanks

NOTE

If you are installing an OEM replacement fuel tank on 1991 FLH, FLT and FXR California models, refer to ***Fuel Tank Vent Modification (1991 FLH, FLT and FXR California Models)*** *in this chapter prior to installing the new tank.*

a. Position the fuel tank on the frame tube and install the washers, bolts and nuts in the original mounting positions.
b. Secure the fuel hose with a *new* hose clamp. Make sure the insulator is placed over the fuel hose before reconnecting it.
c. Refill the tank and check for leaks.

Removal/Installation (FXWG, FXSB and FXEF Models)

Refer to **Figure 139**.

1. Disconnect the negative battery cable from the battery.
2. Drain the fuel from the fuel tank as described under *Fuel Tank Draining* in this section.
3. Remove the instrument panel as described in Chapter Nine.
4. Remove the seat as described in Chapter Fifteen.
5. Remove the choke knob and nuts, if so equipped.

6. Remove the trim panel at the bottom of the tanks.

NOTE
Residual fuel will drain from both sides of the fuel tank when the crossover fuel hose is disconnected. Have several golf tees or bolts ready to plug the hose end and fuel tank fitting.

7. Disconnect the crossover hose (**Figure 140**) from the fuel tank. Plug the hose and tank openings.
8. Remove the front upper and lower mounting bolts, washers and nuts.
9. Remove the rear bolts, washers and spacers securing both fuel tanks to the frame.
10. Disconnect the upper vent line from both fuel tanks.
11. Check and remove any remaining fasteners. Then remove the tank assembly from the frame.

NOTE
After removing the tank assembly, store it in a safe place away from open flame or objects that could fall and damage it.

12. Drain any remaining fuel left in the tanks into the storage tank.
13. Install by reversing these removal steps while noting the following:
   a. Position the fuel tank assembly on the frame tubes and install the washers, bolts and nuts in the original mounting positions. The large inner diameter washers fit over the left and right ends on the upper bracket spacer tube and over the tapped anchor insert at the rear tank brackets.
   b. Route the crossover hose over the lower front tank bracket and reconnect it at the other tank.
   c. Secure the fuel hose with a *new* hose clamp. Make sure the insulator is placed over the fuel hose before reconnecting it.
   d. Refill the tanks and check for leaks.

Removal/Installation (FLH and FLT Series Models)

Refer to **Figure 141** and **Figure 142**, typical.
1. Disconnect the negative battery cable from the battery.
2. Drain the fuel from the fuel tank as described under *Fuel Tank Draining* in this section.
3. Disconnect the hoses from the fuel tank.
4. Remove the seat as described in Chapter Fifteen.
5. On models so equipped, remove the fuel tank console as described in this chapter.

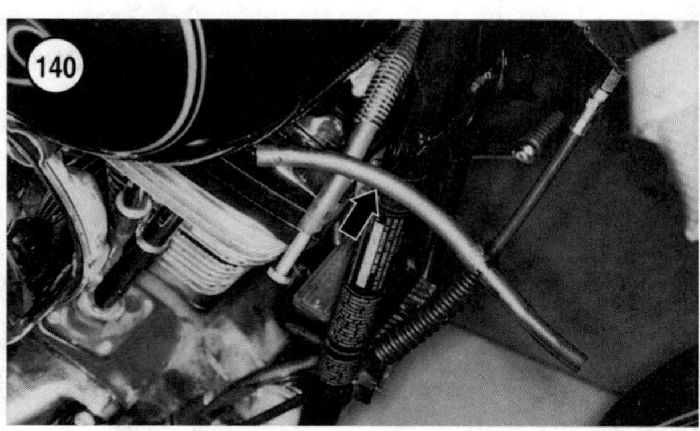

6. Under the fuel tank, disconnect the fuel gauge electrical connector.

NOTE
Residual fuel will drain from both sides of the fuel tank when the crossover fuel hose is disconnected. Have several golf tees or bolts ready to plug the hose end and fuel tank fitting.

7. Disconnect the crossover hose from the fuel tank. Plug the hose and tank openings.
8. Remove the bolt, washers, lockwasher and nut securing the front of the fuel tank.
9. Remove the screws and lockwashers securing the rear of the fuel tank.
10. Carefully lift and remove the fuel tank from the frame.
11. Drain any remaining fuel in the tank into the fuel storage tank.
12. Install by reversing these removal steps while noting the following:

NOTE
*If installing an OEM replacement fuel tank on 1991 FLH, FLT and FXR California models, refer to **Fuel Tank Vent Modification (1991 FLH, FLT and FXR California Models)** in this chapter prior to installing the new tank.*

   a. Position the fuel tank on the frame tubes and install the washers, bolts and nuts in the original mounting positions.
   b. Secure the fuel hose with a *new* hose clamp. Make sure the insulator is placed over the fuel hose before reconnecting it.
   c. Refill the tanks and check for leaks.

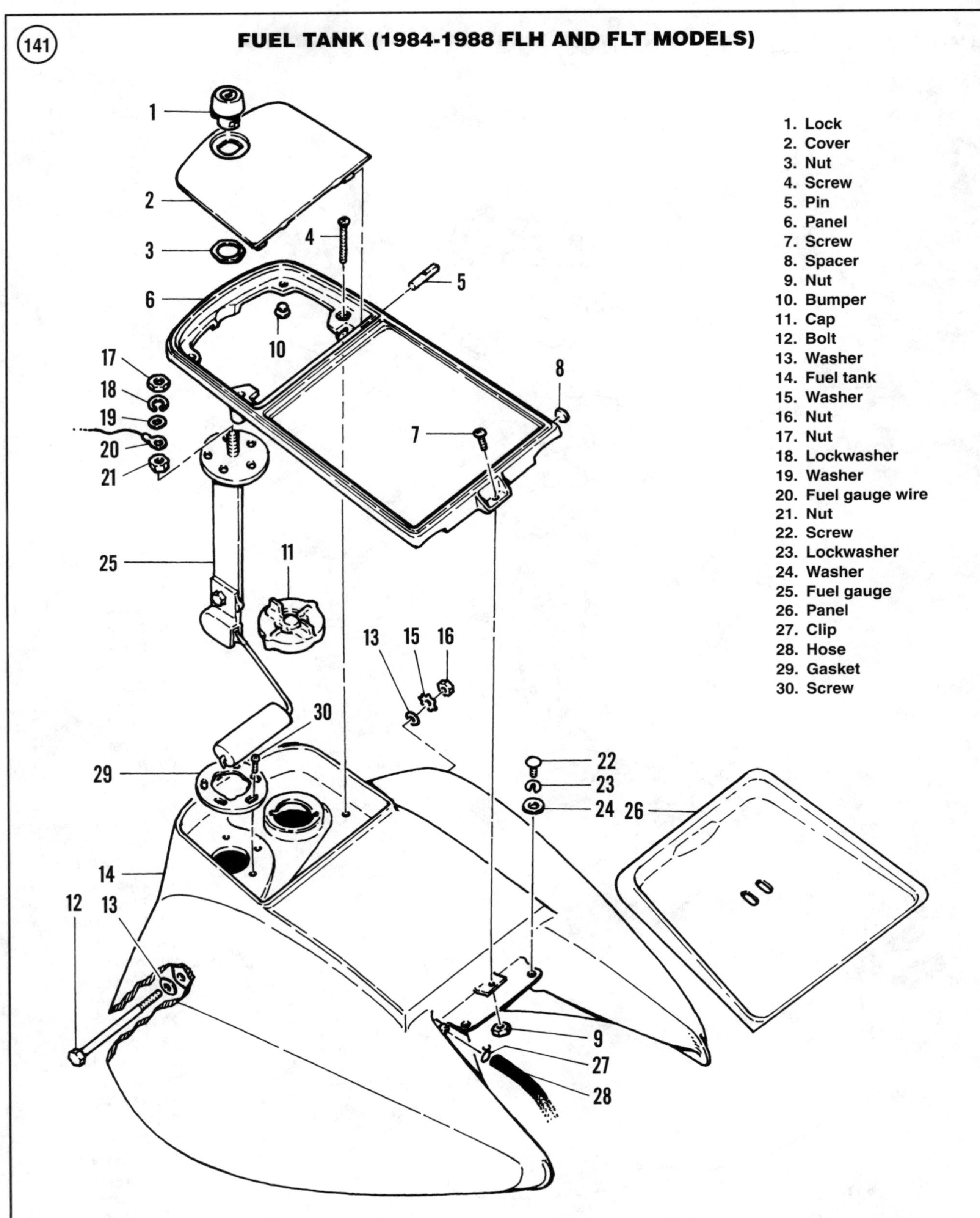
141
FUEL TANK (1984-1988 FLH AND FLT MODELS)
1. Lock
2. Cover
3. Nut
4. Screw
5. Pin
6. Panel
7. Screw
8. Spacer
9. Nut
10. Bumper
11. Cap
12. Bolt
13. Washer
14. Fuel tank
15. Washer
16. Nut
17. Nut
18. Lockwasher
19. Washer
20. Fuel gauge wire
21. Nut
22. Screw
23. Lockwasher
24. Washer
25. Fuel gauge
26. Panel
27. Clip
28. Hose
29. Gasket
30. Screw

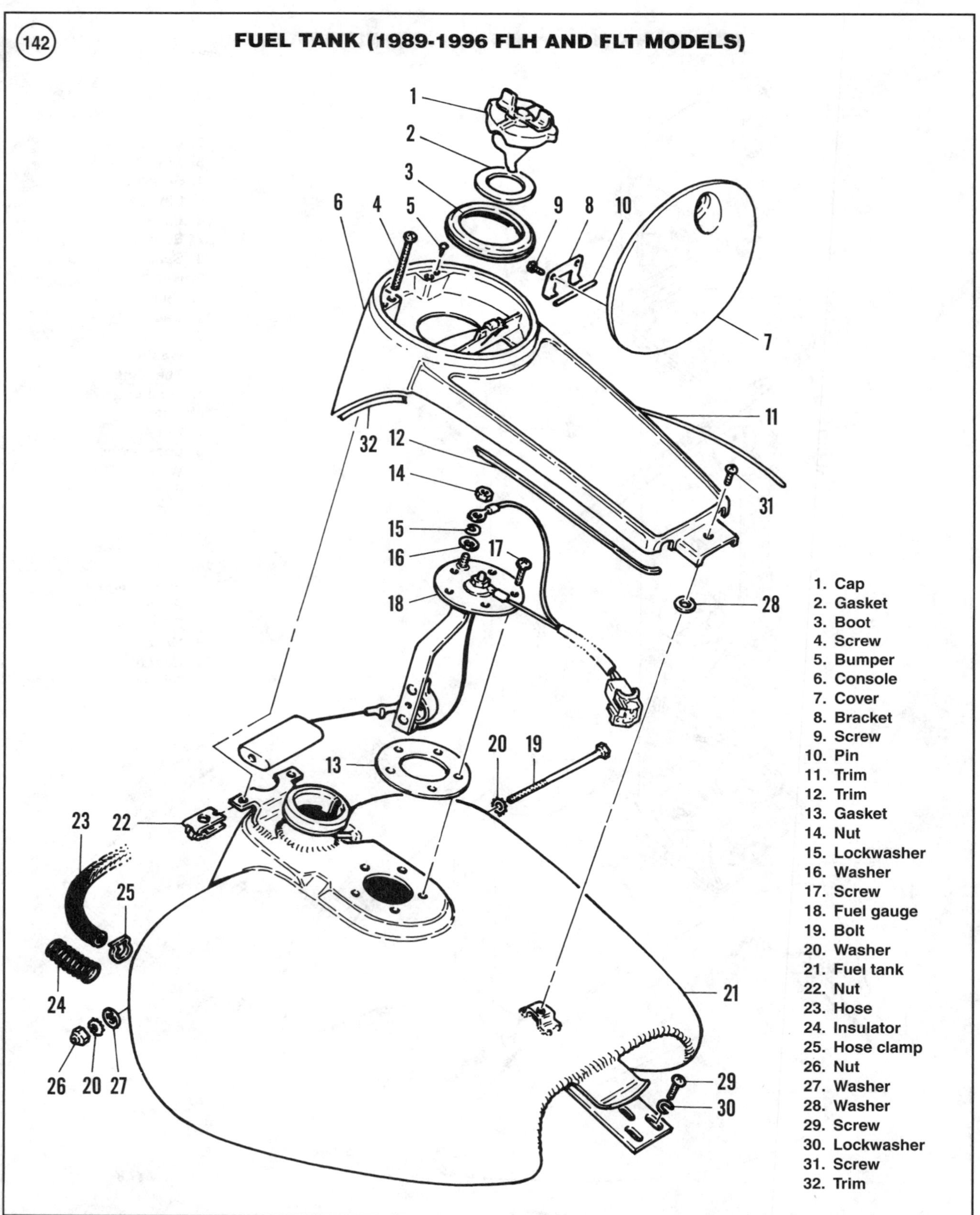
142
FUEL TANK (1989-1996 FLH AND FLT MODELS)
1
2
3
6
4
5
9
8
10
7
11
32
12
14
31
15
16
17
18
28
20
19
13
23
22
25
24
21
26
20
27
29
30
1. Cap
2. Gasket
3. Boot
4. Screw
5. Bumper
6. Console
7. Cover
8. Bracket
9. Screw
10. Pin
11. Trim
12. Trim
13. Gasket
14. Nut
15. Lockwasher
16. Washer
17. Screw
18. Fuel gauge
19. Bolt
20. Washer
21. Fuel tank
22. Nut
23. Hose
24. Insulator
25. Hose clamp
26. Nut
27. Washer
28. Washer
29. Screw
30. Lockwasher
31. Screw
32. Trim

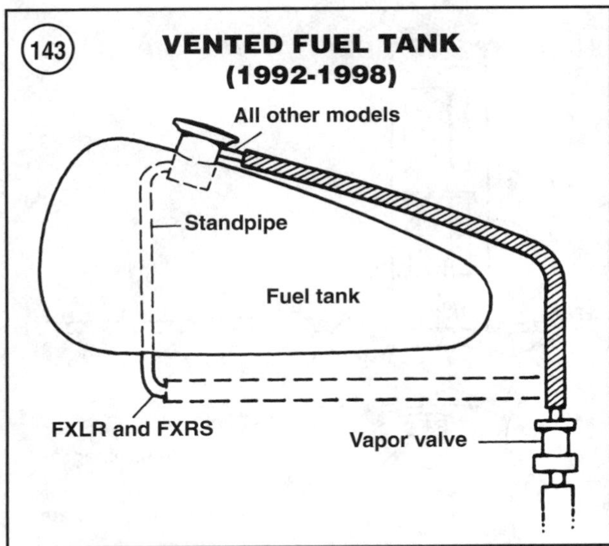

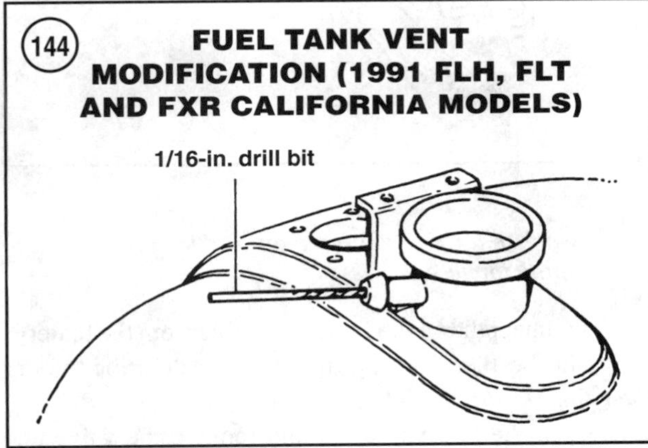

FUEL TANK VENTING (CARBURETED MODELS)

Fuel Tank Venting (1984-1991 Models)

On 1984-1991 models, the fuel tank(s) are vented through the fuel cap.

Fuel Tank Venting (1992-1998 Models)

All 1992-1998 fuel tanks are vented through a vapor valve. On 1992-1998 FXLR and 1992 FXRS models, the vent tube is connected to a standpipe mounted in the bottom of the fuel tank. On all other models, a vent nozzle is installed in the tank filler neck (**Figure 143**).

The vapor valve prevents fuel from flowing through the vent opening if the motorcycle is dropped or positioned at a low angle.

When replacing the vapor valve, note the following:

1. The vapor valve must be installed in a vertical position.
2. The vapor valve has two different end fittings. The long fitting must be installed at the top.

CAUTION

If the vapor valve is installed incorrectly, excessive pressure might build in the fuel tank.

Fuel Tank Vent Modification (1991 FLH, FLT Series and FXR Series California Models)

NOTE

Do not perform this procedure on FXLR and FXRS models equipped with the vapor tube attached to the front right side of the fuel tank.

When installing an OEM replacement fuel tank, a 0.03-0.06 in. (0.76-1.5 mm) hole must be drilled through the vapor tube cap. Confirm this with a Harley-Davidson dealership when purchasing the new fuel tank.

Drill the cap as follows:

1. First center punch the cap and drill through the cap with a 1/16-in. drill bit (**Figure 144**).
2. Remove the fuel cap and use compressed air to remove all chips from the fuel tank.
3. Reinstall the fuel cap.

NON-VACUUM-OPERATED FUEL SHUTOFF VALVE

A three-way fuel shutoff valve is mounted onto the left fuel tank. A replaceable fuel strainer is mounted at the top of the shutoff valve.

Removal/Installation and Filter Cleaning

Refer to **Figure 145**.

WARNING

Some fuel might spill from the fuel tank hose(s) during these procedures. Because gasoline is extremely flammable and explosive, perform this procedure away from all open flames (including appliance pilot lights) and sparks. Do not smoke or allow anyone to smoke in the work area because an explosion and fire can occur. Always

8

work in a well-ventilated area. Wipe up any spills immediately.

1. Disconnect the negative battery cable from the battery.
2. Drain the fuel from the fuel tank as described under *Fuel Tank Draining* in this section.
3. Loosen the fuel valve nut and remove the valve and gasket from the fuel tank. Catch any residual gas that may drain from the fuel tank after the valve is removed.
4. Check the fuel strainer for contamination or damage. If the strainer cannot be thoroughly cleaned, replace it. Install a *new* gasket when installing a *new* strainer.
5. Inspect the condition of the gasket; replace if necessary.
6. Clean the fuel tank threads of all sealant residue.
7. Coat the shutoff valve threads with Loctite Pipe Sealant with Teflon and insert the valve into the tank. Tighten the valve nut as follows:
   a. On 1993-1994 FXR series models, tighten the valve nut to 18 ft.-lb. (24 N•m).

WARNING
On 1993-1994 FXR series models, do not turn the fuel valve nut more than two turns, or the nut will bottom out on the fuel tank threads. This may cause the fuel valve to leak gasoline and create a fire hazard.

   b. On all other models, securely tighten the fuel valve nut.
8. Remove the drain tube from the fuel tank and reconnect the fuel line. Secure the fuel line with a *new* hose clamp. Make sure the insulator is placed over the fuel line before reconnecting the fuel line.
9. Refill the fuel tanks.
10. Check the area around the fuel valve and hoses carefully to make sure no fuel is leaking.

VACUUM-OPERATED FUEL VALVE (1994-1998 FLH AND FLT SERIES MODELS)

Removal/Installation and Filter Cleaning

Refer to **Figure 146**.

WARNING
Some fuel might spill from the fuel tank hose(s) during these procedures. Because gasoline is extremely flammable and explosive, perform this procedure away from all open flames (including appliance pilot lights) and sparks. Do not smoke or allow anyone to smoke in the work area because an explosion and fire can occur. Always

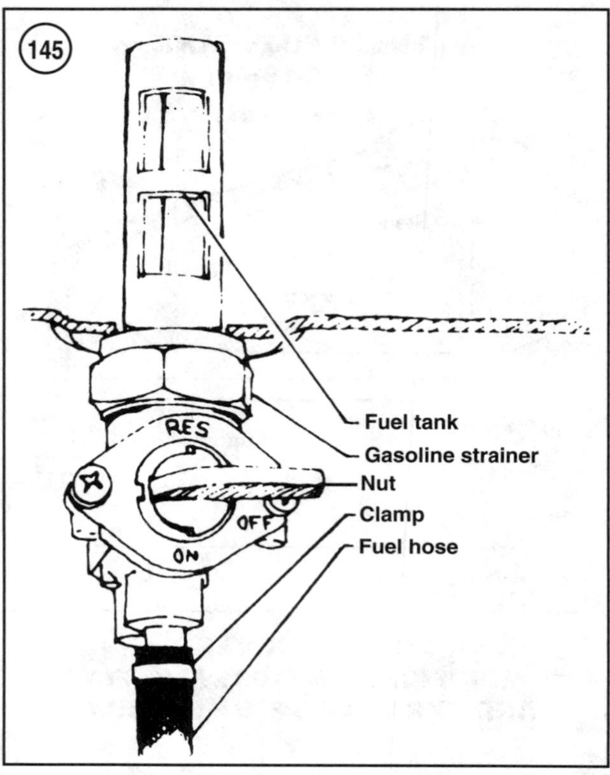

work in a well-ventilated area. Wipe up any spills immediately.

1. Disconnect the negative battery cable from the battery.
2. Drain the fuel from the fuel tank as described under *Fuel Tank Draining* in this section.
3. Loosen the fuel valve nut and remove the valve and gasket from the fuel tank. Catch any fuel that might leak from the fuel tank after the valve is removed.
4. Check the fuel strainer for contamination or damage. If the strainer cannot be thoroughly cleaned, replace it. Install a new gasket when installing a new strainer.

NOTE
If the strainer is contaminated, the fuel tank might require cleaning and flushing.

5. Inspect the fuel valve gasket; replace if necessary.
6. Clean the fuel tank threads of all sealant.
7. Coat the shutoff valve threads with Loctite Pipe Sealant with Teflon and insert the valve into the tank. Tighten the valve nut to 18 ft.-lb. (24 N•m).

WARNING
Do not turn the fuel valve nut more than two turns after initial thread engagement, or the nut will bottom out on the fuel tank threads.

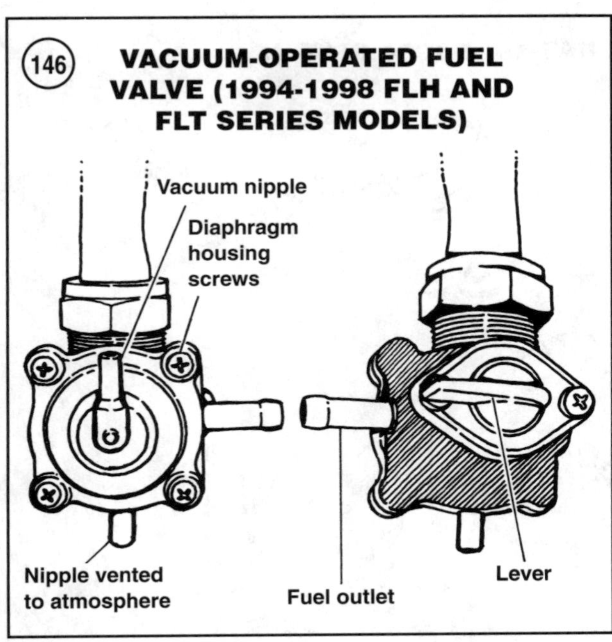

This can cause the fuel valve to leak gasoline and create a fire hazard.

8. Reconnect the vacuum and fuel lines at the fuel shutoff valve. Secure both lines with new hose clamps. Make sure the insulator is placed over the fuel line before reconnecting the fuel line.
9. Refill the fuel tank.
10. Check the area around the fuel valve and hoses carefully to make sure no fuel is leaking.

FUEL TANK (FUEL-INJECTED MODELS)

WARNING
Some fuel might spill from the fuel tank hose(s) during these procedures. Because gasoline is extremely flammable and explosive, perform this procedure away from all open flames (including appliance pilot lights) and sparks. Do not smoke or allow anyone to smoke in the work area because an explosion and fire can occur. Always work in a well-ventilated area. Wipe up any spills immediately.

WARNING
Make sure to route the fuel tank vapor hoses so that they cannot contact any hot engine or exhaust component. These hoses contain flammable vapors. If a hose melts from contacting a hot part, leaking vapors can ignite and cause a fire.

WARNING
Gasoline is a known carcinogen, as well as an extremely flammable liquid, and must be handled carefully. Wear latex gloves to avoid contact. If gasoline does contact skin, immediately and thoroughly wash the area with soap and warm water.

The fuel hoses are secured to the fuel tank with a nonreusable clamp. If the same type of clamp is going to be reinstalled, purchase *new* ones before servicing the fuel tank.

When removing the fuel tank in the following procedures, keep track of all fasteners and rubber bushings to avoid losing them or mixing them up during installation.

8

Fuel Tank Draining

1. Depressurize the fuel system as described under *Depressurizing the Fuel System* in this chapter.
2. Make a drain hose from 5/16-in. inner diameter hose and plug one end of it. Make it long enough to go from the fuel tank crossover hose fitting to an empty fuel can.
3. Disconnect the crossover hose from one of the fittings on the fuel tank. Immediately connect the drain hose made in Step 2 to the fuel tank fitting.
4. Place the plugged end of the drain hose into the fuel can and remove the plug. Drain the fuel from that side of the fuel tank.
5. Disconnect the drain hose and reinstall the plug into one end of it.
6. Repeat for the other side of the fuel tank.
7. Plug the fuel tank crossover fittings to prevent the draining of fuel.

Fuel Tank Removal/Installation

The crossover fuel hose is secured to the fuel tank with nonreusable clamps. If the same type of clamp is going to be reinstalled, purchase *new* ones before servicing the fuel tank.

Refer to **Figure 147** and **Figure 148**.

1. Depressurize the fuel system as described under *Depressurizing the Fuel System* in this chapter.
2. Remove the seat as described in Chapter Fifteen.
3. Remove the fuel tank console as described in this chapter.

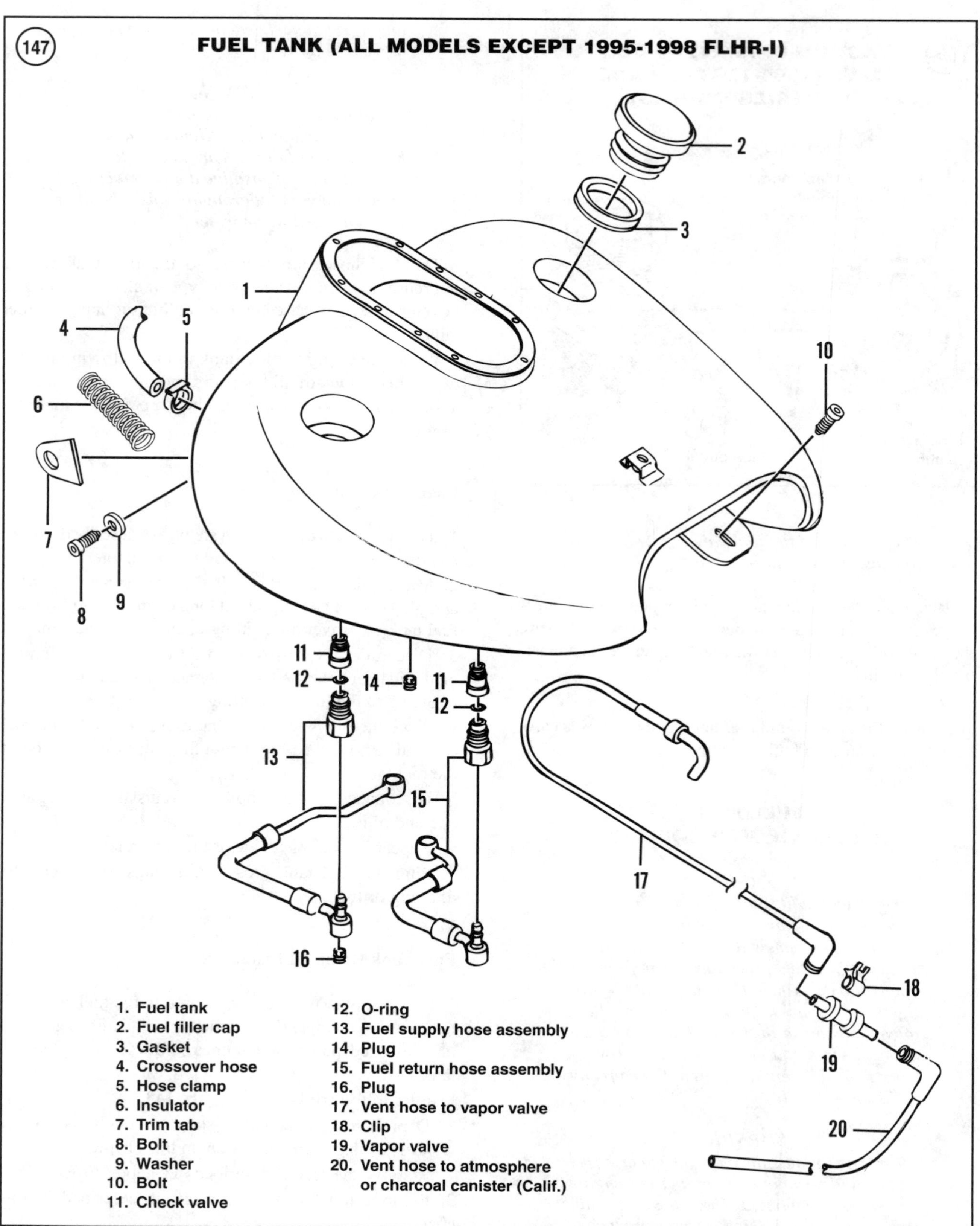
147
FUEL TANK (ALL MODELS EXCEPT 1995-1998 FLHR-I)
1
2
3
4
5
6
7
8
9
10
11
12
13
14
15
16
17
18
19
20
1. Fuel tank
2. Fuel filler cap
3. Gasket
4. Crossover hose
5. Hose clamp
6. Insulator
7. Trim tab
8. Bolt
9. Washer
10. Bolt
11. Check valve
12. O-ring
13. Fuel supply hose assembly
14. Plug
15. Fuel return hose assembly
16. Plug
17. Vent hose to vapor valve
18. Clip
19. Vapor valve
20. Vent hose to atmosphere or charcoal canister (Calif.)

148

FUEL TANK (1995-1998 FLHR-I MODELS)

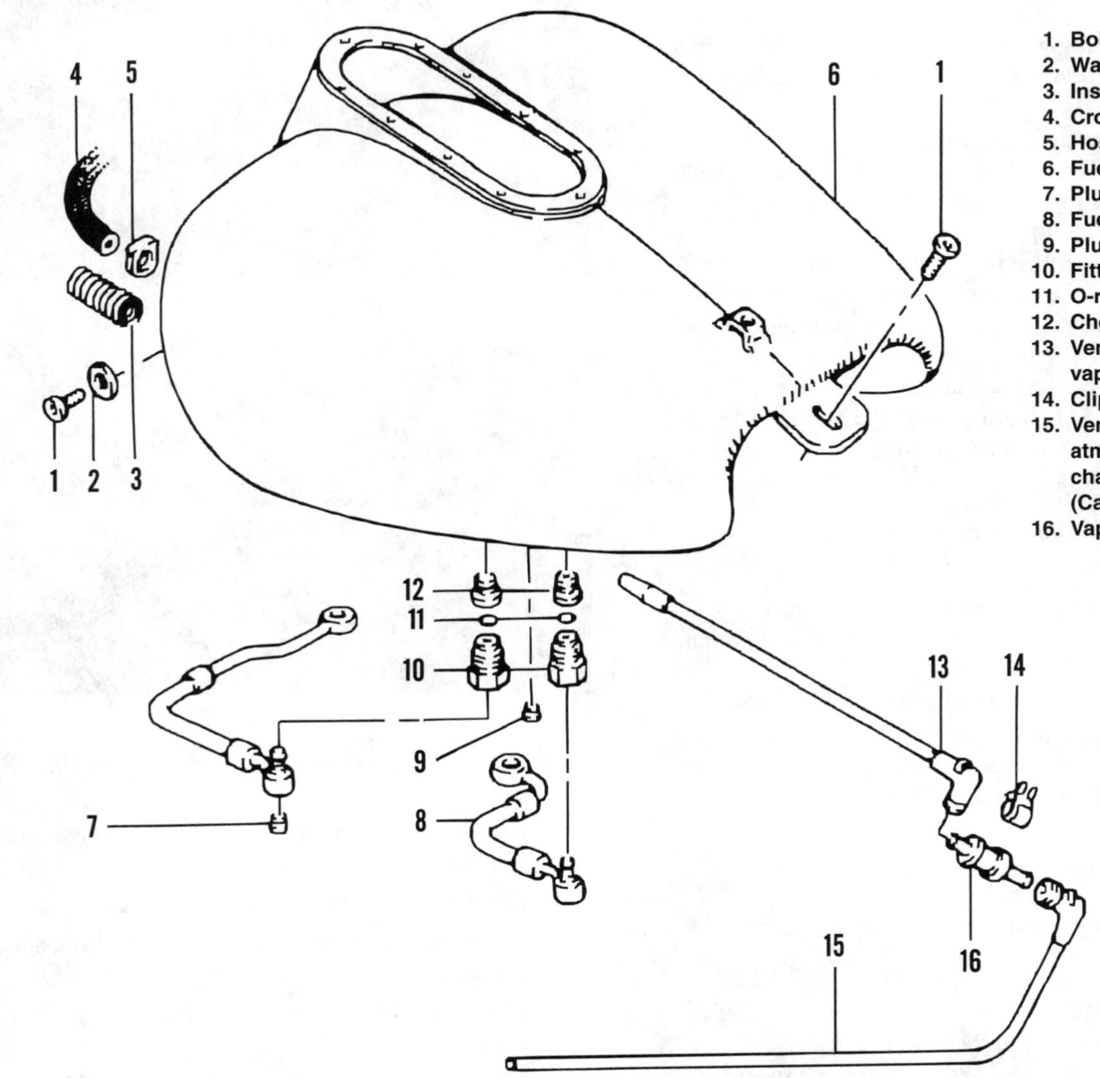

1. Bolt
2. Washer
3. Insulator
4. Crossover hose
5. Hose clamp
6. Fuel tank
7. Plug
8. Fuel hose
9. Plug
10. Fitting
11. O-ring
12. Check valve
13. Vent hose to vapor valve
14. Clip
15. Vent hose to atmosphere or charcoal canister (Calif).
16. Vapor valve

4. Disconnect the crossover hose (**Figure 149**) from one of the fittings on the fuel tank. Drain the fuel tank as described in this chapter.

5. Carefully cut the tie-wraps securing the electrical harness to the left frame tube.

6. Disconnect the vent hose from the fuel tank.

WARNING
A small amount of fuel will drain out of the fuel tank when the fuel lines are disconnected from the base of the tank. Place several shop cloths under the fuel line fittings

to catch any spilled fuel prior to disconnecting them. Discard the shop cloths in a suitably safe manner.

7. On the front fitting, unscrew the hex nut on the fuel line fitting and disconnect the fuel supply line from the fuel tank.
8. On the rear fitting, unscrew the hex nut on the fuel line fitting and disconnect the fuel return line from the fuel tank.
9. Remove the O-ring seal from both fittings.
10. On models so equipped, remove the fairing lower cap on each side as described in Chapter Fifteen.
11. At the front of the fuel tank, remove the T40 Torx bolt and washer (**Figure 150**) on each side securing the fuel tank to the frame.
12. At the rear of the fuel tank, remove the bolt and washer (**Figure 151**) securing the fuel tank to the frame.
13. Lift off and remove the fuel tank from the frame.

NOTE
Store the fuel tank in a safe place away from open flames or where it could be damaged.

14. Drain any remaining fuel left in the tank into a gas can.
15. Installation is the reverse of these steps while noting the following:
   a. Securely tighten the front and rear bolts and nuts.
   b. Install a *new* O-ring seal onto each fuel line fitting and apply clean engine oil to it. Tighten the hex nut fitting to 20-24 ft.-lb. (27-33 N•m).

FUEL PUMP AND FUEL FILTER

Canopy Assembly Removal/Installation

Refer to **Figure 152** and **Figure 153**.

1. Depressurize the fuel system as described under *Depressurizing the Fuel System* in this chapter.
2. Remove the seat as described in Chapter Fifteen.
3. Remove the fuel tank console as described in this chapter.
4. Drain the fuel tank as described in this chapter.
5. Carefully cut the tie-wraps securing the electrical harness to the left frame tube.
6. Disconnect the three individual electrical connectors from the fuel gauge sending unit spade terminals.

7A. On FLHR-I models, perform the following:
   a. Remove the T20 Torx bolts securing the top plate to the top of the fuel tank.
   b. Partially lift the top plate away from the fuel tank and disconnect the yellow/green ground wire from the spade terminal on the under side of the top plate.
   c. Remove the top plate.

7B. On all models except FLHR-I models, perform the following:
   a. Remove the T20 Torx bolts securing the canopy assembly to the top of the fuel tank.
   b. Partially lift the canopy away from the fuel tank.
   c. Disconnect the black ground wire from the spade terminal on the underside of the canopy.
   d. Disconnect the yellow/green wire from the spade terminal.
   e. Carefully pull the canopy assembly straight up and out of the fuel tank. Do not damage the fuel gauge sending unit float during removal.

8. Remove the top plate or canopy gasket and discard it. A *new* gasket must be installed.
9. Installation is the reverse of these removal steps while noting the following:
   a. The top plate or canopy gasket is wider at one end. Place the wider end at the front of the fuel tank, install the *new* gasket and align the bolt holes.
   b. Attach the electrical connector(s) to the spade terminals. The spade terminals are different sizes to eliminate improper connections.
   c. Securely tighten the mounting T20 Torx bolts.

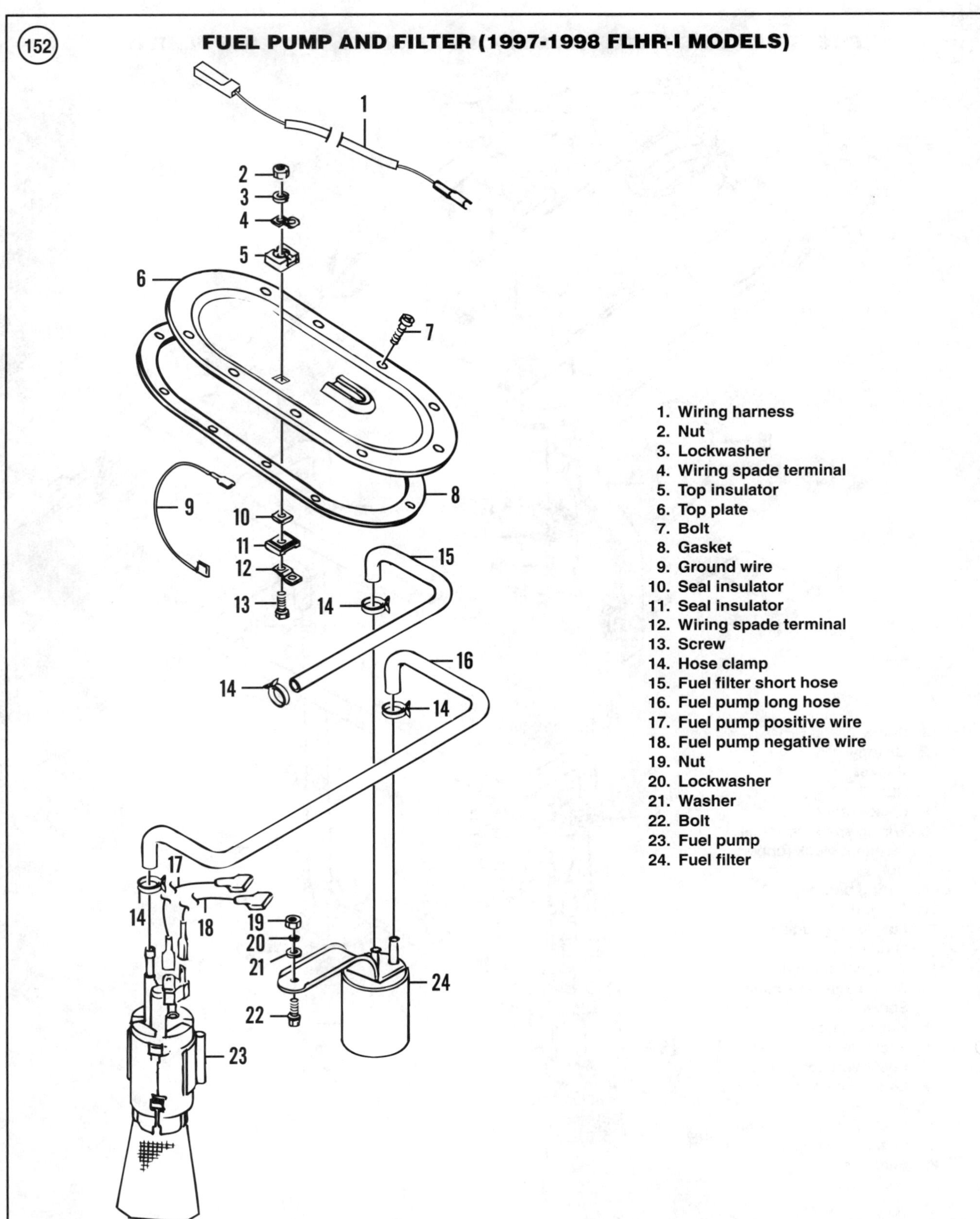
152
FUEL PUMP AND FILTER (1997-1998 FLHR-I MODELS)
1
2
3
4
5
6
7
8
9
10
11
12
13
14
15
16
17
18
19
20
21
22
23
24
1. Wiring harness
2. Nut
3. Lockwasher
4. Wiring spade terminal
5. Top insulator
6. Top plate
7. Bolt
8. Gasket
9. Ground wire
10. Seal insulator
11. Seal insulator
12. Wiring spade terminal
13. Screw
14. Hose clamp
15. Fuel filter short hose
16. Fuel pump long hose
17. Fuel pump positive wire
18. Fuel pump negative wire
19. Nut
20. Lockwasher
21. Washer
22. Bolt
23. Fuel pump
24. Fuel filter

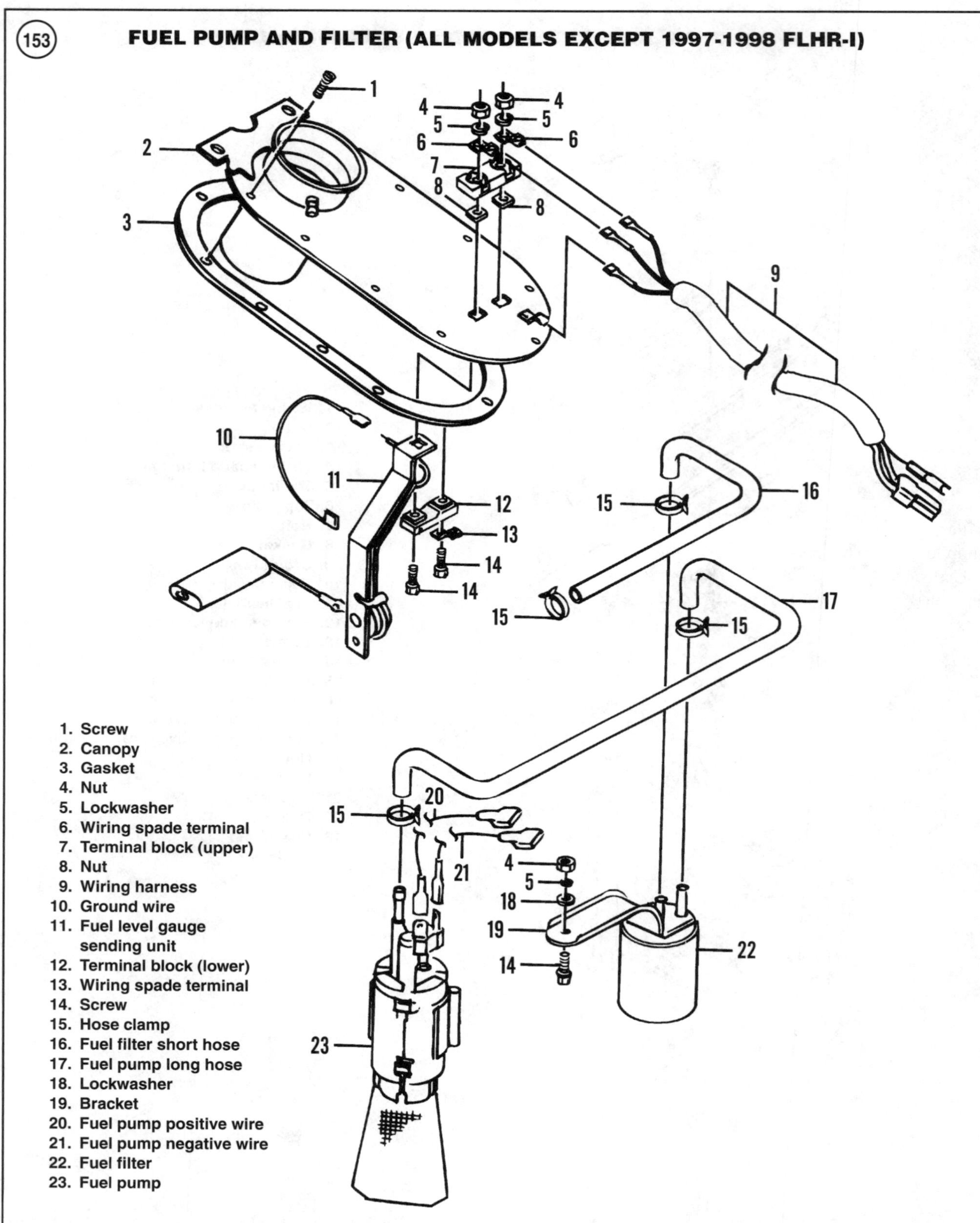
153
FUEL PUMP AND FILTER (ALL MODELS EXCEPT 1997-1998 FLHR-I)
1. Screw
2. Canopy
3. Gasket
4. Nut
5. Lockwasher
6. Wiring spade terminal
7. Terminal block (upper)
8. Nut
9. Wiring harness
10. Ground wire
11. Fuel level gauge sending unit
12. Terminal block (lower)
13. Wiring spade terminal
14. Screw
15. Hose clamp
16. Fuel filter short hose
17. Fuel pump long hose
18. Lockwasher
19. Bracket
20. Fuel pump positive wire
21. Fuel pump negative wire
22. Fuel filter
23. Fuel pump

Fuel Filter Removal/Installation

1. Remove the canopy or top plate assembly as described in this section.

WARNING
The fuel tank opening might have some sharp edges. Protect hands accordingly.

2. Use side-cutting pliers, cut the hose clamp, and remove the fuel filter short hose from the fuel tank inlet supply tube.

CAUTION
Do not drop the nut, lockwasher and washer in the following step because they will fall to the bottom of the fuel tank.

3. Loosen the nut securing the fuel filter bracket to the bolt on top of the fuel tank tunnel. Remove the nut. Then use a magnetic tool and remove the lockwasher and washer from the bolt.
4. Release the fuel filter bracket from the fuel tank tunnel.
5. Partially withdraw the fuel filter along with the fuel pump long hose from the fuel tank.
6. Use side-cutting pliers, cut the hose clamp, and remove the fuel filter long hose from the fuel tank outlet supply tube.
7. Use side-cutting pliers, cut the remaining hose clamp, and remove the fuel filter short hose from the fuel filter inlet supply tube.
8. Remove the fuel filter.
9. Installation is the reverse of removal while noting the following:
   a. Use *new* hose clamps.
   b. Install the short hose onto the *new* fuel filter outlet port so the initial bend runs parallel to the fuel filter bracket. Crimp the hose clamp.
   c. Slide a *new* hose clamp onto the free end of the long hose. Install the hose onto the inlet port so it runs parallel to the short hose. Crimp the clamp.

Fuel Pump Removal/Installation

1. Remove the canopy or top plate assembly as previously described in this section.

WARNING
The fuel tank opening might have some sharp edges. Protect hands accordingly.

2. Lift the fuel pump off the two posts on the left side of the fuel tank. Remove the fuel pump assembly from the fuel tank.
3. Use side-cutting pliers, cut the hose clamp on the long hose, and disconnect it from the outlet port.
4. Disconnect the black and yellow/green wires from the fuel pump.

CAUTION
Do not replace the special Teflon-coated wires with ordinary wire because the insulation can deteriorate when exposed to gasoline.

5. Inspect the fuel pump wires and replace with *new* Teflon-coated wires if necessary.
6. Discard the fuel pump.
7. Installation is the reverse of removal while noting the following:
   a. Use *new* hose clamps.
   b. Attach the electrical connectors to the fuel pump terminals. The terminals are different sizes to eliminate improper connections.

FUEL TANK INSPECTION (ALL MODELS)

1. Inspect all of the fuel and vent lines for cracks, age deterioration or damage. Replace damaged lines with the same type and size of material. The fuel line must be flexible and strong enough to withstand engine heat and vibration.
2. Check the fuel line insulator for damage.
3. Check for damaged or missing rubber dampers.
4. Remove the fuel tank cap(s) and inspect the inside of the tank for rust or contamination. If there is a rust buildup inside the tank, clean and flush the tank as described in this chapter.
5. Inspect the fuel tank for leaks. If fuel was noted on the outside of the tank, and it was not spilled during refilling, the tank is leaking. If the leakage point is small, repair the leak as described in this chapter. If the leak is large, or if it cannot be repaired with a tank sealant, replace the fuel tank.

EXHAUST SYSTEM

Removal

Refer to **Figures 154-156**.

NOTE
If the system joints are corroded or rusty, spray all connections with WD-40 or an equivalent and allow the penetrating oil to soak in sufficiently to free the rusted joints.

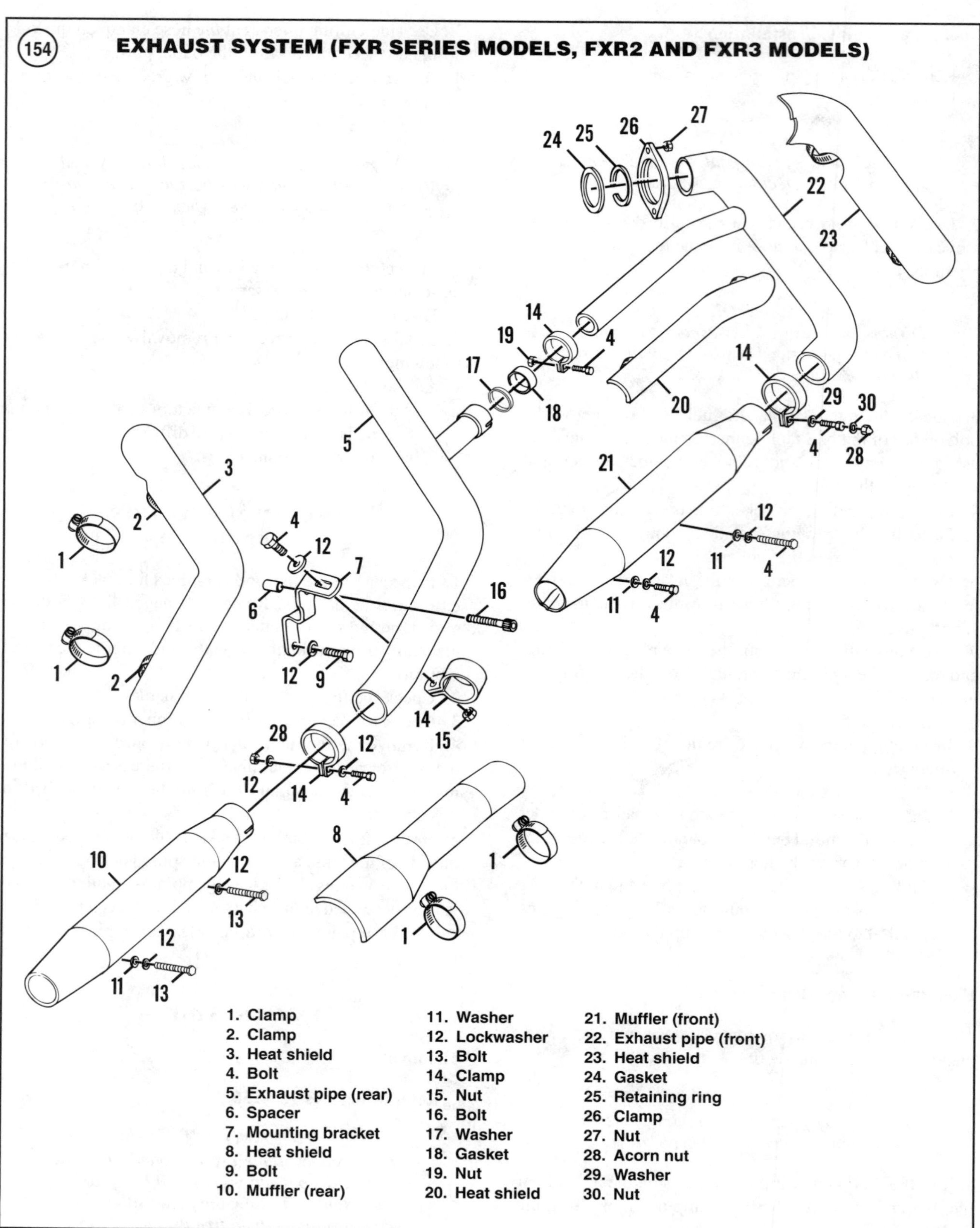
154
EXHAUST SYSTEM (FXR SERIES MODELS, FXR2 AND FXR3 MODELS)
1. Clamp
2. Clamp
3. Heat shield
4. Bolt
5. Exhaust pipe (rear)
6. Spacer
7. Mounting bracket
8. Heat shield
9. Bolt
10. Muffler (rear)
11. Washer
12. Lockwasher
13. Bolt
14. Clamp
15. Nut
16. Bolt
17. Washer
18. Gasket
19. Nut
20. Heat shield
21. Muffler (front)
22. Exhaust pipe (front)
23. Heat shield
24. Gasket
25. Retaining ring
26. Clamp
27. Nut
28. Acorn nut
29. Washer
30. Nut

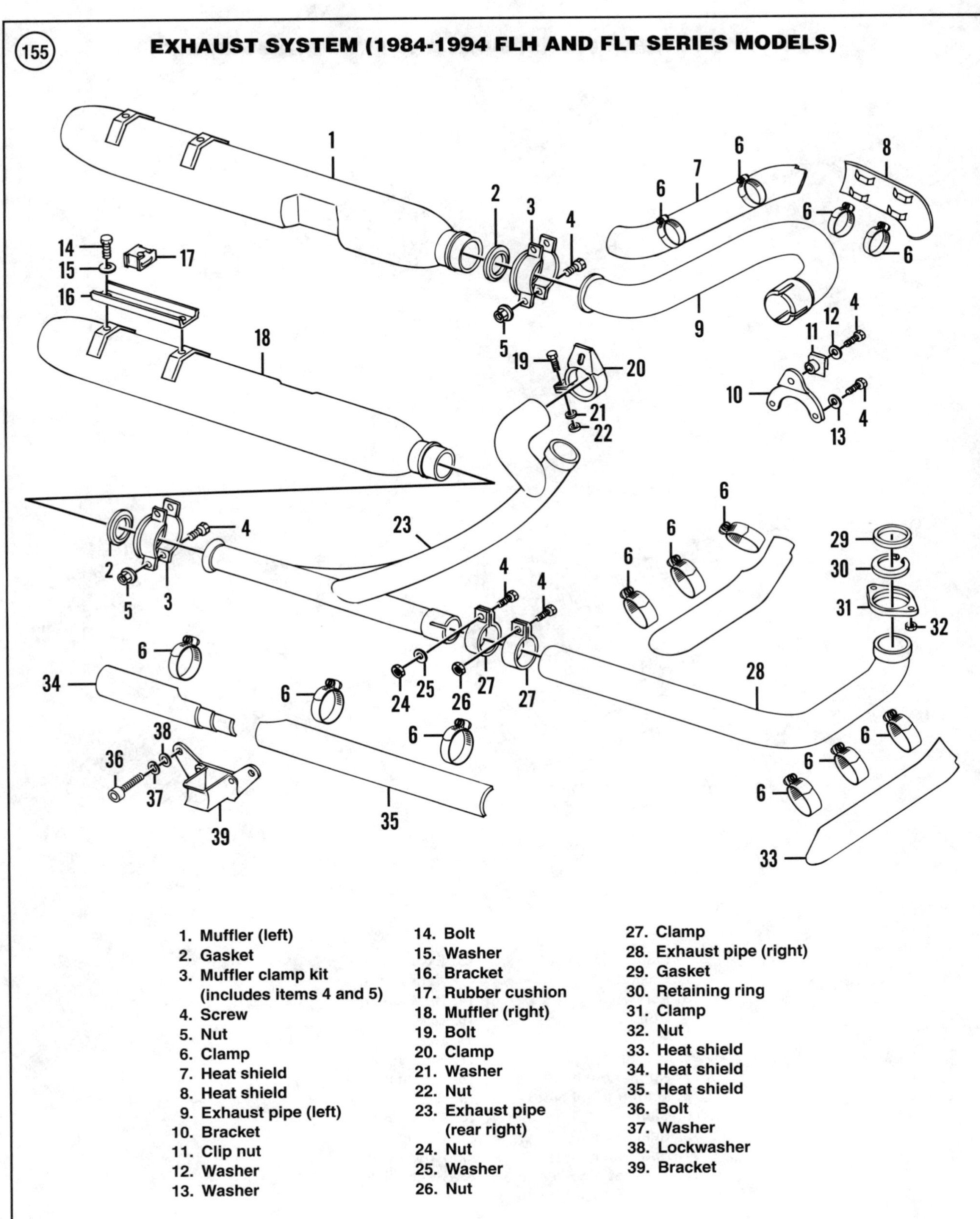

1. Muffler (left)
2. Gasket
3. Muffler clamp kit (includes items 4 and 5)
4. Screw
5. Nut
6. Clamp
7. Heat shield
8. Heat shield
9. Exhaust pipe (left)
10. Bracket
11. Clip nut
12. Washer
13. Washer
14. Bolt
15. Washer
16. Bracket
17. Rubber cushion
18. Muffler (right)
19. Bolt
20. Clamp
21. Washer
22. Nut
23. Exhaust pipe (rear right)
24. Nut
25. Washer
26. Nut
27. Clamp
28. Exhaust pipe (right)
29. Gasket
30. Retaining ring
31. Clamp
32. Nut
33. Heat shield
34. Heat shield
35. Heat shield
36. Bolt
37. Washer
38. Lockwasher
39. Bracket

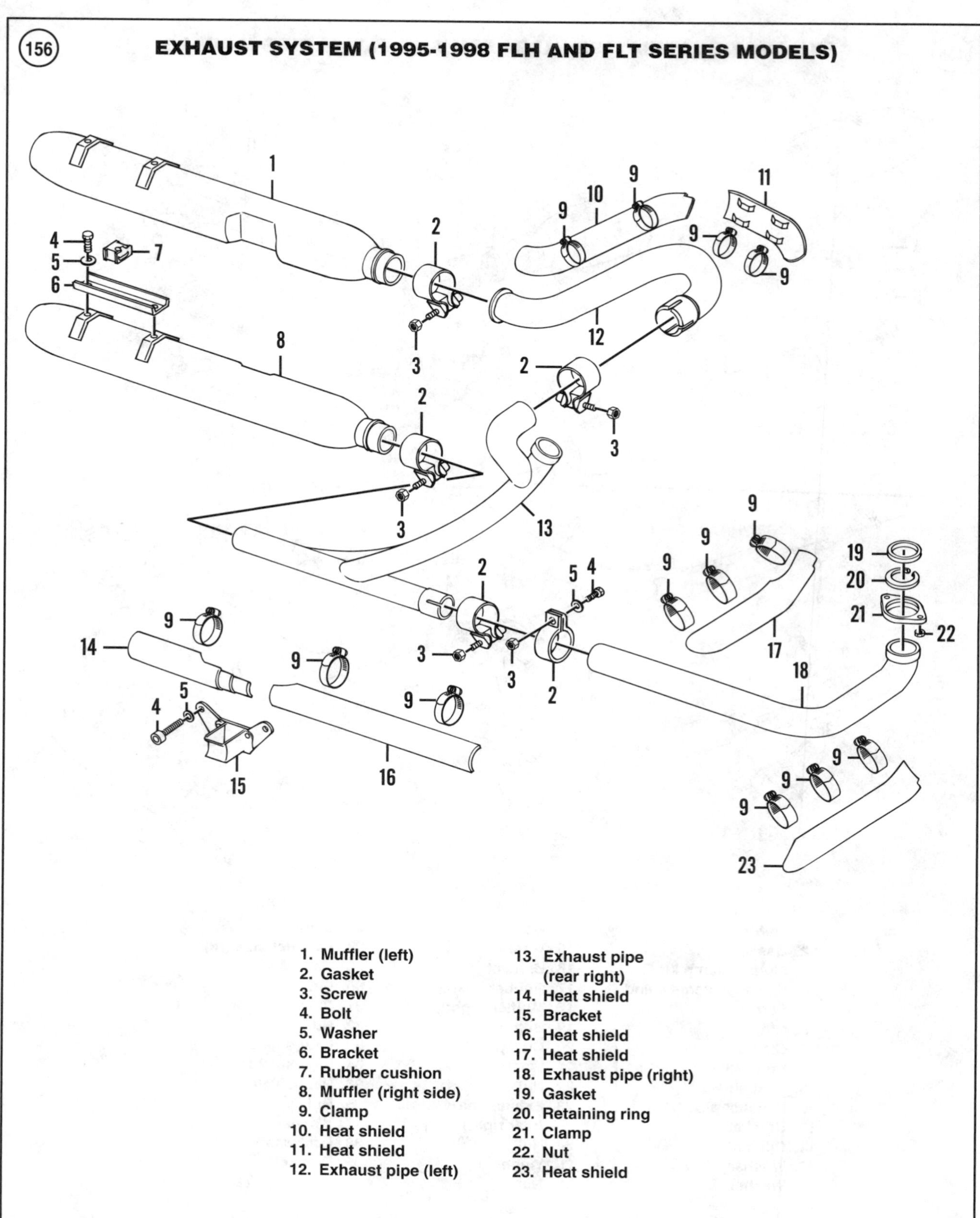
156
EXHAUST SYSTEM (1995-1998 FLH AND FLT SERIES MODELS)
1. Muffler (left)
2. Gasket
3. Screw
4. Bolt
5. Washer
6. Bracket
7. Rubber cushion
8. Muffler (right side)
9. Clamp
10. Heat shield
11. Heat shield
12. Exhaust pipe (left)
13. Exhaust pipe (rear right)
14. Heat shield
15. Bracket
16. Heat shield
17. Heat shield
18. Exhaust pipe (right)
19. Gasket
20. Retaining ring
21. Clamp
22. Nut
23. Heat shield

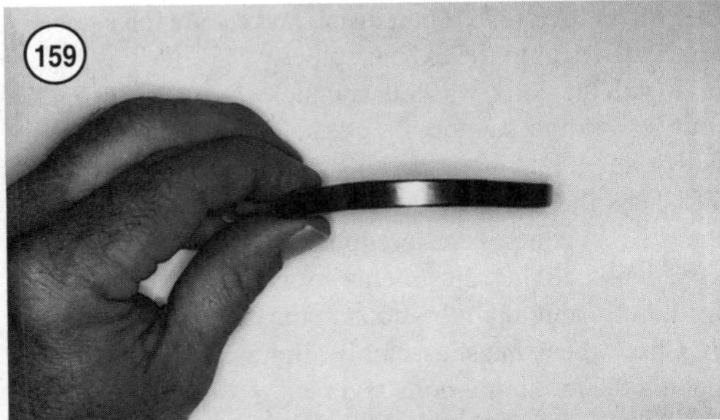

1. Support the motorcycle on a work stand. See *Motorcycle Stands* in Chapter Ten.
2. On models so equipped, remove both saddlebags as described in Chapter Fifteen.
3. On models so equipped, remove the footboards as described in Chapter Fifteen.
4. Identify the heat shields prior to removal. This will aid during installation. They look very similar, but all have slight differences. Use the numbers assigned to these parts in **Figures 154-156**.
5. Loosen the hose clamps and remove all heat shields.
6. Loosen the clamps securing the mufflers to the exhaust pipes.
7. Remove the bolts, washers and lockwashers securing the mufflers to the support brackets.
8. Pull toward the rear and disconnect the muffler from the exhaust pipe and remove the muffler. Slightly rotate the muffler during removal.
9. At each cylinder head, loosen and remove the two flange nuts securing both the front and rear (**Figure 157**) exhaust pipes to the cylinder heads.
10. Slide the flange off the cylinder head port studs on both cylinders.

CAUTION

*If the exhaust flanges (**Figure 158**) did not slide off of the cylinder head studs easily in Step 10, the flange plate is distorted or bowed (**Figure 159**). If a flange is severely distorted, perform Step 11.*

11. If a flange is severely distorted, the distance between the flange holes is reduced, which causes the flange to wedge against the stud and damage the threads. If a flange is tight, remove one of the cylinder head studs using the two-nut technique described in Chapter One.

12A. On FXR series models, perform the following:
   a. Loosen the clamp securing the rear exhaust pipe to the front exhaust pipe.
   b. Remove the bolt, washer and nut securing the rear exhaust pipe to the mounting bracket.
   c. Carefully remove the rear exhaust pipe (A, **Figure 160**) from the cylinder head and frame.
   d. Remove the front exhaust pipe (B, **Figure 160**) from the cylinder head and frame.

12B. On FLH and FLT series models, perform the following:
   a. Loosen the clamp on the left exhaust pipe. Remove the left exhaust pipe from the right rear exhaust pipe.
   b. Loosen the clamps securing the right rear exhaust pipe to the right front exhaust pipe.

c. Remove the right rear exhaust pipe from the right front exhaust pipe. Remove the right rear exhaust pipe from the engine and frame.
d. Remove the right front exhaust pipe from the engine.

13. Remove the retaining ring and gasket (**Figure 161**) from each exhaust port. Discard the gaskets.
14. Place a clean rag into the exhaust port openings.
15. Inspect the exhaust system as described in this chapter.
16. Store the exhaust system components in a safe place until they are reinstalled.

Installation

NOTE
New clamps must be installed to ensure correct sealing integrity. The new clamps eliminate the need for graphite or silicone tape during installation of the mufflers.

NOTE
To eliminate exhaust leaks, do not tighten any of the mounting bolts and nuts or the clamps until all of the exhaust components are in place.

1. Before installing the *new* exhaust port gaskets, scrape the exhaust port surfaces (**Figure 162**) to remove all carbon residue. Removing the carbon will ensure a good gasket fit. Then wipe the port with a rag.
2. Correctly position all clamps onto the exhaust pipes prior to installation.
3. Install a *new* exhaust port gasket into each exhaust port with the tapered side facing out. Install the retaining ring to secure the gasket in place.

4A. On FXR series models, perform the following:
a. Install the front exhaust pipe (B, **Figure 160**) into the frame and onto the cylinder head studs. Install the flange nuts and tighten finger-tight.
b. Install the washer and *new* gasket into the rear exhaust pipe where it joins to the crossover pipe of the front exhaust pipe.
c. Carefully insert the rear exhaust pipe (A, **Figure 160**) into the front cylinder crossover pipe and onto the cylinder head studs. Install the flange nuts finger-tight.
d. Move the crossover pipe clamp into position and tighten the bolt and nut finger-tight.
e. Move the rear exhaust pipe to the mounting bracket into place and tighten the bolt and nut finger-tight.

4B. On FLH and FLT series models, perform the following:
a. Install the right front exhaust pipe into the frame and onto cylinder head studs. Install the flange nuts and tighten finger-tight.
b. Install the right rear exhaust pipe into the frame, onto the right front exhaust pipe and onto the cylinder head studs. Install the flange nuts and tighten finger-tight.
c. Install the left exhaust pipe into the frame and onto the right rear exhaust pipe. Tighten the clamp bolt and nut finger-tight.

5. Protect the finish. Then install and secure the right and left mufflers onto the exhaust pipes.
6. Install the bolts, washers and lockwashers securing the mufflers to the support brackets. Tighten the bolts finger-tight.
7. Check the entire exhaust system to make sure none of the exhaust components are touching the frame. If necessary, make slight adjustments to avoid any contact that would transmit any vibrations to the rider via the frame.
8. Check the exhaust assembly alignment. Then securely tighten the mounting bolts and nuts.
9. Tighten the cylinder flange nuts to 142 in.-lb. (16 N•m).
10. Securely tighten all clamp bolts and nuts.
11. Completely open the heat shield clamps. Position the clamp so the screw is on the outboard side in the most accessible position. Install the heat shields in the locations marked during removal. Tighten the clamps securely.
12. Check all heat shields to make sure none are touching the frame. If necessary, make slight adjustments to avoid any contact that would transmit vibrations to the rider via the frame.
13. Start the engine and check for leaks.
14. On models so equipped, install the saddlebags and floorboards as described in Chapter Fifteen.

Inspection

1. Check the exhaust pipe for cracks or spots that have rusted through it. A damaged or leaking pipe should be replaced.
2. Remove all rust from all pipe and muffler mating surfaces.
3. Check the hose clamps for damage or severe rusting. Clean or repair clamps as required.
4. If the exhaust flange is distorted, repair or replace it before reinstalling it. Perform the following:
   a. Each exhaust flange is secured to the exhaust pipe with a retaining ring. Pry the ring out of the groove and remove the flange. Discard the ring.
   b. Examine the flange for distortion or other damage; the flange must be flat to fit properly onto the exhaust studs. If the flange is not severely distorted, flatten it with a hammer or press it flat. Do not damage the edges or holes in the flange when straightening it.
   c. If the flange has been straightened, install it onto the exhaust studs to ensure it will fit prior to installing it onto the exhaust pipe.
   d. Clean the end of the pipe to remove all rust and other debris. If reinstalling a used flange, thoroughly clean the inside of the flange.
   e. Slide the flange on the exhaust pipe so that the shoulder on the flange faces toward the retaining ring groove. Install a new retaining ring and check the fit; it must be secure in the groove.
   f. Repeat for the other exhaust pipe and flange, if required.
5. Replace worn or damaged heat shield hose clamps as required.
6. Store the exhaust pipes in a safe place until they are reinstalled.

EVAPORATIVE EMISSION CONTROL SYSTEM (1985-1991 CALIFORNIA MODELS)

All 1985 and later models sold in California are equipped with an evaporative emission control system.

When the engine is not running, the system directs the fuel vapor from the fuel tank through the vapor valve and into the charcoal canister. Also, when the engine is not running, the gravity-operated trap door in the air filter back plate blocks the inlet port of the air filter. This prevents hydrocarbon vapors from emanating from the carburetor venturi, or fuel injection induction module, and escaping into the atmosphere.

When the engine is running, these vapors are drawn through a purge hose and into the carburetor, or fuel injection induction module, where they burn in the combustion chambers. The vapor valve also prevents gasoline vapor from escaping from the carbon canister if the motorcycle falls onto its side.

During the 1988 model year, a set of reed valves and a vacuum-operated valve (VOV) were added to the system. The reed valves are installed in the carburetor back plate to prevent vapors from the carbon canister from escaping into the atmosphere when the engine is not running. The VOV vents fuel vapors from the carburetor float bowl to the atmosphere when the engine is not running; when the engine is turned off, the VOV closes off the carburetor vent tube, preventing vapors from escaping into the atmosphere. A damaged VOV can cause the engine to run lean at high speeds. If a 1988 or later model engine is running lean at high speeds, test the VOV as described in this section.

Inspection/Replacement (All Models)

Refer to **Figures 163-167**.

1. Mark the hose and the fitting prior to removing the hoses from any of the components. This will ensure the correct connection of all hoses.
2. Check all emission control lines or hoses to make sure they are correctly routed and properly connected.
3. Make sure that there are no kinks in the lines or hoses and that there are no signs of excessive wear or burning on lines that are routed near engine hot spots.
4. Check all lines and hoses for cuts, tears or loose connections. These lines and hoses are subjected to various temperature and operating conditions and eventually become brittle and crack. Replace all damaged lines or hoses.
5. Check all components in the emission control system for damage, such as broken fittings or broken nipples on the component.

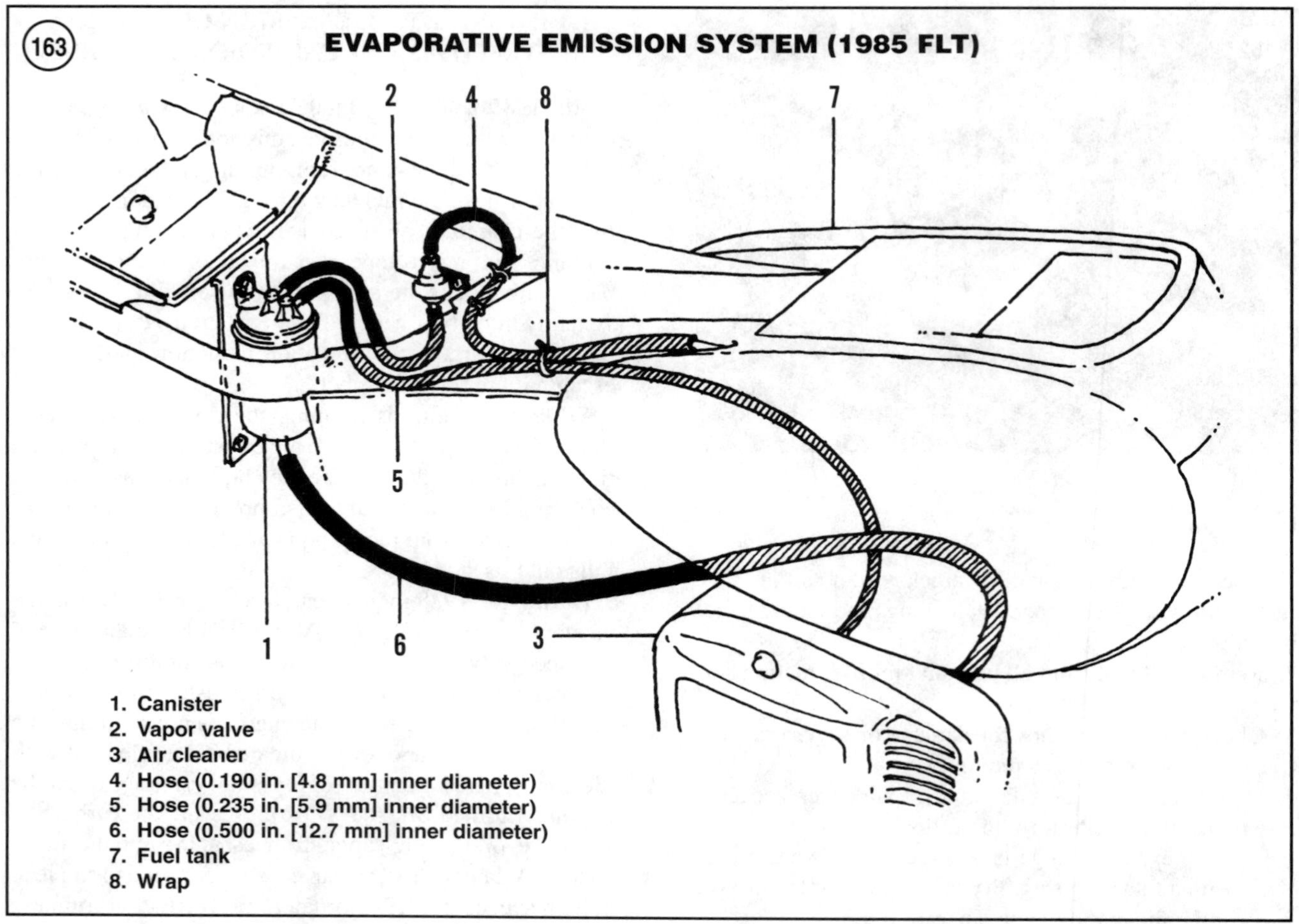

6. When replacing one or more lines or hoses, refer to the diagram for the model being worked on.
7. Disconnect one end of the line from the component. Then connect one end of the *new* line to the component fitting. Disconnect the other end of the line and connect the other end of the new line. At the same time, correct any improper previous placement where the line can rub and wear or be burned by hot components.

NOTE
Emission control hoses have different inside diameters and come in bulk lengths. To find correct replacement hoses, take the existing hose(s) to the Harley-Davidson dealership and automotive parts stores and compare the different sizes and lengths needed.

Vapor Valve Replacement

Refer to **Figures 163-167**.
1. Remove the seat as described in Chapter Fifteen.
2. Mark the hose and the fitting prior to removing the hoses from the vapor valve. Then disconnect them.
3. Note that one end of the vapor valve is longer than the other end. The longer end must face up.
4. Insert a flat-blade screwdriver into the vertical slot of the vapor valve and carefully remove the vapor valve from the bracket or T-stud on the battery box or frame rail (**Figure 168**, typical).

CAUTION
The vapor valve must be installed in a vertical position with the longer end facing upward, or excessive pressure will build in the fuel tank.

5. Install the vapor valve into the bracket or T-stud in a vertical position.
6. Install the hoses onto the correct fittings on the vapor valve.
7. Install the seat as described in Chapter Fifteen.

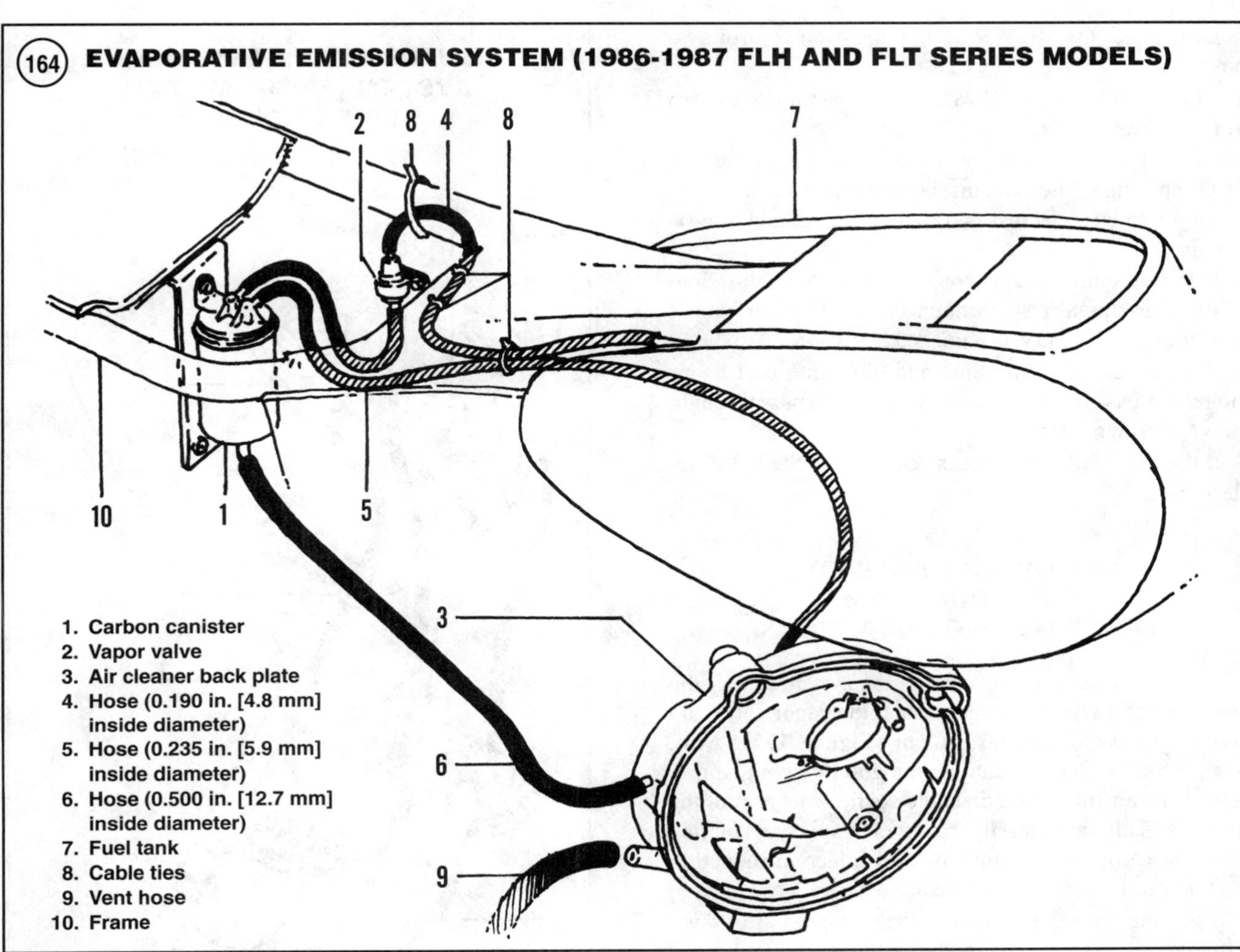

Carbon Canister Replacement

Refer to **Figures 163-167**.

1. Mark the hose and the fitting prior to removing the hoses from the charcoal canister, then disconnect them.
2. Remove the canister mounting brackets and clamps. Remove the canister.
3. Install by reversing these steps.

CAUTION
Do not alter the carbon canister position. The canister must be mounted below the carburetor to work correctly.

Reed Valves (1988-1991 Models)

Whenever the air filter assembly is removed, check the reed valve assembly for broken reed valves. To replace damaged reed valves, perform the following:

1. Remove the air filter and back plate as described in this chapter.
2. Remove the screw and lockwasher securing the reed stop to the back plate. Remove the top and bottom reeds (**Figure 169**).
3. Install the reeds in the order shown in **Figure 169**. Install the screws and lockwashers and tighten securely.

Vacuum-Operated Valve (1988-1991 Models)

During engine operation, the vacuum-operated valve (VOV) vents fuel vapors from the carburetor float bowl to the atmosphere. When the engine is turned off, the VOV closes off the carburetor vent tube to prevent vapors from escaping into the atmosphere. If the diaphragm in the VOV should become damaged and leak, a vacuum leak would occur and cause the engine to run lean at high speeds.

1. Disconnect the VOV from the emission control system.
2. Attach a hand-operated vacuum pump (**Figure 170**) to port A in **Figure 171**.
3. Apply 1-2 in. Hg vacuum to the valve while watching the pump gauge. The vacuum should remain steady. If the vacuum reading decreases rapidly, the diaphragm is damaged.
4. If the vacuum remains constant in Step 3, blow into port C. Air should pass through the VOV. If air cannot pass through, the VOV is damaged.
5. Remove the vacuum pump and blow into port B; air should not pass through the VOV. If air can pass through, the VOV is damaged.
6. If the VOV failed to react as described in Steps 3-5, replace it.

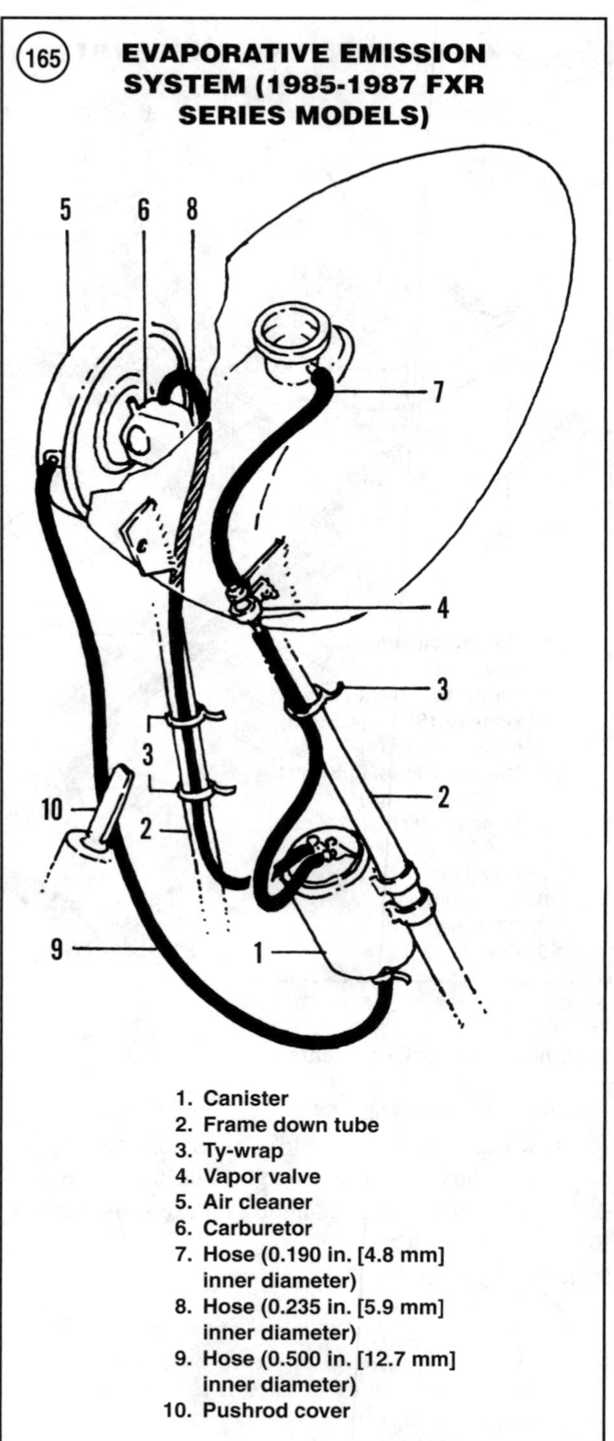

165 **EVAPORATIVE EMISSION SYSTEM (1985-1987 FXR SERIES MODELS)**

1. Canister
2. Frame down tube
3. Ty-wrap
4. Vapor valve
5. Air cleaner
6. Carburetor
7. Hose (0.190 in. [4.8 mm] inner diameter)
8. Hose (0.235 in. [5.9 mm] inner diameter)
9. Hose (0.500 in. [12.7 mm] inner diameter)
10. Pushrod cover

EVAPORATIVE EMISSION CONTROL SYSTEM (1992-1998 CALIFORNIA MODELS)

When the engine is not running, the system directs the fuel vapor from the fuel tank through the vapor valve and into the charcoal canister system (**Figure 172**). Also, when the engine is not running, the gravity-operated trap door in the air filter back plate blocks the inlet port of the air filter. This prevents hydrocarbon vapors emanating from the carburetor venturi, or fuel injection induction module, from escaping into the atmosphere.

When the engine is running, these vapors are drawn through a purge hose and into the carburetor, or fuel injection induction module, where they burn in the combustion chambers. The vapor valve also prevents gasoline vapor from escaping from the carbon canister if the motorcycle falls onto its side.

Solenoid-Operated Butterfly Valve Troubleshooting (1992-1998 Models)

On 1992-1998 California models, a solenoid-operated butterfly valve (**Figure 173**) is installed in the air filter back plate to seal off the back plate when the ignition switch is turned off to prevent fuel vapors from escaping into the atmosphere. Turning on the ignition switch energizes the solenoid hold-in windings. When the start switch is operated, the solenoid pull-in windings are energized. The hold-in windings will keep the butterfly valve open until the ignition switch is turned off.

Test the solenoid-operated butterfly valve if the engine suffers from sluggish acceleration and the motorcycle speed tops out at 40 mph.

1. First check that all of the hoses are properly connected; see **Figure 172**. If the hoses are good, proceed with Step 2.
2. If the butterfly valve is not opening due to an electrical malfunction:

166

EVAPORATIVE EMISSION SYSTEM (1985-1986 FXWG, FXSB AND FXEF MODELS)

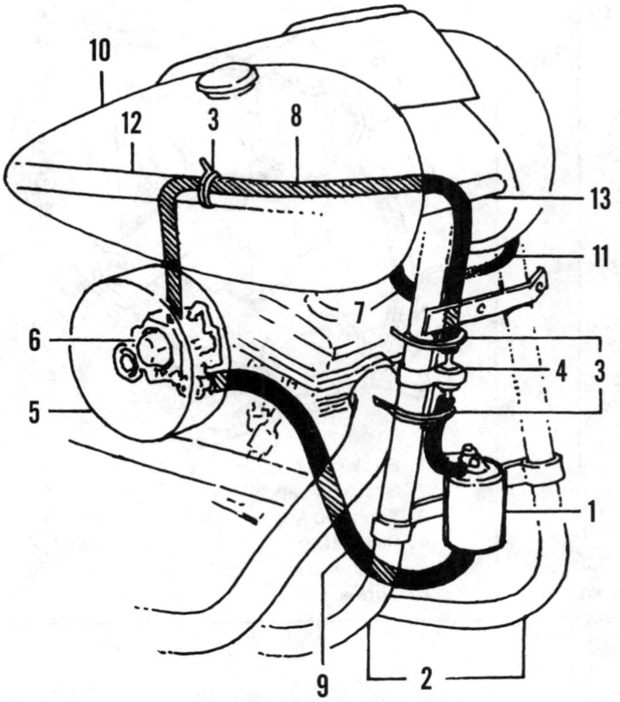

1. Canister
2. Frame
3. Wrap
4. Vapor cleaner
5. Air cleaner
6. Carburetor
7. Hose (0.190 in. [4.8 mm] inner diameter)
8. Hose (0.235 in. [5.9 mm] inner diameter)
9. Hose (0.500 in. [12.7 mm] inner diameter)
10. Fuel tank
11. Crossover hose
12. Frame
13. Bracket

167

CALIFORNIA EVAPORATIVE EMISSION CONTROL SYSTEM (1988-1998)

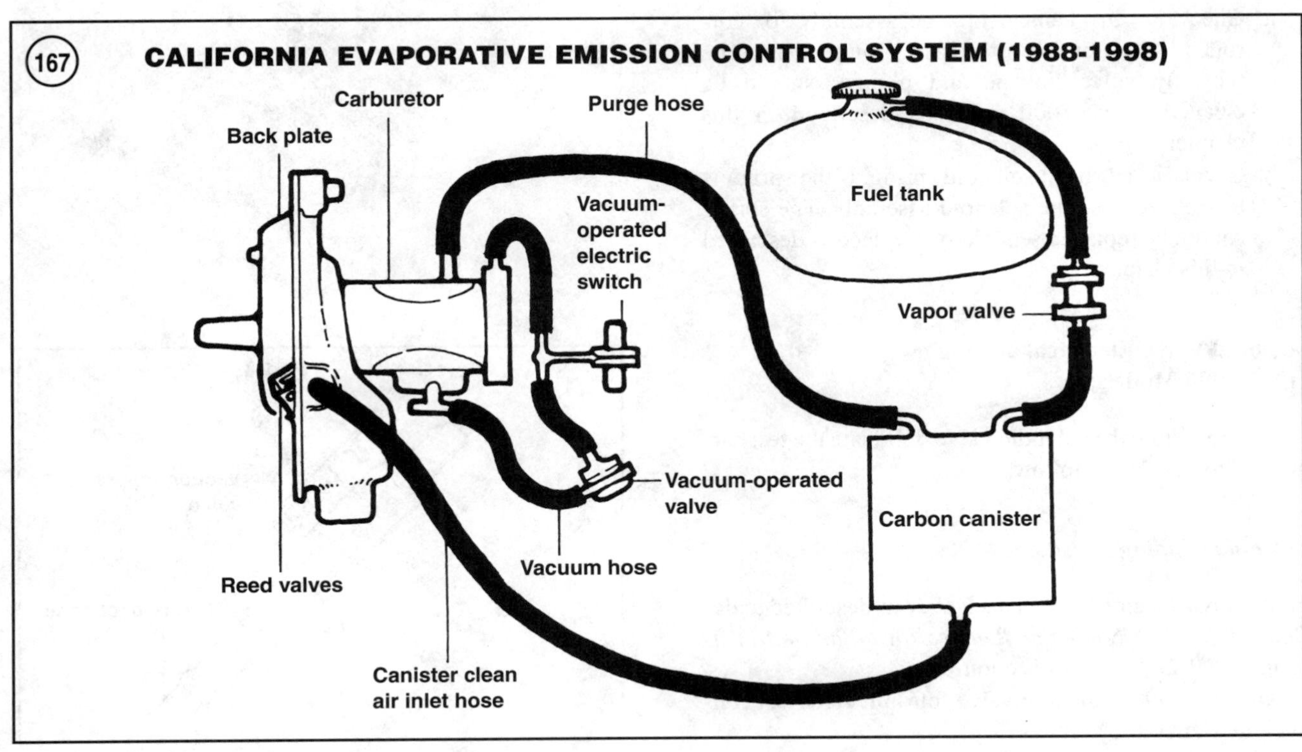

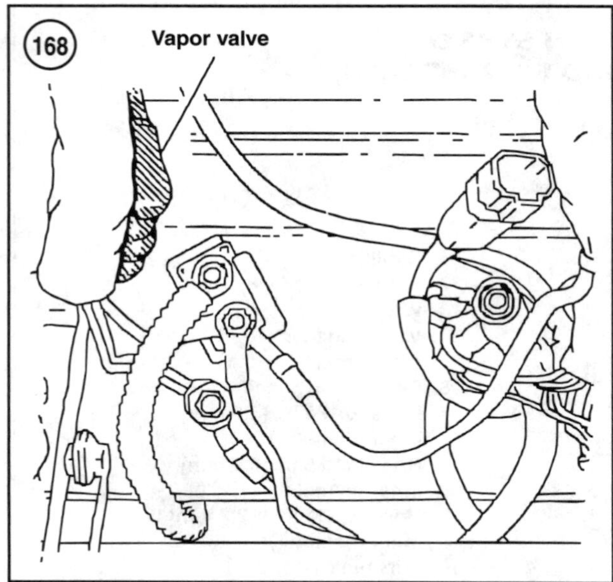

a. Check that the solenoid valve electrical connector is properly connected. If the connection is good, disconnect the connector and check for dirty or loose-fitting terminals; clean and repair as required. If good, continue with substep b.
b. Test the solenoid as described in this section.

3. If the butterfly valve is not opening and closing properly due to a mechanical problem:

a. Check the mechanical linkage assembly for corroded, loose, broken or missing components. The butterfly valve linkage and plunger should be cleaned every 5000 miles as described in this chapter.
b. Check for a broken solenoid spring. If the spring is broken, replace the solenoid assembly. The spring cannot be replaced separately. Replace as described in this chapter.

Solenoid Valve Electrical Testing (1992-1996 Models)

Prior to testing the solenoid valve, fabricate the test harness (**Figure 174**) as follows:

Solenoid winding resistance test

1. Remove the air filter and back plate as described under *Butterfly Valve Solenoid Removal/Installation/Adjustment (1992-1998)* in this section.
2. Disconnect the solenoid valve four-pin electrical connector (**Figure 173**).

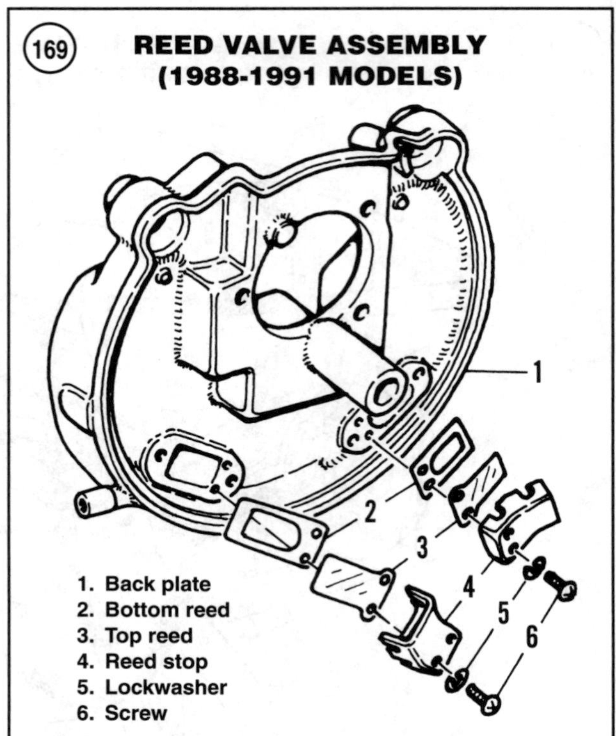

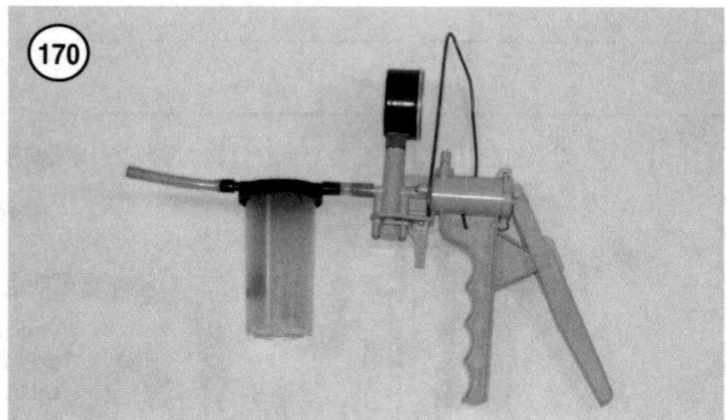

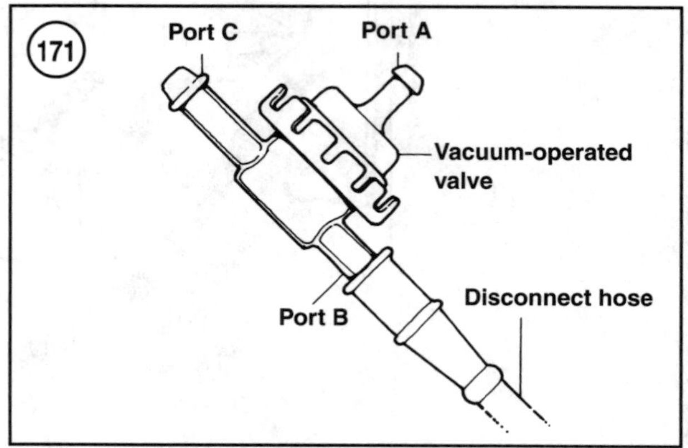

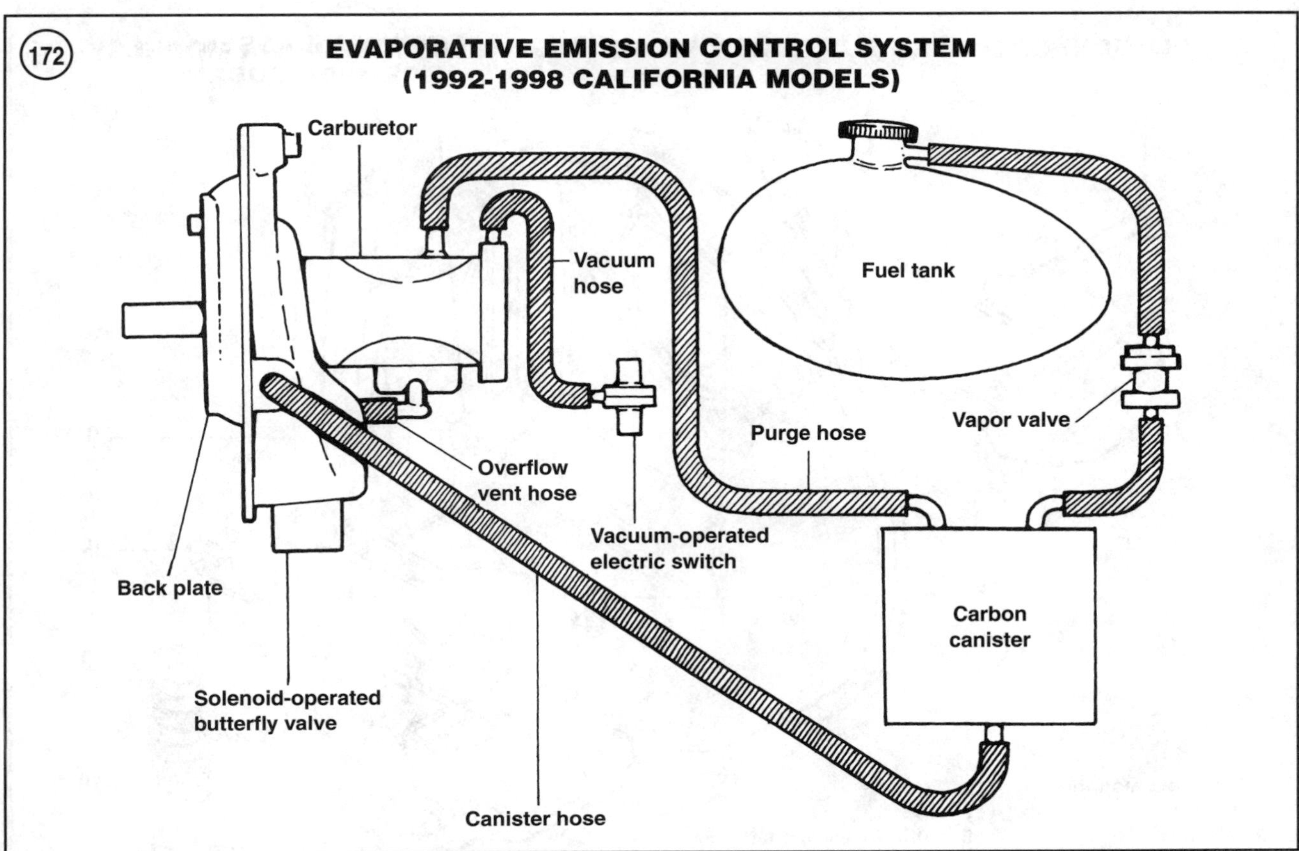

3. Check for dirty or loose-fitting terminals and connectors.

4. Connect the solenoid test connector to the solenoid connector (**Figure 175**).

5. Refer to **Figure 176** for test connections and values and compare the meter readings to the stated values. If any of the meter readings differ from the stated values, replace the solenoid as described in this section.

6. If the resistance readings are correct, proceed with the following dynamic tests.

Pull-in coil test

A fully charged 12-volt battery is required for this test.

1. Remove the air filter and back plate as described under *Butterfly Valve Solenoid Removal/Installation/Adjustment (1992-1998)* in this section.

2. Disconnect the solenoid valve four-pin electrical connector (**Figure 173**).

3. Check for dirty or loose-fitting terminals and connectors.

4. Connect the solenoid test connector to the solenoid connector (**Figure 175**).

5. Connect a 12-volt battery to the two solenoid test connector wires shown in **Figure 177**. The butterfly valve should open when battery voltage is applied. Disconnect the battery connections and note the following:

   a. If the butterfly valve now opens but did not open when originally connected to the wiring harness, perform Step 6.

   b. If the butterfly valve did not open, check the linkage for corroded, missing or damaged parts. If the linkage is in good condition, retest with a new solenoid.

6. Perform the following:

   a. Check for ground with an ohmmeter at the gray/black or black connector pin in the solenoid four-pin connector. The ohmmeter should read 1 ohm or less.

   b. Reconnect the solenoid four-prong connector.

   c. Connect the positive voltmeter lead to the black/red (1992-1993 models) or green (1994-1996 models) lead in the four-pin connector and the negative probe to a good engine ground. Press the start but-

8

173 SOLENOID-OPERATED BUTTERFLY VALVE (1992-1998 CALIFORNIA MODELS)

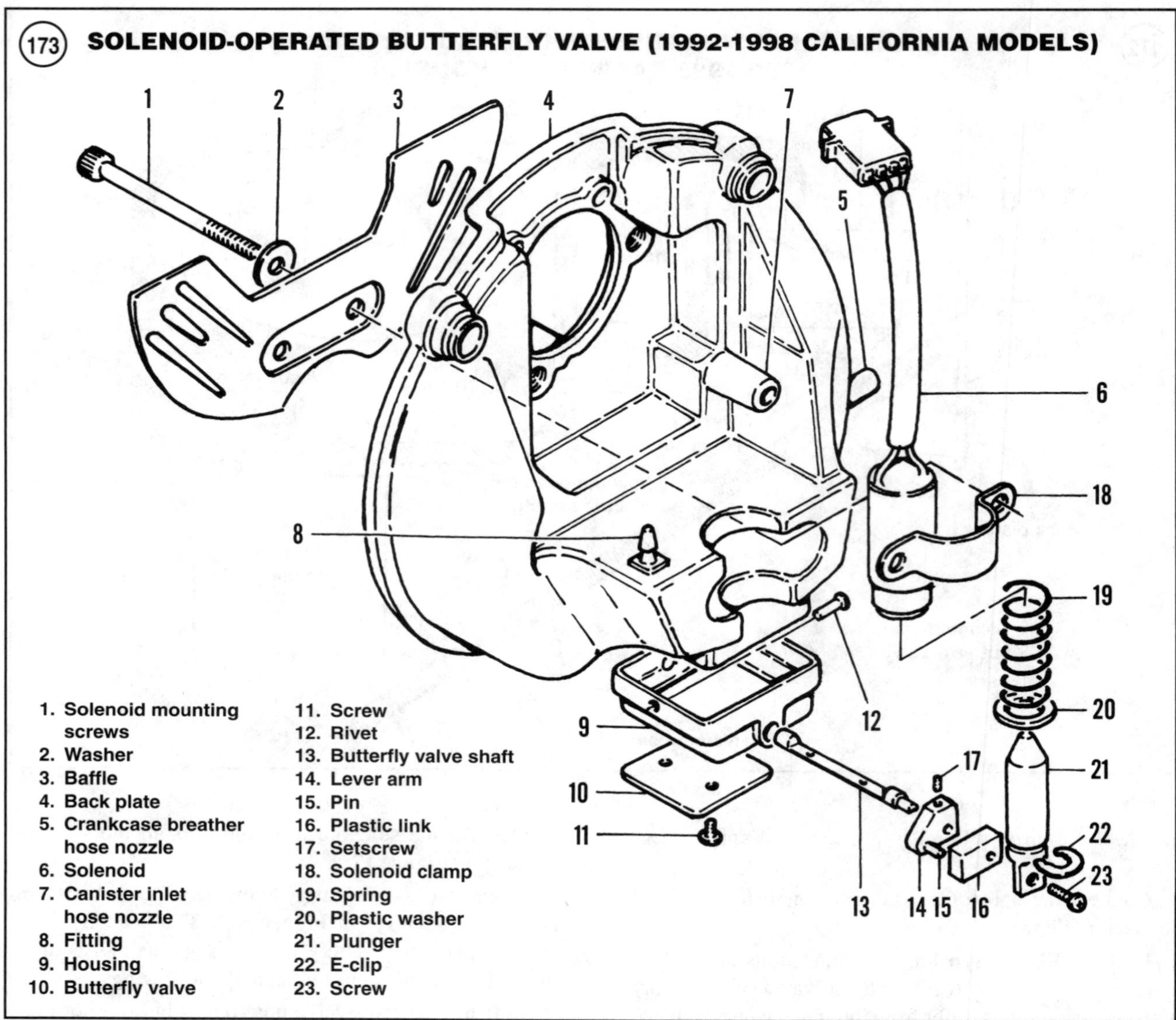

1. Solenoid mounting screws
2. Washer
3. Baffle
4. Back plate
5. Crankcase breather hose nozzle
6. Solenoid
7. Canister inlet hose nozzle
8. Fitting
9. Housing
10. Butterfly valve
11. Screw
12. Rivet
13. Butterfly valve shaft
14. Lever arm
15. Pin
16. Plastic link
17. Setscrew
18. Solenoid clamp
19. Spring
20. Plastic washer
21. Plunger
22. E-clip
23. Screw

ton while reading the voltage indicated on the voltmeter. It should be 12 volts.

7. If any of the readings differ from those specified in Step 6, there is a problem in the solenoid wiring harness. Use voltage and resistance checks to locate the damaged wire(s). After repairing the wire(s), repeat the above checks.

8. If the readings were correct as performed in Step 7, perform the *Hold-in coil test.*

Hold-in coil test

A fully charged 12-volt battery is required for this test.

1. Remove the air filter and back plate as described under *Butterfly Valve Solenoid Removal/Installation/Adjustment (1992-1998)* in this section.

2. Disconnect the solenoid valve four-pin electrical connector (**Figure 173**).

3. Check for dirty or loose-fitting terminals and connectors.

4. Connect the solenoid test connector to the solenoid connector (**Figure 175**).

5. Connect a 12-volt battery to the two solenoid test connector wires shown in **Figure 178** and perform the following:

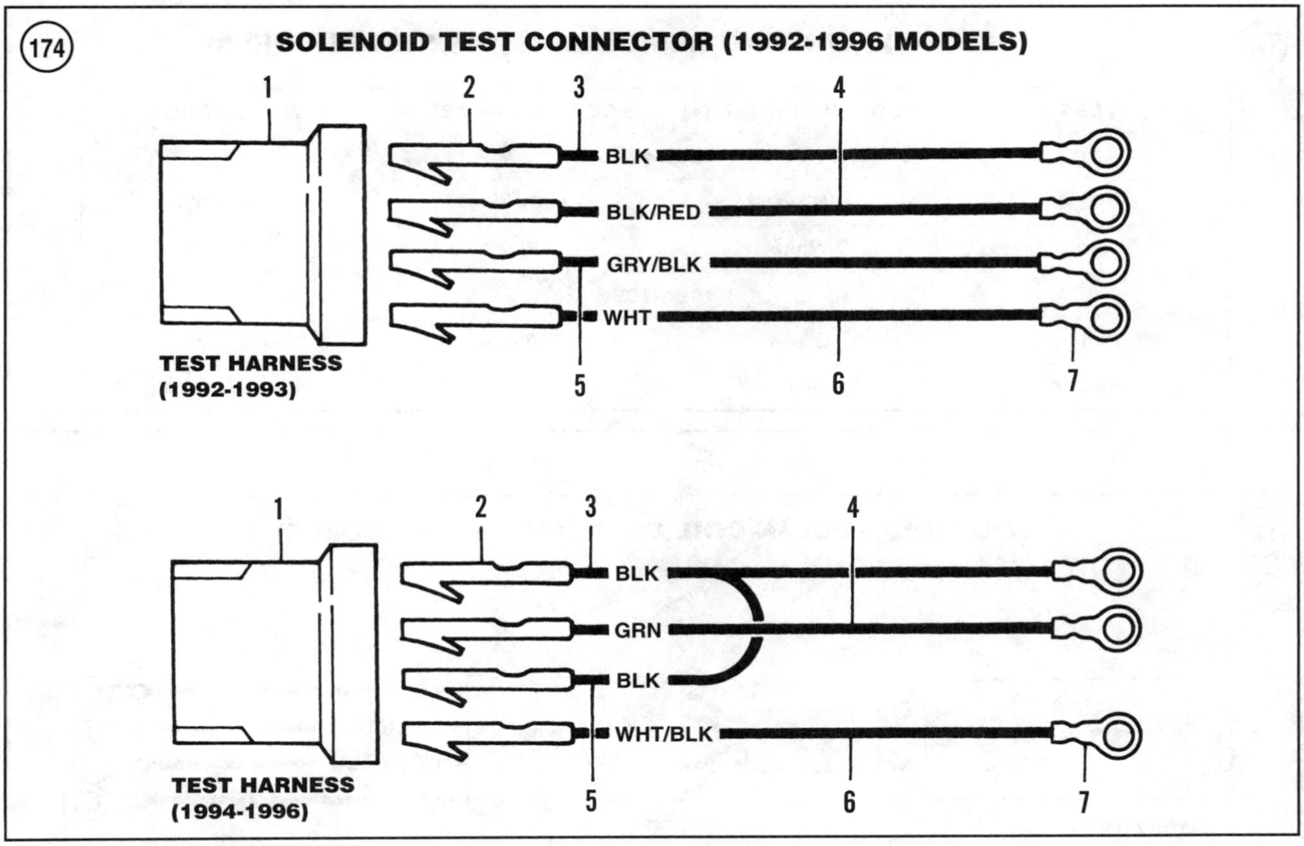

174
SOLENOID TEST CONNECTOR (1992-1996 MODELS)
1
2
3
4
BLK
BLK/RED
GRY/BLK
WHT
TEST HARNESS
(1992-1993)
5
6
7
1
2
3
4
BLK
GRN
BLK
WHT/BLK
TEST HARNESS
(1994-1996)
5
6
7

175
WINDING RESISTANCE TEST (1992-1996 MODELS)
Four-place socket connector
Solenoid
Solenoid test
connector
BLK
BLK/RED
GRY/BLK
WHT
1992-1993
Solenoid
Solenoid test
connector
BLK
GRN
BLK
WHT/BLK
1994-1996
4
3
2
1
WHT/BLK
BLK
GRN
BLK
A
To cycle
harness

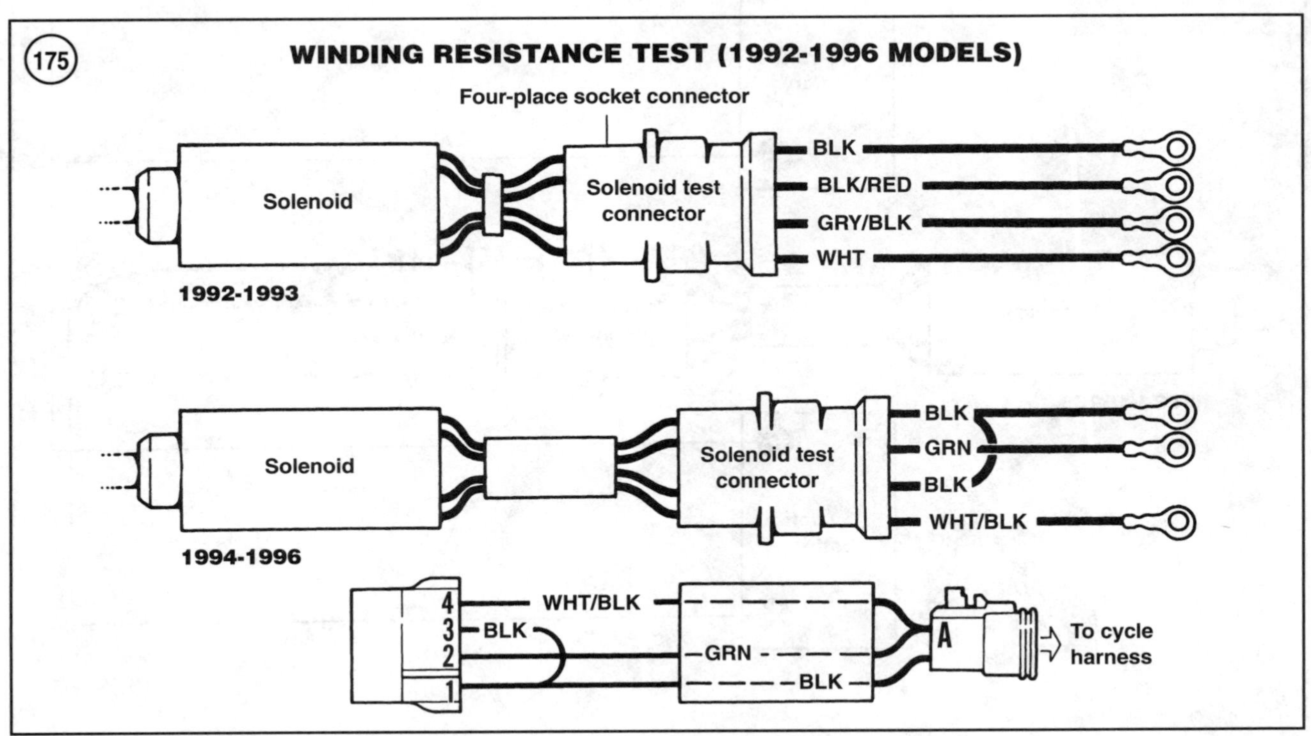

(176)

SOLENOID WINDING RESISTANCE (1992-1996 MODELS)

TEST	POSITIVE PROBE (+)	NEGATIVE PROBE (–)	RESISTANCE
1992-1993			
Pull-in	Black/Red	Gray/Black	4-6 ohms
Hold-in	White	Black	21-27 ohms
1994-1996			
Pull-in	Green	Black	4-6 ohms
Hold-in	White/Black	Black	21-27 ohms

(177)

SOLENOID PULL-IN COIL TEST (1992-1996 MODELS)

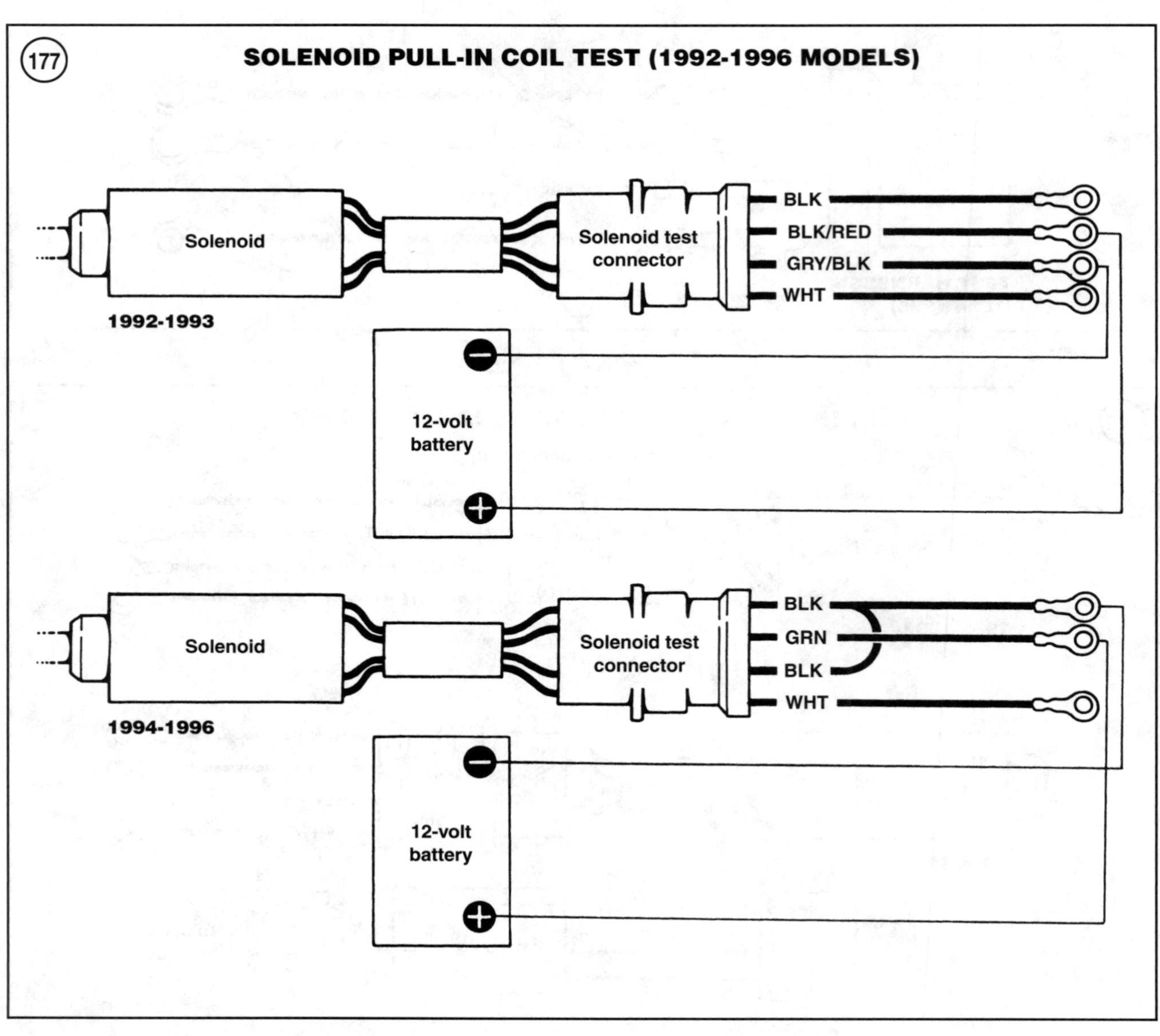

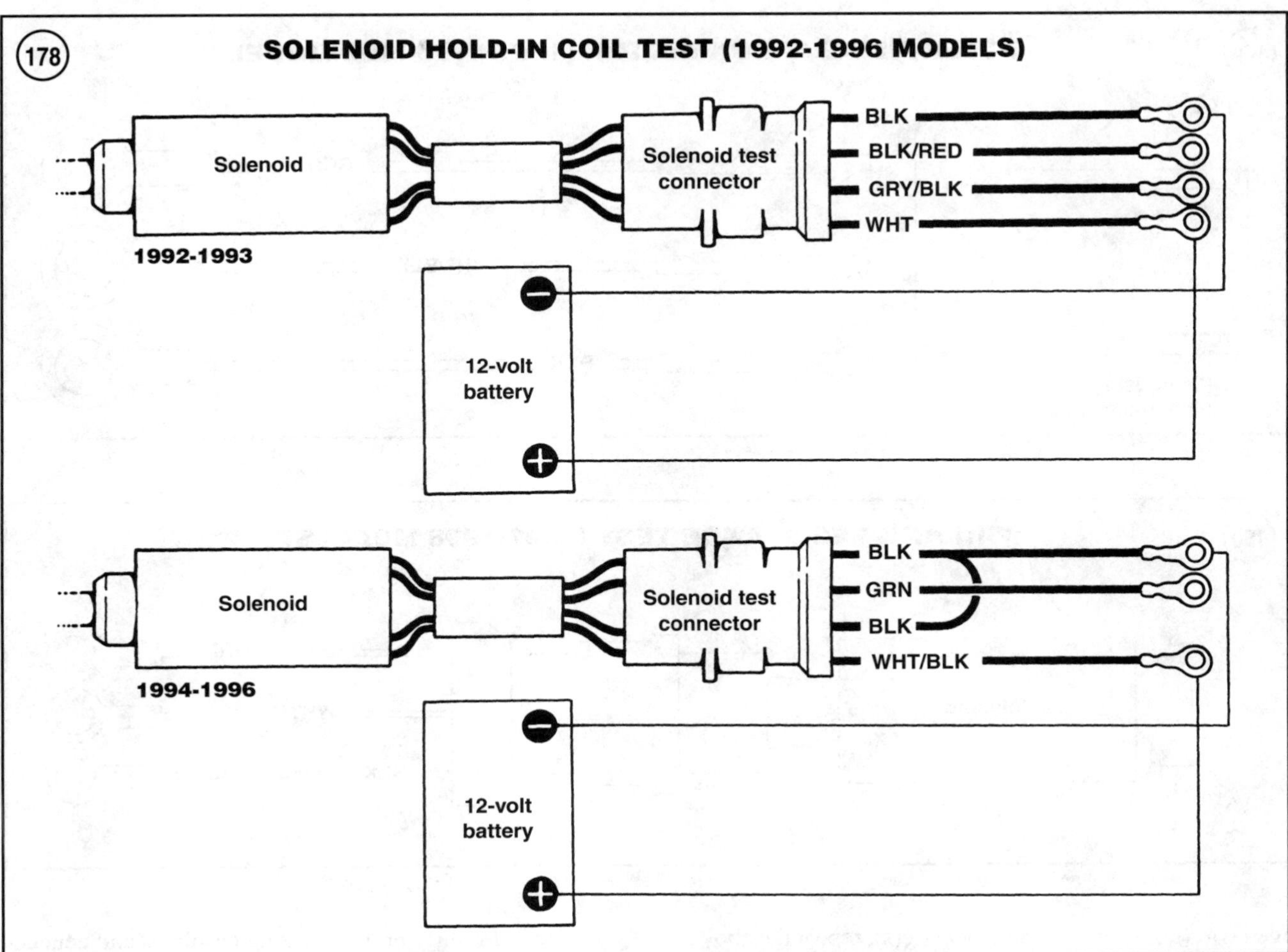

a. Open the butterfly valve carefully with a screwdriver by pushing inward on the left side of the butterfly valve.

b. Remove the screwdriver. The butterfly valve should remain open as long as the solenoid hold-in windings are energized.

c. Disconnect the negative battery cable from the solenoid test connector. The butterfly valve should close.

d. If the butterfly valve operated as described in substeps b and c, the solenoid hold-in windings are operating correctly.

e. If the butterfly valve failed to operate properly, perform Step 6.

f. Disconnect the positive battery cable from the solenoid test connector.

6. If the butterfly valve did not remain open in Step 5, substep b, perform the following:

a. Check for ground with an ohmmeter at the black connector pin in the solenoid four-prong connector. The ohmmeter should read 1 ohm or less.

NOTE
On 1994-1996 FLH and FLT models, make sure the four-pin Deutsch connector is secure.

b. Reconnect the solenoid four-pin connector.

c. Connect the positive voltmeter lead to the white (1992-1993 models) or white/black (1994-1996 models) lead in the four-pin connector and the negative probe to a good engine ground. Turn the ignition switch on and read the voltmeter. It should be 12 volts.

7. If any of the meter readings differ from those specified in Step 6, there is a problem in the solenoid wiring harness. Use voltage and resistance checks to locate the dam-

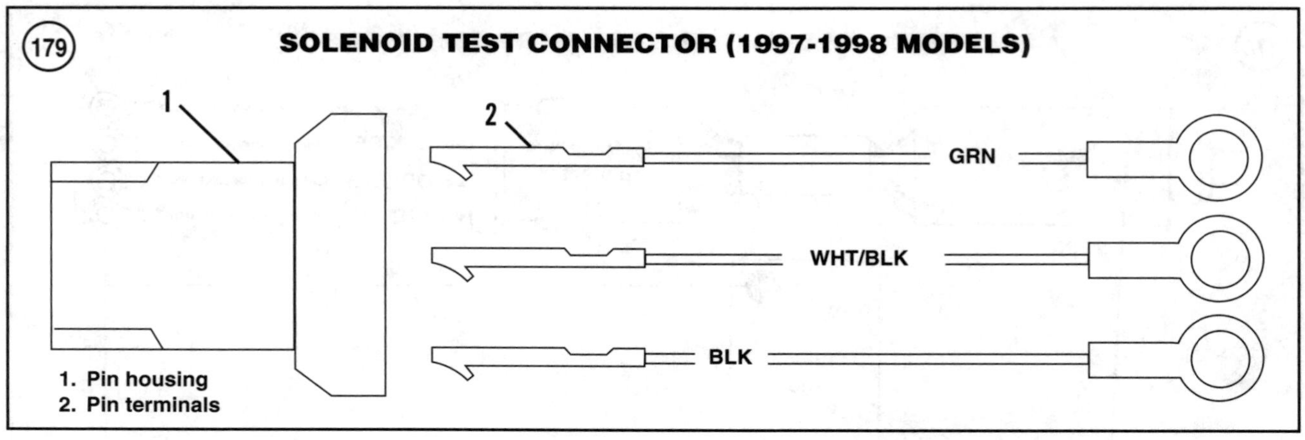

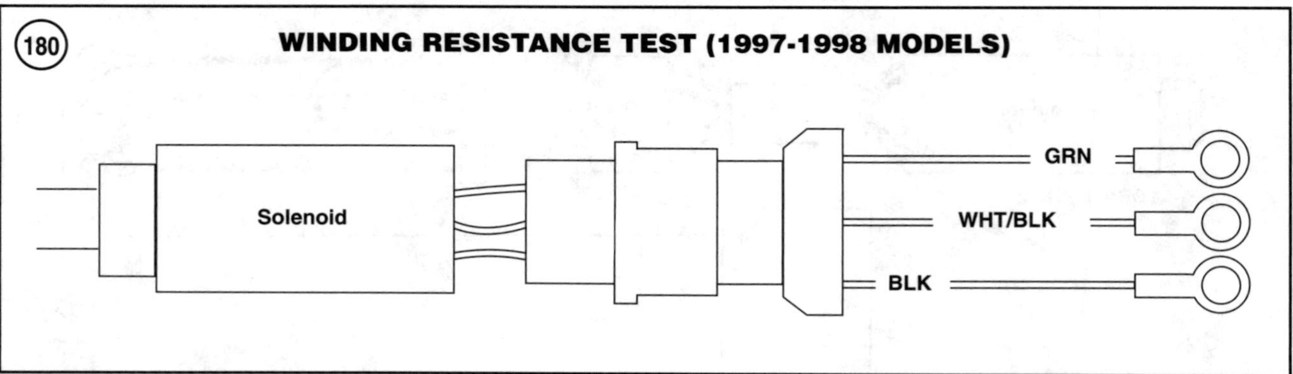

aged wire(s). After repairing the wire(s), repeat the above checks.

8. If the solenoid test readings were correct but the butterfly valve does not work properly, perform Step 3 under *Solenoid-Operated Butterfly Valve Troubleshooting (1992-1998)*.

9. Remove all test equipment and reconnect the solenoid four-prong connector.

Solenoid Valve Electrical Testing (1997-1998 Models)

Prior to testing the solenoid valve, fabricate the test harness (**Figure 179**) as follows:

Solenoid winding resistance test

1. Remove the air filter and back plate as described under *Butterfly Valve Solenoid Removal/Installation/Adjustment (1992-1998)* in this section.

2. Disconnect the solenoid valve four-pin electrical connector (**Figure 173**).

3. Check for dirty or loose-fitting terminals and connectors.

4. Connect the solenoid test connector to the solenoid connector (**Figure 180**).

5. Measure the resistance of the solenoid windings as follows:

   a. Connect the positive test lead to the green wire and the negative test lead to the black wire. The specified resistance is 4-6 ohms.

   b. Connect the positive test lead to the white/black wire and the negative test lead to the black wire. The specified resistance is 21-27 ohms.

   c. If any of the meter readings differ from the stated values, replace the solenoid as described in this section.

6. If the resistance readings are correct, proceed with the following dynamic tests.

Pull-in coil test

A fully charged 12-volt battery is required for this test.

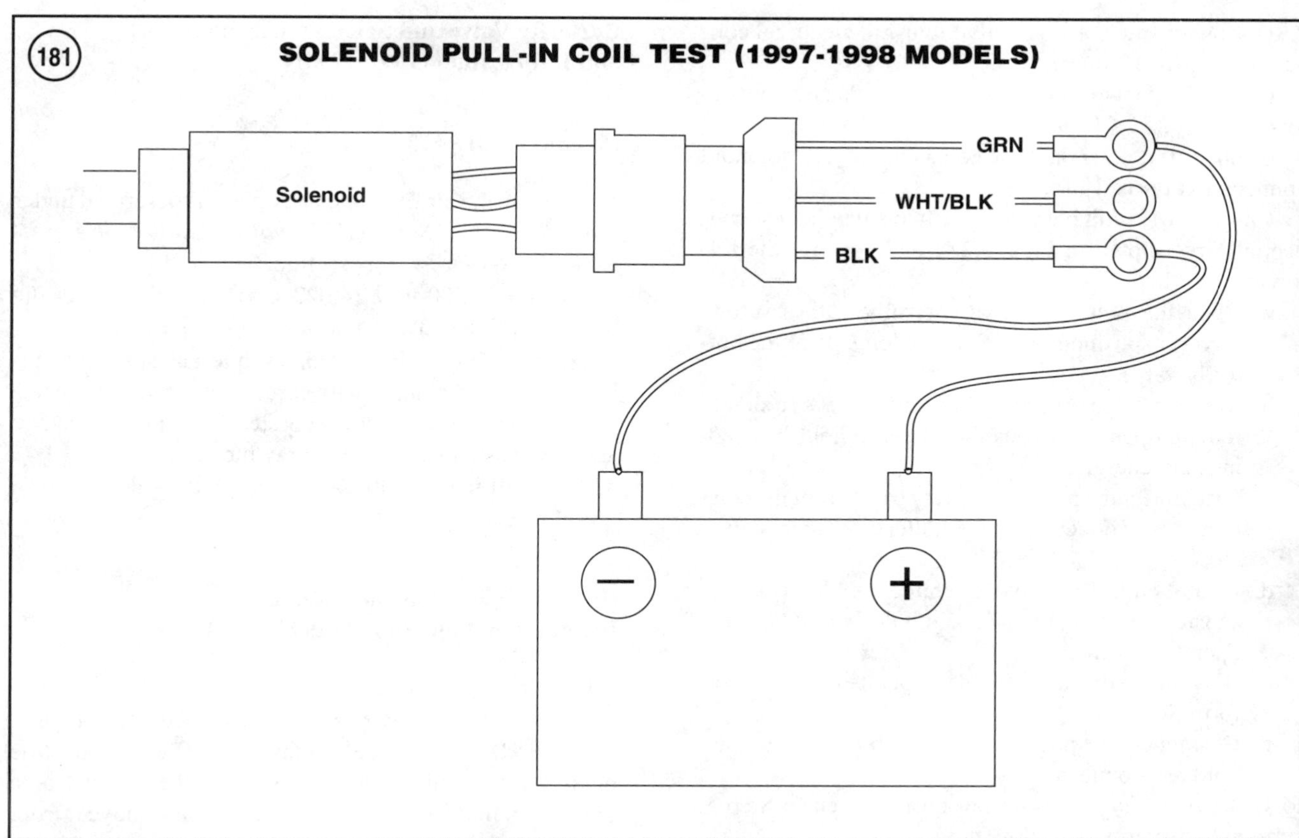

1. Remove the air filter and back plate as described under *Butterfly Valve Solenoid Removal/Installation/Adjustment (1992-1998)* in this chapter.

2. Disconnect the solenoid valve four-pin electrical connector (**Figure 173**).

3. Check for dirty or loose-fitting terminals and connectors.

4. Connect the solenoid test connector to the solenoid connector (**Figure 180**).

5. Connect a 12-volt battery to the two solenoid test connector wires shown in **Figure 181**. The butterfly valve should open when battery voltage is applied. Disconnect the battery connections and note the following:

   a. If the butterfly valve now opens but did not open when originally connected to the wiring harness, perform Step 6.

   b. If the butterfly valve did not open, check the linkage for corroded, missing or damaged parts. If the linkage is in good condition, retest with a new solenoid.

6. Perform the following:

   a. Check for ground with an ohmmeter at the black connector pin in the solenoid four-pin connector. The ohmmeter should read 1 ohm or less.

   b. Reconnect the solenoid four-pin connector.

   c. Connect the positive voltmeter lead to the green lead in the three-pin connector and the negative probe to a good engine ground. Press the start button while reading the voltmeter. It should be 12 volts.

7. If any of the meter readings differ from those specified in Step 6, there is a problem in the solenoid wiring harness. Use voltage and resistance checks to locate the damaged wire(s). After repairing the wire(s), repeat the above checks.

8. If the meter readings were correct as performed in Step 7, perform the *Hold-in coil test*.

Hold-in coil test

A fully charged 12-volt battery is required for this test.

1. Remove the air filter and back plate as described under *Butterfly Valve Solenoid Removal/Installation/Adjustment (1992-1998)* in this section.

2. Disconnect the solenoid valve four-pin electrical connector (**Figure 173**).
3. Check for dirty or loose-fitting terminals and connectors.
4. Connect the solenoid test connector to the solenoid connector (**Figure 180**).
5. Connect a 12-volt battery to the two solenoid test connector wires shown in **Figure 182** and perform the following:
   a. Open the butterfly valve carefully with a screwdriver by pushing inward on the left side of the butterfly valve.
   b. Remove the screwdriver. The butterfly valve should remain open as long as the solenoid hold-in windings are energized.
   c. Disconnect the negative battery cable from the solenoid test connector. The butterfly valve should close.
   d. If the butterfly valve operated as described in substeps b and c, the solenoid hold-in windings are operating correctly.
   e. If the butterfly valve failed to operate properly, perform Step 6.
   f. Disconnect the positive battery cable from the solenoid test connector.
6. If the butterfly valve did not remain open in Step 5, substep b, perform the following:
   a. Check for ground with an ohmmeter at the black connector pin in the solenoid four-prong connector. The ohmmeter should read 1 ohm or less.

NOTE
Make sure the three-pin Deutsch connector is secure; refer to wiring diagrams at end of the manual.

   b. Reconnect the solenoid four-pin connector.
   c. Connect the positive voltmeter lead to the white/black lead in the three-pin connector and the negative probe to a good engine ground. Turn the ignition switch on and read the voltmeter. It should be 12 volts.
7. If any of the meter readings differ from those specified in Step 6, there is a problem in the solenoid wiring harness. Use voltage and resistance checks to locate the damaged wire(s). After repairing the wire(s), repeat the above checks.
8. If the solenoid test readings were correct, but the butterfly valve does not work properly, perform Step 3 under *Solenoid-Operated Butterfly Valve Troubleshooting (1992-1998)*.
9. Remove all test equipment and reconnect the solenoid four-pin connector.

Butterfly Valve and Solenoid Cleaning and Lubrication (1992-1998)

Refer to **Figure 173**.

1. Remove the air filter and back plate as described under *Butterfly Valve Solenoid Removal/Installation/Adjustment (1992-1998)* in this section.
2. At every 2500-mile (4,022 km) interval, inspect the butterfly valve and solenoid for proper operation.
3. At every 5000-mile (8,045 km) interval, spray the butterfly valve and plunger with carburetor cleaner. Then, after the carburetor cleaner evaporates, lubricate the linkage and plunger with a dry film spray lubricant.
4. Reinstall the air filter and back plate as described in this chapter.

Butterfly Valve Solenoid Removal/ Installation/Adjustment (1992-1998)

Refer to **Figure 173**.

1. Remove the air filter as described in Chapter Three.
2. On FXR series models, additional clearance must be made for back plate removal. Loosen the exhaust pipe crossover shield and pivot it downward or remove it from the exhaust pipe.
3. Disconnect the solenoid harness connector.
4. Disconnect the overflow hose from the back plate fitting.
5. Disconnect the canister inlet hose from the back plate fitting.
6. Remove the back plate mounting screws and back plate as follows (**Figure 173**):
   a. Remove the back plate mounting screws.
   b. Loosen the back plate-to-carburetor mounting screws in small amounts in a crisscross pattern. Continue until all of the screws are loose. Then remove the back plate and gasket.
7. To remove the solenoid:
   a. Remove the small screw securing the plunger to the plastic link.
   b. Remove the two long screws and washers securing the solenoid clamp to the back plate.
   c. Remove the solenoid assembly.
8. Clean the back plate and lubricate the butterfly valve linkage as described under *Butterfly Valve and Solenoid Cleaning and Lubrication (1992-1998)* in this section.
9. Assemble the plastic link to the plunger screw as follows:
   a. Apply Loctite 222 (purple) to the plunger screw.

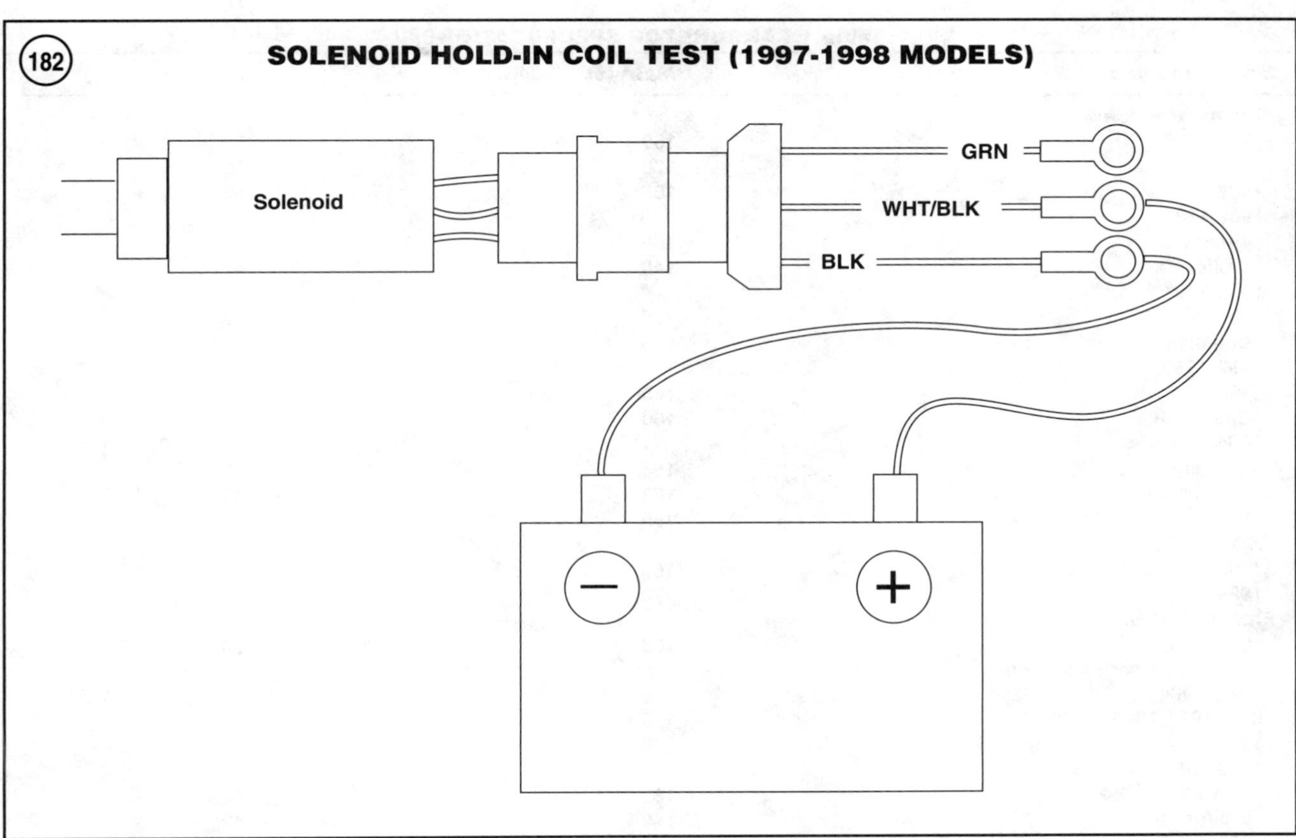

b. Then secure the plastic link to the deep side of the plunger with the plunger screw. When doing so, the link slot must face toward the pin on the lever arm.

c. Securely tighten the plunger screw.

10. Install the solenoid into the back plate groove and install the lever arm pin into the plastic link.

NOTE

Prior to installing the solenoid mounting screws, make sure the bottom of the baffle is mounted behind the rib in the back plate. Otherwise, the solenoid plunger might bind when the mounting screws are tightened.

11. Apply Loctite 222 (purple) to the solenoid mounting screws prior to installation. Install the screws, washers and clamp as shown in **Figure 173**. Do not tighten the screws at this time.

12. Adjust the solenoid plunger as follows:

a. Push the solenoid plunger into the solenoid until it bottoms out. Hold it in this position.

b. Check that the butterfly valve plate is in the full-open position. Tighten the solenoid mounting screws to 20-22 in.-lbs. (2.3-2.5 N•m).

CAUTION

Do not overtighten the solenoid mounting screws; otherwise, the plunger may bind in the solenoid.

c. Release the solenoid plunger and check the butterfly valve plate is closed.

13. Install by reversing Steps 1-6.

Tables 1 through 3 are on the following pages.

Table 1 CARBURETOR SPECIFICATIONS

Model and year	Main jet	Pilot jet
FXR series models		
1984-1985	160	50
1986	170	50
1987	165	50
1988-1989		
49-state	165	52
California	140	42
1990-1991		
49-state	185	52
California	165	42
1992-1993		
49-state	165	40
California	160	40
1994		
49-state	165	42
California	165	42
HDI*	165	40
FXWG		
1985	165	50
1986	170	50
FXEF and FXSB		
1985	165	50
FLH and FLT series models		
Early 1984	165	50
Late 1984-1986	175	50
1987	170	50
1988-1989		
49-state	165	52
California	140	42
1990-1991		
49-state	185	45
California	165	42
1992-1993		
49-state	175	40
California	160	40
1994		
49-state	175	42
California	165	42
HDI*	175	40
1995		
49-state	175	42
California	175	42
HDI*	180	42
Swiss HDI*	175	40
1996		
49-state	175	42
California	180	42
HDI*	175	42
Swiss HDI*	175	40
1997-1998		
49-state	175	42
California	180	42
HDI*	180	42
Swiss HDI*	180	42
1999		
49-state	170	N.A.
California	175	N.A.
Float level	See text	

*HDI indicates International models.

Table 2 FUEL SYSTEM TORQUE SPECIFICATIONS

Item	ft.-lb.	in.-lb.	N•m
Butterfly valve solenoid screw (1992-1998)	–	20-22	2.3-2.5
Fuel line hex fittings (EFI)	20-24	–	27-33
Fuel shutoff valve			
Nut (1993-1998)	18	–	24
Diaphragm cover screws	–	18.5	2.1
Fuel tank mounting bolts			
Front			
Rear			
Intake manifold bolts (carbureted)	–	71-124	8-14
Induction module bolts (EFI)	–	71-124	8-14

Table 3 EXHAUST SYSTEM TORQUE SPECIFICATIONS

Item	ft.-lb.	in.-lb.	N•m
Exhaust flange nuts	–	142	16

CHAPTER NINE

ELECTRICAL SYSTEM

This chapter contains service and test procedures for electrical and ignition system components. Spark plug maintenance is covered in Chapter Three.

The electrical system includes the following systems:

1. Charging system.
2. Ignition system.
3. Starting system.
4. Lighting system.
5. Switches and other electrical components.

Refer to **Tables 1-14** at the end of the chapter for specifications. Wiring diagrams are at the end of the manual.

ELECTRICAL COMPONENT REPLACEMENT

Most motorcycle dealerships and parts suppliers will not accept the return of any electrical part. If you cannot determine the *exact* cause of any electrical system malfunction, have a dealership retest that specific system to verify your test results. If you purchase a new electrical component(s), install it and then find that the system still does not work properly, you will probably be unable to return the unit for a refund.

Consider any test results carefully before replacing a component that tests only *slightly* out of specification, especially resistance. A number of variables can affect test results dramatically. These include: the testing meter internal circuitry, ambient temperature and conditions under which the machine has been operated. All instructions and specifications have been checked for accuracy; however, successful test results depend to a great degree upon individual accuracy.

Electrical Connectors

Many electrical troubles can be traced to damaged wiring or to contaminated or loose connectors.

The locations of the connectors vary by model. Also, if the motorcycle has been serviced previously, the connectors might be in different locations.

The electrical system uses three types of connectors. If individual wires or terminals of a particular connector require repair or replacement, refer to *Electrical Connectors* at the end of this chapter.

Always check the wire colors listed in the procedure or wiring diagrams to verify that the correct component has been identified.

Perform the following steps first if an electrical system fault is encountered.

1. Inspect all wiring for fraying, burning and any other visual damage.
2. Check the main fuse and make sure it is not blown. Replace it if necessary.
3. Check the individual fuse(s) for each circuit. Make sure it is not blown. Replace it if necessary.
4. Inspect the battery as described in this chapter. Make sure it is fully charged and that the battery cables are clean and securely attached to the battery terminals.
5. Clean connectors with an aerosol electrical contact cleaner. After a thorough cleaning, pack multipin electrical connectors with dielectric grease to seal out moisture.
6. Disconnect electrical connectors in the suspect circuits and check for bent terminals on both sides of the electrical connector. A bent terminal will not connect to its mate and will cause an open circuit.
7. Make sure that each terminal is pushed all the way into the connector. If not, carefully push it in with a narrow-blade screwdriver.
8. After everything is checked, push the connectors together and make sure they are fully engaged and locked together.
9. Never pull the electrical wires when disconnecting an electrical connector. Only pull on the connector housing.

BATTERY

The battery is an important component in the motorcycle electrical system, yet most electrical system troubles can be traced to battery neglect. Clean and inspect the battery at periodic intervals.

On all models covered in this manual, the negative side is the ground. When removing the battery, disconnect the negative (–) cable first and then the positive (+) cable. This minimizes the chance of a tool shorting to ground when disconnecting the battery positive cable.

Always wear safety glasses whenever servicing a battery. Protect eyes, skin and clothing. Electrolyte can leak from a cracked battery case. Electrolyte is very corrosive and can cause severe burns as well as permanent injury. If electrolyte spills onto clothing or skin, immediately neutralize the electrolyte with a solution of baking soda and water. Then flush the area with an abundance of clean water.

WARNING

Electrolyte splashed into the eyes is extremely harmful. Always wear safety glasses when servicing a battery. If electrolyte enters the eyes, call a physician immediately. Force the eyes open and flush them with cool, clean water for approximately 15 minutes or until medical help arrives.

Negative Cable

9

Some of the component replacement procedures and some of the test procedures in this chapter require disconnecting the negative battery cable as a safety precaution.

1. Remove the seat as described in Chapter Fifteen.
2. Remove the bolt (A, **Figure 1**, typical) securing the negative cable to the frame. Move the cable away from the battery to avoid making accidental contact with the battery post.
3. Connect the negative cable to the frame post, reinstall the bolt, and tighten securely.
4. Install the seat.

Cable Service

To ensure good electrical contact between the battery and the electrical cables, the cables must be clean and free of corrosion.

1. If the electrical cable terminals are badly corroded, disconnect them from the motorcycle electrical system.
2. Thoroughly clean each connector with a wire brush and then with a baking soda solution. Rinse thoroughly with clean water and wipe dry with a clean cloth.
3. After cleaning, apply a thin layer of dielectric grease to the battery terminals before reattaching the cables.
4. Reconnect the electrical cables to the electrical system if they were disconnected.
5. After connecting the electrical cables, apply a light coat of dielectric grease to the terminals to retard corrosion and decomposition of the terminals.

Removal/Installation

1A. On 1984-1992 FLH and FLT series models, remove the right saddlebag and the right side cover as described in Chapter Fifteen.
1B. On all other models, remove the seat as described in Chapter Fifteen.
2. Disconnect the negative battery cable (A, **Figure 1**, typical) from the battery.
3. Disconnect the positive battery cable (B, **Figure 1**, typical) from the battery.
4. Remove the battery hold-down strap (C, **Figure 1**) and disconnect the battery vent tube (D) at the battery.
5. Carefully remove the battery from the frame.
6. Check the entire battery case for cracks or other damage.
7. Inspect the battery tray and cushion for contamination or damage. Clean with a solution of baking soda and water.
8. Check the battery hold-down strap for age deterioration, cracks or other signs of damage. Replace strap if required.
9. Reposition the battery in the battery tray. If used, make sure the rubber cushion is installed in the bottom of the tray before installing the battery. Install the battery strap to secure the battery.
10. Reinstall the positive battery cable (B, **Figure 1**) and then the negative battery cable (A).

WARNING
*After installing the battery, make sure the vent tube (D, **Figure 1**) is not pinched. A pinched or kinked tube will allow high pressure to accumulate in the battery and cause the electrolyte to overflow. Replace a plugged or damaged vent tube.*

11. After connecting the electrical cables, apply a light coat of dielectric grease to the terminals to retard corrosion and decomposition of the terminals.

Electrolyte Level Check

1. The electrolyte level should be maintained between the two marks on the battery case (**Figure 2**).
2. If the electrolyte level must be adjusted, remove the battery from the frame as described in this section. Do not add water while the battery is still in the frame as any spilled water along with electrolyte will flow onto the rear frame and result in corrosion.
3. Make sure all cell caps are in place and are tight; tighten if necessary.
4. If the electrolyte level is correct, reinstall the battery.

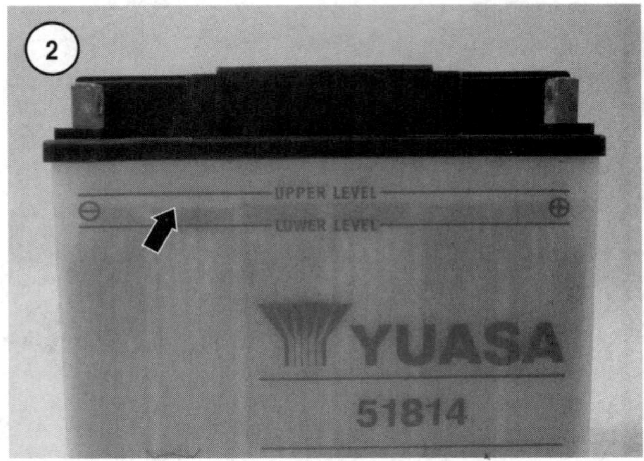

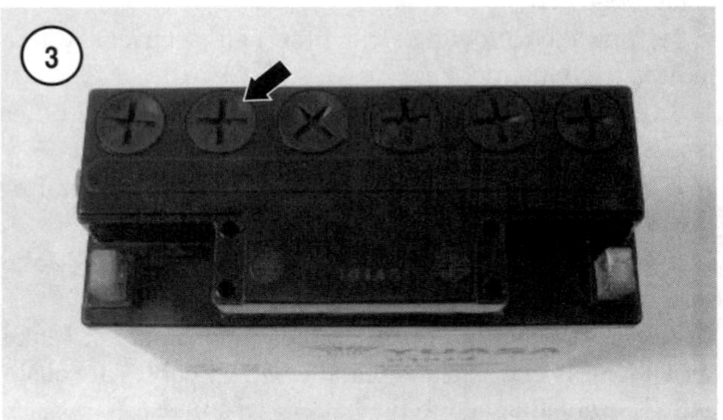

Cleaning, Inspection and Adding Water

1. Remove the battery as described in this section.
2. Inspect the battery tray for contamination or damage. Clean with a solution of baking soda and water.
3. Check the entire battery case for cracks or other damage. If the battery case is warped, is discolored or has a raised top, the battery has been suffering from overcharging or overheating.
4. Check the battery terminal bolts, spacers and nuts for corrosion, deterioration or damage. Clean parts thoroughly with a solution of baking soda and water. Replace severely corroded or damaged parts.

NOTE
Keep cleaning solution out of the battery cells, or the electrolyte level will be seriously weakened.

5. Clean the top of the battery with a stiff bristle brush using the baking soda-and-water solution. Thoroughly rinse off all baking soda residue with fresh water.
6. Check the battery cable clamps for corrosion and damage. If corrosion is minor, clean the battery cable clamps

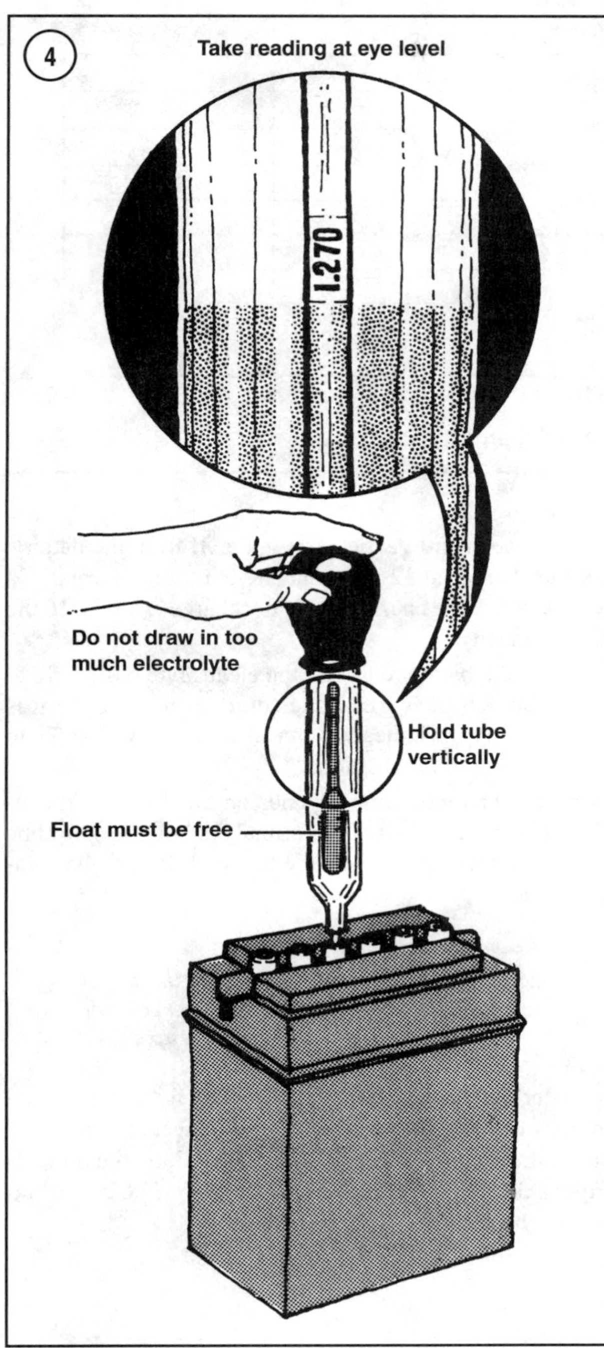

with a stiff wire brush. Replace severely worn or damaged cables.

NOTE
Do not overfill the battery cells in Step 7. The electrolyte expands due to heat from charging and will overflow if the level is above the upper level line.

7. Remove the fill caps (**Figure 3**) from the battery cells and check the electrolyte level in each cell. Add distilled water, if necessary, to bring the level within the upper and lower level lines on the battery case. Install the caps and tighten securely.

CAUTION
Adding water to the cells will dilute the electrolyte. The diluted electrolyte can freeze and destroy the battery during subfreezing temperatures. Therefore, during cold weather, charge the battery after adding water to the cells.

Testing

Checking the specific gravity of the battery electrolyte is the best way to check the state of charge of the battery. Specific gravity is the density of the electrolyte as compared to pure water. To check the specific gravity, use a hydrometer with numbered graduations from 1.100 to 1.300 rather than one with color-coded bands. To use the hydrometer, squeeze the rubber ball, insert the tip into the cell and release the ball (**Figure 4**).

9

NOTE
Adding water to the cells will lower the specific gravity (density) of the electrolyte. After adding water, charge the battery for 15-20 minutes at a rate high enough to cause vigorous gassing.

Draw sufficient electrolyte to float the weighted float inside the hydrometer. When using a temperature-compensated hydrometer, release the electrolyte and repeat this process several times to make sure the thermometer has had time to adjust to the electrolyte temperature before taking the reading.

Hold the hydrometer vertically and note the number in line with the surface of the electrolyte (**Figure 4**). This is the specific gravity for this cell. Return the electrolyte to the cell from which it came. The specific gravity of the electrolyte in each battery cell is an excellent indication of the condition of the cell. Refer to **Figure 5**. Charging is necessary if the specific gravity is low or varies more than 0.050 from cell to cell. After charging, if the specific gravity still varies more than 0.050, the battery has failed.

NOTE
If a temperature-compensated hydrometer is not used, add 0.004 to the specific gravity reading for every 10° above 80° F (25° C). For every 10° below 80° F (25° C), subtract 0.004.

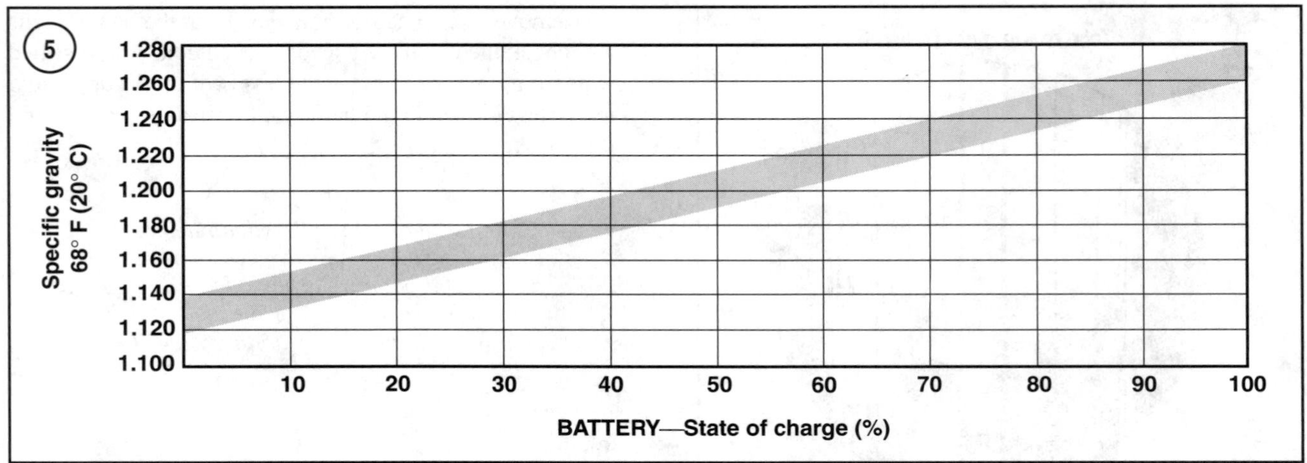

Charging

A good battery should only self-discharge approximately one percent of its given capacity each day. If a battery not in use and without any loads connected loses its charge within a week of being fully charged, the battery is defective.

If the motorcycle is not used for long periods of time, an automatic charger with variable voltage and amperage outputs is recommended for optimum battery service life.

WARNING
During charging, highly explosive hydrogen gas is released from the battery. Only charge the battery in a well-ventilated area away from open flames, including pilot lights on some gas home appliances. Do not allow smoking in the area. Never check the charge of the battery by arcing across the terminals; the resulting spark can ignite the hydrogen gas.

CAUTION
Always remove the battery from the motorcycle before connecting the charging equipment.

1. Remove the battery from the motorcycle as described in this section.
2. Set the battery on a stack of newspapers or shop cloths to protect the surface of the workbench.
3. Make sure the battery charger is turned off prior to attaching the charger leads to the battery.
4. Connect the positive charger lead to the positive battery terminal and the negative charger lead to the negative battery terminal.
5. Remove all fill/vent caps (**Figure 3**) from the battery. Set the charger at 12 volts and switch it on. Normally, a battery should be charged at a slow charge rate of 1/10 the given capacity.
   a. As the battery charges, the electrolyte will begin to bubble (gassing). If one cell does not bubble, it is usually an indication that it is defective. Refer to *Testing* in this section.
   b. The charging time depends on the discharged condition of the battery. Normally, a battery should be charged at a slow charge rate of 1/10 the given capacity.

CAUTION
Maintain the electrolyte level at the upper level during the charging cycle; check and refill with distilled water as necessary.

6. After the battery has been charged for the predetermined time, turn off the charger, disconnect the leads, and check the specific gravity. It should be within the limits in **Figure 5**. If it is and remains stable for one hour, the battery is charged.

Initialization

A new battery must be *fully* charged to a specific gravity of 1.260-1.280 before installation. To bring the battery to a full charge, give it an initial charge. Using a new battery without an initial charge will cause permanent battery damage. That is, the battery will never be able to hold more than an 80 percent charge. Charging a new battery after it has been used will not bring its charge to 100 percent. When purchasing a new battery, verify its charge status.

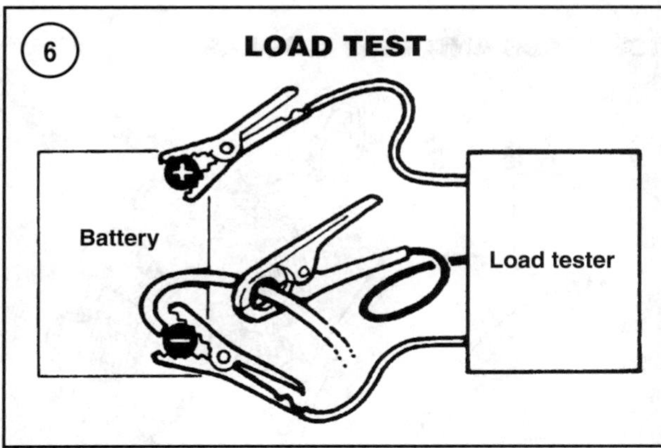

NOTE
***Recycle the old battery**. When a new battery is purchased, turn in the old one for recycling. Most motorcycle dealerships will accept the old battery in trade when purchasing a new one. Never place an old battery in the household trash because it is illegal, in most states, to place any acid or lead (heavy metal) contents in landfills.*

Load Testing

A load test checks the battery performance under full current load and is the best indication of battery condition.

A battery load tester is required for this procedure. When using a load tester, follow the manufacturer's instructions. **Figure 6** shows a typical load tester and battery arrangement.

1. Remove the battery from the motorcycle as described in this section.

NOTE
Let the battery stand for at least one hour after charging prior to performing this test.

2. The battery must be fully charged before beginning this test. If necessary, charge the battery as described in this section.

WARNING
The battery load tester must be turned off prior to connecting or disconnecting the test cables to the battery. Otherwise, a spark could cause the battery to explode.

CAUTION
To prevent battery damage during load testing, do not load-test a discharged battery and do not load-test the battery for more than 20 seconds. Performing a load test on a discharged battery can result in permanent battery damage.

3. Load test the battery as follows:
   a. Connect the load tester cables to the battery following the manufacturer's instructions.
   b. Load the battery at 50 percent of the cold-cranking amperage (CCA).
   c. After 15 seconds, the voltage reading with the load still applied must be 9.6 volts or higher at 70° F (21° C). Now quickly remove the load and turn off the tester.
4. If the voltage reading is 9.6 volts or higher, the battery output capacity is good. If the reading is below 9.6 volts, the battery is defective.
5. With the tester off, disconnect the cables from the battery.
6. Install the battery as described in this section.

CHARGING SYSTEM

The charging system consists of the battery, alternator and a voltage regulator/rectifier. Refer to **Figures 7-9**. Alternating current generated by the alternator is rectified to direct current. The voltage regulator maintains the voltage to the battery and additional electrical loads, such as the lights and ignition system, at a constant voltage regardless of variations in engine speed and load.

A malfunction in the charging system generally causes the battery to remain undercharged. To prevent damage to the alternator and the regulator/rectifier when testing and repairing the charging system, note the following precautions:

1. Always disconnect the negative battery cable, as described in this chapter, before removing a component from the charging system.
2. When it is necessary to charge the battery, remove the battery from the motorcycle and recharge it as described in this chapter.
3. Inspect the battery case. Look for bulges or cracks in the case, leaking electrolyte or corrosion build-up.
4. Check the charging system wiring for signs of chafing, deterioration or other damage.
5. Check the wiring for corroded or loose connections. Clean, tighten or reconnect as required.

Current Draw Test

Perform this test prior to performing the output test.

1. Turn the ignition switch off.
2. Remove the seat as described in Chapter Fifteen.

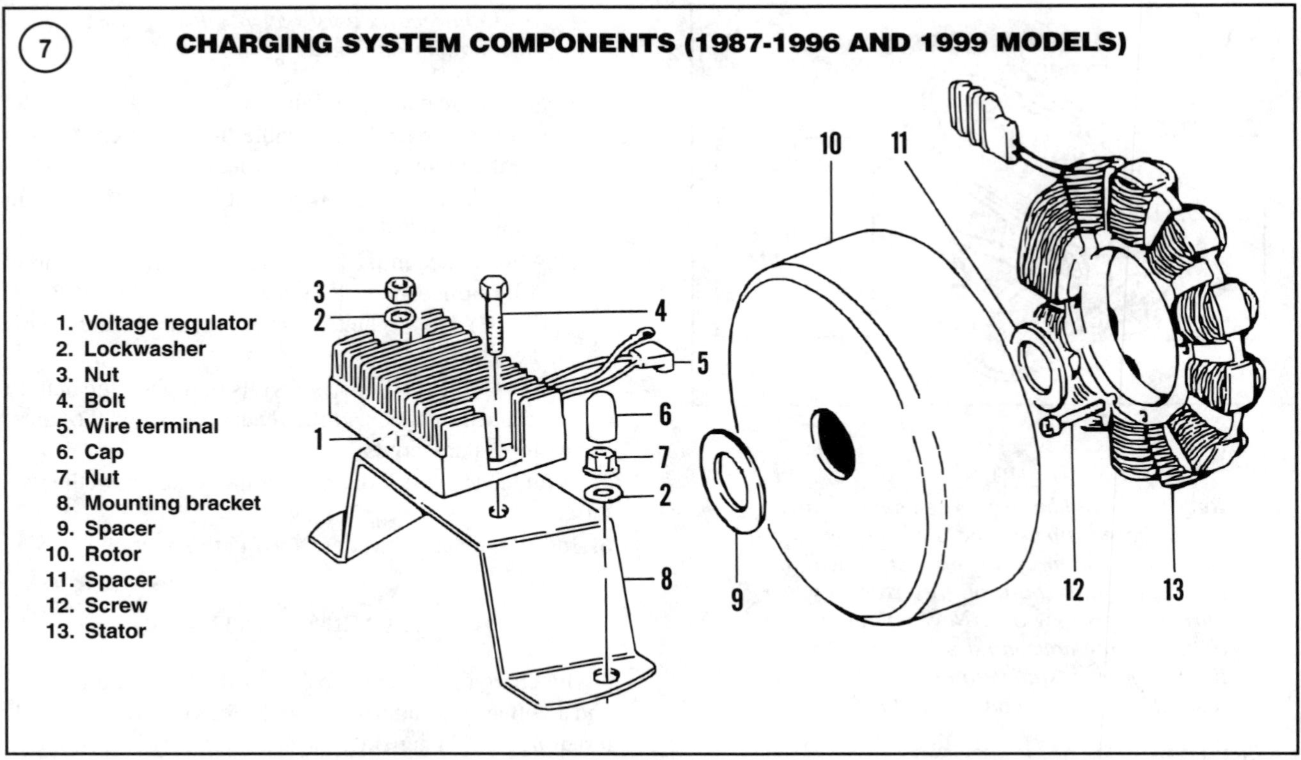

3. Disconnect the negative battery cable as described in this chapter.
4. Switch the ammeter function on a multimeter from the highest to lowest amperage scale while reading the meter scale.

CAUTION
Before connecting the multimeter to the circuit in Step 4, set the meter to the highest amperage scale. This will prevent a possible large current flow from damaging the meter or blowing the meter fuse, if so equipped.

5. Connect the multimeter between the negative battery cable and the negative terminal of the battery (**Figure 10**). If the needle swings even the slightest amount when the meter is connected, there is a current draw in the system that will discharge the battery.
6. If the current draw is excessive, the probable causes are:
   a. Damaged battery.
   b. Short circuit in the system.
   c. Loose, dirty or faulty electrical system connectors in the charging system wiring harness system.
7. Disconnect the multimeter test leads and reconnect the battery negative lead.

Testing

A malfunction in the charging system generally causes the battery to remain undercharged. Perform the following visual inspection to determine the cause of the problem. If the visual inspection proves satisfactory, test the charging system as described under *Charging System* in Chapter Two.

1. Make sure the battery cables are connected properly (**Figure 11**). If polarity is reversed, check for a damaged voltage regulator/rectifier.
2. Inspect the terminals for loose or corroded connections. Tighten or clean as required.
3. Inspect the battery case. Look for bulges or cracks in the case, leaking electrolyte or corrosion buildup.
4. Carefully check all connections at the alternator to make sure they are clean and tight.
5. Check the circuit wiring for corroded or loose connections. Clean, tighten or connect as required.

Alternator Rotor (All Models) Removal/Installation

Refer to **Figures 7-9**.

1. Disconnect the negative battery cable from the battery.

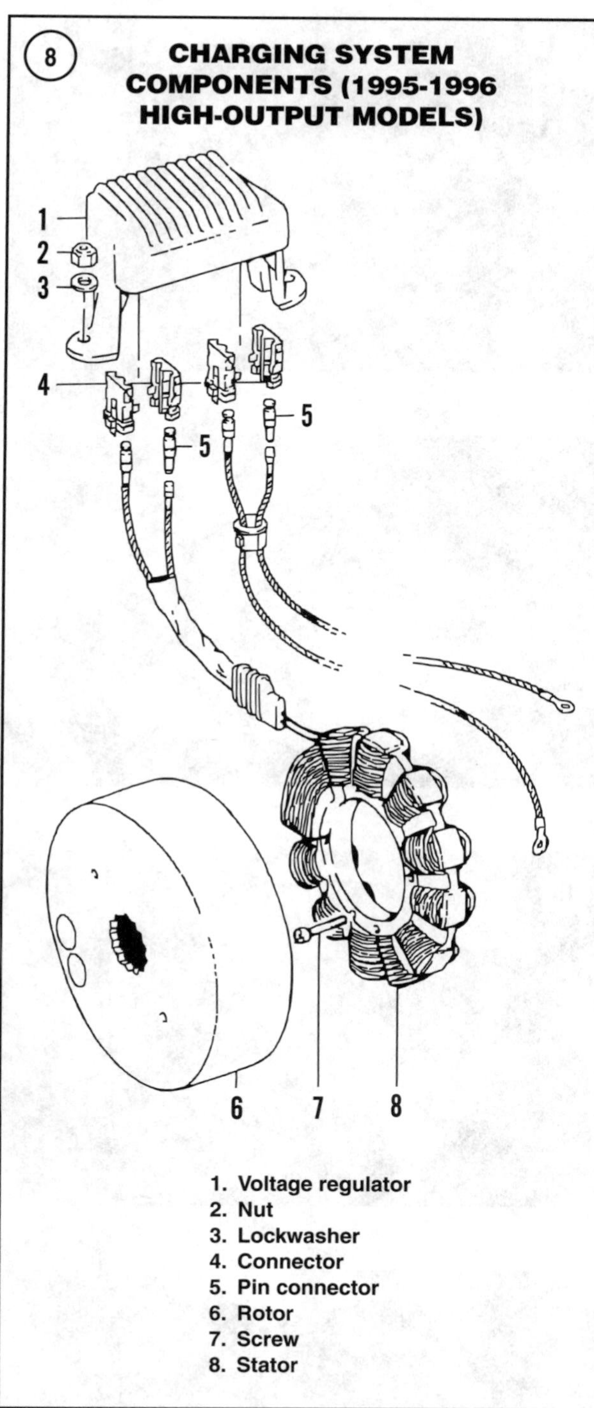

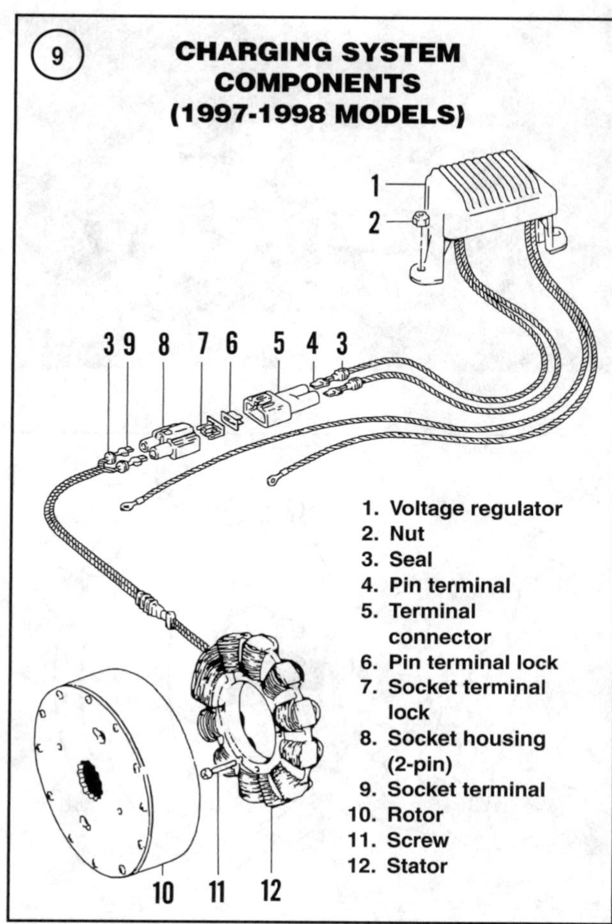

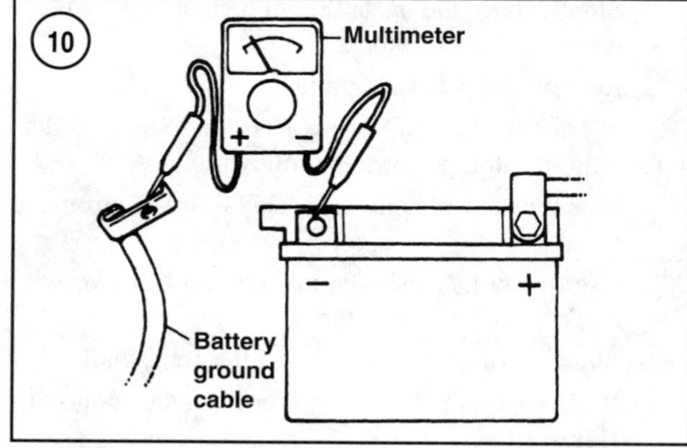

2. Remove the primary chaincase cover and outer housing as described in Chapter Five.

3. Remove the primary chain, clutch assembly, chain tensioner assembly and compensating sprocket components as an assembly. Refer to Chapter Five.

4. If still in place, remove the shaft extension and washer from the crankshaft.

5A. On rotors with an internally splined boss, perform the following:

a. Screw the rotor puller (HD part No. HD-95960-52B) or an equivalent onto the rotor (**Figure 12**).

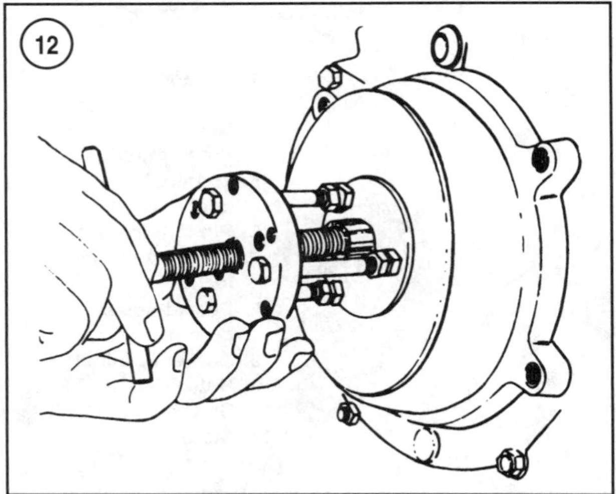

b. Slowly turn the rotor puller center bolt with a wrench until the rotor is free.

c. Remove the rotor and puller.

5B. On later models and up to 1996 and 1999 models with a slip fit rotor, perform the following:

a. Remove the large outer spacer (**Figure 13**) from the rotor.

b. Use two bolts as shown in **Figure 14** or two wire hooks into the face of the rotor.

c. Slide the rotor (**Figure 15**) off the crankshaft.

d. Remove the small inner spacer from the crankshaft (**Figure 16**).

5C. On 1997-1998 fuel-injected models, perform the following:

a. If still in place, remove the spacer (**Figure 17**) from the crankshaft.

b. Use the special tool (JIMS part No. 1147) (**Figure 18**) or a bearing puller and two 5/16 in. × 3 in. course thread bolts (**Figure 19**).

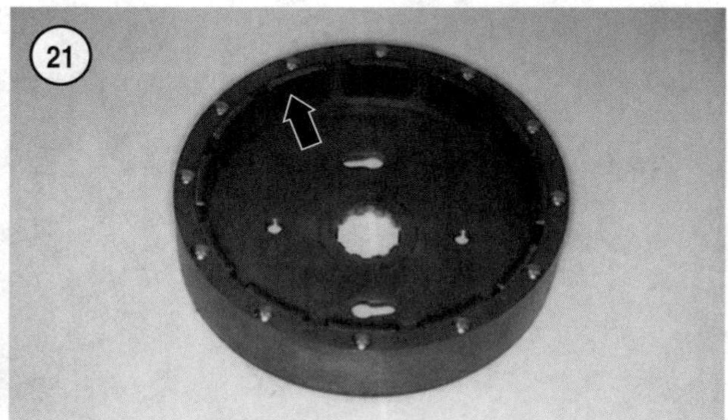

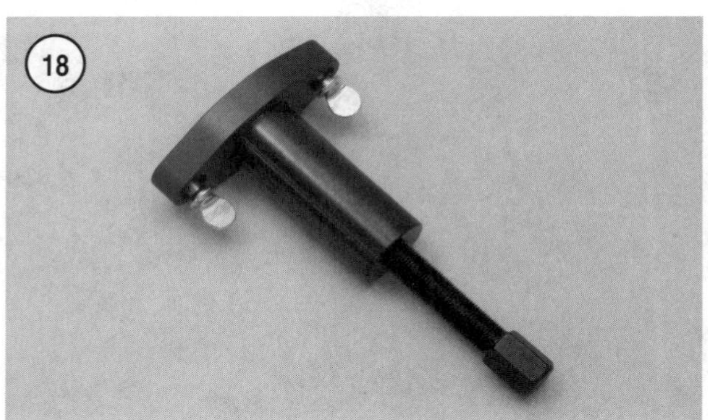

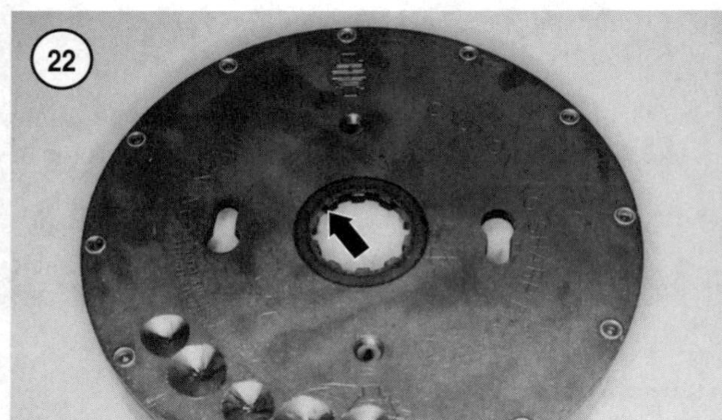

c. Protect the end of the crankshaft with a sleeve or duct tape.

d. Install the rotor remover over the crankshaft and against the rotor.

e. Secure the rotor remover to the rotor with the two bolts (**Figure 20**).

f. Slowly turn the center bolt and withdraw the rotor from the stator coils.

g. Remove the rotor and special tool. Separate the tool from the rotor.

6. Inspect the rotor magnets (**Figure 21**, typical) for small bolts, washers or other metal objects that might have been picked up by the magnets. This debris can cause severe damage to the alternator stator assembly.

7. On models so equipped, check the inner splines (**Figure 22**, typical) for wear or damage. Replace the rotor if necessary.

8. Install by reversing these removal steps while noting the following:

WARNING

On 1997-1998 fuel-injected models, do ***not*** *try to install the rotor without the special tool. The magnets will quickly pull the rotor into place trapping your fingers between the*

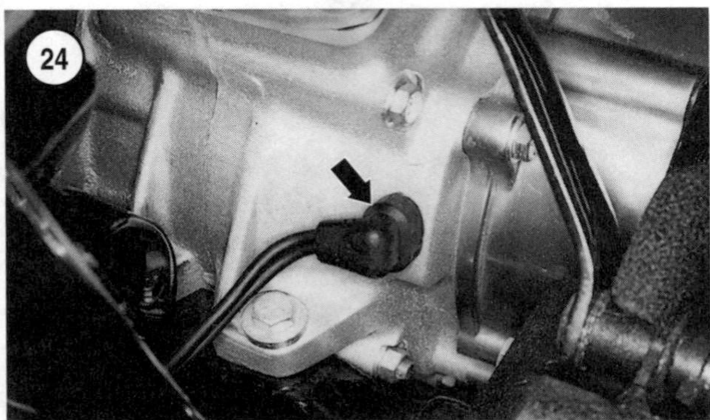

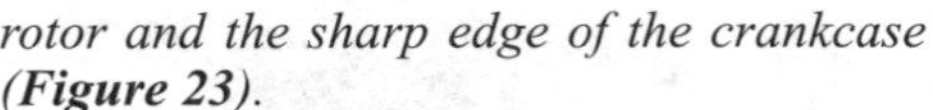

*rotor and the sharp edge of the crankcase (**Figure 23**).*

a. On 1997-1998 fuel-injected models, use the same tool setup used for removal and install the rotor in reverse order.
b. Align the rotor splines with the crankshaft splines.
c. On models so equipped, install both the small inner and large outer spacers.

Alternator Stator Removal/Installation (1984-1996 and 1999 FXR2/3 Models)

1. Remove the rotor as described in this section.
2. Disconnect the electrical connector at the stator (**Figure 24**).
3. Push the connector through the engine crankcase (**Figure 25**).
4A. On early models, bend the lockplates away from the stator screws. Then remove the screws and lockplates.
4B. On later models, remove and discard the stator plate Torx screws (**Figure 26**).
5. Remove the stator assembly (**Figure 27**).
6. Inspect the stator wires (**Figure 28**) for fraying or damage. Check the stator connector pins for looseness or damage. Replace the stator if necessary.
7. Install by reversing these steps while noting the following:

a. On early models, install *new* lockplates.

CAUTION
On later models, new Torx screws must be installed. The threadlocking compound originally applied to the Torx screws is sufficient for one use only. If a used Torx screw is installed, it can work loose and cause engine damage.

b. On later models, install *new* Torx screws (**Figure 26**). Tighten the screws securely.

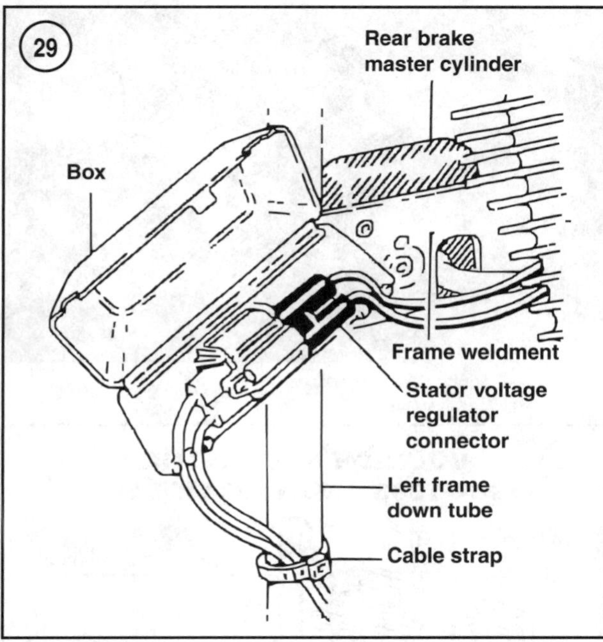

c. Install the rotor as described in this section.

Alternator Stator Removal (1997-1998 Models)

NOTE
Some of the photographs in this procedure are shown with the engine removed to illustrate the steps better.

1. Remove the rotor as described in this section.
2. On the left side of the frame next to the rear master cylinder reservoir, perform the following:
   a. Release the latch on the inboard side of the connector box and open it (**Figure 29**).
   b. Release the 2-pin electrical connector from the mounting tabs in the box.
   c. Cut the cable strap securing the stator coil/voltage regulator 2-pin electrical connector to the left frame down tube.
   d. Depress the external latch, use a rocking motion and separate the socket connector.
3. Insert a small screwdriver between the socket housing side of the connector going to the alternator stator and the locking wedge on the socket housing. Gently pivot the screwdriver tip and pop the wedge loose.
4. Lift the terminal latches inside the socket housing and back the sockets through the wire end of the connector.
5. Remove the Phillips screws from the retainer and remove the retainer from the crankcase.
6. Remove the Torx screws securing the stator assembly to the crankcase. New Torx screws must be used on installation.

NOTE
If necessary, spray electrical contact cleaner or glass cleaner around the wiring harness grommet to help ease it out of the crankcase boss receptacle.

7. Using an awl, carefully lift the capped lip on the grommet (**Figure 30**) away from the crankcase and push it into the bore.
8. Carefully push the stator wires and grommet out through the crankcase bore.
9. Remove the stator assembly.
10. Inspect the stator mounting surface on the crankcase for any oil residue that may have passed by a damaged oil seal. Clean off if necessary.
11. Inspect the stator wires (A, **Figure 31**) for fraying or damage.
12. Inspect the rubber grommet (B, **Figure 31**) for deterioration or hardness.

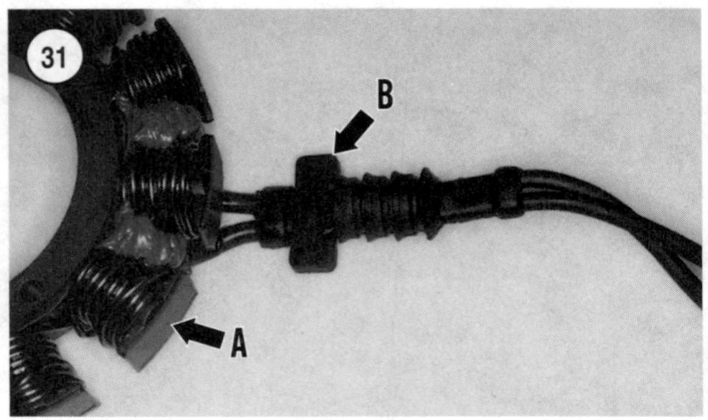

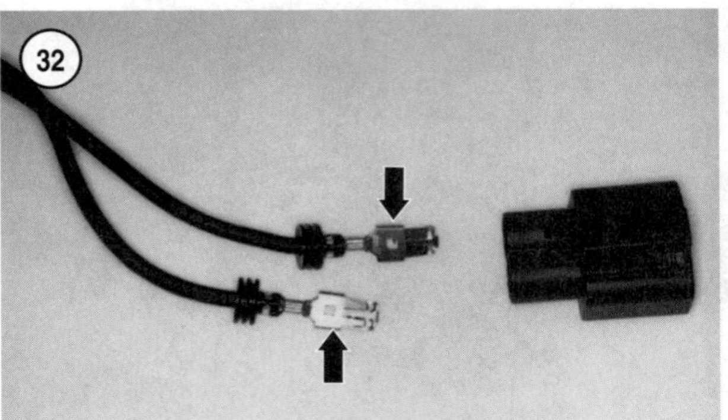

13. Check the stator connector pins (**Figure 32**) for looseness or damage.

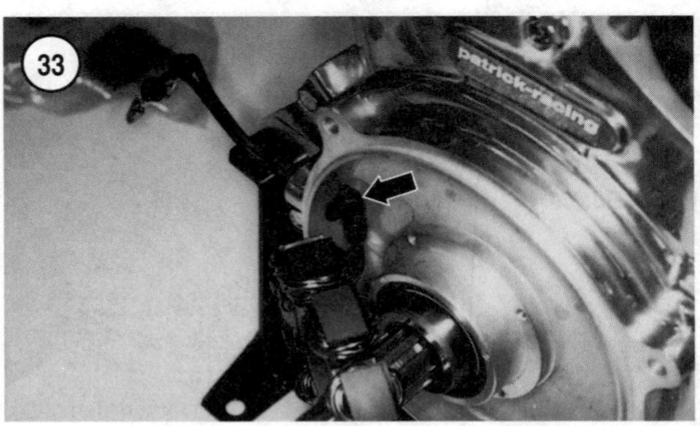

Alternator Stator Installation (1997-1998 Models)

1. Apply a light coat of electrical contact cleaner or glass cleaner to the wiring harness grommet to help ease it into the crankcase boss receptacle.

NOTE
***Figure 33** is shown with the engine removed to illustrate the step better.*

2. Carefully insert the electrical harness and grommet into the crankcase boss receptacle and carefully pull it through until the grommet is correctly seated (**Figure 33**).

CAUTION
New Torx screws must be installed. The threadlocking compound originally applied to the Torx screws is sufficient for one use only. If a used Torx screw is installed, it can work loose and cause engine damage.

3. Move the stator into position on the crankcase and install four *new* T27 Torx screws. Tighten the screws securely.
4. Clean the retainer screws and apply a medium-strength threadlocking compound to the screw threads. Install the retainer onto the crankcase and tighten the screws securely.
5. Move the wires to the left side of the motorcycle.
6. Apply a light coat of dielectric compound to the electrical connector prior to assembling it. Reassemble the electrical connector socket by reversing Steps 3-4 of removal. Make sure it has locked together securely.
7. Position the electrical wires and connector on the inboard side of the left frame rail. Secure it to the frame with a *new* cable strap.

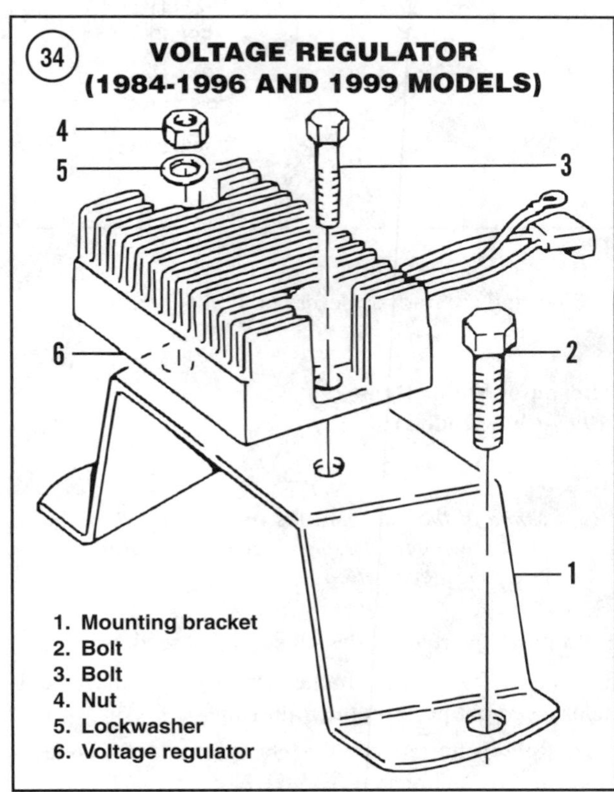

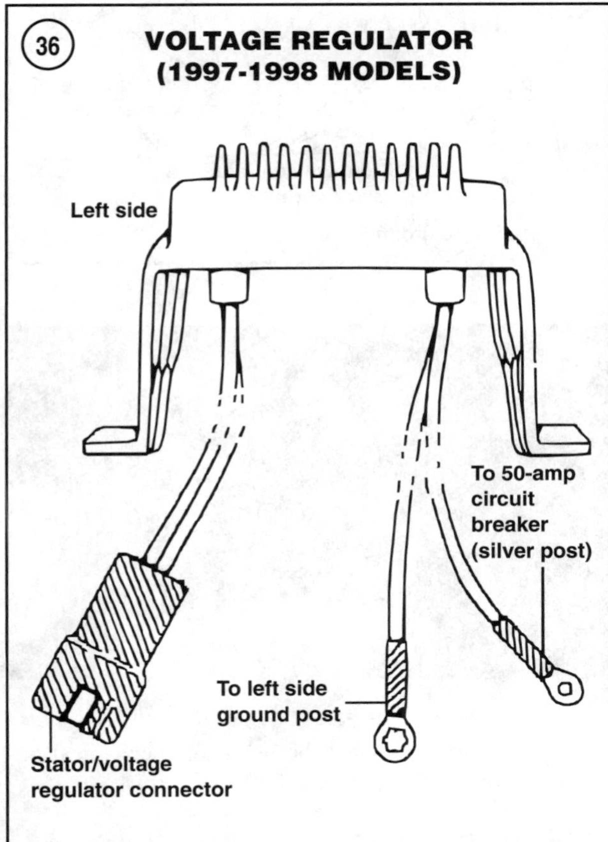

8. On the left side of the frame next to the rear master cylinder reservoir, perform the following:
   a. Install a *new* cable strap securing the stator coil/voltage regulator 2-pin electrical connector to the left frame down tube.
   b. Insert the 2-pin electrical connector onto the mounting tabs in the box. Make sure it is locked into place.
   c. Close the box door and lock it.
9. Install the alternator rotor as described in this section.

Voltage Regulator Removal/Installation

1984-1996 and 1999 models

Refer to **Figure 34**.

NOTE
Before disconnecting and removing the voltage regulator electrical connectors, note the wire routing and tag the electrical connectors so that they will be installed in the correct locations.

1. Disconnect the battery negative cable from the battery.
2. Unplug the voltage regulator from the alternator stator at the crankcase (**Figure 24**).
3. Disconnect the voltage regulator electrical connectors from the main circuit breaker. Refer to *Circuit Breakers* in this chapter for locations.
4. Remove all cable straps securing the wires and connector to the frame.
5. Remove the bolts or nuts and washers (A, **Figure 35**, typical) securing the voltage regulator to the frame bracket or frame crossmember.
6. Remove the voltage regulator (B, **Figure 35**, typical).
7. Install by reversing these removal steps while noting the following:
   a. Apply a light coat of dielectric compound to the electrical connector prior to connecting it to the alternator stator.
   b. Securely tighten the bolts and/or nuts.

9

1997-1998 models

Refer to **Figure 36**.

NOTE
Before disconnecting and removing the voltage regulator electrical connectors, note the wire routing and tag the electrical connectors so that they will be installed in the correct locations.

1. Remove the seat as described in Chapter Fifteen.
2. Remove the battery as described in this chapter.

NOTE
After releasing the cable straps, leave them in place on the frame. This will indicate the path of the wiring during installation.

3. Release the cable clips securing the voltage regulator electrical wires to the right frame rail and at the front of the battery box. Release the wires from the clips.
4. Refer to **Figure 37** and perform the following:

   a. Remove the nut from the left ground post in front of the battery box.
   b. From the post, remove the internal tooth ring terminal with the black shrink wrap tube.
   c. Remove the nut securing the silver post on the circuit breaker. Remove the ring terminal with the yellow shrink wrap tube.
   d. Release the cables from the clip at the front of the battery box.
5. On the left side of the frame next to the rear master cylinder reservoir, perform the following:
   a. Release the latch on the inboard side of the connector box and open it (**Figure 29**).
   b. Release the 2-pin electrical connector from the mounting tabs in the box.
   c. Cut the cable strap securing the stator coil/voltage regulator 2-pin electrical connector to the left frame down tube.
   d. Depress the external latch, use a rocking motion and separate the socket connector.
6. Remove the flange locknuts (A, **Figure 38**) on each side securing the voltage regulator to the lower frame crossmember studs.
7. Remove the voltage regulator (B, **Figure 38**) and related wiring (**Figure 36**) from the frame.
8. Install by reversing these removal steps while noting the following:
   a. When installing the voltage regulator onto the lower frame member studs, move the electrical wires away from the studs. Make sure they are not pinched between the frame member and the voltage regulator flange.
   b. Securely tighten the flange locknuts.
   c. Apply a light coat of dielectric compound to the electrical connectors prior to installing them.
   d. Install *new* cable straps and secure the electrical wires to the three cable clips. The cable clips also secure the engine sensor harness conduit as well as the rear brake line.

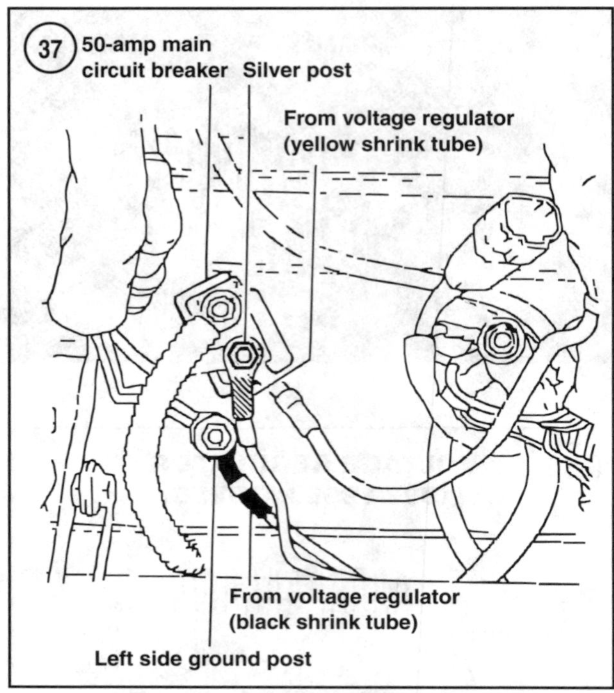

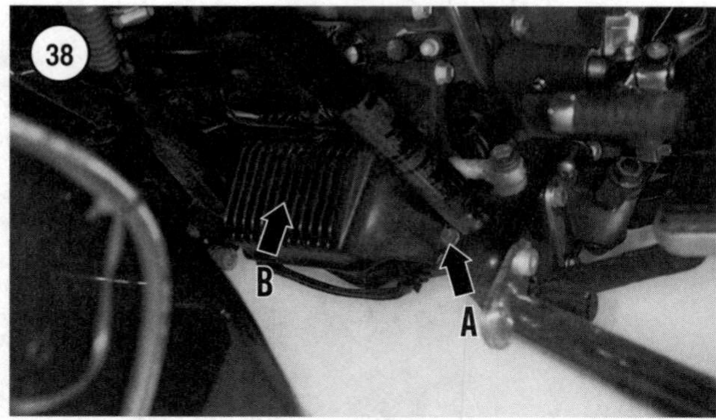

IGNITION SYSTEM (CARBURETED MODELS)

The ignition system consists of a single ignition coil, two spark plugs, an inductive pickup unit, an ignition module and a vacuum-operated electric switch (VOES). Refer to **Figure 39** and **Figure 40**. This system has a full electronic advance. The inductive pickup unit is driven by the engine and generates pulses that are routed to the solid-state ignition control module. This control module computes the ignition timing advance and ignition coil dwell time and eliminates the need for mechanical advance and routine ignition service.

The vacuum-operated electric switch (VOES) senses intake manifold vacuum through a carburetor body opening. The switch is open when the engine is in low vacuum situations such as acceleration and high load. The switch is closed when engine vacuum is high during a low engine load condition. The VOES allows the ignition system to follow two spark advance curves. A maximum spark curve can be used during a high vacuum condition to provide improved fuel economy and performance. During heavy engine load and acceleration (low vacuum) conditions, the spark can be retarded to minimize ignition knock and still maintain performance.

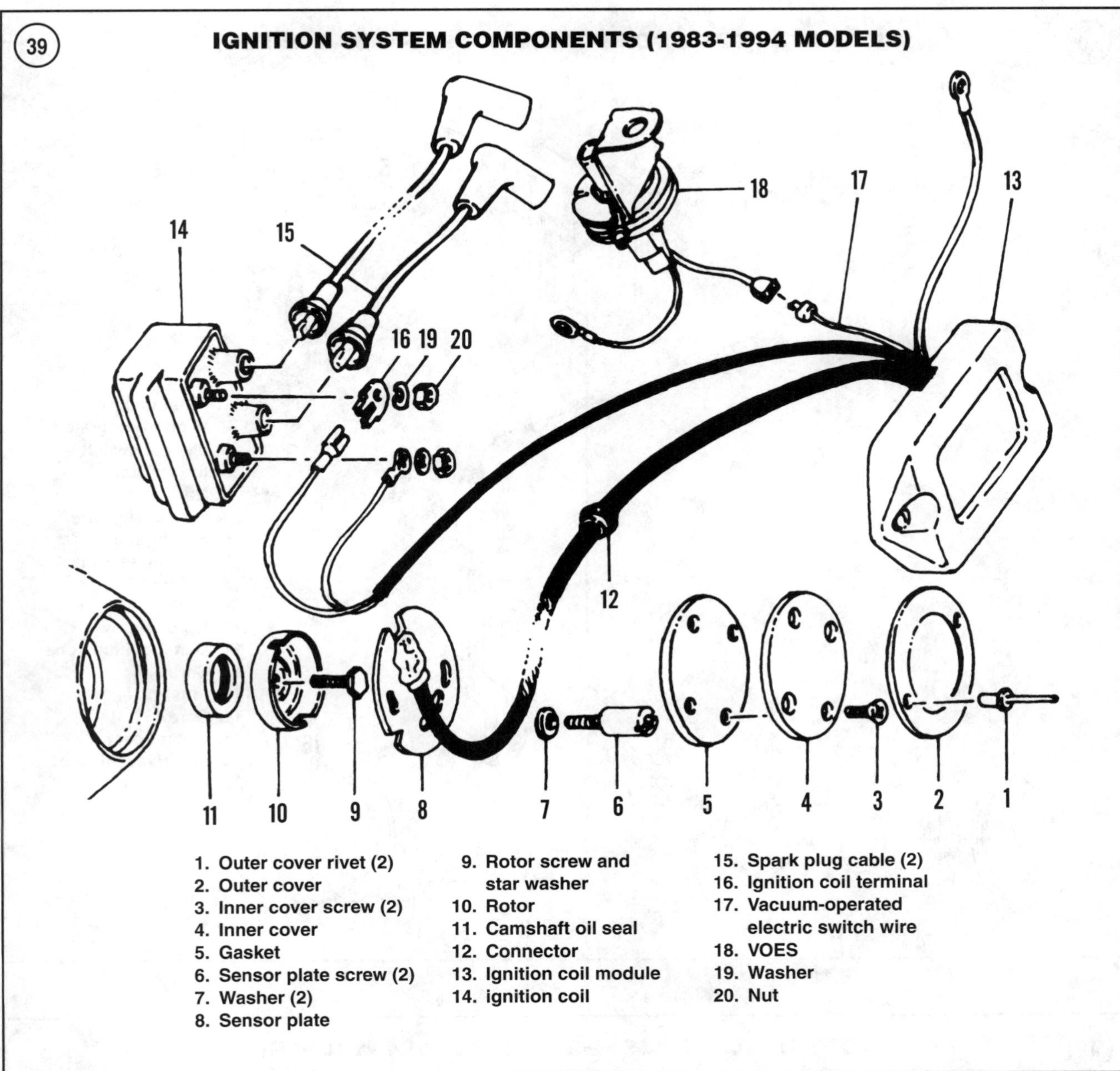

(39) **IGNITION SYSTEM COMPONENTS (1983-1994 MODELS)**

1. Outer cover rivet (2)
2. Outer cover
3. Inner cover screw (2)
4. Inner cover
5. Gasket
6. Sensor plate screw (2)
7. Washer (2)
8. Sensor plate
9. Rotor screw and star washer
10. Rotor
11. Camshaft oil seal
12. Connector
13. Ignition coil module
14. ignition coil
15. Spark plug cable (2)
16. Ignition coil terminal
17. Vacuum-operated electric switch wire
18. VOES
19. Washer
20. Nut

The leading and trailing edges of the two rotor slots trigger the timing sensor. As the engine speed increases, the control module advances the timing in three stages.

Stator Plate Removal

Refer to **Figure 41** and **Figure 42**.

1. Disconnect the negative battery cable from the battery.
2. Drill out the outer cover rivets with a 3/8-in. (9.5 mm) drill bit (**Figure 43**).
3. Using a punch, tap the rivets through the outer cover and remove the outer cover (**Figure 44**). Then remove the rivets.
4. Remove the screws securing the inner cover (**Figure 45**) and remove the inner cover and the gasket (**Figure 46**).
5. Make an alignment mark across the sensor plate mounting screws on the sensor plate so the sensor plate can be reinstalled in the original location.
6. Remove the screws securing the sensor plate (**Figure 47**) to the crankcase.

(40)

IGNITION SYSTEM COMPONENTS (1995-1998 MODELS)

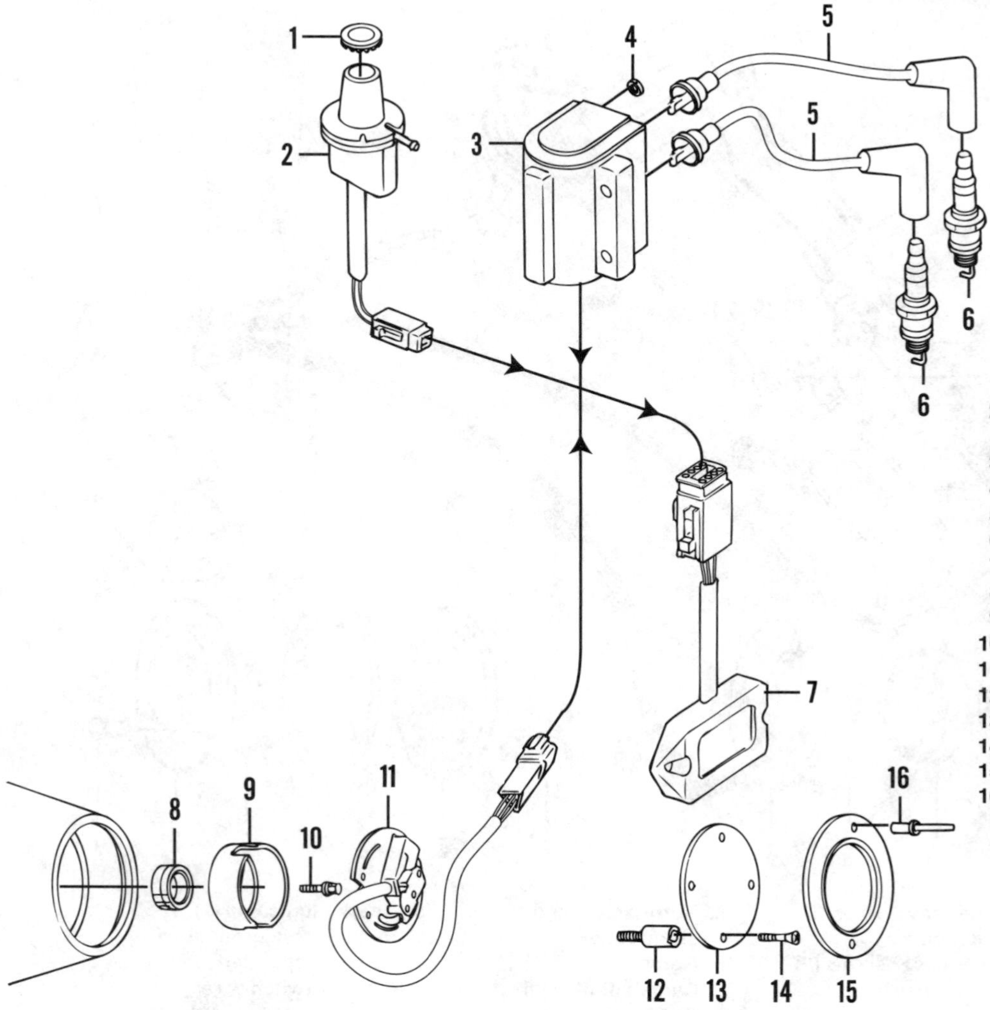

1. Retaining ring
2. Vacuum-operated electric switch
3. Igntion coil
4. Nut
5. Spark plug wire
6. Spark plug
7. Ignition module
8. Oil seal
9. Rotor
10. Rotor screw
11. Cam position sensor
12. Screw
13. Inner cover
14. Screw
15. Outer cover
16. Pop river (HD part No. 8699 only)

(41)

STATOR PLATE ASSEMBLY (1983-1994 MODELS)

1. Oil seal
2. Rotor
3. Rotor screw and star washer
4. Sensor plate
5. Washer
6. Screw
7. Gasket
8. Inner cover
9. Screw
10. Outer cover
11. Outer cover rivet

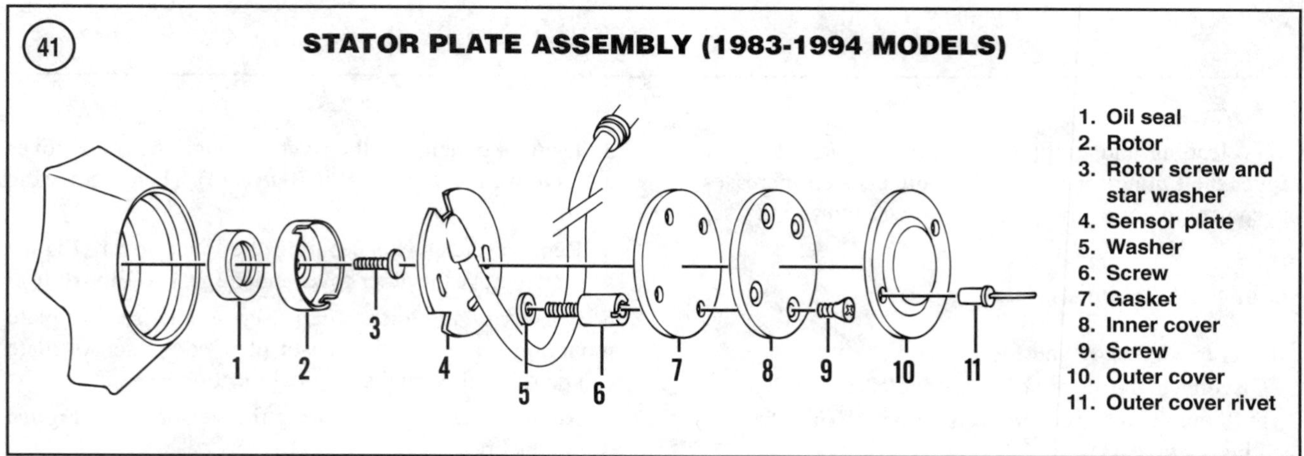

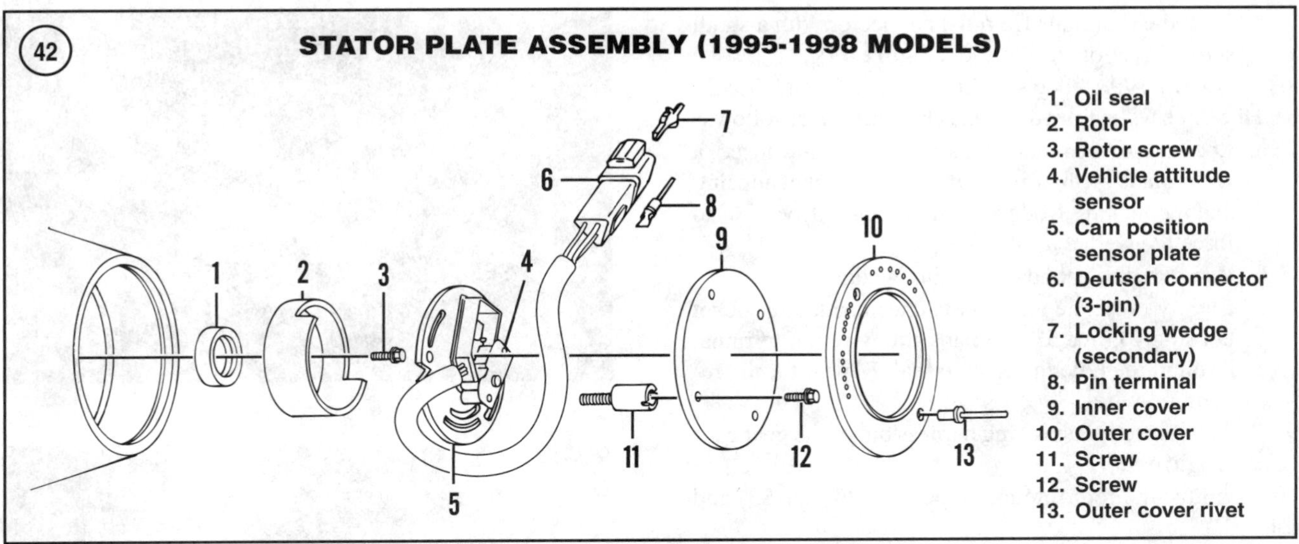

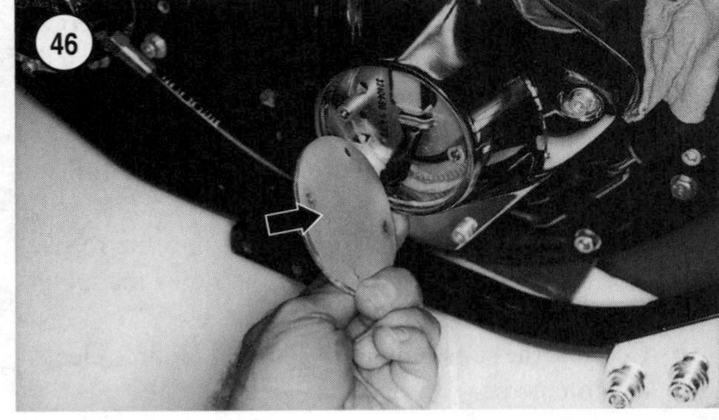

7. Pull the sensor plate away from the rotor. If the sensor plate is going to be removed, perform Step 8. If not, proceed to Step 9.

8A. To remove the sensor plate on 1984-1994 and 1999 models, perform the following:

a. Disconnect the sensor plate-to-ignition module electrical connector.

b. Record the position of each sensor plate wiring terminal in the end of the connector (**Figure 48**). Also refer to the wiring diagram at the end of this manual for the model being worked on.

c. Push the terminals from the connector with a small screwdriver or similar tool (**Figure 49**).

8B. On 1995-1998 models, refer to **Figure 50** and disconnect the three wires from the Deutsch connector as follows:

a. Locate the secondary locking wedge and insert a wide-blade screwdriver between the socket housing and the locking wedge. Turn the screwdriver 90° to force the wedge up.
b. Remove the secondary locking wedge.
c. Lightly press the terminal latches inside the socket housing **Figure 51** and back the wire pin terminal through the hole in the wire seal. Repeat for the remaining wires.

9. Pull the sensor plate wiring harness out of the gear case cover (**Figure 52**).

10. Remove the rotor mounting bolt (A, **Figure 53**) and rotor (B).

11. Remove the two loose rivets from the gearcase cover.

Stator Plate Installation

Refer to **Figure 41** and **Figure 42**.

1. To install the sensor plate, perform the following:

a. Align the tab on the back of the rotor (**Figure 54**) with the notch in the end of the crankshaft (A, **Figure 55**) and install the rotor (B, **Figure 53**).
b. Apply a medium-strength threadlocking compound to the rotor bolt and install the bolt (A, **Figure 53** and tighten to 43-48 in.-lb. (4.8-5.4 N•m).

2. Insert the sensor plate wiring harness into the gearcase cover (**Figure 52**) and route the wiring harness along its original path.

3. Position the sensor plate against the gearcase cover. Then install the sensor plate screws (**Figure 47**). Align the index mark made prior to removal.

4A. On 1984-1994 models, to install and reconnect the sensor plate electrical connector, perform the following:

a. Install the connectors (**Figure 49**) into the respective terminal holes, following the notes made during removal (**Figure 48**).
b. Connect the sensor plate-to-ignition module electrical connector.

4B. On 1995-1999 models, refer to **Figure 50** and connect the three wires into the Deutsch connector as follows:

a. Hold the socket housing and insert the socket terminals through the holes in the wire seal so that they enter the correct chamber hole (**Figure 56**). Continue until the socket terminal locks into place. Then lightly tug on the wire to make sure that it is locked into place. Repeat for the remaining wires.

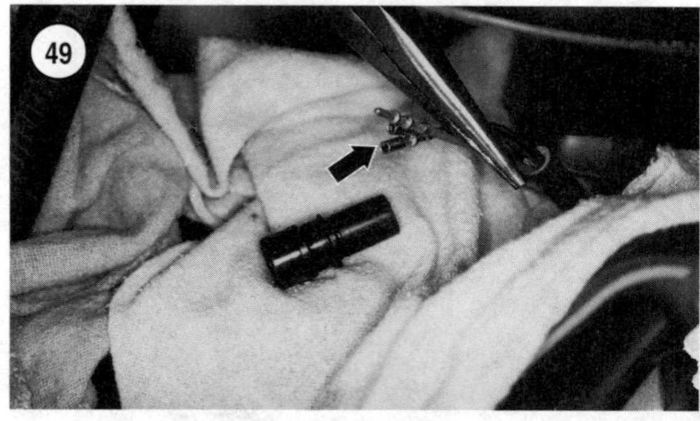

b. Set the terminal seal onto the socket housing if it was removed.
c. Assemble the 3-pin connector with the arrow on the secondary locking wedge pointing toward the external latch as shown in **Figure 57**.

NOTE

If the secondary locking wedge does not slide into position easily, one or more of the socket terminals are not installed correctly. Correct the problem at this time.

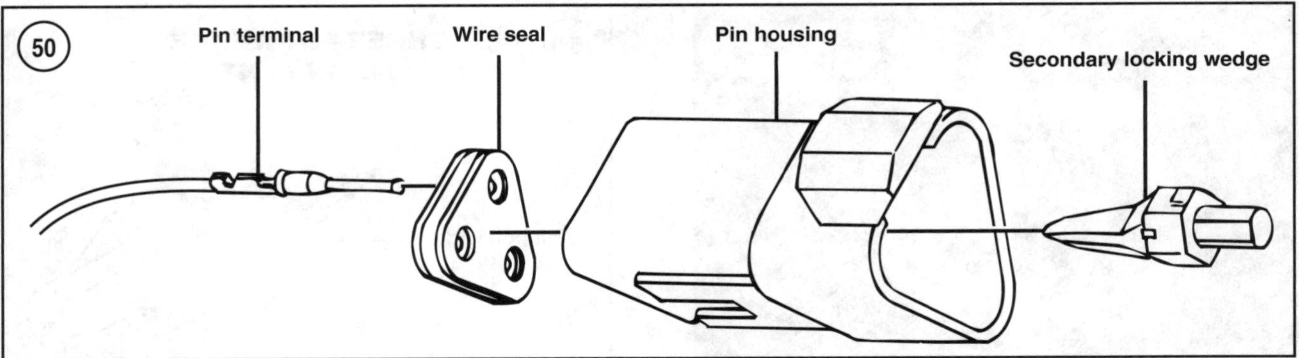

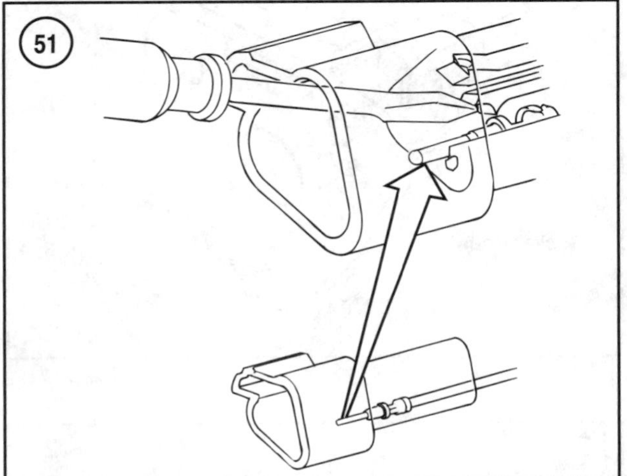

d. Install the secondary locking wedge into the socket housing as shown in **Figure 50**. Press the secondary locking wedge down until it is locked into place.

5. Before riveting the cover in place, check the ignition timing as described in Chapter Three.

6. Install the inner cover and gasket (**Figure 45**). Install the screws and tighten securely.

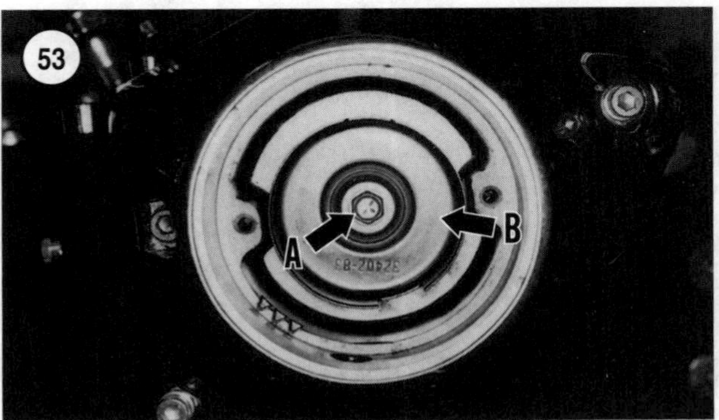

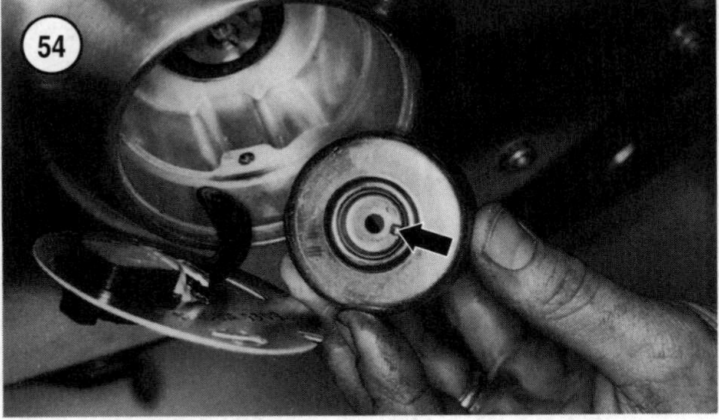

7. Use only OEM timing cover rivets (H-D part No. 8699) (**Figure 58**). Rivet the cover to the inner cover (**Figure 59**). The rivets must be flush against the outer cover (**Figure 60**).

8. Connect the negative battery cable.

Stator Plate Inspection (All Models)

1. If necessary, troubleshoot the ignition system as described in Chapter Two.

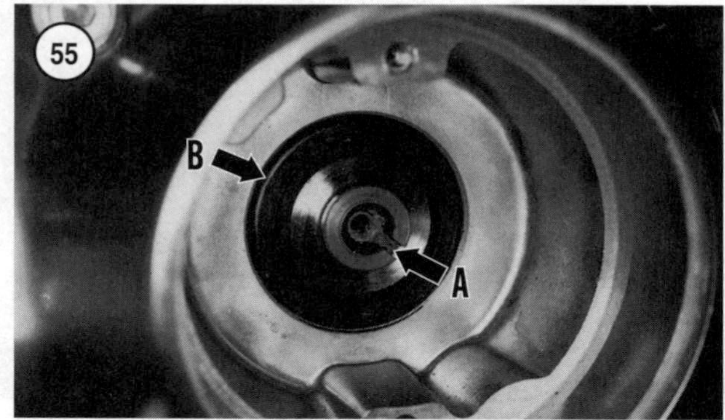

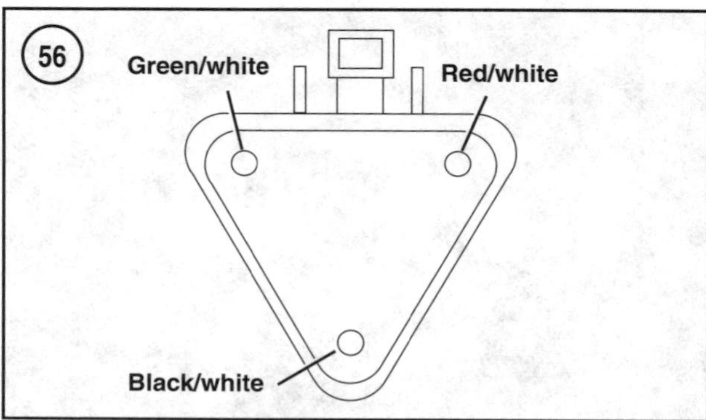

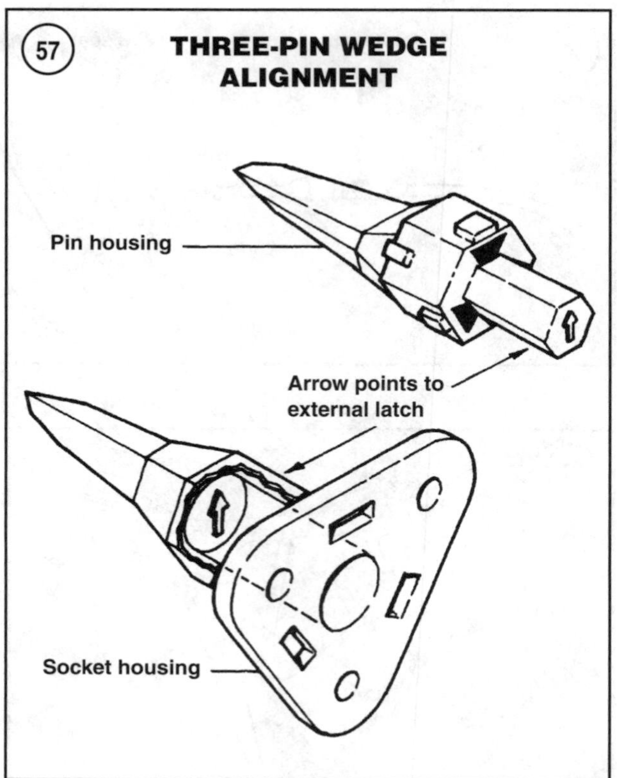

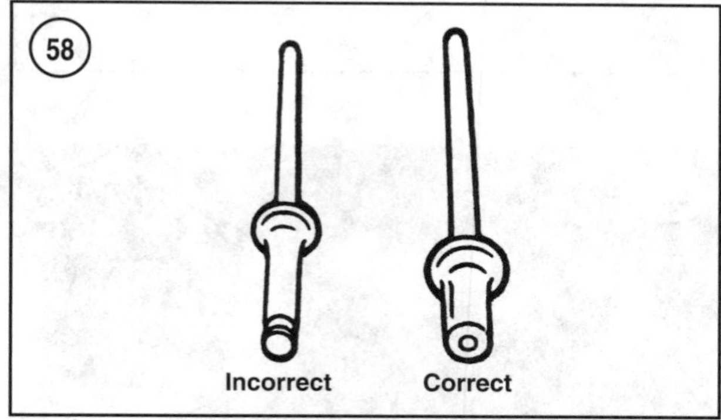

2. Check the sensor plate and connectors for damage (**Figure 61**).

3. Check the ignition compartment for oil leaks. If oil is present, replace the gearcase oil seal (B, **Figure 55**).

IGNITION SYSTEM (FUEL-INJECTED MODELS)

The ignition system consists of an ignition coil, two spark plugs, electronic control module, crankshaft position sensor, barometric pressure sensor, camshaft position sensor, crankshaft position sensor, engine temperature sensor and the attitude sensor.

The electronic control module (ECM) is located behind the right frame cover. It determines the spark advance for correct ignition timing based signals from the various sensors. The ignition system fires the spark plugs near top dead center for starting and then varies the spark advance from 0° to 50° depending on engine speed, crankshaft position and intake manifold pressure. It also regulates the low-voltage circuits between the battery and the ignition coil. The ignition module is a nonrepairable item and, if defective, must be replaced.

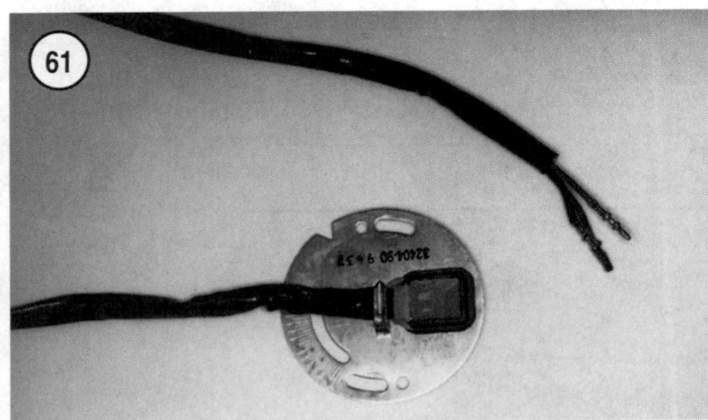

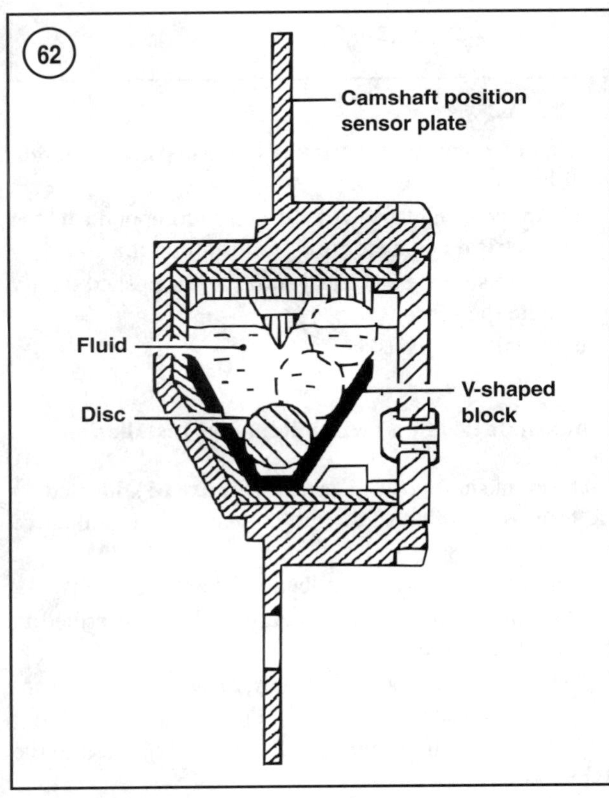

The barometric pressure sensor is located next to the ECM behind the right frame cover. This sensor monitors atmospheric pressure and allows for altitude compensation.

The rotor and camshaft position sensor are located in the camshaft cover on the right side of the crankcase. The raised ridge on the rotor operates at one-half crankshaft speed, and it breaks the magnetic field of the Hall-effect device on the camshaft position sensor. This signal provides accurate timing information to the ignition module.

The attitude sensor mounts on the camshaft position sensor plate under the gearcase cover on the right side of the engine. The sensor consists of a small magnetic disc that rides within a V-shaped channel (**Figure 62**). If the motorcycle is tilted over at an angle of 80° for more than one second, the ignition system is shut off. Once the sensor is activated, the motorcycle must stand upright, and the ignition must be turned off and then on. Once this is done, the ignition system is operational and the engine can be restarted.

When servicing the ignition system, refer to the wiring diagrams, located at the end of the manual.

Barometric Pressure Sensor Removal/Installation

The barometric pressure sensor is located next to the ECM under the right frame cover (**Figure 63**).

1. Disconnect the negative battery cable as described in this chapter.
2. Remove the right saddlebag as described in Chapter Fifteen.
3. Remove the right frame cover.
4. Depress and release the wire latch. Use a rocking motion to disconnect the electrical connector from the sensor.
5. Remove the nuts securing the sensor to the ECM mounting bracket and remove the sensor.
6. Install the sensor by reversing these steps while noting the following:
   a. Apply a light coat of dielectric compound to the electrical connector prior to installing them.
   b. Make sure the electrical connector is pushed tightly onto the sensor.

Throttle Position Sensor Removal/Installation

Located on the front of the induction module and attached directly to the throttle shaft, the throttle position sensor indicates throttle angle. Refer to **Figure 64**.

Replacement of the throttle position sensor must be entrusted to a Harley-Davidson dealership. After installa-

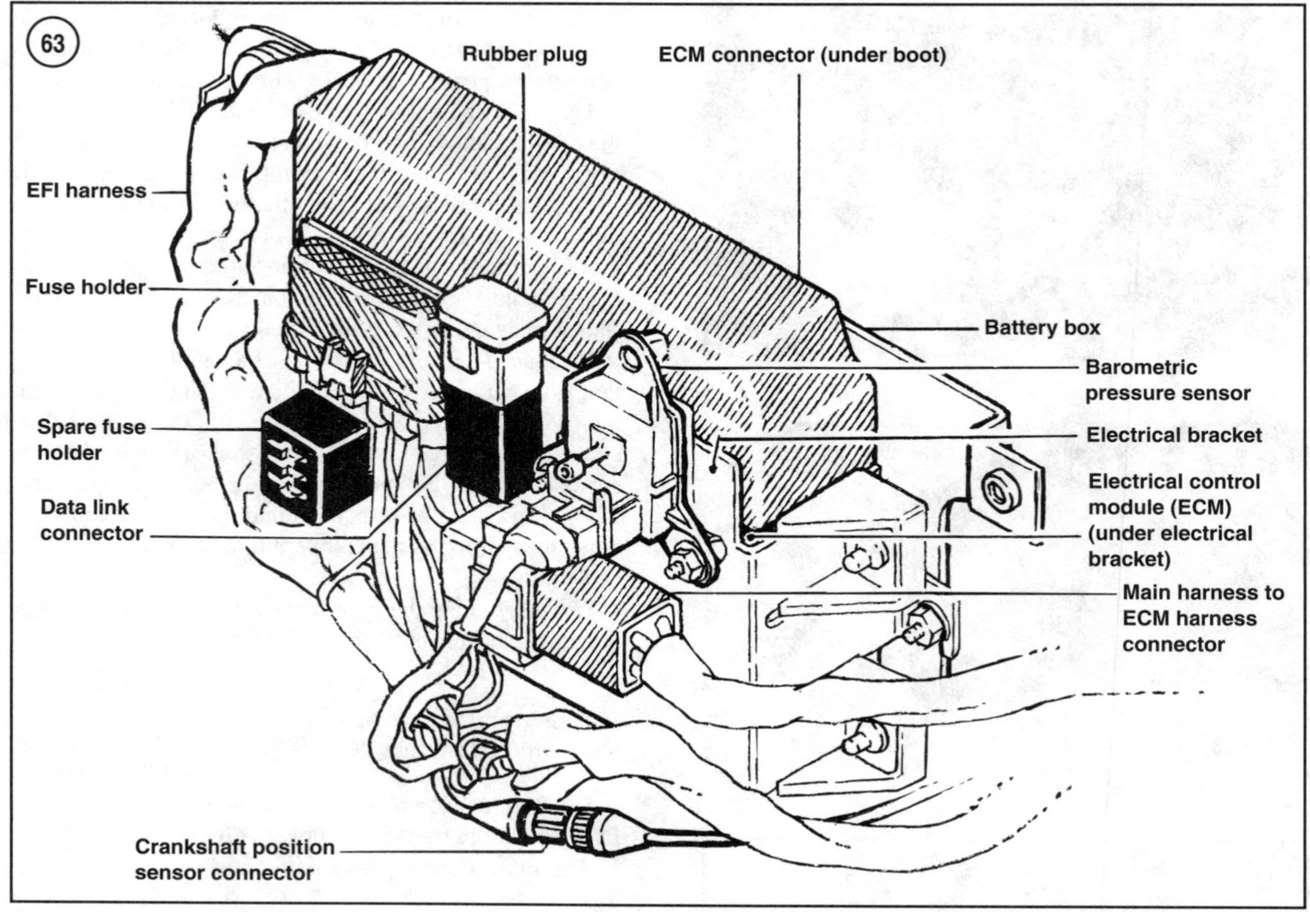

tion, the sensor must be adjusted using the diagnostic tools that are not available to the home mechanic.

Intake Air Temperature Sensor Removal/Installation

The intake air temperature sensor is located inside the induction module (rear cylinder intake runner). Refer to **Figure 64**.

1. Disconnect the negative battery cable as described in this chapter.
2. Remove the air filter element and back plate assembly as described in Chapter Eight.
3. Pull out the latch on each side of the connector. Use a rocking motion to disconnect the electrical connector from the sensor.
4. Remove the screws securing the sensor to the induction module.
5. Remove the sensor and gasket from the induction module.
6. Install the sensor by reversing these steps while noting the following:
   a. Apply a light coat of dielectric compound to the electrical connector prior to installing it.
   b. Make sure the electrical connector is pushed tightly onto the sensor.
   c. Install a *new* gasket.

Crankshaft Position Sensor Removal/Installation

The crankshaft position sensor (**Figure 65**), located on the forward position of the left crankcase is an inductive sensor.

1. Remove the seat as described in Chapter Fifteen.
2. Disconnect the negative battery cable as described in this chapter.
3. At the electrical bracket assembly, rotate the ring and separate the electrical connector from the sensor (**Figure 63**).
4. Unhook the clip securing the electrical harness to the frame down tube.

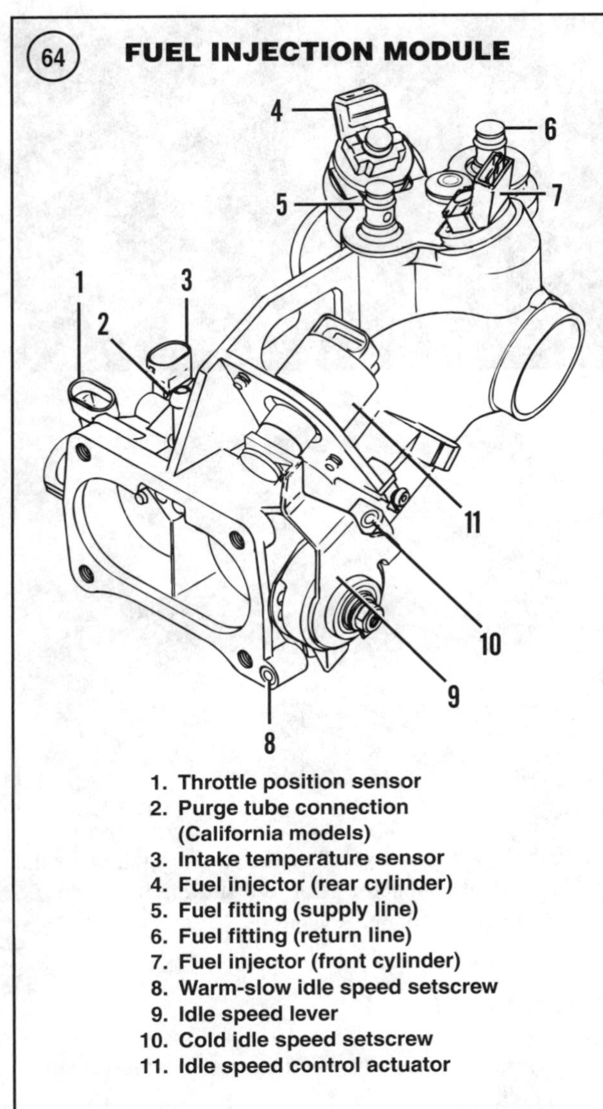

1. Throttle position sensor
2. Purge tube connection (California models)
3. Intake temperature sensor
4. Fuel injector (rear cylinder)
5. Fuel fitting (supply line)
6. Fuel fitting (return line)
7. Fuel injector (front cylinder)
8. Warm-slow idle speed setscrew
9. Idle speed lever
10. Cold idle speed setscrew
11. Idle speed control actuator

NOTE
Do not loosen the crankcase bolts in Step 5 because this can result in an oil leak.

5. Open the clamps on the crankcase lower three bolts located behind the primary chaincase inner cover. Release the electrical harness from these clamps.
6. Remove the Phillips screws securing the sensor to the crankcase.
7. Remove the sensor, sensor mount and O-ring seal from the crankcase.
8. Tie a piece of string to the electrical connector. Tie the other end of the string to the frame crossmember. If necessary, make a drawing of the wire routing through the

frame. It is easy to forget the routing path after removing the wire.
9. Carefully pull the sensor and electrical harness from the frame.
10. Untie the string from the electrical harness.
11. Install by reversing these removal steps while noting the following:
   a. Tie the string to the wiring harness and connector(s).
   b. Carefully pull the string and the electrical harness and connector through the left side of the frame and into position. Untie and remove the string.
   c. Apply a light coat of dielectric compound to the electrical connector prior to installing it.
   d. Apply clean engine oil to the *new* O-ring on the sensor prior to installation. Install the sensor and tighten the Allen screws to 40 in.-lb. (4.5 N•m).

9

Camshaft Position Sensor Removal/Installation

The camshaft position sensor, located in the chaincase cover on the right side, is an inductive sensor. The sensor is located in the same position on carbureted models.

To replace the sensor, refer to *Ignition System (Carbureted Models), Stator Plate Removal and Installation* in this chapter.

Engine Temperature Sensor Removal/Installation

The engine temperature sensor (**Figure 66**) is located on the front cylinder head.

1. Remove the seat as described in Chapter Fifteen.
2. Disconnect the negative battery cable as described in this chapter.
3. On the left side of the front cylinder head, pull the rubber boot back off the sensor (**Figure 66**).
4. Pull the external latch and disconnect the electrical connector from the sensor.

5. Use a 3/4 in. deep socket and loosen the sensor. When the socket turns easily, remove the socket and completely unscrew the sensor by hand.
6. Install a *new* sensor and start it by hand. Using the socket, tighten the sensor to 124-142 in.-lb. (14-16 N•m).
7. Apply a light coat of dielectric compound to the electrical connector prior to installing it.
8. Install the electrical connector and push it on until it locks into place.
9. Move the rubber boot back over the electrical connector.
10. Attach the negative battery cable.
11. Install the seat as described in Chapter Fifteen.

Attitude Sensor Removal/Installation

The attitude sensor is located within the camshaft position sensor assembly and is an integral part of the stator plate assembly. It cannot be replaced separately.

To replace the sensor, refer to *Ignition System (Carbureted Models), Stator Plate Removal and Installation* in this chapter.

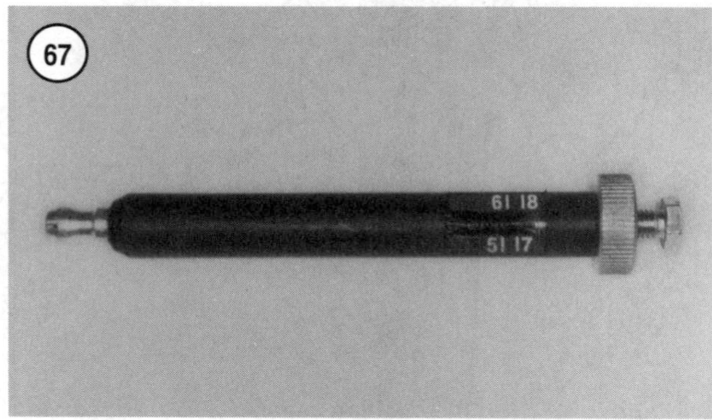

IGNITION MODULE (CARBURETED MODELS)

Removal/Installation

1984-1990 models

1. Disconnect the negative battery cable as described in this chapter.
2A. On FXR series models, remove the right frame cover.
2B. On FLH and FLT series models, remove the inner fairing as described in Chapter Fifteen.
3. Follow the wiring harness from the ignition module to where it connects to the sensor plate. Disconnect the electrical connector.
4. Remove the ignition module ground wire.
5. Disconnect the wire harness connections from the ignition coil and the VOES unit.

NOTE
On 1985 FXWG, FXSB and FXEF models, the ignition module is located behind the voltage regulator. On 1986 FXWG models, it is located under the oil tank.

6. Disconnect the fasteners securing the ignition module and remove the ignition module assembly.
7. Install by reversing these removal steps while noting the following:
   a. Clean the ground wire connector at the frame.
   b. Apply a light coat of dielectric compound to the electrical connector prior to installing it.
   c. Tighten the fasteners securely.

1991-1994 models

1. Disconnect the negative battery cable as described in this chapter.
2A. On FXR series models, remove the right frame cover.
2B. On FLH and FLT series models, remove the inner fairing as described in Chapter Fifteen.
3. Follow the wiring harness from the ignition module to where it connects to the sensor plate. Disconnect the electrical connector.
4. Remove the ignition module ground wire.
5. Disconnect the wire harness connections from the ignition coil and the VOES unit.
6. Disconnect the fasteners securing the ignition module to the left side of the steering head or to the left fairing bracket. Remove the ignition module assembly.
7. Install by reversing these removal steps while noting the following:
   a. Clean the ground wire connector at the frame.

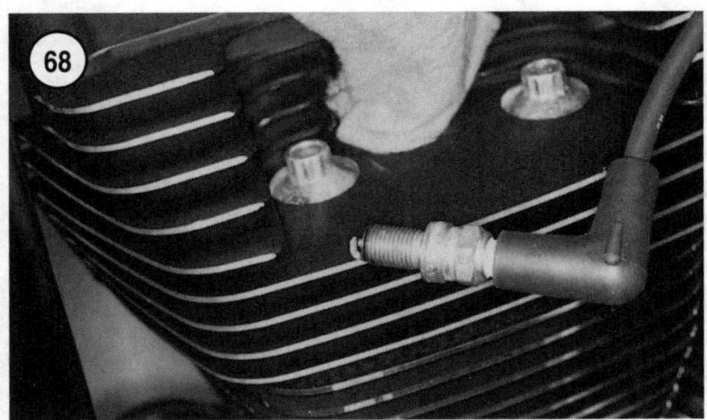

b. Apply a light coat of dielectric compound to the electrical connector prior to installing them.
c. Tighten the fasteners securely.

1995-1998 models

1. Disconnect the negative battery cable as described in this chapter.
2. Remove the right saddlebag as described in Chapter Fifteen.
3. Remove the right frame cover.
4. Push the 8-place Deutsch connector downward and unsnap the clip from the T-stud on the side of the battery box.
5. Depress the latches on the side of the connector housing and separate the connector.
6. Remove the screws securing the ignition module to the side of the battery box. Remove the ignition module assembly.
7. Install by reversing these removal steps while noting the following:
   a. Apply a light coat of dielectric compound to the electrical connector prior to installing it.
   b. Tighten the screws securely.

ELECTRONIC CONTROL MODULE (FUEL-INJECTED MODELS)

Removal/Installation

The electronic control module (ECM) is located under the right frame cover on the electrical bracket.

1. Disconnect the negative battery cable as described in this chapter.
2. Remove the seat and the right saddlebag as described in Chapter Fifteen.
3. Remove the right frame cover.
4. Remove the nuts securing the electrical bracket assembly and the ECM to the side of the battery box.
5. Carefully pull the assembly away from the battery box and place it on the rear footboard.
6. Pull the rubber boot away from the 35-pin electrical connector on the ECM.
7. Disengage the locking tab on the ECM and work that side of the connector free.
8. Disengage the hook on the opposite side of the connector and disconnect it from the ECM.
9. Remove the mounting tabs on the ECM from the boots attached to the electrical bracket and remove the ECM.
10. Install the ECM by reversing these steps while noting the following:
    a. Apply a light coat of dielectric compound to the 35-pin electrical connector prior to installing it.
    b. To avoid pin damage, always connect the 35-pin connector to the ECM prior to attaching the ECM to the electrical bracket.

9

IGNITION COIL

Performance Test

1. Disconnect the plug wire and remove one of the spark plugs as described in Chapter Three.

NOTE

A spark tester is a useful tool for testing the ignition system spark output. ***Figure 67*** *shows the Motion Pro Ignition System Tester (part No. 08-0122). This tool is inserted in the spark plug cap, and the base is grounded against the cylinder head. The air gap is adjustable, and it allows the visual inspection of the spark while testing the intensity of the spark.*

2. Insert a clean shop cloth into the spark plug hole in the cylinder head to lessen the chance of gasoline vapors being emitted from the hole.
3. Insert the spark plug (**Figure 68**) or spark tester (**Figure 69**) into the cap. Touch the spark plug base against the cylinder head to ground it. Position the spark plug so the electrode is visible.

WARNING

Mount the spark plug or tester away from the spark plug hole in the cylinder so that the spark or tester cannot ignite the gasoline vapors in the cylinder. If the engine is flooded, do not perform this test. The firing of the spark plug can ignite fuel that is ejected through the spark plug hole.

NOTE

If not using a spark tester, always use a new spark plug for this test procedure.

4. Turn the engine over with the kickstarter or electric starter. A fat blue spark should appear across the spark plug electrode or spark tester. If there is strong sunlight on the plug or tester, shade it so the spark is more visible. Repeat for the other cylinder.

WARNING

*If necessary, hold the spark plug wire with a pair of insulated pliers. Do **not** hold the spark plug, wire or connector, or a serious electrical shock can result.*

5. If a fat blue spark appears, the ignition coil is good. If not, perform the following resistance test.

Resistance Test

1. Remove the ignition coil as described in this section.
2. Disconnect the secondary wires from the ignition coil.
3. Measure the primary coil resistance between terminals A and B and then terminals B and C (**Figure 70**) at the back side of the ignition coil. The specified resistance is in **Table 4**.
4. Measure the secondary coil resistance between the spark plug leads of the secondary coil terminals (**Figure 70**). The specified resistance is in **Table 4**.
5. If the resistance is less than specified, there is most likely a short in the coil windings. Replace the coil.
6. If the resistance is more than specified, this might indicate corrosion or oxidation of the coil terminals. Thoroughly clean the terminals. Then spray them with an aerosol electrical contact cleaner. Repeat Step 3 and Step 4, and if the resistance is still high, replace the coil.
7. If the coil exhibits visible damage, it should be replaced as described in this section.
8. Install the ignition coil as described in this section.

Removal/Installation

1. Disconnect the negative battery cable as described in this chapter.
2. Remove the fuel tank as described in Chapter Eight.
3. On the left side, remove the ignition coil cover.
4. Loosen the ignition coil mounting bolts (**Figure 71**).

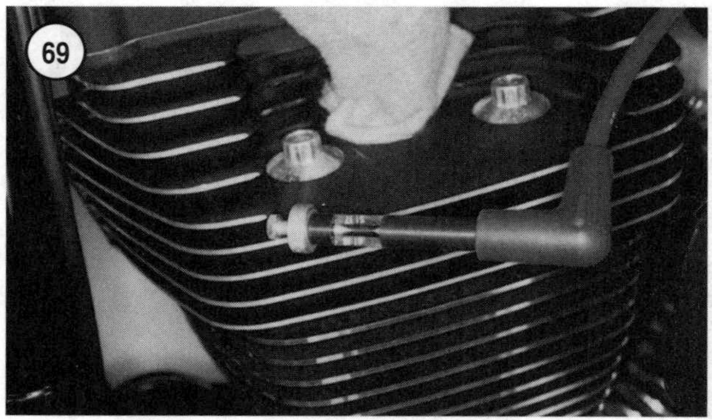

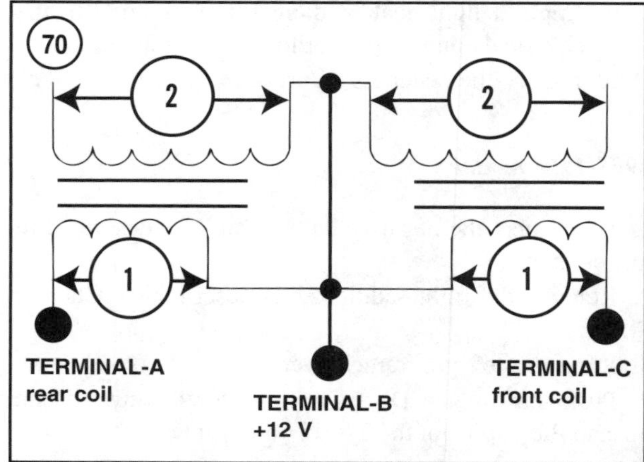

NOTE

Label all wiring connectors prior to disconnecting them in the following steps.

5. Disconnect the primary wire connector (A, **Figure 72**) from the ignition coil.
6. Grasp the rubber boot (B, **Figure 72**) at the end of the spark plug cable as close to the ignition coil as possible and disconnect the secondary cable from the ignition coil.

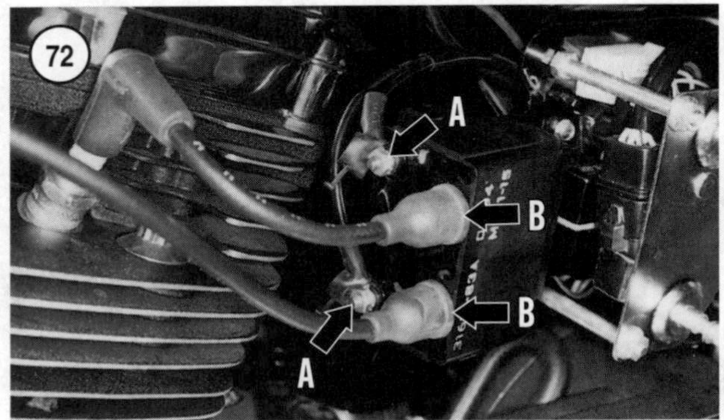

7. Remove the bolts loosened in Step 4. Remove the nut plate located behind the ignition coil.

8. Remove the ignition coil.

9. Install by reversing these removal steps. Make sure all electrical connectors are corrosion-free and tight.

CAUTION
When replacing an ignition coil on older models, make sure the coil is marked ELECTRONIC ADVANCE. Installing an older ignition coil could damage electronic ignition components.

SPARK PLUG CABLES

Resistance Check

1. Remove the secondary spark plug cables from the ignition coil and spark plugs.
2. Check the resistance of the cables as follows:
   a. Cable length of 4.5 in. (114 mm) (carbureted models): 1125-2624 ohms.
   b. Cable length of 6.5 in. (165 mm) (fuel-injected models): 1625-3790 ohms.
   c. Cable length of 19 in. (483 mm) (all models): 4750-11,077 ohms.
3. Replace cables that are worn or damaged or that do not meet the resistance specifications. Install only exact replacement cables for best results.
4. Install the spark plug cables to the ignition coil and spark plugs. Push the rubber boots on the secondary cable against the ignition coil posts to ensure a moisture-proof seal.

STARTING SYSTEM

When servicing the staring system, refer to the wiring diagrams located at the end of this manual.

CAUTION
Do not operate the starter for more than five seconds at a time. Let it cool approximately ten seconds before operating it again.

Troubleshooting

Refer to Chapter Two.

Starter Removal/Installation (1984-1988 FXR, FLH and FLT Series Models)

1. Disconnect the negative battery cable as described in this chapter.
2. Disconnect the solenoid cable at the starter (**Figure 73**).
3. Remove the bolts securing the starter to the transmission side door.
4. Remove the starter throughbolts.

NOTE
Because the throughbolts are no longer holding the starter assembly together, hold the starter and both end covers to prevent the starter from falling apart when removing it in Step 5.

5. Remove the starter housing and drive gear as an assembly (**Figure 74**) from the primary chaincase.

6. Install by reversing these steps while noting the following:
   a. First install the drive gear onto the drive shaft and then install the starter motor onto the primary chaincase.
   b. On FXR models, install the negative battery cable onto the right mounting stud.
   c. On FLH and FLT models, install the negative battery cable onto the left mounting stud.
   d. Tighten starter bolts or nuts to 124-142 in.-lbs. (14-16 N•m).
   e. Tighten mounting bracket nuts to 20-25 in.-lbs. (2-3 N•m).
   f. Tighten the solenoid cable nut to 65-80 in.-lbs. (7-9 N•m).

Starter Removal/Installation (1985-1986 FXWG, FXEF and FXSB Models)

1. Disconnect the negative battery cable as described in this chapter.
2. Disconnect the solenoid cable at the starter.
3. Remove the fasteners securing the master cylinder reservoir bracket to the transmission housing.
4. Remove the starter bracket throughbolts (**Figure 75**) at the rubber mount stud.
5. Remove the starter throughbolts.

NOTE

Because the throughbolts are no longer holding the starter assembly together, hold the starter and both end covers to prevent the starter from falling apart when removing it in Step 6.

6. Remove the starter.
7. Install by reversing these removal steps while noting the following:
   a. Starter through-bolts: 20-25 in.-lbs. (2-3 N•m).
   b. Starter terminal nut: 65-80 in.-lbs. (7-9 N•m).
   c. Outer through-bolt nut (**Figure 75**): 20-25 in.-lbs. (2-3 N•m). Install a new nut during assembly.
   d. Rubber mount stud: 71 in.-lbs. (8 N•m).
   e. Master cylinder reservoir bracket: 13-16 ft.-lbs. (18-22 N•m).

Starter Removal (1989-1998 Models)

1. Remove the seat as described in Chapter Fifteen.
2. Disconnect the negative battery cable as described in this chapter.

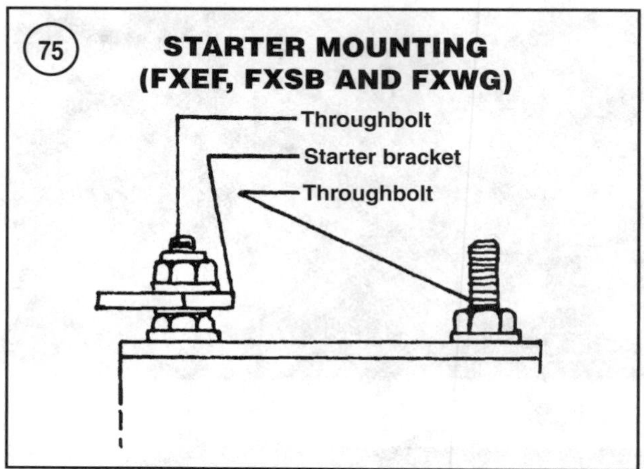

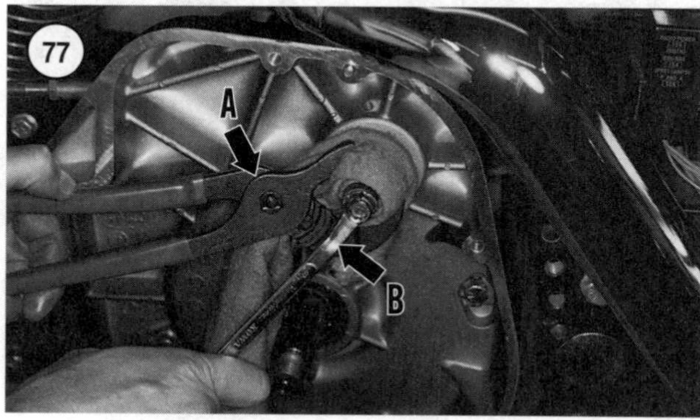

3. Remove the primary drive cover as described in Chapter Five.
4. Straighten the tab on the lockplate (**Figure 76**).
5. Wrap the pinion gear with a cloth to protect the finish. Then secure it with pliers (A, **Figure 77**).
6. Loosen and remove the bolt (B, **Figure 77**), lockplate and thrust washer from the starter jackshaft assembly and the end of the starter.

7. Remove the pinion gear (**Figure 78**) and spring from the jackshaft.
8. Remove the jackshaft assembly and the coupling from the inner housing.
9. Remove the rear exhaust pipe (A, **Figure 79**) as described in Chapter Seven.
10. Remove the bolt and the cover from the end of the starter.
11. Disconnect the solenoid electrical connector (B, **Figure 79**) from the starter.
12. Slide back the rubber boot, remove the nut, and disconnect the positive cable from the starter terminal.
13. Remove the starter mounting bolts and washers. Note the location of the negative ground cable under the front bolt and washer.
14. Pull the starter straight out of the crankcase and remove it.

NOTE
On 1989-1993 models, the jackshaft-to-starter coupling might come off with the starter, or it might stay attached to the jackshaft. If the coupling comes off with the starter, place it back onto the jackshaft. The coupling on 1989 models is symmetrical; either coupling end can be installed over the jackshaft. The coupling on 1990-1993 models is asymmetrical; install the coupling so that the end with the counterbore faces the jackshaft. On 1994-1998 models, the coupling will stay on the starter shaft.

15. If necessary, service the starter as described in this chapter.

Starter Installation (1989-1998 Models)

1. Install the jackshaft (**Figure 80**) into the inner housing if it was removed. Push it in until it stops.
2. On 1989-1993 models, position the coupling with its counterbore facing toward the jackshaft. On all models, install the coupling (**Figure 81**) into the inner housing bushing.
3. Install the spring (**Figure 82**) onto the jackshaft.
4. Install the pinion gear (**Figure 83**) onto the jackshaft.
5. Push in on the pinion gear (A, **Figure 84**) and install the bolt, lockplate and thrust washer (B) onto the jackshaft.
6. Push the assembly on until it bottoms.
7. Align the lockplate tab with the thrust washer. Then insert the tab into the notch in the end of the jackshaft.
8. Screw the bolt into the starter shaft by hand.

9. Wrap the pinion gear with a cloth to protect the finish. Then secure it with pliers (A, **Figure 77**).

10. Tighten the bolt (B, **Figure 77**) onto the starter shaft to 84-108 in.-lbs. (9-12 N•m). Bend the outer lockplate tab against the bolt head (**Figure 76**).

11. To make sure that the components have been installed correctly, perform the following:

   a. Install the clutch shell onto the transmission mainshaft.
   b. With the starter not engaged, the pinion gear (A, **Figure 85**) must not engage the clutch shell gear (B).
   c. To check for proper engagement, pull out the pinion gear and engage it with the clutch shell gear. Then rotate the clutch shell in either direction and make sure the pinion gear rotates with it.
   d. If engagement is incorrect, remove the clutch shell and correct the problem.
   e. Remove the clutch shell.

12. Install the primary cover as described in Chapter Five.

13. Install the rear exhaust pipe as described in Chapter Eight.

14. Connect the negative battery cable.

15. Install the seat.

Starter Disassembly (1984-1988 Models)

Refer to **Figure 86**.

1. Clean all grease, dirt and carbon from the case and end covers.

2. Remove the starter housing bolts (if they were reinstalled after removing the starter from the motorcycle).

3. Remove the rear cover screws and remove the rear cover. The rear cover screws secure the brush holder to the rear cover.

4. Use a piece of wire and lift the brush springs away from the brushes. Remove the brushes from the brush holder.

NOTE

Note the number of thrust washers on the shaft next to the commutator. Install the same number when reassembling the starter.

5. Remove the armature and field frame.

6. Inspect the starter assembly as described in this chapter.

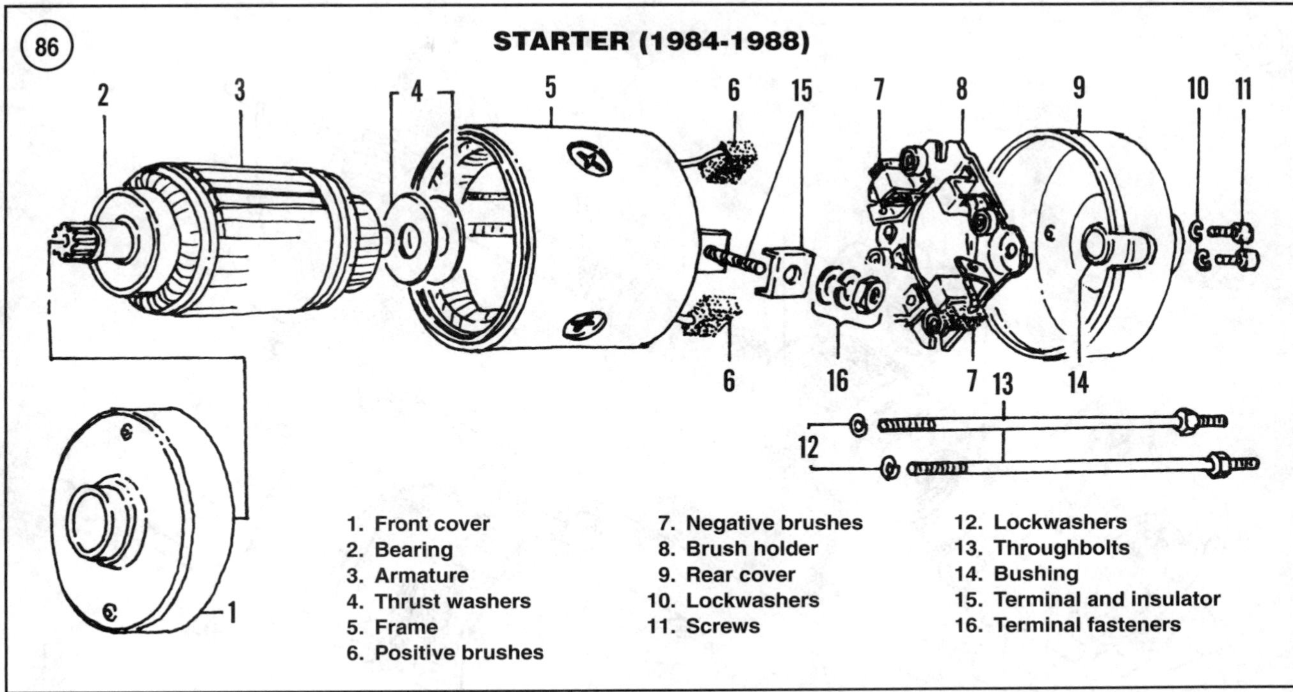

Starter Assembly (1984-1988 Models)

Refer to **Figure 86**.

1. Position the armature with the commutator side facing down toward the brush holder side and install the armature into the frame.
2. Install the front cover over the armature shaft and engage it with the frame.
3. Install the brush holder into the frame.
4. Install the two positive brushes as follows:
   a. The positive brushes are soldered to the field coil assembly.
   b. Make a small hook from a piece of wire and pull a positive brush spring out of its brush holder.
   c. Insert the positive brush into its brush holder.
   d. Release the spring so that tension is applied against the brush. Remove the hook.
   e. Repeat for the other positive brush.
5. Install the two negative brushes as follows:
   a. The negative brushes are mounted onto the brush holder.
   b. Make a small hook from a piece of wire and pull a negative brush spring out of its brush holder.
   c. Insert the negative brush into its brush holder.
   d. Release the spring so that tension is applied against the brush. Remove the hook.
   e. Repeat for the other negative brush.
6. Install the thrust washers onto the armature shaft.
7. Align the slot in the rear cover with the terminal in the frame and install the rear cover. Install the throughbolts through the starter assembly.
8. Secure the brush holder to the rear cover with the two screws and washers. Tighten the screws securely.

Starter Disassembly (1989-1998 Models)

Refer to **Figure 87**.

NOTE
*If only the solenoid assembly requires service, refer to **Starter Solenoid** in this chapter.*

1. Clean all grease, dirt and carbon from the exterior of the starter assembly.
2. Remove the two throughbolts (**Figure 88**).
3. Remove the two drive housing Phillips screws (**Figure 89**) and lockwashers.
4. Tap the drive housing and remove it from the starter assembly (**Figure 90**).
5. Disconnect the *C* terminal field wire (A, **Figure 91**) from the solenoid housing.
6. Separate the field coil (B, **Figure 91**) from the solenoid housing (C).
7. Remove the end cap screws, washers and O-rings (A, **Figure 92**). Then remove the end cap (B, **Figure 92**).

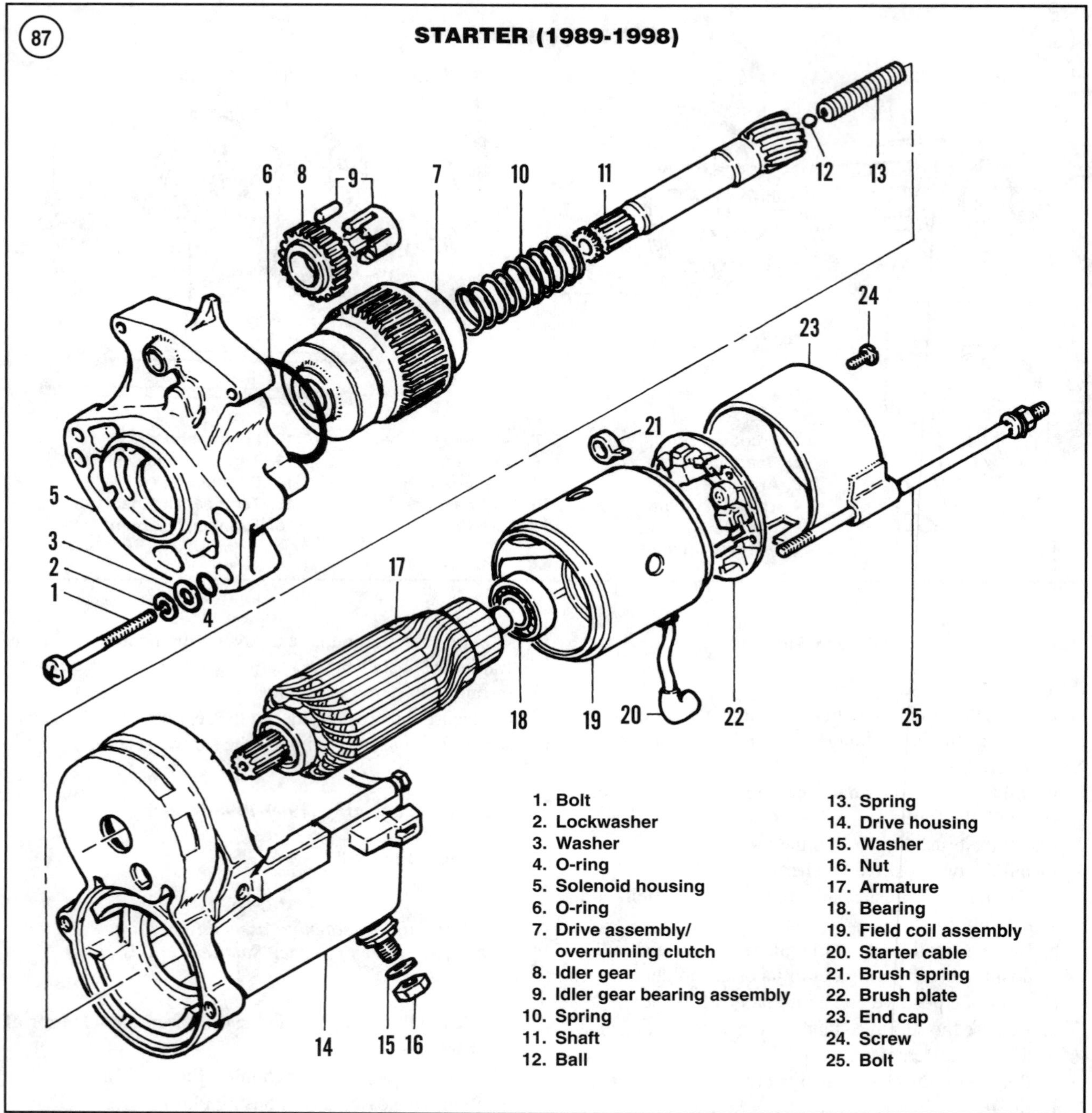

8. Pull the brush holder (A, **Figure 93**) away from the commutator and remove the armature (B) from the field coil assembly.

9. Remove the two field coil brushes from the brush holder (**Figure 94**).

10. Clean all grease, dirt and carbon from the armature, field coil assembly and end covers.

CAUTION

Be extremely careful when selecting a solvent to clean the electrical components. Do not immerse any of the wire windings in solvent because the insulation can be damaged. Wipe the windings with a cloth lightly moistened with solvent. Then allow the solution to dry thoroughly.

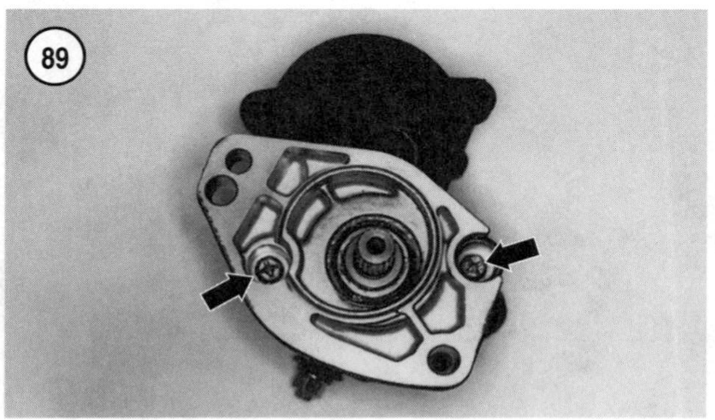

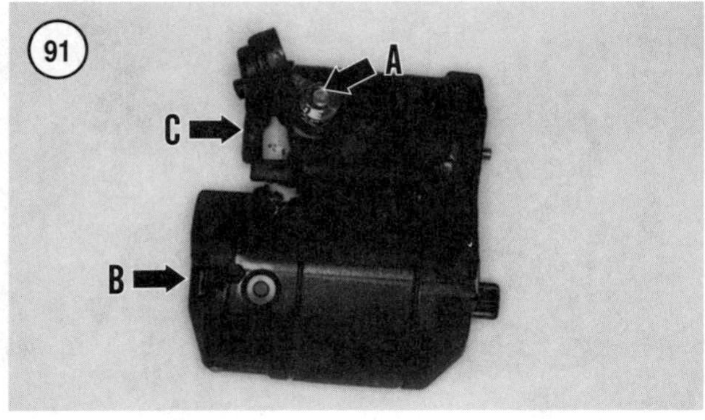

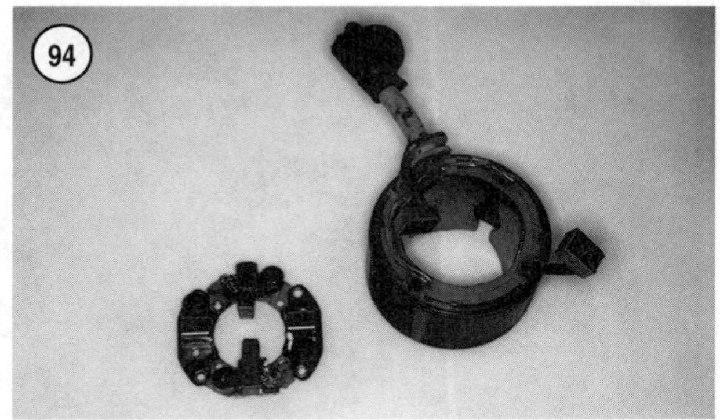

11. To service the drive housing assembly, refer to *Starter Drive Housing Disassembly/Inspection/Assembly* in this section.

12. To service the solenoid housing, refer to *Starter Solenoid Disassembly/Inspection/Assembly* in this chapter.

Starter Assembly

1. If serviced, assemble the drive housing as described in this section.

95

98

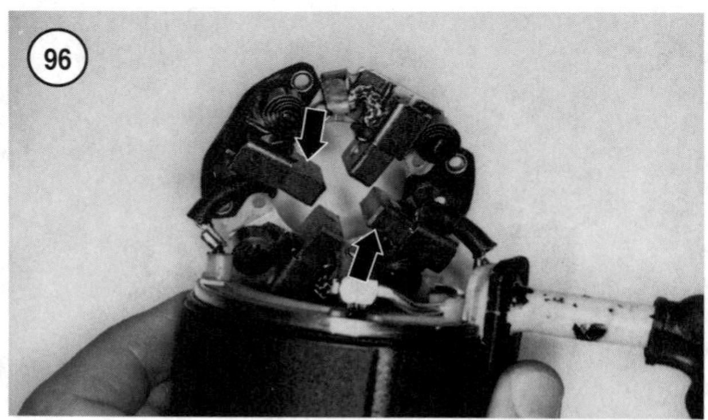

96

99

97

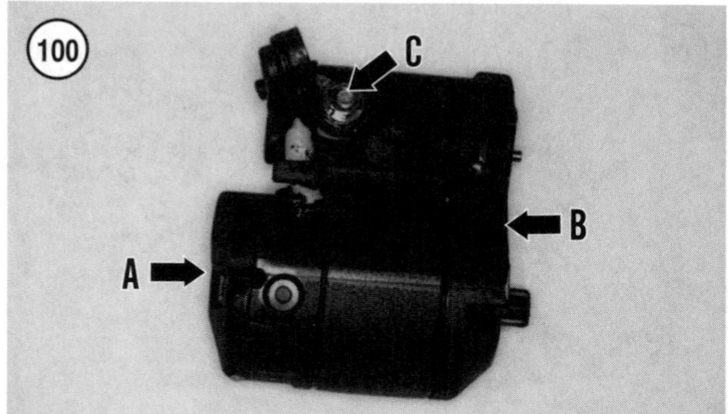

100

101

2. If serviced, assemble the solenoid housing as described in this chapter.

3. Lubricate the armature bearings with high-temperature grease.

4. Install two *new* O-rings onto the field coil shoulders (**Figure 95**).

5. Install the two field coil brushes into the brush plate holders (**Figure 96**).

6. Install the armature partway through the field coil as shown in A, **Figure 93**. Then pull the brushes back and push the armature forward so that when released, all of the

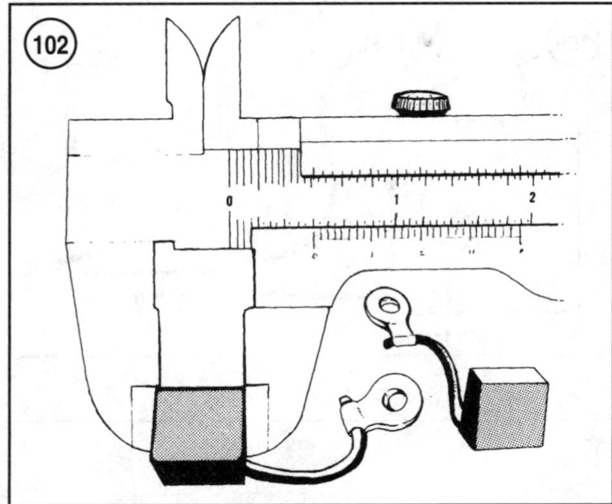

102

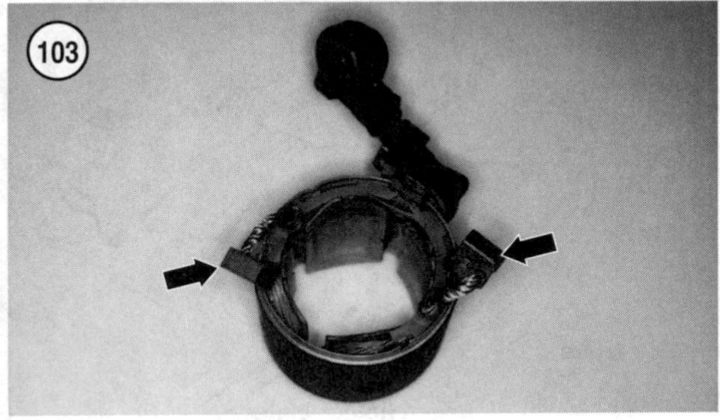

103

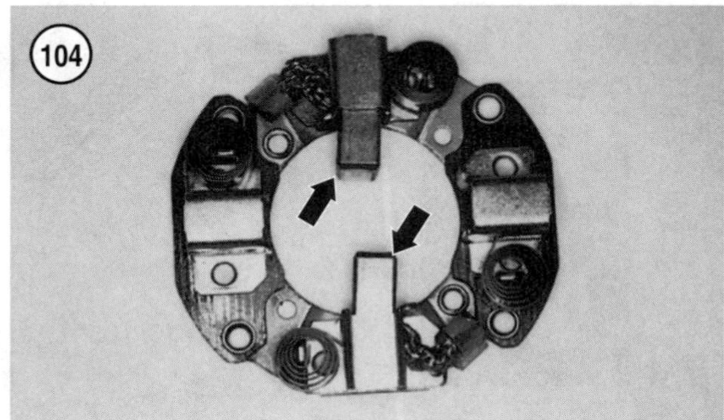

104

105

brushes contact the commutator as shown in **Figure 97** and **Figure 98.**

7. Install the end cap (**Figure 99**) and the two screws, washers and O-rings. Tighten the screws securely.
8. Align the field coil (A, **Figure 100**) with the solenoid housing (B) and assemble both housings. Hold the assembly together while installing the drive housing in Step 9.
9. Align the drive housing (**Figure 101**) with the field coil and solenoid housing assembly and install it. Install the two drive housing screws and lockwashers (**Figure 89**) and tighten securely.
10. Install the two throughbolts, washers and O-rings (**Figure 88**) and tighten securely.
11. Reconnect the *C* terminal field wire (C, **Figure 100**) at the solenoid housing.

Starter Inspection (All Years)

1. Measure the length of each brush with a vernier caliper (**Figure 102**). If the length is less than the minimum specified in **Table 5**, replace all of the brushes as a set. See **Figure 103** for the field coil and **Figure 104** for the brush holder.

NOTE
*The field coil brushes (**Figure 103**) are soldered in position. To replace, unsolder the brushes by heating their joints with a soldering gun, then pull them out with a pair of pliers. Position the new brushes and solder in place with rosin core solder. Do not use acid core solder.*

2. Inspect the commutator. The mica should be below the surface of the copper commutator segments. If the commutator bars are worn to the same level as the mica insulation, have the commutator serviced by a dealership or electrical repair shop.
3. Inspect the commutator copper segments for discoloration. If the commutator segments are rough, discolored or worn, have the commutator serviced by a dealership or electrical repair shop.
4. On 1991-1998 models, measure the outer diameter of the commutator with a vernier caliper (**Figure 105**). Replace the armature if worn to the service limit in **Table 5**.
5. Perform the following:

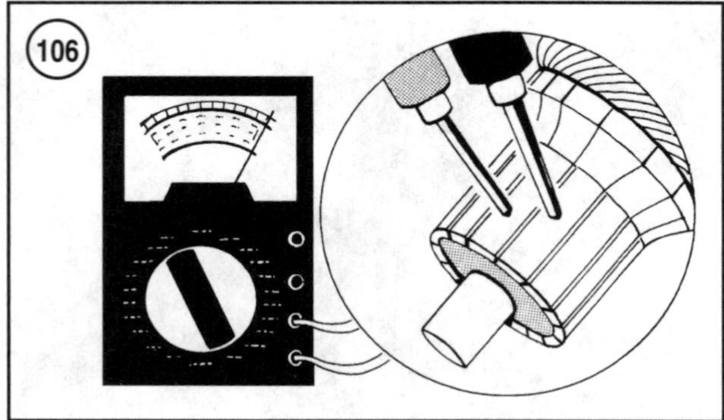

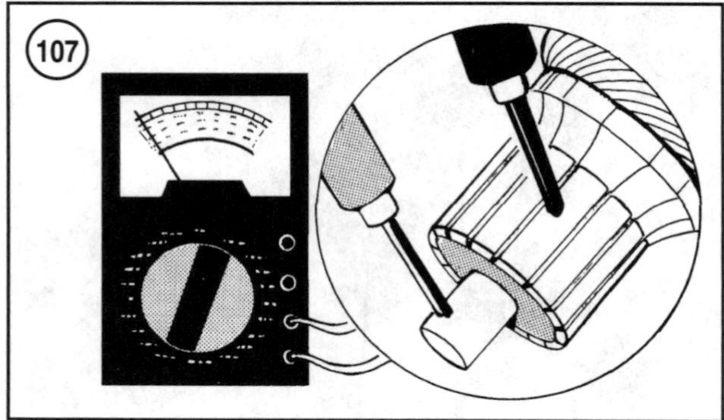

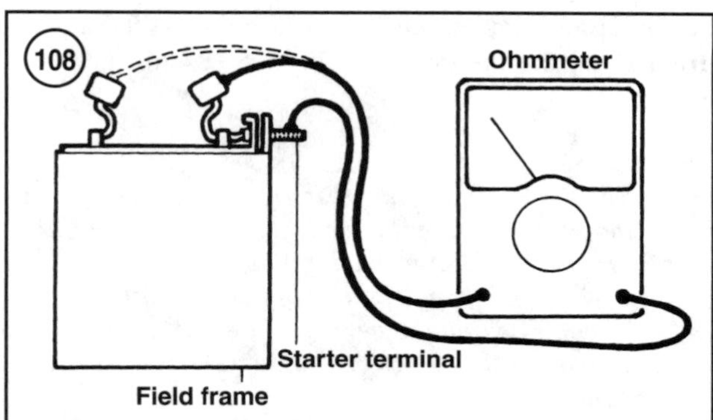

a. Check for continuity between the commutator bars (**Figure 106**); there must be continuity between pairs of bars.
b. Check for continuity between any commutator bar and the shaft (**Figure 107**). There must be no continuity.
c. If the unit fails either of these tests, replace the armature.

6. Perform the following:
   a. Check for continuity between the starter cable terminal and each field frame brush (**Figure 108**); there must be continuity.

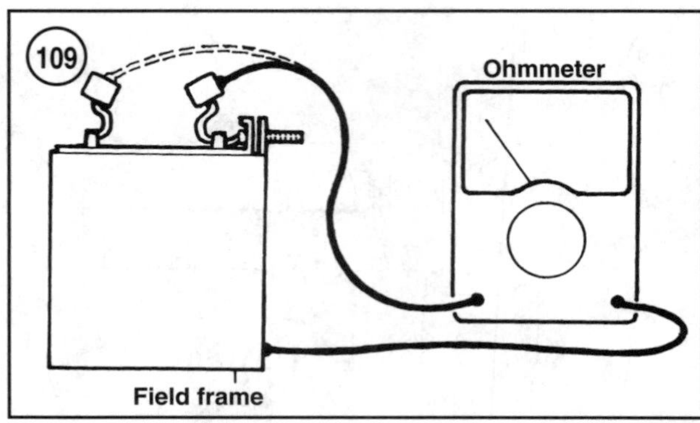

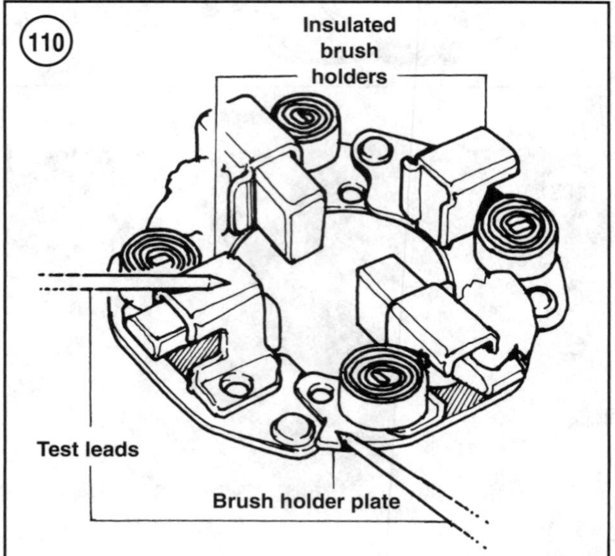

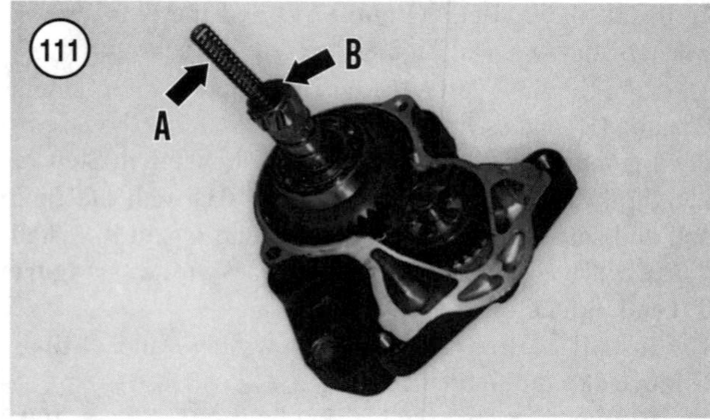

   b. Check for continuity between the field frame housing and each field frame brush (**Figure 109**); there must be no continuity.
   c. If the unit fails either of these tests, replace the field frame assembly.

112

113

114

115

116

7. Check for continuity between the brush holder plate and each brush holder (**Figure 110**); there must be no continuity. If the unit fails this test, replace the brush holder plate.
8. Service the armature bearings as follows:
   a. Check the bearings on the armature shaft. Replace worn or damaged bearings.

NOTE
The armature shaft bearings have different part numbers. Identify the old bearings before removing them.

   b. Check the bearing bores in the end cover and solenoid housing. Replace the cover or housing if the area is worn or cracked.

9

Starter Drive Housing Disassembly/ Inspection/Assembly

The drive housing was removed during starter disassembly.
1. Remove the return spring (A, **Figure 111**), ball, clutch shaft (B) and drive spring from the drive assembly.
2. Remove the idler gear (**Figure 112**) from the drive housing.
3. Remove the idler gear bearing and cage assembly (A, **Figure 113**). There are five individual bearing rollers (**Figure 114**).
4. Remove the drive assembly (B, **Figure 113**).
5. Replace the drive housing O-ring (**Figure 115**) if worn or damaged. Lubricate the O-ring with high-temperature grease.
6. Inspect the idler gear bearing and cage assembly (**Figure 114**) for worn or damaged parts.

CAUTION
*The drive assembly (**Figure 116**) is a sealed unit. Do not clean or soak it in any type of solvent.*

7. Inspect the drive assembly and its bearings (**Figure 116**) for worn or damaged parts. If the bearings are worn or damaged, replace the drive assembly and bearings as a set.
8. Assemble the drive housing by reversing these steps, while noting the following.
9. Lubricate the following components with high-temperature grease:
   a. Idler gear bearing and cage assembly (**Figure 114**).
   b. Drive housing O-ring and shaft (**Figure 115**).
   c. Drive assembly (**Figure 116**).
   d. Clutch shaft, drive spring, return spring and ball.
10. Install the idler gear bearing and cage assembly so that the open side of the cage (A, **Figure 113**) faces toward the solenoid housing.

STARTER SOLENOID

1984-1988 Models

The solenoid is separate from the starter.

Removal/installation

1. Disconnect the negative battery cable as described in this chapter.

NOTE
Refer to the following illustrations to make sure the wiring cables at the solenoid correspond to those on the motorcycle.

2. Label and disconnect the wiring cables from the solenoid terminals. Refer to **Figures 117-121**.
3. Remove the solenoid mounting bolts and remove the solenoid, spacer, spring and gasket.
4. Install by reversing these removal steps. Tighten the mounting bolts securely.

Disassembly/assembly

Refer to **Figure 122**.
1. Clean the solenoid housing of all dirt and residue before disassembling it.
2. Remove the nut and lockwasher from the short large terminal.
3. Remove the nut and lockwasher from the small outer diameter terminal.
4. Remove the two screws and washers securing the solenoid cover to the solenoid and remove the cover.

117 SOLENOID (1984 AND LATE 1985-1988 FLH AND FLT)

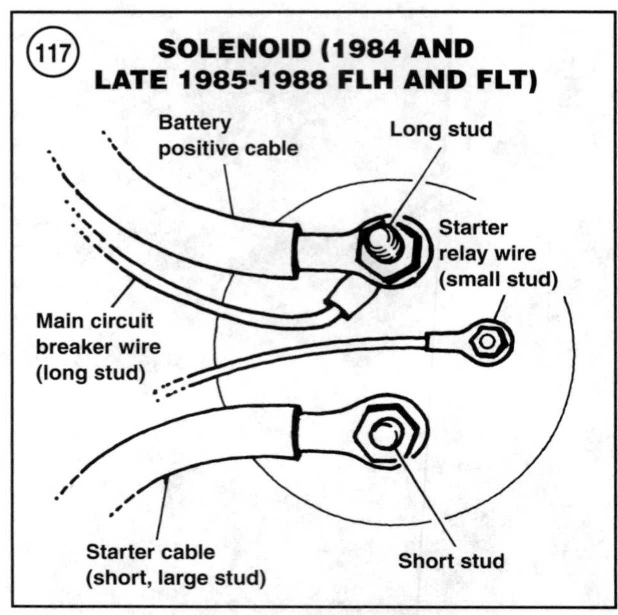

118 SOLENOID (1984 AND LATE 1985-1988 FXR SERIES)

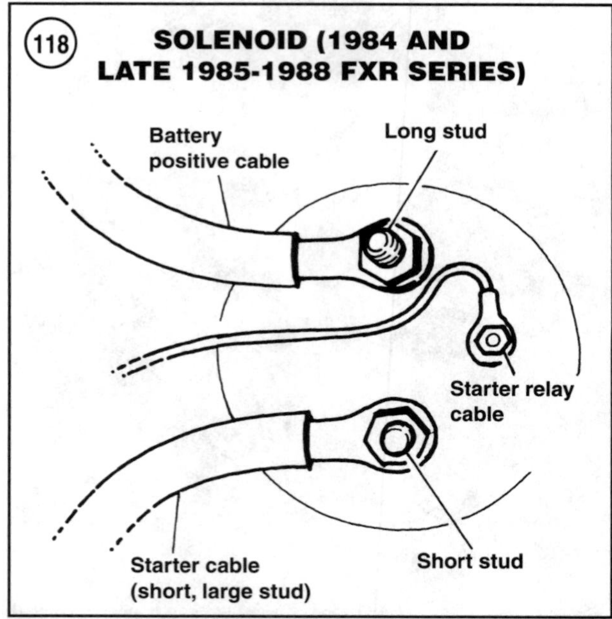

NOTE
When disassembling the inner plunger assembly in Step 5, note the position and condition of the copper washer as it is installed on the plunger between the plastic washer and seat. If one side of the copper washer is grooved or burnt, label the washer as to how it is positioned on the plunger and then turn it around during assembly so that the worn side is facing in the opposite direction.

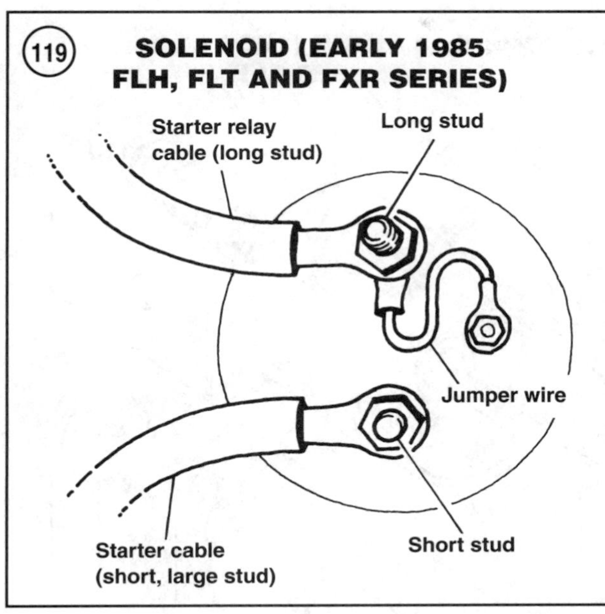

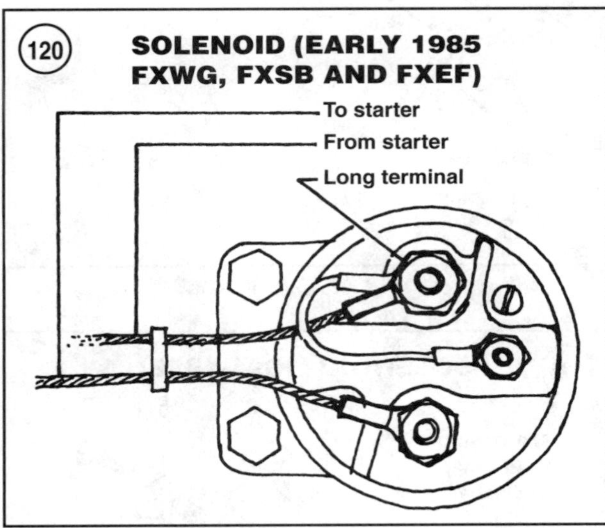

Because the inner plunger assembly components are not available separately, this will extend the life of the copper washer.

5. Refer to **Figure 122**, disassemble the solenoid assembly, keeping the outer and inner plunger parts separate.

6. Clean and inspect the solenoid components as described in this section.

7. Assembly is the reverse of these steps. Note the following.

8. Apply a light coat of Lubriplate 110 to the plunger and the plunger bore.

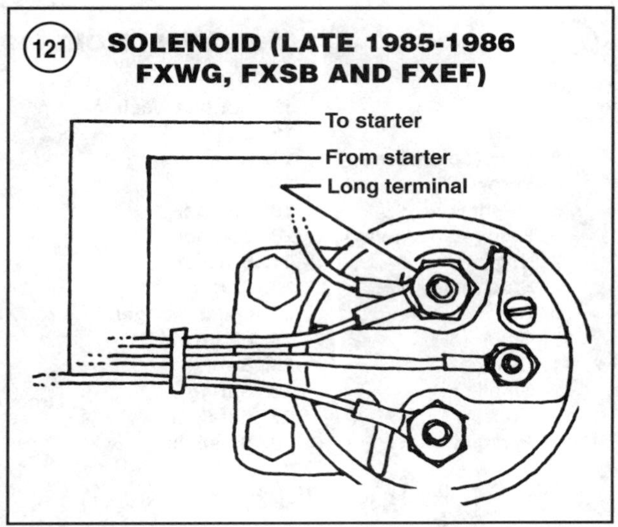

9. Assemble the inner plunger assembly as follows:
   a. Lay out the inner plunger components in the order shown in **Figure 122**. Note that the plunger has two grooves; these are identified as groove No. 1 and groove No. 2 in **Figure 122**. Note also that the two collars are identical.
   b. Install the collar into the No. 2 plunger groove so that the collar spring seat faces toward the No. 1 plunger groove.
   c. Slide the large spring over the plunger and seat it against the collar.
   d. Slide the seat over the plunger with the seat shoulder facing the No. 1 plunger groove.
   e. Slide the copper washer over the plunger and center it onto the seat shoulder installed in sub-step d.
   f. Slide the plastic washer over the plunger and seat it against the copper washer.
   g. Install the remaining collar into the No. 1 plunger groove so that the collar spring seat faces away from the assembled parts installed in sub-steps a-f.

10. Insert the plunger assembly into the plunger bore in the solenoid housing.

11. Stand the solenoid housing upright and slide the small spring over the plunger and seat it against the collar.

12. Install the gasket onto the solenoid housing.

CAUTION

When installing the solenoid cover in Step 13, route the internal solenoid wires so that they cannot contact the copper washer as it travels with the plunger during solenoid operation. Contact of these parts will eventually wear away the wire insulation and cause the circuit to remain closed.

9

(122) SOLENOID (1984-1988; TYPICAL)

1. Nut
2. Plate
3. Stud (postive relay)
4. Screw
5. Washer
6. Stud (starter relay)
7. Nut
8. Stud (starter)
9. Nut
10. Cover
11. O-ring
12. Small spring
13. Collar
14. Plastic washer
15. Contact washer
16. Seat
17. Large spring
18. Collar
19. Plunger
20. Solenoid
21. Bracket
22. Spring
23. Outer plunger
24. Large pin
25. Boot
26. Spring
27. Retainer
28. Small pin

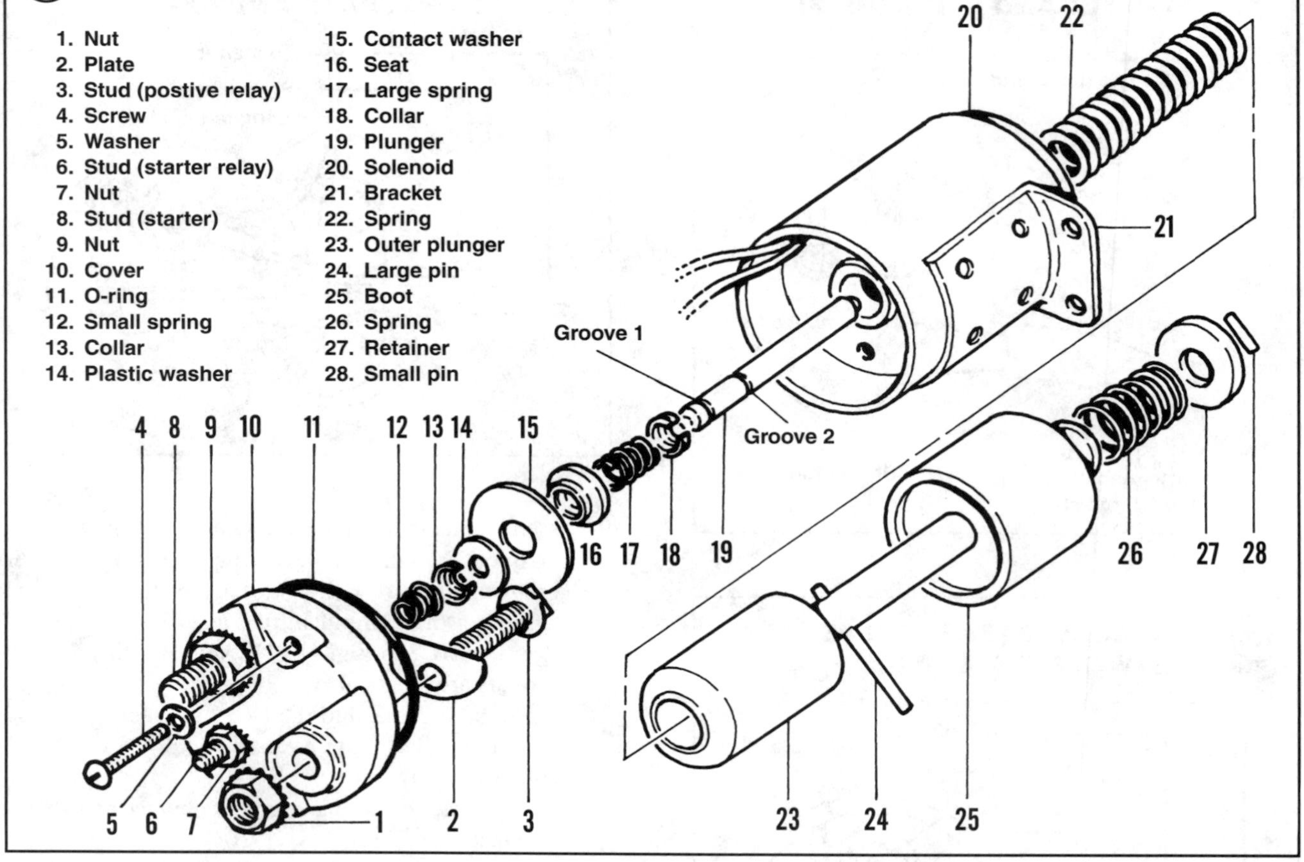

Groove 1

Groove 2

13. Align the solenoid cover with the solenoid housing and place it into position while making sure the small plunger spring, plunger and terminal enter the cover bore properly.
14. Slide a washer onto each of the screws and install the screw through the cover and into the solenoid housing. Tighten the screws securely. Install the terminal nuts and washers previously removed.

Cleaning and inspection

1. Clean all parts thoroughly.
2. Visually check all parts for wear, cracks or other damage. Replace all worn or damaged parts, if available, as required. If necessary, the contact washer can be turned around. Refer to *Disassembly/assembly.*

1989-1990 Models

Service procedures are not available for these model years.

(123) SOLENOID (1991-1998)

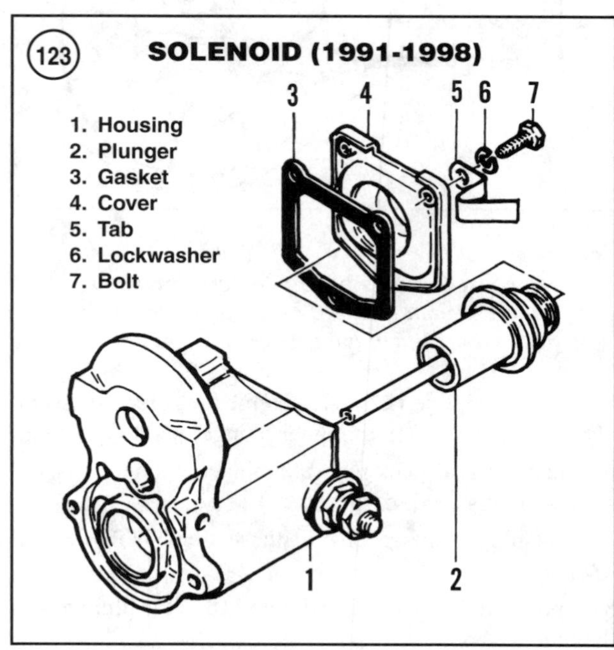

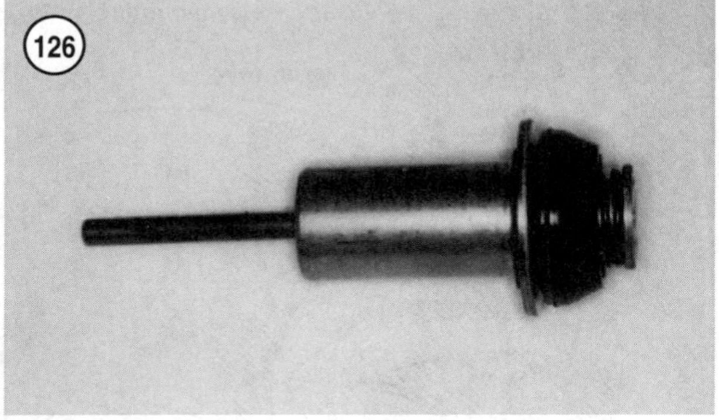

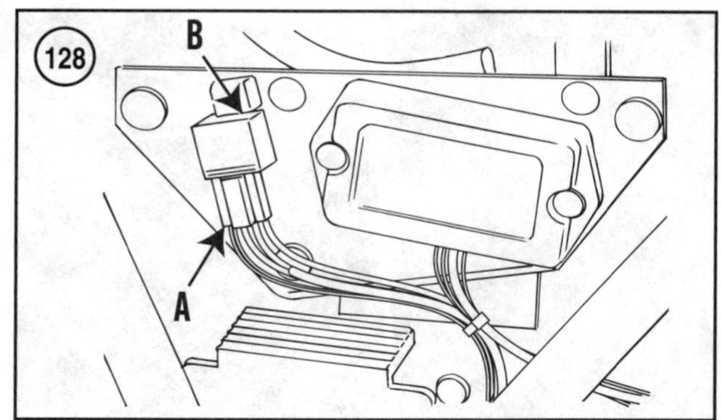

1991-1998 Models

Disassembly/inspection/assembly

1. Remove the solenoid housing (**Figure 123**) as described during starter disassembly.
2. Remove the screws, washers and clip securing the end cover to the solenoid housing. Then remove the end cover (**Figure 124**) and the gasket.
3. Remove the plunger assembly (**Figure 125**).
4. Inspect the plunger (**Figure 126**) for scoring, deep wear marks or other damage.
5. Inspect the solenoid housing (**Figure 127**) for wear, cracks or other damage.
6. The solenoid housing is a separate assembly and cannot be serviced. If any part is defective, the solenoid housing must be replaced as an assembly.
7. Assemble the solenoid housing by reversing these steps. Lubricate the solenoid plunger with high-temperature grease.

STARTER RELAY

Removal/Installation

1A. On 1984-1994 and 1999 FXR series models, perform the following:

a. Remove the right side cover.

NOTE

On early 1985 models, label the wiring at the starter relay before disconnecting it.

b. Disconnect the wiring or the electrical connector (A, **Figure 128**) at the starter relay (B). Remove the starter relay (**Figure 129**).

1B. On FXWG, FXSB and FXEF models, perform the the following:

a. Remove the right side cover.

b. Disconnect the wiring or the electrical connector at the starter relay. Remove the starter relay.

1C. On 1984-early 1986 FLH and FLT series models, perform the following:

a. Remove the seat as described in Chapter Fifteen.

NOTE
On early 1985 models, label the wiring at the starter relay before disconnecting it.

b. Disconnect the wiring or the electrical connector (A, **Figure 130**) at the starter relay (B). Remove the starter relay.

c. On early 1985 FLH and FLT series models, remove the fasteners (**Figure 131**) securing the relay. Remove the starter relay.

1D. On late 1986-1993 FLH and FLT series models, perform the following:

a. Remove the right side cover.

b. Disconnect the wiring or the electrical connector (A, **Figure 132**) at the starter relay (B) and remove the starter relay.

1E. On 1994 FLH and FLT series models, perform the following:

a. Remove the headlight(s) assembly as described in Chapter Nine.

b. Disconnect the wiring or the electrical connector at the starter relay. Remove the starter relay.

1F. On 1995-1996 FLH and FLT series models, perform the following:

a. Remove the right side cover.

b. Disconnect the wiring or the electrical connector (A, **Figure 133**) at the starter relay (B). Remove the starter relay.

1G. On 1997-1998 FLH and FLT series models, perform the following:

a. Remove the seat as described in Chapter Fifteen.

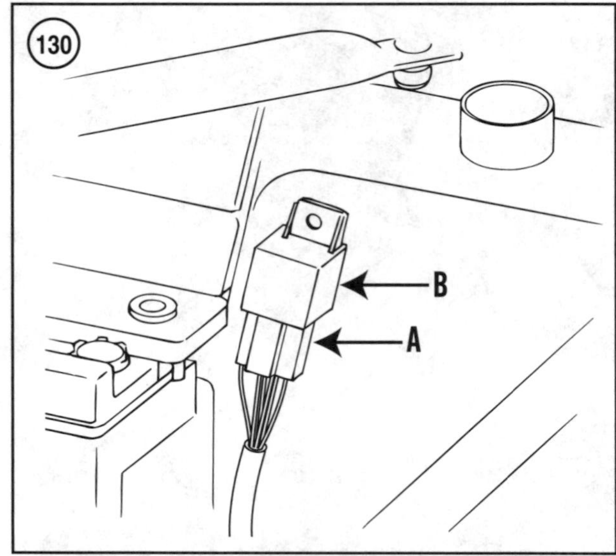

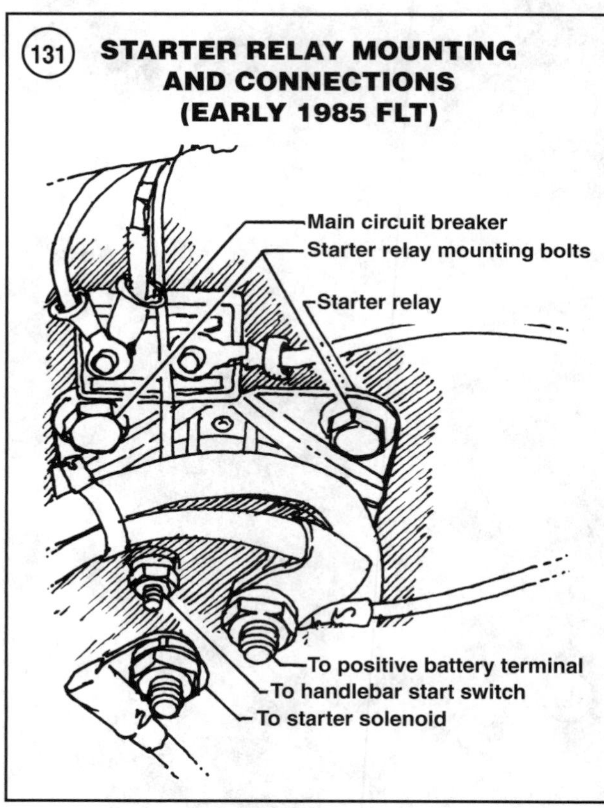

b. Use needlenose pliers and carefully pull on the starter relay tab and release it from the rubber molding (**Figure 134**).

c. Disconnect the electrical connectors from the base of the relay and remove the relay.

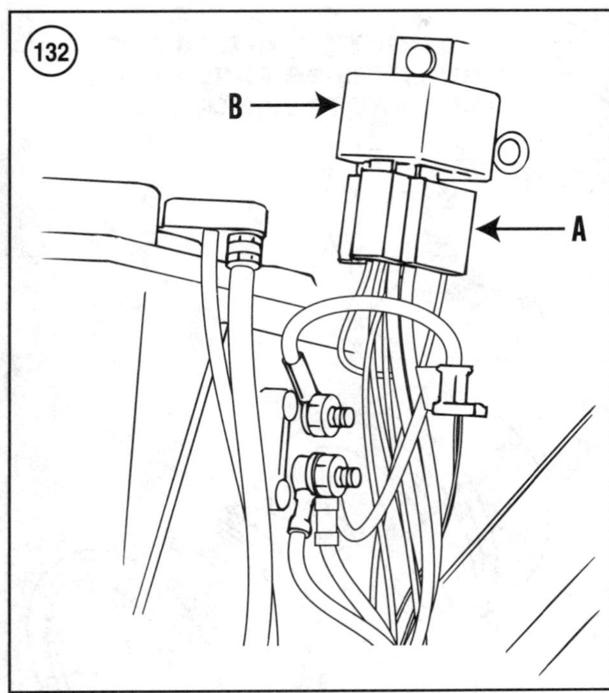

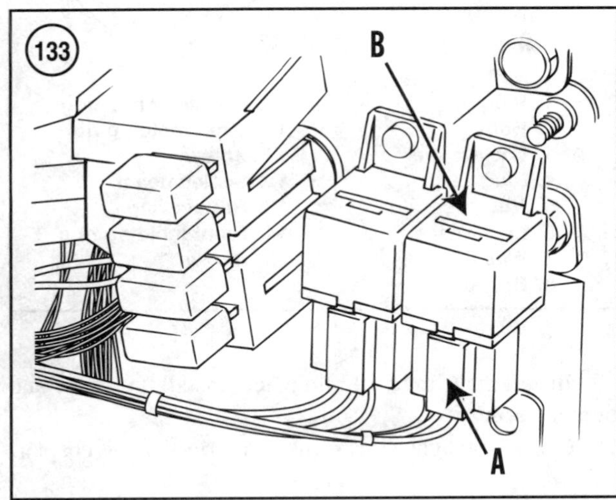

2. Install by reversing these removal steps while noting the following:
   a. Clean the wire or connector pins thoroughly with electrical contact cleaner before assembly.
   b. Install the side cover or seat.

LIGHTING SYSTEM

The lighting system consists of a headlight, passing lamps, taillight/brake light combination and turn signals.

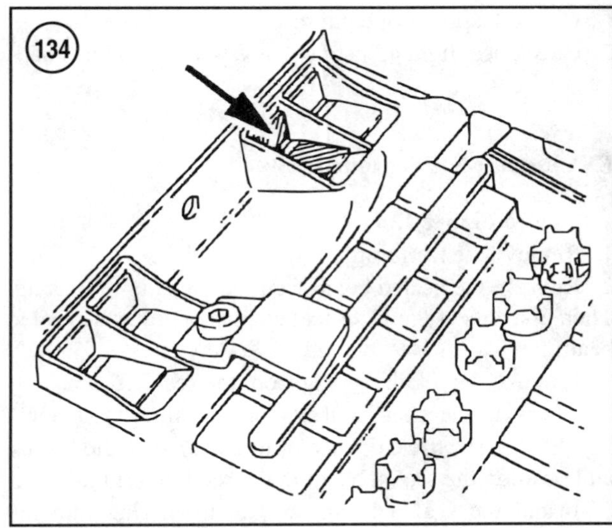

Always use a bulb with the correct wattage. The use of a higher-wattage bulb will give a dim light, and a lower-wattage bulb will burn out prematurely. Refer to **Table 6** and **Table 7** for replacement bulb specifications.

WARNING
If the headlight has just burned out or turned off, it will be hot. To avoid burned fingers, allow the bulb to cool prior to removal.

CAUTION
All models are equipped with a quartz-halogen headlight bulb. Do not touch the bulb glass. Traces of oil on the bulb will drastically reduce the life of the bulb. Clean all traces of oil from the bulb glass with a cloth moistened in alcohol or lacquer thinner.

HEADLIGHT REPLACEMENT

FXR, FXRS, FXRS-SP, FXRS-Con, FXSB and FXEF Models

Refer to **Figure 135**.

1. Remove the front molding ring clamp screw and remove the front molding ring.
2. Remove the sealed beam from the rubber ring. Then disconnect the electrical connector from the sealed beam.
3. Check the electrical contacts for corrosion or damage.
4. Plug the electrical connector into the *new* sealed beam and position the sealed beam in the rubber ring in the headlight housing.
5. Install the front folding ring and secure it with the screw. Tighten the screw securely.

9

6. Check headlight operation.
7. Check headlight adjustment as described in this chapter.

FXLR and FXWG Models

Refer to **Figure 136**.

1. Remove the trim ring.
2. Remove the sealed beam from the headlight housing. Then disconnect the electrical connector from the sealed beam.
3. Remove the retaining ring from the sealed beam.
4. Check the electrical contacts for corrosion or damage.
5. Plug the electrical connector into the *new* sealed beam and position the sealed beam in the retaining ring.
6. Install the sealed beam and retaining ring into the headlight housing.
7. Install the trim ring and secure it with the screw. Tighten the screw securely.
8. Check headlight operation.
9. Check headlight adjustment as described in this chapter.

1986-1994 FLHT Series Models

Refer to **Figure 137**.

1. Remove the screw securing the trim bezel and remove the bezel.
2. Remove the screws securing the retaining ring and remove the retaining ring.
3. Pull the lens assembly out slightly.
4. Disconnect the electrical connector from the bulb and remove the headlight assembly.
5. Remove the rubber boot at the back of the lens. Then press the wire clip together and remove the bulb.
6. Unhook the light bulb retaining clip and pivot it out of the way.
7. Remove and discard the blown bulb.
8. Align the tangs on the new bulb with the notches in the headlight lens and install the bulb.
9. Securely hook the retaining clip onto the bulb.
10. Install the rubber boot and makes sure it is correctly seated against the bulb and the retainer.
11. Correctly align the electrical plug terminals with the bulb and connect it. Push it *straight on* until it bottoms on the bulb and the rubber cover.
12. Check headlight operation.
13. Insert the headlight lens into the headlight housing and seat it correctly.
14. Install the retaining ring and screws and tighten securely.

135 **HEADLIGHT (1991-1998 FXR, FXRS, FXRS-SP, FXRS-CON, FXSB AND FXEF MODELS)**

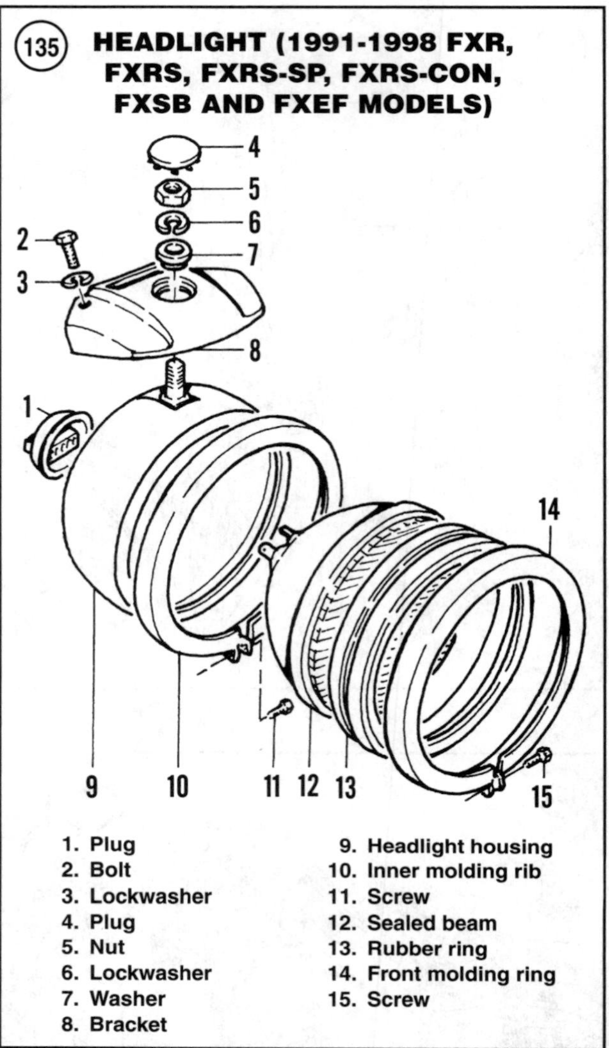

1. Plug
2. Bolt
3. Lockwasher
4. Plug
5. Nut
6. Lockwasher
7. Washer
8. Bracket
9. Headlight housing
10. Inner molding rib
11. Screw
12. Sealed beam
13. Rubber ring
14. Front molding ring
15. Screw

15. Install the trim bezel into place. Install the screw and tighten securely.
16. Check headlight adjustment as described in this chapter.

FLHR Series Models and 1995-1998 FLHT Series Models

Refer to **Figure 138** and **Figure 139**.

1. Remove the screw (A, **Figure 140**) at the base of the trim bezel (B) and remove the trim bezel from the headlight lens assembly. Do not lose the two springs on the trim bezel. Do not lose the gasket on FLHT series models.
2. Remove the screw-securing retaining ring (**Figure 141**) while holding the headlight lens assembly in place.
3. Pull the lens assembly (**Figure 142**) out of the front fairing, or headlight nacelle.

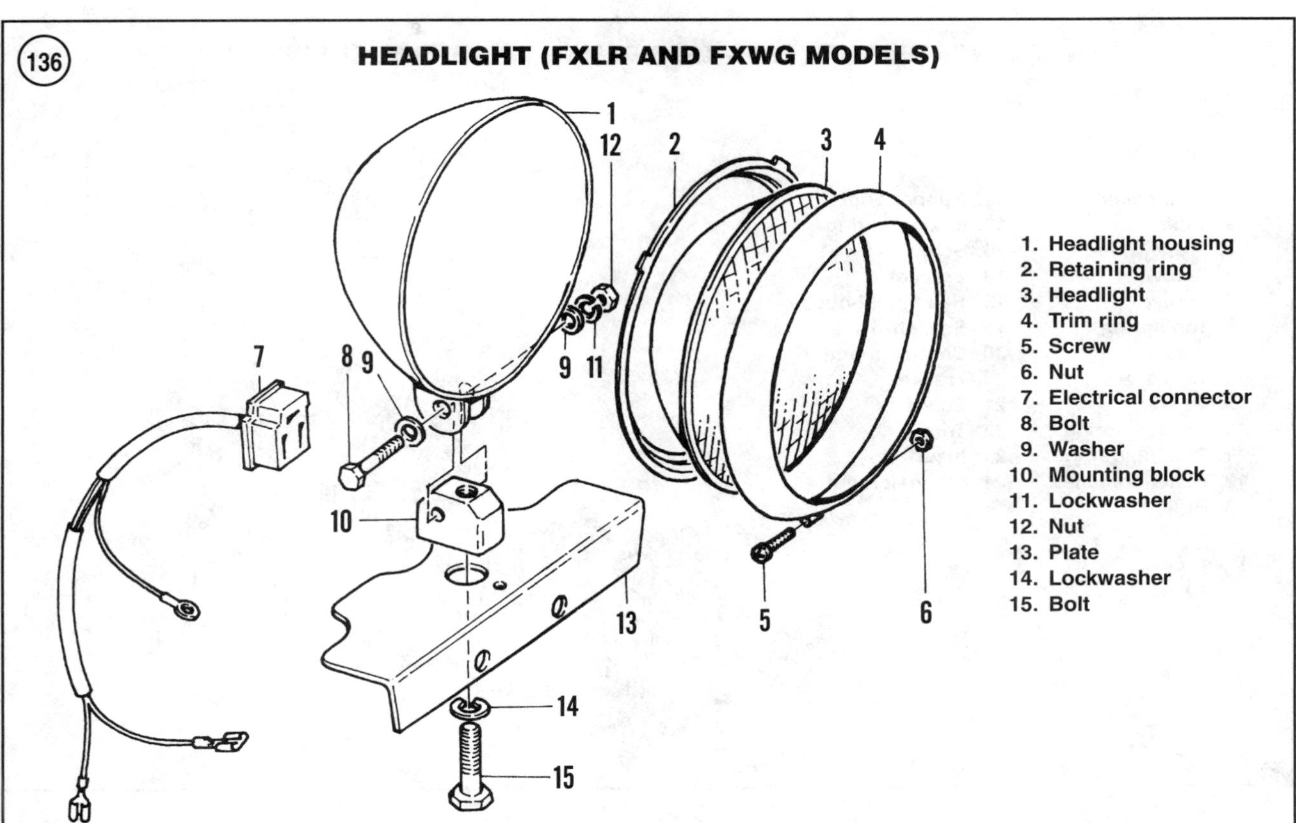

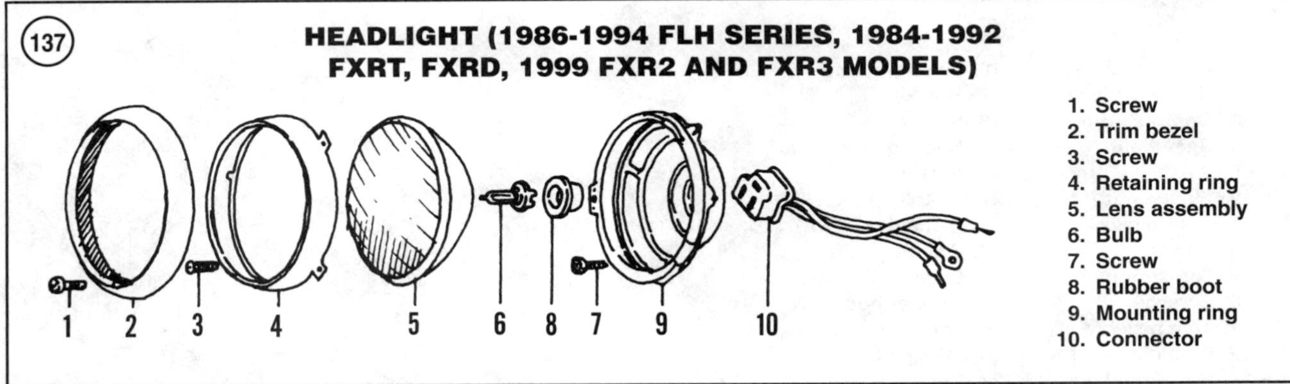

9

4. On models so equipped, squeeze the two external tabs to release the electrical connector from the lens assembly.

5. Pull *straight out*, disconnect the electrical connector from the bulb (**Figure 143**), and remove the headlight assembly.

6. Remove the rubber cover (**Figure 144**) from the back of the headlight lens. Check the rubber boot for tears or deterioration; replace if necessary.

7. Unhook the light bulb retaining clip (**Figure 145**) and pivot it out of the way.

8. Remove and discard the blown bulb (**Figure 146**).

9. Align the tangs on the new bulb with the notches in the headlight lens and install the bulb.

10. Securely hook the retaining clip onto the bulb (**Figure 145**).

11. Install the rubber boot (**Figure 144**) and make sure it is correctly seated against the bulb and the retainer.

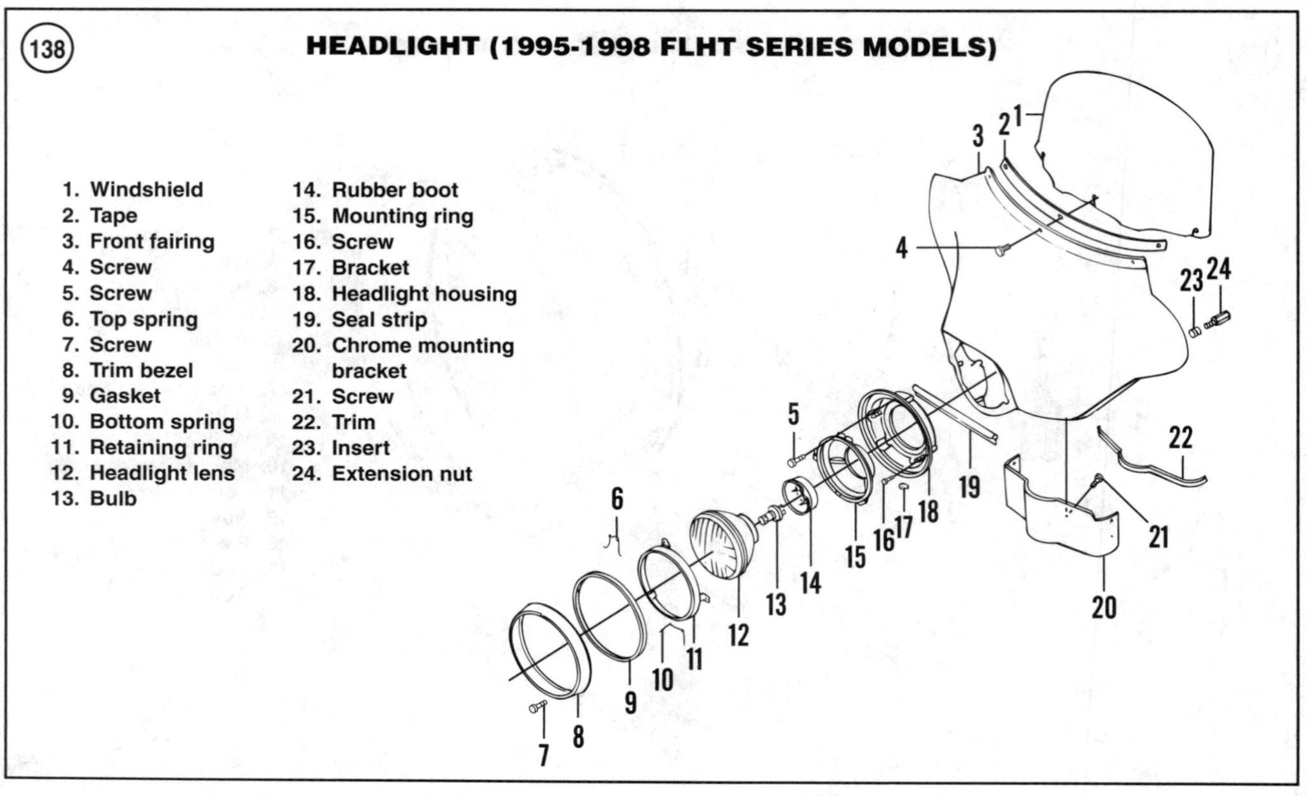
138
HEADLIGHT (1995-1998 FLHT SERIES MODELS)
1. Windshield
2. Tape
3. Front fairing
4. Screw
5. Screw
6. Top spring
7. Screw
8. Trim bezel
9. Gasket
10. Bottom spring
11. Retaining ring
12. Headlight lens
13. Bulb
14. Rubber boot
15. Mounting ring
16. Screw
17. Bracket
18. Headlight housing
19. Seal strip
20. Chrome mounting bracket
21. Screw
22. Trim
23. Insert
24. Extension nut

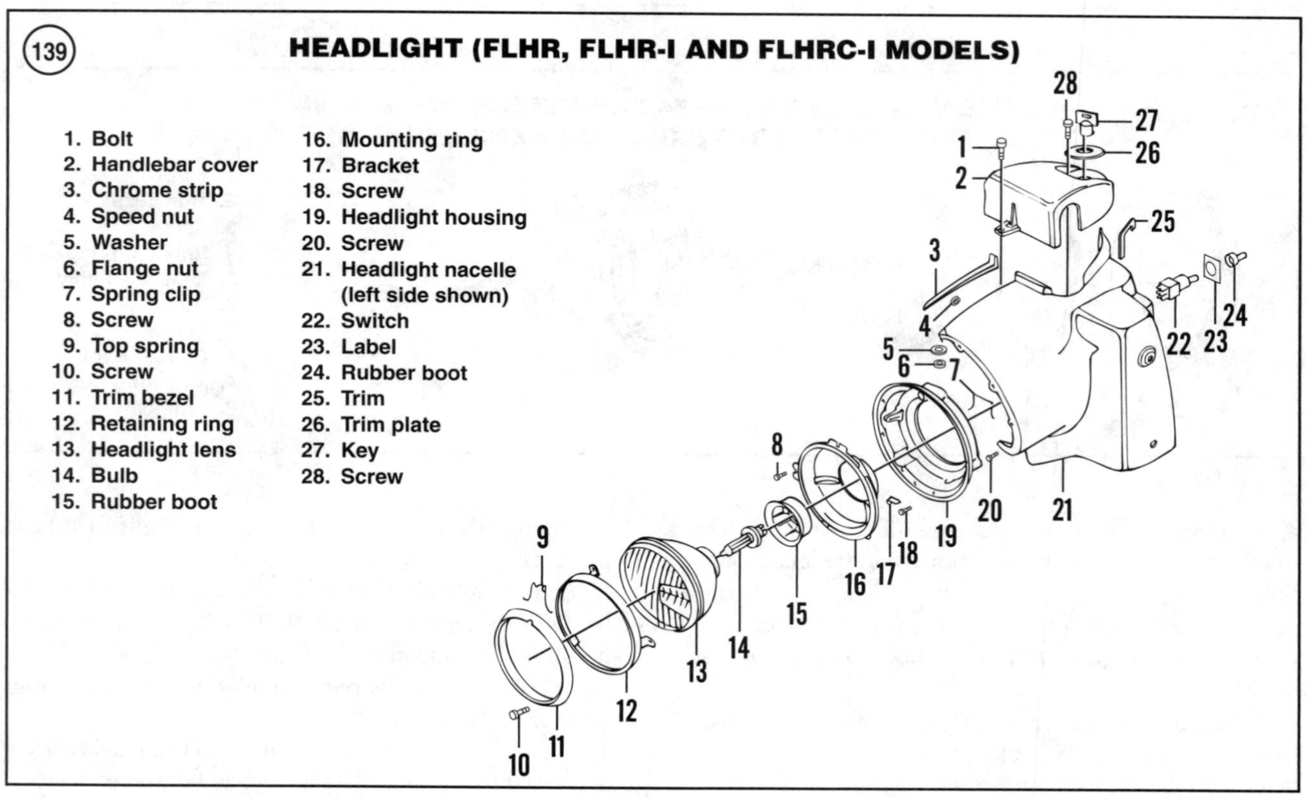
139
HEADLIGHT (FLHR, FLHR-I AND FLHRC-I MODELS)
1. Bolt
2. Handlebar cover
3. Chrome strip
4. Speed nut
5. Washer
6. Flange nut
7. Spring clip
8. Screw
9. Top spring
10. Screw
11. Trim bezel
12. Retaining ring
13. Headlight lens
14. Bulb
15. Rubber boot
16. Mounting ring
17. Bracket
18. Screw
19. Headlight housing
20. Screw
21. Headlight nacelle (left side shown)
22. Switch
23. Label
24. Rubber boot
25. Trim
26. Trim plate
27. Key
28. Screw

12. Correctly align the electrical plug terminals with the bulb and connect it. Push it *straight on* until it bottoms on the bulb and the rubber cover (**Figure 143**).

13. Check headlight operation.

14. Insert the lens (**Figure 142**) into the headlight housing and seat it correctly.

15. Install the retaining ring (**Figure 141**) and screws and tighten securely.

16. Install the square portion of the top spring (**Figure 147**) into the slot in the trim bezel and snap the trim bezel into place. Install the screw and tighten securely.

17. Check headlight adjustment as described in this chapter.

1984-1996 FLTC, FLTC-U and FLTC-UI Models

Refer to **Figure 148**.

1. Remove the headlight cover plate screws and remove the cover plate. Do not lose the spacers at the upper corners.
2. Loosen the retaining ring screws. Then rotate the retaining ring and remove it.
3. Pull the headlight lens out of the headlight housing.
4. On models so equipped, squeeze the two external tabs to release the electrical connector from the lens assembly.
5. Pull *straight out* and disconnect the electrical connector from the bulb and remove the headlight assembly.
6. Remove the rubber cover from the back of the headlight lens. Check the rubber boot for tears or deterioration; replace if necessary.
7. Unhook the light bulb retaining clip and pivot it out of the way.
8. Remove and discard the blown bulb.
9. Align the tangs on the new bulb with the notches in the headlight lens and install the bulb.
10. Securely hook the retaining clip onto the bulb.
11. Install the rubber boot and make sure it is correctly seated against the bulb and the retainer.
12. Correctly align the electrical plug terminals with the bulb and connect it. Push it *straight on* until it bottoms on the bulb and the rubber cover.
13. Check headlight operation.
14. If necessary, repeat for the other headlight lens assembly.
15. Insert the lens into the headlight housing and seat it correctly.
16. Install the retaining ring, rotate it into position and tighten the screws.
17. Install the spacers at the upper corners. Then install the headlight cover plate screws. Tighten the screws securely.
18. Check headlight adjustment as described in this chapter.

1998 FLTR and FLTR-I Models

Refer to **Figure 149**.

1. Remove the front fairing and windshield assembly as described in Chapter Fifteen.
2. Place the front fairing on a workbench covered with several towels to protect the finish.

3. Squeeze the two external tabs, pull *straight out*, and disconnect the electrical connector from the bulb terminals.
4. Remove the rubber cover from the back of the lens assembly. Check the rubber boot for tears or deterioration; replace if necessary.
5. Rotate the bulb retainer *counterclockwise* and remove it from the lens assembly.
6. Remove and discard the blown bulb.
7. Position the new bulb with the wider tab at the top. Then push the bottom of the bulb flange so the lower two tabs fit snugly in the slot of the bulb housing.
8. Place the bulb retainer and carefully rotate it *clockwise* until it is secure in the lens assembly.
9. Install the rubber boot and make sure it is correctly seated against the bulb and the retainer.
10. Correctly align the electrical plug terminals with the bulb and connect it. Push it *straight on* until it bottoms on the bulb and the rubber cover.
11. Repeat for the other bulb if necessary.
12. Install the front fairing and windshield assembly as described in Chapter Fourteen.
13. Check headlight operation.
14. Check headlight adjustment as described in this chapter.

HEADLIGHT ADJUSTMENT

Headlight adjustment will depend on the type of headlight assembly that is installed. If the headlight lens has NAL (North American Lighting) on the front of the lens (**Figure 150**), perform the steps for NAL headlights in the following procedures. If the headlight is not marked as described, refer to the *all other models* procedures.

NOTE

The 1999 FXR2 and FXR3 models are not equipped with the NAL headlight lens but are adjusted following the NAL format.

(148) **1994-1996 FLTC, FLTC-U AND FLTC-UI MODELS**

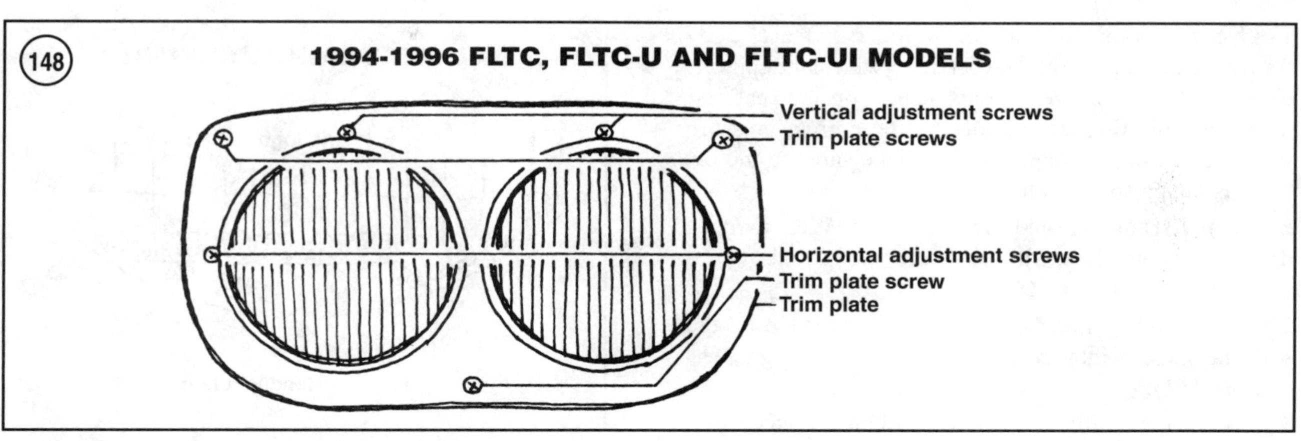

(149) **HEADLIGHT AND TURN SIGNAL ASSEMBLY (1998 FLTR AND FLTR-I MODELS)**

1. Windshield
2. Trim
3. Decal
4. Front fairing
5. Acorn nut
6. Cover plate
7. Rubber boot
8. Bulb retainer
9. Bulb
10. Lens assembly
11. Trim
12. Bezel
13. Adjust stud
14. Mounting clip
15. Wiring harness
16. Screw
17. Lens
18. Bulb
19. Turn signal base
20. Wiring harness
21. Clip
22. Well nut
23. Spacer
24. Screw
25. Trim
26. Mounting bracket
27. Stud plate
28. Plastic washer

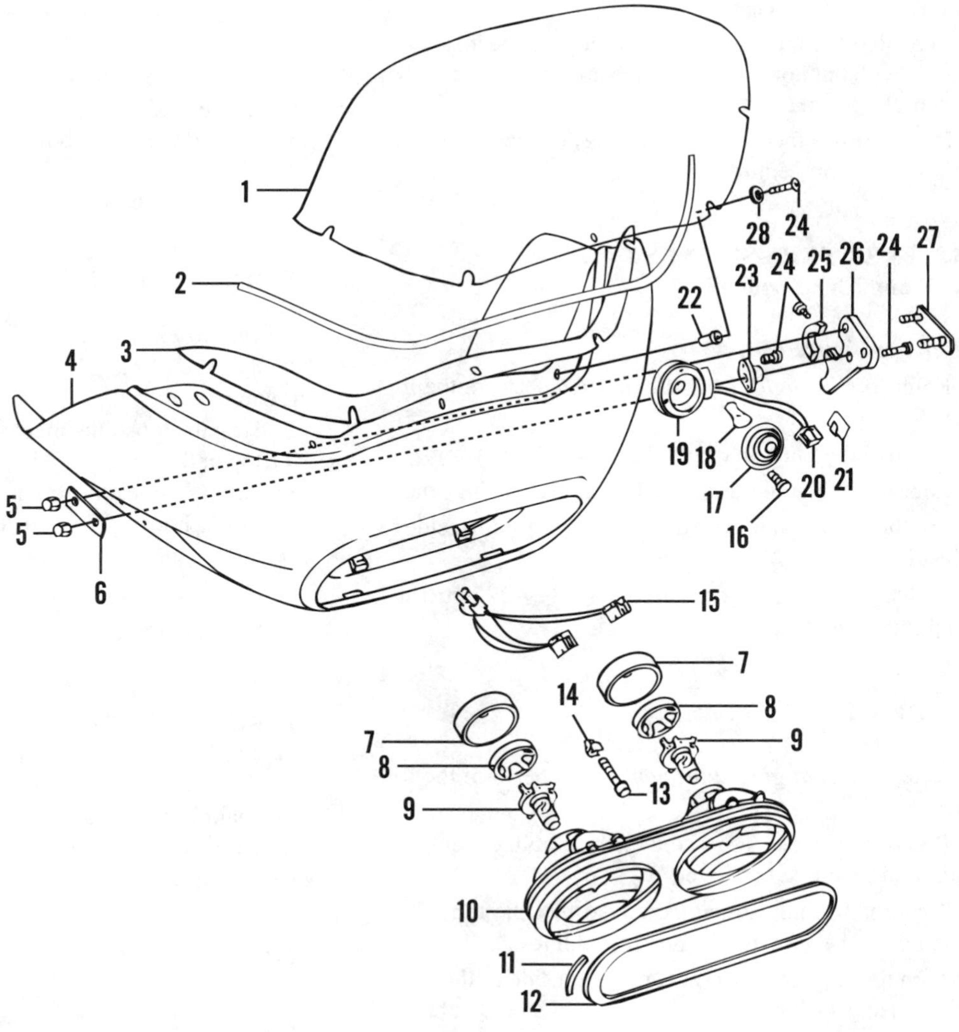

1. Place the motorcycle on a level surface 25 feet (7.6 M) from a wall (test pattern). Have a rider (with same approximate weight as the vehicle owner) sit on the seat and make sure the tires are inflated to the correct pressure when performing this adjustment. Make sure the motorcycle is facing straight ahead.

2A. On NAL models and the FXR2 and FXR3 models, draw a horizontal line, which is 35 in. (0.89 M) above the floor on a wall (**Figure 151**).

2B. On all other models, draw a horizontal line on the wall the same height as the center of the headlight lens (**Figure 152**).

3. Turn on the headlight. Switch headlight to high beam.

4A. On NAL models and the FXR2 and FXR3 models, the main bean should be centered on the horizontal line with equal areas of light above and below line as shown in **Figure 151**. There should also be equal areas of light to the left and right of center.

4B. On all other models, the top of the main beam should be even with but not higher than the horizontal line drawn in Step 2B (**Figure 152**).

5. If the beam is incorrect, adjust it as described in one of the following procedures.

FXR, FXRS, FXRS-SP, FXRS-Con, FXSB and FXEF Models

Refer to **Figure 136**.

1. Refer to *Headlight Adjustment*. Then perform the following.
2. Remove the plug on top of the headlight housing.
3. Loosen the clamp nut on the headlight housing stud.
4. Tilt the headlight up and down and from side to side to adjust it.
5. Tighten the clamp nut to 10-20 ft.-lb. (14-27 N•m) and install the snap plug.

FXRT and FXRD Models

1. Refer to *Headlight Adjustment*. Then perform the following.
2. Remove the screws securing the headlight cover to the fairing and remove the cover.
3. Turn the top adjustment screw so that the top of the main beam is even with the horizontal line.
4. Turn the adjustment screw on the left side of the headlight housing so that the light beam shines straight ahead.
5. Install the headlight cover.

(150) **NAL HEADLIGHT ASSEMBLY**

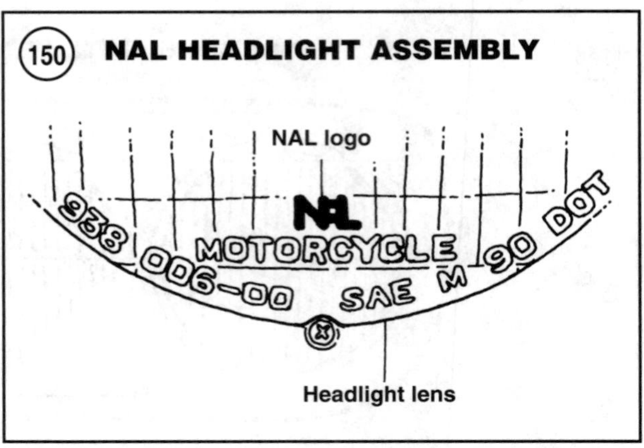

FXLR and FXWG Models

Refer to **Figure 153**.

1. Refer to *Headlight Adjustment*. Then perform the following.
2. Loosen the bottom bolt to move the headlight beam from side to side.
3. Loosen the upper bolt to move the headlight beam up and down.
4. Tighten all bolts securely.

FLH Series Models

Refer to **Figure 137**.

1. Refer to *Headlight Adjustment*. Then perform the following.
2. Turn the top adjustment screw (A, **Figure 154**) so that the top of the main beam is even with the horizontal line.
3. Turn the side adjustment screw (B, **Figure 154**) of the headlight housing so that the light beam shines straight ahead.

FLT Series Models

Refer to **Figure 148**.

1. Refer to *Headlight Adjustment*. Then perform the following.
2. Turn the vertical adjustment screws so that the top of the main beam is even with the horizontal line.
3. Turn the horizontal adjustment screws so that the light beam shines straight ahead.

1998 FLTR and FLTR-I Models

Refer to **Figure 149**.

1. Refer to *Headlight Adjustment*. Perform the following.

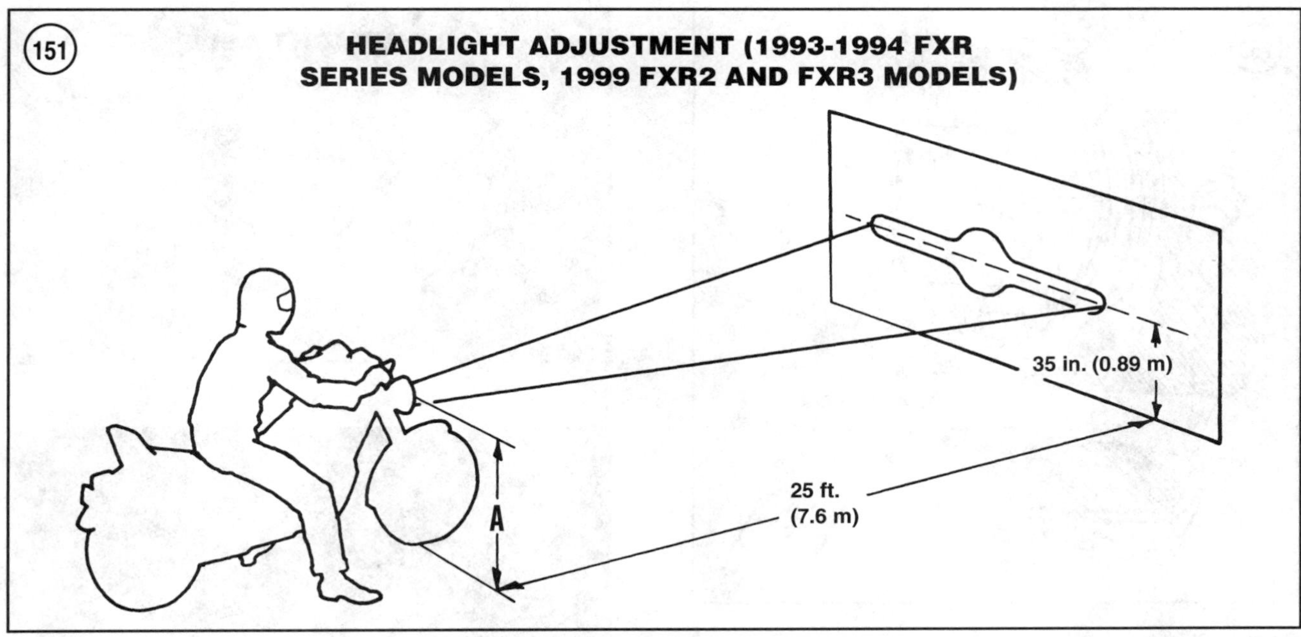

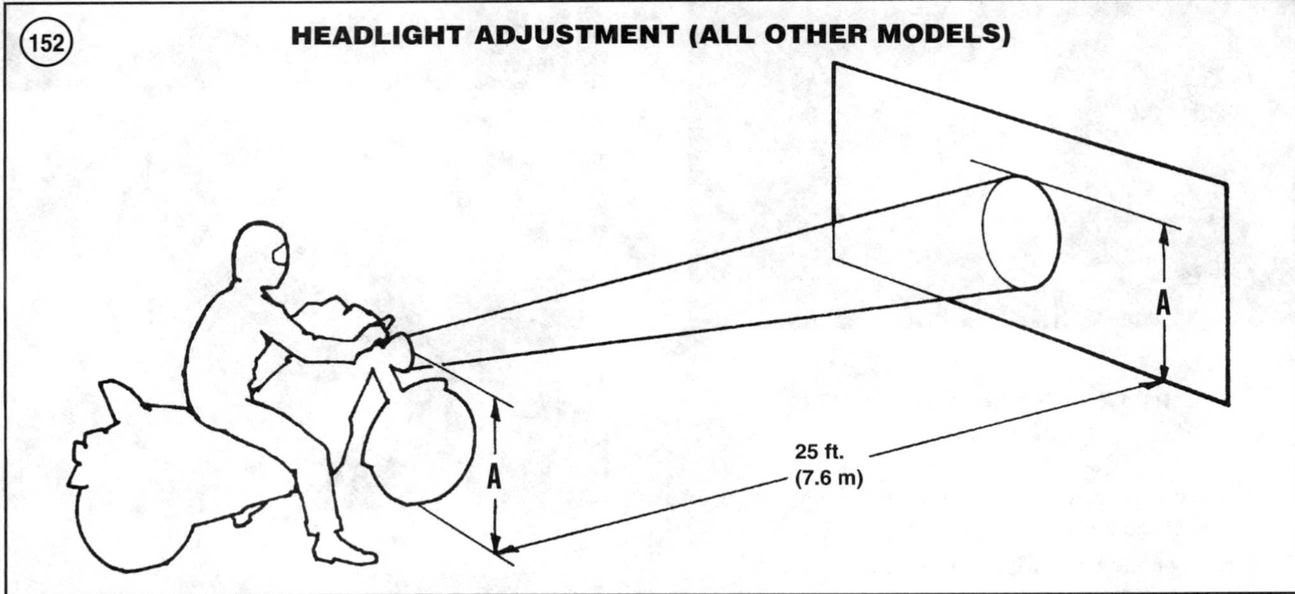

NOTE
The hex adjusters are located on each side of the lower inner surface of the front fairing.

2. Use a 4.5-mm socket on a flexible extension to adjust the hex adjusters.

3. Refer to **Table 8** for the correct rotation of the adjusters to achieve correct headlight aim.

TAILLIGHT/BRAKE LIGHT REPLACEMENT

1. Remove the screws securing the lens. Remove the lens and gasket (**Figure 155**).
2. Push in on the bulb (**Figure 156**) and remove it.
3. Replace the bulb and install the lens.
4. Securely tighten the screws. Do not overtighten the screws because the lens might crack.

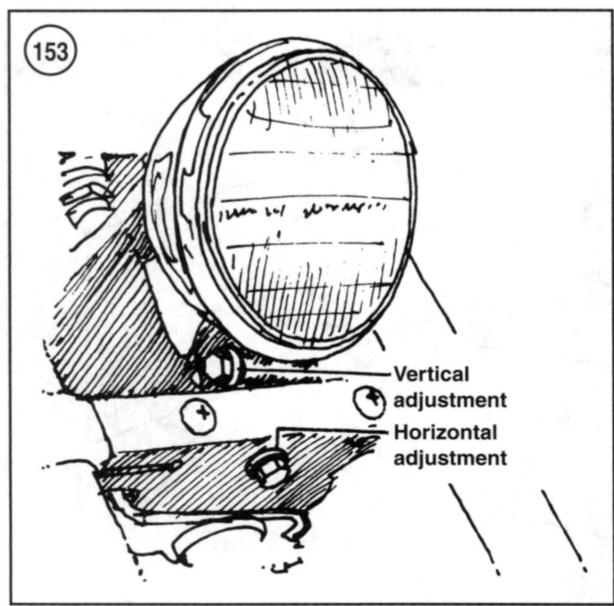

REAR TURN SIGNAL LIGHT REPLACEMENT

1. Remove the screws securing the turn signal lens. Remove the lens and gasket (**Figure 157**).
2. Push in on the bulb (**Figure 158**) and remove it.
3. Replace the bulb and install the lens.
4. Securely tighten the screws. Do not overtighten the screws because the lens might crack.

PASSING LIGHT AND FRONT TURN SIGNAL REPLACEMENT AND ADJUSTMENT

Refer to **Figure 159**.

1. To remove the passing light bulb, perform the following:

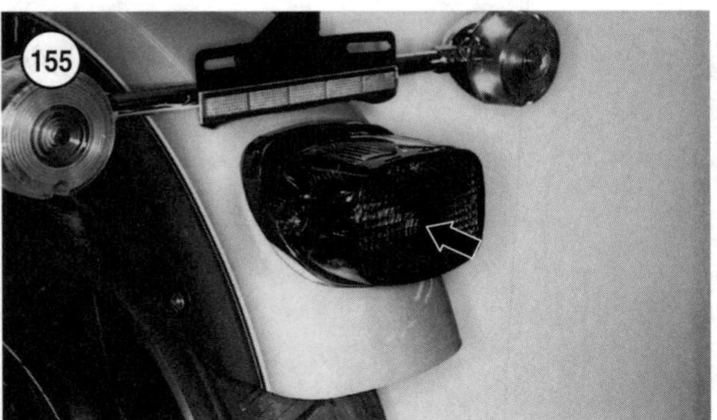

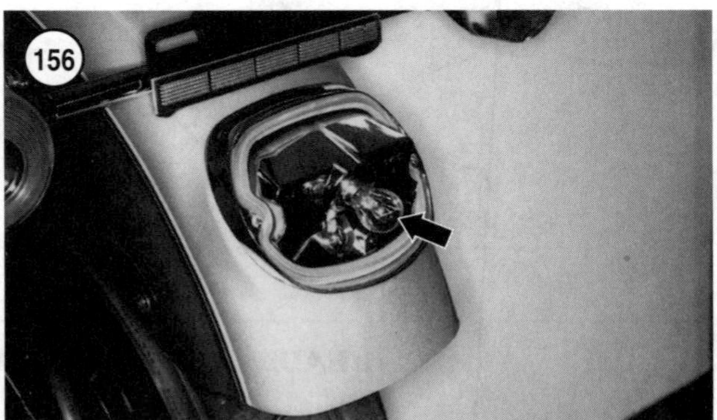

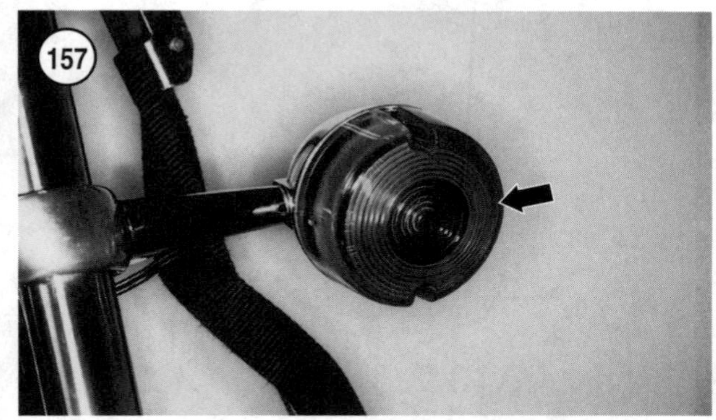

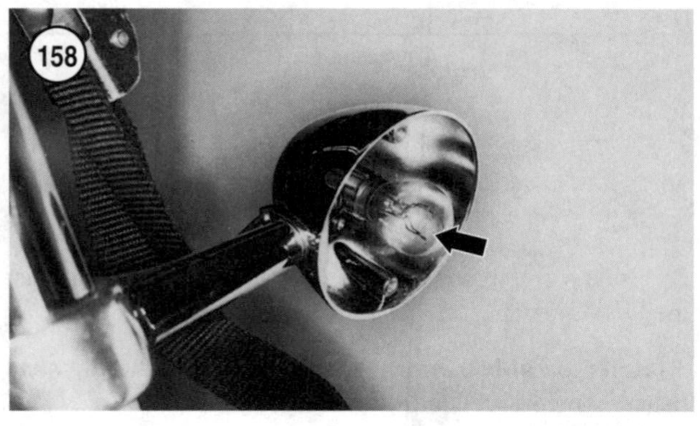

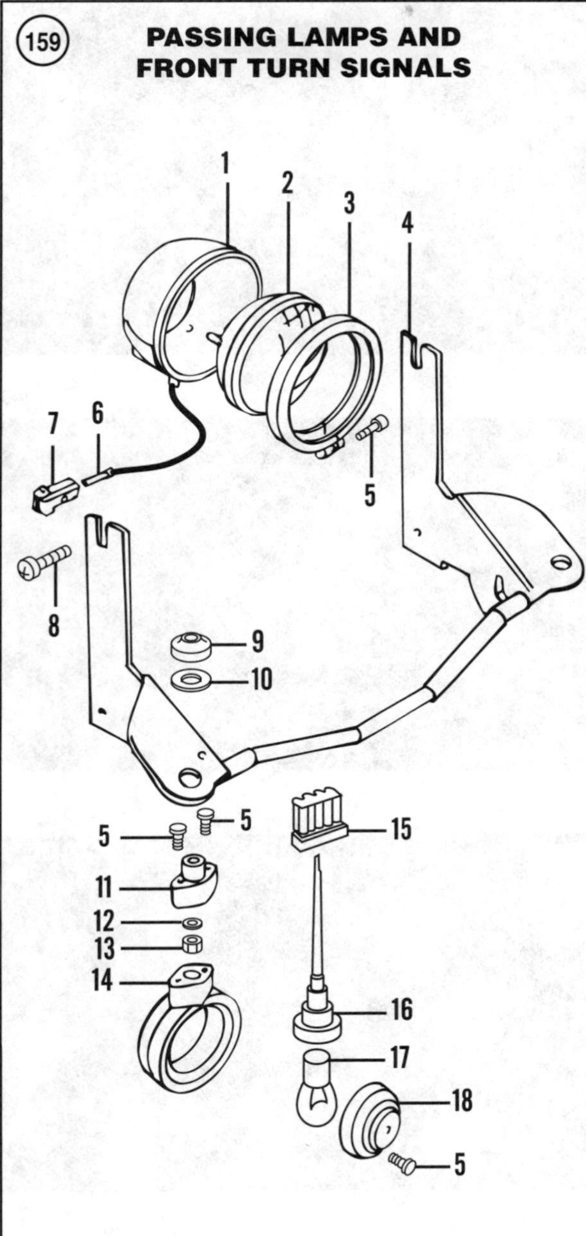

1. Passing lamp housing
2. Passing lens assembly
3. Trim bezel
4. Mounting bracket
5. Screw
6. Wiring harness
7. Socket assembly
8. Bolt
9. Swivel block
10. Dished washer
11. Mounting bracket
12. Clamp block
13. Locknut
14. Turn signal housing
15. Socket connector
16. Bulb socket
17. Turn signal bulb
18. Turn signal lens

a. Remove the screw (**Figure 160**) at the base of the trim bezel and remove the trim bezel from the passing light housing.

b. Carefully pull the bulb/lens assembly partially out of the housing.

c. Loosen the two screws securing the wiring harness (**Figure 161**) to the bulb/lens assembly and remove it.

d. Connect the wiring harness to the *new* bulb/lens assembly and tighten the screws securely.

e. Push the bulb/lens assembly into the housing and install the trim bezel.

f. Tighten the screw securely.

2. To remove the front turn signal bulb, perform the following:

a. Remove the screws securing the lens (**Figure 162**).

b. Push in on the bulb and rotate it and remove the blown bulb (**Figure 163**).

c. Install a new bulb and lens.

d. Securely tighten the screws. Do not overtighten the screws because the lens might crack.

3. Adjust the passing light as follows:

a. Remove the turn signal bracket screws and lift the turn signal off the bracket.

9

b. Loosen the nut on the inside of the turn signal bracket and turn the light so that it shines straight ahead and the top of the light is just below a line on a wall 25 ft. (7.62 m) away. The line should be the same height as the center of the headlight.
c. Hold the light in position and tighten the nut securely.
d. Reinstall the turn signal assembly and tighten the screws securely.

REAR TURN SIGNAL LIGHT REPLACEMENT

1. Remove the screws securing the turn signal lens. Remove the lens and gasket (**Figure 164**).
2. Push in on the bulb (**Figure 165**) and remove it.
3. Replace the bulb and install the lens.
4. Securely tighten the screws. Do not overtighten the screws because the lens might crack.

INSTRUMENTS AND INDICATOR LIGHTS

Speedometer Removal/Installation

FXR and FXLR models

Refer to **Figure 166**.

1. Disconnect the negative battery cable as described in this chapter.
2. Unscrew the odometer trip knob from the speedometer.
3. Disconnect the speedometer cable from the back side of the speedometer.
4. Remove the acorn nuts and remove the speedometer partway out from the cover.
5. Remove the bulb holders from the back side of the speedometer.
6. If necessary, remove the bulbs from the holders and install *new* bulbs.
7. To replace the speedometer, perform the following:
   a. Remove the nuts securing the speedometer to the bracket.
   b. Separate the speedometer, cushion and mounting ring from the bracket.
8. Install by reversing these removal steps. Install the odometer trip knob onto the speedometer.

FXRS, FXRS-SP and FXRS-Con models

Refer to **Figure 167** and **Figure 168**.

1. Disconnect the negative battery cable as described in this chapter.

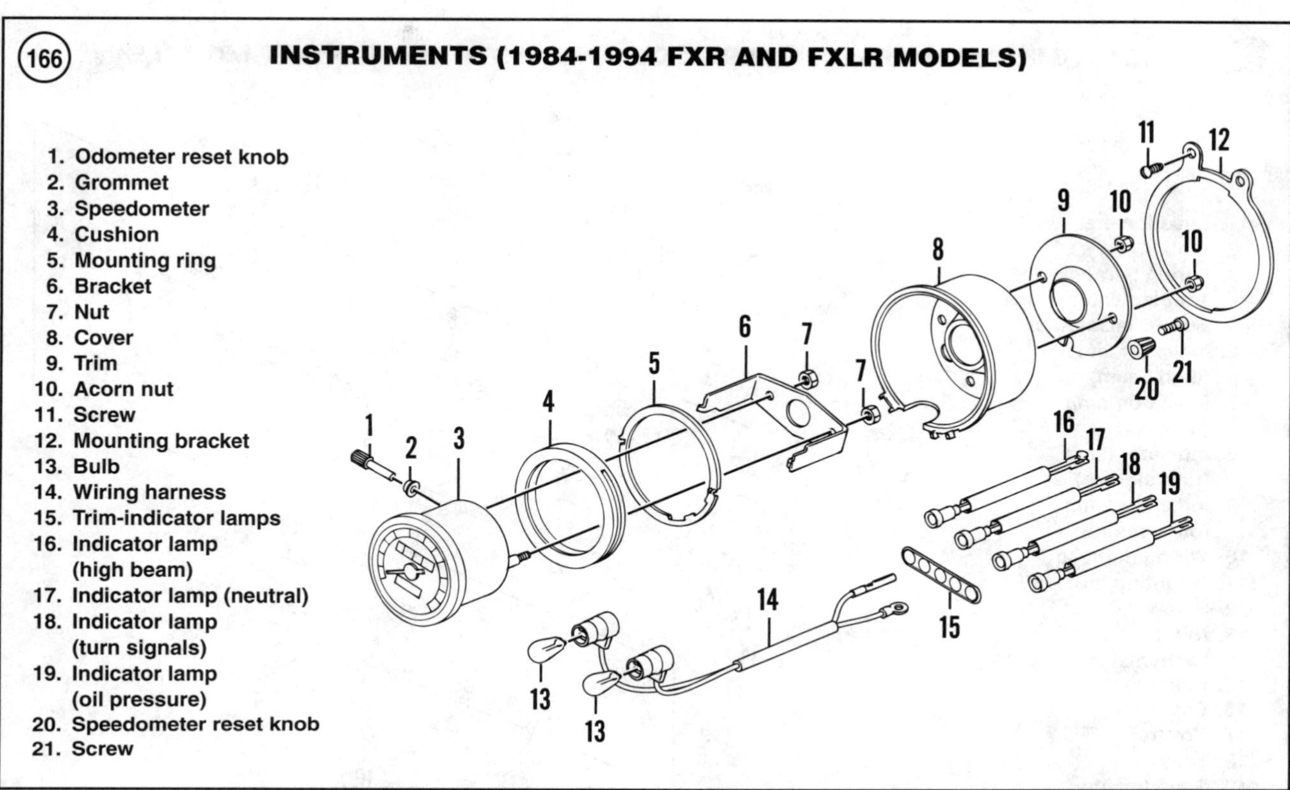
166
INSTRUMENTS (1984-1994 FXR AND FXLR MODELS)
1. Odometer reset knob
2. Grommet
3. Speedometer
4. Cushion
5. Mounting ring
6. Bracket
7. Nut
8. Cover
9. Trim
10. Acorn nut
11. Screw
12. Mounting bracket
13. Bulb
14. Wiring harness
15. Trim-indicator lamps
16. Indicator lamp (high beam)
17. Indicator lamp (neutral)
18. Indicator lamp (turn signals)
19. Indicator lamp (oil pressure)
20. Speedometer reset knob
21. Screw

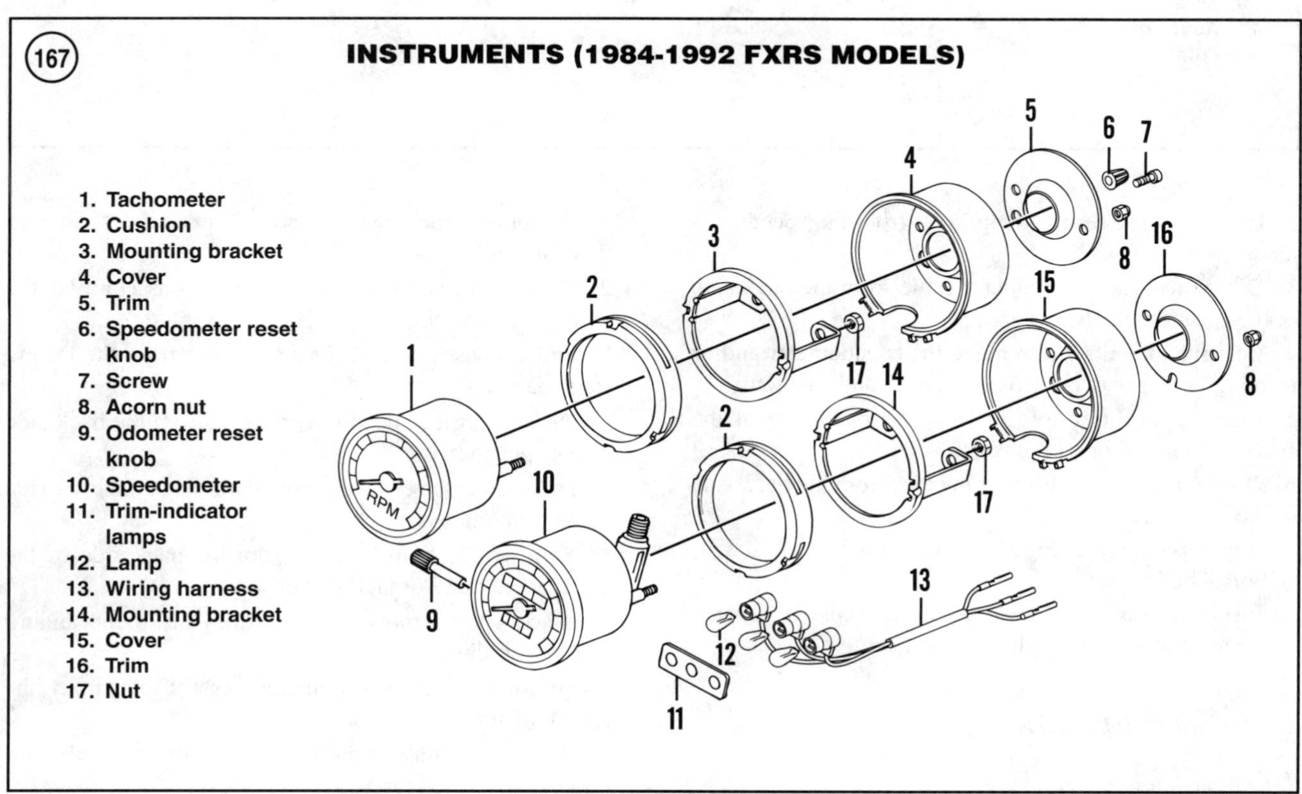
167
INSTRUMENTS (1984-1992 FXRS MODELS)
1. Tachometer
2. Cushion
3. Mounting bracket
4. Cover
5. Trim
6. Speedometer reset knob
7. Screw
8. Acorn nut
9. Odometer reset knob
10. Speedometer
11. Trim-indicator lamps
12. Lamp
13. Wiring harness
14. Mounting bracket
15. Cover
16. Trim
17. Nut
RPM

9

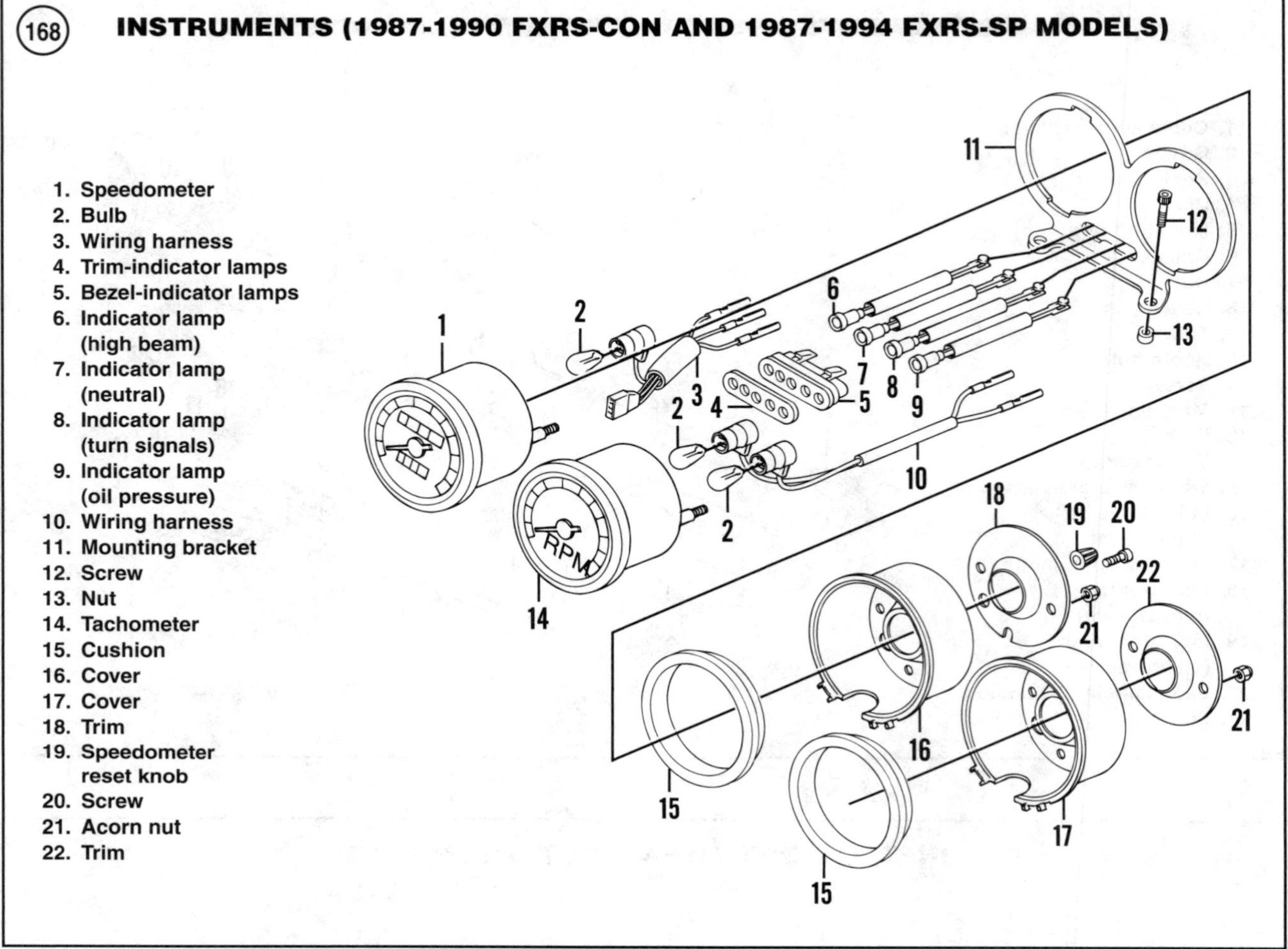

2. Unscrew the odometer trip knob from the speedometer.
3. Disconnect the speedometer cable from the back side of the speedometer.
4. Remove the nuts and remove the speedometer and/or tachometer partway out from the cover and cushions.
5. Remove the bulb holders from the back side of the speedometer and/or tachometer.
6. Disconnect the electrical connector from the back side of the tachometer.
7. If necessary, remove the bulbs from the holders and install *new* bulbs.
8. Install by reversing these removal steps. Install the odometer trip knob onto the speedometer.

FXRD and FXRT models

Refer to **Figure 169**.

1. Disconnect the negative battery cable as described in this chapter.
2. Remove the screws securing the visor assembly to the firing inner panel.
3. Pull the visor assembly partway out from the fairing inner panel.
4. Disconnect the speedometer cable from the back side of the speedometer.
5. Disconnect the electrical connector from the back side of the tachometer.
6. Remove the bulb holders from the back side of the speedometer and/or tachometer.
7. If necessary, remove the bulbs from the holders and install *new* bulbs.
8. Disconnect the speedometer reset cable from the speedometer.
9. Remove the nuts securing the speedometer and/or tachometer to the visor.

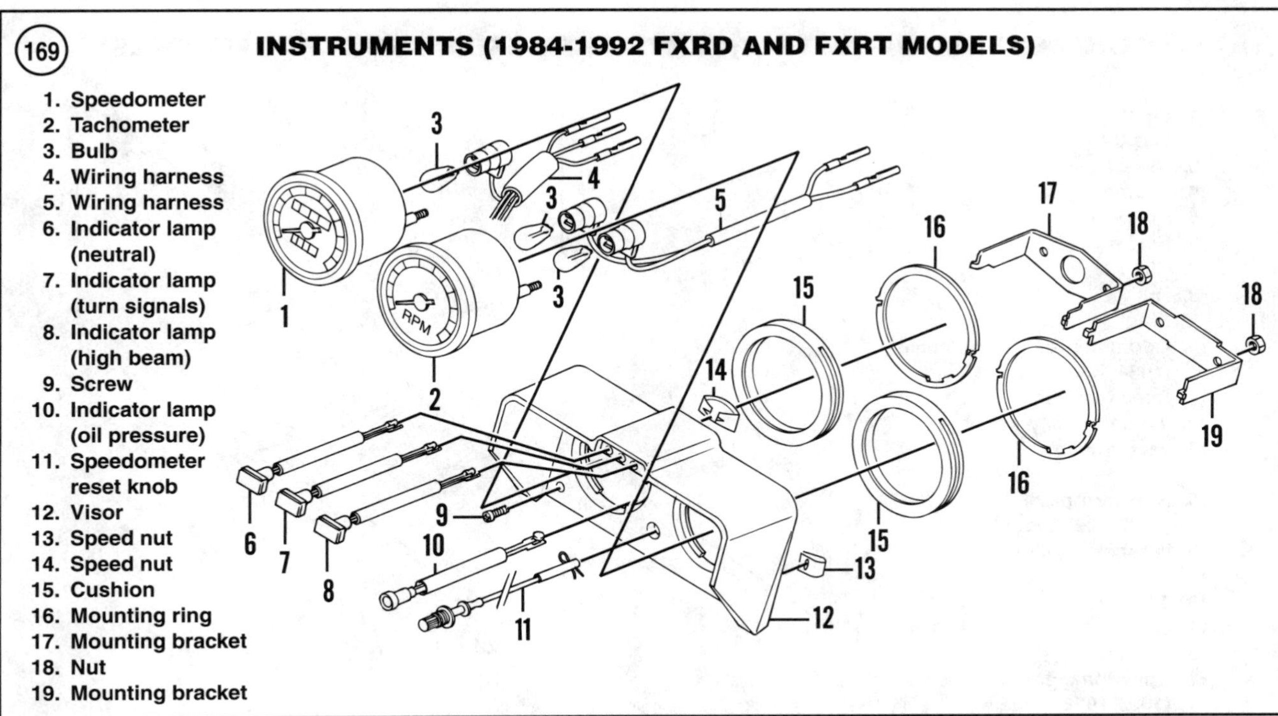

10. Remove the speedometer and/or tachometer from the cushion and mounting ring and remove from the visor.

11. If necessary, remove the indicator light assemblies from the visor.

12. Install by reversing these removal steps.

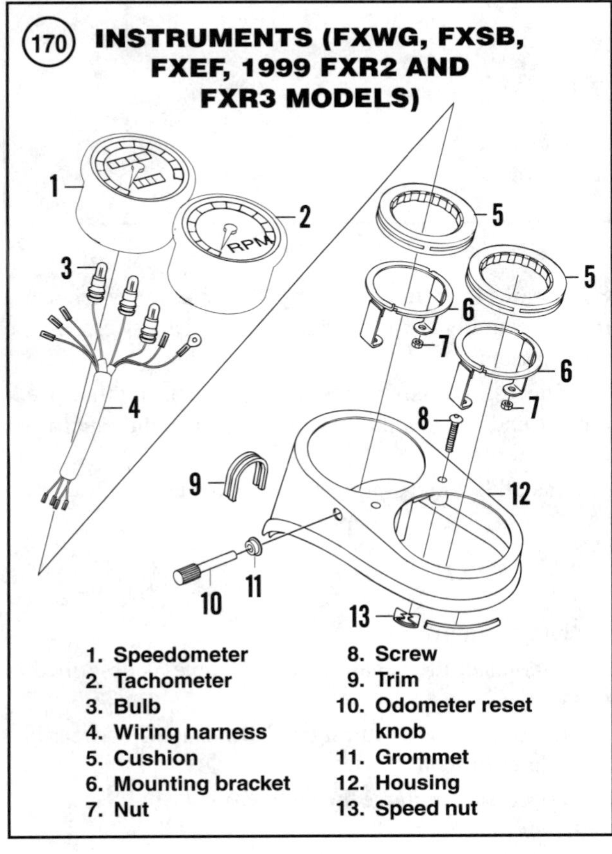

FXWG, FXSB, FXEF, 1999 FXR2 and FXR3 models

Refer to **Figure 170**.

1. Disconnect the negative battery cable as described in this chapter.

2. Remove the fuel tank as described in Chapter Eight.

3. Remove the bolts securing the housing to the top of the fuel tank and remove the housing assembly.

4. Remove the bulb holders from the back side of the speedometer and/or tachometer.

5. If necessary, remove the bulbs from the holders and install *new* bulbs.

6. Remove the nuts securing the speedometer and/or tachometer to the housing.

7. Remove the speedometer and/or tachometer from the housing, cushion and mounting bracket.

8. Install by reversing these removal steps.

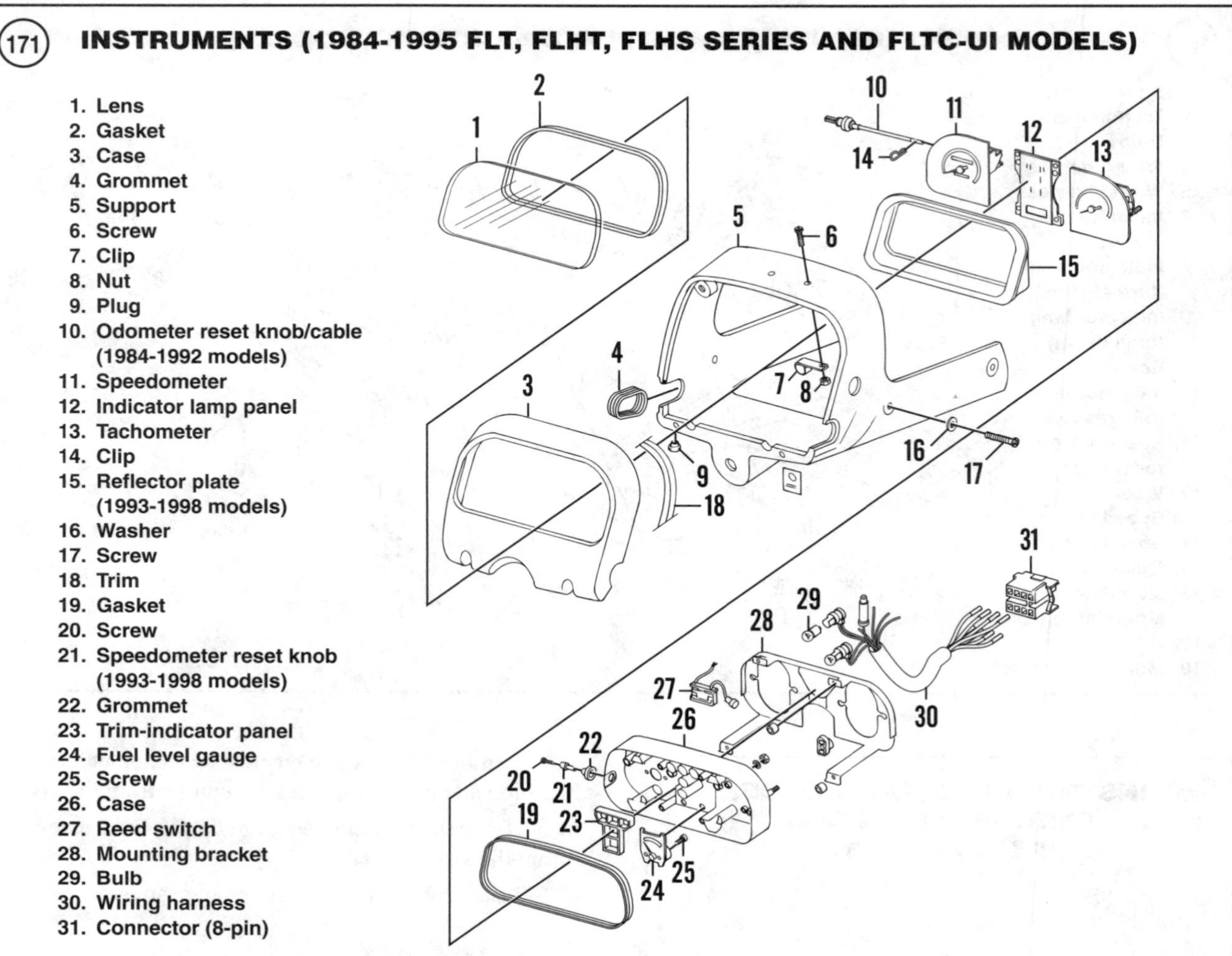

(171) **INSTRUMENTS (1984-1995 FLT, FLHT, FLHS SERIES AND FLTC-UI MODELS)**

1984-1995 FLT, FLHT, FLHS series and FLTC-UI models

Refer to **Figure 171**.

1. Disconnect the negative battery cable as described in this chapter.
2. Remove the speedometer reset knob.
3. Disconnect the speedometer cable from the front wheel.
4. Remove the screws securing the case assembly to the support and lift the case assembly partway off the handlebar.
5. Disconnect the speedometer cable from the back side of the speedometer.
6. Disconnect the wire harness connectors from the meters.
7. Turn the case assembly upside down on the workbench.
8. Remove the screws securing the mounting bracket and meter assembly to the back side of the case. Remove the meter assembly.
9. If necessary, remove the fasteners securing the speedometer and/or tachometer and indicator light panel from the case.
10. Install by reversing these removal steps.

1996-1998 FLHT series models

Refer to **Figure 172**.

1. Disconnect the negative battery cable as described in this chapter.
2. Remove the outer fairing and windshield as described in Chapter Fifteen.
3. If necessary, remove the bulbs from the holders and install *new* new bulbs.

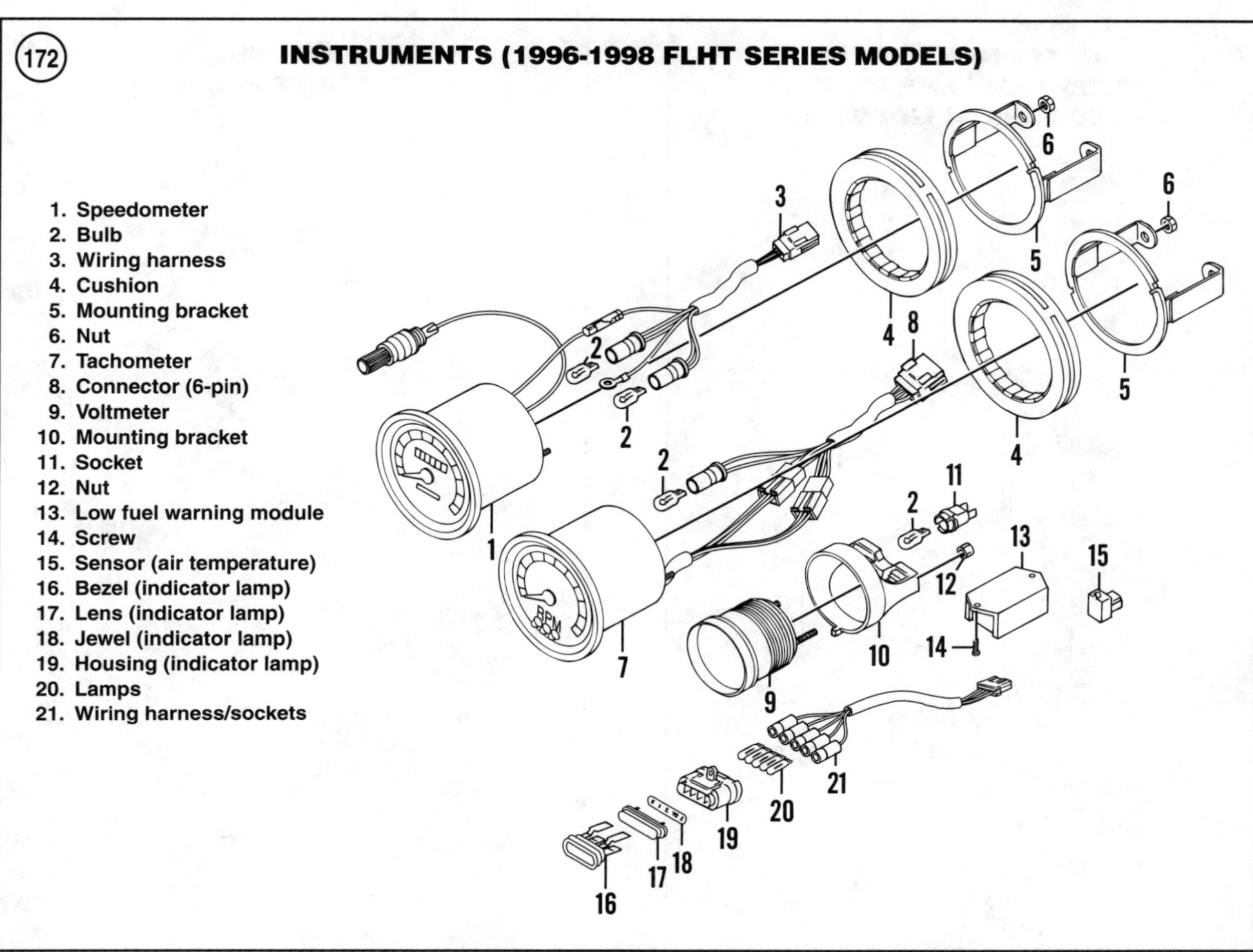

(172) **INSTRUMENTS (1996-1998 FLHT SERIES MODELS)**

4. Carefully pull the wiring harness connectors from the speedometer and/or tachometer.
5. Repeat Step 4 for any remaining gauges requiring removal.
6. Remove the hex nuts securing the mounting bracket and meter to the back side of the inner fairing.
7. Remove the meter(s) and/or gauges from the inner fairing.
8. If necessary, remove the indicator light panel from the case.
9. Install by reversing these removal steps.

1995-1998 FLHR series, FLHR-I and FLHRC-I models

Refer to **Figure 173**.

1. Remove the fuel tank console as described under *Fuel Tank Console (1997-1998 FLHTC-I, FLHTC-UI and FLHR-I Models)* in Chapter Eight.
2. Turn the fuel tank console upside down on towels on the workbench.
3. Bend back the clips and release the wiring harness from the back side of the instrument panel.
4. Carefully withdraw the indicator lamp assembly from the mounting bracket.
5. Hold onto the function switch wires on the left side of the console to keep the switch from turning. Remove the switch rubber cover. Then remove the switch from the console.
6. Carefully pry the latches up on the lockring and release the speedometer from the instrument panel.
7. Turn over the console on the workbench.
8. Remove the speedometer and wiring harness from the top of the console.
9. Install by reversing these removal steps.

FLTR series models

Refer to **Figure 174**.

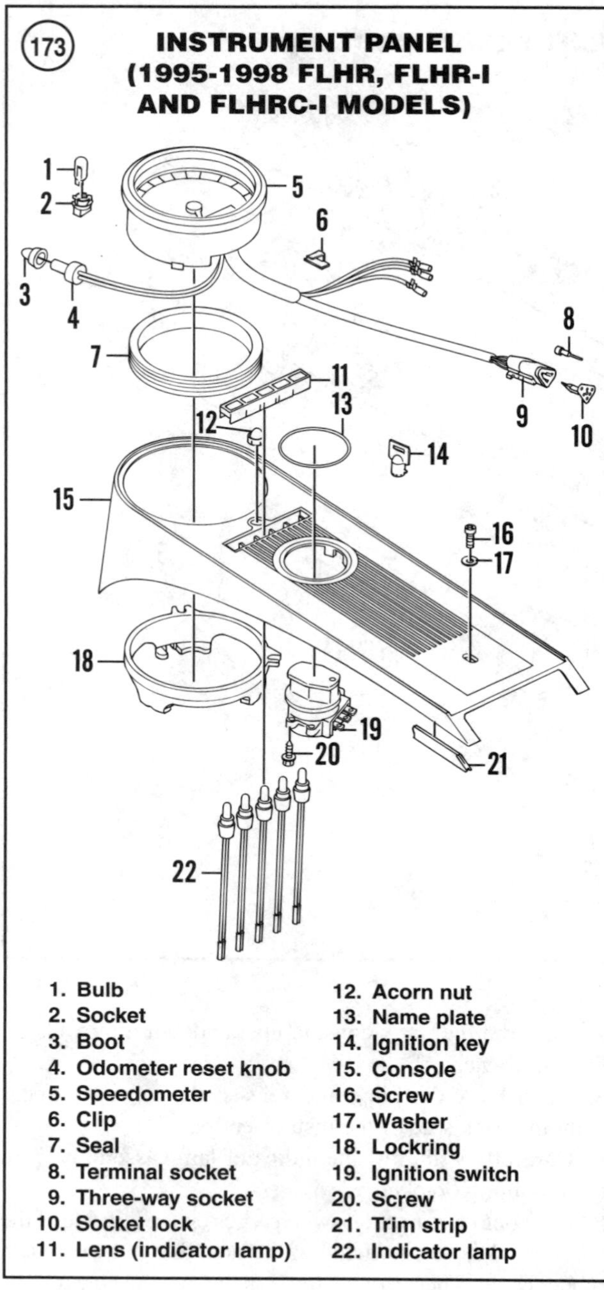

(173) INSTRUMENT PANEL (1995-1998 FLHR, FLHR-I AND FLHRC-I MODELS)

1. Bulb
2. Socket
3. Boot
4. Odometer reset knob
5. Speedometer
6. Clip
7. Seal
8. Terminal socket
9. Three-way socket
10. Socket lock
11. Lens (indicator lamp)
12. Acorn nut
13. Name plate
14. Ignition key
15. Console
16. Screw
17. Washer
18. Lockring
19. Ignition switch
20. Screw
21. Trim strip
22. Indicator lamp

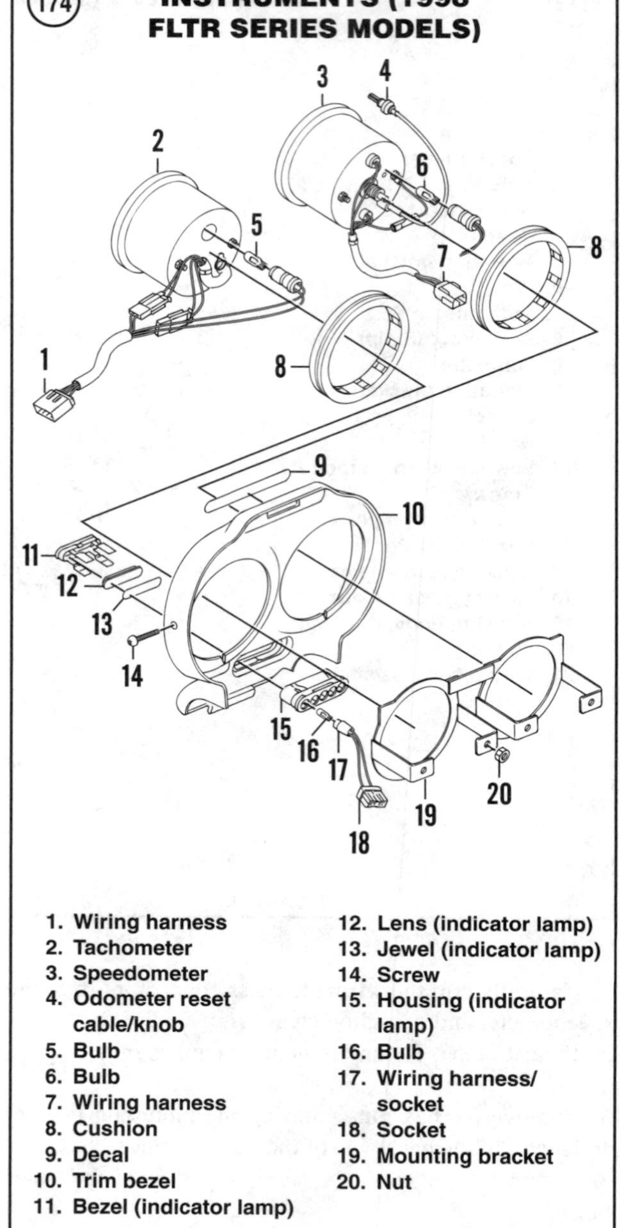

(174) INSTRUMENTS (1998 FLTR SERIES MODELS)

1. Wiring harness
2. Tachometer
3. Speedometer
4. Odometer reset cable/knob
5. Bulb
6. Bulb
7. Wiring harness
8. Cushion
9. Decal
10. Trim bezel
11. Bezel (indicator lamp)
12. Lens (indicator lamp)
13. Jewel (indicator lamp)
14. Screw
15. Housing (indicator lamp)
16. Bulb
17. Wiring harness/socket
18. Socket
19. Mounting bracket
20. Nut

1. Disconnect the negative battery cable as described in this chapter.
2. Remove the Torx screw on each side securing the trim bezel assembly to the inner fairing.
3. Use both thumbs and press on the trim bezel to release it from the slots above the ignition switch.
4. Carefully raise the trim bezel until the tabs on both sides are free from the slot at the top of the bezel (the slot is hidden under the decorative trim strip).
5. Reach under the trim bezel assembly and unscrew the speedometer cable from the speedometer.
6. On the lower right side, remove the knurled nut from the odometer reset knob. Remove the reset knob and rubber washer.
7. Carefully move the trim bezel assembly away from the instrument nacelle and disconnect the three multi-pin electrical connectors.

175

IGNITION SWITCH

POSITION \ SWITCH	WHITE	RED	GREEN
Off		•	
Ignition	•———	———•	
Lights	•———	———•———	———•

8. Remove the trim bezel assembly from the instrument nacelle and inner fairing.
9. If necessary, remove the bulbs from the holders and install *new* bulbs.
10. Remove the nuts securing the speedometer and/or tachometer to the mounting bracket.
11. Remove the speedometer and/or tachometer from the trim bezel and mounting bracket.
12. Install by reversing these removal steps.

HANDLEBAR SWITCHES (1984-1995 MODELS)

Test the switches for continuity at the switch connector plug by operating the switch in each of the operating positions. Compare the results with the switch operating diagrams. For example, **Figure 175** shows a continuity diagram for a *typical* ignition switch. It shows which terminals should show continuity when the switch is in a given position.

When the ignition switch is in the IGNITION position, there should be continuity among the white, red and green terminals. The line on the continuity diagram indicates this. An ohmmeter connected among these three terminals should indicate little or no resistance, or a test light should light. When the switch is OFF, there should be no continuity between the same terminals.

When testing the switches, note the following:

1. Check the battery as described under *Battery* in this chapter; if necessary, charge or replace the battery.
2. Disconnect the negative battery cable as described in this chapter before checking the continuity of any switch.
3. Detach all connectors located between the switch and the electrical circuit.

CAUTION
Do not attempt to start the engine with the battery disconnected.

4. When separating two connectors, pull the connector housings and not the wires.
5. After locating a defective circuit, check the connectors to make sure they are clean and properly connected. Check all wires going into a connector housing to make sure each wire is positioned properly and that the wire end is not loose.
6. To reconnect connectors properly, push them together until they click or snap into place.
7. If the switch or button does not perform properly, replace it.

Handlebar Switch Replacement (Non-Sound System Models)

Refer to **Figure 176**.

1. Remove the screws securing the switch housing to the handlebar. Then carefully separate the switch housing to access the defective switch.
2. Remove the switch screw and pull the switch out of the housing. Cut the switch wires at the switch and discard the switch.
3. Strip the new switch wire 3/4 in. (19.05 mm) from the switch. Do not cut into the wire strands.
4. Install the switch into the housing and secure it with the mounting screw.
5. Cut a piece of shrink tubing to length and slide it over one of the wires.

NOTE
Make sure the heat shrink is positioned away from the soldering gun when soldering the wires in Step 6.

6. Solder the ends to the new switch. Then shrink the tubing over the wire(s). Test the new switch.
7. Install the switch by reversing these steps while noting the following:

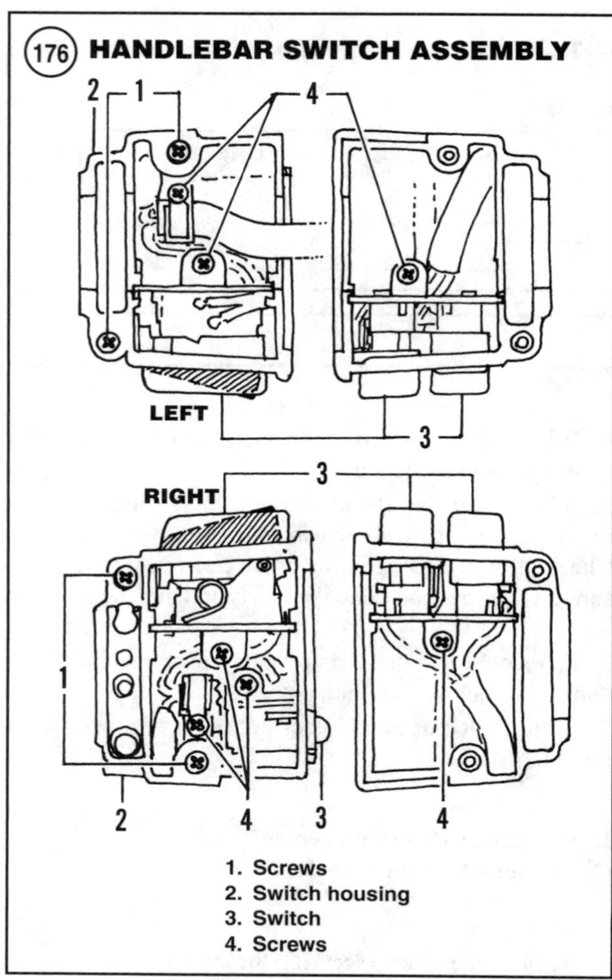

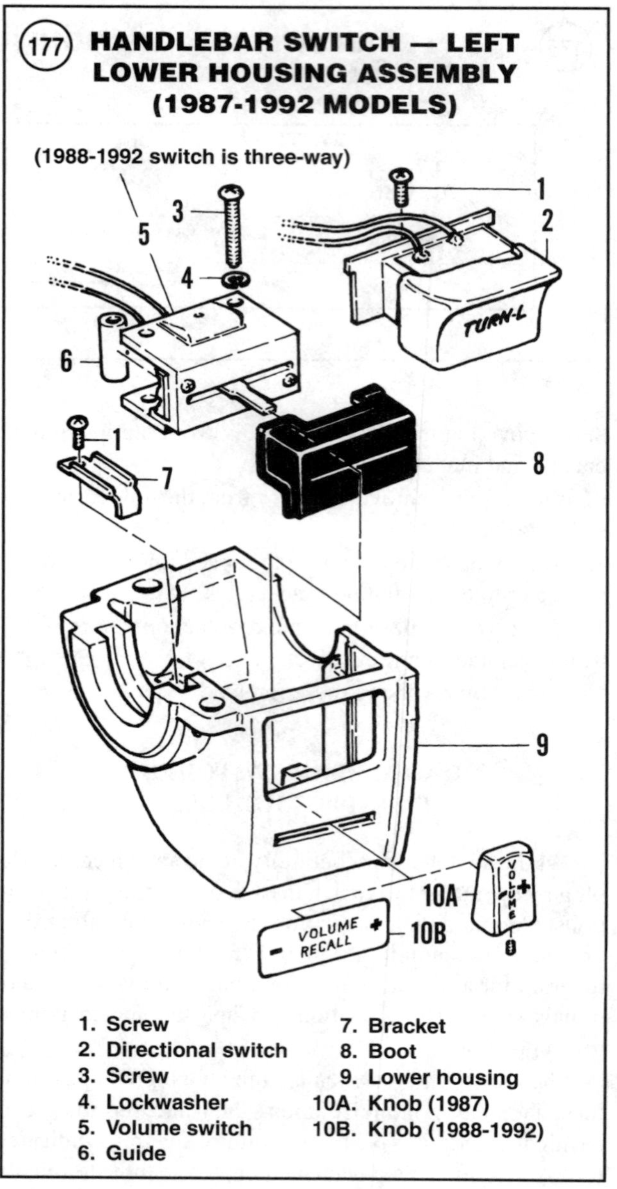

a. When clamping the switch housing onto the handlebar, check the wiring harness routing position to make sure it is not pinched between the housing and handlebar.

b. To install the right switch housing, refer to *Throttle and Idle Cable Replacement* in Chapter Eight.

c. Check throttle control and brake light operation.

Left Switch Replacement (Sound System Models)

Refer to **Figure 177** or **Figure 178**.

1. Remove the switch screws and separate the switch halves.

2. If equipped with a volume control switch, first remove the setscrew and knob from the switch.

3. Remove the screws securing the left directional switch and the volume switch, and remove the switches.

4. Cut the switch wire at the defective switch and discard the switch.

5. Take the volume control switch and install the guides between the switch surfaces so that the hole in the guides line up with the holes in the switch surfaces. Slide the rubber boot over the front switch arm and place the switch into the housing. Install the switch so that the boss on top of the switch faces up as shown in **Figure 177** or **Figure 178**. Secure the switch with the screws and washers.

6. Place the directional switch on top of the volume control switch and secure it with the attaching screws.

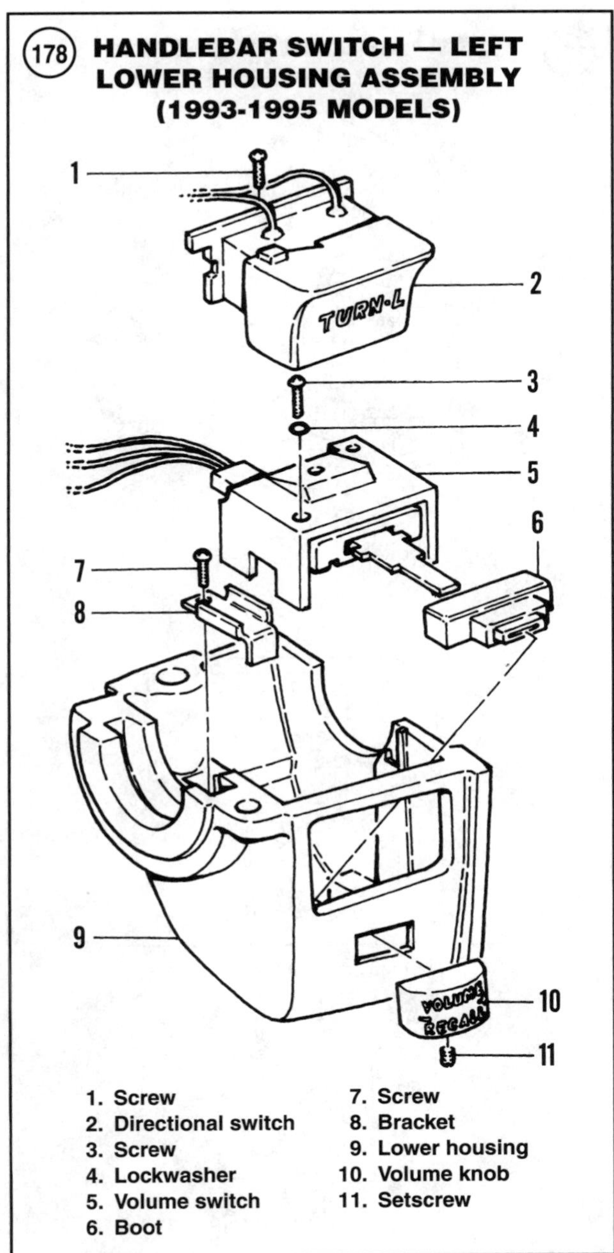

(178) **HANDLEBAR SWITCH — LEFT LOWER HOUSING ASSEMBLY (1993-1995 MODELS)**

1. Screw
2. Directional switch
3. Screw
4. Lockwasher
5. Volume switch
6. Boot
7. Screw
8. Bracket
9. Lower housing
10. Volume knob
11. Setscrew

7. Route the volume control and directional switch wires together following the same routing path through the right side of the switch housing. Secure the wires with the bracket and screw.
8. Install the switch housings onto the handlebar and secure with the mounting screws.
9. Install the volume knob onto the switch lever (if used) and secure it with the setscrew.
10. Strip the new switch wire 3/4 in. (19.05 mm) from the switch. Do not cut into the wire strands.

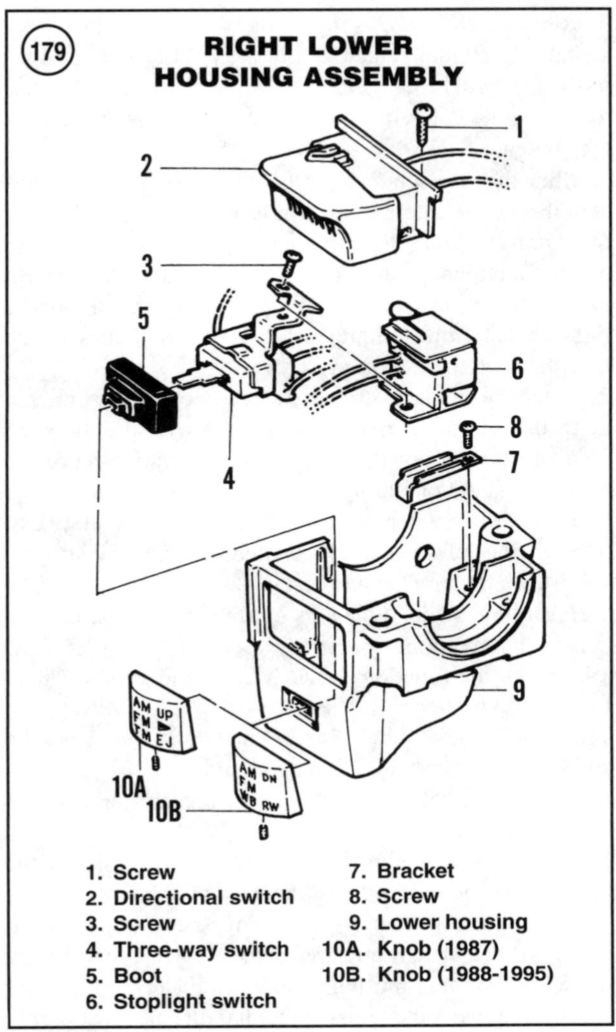

(179) **RIGHT LOWER HOUSING ASSEMBLY**

1. Screw
2. Directional switch
3. Screw
4. Three-way switch
5. Boot
6. Stoplight switch
7. Bracket
8. Screw
9. Lower housing
10A. Knob (1987)
10B. Knob (1988-1995)

11. Cut a piece of shrink tubing to length and slide it over one of the wires.
12. Solder the ends to the new switch. Then shrink the tubing over the wire(s). Test the new switch.
13. Install the switch by reversing these steps. When clamping the switch housing onto the handlebar, check the wiring harness routing position to make sure it is not pinched between the housing and handlebar.

Right Switch Replacement (Sound System Models)

Refer to **Figure 179**.

1. Remove the switch screws and separate the switch halves.
2. If equipped with a radio control switch, first remove the setscrew and knob from the switch.

3. Remove the screws securing the right directional switch, functional switch and brake light switch, and remove the switches.
4. Cut the switch wire at the defective switch and discard the switch.
5. Slide the rubber boot over the functional switch and install the switch into the lower housing.
6. Install the brake light switch so that the mounting tab on the functional switch is placed on top of the brake light switch mounting tab. This alignment prevents the brake light switch from binding. Secure both switches to the housing with the mounting screws.
7. Place the right directional switch into the housing and align the mounting tab on the switch with the threaded hole in the functional switch mounting tab. Secure the switch with the mounting screw.
8. Route the switch wires together so that they exit through the left side of the switch housing. Secure the wires with the bracket and screw.
9. Install the switch housings onto the handlebar and secure with the mounting screws.
10. Install the functional switch knob and secure it with the setscrew.
11. Strip the new switch wire 3/4 in. (19.05 mm) from the switch. Do not cut into the wire strands.
12. Cut a piece of shrink tubing to length and slide it over one of the wires.
13. Solder the ends to the new switch. Then shrink the tubing over the wire(s). Test the new switch.
14. Install the switch by reversing these steps. When clamping the switch housing onto the handlebar, check the wiring harness routing position to make sure it is not pinched between the housing and handlebar.
15. Check the throttle control and brake light operation.

HANDLEBAR SWITCHES (1996-1998 MODELS)

Testing

Test the switches for continuity at the switch connector plug by operating the switch in each of the operating positions. Compare the results with the switch operating diagrams. For example, **Figure 175** shows a continuity diagram for a *typical* ignition switch. It shows which terminals should show continuity when the switch is in a given position.

When the ignition switch is in the IGNITION position, there should be continuity among the white, red and green terminals. The line on the continuity diagram indicates this. An ohmmeter connected among these three terminals should indicate little or no resistance, or a test light should

180 LEFT HANDLEBAR SWITCH (1996-1998 MODELS)

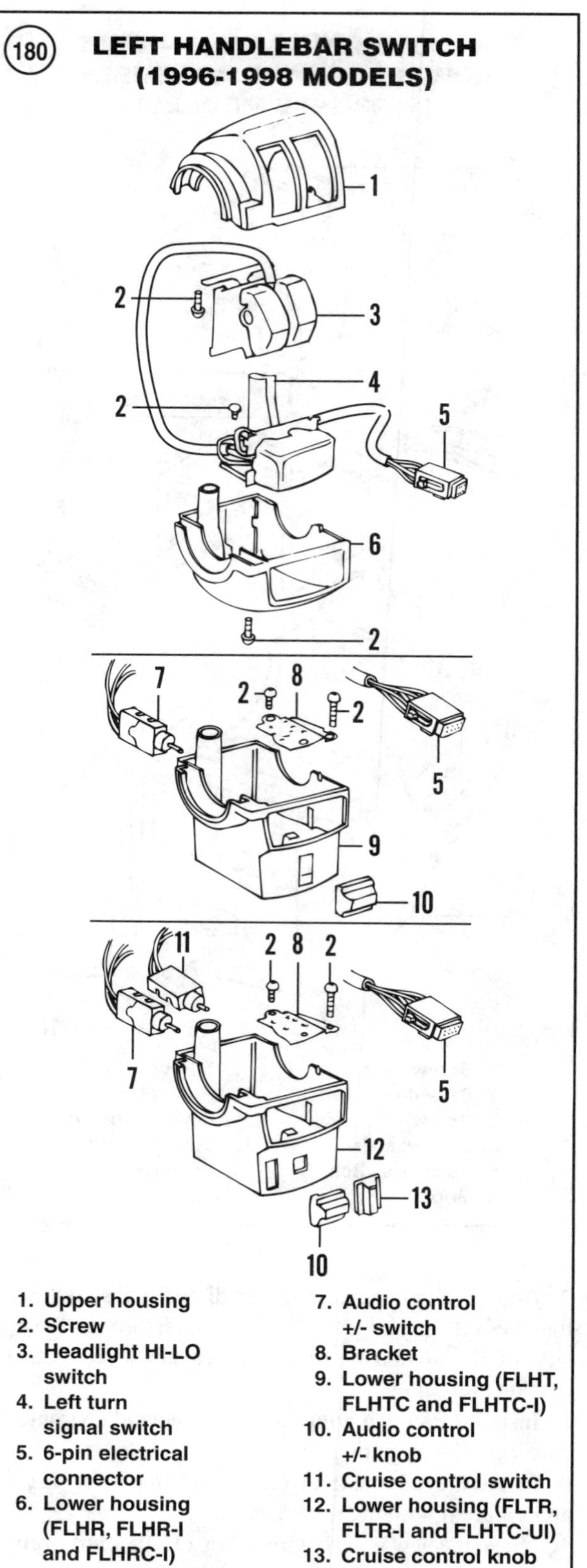

1. Upper housing
2. Screw
3. Headlight HI-LO switch
4. Left turn signal switch
5. 6-pin electrical connector
6. Lower housing (FLHR, FLHR-I and FLHRC-I)
7. Audio control +/- switch
8. Bracket
9. Lower housing (FLHT, FLHTC and FLHTC-I)
10. Audio control +/- knob
11. Cruise control switch
12. Lower housing (FLTR, FLTR-I and FLHTC-UI)
13. Cruise control knob

181 RIGHT HANDLEBAR SWITCH (1996-1998 MODELS)

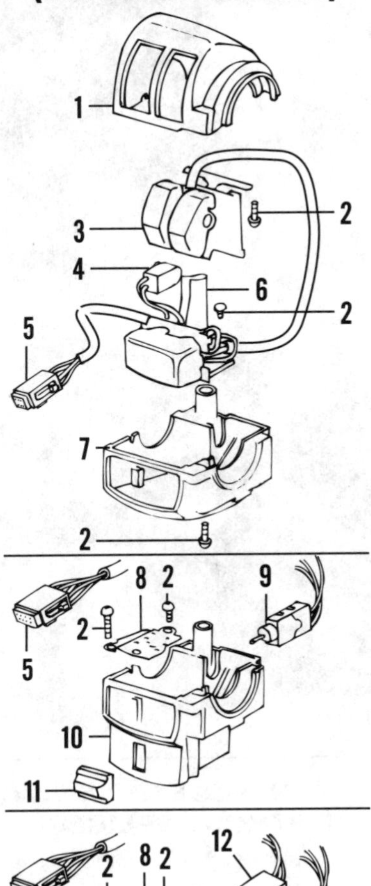

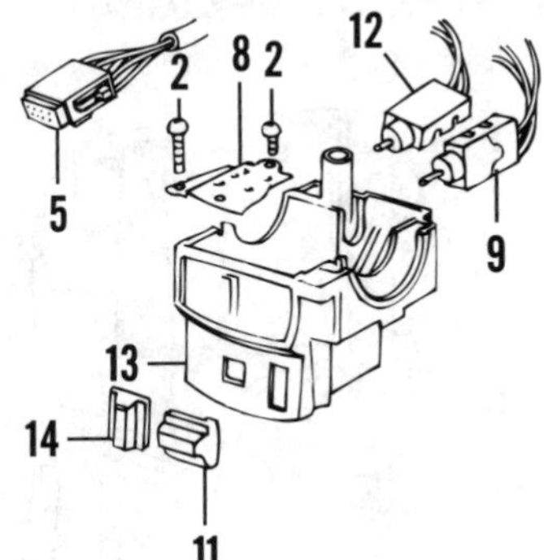

1. Upper housing
2. Screw
3. Engine stop/run/ start switch
4. Front brake light switch
5. Electrical connector
6. Right turn signal switch
7. Lower housing (FLHR, FLHR-I and FLHRC-I)
8. Bracket
9. Mode select UP/DN switch
10. Lower housing (FLHT, FLHTC and FLHTC-I)
11. Mode select UP/DN knob
12. Cruise control set/resume switch
13. Lower housing (FLTR, FLTR-I and FLHTC-UI)
14. Cruise control set/resume knob

light. When the switch is OFF, there should be no continuity between the same terminals.

When testing the switches, note the following:

1. Check the battery as described under *Battery* in this chapter; if necessary, charge or replace the battery.
2. Disconnect the negative battery cable (see this chapter) before checking the continuity of any switch.
3. Detach all connectors located between the switch and the electrical circuit.

CAUTION
Do not attempt to start the engine with the battery disconnected.

4. When separating two connectors, pull the connector housings and not the wires.
5. After locating a defective circuit, check the connectors to make sure they are clean and properly connected. Check all wires going into a connector housing to make sure each wire is positioned properly and that the wire end is not loose.
6. To reconnect connectors properly, push them together until they click or snap into place.
7. If the switch or button does not perform properly, replace it.

9

Handlebar Switches (Non-Sound and Non-Cruise Control Models)

Left handlebar switch description

The left handlebar switch housing (**Figure 180**) is equipped with the following switches:

1. Headlight HI-LO beam.
2. Horn.
3. Left turn signal.

Right handlebar switch description

The right handlebar switch housing (**Figure 181**) is equipped with the following switches:

1. Engine stop/run.
2. Start button.
3. Right turn signal.
4. Front brake light.

Handlebar switch replacement

1. Remove the screws securing the left side switch housing (**Figure 182**) to the handlebar. Then carefully separate the switch housing to access the defective switch.

2. Remove the screws securing the right switch housing (**Figure 183**) to the handlebar. Then carefully separate the switch housing to see the defective switch.

NOTE
*To service the front brake light switch, refer to **Front Brake Light Switch Replacement** in this chapter.*

3A. On models without splices, remove the screw and bracket.
3B. On models with splices, remove the cable strap.
4. Pull the switch(es) out of the housing.
5. Cut the switch wire(s) from the defective switch(es).
6. Slip a piece of heat shrink tubing over each wire cut in Step 2.
7. Solder the wire end(s) to the new switch. Then shrink the tubing over the wire(s). Test the new switch.
8. Install the switch by reversing these steps while noting the following:
   a. When clamping the switch housing onto the handlebar, check the wiring harness routing position to make sure it is not pinched between the housing and handlebar.
   b. To install the right switch housing, refer to *Throttle and Idle Cable Replacement* in Chapter Eight.

WARNING
Do not ride the motorcycle until the throttle cables are properly adjusted. Also, the cables must not catch or pull when the handlebars are turned. Improper cable routing and adjustment can cause the throttle to stick open. This could cause loss of control.

Handlebar Switches (Sound and Cruise Control Models)

Left handlebar switch description

The left handlebar switch housing (**Figure 180**) is equipped with the following switches:
1. Headlight HI-LO beam.
2. Horn.
3. Left turn signal.

Right handlebar switch description

The right handlebar switch housing (**Figure 183**), on models without splices (**Figure 184**) or models with splices (**Figure 185**) is equipped with the following switches:
1. Engine stop/run.

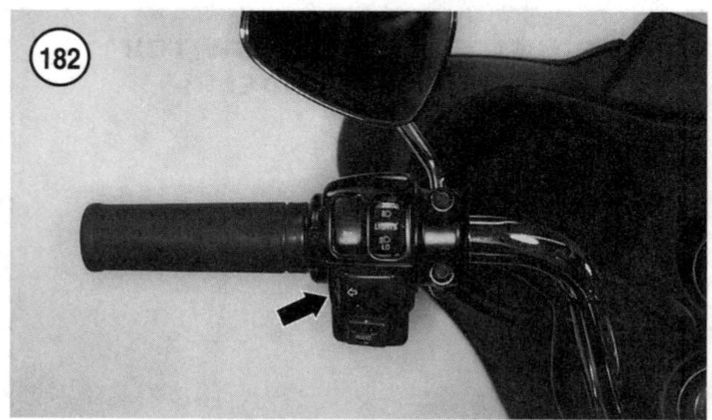

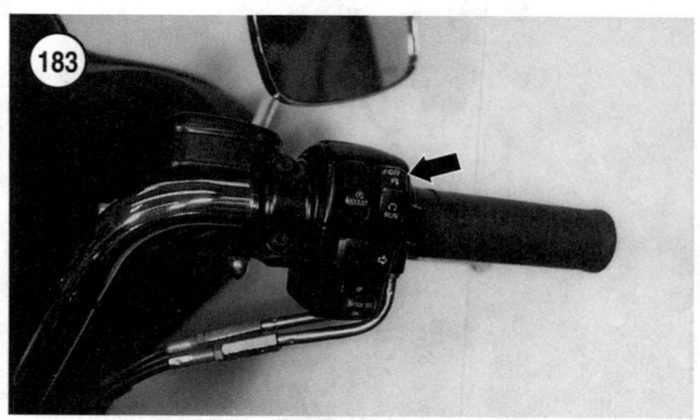

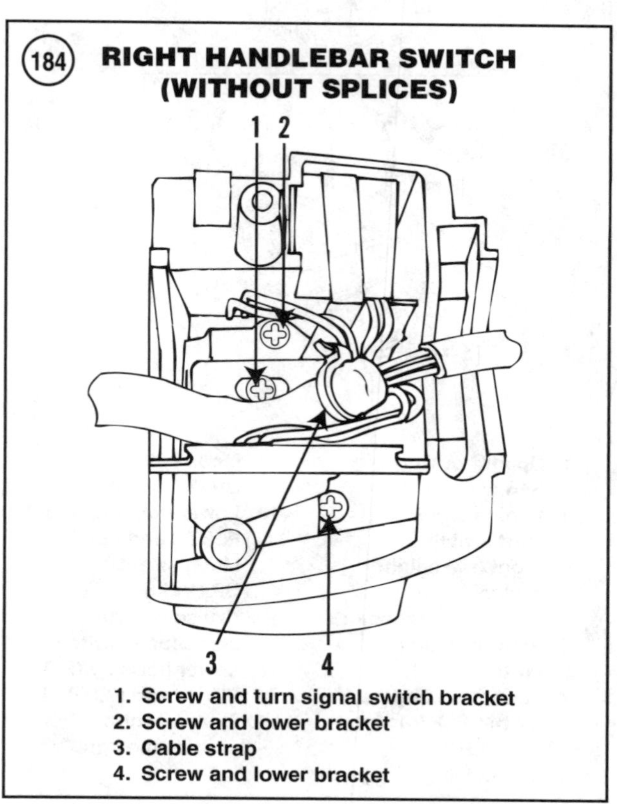

1. Screw and turn signal switch bracket
2. Screw and lower bracket
3. Cable strap
4. Screw and lower bracket

185 RIGHT HANDLEBAR SWITCH (WITH SPLICES)

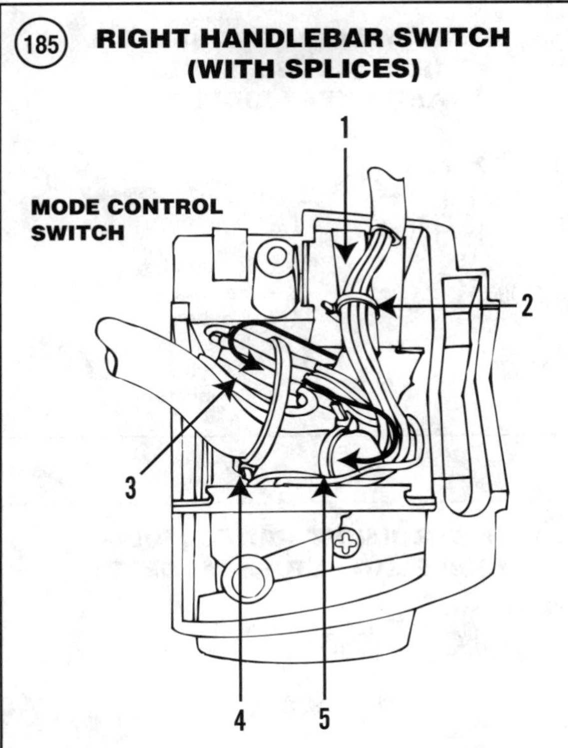

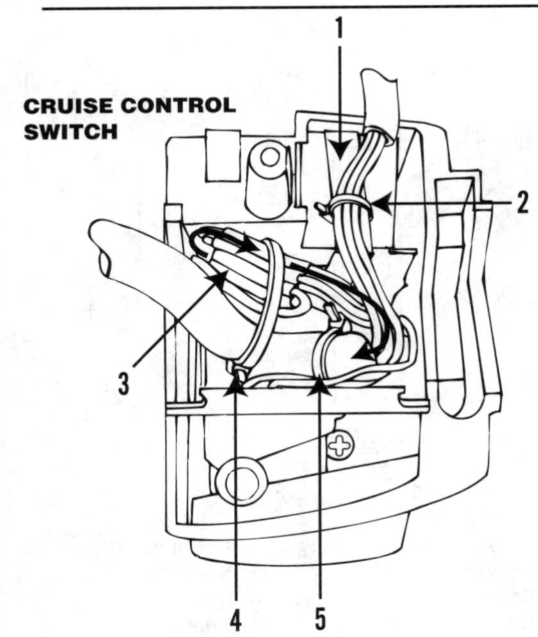

1. Angular arm
2. Cable strap
3. Splices
4. Splices-to-conduit cable strap
5. Conduit-to-bracket cable strap

2. Start button.
3. Right turn signal.
4. Front brake light.
5. On sound models, mode select switch UP/DN.
6. On sound and cruise models, mode select switch UP/DN and cruise control switch.

Handlebar switch replacement

1. Remove the screws securing the left switch housing (**Figure 182**) to the handlebar. Then carefully separate the switch housing to access the defective switch.
2. Remove the screws securing the right switch housing (**Figure 183**) to the handlebar. Then carefully separate the switch housing to see the defective switch.

NOTE
*To service the front brake light switch, refer to **Front Brake Light Switch Replacement** in this chapter.*

3A. On models without splices, remove the three screws and brackets.
3B. On models with splices, remove the cable straps.
4. Pull the switch(es) out of the housing.
5. Cut the switch wire(s) from the defective switch(es).
6. Slip a piece of heat shrink tubing over each wire cut in Step 2.
7. Solder the wire end(s) to the new switch. Then shrink the tubing over the wire(s). Test the new switch.
8. Install the switch by reversing these steps while noting the following:
   a. When clamping the switch housing onto the handlebar, check the wiring harness routing position to make sure it is not pinched between the housing and handlebar.
   b. To install the right switch housing, refer to *Throttle and Idle Cable Replacement* in Chapter Seven.

WARNING
Do not ride the motorcycle until the throttle cables are properly adjusted. Also, the cables must not catch or pull when the handlebars are turned. Improper cable routing and adjustment can cause the throttle to stick open. This could cause lose of control.

IGNITION/LIGHTING SWITCH

Side-Mounted Switch Removal/Installation (FXR Series, FXSB and FXEF Models)

Refer to **Figure 186**.

1. Disconnect the negative battery cable as described in this chapter.
2. Turn the ignition switch off and remove the ignition key.
3A. On FXR series models, perform the following:
   a. Loosen and remove the nut, washer and label securing the ignition switch to the mounting plate.
   b. Push the ignition switch through the cover (toward the inside) and remove it from the mounting plate.
3B. On FXSB and FXEF models, perform the following:
   a. Loosen and remove the nut, washer and label securing the ignition switch to the mounting bracket.
   b. Remove the switch from the mounting bracket.
4. Disconnect the electrical connectors from the ignition switch and remove the ignition switch.
5. Install by reversing these removal steps.

Removal/Installation (FXWG Models)

1. Disconnect the negative battery cable as described in this chapter.
2. Turn the ignition switch off and remove the ignition key.
3. Remove the bolt securing the speedometer trim panel to the base and remove the trim panel.
4. Disconnect the electrical connectors from the ignition switch
5. Remove the screws and washers securing the ignition switch to the base and remove the ignition switch.
6. Install by reversing these removal steps.

Removal/Installation (FLT and FLH Series Models)

1. Disconnect the negative battery cable as described in this chapter.
2. Turn the ignition switch off and remove the ignition key.
3. Remove the fuel tank as described in Chapter Eight.
4. Remove the instrument assembly as described in this chapter.
5. Remove the handlebar assembly as described in Chapter Eleven.
6. Remove the ignition switch tamper shield.
7. Use needlenose pliers and pull on the ignition switch pin located under the support housing. Remove the ignition switch knob.
8. Remove the fork lock adjusting screw, jam nut, spring and washers.
9. Remove the screws securing the instrument panel support housing to the upper and lower fork brackets. Move

(186) IGNITION/LIGHTING SWITCH (FXR SERIES, FXSB AND FXEF MODELS)

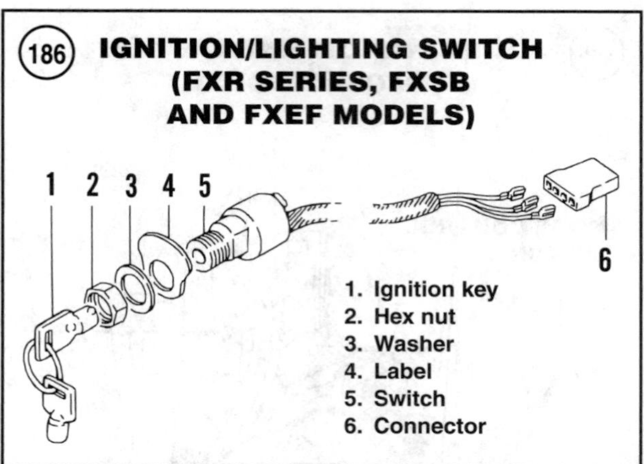

1. Ignition key
2. Hex nut
3. Washer
4. Label
5. Switch
6. Connector

(187) INSTRUMENT PANEL (1994-1998 FLHR SERIES MODELS)

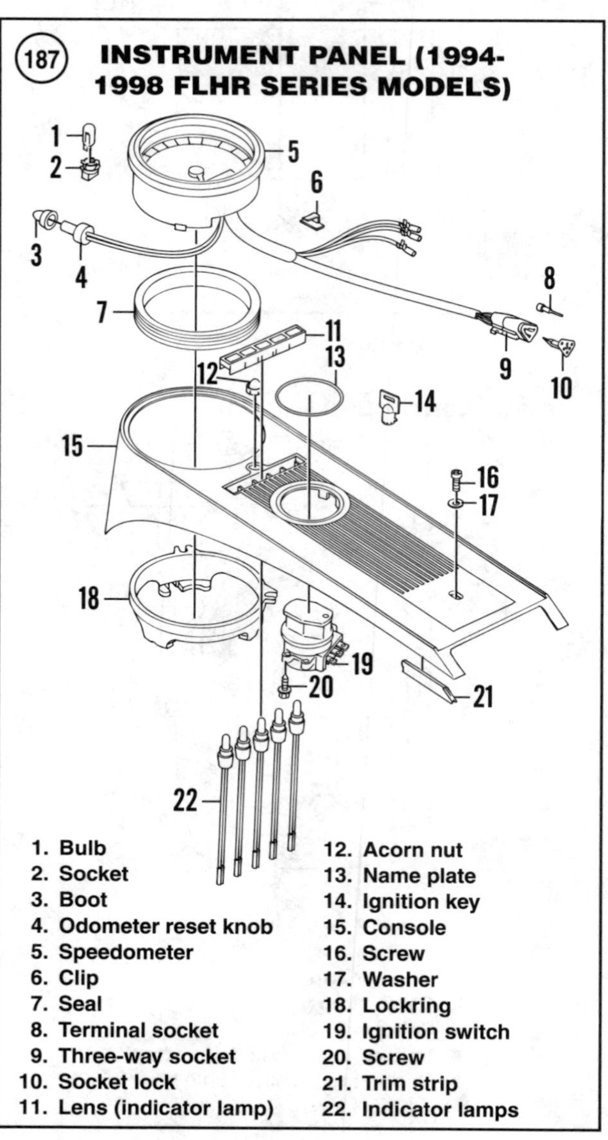

1. Bulb
2. Socket
3. Boot
4. Odometer reset knob
5. Speedometer
6. Clip
7. Seal
8. Terminal socket
9. Three-way socket
10. Socket lock
11. Lens (indicator lamp)
12. Acorn nut
13. Name plate
14. Ignition key
15. Console
16. Screw
17. Washer
18. Lockring
19. Ignition switch
20. Screw
21. Trim strip
22. Indicator lamps

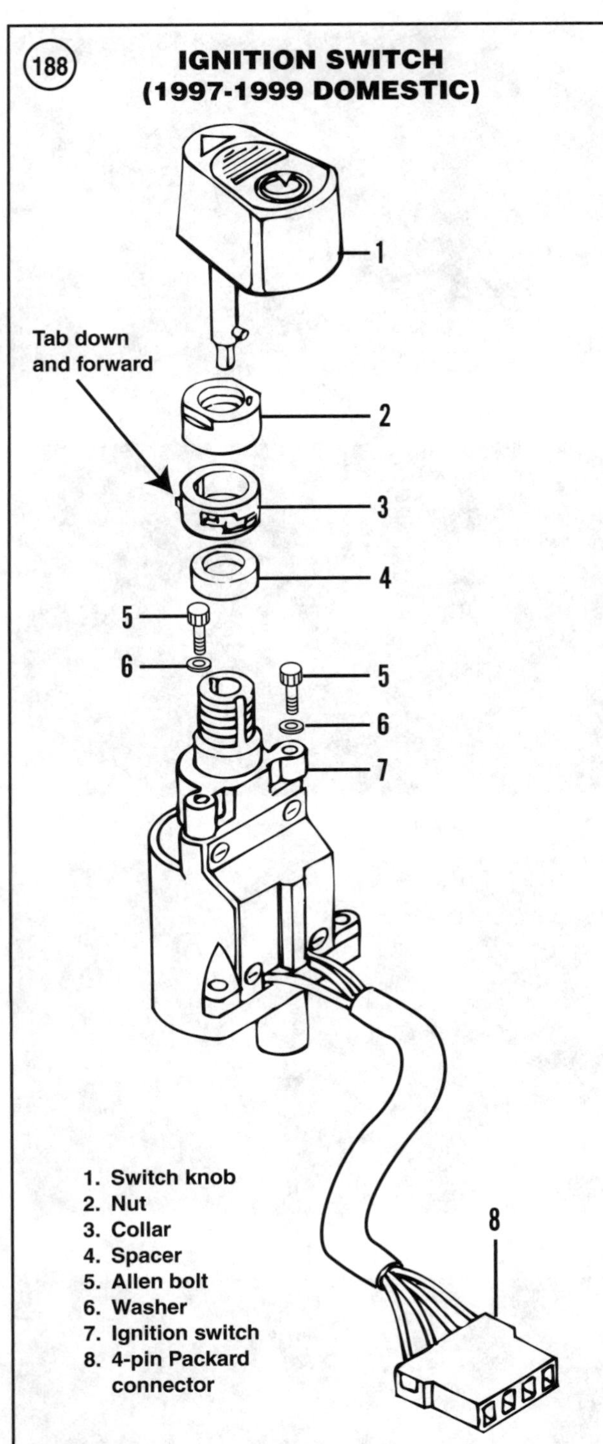

the support housing out of the way to gain access to the ignition switch.

10. Disconnect the electrical wires from the ignition switch.

11. Remove the switch housing head nut and spacer from the top of the ignition switch.
12. Push down on the threaded shaft and withdraw the ignition switch from beneath it. Then remove the ignition switch.
13. Install by reversing these removal steps.

Removal/Installation
(1994-1998 FLHR Series Models)

9

Refer to **Figure 187**.

1. Remove the fuel tank console as described under *Fuel Tank Console (1997-1998 FLHTC-I, FLHTC-UI, FLHR and FLHR-I Models)* in Chapter Eight.
2. Turn the fuel tank console upside down on towels on the workbench.
3. Disconnect the electrical connectors from the ignition switch.
4. Remove the screws securing the ignition switch to the back side of the instrument panel.
5. Remove the ignition switch.
6. Install by reversing these removal steps.

Ignition/Light Switch Removal/Installation
(1997-1999 Domestic Models)

Refer to **Figure 188**.

1. Remove the outer fairing as described in Chapter Fifteen.
2. To remove the ignition switch knob, perform the following:
   a. Using the ignition key, turn the ignition switch to the UNLOCK position.
   b. Turn the ignition switch knob to the ACCESS position.
   c. Insert a small flat-blade screwdriver under the left side of the switch knob (A, **Figure 189**) and depress the release button. Keep it depressed.

d. Push the ignition key down, turn the ignition key 60° *counterclockwise* (B, **Figure 189**), and lift up and remove the switch knob.

3. Use a 7/8-in. open-end wrench and loosen the ignition switch nut (**Figure 190**). Unscrew and remove the nut from the threaded post.

4. Remove the collar and spacer (**Figure 191**) from the threaded post.

5. Pull on the tabs and remove the decal plate (**Figure 192**) from the slots in the fairing cap.

6. Remove the T27 Torx screws and washers (**Figure 193**) on each side securing the fairing cap on each side of the inner fairing.

7. Carefully disengage the fairing cap (**Figure 194**) and pull it down. Disconnect the auxiliary switch electrical connector from the harness (A, **Figure 195**).

8. Carefully remove the auxiliary switch wiring harness (B, **Figure 195**) from around the ignition switch and remove the fairing cap from the front fairing inner panel.

9. Working at the front of the motorcycle, locate the ignition switch black four-pin Packard electrical connector next to the fork bracket. Disconnect the four-pin connector.

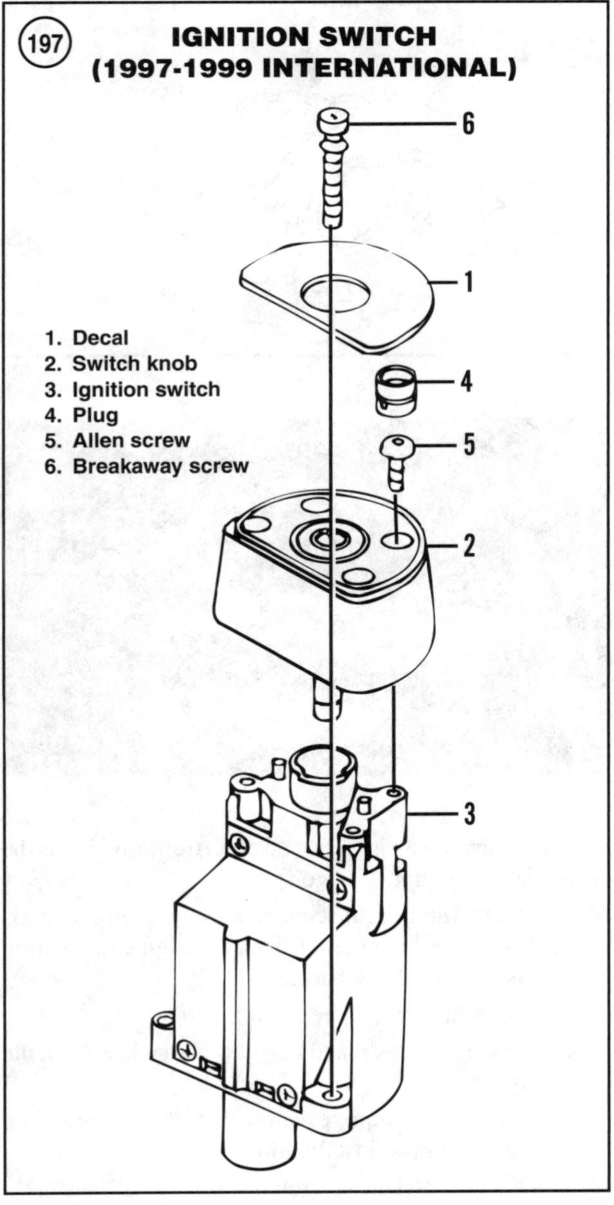

10. Remove the Allen screws and washers (A, **Figure 196**) securing the ignition switch to the upper fork bracket.

11. Carefully remove the ignition switch (B, **Figure 196**) and wiring harness from the inner fairing.

12. Installation is the reverse of removal. Note the following:
   a. Apply a light coat of dielectric compound to the electrical connectors prior to connecting them.
   b. Install the ignition switch to the upper fork bracket and tighten the Allen screws to 40-50 in.-lb. (5-6 N•m).
   c. Check the switch in each of the operating positions.

Ignition/Light Switch Removal/Installation (1997-1999 International Models)

Refer to **Figure 197**.

1. Remove the outer fairing as described in Chapter Fifteen.

2. To remove the ignition switch knob, perform the following:
   a. Remove the decal on top of the ignition switch knob.
   b. Remove the plug above each Allen screw with a screw extractor or Easy-Out. Refer to Chapter One.
   c. Remove the four Allen screws securing the knob and remove the knob.

3. Remove the T27 Torx screws and washers (**Figure 193**) on each side securing the fairing cap on each side of the inner fairing.

4. Carefully disengage the fairing cap (**Figure 194**) and pull it down. Disconnect the auxiliary switch electrical connector from the harness (A, **Figure 195**).

5. Carefully remove the auxiliary switch wiring harness (B, **Figure 195**) from around the ignition switch and remove the fairing cap from the front fairing inner panel.

6. At the front of the motorcycle, locate the ignition switch black 4-pin Packard electrical connector next to the fork bracket. Disconnect the 4-pin connector.

7. Carefully working within the inner fairing, use a long-shank 3/16-in. drill to drill out the two breakaway screws at the base of the ignition switch securing the ignition switch to the upper fork bracket.

8. Carefully remove the ignition switch and wiring harness from the inner fairing.

9. Use pliers to remove the remaining portions of the breakaway screws from the upper fork bracket.

10. Install by reversing these removal steps. Note the following:
   a. Apply a light coat of dielectric compound to the electrical connectors prior to connecting them.

b. Install the new ignition switch to the upper fork bracket. Install new breakaway screws and tighten until the heads break off.
c. Install new plugs over the breakaway screws.
d. Check the switch in each of the operating positions.

OIL PRESSURE SWITCH

Operation

The oil pressure switch is located on the right crankcase next to the rear tappet guide (**Figure 198**). The electrical wire is connected to the switch with a lockwasher and nut.

A pressure-actuated diaphragm oil pressure switch is used. When the oil pressure is low, or when oil is not circulating through a running engine, spring tension inside the switch holds the switch contacts closed. This completes the signal light circuit and causes the oil pressure indicator lamp to light.

The oil pressure signal light should turn on when any of the following occurs:

1. The ignition switch is turned on prior to starting the engine.
2. The engine idle is below idle speed specified in Chapter Three.
3. The engine is operating with low oil pressure.
4. Oil is not circulating through the running engine.

NOTE

The oil pressure indicator light might not come on when the ignition switch is turned off and then back on immediately. This is due to the oil pressure retained in the oil filter housing. The following steps test the electrical part of the oil pressure switch. If the oil pressure switch, indicator lamp and related wiring are in good condition, inspect the lubrication system as described in Chapter Two.

198

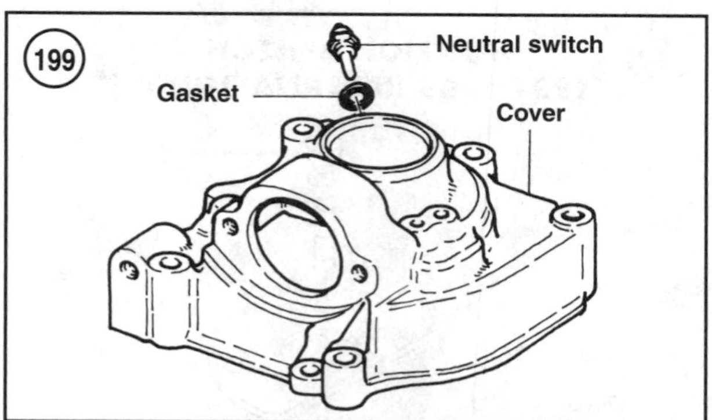

199

200

Testing/Replacement

1. Remove the rubber boot and disconnect the electrical connector from the switch.
2. Turn the ignition switch on.
3. Ground the switch wire to the engine.
4. The oil pressure indicator lamp on the instrument panel must light.
5. If the indicator lamp does not light, check for a defective indicator lamp and inspect all wiring between the switch or sender and the indicator lamp.

6A. If the oil pressure warning light operates properly, attach the electrical connector to the pressure switch. Make sure the connection is tight and free from oil. Slide the rubber boot back into position.

6B. If the warning light remains on when the engine is running, shut the engine off. Check the engine lubrication system as described in Chapter Two.

7. To replace the switch, perform the following:
   a. Use a deep socket and unscrew the switch from the engine.
   b. Apply Loctite pipe sealant with Teflon to the switch threads prior to installation.
   c. Install the switch securely.

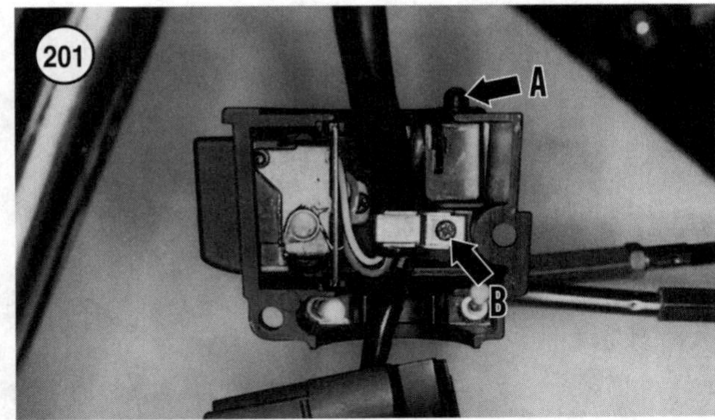

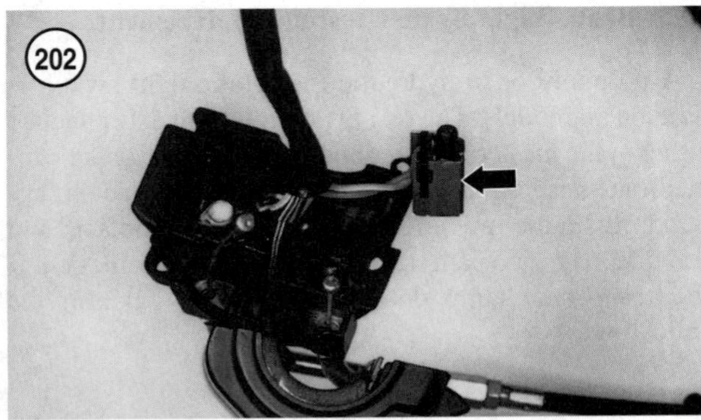

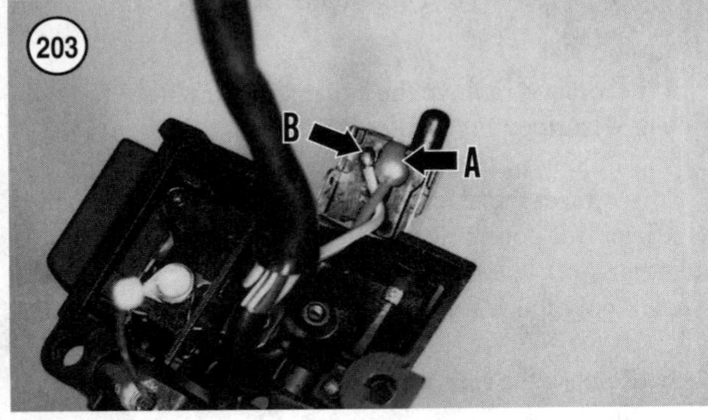

d. Test the new switch as described in Steps 1-4.

NEUTRAL INDICATOR SWITCH TESTING/REPLACEMENT

The neutral indicator switch is mounted on the shifter cover on four-speed models (**Figure 199**) and on top of the transmission cover on five-speed models (**Figure 200**). The neutral indicator light on the instrument panel should light when the ignition is turned on and the transmission is in neutral.

1. Slide the rubber boot up the neutral switch wire and disconnect the electrical connector to the switch.
2. Turn the ignition switch on.
3. Ground the switch wire to the transmission housing.
4. The neutral indicator light on the instrument panel should light.
5. If the neutral indicator lamp lights, the neutral switch is defective. Replace the neutral indicator switch and retest.
6. If the neutral indicator lamp does not light, check for a defective indicator lamp, faulty wiring or a loose or corroded connection.

7A. If the neutral switch operates correctly, attach the electrical connector to the neutral switch. Make sure the connection is tight and free from oil.

7B. If the neutral switch is defective, replace the neutral indicator switch.

8. To replace the old switch, perform the following:
   a. Shift the transmission into neutral.
   b. Unscrew and remove the old switch and O-ring.
   c. Apply clean transmission oil to the *new* O-ring seal.
   d. Install the new switch and tighten securely.

BRAKE LIGHT SWITCH

Front Brake Light Switch Replacement

1984-1995 models

The front brake light switch (A, **Figure 201**) is mounted in the lower right switch housing.

1. Separate the right switch housing as described under *Handlebar Switch Replacement* in this chapter.
2. Remove the wire clamp screw (B, **Figure 201**).
3. Push the switch button and slide the switch out of the housing (**Figure 202**).
4. Scrape the silicone off the red or red/yellow wire connection (A, **Figure 203**) at the switch.
5. Heat the two soldered wire connections and pull the wires away from the switch. Then discard the switch.
6. Slip a piece of heat shrink tubing over each wire.
7. Solder the red/yellow (A, **Figure 203**) and orange/white (B) wires to the *new* switch. Then shrink the tubing over the wires. Test the new switch.
8. After the soldered connections are completely cool, apply a small amount of silicone to the red/yellow wire connection at the switch (A, **Figure 203**).

NOTE

Allow the silicone to cure prior to assembling the switch halves onto the handlebar.

9. Push the switch button and slide the switch onto the housing (**Figure 202**).

10. Rotate the brake switch wires through the half-moon guide in the bottom of the switch housing. Install the wire clamp and screw (B, **Figure 201**).

11. Check the wiring harness routing position to make sure it is not pinched between the housing and the handlebar.

12. Assemble and install the right switch housing as described under *Handlebar Switch Replacement* in this chapter.

WARNING
Do not ride the motorcycle until the throttle cables are properly adjusted. Likewise, the cables must not catch or pull when the handlebars are turned. Improper cable routing and adjustment can cause the throttle to stick open. This could cause loss of control.

1996-1998 models

The front brake light switch (**Figure 204**) is mounted in the lower right switch housing.

1. Separate the right side switch housing as described under *Handlebar Switch Replacement* in this chapter.
2. If still in place, remove the wedge between the switch and the switch housing.
3. While depressing the switch plunger, slowly rotate the switch upward, rock it slightly, and remove it from the switch housing.
4. Cut the switch wires from the defective switch.
5. Slip a piece of heat shrink tubing over each wire cut in Step 4.
6. Solder the wire ends to the new switch. Then shrink the tubing over the wires. Test the new switch.
7. Install the switch by reversing these steps and performing the following.
8. When clamping the switch housing onto the handlebar, check the wiring harness routing position to make sure it is not pinched between the housing and handlebar.
9. Assemble the right switch housing as described under *Handlebar Switch Replacement* in this chapter.

WARNING
Do not ride the motorcycle until the throttle cables are properly adjusted. Likewise, the cables must not catch or pull when the handlebars are turned. Improper cable routing and adjustment can cause the throttle to stick open. This could cause loss of control.

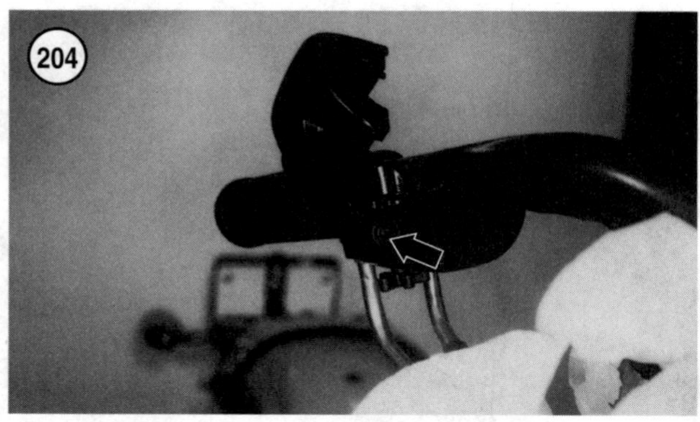

Rear Brake Light Switch Testing/Replacement

A normally open hydraulic rear brake light switch is used on all models. The rear brake light switch is attached either to the master cylinder body or to the rear brake caliper brake hose assembly. When the rear brake pedal is applied, hydraulic pressure closes the switch contacts and provides a ground path so the rear brake lamp comes on. If the rear brake lamp does not come on, perform the following.

NOTE
Removal of the exhaust system is not necessary, but it does provide additional work room for this test and replacement, if necessary.

1. If necessary, remove the exhaust system from the right side as described in Chapter Seven.
2. Turn the ignition switch off.
3. Disconnect the electrical connector from the switch.
4. Check for continuity between the switch terminals as follows:
   a. Apply the rear brake pedal. There must be continuity.
   b. Release the rear brake pedal. There must be no continuity.
   c. If the switch fails either of these tests, replace the switch.
5. Place a drip pan under the switch because some brake fluid will drain out when the switch is removed.

6A. On 1984-1986 FXR series models and 1984-1991 FLT series models, remove the switch from the rear left side of the rear master cylinder.

6B. On all other models, remove the switch from the rear brake line fitting.

7. Thread the new switch into the fitting and tighten securely.
8. Reconnect the switch electrical connectors.
9. Bleed the rear brake as described in Chapter Thirteen.

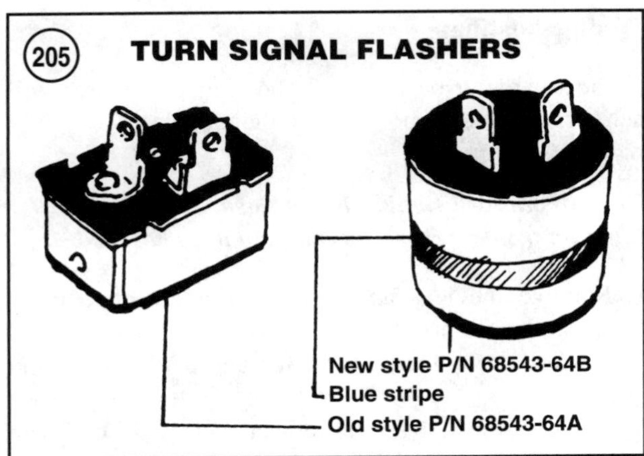

10. Check the rear brake light operation. Turn the ignition switch on and apply the rear brake. The light must come on.

HORN

Testing

1. Remove the seat as described in Chapter Fifteen.
2. Disconnect the electrical connector from the back side of the horn.
3. Check for voltage as follows:
   a. Positive test lead to the electrical connector.
   b. Negative test lead to ground.
4. Turn the ignition switch on.
5. Depress the horn button. If battery voltage is present, the horn is faulty or is not grounded properly. If there is no battery voltage, either the horn switch or the horn wiring is faulty.
6. Check the resistance across both horn terminals. The correct resistance is 45-66 ohms. If the circuit is open, the horn is defective.
7. Replace the horn or horn switch as necessary.

Replacement

1. Remove the seat as described in Chapter Fifteen.
2. Disconnect the negative battery cable as described in this chapter.
3. Remove the long acorn nut securing the horn assembly bracket to the frame post.
4. Move the horn assembly to the frame and engine and disconnect the electrical connectors from the horn spade terminals.
5. Remove the screw and nut securing the horn to the mounting bracket and remove the horn.
6. Install the horn by reversing these removal steps. Note the following:
   a. Make sure the electrical connectors and horn spade terminals are free of corrosion.
   b. Connect the wires to the horn top spade terminals.
   c. Check that the horn operates correctly.

TURN SIGNAL AND FOUR-WAY FLASHERS (1984-1990 FXR SERIES MODELS AND 1984-1988 FLH AND FLT SERIES MODELS)

The FXR series models are only equipped with a single turn signal flasher. The FLH and FLT series models are equipped with a turn signal flasher and a four-way flasher.

NOTE
On 1986 models, if the turn signals do not work, check to see whether both the left and right turn signal switches are turned on at the same time. This will overload the flasher and prevent it from operating properly.

NOTE
*The 1984-early 1986 models are equipped with a rectangular flasher. The late 1986 and later models are equipped with a round flasher with a blue stripe (**Figure 205**). Do not use a replacement round flasher that does not have the blue stripe because it will cause incorrect turn signal operation.*

Replacement (All FXR Models Except FXLR, FXRD and FXRT)

1. Remove the headlight sealed beam.
2. Remove the flasher and install a *new* one.
3. Reverse to install. Make sure the flasher is positioned in the headlight housing so that the electrical terminals on the flasher face the rear of the motorcycle.

CAUTION
If the flasher is installed with the electrical terminals facing forward, the terminals can become damaged from contact with the sealed beam unit.

4. Check headlight adjustment as described in this chapter. Check flasher operation.

Replacement (FXLR Models)

The flasher is mounted on the upper engine mount stabilizer bracket above the carburetor. Remove wires and install a *new* flasher. Check flasher operation.

9

Replacement (FXRT and FXRD Models)

The flasher is mounted inside the fairing above the headlight.

1. Remove the instrument panel.
2. Working through the instrument panel opening, disconnect the flasher and install a *new* flasher.
3. Install by reversing these steps.

Replacement (1984-1988 FLT and FLH Series Models)

NOTE

The turn signal and four-way flashers must be installed in the original mounting positions. To prevent confusion when removing both flashers, record the flasher positions prior to removing them.

1A. On FLHTC models, the turn signal and four-way flashers are mounted on a bracket attached to the fork stem. Perform the following:

   a. Remove the headlight assembly.
   b. Working through the headlight opening, disconnect the wires from the flasher and remove the flasher from its mounting clip.

1B. On FLTC and FLHS models, the turn signal and four-way flashers are mounted on a bracket attached to the fork stem. Perform the following:

   a. Remove the instrument panel.
   b. Working through the instrument panel opening, disconnect the wires from the flasher and remove the flasher from its mounting clip.

2. Install a new flasher in the original mounting position by reversing these steps. Check headlight adjustment on FLHTC models as described in this chapter. Check flasher operation.

TURN SIGNAL MODULE (1989-1994 MODELS)

The turn signal module (TSM) is an electronic microprocessor that controls the turn signals and the four-way hazard flasher. The turn signal module receives its information from the speedometer and turn signal switches.

The turn signal module is mounted to the frame panel under the right side cover on FXR series models and onto the right upper fork tube on FLH and FLT series models.

If the following tests do not locate the problem, refer TSM testing to a Harley-Davidson dealership.

Troubleshooting

The following basic troubleshooting procedures will help isolate specific problems to the module.

One or both turn signals do not flash.
Light on front or rear side is lit, but does not flash

1. Remove the lens and check for a defective bulb. Replace if necessary.
2. If the bulb is good, check for one of the following problems:
   a. Check the bulb socket contacts for corrosion. Clean contacts and recheck. If there is a problem with corrosion building on the contacts, wipe the contacts with a dielectric grease before installing the bulb.
   b. Check for a damaged electrical wire. Repair wire or connector.
   c. Check for a loose bulb socket where it is staked to the housing. If the bulb socket is loose, replace the light assembly.
   d. Check for a poor ground connection. If necessary, scrape the ground mounting area or replace damaged ground wire(s).

Turn signals do not operate on one side

1. Perform the checks listed under *One or both turn signals do not flash. Light on front or rear side is lit, but does not flash.* If these checks do not locate the problem, proceed to Step 2.
2. Inspect the handlebar directional switch as follows:
   a. Turn the ignition switch on.
   b. Disconnect the turn signal module electrical connector.
   c. Referring to **Figure 206**, locate pin No. 6 or No. 7 for 1994 FLH and FLT models or pin No. 8 or No. 10 for all other models.
   d. Connect the voltmeter negative lead to a good ground and the positive lead to pin No.6 or No. 7 (1994 FLH and FLT models) or pin No. 8 or No. 10 (all other models) and press the turn signal switch. The meter should indicate 12 volts when the switch is pressed in.
   e. If the voltage is correct, proceed to Step 3.
   f. If the voltage reading is incorrect, proceed to Step 4.
3. If 12 volts were recorded in Step 2, and the lights and connecting wires are in good condition, the module might be damaged. Replace the module and retest.
4. A damaged directional switch wire circuit is possible. If no voltage was recorded in Step 2, check the handlebar

206

TURN SIGNAL MODULE

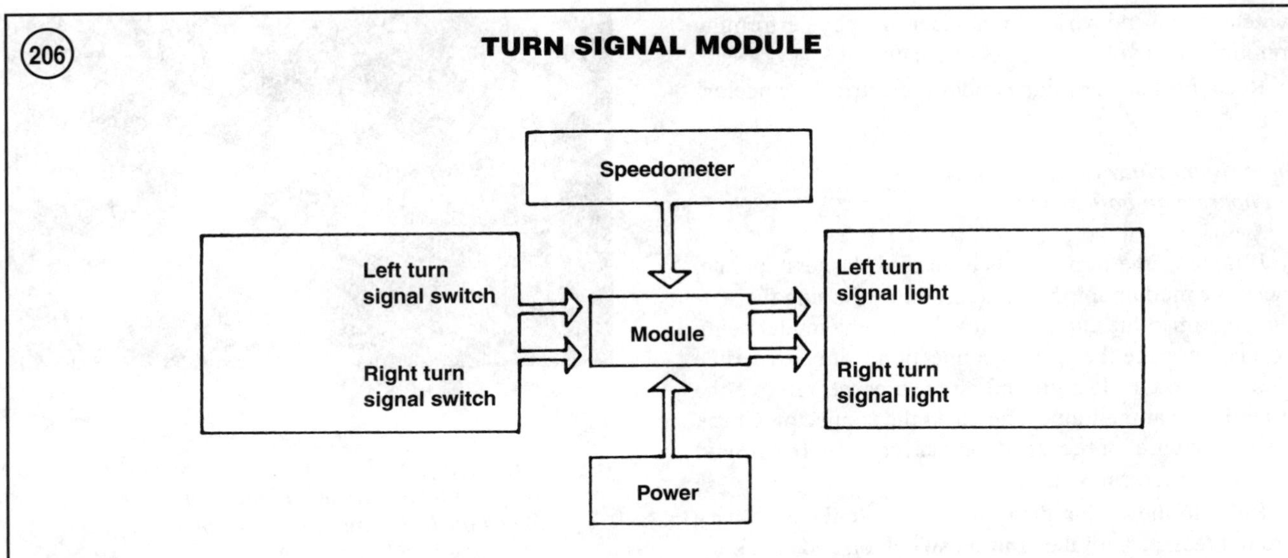

1989-1993 FLH, FLT AND 1991-1998 FXR CONNECTOR BLOCK

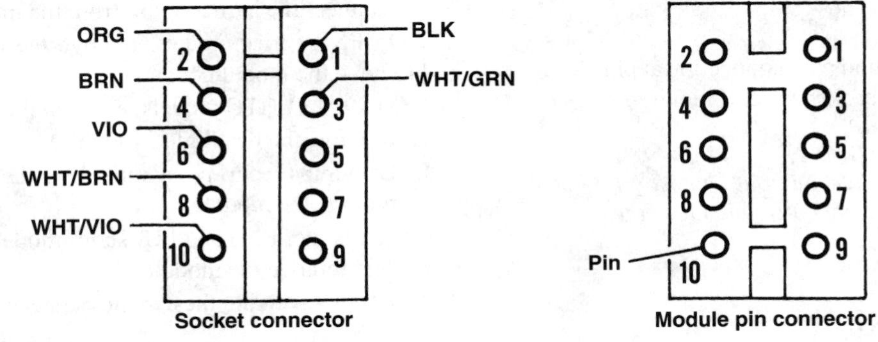

1994 FLH AND FLT CONNECTOR 30A

Pin No.	1	2	3	4	5	6	7	8
Color code	BLK	ORG WHT	WHT GRN	BRN	VIO	WHT BRN	WHT VIO	OPEN

9

switch and related wiring for damage. Test by performing continuity and voltage checks of the circuit.

5. Reconnect the turn signal module electrical connector.

Turn signals/hazard lights do not operate on both sides

1. If none of the turn signals or hazard flashers operate, check the module for ground (continuity). Using the wiring diagram at the end of the manual for the model being worked on, trace the ground connection from the module to the frame tab. If a ground is not present, remove the ground wire at the frame, and clean the connector. Check the ground wire for breaks. Repair as required. If a ground is present, perform Step 2.

2. Refer to the wiring diagram and locate the accessory circuit breaker. Turn the ignition switch on and check for voltage on the hot or load side of the circuit breaker. If there is no voltage, check the following components:

   a. Accessory circuit breaker.
   b. Main circuit breaker.
   c. Starter relay.
   d. Ignition switch.
   e. Circuit wiring.

3. Check for an open ground wire connection at pin No. 1 (**Figure 206**). Repair the broken wire, if required.

CAUTION
Operating the module without pin No. 1 grounded will permanently damage the module.

Turn signals do not cancel

1. Support the motorcycle with the front wheel off the ground. Refer to *Motorcycle Stands* in Chapter Ten.

2. Connect an ohmmeter to the white/green speedometer switch wire and ground. Spin the front wheel and observe the readings. The ohmmeter should alternate between 0 ohm and infinity.

   a. If the reading is correct, disconnect the module pin connector. Connect the voltmeter negative lead to a good ground and the positive lead to the No. 3 pin socket connector. There should be 12 volts. If resistance and voltage readings are correct, the module is damaged.
   b. If resistance reading is incorrect, check for damaged wiring from the white/green speedometer switch wire to the module. If the wiring is good, the reed switch in the speedometer might be damaged.

NOTE
The reed switch signal also controls the sound system volume and the cruise control speed on 1990 and later Ultra models.

Removal/Installation

The turn signal module is mounted onto the right upper fork tube on FLT models and to the frame panel underneath the right side cover on FXR models.

1. Disconnect the harness plug from the module.

2A. On FXR series models, remove the mounting bolt and remove the module.

2B. On 1994 FLHTC models, perform the following:

   a. Remove the headlight assembly.
   b. Cut straps securing the module to the fork tube and remove the module.

2C. On all other FLH and FLT series models, cut harness straps and remove the module.

3. Install by reversing these removal steps.

TURN SIGNAL MODULE (1995-1998 MODELS)

The turn signal module (TSM) is an electronic microprocessor that controls the turn signals and the four-way hazard flashers. The turn signal module receives its information from the speedometer and turn signal switches.

The turn signal module is located under the seat within the cavity in the frame backbone.

If the following tests do not locate the problem with the TSM, have the unit tested by a Harley-Davidson dealership.

Operation

Refer to **Figure 207**.

1. When the left turn signal switch is pressed, a momentary 12-VDC pulse goes to pin No. 8 (input) on the TSM. The module responds to this signal by sending a series of 12-VDC pulses to pin No. 4 (output) to flash the left front and rear turn signal lamps.

2. The TSM then monitors the number of motorcycle sensor pulses sent from the speedometer sending unit to Pin No. 5. These pulses indicate the distance the bike has traveled. When the number of speedometer pulses is equal to the quantity preset in the module program, the turn signal is canceled.

NOTE

If the turn signal switch is pressed and held in, the turn signal will flash indefinitely until the switch is released.

3. When the right turn signal switch is pressed, a momentary 12-VDC pulse goes to pin No. 7 (input) on the TSM and an output signal at pin No. 3 (output). The remaining signal process is identical to the left turn signal operation.

Preliminary Troubleshooting

If one of the turn signals does not flash, perform the following:

1. Remove the lens and check for a defective bulb(s). Replace the bulb(s) if necessary.

2. If the bulb(s) is good, check for one of the following problems:

   a. Check the bulb socket contacts for corrosion. Clean the contacts and recheck. If there is a problem with corrosion building on the contacts, wipe the contacts with a dielectric grease before reinstalling the bulb.

   b. Check for a damaged wire within the circuit. Repair the wire(s) or connector(s).

   c. Check for a loose bulb socket where it is staked to the housing. If the bulb socket is loose, replace the light assembly.

   d. Check for a poor ground connection. If the ground is poor, clean the ground mounting area or replace damaged ground wire(s), as required.

   e. Stuck turn signal button.

3. Remove the TSM as described in this section.

4. Disconnect the electrical connector from the TSM.

5. Check the electrical connectors in the TSM and in the wiring harness for corrosion. Clean off if necessary.

Distance Test

The turn signal module (TSM) recognizes four different speed ranges and uses these distances to activate the cancellation action. Refer to the speed ranges listed in **Table 9**.

1. Ride the bike at the midpoint of speed range No. 1.
2. Press and release the right turn button and closely check the motorcycle speed and the odometer at the time the button is released and the time the turn signal is canceled.
3. Repeat Step 1 and Step 2 for right and left turns at the midpoint of speed ranges No. 2 through No. 4.
4. If the distances observed in Steps 1-3 are not correct, check the following steps:
   a. Check the TSM ground connection and module pin connections for corrosion.
   b. Check all lamps and lamp connections.
   c. Check the motorcycle speed sensor connections and ground for corrosion.

9

Time Test

This is an alternate test to the previously described *Distance Test* to check whether the TSM is operating correctly. Measure the turn signal on time at the four indicated constant speeds listed in **Table 10**.

If the TSM fails this test, replace the TSM and repeat with a good module.

Rider Preference Setting

If the rider desires the turn signals to flash for a longer or shorter distance that the preset time, perform the following:

1. Longer distance cycle: Hold the turn signal longer and release it closer to the turning point.
2. Shorter distance cycle: Press the button a second time to cancel the turn signals.

Turn Signal Module (TSM) Removal/Installation

1. Remove the seat as described in Chapter Fifteen.
2. Turn the ignition switch off.

3A. On 1995 FLHT series models, perform the following:
   a. Remove the headlight assembly as described in this chapter.
   b. Disconnect the 8-place Deutsch connector from the TSM located just below the radio.

c. Remove the cable strap securing the TSM to the lower fork tube.
d. Install the *new* TSM and secure with cable straps.

3B. On 1996-1998 FLHT series models, perform the following:
a. Remove the outer fairing as described in Chapter Fifteen.
b. Disconnect the 8-place Deutsch connector from the TSM located just below the radio.
c. Remove the nut, flat washer and rubber washer. Then remove the TSM from the threaded bracket stud.
d. Position the *new* TSM with the flat side up and install it on the threaded stud.
e. Install the rubber washer, flat washer and nut, and tighten the nut securely.

3C. On FLHR series models, perform the following:
a. Remove the headlight assembly as described in this chapter.

NOTE
The connector bracket also serves as the locking plate for the steering stem nut.

b. On the left side, reach under the headlight nacelle, or shroud, and remove the bolt, flat washer and rubber washer. Then remove the TSM from the connector bracket.
c. Use a rocking motion, depress the external latches, and remove the connector from the TSM.
d. Install the connector onto the *new* TSM.
e. Install the rubber washer and flat washer onto the bolt.
f. Align the TSM bolt hole with the hole in the connector bracket and install the bolt. Tighten the bolt securely.
g. Install the headlight assembly as described in this chapter.

4. Check that the turn signal and flasher systems work properly.

SPEEDOMETER SPEED SENSOR (1996-1998 MODELS)

These models are equipped with an electronic speedometer assembly that consists of the speedometer, speed sensor and a function switch.

The speed sensor mounts directly over fifth gear on top of the transmission housing.

Performance Check

The Harley-Davidson Speedometer Tester must be used to check the performance of the speedometer.

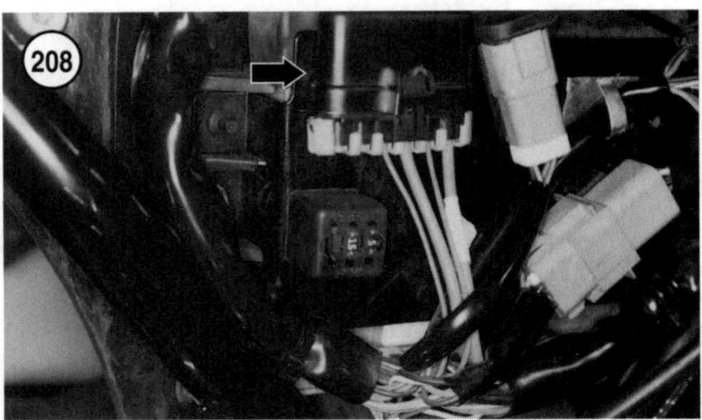

NOTE
This test cannot be used to verify the calibration of the speedometer and will not verify the speedometer function to support legal proceedings. The test will verify speedometer function when performing service diagnosis or repair and to verify whether the speedometer requires replacement.

Speedometer Speed Sensor Removal/Installation

The speedometer speed sensor mounts on top of the transmission case.

1. Remove the seat as described in Chapter Fifteen.
2. Disconnect the negative battery cable as described in this chapter.
3. Remove the Allen screw and remove the speed sensor from the transmission case.
4. Disconnect the 3-pin Mini-Deutsch connector containing one red, one black and one white wire in front of the battery box.
5. Carefully pull the electrical connector out from under the frame crossmember. Disconnect the secondary locks on the Mini-Deutsch connector and disconnect the connector.
6. Tie a piece of string to the electrical connector. Tie the other end of the string to the frame crossmember.
7. Carefully pull the wiring harness and connector out of the frame on the right side. If the wire becomes tight or stuck, do not force it. If necessary, make a drawing of the wire routing through the frame. It is easy to forget the routing path after removing the wire.
8. Untie the string from the wiring harness.
9. Install by reversing these removal steps while noting the following:
a. Tie the string to the wiring harness and connector.
b. Carefully pull the string and the wiring harness and connector through the right side of the frame and

into position under the seat. Untie and remove the string.

c. Apply a light coat of dielectric compound to the electrical connector(s) prior to installing them.

d. Apply clean engine oil to the *new* O-ring on the speedometer sensor prior to installation. Install the sensor and tighten the Allen screw securely.

RADIO, CB AND INTERCOM SYSTEMS

Refer all service related to the radio, CB and intercom systems to a Harley-Davidson dealership.

ELECTRICAL CIRCUIT PROTECTION

Fuses

The 1994-1998 FLH and FLT series models and 1999 FXR2 and FXR3 models are equipped with a series of fuses to protect the electrical system. The number of fuses varies depending on the year and model. The fuse ratings are listed in **Table 11**.

The fuel injection fuel pump and electronic control module fuses are located under the right frame cover. All other fuses are located under the left frame cover. If there is an electrical failure, first check for a blown fuse. A blown fuse will have a break in the element.

Whenever the fuse blows, find out the reason for the failure before replacing the fuse. Usually, the trouble is a short circuit in the wiring. This may be caused by worn-through insulation or a disconnected wire shorted to ground. Check the circuit the fuse protects.

Fuse Replacement

The 1994-1998 FLH and FLT series models are equipped with fuses to protect the electrical circuits. **Table 11** lists the fuse ratings and color code designation.

1. Disconnect the negative battery cable as described in this chapter.

2. Remove the right or left saddlebag and right or left frame cover as described in Chapter Fifteen.

3A. On fuel-injected models, depress the latch and remove the fuse block cover (**Figure 208**). Remove the fuse for the ECM and fuel pump.

3B. On 1994-1996 and 1999 models, remove the fuse block cover.

3C. On 1997-1998 models, depress the latches and remove the fuse block cover (**Figure 209**).

WARNING
For continued protection against risk of fire, replace old fuse only with the same type of fuse and rating.

4. Locate the blown fuse (**Figure 210**, typical 1997-1988 models) and install a new one of the *same* amperage.

NOTE
Always carry spare fuses.

CIRCUIT BREAKER

All models use a single circuit breaker to protect the electrical circuits. **Table 12** and **Table 13** list the circuit breaker ratings.

Whenever a failure occurs in any part of the electrical system, the circuit breaker is self-resetting and will automatically return power to the circuit when the electrical fault is found and corrected.

CAUTION
If the electrical fault is not found and corrected, the circuit breaker will cycle on and off continuously. This will cause the motorcycle to run erratically.

9

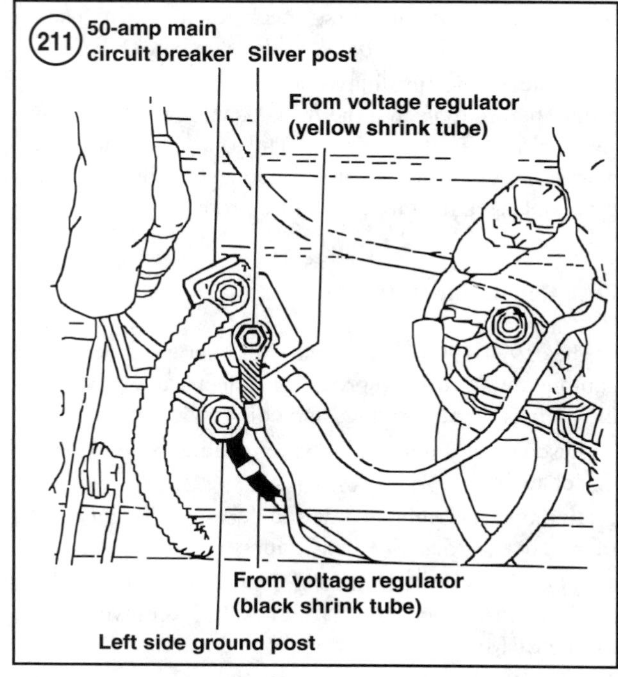

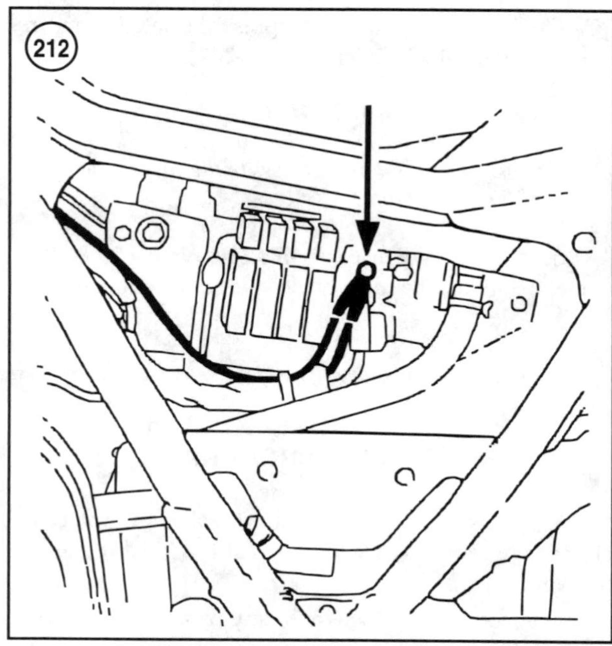

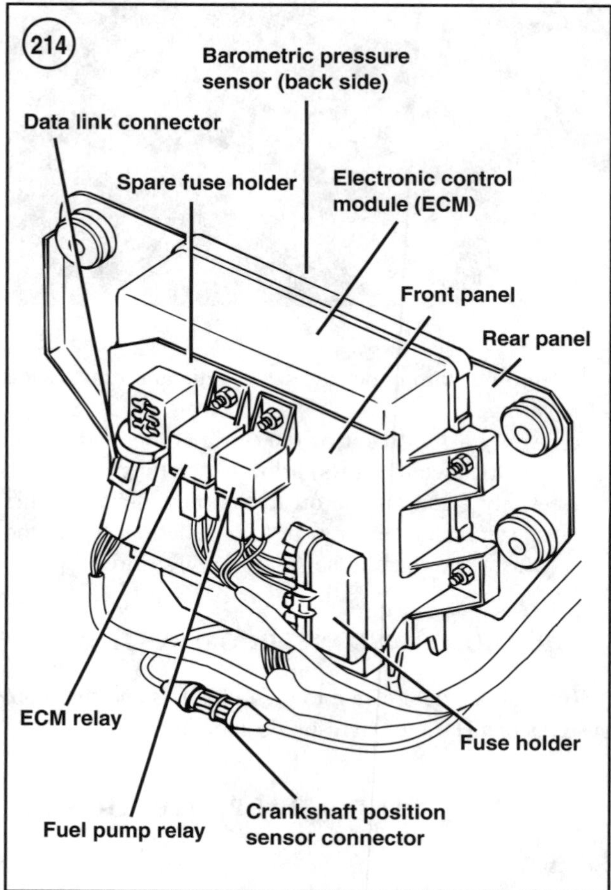

Refer to the wiring diagrams at the back of the manual to determine which circuits are protected by the breaker. Inspect the wiring and connectors for damage.

Do not ignore a tripped circuit breaker; it indicates that something is wrong in the electrical system requiring immediate attention.

Replacement

The circuit breaker is located under the seat or front fairing.

1. Disconnect the negative battery cable as described in this chapter.

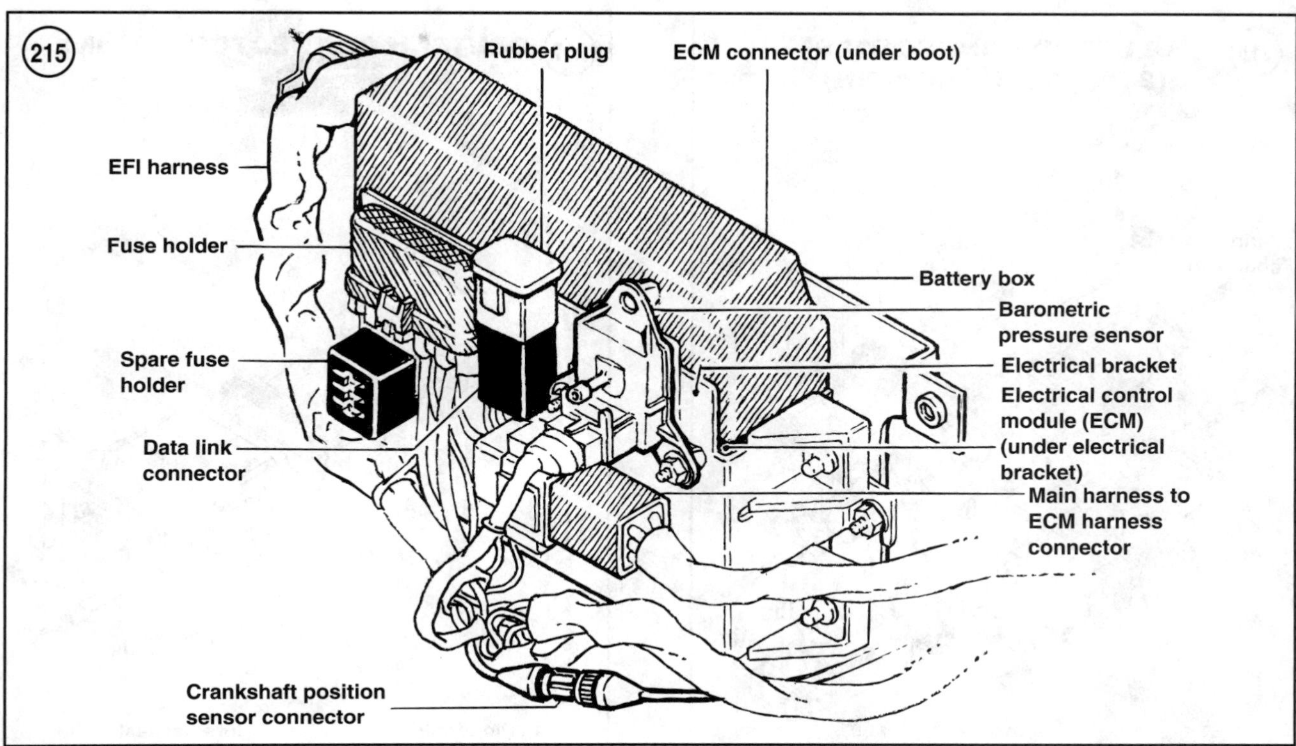

2. Remove the seat as described in Chapter Fifteen.
3. Remove the right or left cover as described in Chapter Fifteen.
4. On FLTCU models, remove the front fairing as described in Chapter Fifteen.

NOTE
Record the wire colors and the terminal to which they are connected. The wires must be reinstalled onto the correct terminals.

5A. On 1997-1998 models, remove the nuts and wire connections at the circuit breaker (**Figure 211**).
5B. On 1999 FXR2 and FXR3 models, remove the nuts and wire connections at the circuit breaker (**Figure 212**).
5C. On all other models, remove the nuts and wire connections at the circuit breaker on the electrical panel (**Figure 213**).
6. Remove the circuit breaker from the mounting bracket.
7. Install the circuit breaker by reversing these steps.

ELECTRICAL PANEL

The electrical panel is mounted on the right side of the motorcycle under the side cover. The panel assembly houses the circuit breaker(s), fuses (certain models) and, depending on model and year, various additional electrical connectors and components.

Refer to **Figures 213-215**.

1. Disconnect the negative battery cable as described in this chapter.
2. Remove the right or left side cover as described in Chapter Fifteen.
3. On models so equipped, remove the panel cover.
4. Install the panel cover if it was removed.
5. Connect the battery negative cable.

ELECTRICAL CONNECTORS

There are a variety of electrical connectors used throughout the electrical system. The following procedures are included in the event that the connector must be disassembled to replace an individual electrical wire within the connector.

Deutsch Socket Terminal Connectors

This procedure shows how to remove and install the socket terminals from the socket housing connector half. This procedure is shown on a 12-pin Deutsch connector

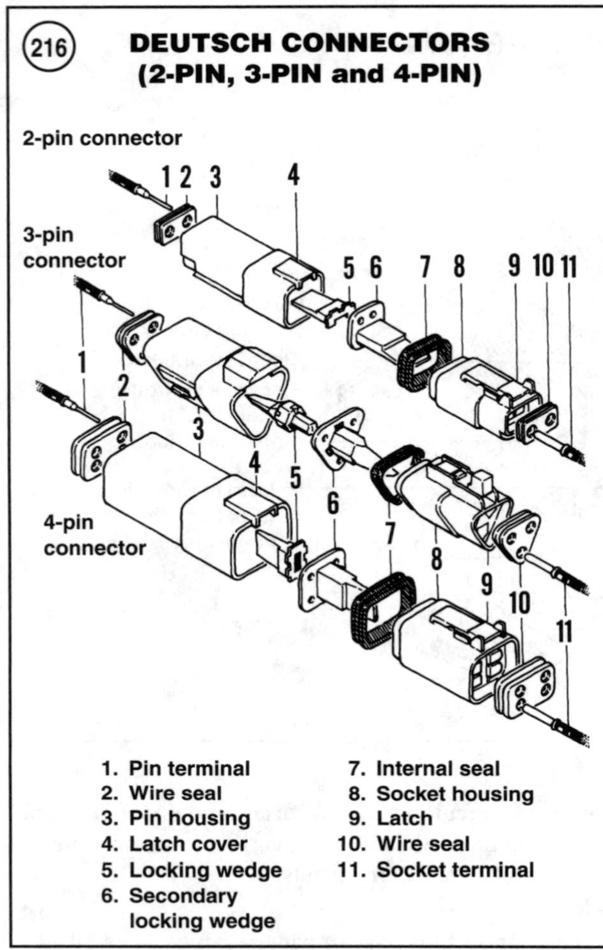

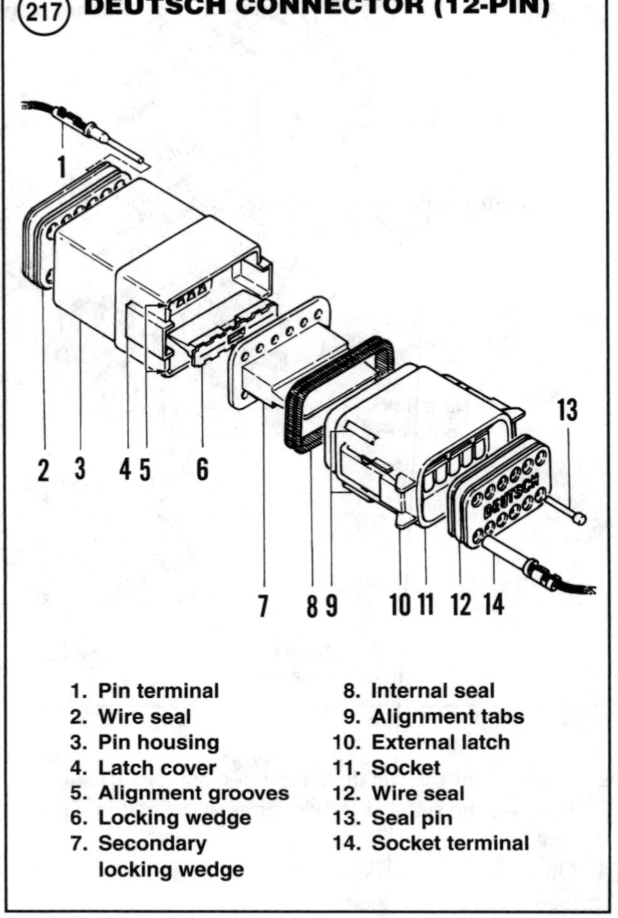

and relates to all of the Deutsch connectors (2-, 3-, 4- and 6-pin) connectors.

Refer to **Figure 216** and **Figure 217**.

1. Remove the seat as described in Chapter Fifteen.
2. Disconnect the negative battery cable as described in this chapter.
3. Disconnect the connector housing. Note the positions and colors of the wires before removing them.
4. Remove the secondary locking wedge (7, **Figure 217**) as follows:
   a. Locate the secondary locking wedge.
   b. Insert a wide-blade screwdriver between the socket housing and the locking wedge. Turn the screwdriver 90° to force up the wedge (**Figure 218**).
   c. Remove the secondary locking wedge (7, **Figure 217**).
5. Lightly press the terminal latches inside the socket housing and remove the socket terminal (14, **Figure 217**) through the holes in the rear wire seal.
6. Repeat Step 5 for each socket terminal.
7. If necessary, remove the wire seal (12, **Figure 217**).
8. Install the wire seal (12, **Figure 217**) into the socket housing if it was removed.
9. Refer to the notes made in Step 3. Hold the socket housing. Insert the socket terminals (14, **Figure 217**) through the holes in the wire seal so they enter the correct chamber holes. Continue until the socket terminal locks into place. Then lightly tug on the wire to make sure that it is locked in place.
10. Set the terminal seal (8, **Figure 217**) onto the socket housing if it was removed.

NOTE

With the exception of the 3-pin Deutsch connector, all of the secondary locking wedges are symmetrical. When assembling the 3-pin connector, the arrow on the secondary locking wedge must be installed so that it is

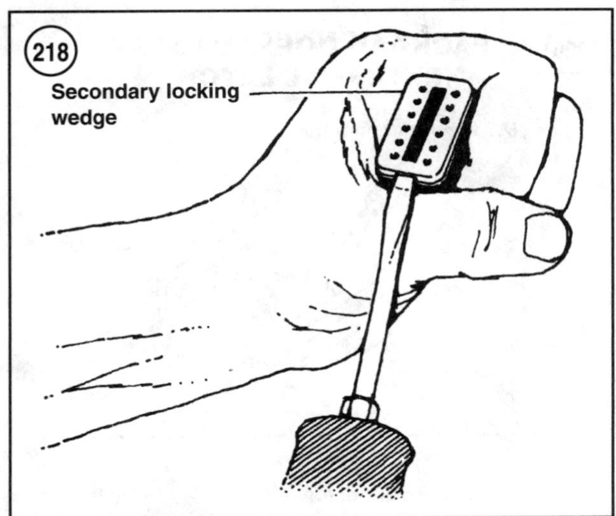

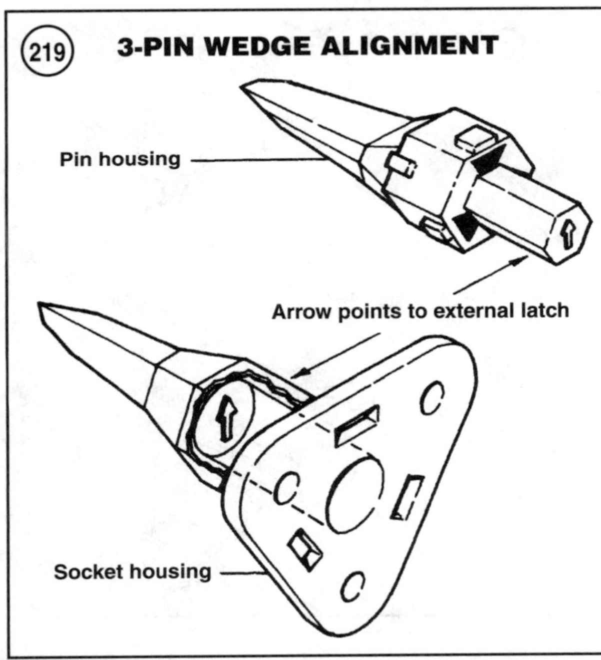

*pointing toward the external latch as shown in **Figure 219**.*

NOTE

If the secondary locking wedge does not slide into position easily, one or more of the socket terminals are not installed correctly. Correct the problem at this time.

11. Install the secondary locking wedge into the socket housing as shown in **Figure 216** or **Figure 217**. Press the secondary locking wedge down until it locks into place.

Deutsch Connector Terminal Pin

This procedure shows how to remove and install the pin terminals from the pin housing connector half (**Figure 216** and **Figure 217**). The procedure is shown on a 12-pin Deutsch connector and relates to all of the Deutsch connectors (2-, 3-, 4- and 6-pin) connectors.

1. Remove the seat as described in Chapter Fifteen.
2. Disconnect the negative battery cable as described in this chapter.
3. Disconnect the connector housing.
4. Use needlenose pliers to remove the secondary locking wedge (6, **Figure 217**)
5. Lightly press the terminal latches inside the pin housing and remove the pin terminal(s) (1, **Figure 217**) through the holes in the rear wire seal.
6. Repeat Step 5 for each socket terminal.
7. If necessary, remove the wire seal (2, **Figure 217**).
8. Install the wire seal (2, **Figure 217**) into the socket housing if it was removed.
9. Hold onto the pin housing and insert the pin terminals (1, **Figure 217**) through the holes in the wire seal so that they enter the correct chamber holes. Continue until the pin terminal locks in place. Then lightly tug on the wire to make sure that it is locked in place.
10. Set the terminal seal (8, **Figure 217**) onto the socket housing if it was removed.

NOTE

*With the exception of the 3-pin Deutsch connector, all of the secondary locking wedges are symmetrical. When assembling the 3-pin connector, the arrow on the secondary locking wedge must be installed so that it is pointing toward the external latch as shown in **Figure 219**.*

NOTE

If the secondary locking wedge does not slide into position easily, one or more of the socket terminals are not installed correctly. Correct the problem at this time.

11. Install the secondary locking wedge into the pin housing as shown in **Figure 216** or **Figure 217**. Press the secondary locking wedge down until it locks into place. When properly installed, the wedge will fit into the pin housing center groove.

Packard External Latch Connectors

This procedure shows how to remove and install the electrical terminals from external latch connectors with pull-to-seat terminals (**Figure 220**).

1. Remove the seat as described in Chapter Fifteen.
2. Disconnect the negative battery cable as described in this chapter.
3. Bend back the external latch(es) slightly and separate the connector.
4. Look into the mating end of the connector and locate the locking tang (1, **Figure 221**) located in the middle chamber and on the external latch side of connector. On locking ear connectors, the tang is on the side opposite the ear.
5. Insert the point of a 1-in. safety pin about 1/8 in. into the middle chamber (2, **Figure 221**). Pivot the end of the safety pin up toward the terminal body until a click is heard. Repeat this step several times. The click represents the tang returning to the locked position as it slips from the point of the safety pin. Continue to pick at the tang until the clicking stops and the safety pin seems to slide in at a slightly greater depth indicating the tang has been depressed.
6. Remove the safety pin, push the wire end of the lead, and remove the lead from the connector (3, **Figure 221**). If additional slack is necessary, pull back on the harness conduit and remove the wire seal at the back of the connector.
7. To install the terminal and wire back into the connector, use the thin flat blade of an X-Acto knife and carefully bend the tang outward away from the terminal (4, **Figure 221**).
8. Carefully pull the lead and terminal into the connector until a click is heard indicating the terminal is seated correctly within the connector. Gently push on the lead to make sure the terminal is correctly seated.
9. If necessary, install the wire seal and push the harness conduit back into position on the back side of the connector.
10. Push the socket halves together until the latch(es) are locked together.

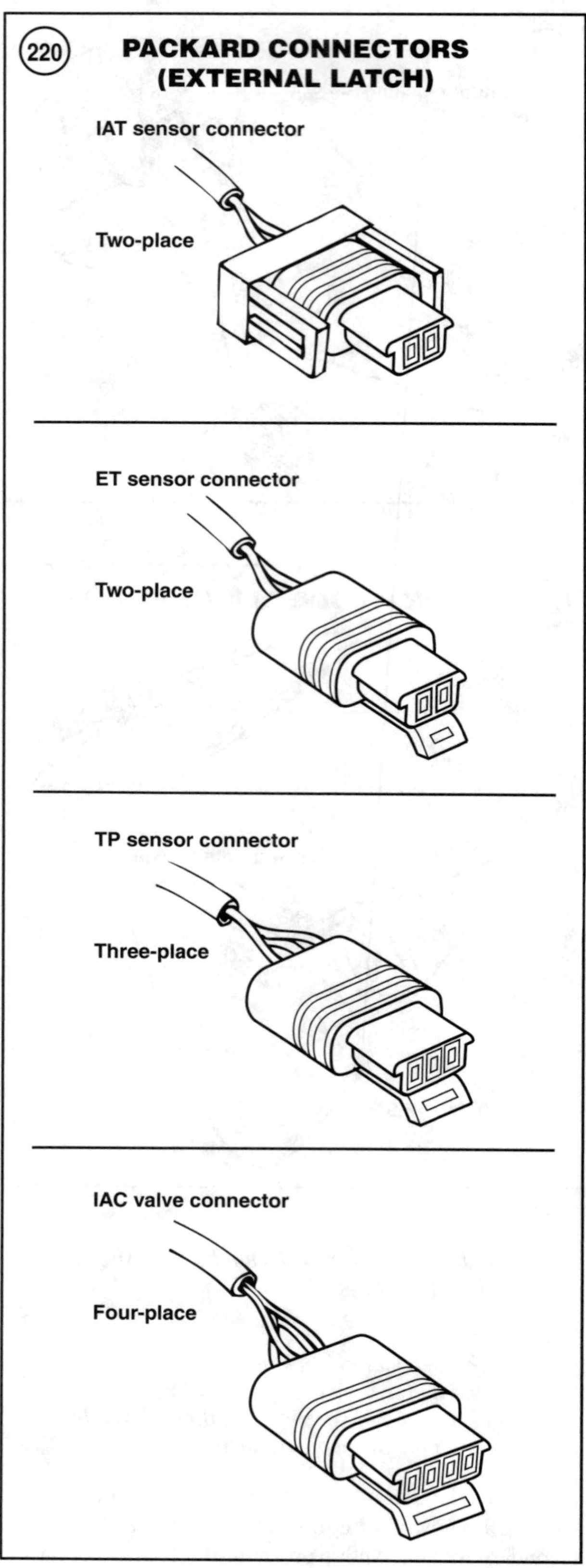

Packard Wire Form Connectors

This procedure shows how to remove and install the electrical terminals from wire form connectors with pull-to-seat terminals (**Figure 222**).

1. Remove the seat as described in Chapter Fifteen.
2. Disconnect the negative battery cable as described in this chapter.
3. Depress the wire form and separate the connector.
4. Hold the connector so the wire form is facing down.
5. Look into the mating end of the connector and locate the plastic rib that separates the wire terminals. The terminal is located on each side of the rib with the tang located at the rear.
6. Use the thin flat blade of an X-Acto knife to depress the tang. Tilt the blade at an angle and place the tip at the inboard edge of the terminal. Push down slightly until the

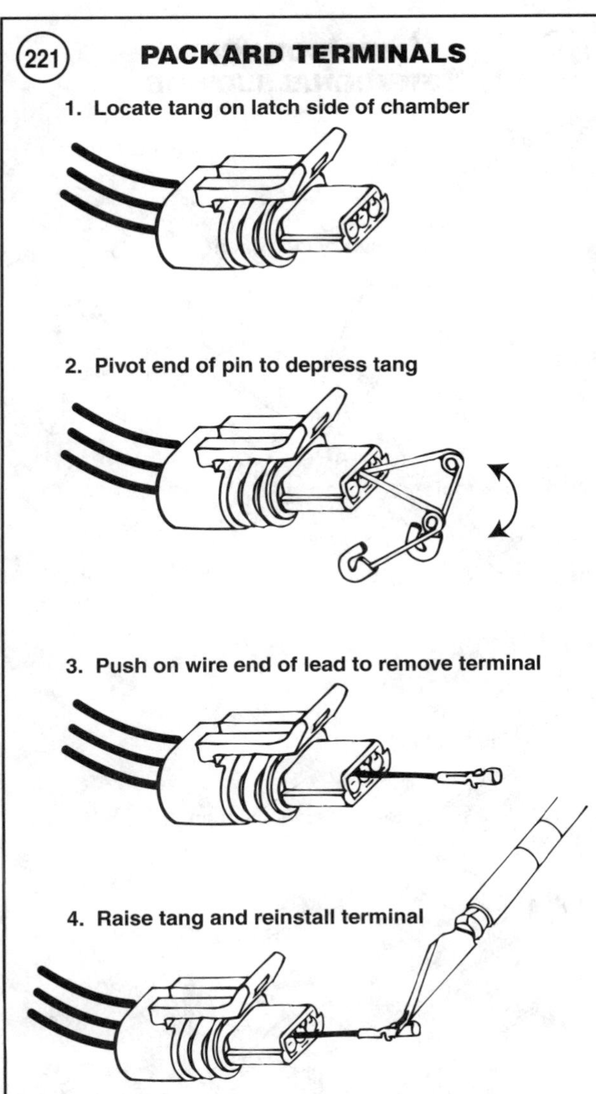

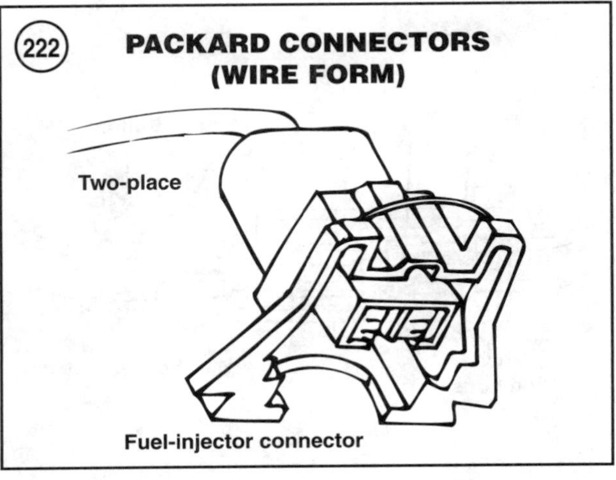

spring tension is relieved and a click is heard. Repeat this step several times. The click represents the tang returning to the locked position as it slips from the point of the knife blade. Continue to push down until the clicking stops indicating the tang has been depressed.

7. Remove the knife blade and push the wire end of the lead and remove the lead from the connector. If additional slack is necessary, pull back on the harness conduit and remove the wire seal at the back of the connector.

8. To install the terminal and wire back into the connector, use a thin flat blade of an X-Acto knife and carefully bend the tang outward away from the terminal.

9. Carefully pull the lead and terminal into the connector until a click is heard indicating the terminal is seated correctly within the connector. Gently pull on the lead to make sure the terminal is correctly seated.

10. If necessary, install the wire seal and push the harness conduit back into position on the back side of the connector.

11. Push the socket halves together until the latch(es) are locked together.

Amp Electrical Connectors

This procedure shows how to remove and install the socket and pin terminals from the pin and socket housing connector. This procedure relates to all 3-, 6- and 10-pin connectors (**Figure 223**).

1. Remove the seat as described in Chapter Fifteen.
2. Disconnect the negative battery cable as described in this chapter.
3. Depress the button on the socket on the terminal side and pull apart the connector.
4. Slightly bend back the latch and free one side of the secondary lock. Repeat for the other side.
5. Rotate the secondary lock (1, **Figure 224**) out on the hinge to access the terminals within the connector.

NOTE
Do not pull too hard on the wire until the tang is released or the terminal will be difficult to remove.

6. Insert a pick tool (2, **Figure 224**) into the flat edge of the terminal cavity until it stops. Pivot the pick tool away (3, **Figure 224**) from the terminal and gently pull on the wire to pull the terminal (4) from the terminal cavity. Note the wire location number on the connector (**Figure 225**) and from which chamber the wire was removed.

NOTE
The release button used to separate the connectors is located at the top of the connector.

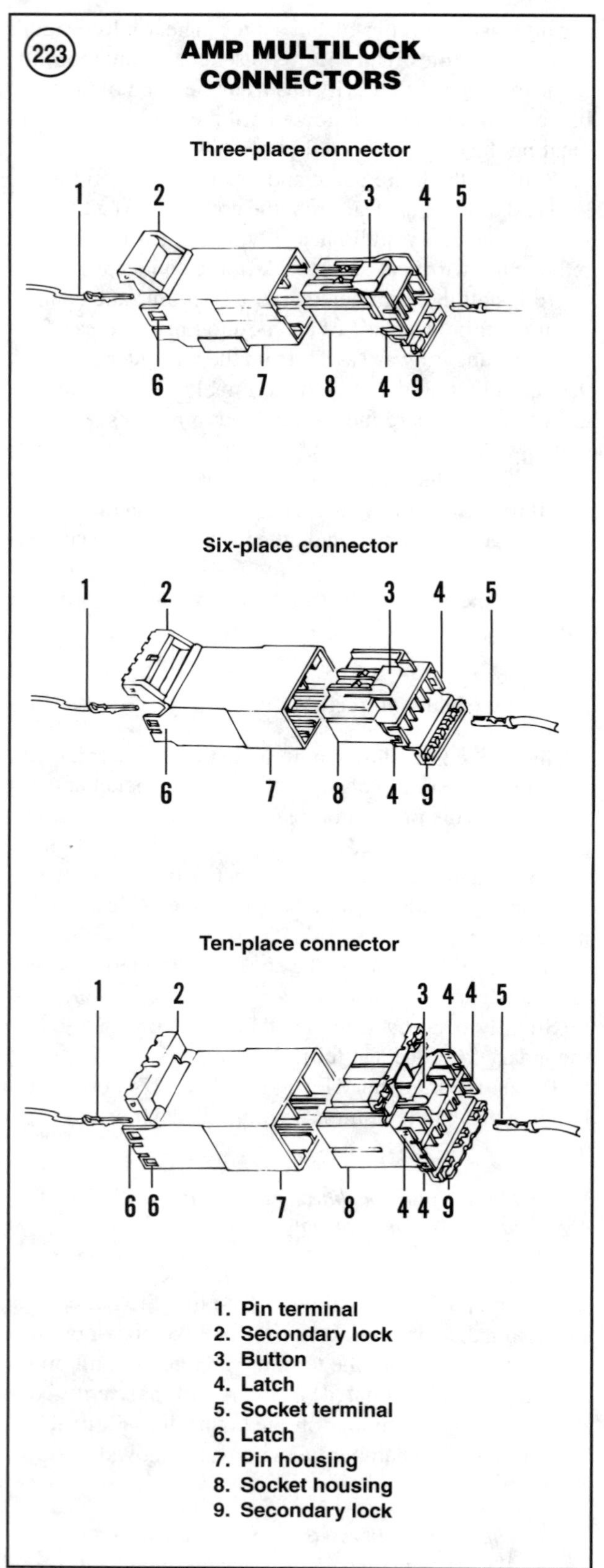
223
AMP MULTILOCK
CONNECTORS
Three-place connector
1
2
3
4
5
6
7
8
4
9
Six-place connector
1
2
3
4
5
6
7
8
4
9
Ten-place connector
1
2
3
4
4
5
6
6
7
8
4
4
9
1. Pin terminal
2. Secondary lock
3. Button
4. Latch
5. Socket terminal
6. Latch
7. Pin housing
8. Socket housing
9. Secondary lock

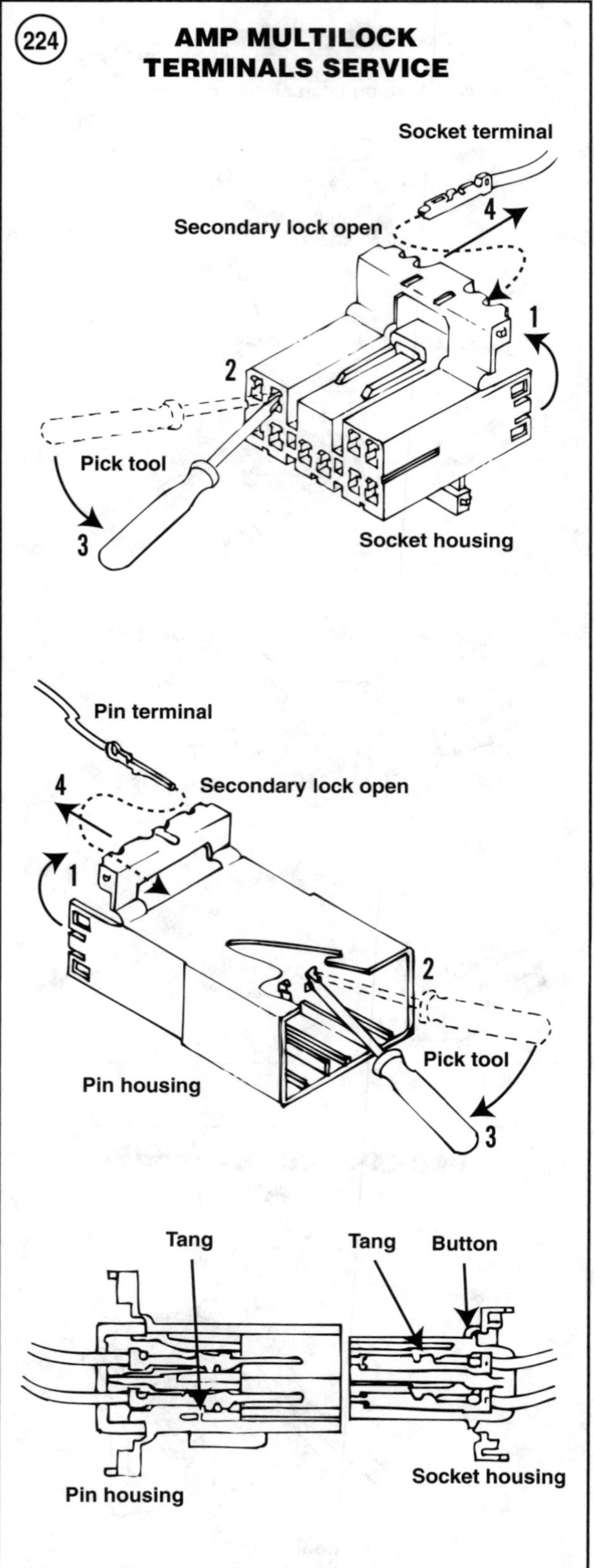
224
AMP MULTILOCK
TERMINALS SERVICE
Socket terminal
Secondary lock open
4
1
2
Pick tool
3
Socket housing
Pin terminal
4
Secondary lock open
1
2
Pick tool
Pin housing
3
Tang
Tang
Button
Pin housing
Socket housing

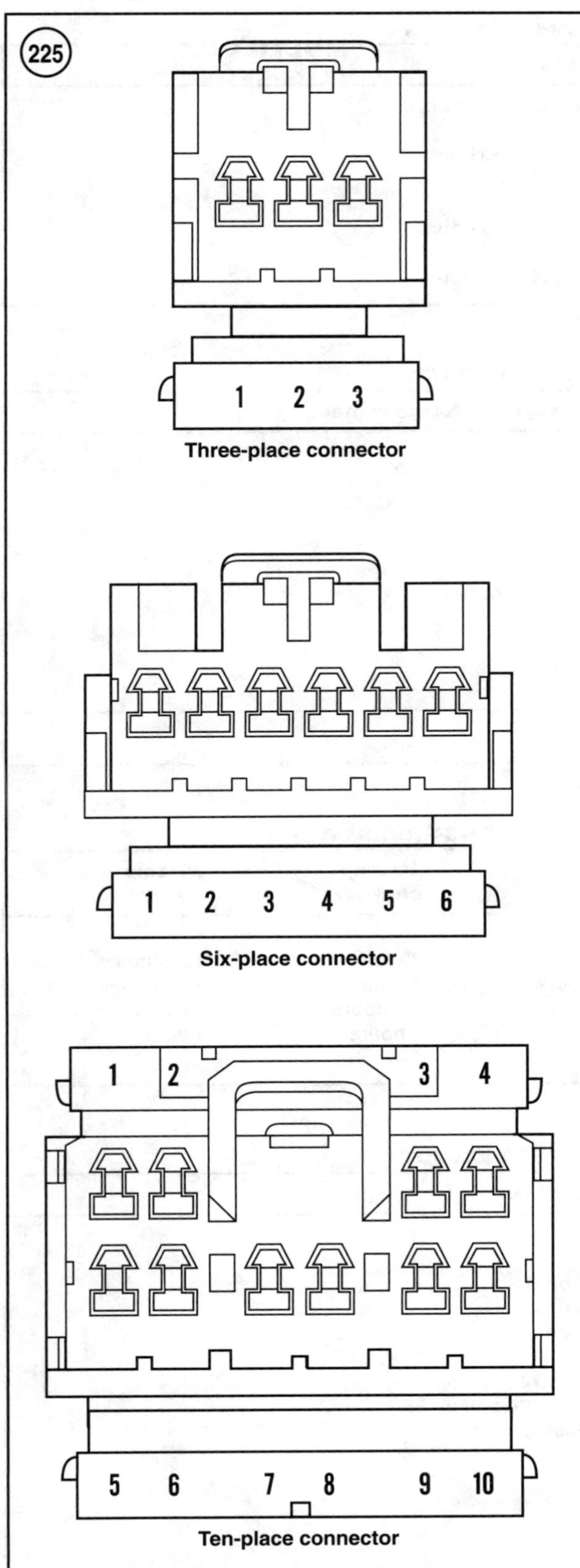

Three-place connector

Six-place connector

Ten-place connector

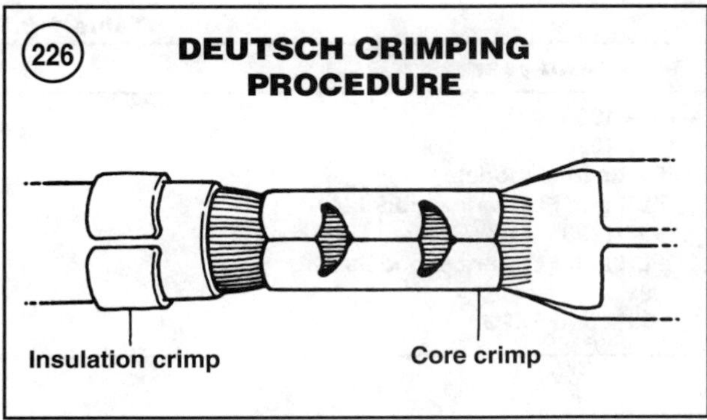

7. The tang within the chamber engages the pin terminal slot to lock the terminal into position. The tangs (**Figure 224**) are located as follows:
   a. On the pin housing side, the tangs are located at the bottom of each chamber. The pin terminal slot, on the side opposite the crimp tails, must face downward.
   b. On the socket housing side, the tangs are located at the top of each chamber. The pin terminal slot, on the same side as the crimp tails, must face upward.
8. On the secondary lock side of the connector, insert the wire and terminal into the correct location until it snaps into place. Gently pull on the lead to make sure the terminal is seated correctly.
9. Rotate the hinged secondary lock down and inward until the tabs are fully engaged with the latches on both sides of the connector. Pull upward to make sure the tabs are locked in place.
10. Insert the socket housing into the pin housing and push it until it locks into place.

9

Deutsch Pin and Socket Crimping Procedures

The Harley-Davidson electrical terminal crimp tool (part No. HD-39965) is required to install new pin (1, **Figure 217**) and socket (14, **Figure 217**) terminals. Use the instructions included with the crimp tool.

When stripping the wire insulation prior to installing the socket or pin terminals, strip away 5/32 in. (3.96 mm) of wire insulation. This ensures that the exposed wires will fill the terminal barrel.

After crimping the terminal and wire, tug lightly on the wire to make sure the crimp holds. **Figure 226** shows a properly crimped terminal and wire.

WIRING DIAGRAMS

Wiring diagrams are located at the end of this manual.

Table 1 BATTERY CAPACITY

Model and year	Capacity
1984-1990	12 volts, 19 amp hours
1991-1996	
FXR series models	12 volts, 19 amp hours
FLH and FLT series models	12 volts, 20 amp hours
1997-1998	
FLH and FLT series models	12 volts, 30 amp hours
1999	
FXR2 and FXR3	12 volts, 19 amp hours

Table 2 BATTERY STATE OF CHARGE*

Specific gravity reading	Percentage of charge remaining
1.120-1.140	0
1.135-1.155	10
1.150-1.170	20
1.160-1.180	30
1.175-1.195	40
1.190-1.210	50
1.205-1.225	60
1.215-1.235	70
1.230-1.250	80
1.245-1.265	90
1.260-1.280	100

*At 80° F.

Table 3 BATTERY CHARGING RATES/TIMES (APPROXIMATE)

Voltage	Percentage of full charge	3-amp charger	6-amp charger	10-amp charger	20-amp charger
12.8	100%	–	–	–	–
12.6	75%	1.75 hours	50 minutes	30 minutes	15 minutes
12.3	50%	3.5 hours	1.75 hours	1 hour	30 minutes
12.0	25%	5 hours	2.5 hours	1.5 hours	45 minutes
11.8	0%	6 hours and 40 minutes	3 hours and 20 minutes	2 hours	1 hour

Table 4 IGNITION SYSTEM SPECIFICATIONS

Item	Specification
Ignition coil	
Primary resistance	
1984-1994	2.5-3.1 ohms
1995-1998 (carbureted)	2.5-3.1 ohms
1995-1998 (EFI)	0.4-0.6 ohm
Secondary resistance	
1984-1994	11,250-13,740 ohms
1995-1998 (carbureted)	10,000-12,500 ohms
1995-1998 (EFI)	5000-6000 ohms
Spark plug wire resistance	
Cable length 4.5 in. (114 mm)	
carbureted models	1125-2624 ohms

(continued)

Table 4 IGNITION SYSTEM SPECIFICATIONS (continued)

Item	Specification
Spark plug wire resistance (continued)	
Cable length 6.5 in. (165 mm)	
EFI models	1625-3790 ohms
Cable length 19 in. (483 mm)	
all models	4750-11,077 ohms

Table 5 STARTER SPECIFICATIONS

Model and year	in.	mm
Commutator outer diameter service limit (1991-1998)	1.141	29.0
Starter brush length (minimum)		
1984-1988	0.438	11.1
1989-1990	0.354	9.0
1991-1992	0.413	10.5
1993-1994	0.354	9.0
1995-1999	0.433	11.0

Table 6 REPLACEMENT BULBS (1984-1994 MODELS)

Item	Size-amperage (all 12-volt) × quantity
Headlight	
FXWG, FXSB and FXEF	3.9
FLTC	3.57/2.5 × 2
FLHTC and FLHS	4.28/3.93
Passing lamp	2.34 × 2
Instrument panel/gauges lamps	
FXSB and FXEF	0.27 × 5
FXWG	
High beam	0.04
Oil pressure	0.08
Neutral indicator	0.08
Speedometer	0.27
FLT series	0.12 × 9
FXRT	
Fuel gauge	
1984-1990	0.27
1991-1992	0.12
High beam indicator	0.12
Neutral indicator	0.08
Oil pressure gauge	0.08
Speedometer	0.12 × 2
Tachometer	0.12
Turn signal indicator	0.27
FXR, FXLR, FXRS-SP and FXRS-Con	
Fuel gauge	0.12
High beam indicator	0.27
Neutral indicator	0.08
Oil pressure gauge	0.08
Speedometer	0.27
Tachometer	0.27
Turn signal indicator	0.27 × 2

(continued)

Table 6 REPLACEMENT BULBS (1984-1994 MODELS) (continued)

Item	Size-amperage (all 12-volt) × quantity
Tail lamp	0.59
Stop lamp	
FXR, FXLR, FSRS-SP and FXRS-Con	2.25
All other models	2.1
Front turn signal/running	
FXWG, FXSB and FXEF	2.1 × 2
All other models	0.59/2.25 × 2
Rear turn signal	
FXR, FXLR, FXRS-SP and FXRS-Con	2.25 × 2
All other models	2.1 × 2
Tour-Pak lamps	0.10 × 4
Fender tip lamp	0.10 × 2

Table 7 REPLACEMENT BULBS (1995-1998 MODELS)

Item	Size-wattage (all 12-volt) × quantity
Headlight	
FLTCU-I and FLTR	55/60 × 2
All other models	55/60
Passing lamp	
Domestic	30 × 2
HDI	35 × 2
Position lamp (HDI)	3.9
Instrument panel/gauges lamps	
1995-1997 FLHR	
Engine check light (EFI)	2.1
Fuel gauge	2.7
High beam indicator	2.1
Neutral indicator	2.1
Oil pressure gauge	2.1
Speedometer	3.7 × 2
Odometer	2.7
Turn signal indicator	2.1 × 2
1995 FLTC-U, FLHT, FLHTC, FLHTC-U and 1996 FLHTC-UI	
Cruise	2.7
Engine check light (EFI)	3.7
Fuel gauge	2.7
High beam indicator	2.7
Neutral indicator	3.7
Odometer	2.7
Oil pressure gauge	2
Speedometer	3.7 × 2
Tachometer	3.7 × 2
Turn signal indicator	3.7 × 2
Voltmeter	2
1996-1998 FLHT, FLHTC, FLHTC-U and FLHTC-UI	
Air temperature gauge (EFI)	3.4
Engine check light (EFI)	2.1
Fuel gauge	3.4
High beam indicator	2.1
Neutral indicator	2.1
Odometer	2.7
Oil pressure gauge	3.4
Speedometer	1.7 × 2
Tachometer	3.4

(continued)

Table 7 REPLACEMENT BULBS (1995-1998 MODELS) (continued)

Item	Size-wattage (all 12-volt) × quantity
Instrument panel/gauges lamps	
1996-1998 FLHT, FLHTC, FLHTC-U and FLHTC-UI (continued)	
Turn signal indicator	2.1 × 2
Voltmeter	3.4
1998 FLTR and FLTR-I	
Air temperature gauge (EFI)	3.4
Engine check light (EFI)	2.1
Fuel gauge	3.4
High beam indicator	2.1
Neutral indicator	2.1
Oil pressure gauge	3.4
Speedometer	1.7 × 2
Tachometer	3.4
Turn signal indicator	2.1 × 2
1999 FXR2 and FXR3	
Fuel gauge	2.7
High beam indicator	1.1
Neutral indicator	1.1
Odometer	2.7
Oil pressure gauge	1.1
Speedometer	3.7
Tachometer	4.9
Turn signal indicator	1.1 × 2
Tail lamp	
Domestic	7
HDI	5
Stop lamp	
Domestic	27
HDI	21
Front turn signal/running	27/7
Rear turn signal	
Domestic	27
HDI	21
License plate lamp (HDI)	5.2
Fender tip lamp	3.7 × 2
Tour-Pak	3.7 × 4

9

Table 8 HEADLIGHT AIM ADJUSTMENTS (FLTR MODELS)

Hex adjuster	Rotation	Beam movement
Left bulb	Clockwise	To the right
Right bulb	Counterclockwise	To the right
Left bulb	Counterclockwise	To the left
Right bulb	Clockwise	To the left
Left and right bulb equally	Clockwise	Upward
Left and right bulb equally	Counterclockwise	Downward

Table 9 TURN SIGNAL SPEED/DISTANCE TEST

Range	1	2	3	4
MPH	0-34	35-44	45-60	61+
KMH	0-56	56-71	72-97	98+
Feet	221	339	680	1051
Miles	0.04	0.06	0.13	0.20
Meters	67	103	207	320

Table 10 TURN SIGNAL SPEED/DISTANCE TEST

Constant speed mph	km/h	Turn signal on time in seconds
25	40	5-7
38	61	5-7
52	84	8-10
65	105	10-12

Table 11 BLADE-TYPE FUSES (1994-1998 FLH AND FLT SERIES MODELS)

Circuit	Rating (amps)	Color code
CB power	3	Violet
CB memory	1	Charcoal
Cruise and brake (1997-1998)	15	Blue
Fender tip light		
1994-1998 FLHT and FLHR series models	1	Charcoal
Instruments (1997-1998)	15	Blue
P & A (1997-1998)	10	Red
Pod power	5	Tan
Radio (Ultra models)	10	Red
Radio memory	1	Charcoal
Fuel pump (EFI)	15	Blue
Electronic control module (EFI)	5	Tan

Table 12 CIRCUIT BREAKER RATINGS (1983-1993 MODELS AND 1994 FXR MODELS)

Circuit	Rating (amps)
Main (battery)	30
Ignition	15
Lights	15
Accessories	
All models except FLHS	15
FLHS only	10
Cruise (models so equipped)	15

Table 13 CIRCUIT BREAKER RATINGS (1994-1996 FLH AND FLT SERIES MODELS)

Circuit	Ratings (amps)	Color code	Terminal
Main	50	None	Threaded
Lights	15	Blue	Blade-type
Accessory	15	Blue	Blade-type
Ignition	15	Blue	Blade-type
Constant	15	Blue	Blade-type

Table 14 ELECTRICAL SYSTEM TORQUE SPECIFICATIONS

Item	ft.-lb.	in.-lb.	N•m
Fuel-injected models			
Crankshaft position sensor Allen screw	–	40	4.5

(continued)

Table 14 ELECTRICAL SYSTEM TORQUE SPECIFICATIONS (continued)

Item	ft.-lb.	in.-lb.	N•m
Fuel-injected models (continued)			
Engine temperature sensor	–	124-142	14-16
Ignition system			
Stator plate rotor bolt	–	43-48	4.8-5.4
Headlamp clamp nut (FXR, FXRS, FXRS-SP, FXRS-Con, FXSB and FXEF)	10-20	–	14-27
Ignition switch (1997-1998 domestic models)			
Allen screws	–	40-50	5-6
Starter			
1984-1988 FXR, FLH and FLT series models			
Starter mount bolts or nuts	–	124-142	14-16
Mount bracket nuts	–	20-25	2-3
Solenoid cable nut	–	65-80	7-9
1985-1986 FXWG, FXEF and FXSB models			
Starter throughbolts	–	20-25	2-3
Outer throughbolt nut	–	20-25	2-3
Starter terminal nut	–	65-80	7-9
Rubber mount stud	–	71	8
Master cylinder reservoir bracket	13-16	–	18-22
1989-1998 models			
Mount bolt	13-20	–	18-27
Jackshaft lockplate bolt	–	84-108	9-12

CHAPTER TEN

WHEELS, HUBS AND TIRES

This chapter describes disassembly and repair of the front and rear wheels and hubs as well as tire service. Refer to Chapter Three for routine maintenance.

Tables 1-5 are at the end of the chapter.

MOTORCYCLE STANDS

Many procedures in this chapter require that the front or rear wheel be lifted off the ground. To do this, a motorcycle front end stand (**Figure 1**), or swing arm stand, or suitable size jack is required. Before purchasing or using a stand, check the manufacturer's instructions to make sure the stand will work with the specific model being worked on. If any adjustments to the motorcycle and/or stand or accessories are required, perform the necessary adjustments or install the correct parts before lifting the motorcycle. When using the stand, have an assistant standing by to help. Some means to tie down one end of the motorcycle might also be required. After lifting it onto a stand, make sure the motorcycle is properly supported.

If a motorcycle stand is not available, use a scissor jack (**Figure 2**) with adapters that securely fit onto the frame tubes (**Figure 3**).

FRONT WHEEL

Removal

NOTE

Due to the number of models and years covered in this manual, this procedure represents a typical front wheel removal and installation.

1. Support the motorcycle with the front wheel off the ground. Refer to *Motorcycle Stands* in this chapter.
2. Remove the front caliper as described in Chapter Thirteen. On models so equipped, repeat for the opposite brake caliper.

NOTE

Prior to removing the front axle nut, record the side from which the front axle is installed. The axle must be reinstalled through the same side.

3. Remove the axle nut (**Figure 4**), lockwasher and flat washer.

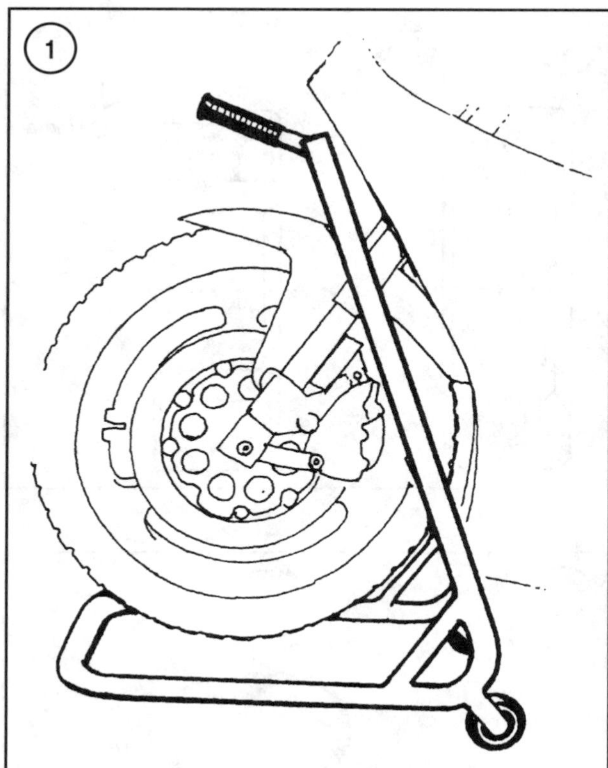

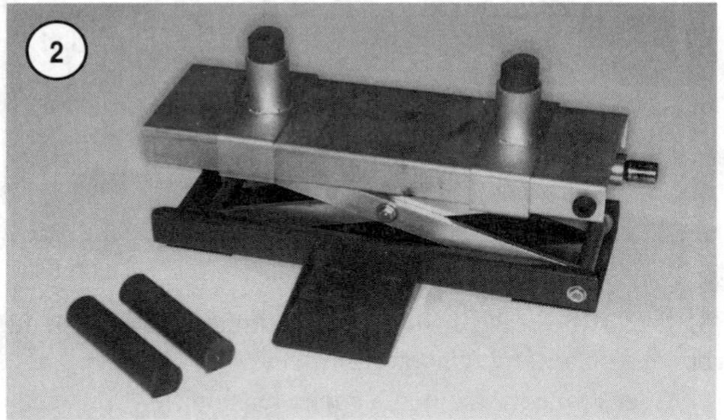

4. Loosen the fork slider cap nuts (**Figure 5**). It is not necessary to remove the nuts and slider cap.

5. Prior to removing the front axle, note the locations of the right and left spacers. The spacers must be reinstalled on the correct sides during installation.

6. Tap the end of the axle with a soft-faced mallet and remove it from the wheel.

7. Pull the wheel away from the fork sliders slightly and remove the speedometer drive gear from the wheel. Remove the rubber washer seal installed between the speedometer drive and oil seal, if so equipped.

CAUTION
Do not set the wheel down on the brake disc surface because it can be damaged.

8. Install the axle spacers, fasteners and the speedometer drive assembly onto the axle to avoid misplacing them.

9. Inspect the front wheel assembly as described in this section.

Installation

1. Clean the axle in solvent and dry thoroughly. Make sure the axle bearing surfaces on both fork sliders and the axle are free from burrs and nicks.
2. Apply an antiseize lubricant to the axle shaft prior to installation.
3. If the front wheel oil seals or bearings were replaced, confirm front axle spacer alignment as described under *Front Hub* in this chapter.
4. Install the rubber washer seal between the speedometer drive and wheel, if so equipped.
5. Align the speedometer drive dogs with the wheel gearcase notches and install the speedometer drive into the wheel.
6. Hold the speedometer drive in position and install the wheel between the fork tubes.
7. Insert the axle through the front fork and wheel from the same side noted during removal. After installation through the wheel and fork, install the flat washer, lockwasher and axle nut finger-tight.
8. Tighten the fork slider cap nuts (**Figure 5**) securely to prevent the axle from turning.
9. Tighten the axle nut to the specification listed in **Table 2**. Loosen the slider cap nuts and then retighten to the specification listed in **Table 4**. Make sure gap between the slider cap and fork slider is equal on both sides.
10. Perform the *Front Axle End Play Check* in this chapter.
11. Install the front brake caliper(s) as described in Chapter Thirteen.
12. After the wheel and brake are completely installed, rotate the wheel several times and apply the front brake a couple of times to make sure the wheel rotates freely and that the brake pads seat against the disc correctly.

Inspection

Replace worn or damaged parts as described in this section.

1. Turn each bearing inner race by hand. The bearing should turn smoothly. Some axial play (end play) is normal, but radial play (side play) should be negligible. See **Figure 6**. If one bearing is damaged, replace both bearings as a set. Refer to *Front Hub* in this chapter.
2. Clean the axle and axle spacers in solvent to remove all grease and dirt. Make sure the axle contact surfaces are clean and free of dirt and old grease.
3. Check the axle runout with a set of V-blocks and a dial indicator (**Figure 7**).
4. Check the spacers for wear, burrs and damage. Replace as necessary.

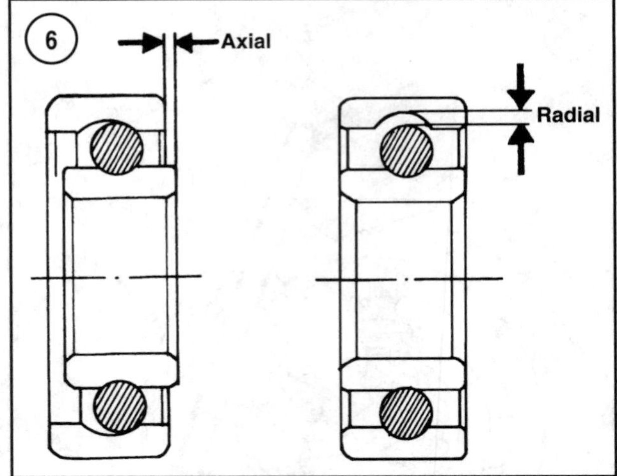

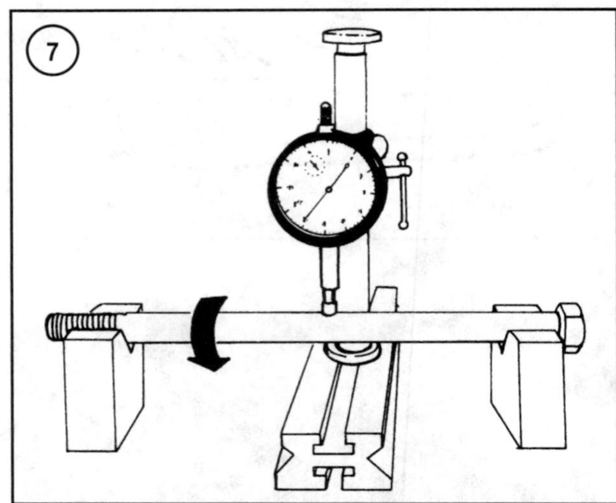

5. Check the brake disc bolts for tightness. To service the brake disc, refer to Chapter Thirteen.
6. Check wheel runout and spoke tension (laced wheels) as described in this chapter.

Front Wheel Bearing End Play Check/Adjustment (1984-Early 1990 FXR, FXWG, FXSB and FXEF Models)

Wheel bearing end play is controlled by the length of the center hub spacer. Check the end play every time the front wheel is removed or whenever unstable handling is noticed.

1. Support the motorcycle with the front wheel off the ground. Refer to *Motorcycle Stands* in this chapter.
2. Tighten the front axle nut to the specification in **Table 4**.
3. Tighten the slider cap nuts to the specification in **Table 4**.

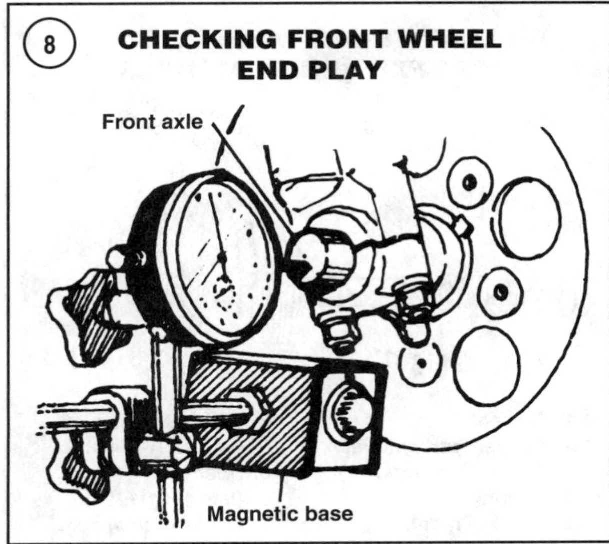

8 CHECKING FRONT WHEEL END PLAY

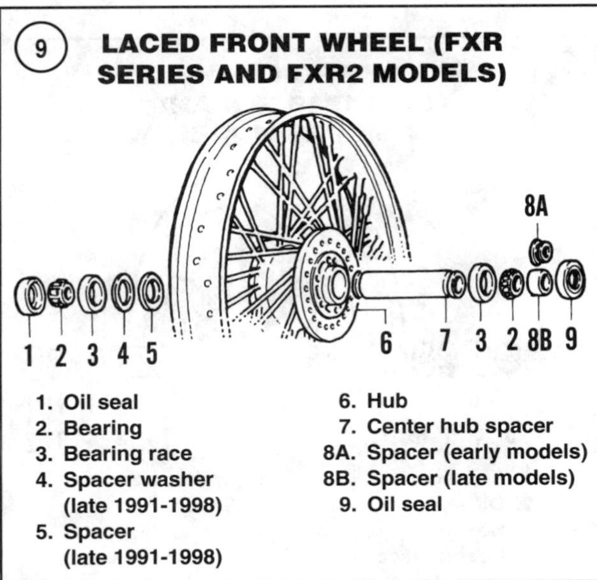

9 LACED FRONT WHEEL (FXR SERIES AND FXR2 MODELS)

1. Oil seal
2. Bearing
3. Bearing race
4. Spacer washer (late 1991-1998)
5. Spacer (late 1991-1998)
6. Hub
7. Center hub spacer
8A. Spacer (early models)
8B. Spacer (late models)
9. Oil seal

4. Mount a dial indicator so that the plunger contacts the end of the axle (**Figure 8**). Grasp the wheel and move it back and forth by pushing and pulling it along the axle centerline. Note the axle end play and refer to **Table 1** for specifications.
5. If the end play is incorrect, replace the center hub spacer. Refer to *Front Hub* in this chapter. Install a longer spacer for less end play and a shorter spacer for more end play. Three spacers with different lengths are available from a Harley-Davidson dealership as follows:
   a. Violet color: 2.564 in. (65.1 mm).
   b. Pink color: 2.550 in. (64.77 mm).
   c. Gold color: 2.536 in. (64.41 mm).
6. Install a new spacer and recheck the end play.

Front Wheel Bearing End Play Check/Adjustment (FLH, FLT and Late 1991-1998 FXR Models)

Wheel bearing end play is controlled by the length of the center hub spacer. Check the end play every time the front wheel is removed or whenever unstable handling is noticed.

1. Support the motorcycle with the front wheel off the ground. Refer to *Motorcycle Stands* in this chapter.
2. Tighten the front axle nut to the torque specification in **Table 4**.
3. Tighten the slider cap nuts to the torque specification in **Table 4**.
4. Mount a dial indicator so that the plunger contacts the end of the axle (**Figure 8**). Grasp the wheel and move it back and forth by pushing and pulling it along the axle centerline. Note the axle end play and refer to **Table 1** for specifications.
5. If the end play is incorrect, replace the spacer washer. Refer to *Front Hubs* in this chapter. Install a thicker spacer washer for less end play and a thinner spacer washer for more end play. Spacer washers with five different thicknesses are available from a Harley-Davidson dealership as follows:
   a. 0.030-0.033 in. (0.76-0.84 mm).
   b. 0.015-0.017 in. (0.38-0.43 mm).
   c. 0.0075-0.0085 in. (0.190-0.216 mm).
   d. 0.0035-0.0045 in. (0.089-0.114 mm).
   e. 0.0015-0.0025 in. (0.038-0.064 mm).
6. Install a new spacer washer and recheck the end play.

10

FRONT HUB

Tapered roller bearings are installed on each side of the hub. A center hub spacer installed between the bearings maintains front wheel bearing end play within a specified range.

The bearing races are pressed into the hub and should not be removed unless they require replacement.

Disassembly/Inspection/Assembly

Refer to **Figures 9-15**.

NOTE
If only the axle spacer is going to be replaced or exchanged, remove the bearing

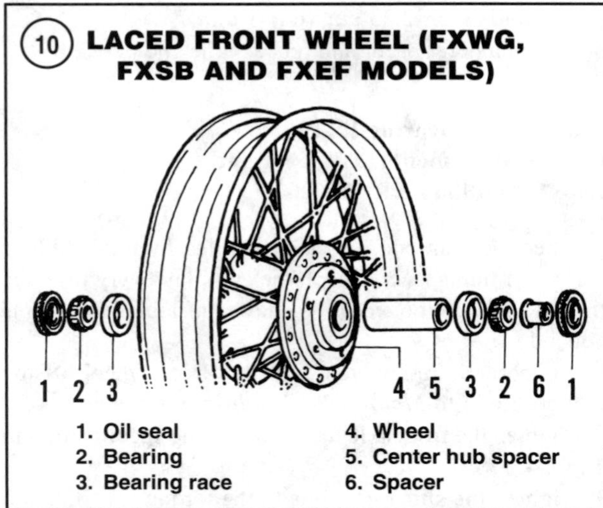

(10) LACED FRONT WHEEL (FXWG, FXSB AND FXEF MODELS)

1. Oil seal
2. Bearing
3. Bearing race
4. Wheel
5. Center hub spacer
6. Spacer

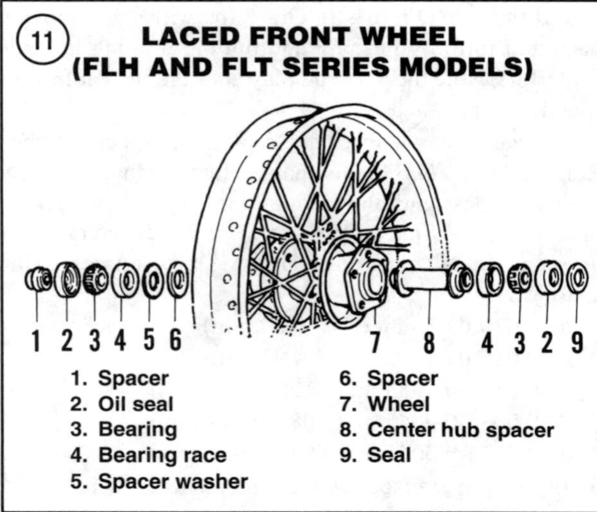

(11) LACED FRONT WHEEL (FLH AND FLT SERIES MODELS)

1. Spacer
2. Oil seal
3. Bearing
4. Bearing race
5. Spacer washer
6. Spacer
7. Wheel
8. Center hub spacer
9. Seal

opposite the brake disc (single-disc models).

NOTE

The bearings and races are matched. Keep the parts separate and label them to ensure correct installation.

1. Remove the front wheel as described in this chapter.
2. Remove the axle spacers from each side of the hub if they are still in place. Note the locations on the hub to ensure correct installation.
3. If necessary, remove the brake disc as described in Chapter Thirteen.
4. On models so equipped, remove the shouldered spacer from the oil seal.

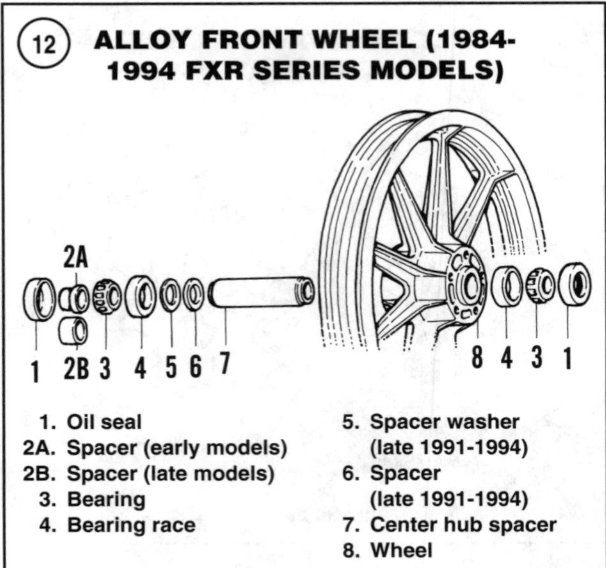

(12) ALLOY FRONT WHEEL (1984-1994 FXR SERIES MODELS)

1. Oil seal
2A. Spacer (early models)
2B. Spacer (late models)
3. Bearing
4. Bearing race
5. Spacer washer (late 1991-1994)
6. Spacer (late 1991-1994)
7. Center hub spacer
8. Wheel

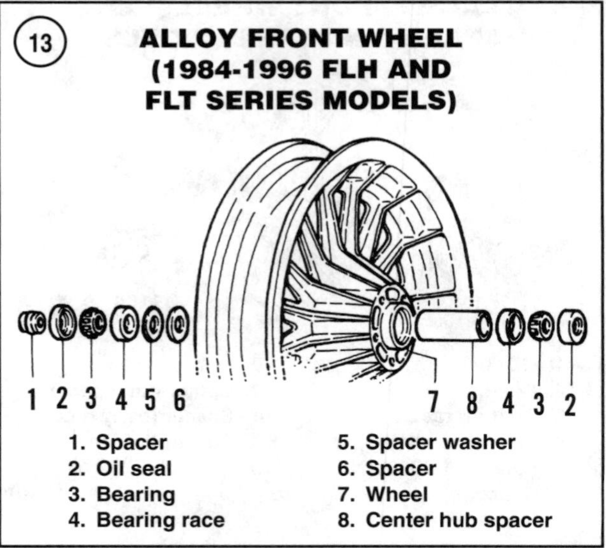

(13) ALLOY FRONT WHEEL (1984-1996 FLH AND FLT SERIES MODELS)

1. Spacer
2. Oil seal
3. Bearing
4. Bearing race
5. Spacer washer
6. Spacer
7. Wheel
8. Center hub spacer

5. Carefully pry one of the oil seals out of the hub (**Figure 16**). Place a rag underneath the pry tool to protect the hub surface.
6. Remove the bearing (**Figure 17**) from the race and note the location.

7A. On FLH, FLT and late 1991-1998 FXR series models, remove the spacer washer, spacer and the center hub spacer from the hub. Note that the spacer washer has a shoulder.

7B. On all other models, remove the center hub spacer (**Figure 18**) from the hub.

8. Repeat Step 6 and remove the opposite bearing and note the location.

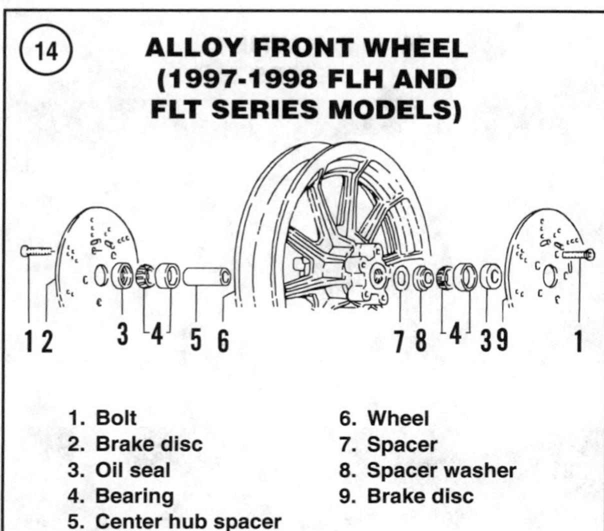

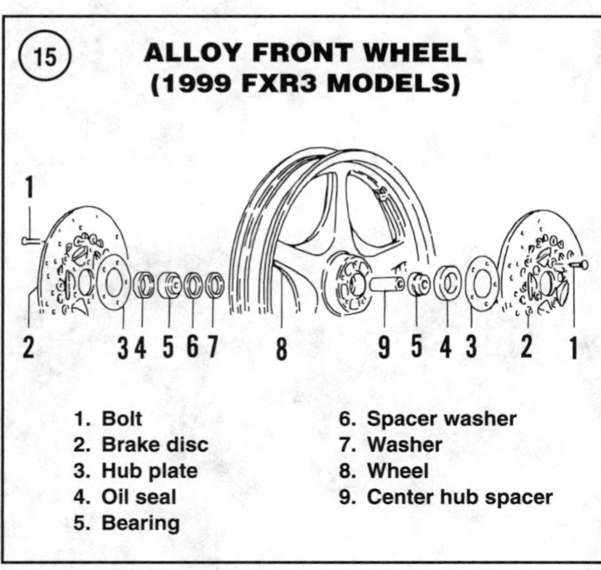

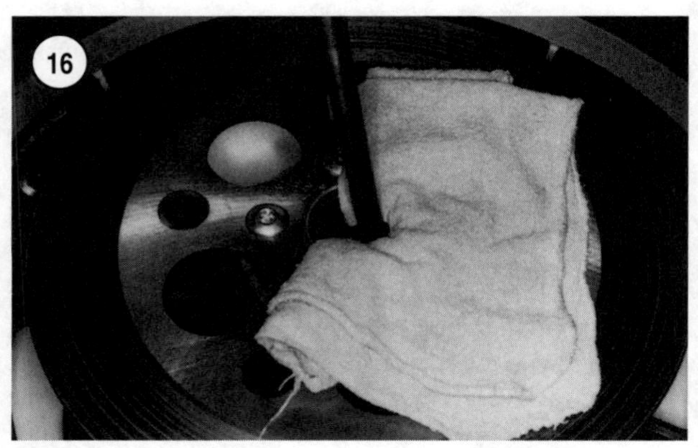

9. Wash the bearings thoroughly in clean solvent and dry with compressed air. Wipe the bearing races off with a clean rag dipped in solvent.

10. Then check the roller bearings and races for wear, pitting or excessive heat (bluish tint). Replace the bearings and races as a complete set. Replace the bearing races as described in Step 11. If the bearing and the race do not require replacement, proceed to Step 12. If reinstalling the original bearing(s), pack the bearing thoroughly with grease and wrap it in a clean, lint-free cloth or wax paper. Wipe a film of grease across the bearing race (**Figure 19**).

The bearings and races must be lubricated after cleaning them so they will not rust.

11. Replace the bearing races (**Figure 19**) as follows:
   a. To protect the front hub from damage, remove the bearing races with a wheel bearing race remover and installer tool (JIMS part No. 33071-73) (**Figure 20**).
   b. If the special tool is not available, insert a drift punch through the hub and tap the opposite race out of the hub with a hammer. Move the punch around the race to make sure the race is driven squarely out of the hub. Do not allow the race to bind in the hub because this can damage the race bore in the hub. Damage to the race bore will require replacement of the hub.
   c. Thoroughly clean the inside and outside of the hub with solvent. Dry with compressed air.
   d. Apply oil to the outside of the new race and align it with the hub. Install the bearing race with the same driver or socket. Drive the race into the hub until it bottoms out on the hub shoulder.

CAUTION

When installing the race, stop and check the alignment of the bearing race to make sure the race is square with the hub bore. Do not allow the race to bind during installation, or the hub race bore will be damaged.

12. Blow any dirt out of the hub prior to installing the bearings.

13A. On FLH, FLT and late 1991-1998 FXR models, perform the following:
   a. Apply grease to the ends of the center hub spacer and install it into the hub.
   b. Install the spacer and spacer washer as shown in **Figure 9** and **Figures 11-15**. Install the spacer washer so that the shoulder faces away from the spacer and toward the bearing.

13B. On all other models, apply grease to the ends of the center hub spacer and install it into the hub.

NOTE

If performing this procedure to correct wheel bearing end play, make sure to install the center hub spacer with the correct length.

14. Apply grease to each bearing race.

15. Pack each bearing with grease. Then install each bearing in the respective bearing race. Pack the area between the bearing and oil seal (to be installed later) with grease; repeat for both sides.

16. Pack the seal lip cavity of each seal with grease.

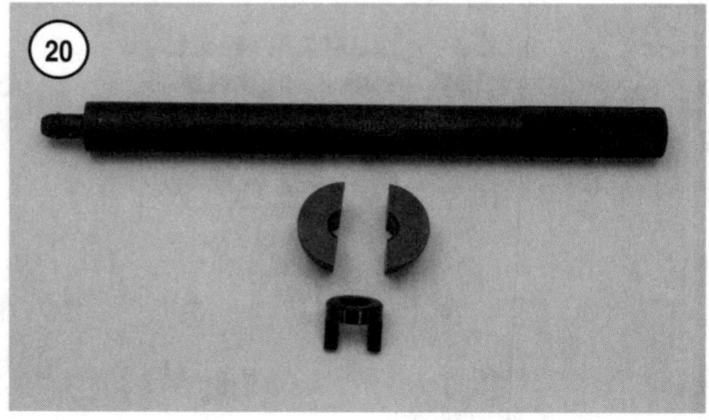

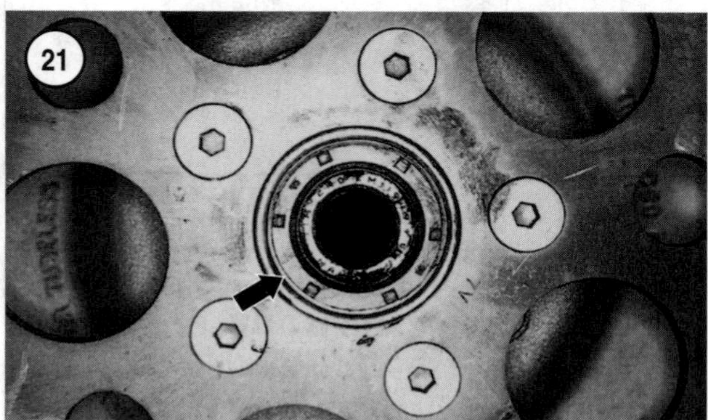

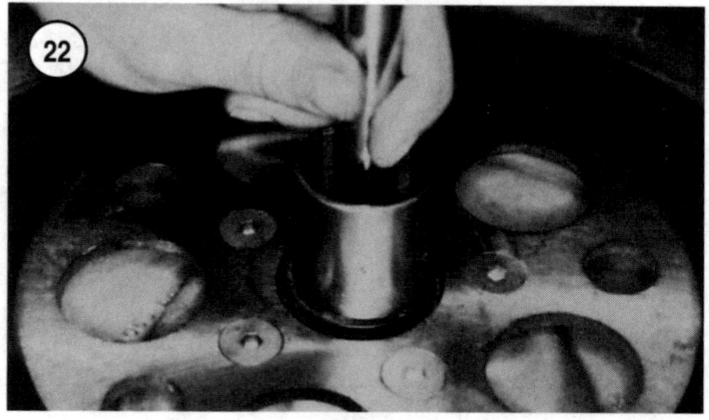

17A. On 1984-1990 FLH and FLT series models, install the oil seals and the two outer axle spacers as follows:
   a. One of the outer axle spacers is longer than the other one. Install the longer axle spacer into the valve stem side of the wheel. Install the shorter spacer into the opposite side.
   b. Install the oil seals over the axle spacers and drive them into the hub while aligning the hole in the oil seal with the spacer shaft, until they are 13/64-7/32 in. (5.16-5.55 mm) below the outside edge of the hub.

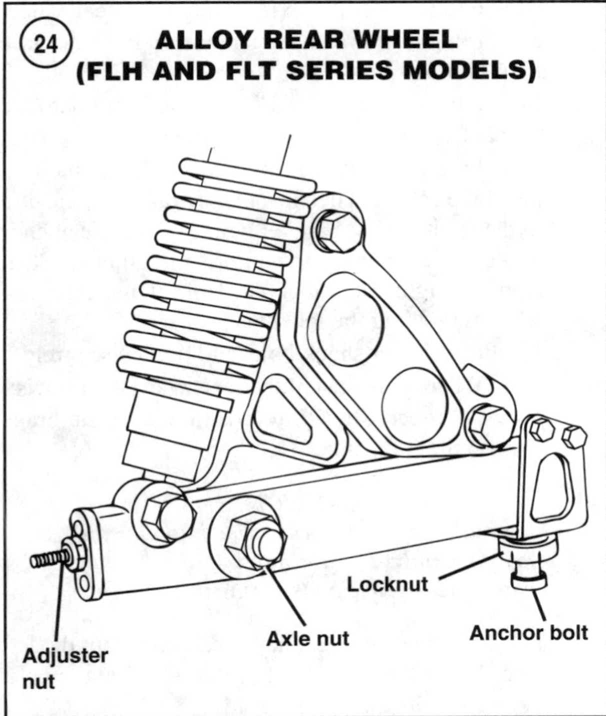

17B. On 1991-1998 FLH and FLT series models, install the oil seals and the two outer axle spacers as follows:

a. The two outer axle spacers are different. Install the outer axle spacer with the large chamfered end into the valve-stem side of the wheel. Position the spacer so that the chamfered end faces toward the bearing. Install the other spacer into the opposite side.
b. Install the oil seals over the axle spacers and drive them into the hub while aligning the hole in the oil seal with the spacer shaft. On alloy wheels, the oil seals should be driven into the hub so that the seal is flush or within 0.04 in. (1.0 mm) below the outside edge of the hub. On laced wheels, the oil seals must be installed so that they are flush or within 0.02 in. (0.51 mm) below the outside edge of the hub.

17C. On all other models, install the oil seals and the right outer axle spacer as follows:

NOTE
On 1984-1986 FXR and 1985-1986 FXWG, FXSB and FXEF models, the right axle spacer has a shoulder. The axle spacer on 1987 and later FXR models does not. On models with the axle spacer having a shoulder, install it with the shoulder facing against the right bearing.

a. Install the right axle spacer through a new oil seal and align the oil seal with the right side of the hub. Install the other oil seal into the left side (**Figure 21**).
b. Use a bearing driver or socket with an outside diameter slightly smaller than the oil seals (**Figure 22**). Carefully drive the oil seals into the hub until they are flush with the hub. On FXWG, FXSB and FXEF models, the oil seal may be installed so that the upper surface is flush or within 0.015 in. (0.38 mm) below the outside edge of the hub.

18. If removed, install the brake disc as described in Chapter Thirteen.
19. After installing the wheel, check the bearing end play as described in this section.

10

REAR WHEEL

Removal/Installation (FLH, FLT and FXRT Models with Enclosed Sprocket)

Removal without disconnecting sprocket

1. Support the motorcycle on a swing arm stand with the rear wheel off the ground a minimum of 4 in.
2. On models so equipped, remove the saddlebags as described in Chapter Fifteen.
3. On FLH and FLT series models, remove the mufflers as described in Chapter Eight.
4. Unscrew and remove the plug and O-ring (**Figure 23**) from the sprocket housing.
5. Use a 3/8-in. Allen wrench and remove the bolts securing the sprocket and spacer to the rear hub.

6A. On FLH and FLT series models, refer to **Figure 24** and perform the following:

a. Remove the shock absorber (**Figure 25**) lower mounting bolts and lower the wheel to the ground.
b. Remove the brake anchor bracket bolts and anchor.
c. Remove the axle nut, lockwasher and washer.

d. Tap the axle out of the wheel far enough so that the axle clears the wheel but still supports the sprocket and drive chain housing.
e. Move the brake caliper and carrier up and away from the wheel.
f. Separate the rear wheel from the sprocket and chain housing. Remove the rear wheel.

6B. On FXRT models, perform the following:
a. Remove the axle nut.
b. Tap the axle out of the wheel far enough so that the axle clears the wheel but still supports the sprocket and left chain adjuster.
c. Remove the spacer located between the brake caliper bracket and the swing arm.
d. Slide the caliper bracket to the right and lower the rear wheel to the ground.

CAUTION
Do not set the wheel down on the brake disc surface because it can be damaged.

NOTE
Place a plastic or wooden spacer between the brake pads. Then, if the brake lever is inadvertently applied, the piston will not be forced out of the cylinder. If the piston is forced out, disassemble the caliper to reseat the piston.

Installation without disconnected sprocket

1. Remove the spacer from the brake pads in the rear brake caliper.
2. Apply a light coat of multipurpose grease to the rear axle prior to installation.

3A. On FLH and FLT series models (**Figure 24**), install the rear wheel as follows:
a. Make sure the right axle spacer is installed through the oil seal.
b. Move the rear wheel into position with the brake disc on the right side.

CAUTION
Carefully insert the brake disc into the caliper assembly. Do not damage the leading edges of the brake pads during installation.

c. Move the brake caliper into position between the wheel and swing arm.
d. Lift the wheel and slowly install the rear axle from the left side while aligning the spacer and sprocket with the rear wheel.

e. Continue to push the axle through the rear wheel and through the brake caliper carrier. Push the axle in until it bottoms.
f. Install the washer, lockwasher and axle nut onto the rear axle. Tighten the axle nut finger-tight.
g. Install the brake anchor and the bracket bolts onto the brake caliper. Then install the brake line and clip to the front anchor bracket bolt. Tighten the anchor bolt until it just starts to compress the rubber. Then stop and tighten the locknut. Hold the anchor bolt when tightening the locknut.
h. Install the lower shock bolts and tighten securely.

3B. On FXRT models, install the rear wheel as follows:
a. Move the rear wheel into position with the brake disc on the right side.

CAUTION
Carefully insert the brake disc into the caliper assembly. Do not damage the leading edges of the brake pads during installation.

b. Lift the wheel and install the rear axle from the left side. Insert the axle through the wheel and stop it before it exits the opposite side.
c. Align the right axle spacer with the brake caliper and swing arm and push the axle through the wheel, axle spacer and brake caliper until it bottoms out.
d. Install the washer, lockwasher and axle nut onto the rear axle. Tighten the axle nut finger-tight.

4. Align the holes in the hub with the sprocket.
5. Apply clean engine oil to the sprocket bolts and tighten to the specification listed in **Table 5**.
6. Install the plug and *new* O-ring (**Figure 23**) onto the sprocket housing. Tighten the plug securely.
7. Perform *Rear Wheel Bearing End Play Check/Adjustment* in this section.
8. Adjust the drive chain as described in Chapter Three.
9. Tighten the axle nut to 60-65 ft.-lb. (80-88 N•m).
10. Adjust the rear brake as described in Chapter Three.

11. Rotate the wheel several times to make sure it rotates freely and that the rear brake works properly.
12. On FLH and FLT series models, install the mufflers as described in Chapter Eight.
13. On models so equipped, install the saddlebags as described in Chapter Fifteen.

WARNING
Do not ride the motorcycle until the rear brake is operating correctly with full hydraulic advantage.

Wheel removal with sprocket

Refer to **Figure 26**.

1. Support the motorcycle on a swing arm stand with the rear wheel off the ground a minimum of 4 in.
2. On models so equipped, remove the saddlebags as described in Chapter Fifteen.
3. On FLH and FLT series models, remove the mufflers as described in Chapter Eight.
4. Remove the screws and disconnect the upper and lower rubber boots from the rear wheel sprocket housing.
5. Move the boots away from the sprocket housing to gain access to the drive chain.
6. Rotate the rear wheel until the master link is visible. Disconnect the rear drive chain master link. A chain breaker might be required to separate the chain.
7. Remove the bolts and washers securing the swing arm bracket to the sprocket housing and remove the bracket.
8. Loosen and remove the axle nut, lockwasher and washer.
9. Tap the axle out of the wheel far enough so that the axle almost clears the wheel.
10. On FXRT models, remove the spacer located between the brake caliper bracket and the swing arm.
11. Slide the caliper bracket to the right and lower the rear wheel to the ground.
12. Remove the rear wheel and the rear wheel sprocket housing.

CAUTION
Do not set the wheel down on the brake disc surface because it can be damaged.

NOTE
Place a plastic or wooden spacer between the brake pads. Then, if the brake lever is inadvertently applied, the piston will not be forced out of the cylinder. If the piston is forced out, disassemble the caliper to reseat the piston.

13. If necessary, disassemble the sprocket housing assembly as described in this chapter.

Wheel installation with sprocket

Refer to **Figure 26**.

1. Remove the spacer from the brake pads.
2. Apply a light coat of multipurpose grease to the rear axle prior to installation.

CAUTION
Carefully insert the brake disc into the caliper assembly. Do not damage the leading edges of the brake pads during installation.

3A. On FLH and FLT series models, install the rear wheel as follows:
   a. Make sure the right axle spacer is in place within the oil seal.
   b. Move the rear wheel into position with the brake disc on the right side and with the sprocket housing opening facing forward.

CAUTION
Carefully insert the brake disc into the caliper assembly. Do not damage the leading edges of the brake pads during installation.

   c. Lift the wheel and install the rear axle from the left side. Insert the axle through the wheel and stop it before it exits the opposite side.
   d. Align the right axle spacer with the brake caliper and swing arm and push the axle through the wheel, axle spacer and brake caliper until it bottoms out.
   e. Install the washer, lockwasher and axle nut onto the rear axle. Tighten the axle nut finger-tight.

3B. On FXRT series models, install the rear wheel as follows:
   a. Move the rear wheel into position with the brake disc on the right side and with the sprocket housing opening facing forward.

CAUTION
Carefully insert the brake disc into the caliper assembly. Do not damage the leading edges of the brake pads during installation.

   b. Lift the wheel and install the rear axle from the left side. Insert the axle through the wheel and stop it before it exits the opposite side.
   c. Align the right axle spacer with the brake caliper and swing arm and push the axle through the wheel, axle spacer and brake caliper until it bottoms out.

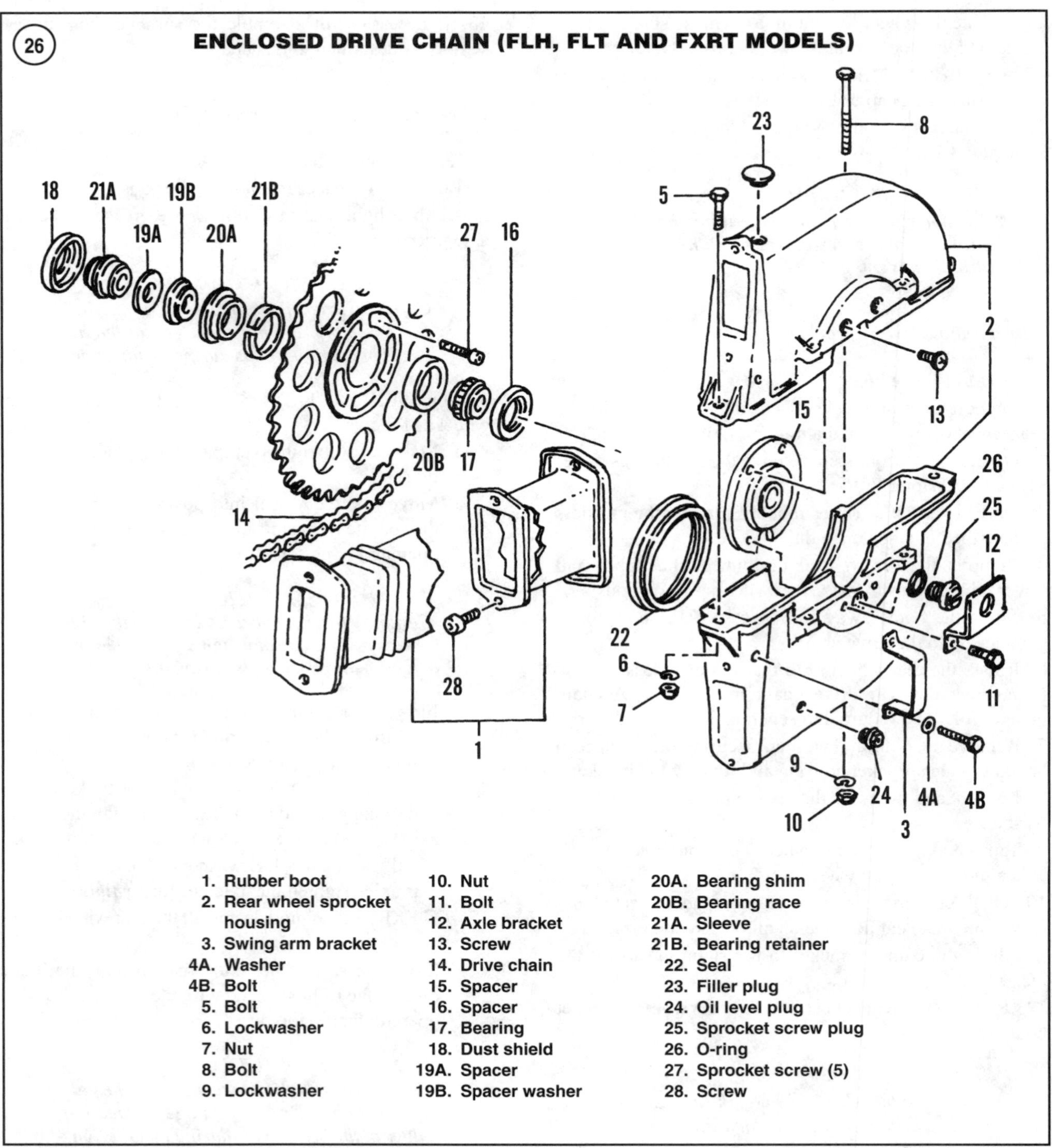

d. Install the washer, lockwasher and axle nut onto the rear axle. Tighten the axle nut finger-tight.

4. Tighten the axle nut to 60-65 ft.-lb. (81-88 N•m).

5. Perform *Rear Wheel Bearing End Play Check/Adjustment* as described in this chapter.

6. After performing Step 5, loosen the rear axle nut and reconnect the drive chain with a new master link. Attach the master link open clip so that the closed end faces in the direction of chain travel (**Figure 27**).

7. Adjust the drive chain as described in Chapter Three.

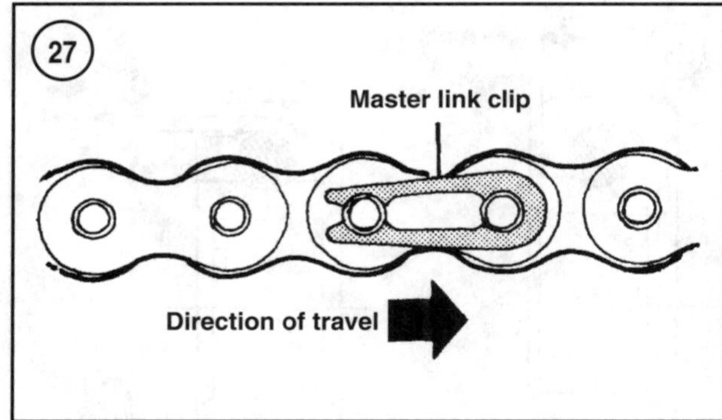

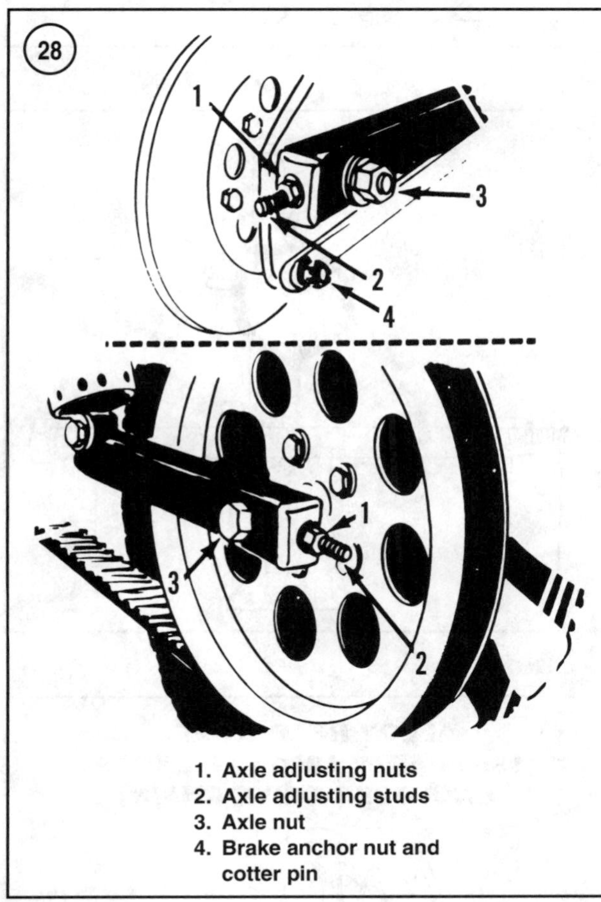

1. Axle adjusting nuts
2. Axle adjusting studs
3. Axle nut
4. Brake anchor nut and cotter pin

8. Tighten the axle nut to 60-65 ft.-lb. (81-88 N•m).

9. Adjust the rear brake as described in Chapter Three.

10. Apply a coating of RTV silicone sealant to the rubber chain cover boots and to the chain housing mating surfaces.

11. Slide the boots onto the sprocket housing and secure with the screws.

12. Rotate the wheel several times to make sure it rotates freely and that the rear brake works properly.

WARNING
Do not ride the motorcycle until the rear brake is operating correctly with full hydraulic advantage.

Removal (Open Drive Chain or Drive Belt Models)

NOTE
Due to the number of models and years covered in this manual, this procedure represents a typical rear wheel removal and installation.

1. Support the motorcycle on a swing arm stand with the rear wheel off the ground a minimum of 4 in.
2. Remove the bolts securing the drive belt or chain guard. Remove the guard.
3. On models so equipped, remove the saddlebags as described in Chapter Fifteen.
4. On models so equipped, remove the rear axle cotter pin.
5. Loosen the drive chain or belt-adjusting locknuts and adjuster bolts (**Figure 28**, typical).
6. Loosen and remove the axle nut and washers.
7. Slide the axle out of the wheel and lower the wheel to the ground.
8. Remove the axle spacer.
9. Lift the drive chain or belt off of the sprocket and remove the rear wheel.

CAUTION
Do not set the wheel down on the brake disc surface because it can be damaged.

NOTE
Place a plastic or wooden spacer between the brake pads. Then, if the brake pedal is inadvertently applied, the piston will not be forced out of the cylinder. If the piston is forced out, disassemble the caliper to reseat the piston.

10. Inspect the rear wheel assembly as described in this chapter.

Installation

1. Remove the spacer from the brake pads in the rear brake caliper.

2. Apply a light coat of multipurpose grease to the rear axle prior to installation.

CAUTION

Carefully insert the brake disc into the caliper assembly. Do not damage the leading edges of the brake pads during installation.

CAUTION

When installing the rear wheel in Step 3, carefully insert the brake disc into the caliper assembly. Do not damage the brake pad leading edges during installation.

3A. On 1984-1990 FLH, FLT and FXR chain drive models, perform the following:

   a. Position the rear wheel into the swing arm and install the axle spacer.
   b. Install the axle through the left side.
   c. Install the washer, lockwasher and axle nut.

3B. On 1984-1990 FLH, FLT and FXR belt drive models, perform the following:

   a. Position the rear wheel into the swing arm and through the drive belt. Install the axle spacer.
   b. Install the axle through the left side.
   c. Install the washer and lockwasher (1984-1988 models) and the axle nut.

3C. On 1985-1986 FXWG, FXSB and FXEF models, perform the following:

   a. Position the rear wheel into the swing arm and through the drive belt. Install the axle spacer.
   b. Install the axle through the left (laced wheel) or right (alloy wheel) side.
   c. Install the washer, lockwasher (if so equipped) and the axle nut.

3D. On 1991 FLH and FLT models, perform the following:

   a. Position the rear wheel into the swing arm and through the drive belt. Install the axle spacer.
   b. Install the axle through the left side.
   c. Install the washer and the axle nut.

3E. On 1991 FXR models, perform the following:

   a. Position the rear wheel into the swing arm and through the drive belt. Install the axle spacer.
   b. Install the axle through the right side.
   c. Install the washer and the axle nut.

4. Perform *Rear Wheel Bearing End Play Check/Adjustment* in this chapter.

NOTE

If it is necessary to tighten the axle nut a bit more to line up the axle nut slot with the cotter pin hole in the axle, make sure you do not exceed the maximum torque specification listed in ***Table 5****.*

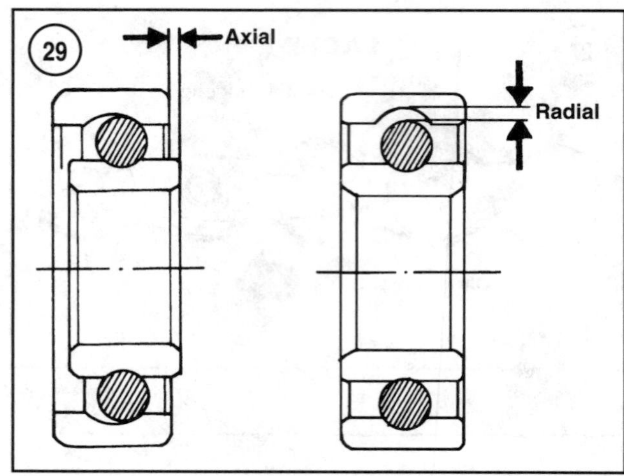

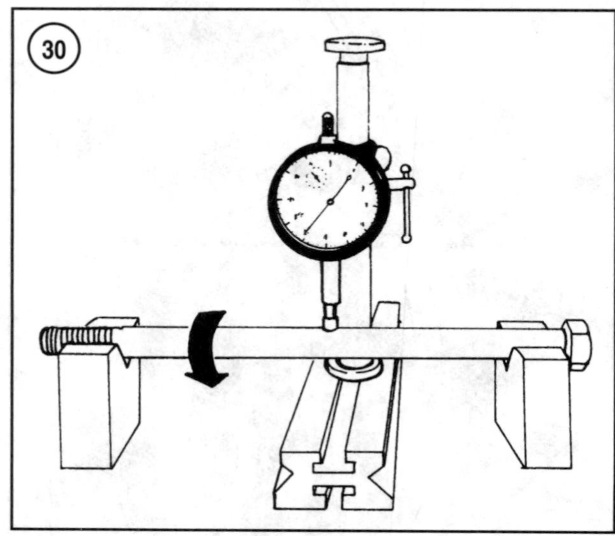

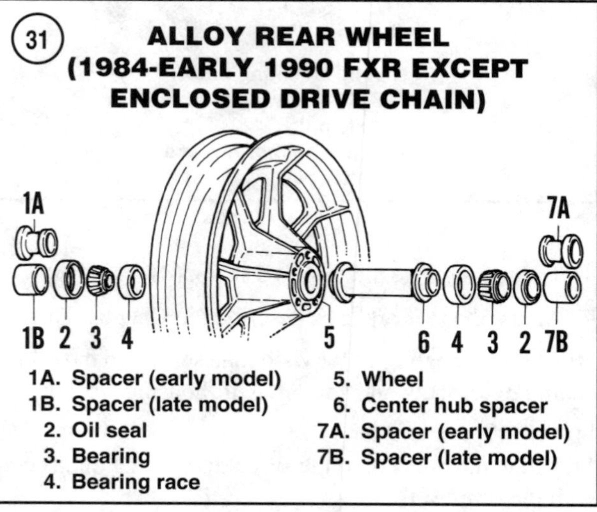

ALLOY REAR WHEEL (1984-EARLY 1990 FXR EXCEPT ENCLOSED DRIVE CHAIN)

1A. Spacer (early model)
1B. Spacer (late model)
2. Oil seal
3. Bearing
4. Bearing race
5. Wheel
6. Center hub spacer
7A. Spacer (early model)
7B. Spacer (late model)

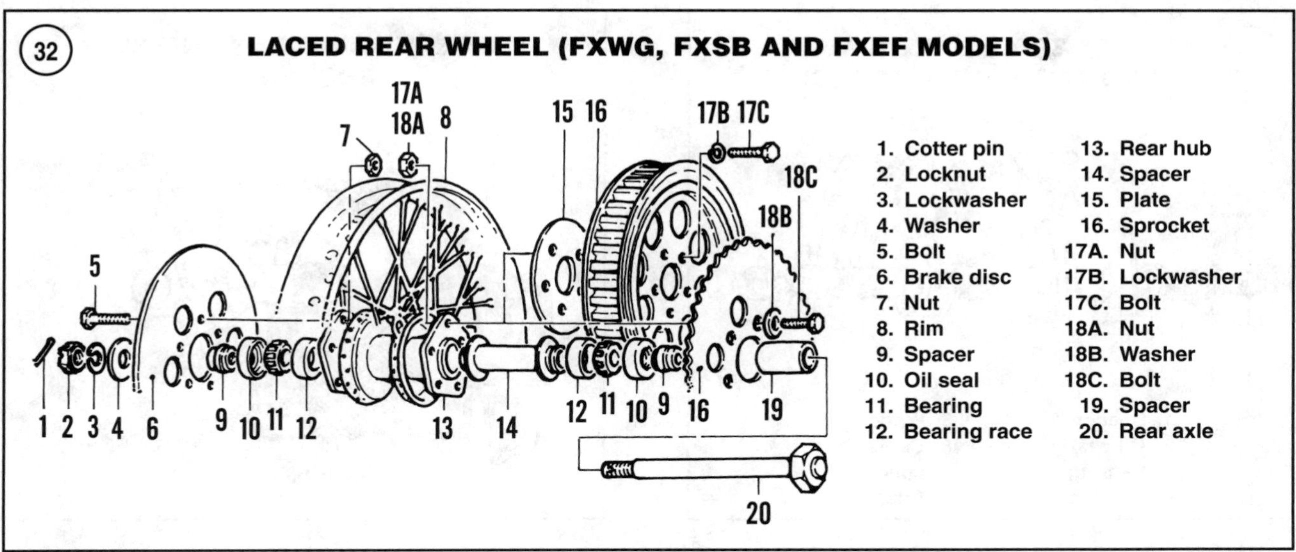

5A. On drive chain models, perform the following:
   a. After performing Step 4, loosen the rear axle nut and reconnect the drive chain with a new master link. Attach the master link open clip so that the closed end faces in the direction of chain travel (**Figure 27**).
   b. Adjust the drive chain as described in Chapter Three.
   c. Tighten the axle nut to 60-65 ft.-lb. (81-88 N•m).
   d. On models so equipped, install a *new* cotter pin and bend the ends over completely.

5B. On belt drive models, perform the following:
   a. Adjust the drive belt as described in Chapter Three.
   b. Tighten the axle nut to 60-65 ft.-lb. (81-88 N•m).
   c. On models so equipped, install a *new* cotter pin and bend the ends over completely.

6. Adjust the rear brake as described in Chapter Three.
7. Install the drive belt or chain guard and tighten the bolts securely.
8. On models so equipped, install the saddlebags as described in Chapter Fifteen.
9. Rotate the wheel several times to make sure it rotates freely and that the rear brake works properly.

WARNING

Do not ride the motorcycle until the rear brake is operating correctly with full hydraulic advantage.

Inspection (All Models)

Replace worn or damaged parts as described in this section.

1. Turn each inner bearing race by hand. The bearing should turn smoothly. Some axial play (end play) is normal, but radial play (side play) should be negligible. See **Figure 29**. If one bearing is damaged, replace both bearings as a set. Refer to *Front and Rear Hubs* in this chapter.
2. Clean the axle and axle spacers in solvent to remove all grease and dirt. Make sure the axle contact surfaces are clean and free of dirt and old grease.
3. Check the axle runout with a set of V-blocks and a dial indicator (**Figure 30**).
4. Check the spacers for wear, burrs and damage. Replace as necessary.
5. Check the brake disc bolts for tightness. To service the brake disc, refer to Chapter Thirteen.
6. Check wheel runout and spoke tension (laced wheels) as described in this chapter.
7. While the wheel is off, check the tightness of the brake disc bolts. Refer to the torque listed at the end of Chapter Thirteen.

Rear Wheel Bearing End Play Check/Adjustment (1984-Early 1990 FXR, FXWG, FXSB and FXEF Models)

Wheel bearing end play is controlled by the length of the center hub spacer. Refer to **Figures 31-33**. Check the end play every time the rear wheel is removed or whenever unstable handling is noticed.

1. Support the motorcycle on a swing arm stand with the rear wheel off the ground.
2. Tighten the axle nut to 60-65 ft.-lb. (81-88 N•m).

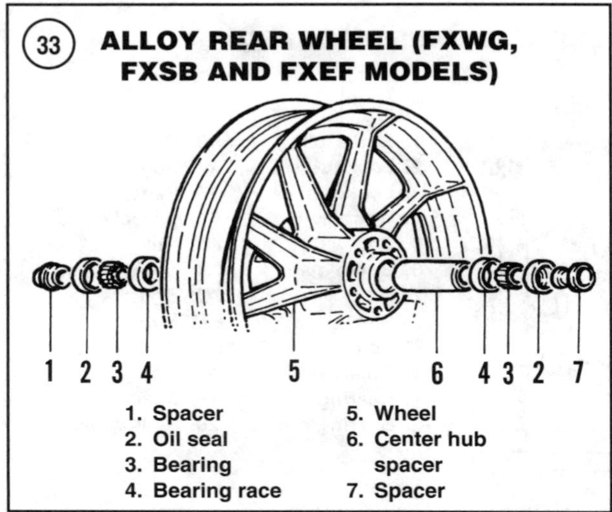

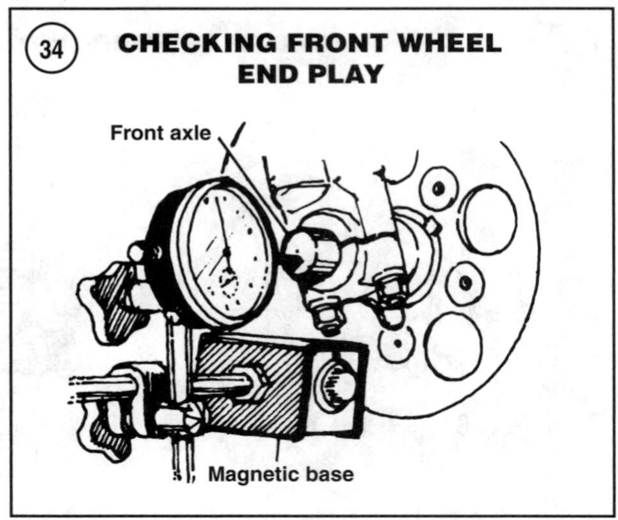

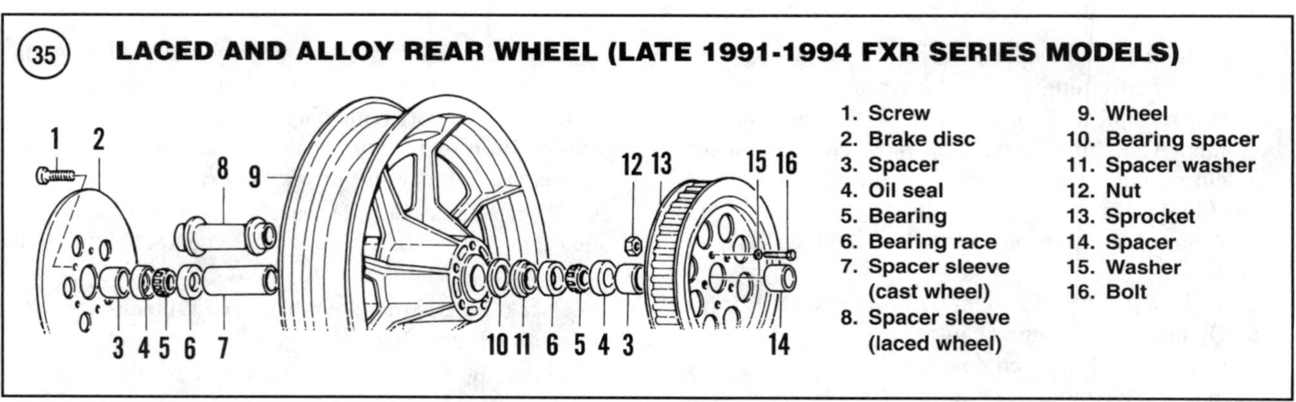

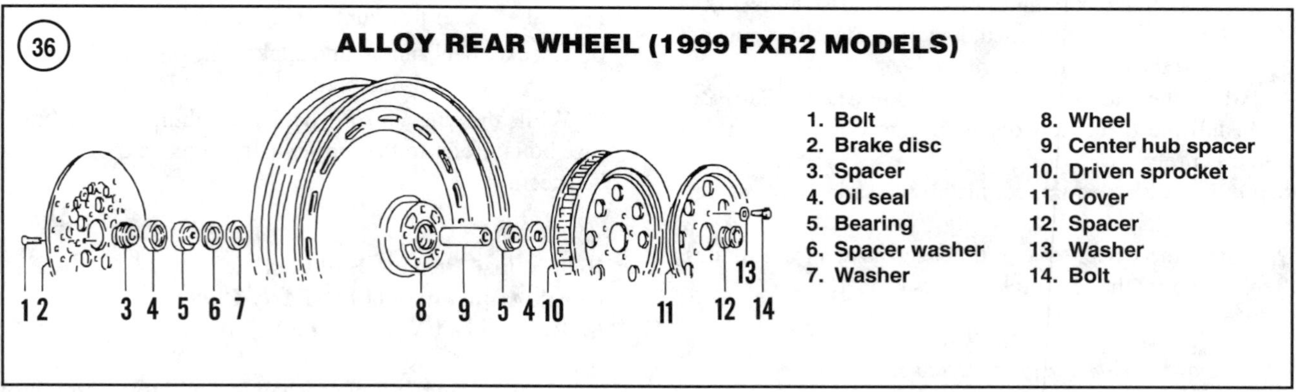

3. Mount a dial indicator so that the plunger contacts the end of the axle (**Figure 34**). Grasp the wheel and move it back and forth by pushing and pulling it along the axle centerline. Note the axle end play and refer to **Table 1** specifications.

4. If the end play is incorrect, replace the center hub spacer. Refer to **Figures 31-33**. Install a longer spacer for less end play and a shorter spacer for more end play. Spacers with three different lengths are available from a Harley-Davidson dealership as follows:

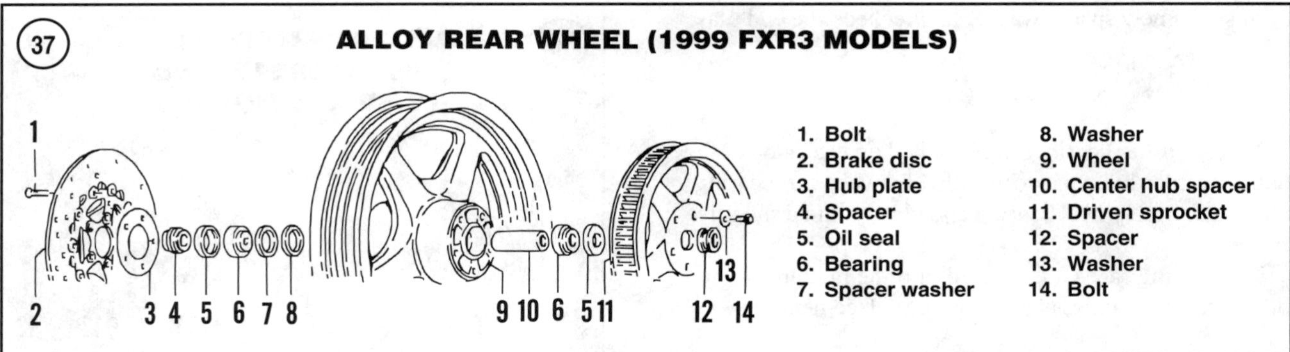

37 ALLOY REAR WHEEL (1999 FXR3 MODELS)

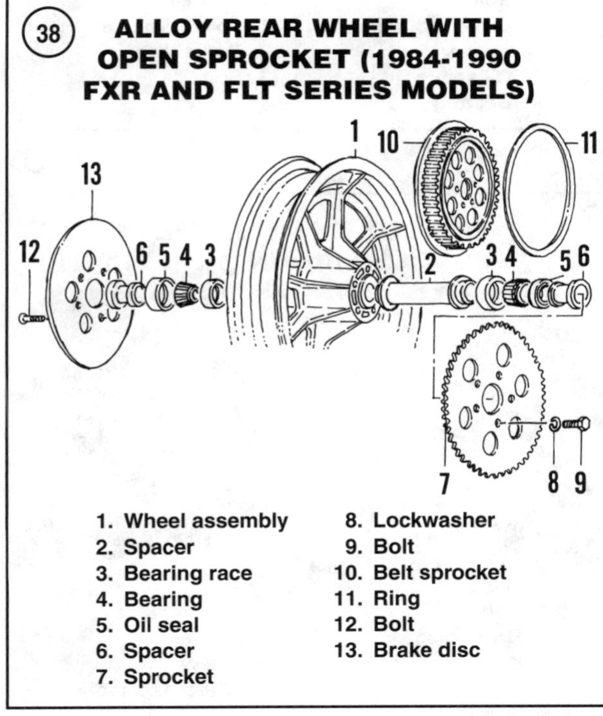

38 ALLOY REAR WHEEL WITH OPEN SPROCKET (1984-1990 FXR AND FLT SERIES MODELS)

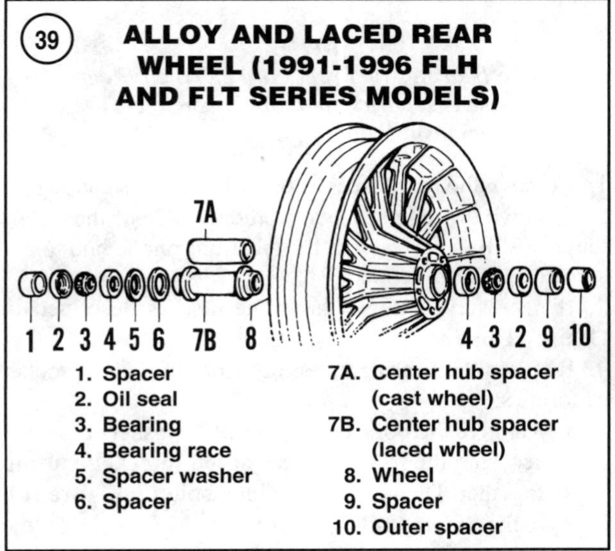

39 ALLOY AND LACED REAR WHEEL (1991-1996 FLH AND FLT SERIES MODELS)

a. Orange color: 4.420 in. (112.27 mm).
b. Yellow color: 4.434 in. (112.62 mm).
c. White color: 4.448 in. (112.98 mm).

5. Install a new spacer and recheck the end play.

Rear Wheel Bearing End Play Check/Adjustment (Late 1991-1998 FXR Series, FXR2 and FXR3 Models and FLH and FLT Series Models)

Wheel bearing end play is controlled by the length of the center hub spacer. Refer to **Figures 35-41**. Check the end play every time the rear wheel is removed or whenever unstable handling is noticed.

1. Support the motorcycle on a swing arm stand with the rear wheel off the ground.
2. Tighten the axle nut to 60-65 ft.-lb. (81-88 N•m).
3. Mount a dial indicator so that the plunger contacts the end of the axle (**Figure 34**). Grasp the wheel and move it back and forth by pushing and pulling it along the axle centerline. Note the axle end play and refer to **Table 1** for specifications.
4. If the end play is incorrect, replace the spacer washer. Refer to **Figures 35-41**. Install a thicker spacer washer for less end play and a thinner spacer washer for more end play. Spacer washers with five different thicknesses are available from a Harley-Davidson dealership as follows:
   a. 0.030-0.033 in. (0.76-0.84 mm).
   b. 0.015-0.017 in. (0.38-0.43 mm).
   c. 0.0075-0.0085 in. (0.190-0.216 mm).
   d. 0.0035-0.0045 in. (0.089-0.114 mm).
   e. 0.0015-0.0025 in. (0.038-0.064 mm).

5. Install a new spacer washer and recheck the end play.

REAR HUB

Tapered roller bearings are installed on each side of the hub. A center hub spacer installed between the bearings maintains front wheel bearing end play within a specified range.

The bearing races are pressed into the hub and should not be removed unless they require replacement.

Disassembly/Inspection/Assembly (Enclosed Drive Chain)

NOTE

The bearings and races are matched. Keep the parts separate and label them to ensure correct installation.

1. Remove the rear wheel as described in this chapter.
2. Remove the axle spacers from each side of the hub if they are still in place. Note the locations on the hub to ensure correct installation.
3. If necessary, remove the brake disc as described in Chapter Thirteen.
4. Remove the bearing assembly from the rear sprocket as follows:
   a. Remove the bolts (5, **Figure 26**), washers and nuts securing the front and rear of the sprocket housing together. Then remove the long bolts (8, **Figure 26**), lockwashers and nuts from the right side of the housing.
   b. Remove the bolts, axle bracket (12, **Figure 26**) and screws from the left side of the housing. Separate the two housings.
   c. Remove the sprocket assembly and spacer (15, **Figure 26**) from the wheel.
   d. Carefully pry the left seals out of the sprocket. Place a rag under the pry tool to protect the sprocket surface.
   e. Then remove the bearing (17, **Figure 26**), spacer washer (19) and sleeve (21A) from the left side.
   f. Remove the dust shield from the right side of the hub.
5. Remove the bearing assembly from the rear hub as follows:
   a. Remove the right axle spacer.
   b. Carefully pry the right seals out of the hub. Place a rag under the pry tool to protect the hub surface (**Figure 42**).
   c. Remove the bearing (**Figure 43**), hub spacer and sleeve (**Figure 44**) from the hub.

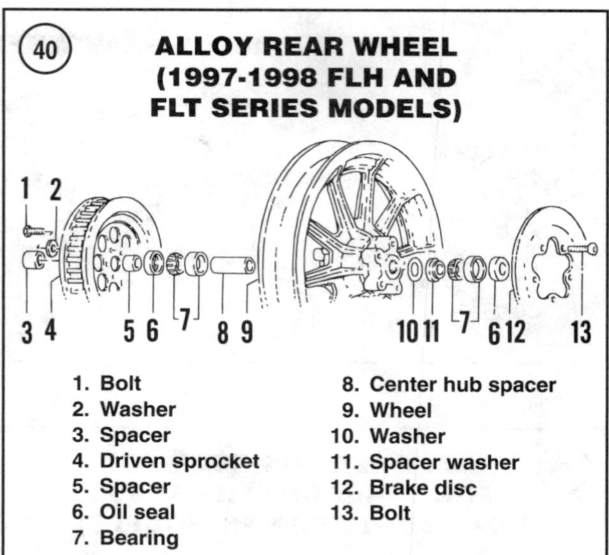

40 **ALLOY REAR WHEEL (1997-1998 FLH AND FLT SERIES MODELS)**

1. Bolt
2. Washer
3. Spacer
4. Driven sprocket
5. Spacer
6. Oil seal
7. Bearing
8. Center hub spacer
9. Wheel
10. Washer
11. Spacer washer
12. Brake disc
13. Bolt

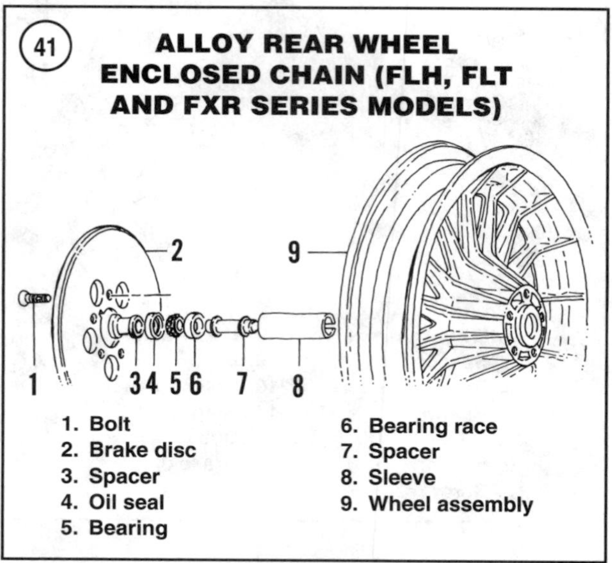

41 **ALLOY REAR WHEEL ENCLOSED CHAIN (FLH, FLT AND FXR SERIES MODELS)**

1. Bolt
2. Brake disc
3. Spacer
4. Oil seal
5. Bearing
6. Bearing race
7. Spacer
8. Sleeve
9. Wheel assembly

6. Wash the bearings thoroughly in clean solvent and dry with compressed air. Wipe off the bearing races with a clean rag dipped in solvent.

7. Then check the roller bearings and races for wear, pitting or excessive heat (bluish tint). Replace the bearings and races as a complete set. Replace the bearing races as described in Step 8. If the bearing and the race do not require replacement, proceed to Step 9. If reinstalling the original bearing(s), pack the bearing thoroughly with grease and wrap it in a clean, lint-free cloth or wax paper. Wipe a film of grease across the bearing race so it will not rust.

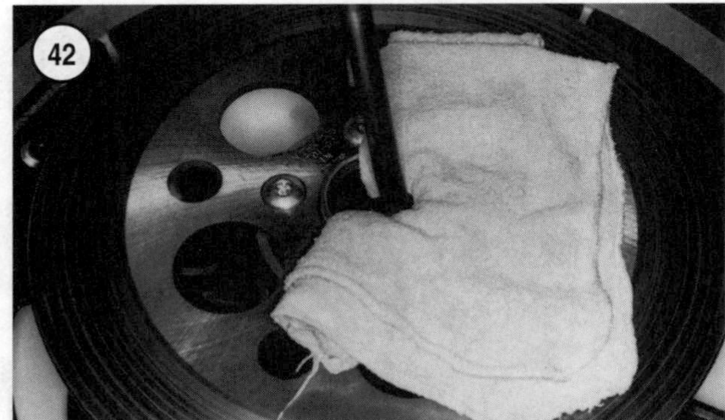

8A. To replace the sprocket bearing race, perform the following:

a. Support the sprocket on a wooden block.

b. Insert a drift punch through the sprocket and tap the opposite race out of the sprocket hub with a hammer. Move the punch around the race to make sure the race is driven squarely out of the sprocket hub. Do not allow the race to bind in the sprocket hub because this can damage the race bore in the sprocket hub. Damage to the race bore will require replacement of the sprocket.

c. Thoroughly clean the inside and outside of the hub with solvent. Dry with compressed air.

d. Apply oil to the outside of the new race and align it with the sprocket hub.

e. Use a bearing driver or socket with an outside diameter slightly smaller than the bearing race to drive the race into the sprocket hub until it bottoms out on the hub shoulder.

NOTE

When installing the race, stop and check the alignment of the bearing race to make sure the race is square with the sprocket hub bore. Do not allow the race to bind during installation, or the sprocket hub race bore will be damaged.

8B. To replace the hub bearing race, perform the following:

a. To protect the front hub from damage, remove the bearing races with a wheel bearing race remover and installer tool (JIMS part No. 33071-73) (**Figure 20**).

b. If the special tool is not available, insert a drift punch through the hub and tap the opposite race out of the hub with a hammer. Move the punch around the race to make sure the race is driven squarely out of the hub. Do not allow the race to bind in the hub because this can damage the race bore in the hub. Damage to the race bore will require replacement of the hub.

c. Thoroughly clean the inside and outside of the hub with solvent. Dry with compressed air.

d. Wipe the outside of the new race with oil and align it with the hub. Install the bearing race with the same tool, bearing driver or socket. Drive the race into the hub until it bottoms out on the hub shoulder.

CAUTION

When installing the race, stop and check the alignment of the bearing race to make sure the race is square with the hub bore. Do not allow the race to bind during installation, or the hub race bore will be damaged.

9A. To assemble the sprocket assembly, perform the following:

a. Pack the bearing with bearing grease.

b. Wipe the bearing race with grease.

c. Pack the seal lip cavity of each seal with grease.

d. Assemble the bearing assembly in the order shown in **Figure 41**.

9B. To assemble the hub assembly, perform the following:

a. Blow any dirt out of the hub prior to installing the bearing.
b. Wipe the ends of the bearing spacer with grease. Install the sleeve and spacer into the hub.

NOTE
If this procedure is being performed to correct wheel bearing end play, install the center hub sleeve of the correct length.

c. Wipe the bearing race with grease.
d. Pack the bearing with grease and install it into the bearing race.
e. Pack the seal lip cavity with grease.
f. Install the seal so that it is flush with the hub bearing bore surface.
g. Wipe the seal lip with oil and install the axle spacer into the seal.

10. If the brake disc was removed, install it as described in Chapter Thirteen.
11. Install the axle spacers into the correct side of the hub as noted during removal.
12. Install the rear wheel as described in this chapter.
13. Check the bearing end play as described in this chapter.

45

46

Disassembly/Inspection/Assembly (All Models Except Enclosed Drive Chain)

Refer to **Figures 31-40**.

NOTE
If only the axle spacer is going to be replaced or exchanged, remove the bearing opposite the brake disc.

NOTE
The bearings and races are matched. Keep the parts separate and label them to ensure correct installation.

1. Remove the rear wheel as described in this chapter.
2. Remove the axle spacers from each side of the hub if they are still in place. Refer to **Figure 45** and **Figure 46**. Note the locations on the hub to ensure correct installation.
3. If necessary, remove the brake disc as described in Chapter Thirteen.
4. If necessary, remove the driven sprocket as described in this chapter.
5. Carefully pry one of the seals out of the hub (**Figure 42**). Place a rag under the pry tool to protect the hub surface.

6A. On 1991-1998 FLH and FLT series models, remove the bearing (**Figure 43**), spacer washer, spacer and center hub spacer from the hub. Note that the spacer washer has a shoulder. Wash these parts thoroughly in solvent and dry with compressed air.

6B. On all other models, remove the bearing (**Figure 43**) from the race. Then remove the center hub spacer from the hub and wash it thoroughly in solvent. Dry with compressed air.

7. Remove the opposite bearing.

8. Wash the bearings thoroughly in clean solvent and dry with compressed air. Wipe the bearing races off with a clean rag dipped in solvent.

9. Then check the roller bearings and races for wear, pitting or excessive heat (bluish tint). Replace the bearings and races as a complete set. Replace the bearing races as described in Step 10. If the bearing and the race do not require replacement, proceed to Step 11. If reinstalling the original bearing(s), pack the bearing thoroughly with grease and wrap it in a clean, lint-free cloth or wax paper. Wipe a film of grease across the bearing race (**Figure 47**). The bearings and races must be lubricated after cleaning, so they will not rust.

10. Replace the bearing races (**Figure 47**) as follows:

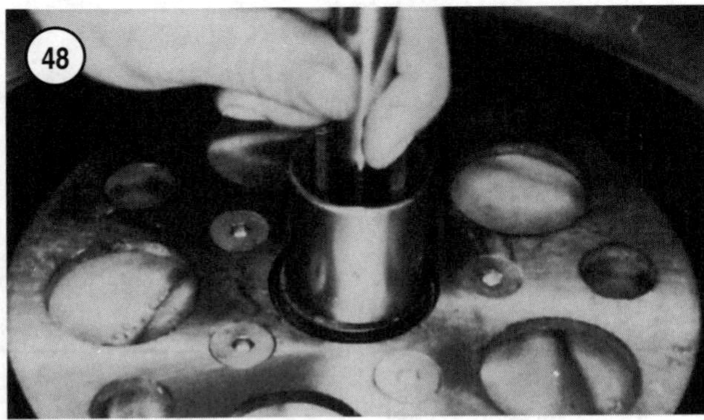

a. To protect the front hub from damage, remove the bearing races with a wheel bearing race remover and installer tool (JIMS part No. 33071-73) (**Figure 20**).

b. If the tool is not available, insert a drift punch through the hub and tap the opposite race out of the hub with a hammer. Move the punch around the race to make sure the race is driven squarely out of the hub. Do not allow the race to bind in the hub because this can damage the race bore in the hub. Damage to the race bore will require replacement of the hub.

c. Thoroughly clean the inside and outside of the hub with solvent. Dry with compressed air.

d. Wipe the outside of the new race with oil and align it with the hub. Install the bearing race with the same tool, bearing driver or socket. Drive the race into the hub until it bottoms out on the hub shoulder.

CAUTION

When installing the race, stop and check the alignment of the bearing race to make sure the race is square with the hub bore. Do not allow the race to bind during installation, or the hub race bore will be damaged.

11. Blow any dirt out of the hub prior to installing the bearings.

NOTE

If performing this procedure to correct wheel bearing end play, make sure you install the center hub spacer with the correct length.

12A. On 1991-1998 FLH and FLT and late 1991-1998 FXR series models, perform the following:

a. Apply grease to the ends of the center hub spacer and install it into the hub.

b. Install the spacer and spacer washer as shown in **Figure 33** or **Figure 39**.

c. Position the spacer washer with the smaller diameter facing outward toward the bearing and install it on the disc brake side.

WARNING

On FXLR models with alloy disc wheels, the spacer washer and spacer must be installed on the sprocket side of wheel. Installing these parts on the brake disc side will reduce wheel bearing end play that could cause bearing seizure and rear wheel lockup.

CAUTION

If the spacer washer is installed with the large diameter facing the bearing it could contact the bearing rollers and damage the bearing.

12B. On all other models, apply grease to the ends of the spacer and install it into the hub.

13. Apply grease to each bearing race.

14. Pack both bearings with grease and install them into the correct bearing race noted during removal.

15. Pack the seal lip cavity of each seal with grease.

NOTE

*When installing the seals in Step 14, use a bearing driver or socket with an outer diameter slightly smaller than the seal (**Figure 48**) and carefully drive the seals into the hub. Install all seals so that the closed sides face out.*

16A. On 1990 and earlier FLH and FLT series models, install both seals so that the outer surfaces are flush with the outer hub surface.

16B. On 1991 FLH and FLT series models, install the seals as follows:

a. On alloy wheels, install the right seal so that the outer surface is flush with the outer hub surface. Install the left seal until the outer surface is 0.031 in. (0.79 mm) below the outer hub surface.

b. On laced wheels, install both oil seals so that the outer surfaces are flush with the outer hub surface.

16C. On 1984-1990 FXR series models, install both seals so that the outer surfaces are 19/64-5/16 in. (7.54-7.94 mm) below the outer hub surface.

16D. On 1991-1994 FXLR models with alloy disc wheels, install the seals as follows:

a. Install the right seal so that the outer surface is flush with the outer hub surface.

b. Install the left seal until the outer surface is 0.31 in. (7.9 mm) below the outer hub surface.

16E. On all other 1991-1998 FXR series models, install the seals as follows:

a. On alloy wheels, install both seals so that the outer surfaces are 0.31 in. (7.9 mm) below the outer hub surface.

b. On laced wheels, install both seals so that the outer surfaces are 0.26-0.28 in. (6.6-7.1 mm) below the outer hub surface.

16F. On FXWG, FXSB and FXEF models, install the seals as follows:

a. On alloy wheels, install both seals so that the outer surfaces are 0.31 in. (7.9 mm) below the outer hub surface.

b. On laced wheels, install both seals so that the outer surfaces are 0.203-0.219 in. (5.16-5.56 mm) below the outer hub surface.

17. If the brake disc was removed, install it as described in Chapter Thirteen.

18. If the driven sprocket was removed, install it as described in this chapter.

19. After the wheel is installed on the motorcycle and the rear axle tightened to the specified torque specification, the bearing end play should be checked as described in this chapter.

DRIVEN SPROCKET ASSEMBLY (CHAIN-DRIVEN MODELS)

Removal/Installation

1A. On closed drive chain models, remove the rear wheel and sprocket as described in this chapter.

1B. On open drive chain models, perform the following:

a. Remove the rear wheel as described in this chapter.

b. Remove the bolts and nuts (**Figure 49**) securing the sprocket to the hub and remove the sprocket.

c. On models so equipped, remove the sprocket spacer.

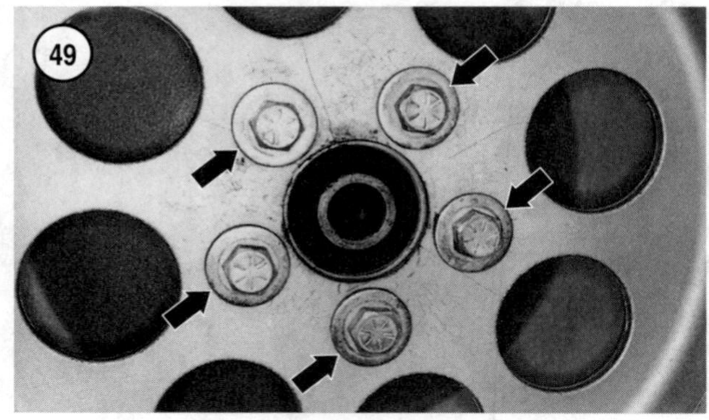

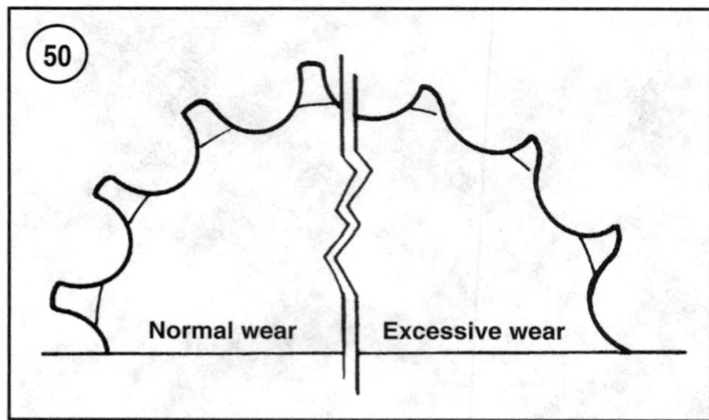

2. Installation is the reverse of these steps. Apply clean engine oil to the sprocket bolts and tighten to the specification listed in **Table 5**.

WARNING
If replacing sprocket bolts, replace with the same grade bolt.

Inspection

Inspect the driven sprocket teeth. If the teeth are visibly worn or undercut (**Figure 50**), replace the driven sprocket as described in this section.

CAUTION
If the driven sprocket requires replacement, also replace the engine drive sprocket and the drive chain. Never install a new drive chain over worn sprockets or a worn drive chain over new sprockets. The old parts will prematurely wear out the new part.

If the rear sprocket requires replacement, also inspect the drive chain as described in Chapter Three and the engine sprocket as described in Chapter Six. They also might be worn and need replacing.

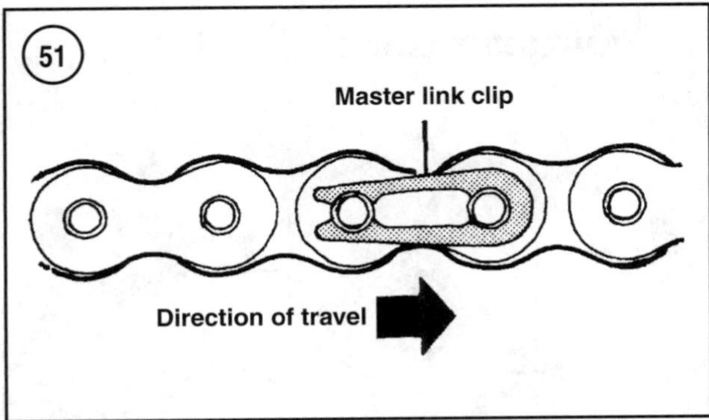

DRIVE CHAIN

Removal/Installation

1. Support the motorcycle on a swing arm stand with the rear wheel off the ground.
2. Loosen the rear axle nut, chain adjuster nuts and the anchor bolt (if so equipped).
3. Push the rear wheel as far forward in the swing arm as possible.
4. On enclosed drive chain models, perform the following:
   a. Remove the bolts, washers and nuts securing the upper chain cover in place.
   b. Slide the cover forward to expose as much of the upper chain run as possible.
   c. Secure the cover with a bungee cord.
5. Turn the rear wheel and locate the drive chain master link on the rear sprocket.
6. Remove the master link spring clip and separate the chain. A chain breaker might be required to separate the chain.
7. If installing a new drive chain, perform the following:
   a. Connect the new chain to the old chain with the old master link.
   b. Pull the new chain through the front sprocket. If the original chain is to be reinstalled, connect it to an old chain or tie a piece of wire approximately 20 in. (50.8 cm) long to the drive chain.
   c. Pull the chain so that the old chain or wire is routed around the front sprocket. Disconnect the old chain and remove it.
8. Install by reversing these removal steps while noting the following:
   a. Install a *new* drive chain master link spring clip with the closed end facing in the direction of chain travel (**Figure 51**).
   b. Adjust the drive chain as described in Chapter Three.
   c. Tighten the axle nut to 60-65 ft.-lb. (80-88 N•m).
   d. On enclosed drive chain models (**Figure 52**), apply a coating of RTV silicone sealant to the rubber chain cover and to the chain housing mating surfaces. Secure the boots with its screws, nuts and washers.
   e. Rotate the wheel several times to make sure it rotates smoothly. Apply the brake several times to make sure it operates correctly.
   f. Adjust the rear brake as described in Chapter Three.

Lubrication

Refer to Chapter Three for drive chain lubrication.

DRIVEN SPROCKET ASSEMBLY (BELT-DRIVEN MODELS)

Inspection

Inspect the sprocket teeth (**Figure 53**). If the teeth are visibly worn, replace the drive belt and both sprockets.

10

Removal/Installation

1. Remove the rear wheel as described in this chapter.
2. Remove the bolts and washers (**Figure 54**, typical) securing the driven sprocket to the hub and remove the sprocket.
3. Position the driven sprocket onto the rear hub.
4. Apply a light coat of medium-strength threadlocking compound to the bolts prior to installation.
5. Install the bolts and washers and tighten the bolts to 55-65 ft.-lb. (75-88 N•m).

DRIVE BELT

CAUTION
When handling the drive belt, never wrap it in a loop smaller than 5 in. (130 mm) or bend it sharply. This will weaken or break the belt fibers and cause premature belt failure.

Removal

NOTE
If the existing drive belt is being reinstalled, install it so it travels in the same direction. Before removing the belt, draw an arrow on the top surface of the belt facing forward.

(52) **ENCLOSED DRIVE CHAIN (FLH, FLT AND FXRT MODELS)**

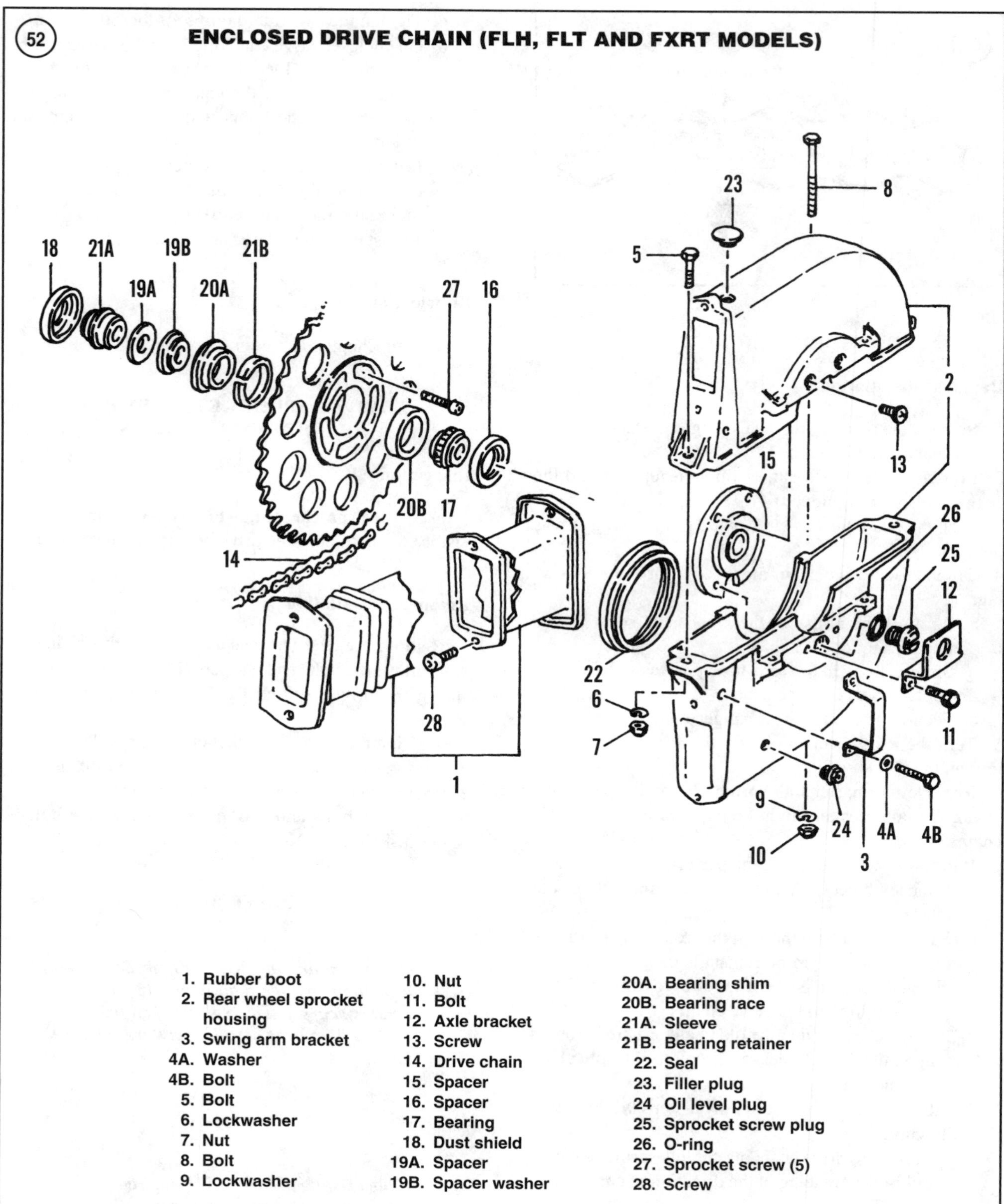

1. Rubber boot
2. Rear wheel sprocket housing
3. Swing arm bracket
4A. Washer
4B. Bolt
5. Bolt
6. Lockwasher
7. Nut
8. Bolt
9. Lockwasher
10. Nut
11. Bolt
12. Axle bracket
13. Screw
14. Drive chain
15. Spacer
16. Spacer
17. Bearing
18. Dust shield
19A. Spacer
19B. Spacer washer
20A. Bearing shim
20B. Bearing race
21A. Sleeve
21B. Bearing retainer
22. Seal
23. Filler plug
24 Oil level plug
25. Sprocket screw plug
26. O-ring
27. Sprocket screw (5)
28. Screw

53

54

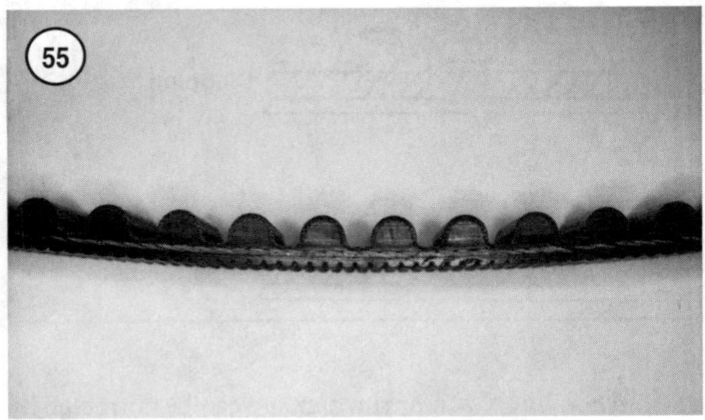
55

1. Remove the exhaust system as described in Chapter Eight.
2. Install wooden blocks or a floor jack under the transmission and engine assembly.
3. Remove the compensating sprocket and clutch as described in Chapter Five.
4. Remove the primary chain inner housing as described in Chapter Five.
5. Remove the rear wheel as described in this chapter.
6. Remove the swing arm as described in Chapter Twelve.
7. Remove the drive belt from the drive sprocket and remove the drive belt from the frame.

Installation

NOTE
If the existing drive belt is being reinstalled, install it so it travels in the same direction as noted prior to removal. If a new drive belt is being installed, it can be installed in either direction.

1. Install the drive belt onto the drive sprocket.
2. Correctly position the drive belt and install the swing arm as described in Chapter Twelve.
3. Install the rear wheel as described in this chapter.
4. Remove the wooden blocks or floor jack from under the transmission and engine assembly.
5. Install the primary chain inner housing as described in Chapter Five.
6. Install the compensating sprocket and clutch as described in Chapter Five.
7. Install the exhaust system as described in Chapter Seven.

Inspection

Do not apply any type of lubricant to the drive belt. Inspect the drive belt and teeth (**Figure 55**) for severe wear, damage or oil contamination.

Refer to **Figure 56** for various types of drive belt wear or damage. Replace the drive belt if it is worn or damaged.

WHEEL RUNOUT

1. Remove the front or rear wheel as described in this chapter.
2. Install the wheel in a wheel truing stand and check the wheel for excessive wobble or runout.
3. If the wheel is not running true, remove the tire from the rim as described in this chapter. Then remount the wheel into the truing stand and measure axial and lateral runout (**Figure 57**) with a pointer or dial indicator. Compare actual runout readings with the service limit specification in **Table 1**. Note the following:
   a. On disc or alloy wheels, if the runout meets or exceeds the service limit in **Table 1**, check the wheel bearings as described under *Front and Rear Hub* in this chapter. If the wheel bearings are acceptable, replace the alloy or disc wheel because it cannot be

serviced. Inspect the wheel for cracks, fractures, dents or bends. Replace a damaged wheel.

WARNING

Do not try to repair damage to a disc wheel because it will result in an unsafe riding condition.

b. On laced wheels, if the wheel bearings, spokes, hub and rim assembly are not damaged, the runout can be corrected by truing the wheel. Refer to *Rim and Laced Wheel Service* in this chapter. If the rim is dented or damaged, replace the rim and rebuild the wheel.

4. While the wheel is off, perform the following:
   a. Check the brake disc mounting bolts (**Figure 49**) for tightness as described in Chapter Thirteen.
   b. On the rear wheel, check the driven sprocket bolts for tightness as described in this chapter.

RIM AND LACED WHEEL SERVICE

The laced wheel assembly consists of a rim, spokes, nipples and hub containing the bearings, and spacer collar.

Component Condition

Wheels are subjected to a significant amount of punishment. Inspect the wheel regularly for lateral (side-to-side) and radial (up-and-down) runout and even spoke tension and visible rim damage. When a wheel has a noticeable wobble, it is out of true. This is usually cause by loose spokes, but it can be caused by an impact-damaged rim.

Truing a wheel corrects the lateral and radial runout to bring the wheel back into specification. The condition of the individual wheel components will effect the ability to successfully true the wheel. Note the following:

1. Spoke condition. Do not attempt to true a wheel with bent or damaged spokes. Doing so places an excessive amount of tension on the spoke and rim. The spoke might break and/or pull through the spoke nipple hole in the rim. Inspect the spokes carefully and replace any spokes that are damaged.
2. Nipple condition. When truing the wheels, the nipples should turn freely on the spoke. It is common for the spoke threads to become corroded and make turning the nipple difficult. Spray a penetrating liquid onto the nipple and allow sufficient time for it to penetrate before trying to force the nipple loose. Work the spoke wrench in both directions and continue to apply penetrating liquid. If the spoke wrench rounds off the nipple, remove the tire from the rim and cut the spoke(s) out of the wheel.

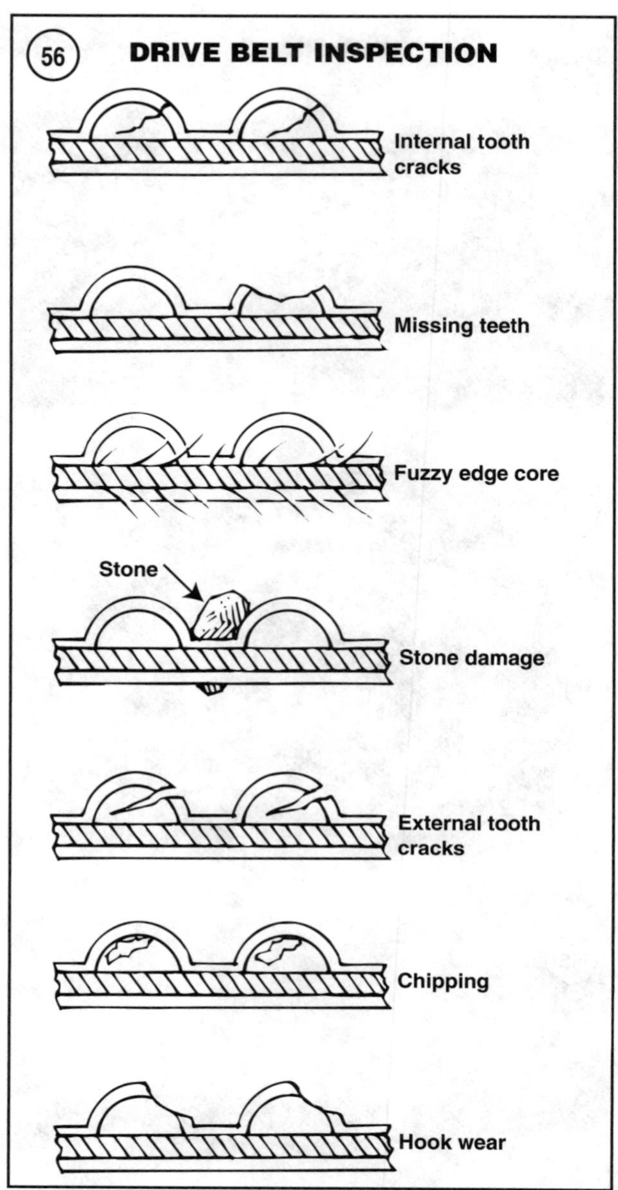

3. Rim condition. Minor rim damage can be corrected by truing the wheel; however, trying to correct excessive runout caused by impact damage causes hub and rim damage due to spoke overtightening. Inspect the rims for cracks, flat spots or dents. Check the spoke holes for cracks or enlargement. Replace rims with excessive damage.

Wheel Truing Preliminaries

Before checking runout and truing the wheel, note the following:

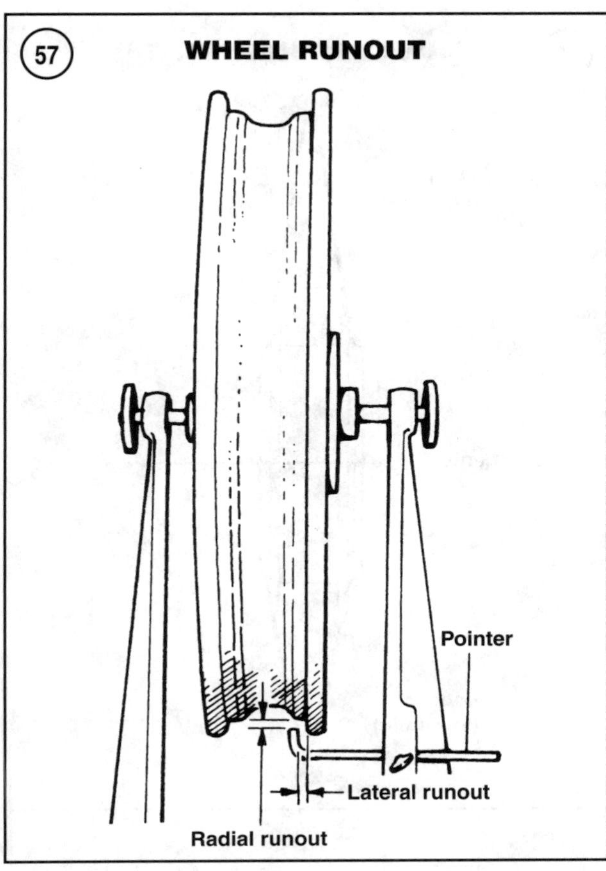

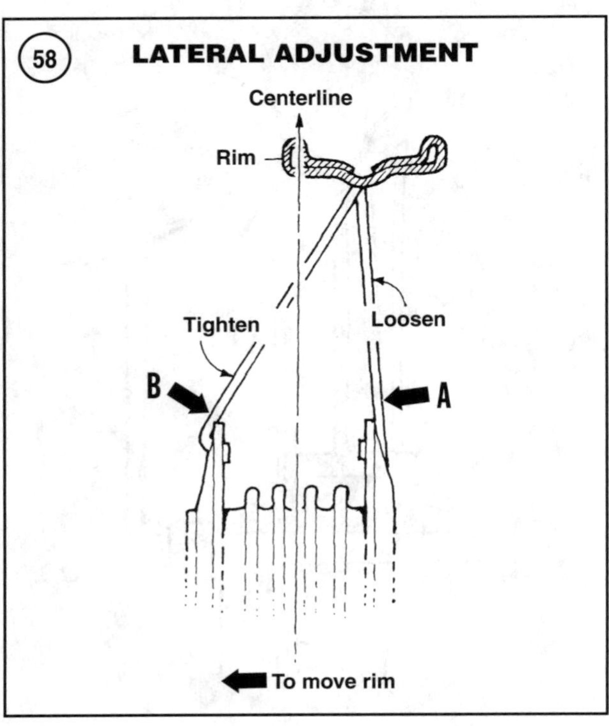

1. Make sure the wheel bearings are in good condition. Refer to *Front and Rear Hubs* in this chapter.
2. A small amount of wheel runout is acceptable. Do not try to true the wheel to a perfect zero reading. Doing so causes excessive spoke tension and possible rim and hub damage. **Table 1** lists the lateral (side-to-side) and radial (up-and-down) runout limit specifications.
3. The runout can be checked on the motorcycle by mounting a pointer against the fork or swing arm and slowly rotating the wheel.
4. Perform major wheel truing with the tire removed and the wheel mounted in a truing stand (**Figure 57**). If a stand is not available, mount the wheel on the motorcycle with spacers on each side of the wheel to prevent it from sliding on the axle.
5. Use a spoke nipple wrench of the correct size. Using the wrong type of tool or one that is the incorrect size will round off the spoke nipples and make adjustment difficult. Quality spoke wrenches have openings that grip the nipple on four corners to prevent nipple damage.
6. Refer to the spoke nipple torque specifications in **Table 4** or **Table 5** when using a torque wrench.

10

Wheel Truing Procedure

1. Position a pointer facing toward the rim (**Figure 57**). Then spin the wheel slowly and check the lateral and radial runout. If the rim is out of adjustment, continue with Step 2.

NOTE
If there is a large number of loose spokes, make sure the hub is centered in the rim. This must be done visually as there are no hub and rim centering specifications for these models.

NOTE
The number of spokes to loosen and tighten in Steps 2 and 3 depends on how far the runout is out of adjustment. As a minimum, always loosen two or three spokes. Then tighten the opposite two or three spokes. If the runout is excessive and affects a greater area along the rim, a greater number of spokes will require adjustment.

2. If the lateral (side-to-side) runout is out of specification, adjust the wheel by using **Figure 58** for an example. To move the rim to the right in **Figure 58**, loosen spoke A and tighten spoke B. Always loosen and tighten the spokes an equal number of turns.
3. If the radial (up and down) runout is out of specification, the hub is not centered in the rim. Draw the high

point of the rim toward the centerline of the wheel by loosening the spokes in the area of the high point and on the same side as the high point, and tightening the spokes on the side opposite the high point (**Figure 59**). Tighten spokes in equal amounts to prevent distortion.

4. After truing the wheel, seat each spoke in the hub by tapping it with a flat nose punch and hammer. Then recheck the spoke tension and wheel runout. Readjust if necessary.

5. Check the ends of the spokes where they are threaded in the nipples. Grind off ends that protrude through the nipples.

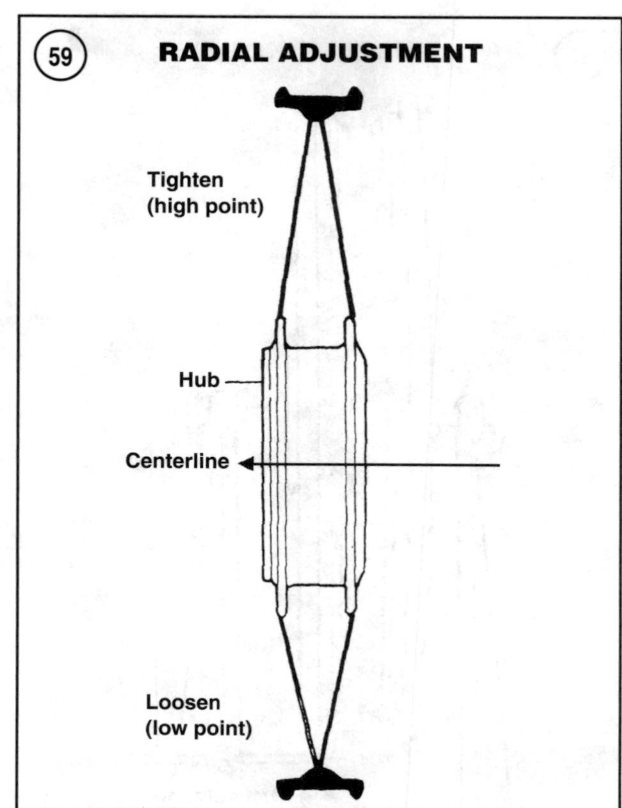

DISC AND ALLOY WHEELS

Disc and alloy wheels consist of a single assembly equipped with bearings and a spacer sleeve.

Although these wheels are virtually maintenance free, they must be checked for damage at the maintenance intervals in Chapter Three. Also, check the wheel prior to installing a new tire. Wheel bearing service is described in this chapter.

Inspection

Before checking runout and truing the wheel, note the following:

1. Make sure the wheel bearings are in good condition.
2. Perform wheel runout with the tire removed and the wheel mounted in a truing stand (**Figure 60**). If a stand is not available, mount the wheel on the motorcycle with spacers on each side of the wheel to prevent it from sliding on the axle.
3. The maximum axial (end play) and radial (side play) runout is listed in **Table 1**.

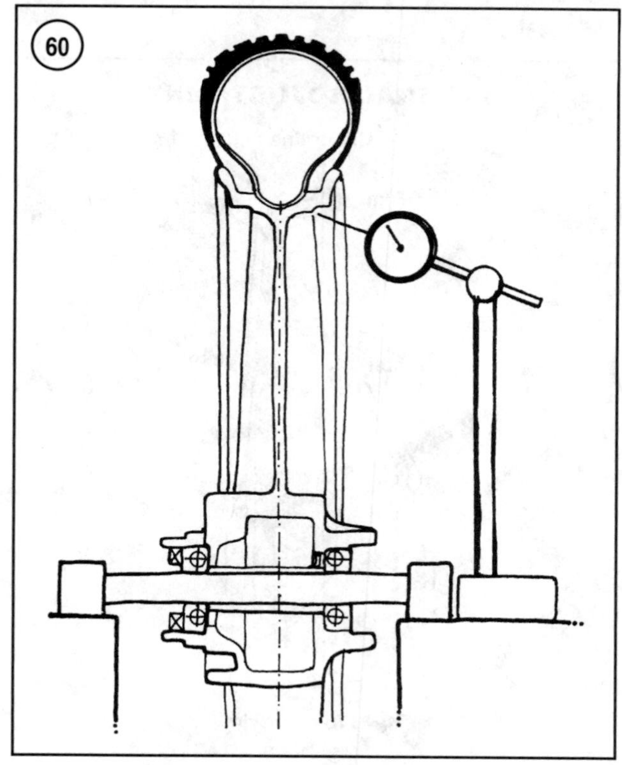

WARNING
Do not try to repair any damage to a disc or alloy wheel because it will result in an unsafe riding condition.

WHEEL BALANCE

An unbalanced wheel is unsafe. Depending on the degree of unbalance and the speed of the motorcycle, the rider might experience anything from a mild vibration to a violent shimmy that can cause loss of control.

On alloy or disc wheels, weights are attached to the flat surface on the rim (**Figure 61**). On laced wheels, the weights are attached to the spoke nipples (**Figure 62**).

61

62

63

Before attempting to balance the wheel, make sure the wheel bearings are in good condition and properly lubricated. The wheel must rotate freely.

1A. Remove the front wheel as described in this chapter.

1B. Remove the rear wheel as described in this chapter.

2. Mount the wheel on a fixture (**Figure 63**) so it can rotate freely.

3. Spin the wheel and let it coast to a stop. Mark the tire at the lowest point.

4. Spin the wheel several more times. If the wheel keeps coming to rest at the same point, it is out of balance.

5A. On alloy or disc wheels, tape a test weight to the upper or light side of the wheel (**Figure 61**).

5B. On laced wheels, attach a weight to the spoke (**Figure 62**) on the upper or light side of the wheel.

6. Experiment with different weights until the wheel comes to a stop at a different position every time it is spun.

7. On disc or alloy wheels, remove the test weight and install the correct weight.

   a. Attach the weights to the flat surface on the rim (**Figure 61**). Clean the rim of all road debris before installing the weights; otherwise, the weights might fall off.
   b. Add weights in 1/4 oz. (7g) increments. If 1 oz. (28 g) or more must be added to one location, apply half the amount to each side of the rim.
   c. To apply OEM wheel weights, remove the paper backing from the weight and apply three drops of Loctite 420 Superbonder to the bottom of the weight. Position the weight on the rim, press it down and hold in position for 10 seconds. To allow the adhesive to cure properly, do not use the wheel for eight hours.

8. When fitting weights on laced wheels for the final time, crimp the weights (**Figure 62**) onto the spoke with slip-joint pliers.

TIRES

Tire Safety

Maintain the tire inflation pressure at the specification in **Table 2** and **Table 3**. If a different brand of tire is used, follow the inflation recommendation provided by the tire manufacturer. Tire inflation specifications are cold inflation specifications. Do not check/adjust tire pressure after riding the motorcycle.

Always allow the tires to warm up by riding before subjecting them to high cornering loads. Warm tires provide more adhesion.

New tires provide significantly less adhesion until they are broken in. Do not subject new tires to high speed or high cornering forces for at least 60 miles (100 km). Be especially careful when encountering wet conditions with new tires.

TIRE CHANGING

The alloy or disc wheels can easily be damaged during tire removal. Take special care with tire irons when changing a tire to avoid scratches and gouges to the outer rim surface. Insert scraps of leather between the tire iron and the rim to protect the rim from damage. All original equipment alloy or disc wheels are designed for use with tubeless tires only. All laced wheels use a tube and tire combination.

When removing a tubeless tire, take care not to damage the tire beads, inner liner of the tire or the wheel rim flange. Use tire levers or flat handle tire irons with rounded heads.

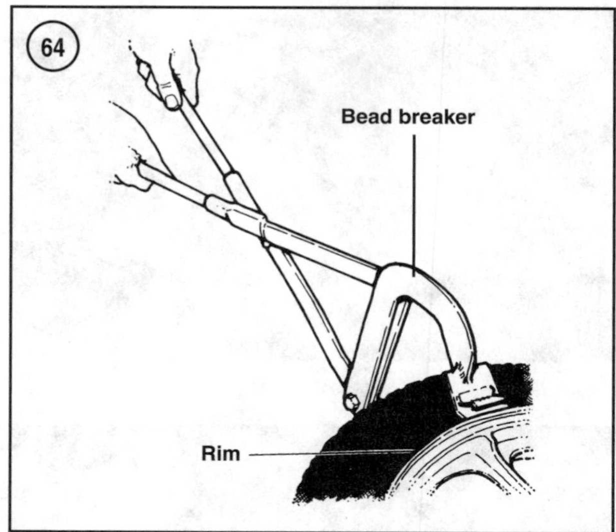

Tire Removal

CAUTION
To avoid damage when removing the tire, support the wheel on two wooden blocks so neither the brake disc nor the driven sprocket contacts the floor.

NOTE
To make tire removal easier, warm the tire to make it softer and more pliable. Place the wheel and tire assembly in the sun. If possible, place the wheel assembly and the new tire in a closed vehicle.

1A. Remove the front wheel as described in this chapter.
1B. Remove the rear wheel as described in this chapter.
2. If not already marked by the tire manufacturer, mark the valve stem location on the tire, so the tire can be installed in the same location for easier balancing.
3. Remove the valve cap and unscrew the core from the valve stem and deflate the tire or tube.

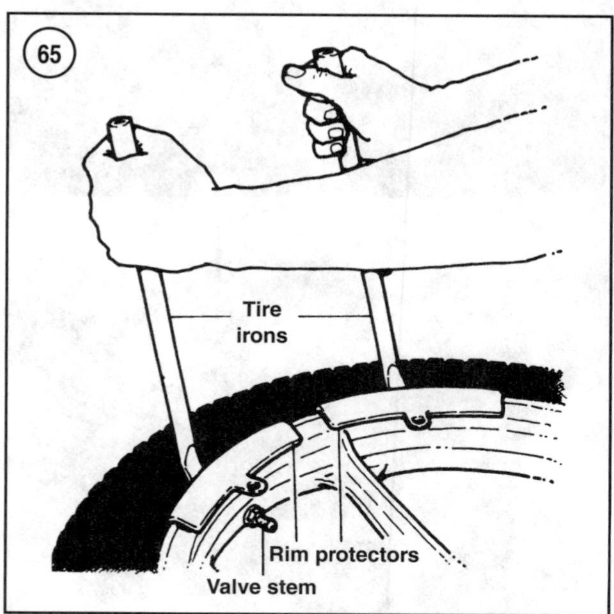

CAUTION
The inner rim and tire bead areas are the sealing surfaces on the tubeless tire. Do not scratch the inside of the rim or damage the tire bead.

NOTE
*Removal of tubeless tires from the rims can be difficult because of the exceptionally tight tire bead-to-rim seal. Breaking the bead seal may require a special tool (**Figure 64**). If unable to break the seal loose, take the wheel to a motorcycle dealership or tire repair shop, and have a professional break it loose on a tire changing machine.*

4. Press the entire bead on both sides of the tire away from the rim and into the center of the rim. If the bead is tight, use a bead breaker.
5. Lubricate both beads with soapy water.

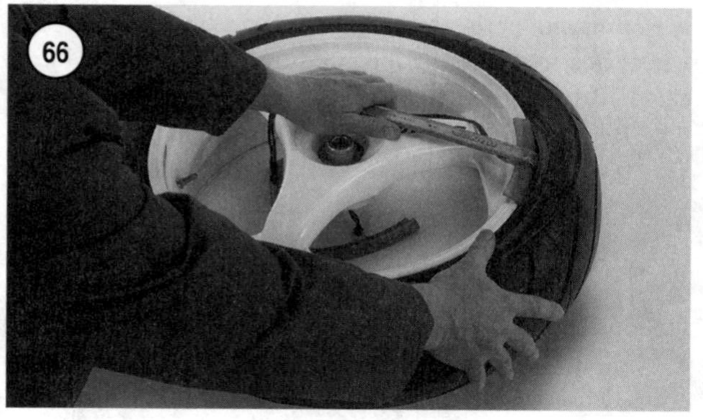

CAUTION
*Use rim protectors (part No. HD-01289) or an equivalent (**Figure 65**) or insert scraps*

67

68

of leather between the tire iron and the rim to protect the rim from damage. Use only quality tire irons without sharp edges. If necessary, file the ends of the tire irons to remove rough edges.

6. Insert a tire iron under the top bead next to the valve stem (**Figure 66**, typical). Force the bead on the opposite side of the tire into the center of the rim and pry the bead over the rim with the tire iron.
7. Insert a second tire iron next to the first iron to hold the bead over the rim. Then work around the tire with the first tire iron and pry the bead over the rim (**Figure 67**, typical). On tube tires, be careful not to pinch the inner tube with the tools.
8. On tube tires, use a thumb and push the valve stem from its hole in the rim to the inside of the tire. Carefully pull the tube out of the tire and lay it aside.

NOTE

Step 9 is necessary only if it is necessary to remove the tire from the wheel completely for tire replacement or tubeless tire repair, for example.

9. Stand the wheel upright. Insert a tire iron between the back bead and the side of the rim that the top bead was pried over (**Figure 68**, typical). Force the bead on the opposite side from the tire iron into the center of the rim. Work around the tire and pry the back bead off the rim. On tube tires, remove the rim band.
10. Inspect the valve stem seal. Because rubber deteriorates with age, replace the valve stem when replacing the tire.
11. On tubeless tires, remove the old valve stem and discard it. Inspect the valve stem hole in the rim. Remove any dirt or corrosion from the hole and wipe it dry with a clean cloth. Install a new valve stem and make sure it is properly seated in the rim.
12. Carefully inspect the tire and wheel rim for damage as described in the following section.

Tire and Wheel Rim Inspection

1. Wipe off the inner surfaces of the wheel rim. Clean off any rubber residue or oxidation.

WARNING

Carefully consider whether a tire should be replaced. If there is any doubt about the quality of the existing tire, replace it with a new one. Do not take a chance on a tire failure at any speed.

2. On tubeless tires, inspect the valve stem rubber grommet for deterioration. If replacement is necessary, install only the OEM valve stem assembly.

WARNING

Install only OEM tire valves and valve caps. A valve or valve/cap combination that is too long or heavier than OEM parts can interfere with adjacent components when the motorcycle is under way. Damage to the valve will cause rapid tire deflation and loss of control.

3. If any of the following conditions are observed, replace the tire.
   a. A puncture or split whose total length or diameter exceeds 0.44 in. (6 mm).
   b. A scratch or split on the side wall.
   c. Any type of ply separation.
   d. Tread separation or excessive abnormal wear pattern.
   e. Tread depth of less than 1/16 in. (1.6 mm) on original equipment tires. Tread depth minimum might vary on aftermarket tires.

f. Scratches on either sealing bead.
g. The cord is cut in any place.
h. Flat spots in the tread from skidding.
i. Any abnormality in the inner liner.

Tire Installation

1. A new tire might have balancing rubbers inside. These are not patches. Do not remove them. Most tires are marked with a colored spot near the bead (**Figure 69**) that indicates a lighter point on the tire. This should be placed next to the valve stem.
2. On tube tires, install the rim band over the wheel and align the hole in the rim band with the hole in the rim. If installing a new rim band, make sure it is the correct diameter and width for the wheel.
3. Lubricate both beads of the tire with soapy water.
4. When installing the tire on the rim, make sure the correct tire (either front or rear) is installed on the correct wheel. Also make sure the direction arrow faces the direction of wheel rotation.
5. When remounting the old tire, align the mark made in Step 2 of *Removal* with the valve stem (**Figure 69**).
6. Place the back side of the tire onto the rim so the lower bead sits in the center of the rim while the upper bead remains outside the rim (**Figure 70**, typical). Work around the tire in both directions and press the lower bead by hand into the center of the rim. Use a tire iron for the last few inches of the bead.
7. On tube tires, perform the following:
   a. Dust the inner tube with talcum powder before installing it in the tire. The talcum powder will prevent the tube from sticking to the tire.
   b. Inflate the tube just enough to round it out. Too much air will make installation difficult.
   c. Place the tube on top of the tire. Aligning the valve stem with the matching hole in the rim. Insert the tube into the tire.
   d. Lift the upper bead away from the rim with a hand and insert the tube valve stem through the rim hole. Check to make sure that the valve stem is straight up (90°) and not cocked to one side. If necessary, reposition the tube in the tire. If the valve stem wants to slide out of the hole and back into the tire, install the valve stem nut at the top of the valve; do not tighten the nut at this time.
8. Press the upper bead into the rim opposite the valve stem. Working on both sides of this initial point, pry the bead into the rim with the tire tool. Work around the rim to the valve stem (**Figure 71**, typical). On tube tires, do not pinch the inner tube during the last few inches. If the tire wants to pull up on one side, either use another tire iron or one knee to hold the tire in place. The last few inches are usually the toughest to install. Continue to push the tire into the rim by hand. Relubricate the bead if necessary. If the tire bead pulls out from under the rim, use both knees to hold the tire in place. If necessary, use a tire iron for the last few inches (**Figure 72**, typical).
9. On tube tires, check to make sure that the valve stem is straight up (90°) and not cocked to one side (**Figure 73**,

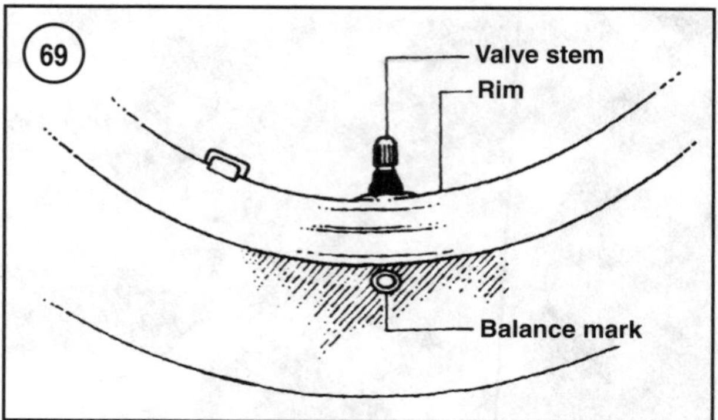

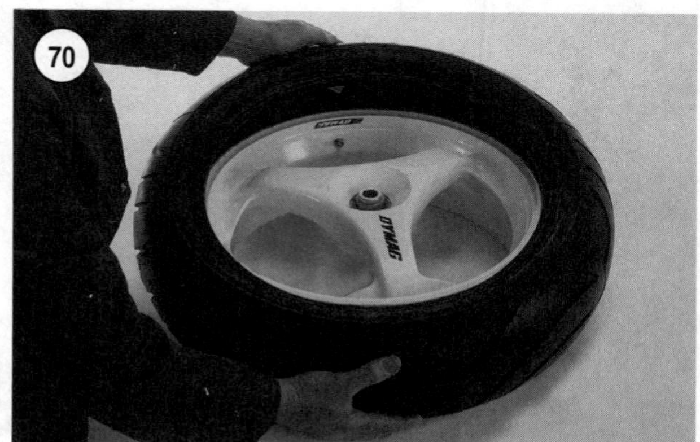

72

73

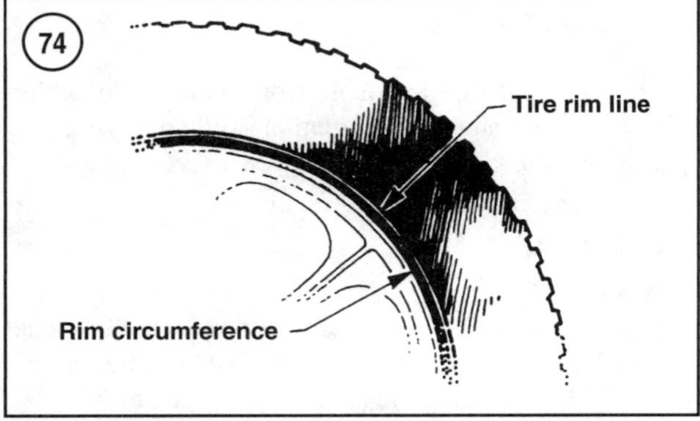

74

typical). If necessary, slide the tire along the rim in either direction while holding the rim securely. When the valve stem is straight up, tighten the valve stem nut at the top of the valve; do not tighten it against the rim at this time. Check that the tube was not forced outward so that it rests between the tire bead and the rim. If necessary, push the tube back into the tire.

10. Bounce the wheel several times, rotating it each time. This will force the tire bead against the rim flanges. After the tire beads are in contact with the rim, inflate the tire to seat the beads.

11A. On tube tires, perform the following:
   a. Inflate the tube to the maximum tire pressure to seat the tire beads in the rim.
   b. After inflating the tire, make sure the beads are fully seated and the rim lines are the same distance from the rim all the way around the tire (**Figure 74**).
   c. If the tire beads do not seat properly, release the air pressure and relubricate the tire beads.
   d. When the tire is seated correctly, remove the valve core and deflate the tire allowing the tube to straighten out within the tire.
   e. Install the valve core and inflate the tire to the pressure in **Table 2**.
   f. Tighten the valve stem nut securely and install the valve stem cap.

11B. On tubeless tires, perform the following:
   a. Place an inflatable band around the circumference of the tire. Slowly inflate the band until the tire beads are pressed against the rim. Inflate the tire enough to make it seat, deflate the band, and remove it.

WARNING
In the next step, never exceed 40 psi (276 kPa) inflation pressure because the tire could burst and cause severe injury. Never stand directly over a tire while inflating it.

   b. After inflating the tire, make sure the beads are fully seated and the rim lines are the same distance from the rim all the way around the tire (**Figure 74**). If the beads will not seat, deflate the tire and lubricate the rim and beads with soapy water.
   c. Reinflate the tire to the pressure in **Table 2** or **Table 3**. Install the valve stem cap.

12. Check tire runout as described in this chapter.
13. Balance the wheel as described in this chapter.

14A. Install the front wheel as described in this chapter.

14B. Install the rear wheel as described in this chapter.

TIRE REPAIRS (TUBELESS)

WARNING
Do not install an inner tube inside a tubeless tire. The tube will cause abnormal heat buildup in the tire.

NOTE
Changing or patching on the road is very difficult. A can of pressurized tire inflator

and sealer can inflate the tire and seal the hole, but this is only a temporary fix.

Tubeless tires have the word TUBELESS molded into the sidewall, and the rims have SUITABLE FOR TUBELESS TIRES or equivalent stamped or alloyed on them.

If the tire is punctured, remove it from the rim to inspect the inside of the tire and apply a combination plug/patch from inside the tire (**Figure 75**). Never attempt to repair a tubeless motorcycle tire using a plug or cord patch applied from outside the tire.

After repairing a tubeless tire, do not exceed 50 mph (80 km/h) for the first 24 hours.

As soon as possible, replace the patched tire with a new one.

Repair

Do not rely on a plug or cord patch applied from outside the tire. Use a combination plug/patch applied from inside the tire (**Figure 75**).

1. Remove the tire from the wheel rim as described in this chapter.
2. Inspect the rim inner flange. Smooth scratches on the sealing surface with emery cloth. If a scratch is deeper than 0.020 in. (0.5 mm), replace the wheel.
3. Inspect the inside and outside of the tire. Replace a tire if any of the following conditions are found.
   a. A puncture larger than 1/8 in. (3 mm) in diameter.
   b. A punctured or damaged side wall.
   c. More than two punctures in the tire.
4. Apply the plug/patch following the manufacturer's instructions with the patch kit.
5. As soon as possible, replace the patched tire with a new one.

TIRE REPAIRS (TUBE)

NOTE

Changing or patching on the road is very difficult. A can of pressurized tire inflator and sealer can inflate the tire and seal the hole, but this is only a temporary fix.

Patching a motorcycle tube is only a temporary fix. A motorcycle tire flexes too much and a patch can rub right off. As soon as possible, replace the tube with a new one.

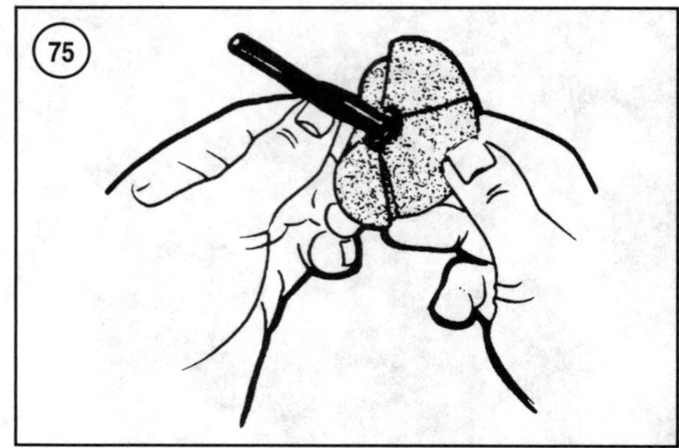

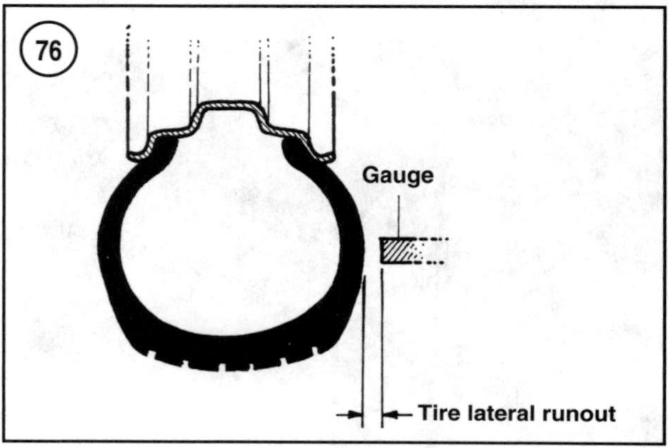

Tube Repair Kits

Tire repair kits are available from motorcycle dealerships and some auto supply retailers. When buying one, specify that the kit is for a motorcycle tire.

There are two types of tube repair kits:

a. Hot patch.
b. Cold patch.

Hot patches are stronger because they actually vulcanize to the tube, becoming part of it. Cold patches are not vulcanized to the tube; they are simply glued to it.

Purchase the repair kit and follow the manufacturer's instructions.

TIRE RUNOUT

Check the tires for excessive lateral and radial runout after a wheel has been mounted or if the motorcycle develops a wobble that cannot be traced to another component. Mount the wheels on the axles when making the following checks.

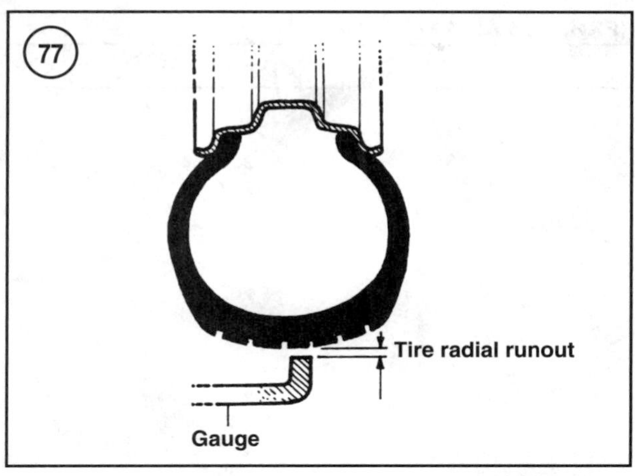

1. For lateral runout, check the tire for excessive side-to-side play as follows:
   a. Position a fixed pointer next to the tire sidewall as shown in **Figure 76**. Position the pointer tip so it is not directly in line with the molded tire logo or any other raised surface.
   b. Rotate the tire and measure lateral runout.
   c. The lateral runout should not exceed 0.080 in. (2.03 mm). If runout is excessive, remove the tire from the wheel and recheck the lateral runout as described in this chapter. If the runout is excessive, the wheel must be trued (laced wheels) or replaced (alloy wheels). If wheel runout is correct, the tire runout is excessive and the tire must be replaced.
2. For radial runout, check the tire for excessive up-and-down play as follows:
   a. Position a fixed pointer at the center bottom of the tire tread as shown in **Figure 77**.
   b. Rotate the tire and measure the amount of radial runout.
   c. The radial runout should not exceed 0.090 in. (2.29 mm). If runout is excessive, remove the tire from the wheel and recheck the radial runout as described in this chapter. If runout is excessive, true (laced wheel) or replace the wheel. If wheel runout is correct, the tire runout is excessive, and the tire must be replaced.

Table 1 WHEEL SPECIFICATIONS

Item	Specification in. (mm)
Alloy rim runout	
Lateral runout	
FXWG, FXSB and FXEF	0.047 (1.19)
FLT and FXR model series	0.040 (1.02)
Radial runout	
FXWG, FXSB and FXEF	0.030 (0.76)
FLT and FXR model series	0.031 (0.79)
Laced rim runout	0.031 (0.79)
Wheel bearing end play	
FXR series models	
1984-early 1991	
1984 FXRT (enclosed drive chain models)	
Front	0.004-0.018 (0.10-0.46)
Rear	0.002-0.006 (0.05-0.15)
All other models (front and rear)	0.004-0.018 (0.10-0.46)
Late 1991-1998	
Front and rear	0.002-0.006 (0.05-0.15)
FXWG, FXSB and FXEF	
Front and rear	0.004-0.018 (0.10-0.46)
FLH and FLT series models	
Front wheel	0.002-0.006 (0.05-0.15)
Rear wheel	
Enclosed drive chain models	0.002-0.006 (0.05-0.15)
All other models	
1984-early1991	0.004-0.018 (0.10-0.46)
Late 1991-1998	0.002-0.006 (0.05-0.15)

Table 2 TIRE INFLATION PRESSURE (FXR, FLH AND FLT [COLD])[1]

Item	psi	kPa
Front (rider only)		
1984-1985		
FXRS (K291T[2])	30	207
FXRT (K291T[2])	30	207
FLT/FLTC	–	–
FLHT/FLHTC (K101A[2])	28	193
1996-1998		
FXR series models	30	207
FLH and FLT series models	36	248
Front (rider with one passenger)		
1984-1985		
FXRS	30	207
FXRT	30	207
FLT/FLTC and FLHT/FLHTC	28	193
FLT with sidecar	28	193
1996-1998		
FXR series models	30	207
FLH and FLT series models	36	248
Rear (rider only)		
1984-1985		
FXRS (K291T[2])	36	248
FXRT (K291T[2])	36	248
FLT/FLTC	36	248
FLHT/FLHTC (K101A[2])	36	248
1996-1998		
FXR series	36	248
FLH and FLT series models	36	248
Rear (rider with one passenger)		
1984-1985		
FXRS	40	275
FXRT	40	275
FLT/FLTC and FLHT/FLHTC	36	248
FLT with sidecar	40	275
1996-1998		
FXR series models	40	275
FLH and FLT series models	40	275

1. Tire inflation pressure is for OEM tires. Aftermarket tires might require different inflation pressure. The use of tires other than those specified by Harley-Davidson can cause instability.
2. Indicates the OEM Dunlop tire designation.

Table 3 TIRE INFLATION PRESSURE (FXWG, FXSB AND FXEF [COLD])[1]

Item	psi	kPa
Front (rider only)		
FXWG	30	207
FXEF and FXSB		
K181[2]	30	207
K291T[2]	36	248
Front (rider with one passenger)		
FXWG		
F rib	30	207
K101A[3]	–	–
FXEF and FXSB		
K181[2]	30	207
K291T[2]	36	248

(continued)

Table 3 TIRE INFLATION PRESSURE (FXWG, FXSB AND FXEF [COLD])[1] (continued)

Item	psi	kPa
Rear (rider only)		
FXWG	32	221
FXEF and FXSB		
K181[2]	32	221
K291T[2]	36	248
Rear (rider with one passenger)		
FXWG		
F rib	32	221
K101A[3]	28	193
FXEF and FXSB		
K181[2]	32	221

1. Tire inflation pressure is for OEM tires. Aftermarket tires might require different inflation pressure. The use of tires other than those specified by Harley-Davidson can cause instability.
2. Indicates the OEM Dunlop tire designation.
3. Early 1985 models.

Table 4 FRONT WHEEL TORQUE SPECIFICATIONS

Item	ft.-lb.	in.-lb.	N•m
Axle nut			
FXR series models			
1984-1992	50	–	68
1993-1998	50-55	–	68-75
FXWG, FXSB and FXEF	50-55	–	68-75
FLH and FLT series models	50-55	–	68-75
Axle slider cap nuts			
FXR series models			
FXLR	–	85-110	10-12
All other models	–	106-156	12-18
FXWG, FXSB and FXEF	–	106-156	12-18
FLH and FLT series models	–	106-156	12-18
Front brake caliper	25-30	–	34-41
Spoke nipple	–	40-50	4-6

10

Table 5 REAR WHEEL TORQUE SPECIFICATIONS

Item	ft.-lb.	in.-lb.	N•m
Axle nut	60-65	–	80-88
Driven sprocket bolts (belt drive)	55-65	–	75-88
Driven sprocket bolts (chain drive)			
FXR, FLH and FLT series models			
1984-1991			
Grade No. 5 bolts	45-50	–	61-68
Grade No. 8 bolts	65-70	–	88-95
1992	45-55	–	61-75
1993-1998	55-65	–	75-88
FXWG, FXSB and FXEF			
Laced wheel			
FXWG	40-55	–	54-75
FXSB and FXEF	35	–	47
Alloy wheel			
Grade No. 5 bolts	45-50	–	61-68
Grade No. 8 bolts	65-70	–	88-95
Spoke nipple	–	40-50	4-6

CHAPTER ELEVEN

FRONT SUSPENSION AND STEERING

This chapter covers the handlebar, steering head and front fork assemblies.

Tables 1-5 are found at the end of the chapter.

HANDLEBAR

Removal/Installation

Refer to **Figure 1**, typical.

1A. On all FLHT series models, refer to Chapter Fifteen and perform the following:

a. Remove the outer faring.
b. Partially remove the inner faring (A, **Figure 2**) until the handlebar forward mounting bolts are accessible. It is not necessary to completely remove the inner fairing.

1B. On all FLHR series models, remove the headlight nacelle as described in Chapter Nine.

2. Support the motorcycle with the front wheel off the ground. Refer to *Motorcycle Stands* in Chapter Ten.

CAUTION

Cover the fuel tank with a heavy cloth or plastic tarp to protect it from accidental scratches or dents when removing the handlebar.

NOTE

Before removing the handlebar, make a drawing of the clutch and throttle cable routing from the handlebar and through the frame. This information will prove helpful when reinstalling the handlebar and connecting the cables.

3. On the right side of the handlebar, perform the following:

a. Unscrew and remove the mirror (A, **Figure 3**).
b. Remove the screws securing the master cylinder (B, **Figure 3**). Do not disconnect the hydraulic brake line.
c. Remove the screws securing the right switch assembly together (C, **Figure 3**) and separate the housing halves.

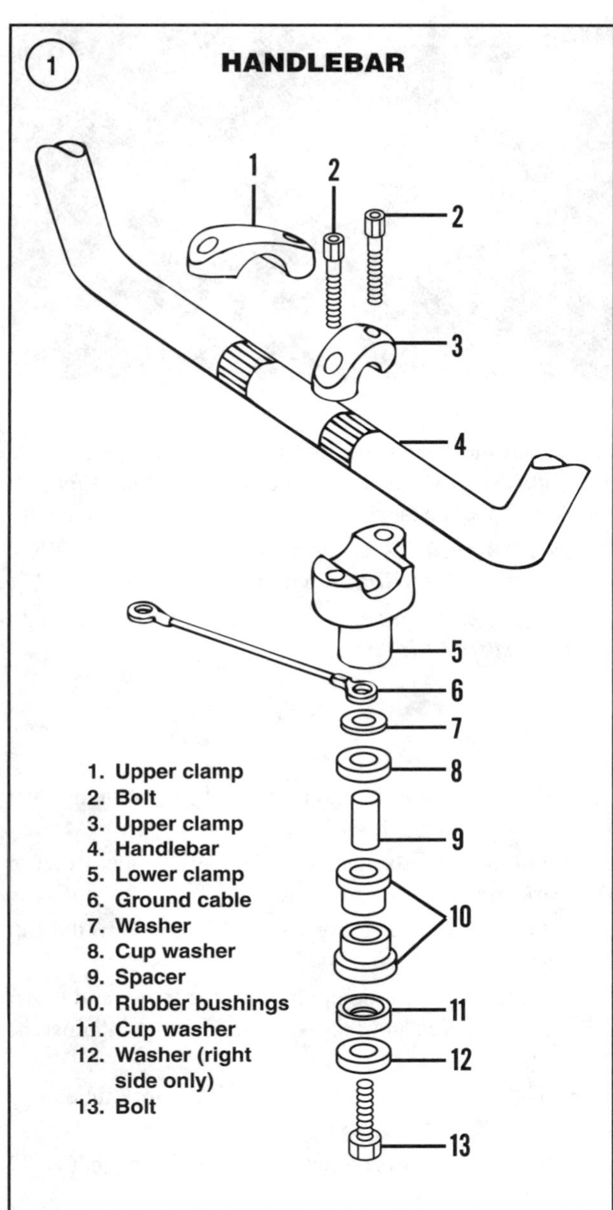

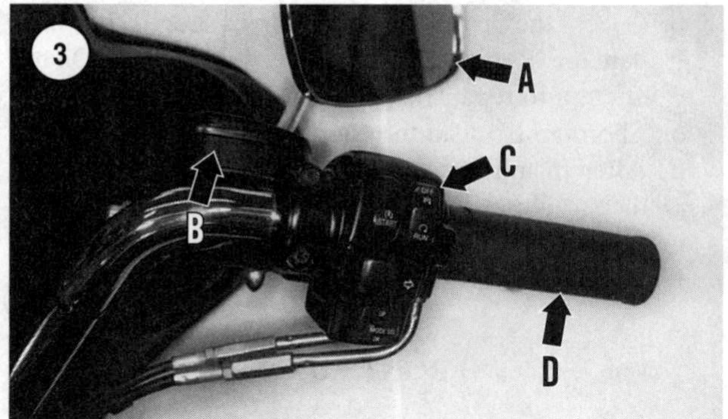

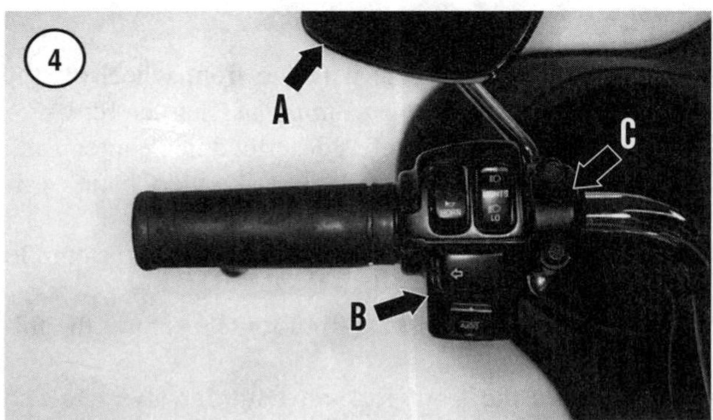

d. Slide the throttle housing assembly (D, **Figure 3**) off the handlebar.

4. On the left side of the handlebar, perform the following:

a. Unscrew and remove the mirror (A, **Figure 4**).

b. Remove the screws securing the left switch assembly together (B, **Figure 4**) and separate the housing halves.

c. Remove the clutch lever clamp (C, **Figure 4**) mounting screws and washers and separate the clamp halves.

5. Disconnect or remove any wiring harness clamps at the handlebar.

6A. On all FLHT series models, remove the two front handlebar clamp bolts and then the rear clamp bolts (B, **Figure 2**). Remove the holders and handlebar (C, **Figure 2**).

6B. On models other than FLHT, remove the two front handlebar clamp bolts and then the two rear clamp bolts (**Figure 5**). Remove the clamp and the handlebar.

7. Install the handlebar by reversing these steps while noting the following:

a. Check the knurled rings on the handlebar for galling and bits of aluminum. Clean the knurled section with a wire brush.

b. Check the handlebar for cracks, bends or other damage. Replace the handlebar if necessary. Do not attempt to repair it.
c. Thoroughly clean the clamp halves of all residue.
d. After installing the handlebar, reposition the handlebar while sitting on the motorcycle.
e. Securely tighten the handlebar clamp bolts.
f. Adjust the mirrors.

FRONT FORK

FXR Series Models

Removal

1. Support the motorcycle with the front wheel off the ground. Refer to *Motorcycle Stands* in Chapter Ten.
2. Remove the front wheel as described in Chapter Ten.
3. Remove the front fender as described in Chapter Fifteen.
4. Remove the headlight bracket and attach it to a cord to prevent the wires from pulling loose.
5. On models with air-assist front forks, perform the following:
   a. Remove the front fork air control valve cap and bleed the air control system as described in this chapter.
   b. Remove the banjo bolts attaching the air control system to the front fork tubes.
6. On 1984-1987 FXR, except 1987 FXLR and FXRS, models, perform the following:
   a. Loosen the upper bracket pinch bolts.
   b. Remove the lower bracket cover screws. Move the cover to expose the lower bracket pinch bolts.
   c. Loosen the fork cap bolt two complete turns.
   d. Tap the fork cap bolts squarely with a plastic hammer and loosen the fork tube-to-upper bracket taper fit.

WARNING
The fork cap bolt is under spring pressure. Be careful when removing it.

   e. When the taper fit is loosened, carefully remove the fork cap bolt from the fork tube.

NOTE
On 1987 FXLR and FXRS and all 1988 and later FXR series models, removal of the fork cap bolt is not required for fork removal.

7. If removing both fork assemblies, mark them with an *R* (right side) and *L* (left side) so the assemblies will be reinstalled on the correct sides.

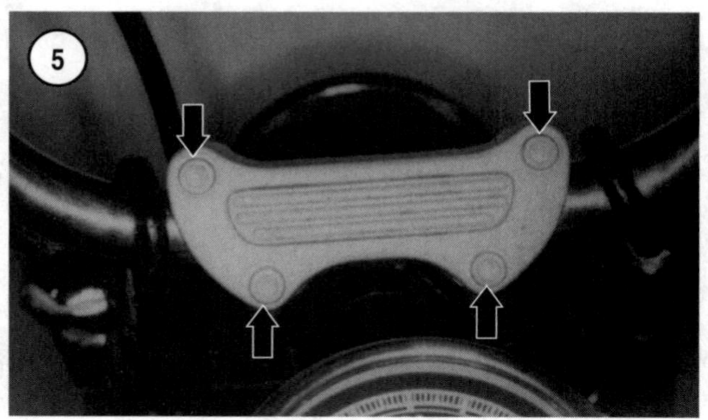

8. Loosen the upper and lower fork bracket pinch bolts and slide the fork tube out of the fork brackets. It may be necessary to rotate the fork tube slightly while removing it.
9. On 1984-1987 FXR, except 1987 FXLR and FXRS, models, reinstall the fork cap bolt.
10. If fork service is required, refer to *Fork Service (All Models Except FLH and FLT)*.

Installation

1. Clean off any corrosion or dirt on the upper and lower fork bracket receptacles.
2. Install the fork assemblies in the correct side. Refer to the marks made during removal.

3A. On 1984-1987 FXR series models, perform the following:
   a. Slide the fork tube up through the lower and upper fork brackets until the fork tube bottoms against the upper bracket.
   b. Tighten the fork cap bolt to pull the fork tube taper into the upper bracket.
   c. Tighten the lower pinch bolts to 30-35 ft.-lb. (41-47 N•m).
   d. If the fork oil was previously drained, remove the fork cap bolt. Refill the fork tube with HD type E, or equivalent, fork oil. Refer to **Table 1** for specified quantity.
   e. Install and tighten the fork cap.
   f. Tighten the upper pinch bolts to 21-27 ft.-lb. (28-37 N•m).

3B. On 1987 FXLR and FXRS and all 1988-1998 FXR series models, perform the following:
   a. Slide the fork tube up through the lower and upper fork brackets so that the fork tube extends 0.42-0.50 in. (10.7-12.7 mm). above the upper fork bracket as shown in **Figure 6**.

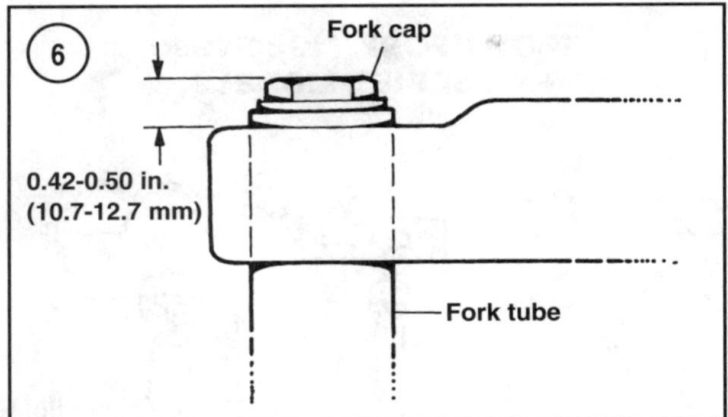

b. Tighten the upper and lower pinch bolts to 25-30 ft.-lb. (34-41 N•m) on FXLR and FXRS models and 30-35 ft.-lb. (41-47 N•m) on FXR models.
c. If the fork oil was previously drained, remove the fork cap and refill the fork tube with HD type E, or equivalent, fork oil. Refer to **Table 1** for specified quantity.

4. On 1984-1987 models, except 1987 FXLR and FXRS models, install the lower bracket cover and tighten the screws securely.
5. On models with air-assist front fork, perform the following:
   a. Move the air control system into position on the front fork tubes and install the banjo bolts. Tighten the bolts securely.
   b. Install the front fork air control valve cap and tighten securely.
   c. Adjust the air pressure as described in this chapter.
6. Install the headlight bracket and tighten the bolts securely.
7. Install the front fender as described in Chapter Fifteen.
8. Install the front wheel as described in Chapter Ten.
9. Apply the front brake and pump the front fork several times to seat the fork tubes and front wheel.

FXWG Models

Removal

1. Support the motorcycle with the front wheel off the ground. Refer to *Motorcycle Stands* in Chapter Ten.
2. Remove the front wheel as described in Chapter Ten.
3. Remove the front fender as described in Chapter Fifteen.
4. Loosen the fork cap from the top of the upper fork bracket. Then remove the cap, washer and oil seal.
5. If removing both fork assemblies, mark them with an *R* (right side) and *L* (left side) so the assemblies will be reinstalled on the correct sides.
6. Loosen the fork bracket pinch bolts and slide the fork tube out of the upper and lower fork brackets. If necessary, rotate the fork tube slightly while removing it.
7. If fork service is required, refer to *Disassembly* in this chapter.

Installation

1. Clean off any corrosion or dirt on the upper and lower fork bracket receptacles.
2. Make sure the fork cap is in place and tightened securely.
3. Install the fork assemblies in the correct side. Refer to the marks made during removal.
4. Slide the fork tube up through the lower and upper fork brackets. Push the fork tube up until the fork tube plug bottoms out on the upper fork bracket.
5. Rotate the fork tube so that one flat on the fork cap faces toward the inside of the fork tube.
6. Slide the washer and oil seal onto the fork cap threads.
7. Install the fork cap onto the fork cap bolt and tighten securely. After tightening the fork cap bolt, check that one flat on the fork cap still faces toward the inside of the fork tube. Readjust if necessary.
8. Tighten the fork bracket pinch bolt to 25-30 ft.-lb. (34-41 N•m).
9. Install the front fender as described in Chapter Fifteen.
10. Install the front wheel and front master cylinder as described in Chapter Ten.
11. Apply the front brake and pump the front fork several times to seat the fork tubes and front wheel.

FXSB AND FXEF Models

Removal

1. Support the motorcycle with the front wheel off the ground. Refer to *Motorcycle Stands* in Chapter Ten.
2. Remove the front wheel as described in Chapter Ten.
3. Remove the front fender as described in Chapter Fifteen.
4. Remove the screw on each side of the fork tube cover. Slide the cover up and secure it in this position to expose the lower bracket pinch bolts.
5. Loosen the upper bracket pinch bolts.
6. Loosen the fork cap bolt two complete turns.
7. Tap the fork cap bolt squarely with a plastic hammer and loosen the fork tube-to-upper bracket taper fit.

WARNING
The fork cap bolt is under spring pressure. Be careful when removing it.

8. When the taper fit is loosened, carefully remove the fork cap bolt from the fork tube.

9. If removing both fork assemblies, mark them with an *R* (right side) and *L* (left side) so the assemblies will be reinstalled on the correct sides.

10. Loosen the lower fork bracket pinch bolts.

11. Slide the fork tube out of the fork brackets. It might be necessary to rotate the fork tube slightly while removing it.

12. Reinstall the fork cap bolt and tighten securely.

13. If fork service is required, refer to *Fork Service (All Models Except FLH and FLT)*.

Installation

1. Clean off any corrosion or dirt on the upper and lower fork bracket receptacles.

2. Install the fork assemblies in the correct sides. Refer to the marks made during removal.

3. Slide the fork tube up through the lower and upper fork brackets until the fork tube bottoms against the upper bracket.

4. Tighten the fork cap bolt to pull the fork tube taper into the upper bracket.

5. Tighten the lower pinch bolts to 30-35 ft.-lb. (41-47 N•m).

6. Remove the fork cap bolt.

7. Refill the fork tube with HD type E, or equivalent, fork oil. Refer to **Table 1** for specified quantity.

8. Install and tighten the fork cap and tighten securely.

9. Tighten the upper pinch bolts to 21-27 ft.-lb. (28-37 N•m).

10. Install the cover and secure it to the lower fork bracket with its attaching screws.

11. Install the front fender as described in Chapter Fifteen.

12. Install the front wheel and front master cylinder as described in Chapter Ten.

13. Apply the front brake and pump the front fork several times to seat the fork tubes and front wheel.

FORK SERVICE (ALL MODELS EXCEPT FLH AND FLT)

These procedures relate to all models, except FLH and FLT series models. Where they occur differences are identified.

Refer to **Figures 7-10**.

7 **FRONT FORK (1984-1990 FXR SERIES MODELS)**

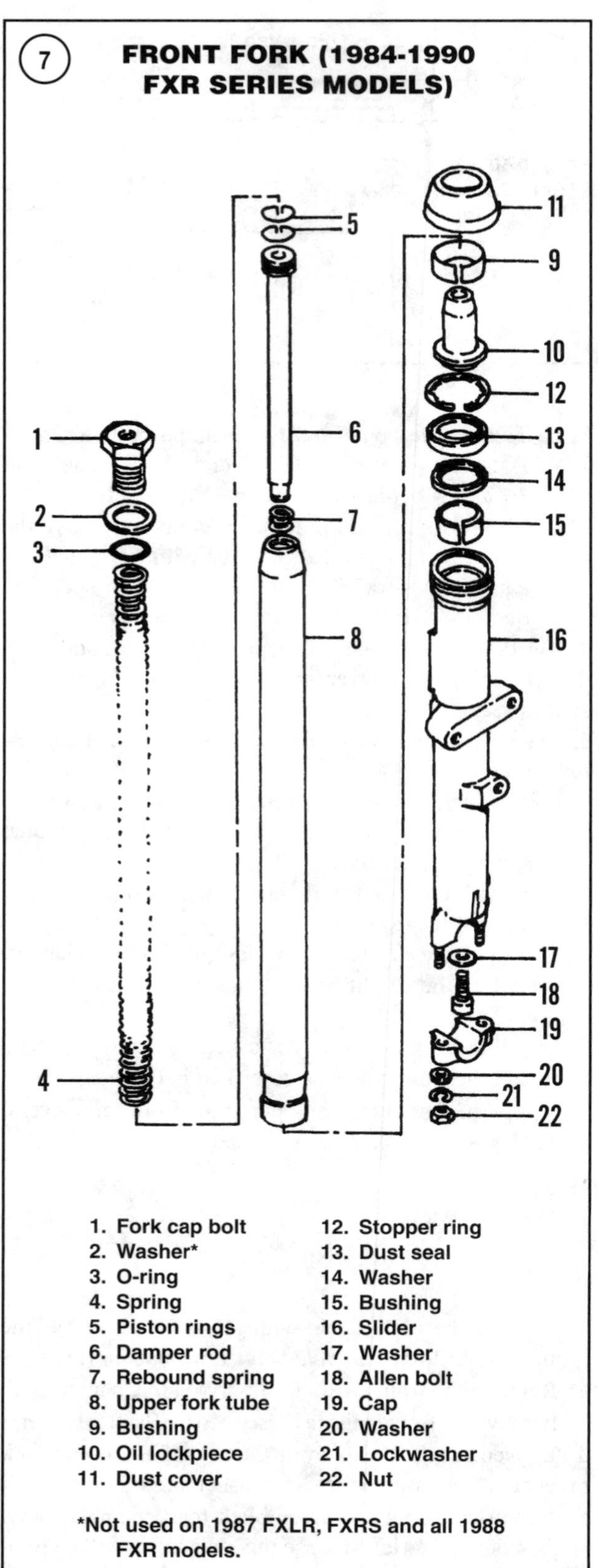

1. Fork cap bolt
2. Washer*
3. O-ring
4. Spring
5. Piston rings
6. Damper rod
7. Rebound spring
8. Upper fork tube
9. Bushing
10. Oil lockpiece
11. Dust cover
12. Stopper ring
13. Dust seal
14. Washer
15. Bushing
16. Slider
17. Washer
18. Allen bolt
19. Cap
20. Washer
21. Lockwasher
22. Nut

*Not used on 1987 FXLR, FXRS and all 1988 FXR models.

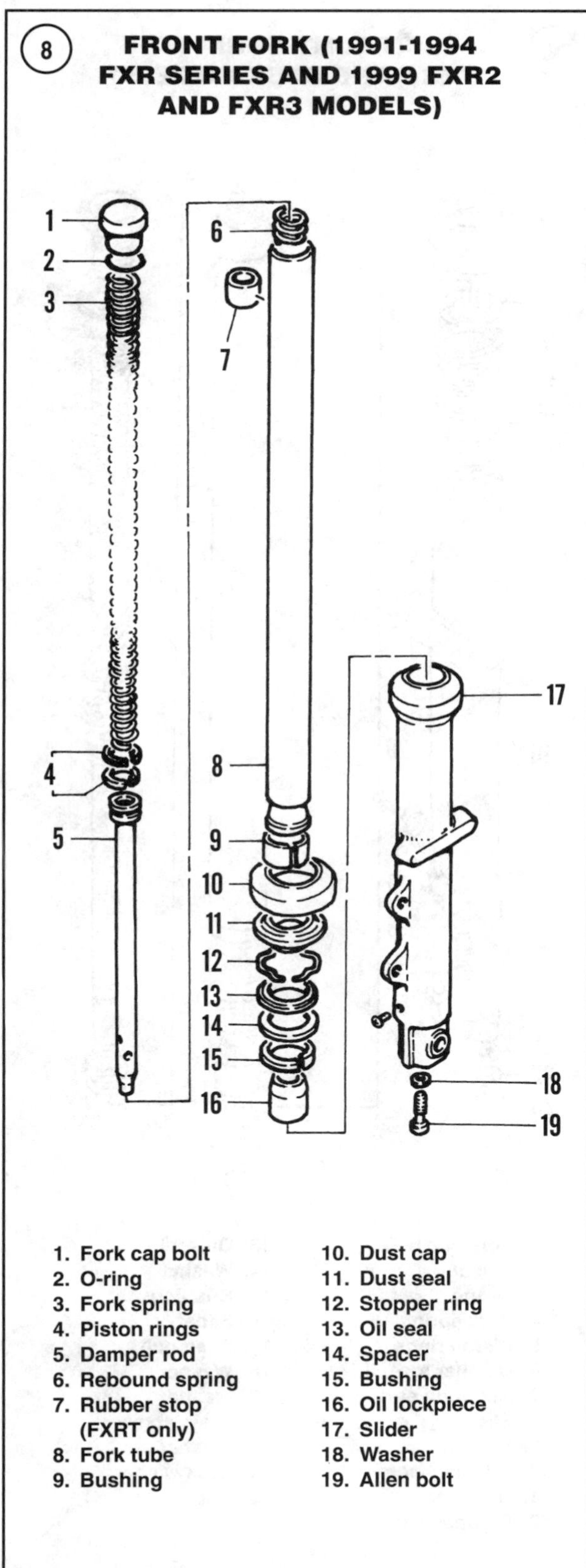
8
FRONT FORK (1991-1994 FXR SERIES AND 1999 FXR2 AND FXR3 MODELS)
1. Fork cap bolt
2. O-ring
3. Fork spring
4. Piston rings
5. Damper rod
6. Rebound spring
7. Rubber stop (FXRT only)
8. Fork tube
9. Bushing
10. Dust cap
11. Dust seal
12. Stopper ring
13. Oil seal
14. Spacer
15. Bushing
16. Oil lockpiece
17. Slider
18. Washer
19. Allen bolt

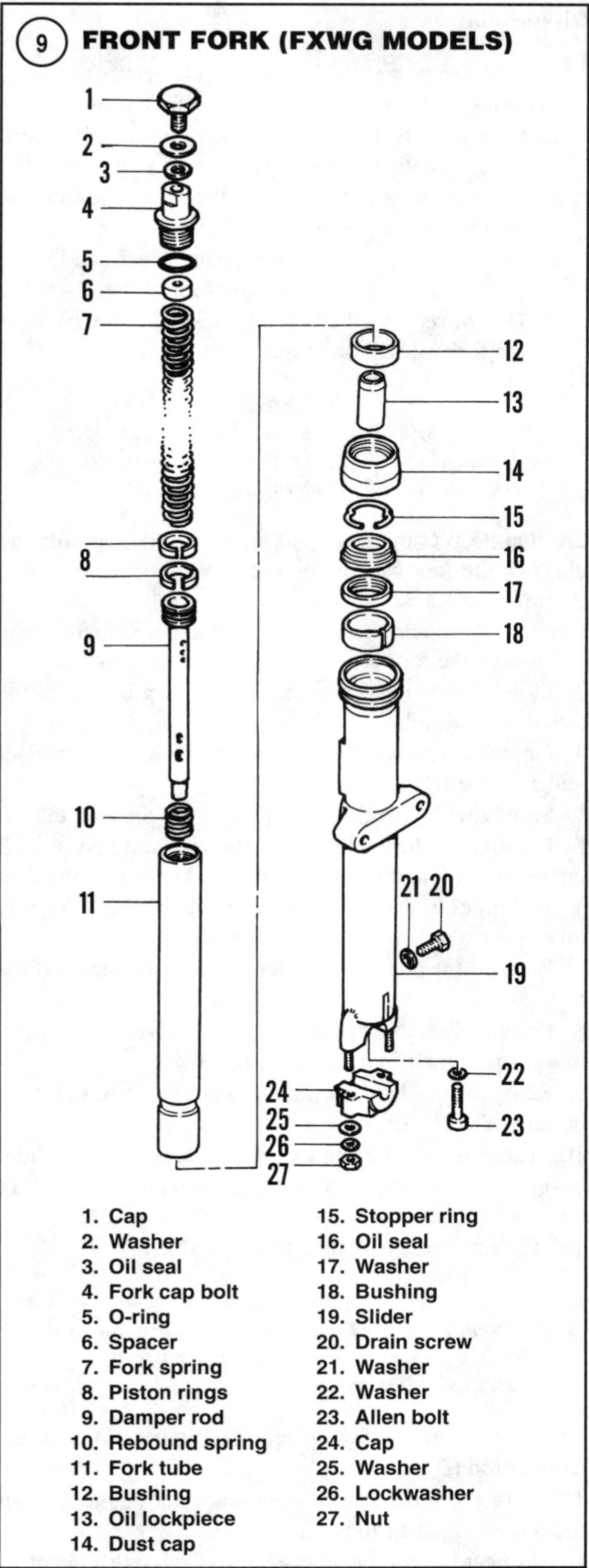
9
FRONT FORK (FXWG MODELS)
1. Cap
2. Washer
3. Oil seal
4. Fork cap bolt
5. O-ring
6. Spacer
7. Fork spring
8. Piston rings
9. Damper rod
10. Rebound spring
11. Fork tube
12. Bushing
13. Oil lockpiece
14. Dust cap
15. Stopper ring
16. Oil seal
17. Washer
18. Bushing
19. Slider
20. Drain screw
21. Washer
22. Washer
23. Allen bolt
24. Cap
25. Washer
26. Lockwasher
27. Nut

Disassembly

1. If the Allen bolt at the base of the slider was not loosened during fork removal, perform the following.
   a. Secure the front axle boss at the bottom of the fork slider in a vise with soft jaws.
   b. Have an assistant compress the fork tube into the slider to place pressure on the damper rod.
   c. Use an Allen wrench and impact driver and loosen the Allen bolt on the bottom of the slider.
   d. Do not remove the Allen bolt at this time because the fork oil will drain out.

WARNING
Be careful when removing the fork cap bolt because the spring is under pressure. Protect eyes and face accordingly.

2A. On FXWG models, hold onto the fork cap bolt and unscrew the fork cap and washer from the fork cap bolt. Remove the oil seal.

2B. On all models except FXWG, hold onto the fork tube and loosen the fork cap bolt.

3. Slowly loosen and remove the fork cap bolt from the top of the fork tube.
4. On models so equipped, remove the washer or spacer under the bolt.
5. Slowly withdraw the fork spring from the fork tube.
6. Remove the fork slider from the vise and pour the oil out of the fork and into a clean container. Pump the fork several times by hand to expel as much of the remaining oil as possible. Discard the oil properly.
7. Remove the dust cover (**Figure 11**) and slide it off the fork tube.
8. Remove the stopper ring (**Figure 12**) from the groove in the top of the slider. See **Figure 13**.
9. Remove the Allen screw and washer (**Figure 14**) at the bottom of the slider.
10. There is an interference fit between the fork slider bushing and the fork tube bushing. Pull hard on the fork tube using quick in-and-out strokes (**Figure 15**).
11. Withdraw the fork tube from the slider.

NOTE
Do not remove the fork tube bushing unless it is going to be replaced. Inspect it as described in this chapter.

12. Remove the oil lock piece (A, **Figure 16**) from the damper rod (B).
13. Turn the fork upside down and remove the damper rod and rebound spring (**Figure 17**).
14. Inspect the components as described in this chapter.

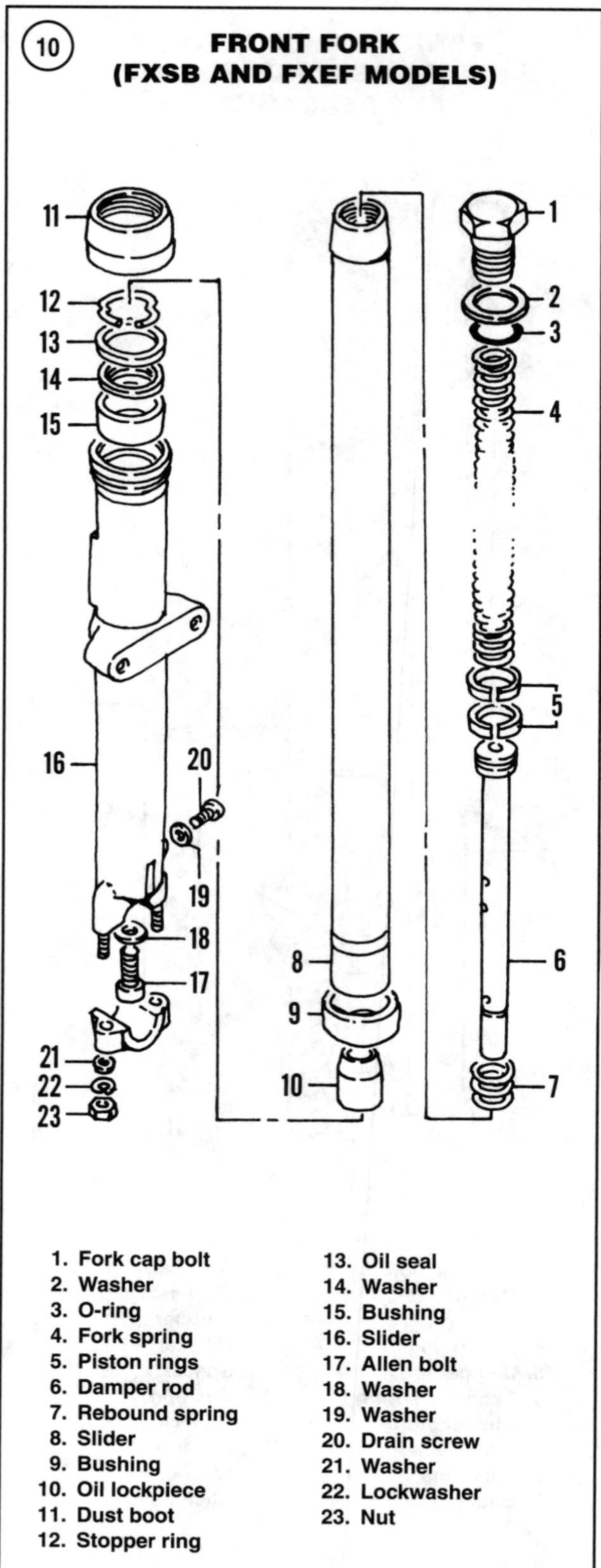

10

FRONT FORK (FXSB AND FXEF MODELS)

1. Fork cap bolt
2. Washer
3. O-ring
4. Fork spring
5. Piston rings
6. Damper rod
7. Rebound spring
8. Slider
9. Bushing
10. Oil lockpiece
11. Dust boot
12. Stopper ring
13. Oil seal
14. Washer
15. Bushing
16. Slider
17. Allen bolt
18. Washer
19. Washer
20. Drain screw
21. Washer
22. Lockwasher
23. Nut

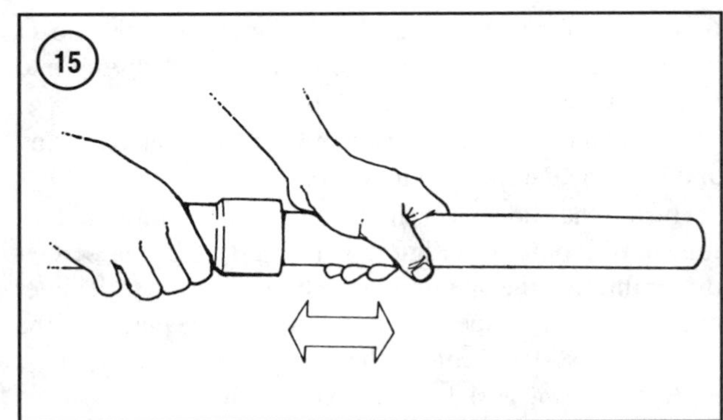

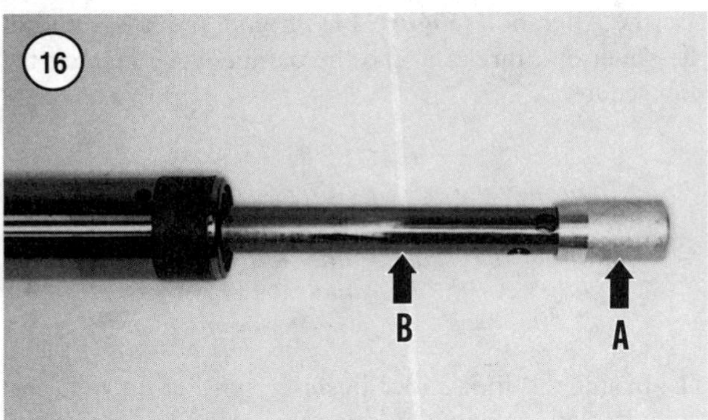

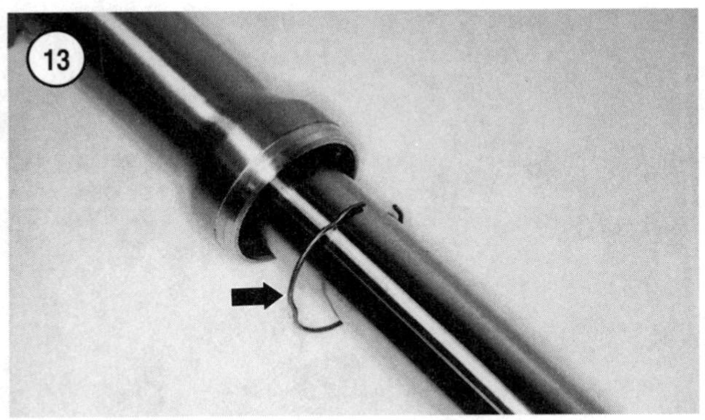

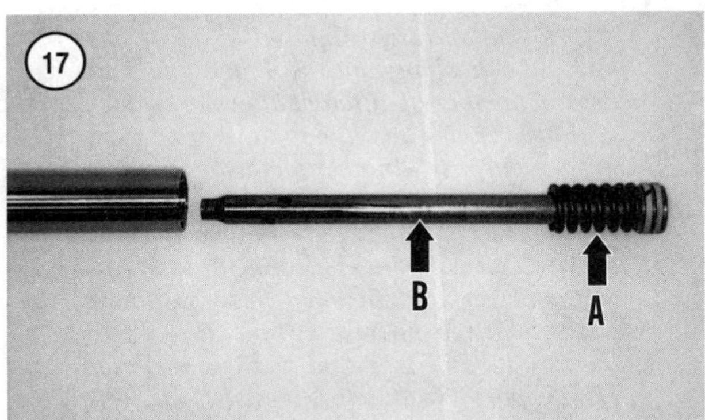

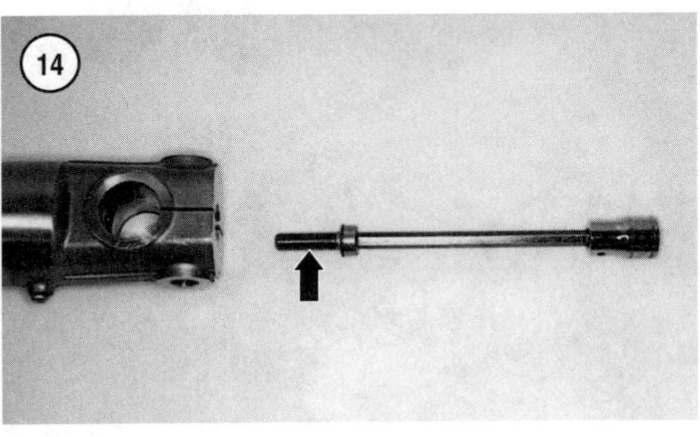

Assembly

1. Install a *new* O-ring onto the fork cap.

2. Coat all parts with Harley-Davidson Type E Fork Oil or an equivalent before assembly.

3. Install the rebound spring (A, **Figure 17**) onto the damper rod (B).

4. Slide the damper rod (B, **Figure 17**) into the fork tube until it extends out the end of the fork tube.

5. Install the oil lock piece (A, **Figure 16**) onto the end of the damper rod (B).

6. Position the fork spring (A, **Figure 18**) with the closer wound coils going in first and install the fork spring into the fork tube.
7. Install the fork cap (B, **Figure 18**) to tension the spring and hold the damper rod in place.
8. Install the slider over the damper rod and into the fork tube until it bottoms (**Figure 19**). Insert a Phillips screwdriver through the opening in the bottom of the fork slider and guide the damper rod end into the receptacle in the base of the slider. Remove the screwdriver.
9. Install a *new* gasket on the Allen bolt.
10. Apply a nonpermanent threadlocking compound to the damper rod Allen bolt threads prior to installation. Insert the Allen bolt (**Figure 14**) through the lower end of the slider and thread it into the damper rod. Tighten the bolt securely.

CAUTION

To protect the oil seal lips, place a thin plastic bag on top of the fork tube. Before installing the seal in the following steps, lightly coat the bag and the seal lips with fork oil.

11. Install the fork slider bushing, washer and oil seal (with the letters facing up) onto the fork tube.

NOTE

A fork seal driver is required to install the fork tube bushing and seal into the fork tube. A number of different aftermarket fork seal drivers are available that can be used for this purpose. Another method is to use a piece of pipe or metal collar with correct dimensions to slide over the fork tube and seat against the seal. When selecting or fabricating a driver tool, it must have sufficient weight to drive the bushing and oil seal into the fork tube. A fork seal and cap installer (JIMS part No. 2046) is used for this procedure.

12. Slide the fork slider bushing (A, **Figure 20**) and washer (B) down into the slider.
13. Slide the fork seal driver down the fork tube and seat it against the oil seal (**Figure 21**).
14. Operate the driver and drive the fork slider bushing and new seal into the fork tube. Continue to operate the driver until the stopper ring groove in the tube is visible above the fork seal. Remove the fork seal driver tool.
15. Install the stopper ring (**Figure 13**) into the slider groove. Make sure the retaining ring seats in the groove (**Figure 12**).
16. Install the fork tube as described in this chapter.

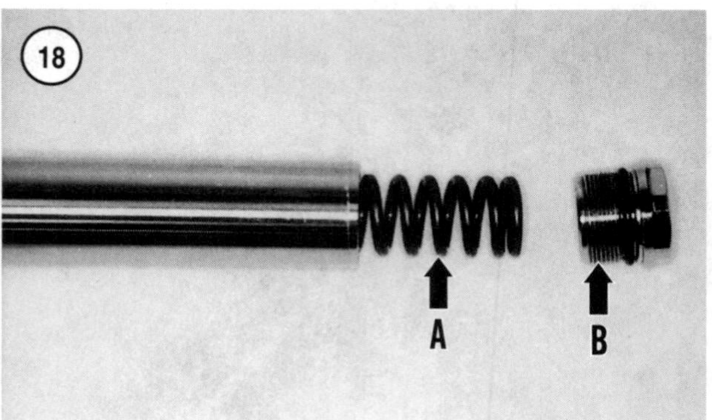

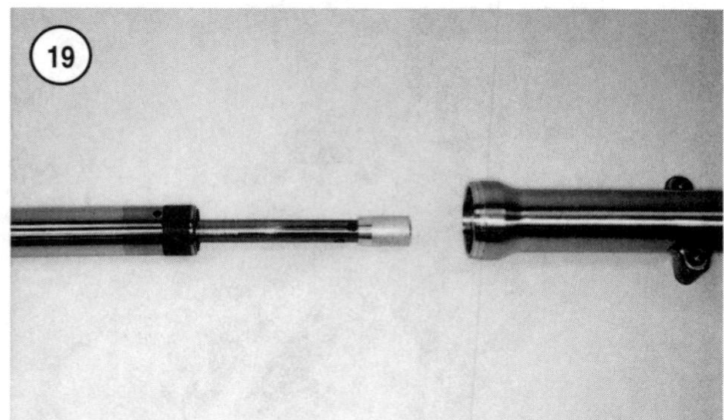

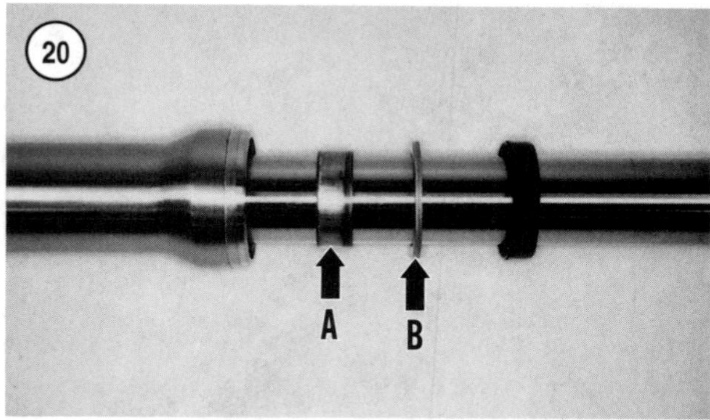

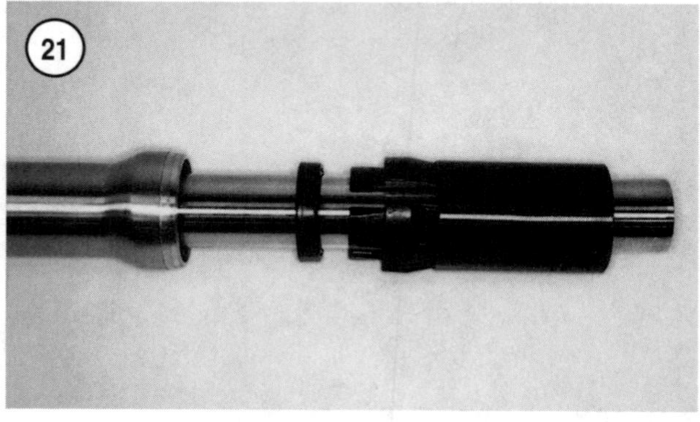

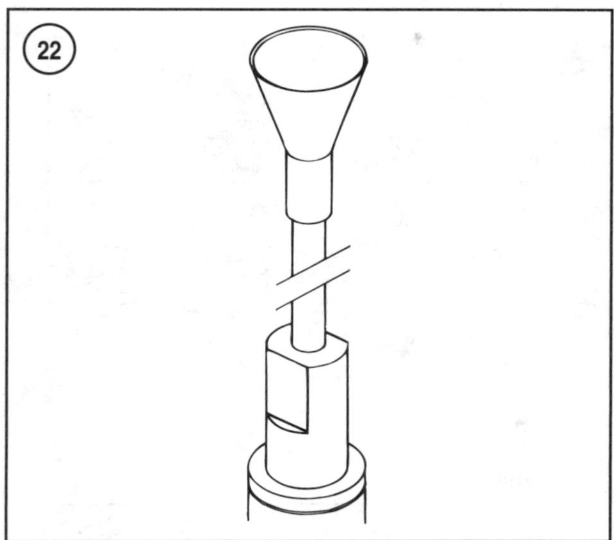

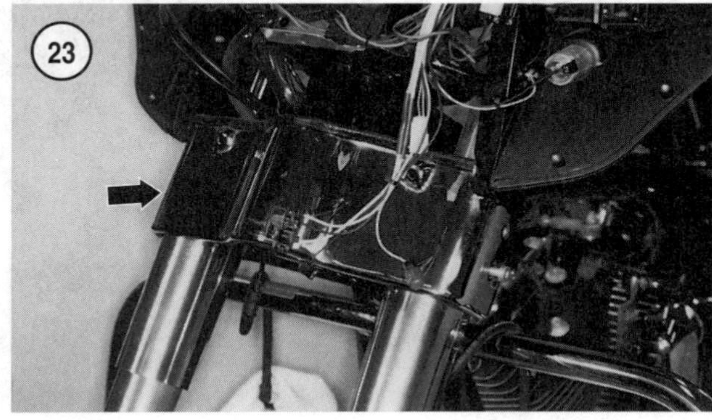

17. If necessary on FXWG models, insert a clear plastic tube into the fork cap bolt opening (**Figure 22**). Attach a funnel to the plastic tube and refill each fork leg with the correct viscosity and quantity of fork oil in **Table 1**. Remove the small funnel and plastic tube. Install the cap, washer and oil seal.

FRONT FORK (FLH AND FLT SERIES MODELS)

Before assuming a fork is malfunctioning, drain the front fork oil and refill with the proper type and quantity fork oil as described in Chapter Three. If there is still a problem, such as poor damping, a tendency to bottom or top out, or leaks around the oil seals, follow the service procedures in this section.

To simplify fork service and to prevent the mixing of parts, remove, service and install the fork legs individually.

Removal (Fork Not To Be Serviced)

1A. On all FLHT series models, remove the outer fairing. On FLHTC series models, also remove the storage box. Refer to Chapter Fifteen.
1B. On all FLHR series models, remove the headlight nacelle as described in Chapter Nine.
2. Remove the passing lamp assembly as described in Chapter Nine.
3. Support the motorcycle with the front wheel off the ground. Refer to *Motorcycle Stands* in Chapter Ten.
4. Remove the front fender and front wheel as described in Chapter Nine.
5. Remove the screws securing the chrome mounting bracket (**Figure 23**) and remove the bracket.
6. If both fork tube assemblies are going to be removed, mark them with an *R* (right side) and *L* (left side) so the assemblies will be reinstalled on the correct sides.
7. On models so equipped, remove the right saddlebag as described in Chapter Fifteen.

WARNING
Use caution when releasing the air from the front fork air valve. Moisture and fork oil may spurt out when the air pressure is released. Protect eyes accordingly.

8. Cover the rear brake assembly and wheel prior to releasing the compressed air from the rear air valve. If necessary, wipe any oil reside that may have been ejected from the air valve.
9. Remove the cap from the front fork air valve (**Figure 24**). Then slowly depress the air valve to evacuate the air from the front fork air pipe system. Unscrew and remove the core from the air valve. Place the air valve core and cap in a reclosable plastic bag to avoid misplacing them.
10. Refer to **Figure 25**. Unscrew and remove the hex bolts (**Figure 26**) securing the banjo bolt on top of each fork tube. Move the air tube assembly out of the way from the fork assemblies.

11. Remove the fork cap bolt (**Figure 27**) from the top of the fork tube.
12. Working at the base of the steering stem, loosen the pinch bolt (**Figure 28**).
13. Slide the fork tube out of the upper fork bracket. Remove the rubber stop (**Figure 29**) from the fork tube.
14. Continue to slide the fork tube out of the lower fork bracket. It may be necessary to rotate the fork tube slightly while pulling it down and out. Remove the fork assembly and take it to the workbench for service. If the fork is not going to be serviced, wrap it in a bath towel or blanket to protect the surface from damage.
15. Repeat for the other fork assembly.

Installation (Fork Was Not Serviced)

1. Install a fork tube through the lower fork bracket and install the rubber fork stop (**Figure 29**).
2. Continue to push the fork tube up through the top fork bracket until it bottoms against the upper fork bracket.
3. Tighten the pinch bolt (**Figure 28**) to 40 ft.-lb. (54 N•m).
4. Install the fork cap bolt (**Figure 27**) onto the top of the fork tube and tighten securely.
5. Install a *new* O-ring onto each hex bolt (**Figure 30**) and apply a light coat of clean engine oil to them.
6. Install the air tube assembly onto the top of the fork assemblies and install the hex bolts through the banjo bolts. Tighten the hex bolts to 97-142 in.-lb. (11-16 N•m).
7. On models so equipped, install the right saddlebag as described in Chapter Fifteen.
8. Install the front fender and front wheel as described in Chapter Nine.
9A. On all FLHT series models, install the outer fairing. On FLHTC series models, also install the storage box. Refer to Chapter Fifteen.
9B. On all FLHR series models, install the headlight nacelle as described in Chapter Nine.
10. Apply the front brake and pump the front fork several times to seat the fork tubes and front wheel.
11. Adjust the front fork air pressure as described in this chapter.

Removal (Fork To Be Serviced)

1A. On all FLHT models, remove the outer fairing. On FLHTC models, also remove the storage box. Refer to Chapter Fifteen.
1B. On all FLHR models, remove the headlight nacelle as described in Chapter Nine.

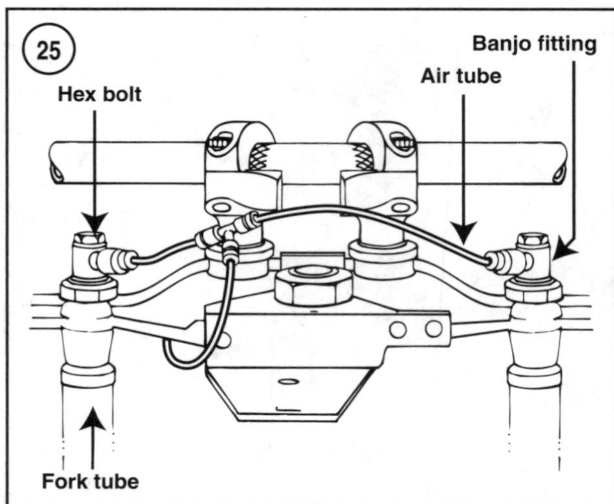

2. Remove the passing lamp assembly as described in Chapter Nine.
3. Support the motorcycle with the front wheel off the ground. Refer to *Motorcycle Stands* in Chapter Ten.
4. Remove the front fender and front wheel.
5. Remove the screws securing the chrome mounting bracket (**Figure 23**) and remove the bracket.

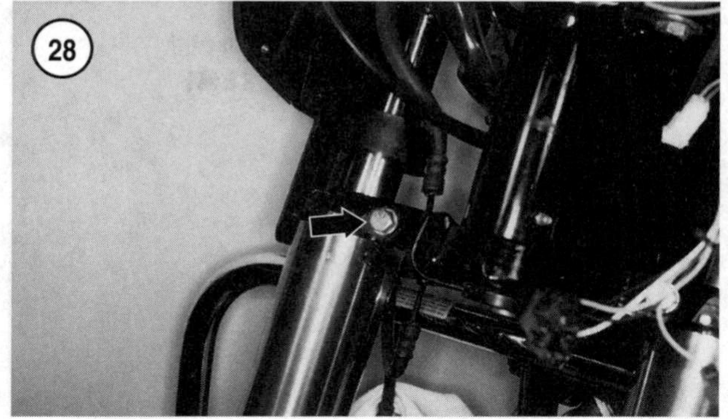

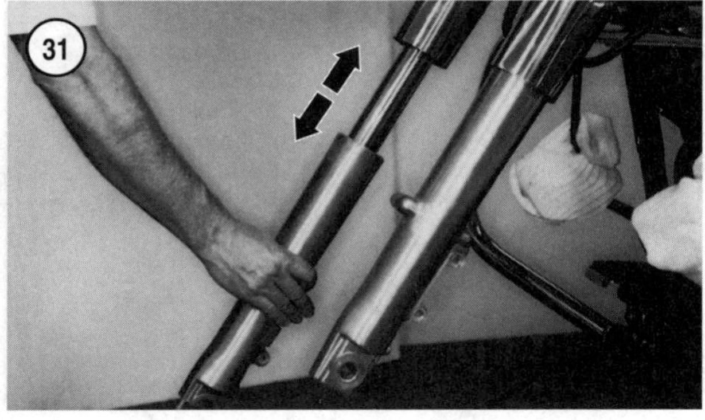

6. If both fork tube assemblies are going to be removed, mark them with an *R* (right side) and *L* (left side) so the assemblies will be reinstalled on the correct side.
7. On models so equipped, remove the right saddlebag as described in Chapter Fifteen.

WARNING

Use caution when releasing the air from the front fork air valve. Moisture and fork oil may spurt out when the air pressure is released. Protect eyes accordingly.

8. Cover the rear brake assembly and wheel prior to releasing the compressed air from the rear air valve. If necessary, wipe any oil residue that might have been ejected from the air valve.
9. Remove the cap from the front fork air valve (**Figure 24**). Then slowly depress the air valve to evacuate the air from the front fork air pipe system. Unscrew and remove the core from the air valve. Place the air valve core and cap in a reclosable plastic bag to avoid misplacing them.
10. Refer to **Figure 25**. Unscrew and remove the hex bolts (**Figure 26**) securing the banjo bolt on top of each fork tube. Move the air tube assembly out of the way from the fork assemblies.
11. Remove the fork cap bolt (**Figure 27**) from the top of the fork tube.
12. Loosen the pinch bolt (**Figure 28**) at the base of the steering stem.
13. Slide the fork assembly part way down and retighten the pinch bolt (**Figure 28**).
14. Place a drain pan under the fork slider to catch the fork oil.
15. Use an 8 mm Allen wrench and impact driver and loosen the damper rod cartridge 8 mm Allen bolt at the base of the slider.
16. Remove the Allen bolt and drain the fork oil. Pump the slider several times to expel most of the fork oil. Reinstall the Allen bolt to keep residual oil in the fork.
17. Remove the stopper ring from the fork slider.
18. Lower the fork slider on the fork tube.

NOTE

It might be necessary to slightly heat the area on the slider around the oil seal prior to removal. Use a rag soaked in hot water; do not directly apply a flame to the fork slider.

19. There is an interference fit between the bushing in the fork slider and the bushing on the fork tube. In order to remove the fork tube from the slider, pull hard on the fork tube using quick in-and-out strokes (**Figure 31**). Doing so will withdraw the bushing and the oil seal from the slider.

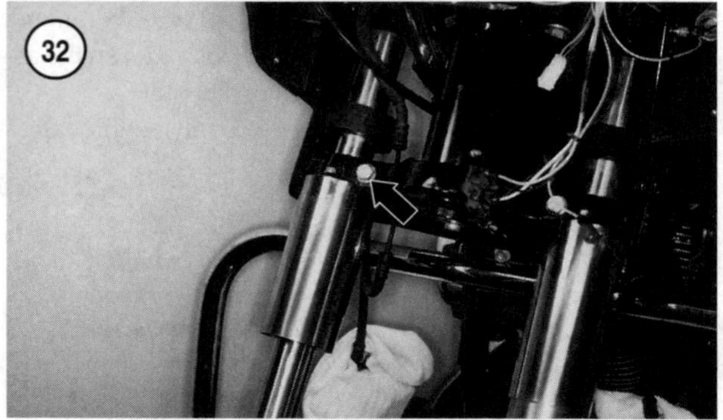

20. Remove the slider from the fork tube. If still in place, remove the oil lock piece from the damper rod.
21. Loosen the pinch bolt (**Figure 32**). Slide the fork tube out of the lower fork bracket and remove the rubber stop (**Figure 29**) from the fork tube. It might be necessary to rotate the fork tube slightly while pulling it down and out. Remove the fork assembly and take it to the workbench for service. If the fork is not going to be serviced, wrap it in a bath towel or blanket to protect the surface from damage.
22. Repeat for the other fork assembly.

Installation (Fork Was Serviced)

1. Assemble the fork as described in this chapter.
2. Install a fork tube through the lower fork bracket and install the rubber fork stop (**Figure 29**).
3. Continue to push the fork tube up through the top fork bracket until it bottoms against the upper fork bracket.
4. Tighten the pinch bolt (**Figure 32**) to 40 ft.-lb. (54 N•m).
5. Install the fork cap bolt (**Figure 27**) onto the top of the fork tube and tighten securely.
6. Install *new* O-rings onto all the hex bolts (**Figure 30**) and apply a light coat of clean engine oil to them.
7. Install the air tube assembly onto the top of the fork assemblies and install the hex bolts through the banjo bolts. Tighten the hex bolts to 97-142 in.-lb. (11-16 N•m).
8. On models so equipped, install the right saddlebag as described in Chapter Fifteen.
9. Install the front fender and front wheel.
10A. On all FLHT series models, install the outer fairing. On FLHTC series models, also install the storage box. Refer to Chapter Fifteen.
10B. On all FLHR series models, install the headlight nacelle as described in Chapter Nine.
11. Apply the front brake and pump the front fork several times to seat the fork tubes and front wheel.

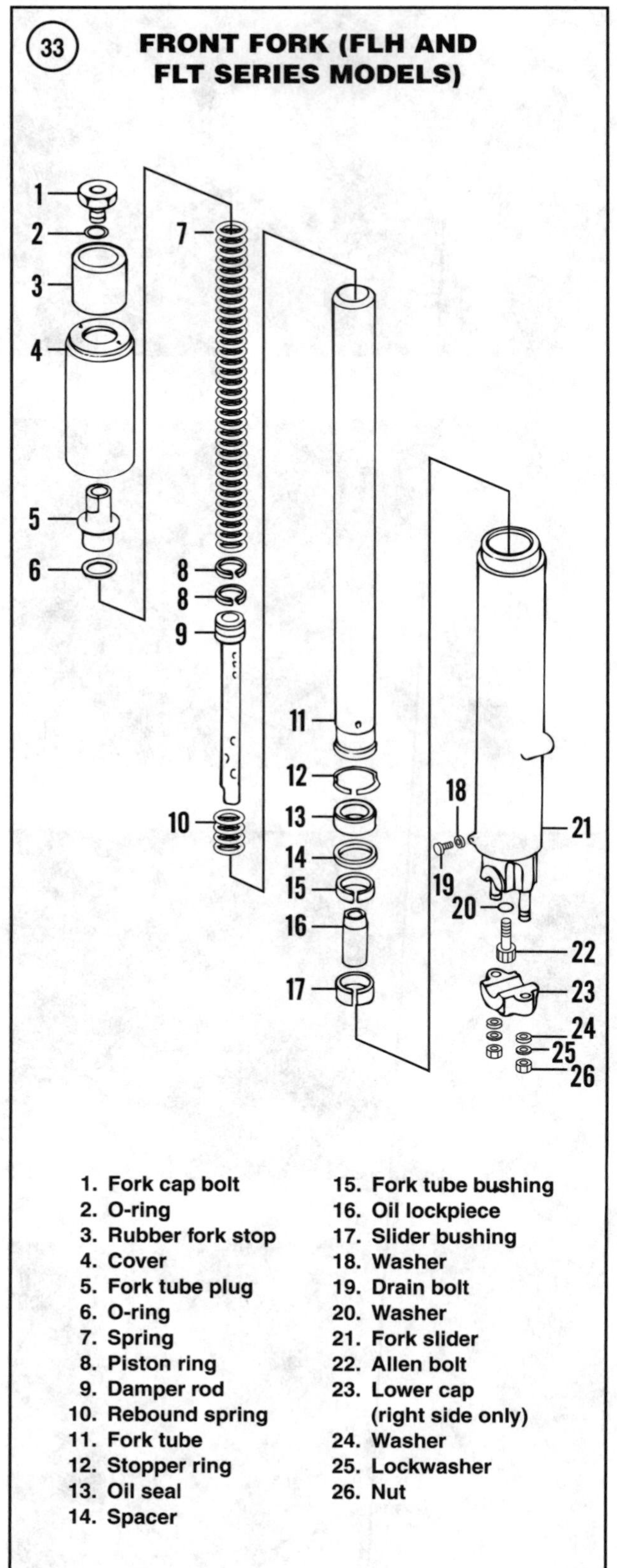

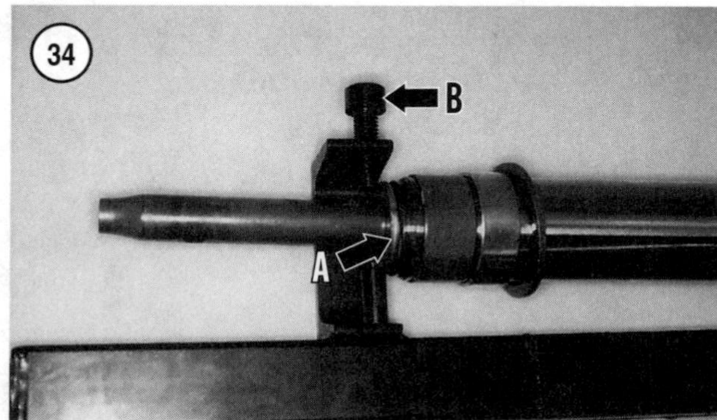

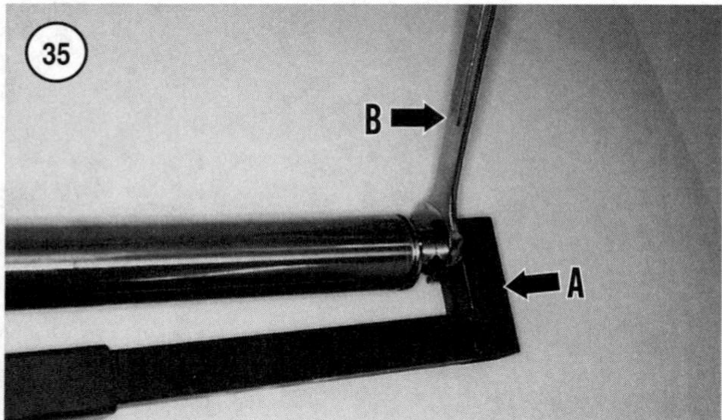

12. Adjust the front forks air pressure as described in this chapter.

Disassembly

Refer to **Figure 33**.

WARNING
A special fork-holding tool is required to disassemble and assemble this fork assembly. The fork spring is so strong that it cannot be compressed sufficiently by hand to loosen and remove the fork tube plug. This special tool is available from motorcycle dealerships.

1. To protect the fork tube, place a steel washer (A, **Figure 34**) over the fork damper rod and against the base of the fork tube.
2. Tighten the lower bolt (B, **Figure 34**) so it seats below the steel washer. Do not overtighten because the damper rod will be damaged. Make sure the tool is indexed properly against the steel washer.
3. Following the manufacturer's instructions, install the special tool upper bolt into the hole in the fork tube plug (A, **Figure 35**). Make sure the tool is indexed properly in the hole in the fork tube plug.

WARNING
Be careful when removing the fork top plug because the spring is under pressure. Protect eyes and face accordingly.

4. Hold onto the fork tube and loosen the fork tube plug (B, **Figure 35**). Slowly loosen the special tool while unscrewing the fork tube plug.
5. When the fork tube plug is completely unscrewed from the fork tube, loosen and remove the special tool from the fork assembly.
6. Remove the fork tube plug and fork spring and drain out any residual fork oil. Dispose of the fork oil properly.
7. Turn the fork tube upside down and remove the damper rod and rebound spring.
8. Inspect all parts as described in this section.

Assembly

1. Install a *new* O-ring onto the fork top plug (**Figure 36**).
2. Install a *new* O-ring onto on the fork cap bolt (**Figure 37**).
3. Before assembly, coat all parts with Harley-Davidson Type E Fork Oil or an equivalent fork oil.

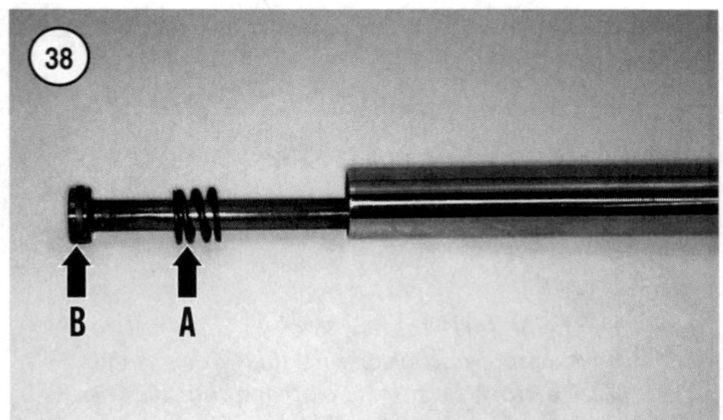

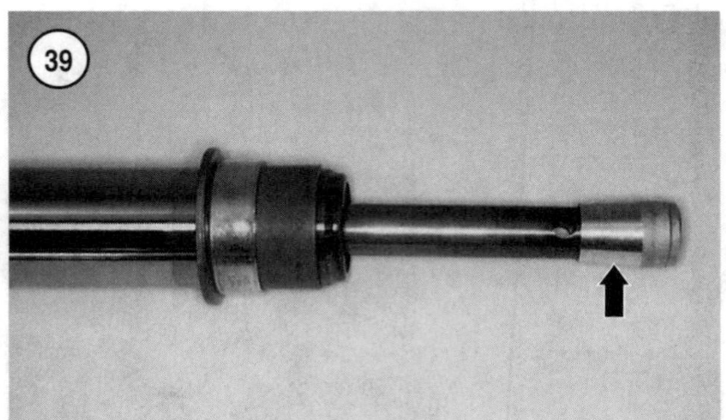

4. Install the rebound spring (A, **Figure 38**) onto the damper rod and slide the damper rod (B) into the fork tube until it extends out the end of the fork tube.

5. Install the oil lock piece (**Figure 39**) onto the end of the damper rod.

6. Position the fork spring with the closer wound coils going in first (**Figure 40**) and install the fork spring into the fork tube.

7. To protect the fork tube, place a steel washer (A, **Figure 34**) over the fork damper rod and up against the base of the fork tube.

8. Tighten the lower bolt (B, **Figure 34**) so it seats below the steel washer. Do not overtighten because the damper rod will be damaged. Make sure the tool is indexed properly against the steel washer.

9. Position the fork tube plug onto the top of the fork spring.

10. Install the special tool upper bolt into the hole in the fork tube plug (A, **Figure 41**) following the manufacturer's instructions. Make sure the tool is indexed properly in the hole in the fork tube plug.

CAUTION

While tightening the special tool, do not jam the fork tube plug into the threaded portion of the fork tube. Doing so will damage the threads on either or both parts.

11. Hold the fork tube plug and slowly tighten the special tool while guiding the fork tube plug into the top of the fork tube (B, **Figure 41**).

12. Place a wrench on the fork tube plug (B, **Figure 35**) and screw the fork tube plug into the fork tube while tightening the special tool. Once the fork tube plug has started to thread into the fork tube, loosen the special tool and remove it from the fork assembly.

13. Place the slider in a vise with soft jaws and securely tighten the fork top plug (**Figure 42**).

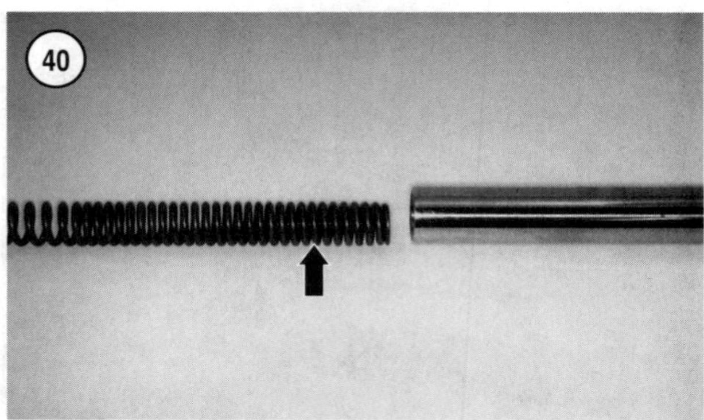

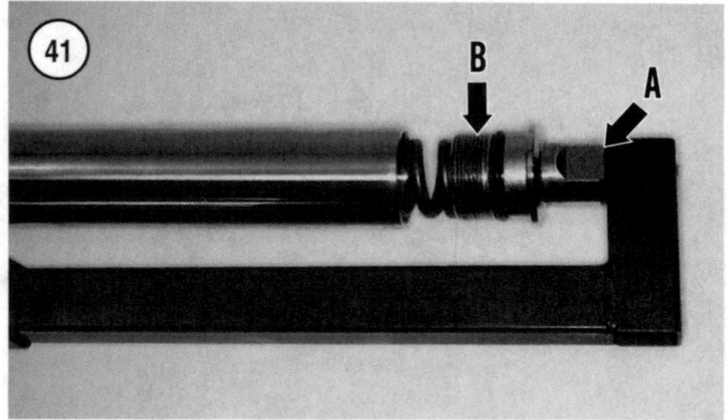

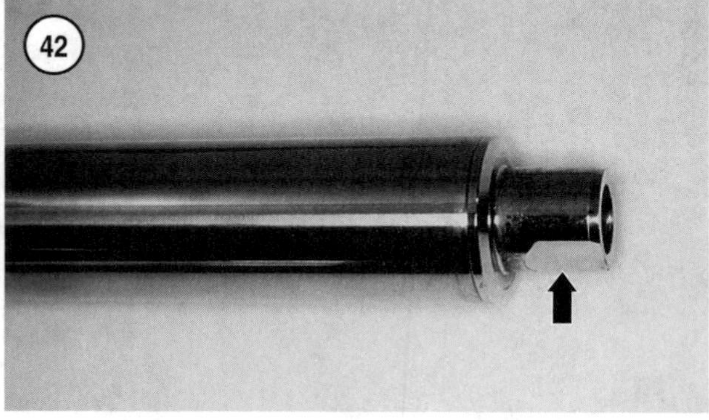

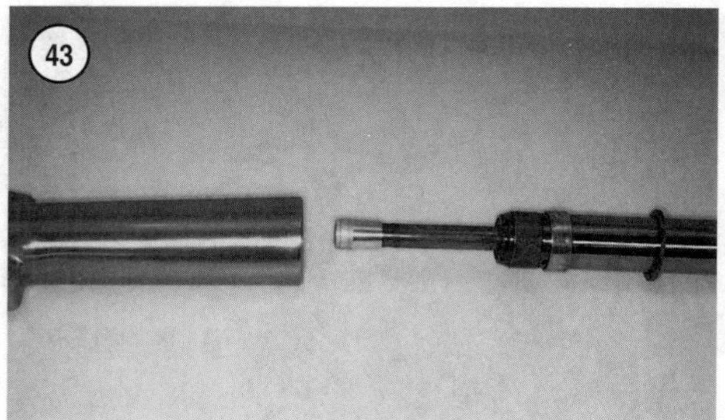

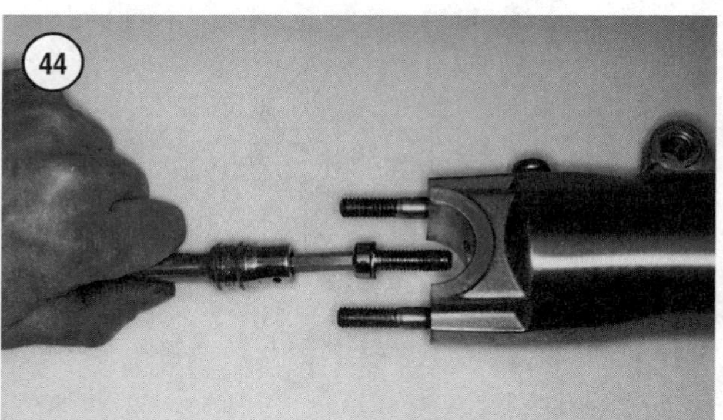

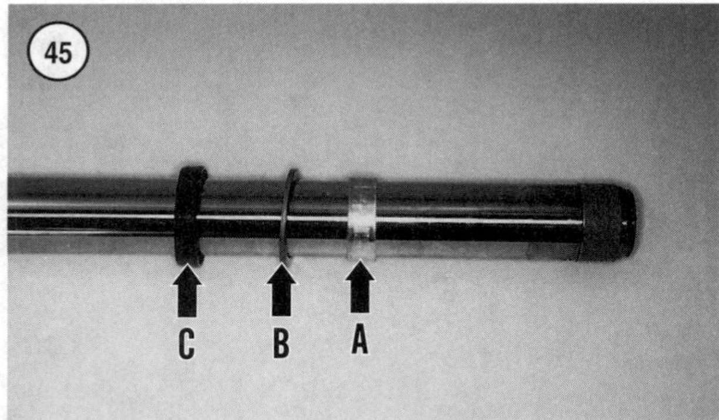

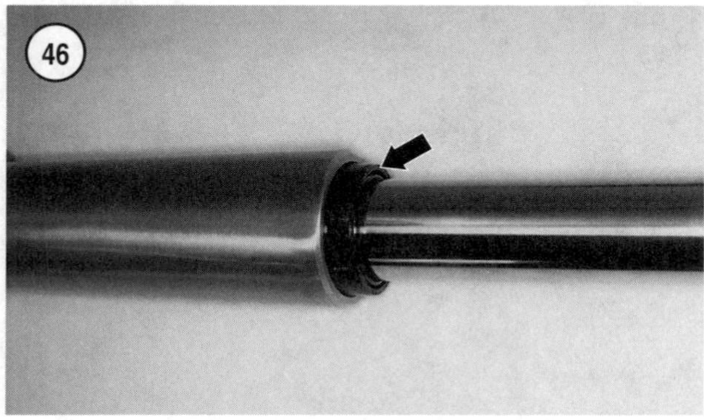

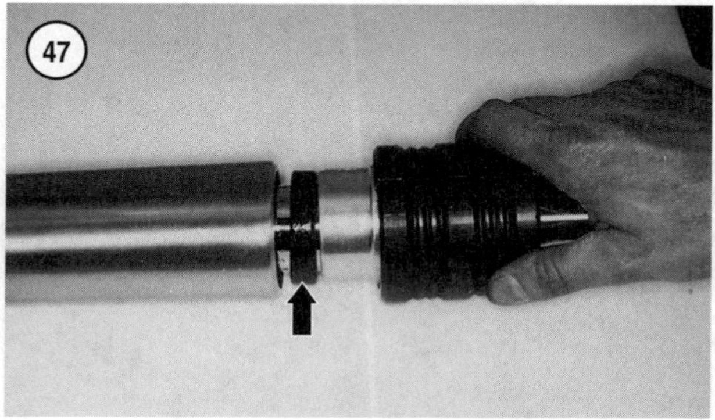

14. Push the fork slider and damper rod (**Figure 43**) into the fork slider. Insert a Phillips screwdriver through the opening in the bottom of the fork slider and guide the damper rod end into the receptacle in the base of the slider. Remove the screwdriver.

15. Install a new washer onto the damper rod Allen bolt.

16. Apply a nonpermanent threadlocking compound to the damper rod Allen bolt threads prior to installation. Insert the Allen bolt (**Figure 44**) through the lower end of the slider and thread it into the damper rod. Tighten the bolt securely.

CAUTION
To protect the oil seal lips, place a thin plastic bag on top of the fork tube. Before installing the seal in the following steps, lightly coat the bag and the seal lips with fork oil.

17. Slide the fork slider bushing (A, **Figure 45**), oil seal spacer (B) and oil seal (C) (with the letters facing up) down into the fork tube receptacle (**Figure 46**).

NOTE
A fork seal driver is required to install the fork tube bushing and seal into the fork tube. A number of different aftermarket fork seal drivers are available that can be used for this purpose. Another method is to use a piece of pipe or metal collar with correct dimensions to slide over the fork tube and seat against the seal. When selecting or fabricating a driver tool, it must have sufficient weight to drive the bushing and oil seal into the fork tube. A fork seal and cap installer (JIMS part No. 2046) is used for this procedure.

18. Slide the fork seal driver down the fork tube and seat it against the oil seal (**Figure 47**).

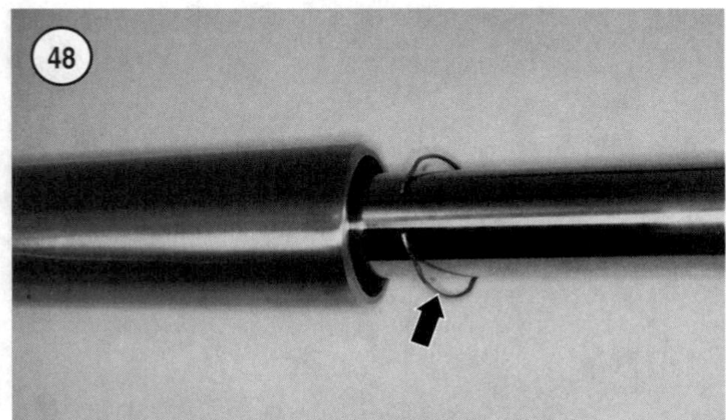

48

50

49

51

19. Operate the driver and drive the fork slider bushing and new seal into the fork tube. Continue to operate the driver until the stopper ring groove in the tube is visible above the fork seal. Remove the fork seal driver tool.

20. Install the stopper ring (**Figure 48**) into the slider groove. Make sure the retaining ring seats in the groove (**Figure 49**).

21. Install the fork tube as described in this chapter.

22. Insert a clear plastic tube into the fork cap bolt opening (**Figure 50**). Attach a funnel to the plastic tube and refill each fork leg with the correct viscosity and quantity of fork oil in **Table 1**. Remove the small funnel and plastic tube.

52

INSPECTION (ALL MODELS)

1. Thoroughly clean all parts in solvent and dry them. Check the fork tube for signs of wear or scratches.

2. Check the fork tube for bending, nicks, rust or other damage. Place the fork tube on a set of V-blocks and check runout with a dial indicator. If the special tools are not available, roll the fork tube on a large plate glass or another flat surface. Harley-Davidson does not provide service specifications for runout.

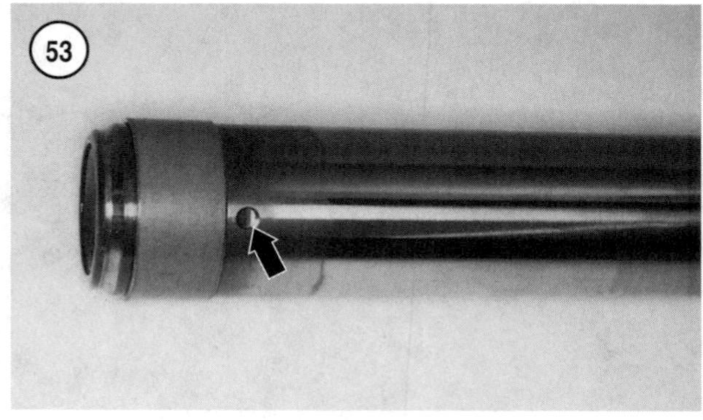

53

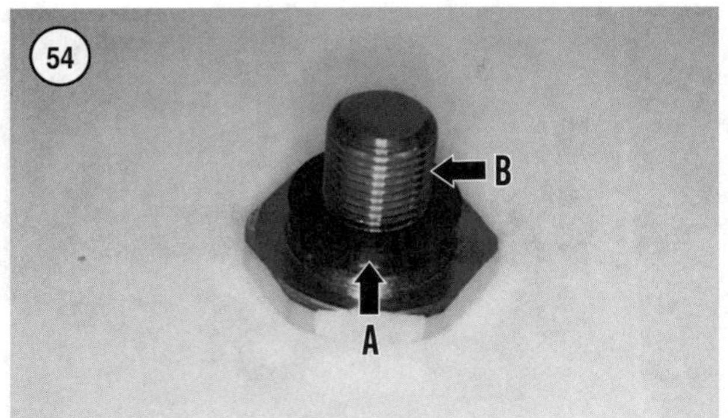

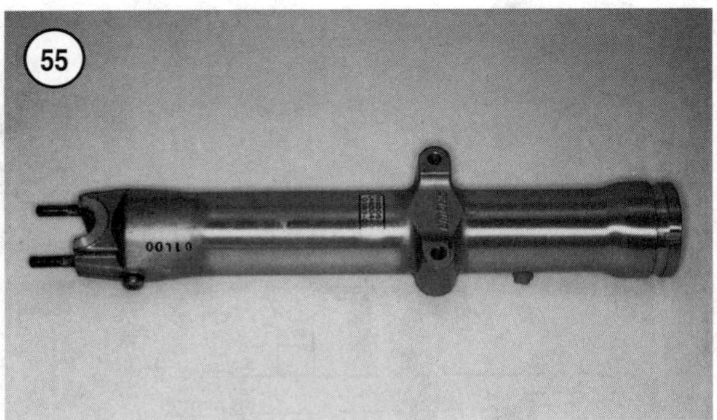

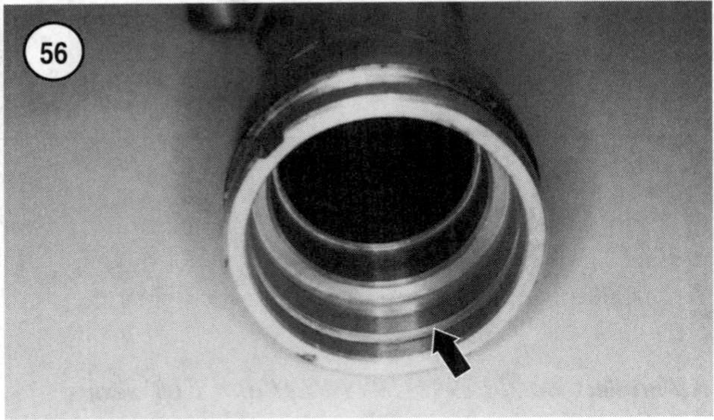

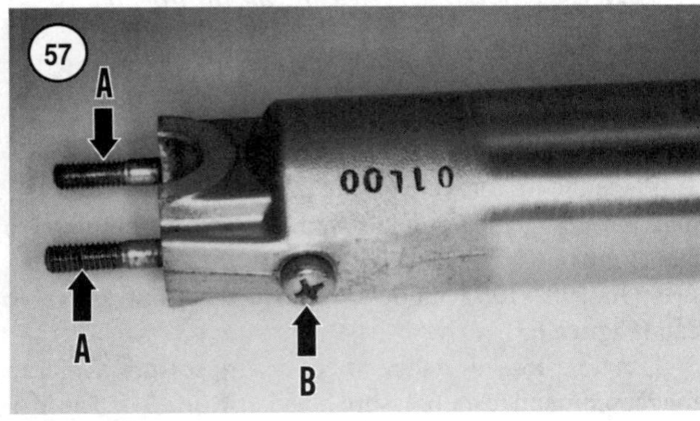

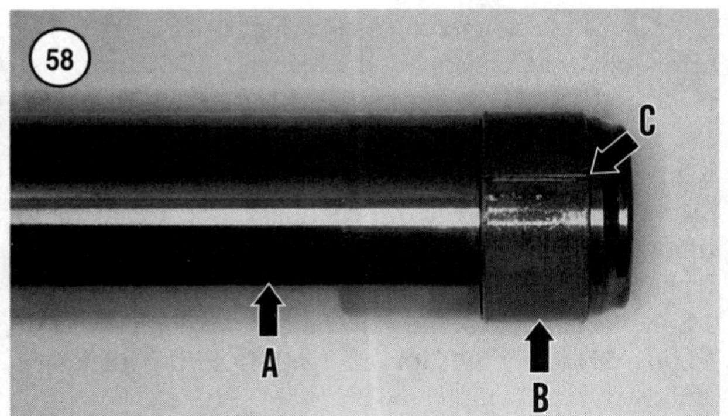

3. Check the internal threads in the top of the fork tube (**Figure 51**) for stripping, cross-threading or sealer residue. Use a tap to true the threads and to remove sealer deposits.

4. Check the fork tube plug O-ring (A, **Figure 52**) for hardness or deterioration. Replace if necessary.

5. Check the external threads on the fork tube plug (B, **Figure 52**) for stripping, cross-threading or sealer residue. Use a die to true the threads and to remove sealer deposits.

6. Make sure the oil passage hole in the fork tube (**Figure 53**) is open. If it is clogged, flush it with solvent and dry it with compressed air.

7. Check the fork cap bolt O-ring (A, **Figure 54**) for hardness or deterioration. Replace if necessary.

8. Check the external threads on the fork cap (B, **Figure 54**) for stripping, cross-threading or sealer residue. Use a die to true the threads and to remove sealer deposits.

9. Check the slider (**Figure 55**) for dents or other exterior damage. Check the retaining ring groove (**Figure 56**) in the top of the slider for cracks or other damage.

10. Check the front caliper mounting bosses for cracks or damage.

11. Check the threaded studs (A, **Figure 57**) on the base of the slider for thread damage. Repair if necessary.

12. Check the drain screw (B, **Figure 57**) and washer for damage.

13. Check the slider (A, **Figure 58**) and fork tube bushings (B) for excessive wear, cracks or damage.

14. Remove the fork tube bushing as follows:
   a. Expand the bushing slit (C, **Figure 58**) with a screwdriver and slide the bushing off the fork tube.
   b. Coat the new bushing with new fork oil.
   c. Install the new bushing by expanding the slit with a screwdriver.
   d. Seat the new bushing into the fork tube groove.

15. Check the damper rod piston rings (A, **Figure 59**) for excessive wear, cracks or other damage. If necessary, replace both rings as a set.

16. Check the damper rod (B, **Figure 59**) for straightness with a set of V-blocks and a dial indicator (**Figure 60**), or by rolling it on a piece of plate glass. Specifications for runout are not available. If the damper rod is not straight, replace it.

17. Make sure the oil passage hole in the damper rod (C, **Figure 59**) is open. If it is clogged, flush it with solvent and dry it with compressed air.

18. Check the internal threads in the bottom of the damper rod for stripping, cross-threading or sealer residue. Use a tap to true the threads and to remove sealer deposits.

19. Check the damper rod rebound spring and the fork spring for wear or damage. Service limit specifications for spring free length are not available. If necessary, replace both fork springs as a set.

20. Replace the oil seal whenever it is removed. Always replace both oil seals as a set.

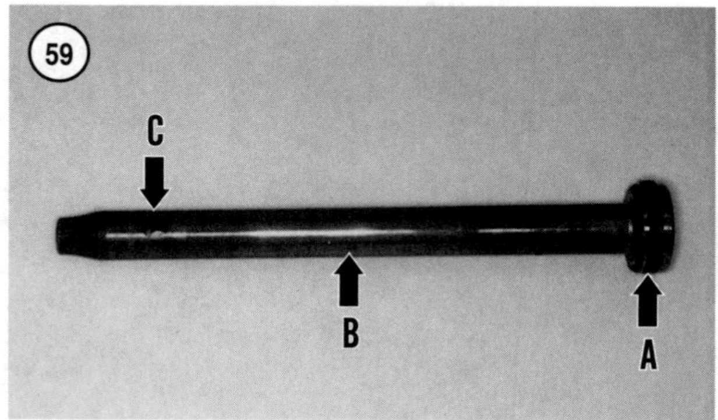

FRONT FORK AIR CONTROL AND ANTIDIVE SYSTEM (ADJUSTMENT AND INSPECTION)

All FLH, FLT and some FXR series models are equipped with a front fork air control/antidive system. This system uses air pressure to reduce fork compression during braking. The amount of antidive is dependent on the amount of air pressure applied to the system.

Air Pressure Adjustment

1996-1998 FLH and FLT series models

WARNING
Use caution when releasing the air from the front fork and the front fork air valve. Moisture and/or fork oil might spurt out when the air pressure is released. Protect eyes accordingly.

1. Place the motorcycle on the jiffy stand.
2. Remove the right saddlebag as described in Chapter Fifteen.
3. Remove the front air valve cap (**Figure 61**).
4. Use a no-loss air gauge to check air pressure. Refer to the recommended air pressure listed in **Table 4**.
5. Increase or decrease air pressure to achieve the desired ride and control.
6. At the same time, check and adjust, if necessary, the air pressure in the rear shock absorbers.
7. Install the air valve cap(s) and the saddlebag.

All models except 1996-1998 FLH and FLT series

WARNING
Use caution when releasing the air from the front fork and the front fork air valve. Moisture and/or fork oil might spurt out when the air pressure is released. Protect eyes accordingly.

1. Place the motorcycle on the jiffy stand.

2A. On 1984-1987 models, remove the front air valve cap (**Figure 62**).

2B. On 1988-1995 models, remove the front air valve cap (**Figure 63**).

3. Use a no-loss air gauge to check air pressure. Refer to the recommended air pressure listed in **Table 3** or **Table 4**.

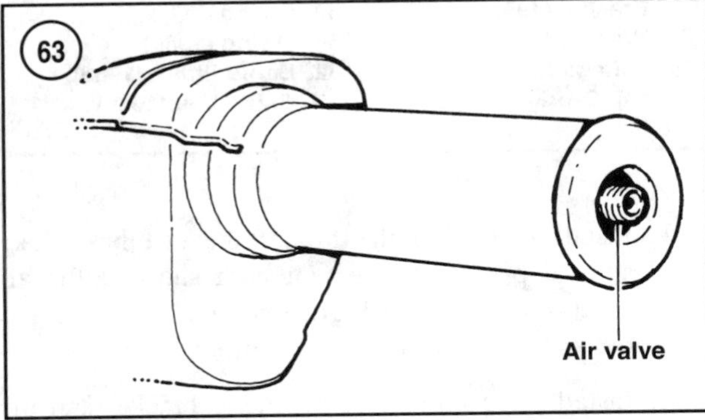

4. Increase or decrease air pressure to achieve the desired ride and control.
5. Install the air valve cap.

System Inspection

All models except 1996-1998 FLH and FLT series

Refer to **Figures 64-66**.

1. Check the tightness of the valve core within the air valve. If the valve core is tight, fill the system once again and put some soapy water on the valve. If air bubbles appear across the face of the valve, the valve might be damaged. If air is not leaking from the valve core, securely tighten all of the air line fittings and recheck.
2. Visually inspect the air lines for cracks or other signs of damage. If tightening the fittings does not stop the leak, remove the assembly and replace worn or damaged parts.
3. On FLH and FLT series models, perform the following:
   a. Check the ground connector screwed onto the air manifold. If the screws are loose, air can leak out of the screw hole.
   b. If the screws are loose or suspect, remove them from the ground connector and apply Loctite Pipe Sealant with Teflon to the screw threads. Reinstall the screws and tighten securely.
   c. Check the system once again for leaks.

NOTE
When removing the air control system as described in this chapter, you should replace all of the O-rings and copper washers (if used) during assembly.

4. Check the antidive solenoid operation as follows:
   a. Turn the ignition switch on.
   b. Apply the front or rear brake while listening to the antidive solenoid. When the brake is applied, a faint click should be heard, or a vibration can be felt on the solenoid.
5. Check the antidive system as follows:
   a. Install a no-loss air gauge on the air control valve fitting. See **Figure 62** and **Figure 63**.
   b. Turn the ignition switch off.
   c. Apply the front brake and bounce the front end while watching the air gauge. The air pressure should fluctuate as the front end moves up and down.
   d. Turn the ignition switch on and repeat substep b. The air pressure should stay constant as the front wheel bounces up and down.
6. If necessary, service the air control/antidive system as described in this chapter.

FRONT FORK AIR CONTROL AND ANTIDIVE SYSTEM (SERVICE AND TESTING)

Removal/Installation

1984-1987 FXRD and FXRT models

Refer to **Figure 64**.

1. Disconnect the negative battery cable from the battery.

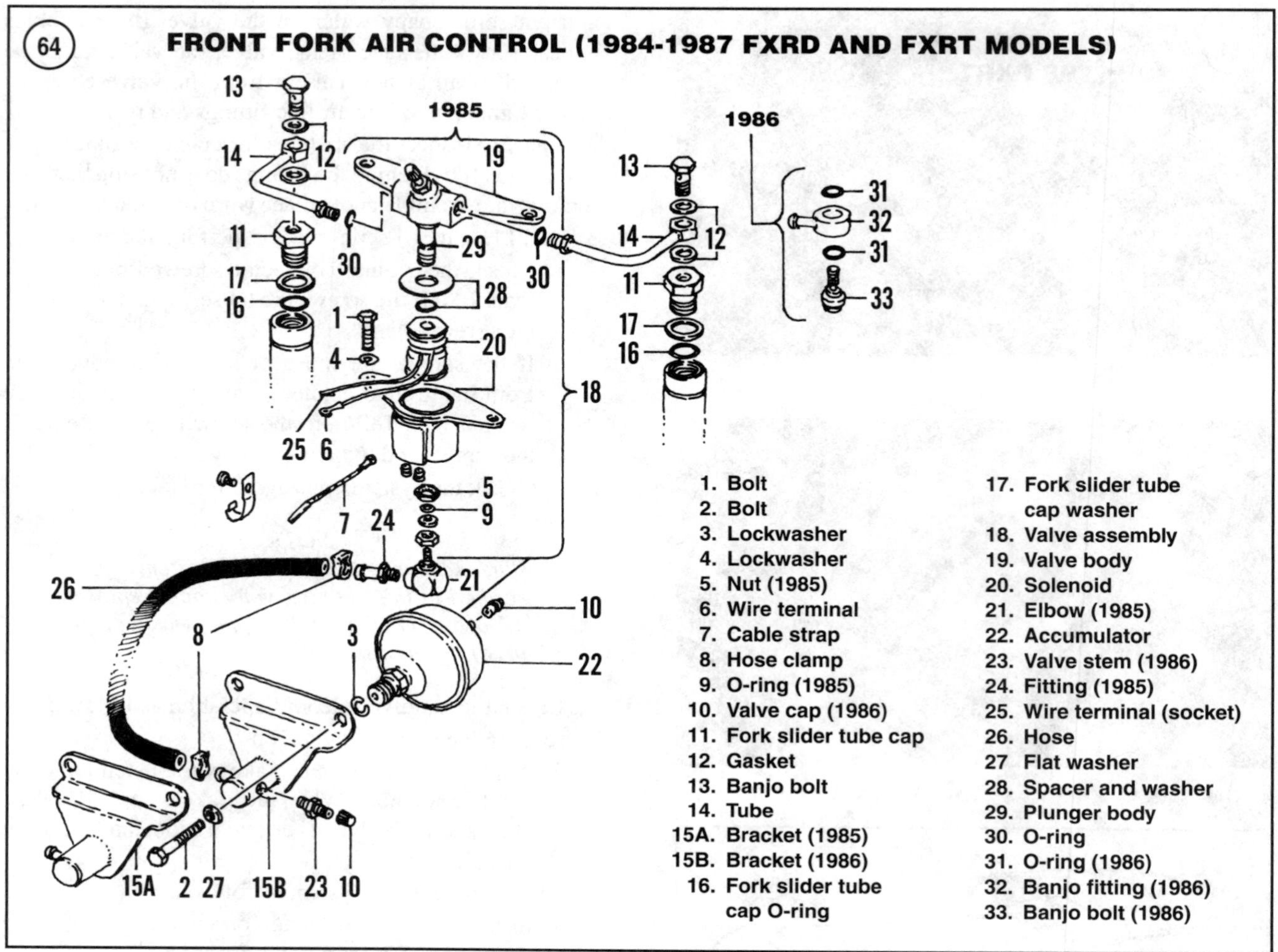

2. Remove the air valve cap, depress the air valve and bleed the system.
3. Remove the instrument from the handlebar as described in Chapter Nine.
4. Remove both banjo bolts and the washers securing the air tubes to the fork cap.
5. Remove the antidive valve solenoid housing bolts and washers.
6. Disconnect the antidive valve electrical connectors.
7. Remove the accumulator bracket bolts and washers.
8. Remove the plastic tie(s) and clamp(s) securing the air hose to the fork tube.
9. Remove any additional plastic ties securing the control assembly.
10. Remove the air control assembly from the front fork.
11. Installation is the reverse of these steps while noting the following:
   a. If removed, install the air tubes to the valve body as described in this chapter.
   b. Install the banjo bolts through the air tubes. Make sure to place a washer on both sides of the air tube(s) as shown in **Figure 64**. Tighten the banjo bolts to 25-30 ft.-lb. (34-41 N•m).
   c. Install the accumulator mounting bracket and the bolts. Place a flat washer so it is positioned between the bolt head and the bracket. Place a lockwasher so that it is positioned between the back of the bracket and the lower fork bracket. Tighten these bolts to 30-35 ft.-lb. (41-47 N•m).
   d. Slide a lockwasher onto the antidive solenoid housing mounting bolts and tighten the bolts to 155-190 in.-lb. (17-21 N•m).
   e. Reconnect the air hose. Make sure to secure both ends of the hose with *new* hose clamps.
   f. Pressurize the system as described in this chapter and check for leaks.

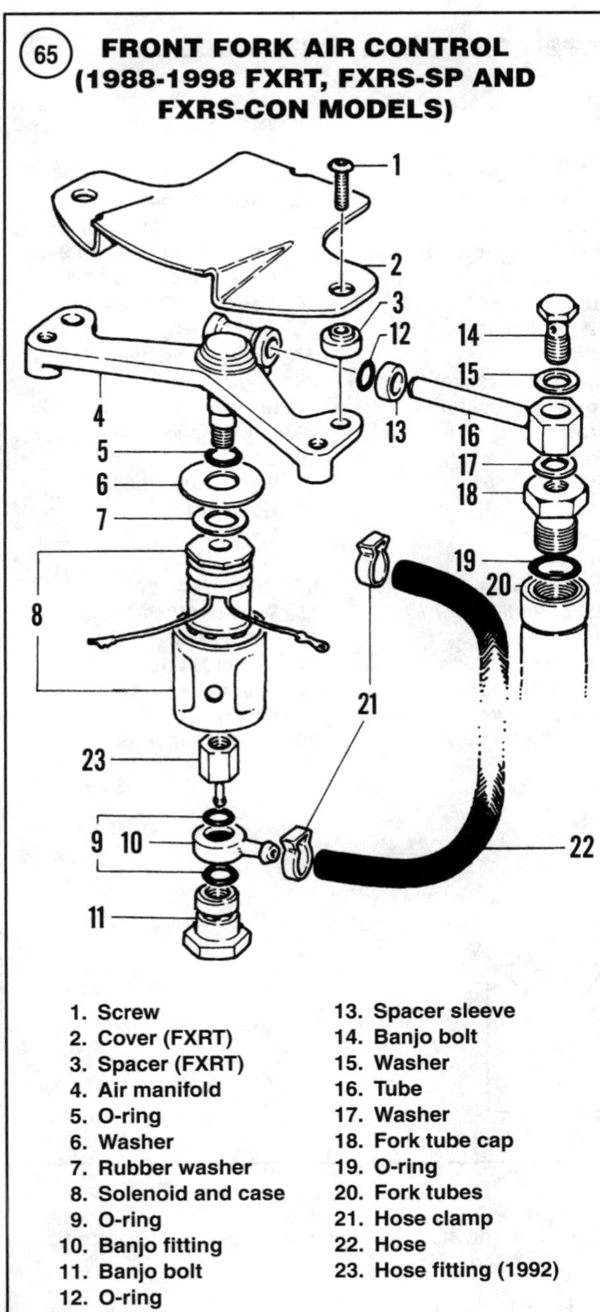

65 FRONT FORK AIR CONTROL (1988-1998 FXRT, FXRS-SP AND FXRS-CON MODELS)

1. Screw
2. Cover (FXRT)
3. Spacer (FXRT)
4. Air manifold
5. O-ring
6. Washer
7. Rubber washer
8. Solenoid and case
9. O-ring
10. Banjo fitting
11. Banjo bolt
12. O-ring
13. Spacer sleeve
14. Banjo bolt
15. Washer
16. Tube
17. Washer
18. Fork tube cap
19. O-ring
20. Fork tubes
21. Hose clamp
22. Hose
23. Hose fitting (1992)

1988-1994 FXRT and FXRS-SP models

Refer to **Figure 65**.

1. Disconnect the negative battery cable as described in Chapter Nine.
2. Remove the air valve cap from the air valve in the left grip. Depress the air valve and bleed the system.
3. Remove the headlight as described in Chapter Nine.
4. On FXRT models, remove the screws securing the cover. Remove the cover and the two spacers.
5. On FXRS-SP models, remove the headlight bracket and the manifold bolts.
6. Remove the banjo bolts and washers securing the air tubes to the fork caps.
7. Disconnect the air hose at the antidive valve connection.
8. Remove the air control assembly from the front fork.
9. Installation is the reverse of these steps while noting the following:
   a. Position the air fork assembly into position on the fork tubes.
   b. Install a *new* O-ring into the valve body/air tube bore.
   c. Insert the flared end of the air tube into the valve body; align the end of the tube with the fork cap. Secure the end of the tube with the O-ring and valve body.
   d. Tighten the flare nut to 17 ft.-lb. (23 N•m).
   e. Install the banjo bolts through the air tubes. Make sure to place a washer on both sides of the air tube(s) as shown in **Figure 65**. Tighten the banjo bolts to 25-30 ft.-lb. (34-41 N•m).
   f. Reconnect the air hose. Secure both ends of the hose with *new* hose clamps.
   g. On FXRT models, install the spacers under the top cover and tighten the screws securely.
   h. Pressurize the system as described in this chapter and check for leaks.
   i. Adjust the headlight as described in Chapter Nine.

All 1984-1996 FLH and FLT series models except 1984-1996 FLHT and FLHTC

Refer to **Figure 66**.

1. Disconnect the negative battery cable as described in Chapter Nine.

CAUTION

When removing the instrument panel in Step 2, do not turn the panel upside down because damping oil in the fuel gauge will run onto the gauge face and stain it.

NOTE

Cover the fuel tank and front fender with a heavy cloth to protect them from accidental scratches or dents when removing the following components.

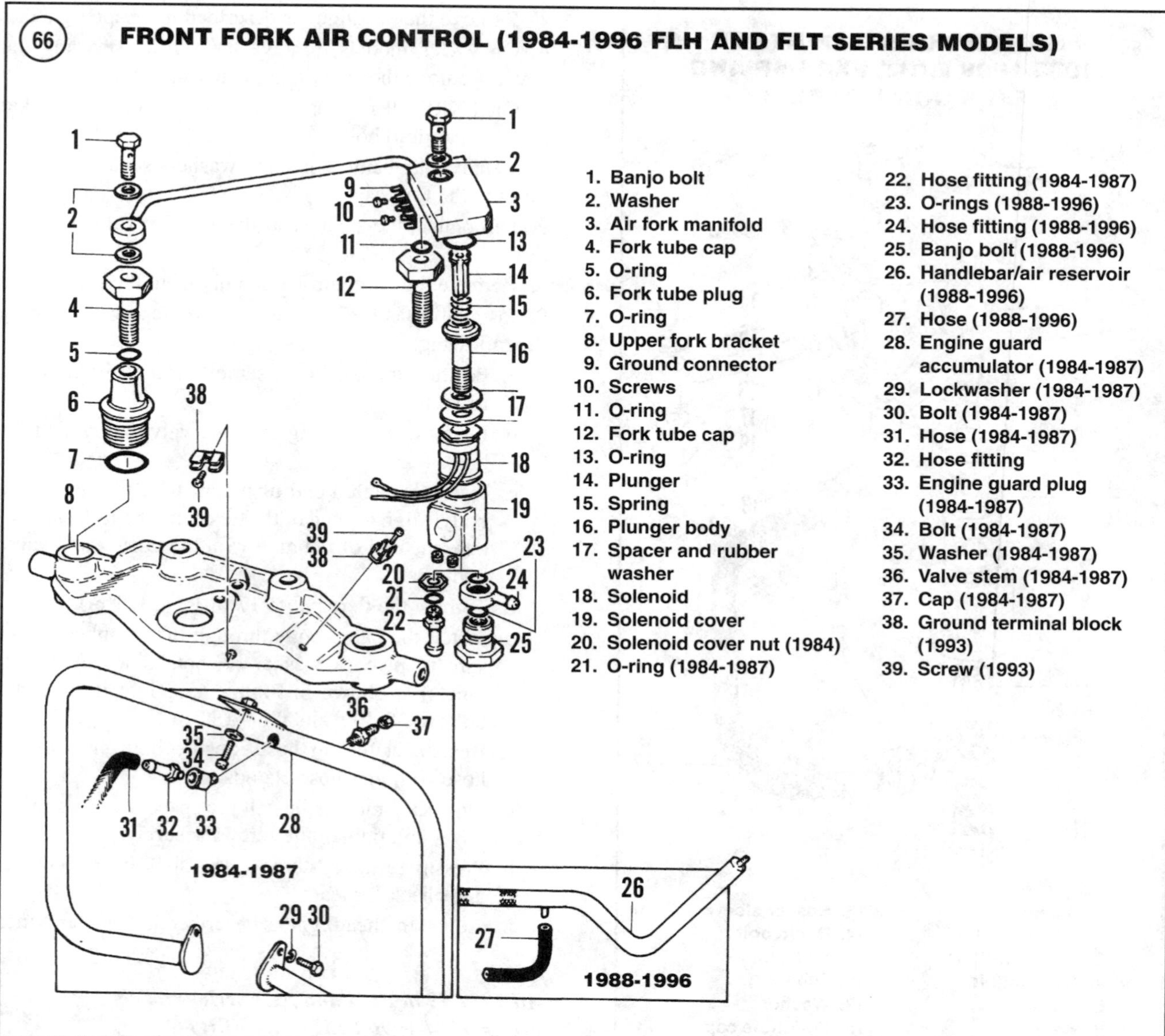

2. Remove the instrument panel as described in Chapter Nine.

3. Remove the air valve cap. Then depress the air valve and bleed the system.

4A. On 1984-1987 models, disconnect the air hose from the engine guard accumulator.

4B. On 1988-1998 models, perform the following:

a. Remove the handlebar riser locknuts from under the fork bracket.
b. Remove the upper clamps and lift the handlebar up slightly.
c. Disconnect the air hose from the fitting on the handlebar.
d. Set the handlebar aside to prevent damaging the control cables.

5. Loosen and remove the air manifold banjo bolts and washers. Disconnect any electrical connectors at the manifold and remove the manifold. Remove and discard the O-rings.

6. If necessary, remove the antidive switch as described in this section.

7. Installation is the reverse of these steps while noting the following:

a. Install a *new* O-ring in the bottom of the air manifold.

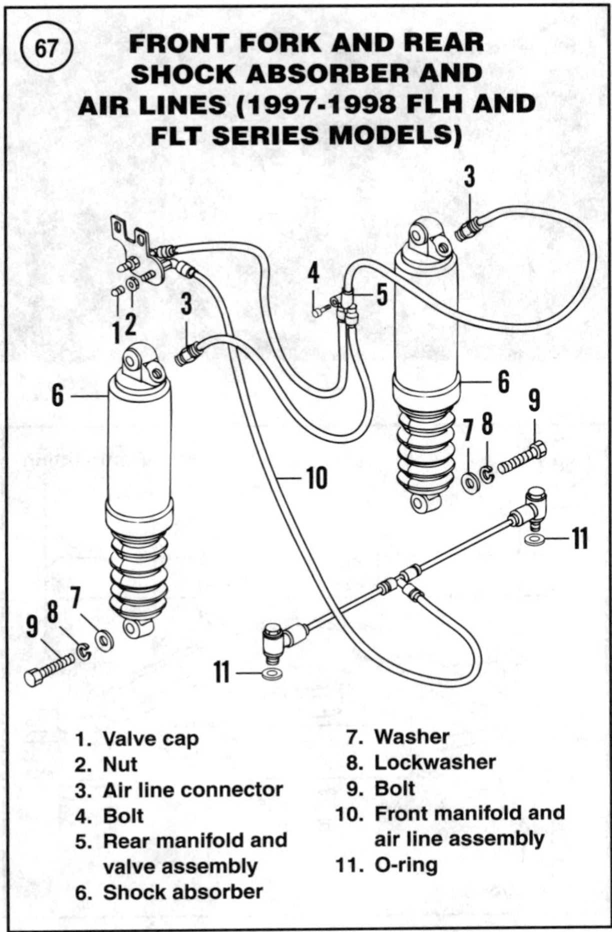

(67) FRONT FORK AND REAR SHOCK ABSORBER AND AIR LINES (1997-1998 FLH AND FLT SERIES MODELS)

1. Valve cap
2. Nut
3. Air line connector
4. Bolt
5. Rear manifold and valve assembly
6. Shock absorber
7. Washer
8. Lockwasher
9. Bolt
10. Front manifold and air line assembly
11. O-ring

b. Position the antidive switch on the forks, if removed, and reconnect the switch electrical leads.

c. Install the upper banjo bolts using new washers. Tighten banjo bolts to 25-30 ft.-lb. (34-41 N•m).

d. Reconnect the air hoses after installing all air control components.

e. Pressurize the system and check for leaks.

1986-1996 FLHT and FLHTC models

Refer to **Figure 66**.

1. Disconnect the negative battery cable as described in Chapter Nine.

NOTE
Cover the fuel tank and front fender with a heavy cloth to protect them from accidental scratches or dents when removing the following components.

2. Remove the passing lamp bracket bolts and remove the bracket from the inner fairing; place the bracket onto the front fender. Reinstall the lower bracket bolts into the inner fairing to hold it in place.
3. Remove the outer fairing as described in Chapter Fifteen.
4. Remove the air valve cap. Then depress the air valve and bleed the system.
5. If necessary, remove the valve as described under *Inspection* in this chapter.
6. On 1988 or later models, disconnect the air hose from the fitting on the handlebar.
7. Remove the handlebar riser nuts and move the handlebar back and lay it on the blanket covering the fuel tank.
8. Remove the ignition/fork lock assembly mounting bolts on the upper fork bracket.
9. If not already removed, disconnect the electrical connectors from the antidive valve.
10. On 1986-1987 models, disconnect the hose from the antidive valve.
11. Loosen and remove the two banjo bolts securing the air fork manifold to the fork tube bolts.
12. Lift the air fork manifold up and remove it. If the manifold contacts the inner fairing, gently push the fairing back by hand to make room for the manifold.
13. Installation is the reverse of these steps while noting the following:

a. Install a *new* O-ring in the bottom of the air manifold.

b. Position the antidive switch on the forks, if removed, and reconnect the switch electrical leads.

c. Install the upper banjo bolts using new washers. Tighten banjo bolts to 25-30 ft.-lb. (34-41 N•m).

d. Reconnect the air hoses after installing all air control components.

e. Pressurize the system and check for leaks.

1997-1998 FLH and FLT series models

Refer to **Figure 67**.

1A. On all FLHT series models, remove the outer faring. On FLHTC series models, also remove the storage box. Refer to Chapter Fifteen.

1B. On all FLHR series models, remove the headlight nacelle as described in Chapter Nine.

2. Remove the passing lamp assembly as described in Chapter Nine.
3. Support the motorcycle with the front wheel off the ground. Refer to *Motorcycle Stands* in Chapter Ten.
4. Remove the front fender and front wheel as described in Chapter Nine.

5. On models so equipped, remove the right saddlebag as described in Chapter Fifteen.

WARNING
Use caution when releasing the air from the front fork air valve. Moisture and fork oil might spurt out when the air pressure is released. Protect eyes accordingly.

6. Cover the rear brake assembly and wheel prior to releasing the compressed air from the rear air valve. If necessary, wipe any oil residue that may have been ejected from the air valve.

7. Remove the cap from the front fork air valve (A, **Figure 68**). Then slowly depress the air valve to evacuate the air from the front fork air pipe system. Unscrew and remove the core from the air valve. Place the air valve core and cap in a reclosable plastic bag to avoid misplacing them.

8. Refer to **Figure 69**. Unscrew and remove the hex bolts (**Figure 70**) securing the banjo bolt on top of each fork tube. Move the air tube assembly out of the way of the fork assemblies.

9. Remove the nut securing the air valve, hose and valve mounting bracket (B, **Figure 68**) on the frame.

10. Make a sketch of the front hose routing through the frame prior to removal. Then remove the hose assembly.

11. Installation is the reverse of these steps while noting the following:

   a. Install a *new* O-ring (**Figure 71**) and apply a light coat of oil to it.
   b. Install the air tube assembly onto the top of the fork assembly and install the hex bolts through the banjo bolts. Tighten the hex bolts to 97-142 in.-lb. (11-16 N•m).
   c. Pressurize the system and check for leaks.

Antidive Solenoid Testing

Refer to **Figures 64-66**.

1. Disconnect the switch leads.

2. Connect the ohmmeter leads to both switch leads. The specified resistance is 10-20 ohms.

3. Connect one ohmmeter lead to one of the antidive solenoid leads. Touch the other lead to the antidive solenoid housing. The resistance should be infinity.

4. Replace the antidive solenoid if it failed either test.

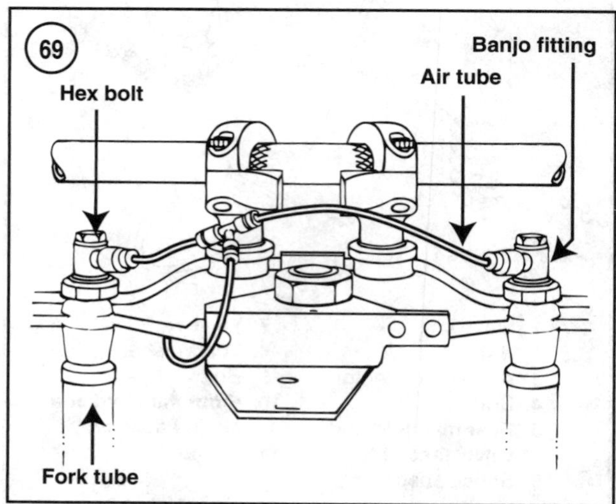

Antidive Solenoid Removal/Installation

1984-1987 FXRT and FXRD models

Refer to **Figure 64**.

1. Remove the front fork air control assembly as described in this chapter.

2A. On 1984-1985 models, disconnect the hose from the hose fitting. Then unscrew and remove the hose fitting, nut, washer and O-ring.

2B. On 1986-1987 models, disconnect the hose from the banjo fitting. Then unscrew and remove the banjo bolt, banjo fitting and O-rings.

3. On early models only, remove the nut from the end of the plunger body.

4. Remove the antidive valve and its housing, O-ring and spacer.

5. Unscrew the air hoses from the valve body. Remove the hoses and the O-rings. Discard the O-rings.

6. Remove the plunger body from the antidive valve as follows:

a. On 1984 models, use a spanner wrench and unscrew the plunger body from the antidive valve. If a spanner wrench is not available, thread two thin jam nuts onto the plunger body and lock them together.

b. On 1985 and later models, use a screwdriver and unscrew and remove the plunger body.

7. After removing the plunger body, remove the spring, plunger and O-ring from the plunger body.

8. To ensure an air-tight system, replace all steel and copper washers and O-rings.

9. Remove all sealer residue from the plunger body and antidive valve threads.

10. Install a *new* O-ring into the air manifold recess.

11. Position the smaller outer diameter of the plunger spring going in first and install the spring onto the plunger.

12. Coat the plunger body threads with Loctite Pipe Sealant with Teflon and thread the plunger body into the air manifold. Tighten the plunger body using the same tool and method used for removal. See Step 6.

13. Install the spacer, washer, antidive valve and valve housing.

14. On early models only, install the nut onto the end of the plunger body.

15A. On 1984-1985 models, perform the following:

a. Install the nut, washer and O-ring onto the hose fitting.

b. Thread the hose fitting into the end of the plunger body.

c. Securely tighten the nut, washer and O-ring.

15B. On 1986-1987 models, perform the following:

a. Install two *new* O-rings into the banjo fitting grooves.

b. Then slide the banjo fitting over the plunger body.

c. Install the banjo bolt and tighten to 97-124 in.-lb. (11-14 N•m).

1988-1998 FXRT, FXRS-SP and FXRS-Con models

Refer to **Figure 65**.

1. Remove the front fork air control assembly as described in this chapter.

2A. On 1988-1991 models, loosen and remove the banjo bolts, banjo fitting and two O-rings.

2B. On 1992-1998 models, loosen and remove the fitting and O-ring.

3. Remove the antidive solenoid and its housing, rubber washer, washer and O-ring.

4. On 1984 models, use a spanner wrench and unscrew the plunger body from the antidive valve. If a spanner wrench is not available, thread two thin jam nuts onto the plunger body and lock them together.

5. Thread two thin jam nuts onto the plunger body and lock them together. Unscrew and remove the plunger body from the bottom of the air manifold.

6. Remove the spring, plunger and O-ring from the plunger body.

7. If necessary, remove the two tubes from the top of the air manifold.

CAUTION

When removing the tube(s) in Step 8, do not remove the spacer sleeves.

8. Carefully pull and remove the air tube from the air manifold. Remove the O-ring installed between the tube and air manifold seat. Repeat for the other air tube and O-ring.

9. Remove all sealer residue from the plunger body and antidive valve threads.

10. Install a *new* O-ring into the air manifold recess.

11. Position the smaller outer diameter of the plunger spring going in first and install the spring onto the plunger.

12. Coat the plunger body threads with Loctite Pipe Sealant with Teflon and thread the plunger body into the air manifold. Securely tighten the plunger body.
13. Slide the washer, rubber washer and antidive solenoid onto the plunger body. Install the housing onto the antidive solenoid.
14. Install a *new* O-ring into the groove above the threads on the plunger body.
15A. On 1988-1991 models, perform the following:
   a. Install two *new* O-rings into the banjo fitting and slide the banjo fitting onto the plunger body. Thread the banjo bolt onto the plunger body until it is finger-tight.
   b. Turn the banjo fitting so that its hose nozzle faces in the direction shown in **Figure 65**. Tighten the banjo bolt to 97-124 in.-lb. (11-14 N•m).
15B. On 1992-1998 models, install the fitting with a *new* O-ring.
16. If the air tubes were removed, install them as follows:
   a. Install a *new* O-ring into the air manifold.
   b. Carefully insert the air tube into the air manifold until the taper on the end of the tube touches the O-ring.
   c. Repeat for the other tube and O-ring.

FLH and FLT series models

Refer to **Figure 66**.
1A. On FLT, 1984-1985 FLHTC and FLHS models, perform Steps 1-7 under *Removal (All 1984-1996 FLH and FLT series models except 1984-1996 FLHT and FLHTC)* in this section.
1B. On 1986-1996 FLHTC models, perform Steps 1-7 under *Removal (1986-1996 FLHT and FLHTC models)* in this section.
2A. On 1984-1987 models, remove the hose fitting and O-ring from the bottom of the antidive solenoid.
2B. On 1988-1996 models, remove the banjo bolt, O-rings and hose fitting from the bottom of the antidive solenoid.
3. If so equipped, remove the antidive valve cover nut.
4. Remove the antidive valve case, antidive valve, spacer and rubber washer.
5. To remove the plunger body from the antidive valve as follows:
   a. On 1984 models, use a spanner wrench and unscrew the plunger body from the antidive valve. If a spanner wrench is not available, thread two thin jam nuts onto the plunger body and lock them together.
   b. On 1985 and later models, use a screwdriver and unscrew and remove the plunger body.

(72) STEERING STEM AND BRACKET (1984-1987 FXR SERIES MODELS)

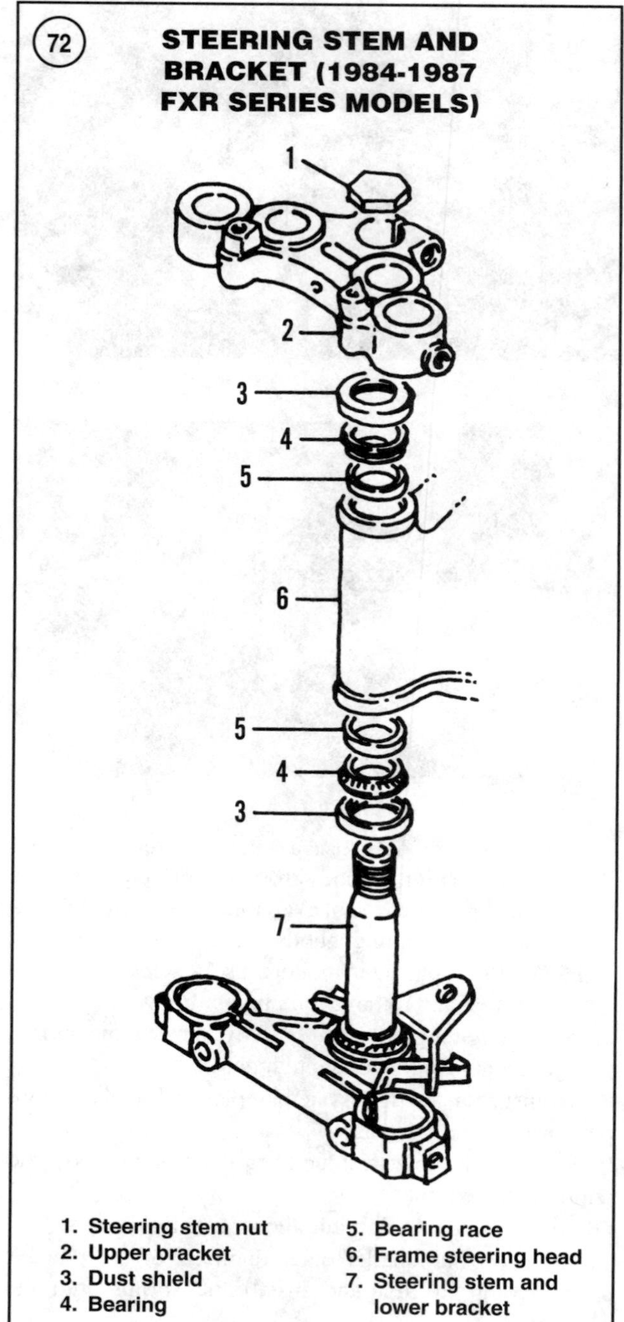

1. Steering stem nut
2. Upper bracket
3. Dust shield
4. Bearing
5. Bearing race
6. Frame steering head
7. Steering stem and lower bracket

6. After removing the plunger body, remove the spring, plunger and O-ring from the plunger body.
7. To ensure an air-tight system, install all *new* steel and copper washers and O-rings.
8. Remove all sealer residue from the plunger body and antidive valve threads.
9. Install a *new* O-ring into the air manifold recess.

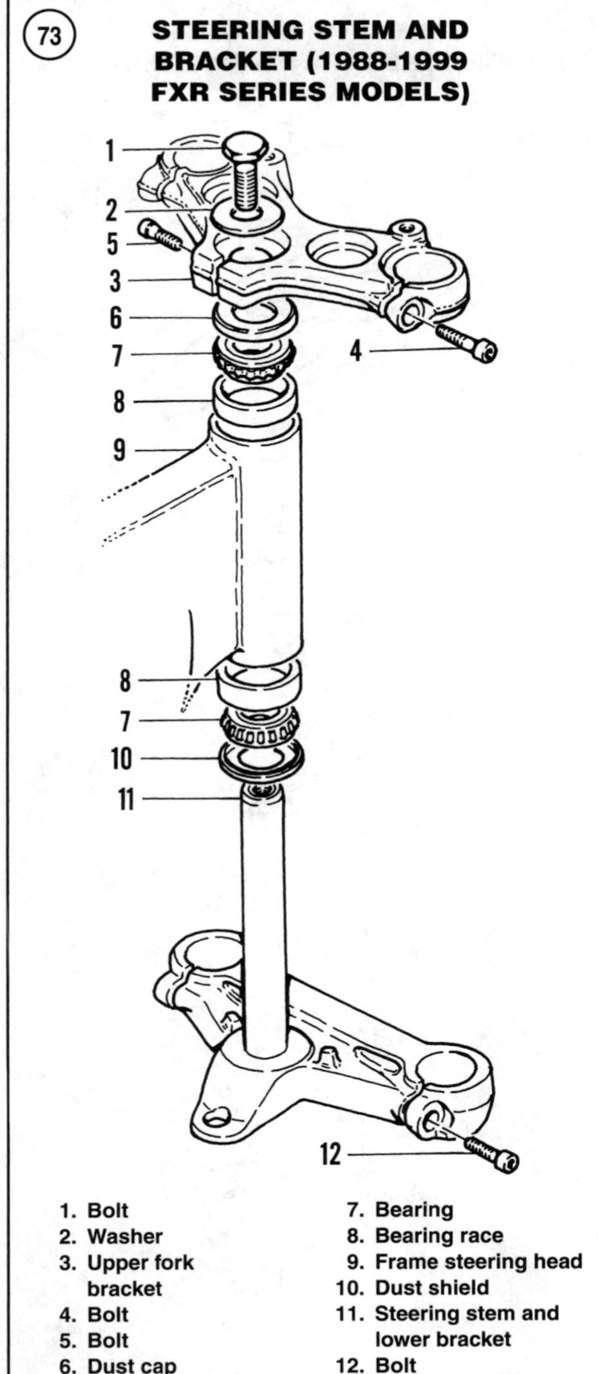

1. Bolt
2. Washer
3. Upper fork bracket
4. Bolt
5. Bolt
6. Dust cap
7. Bearing
8. Bearing race
9. Frame steering head
10. Dust shield
11. Steering stem and lower bracket
12. Bolt

10. Position the smaller outer diameter of the plunger spring going in first and install the spring and install the plunger.

11. Coat the plunger body threads with Loctite Pipe Sealant with Teflon and thread the plunger body into the air manifold. Tighten the plunger body using the same tool and method used in *Removal* in Step 5.

12. Install the spacer, washer, antidive valve and valve housing. On early models only, install the nut onto the end of the plunger body and tighten securely.

13A. On 1984-1987 models, install a *new* O-ring into the groove machined above the plunger body threads. Then install the hose fitting on the plunger body.

13B. On 1986-1987 models, perform the following:

a. Install two *new* O-rings into the banjo fitting grooves.
b. Then slide the banjo fitting over the plunger body.
c. Install the banjo bolt and tighten to 97-124 in.-lb. (11-14 N•m).

14. If the ground connector was removed from the air fork manifold, perform the following:

a. Apply Loctite Pipe Sealant with Teflon to the screw threads before installing the screws.
b. Move the ground connector into position and install the two screws. Tighten the screws securely to prevent an air leak.

STEERING HEAD AND STEM

FXR Series Models

Removal

Refer to **Figure 72** and **Figure 73**.

1. Remove the front wheel as described in Chapter Ten.
2. Remove the fuel tank as described in Chapter Nine.
3. Remove the handlebar assembly as described in this chapter. Position the handlebar so that the control cables are not kinked or damaged.
4. On models with the air control system, remove the air control system from the upper fork bracket as described in this chapter.
5. Loosen the fork stem nut on early models or the steering stem bolt on later models.
6. Remove the front forks as described in this chapter.

NOTE

Hold onto the steering stem when removing the upper fork bracket pinch bolt in Step 7 to prevent the steering stem from falling out.

7. Loosen the steering stem pinch bolt and remove the upper bracket.
8. Carefully lower the steering stem and lower bracket out of the steering head.
9. Remove the upper dust shield from the steering head.
10. Remove the bearing from the upper bearing race in the steering head.

11. Inspect the fork stem assembly as described in this section.

Installation

1. Thoroughly pack both bearings with bearing grease.
2. Make sure the steering head and stem races are properly seated.
3. Apply a light coat of grease to the steering head races.
4. Install the lower dust shield onto the lower bearing on the steering stem.
5. Install the steering stem into the steering head and hold it firmly in place.
6. Install the upper bearing over the fork stem and seat into the upper race.
7. Install the upper dust shield.
8. Install the upper bracket onto the steering stem and tighten the steering stem pinch bolt securely.
9. Install the fork stem nut on early models or the steering stem bolt on later models. Tighten securely.
10. Install the front fork as described in this chapter.
11. Tighten the upper bracket-to-fork stem pinch bolt to the specification in **Table 5**.

CAUTION
Do not overtighten the fork stem nut or bolt in Step 12, or the bearings and races can be damaged.

12. Tighten the fork stem nut or bolt to remove all noticeable play in the fork stem.
13. Install the handlebar assembly as described in this chapter.
14. Install the fuel tank as described in Chapter Nine.
15. Adjust the front steering as described in this chapter.
16. On models with the air control system, install the air control system onto the upper fork bracket as described in this chapter.

FXWG Models

Removal

Refer to **Figure 74**.

1. Remove the front wheel as described in Chapter Ten.
2. Remove the fuel tank as described in Chapter Nine.
3. Remove the handlebar assembly as described in this chapter. Position the handlebar so that the control cables are not kinked or damaged.
4. Remove the front fork as described in this chapter.
5. Remove the headlight and headlight bracket as described in Chapter Nine.

(74) **STEERING STEM AND BRACKET (FXWG MODELS)**

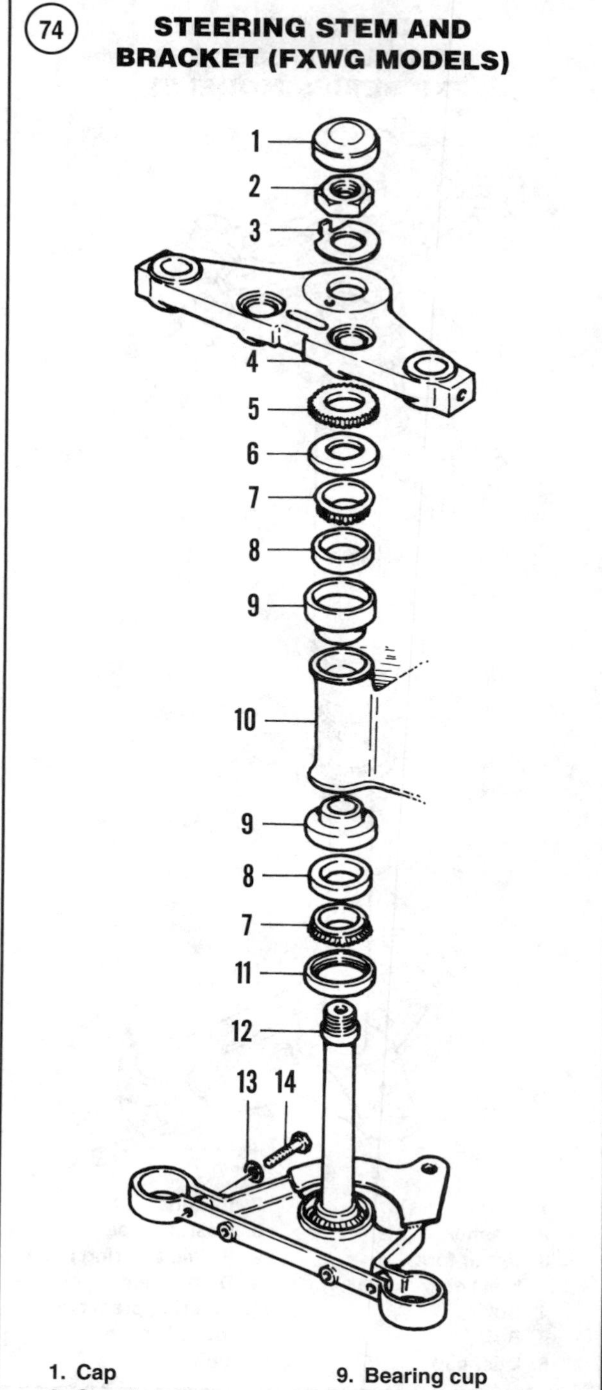

1. Cap
2. Steering stem nut
3. Lockwasher
4. Upper bracket
5. Adjust nut
6. Upper dust shield
7. Bearing
8. Bearing race
9. Bearing cup
10. Frame steering head
11. Lower dust shield
12. Steering stem and lower bracket
13. Washer
14. Bolt

6. Remove the brake hose bracket at the bottom of the fork stem bracket. Do not disconnect the brake hose connection.
7. Disconnect the ground wire at the fork stem bracket.
8. Remove the steering stem cap from the fork stem nut.
9. Straighten the lockwasher tab away from the steering stem nut. Then loosen and remove the nut and lockwasher.
10. Remove the upper steering stem bracket from the steering stem.

NOTE
To prevent the steering stem from falling out, hold onto the steering stem when removing the upper fork bracket pinch bolt in Step 11.

11. Loosen and remove the bearing adjust nut. Then slide the steering stem and bracket out of the steering head.
12. Remove the upper dust shield from the steering head.
13. Remove the bearing from the upper bearing race in the steering head.
14. Inspect the fork stem assembly as described in this section.

Installation

1. Thoroughly pack both bearings with bearing grease.
2. Make sure the steering head and stem races are properly seated.
3. Apply a light coat of grease to the steering head races.
4. Install the lower dust shield onto the lower bearing on the steering stem.
5. Install the steering stem into the steering head and hold it firmly in place.
6. Install the upper bearing over the steering stem and seat into the upper race.
7. Install the upper dust shield.
8. Install the bearing adjust nut and tighten to remove all bearing play.
9. Install the upper bracket over the steering stem.
10. Install a *new* lockwasher over the steering stem and insert the locating pin into the hole in the fork bracket.
11. Install the steering stem nut until it is finger-tight. Check that the lockwasher location pin is still engaged in the hole in the upper bracket.

NOTE
Final tightening of the steering stem nut will occur after the front wheel is installed and the front steering is adjusted as described in this section.

12. Install the brake hose bracket to the lower steering stem bracket and tighten to 133 in.-lb. (15 N•m).
13. Install the headlight bracket and headlight. Adjust the headlight as described in Chapter Nine.
14. Install the front fork as described in this chapter.
15. Install the front wheel as described in Chapter Ten.
16. Adjust the front steering as described in this chapter.
17. Install the fork stem cap over the nut.

FXSB and FXEF Models

Removal

Refer to **Figure 75**.
1. Remove the front wheel as described in Chapter Ten.
2. Remove the fuel tank as described in Chapter Nine.
3. Remove the handlebar assembly as described in this chapter. Position the handlebar so that the control cables are not kinked or damaged.
4. Remove the front fork as described in this chapter.
5. Remove the brake hose bracket at the bottom of the fork stem bracket. Do not disconnect the brake hose connection.

CAUTION
Secure the steering stem before removing the fork stem nut in the following steps, or it will fall to the ground.

6. Loosen and remove the steering stem nut.
7. Loosen the upper bracket pinch bolt.
8. Remove the upper bracket from the steering stem.
9. Lower the fork stem out of the steering head.
10. Remove the upper dust shield.
11. Remove the bearing from the upper bearing race in the steering head cup.
12. Inspect the fork stem assembly as described later in this chapter.

Installation

1. Thoroughly pack both bearings with bearing grease.
2. Make sure the steering head and stem races are properly seated.
3. Apply a light coat of grease to the steering head races.
4. Install the lower dust shield onto the lower bearing on the steering stem.
5. Install the steering stem into the steering head and hold it firmly in place.
6. Install the upper bearing over the steering stem and seat into the upper race.
7. Install the upper dust shield.

8. Install the upper bracket over the steering stem.
9. Install the steering stem nut until it is finger-tight.

NOTE
Final tightening of the steering stem nut will occur after the front wheel is installed and the front steering is adjusted as described in this section.

10. Install the front fork as described in this chapter.
11. Install the brake hose bracket at the bottom of the fork stem bracket.
12. Install the front wheel as described in Chapter Ten.
13. Adjust the front steering as described in this chapter.
14. Install the fork stem cap over the nut.

FLH and FLT Series Models

Removal

Refer to **Figure 76**.

1. Remove the front wheel as described in Chapter Ten.
2. On 1986-1998 FLHTC series models, remove the light bar and outer fairing as described in Chapter Fifteen.
3. On FLTC series models, remove the instrument panel and handlebar.
4. Remove the fuel tank as described in Chapter Nine.
5. Remove the handlebar assembly as described in this chapter. Position the handlebar so that the control cables are not kinked or damaged.
6. On models with the air control system, remove the air control system from the upper fork bracket as described in this chapter.
7. Remove the front fork as described in this chapter.
8. Remove the brake line bracket at the lower fork stem bracket.
9. Disconnect the electrical connectors from the main circuit board.
10. On models so equipped, straighten the lockwasher tab away from the fork stem nut. Then loosen and remove the nut, lockwasher and main circuit board.
11. Remove the upper fork bracket from the steering stem.

NOTE
To prevent the steering stem from falling out, hold onto the steering stem when removing the upper fork bracket pinch bolt in Step 11.

12. Loosen and remove the bearing adjust nut, then slide the steering stem and bracket out of the steering head.
13. Remove the upper dust shield from the steering head.

75 **STEERING STEM AND BRACKET (FXSB AND FXEF MODELS)**

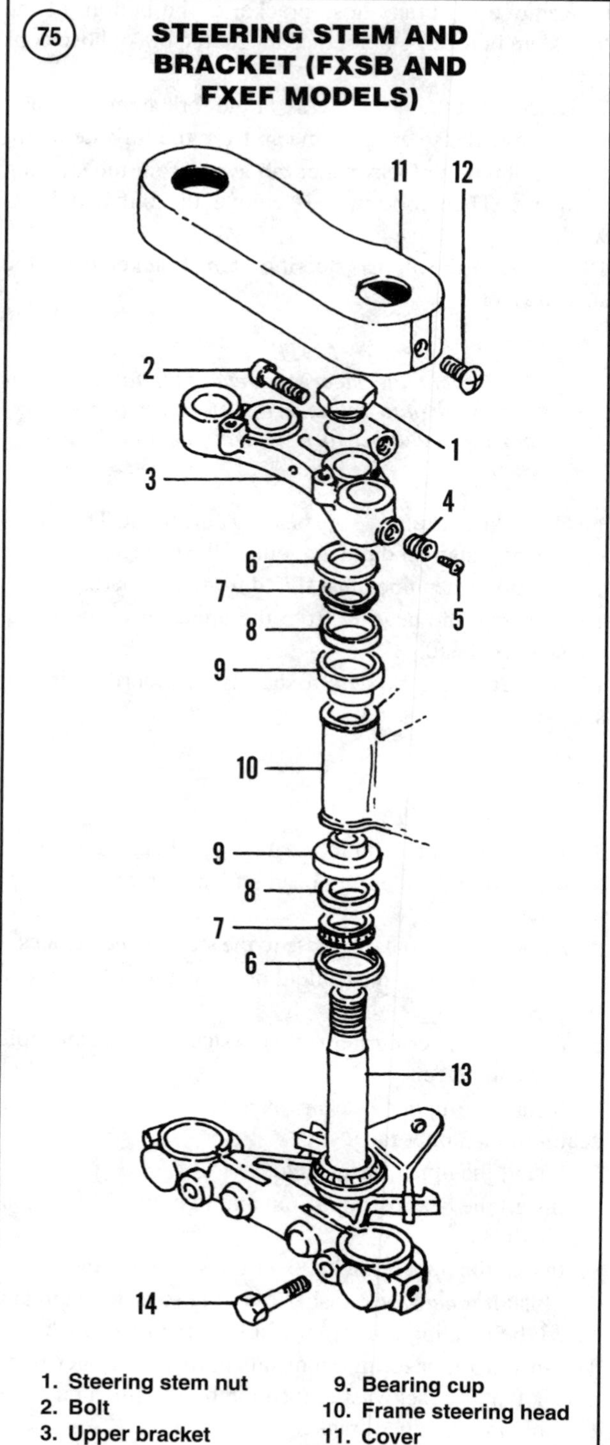

1. Steering stem nut
2. Bolt
3. Upper bracket
4. Insert
5. Screw
6. Dust shield
7. Bearing
8. Bearing race
9. Bearing cup
10. Frame steering head
11. Cover
12. Screw
13. Steering stem and lower bracket
14. Bolt

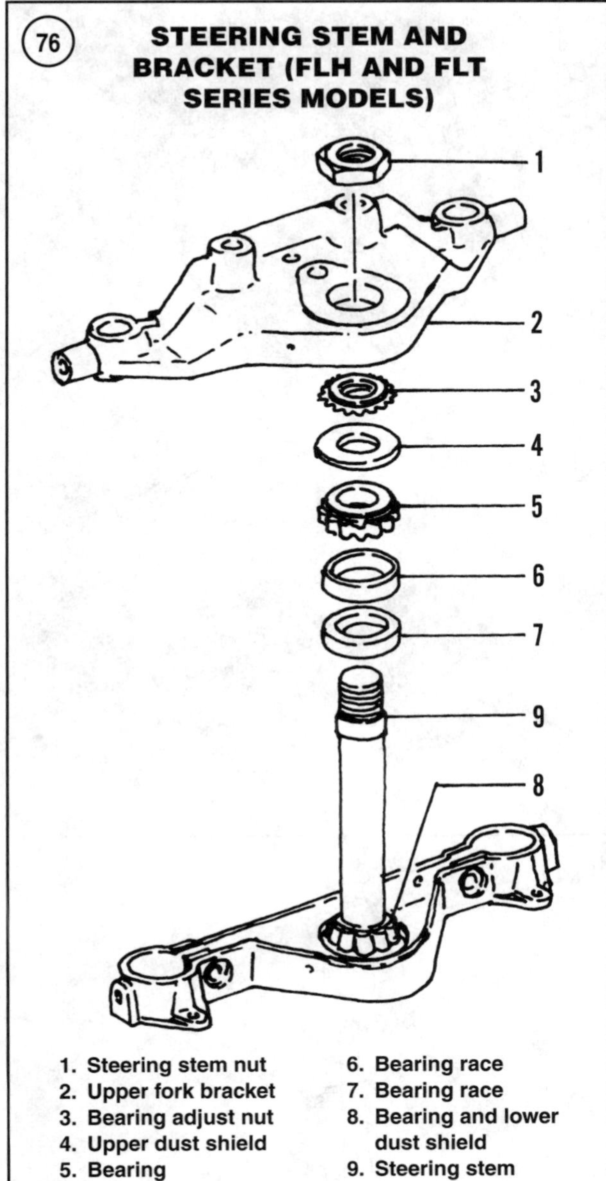

14. Remove the bearing from the upper bearing race in the steering head.
15. Inspect the steering stem assembly as described in this section.

Installation

1. Thoroughly pack both bearings with bearing grease.
2. Make sure the steering head and stem races are properly seated.
3. Apply a light coat of grease to the steering head races.
4. Install the lower dust shield onto the lower bearing on the steering stem.
5. Install the steering stem into the steering head and hold it firmly in place.
6. Install the upper bearing over the steering stem and seat it into the upper race.
7. Install the upper dust shield.
8. Install the bearing adjust nut and tighten to remove all bearing play.
9. Install the upper bracket over the fork stem.
10. Install the main circuit board and align it with the mounting bracket.

CAUTION
Do not overtighten the fork stem nut in Step 11, or the bearings and races can be damaged.

11. Install the steering stem nut and tighten it to 35-40 ft.-lb. (47-54 N•m).
12. On models so equipped, bend the lockwasher tab against one flat on the nut. If necessary, tighten the nut to align it with the lockwasher.
13. On 1991-1998 models, pack the steering head with the same type of bearing grease originally used to pack the bearing during disassembly.
14. Connect the electrical connectors from the main circuit board.
15. Install the brake line bracket onto the lower steering stem bracket.
16. Install the front fork as described in this chapter.
17. On models with the air control system, install the air control system from the upper fork bracket as described in this chapter.
18. Install the handlebar assembly as described in this chapter.
19. Install the fuel tank as described in Chapter Nine.
20. On FLTC series models, install the instrument panel and handlebar.
21. On 1986-1998 FLHTC series models, install the light bar and outer fairing as described in Chapter Fifteen.
22. Install the front wheel as described in Chapter Ten.
23. Adjust steering play as described in this chapter.

Inspection (All Models)

The bearing outer races are pressed into the steering head. Do not remove them unless they are going to be replaced.

1. Wipe the bearing races with a solvent-soaked rag and dry them with compressed air or a lint-free cloth. Check the races in the steering head (**Figure 77**) for pitting,

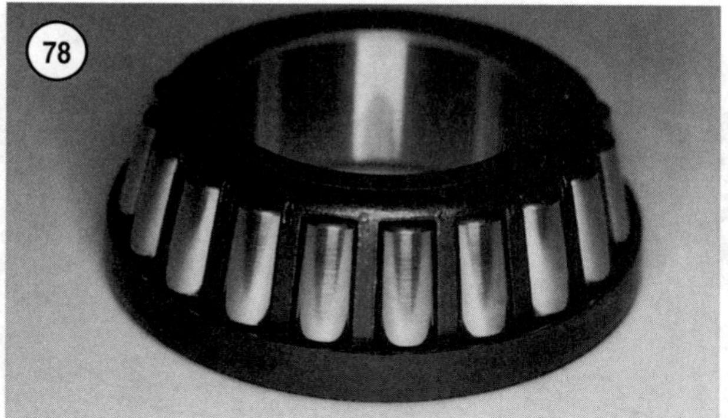

scratches, galling or excessive wear. If any of these conditions exist, replace the races as described in this chapter. If the races are in good condition, wipe each race with grease.

2. Clean the bearings in solvent to remove all of the old grease. Blow the bearing dry with compressed air without allowing the air jet to spin the bearing. Do not remove the lower bearing from the fork stem unless it is to be replaced. Clean the bearing while it is installed in the steering stem.

3. After the bearings are dry, hold the inner race with one hand and turn the outer race with the other hand. Turn the bearing slowly. The bearing should turn smoothly with no roughness. Visually check the bearing (**Figure 78**) for pitting, scratches or visible damage. If the bearings are worn, check the dust covers for wear, damage or improper bearing lubrication. Replace the bearing if necessary. If a bearing is going to be reused, pack it with grease and wrap it with wax paper or some other lint-free material until it is reinstalled. Do not store the bearings for any length of time without lubricating them to prevent rust.

4. Check the steering stem/lower bracket for cracks or damage. Check the threads at the top of the stem for damage. Check the steering stem bolt or nut for damage. Thread it into the steering stem. Make sure the bolt or nut threads easily with no roughness.

5. Replace all worn or damaged parts. Replace bearing races as described in this chapter.

6. Replace the lower steering stem bearing (**Figure 79**) and the dust shield as described in this chapter.

7. Check for broken welds on the frame around the steering head. If any are found, have them repaired by a competent frame shop or welding service familiar with motorcycle frame repair.

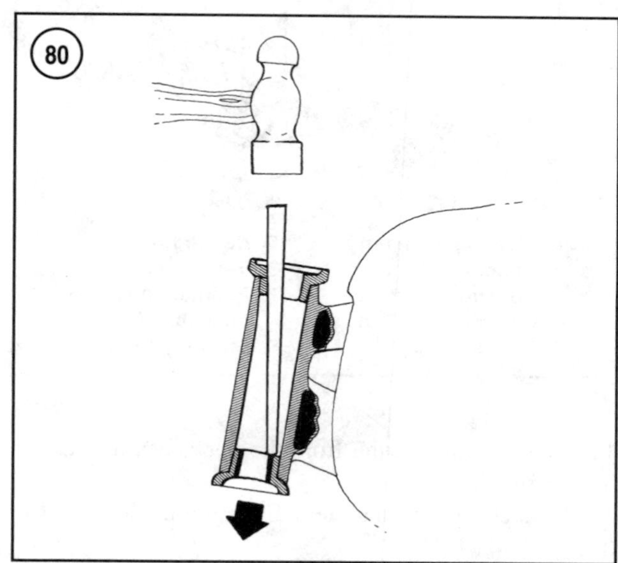

STEERING HEAD BEARING RACE REPLACEMENT

The upper and lower bearing outer races are pressed into the frame. Do not remove the bearing races unless re-

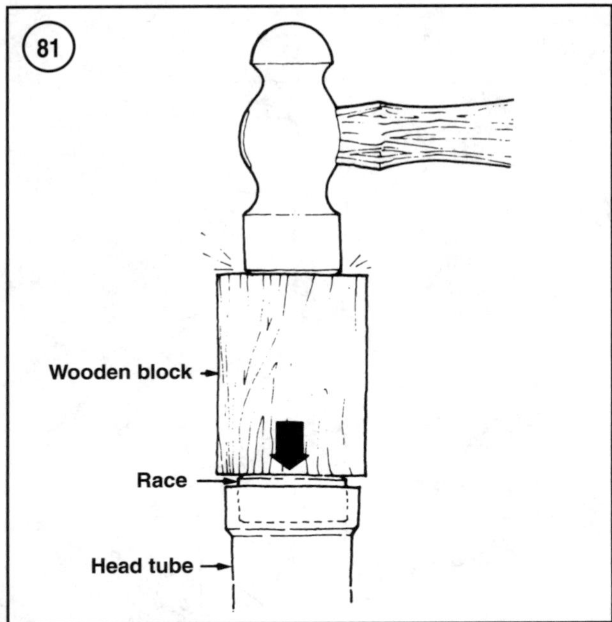

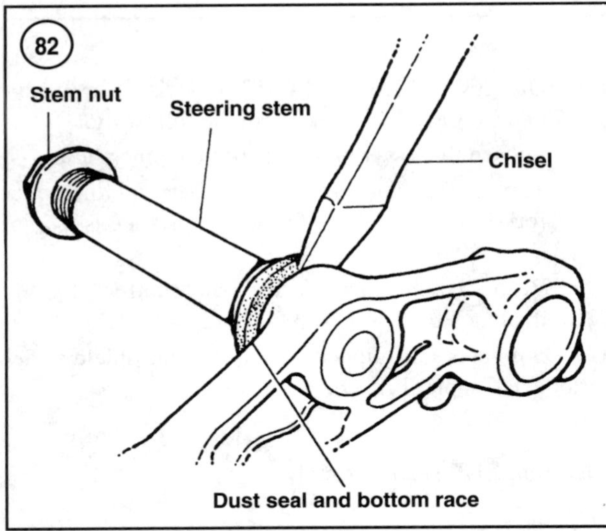

placement is necessary. If they are removed, replace both the outer race and bearing at the same time. Never reinstall an outer race that has been removed as it is no longer true and will damage the bearing.

1. Remove the steering stem as described in this chapter.
2. To remove a race, insert an aluminum or brass rod into the steering head and carefully tap the race out from the inside (**Figure 80**). Tap all around the race so neither the race nor the steering head is bent.
3. Clean the steering head with solvent and dry it thoroughly.

4A. Install the bearing races with the steering head bearing race installer tool (JIMS part No. 1725) following the manufacturer's instructions.

4B. If the special tools are not available, install the bearing races as follows:

   a. Clean the race thoroughly before installing it.
   b. Align the upper race with the frame steering head and tap it slowly and squarely in place (**Figure 81**). Do not contact the bearing race surfaces. Drive the race into the steering head until it bottoms on the bore shoulder.
   c. Repeat substeps a-c to install the lower race into the steering head.

5. Apply bearing grease to the face of each race.

Steering Stem Lower Bearing Replacement

Do not remove the steering stem lower bearing and lower dust seal unless they are going to be replaced. The lower bearing can be difficult to remove. If the lower bearing cannot be removed as described in this procedure, refer the service to a Harley-Davidson dealership.

Never reinstall a lower bearing that has been removed. It is no longer true and will damage the bearing assembly.

1. Install the steering stem bolt or nut onto the top of the steering stem to protect the threads.
2. Loosen the lower bearing from the shoulder at the base of the steering stem with a chisel as shown in **Figure 82**. Slide the lower bearing and lower dust seal off the steering stem.
3. Clean the steering stem with solvent and dry it thoroughly.
4. Position the new lower dust seal with the flange side facing up.
5. Slide a *new* lower dust seal and the lower bearing onto the steering stem until the bearing stops on the raised shoulder.
6. Align the lower bearing with the machined shoulder on the steering stem. Press or drive the lower bearing onto the steering stem until it bottoms (**Figure 83**).

11

STEERING PLAY ADJUSTMENT

If aftermarket accessories have been installed on the steering assembly, they must be removed before attempting to adjust the steering play.

FXR and FX Series Models

1. Use a floor jack centered under the frame. Support the motorcycle with both the front and rear wheels the same

distance off the ground. If necessary, place a wooden block(s) under the rear wheel until the motorcycle is level.

2. On models so equipped, remove the windshield as described in Chapter Fifteen.

3. If any control cable is routed so that it pulls the front end one way or the other, disconnect it.

4. Loosen the lower bracket pinch bolts.

5. Place a piece of masking tape transversely across the leading edge of the front fender.

6. Swing the handlebar so that the front wheel faces straight ahead.

7. Place a pointer on a stand so that the tip points to the center of the fender when the wheel is facing straight ahead.

8. Lightly push the fender toward the right side until the front end starts to turn by itself. Mark this point on the piece of tape.

9. Repeat Step 8 for the left side.

10. Measure the distance between the two marks on the tape. For proper bearing adjustment, the distance should be 1-2 in. (25.4-50.8 mm). If the distance is incorrect, perform Step 11.

NOTE
On FXWG models, adjustment is made by loosening or tightening the fork stem nut or bolt.

NOTE
If the adjustment is less than 1 in. (25.4 mm), slightly tighten the nut, bolt or bearing seat. Loosen the nut, bolt or bearing seat if the adjustment is more than 2 in. (50.8 mm).

11A. On 1984-1987 FXR (except 1987 FXLR, FXRS-SP, FXEF and FXSB) models, refer to **Figure 72** and perform the following:

a. Loosen the upper fork bracket pinch bolt and the lower bracket fork tube pinch bolts.
b. Loosen or tighten the fork stem nut until the fall-away distance is 1-2 in. (25.4-50.8 mm).
c. Recheck adjustment. Then, when correct, tighten the pinch bolts to 21-27 ft.-lb. (28-37 N•m).

11B. On 1987 FXLR and FXRS-SP and all 1988-1998 FXR models, refer to **Figure 73** and perform the following:

a. Loosen the upper fork bracket pinch bolt and the lower bracket fork tube pinch bolts.
b. Loosen or tighten the fork stem bolt until the fall-away distance is 1-2 in. (25.4-50.8 mm).
c. Recheck adjustment. Then, when correct, tighten the pinch bolts to 25-30 ft.-lb. (34-41 N•m).

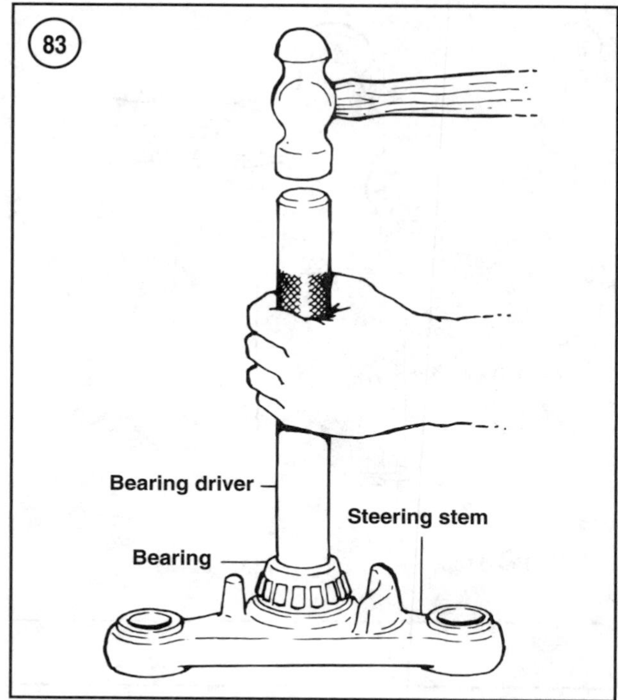

11C. On FXWG, FXSB and FXEF models, refer to **Figure 74** and **Figure 75** and perform the following:

a. Loosen the lower bracket fork tube pinch bolts.
b. Turn the bearing seat located underneath the upper fork bracket until the fall-away distance is 1-2 in. (25.4-50.8 mm).
c. Recheck adjustment. Then, when correct, tighten the pinch bolts to 25-30 ft.-lb. (34-41 N•m).

12. On models so equipped, install the windshield as described in Chapter Fifteen.

FLH and FLT Series Models

1. Use a floor jack centered under the frame. Support the motorcycle with both the front and rear wheels the same distance off the ground. If necessary, place a wooden block(s) under the rear wheel until the motorcycle is level.

2. Remove the windshield (if so equipped) and all other accessory weight from the handlebar and front forks that could affect this adjustment.

3. If any control cable is routed so that it pulls the front end one way or the other, disconnect it.

4. Turn the wheel to the left as far as it will go and then let it go. If the steering adjustment is correct, the front wheel will swing from left to right three times and then stop near the center or straight-ahead position. If the adjustment is

incorrect (the number of swings past center is fewer or more than three times), perform the following.

5. Loosen the lower bracket pinch bolts.
6. Slide both rubber fork stops a few inches up the respective fork tubes.
7. Straighten the lockwasher tab away from the fork stem nut and loosen the nut.
8. Insert a drift punch into a notch in the bearing adjust nut (**Figure 74**). Tighten the nut to decrease the number of swings or loosen the nut to increase the number of swings.
9. Tighten the lower bracket pinch bolts to the specification in **Table 5**.
10. Tighten the fork stem nut to the specification in **Table 5**. Bend the lockwasher tab against one flat on the nut; tighten the nut, if required, to align the nut flat and lockwasher tab.
11. Recheck the bearing adjustment.
12. When the adjustment is correct, reposition the rubber fork stops.
13. Reinstall all parts previously removed.

Table 1 FRONT FORK OIL CAPACITY

Model and year	Oil Change oz.	Oil Change cc	Rebuild oz.	Rebuild cc
FXR				
1984-1987 FXR and FXRS	6.25	184.8	7.0	206.9
1984-1987 FXRD and FXRT	7.0	206.9	7.75	229.2
1987-1994 FXLR	9.2	272	10.2	300.9
1988-1994 FXR and FXRS	9.2	272	10.2	300.9
1988-1994 FXRT and FXRS-SP and FXRS-Con	10.5	310.5	11.5	339.2
1999 FXR2 and FXR3	9.2	272	10.2	300.9
FXWG	10.2	300.9	11.2	330.4
FXSB	7.5	221.8	6.75	199.6
FXEF	5.0	147.8	6.5	192.2
FLT and FLH series models	7.75	229.2	8.5	251.3

11

Table 2 FRONT FORK AIR CONTROL (1984-1994 FXR SERIES MODELS)

Vehicle load	Recommended air pressure psi (kPa) Front fork	Accumulator 1984-1987 FXRD and FXRT
Rider weight not exceeding 150 lbs. (68 kg)	4-8 (28-55)	5-30 (34-207)
Each additional 25 lbs. (11 kg), add	2 (14)	
Passenger weight: For each 50 lbs. (23 kg), add	1 (7)	
Maximum pressure	20 (138)	30 (207)

Table 3 FRONT FORK AIR CONTROL (1984-1994 FLH AND FLT SERIES MODELS)

Ride	Amount of antidive	Recommended pressure psi (kPa)
Firm	Stiff	20 (138)
Normal	Normal	15 (103)
Soft	Soft	10 (69)

Table 4 AIR SUSPENSION ADJUSTMENTS (1995-1998 FLH AND FLT SERIES MODELS)

Load	Recommended pressure psi (kPa) Front fork	Rear shock absorber
Rider weight		
Up to 150 lbs. (68 kg), add	–	–
For each additional 25 lbs. (11 kg), add	1 (7)	1 (7)
Passenger weight: For each additional 50 lbs. (23 kg), add	–	1.5 (10)
Luggage weight: For each additional 10 lbs. (4.5 kg), add	1 (7)	3 (21)
Maximum pressure	25 (172)	35 (241)

Table 5 FRONT SUSPENSION TORQUE SPECIFICATIONS

Item	ft.-lb.	in.-lb.	N•m
Fork air control system			
Air tubes banjo bolts			
1984-1994 FXRD, FXRT and FXRS-SP models	25-30	–	34-41
Air accumulator bracket bolts			
1984-1987 FXRD and FXRT models	30-35	–	41-47
Antidive solenoid housing bolts			
1984-1987 FXRD and FXRT models	–	155-190	17-21
Air tubes flange nuts			
1988-1994 FXRT and FXRS-SP	17	–	23
Antidive switch bolts			
1986-1996 FLH and FLT series models	25-30	–	34-41
1986-1996 FLHT and FLHTC models	25-30	–	34-41
Air tube assembly hex bolts			
1997-1998 FLH and FLT series models	–	97-142	11-16
Antidive solenoid banjo bolts	–	97-124	11-14
Fork tube pinch bolts			
FXR series models			
1984-1987 FXR, FXRS, FXRD and FXRT			
Upper	21-27	–	28-37
Lower	30-35	–	41-47
1987 FXLR, FXRS and 1988-1992 FXR			
Upper and lower	25-30	–	34-41
1993-1994 FXR, 1999 FXR2 and FXR3			
Upper and lower	30-35	–	41-47
FXWG, FXSB and FXEF	25-30	–	34-41
FLH and FLT series models			
1984-1990	25	–	34
1991-1998	40	–	54
Fork tube plug (FLH and FLT series models)	50-55	–	68-75
Fork stem and bracket			
FXR series models			
Fork stem nut or bolt	See text		
Upper bracket-to-fork stem pinch bolt			
1984-1987 FXR, FXRS, FXRD and FXRT	21-27	–	28-37
1987 FXLR, FXRS and 1988-1992 FXR	25-30	–	34-41
1993-1994 FXR	30-35	–	41-47
FXWG, FXR2 and FXR3			
Fork stem nut	35-40	–	47-54
Brake hose-to-lower steering stem bracket	–	133	15
FXSB and FXEF			
Fork stem nut	See text		
Upper bracket-to-fork stem pinch bolt	20-25	–	27-34
FLH and FLT series models			
Fork stem nut	35-40	–	47-54
Steering stem nut			
FLH and FLT	35-40	–	41-54

CHAPTER TWELVE

REAR SUSPENSION

This chapter includes repair and replacement procedures for the rear suspension components. **Tables 1-5** are located at the end of this chapter.

WARNING
All nuts and bolts used on the rear suspension must be replaced with the same type of parts. Do not use a replacement part of lesser quality or substitute design because it might affect the performance of the rear suspension or fail and lead to loss of control of the motorcycle. The torque specifications listed in ***Table 5*** *must be used during installation to ensure proper retention of these components.*

SHOCK ABSORBERS

Removal/Installation

When servicing the rear shock absorbers, remove one shock at a time. If it is necessary to remove both shocks, support the motorcycle with the rear wheel off the ground on a suitable floor jack.

1. Support the motorcycle on a swing arm stand with the rear wheel off the ground a minimum of four inches.
2. Slide a wooden block between the rear tire and floor so that it just touches the tire.
3. On models so equipped, remove the saddlebags as described in Chapter Fifteen.
4. If necessary, remove the muffler to access the bottom shock mounting bolt. Refer to Chapter Eight.

NOTE
A rear shock absorber system is a split system used on 1985 and later FXRT models. The shock absorber installed on the left side is a nonadjustable hydraulically damped shock. The right side is equipped with an air shock similar to the air shocks used on some FLH and FLT models.

5. On air shocks, bleed the air shock of all air pressure. Then disconnect the air line at the compression fitting.

NOTE
Note the location of the washers used on each of the shock absorber bolts or studs so they can be reinstalled in the original positions.

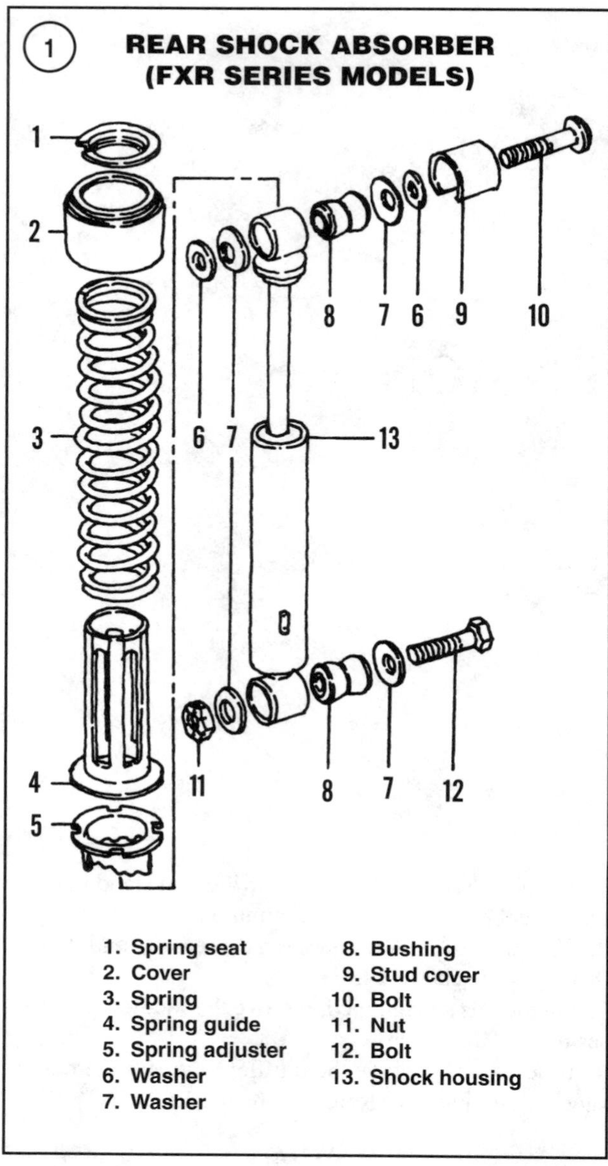

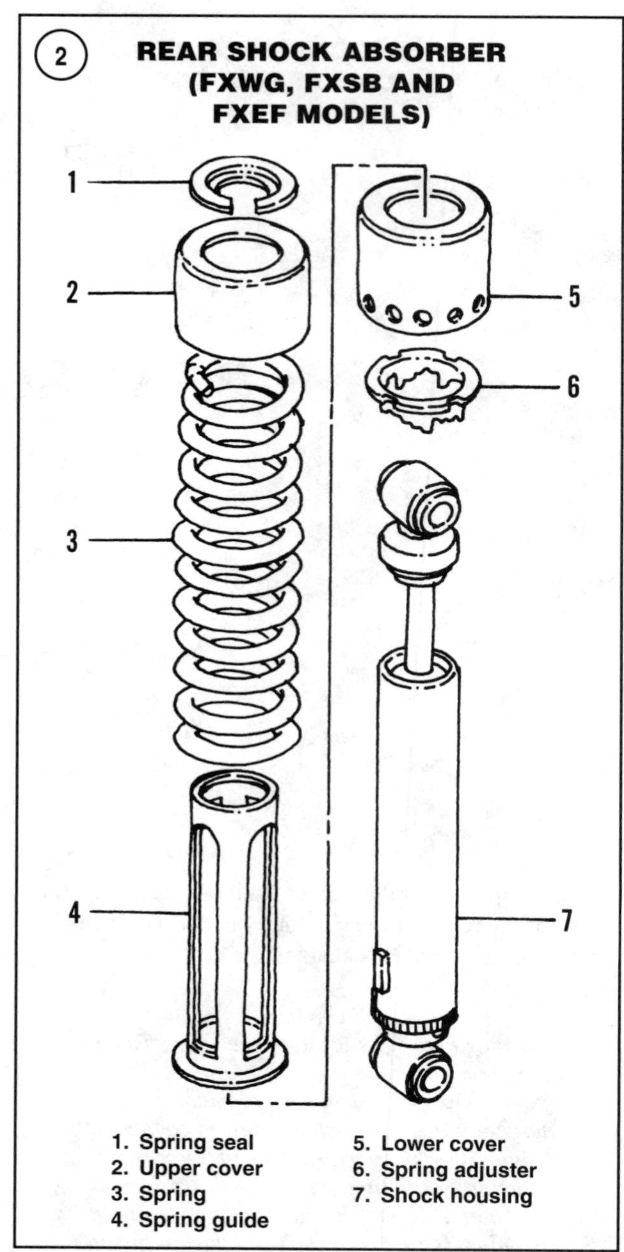

6. Remove the upper and lower bolts or nuts.
7. Pull the shock off of the frame and swing arm. Remove it.
8. Inspect the shock absorbers and the mounting fasteners as described in this chapter.
9. Install by reversing these removal steps while noting the following:
   a. Apply a medium-strength threadlocking compound to the shock mounting bolt or stud threads.
   b. Tighten the upper and lower shock fasteners to the specification in **Table 5**.
   c. On air shock models, adjust the shock absorber air pressure as described in this chapter.
   d. Lower the motorcycle and test ride it to make sure the rear suspension is working properly.

Disassembly/Inspection/Assembly (Hydraulically Dampened Shocks)

The damper unit cannot be serviced. All remaining components can be replaced. Check with a Harley-Davidson dealership for parts availability prior to disassembling the shock absorber.

(3) REAR SHOCK ABSORBER (1999 FXR2 AND FXR3 MODELS)

1. Bolt
2. Lockwasher
3. Washer
4. Spacer
5. Bushing
6. Stud (shock mount)
7. Shock absorber
8. Bushing
9. Bolt
10. Acorn nut
11. Preload adjust collar
12. Retaining clip
13. Spring guide
14. Spring
15. Lower retainer
16. Snap ring

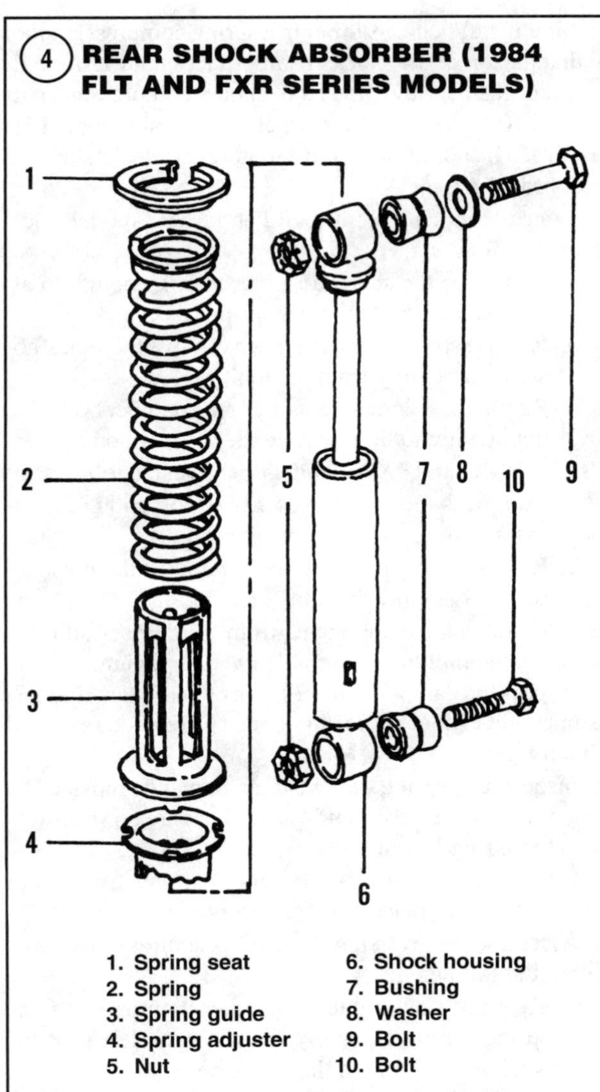

(4) REAR SHOCK ABSORBER (1984 FLT AND FXR SERIES MODELS)

1. Spring seat
2. Spring
3. Spring guide
4. Spring adjuster
5. Nut
6. Shock housing
7. Bushing
8. Washer
9. Bolt
10. Bolt

Refer to **Figures 1-4**.

1. Remove the shock absorber as described in this chapter.

2. Check the shock fastener threads for stripping, cross-threading or deposit buildup. If necessary, use a tap or die to true up the threads and to remove any deposits.

3. Check the washers for cupping, deformation, cracks or other damage. Replace the washers with the same size and thickness, if necessary.

WARNING

Do not attempt to remove the shock springs without the proper spring compression tools.

4. Mount the shock absorber in a spring compression tool so that the top of the shock absorber faces up. **Figure 5** illustrates the Harley-Davidson shock compressor (part No. 97010-52A). An aftermarket compression tool (**Figure 6**) can be purchased from a motorcycle dealership and mail-order houses.

5A. On all models except FXR2 and FXR3 models, perform the following:

a. Compress the shock absorber spring enough to allow removal of the upper spring seat.
b. Release spring pressure. Then remove the shock absorber assembly from the tool.
c. Remove the components from the damper body. Do not attempt to disassemble the damper body.

5B. On FXR2 and FXR3 models, perform the following:

a. Compress the shock absorber spring enough to allow removal of the lower snap ring.
b. Release spring pressure. Then remove the shock absorber assembly from the tool.
c. Remove the components from the damper unit. Do not attempt to disassemble the damper unit.

6. Inspect the damper unit for leaks or shaft damage. The damper unit cannot be rebuilt; it must be replaced as a unit if faulty.
7. Inspect the spring for wear or damage; replace the spring if it is cracked or deformed. There are no specifications for spring length.
8. Check all components for abnormal wear, cracks or other damage. Replace damaged parts as required.
9. Assemble by reversing these disassembly steps while noting the following:

a. To reduce spring tension when compressing the spring during assembly, set the cam detent to the weakest position on the shock body.
b. Install all parts in the reverse order of removal.
c. After the spring has been installed, make sure the spring seat or snap ring engages the damper unit groove and is correctly seated. Then slowly release tension on the tool and allow the parts to seat together.
d. Before removing the tool, check the fit of the parts, especially at the top of the shock.

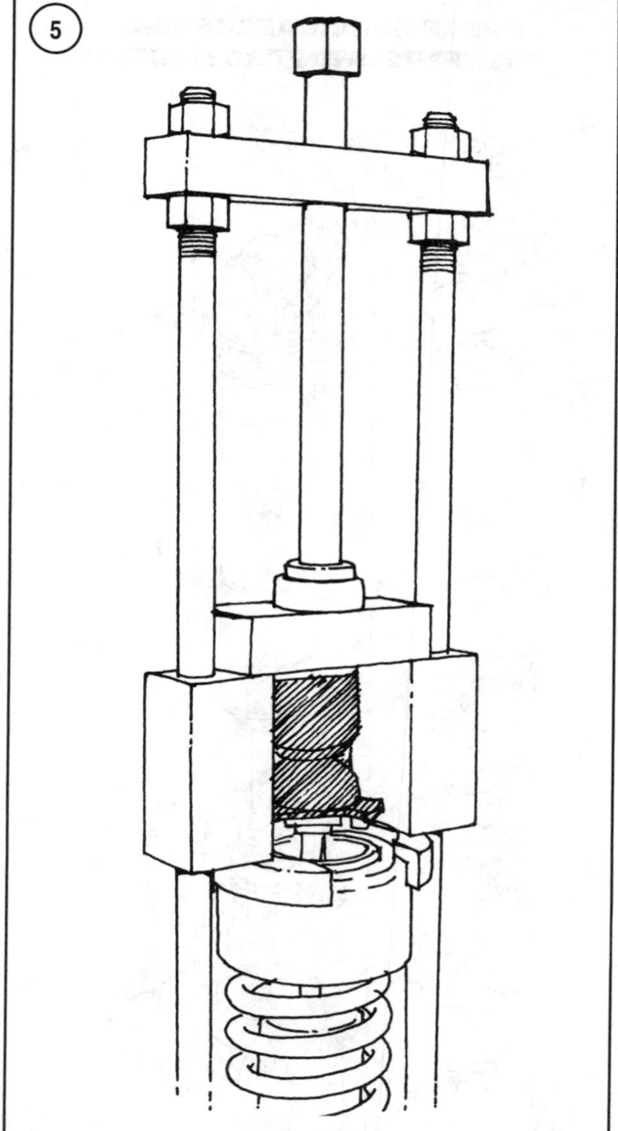

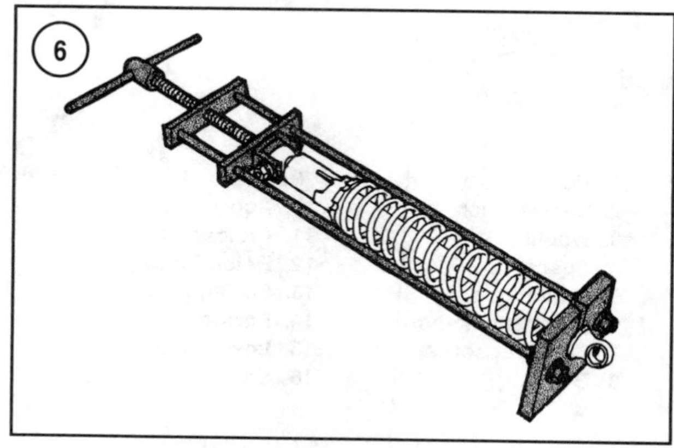

Shock Bushing Replacement

On models so equipped, the shock bushings should be replaced as a set when they become worn or damaged.

1. Before removing the bushings from the shock absorbers, purchase new bushings ahead of time.
2. Support the shock absorber in a press and press the bushing out of the eyelet.

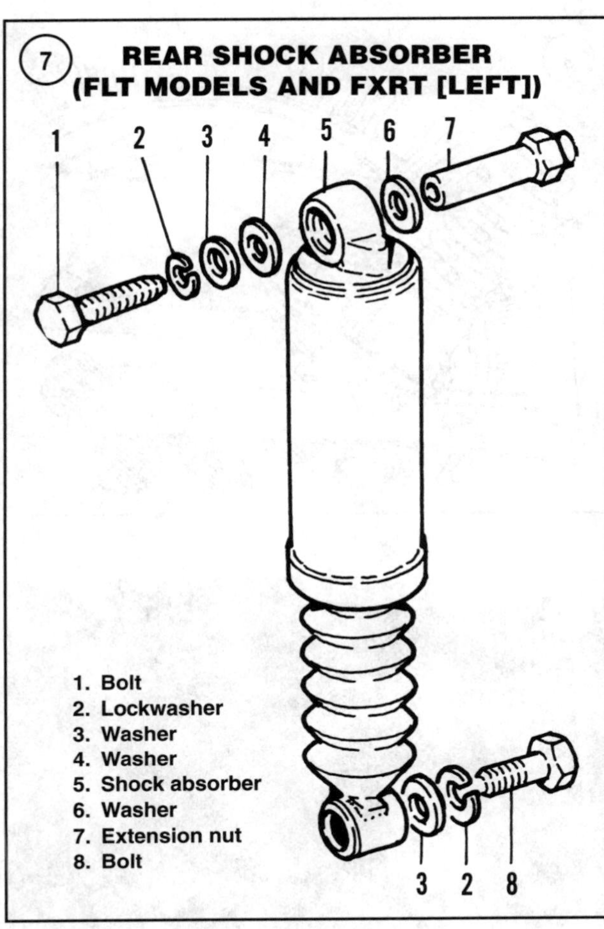

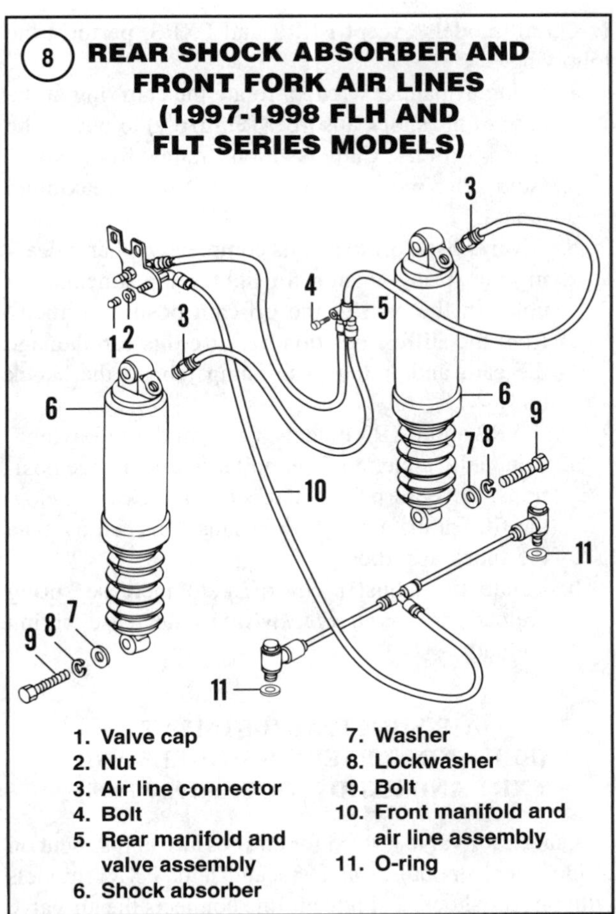

12

3. Clean the eyelet thoroughly before installing the new bushing.
4. Press the new bushing into the shock eyelet.
5. Repeat for each bushing.

Inspection (Air Shocks)

The shock absorbers are not serviceable (**Figure 7** and **Figure 8**). The only replacement parts available are the mounting hardware.

1. Visually inspect the shock for leaks or shaft damage. Check the rubber boot for deterioration, tears or other damage. If necessary, replace the shock absorber.
2. Check the shock fastener threads for stripping, cross-threading or deposit buildup. If necessary, use a tap or die to true the threads and to remove any deposits.
3. If the air fittings on the shocks were removed, or if they appear to be leaking, clean the fitting threads thoroughly to remove all sealant residue. Apply Loctite Pipe Sealant with Teflon to the fitting threads. Then install the fitting into the shock body and tighten securely.

SPRING PRELOAD ADJUSTMENT (NONAIR TYPE)

NOTE
A split rear shock absorber system is used on 1985 and later FXRT models. The shock absorber installed on the left side is a nonadjustable hydraulically damped shock. The right side is equipped with an air shock similar to the air shocks used on some FLH and FLT models.

The shock absorber spring preload can be adjusted to compensate for the weight the motorcycle is to carry.

WARNING
The cam ring must be set to the same setting on both sides, or it will result in an unsafe riding condition.

1. On all models except FXR2 and FXR3, perform the following:
   a. Using a spanner wrench, rotate the cam ring at the base of the shock absorber (**Figure 9**) to one of the five positions. Cam positions range from No. 1 (solo rider with no luggage) to No. 5 (maximum loads).
   b. Always back off the cams completely when releasing the spring tension for lighter adjustments. Do not turn the cam to the off-cam position directly from the stiffest position because this can damage the cam and/or the positioning tab on the shock body.
2. On FXR2 and FXR3 models, perform the following:
   a. Rotate the upper adjuster collar to one of five positions. Never turn the collar *counterclockwise* below the fifth adjustment mark because this can damage the shock absorber.
   b. Rotate the adjuster *clockwise* to increase spring preload or *counterclockwise* to decrease spring preload.

AIR SHOCK ADJUSTMENT (FLH AND FLT SERIES MODELS AND FXRT AND FXRD MODELS 1984-1998)

A single air valve is used for air pressure adjustment on all air shock models. On 1985 and later FXRT models with one air shock, a single air line connects the air valve to the shock body. On all other models, separate air lines leading out from the air valve connect to the separate shock absorbers.

NOTE
*The air chambers in the rear shock are small and fill rapidly. Do not use compressed air. Only use a small hand-held or foot-operated air pump. The maximum air pressure specification listed in **Tables 1-4** should not be exceeded, or damage to the air shock or air lines might occur.*

1. Locate and remove the air valve cap:
   a. On 1984 FXRT models, the air valve is located under the seat.
   b. On 1985-1992 FXRT and FXRD models, the air valve is located under the right saddlebag.
   c. On 1984-1996 FLH and FLT series models, the air valve is located on the left side cover.
   d. On 1997-1998 FLH and FLT series models, the air valve (**Figure 10**) is located under the right saddlebag.
2. Place the motorcycle on the jiffy stand.
3. On models so equipped, remove the saddlebag as described in Chapter Fifteen.
4. Remove the air valve cap.
5. Use a no-loss air pressure gauge. Refer to the recommended air pressure in **Tables 1-4**.
6. Increase or decrease air pressure to achieve the desired ride and control.
7. On 1997-1998 FLH and FLT series models, check and, if necessary, adjust the air pressure in the front fork at the same time.
8. Reinstall the air valve cap.

SWING ARM (FXR, FLH AND FLT SERIES MODELS EXCEPT FXWG, FXEF AND FXSB)

In time, the cleavebloc bushings installed in the swing arm will wear and require replacement. Worn or damaged bushings can greatly affect handling performance, and if worn parts are not replaced, they can produce erratic and

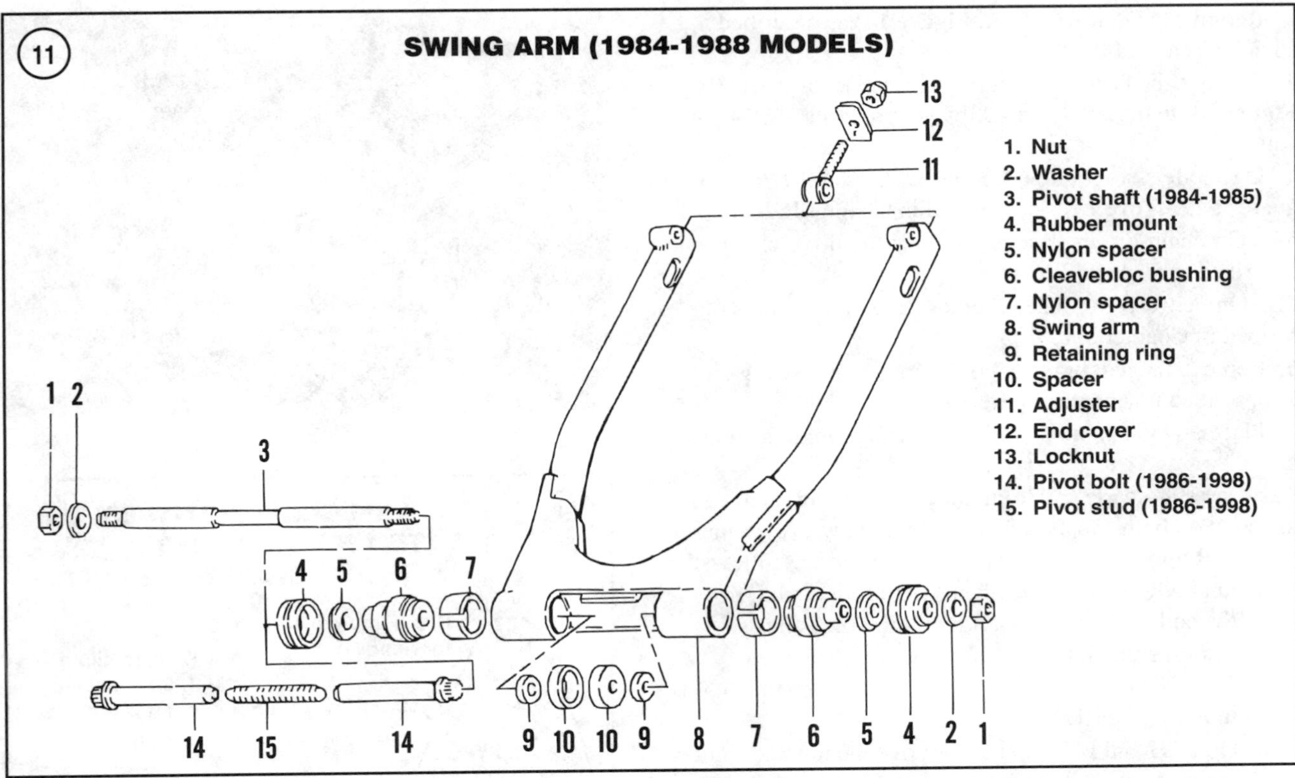

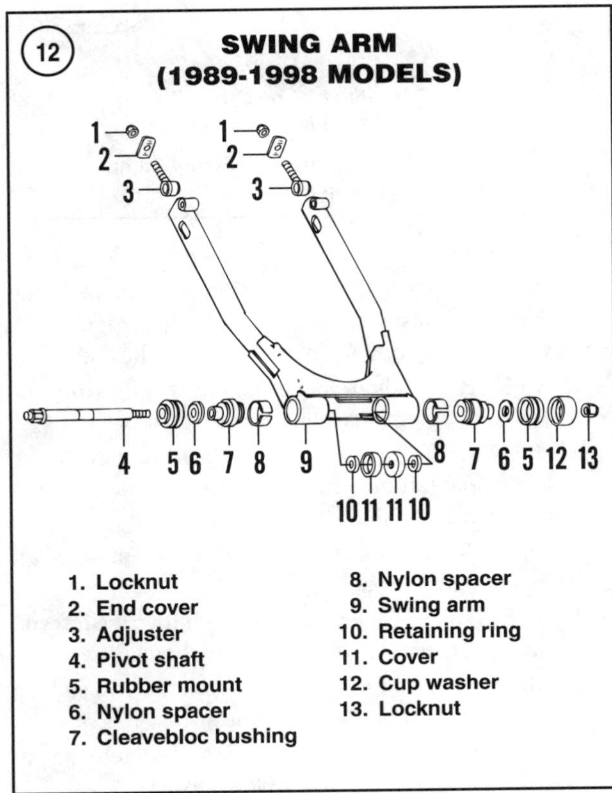

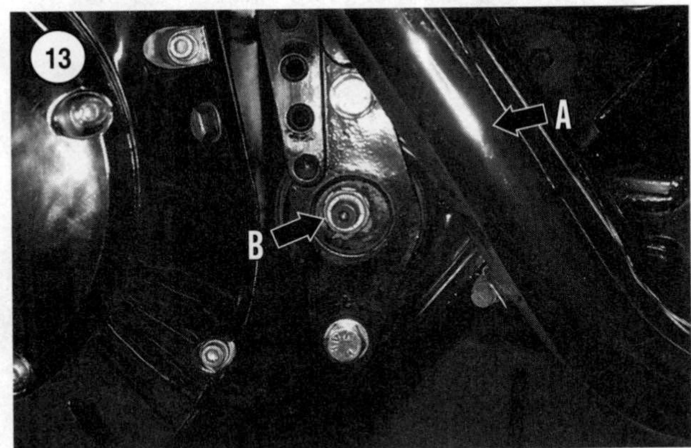

dangerous handling. Common symptoms are wheel hop, pulling to one side during acceleration and pulling to the other side during braking.

Removal

Refer to **Figure 11** and **Figure 12**.

1. Remove the exhaust system (A, **Figure 13**) as described in Chapter Eight.

2. Remove the rear wheel (A, **Figure 14**) as described in Chapter Ten.
3. Remove the fasteners securing the shock absorbers (B, **Figure 14**) to the swing arm. Move them up and out of the way.
4. On models so equipped, remove the saddlebags and guards (C, **Figure 14**) as described in Chapter Fifteen.
5A. On chain-driven models, remove the drive chain as described in Chapter Ten.
5B. On belt-driven models, remove the drive belt as described in Chapter Ten.
6. Remove the rear brake caliper from the rear swing arm as described in Chapter Thirteen.
7. Place a wooden block under the swing arm to support it.
8A. On 1984-early 1986 models, the pivot shaft is threaded on both ends; each end is secured with a washer and nut. Remove the pivot shaft and swing arm as follows:
   a. On FXR series models, remove the cover plug from the end of the pivot shaft mounting brackets.
   b. Remove the right pivot shaft nut and spacer.
   c. On FXR series models, remove the pivot shaft mounting brackets.
   d. On FLH and FLT models, remove the left and right passenger footpeg mounting brackets.
   e. Use an aluminum or brass rod and tap the pivot shaft out of the swing arm.
   f. Remove the pivot shaft and the swing arm. Note the location of the rubber and nylon washers.

8B. On late 1986-1988 models, a dual pivot shaft assembly is used. The left and right pivot shafts screw onto a center stud (**Figure 11**). Remove the swing arm and pivot shafts as follows:
   a. On FXR series models, remove the cover plug from the end of the pivot shaft mounting brackets. On late 1987 and 1988 models, remove the spring clips installed inside the mounting bracket access hole on both sides (**Figure 15**).
   b. Hold the left pivot bolt with a wrench and loosen the right pivot bolt.
   c. On FXR series models, remove the pivot shaft mounting brackets.
   d. On FLH and FLT series models, remove the left and right passenger footpeg mounting brackets.
   e. Select the properly sized outer diameter aluminum or brass rod. Insert the rod through the swing arm from the right side. Center it against the center stud and carefully tap the center stud and left pivot shaft out of the swing arm.
   f. Remove the swing arm assembly from the frame. Note the positions of the rubber and nylon washers.

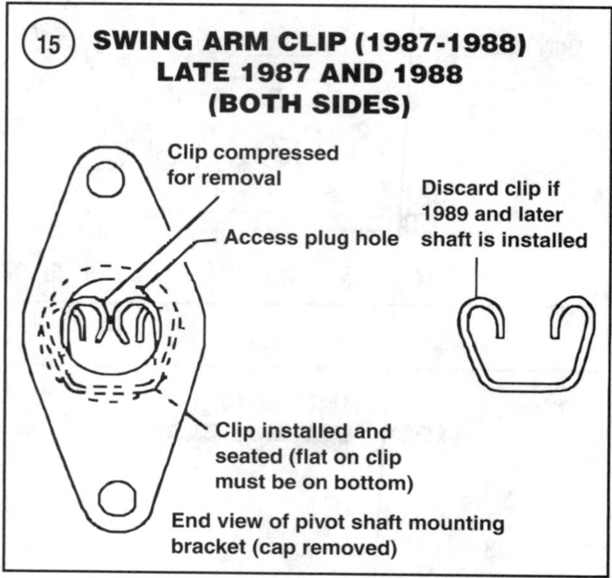

8C. On 1989-1998 models, the swing arm pivots on the pivot shaft that is installed from the right side (**Figure 12**). Remove the swing arm and pivot shaft as follows:
   a. On FXR models, remove the cover plug from the end of the pivot shaft mounting brackets.
   b. Hold the right pivot shaft nut with a wrench and loosen the left nut (B, **Figure 13**). Remove the nut and the cup washer.
   c. On FXR series models, remove the pivot shaft mounting brackets.
   d. On FLH and FLT series models, remove the left and right passenger footpeg mounting brackets.
   e. Align the end of an aluminum or brass rod and tap the pivot shaft out of the swing arm.
   f. Remove the pivot shaft and swing arm. Note the positions of the rubber and nylon washers.

16

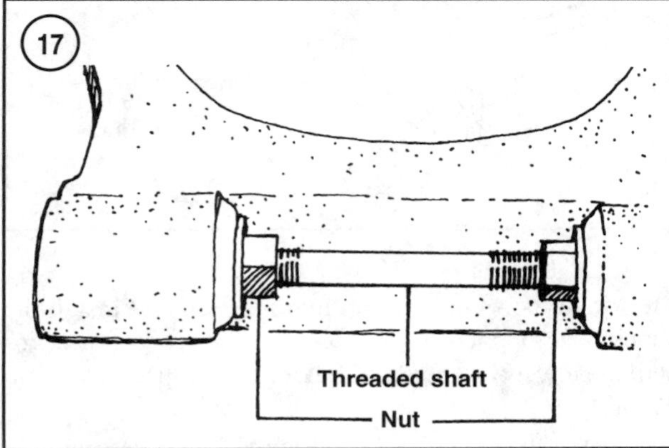

17

9. Inspect the swing arm and pivot shaft assembly as described in this chapter.

Installation

1. Apply an antiseize lubricant or an appropriate grease to the pivot shaft.
2. Correctly position the drive chain or drive belt over the drive sprocket before installing the swing arm. Leave the drive chain open; connect it later.
3. Install the swing arm at the back of the transmission. If the swing arm will not fit into the transmission, it will be necessary to spread the bushings apart as follows:
   a. Remove the swing arm from the transmission case.
   b. Place the swing arm on a workbench.
   c. Install the bushing spreading tool (JIMS part No. 1707) (**Figure 16**) between the bushings as shown in **Figure 17**.

NOTE

If the special tool is not available, a substitute tool of threaded rod, two large washers and two nuts may be used.

   d. Install the special tool or assemble the threaded rod, nuts and washers between the bushings as shown in **Figure 17**. Then turn the nuts with a wrench to spread the bushings apart approximately 4 9/16 in. (115.9 mm).
   e. Remove the tool and check whether the swing arm fits into the transmission case.
   f. If necessary, repeat this step until the swing arm fits into the transmission case.

4A. On 1984-early 1986 models, install the pivot shaft assembly as follows:
   a. Lay out the pivot shaft assembly in the order shown in **Figure 11**.
   b. Identify the left side of the pivot shaft and slide the left rubber mount (with shoulder facing outward) onto the pivot shaft. Then install the washer and nut onto the pivot shaft; tighten the nut until it bottoms out on the shaft threads.
   c. Slide the nylon washer onto the pivot shaft and seat it against the rubber mount so that the smaller washer diameter faces inboard.
   d. Wipe the pivot shaft with antiseize lubricant or equivalent.
   e. Install the pivot shaft through the swing arm from the left side.
   f. Install the right-hand nylon washer (small washer diameter facing inward), rubber mount (shoulder facing outward), washer and nut. Tighten the nut finger-tight at this time.

NOTE

If working on a late 1986-1988 model, and the swing arm pivot shaft assembly was replaced with a 1989 or later pivot shaft assembly, perform Step 4C.

4B. On late 1986-1988 models, install the pivot shaft assembly as follows:
   a. Lay out the pivot shaft assembly in the order shown in **Figure 11**.
   b. Install the left pivot shaft onto the center stud.
   c. Coat the pivot shaft and center stud with antiseize lubricant or equivalent.
   d. Slide the left rubber mount (with shoulder facing outward) onto the pivot shaft.
   e. Slide the nylon washer onto the pivot shaft and seat it against the rubber mount so that the small washer diameter faces inboard.
   f. Install the pivot shaft through the swing arm from the left side.
   g. Coat the right pivot shaft with antiseize lubricant or equivalent. Install the right nylon washer (small washer diameter facing inboard) and the right rub-

12

ber mount (shoulder facing outward) onto the pivot shaft.

h. Insert the right pivot shaft through the swing arm and thread it into the center stud finger-tight.

4C. On 1989-1998 models, install the pivot shaft assembly as follows:

a. Lay out the pivot shaft assembly in the order shown in **Figure 12**.
b. Wipe the pivot shaft with antiseize lubricant or equivalent.
c. Slide the right rubber mount (with shoulder facing outward) onto the pivot shaft.
d. Slide the right nylon washer (with small washer diameter facing inward) onto the pivot shaft.
e. Insert the pivot shaft through the swing arm from the right side.
f. Install the left nylon washer (small diameter facing inward), rubber mount (shoulder facing outward) and cup washer onto the pivot shaft. Install the pivot shaft nut and tighten finger-tight.

5. On FLH and FLT series models, install the passenger footpeg mounting bracket. Make sure the roll pin in each bracket engages the hole in the rubber mount.

6. On FXR series models, install the pivot shaft mounting brackets. Make sure roll pin in each bracket engages hole in rubber mount.

7. On 1984-early 1986 models, make sure the flat on the pivot shaft engages the flat on the right rubber mount.

8. If the passenger footpegs were removed, position the footpegs so that they fold at a 45° angle. Tighten the mounting nuts to 20-25 ft.-lb. (27-34 N•m).

9A. On 1984-early 1986 models, hold the left pivot shaft nut with a wrench and tighten the right nut to 45 ft.-lb. (61 N•m).

NOTE

*If a 1989 or later pivot shaft assembly was installed on a late 1986-1988 model (to replace the three-piece pivot shaft assembly), do **not** install the clips into the mounting brackets as described in Step 9B.*

9B. On late 1986-1988 models, hold the left pivot bolt with a wrench and tighten the right pivot bolt to 85 ft.-lb. (115 N•m). After tightening the pivot bolts, install the clip into each mounting bracket so that the flat on the clip faces toward the bottom of the bracket; see **Figure 15**.

9C. On 1989-1998 models, hold the right pivot nut with a wrench and tighten the left nut to 45 ft.-lb. (61 N•m).

10. After tightening the pivot shaft(s), move the swing arm up and down by hand. It should move smoothly with no sign of roughness or tightness.

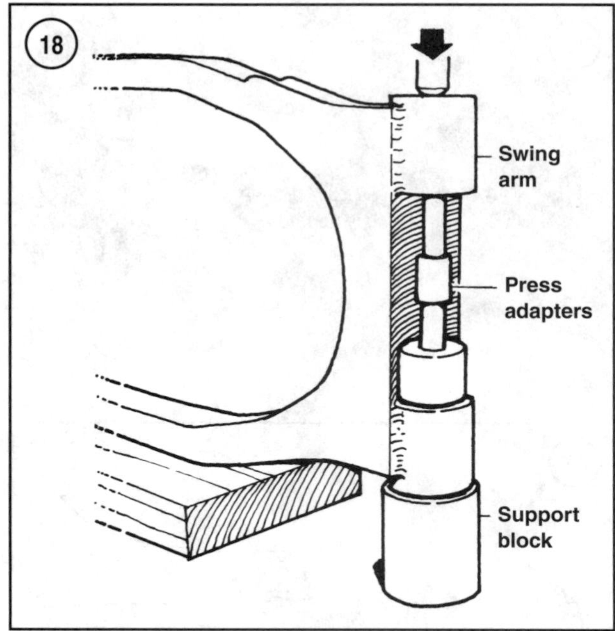

11. Move the swing arm up into position and install the shock absorbers (B, **Figure 14**) onto the swing arm. Install the lower fasteners and tighten to the specification in **Table 5**.

12. Install the rear wheel (A, **Figure 14**) as described in Chapter Ten.

13. Install the rear brake caliper as described in Chapter Thirteen.

14A. On chain-driven models, install the drive chain as described in Chapter Ten.

14B. On belt-driven models, install the drive belt as described in Chapter Ten.

15. On models so equipped, install the saddlebags and guards (C, **Figure 14**) as described in Chapter Fifteen.

16. Install the exhaust system (A, **Figure 13**) as described in Chapter Eight.

NOTE

Check the pivot shaft torque every 5000 miles (8000 km).

Inspection

1. Remove the rubber mounts from the outside of the swing arm. Then remove the left and right nylon washers from the outboard side of each bushing.

2. Wash the swing arm in solvent and dry with compressed air.

3. Inspect the swing arm for cracks or other damage.

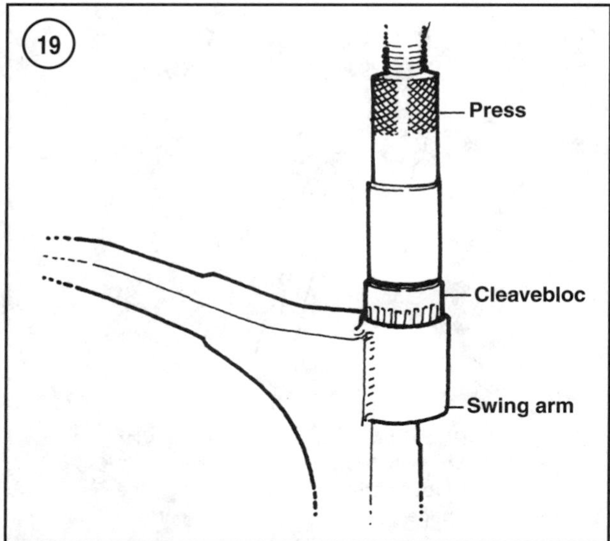

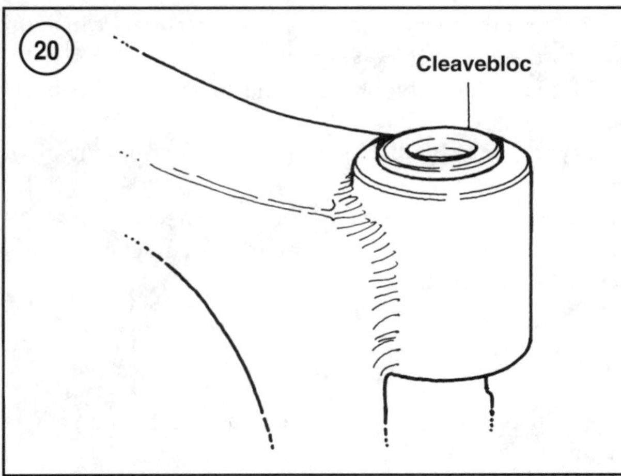

4. Replace the rubber mounts if severely worn or damaged.

5. Inspect the pivot shaft(s) surface for cracks, deep scoring, excessive wear or heat discoloration.

6. Check the pivot shaft and center stud (late 1986-1988 models) threads for stripping, cross-threading or damage.

7. Check the pivot bolts on late 1986-1988 models for deposit buildup in the end of the shafts. These areas should be blown out with compressed air. If necessary, use a tap or die to true up the threads and to remove any deposits.

8. The cleavebloc bushings are filled with silicone. If a bushing is leaking or punctured, replace it as described in this chapter.

9. Replace worn or damaged pivot shaft(s).

NOTE
Replacement parts on some of the older models are no longer available. If necessary, install a late model pivot shaft assembly. Discuss this with a Harley-Davidson dealership for further information.

Bushing Replacement (with Harley-Davidson Tool and Hydraulic Press)

Replacement of the bushing requires a swing arm assembly tool (Harley-Davidson part No. HD-96200-80).

1. Remove the rubber mounts and nylon washers from the outside surface on each side of the swing arms pivot point.
2. Pry out the cover and retaining ring from the inside surface on each side of the swing arms pivot point.

CAUTION
Do not apply pressure against the swing arm without supporting the lower pivot point as described in Step 3. If not properly supported, the swing arm will distort and need to be replaced.

3. Support the swing arm on the press bed and align both pivot points with the press ram. Place the support block (**Figure 18**) under the lower pivot point.
4. Use a long extension and the press collar adapter, or a 1 1/4 in. socket, on the swing arm and on the outside diameter of the bushing (**Figure 18**).
5. Support the swing arm and slowly press out the bushing from the lower pivot point.
6. Remove the swing arm from the press. Repeat Steps 3-5 and remove the bushing from the opposite side of the swing arm.
7. Thoroughly clean the pivot areas with solvent and dry with compressed air.
8. Inspect the pivot areas for burrs or other internal damage. Clean out if necessary.
9. Install the new nylon spacer onto the new bushing. Install these two parts at the same time.
10. Support the swing arm on the press bed and align both pivot points with the press ram.
11. Center the bushing on the swing arm pivot point and start it in by hand.
12. Place the press plug onto the outside diameter of the bushing.
13. Support the swing arm and slowly press the cleavebloc bushing into the pivot area (**Figure 19**).
14. Press the bushing into the swing arm until the outer diameter shoulder is flush with the swing arm outer surface (**Figure 20**).

15. Remove the swing arm from the press. Repeat Steps 9-14 and install the cleavebloc bushing into the opposite side of the swing arm.
16. Install a new cover and retaining ring onto the inside surface on each side of the swing arm pivot point.
17. Install the nylon washer and the rubber mounts onto the outside surface on each side of the swing arm pivot point.

Bushing Replacement (with JIMS Tool)

Replacement of the bushing requires the use of a bushing assembly rear swing arm assembly tool (JIMS part No. 1743). This tool does not require the use of a hydraulic press.

1. Remove the rubber mounts and nylon washers from the outside surface on each side of the swing arm pivot point.
2. Pry out the cover and retaining ring from the inside surface on each side of the swing arm pivot point.
3. Following the manufacturer's instructions, install the tool assembly onto the swing arm.
4. Remove the bushing from each side of the swing arm.
5. Thoroughly clean the pivot areas with solvent and dry with compressed air.
6. Inspect the pivot areas for burrs or other internal damage. Clean out if necessary.
7. Install the new nylon spacer onto the new bushing. Install these two parts at the same time.
8. Following the manufacturer's instructions, install the tool assembly onto the swing arm.
9. Install the cleavebloc bushing into each side of the swing arm until the outer diameter shoulder is flush with the swing arm outer surface (**Figure 20**).
10. Install a new cover and retaining ring onto the inside surface on each side of the swing arm pivot point.
11. Install the nylon washer and the rubber mounts onto the outside surface on each side of the swing arm pivot point.

SWING ARM (FXWG, FXEF AND FXSB)

Removal

Refer to **Figure 21**.

1. Remove the exhaust system as described in Chapter Eight.
2. Remove the rear wheel as described in Chapter Ten.
3. Remove the fasteners securing the shock absorbers to the swing arm. Move them up and out of the way.
4. Remove the drive chain as described in Chapter Ten.

21 **REAR SWING ARM (FXWG, FXEF AND FXSB)**

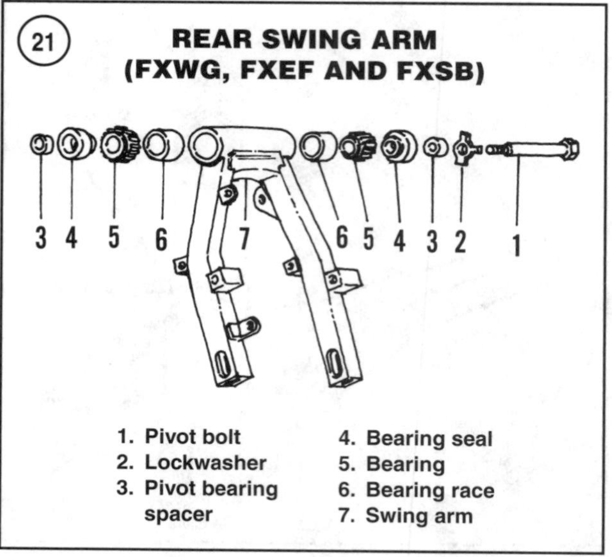

1. Pivot bolt
2. Lockwasher
3. Pivot bearing spacer
4. Bearing seal
5. Bearing
6. Bearing race
7. Swing arm

5. Remove the rear brake caliper from the rear swing arm as described in Chapter Thirteen.
6. Place a wooden block under the swing arm to support it.
7. Pry the pivot bolt lockwasher tab away from the pivot bolt.
8. Loosen and remove the pivot bolt and swing arm.
9. Inspect the swing arm and pivot shaft assembly as described in this section.

Installation

1. Clean the swing arm mounting holes in the frame thoroughly before installing the swing arm.
2. Install a *new* lockwasher onto the pivot bolt.
3. Apply an antiseize lubricant or an appropriate grease to the pivot bolt.
4. Install the left and right spacers into the swing arm.
5. Correctly position the drive chain over the drive sprocket before installing the swing arm. Leave the drive chain open; it can be connected later.
6. Position the swing arm into the frame and install the pivot shaft from the right side. Thread the pivot shaft into the frame so that it supports the swing arm, but do not tighten the pivot shaft.
7. Preload the swing arm bearings as follows:
   a. Attach a spring scale to the rear of the swing arm.
   b. Lift the spring scale and note the reading on the scale as the swing arm is raised past horizontal.
   c. Tighten the pivot shaft to preload bearings 1-2 lbs. (0.45-0.90 kg). For example, if the scale reading is 5 lbs. (2.3 kg) when the swing arm is raised in substep

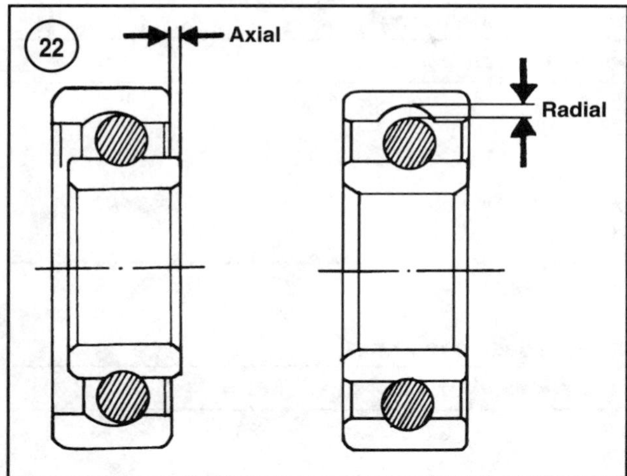

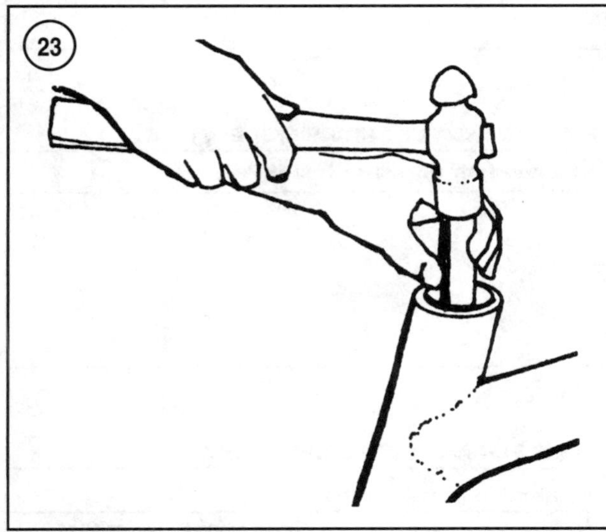

a, tighten the pivot shaft until the spring scale reads 6-7 lbs. (2.7-3.1 kg) when the swing arm is raised past horizontal.

d. When preload is set, bend the lockwasher tab against the pivot bolt head.

8. After preloading the bearings in Step 5, use a grease gun and fill the area between the bearings with bearing grease through the swing arm grease nipple. Wipe off excess grease.
9. Install the shock absorbers as described in this chapter.
10. Install the rear brake caliper as described in Chapter Thirteen.
11. Install the rear wheel and reconnect the drive chain as described in Chapter Ten.
12. Adjust the drive chain as described in Chapter Three.

Inspection

NOTE
Mark each bearing as it is removed from the swing arm to ensure the bearings will be installed in the correct location.

1. Tap a spacer and oil seal out of the swing arm with a long drift. Then remove the bearing from the race. Repeat to remove the opposite spacer, oil seal and bearing.
2. Turn the bearing by hand. The bearing should turn smoothly. Some axial play (end play) is normal, but radial play (side play) should be negligible. See **Figure 22**. If one bearing is damaged, replace both bearings as a set.
3. Inspect the pivot bolt surface for cracks, deep scoring, excessive wear or heat discoloration.
4. Pack the bearings with grease.
5. Place one bearing within the race. Then install the oil seal and the spacer. Repeat for the opposite bearing.

Bearing Race Replacement

Refer to **Figure 21**.
1. Secure the swing arm in a vise with soft jaws.
2. Remove the bearing spacers and oil seals if they were not previously removed.
3. Drive a bearing race out of the swing arm from the opposite side with an aluminum or brass drift (**Figure 23**).
4. Repeat Step 3 to remove the opposite bearing race.
5. Clean the swing arm with solvent and allow to dry thoroughly.
6. Pack the new bearings thoroughly with grease before installing them.
7. Press the new bearing races into the swing arm. Support the swing arm when installing the races.

Tables 1-5 are on the following pages.

Table 1 REAR SHOCK AIR CONTROL (1984 FXRT)

Vehicle load	Recommended air pressure (psi [kPa])
Rider weight not exceeding 150 lbs. (68 kg)	4-8 (28-55)
Each additional 25 lbs. (11 kg), add	3 (20.6)
Passenger weight: For each 50 lbs. (23 kg), add	1 (6.8)
For each additional 10 lbs. (4.5 kg)	
luggage weight, add	2 (13.8)
Maximum pressure	40 (276)

Table 2 REAR SHOCK AIR CONTROL (1985-1992 FXRT)

Vehicle load	Recommended air pressure (psi [kPa])
Rider weight not exceeding 150 lbs. (68 kg)	0-5 (0-34)
Each additional 25 lbs. (11 kg), add	5 (34)
Passenger weight: For each 50 lbs. (23 kg), add	10 (69)
For each additional 10 lbs. (4.5 kg)	
luggage weight, add	3 (21)
Maximum pressure	60 (414)

Table 3 REAR SHOCK AIR CONTROL (1984-1996 FLH AND FLT SERIES MODELS)

Vehicle load	Recommended air pressure (psi [kPa])
Solo rider	0 (0)
Rider and passenger	5 (34)
Rider, passenger and maximum luggage load	10 (69)
Maximum pressure	
1984-1992	20 (138)
1993-1996	35 (241)

Table 4 AIR SUSPENSION ADJUSTMENTS (1997-1998 FLH AND FLT SERIES MODELS)

	Recommended pressure (psi [kPa])	
Load	Front fork	Rear shock absorbers
Rider weight		
Up to 150 lbs. (68 kg) add:		
For each additional 25 lbs. (11 kg)	1 (7)	1 (7)
Passenger weight: For each additional 50 lbs. (23 kg)	–	1.5 (10)
Luggage weight: For each additional 10 lbs. (4.5 kg)	1 (7)	3 (21)
Maximum pressure	25 (172)	35 (241)

Table 5 REAR SUSPENSION TORQUE SPECIFICATIONS

Item	ft.-lb.	in.-lb.	N•m
Swing arm pivot bolt			
FXR, FLH and FLT series models			
1984-early 1986 pivot shaft nut	45	–	61
Late 1986-1988 pivot bolt	85	–	115
1989-1998 pivot shaft nut	45	–	61
FXWG, FXSB and FXEF	See text		

(continued)

Table 5 REAR SUSPENSION TORQUE SPECIFICATIONS (continued)

Item	ft.-lb.	in.-lb.	N•m
Rear axle nut	60-65	–	81-88
Rear shock absorber bolts or nuts			
FXR series models			
1984	N.A.		
1985-1998			
Upper and lower	33-35	–	45-47
FXWG, FXSB and FXEF	N.A.		
FLH and FLT series models			
Upper			
1984-early 1988	35-40	–	47-54
Late 1988-1998	33-35	–	45-47
Lower	35-40	–	47-54
Passenger footpeg bolts	20-25	–	27-34

CHAPTER THIRTEEN

BRAKES

This chapter includes repair and replacement procedures for all brake system components.

Refer to **Table 1** and **Table 2** located at the end of this chapter.

BRAKE SERVICE

WARNING
*Do not use brake fluid labeled **DOT 5.1**. This is a glycol-based fluid that is **not compatible** with silicone-based DOT 5. DOT 5 brake fluid is purple while DOT 5.1 is amber/clear. Do not mix these two different types of brake fluid. It will lead to brake component damage and possible brake failure.*

WARNING
Do not mix DOT 3, DOT 4, or DOT 5.1 brake fluids because they are not silicone-based. Using nonsilicone brake fluid in these models can cause brake failure.

WARNING
*When working on the brake system, do **not** inhale brake dust. It might contain asbestos, which is a known carcinogen. Do **not** use compressed air to blow off brake dust. Use an aerosol brake cleaner. Wear a facemask and wash thoroughly after completing the work.*

The disc brake system transmits hydraulic pressure from the master cylinders to the brake calipers. This pressure is transmitted from the caliper(s) to the brake pads, which grip both sides of the brake disc(s) and slow the motorcycle. As the pads wear, the pistons move out of the caliper bores to compensate automatically. As this occurs, the fluid level in the master cylinder reservoir goes down. Compensate for this by occasionally adding fluid.

The proper operation of this system depends on a supply of clean brake fluid (DOT 5) and a clean work environment when performing any service. Any particle of debris that enters the system can damage the components and cause poor brake performance.

Brake fluid is hygroscopic (easily absorbs moisture), and moisture in the system reduces brake performance. Purchase brake fluid in small containers and properly discard small quantities that remain. Small quantities of fluid will quickly absorb the moisture in the container. Only use fluid clearly marked DOT 5. If possible, use the same brand of fluid. Do not replace the fluid with a nonsilicone fluid. It is not possible to remove all of the old fluid. Other types are not compatible with DOT 5. Do not reuse drained fluid. Discard old fluid properly. Do not combine brake fluid with fluids for recycling.

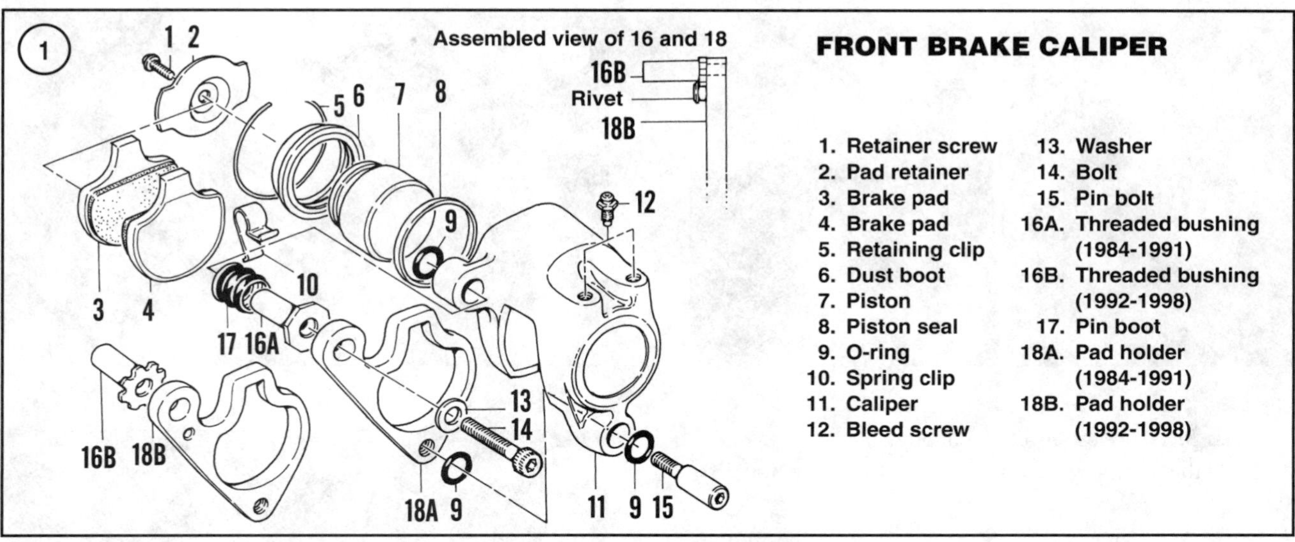

Carefully perform service procedures. Do not use sharp tools inside the master cylinders or calipers on the pistons. Damage to these components can cause a loss in the ability of the system to maintain hydraulic pressure. If there is any doubt in the ability to correctly and safely service the brake system, have a professional technician perform the task.

Consider the following when servicing the brake system:

1. The hydraulic components rarely require disassembly. Make sure disassembly is necessary.
2. Keep the reservoir covers in place to prevent the entry of moisture and debris.
3. Clean parts with an aerosol brake part cleaner or isopropyl alcohol. Never use petroleum-based solvents on internal brake system components. They will cause seals to swell and distort.
4. Do not allow brake fluid to contact plastic, painted or plated parts. It will damage the surfaces.
5. Dispose of brake fluid properly.
6. If the hydraulic system, not including the reservoir cover, has been opened, bleed the system to remove air from it. Refer to *Bleeding the System* in this chapter.
7. The manufacturer does not provide wear limit specifications for the caliper and master cylinder assemblies. Use good judgment when inspecting these components or consult a professional technician for advice.

PREVENTING BRAKE FLUID DAMAGE

Brake fluid will damage most surfaces on the motorcycle. To prevent damage, note the following:

1. Protect the motorcycle before beginning any service requiring draining, bleeding or handling of brake fluid. Anticipate which parts are likely to leak brake fluid and use a large tarp or piece of plastic to cover the areas beneath those parts. Even a few drops of brake fluid can extensively damage painted or plastic surfaces.
2. Keep a bucket of water close to the motorcycle while working on the brake system. If brake fluid spills on any surface, immediately wash the area with soap and water. Then rinse it thoroughly.
3. To help control the flow of brake fluid when refilling the reservoirs, punch a small hole into the edge of the fluid container seal to help the pour spout.

FRONT BRAKE PAD REPLACEMENT

There is no recommended mileage interval for changing the brake pads. Pad wear depends on riding habits and conditions. Frequently check the brake pads for wear. Increase the inspection interval when the wear indicator reaches the edge of the brake disc. After removal, measure the thickness of each brake pad with a vernier caliper or ruler and compare measurements to the dimensions in **Table 1**. 13

Always replace both pads in the caliper at the same time to maintain even brake pressure on the disc. Do not disconnect the hydraulic brake hose from the brake caliper for brake pad replacement. Only disconnect the hose if the caliper assembly is going to be removed.

CAUTION

Check the pads more frequently when the lining approaches the pad metal back plate. If pad wear is uneven for some reason, the back plate can come in contact with the disc and cause damage.

Refer to **Figure 1**.

2

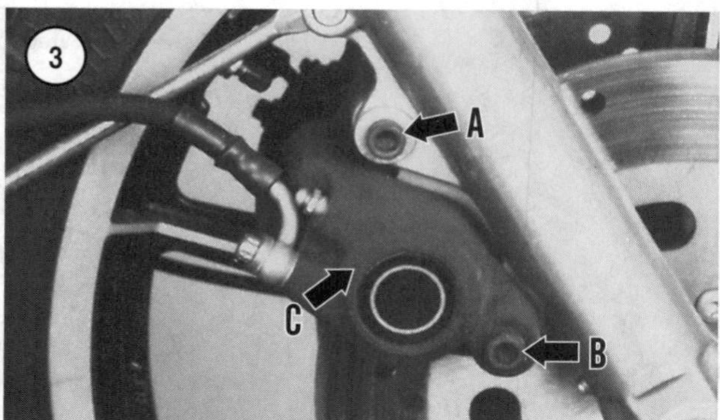

3

1. Read *Brake Service* in this chapter.
2. Park the motorcycle on a level surface on the jiffy stand.
3. To prevent the front brake lever from being applied, place a spacer between the brake lever and the throttle grip and secure it in place. Then if the brake lever is inadvertently squeezed, the piston will not be forced out of the cylinder.
4. To prevent the reservoir from overflowing while repositioning the piston in the caliper, perform the following:
   a. Remove the screws securing the cover (**Figure 2**) and remove the cover and diaphragm.
   b. Use a shop syringe and remove about 50 percent of the brake fluid from the reservoir. Do *not* remove more than 50 percent of the brake fluid or air will enter the system. Discard the brake fluid properly.
5. Remove the upper mounting bolt and washer (A, **Figure 3**) and lower mounting pin (B) securing the caliper to the front fork slider.
6. Carefully slide the brake caliper (C, **Figure 3**) off of the brake disc.
7. Remove the outer pad, pad holder and spring clip as an assembly (**Figure 4**).
8. Remove the screw (A, **Figure 5**), pad retainer (B) and inner pad (**Figure 6**).
9. Push the outer pad (A, **Figure 7**) free of the spring clip (B) and remove it.
10. Check the brake pads (**Figure 8**) for wear or damage. Measure the thickness of the brake pad material (**Figure 9**). Replace the brake pads if they are worn to 1/16 in. (1.6 mm) or less. Replace both pads as a set. On dual caliper models, replace the brake pads in both calipers at the same time.
11. Inspect the upper mounting bolt and lower mounting pin (**Figure 10**). Replace if damaged or badly corroded.
12. Check the pad retainer (**Figure 11**) for damage. Replace if necessary.
13. Check the piston dust boot in the caliper. Remove and overhaul the caliper if the boot is swollen or damaged, or

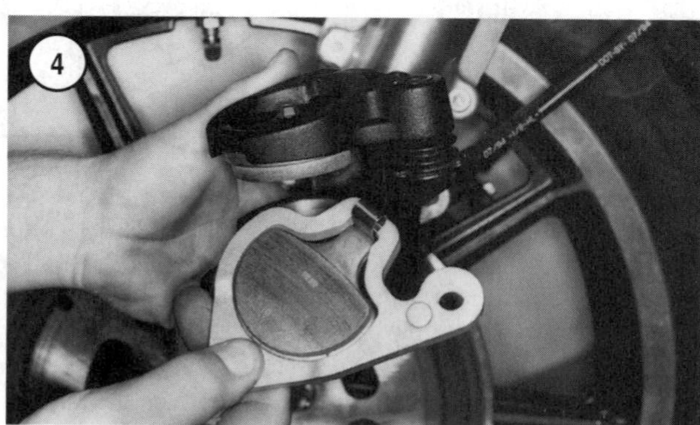
4

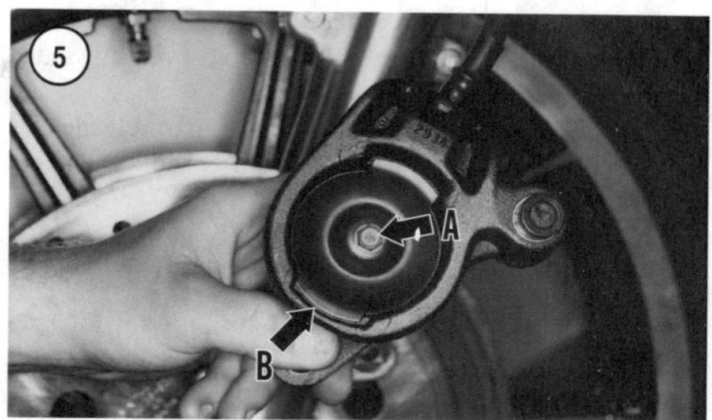

5

6

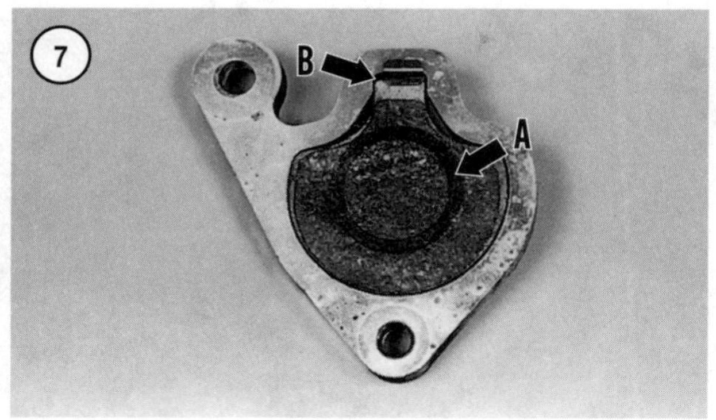

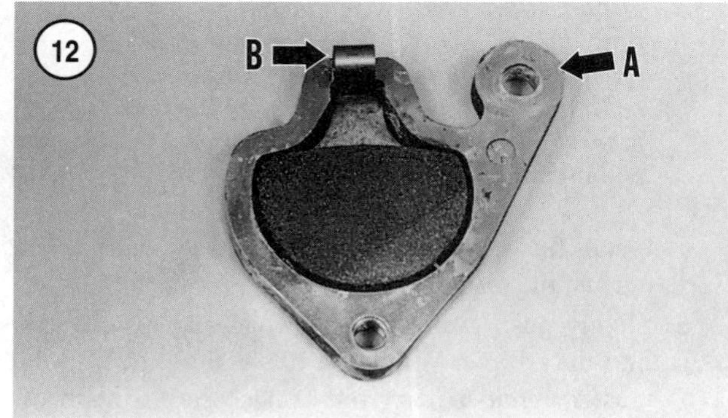

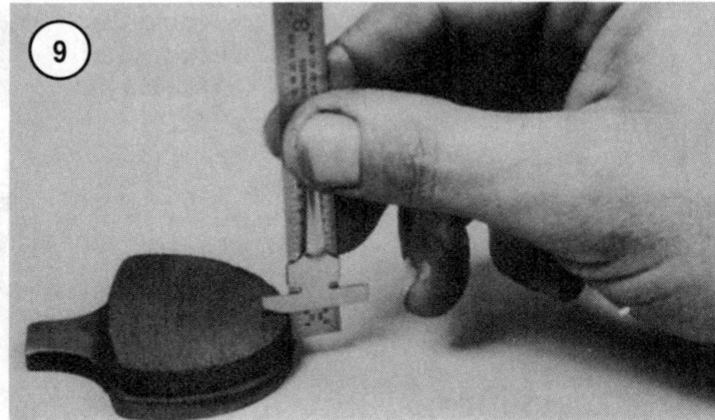

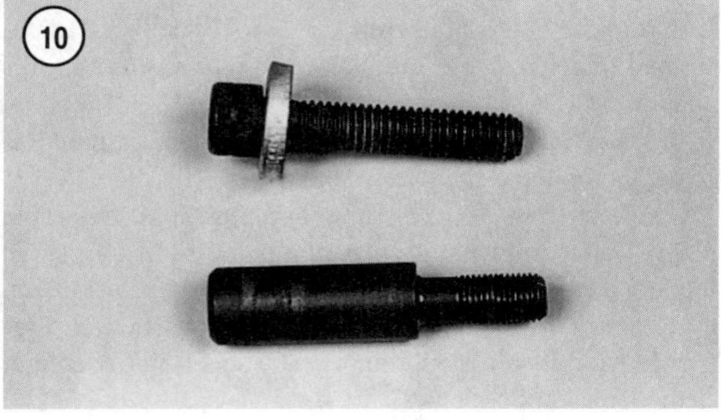

if the brake fluid is leaking from the caliper. Refer to *Front Brake Caliper* in this chapter.

14. Remove all corrosion from the pad holder.

15. Replace the spring clip if it is damaged or badly corroded.

16. Check the brake disc for wear as described under *Brake Disc* in this chapter. Service the brake disc if necessary.

17. Assemble the pad holder, spring clip and outboard brake pad as follows:

   a. Lay the pad holder on a workbench so the upper mounting screw hole is positioned at the upper right as shown in A, **Figure 12**.
   b. Install the spring clip (B, **Figure 12**) at the top of the pad holder so the spring loop faces in the direction shown in B, **Figure 12**.
   c. The outboard brake pad has an insulator pad mounted on its back side (A, **Figure 7**).
   d. Center the outboard brake pad into the pad holder so the lower end of the pad rests inside the pad holder. Push the upper end of the brake pad past the spring clip and into the holder.

NOTE

Step 18 is not necessary if Step 4 was not performed.

18. After the installation of new brake pads, the caliper piston must be relocated into the caliper before the caliper is installed over the brake disc. This will force brake fluid back into the reservoir. To prevent the reservoir from overflowing, perform the following:

a. Remove the screws securing the cover (**Figure 2**) and remove the cover and diaphragm.
b. Use a shop syringe and remove about 50 percent of the brake fluid from the reservoir. Do *not* drain more than 50 percent of the brake fluid, or air will enter the system. Discard the brake fluid properly.

CAUTION
Do not allow the master cylinder to overflow during this step. Wash brake fluid off any painted, plated or plastic surfaces immediately because it will damage most surfaces it contacts. Use soapy water and rinse completely.

c. Install the old outer brake pad into the caliper and against the piston.
d. Slowly push the outer brake pad and piston back into the caliper. Watch the brake fluid level in the master cylinder reservoir. If necessary, siphon off fluid before it overflows.
e. Remove the old brake pad.
f. Temporarily install the diaphragm and cover. Install the screws finger-tight at this time.

19. Install the inner brake pad (without the insulator backing) in the caliper recessed seat (**Figure 6**).

20. Insert the pad retainer (B, **Figure 5**) within the counterbore inside the caliper. Install the self-tapping screw (A, **Figure 5**) through the pad retainer and thread into the brake pad. Tighten the screw securely.

21. Coat the lower mounting bolt with Dow Corning Moly 44 grease.

22. Install the caliper as follows:

a. Install the caliper (C, **Figure 3**) over the brake disc while making sure the friction surface on each pad faces the disc.

CAUTION
*On 1992-1998 models, the splined head on the threaded bushing (16B, **Figure 1**) must be installed between the rivet head and the pad holder as shown in **Figure 1**. Also, one of the bushing head splined notches must engage the rivet head as shown in **Figure 1**. If the bushing is installed incorrectly, the rivet will be damaged when the caliper mounting bolts are tightened.*

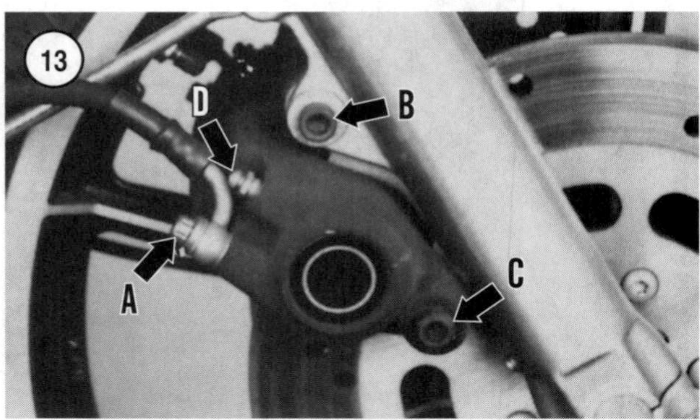

b. Align the two mounting holes in the caliper with the slider mounting lugs.
c. Install the washer and upper mounting bolt (A, **Figure 3**) and tighten finger-tight.
d. Insert the lower mounting pin (B, **Figure 3**) and tighten finger-tight.
e. Tighten the upper mounting bolt and lower mounting pin to 25-30 ft.-lb. (34-41 N•m).

23. If necessary, refill the master cylinder reservoir to maintain the correct fluid level. Install the diaphragm and top cap.

WARNING
Use brake fluid clearly marked DOT 5 from a sealed container. Other types can vaporize and cause brake failure. Always use the same brand name; do not mix because many brands are not compatible.

WARNING
Do not ride the motorcycle until the front brakes are operating correctly with full hydraulic advantage. If necessary, bleed the brake system as described in this chapter.

FRONT BRAKE CALIPER

Removal

1. Drain the brake fluid from the front brake hose as described under *Brake Hose and Line Replacement* in this chapter.
2. Loosen the banjo bolt (A, **Figure 13**) at the caliper. Remove the bolt and the two washers.
3. Place the loose end of the brake hose in a reclosable plastic bag to prevent the entry of moisture and debris. Tie the loose end of the hose out of the way.
4. Remove the upper mounting bolt and washer (B, **Figure 13**) and lower mounting pin (C) securing the caliper to the front fork slider.

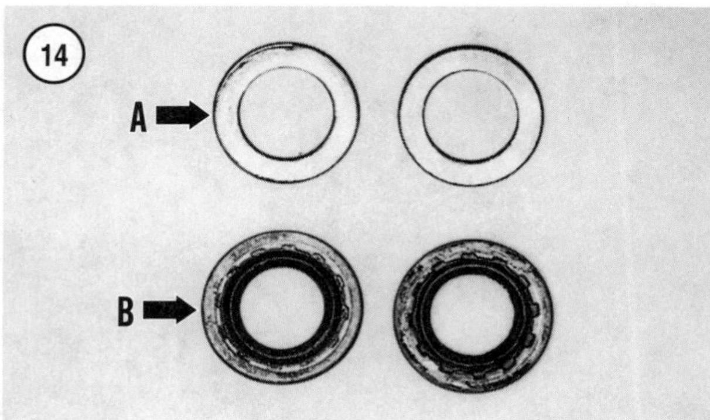

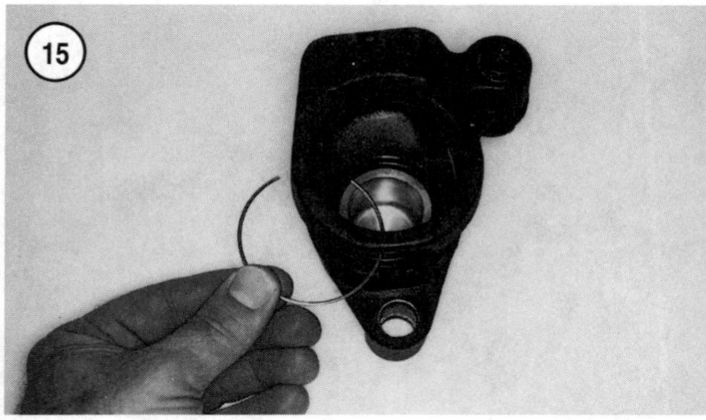

5. Carefully slide the brake caliper off the brake disc.

6. If the brake caliper is not going to be serviced, place it in a plastic bag to keep it clean.

Installation

1. If removed, install the brake pads into the caliper as described in this chapter.

2. Coat the lower mounting pin with Dow Corning Moly 44 grease.

3. Install the caliper over the brake disc, making sure the friction surface on each pad faces against the disc.

4. Align the two mounting holes in the caliper with the slider mounting lugs.

5. Install the washer and upper mounting bolt and tighten finger-tight.

6. Insert the lower mounting pin and tighten the mounting bolt finger-tight.

7. Tighten the upper mounting bolt and lower mounting pin to 25-30 ft.-lb. (34-41 N•m).

8. Tighten the bleed screw (D, **Figure 13**) if it was previously loosened.

WARNING

*There are two different type of sealing washers used with the banjo bolts. Early models are copper with a zinc coating (A, **Figure 14**). Late models are steel with a rubber O-ring (B, **Figure 14**). The banjo bolts must be used with the specific sealing washers. Make sure that the banjo bolts and washers match the original parts. A mismatch of these parts will result in a brake fluid leak and possible complete loss of brake operation.*

9. Install the brake line onto the caliper with a *new* washer on both sides of the brake line fitting. Then secure the fitting to the caliper with the banjo bolt. Tighten the banjo bolt as follows:
   a. Banjo bolt with copper sealing washer: 35 ft.-lb. (47 N•m).
   b. Banjo bolt with steel/rubber sealing washer: 17-22 ft.-lb. (23-30 N•m).

10. Refill the master cylinder reservoir with DOT 5 brake fluid.

11. Apply the front brake lever several times to seat the pads against the disc.

WARNING

Do not ride the motorcycle until the front brake operates correctly with full hydraulic advantage.

12. Bleed the brakes as described in this chapter.

Disassembly

Refer to **Figure 1**.

1. Partially remove the piston from the caliper as described during caliper inspection in this chapter.

WARNING

Compressed air will force the piston out of the caliper under considerable force. Do not block the piston by hand because injury will occur.

2. Insert a small screwdriver into the notched groove machined in the bottom of the piston bore. Then pry the retaining ring (**Figure 15**) out of the caliper body.

3. If the piston did not partially come out of the caliper bore, perform the following:
   a. Place a rag and a piece of wood in the caliper (**Figure 16**). Keep fingers out of the way of the piston.
   b. Apply compressed air through the brake hose port and force the piston out of the caliper.

4. Remove the piston and dust boot assembly (**Figure 17**).

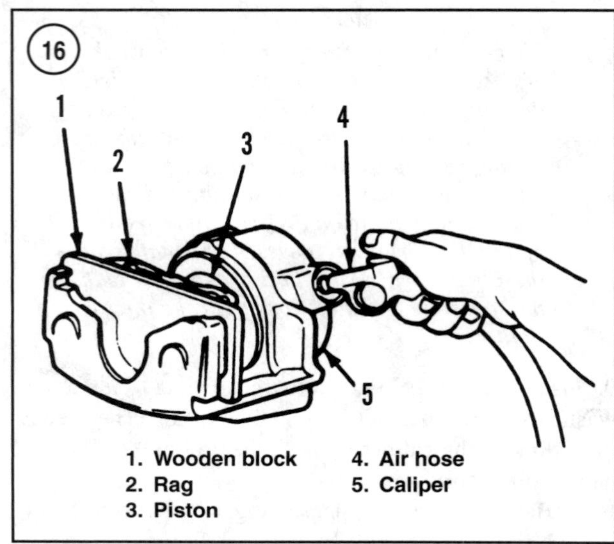

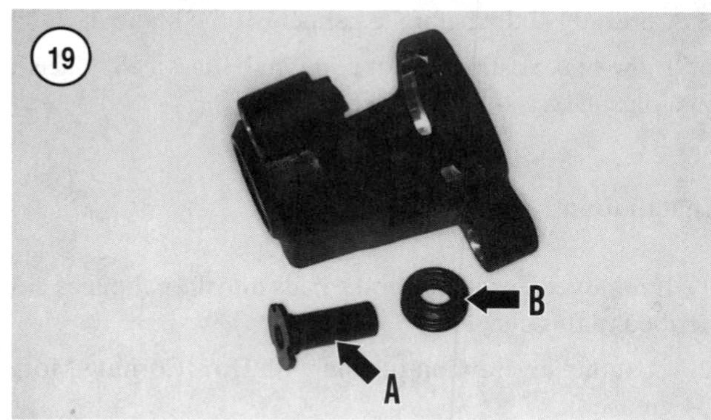

5. Remove the piston seal (**Figure 18**) from the groove in the caliper body.
6. Pull the threaded bushing (A, **Figure 19**) out of the caliper. Then remove the pin boot (B, **Figure 19**).
7. Remove the O-rings from the caliper body (**Figure 20**).

Assembly

1. A Harley-Davidson rebuild kit (part No. 44020-83) includes a piston seal (A, **Figure 21**), piston (B), dust boot (C) and retaining ring (D).

WARNING
Never reuse an old dust boot or piston seal. Very minor damage or age deterioration can make the boot and seal ineffective.

2. Soak the new dust boot and piston seal in clean DOT 5 brake fluid.
3. Carefully install the *new* piston seal into the groove. Make sure the seal is properly seated in the groove.
4. Install *new* O-rings into the caliper grooves.
5. Wipe the inside of the pin boot with Dow Corning Moly 44 grease. Then insert the boot into the bushing bore with the flange end seating in the bore groove (**Figure 22**).
6. Insert the threaded bushing into the boot (**Figure 23**).
7. Install the piston dust boot on the piston before the piston is installed in the caliper bore. Perform the following:
   a. Place the piston on the workbench with the open side facing up.
   b. Align the piston dust boot with the piston so the shoulder on the dust boot faces up.

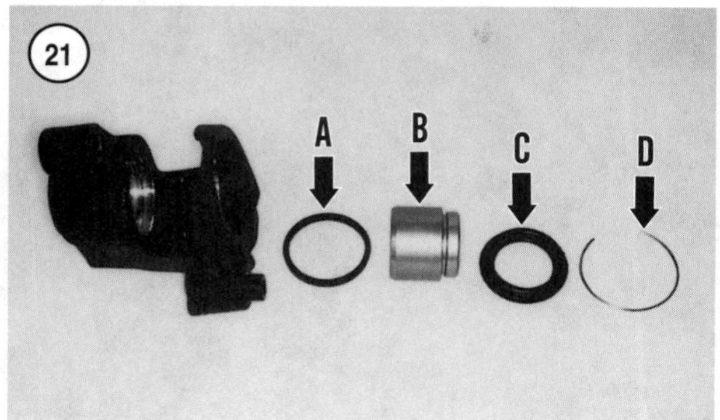

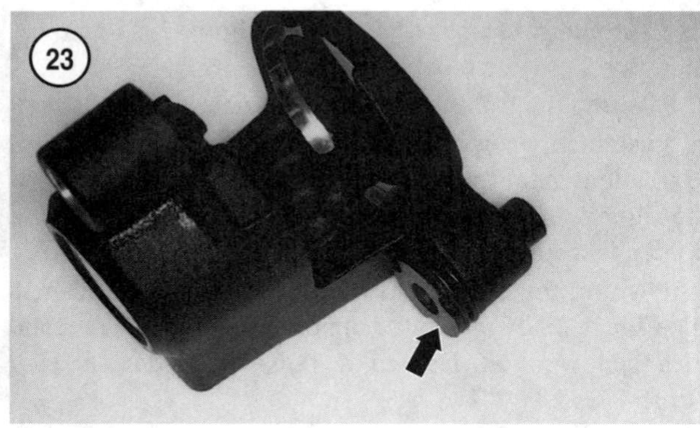

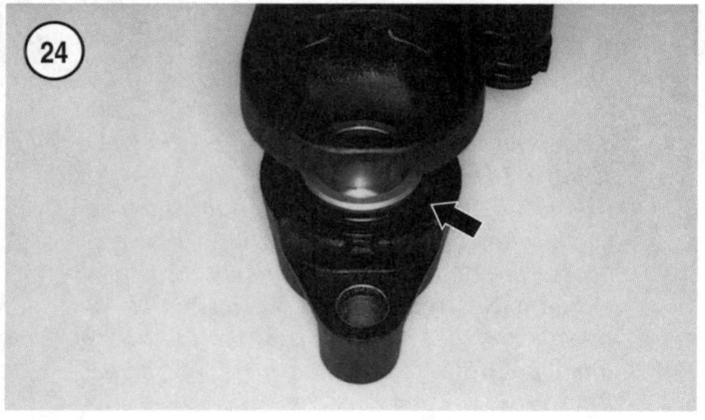

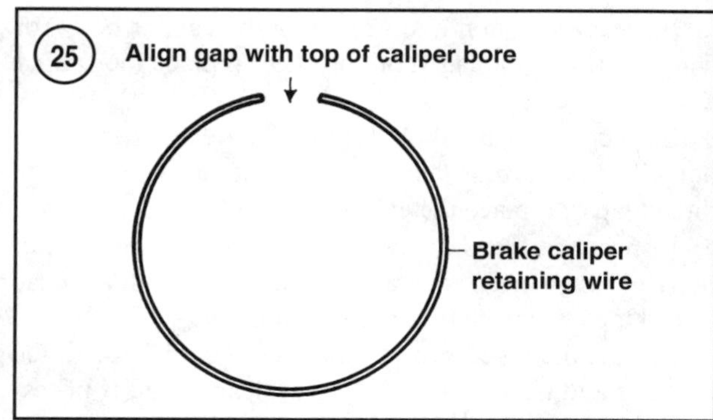

   c. Slide the piston dust boot onto the piston until the inner lip on the dust boot seats in the piston groove (**Figure 17**).

8. Coat the piston and the caliper bore with DOT 5 brake fluid.
9. Align the piston with the caliper bore so the open end faces out (**Figure 17**). Then push the piston in until it bottoms.
10. Seat the piston dust boot (**Figure 24**) into the caliper bore.
11. Locate the retaining ring groove in the top end of the caliper bore. Align the retaining ring so the gap (**Figure 25**) is at the top of the caliper bore. Install the ring into the ring groove. Make sure the retaining ring is correctly seated in the groove.
12. Apply a light coat of Dow Corning Moly 44 grease to the caliper mounting lug bores.
13. If the bleed screw assembly was removed, install it and tighten it to the following:
   a. 1984-1990 models: 32-40 in.-lb. (3.6-4.5 N•m).
   b. 1991-1998 models: 80-100 in.-lb. (9-11 N•m).
14. Install the caliper and brake pads as described in this chapter.
15. Bleed the brakes as described under *Bleeding the System* in this chapter.

Inspection

Service specifications for the front caliper components are not available. Replace worn, damaged or questionable parts.

1. Clean the caliper body and piston in clean DOT 5 brake fluid or isopropyl alcohol. Dry them with compressed air.
2. Make sure the fluid passageway in the base of the piston bore is clear. Apply compressed air to the opening to make sure it is clear. Clean it out, if necessary, with clean brake fluid.

3. Inspect the piston seal groove in the caliper body for damage. If it is damaged or corroded, replace the caliper assembly.
4. Inspect the banjo bolt threaded hole in the caliper body. If it is worn or damaged, clean it out with a metric thread tap or replace the caliper assembly.
5. Inspect the bleed screw threaded hole in the caliper body. If it is worn or damaged, clean it out with a metric thread tap or replace the caliper assembly.
6. Inspect the bleed screw. Apply compressed air to the opening and make sure it is clear. Clean it out, if necessary, with clean brake fluid. Install the bleed screw and tighten it to the following:
   a. 1984-1990: 32-40 in.-lb. (3.6-4.5 N•m).
   b. 1991-1998: 80-100 in.-lb. (9-11 N•m).
7. Inspect the caliper body for damage.
8. Inspect the cylinder wall (A, **Figure 26**) and piston (B) for scratches, scoring or other damage.

FRONT MASTER CYLINDER

1984-1995 Models

Removal/installation

Refer to **Figure 27**.

CAUTION
Cover the fuel tank and front fender with a heavy cloth or plastic tarp to protect them from accidental brake fluid spills. Wash brake fluid off painted, plated or plastic surfaces immediately because it will destroy most surfaces it contacts. Use soapy water and rinse completely.

1. On models so equipped, remove the windshield as described in Chapter Fifteen.
2. Remove the mirror (A, **Figure 28**) from the master cylinder.
3. Clean the top of the master cylinder of all dirt and debris.
4. Remove the screws securing the cover (B, **Figure 28**), and remove the cover and diaphragm.
5. Use a shop syringe to draw all of the brake fluid out of the master cylinder reservoir. Temporarily reinstall the diaphragm and the cover. Tighten the screws finger-tight.
6. Remove the banjo bolt and sealing washers (C, **Figure 28**) securing the brake hose to the master cylinder.
7. Place the loose end of the brake hose in a reclosable plastic bag to prevent the entry of moisture and debris. Tie the loose end of the hose to the handlebar.
8. Remove the screw securing the right switch together and separate the switch.
9. Remove the bolts and washers (D, **Figure 28**) securing the clamp and master cylinder to the handlebar.
10. Remove the master cylinder assembly from the handlebar.
11. Drain any residual brake fluid from the master cylinder and dispose of it properly.
12. If the master cylinder assembly is not going to be serviced, reinstall the clamp and Torx bolts to the master cylinder. Place the assembly in a reclosable plastic bag to protect it from debris.

Installation

1. Thoroughly clean the banjo bolt (**Figure 29**) fluid passageway. Dry with compressed air.
2. Position the front master cylinder onto the handlebar.
3. Push the master cylinder all the way onto the handlebar. Hold it in this position and install the upper portion of the right switch. Install the switch clamping screw and tighten it securely.
4. Position the clamp and install the bolts and washers (D, **Figure 28**). Tighten the upper mounting bolt first and then the lower bolt. Tighten the bolts to 70-80 in.-lb. (8-9 N•m).
5. Apply clean DOT 5 brake fluid to the rubber portions of the new sealing washers prior to installation.

WARNING
*There are two different types of sealing washers used with the banjo bolts. Early models are copper with a zinc coating (A, **Figure 14**). Late models are steel with a rubber O-ring (B). The banjo bolts must be used with the specific sealing washers. Make sure that the banjo bolts and washers match the original parts. A mismatch of these parts will result in a brake fluid leak and possible complete loss of brake operation.*

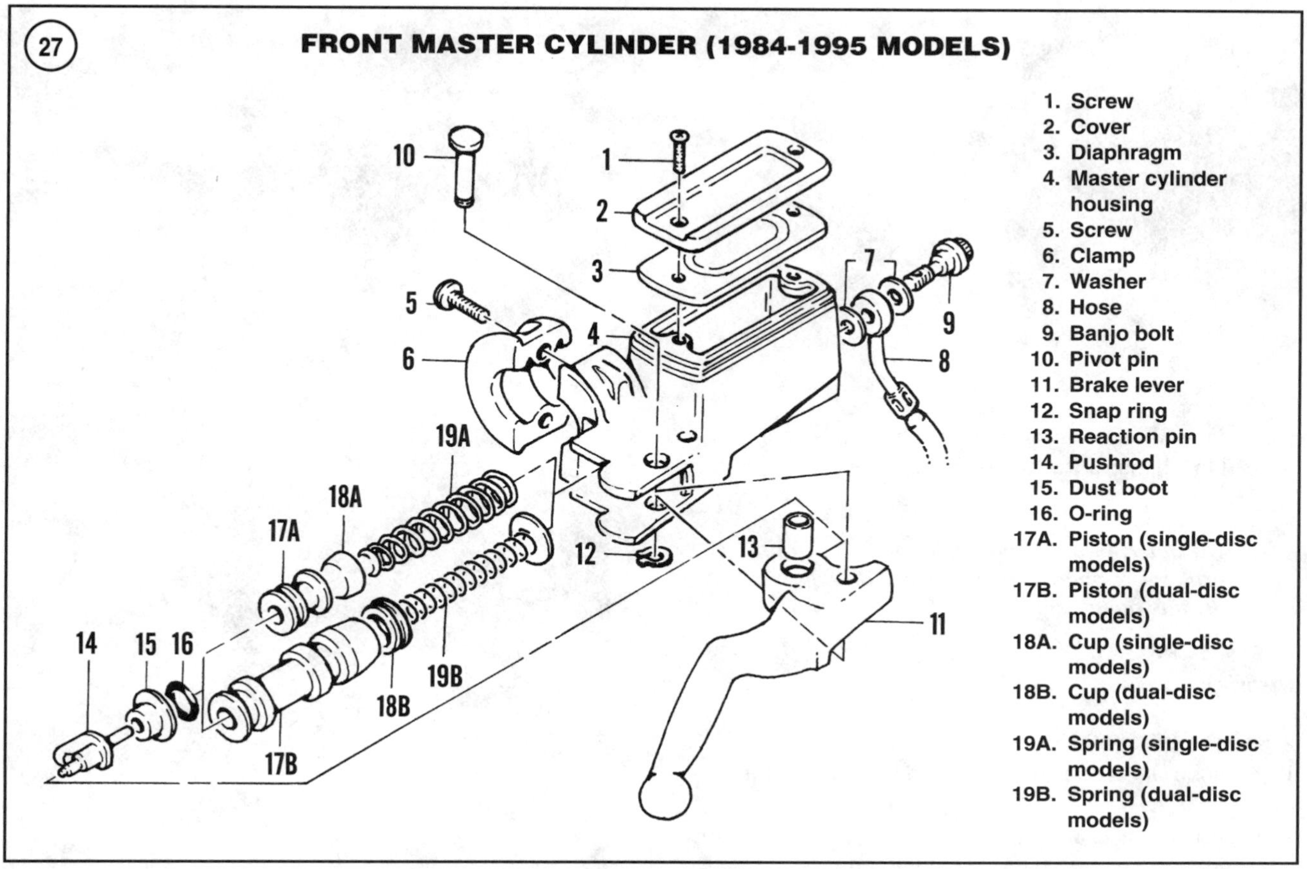

27

FRONT MASTER CYLINDER (1984-1995 MODELS)

1. Screw
2. Cover
3. Diaphragm
4. Master cylinder housing
5. Screw
6. Clamp
7. Washer
8. Hose
9. Banjo bolt
10. Pivot pin
11. Brake lever
12. Snap ring
13. Reaction pin
14. Pushrod
15. Dust boot
16. O-ring

17A. Piston (single-disc models)
17B. Piston (dual-disc models)
18A. Cup (single-disc models)
18B. Cup (dual-disc models)
19A. Spring (single-disc models)
19B. Spring (dual-disc models)

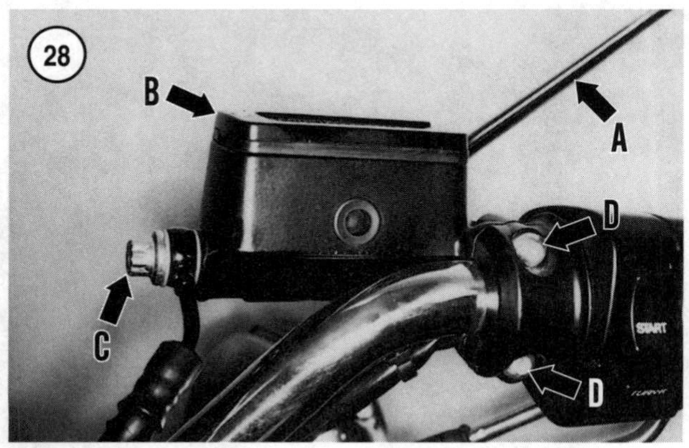

13

6. Install the brake line onto the master cylinder with a *new* washer on both sides of the brake line fitting. Then secure the fitting to the caliper with the banjo bolt (C, **Figure 28**). Tighten the banjo bolt as follows:
   a. Banjo bolt with copper sealing washer: 35 ft.-lb. (47 N•m).
   b. Banjo bolt with steel/rubber sealing washer: 17-22 ft.-lb. (23-30 N•m).

7. Temporarily install the diaphragm and top cover (B, **Figure 28**) onto the reservoir. Tighten the screws finger-tight at this time.

8. Install the mirror (A, **Figure 28**) onto the master cylinder.

9. Refill the master cylinder reservoir and bleed the brake system as described under *Bleeding the System* in this chapter.

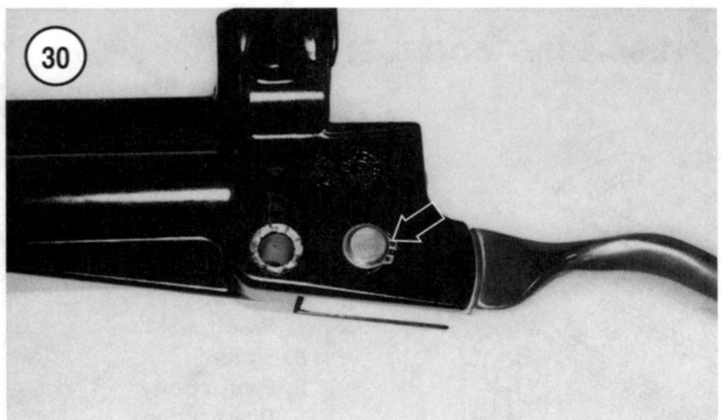

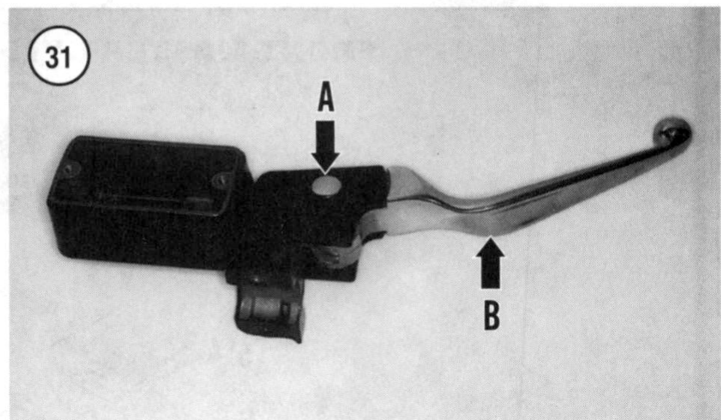

10. On models so equipped, install the windshield as described in Chapter Fifteen.

WARNING
Do not ride the motorcycle until the front brakes are operating correctly with full hydraulic advantage.

Disassembly

Refer to **Figure 27**.

1. Remove the master cylinder as described in this section.
2. If still in place, remove the screws securing the top cover and remove the cover and diaphragm.
3. Remove the brake lever assembly as follows:
   a. Remove the snap ring (**Figure 30**) from the pivot pin.
   b. Push out the pivot pin (A, **Figure 31**) and remove the brake lever (B) assembly.
   c. Remove the reaction pin (A, **Figure 32**) from the brake lever.
   d. Remove the pushrod (B, **Figure 32**) from the piston assembly.
4. Remove the piston assembly as follows:
   a. Remove the dust boot (A, **Figure 33**).
   b. Remove the piston and spring assembly (B, **Figure 33**).
5. If damaged, remove the grommet and sight glass from the rear side of the master cylinder housing.

Assembly

The piston assembly on single-disc and dual-disc brakes are different as shown in (**Figure 27**).

1A. If installing the OEM master cylinder rebuild kit, use the lubricant supplied with the rebuild kit to coat the master cylinder bore and piston components.

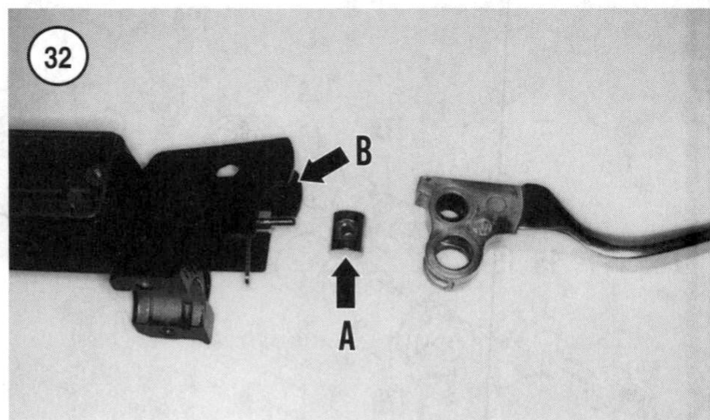

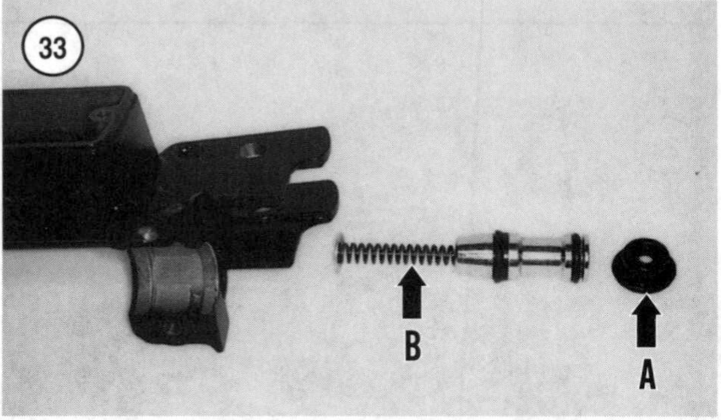

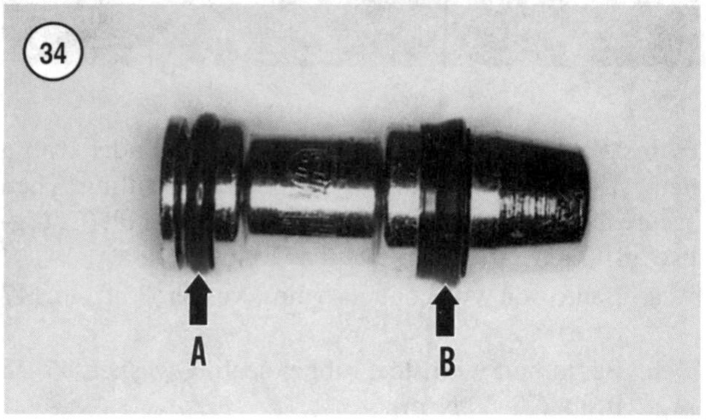

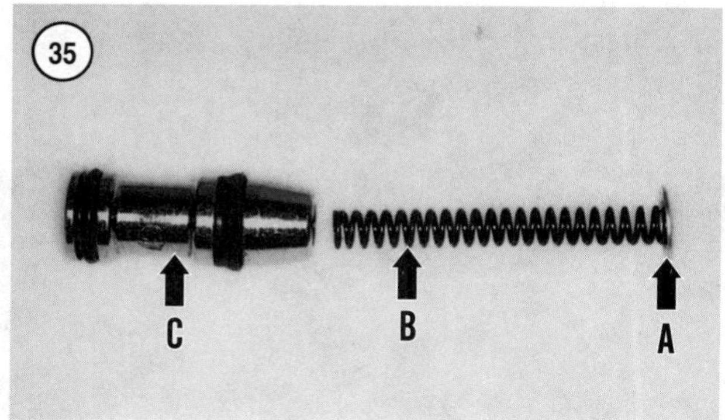

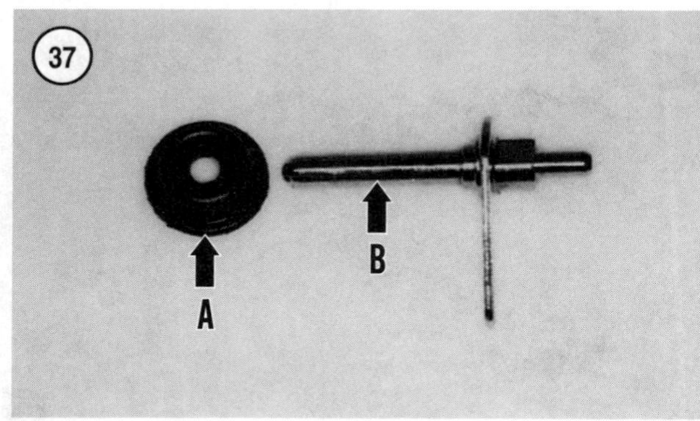

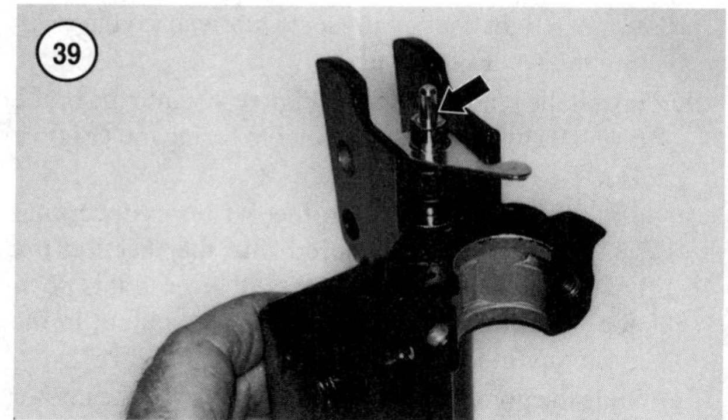

1B. If not installing the OEM master cylinder rebuild kit, soak the piston O-ring and cup in fresh DOT 5 prior to installation. Apply a thin coat of brake fluid to the cylinder bore prior to assembly.

2. Install the grommet and sight glass if removed.
   a. Install the cup onto the narrow end of the spring.
   b. Install the O-ring onto the piston.
3. On dual disc models, assemble the piston assembly as follows:
   a. Install the O-ring (A, **Figure 34**) and cup (B) onto the piston. Make sure both parts are seated correctly on the piston.
   b. Make sure the small plate is installed onto the piston spring as shown in A, **Figure 35**.

4A. On single-disc models, install the piston assembly as follows:

   a. Position the spring with the wide end first and install the spring into the master cylinder.
   b. Position the piston with the O-ring end going in last and install the piston into the master cylinder.

13

4B. On dual-disc models, install the piston assembly as follows:

   a. Install the spring (B, **Figure 35**) onto the piston (C) with the plate end of the spring facing away from the piston.
   b. Install the spring and piston into the master cylinder (**Figure 36**).

5. Slide the dust boot (A, **Figure 37**) onto the pushrod (B) as shown in **Figure 38**.
6. Assemble the brake lever as follows:
   a. Slide the long end of the pushrod into the piston (**Figure 39**) with the dust boot facing the piston. Turn the pushrod so the arm faces the master cylinder (**Figure 39**).

NOTE

Do not seat the dust boot into the master cylinder at this time.

b. Apply a light coat of antiseize lubricant to the reaction pin (A, **Figure 40**).
c. Install the reaction pin (A, **Figure 40**) into the brake lever (B) with the square pinhole facing out (**Figure 41**).
d. Slide the brake lever into the master cylinder and seat the end of the pushrod into the reaction pin hose (**Figure 42**). Hold the brake lever in this position. Install the pushrod arm into the cutout in the master cylinder.
e. Slide the pivot pin (A, **Figure 31**) though the master cylinder and brake lever (B) pivot holes.
f. Turn the master cylinder over and install the snap ring (**Figure 30**) into the pivot pin groove. Make sure the snap ring is seated correctly in the groove.
g. Apply the brake lever once to seat the dust seal into the master cylinder bore (**Figure 43**).

7. Apply the brake lever several times. There must be no binding or excessive play. Check that the pushrod is seated in the reaction pinhole (**Figure 43**). If the brake lever does not operate correctly, repeat this procedure and correct the problem.

WARNING

If the assembled pushrod and reaction pin are not operating correctly, the front master may cause the front brake to lock up and/or result in the complete loss of front brake operation.

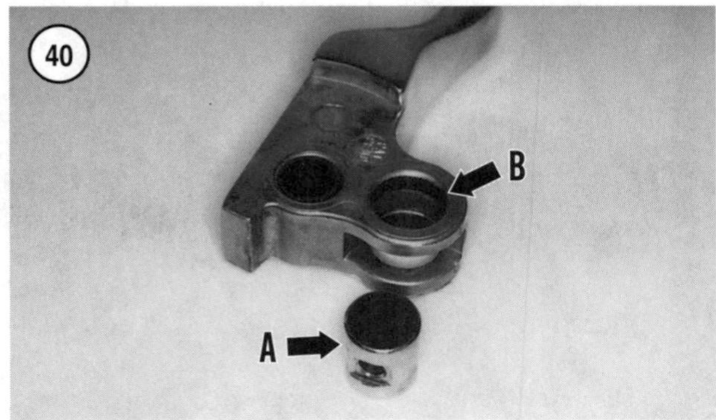

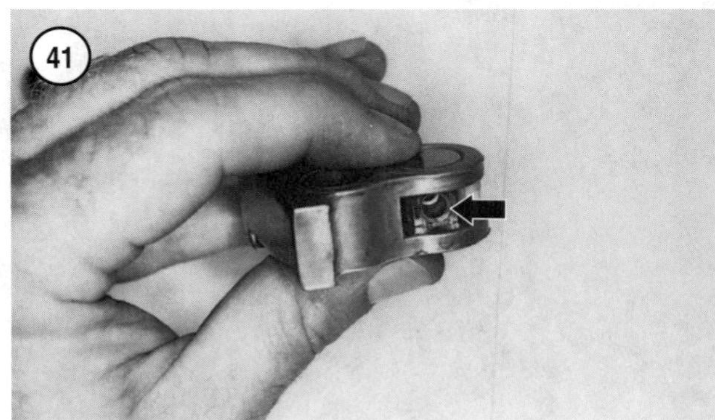

Inspection

Replace worn or damaged parts as described in this section. It is recommended that a new piston kit be installed every time the master cylinder is disassembled.

1. Clean all parts in isopropyl alcohol or clean DOT 5 brake fluid. Inspect the body cylinder bore surface for signs of wear and damage. If it is less than perfect, replace the master cylinder assembly. The body cannot be replaced separately.
2. The piston assembly consists of the dust boot, O-ring, piston, cup and spring. Inspect the rubber parts (**Figure 34**) for wear, cracks, swelling or other damage. Check the piston for severe wear or damage. If any one part of the piston assembly is damaged, replace the entire piston assembly as a kit.
3. Inspect the master cylinder bore for scratches or wear grooves.
4. Clean the vent hole in the cover if plugged.
5. Check the banjo bolt threads in the master cylinder. If the threads are slightly damaged, true them with the properly sized thread tap. If the threads are severely worn or damaged, replace the master cylinder body.
6. Inspect the piston bore in the master cylinder for wear, corrosion or damage. Replace the master cylinder if necessary.

NOTE

If you use a tap to clean the threads in the master cylinder, flush the master cylinder thoroughly and blow dry.

7. Make sure the banjo bolt passage hole is clear.

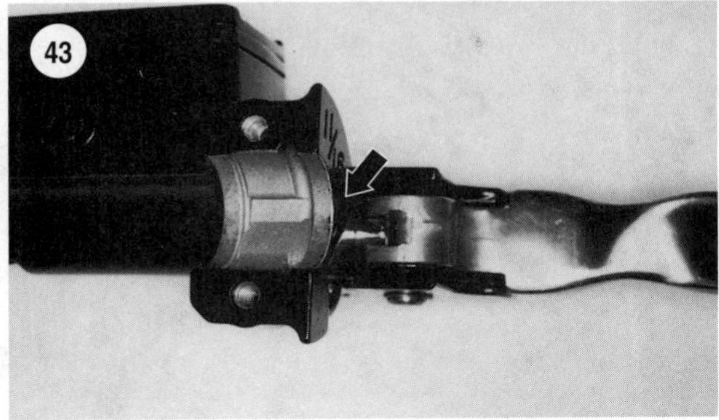

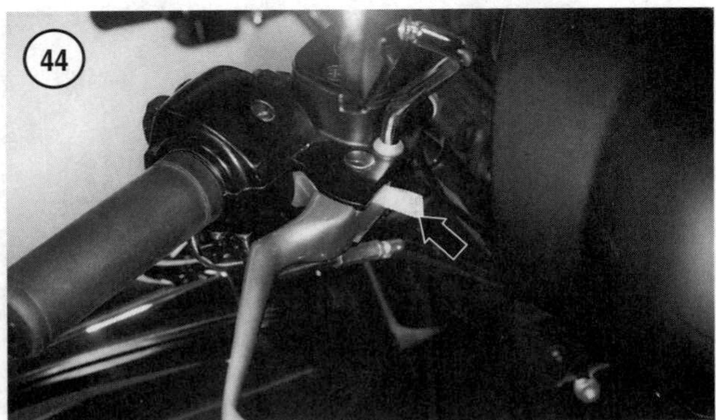

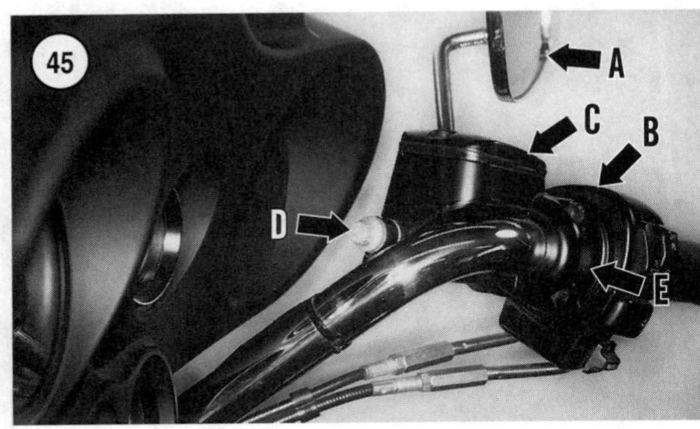

8. Check the reaction pin and pivot pin for severe wear or damage. Check the fit of each pin in the brake lever. Replace worn or damaged parts as required.
9. Replace the pivot pin snap ring if weak or damaged.

1996-1999 Models

Removal

CAUTION
Cover the fuel tank and front fender with a heavy cloth or plastic tarp to protect them from accidental brake fluid spills. Wash brake fluid off painted, plated or plastic surfaces immediately because it will damage most surfaces it contacts. Use soapy water and rinse completely.

1. On models so equipped, remove the windshield or front fairing as described in Chapter Fifteen.

CAUTION
Failure to install the spacer in Step 2 will result in damage to the rubber boot and plunger on the front brake switch.

2. Insert a 5/32 in. (4 mm) thick spacer (**Figure 44**) between the brake lever and lever bracket. Make sure the spacer stays in place during the following steps.
3. Remove the mirror (A, **Figure 45**) from the master cylinder.
4. Remove the screw securing the right switch (B, **Figure 45**) together and separate the switch.
5. Clean the top of the master cylinder of all dirt and debris.
6. Remove the screws securing the cover (C, **Figure 45**), and remove the cover and diaphragm.
7. Use a shop syringe to draw all of the brake fluid out of the master cylinder reservoir. Temporarily reinstall the diaphragm and the cover. Tighten the screws finger-tight.
8. Remove the banjo bolt and sealing washers (D, **Figure 45**) securing the brake hose to the master cylinder.
9. Place the loose end of the brake hose in a reclosable plastic bag to prevent the entry of moisture and debris. Tie the loose end of the hose to the handlebar.
10. Remove the T27 Torx bolts and washers securing the clamp (E, **Figure 45**) and master cylinder to the handlebar.
11. Remove the master cylinder assembly from the handlebar.
12. Drain any residual brake fluid from the master cylinder and dispose of it properly.
13. If the master cylinder assembly is not going to be serviced, reinstall the clamp and Torx bolts to the master cylinder. Place the assembly in a reclosable plastic bag to protect it from debris.

Installation

1. If removed, insert the 5/32 in. (4 mm) thick spacer between the brake lever and lever bracket. Make sure the spacer stays in place during the following steps.

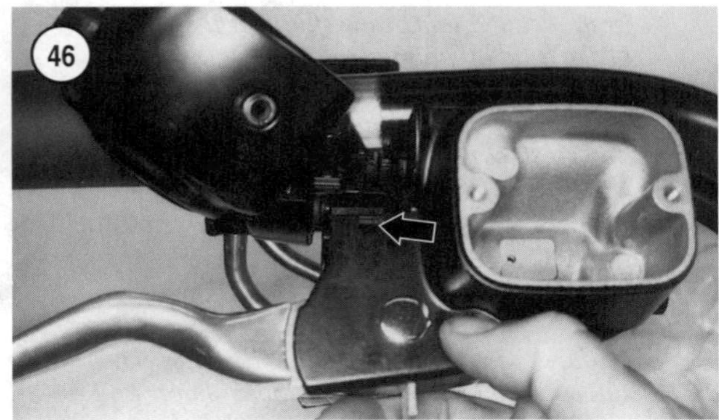

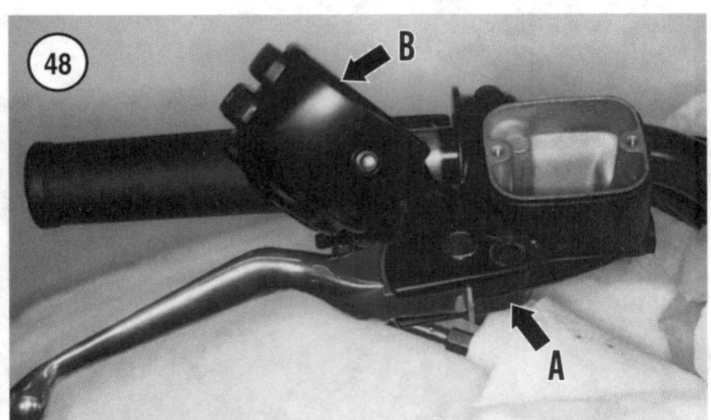

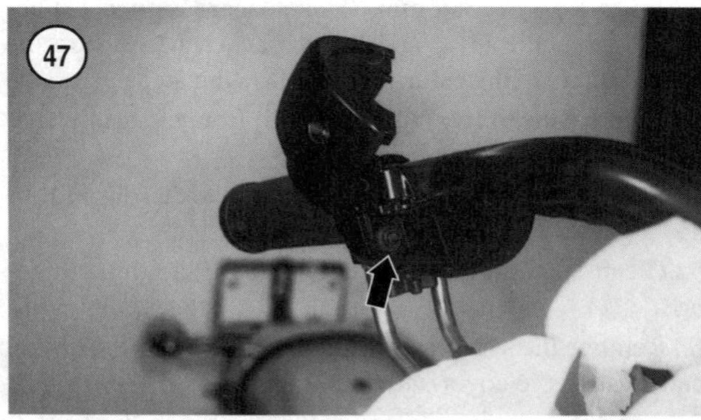

2. Position the front master cylinder onto the handlebar. Align the master cylinder notch (**Figure 46**) with the locating tab on the lower portion of the right switch.

CAUTION
*Do not damage the front brake light switch and rubber boot (**Figure 47**, typical) when installing the master cylinder in Step 3.*

3. Push the master cylinder all the way onto the handlebar (A, **Figure 48**). Hold it in this position and install the upper portion of the right switch (B, **Figure 48**). Install the switch clamping screw and tighten it securely.
4. Position the clamp (E, **Figure 45**) and install the bolts and washers. Tighten the upper mounting bolt. Then tighten the lower bolt. Tighten the bolts to 70-80 in.-lb. (8-9 N•m).
5. Prior to installation, apply clean DOT 5 brake fluid to the rubber portions of the new sealing washers.
6. Install *new* sealing washers and the banjo bolt (D, **Figure 45**) securing the brake hose to the master cylinder. Tighten the banjo bolt to 17-22 ft.-lb. (23-30 N•m).
7. Remove the spacer from the brake lever.
8. Temporarily install the diaphragm and top cover (C, **Figure 45**) onto the reservoir. Tighten the screws finger-tight at this time.

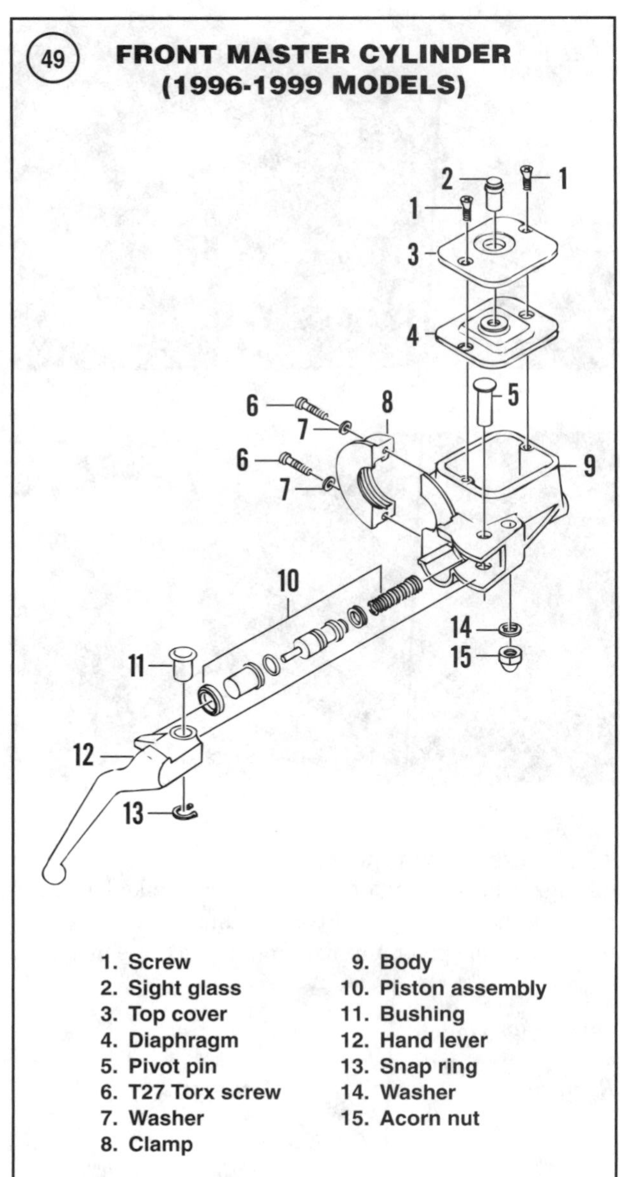

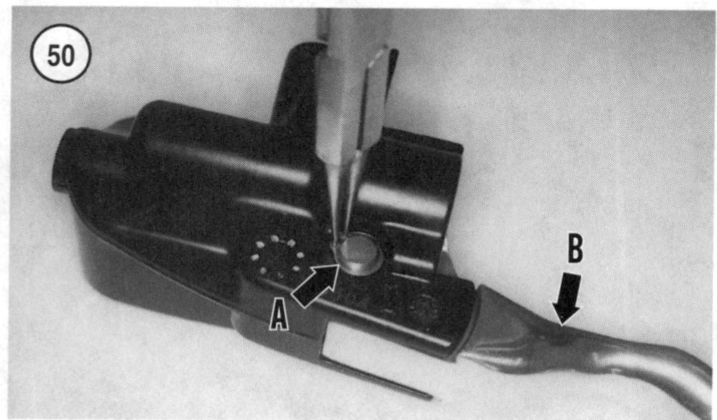

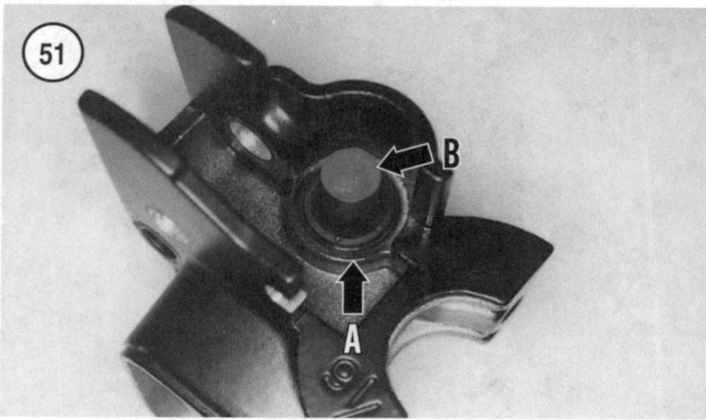

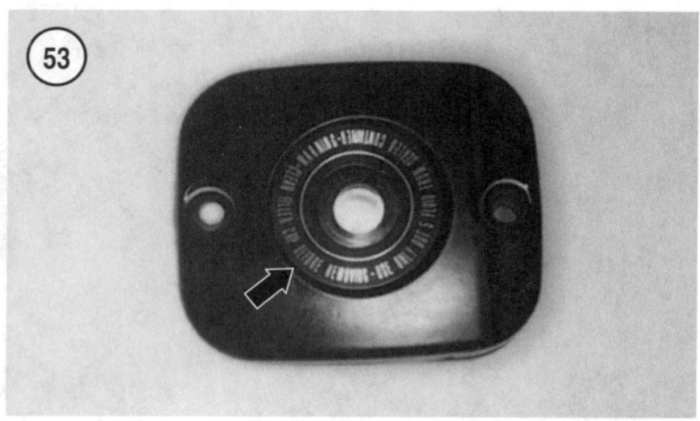

9. Install the mirror (A, **Figure 45**) onto the master cylinder.

10. Refill the master cylinder reservoir and bleed the brake system as described in this chapter.

11. On models so equipped, install the windshield or front fairing as described in Chapter Fifteen.

WARNING

Do not ride the motorcycle until the front brakes are operating correctly with full hydraulic advantage.

Disassembly

1. Store the master cylinder components (**Figure 49**) in a divided container, such as a restaurant-sized egg carton, to help maintain the correct alignment positions.

2. Remove the screws securing the top cover if they are still in place. Remove the top cover and the diaphragm from the master cylinder.

3. Remove the master cylinder assembly as described in this chapter.

4. Remove the snap ring (A, **Figure 50**) and pivot pin securing the hand lever to the master cylinder. Remove the hand lever (B, **Figure 50**).

5. Remove the retainer (A, **Figure 51**) and the rubber boot (B) from the area where the hand lever actuates the piston assembly.

6. Remove the piston assembly (**Figure 52**) and the spring.

7. Inspect all parts as described in this section.

Assembly

CAUTION

The cover and diaphragm must be assembled as described. If the sight glass is not installed correctly through the cover and diaphragm neck, brake fluid will leak past these components.

NOTE

When installing a new piston assembly, coat all parts with the lubricant provided with the Harley-Davidson parts kit. When installing existing parts, coat them with DOT 5 brake fluid.

1. If the cover and the diaphragm were disassembled, assemble them as follows:

   a. Install the trim plate (**Figure 53**) onto the cover if it was removed.

b. Insert the neck of the diaphragm into the cover. Press it in until it seats correctly and the outer edges are aligned with the cover.
c. Push the sight glass (**Figure 54**) straight down through the cover and the neck of the diaphragm (**Figure 55**) until it snaps into place. The sight glass must lock these two parts together to avoid a brake fluid leak.

2. Soak the *new* cup, O-ring and piston assembly in clean DOT 5 brake fluid for 15 minutes to make them pliable. Coat the inside of the cylinder bore with clean brake fluid prior to the assembly of parts.

CAUTION
When installing the piston assembly, do not allow the cup to turn inside out because it will be damaged and allow brake fluid leaks within the cylinder bore.

3. Install the spring and piston assembly into the cylinder (**Figure 56**). Push them in until they bottom in the cylinder (**Figure 52**).
4. Position the retainer with the flat side going on first, and install the piston cap and retainer onto the piston end.
5. Push down on the piston cap (**Figure 57**). Hold it in place and press the retainer down until it correctly seats in the cylinder groove (A, **Figure 51**).
6. Make sure the bushing is in place in the hand lever pivot area.
7. Install the hand lever (B, **Figure 50**) into the master cylinder. Install the pivot pin and secure it with the snap ring. Make sure the snap ring is correctly seated in the pivot pin groove (A, **Figure 50**).
8. Slowly apply the lever to make sure it pivots freely.
9. Install the master cylinder as described in this chapter.

Inspection

Replace worn or damaged parts as described in this section. It is recommended that a new piston kit assembly be installed every time the master cylinder is disassembled.

1. Clean all parts in isopropyl alcohol or clean DOT 5 brake fluid. Inspect the cylinder bore surface for signs of wear and damage. If it is less than perfect, replace the master cylinder assembly. The body cannot be replaced separately.
2. Inspect the piston cup (A, **Figure 58**) and O-ring (B) for signs of wear and damage.
3. Make sure the fluid passage (**Figure 59**) in the bottom of the master cylinder reservoir is clear. Clean it out if necessary.

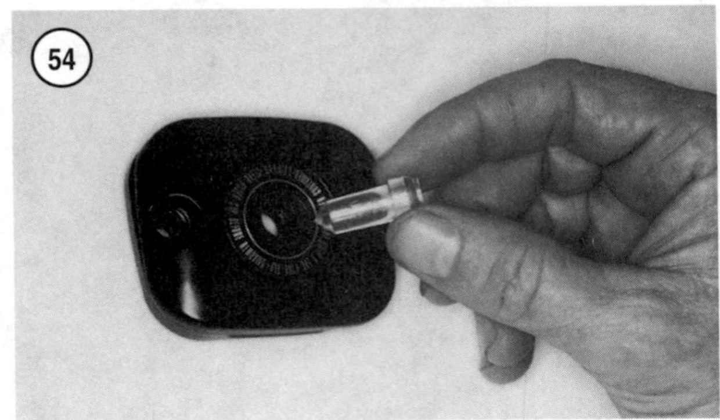
54

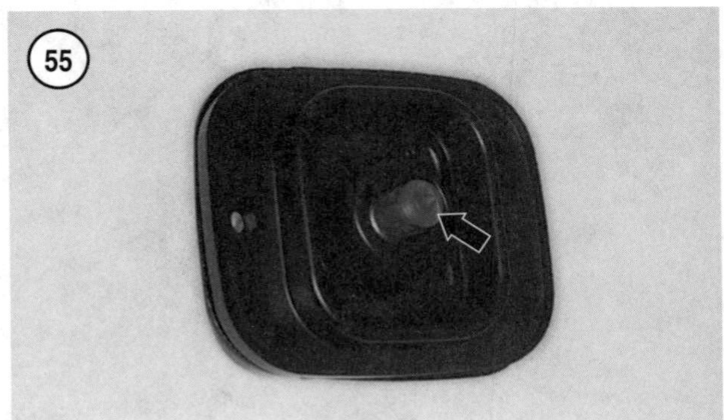
55

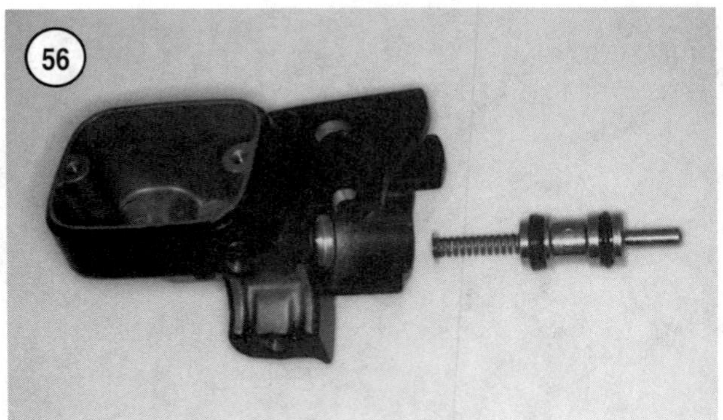
56

57

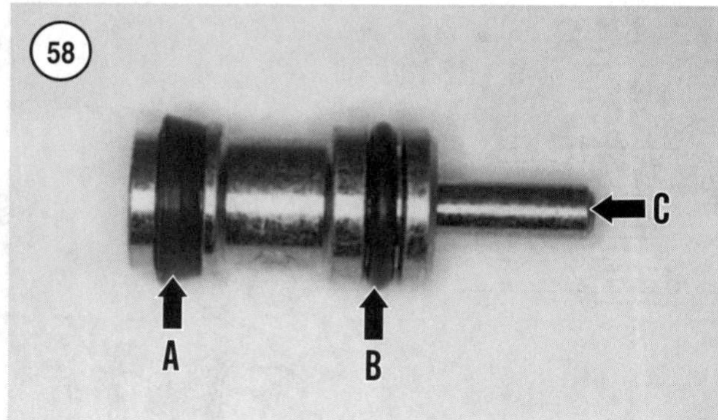

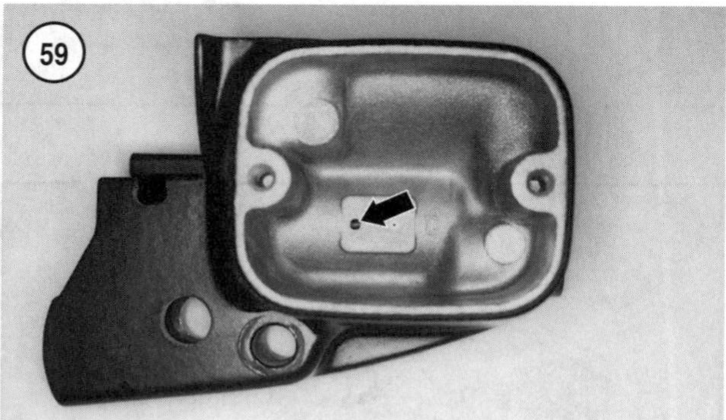

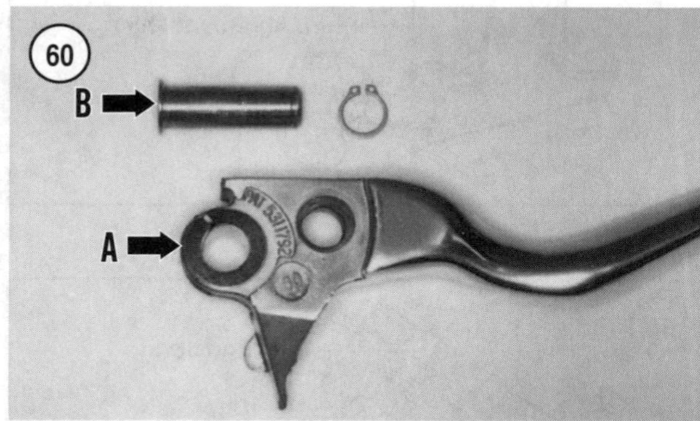

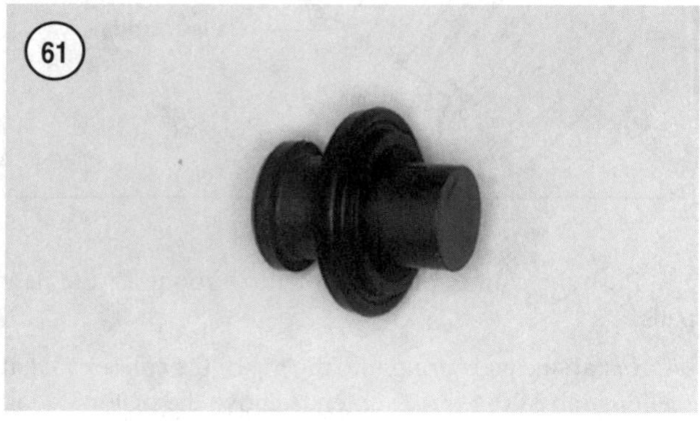

4. Inspect the piston contact surface for signs of wear and damage.
5. Check the end of the piston (C, **Figure 58**) for wear caused by the hand lever.
6. Check the hand lever pivot lugs in the master cylinder body for cracks or elongation.
7. Inspect the hand lever pivot hole and bushing (A, **Figure 60**), and the pivot pin (B) for wear, cracks or elongation.
8. Inspect the piston cap and retainer (**Figure 61**) for wear or damage.
9. Inspect the threads in the bore for the banjo bolt. If they are worn or damaged, clean them out with a thread tap or replace the master cylinder assembly.
10. Check the top cover and diaphragm for damage or deterioration.
11. If necessary, separate the cover from the diaphragm as follows:
   a. Pull straight up on the sight glass (**Figure 54**) and remove it from the cover and diaphragm.
   b. Separate the diaphragm from the cover.
   c. The trim plate might separate from the cover.

REAR BRAKE PAD REPLACEMENT

There is no recommended mileage interval for changing the brake pads. Pad wear depends greatly on riding habits and conditions. The pads should be checked for wear initially at 500 miles (800 km) and then every 2500 miles (4000 km). Replace the pads when the lining thickness reaches 1/16 in. (1.6 mm) from the brake pad back plate. To maintain even brake pressure on the disc, always replace both pads in the caliper at the same time.

1984-Early 1987 FXR and FXWG, FXSB and FXEF Models

Refer to **Figure 62**.
1. Read *Brake Service* in this chapter.
2. Park the motorcycle on level ground.
3. Tie the end of the brake pedal to the frame. If the brake pedal is inadvertently applied, this will prevent the piston from being forced out of the cylinder.
4. On models so equipped, remove the right saddlebag as described in Chapter Fifteen.
5. Clean the top of the rear master cylinder of all dirt and debris.
6. Remove the screws securing the cover. Remove the cover and diaphragm.
7. Use a shop syringe to remove about 50 percent of the brake fluid from the reservoir. This will prevent the mas-

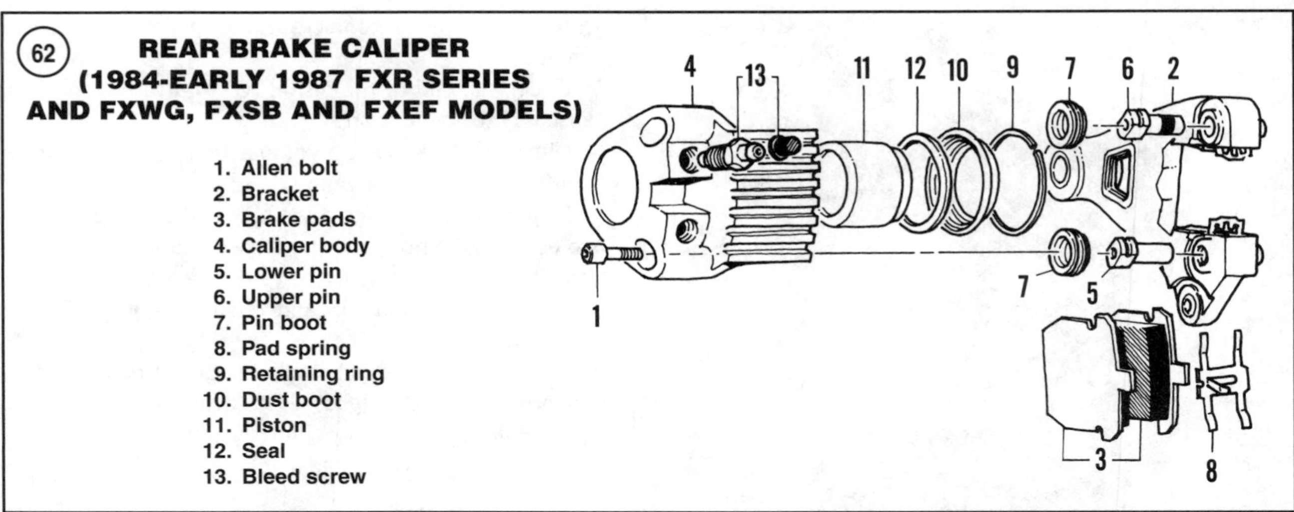

ter cylinder from overflowing when the piston is compressed for reinstallation. Do *not* drain more than 50 percent of the brake fluid, or air will enter the system. Discard the brake fluid.

8. Remove the Allen bolts securing the caliper and carefully lift the caliper off of the brake disc. Do not disconnect the brake hose at the caliper.
9. Remove the brake pads from the caliper body or caliper bracket.
10. Remove the pad spring from inside the caliper.
11. Check the abutment shims in the caliper bracket (**Figure 63**). If they are worn or damaged, replace them as follows:
   a. Pry the abutment shims away from the caliper bracket.
   b. Remove all adhesive residue from the caliper bracket surface where the abutment shims were located.
   c. Clean the abutment shim surface with denatured alcohol.
   d. Apply silicone sealant to the abutment shim surface on the caliper bracket and install both abutment shims. Hold the shims in position by installing the brake pads in the caliper bracket.
   e. Allow the silicone sealant to dry thoroughly before completing brake pad installation.
   f. Check that the brake pads slide freely in the caliper bracket.
   g. Remove the brake pads after the silicone sealant has dried.
12. Check the brake pads for wear or damage. Replace the brake pads if they are worn to 1/16 in. (1.6 mm) or less. Replace both pads as a set.

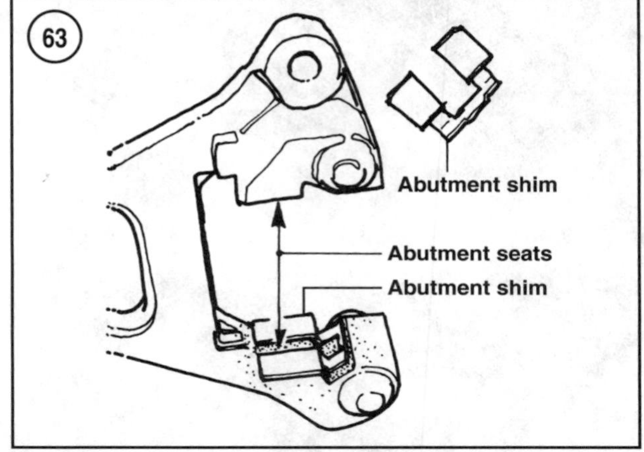

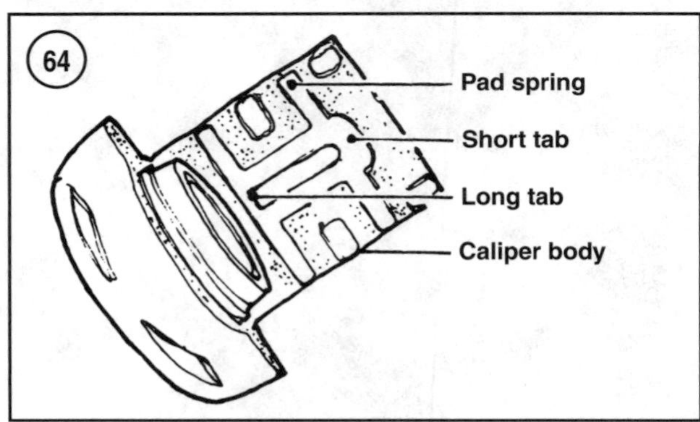

13. Push the caliper piston in to allow room for the new pads.

14. Install the pad spring into the top of the caliper so that the long tab of the spring extends above the piston. Hook

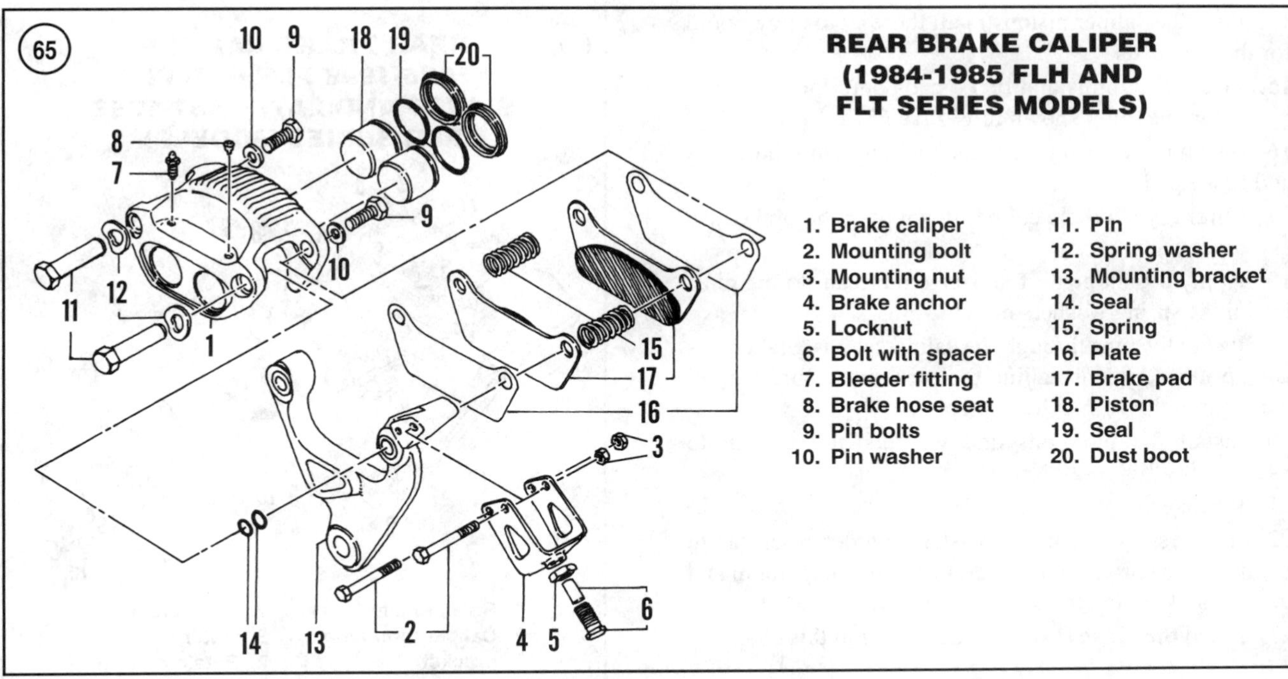

the short tab above the ridge on the caliper casting opposite the piston (**Figure 64**).

15. If removed, install the upper and lower pins and boots into the caliper bracket. Position the flat side on each pin so it is parallel with the caliper bracket opening.
16. Install both brake pads onto the caliper bracket.
17. Install the caliper body over the brake pads and onto the bracket. Make sure the upper and lower pins do not rotate when installing the caliper body. Readjust if necessary. Refer to Step 15.
18. Install the Allen bolts and tighten to 12-15 ft.-lb. (16-20 N•m).
19. Release the rear brake pedal.
20. If necessary, refill the master cylinder reservoir to maintain the correct fluid level. Install the diaphragm and top cap and tighten the screws securely.
21. Bleed the brake system as described in this chapter.
22. On models so equipped, install the right saddlebag as described in Chapter Fifteen.

WARNING

Do not ride the motorcycle until the rear brake is operating correctly with full hydraulic advantage.

1984-1985 FLH and FLT Series Models

Refer to **Figure 65**.

1. Read *Brake Service* in this chapter.
2. Park the motorcycle on level ground.
3. Tie the end of the brake pedal to the frame. If the brake pedal is inadvertently applied, this will prevent the piston from being forced out of the cylinder.
4. On models so equipped, remove the right saddlebag as described in Chapter Fifteen.
5. Clean the top of the rear master cylinder of all dirt and debris.
6. Remove the screws securing the cover, and remove the cover and diaphragm.
7. Use a shop syringe to remove about 50 percent of the brake fluid from the reservoir. This will prevent the master cylinder from overflowing when the piston is compressed for reinstallation. Do *not* drain more than 50 percent of the brake fluid, or air will enter the system. Discard the brake fluid.
8. Remove both bolts and washers securing the caliper to the mounting bracket.
9. Withdraw both pins and spring washers from the mounting bracket.
10. Remove both seals from the mounting bracket.
11. Carefully lift the caliper off of the brake disc. Secure the caliper to the frame with wire or bungee cord.
12. Remove the shims, brake pads and springs from the mounting bracket.
13. Inspect the brake pads for wear or damage. Replace the brake pads if they are worn to 1/16 in. (1.6 mm) or less. Replace both pads as a set.

14. Push the caliper pistons in all the way to allow room for the new pads.
15. Install the shims and brake pads onto the mounting bracket in the order shown in **Figure 65**.
16. Install both springs and line them up with the shims and brake pad holes.
17. Carefully slide the caliper down over the brake disc and brake pads.
18. Apply a light coat of antiseize lubricant to the pins. Install the spring washers onto the pins.
19. Install the pins through the caliper, shims, brake pads and springs. After installing the pins, make sure that all parts are in the correct locations.
20. Install the pin bolts and washers and tighten to 142-177 in.-lb. (16-20 N•m).
21. Release the rear brake pedal.
22. If necessary, refill the master cylinder reservoir to maintain the correct fluid level. Install the diaphragm and top cap and tighten the screws securely.
23. Bleed the brake system as described in this chapter.

WARNING
Use brake fluid clearly marked DOT 5 from a sealed container. Other types can vaporize and cause brake failure. Always use the same brand name; do not mix because many brands are not compatible.

WARNING
Do not ride the motorcycle until the rear brake is operating correctly with full hydraulic advantage.

1986-1998 FLH and FLT Series and Late 1987-1999 FXR Models

Refer to **Figure 66**.

Brake pad/pad shim identification

There was a design change between late 1987-early 1991 and late 1991-1998 models regarding the brake pads and pad shims. When purchasing replacement parts, note the following while referring to **Figure 67** (late 1987-early 1991 models) or **Figure 68** (late 1991-1998 models):

1. On late 1987-early 1991 models, pad shim thickness is 0.015 in. (0.38 mm).
2. On late 1991-1999 models, pad shim thickness is 0.030 in. (0.76 mm).
3. On late 1987-early 1991 models, pad shims have a tab in the middle of each long side.

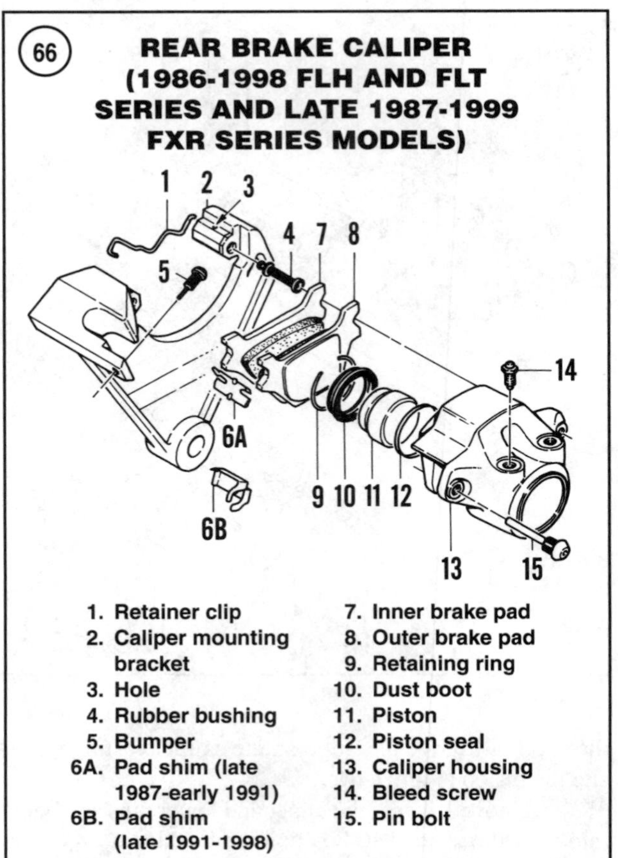

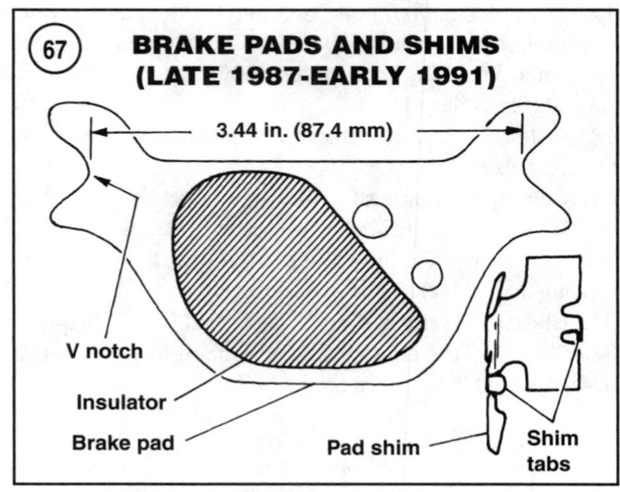

4. On late 1991-1999 models, pad shims have an open loop at one end of the shim.
5. On late 1987-early 1991 models, brake pads measure approximately 3.44 in. (87.4 mm) between the *V* notches as shown in **Figure 67**. On late 1991-1999 models, brake

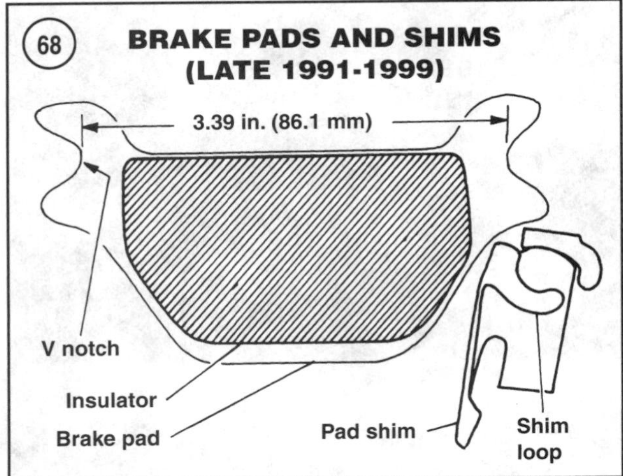

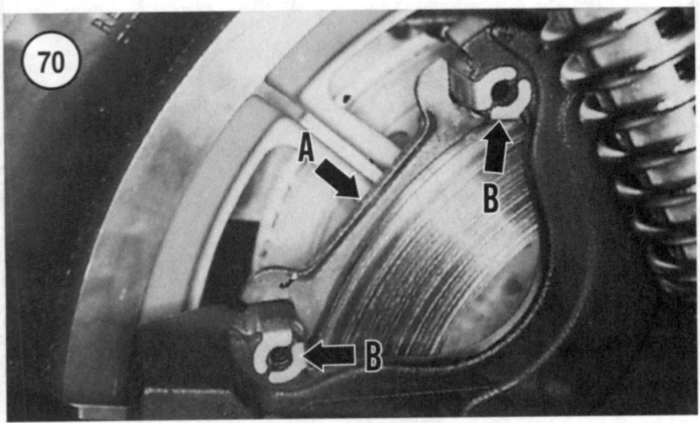

pads measure approximately 3.39 in. (86.1 mm) as shown in **Figure 68**.

6. On late 1987-early 1991 models, the outboard brake pads have an angle-cut, half-size insulator mounted on the back of the pad. The inboard brake pad has a full-size insulator.

7. On late 1991-1999 models, the brake pads have full-size insulators mounted on the back of each pad.

Replacement

WARNING

When replacing brake pads, do not mix late 1987-early 1991 and late 1991-1999 brake pads and pad shims. If the wrong pads and shims are installed, the rear brake will not operate correctly and will result in brake failure. When purchasing new brake pads, verify the exact year and model being worked on (refer to frame serial and/or VIN number).

1. Read *Brake Service* in this chapter.
2. Park the motorcycle on level ground.
3. Tie the end of the brake pedal to the frame. If the brake pedal is inadvertently applied, this will prevent the piston from being forced out of the cylinder.
4. On FLH and FLT series models: perform the following:
   a. Remove the right saddlebag; see Chapter Fifteen.
   b. Remove the right side cover.
   c. Disconnect the negative and then the positive battery cables. Remove the battery and the battery carrier.
5. Clean the top of the rear master cylinder of all dirt and debris.
6. Remove the screws securing the cover and remove the cover and diaphragm.
7. Use a shop syringe to remove about 50 percent of the brake fluid from the reservoir. This will prevent the master cylinder from overflowing when the piston is compressed for reinstallation. Do *not* drain more than 50 percent of the brake fluid, or air will enter the system. Discard the brake fluid.
8. Remove the caliper pin bolts (A, **Figure 69**) and lift the caliper (B) off of the mounting bracket. Do not disconnect the brake hose at the caliper. 13
9. Pull the retainer clip (A, **Figure 70**) over the mounting bracket and remove it.
10. Slide the outer brake pad off the mounting bracket.
11. Slide the inner brake pad (**Figure 71**) toward the wheel and off the mounting bracket.
12. Remove the pad shims from the mounting bracket.
13. Check the brake pads (**Figure 72**) for wear or damage. Replace the brake pads if they are worn to 1/16 in. (1.6 mm) or less. Replace both pads as a set.
14. Thoroughly clean the pad shims and check for cracks or damage. Replace if necessary.
15. Thoroughly clean the shim mounting area on the mounting bracket.
16. Check the pad clip for damage; replace if necessary.
17. Push the caliper piston in all the way to allow room for the new pads.

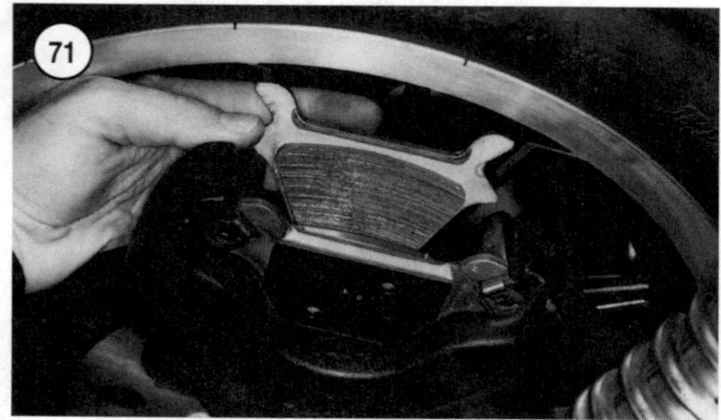

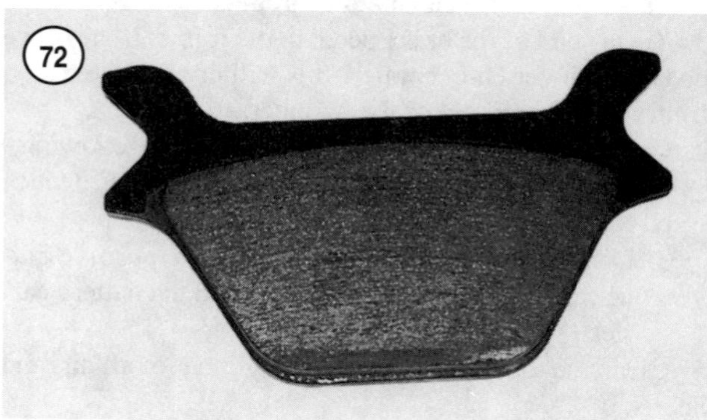

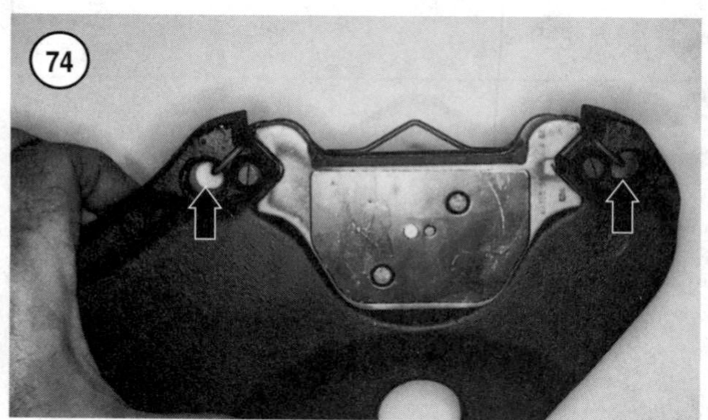

18. Install the pad shims onto the caliper mounting bracket rails as follows:
   a. On late 1987-early 1991 models, insert the pad shim tabs (**Figure 67**) into the caliper bracket shim holes (No. 3, **Figure 66**).
   b. On late 1991-1999 models, install the pad shims (**Figure 68**) so that the retaining loops face the outer caliper mounting bracket rails as shown in B, **Figure 70** and **Figure 73**.
   c. On all models, hold the pad shims in place when installing the inner brake pad in Step 20.
19. Install the inner brake pad and slide it over the pad shims so that it contacts the inside brake disc surface.
20. Install the outer brake pad and slide it over the pad shims so that it contacts the outside brake disc surface.
21. Working on the inside of the mounting bracket, insert the ends of the pad clip into the two large holes (**Figure 74**) in the mounting bracket. Pivot the clip over the top of the brake pads until it seats against the outer brake pad as shown in **Figure 75**.

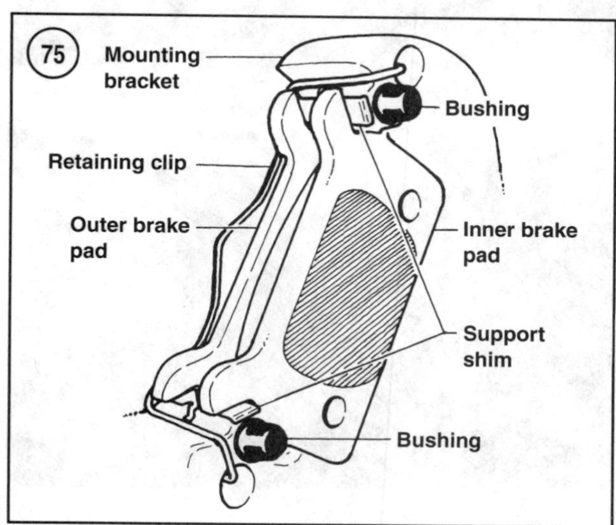

WARNING

*After installing the pad clip, check that the outer brake pad is still contacting both pad support shims (**Figure 75**). Failure of the outer pad to contact both pad shims can result in irregular pad wear, brake drag or mounting bracket damage.*

NOTE

Carefully install the caliper over the brake pads so it does not knock against the brake pads and dislodge the pad shims.

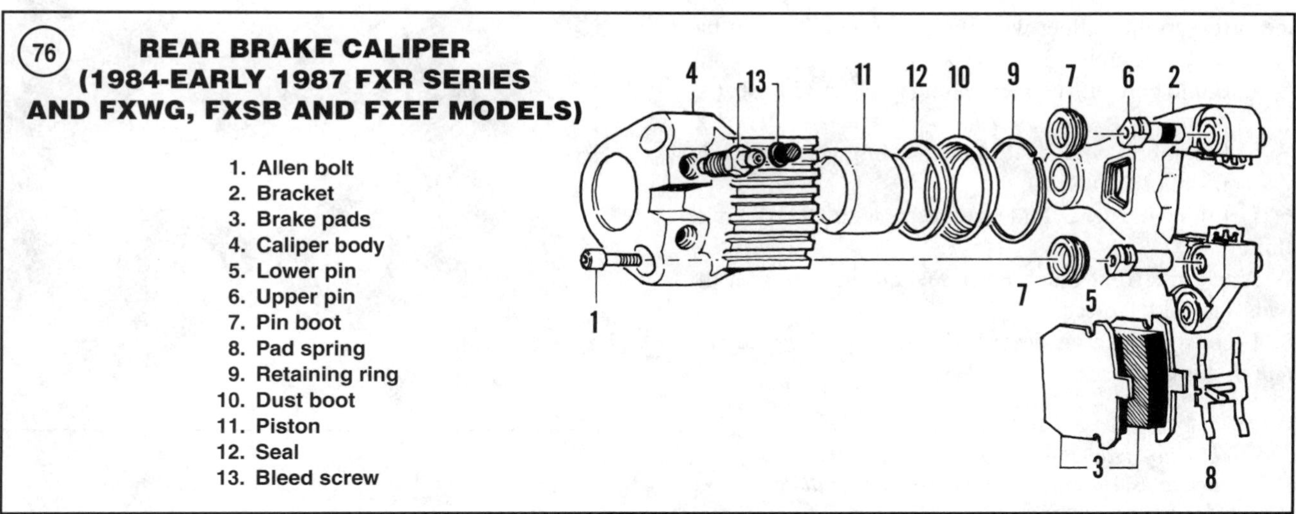

76 REAR BRAKE CALIPER (1984-EARLY 1987 FXR SERIES AND FXWG, FXSB AND FXEF MODELS)

22. Align the caliper with the brake pads and carefully install it over the pads.
23. Align the holes in the caliper with the threaded holes in the mounting bracket and install both pin bolts.
24. Start the bolts by hand. Then tighten to 15-20 ft.-lb. (20-27 N•m).
25. Release the rear brake pedal.
26. If necessary, refill the master cylinder reservoir to maintain the correct fluid level. Install the diaphragm and top cap and tighten the screws securely.
27. Bleed the brake system as described in this chapter.

WARNING
Do not ride the motorcycle until the rear brake is operating correctly with full hydraulic advantage.

REAR BRAKE CALIPER

1984-Early 1987 FXR and FXWG, FXEF and FXSB Models

Refer to **Figure 76**.

Removal

1. Drain the brake fluid from the rear brake hose as described under *Brake Hose and Line Replacement* in this chapter.
2. Loosen the banjo bolt at the caliper. Remove the banjo bolt and the two washers.
3. Place the loose end of the brake hose in a reclosable plastic bag to prevent the entry of moisture and debris. Tie the loose end of the hose out of the way.
4. Remove the Allen bolts securing the caliper to the mounting bracket.
5. Carefully slide the brake caliper off of the brake disc.
6. If the brake caliper is not going to be serviced, place it in a plastic bag to keep it clean.

Installation

1. If removed, install the brake pads as described in this chapter.
2. If removed, install the upper and lower pins and boots into the caliper bracket. Position the flat side on each pin parallel with the caliper bracket opening.
3. Install the caliper body over the brake pads and onto the bracket. Make sure the upper and lower pins do not rotate when installing the caliper body. Readjust if necessary.
4. Install the Allen bolts and tighten to 142-177 in.-lb. (16-20 N•m).

WARNING
*There are two different types of sealing washers used with the banjo bolts. Early models are copper with a zinc coating (A, **Figure** 77). Late models are steel with a rubber O-ring (B, **Figure** 77). The banjo bolts must be used with the specific sealing washers. Make sure that the banjo bolts and washers match the original parts. A mismatch of these parts will result in a brake fluid leak and possible complete loss of brake operation.*

5. Install the brake hose onto the caliper with a *new* washer on both sides of the brake line fitting. Then secure

the fitting to the caliper with the banjo bolt. Tighten the banjo bolt as follows:

a. Banjo bolt with copper sealing washer: 35 ft.-lb. (47 N•m).
b. Banjo bolt with steel/rubber sealing washer: 17-22 ft.-lb. (23-30 N•m).

6. Refill the master cylinder reservoir with DOT 5 brake fluid.
7. Apply the front brake lever several times to seat the pads against the disc.
8. Bleed the brakes as described under *Bleeding the System* in this chapter.

WARNING
Do not ride the motorcycle until the rear brake is operating correctly with full hydraulic advantage.

Disassembly

1. Remove the brake pads as described in this chapter.
2. Insert a small screwdriver into the notched groove machined in the bottom of the piston bore. Then pry the retaining ring out of the caliper body.
3. Remove the dust boot from the groove at the top of the piston.
4. Remove the piston from the caliper.

WARNING
Compressed air will force the piston out of the caliper under considerable force. Do not block the piston by hand because injury will occur.

5. If the piston did not come partially out of the caliper bore, perform the following:
   a. Place a rag and a piece of wood in the caliper (**Figure 78**). Keep fingers out of the way of the piston.
   b. Apply compressed air through the brake hose port and force the piston out of the caliper.
6. Carefully pry the piston seal out of the caliper bore groove and remove it.
7. Remove the upper and lower pins and their rubber boots.

Assembly

WARNING
Never reuse an old dust boot or piston seal. Very minor damage or age deterioration can make the boot and seal ineffective.

1. Install the *new* piston seal into the caliper body groove.

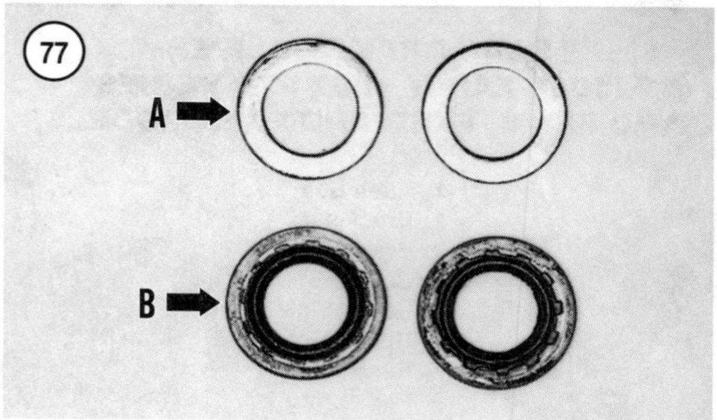

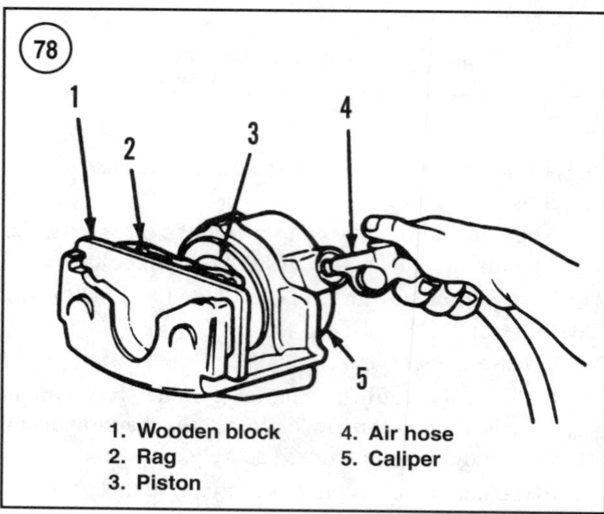

1. Wooden block
2. Rag
3. Piston
4. Air hose
5. Caliper

2. Coat the piston and the caliper bore with DOT 5 brake fluid.
3. Align the piston with the caliper bore so that the open end faces out. Then push in the piston until it bottoms.
4. Install the *new* piston dust boot onto the end of the piston.
5. Locate the retaining wire groove in the end of the caliper bore and install the wire into the wire groove. Make sure that the retaining wire is seated completely in the groove and that it is pushing against the piston dust boot.
6. Install the boot onto the upper and lower pins. Then apply silicone grease to the pin shafts and the pin bores in the mounting bracket.
7. Insert the pins into the pin bores. Install the pin with the nylon sleeve into the top mounting bracket hole. Make sure the boot shoulder on each boot fits onto their respective boss. Rotate the pins so that flats on both pins are parallel with the bracket opening.
8. Install the brake pads and abutment shims as described in this chapter.

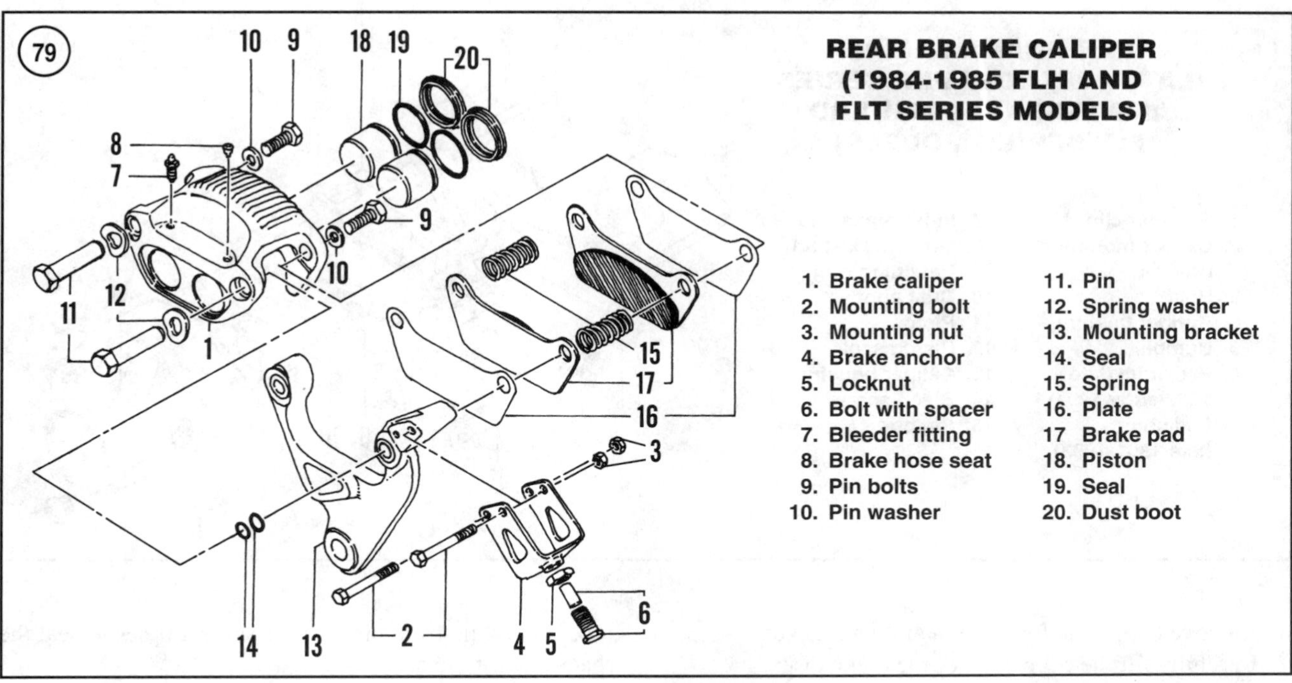

Inspection

Service specifications for the rear caliper components are not available. Replace worn, damaged or questionable parts.

1. Clean the caliper body and piston in clean DOT 5 brake fluid or isopropyl alcohol. Dry them with compressed air.
2. Make sure the fluid passageway in the base of the piston bore is clear. Apply compressed air to the opening to make sure it is clear. Clean it out, if necessary, with clean brake fluid.
3. Inspect the piston seal groove in the caliper body for damage. If it is damaged or corroded, replace the caliper assembly.
4. Inspect the banjo bolt threaded hole in the caliper body. If it is worn or damaged, clean it out with a thread tap or replace the caliper assembly.
5. Inspect the bleed screw threaded hole in the caliper body. If it is worn or damaged, clean it out with a thread tap or replace the caliper assembly.
6. Inspect the bleed screw. Apply compressed air to the opening and make sure it is clear. Clean it out, if necessary, with clean brake fluid. Install the bleed screw and tighten it to the following:
   a. 1984-1990: 32-40 in.-lb. (3.6-4.5 N•m).
   b. 1991-1998: 80-100 in.-lb. (9-11 N•m).
7. Inspect the caliper body for damage.
8. Inspect the cylinder wall and piston for scratches, scoring or other damage.
9. Check the mounting bracket for cracks or damage. Check the threads in the plate for damage. If the threads are slightly damaged, clean them up with the properly sized thread tap. If the threads are worn or damaged beyond repair, replace the mounting bracket.
10. Check the mounting pin shoulder for deep scoring or excessive wear; replace if necessary.
11. Check the pad retainer for cracks or damage.

13

1984-1985 FLH and FLT Series Models

Removal

Refer to **Figure 79**.

1. Drain the brake fluid from the rear brake hose as described under *Brake Hose and Line Replacement* in this chapter.
2. Loosen the banjo bolt at the caliper. Remove the banjo bolt and the two washers.
3. Place the loose end of the brake hose in a reclosable plastic bag to prevent the entry of moisture and debris. Tie the loose end of the hose to the handlebar.
4. Remove both bolts and washers securing the caliper to the mounting bracket.
5. Withdraw both pins and spring washers from the mounting bracket.

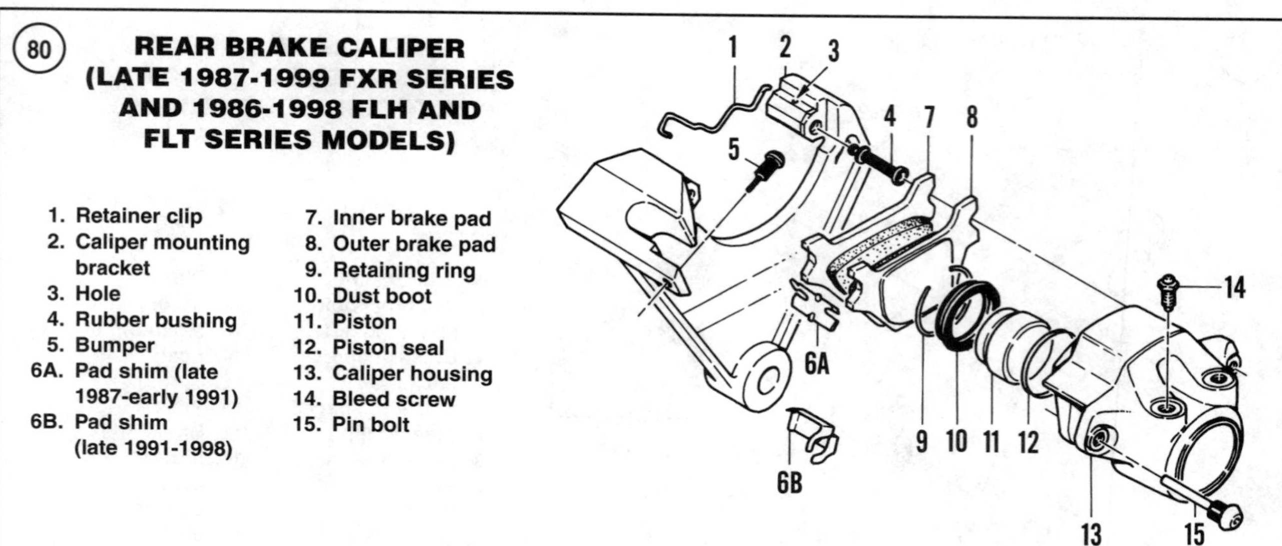

REAR BRAKE CALIPER (LATE 1987-1999 FXR SERIES AND 1986-1998 FLH AND FLT SERIES MODELS)

6. Remove both seals from the mounting bracket.
7. Carefully lift the caliper off of the brake disc.
8. If the brake caliper is not going to be serviced, place it in a plastic bag to keep it clean.

Installation

1. If removed, install the brake pads as described in this chapter.
2. Install the shims and brake pads onto the mounting bracket in the order shown in **Figure 79**.
3. Install both springs and line them up with the shims and brake pad holes.
4. Carefully slide the caliper down over the brake disc and brake pads.
5. Apply a light coat of antiseize lubricant to the pins. Install the spring washers onto the pins.
6. Install the pins through the caliper, shims, brake pads and springs. After installing the pins, make sure that all parts are in the correct locations.
7. Install the pin bolts and washers and tighten to 142-177 in.-lb. (16-20 N•m).
8. Install the brake hose onto the caliper with a *new* washer on both sides of the brake line fitting. Then secure the fitting to the caliper with the banjo bolt. Tighten the banjo bolt as follows:
   a. Banjo bolt with copper sealing washer: 35 ft.-lb. (47 N•m).
   b. Banjo bolt with steel/rubber sealing washer: 17-22 ft.-lb. (23-30 N•m).
9. Refill the master cylinder reservoir with DOT 5 brake fluid.
10. Apply the front brake lever several times to seat the pads against the disc.
11. Bleed the brakes as described in this chapter.

WARNING
Do not ride the motorcycle until the rear brake is operating correctly with full hydraulic advantage.

Disassembly

1. Remove the brake pads as described in this chapter.

NOTE
Before removing the pistons, mark the locations within the caliper. The pistons must be reinstalled in the original cylinders.

2. Remove the dust boots from the caliper.
3. Remove the pistons from the caliper.

WARNING
Compressed air will force the piston out of the caliper under considerable force. Do not block the piston by hand as injury will occur.

4. If the pistons did not come partially out of the caliper bore, perform the following:
   a. Place a rag and a piece of wood in the caliper (**Figure 78**). Keep fingers out of the way of the pistons.
   b. Apply compressed air through the brake hose port and force the pistons out of the caliper.

5. Carefully pry the piston seal out of each caliper bore groove.

Assembly

1. Install a *new* piston seal in each cylinder bore wall groove. Make sure the seals seat squarely in the grooves.
2. Coat the pistons and the caliper bores with DOT 5 brake fluid.
3. Install the pistons into the correct caliper bores as noted during *Disassembly*.
4. Position the piston into the caliper bore with the open end facing out.
5. Push in the piston until it bottoms out. Repeat for the other piston.
6. Install a *new* piston dust boot onto the end of the piston. Make sure the seals seat squarely in the grooves. Repeat for the other piston.
7. Install the brake pads as described in this chapter.

Inspection

Service specifications for the front caliper components are not available. Replace worn, damaged or questionable parts.

1. Clean the caliper body and pistons in clean DOT 5 brake fluid or isopropyl alcohol. Dry them with compressed air.
2. Make sure the fluid passageway in the base of the piston bore is clear. Apply compressed air to the opening to make sure it is clear. Clean it out, if necessary, with clean brake fluid.
3. Inspect the piston seal grooves in the caliper body for damage. If they are damaged or corroded, replace the caliper assembly.
4. Inspect the banjo bolt threaded hole in the caliper body. If it is worn or damaged, clean it out with a metric thread tap or replace the caliper assembly.
5. Inspect the bleed screw threaded hole in the caliper body. If it is worn or damaged, clean it out with a metric thread tap or replace the caliper assembly.
6. Inspect the bleed screw. Apply compressed air to the opening and make sure it is clear. Clean it out, if necessary, with clean brake fluid. Install the bleed screw and tighten it to the following:
   a. 1984-1990: 32-40 in.-lb. (3.6-4.5 N•m).
   b. 1991-1998: 80-100 in.-lb. (9-11 N•m).
7. Inspect the caliper body for damage.
8. Inspect the cylinder walls and pistons for scratches, scoring or other damage.
9. Check the mounting bracket for cracks or damage. Check the threads in the bracket for damage. If the threads are slightly damaged, clean them up with a properly sized thread tap. If the threads are worn or damaged beyond repair, replace the mounting bracket.

1986-1998 FLH, FLT and Late 1987-1999 FXR Series Models

Refer to **Figure 80**.

Removal

1. Drain the brake fluid from the rear brake hose as described under *Brake Hose and Line Replacement* in this chapter.
2. Loosen and remove the banjo bolt holding the brake line to the caliper (**Figure 81**). Remove the bolt and the two washers. Place the end of the brake line in a plastic bag and secure the bag against the brake line with a plastic tie to prevent brake fluid from dripping onto the rear wheel.
3. Remove the brake pads (and caliper) as described in this chapter.
4. If the brake caliper is not going to be serviced, place it in a plastic bag to keep it clean.

Installation

1. If removed, install the brake pads (and caliper) as described in this chapter.
2. Install the caliper bolts and tighten to 15-20 ft.-lb. (20-27 N•m).

WARNING

There are two different types of sealing washers used with the banjo bolts. Early models are copper with a zinc coating (A, ***Figure*** *77). Late models are steel with a rubber O-ring (B). The banjo bolts must be*

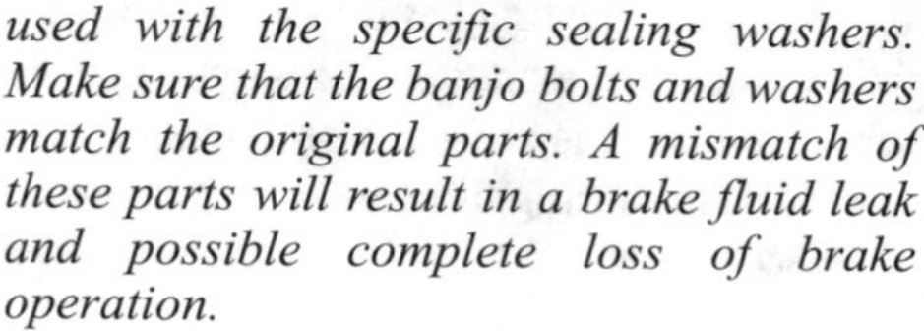
used with the specific sealing washers. Make sure that the banjo bolts and washers match the original parts. A mismatch of these parts will result in a brake fluid leak and possible complete loss of brake operation.

3. Install the brake line onto the caliper with a *new* washer (**Figure 82**) on both sides of the brake line fitting. Then secure the fitting to the caliper with the banjo bolt. Tighten the banjo bolt as follows:
   a. Banjo bolt with copper sealing washer: 35 ft.-lb. (47 N•m).
   b. Banjo bolt with steel/rubber sealing washer: 17-22 ft.-lb. (23-30 N•m).
4. Refill the master cylinder reservoir with DOT 5 brake fluid.
5. Apply the front brake lever several times to seat the pads against the disc.
6. Bleed the brakes as described in this chapter.

WARNING
Do not ride the motorcycle until the front brake operates correctly with full hydraulic advantage.

Disassembly

1. Remove the brake pads as described in this section.
2. Insert a small screwdriver placed in the caliper notch (**Figure 83**) and carefully pry the retaining ring (**Figure 84**) out of the caliper body.
3. Remove the piston dust boot from the groove at the top of the piston (**Figure 85**).
4. Remove the piston from the caliper.

WARNING
Compressed air will force the piston out of the caliper under considerable force. Do

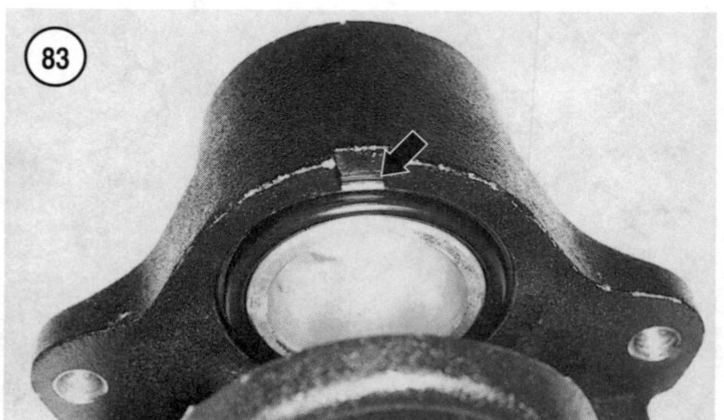

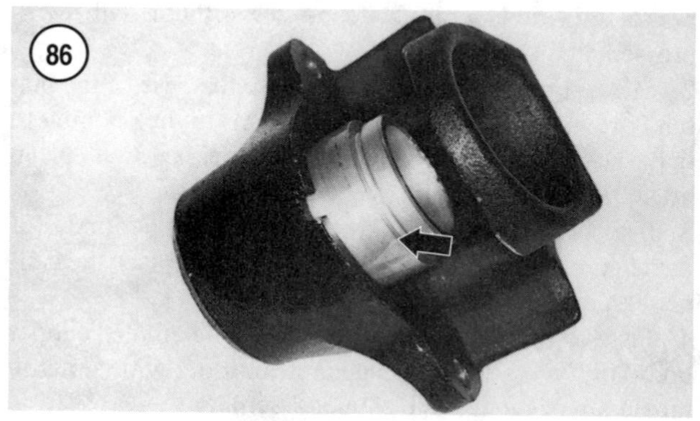

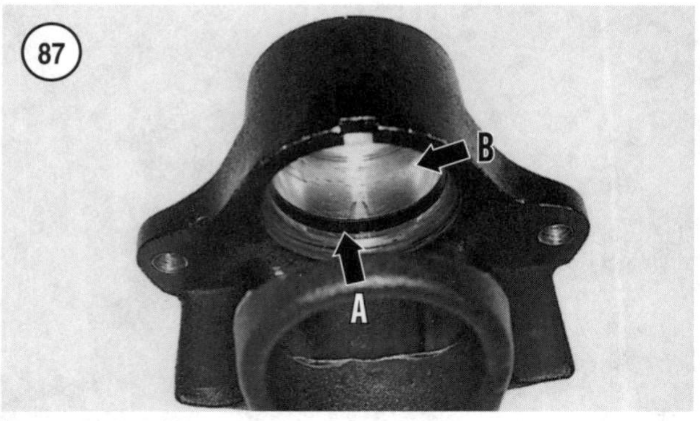

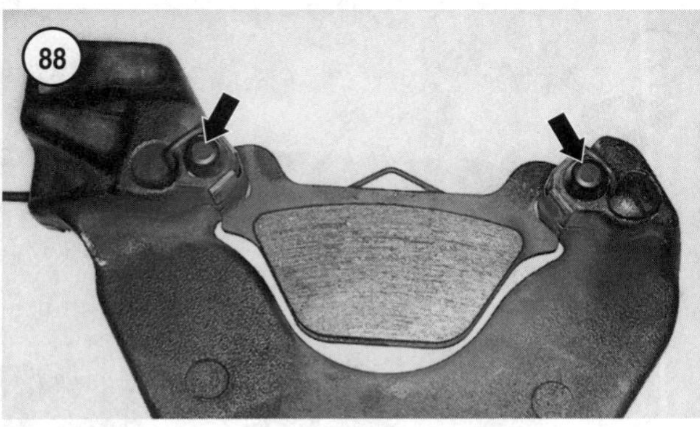

not block the piston by hand because injury will occur.

5. If the piston did not come partially out of the caliper bore, perform the following:
   a. Place a rag and a piece of wood in the caliper (**Figure 78**). Keep fingers out of the way of the piston.
   b. Apply compressed air through the brake hose port and force the piston out of the caliper (**Figure 86**).
6. Remove the piston seal (A, **Figure 87**) from the groove in the caliper body and discard it.
7. Replace the rubber bushings (**Figure 88**) in the mounting bracket if worn or damaged.

Assembly

1. Install the *new* piston seal (A, **Figure 87**) into the caliper body groove.
2. Coat the piston and the caliper bore with DOT 5 brake fluid.
3. Position the piston with the open end facing out and install it into the caliper bore (**Figure 86**). Then push the piston in until it bottoms.
4. Install the *new* piston dust boot (**Figure 85**) onto the end of the piston.
5. Locate the retaining wire groove in the end of the caliper bore and install the wire into the wire groove (**Figure 84**). Make sure that the retaining wire is seated completely in the groove and that it is pushing against the piston dust boot.
6. Install *new* rubber bushings (**Figure 88**) into the mounting bracket if worn or damaged.
7. Install the brake pads and pad shims as described in this chapter.

Inspection

Service specifications for the rear caliper components are not available. Replace worn, damaged or questionable parts.

1. Inspect the caliper body for damage; replace the caliper body if necessary.
2. Inspect the hydraulic fluid passageways in the caliper body (**Figure 89**). Make sure they are clean and open.
3. Inspect the cylinder wall (B, **Figure 87**) and the piston (**Figure 90**) for scratches, scoring or other damage. Replace worn, corroded or damaged parts. Do not bore or hone the caliper cylinder.
4. Inspect the banjo bolt and bleed valve threads in the caliper body. If the threads are slightly damaged, clean them up with a properly sized thread tap. If the threads are worn or damaged beyond repair, replace the caliper body.

5. Make sure the hole in the bleed valve screw (**Figure 91**) is clean and open.
6. Check the mounting bracket for cracks or damage. Check the threads in the plate for damage. If the threads are slightly damaged, clean them up with a properly sized thread tap. If the threads are worn or damaged beyond repair, replace the mounting bracket.
7. Check the pin bolt shoulder for deep scoring or excessive wear; replace if necessary.
8. Check the pad retainer for cracks or damage.
9. Check the brake pads (**Figure 92**) for wear or damage. Replace the brake pads if they are worn to 1/16 in. (1.6 mm) or less. Replace both pads as a set.

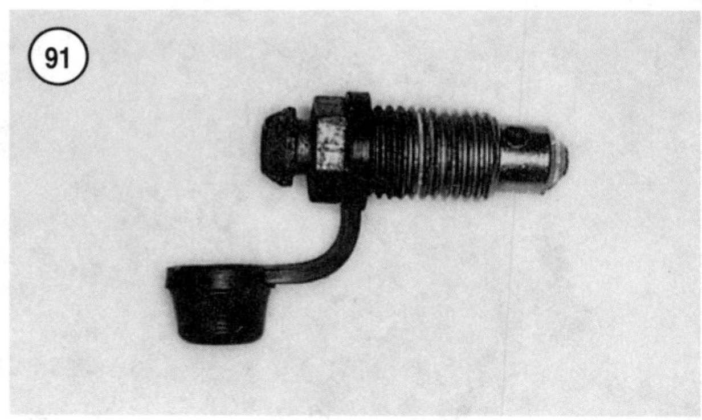

91

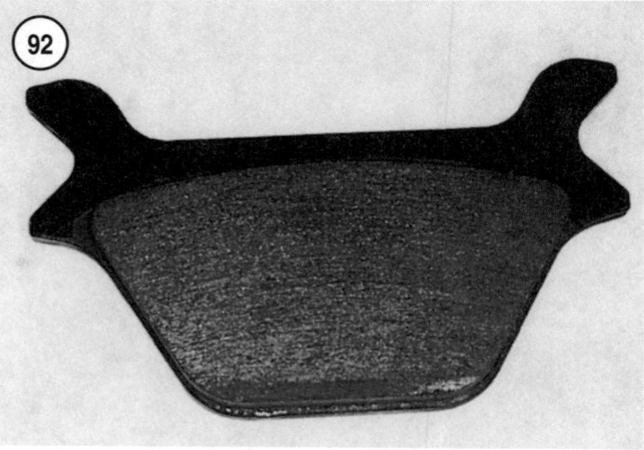

92

REAR MASTER CYLINDER AND RESERVOIR

1984-Early 1987 FXR Series Models

Refer to **Figure 93**.

Removal

1. Drain the brake fluid from the rear brake hose as described under *Brake Hose and Line Replacement* in this chapter.
2. To disconnect the master cylinder reservoir, cut the reservoir hose clamp at the master cylinder and disconnect the hose. Do not twist the hose back and forth sharply because the hose nipple on the master cylinder can be damaged. Plug the hose opening.
3. Use a flare nut wrench and remove the caliper brake hose at the master cylinder. Pull the hose away from the master cylinder.

NOTE
Place the end of the brake hose in a plastic bag.

4. Disconnect the electrical connector from the brake switch mounted on the master cylinder.
5. Remove the bolts and washers securing the master cylinder to the frame.
6. Slowly pull the master cylinder back and disconnect it from the pushrod. Install the boot onto the pushrod if it came off when removing the master cylinder.

Installation

1. If necessary, install the boot onto the pushrod.
2. Insert the pushrod into the piston in the end of the master cylinder and position the master cylinder onto the frame. Install the bolts and washers and tighten to 13-16 ft.-lb. (18-22 N•m).
3. Connect the caliper brake hose to the master cylinder port. Tighten the fitting to 70-80 in.-lb. (8-9 N•m).
4. Slide a *new* hose clamp onto the hose and fit the hose onto the hose reservoir nipple. Slide the clamp down so that it is against the hose where the hose fits onto the nipple. Close the hose clamp so that it is tight against the hose.

NOTE
Figure 94 *shows the type of pliers required to close the hose clamp.*

5. Fill the reservoir with new DOT 5 hydraulic brake fluid. Bleed brake system as described in this chapter.
6. Install the reservoir gasket and cover. Tighten the screws securely.

WARNING
Do not ride the motorcycle until the rear brake is operating correctly with full hydraulic advantage.

(93) **REAR BRAKE MASTER CYLINDER (1984-EARLY 1987 FXR SERIES MODELS)**

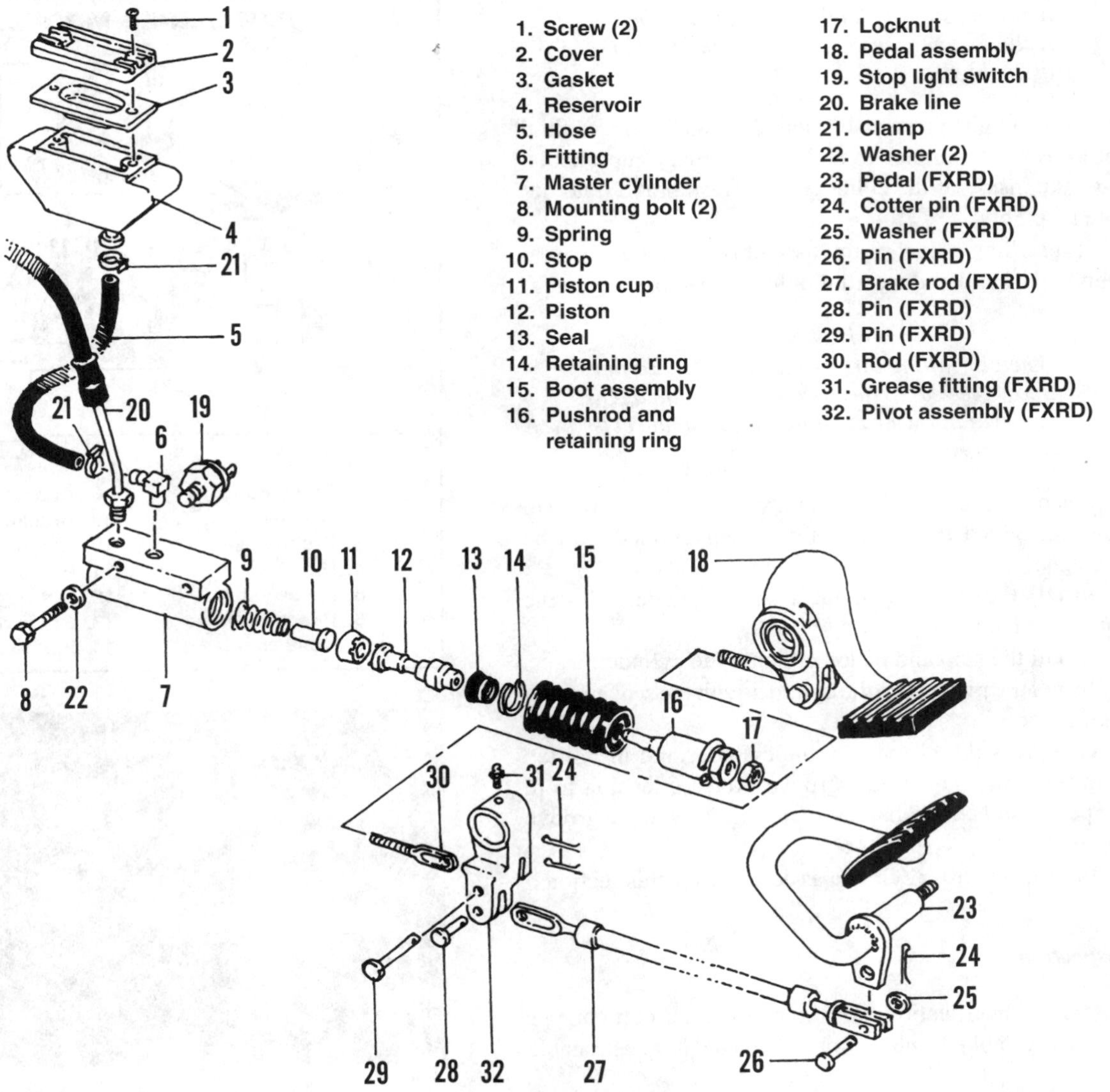

1. Screw (2)
2. Cover
3. Gasket
4. Reservoir
5. Hose
6. Fitting
7. Master cylinder
8. Mounting bolt (2)
9. Spring
10. Stop
11. Piston cup
12. Piston
13. Seal
14. Retaining ring
15. Boot assembly
16. Pushrod and retaining ring
17. Locknut
18. Pedal assembly
19. Stop light switch
20. Brake line
21. Clamp
22. Washer (2)
23. Pedal (FXRD)
24. Cotter pin (FXRD)
25. Washer (FXRD)
26. Pin (FXRD)
27. Brake rod (FXRD)
28. Pin (FXRD)
29. Pin (FXRD)
30. Rod (FXRD)
31. Grease fitting (FXRD)
32. Pivot assembly (FXRD)

(94)

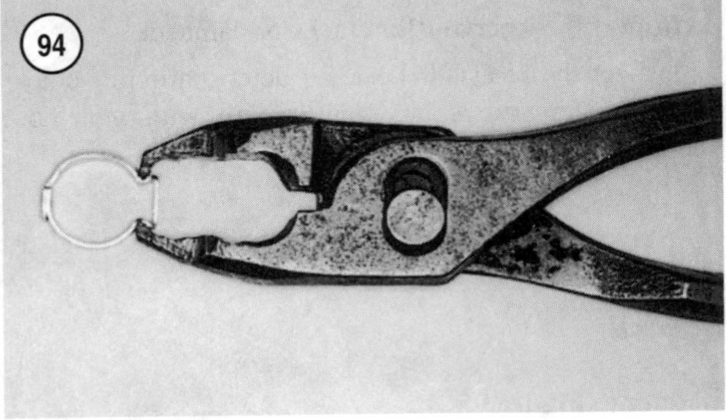

Disassembly

1. Remove the master cylinder as described in this section.
2. Place the master cylinder in a vise with soft jaws.
3. Insert a rod into the end of the piston and compress the piston to remove tension against the snap ring.
4. Remove the snap ring and slowly remove tension from the piston.
5. Remove the piston assembly, stop and spring from the master cylinder.

Assembly

WARNING
A new master cylinder repair kit must be installed whenever the master cylinder is disassembled.

1. Soak the piston assembly in fresh DOT 5 brake fluid for at least 15 minutes to make the primary cup pliable. Coat the inside of the cylinder with fresh brake fluid before assembly.
2. If installing a new piston assembly, coat the new seal with brake fluid and install it onto the piston.

WARNING
When installing the piston assembly, do not allow the seal to turn inside out. A damaged seal will allow brake fluid to leak in the cylinder bore.

3. Place the master cylinder in a vise with soft jaws. Do not overtighten the jaws or the master cylinder can be damaged.
4. Install the spring into the master cylinder with the small end facing out.
5. Install the stop and piston cup into the cylinder.
6. Install the piston into the cylinder with the seal end facing out.
7. Compress the piston into the cylinder and install the snap ring into the cylinder groove. Release tension from the piston and check that the snap ring seats in the groove completely.
8. Install the master cylinder as described in this section.

Inspection

Service specifications for the rear caliper components are not available. Replace worn, damaged or questionable parts.
1. Clean all rubber parts in isopropyl alcohol or fresh DOT 5 brake fluid.
2. Apply compressed air to all openings in the master cylinder body and dry it thoroughly.
3. Inspect the cylinder bore and the piston contact surfaces for signs of wear and damage. If either part is less than perfect, replace it.
4. Replace the piston assembly if the cup and seal are damaged. The cup and seal cannot be replaced individually.
5. Check the end of the piston assembly for wear caused by the pushrod.
6. Inspect the rubber boot for deterioration, cracking and wear.

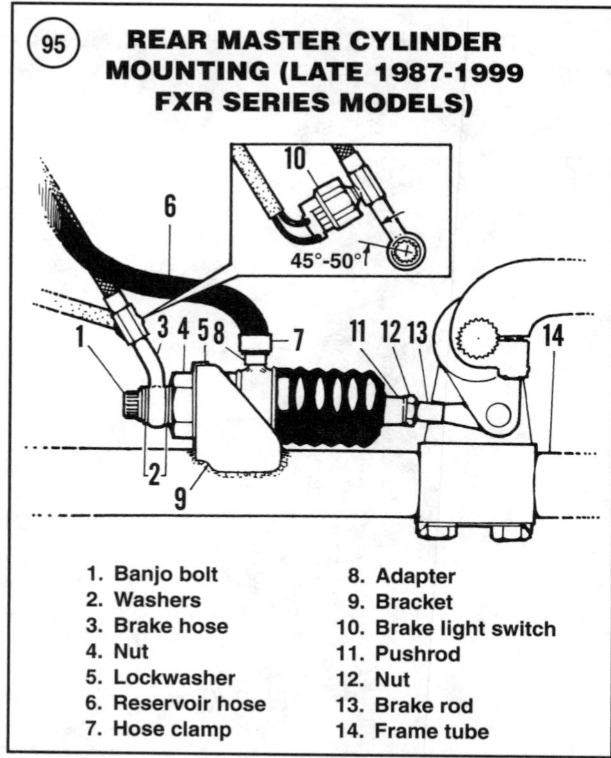

7. Remove the cover and gasket from the reservoir. Inspect the gasket for wear, deterioration or damage.
8. Inspect the reservoir for cracks or damage.
9. Inspect the reservoir hose for deterioration or cracking. If necessary, replace and secure with *new* hose clamps.

Late 1987-1999 FXR Series Models

Removal

Refer to **Figure 95**.

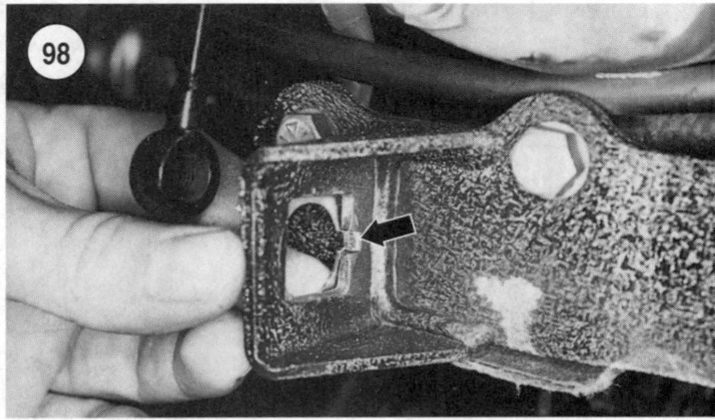

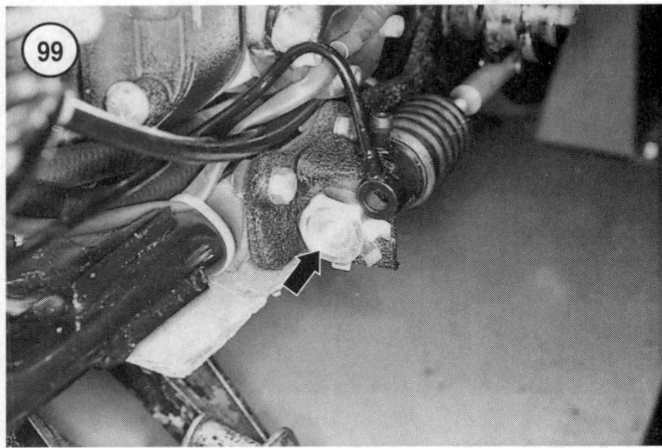

1. Drain the brake fluid from the rear brake hose as described under *Brake Hose and Line Replacement* in this chapter.

2. To disconnect the master cylinder reservoir, cut the reservoir hose clamp at the master cylinder and disconnect the hose. Do not twist the hose back and forth sharply because the hose nipple on the master cylinder can be damaged. Plug the hose opening.

3. Remove the exhaust system as described in Chapter Eight.

4. Remove the cotter pin and pin. Then disconnect the brake pedal from the brake pedal rod.

CAUTION
Follow the procedure in Step 5 to prevent damage to the metal brake line.

5. Loosen the metal brake line banjo bolt as follows:
   a. Have an assistant hold onto the brake line to keep it from rotating when loosening the banjo bolt.
   b. Use an air wrench or impact driver and carefully loosen the banjo bolt (**Figure 96**) securing the metal brake line to the cartridge body.
6. Remove the banjo bolt and two sealing washers from the cartridge body. Place the open end of the hose in a plastic bag.
7. Bend the lockplate tab away from the cartridge body.
8. Remove the nut (**Figure 97**) and lockplate and remove the cartridge body.

Installation

1. If the reservoir was removed, place it into position and secure it with the screws and washers. Install the hose onto the reservoir nipple and secure the hose with a new hose clamp.

CAUTION
Handle the cartridge body carefully when installing it as the hose reservoir can be easily cracked or broken off.

2. Align the tab on the lockwasher with the notch in the master cylinder mounting bracket and install the lockwasher (**Figure 98**).
3. Position the brake pedal away from the cartridge body frame mounting bracket.
4. Position the cartridge body with the brake hose nipple facing up.
5. Carefully insert the threaded end of the cartridge body through the frame mounting bracket. Insert the square portion of the cartridge body into the square hole in the mounting bracket.
6. Install the cartridge body nut (**Figure 99**) onto the cartridge body and tighten to 30-40 ft.-lb. (41-54 N•m). Bend the lockwasher tab over the nut to lock it.

WARNING
There are two different types of sealing washers used with the banjo bolts. Early models are copper with a zinc coating (A, ***Figure 100****). Late models are steel with a rubber O-ring (B,* ***Figure 100****). The banjo bolts must be used with the specific sealing*

washers. Make sure that the banjo bolts and washers match the original parts. A mismatch of these parts will result in a brake fluid leak and possible complete loss of brake operation.

7. Install the brake line onto the cartridge body with a *new* washer (**Figure 101**) on both sides of the brake line fitting. Then secure the fitting to the caliper with the banjo bolt.
8. Correctly position the brake line so that it is at a 45-50° angle from horizontal (**Figure 95**). When the brake line is angled properly, tighten the banjo bolt as follows:
   a. Banjo bolt with copper sealing washer: 35 ft.-lb. (47 N•m).
   b. Banjo bolt with steel/rubber sealing washer: 17-22 ft.-lb. (23-30 N•m).
9. Slide a *new* hose clamp (A, **Figure 102**) up onto the reservoir hose.
10. Install the reservoir hose (B, **Figure 102**) onto the fitting on the adapter and push it on until it bottoms on the fitting.

NOTE
***Figure 94** shows the type of pliers required to close the hose clamp.*

11. Slide the clamp down so that it is against the hose where the hose fits onto the nipple. Close the hose clamp so that it is tight against the hose (**Figure 103**).
12. Move the brake pedal into position and attach the pedal rod to the brake pedal (**Figure 95**) with the pin. Secure with a *new* cotter pin. Bend the ends over completely.
13. Adjust the brake pedal as described in Chapter Three.
14. Fill the reservoir with new DOT 5 hydraulic brake fluid. Bleed the brake system as described under *Bleeding the System* in this chapter.
15. Install the reservoir gasket and cover after bleeding the brakes. Tighten the screws securely.

WARNING
Do not ride the motorcycle until the rear brake is operating correctly with full hydraulic advantage.

Disassembly

Refer to **Figure 104**.
1. Remove the master cylinder as described in this section.
2. Clean all rubber parts in isopropyl alcohol or fresh DOT 5 brake fluid.
3. Screw the banjo bolt into the end of the cartridge body to protect the end of the cartridge when removing it.

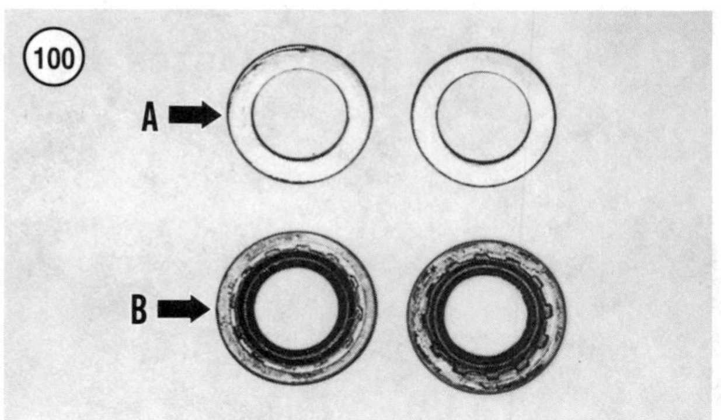

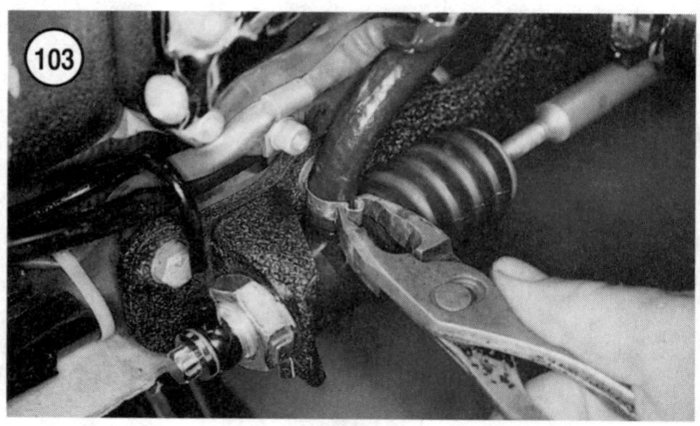

104

REAR MASTER CYLINDER (LATE 1987-1998 FXR)

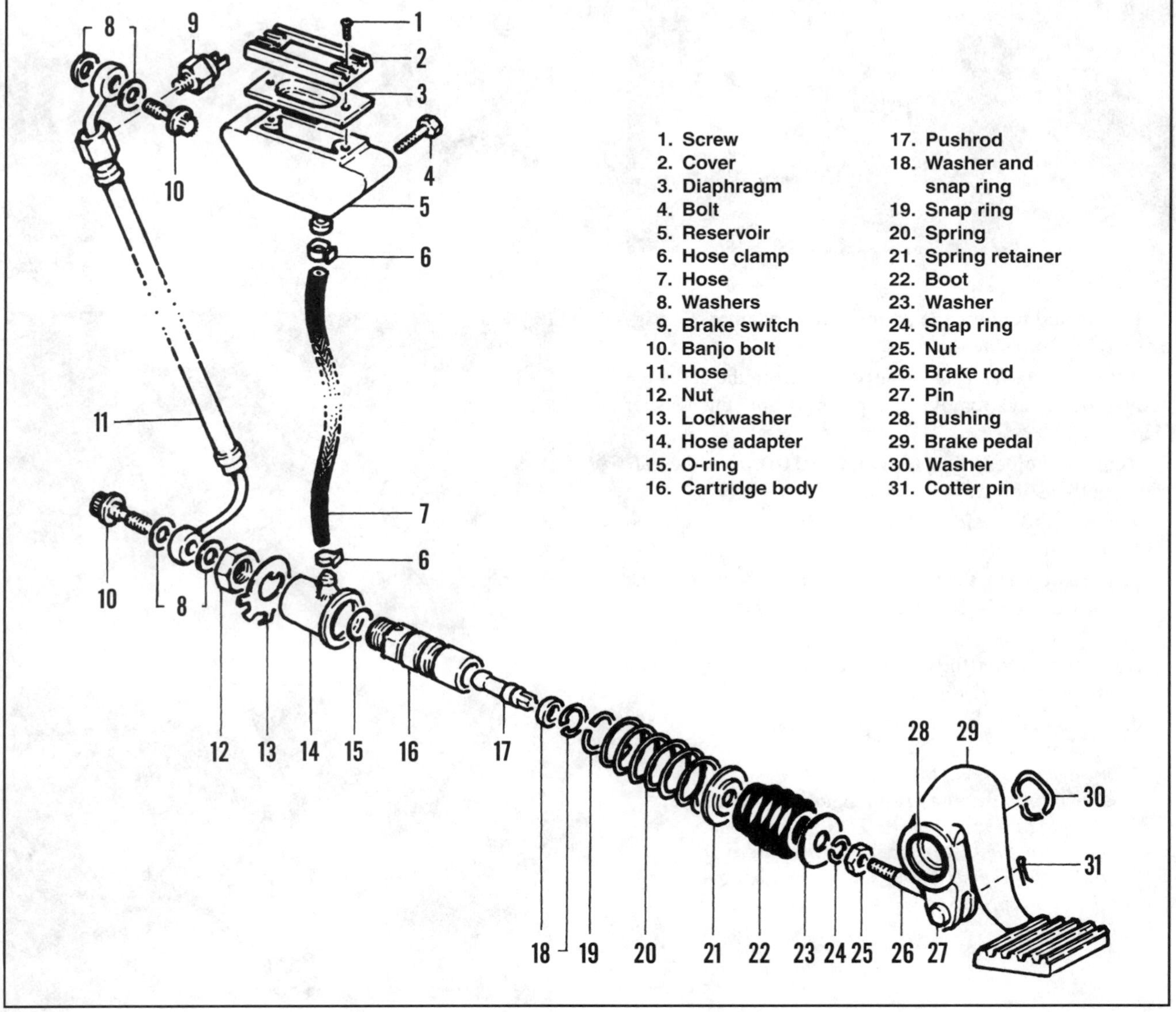

1. Screw
2. Cover
3. Diaphragm
4. Bolt
5. Reservoir
6. Hose clamp
7. Hose
8. Washers
9. Brake switch
10. Banjo bolt
11. Hose
12. Nut
13. Lockwasher
14. Hose adapter
15. O-ring
16. Cartridge body
17. Pushrod
18. Washer and snap ring
19. Snap ring
20. Spring
21. Spring retainer
22. Boot
23. Washer
24. Snap ring
25. Nut
26. Brake rod
27. Pin
28. Bushing
29. Brake pedal
30. Washer
31. Cotter pin

105

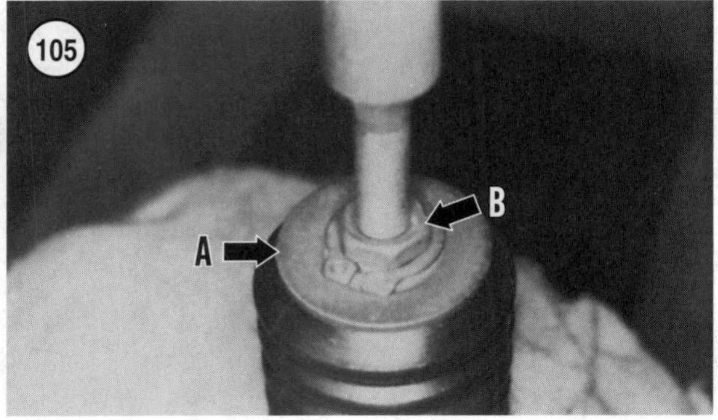

4. Press down on the large washer (A, **Figure 105**) and compress the spring.

5. Put a wrench across the flat on the pushrod (A, **Figure 106**). Then use another wrench to loosen the pushrod locknut (B, **Figure 106**) on the pedal rod and unscrew the rod from the end of the pushrod.

6. Set the cartridge body upright so that it rests on the banjo bolt. Then compress the large washer (A, **Figure 105**) in the end of the cartridge body and remove the snap ring from the groove in the pushrod. Release the washer and remove the washer, boot (A, **Figure 107**) and spring (B).

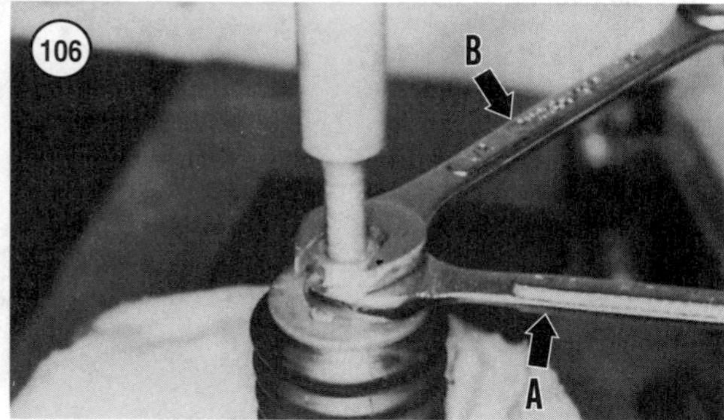

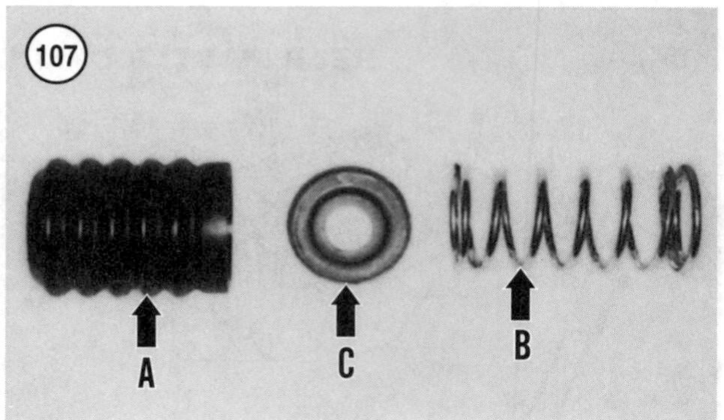

7. Locate and remove the spring return retainer (C, **Figure 107**) from inside the boot.
8. Remove the snap ring (**Figure 108**) from the cartridge body groove and remove the pushrod and the washer (**Figure 109**).
9. Remove the hose adapter (**Figure 110**) from the cartridge body as follows:
   a. Stand the cartridge body upright so that it rests on the banjo bolt.
   b. Push down on the hose adapter and slide it off of the cartridge body. Protect the cartridge body while it is exposed.
   c. Do not remove the O-rings (**Figure 111**) unless they are going to be replaced.
   d. Remove the outer cartridge body snap ring.

CAUTION
*Do not remove the piston assembly from the cartridge body (**Figure 112**). Replacement parts for the piston assembly are not available. If the piston and seals are damaged, the cartridge body assembly must be replaced.*

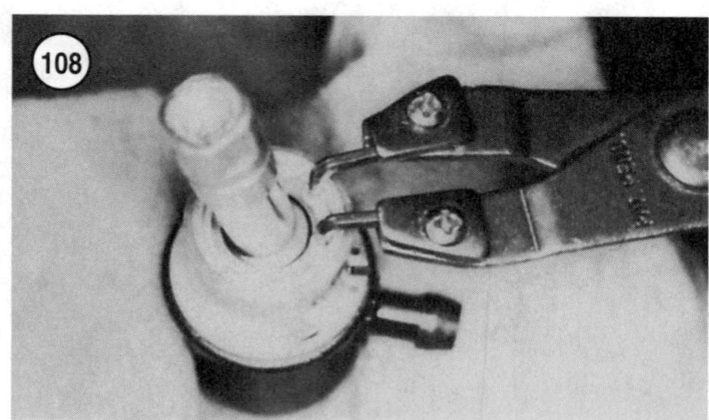

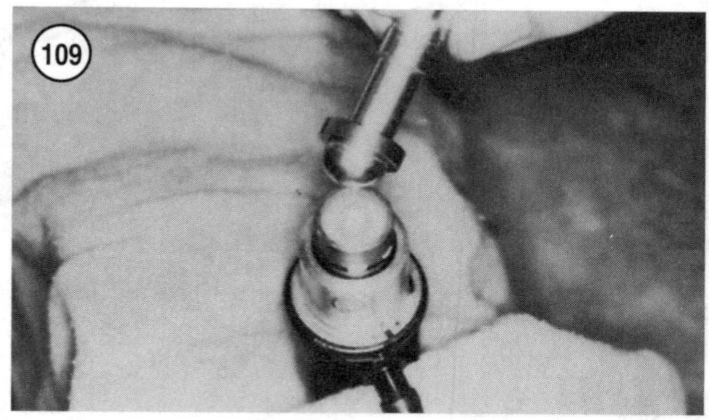

Assembly

1. Assemble the hose reservoir adapter, if removed, as follows:
   a. If new O-rings are being installed, soak them in DOT 5 brake fluid.
   b. Install the O-rings into the cartridge body grooves (**Figure 111**).
   c. Coat the interior of the adapter with DOT 5 brake fluid.
   d. Using hand pressure only, slide the hose reservoir adapter over the cartridge body. Engage the tab in the hose reservoir adapter (A, **Figure 113**) with the notch (B) in the cartridge body (**Figure 114**).

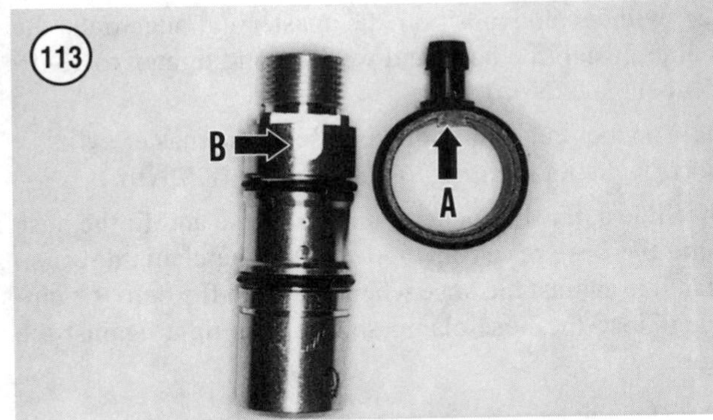

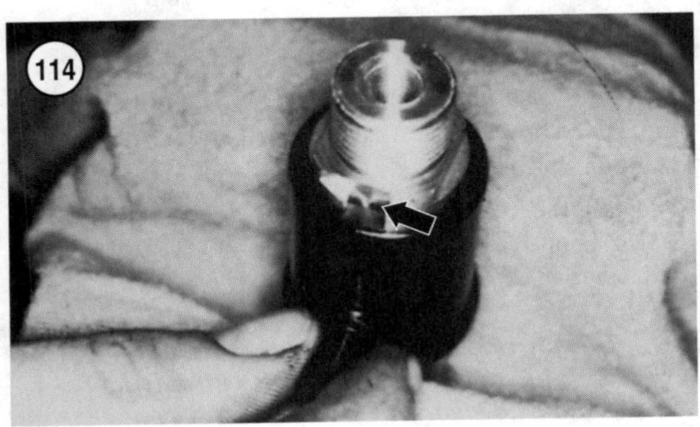

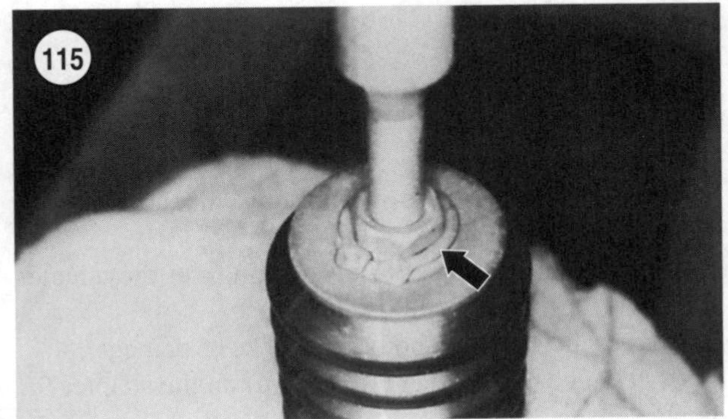

CAUTION

Do not force the cartridge into the cartridge body. If the parts do not assemble easily, the cartridge and cartridge body are not properly aligned. Forcing these parts together will damage both parts.

2. Install the banjo bolt into the end of the cartridge body and stand the assembly up so that it rests on the banjo bolt.
3. Install the washer onto the pushrod (opposite ball end) (**Figure 109**).
4. Insert the pushrod (ball end first) into the cartridge until the pushrod washer is seated in the cartridge body bore. Then install the snap ring into the cartridge body groove to secure the pushrod (**Figure 108**). Make sure the snap ring seats in the groove completely. After installing the snap ring, rotate the pushrod by hand; it should turn freely. If the pushrod is tight, disassemble the cartridge body to locate the damaged or improperly installed part.
5. Install the return spring (B, **Figure 107**) and spring retainer (C) onto the pushrod. Install the spring retainer so that the shoulder on the retainer faces away from the spring.
6. Install the dust boot (A, **Figure 107**) over the pushrod and turn it so the drain hole in the boot faces down. Seat the lip on the dust boot into the groove in the hose reservoir.
7. Install the large washer over the end of the pushrod.
8. Push the washer down to compress the return spring and install the snap ring onto the end of the pushrod. Make sure the snap ring seats in the groove completely (**Figure 115**).
9. Thread the locknut onto the pedal rod and thread the rod into the pushrod. Do not tighten the locknut because it will be tightened after adjusting the rear brake pedal in Chapter Three.

Inspection

Service specifications for the rear master cylinder components are not available. Replace worn, damaged or questionable parts.

1. Clean all rubber parts in isopropyl alcohol or fresh DOT 5 brake fluid.
2. Apply compressed air to all openings in the adapter and dry it thoroughly.
3. Inspect the cartridge body for cracks or damage.
4. Check the hose fitting (**Figure 116**) on the adapter for damage.
5. Inspect the O-rings (**Figure 111**) on the cartridge body for wear or damage. Replace the O-rings, if worn, along with adapter.
6. Check the threads on the cartridge body, banjo bolt and pushrod.
7. Check the dust boot (A, **Figure 107**) for cracks, age deterioration or other damage. Replace if necessary.
8. Remove the cover and gasket from the reservoir. Inspect the gasket for wear, deterioration or damage.
9. Inspect the reservoir for cracks or damage.
10. Inspect the reservoir hose for deterioration or cracking. Replace if necessary and secure with *new* hose clamps.

FXWG, FXSB and FXEF Models

Refer to **Figure 117**.

Removal

1. Drain the brake fluid from the rear brake hose as described under *Brake Hose and Line Replacement* in this chapter.
2. To disconnect the master cylinder reservoir, cut the reservoir hose clamp at the master cylinder and disconnect the hose. Do not twist the hose back and forth sharply as the hose nipple on the master cylinder can be damaged. Plug the hose opening.
3. Use a flare nut wrench and remove the caliper brake hose at the master cylinder. Pull the hose away from the master cylinder.

NOTE
Place the end of the brake hose in a plastic bag.

4. Remove the bolts and washers securing the master cylinder to the frame.
5. Slowly pull the master cylinder back and disconnect it from the pushrod.

6A. On FXWG models, remove the boot, spring and spring washer.

6B. On FXSB and FXEF models, remove the boot.

Installation

1A. On FXWG models, install the spring and spring washer over the small end of the pushrod. Install the boot over the pushrod.

1B. On FXSB and FXEF models, install the boot onto the pushrod.

2. Insert the pushrod into the piston in the end of the master cylinder and position the master cylinder onto the frame. Install the bolts and washers and tighten to 13-16 ft.-lb. (18-22 N•m).
3. Connect the caliper brake hose to the master cylinder port. Tighten the fitting to 70-80 in.-lb. (8-9 N•m).
4. Slide a *new* hose clamp onto the hose and fit the hose onto the hose reservoir nipple. Slide the clamp down so that it is against the hose where the hose fits onto the nipple. Close the hose clamp so that it is tight against the hose.

NOTE
Figure 94 *shows the type of pliers required to close the hose clamp.*

5. Fill the reservoir with new DOT 5 hydraulic brake fluid. Bleed brake system as described under *Bleeding the System* in this chapter.
6. Install the reservoir gasket and cover. Tighten the screws securely.

WARNING
Do not ride the motorcycle until the rear brake is operating correctly with full hydraulic advantage.

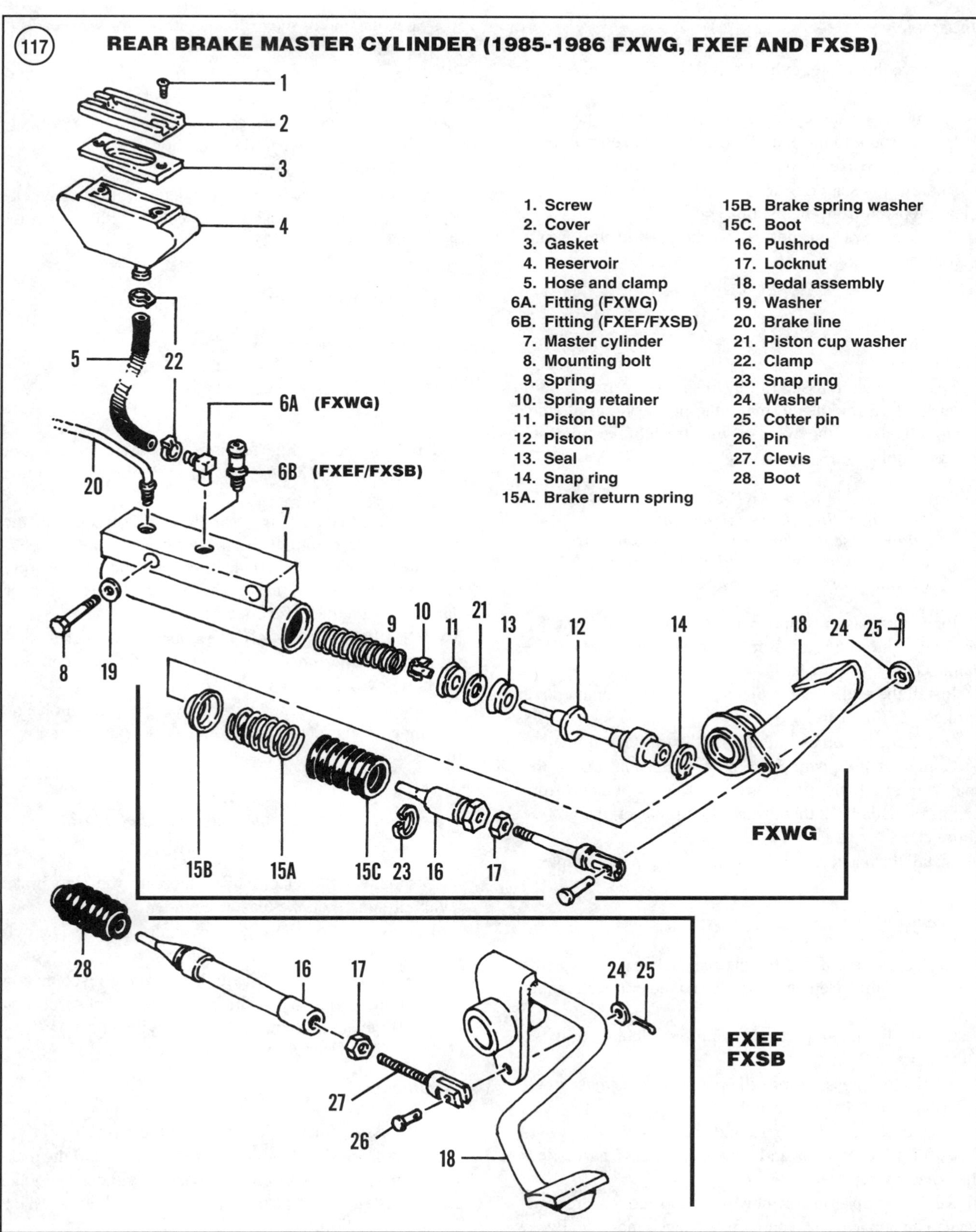
117
REAR BRAKE MASTER CYLINDER (1985-1986 FXWG, FXEF AND FXSB)
1. Screw
2. Cover
3. Gasket
4. Reservoir
5. Hose and clamp
6A. Fitting (FXWG)
6B. Fitting (FXEF/FXSB)
7. Master cylinder
8. Mounting bolt
9. Spring
10. Spring retainer
11. Piston cup
12. Piston
13. Seal
14. Snap ring
15A. Brake return spring
15B. Brake spring washer
15C. Boot
16. Pushrod
17. Locknut
18. Pedal assembly
19. Washer
20. Brake line
21. Piston cup washer
22. Clamp
23. Snap ring
24. Washer
25. Cotter pin
26. Pin
27. Clevis
28. Boot
6A (FXWG)
6B (FXEF/FXSB)
FXWG
FXEF
FXSB

13

Disassembly

1. Remove the master cylinder as described in this chapter.
2. Mount the master cylinder in a vise with soft jaws.
3. Insert a rod into the end of the piston and compress the piston to remove tension against the snap ring.
4. Remove the snap ring with snap ring pliers and slowly release tension from the piston.
5. Remove the piston and seal, washer, piston cup, spring retainer and spring.
6. Remove the seal from the piston.

Assembly

1. Soak the piston assembly in fresh DOT 5 brake fluid for at least 15 minutes to make the primary cup pliable. Coat the inside of the cylinder with fresh brake fluid before assembly.

WARNING
When installing the piston assembly, do not allow the seal to turn inside out. A damaged seal will allow brake fluid to leak inside the cylinder bore.

2. Place the master cylinder in a vise with soft jaws. Do not overtighten the jaws, or the master cylinder can be damaged.
3. Install the seal, washer, piston cup, spring retainer and spring onto the piston.
4. Install the piston assembly into the master cylinder.
5. Compress the piston into the cylinder and install the snap ring into the cylinder groove. Release tension from the piston and check that the snap ring seats in the groove completely.
6. Install the master cylinder as described in this chapter.

Inspection

Service specifications for the rear caliper components are not available. Replace worn, damaged or questionable parts.

1. Clean all rubber parts in isopropyl alcohol or fresh DOT 5 brake fluid.
2. Apply compressed air to all openings in the master cylinder body and dry it thoroughly.
3. Inspect the cylinder bore and the piston contact surfaces for signs of wear and damage. If either part is less than perfect, replace it.
4. Replace the piston assembly if the cup and seal are damaged. The cup and seal cannot be replaced individually.
5. Check the end of the piston assembly for wear caused by the pushrod.
6. Inspect the rubber boot for deterioration, cracking and wear.
7. Remove the cover and gasket from the reservoir. Inspect the gasket for wear, deterioration or damage.
8. Inspect the reservoir for cracks or damage.
9. Inspect the reservoir hose for deterioration or cracking. Replace if necessary and secure with *new* hose clamps.

1984-1991 FLH and FLT Series Models

Refer to **Figure 118**.

Removal

1. Drain the brake fluid from the rear brake hose as described under *Brake Hose and Line Replacement* in this chapter.
2. To disconnect the master cylinder reservoir, cut the reservoir hose clamp at the master cylinder and disconnect the hose. Do not twist the hose back and forth sharply because the hose nipple on the master cylinder can be damaged. Plug the hose opening.

3A. On 1984-1985 models, use a flare nut wrench and remove the caliper brake hose at the master cylinder. Pull the hose away from the master cylinder.

3B. On 1986-1998 models, remove the banjo bolt and sealing washers securing the brake hose to the master cylinder.

NOTE
Place the end of the brake hose in a plastic bag.

4. Disconnect the electrical connector from the brake switch mounted on the master cylinder.
5. Remove the bolts and washers securing the master cylinder to the frame.
6. Slowly pull the master cylinder back and disconnect it from the pushrod. Install the boot onto the pushrod if it came off when removing the master cylinder.

Installation

1. If necessary, install the boot onto the pushrod.
2. Insert the pushrod into the piston in the end of the master cylinder and position the master cylinder onto the frame. Install the bolts and washers and tighten to 13-16 ft.-lb. (18-22 N•m).

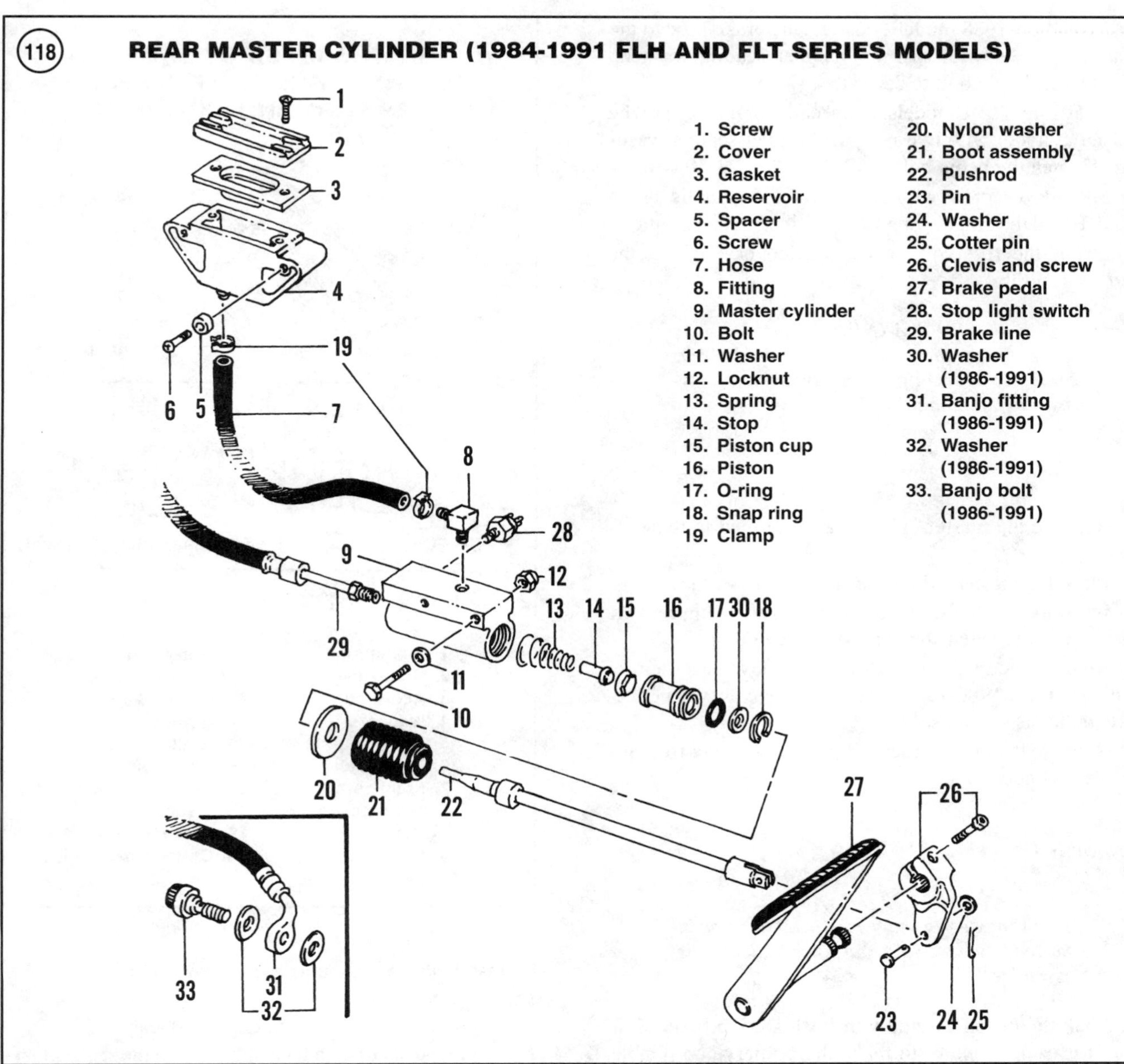

3. Connect the caliper brake hose to the master cylinder port. Tighten the fitting to 70-80 in.-lb. (8-9 N•m).

4A. On 1984-1985 models, slide a *new* hose clamp onto the hose and fit the hose onto the hose reservoir nipple. Slide the clamp down so that it is against the hose where the hose fits onto the nipple. Close the hose clamp so that it is tight against the hose.

WARNING

There are two different types of sealing washers used with the banjo bolts. Early models are copper with a zinc coating (A, ***Figure 110****). Late models are steel with a rubber O-ring (B,* ***Figure 110****). The banjo bolts must be used with the specific sealing washers. Make sure that the banjo bolts and washers match the original parts. A mismatch of these parts will result in a brake fluid leak and possible complete loss of brake operation.*

NOTE

Figure 94 *shows the type of pliers required to close the hose clamp.*

13

4B. On 1986-1988 models, connect the brake hose to the master cylinder with two *new* copper sealing washers. Tighten the banjo bolt to 35 ft.-lb. (47 N•m).

4C. On 1989-1991 models, connect the brake hose to the master cylinder with two *new* steel/rubber sealing washers. Tighten the banjo bolt to 17-22 ft.-lb. (23-30 N•m).

5. Fill the reservoir with new DOT 5 hydraulic brake fluid. Bleed the brake system as described in this chapter.

6. Install the reservoir gasket and cover. Tighten the screws securely.

WARNING
Do not ride the motorcycle until the rear brake is operating correctly with full hydraulic advantage.

Disassembly

1. Remove the master cylinder as described in this section.
2. Place the master cylinder in a vise with soft jaws.
3. Insert a rod into the end of the piston and compress the piston to remove tension against the snap ring.
4. Remove the snap ring and slowly remove tension from the piston. On 1986-1998 models, remove the washer between the piston and snap ring.
5. Remove the piston assembly, stop and spring from the master cylinder.

Assembly

NOTE
A new master cylinder repair kit must be installed whenever the master cylinder is disassembled.

1. Soak the piston assembly in fresh DOT 5 brake fluid for at least 15 minutes to make the primary cup pliable. Coat the inside of the cylinder with fresh brake fluid before assembly.
2. If installing a new piston assembly, coat the new seal with brake fluid and install it onto the piston.

WARNING
When installing the piston assembly, do not allow the seal to turn inside out. A damaged seal will allow brake fluid to leak in the cylinder bore.

3. Place the master cylinder in a vise with soft jaws. Do not overtighten the jaws or the master cylinder can be damaged.

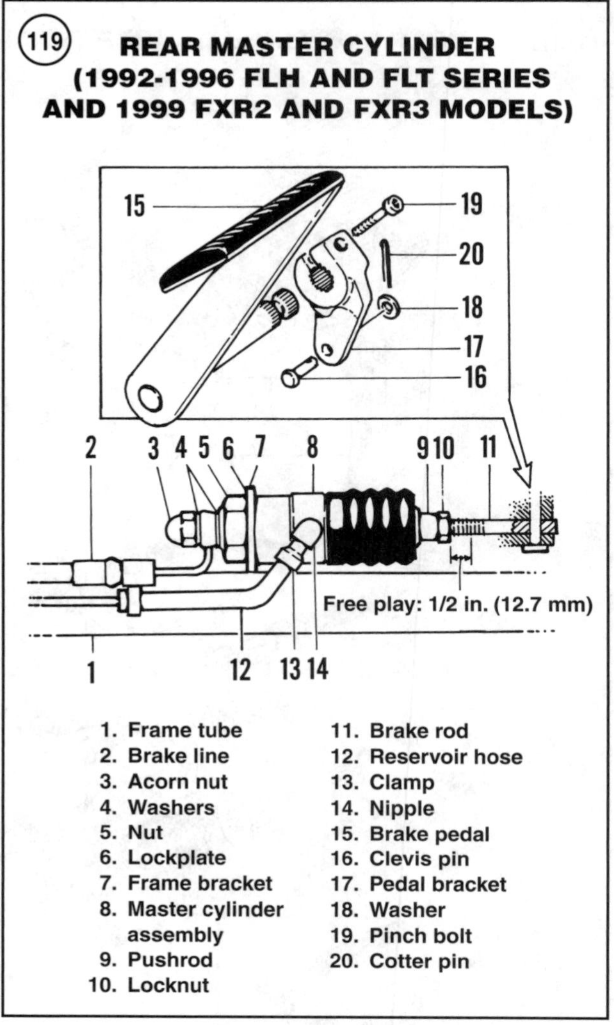

REAR MASTER CYLINDER (1992-1996 FLH AND FLT SERIES AND 1999 FXR2 AND FXR3 MODELS)

1. Frame tube
2. Brake line
3. Acorn nut
4. Washers
5. Nut
6. Lockplate
7. Frame bracket
8. Master cylinder assembly
9. Pushrod
10. Locknut
11. Brake rod
12. Reservoir hose
13. Clamp
14. Nipple
15. Brake pedal
16. Clevis pin
17. Pedal bracket
18. Washer
19. Pinch bolt
20. Cotter pin

4. Install the spring into the master cylinder with the small end facing out.
5. Install the stop and piston cup into the cylinder.
6. Install the piston into the cylinder with the seal end facing out.
7. On 1986-1991 models, install the washer onto the piston.
8. Compress the piston into the cylinder and install the snap ring into the cylinder groove. Release tension from the piston and check that the snap ring seats in the groove completely.
9. Install the master cylinder as described in this section.

Inspection

Service specifications for the rear master cylinder components are not available. Replace worn, damaged or questionable parts.

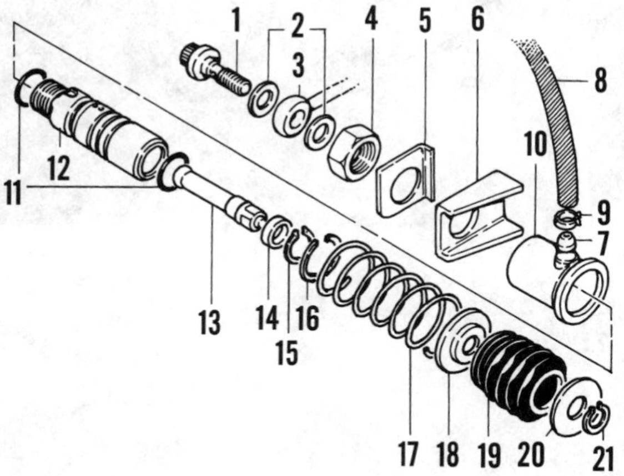

(120) REAR MASTER CYLINDER (1992-1996 FLH AND FLT SERIES AND 1999 FXR2 AND FXR3 MODELS)

1. Banjo bolt
2. Washers
3. Brake line
4. Nut
5. Lockplate
6. Frame mounting bracket
7. Nipple
8. Reservoir hose
9. Clamp
10. Reservoir adapter
11. O-rings
12. Cartridge body
13. Pushrod
14. Washer
15. Snap ring
16. Snap ring
17. Spring
18. Spring retainer
19. Boot
20. Washer
21. Snap ring

1. Clean all rubber parts in isopropyl alcohol or fresh DOT 5 brake fluid.
2. Apply compressed air to all openings in the master cylinder body and dry it thoroughly.
3. Inspect the cylinder bore and the piston contact surfaces for signs of wear and damage. If either part is less than perfect, replace it.
4. Replace the piston assembly if the cup and seal are damaged. The cup and seal cannot be replaced individually.
5. Check the end of the piston assembly for wear caused by the pushrod.
6. Inspect the rubber boot for deterioration, cracking and wear.
7. Remove the cover and gasket from the reservoir. Inspect the gasket for wear, deterioration or damage.
8. Inspect the reservoir for cracks or damage.
9. Inspect the reservoir hose for deterioration or cracking. Replace if necessary and secure with *new* hose clamps.

1992-1996 FLH, FLT Series, 1999 FXR2 and FXR3 Models

Refer to **Figure 119**.

Removal

1. Drain the brake fluid from the rear brake hose as described under *Brake Hose and Line Replacement* in this chapter.
2. To disconnect the master cylinder reservoir, cut the reservoir hose clamp at the master cylinder and disconnect the hose. Do not twist the hose back and forth sharply because the hose nipple on the master cylinder can be damaged. Plug the hose opening.
3. Remove the exhaust system as described in Chapter Eight.
4. Remove the cotter pin and pin. Then disconnect the brake pedal from the brake pedal rod.
5. Remove the banjo bolt and two sealing washers from the cartridge body. Place the open end of the hose in a plastic bag.
6. Bend the lockplate tab away from the cartridge body.
7. Loosen and remove the mounting nut and lockplate and remove the cartridge body.
8. Remove the brake pedal clevis pinch bolt and remove the brake pedal from the clevis.
9. Loosen the pushrod locknut and turn the pushrod to disconnect it from the brake rod.
10. Pull the master cylinder out of the mounting bracket and remove it.

Installation

1. If the reservoir was removed, place it into position and secure it with the screws and washers. Install the hose onto the reservoir nipple and secure the hose with a new hose clamp.
2. Align the master cylinder square body with the square hole in the frame mounting bracket and install the master cylinder. The hose nipple should be facing as shown in **Figure 120**.
3. Thread the pushrod onto the brake rod. Do not tighten the locknut at this time.
4. Align the tab on the lockwasher with the notch in the master cylinder mounting bracket and install the lockwasher.
5. Install the master cylinder nut and tighten to 30-40 ft.-lb. (41-54 N•m). Bend the lockwasher tab against a flat on the nut.

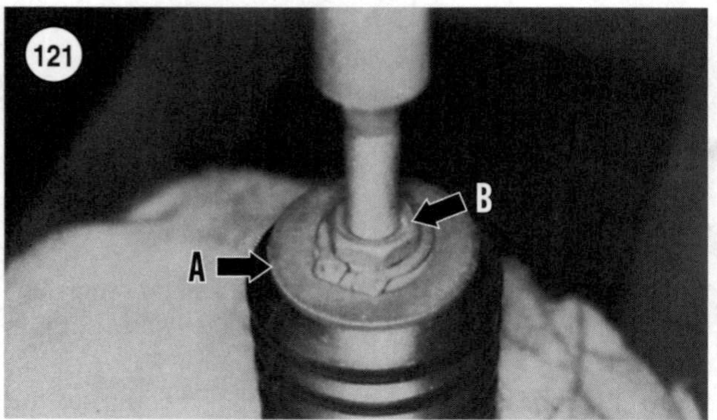

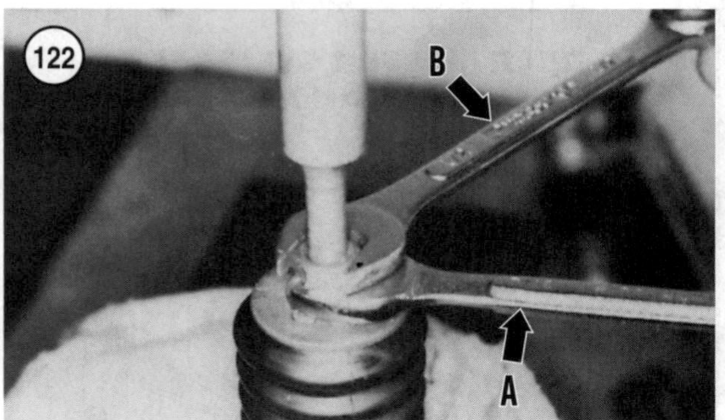

6. Install the brake line onto the master cylinder using the Acorn nut and two *new* washers. Tighten the Acorn nut to 17-22 ft.-lb. (23-30 N•m).
7. Slide a *new* hose clamp up onto the reservoir hose.
8. Install the reservoir hose onto the fitting on the adapter and push it on until it bottoms on the fitting.

NOTE
***Figure 94** shows the type of pliers required to close the hose clamp.*

9. Slide the clamp down so that it is against the hose where the hose fits onto the nipple. Close the hose clamp so that it is tight against the hose.
10. Slide the clevis onto the brake pedal. Install the pinch bolt and tighten securely.
11. Adjust the brake pedal height as described under *Rear Brake Adjustment* in Chapter Three.
12. Fill the reservoir with new DOT 5 hydraulic brake fluid. Bleed the brake system as described in this chapter.
13. Install the reservoir gasket and cover after bleeding the brakes. Tighten the screws securely.

WARNING
Do not ride the motorcycle until the rear brake is operating correctly with full hydraulic advantage.

Disassembly

Refer to **Figure 120**.

1. Remove the master cylinder as described in this chapter.
2. Clean the master cylinder cartridge body with isopropyl alcohol.
3. Screw the banjo bolt into the end of the cartridge body to protect the end of the cartridge when removing it.
4. Press down on the large washer (A, **Figure 121**) and compress the spring.

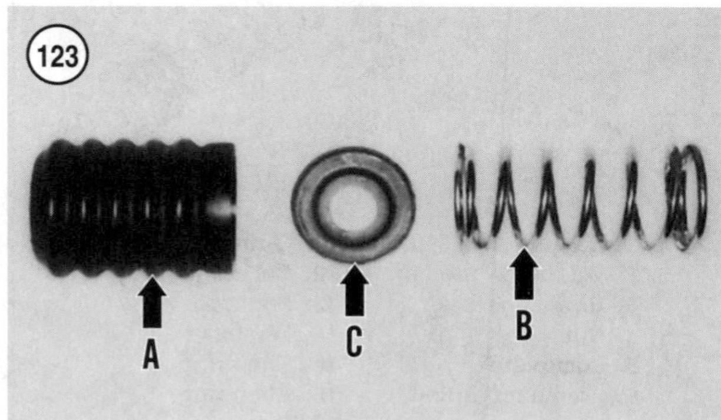

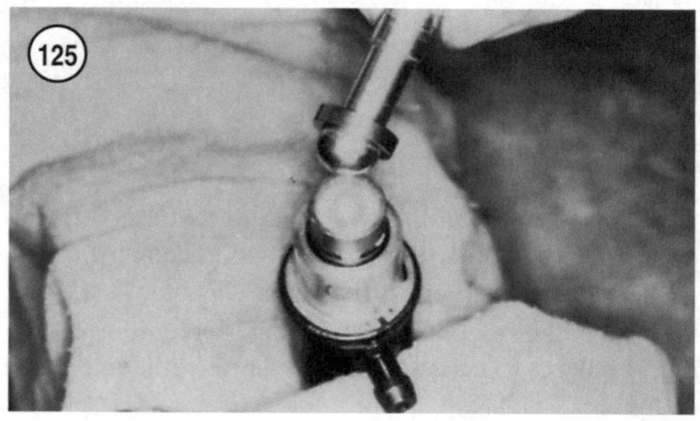

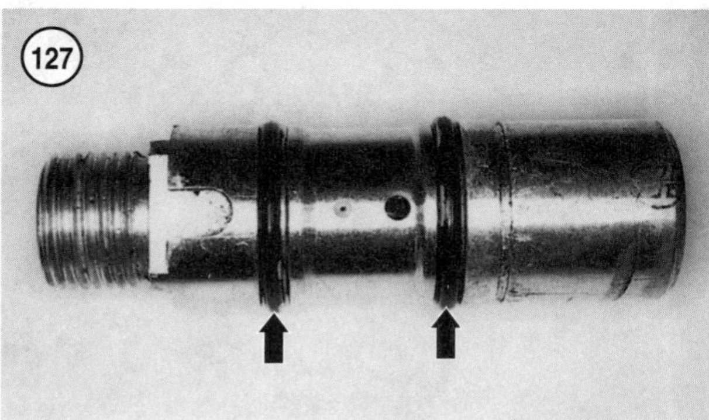

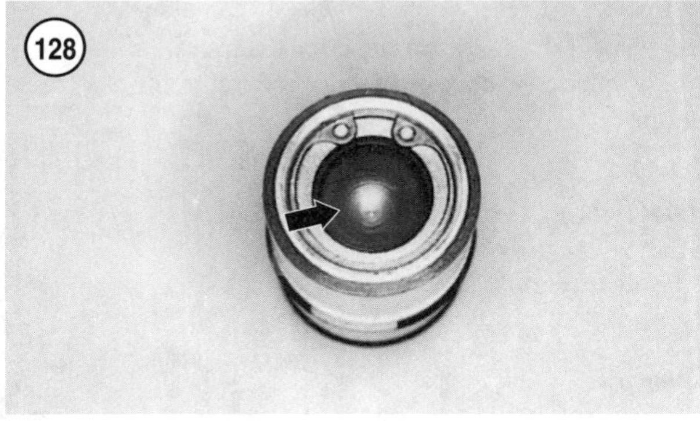

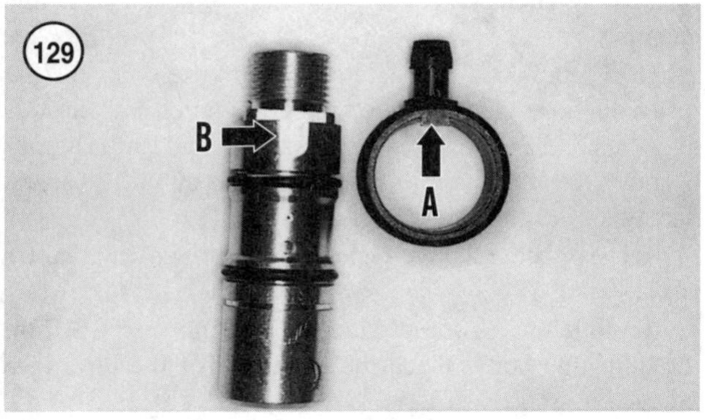

5. Put a wrench across the flat on the pushrod (A, **Figure 122**). Then use another wrench to loosen the pushrod locknut (B, **Figure 121**) on the pedal rod and unscrew the rod from the end of the pushrod.
6. Set the cartridge body upright so that it rests on the banjo bolt. Then compress the large washer (A, **Figure 121**) in the end of the cartridge body and remove the snap ring from the groove in the pushrod. Release the washer and remove the washer, boot (A, **Figure 123**) and spring (B).
7. Locate and remove the spring return retainer (C, **Figure 123**) from inside the boot.
8. Remove the snap ring (**Figure 124**) from the cartridge body groove and remove the pushrod and its washer (**Figure 125**).
9. Remove the hose adapter (**Figure 126**) from the cartridge body as follows:
   a. Stand the cartridge body upright so that it rests on the banjo bolt.
   b. Push down on the hose adapter and slide it off of the cartridge body. Protect the cartridge body while it is exposed.
   c. Do not remove the O-rings (**Figure 127**) unless they are going to be replaced.
   d. Remove the outer cartridge body snap ring.

CAUTION
*Do not remove the piston assembly from the cartridge body (**Figure 128**). Replacement parts for the piston assembly are not available. If the piston and seals are damaged, the cartridge body assembly must be replaced.*

13

Assembly

1. Assemble the hose reservoir adapter, if removed, as follows:
   a. If new O-rings are being installed, soak them in DOT 5 brake fluid.
   b. Install the *new* O-rings into the cartridge body grooves (**Figure 127**).
   c. Coat the interior of the hose adapter with DOT 5 brake fluid.
   d. Using hand pressure only, slide the hose reservoir adapter over the cartridge body. Engage the tab in the hose adapter (A, **Figure 129**) with the notch (B) in the cartridge body (**Figure 130**).

CAUTION
Do not force the cartridge into the cartridge body. If the parts do not assemble easily, the cartridge and cartridge body are not prop-

erly aligned. Forcing these parts together will damage both parts.

2. Install the banjo bolt into the end of the cartridge body and stand the assembly up so that it rests on the banjo bolt.
3. Install the washer onto the pushrod (opposite ball end) (**Figure 125**).
4. Insert the pushrod (ball end first) into the cartridge until the pushrod washer is seated in the cartridge body bore. Then install the snap ring into the cartridge body groove to secure the pushrod (**Figure 124**). Make sure the snap ring seats in the groove completely. After installing the snap ring, rotate the pushrod by hand; it should turn freely. If the pushrod is tight, disassemble the cartridge body to locate the damaged or improperly installed part.
5. Install the return spring (B, **Figure 123**) and spring retainer (C) onto the pushrod. Install the spring retainer so that the shoulder on the retainer faces away from the spring.
6. Install the dust boot (A, **Figure 123**) over the pushrod and turn it so the drain hole in the boot faces down. Seat the lip on the dust boot into the groove in the hose reservoir.
7. Install the large washer over the end of the pushrod.
8. Push the washer down to compress the return spring and install the snap ring onto the end of the pushrod. Make sure the snap ring seats in the groove completely (**Figure 131**).
9. Thread the locknut onto the pedal rod and thread the rod into the pushrod. Do not tighten the locknut because it will be tightened after adjusting the rear brake pedal in Chapter Three.

Inspection

Service specifications for the rear caliper components are not available. Replace worn, damaged or questionable parts.

1. Clean all rubber parts in isopropyl alcohol or fresh DOT 5 brake fluid.
2. Apply compressed air to all openings in the adapter and dry it thoroughly.
3. Inspect the cartridge body for cracks or damage.
4. Check the hose fitting on the adapter for damage.
5. Inspect the O-rings (**Figure 127**) on the cartridge body for wear or damage. Replace the O-rings if worn along with adapter.
6. Check the threads on the cartridge body, banjo bolt and pushrod.
7. Check the dust boot (A, **Figure 123**) for cracks, age deterioration or other damage. Replace if necessary.
8. Remove the cover and gasket from the reservoir. Inspect the gasket for wear, deterioration or damage.

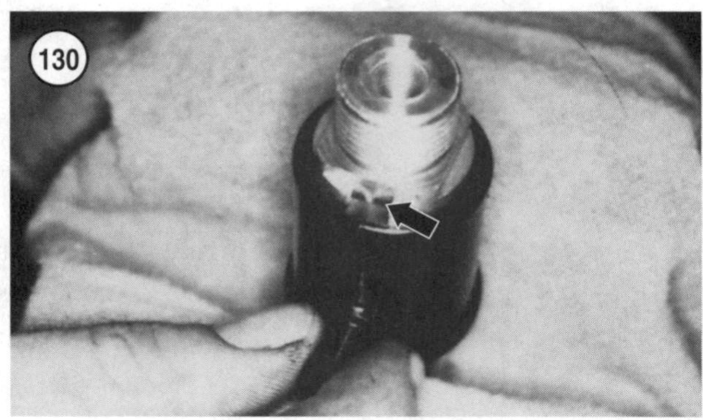

9. Inspect the reservoir for cracks or damage.
10. Inspect the reservoir hose for deterioration or cracking. Replace if necessary and secure with *new* hose clamps.

1997-1998 FLH and FLT Series Models

Refer to **Figure 132**.

Removal

1. Drain the brake fluid from the rear brake hose as described under *Brake Hose and Line Replacement* in this chapter.
2. To disconnect the master cylinder reservoir, cut the reservoir hose clamp at the master cylinder and disconnect the hose. Do not twist the hose back and forth sharply because the hose nipple on the master cylinder can be damaged. Plug the hose opening.
3. Remove the exhaust system as described in Chapter Eight.
4. Remove the banjo bolt and two sealing washers from the cartridge body. Place the open end of the hose in a plastic bag.

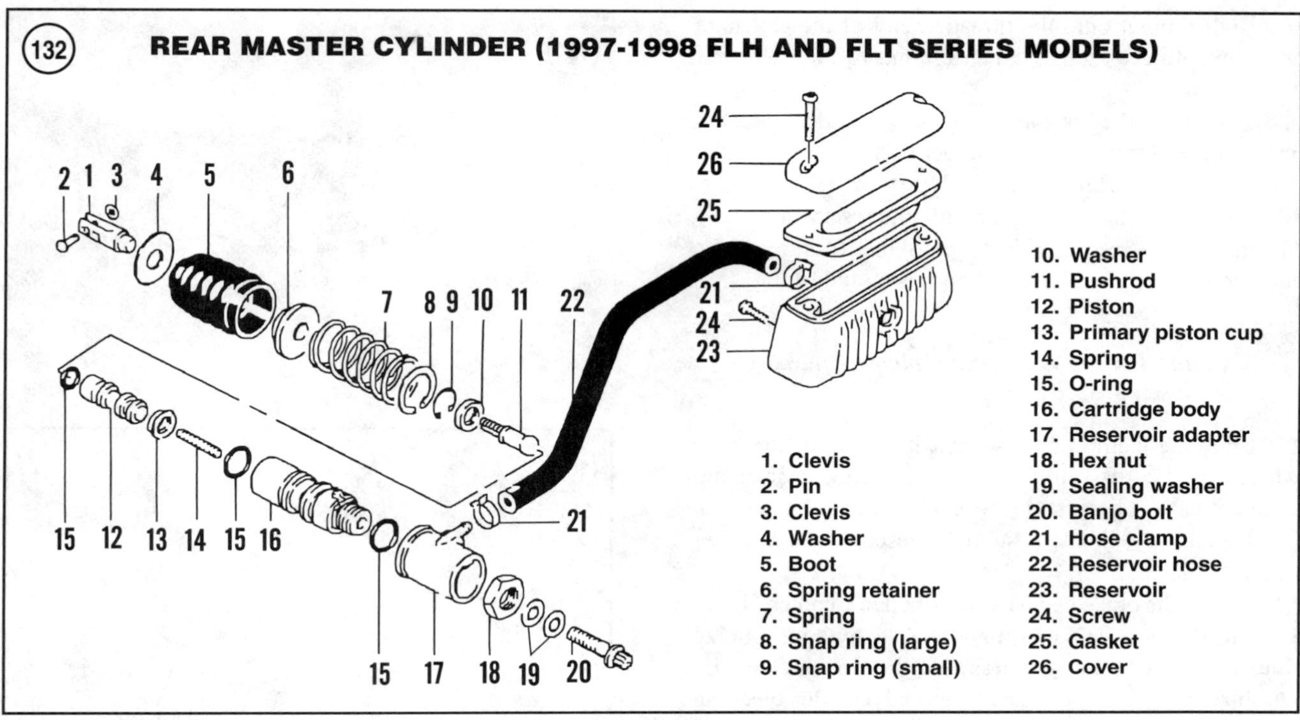

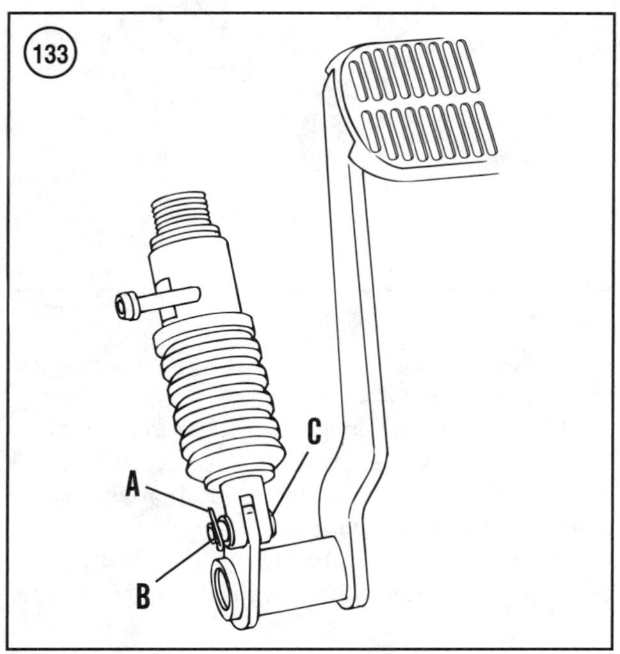

5. Remove the hex nut securing the brake pedal/master cylinder assembly to the frame mounting bracket.

6. Remove the hex nut and flat washer securing the brake pedal/master cylinder assembly to the frame pivot post. Remove the assembly from the frame pivot post.

7. Remove the cotter pin (A, **Figure 133**) and flat washer (B) from the clevis pin (C).

8. Support the brake pedal/master cylinder assembly in a vise with soft jaws.

9. Use an appropriately sized drift and carefully tap out and remove the clevis pin. Separate the master cylinder assembly from the brake pedal.

Installation

1. If the reservoir was removed, place it into position and secure it with the screws and washers. Install the hose onto the reservoir nipple and secure the hose with a new hose clamp.

2. Install the brake pedal in a vise with soft jaws.

3. Position the master cylinder assembly so the reservoir hose fitting is facing away from the brake pedal assembly. Install the master cylinder onto the brake pedal.

4. Use an appropriately sized drift and carefully tap the clevis pin (C, **Figure 133**) into position.

5. Install the flat washer (B, **Figure 133**) and *new* cotter pin (A). Completely bend over the ends of the cotter pin.

6. Move the brake pedal/master cylinder assembly to the square-shaped hole in the frame mounting bracket.

7. Apply a light coat of medium-strength threadlocking compound to the nut threads.

8. Install the nut onto the threaded end of the cartridge body until finger-tight. Tighten the nut to 50 ft.-lb. (68 N•m).
9. Install the brake line onto the master cylinder using the banjo bolt and two *new* steel/rubber washers. Tighten the banjo bolt to 17-22 ft.-lb. (23-30 N•m).
10. Slide a *new* hose clamp up onto the reservoir hose.
11. Install the reservoir hose onto the fitting on the adapter and push it on until it bottoms on the fitting.

NOTE
***Figure 134** shows the type of pliers required to close the hose clamp.*

12. Slide the clamp down so that it is against the hose where the hose fits onto the nipple. Close the hose clamp so that it is tight against the hose.
13. Install the exhaust system as described in Chapter Eight.
14. Adjust the brake pedal as described in Chapter Three.
15. Fill the reservoir with new DOT 5 hydraulic brake fluid. Bleed the brake system as described in this chapter.
16. Install the reservoir gasket and cover after bleeding the brakes. Tighten the screws securely.

WARNING
Do not ride the motorcycle until the rear brake is operating correctly with full hydraulic advantage.

Disassembly

Refer to **Figure 132**.
1. Remove the master cylinder as described in this chapter.
2. Clean the master cylinder cartridge body with isopropyl alcohol.
3. Remove the spring pin from the clevis.
4. Screw the banjo bolt into the end of the cartridge body to protect the end of the cartridge when removing it.
5. Lay several shop cloths on the workbench.
6. Set the cartridge body upright so that it rests on the banjo bolt and shop cloths (A, **Figure 135**).
7. Then compress the large washer and compress the spring.
8. While holding the spring compressed, unscrew and remove the clevis (B, **Figure 135**) from the pushrod. Carefully release the spring.
9. Remove the large washer, boot, spring and spring retainer from the push rod end of the cartridge body.
10. Push on the threaded end of the cartridge body (A, **Figure 136**) and remove it from the reservoir adapter (B).

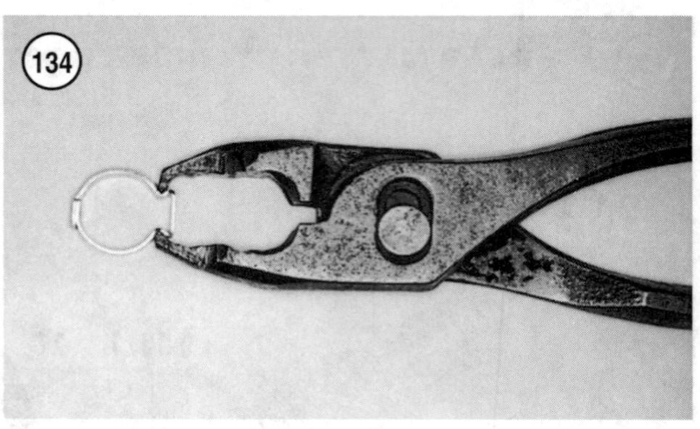

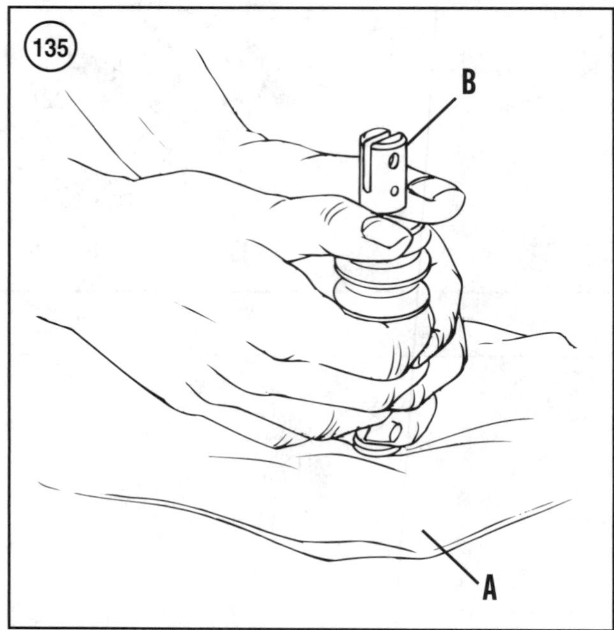

11. Remove the large snap ring from the groove closest to the pushrod end of the cartridge body.
12. Remove the two O-rings from the cartridge body.
13. Hold a finger over the end of the pushrod as it is spring-loaded. Then remove the small snap ring from the pushrod end of the cartridge body.
14. Remove the pushrod from the cartridge body.
15. Remove the small snap ring and washer from the pushrod.

CAUTION
*Do not remove the piston assembly from the cartridge body (**Figure 128**). Replacement parts for the piston assembly are not available. If the piston and seals are damaged, the cartridge body assembly must be replaced.*

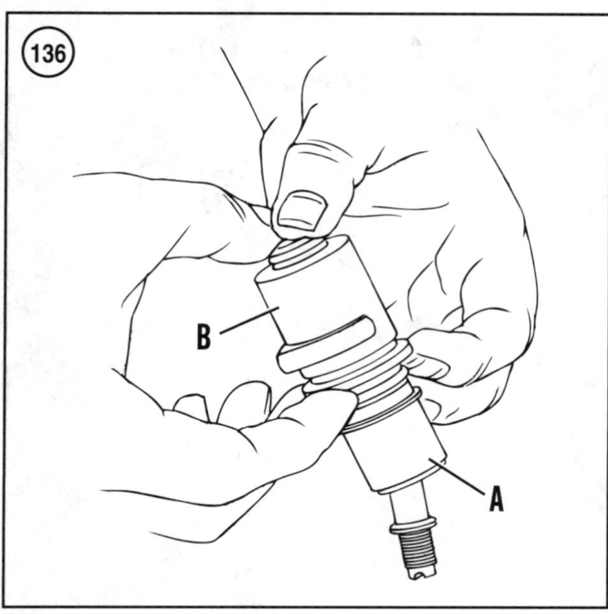

Assembly

1. Slide the washer and small snap ring over the threaded end of the *new* pushrod.
2. If the cartridge body is removed, lay several shop cloths on the workbench.
3. Set the cartridge body upright so that it rests on the banjo bolt sealing surface and the shop cloths.
4. Insert the ball end of the pushrod into the piston cup.
5. Push down on the pushrod and compress the spring.
6. Install the small retaining ring in the groove of the cartridge body bore. Make sure it is properly seated in the groove. After installing the snap ring, rotate the pushrod by hand; it should turn freely. If the pushrod is tight, disassemble the cartridge body to locate the damaged or improperly installed part.
7. Lubricate the two *new* O-rings and carefully install them into the cartridge body grooves.
8. Coat the interior of the adapter with clean DOT 5 brake fluid.
9. Install the large snap ring into the groove closest to the pushrod end of the cartridge body. Make sure it is properly seated in the groove.
10. Using hand pressure only, slide the cartridge body over the adapter. Engage the tab in the adapter with the notch in the cartridge body. The cartridge body is installed correctly when the adapter contacts the large snap ring.
11. Stand the assembly cartridge body assembly upright on the banjo bolt sealing surface and the shop cloths.
12. Install the spring over the pushrod end of the cartridge body until it rests on the large snap ring.
13. Position the spring retainer with the shoulder side facing up away from the spring and rest it on the spring.
14. Slide the boot over the spring and spring retainer and push it down until it stops.
15. Place the large washer on top of the spring retainer and boot.
16. Push down on the large washer and compress the spring.
17. While holding the spring compressed, screw the clevis on the pushrod until it bottoms on the pushrod.
18. Pull the boot down until the sealing lips seat in the adapter groove. Make sure the boot seats around the circumference of the adapter.
19. Rotate the boot until the drain hole is opposite the index tab on the adapter.
20. Align the groove on the threaded end of the pushrod with the spring pinhole of the clevis. If not aligned correctly, back off the clevis slightly but do not exceed one-half turn.
21. Support the pushrod end and carefully tap the spring pin into the clevis and through the pushrod groove.

Inspection

Service specifications for the rear caliper components are not available. Replace worn, damaged or questionable parts.

1. Clean all rubber parts in isopropyl alcohol or fresh DOT 5 brake fluid.
2. Apply compressed air to all openings in the adapter and dry it thoroughly.
3. Inspect the cartridge body for cracks or damage.
4. Check the hose fitting on the reservoir adapter for damage.
5. Inspect the O-rings (**Figure 127**) on the cartridge body for wear or damage. Replace the O-rings, if worn, along with the adapter.
6. Check the threads on the cartridge body, banjo bolt and pushrod.
7. Check the dust boot for cracks, age deterioration or other damage. Replace if necessary.
8. Remove the cover and gasket from the reservoir. Inspect the gasket for wear, deterioration or damage.
9. Inspect the reservoir for cracks or damage.
10. Inspect the reservoir hose for deterioration or cracking. Replace if necessary and secure with *new* hose clamps.

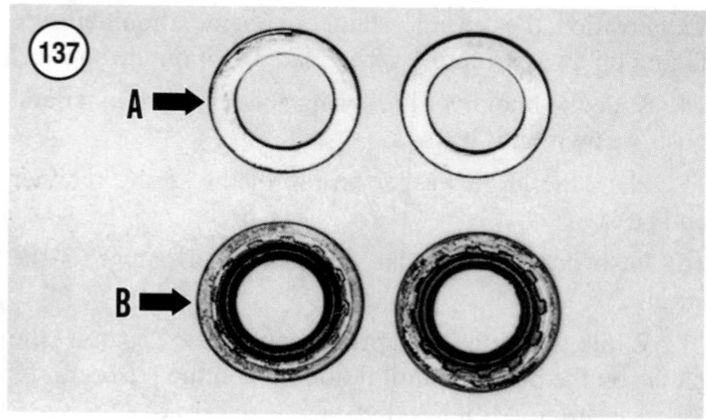

BRAKE HOSE AND LINE REPLACEMENT

A combination of steel and flexible brake lines connect the master cylinder to the brake caliper(s). Banjo fittings and bolts connect brake hoses to the master cylinder and brake calipers. Sealing washers should be replaced when there is an indication of brake fluid leakage at any connection.

WARNING
*There are two different types of sealing washers used with the banjo bolts on 1986 and later FLH and FLT models and late 1987 and later FXR series models. Early models are copper with a zinc coating (A, **Figure 137**). Later models are steel with a rubber O-ring (B, **Figure 137**). The banjo bolts must be used with the specific sealing washers. Make sure that the banjo bolts and washers match the original parts. A mismatch of these parts will result in a brake fluid leak and possible complete loss of brake operation.*

Replace a hose/line assembly if the flexible portion is swelling, cracking or damaged. Replace the brake hose/line assembly if the metal portion leaks or if there are dents or cracks.

Front Brake Hose Removal/Installation

A combination steel/flexible brake hose connects the front master cylinder to the front brake caliper(s). Refer to **Figure 138** or **Figure 139**. When purchasing a new hose/line assembly, compare it to the old hose/line assembly to make sure the length and angle of the steel hose portion are correct. Install *new* banjo bolt washers at both ends.

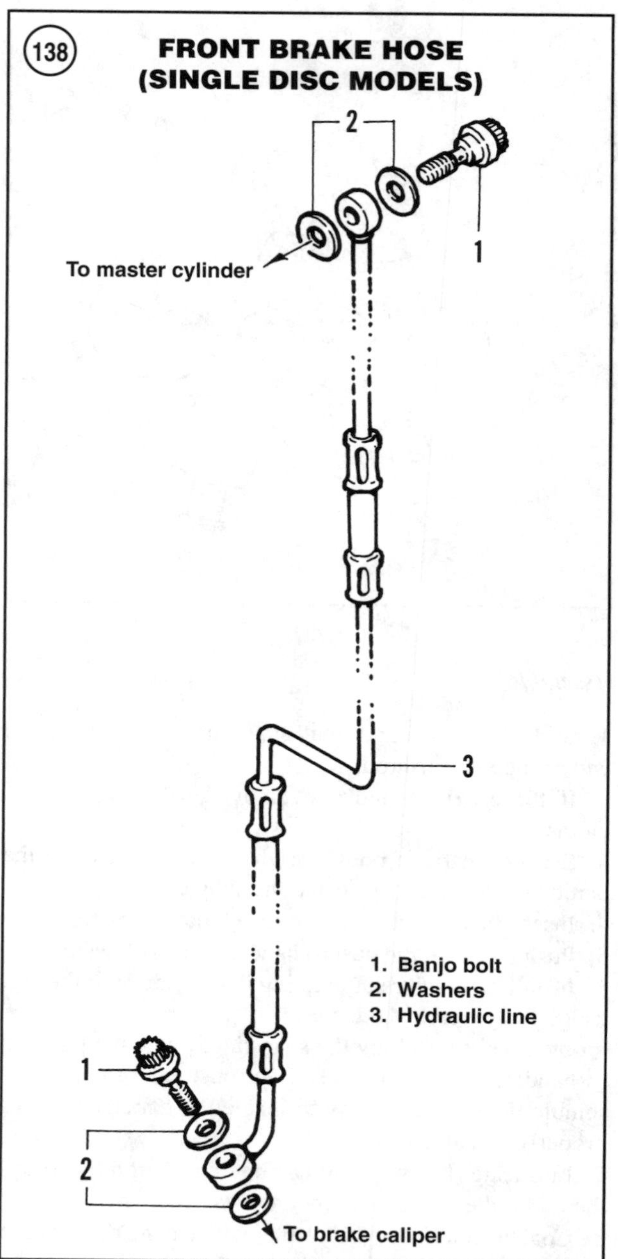

CAUTION
Do not spill brake fluid on the front fork or front wheel. Wash brake fluid off painted, plated or plastic surfaces immediately because it will damage most surfaces it contacts. Use soapy water and rinse completely.

1. On models so equipped, remove the windshield assembly and/or front fairing as described in Chapter Fifteen.

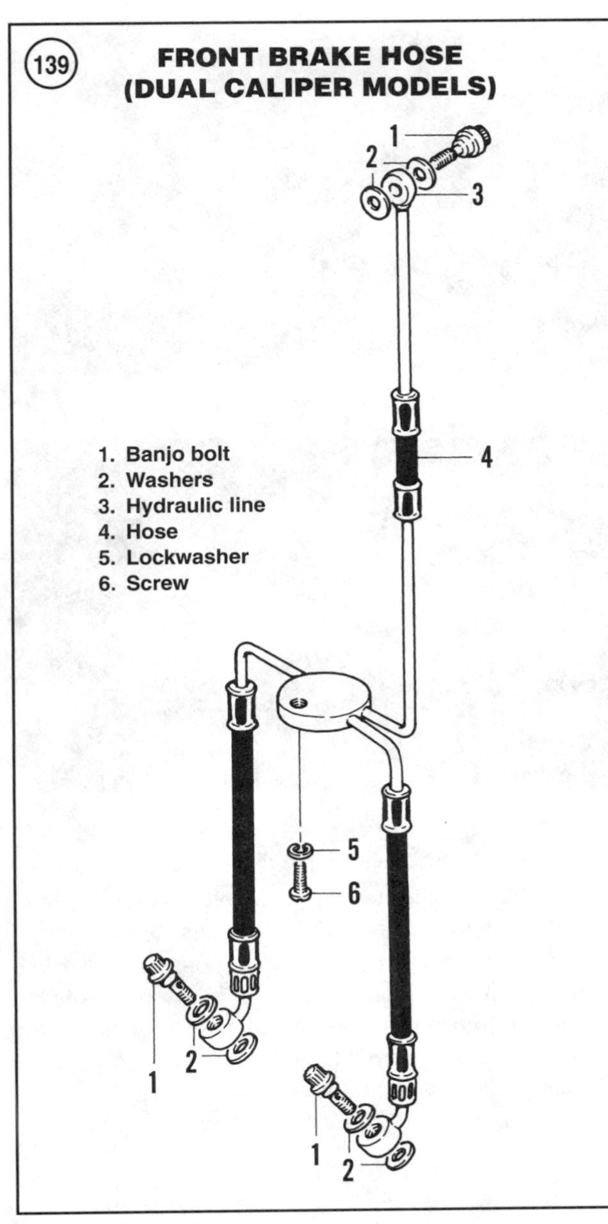

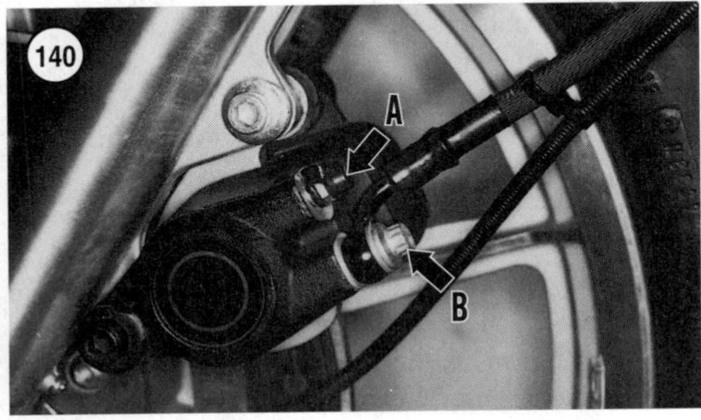

2. Drain the front brake system as follows:
   a. Connect a hose over the bleed valve (A, **Figure 140**).
   b. Insert the loose end of the hose into a container to catch the brake fluid.
   c. Open the bleed valve and apply the front brake lever to pump the fluid out of the master cylinder and brake line. Continue until the fluid is removed.
   d. Close the bleed valve and disconnect the hose.
   e. Dispose of the brake fluid. Never reuse brake fluid. Contaminated brake fluid will cause brake failure.
   f. On dual-disc models, repeat for the remaining caliper.
3. Before removing the brake line assembly, note the brake line routing from the master cylinder to the caliper(s). Note the number and position of metal hose clamps and/or plastic ties used to hold the brake line in place.
4. Remove any metal clamp or cut any plastic ties.
5. On models so equipped, remove the bolt securing the brake hose and mounting plate to the lower steering stem. On models so equipped, do not lose the guide plate between the hose mounting plate and the steering stem.
6. Remove the screw or nut securing the metal clamps around the brake line. Spread the clamp and remove it from the brake line.
7. Remove the banjo bolt (B, **Figure 140**) and washers securing the hose to the brake caliper.
8. Remove the banjo bolt (A, **Figure 141**) and washers securing the hose to the front master cylinder.
9. Cover the ends of the brake hose to prevent brake fluid from leaking out.
10. Remove the brake hose assembly (B, **Figure 141**) from the motorcycle.
11. If the existing brake hose assembly is going to be reinstalled, inspect it as follows:
    a. Check the metal pipes where they enter and exit at the flexible hoses. Check the crimped clamp for looseness or damage.
    b. Check the flexible hose portions for swelling, cracks or other damage.

c. If wear or damage is found, replace the brake hose assembly.

12. Install the brake hose, *new* sealing washers and banjo bolts in the reverse order of removal. Note the following:

a. Install *new* sealing washers against the side of each hose fitting.

b. Carefully install the clips and guides to hold the brake hose in place.

c. Tighten the banjo bolts with *new* copper sealing washers to 35 ft.-lb. (47 N•m).

d. Tighten the banjo bolts with *new* steel/rubber sealing washers to 17-22 ft.-lb. (23-30 N•m).

e. Refill the front master cylinder with clean brake fluid clearly marked DOT 5. Bleed the front brake system as described in this chapter.

WARNING

Do not ride the motorcycle until the front brakes operate correctly with full hydraulic advantage.

Rear Brake Hose Removal/Installation

A single steel-and-rubber combination brake hose connects the rear master cylinder to the rear brake caliper. On some models, the rear brake switch is installed in the rear brake hose. When buying a new hose, compare it to the old hose. Make sure the length and angle of the steel hose portion are correct. Install *new* banjo bolt washers at both hose ends.

CAUTION

Do not spill brake fluid on the swing arm, frame or rear wheel. Wash brake fluid off any painted, plated or plastic surfaces immediately because it will damage most surfaces it contacts. Use soapy water and rinse completely.

1. Remove the exhaust system as described in Chapter Eight.

2. On models so equipped, remove the right saddlebag as described in Chapter Fifteen.

3. Drain the hydraulic brake fluid from the rear brake system as follows:

a. Connect a hose to the rear caliper bleed valve (A, **Figure 142**).

b. Insert the loose end of the hose in a container to catch the brake fluid.

c. Open the caliper bleed valve and operate the rear brake pedal to pump the fluid out of the master cylinder and brake line. Continue until all of the fluid is removed.

d. Close the bleed valve and disconnect the hose.

e. Dispose of the brake fluid. Never reuse brake fluid. Contaminated brake fluid will cause brake failure.

4. Before removing the brake line, note the brake line routing from the master cylinder to the caliper. Note the number and position of the metal hose clamps, plastic clips and plastic ties used to hold the brake line in place. The metal clamp and plastic clips can be reused.

NOTE

To open the cable clips, insert a small screwdriver into the gap at the side of the clip and carefully rotate the screwdriver.

5. Open the cable clips on the lower frame tube.

6. At the rear brake light switch, cut the plastic tie securing the rear brake light switch wires, voltage regulator wires and the engine sensor harness to the frame lower tube.

7. On models with the rear brake light switch attached to the rear brake line, perform the following:

a. Disconnect the electrical connector from the rear brake switch.

b. Remove the bolt securing the brake light switch to the frame bracket.

8. Remove the banjo bolt and washers (B, **Figure 142**) securing the hose to the brake caliper.
9. Remove the brake hose (**Figure 143**, typical) from the master cylinder. Refer to the rear master cylinder replacement procedure, in this chapter, for the year and model being worked on.
10. Carefully move the rear brake line assembly forward and away from the rear swing arm bracket. Remove the brake hose assembly from the motorcycle.
11. If the existing brake hose assembly is going to be reinstalled, inspect it as follows:
   a. Check the metal pipe where it enters and exits the flexible hose. Check the crimped clamp for looseness or damage.
   b. Check the flexible hose portion for swelling, cracks or other damage.
   c. If wear or damage is found, replace the brake hose.
12. If replacement is necessary, remove the brake light switch from the rear brake hose fitting.
13. Installation is the reverse of removal. Note the following:
   a. On models so equipped, install and tighten the brake light switch securely.
   b. Install *new* sealing washers against the side of each hose fitting.
   c. Carefully install the clips and guides to hold the brake hose in place.
   d. Tighten the banjo bolts with *new* copper sealing washers to 35 ft.-lb. (47 N•m).
   e. Tighten the banjo bolts with *new* steel/rubber sealing washers to 17-22 ft.-lb. (23-30 N•m).
   f. Refill the master cylinder with clean brake fluid clearly marked DOT 5. Bleed the rear brake system as described in this chapter.

WARNING

Do not ride the motorcycle until the rear brake is operating correctly with full hydraulic advantage.

BRAKE DISC (FRONT AND REAR)

Check brake discs for runout and thickness. The minimum disc thickness is stamped on Harley-Davidson brake discs. **Table 1** lists disc brake specifications.

The brake discs are separate from the wheel hubs and can be removed once the wheel is removed from the motorcycle.

Inspection

It is not necessary to remove the disc from the wheel to inspect it. Small nicks and marks on the disc are not important, but radial scratches deep enough to snag a fingernail reduce braking effectiveness and increase brake pad wear. If these grooves are present, and the brake pads are wearing rapidly, replace the disc.

The specifications for the standard and service limits on some models are in **Table 1**. Each disc is also marked with the minimum (MIN) thickness. If the specification marked on the disc differs from the one in **Table 1**, use the specification on the disc.

When servicing the brake discs, do not have the discs machined to compensate for warp. The discs are thin, and machining will only reduce the thickness and cause them to warp rapidly. A warped disc can be caused by the brake pads dragging on the disc, due to a faulty caliper, and overheating the disc. Overheating can also be caused by unequal pad pressure on the disc.

1. Measure the thickness of the disc at several locations around the disc with a vernier caliper or a micrometer (**Figure 144**). Replace the disc if the thickness in any area is less than that specified in **Table 1** or the marked MIN dimension on the disc (**Figure 145**).

2. Make sure the disc mounting bolts are tight prior to running this check. Check the disc runout with a dial indicator as shown in **Figure 146**.

NOTE
When checking the front disc, turn the handlebar all the way to one side and then to the other side.

3. Slowly rotate the wheel and watch the dial indicator. If the runout exceeds the specification in **Table 1**, replace the disc.
4. Clean the disc of any rust or corrosion and wipe it clean with brake cleaner. Never use an oil-based solvent that can leave an oil residue on the disc.

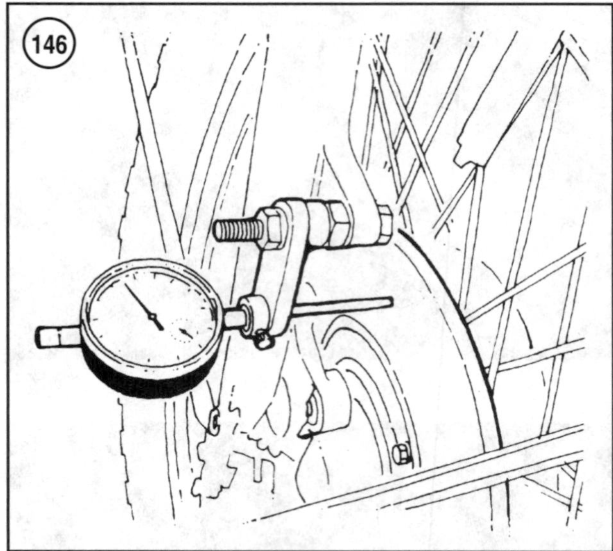

Removal/Installation

1. Remove the front or rear wheel as described in Chapter Nine.
2. Remove the Torx bolts (**Figure 147**) securing the brake disc to the hub and remove the disc.
3. Check the brake disc bolts for thread damage. Replace worn or damaged fasteners.
4. Check the threaded bolt holes for the brake disc in the wheel hub for thread damage. True them with a tap if necessary.
5. Clean the disc and the disc mounting surface thoroughly with brake cleaner. Allow the surfaces to dry before installation.
6. Install the disc onto the wheel hub.
7. Apply a drop of medium-strength threadlocking compound to the threads of *new* Torx bolts prior to installation.
8. Install the bolts and tighten for the specification in **Table 2**.

BLEEDING THE SYSTEM

If air enters the brake system, the brake will feel soft or spongy and braking pressure will reduce. Bleed the system to remove the air. Air can enter the system if there is a leak in the system, the brake fluid level in a master cylinder runs low, a brake line is opened, or the brake fluid is replaced.

The brakes can bleed with a brake bleeder or manually. This section includes procedures for both.

Before bleeding the brake system:

1. Check the brake lines to make sure all fittings are tight.
2. Make sure the caliper piston does not stick or bind in the bore.
3. Check piston movement in each master cylinder. Operate the lever or brake pedal and make sure there is no binding or other abnormal condition.

Brake Bleeder Process

This procedure uses the Mityvac hydraulic brake bleeding kit (**Figure 148**) available from motorcycle or automotive supply stores.

NOTE
This procedure is shown on the rear wheel and relates to the front wheel as well.

1. Remove the dust cap from the caliper bleed valve.
2. Place a clean shop cloth over the caliper to protect it from accidental brake fluid spills.
3. Open the bleed screw approximately a half turn.

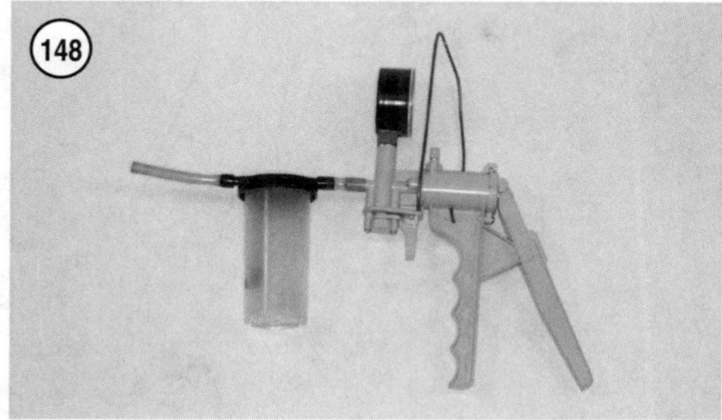

148

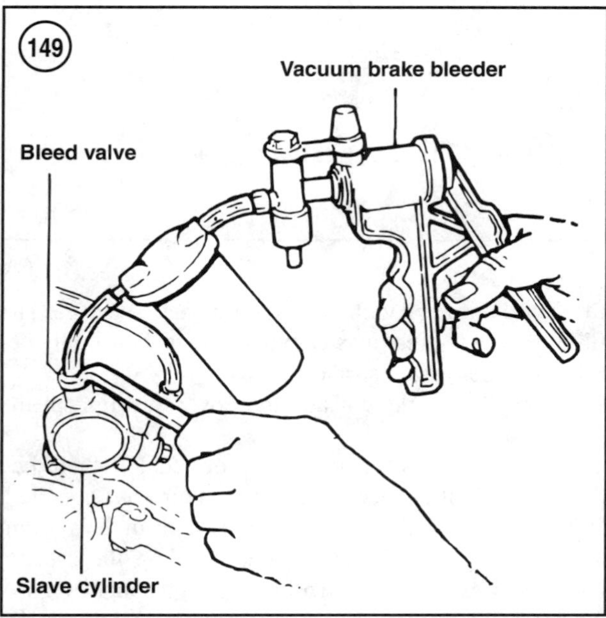

149

4. Assemble the brake bleeder according to the manufacturer's instructions. Secure it to the caliper bleed valve.
5. Clean the top of the master cylinder of all dirt and debris.
6. Remove the screws securing the master cylinder top cover and remove the cover and rubber diaphragm.
7. Fill the reservoir almost to the top with DOT 5 brake fluid and reinstall the diaphragm and cover. Leave the cover in place during this procedure to prevent the entry of dirt.

WARNING
Do not mix DOT 3, DOT 4 or DOT 5.1 brake fluids because they are not silicone-based. Nonsilicone brake fluid used in these models can cause brake failure.

8. Operate the pump several times to create a vacuum in the line (**Figure 149**). Brake fluid will quickly flow from the caliper into the pump reservoir. Tighten the caliper bleed valve before the fluid stops flowing through the hose. To prevent air from being drawn through the master cylinder, add fluid to maintain the level at the top of the reservoir.

NOTE
Do not allow the master cylinder reservoir to empty during the bleeding operation or more air will enter the system. If this occurs, the procedure must be repeated.

9. Continue the bleeding process until the fluid drawn from the caliper is bubble-free. If bubbles are in the brake fluid, more air is trapped in the line. Repeat Step 8 and make sure to refill the master cylinder to prevent air from being drawn into the system.
10. When the brake fluid is free of bubbles, tighten the bleed valve and remove the brake bleeder assembly. Reinstall the bleed valve dust cap.
11. If necessary, add fluid to correct the level in the master cylinder reservoir. When topping off the front master cylinder, turn the handlebar until the reservoir is level. Add fluid until it is level with the reservoir gasket surface. The fluid level in the rear master cylinder must be slightly below the upper gasket surface.
12. Reinstall the reservoir diaphragm and cover. Install the screws and tighten securely.
13. Test the feel of the brake lever or pedal. It should be firm and offer the same resistance each time it is operated. If it feels spongy, there is probably still air in the system. Bleed the system again. After bleeding the system, check for leaks and tighten all fittings and connections as necessary.

WARNING
Do not ride the motorcycle until the front and/or rear brakes are operating correctly with full hydraulic advantage.

Without a Brake Bleeder

1. Connect a length of clear tubing to the bleed valve on the caliper. Place the other end of the tube into a clean container. Fill the container with enough clean DOT 5 brake fluid to keep the end of the tube submerged. The tube must be long enough so a loop can be made higher than the bleeder valve to prevent air from being drawn into the caliper during bleeding.
2. Clean the top of the master cylinder of all debris.
3. Remove the screws securing the master cylinder top cover and remove the cover and diaphragm.

4. Fill the reservoir almost to the top with DOT 5 brake fluid and reinstall the diaphragm and cover. Leave the cover in place during this procedure to prevent the entry of dirt.

WARNING
Do not mix DOT 3, DOT 4 or DOT 5.1 brake fluids because they are not silicone-based. Nonsilicone brake fluid used in these models can cause brake failure.

NOTE
During this procedure, check the fluid level in the master cylinder reservoir often. If the reservoir runs dry, air will enter the system.

5. Slowly apply the brake lever several times. Hold the lever in the applied position and open the bleed valve about a half turn (**Figure 150**). Allow the lever to travel to the limit. When the limit is reached, tighten the bleed valve. Then release the brake lever. As the brake fluid enters the system, the level will drop in the master cylinder reservoir. Maintain the level at the top of the reservoir to prevent air from being drawn into the system.
6. Continue the bleeding process until the fluid emerging from the hose is completely free of air bubbles. If the fluid is being replaced, continue until the fluid emerging from the hose is clean.

NOTE
If bleeding is difficult, allow the fluid to stabilize for a few hours. Repeat the bleeding procedure when the bubbles in the system dissipate.

7. Hold the lever in the applied position and tighten the bleed valve. Remove the bleed tube and install the bleed valve dust cap.
8. If necessary, add fluid to correct the level in the master cylinder reservoir. When topping off the front master cylinder, turn the handlebar until the reservoir is level. Add fluid until it is level with the reservoir gasket surface. The fluid level in the rear master cylinder must be slightly below the upper gasket surface.
9. Install the diaphragm and top cover and tighten the screws securely.
10. Test the feel of the brake lever or pedal. It should be firm and offer the same resistance each time it is operated. If it feels spongy, there is probably still air in the system, and it must be bled again. After bleeding the system, check for leaks and tighten all fittings and connections as necessary.

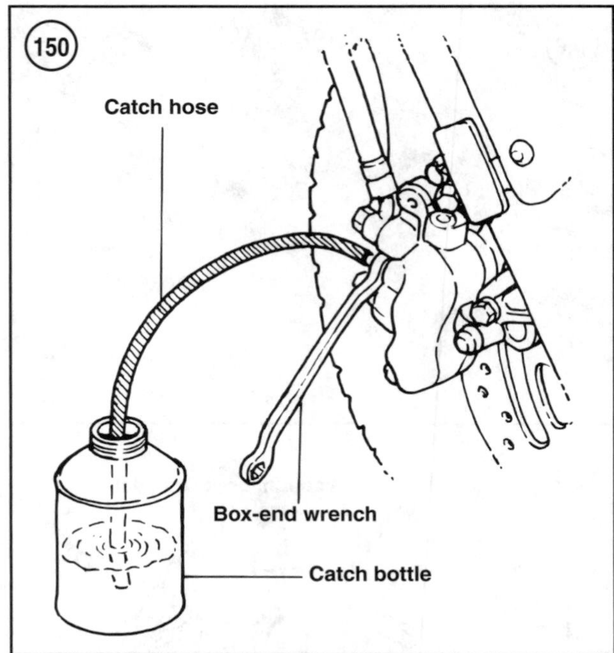

WARNING
Do not ride the motorcycle until the front and/or rear brakes are operating correctly with full hydraulic advantage.

Table 1 BRAKE SPECIFICATIONS

Item	in.	mm
Brake pad minimum thickness		
Front and rear	0.062	1.6
Brake disc		
FXR, FLH and FLT series models	See stamped mark on disc	
FXWG, FXSB and FXEF		
Minimum thickness	0.20	5.08
Outside diameter	11.50	292.1
Brake disc runout (maximum)	0.008	0.2

Table 2 BRAKE TORQUE SPECIFICATIONS

Item	ft.-lb.	in.-lb.	N•m
Brake disc mount bolts			
FXR series models			
Front			
1984-1990	16-18	–	22-24
1991-1998	16-24	–	22-32
Rear			
1984-1990	23-27	–	31-37
1991-1998	30-45	–	41-61
FLH and FLT series models			
Front			
1984-1990	16-18	–	22-24
1991-1998	16-24	–	22-32
Rear			
1984-1990	24-30	–	32-41
1991-1998	30-45	–	41-61
FXWG, FXSB and FXEF			
Front	16-18	–	22-24
Rear	23-27	–	31-37
Banjo bolts*			
Copper sealing washers	35	–	47
Steel/rubber sealing washers	17-22	–	23-30
Brake bleeder screw			
1984-1990	–	32-40	3.6-4.5
1991-1998	–	80-100	9-11
Brake line fitting at rear caliper			
FXR 1984-early 1987	–	70-80	8-9
FXR2 and FXR3	17-22	–	23-30
FLH and FLT			
1984-1991	–	70-80	8-9
1992-1996 Acorn nut	17-22	–	23-30
1997-1998 banjo bolt	17-22	–	23-30
Front brake caliper mounting bolts	25-30	–	34-41
Front master cylinder clamp bolts	–	70-80	8-9
Rear brake caliper mounting bolts			
FXR series models	15-20	–	20-27
FLH and FLT series models			
1984-1985	–	142-177	16-20
1986-1998	15-20	–	20-27
FXWG, FXSB and FXEF	–	142-177	16-20
Rear master cylinder cartridge body hex nut			
1997-1998 FLH and FLT series models	50	–	68
Rear master cylinder mounting bolts			
1984-early 1987 FXR series models	13-16	–	18-22
FXWG, FXSB and FXEF models	13-16	–	18-22
1984-1991 FLH and FLT series models	13-16	–	18-22
Rear master cylinder mounting nut			
1992-1998 FLH and FLT and 1999 FXR2 and FXR3 models	30-40	–	41-54

*Refer to text for additional information regarding sealing washer use.

CHAPTER FOURTEEN

CRUISE CONTROL

The cruise control system uses mechanical and electrical equipment to maintain a select speed set by the rider. This chapter covers service and troubleshooting procedures for the cruise control system installed on 1989-1998 FLTC-U and FLHT series models.

WARNING
When testing and servicing the cruise control system, do not ride the motorcycle until the system is working correctly. If necessary, have the system diagnosed by a Harley-Davidson dealership.

CRUISE CONTROL COMPONENTS (1989-1996 MODELS)

1989-1992 Models

The cruise control system consists of a cruise module, bellcrank system (1989 models), switches and related wiring. Refer to **Figure 1** and **Figure 2**.

The cruise module receives command signals from the cruise ON/OFF switch. The cruise module receives information on operating conditions from the tachometer, SET (1989 models) or RES/SET (1990-1992 models) switches, both brake light switches, throttle position and speedometer reed switch (1990-1992 models).

The cruise control will set and automatically maintain a speed starting at 40 mph (64 km/h). To set the cruise control, turn the cruise switch to the ON position (**Figure 3** or **Figure 4**). Power is then supplied through the 2-amp fuse leading from the cruise module. After reaching the desired speed (minimum 40 mph [64 km/h]), momentarily press the SET switch on 1989 models or flip down the RES/SET switch on 1990-1992 models and release it. The cruise module receives a signal input reading from the tachometer on 1989 models or from the reed switch on 1990-1992 models. The cruise module then sends a signal to actuate the servo motor.

During operation, the cruise module on 1989 models monitors engine rpm via the tachometer input. On 1990-1992 models, the tachometer and speedometer reed switch signals are used. The input received from the cruise module signals the servo motor to vary the throttle position. Cruise disengagement occurs if engine rpm changes to a nondesired speed.

The cruise control system can be canceled by applying the front or rear brake, closing the throttle or disengaging

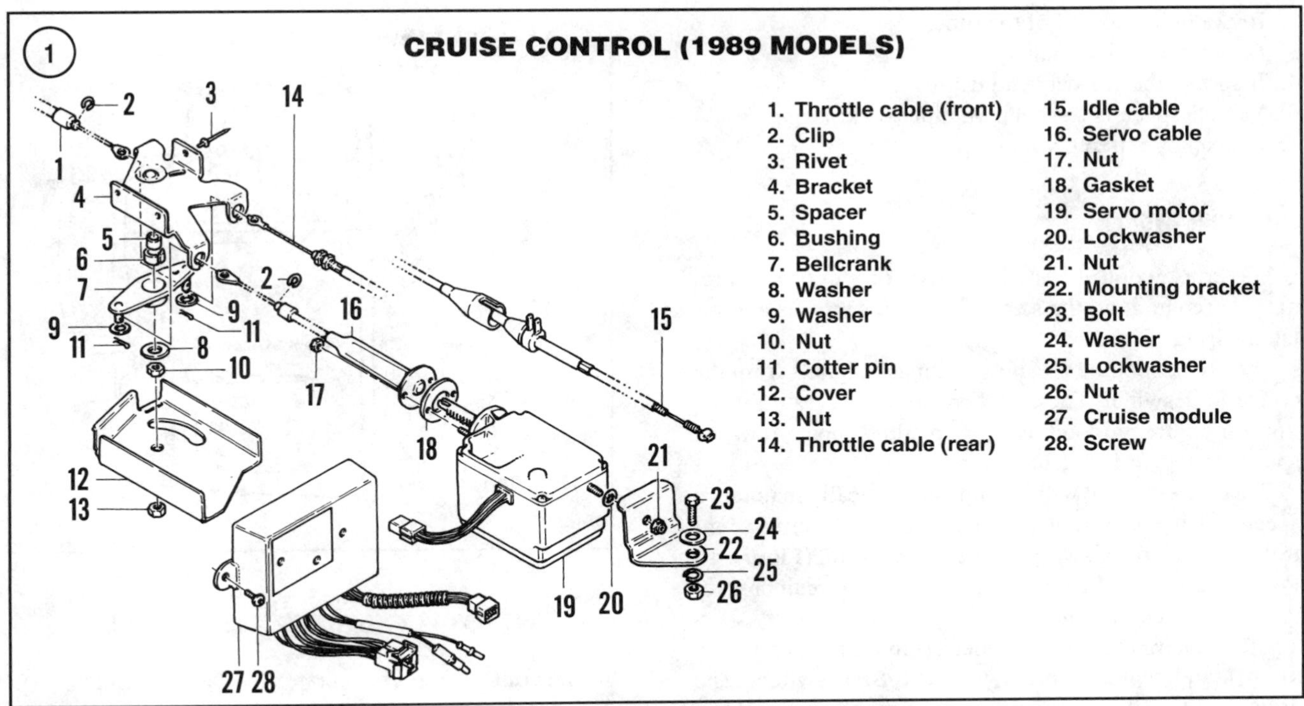

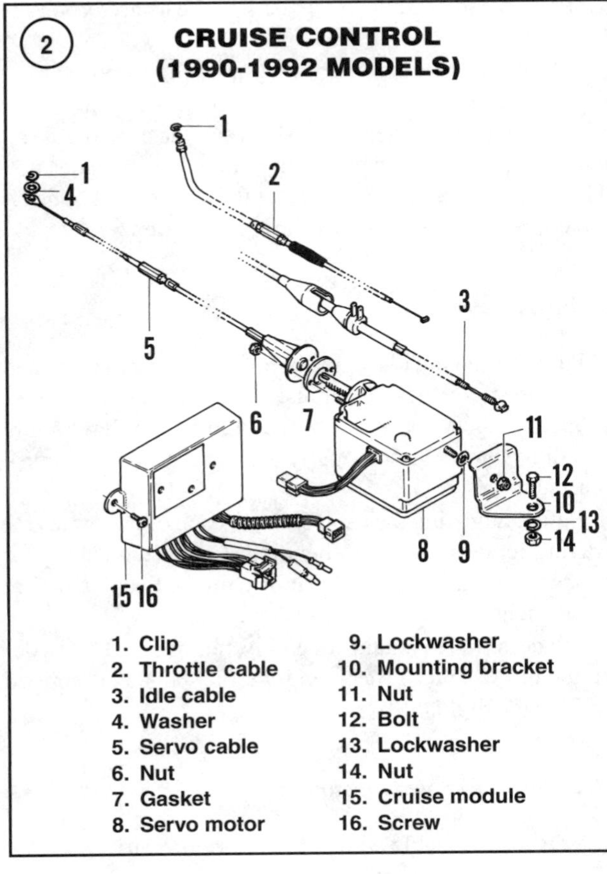

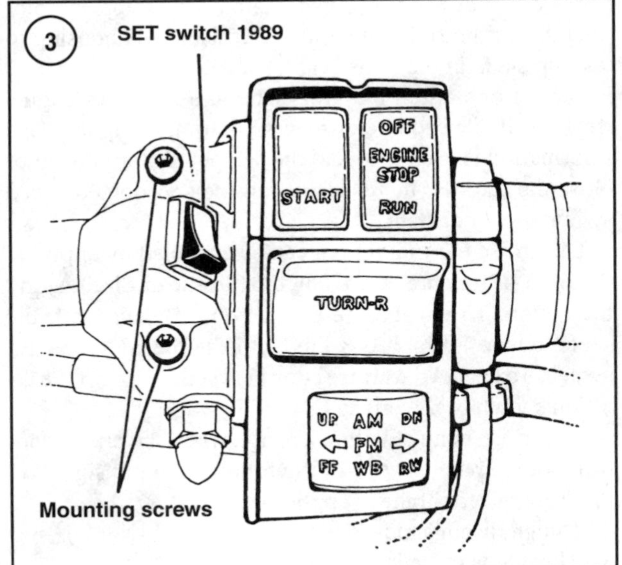

the clutch. To engage the cruise control again with the speed above 40 mph (64 km/h), press the SET or RES switch. To cancel the cruise control system, turn off the ignition switch or the cruise ON/OFF switch.

The cruise control system will not work if one or more of the following conditions occur:

1. Incorrect rear brake light switch adjustment.

14

2. Brake light is on all of the time.
3. Blown brake light bulbs.
4. Incorrect throttle cable adjustment.
5. Vehicle speed is less than 40 mph (64 km/h).
6. A steep or extremely long uphill grade.

1993-1996 Models

The cruise control system consists of a cruise control module (containing the stepper motor), switches and related wiring (**Figure 5**).

The cruise module receives command signals from the cruise SET switch. The cruise module receives information on operating conditions by reading input from the speedometer reed switch.

The cruise control will set and automatically maintain a speed starting at 30 mph (48 km/h). To set the cruise control, turn the cruise switch to the ON position (**Figure 4**). Power is then supplied through the 15-amp circuit breaker to the cruise control module.

After reaching the desired speed (minimum 30 mph [48 km/h]), momentarily press the RES/SET switch. The cruise module then receives a signal input reading from the speedometer reed switch. The cruise module then sends a signal to the stepper motor. The stepper motor then drives the ribbon reel in the cruise cable housing to take up slack in the cruise cable.

During operation, the cruise module monitors engine rpm and the speedometer reed switch input signal. This information is used to signal the stepper motor to open or close the throttle, thereby keeping the speedometer reed switch input constant.

The cruise control system can be canceled by applying the front or rear brake, closing the throttle or disengaging the clutch. To engage the cruise control again with the speed above 30 mph (48 km/h), press the SET or RES switch. To cancel the cruise control system, turn off the ignition switch or the cruise ON/OFF switch.

The cruise control will disengage when the cruise control module receives one of the following input signals:

1. Front or rear brake is applied.
2. Clutch disengaged.
3. Throttle is closed.
4. Cruise switch turned OFF.
5. Engine stop switch turned OFF.
6. RES/SET switch is pressed and held in this position for more than 6 seconds.
7. The RES/SET switch is pressed into the SET position and held until the vehicle speed drops below 30 mph (48 km/h). However, if the switch is released with vehicle speed above 30 mph (48 km/h), the system will re-engage cruise control.

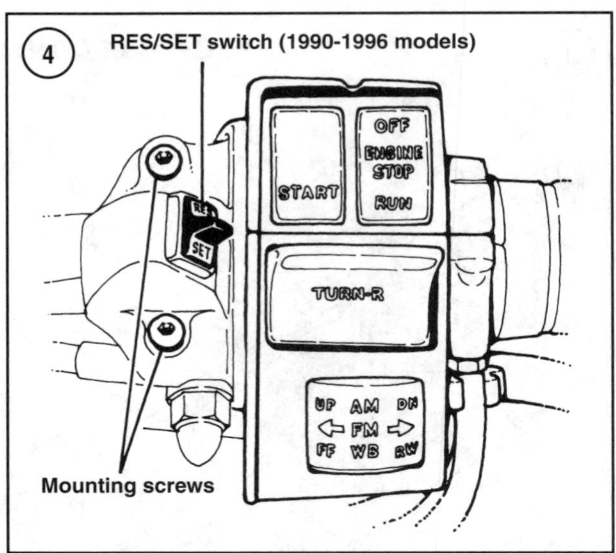

THROTTLE CABLES (1989 MODELS)

The cruise control is operated by the following:

1. Front throttle cable: Connects the throttle grip to the bellcrank.
2. Rear throttle cable: Connects the carburetor to the bellcrank.
3. Idle cable: Connects throttle grip to the carburetor.
4. Servo cable: Connects bellcrank to servo motor.

The front and rear throttle cables and the servo cable all attach to the bellcrank assembly. The idle cable does not. The bellcrank is mounted under the frame backbone. A cover protects the bellcrank during operation.

Cable Adjustment

Fully loosen the idle cable before adjusting the rear and front throttle cables. To adjust the cruise control cables properly, adjust the cables in the following order. Failure to adjust the cables properly can cause cruise control malfunction.

Before adjusting the cables, check each of the cables for fraying, cracks or severe bending. Check the cables for proper routing. Replace worn or damaged cables before adjustment as described in this chapter.

To access the bellcrank assembly, remove the seat as described in Chapter Fifteen and the fuel tank as described in Chapter Eight.

Rear throttle cable adjustment

Rear throttle cable adjustment is required if:

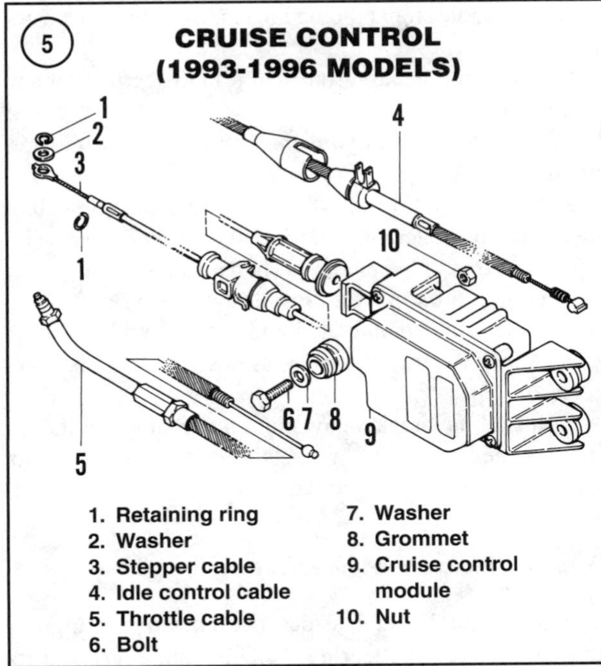

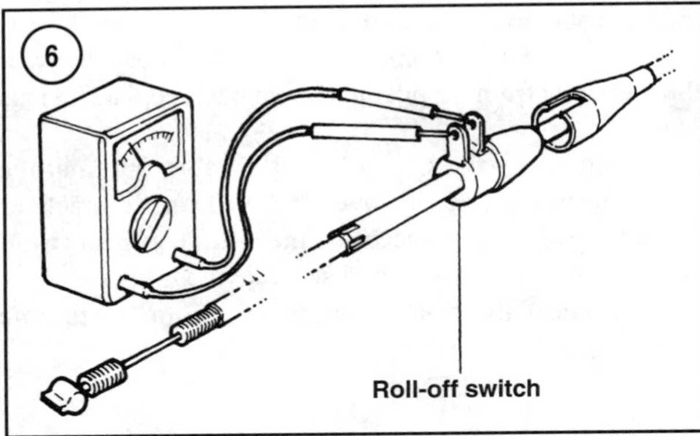

1. The rear throttle cable has been replaced.
2. The carburetor was removed from the motorcycle.

Refer to the following *Front throttle cable* section for adjustment.

Front throttle cable adjustment

The front and rear throttle cables are connected together at the bellcrank (**Figure 1**). The front throttle cable is attached to the bellcrank bracket with an E-clip. The rear throttle cable is inserted through the bellcrank bracket and held in position by two adjust nuts. These nuts are used to adjust the front and rear throttle cables.

1. Make sure all cables are properly installed.

NOTE
Because the front and rear throttle cables are connected together, they are referred to as the pull-open cable in the following steps.

2. Loosen the idle cable adjuster locknuts and turn the adjuster to gain as much slack in the idle cable as possible.
3. Position the handlebar so that the front wheel faces straight ahead.
4. Turn the throttle grip to the wide-open throttle position.
5. The carburetor must be at the wide-open throttle position. If not, adjust the pull-open cable until the throttle opening at the carburetor is completely open. Tighten the cable adjuster locknuts. Release the throttle and then open it again to the wide-open throttle position and recheck the adjustment.
6. Twist the throttle grip until the throttle is completely open. Then close the throttle grip without releasing it; do not release it so that it snaps back to the closed position. Check the idle stop screw; it must be touching the stop on the carburetor with the front wheel facing straight ahead. Then turn the handlebar from side to side (lock to lock). The idle stop screw must still be touching its stop on the carburetor. If the idle stop screw is not touching the idle stop on the carburetor, perform the following:
   a. First check that the cables are properly routed. If cables are properly routed, perform substep b.
   b. Loosen the pull-open cable adjuster just enough so that the idle stop screw touches the stop on the carburetor when the handlebars are turned from side to side. Tighten the cable adjuster locknuts and recheck the adjustment. When the idle stop screw touches the stop on the carburetor when the handlebars are turned from side to side, perform substep c.
   c. Turn the throttle grip so that it is at wide-open throttle position and hold it in this position. Measure the gap from the throttle cam stop to the carburetor stop boss. The specified maximum distance is 1/8 in. (3.2 mm) from the cam stop to the stop boss when the throttle grip is at wide-open throttle position.
7. Make sure the pull-open cable adjuster locknuts are tight.
8. Perform the *Idle cable adjustment* in this section.

14

Idle cable adjustment

The idle cable and roll-off switch are an integrated unit. If one part of the cable is damaged, the entire cable/switch assembly must be replaced.

1. Disconnect the wire connectors from the roll-off switch. Check for continuity at the two switch contacts (**Figure 6**). There should be no continuity. If there is con-

tinuity, replace the idle cable/roll-off switch assembly as described in this chapter. If there is no continuity, proceed to Step 2.
2. Position the handlebar so that the front wheel faces straight ahead.
3. Adjust the idle cable adjuster until there is approximately 0.06 in. (1.5 mm) of free play at the throttle grip. Tighten the idle cable adjuster locknuts and recheck adjustment. When adjustment is correct, proceed to Step 4.
4. Rotate the throttle grip toward the closed throttle position. There should be continuity. If there is no continuity, loosen the idle cable adjuster locknut and slowly turn the adjuster to decrease cable free play until continuity is achieved. The throttle grip must still have some free play. Tighten the idle cable adjuster locknut and recheck adjustment. When continuity is indicated as described, proceed to Step 5.
5. Hold the throttle grip in the completely closed position (remove all free play) and then turn the handlebar from side to side (lock to lock). The multimeter must indicate continuity. If not, repeat Step 4.
6. Position the handlebar so that the front wheel faces straight ahead. Rotate the throttle grip until it is at wide-open throttle and release it. Throttle must return to idle position (idle stop screw touching the carburetor stop). Repeat with the handlebar turned all the way to the left and then all the way to the right. Again, throttle must return to the idle position.
7. If the idle stop screw does not return properly when performing Step 6, repeat Steps 2-6.

Servo cable adjustment

There is no adjustment for the servo cable.

Throttle Cable Replacement

The bellcrank assembly is located on the left side of the frame under the fuel tank.

Rear throttle cable replacement

Refer to **Figure 1**.
1. Remove the fuel tank as described in Chapter Eight.
2. Remove the nut securing the bellcrank cover and remove the cover.
3. Loosen the locknuts securing the rear throttle cable to the bellcrank bracket.
4. Remove the cotter pin and washer securing the front throttle cable to the bellcrank. Then slip the front and rear throttle cables off of the bellcrank pin.
5. Cut the cable strap holding the rear throttle cable in position.
6. Disconnect the rear throttle cable at the carburetor and remove the cable.
7. Install a new cable by reversing these steps while noting the following:
   a. When installing the front and rear throttle cables onto the bellcrank pin, the rear cable end must be installed onto the pin first. Then install the front cable end onto the pin and install the washer and a *new* cotter pin. Completely bend over the ends.
   b. Adjust the throttle cables as described in this chapter.
   c. Install the bracket cover and make sure that the tab on the front of the brackets extends through the slot in the front of the cover.

Front throttle cable replacement

1. Remove the fuel tank as described in Chapter Eight.
2. Remove the nut securing the bellcrank cover and remove the cover.
3. Remove the cotter pin and washer securing the front throttle cable to the bellcrank. Then slip the front throttle cable off of the bellcrank pin. Do not remove the rear throttle cable from the pin unless rear cable replacement is required.
4. Carefully pry the E-clip from the cable fitting at the rear of the bracket and remove the cable from the bracket.
5. Remove the screws securing the throttle grip and right switch housing assembly and separate them.
6. Disconnect the front throttle cable from the throttle grip. Do not lose the ferrule onthe end of the cable.

NOTE
Note how the front throttle cable is routed so it is possible to install the new cable following the original cable path.

7. Remove the old front throttle cable.
8. Install a *new* cable by reversing these steps while noting the following:
   a. The front throttle cable must be installed onto the bellcrank pin so that it is positioned under the rear throttle cable (**Figure 1**). After both cables are installed on the bellcrank pin, install the washer and a *new* cotter pin. Completely bend over the ends.
   b. Adjust the throttle cables as described in this chapter.
   c. Install the bracket cover and make sure that the tab on the front of the brackets extends through the slot in the front of the cover.

Idle cable replacement

1. Remove the fuel tank as described in Chapter Eight.
2. Remove the screws securing the throttle grip and right switch housing assembly and separate them.
3. Disconnect the idle cable from the throttle grip. Do not lose the ferrule on the end of the cable.

NOTE
Note how the idle cable is routed so that it is possible to install the new cable following the original cable path.

4. Cut or remove all clamps holding the idle cable in position.
5. Disconnect the idle cable at the carburetor.
6. Remove the old idle cable.
7. Installation is the reverse of these steps. Adjust the throttle cables as described in this chapter.

Servo cable replacement

The servo cable connects the bellcrank to the servo motor.

1. Remove the fuel tank as described in Chapter Eight.
2. Remove the cotter pin and washer securing the servo cable to the pin. Disconnect the servo cable at the bellcrank pin.
3. Pry the servo cable E-clip out of the cable conduit groove.
4. Remove the nuts securing the servo cable to the servo motor. Then pull the servo cable forward to disconnect the cable from the servo motor rack and remove the cable and the gasket.
5. Installation is the reverse of these steps. Note the following:
   a. Replace the servo cable gasket if the old gasket is worn or damaged.
   b. Use a *new* E-clip securing the servo cable to the bellcrank bracket. Make sure the E-clip seats in the cable conduit groove completely.
   c. After attaching the servo cable to the bellcrank pin, install the washer and a *new* cotter pin. Completely bend over the ends.

THROTTLE CABLES (1989-1996 MODELS)

The cruise control is operated by the following:

1. Throttle cable: Connects the throttle grip to the carburetor.
2. Idle cable: Connects throttle grip to the carburetor.
3. Servo cable (1990-1992 models): Connects servo motor to carburetor.
4. Cruise cable (1993-1996 models): Connects stepper motor (cruise control module) to carburetor.

Cable Adjustment

Fully loosen the idle cable before adjusting the cruise control cables. To adjust these cables properly, perform the adjustments in the following order. Failure to adjust the cables properly can cause cruise control malfunction.

Before adjusting the cables, check each of the cables for fraying, cracks or severe bending. Check the cables for proper routing. Replace worn or damaged cables before adjustment as described in this chapter.

Throttle cable

1. Remove the fuel tank as described in Chapter Eight.
2. Loosen the idle cable adjuster locknuts and turn the adjuster to gain as much slack in the idle cable as possible.
3. Position the handlebar so that the front wheel faces straight ahead.
4. Turn the throttle grip so that it is at wide-open throttle position.
5. The carburetor throttle valve should be at wide-open throttle position. If not, adjust the throttle cable adjuster until the carburetor throttle valve is completely open. Tighten the cable adjuster. Release the throttle and then open it again to wide-open throttle position and recheck the adjustment.
6. Twist the throttle grip by hand until the throttle is completely open. Then close the throttle grip without releasing it; do not release it so that it snaps back. Check the idle stop screw; it should be touching the stop on the carburetor with the front wheel facing straight ahead. Then turn the handlebar from side to side (lock to lock). The idle stop screw should still be touching the carburetor. If the idle stop screw is not touching the carburetor, perform the following:
   a. First check that the cables are properly routed. If cables are properly routed, perform substep b.
   b. If the servo cable does not have enough slack, it will open the throttle cable. Loosen the servo cable adjuster locknut and loosen the cable, if necessary. Tighten the cable adjuster locknut and recheck adjustment. If the servo cable is not causing the problem, perform substep c.
   c. Loosen the throttle cable adjuster just enough so that the idle stop screw touches the carburetor when the handlebars are turned from side to side. Tighten

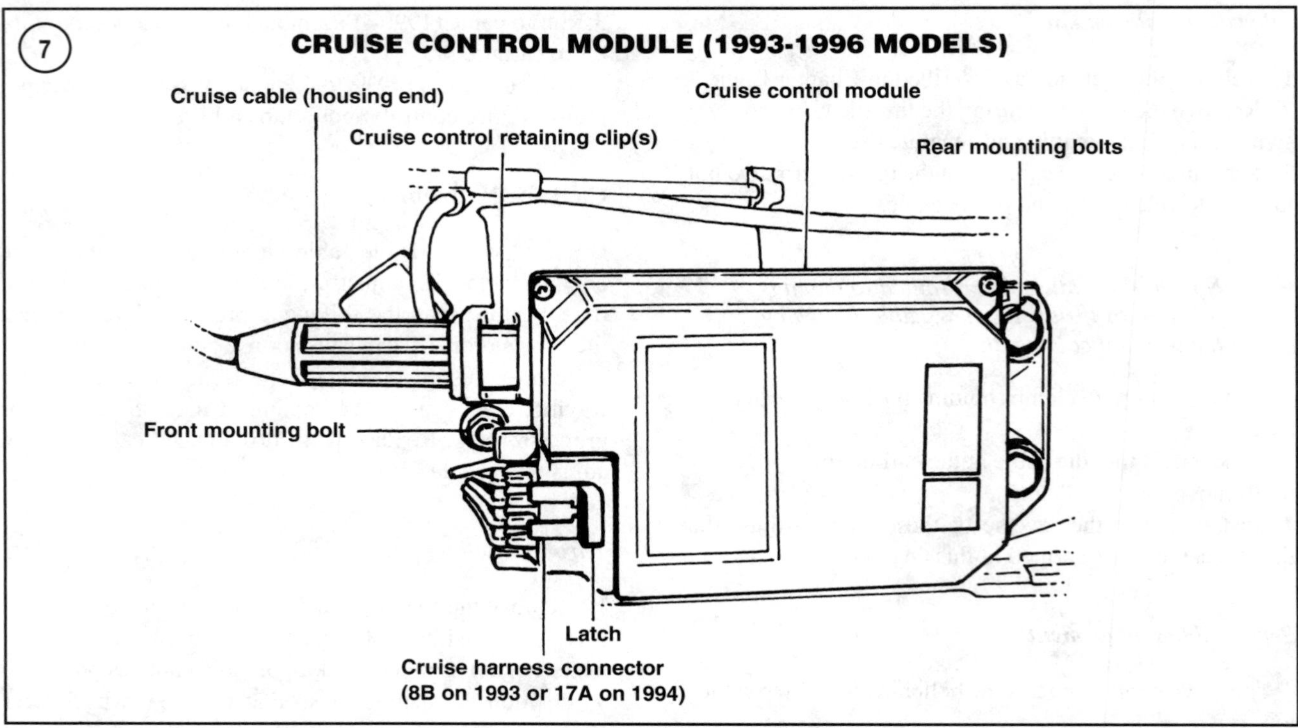

the cable adjuster locknut and recheck the adjustment.

7. Perform the *Idle cable adjustment*.

Idle cable adjustment (1989-1992 models)

The idle cable and roll-off switch are an integrated unit. If one part of the cable is damaged, the entire cable/switch assembly must be replaced.

1. Remove the fuel tank as described in Chapter Eight.
2. Disconnect the wire connectors from the roll-off switch. Check for continuity at the two switch contacts (**Figure 6**). There should be no continuity. If there is continuity, replace the idle cable/roll-off switch assembly as described in this chapter. If there is no continuity, proceed to Step 2.
3. Position the handlebar so that the front wheel faces straight ahead.
4. Adjust the idle cable adjuster until there is approximately 0.06 in. (1.5 mm) of free play at the throttle grip. Tighten the idle cable adjuster locknuts and recheck adjustment. When adjustment is correct, proceed to Step 5.
5. Rotate the throttle grip toward the closed throttle position. There should be continuity. If there is no continuity, loosen the idle cable adjuster locknut and slowly turn the adjuster to decrease cable free play until continuity is achieved. The throttle grip must still have some free play. Tighten the idle cable adjuster locknut and recheck adjustment. When continuity is indicated as described, proceed to Step 6.
6. Hold the throttle grip in the completely closed position (remove all free play) and then turn the handlebar from side to side (lock to lock). The multimeter must indicate continuity. If not, repeat Step 5.
7. Position the handlebar so that the front wheel faces straight ahead. Rotate the throttle grip until it is at wide-open throttle and release it. Throttle must return to idle position (idle stop screw touching carburetor stop). Repeat with the handlebar turned all the way to the left and then all the way to the right. Again, throttle must return to the idle position.
8. If the idle stop screw does not return properly when performing Step 7, repeat Steps 2-7.
9. Perform the *Servo cable adjustment (1990-1992 models)*.

Idle cable adjustment (1993-1996 models)

1. Remove the fuel tank as described in Chapter Eight.
2. Remove the left side cover.
3. Disconnect the cruise harness connector at the cruise control module (**Figure 7**) and perform the following:

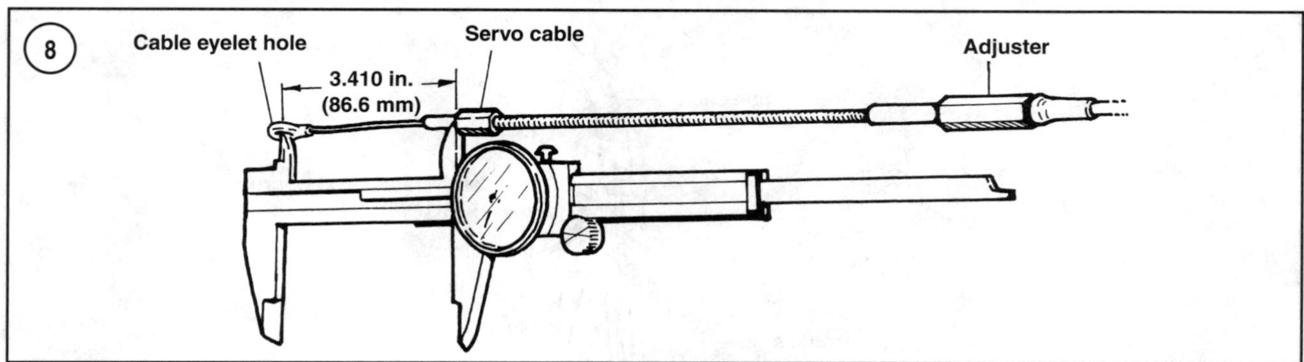

a. On 1993 models, connect a multimeter to the black/red and black/orange leads on the cruise harness connector.

b. On 1994 models, connect an ohmmeter to the violet/yellow and orange/violet leads on cruise harness connector.

4. There should be no continuity. If the multimeter shows continuity, the roll-off switch is damaged. If necessary, replace the idle cable assembly as described in this chapter.

NOTE
Leave the meter leads attached to connectors when performing the following.

5. Position the handlebar so the front tire faces straight ahead.
6. Adjust the idle cable adjuster (at handlebar) until there is approximately 0.06 in. (1.5 mm) of free play at the throttle grip. Tighten the idle cable adjuster locknuts and recheck adjustment. When adjustment is correct, perform Step 7.
7. Rotate the throttle grip toward closed throttle position; there should be continuity. If there is no continuity reading, loosen the idle cable adjuster locknut and turn the adjuster to decrease cable free play; adjust until the ohmmeter indicates continuity while there is some free play at throttle grip. Tighten the idle cable adjuster locknut and recheck adjustment. When continuity is indicated as described, perform Step 8.
8. Hold the throttle grip in the completely closed position (remove all free play) and then turn the handlebar from side to side (lock to lock). The multimeter must indicate continuity. If not, repeat Step 7.
9. Position the handlebar so that the front wheel faces straight ahead. Rotate the throttle grip until it is at wide-open throttle and release it. Throttle must return to idle position. Repeat with handlebar turned all the way to the left and then all the way to the right. Again, throttle must return to the idle position.
10. If throttle does not return properly when performing Step 9, repeat Steps 5-9.
11. Perform *Cruise cable adjustment (1993-1996 models)* as described in this chapter.

Servo cable adjustment (1989-1992 models)

Refer to **Figure 2**.

1. Remove the fuel tank as described in Chapter Eight.
2. Adjust the throttle and idle cables as described in the previous procedures.
3. Remove the E-clips, one at the carburetor pin and one at the carburetor cable bracket. Disconnect the servo cable at the carburetor.

NOTE
When performing the following procedures, the servo cable must be attached to the servo motor with the motor rack fully extended.

4. Measure the servo cable with a vernier or dial caliper as follows:
   a. Insert the front caliper arm into the servo cable eyelet hole and the opposite caliper arm against the cable shoulder (**Figure 8**).
   b. The cable length should be 3.410 in. (86.6 mm).
   c. If the cable length is incorrect, loosen the servo cable adjuster locknut and turn the cable adjuster as required to obtain the correct length adjustment. Tighten the adjuster locknut and recheck the adjustment length.
5. If the servo cable was removed from the mounting position, insert the cable through the two mounting retainers. Then route the cable over the top of the engine stabilizer and drop it between the cylinder heads and toward the carburetor.
6. Insert the servo cable conduit into the cable bracket on the carburetor. Secure the cable in the conduit cable

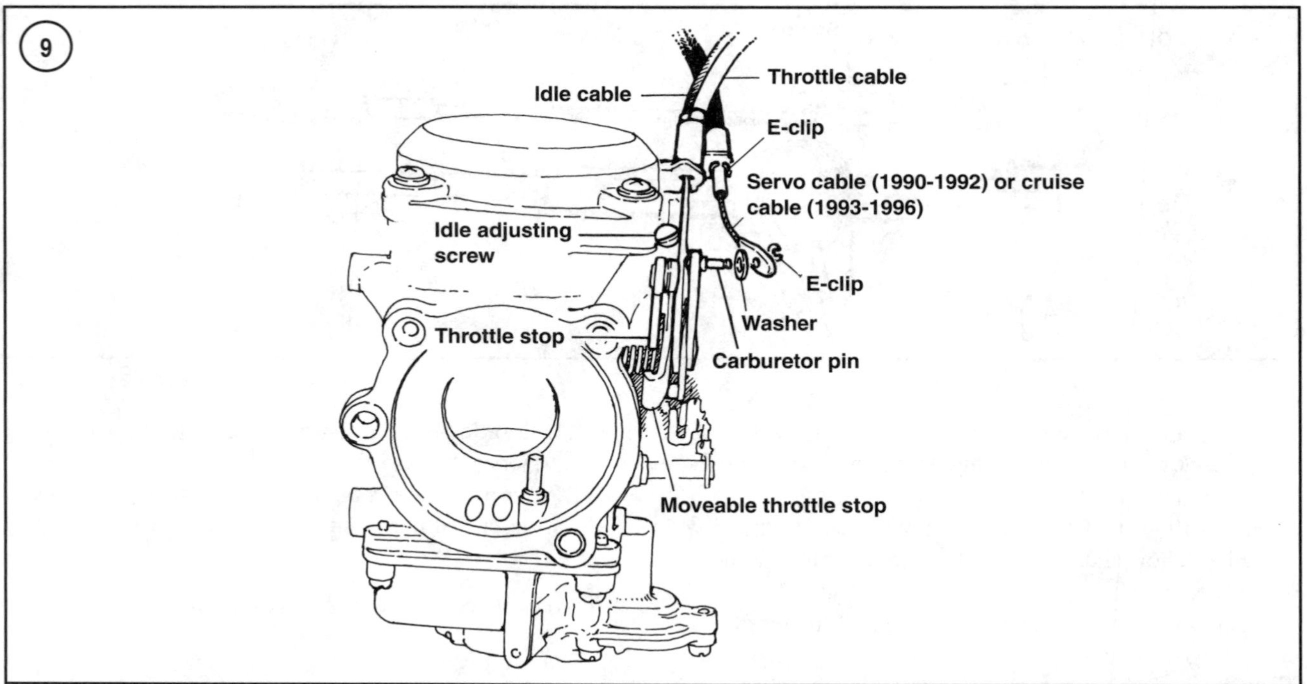

groove with a *new* E-clip. Make sure the E-clip seats correctly in the groove.

7. Fit the servo cable eyelet over the carburetor pin (**Figure 9**). Then visually check the cable fit on the pin. For the servo cable adjustment to be correct, the eyelet must fit against the pin so that the cable slack is at the back of the pin (a visible distance that is equal to one-third the eyelet hole diameter) (**Figure 10**). If necessary, loosen the servo cable adjuster and change the cable length until the specified clearance is obtained. Tighten the adjuster locknut and recheck adjustment.
8. Install the cable washer on the carburetor pin. Then secure the cable onto the pin with a *new* E-clip. Make sure the E-clip seats correctly in the pin groove.
9. Once the servo cable is installed and secured with the E-clip, snap the throttle grip a few times while turning the handlebars from side to side. Then release the throttle grip and check that the idle adjusting screw touches the carburetor idle stop. If not, readjust the cable length.

NOTE
Proper servo cable adjustment is critical to cruise control and idle speed adjustment. If the servo cable adjustment is too loose, the servo motor will run nonstop when the cruise and ignition switches are turned ON as well as cause the overall speed of the motorcycle to drop a few mph after the cruise control is set to run at a specified speed. If the servo cable adjustment is too tight, it will be difficult to adjust and maintain a correct idle speed. The motorcycle will also gain an additional 1-2 mph (1.6-3.2 km) when the cruise control RES/SET switch is switched to SET speed.

Cruise cable adjustment (1993-1996 models)

Cruise cable adjustment is only required if the cruise control module or cruise cable have been replaced.

1. Remove the fuel tank as described in Chapter Eight.
2. Adjust the throttle and idle cables as previously described.
3. Disconnect the cruise cable at the carburetor (**Figure 9**). Remove the two cable E-clips, one at the carburetor pin and one at the carburetor cable bracket.

NOTE
*The cruise cable must be attached to the cruise control module (**Figure** 7) when performing the following; refer to **Cruise cable replacement (1993-1996 models)** in this chapter.*

4. Set cruise cable length as follows:
   a. Push the square locking button on the cruise cable adjuster (**Figure 11**) and move the upper cruise ca-

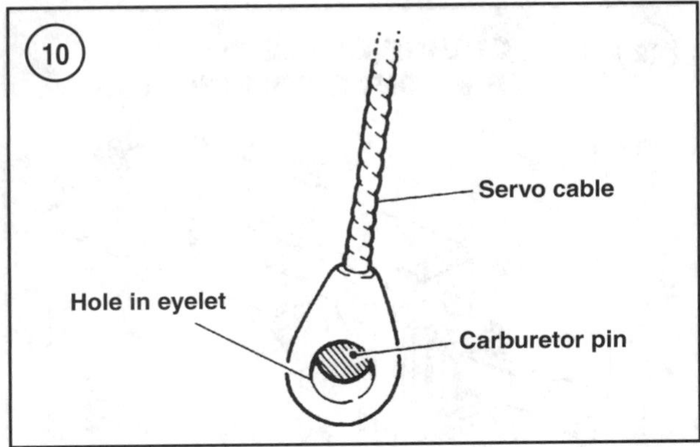

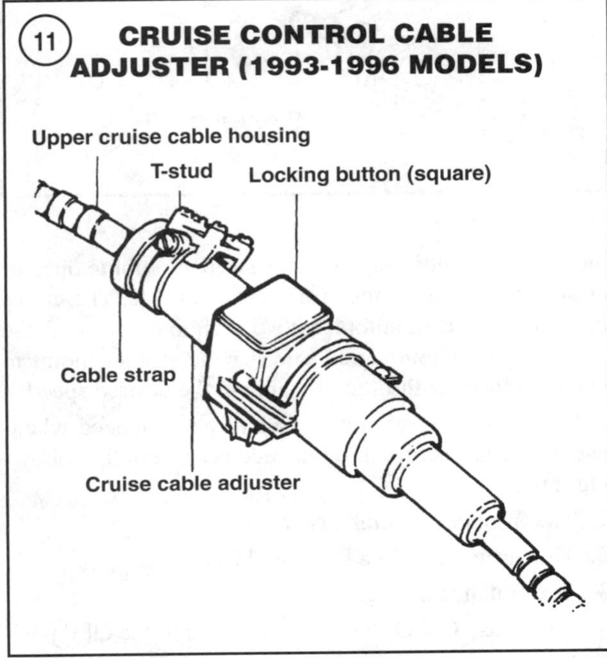

ble housing in or out so the cable eyelet can be slipped on the carburetor pin as shown in **Figure 9**.

b. For the cruise cable adjustment to be correct, the eyelet must fit against the pin so that the cable slack is at the back of the pin, a distance that is equal to one-third the eyelet hole diameter (**Figure 10**).

5. Install the cable washer on the carburetor pin. Then secure the cable onto the pin with a *new* E-clip. Make sure the E-clip seats correctly in the pin groove.
6. Once the cruise cable is installed and secured with the E-clip, snap the throttle grip a few times while turning the handlebar from side to side. Then release the throttle grip and check that the idle adjusting screw touches the carburetor idle stop (**Figure 9**). If not, readjust the cable length.

NOTE
Proper cruise cable adjustment is critical to cruise control and idle speed adjustment. If the cruise cable adjustment is too loose, the SET speed may be 1-2 mph (1.6-3.2 km/h) lower than the speed present when cruise was SET. If cruise cable adjustment is too tight, it will be difficult to adjust and maintain a correct idle speed. The motorcycle will also gain an additional 1-2 mph when the cruise control RES/SET switch is switched to SET speed.

Throttle and idle cable replacement (1989-1996 models)

Throttle and idle cable replacement are the same as for noncruise control FLH and FLT models. Refer to Chapter Eight.

Servo cable replacement (1989-1992 models)

Refer to **Figure 2**.

1. Remove the fuel tank as described in Chapter Eight.
2. Remove the seat as described in Chapter Fifteen.
3. Remove the E-clip securing the servo cable eyelet to the carburetor pin. Remove the washer and slide the eyelet off of the pin.
4. Remove the E-clip securing the servo cable to the carburetor cable bracket.
5. Discard both E-clips.
6. Remove the nuts securing the servo cable to the servo motor. Then pull the servo cable forward to disconnect the cable from the servo motor rack and remove the cable and the gasket.
7. Replace the servo cable gasket if the old gasket is worn or damaged.
8. Align the gasket with the servo cable and attach the cable to the servo motor rack. Secure the cable to the motor with the mounting nuts.
9. Complete installation by performing the steps described under *Servo cable adjustment* for 1990-1992 models in this section. Install *new* E-clips.

Cruise cable replacement (1993-1996 models)

1. Remove the fuel tank as described in Chapter Eight.
2. Remove the air filter and back plate as described in Chapter Eight.
3. Remove the E-clip securing the cruise cable to the carburetor pin (**Figure 9**). Slide the cruise eyelet off the pin and remove the washer.

4. Remove the E-clip securing the cruise cable to the carburetor cable bracket.
5. Remove the left saddlebag as described in Chapter Fifteen.
6. Remove the left side cover mounting screw and remove the side cover.
7. Remove the T-stud mount strap securing the cruise cable to the frame (**Figure 11**). Then press the square button on the cruise cable and push the carburetor end of the cable conduit into the cable adjuster to increase cable slack.
8. Lift the cruise harness connector latch at the cruise control module and disconnect the connector from the module (**Figure 7**).
9. Pull the cruise cable out and disconnect the cable end from the ribbon (**Figure 12**).
10. Pull the ribbon out so that it is not twisted and connect the new cruise cable to it.

CAUTION
Make sure the ribbon is not twisted when reconnecting the cable end.

11. Push the cruise cable housing end (**Figure 7**) into the cruise control module. Make sure the latches securely lock the housing end.
12. Complete installation by performing the steps described under *Cruise cable adjustment* for 1993-1996 models in this section. Install *new* E-clips.

CRUISE CONTROL COMPONENTS (1997-1998 MODELS)

The cruise control system consists of a cruise control module containing the stepper motor, switches and related wiring. The stepper motor actuates the cruise control cable through a gear train and ribbon reel.

The cruise control module receives command signals from the cruise control SET/RESUME switch on the right handlebar switch. The cruise control module receives information on operating conditions from the speedometer output signal.

The cruise control system will set and automatically maintain any speed between 30-85 mph (48-137 km/h). To set the cruise control, turn the front fairing cap cruise ON/OFF switch to the ON position. Power is then supplied to the cruise control module through the 15-amp fuse located in the fuse block under the frame left side cover.

After reaching the desired speed, momentarily push the cruise SET/RESUME switch to the SET position. The cruise control module will then receive a signal input from the speedometer output signal. The cruise control module then sends a signal to the steeper motor to open or close the throttle via the cruise control cable. The cruise control module monitors both the engine rpm and the speedometer output signal to order the steeper motor to open or close the throttle to maintain the desired speed.

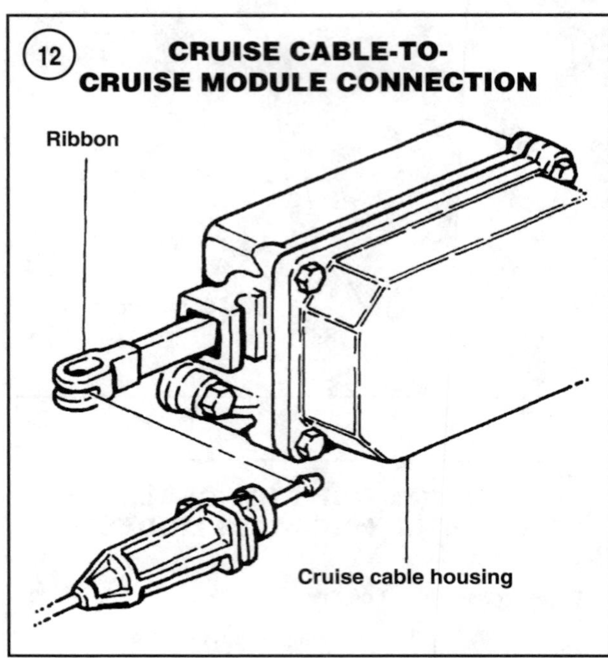

The cruise control is automatically disengaged whenever the cruise control module receives one of the following inputs:

1. The front or rear brake is applied.
2. The throttle is rolled back or closed.
3. The clutch is disengaged.
4. The cruise ON/OFF switch is moved to the OFF position.
5. The engine stop switch is moved to the OFF position.
6. The handlebar cruise SET/RESUME switch is moved to the SET position and held in that position until the motorcycle speed drops below 30 mph (48 km/h).

CONTROL CABLES (1997-1998 MODELS)

Throttle and Idle Cables Adjustment

The throttle and idle cable adjustment must be performed at a Harley-Davidson dealership equipped with the Scanalyzer tool. The engine must be at a specific temperature during this procedure and must be monitored to assure correct adjustment.

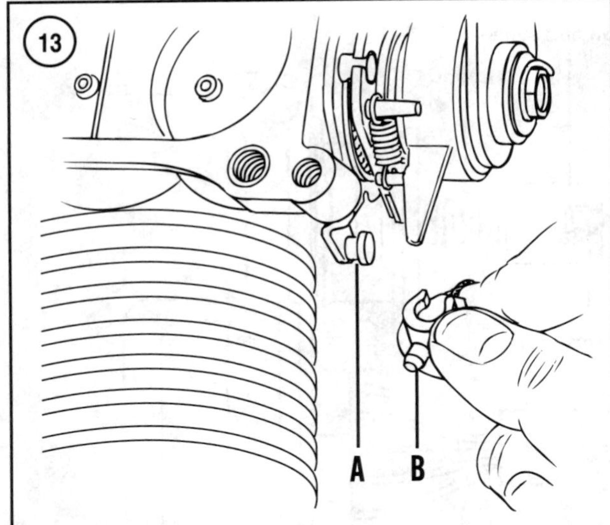

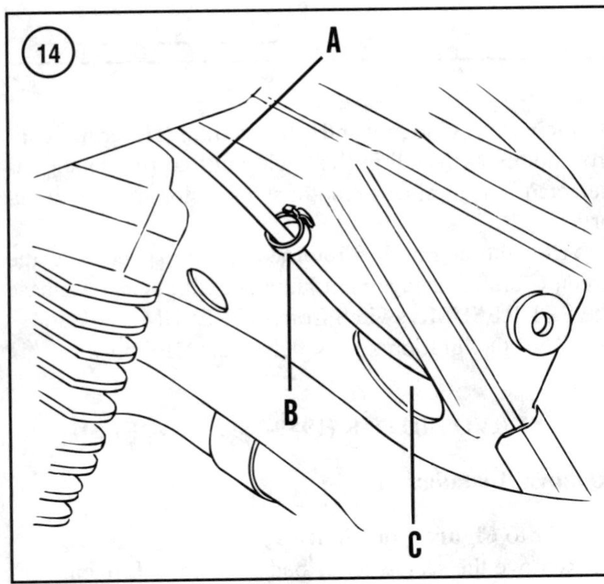

Cruise Control Cable Adjustment

The cruise control cable only requires adjustment if the cruise control module or cruise control cable are removed or replaced. If necessary, adjust the cruise control cable using the *Cable Lash Initialization* in this chapter.

Removal

1. Remove the fuel tank as described in Chapter Eight.
2. Remove the left saddlebag as described in Chapter Fifteen.
3. Remove the frame left side cover.
4. Remove the air filter and back plate as described in Chapter Eight.
5. Remove the E-clip and release the cable housing from the induction module.
6. At the outboard side pin wheel (A, **Figure 13**), push on the plastic end fitting (B) and remove it from the pin wheel.
7. Remove the cruise cable (A, **Figure 14**) from the cable clip (B) on the frame.
8. Make a drawing of the cable routing from the cruise control module through to the induction module.
9. Carefully remove the cruise cable out from under the fuel tank.
10. Rotate the cruise cable connector in a *counterclockwise* direction and detach it from the cruise control module.
11. Pull the cable out of the connector and remove the cable end bead from the ribbon end eyelet.
12. Pull the cruise control cable and connector from the hole (C, **Figure 14**) in the frame crossmember and remove it from the frame.

Installation

1. On the left side, route the new cruise control cable forward and over the top of the engine top stabilizer and then down between the cylinder heads to the induction module.
2. On the right side, position the new cruise control cable housing into the cable guide. Install a *new* E-clip on the cable housing and lock the cable into place.
3. Route the cruise control cable through the hole in the frame (C, **Figure 14**).
4. Position the hole in the ribbon end eyelet and flat on the cable connector facing outward. Insert the cable end bead into the ribbon end eyelet (**Figure 15**). Make sure it is secure in the eyelet.
5. Make sure the cable end bead, the eyelet and the ribbon are lined up correctly. At the induction end of the cable, gently pull on the end fitting to remove cable slack.
6. Insert the cruise control connector into the cruise control module, rotate it *clockwise* until the connector tabs are fully engaged with the detents in the cruise control module. Carefully pull on the connector to make sure it is secured correctly.
7. Attach the cruise cable (A, **Figure 14**) to the frame with a *new* cable clip (B).
8. Adjust the cruise control cable as described in this chapter.
9. Hold onto the cam lever assembly to prevent it from rotating. Install the cruise control cable and plastic end fit-

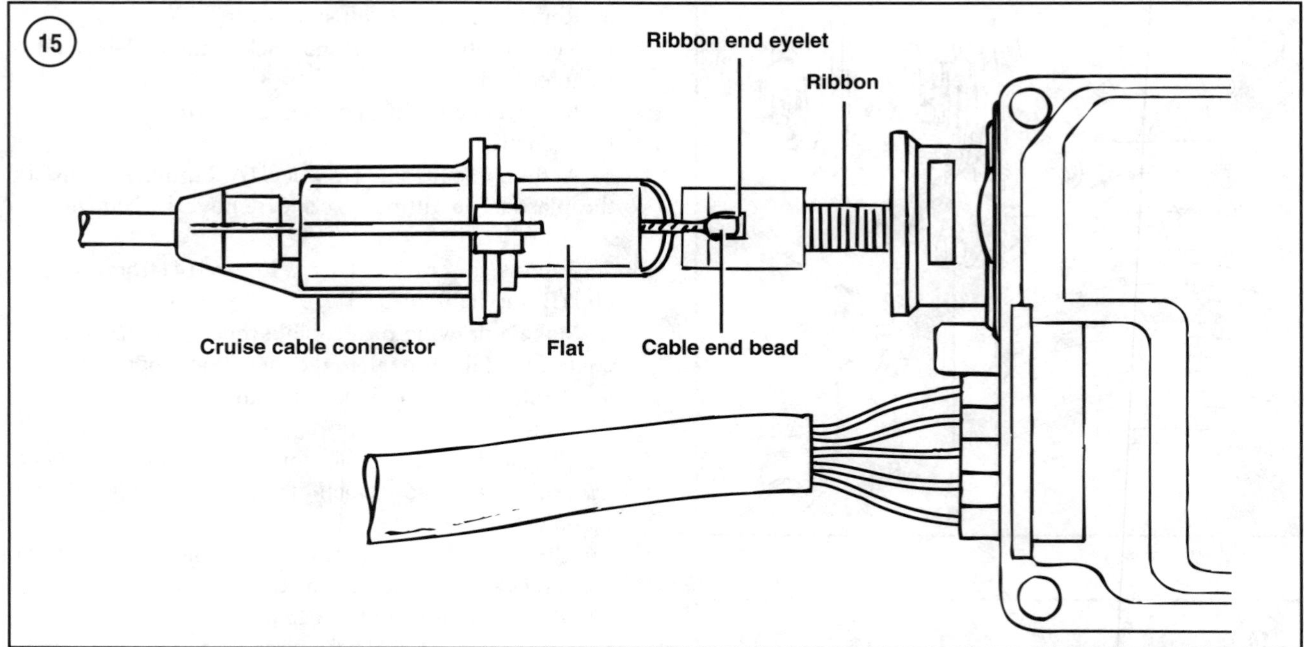

ting (B, **Figure 13**) on the pin wheel (A). Push the end fitting until it locks into place.

10. Install the back plate and the air filter as described in this chapter.
11. Install the frame left side cover.
12. Install the left saddlebag.
13. Install the fuel tank as described in this chapter.

Cable Lash Initialization

This is not a routine adjustment and is only necessary if the cruise control module or cruise control cable are removed or replaced.

1. Start the engine and allow it to reach normal operating temperature. Shut off the engine.
2. On the right handlebar switch, push the cruise control SET/RESUME switch to the RESUME position and hold it on.
3. On the front fairing cap turn the cruise control ON/OFF switch to the ON position.
4. Turn the ignition/key switch to the ON position.
5. Start the engine and allow it to idle. The green *C* cruise engagement lamp on the tachometer face will illuminate. Wait for three seconds for the lamp to go off.
6. Release the SET/RESUME switch from the RESUME position.
7. On the right handlebar switch, push the cruise control SET/RESUME switch to the RESUME position and hold it on.
8. Increase engine rpm and return to idle. The cruise control module will pull in the cable until an rpm change is detected. The number of motor steps is stored in the memory.
9. After the engine has returned to idle speed, and the green *C* cruise engagement lamp is extinguished, release the SET/RESUME switch from the RESUME position.
10. Turn the ignition/key switch to the OFF position.

SERVO MOTOR (1989-1992 MODELS)

Removal/Installation

Refer to **Figure 1** or **Figure 2**.

1. Remove the seat as described in Chapter Fifteen.
2. Disconnect the 6-pin servo motor electrical connector.
3. Remove the nuts securing the servo cable to the servo motor. Then pull the servo cable forward, disconnect the cable from the servo motor rack, and remove the cable and the gasket.
4. Remove the nut securing the servo motor to the bracket. Remove the servo motor and the external tooth lockwasher.

NOTE
The lockwasher is installed between the servo motor and the mounting bracket.

5. Installation is the reverse of these steps while noting the following:

a. Replace the servo cable gasket if damaged.
b. Replace the external tooth lockwasher if worn or damaged.
c. Make sure the external tooth lockwasher is installed between the servo motor and the mounting bracket when installing the motor into position. Refer to 20, **Figure 1**, or 9, **Figure 2**. Tighten the nut securely.
d. Clean the servo motor and servo module electrical connectors with electrical contact cleaner. After the cleaner evaporates, apply a dielectric electrical grease to the connector halves before connecting them.
e. On 1990-1992 models, adjust the servo cable as described in this chapter. On 1989 models, servo cable adjustment is not required.

CRUISE MODULE (1989-1992 MODELS)

Removal/Installation

Refer to **Figure 1** or **Figure 2**.

1. Remove the seat as described in Chapter Fifteen.
2. Disconnect all of the electrical connectors at the cruise module.
3. Remove the screws securing the module and remove the module.
4. Installation is the reverse of these steps while noting the following:
   a. Clean the cruise module electrical connectors with contact cleaner and apply dielectric compound to the connector halves prior to connecting them.
   b. Make sure the cruise module wire connector leads are properly connected.

CRUISE CONTROL MODULE

Removal/Installation

1993-1996 models

1. Remove the battery as described in Chapter Nine.
2. Remove the air filter and back plate as described in Chapter Eight.
3. Remove the left saddlebag as described in Chapter Fifteen.
4. Remove the left side cover mounting screw and remove the side cover.
5. Remove the T-stud mount strap securing the cruise cable to the frame (**Figure 11**).
6. Disconnect the cruise control cable at the cruise control module as described under *Cruise cable replacement (1993-1996 models)* in this chapter.
7. Lift the cruise harness connector latch at the cruise control module and disconnect the connector from the module.
8. Loosen and then remove the cruise control module rear mounting bolts.
9. Loosen the front cruise control module mounting bolt until tension is released from the front module mount grommet.
10. Remove the cruise control module.
11. If replacing the cruise control module, transfer the grommets from the old module to the new one.
12. Install the module into position on the frame. Install the rear mounting bolts. Tighten all mounting bolts to 9-11 ft.-lb. (12-15 N•m).
13. Reconnect the cruise harness connector.
14. Reconnect and adjust the cruise cable as described in this chapter.
15. Install the left side cover and the mounting bolt.
16. Install the left saddlebag as described in Chapter Fifteen.
17. Install the battery as described in Chapter Nine.
18. Install the air filter and back plate as described in Chapter Eight.

Removal/Installation

1997-1998 models

1. Remove the battery as described in Chapter Eight.
2. Disconnect the cruise control cable from the module as described in this chapter.
3. Disconnect the cruise control electrical connector from the module.
4. Working within the battery box, remove the locknuts from the cruise control mounting studs.
5. Carefully remove the cruise control module from the outer surface of the battery box. Do not lose the rubber grommet on each mounting stud.
6. Install by reversing these removal steps while noting the following:
   a. Install the rubber grommet onto each mounting stud.
   b. Securely tighten the mounting locknuts.

14

CRUISE CONTROL SWITCH REPLACEMENT (1989-1996 MODELS)

ON/OFF Switch

On FLHT series models, the ON/OFF switch is mounted on the far right side of the inner fairing. To remove the switch, carefully pry it out of the fairing. Then disconnect the connector leads from the switch. Reverse to install a new switch.

On FLTC-U models, the ON/OFF switch is mounted on the right front side of the instrument panel. Remove the instrument panel to access the switch. Remove the switch and disconnect the connector leads from the back of the switch. Reverse to install a new switch.

Set Switch (1989 Models)

The set switch is mounted onto the right handlebar (**Figure 3**).

1. Remove the mounting screws securing the switch housing to the handlebar.
2. Disconnect the switch wires and remove the switch.
3. Install a new set switch by reversing these removal steps. Refer to **Figure 16** for wire-connecting locations.

Set/Resume Switch

1990-1992 models

The set/resume switch is mounted onto the right handlebar (**Figure 4**).

1. Remove the mounting screws securing the switch to the handlebar.
2. Disconnect the switch wires and remove the switch.
3. Install a new set switch by reversing these steps. Refer to **Figure 17** for wire-connecting locations.

1993-1996 models

The set/resume switch is mounted on the right handlebar (**Figure 4**).

1A. On FLTC-U models, remove the instrument housing as described in Chapter Nine.

1B. On FLHT series models, remove the headlight assembly as described in Chapter Nine.

2. On 1994 models, remove the 3-pin set/resume connector from the T-stud mount.
3. Disconnect the 3-pin connectors. Then remove the terminals from the connector housing.
4. Remove the screws securing the set/resume switch to the handlebar and remove the switch.
5. Install the new switch onto the handlebar. Check and adjust the front brake lever position prior to tightening the set/resume switch screws. Then securely tighten the switch screws.
6. Cut the new switch wires to length. Route the wires from the harness through the handlebar grommet. Crimp new connectors onto wires and reconnect. Test the new switch.

7A. On FLTC-U models, install the instrument housing as described in Chapter Nine.

(16) **1989 MODELS**

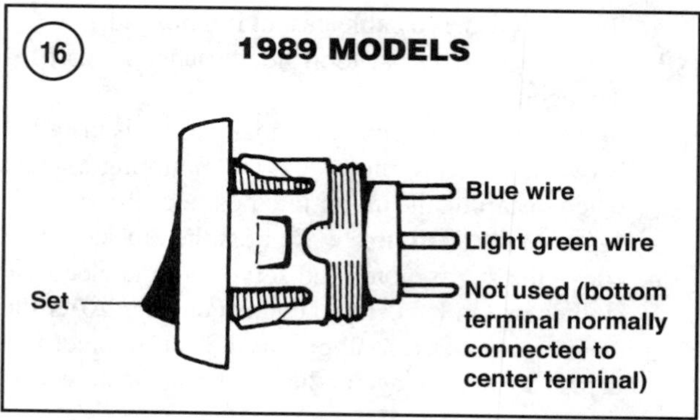

(17) **1990-1992 MODELS**

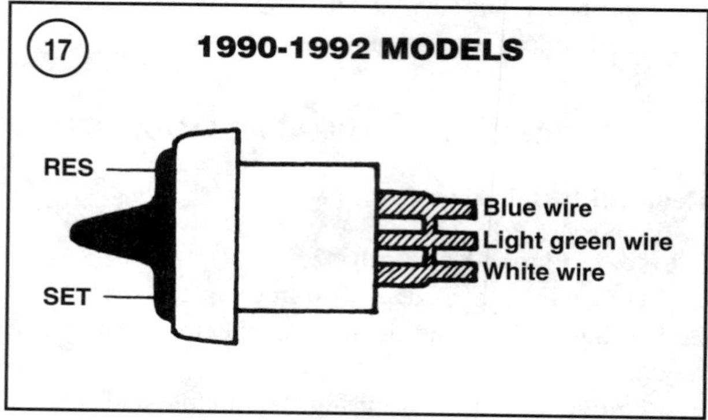

7B. On FLHT series models, install the headlight assembly as described in Chapter Nine.

8. Check switch operation.

CRUISE CONTROL SWITCH REPLACEMENT (1997-1998 MODELS)

ON/OFF Switch

1. Remove the front fairing inner fairing cap as described in Chapter Fifteen.

NOTE

The black/green cruise control ON/OFF switch wire is interconnected to the speaker switch. This wire is permanently attached to both switches and must be cut to remove either switch.

2. Cut the black/green wire halfway between the ON/OFF and the speaker switches.

NOTE

Note the switch terminals to which the following wires connect. They must reconnect to the same terminals.

(18) CRUISE CONTROL WIRING DIAGRAM (1989)

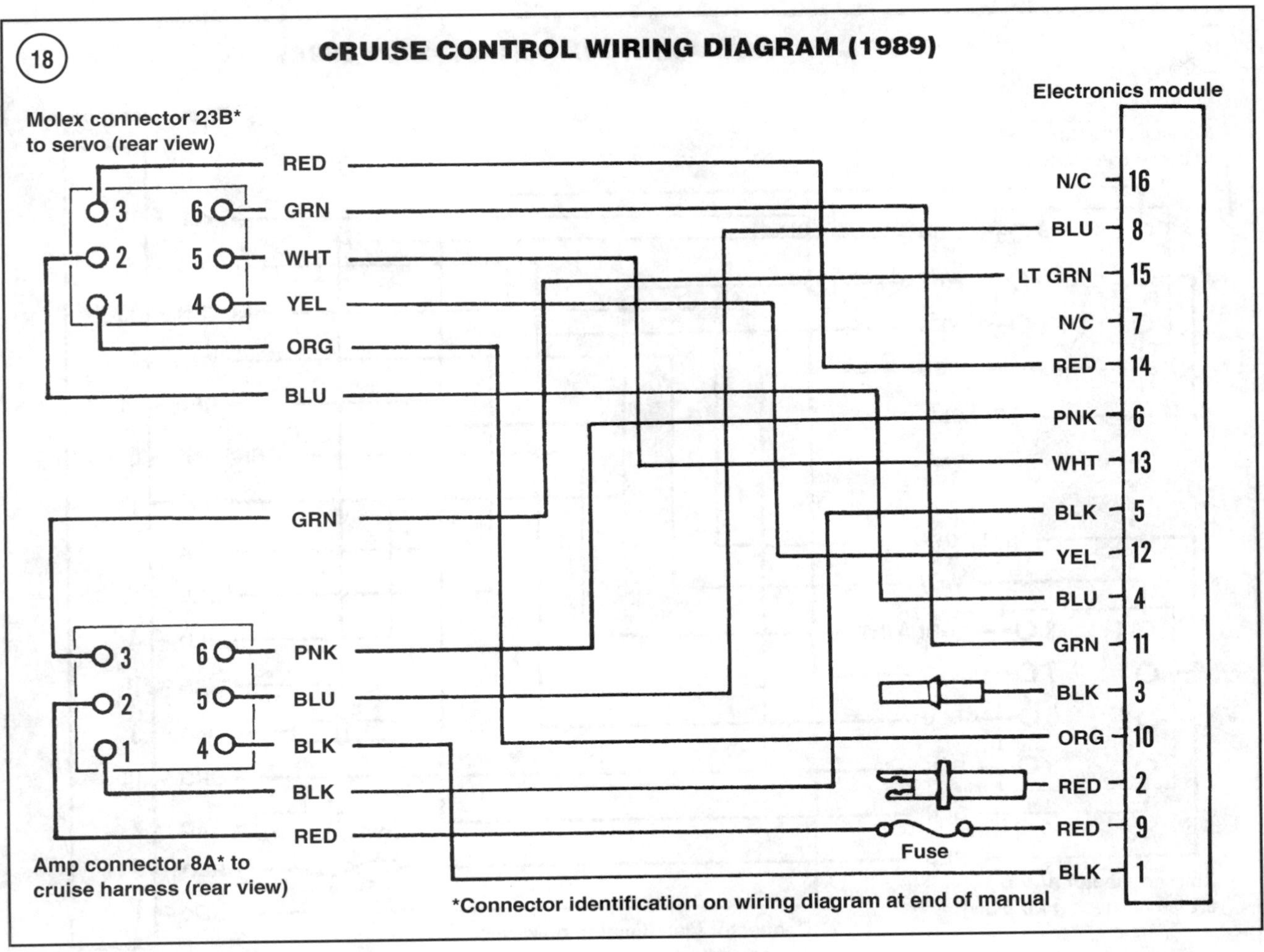

3. Disconnect the orange/violet and the red/green wire terminal connectors from the back side of the switch.
4. Remove the screws securing the switch mounting bracket and remove the switch.
5. Install by reversing these removal steps while noting the following:
   a. Butt splice the black/green wire between the ON/OFF and the speaker switches.
   b. Make sure the other wires are connected to the correct switch terminals and pushed on securely.

SET/RESUME Switch

1. Disassemble the right switch assembly as described under *Handlebar Switch Replacement* in Chapter Nine.
2. Locate the switch and partially remove it from the switch housing.
3. Cut the wires about 1 1/2 in. from the old SET/RESUME switch. Discard the old switch.

NOTE
New replacement switch wires are cut to a length of 2 in., and the insulation is partially stripped.

4. Slide a 1-in. piece of dual wall heat shrink tubing, supplied with the new switch, over the wire.
5. Securely splice the new switch onto the existing wires and solder the connection.
6. Cover the splice with the dual wall heat shrink tubing.
7. Assemble the right switch.

TROUBLESHOOTING (1989-1992 MODELS)

Wiring Diagrams

Refer to **Figure 18** or **Figure 19**. Diagrams for the entire electrical system are located in Chapter Seventeen.

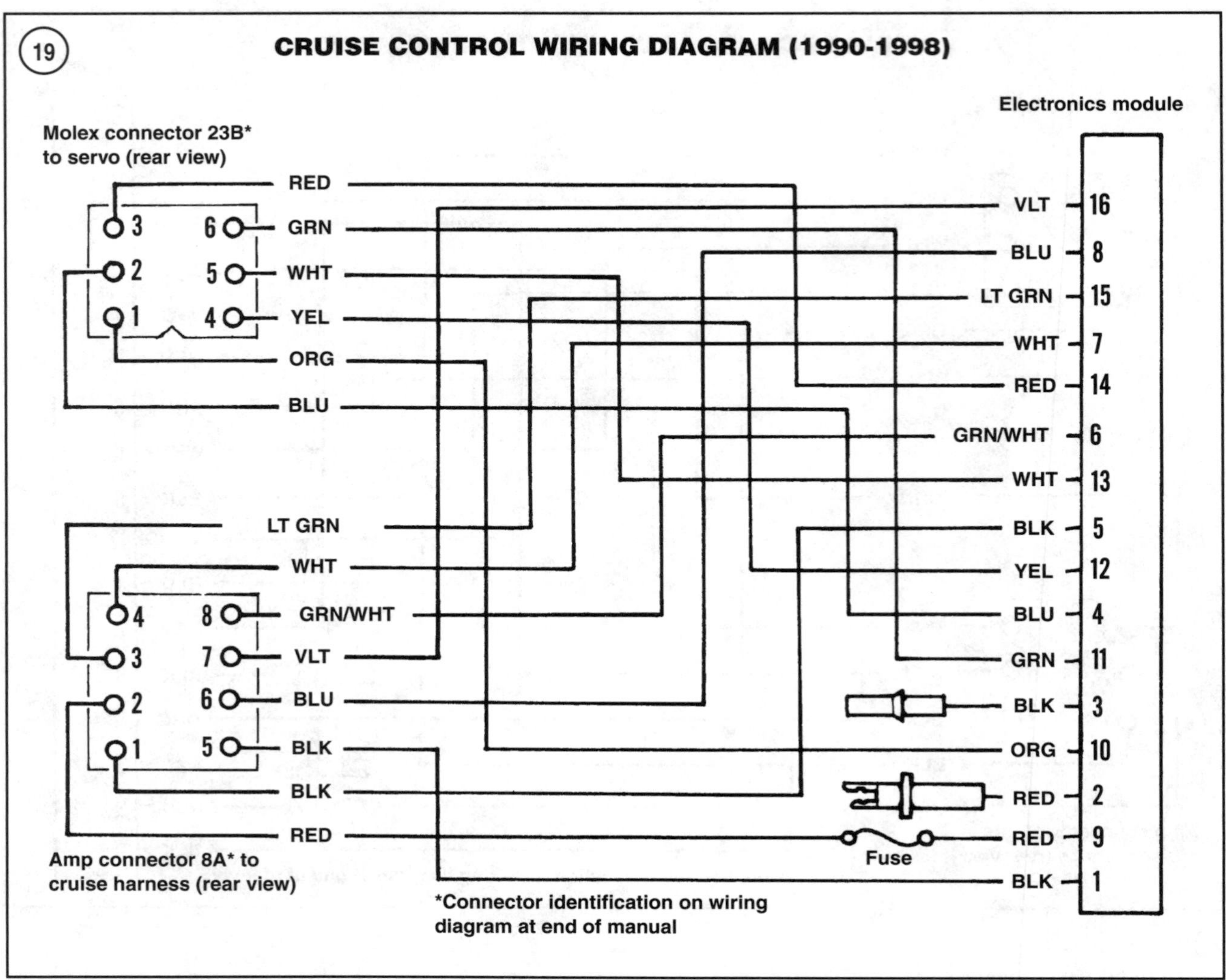

System Inspection

A malfunction in the cruise control system will cause the system to be inoperative. Perform the following visual inspection to determine the cause of the problem. If the visual inspection fails to locate the problem, identify the complaint by the following headings and perform the steps in order to locate the problem.

1. Make sure the battery is fully charged and that the cables are connected properly.

2. Inspect the battery terminals for loose or corroded terminals. Tighten or clean as required.

3. Carefully check the wiring leading to and within the cruise control system. Check the wiring for corroded, loose or disconnected connections. Clean, tighten or connect as required.

Test Procedures

Locate the applicable test procedure and read through the test before starting.

If the problem cannot be located and repaired safely, refer service to a Harley-Davidson dealership.

WARNING
When testing or servicing the cruise control system, do not ride the motorcycle until the system is working correctly.

1. Test 1: Indicator light does not come on.
2. Test 2: Cruise control will not stay in SET position.
3. Test 3: Cruise control will not stay in RES position (1990-1992 models).
4. Test 4: Cruise control will not stay in SET or RES position.

5. Test 5: Engine speed changes after being SET; vehicle surges constantly.
6. Test 6: Fast engine idle and/or engine speed increases when cruise control SET (1990-1992 models).
7. Test 7: Servo motor runs continuously with ignition and cruise switch ON and engine at idle (1990-1992 models).

Test 1: Indicator light does not come on

1. If the cruise ON/OFF indicator light does not come on, but the cruise control system works:
   a. Check for a burned out indicator light filament. On FLHTCU models, replace the rocker switch. On FLTC Ultra models, replace the indicator assembly.
   b. If the indicator light filament is good, check the indicator bulb circuit with a test light or ohmmeter. If the test lamp does not light or if the ohmmeter shows infinite resistance, there is an open in the indicator light wiring circuit.
2. If the cruise ON/OFF indicator light does not come on, and the cruise control system does not work:
   a. Remove the seat as described in Chapter Fifteen.
   b. Connect a voltmeter to a good ground and the servo connector 6-pin connector red wire.
   c. Turn both the ignition switch and the cruise ON/OFF switch ON. The voltmeter should read 9-12 volts. Turn the cruise ON/OFF switch OFF. The voltmeter should read 0 volts.
   d. If the reading is incorrect, remove the cruise ON/OFF switch to access the wiring connectors at the switch. If the switch was recently replaced, confirm that the switch is wired properly; compare actual wiring with the wiring diagram at end of book. If the switch is wired properly, test the switch with an ohmmeter or test light. There should be continuity when the switch is in the ON position and no continuity in the OFF position.
   e. Replace the switch if damaged.
   f. If the switch is good, check the switch wiring circuit.

Test 2: Cruise control will not stay in SET position

1. First check the 2-amp electronic module fuse. If the fuse is blown, and a new one blows when installed, look for a short to ground in the wire circuit.
2. Turn on the lights and check for a blown taillight bulb. If this bulb is blown, also check the bulbs installed in the Tour-Pak. If all three bulbs are blown, the cruise control system will be inoperative. Replace bulbs as required.
3. If the brake light stays on constantly, check for a shorted front or rear brake light switch; refer to Chapter Nine for switch testing. If both switches are good, check the front brake light switch for binding in the brake lever. Refer to *Front Brake Caliper* in Chapter Thirteen for service procedures.
4. One way to deactivate the cruise control system under normal riding conditions is to fully close the throttle. If the idle cable does not have enough free play, the roll-off switch (mounted in the idle cable) will close and simulate a closed throttle position. Check the idle throttle cable adjustment as described in this chapter.
5. Check the electronic module return ground as follows:
   a. Connect an ohmmeter to a good ground. Then probe the No. 3 electronic module pin (black wire bullet connector). There should be continuity (0.5 ohm or less).
   b. If there is more than 0.5 ohm, check the electronic module ground wire for a loose or damaged connection.
6. Check the servo motor return ground as follows:
   a. Connect an ohmmeter to a good ground. Then probe the No. 11 electronic module pin (green wire). There should be continuity (0.5 ohm or less).
   b. If there is more than 0.5 ohm, check the green wire from the electronic module, through the 23A and 23B connectors and to the servo motor. Check the wire for damage. Check the connectors for contamination or a damaged mating pin and socket.

7A. On 1989 models, check the coil signal speed sense circuit as follows:
   a. Turn the ignition switch ON but do not start the engine.

NOTE

The ignition switch must be turned to IGNITION (ON). Do not perform the following test with the ignition switch turned to ACCESS. Refer to ***Figure 20*** *for switch contact identification.*

   b. Connect a voltmeter to a good ground. Then probe the pink wire at the back of the 6-pin 8B connector. There should be 9-12 volts.
   c. If the voltage reading is incorrect, the rotor might be perfectly aligned with the sensor. Turn the engine over with the starter button and recheck. If a reading of 9-12 volts is now obtained, proceed to Step 9.
   d. If there was no recorded voltage in substep c, check for voltage at the pink wire connection on the ignition coil. If voltage is recorded, check the 8A and

8B connectors for contamination or a damaged pin socket and pin connection. If these are good, check the pink 1-pin connector for a loose or damaged connection. If necessary, continue to check the pink wire from the 1-pin connector to the cruise module.

7B. On 1990-1992 models, check the coil signal speed sense circuit as follows:

a. Turn the ignition switch to ON but do not start the engine.

NOTE
*The ignition switch must be turned to IGNITION (ON). Do not perform the following test with the ignition switch turned to ACCESS. See **Figure 20** for switch contact identification.*

b. Connect a voltmeter lead to a good ground. Then probe the pink wire at the back of the 8-pin 8B connector. There should be 9-12 volts.
c. If the voltage reading is incorrect, the rotor might be perfectly aligned with the sensor. Turn the engine over with the starter button and recheck. If a reading of 9-12 volts is now obtained, proceed to Step 8.
d. If there was no recorded voltage in substep c, check for voltage at the pink wire connection on the ignition coil. If voltage is recorded, check the 8A and 8B connectors for contamination or a damaged pin socket and pin connection. If these are good, check the pink 1-pin connector for a loose or damaged connection. If necessary, continue to check the pink wire from the 1-pin connector to the cruise module.

8. On 1990-1992 models, check the reed switch signal as follows:

a. Support the motorcycle so that the front wheel is off the ground. Refer to *Motorcycle Stands* in Chapter Ten.
b. Connect an ohmmeter to a good ground. Then connect the red lead to the white/green wire at the 8A connector.
c. Spin the front wheel to operate the speedometer. The ohmmeter needle should fluctuate between 0 ohms and infinity.
d. If the ohmmeter needle does not fluctuate as described, check the white/green 20A and 20B connectors for a loose or damaged connection. If the wire connection is good, the reed switch, mounted in the instrument panel, might be damaged. Refer further testing to a Harley-Davidson dealership.

9. Inspect the SET portion of the SET (1989 models) or the RES/SET (1990-1992 models) switch and the wiring as follows:

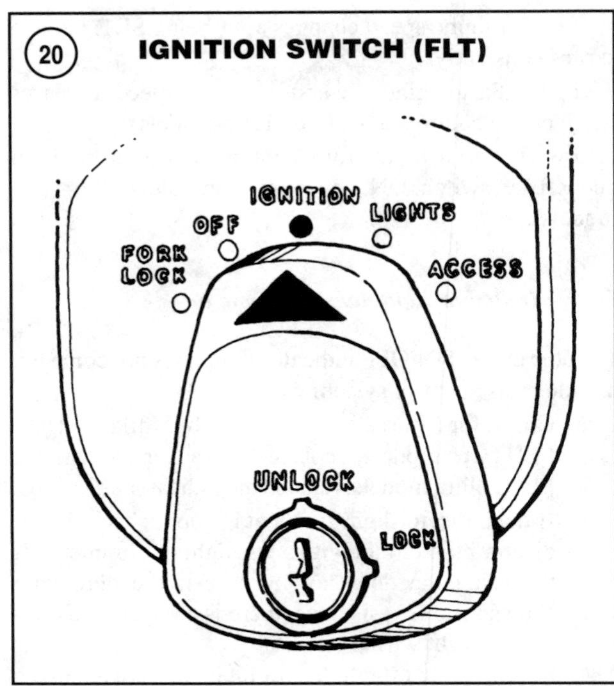

a. Connect an ohmmeter between the light green and blue wire wires at the 8A connector. There should be 0.5 ohm or less when the switch is pressed down on 1989 models (**Figure 3**) or set to the SET position on 1990-1992 models (**Figure 4**).
b. If the ohmmeter reading was higher than specified, check the 17A and 17B connectors for proper connection. Disconnect the 17A and 17B connectors and clean the connector plugs and sockets with electrical contact cleaner and retest. If the reading is still excessive, disconnect the connectors once again and check the switch operation with an ohmmeter.
c. To test the switch, connect the ohmmeter leads to the blue and light green wire switch terminals (1989 models) or between the blue and light green switch terminals (1990-1992 models). There should be continuity when the switch is in the SET position, and no continuity in the OFF position. Replace the switch if necessary.

Test 3: Cruise control will not stay in RES position (1990-1992 models)

1. Inspect the RES portion of the SET/RES switch and the wiring as follows:

a. Connect an ohmmeter between the light green and white wires at the 8A connector. There should be

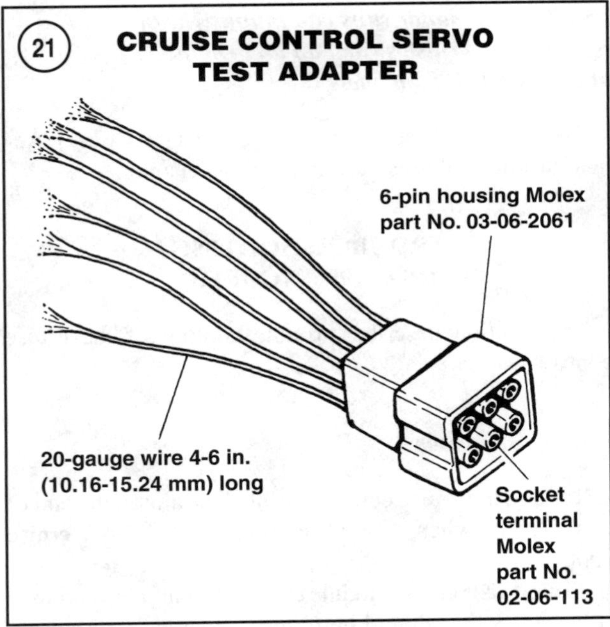

0.5 ohm or less when the switch is set at the RES position.

b. If the ohmmeter reading was higher than specified, check the 17A and 17B connectors for proper connection. Disconnect the 17A and 17B connectors, clean the connector plugs and sockets with electrical contact cleaner, and retest. If the reading is still excessive, disconnect the connectors once again and check switch operation with an ohmmeter.

c. To test the switch, connect the meter leads between the light green and white wire terminals. There should be continuity when the switch is in the RES position and no continuity in the OFF position. Replace the switch if necessary.

2. Replace the switch if necessary and retest.

Test 4: Cruise control will not stay in SET or RES position

1. On 1990-1992 models, consider the following when troubleshooting this complaint:

a. The cruise control will not engage if vehicle speed is below 40 mph (64 km/h). Increase speed to above 40 mph (64 km/h) and reset control.

b. If the motorcycle speed was increased or decreased by more than 10 mph (16 km/h) since the last SET speed was set, the RES system will not activate. For the system to activate, you must increase or decrease the motorcycle speed to within 10 mph (16 km/h) of the last SET speed.

c. If the above situations do not account for system malfunction, proceed to Step 2.

2. Remove the seat and check that the 6-pin servo connector is not disconnected. If the connector halves are properly pushed together, disconnect them and clean both connectors with electrical contact cleaner. Check that all of the pins are straight and that the wires leading into both connector halves are tight. Assemble the connectors by pushing them together until they click into place.

3. If the brake light does not operate, remove the lens and check for a burned out bulb. If the bulb is good, reinstall it and perform the following:

a. Refer to the wiring diagram, at the end of the manual, for the model being worked on. Locate the red 1-pin connector leading from the rear brake light. Connect a voltmeter to a good ground and the red 1-pin connector. There should be 9-12 volts with the ignition switch ON while applying either the front or rear brake.

b. If there is no voltage reading, check the red brake wire for damage.

4. A malfunctioning servo motor can cause this complaint. Test the motor as follows:

NOTE

*Assemble a test adapter as shown in **Figure 21**. The 20 gauge wires installed in the test adapter should be the same color and placed in the same position as the cruise module-to-servo connector. See **Figure 18** (1989 models) or **Figure 19** (1990-1992 models) for servo motor connector wire colors.*

a. Disconnect the 6-pin cruise module-to-servo motor connector.

b. Connect the test adapter to the 6-pin servo motor connector.

c. Connect an ohmmeter to the red and white test adapter wires. With the throttle closed (servo motor cable rack extended), there should be 5000-8000 ohms.

d. Rotate the throttle grip until it is completely open and wire it so that it will stay in this position. Then remove the servo cable at the servo motor; see throttle cable information in this chapter. Using a stiff piece of wire, push the servo motor rack into the servo motor. With the rack all the way in and the throttle all the way open, there should be 1500-2500 ohms.

CAUTION

Read through the following test procedures before testing. When battery voltage is applied, turn the voltage off after the servo mo-

tor rack travels approximately 1/2 in. (12.7 mm). If voltage input is continued, damage to the servo or throttle linkage can occur.

NOTE

When performing the following tests, four jumper cables with alligator clips are necessary. A fully charged 12-volt battery is also required.

e. With the cruise control adapter still connected to the 6-pin cruise control connector, connect the blue test adapter wire to the positive battery terminal and the green test adapter wire to the negative battery terminal. Then connect the orange test adapter wire to the positive battery terminal and the yellow test adapter wire to the negative battery terminal. The servo rack should move in and simulate throttle opening. Disconnect the test leads.

f. Connect the orange test adapter lead to the positive battery terminal and the yellow test adapter lead to the negative battery terminal. The servo rack should extend and simulate the throttle returning to idle. Disconnect the test leads.

g. Replace the servo motor if it failed to operate as described in these tests. If the servo motor tested correctly, the cruise control module is damaged; replace it as described in this chapter.

Test 5: Engine speed changes after being SET; vehicle surges constantly

1. First check for proper cruise control operation as follows:
   a. On 1989 models, this condition can occur if the SET switch is pressed down and held too long.
   b. On 1990-1992 models, this condition can occur if the RES/SET switch is held up (increased acceleration) or held down (decreased acceleration).
   c. Refer to the owner's manual for proper operation.
2. Incorrect throttle cable adjustment. Adjust cables as described in this chapter.
3. If condition continues after performing Steps 1 and 2, the cruise module might be damaged.

Test 6: Fast engine idle and/or engine speed increases when cruise control is SET (1990-1992 models)

The servo cable adjustment is incorrect (too tight). Adjust throttle cables as described in this chapter.

Test 7: Servo motor runs continuously with ignition and cruise switch on and engine at idle (1990-1992 models)

The servo cable adjustment is incorrect (too loose). Adjust throttle cables as described in this chapter.

TROUBLESHOOTING (1993-1996 MODELS)

This section describes troubleshooting of the cruise control system.

Wiring Diagrams

Refer to the cruise control wiring diagrams at the end of this manual when troubleshooting a 1993-1996 cruise control system.

Table 1 lists cruise module connector numbers and wire color codes that should be referred to along with wiring diagrams at the end of this manual.

Cruise Control System Check

For the following system check to be accurate, the steps must be followed in order and with the engine turned off.

1. Turn the ignition switch OFF.
2. Turn the cruise main switch ON.
3. Press the SET switch (**Figure 4**) down and turn the ignition switch to the ON position. The green cruise light should come on and stay on as long as the SET switch is held down. If the green cruise light stays on after releasing the SET switch, the SET switch and/or the wiring is shorted. Proceed to Step 4 if the light operates properly. If the cruise light did not come on after pressing the SET switch down, one or more of the following conditions might be causing the cruise light malfunction:
   a. SET/RES switch shorted.
   b. Damaged SET/RES switch wires and/or connectors.
   c. Blown cruise light.
   d. Damaged cruise light wires and/or connectors.
   e. Cruise harness connector (**Figure 7**) is disconnected or damaged.
   f. Damaged cruise main switch.
   g. Damaged cruise main switch wires and/or connectors.
   h. Incorrect throttle cable adjustment.
   i. Faulty module ground wire connection at terminal E in 10-pin connector.
   j. Brake light stays on constantly.

4. With the ignition switch in the ON position, press the RES switch (**Figure 4**) upward. The green cruise light should come on and stay on as long as the RES switch is pressed up. Proceed to Step 5 if the light operates properly. If the green cruise light did not come on after pressing the RES switch up, one or more of the following conditions might be causing the cruise light malfunction:

  a. RES switch wired incorrectly.
  b. Loose or damaged wire to RES switch or cruise module.

5. To check the throttle grip switch, turn the throttle grip so that it is tightly closed. With the ignition switch turned ON, the green cruise light should light when the throttle switch is tightly closed and should turn off when the throttle grip returns to the free (relaxed with no hand pressure) position. Proceed to Step 6 if the light operates properly. If the green cruise light did not come on as described, one or more of the following conditions might be causing the cruise light malfunction:

  a. Throttle grip switch wires are damaged, or switch is wired incorrectly.
  b. Damaged throttle grip switch or cruise module wire or wire connector.
  c. Faulty throttle grip switch.

6. Apply the front brake lever. With the ignition switch turned ON, the green cruise light should come on and remain on as long as the brake lever is applied. Proceed to Step 7 if the light operates properly. If the green cruise light did not come on as described, one or more of the following conditions might be causing the cruise light to malfunction:

  a. All brake light bulbs are disconnected (or burned out).
  b. Faulty or damaged front brake light switch.
  c. Faulty brake relay.
  d. Damaged cruise module wire or wire connector.
  e. Brake relay wires are damaged, or component is wired incorrectly.

7. Press the rear brake pedal and hold it in this position for at least 5 seconds. Then release it. The green cruise light should come on when the rear brake pedal is pressed and should turn off after 5 seconds. Then, when the brake pedal is released, the cruise module will momentarily pull the throttle open for approximately 20 percent of travel. If the brake is applied with the throttle pulled open, the throttle should stop turning immediately. Proceed to Step 8 if the light and throttle grip operate as described. If not, one or more of the following conditions might be causing the malfunction:

NOTE

If the green cruise light failed to operate properly, refer to substeps a, b and c. If the throttle did not operate properly, refer to substeps d and e.

  a. Faulty rear brake light switch.
  b. Damaged relay wires.
  c. Rear brake light switch and/or relay is incorrectly wired.
  d. Incorrect throttle cable adjustment.
  e. Faulty cruise control module.

8. While straddling the motorcycle and with the transmission in neutral, roll the motorcycle forward and then backward to activate the reed switch (mounted in speedometer). The green cruise light should come on. Proceed to Step 9 if the light operates as described. If not, note the following:

  a. Speedometer cable/drive is damaged.
  b. Reed switch is wired incorrectly, or wires are damaged.
  c. Faulty reed switch.
  d. Disconnected reed switch ground wire.

9. Perform the following tests to simulate ignition sensor plate input:

  a. Turn the main cruise switch OFF.
  b. Disconnect the 3-pin ignition sensor-to-ignition module electrical connector.
  c. Momentarily place a screwdriver across the black/white and green or green/white ignition module wire connectors (on ignition module side) while watching the green cruise light. Then repeat this step ten times. The cruise light should flash on the fifth through tenth attempts. If the cruise light fails to operate properly, refer further service to a Harley-Davidson dealership.

10. Terminate check procedure by turning the ignition switch OFF. If this procedure has failed to locate the cruise control system malfunction, refer service to a Harley-Davidson dealership.

Cruise Control Malfunctions

If the cruise control is not working properly, consider one of the following malfunctions that most closely resembles the vehicle condition.

Vehicle gains speed

Cruise cable is too tight. Readjust cable as described in this chapter.

Vehicle loses speed

The cruise cable is too loose, or the set switch was held on too long.

Speed surges

1. Reed switch is defective.
2. Cruise module is defective.
3. Poor ground connection at reed switch or cruise control module (**Figure 7**).

NOTE
If surging occurs when the cruise control is turned off, the air/fuel mixture might be too lean.

Cruise disengages with RES switch in on position

The RES switch is being held on for longer than 6 seconds.

TROUBLESHOOTING (1997-1998 MODELS)

The cruise control system provides on-board diagnostics to help isolate any problems that can occur within the system. Refer to *Cruise Control Diagnostic Codes* in Chapter Two.

During normal operation, the *C* cruise engagement lamp illuminates only when the cruise control is in operation.

Table 1 MODULE CONNECTORS AND WIRE COLORS

Terminal letter for connector 8A (1993) and connector 17A (1994)*	Wire color	
	1993	1994
A	Red/blue	Red/green
B	Blue	Blue/black
C	White	White/blue
D	Black/red	Violet/yellow
E	Black	Black
F	Black/orange	Orange/violet
G	Red/white	Red/yellow
H	Pink	Pink
J	Green	Green/red
K	White/green	White/green

*Terminal letters are printed on connectors next to wires.

CHAPTER FIFTEEN

BODY

This chapter describes the removal and installation of the body components. Most of these components are fragile and must be handled carefully, and the finish must be protected during handling. If a component will be left off for a period of time, wrap it with a blanket or towels and place it in a safe location. Refer to **Table 1** at the end of the chapter for specifications.

SEAT

Removal/Installation

FXR series models: fixed seat

1. Place the motorcycle on the jiffy stand.
2. Remove the rear fender pad screws, lockwashers and plastic washer.
3. Pull the seat back to clear the frame mounting bracket and remove the seat.
4. Install by reversing these removal steps. Install the plastic washer between the seat mounting bracket and the fender. Tighten the screws securely.
5. Pull up on the front of the seat to ensure the seat is secured in place.

FXR series models: hinged seat

1. Place the motorcycle on the jiffy stand.
2. Raise the rider seat and remove the seat stop cord from the battery bracket bolt.
3. Remove the plastic sleeve from the seat pins. Then slide the seat forward and remove it.
4. To remove the passenger seat, perform the following:
   a. Remove the rear bolt, slide the seat back and off the rear fender, and remove it.
   b. If equipped with a backrest bar, remove the front mounting bolts before removing the seat.
5. Install by reversing these removal steps while noting the following:
   a. Tighten the bolts securely.
   b. Pull up on the front of the seat to make sure the seat is secured in place.

FXWG, FXSB and FXEF models

1. Place the motorcycle on the jiffy stand.
2. Remove the bolt(s) securing the seat to the rear fender and remove the seat.

3. Install the seat and tighten the bolt(s) securely.
4. Pull up on the front of the seat to make sure the seat is secured in place.

1984-1994 FLH and FLT series models

1. Place the motorcycle on the jiffy stand.
2A. On 1984-1990 models, remove the bolts and washers securing the seat to the handrail. Then pull the seat up and back and remove it.
2B. On 1991-1994 models, perform the following:
   a. Open the Tour-Pak cover. Move the Tour-Pak to the most rearward position.
   b. Remove the bolt securing the seat to the luggage rack.
   c. Remove the seat.
3. Install by reversing these removal steps while noting the following:
   a. Tighten the bolts securely.
   b. Pull up on the front of the seat to make sure the seat is secured in place.

1995-1998 FLHR models

1. Place the motorcycle on the jiffy stand.
2. Remove the passenger seat as follows:
   a. Remove the bolt, lockwasher and nylon washer at the rear of the seat.
   b. Slide the seat toward the rear and release it from the two 5/8-in. hex studs on the rear fender and remove it.
3. To remove the rider seat, perform the following:
   a. Remove the 5/8 in. hex studs securing the seat to the rear fender.
   b. Slide the seat toward the rear and remove it.
4. Install by reversing these removal steps while noting the following:
   a. Tighten the bolts securely.
   b. Pull up on the fronts of the seats to make sure the seats are secured in place.

All 1995-1996 models except FLHR models

1. Place the motorcycle on the jiffy stand.
2. Open the Tour-Pak cover and move the passenger seat backrest out of the way.
3. Remove the bolt securing the seat bracket to the backrest.
4. Slide the seat toward the rear and remove it.
5. Install by reversing these removal steps while noting the following:
   a. Tighten the bolts securely.
   b. Pull up on the front of the seat to make sure the seat is secured in place.

1997-1998 FLHRC models

1. Place the motorcycle on the jiffy stand.
2. Remove the left saddlebag as described in this chapter.
3. Remove the bolt and washer on each side securing the passenger seat strap to the frame tube cover.
4. Remove the Phillips screw securing the rear of the seat to the fender.
5. Pull the seat toward the rear and disengage the locating tongue from the slot in the frame backbone. Remove the seat.
6. Install the seat and push it downwards and toward the front and engage the locating tongue into the slot in the frame backbone. Tighten the Phillips screw securely.

WARNING
If the seat retention nut(s) is damaged, replace it as described in this section.

7. Install the bolt and washer on each side securing the passenger seat strap to the frame tube cover. Tighten the bolts securely. Do not overtighten.
8. Pull up on the front of the seat to make sure the seat is secured in place.
9. Install the left saddlebag as described in this chapter.

1997-1998 FLHT models

1. Place the motorcycle on the jiffy stand.
2. Remove the Phillips screw securing the rear of the seat to the fender.
3. Pull the seat toward the rear and disengage the locating tongue from the slot in the frame backbone. Remove the seat.
4. Install the seat and push it down and toward the front and engage the locating tongue into the slot in the frame backbone.
5. Tighten the Phillips screw securely.
6. Pull up on the front of the seat to make sure the seat is secured in place.

1997-1998 FLHTC and FLHTC-U models

1. Place the motorcycle on the jiffy stand.
2. Open the Tour-Pak cover and move the passenger backrest out of the way.
3. Remove the Phillips screw securing the seat bracket to the fender.

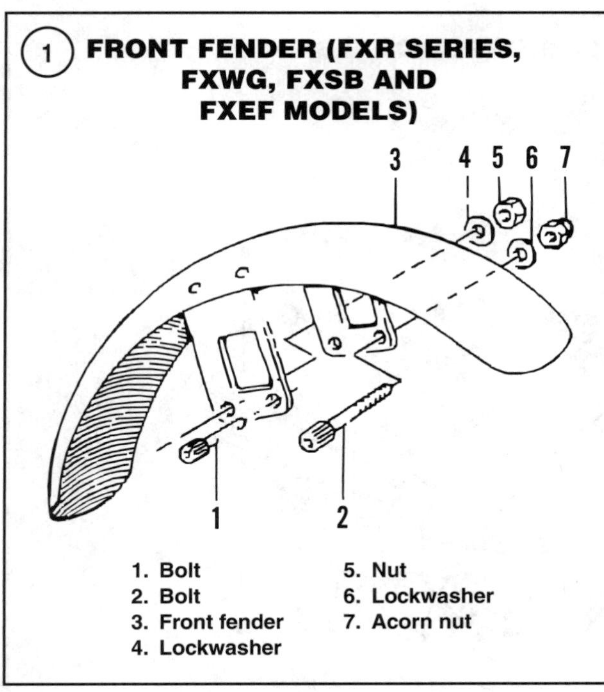

1 FRONT FENDER (FXR SERIES, FXWG, FXSB AND FXEF MODELS)

1. Bolt
2. Bolt
3. Front fender
4. Lockwasher
5. Nut
6. Lockwasher
7. Acorn nut

4. Cover the mounting bracket with a shop cloth or hand to protect the Tour-Pak in Step 5.
5. Push the seat forward. Raise the rear of the seat until it clears the top of the Tour-Pak.
6. Pull the seat toward the rear and disengage the locating tongue from the slot in the frame backbone. Remove the seat.
7. Install the seat and push it down and toward the front and engage the locating tongue into the slot in the frame backbone.
8. Tighten the Phillips screw securely.
9. Pull up on the front of the seat to make sure the seats are secured in place.
10. Move the passenger backrest back into position and close the Tour-Pak cover.

1997-1998 FLTR models

1. Place the motorcycle on the jiffy stand.
2. Remove the left saddlebag as described in this chapter.
3. Remove the bolt and washer securing the passenger seat strap and saddlebag front mounting bracket to the frame tube cover on each side.
4. Remove the Phillips screw securing the rear of the seat to the fender.
5. Pull the seat toward the rear and disengage the locating tongue from the slot in the frame backbone. Remove the seat.
6. Install the seat and push it down and toward the front and engage the locating tongue into the slot in the frame backbone. Tighten the Phillips screw securely.

WARNING
If the seat retention nut(s) is damaged, replace it as described in this section.

7. Install the bolt and washer securing the passenger seat strap to the frame tube cover on each side. Tighten the bolts securely. Do not overtighten.
8. Pull up on the front of the seat to make sure the seat is secured in place.
9. Install the left saddlebag as described in this chapter.

Seat Retention Nut Replacement

1997-1998 FLTR and FLHRC models

1. Slide the retention nut over the tapered end of the cable strap so the larger outer diameter of the nut rests on the cable strap eyelet.
2. Working under the rear fender, feed the cable strap up and through the hole in the fender.
3. With the tab on the retention nut seated in the notch of the fender hole, pull up on the cable strap to hold the nut snugly against the underside of the rear fender.
4. From the side opposite the tab, slide the retention washer and lock the location of the retention nut.

FRONT FENDER

Removal/Installation

FXR series, FXWG, FXSB and FXEF models

Refer to **Figure 1**.

1. Support the motorcycle with the front wheel off the ground. Refer to *Motorcycle Stands* in Chapter Ten.
2. Disconnect the speedometer cable from the front hub and move it out of the way.
3. Remove the front wheel as described in Chapter Ten.
4. Remove the bolt, lockwasher and nut securing the front fender to the fork slider.
5. Be careful not to scratch the paint and remove the front fender from the fork sliders.
6. Install by reversing these removal steps. Securely tighten the bolts and nuts.

FLH and FLT series models

Refer to **Figure 2**.

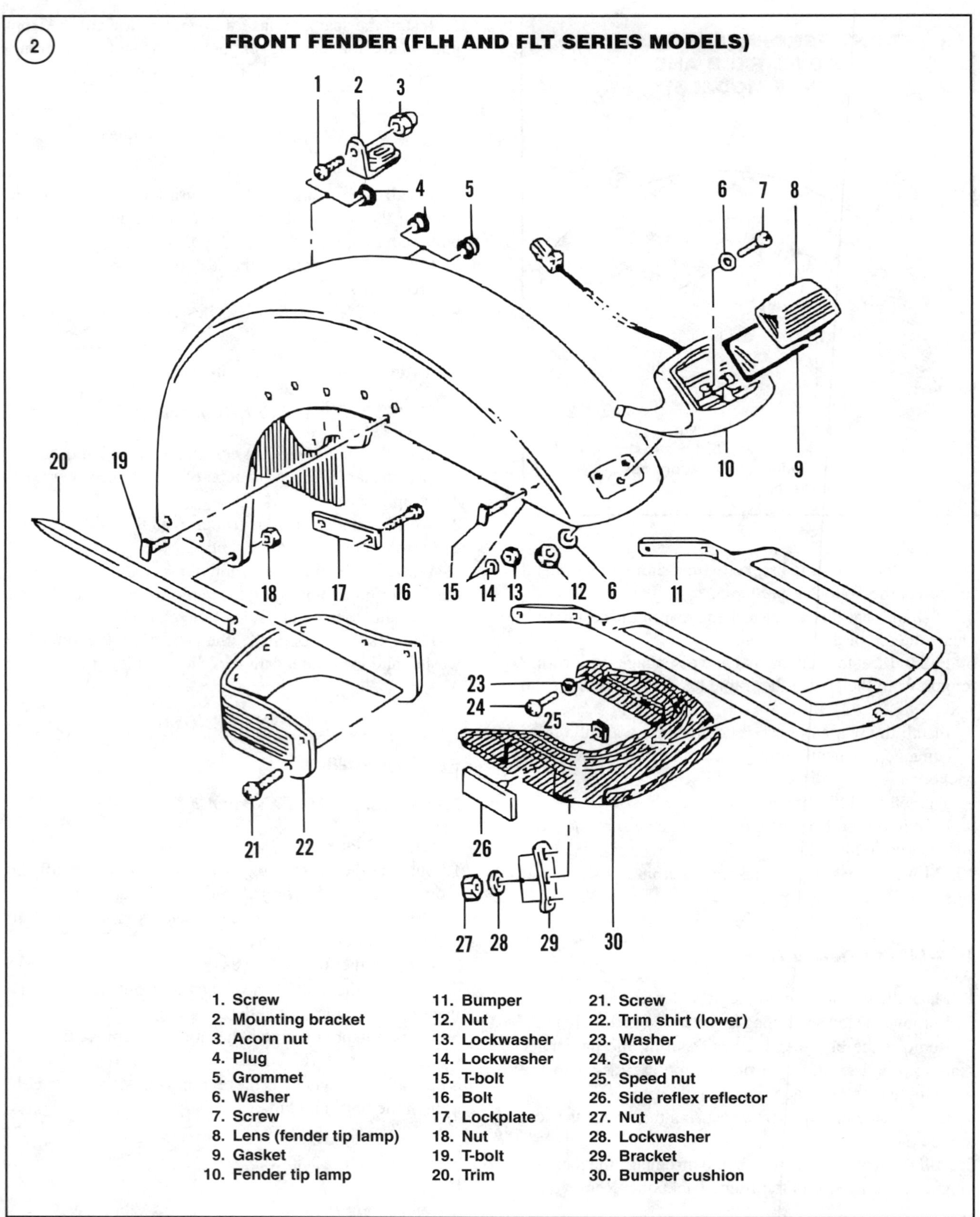
2
FRONT FENDER (FLH AND FLT SERIES MODELS)
1
2
3
4
5
6
7
8
9
10
11
12
13
14
15
16
17
18
19
20
21
22
23
24
25
26
27
28
29
30
1. Screw
2. Mounting bracket
3. Acorn nut
4. Plug
5. Grommet
6. Washer
7. Screw
8. Lens (fender tip lamp)
9. Gasket
10. Fender tip lamp
11. Bumper
12. Nut
13. Lockwasher
14. Lockwasher
15. T-bolt
16. Bolt
17. Lockplate
18. Nut
19. T-bolt
20. Trim
21. Screw
22. Trim shirt (lower)
23. Washer
24. Screw
25. Speed nut
26. Side reflex reflector
27. Nut
28. Lockwasher
29. Bracket
30. Bumper cushion

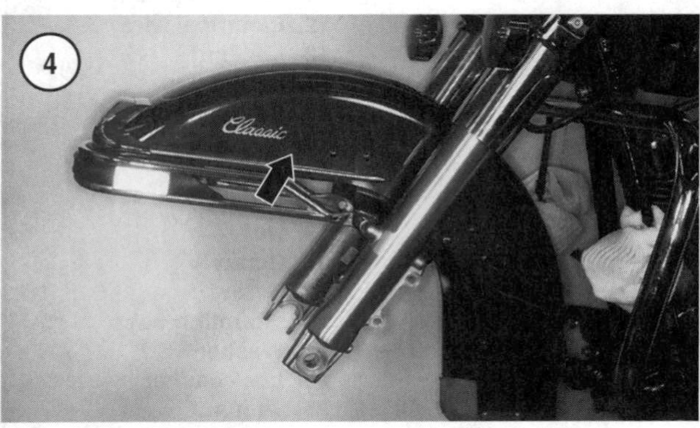

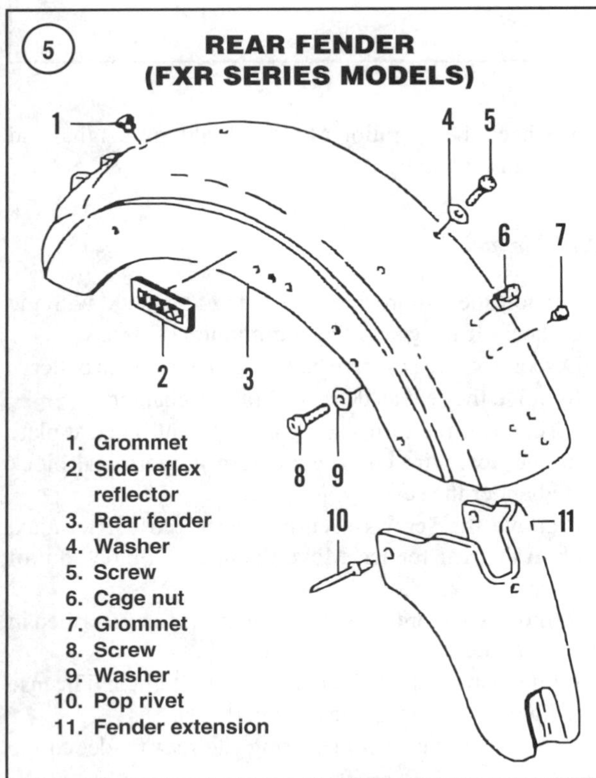

1. Support the motorcycle with the front wheel off the ground. Refer to *Motorcycle Stands* in Chapter Ten.
2. Disconnect the speedometer cable from the front hub and move it out of the way.
3. Disconnect the negative battery cable from the battery.

4A. On all FLH series models, perform the following:
  a. Remove the headlight unit as described in Chapter Nine.
  b. Within the headlight case, locate and disconnect the 2-pin front fender tip lamp electrical connector (one black and one orange/white wire).
  c. Carefully pull the electrical connector free from the headlight case.

4B. On all FLT series models, perform the following:
  a. Remove the outer portion of the front fairing as described in this chapter.
  b. On the left side of the inner front fairing, locate and disconnect the 2-pin front fender tip lamp electrical connector.
  c. Carefully pull the electrical connector free from the inner front fairing.

5. Carefully cut the cable strap securing the fender tip lamp wire to the front brake line.
6. Remove the front wheel as described in Chapter Ten.
7. Straighten the locking tabs away from the front fender mounting bolts (**Figure 3**).
8. Remove the mounting bolts and lockplates securing the front fender to the fork sliders.
9. Be careful not to scratch the paint and remove the front fender (**Figure 4**) from the fork sliders.
10. Install by reversing these removal steps while noting the following:
  a. Install the lockplates and tighten the bolts securely.
  b. Bend the locking tabs up against the bolt heads.

REAR FENDER

Removal/Installation

FXR series models

Refer to **Figure 5**.

1. Support the motorcycle on a swing arm stand with the rear wheel off the ground by a minimum of 4 in.
2. Disconnect the negative battery cable from the battery.
3. Remove the seat and left side cover.
4. Disconnect the taillight terminal block from the mounting plate. Then disconnect two gray wires from the terminal block. Use the pin terminal tool (part No. HD-97363-71) or an equivalent.
5. Place wooden blocks under the rear wheel.

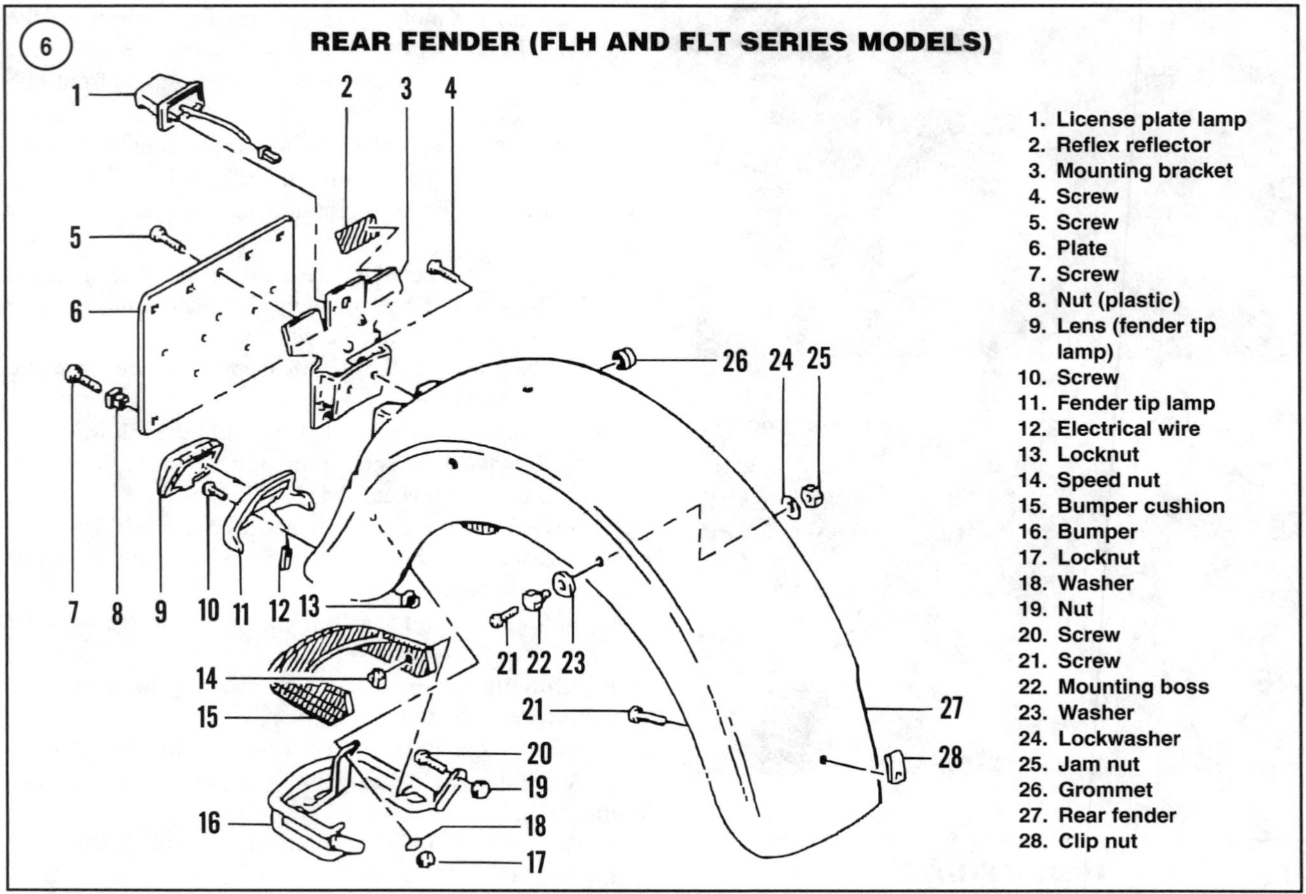

6. Remove the shock absorbers upper mounting bolt on both sides as described in Chapter Twelve. Remove the blocks and lower the rear wheel to the ground.
7. Remove the rear turn signal assemblies as described in Chapter Nine.
8. Remove the side plate-to-rear fender mounting screws on both sides.
9. Working under the rear fender, perform the following:
   a. Remove the rear fender-to-frame rail mounting bolts.
   b. Remove the remaining mounting bolts and partially remove the fender and sissy bar side plates on models so equipped.
10. Remove the two speed nuts securing the taillight to the rear fender.
11. Remove the three nuts securing the license plate bracket to the rear fender.
12. Remove the rear fender from the frame.
13. Install by reversing these removal steps while noting the following:
   a. Securely tighten all bolts and nuts.
   b. Check the operation of the taillight, turn signal and license plate light.

FXWG models

1. Support the motorcycle on a swing arm stand with the rear wheel off the ground by a minimum of 4 in.
2. Disconnect the negative battery cable from the battery.
3. Remove the seat as described in this chapter.
4. Disconnect the turn signal, taillight and license plate light electrical wire connectors from the terminal block located under the seat.
5. Remove the screws securing the electrical terminal block to the rear fender. Move the terminal block out of the way.
6. Remove the rear turn signal assemblies as described in Chapter Nine.
7. Remove the fasteners securing the taillight and license plate light bracket to the rear fender.
8. Remove the fasteners securing the rear fender to the frame.

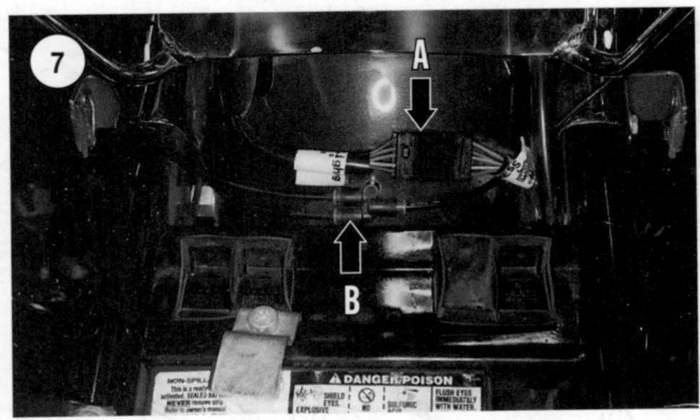

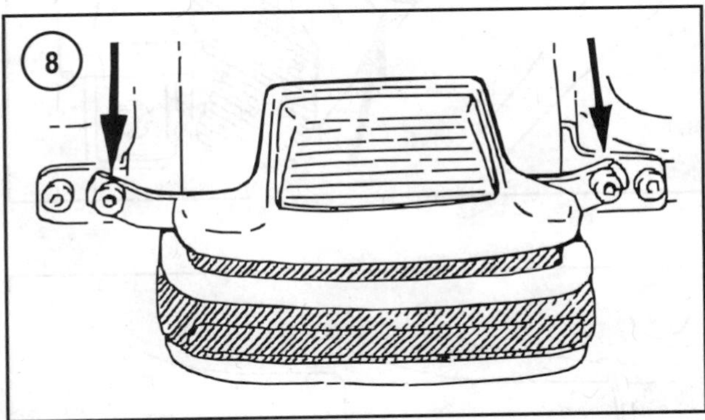

9. Partially remove the rear fender from the frame. Then carefully pull the electrical wires and connector free from the frame. Remove the rear fender from the frame.
10. Install by reversing these removal steps while noting the following:
   a. Tighten all fasteners securely.
   b. Check the operation of the taillight, turn signal and license plate light.

FXSB and FXEF models

1. Support the motorcycle on a swing arm stand with the rear wheel off the ground by a minimum of 4 in.
2. Disconnect the negative battery cable from the battery.
3. Remove the seat as described in this chapter.
4. Located under the seat area, disconnect the taillight wire harness connector. Also remove the circuit breakers from the retaining clips.
5. Remove the Acorn nuts securing the rear fender to the mounting bracket on both sides.
6. Partially remove the rear fender and remove the taillight electrical wiring pins at the connector. Pull the electrical wires through the rear fender.
7. Remove the speed nuts securing the taillight assembly to the rear fender.
8. Install by reversing these removal steps while noting the following:
   a. If installing a new fender, transfer all old components to the new fender.
   b. Tighten all fasteners securely.
   c. Check the operation of the taillight, turn signal and license plate light.

FLH and FLT series models

Refer to **Figure 6**.

CAUTION
The rear of the motorcycle must be elevated sufficiently to allow the rear fender to roll back and over the rear wheel as well as clear the frame rear crossmember.

1. Raise the motorcycle on a center lift with the rear wheel off the ground. Secure the motorcycle in the raised position.
2. Remove the seat as described in this chapter.
3. On models so equipped, remove the Tour-Pak assembly as described in this chapter.
4. Remove both saddlebags as described in this chapter.
5. On models so equipped, disconnect the rear fender lights electrical connector (A, **Figure 7**, typical) from the top of the rear fender.
6. On 1984-1998 models, release the rear shock absorber air inlet T-fitting (B, **Figure 7**) from the top of the rear fender.
7. Remove both frame side covers.
8A. On early models, remove the bolt and nut securing the front section of the rear fender to the frame crossmember.
8B. On later models on the left side, remove the T40 Torx bolt securing the rear fender to the battery box.
9. Remove two bolts and lockwashers securing the muffler clamp to the saddlebag lower support rail. Carefully pull the muffler toward the outboard side of the support rail. Repeat for the other side.
10. Remove the shock absorber lower mounting bolt, lockwasher and washer securing the shock absorber to the swing arm. Repeat for the other side.
11A. On early models, remove the bolts, lockwashers and nuts securing the saddlebag lower guard to the fender bumper.
11B. On later models at the rear, remove the inside bolt and flange nut securing the rear bumper support rail to the saddlebag support bracket and saddlebag support rail (**Figure 8**). Repeat for the other side.

12. Working under the rear bumper, remove the nut with the flat washer and release the bumper bracket from the fender weld nut. Remove the rear bumper and rear bumper cushion.

13. Remove the T40 Torx bolt securing the fender side mounting bolt adjacent to the frame side cover rubber grommet (**Figure 9**). Repeat for the other side (**Figure 10**).

14. Remove the hex bolts or T40 Torx rear bolt (A, **Figure 11**) securing the saddlebag support to the frame support. Repeat for the other side.

CAUTION
Hold onto the rear fender because it will drop down slightly when the following front bolt is removed.

15. Hold onto the rear fender and remove the T40 Torx upper front bolt (B, **Figure 11**) securing the saddlebag support to the frame support.

16. Be careful not to scratch the fender paint on any of the surrounding brackets. Have an assistant spread the saddlebag supports outward. Slowly roll the rear fender back and off the rear wheel (**Figure 12**), staying away from the saddlebag supports and mufflers.

17. Install by reversing these removal steps. Securely tighten all bolts and nuts.

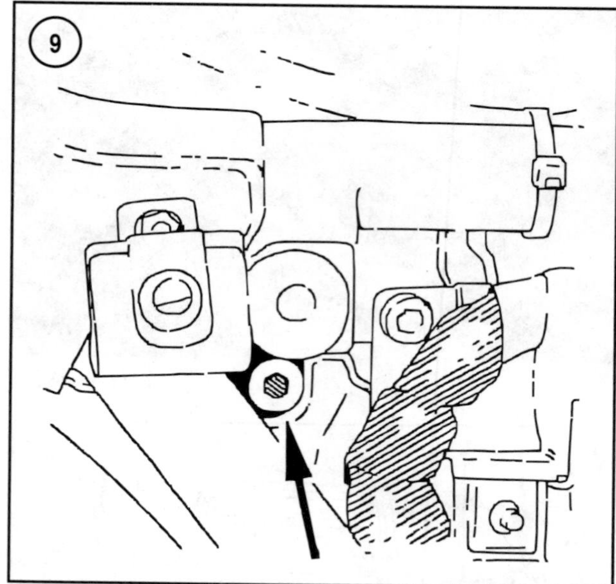

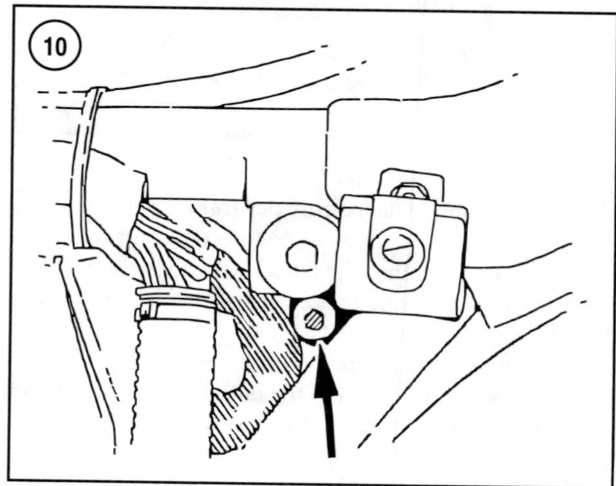

FAIRING AND WINDSHIELD (1984-1992 FXRT AND FXRD MODELS)

Windshield Removal/Installation

Refer to **Figure 13**.

1. Remove the screws and nylon washers securing the windshield to the fairing. Then lift the windshield and remove it.
2. Install by reversing these removal steps while noting the following:
   a. Install a nylon washer on each side of the screw and install all screws finger-tight.
   b. Starting at the center of the windshield and working outward, tighten each screw securely. Do not overtighten because the windshield can fracture.

Fairing Removal (All Years)

Refer to **Figure 13**.

1. Place the motorcycle on the jiffy stand.
2. On 1996-1998 models, disconnect the speedometer cable from the front hub.
3. Remove the upper and lower fairing mounting bolts, washers and nuts. Store the bolts, washers and nuts in separate containers to keep them in order of removal.
4. Remove the bolts securing the fairing bracket to the steering head.
5. Have an assistant slide the fairing forward to gain access to the 12-pin electrical connector.
6. Disconnect the electrical connector. Then carefully remove the fairing from the motorcycle.

CAUTION
Do not allow the fairing to rest on the speedometer cable because it can kink the cable and damage it.

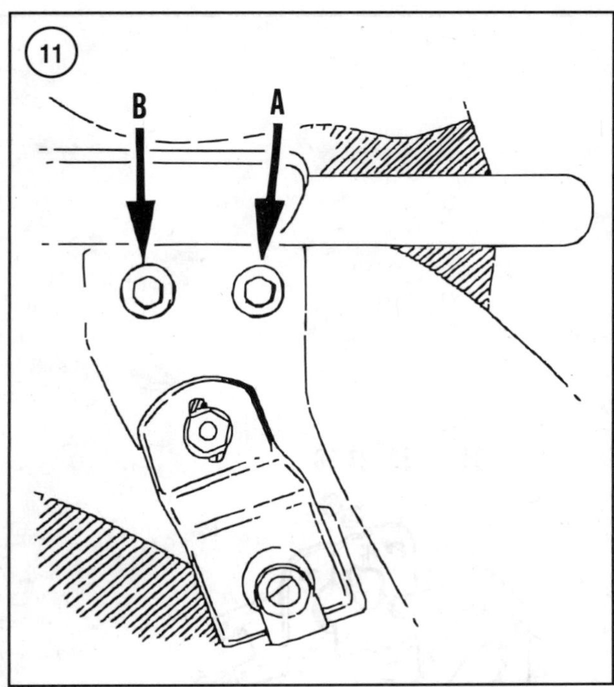

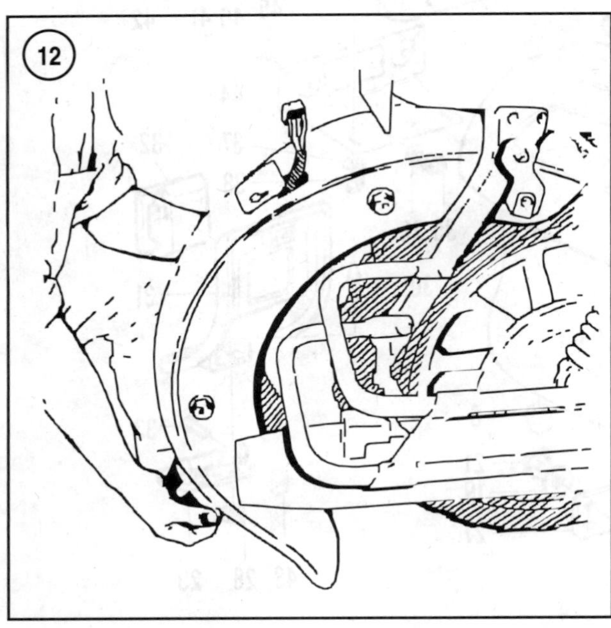

Installation

1. Clean the electrical connector with contact cleaner. Then apply dielectric grease to both sides of the connector.

2. Have an assistant hold the fairing partway in place. Then connect the 12-pin electrical connector. Push the connector together until it locks in place.

3. Move the throttle and choke cables into the correct location.

4. Place the fairing onto the mounting bracket lugs with the steering head threaded bushings.

5. Install the washers onto the 5/16 × 5/8 in. hex bolts and install the bolts through the mounting bracket and into the mounting holes in the steering head. Start the bolts and tighten finger-tight.

6A. On 1984-1985 models, install the lower mounting support bolts as follows:

a. Install the flat washers onto the 1/4-in. bolts.
b. Place one nylon washer between the bottom of the fairing and the top of the lower mounting support at each hole in the support.
c. Install the bolts while making sure they pass through the nylon washers installed in substep b.
d. Install all nuts and tighten finger-tight.
e. Secure the bolt with a wrench and tighten the nut to 97 in.-lb. (11 N•m). Repeat for all remaining nuts.

6B. On 1986-1992 models, install the lower mounting support bolts as follows:

CAUTION
The following washers have one plastic side and one metal side. Install the washer with the metal side facing the bolt head.

a. Install the washers onto the lower mounting support bolts.
b. Position the washers between the bottom of the fairing and the top of the lower mounting support with the metal side facing the lower mounting support.
c. Insert the bolts through the lower support bracket and into the weld nuts inside the fairing. Make sure the bolts pass through the washers installed in substep b.
d. Tighten each bolt to 97 in.-lb. (11 N•m).

7. Tighten the 5/16-in. bolts, installed in Step 5, to 19 ft.-lb. (26 N•m).

8. Align the fairing brace with the corresponding hole in the fairing on one side. Install two 1/4 in. × 3/4 in. screws through the fairing and into the fairing brace holes. Install the lockwasher and nut to 124 in.-lb. (14 N•m).

9. Connect the speedometer cable to the front hub.

10. Adjust the throttle and clutch cables as described in Chapter Three.

11. Slowly test-ride the motorcycle to make sure routing of the throttle and choke cables is correct.

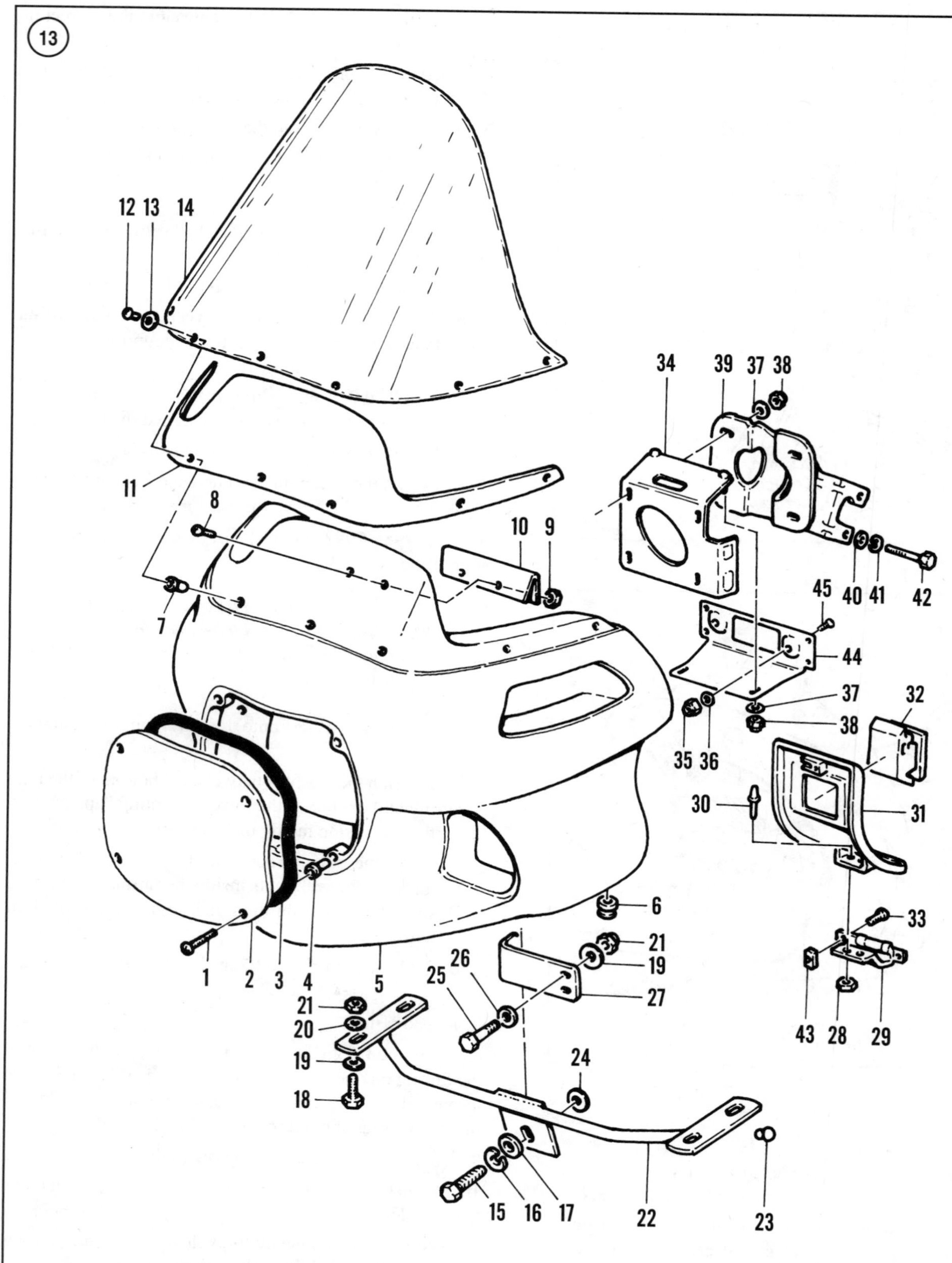
13
12 13 14
34 39 37 38
11
8
10 9
7
45 40 41 42
44
37
32
35 36
38
30
31
6
33
21
19
1 2 3 4 5
26
25
27
21
20
19
18
24
43 28 29
15 16 17 22 23

FRONT FAIRING AND WINDSHIELD (1984-1992 FXRT AND FXRD MODELS)

1. Screw
2. Cover
3. Seal
4. Screw
5. Fairing
6. Grommet
7. Well nut
8. Screw
9. Locknut
10. Bracket
11. Windshield seal
12. Screw
13. Washer
14. Windshield
15. Bolt
16. Lockwasher
17. Washer
18. Bolt
19. Washer
20. Washer
21. Nut
22. Mounting bracket
23. Plug
24. Washer
25. Bolt
26. Washer
27. Bracket support
28. Washer
29. Latch
30. Rivet
31. Fairing door
32. Door latch
33. Screw
34. Radio support bracket
35. Locknut
36. Washer
37. Washer
38. Nut
39. Bracket
40. Washer
41. Lockwasher
42. Bolt
43. Speed nut
44. Mounting bracket
45. Screw

WINDSHIELD (FXRS-CON)

Removal/Installation

Refer to **Figure 14**.

1. Support the motorcycle on level ground on the jiffy stand.
2. Cover the headlight housing and front turn signals with a towel or blanket.
3. Sufficiently loosen the toggle bolt within the hinge to slip the toggle stop out of the notch in the hinge. Repeat for the other side.
4. Support the windshield. Then disconnect the hinge from the fork tube. The toggle stop and bolt will remain with the hinge. Repeat for the other side.
5. Remove the windshield from the motorcycle.
6. Position the lower portion of the windshield behind the front turn signals and onto the front fork.

CAUTION
Do not allow the hinge to close against the wiring harness or cable in Step 7.

7. Wrap both hinges around the fork tubes and close them.
8. Move the toggle stop on the toggle bolt onto the notch in the hinge so that the lip on the stop faces out. Tighten the toggle bolt finger-tight. Repeat for the other side.
9. Check the position of the windshield. Make sure that no part of the windshield comes in contact with any part of the motorcycle. Reposition the windshield as necessary.
10. To obtain the maximum clamping load on the fork tubes, the toggle bolt must be tightened to a snug fit. If they are overtightened, the toggle bolt will cause the hinge to loosen, and the windshield will vibrate.
11. If minor adjustment is necessary, loosen the Allen bolt securing the hinge to the bracket on each side. Move the windshield and tighten the Allen bolts securely.

FAIRING AND WINDSHIELD (1984-1994 FLHTC, FLHTC-U AND FLHS MODELS)

Outer Fairing Removal

Refer to **Figure 15**.

1. Support the motorcycle with the front wheel off the ground. Refer to *Motorcycle Stands* in Chapter Ten.
2. Cover the front fender with a blanket or several towels to protect the finish.
3. Remove the headlight lens assembly as described in Chapter Nine.

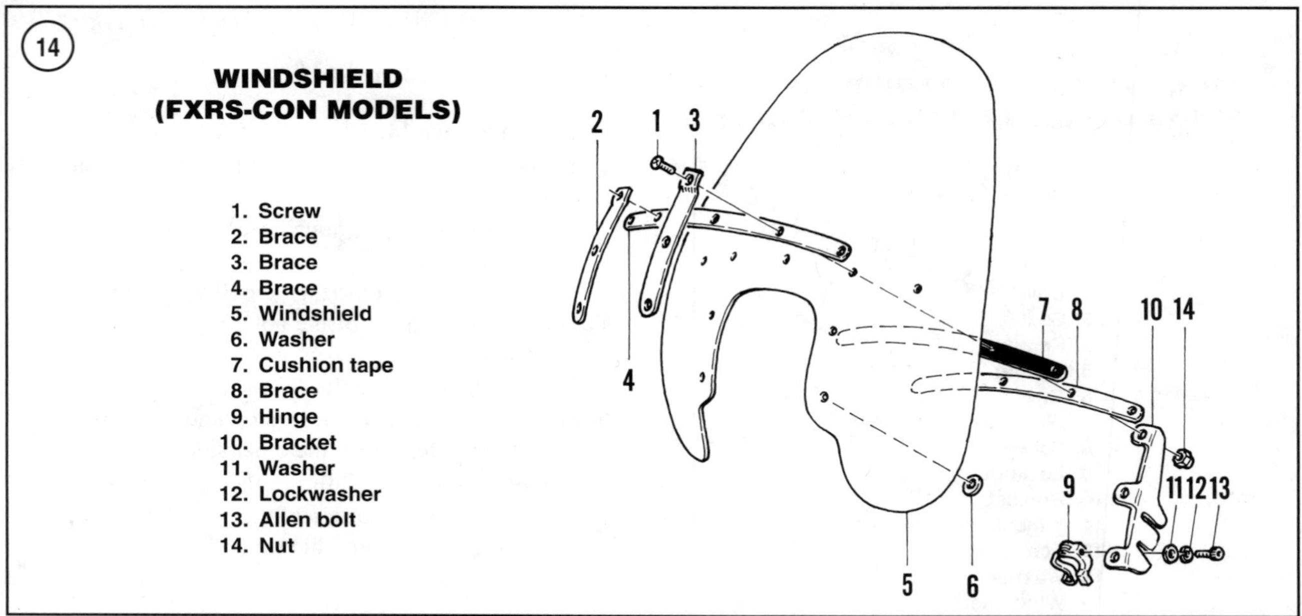

4. Remove the bolts, nuts and washers securing the outer fairing to the windshield and inner fairing.

5. On each side, loosen the bolts securing the light bracket and outer fairing to the fork bracket.

6. Remove the lower bracket bolt from each side. Then lower the bracket and rest it on the front fender.

7. Remove the screws securing the headlight assembly to the outer fairing. Remove the headlight assembly as described in Chapter Nine.

8. Working within the headlight opening in the fairing, loosen the locknuts securing the fairing studs to the fairing mounting bracket. With the locknuts loose, pull the fairing forward sliding the mounting studs off the mounting bracket slots.

9. Carefully remove the outer fairing.

Windshield Removal

Refer to **Figure 15** and **Figure 16**.

1. Remove the outer fairing as described in this section.

2. Remove the Acorn nuts, lockwashers, flat washers, nylon washers and screws securing the windshield to the inner fairing.

3. Carefully lift the windshield off the inner fairing.

Outer Fairing/Windshield Installation

1. Install the inner fairing as described in this section.

2. Install the windshield as follows:

   a. Set the windshield into position on the inner fairing and align the holes with the corresponding holes in the inner fairing.

   b. Install a nylon washer and screw through the outer end of the windshield and inner fairing.

   c. From the opposite side, install a washer, lockwasher and Acorn nut onto the screw.

   d. Tighten the screw and nut finger-tight.

   e. Repeat substeps b-d at the opposite outer end of the windshield.

   f. Install the remaining fasteners onto the windshield.

3. Install the outer fairing into position and install the remaining sets of windshield fasteners. Tighten the screws and nuts finger-tight.

4. Push the fairing toward the rear and slide the mounting studs onto the mounting bracket slots.

5. Working within the headlight opening in the faring, install the locknuts securing the fairing studs to the fairing mounting bracket. Tighten the locknuts finger-tight.

6. Make sure that the outer fairing is positioned correctly. Then securely tighten the locknuts.

7. Move the light bracket into position and align the slots in the top of the bracket with the bolts installed on the lower fork bracket.

8. Prior to tightening the outer fairing mounting bolts, make sure the rubber seal is positioned evenly around the inner fairing.

9. Install the mounting bolts and tighten to 142-168 in.-lb. (16-19 N•m).

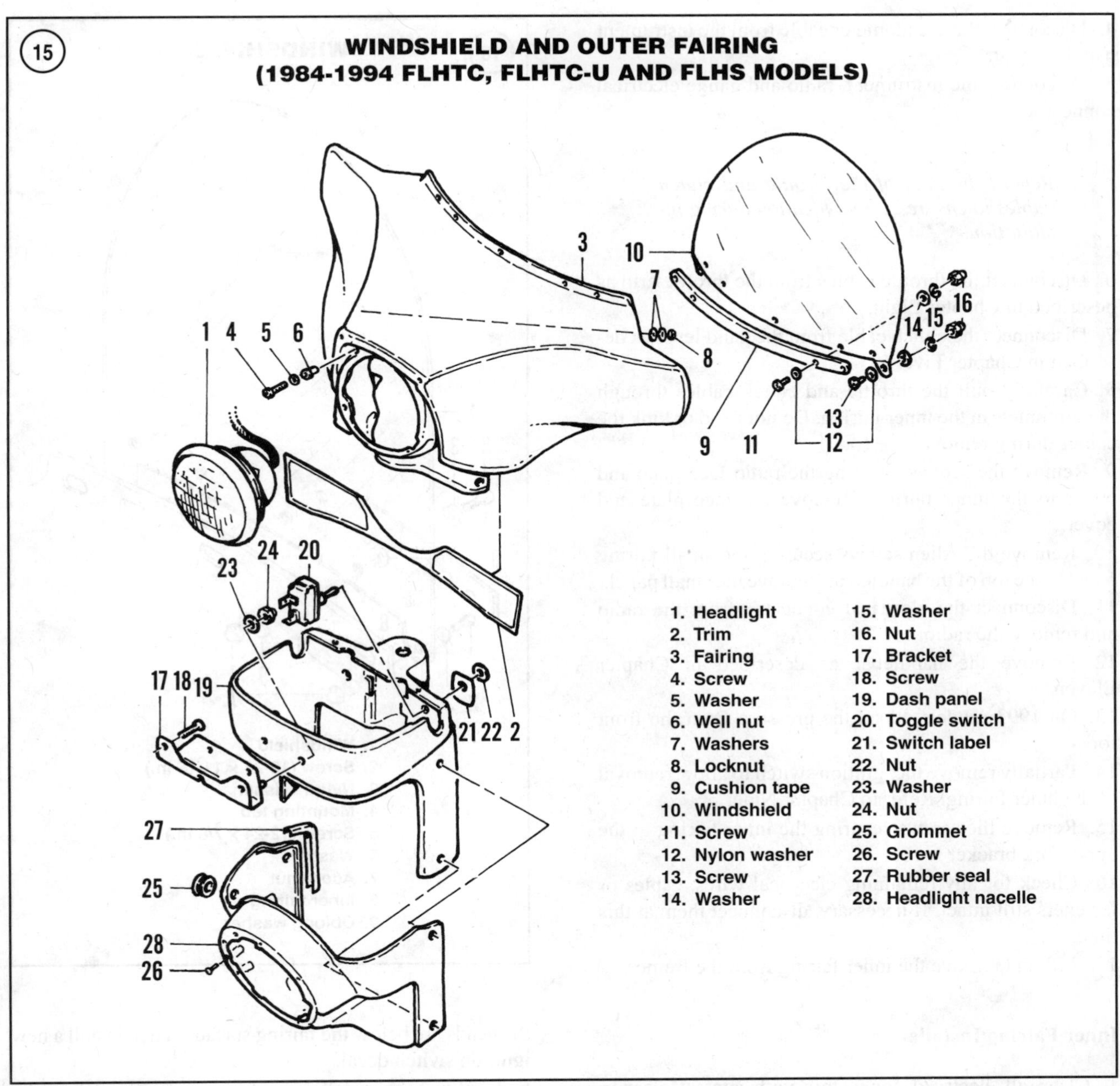

10. Starting at the center of the windshield and working outward, securely tighten each screw and Acorn nut. Do not overtighten because the windshield can fracture.

11. Install the headlight and lens assembly as described in Chapter Nine.

12. Adjust the throttle and clutch cables as described in Chapter Three.

13. Slowly test-ride the motorcycle to make sure routing of the throttle and choke cables is correct.

Inner Fairing Removal

Refer to **Figure 17**.

1. Disconnect the negative battery cable from the battery.
2. Remove the outer fairing and windshield as described in this section.
3. Remove the fuel tank as described in Chapter Eight. This step is not required, but it will prevent accidental damage to the fuel tank.

4. Disconnect the speedometer cable from the instrument panel.
5. Disconnect the instrument, radio and gauge electrical connectors.

NOTE
Record the path of the throttle and clutch cables to ensure correct location during installation.

6. Disconnect the throttle cables from the throttle grip as described in Chapter Eight.
7. Disconnect the clutch cable from the hand lever as described in Chapter Five.
8. Carefully pull the throttle and clutch cables through the grommets in the inner fairing. Do not bend or kink the cables during removal.
9. Remove the screws securing the radio face plate and cover to the inner fairing. Remove the face plate and cover.
10. Remove the Allen screws securing the small fairing panel to the top of the handlebar. Remove the small panel.
11. Disconnect the electrical connector from the radio and remove the radio.
12. Remove the handlebar as described in Chapter Eleven.
13. On 1993 models, bleed the pressure from the front forks.
14. Partially remove the ignition switch to allow removal of the inner fairing. Refer to Chapter Nine.
15. Remove the screws securing the inner fairing to the upper fork bracket.
16. Check for any remaining electrical wires, cables or fasteners still intact. If necessary, disconnect them at this time.
17. Lift and remove the inner fairing from the frame.

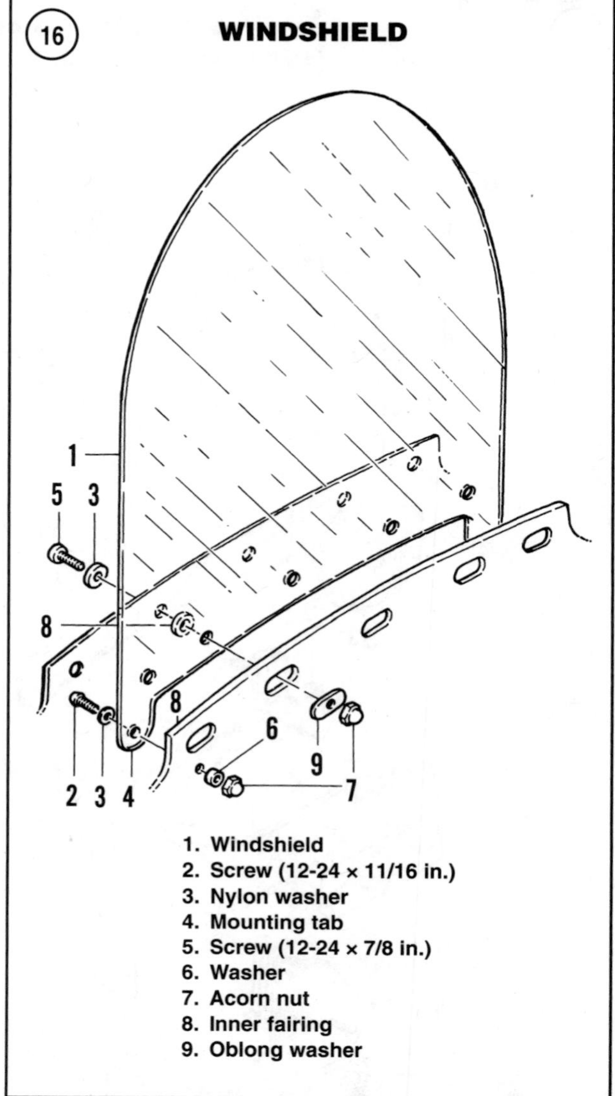

Inner Fairing Installation

1. Clean all electrical connectors with contact cleaner. Then apply dielectric grease to both sides of the connectors.
2. Lift the inner fairing partway onto the frame.
3. Carefully insert and pull the throttle and clutch cables through the grommets in the inner fairing. Do not bend or kink the cables during installation.
4. Place the inner fairing over the ignition switch and snap the inner fairing support brackets into the bushings on the lower fork bracket.
5. Install the screws securing the inner fairing to the ignition switch bracket. Tighten the screws (**Figure 18**) until the heads are below the fairing surface. Then install a new ignition switch decal.
6. Continue the installation of the ignition switch as described in Chapter Nine.
7. Install the inner fairing-to-upper fork bracket bolts. Tighten finger-tight.
8. Install the handlebar as described in Chapter Eleven.
9. Install the radio and connect the electrical connector.
10. Install the small fairing panel onto the handlebar. Install the radio faceplate and cover and tighten the screws securely.
11. Reconnect all remaining electrical connectors.
12. Connect the speedometer cable to the instrument panel.

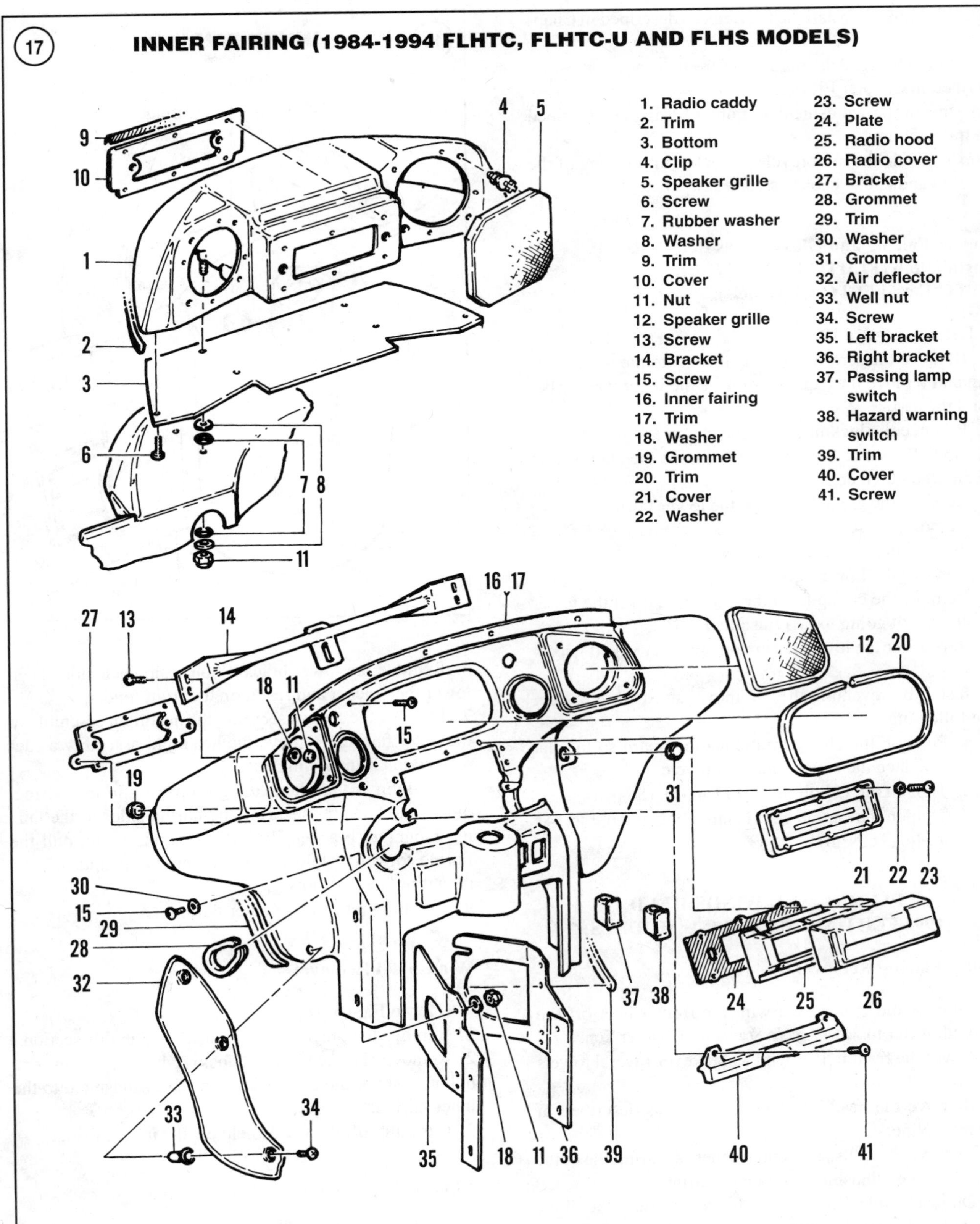
17
INNER FAIRING (1984-1994 FLHTC, FLHTC-U AND FLHS MODELS)
1. Radio caddy
2. Trim
3. Bottom
4. Clip
5. Speaker grille
6. Screw
7. Rubber washer
8. Washer
9. Trim
10. Cover
11. Nut
12. Speaker grille
13. Screw
14. Bracket
15. Screw
16. Inner fairing
17. Trim
18. Washer
19. Grommet
20. Trim
21. Cover
22. Washer
23. Screw
24. Plate
25. Radio hood
26. Radio cover
27. Bracket
28. Grommet
29. Trim
30. Washer
31. Grommet
32. Air deflector
33. Well nut
34. Screw
35. Left bracket
36. Right bracket
37. Passing lamp switch
38. Hazard warning switch
39. Trim
40. Cover
41. Screw

13. If removed, install the fuel tank as described in Chapter Eight.
14. On 1993 models, inflate the front suspension as described in Chapter Eleven.
15. Install the windshield and outer fairing as described in this section.
16. Test-ride the motorcycle to make sure routing of the throttle and choke cables is correct.

Lower Fairing and Glove Boxes Removal/ Installation (FLHTC-U, FLHTC-UI, FLTC-U and FLTC-UI Models)

Refer to **Figure 19**.

1. Remove the screws securing the cap to the lower fairing and remove the cap. Do not lose the inner washer behind the cap.
2. Remove the locknuts from the clamp and the bracket.
3. Open the glove box door and remove the clamp from within the glove box.
4. Remove the glove box from the lower fairing.
5. Remove the screw and washers securing the clamp to the base of the lower fairing.
6. Remove the lower fairing.
7. Remove the clamp from the engine guard if the lower fairing is not going to be reinstalled.
8. Repeat for the lower fairing on the other side if necessary.
9. Install by reversing these removal steps while noting the following:
   a. Position the clamp on the engine guard so the flat tabs face the rear of the motorcycle.
   b. Tighten the U-bolt nuts to 71 in.-lb. (8 N•m).
   c. Tighten the engine guard clamp bolt and nut to 142 in.-lb. (16 N•m).

FAIRING AND WINDSHIELD (1994 FLHTC AND FLHTC-U MODELS)

Outer Fairing Removal

1. Support the motorcycle with the front wheel off the ground. Refer to *Motorcycle Stands* in Chapter Ten.
2. Cover the front fender with a blanket or several towels to protect the finish.
3. Remove the headlight lens assembly as described in Chapter Nine.
4. Remove the bolts, nuts and washers securing the outer fairing to the windshield and inner fairing.
5. On each side, loosen the bolts securing the light bracket and outer fairing to the fork bracket.

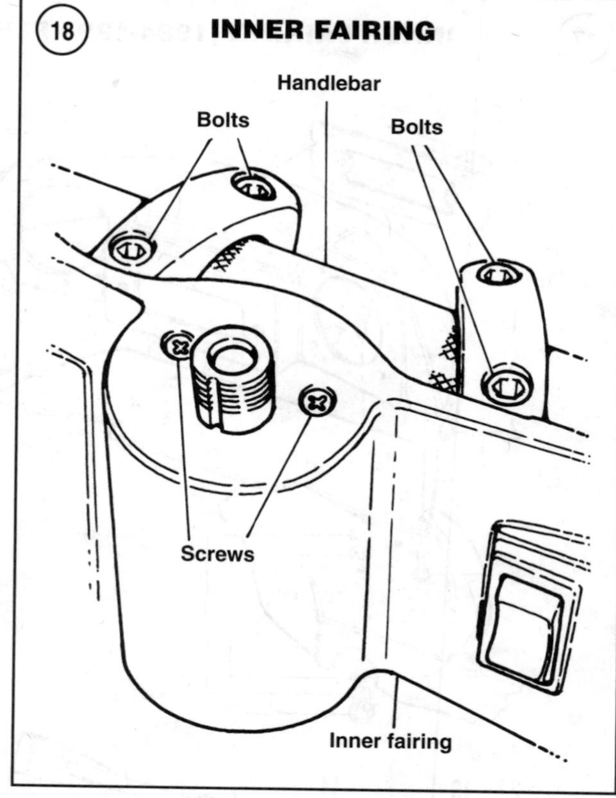

6. Remove the lower bracket bolt from each side. Then lower the bracket and rest it on the front fender.
7. Remove the screws securing the headlight assembly to the outer fairing. Remove the headlight assembly as described in Chapter Nine.
8. Working within the headlight opening in the fairing, loosen the locknuts securing the fairing studs to the fairing mounting bracket. With the locknuts loose, pull the fairing forward while sliding the mounting studs off the mounting bracket slots.
9. Carefully remove the outer fairing.

Windshield Removal

Refer to **Figure 16**.

1. Remove the outer fairing as described in this section.
2. Remove the Acorn nuts, lockwashers, flat washers, nylon washers and screws securing the windshield to the inner fairing.
3. Carefully lift the windshield off the inner fairing.

Outer Fairing/Windshield Installation

1. Install the inner fairing as described in this section.

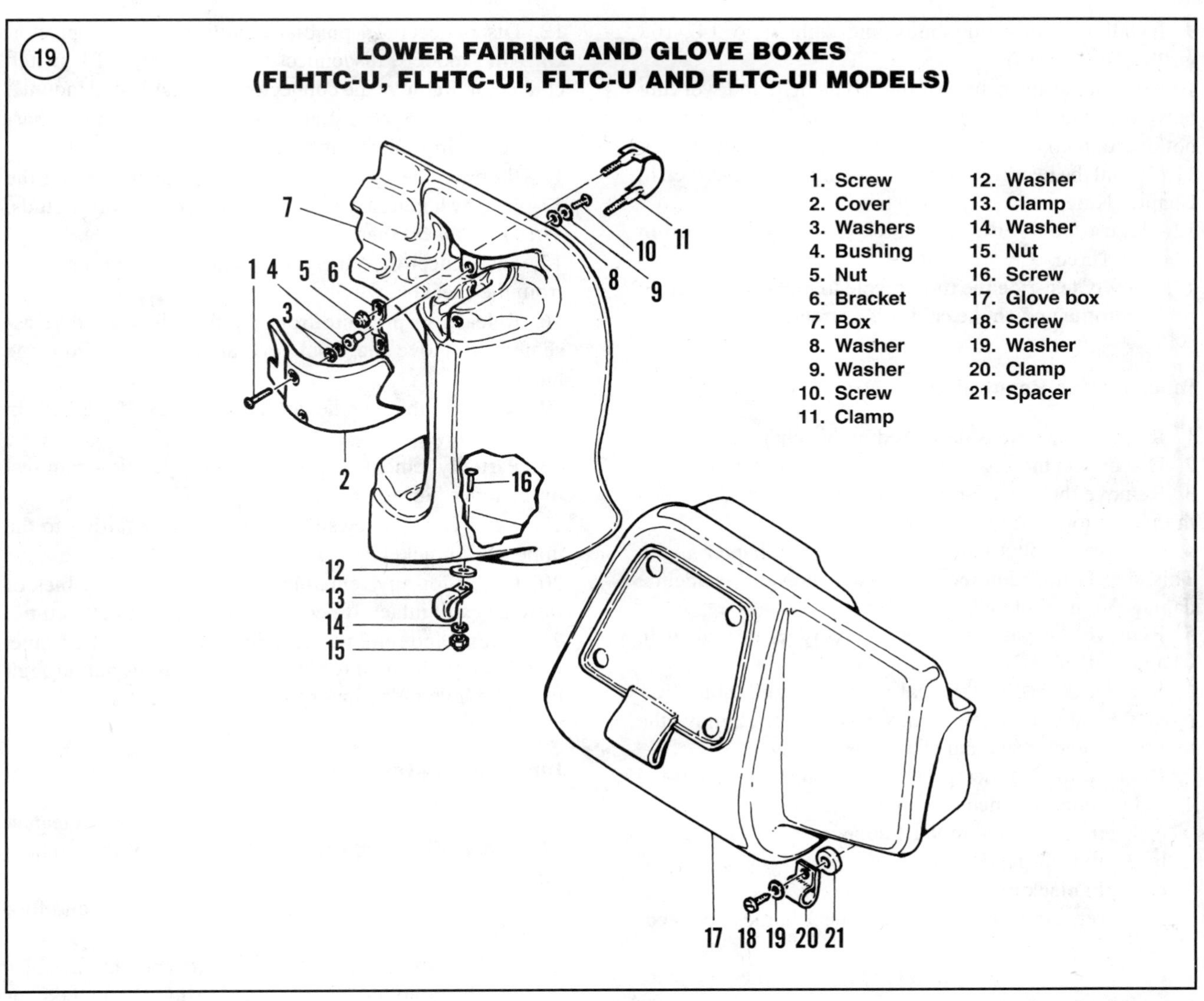

2. Install the windshield as follows:
   a. Set the windshield into position on the inner fairing and align the holes with the corresponding holes in the inner fairing.
   b. Install a nylon washer and screw through the outer end of the windshield and inner fairing.
   c. From the opposite side, install a washer, lockwasher and Acorn nut onto the screw.
   d. Tighten the screw and nut finger-tight.
   e. Repeat substeps b-d at the opposite outer end of the windshield.
   f. Install the remaining fasteners onto the windshield.
3. Install the outer fairing into position and install the remaining sets of windshield fasteners. Make sure to install the washers between the windshield and the inner fairing as shown in **Figure 16**. Tighten the screws and nuts finger-tight.
4. Push the fairing toward the rear and slide its mounting studs onto the mounting bracket slots.
5. Working within the headlight opening in the fairing, install the locknuts securing the fairing studs to the fairing mounting bracket. Tighten the locknuts finger-tight.
6. Make sure that the outer fairing is positioned correctly. Then tighten the locknuts securely.
7. Move the light bracket into position and align the slots in the top of the bracket with the bolts installed on the lower fork bracket.
8. Prior to tightening the outer fairing mounting bolts, make sure the rubber seal is positioned evenly around the inner fairing.

9. Install the mounting bolts and tighten to 142-168 in.-lb. (16-19 N•m).
10. Starting at the center of the windshield and working outward, securely tighten each screw and Acorn nut. Do not overtighten because the windshield can fracture.
11. Install the headlight and lens assembly as described in Chapter Nine.
12. Adjust the throttle and clutch cables as described in Chapter Three.
13. Slowly test-ride the motorcycle to make sure routing of the throttle and choke cables is correct.

Inner Fairing Removal

1. Remove the seat as described in this chapter.
2. Disconnect the negative battery cable from the battery.
3. Remove the outer fairing and windshield as described in this section.
4. Remove the fuel tank as described in Chapter Eight. This step is not required, but it will prevent accidental damage to the fuel tank.
5. Remove the passing lamp assembly as described in Chapter Nine.
6. Remove the radio electrical connectors and cables. Remove the radio, mounting bracket and panel. Remove the mounting bracket and panel as an assembly.
7. Remove the following electrical connectors from the T-stud mounts and then disconnect:
   a. 8-pin turn signal module connector.
   b. 3-pin front fender connector.
   c. 3-pin black main power connector.
   d. 12-pin gray main-to-interconnect harness connector.
   e. 12-pin black main-to-interconnect harness connector.
8. Remove the fairing cross bracket fasteners and remove the fairing cross bracket.
9. Remove the 6-pin gray handlebar switch connector from the T-stud. Then disconnect it.
10A. On non-Ultra models, remove the 6-pin black radio control-to-interconnect harness connector from the T-stud. Then disconnect it.
10B. On Ultra models, remove the following electrical connectors from the T-stud mounts. Then disconnect them:
   a. 3-pin gray SET/RESUME switch connector.
   b. 6-pin black radio overlay-to-radio control wiring harness.
   c. 6-pin black interconnect-to-radio overlay wiring harness.
11. On Ultra models, disconnect the red/green cruise switch terminal wire from the front interconnect harness.
12. Disconnect the 4-pin black ignition switch connector. On Ultra models, disconnect the 2-pin gray PTT switch connector. Remove the connector from the T-stud mount.
13. Remove the cable strap securing the interconnect harness to the front fork antidive cross tube.
14. Remove the 2-pin black antidive connector and the 12-pin gray handlebar switch connector from the T-studs. Then disconnect them.
15. Disconnect the blue/yellow and yellow/violet wires from the speaker switch.
16. Release air pressure from the front fork antidive assembly. Remove the front fork antidive hose from the handlebar.
17. Remove the handlebar assembly as described in Chapter Eleven.
18. Partially remove the ignition switch to allow removal of the inner fairing. Refer to Chapter Nine.
19. Remove the screws securing the inner fairing to the upper fork bracket.
20. Check for any remaining electrical wires, cables or fasteners still intact. If necessary, disconnect at this time.
21. Lift up and remove the inner fairing from the frame. Carefully guide the throttle and clutch cables out through the radio hole in the inner fairing.

Inner Fairing Installation

1. Clean all electrical connectors with contact cleaner. Then apply dielectric grease to both sides of the connectors.
2. Lift the inner fairing partway onto the frame and fork brackets.
3. Carefully insert and pull the throttle and clutch cables through the radio hole in the inner fairing. Do not bend or kink the cables during installation.
4. Install the upper inner fairing-to-upper fork bracket mounting bolts. Tighten the bolts finger-tight.
5. Install and securely tighten the inner fairing bracket bolts.
6. Install the screws securing the inner fairing to the ignition switch bracket. Tighten the screws (**Figure 18**) until the heads are below the fairing surface. Then install a new ignition switch decal.
7. Continue the installation of the ignition switch as described in Chapter Nine.
8. Install the handlebar as described in Chapter Eleven.
9. Install the radio and connect the electrical connector.
10. Connect the following connectors and secure them to the T-stud mounts:
   a. 2-pin black antidive connector.
   b. 2-pin gray handlebar switch connector.

c. Route these wires behind the clutch cable prior to connecting to the connector blocks.
11. Connect the speaker wires (blue/yellow and yellow/violet).
12. Install the speaker switch into position.
13. Connect the 4-pin black ignition switch connector. Insert the wires between the handlebar risers.
14. On Ultra models, connect the 2-pin gray PTT switch connector and secure it to the T-stud mount.
15. Secure the interconnect harness to the front fork antidive crossover tube.
16. Install the radio mounting bracket and fasteners. Tighten to 48-71 in.-lb. (5-8 N•m).
17. On Ultra models, connect the red/green wire (leading from the front interconnect harness) to the cruise control switch terminal. Install the cruise control switch.
18. On Ultra models, connect the following connectors and attach them to the T-stud mounts:
   a. 3-pin gray SET/RESUME switch connector.
   b. 6-pin black radio overlay-to-radio control harness connector.
   c. 6-pin black interconnect-to-radio overlay connector.
19. On non-Ultra models, connect the six-pin black radio control-to-interconnect harness connector.
20. Install the fairing cross bar and tighten the bolts finger-tight.
21. Connect the following connectors and then attach to the T-stud mounts:
   a. 8-pin gray turn signal module connector.
   b. 3-pin front fender light connector.
   c. 3-pin gray main harness-to-interconnect harness connector.
   d. 12-pin black main harness-to-interconnect harness connector.
22. Install the radio. Then connect the following connectors:
   a. 8-pin black.
   b. 12-pin black.
   c. DIN cable.
   d. Antenna cable.

   Connect each of the connectors to the T-stud mounts.
23. Securely tighten the fairing cross brace bolts.
24. Inflate the front fork antidive as described in Chapter Eleven.
25. If removed, install the fuel tank as described in Chapter Eight.
26. Install the passing lamp assembly as described in Chapter Nine.
27. Install the windshield and outer fairing as described in this section.
28. Connect the negative battery cable to the battery.
29. Slowly test-ride the motorcycle to make sure routing of the throttle and choke cables is correct.

Lower Fairing and Glove Boxes Removal/Installation (FLHTC-U and FLHTC-UI Models)

Refer to **Figure 19**.
1. Remove the screws securing the cap to the lower fairing and remove the cap. Do not lose the inner washer behind the cap.
2. Remove the locknuts from the clamp and the bracket.
3. Open the glove box door and remove the clamp from within the glove box.
4. Remove the glove box from the lower fairing.
5. Remove the screw and washers securing the clamp to the base of the lower fairing.
6. Remove the lower fairing.
7. Remove the clamp from the engine guard if the lower fairing is not going to be reinstalled.
8. Repeat for the lower fairing on the other side if necessary.
9. Install by reversing these removal steps while noting the following:
   a. Position the clamp on the engine guard so the flat tabs face the rear of the motorcycle.
   b. Tighten the U-bolt nuts to 71 in.-lb. (8 N•m).
   c. Tighten the engine guard clamp bolt and nut to 142 in.-lb. (16 N•m).

FRONT FAIRING (1995-1998 FLHT, FLHTC, FLHTC-U AND FLHTC-UI MODELS)

Front Outer Fairing Removal/Installation

Refer to **Figure 20**.
1. Place the motorcycle on the jiffy stand.
2. Remove the seat as described in this chapter.
3. Disconnect the negative battery cable from the battery.
4. Cover the front fender with towels or a blanket to protect the painted finish.

NOTE
The windshield will stay with the front outer fairing with the cushion tape.

5. At the front of the front outer fairing, locate the three T27 Torx screws (**Figure 21**) securing the windshield and the outer fairing to the inner fairing. Using an alternating pattern, loosen and remove the three screws.
6. Working on the inner fairing side, remove the T25 Torx screw at the corner (**Figure 22**) on each side of the inner fairing.

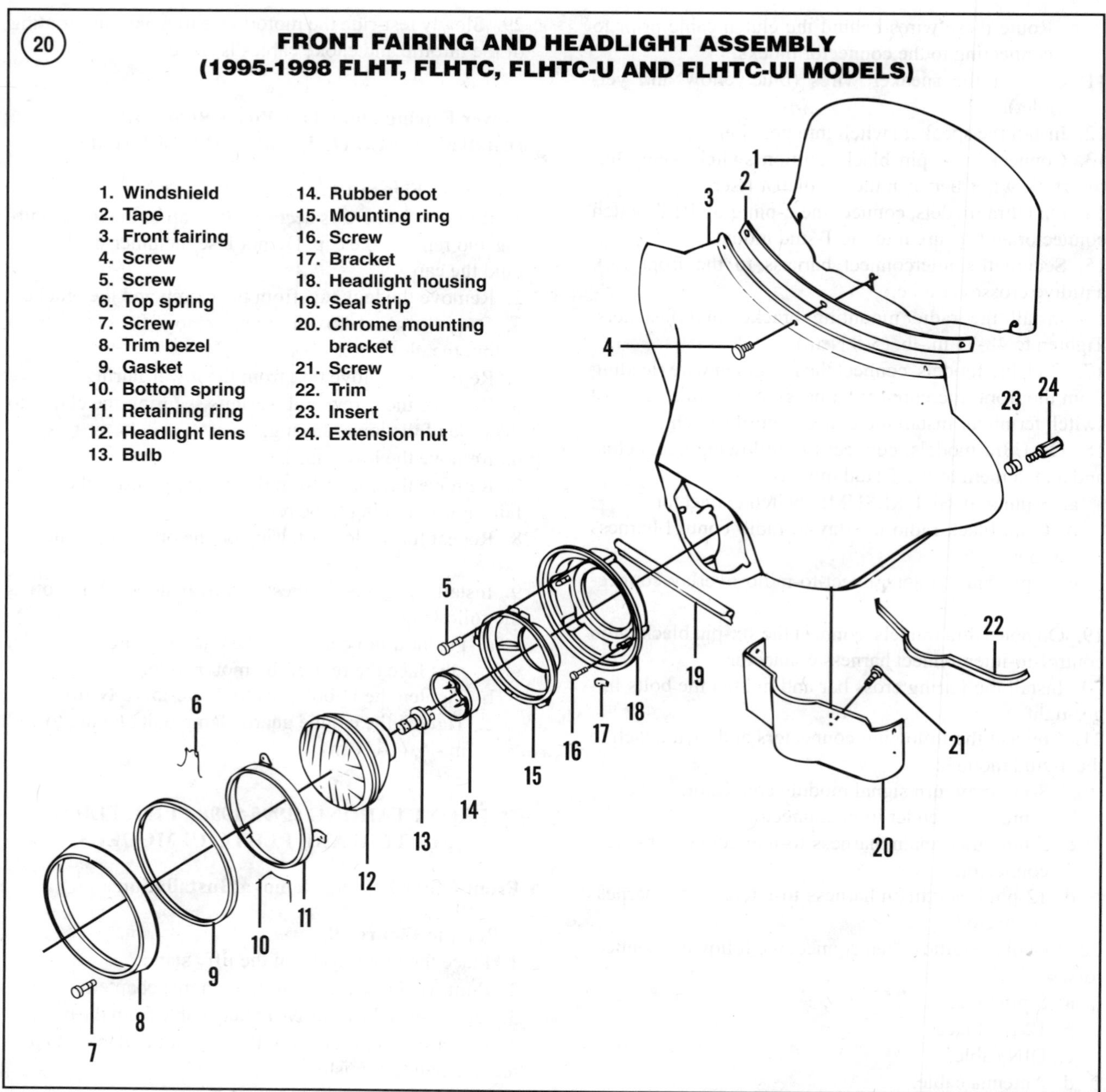

7. Turn the front wheel all the way to the left. Working below the fairing cap, remove the screw (**Figure 23**) securing the front outer fairing to the mounting bracket.

8. Have an assistant hold onto the front outer fairing because it will be loose after removal of the fasteners in the following step.

9. Turn the front wheel all the way to the right. Below the fairing cap, remove the other screw securing the front outer fairing to the mounting bracket.

CAUTION

*The windshield is **not** mechanically attached to the front outer fairing and can fall off during outer fairing removal. The windshield can remain attached to the fairing with the cushion tape securing it to the front outer fairing.*

10. Pull the front outer fairing forward and disconnect the electrical connector from the headlight assembly.

21

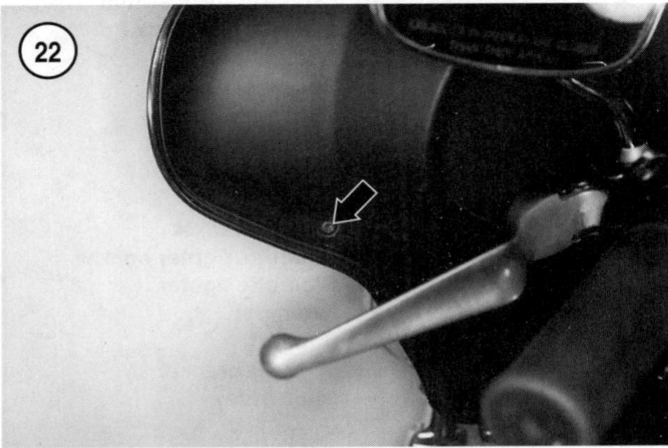
22

23

11. Remove the front outer fairing and windshield and store them in a safe place. If necessary, remove the windshield from the front outer fairing.

12. Install by reversing these removal steps. Starting with the center screw and alternating from side to side, tighten the three screws securely. Do not overtighten because the area surrounding the screw might fracture.

Front Inner Fairing Cap Removal/Installation

The inner fairing cap is removed when the ignition switch is removed. Refer to *Ignition/Light Switch Removal/Installation (1997-1998 Domestic Models)* in Chapter Nine.

Front Inner Fairing Removal/Installation

Refer to **Figure 24**.

1. Place the motorcycle on the jiffy stand.
2. Remove the front outer fairing and windshield as previously described in this section.
3. On the left side of the inner fairing, unscrew the rubber boot and remove the odometer reset switch from the housing.
4. On the lower left side, disconnect the 6-pin electrical connector (A, **Figure 25**) for the turn signal lamps.
5. Remove the passing lamp assembly as described in Chapter Nine.
6. Remove the front inner fairing cap as previously described in this section.
7. Remove the screws securing the chrome mounting skirt (**Figure 26**) and remove it.
8. Disconnect the clutch cable from the clutch lever as described under *Clutch Cable Replacement* in Chapter Five.
9. Withdraw the clutch cable from the inner fairing rubber grommet (**Figure 27**). Move the clutch cable forward and out of the way. Remove the rubber grommet.
10. Remove the front brake master cylinder from the handlebar as described in Chapter Thirteen.
11. Separate the right switch housing as described in Chapter Nine.
12. Disconnect both the throttle and idle cables from the throttle grip as described in Chapter Eight.
13. Withdraw the throttle and idle cables from the inner fairing rubber grommet. Move the idle and throttle cables forward and out of the way. Remove the rubber grommet.
14. Disconnect the electrical terminals from the cigarette lighter (B, **Figure 25**) and both speakers (C).
15. Remove the T25 Torx screws securing the speaker adapters (D, **Figure 25**) to the inner fairing.
16. Remove the cigarette lighter from the socket. Hold onto the socket and unscrew the outer shell. Remove the outer shell from the inner fairing.
17. Disconnect the electrical terminals from the voltmeter and the fuel gauge.
18. Carefully cut the cable strap securing the indicator lamp connector between the speedometer and tachometer brackets.
19. Disconnect the following electrical connectors:

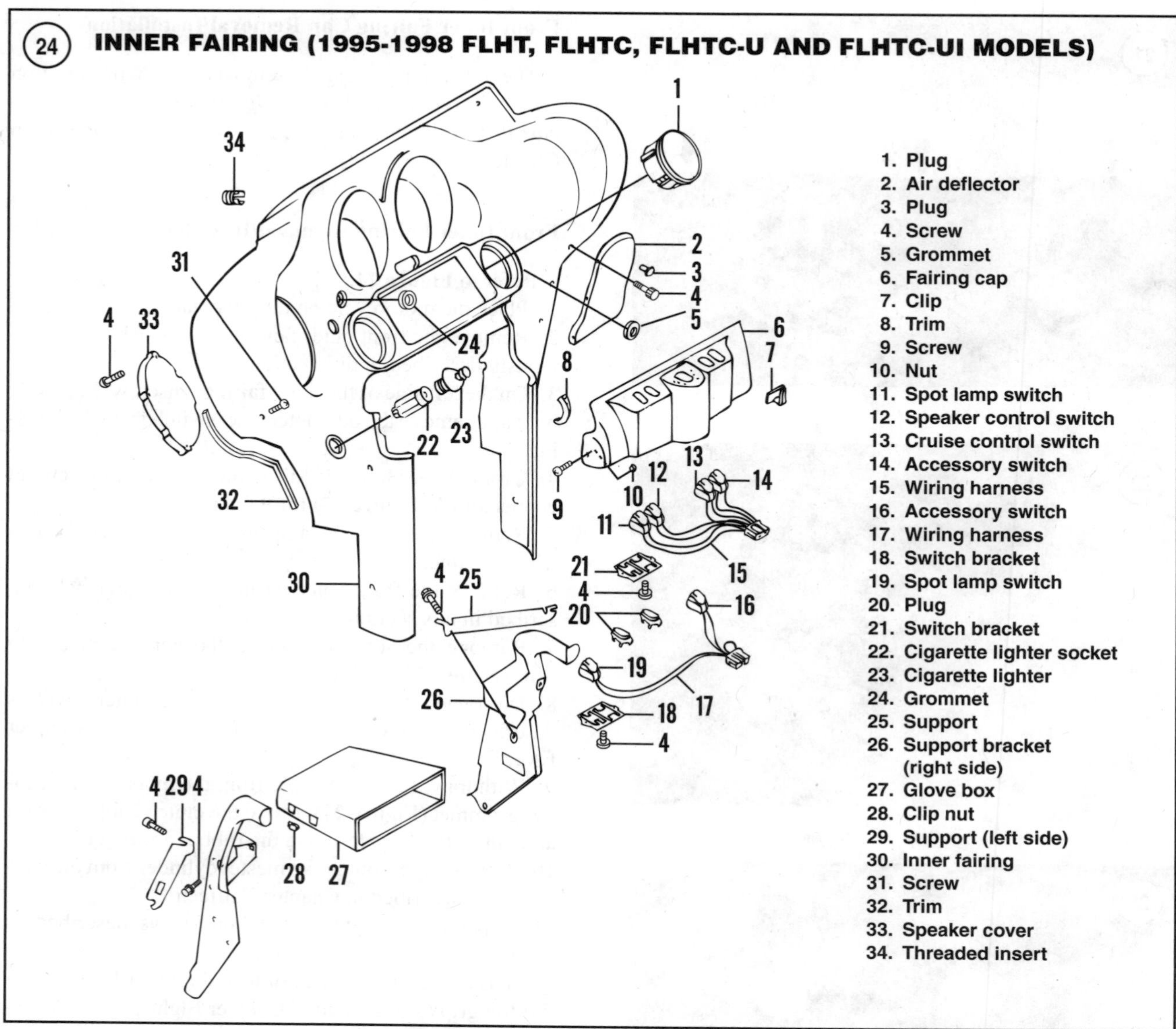

(24) **INNER FAIRING (1995-1998 FLHT, FLHTC, FLHTC-U AND FLHTC-UI MODELS)**

a. Speedometer 12-pin Packard electrical connector.
b. Tachometer 6-pin Packard electrical connector.
c. Indicator lamps 10-pin electrical connector.

20. Remove the screws securing the speedometer and tachometer (**Figure 28**) to the mounting brackets. Remove the speedometer and tachometer from the inner fairing.
21. Remove the hex nuts securing the voltmeter and fuel level gauges to the mounting brackets. Remove the voltmeter and fuel level gauge from the inner fairing.
22. Release the four paddles and free the indicator bulb housing from the lens assembly. Remove the lens assembly from the inner fairing.
23. Spread the lower legs of the inner fairing and the support brackets outward and disengage the lower legs from the locating dowels on the lower fork brace. Raise the lower fairing and support brackets high enough to gain access to the lower row of gauges.
24. On FLHTC, FLHTC-I and FLHTC-UI models, perform the following:

a. Disconnect the electrical connectors from the oil pressure gauge and the ambient air temperature gauge.
b. Remove the hex nuts securing the oil pressure gauge and the ambient air temperature gauges to the mounting brackets. Remove the oil pressure gauge and the ambient air temperature gauges from the inner fairing.

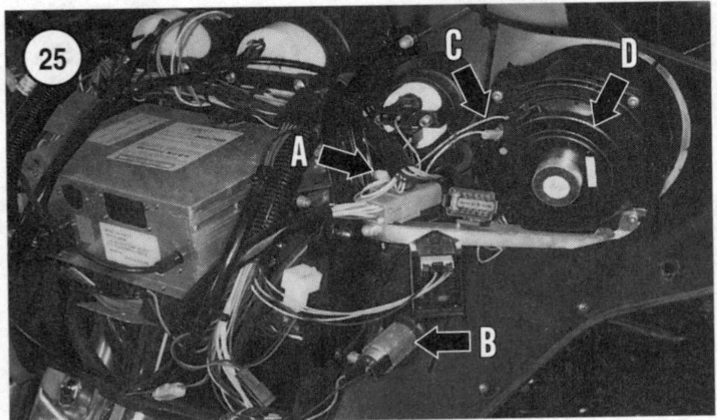

25. Remove the four Allen bolts securing the inner fairing to the fairing mounting bracket.

26. Raise the inner fairing and the support brackets farther up, tilt the inner fairing toward the rear of the motorcycle, and free the fairing from the radio nose seal.

27. Remove the front inner fairing from the mounting bracket. The radio and the interconnecting harness will remain with the frame.

28. Install by reversing these removal steps.

Lower Fairing and Glove Boxes (FLHTC-UI Models) Removal/Installation

Refer to **Figure 29**.

1. Place the motorcycle on the jiffy stand.
2. Remove the two screws securing the lower cap on the right side. Remove the lower cap.
3. Secure the locknut on the base of the lower fairing. Unscrew the T40 Torx screw from the clamp and locknut. Remove the clamp and rubber washer.
4. Have an assistant hold onto the lower fairing.
5. Remove the two locknuts securing the U-bolt and retainer to the engine guard. Remove the U-bolt and retainer. Remove the lower fairing and storage box from the frame.
6. Repeat for the other side if necessary.
7. Install by reversing these removal steps.

WINDSHIELD AND HEADLIGHT NACELLE (1994-1998 FLHR AND FLHR-I MODELS)

Windshield Only Removal/Installation

1. Place the motorcycle on the jiffy stand.
2. Use a finger and lift the wire form latch spring on each side of the windshield next to the headlight nacelle.
3. Straddle the front wheel and hold onto the windshield. Gently pull straight up on the top of the windshield until the upper notches on the side brackets are free of the upper grommets on the passing lamp support.
4. Continue to raise the windshield until the side bracket lower notches are free from the lower grommets and remove the windshield.
5. Install by reversing these removal steps while noting the following:
   a. Lower the windshield until the latches are seated on the grommets.
   b. Push down on the wire form latch springs until they hang over the upper grommets.
   c. Make sure the windshield is securely in place prior to the first ride.

(29)

LOWER FAIRING AND GLOVE BOXES (1995-1998 FLHTC-UI MODELS)

1. Bolt
2. Fairing lower cap
3. Crimp nut
4. Flange nut
5. Retainer
6. Lower fairing (right side shown)
7. U-hook
8. Storage box
9. Door
10. Nut
11. Clamp
12. Rubber washer
13. Bolt

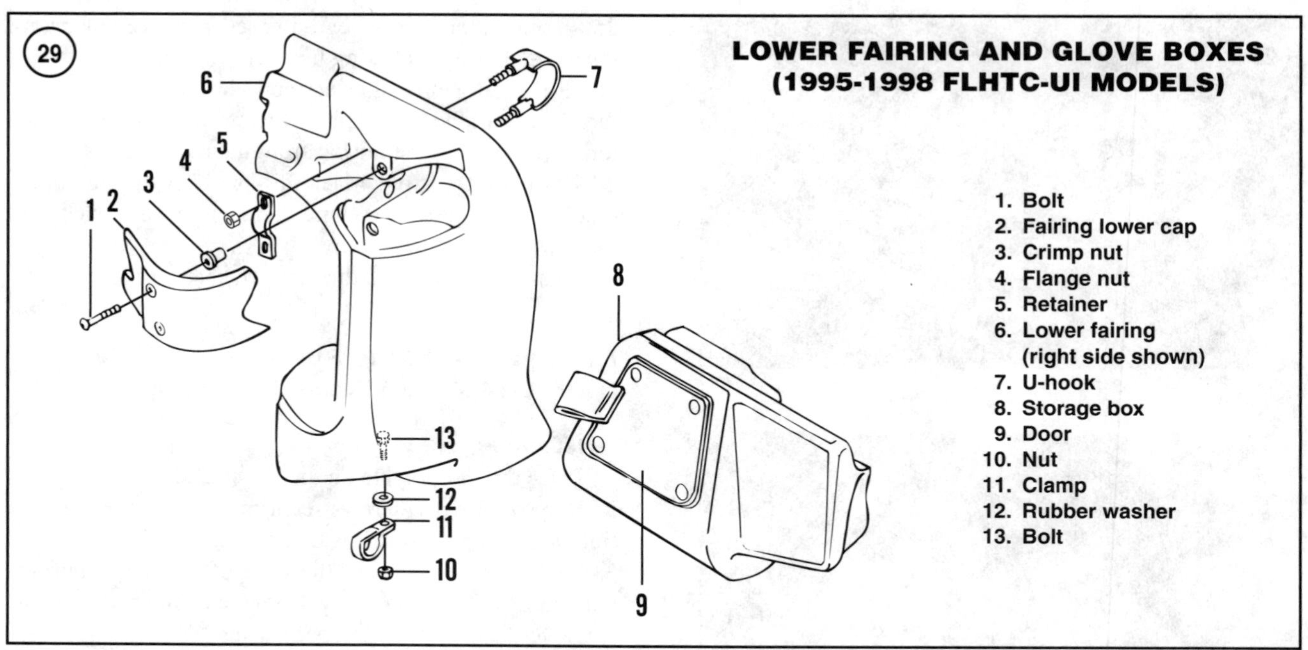

(30)

HEADLIGHT AND NACELLE (1994-1998 FLHR AND FLHR-I MODELS)

1. Bolt
2. Handlebar cover
3. Chrome strip
4. Speed nut
5. Washer
6. Flange nut
7. Spring clip
8. Screw
9. Top spring
10. Screw
11. Trim bezel
12. Retaining ring
13. Headlight lens
14. Bulb
15. Rubber boot
16. Mounting ring
17. Bracket
18. Screw
19. Headlight housing
20. Screw
21. Headlight nacelle (left side shown)
22. Switch
23. Label
24. Rubber boot
25. Trim
26. Trim plate
27. Key
28. Screw

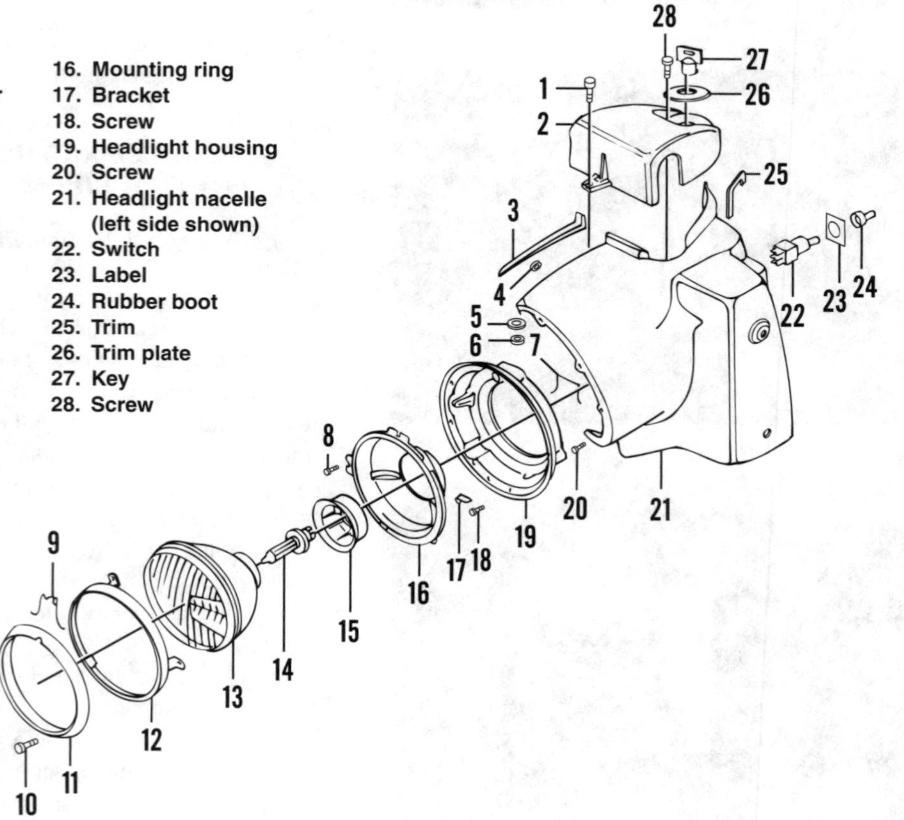

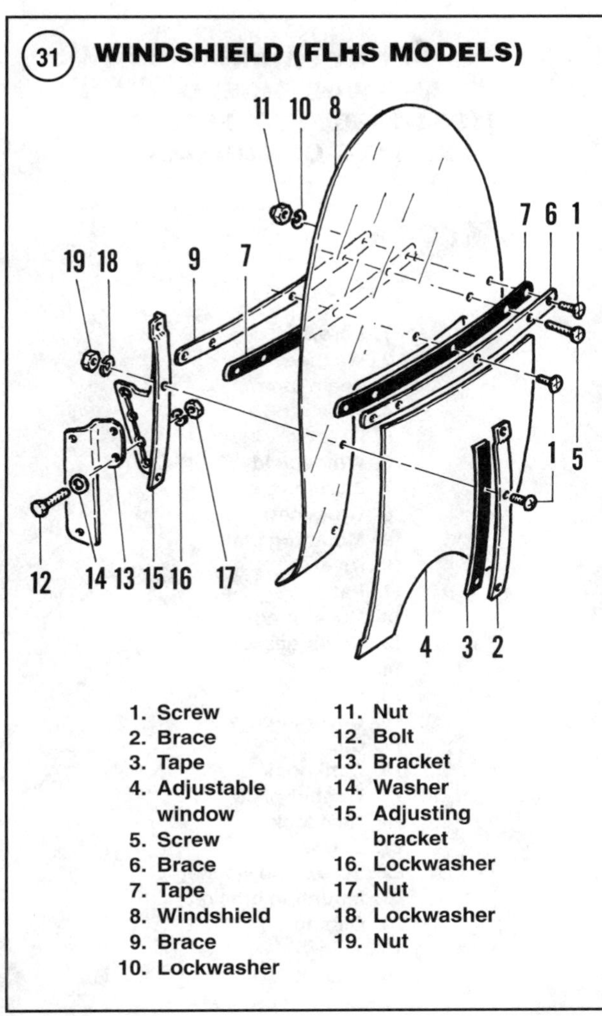

(31) **WINDSHIELD (FLHS MODELS)**

1. Screw
2. Brace
3. Tape
4. Adjustable window
5. Screw
6. Brace
7. Tape
8. Windshield
9. Brace
10. Lockwasher
11. Nut
12. Bolt
13. Bracket
14. Washer
15. Adjusting bracket
16. Lockwasher
17. Nut
18. Lockwasher
19. Nut

Headlight Nacelle Removal/Installation

Refer to **Figure 30**.

1. Place the motorcycle on the jiffy stand.
2. Remove the seat as described in this chapter.
3. Disconnect the battery negative lead from the battery.
4. Remove the windshield as described in this section.
5. Remove the screw securing the trim bezel and remove the bezel.
6. Remove the seven screws securing the headlight assembly to the nacelle.
7. Partially remove the headlight assembly from the nacelle. Then disconnect the electrical connector from the backside of the headlight lens assembly. Remove the headlight assembly.
8. Working within the headlight nacelle, remove the speed nut and washer securing the center chrome strip. Remove the chrome strip.
9. Carefully pry off the fork lock trim plate.
10. Loosen, but do not remove, the screw on the handlebar cover front mounting tab.
11. On each side, remove the two Acorn nuts securing the right and left headlight nacelles to the fork tube studs.
12. Cover the front fender with towels or a blanket to protect the painted finish.
13. Remove the passing lamp assembly as described in Chapter Nine.
14. Remove the rubber grommets and clutch cable clamp from both fork tubes.
15. Slightly raise the handlebar cover and carefully spread the rear of the nacelle halves from the fork tube studs.
16. Disconnect the accessory switch and passing lamp switch connectors.
17. Remove the nacelle halves from the front forks and store them in safe place.
18. Install by reversing these removal steps.

WINDSHIELD (FLHS MODELS)

Refer to **Figure 31**.

1. Remove the shoulder bolts, flat washers, lockwashers and nuts securing the windshield and adjust bracket to the mounting brackets.
2. Remove the windshield from the motorcycle.
3. Install the windshield as follows:
   a. Position the windshield between the mounting brackets.
   b. Align the slots in the adjusting brackets with the holes in the mounting brackets.
   c. Install the shoulder bolt, flat washer, lockwasher and nut on each side. Install the shoulder bolt into the same hole in the mounting brackets on both sides. Tighten the nuts finger-tight.
4. Adjust the windshield as follows:
   a. Adjust the height of the windshield so the rider sitting on the seat can see over the top of the windshield.
   b. Reposition the windshield as necessary. Then tighten the nuts securely.
   c. The lower edge of the adjustable window must align with the bottom of the instrument panel.

CAUTION
The windshield must not contact the headlight housing.

FAIRING AND WINDSHIELD (1984-1996 FLTC, FLTC-U AND FLTC-UI)

Windshield and Fairing Removal

Refer to **Figure 32**.

1. Support the motorcycle with the front wheel off the ground. Refer to *Motorcycle Stands* in Chapter Ten.
2. Cover the front fender with a blanket or several towels to protect the finish.
3. Disconnect the negative battery cable from the battery.
4. To remove the windshield, perform the following:
   a. Remove the screws and washers securing the windshield to the fairing. The well nut should stay within the fairing.
   b. Remove the windshield from the fairing.

5A. On 1984-1985 models, disconnect the electrical connector at the back of the fairing.
5B. On 1986-1996 models, disconnect the two electrical connectors at the back of the fairing.
6. Remove the headlight housing assembly as described in Chapter Nine.
7. Remove the bolts securing each clamp to the support bracket on the engine guard (**Figure 33**).
8. Check for any remaining electrical wires or fasteners still intact. If necessary, remove them at this time.
9. Have an assistant hold the fairing.
10. Remove the bolts located behind the headlight housing (**Figure 33**) and remove the fairing.

Installation

1. Clean all electrical connectors with contact cleaner. Then apply dielectric grease to both sides of the connectors.
2. Have an assistant hold the fairing in place while making sure not to pinch or interfere with the control cables and wires.
3. Install the bolts located behind the headlight housing (**Figure 33**) and tighten securely.
4. Align the clamp with the support bracket and align it on the engine guard. Install the bolts and tighten finger-tight. Repeat for the clamp on the other side.
5. Correctly align the clamps on the engine guard. Then tighten the screws securely.
6. Install the headlight housing as described in Chapter Nine.
7. Connect the electrical connector(s).
8. Make sure all windshield attachment well nuts are in place in the fairing.
9. Align the groove in the bottom of the windshield with the fairing and place the windshield into position.

FRONT FAIRING AND WINDSHIELD (1984-1996 FLTC, FLTC-U AND FLTC-UI MODELS)

1. Screw
2. Washer
3. Foam tape
4. Well nut
5. Decal
6. Windshield
7. Fairing
8. Grommet
9. Mounting plate
10. Rivet
11. Pad
12. Cover hinge
13. Cover gasket
14. Cover
15. Rivets
16. Cover latch
17. Clip
18. Cam hook
19. Washer plate
20. Cam lock
21. Screw
22. Screw and washer
23. Mounting bracket
24. Clip nut
25. Screw
26. Gasket
27. Support bracket
28. Clamp
29. Support bracket
30. Bolt
31. Nut
32. Screw
33. Nut
34. Upper mounting bracket
35. Washer
36. Bolt
37. Washer
38. Locknut
39. Washer
40. Rubber pad

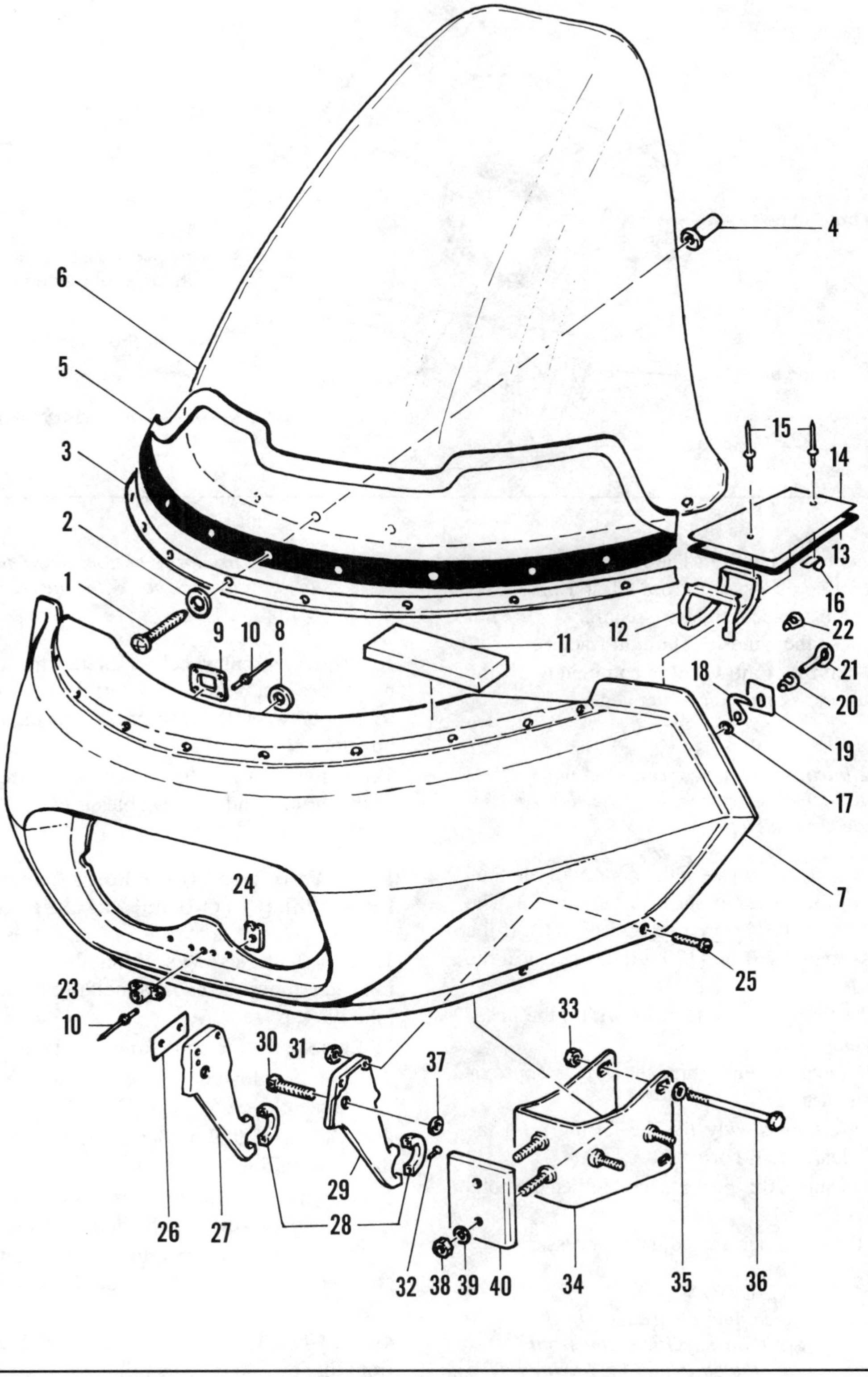
1
2
3
4
5
6
7
8
9
10
11
12
13
14
15
16
17
18
19
20
21
22
23
24
25
26
27
28
29
30
31
32
33
34
35
36
37
38
39
40

15

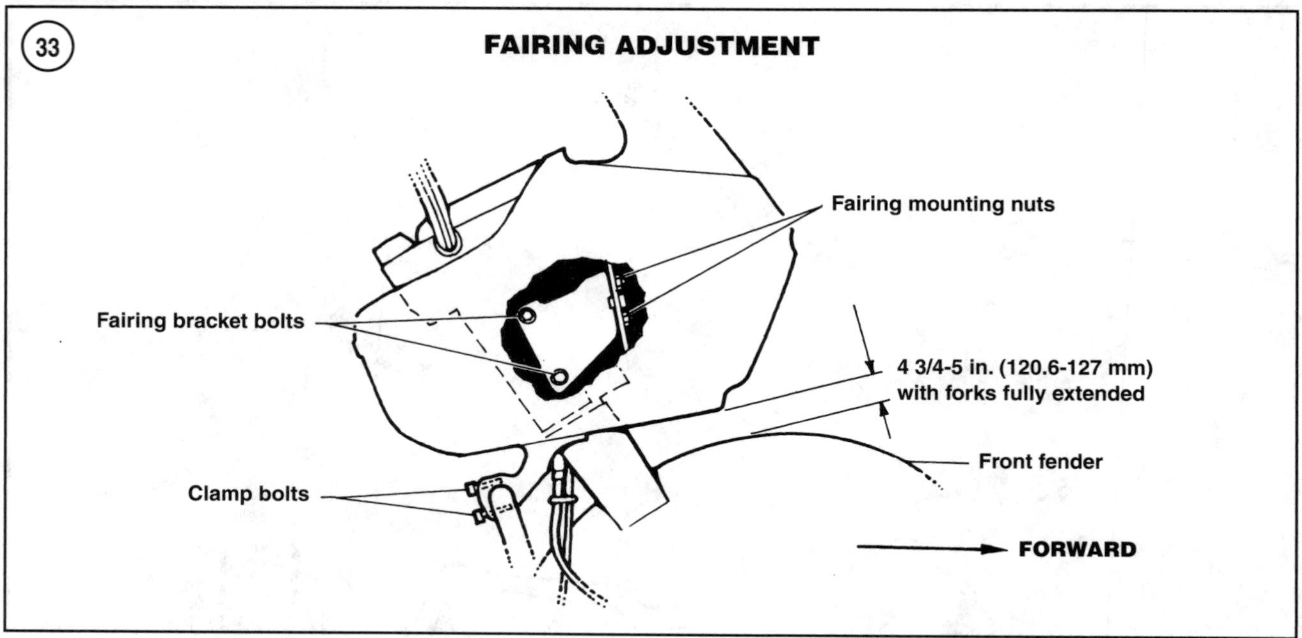

10. Install the center screw first. Then install the remaining screws in a crisscross pattern from left to right. After all screws are in place, tighten securely. Do not overtighten because the windshield might fracture.
11. Make sure that the front wheel is completely off the ground with the forks completely extended.

NOTE
All of the fairing mounting screws and bolts must be tightened prior to making the clearance inspection in Step 12.

12. Measure the distance between the bottom of the fairing and the top of the fender as shown in **Figure 33**. The specified clearance is 4 3/4-5 in. (120.6-127 mm). If the clearance is less than 4 3/4 in. (120.6 mm), perform the following:
   a. Loosen the firing mounting bolts within the headlight housing.
   b. Loosen the engine guard bracket screws approximately one turn.
   c. Have an assistant slowly lift the fairing until the specified clearance is correct.
   d. Hold the fairing in this position and tighten the bolts and screws securely.
   e. Recheck the clearance and adjust if necessary.

CAUTION
Maintain this specified clearance. If the clearance is less than specified, the front fender will contact the bottom of the fairing when the front fork bottom out. This will result in damage to both the fender and fairing.

13. Turn the front wheel completely from left to right and make sure that there is no interference with throttle cable routing between the instrument housing and fairing. Reposition the cable if necessary.
14. Slowly test-ride the motorcycle to make sure routing of the throttle and choke cables is correct.

Lower Fairing and Glove Boxes Removal/ Installation (FLTC-U and FLTC-UI Models)

1. Remove the screws securing the cap to the lower fairing and remove the cap. Do not lose the inner washer behind the cap.
2. Remove the locknuts from the clamp and the bracket.
3. Open the glove box door and remove the clamp from within the glove box.

4A. On early 1989 models, remove the glove box from the lower fairing as follows:
   a. Remove the screw, lockwasher and clamp securing the clutch cable to the left side lower fairing.
   b. Remove the screw, lockwasher and flat washer securing the left glove box. Then remove the glove box.

4B. On late 1989-1998 models, remove the glove box from the lower fairing as follows:

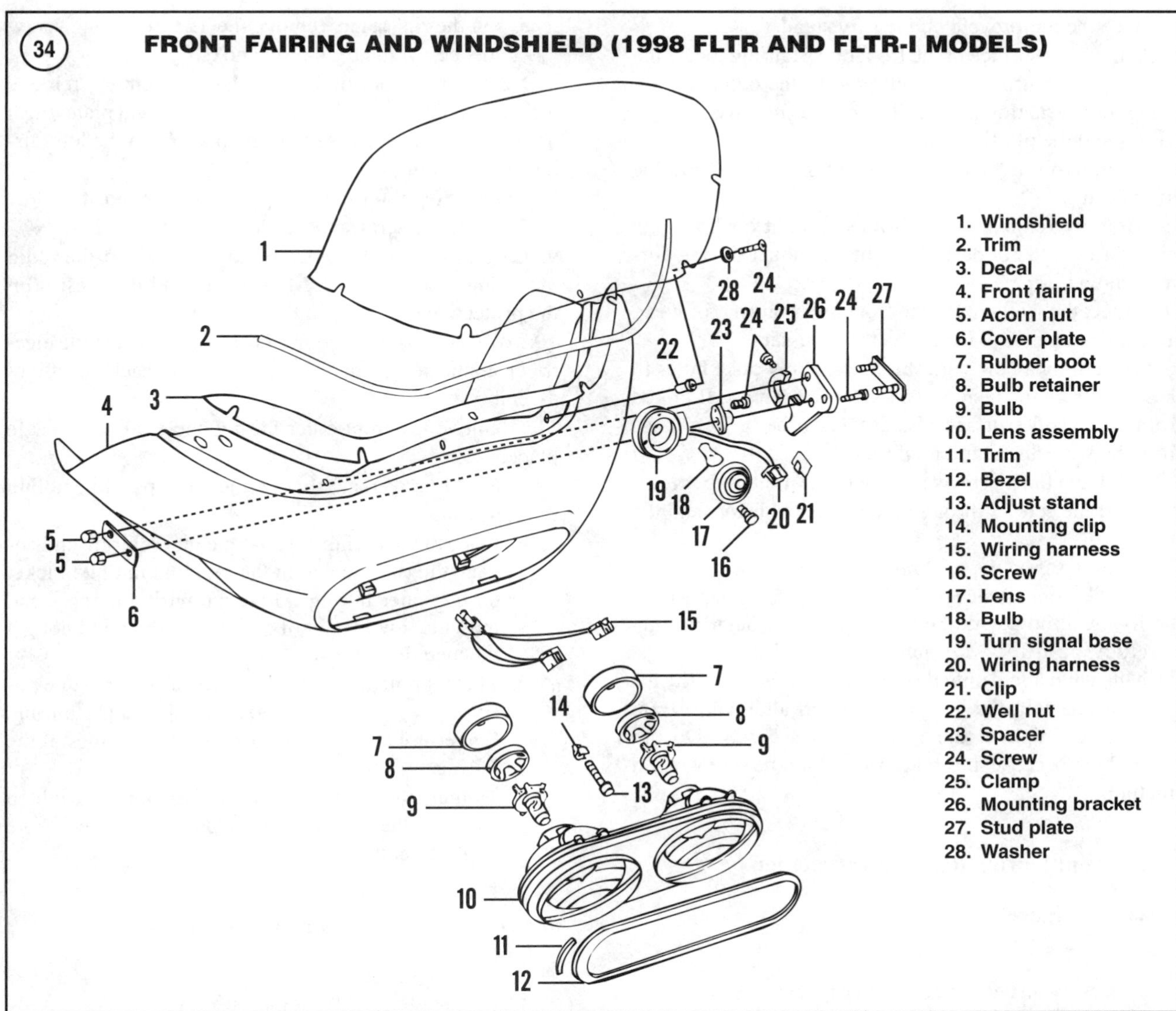

(34) **FRONT FAIRING AND WINDSHIELD (1998 FLTR AND FLTR-I MODELS)**

a. Remove the screws securing the lower cap to the left lower fairing. Remove the lower cap.

b. Remove the screw, lockwasher and clamp securing the clutch cable to the left lower fairing.

c. Working through the front of the lower fairing, remove the screws securing the left glove box to the lower fairing. Remove the glove box.

5. Remove the screw and washers securing the clamp to the base of the lower fairing.

6. Remove the lower fairing.

7. Remove the clamp from the engine guard if the lower fairing is not going to be reinstalled.

8. Repeat for the lower fairing on the other side if necessary.

9. Install by reversing these removal steps while noting the following:

a. Position the clamp on the engine guard so the flat tabs face the rear of the motorcycle.

b. Tighten the U-bolt nuts to 72 in.-lb. (8 N•m).

c. Tighten the engine guard clamp bolt and nut to 12 ft.-lb. (16 N•m).

WINDSHIELD AND FRONT FAIRING (1998 FLTR AND FLTR-I MODELS)

Windshield Only Removal/Installation

Refer to **Figure 34**.

1. Place the motorcycle on the jiffy stand.
2. At the front surface of the front outer fairing, locate the five screws securing the windshield to the outer fairing. Using an alternating pattern, loosen and remove the five screws and the plastic washers.
3. Carefully pull the windshield and trim away from the outer fairing.
4. Carefully remove the well-nuts straight out from the outer faring. Do not push them into the inner fairing during removal.
5. Inspect the well nuts in the front outer fairing for wear, cuts or damage. Replace as a set if necessary.
6. If installing a new windshield, carefully poke holes in the decal from the inside surface for the screws. If poked from the outside surface, the decal will be broken loose from the windshield and might tear.
7. Install the flat plastic washer onto the mounting screw.
8. Insert the screws through the windshield slots and the decal.
9. Partially screw the well nuts onto the screws.
10. At the front surface of the front outer fairing, position the five well nuts with the openings in the outer fairing. Carefully push the well nuts into the fairing openings. Push the windshield onto the outer fairing until it is flush.
11. Starting with the center screw and alternating from side to side, tighten the five screws securely. Do not overtighten because the area surrounding the screw might fracture.

Outer Front Fairing Removal/Installation

Refer to **Figure 34**.

NOTE
It is not necessary to remove the windshield when removing the outer fairing.

1. Place the motorcycle on the jiffy stand.
2. Remove the seat as described in this chapter.
3. Disconnect the negative battery cable from the battery.
4. Cover the front fender with towels or a blanket to protect the painted finish.
5. Remove the screws securing the outer fairing to the inner fairing in the following order:
   a. On the left side, remove the T25 Torx long screw just below the left glove box.
   b. On the left side, remove the screw at the edge of the fairing next to the left speaker.
   c. Loosen, but do not remove, the top left and right screws outboard of the fuel and volt gauges.
   d. On the right side, remove the screw at the edge of the fairing next to the right speaker.
   e. On the right side, remove the T25 Torx long screw just below the right glove box.
6. Next to the front turn signal lamp assembly, remove the two Acorn nuts and washers from the stud plate. Push on both studs and release the stud plate from the left fairing support.
7. Repeat Step 6 for the stud plate on the opposite side.
8. Remove the screws loosened in Step 5c.
9. Carefully raise the outer fairing up and off the radio mounting bracket hooks. Move it out and then rest it on the protective covering on the front fender.
10. Working inside the outer fairing, disconnect the electrical connector from the back side of each headlight assembly.
11. Remove the front outer fairing and store it in a safe place.
12. Install by reversing these removal steps while noting the following:
   a. Place the outer fairing onto the inner fairing and engage the two slots with the radio mounting bracket on the inner fairing. Move the wiring harness and individual wires out of the way so they will not get pinched during installation.
   b. The alignment tabs on the inner fairing must be positioned outboard of those on the outer fairing. Make sure this condition exists on both sides of the fairing.
   c. Tighten the screws securely. Do not overtighten because the plastic surrounding the screw hole might fracture.

Instrument Bezel Housing Removal/Installation

Refer to **Figure 35**.

1. Place the motorcycle on the jiffy stand.
2. Remove the seat as described in this chapter.
3. Disconnect the battery negative cable from the battery.
4. On the lower right side of the housing, unscrew the rubber boot and remove the odometer reset switch from the housing.
5. Remove the instruments and bezel as described in Chapter Nine.
6. Remove the throttle cable clip for the hole on the upper right housing.
7. Remove the ignition switch knob, nut, collar and washer as described in Chapter Nine.
8. Disconnect the speaker switch from the wiring harness.
9. Remove the two T40 Torx bolts and washers securing the left housing to the fork assembly. Carefully remove the left housing from the frame and store it in a safe place.

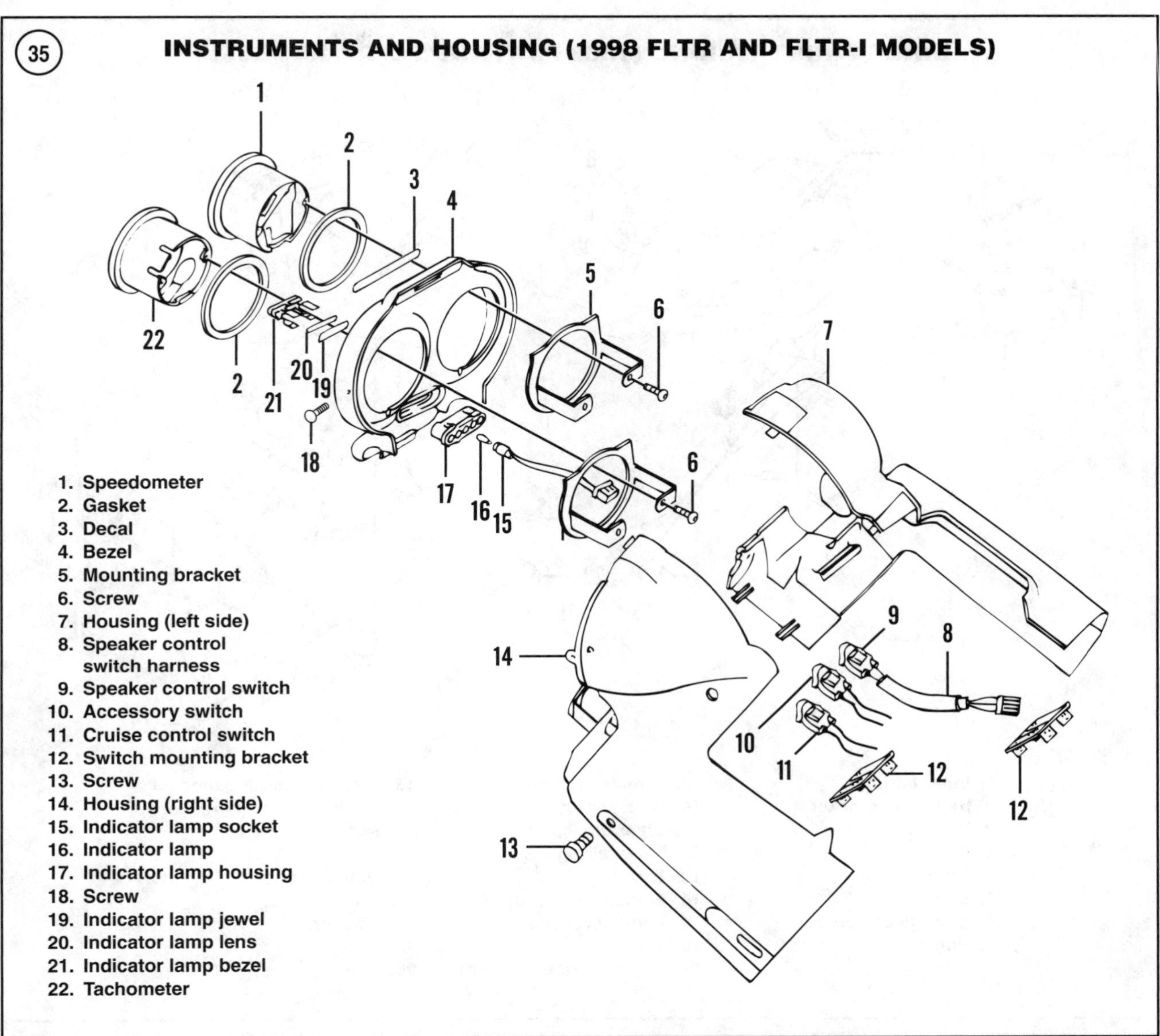

10. Remove the outer front fairing as described in this chapter.

11. Carefully pull the electrical wire bundles and conduit from the funnel of the fairing bracket and allow them to hang down. If necessary, cut the cable strap securing the interconnect harness to the front corners of the radio mounting bracket.

12. At the front portion of the bezel housing, disconnect the ten-pin electrical connector for the indicator lamps and the 12-pin electrical connector for the instrument nacelle.

13. Remove two T40 Torx bolts and washers securing the right housing to the front fork.

14. Pull the free end of the jumper cable harness through the tunnel of the fairing bracket and remove the right housing from the frame. Store it in a safe place.

15. Install by reversing these removal steps.

Inner Front Fairing Removal/Installation

Refer to **Figure 36**.

1. Place the motorcycle on the jiffy stand.
2. Remove the seat as described in this chapter.
3. Disconnect the negative battery cable from the battery.
4. Cover the front fender with towels or a blanket to protect the painted finish.

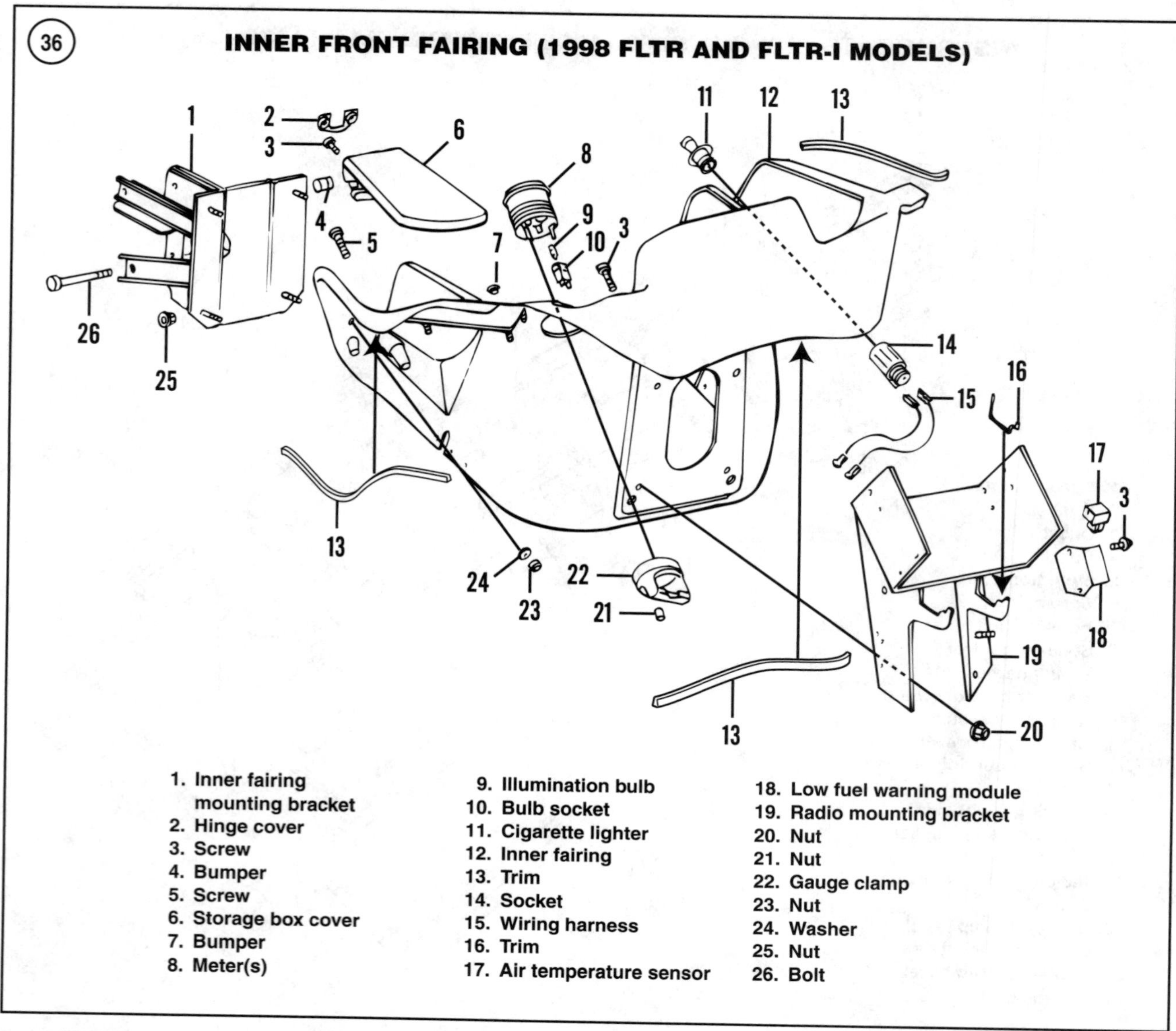

5. Remove the instrument bezel housing as previously described in this section.

6. Remove the outer front fairing as previously described in this section.

NOTE

Due to the number of electrical connectors to be disconnected in the following steps, be sure to identify each mating half of the connectors to assist during installation.

7. Disconnect the main harness from the interconnect harness electrical connectors as follows:

a. The interconnect black 12-pin Deutsch electrical connector below the radio on the right side.

b. The main-to-interconnect harness gray 12-pin Deutsch electrical connector secured to the T-stud on the radio right side bracket.

c. The main power black 2-pin Packard electrical connector on the back left side of the radio.

d. The radio antenna cable connector on the left side of radio.

8. Disconnect the black 4-pin Packard ignition switch connector from the main harness at the inside surface of the left fairing bracket.

9. On FLHTC-UI Ultra models, disconnect the black 12-pin Deutsch overlay harness from the interconnect harness secured to the T-stud on the radio left side bracket.

10. Disconnect the handlebar switch controls and radio ground from the interconnect harness as follows:
   a. The gray 12-pin Deutsch left handlebar switch electrical connector secured to the T-stud on the radio left side bracket.
   b. The black 12-pin Deutsch right handlebar switch electrical connector secured to the T-stud on the radio right side bracket.
   c. The front turn signal 6-pin connector below the right side of the radio.
   d. The radio ground single spade and socket terminal.
11. Double check to make sure all electrical connectors have been disconnected.
12. Unhook the turn signal conduit from the flexible clips on both sides of the inner fairing. Carefully pull the conduit down to free it from the slots at the bottom of the inner fairing.
13. Release the jumper harness, main harness, FLHTC-UI Ultra models overlay harness and handlebar switch control conduit from the interconnect harness. Carefully cut and remove any cable straps if necessary.
14. Carefully pull all of the disconnected harnesses and electrical connectors forward and away from the front opening in the inner fairing. Wrap the harness bundle tightly with shop cloths and secure them with tape or string. This bundle of wires must pass through the front opening in the inner fairing.
15. Hold the front inner fairing and remove the four locknuts securing the front inner fairing and radio mounting bracket to the fairing mounting bracket. Remove the front inner fairing and radio mounting bracket from the frame. Store it in a safe place.
16. Install by reversing these removal steps. Correctly reconnect all electrical connectors.

TOUR-PAK (FLH AND FLT SERIES MODELS)

Removal/Installation

Refer to **Figure 37**.

1. Place the motorcycle on the jiffy stand.
2. Remove the seat as described in this chapter.
3. Disconnect the negative battery cable from the battery.
4. Remove both saddlebags as described in this chapter.
5. Open the cover and remove the rubber mat. Leave the cover open for the remainder of this procedure.
6. On FLHTC-U models, perform the following:
   a. Open the map pocket and remove the Acorn nuts and flat washers securing the molded inner liner to the lower case. Remove the molded liner.
   b. Depress the latch, rotate the housing, and release the bulb socket from the left side of the lower case.
7. Rotate the knurled locking ring *counterclockwise* and disconnect the radio antenna cable connector. Release the cable from the two clips at the base of the lower case.
8. Pull the grommet into the lower case and remove it from the wire harness.
9. On FLHTC-U models, separate the 3-pin electrical connector for the Tour-Pak light harness. Pull the grommet into the lower case and remove it from the wire harness.
10. Feed the wire harness down and through the opening in the base of the lower case.
11. On FLHTC-U models, perform the following:
   a. Release the headrest receptacle from the bottom of the left speaker box.
   b. Release the wire harness from the clamp at the front corner of the lower case.
   c. On the right side, disconnect the CB antenna cable connector and release the cable from the two clips on the bottom of the lower case. Disconnect the cable connector.
   d. Feed the CB antenna down and through the opening in the bottom of the lower case.
   e. Remove the T40 mounting bolt at the front right corner and release the ground wire ring terminal from the rear passenger controls.
   f. Pull the right side grommet surrounding the CB antenna cable into the lower case and remove it from the cable.
   g. Feed the CB antenna cable and ground wire through the opening in the lower case.

NOTE

The Tour-Pak is adjustable fore and aft to adjust the passenger backrest position. Prior to removing the bolts and nuts, note the present bolt locations within the luggage rack to ensure original installation locations.

12. Have an assistant hold the Tour-Pak during bolt and nut removal. With the cover open, the Tour-Pak is top heavy on the left side.
13. Secure the locknut below each mounting bolt and remove the bolts and nuts securing the lower Tour-Pak case to the luggage rack.
14. Lift the Tour-Pak off the luggage rack and release the cable from the clamp at the front corner of the lower case. Remove the Tour-Pak from the luggage rack.
15. Remove the spacers from the luggage rack and place them in a plastic bag.
16. Install by reversing these removal steps. Securely tighten the bolts and nuts.

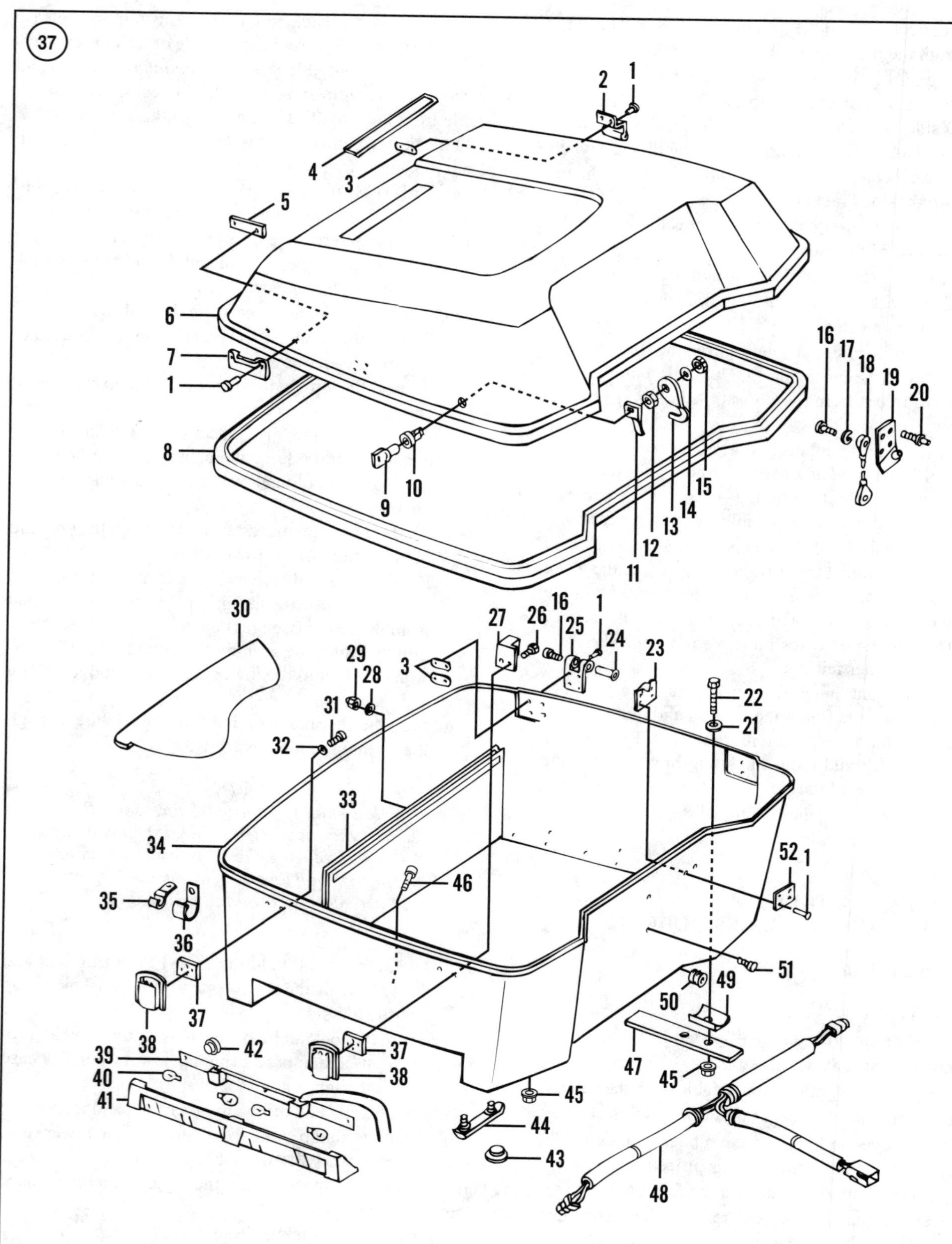
37
2
1
4
3
5
6
7
1
8
9
10
11
12
13
14
15
16
17
18
19
20
30
27
26
16
1
25
24
23
3
29
28
31
32
22
21
33
34
52
1
35
46
36
51
37
49
50
38
47
39
42
37
40
38
45
41
45
44
43
48

TOUR-PAK (FLH AND FLT SERIES MODELS)

1. Rivet
2. Hinge
3. Back plate
4. Nameplate
5. Back plate
6. Cover
7. Upper catch
8. Gasket
9. Key
10. Lock
11. Lock guide
12. Nut
13. Cam hook
14. Lockwasher
15. Nut
16. Screw
17. Spring washer
18. Cable brace
19. Bracket
20. Nylon rivet
21. Washer
22. Screw
23. Bracket
24. Hinge pin
25. Hinge
26. Screw
27. Lower catch
28. Washer
29. Nut
30. Rubber mat
31. Screw
32. Washer
33. Pouch
34. Lower case
35. Antenna cable clip
36. Clamp
37. Spacer
38. Catch body
39. Mounting bracket
40. Bulb
41. Side marker lens
42. Eyelet
43. Grommet
44. Bumper
45. Nut
46. Screw
47. Gasket
48. Wiring harness
49. Spacer
50. Grommet
51. Screw
52. Back plate

Passenger Backrest Removal/Installation

1. Remove the seat as described in this chapter.
2. Open the Tour-Pak cover.
3. Remove the locknuts, back plates and cushion plates securing the backrest to the Tour-Pak.
4. Move the backrest forward and remove it.
5. Install by reversing these removal steps. Tighten the locknuts securely.

SADDLEBAGS AND GUARDS

Removal/Installation

FXRS-Con models

Refer to **Figure 38**.

1. Place the motorcycle on the jiffy stand.
2. Pull the saddlebag handle out from under the fender brace.
3. Secure the saddlebag. Then remove the knobbed screws securing the saddlebag to the fender brace mounting sockets. The well nuts will remain on the knobbed screws after removal.
4. Install the knobbed screws into the fender brace or insert the caps into the frame mounting sockets.
5. Install by reversing these removal steps. Tuck the saddlebag handles under the fender brace. Then install the knobbed screws.

WARNING

The saddlebag handles are not designed as passenger grab handles. Do not allow a passenger to grab the handles because they will break off. Be sure to tuck the handles under the fender brace.

FXRT and FXRD models

Refer to **Figure 39**.

1. Place the motorcycle on the jiffy stand.
2. Unlock the outer cover and hinge it down.
3. Remove the bolts, washers, lockwashers and nuts securing the saddlebag to the support bracket. Remove the saddlebag.
4. Install by reversing these removal steps while noting the following:
   a. Position the rubber washers so they seat next to the saddlebag surface. Install the bolts, washers, lockwashers and nuts.
   b. Tighten all bolts finger-tight. Then tighten securely.

15

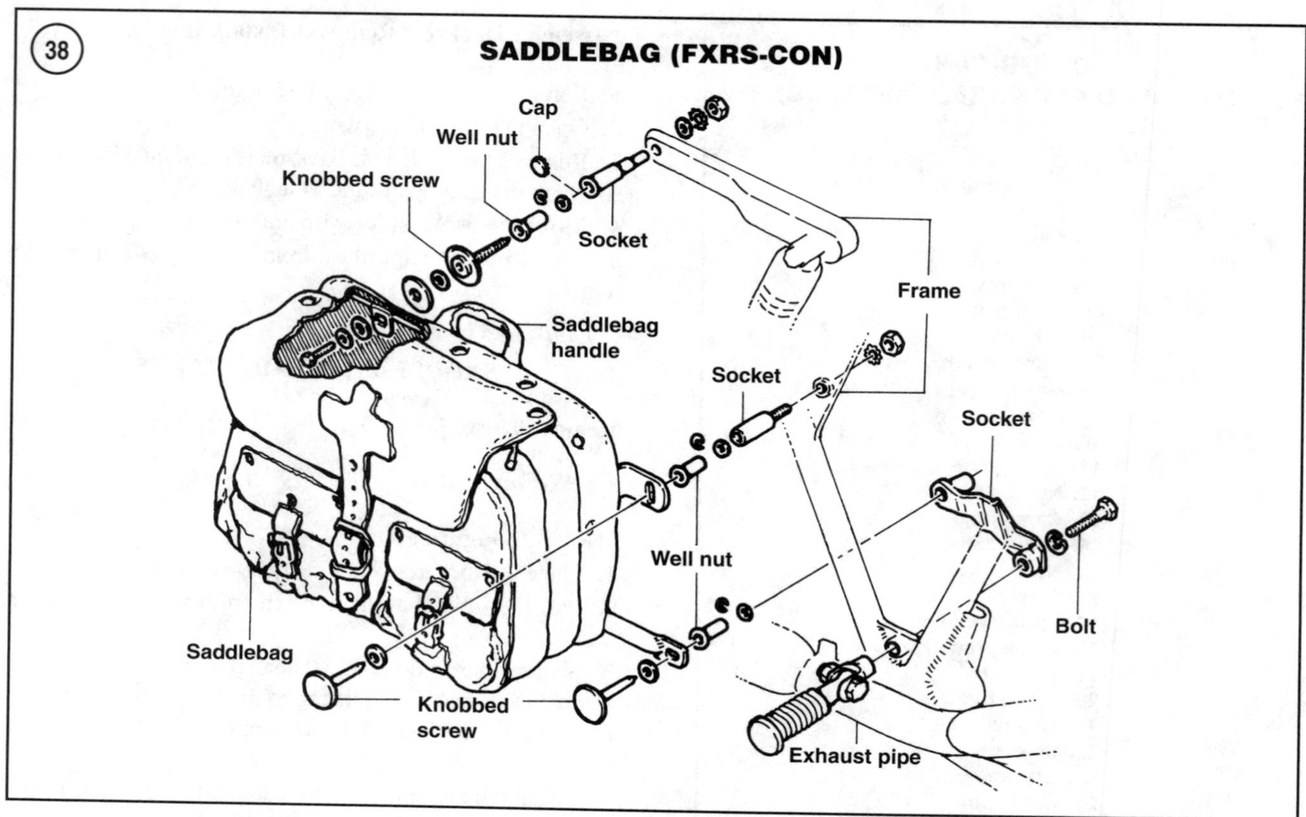

FLH and FLT series models

Refer to **Figures 40-42**.

1. Place the motorcycle on the jiffy stand.

2A. On 1984-1992 models, unlock the cover and remove it from the saddlebag.

2B. On 1999 FLHRC-I models, perform the following:

   a. Lift the decorative buckle, press in on the tabs, and release the catch from the receptacle.
   b. Rotate the hinge on the outboard side of the saddlebag and open the lid.

2C. On all other models, perform the following:

   a. Unlock the handle latch.
   b. Pull on the bottom of the latch (**Figure 43**) and open the lid.

3. Within the saddlebag case, grasp the latch bail wire (**Figure 44**), rotate the latch stud one-quarter turn counterclockwise, and release the stud from the mounting bracket (**Figure 45**).

4. Repeat for the other latch stud.

5. Carefully pull the saddlebag up and out of the bracket or guards.

6. Inspect the latch mounting brackets (**Figure 46**) for damage.

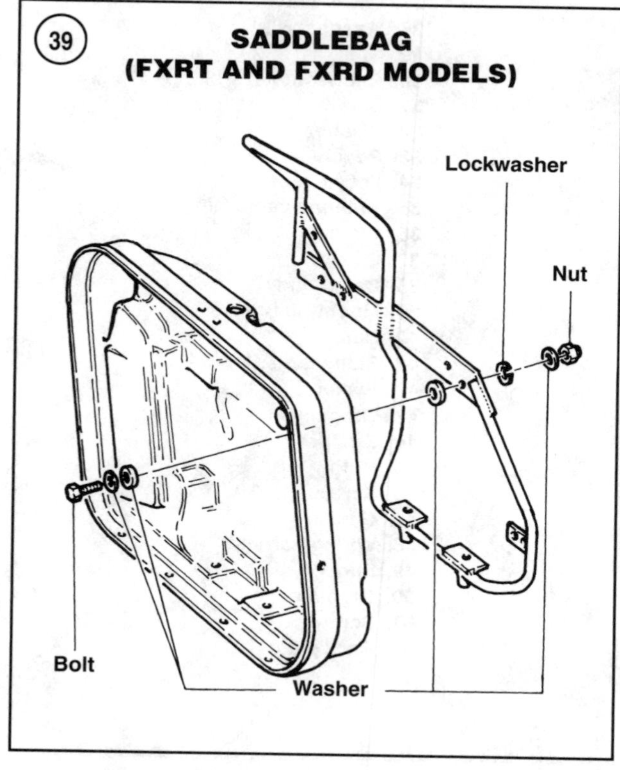

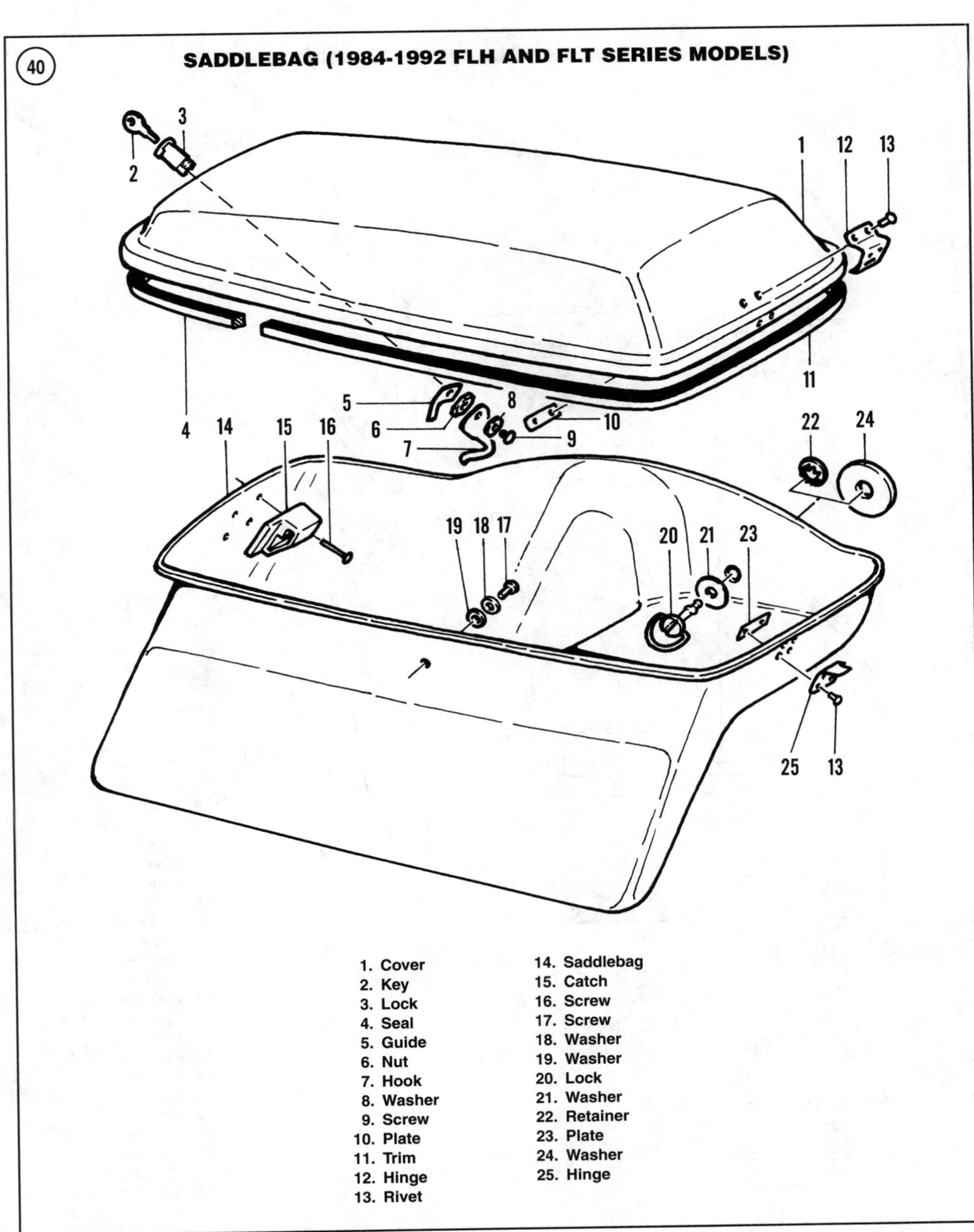
40
SADDLEBAG (1984-1992 FLH AND FLT SERIES MODELS)
1
2
3
4
5
6
7
8
9
10
11
12
13
14
15
16
17
18
19
20
21
22
23
24
25
13
1. Cover
2. Key
3. Lock
4. Seal
5. Guide
6. Nut
7. Hook
8. Washer
9. Screw
10. Plate
11. Trim
12. Hinge
13. Rivet
14. Saddlebag
15. Catch
16. Screw
17. Screw
18. Washer
19. Washer
20. Lock
21. Washer
22. Retainer
23. Plate
24. Washer
25. Hinge

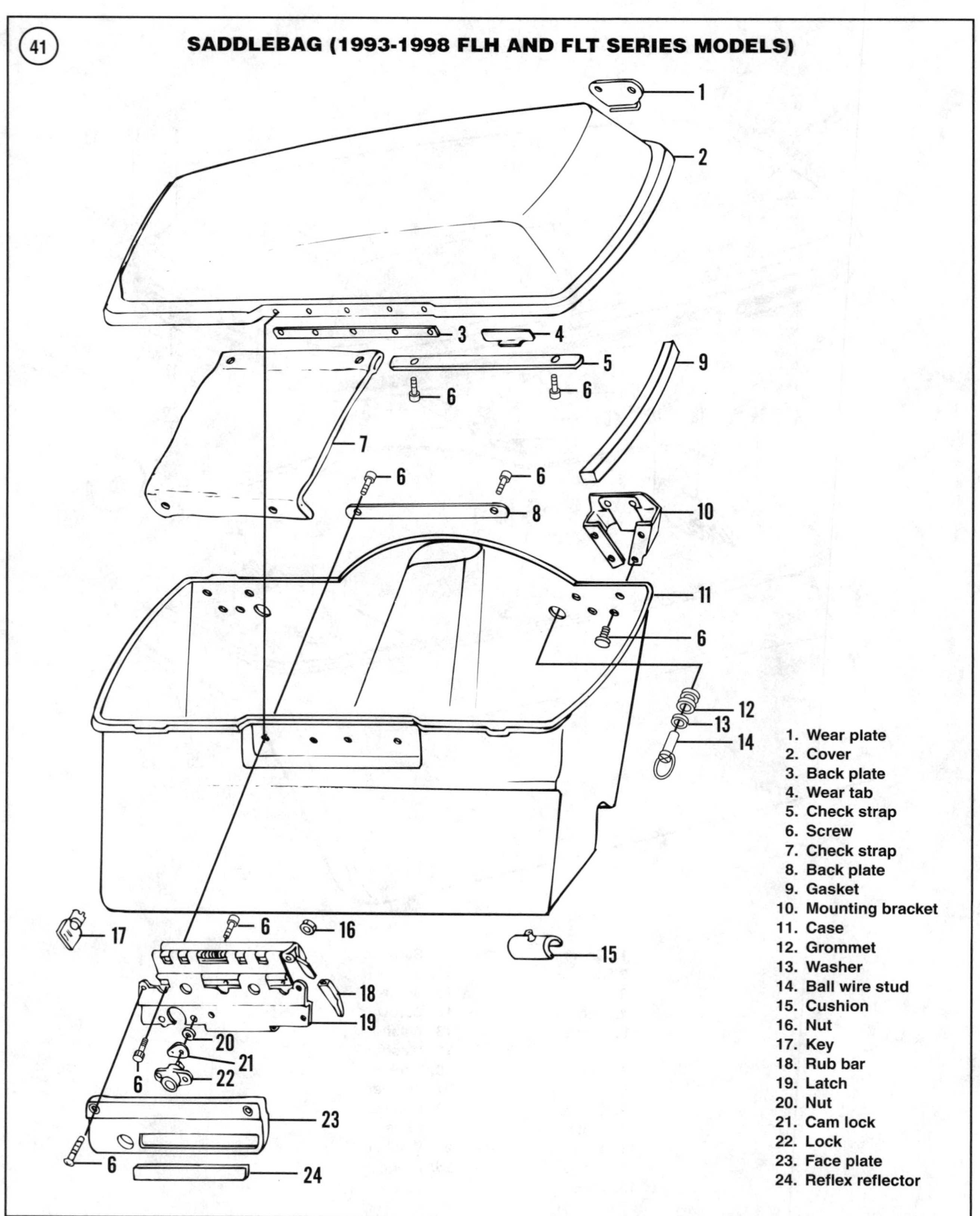
41
SADDLEBAG (1993-1998 FLH AND FLT SERIES MODELS)
1
2
3
4
5
6
7
8
9
10
11
12
13
14
15
16
17
18
19
20
21
22
23
24
1. Wear plate
2. Cover
3. Back plate
4. Wear tab
5. Check strap
6. Screw
7. Check strap
8. Back plate
9. Gasket
10. Mounting bracket
11. Case
12. Grommet
13. Washer
14. Ball wire stud
15. Cushion
16. Nut
17. Key
18. Rub bar
19. Latch
20. Nut
21. Cam lock
22. Lock
23. Face plate
24. Reflex reflector

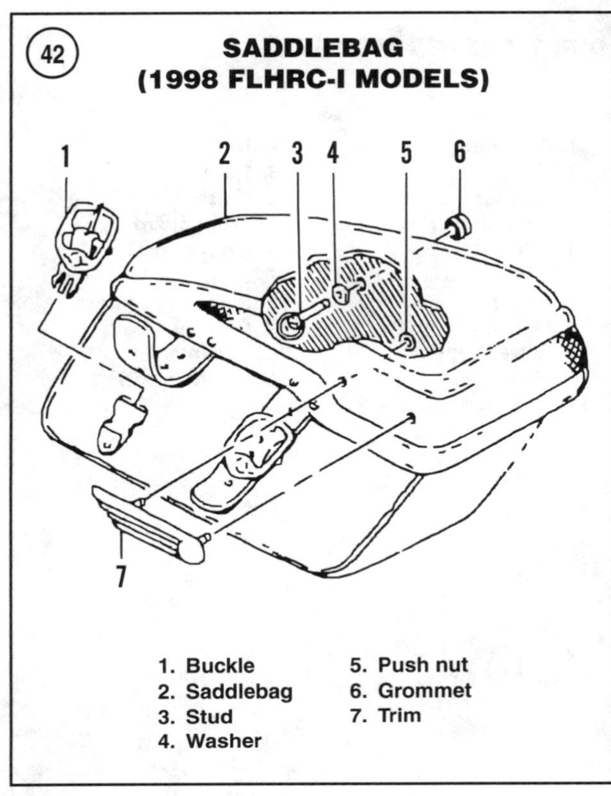

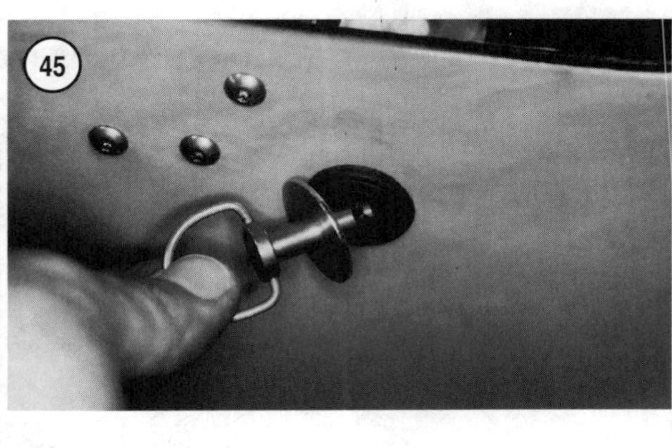

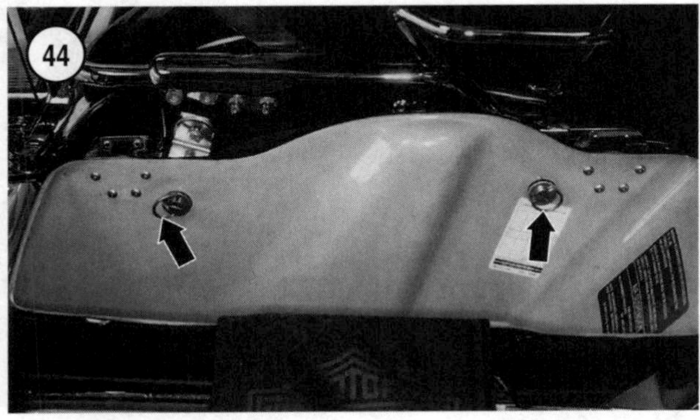

7. Install by reversing these removal steps. Make sure the saddlebag is locked in place.

Saddlebag Guards Removal/Installation

Refer to **Figure 47**.

1. Place the motorcycle on level ground on the jiffy stand.
2. Remove the saddlebag as described in this section.
3. Remove the front lower bolt and locknut securing the front guard to the frame bracket.
4. Remove the bolts and lockwashers (A, **Figure 48**) securing the muffler to the lower support. Remove the support bracket and rubber cushion.
5. Remove one of the bolts (B, **Figure 48**) securing the rear support bracket to the frame bracket. Loosen the other one at this time but leave it in place.
6. Hold the saddlebag support and remove the front upper bolt (**Figure 49**) securing the front guard to the frame.
7. Remove the saddlebag guard assembly (**Figure 50**) from the frame.
8. Support the rear of the muffler to the frame with a bungee cord or rope.
9. Install by reversing these removal steps. Securely tighten all bolts and nuts.

47 SADDLEBAG GUARDS (FLH AND FLT SERIES MODELS)

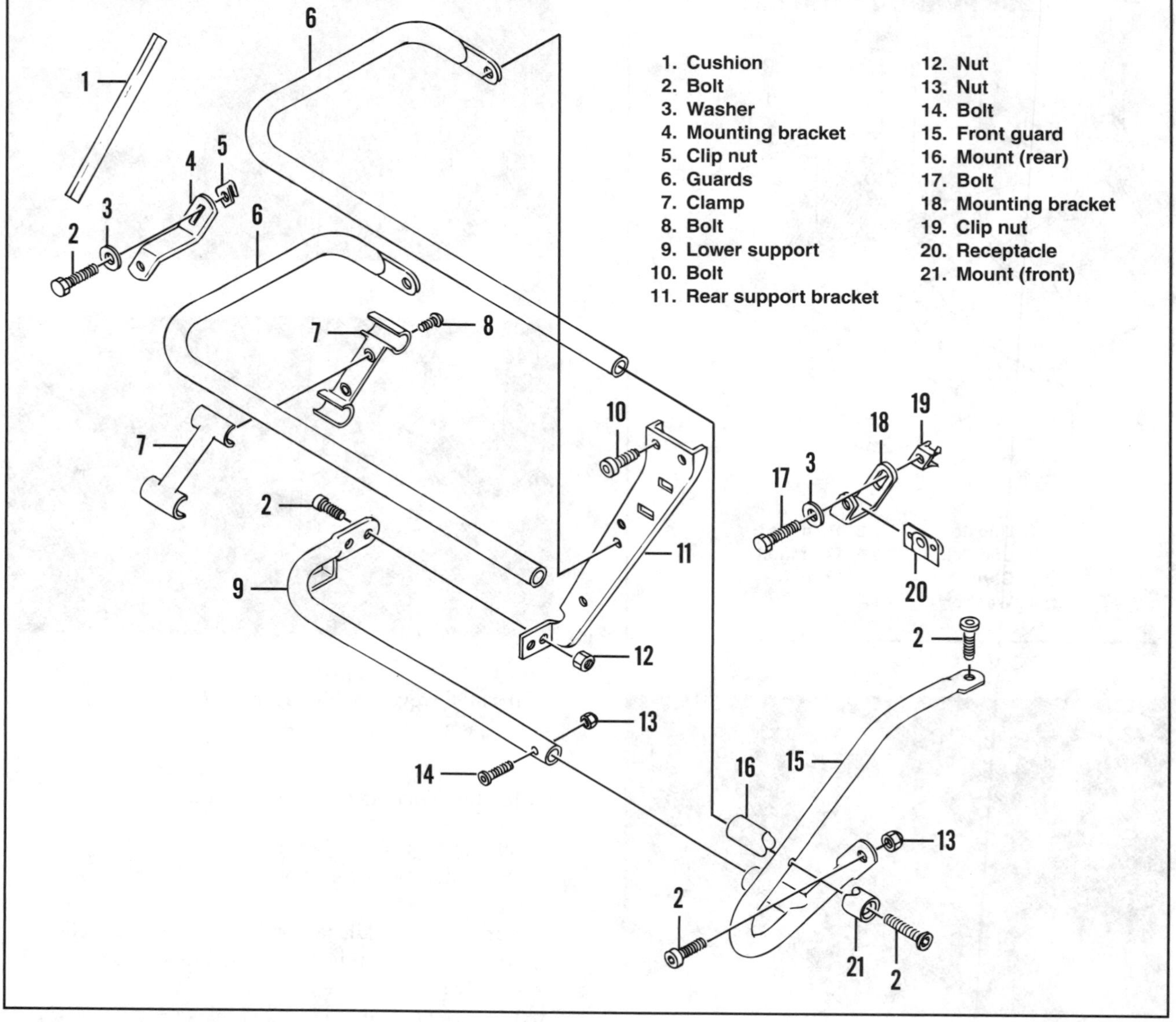

1. Cushion
2. Bolt
3. Washer
4. Mounting bracket
5. Clip nut
6. Guards
7. Clamp
8. Bolt
9. Lower support
10. Bolt
11. Rear support bracket
12. Nut
13. Nut
14. Bolt
15. Front guard
16. Mount (rear)
17. Bolt
18. Mounting bracket
19. Clip nut
20. Receptacle
21. Mount (front)

FOOTBOARDS (FLH AND FLT SERIES MODELS)

Driver Footboard Removal/Installation

Refer to **Figure 51**.

1. Place the motorcycle on the jiffy stand.

2A. On the right side, perform the following:

a. Working on the inner side of the frame side rail, loosen and remove the Allen bolt, lockwasher and washer securing the front mounting bracket to the frame.

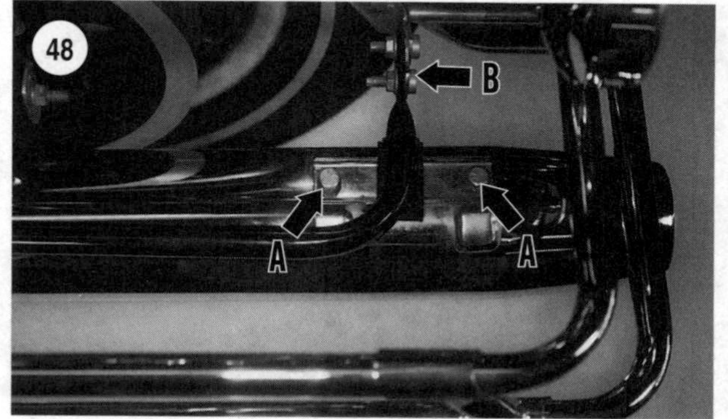

51

FOOTBOARDS (FLH AND FLT SERIES MODELS)

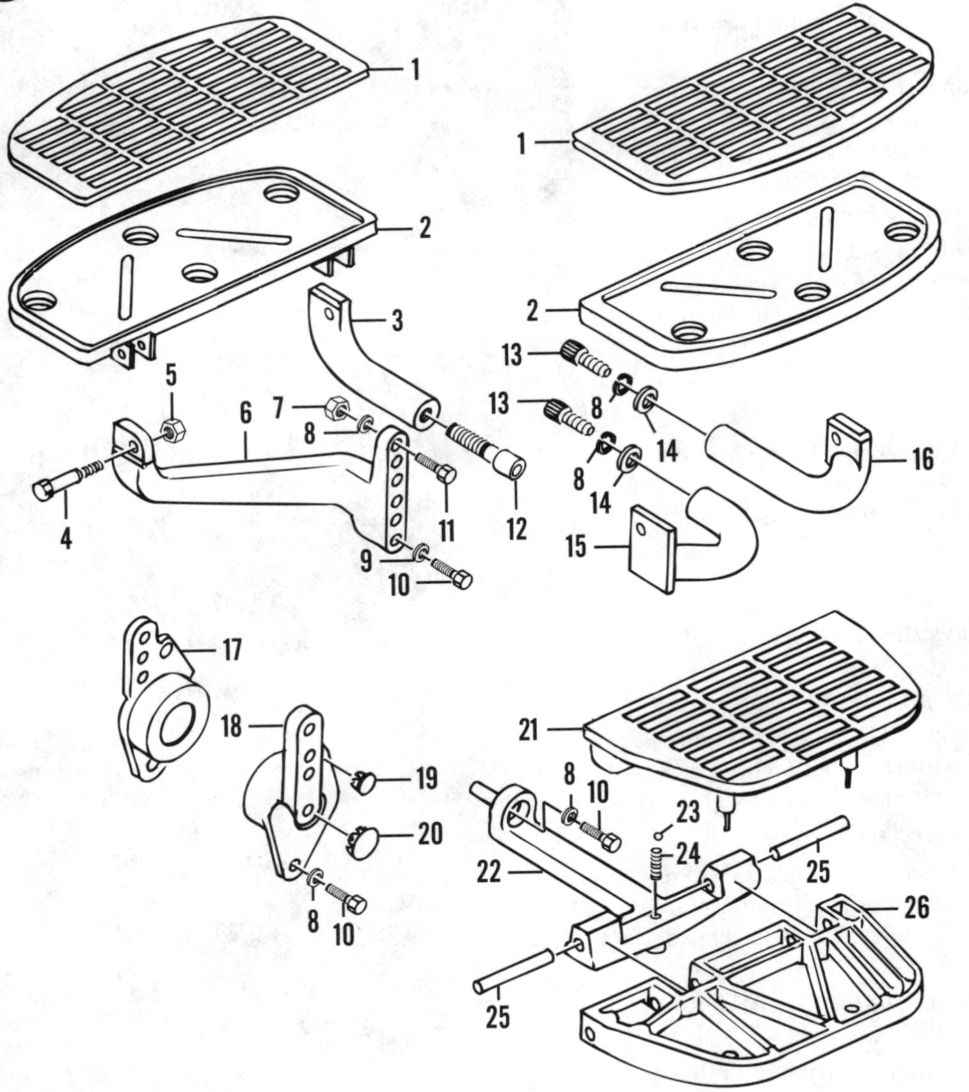

1. Driver rubber mat
2. Driver footboard
3. Front bracket (left side)
4. Pivot bolt
5. Nut
6. Rear bracket (left side)
7. Nut
8. Lockwasher
9. Lockwasher
10. Hex bolt
11. Hex bolt
12. Allen bolt
13. Allen bolt
14. Washer
15. Rear mounting bracket (right side)
16. Front mounting bracket (right side)
17. Bracket (left side)
18. Bracket (right side)
19. Plug
20. Plug
21. Passenger rubber pad*
22. Mounting bracket*
23. Steel ball*
24. Spring*
25. Pivot pin*
26. Passenger footboard*

*Items shown are for right side. Left side is identical.

15

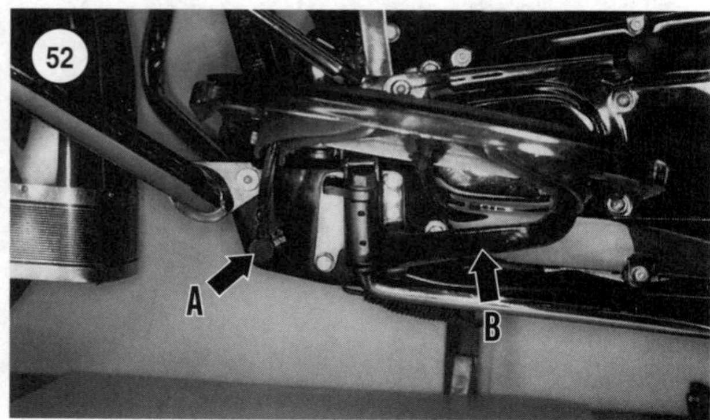

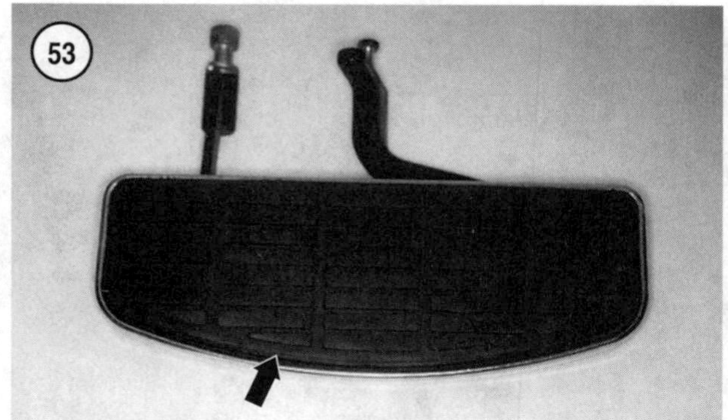

b. Working on the inner side of the frame side rail, loosen and remove the upper hex bolt, lockwasher and washer as well as the lower hex bolt and lockwasher securing the rear mounting bracket to the frame.

2B. On the left side, working on the inner side of the frame side rail, loosen and remove the Allen bolts, lockwashers and washers securing the front (A, **Figure 52**) and rear mounting brackets (B) to the frame.

3. Remove the footboard assembly from the frame.

4. If necessary, remove the rubber pad (**Figure 53**) from the footboard and install a new one. Push the locating pins all the way through the footboard to secure the rubber pad in place.

5. Inspect the pivot bolts and nuts for looseness. Replace if necessary.

6. Inspect the footboard and the mounting brackets for damage and fractures. Replace as necessary.

7. Install the footboard onto the frame and securely tighten the Allen and hex bolts.

Passenger Footboard Removal/Installation

1. Place the motorcycle on the jiffy stand.

2. Remove the upper Allen bolt and lockwasher (**Figure 54**) and the lower hex bolt and lockwasher securing the passenger footpeg to the frame. Remove the footpeg.

3. Repeat for the other side if necessary.

4. If necessary, remove the rubber pad (**Figure 55**) from the footboard and install a new one. Push the locating pins all the way through the footboard to secure the rubber pad in place.

5. Inspect the pivot pins (**Figure 56**) for looseness. Replace if necessary.

6. Install the footboard onto the frame and tighten the hex bolt securely.

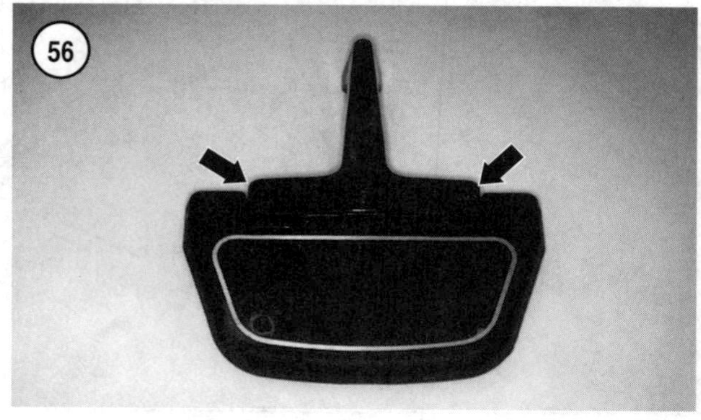

Table 1 BODY TORQUE SPECIFICATIONS

Item	in.-lb.	ft.-lb.	N•m
Engine guard clamp bolt and nut	142	–	16
Fairing mounting bolts (1984-1992 FXRT and FXRD)			
1/4 in. bolts	97	–	11
5/16 in. bolts	–	19	26
Fairing brace bolts	124	–	14
Lower fairing U-bolt nuts	71	–	8
Outer fairing mounting bolts	142-168	–	16-19
Passenger footpegs	–	20-25	27-34
Radio mounting bracket screws	48-71	–	5-8

Index

D

E

F

G

H

I

K

L

M

N

O

P

R

S

T

NOTES

Wiring Diagrams

1984-1985 FLHTC MODELS

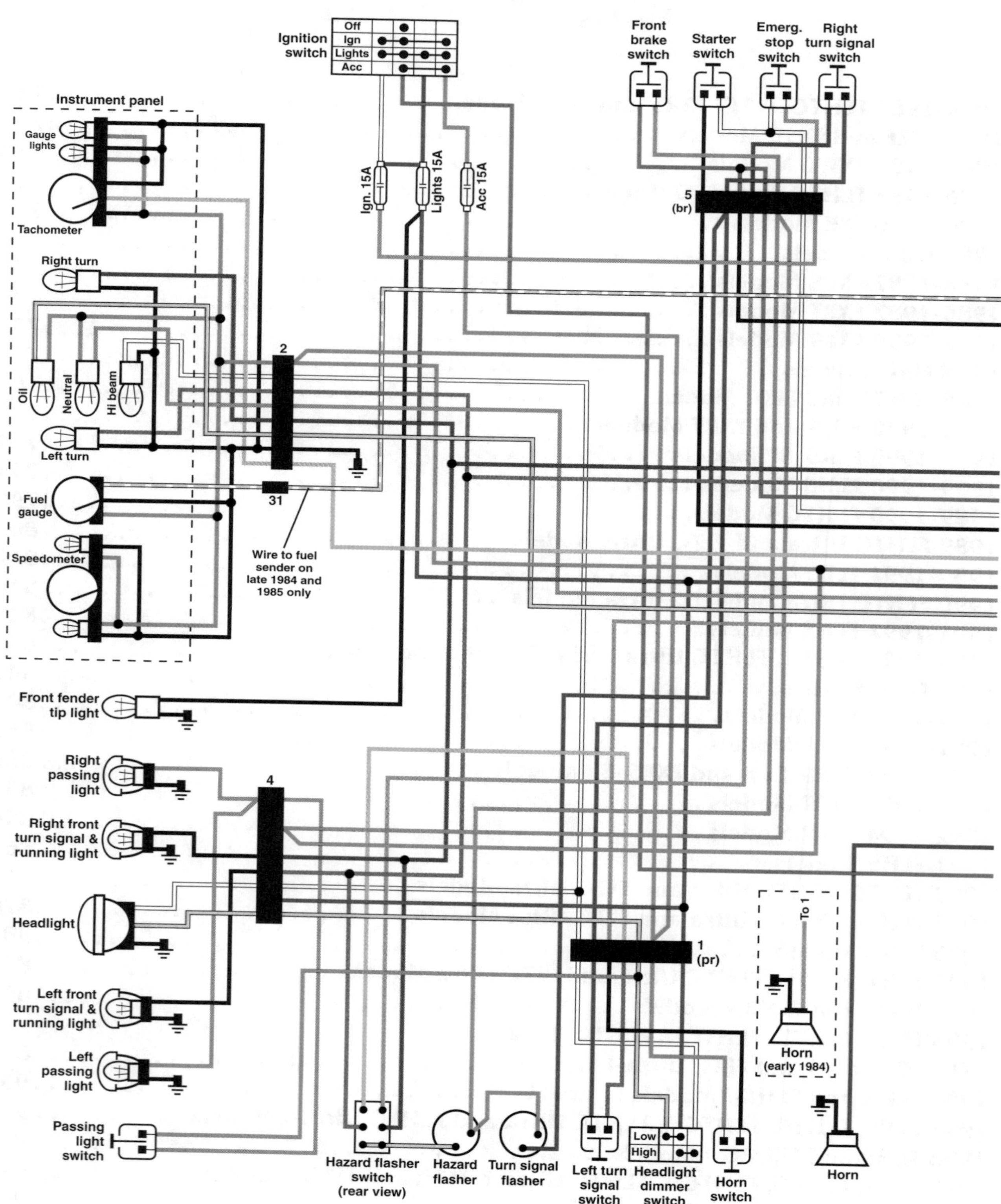

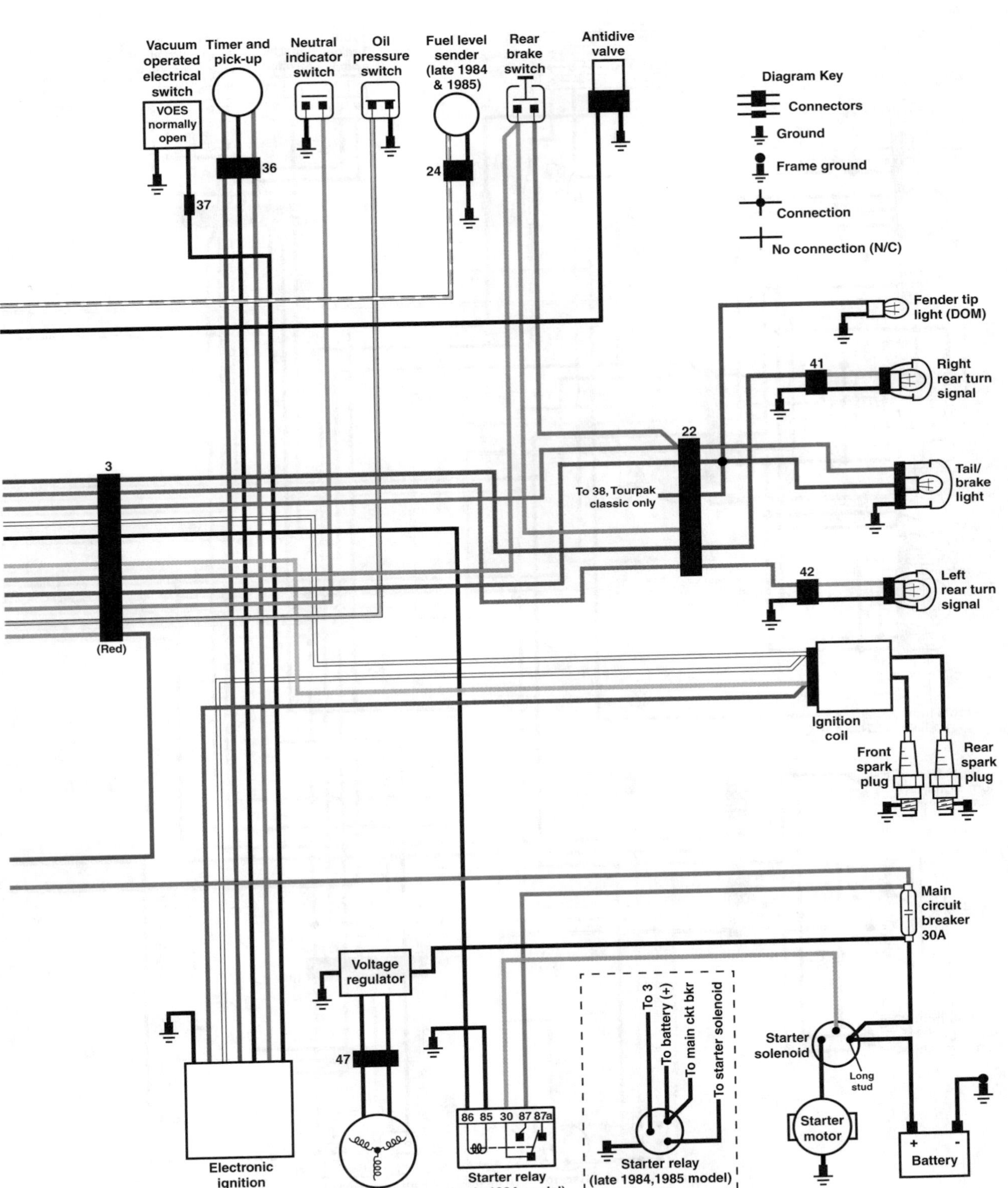
Vacuum operated electrical switch
VOES normally open
Timer and pick-up
Neutral indicator switch
Oil pressure switch
Fuel level sender (late 1984 & 1985)
Rear brake switch
Antidive valve
Diagram Key
Connectors
Ground
Frame ground
Connection
No connection (N/C)
36
37
24
3
(Red)
22
To 38, Tourpak classic only
41
42
Fender tip light (DOM)
Right rear turn signal
Tail/ brake light
Left rear turn signal
Ignition coil
Front spark plug
Rear spark plug
Main circuit breaker 30A
Voltage regulator
47
Electronic ignition module
Stator
86 85 30 87 87a
Starter relay (early 1984 model)
To 3
To battery (+)
To main ckt bkr
To starter solenoid
Starter relay (late 1984,1985 model)
Starter solenoid
Long stud
Starter motor
Battery

1984-1985 FLTC MODELS

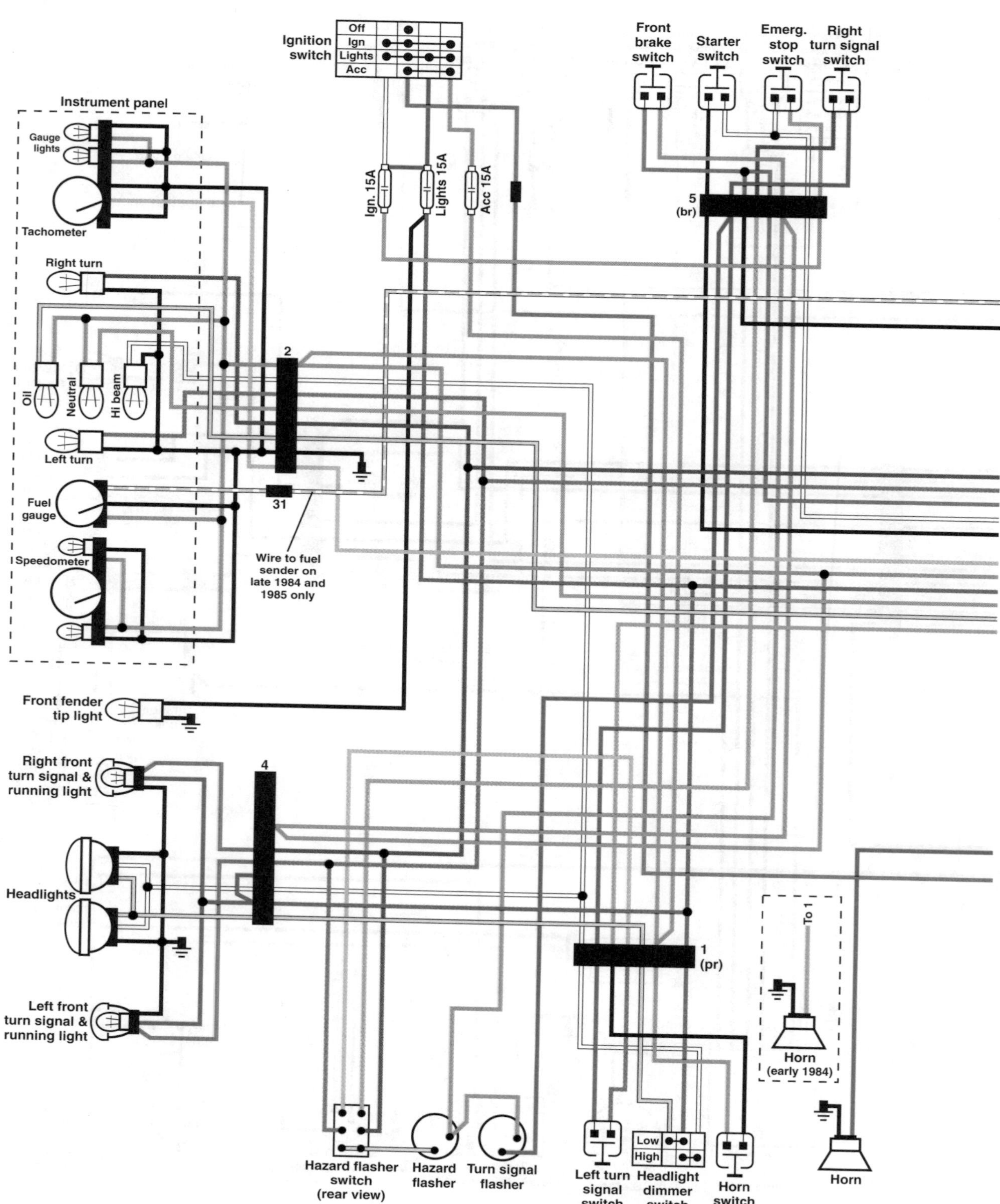

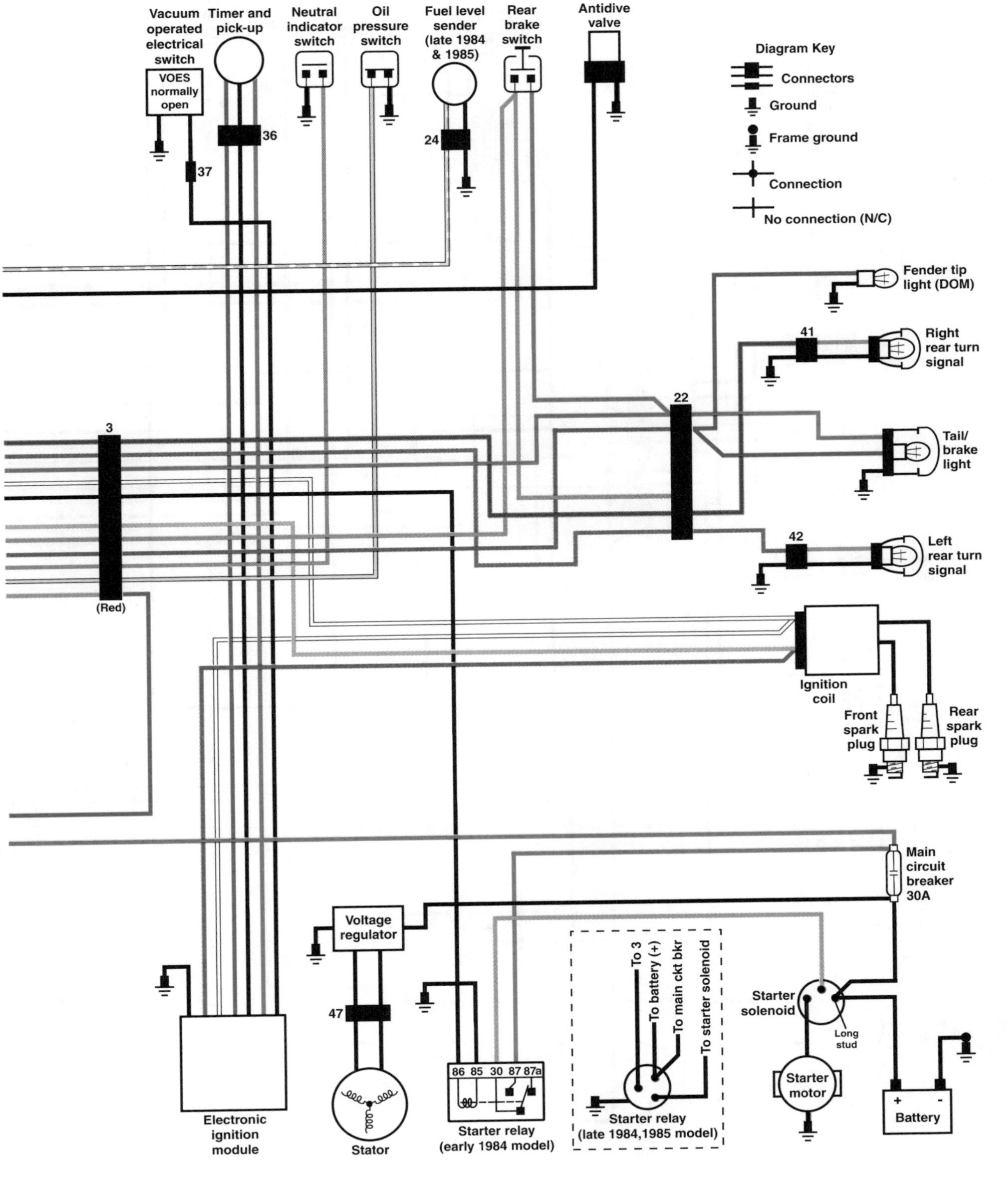

Vacuum operated electrical switch
VOES normally open
Timer and pick-up
Neutral indicator switch
Oil pressure switch
Fuel level sender (late 1984 & 1985)
Rear brake switch
Antidive valve
36
37
24

Diagram Key
Connectors
Ground
Frame ground
Connection
No connection (N/C)

Fender tip light (DOM)
41
Right rear turn signal
22
Tail/ brake light
3
42
Left rear turn signal
(Red)
Ignition coil
Front spark plug
Rear spark plug

Main circuit breaker 30A
Voltage regulator
47
To 3
To battery (+)
To main ckt bkr
To starter solenoid
Starter solenoid
Long stud
Starter motor
Battery
86 85 30 87 87a
Electronic ignition module
Stator
Starter relay (early 1984 model)
Starter relay (late 1984,1985 model)

1984-1985 FXRS MODELS

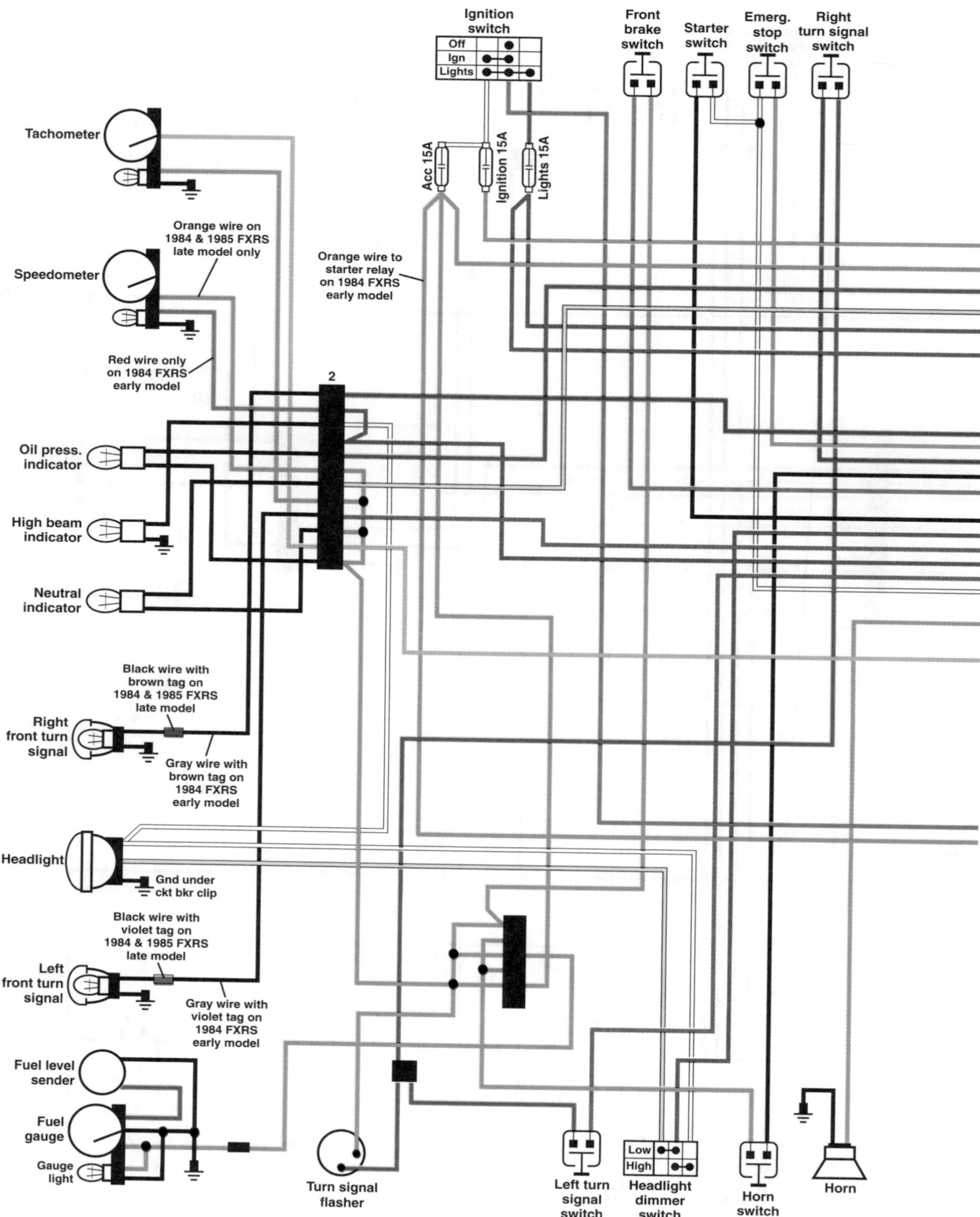

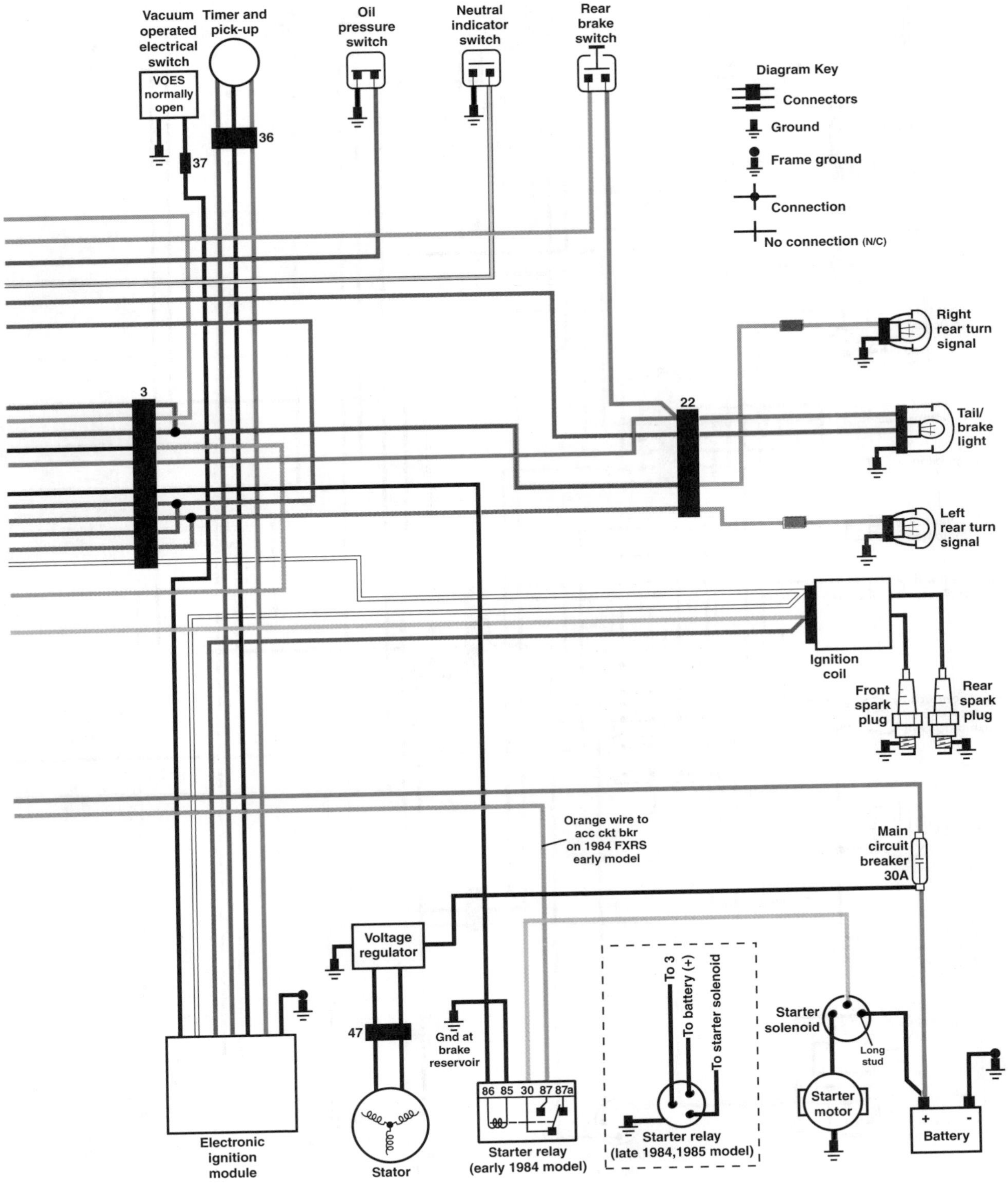

Vacuum operated electrical switch
VOES normally open
Timer and pick-up
36
37
Oil pressure switch
Neutral indicator switch
Rear brake switch

Diagram Key
Connectors
Ground
Frame ground
Connection
No connection (N/C)

3
22
Right rear turn signal
Tail/ brake light
Left rear turn signal
Ignition coil
Front spark plug
Rear spark plug
Orange wire to acc ckt bkr on 1984 FXRS early model
Main circuit breaker 30A
Voltage regulator
47
Gnd at brake reservoir
86 85 30 87 87a
To 3
To battery (+)
To starter solenoid
Starter solenoid
Long stud
Starter motor
Battery
Electronic ignition module
Stator
Starter relay (early 1984 model)
Starter relay (late 1984,1985 model)

17

1984-1985 FXRT MODELS

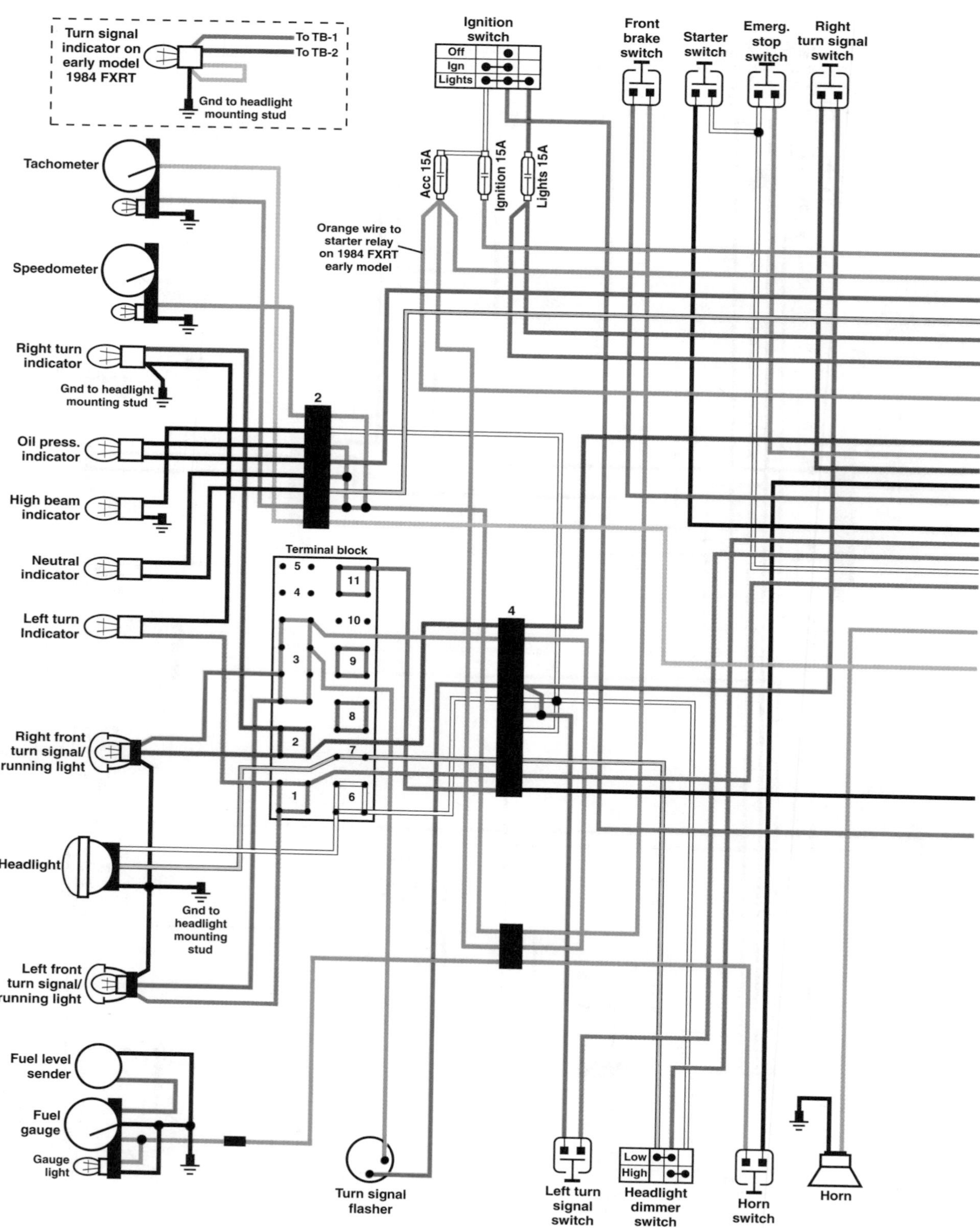

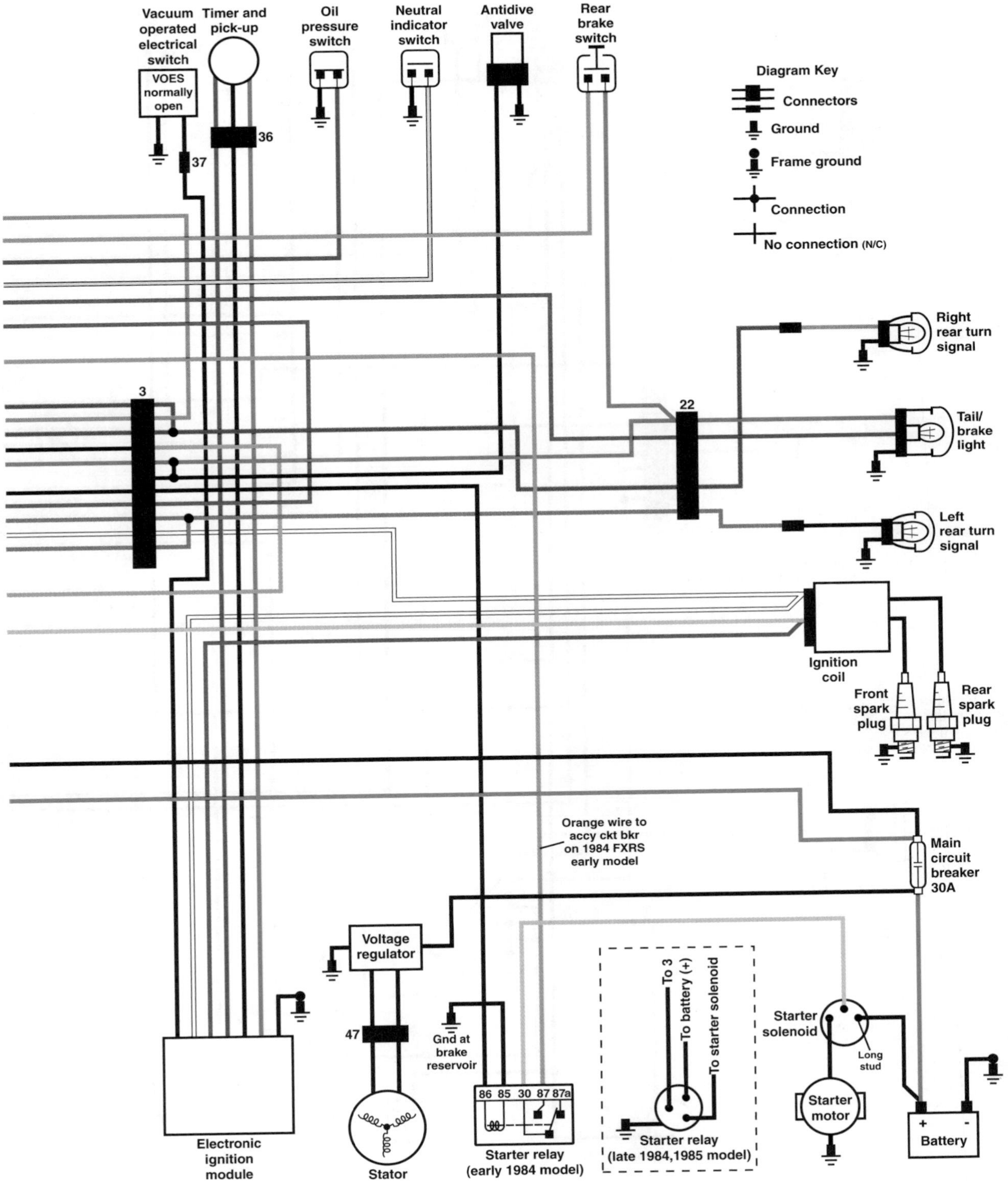

Vacuum operated electrical switch

VOES normally open

37

Timer and pick-up

36

Oil pressure switch

Neutral indicator switch

Antidive valve

Rear brake switch

Diagram Key

Connectors

Ground

Frame ground

Connection

No connection (N/C)

Right rear turn signal

3

22

Tail/ brake light

Left rear turn signal

Ignition coil

Front spark plug

Rear spark plug

Orange wire to accy ckt bkr on 1984 FXRS early model

Main circuit breaker 30A

Voltage regulator

47

Gnd at brake reservoir

To 3

To battery (+)

To starter solenoid

Starter solenoid

Long stud

Starter motor

+ -

Battery

86 85 30 87 87a

Electronic ignition module

Stator

Starter relay (early 1984 model)

Starter relay (late 1984,1985 model)

1985 FXEF AND FXSB MODELS

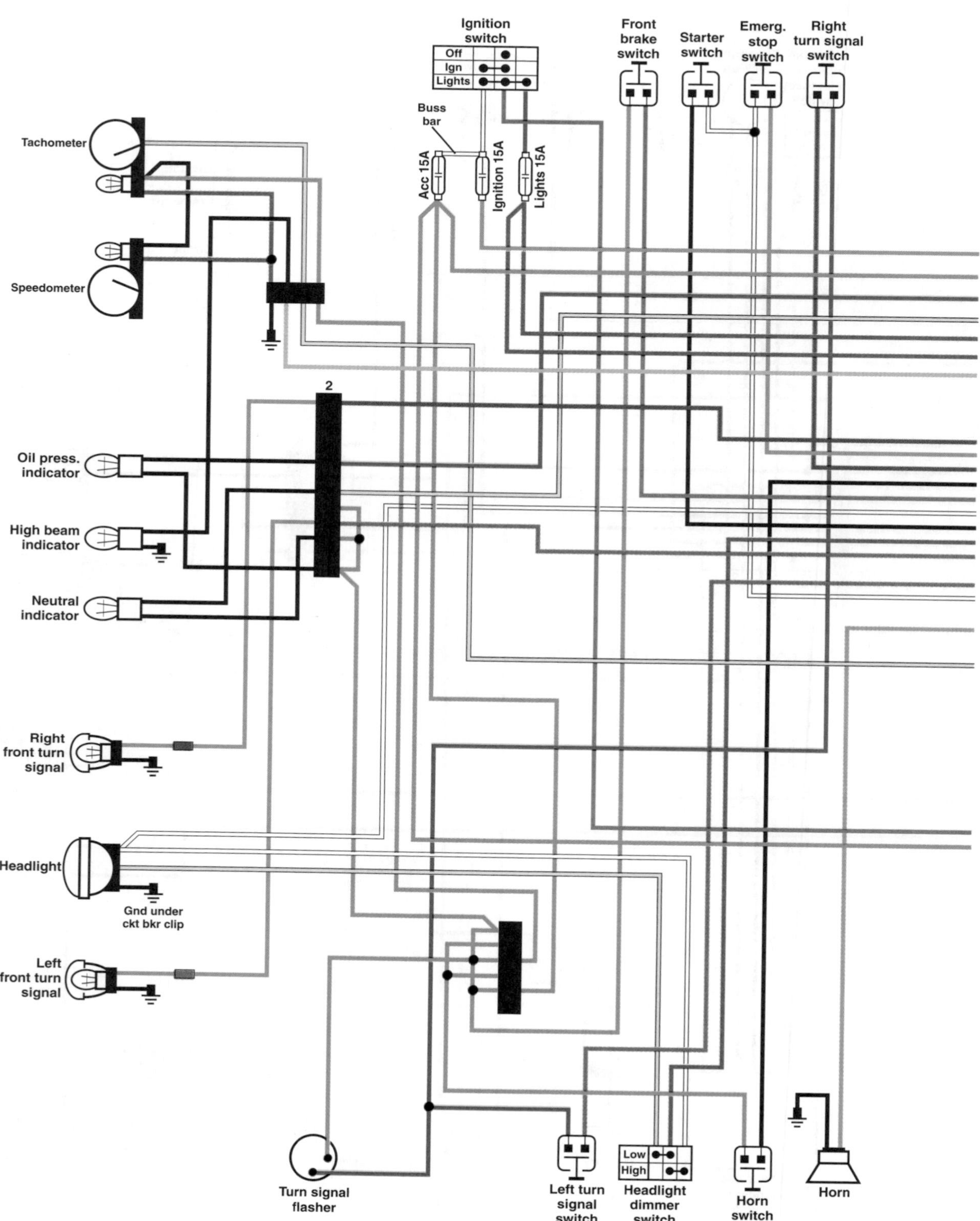

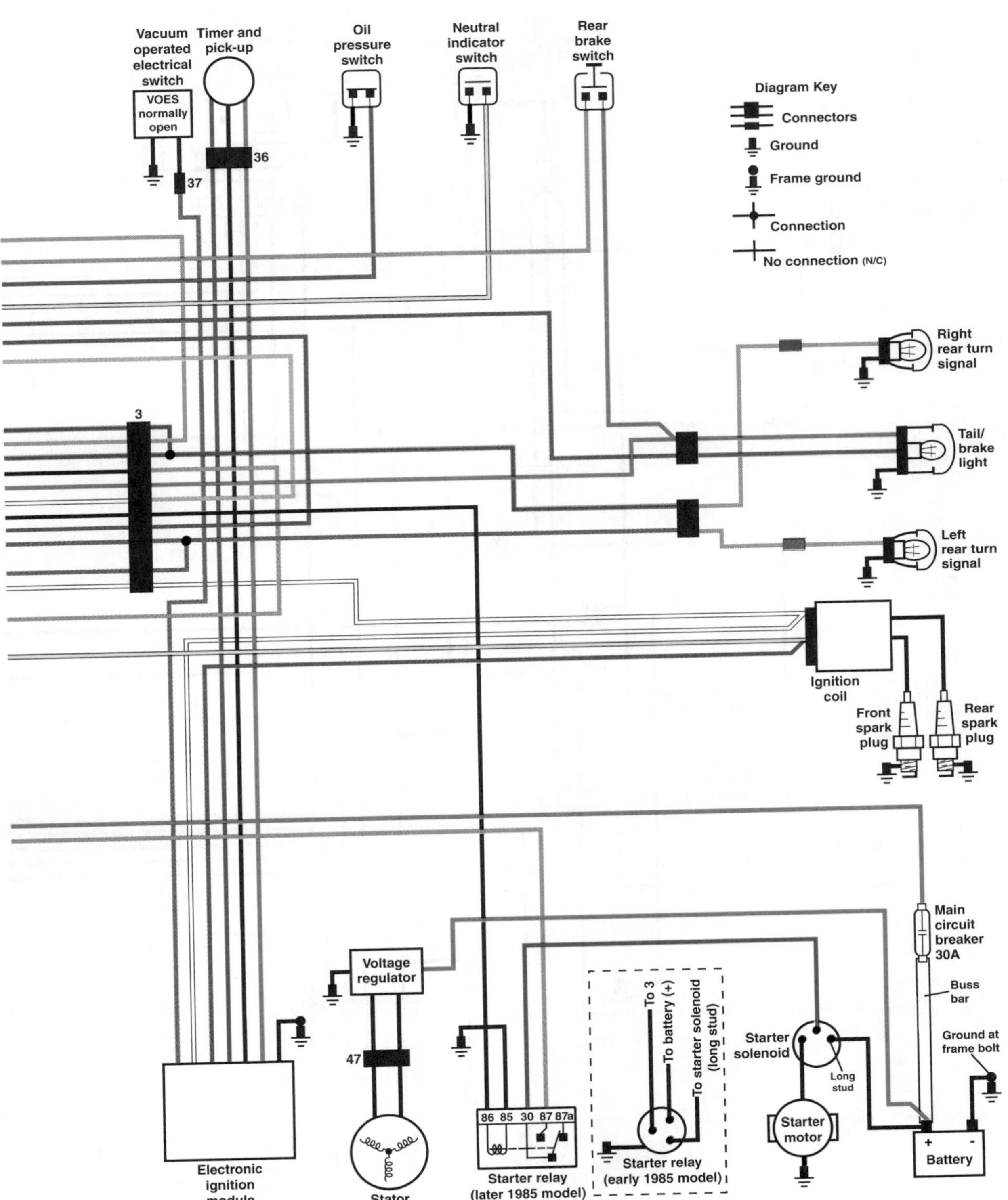
Vacuum operated electrical switch
VOES normally open
37
Timer and pick-up
36
Oil pressure switch
Neutral indicator switch
Rear brake switch
Diagram Key
Connectors
Ground
Frame ground
Connection
No connection (N/C)
Right rear turn signal
3
Tail/ brake light
Left rear turn signal
Ignition coil
Front spark plug
Rear spark plug
Main circuit breaker 30A
Buss bar
Ground at frame bolt
Voltage regulator
47
To 3
To battery (+)
To starter solenoid (long stud)
Starter solenoid
Long stud
Starter motor
86 85 30 87 87a
Electronic ignition module
Stator
Starter relay (later 1985 model)
Starter relay (early 1985 model)
Battery

1985-1986 FXWG MODELS

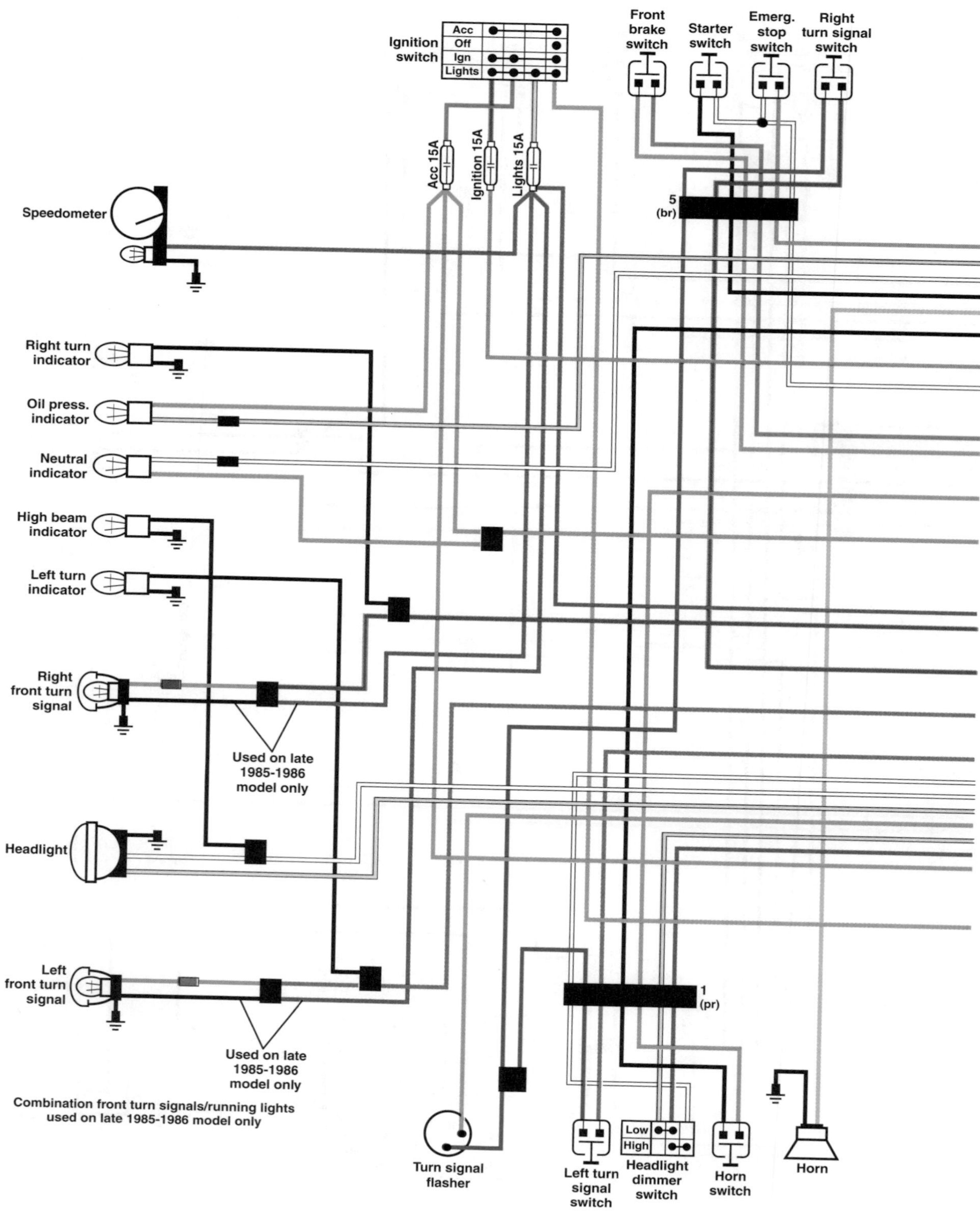

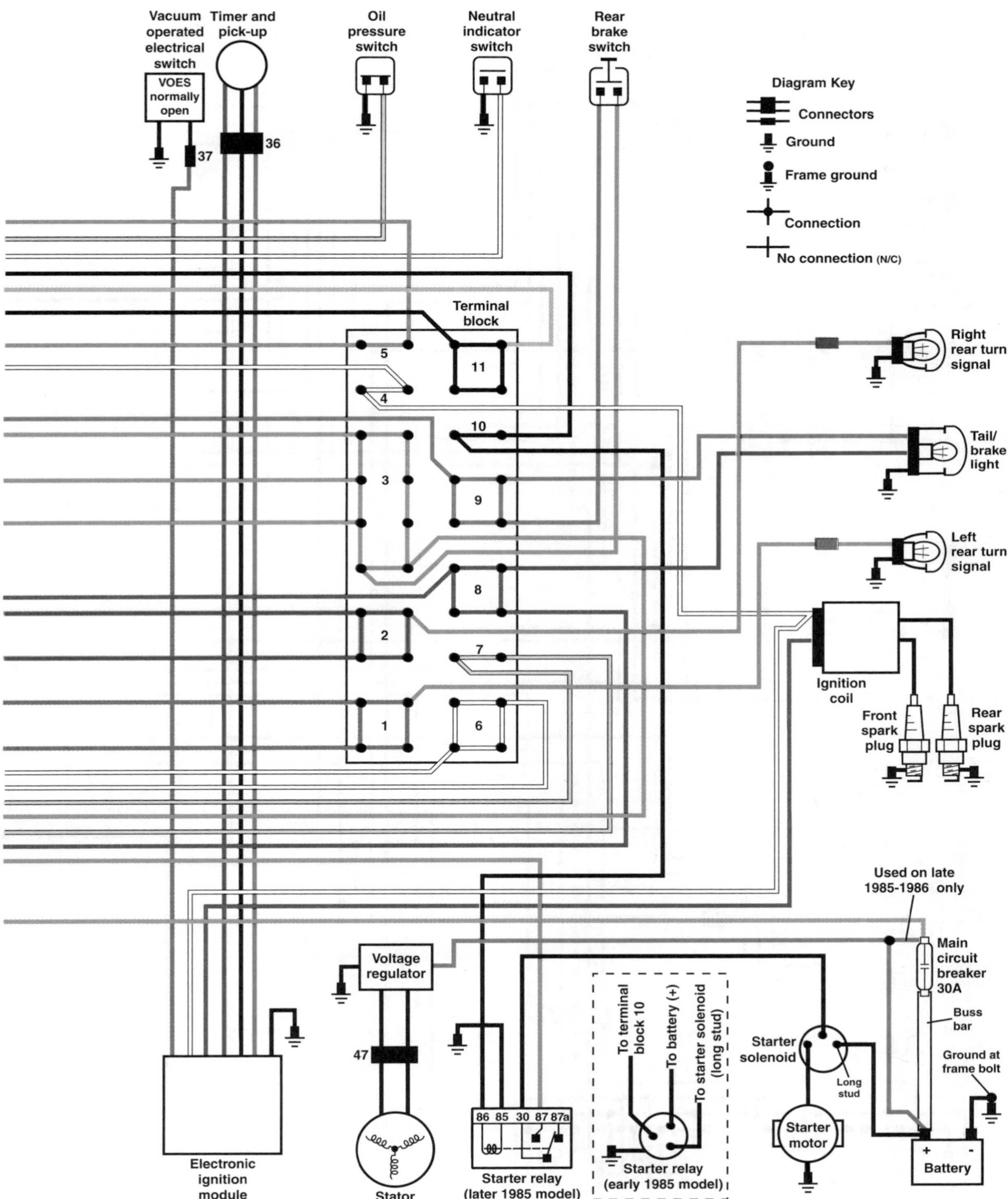
Vacuum operated electrical switch
VOES normally open
37
Timer and pick-up
36
Oil pressure switch
Neutral indicator switch
Rear brake switch
Diagram Key
Connectors
Ground
Frame ground
Connection
No connection (N/C)
Terminal block
5
4
11
10
3
9
8
2
7
1
6
Right rear turn signal
Tail/ brake light
Left rear turn signal
Ignition coil
Front spark plug
Rear spark plug
Used on late 1985-1986 only
Main circuit breaker 30A
Buss bar
Ground at frame bolt
Battery
Starter solenoid
Long stud
Starter motor
To terminal block 10
To battery (+)
To starter solenoid (long stud)
Starter relay (early 1985 model)
86 85 30 87 87a
Starter relay (later 1985 model)
Voltage regulator
47
Stator
Electronic ignition module

1986-1987 FLHTC MODELS

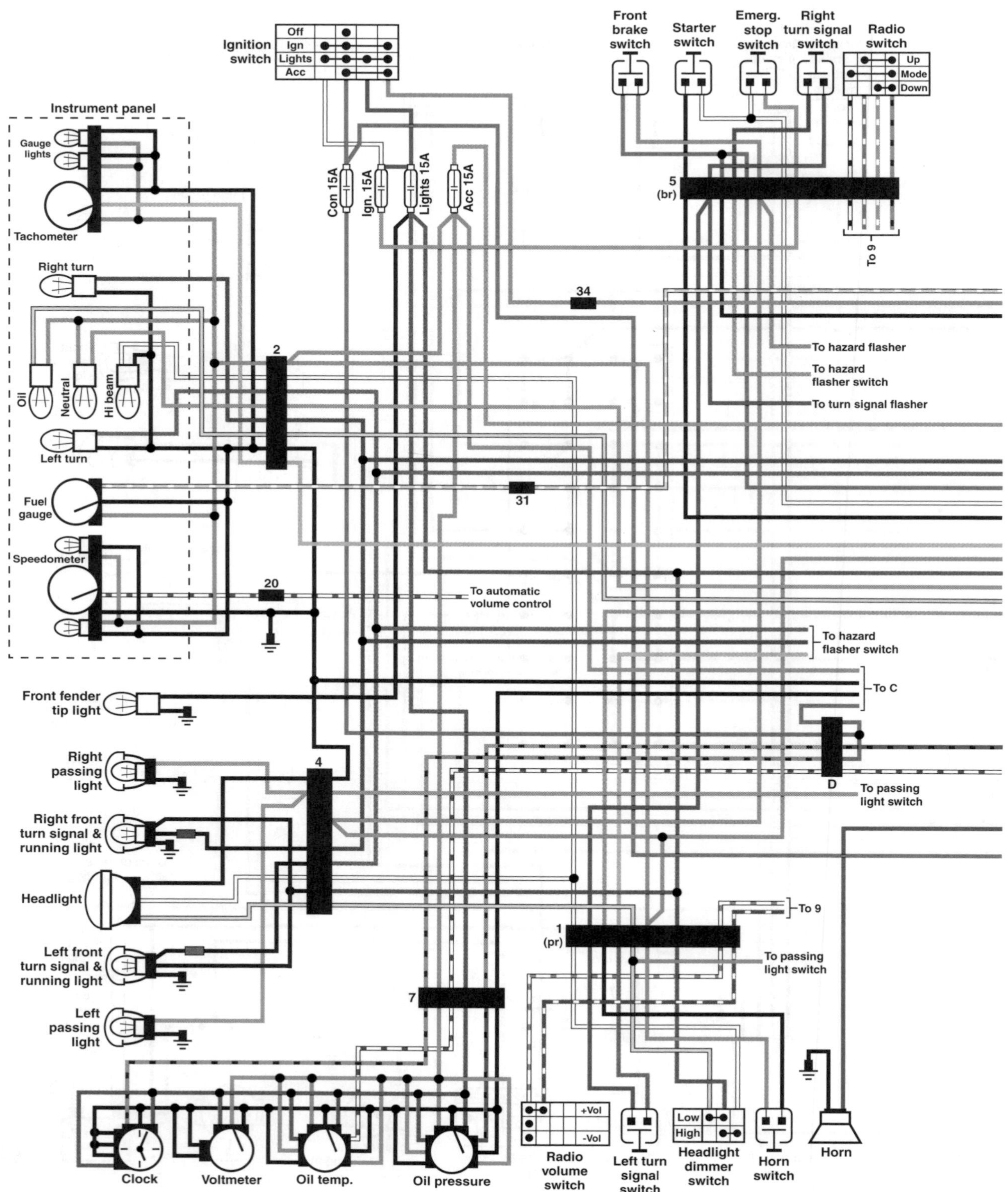

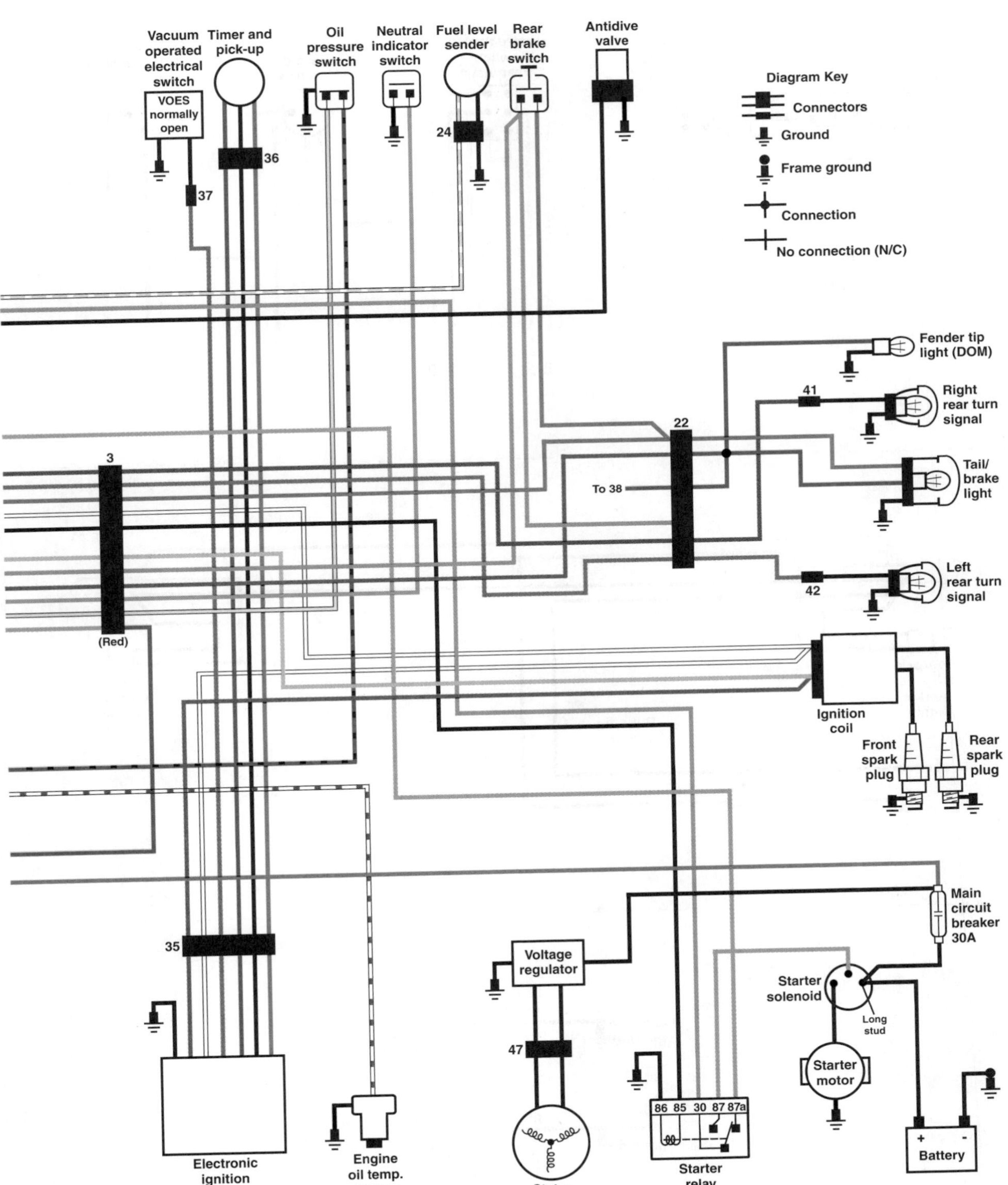
Vacuum operated electrical switch
VOES normally open
Timer and pick-up
Oil pressure switch
Neutral indicator switch
Fuel level sender
Rear brake switch
Antidive valve
Diagram Key
Connectors
Ground
Frame ground
Connection
No connection (N/C)
36
37
24
Fender tip light (DOM)
41
Right rear turn signal
22
Tail/ brake light
To 38
3
(Red)
Left rear turn signal
42
Ignition coil
Front spark plug
Rear spark plug
Main circuit breaker 30A
35
Voltage regulator
47
Starter solenoid
Long stud
Starter motor
86 85 30 87 87a
Battery
Electronic ignition module
Engine oil temp. sensor
Stator
Starter relay

1986-1987 FLHTC MODELS SPOTLIGHT SWITCH, HAZARD SWITCH, TURN SIGNAL AND HAZARD FLASHERS, TOURPAK AND GROUNDS

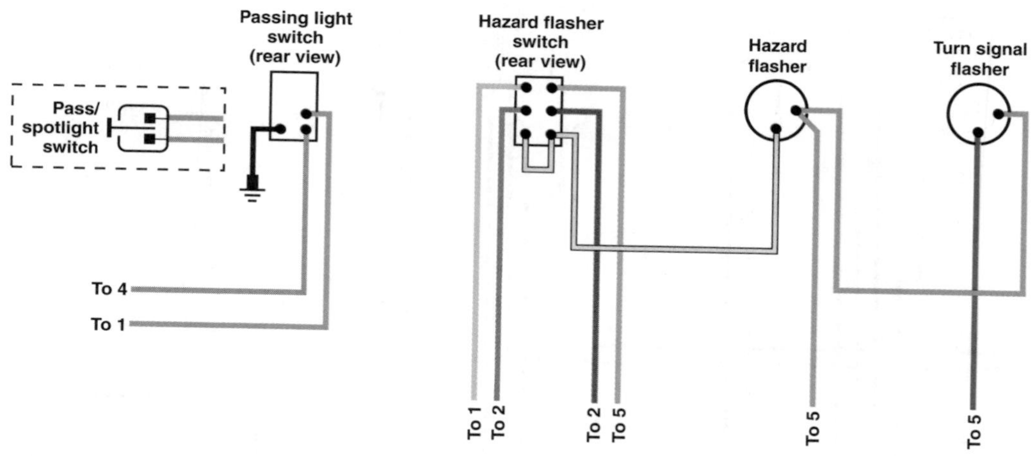

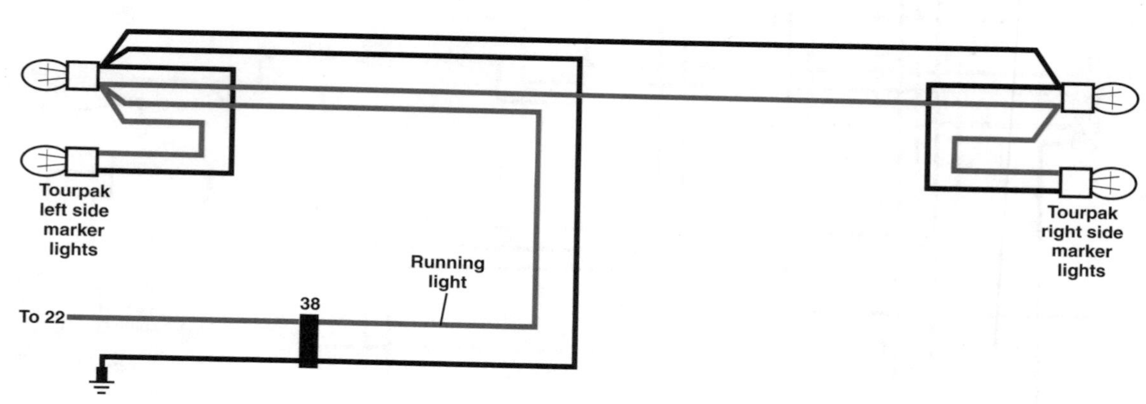

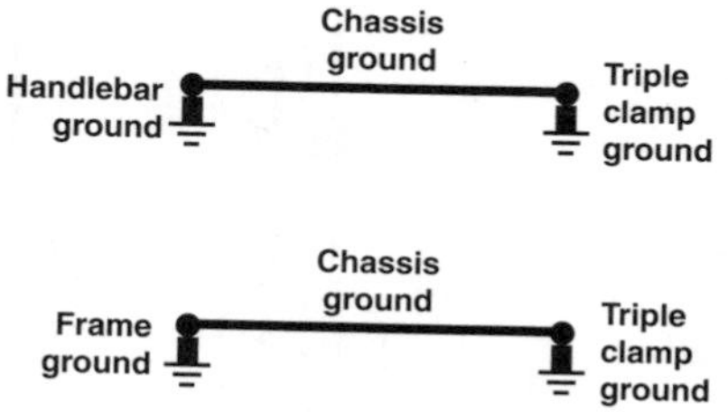

1986-1987 FLHTC MODELS RADIO AND HARNESS CONNECTORS

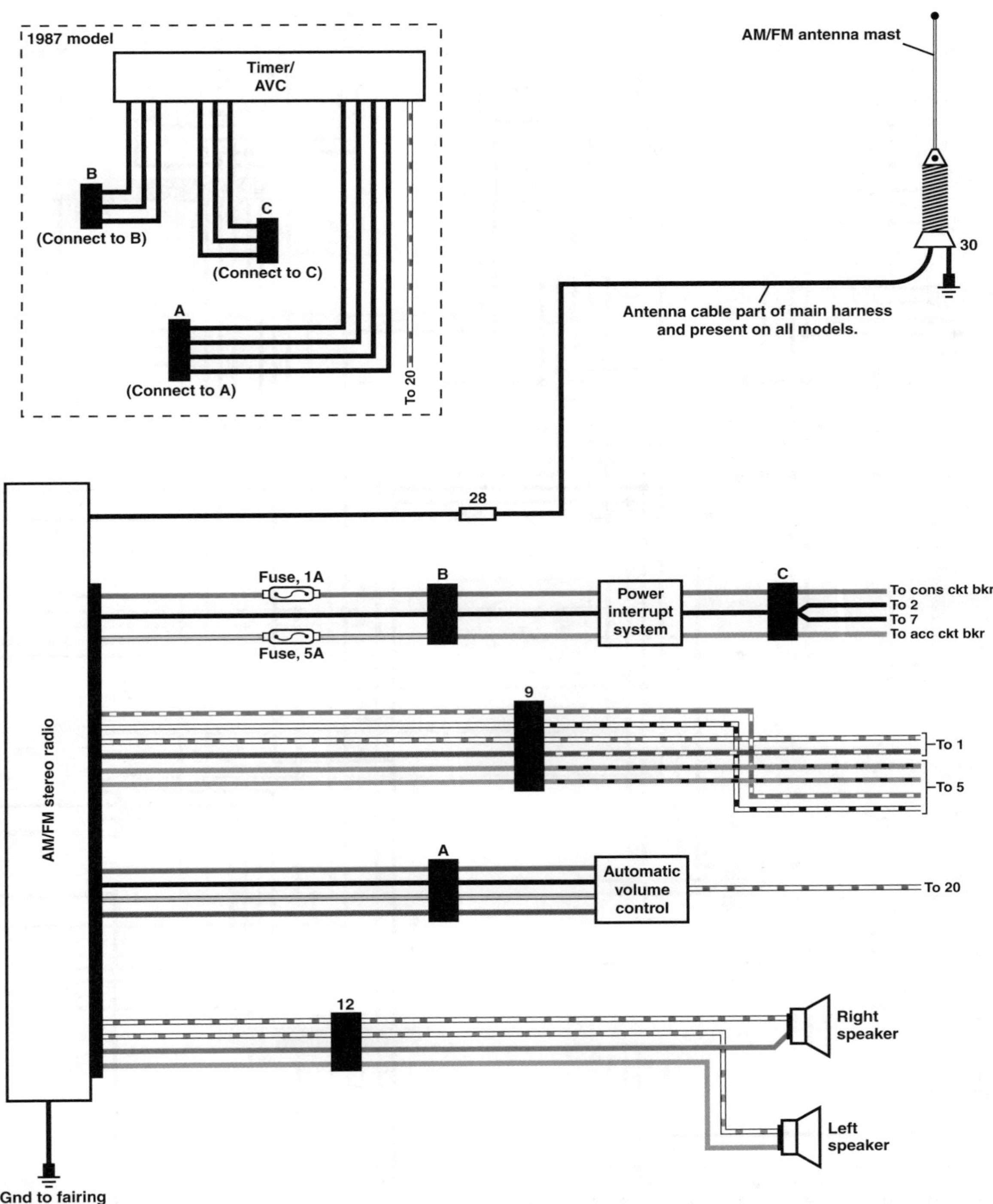

1986-1987 FLTC MODELS

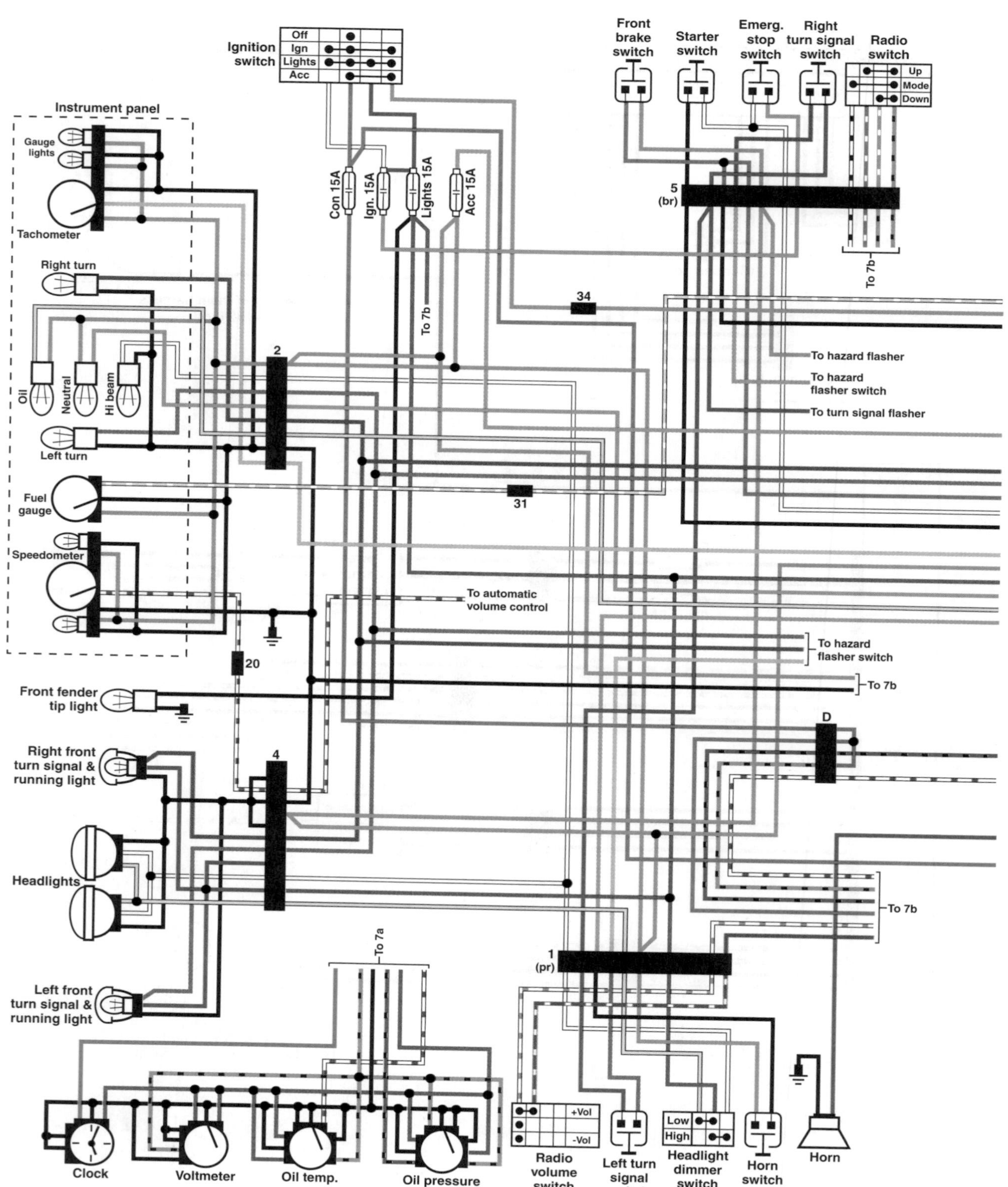

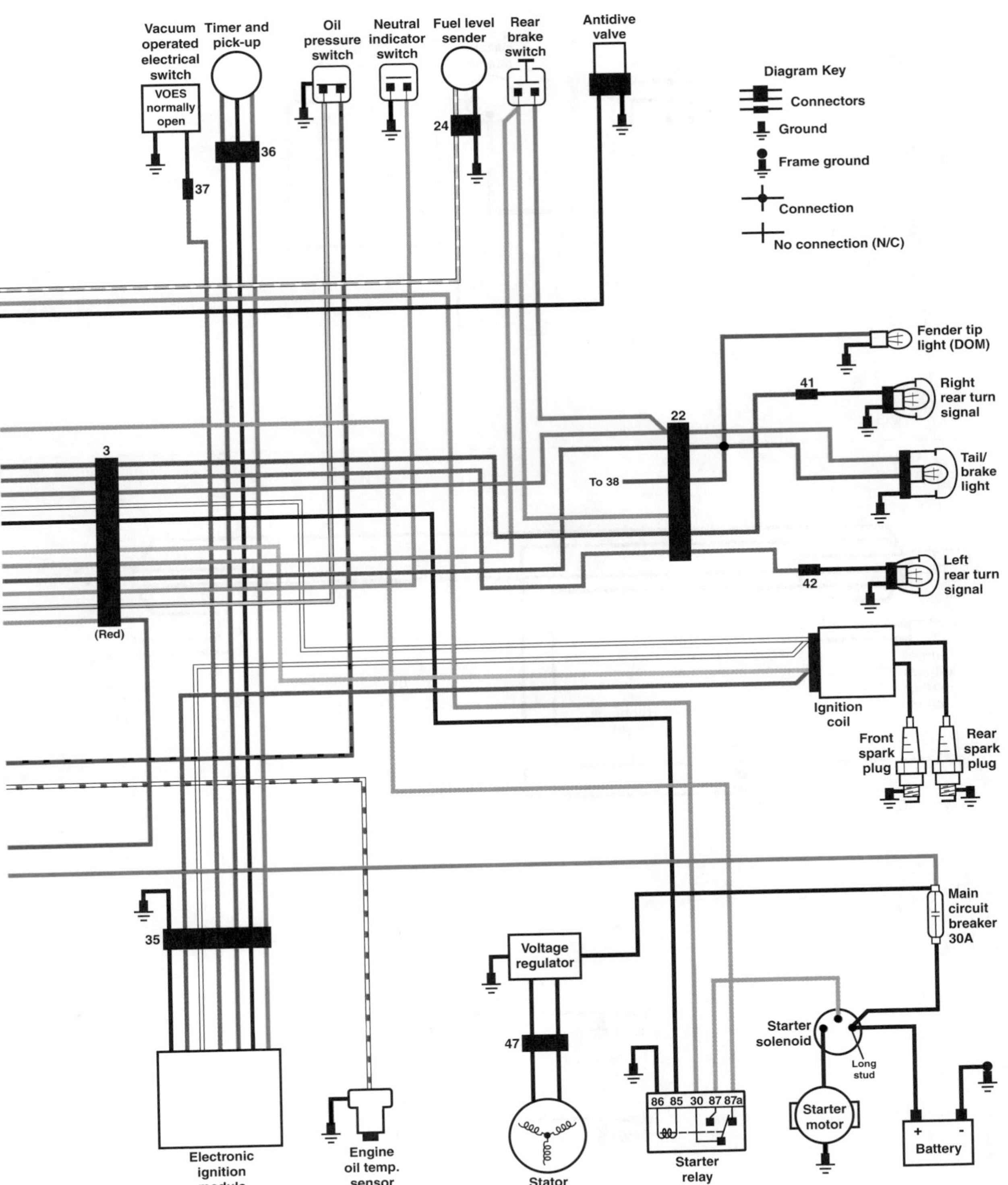
Vacuum operated electrical switch
VOES normally open
Timer and pick-up
Oil pressure switch
Neutral indicator switch
Fuel level sender
Rear brake switch
Antidive valve
Diagram Key
Connectors
Ground
Frame ground
Connection
No connection (N/C)
36
37
24
Fender tip light (DOM)
41
Right rear turn signal
22
Tail/ brake light
3
To 38
Left rear turn signal
42
(Red)
Ignition coil
Front spark plug
Rear spark plug
Main circuit breaker 30A
35
Voltage regulator
47
Starter solenoid
Long stud
Starter motor
Battery
86 85 30 87 87a
Starter relay
Stator
Electronic ignition module
Engine oil temp. sensor

17

1986-1987 FLTC MODELS HAZARD SWITCH, TURN SIGNAL AND HAZARD FLASHERS, TOURPAK AND GROUNDS

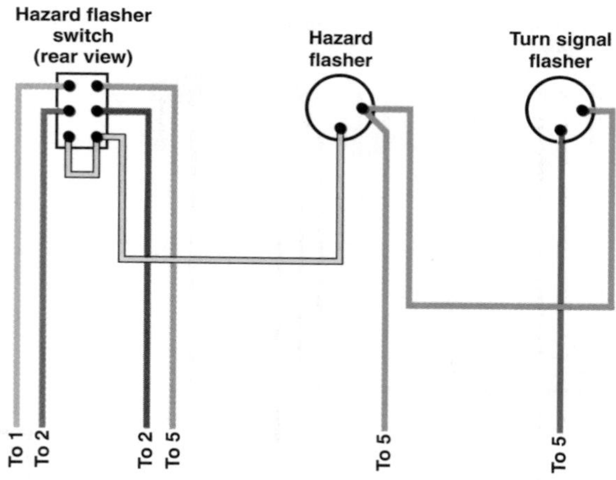

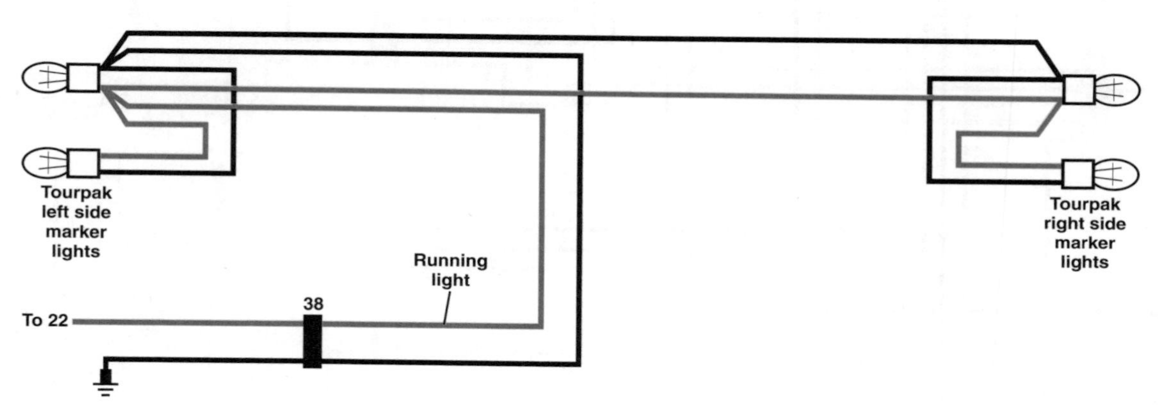

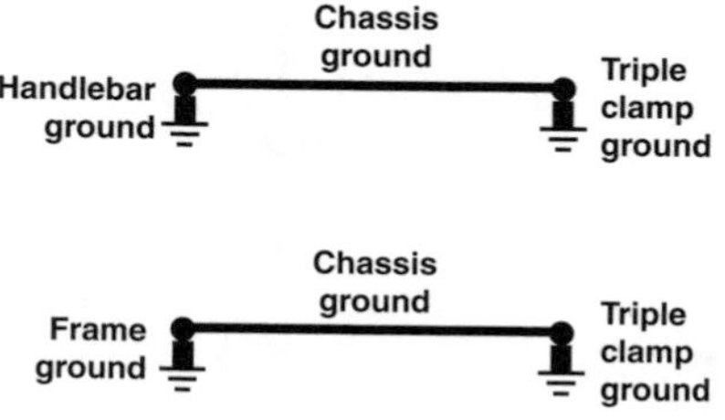

1986-1987 FLTC MODELS RADIO AND HARNESS CONNECTORS

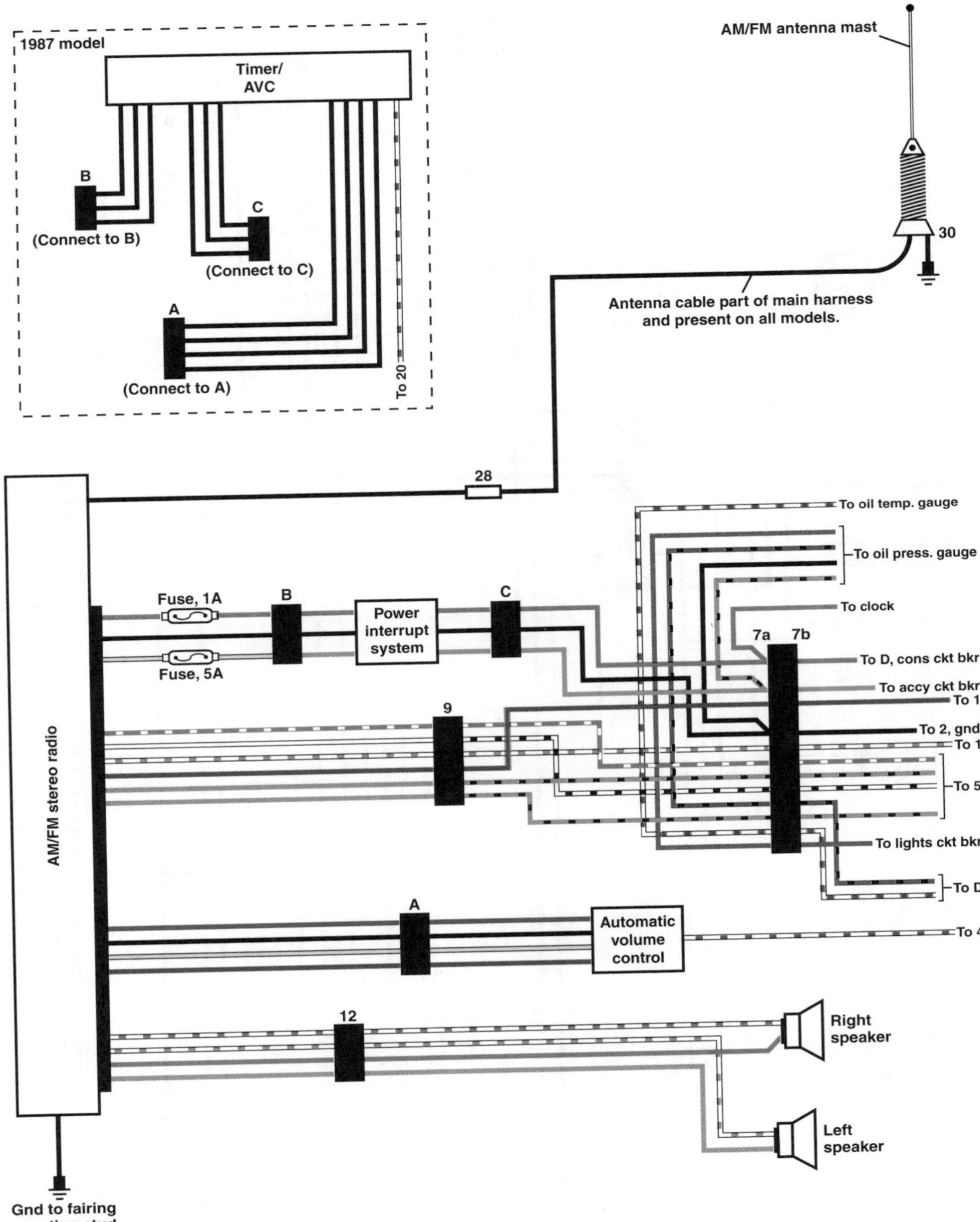

17

1986-1990 FXR MODELS

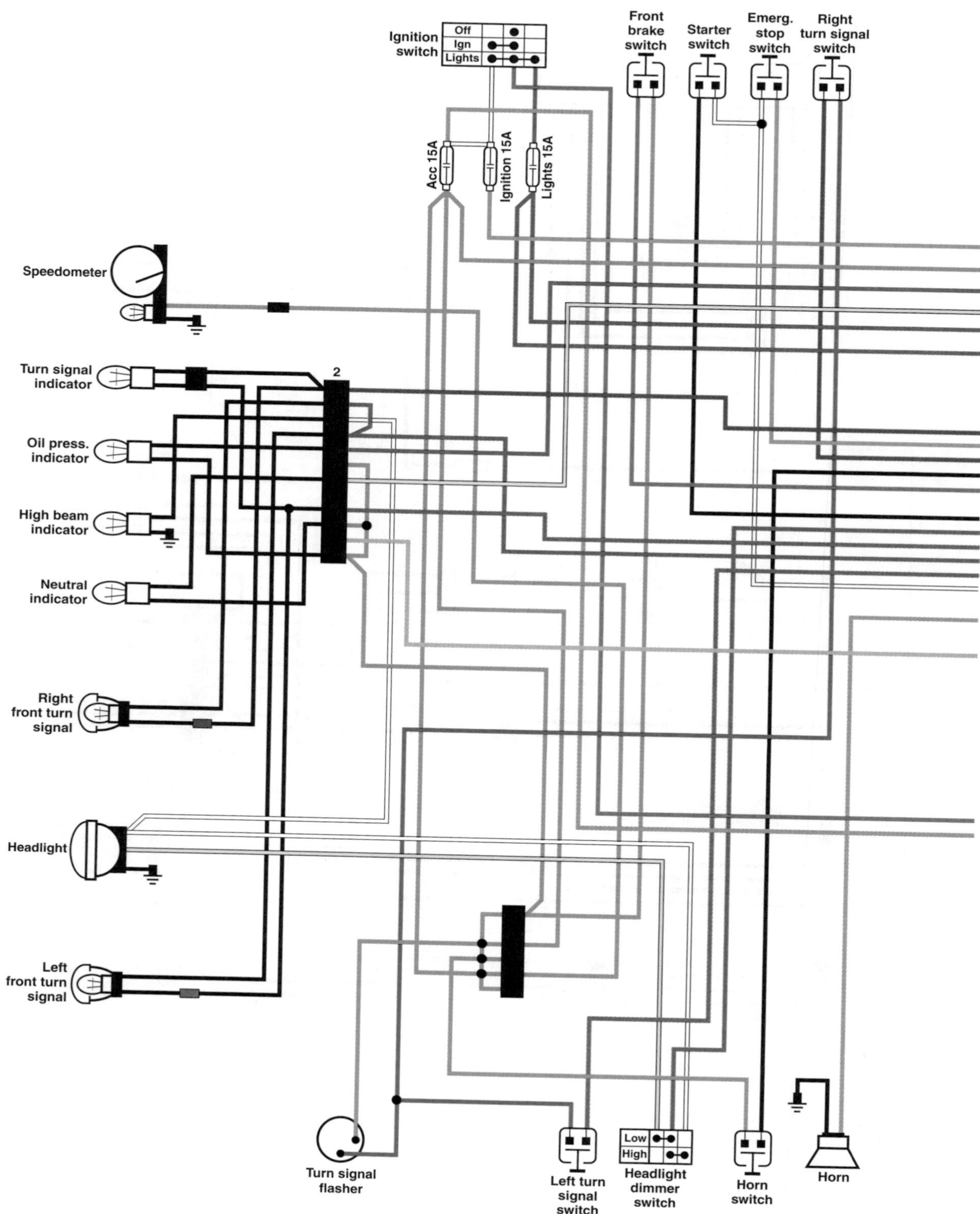

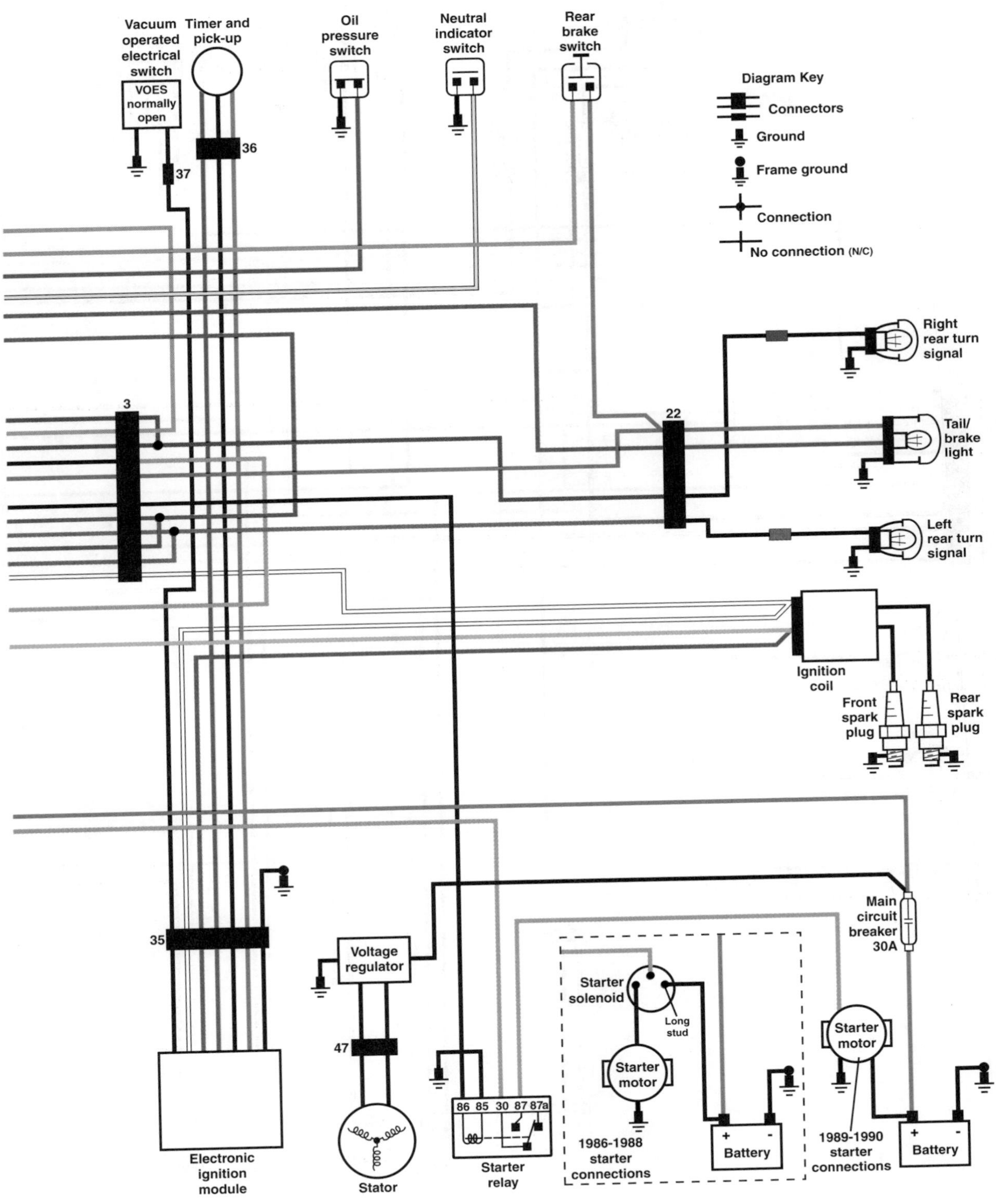
Vacuum operated electrical switch
VOES normally open
Timer and pick-up
Oil pressure switch
Neutral indicator switch
Rear brake switch
Diagram Key
Connectors
Ground
Frame ground
Connection
No connection (N/C)
36
37
3
22
Right rear turn signal
Tail/ brake light
Left rear turn signal
Ignition coil
Front spark plug
Rear spark plug
Main circuit breaker 30A
35
Voltage regulator
47
Starter solenoid
Long stud
Starter motor
Starter motor
86 85 30 87 87a
Electronic ignition module
Stator
Starter relay
1986-1988 starter connections
Battery
1989-1990 starter connections
Battery

1986 FXRD AND 1986-1987 FXRT MODELS

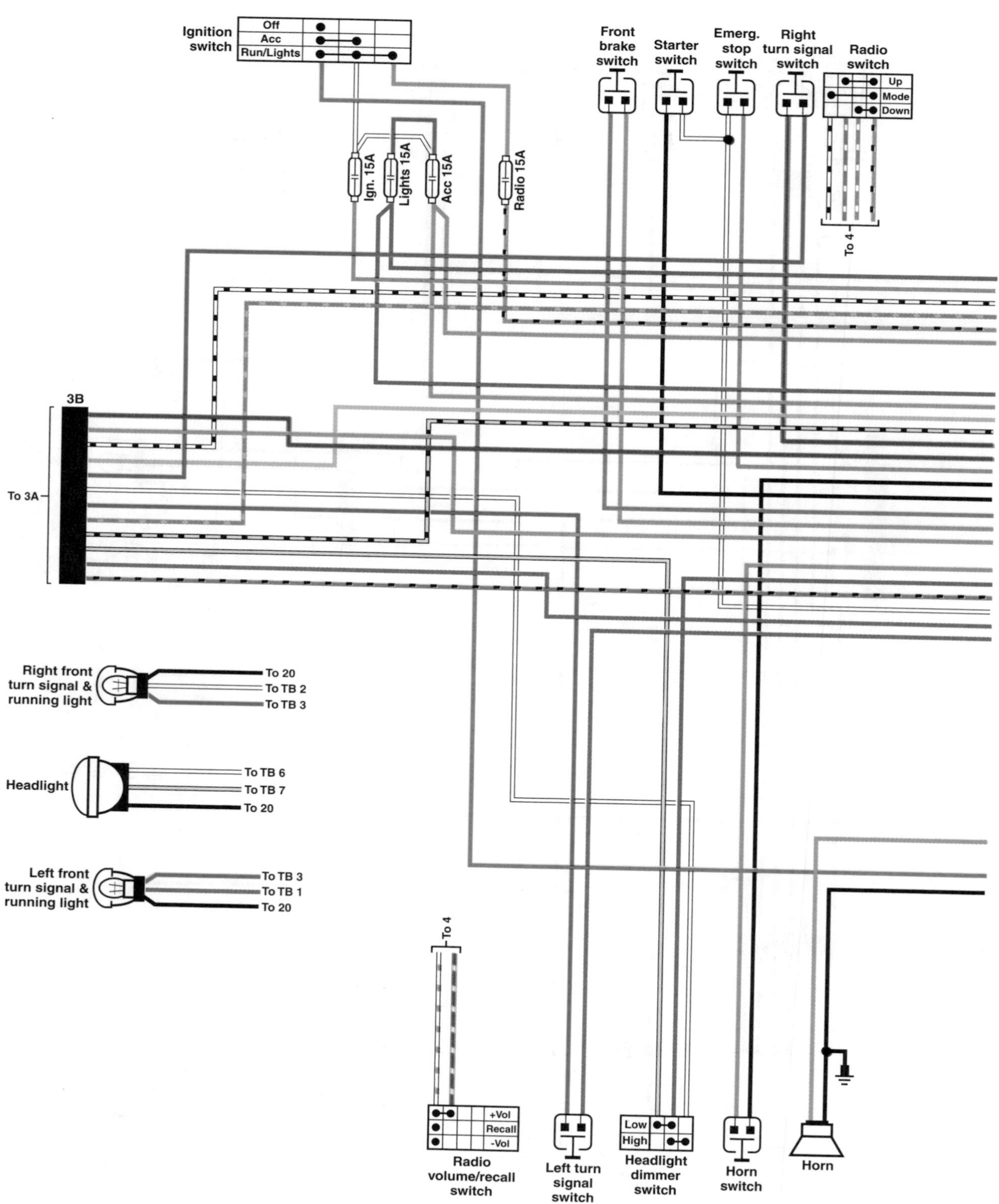

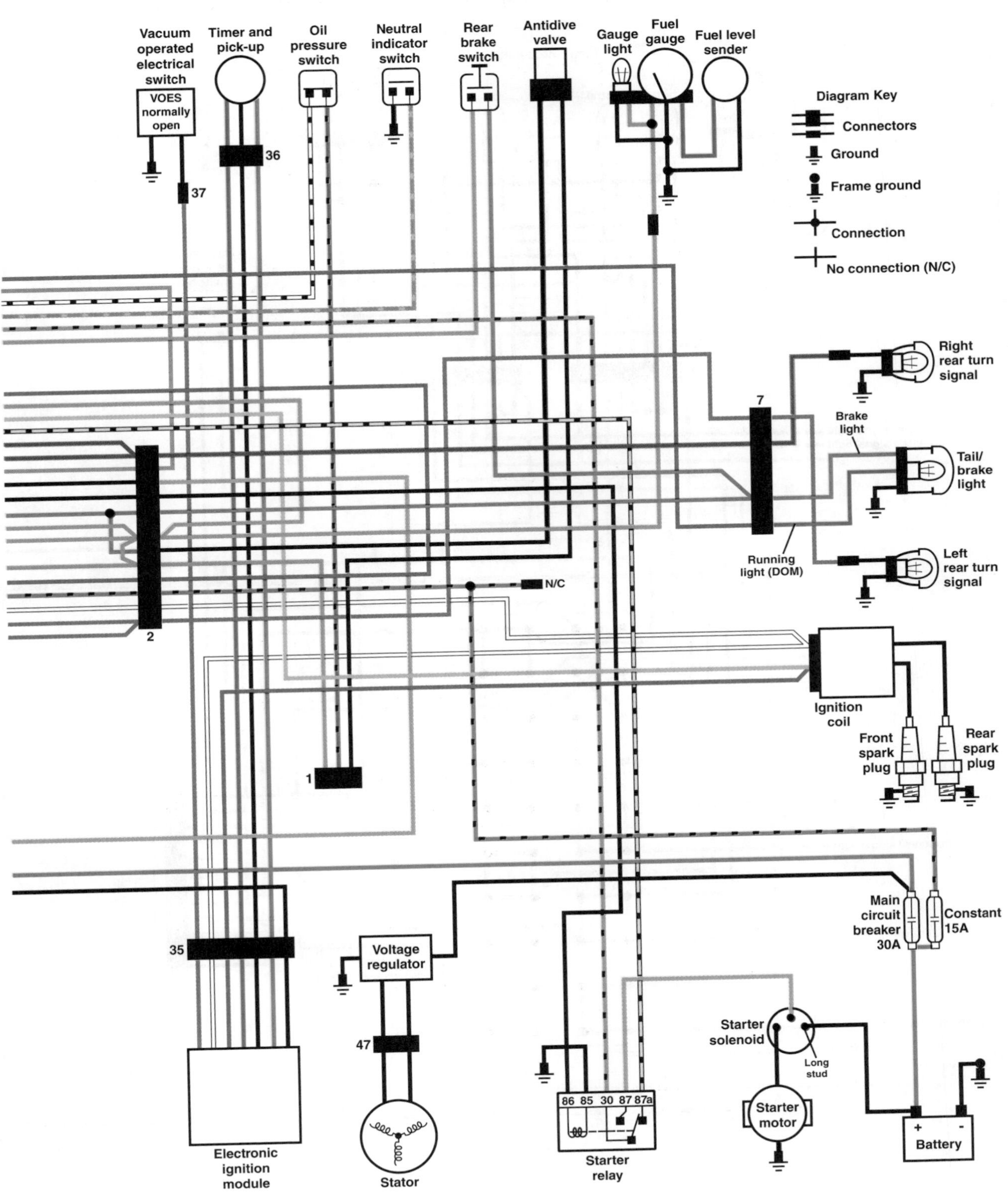
Vacuum operated electrical switch
VOES normally open
Timer and pick-up
Oil pressure switch
Neutral indicator switch
Rear brake switch
Antidive valve
Gauge light
Fuel gauge
Fuel level sender
Diagram Key
Connectors
Ground
Frame ground
Connection
No connection (N/C)
36
37
Right rear turn signal
7
Brake light
Tail/ brake light
Running light (DOM)
Left rear turn signal
N/C
2
Ignition coil
Front spark plug
Rear spark plug
1
Main circuit breaker 30A
Constant 15A
35
Voltage regulator
47
Starter solenoid
Long stud
Starter motor
86 85 30 87 87a
Starter relay
Battery
Electronic ignition module
Stator

1986 FXRD AND 1986-1987 FXRT MODELS INSTRUMENT PANEL, TERMINAL BLOCK, RADIO AND ANTENNA

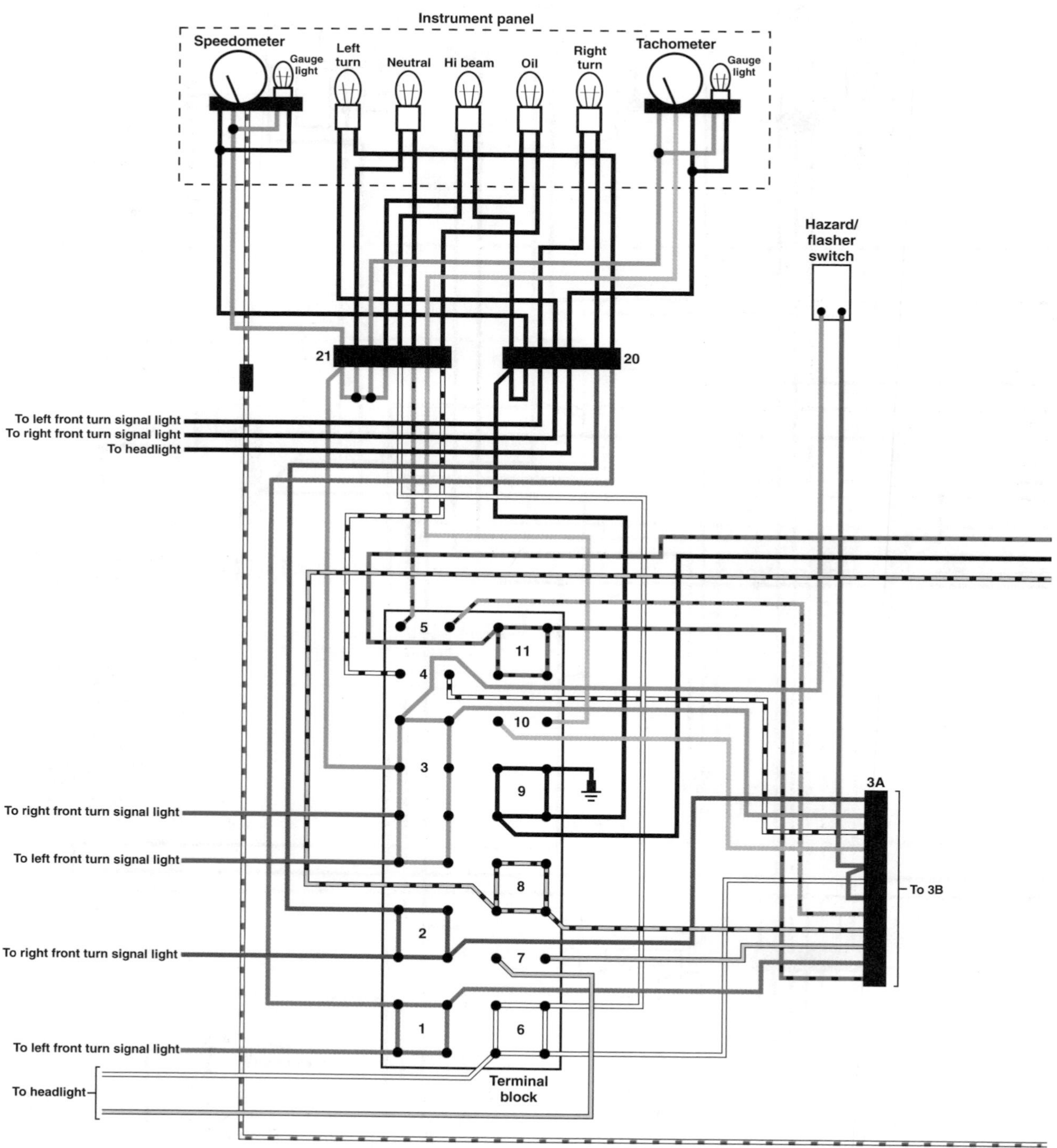

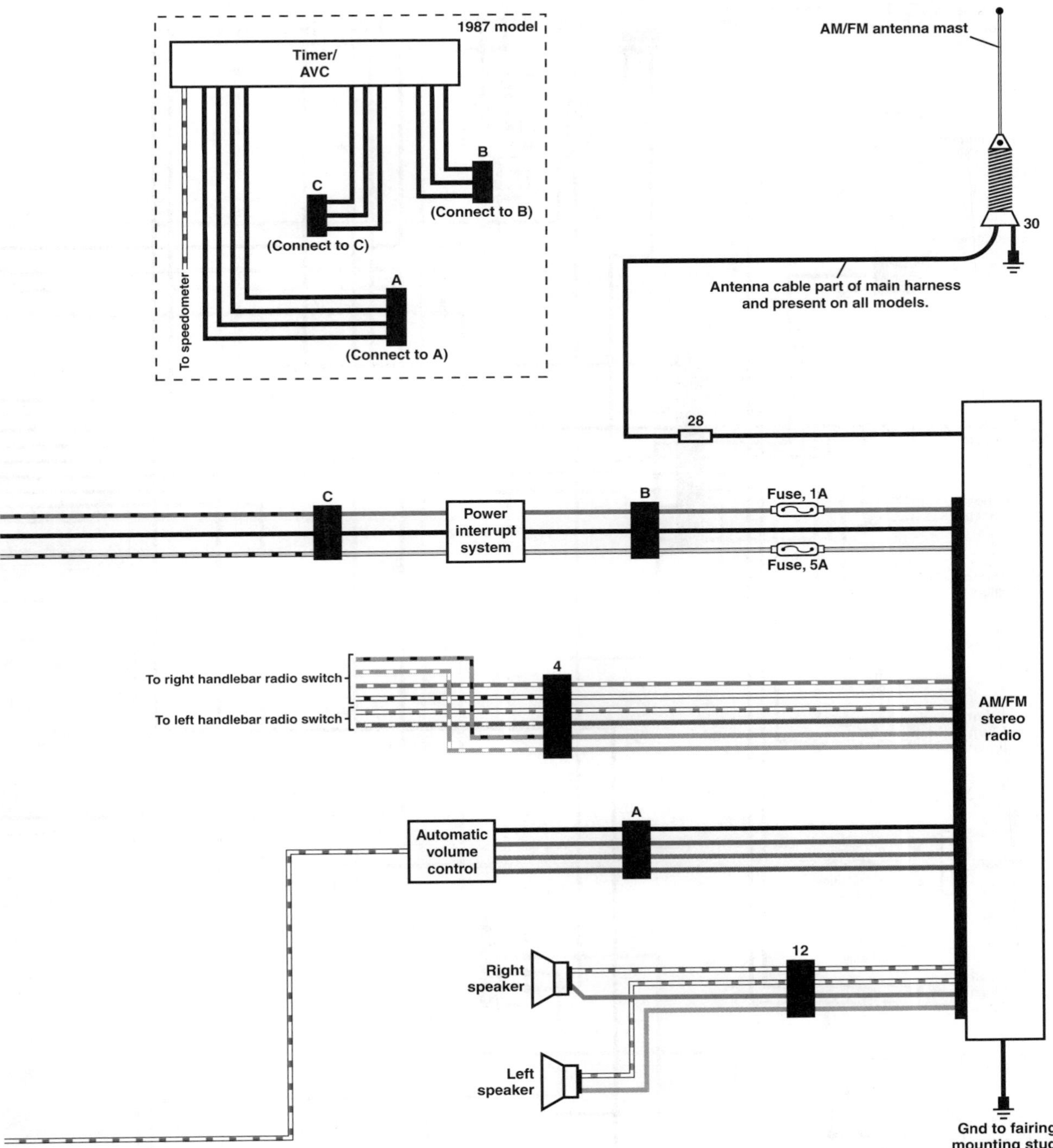
1987 model
Timer/
AVC
B
C
(Connect to B)
(Connect to C)
A
To speedometer
(Connect to A)
AM/FM antenna mast
30
Antenna cable part of main harness
and present on all models.
28
C
B
Fuse, 1A
Power
interrupt
system
Fuse, 5A
4
To right handlebar radio switch
To left handlebar radio switch
AM/FM
stereo
radio
A
Automatic
volume
control
12
Right
speaker
Left
speaker
Gnd to fairing
mounting stud

17

1986-1987 FXRS AND 1988-1990 FXRS-SP MODELS

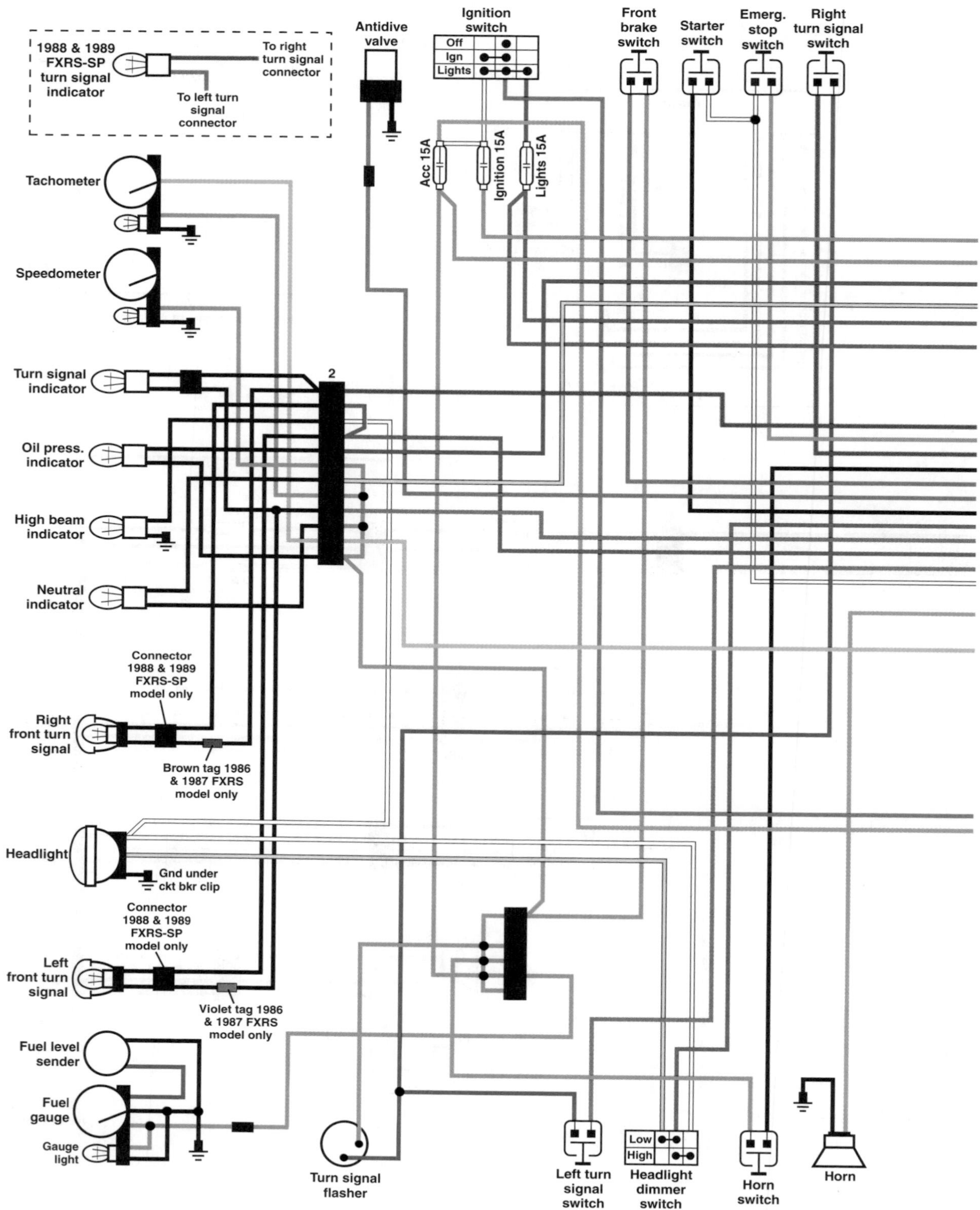

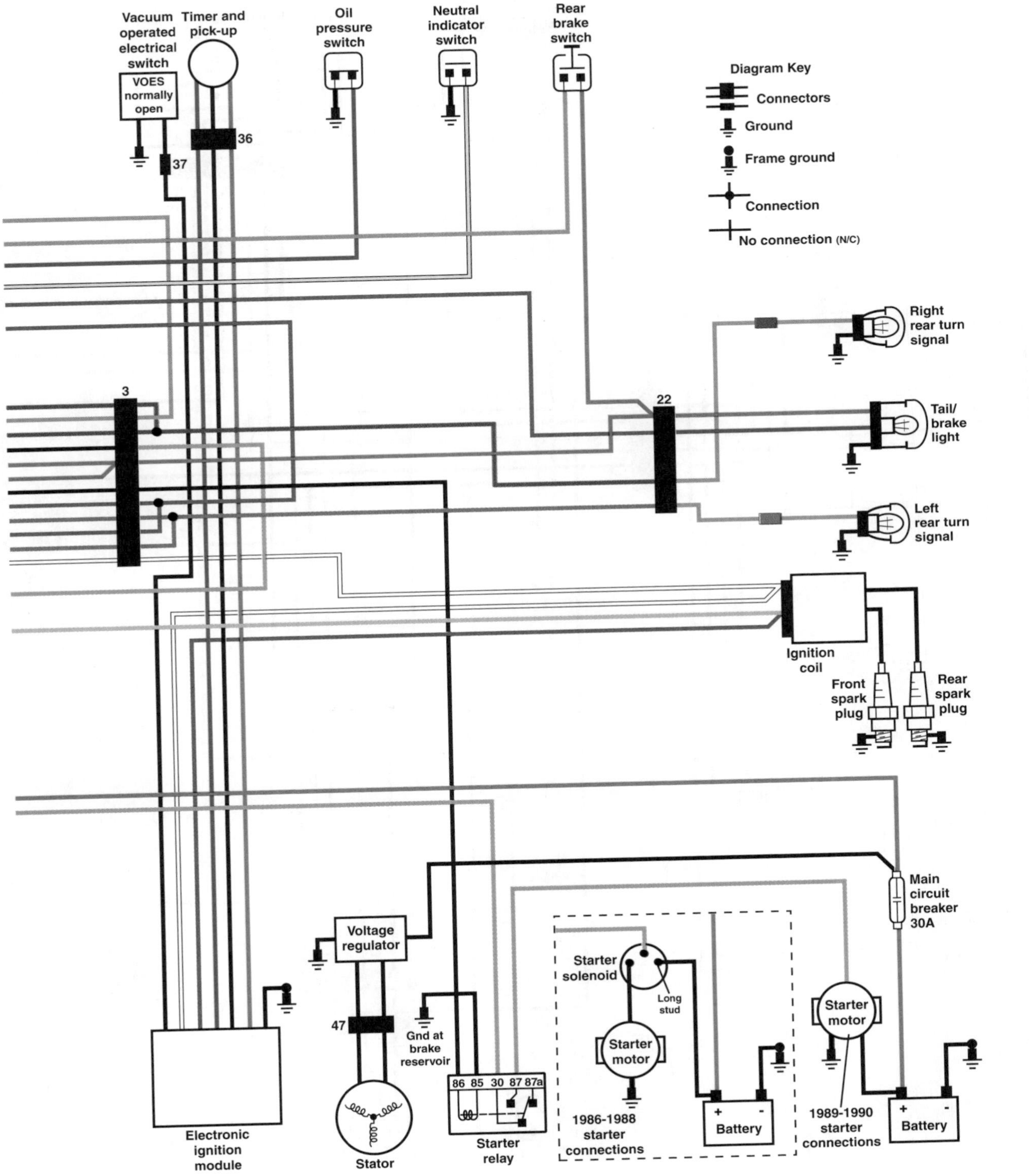

Vacuum operated electrical switch
VOES normally open
Timer and pick-up
Oil pressure switch
Neutral indicator switch
Rear brake switch

Diagram Key
Connectors
Ground
Frame ground
Connection
No connection (N/C)

36
37
3
22

Right rear turn signal
Tail/ brake light
Left rear turn signal
Ignition coil
Front spark plug
Rear spark plug
Main circuit breaker 30A
Voltage regulator
47
Gnd at brake reservoir
86 85 30 87 87a
Starter relay
Stator
Electronic ignition module
Starter solenoid
Long stud
Starter motor
1986-1988 starter connections
+ - Battery
Starter motor
1989-1990 starter connections
+ - Battery

1987-1990 FXLR MODELS

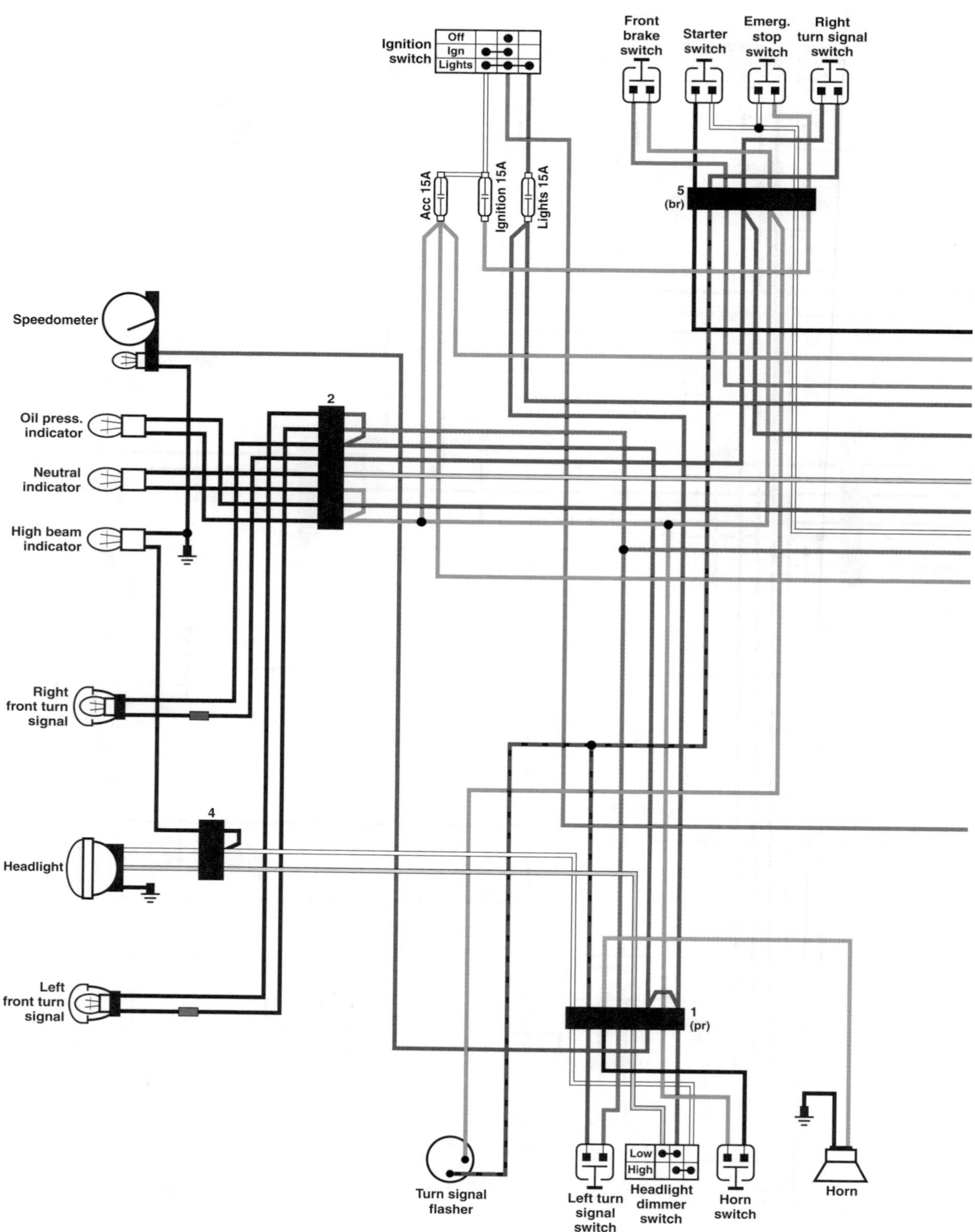

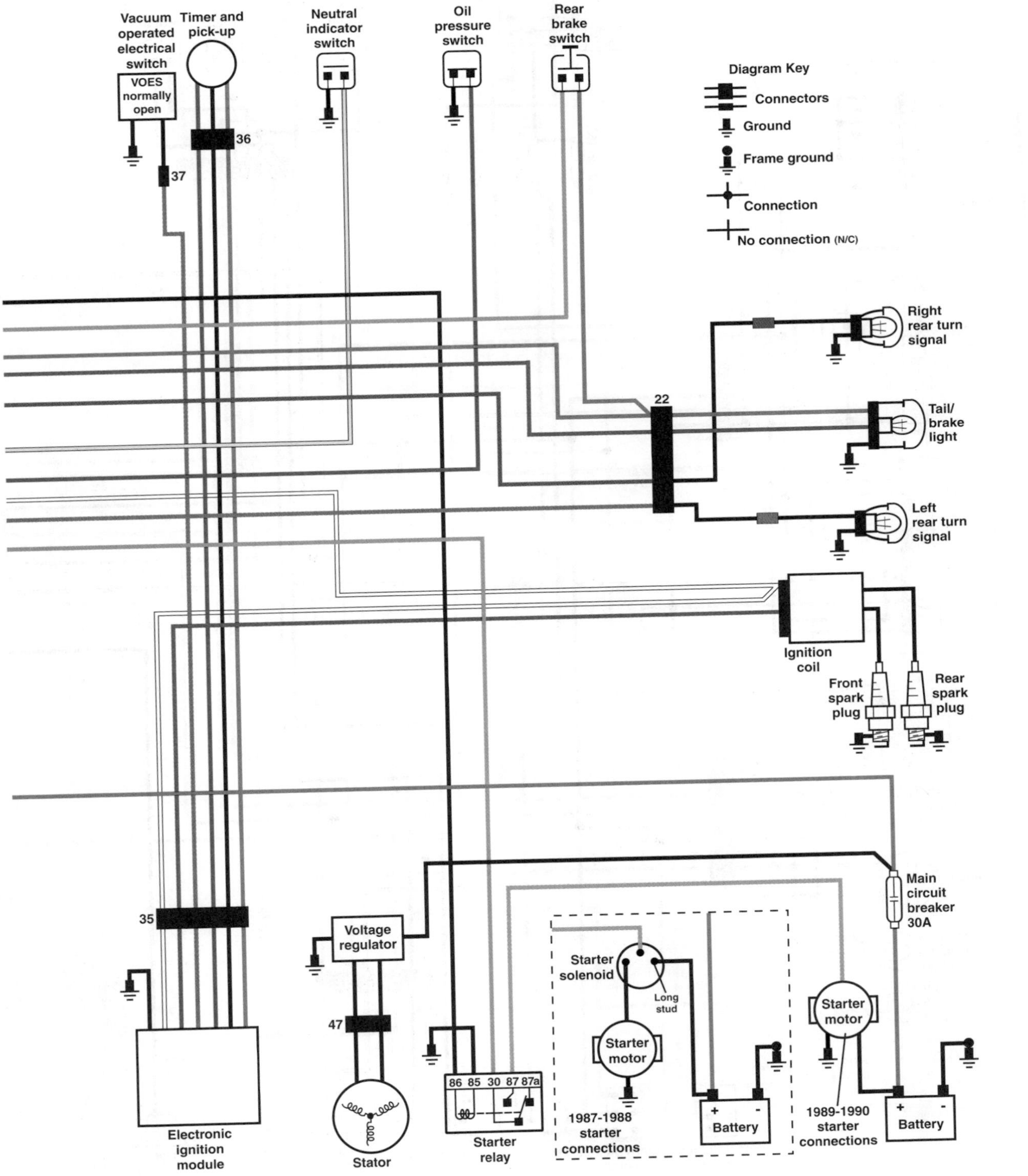

Vacuum operated electrical switch
VOES normally open
Timer and pick-up
Neutral indicator switch
Oil pressure switch
Rear brake switch
Diagram Key
Connectors
Ground
Frame ground
Connection
No connection (N/C)
36
37
Right rear turn signal
22
Tail/ brake light
Left rear turn signal
Ignition coil
Front spark plug
Rear spark plug
Main circuit breaker 30A
35
Voltage regulator
47
Starter solenoid
Long stud
Starter motor
86 85 30 87 87a
1987-1988 starter connections
Battery
Starter motor
1989-1990 starter connections
Battery
Electronic ignition module
Stator
Starter relay

1988 FLHS MODELS

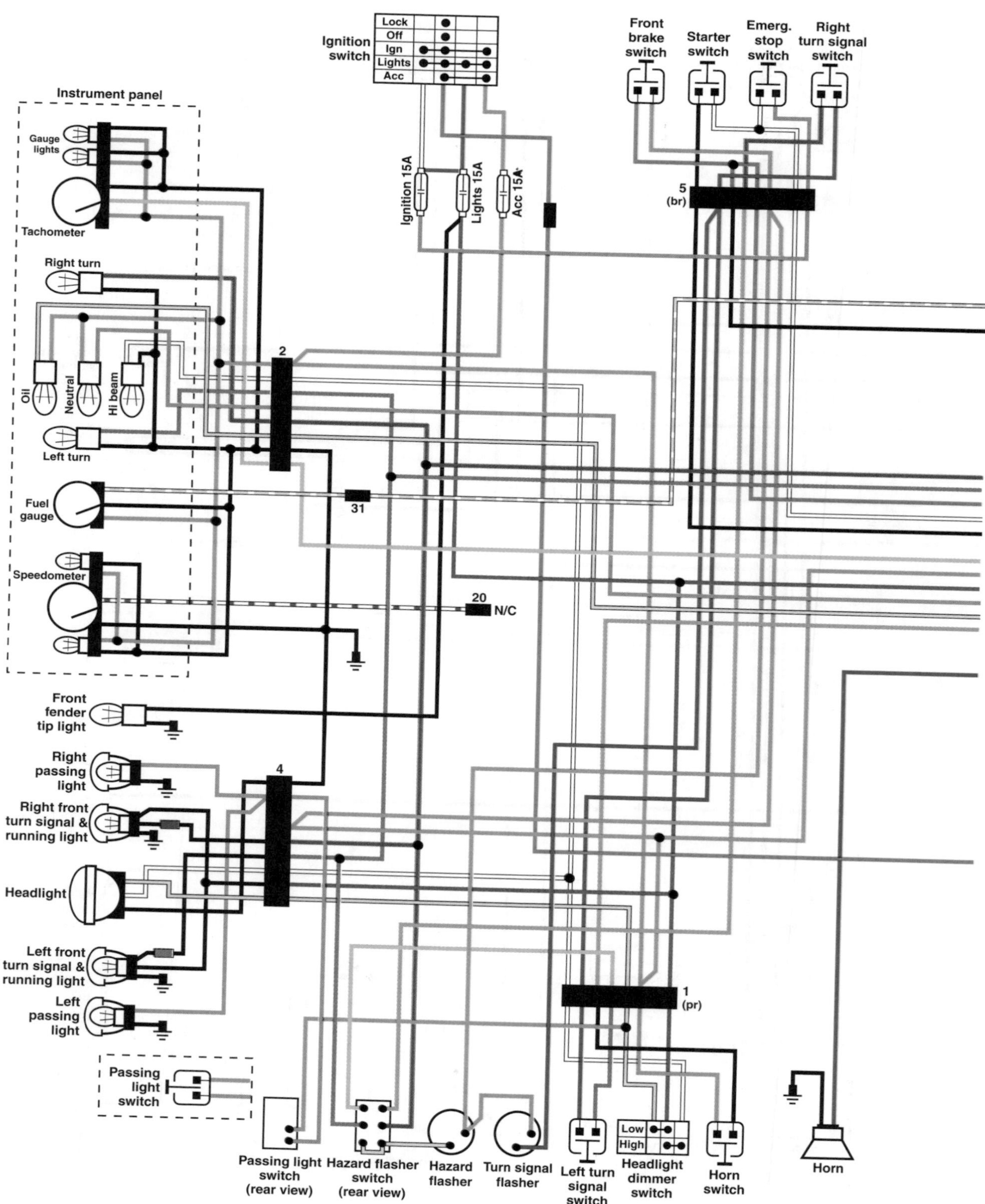

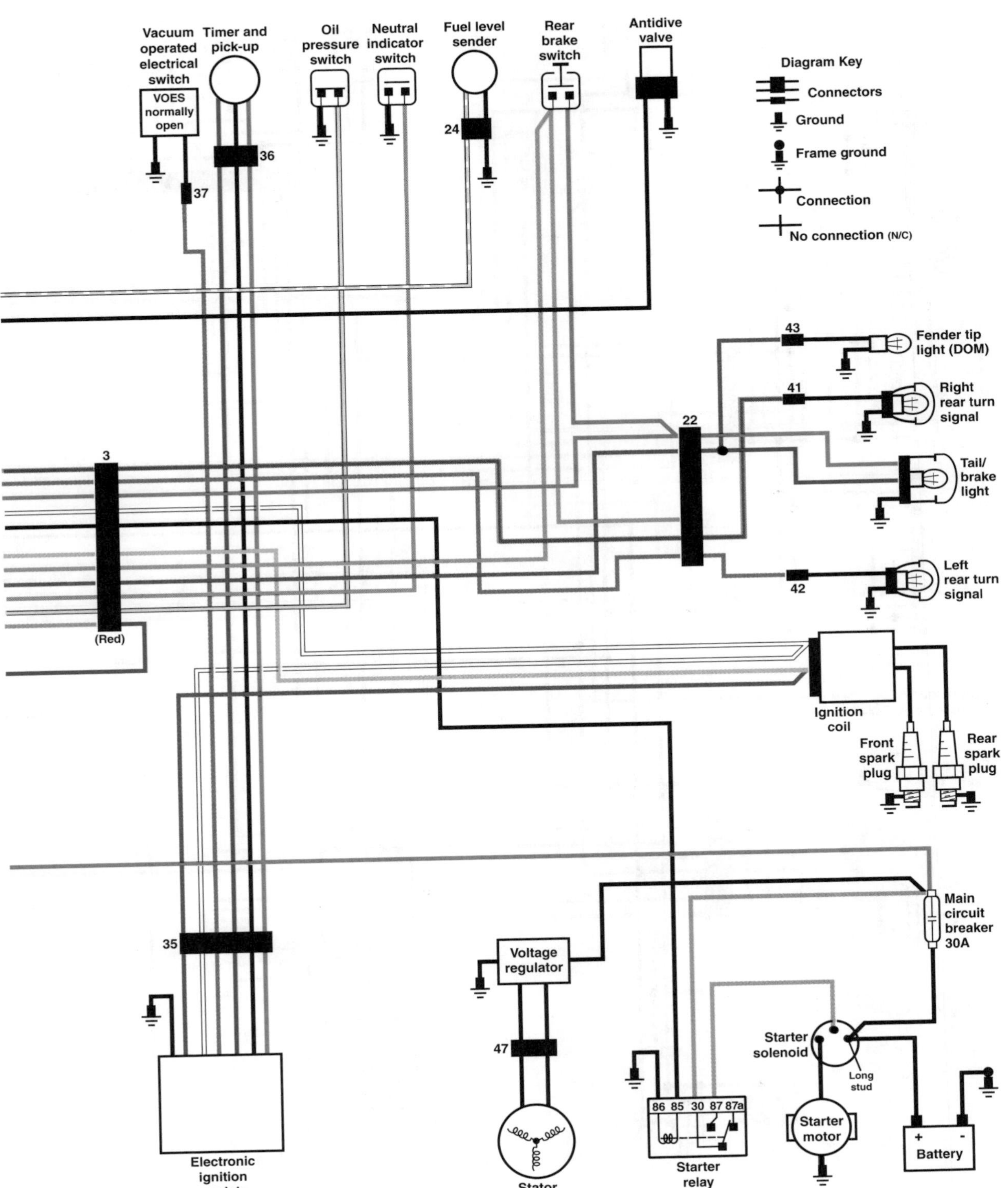
Vacuum operated electrical switch
VOES normally open
Timer and pick-up
Oil pressure switch
Neutral indicator switch
Fuel level sender
Rear brake switch
Antidive valve
Diagram Key
Connectors
Ground
Frame ground
Connection
No connection (N/C)
36
37
24
43
Fender tip light (DOM)
41
Right rear turn signal
22
Tail/ brake light
3
(Red)
42
Left rear turn signal
Ignition coil
Front spark plug
Rear spark plug
Main circuit breaker 30A
35
Voltage regulator
47
Starter solenoid
Long stud
86 85 30 87 87a
Starter relay
Starter motor
Battery
Electronic ignition module
Stator

17

1988 FLHTC MODELS

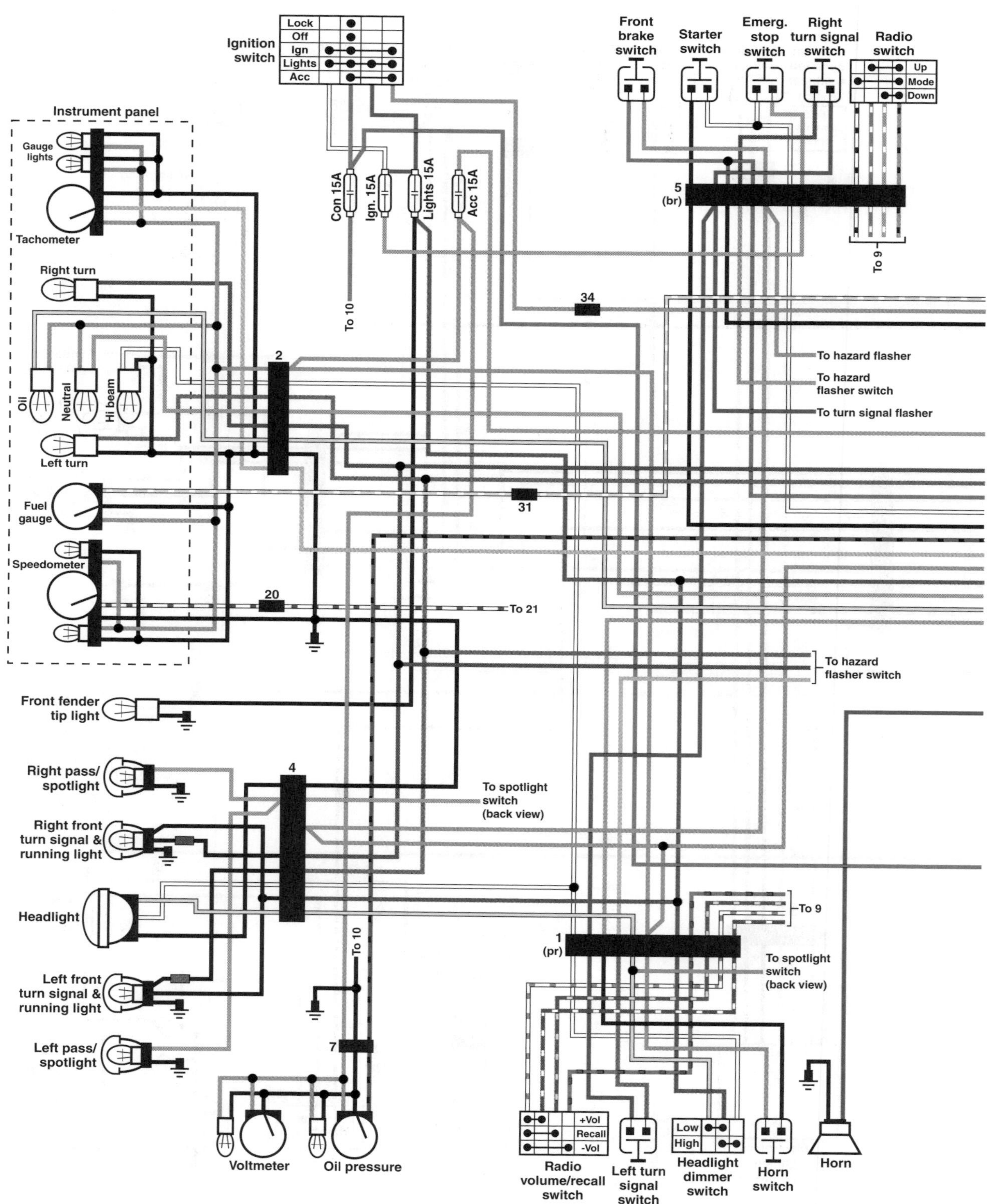

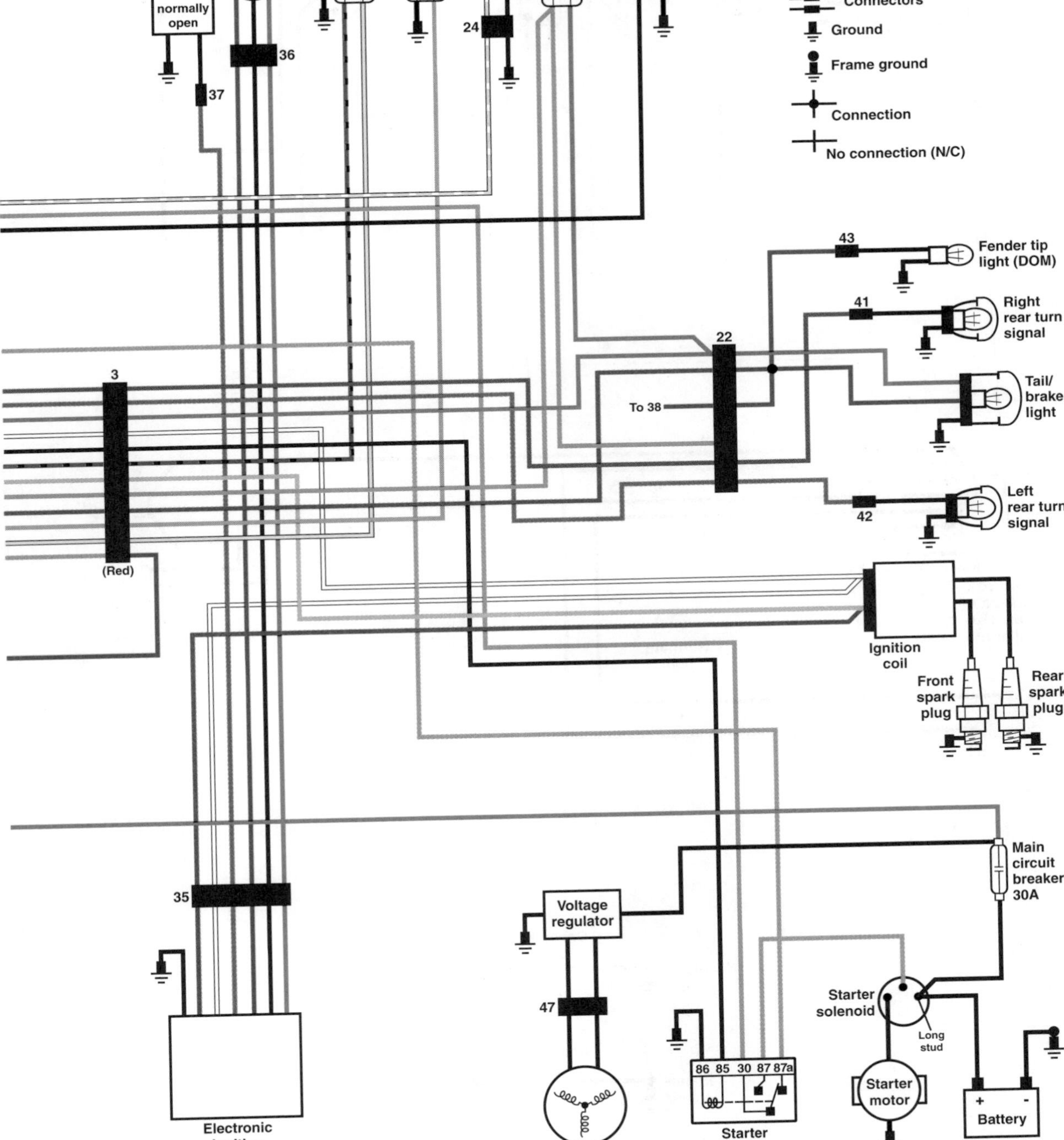

Vacuum operated electrical switch
VOES normally open
Timer and pick-up
Oil pressure switch
Neutral indicator switch
Fuel level sender
Rear brake switch
Antidive valve
Diagram Key
Connectors
Ground
Frame ground
Connection
No connection (N/C)
36
37
24
43
Fender tip light (DOM)
41
Right rear turn signal
22
Tail/ brake light
3
To 38
42
Left rear turn signal
(Red)
Ignition coil
Front spark plug
Rear spark plug
Main circuit breaker 30A
35
Voltage regulator
47
Starter solenoid
Long stud
86 85 30 87 87a
Starter motor
Battery
Electronic ignition module
Stator
Starter relay

1988 FLHTC MODELS SPOTLIGHT SWITCH, HAZARD SWITCH, TURN SIGNAL AND HAZARD FLASHERS, TOURPAK AND GROUNDS

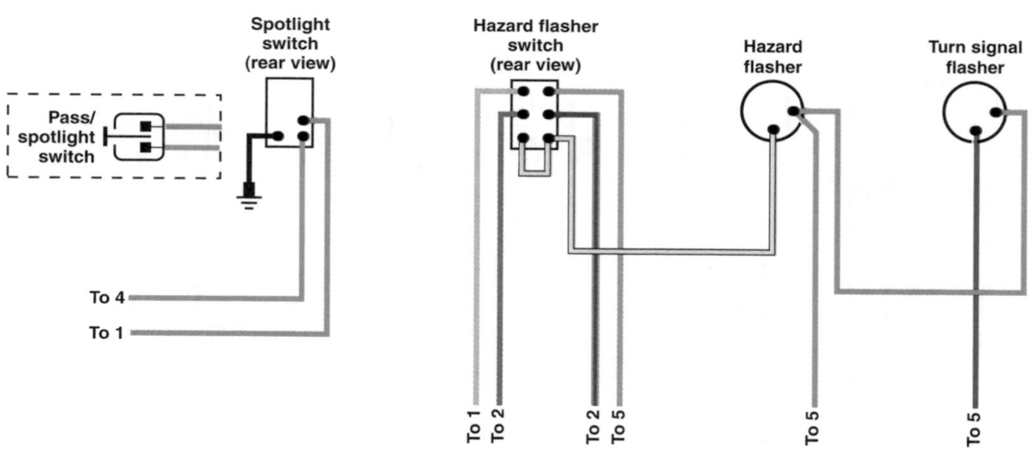

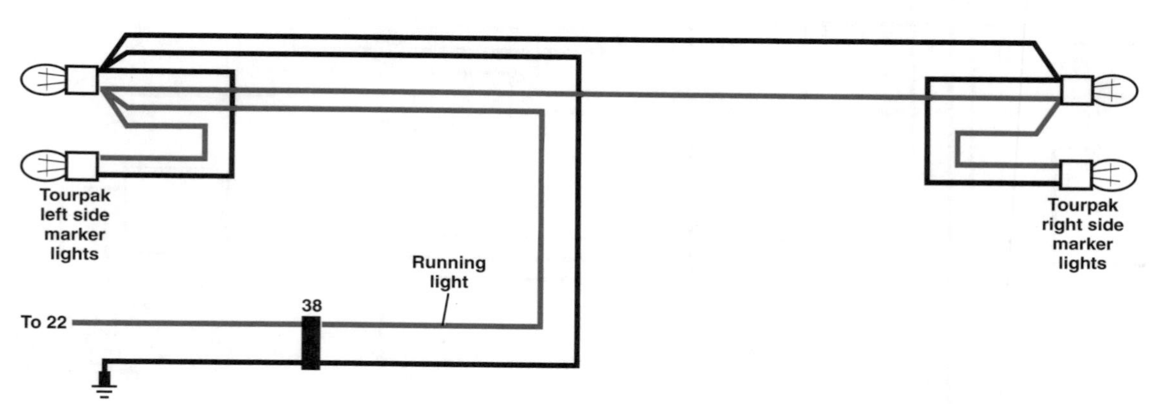

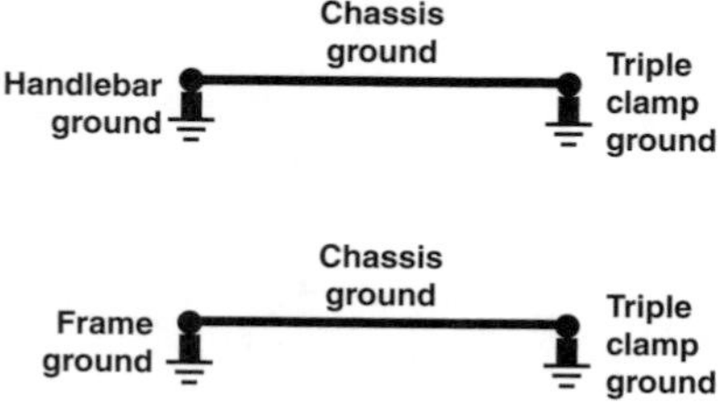

1988 FLHTC MODELS RADIO AND HARNESS CONNECTORS

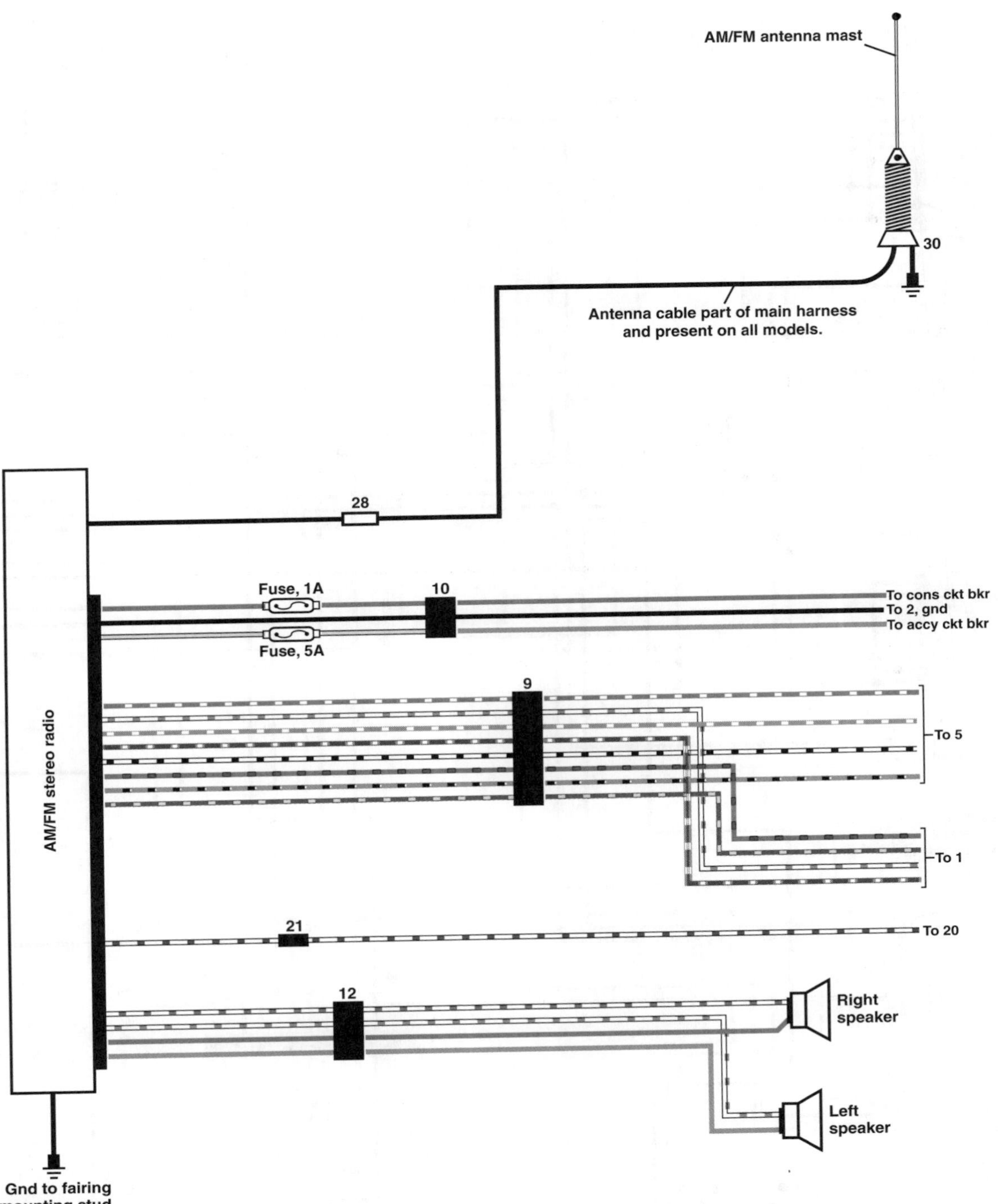

1988 FLTC MODELS

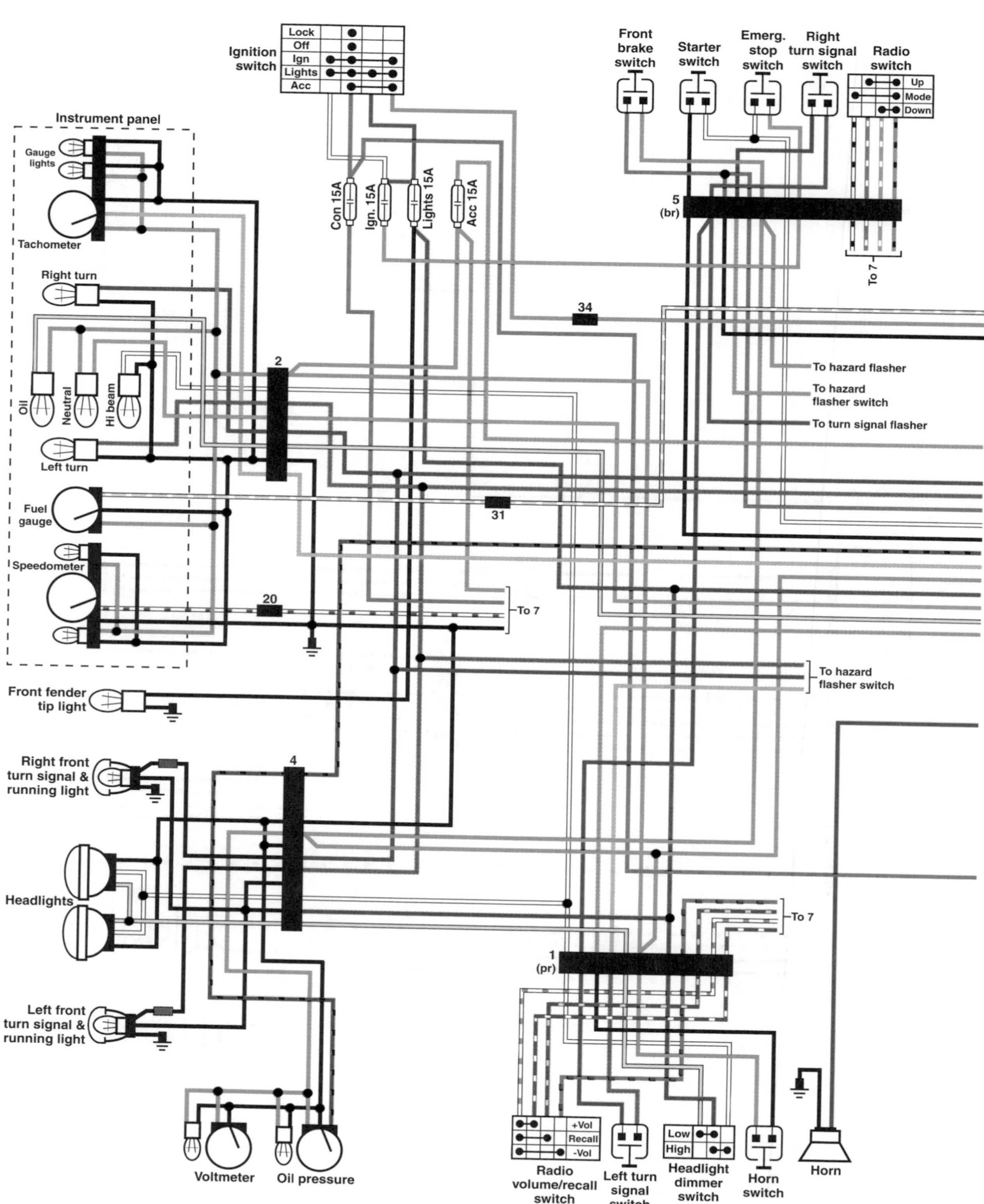

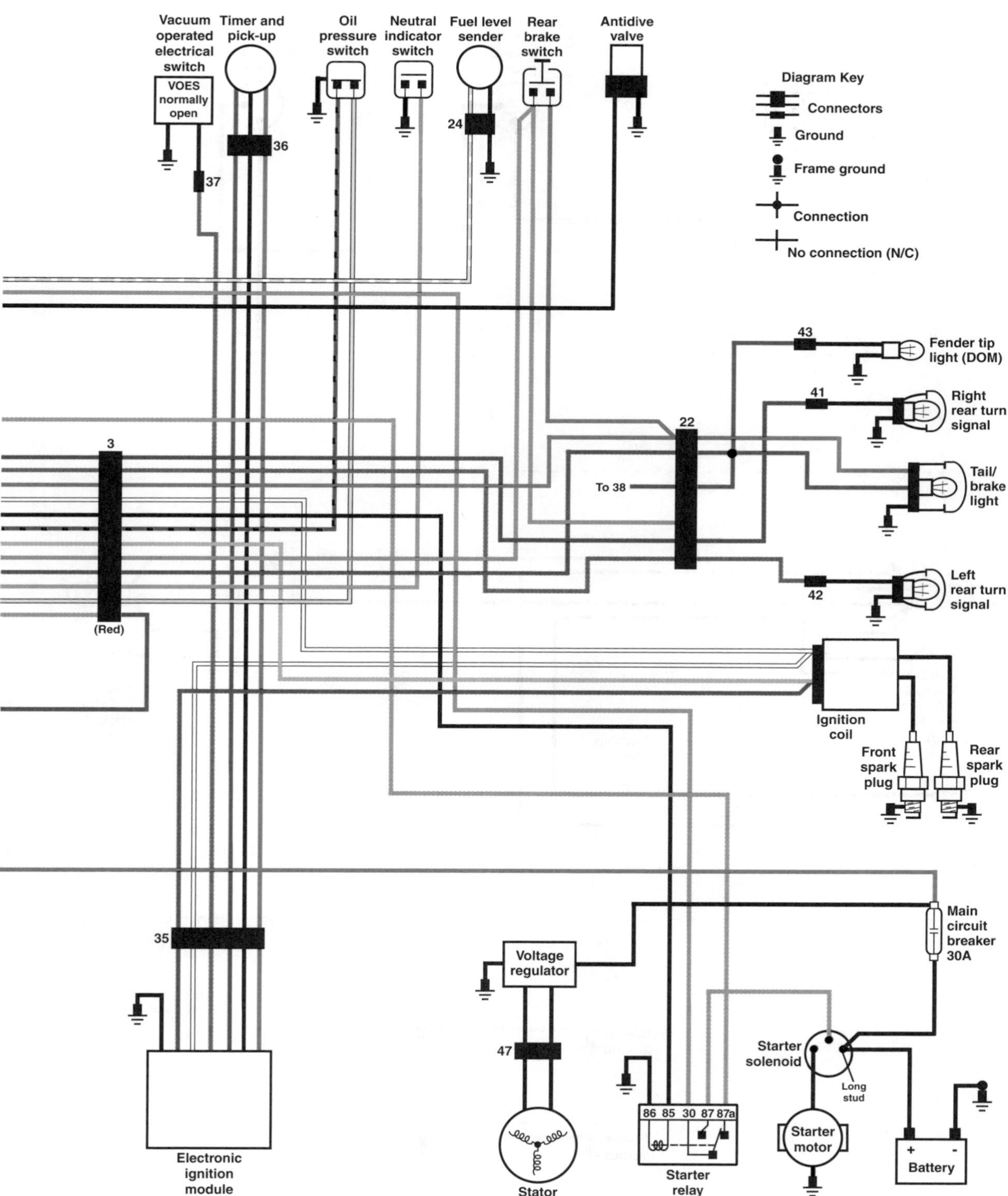
Vacuum operated electrical switch
VOES normally open
Timer and pick-up
Oil pressure switch
Neutral indicator switch
Fuel level sender
Rear brake switch
Antidive valve
Diagram Key
Connectors
Ground
Frame ground
Connection
No connection (N/C)
36
37
24
43
Fender tip light (DOM)
41
Right rear turn signal
22
3
To 38
Tail/ brake light
42
Left rear turn signal
(Red)
Ignition coil
Front spark plug
Rear spark plug
35
Main circuit breaker 30A
Voltage regulator
47
Starter solenoid
Long stud
86 85 30 87 87a
Starter relay
Starter motor
Battery
Electronic ignition module
Stator

1988 FLTC MODELS HAZARD SWITCH, TURN SIGNAL AND HAZARD FLASHERS, TOURPAK AND GROUNDS

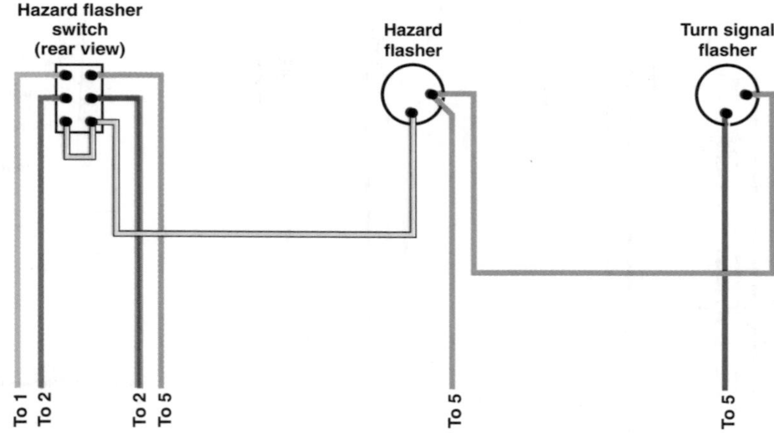

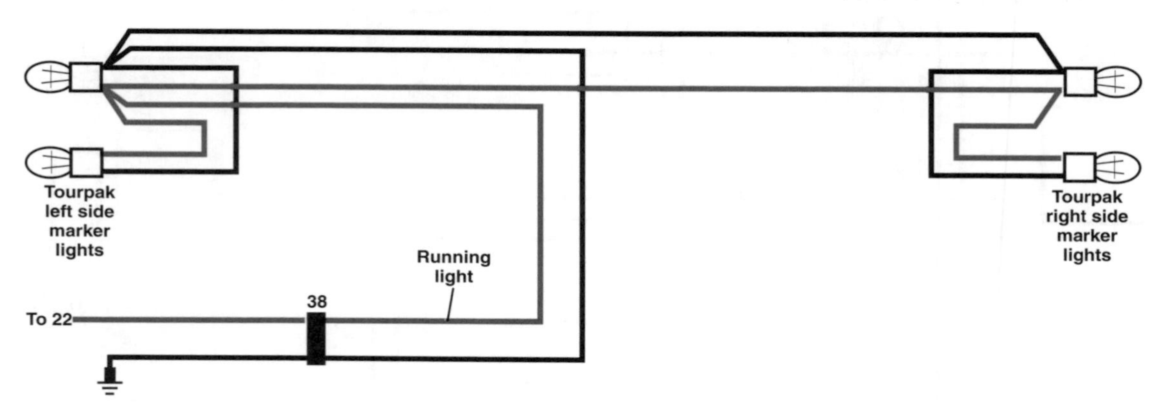

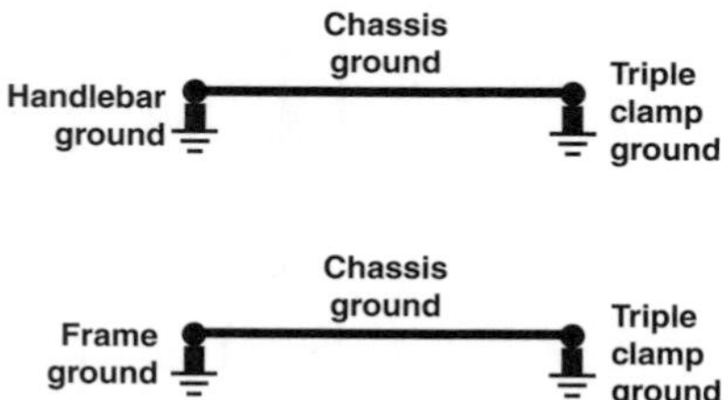

1988 FLTC MODELS RADIO AND HARNESS CONNECTORS

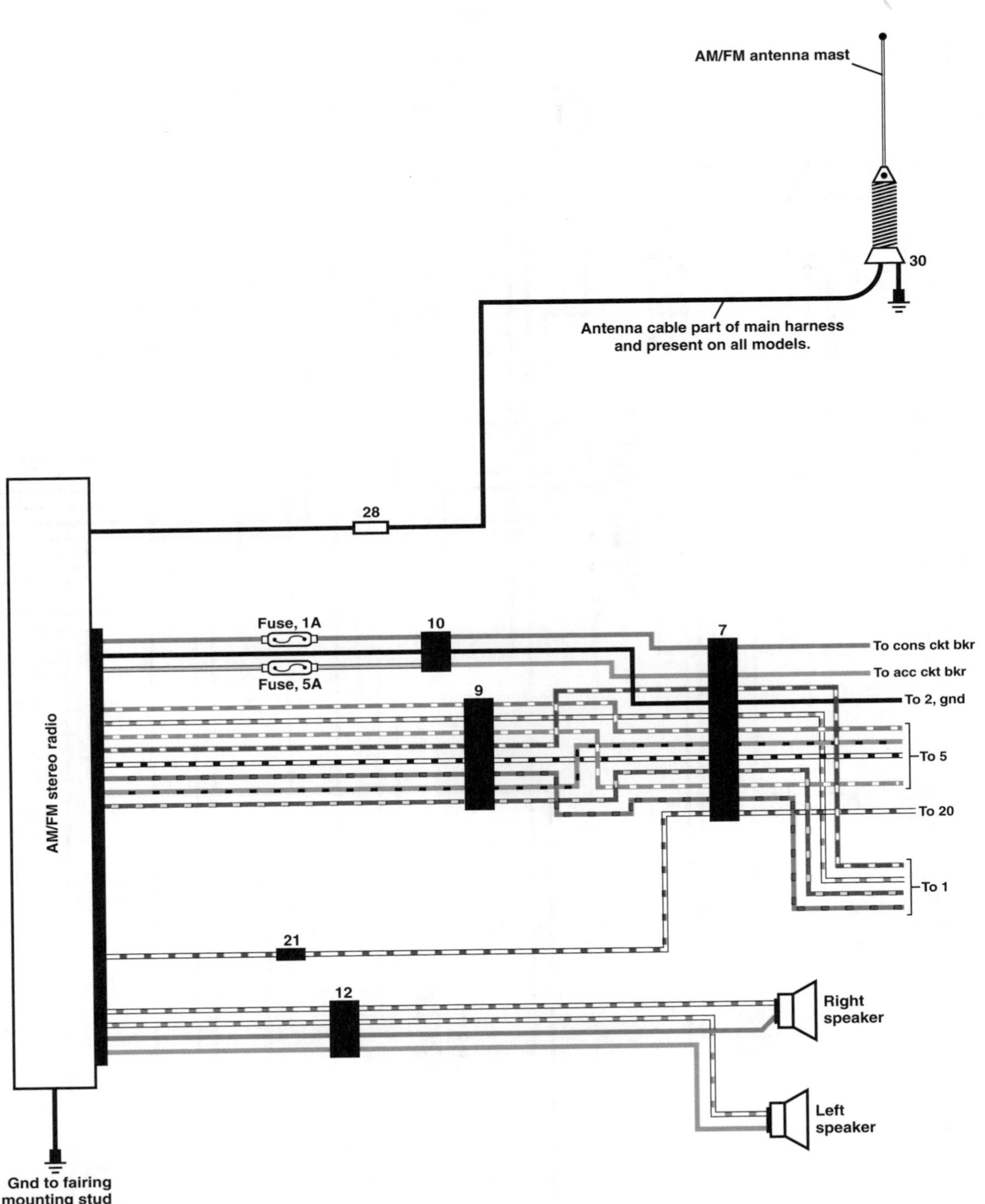

1988-1990 FXRS MODELS

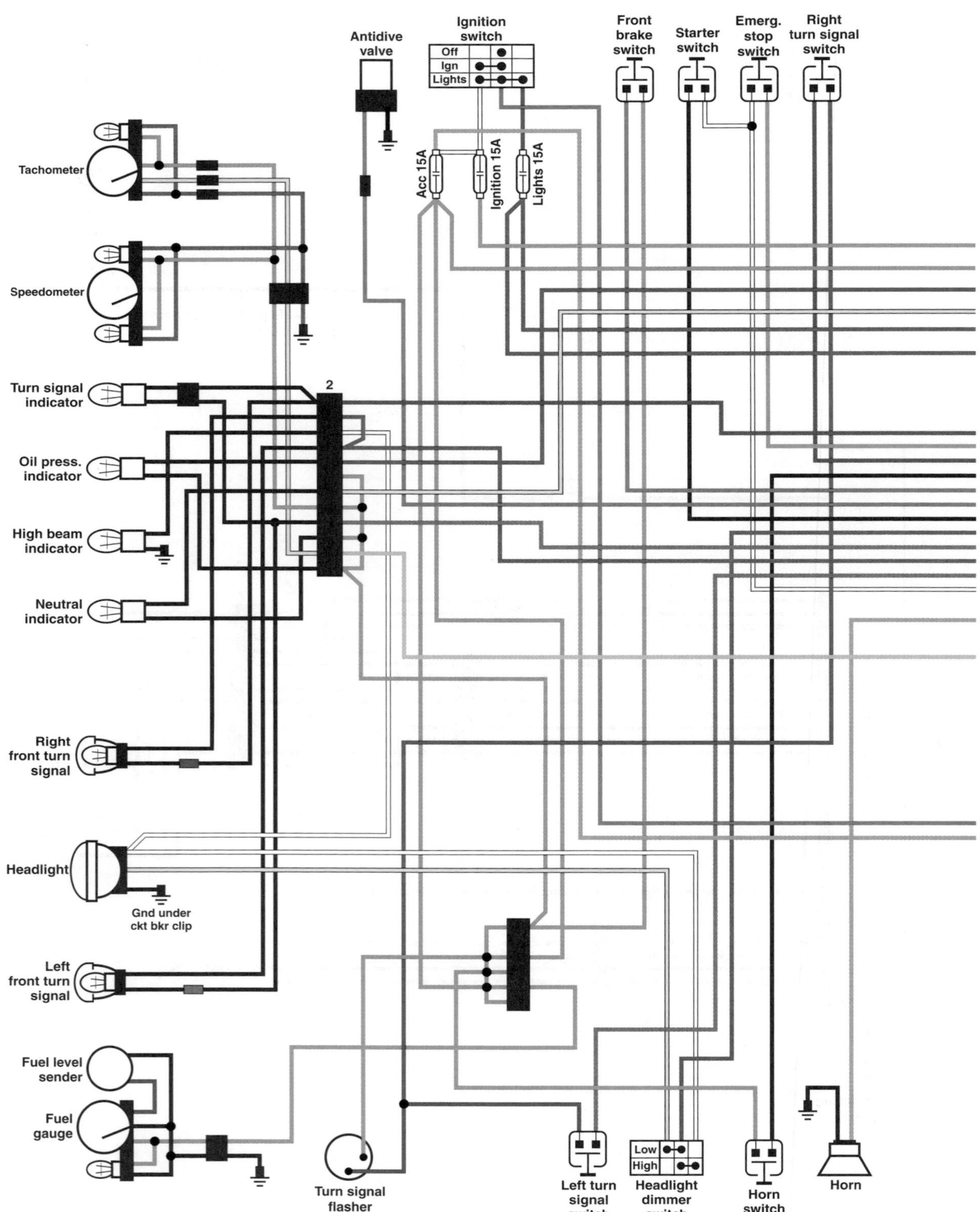

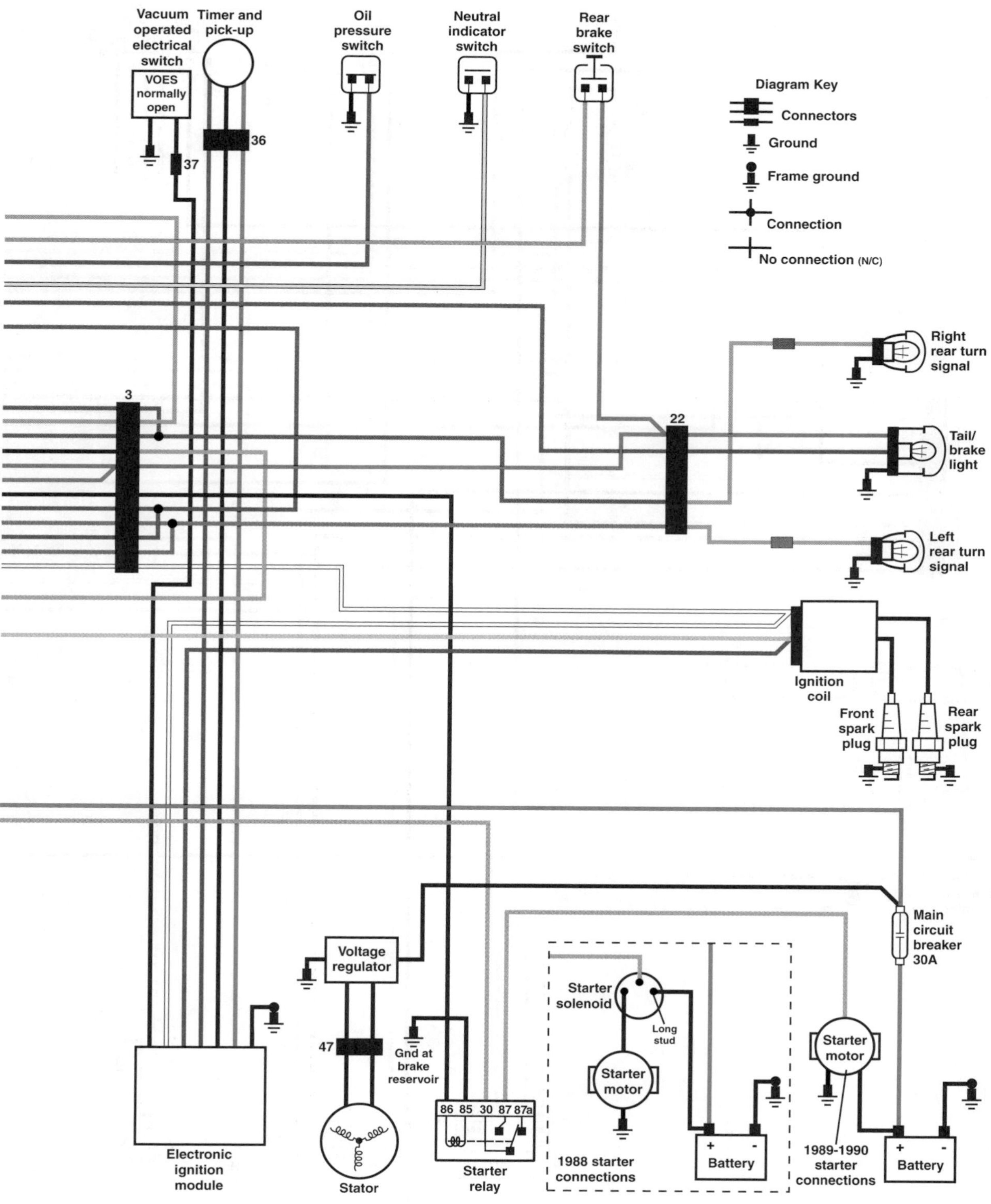

Vacuum operated electrical switch
VOES normally open
Timer and pick-up
Oil pressure switch
Neutral indicator switch
Rear brake switch
Diagram Key
Connectors
Ground
Frame ground
Connection
No connection (N/C)
36
37
3
22
Right rear turn signal
Tail/ brake light
Left rear turn signal
Ignition coil
Front spark plug
Rear spark plug
Main circuit breaker 30A
Voltage regulator
47
Gnd at brake reservoir
86 85 30 87 87a
Starter relay
Starter solenoid
Long stud
Starter motor
Battery
1988 starter connections
Starter motor
1989-1990 starter connections
Battery
Electronic ignition module
Stator

1988-1990 FXRT MODELS

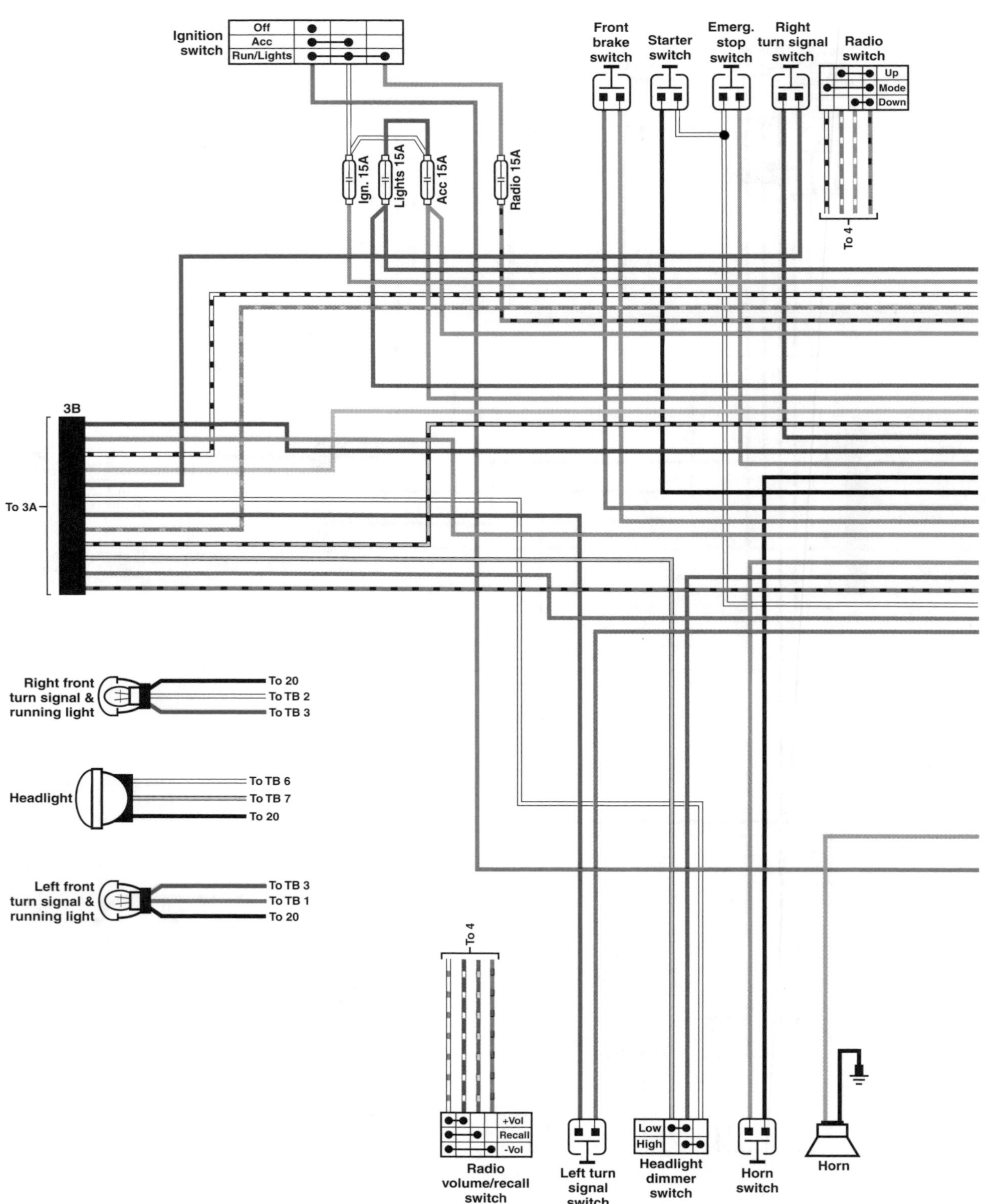

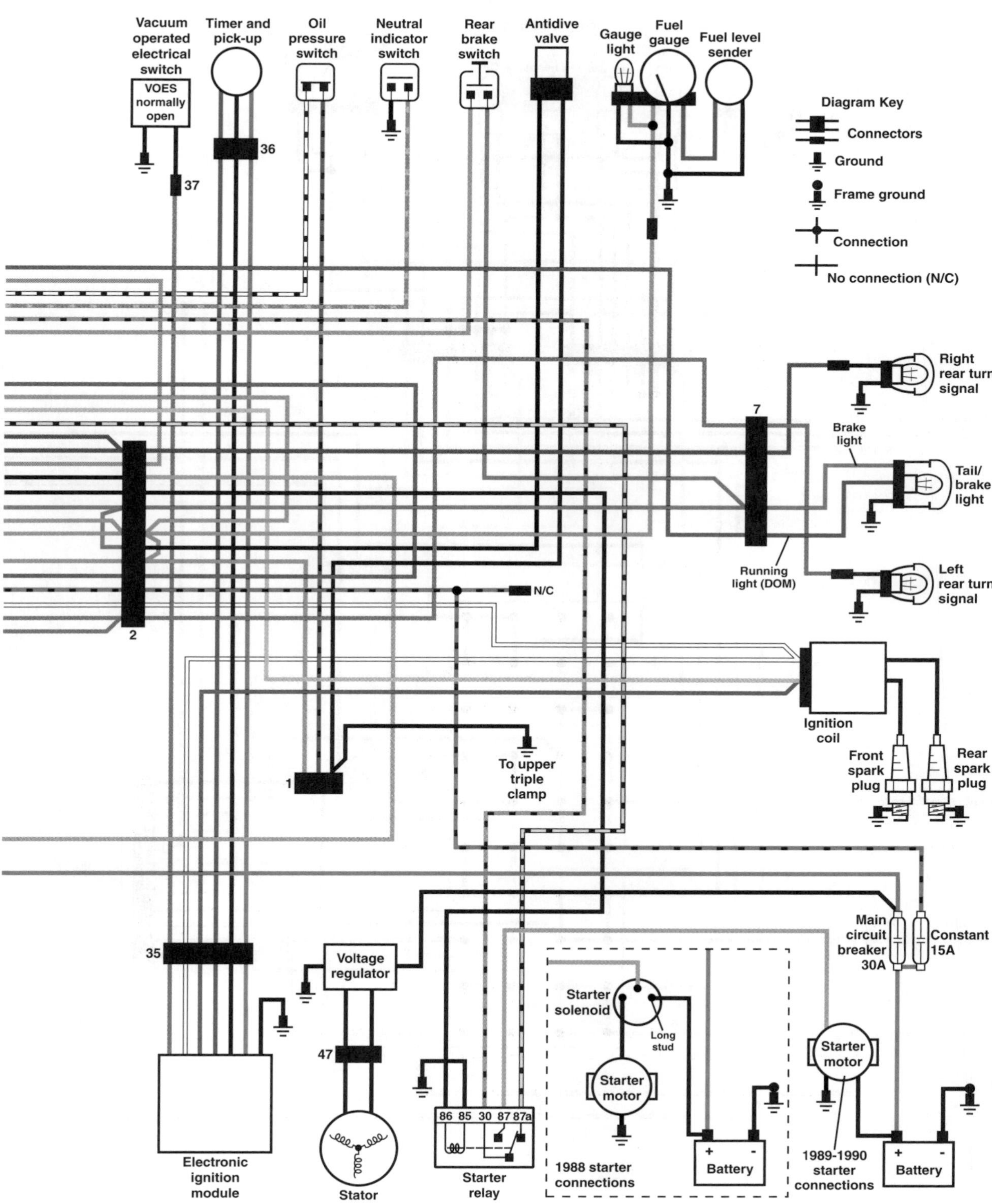
Vacuum operated electrical switch
VOES normally open
Timer and pick-up
Oil pressure switch
Neutral indicator switch
Rear brake switch
Antidive valve
Gauge light
Fuel gauge
Fuel level sender
Diagram Key
Connectors
Ground
Frame ground
Connection
No connection (N/C)
36
37
Right rear turn signal
7
Brake light
Tail/ brake light
Running light (DOM)
Left rear turn signal
N/C
2
Ignition coil
Front spark plug
Rear spark plug
1
To upper triple clamp
Main circuit breaker 30A
Constant 15A
35
Voltage regulator
47
Starter solenoid
Long stud
Starter motor
Starter motor
86 85 30 87 87a
Electronic ignition module
Stator
Starter relay
1988 starter connections
Battery
1989-1990 starter connections
Battery

1988-1990 FXRT MODELS INSTRUMENT PANEL, TERMINAL BLOCK AND RADIO

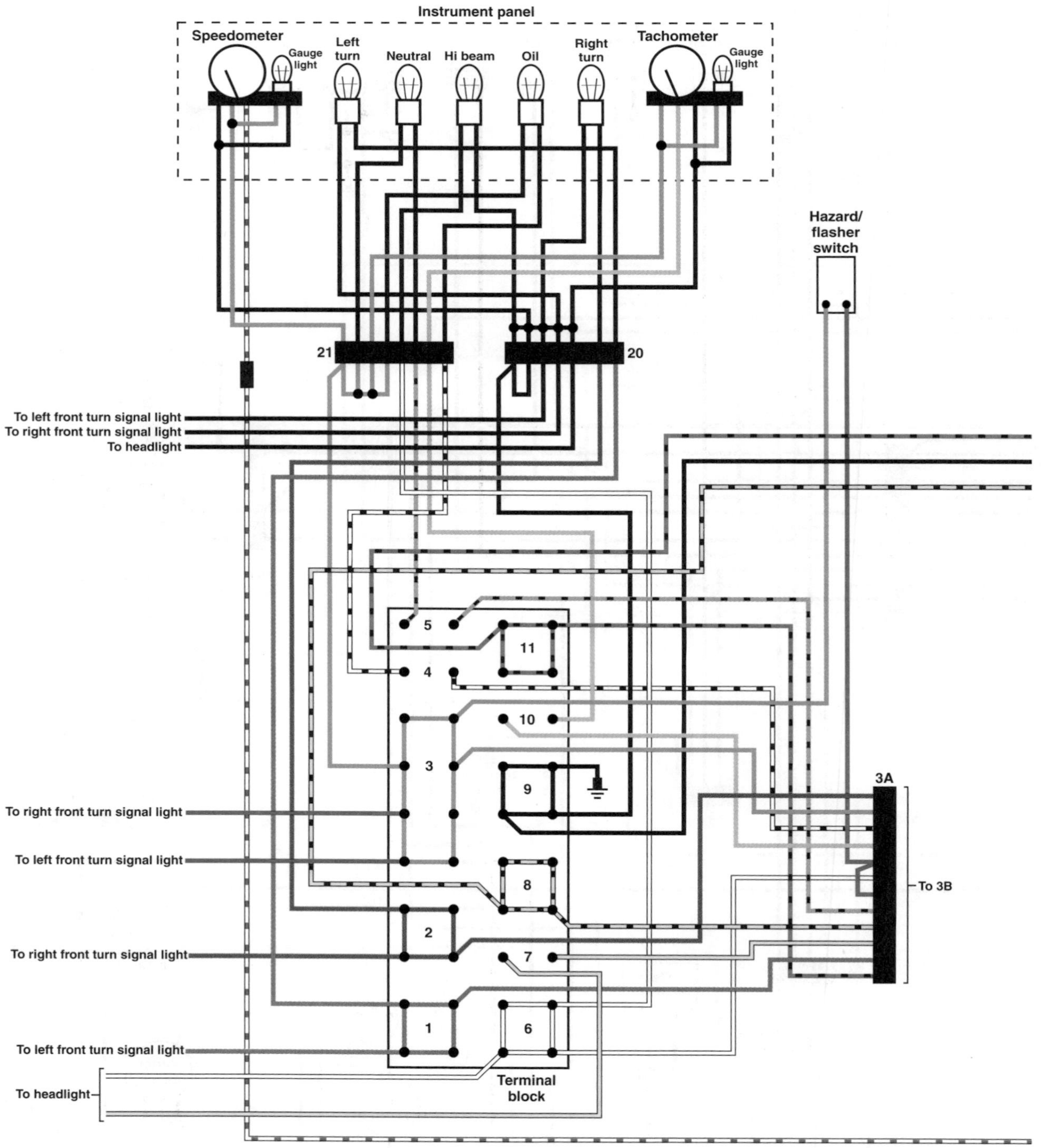

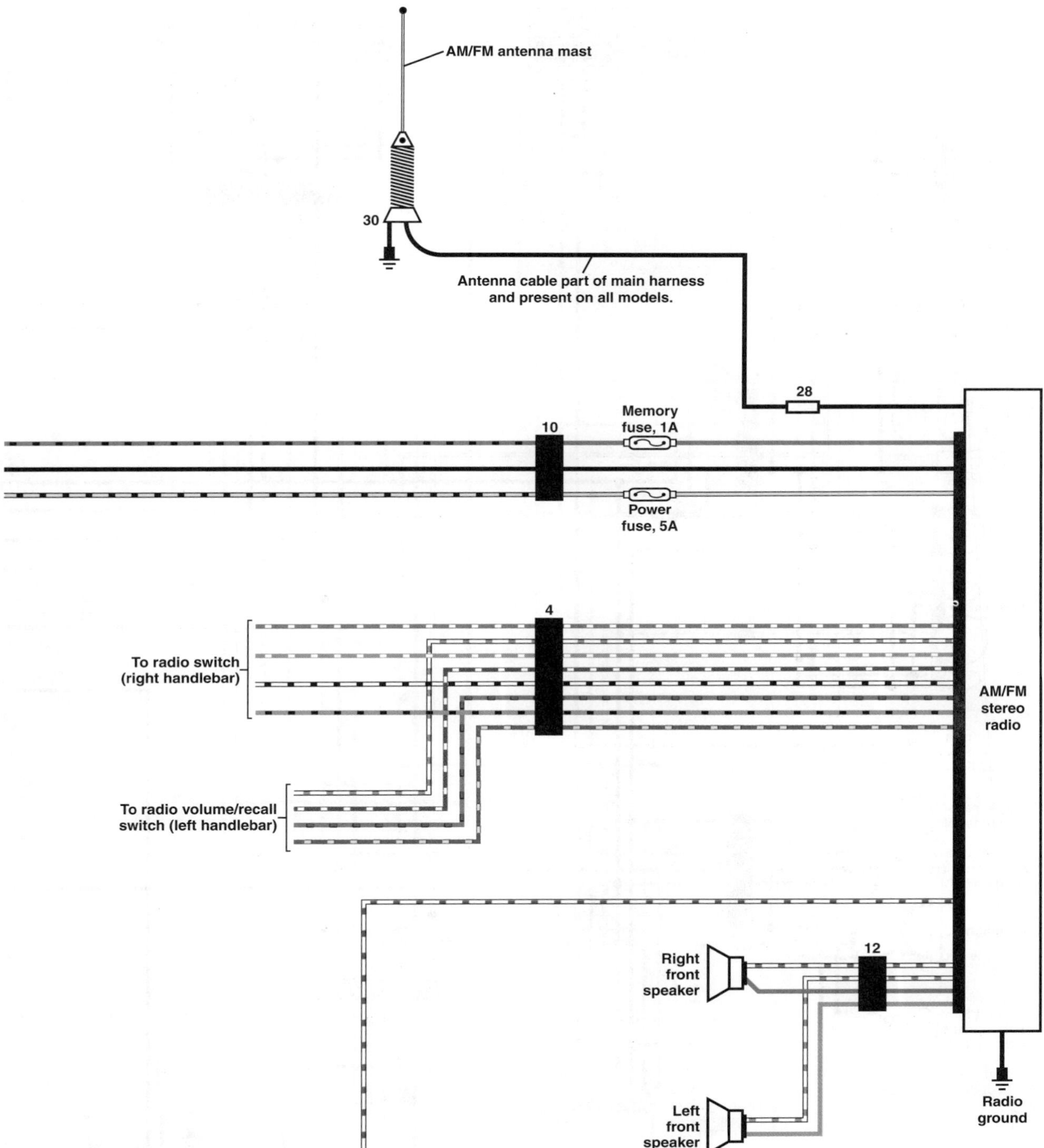
AM/FM antenna mast
30
Antenna cable part of main harness
and present on all models.
28
Memory
fuse, 1A
10
Power
fuse, 5A
4
To radio switch
(right handlebar)
AM/FM
stereo
radio
To radio volume/recall
switch (left handlebar)
12
Right
front
speaker
Left
front
speaker
Radio
ground

1989-1990 FLHS MODELS

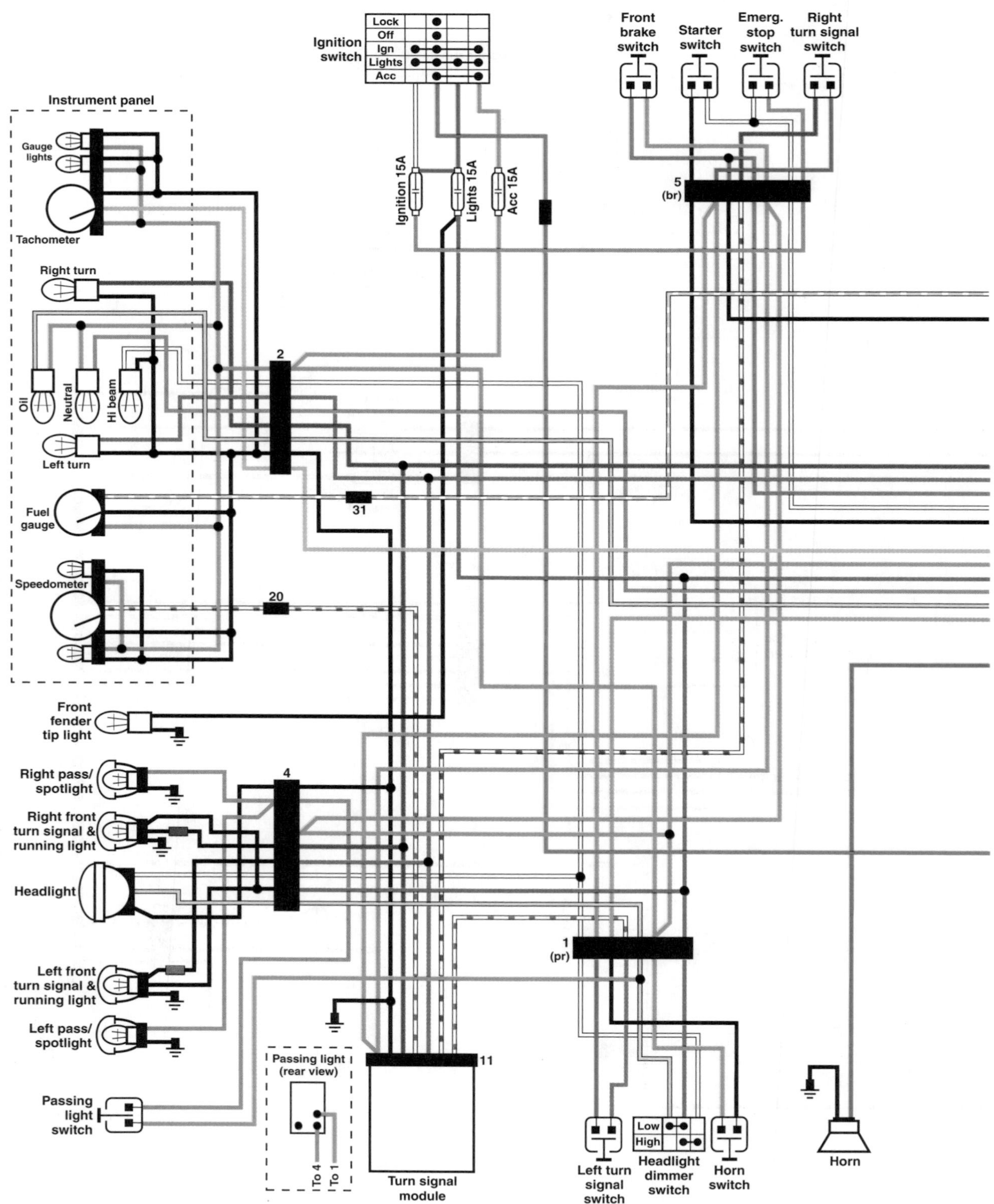

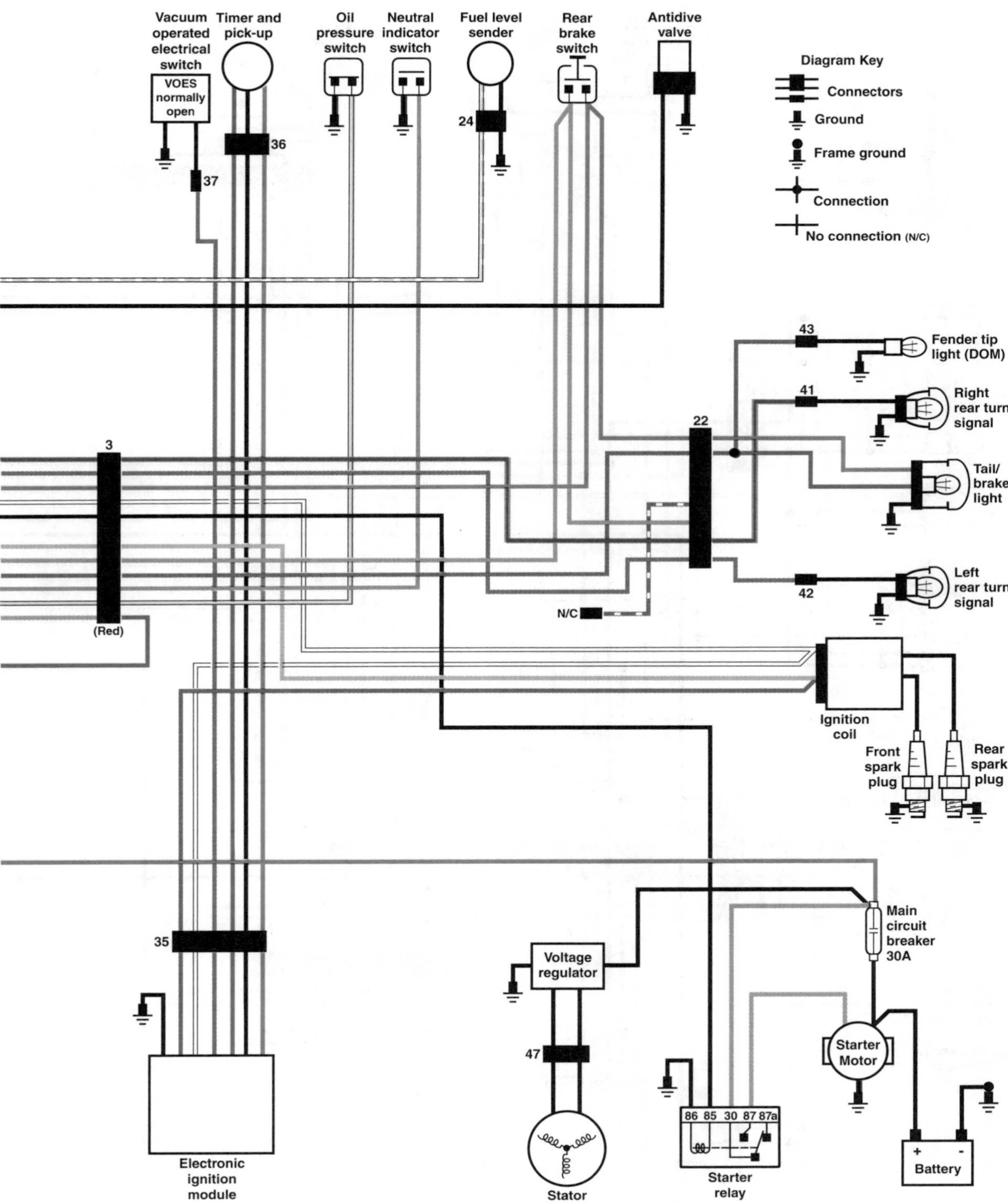
Vacuum operated electrical switch
VOES normally open
Timer and pick-up
Oil pressure switch
Neutral indicator switch
Fuel level sender
Rear brake switch
Antidive valve
Diagram Key
Connectors
Ground
Frame ground
Connection
No connection (N/C)
36
37
24
43
Fender tip light (DOM)
41
Right rear turn signal
22
3
Tail/ brake light
42
Left rear turn signal
N/C
(Red)
Ignition coil
Front spark plug
Rear spark plug
Main circuit breaker 30A
35
Voltage regulator
47
Starter Motor
86 85 30 87 87a
Electronic ignition module
Stator
Starter relay
Battery

1989-1990 FLHTC MODELS

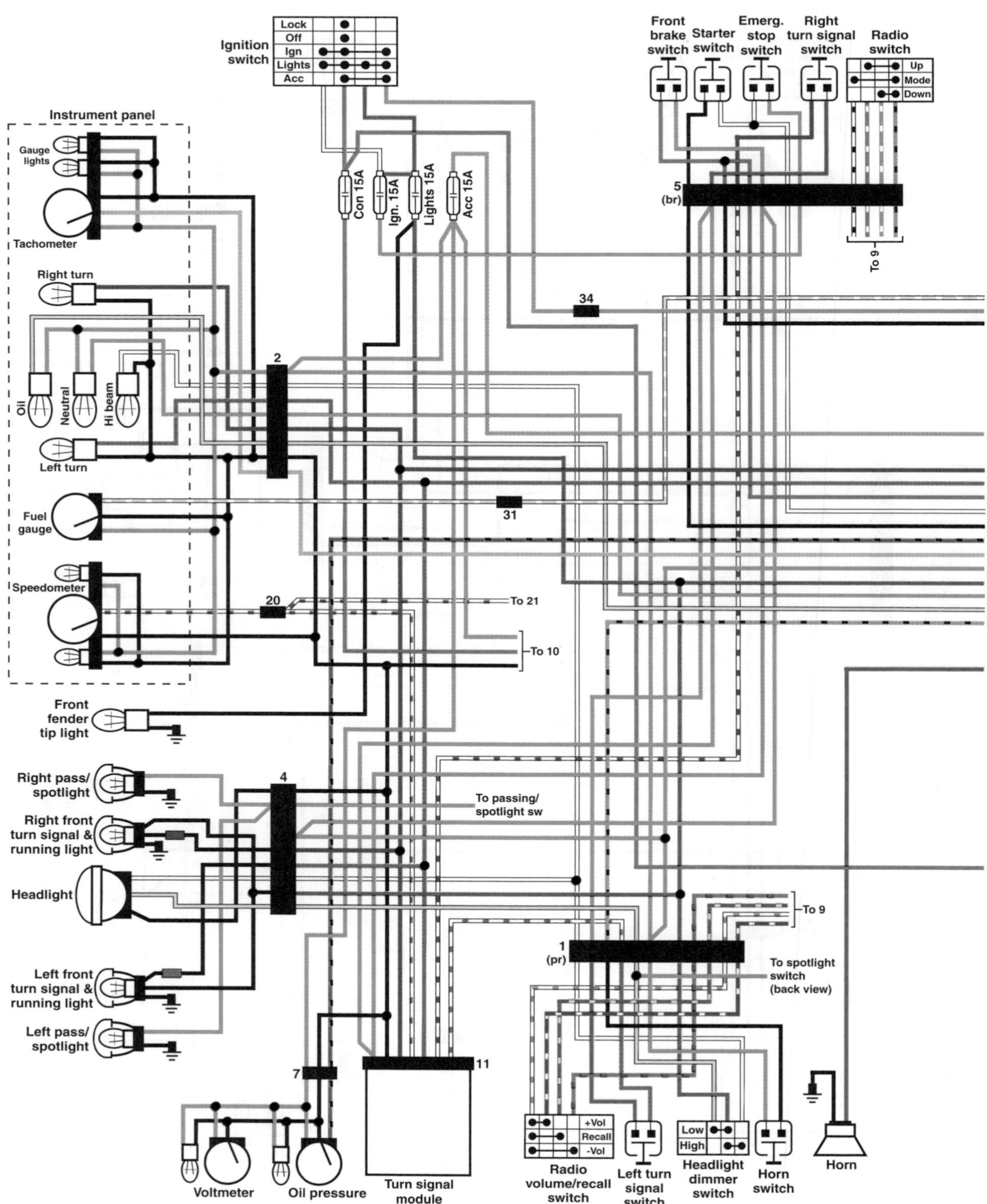

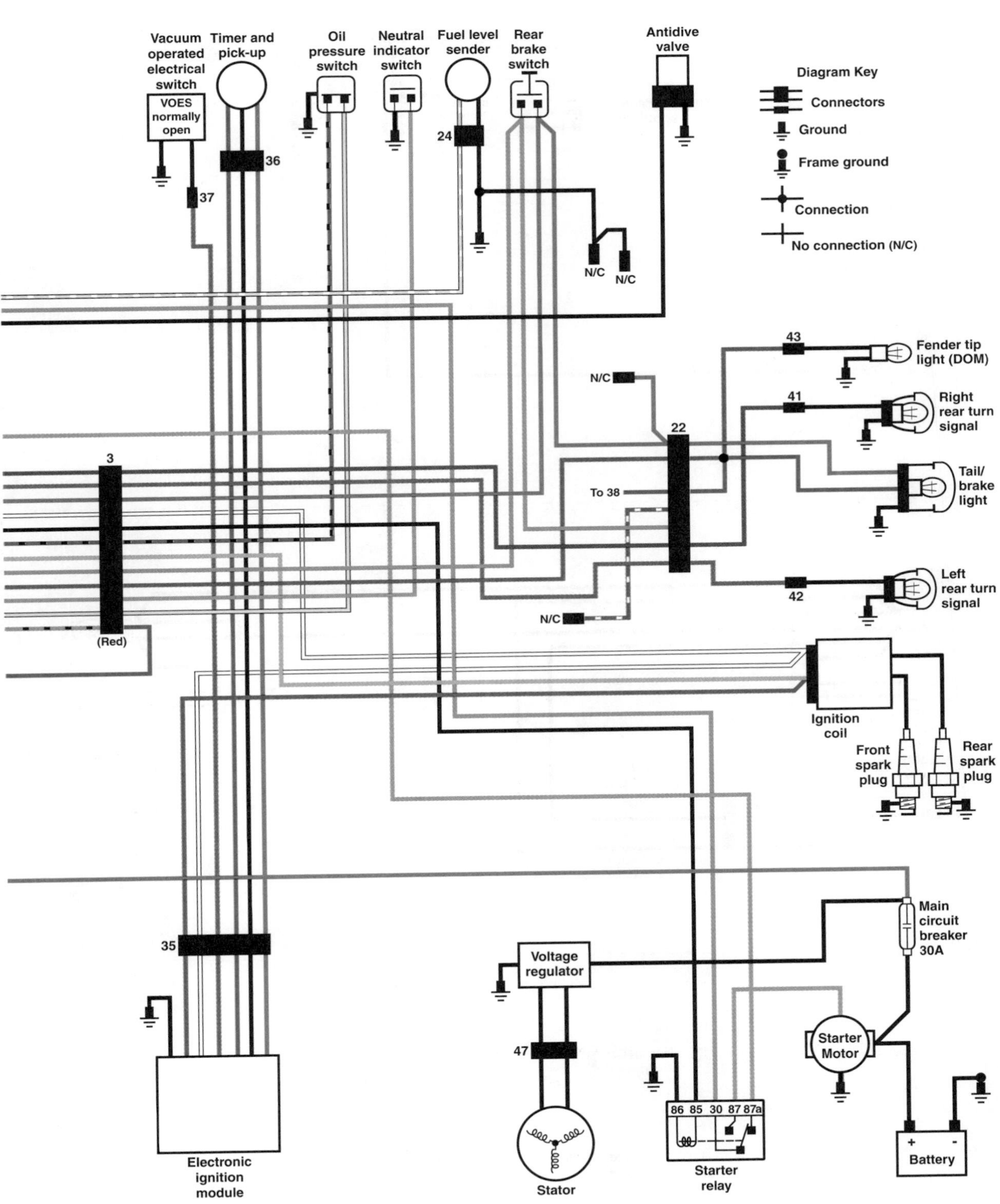
Vacuum operated electrical switch
VOES normally open
Timer and pick-up
Oil pressure switch
Neutral indicator switch
Fuel level sender
Rear brake switch
Antidive valve
Diagram Key
Connectors
Ground
Frame ground
Connection
No connection (N/C)
36
37
24
N/C
N/C
43
Fender tip light (DOM)
N/C
41
Right rear turn signal
22
Tail/ brake light
3
To 38
42
Left rear turn signal
N/C
(Red)
Ignition coil
Front spark plug
Rear spark plug
Main circuit breaker 30A
35
Voltage regulator
47
Starter Motor
86 85 30 87 87a
Battery
Electronic ignition module
Stator
Starter relay

17

1989-1990 FLHTC MODELS DASH SWITCHES, TOURPAK AND GROUNDS

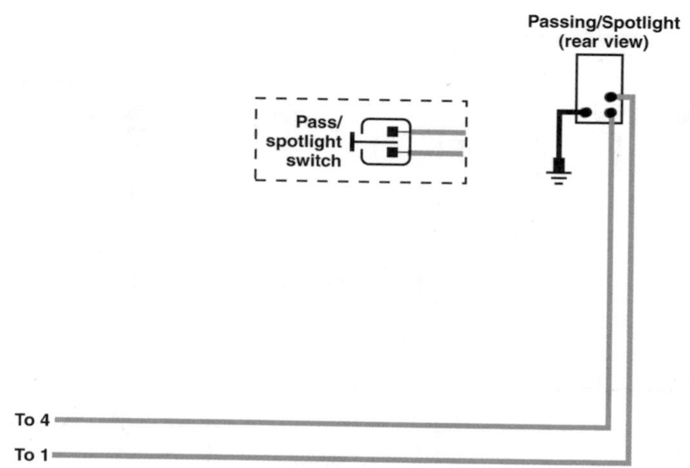

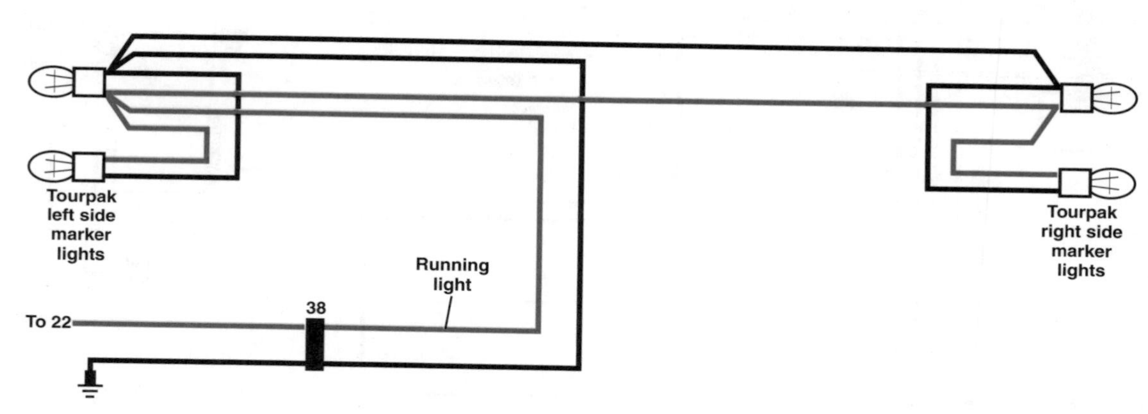

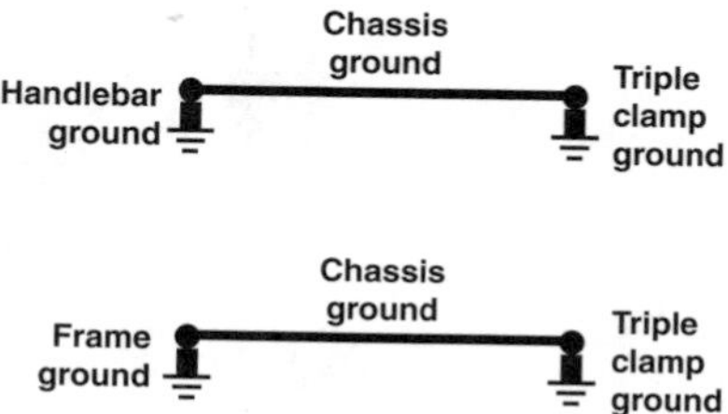

1989-1990 FLHTC MODELS RADIO, HARNESS CONNECTORS AND ANTENNA

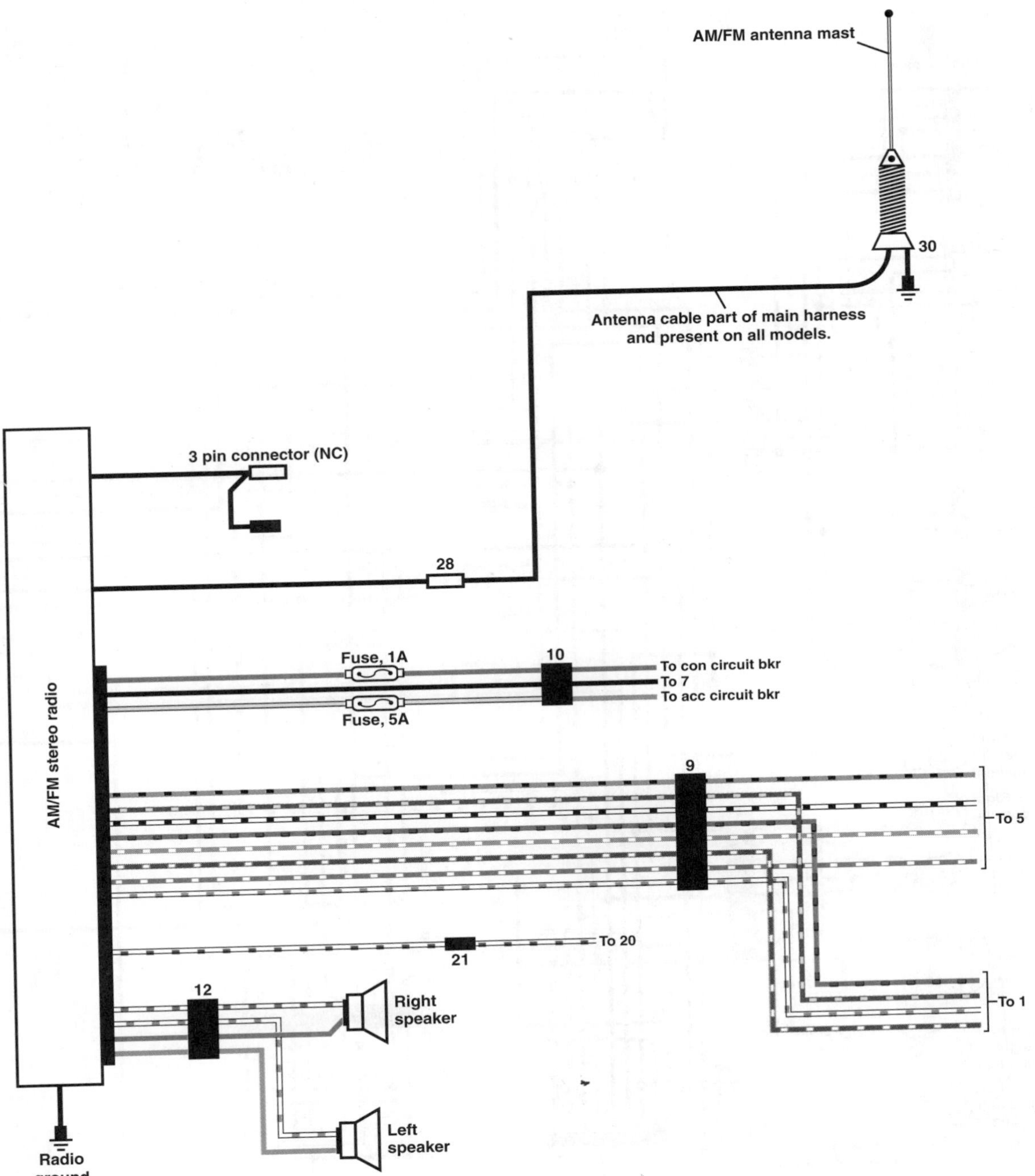

1989 FLHTC ULTRA MODELS

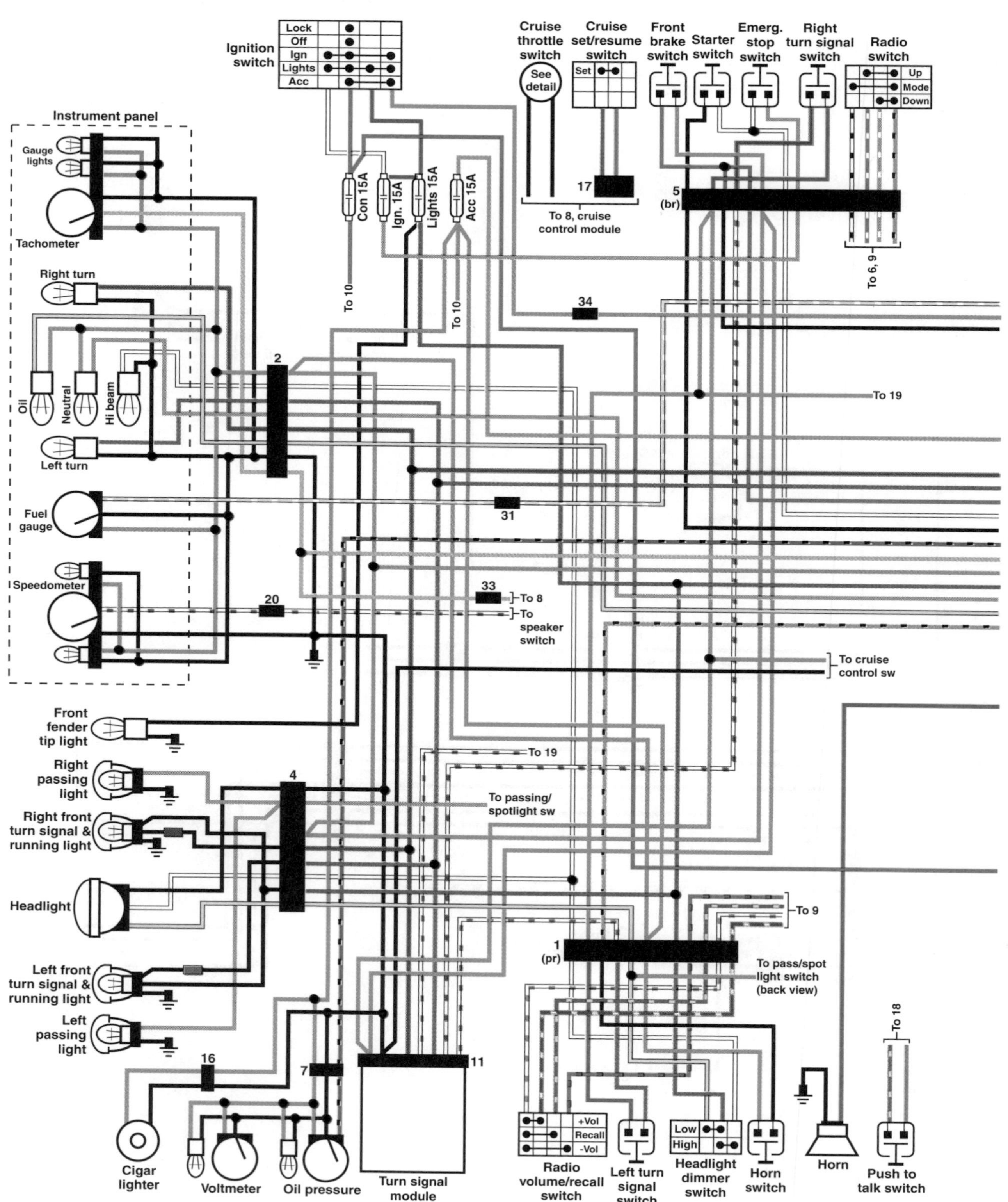

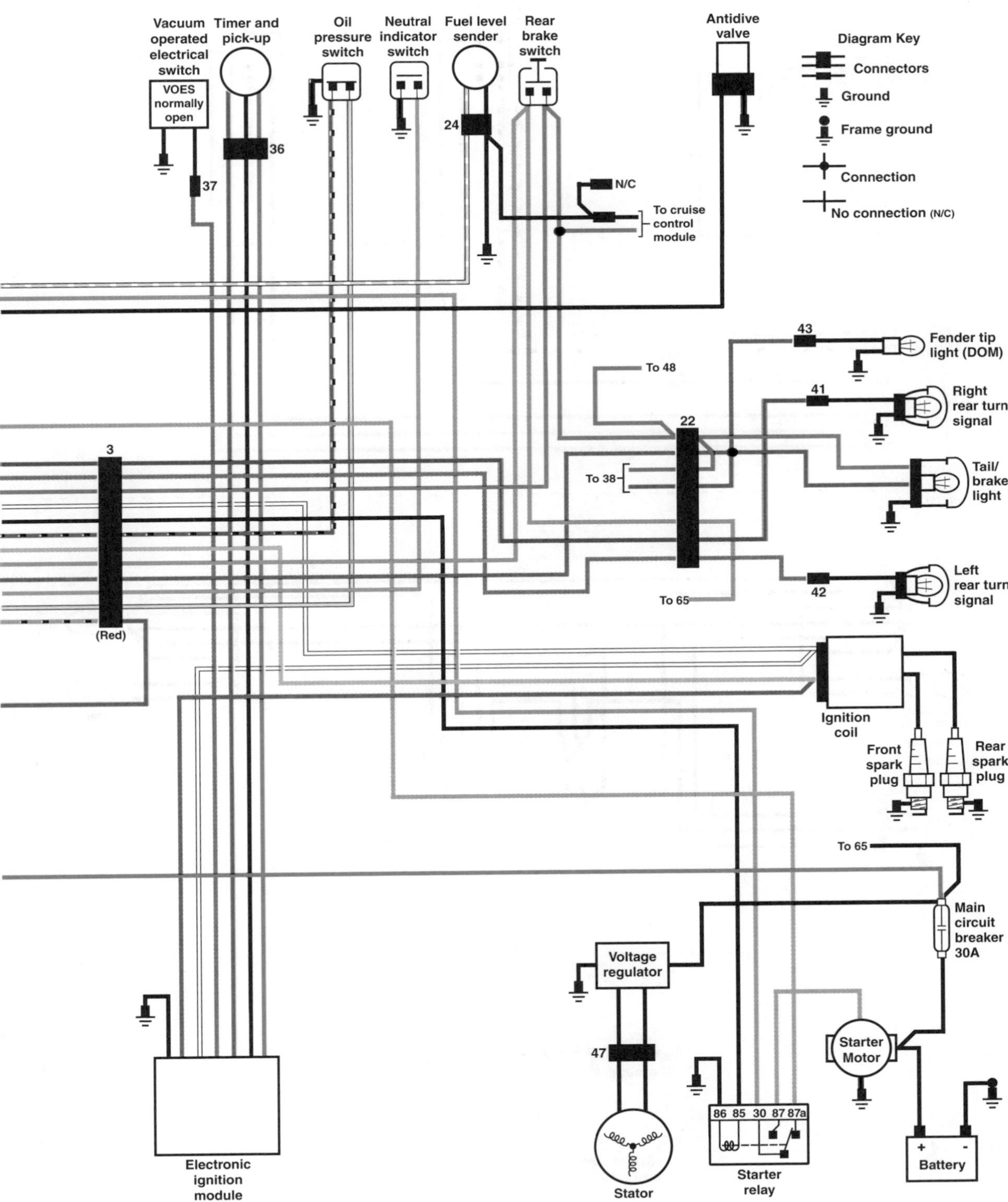
Vacuum operated electrical switch
VOES normally open
Timer and pick-up
Oil pressure switch
Neutral indicator switch
Fuel level sender
Rear brake switch
Antidive valve
Diagram Key
Connectors
Ground
Frame ground
Connection
No connection (N/C)
36
37
24
N/C
To cruise control module
43
Fender tip light (DOM)
To 48
41
Right rear turn signal
22
3
Tail/ brake light
To 38
Left rear turn signal
42
To 65
(Red)
Ignition coil
Front spark plug
Rear spark plug
To 65
Main circuit breaker 30A
Voltage regulator
47
Starter Motor
86 85 30 87 87a
+ -
Battery
Electronic ignition module
Stator
Starter relay

1989 FLHTC ULTRA MODELS DASH SWITCHES, TOURPAK AND GROUNDS

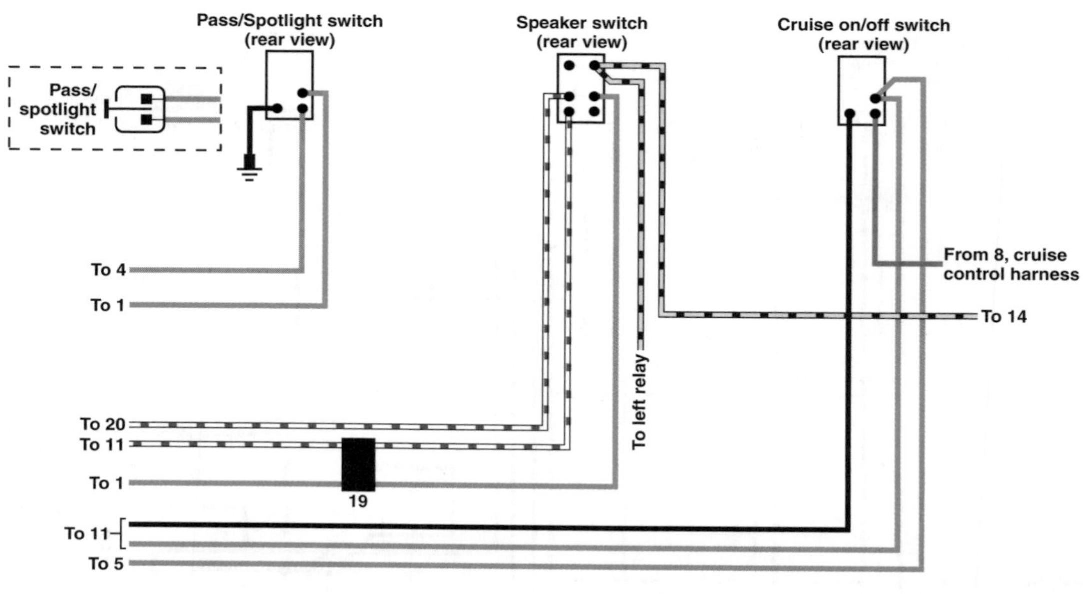

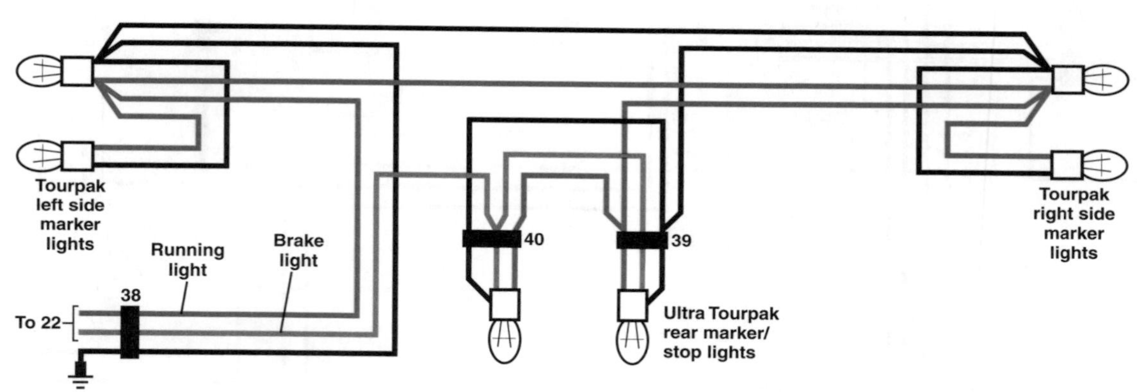

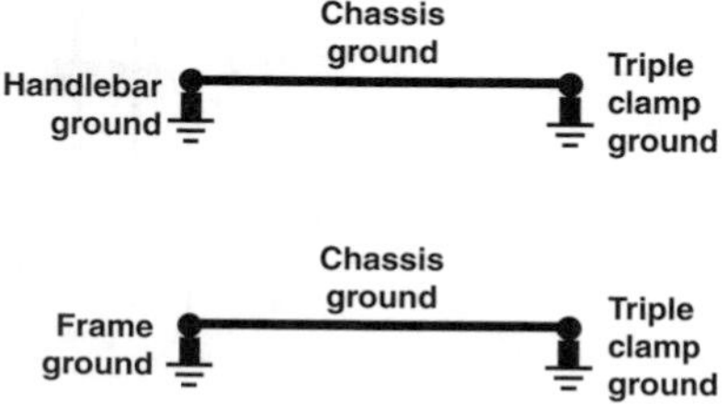

1989 FLHTC ULTRA MODELS RADIO, HARNESS CONNECTORS AND CRUISE CONTROL CONNECTIONS

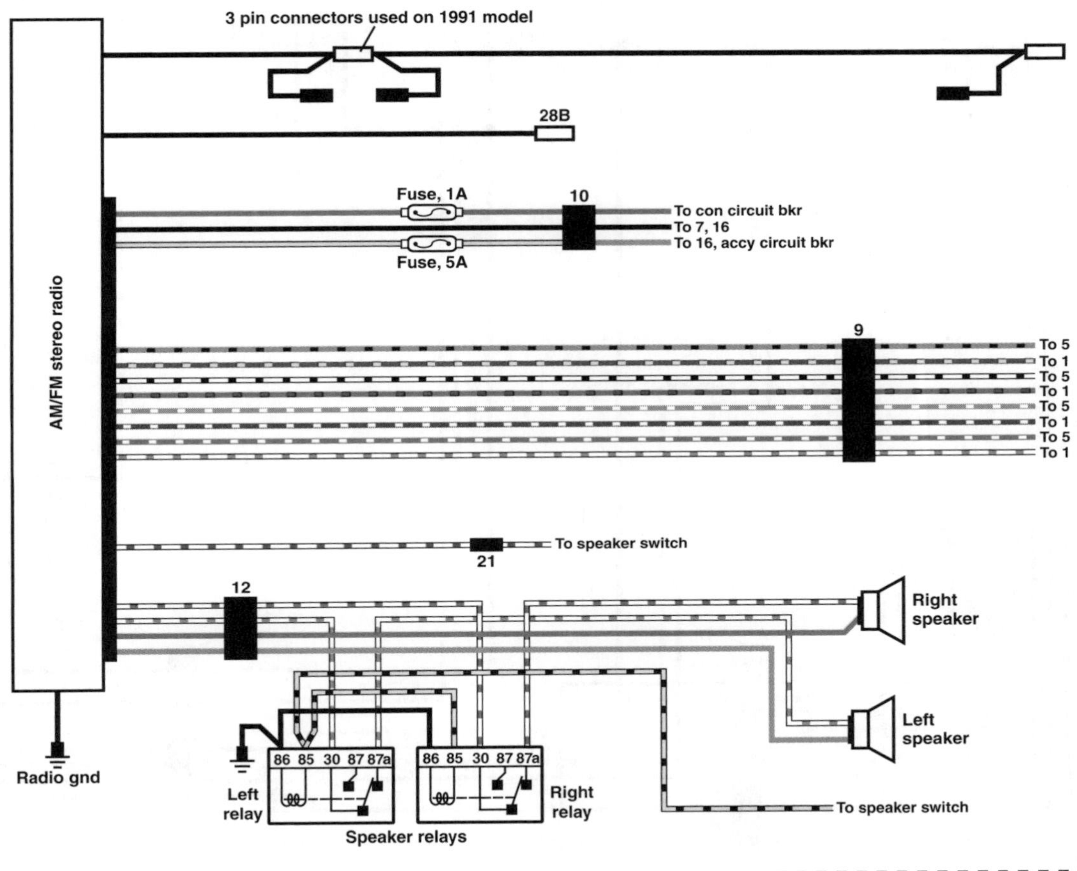

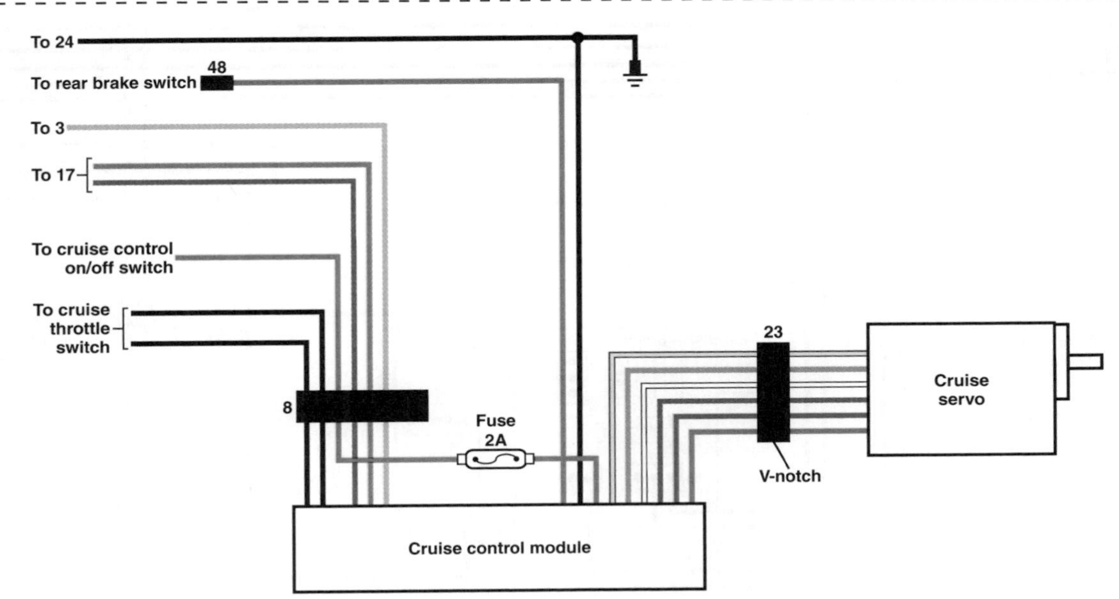

1989 FLHTC ULTRA MODELS RADIO CB/INTERCOM, REAR SPEAKERS AND ANTENNAS

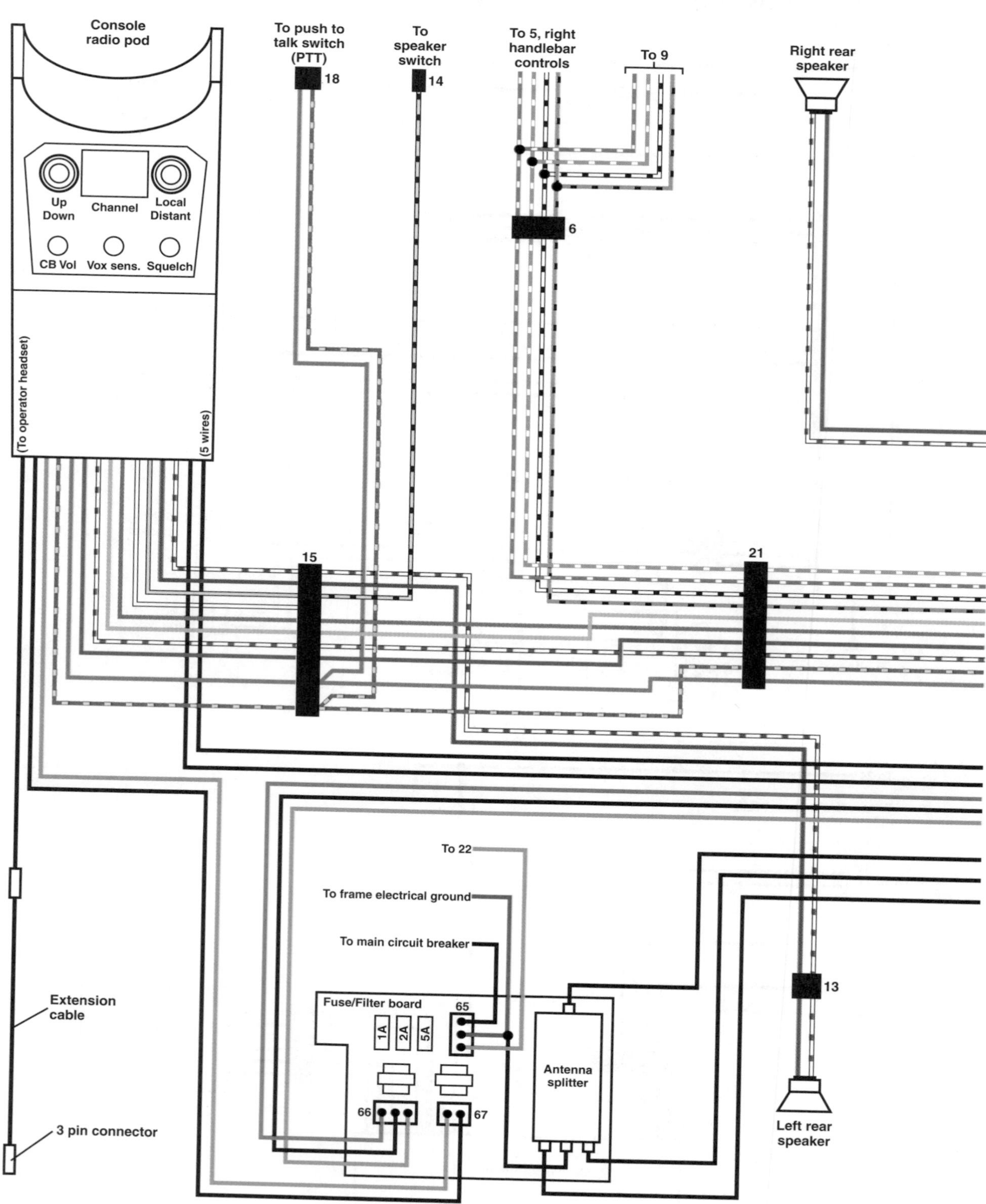

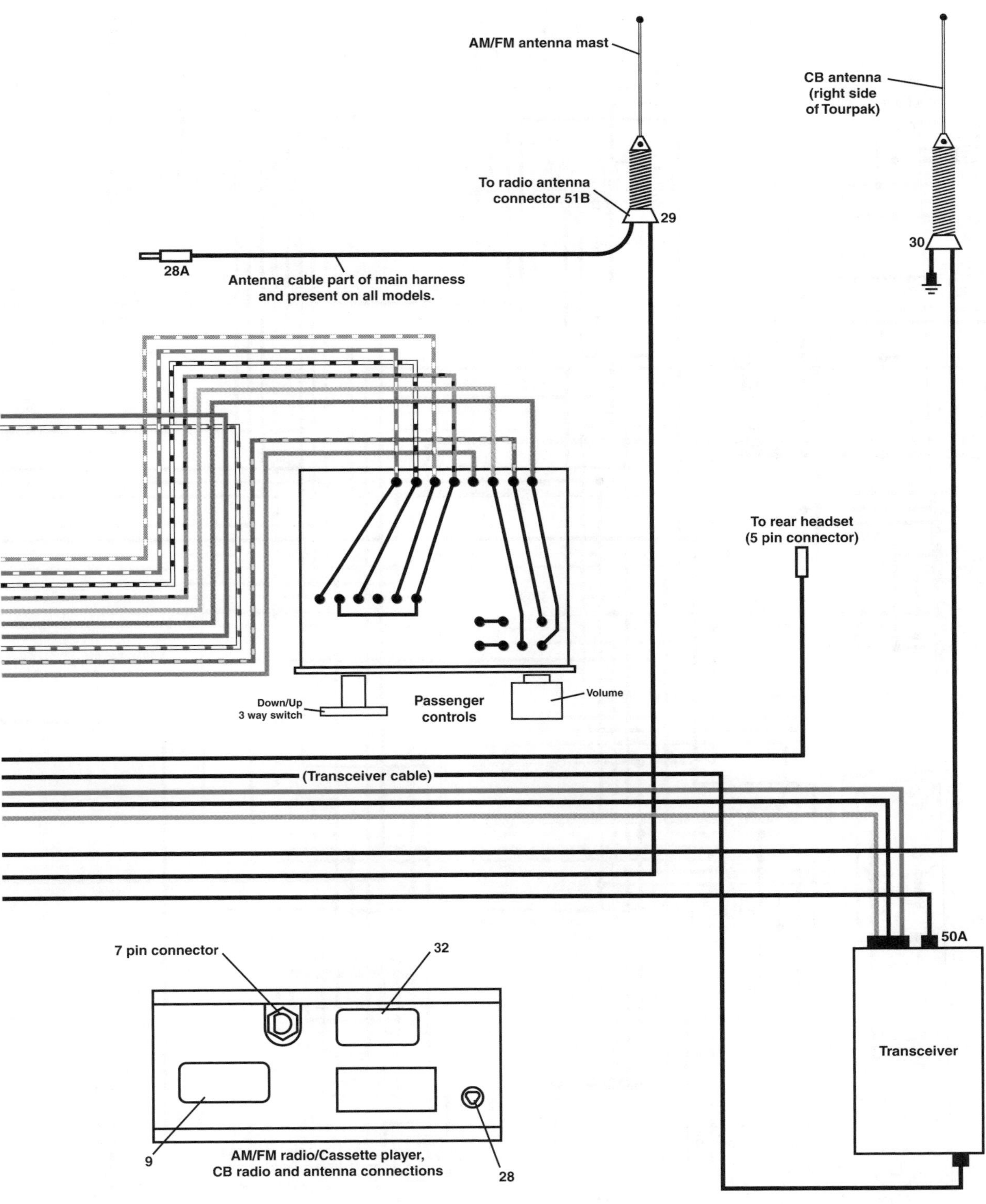
AM/FM antenna mast
CB antenna
(right side
of Tourpak)
To radio antenna
connector 51B
29
30
28A
Antenna cable part of main harness
and present on all models.
To rear headset
(5 pin connector)
Down/Up
3 way switch
Passenger
controls
Volume
(Transceiver cable)
7 pin connector
32
50A
Transceiver
9
AM/FM radio/Cassette player,
CB radio and antenna connections
28

1989 FLTC ULTRA MODELS

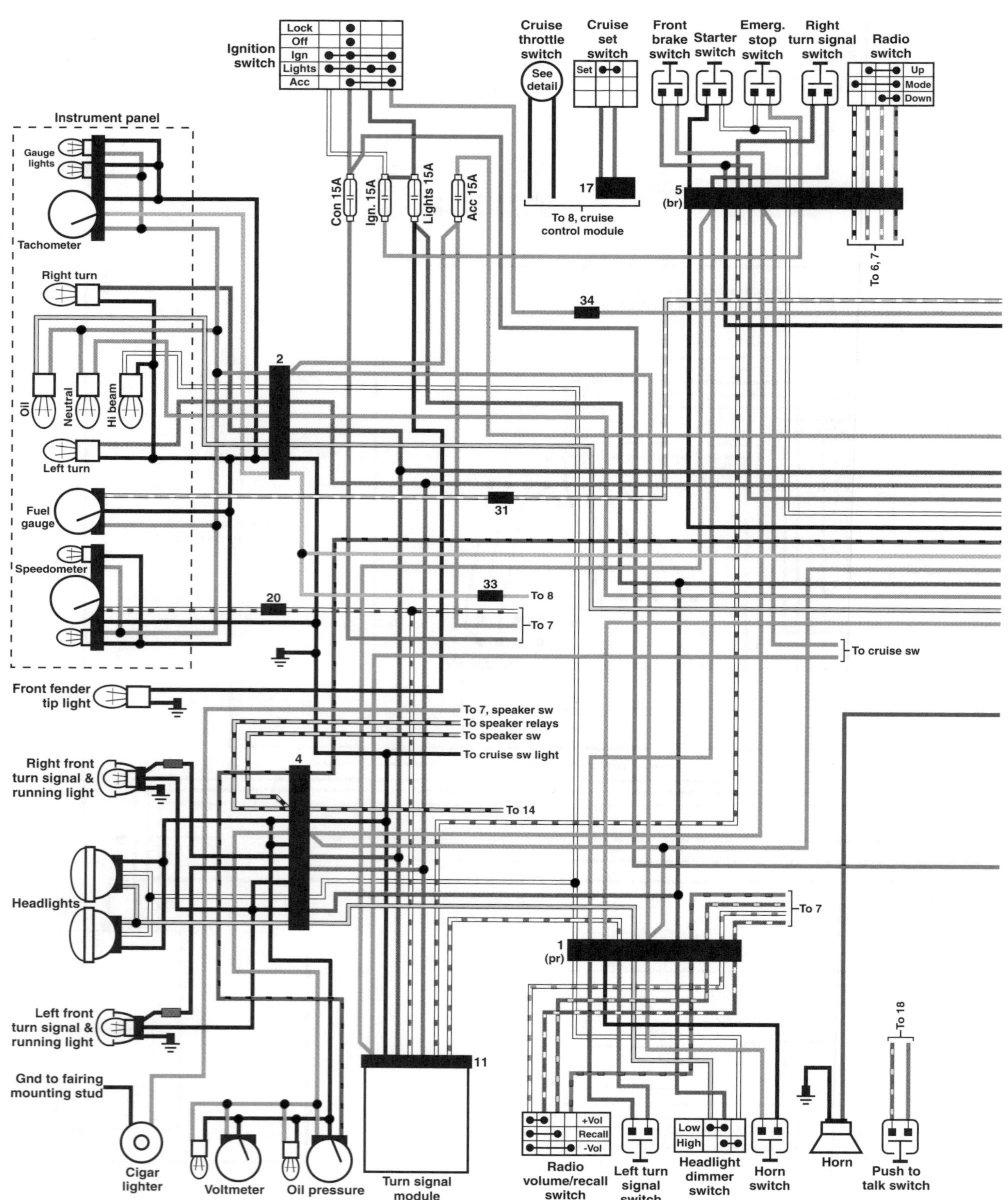

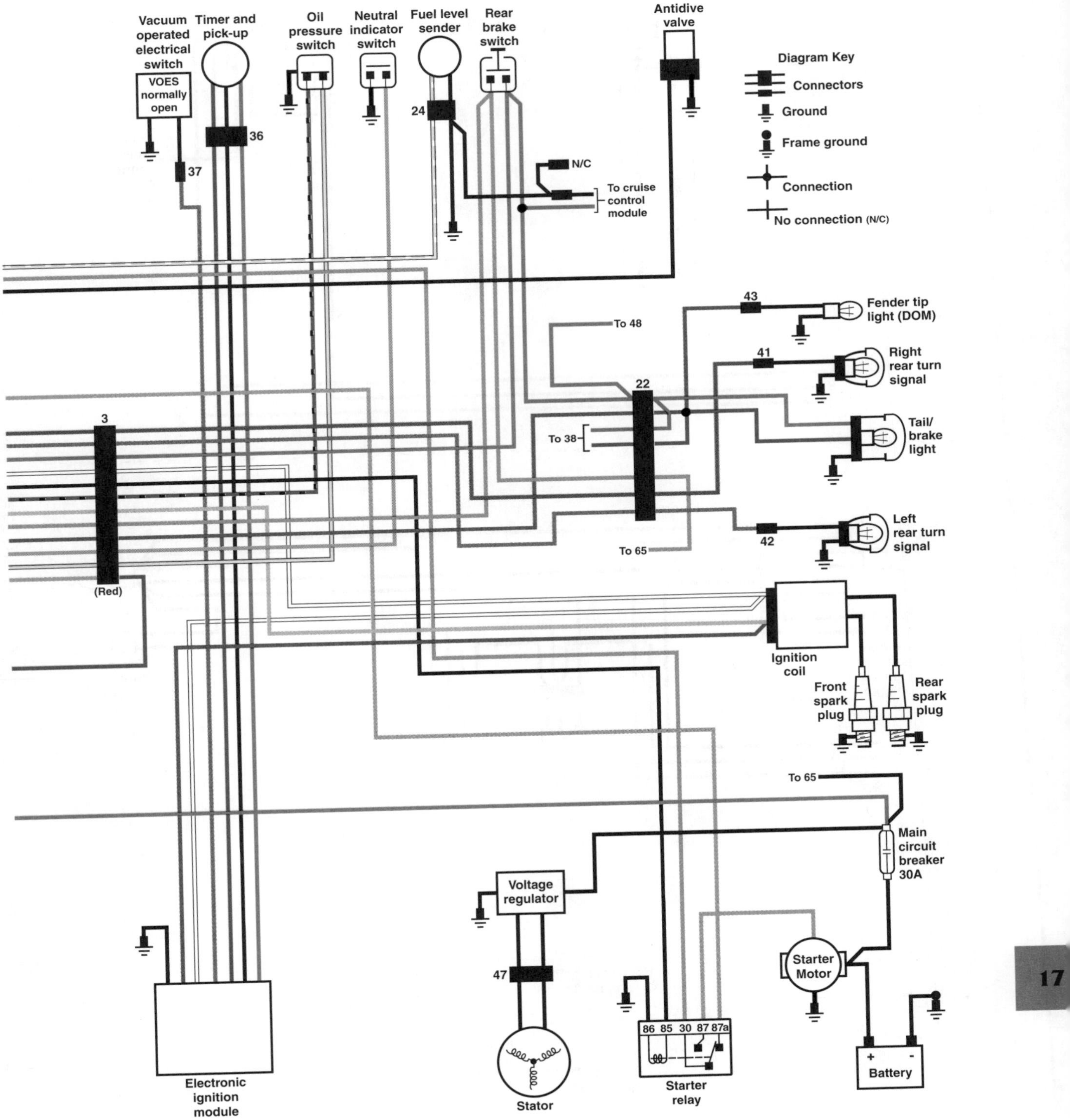

Vacuum operated electrical switch

VOES normally open

Timer and pick-up

Oil pressure switch

Neutral indicator switch

Fuel level sender

Rear brake switch

Antidive valve

Diagram Key

Connectors

Ground

Frame ground

Connection

No connection (N/C)

36

37

24

N/C

To cruise control module

43

Fender tip light (DOM)

To 48

41

Right rear turn signal

22

Tail/ brake light

To 38

3

Left rear turn signal

42

To 65

(Red)

Ignition coil

Front spark plug

Rear spark plug

To 65

Main circuit breaker 30A

Voltage regulator

47

Starter Motor

86 85 30 87 87a

+ -

Battery

Electronic ignition module

Stator

Starter relay

1989 FLTC ULTRA MODELS DASH SWITCHES, TOURPAK AND GROUNDS

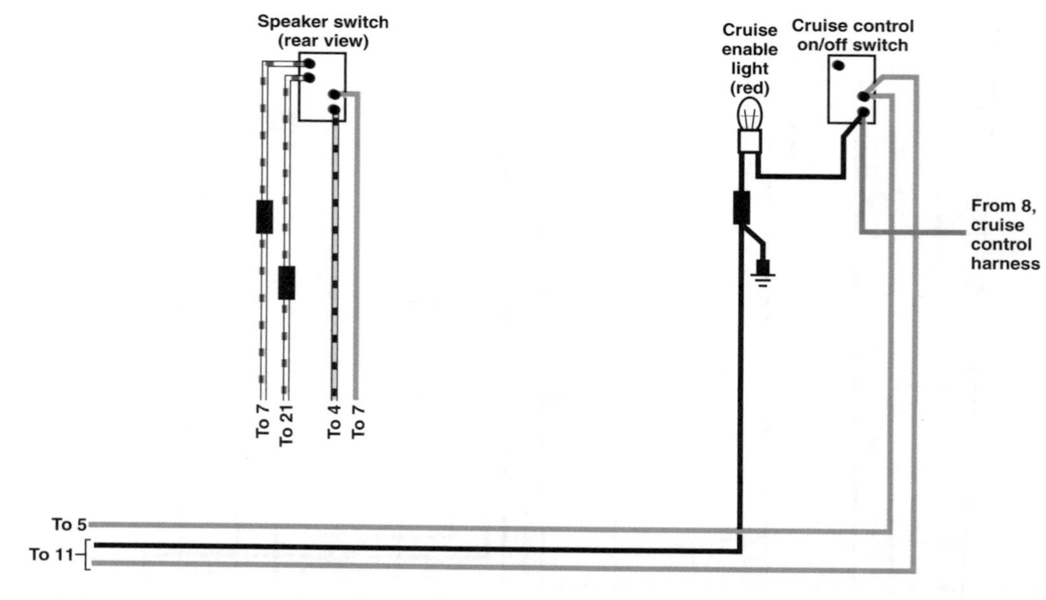

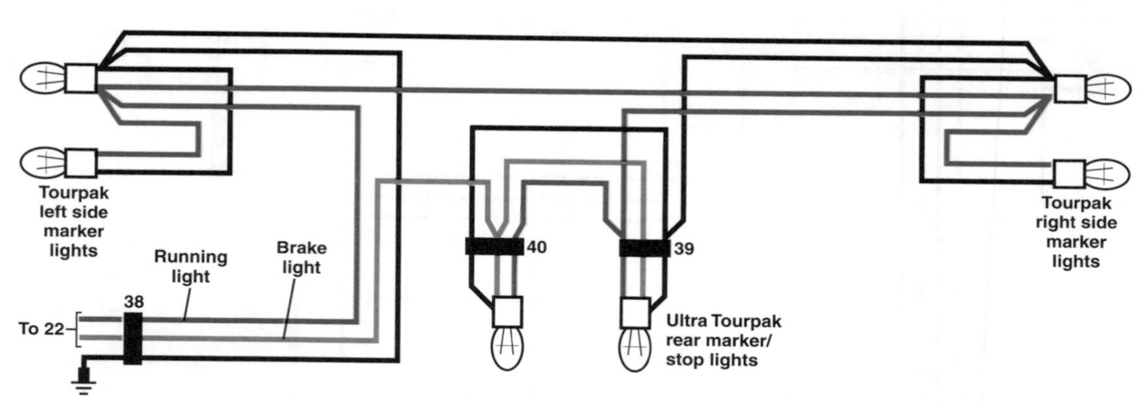

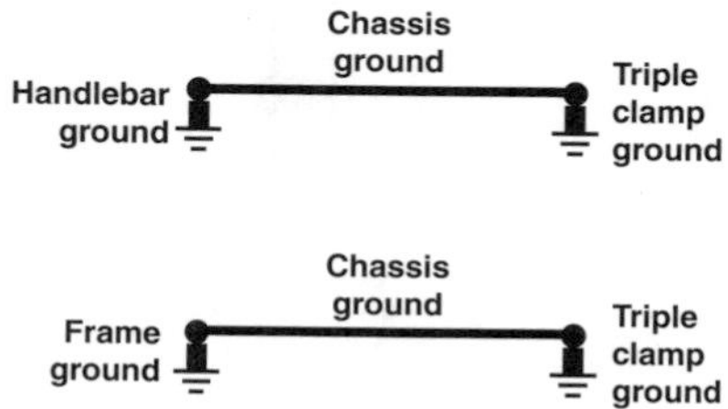

1989 FLTC ULTRA MODELS RADIO, HARNESS CONNECTORS AND CRUISE CONTROL CONNECTIONS

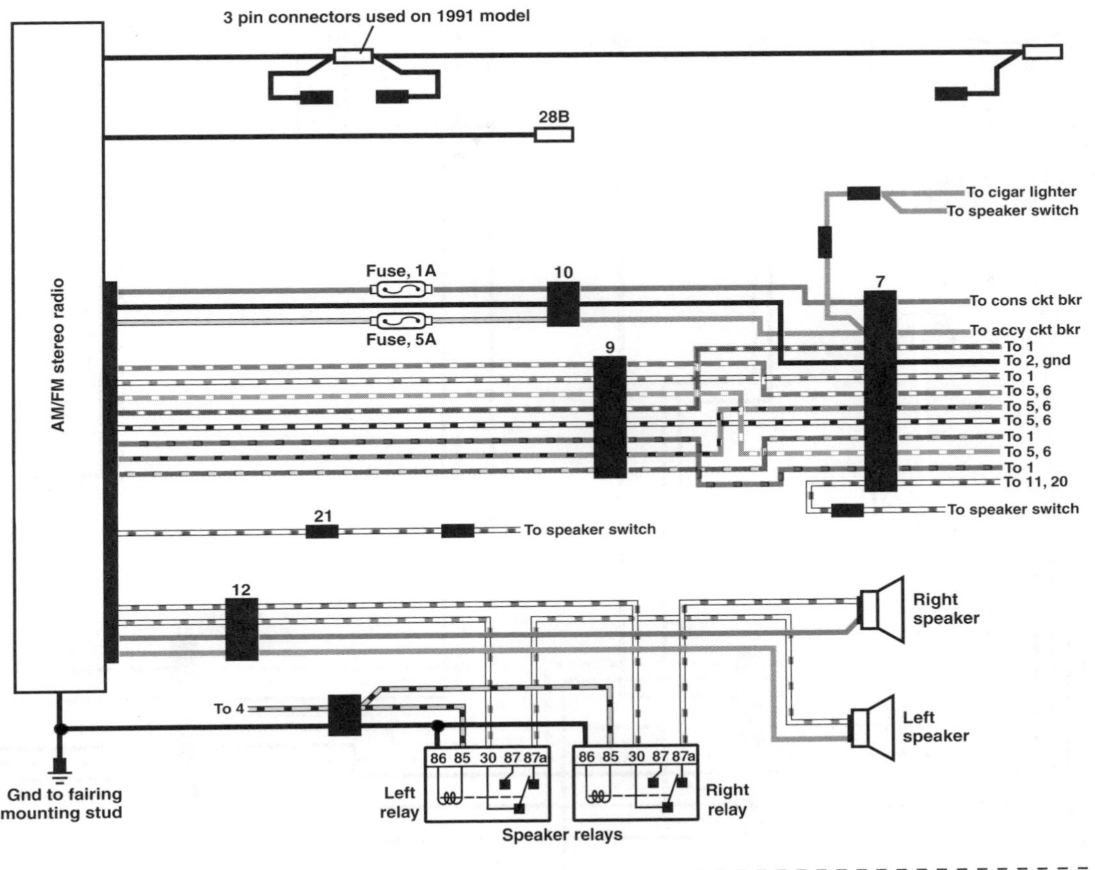

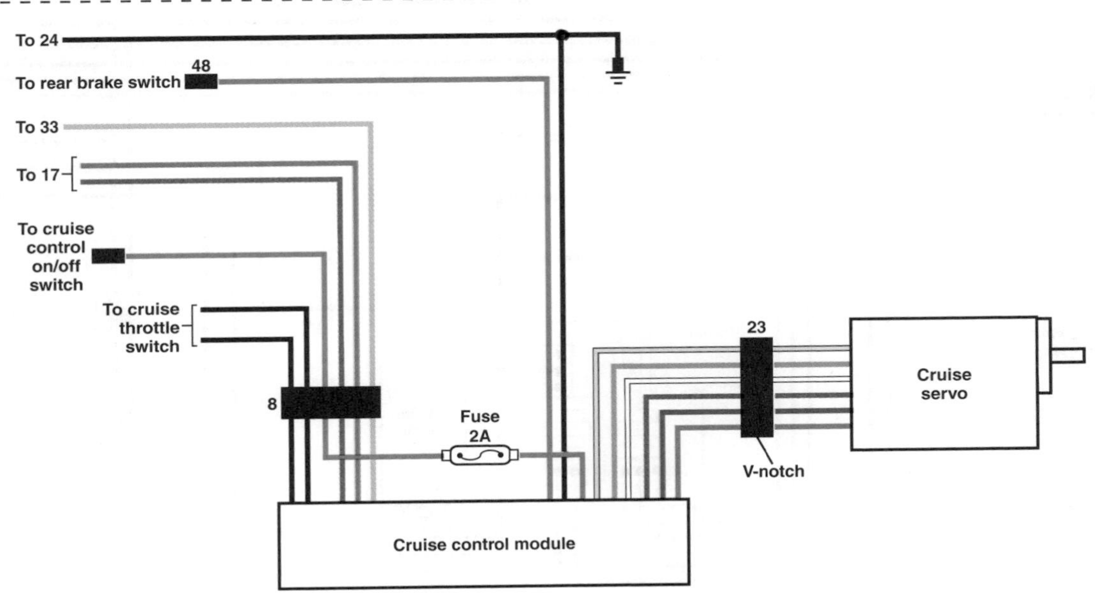

1989 FLTC ULTRA MODELS RADIO CB/INTERCOM, REAR SPEAKERS AND ANTENNAS

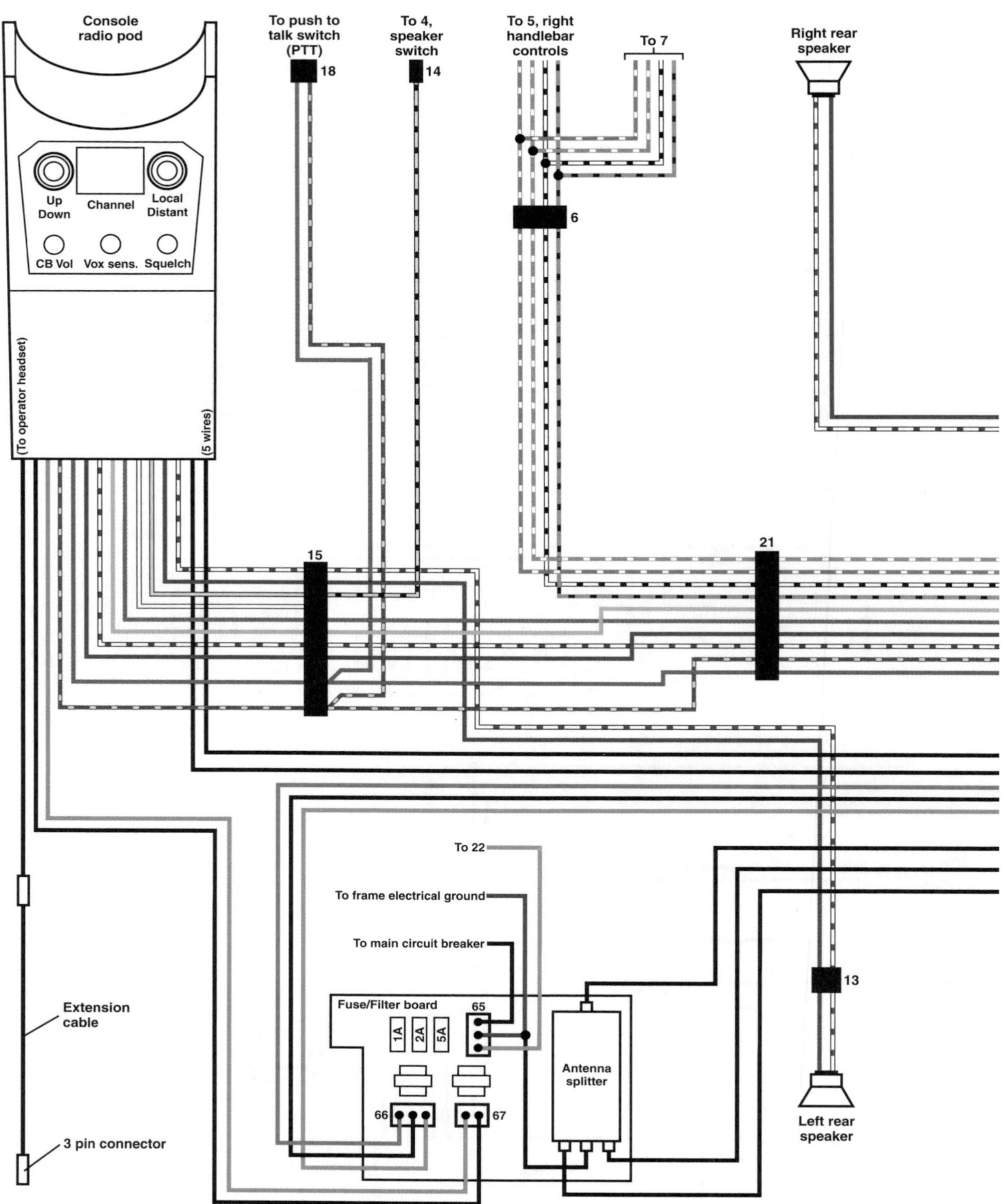

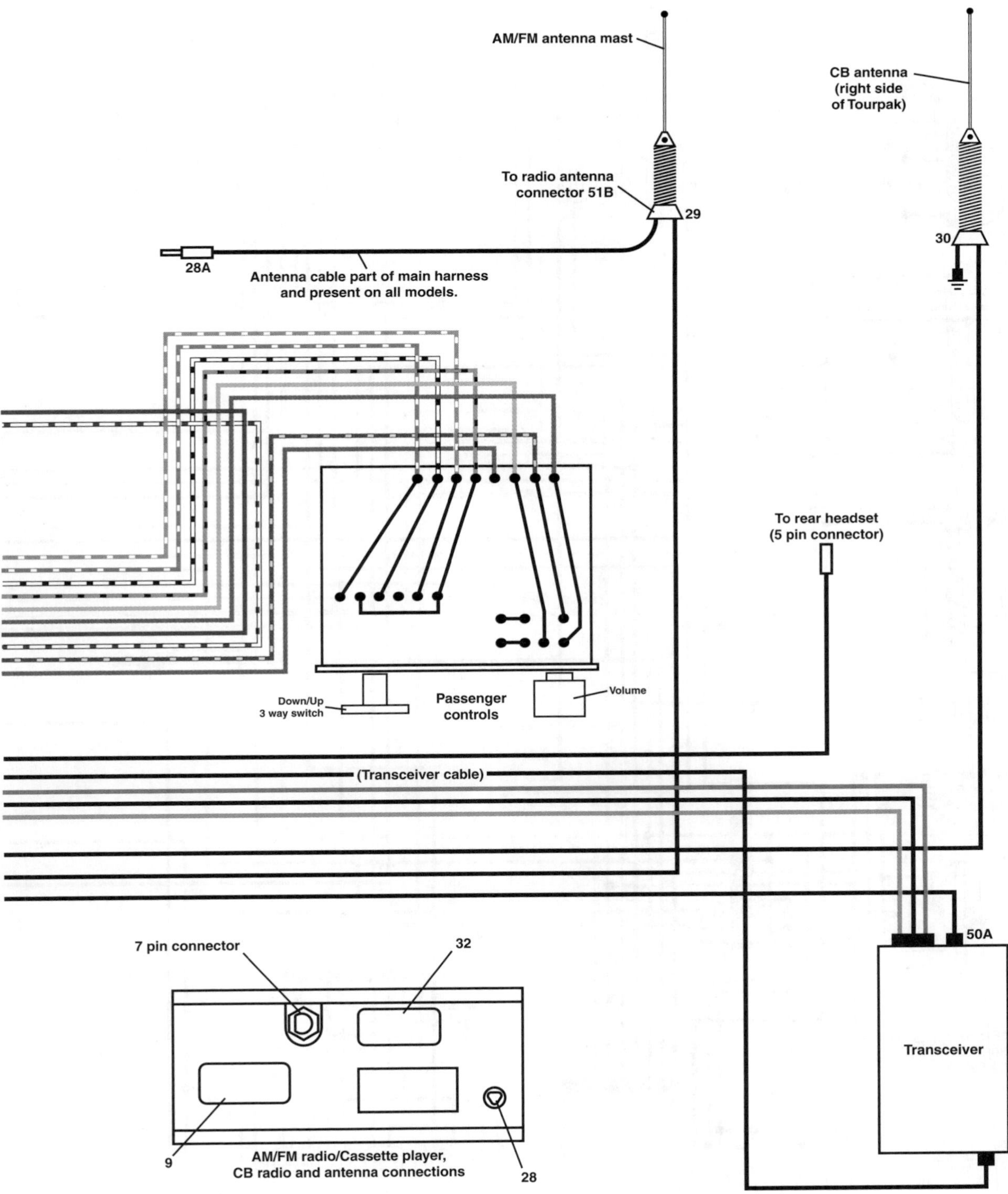
AM/FM antenna mast
CB antenna (right side of Tourpak)
To radio antenna connector 51B
29
30
28A
Antenna cable part of main harness and present on all models.
To rear headset (5 pin connector)
Down/Up 3 way switch
Passenger controls
Volume
(Transceiver cable)
50A
7 pin connector
32
Transceiver
9
28
AM/FM radio/Cassette player, CB radio and antenna connections

1989-1991 FLTC MODELS

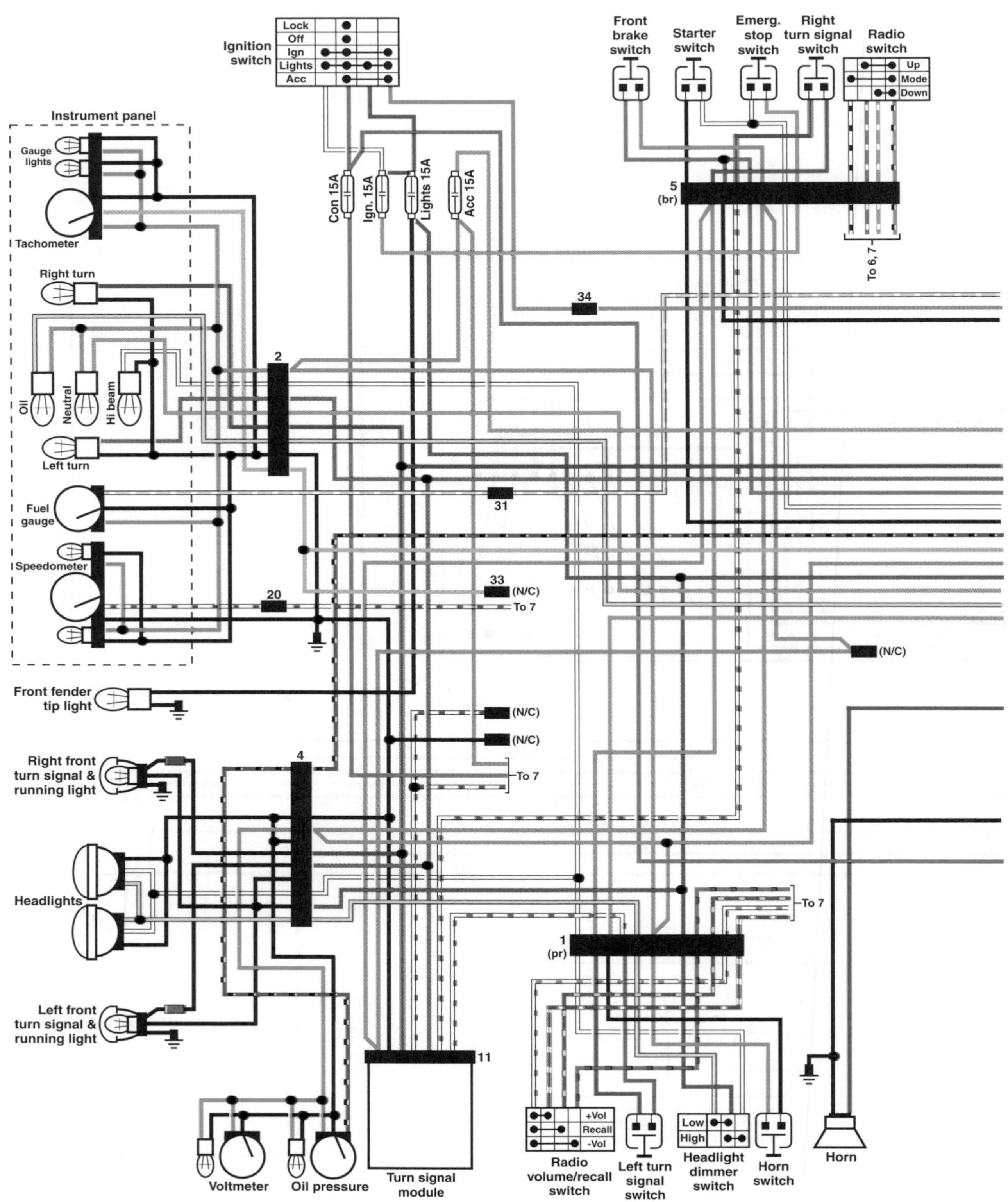

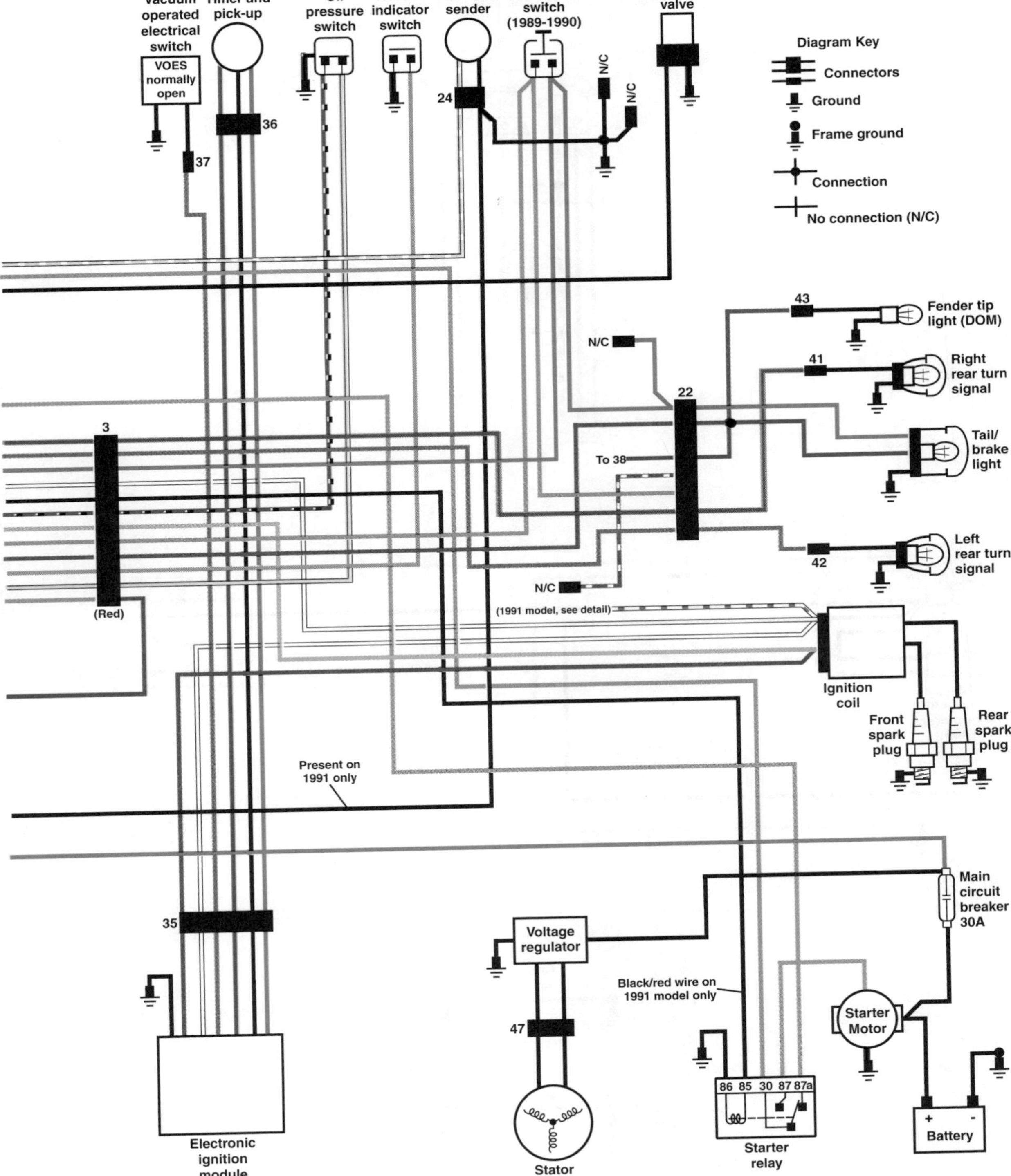
Vacuum operated electrical switch
VOES normally open
Timer and pick-up
Oil pressure switch
Neutral indicator switch
Fuel level sender
Rear brake switch (1989-1990)
Antidive valve
N/C
N/C
Diagram Key
Connectors
Ground
Frame ground
Connection
No connection (N/C)
36
37
24
43
Fender tip light (DOM)
N/C
41
Right rear turn signal
22
Tail/ brake light
3
To 38
42
Left rear turn signal
N/C
(Red)
(1991 model, see detail)
Ignition coil
Front spark plug
Rear spark plug
Present on 1991 only
Main circuit breaker 30A
35
Voltage regulator
Black/red wire on 1991 model only
Starter Motor
47
86 85 30 87 87a
Electronic ignition module
Stator
Starter relay
Battery

1989-1991 FLTC MODELS REAR BRAKE SWITCH AND RELAY, TOURPAK AND GROUNDS

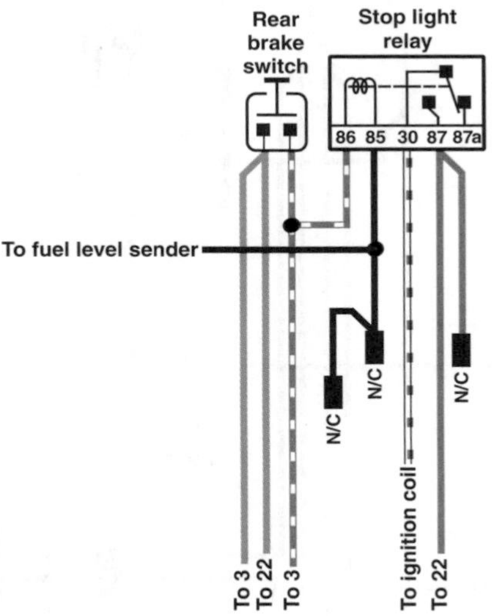

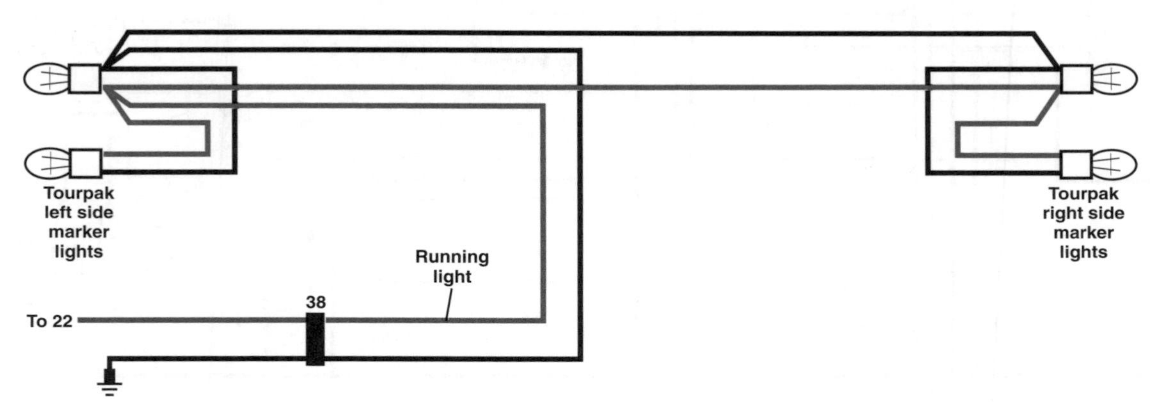

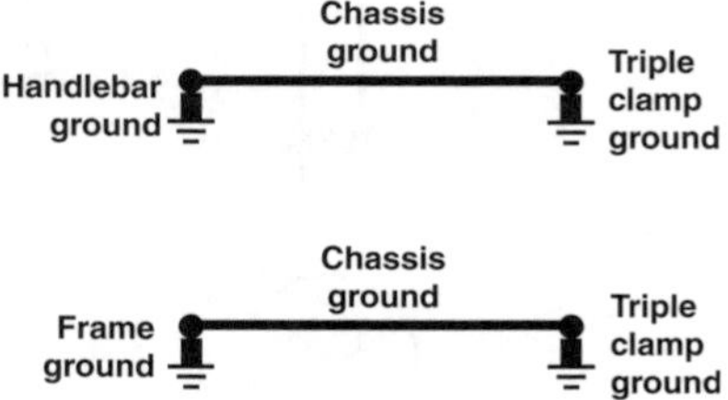

1989-1991 FLTC MODELS RADIO AND HARNESS CONNECTORS

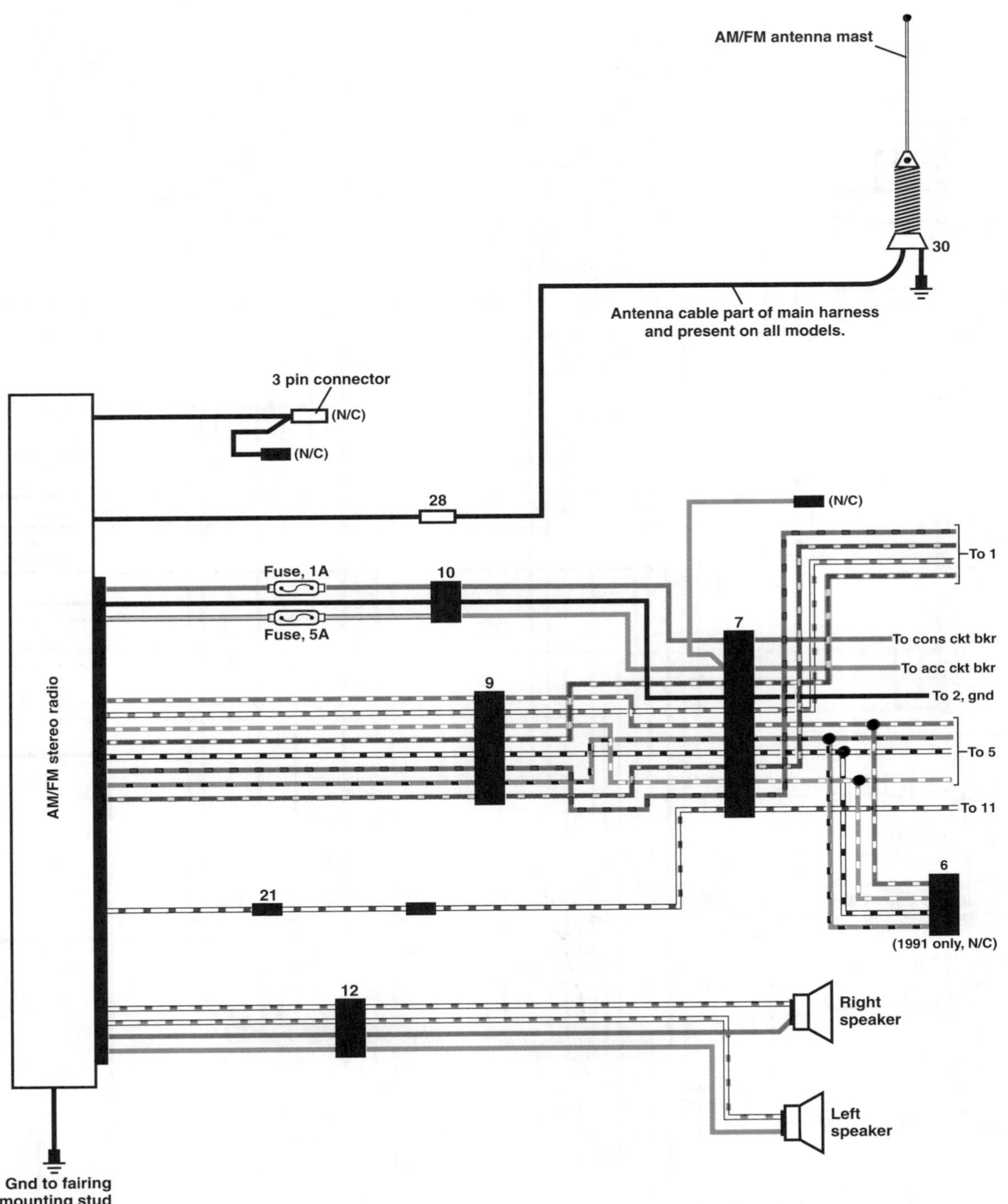

1990 FLHTC ULTRA MODELS

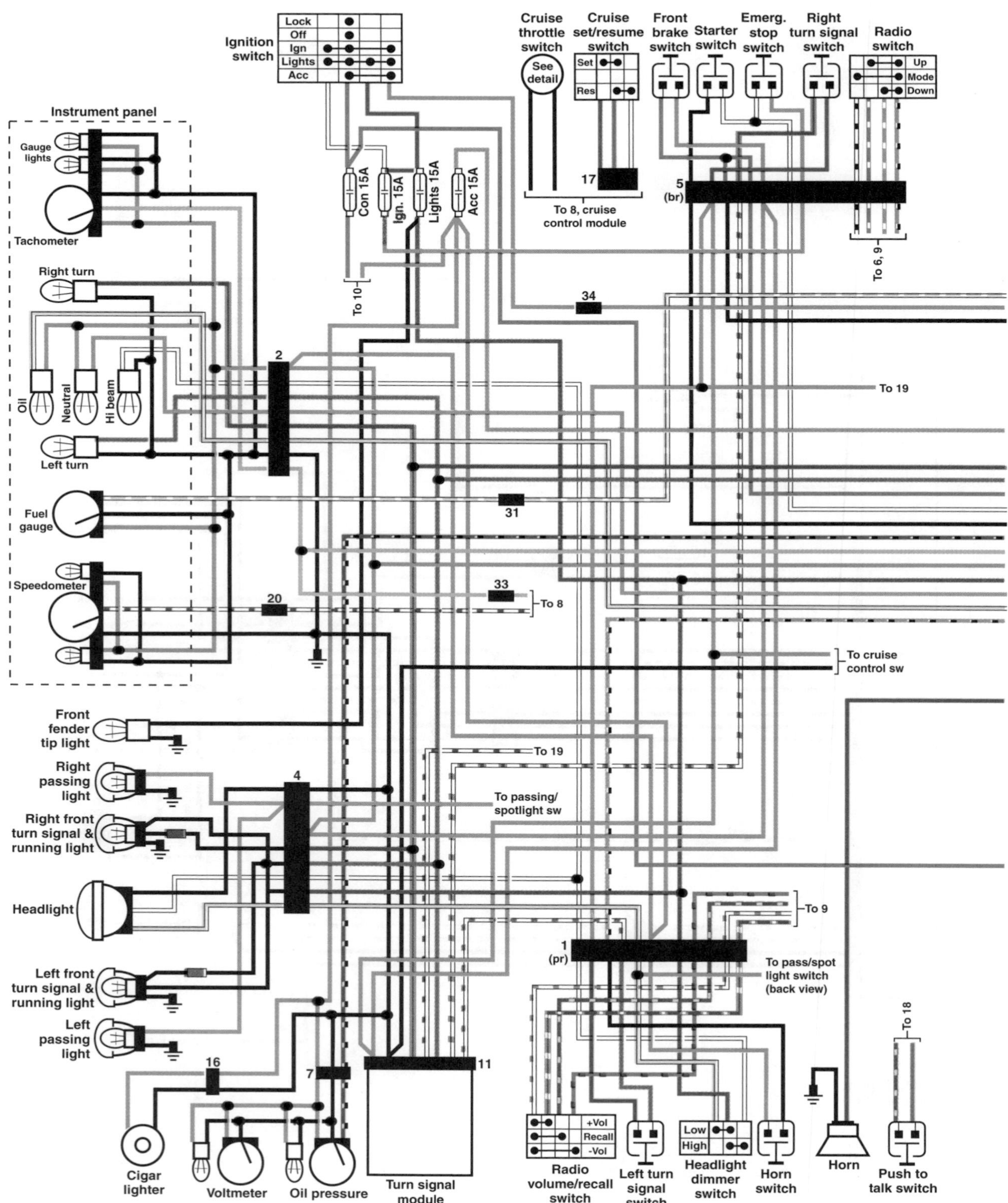

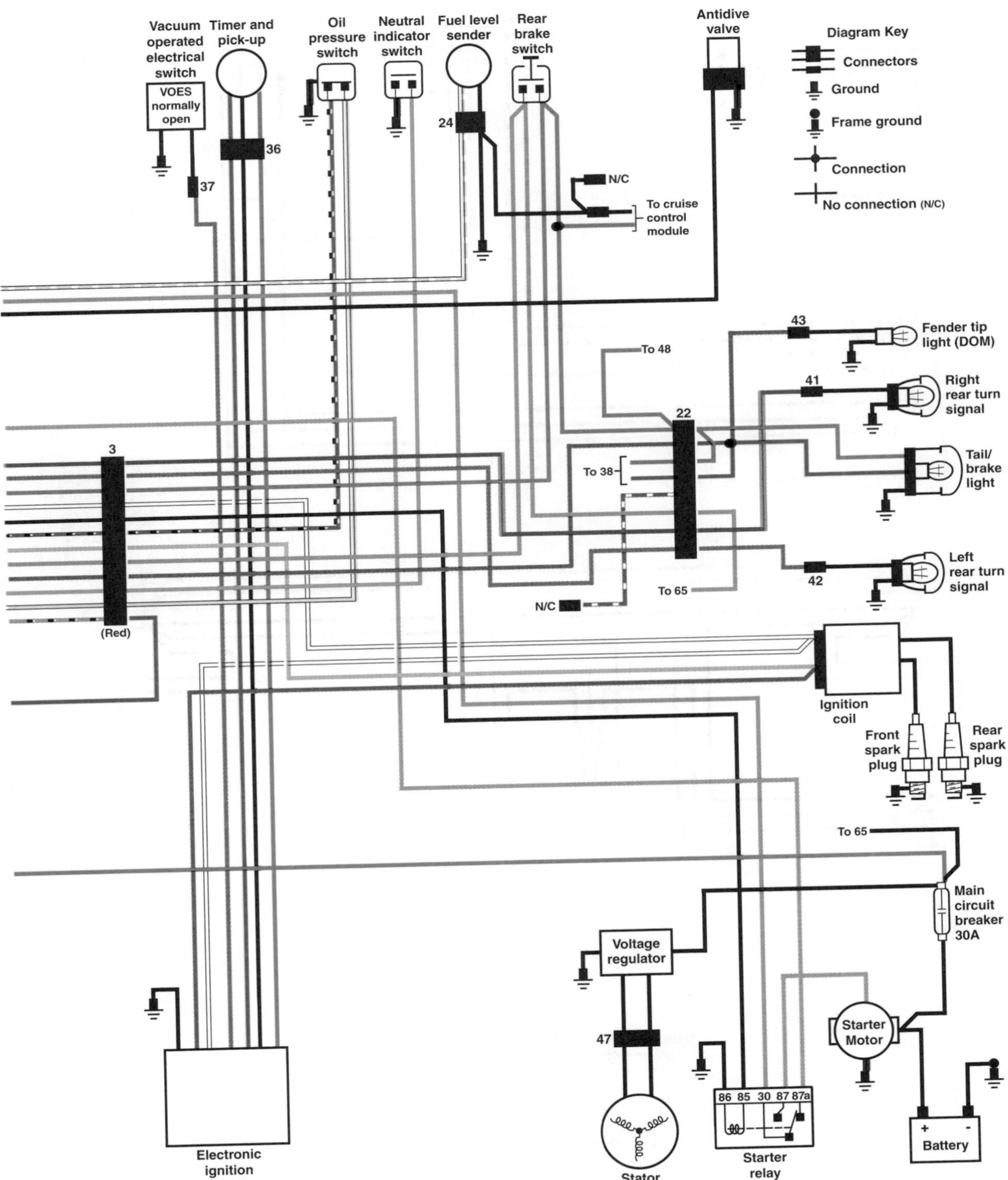

Vacuum operated electrical switch
VOES normally open
Timer and pick-up
Oil pressure switch
Neutral indicator switch
Fuel level sender
Rear brake switch
Antidive valve
Diagram Key
Connectors
Ground
Frame ground
Connection
No connection (N/C)
36
37
24
N/C
To cruise control module
43
Fender tip light (DOM)
To 48
41
Right rear turn signal
22
Tail/ brake light
3
To 38
Left rear turn signal
42
To 65
N/C
(Red)
Ignition coil
Front spark plug
Rear spark plug
To 65
Main circuit breaker 30A
Voltage regulator
47
Starter Motor
86 85 30 87 87a
Electronic ignition module
Stator
Starter relay
Battery

1990 FLHTC ULTRA MODELS DASH SWITCHES, TOURPAK AND GROUNDS

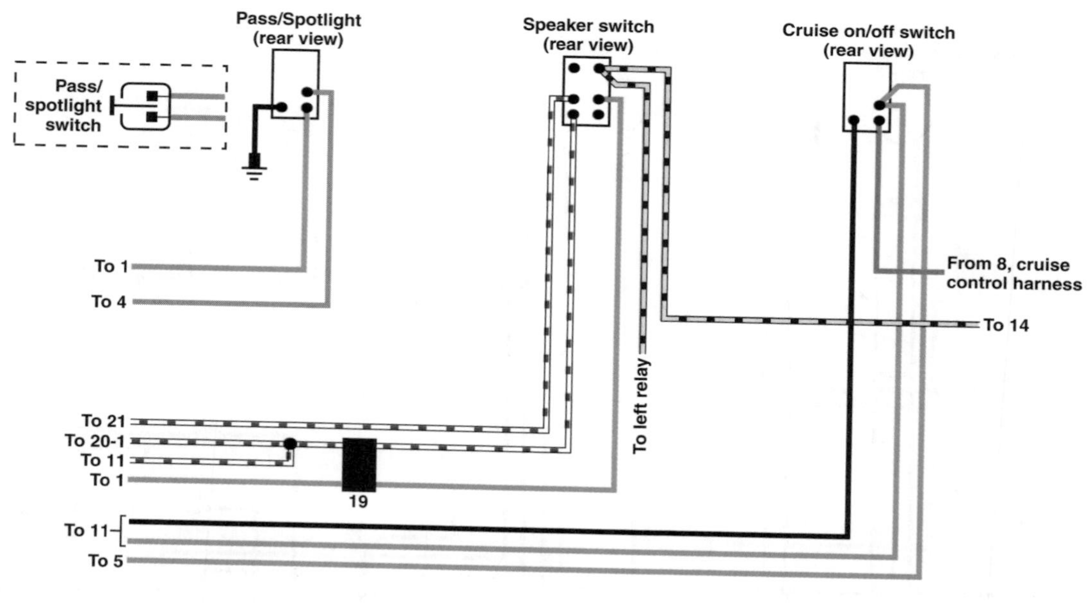

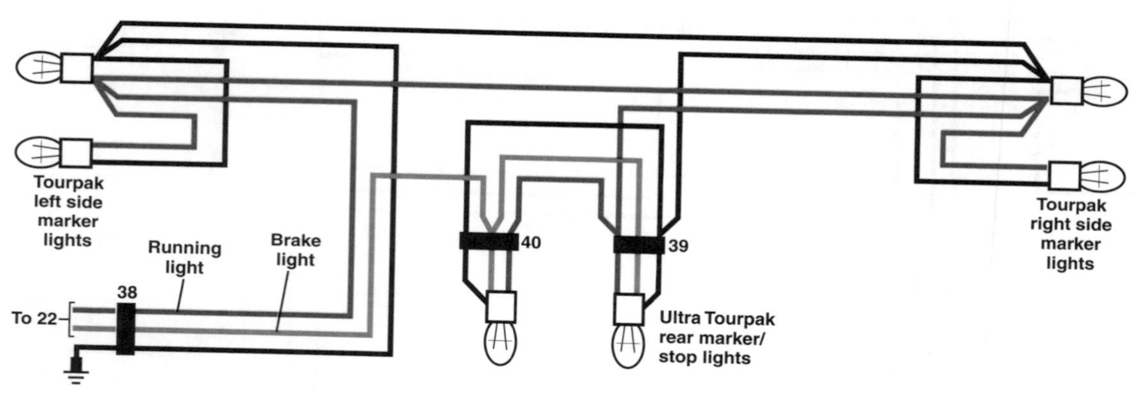

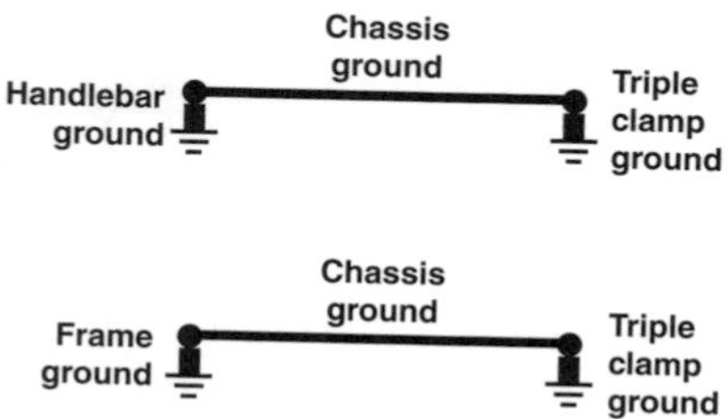

1990 FLHTC ULTRA MODELS RADIO, HARNESS CONNECTORS AND CRUISE CONTROL CONNECTIONS

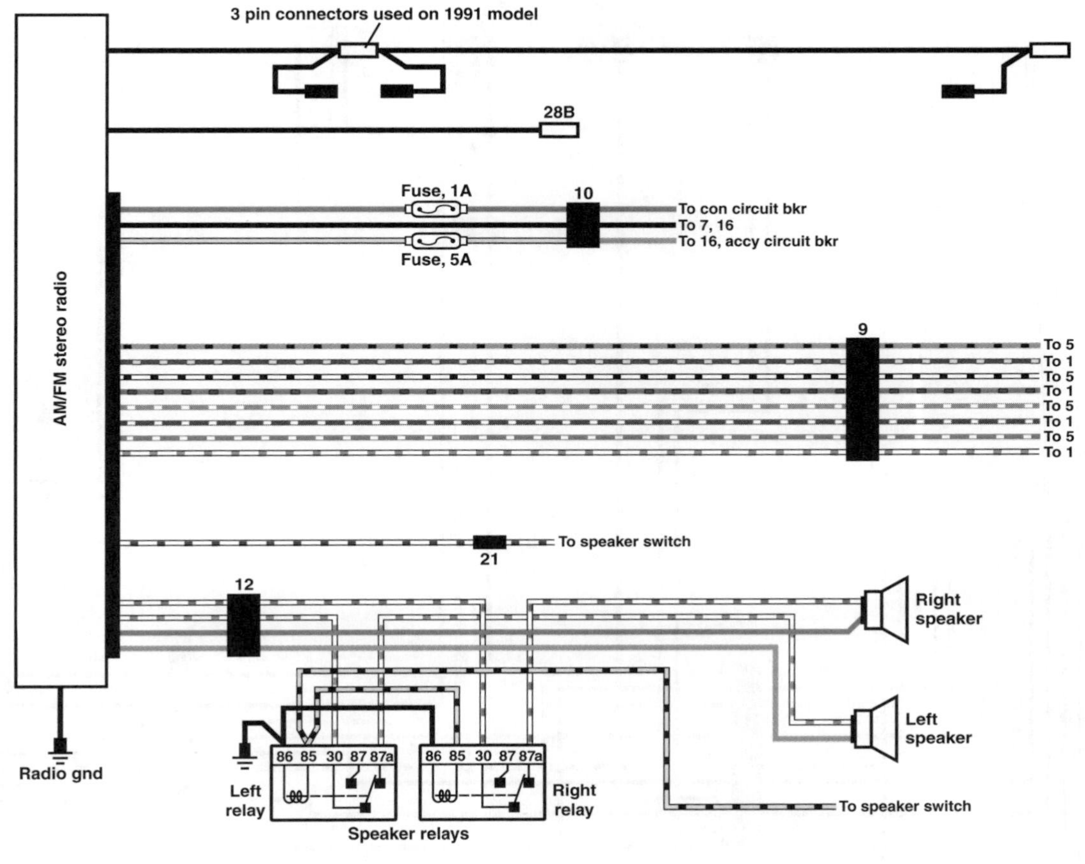

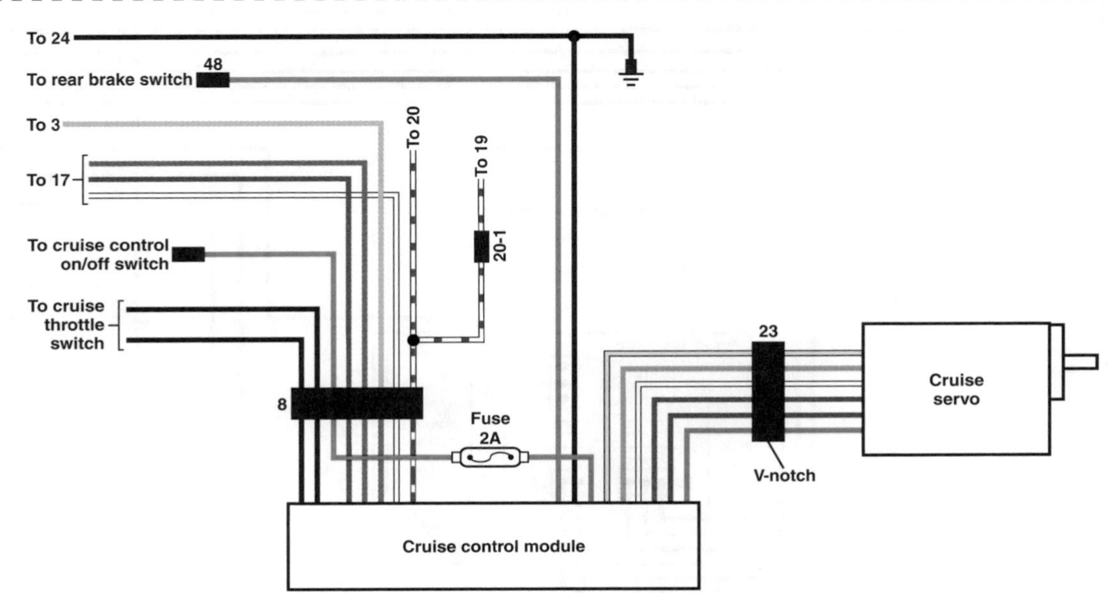

1990 FLHTC ULTRA MODELS RADIO CB/INTERCOM, REAR SPEAKERS AND ANTENNAS

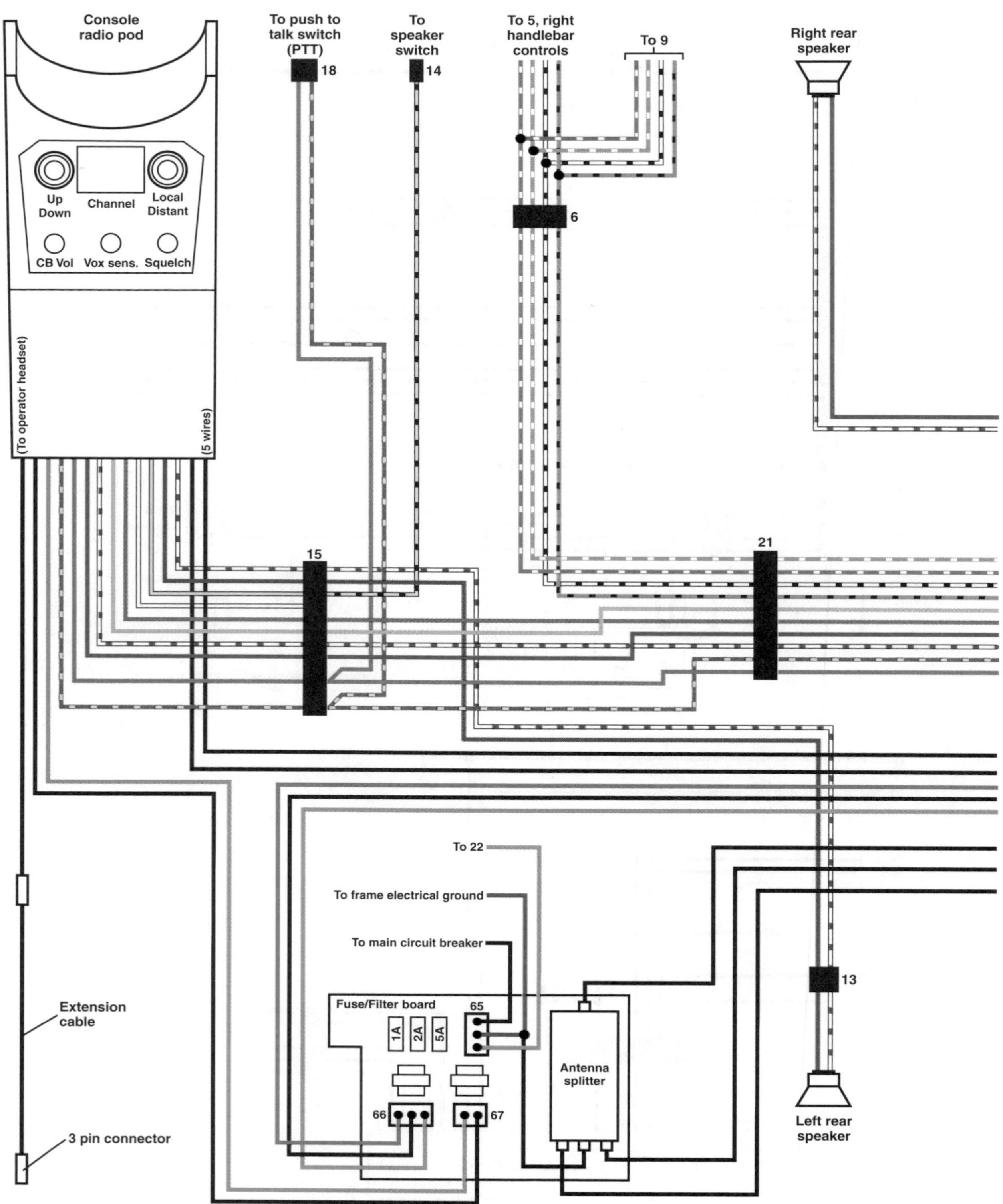

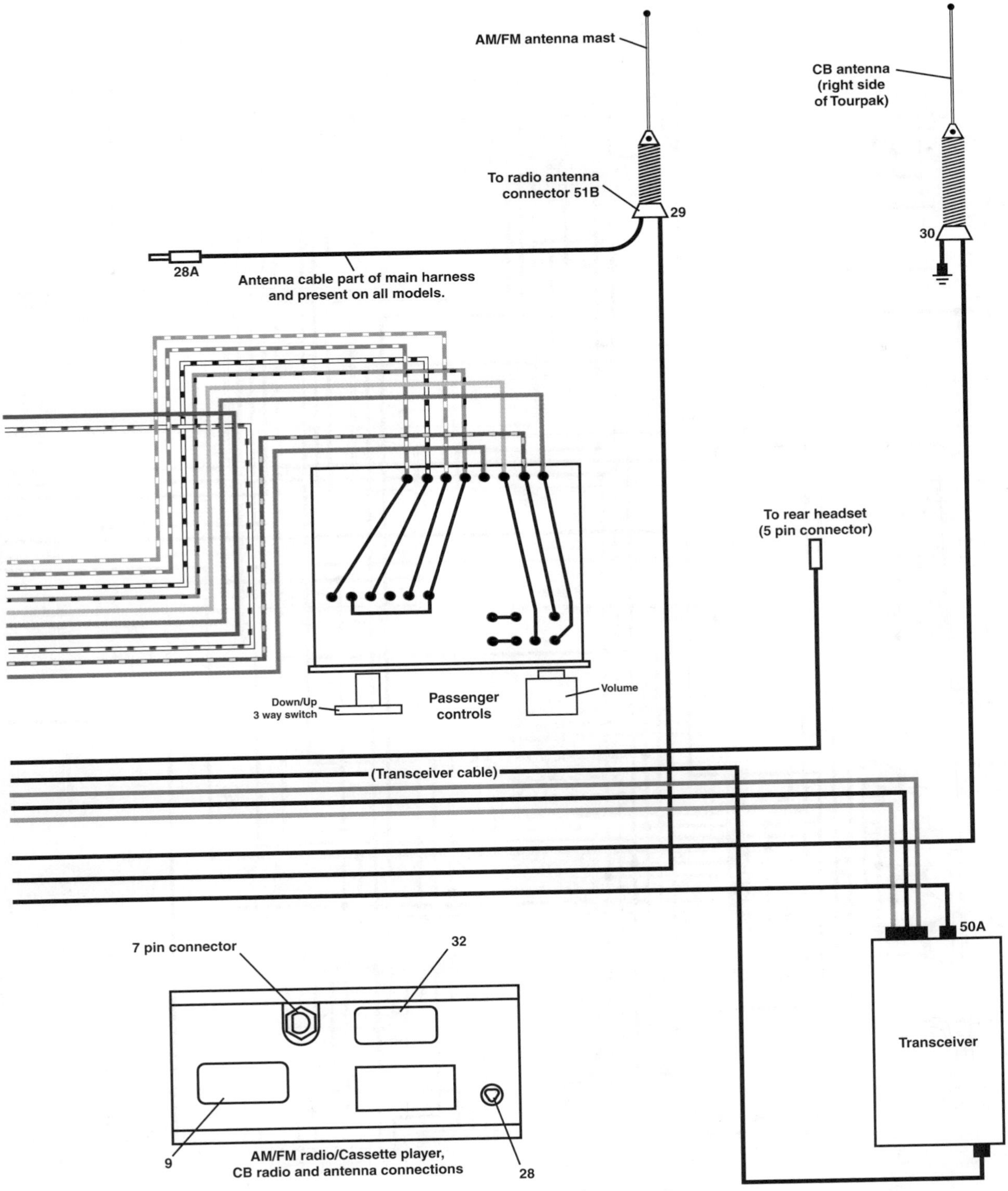

AM/FM antenna mast
CB antenna (right side of Tourpak)
To radio antenna connector 51B
29
30
28A
Antenna cable part of main harness and present on all models.
To rear headset (5 pin connector)
Down/Up 3 way switch
Passenger controls
Volume
(Transceiver cable)
50A
7 pin connector
32
Transceiver
9
28
AM/FM radio/Cassette player, CB radio and antenna connections

1990 FLTC ULTRA MODELS

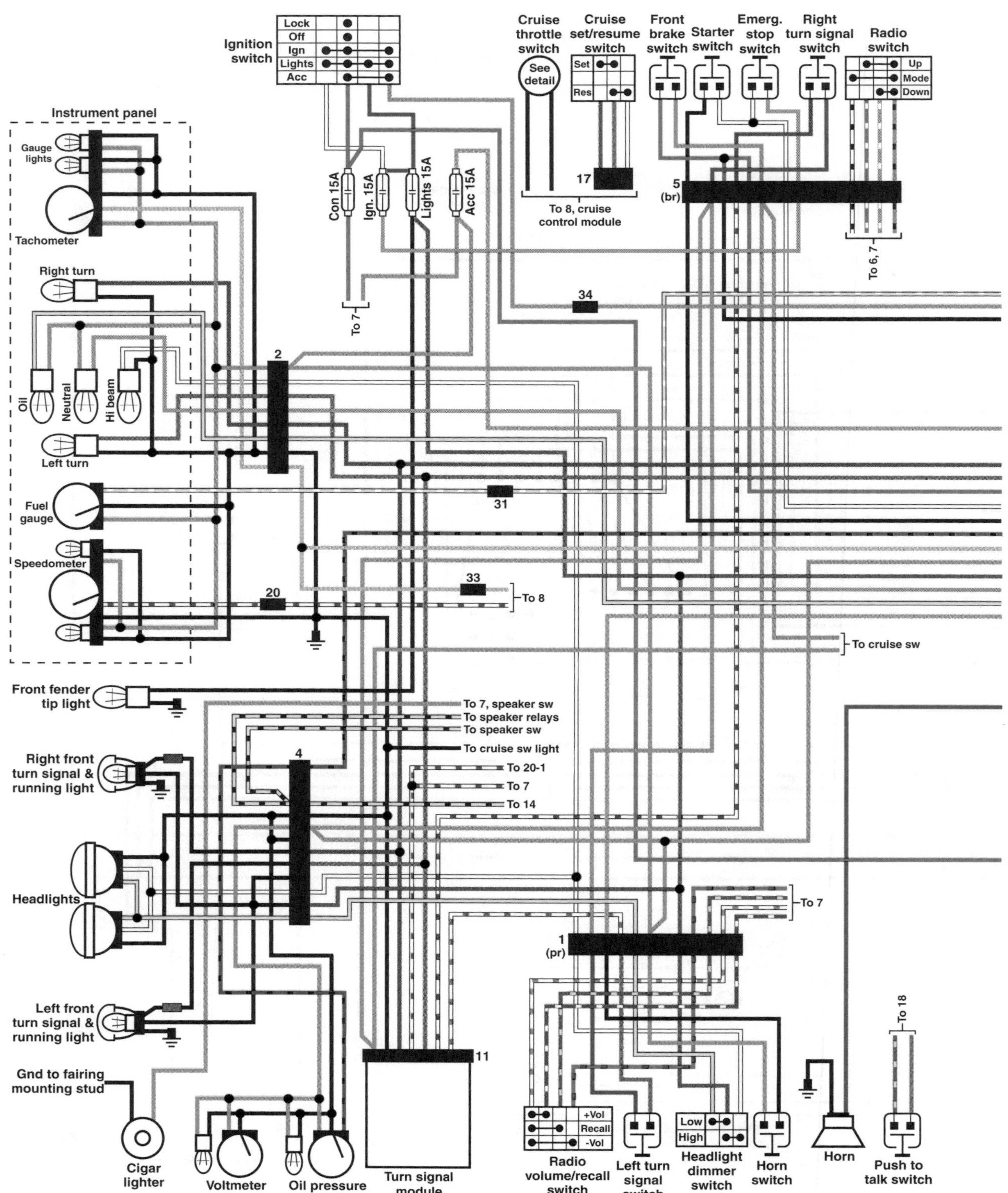

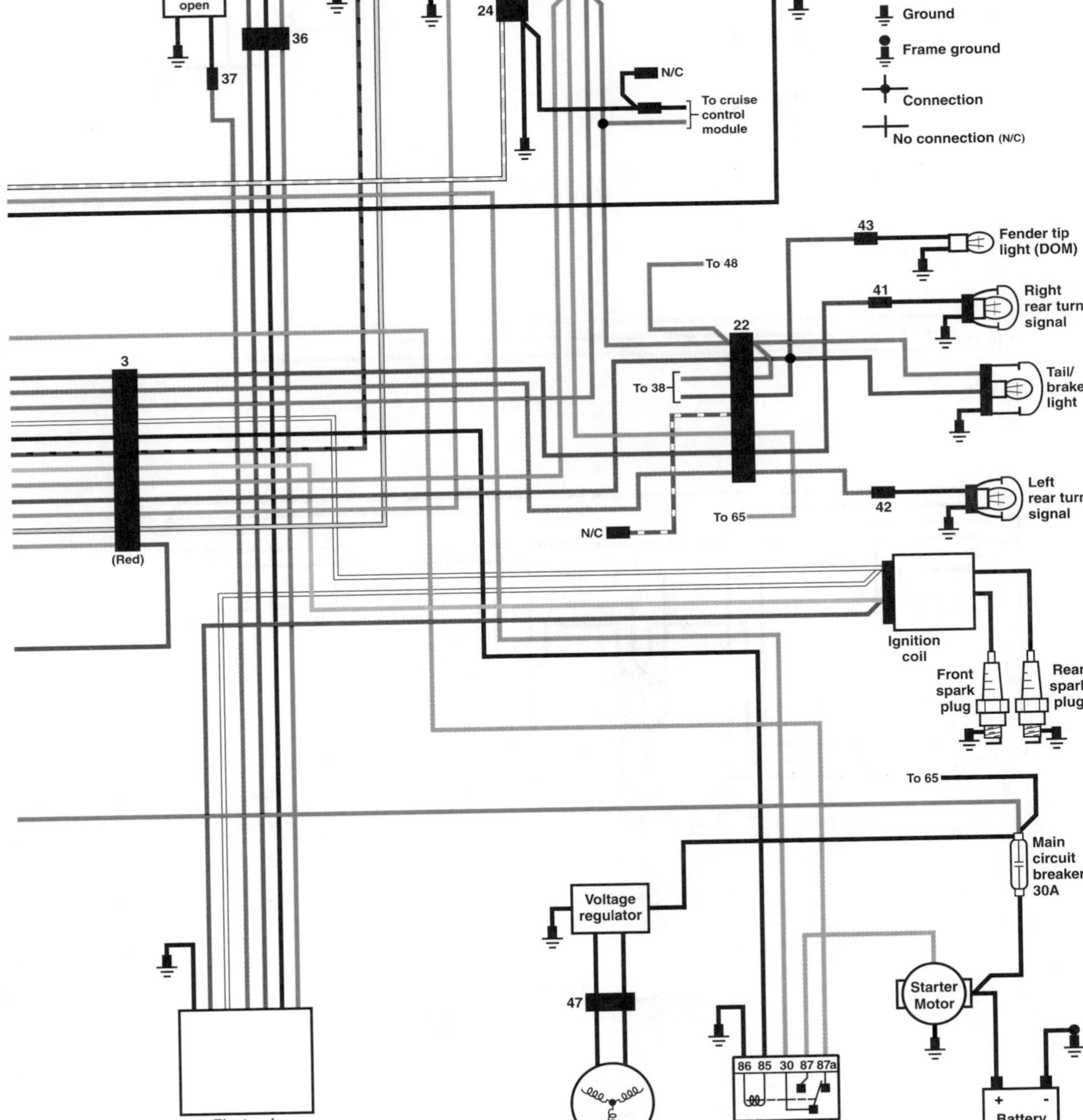
Vacuum operated electrical switch
VOES normally open
Timer and pick-up
Oil pressure switch
Neutral indicator switch
Fuel level sender
Rear brake switch
Antidive valve
Diagram Key
Connectors
Ground
Frame ground
Connection
No connection (N/C)
36
37
24
N/C
To cruise control module
43
Fender tip light (DOM)
To 48
41
Right rear turn signal
22
3
To 38
Tail/ brake light
Left rear turn signal
42
To 65
N/C
(Red)
Ignition coil
Front spark plug
Rear spark plug
To 65
Main circuit breaker 30A
Voltage regulator
47
Starter Motor
86 85 30 87 87a
Starter relay
Battery
Electronic ignition module
Stator

1990 FLTC ULTRA MODELS DASH SWITCHES, TOURPAK AND GROUNDS

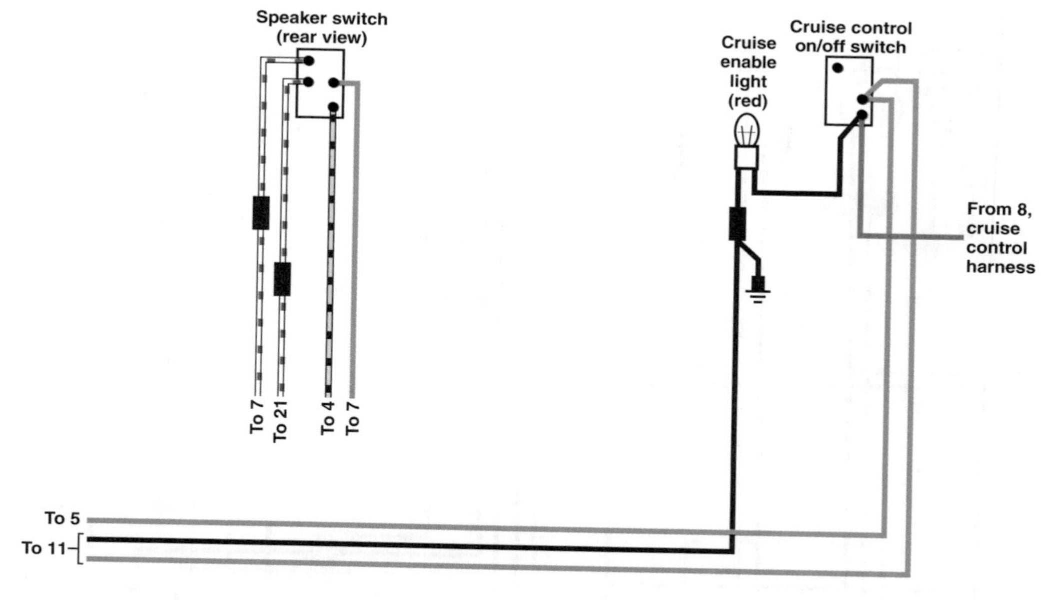

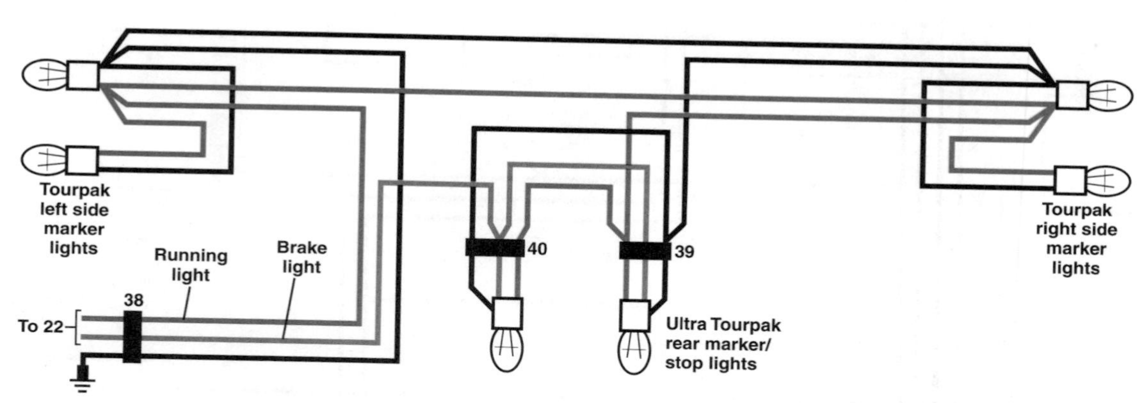

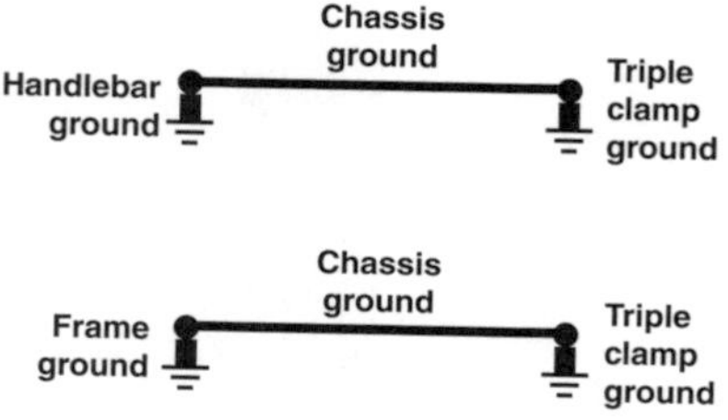

1990 FLTC ULTRA MODELS RADIO, HARNESS CONNECTORS AND CRUISE CONTROL CONNECTIONS

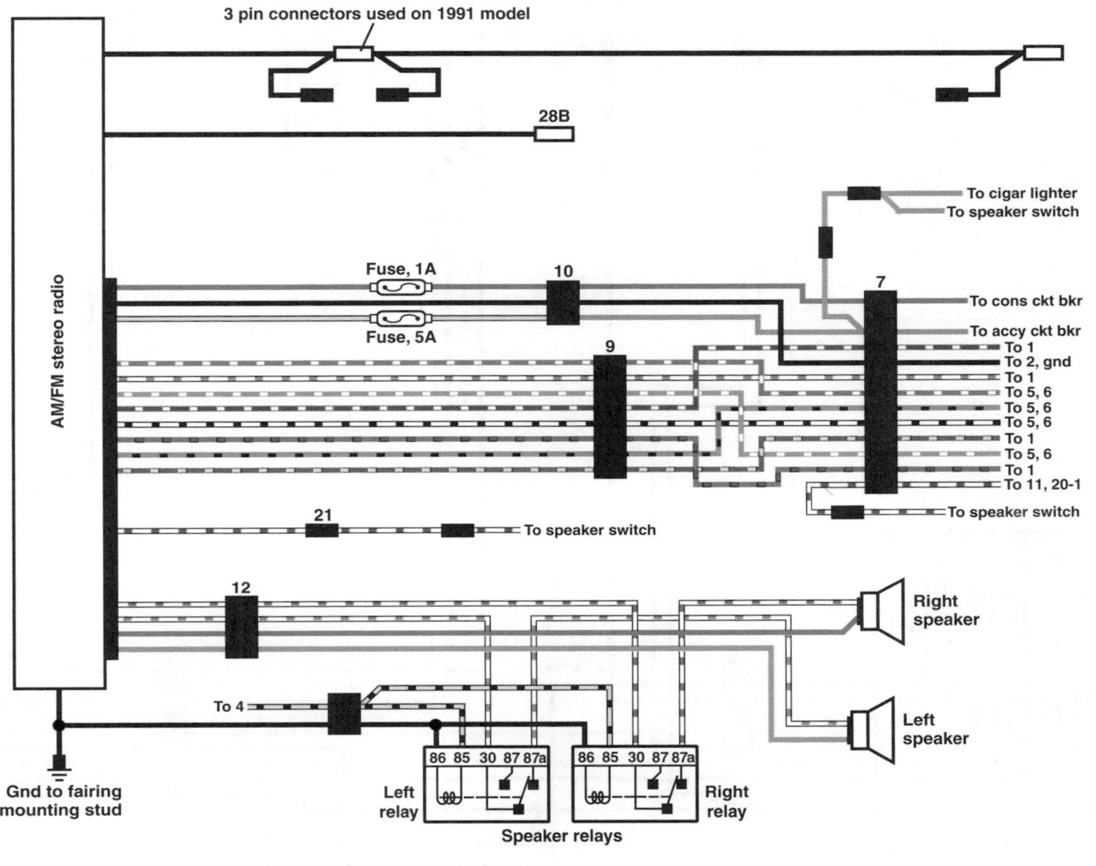

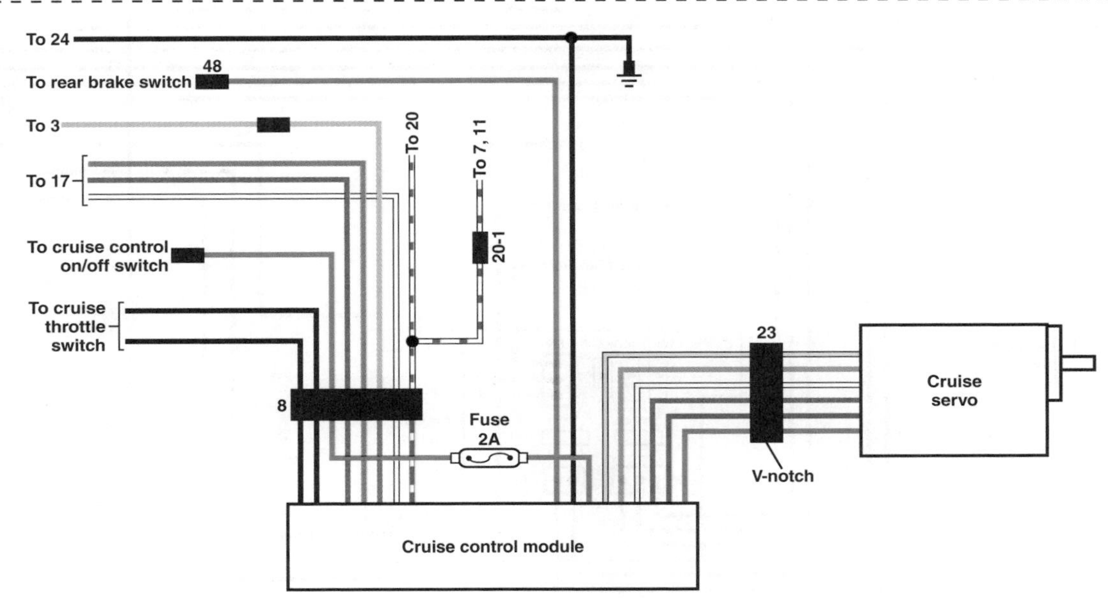

17

1990 FLTC ULTRA MODELS RADIO CB/INTERCOM, REAR SPEAKERS AND ANTENNAS

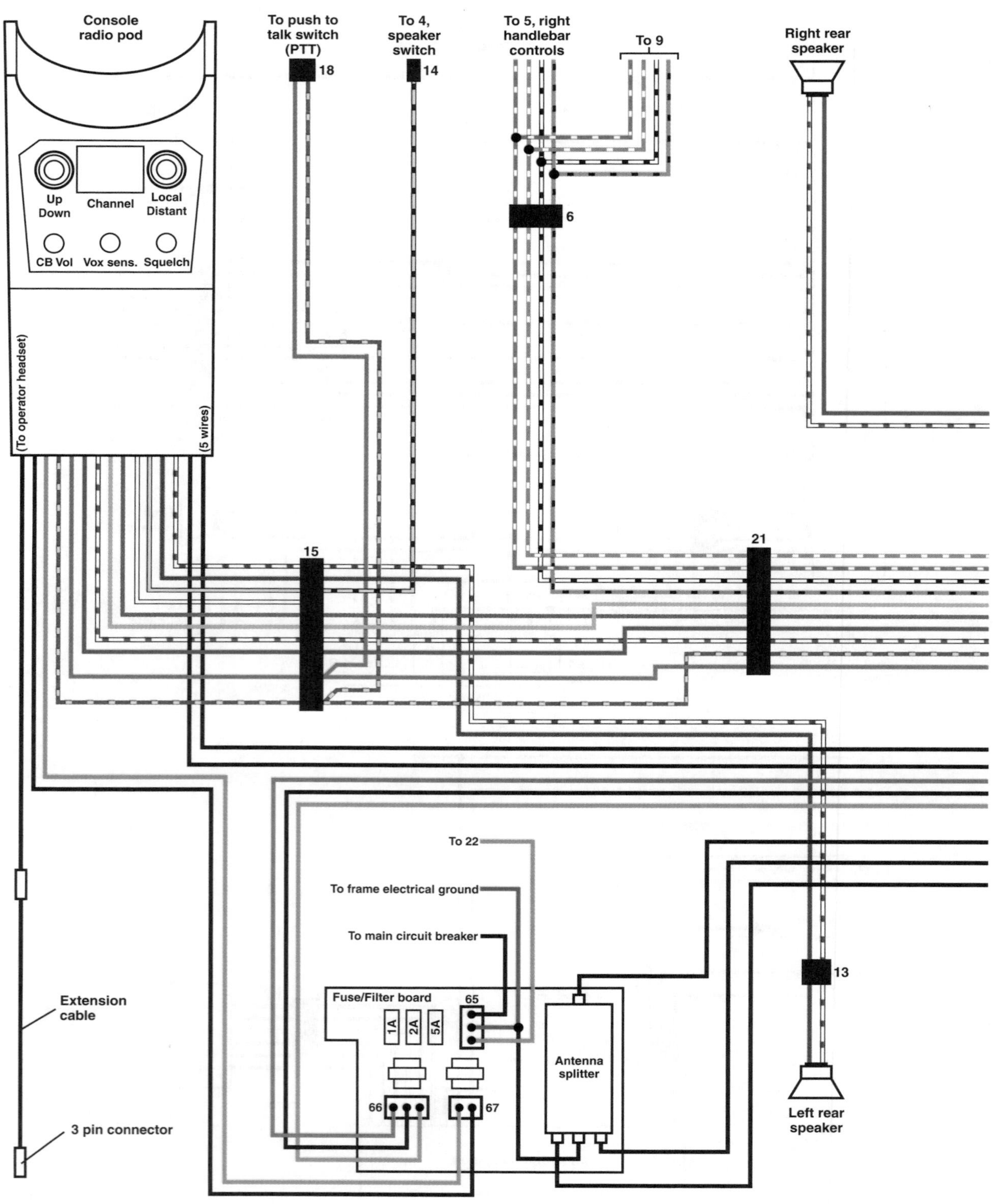

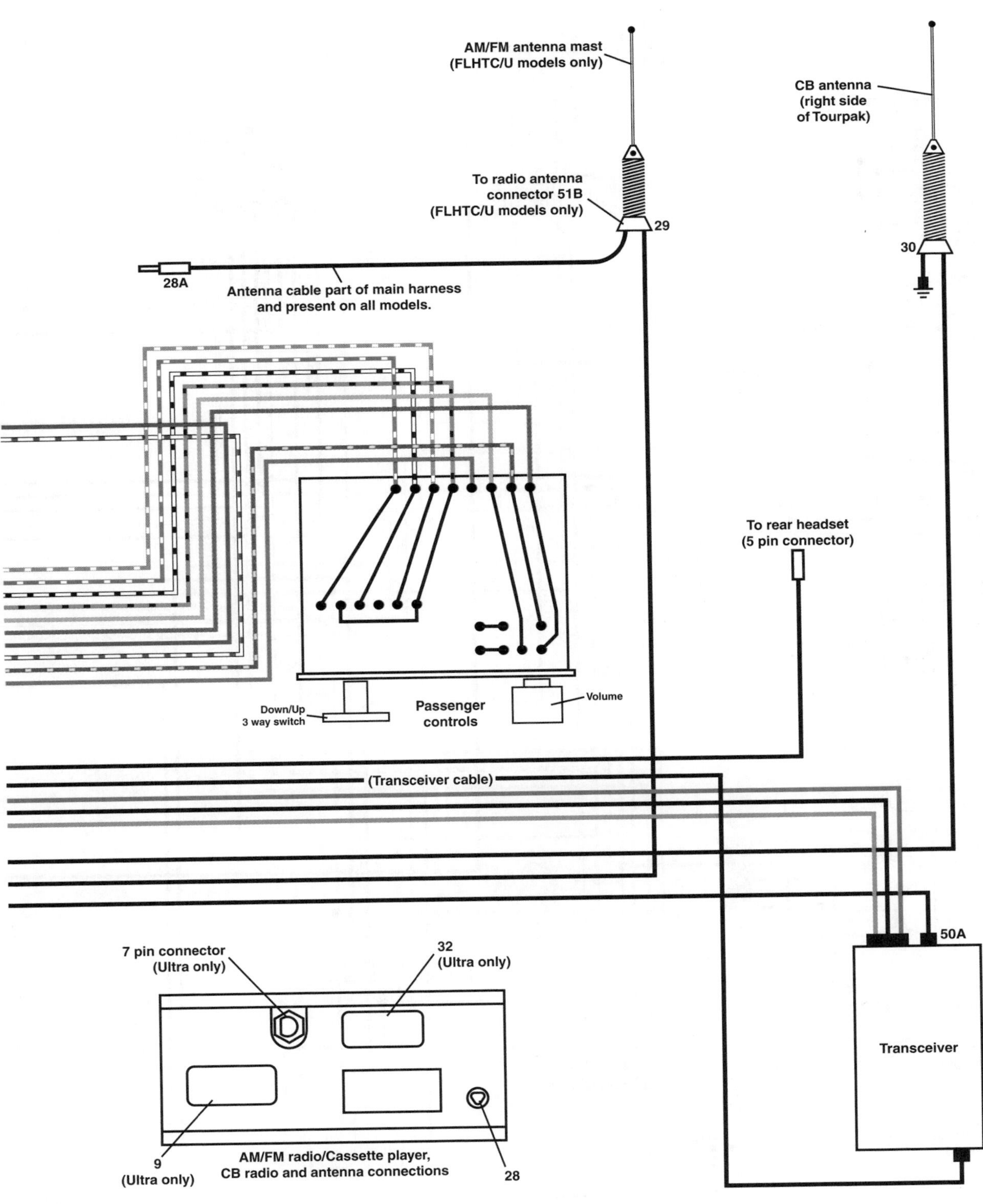
AM/FM antenna mast
(FLHTC/U models only)
CB antenna
(right side
of Tourpak)
To radio antenna
connector 51B
(FLHTC/U models only)
29
30
28A
Antenna cable part of main harness
and present on all models.
To rear headset
(5 pin connector)
Down/Up
3 way switch
Passenger
controls
Volume
(Transceiver cable)
50A
7 pin connector
(Ultra only)
32
(Ultra only)
Transceiver
9
(Ultra only)
AM/FM radio/Cassette player,
CB radio and antenna connections
28

1991-1992 FLHS MODELS

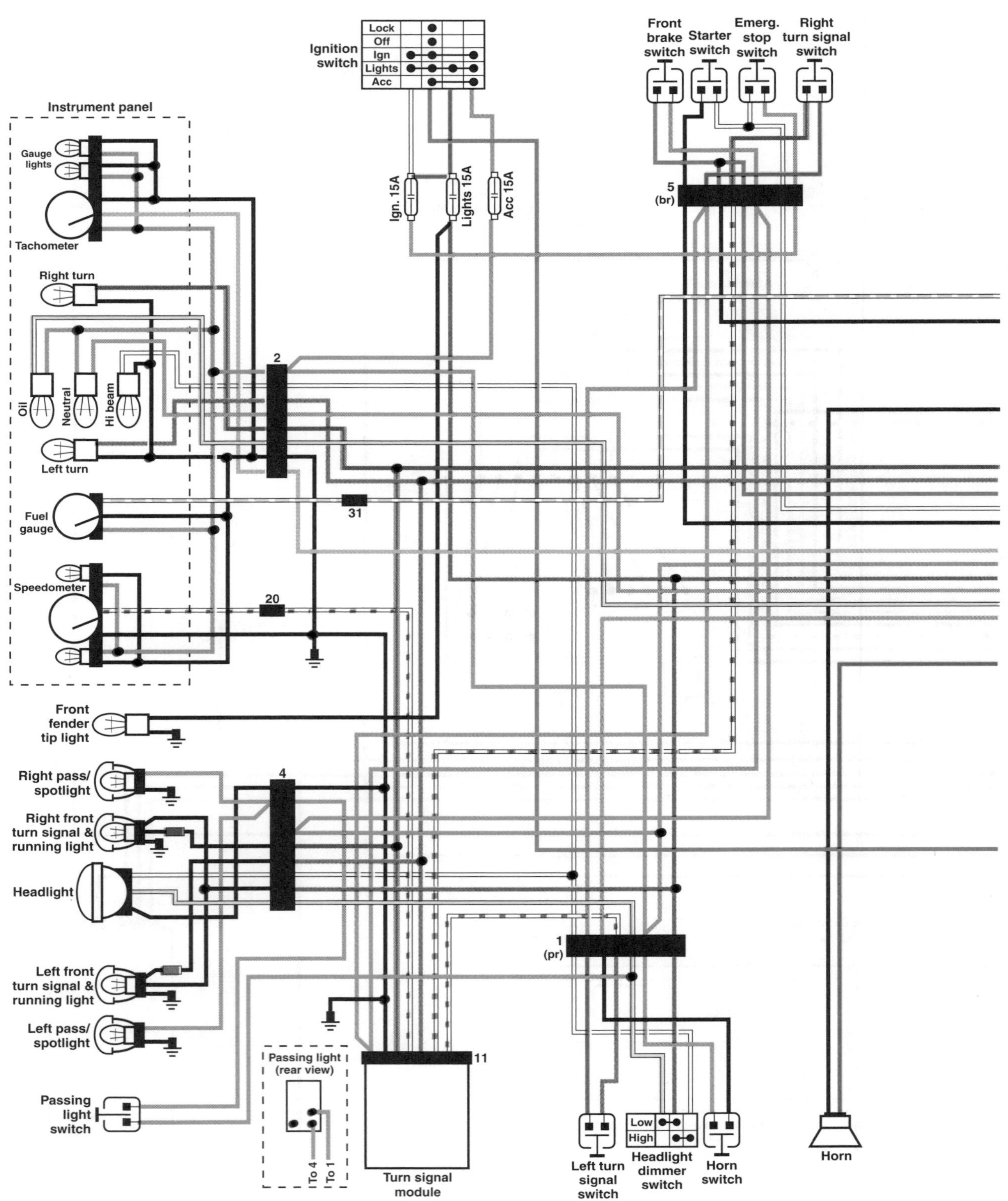

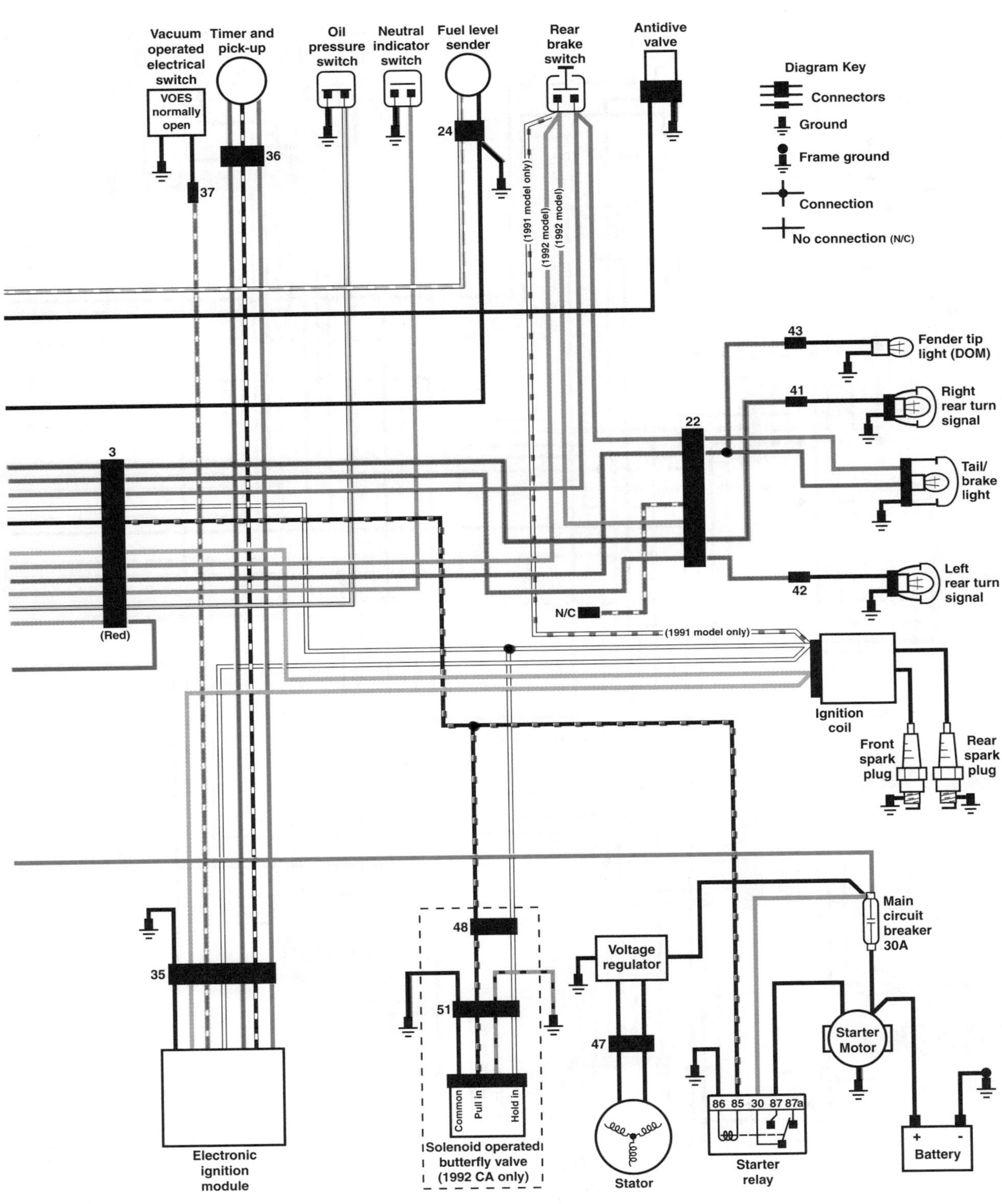
Vacuum operated electrical switch
VOES normally open
Timer and pick-up
Oil pressure switch
Neutral indicator switch
Fuel level sender
Rear brake switch
Antidive valve
Diagram Key
Connectors
Ground
Frame ground
Connection
No connection (N/C)
(1991 model only)
(1992 model)
(1992 model)
Fender tip light (DOM)
Right rear turn signal
Tail/ brake light
Left rear turn signal
(Red)
N/C
(1991 model only)
Ignition coil
Front spark plug
Rear spark plug
Main circuit breaker 30A
Voltage regulator
Starter Motor
Common
Pull in
Hold in
Solenoid operated butterfly valve (1992 CA only)
86 85 30 87 87a
Battery
Electronic ignition module
Stator
Starter relay

1991-1992 FLHTC MODELS

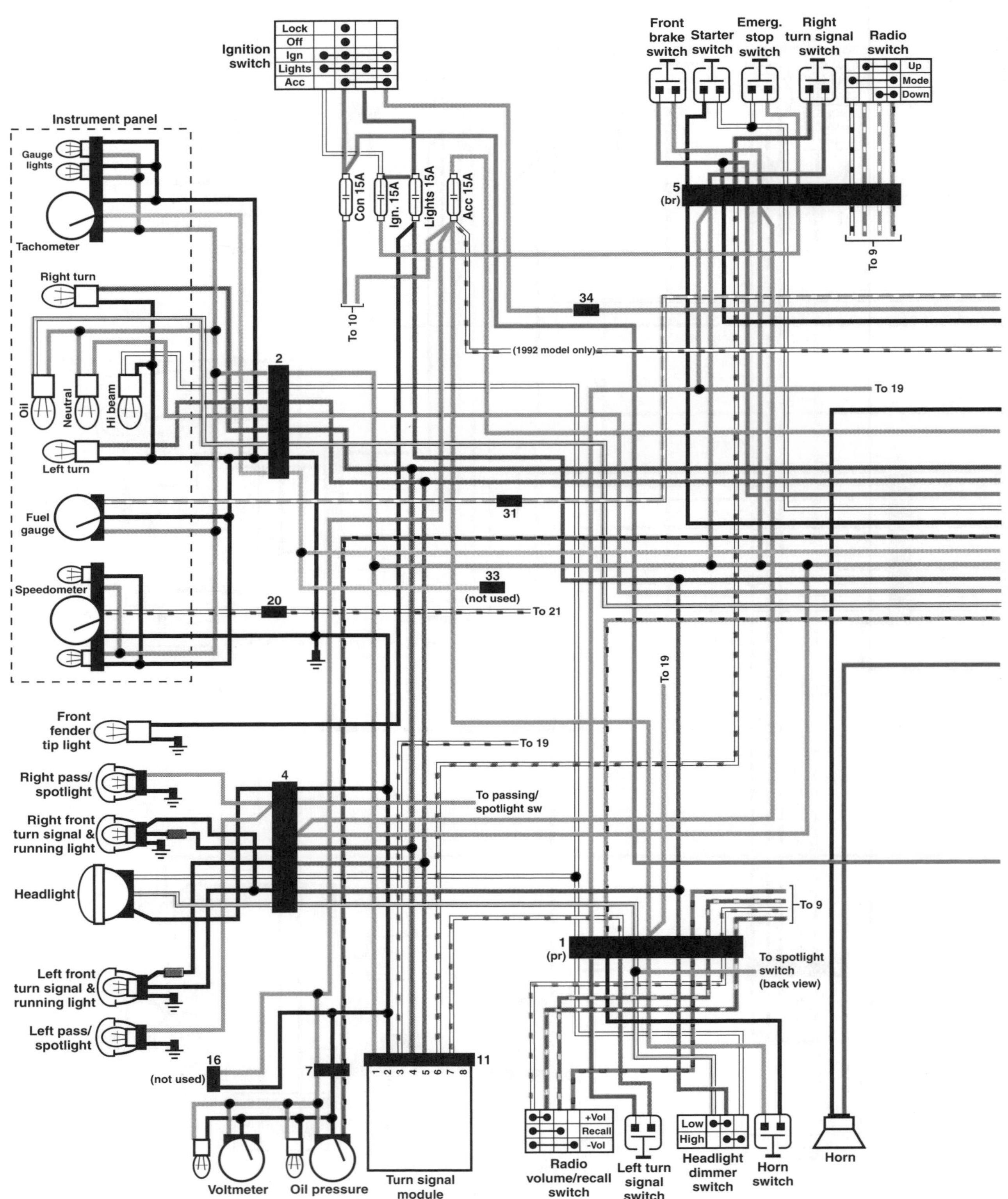

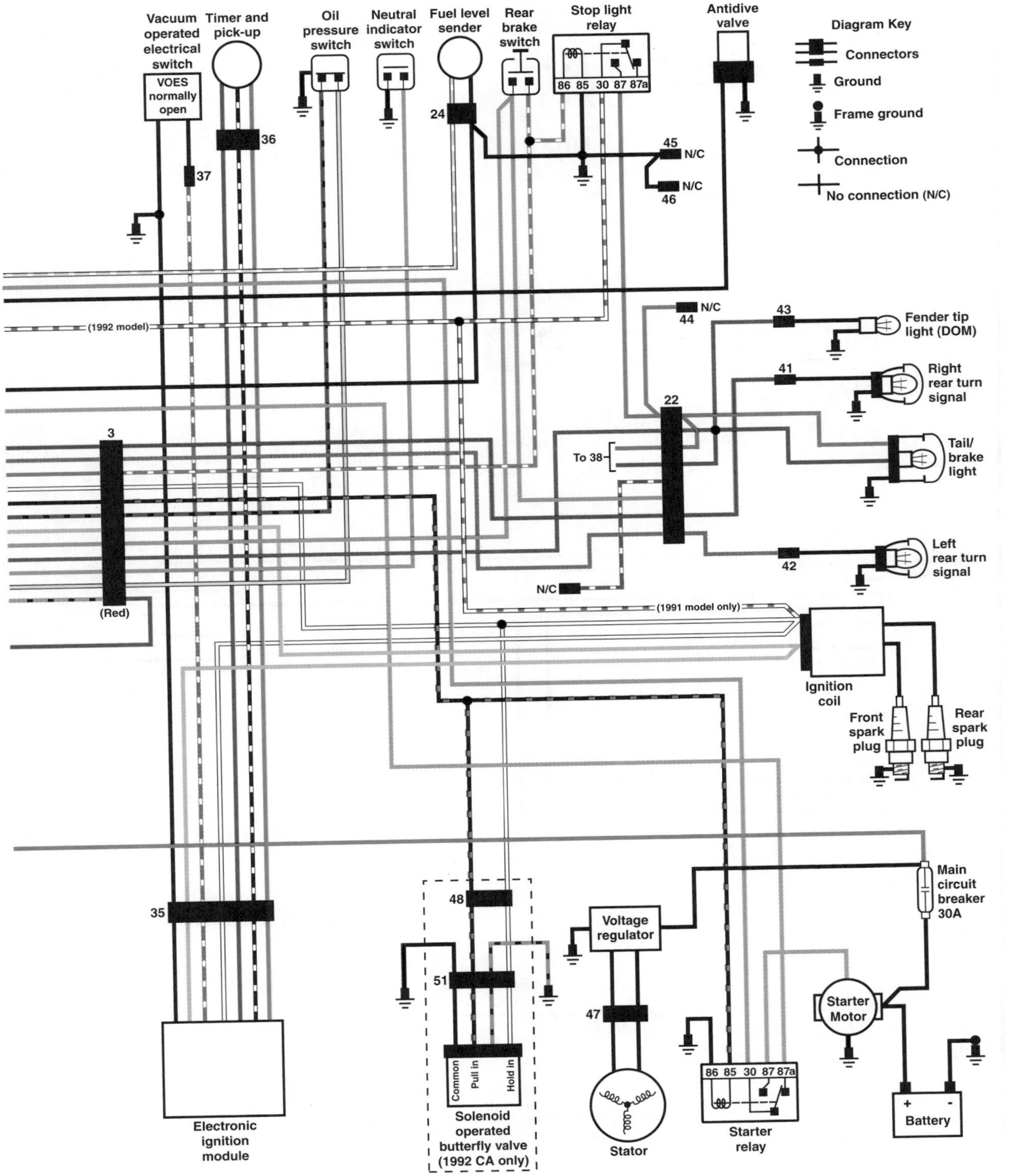

Vacuum operated electrical switch
VOES normally open
Timer and pick-up
Oil pressure switch
Neutral indicator switch
Fuel level sender
Rear brake switch
Stop light relay
86 85 30 87 87a
Antidive valve
Diagram Key
Connectors
Ground
Frame ground
Connection
No connection (N/C)
36
37
24
45
N/C
46
N/C
(1992 model)
44
N/C
43
Fender tip light (DOM)
41
Right rear turn signal
22
3
To 38
Tail/ brake light
Left rear turn signal
42
N/C
(Red)
(1991 model only)
Ignition coil
Front spark plug
Rear spark plug
Main circuit breaker 30A
35
48
51
Voltage regulator
47
Starter Motor
Common
Pull in
Hold in
Solenoid operated butterfly valve (1992 CA only)
86 85 30 87 87a
Starter relay
Battery
Electronic ignition module
Stator

1991-1992 FLHTC MODELS DASH SWITCHES, TOURPAK AND GROUNDS

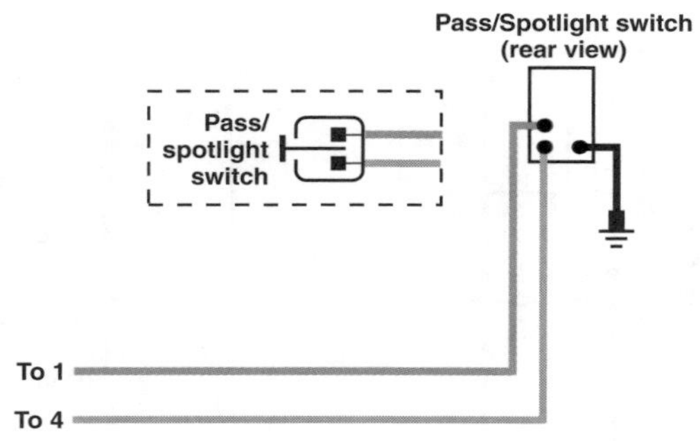

Tourpak
left side
marker
lights

Tourpak
right side
marker
lights

Running
light

38

To 22

Chassis
ground

Handlebar
ground

Triple
clamp
ground

Chassis
ground

Frame
ground

Triple
clamp
ground

1991-1992 FLHTC MODELS RADIO, HARNESS CONNECTORS AND ANTENNA

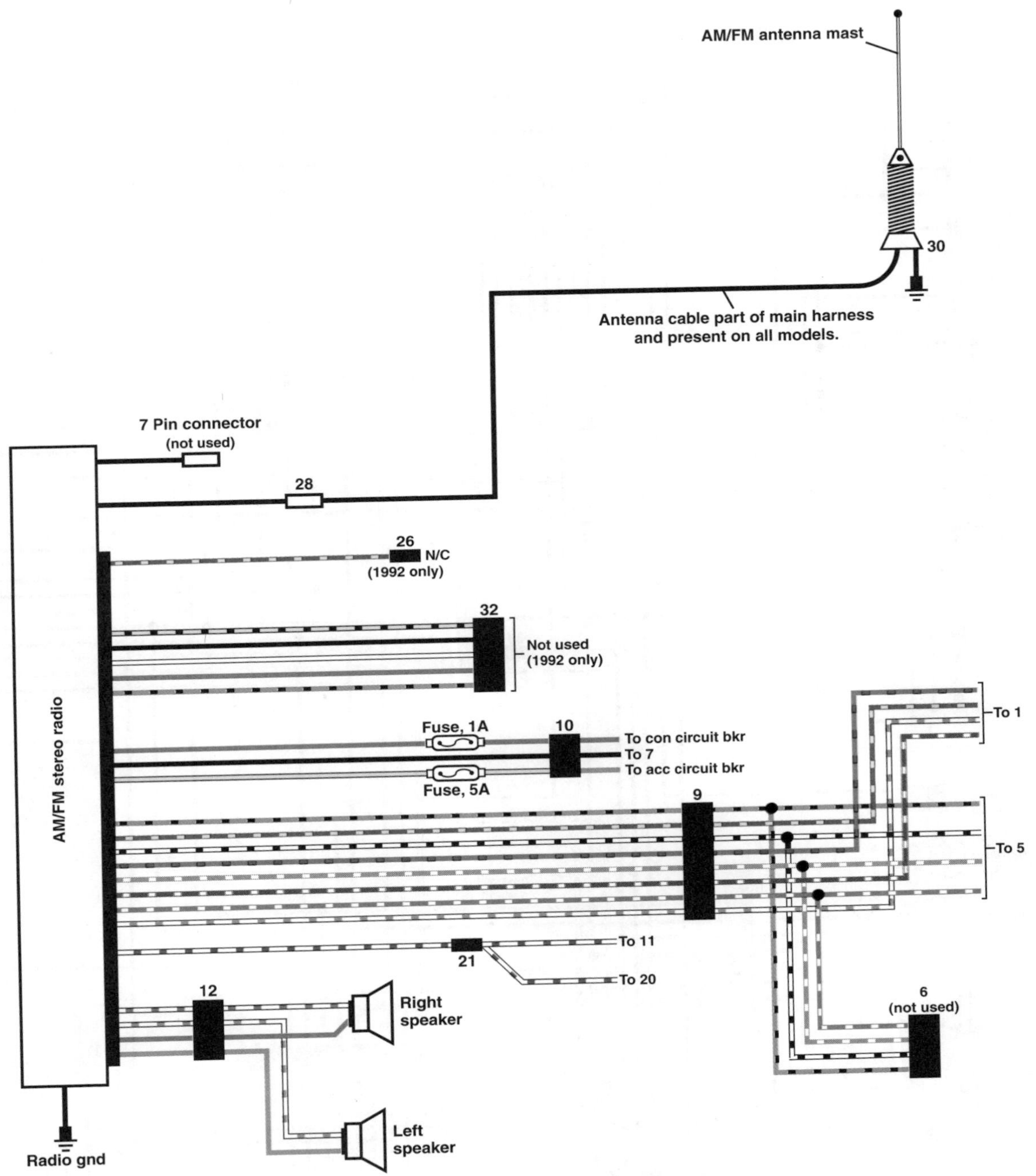

1991-1992 FLHTC ULTRA MODELS

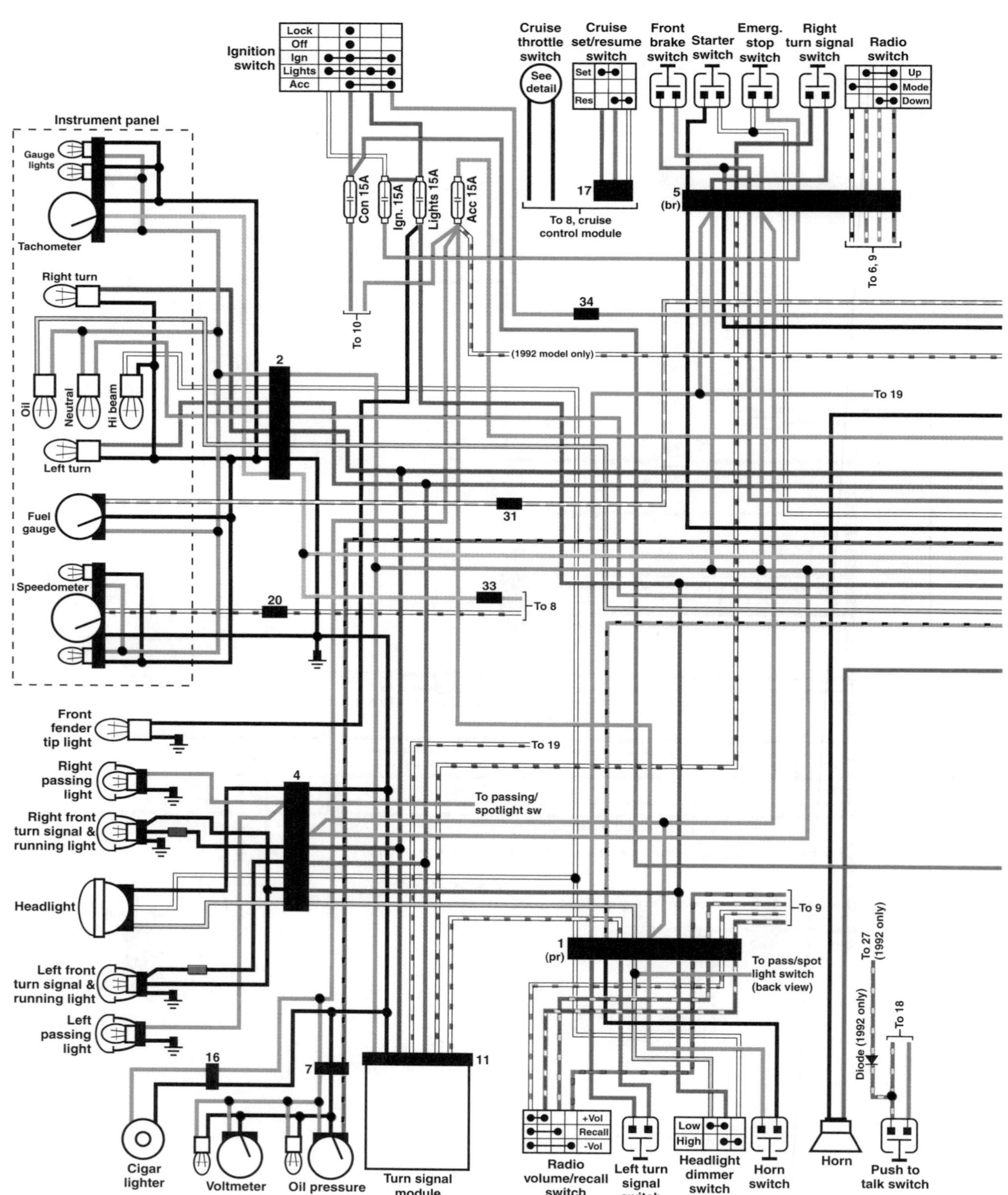

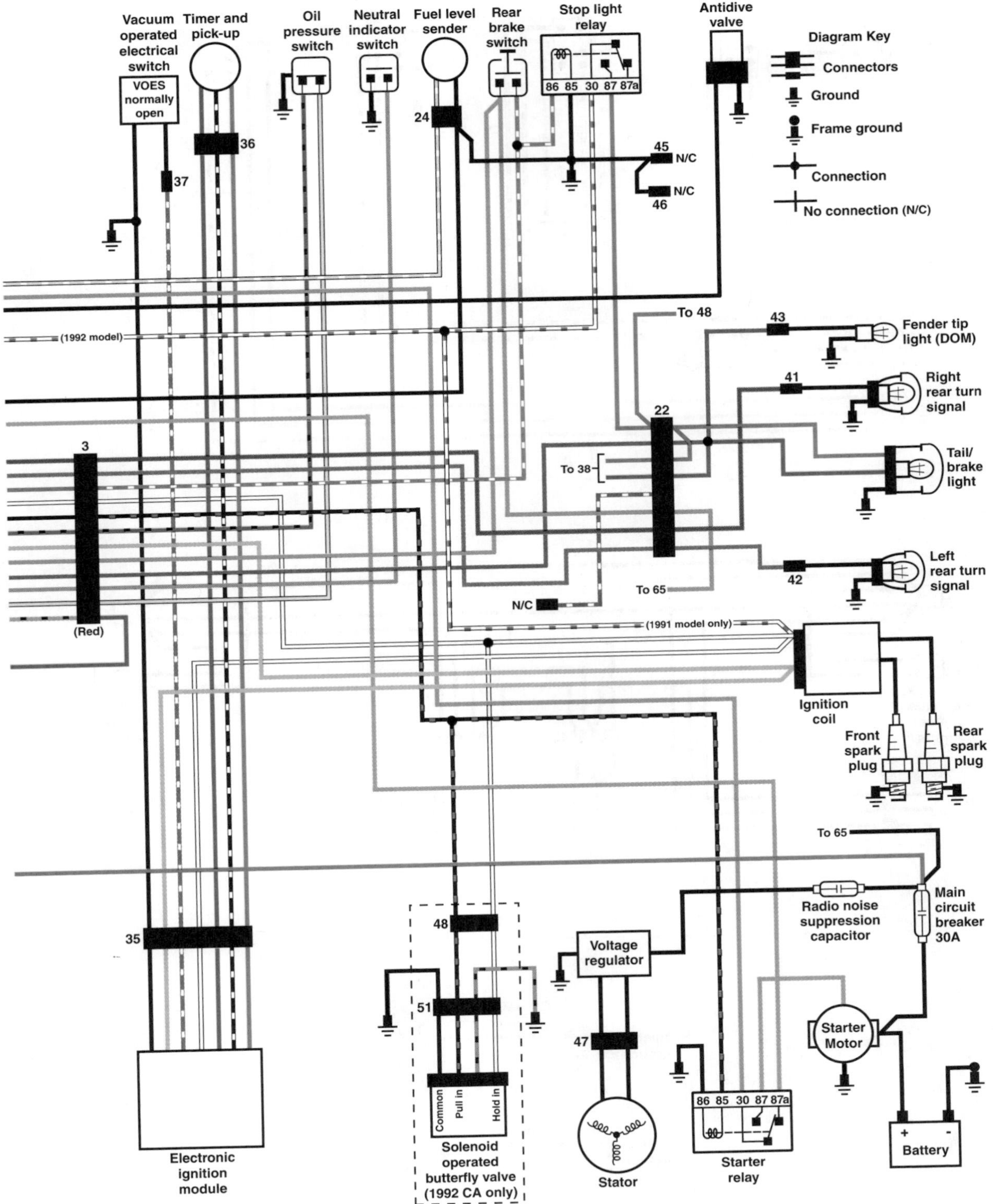

Vacuum operated electrical switch
VOES normally open
Timer and pick-up
Oil pressure switch
Neutral indicator switch
Fuel level sender
Rear brake switch
Stop light relay
86 85 30 87 87a
Antidive valve
Diagram Key
Connectors
Ground
Frame ground
Connection
No connection (N/C)
36
37
24
45
N/C
46
N/C
(1992 model)
To 48
43
Fender tip light (DOM)
41
Right rear turn signal
22
Tail/ brake light
To 38
3
Left rear turn signal
42
To 65
N/C
(Red)
(1991 model only)
Ignition coil
Front spark plug
Rear spark plug
To 65
Main circuit breaker 30A
Radio noise suppression capacitor
35
48
Voltage regulator
51
47
Starter Motor
Common
Pull in
Hold in
Solenoid operated butterfly valve (1992 CA only)
Electronic ignition module
Stator
86 85 30 87 87a
Starter relay
Battery

17

1991-1992 FLHTC ULTRA MODELS DASH SWITCHES, TOURPAK AND GROUNDS

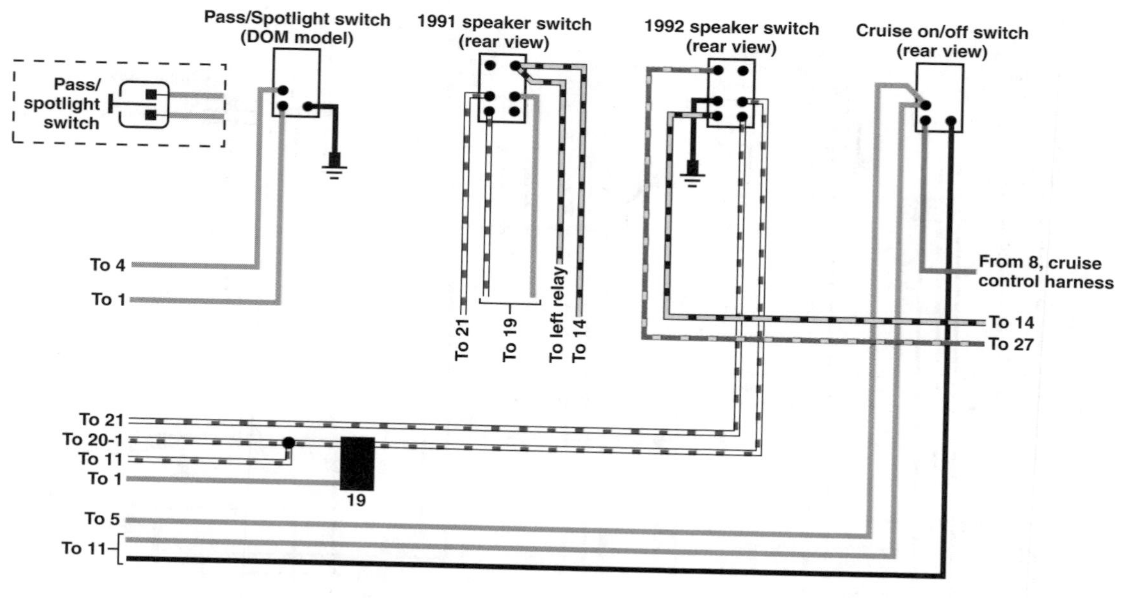

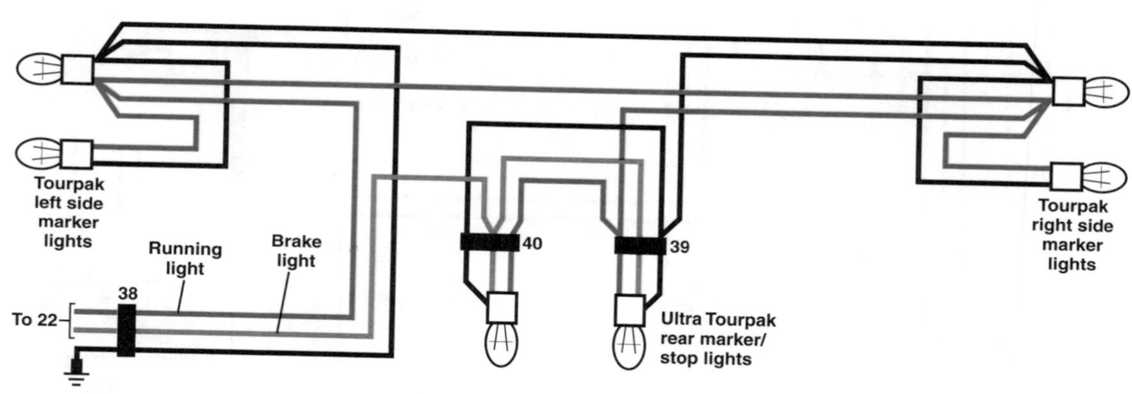

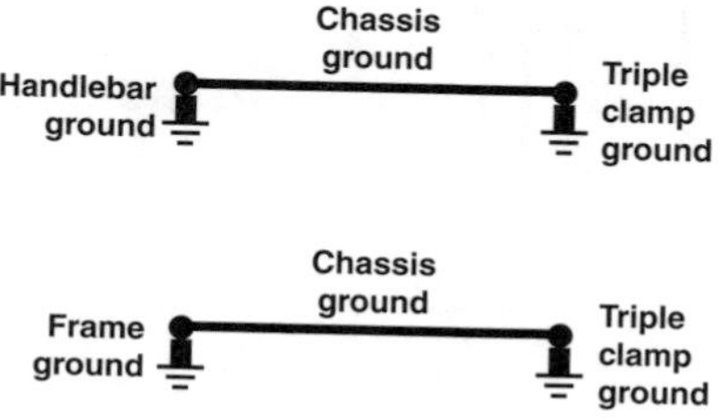

1991-1992 FLHTC ULTRA MODELS RADIO, HARNESS CONNECTORS AND CRUISE CONTROL CONNECTIONS

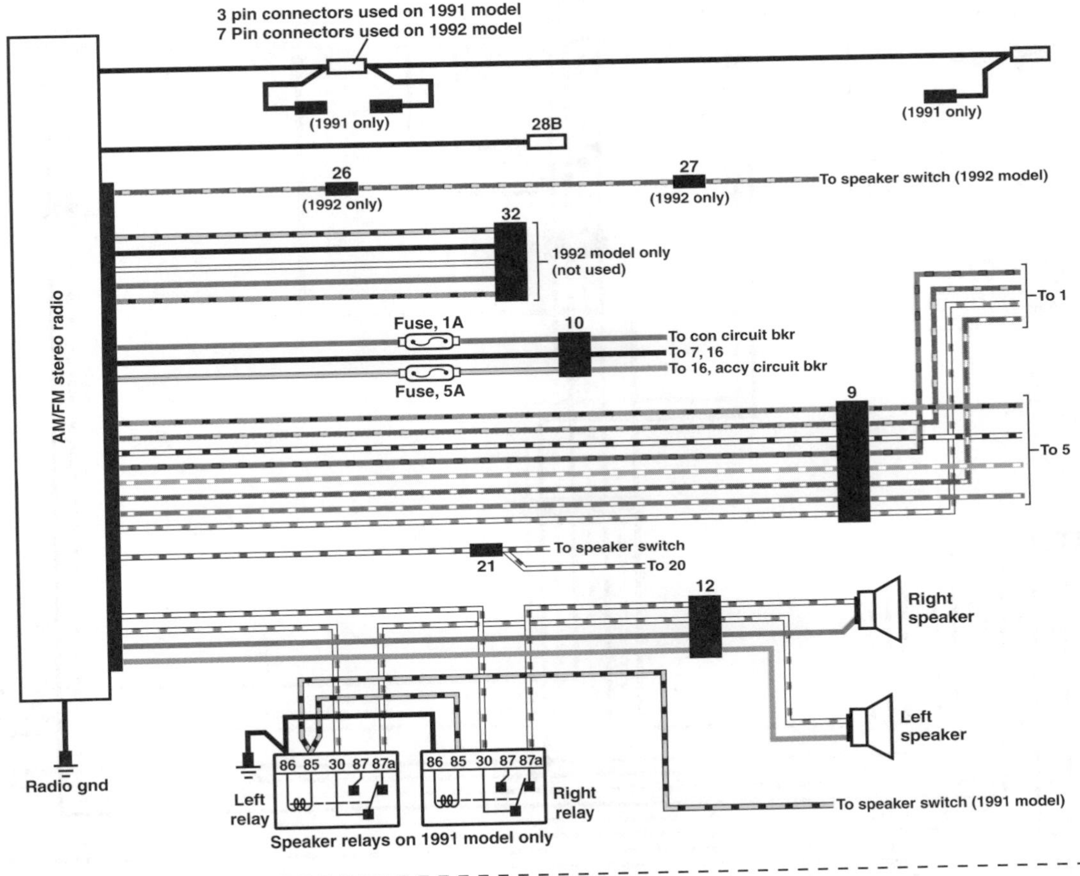

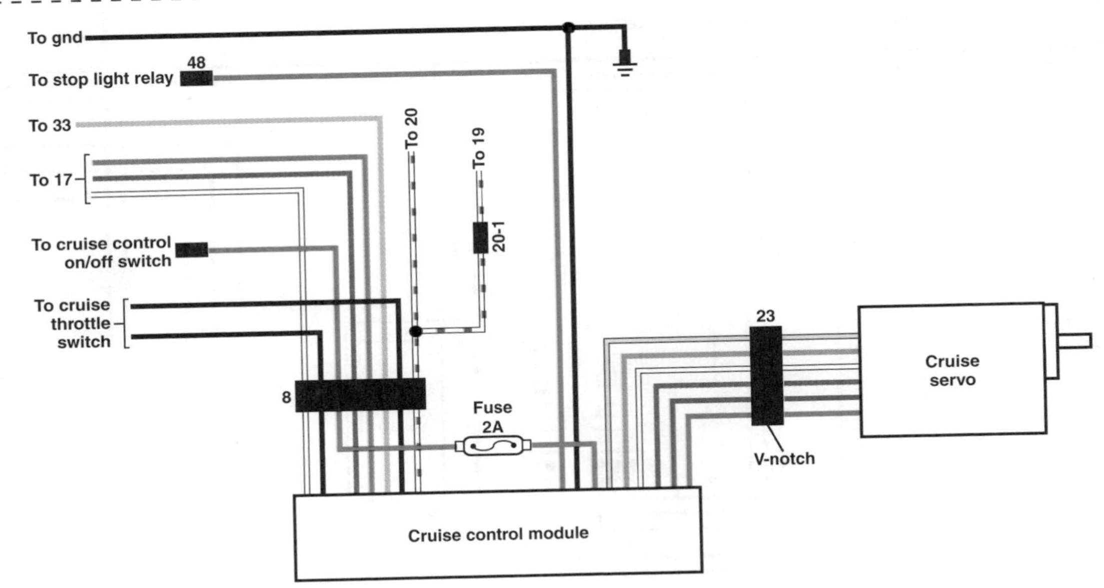

17

1991-1992 FLHTC ULTRA MODELS RADIO CB/INTERCOM, REAR SPEAKERS AND ANTENNAS

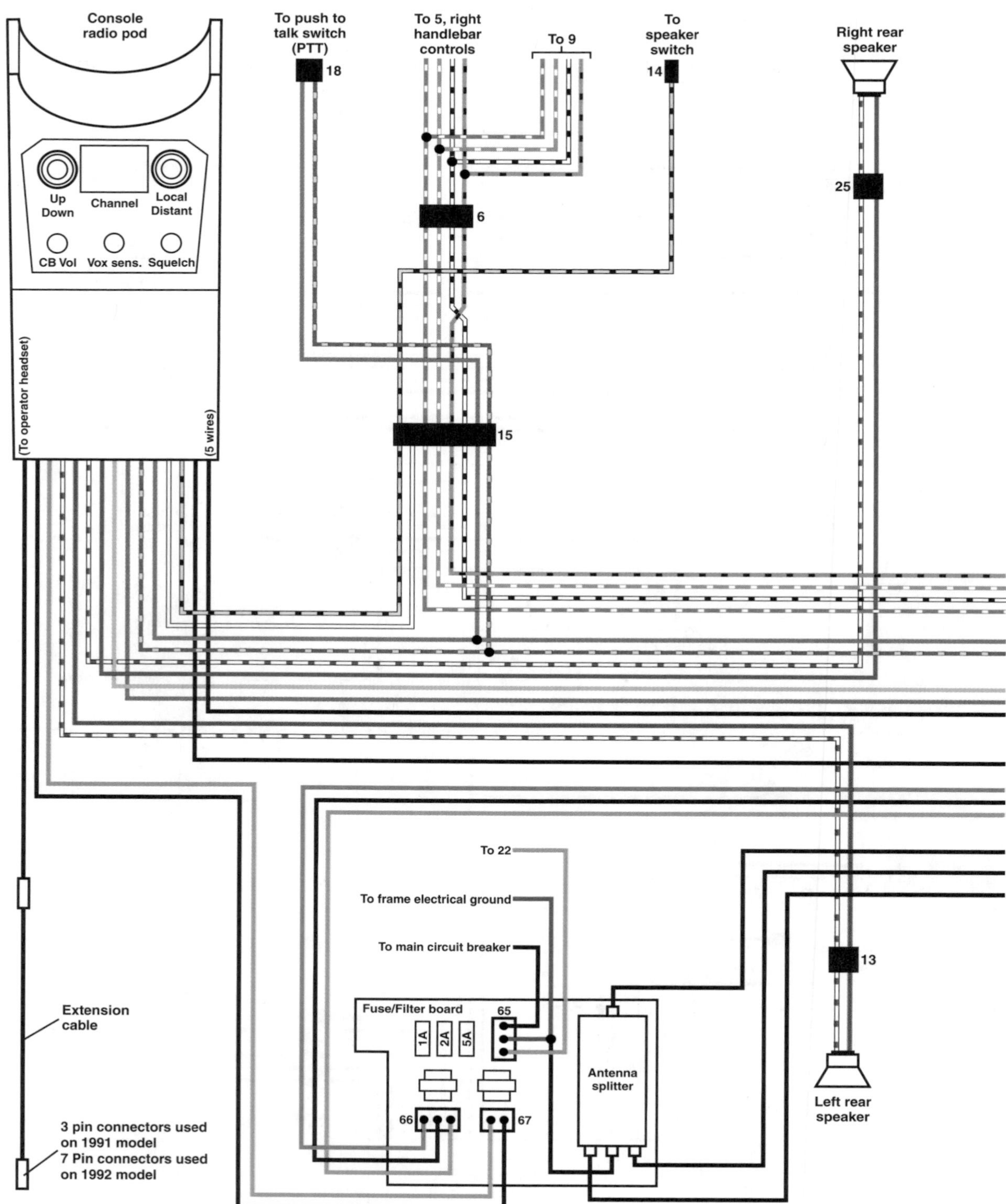

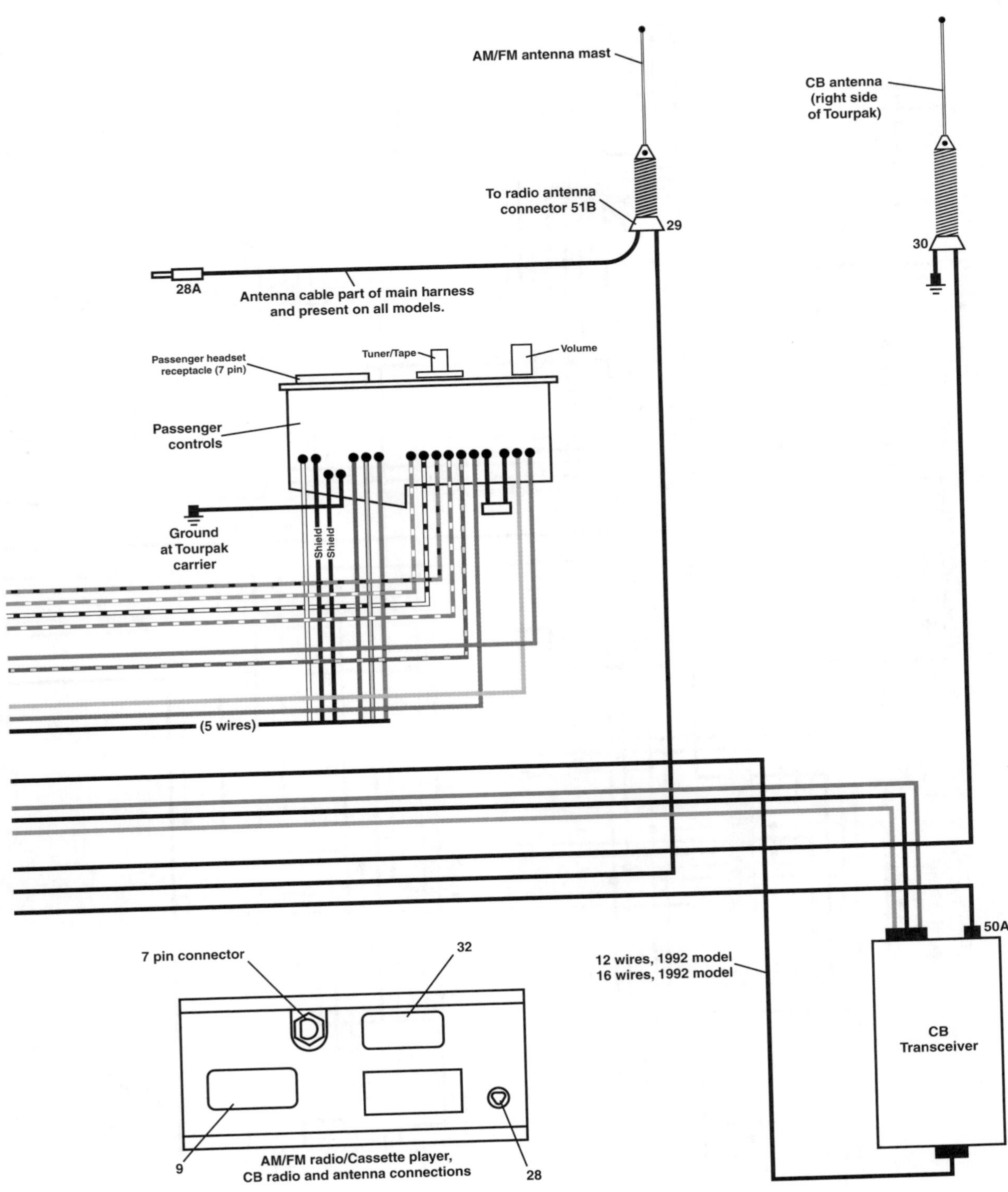
AM/FM antenna mast
CB antenna
(right side
of Tourpak)
To radio antenna
connector 51B
29
30
28A
Antenna cable part of main harness
and present on all models.
Passenger headset
receptacle (7 pin)
Tuner/Tape
Volume
Passenger
controls
Ground
at Tourpak
carrier
Shield
Shield
(5 wires)
50A
7 pin connector
32
12 wires, 1992 model
16 wires, 1992 model
CB
Transceiver
9
28
AM/FM radio/Cassette player,
CB radio and antenna connections

1991-1992 FLTC ULTRA MODELS

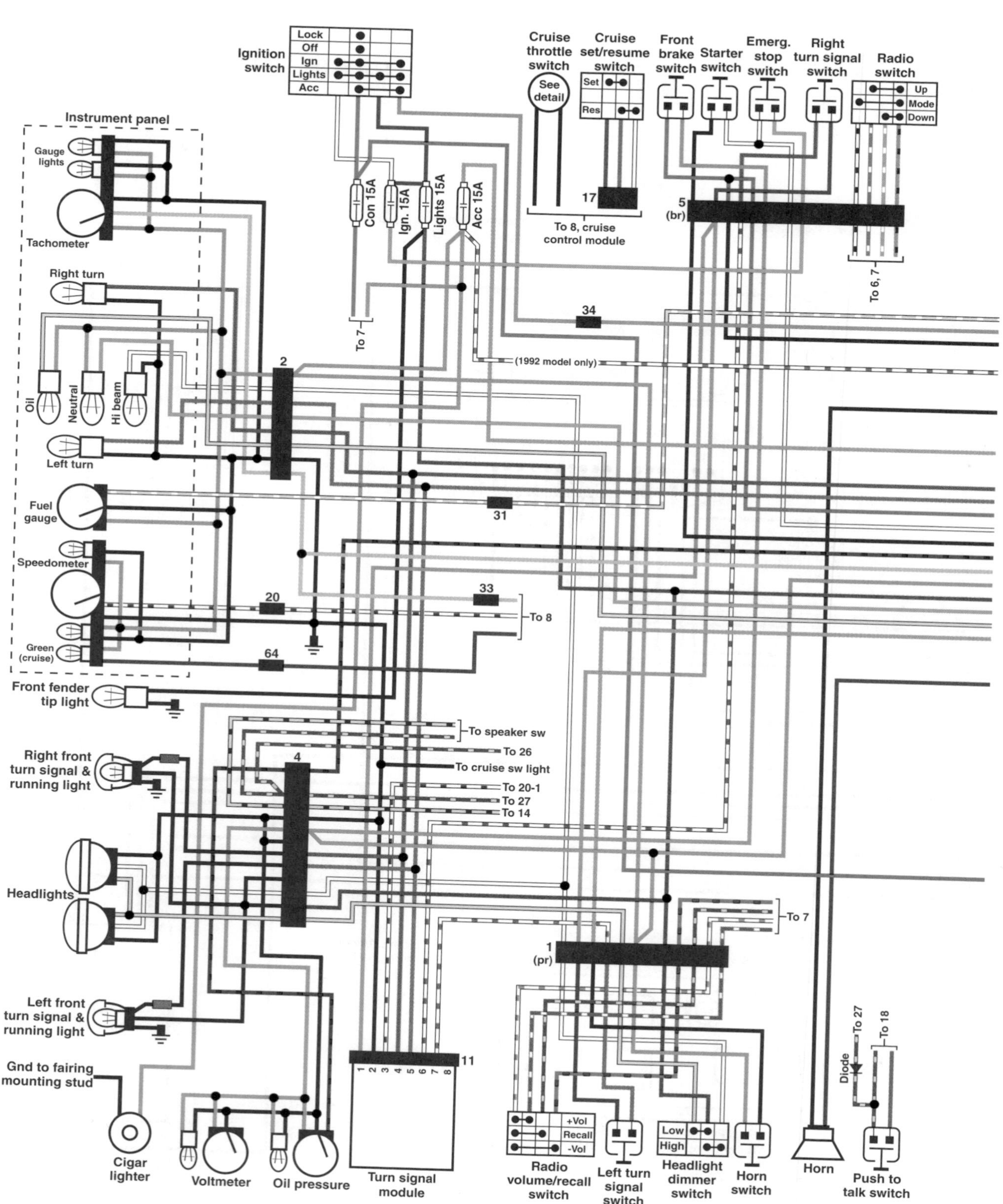

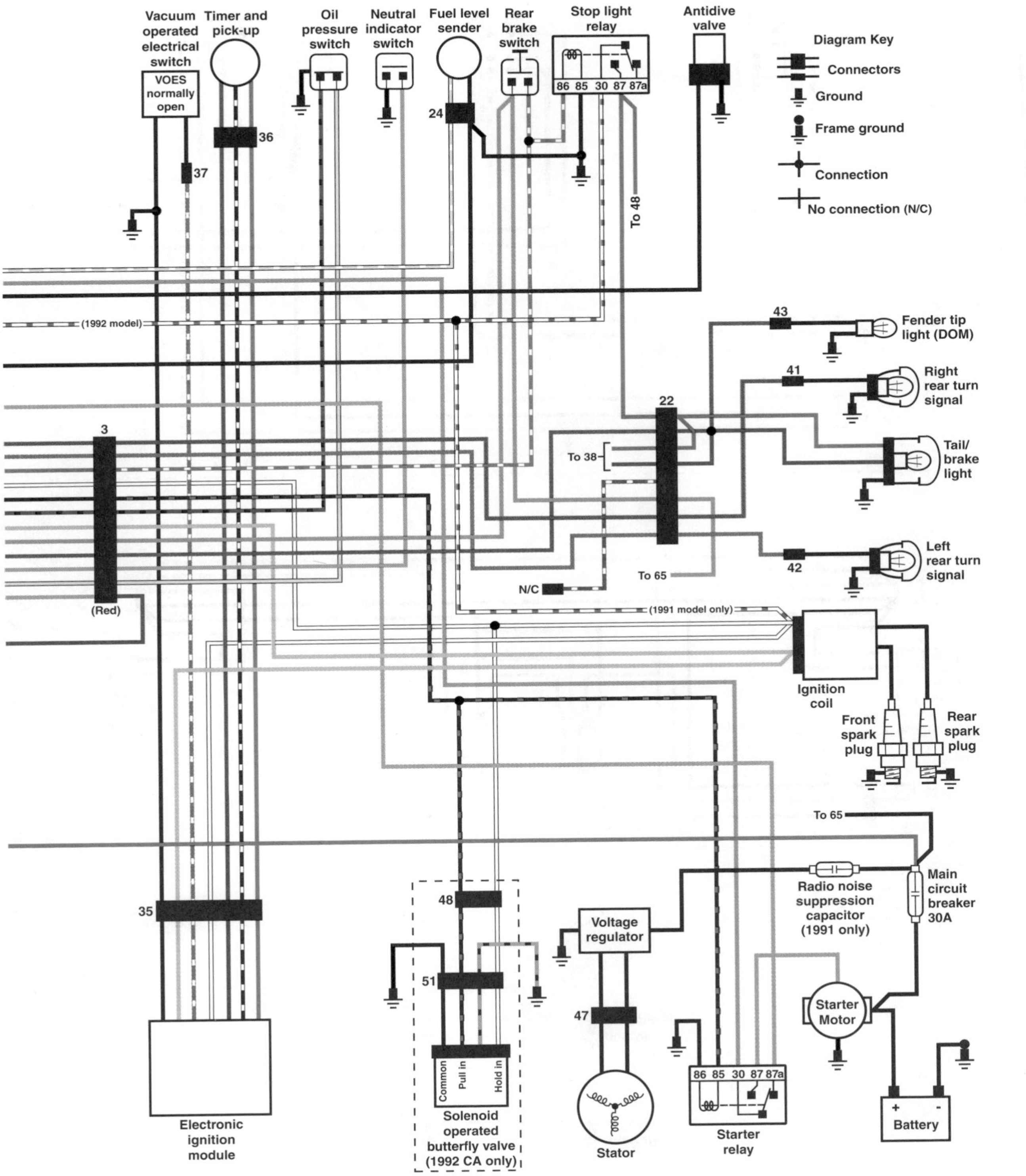

Vacuum operated electrical switch
VOES normally open
Timer and pick-up
Oil pressure switch
Neutral indicator switch
Fuel level sender
Rear brake switch
Stop light relay
86 85 30 87 87a
Antidive valve

Diagram Key
Connectors
Ground
Frame ground
Connection
No connection (N/C)

36
37
24
To 48
(1992 model)
43
Fender tip light (DOM)
41
Right rear turn signal
22
3
To 38
Tail/ brake light
(Red)
To 65
N/C
42
Left rear turn signal
(1991 model only)
Ignition coil
Front spark plug
Rear spark plug
To 65
Main circuit breaker 30A
Radio noise suppression capacitor (1991 only)
35
48
Voltage regulator
51
47
Starter Motor
Common
Pull in
Hold in
86 85 30 87 87a
Battery
Electronic ignition module
Solenoid operated butterfly valve (1992 CA only)
Stator
Starter relay

17

1991-1992 FLTC ULTRA MODELS DASH SWITCHES, TOURPAK AND GROUNDS

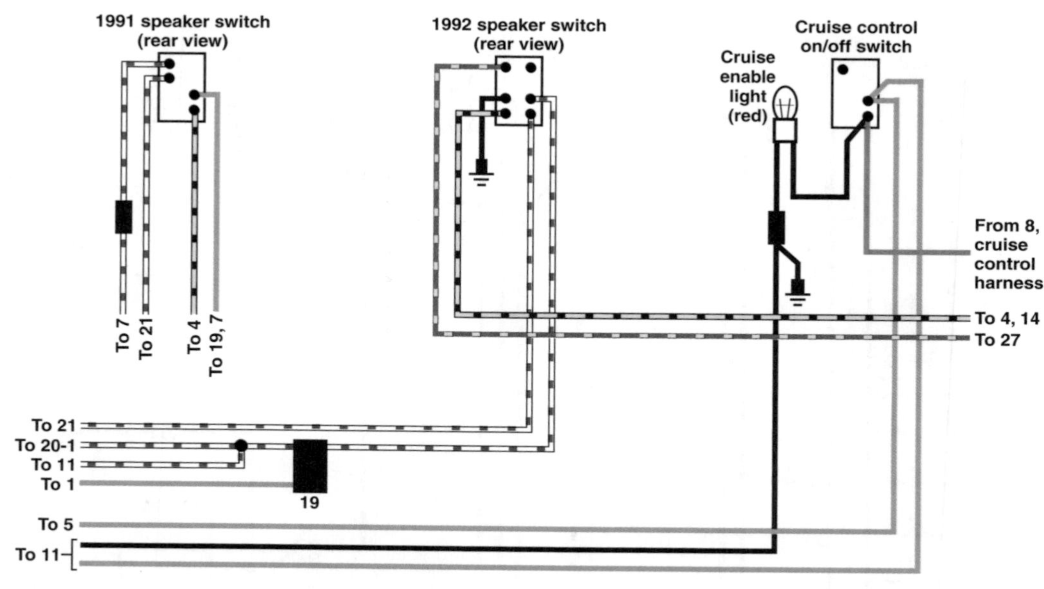

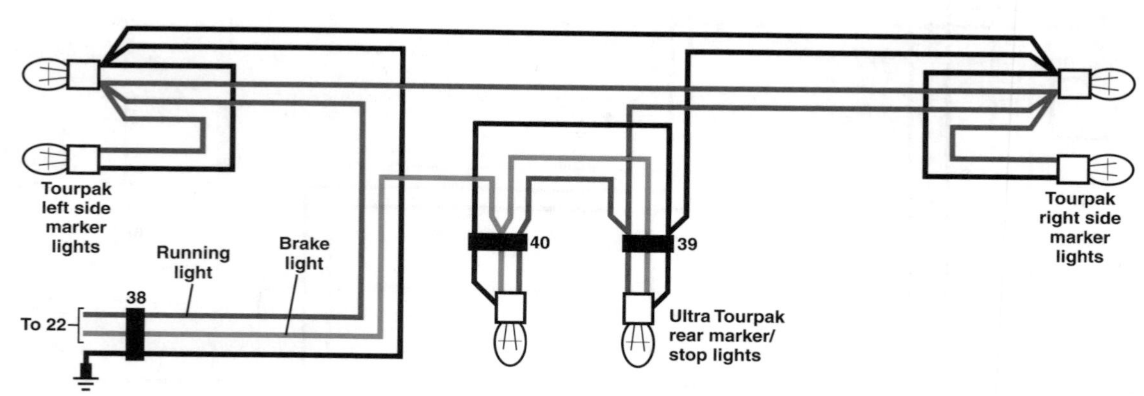

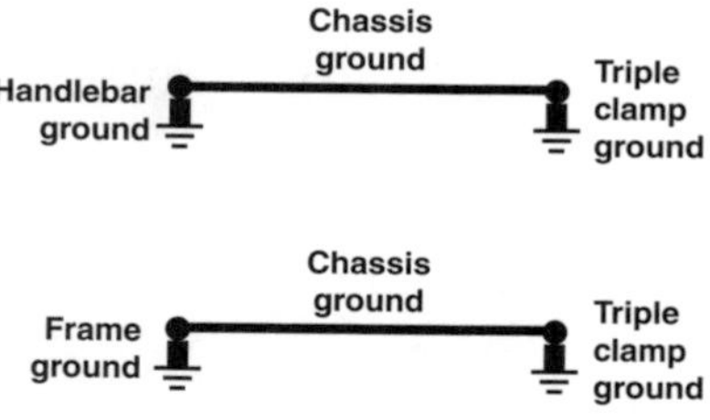

1991-1992 FLTC ULTRA MODELS RADIO, HARNESS CONNECTORS AND CRUISE CONTROL CONNECTIONS

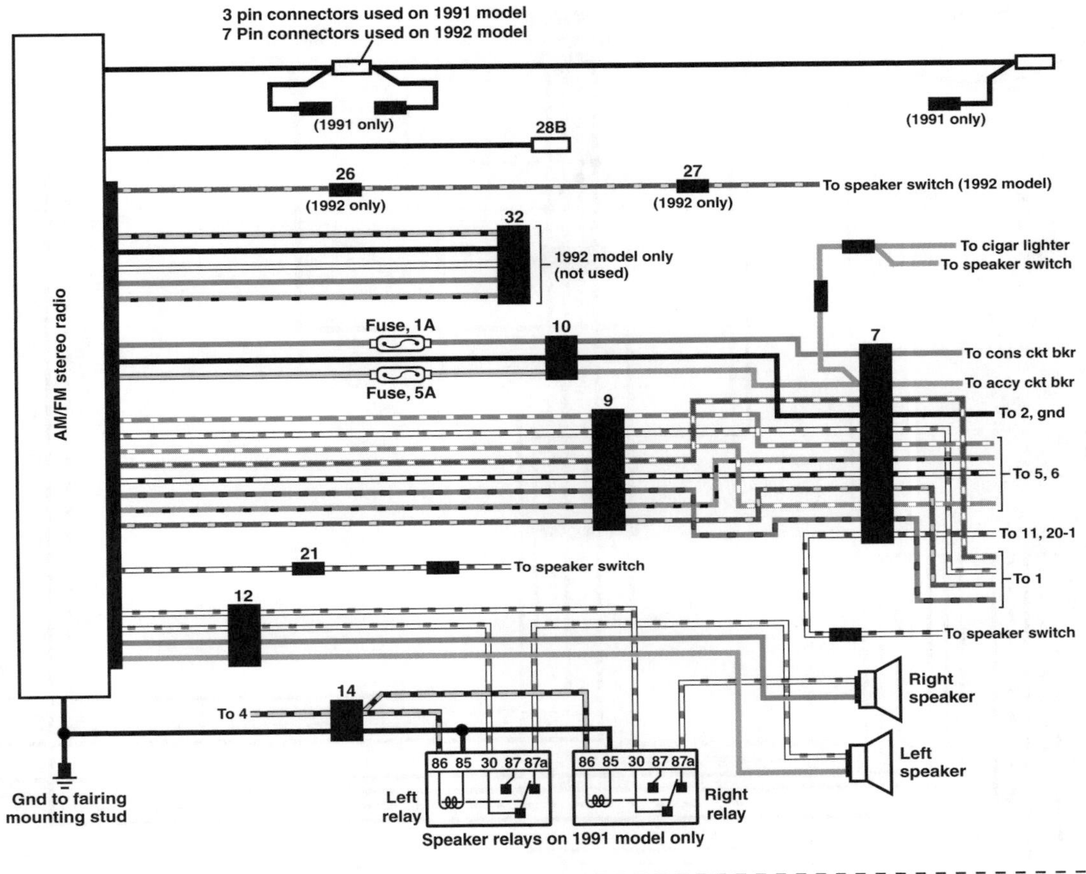

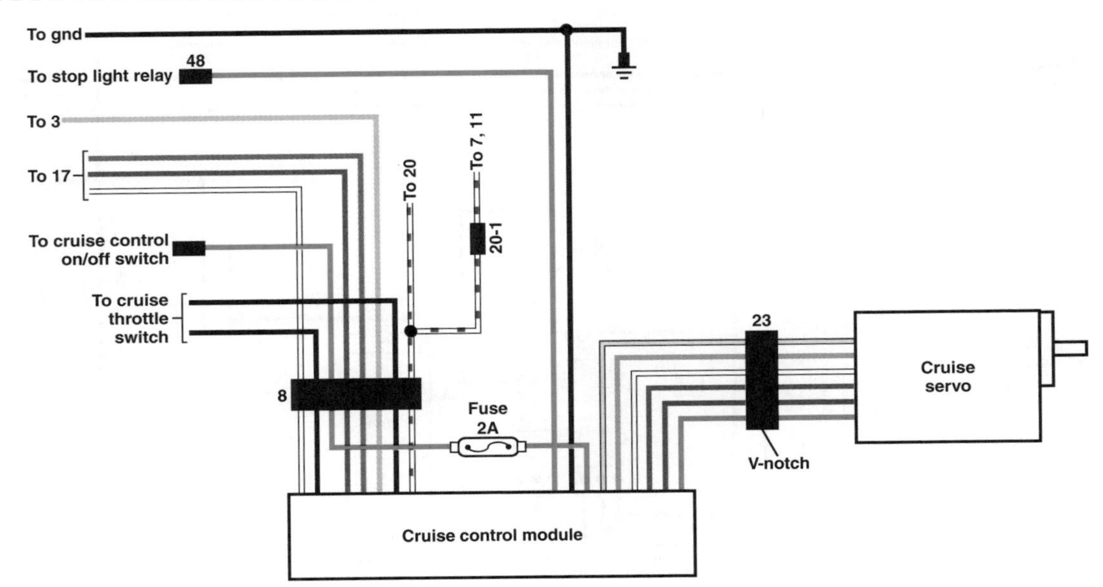

17

1991-1992 FLTC ULTRA MODELS RADIO CB/INTERCOM, REAR SPEAKERS AND ANTENNAS

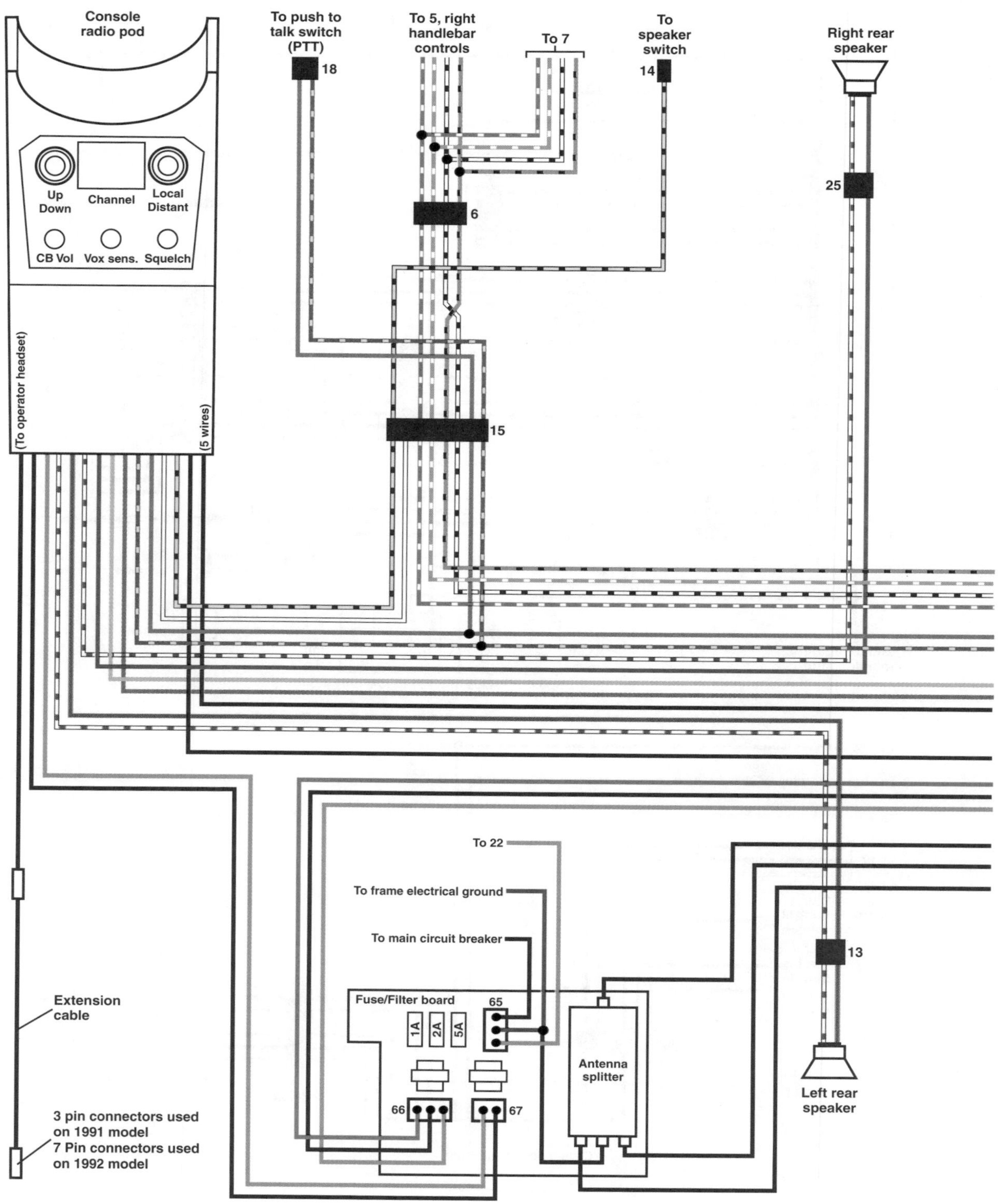

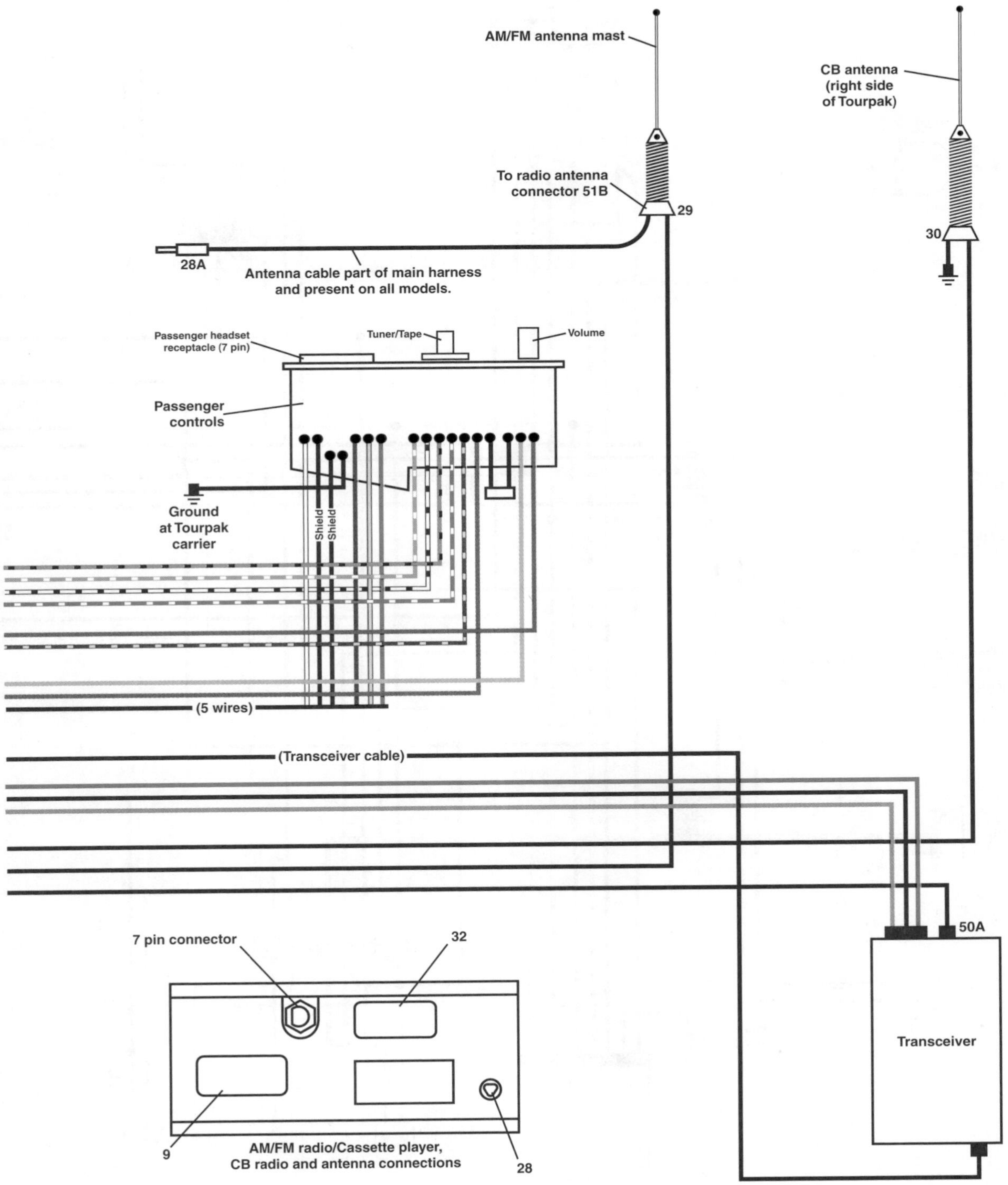

AM/FM antenna mast

CB antenna (right side of Tourpak)

To radio antenna connector 51B

29

30

28A

Antenna cable part of main harness and present on all models.

Passenger headset receptacle (7 pin)

Tuner/Tape

Volume

Passenger controls

Ground at Tourpak carrier

Shield

Shield

(5 wires)

(Transceiver cable)

50A

Transceiver

7 pin connector

32

9

28

AM/FM radio/Cassette player, CB radio and antenna connections

1991 FXLR MODELS

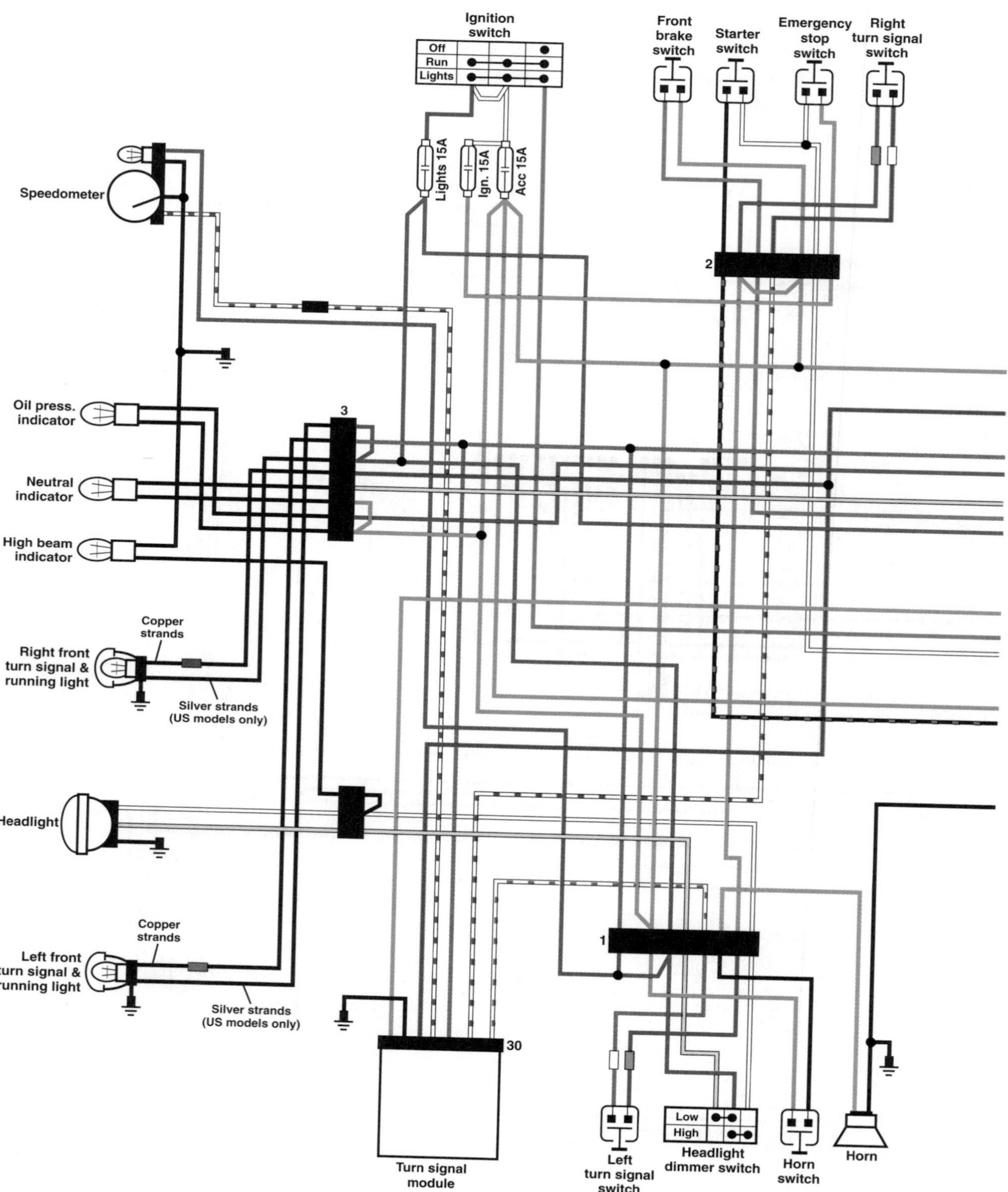

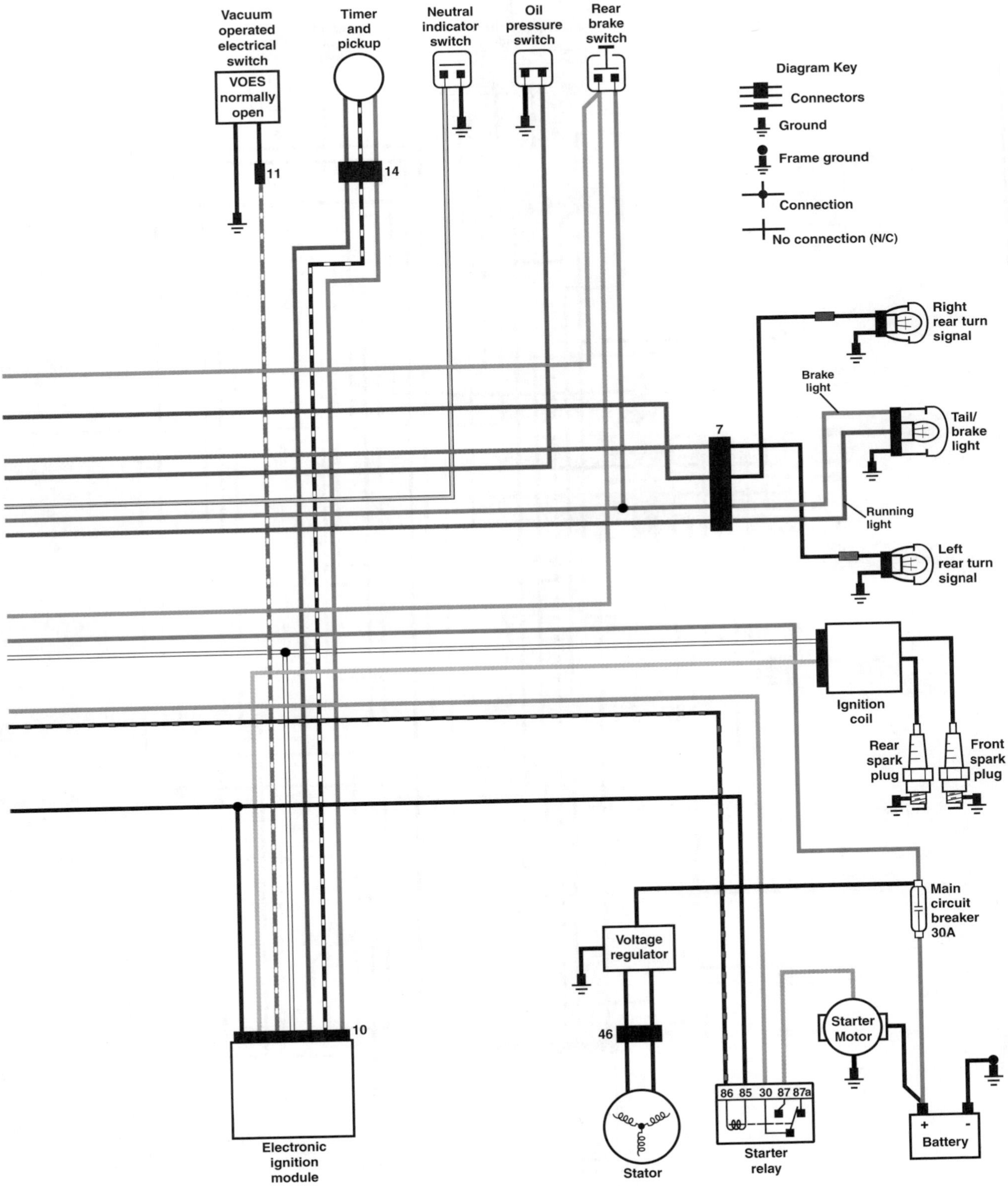

Vacuum operated electrical switch
VOES normally open
11
Timer and pickup
14
Neutral indicator switch
Oil pressure switch
Rear brake switch

Diagram Key
Connectors
Ground
Frame ground
Connection
No connection (N/C)

Right rear turn signal
Brake light
Tail/ brake light
7
Running light
Left rear turn signal

Ignition coil
Rear spark plug
Front spark plug

Main circuit breaker 30A
Voltage regulator
46
Starter Motor
10
86 85 30 87 87a
Battery
+ -

Electronic ignition module
Stator
Starter relay

1991-1994 FXR MODELS

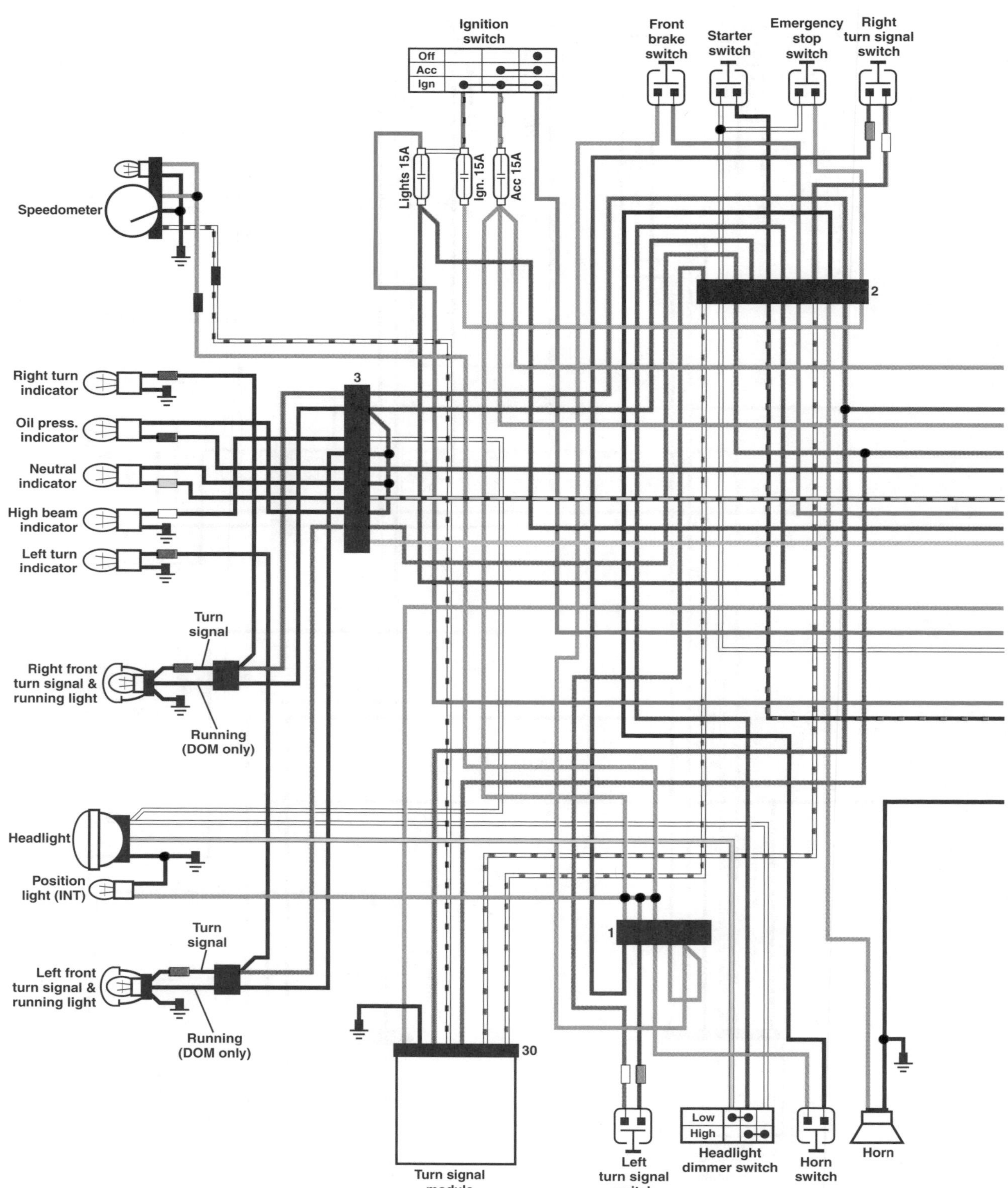

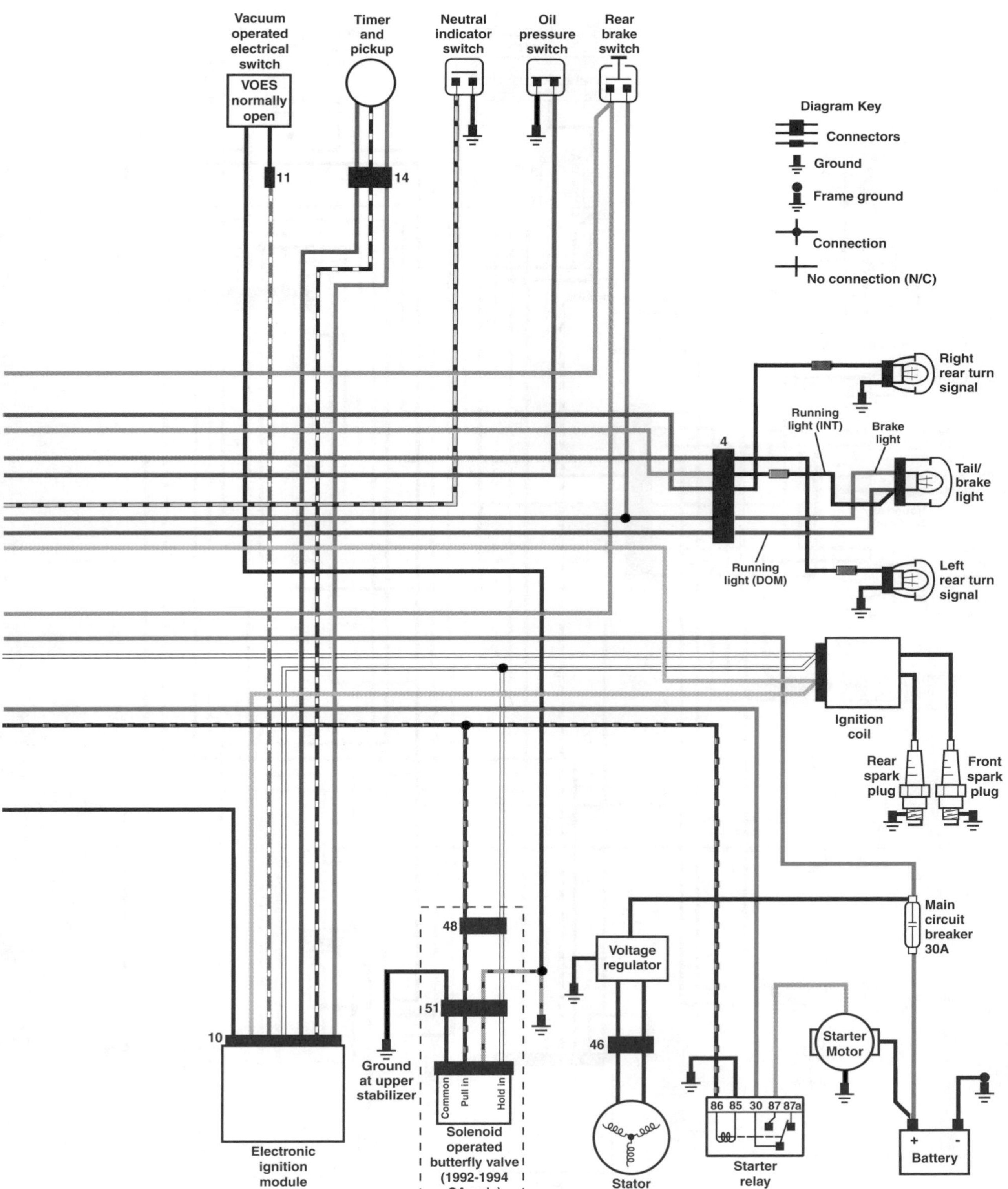

Vacuum operated electrical switch
VOES normally open
Timer and pickup
Neutral indicator switch
Oil pressure switch
Rear brake switch
Diagram Key
Connectors
Ground
Frame ground
Connection
No connection (N/C)
11
14
Right rear turn signal
Running light (INT)
Brake light
4
Tail/ brake light
Running light (DOM)
Left rear turn signal
Ignition coil
Rear spark plug
Front spark plug
Main circuit breaker 30A
48
Voltage regulator
51
10
46
Starter Motor
Ground at upper stabilizer
Common
Pull in
Hold in
86 85 30 87 87a
+ -
Battery
Electronic ignition module
Solenoid operated butterfly valve (1992-1994 CA only)
Stator
Starter relay

1991-1992 FXRS MODELS

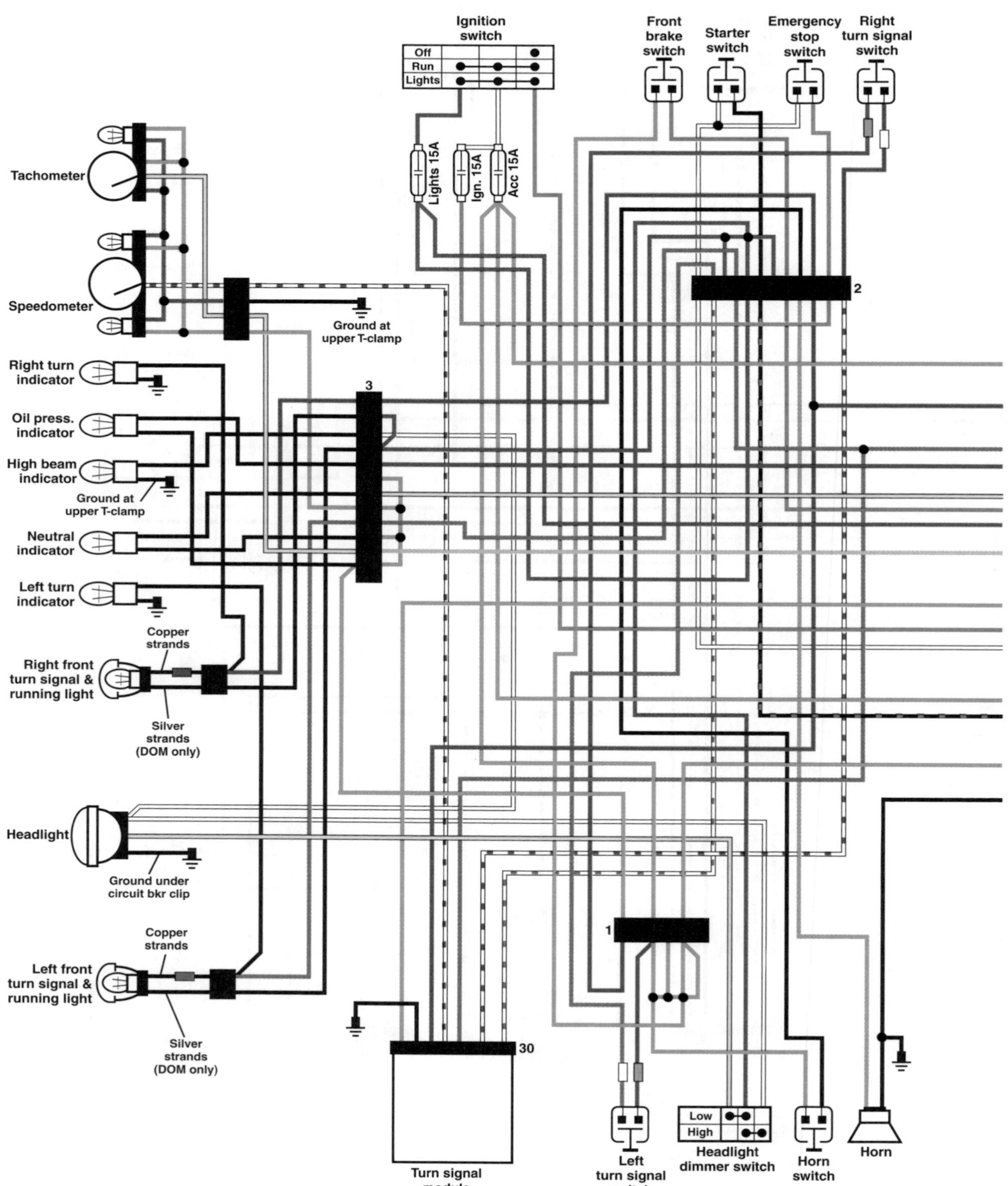

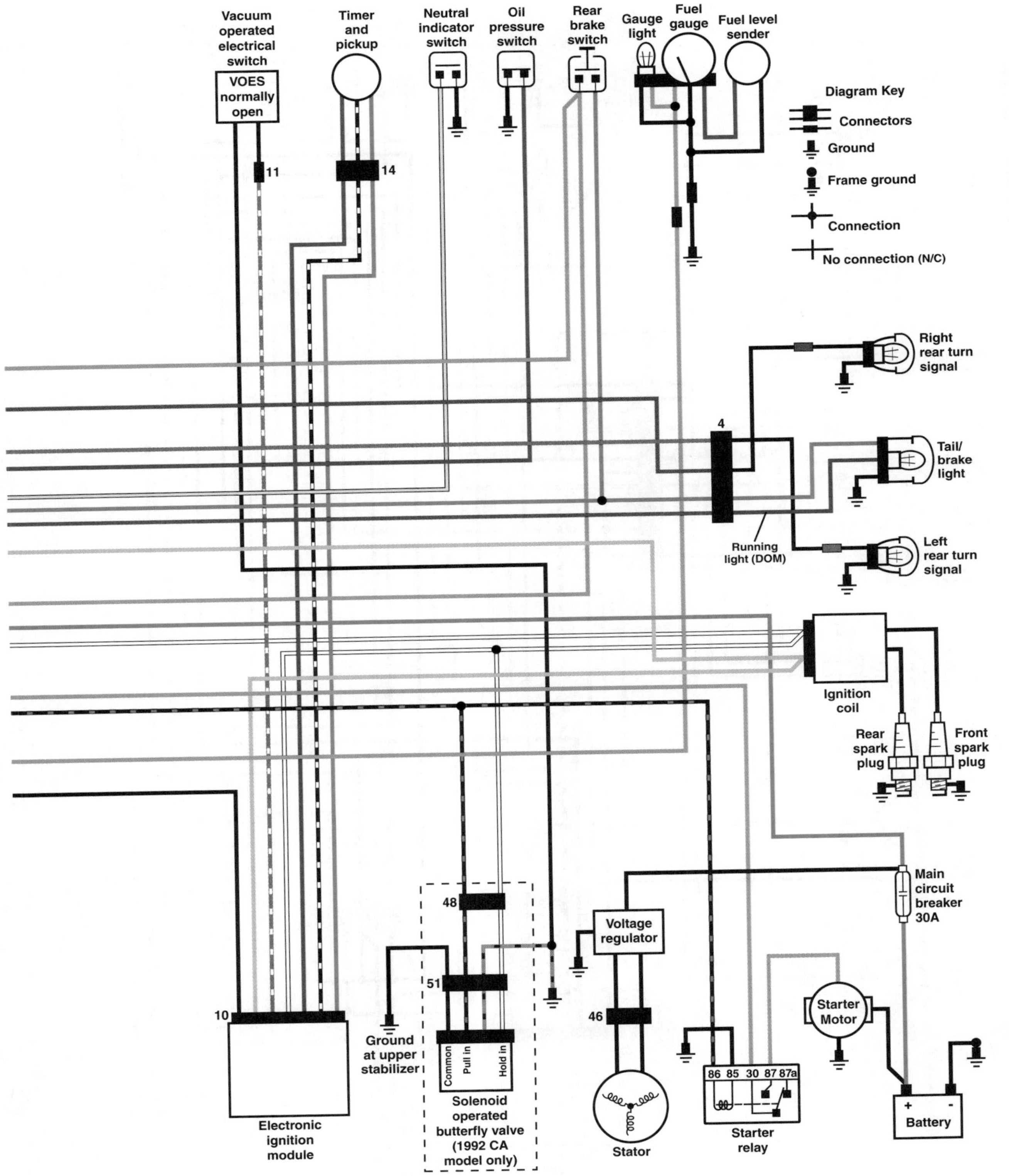

Vacuum operated electrical switch
VOES normally open
Timer and pickup
Neutral indicator switch
Oil pressure switch
Rear brake switch
Gauge light
Fuel gauge
Fuel level sender
Diagram Key
Connectors
Ground
Frame ground
Connection
No connection (N/C)
11
14
Right rear turn signal
4
Tail/ brake light
Running light (DOM)
Left rear turn signal
Ignition coil
Rear spark plug
Front spark plug
Main circuit breaker 30A
48
51
10
Ground at upper stabilizer
Common
Pull in
Hold in
Solenoid operated butterfly valve (1992 CA model only)
Electronic ignition module
Voltage regulator
46
Stator
86 85 30 87 87a
Starter relay
Starter Motor
Battery

1991-1993 FXRS-CON AND FXRS-SP MODELS

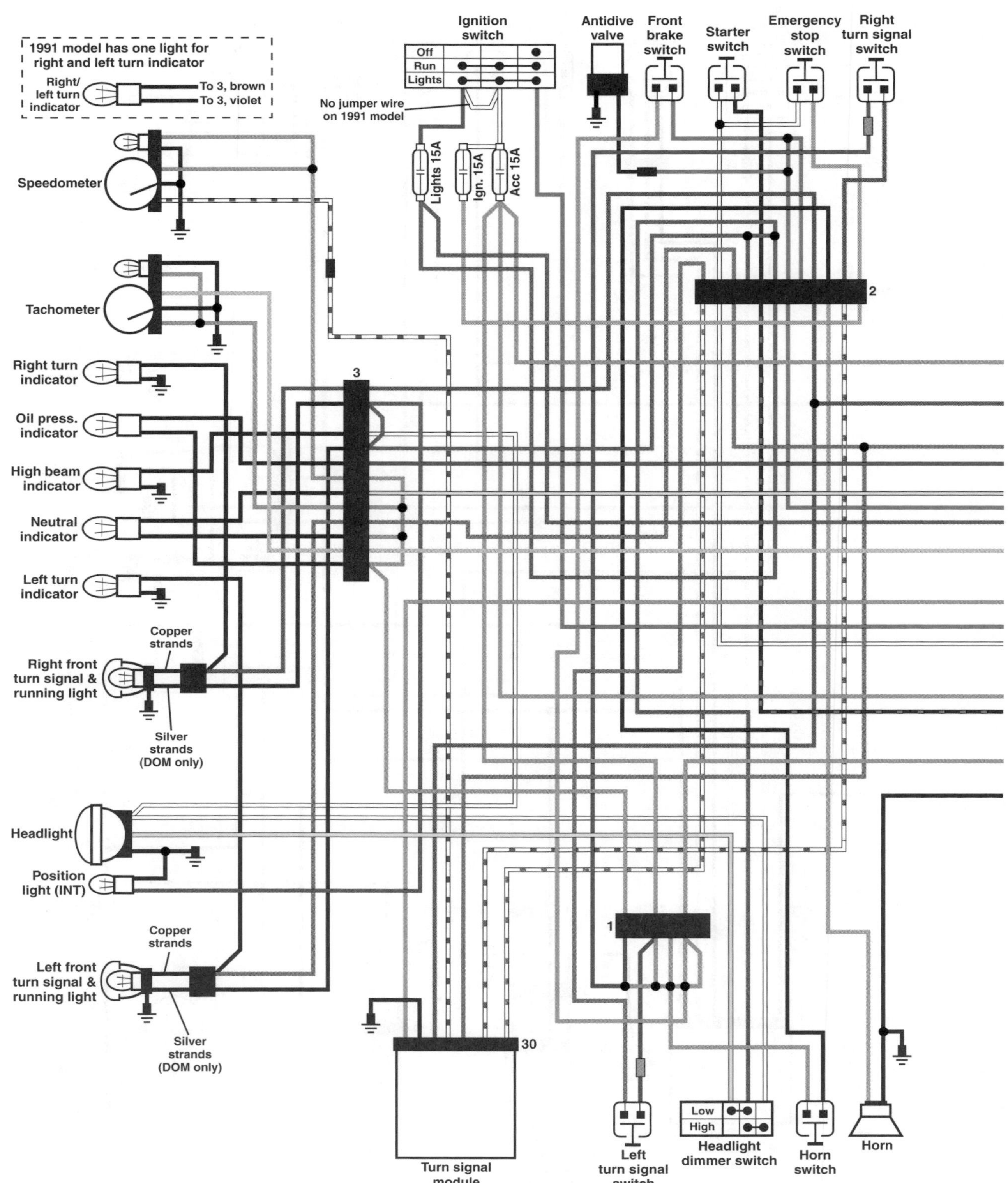

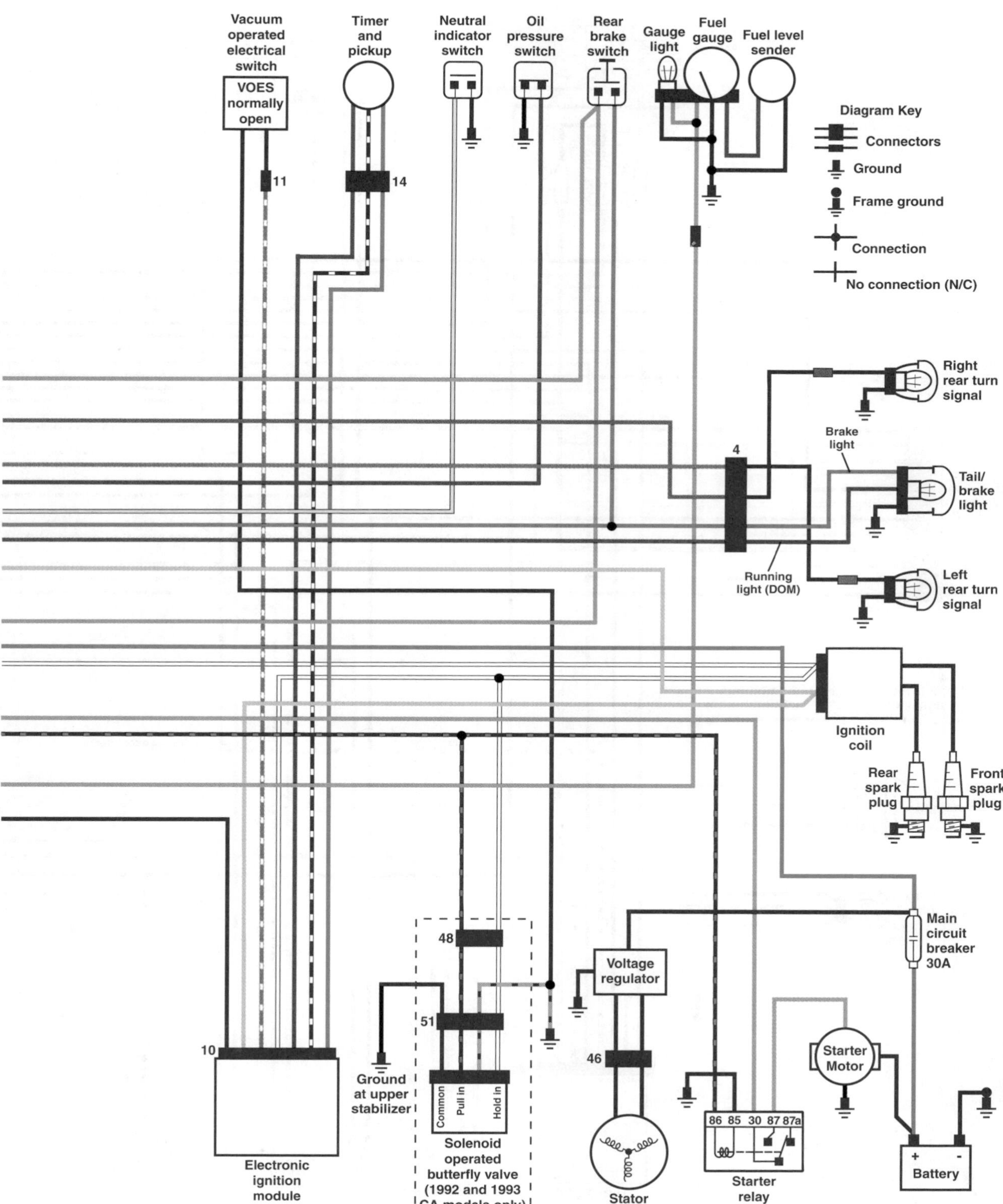
Vacuum operated electrical switch
VOES normally open
Timer and pickup
Neutral indicator switch
Oil pressure switch
Rear brake switch
Gauge light
Fuel gauge
Fuel level sender
Diagram Key
Connectors
Ground
Frame ground
Connection
No connection (N/C)
11
14
Right rear turn signal
Brake light
4
Tail/ brake light
Running light (DOM)
Left rear turn signal
Ignition coil
Rear spark plug
Front spark plug
Main circuit breaker 30A
48
Voltage regulator
51
46
10
Starter Motor
Common
Pull in
Hold in
Ground at upper stabilizer
86 85 30 87 87a
+ -
Battery
Electronic ignition module
Solenoid operated butterfly valve (1992 and 1993 CA models only)
Stator
Starter relay

1991-1992 FXRT MODELS

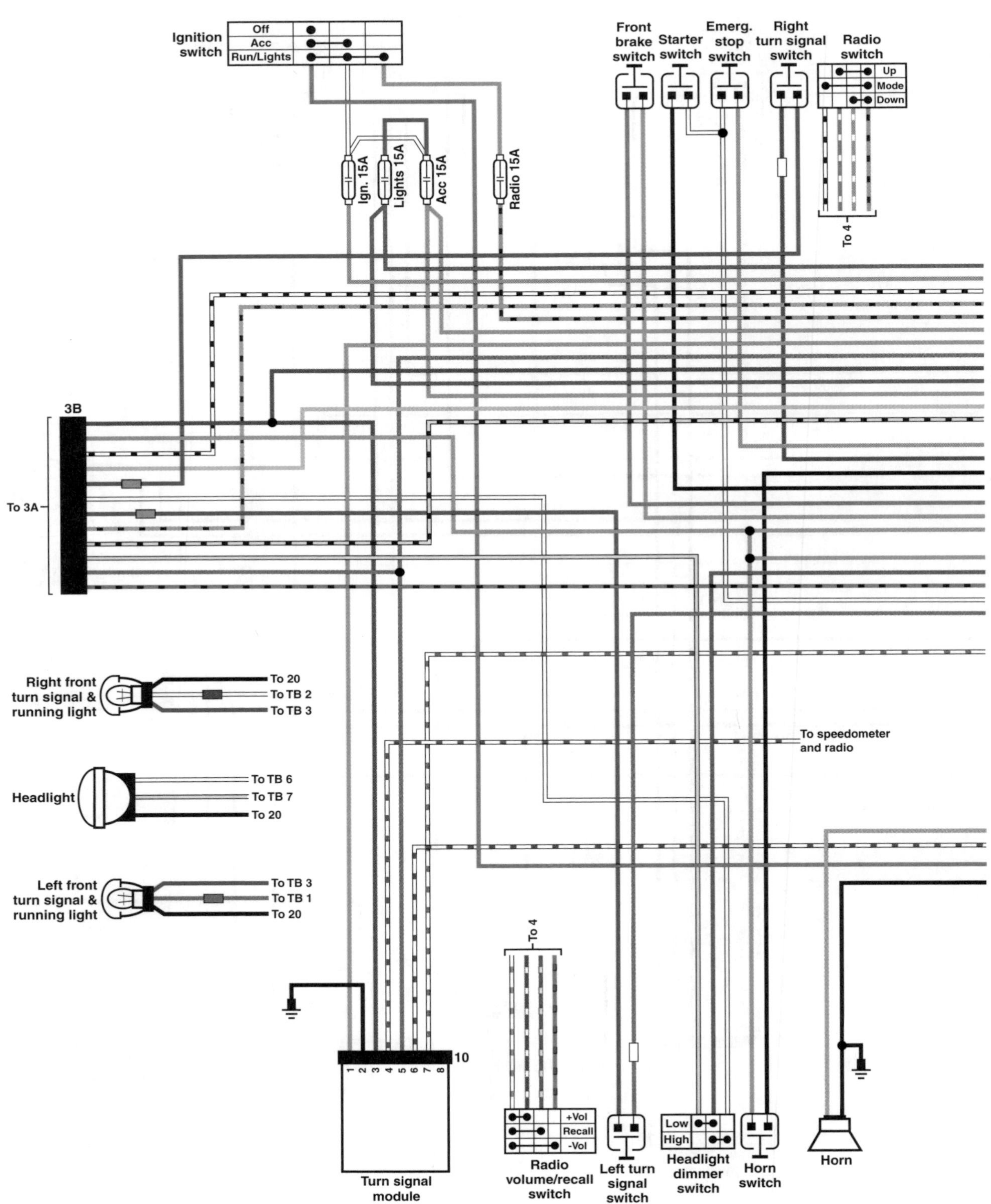

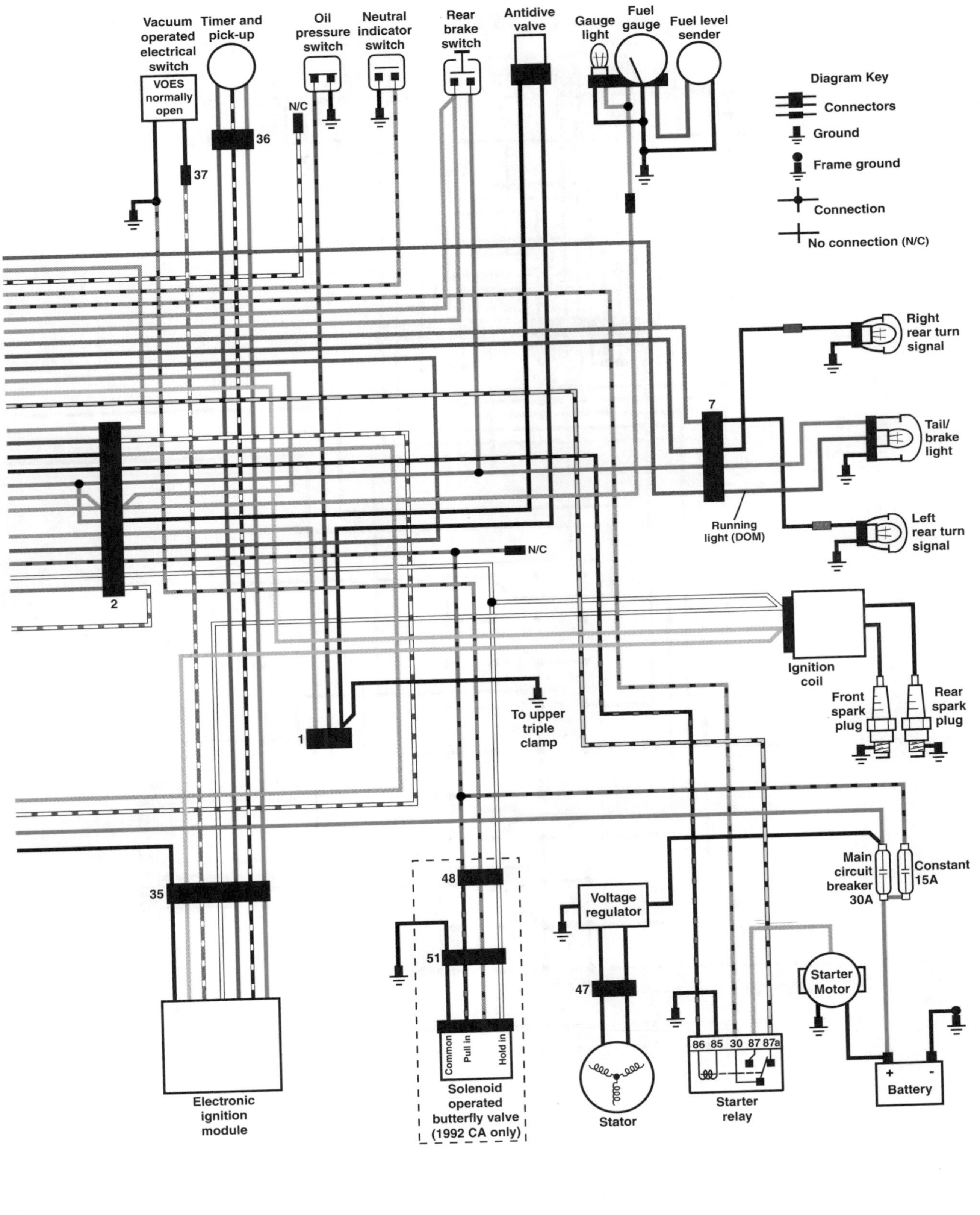

Vacuum operated electrical switch
VOES normally open
Timer and pick-up
Oil pressure switch
Neutral indicator switch
Rear brake switch
Antidive valve
Gauge light
Fuel gauge
Fuel level sender
N/C
36
37

Diagram Key
Connectors
Ground
Frame ground
Connection
No connection (N/C)

Right rear turn signal
7
Tail/ brake light
Running light (DOM)
Left rear turn signal
2
N/C
Ignition coil
Front spark plug
Rear spark plug
1
To upper triple clamp
35
48
51
47
Main circuit breaker 30A
Constant 15A
Voltage regulator
Starter Motor
Common
Pull in
Hold in
86 85 30 87 87a
Electronic ignition module
Solenoid operated butterfly valve (1992 CA only)
Stator
Starter relay
Battery
+
-

1991-1992 FXRT MODELS INSTRUMENT PANEL, TERMINAL BLOCK AND RADIO

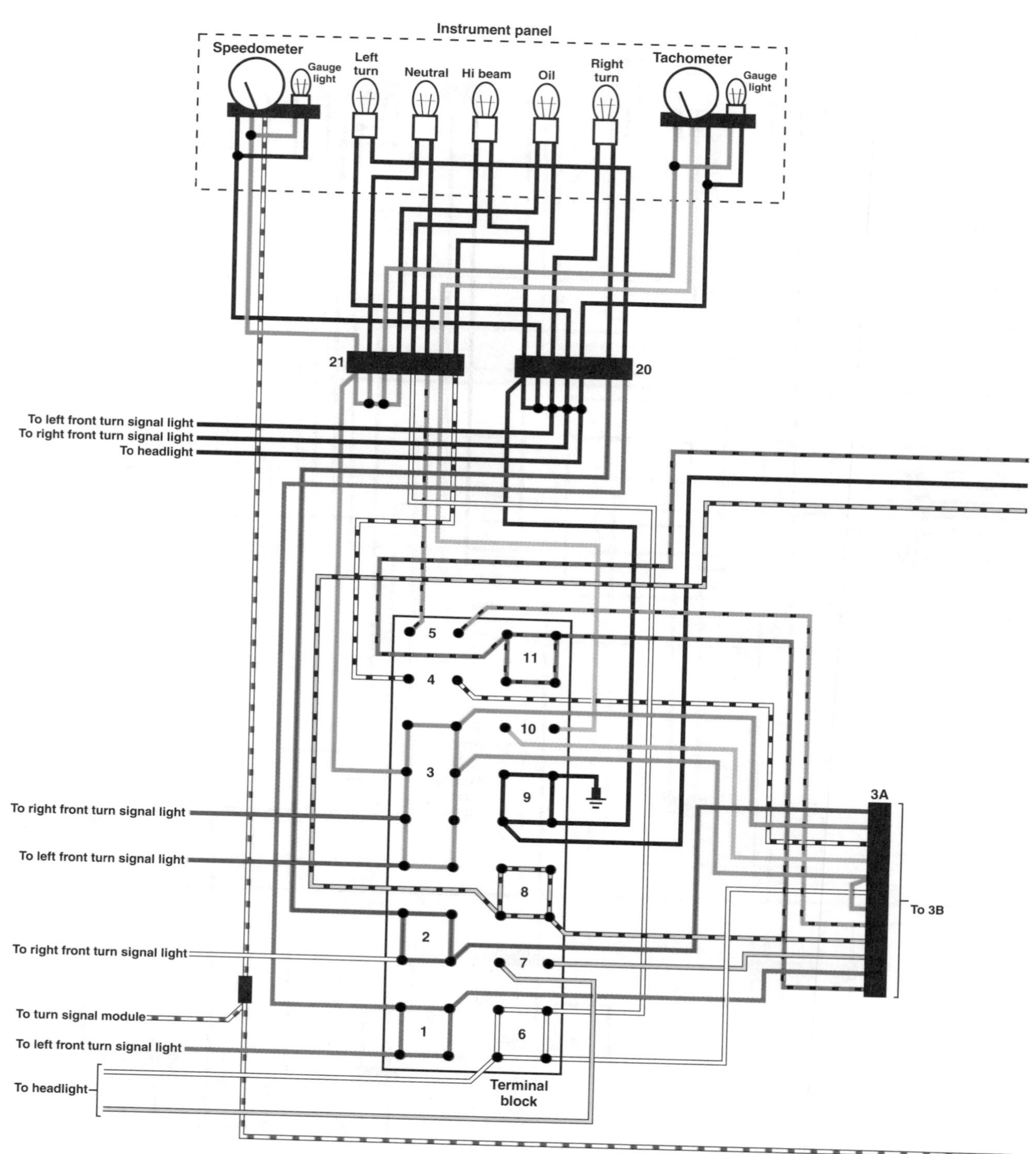

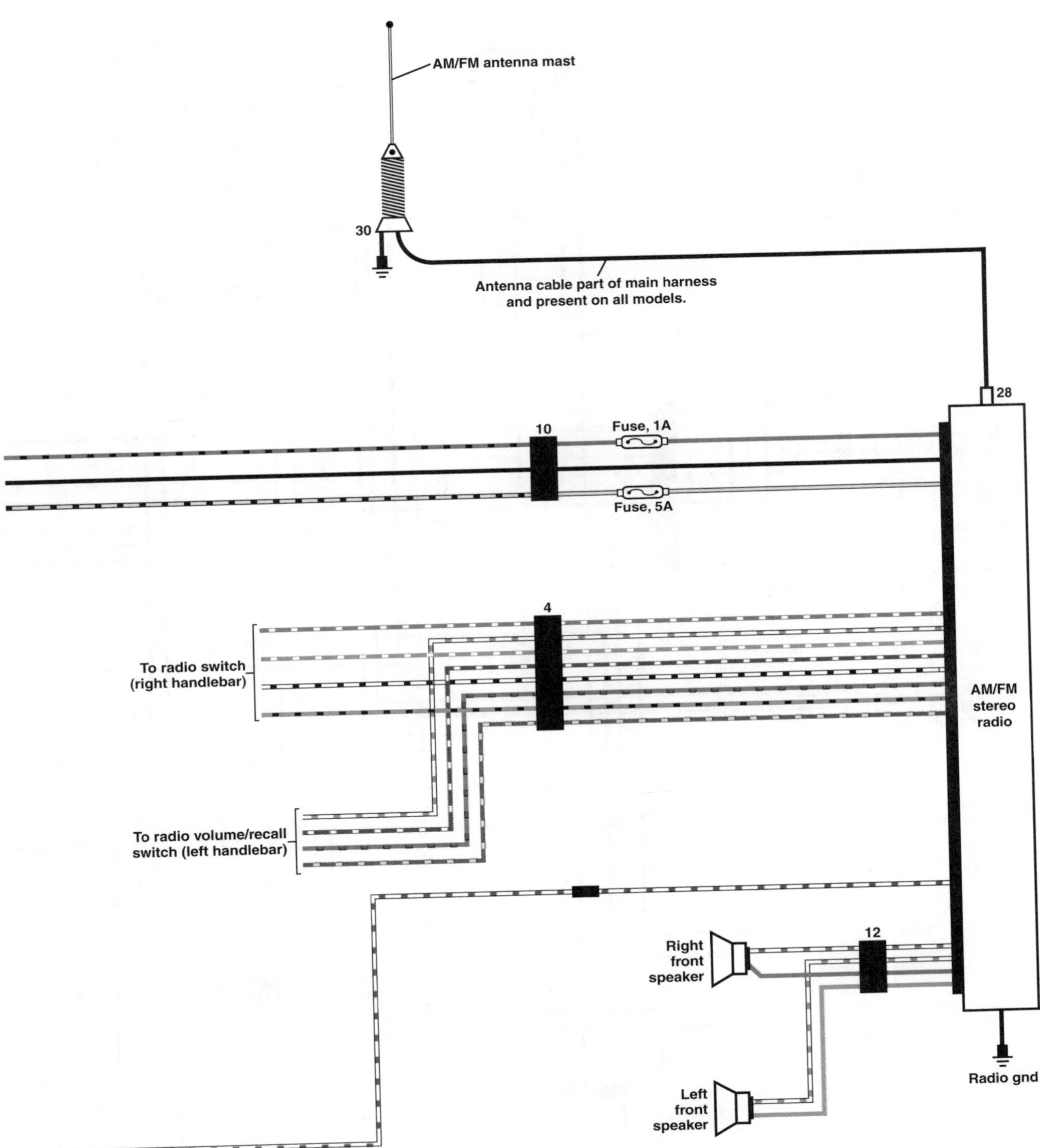
AM/FM antenna mast
30
Antenna cable part of main harness
and present on all models.
28
10
Fuse, 1A
Fuse, 5A
4
To radio switch
(right handlebar)
AM/FM
stereo
radio
To radio volume/recall
switch (left handlebar)
12
Right
front
speaker
Left
front
speaker
Radio gnd

1992-1994 FXLR MODELS

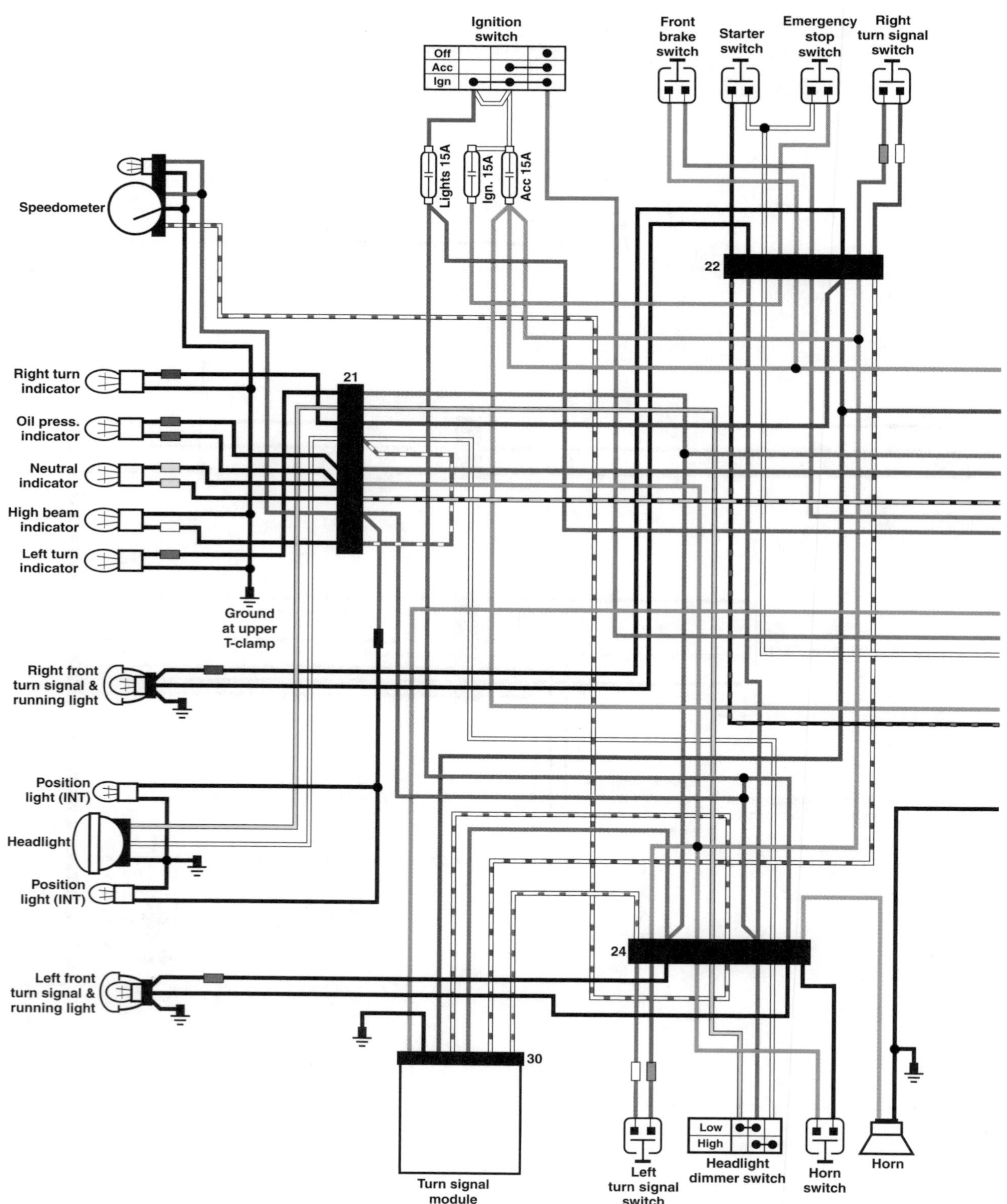

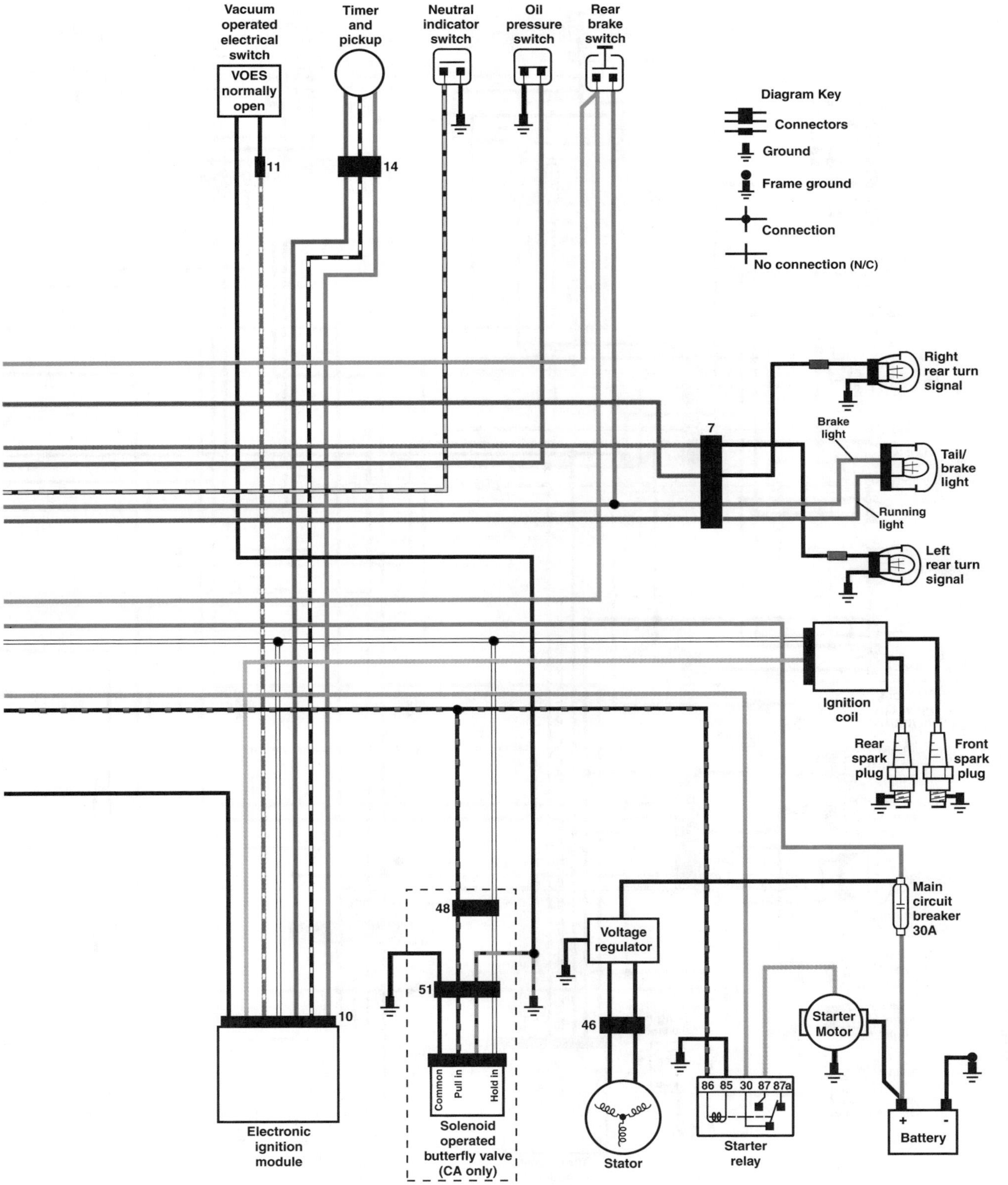

Vacuum operated electrical switch
VOES normally open
Timer and pickup
Neutral indicator switch
Oil pressure switch
Rear brake switch

Diagram Key
Connectors
Ground
Frame ground
Connection
No connection (N/C)

11
14
7
Right rear turn signal
Brake light
Tail/ brake light
Running light
Left rear turn signal
Ignition coil
Rear spark plug
Front spark plug
Main circuit breaker 30A
48
51
Common
Pull in
Hold in
Solenoid operated butterfly valve (CA only)
10
Electronic ignition module
Voltage regulator
46
Stator
Starter Motor
86 85 30 87 87a
Starter relay
+ -
Battery

1993 FLHS MODELS

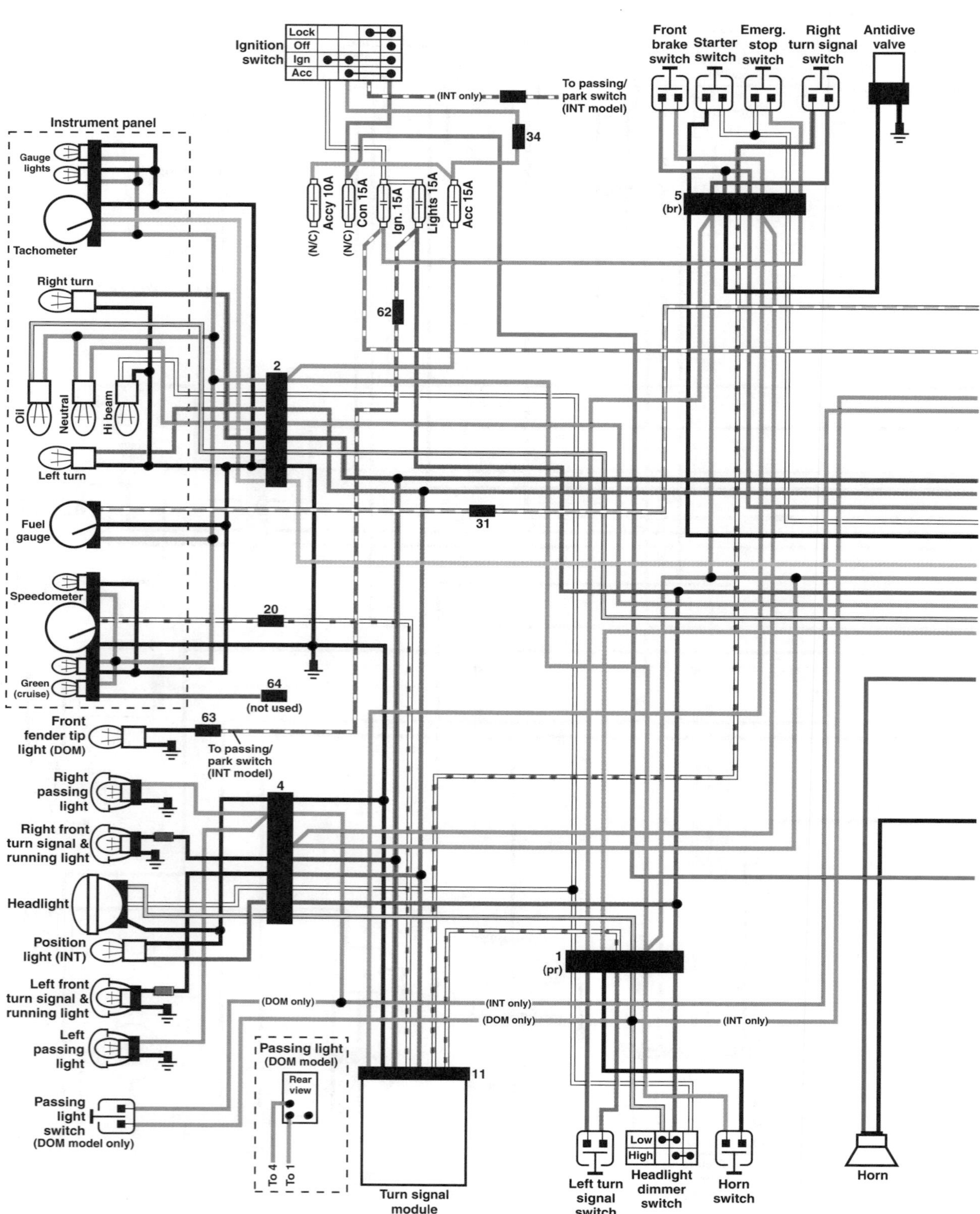

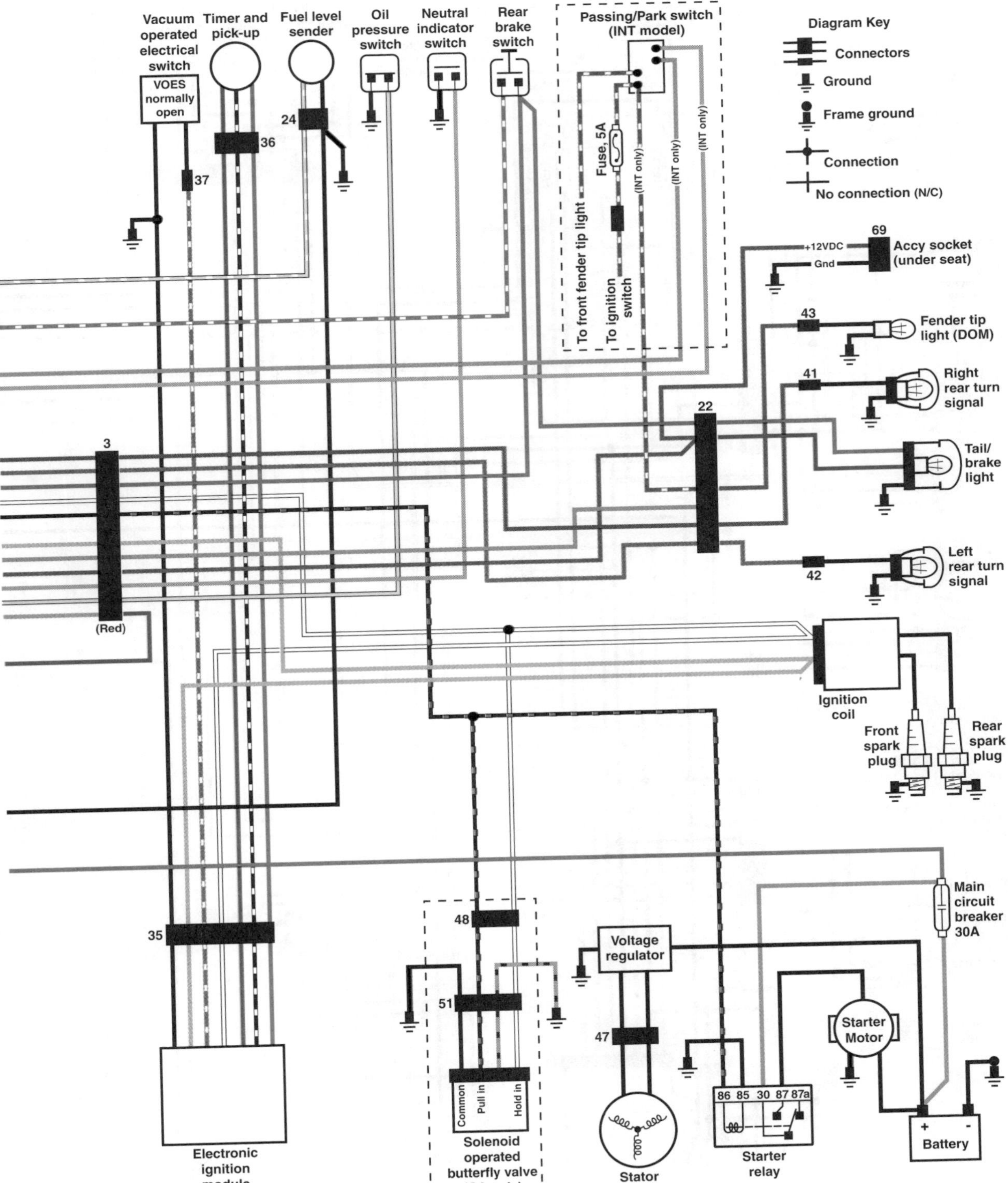
Vacuum operated electrical switch
VOES normally open
Timer and pick-up
Fuel level sender
Oil pressure switch
Neutral indicator switch
Rear brake switch
Passing/Park switch (INT model)
Fuse, 5A
(INT only)
(INT only)
(INT only)
To front fender tip light
To ignition switch
Diagram Key
Connectors
Ground
Frame ground
Connection
No connection (N/C)
+12VDC
Gnd
69
Accy socket (under seat)
43
Fender tip light (DOM)
41
Right rear turn signal
22
Tail/ brake light
42
Left rear turn signal
3
(Red)
24
36
37
Ignition coil
Front spark plug
Rear spark plug
Main circuit breaker 30A
35
48
51
47
Voltage regulator
Starter Motor
Common
Pull in
Hold in
Solenoid operated butterfly valve (CA only)
Electronic ignition module
Stator
86 85 30 87 87a
Starter relay
Battery
+
-

17

1993 FLHTC MODELS

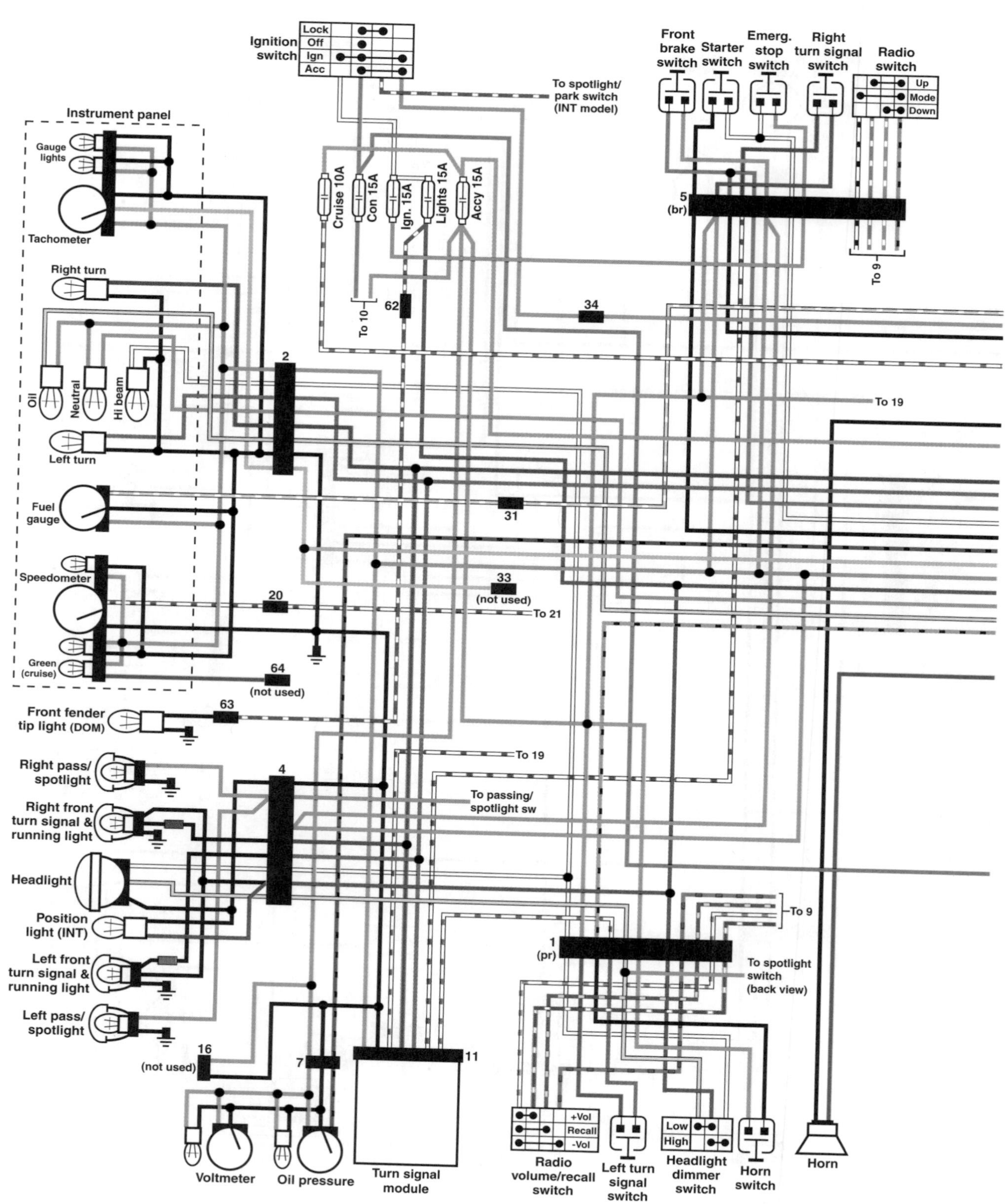

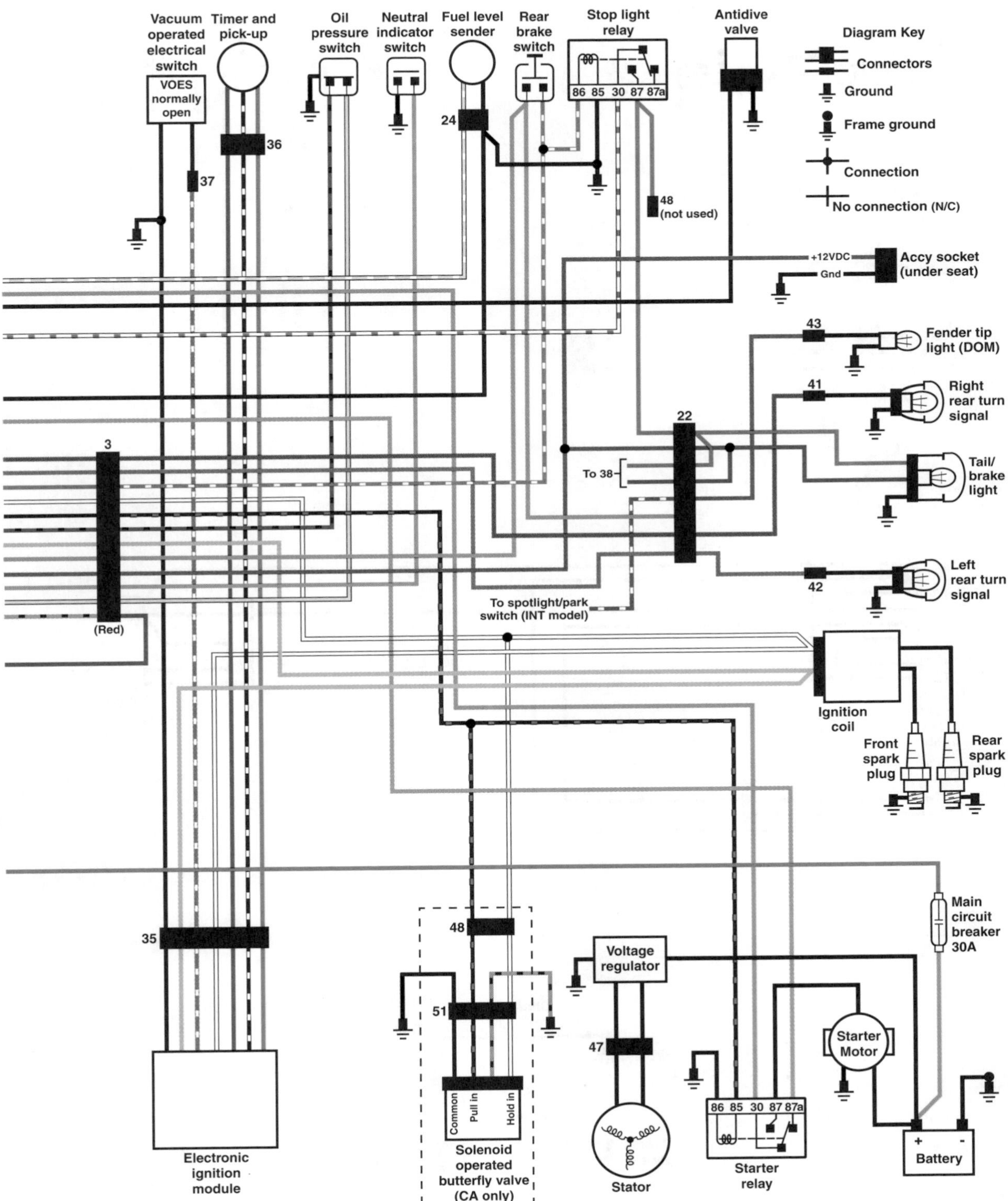

Vacuum operated electrical switch
VOES normally open
Timer and pick-up
Oil pressure switch
Neutral indicator switch
Fuel level sender
Rear brake switch
Stop light relay
86 85 30 87 87a
Antidive valve
Diagram Key
Connectors
Ground
Frame ground
Connection
No connection (N/C)
36
37
24
48 (not used)
+12VDC
Gnd
Accy socket (under seat)
43
Fender tip light (DOM)
41
Right rear turn signal
22
3
To 38
Tail/ brake light
42
Left rear turn signal
To spotlight/park switch (INT model)
(Red)
Ignition coil
Front spark plug
Rear spark plug
Main circuit breaker 30A
35
48
51
Common
Pull in
Hold in
Solenoid operated butterfly valve (CA only)
Voltage regulator
47
Stator
Starter relay
Starter Motor
Battery
Electronic ignition module

1993 FLHTC MODELS DASH SWITCHES, TOURPAK AND GROUNDS

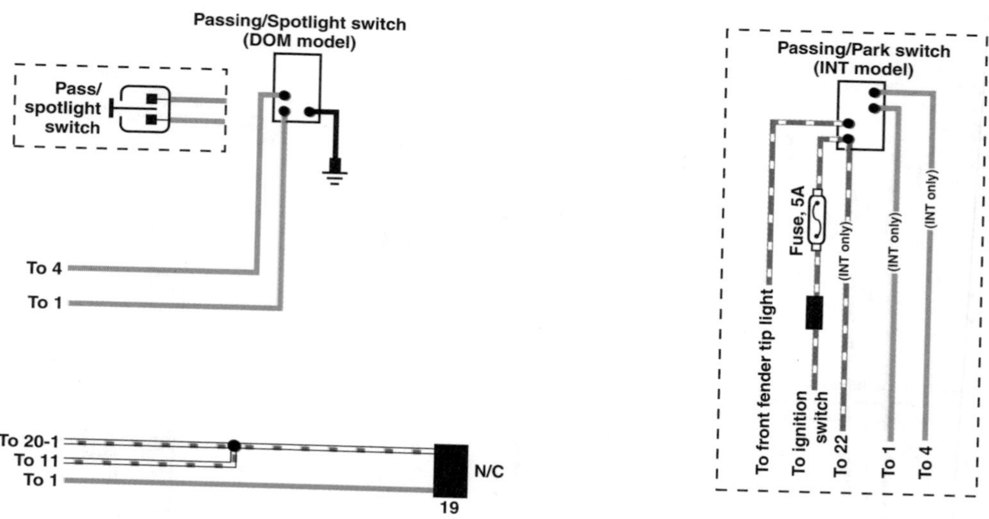

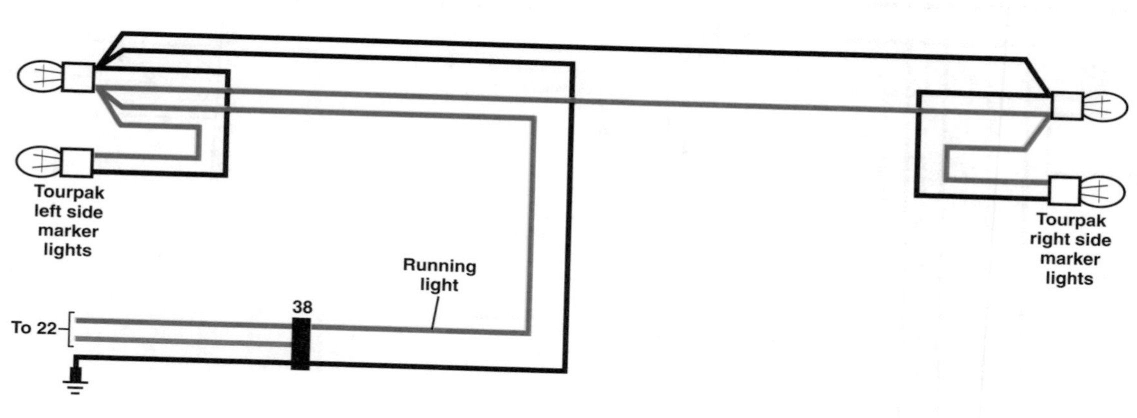

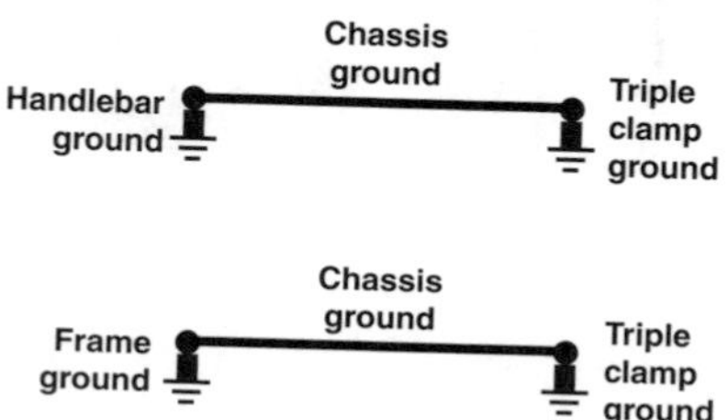

1993 FLHTC MODELS RADIO, HARNESS CONNECTORS AND ANTENNA

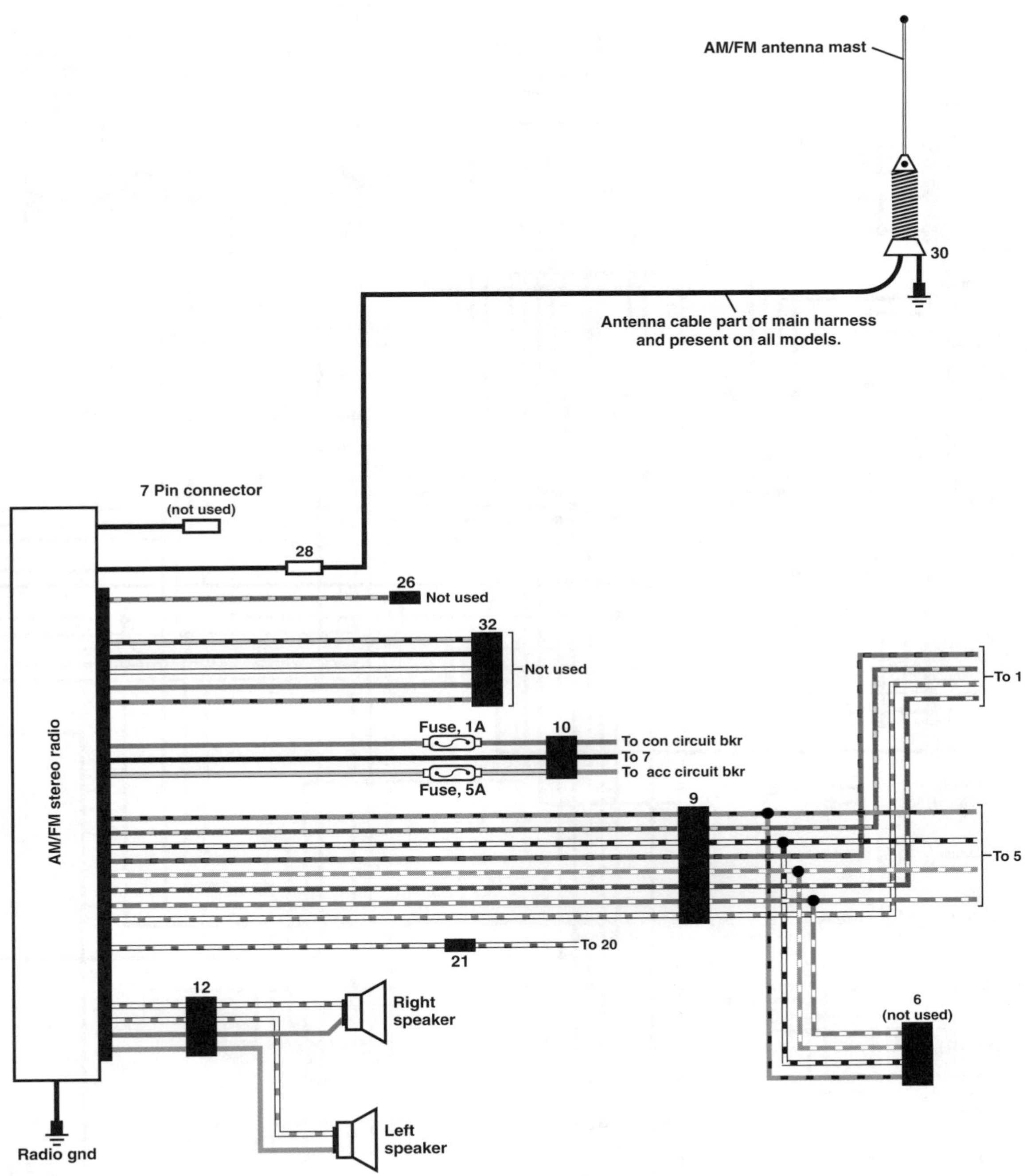

1993 FLHTC ULTRA MODELS

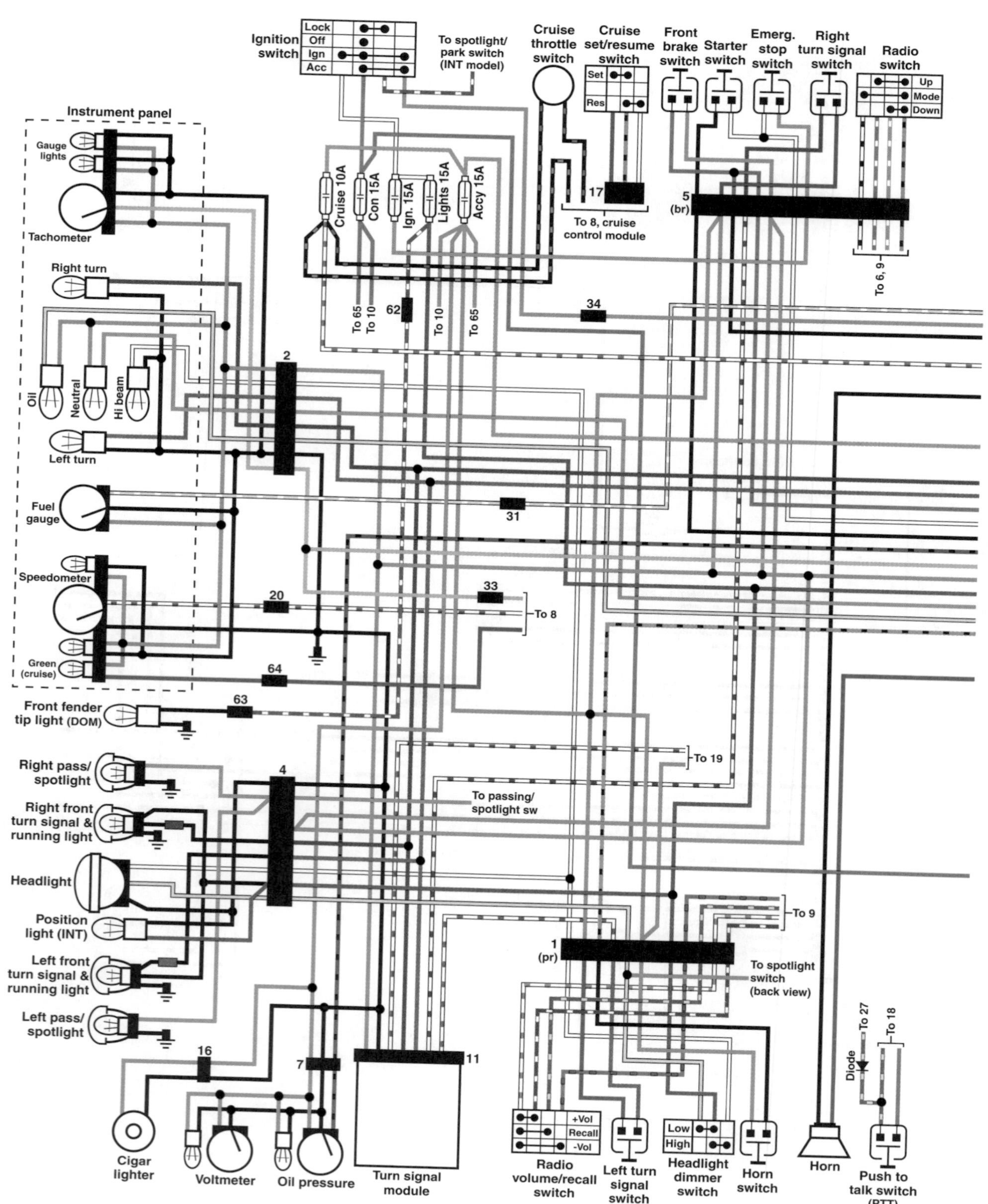

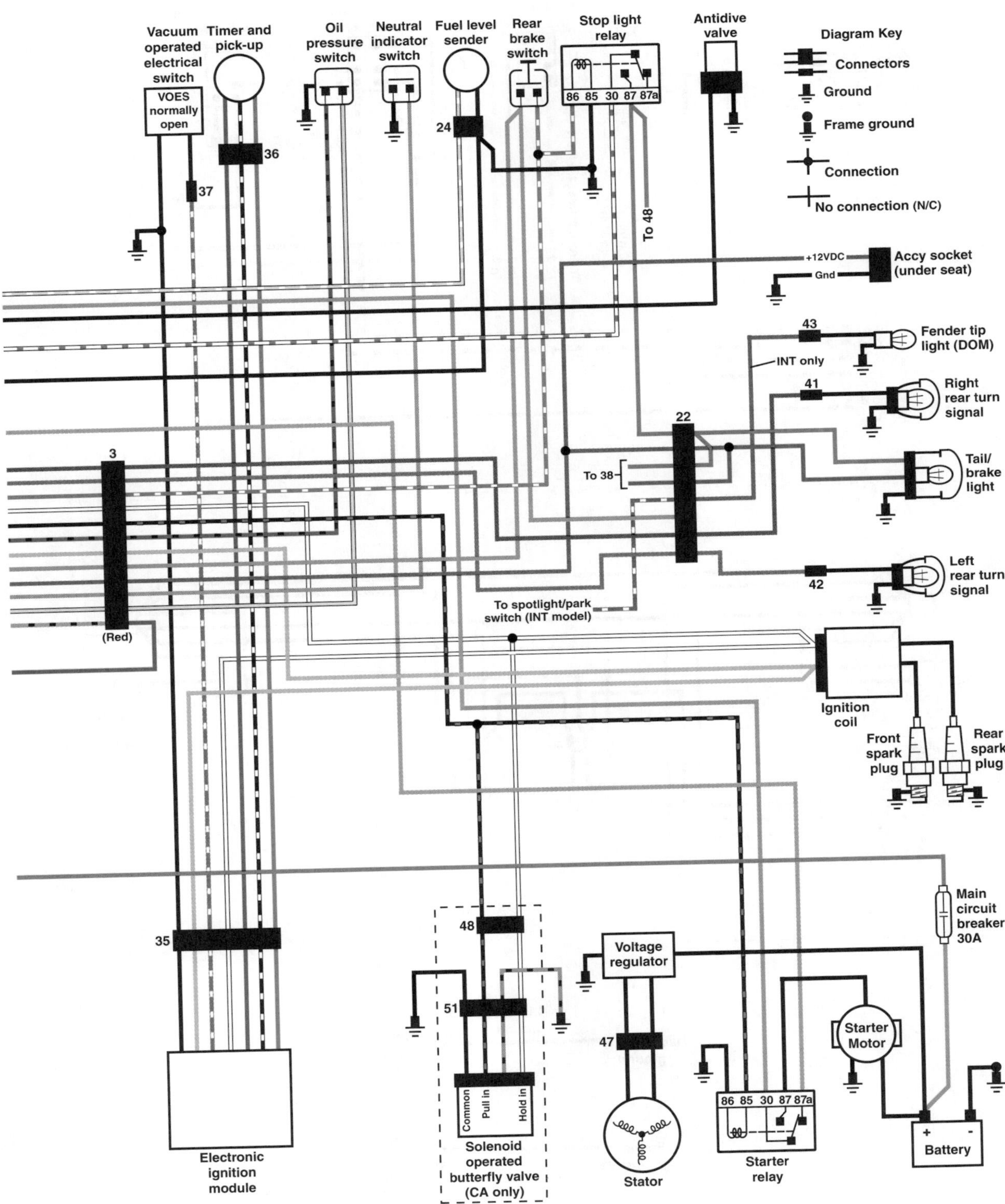
Vacuum operated electrical switch
VOES normally open
Timer and pick-up
Oil pressure switch
Neutral indicator switch
Fuel level sender
Rear brake switch
Stop light relay
86 85 30 87 87a
Antidive valve
Diagram Key
Connectors
Ground
Frame ground
Connection
No connection (N/C)
+12VDC
Gnd
Accy socket (under seat)
To 48
43
Fender tip light (DOM)
INT only
41
Right rear turn signal
22
Tail/ brake light
To 38
3
Left rear turn signal
42
To spotlight/park switch (INT model)
(Red)
Ignition coil
Front spark plug
Rear spark plug
Main circuit breaker 30A
24
36
37
35
48
51
47
Voltage regulator
Starter Motor
Common
Pull in
Hold in
Solenoid operated butterfly valve (CA only)
Electronic ignition module
Stator
86 85 30 87 87a
Starter relay
Battery

1993 FLHTC ULTRA MODELS DASH SWITCHES, TOURPAK AND GROUNDS

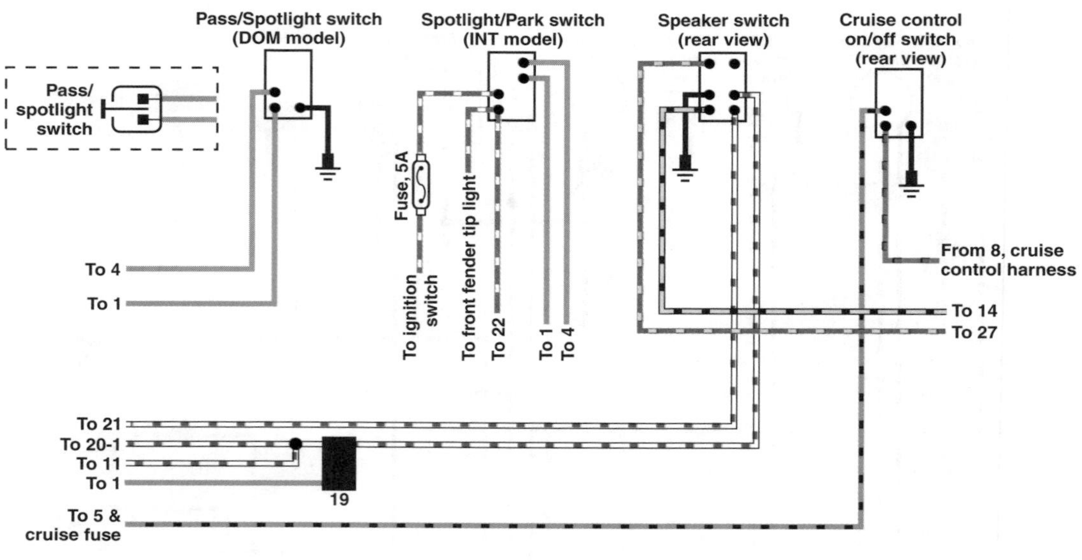

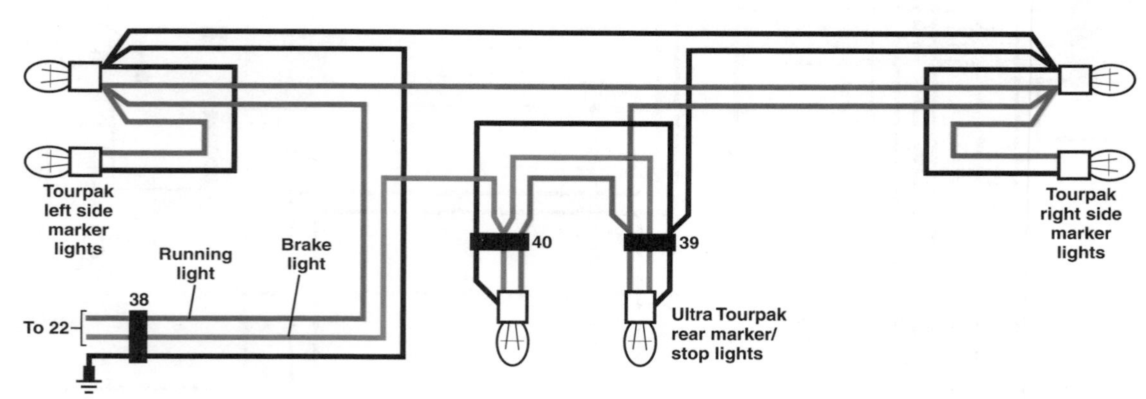

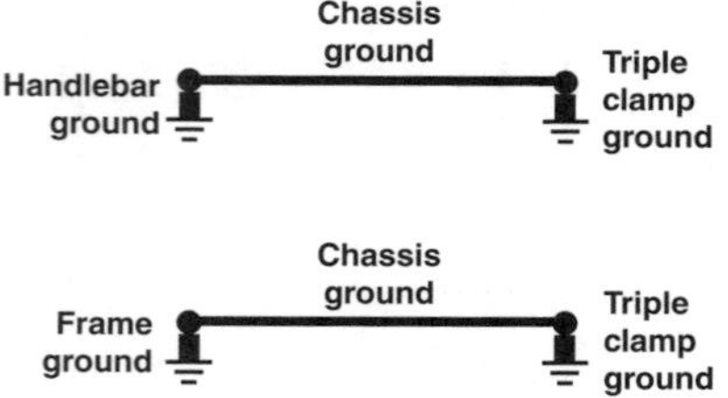

1993 FLHTC ULTRA MODELS RADIO, HARNESS CONNECTORS AND CRUISE CONTROL CONNECTIONS

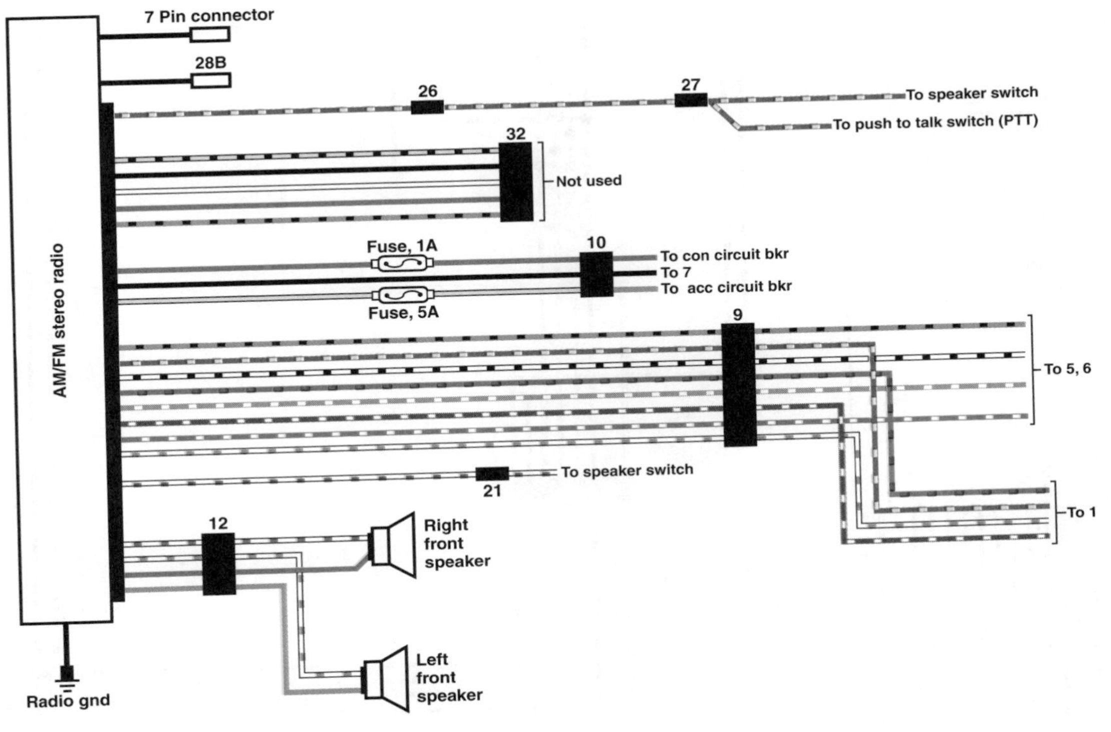

48
To stop light relay
To cruise circuit bkr
To 17
To gnd
R1
270 ohm, 3W
R2
270 ohm, 3W
To cruise control on/off switch
To cruise throttle switch
To 33
To 64
To 20
To 19
20-1
8
A On/Off
B Set/Coast
C Resume/Accel
D Throttle roll-off
E Ground
F Ignition
G Brake signal
H Engine speed
J Set light
K Speed signal
Cruise control module

1993 FLHTC ULTRA MODELS RADIO CB/INTERCOM, REAR SPEAKERS AND ANTENNAS

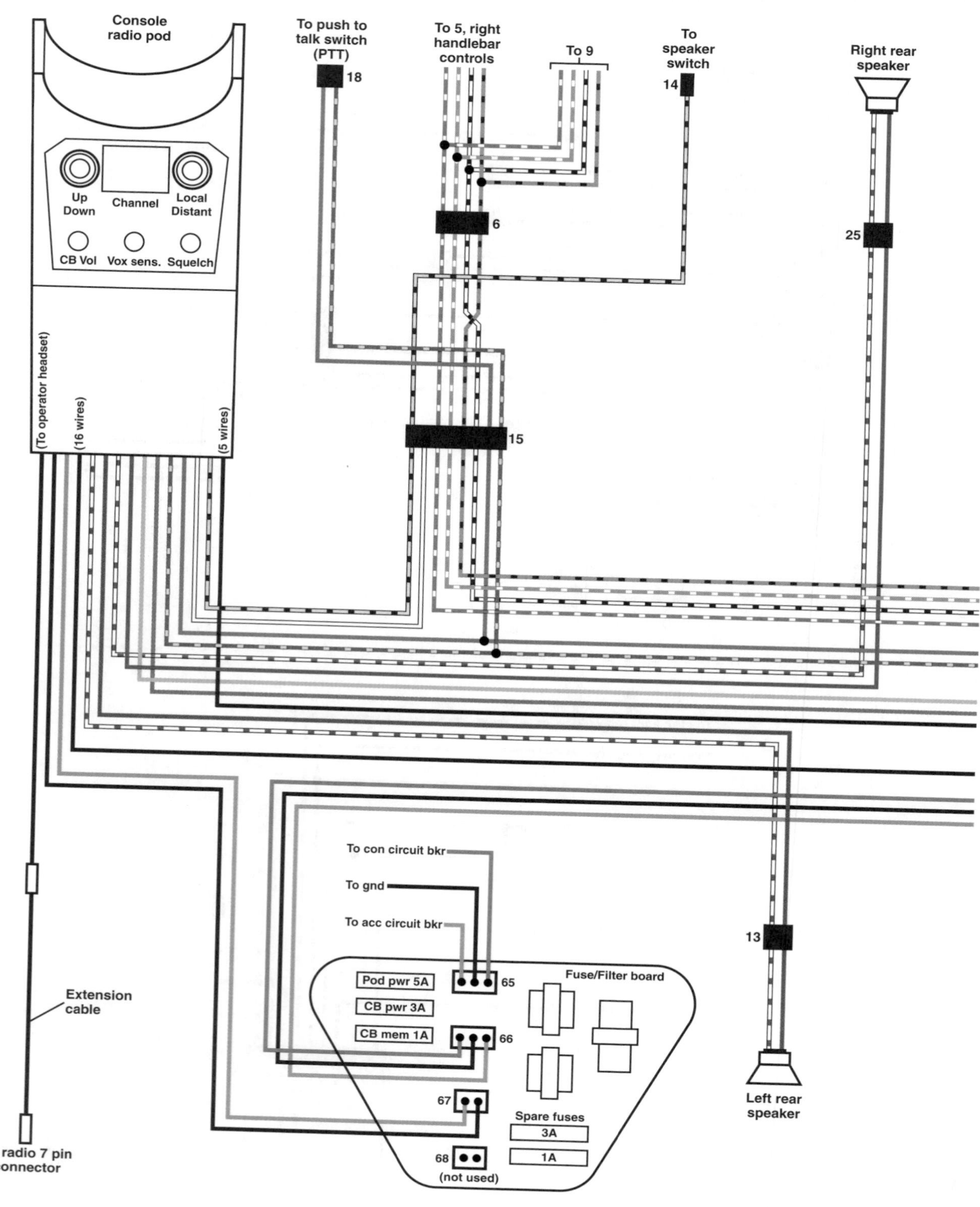

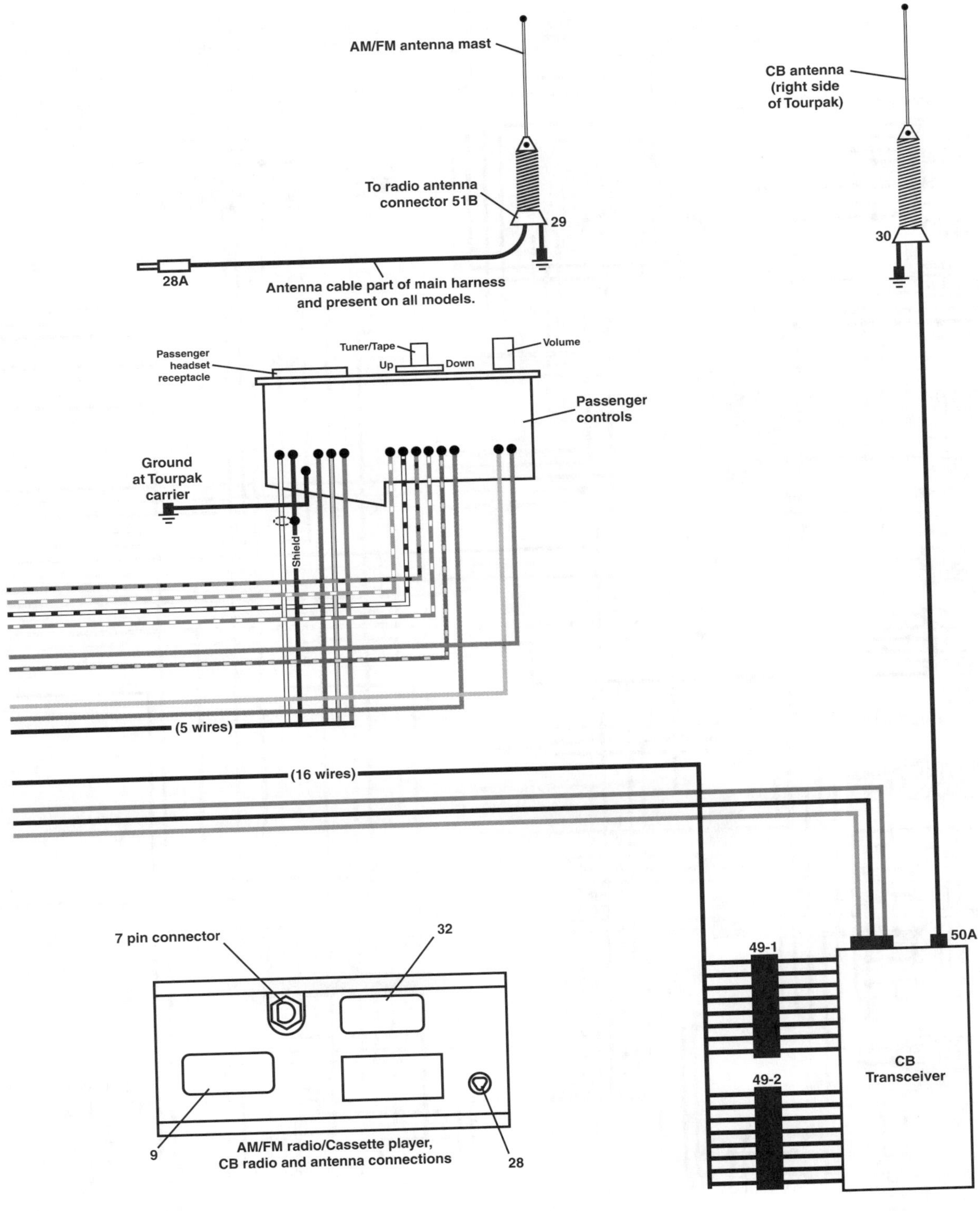

AM/FM radio/Cassette player,
CB radio and antenna connections

1993 FLTC ULTRA MODELS

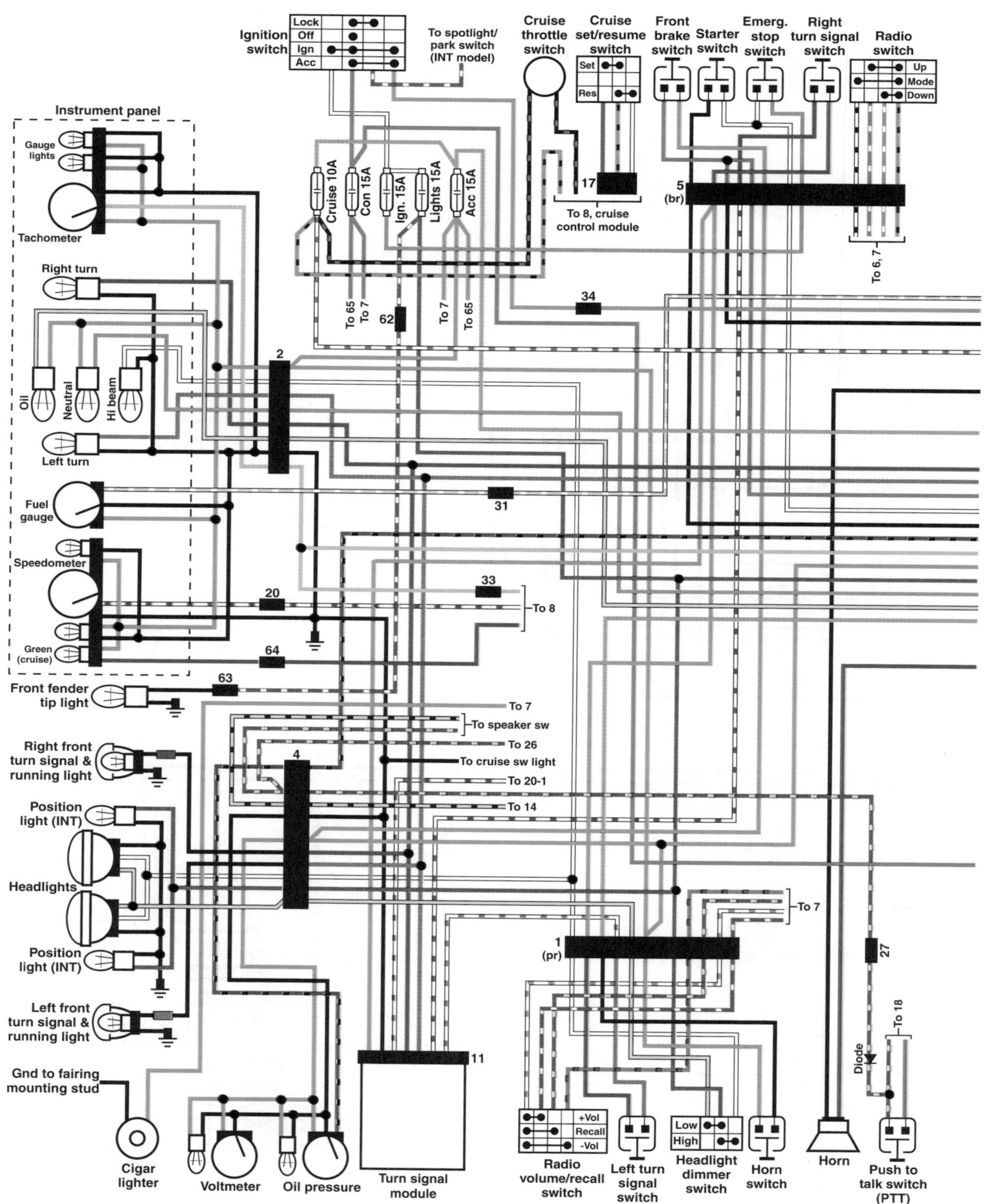

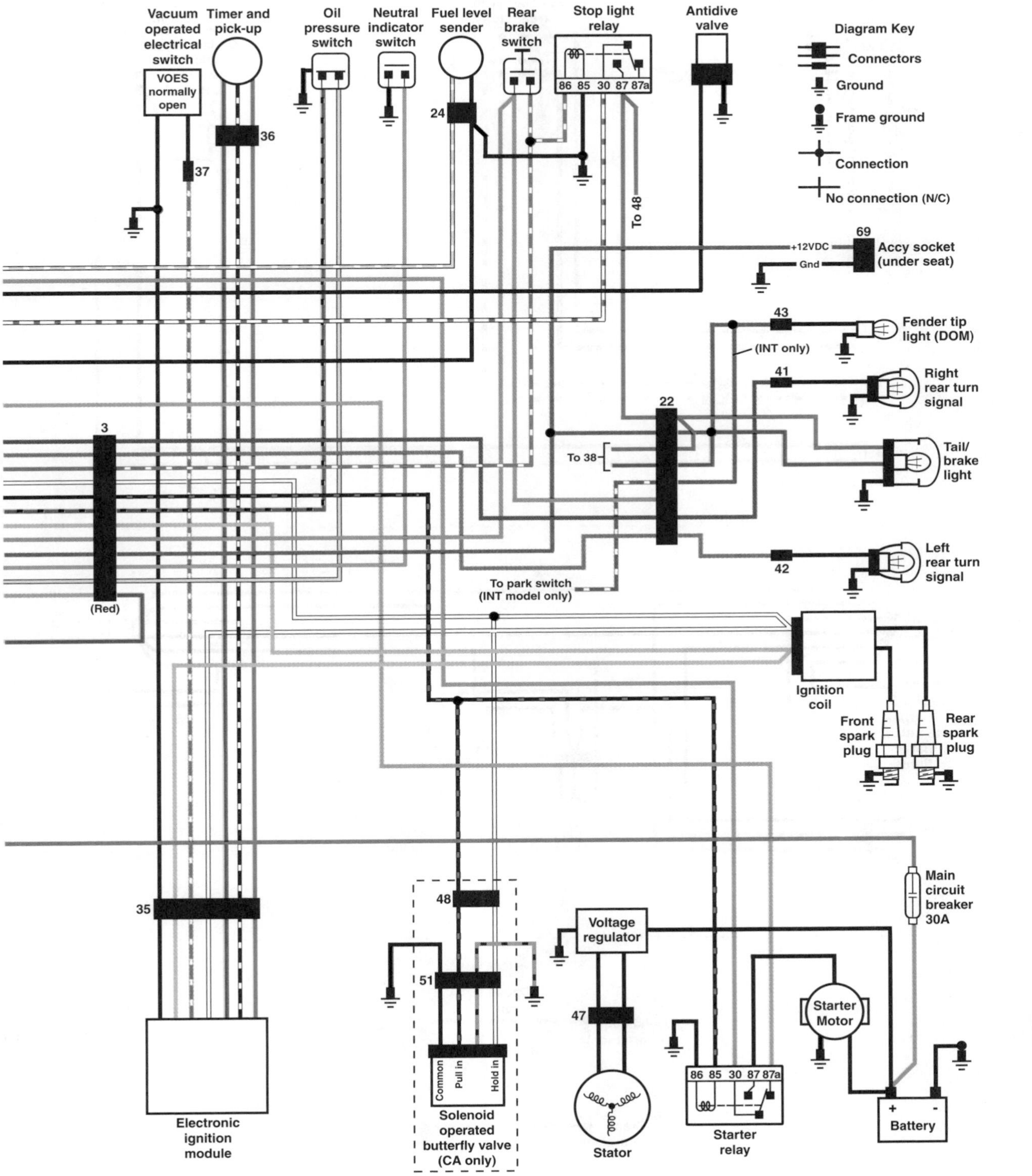

Vacuum operated electrical switch
VOES normally open
Timer and pick-up
Oil pressure switch
Neutral indicator switch
Fuel level sender
Rear brake switch
Stop light relay
86 85 30 87 87a
Antidive valve
Diagram Key
Connectors
Ground
Frame ground
Connection
No connection (N/C)
36
37
24
To 48
69
+12VDC
Gnd
Accy socket (under seat)
43
Fender tip light (DOM)
(INT only)
41
Right rear turn signal
22
Tail/ brake light
To 38
3
Left rear turn signal
42
(Red)
To park switch (INT model only)
Ignition coil
Front spark plug
Rear spark plug
Main circuit breaker 30A
35
48
Voltage regulator
51
47
Starter Motor
86 85 30 87 87a
Common
Pull in
Hold in
Electronic ignition module
Solenoid operated butterfly valve (CA only)
Stator
Starter relay
Battery

17

1993 FLTC ULTRA MODELS DASH SWITCHES, TOURPAK AND GROUNDS

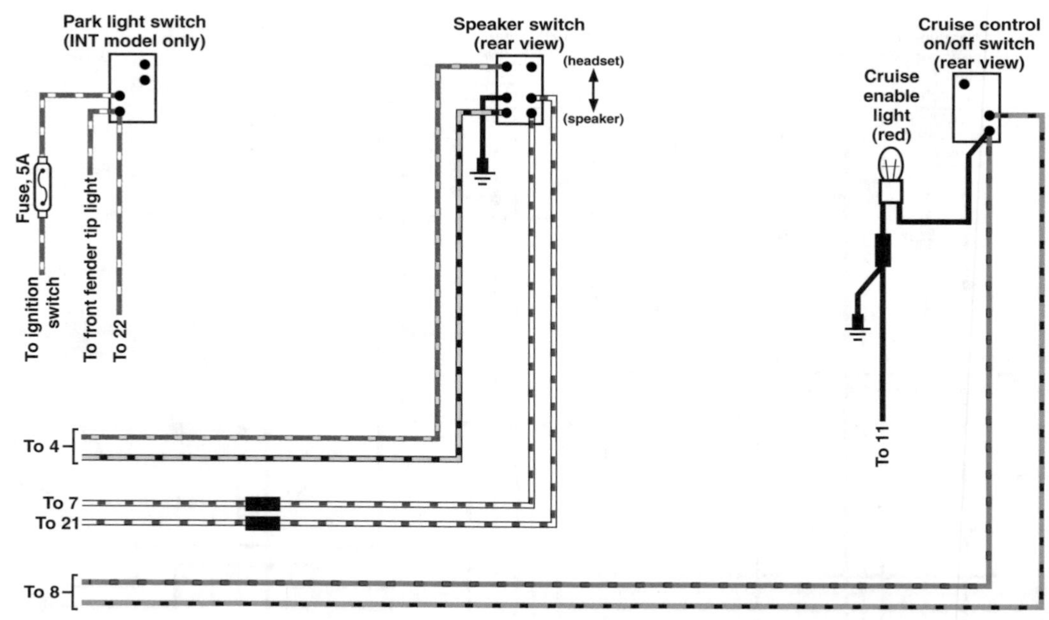

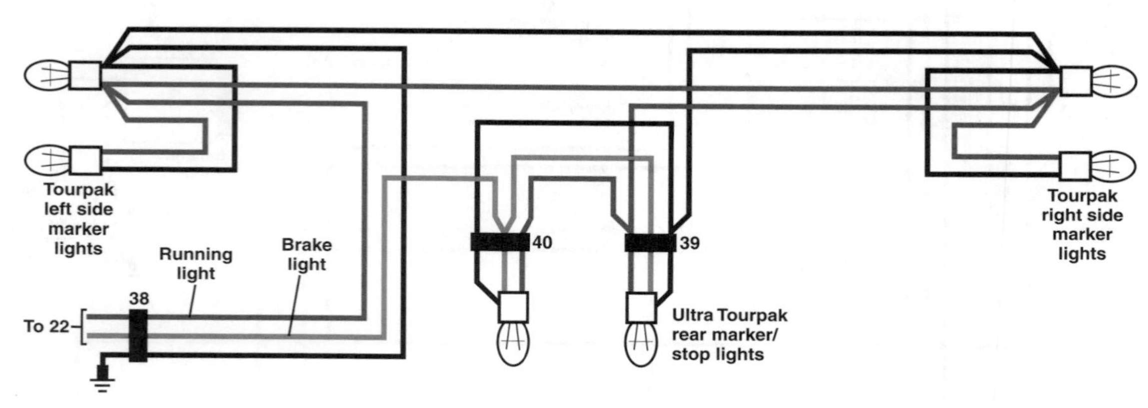

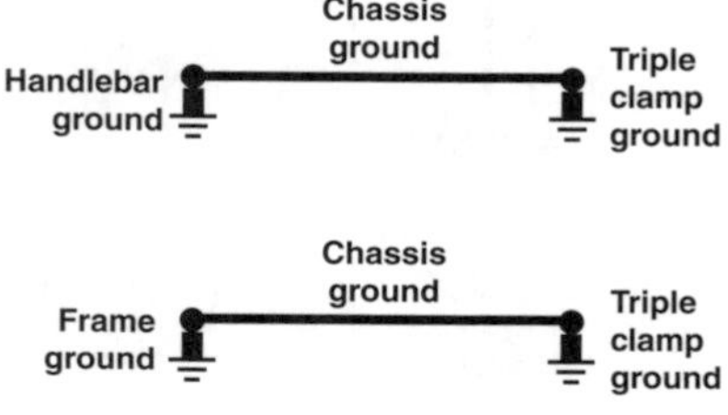

1993 FLTC ULTRA MODELS RADIO, HARNESS CONNECTORS AND CRUISE CONTROL CONNECTIONS

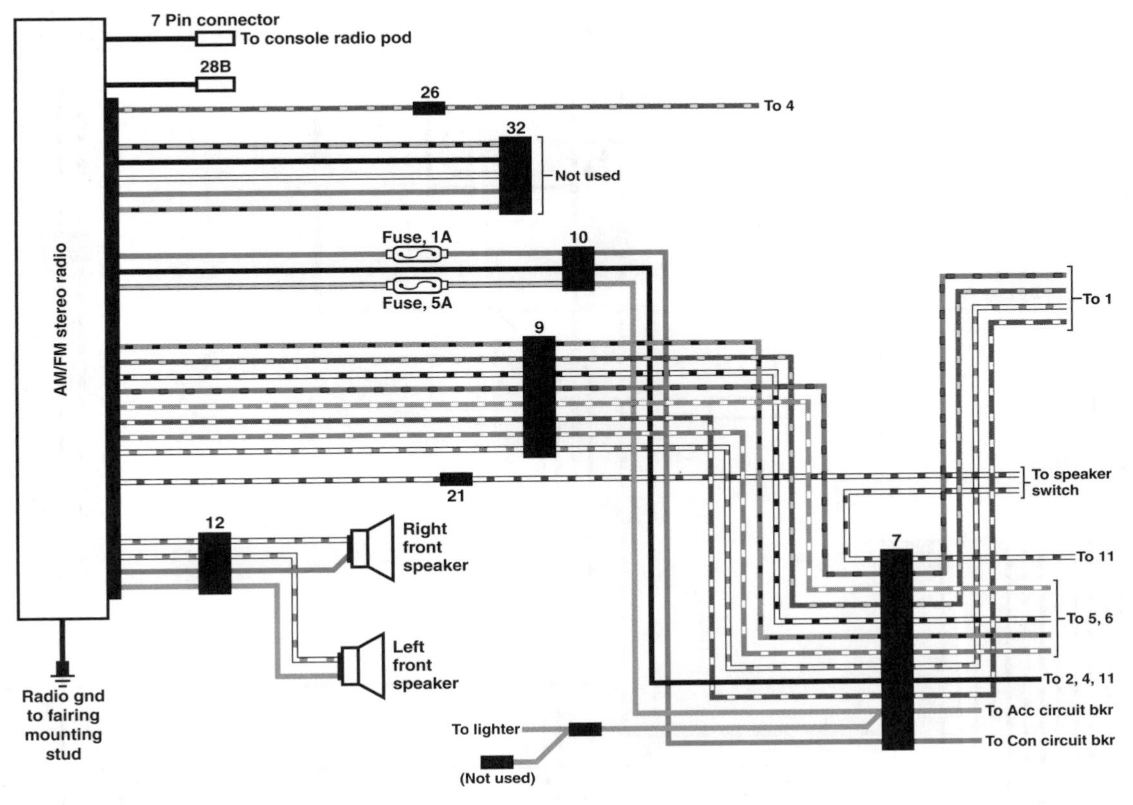

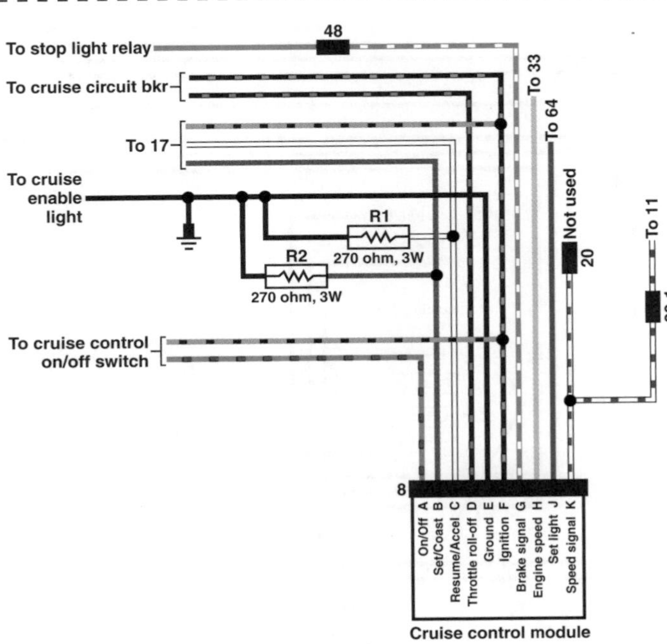

1993 FLTC ULTRA MODELS RADIO CB/INTERCOM, REAR SPEAKERS AND ANTENNAS

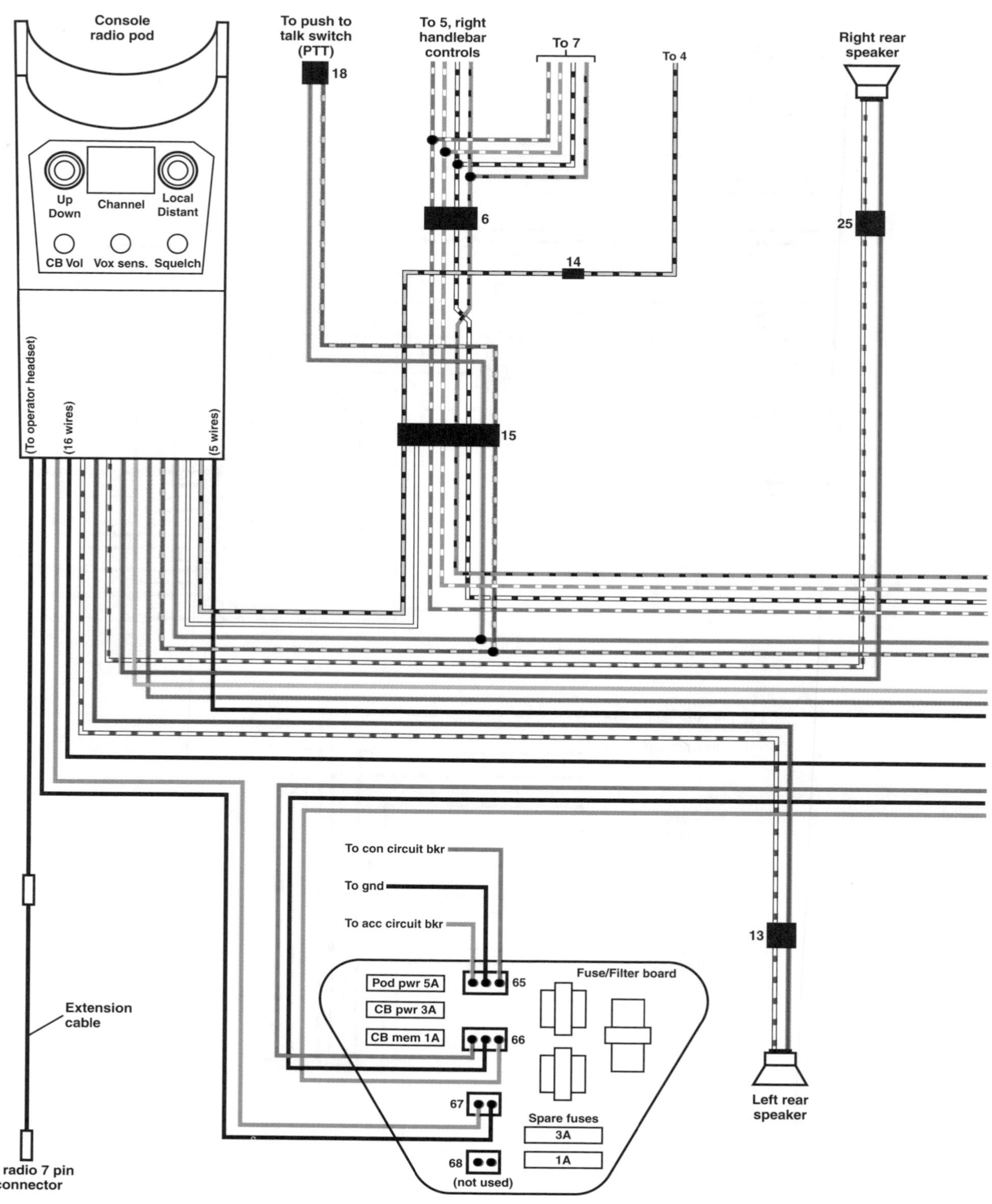

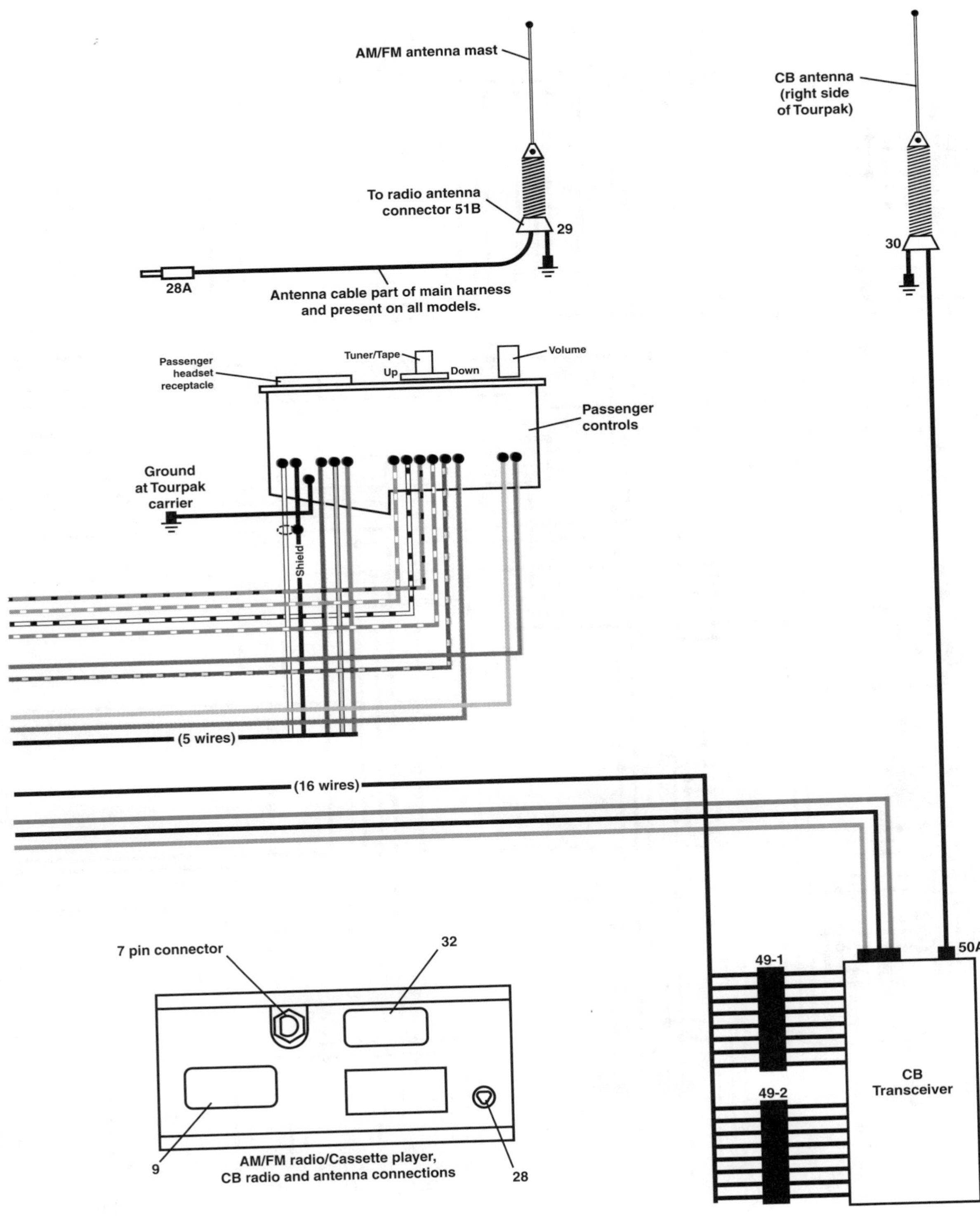
AM/FM antenna mast
CB antenna
(right side
of Tourpak)
To radio antenna
connector 51B
29
30
28A
Antenna cable part of main harness
and present on all models.
Passenger
headset
receptacle
Tuner/Tape
Up
Down
Volume
Passenger
controls
Ground
at Tourpak
carrier
Shield
(5 wires)
(16 wires)
7 pin connector
32
50A
49-1
49-2
CB
Transceiver
9
AM/FM radio/Cassette player,
CB radio and antenna connections
28

1994 FLHTC, FLHTC ULTRA AND FLTC ULTRA MODELS

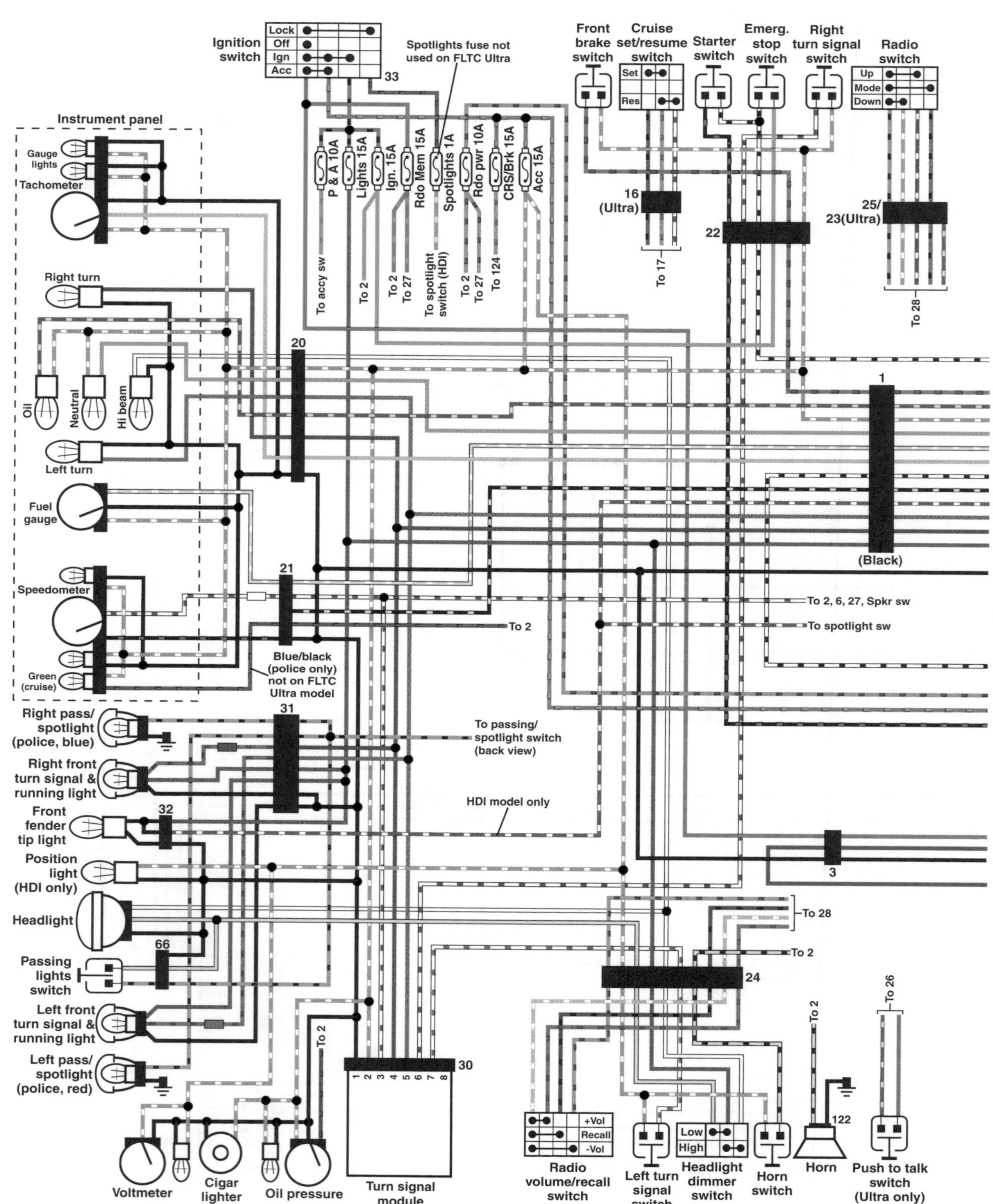

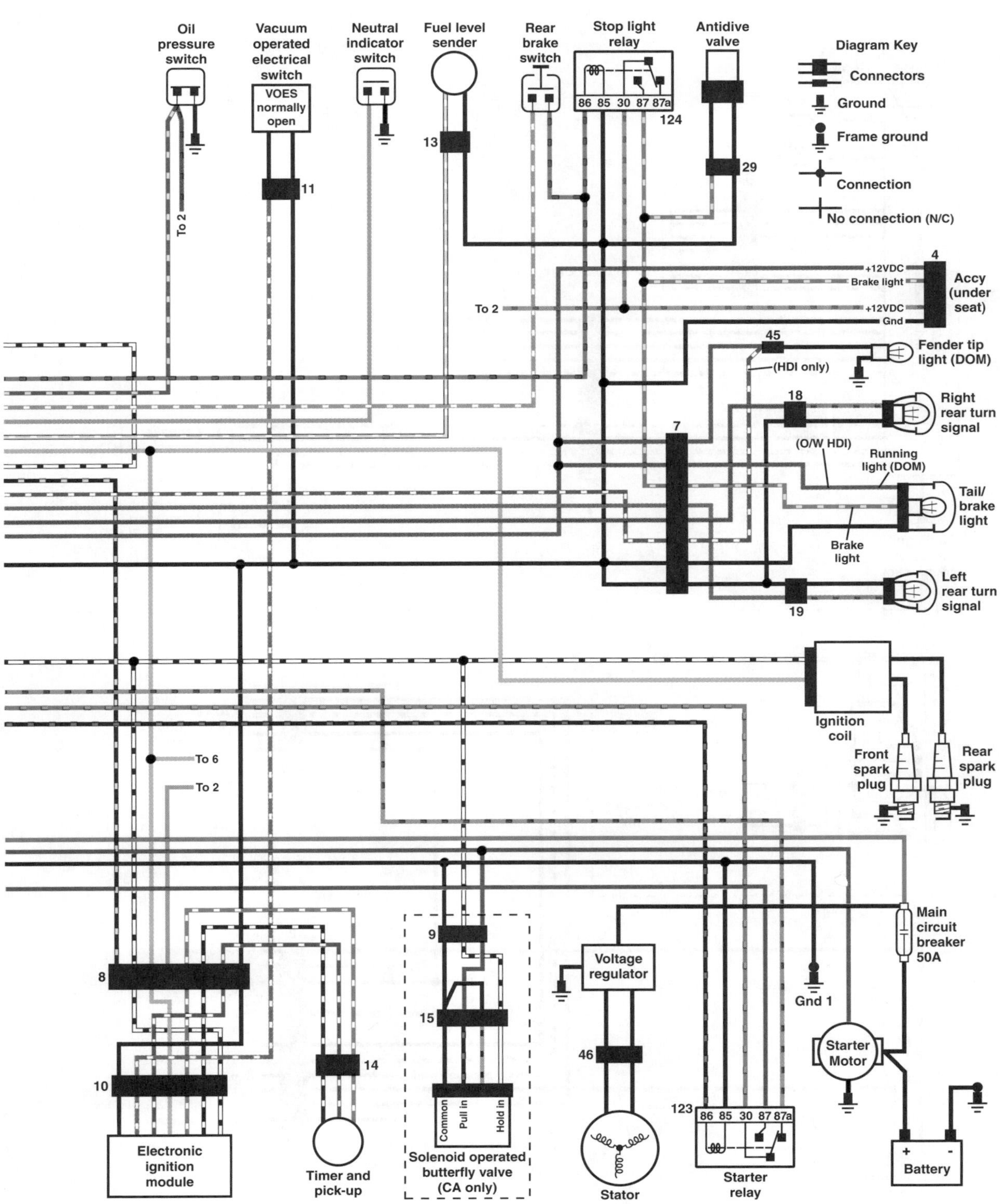

Oil pressure switch
Vacuum operated electrical switch
VOES normally open
Neutral indicator switch
Fuel level sender
Rear brake switch
Stop light relay
86 85 30 87 87a
124
Antidive valve
Diagram Key
Connectors
Ground
Frame ground
Connection
No connection (N/C)
To 2
11
13
29
4
+12VDC
Brake light
+12VDC
Gnd
Accy (under seat)
To 2
45
(HDI only)
Fender tip light (DOM)
18
Right rear turn signal
7
(O/W HDI)
Running light (DOM)
Tail/ brake light
Brake light
Left rear turn signal
19
Ignition coil
Front spark plug
Rear spark plug
To 6
To 2
Main circuit breaker 50A
9
15
8
Voltage regulator
Gnd 1
Starter Motor
46
14
10
Common
Pull in
Hold in
123
86 85 30 87 87a
Electronic ignition module
Timer and pick-up
Solenoid operated butterfly valve (CA only)
Stator
Starter relay
Battery

1994 FLHTC, FLHTC ULTRA AND FLTC ULTRA MODELS RADIO, FAIRING HEADLIGHTS AND HARNESS CONNECTORS

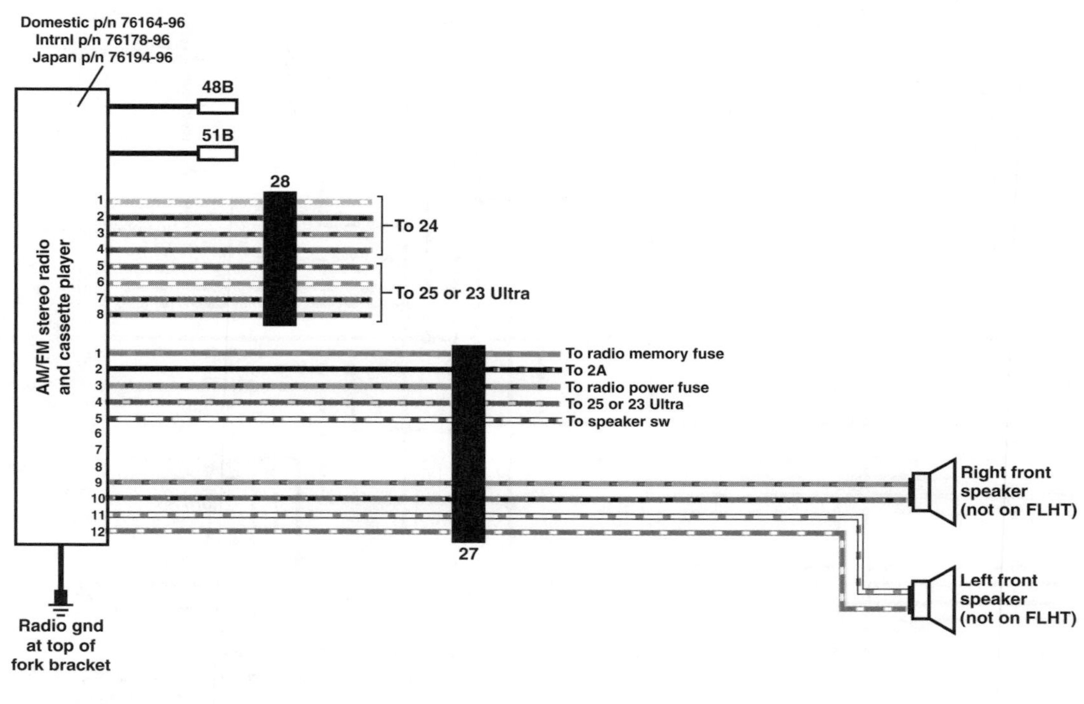

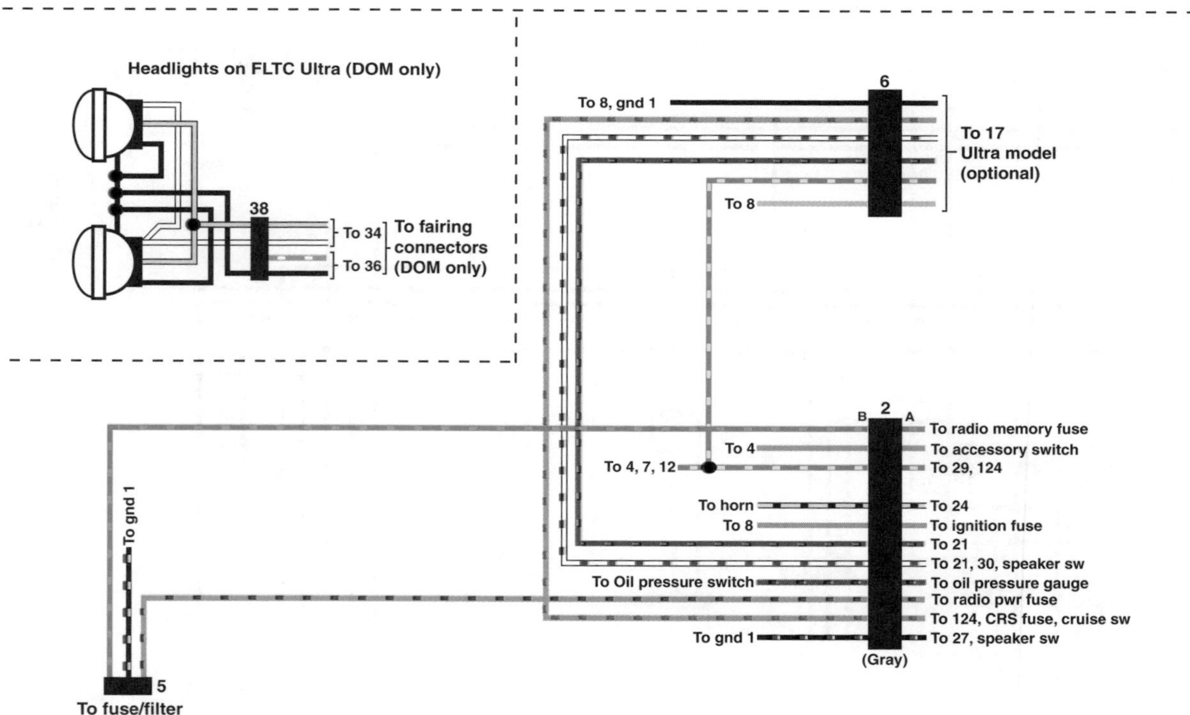

1994 FLHTC, FLHTC ULTRA AND FLTC ULTRA MODELS DASH SWITCHES, GROUNDS, CRUISE CONTROL AND TOURPAK

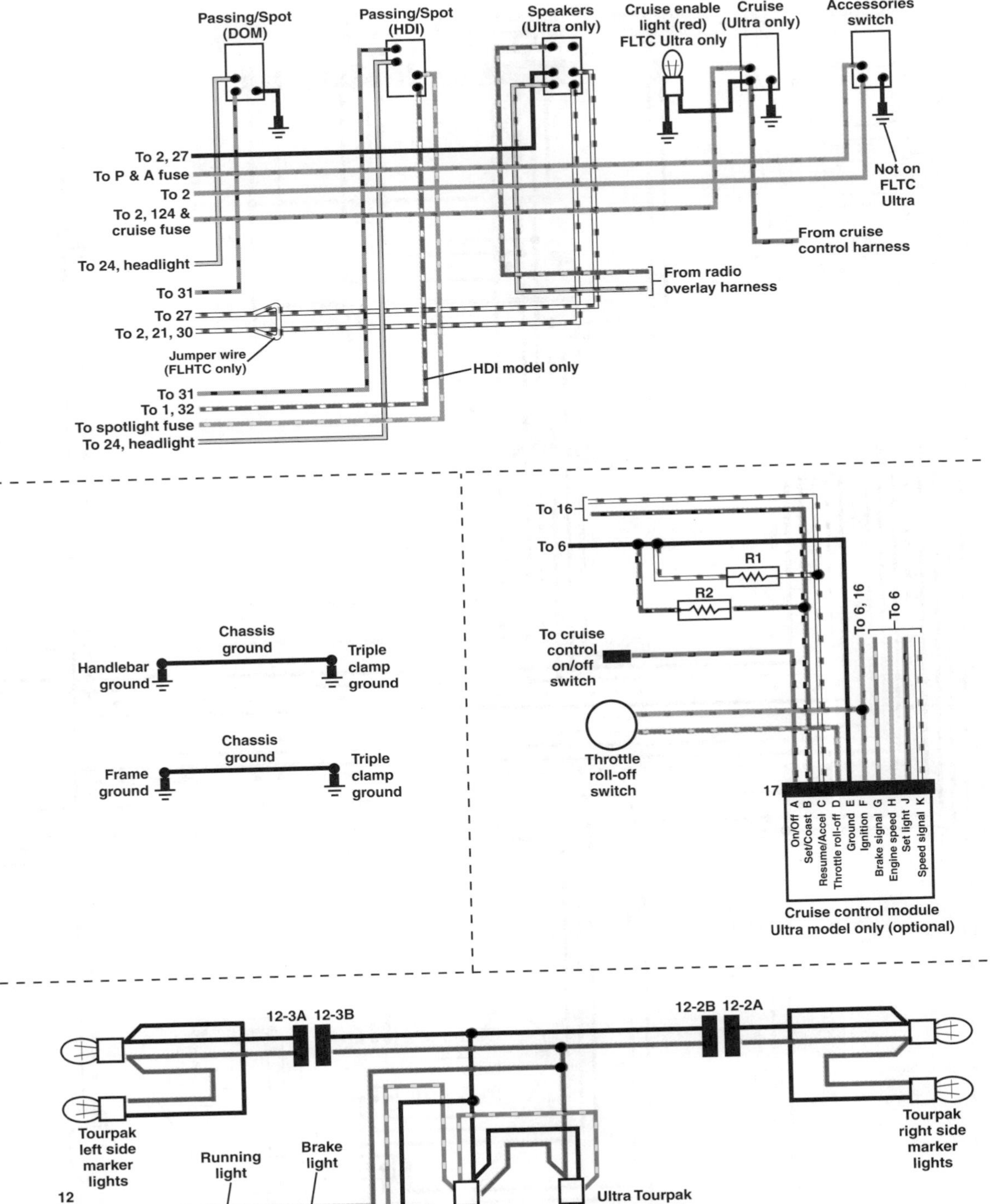

17

1994 FLHTC, FLHTC ULTRA AND FLTC ULTRA MODELS RADIO CB/INTERCOM, REAR SPEAKERS AND ANTENNAS

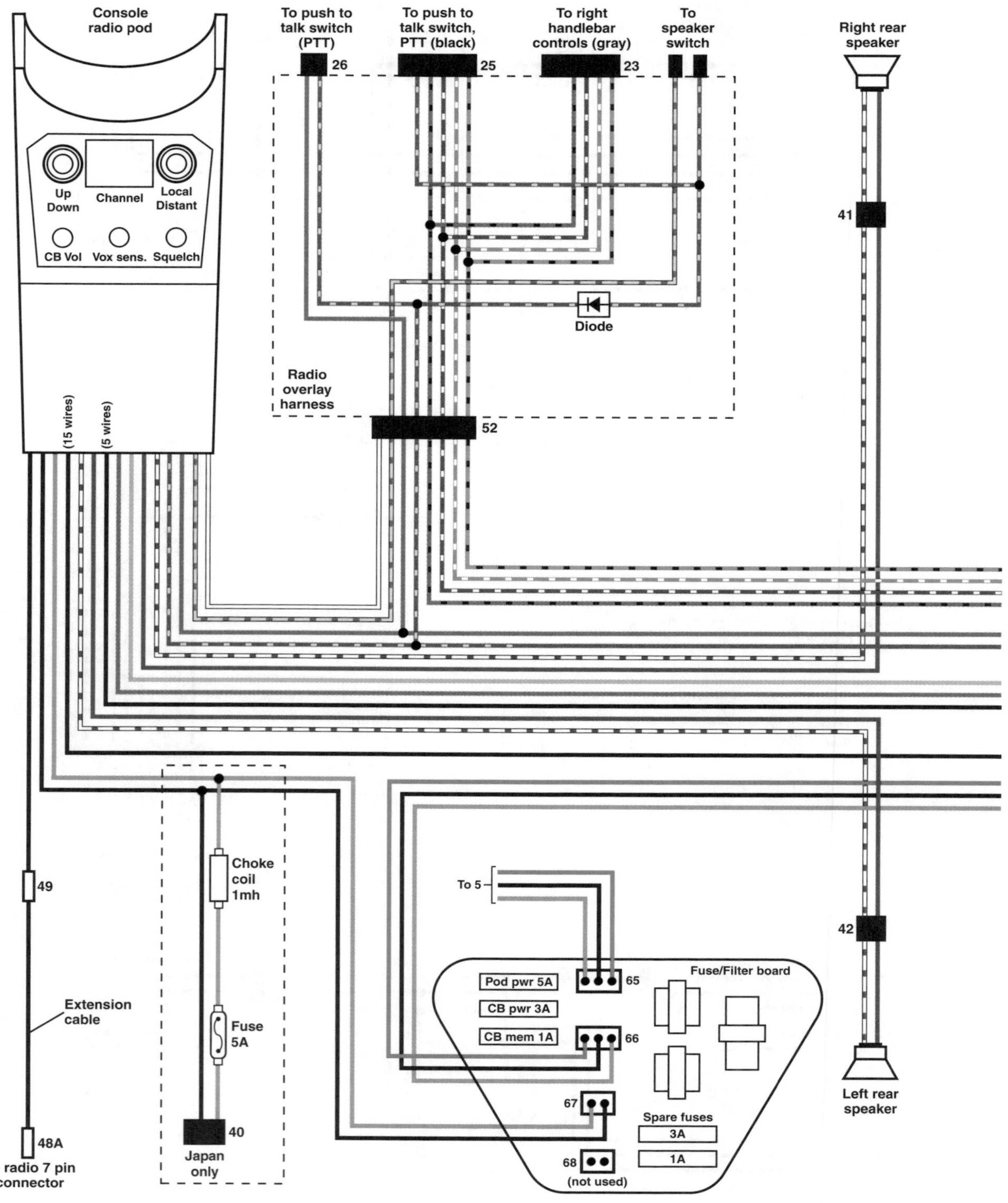

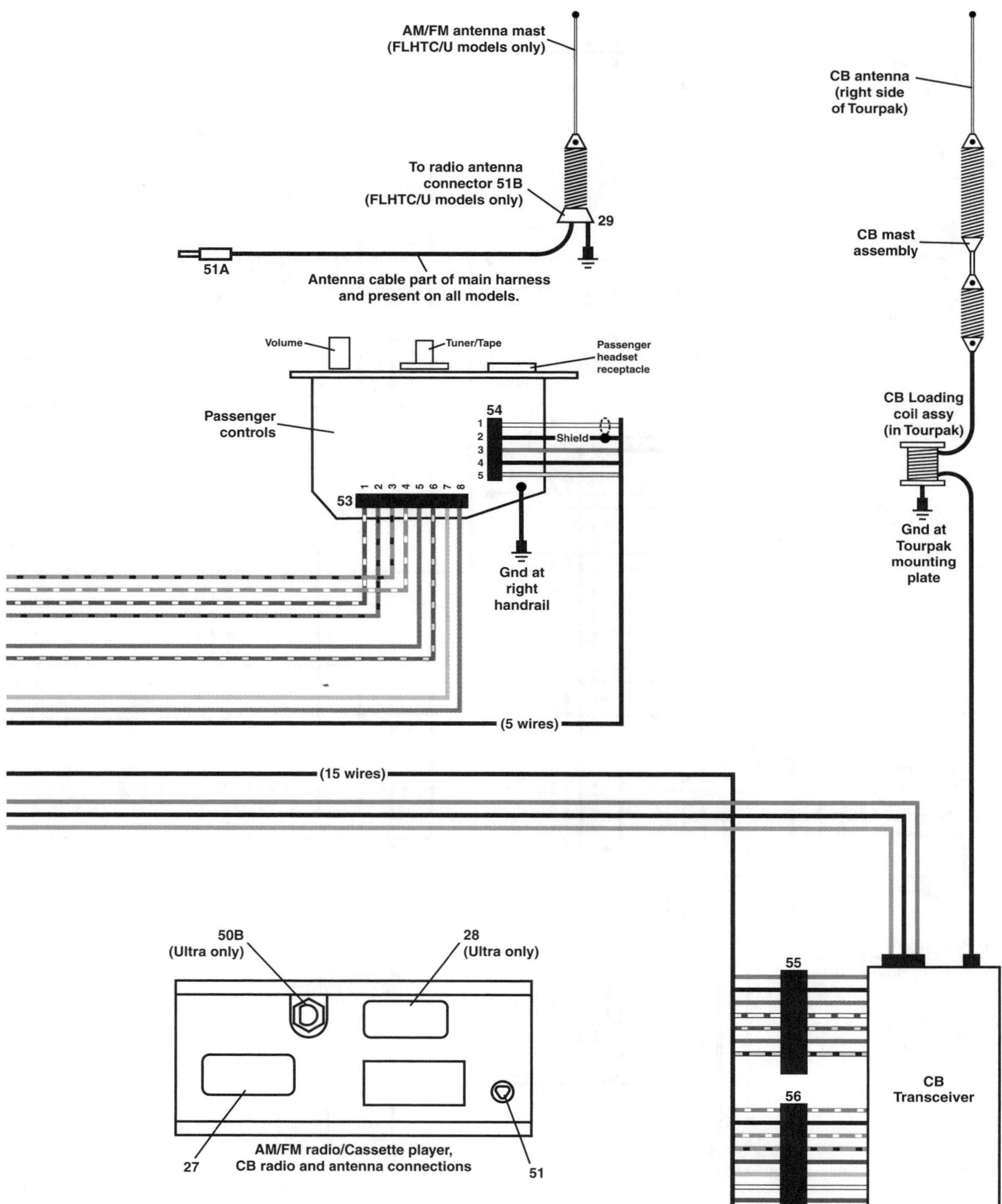
AM/FM antenna mast
(FLHTC/U models only)
To radio antenna
connector 51B
(FLHTC/U models only)
29
51A
Antenna cable part of main harness
and present on all models.
CB antenna
(right side
of Tourpak)
CB mast
assembly
CB Loading
coil assy
(in Tourpak)
Gnd at
Tourpak
mounting
plate
Volume
Tuner/Tape
Passenger
headset
receptacle
Passenger
controls
54
1
2
3
4
5
Shield
53
1 2 3 4 5 6 7 8
Gnd at
right
handrail
(5 wires)
(15 wires)
50B
(Ultra only)
28
(Ultra only)
27
AM/FM radio/Cassette player,
CB radio and antenna connections
51
55
56
CB
Transceiver

1995 FLHR MODELS

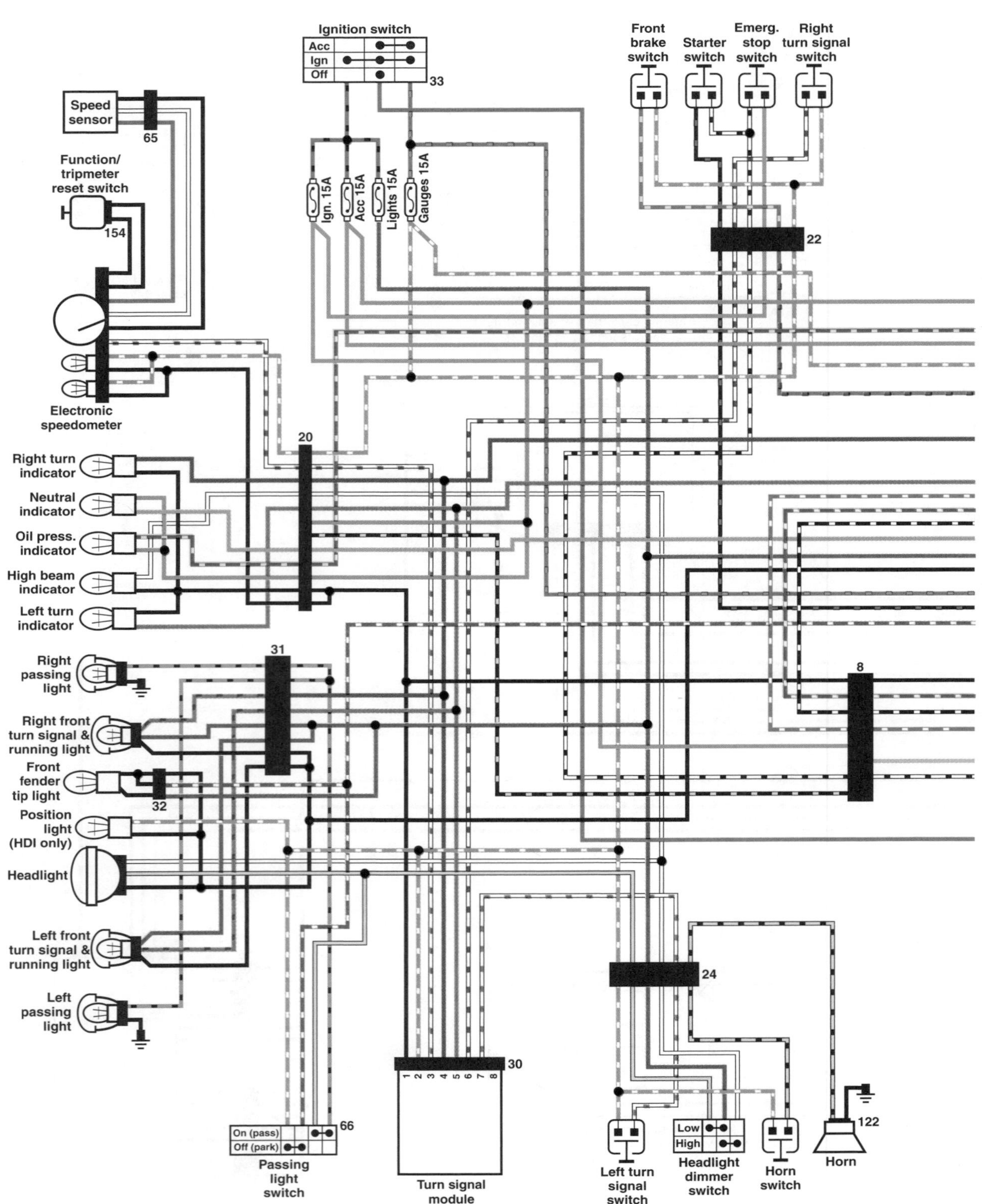

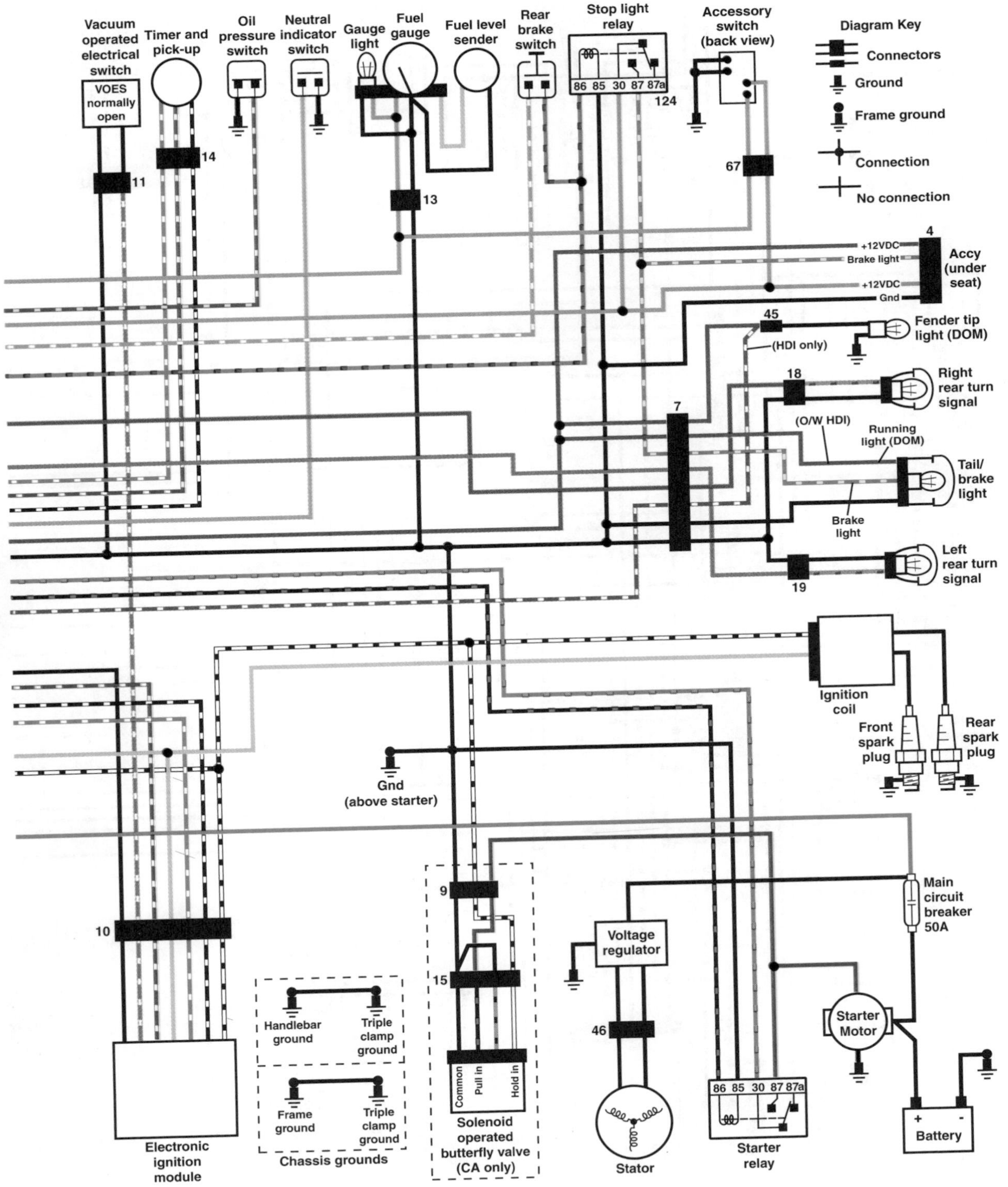

Vacuum operated electrical switch
VOES normally open
Timer and pick-up
Oil pressure switch
Neutral indicator switch
Gauge light
Fuel gauge
Fuel level sender
Rear brake switch
Stop light relay
86 85 30 87 87a
124
Accessory switch (back view)
Diagram Key
Connectors
Ground
Frame ground
Connection
No connection
11
14
13
67
4
Accy (under seat)
+12VDC
Brake light
+12VDC
Gnd
45
Fender tip light (DOM)
(HDI only)
18
Right rear turn signal
7
(O/W HDI)
Running light (DOM)
Tail/ brake light
Brake light
19
Left rear turn signal
Ignition coil
Front spark plug
Rear spark plug
Gnd (above starter)
Main circuit breaker 50A
9
10
15
Voltage regulator
46
Starter Motor
Handlebar ground
Triple clamp ground
Frame ground
Triple clamp ground
Chassis grounds
Common
Pull in
Hold in
Solenoid operated butterfly valve (CA only)
86 85 30 87 87a
Starter relay
Stator
Battery
Electronic ignition module

1995 FLHT, FLHTC, FLHTC ULTRA AND FLTC ULTRA MODELS

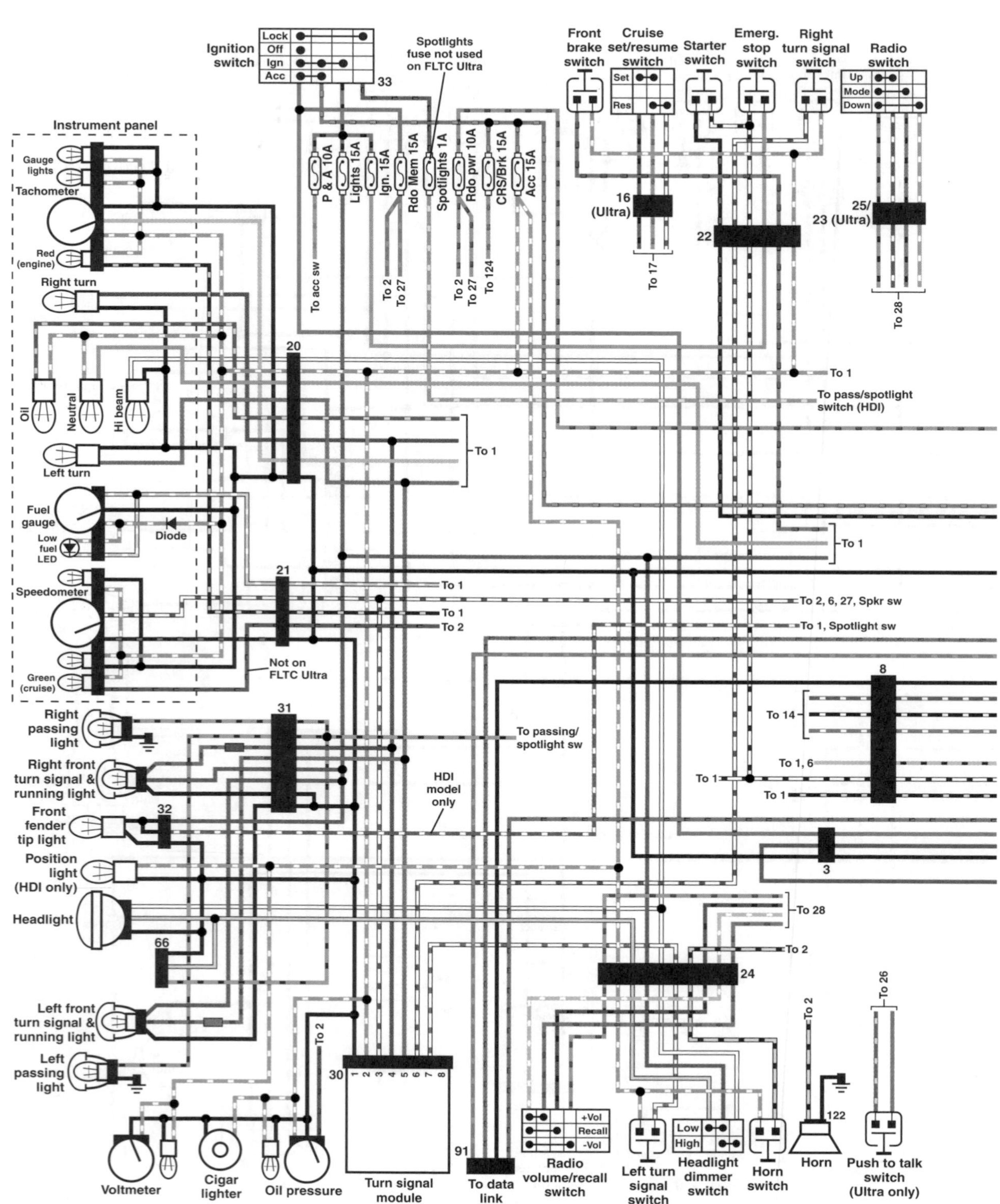

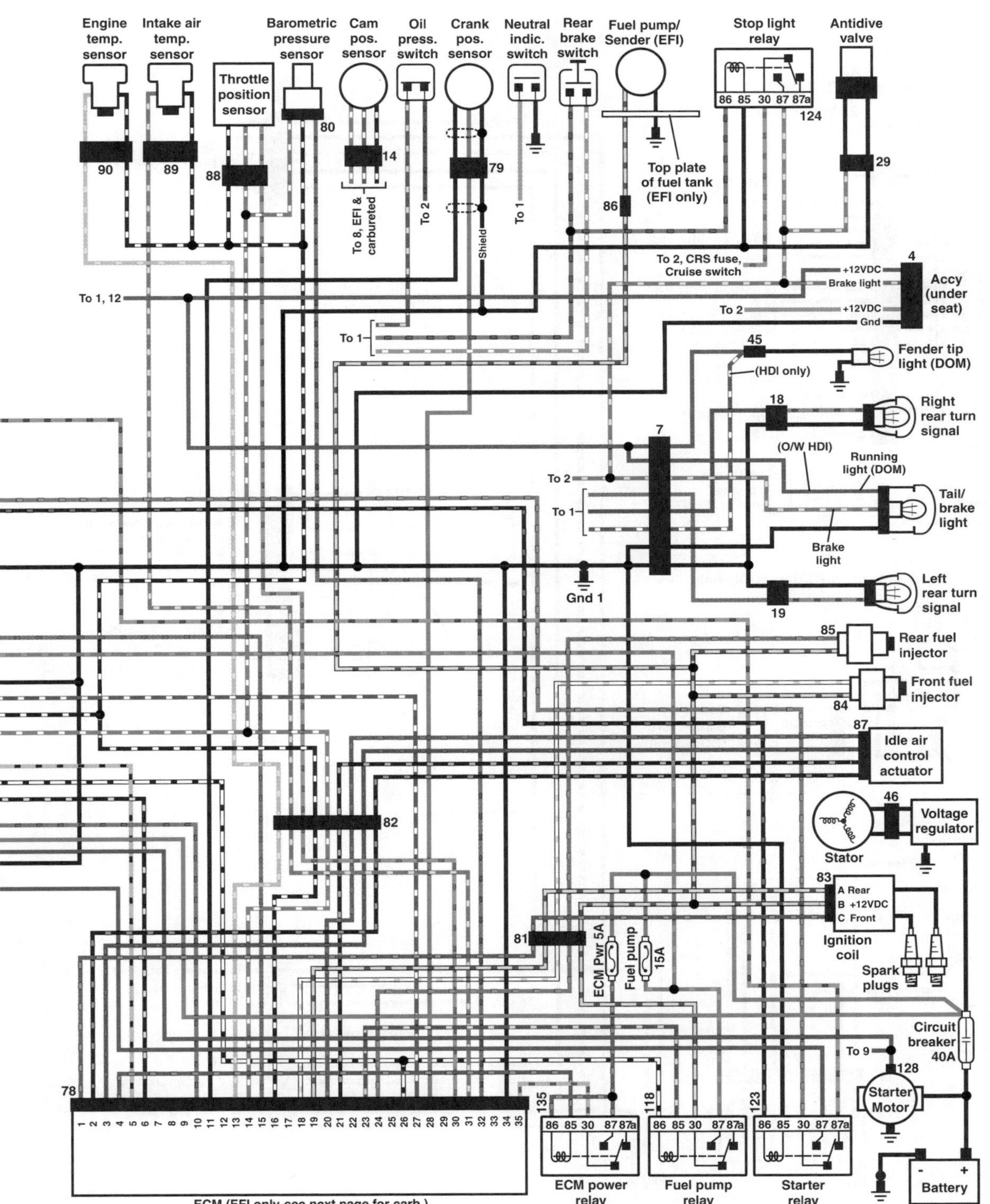
Engine temp. sensor
Intake air temp. sensor
Throttle position sensor
Barometric pressure sensor
Cam pos. sensor
Oil press. switch
Crank pos. sensor
Neutral indic. switch
Rear brake switch
Fuel pump/ Sender (EFI)
Stop light relay
Antidive valve
Top plate of fuel tank (EFI only)
To 8, EFI & carbureted
To 2
Shield
To 1
To 2, CRS fuse, Cruise switch
Accy (under seat)
+12VDC
Brake light
Gnd
To 1, 12
Fender tip light (DOM)
(HDI only)
Right rear turn signal
(O/W HDI)
Running light (DOM)
Tail/ brake light
Brake light
Left rear turn signal
Gnd 1
Rear fuel injector
Front fuel injector
Idle air control actuator
Stator
Voltage regulator
A Rear
B +12VDC
C Front
Ignition coil
Spark plugs
ECM Pwr 5A
Fuel pump 15A
Circuit breaker 40A
To 9
Starter Motor
Battery
ECM power relay
Fuel pump relay
Starter relay
ECM (EFI only-see next page for carb.)

1995 FLHT, FLHTC, FLHTC ULTRA AND FLTC ULTRA MODELS RADIO, HEADLIGHTS, CRUISE CONTROL MODULE AND HARNESS CONNECTORS

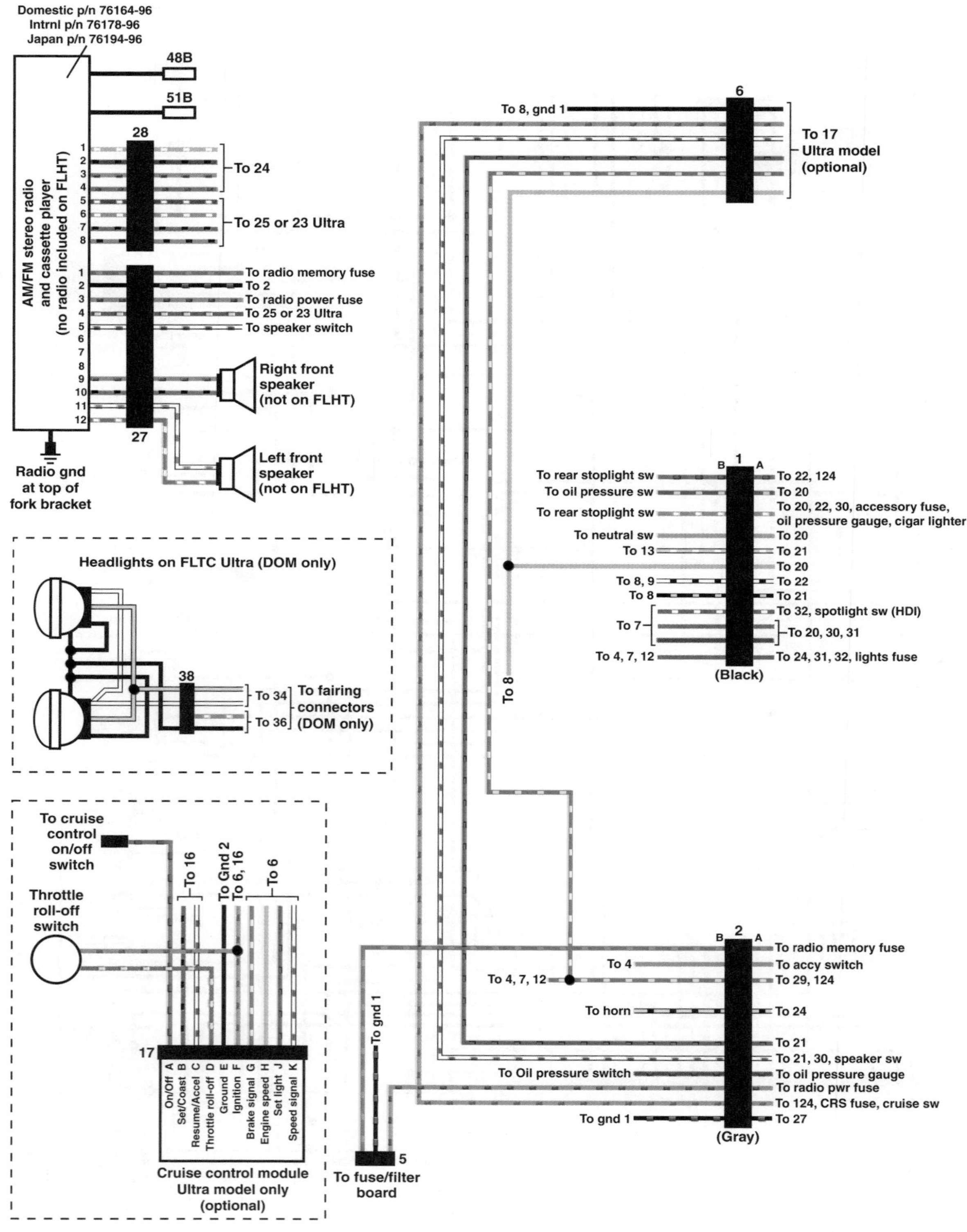

1995 FLHT, FLHTC, FLHTC ULTRA AND FLTC ULTRA MODELS CARBURETED IGNITION, DASH SWITCHES AND TOURPAK

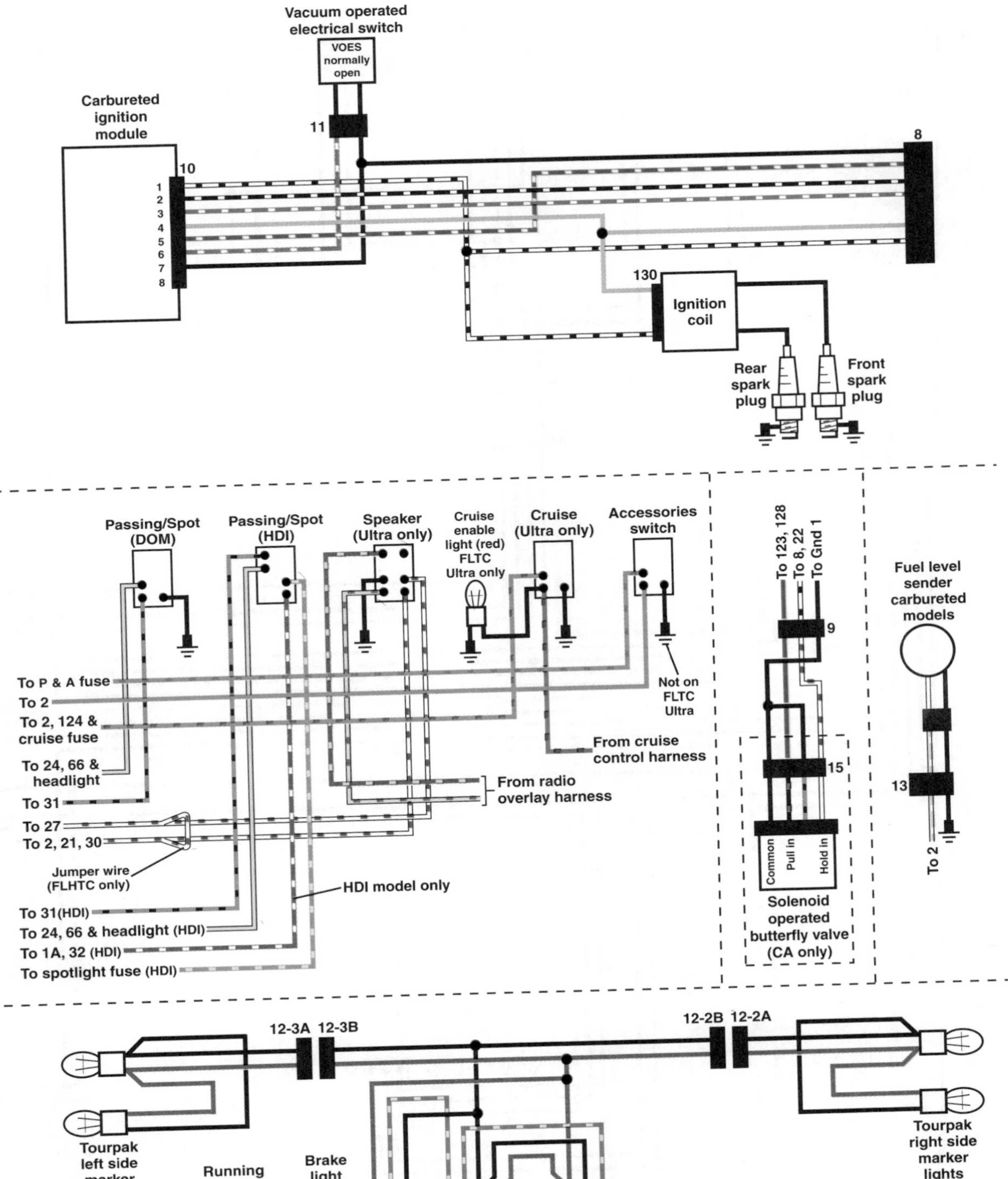

1995 FLHT, FLHTC, FLHTC ULTRA AND FLTC ULTRA MODELS RADIO CB/INTERCOM, REAR SPEAKERS AND ANTENNAS

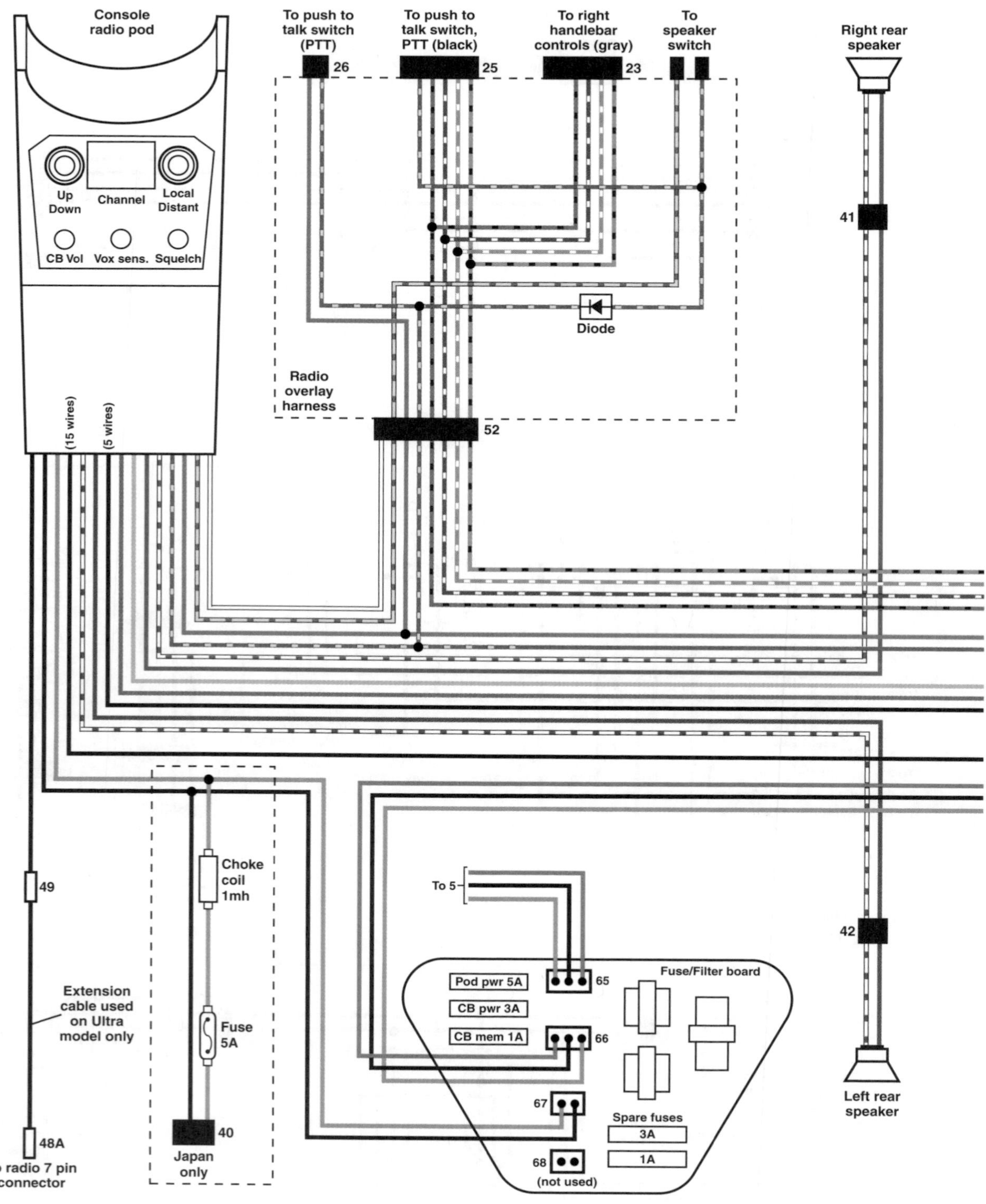

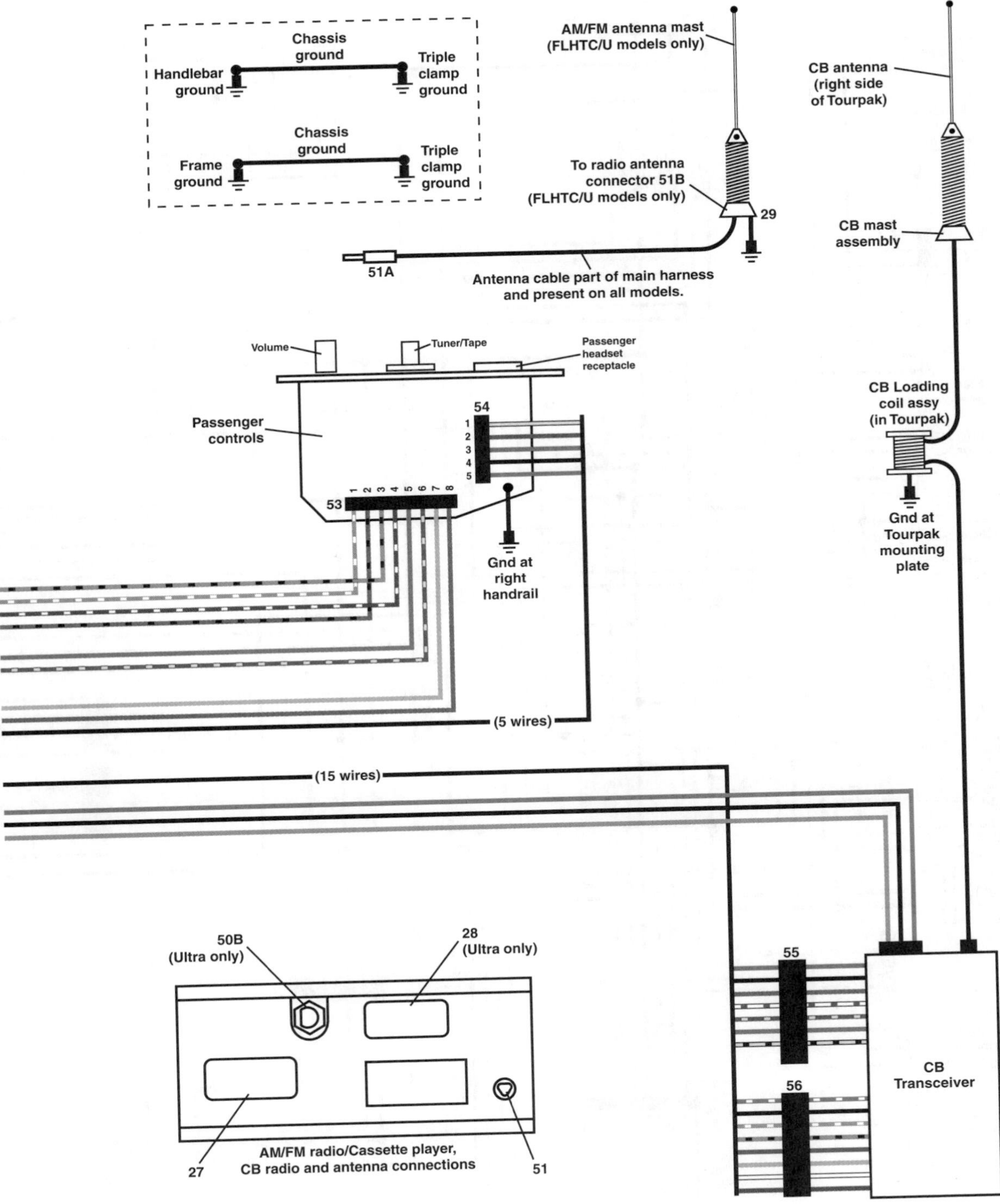
Handlebar ground
Chassis ground
Triple clamp ground
Frame ground
Chassis ground
Triple clamp ground
AM/FM antenna mast (FLHTC/U models only)
To radio antenna connector 51B (FLHTC/U models only)
29
51A
Antenna cable part of main harness and present on all models.
CB antenna (right side of Tourpak)
CB mast assembly
Volume
Tuner/Tape
Passenger headset receptacle
Passenger controls
54
53
Gnd at right handrail
CB Loading coil assy (in Tourpak)
Gnd at Tourpak mounting plate
(5 wires)
(15 wires)
50B (Ultra only)
28 (Ultra only)
55
56
CB Transceiver
27
AM/FM radio/Cassette player, CB radio and antenna connections
51

1996 FLHR AND FLHR-I MODELS

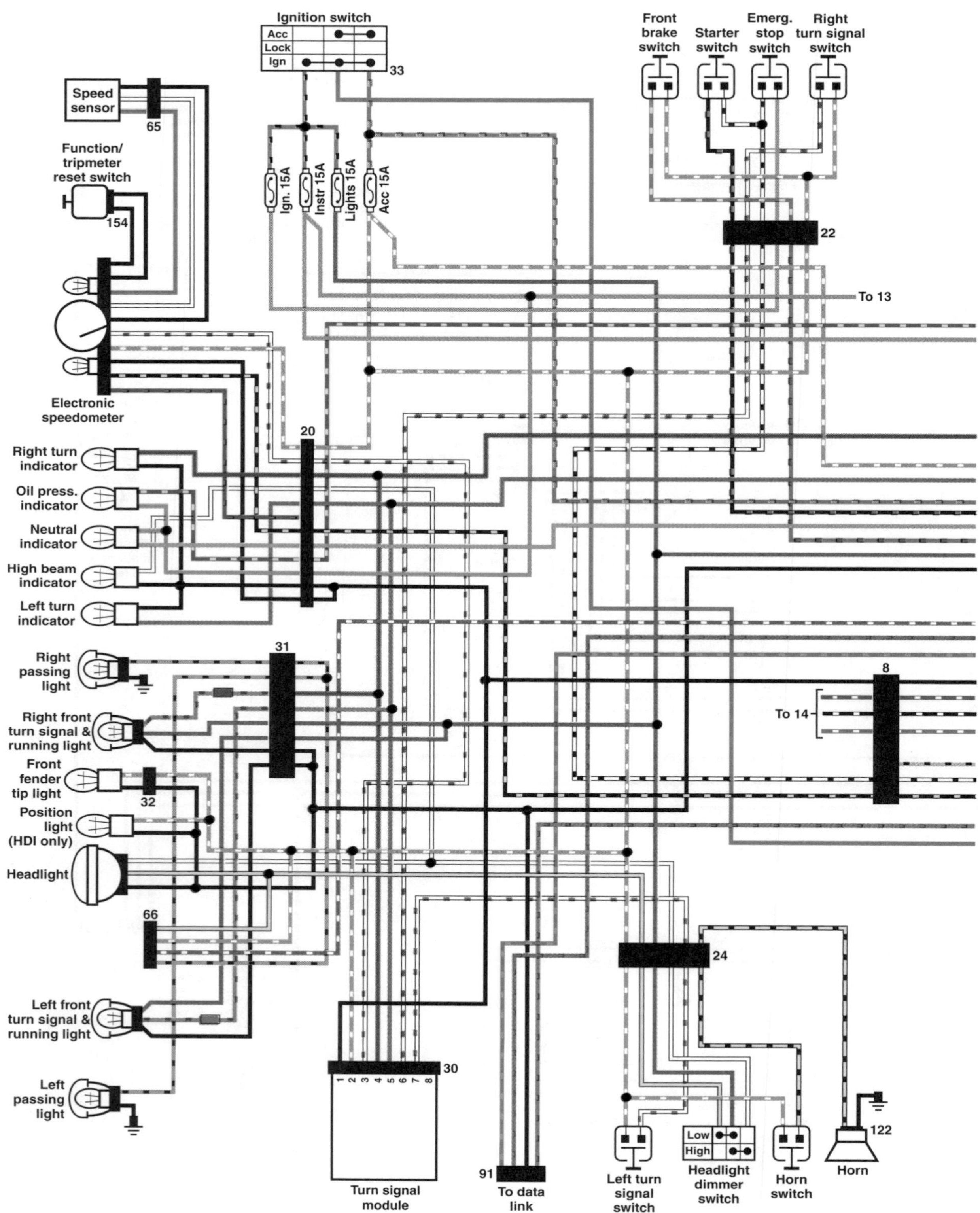

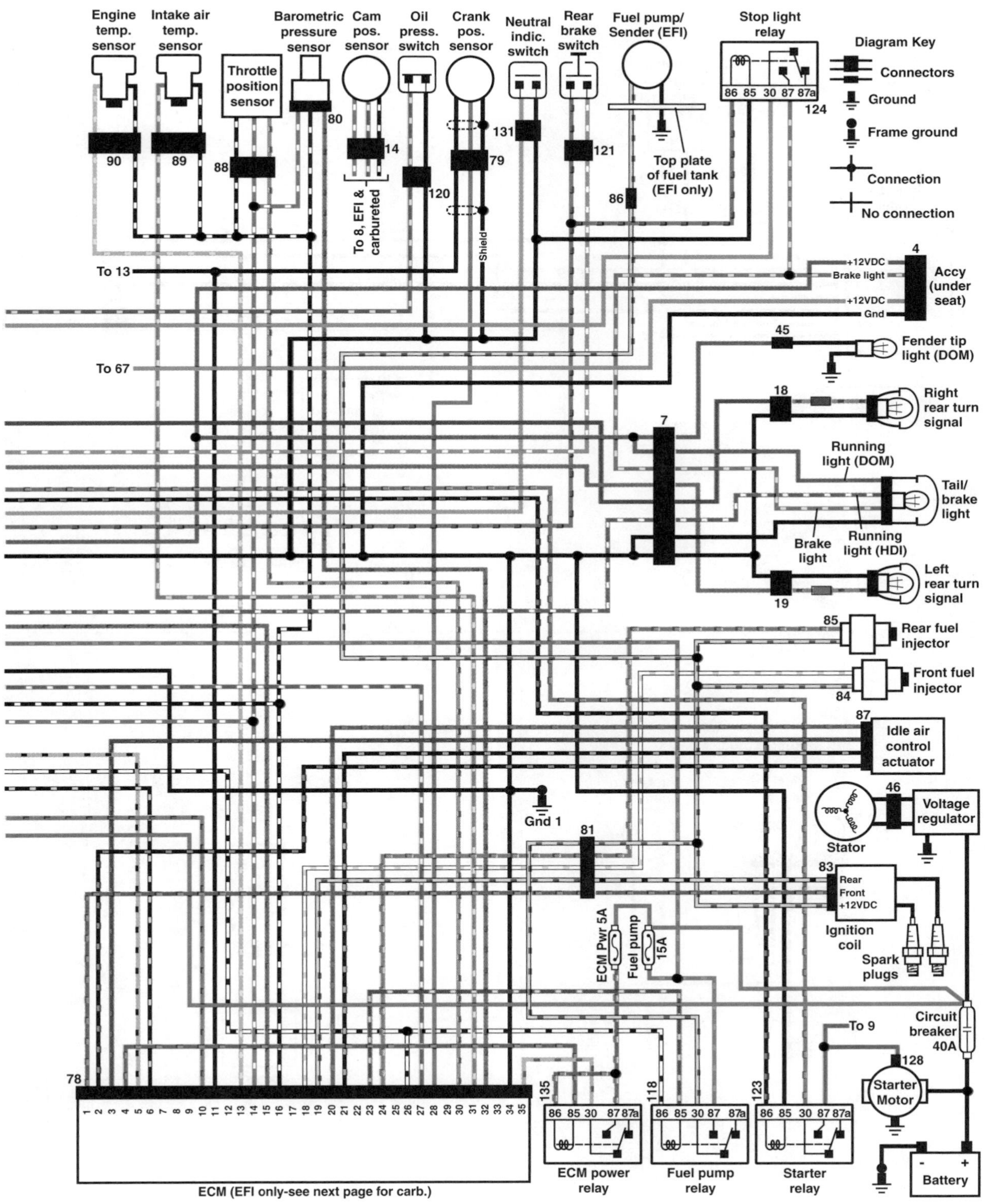
Engine temp. sensor
Intake air temp. sensor
Throttle position sensor
Barometric pressure sensor
Cam pos. sensor
Oil press. switch
Crank pos. sensor
Neutral indic. switch
Rear brake switch
Fuel pump/ Sender (EFI)
Stop light relay
Diagram Key
Connectors
Ground
Frame ground
Connection
No connection
Top plate of fuel tank (EFI only)
To 8, EFI & carbureted
Shield
To 13
To 67
Accy (under seat)
+12VDC
Brake light
Gnd
Fender tip light (DOM)
Right rear turn signal
Running light (DOM)
Tail/ brake light
Brake light
Running light (HDI)
Left rear turn signal
Rear fuel injector
Front fuel injector
Idle air control actuator
Voltage regulator
Stator
Gnd 1
Rear
Front
Ignition coil
Spark plugs
ECM Pwr 5A
Fuel pump 15A
Circuit breaker 40A
To 9
Starter Motor
Battery
ECM (EFI only-see next page for carb.)
ECM power relay
Fuel pump relay
Starter relay

1996 FLHR AND FLHR-I MODELS

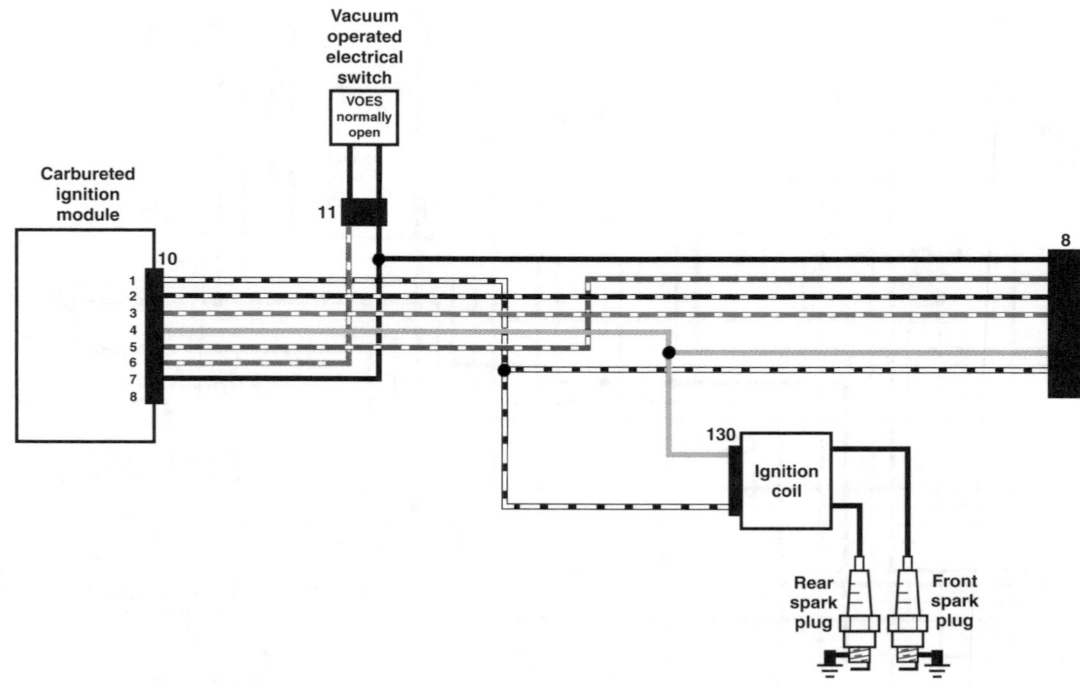

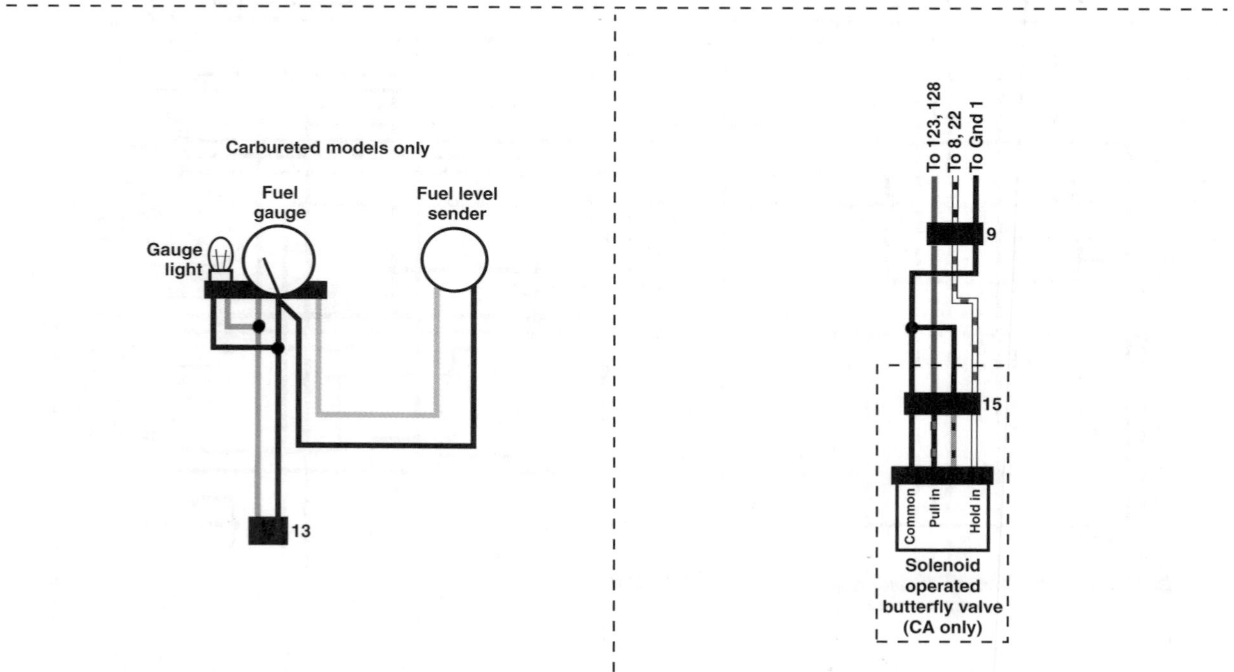

1996 FLHR AND FLHR-I MODELS

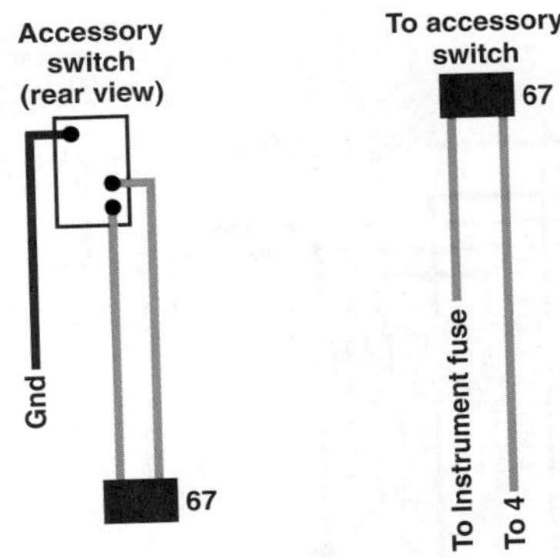

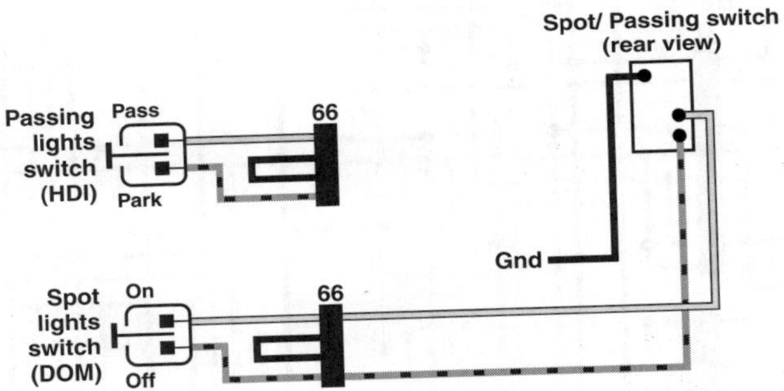

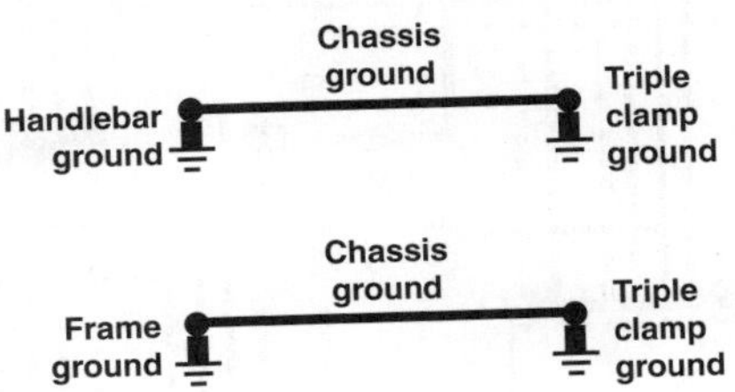

1996 FLHT, FLHTC, FLHTC-I, FLHTC ULTRA, FLHTC ULTRA-I AND FLTC ULTRA-I MODELS

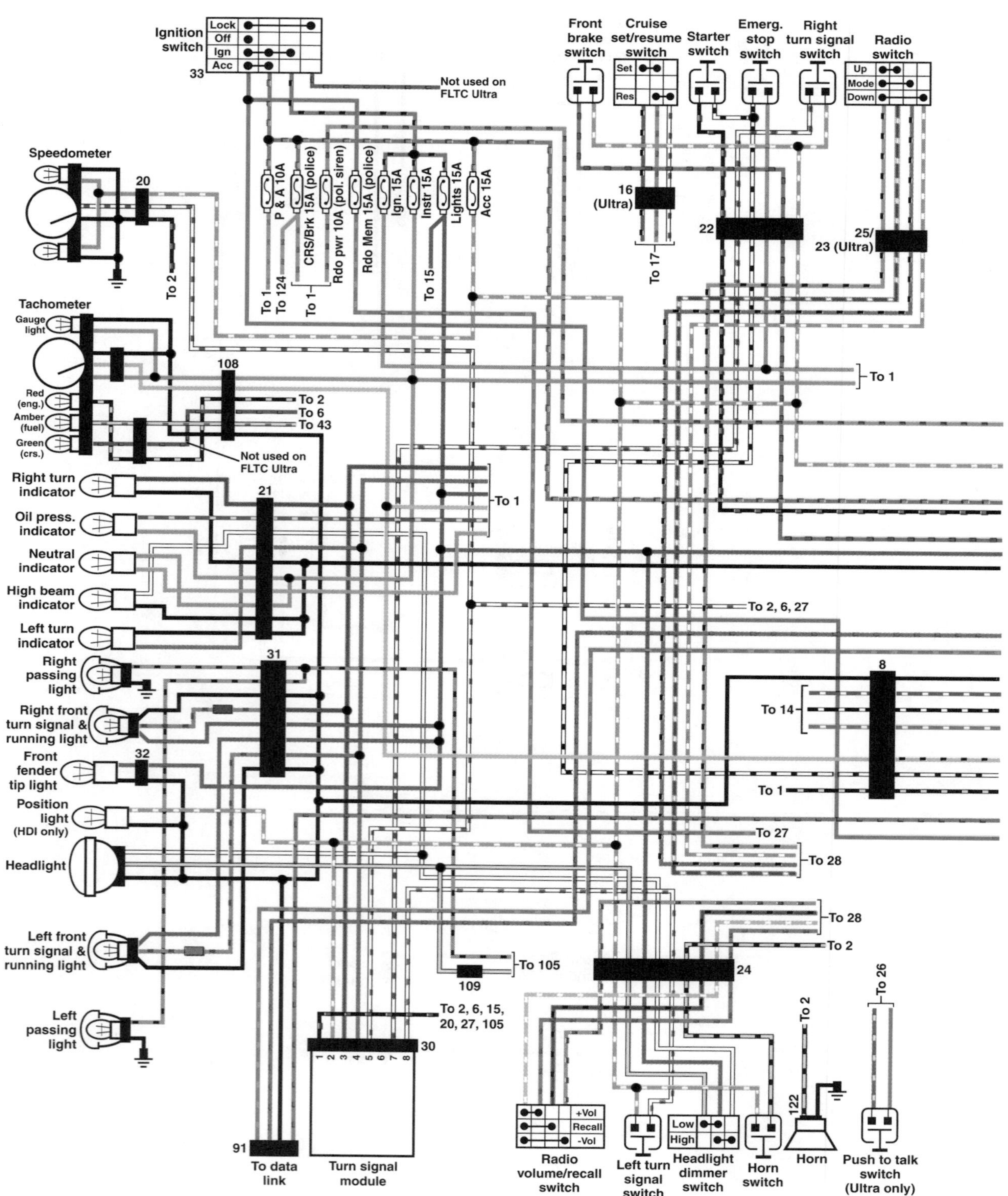

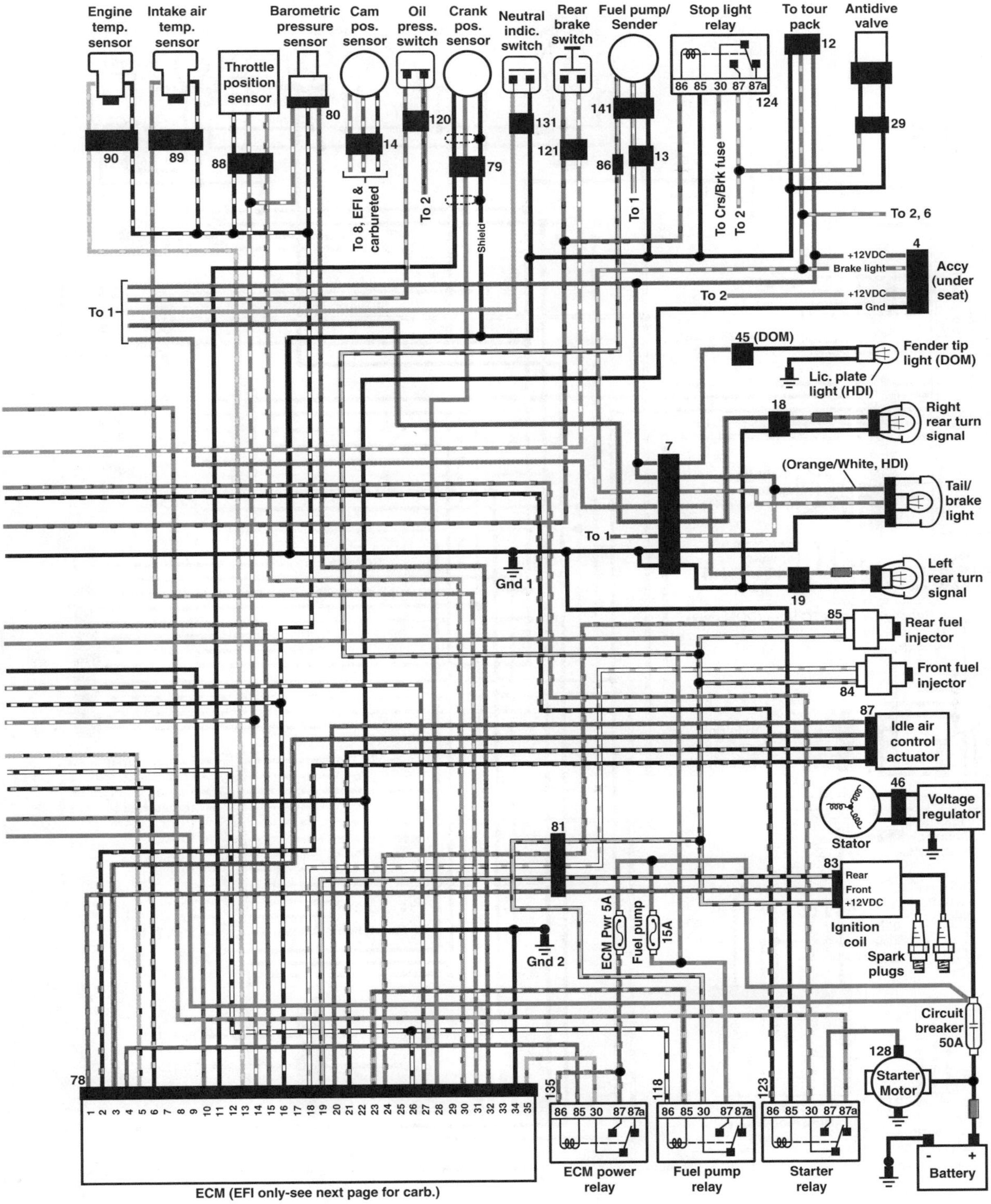

Engine temp. sensor
Intake air temp. sensor
Throttle position sensor
Barometric pressure sensor
Cam pos. sensor
Oil press. switch
Crank pos. sensor
Neutral indic. switch
Rear brake switch
Fuel pump/ Sender
Stop light relay
To tour pack
Antidive valve

90 89 88 80 14 120 79 131 121 141 86 13 124 12 29

To 8, EFI & carbureted
To 2
Shield
To 1
To Crs/Brk fuse
To 2
To 2, 6

86 85 30 87 87a

+12VDC
Brake light
+12VDC
Gnd
4 Accy (under seat)
To 2
To 1

45 (DOM)
Fender tip light (DOM)
Lic. plate light (HDI)
18 Right rear turn signal
7
(Orange/White, HDI)
Tail/ brake light
To 1
Gnd 1
19 Left rear turn signal
85 Rear fuel injector
84 Front fuel injector
87 Idle air control actuator
46 Voltage regulator
Stator
81
83 Rear Front +12VDC
Ignition coil
Spark plugs
Gnd 2
ECM Pwr 5A
Fuel pump 15A
Circuit breaker 50A
128 Starter Motor
Battery

78
1 2 3 4 5 6 7 8 9 10 11 12 13 14 15 16 17 18 19 20 21 22 23 24 25 26 27 28 29 30 31 32 33 34 35
ECM (EFI only-see next page for carb.)

135 86 85 30 87 87a
ECM power relay
118 86 85 30 87 87a
Fuel pump relay
123 86 85 30 87 87a
Starter relay

17

1996 FLHT, FLHTC, FLHTC-I, FLHTC ULTRA, FLHTC ULTRA-I AND FLTC ULTRA-I MODELS RADIO, GAUGES, HEADLIGHTS AND CRUISE CONTROL

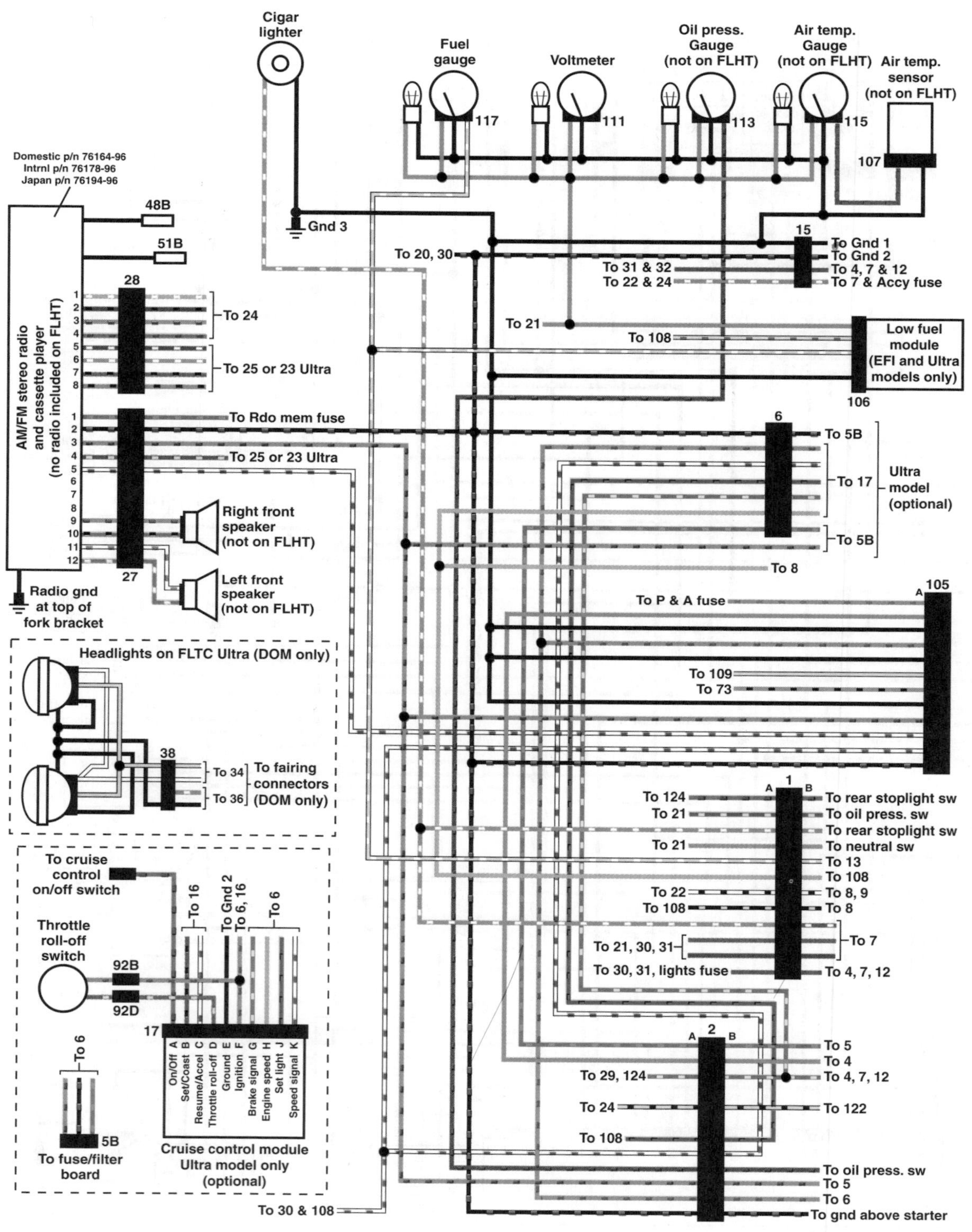

1996 FLHT, FLHTC, FLHTC-I, FLHTC ULTRA, FLHTC ULTRA-I AND FLTC ULTRA-I MODELS CARBURETED IGNITION, DASH SWITCHES AND TOURPAK

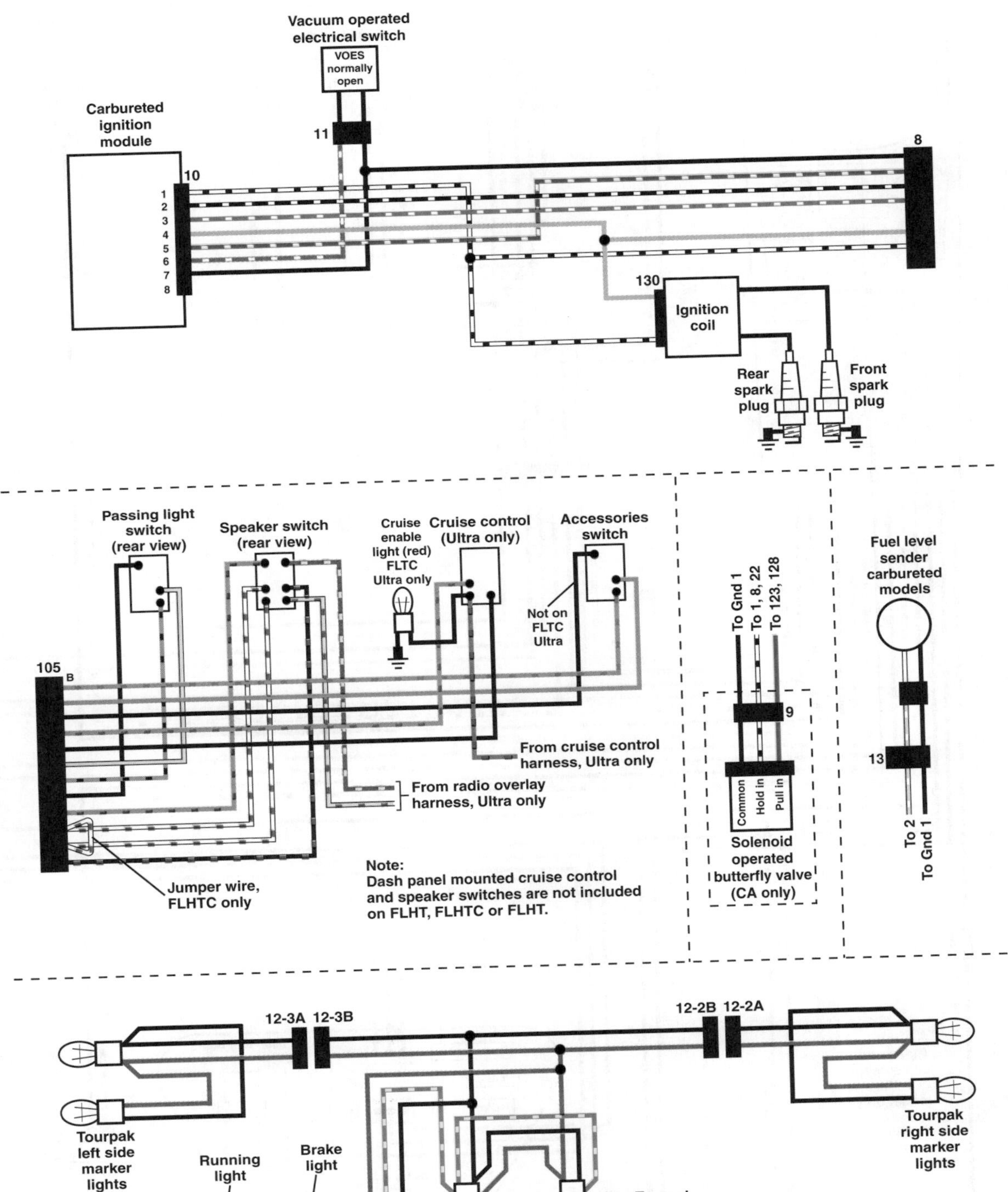

17

1996 FLHT, FLHTC, FLHTC-I, FLHTC ULTRA, FLHTC ULTRA-I AND FLTC ULTRA-I MODELS RADIO CB/INTERCOM, REAR SPEAKERS AND ANTENNAS

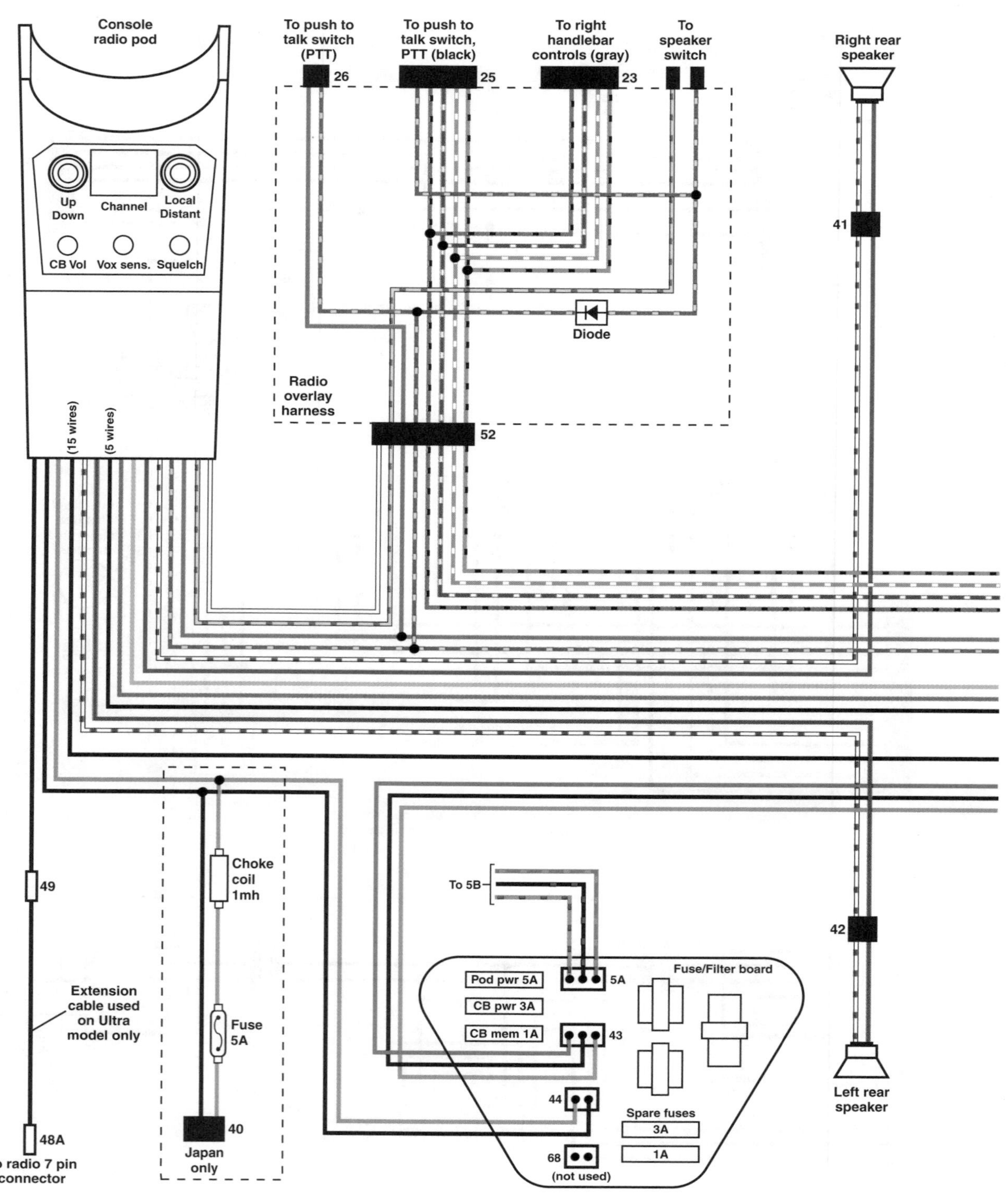

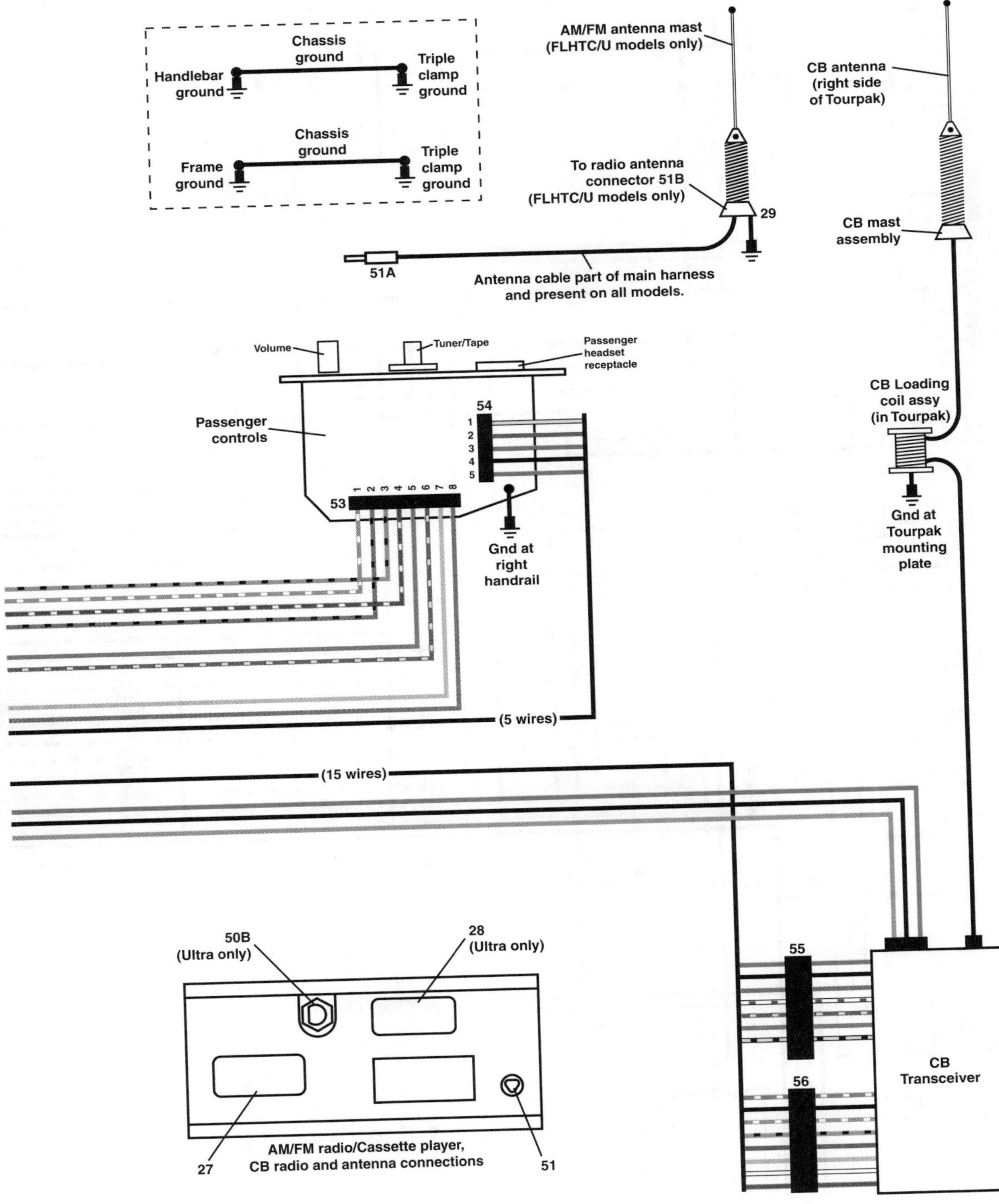
Chassis ground
Handlebar ground
Triple clamp ground
Chassis ground
Frame ground
Triple clamp ground
AM/FM antenna mast (FLHTC/U models only)
To radio antenna connector 51B (FLHTC/U models only)
29
51A
Antenna cable part of main harness and present on all models.
CB antenna (right side of Tourpak)
CB mast assembly
Volume
Tuner/Tape
Passenger headset receptacle
Passenger controls
54
1
2
3
4
5
53
1 2 3 4 5 6 7 8
Gnd at right handrail
CB Loading coil assy (in Tourpak)
Gnd at Tourpak mounting plate
(5 wires)
(15 wires)
50B (Ultra only)
28 (Ultra only)
27
AM/FM radio/Cassette player, CB radio and antenna connections
51
55
56
CB Transceiver

1997 FLHR AND FLHR-I MODELS

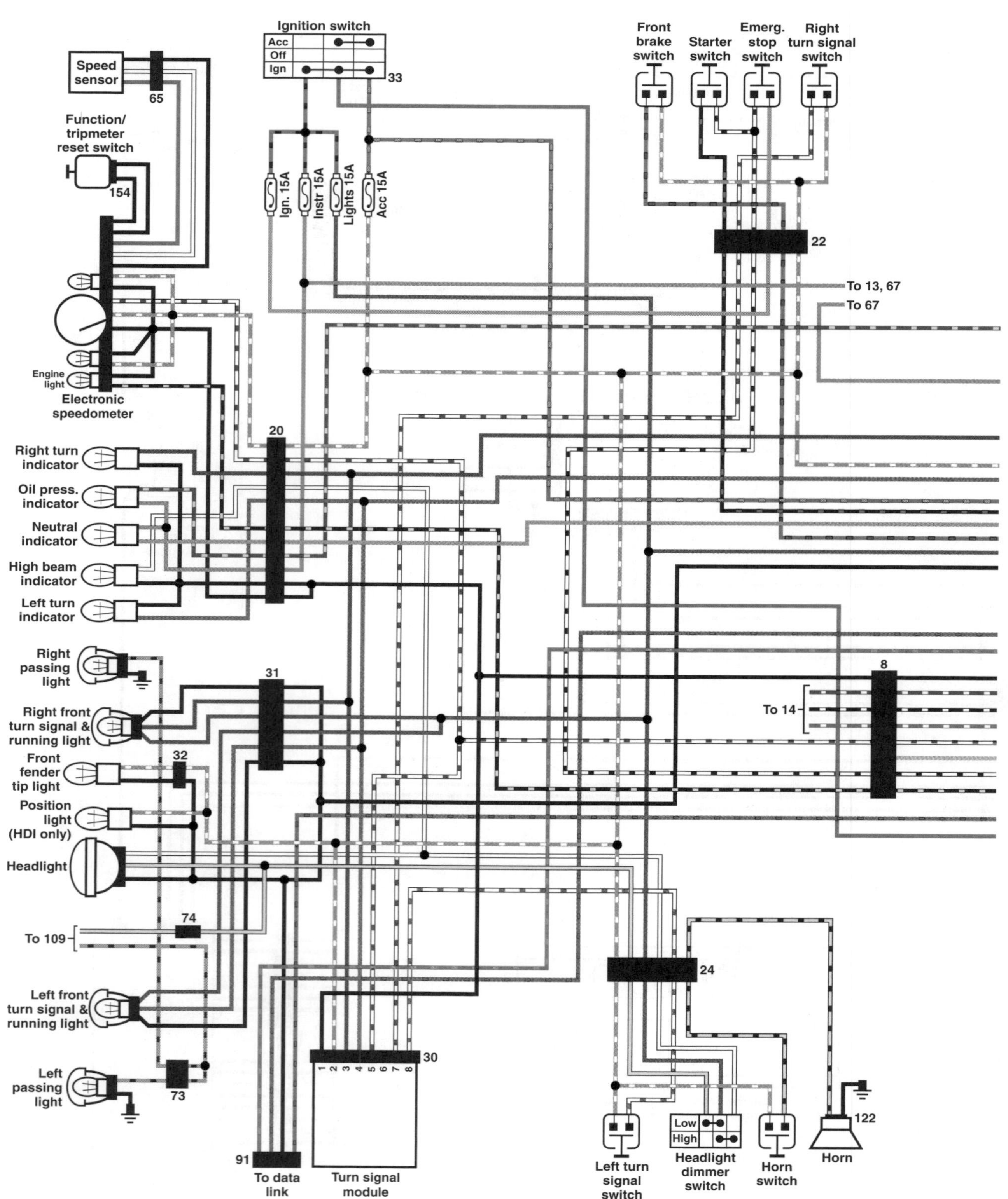

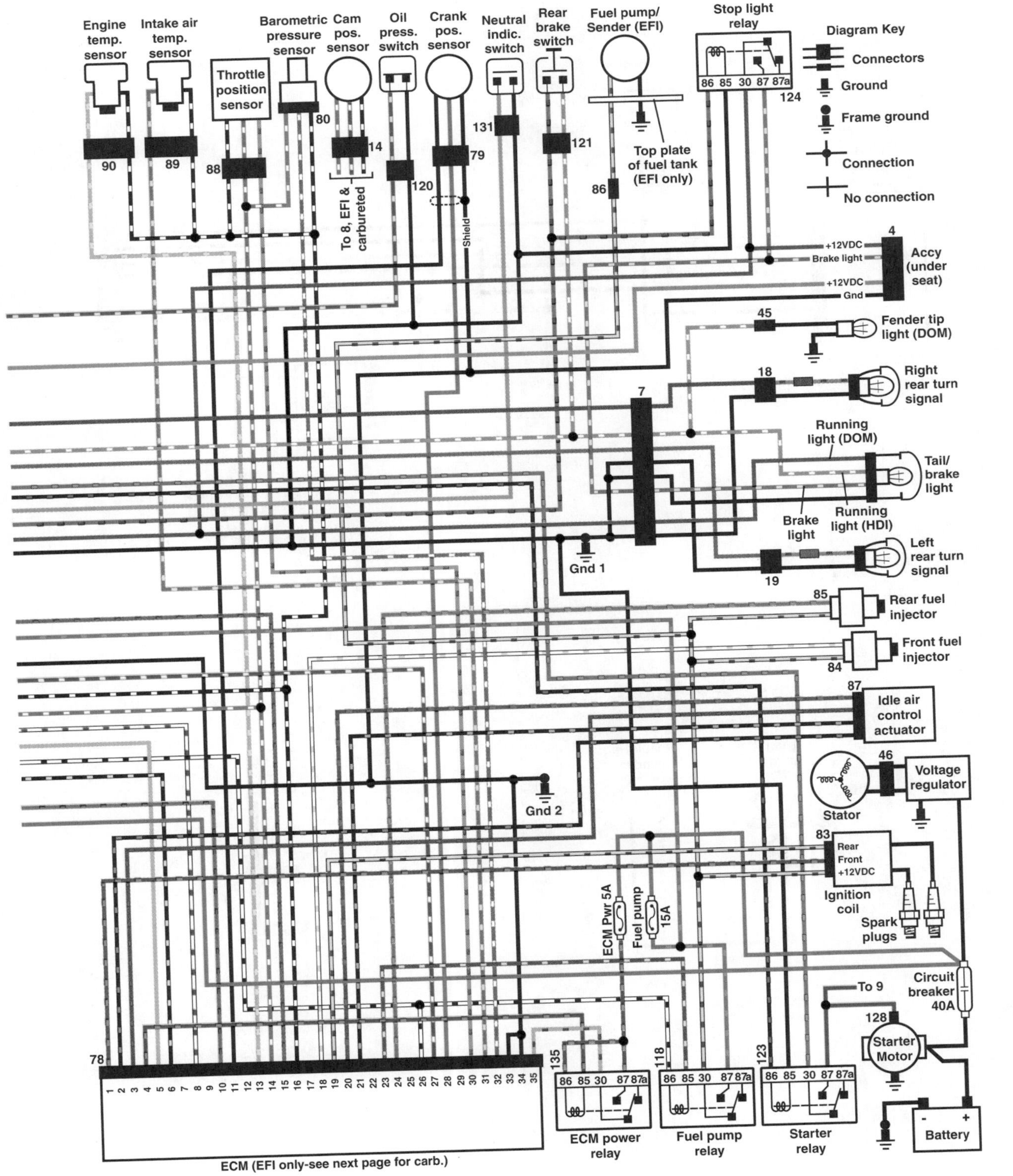

Engine temp. sensor
Intake air temp. sensor
Throttle position sensor
Barometric pressure sensor
Cam pos. sensor
Oil press. switch
Crank pos. sensor
Neutral indic. switch
Rear brake switch
Fuel pump/ Sender (EFI)
Stop light relay
86 85 30 87 87a
124
Diagram Key
Connectors
Ground
Frame ground
Connection
No connection
90
89
88
80
14
To 8, EFI & carbureted
120
79
Shield
131
121
86
Top plate of fuel tank (EFI only)
4
+12VDC
Brake light
+12VDC
Gnd
Accy (under seat)
45
Fender tip light (DOM)
18
Right rear turn signal
7
Running light (DOM)
Tail/ brake light
Brake light
Running light (HDI)
Gnd 1
19
Left rear turn signal
85
Rear fuel injector
Front fuel injector
84
87
Idle air control actuator
46
Voltage regulator
Stator
Gnd 2
83
Rear
Front
+12VDC
Ignition coil
Spark plugs
ECM Pwr 5A
Fuel pump 15A
Circuit breaker 40A
To 9
128
Starter Motor
Battery
78
1 2 3 4 5 6 7 8 9 10 11 12 13 14 15 16 17 18 19 20 21 22 23 24 25 26 27 28 29 30 31 32 33 34 35
ECM (EFI only-see next page for carb.)
135
86 85 30 87 87a
ECM power relay
118
86 85 30 87 87a
Fuel pump relay
123
86 85 30 87 87a
Starter relay

1997 FLHR AND FLHR-I MODELS

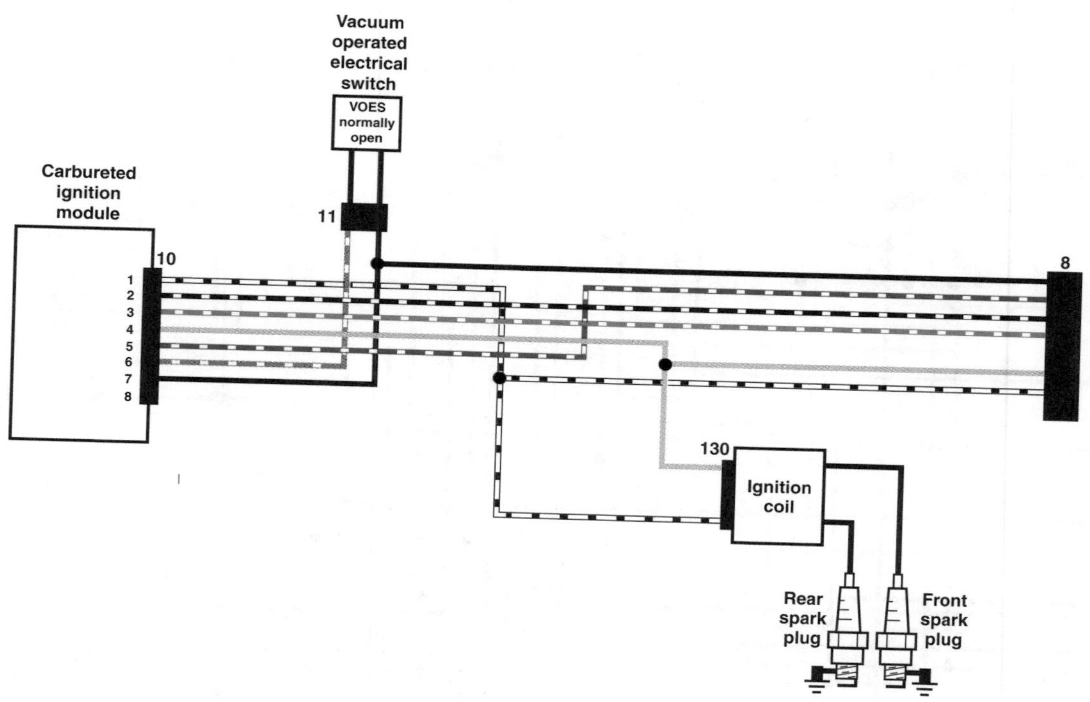

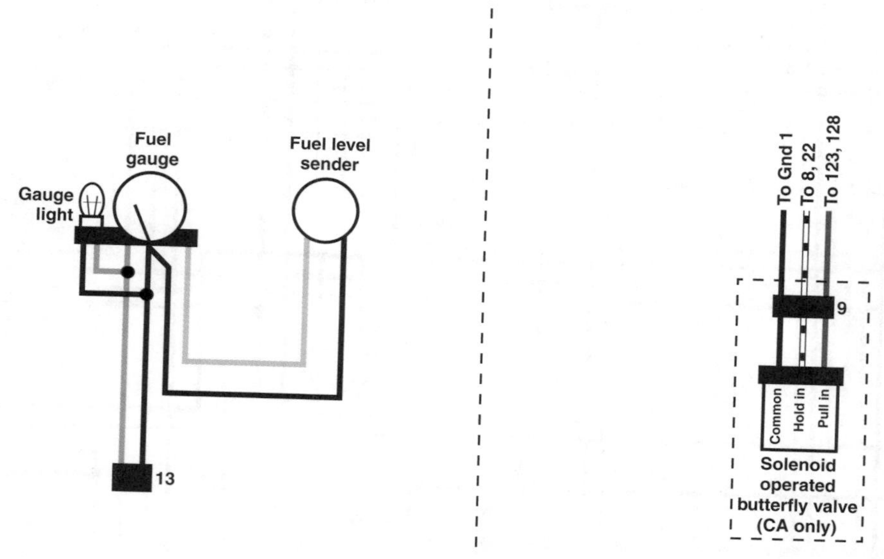

1997 FLHR AND FLHR-I MODELS

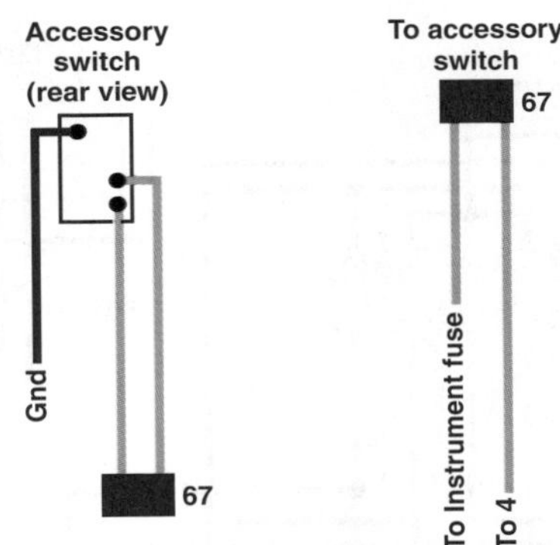

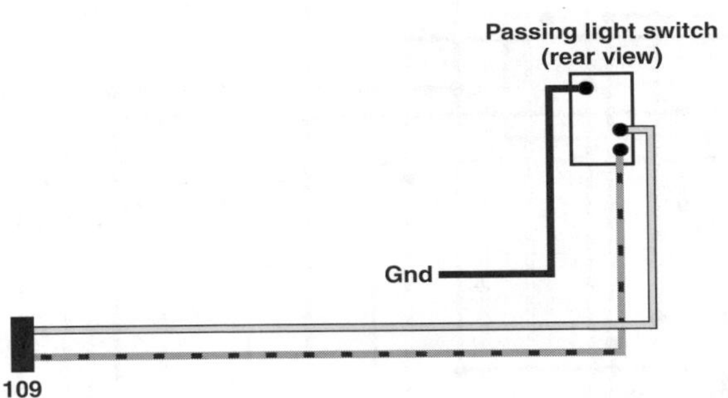

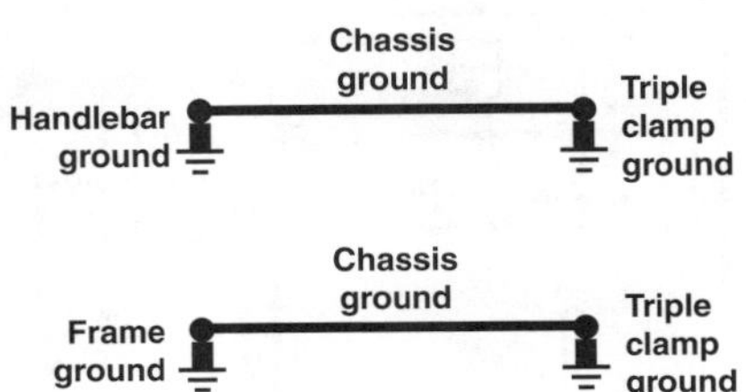

1997 FLHT, FLHTC, FLHTC-I, FLHTC ULTRA AND FLHTC ULTRA-I MODELS

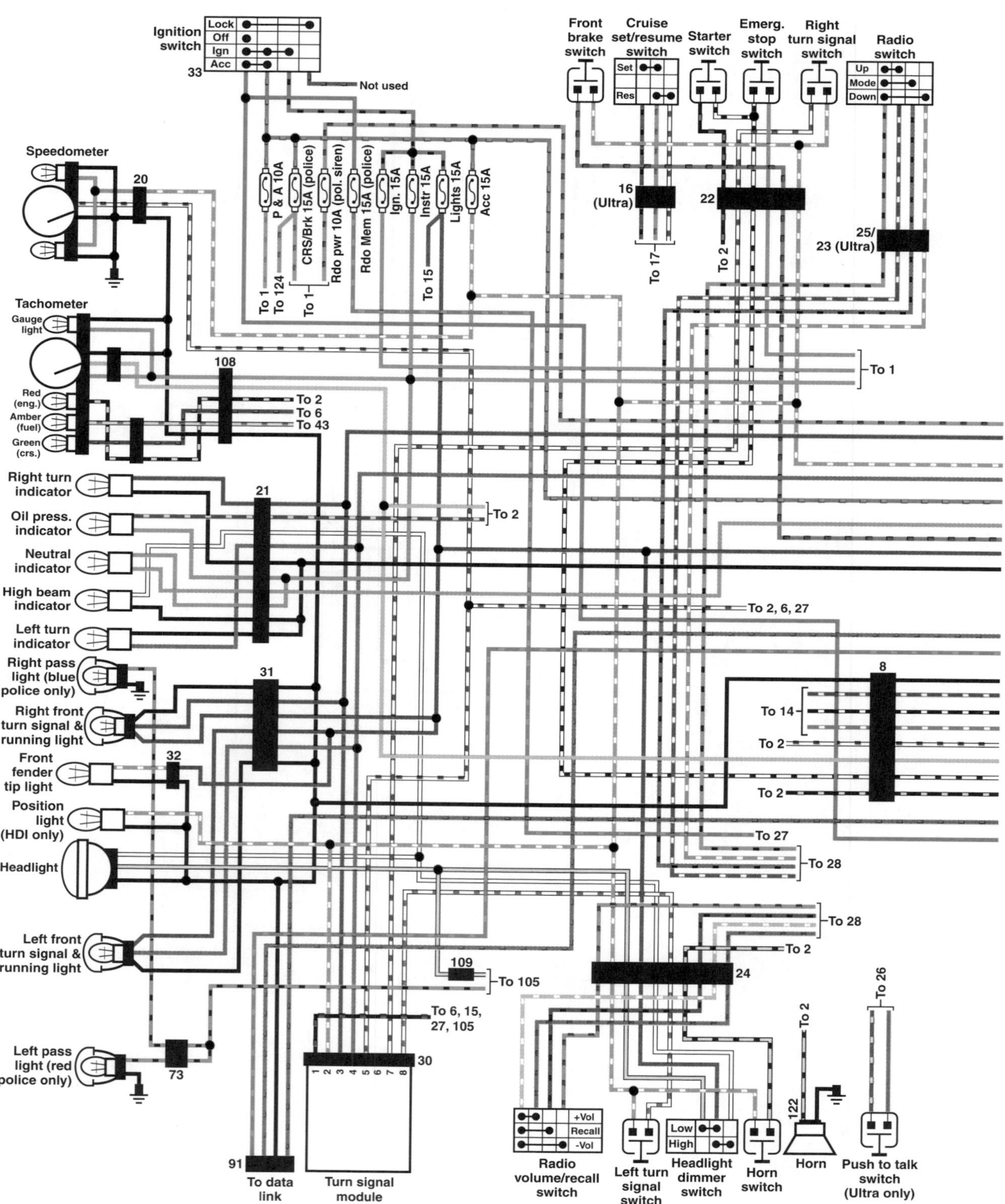

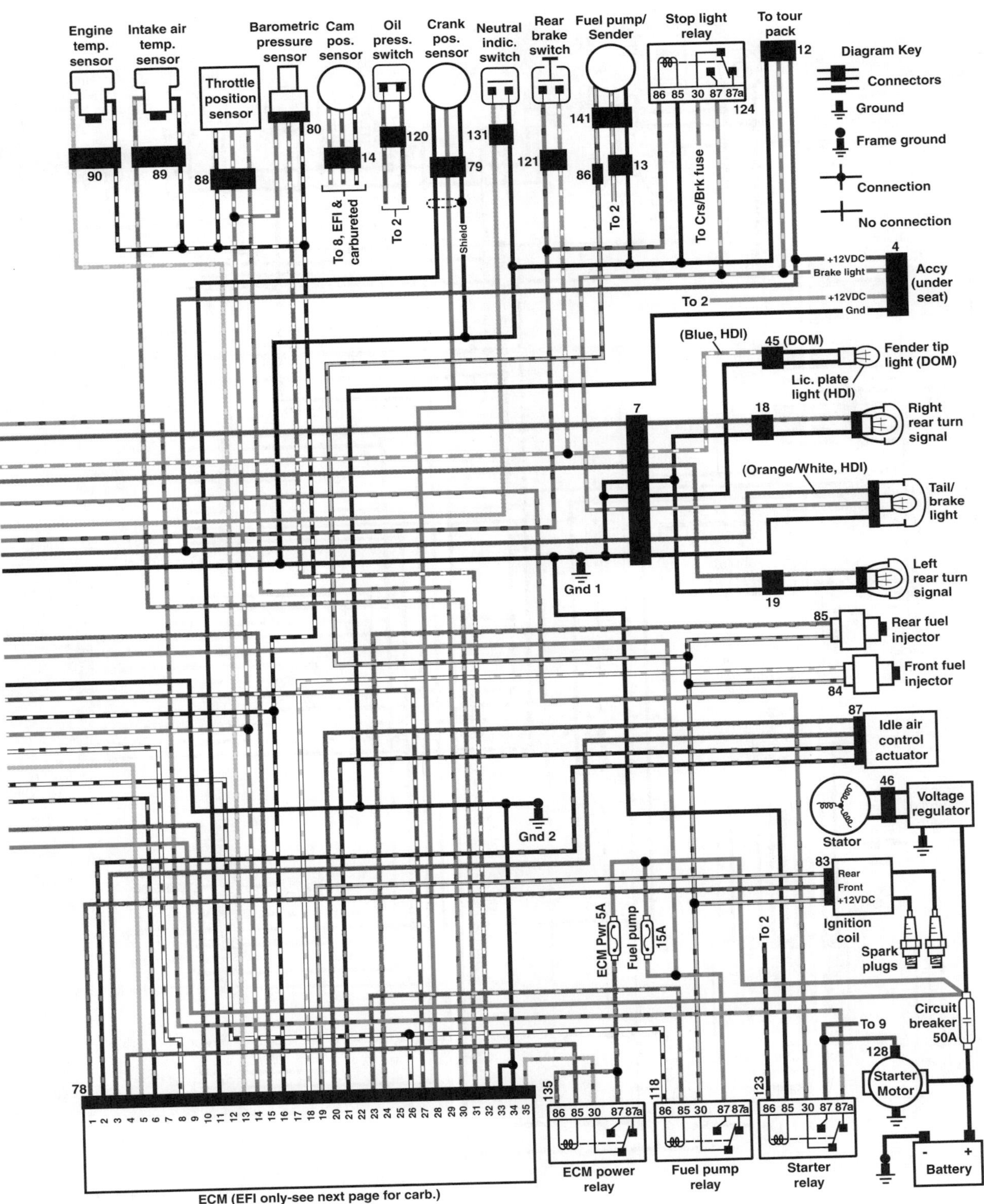
Engine temp. sensor
Intake air temp. sensor
Throttle position sensor
Barometric pressure sensor
Cam pos. sensor
Oil press. switch
Crank pos. sensor
Neutral indic. switch
Rear brake switch
Fuel pump/ Sender
Stop light relay
To tour pack
Diagram Key
Connectors
Ground
Frame ground
Connection
No connection
To 8, EFI & carbureted
To 2
Shield
To Crs/Brk fuse
Accy (under seat)
+12VDC
Brake light
Gnd
(Blue, HDI)
45 (DOM)
Fender tip light (DOM)
Lic. plate light (HDI)
Right rear turn signal
(Orange/White, HDI)
Tail/ brake light
Left rear turn signal
Gnd 1
Rear fuel injector
Front fuel injector
Idle air control actuator
Stator
Voltage regulator
Gnd 2
Rear
Front
Ignition coil
Spark plugs
ECM Pwr 5A
Fuel pump 15A
Circuit breaker 50A
To 9
Starter Motor
Battery
ECM power relay
Fuel pump relay
Starter relay
ECM (EFI only-see next page for carb.)

17

1997 FLHT, FLHTC, FLHTC-I, FLHTC ULTRA AND FLHTC ULTRA-I MODELS RADIO, GAUGES AND CRUISE CONTROL

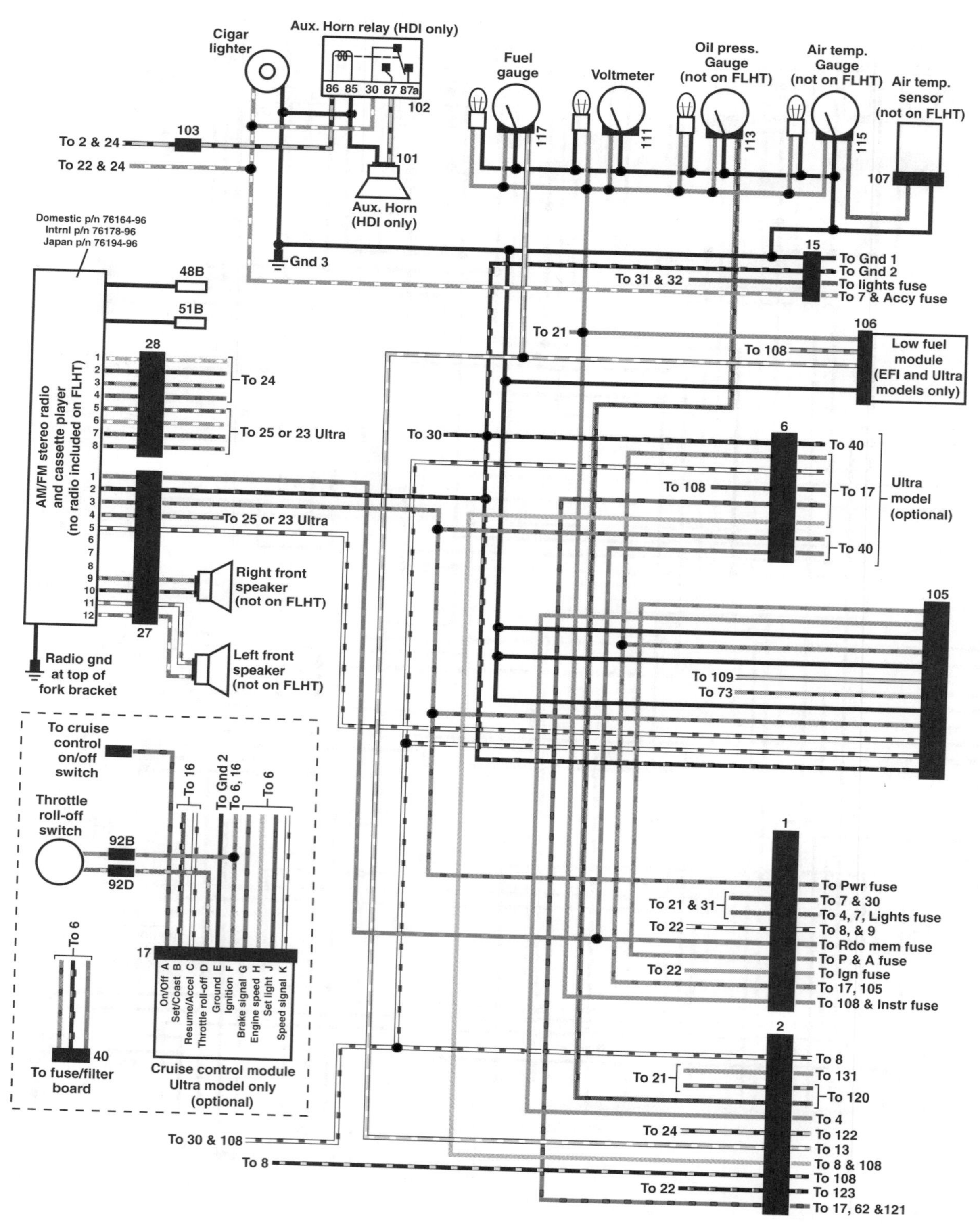

1997 FLHT, FLHTC, FLHTC-I, FLHTC ULTRA AND FLHTC ULTRA-I MODELS CARBURETED IGNITION, DASH SWITCHES AND TOURPAK

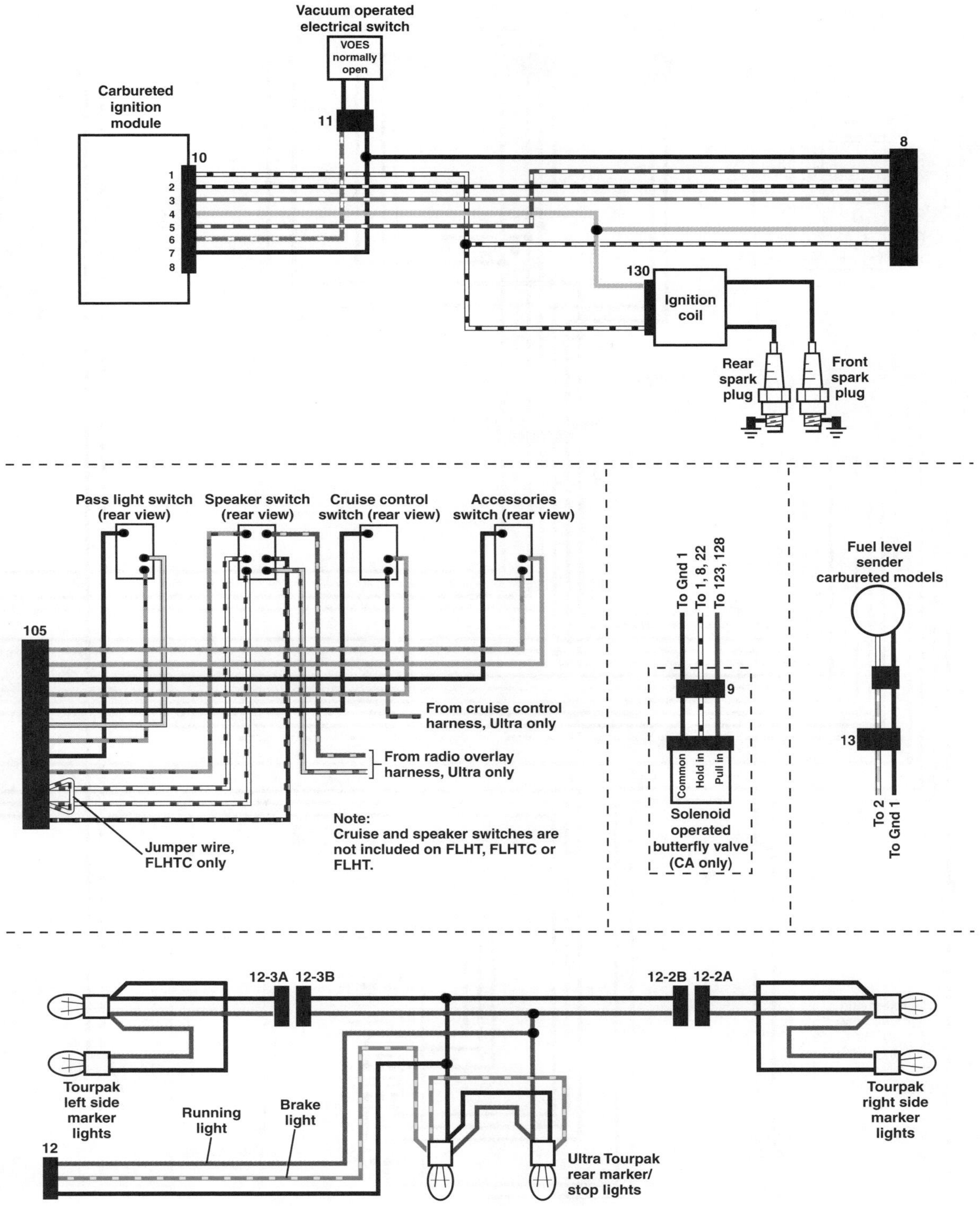

Vacuum operated electrical switch
VOES normally open
Carbureted ignition module
11
10
1
2
3
4
5
6
7
8
8
130
Ignition coil
Rear spark plug
Front spark plug
Pass light switch (rear view)
Speaker switch (rear view)
Cruise control switch (rear view)
Accessories switch (rear view)
105
From cruise control harness, Ultra only
From radio overlay harness, Ultra only
Jumper wire, FLHTC only
Note:
Cruise and speaker switches are not included on FLHT, FLHTC or FLHT.
To Gnd 1
To 1, 8, 22
To 123, 128
9
Common
Hold in
Pull in
Solenoid operated butterfly valve (CA only)
Fuel level sender carbureted models
13
To 2
To Gnd 1
12-3A
12-3B
12-2B
12-2A
Tourpak left side marker lights
Running light
Brake light
12
Ultra Tourpak rear marker/ stop lights
Tourpak right side marker lights

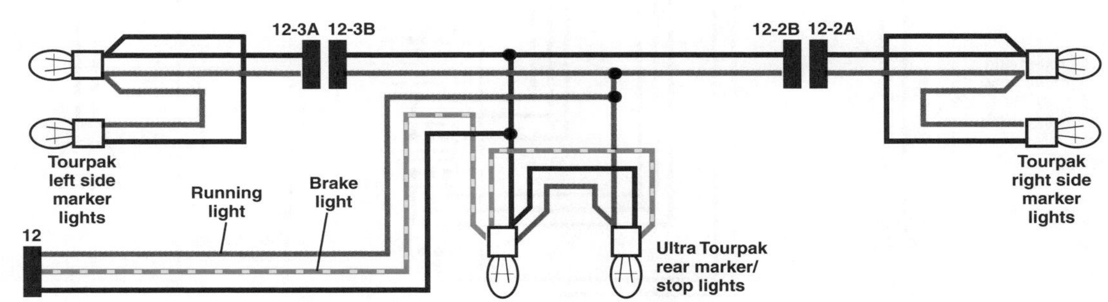

1997 FLHT, FLHTC, FLHTC-I, FLHTC ULTRA AND FLHTC ULTRA-I MODELS CB/INTERCOM, REAR SPEAKERS, RADIO AND ANTENNAS

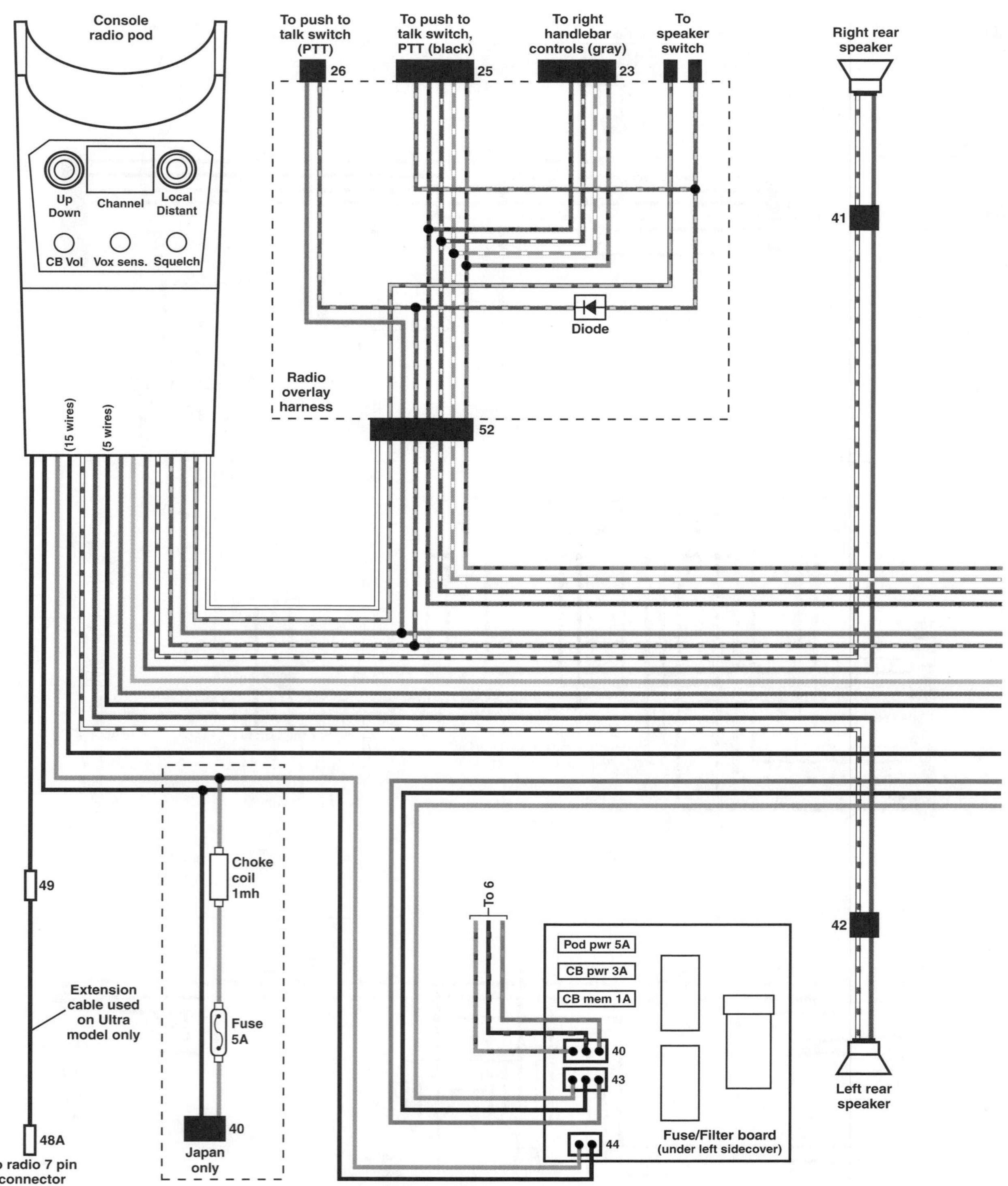

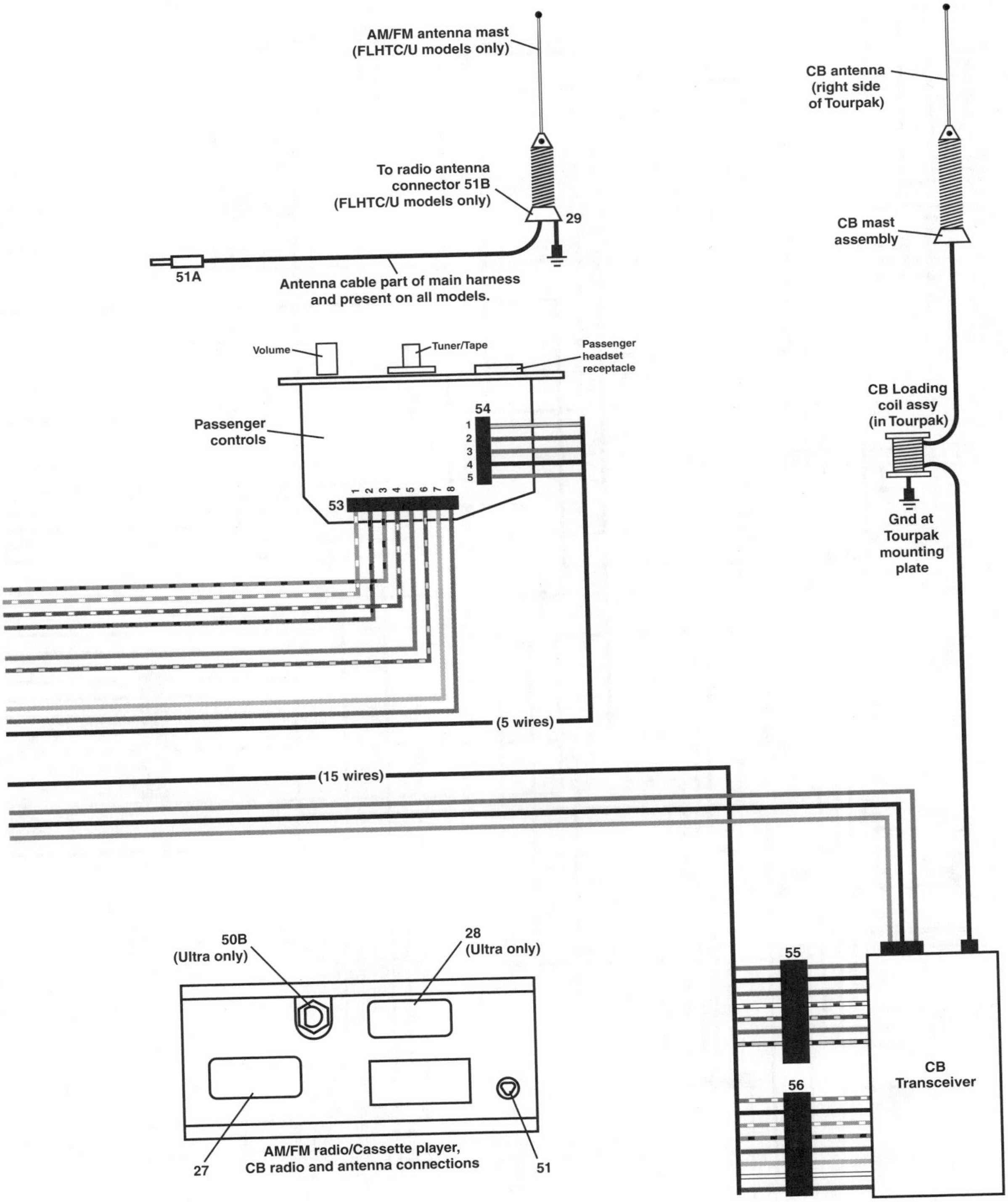

AM/FM antenna mast
(FLHTC/U models only)

CB antenna
(right side
of Tourpak)

To radio antenna
connector 51B
(FLHTC/U models only)

29

CB mast
assembly

51A

Antenna cable part of main harness
and present on all models.

Volume

Tuner/Tape

Passenger
headset
receptacle

54

1
2
3
4
5

Passenger
controls

CB Loading
coil assy
(in Tourpak)

Gnd at
Tourpak
mounting
plate

53

1 2 3 4 5 6 7 8

(5 wires)

(15 wires)

50B
(Ultra only)

28
(Ultra only)

55

56

CB
Transceiver

27

AM/FM radio/Cassette player,
CB radio and antenna connections

51

1

1998 FLHR AND FLHRC-I MODELS

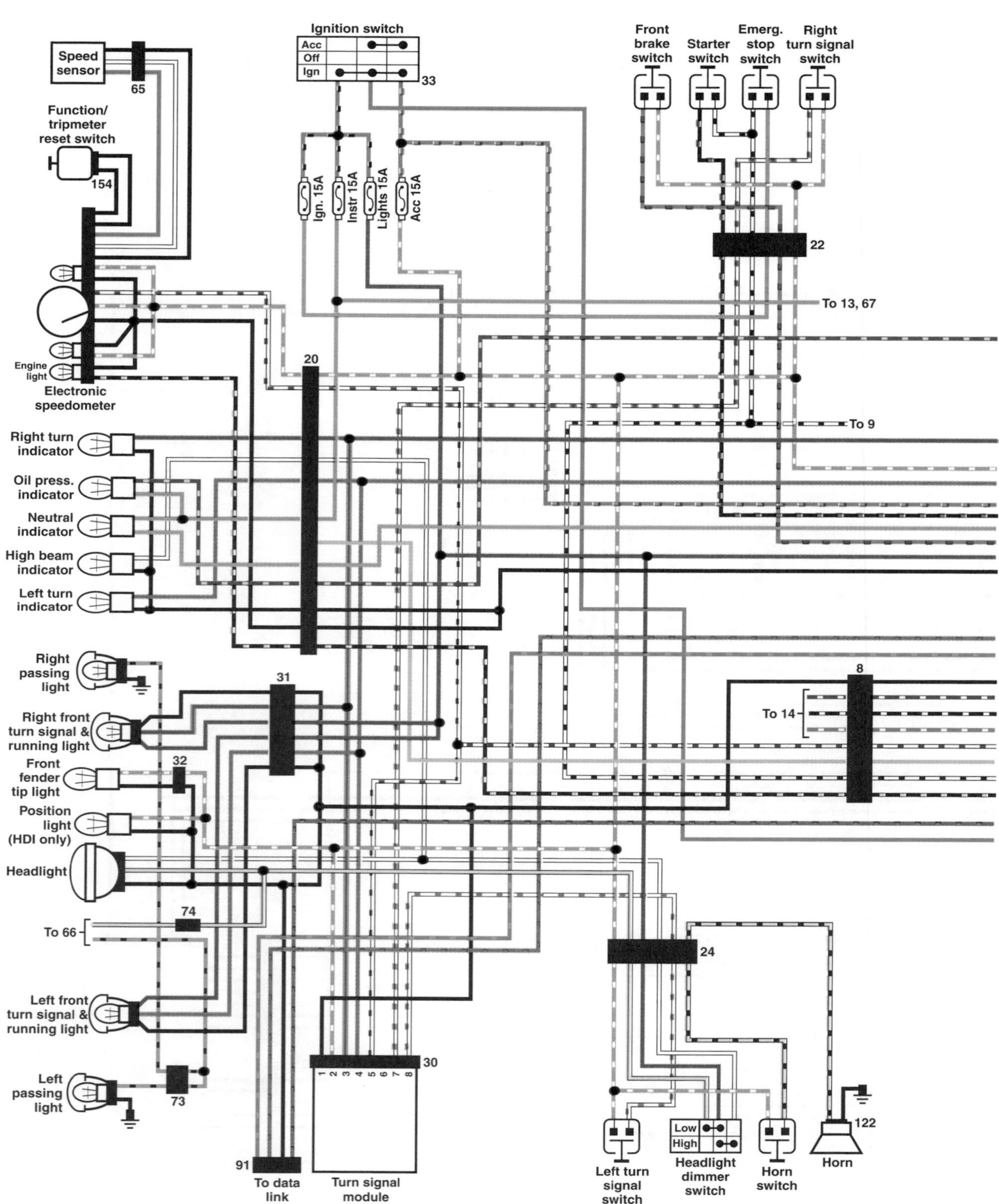

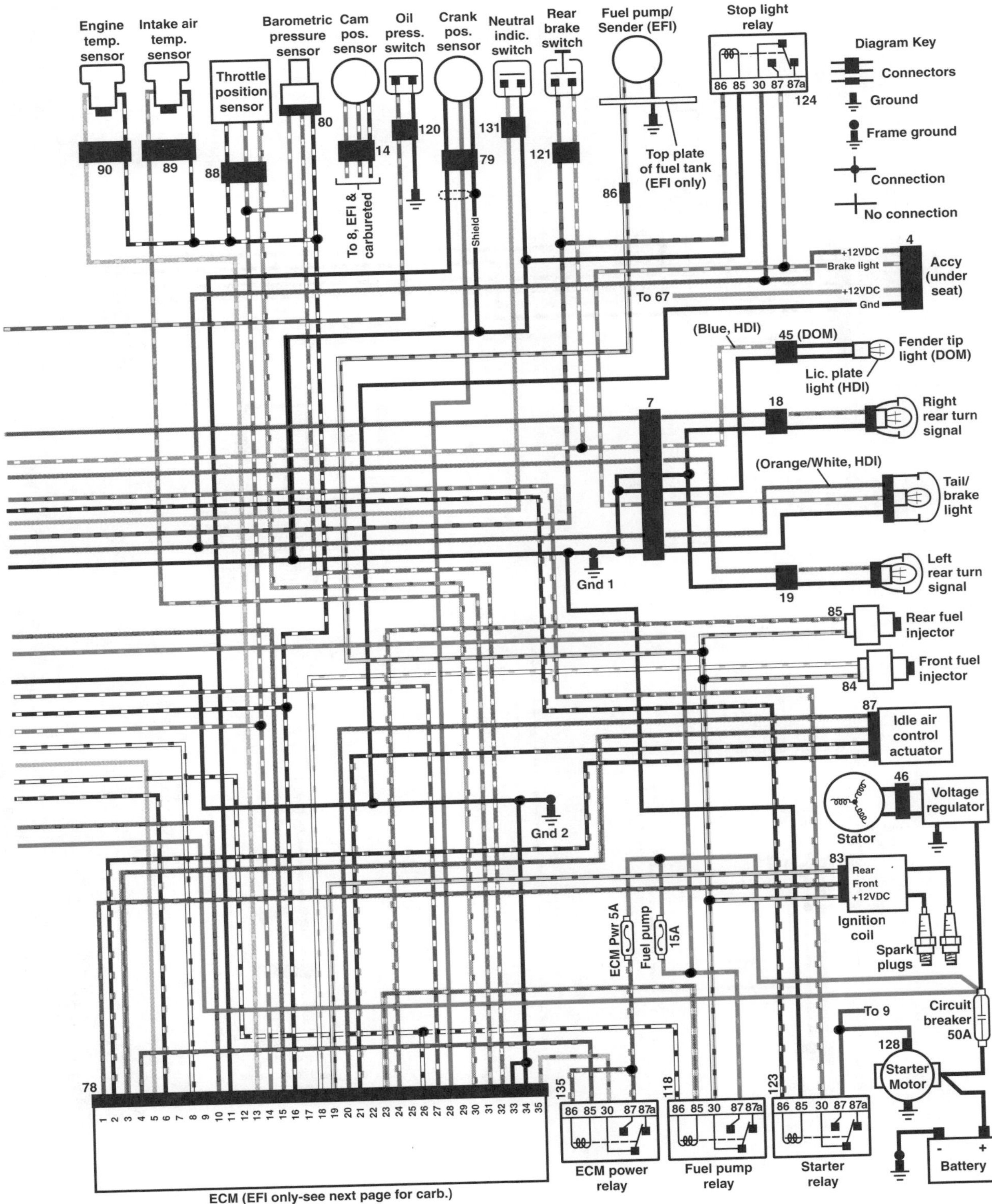
Engine temp. sensor
Intake air temp. sensor
Throttle position sensor
Barometric pressure sensor
Cam pos. sensor
Oil press. switch
Crank pos. sensor
Neutral indic. switch
Rear brake switch
Fuel pump/ Sender (EFI)
Stop light relay
86 85 30 87 87a
124
Diagram Key
Connectors
Ground
Frame ground
Connection
No connection
90
89
88
80
14
120
79
131
121
86
To 8, EFI & carbureted
Shield
Top plate of fuel tank (EFI only)
4
+12VDC
Brake light
+12VDC
Gnd
Accy (under seat)
To 67
(Blue, HDI)
45 (DOM)
Fender tip light (DOM)
Lic. plate light (HDI)
7
18
Right rear turn signal
(Orange/White, HDI)
Tail/ brake light
Gnd 1
19
Left rear turn signal
85
Rear fuel injector
Front fuel injector
84
87
Idle air control actuator
46
Voltage regulator
Stator
Gnd 2
83
Rear
Front
+12VDC
Ignition coil
Spark plugs
ECM Pwr 5A
Fuel pump 15A
Circuit breaker 50A
To 9
128
Starter Motor
78
1 2 3 4 5 6 7 8 9 10 11 12 13 14 15 16 17 18 19 20 21 22 23 24 25 26 27 28 29 30 31 32 33 34 35
ECM (EFI only-see next page for carb.)
135
118
123
86 85 30 87 87a
ECM power relay
Fuel pump relay
Starter relay
Battery

1998 FLHR AND FLHRC-I MODELS

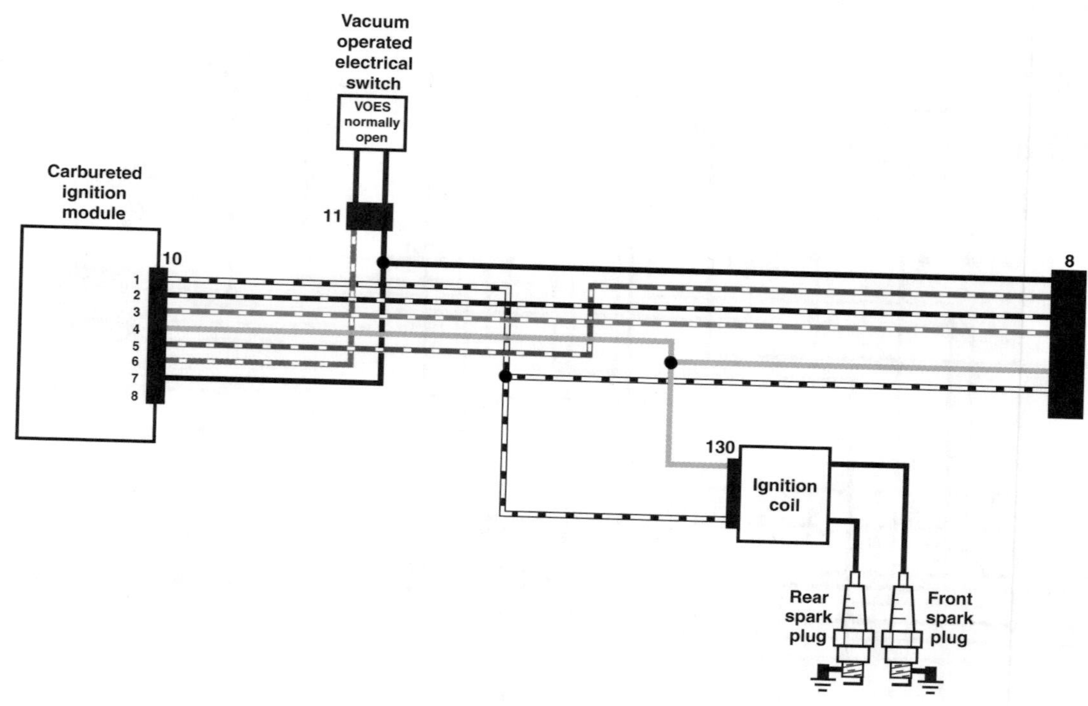

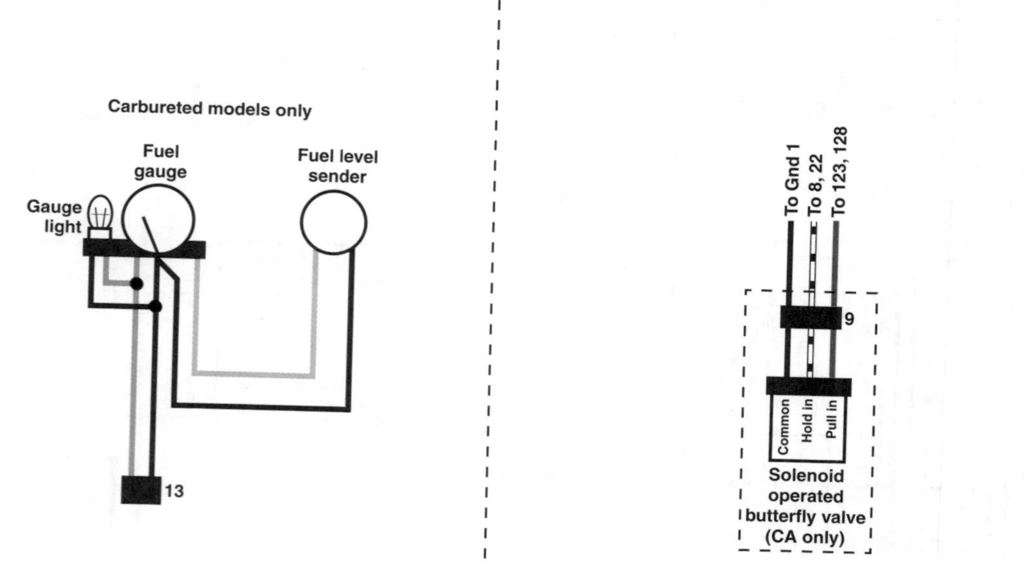

1998 FLHR AND FLHRC-I MODELS

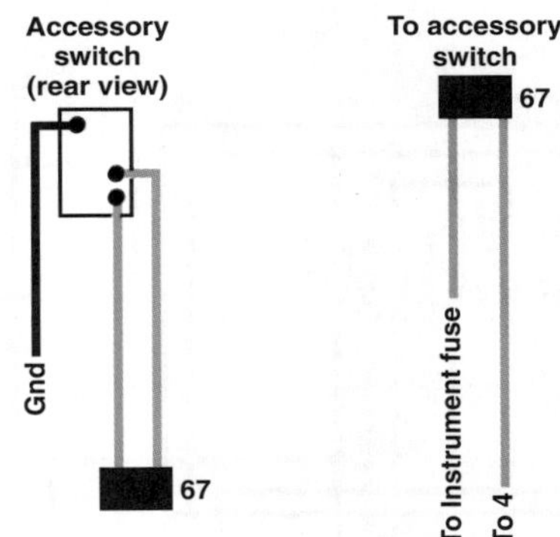

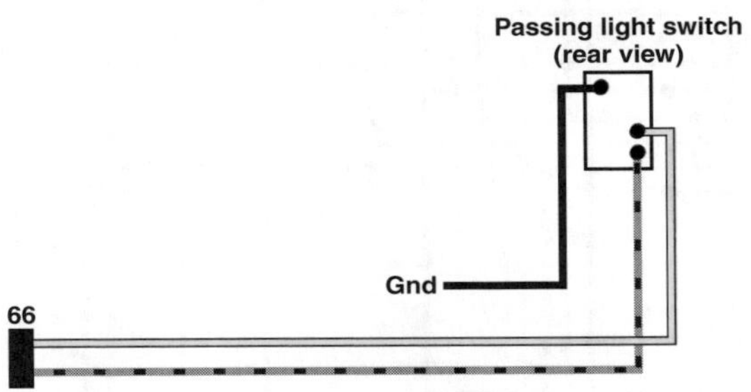

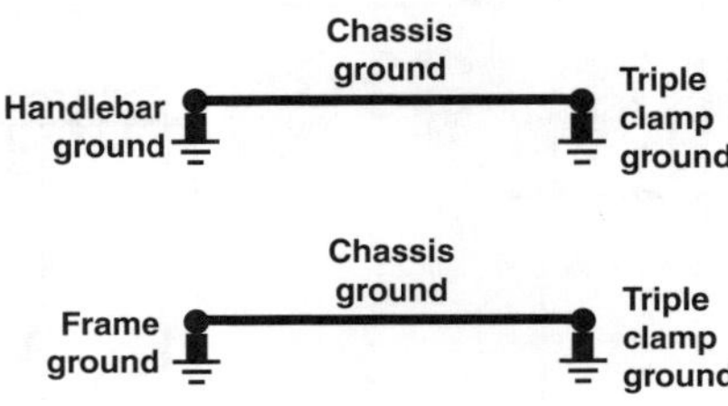

1998 FLHT, FLHTC, FLHTC-I, FLHTC ULTRA-I, FLTR AND FLTR-I MODELS

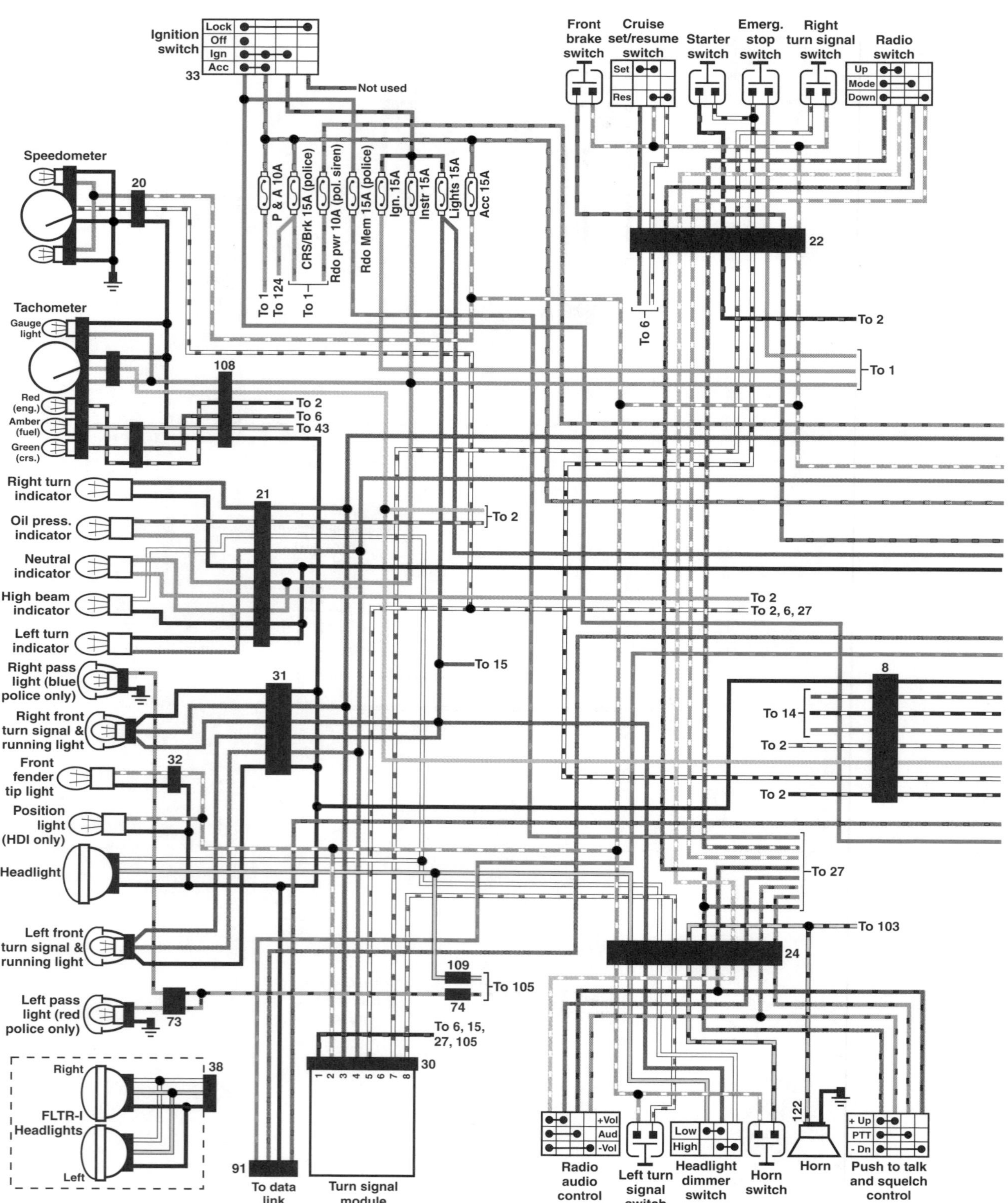

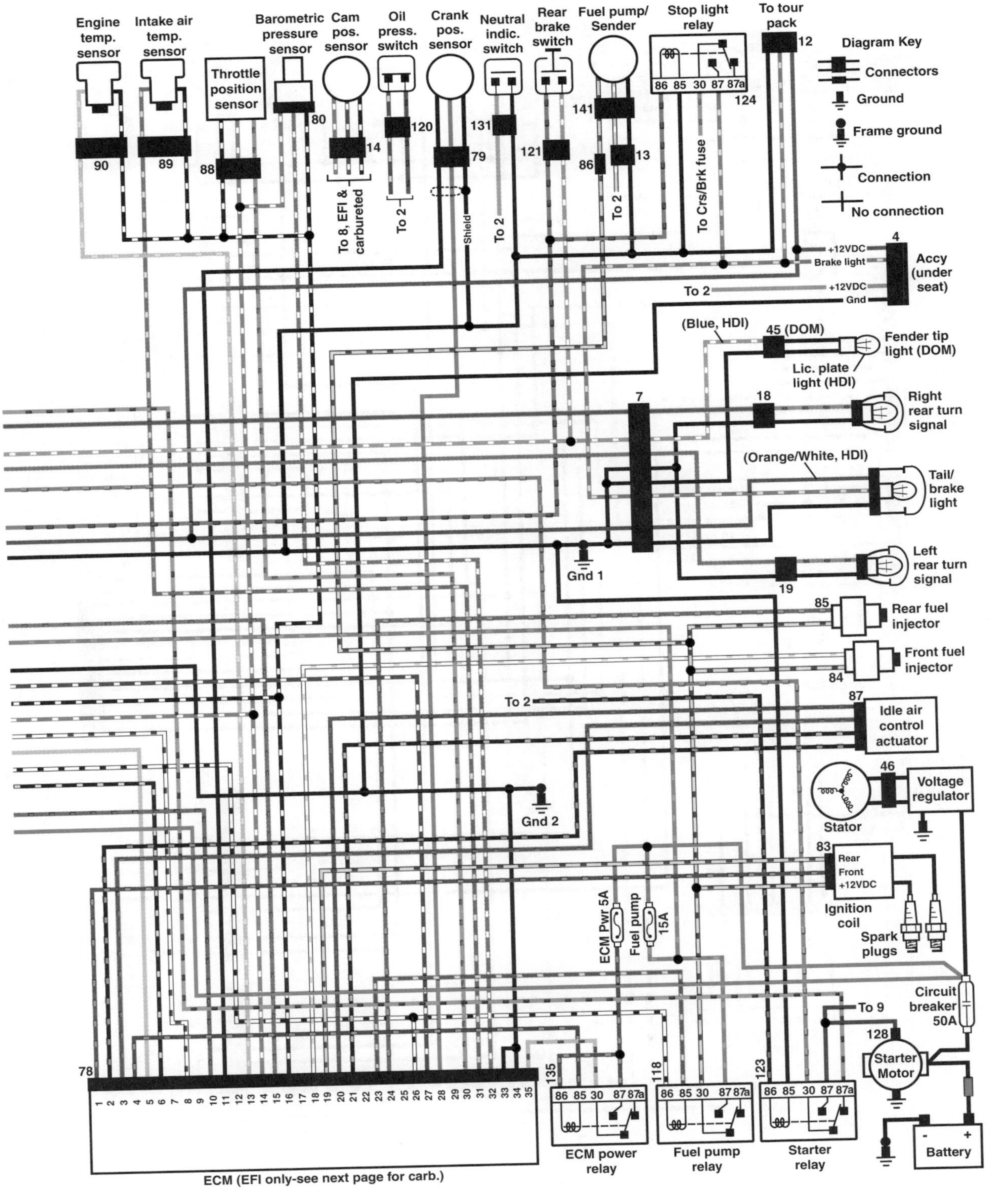

Engine temp. sensor
Intake air temp. sensor
Throttle position sensor
Barometric pressure sensor
Cam pos. sensor
Oil press. switch
Crank pos. sensor
Neutral indic. switch
Rear brake switch
Fuel pump/ Sender
Stop light relay
To tour pack
12
Diagram Key
Connectors
Ground
Frame ground
Connection
No connection
86 85 30 87 87a
124
141
80
14
120
131
79
121
86
13
90
89
88
To 8, EFI & carbureted
To 2
Shield
To 2
To 2
To Crs/Brk fuse
4
+12VDC
Brake light
To 2
+12VDC
Gnd
Accy (under seat)
(Blue, HDI)
45 (DOM)
Fender tip light (DOM)
Lic. plate light (HDI)
7
18
Right rear turn signal
(Orange/White, HDI)
Tail/ brake light
Gnd 1
19
Left rear turn signal
85
Rear fuel injector
Front fuel injector
84
To 2
87
Idle air control actuator
46
Voltage regulator
Stator
Gnd 2
83
Rear
Front
+12VDC
Ignition coil
Spark plugs
ECM Pwr 5A
Fuel pump 15A
Circuit breaker 50A
To 9
128
Starter Motor
78
1 2 3 4 5 6 7 8 9 10 11 12 13 14 15 16 17 18 19 20 21 22 23 24 25 26 27 28 29 30 31 32 33 34 35
135
86 85 30 87 87a
118
86 85 30 87 87a
123
86 85 30 87 87a
- +
Battery
ECM (EFI only-see next page for carb.)
ECM power relay
Fuel pump relay
Starter relay

17

1998 FLHT, FLHTC, FLHTC-I, FLHTC ULTRA-I, FLTR AND FLTR-I MODELS RADIO, GAUGES AND CRUISE CONTROL

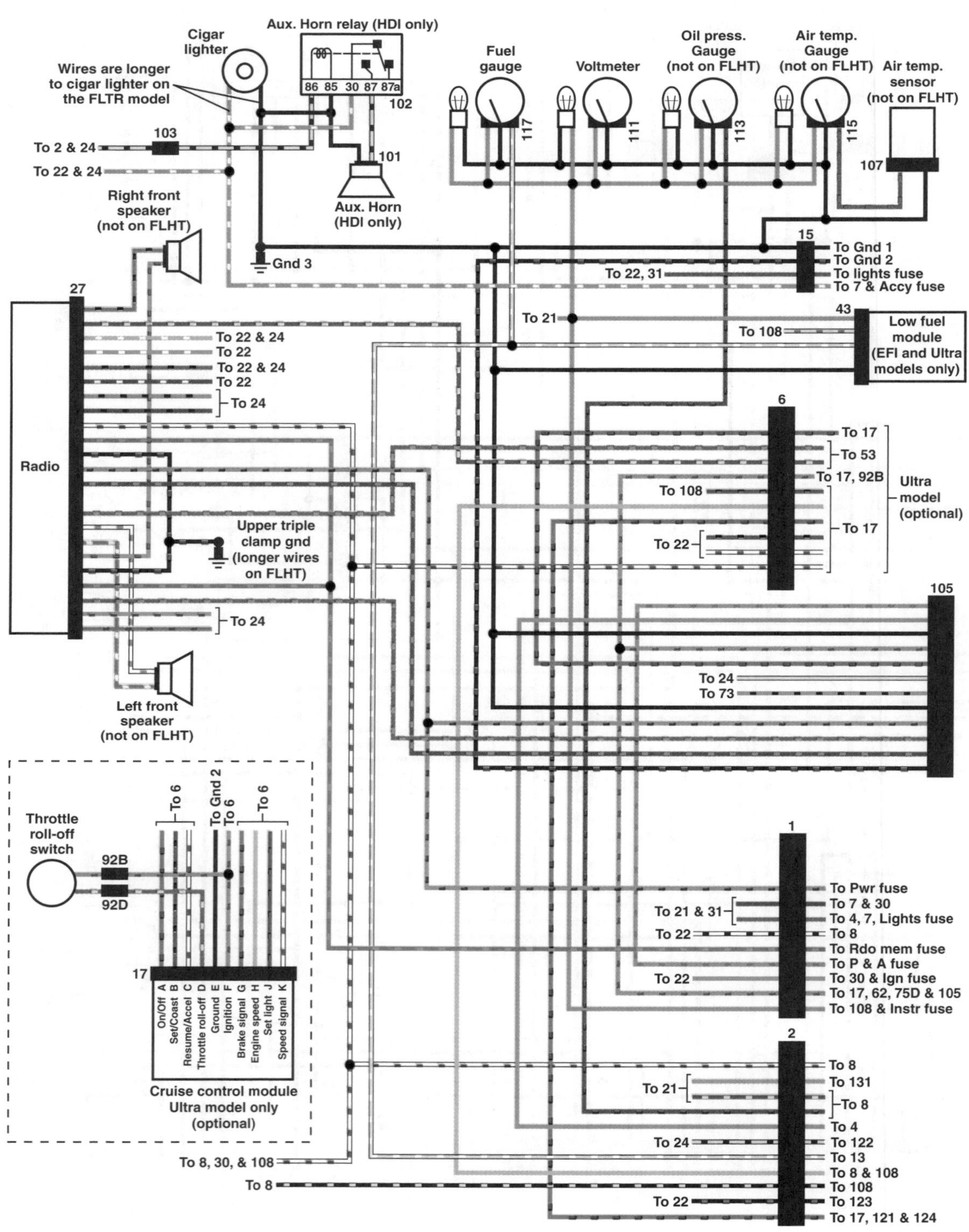

1998 FLHT, FLHTC, FLHTC-I, FLHTC ULTRA-I, FLTR AND FLTR-I MODELS CARBURETED IGNITION, DASH SWITCHES AND TOURPAK

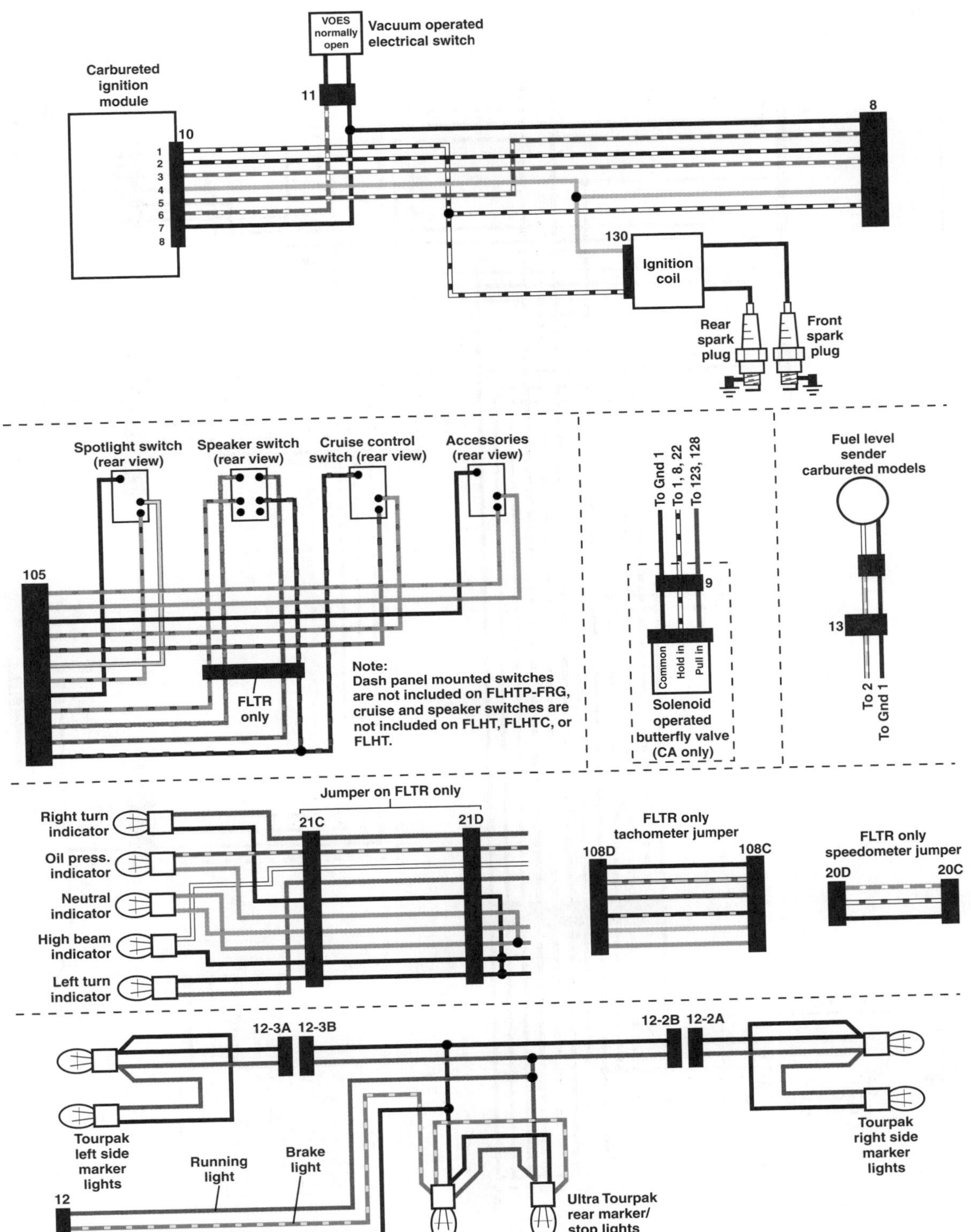

1998 FLHT, FLHTC, FLHTC-I, FLHTC ULTRA-I, FLTR AND FLTR-I MODELS RADIO, CB/INTERCOM AND REAR SPEAKERS

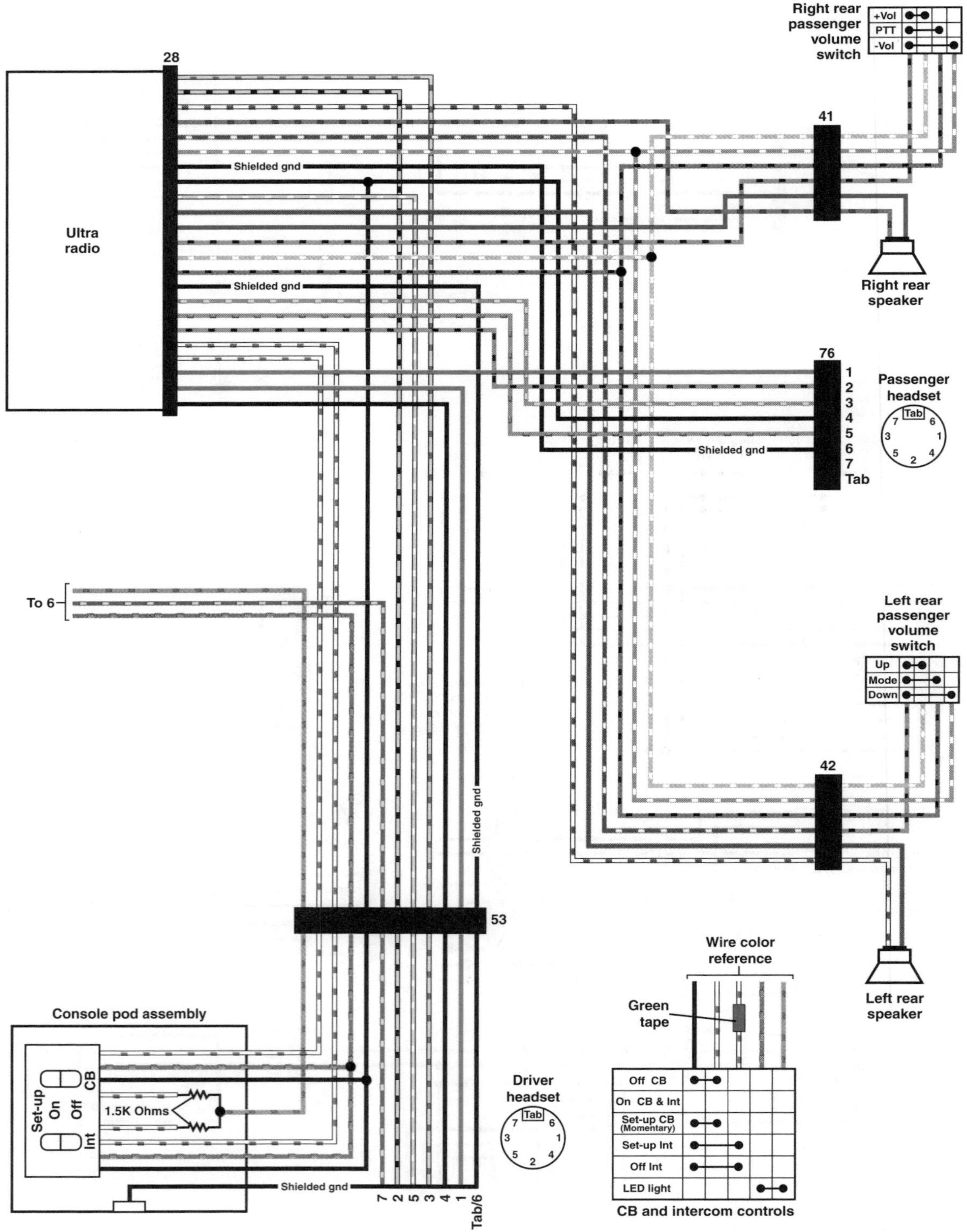

1998 FLHT, FLHTC, FLHTC-I, FLHTC ULTRA-I, FLTR AND FLTR-I MODELS RADIO, CB/INTERCOM AND ANTENNAS

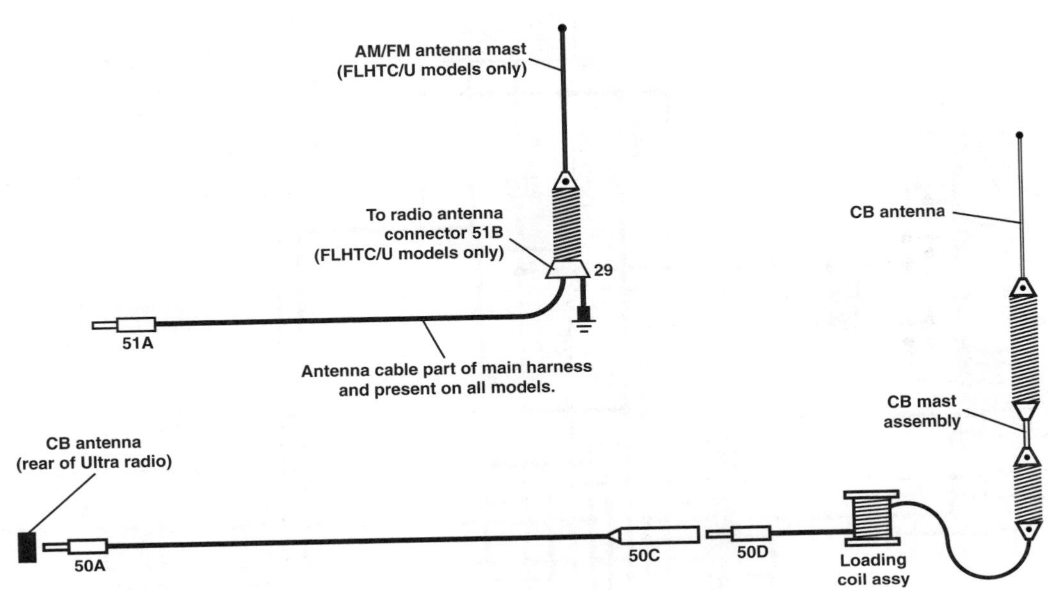

Ultra radio pinouts 28

Function	Pin
Rt front headset (+)	1
Front headset common	2
Left rear speaker	3
Right rear speaker	4
C4 (rear control matrix)	5
R1 (rear control matrix)	6
Rear mic shield	7
Rear mic common	8
Left front headset	9
Left rear speaker (+)	10
Right rear speaker (+)	11
C3 (rear control matrix)	12
R0 (rear control matrix)	13
R2 (rear control matrix)	14
Front mic shield	15
Right rear headset (+)	16
Left rear headset (+)	17
Rear headset common	18
N/C	19
N/C	20
Rear mic	21
Front mic	22
Front mic common	23

Handlebar matrix

	C0	C1	C2	C3	C4
R0	Vol. up	Vol. dwn	Menu		Up tune/fast fwd
R1					Dwn tune/rewind
R2		Squelch up	Squelch dwn	Push to talk	Band

Rear control matrix

	C3	C4
R0	Rear vol. up	Up tune/fast fwd
R1	Rear vol. dwn	Dwn tune/rewind
R2	Push to talk	Band

Base radio 27

Function	Pin
Rt front speaker (+)	1
Push to talk (mic)	2
R0 (handlebar matrix)	3
R1 (handlebar matrix)	4
R2 (handlebar matrix)	5
C4 (handlebar matrix)	6
C3 (handlebar matrix)	7
C2 (handlebar matrix)	8
Vehicle speed signal	9
Battery	10
Ground	11
Ignition	12
Headset speakers B	13
N/C	14
N/C	15
Left front speaker (+)	16
Left rear headset (-)	17
Right front speaker (+)	18
Ground	19
Battery	20
Headset speakers A	21
C1 (handlebar matrix)	22
C0 (handlebar matrix)	23

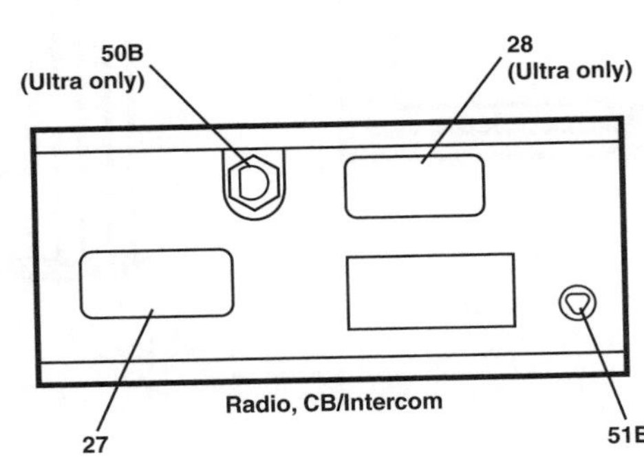

17

1999 FXR2 AND FXR3 MODELS

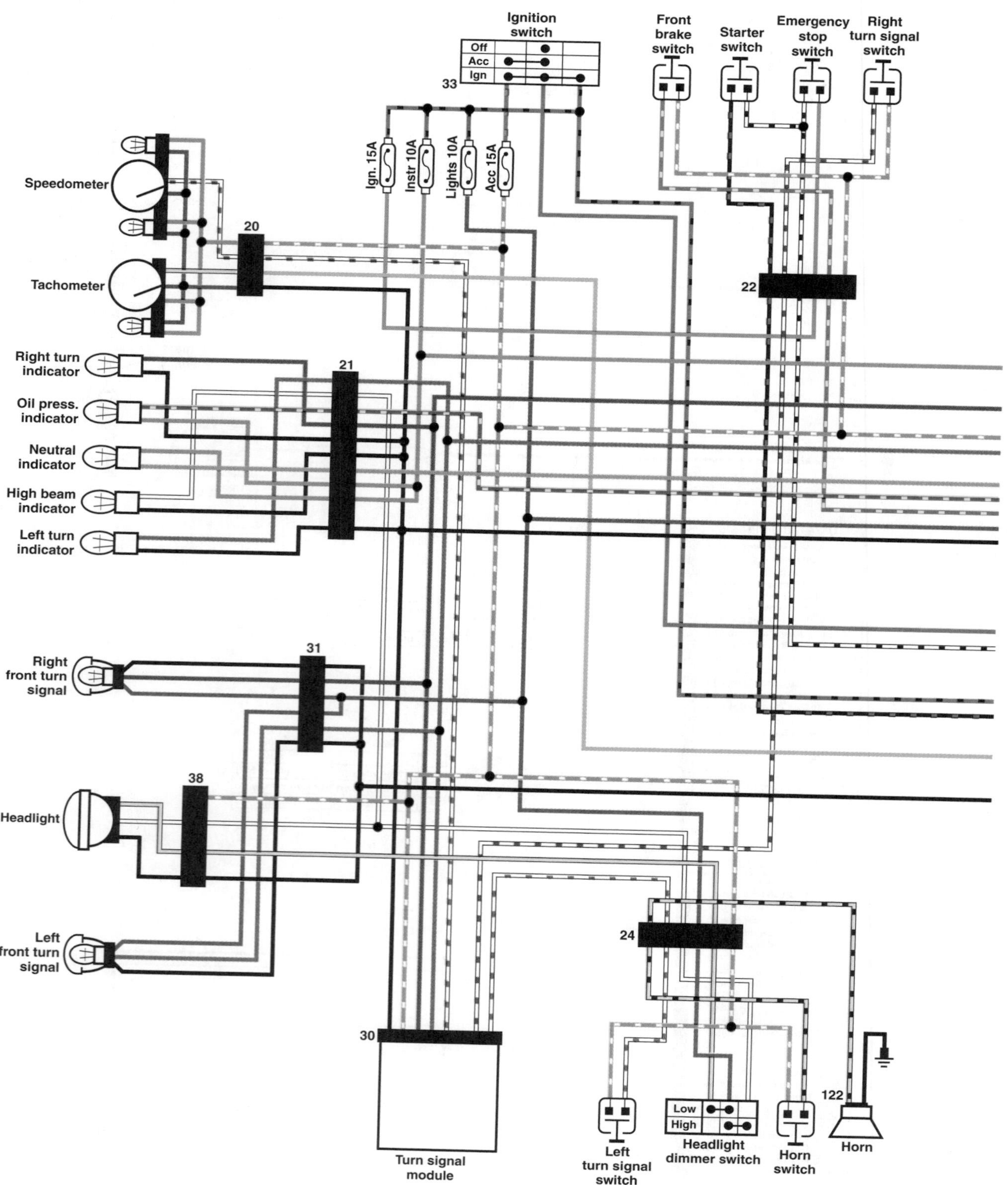

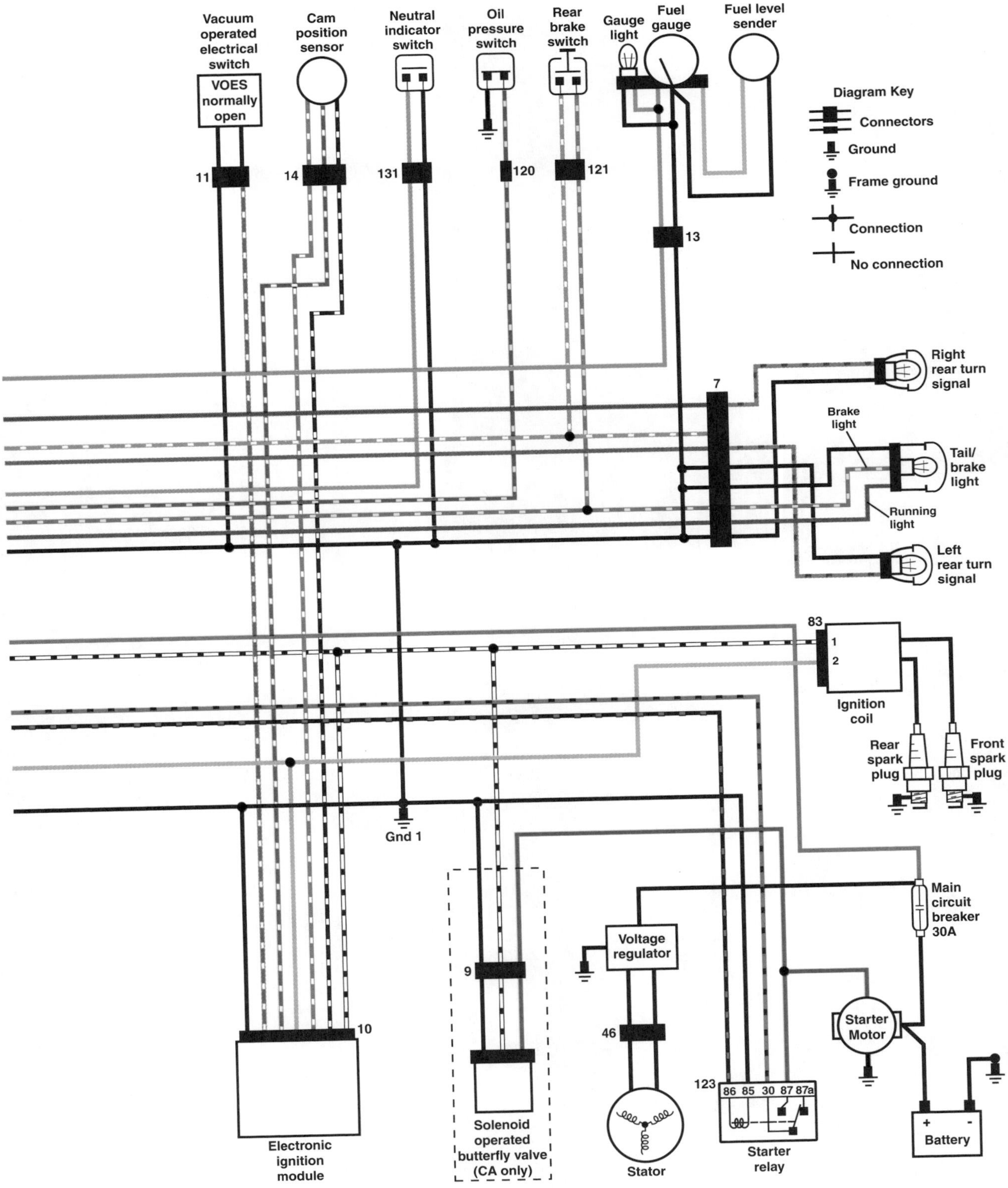

Vacuum operated electrical switch
VOES normally open
Cam position sensor
Neutral indicator switch
Oil pressure switch
Rear brake switch
Gauge light
Fuel gauge
Fuel level sender

Diagram Key
Connectors
Ground
Frame ground
Connection
No connection

11
14
131
120
121
13
7

Right rear turn signal
Brake light
Tail/ brake light
Running light
Left rear turn signal

83
1
2
Ignition coil
Rear spark plug
Front spark plug

Gnd 1
Main circuit breaker 30A
9
Voltage regulator
46
10
123
86 85 30 87 87a
Starter Motor
Battery
Electronic ignition module
Solenoid operated butterfly valve (CA only)
Stator
Starter relay

NOTES

MAINTENANCE LOG

Date	Miles	Type of Service